The
Concise Dictionary
of
National Biography

The
Concise Dictionary
of
National Biography

From earliest times to 1985

Volume II: G–M

Oxford   New York

OXFORD UNIVERSITY PRESS

1992

Oxford University Press, Walton Street, Oxford OX2 6DP

Oxford New York Toronto
Delhi Bombay Calcutta Madras Karachi
Petaling Jaya Singapore Hong Kong Tokyo
Nairobi Dar es Salaam Cape Town
Melbourne Auckland
and associated companies in
Berlin Ibadan

Oxford is a trade mark of Oxford University Press

© *Oxford University Press 1992*

British Library Cataloguing in Publication Data
Data available
ISBN 0–19–865305–0

Library of Congress Cataloging in Publication Data
Data available
ISBN 0–19–865305–0

Datacapture by Alliance Phototypesetters
Typeset by Promenade Graphics
Printed in Great Britain by
The Bath Press Ltd.
Bath, Avon

NOTE TO THE READER

ENTRIES are arranged in strict alphabetical order of their headword, except that names beginning with Mc and M' are treated as if they were spelled Mac, and names beginning with St are treated as Saint. Identical headwords are arranged in chronological sequence by date of birth.

Within the text, an asterisk (*) in front of a name or part of a name indicates that an entry for the person in question can be found in the dictionary. With very few exceptions, individuals are entered under their original family name and signpost entries, using small capitals, are therefore provided for titles involving name changes, and for aliases, pseudonyms, religious names, bardic names, and in some cases for maiden names, to direct the reader to the main entry. Alternative spellings for early names are not invariably cross-referred. Following *DNB* tradition, there are no cross-references to English monarchs from William I onwards or to British prime ministers, it being deemed obvious that all have an entry. For the same reason there are no cross-references to Shakespeare.

G

GABELL, Henry Dison (1764–1831), headmaster of Winchester; fellow of New College, Oxford, 1782–90; BA, 1786; MA, Cambridge, 1807; headmaster of Winchester, 1810–23; published pamphlets.

GABOR, Dennis (1900–1979), electrical engineer, physicist, and inventor; born in Hungary as Gábor Dénes; served in the army during the 1914–18 war; studied mechanical engineering at Technical University of Budapest; left Hungary to study electrical engineering at Charlottenburg; graduated, 1924; did research on lamps with the Siemens Company, 1928–33; emigrated to England to work in the British Thomson-Houston Co., Rugby, 1934; anglicized his name and became naturalized, 1946; with BTH Co. worked on the properties of electron beams in lamps, in television tubes, and electron microscopes, on a system for three-dimensional image projection for cinemas, and on a scheme for detecting heat from the exhaust of an aeroplane, 1937–48; invented holography, 1947; reader in electronics, Imperial College, London, 1949–58; produced working model of flat television tube; professor, 1958–67; published *Inventing the Future* (1963); holography leaped ahead with invention of the laser, 1961; Gabor produced many valuable patents; joined CBS Laboratories, Stamford, Connecticut, working on holography 1967; published *The Mature Society* (1972) and *Beyond the Age of Waste* (1978); FRS, 1956; D.Sc., London, 1964; CBE, 1970; number of honorary degrees; Nobel Prize for physics, 1971.

GABRIEL (afterwards MARCH), Mary Ann Virginia (1825–1877), musical composer; published songs, operettas, and cantatas, including *Evangeline*, 1873.

GACE, William (*fl.* 1580), translator; BA, Clare Hall, Cambridge, 1573; Englished N. Hemminge's *Commentary on the Epistle of St. James* (1577), selected sermons of Martin Luther (1578), and Luther's treatise to Duke Frederick of Saxony when sick (1580).

GADBURY, John (1627–1704), astrologer; educated at Oxford; defended *Lilly and other astrologers in *Philastrogus' Knavery Epitomized* (1652); published also *Genethlialogia, or the Doctrine of Nativities* (1658), and nativities of Charles I, the king of Sweden, and Sir Matthew Hales; produced *De Cometis . . . with an Account of the three late Comets in 1664 and 1665* (1665), *Vox Solis; or a Discourse of the Sun's Eclipse, 22 June 1666, Obsequium Rationabile* (1675), describing Lilly as an impostor, and *A Ballad upon the Popish Plot* (1679); he received compensation (1681) for 'wrongous imprisonment' at the time of the Popish Plot; falsely accused of complicity in a plot against William III, 1690.

GADDERAR, James (1655–1733), restorer of Scottish episcopacy; MA, Glasgow, 1675; minister of Kilmalcolm, 1682; 'rabbled' out, 1688; consecrated Scottish bishop, 1712, but lived in London; with Bishop Archibald *Campbell (d. 1744) came to Scotland as his 'vicar', 1721; obtained sanction of 'the usages' at Holy Communion; confirmed bishop of Aberdeen, 1724; elected to see of Moray, 1725.

GADDESDEN, John of (1280?–1361), physician; member of Merton College, Oxford; practised in London, and treated a son of Edward I for smallpox; his treatise, *Rosa Medicinae* or *Rosa Anglica*, first printed at Pavia (1492); prebendary of St Paul's, 1332; the 'Gatesden' of *Chaucer's prologue.

GADDUM, Sir John Henry (1900–1965), pharmacologist; educated at Rugby and Trinity College, Cambridge; first class, part i, mathematical tripos, 1920; entered University College Hospital, London, 1922; qualified, 1924; failed Cambridge MB, but later awarded Sc.D.; began pharmacological research at Wellcome Research Laboratories, 1925; assistant to (Sir) Henry *Dale at National Institute for Medical Research, 1928–34; professor of pharmacology, Cairo University, 1934–5; professor of pharmacology, University College, London, 1935; professor, College of the Pharmaceutical Society, London, 1938; during 1939–45 war, worked at Chemical Defence Research Station, Porton; professor of materia medica, Edinburgh University, 1942–58; director, Institute of Animal Physiology, Cambridge, 1958; FRS, 1945; fellow, Royal Society of Edinburgh; knighted, 1964; hon. LL D, Edinburgh; did important research on the development of specific and sensitive methods of biological assay; publications include textbook on pharmacology (1940), translated into German, Spanish, and Japanese; Gaddum

Memorial Trust created by British Pharmacological Society, 1966.

GADSBY, Henry Robert (1842–1907), musician; professor of harmony at Guildhall School of Music from 1880; published choral and orchestral cantatas, part songs, and anthems, and textbooks on harmony (1883) and sight singing (1897).

GADSBY, William (1773–1844), Particular Baptist minister; pastor of Back Lane Chapel, Manchester, from 1805; wrote hymns; his pamphlets and sermons published by his son, 1851 and 1854.

GAGE, Francis (1621–1682), president of Douai College, 1676; half-brother of Sir Henry *Gage; studied at Douai and Tournay College, Paris, under William *Clifford; DD of the Sorbonne, 1654; agent to the English chapter at Rome, 1659–61; left in manuscript a journal of his life.

GAGE, George (fl. 1614–1640), Roman Catholic agent; half-brother of Francis *Gage; friend of Sir Toby *Matthew; sent by James I to Rome, 1621, to obtain dispensation for marriage of the Spanish Infanta with Prince Charles; failed after three years' negotiations.

GAGE, Sir Henry (1597–1645), Royalist; great-grandson of Sir John *Gage; educated in Flanders and in Italy under Piccolomini; in Spanish service at Antwerp; commanded company in Argyll's regiment at Bergen-op-Zoom, 1622, and Breda, 1624; defended St Omer, 1638; intercepted parliament's supplies from Flanders; during the Rebellion was prominent in defence of Oxford, captured Borstall House, and relieved Basing House, 1644; knighted, 1644; governor of Oxford; mortally wounded at Abingdon.

GAGE, Sir John (1479–1556), statesman and military commander; governor of Guisnes and comptroller of Calais, 1522; vice-chamberlain to the king, 1528–40; KG, 1532; commissioner for surrender of religious houses; constable of the Tower, comptroller of the household, 1540, and chancellor of the duchy of Lancaster on fall of *Cromwell; commanded the expedition against Scotland, 1542; with *Suffolk conducted siege of Boulogne; expelled from Privy Council by *Somerset; joined *Southampton; created lord chamberlain by Queen Mary and restored to the constableship of the Tower, where he received Elizabeth, 1555, having afterwards charge of her at her own house.

GAGE, John (1786–1842), antiquary. See ROKEWODE, JOHN GAGE.

GAGE, Joseph (or **Joseph Edward**), Count Gage (or De Gages) (1678?–1753?), grandee of Spain; uncle of Thomas *Gage (1721–1787); went to Spain after losing a great fortune in Mississippi stock; commanded Spanish troops in Italy, 1743–6, and was promoted grandee of the first class, receiving also from the king of Naples the order of St Januarius and a pension.

GAGE, Thomas (d. 1656), traveller; brother of Sir Henry *Gage; when a Spanish Dominican lived for some time among the Indians of Central America; crossed Nicaragua, reached Panama, and, traversing the isthmus, sailed from Portobello; reached Europe, 1637; after a visit to Loreto renounced Catholicism and came to England, 1641; preached recantation sermon at St Paul's (published, 1642); joined Parliamentarians and became rector of Acrise, 1642, and Deal, c.1651; died in Jamaica, as chaplain to *Venables. His great work, *The English-American his Travail by Sea and Land* (1648), was translated into French by order of Colbert, 1676, also into Dutch and German; portions concerning *Laud and rules for learning Central American languages appeared separately.

GAGE, Thomas (1721–1787), general; aide-de-camp to Lord *Albemarle in Flanders, 1747–8; as lieutenant-colonel of the 44th served in America under *Braddock, 1751–6; raised 80th Foot and commanded light infantry at Ticonderoga, 1758; as brigadier-general commanded rearguard of *Amherst; governor of Montreal, 1759–60; major-general, 1761; commander-in-chief in America, 1763–72; lieutenant-general, 1770; governor of Massachusetts, 1774–5; superseded by *Howe, Oct. 1775.

GAGE, Sir William Hall (1777–1864), admiral of the fleet; youngest son of Thomas *Gage (1721–1787); entered navy, 1789; engaged off Toulon, 1795, against the Sabina, 1796, and at St Vincent, 1797; commanded the *Terpsichore* at blockade of Malta, and was in the action with the Danish *Freja*; commanded the *Thetis*, 1805–8, and the *Indus*, 1813–14; rear-admiral, 1821; commander in East Indies, 1825–30, at Plymouth, 1848–51; member of Board of Admiralty, 1842–6; admiral, 1846; GCB, 1860; admiral of the fleet, 1862.

GAGER, William (fl. 1580–1619), Latin dramatist; educated at Westminster and Christ Church, Oxford; MA, 1580; DCL, 1589; chancellor of Ely, 1606, and vicar-general to Bishop *Andrewes, 1613, 1616, and 1618; defended performance of plays at Oxford against John *Rainolds; wrote five Latin plays acted at Oxford; ranked among comic dramatists in *Meres's *Palladis Tamia* (1598).

GAGNIER, John (1670?–1740), orientalist; born at Paris; studied Hebrew and Arabic at the Collège de Navarre; MA, Cambridge, 1703; settled at Oxford under patronage of Bishop William *Lloyd, taught Hebrew, and became professor of Arabic, 1724; published editions of Ben Gorion's *History of the Jews* (1706), and of Abu Al-Fida's *Life of Mahomet* (1723), also a translation of the Arabic treatise of Rhazes on the smallpox.

GAHAGAN, Usher (d. 1749), classical scholar; edited Latin authors for Brindley's classics; rendered in Latin verse *Pope's *Essay on Criticism* (1747), and *Messiah* and *Temple of Fame* (1749); hanged for coining.

GAHAN, William (1730–1804), Irish ecclesiastic and author; graduated at Louvain; received back into the Roman Church John *Butler, twelfth Lord Dunboyne; imprisoned, 1802, for refusing to reveal to the court of assize details of his relations with John Butler; published *Sermons and Moral Discourses* and popular devotional works.

GAIMAR, Geoffrey (*fl.* 1140?), author of *Lestorie des Engles*, probably a Norman resident at Scampton, Lincolnshire.

GAINFORD, first Baron (1860–1943), politician and man of business. See PEASE, JOSEPH ALBERT.

GAINSBOROUGH, Thomas (1727–1788), painter; youngest son of a Sudbury wool manufacturer; studied under *Gravelot and Francis *Hayman in London; married and lived at Ipswich, 1746–60, where he became acquainted with John Joshua *Kirby and Philip *Thicknesse; painted *Gainsborough's Forest* (National Gallery) and portraits of Admiral *Vernon and others; resided at Bath, 1760–74; during those years contributed eighteen pictures to the Society of Artists; elected an original member of the Royal Academy, 1768, and exhibited there, 1769–72, as well as, after a misunderstanding with *Reynolds, at the Free Society; settled in London, 1774; resumed exhibiting at Academy, 1779–83, but in consequence of a dispute about hanging three portraits, withdrew all his works, 1784, and henceforth showed his pictures in his own house. To the Bath period are assigned his two portraits of *Garrick, those of *Quin, *Foote, Orpin (National Gallery), Lord *Camden, *Richardson, *Sterne, and *Chatterton, and *The Harvest Waggon*; to the London period belong two portraits of the duchess of *Devonshire (including that stolen in 1876), the full-length known as *The Blue Boy*, Mr Bate, Mrs *Siddons (both in the National Gallery), and Colonel St Leger (Hampton Court), *The View in the Mall of St James's Park*, *Girl with Pigs* (bought by Reynolds), and many fine landscapes. Among his intimate friends were *Burke and *Sheridan, and he was reconciled to Reynolds on his deathbed.

GAINSBOROUGH, William (d. 1307), ecclesiastic; when divinity lecturer of the Franciscans at Oxford one of the embassy sent by Edward I to Philip IV of France and Pope Boniface VIII; reader in theology to the pope, 1300; appointed to the see of Worcester by 'provision', 1302; one of the embassy to Clement V, 1305; sent, 1307, to arrange for the marriage of Prince Edward with *Isabella of France; died at Beauvais.

GAINSFORD, Thomas (d. 1624?), author; served in Ireland against the Spaniards (1601) and Tyrone; published *Vision and Discourse of Henry the seventh concerning the unitie of Great Britaine* (1610), *The Historie of Trebizond* (1616), and other works.

GAIRDNER, James (1828–1912), historian; son of John *Gairdner; clerk in Public Record Office, 1846–93; joint editor of *Calendar of Letters and Papers of the Reign of Henry VIII*; edited *Paston Letters*, etc.

GAIRDNER, John (1790–1876), medical reformer; MD, Edinburgh, 1811; studied anatomy under Bell; president of the Edinburgh College of Surgeons, 1830–2; obtained leave for medical students to attend extra-academical lectures, and was active in obtaining by the act of 1859 legal status for every licensed practitioner in Great Britain; published lectures on Edinburgh medical history; his *Burns and the Ayrshire Moderates* published posthumously.

GAIRDNER, William (1793–1867), physician; brother of John *Gairdner; MD, Edinburgh, 1813; LRCP, 1823; died at Avignon; published treatise on gout (1849).

GAIRDNER, Sir William Tennant (1824–1907), professor of medicine at Glasgow; son of John *Gairdner; MD, Edinburgh, 1845; hon. LL D, 1883; pathologist and physician to Royal Infirmary there; professor of medicine at Glasgow University, 1862–90; medical officer of health, Glasgow, 1863–72; attractive lecturer; made many original researches in connection with heart and lung diseases; FRS, 1892; KCB, 1898; works include *Clinical Medicine* (1862) and *The Physician as Naturalist* (1889).

GAISFORD, Thomas (1779–1855), dean of Christ Church, Oxford; student of Christ Church, 1800; MA, 1804; appointed regius professor of Greek, 1812; canon of Llandaff and St Paul's, 1823, Worcester, 1825, Durham, 1831; dean of Christ Church, Oxford, 1831–55; edited the *Tusculan Disputations* (1805) and *De Oratore* of Cicero (1809); the works of Euripides, Sophocles, and Herodotus (1824), *Hephaestion de Metris* (1810), *Poetae Graeci Minores* (1814–20), *Suidae Lexicon* (1834), *Etymologicon Magnum* (1848), several works of Eusebius and Theodoret, and an edition of the Septuagint (1848). The Gaisford prizes at Oxford for Greek prose and verse were founded, 1856.

GAITSKELL, Hugh Todd Naylor (1906–1963), politician; educated at Winchester and New College, Oxford; first class, philosophy, politics, and economics, 1927; tutored by G. D. H. *Cole; joined Labour party as an undergraduate; lecturer in political economy, University College, London, 1928–38; head of department and university reader, 1938; temporary civil servant, during 1939–45 war, in Ministry of Economic Warfare, and Board of Trade; Labour MP, South Leeds, 1945–63; parliamentary secretary, Ministry of Fuel and Power, 1946; minister and PC, 1947; minister of state for economic affairs, 1950; chancellor of the Exchequer, 1950–1; opposed to policies of Aneurin *Bevan; defeated Bevan and Herbert *Morrison (later Lord Morrison of Lambeth) for party leadership, 1955; defeated at general election, 1959; opposed party resolution in favour of unilateral disarmament; opposed British entry into EEC, 1962; CBE, 1945; hon. DCL, Oxford, 1958.

GALBRAITH, Robert (d. 1543), Scottish judge; advocate to Queen *Margaret Tudor; one of the original lords of the College of Senators, 1537; murdered by John Carkettle of Edinburgh.

GALBRAITH, Vivian Hunter (1889–1976), historian; educated at Highgate School and Manchester University; first class, modern history, 1910; awarded Brackenbury scholarship to Balliol College, Oxford; won Stanhope Prize, 1911; first class, modern history, 1914; Langton research fellow; served in the Queen's Regiment, 1917–18; assistant keeper, Public Record Office, 1921; edited the Anonimalle Chronicle of St Mary's, York, 1927; succeeded R. L. *Poole as reader in diplomatic, Oxford; tutorial fellow of Balliol, 1928; published *Introduction to the Use of Public Records* (1934); edited the St Alban's Chronicle, 1406–20 (1937); appointed professor of history, Edinburgh, 1937; FBA, 1939; Ford's lecturer, Oxford, 1940; succeeded A. F. *Pollard as director of the Institute of Historical Research, 1944; regius professor, Oxford, 1948–57; made detailed study of Domesday Book and published *Domesday Book: its Place in Administrative History* (1974); received many honorary degrees; hon. fellow, Balliol, 1957 and Oriel College, Oxford, 1958.

GALDRIC (GUALDRIC or **WALDRIC)** (d. 1112), bishop of Laon; chancellor of Henry I;

captured Duke *Robert of Normandy at Tenchebrai, 1106; bishop of Laon, 1106; expelled from his diocese after the murder by his brother of Gerard, castellan of Laon, but restored by Louis VI, 1109; having attempted to abolish the 'commune' granted in his absence, was murdered in the cellars of his cathedral.

GALE, Dunstan (*fl.* 1596), poet; author of *Pyramus and Thisbe* (1597).

GALE, Frederick (1823–1904), cricketer and writer on cricket under the pseudonym of 'Old Buffer'; works include *Public School Matches and those we meet there* (1853) and *The Game of Cricket* (1887); brother-in-law of Walter *Severn and a friend of *Ruskin.

GALE, George (1797?–1850), aeronaut; played Mazeppa in New York, 1831; joined a tribe of Indians, with six of whom he was exhibited at the Victoria Theatre, London; made his first ascent from Peckham, 1848; perished at the 114th ascent made in the Royal Cremorne, near Bordeaux.

GALE, Sir Humfrey Myddelton (1890–1971), lieutenant-general; educated at St Paul's School and studied at the Architectural School, Westminster, 1908–10; served, as Territorial, with the Artist's Rifles; accepted for Royal Military College, Sandhurst, 1910; gazetted in Army Service Corps, 1911; served in France during 1914–18 war; MC; instructor at Staff College, Camberley, 1934; staff colonel, War Office, 1937; brigadier, DAQMG III Corps in France, 1940; responsible for administrative arrangements for withdrawal of 70,000 men to Dunkirk; CBE; in charge of administration for all home forces, 1941; chief administrative officer to General Eisenhower for north-west Africa campaign, 1942; CB; CVO, 1943; US Legion of Merit; deputy chief of staff (administration) for invasion of Sicily and Italy; KBE, 1943; advised Eisenhower on all administrative problems concerned with invasion of Normandy, 1944; US Distinguished Service Medal, 1945; European director of Unrra, 1945–7; chairman, Basildon New Town Development Corporation, 1954–64; colonel commandant, RASC, 1944–54, and Army Catering Corps 1946–58; received awards from France, Panama, and Morocco.

GALE, John (1680–1721), General Baptist minister; MA and Ph.D., Leiden, 1699; chairman of *Whiston's 'society for promoting primitive christianity', 1715–16; took liberal side at Salters' Hall dispute, 1719; introduced by Shute to Whig bishops; published *Reflections on Mr. Wall's History of Infant Baptism* (1711).

GALE, Miles (1647–1721), antiquary; MA, Trinity College, Cambridge, 1670; rector of

Keighley, 1680–1721; published *Memoirs of the Family of Gale* (1703) and *Description of the Parish of Keighley*.

GALE, Sir **Richard Nelson** (1896–1982), general; educated at Merchant Taylors' School, Aldenham, and the Royal Military College, Sandhurst; gazetted to Worcestershire Regiment, 1915; transferred to Machine Gun Corps; took part in major battles in France and Flanders; MC, 1918; served in India, 1919–36; attended Staff College, Quetta, 1930–2; captain in Duke of Cornwall's Light Infantry, 1930; major in Royal Inniskilling Fusiliers, 1938; general staff officer in War Office, 1938–40; given command of 5th Leicesters, 1940; promoted to command, 1st Parachute brigade, 1941; director of airborne forces, War Office, 1942; in command of 6th Airborne division, 1943; responsible for airborne success in Normandy landings, against German Ardennes offensive, and in Rhine crossings, 1944–5; commanded 1st division in Palestine, 1946–7, and British troops in Egypt, 1948–9; director-general of military training, 1949–52; general, 1952; commander-in-chief, British Army of the Rhine and NATO Northern Army Group, 1952–6; deputy to supreme Allied commander in Europe, 1958–60; CB, 1945; KCB, 1953; GCB, 1954; KBE, 1950; DSO, 1944; commander, Legion of Merit (US); Croix de Guerre (with palm); ADC (general) to the Queen, 1954–7; colonel, the Worcestershire Regiment, 1950–61; colonel-commandant, Parachute Regiment, 1956–67; published autobiography *Call to Arms* (1968).

GALE, Roger (1672–1744), antiquary; eldest son of Thomas *Gale (1635?–1702); educated at St Paul's School and Trinity College, Cambridge; fellow, 1697; MA, 1698; MP, Northallerton, 1705–13; commissioner of excise, 1715–35; friend of *Stukeley, *Willis, and *Hearne; first vice-president of Society of Antiquaries; FRS, 1717, later treasurer; left manuscripts to Trinity College and coins to the University Library; his topographical papers collected in *Bibliotheca Topographica Britannica* (1781).

GALE, Samuel (1682–1754), antiquary; brother of Roger *Gale; educated at St Paul's School; first treasurer of revived Society of Antiquaries, 1718; travelled about in England incognito with Dr *Ducarel; published (1715) *History of Winchester Cathedral*, begun by Henry, earl of *Clarendon.

GALE, Theophilus (1628–1678), Nonconformist tutor; fellow of Magdalen College, Oxford, 1650–60; MA, 1652; tutor to Thomas (afterwards Marquis) *Wharton and his brother,

1662–5; tutor and Independent minister at Newington Green; left his library to Harvard College; published *The Court of the Gentiles* (1669–77), *A True Idea of Jansenisme* (1669), and other theological works.

GALE, Thomas (1507–1587), surgeon; served with the army of Henry VIII in France, 1544, and with that of Philip II at St Quentin, 1557; master of the Barber-Surgeons' Company, 1561; published a volume on surgery (1563), containing the prescription for his styptic powder.

GALE, Thomas (1635?–1702), dean of York; educated at Westminster and Trinity College, Cambridge; MA, 1662; fellow, 1669; Cambridge professor of Greek, 1672; high master of St Paul's, 1672–97; active member of the Royal Society from 1677; dean of York, 1697–1702; edited *Opuscula Mythologica, ethica et physica* (1671), *Historiae Poeticae Scriptores Antiqui* (1675), *Rhetores Selecti* (1676), vol. ii of *Historiae Anglicanae Scriptores* (1687), *Historiae Britannicae, Saxonicae, Anglo-Danicae Scriptores* (1691), and *Antonini Iter Britanniarum* (1709).

GALENSIS, John (*fl.* 1215), Franciscan. See WALLENSIS.

GALEON, William (d. 1507), Augustinian; provincial in England; various theological works ascribed to him.

GALEYS, Sir **Henry le** (d. 1302?), mayor of London. See WALEYS.

GALFRIDUS. See GEOFFREY OF MONMOUTH.

GALGACUS (or **CALGACUS)** (*fl. c.*84), Caledonian chieftain; commander of the tribes defeated at Grampius by Agricola.

GALIGNANI, John Anthony (1796–1873), publisher in Paris; born in London; issued, with his brother William *Galignani till 1852, in Paris, reprints of English books; carried on *The Messenger* founded by his father, 1815; erected at Neuilly a hospital (now orphanage) for indigent British.

GALIGNANI, William (1798–1882), publisher in Paris; brother of John Anthony *Galignani, in all whose undertakings he took part.

GALL, Saint (550?–645?), originally named Cellach or Caillech, abbot and apostle of the Suevi and Alemanni; reputed son of a noble Irishman and a queen of Hungary; educated by St *Columban at Bangor; followed St Columban to Gaul, *c.* 585, and at Arbon and Bregenz preached to the people in their own tongue; built cell on the Steinach river, which became the nucleus of the monastery of St. Gall; died at Arbon; commemorated 16 Oct. and 20 Feb.

GALL, Richard (1776–1801), Scottish poet; friend of *Burns and *Campbell; his *Poems and Songs* published (1819).

GALLACHER, William (1881–1965), working-class agitator and politician; left school at 12 and worked as grocer's delivery boy; apprenticed as brass-finisher, 1895; worked as ship's steward, 1909–10; joined Social Democratic Federation, 1906; chairman, Clyde Workers' Committee; sentenced to imprisonment for sedition, 1916, and for rioting, 1919; supported Russian Revolution and Soviet Union, 1917; published (with J. R. Campbell) *Direct Action* (1919); after personal discussion with Lenin, accepted view that workers should take part in parliamentary politics; helped to found British Communist party, 1920–1; served further periods of imprisonment for sedition, 1921 and 1925; Communist MP, West Fife, 1935–50; publicly opposed the Munich Agreement, 1938; chairman, Communist party 1943–56; president, 1956–63; publications include *The Chosen Few: a Sketch of Men and Events in Parliament* (1940), *The Case for Communism* (1949), and *The Tyrants' Might is Passing* (1954).

GALLAGHER, James (d. 1751), Roman Catholic bishop of Raphoe, 1725, and Kildare, 1737; published *Irish Sermons, in an easy and familiar style* (1735).

GALLAN, Saint (*fl.* 500). See GRELLAN.

GALLENGA, Antonio Carlo Napoleone (1810–1895), author and journalist; born and educated at Parma; took part in political agitation in Italy, 1830, and was compelled to live in exile, assuming name of Luigi Mariotti; successful lecturer, teacher, and writer for magazines in New York, 1836; came to England, 1839; teacher and translator; professor of modern languages at King's College, Windsor, Nova Scotia, *c.*1841–3; returned to England, 1843; naturalized, 1846; professor of Italian language and literature, University College, London, 1848–59; chargé d'affaires at Frankfurt, 1848; resided in Italy, 1854–7; deputy in Piedmontese parliament, and correspondent of *Daily News*; *The Times* correspondent in Italy, 1859–64; deputy of Italian chamber, 1859–64; *The Times* war correspondent in United States, 1863, and Denmark, 1864; leader-writer for *The Times*, 1866–73, and correspondent in Spain, 1874 and 1879, and at Constantinople, 1875–7. His publications include *Italy: General views of its History and Literature* (1841, reprinted as *Italy, Past and Present*, 1846) and an Italian grammar (1858).

GALLEN-RIDGEWAY, first Baron (1565?–1631). See RIDGEWAY, Sir THOMAS, earl of Londonderry.

GALLIARD, John Ernest (1687?–1749), musical composer; son of a hairdresser at Zell; said to have been chamber-musician to Prince *George of Denmark; set *Hughes's *Calypso and Telemachus*, 1712; provided music for pantomimes and farces at Covent Garden and Lincoln's Inn Fields, 1717–36; composed six cantatas to *Congreve's, *Prior's, and Hughes's words, sonatas for flute, bassoon, and violin, and a setting of the morning hymns from *Paradise Lost*; translated Tosi's *Opinioni di Cantori Antichi e Moderni* (1742).

GALLINI, Giovanni Andrea Battista (1728–1805), called Sir John; dancing-master; came to England, *c.*1753; director of dances and stage-manager at Haymarket opera-house; had great vogue as a dancing-master; married Lady Elizabeth Peregrine Bertie, eldest daughter of third earl of Abingdon; created knight of the Golden Spur by the pope; built Hanover Square concert-rooms; published treatises on callisthenics.

GALLOWAY, Sir Alexander (1895–1977), lieutenant-general; educated at King William's College, Isle of Man; served with 4th King's Own Scottish Borderers at Gallipoli and in campaigns in Egypt and Palestine and on the Western Front; MC, 1918; entered Staff College, Camberley, 1928; instructor, 1938; commander, Staff College, Haifa, 1940; chief staff officer to Sir H. M. (later Lord) *Wilson in Western Desert, 1940; and to Lt.-Gen. Sir Alan *Cunningham, 1941; risked court martial by withholding Cunningham's order to withdraw from battle in Operation Crusader; appointed director of staff duties under General Sir Alan *Brooke (later Viscount Alanbrooke); CBE and DSO, 1941; with 1st Armoured division, Mediterranean, 1944; commanded 4th Indian division at Casino; served in north-west Europe and Malaya; CB, 1946; high commissioner and commander-in-chief, British forces in Austria, 1947–9; KBE; awarded military honours by Greece, Czechoslovakia, and the Netherlands.

GALLOWAY, Sir Archibald (1780?–1850), major-general; entered Bengal Native Infantry, 1800; colonel of the 58th, 1836; major-general, 1841; KCB, 1848; chairman of the East India Company, 1849; published works, including *Notes on Siege of Delhi* (1804) and *On Sieges of India*.

GALLOWAY, Joseph (1730–1803), lawyer; born in Maryland; as speaker of Pennsylvania supported the popular against the proprietary interest, and was challenged (1764) by John Dickinson; when member of the first Congress proposed and published (1775) plan for union between Great Britain and the colonies; joined British, 1776; gave evidence before parliament, 1778; published pamphlets, including attacks on the Howes for their conduct of the war.

GALLOWAY, Patrick (1551?–1626?), Scottish divine; preached against the first duke of *Lennox at Perth, and was suspected of being privy to the raid of *Ruthven, 1582; fled to England, 1584; minister of the royal household of Scotland and moderator of the general assembly, 1590; rebuked James VI for recalling *Arran, 1592, and refused to take the 'band' of 1596; again moderator, 1602; present at Hampton Court Conference, 1604; minister of St Giles's, Edinburgh, 1607; member of the High Commission court; signed protestation for liberties of the kirk, 1617, but supported five articles of Perth; edited works by James VI.

GALLOWAY, Thomas (1796–1851), mathematician; MA, Edinburgh; teacher of mathematics at Sandhurst, 1823; registrar of Amicable Life Assurance Company, 1833; FRS and FRAS, 1829; contributed to seventh edition of *Encyclopaedia Britannica* and *Edinburgh Review*.

GALLOWAY, Sir **William** (1840–1927), mining engineer; researched into causes of mine explosions, which he came to believe largely depended on floating coal-dust; this view, at first considered unorthodox, was finally confirmed by other investigators; professor of mining, University College, Cardiff, 1891–1902; knighted, 1924.

GALLWEY, Peter (1820–1906), Jesuit preacher and writer; studied at Stonyhurst; entered Society of Jesus, 1836; in charge of Farm Street Church, London, 1857–69 and 1877–1906; provincial of Jesuits in England, 1873–6; published *Lectures on Ritualism* (2 vols., 1879), pamphlets, and sermons.

GALLY, Henry (1696–1769), divine and scholar; MA, Corpus Christi College, Cambridge, 1721; DD, 1728; chaplain to Lord King, 1725; prebendary of Gloucester, 1728, of Norwich, 1731; rector of St Giles-in-the-Fields, 1732; chaplain to George II, 1735; edited Theophrastus, with an essay on 'Characteristic Writings', 1725; published pamphlets on tenure of corporate estates (1731) and on clandestine marriages (1750) and essays against pronouncing Greek according to accent.

GALMOY, third Viscount (1652–1740). See BUTLER, PIERCE.

GALPINE, John (d. 1806), author of *Synoptical Compend of the British Flora* (1806).

GALSWORTHY, John (1867–1933), playwright and novelist; educated at Harrow and New College, Oxford; called to bar (Lincoln's Inn), 1890; published early novels under pseudonym John Sinjohn; *The Man of Property* (1906) began the *Forsyte Saga* sequence (published collectively, 1922) in which he wrote with an exact and not unsympathetic observation of Victorian upper-class commercial society, continuing the story of its supersession by a more easy-going generation in the trilogy *A Modern Comedy* (1929); his remarkably successful plays (including *The Silver Box*, 1906, *Justice*, 1910, and *The Skin Game*, 1920) state a theme with great simplicity of construction and dialogue; OM, 1929; Nobel Prize, 1932.

GALT, Sir **Alexander Tilloch** (1817–1893), finance minister of Canada; son of John *Galt; settled in Sherbrooke, Lower Canada, 1835; commissioner in British-American Land Company, 1844; active promoter of railways; Liberal MP for county of Sherbrooke, 1849 and 1853–72; inspector-general, 1858–62 and 1864–5; delegate to Charlottetown and Quebec conferences, 1864; first minister of finance on inauguration of Dominion of Canada, 1867–72; nominee of Canada on Halifax Commission, 1877; high commissioner for the dominion in England, 1880–3; GCMG, 1878; hon. LL D, Edinburgh, 1878; published pamphlets on political questions.

GALT, John (1779–1839), novelist; employed in Greenock Custom-House and in a mercantile house; came to London, *c.*1803, and published a poem on the *Battle of Largs*; entered at Lincoln's Inn; while on a commercial mission to the continent (1809) travelled with *Byron from Gibraltar to Malta, visited Constantinople and Greece; published (1812) an account of his travels and a life of *Wolsey; edited the *New British Theatre*, 1814–15, containing his play *The Witness*; compiled *Life . . . and Studies of Benjamin West* (1816–20); published *The Majolo* (1816); compiled *Voyages* under pseudonym S. Prior, and *Tour of Asia* and *The Wandering Jew* as Revd T. Clark; produced novels, *The Ayrshire Legatees* (1820), *Annals of the Parish* (1821), *Sir Andrew Wylie* (1822), and *The Entail* (1824); visited Canada, 1824 and 1826, as secretary to a company formed for the purchase of crown land; founded town of Guelph; imprisoned for debt after his return, 1829; published *Lawrie Todd* and *Life of Byron* (1830), and *Lives of the Players*; met *Carlyle; issued his *Autobiography* (1833) and *Literary Life* (1834), for which William IV sent him £200; paralysed, 1834, but continued literary work.

GALTON, Sir **Douglas Strutt** (1822–1899), man of science and captain, Royal Engineers; educated at Rugby and Royal Military Academy,

Woolwich; lieutenant, Royal Engineers, 1843; first captain, 1855; served in Mediterranean; joined Ordnance Survey, 1846; secretary to Railway Commission, 1847, and to Royal Commission on Application of Iron to Railway Structures; secretary to railway department of Board of Trade, 1854; chairman of committee to investigate question of electric submarine telegraph cables, 1859–61; assistant permanent under-secretary for war, 1862–9; CB, 1865; director of public works and buildings, 1869–75; president of British Association, 1895; president of senate of University College, London; KCB, 1887; hon. MICE, 1894; hon. DCL, Oxford, 1875; FRS, 1859; published works on sanitary and educational questions.

GALTON, Sir Francis (1822–1911), founder of the science of 'eugenics'; born at Birmingham; entered Trinity College, Cambridge, 1840; travelled in Syria and Egypt, 1844; published account of exploration, into interior of Damaraland, in *Tropical South Africa*, 1853; FRS, 1856; general secretary of British Association, 1863–7; in *Meteorographica* (1863) he pointed out importance of 'anticyclones', a word coined by himself; began researches into laws of heredity, 1865; initiated anthropometric laboratory at Health Exhibition, 1884–5, collecting impressions of fingers; proved permanence of fingerprints; published *Finger Prints* (1893) and *Finger Print Directory* (1895); influenced by his cousin Charles *Darwin's *Origin of Species* he investigated the heritability of genius; published his results in *Hereditary Genius* (1869), *English Men of Science* (1874), *Human Faculty* (1883), *Natural Inheritance* (1889), and *Noteworthy Families* (1906); founded eugenics laboratory, 1904, and research fellowship and scholarship, 1907, at University College, London; initiated quarterly journal, *Biometrika*, 1901; knighted, 1909; by will left £45,000 for foundation of chair of eugenics in London University; wrote *Memories of My Life* (1908).

GALTON, Mary Anne (1778–1856), author. See SCHIMMELPENNINCK.

GALWAY, earl of (1648–1720). See MASSUE DE RUVIGNY, HENRI DE.

GAM, David (d. 1415), Welsh warrior; real name Davydd ab Llewelyn; rewarded for fidelity to Henry IV during revolt of *Glendower by confiscated lands in South Wales, 1401; captured by Glendower; followed Henry V to France and fell at Agincourt.

GAMBIER, Sir Edward John (1794–1879), chief justice of Madras; nephew of James, Baron *Gambier; fellow of Trinity College, Cambridge; MA, 1820; barrister, Lincoln's Inn, 1822; municipal corporation commissioner, 1833; recorder of Prince of Wales Island, 1834; chief justice at Madras, 1842–9; published *Treatise on Parochial Settlement* (1828).

GAMBIER, James (1723–1789), vice-admiral; uncle of James, Baron *Gambier; present at capture of Louisbourg, 1758, Guadaloupe, 1759, and the Battle of Quiberon Bay, 1759; commander-in-chief on North American Station, 1770–3; second-in-command under Lord *Howe at New York; vice-admiral, 1780; commander at Jamaica, 1783–4.

GAMBIER, James, first Baron Gambier (1756–1833), admiral of the fleet; captured by D'Estaing in the *Thunder* bomb; took part in relief of Jersey, 1779, and capture of Charlestown, 1780; in the *Defence* first to break enemy's line in *Howe's victory of 1 June 1794; a lord of the Admiralty, 1795–1801 and 1804–6; rear-admiral and vice-admiral, 1799; governor of Newfoundland, 1802–4; admiral, 1805; led the fleet at bombardment of Copenhagen, the Danish fleet being surrendered, 1807; created Baron Gambier; commanded Channel Fleet, 1808–11; blockaded French fleet in Basque roads and destroyed it by fireships; a commissioner for treaty with United States, 1814; GCB, 1815; admiral of the fleet, 1830.

GAMBLE, John (d. 1687), musician in Chapel Royal and composer; published *Ayres and Dialogues to be sung to the theorbo, lute, or base violl* (1656) and *Ayres and Dialogues, for one, two, and three voyces* (1659).

GAMBLE, John (d. 1811), writer on telegraphy; fellow of Pembroke College, Cambridge; MA, 1787; chaplain to the duke of *York, and chaplain-general of the forces; published *Observations on Telegraphic Experiments* (1795) and *Essay on the different Modes of Communication by Signals* (1797).

GAMBOLD, John (1711–1771), bishop of the Unitas Fratrum; while at Christ Church, Oxford, was a member of the *Wesleys' 'Holy Club'; vicar of Stanton-Harcourt, 1735–42; formed Anglican branch of Moravians, 1749, and was consecrated a bishop, 1753; prominent at synod of Marienborn, 1764; founded community at Cootehill, Co. Cavan, 1765; translated Count Zinzendorf's *Maxims* into English in 1751; published also *Collection of Hymns* (1754) and posthumous *Poems* (1816); edited *Bacon (1765).

GAME, Sir Philip Woolcott (1876–1961), air vice-marshal, governor of New South Wales, and commissioner of the Metropolitan Police; educated at Charterhouse and Royal Military Academy, Woolwich; joined Royal Artillery, 1895; served in South Africa, 1901–2; attended Staff

College, 1910; served in France, 1914–16; DSO, 1915; served on Royal Flying Corps staff of Brigadier-General (later Viscount) *Trenchard, 1916; joined Royal Air Force, 1918; director of training and organization (air commodore), 1919; air vice-marshal, 1922; air member for personnel, Air Ministry, 1923–9; governor, New South Wales, 1930–5, dimissed Labour party premier, J. T. Lang, a controversial decision; succeeded Lord Trenchard as commissioner, Metropolitan Police, 1935–45; CB, 1919; KCB, 1924; GBE, 1929; KCMG, 1935; GCVO, 1937; GCB, 1945.

GAMELINE (d. 1271), lord-chancellor of Scotland, 1250–63; chaplain of Innocent IV, 1254; bishop of St Andrews, 1255; banished from Scotland for prohibiting Alexander III from seizing church property; died in Scotland.

GAMGEE, Arthur (1841–1909), physiologist; born at Florence; brother of Joseph *Gamgee (1828–86); MD, Edinburgh University, 1862; lecturer on physiology at Royal College of Surgeons, Edinburgh, 1863–9; fellow, 1872; studied under Kühne at Heidelberg and Ludwig at Leipzig, 1871; FRS, 1872; FRCP, London, 1896; first Brackenbury professor of physiology in Owens College, Manchester, 1873–85; practised in Switzerland from 1889; visited America, 1902 and 1903; extended knowledge of physical and chemical properties of haemoglobin; made elaborate research on diurnal variations of temperature of human body; works include *Textbook of Physiological Chemistry* (2 vols., 1880–93); died in Paris.

GAMGEE, Joseph Sampson (1828–1886), surgeon; born and educated in Italy; Liston prizeman, University College, 1853; surgeon to British-Italian legion, 1855, to Queen's Hospital, Birmingham, 1857–81; published *On the Advantages of the Starched Apparatus in the Treatment of Fractures* (1853), *On the Treatment of Wounds and Fractures* (1883), *On Absorbent and Antiseptic Surgical Dressings* (1880), and other works.

GAMMAGE, Robert George (1815–1888), Chartist; deputy from Northampton to National Convention of 1838; opposed Feargus *O'Connor; published *History of the Chartist Movement* (1854).

GAMMON, James (*fl.* 1660–1670), engraver of portraits valued for their rarity.

GAMON (or GAMMON), Hannibal (*fl.* 1642), Puritan divine; MA, Broadgates Hall (Pembroke College), Oxford, 1607; rector of Mawgan-in-Pyder, Cornwall, 1619, which county he represented in the Westminster assembly, 1642.

GANDELL, Robert (1818–1887), professor of Arabic at Oxford; BA, The Queen's College, Oxford, 1843; Michel fellow of The Queen's College, 1845–50; professor of Arabic, 1861; canon of Wells, 1880; edited *Lightfoot's *Horae Hebraicae* (1859) and contributed to *Speaker's Commentary*.

GANDHI, Indira Priyadarshani (1917–1984), prime minister of India; only child of Jawaharlal *Nehru; educated in schools at Geneva, Allahabad, Poona, Bombay, and at Badminton School, near Bristol, and Somerville College, Oxford; married Feroze Gandhi, 1942; acted as official hostess to her father when he was prime minister from 1947 to 1964; member of Congress Working Committee, 1955; president, Congress Party, 1959; prime minister, 1965–77; 1977 defeat largely caused by influence and activity of her younger son Sanjay; re-elected, 1980; Sanjay killed in air crash, 1980; faced with Sikh militancy, Indira Gandhi ordered Indian army to enter Golden Temple in Amritsar, and caused widespread outrage in Sikh community, 1984; assassinated by two Sikh members of her bodyguard; succeeded by her elder son Rajiv; recipient of many honorary doctorates and international awards, including Lenin Prize awarded posthumously, 1985.

GANDHI, Mohandas Karamchand, the mahatma (1869–1948), Indian political leader and social reformer; son of chief minister in Porbandar; of Vaisya sub-caste of merchants; called to bar (Inner Temple), 1891; studied many religious works; influenced especially by the *Bhagavad Gita* and New Testament; experimented in asceticism and in 1906 took vow of complete sexual abstinence; in South Africa (1893–1914) a prosperous lawyer and leader of Indian opposition to racial discrimination; evolved technique of passive resistance or 'Satyagraha' (truthforce); secured compromise agreement with Smuts, 1914; raised Indian ambulance units in South African War, Zulu expedition, and in 1914; returned to India, 1915; conducted recruiting campaign, 1918; established *ashram* at Sabarmati; moved to Wardha, near Nagpur, 1933; in opposition to Rowlatt Act, 1919, introduced the *hartal* (strike with prayer and fasting); extended activities of Indian National Congress to the villages; secured its acceptance of non-cooperation policy, 1920; discontinued civil disobedience for fear of violence, 1922; imprisoned, 1922–4; undertook first major fast, for Hindu–Moslem unity, 1924; withdrawing from politics travelled country preaching hand-spinning, Hindu–Moslem unity, and abolition of untouchability; adopted loincloth, shawl, and sandals and became widely known as the mahatma and regarded as a saint; marched to sea to break salt law and imprisoned, 1930; released for talks with Lord Irwin, later the earl of *Halifax, 1931; attended second Round Table Conference in London, 1931; attracted much publicity but proved unsuccessful in conference; threatened further civil disobedience and imprisoned, 1932; fasted to prevent separate electorates for depressed classes and obtained alternative suggestions, 1932; released at beginning of 21-day self-purification fast, 1933; resigned from Congress (1934), but remained its mentor; persuaded it to accept office, 1937; resumed leadership, 1940–1; opposed force even in defence of India; imprisoned after 'Quit India' motion, 1942–4; failed to reach agreement on Hindu–Moslem problems with M. A. *Jinnah; totally opposed to but unable to prevent partition (1947); fasted in Calcutta (1947) and Delhi (1948) to obtain communal harmony; shot dead by militant Hindu.

GANDOLPHY, Peter (1779–1821), Jesuit; educated at Liège and Stonyhurst; celebrated as a preacher at the Spanish Chapel, Manchester Square; suspended and censured by Bishop Poynter for his *Liturgy* (1812) and *Defence of the Ancient Faith* (1813–15).

GANDON, James (1743–1823), architect; articled to Sir William *Chambers; with J. Woolfe published continuation of *Campbell's *Vitruvius Britannicus* (1767–71); won first Gold Medal for architecture at Royal Academy, 1768, and exhibited drawings, 1774–80; designed at Dublin many public works, including portico and screen wall to Parliament House, 1785, Four Courts, 1786, and King's Inns, 1795–9; original member of Royal Irish Academy.

GANDY, Henry (1649–1734), nonjuring bishop; educated at Merchant Taylors' School and Oriel College, Oxford; MA, 1674; fellow, 1670; proctor, 1683; deprived of fellowship for refusing oath of allegiance, 1690; consecrated bishop, 1716, by Jeremy *Collier, Nathaniel *Spinckes, and Samuel Hawes (d. 1722); published theological works.

GANDY, James (1619–1689), portrait painter; pupil of *Van Dyck, many of whose portraits he copied for the duke of *Ormonde.

GANDY, John Peter (1787–1850), architect. See DEERING.

GANDY, Joseph Michael (1771–1843), architect; pupil of *Wyatt; received the Pope's Medal for architecture, 1795; exhibited at the Academy, 1789–1838; ARA, 1803; executed many drawings for Sir John *Soane; designed Phoenix and Pelican Insurance Offices, Charing Cross; contributed illustrations to *Britton's *Architectural Antiquities*.

GANDY, Michael (1778–1862), architect; brother of Joseph Michael *Gandy; employed in Indian Naval Service and by Sir Jeffrey *Wyatville; exhibited at Academy *Burning of Onrust and Kupers Island, Batavia*, 1812.

GANDY, William (d. 1729), portrait painter; son of James *Gandy. His pictures, most of which are to be found in the west of England, were much admired by *Reynolds and *Northcote.

GANN, Thomas William Francis (1867–1938), archaeologist; educated at King's School, Canterbury, and Middlesex Hospital; medical officer, British Honduras, 1894–1923; excavated remains of ancient Maya civilization notably at Lubaantun (1904), Coba and Ichpaatun (1926), Tzibanche (1927), and Noh Mul (1936, 1938); lecturer in Central American archaeology, Liverpool, 1919–38.

GARBET, Samuel (d. 1751?), author of *History of Wem* (published 1818), second master at Wem School, 1712–42; MA, Christ Church, Oxford, 1707; translated Phaedrus, Books i and ii, 1715.

GARBETT, Cyril Forster (1875–1955), archbishop of York; son of a clergyman and nephew of *Edward and James *Garbett; educated at Farnham and Portsmouth grammar schools; Gomm scholar, Keble College, Oxford; president of Union, 1898; at Cuddesdon acquired fidelity to a strict rule of life; deacon, 1899; priest, 1901; curate (1899–1909) and vicar (1909–19), St Mary's, Portsea; as bishop of Southwark, 1919–32, was an indefatigable visitor, became expert on problems of bad housing and malnutrition, and provided diocese with twenty-five new churches; chairman, BBC Religious Advisory Committee, 1923–45; until outbreak of war had more relaxed life as bishop of Winchester, 1932–42; archbishop of York, 1942–55; assiduously attended House of Lords; used broadcasting and the press to interpret the Church to the nation; publications include *The Claims of the Church of England* (1947), *Church and State in England* (1950), and *In an Age of Revolution* (1952); in 1943–55 visited Russia, North America, Malaya, Australia, many European countries, and the Holy Land; a stern disciplinarian and inhibited by shyness, he was formidable to his clergy but mellowed in later life; not an original thinker but very widely read and a talented synthesis whose purpose was to build a bridge between the secular and sacred views of life; much trusted by the laity whose problems he understood and who respected his common sense and sanctity; PC, 1942.

GARBETT, Edward (1817–1887), divine; MA, Brasenose College, Oxford, 1847; editor of the *Record* 1854–67; incumbent of Christ Church, Surbiton, 1863, of Barcombe, 1877; Bampton lecturer, 1867; published Boyle Lectures (1860 and 1863), Bampton Lectures (1867), and other works.

GARBETT, James (1802–1879), professor of poetry at Oxford; brother of Edward *Garbett; fellow of The Queen's College, Oxford, 1824–5, of Brasenose, 1825–36; MA, 1825; incumbent of Clayton-cum-Keymer, 1835–79; Bampton lecturer, 1842; professor of poetry, 1842–52; archdeacon of Chichester, 1851; published anti-Tractarian Bampton lectures and *De Rei Poeticae Idea* (1843).

GARBRAND, Herks (*fl.* 1556), Dutch Protestant refugee; bookseller, and also, after 1546, wine-seller at Oxford.

GARBRAND (or HERKS), John (1542–1589), divine; son of Herks *Garbrand; educated at Winchester and New College, Oxford; fellow, 1562; MA, 1567; MA, Cambridge, 1568; DD, Oxford, 1582; prebendary of Salisbury, 1565, and of Wells; rector of North Crawley and Farthingstone; edited three works of his patron, Bishop *Jewel.

GARBRAND, John (*fl.* 1695), writer of pamphlets 'to clear the duke of York from being a papist'; son of Tobias *Garbrand (d. 1689); BA, New Inn Hall, Oxford, 1667; barrister, Inner Temple.

GARBRAND, Tobias (1579–1638), probably grandfather of John *Garbrand (*fl.* 1695); vice-president of Magdalen College, Oxford, 1618, and vicar of Finden, Sussex, 1618–38.

GARBRAND, Tobias (d. 1689), principal of Gloucester Hall, Oxford, 1648–60; MD, Oxford.

GARCIA, Manuel Patricio Rodriguez (1805–1906), singer and teacher of singing; born at Zafra, Spain; studied harmony in Paris; as professor at Paris Conservatoire he taught Jenny *Lind; published famous *Traité complet de l'art du chant* (1847); professor of singing at Royal Academy of Music, London, 1848–95; invented laryngoscope (1854), which became universally used in medicine and surgery; made CVO on hundredth birthday, 1905.

GARDELLE, Theodore (1721–1761), miniature painter and murderer; born at Geneva; executed for the murder of Anne King; his portrait by Hogarth engraved in *Ireland's *Graphic Illustrations*.

GARDEN, Alexander, the elder (1730–1791), botanist; born at Biroe, Aberdeenshire; MD,

Edinburgh; pupil of *Alston; corresponded with Peter *Collinson, Gronovius, and Linnaeus, in whose *Systema Naturae* his name is appended to new species of fish and reptiles; settled in England, 1783, and became vice-president of the Royal Society; introduced many plants; the Cape Jessamine named *Gardenia* after him.

GARDEN, Alexander, the younger (1757–1829), author; son of Alexander *Garden the elder; published *Anecdotes of the Revolutionary War* (1822).

GARDEN, Francis, Lord Gardenstone (1721–1793), Scottish judge; educated at Edinburgh University; admitted advocate, 1744; sheriff-depute of Kincardineshire, 1748; joint solicitor-general, 1760; employed in the Douglas cause; lord of session, 1764–93; lord of justiciary, 1776–87; founded Lawrence Kirk, Kincardineshire; published notes of travel.

GARDEN, Francis (1810–1884), theologian; MA, Trinity College, Cambridge, 1836; intimate of Richard Chenevix *Trench, Frederick Denison *Maurice, and John *Sterling; subdean of the Chapel Royal, 1859–84; editor of *The Christian Remembrancer*, 1841; published *Dictionary of English Philosophical Terms* (1878) and other works.

GARDEN, George (1649–1733), Scottish divine; professor at King's College, Aberdeen, 1673; minister of Old Machar, Aberdeen, 1679, of St Nicholas, 1683; 'laid aside', 1692, as a nonjuror; deposed, 1701, in connection with his *Apology for Madame Bourignon*, but continued to officiate; imprisoned after rebellion of 1715; edited the works of John *Forbes (1593–1648), and wrote pamphlets on behalf of the Scots Episcopal clergy.

GARDEN, James (1647–1726), professor of divinity, Aberdeen; brother of George *Garden; deprived of professorship, 1696, for refusing to sign Westminster Confession; published *Comparative Theology*.

GARDENSTONE, Lord (1721–1793). See GARDEN, FRANCIS.

GARDINER. See also GARDNER.

GARDINER, Sir Alan Henderson (1879–1963), Egyptologist and linguist; brother of H. B. *Gardiner, the composer; educated at Charterhouse, the Sorbonne, and The Queen's College, Oxford; first class, Hebrew and Arabic, 1901; co-operated in preparation of Egyptian dictionary in Berlin, 1902–12; reader in Egyptology, Manchester, 1912–14; publications include *The Admonitions of an Egyptian Sage* (1909), *Notes on the Story of Sinuhe* (1916), *Egyptian Letters to the Dead* (1928), *Late-Egyptian Stories* (1932), *Ancient*

Egyptian Onomastica (3 vols., 1947), and *Egyptian Grammar* (1927); edited the *Journal of Egyptian Archaeology*, 1916–21, 1934, and 1941–6; discovered pictographic ancestor of Phoenician alphabet, 1915; also published *The Theory of Speech and Language* (1932), *The Theory of Proper Names* (1940), and *Egypt of the Pharaohs* (1961); D.Litt., Oxford, 1910; FBA, 1929; honorary degrees, Durham and Cambridge; hon. fellow, The Queen's College, Oxford, 1935; knighted, 1948.

GARDINER, Alfred George (1865–1946), author and journalist; joined *Northern Daily Telegraph*, 1886; editor, *Daily News*, 1902–19; supporter of Liberal political and social reforms and of Asquith's conduct of war; in sharp disagreement with Lloyd George and severe critic of Versailles Treaty; publications include life of Sir William *Harcourt (2 vols., 1923) and volumes of portrait sketches.

GARDINER, Allen Francis (1794–1851), missionary to Patagonia; served in navy; lieutenant, 1844; tried to establish Christian churches in Zululand, 1834–8; laboured among Chile Indians, 1838–43; attempted to establish mission in Patagonia, 1844–5; visited Bolivia, 1845–6; surveyed Tierra del Fuego, 1848; died of starvation there; published *Outlines of a Plan for Exploring the Interior of Australia* (1833) and books describing his missionary travels.

GARDINER, Arthur (1716?–1758), captain in the navy; served with *Byng in the Mediterranean and (1756) gave unwilling testimony against him at his trial; captured the *Foudroyant* off the Spanish coast, but fell in the action.

GARDINER, Bernard (1668–1726), warden of All Souls College, Oxford; ejected from demyship of Magdalen by James II; BA, 1688; DCL, 1698; fellow of All Souls, 1689; warden, 1702–26; vice-chancellor, 1712–15; checked Jacobitism and suppressed the *terrae filius* (elected undergraduate).

GARDINER, George (1535?–1589), dean of Norwich; BA, Christ's College, Cambridge, 1554; fellow of Queens' College, Cambridge, 1558–61; MA, 1558; minister of St Andrew's, Norwich, 1562; prebendary of Norwich, 1565; one of those who broke down the cathedral organ, 1570; rector of St Martin Outwich, London, 1571; dean of Norwich, 1573–89.

GARDINER, Henry Balfour (1877–1950), composer; educated at Charterhouse and New College, Oxford; studied under Ivan Knorr at Frankfurt; compositions include *Shepherd Fennel's Dance* and (for chorus and orchestra) *News from Whydah* and *April* (1912) and *Philomena* (1923); finding post-war musical atmosphere uncongenial ceased composition, 1924; generous benefactor of contemporary musicians.

GARDINER, James, the elder (1637–1705), bishop of Lincoln; MA, Emmanuel College, Cambridge, 1656; DD, 1669; chaplain to *Monmouth and incumbent of Epworth, 1660; bishop of Lincoln, 1695–1705; assisted Simon *Patrick to decipher Peterborough charters and muniments.

GARDINER, James, the younger (d. 1732), sub-dean of Lincoln; son of James *Gardiner the elder; BA, Emmanuel College, Cambridge, 1699; fellow of Jesus College, 1700; master of St John's Hospital, Peterborough, 1707; published sermons.

GARDINER, James (1688–1745), colonel of dragoons; wounded at Blenheim, 1704; headed storming party at Battle of Preston; lieutenant-colonel, Inniskilling Dragoons, 1730; colonel in command of Light Dragoons (now 13th Hussars), 1743–5; deserted by most of his men at Prestonpans, and mortally wounded; 'converted', after a dissolute life; commemorated in *Life* by Philip *Doddridge, and song by Sir Gilbert *Elliot (1722–1777).

GARDINER, Marguerite, countess of Blessington (1789–1849). See BLESSINGTON.

GARDINER, Richard (1591–1670), divine; deputy-orator at Oxford before 1620; canon of Christ Church, Oxford, 1629; MA, 1614; DD, 1630; deprived, 1647, reinstated, 1660; chaplain to Charles I, 1630; a brilliant, quaint preacher; published *Specimen Oratorium* (1653).

GARDINER, Richard (1723–1781), author; educated at Eton and St Catharine's Hall, Cambridge; published *History of Pudica . . . with an account of her five Lovers* (1754), in which 'Dick Merryfellow' is himself, and *Account of the Expedition . . . against Martinico, Guadeloupe, and other the Leeward Islands* (1759); commanded the marines in the Leeward Islands.

GARDINER, Sir Robert William (1781–1864), general; entered Royal Artillery, 1797; brevet-lieutenant-colonel, 1814; major-general, 1841; general and colonel-commandant, 1853–4; aide-de-camp to Sir John *Moore in Sicily, 1806–7, and brigade-major at Corunna, 1809; served in the Peninsula and (1809) Walcheren expedition; prominent at Barossa and Badajoz; commanded field-battery at Salamanca, 1812; commanded E troop, Royal Horse Artillery at Vittoria, 1813, and succeeding battles, and at Waterloo; KCB, 1814; governor of Gibraltar, 1848–55; published life of Admiral Sir Graham *Moore and valuable professional papers.

GARDINER, Samuel (*fl.* 1606), chaplain to Archbishop *Abbot and author of *A Booke of Angling or Fishing. Wherein is shewed . . . the agreement betweene the Fishermen . . . of both natures, Temporall and Spirituall* (1606); DD.

GARDINER, Samuel Rawson (1829–1902), historian; BA, Christ Church, Oxford, 1851; married daughter of Edward *Irving, 1856; settled in London to study history of Puritan revolution, supporting himself meanwhile by teaching; lecturer (1872–7) and professor of modern history (1877–85) at King's College, London; published first instalment of his *History of England (1603–42)* in 1863, and last in 1882; collective edition in 10 vols., 1883–4; there followed *The Great Civil War* (3 vols., 1886–91) and *The History of the Commonwealth and Protectorate* (3 vols., 1895–1901); his unfinished *Last Years of the Protectorate* was completed by (Sir) Charles *Firth (2 vols., 1909); his historical work shows scientific arrangement of material, minute accuracy, impartiality, but lacks the picturesque style of *Froude or *Macaulay; wrote also *The Thirty Years War* (1874) and *The Puritan Revolution* (1876) for 'Epochs of English History' series; *Student's History of England* (3 vols., 1890); edited *Constitutional Documents of the Puritan Revolution*, 1889; was editor of *English Historical Review*, 1891–1901; director of Camden Society, 1869–97, he edited 12 of its volumes, and also contributed to publications of Navy Records Society, Scottish History Society, and to this Dictionary; awarded civil list pension, 1882; research fellow of All Souls, Oxford, 1884–92, and of Merton, 1892–1902; received many honorary distinctions at home and abroad and was Ford's lecturer, Oxford, 1896.

GARDINER, Stephen (1483?–1555), bishop of Winchester; educated at Trinity Hall, Cambridge; fellow; doctor of civil law, 1520, of canon law, 1521; Rede lecturer, 1524; tutor to duke of Norfolk's son; master of Trinity Hall, 1525–49, re-elected, 1553; private secretary to *Wolsey; obtained Clement VII's consent to a second commission in the royal divorce question, 1527; attempted to obtain from Cambridge opinions favourable to the divorce, 1530; though taking up a 'middle course', compiled reply to Catherine's counsel at Rome; after Wolsey's fall acted as secretary to Henry VIII till 1534; bishop of Winchester, 1531; ambassador in France, 1531–2; prepared reply of the ordinaries to the House of Commons' address to the king, stoutly defending his order; member of the court which invalidated Queen *Catherine's marriage, 1533; signed renunciation of obedience to Roman jurisdiction, and published oration, *De vera Obedientia*, repudiating it, and maintaining supremacy of secular

princes over the church (1535); chancellor of Cambridge University, 1540–51; opposed *Cromwell and *Cranmer; fell temporarily out of favour; after the fall of Cromwell had supreme political influence, inspiring the Six Articles, 1539; constantly employed in negotiations with the emperor; imprisoned in the Tower during the greater part of the reign of Edward VI on account of his opposition to doctrinal changes, and (1551) deprived of his see; reinstated and made lord chancellor on Mary's accession; procured (1554) re-enactment of 'De Haeretico Comburendo' and took part against *Bradford and *Rogers, but tried to save Cranmer and *Northumberland, and protected Thomas Smith and *Peter Martyr; opposed the Spanish marriage, but advocated great severity towards Elizabeth, whom he caused to be declared illegitimate by act of parliament; published controversial works against Martin *Bucer and Latin letters to John *Cheke on the pronunciation of Greek (1555).

GARDINER, Thomas (*fl.* 1516), monk of Westminster; compiled *The Flowers of England*, a chronicle.

GARDINER, Sir Thomas (1591–1652), recorder of London, 1636; barrister, Inner Temple, 1618; bencher, 1635, treasurer, 1639; MP for Callington in Short Parliament, 1640; unsuccessful Royalist candidate for the City of London; leading counsel to Sir Edward *Herbert, when impeached, 1642; himself impeached soon after for his support of ship money; solicitor-general to the king at Oxford, 1643; commissioner at Uxbridge and Royalist attorney-general, 1645; pardoned by parliament on payment of fine, 1647.

GARDINER, Sir Thomas Robert (1883–1964), civil servant; educated at Lurgan College, County Armagh, Royal High School, Edinburgh, and Edinburgh University; MA; first class, history and economic science, 1905; entered Post Office, 1906; private secretary to the secretary of the Post Office, (Sir) Q. E. C. Murray, 1914–17; controller, London Postal Service, 1926–34; deputy director-general, Post Office, 1934–6; director-general, 1936–9 and 1940–5; permanent secretary, Ministry of Home Security, 1939–40; chairman, Stevenage New Town Development Corporation, 1947–8; chairman, National Dock Labour Board; government director, Anglo-Iranian Oil Co., 1950–3; member of a number of public committees and commissions; KBE, 1936; KCB, 1937; GBE, 1941; GCB, 1954; hon. LL D, Edinburgh, 1949.

GARDINER, William (or William Neville) (1748–1806), diplomat; lieutenant-general; served in America, 1775–6; wounded at Freehold, New Jersey, 1778; lieutenant-colonel, 45th Foot (Sherwood Foresters), 1778; special envoy at Brussels, 1789–92; plenipotentiary at Warsaw, 1792–5; major-general, 1793; lieutenant-general, 1799; MP, Thomastown, in Irish parliament; commander of north inland district of Ireland, 1803–5; commander-in-chief of Nova Scotia, 1805.

GARDINER, William (1770–1853), musical composer; member of the Adelphi Philosophical Society, 1790–2; composed songs and compiled *Sacred Melodies from Haydn, Mozart and Beethoven . . . adapted to the best English Poets* (1812–15) and *Judah* (1821), an oratorio culled from the same masters; edited Berry's version of Bombet's *Life of Haydn* and Brewin's version of Schlichtergroll's *Life of Mozart* (1817); published popular works on music.

GARDINER, William Nelson (1766–1814), engraver and bookseller; employed in London by Edward *Harding and Silvester *Harding, and *Bartolozzi; BA, Corpus Christi College, Cambridge, 1797; the Mustapha of Dibdin's *Bibliomania*; committed suicide.

GARDNER. See also GARDINER.

GARDNER, Mrs (*fl.* 1763–1782), actress; as Miss Cheney played Miss Prue in *Love for Love* at Drury Lane, and Rose in *The Recruiting Officer*, 1763–4; made her reputation in *Foote's pieces at the Haymarket, 1768–74; her comedy, *Advertisement, or a Bold Stroke for a Husband*, played there for her benefit, 1777.

GARDNER, Alan, first Baron Gardner (1742–1809), admiral; present at Quiberon Bay in the *Dorsetshire*; carried to *Howe first news of the French approach, and captured on North American coast large French merchant ship, 1778; commanded the *Sultan* at Grenada, 1779; with *Rodney in the *Duke* in the victory of 1782; commander in Jamaica, 1786–9; lord of the Admiralty, 1790–5; created a baronet for his services in Howe's victory, 1794; interviewed mutineers at Spithead, 1797; admiral of the blue, 1799; MP, Plymouth, 1790–6, and Westminster, 1796–1806; created Baron Gardner in Irish peerage, 1800; peer of the United Kingdom, 1806.

GARDNER, Daniel (1750?–1805), portrait painter; celebrated for small pictures in oil and crayons.

GARDNER, Ernest Arthur (1862–1939), classical scholar and archaeologist; brother of Percy *Gardner; educated at City of London School and Gonville and Caius College, Cambridge; first classes, classical tripos, 1882–4; director, British School of Archaeology, Athens, 1887–95; professor of archaeology, London, 1896–1929; vice-chancellor, 1924–6; works include *Handbook of Greek Sculpture* (1896–7).

GARDNER, George (1812–1849), botanist; collected in Brazil many thousand specimens of plants, 1836–40; FLS, 1842; died in Ceylon, superintendent of botanical garden; published *Travels in the Interior of Brazil* (1846).

GARDNER, John (1804–1880), medical writer; LRCP, Edinburgh, 1860; MD, Giessen, 1847; translated Liebig's *Familiar Letters on Chemistry* (1843); first secretary to Royal College of Chemistry and professor of chemistry to General Apothecaries' Company; published *The Great Physician* (1843), *Household Medicine*, and *Longevity*.

GARDNER, Percy (1846–1937), classical archaeologist and numismatist; brother of E. A. *Gardner; educated at City of London School and Christ's College, Cambridge; first classes in classical and moral sciences triposes, 1869; assistant in department of coins and medals, British Museum, 1871; Disney professor of archaeology, Cambridge, 1880; editor, *Journal of Hellenic Studies*, 1880–96; professor of classical archaeology, Oxford, 1887–1925; works include *New Chapters in Greek History* (1892), *History of Ancient Coinage 700–300 B.C.* (1918), and *New Chapters in Greek Art* (1926); FBA, 1903; exponent of 'evolutional' Christianity in *Exploratio Evangelica* (1899), etc.

GARDNER, Thomas (1690?–1769), Southwold antiquary; published *Historical Account of Dunwich . . . Blithburgh . . . Southwold* (1754).

GARDNER, William (1844–1887), inventor of the Gardner machine-gun, 1876, and of a quick-firing cannon; a native of Ohio.

GARDNER, William Linnaeus (1771–1835), Indian officer; nephew of Alan, first Baron *Gardner; ensign in India, 1789; captain, 30th Foot, 1794; employed by the Mahratta Jeswunt Rao Holkar; married a princess of Cambay; escaped to General Lake disguised as a grass-cutter, 1804; commanded irregular horse in Kamaun and Rajputana; lieutenant-colonel in Indian Army, 1819, commanding Gardner's Horse.

GARDNOR, John (1729–1808), painter; vicar of Battersea, 1778–1808; exhibited landscapes at Royal Academy, 1782–96; published views of the Rhine country, engraved in aquatint by himself and others.

GARDNOR, Richard (*fl.* 1766–1793), painter; nephew and assistant of John *Gardnor; exhibited with Free Society and at the Academy, 1786–93.

GARDYNE, Alexander (1585?–1634?), Scots poet; published *Garden of Grave and Godlie Flowers* (1609) and *Theatre of Scotish Kings*.

GARENCIÈRES, Theophilus (1610–1680), physician; MD, Caen, 1636; incorporated MD, Oxford, 1657; published *Angliae Flagellum seu Tabes Anglica* (1647) and a book of prescriptions for the plague (1665); translated Nostradamus, 1672.

GARGAN, Denis (1819–1903), president of Maynooth College; ordained, 1843; professor of humanity, 1845, and of ecclesiastical history, 1859; vice-president, 1885, and president, 1894, of Maynooth; received King Edward VII there, 1903; published *The Ancient Church of Ireland* (1864).

GARGRAVE, George (1710–1785), mathematician; contributed to the *Gentleman's Magazine* papers on the transit of Venus (1761 and 1769) and (1781) memoirs of Abraham *Sharp the mathematician.

GARGRAVE, Sir Thomas (1495–1579), speaker and (1560) vice-president of the Council of the North; MP for York, 1547–55, Yorkshire, 1555; speaker, 1559; active in suppressing rising of 1569.

GARLAND, Augustine (*fl.* 1660), regicide; of Emmanuel College, Cambridge, and Lincoln's Inn; MP, Queenborough, 1648; presided over the committee to consider method of the king's trial, and signed death-warrant; condemned to death, 1660, but suffered only confiscation and imprisonment.

GARLAND, John (*fl.* 1230), grammarian and alchemist; often confused with Gerlandus, a French writer of twelfth century, and others; studied at Oxford and Paris; master of grammar at Toulouse University, 1229–31; wrote *Dictionarius Scolasticus* and many other grammatical treatises, *Compendium Alchymiae cum Dictionario, Liber de Mineralibus*, and similar works; author of treatises on counterpoint, plainsong, and other musical subjects; some verses by him, including the autobiographical 'De Triumphis Ecclesiae' and 'De Contemptu Mundi', wrongly ascribed to St Bernard.

GARNEAU, François Xavier (1809–1866), historian of Canada; native of Canada; greffier of Quebec, 1844–64; president of Canadian Institute, 1855; member of council of education, 1857; published *Histoire du Canada* (1845–6) and *Voyage en Angleterre et en France* (1855).

GARNER, (Joseph John) Saville, Baron Garner (1908–1983), civil servant and diplomat; educated at Highgate School, London, and Jesus College, Cambridge; first class, modern and medieval languages tripos, 1929; assistant principal, Dominions Office, 1930; assistant private secretary, 1935; principal private secretary, 1939–42; deputy high commissioner, Ottawa, 1943–8; assistant under-secretary of state, Dominions Office, 1948–51; deputy high commissioner, Delhi, 1951–3; deputy permanent under-secretary of state, Commonwealth Relations Office, 1953–6; high commissioner, Canada, 1956–62; permanent under-secretary of state, Commonwealth Relations Office, 1962–5; permanent under-secretary, Commonwealth office, and Head of HM Diplomatic Service, 1965–8; chairman, Commonwealth Institute, 1968–74, Commonwealth scholarship commission for the UK, 1968–77, and Institute of Commonwealth Studies, 1971–9; member, Security Commission, 1968–73; CMG, 1948; KCMG, 1954; GCMG, 1965; life peer, 1969; hon. LL D, British Columbia University, 1958, and Toronto, 1959; hon. fellow, Jesus College, Cambridge, 1967; published *The Commonwealth Office 1925–1968* (1978).

GARNER, Thomas (1789–1868), engraver; pupil of Samuel *Lines; a founder of Birmingham Society of Artists.

GARNER, Thomas (1839–1906), architect; fellow pupil of Sir George Gilbert *Scott with G. F. *Bodley, whose partner he became, 1869–97; did much ecclesiastical, domestic, and collegiate architecture in Oxford, Cambridge, and London; in later life joined Church of Rome; joint author of *The Domestic Architecture of England during the Tudor Period* (1908).

GARNER, William Edward (1889–1960), chemist; educated at Market Bosworth Grammar School and Birmingham (honours in chemistry, 1912) and Göttingen universities; appointed lecturer, University College, London, 1919; reader in physical chemistry, 1924; Leverhulme professor of physical and inorganic chemistry, Bristol, 1927–54; carried out systematic study of kinetics of solid reactions and of heterogeneous catalysis; in 1939–45 associated with notable developments in armaments and munitions; CBE, 1946; FRS, 1937.

GARNETT, Arthur William (1829–1861), engineer; younger son of William *Garnett; entered Bengal Engineers, 1846; wounded at Multan, 1849; held fords of the Chenab at Gujerat, 1849; designed forts on Afghan frontier; buried in Calcutta Cathedral.

GARNETT, Constance Clara (1861–1946), translator of Russian classics; born Black; educated at Brighton High School and Newnham College, Cambridge; married (1889) Edward Garnett; translations include whole of Turgenev,

Dostoevsky, Gogol, and (virtually) Chekhov, and two novels of Tolstoy.

GARNETT, David (1892–1981), writer, editor, and publisher; son of Edward and Constance *Garnett; educated at University College School and Royal College of Science, South Kensington; from boyhood associated with the Bloomsbury Group; during 1914–18 war in France with War Victims' Relief Mission; postwar, opened bookshop in Bloomsbury with Francis Birrell; published *Lady into Fox* (1922) which won Hawthornden and James Tait Black Memorial prizes, 1923; produced further novels, including *The Sailor's Return* (1925), *Aspects of Love* (1955), and *Up She Rises* (1977); published autobiographical *A Rabbit in the Air* (1932), *The Golden Echo* (1953), and *Great Friends* (1979); edited *The Letters of T. E. Lawrence* (1938), *The Novels of Thomas Love Peacock* (1948), and Dora Carrington's *Letters and Extracts from her Diaries* (1970); involved in publishing with (Sir) Francis *Meynell, 1923, and Rupert Hart-Davis Ltd., 1946; literary editor, *New Statesman*, 1939; during 1939–45 war worked in Air Ministry and Political Warfare Executive; *Lady into Fox* (1939) and *The Sailor's Return* (1947) produced as ballets, and the latter and *A Man in the Zoo* (1928) made into films; CBE, 1952; fellow, Imperial College of Science and Technology, 1956; C.Lit., 1977; hon. D.Litt., Birmingham, 1977; married Rachel Alice ('Ray') Marshall, 1921 (d. 1940); married Angelica Vanessa, daughter of Duncan *Grant and Vanessa *Bell, 1942.

GARNETT, Henry (1555–1606), Jesuit; educated at Winchester, 1567; two years corrector of the press to *Tottel, the law printer; went to Spain and Italy; Jesuit novice, 1575; professor of Hebrew in the college at Rome; superior of the English province, 1587–1606; professed of the four vows, 1598; accused of complicity in Gunpowder Plot; arrested after three days' search at Hindlip Hall; imprisoned in the Tower; twenty-three times examined before the Privy Council; condemned on his admission of conversations with *Catesby, and executed; published a translation, with supplements, of *Summa Canisii* (1590), *A Treatise on Schism*, and other theological works.

GARNETT, James Clerk Maxwell (1880–1958), educationist and secretary of League of Nations Union; scholar of St Paul's and Trinity College, Cambridge; sixteenth wrangler, 1902; called to bar (Inner Temple), 1908; examiner, Board of Education, 1904–12; principal, Manchester College of Technology, 1912–20; secretary, League of Nations Union, 1920–38; impelled by strong sense of Christian service;

publications include *World Loyalty* (1928); CBE, 1919.

GARNETT, Jeremiah (1793–1870), journalist; brother of Richard *Garnett; co-founder of the *Manchester Guardian*, 1821; sole editor, 1844–61; obtained defeat of Thomas Milner *Gibson and John *Bright, 1857.

GARNETT, John (1709–1782), bishop of Clogher; fellow of Sidney Sussex College, Cambridge; MA, 1732; bishop of Ferns, 1752–8, of Clogher, 1758; patron of Philip *Skelton; published *Dissertation on Job* (1749).

GARNETT, John (d. 1813), dean of Exeter, 1810; son of John *Garnett (1709–1782).

GARNETT, Richard (1789–1850), philologist; became priest-vicar of Lichfield Cathedral, 1829; incumbent of Chebsey, near Stafford, 1836–8; assistant keeper of printed books, British Museum, 1838; his philological essays edited by his eldest son, 1859.

GARNETT, Richard (1835–1906), man of letters and keeper of printed books in the British Museum; elder son of Richard *Garnett; privately educated; early developed linguistic and literary aptitudes; entered British Museum library, 1857, and won favour of Sir Anthony *Panizzi; assistant keeper of printed books and superintendent of the reading room, 1875–90; superintended printing of catalogue; keeper of printed books, 1890–9; his chief acquisitions noticed in *A Description of 300 Notable Books* (privately printed, 1899); president of Library Association, 1892–3; engaged through life in literary work, poetic, critical, and biographical; his most important publications were hitherto unpublished *Relics of Shelley* (1862) and *The Twilight of the Gods* (1888, new edn., 1903), apologues of pleasantly cynical flavour in Lucian's vein; other writings include *Io in Egypt and other Poems* (1859, new edn., 1893); brief biographies of *Milton and *Carlyle (1877), Emerson (1888), Edward Gibbon *Wakefield (1898), and a *History of Italian Literature* (1897); a contributor to this Dictionary; hon. LL D, Edinburgh, 1883; CB, 1895.

GARNETT, Thomas (1575–1608), Jesuit; nephew of Henry *Garnett; Jesuit, 1604; imprisoned in the Tower and banished for life, 1606; executed on his return.

GARNETT, Thomas (1766–1802), physician and natural philosopher; MD, Edinburgh, 1788; practised at Bradford, Knaresborough, and Harrogate; published first analysis of Harrogate waters; professor of natural philosophy at Anderson's Institution, Glasgow, of natural philosophy and chemistry at Royal Institution, 1799–1801;

anticipated modern theory of a quasi-intelligence in plants; published *Highland Tour* (1800); his *Zoonomia* published (1804).

GARNETT, Thomas (1799–1878), naturalist; brother of Richard and Jeremiah *Garnett; wrote on pisciculture and experimented with guano; his papers privately printed (1883).

GARNETT, William (1793–1873), civil servant; deputy-registrar and registrar of land tax, 1819–41; inspector-general of stamps and taxes, 1842; published *Guide to Property and Income Tax*.

GARNEYS (or GARNYSSHE), Sir Christopher (d. 1534), chief porter of Calais, 1526–34; favourite of Henry VIII, who knighted him at Tournay, 1513.

GARNIER (or WARNER) (*fl.* 1106), monk of Westminster. See WARNER.

GARNIER, Thomas, the elder (1776–1873), dean of Winchester; educated at Winchester and Worcester College, Oxford; fellow of All Souls, 1796; rector of Bishopstoke, 1807; DCL, 1850; dean of Winchester, 1840–72; friend of Palmerston.

GARNIER, Thomas, the younger (1809–1863), dean of Lincoln; of Winchester and Worcester College, Oxford; BA, 1830; fellow of All Souls, 1830; BCL, 1833; chaplain of House of Commons, 1849; incumbent, Holy Trinity, Marylebone, 1850; dean of Ripon, 1859, of Lincoln, 1860; published sermons.

GARNOCK, Robert (d. 1681), Covenanter; executed for declining the king's authority; his head discovered in 1728; extracts from his autobiography contained in *Howie's *Biographia Scoticana*, and dying testimony in *Cloud of Witnesses*.

GARRAN (formerly GAMMAN), Andrew (1825–1901), Australian journalist and politician; BA, London, 1845; MA, 1848; migrated to Adelaide, 1851; assistant editor (1856) and editor (1873–85) of *Sydney Morning Herald*; member of Legislative Council of New South Wales, 1887; president of Royal Commission on Strikes, 1890, whose report led to Trades Disputes Conciliation Act, 1892; president of Arbitration Council, 1892; vice-president of Executive Council, 1895–8; edited *Picturesque Atlas of Australasia* (1886).

GARRARD, Apsley George Benet Cherry- (1886–1959), polar explorer. See CHERRY-GARRARD.

GARRARD, George (1760–1826), animal painter and sculptor; pupil of Sawrey *Gilpin; exhibited *View of a Brewhouse Yard*, 1784, *Sheepshearing at Aston Clinton*, 1793; published description of British oxen (1800); instrumental in

obtaining act of 1798 securing copyright in works of plastic art; ARA, 1800.

GARRARD, Marcus (1561–1635), painter. See GHEERAERTS.

GARRARD, Sir Samuel (1650–1724), lord mayor of London; succeeded as baronet, 1700; sheriff of London, 1702; lord mayor, 1709–10; warden of the Grocers' Company, 1701–2; MP, Agmundesham (Amersham), 1702–14; president of Bridewell and Bethlehem hospitals, 1721.

GARRARD, Thomas (1787–1859), biographer; treasurer of Bristol, 1836–56; published life of Edward *Colston (1852).

GARRAWAY, Sir Henry (1575–1646), lord mayor of London; governor of Greenland, Russia, and Turkey companies, 1639; master of the Drapers' Company, 1627 and 1639; sheriff of London, 1627; lord mayor of London, 1639; knighted, 1640; assisted the king to raise money in the City; expelled from court of aldermen for Royalism, 1643; imprisoned; his speech (1642) in answer to *Pym's address to the citizens frequently reprinted.

GARRETT, Fydell Edmund (1865–1907), publicist; BA, Trinity College, Cambridge, and president of Union, 1887; joined staff of *Pall Mall Gazette*; sent for phthisis cure to South Africa, 1889; intimate of Cecil *Rhodes and President Kruger; described experiences in *In Afrikanderland* (1891); returned to London, writing for *Pall Mall* and *Westminster* gazettes, 1891–5; translated Ibsen's *Brand*, 1894; as editor of *Cape Times*, 1895–1900, he influenced public affairs in South Africa; member of Cape parliament, 1898–1902; advocated united autonomous South Africa; settled in Devonshire, 1904; wrote also *The Story of an African Crisis* (1897).

GARRETT, Jeremiah Learnoult (*fl.* 1809), Dissenting minister; preached in the fields near London; laid foundation stone of Islington Chapel, 1788; ejected for heresy from Lady *Huntingdon's Connection; carried on controversies with Joanna *Southcott and William *Huntington; published *Songs of Sion* and other works.

GARRETT, Sir Robert (1794–1869), lieutenant-general; educated at Harrow; ensign, 2nd Queen's Foot, 1811; wounded at Salamanca, 1812; severely wounded in the Pyrenees, 1814; lieutenant-colonel, 1846; led 46th Foot in the Crimea, where he commanded first a brigade and subsequently the 4th division; brigadier in China, 1857; lieutenant-general, 1866; KCB.

GARRETT ANDERSON, Elizabeth (1836–1917), physician. See ANDERSON.

GARRICK, David (1717–1779), actor; Dr *Johnson's first pupil at Edial; with him left Lichfield for London, 1737; started a wine business with his brother Peter; introduced by Johnson to *Cave; wrote in the *Gentleman's Magazine*; his *Lethe* performed at Drury Lane, 1740; became attached to Margaret ('Peg') *Woffington, to whom he afterwards offered marriage; under name Lyddal made first appearance at Ipswich in *Oroonoko*, 1741; made his reputation at Goodman's Fields in *Richard III*, 1741; played Bayes and King Lear, 1742; highly successful at Dublin in *Hamlet* and *The Recruiting Officer*, 1742; at Drury Lane played Abel Drugger and other parts, but quarrelled with *Macklin, 1742–3; acted Macbeth 'as written by Shakespeare', 1744, Sir John Brute (*Provoked Wife*) and Othello, 1744–5, played Faulconbridge and Iago at Dublin, 1745; first appeared at Covent Garden in Shakespearean parts, 1746; joined Lacy in management of Drury Lane, 1747; played Benedick and Romeo (his own version), 1748, and Demetrius in Johnson's *Mahomet and Irene*, 1749; his marriage resented by Mrs *Cibber, *Quin, Macklin, and *Barry; with Miss *Bellamy played Romeo and Lear against the same parts by Barry with Mrs Cibber at Covent Garden, 1750; appeared as Kitely in *Every Man in his Humour*, 1751; rejoined by Mrs Cibber and joined by *Foote, 1754, when he produced his version of *Taming of the Shrew* and *Coriolanus*; threatened to retire from the stage in consequence of riots against French dancers, 1755; appeared in his adaptation of *Winter's Tale*, 1756; played Don Felix in *The Wonder*, 1756; produced Foote's *Author*, 1756; produced his adaptation of *Cymbeline*, 1761; Sciolto in the *Fair Penitent*, his last new part, 1763, during which season riots occurred at Drury Lane in consequence of alterations in prices; travelled with his wife in France and Italy, 1763–4; made free of the Comédie Française; met Diderot, Beaumarchais, Marivaux, Marmontel, and Mlle Clairon; reappearing at Drury Lane as Benedick, 1765, introduced the system of invisible lighting; produced *The Clandestine Marriage*, written by himself and *Colman, 1766; produced his *Peep Behind the Curtain*, 1767; designed and carried out the Shakespeare jubilee at Stratford, 1769, and produced the *Jubilee* at Drury Lane; produced *Cumberland's *West Indian* and *Dryden's *King Arthur*, 1770; produced his version of *Hamlet*, 1772, and his *Bon Ton, or High Life above Stairs*, 1775; made last appearance as Don Felix, 10 June 1776, selling moiety of his patent to *Sheridan and two others for £35,000; wrote prologue to the *School for Scandal* and *All the World's a Stage*, and prologue and epilogue for *Fielding's *Fathers*; made a larger fortune than any actor except *Alleyn; last actor buried in Westminster Abbey; his poetical works published (1785), his dramatic works (sixteen plays, 1768). His portrait was painted by *Reynolds, *Hogarth, and *Gainsborough.

GARROD, Sir Alfred Baring (1819–1907), physician; studied medicine at University College Hospital; MD, 1843; physician and professor of materia medica and therapeutics and a professor of clinical medicine at University College Hospital, 1849–63, and at King's College Hospital, 1863–74; FRCP, 1856; Gulstonian lecturer, 1857; Lumleian lecturer, 1883; FRS, 1858; knighted, 1887; made valuable researches into gout; wrote *Treatise on Gout and Rheumatic Gout* (1859).

GARROD, Sir (Alfred) Guy (Roland) (1891–1965), air chief marshal; educated at Bradfield College and University College, Oxford; leading member of OUDS; commissioned in Leicestershire Regiment, 1914; seconded to Royal Flying Corps, 1915; DFC; MC; permanently commissioned in Royal Air Force, 1919; filled number of Staff College appointments, 1919–39; air commodore, 1936; air vice-marshal, 1939; director of equipment, Air Ministry; air member for training on Air Council, 1940–3; deputy Allied air commander-in-chief, South-East Asia, 1943; commander-in-chief, RAF, Mediterranean and Middle East, 1945; head of RAF delegation, Washington; air chief marshal; retired, 1948; held several business posts; warden, Bradfield, 1959; hon. fellow, University College, Oxford (1917); hon. LL D, Aberdeen; OBE, 1932; GBE, 1948; CB, 1941; KCB, 1943.

GARROD, Alfred Henry (1846–1879), zoologist; studied at University College, London; thrice won medical scholarship at King's College, London; senior in natural science tripos, Cambridge, 1871; prosector of Cambridge Zoological Society, 1871; fellow of St John's College, Cambridge, 1873; professor of comparative anatomy at King's College, London, 1874–9; Fullerian professor of physiology, Royal Institution, 1875; FRS, 1876; made important researches in the anatomy and myology of birds and ruminants; edited Bell's version of Müller on the vocal organs of passerines, and contributed to *Cassell's *Natural History*.

GARROD, Sir Archibald Edward (1857–1936), physician and biochemist; son of Sir A. B. *Garrod; educated at Marlborough, Christ Church, Oxford, and St Bartholomew's Hospital; assistant physician, 1903; full physician, 1912; consulting physician to Mediterranean forces, 1915–19; KCMG, 1918; regius professor of medicine, Oxford, 1920–7; works include

Inborn Errors of Metabolism (1909) and *The Inborn Factors in Disease* (1931); FRS, 1910.

GARROD, Heathcote William (1878–1960), scholar; educated at Bath College and Balliol College, Oxford; first class, Lit. Hum., and Newdigate Prize, 1901; tutor at Merton College, 1904–25; fellow of Merton from 1901, his rich, uncommon personality made him a presiding genius there; professor of poetry, 1923–8; publications include edition of Statius (1906); *The Oxford Book of Latin Verse* (1912); *Wordsworth: Lectures and Essays* (1923); edited *Keats for Oxford English Texts, 1939; with Mrs Allen completed edition by P. S. *Allen of *Letters of Erasmus*; original works include *Oxford Poems* (1912) and *Epigrams* (1946); CBE, 1918; FBA, 1931; hon. fellow, Merton College; hon. D.Litt., Durham, and LL D, Edinburgh.

GARROD, Lawrence Paul (1895–1979), clinical bacteriologist; educated at Sidcot School and King's College, Cambridge; entered St Bartholomew's Hospital, 1916; served as surgeon sublieutenant, RNVR, 1917–18; Brackenbury scholar in medicine, Bart's, 1919; MRCS (Eng.) and LRCP (Lond.), 1920; MA, MB, and B.Chir., 1921; MRCP, 1923; MD, 1938; became premier British authority on antimicrobial chemotherapy; senior demonstrator of pathology at Bart's, 1925; reader in bacteriology, 1934; professor of bacteriology, 1937–61; FRCP, 1936; hon. consultant in chemotherapy, Royal Postgraduate Medical School, 1961; member of Penicillin Clinical Trials Committee of Medical Research Council; chairman, MRC Antibiotics Clinical Trials Committee; chairman, antibiotics panel of Committee on Medical Aspects of Food Policy, 1965–70; publications include five editions of *Recent Advances in Pathology* (1st edn., 1932), *Hospital Infection* (two edns., 1st 1960), and *Antibiotic and Chemotherapy* (five edns., 1st 1963); wrote 200 scientific papers and over 600 unsigned editorials for *British Medical Journal*; editor, *British Journal of Experimental Pathology*, 1951–7; bacteriologist, Bart's, 1934–61; bacteriologist to City of London, 1936; consultant in antibiotics to the army, 1948; president, Institute of Medical Laboratory Technology, 1949–53; vice-president, BMA; honorary degrees and hon. fellow, Royal College of Pathologists, 1979.

GARROW, Sir William (1760–1840), baron of the Exchequer; barrister, Lincoln's Inn, 1783; made reputation by prosecution of Aikles for stealing bill of exchange, 1784; acted for *Fox in Westminster scrutiny; KC, 1793; MP, Gatton, 1805, Callington, 1806, and Eye, 1812; solicitor-general, 1812; knighted, 1812; attorney-general, 1813; chief justice of Chester, 1814; baron of Exchequer, 1817–32; privy councillor, 1832.

GARSIDE, Charles Brierley (1818–1876), Roman Catholic divine; educated at Manchester School; MA, Brasenose College, Oxford, 1844; Anglican curate, 1842–50; graduated at the Collegio Romano, and was ordained Romanist priest, 1854; chaplain to earl of Shrewsbury, 1855; afterwards assistant priest in Chelsea and Oxford; died at Posilippo, Italy; published theological works.

GARSTANG, John (1876–1956), archaeologist; educated at Blackburn Grammar School and Jesus College, Oxford; reader in Egyptian archaeology, Liverpool, 1902; professor of methods and practice of archaeology, 1907–41; organized Institute of Archaeology; director, Jerusalem School of Archaeology, 1919–26, and Palestine Department of Antiquities, 1920–6; founded British Institute of Archaeology at Ankara, 1948; excavated in Egypt, Asia Minor, and Sudan; in Jericho, 1930–6; thereafter in Turkey; publications include *The Land of the Hittites* (1910), *Joshua, Judges* (1931), *The Heritage of Solomon* (1934), and *Prehistoric Mersin* (1953); CBE, 1949; hon. LL D, Aberdeen.

GARSTIN, Sir William Edmund (1849–1925), engineer; born in India; entered Indian Public Works Department, 1872; joined group of Indian engineers appointed to reorganize irrigation system of Egypt, 1885; inspector-general of irrigation, Egypt, 1892; under-secretary of state in Ministry of Public Works, 1892; his notable system of water storage and control comprised construction of great dam at Aswan and barrages at Assiut, Esna, and Zifta; after freeing of Sudan from Dervish rule (1898) cleared Bahr el Jebel and Bahr el Ghazal from 'sudd'; responsible for formation of Sudan Irrigation Service; supervised care of buildings and antiquities of Egypt; adviser to Public Works Department, 1905–8; KCMG, 1897; earned profound gratitude of Egyptian people for his irrigation work.

GARTER, Bernard (*fl.* 1570), anti-papist poet; published *The tragicall and true historie which happened betweene two English lovers, 1563* (1565) and *A New Yeares Gifte* (1579).

GARTH, John (*fl.* 1757), musical composer; adapted the *First Fifty Psalms of Marcello* to the English version, 1757–65.

GARTH, Sir Richard (1820–1903), chief justice of Bengal, 1875–86; educated at Eton and Christ Church, Oxford; in university cricket XI, 1839–42; called to bar, 1847; QC, 1866; Conservative MP for Guildford, 1866–8; knighted, 1875; able judge but partisan controversialist; opposed to Bengal Tenancy Bill; promoted Legal Practitioners Act, 1879; PC, 1888; supported

Indian National Congress in *A Few Plain Truths about India* (1888).

GARTH, Sir Samuel (1661–1719), physician and poet; MA, Peterhouse, Cambridge, 1684; MD, 1691; FRCP, 1693; Gulstonian lecturer, 1694; Harveian orator, 1697; FRS, 1706; knighted, 1714; physician-in-ordinary to George I, and physician-general to the army; made a Latin oration over the body of *Dryden as it lay in state at the College of Physicians, 1700; wrote much occasional verse, and was a member of the Kit-cat Club; ridiculed in his poem *The Dispensary* (1699) the opposition of the apothecaries and their allies to the scheme of out-patient rooms.

GARTHSHORE, Maxwell (1732–1812), physician; MD, Edinburgh, 1764; LRCP, 1764; FRS and FSA; physician to British Lying-in Hospital; bore striking likeness to great Lord Chatham; provided for widow of John *Hunter (1728–1793); published works on obstetrics.

GARTHSHORE, William (1764–1806), lord of the Admiralty; son of Maxwell *Garthshore; educated at Westminster; MA, Christ Church, Oxford, 1789; private secretary to *Dundas, 1794; MP, Launceston, 1795, Weymouth, 1797–1806; a lord of the Admiralty, 1801–4.

GARVEY, Edmund (d. 1813), landscape painter; exhibited at Dublin, the Free Society of Artists, and (1769–1808) at the Royal Academy; RA, 1783.

GARVEY, John (1527–1595), archbishop of Armagh; graduated at Oxford; dean of Ferns, 1558, of Christ Church, Dublin, 1565; privy councillor of Ireland; bishop of Kilmore, 1585; archbishop of Armagh, 1589–95.

GARVIE, Alfred Ernest (1861–1945), theologian and Church leader; first class, theology, Mansfield College, Oxford, 1892; professor at Hackney and New colleges, London, 1903; principal, New College, 1907; Hackney, 1922; of combined colleges, 1924–33; publications include *The Ritschlian Theology* (1899), *The Christian Doctrine of the Godhead* (1925), *The Christian Ideal for Human Society* (1930), and *The Christian Belief in God* (1932).

GARVIN, James Louis (1868–1947), editor of the *Observer*; joined *Newcastle Chronicle*, 1891; *Daily Telegraph*, 1899; wrote as 'Calchas' in *Fortnightly Review*; advocated military preparedness and tariff reform; edited *Outlook*, 1905–6; *Pall Mall Gazette*, 1912–15; *Observer*, 1908–42; established remarkable personal influence; made *Observer* financial success, strong political force, and new pattern of Sunday paper, combining news with full treatment of arts; supported Lloyd George's war policy; criticized Versailles Treaty

and in *The Economic Foundations of Peace* (1919) sought system Germany could enter as an equal; favoured negotiation with Hitler from strength but insisted Munich must be last concession; strong supporter of 'National' government (1931) and lifelong advocate of coalitions in emergency; wrote for *Sunday Express*, 1942–5; *Daily Telegraph*, 1945–7; edited 13th and 14th editions of *Encyclopaedia Britannica*; published *Life of Joseph Chamberlain* (3 vols., 1932–4); CH, 1941.

GARWAY, Sir Henry (1575–1646), lord mayor of London. See GARRAWAY.

GASCAR, Henri (1635–1701), portrait painter; born at Paris; protégé of Louise de *Keroualle, duchess of Portsmouth; in England, 1674; returned to France, 1680; died at Rome. His portraits include Charles II, the duchesses of Portsmouth and *Cleveland, and Nell (Eleanor) *Gwyn.

GASCOIGNE, Sir Bernard (1614–1687), soldier and diplomat; born at Florence; saw military service in Italy and Germany; originally named Bernardo or Bernardino Guasconi; captured Parliamentarian officers in Cornwall, 1644; commanded a regiment of horse at Colchester, 1648; granted denization as Sir Bernard Gascoigne, 1661; FRS, 1667; envoy to Vienna to negotiate marriage of duke of York with a daughter of the archduke of Austria, 1672; his memoirs printed at Florence (1886); his 'Description of Germany' printed in *Miscellanea Aulica* (1702).

GASCOIGNE, Sir Crisp (1700–1761). See GASCOYNE.

GASCOIGNE, George (1542–1577), poet; a descendant of Sir William *Gascoigne (1350?–1419); probably educated at Trinity College, Cambridge; ancient of Gray's Inn, *c.*1557; MP, Bedford, 1557–9; his *Supposes*, an adaptation of Ariosto's comedy, acted at Gray's Inn, 1566; married the mother of Nicholas *Breton, *c.*1566; MP, Midhurst, 1572; went to Holland to avoid his creditors, 1572; saw military service in Holland, 1572–5; captured by the Spaniards; an unauthorized book of poems by him published in his absence; issued the *Posies of G. Gascoigne, corrected, perfected, and augmented* (1575), containing 'Jocasta', the second earliest tragedy in English in blank verse, and 'Certayne Notes of Instruction concerning the making of verse or ryme in English', the earliest English critical essay; published his 'tragicall comedie', *The Glasse of Government* (1575); visited Kenilworth with Queen Elizabeth and Leicester, 1575; contributed to *The Princelye Pleasures* (1576). His other works include *The Steele Glas* (1576), *The Droomme of Doomesday*, and the posthumously published *Tale of Hemetes* *the heremyte*, in English, French, Latin, and Italian. He was praised by *Meres, *Nash, and other contemporaries.

GASCOIGNE, John (*fl.* 1381), doctor of canon law at Oxford; signatory of the chancellor's condemnation of *Wycliffe's views on the Sacrament, 1381; credited by *Pits with authorship of a treatise, *Contra Wiclevum*.

GASCOIGNE, Richard (1579–*c.*1663), antiquary; BA, Jesus College, Cambridge, 1599; left books to Jesus College, Cambridge; compiled pedigrees of Gascoigne, Wentworth, and other families.

GASCOIGNE, Richard (d. 1716), Jacobite; joined the rebels at Preston, 1715; captured and hanged at Tyburn.

GASCOIGNE, Thomas (1403–1458), theologian; resided in Oriel College, Oxford; DD, 1434; chancellor of the university, 1444–5, and frequently *cancellarius natus* and vice-chancellor; an active preacher and denouncer of lollardy, but zealous against pluralities and other ecclesiastical abuses; benefactor of Oriel, Balliol, and other colleges; his 'Dictionarium Theologicum' (from which extracts were printed by J. E. T. *Rogers, 1881) preserved at Lincoln College. Other works attributed to him include *The Myroure of our Ladye* (ed. J. H. *Blunt, 1873), and a life of St Bridget of Sweden.

GASCOIGNE, Sir Thomas (1593?–1686), alleged conspirator; succeeded as baronet of Nova Scotia, 1637; endowed convent near Fountains Abbey, 1678; sent to the Tower on a charge of plotting with other members of his family to murder Charles II, 1679; acquitted, 1679; retired to his brother's monastery at Lambspring, Germany, where he died.

GASCOIGNE, Sir William (1350?–1419), judge; reader at Gray's Inn; king's serjeant, 1397, and attorney to the duke of Hereford (Lancaster) on his banishment; chief justice of King's Bench, 1400; raised forces against *Northumberland, 1403, and received the submission of his adherents, 1405; probably a member of the court which tried them; improbably said to have refused to try Archbishop *Scrope; ceased to be chief justice soon after Henry V's accession. The story taken by *Hall from Sir T. *Elyot's *Governour* (1531) of his committing Henry V when prince of Wales is without foundation.

GASCOIGNE, William (1612?–1644), inventor of the micrometer; corresponded with *Horrocks and *Crabtree; his invention of the micrometer not published till Auzout's announcement (1666) of his own; killed on Royalist side at Marston Moor.

GASCOYNE, Bamber (1725–1791), lord of the Admiralty; eldest son of Sir Crisp *Gascoyne; MP, Malden, 1761–3, Midhurst, 1765–70, Weobly, 1770–4, Truro, 1774–84, Bossiney, 1784–6; receiver-general of customs.

GASCOYNE, Sir Crisp (1700–1761), lord mayor of London; master of the Brewers' Company, 1746–7; sheriff of London, 1747–8; passed in common council act for relief of city orphans, 1748; lord mayor, 1752–3; knighted, 1752; first mayor who occupied Mansion House; convicted alleged kidnappers of Elizabeth *Canning, but afterwards proved her information to be false.

GASCOYNE, Isaac (1770–1841), general; third son of Bamber *Gascoyne; served with Coldstream Guards in Flanders, 1793–4, and commanded them in Ireland, 1798; major-general on the staff, 1802–8; general, 1819; MP, Liverpool, 1802–30.

GASELEE, Sir Alfred (1844–1918), general; joined army, 1863; served chiefly in Indian wars and expeditions, 1863–1900; CB, 1891; KCB, 1898; commanded British Expeditionary Force for relief of legations in Peking, 1900; full general, 1906; commanded Northern Army in India, 1907–8; GCB, 1909.

GASELEE, Sir Stephen (1762–1839), judge; barrister, Gray's Inn, 1793; pupil of Sir Vicary *Gibbs; went the western circuit; KC, 1819; knighted, 1825; justice of common pleas, 1824–37; supposed original of *Dickens's Justice Stareleigh.

GASELEE, Stephen (1807–1883), serjeant-at-law; son of Sir Stephen *Gaselee; educated at Winchester and Balliol College, Oxford; MA, 1832; barrister, Inner Temple, 1832; serjeant-at-law, 1840; MP, Portsmouth, 1865–8.

GASELEE, Sir Stephen (1882–1943), librarian, scholar, and connoisseur; scholar of Eton and King's College, Cambridge; Pepysian librarian, Magdalene College, 1908–19; fellow, 1909–43; served in Foreign Office, 1916–19; librarian and keeper of the papers there, 1920–43; honorary librarian, Athenaeum, 1928–43; publications include Coptic texts; text of Petronius' *Satyricon* (1910); editions of Apuleius (1915), Parthenius (1916), and Achilles Tatius (1917) for Loeb Classical Library; and *The Oxford Book of Medieval Latin Verse* (1928); presented valuable book collections to Cambridge university library; FBA, 1939; KCMG, 1935.

GASK, George Ernest (1875–1951), surgeon; educated at Dulwich College; qualified from St Bartholomew's Hospital, 1898; FRCS, 1901; council member, 1923–39; assistant surgeon to

(Sir) D'Arcy *Power, 1907; consulting surgeon, Fourth Army; DSO, 1917; CMG, 1919; formed surgical professorial unit, Bart's, after 1918; retired 1935; with J. Paterson Ross wrote pioneer study of *The Surgery of the Sympathetic Nervous System* (1934); temporary surgeon, Radcliffe Infirmary, Oxford, 1939–45; succeeded Lord *Moynihan as chairman, editorial committee, *British Journal of Surgery*.

GASKELL, Elizabeth Cleghorn (1810–1865), novelist; daughter of William *Stevenson (1772–1829); brought up by her aunt at Knutsford, the original of *Cranford*; married William *Gaskell, 1832; became an intimate of the *Howitts, 1841; published *Mary Barton* anonymously (1848); praised by Miss *Edgeworth, *Landor, *Carlyle, and *Bamford; attacked by W. R. *Greg and others as hostile to employers; a guest of *Dickens, with Carlyle and *Thackeray, 1849; contributed to *Household Words* from 1850, when she also became acquainted with Charlotte *Brontë; published *Life* of Charlotte Brontë (1857), the first edition being withdrawn because some of its statements were challenged by persons concerned; became an intimate of Madame *Mohl, 1855; organized sewing-rooms during cotton famine of 1862; died suddenly. Her other works include *Lizzie Leigh* (1855), *The Grey Woman* (1865), *My Lady Ludlow* (1859, republished as *Round the Sofa*, 1871), *Mr. Harrison's Confessions* (1865), *Ruth* (1853), *Cranford* (1853), *North and South* (1855), *Sylvia's Lovers* (1863), and *Wives and Daughters* (1865). The first edition of her collected works appeared (1873).

GASKELL, Walter Holbrook (1847–1914), physiologist; born at Naples; BA, Trinity College, Cambridge (26th wrangler), 1869; studied physiology at Leipzig, 1874–5; MD, Cambridge, 1878; FRS, 1882; university lecturer in physiology, 1883; fellow of Trinity Hall, 1889; his physiological researches revolutionized current ideas of action of the heart, and of cardiac disease; aroused great controversy by his theory of the origin of vertebrates.

GASKELL, William (1805–1884), Unitarian minister; MA, Glasgow, 1824; junior minister of Cross Street Chapel, Manchester, 1828, senior, 1854; secretary to Manchester New College, 1840–6, professor of English history and literature, 1846–53, and chairman of committee from 1854; taught logic and literature at Owens College; his 'Lectures on the Lancashire Dialect' (1844) appended to fifth edition of his wife's novel, *Mary Barton* (see GASKELL, ELIZABETH CLEGHORN); some of his hymns included in *Martineau's Hymns of Praise and Prayer* (1874).

GASKIN, George (1751–1829), divine; MA, Trinity College, Oxford, 1778; DD, 1788; for forty-six years lecturer in Islington; incumbent of St Bennet, Gracechurch Street, and secretary, SPCK, 1791; rector of Stoke Newington, 1797; prebendary of Ely, 1822; edited Bishop Dehon's sermons.

GASPARS (JASPERS), Jan Baptist (1620?–1691), portrait painter; native of Antwerp; worked for General *Lambert; assisted *Lely and *Kneller, and became known as 'Lely's Baptist'; painted portraits of Charles II and *Hobbes, and etched *Banquet of the Gods*.

GASPEY, Thomas (1788–1871), journalist and author; for sixteen years on the staff of the *Morning Post*, for which he wrote 'Elegy on Marquis of Anglesey's Leg'; sub-editor of *Courier*; published novels and historical works.

GASQUET, Francis Neil (in religion Dom **Aidan)** (1846–1929), cardinal and historian; entered Benedictine novitiate at Downside Priory, 1866; master at Downside School, 1870; priest, 1874; prior, 1878–85; his priorship turning-point in history of Downside; resigned owing to ill health; engaged in historical research; his publications include *Henry VIII and the English Monasteries* (1888–9); chairman of Papal Commission for Reorganization of English Benedictine Congregation, 1899; president of Papal Commission for Revising Text of Vulgate, 1907; cardinal deacon, 1914; successfully countered propaganda of central powers; prefect of archives of Holy See, 1917; librarian of Holy Roman Church, 1919; cardinal priest, 1924; died in Rome.

GASSIOT, John Peter (1797–1877), scientific writer; chairman of Kew Observatory, which he helped to endow; founder of Royal Society Scientific Relief Fund; proved by experiments with *Grove's cells that the static effect of a battery increases with its chemical action, 1844; proved with delicate micrometers the correctness of Grove's arguments against the contact theory, 1844; discovered stratification of electric discharge, 1852; FRS.

GAST, Luce de (fl. 1190?), lord of the castle of Gast, near Salisbury; reputed author of the first part of the French poem *Tristan*.

GASTER, Moses (1856–1939), scholar and rabbi; born and educated in Bucharest; rabbinical diploma, Breslau, 1881; expelled from Romania for activities on behalf of Jews; naturalized British subject, 1893; chief rabbi of Sephardi Jews in England, 1887–1918; a founder and president of English Zionist Federation; publications include *The Sword of Moses* (1896),

Rumanian Bird and Beast Stories (1915), and *Samaritan Eschatology* (1932).

GASTINEAU, Henry (1791–1876), water-colour painter; member of Society of Painters in Water-colours, 1823; exhibited for fifty-eight years.

GASTRELL, Francis (1662–1725), bishop of Chester; educated at Westminster; MA, Christ Church, Oxford, 1687; DD, 1700; carried on a controversy with *Sherlock on the Trinity, 1696–8; Boyle lecturer, 1697; chaplain to *Harley, when speaker, 1700; canon of Christ Church, 1702; queen's chaplain, 1711; bishop of Chester, 1714; published, among other works, *Christian Institutes* (1707) and *Historical Notices of the Diocese of Chester.*

GATACRE, Thomas (d. 1593), divine; educated at Oxford and Magdalene College, Cambridge; student, Middle Temple, *c.*1553; domestic chaplain to Leicester; rector of St Edmund's, Lombard Street, 1572.

GATACRE, Sir William Forbes (1843–1906), major-general; joined 77th Foot in Bengal, 1862; instructor in surveying at Sandhurst, 1875–9; commanded regiment at Secunderabad, 1884; in command of Bombay district, 1894–7, and 3rd brigade of relief force in Chitral expedition, 1895; CB; received Kaisar-i-Hind Gold Medal for services in Bombay plague, 1897; commanded brigade in advance up Nile for recovery of Khartoum; major-general and KCB; known as 'General Backacher', 1898; in South African War he defended railway from East London to Bethulie, 1899; was forced to retreat at Stormberg (Dec.); joined main army at Bloemfontein, March 1900; occupied Dewetsdorp and sent detachment on to Reddersburg; detachment surrounded and surrendered owing to Gatacre's failure to relieve it (Apr.); removed from command; commanded Eastern district at Colchester, 1900–3; explored rubber forests in Abyssinia, 1905; died of fever at Iddeni.

GATAKER, Charles (1614?–1680), divine; son of Thomas *Gataker; educated at St Paul's School; BA, Sidney Sussex College, Cambridge; MA, Pembroke College, Oxford, 1636; chaplain to Falkland and rector of Hoggeston, Buckinghamshire; published works, including *Animadversions* on *Bull's *Harmonia Apostolica* and *Examination of the Case of the Quakers concerning Oaths* (1675).

GATAKER, Thomas (1574–1654), Puritan divine and critic; son of Thomas *Gatacre; scholar of St John's College, Cambridge; fellow of Sidney Sussex College, 1596; BD, 1603; MA, St John's College, Cambridge; lecturer at Lincoln's Inn, 1601; rector of Rotherhithe, 1611;

active member of the Westminster Assembly; favoured a mixture of prelacy and Presbyterianism; signed address against Charles I's trial; published, besides controversial works and life of William *Bradshaw, *Marci Antonini de Rebus Suis* (1652, Greek text with Latin version and commentary) and commentaries on Isaiah, Jeremiah, and Lamentations.

GATENBY, James Brontë (1892–1960), zoologist; born in New Zealand; educated at Wanganui Collegiate School, St Patrick's College, Wellington, and Jesus College, Oxford; first class, zoology, 1916; professor of zoology and comparative anatomy, Trinity College, Dublin, 1921–59, of cytology, 1959–60; an inspiring teacher; studied cytoplasmic structures in many animals from protozoans to man.

GATER, Sir George Henry (1886–1963), administrator; educated at Winchester and New College, Oxford; diploma in education, Oxford, 1909; assistant director of education, Nottingham, 1912; served in army in Gallipoli, Egypt, and France, 1914–18; DSO and bar; Croix de Guerre; commander of the Legion of Honour; CMG, 1918; director of education, Lancashire, 1919–24; education officer, London County Council, 1924–33; clerk to LCC, 1933–9; succeeded (Sir A. C.) Cosmo *Parkinson as permanent under-secretary of state for the colonies, 1939 and 1942–7; short periods in Ministry of Home Security and Ministry of Supply, 1940–2; chairman, School Broadcasting Council and member, BBC General Advisory Council; hon. fellow, New College and the Royal College of Music; warden of Winchester College, 1951–9; knighted, 1936; KCB, 1941; GCMG, 1944.

GATES, Bernard (1685?–1773), musician; master of Children of the Chapel Royal; member of Westminster Abbey choir and of Academy of Vocal Music; sang air in Dettingen *Te Deum*, 1743; *Handel's *Esther* performed at his house, 1732.

GATES, Horatio (1728–1806), major-general in United States service; served under Prince Ferdinand of Brunswick; captain, 1754; served at Fort Duquesne, 1755, Fort Pitt, 1760, and Martinique, 1762; major, 1762; in Ireland, 1768–9; retired from service and returned to America, 1769; adjutant-general and brigadier in American army on outbreak of war, 1775; major-general and commander of northern army serving in Canada, 1776; defeated Burgoyne at Bemus Heights, and forced him to surrender at Saratoga, 1777; president of Board of War and Ordnance, 1777; defeated at Camden, South Carolina, 1780; superseded in the command, 1780.

GATES, Sir **John** (1504?–1553), statesman; accompanied Henry VIII to Lincolnshire, 1536; received valuable grants in Essex for confidential services; KB, 1547; privy councillor and vice-chamberlain, 1551; chancellor of the duchy of Lancaster, 1552; executed as a partisan of *Northumberland.

GATES, Reginald Ruggles (1882–1962), botanist, geneticist, and anthropologist; born near Middleton, Nova Scotia; ancestors included Sir John *Gates and Major-General Horatio *Gates; educated at Middleton High School and Mount Allison University, Sackville, Nova Scotia; first class, science, 1903; demonstrator in botany, McGill University; senior fellow, Chicago University, Ph.D., 1908; wrote many books on genetics, including *The Mutation Factor in Evolution, with particular reference to Oenothera* (1915); paid first visit to Europe, 1910; worked at Imperial College of Science, London, 1911; lecturer in biology, St Thomas's Hospital, 1912–14; associate professor of zoology, California University, 1915–16; reader, botany department, King's College, London, 1919; professor, 1921–42; FRS, 1931; research fellow in botany and anthropology, Harvard University; made outstanding contributions to anthropology and human genetics as well as to botany and cytology; married Dr Marie Charlotte Carmichael *Stopes; marriage annulled; vice-president, Linnean Society; vice-president, Royal Anthropological Institute; fellow, King's College, London; LL D, Mount Allison; D.Sc., London.

GATES, Sir **Thomas** (*fl.* 1596–1621), governor of Virginia; knighted for service in Cadiz expedition, 1596; served in Netherlands, 1604–8; sailed for Virginia as lieutenant-general of the Colonization Company, 1609; wrecked off the Bermudas; governor, 1611–14, organizing the colony; supposed to have died in East Indies; *Jourdan's and *Purchas's accounts of his adventures in the Bermudas probably groundwork of the *Tempest*.

GATFORD, Lionel (d. 1665), Royalist divine; fellow of Jesus College, Cambridge; MA, 1625; BD, 1633; vicar of St Clement's, Cambridge, 1633; rector of Dennington, 1641–5 and 1660–5; arrested at Cambridge and imprisoned in Ely House, Holborn, for an unpublished work on passive obedience, 1643; minister in Jersey and chaplain to Sir Edward *Hyde, 1647; DD, 1660; vicar of Plymouth, 1661, but never had possession; died of the plague when curate of Yarmouth.

GATHORNE-HARDY, Gathorne, first earl of Cranbrook (1814–1906), statesman; educated at Eton and Oriel College, Oxford; BA, 1836; MA, 1861; hon. fellow, 1894; called to bar, 1840; obtained lead on sessions and at parliamentary bar; Conservative MP for Leominster, 1856–65; under-secretary for Home Department, 1858–9; active champion of Church of England; defeated Gladstone in parliamentary election for Oxford University, 1865; president of the Poor Law Board and PC, 1866; introduced Poor Law Amendment Bill, 1867; home secretary after Hyde Park riots, May 1867–8; dealt firmly with Fenian conspirators; in opposition warmly attacked Irish Church Disestablishment Bill, 1869; secretary of state for war under Disraeli, 1874–8; opposed Public Worship Regulation Bill, 1874; introduced Regimental Exchanges Bill, 1875; supported Disraeli's pro-Turkish policy; succeeded Lord Salisbury as secretary for India, 1878; raised to peerage as Viscount Cranbrook, 1878; sanctioned Vernacular Press Act of 1878; supported Lord *Lytton's forward policy on North-West Frontier; justified coercion of Amir Shere Ali; approved separation of Kandahar from Kabul, 1880; GCSI, 1880; sat on Royal Commission on Cathedral Churches, 1879–85; lord president of the Council, 1885–92; created earl, 1892; denounced Gladstone's Home Rule Bill, 1893; hon. DCL, Oxford, 1865; hon. LL D, Cambridge, 1892; good debater and platform speaker; ardent sportsman and broad churchman.

GATLEY, Alfred (1816–1863), sculptor; his *Hebe* purchased by Art Union; exhibited busts of Espartero, 1846, Archbishop *Sumner, 1848, and S. Christie-Miller, 1850, and executed that of Richard *Hooker in the Temple Church; after 1852 lived at Rome, where he died; his bas-relief, *Overthrow of Pharaoh*, statues of *Echo* and *Night* and marble statuettes of animals exhibited at International Exhibition, 1862.

GATLIFF, James (1766–1831), divine; educated at Manchester Grammar School; perpetual curate of Gorton, Manchester; edited, with life, *Wogan's *Essay on the Proper Lessons* (1818); imprisoned for debt and sequestrated; issued apologetic pamphlet with eccentric title (1820).

GATTIE, Henry (1774–1844), actor; appeared at Bath in vocal characters and old men's parts, 1807–12; at Drury Lane, 1813–33; his best parts, Morbleu in *Monsieur Tonson* and Dr Caius in *Merry Wives.*

GATTY, Alfred (1813–1903), vicar of Ecclesfield and author; BA, Exeter College, Oxford, 1836; MA, 1839; DD, 1860; vicar of Ecclesfield from 1839 till death; sub-dean of York Minster, 1862; published *The Bell: its Origin and History* (1847), *Sheffield Past and Present* (1873), verse, biographies, and sermons.

GATTY, Margaret (1807–1873), writer for children; daughter of Alexander John *Scott, whose life she and her husband published (1842); married Alfred Gatty, DD, 1839; established *Aunt Judy's Magazine*, 1866; published *Parables from Nature* (1855–71), *Aunt Judy's Tales* (1859), and *Aunt Judy's Letters*.

GAU, John (1493?–1553?), translator; MA, St Andrews, 1511; published in Sweden *Richt Vay to the Kingdome of Heuine* (translation from Christiern Pedersen), 1533, the earliest Protestant work in Scottish prose; prebendary of Church of Our Lady, Copenhagen.

GAUDEN, John (1605–1662), bishop of Worcester; MA, St John's College, Cambridge, 1626; entered Wadham College, Oxford; DD, 1641; vicar of Chippenham and chaplain to Robert *Rich, earl of Warwick, 1640; dean of Bocking, 1641; 'shuffled out' of the Westminster Assembly for Episcopalianism; retained benefices during the Commonwealth; wrote against the Army and the Civil Marriage Act and in defence of the church of England; published *Ecclesiae Anglicanae Suspiria* (1659); bishop of Exeter, 1660–2; wrote treatises against the Covenanters, 1660–1; edited *Hooker's *Ecclesiastical Polity* (1662); bishop of Worcester, 1662; claimed the authorship of Εἰκὼν Βασιλική; the *Pourtraicture of His Sacred Majestie in His Solitudes and Sufferings*, attributed by Royalist writers and Bishop Christopher *Wordsworth to Charles I. Gauden's claim was apparently admitted at the Restoration.

GAUGAIN, Thomas (1748–1810?), stipple engraver, native of Abbeville; exhibited paintings at Royal Academy, 1778–82; executed numerous engravings after *Reynolds, *Northcote, *Morland, Maria *Cosway, and *Nollekens's bust of Fox.

GAULE, John (c.1604–1687), divine; studied at Oxford and Cambridge; BA, Magdalene College, Cambridge, 1623–4; chaplain to Lord Camden, 1629; vicar of Great Staughton, 1632; published numerous theological works, including *Select Cases of Conscience touching Witches* (1646).

GAUNT, Elizabeth (d. 1685), the last woman executed for a political offence; burnt at Tyburn for treason in sheltering Burton, a Rye House conspirator and adherent of *Monmouth.

GAUNT, John of, duke of Lancaster (1340–1399). See JOHN.

GAUNT (GANT or PAYNELL), Maurice de (1184?–1230), baron of Leeds; granted charter to burgesses of Leeds, 1208; joined insurgent barons, 1216; captured at Lincoln, 1217; paid scutage for lands in eight counties, 1223; justice-

itinerant for Herefordshire, Staffordshire, Shropshire, Devonshire, Hampshire, and Berkshire, 1227; died in Brittany.

GAUNT, Simon de (d. 1315), bishop of Salisbury. See GHENT.

GAUNTLETT, Henry (1762–1833), divine; vicar of Olney, 1815–33, and friend of Rowland *Hill; published *Exposition of the Book of Revelation* (1821).

GAUNTLETT, Henry John (1805–1876), organist and composer; son of Henry *Gauntlett; played the organ at Olney as a child; organist at St Olave's, Southwark, 1827–46, at Union Chapel, Islington, 1853–61, and St Bartholomew's, Smithfield, 1872–6; introduced enlarged organs on the Haarlem model; patented electrical-action apparatus, 1852; created Mus.Doc. by Archbishop *Howley, 1842; played the *Elijah* at Birmingham, 1846; edited *Musical World*, contributing 'Characteristics of Beethoven' and other papers; composed *St. Alphege, St. Albinus, St. George*, and other hymn-tunes and chants, *The Song of the Soul*, and *Notes, Queries, and Exercises in Science and Practice of Music* (1859). *Encyclopaedia of the Chant* (first published 1885), was largely his work.

GAUVAIN, Sir Henry John (1878–1945), surgeon and specialist in tuberculosis; first class, natural sciences, St John's College, Cambridge, 1902; qualified at St Bartholomew's Hospital, 1906; medical superintendent, Lord Mayor Treloar Cripples' Home (later Orthopaedic Hospital), Alton, 1908–45; established first hospital school (1912), marine branch (1919), private clinics (1925); knighted, 1920.

GAVESTON, Piers, earl of Cornwall (d. 1312), favourite and foster-brother of Edward II; banished by Edward I, 1307, but recalled and created an earl on accession of Edward II; betrothed to sister of the earl of *Gloucester; having offended the barons by his conduct at the coronation was banished, but made lieutenant of Ireland, 1308; recalled, 1309; gave fresh offence by insolence and extravagance; accompanied Edward to Scotland, 1310–11; his banishment again demanded by lords ordainers, 1311; returned secretly from Bruges and joined the king at York; surrendered conditionally to *Pembroke at Scarborough; kidnapped by *Warwick and executed on Blacklow Hill in presence of *Lancaster and other barons.

GAVIN, Antonio (fl. 1726), author of *A Master-Key to Popery*; MA, Saragossa; having become a Protestant, escaped from Spain to London, and was entertained by Lord *Stanhope; officiated as a minister in London and afterwards in Ireland, where his *Master-Key*, containing mendacious revelations, appeared (1724).

GAVIN, Robert (1827–1883), painter; exhibited popular landscapes at the Scottish Academy; ARSA, 1854; travelled in America and Morocco, and lived some years at Tangier; RSA, 1879.

GAWDIE, Sir **John** (1639–1699), painter. See GAWDY.

GAWDY, Framlingham (1589–1654), Parliamentary reporter; MP, Thetford, 1620–1, 1623–4, 1625–6, and 1640; his 'Notes of what passed in Parliament, 1641, 1642', preserved in British Museum.

GAWDY, Sir **Francis** (d. 1606), chief justice of common pleas; half-brother of Sir Thomas *Gawdy; treasurer of the Inner Temple, 1571; MP, Morpeth, 1571; serjeant-at-law, 1577; as queen's serjeant, 1582, took part in proceedings against *Mary Queen of Scots at Fotheringay, and those against William *Davison (1541?–1608); justice of Queen's Bench, 1589; knighted, 1603; member of the courts which tried *Essex and *Ralegh; chief justice of common pleas, 1605.

GAWDY, Sir **John** (1639–1699), painter; grandson of Framlingham *Gawdy; succeeded to baronetcy, 1666.

GAWDY, Sir **Thomas** (d. 1588), judge; matriculated from Trinity Hall, Cambridge, 1545; bencher, Inner Temple, 1551; master of requests, 1551; MP, Arundel, 1553; treasurer of Inner Temple, 1561; serjeant-at-law, 1567; justice of the Queen's Bench, 1574; knighted, 1578; president of commission to determine fishing rights of Yarmouth and the Cinque Ports, 1575; member of the courts which tried Dr *Parry, 1585, William Shelley, 1586, *Mary Queen of Scots at Fotheringay, and the earl of *Arundel, 1589.

GAWEN, Thomas (1612–1684), Roman Catholic writer; educated at Winchester; fellow of New College, Oxford, 1632; MA; met *Milton at Rome; prebendary of Winchester, 1645; rector of Bishopstoke, 1660; having become a Romanist, withdrew to France, being admitted to *Henrietta Maria's household; devotional works published (1686).

GAWLER, George (1796–1869), governor of South Australia; served with 52nd Foot in the Peninsula (being twice wounded) and at Waterloo; governor of South Australia, 1838–41.

GAWLER, John (1765?–1842), botanist. See KER, JOHN BELLENDEN.

GAWLER, William (1750–1809), organist and composer; published collections for piano or harpsichord, with instructions (1780), *Harmonia Sacra* (1781), and other compositions.

GAY, John (1685–1732), poet and dramatist; apprenticed to a London mercer; afterwards lived as a private gentleman; his first poem, *Wine*, denying possibility of successful authorship to water-drinkers, possibly published in 1708; published *Present State of Wit* (1711); secretary to the duchess of Monmouth, 1712–14; issued *Rural Sports* (1713); contributed (1713) to *Steele's *Guardian* and *Poetical Miscellanies*; his *Shepherd's Week* (satirical eclogues directed against Ambrose *Philips), dedicated to *Bolingbroke, 1714; accompanied Lord Clarendon to Hanover as secretary, 1714; his first play, *What-d'ye Call it*, acted at Drury Lane and published, 1715; assisted by *Swift in the poem *Trivia* (1716), and by *Pope and *Arbuthnot in *Three Hours after Marriage*, acted 1717; accompanied William *Pulteney to Aix, 1717; issued *Poems* (1720), with subscriptions from *Burlington, *Chandos, and other noble patrons; lost a fortune in South Sea funds; patronized by the duke and duchess of *Queensberry ('Kitty'); lottery commissioner, 1722–31; offered post of gentleman-usher to the Princess Louisa, 1727; his *Captives* acted at Drury Lane, 1724; the first series of his *Fables* issued, 1727; his *Beggar's Opera* played for two seasons at Lincoln's Inn Fields, 1728, and throughout the British Isles, making much sensation, while its sequel, *Polly*, though prohibited (1728) by the court from being acted, was also published with great success; wrote the libretto for *Handel's *Acis and Galatea*, 1732, and *Achilles*, an opera produced at Covent Garden, 1733; the second series of *Fables* (1738), his principal posthumous work. He was buried in Westminster Abbey.

GAY, John (1699–1745), philosophical writer; MA, Sidney Sussex College, Cambridge, 1725; fellow, 1724–32; vicar of Wilshampstead, Bedfordshire, 1732–45; prefixed to the translation by Edmund *Law of the archbishop of Dublin's *Essay on the Origin of Evil* (1731) a 'Preliminary Dissertation' on utilitarian lines.

GAY, John (1813–1885), surgeon; MRCS, 1834; surgeon to Royal Free Hospital, 1836, and Great Northern, 1856–85; published medical works, including treatise *On Femoral Rupture* (1848).

GAY, Joseph (pseudonym) (1680?–1738). See BREVAL, JOHN DURANT.

GAYER, Arthur Edward (1801–1877), Irish ecclesiastical commissioner for Ireland, 1859–69; BA, Trinity College, Dublin, 1823; LL D, 1830; called to Irish bar, 1827; QC, 1844; chancellor of Ossory, 1848, and of Meath and other dioceses, 1851. His works include *The Catholic Layman* (1862) and *Memoirs of Family of Gayer* (1870).

GAYER, Sir John (d. 1649), lord mayor of London; warden of Fishmongers' Company, 1638; prominent director of East India Company; as sheriff of London, 1635, enforced ship money; knighted, 1641; lord mayor, 1646; impeached for abetting riots against compulsory militia service, 1647–8; president of Christ's Hospital, 1648; benefactor of Christ's Hospital.

GAYER, Sir John (d. 1711?), governor of Bombay; received freedom of East India Company, 1682; knighted, 1693; governor of Bombay under Sir John *Goldsborough, 1693; chief governor on death of latter, 1694; arrested, 1700, and confined several years at Surat, at the instance of Sir Nicholas Waite, representative of the New East India Company; died at Bombay soon after his release.

GAYNESBURGH, William de (d. 1307), ecclesiastic. See GAINSBOROUGH, WILLIAM.

GAYTON, Clark (1720?–1787?), admiral; commanded the *St George* at the attack on Martinique and the reduction of Guadaloupe, 1759; commander on Jamaica Station, 1774–8; rear-admiral, 1770; admiral, 1782.

GAYTON, Edmund (1608–1666), author; educated at Merchant Taylors' School; MA, St John's College, Oxford, 1633; fellow; adopted as a son by Ben *Jonson; expelled from post of superior beadle in arts at Oxford by parliamentary visitors, 1648; lived in great pecuniary distress in London; published, among other works, *Festivous Notes on . . . Don Quixote* (1654) in prose and verse.

GAYWOOD, Richard (*fl.* 1650–1680), engraver and etcher; pupil of Wenceslaus *Hollar and friend of Francis *Barlow.

GEARE, Allan (1622–1662), Nonconformist; MA, Leiden, 1651; incorporated at Oxford; successively minister of St Peter's, Paul's Wharf, chaplain to the earl of Bedford, and minister of St Saviour's, Dartmouth; ejected, 1662.

GEARY, Sir Francis (1710?–1796), admiral; entered navy, 1727; while commanding the *Chester* captured several French and Spanish ships, 1743–5; rear-admiral, 1759; commander of Portsmouth, 1770; admiral of the blue, 1775, of the white, 1778; created baronet, 1782.

GED, William (1690–1749), inventor of stereotyping; patented development of Van der Mey's method, 1725; made successful experiments, but was foiled in London by the dishonesty of his partner and the jealousy of the trade; returned to Edinburgh, and published (1744) his stereotyped Sallust; died in poverty.

GEDDES, Alexander (1737–1802), biblical critic; studied at Scalan and Paris; priest of Auchinhalrig and Preshome, Banffshire, 1769–79; made literary reputation by his verse translation of Horace's *Satires* (1779); LL D, Aberdeen, 1780; suspended for attending a Presbyterian service and hunting; while officiating at the imperial ambassador's chapel in London received from Lord Petre the means to prosecute his scheme for a revised Catholic version of the Bible; encouraged by *Kennicott and Bishop *Lowth; issued *General Answer to Queries, Counsels, and Criticisms* (1790); published the historical books of the Old Testament and Ruth (1792, 1797), and *Critical Remarks on the Hebrew Scriptures* (1800), the rationalistic character of which caused their prohibition and the author's suspension from ecclesiastical functions; his orthodoxy defended by Charles *Butler (1750–1832); maintained that the divinity of Jesus Christ was a primitive tenet of Christianity, 1787; published miscellaneous works.

GEDDES, Andrew (1783–1844), painter; educated at Edinburgh; exhibited at Royal Academy after 1806; ARA, 1832; in Italy, 1828–31; painted chiefly portraits; excelled as an etcher of portraits, landscapes, and copies of old masters.

GEDDES, Auckland Campbell, first Baron Geddes (1879–1954), public servant; brother of Sir Eric *Geddes; educated at George Watson's College and the University, Edinburgh; qualified in medicine, 1903; MD, 1908; professor of anatomy, Royal College of Surgeons, Dublin, 1909; McGill University, Montreal, 1913–14; director of recruiting, War Office, 1916; CB, KCB, and PC, 1917; MP, Basingstoke, 1917–20; minister of national service, 1917–19; president, Board of Trade, 1919–20; ambassador in Washington, 1920–4; GCMG, 1922; chairman, Royal Commission on Food Prices (1924), of Rio Tinto Company, and founding chairman, Rhokana Corporation; baron, 1942; although blind, he wrote *The Forging of a Family* (1952).

GEDDES, Sir Eric Campbell (1875–1937), politician, administrator, and man of business; educated at Merchiston Castle School, Edinburgh; deputy general manager, North Eastern Railway, 1914; inspector-general, transportation, all theatres of war, 1916–17; controller of navy, May–July 1917; first lord of Admiralty, 1917–18; Unionist MP, Cambridge borough, 1917–22; minister of transport, 1919–21; carried through railway amalgamation; chairman of 'Geddes Axe' Committee on national economy, 1921–2; chairman of Dunlop Rubber Company and Imperial Airways; knighted, 1916; PC, 1917; GCB, 1919.

GEDDES, James (d. 1748?), advocate; published *Essay on the Composition and Manner of Writing of the Ancients, particularly Plato* (1748).

GEDDES, Jenny (*fl.* 1637?), supposed name of the woman who threw a stool at the head of Bishop David *Lindsay when attempting to read *Laud's service-book in St Giles's, Edinburgh. Her real name is a very open question.

GEDDES, John (1735–1799), Roman Catholic bishop; educated at the Scots College, Rome; superior of Scalan, 1762–7, of Semple's College in Spain, 1770–9; coadjutor of the Lowlands, with title of Bishop of Morocco, 1779–97; published *Life of St. Margaret, Queen of Scotland* and *Treatise against Duelling*.

GEDDES, Michael (1650?–1713), divine; MA, Edinburgh, 1668; incorporated at Oxford, 1671; one of the first four Scottish students at Balliol College, Oxford, 1672; chaplain to English factory at Lisbon, 1678–88; chancellor of Salisbury, 1691; created LL D by Archbishop *Tenison, 1695; translated Portuguese and Spanish works.

GEDDES, Sir Patrick (1854–1932), biologist, sociologist, educationist, and town planner; educated at Perth Academy; studied under T. H. *Huxley in Paris; microscopy made impossible by attack of blindness; demonstrator in botany, Edinburgh; professor of botany, Dundee, 1889–1914; established 'world's first sociological laboratory' (1892) in Outlook Tower, Castlehill, Edinburgh, where he arranged stories of regional interpretation; interests centred increasingly on civics and town planning; his Cities and Town Planning Exhibition shown in Europe and India; professor of civics and sociology, Bombay, 1920–3; settled (1924) at Montpellier and built an unofficial 'Scots College'; an evolutionist; his concept of the relationship environment–function–organism led to place–work–folk; collaborated with Sir J. A. Thomson in *The Evolution of Sex* (1889), etc.; knighted, 1932.

GEDDES, William (1600?–1694), Presbyterian divine and author; graduated at Aberdeen, 1650; minister at Wick and Urquhart; published *The Saint's Recreation*.

GEDDES, Sir William Duguid (1828–1900), Greek scholar; MA, University and King's Colleges, Aberdeen, 1846; rector of Aberdeen Grammar School, 1853; professor of Greek at University and King's College, 1855, and in United University, 1860–85; principal and vice-chancellor of Aberdeen, 1885; LL D, Edinburgh, 1876; knighted, 1892; published, among other works, an edition of Plato's *Phaedo* (1863).

GEDEN, John Dury (1822–1886), Wesleyan; educated at Kingswood and Richmond College; joint editor of *London Quarterly Review* (established 1853); member of legal hundred, 1868; hon. DD, St Andrews, 1885; Fernley lecturer, 1874; one of the Old Testament revisers.

GEDGE, Sydney (1802–1883), divine; BA, St Catharine's College, Cambridge, 1824; fellow, 1825; second master of King Edward's School, Birmingham, 1835–59; vicar of All Saints', Northampton, 1859–75; active supporter of Church Missionary Society.

GEDY, John (*fl.* 1370), abbot of Arbroath; agreed to make a harbour for the burgh, 1394. *Southey's story that he placed a bell on the Bell Rock to warn sailors of the dangerous nature of the coast is not supported by evidence.

GEDYE, (George) Eric (Rowe) (1890–1970), journalist; educated at Clarence School, Weston-super-Mare, and Queen's College, Taunton; matriculated, London University; served in Gloucestershire Regiment in France, 1914–18; served on Inter-Allied Rhineland High Commission, 1919–22; appointed local correspondent (Cologne) of *The Times* and *Daily Mail*, 1922; 'special correspondent' of *The Times*, 1923–5; Central European correspondent, *The Times*, Vienna, 1925; moved to *Daily Express*, 1926, and to *Daily Telegraph*, 1929; expelled from Austria by Gestapo, 1938; worked for *Daily Telegraph* in Prague; Moscow correspondent of the *New York Times*, 1939; correspondent in Turkey, 1940–1; worked again in Vienna for the *Daily Herald*, the *Observer*, and the *Manchester Guardian*, 1945; MBE, 1946; head of evaluation for Radio Free Europe, 1954–61; publications include *A Wayfarer in Austria* (1928), *The Revolver Republic* (1930), *Heirs to the Hapsburgs* (1932), and *Fallen Bastions* (1939).

GEE, Edward (1565–1618), divine; fellow of Brasenose College, Oxford, 1588; MA, 1590; DD, 1616; chaplain to James I and fellow of Chelsea College; prebendary of Exeter, 1616.

GEE, Edward (1613–1660), Presbyterian divine; nephew of Edward *Gee (1565–1618); MA, Brasenose College, Oxford, 1636; rector of Eccleston, 1643, by choice of the people; prominent member of the Lancashire Presbytery; author of *A Treatise of Prayer* (1653) and *The Divine Right and Originall of Civil Magistrates* (1658).

GEE, Edward (1657–1730), dean of Lincoln; MA, St John's College, Cambridge, 1683; DD after 1701; rector of St Benet's, Paul's Wharf, and chaplain to William III, 1688; prebendary of Westminster and incumbent of St Margaret's, 1701; dean of Lincoln, 1722–30; published Protestant pamphlets, 1687–9.

GEE, John (1596–1639), anti-Catholic writer; nephew of Edward *Gee (1565–1618); MA, Exeter College, Oxford, 1621; beneficed at Newton, 1622, and afterwards at Tenterden; for a short time a Romanist; published on reconversion *The Foot out of the Snare* (1624) and similar works.

GEE, Sir Orlando (1619–1705), registrar of court of Admiralty, 1660; brother of John *Gee, benefactor of Isleworth Church.

GEE, Samuel Jones (1839–1911), physician; studied medicine at University College, London; MB, 1861; MD, 1865; FRCP, 1870; physician and lecturer at St Bartholomew's Hospital from 1868 to death; Gulstonian (1871), Bradshaw (1892), and Lumleian (1899) lecturer at Royal College of Physicians; had wide knowledge of early medical literature; published *Auscultation and Percussion* (1870) and *Medical Lectures and Aphorisms* (1902).

GEERAN (or GUERIN), Thomas (d. 1871), reputed centenarian; his case discredited by W. J. *Thoms, FSA.

GEFFREY, Sir Robert (1613–1703), lord mayor of London; master of Ironmongers' Company, 1667, 1685, 1688; sheriff of London, 1673; knighted, 1673; lord mayor, 1685; president of Bethlehem and Bridewell, 1693; founded school at Landrake; almshouses in Kingsland Road, London, erected from his bequests.

GEIKIE, Sir Archibald (1835–1924), geologist; educated at Edinburgh High School and University; joined Scottish branch of Geological Survey, 1855; director in Scotland, 1867; director-general for Great Britain, 1882; retired, 1901; Murchison professor of geology and mineralogy, Edinburgh, 1871–81; FRS, 1865; knighted, 1891; KCB, 1907; OM, 1913; his greatest contributions to geological science concerned with past volcanic history of Great Britain; furthered study of Scottish glacial deposits; works include *History of Volcanic Action during the Tertiary Period in Britain* (1888) and *Ancient Volcanoes of Great Britain* (1897).

GEIKIE, John Cunningham (1824–1906), religious writer; Presbyterian minister in Canada and in England, 1848–73; hon. LL D, Edinburgh, 1891; awarded Civil List pension, 1898; works include *Life and Words of Christ* (2 vols., 1877) and *Hours with the Bible* (10 vols., 1881–4).

GEIKIE, Walter (1795–1837), painter and draughtsman; a deaf mute from infancy; educated under Thomas *Braidwood; exhibited at Scottish Academy from 1827; RSA, 1834; published *Etchings Illustrative of Scottish Character and Scenery* (1833).

GELASIUS (or GILLA MAC LIAG) (1087–1173), count of Armagh and primate of Ireland; erenach of Derry, 1121; asserted primacy of Armagh by visitations; received the pall at the synod of Kells, 1149; summoned synod of Clane to promote uniformity.

GELDART, Edmund Martin (1844–1885), Unitarian minister; BA, Balliol College, Oxford, 1867; lived for some time at Athens; joined the Unitarians, 1872, and officiated at Hope Street, Liverpool, and at the Croydon Free Christian Church; published works on Modern Greek, a translation of Keim's *Jesus of Nazara* (vol. ii, 1876), *The Gospel according to Paul* (1884), and *A Son of Belial*, i.e. Balliol, (1882); disappeared on voyage to Dieppe.

GELDART, James William (1785–1876), professor of civil law at Cambridge, 1814–47; fellow of St Catharine's Hall, Cambridge, 1808, of Trinity Hall, 1809–21; LL D, 1814; rector of Kirk Deighton, 1840–76; edited Halifax's *Analysis of Civil Law* (1836).

GELDORP, George (*fl.* 1611–1660), portrait painter; came to England from Antwerp before 1623; intimate of *Van Dyck; painted portraits of William *Cecil, second earl of Salisbury (now at Hatfield), and Lord *Totnes.

GELL, Sir James (1823–1905), Manx lawyer and judge; admitted to Manx bar, 1845; edited for government Manx statute laws (1836–48); attorney-general, 1866–98; first deemster, 1898; clerk of the rolls, 1900–5; deputy-governor, 1897–1902; knighted, 1877; CVO, 1902.

GELL, Sir John (1593–1671), Parliamentarian; as sheriff of Derbyshire levied ship money, 1635; created baronet, 1642; raised regiment for the parliament, which was notorious for its plundering, 1642; prominent at capture of Lichfield and Battle of Hopton Heath, 1643; suspected of conniving at escape of the Royalists after Naseby, 1645; imprisoned and fined for plots against the Commonwealth, 1650; signed Derbyshire petition to *Monck, 1660.

GELL, John (d. 1806), admiral; commanded the *Monarca* in actions of Sir Edward *Hughes with De Suffren; rear-admiral, 1793, when he captured a French privateer with the valuable Spanish treasure-ship *Santiago*; took part in occupation of Toulon; admiral, 1799.

GELL, Robert (1595–1665), divine; educated at Westminster and Christ's College, Cambridge; fellow; rector of St Mary, Aldermary, *c.* 1641–65; published *Essay towards the Amendment of the last English Translation of the Bible* (1659).

GELL, Sir William (1778–1836), archaeologist and traveller; fellow of Emmanuel College, Cambridge; his *Topography of Troy* (1804), made in three days, alluded to by *Byron's epithet 'rapid Gell' (originally 'classic'); knighted after mission to Ionian islands, 1803; travelled in Greece with Edward *Dodwell and published *Geography and Antiquities of Ithaca* (1807) and *Itinerary of Greece* (1810); published *Itinerary of the Morea* (1817) and *Journey in the Morea* (1823); gave evidence (1820) in favour of Queen *Caroline, whose chamberlain he had been; after 1820 lived in Italy; published *Pompeiana* (1817–19) and *Topography of Rome* (1834); his original drawings preserved in the British Museum.

GELLIBRAND, Henry (1597–1636), mathematician; MA, Trinity College, Oxford, 1623; friend of Henry *Briggs; Gresham professor of astronomy, 1627; prosecuted by Laud for bringing out an almanac in which Protestant martyrs were substituted for Romish saints; acquitted; completed Briggs's *Trigonometria Britannica* (1633); published other mathematical works and *Epitome of Navigation*.

GELLIBRAND, Sir John (1872–1945), major-general; born in Tasmania; educated at King's School, Canterbury, and Sandhurst; retired (captain) from Manchester Regiment to Tasmania, 1912; served with Australian forces at Gallipoli; brilliant brigade commander in France; commanded 3rd Australian division, 1918; DSO, 1916; KCB, 1919; commissioner of police, Victoria, 1920–2; Nationalist member (Denison, Tasmania), federal parliament, 1925–8.

GEMINI (GEMINIE or GEMINUS), Thomas (*fl.* 1540–1560), engraver and printer; published with copper-plate engravings by himself *Compendiosa totius Anatomie delineatio* (1545), an abridgment of Vesalius's work of 1543; printed works for Leonard *Digges (d. 1571?) and engraved a portrait of Queen Mary (1559).

GENDALL, John (1790–1865), painter, employed by Rudolph *Ackermann; exhibited paintings of Devonshire scenery at the Academy, 1846–63.

GENÉE, Dame Adeline (1878–1970), ballet dancer; born in Jutland of parents named Jensen; came under guardianship of an uncle with stage name, Genée, and trained as dancer; first public appearance in Christiania (Oslo), 1888; danced in Berlin and Munich, where she danced Swanilda in *Coppélia*, 1896; settled in London, appearing at the Empire, Leicester Square, 1897; undertook tours of America, Australia, and New Zealand, and visited Copenhagen and Paris; danced before Edward VII and Queen Alexandra, 1905; danced in London at the Coliseum, Alhambra, and the Albert Hall, 1914–17; first

president, the Association of Operatic Dancing (later the Royal Academy of Dancing), formed to improve standards of teaching, 1920–54; Genée Gold Medal instituted, 1931; sponsored and led the English Ballet Company on visit to Copenhagen, 1932 (first group of British ballet dancers to go abroad); DBE, 1950; commander of the Order of Dannebrog; hon. D.Mus., London.

GENEST, John (1764–1839), dramatic historian; educated at Westminster; MA, Trinity College, Cambridge, 1787; published at Bath *Account of the English Stage, 1660–1830* (1832).

GENINGES, Edmund (1567–1591), Roman Catholic divine; executed at Tyburn for returning to the realm; his life published at St Omer (1614).

GENINGES, John (1570?–1660), provincial of English Franciscans; brother of Edmund *Geninges; first vicar of St Bonaventure, Douai, 1619; co-founder of convent of St Elizabeth, Brussels; published *Institutio Missionariorum* (1651).

GENT, Sir Thomas (d. 1593), judge; barrister, Middle Temple; MP, Malden, 1571; serjeant-at-law, 1584; baron of the Exchequer, 1586; member of High Commission court.

GENT, Thomas (1693–1778), printer and topographer; member of Stationers' Company and admitted to freedom of the City, 1717; employed in Fleet Street by Henry *Woodfall and Samuel *Richardson; settled at York, 1724, being the sole printer in the city and county; printed his own histories of York (1730), Ripon (1734), and Hull (1735); set up the first press at Scarborough; died in great poverty; his autobiography edited by Revd Joseph *Hunter, 1832.

GENTILESCHI, Artemisia (1590–1642?), painter; came to England with her father, Orazio *Gentileschi; painted for Charles I *David and Goliath, Fame*, and a portrait of herself; returned to Italy before 1630; famous for her portraits.

GENTILESCHI, Orazio (1563–1647), painter; native of Pisa; came to England, 1626, from Paris, at invitation of *Van Dyck; painted for *Buckingham and Charles I, who lodged him and gave him an annuity; some of his pictures at Marlborough House and two at Hampton Court.

GENTILI, Alberico (1552–1608), civilian; born at Sanginesio; DCL, Perugia; obliged to leave Italy with his father on account of heretical opinions; arrived in London, 1580; incorporated DCL at Oxford, 1581; consulted by government as to course to be taken with Mendoza, the plotting Spanish ambassador, 1584; accompanied embassy of Pallavicino to Saxony, 1586; regius professor of civil law at Oxford through *Walsingham's influence, 1587; began to practise as an advocate, 1590; admitted at Gray's Inn, 1600; permanent advocate for king of Spain, 1605. His chief works were *De Juris Interpretibus Dialogi sex* (1582) in defence of the older jurists against the 'humanist' school, *De Legationibus* (1585), *De Jure Belli Commentationes Tres* (1589), *De Jure Belli* (1598), and *Hispanicae Advocationis Libri Duo* (1613); fifteen volumes of his manuscripts (D'Orville) acquired by the Bodleian, 1805.

GENTILI, Aloysius (1801–1848), missionary apostolic in England; came to England, 1835, as missioner of Rosmini's Institute of Charity; superior of the college, Prior Park, Bath, till 1839; removed to Loughborough mission, 1842.

GENTILI, Robert (1590–1654?), infant prodigy and translator; eldest son of Alberico *Gentili; spoke French and Latin at 7; matriculated at Christ Church, Oxford, at 9; BA, Jesus College, Oxford, at 13; nominated probationer fellow of All Souls College by Archbishop *Bancroft in eighteenth year; resigned fellowship, 1612, and disappeared till 1637; translated Servita's *History of the Inquisition*, several works of Malvezzi, *Bacon's *Historie of Winds* (1653), and *Le Chemin Abrégé* (1654).

GENTLEMAN, Francis (1728–1784), actor and dramatist; appeared at Dublin in *Oroonoko*; afterwards played in his own pieces in England and Scotland, the best being *The Modish Wife* (1774), produced at Chester; published anonymously *The Dramatic Censor* (1770); often relieved by *Garrick, whom he ridiculed in his *Stratford Jubilee* (1769); edited Bell's acting Shakespeare; played Sir Epicure Mammon in his *Tobacconist*, 1771, an adaptation from the *Alchemist*.

GENTLEMAN, Robert (1746–1795), Dissenting divine; preached and taught school at Shrewsbury, 1765–9; divinity tutor at Carmarthen Academy, 1779–84; minister at Kidderminster, 1784–95; published, among other works, *Young English Scholar's Companion*.

GENTLEMAN, Tobias (*fl.* 1614), author of a work entitled *Way to Wealth* (1614), pointing out advantages of developing herring fisheries.

GEOFFREY (d. 1093), bishop of Coutances, 1048; completed his cathedral, 1056; followed Duke William to England, 1066, and interpreted at his coronation; received vast grants of land, chiefly in the west, where he was active in repressing the rising of 1069; presided at trial of suit between *Lanfranc and *Odo at Pennenden, 1071; attended councils of Winchester and Windsor, 1072, and the ecclesiastical council at St Paul's, 1075; helped to put down rising of *Ralph, earl of Norfolk, and *Roger, earl of Hereford, 1075; took part in the baronial rising

against William II, and held Bristol Castle, but was pardoned; upheld privileges of the clergy at Salisbury, 1088; died at Coutances.

GEOFFREY (d. 1154), first abbot of Dunfermline, 1128; prior of Christ Church, Canterbury, 1126.

GEOFFREY (d. 1178), abbot of Dunfermline, nephew and successor of *Geoffrey (d. 1154); witnessed charters of *Malcolm IV and *William the Lion; wrote in defence of Scottish Church.

GEOFFREY (1158–1186), fourth son of Henry II and count of Brittany; betrothed by his father to Constance, daughter of Count Conan, the Little, and adopted as heir, 1166; with the French king and his own brothers invaded Normandy, 1173, but did homage to his father on a promise of half the revenues of Brittany, 1175; knighted, 1178; upheld Philip II of France against the rebellious lords, and married Constance, 1181; by order of Henry II made war on his brother Richard; invaded Poitou, and refused to desist, occupying Limoges by treachery, 1183; after temporary reconciliation with Richard, joined Prince John against him, 1184; held 'Assize of Count Geoffrey' at Rennes to preserve rights of the lord, 1185; plotted with Philip II for possession of Anjou; died suddenly at Paris, and was buried in Notre Dame.

GEOFFREY (d. 1212), archbishop of York; reputed son of Henry II, at whose accession he was acknowledged and received into the household; made bishop of Lincoln, 1173; took prominent part in suppressing the northern rebellion of 1173–4; remained unconsecrated and resigned under pressure from Pope Alexander III, 1182, but became chancellor of England and treasurer of York; faithful to his father in his last war with Richard and Philip Augustus, 1188–9; named archbishop of York by Richard I, 1189, but opposed by Hubert *Walter and part of the chapter; ordained priest and confirmed in his see after much opposition; retired to Normandy, 1190, and ordered by Richard to remain abroad for three years; consecrated at Tours, 1191, and thereupon returned to England; arrested by William of *Longchamp on the ground of Richard's prohibition of his return to England, but supported by Prince John; released and enthroned; excommunicated Bishop Hugh *Puiset of Durham and other opponents; joined Bishop Hugh against John, 1193; his chapter in open rebellion against him after a demand for contributions for the king's ransom; suspended by the pope and deprived of sheriffdom of Yorkshire by the king, 1195; went to Rome and obtained reversal of sentence from the pope, 1196; temporarily favoured by Richard I, 1198; received with favour at accession of John, 1199; reconciled temporarily with chapter, 1200, but was again involved in disputes; upheld throughout by Innocent III; opposed levy of a tax on church property and fled abroad, 1207; buried at Grandmont, near Rouen.

GEOFFREY (d. 1235?), prior of Coventry, 1216; chosen by his monks to see of Lichfield and Coventry, 1223, but the election quashed by Archbishop Stephen *Langton and Honorius III; suspended for resisting visitation of new bishop, 1232; author of chronicle cited in *Dugdale's *Warwick*.

GEOFFREY, Rufus (d. 1140), chancellor to Henry I. See RUFUS.

GEOFFREY DE MUSCHAMP (d. 1208), bishop of Lichfield and Coventry, 1198; archdeacon of Cleveland, 1189; elected bishop by monks of Coventry at instance of Richard I and Archbishop *Hubert, 1198; said to have fled from England, 1207.

GEOFFREY DE VINSAUF (*fl.* 1200), poet. See VINSAUF.

GEOFFREY GAIMAR (*fl.* 1140?), author of *Lestorie des Engles*. See GAIMAR.

GEOFFREY OF COLDINGHAM (*fl.* 1214), writer of church history. See COLDINGHAM.

GEOFFREY OF GORHAM (d. 1146), abbot of St Albans, 1119–46; native of Maine; while teaching at Dunstable composed a miracle play of St Katharine; built guests' hall, queen's chamber, and a shrine; translated St Alban's body, 1129; founded leper hospital of St Julian, and enlarged nunnery at Sopwell.

GEOFFREY OF MONMOUTH (1100?–1154), bishop of St Asaph and chronicler; probably a canon of St George's in Oxford Castle; studied at Oxford; archdeacon of Llandaff, *c.*1140; bishop of St Asaph, 1152–4; witnessed Treaty of Wallingford, 1153; buried at Llandaff. His *Historia Britonum*, compiled from 'Nennius' and a lost book of Breton legends, tracing the descent of British princes from the Trojans, was translated into Anglo-Norman by *Gaimar and *Wace, and into English by *Layamon and *Robert of Gloucester; first printed in 1508 (Paris), and edited by Dr *Giles in 1844. Geoffrey's *Prophetia Anglicana Merlini Ambrosii Britanni* was first printed (1603).

GEOFFREY THE GRAMMARIAN (*fl.* 1440), alias Starkey a friar; preacher at King's Lynn, Norfolk; his *Promptuarium* [store-house] *Parvulorum Clericorum*, an English–Latin dictionary, valuable as record of fifteenth-century English and East-Anglian dialect, and for elucidation of debased Latin (printed by *Pynson, 1499, and by Wynkyn de *Worde). Other works assigned to Geoffrey by Bale and *Pits include the first Latin–English dictionary printed in England (*Hortus*, W. de Worde, 1500).

GEORGE, duke of Clarence (1449–1478), son of *Richard, duke of York (1411–1460); after his father's death in 1460 was sent for safety to Utrecht, whence he was brought back on his brother Edward IV's accession in 1461 and created duke of Clarence; lord-lieutenant of Ireland, 1462; at Calais married, contrary to Edward's wishes (1469), Isabella, the elder daughter of the earl of Warwick (see NEVILLE, RICHARD); invaded England in company with his father-in-law and made King Edward prisoner at Edgecot, 1469; forced by public opinion to release him; after obtaining an amnesty became implicated with Warwick in an unsuccessful Lancastrian rising in Lincolnshire; fled to France, Mar. 1470; returned to England with Warwick, Sept. 1470, and Edward fled the country; disapproved of the restoration of Henry VI, and in 1471 deserted to his brother at Coventry with four thousand men; fought with Edward at Barnet, 1471, and Tewkesbury, 1471, and assisted in the re-establishment of the York dynasty; became involved in a violent quarrel with his brother, Gloucester, who wished to marry Anne Neville (see ANNE, queen of Richard III) and share her mother's inheritance; reconciled with Gloucester by a parliamentary partition of the Neville estates, 1474; offered himself (1476) as a suitor for the hand of Mary of Burgundy, the successor of Charles the Bold; his scheme vetoed by Edward IV; revenged himself on some of the queen's adherents; charged with compassing the death of the king by necromancy and with other treasonable practices and committed to the Tower; attainted by parliament, Jan. 1478, and sentenced to death; secretly executed within the Tower, 17 or 18 Feb. 1478. The mode of death is uncertain, the statement that he was drowned in a butt of malmsey being perhaps only a London rumour.

GEORGE, prince of Denmark (1653–1708), consort of Queen Anne; married Princess Anne, 1683; deserted James II, 1688, at Andover; rewarded by act of naturalization and a peerage, being created duke of Cumberland, 1689; disliked by William III; on his wife's accession was refused title of king, 1702, but named 'generalissimo' (nominally superior of *Marlborough as captain-general) and lord high admiral, receiving a large annuity and exemption from disabilities under Act of Settlement; voted for Occasional Conformity Bill, 1702; his management of the Admiralty attacked by the Whigs, 1704–8; FRS. A portrait by *Wissing is in the National Portrait Gallery.

GEORGE I (George Lewis) (1660–1727), king of Great Britain and Ireland and elector of Hanover; great-grandson of James I; first saw military service under the empire, 1675; came to England to propose for the hand of the Princess Anne, 1680; married his cousin, Sophia Dorothea of Celle, 1682; took part in Sobieski's relief of Vienna, 1683; distinguished himself in Hungary, 1685, and at Neerwinden, 1693; divorced his wife and imprisoned her for life, 1694; succeeded to Hanover, 1698, admitted to the College of Electors at the Diet, 1708, and named arch-treasurer of the empire, 1710; protected Holstein-Gottorp against Denmark, 1699; joined the Grand Alliance, 1701, contributing 10,000 men and five regiments of horse; formed intimate relations with *Marlborough after his mission of 1704–5; commanded Imperial Army on Upper Rhine, 1707–9; concluded alliances with Poland, 1709, and Denmark, 1710; occupied Verden, 1712; refused to intervene in English politics; reconciled with his son on death (1714) of his mother, Electress Sophia, which made him the next heir after Queen Anne to the English throne; on Queen Anne's death had fresh instrument of regency drawn up for England, 1714; while at The Hague, on his way to fill English throne, displaced *Bolingbroke for *Townshend as secretary of state, having previously named Marlborough captain-general; became king of England, 1714; his first collective Cabinet entirely Whig, with the exception of Nottingham (see FINCH, DANIEL); conformed to the national church, though he was allowed a Lutheran chaplain, but was unpopular on account of his character and the rapacity of his foreign favourites, an attempt on his life being made, 1717; after suppression of Jacobite rebellion of 1715, and passing of Septennial Act, 1716, went to Hanover, where he frequently spent the latter half of each year, his son Prince George being left as regent; formed an alliance with France and the Netherlands, 1717, in which year Townshend was replaced by *Stanhope as chief minister; the Quadruple Alliance formed in 1718, in accordance with his wishes, and Bremen and Verden added to Hanover, the schemes of Charles XII and Alberoni to aid the Jacobites being foiled; granted a slight measure of relief to the Romanists and Dissenters; had Convocation silenced, 1717. Walpole, who was called in to deal with the South Sea crisis, remained chief minister from 1721 till the end of the reign. Under Walpole the 'Atterbury plot' was discovered, 1722, further interference with Sweden checked, the Treaty of Hanover negotiated, 1725, as a countercheck to that of Vienna, and George I induced to assent to it. George I died of apoplexy at Osnabrück and was buried at Hanover. His will was destroyed by George II. A certain brusqueness of manner, in spite of some kingly qualities, prevented him from attaining popularity. Portraits by *Kneller are at Windsor and in the National Portrait Gallery.

GEORGE II (1683–1760), king of Great Britain and Ireland; son of George I; after the divorce of his mother, whom he thought innocent, lived with his grandparents at Hanover; married *Caroline of Brandenburg-Anspach, 1705; created an English peer, 1706; distinguished himself at Oudenarde, 1708; came to England with his father and was created prince of Wales, 1714; on friendly terms with John *Campbell, second duke of Argyll, formed intimacy with Henrietta *Howard (later countess of Suffolk); popular with English, but not with Hanoverians; confined to his room and excluded from St James's on account of his conduct to the king and Newcastle at the baptism of his eldest son, *Frederick, 1717; removed to Leicester House, which became a centre of opposition, 1718; deprived of custody of his children; partially reconciled to the king through Walpole, 1720; succeeded to the throne, 1727; continued Walpole in office after his favourite, Sir Spencer Compton, afterwards Lord Wilmington, had failed to form a ministry, but replaced Lord *Berkeley (who had propounded a scheme for transplanting him to America when prince of Wales) by Sir George *Byng at the Admiralty; went to Hanover to secure possession of his mother's property and that of his uncle, the late bishop of Osnabrück; quarrelled with Frederick William of Prussia, and though reconciled to him by arbitration, 1730, was debarred from carrying out contemplated marriage alliances between the houses of England and Prussia; with difficulty prevented from involving England in the Polish Succession War, 1733; tried to negotiate an alliance between the king of Spain, Philip V, and the emperor Charles VII; concluded treaty with Denmark, 1734; became attached to Countess von *Walmoden, 1735; reluctantly refused alliance with the emperor; negotiated marriage for Frederick, prince of Wales, with Augusta of Saxe-Gotha, 1736; spent most of 1736 in Hanover; was in great danger from a storm in returning; had an open rupture with Frederick, prince of Wales, 1737; created Countess Walmoden Lady Yarmouth, 1738; overcame the pacific policy of Walpole, 1739, and declared war against Spain; concluded treaty with Maria Theresa, for whom he obtained a subsidy, 1741; secured Hanover by neutrality agreement with France; reluctantly parted with Walpole, 1742; made Lord Wilmington (Compton) head of the Treasury, and in *Carteret as secretary of state (1742–5) found a sympathetic foreign minister; probably by advice of Carteret arranged Treaty of Breslau between Frederick the Great of Prussia and Maria Theresa, 1742, and formed defensive alliances with Prussia and Russia, 1742; took Hanoverian troops into British pay and sent them into the Netherlands; personally led the allied troops at Dettingen against the French, the victory recovering him his popularity, 1743; concluded Treaty of Worms with Maria Theresa and Sardinia, 1743; compelled by his other ministers to dismiss Carteret, 1744; made largely responsible for the defence of Bohemia when Frederick the Great declared war upon that country and renewed hostilities with Maria Theresa; compelled by the success of the French and Prussians, and landing of the Young Pretender in Scotland, to extort Maria Theresa's consent to the cession of Silesia, 1745; tried to get rid of his ministers and to recall Carteret (Lord Granville) and Pulteney (Lord Bath); refused to accept Pitt as secretary-at-war; gained over Newcastle to his warlike views, and after Culloden sent more troops to the Netherlands, 1746; after unsuccessful operations obliged to make peace on the basis of mutual restitution, 1748; his scheme for procuring election of Archduke Joseph as king of the Romans defeated by Prussia, 1750; submitted to the Pelhams on the death of Frederick, prince of Wales, 1751; the subsidy treaties arranged by him for the defence of Hanover rejected by the regents, 1755, though next year a treaty was arranged with Prussia guaranteeing the integrity of Germany; obliged by the resignation of Henry *Fox to accept Pitt as secretary of state under Devonshire, 1756, and, though he dismissed him within three months, on *Waldegrave's failure to form a ministry was obliged to reappoint him with Newcastle at the Treasury, 1757. He showed much displeasure with his son, the duke of *Cumberland, after his failure in Germany, and considered the sentence of the court martial on *Sackville too lenient. At the date of his death the French had been driven from Canada, checked in Europe, and successfully attacked in India, Africa, and the West Indies, while the Dutch were ousted from Bengal. He was buried beside Queen Caroline in Henry VII's Chapel, Westminster Abbey. In state affairs he was largely guided by Queen Caroline, to whom he was much attached, in spite of his mistresses. He put Hanover and his continental interests before England. Though a patron of *Handel, he neglected literature and pictorial art. Several portraits of him are in the National Portrait Gallery and at Hampton Court, and a royal group by *Hogarth in the National Portrait Gallery of Ireland.

GEORGE III (George William Frederick) (1738–1820), grandson of George II, and king of Great Britain and Ireland; son of *Frederick Louis, prince of Wales; created prince of Wales, 1751; imbibed political principles from writings of *Bolingbroke and *Blackstone; completely under influence of his mother, and after attainment of his majority (1756) of Bute; said to have been in love with Hannah *Lightfoot, a Quakeress; on coming to the throne, 1760, put forth a proclamation against immorality, and declared that he 'gloried in the name of Briton'; after a flirtation with Lady Sarah Lennox, married *Charlotte Sophia of Mecklenburg-Strelitz, 1761; recommended the extension of judge's tenures beyond the demise of the crown; determined to destroy the party system and to end the French War; dismissed Pitt and Newcastle, and made Bute secretary of state, 1761, and first minister, 1762; dismissed Portland, Rockingham, and other leading Whigs, and concluded peace with France and Spain, 1763; was obliged to part with Bute, but for some time acted on his advice; called in George Grenville, but made constant attempts to get rid of him, though concurring generally in his policy; urged on prosecution of *Wilkes, 1763; approved Grenville's Stamp Act, 1765, but allowed its repeal, 1766; the Regency Act, from which ministers at first excluded name of princess dowager, due to his first mental illness, 1765; negotiated with Pitt and *Lyttelton through *Cumberland; again promised to deny access to Bute, probably keeping his word; obliged to accept Rockingham as minister; intrigued against Rockingham through 'the king's friends'; allowed Pitt to come in with a free hand, creating him earl of Chatham, Grafton being nominal premier, 1766; entreated Chatham to retain office, 1767; urged firmness in dealing with the rioters of 1769 and with Wilkes; insulted by a mob at St James's; induced Charles *Yorke to accept the seals, 1770; made North premier, 1770; remained unmoved by petitions from the City demanding a dissolution; and for twelve years personally directed the government through distribution of patronage, disposal of civil list revenue, and manifestations of feeling at court ceremonials; frequently wrote to North, but sometimes consulted Charles *Jenkinson, afterwards first earl of Liverpool; directed the opposition to *Savile's Nullum Tempus Bill; forbade Cumberland and *Gloucester the court, and promoted the Royal Marriage Bill, which prohibited members of the royal family from marrying under 25 without the king's consent; prevented interference of France between Russia and Turkey; showed hostility to *Clive, 1773; favoured Boston Port Bill, 1774; arranged for Hanoverian garrisons in Gibraltar and Minorca, and negotiated for the hire of Russian troops, 1775; supported the policy which led to outbreak of war with American colonists, and as the war continued, approved 'every means of distressing America'; applied to parliament for a grant to pay his debts, and though presenting imperfect accounts, received a sum for arrears and an addition to the civil list, 1777; refused to allow North to resign or to receive Chatham as chief minister, 1778; allowed North to negotiate with the opposition; contemplated retirement to Hanover; saved London by his conduct during Gordon riots, 1780; spent great sums in elections of 1781, and is said to have personally canvassed against *Keppel at Windsor; applied to Shelburne and Gower on North's resignation, 1782, but was forced again to take Rockingham as minister; through *Thurlow set the Shelburne section against the Rockingham Whigs, and on Rockingham's death (1782) appointed Shelburne as his successor; on Shelburne's resignation applied to the younger Pitt and Gower before submitting to receive the coalition, 1783, whom he overthrew by using his personal influence with the peers against their India Bill, 1783; supported Pitt both before and after the general election, which secured him a majority, the 'king's friends' subsequently disappearing as a party; followed Pitt's advice when premier, though disliking his scheme of parliamentary reform and the trial of Warren *Hastings; his life threatened by the mad Margaret *Nicholson, 1786; suffered second attack of madness, 1788–9; agreed to dismissal of Thurlow, 1792, and recall of duke of *York from Flanders, 1794; remonstrated with Pitt against negotiating with France, 1797; shot at by Hadfield, 1800; caused the resignation of Pitt by declaration against revival of Catholic emancipation, 1801; suffered a third attack of mania, which was abridged by Pitt's promise not to revive the Roman Catholic question; reviewed volunteers in Hyde Park, 1803; became deranged again, 1804, in consequence of the conduct of the prince of Wales; through *Eldon consented to receive Pitt back with the Grenvilles, but without Fox, 1804; opened parliament for last time, 1805; appointed *Manners-Sutton primate instead of Pitt's nominee, 1805; sent for *Hawkesbury (Jenkinson), 1806, and on his failure accepted Grenville as minister with Fox, to whom he became reconciled, but brought about his resignation by demanding a pledge against Catholic emancipation; by his influence kept the Portland ministry together, 1809–12; condemned the duel of Canning and *Castlereagh; became blind and, after 1811, permanently deranged, but retained bodily strength almost till death. He was very popular with the middle classes, and generally with the majority of his subjects, who respected the

decorum of his life, and a firmness which at times verged on obstinacy. He was buried in St George's Chapel, Windsor. Portraits of him are at Windsor, Hampton Court, and in the National Portrait Gallery.

GEORGE IV (1762–1830), king of Great Britain and Ireland; son of George III and Queen *Charlotte; brought up in strict seclusion with his brother *Frederick Augustus, duke of York, at Kew, but well educated; already involved in intrigue with Mary *Robinson ('Perdita'), 1780; came of age, 1783, when he established himself at Carlton House; received £30,000 from parliament to pay debts, and an annual allowance of £50,000 from the king; in close alliance with Charles James *Fox and other Whig leaders; fell in love with Mrs Maria Anne *Fitzherbert and married her, 1785; denied the marriage in order to conciliate parliament and deceived Fox; received an addition to his income and a parliamentary grant of £161,000 for his debts, 1787; plunged into fresh extravagances in company with York, Fox, *Sheridan, and Beau *Brummell; built Brighton Pavilion, 1784, and lived much there; intrigued with *Thurlow and *Loughborough against the queen and Pitt, and openly canvassed for support against the minister's regency resolutions, 1788; drew up a letter of remonstrance in concert with the Whigs against the restrictions on his powers as regent, 1789; received an offer of free powers from Irish parliament; excluded from the king's presence on his recovery; addressed remonstrances to him on conduct of the queen and an apologetic memorial; raised money abroad on Osnabrück bishopric and post-obits; their liability repudiated by the prince's agents after 1792; married *Caroline of Brunswick, 1795, but soon separated from her, and returned to Mrs Fitzherbert, though recently intimate with Lady Jersey; received another grant from parliament; demanded viceroyalty of Ireland, and intervened on behalf of Lord Edward *Fitzgerald, 1797–8; applied for service abroad; under influence of Moira (see HASTINGS, FRANCIS RAWDON-, 1754–1826) made overtures to Pitt, 1801; received a fresh money grant and a commutation of his claims on the duchy of Cornwall, 1803; his application for military employment again refused; negotiated through Sheridan with *Addington, but at the same time suggested to Pitt a junction between him and Fox under the premiership of Moira, 1804; deprived of the care of his daughter, Princess *Charlotte, 1805; obtained commission for examination into charges against Princess Caroline, 1806; practically severed himself from all the Whigs except Sheridan, *Erskine, and Moira; consulted Grey and Grenville upon his answer to Perceval's regency proposals, when the king was permanently disabled by insanity, but acted on the advice given by Sheridan and *Adam, 1811; after further negotiations with the Whigs was induced by influence of Lady Hertford to accept the restricted regency; broke with Mrs Fitzherbert at installation as prince regent; deprived of Perceval's services by his death, 1812, after which complicated negotiations for the formation of a coalition ministry under the Marquis Wellesley or Lord Moira followed, but were rendered fruitless owing to the regent's aversion from Grey and Grenville, on which the Tories returned to office under Liverpool, 1812; became involved in disputes with his wife and daughter; the re-enactment of the act of 1795 for the security of the king's person necessitated by his unpopularity, 1817; succeeded to the throne, 1820; employed *Knighton to deal with his debts; tried to prevent the return of Queen Caroline, and on her arrival excluded her from the coronation, and forced ministers to bring in a Divorce Bill, 1820; visited Ireland and Hanover, 1821, and Scotland, 1822; tried to exclude Canning from office, and thwarted his foreign policy; retired with Lady Conyngham to Brighton and Windsor; strongly opposed Catholic emancipation and the recognition of the Spanish-American republics; wished to take command of the army on Wellington's retirement; under the Goderich ministry, 1827–8, distributed appointments without consulting the ministers; reluctantly accepted the repeal of Test and Corporation Acts, and put many obstacles in the way of the passing of Catholic Emancipation Bill, but finally gave way; latterly suffered from failing health and delusions; the power of the crown much diminished in his reign. He was buried in St George's Chapel, Windsor. Portraits by *Lawrence are at Windsor and in the National Portrait Gallery.

GEORGE V (1865–1936), king of Great Britain, Ireland, and the British Dominions beyond the Seas, emperor of India; born at Marlborough House 3 June 1865, second son of the prince and princess of Wales, later King Edward VII and Queen *Alexandra; at Windsor Castle (7 July) baptized George Frederick Ernest Albert; passed his childhood in an atmosphere of sustained happiness and affection and remained devoted to his parents throughout life; with his elder brother, the duke of *Clarence, joined the *Britannia* as naval cadet, 1877; set his heart upon a naval career; in *Bacchante* made a cruise to the West Indies (1879–80) and to South America, South Africa, Australia, Japan, and China (1880–2); separating for first time from his brother joined corvette *Canada* for service on North America Station, 1883; promoted sub-lieutenant, 3 June

1884; KG, 1884; secured first class in seamanship, gunnery, and torpedo work at Royal Naval College, Greenwich, 1885; served on Mediterranean Station until 1888; received freedom of City of London, June 1889; commanded gunboat *Thrush*, 1890–1; promoted commander, 1891; his naval career ended by death of duke of Clarence, 14 Jan. 1892; created duke of York (1892) and provided with apartments in St James's Palace ('York House') and York Cottage at Sandringham; in Chapel Royal, St James's Palace, 6 July 1893, married Princess Victoria Mary (May) of Teck, who had previously been engaged to his elder brother; their close companionship henceforward exemplified a lofty standard of family life; the following children were born to them: Prince Edward (1894), Prince Albert (1895), Princess Mary (1897), Prince *Henry (1900), Prince *George (1902), and Prince John (1905); on death of Queen Victoria (22 Jan. 1901) became duke of Cornwall and his public duties increased; obtained the services of Sir Arthur *Bigge (later Lord Stamfordham) whose knowledge and devotion proved inestimable asset; with the duchess toured Australia and New Zealand (1901), opening the new Commonwealth parliament in Melbourne (9 May); on return journey visited South Africa and crossed and recrossed Canada; created prince of Wales and earl of Chester, 9 Nov. 1901; maintained uniformly harmonious relations with his father who put state papers at his disposal; formed habit of attending parliamentary debates; played golf and lawn tennis; perfected his shooting, sailed his famous yacht *Britannia*, and collected postage stamps of British Empire; in the last three pastimes he was an expert in his own right; paid several visits to the courts of Europe; with the princess made an extensive tour of India (1905–6); visited Canada (1908).

On death of his father was proclaimed king, 6 May 1910; felt himself ill equipped in face of a complex political situation and little known to his subjects; profoundly impressed by his coronation in Westminster Abbey, 22 June 1911; celebrations in London followed by a review at Spithead of largest naval fleet ever assembled and by visits to Ireland and Wales; left with the queen in Nov. for a state visit to India; at the magnificent coronation durbar (12 Dec.) at Delhi announced that the seat of government was to be transferred there from Calcutta. On 16 Nov. 1910 Asquith and *Crewe obtained from him a 'hypothetical understanding' that should need arise in the next parliament he would agree to create a sufficient number of peers to secure the passage of the Parliament Bill designed to restrict the powers of the House of Lords; when this was revealed the Lords accepted the bill (10 Aug. 1911) in an atmosphere of intense political excitement; the bill had the effect of increasing the responsibility of the king when a bill, thrice rejected by the Lords, came up for royal assent, since he alone must decide whether an appeal to the country would be justified; this situation became imminent in 1913 when the Lords twice rejected the Home Rule Bill; as the Irish situation worsened, the king urged restraint on all in an endeavour to prevent civil strife; invited representatives of all parties to a conference at Buckingham Palace at which the speaker presided, July 1914; conference failed but the controversy was laid aside upon the outbreak of the European war.

In 1912 the king had told Prince Henry of Prussia, the emperor's brother, that in the event of Austria and Germany going to war with Russia and France, England would come to the assistance of the latter; on 26 July 1914 when war seemed imminent he informed Prince Henry that England still hoped not to be drawn in; this was misinterpreted as an assurance of neutrality; resided for most of war at Buckingham Palace where he ordered that no alcohol should be consumed and maintained strict adherence to rationing regulations; paid numerous visits to hospitals, naval and military formations, factories, etc.; distributed 58,000 decorations; paid five visits to Grand Fleet and seven to armies in France and Belgium; fractured his pelvis when thrown from his horse during a visit in 1915; adopted the name of Windsor for royal house and family, 1917; at the end of the war he and the queen were greeted with unparalleled demonstrations of affection.

With queen visited Belfast (June 1921) to open Ulster parliament and earnestly appealed to all Irishmen for forbearance; urged Lloyd George to make fresh overtures, which resulted in a truce; at a critical stage in subsequent negotiations (Sept.) secured a more conciliatory tone in note from Lloyd George to Mr *de Valera and an invitation to Sinn Fein representatives to meet Lloyd George; agreement signed, 6 Dec. On resignation (1923) of Bonar Law, who intimated that he would prefer not to tender advice on his successor, summoned Stanley Baldwin in preference to Lord *Curzon who was in the House of Lords; on sending for Ramsay MacDonald (Jan. 1924), first Labour prime minister, assured him that he might count on his assistance in every way; was immediately at home with the Labour ministers; granted dissolution to MacDonald in Oct.; asked his people to forget all bitterness after General Strike, 1926; by the Statute of Westminster (1931) parliament ceased to control the overseas dominions and the king alone constituted the bond between them and the home country; in broadcasts each Christmas Day from 1932 he sent a personal message of kindliness to British homes throughout the world and asserted a simple faith in the continued guidance of a divine Providence; established singular hold upon the affections of his people; contracted a streptococcal infection (Nov. 1928) which necessitated an operation for drainage of chest (12 Dec.) and for some weeks the issue remained in doubt; although not completely recovered attended a service of thanksgiving in St Paul's Cathedral, 7 July 1929; when MacDonald tendered the resignation of his government owing to internal dissension arising out of the financial crisis (Aug. 1931), urged him to consider an all-party government and called a conference of the party leaders which resulted in the 'National' government; had by now a great store of political experience so that ministers were apt not only to tender but to seek advice; the extent to which he had become the father of his people was demonstrated when he celebrated his Silver Jubilee, 1935; died at Sandringham, 20 Jan. 1936, after an illness which was short and peaceful in its close; the funeral took place at Windsor, 28 Jan.

In person he was neatly made and slightly below middle height; his voice strong and resonant, his eyes arrestingly blue; his naval training had implanted habits of discipline, and his mode of life was extremely regular; he was quick to check infractions of traditional observances and duties; a sound churchman, with the habit of daily Bible reading, he always attended Sunday morning service; keenly interested in all three fighting services and conscientious in his perusal of state documents; in private life his pursuits were those of the English country gentleman; in his mistrust of cleverness, his homespun common sense, dislike of pretension, ready sense of the ludicrous, and devotion to sport, he possessed qualities which appealed to Englishmen of all classes.

GEORGE VI (1895–1952), king of Great Britain, Ireland, and the British Dominions beyond the Seas; born at York Cottage, Sandringham, 14 Dec. 1895; second son of duke and duchess of York, afterwards King George V and Queen Mary; baptized Albert Frederick Arthur George; served in navy, 1909–17; qualified as pilot in RAF, 1919; at Trinity College, Cambridge, 1919–20; became president of Industrial Welfare Society and made industrial areas his special interest; inaugurated Duke of York camps for boys from public schools and industry, 1921; KG, 1916; created Duke of York, 1920; KT, 1923; PC, 1925; married in Westminster Abbey, 26 Apr. 1923, Lady Elizabeth Angela Marguerite Bowes-Lyon, daughter of fourteenth earl of *Strathmore and Kinghorne; together they established a pattern of family life and devotion to duty; two children were born to them; Princess Elizabeth (1926) and Princess Margaret (1930); with Duchess toured New Zealand and Australia, 1927; proclaimed King, 12 Dec. 1936, upon abdication of his elder brother, King Edward VIII; crowned in Westminster Abbey, 12 May 1937; with Queen paid state visit to France, 1938, and visited Canada and United States, 1939; despite speech impediment resumed father's tradition of Christmas Day broadcast to Empire, 1939; entirely confident of outcome of the war; remained in London throughout and was indefatigable in sympathetic visiting of bombed areas; created George Cross and Medal mainly for civilian gallantry, 1940; popularity of monarchy manifest during celebrations at end of European war; with Queen and Princesses visited Southern Africa, 1947; underwent right lumbar sympathectomy operation, 1949; opened Festival of Britain, 3 May 1951; his left lung removed, 23 Sept. 1951; died in his sleep at Sandringham, 6 Feb. 1952; buried in St George's chapel, Windsor; earned respect and affection of nation for courage in assuming monarchy for which he had not been trained; had the simple religious faith and many of the characteristics of his father.

GEORGE, David Lloyd, first Earl Lloyd-George of Dwyfor (1863–1945), statesman. See LLOYD GEORGE.

GEORGE, Sir **Ernest** (1839–1922), architect; articled to London architect; joined Royal Academy Schools and won Gold Medal for architecture, 1859; in partnership with Harold Peto (until 1893), obtained countless commissions for elaborate domestic architecture which he executed in Tudor and Jacobean styles; office became fashionable training-ground for young architects; 'discovered' Netherlands for nineteenth century; skilfully adapted details of Flemish and Dutch work of early Renaissance for use in London; his practice of large-scale domestic architecture ruined by Liberal legislation from 1906 onwards; retired, 1920; knighted, 1911; RA, 1917.

GEORGE, Frances Louise Lloyd, Countess Lloyd-George of Dwyfor (1888–1972), political secretary. See LLOYD GEORGE.

GEORGE, Gwilym Lloyd-, first Viscount Tenby (1894–1967). See LLOYD-GEORGE.

GEORGE, Hereford Brooke (1838–1910), historical writer; BA, New College, Oxford, 1860; MA, 1862; tutor, 1867–91; pioneer of military history at Oxford; published *Battles of English History* (1895), *Napoleon's Invasion of Russia* (1899), *New College, 1856–1906* (1906); made

first ascent of Gross Viescherhorn, 1862; edited *Alpine Journal*, 1863–7; published *The Oberland and its Glaciers* (1866); lost fortune by failure of West of England and South Wales Bank, at Bristol, 1880.

GEORGE, John (1804–1871), Irish judge; MA, Trinity College, Dublin, 1826; barrister, King's Inns, 1826, and Gray's Inn, 1827; QC, 1844; MP for Co. Wexford, 1852–7 and 1859–66; solicitor-general under Lord Derby, 1859; privy councillor of Ireland, and judge of Queen's Bench, 1866.

GEORGE, Lady **Megan Lloyd** (1902–1966), politician. See LLOYD GEORGE.

GEORGE, Thomas Neville (1904–1980), geologist; educated at Swansea Municipal Secondary (Dynevor) School, Swansea Grammar School, and University College of Swansea, of which he was a scholar; first class B.Sc. (Wales) in geology, 1924; M.Sc., 1926; studied at St John's College, Cambridge; Ph.D., 1928; demonstrator in geology, Swansea, 1928–30; appointed to Geological Survey of Great Britain, 1930–3; wrote first editions of British Regional Geology handbooks of *North Wales* (1935) with Bernard Smith and *South Wales* (1973) with J. Pringle; professor of geology and geography, University College, Swansea, 1933–47; professor of geology, Glasgow, 1947–74; published nearly 150 articles; received many academic honours including hon. LL D of Wales, 1970, D.Sc. (Wales) and Sc.D. (Cambridge); FRS, 1963; president, Association of University Teachers (1959–60), Geological Society of London (1968–70), and Palaeontological Association (1962–4).

GEORGE, William (1697–1756), dean of Lincoln; educated at Eton and King's College, Cambridge; MA, 1723; DD, 1728; seventeen years principal of Eton; provost of King's, 1743, and vice-chancellor of Cambridge; dean of Lincoln, 1748–56; his lines on the death of Prince Frederick highly commended by Pope Benedict XIV.

GEORGE-BROWN, Baron (1914–1985), politician. See BROWN, GEORGE ALFRED.

GEORGE EDWARD ALEXANDER EDMUND, duke of Kent (1902–1942), fourth son of King George V; served in navy until 1929; visited Canada (1927), South America (1931), and South Africa (1934); created duke of Kent, 1934; staff officer, Training Command, Royal Air Force, 1940; killed in air crash.

GEORGE WILLIAM FREDERICK CHARLES, second duke of Cambridge, earl of Tipperary and Baron Culloden (1819–1904), field marshal and commander-in-chief of the army; only son of *Adolphus Frederick, first duke; born at Hanover; sent to England, 1830; GCH, 1825; KG, 1835; served in Hanoverian Army, 1836; settled in England on Queen Victoria's accession, 1837; contracted a morganatic marriage, 1840; made brevet-colonel; commanded 17th Lancers at disturbances at Leeds, 1842; commanded troops at Corfu, 1843–5; GCMG and major-general, 1845; commanded Dublin district, 1847–52; succeeded to dukedom, 1850; KP, 1851; commanded a division in Crimea, 1854; present at Alma and Inkerman; GCB, 1855; succeeded Lord *Hardinge as general commanding in chief, 1856; general and PC, 1856; colonel of artillery and engineers, 1861; president of National Rifle Association, 1859; helped to found Staff College; field marshal, 1862; as general commanding in chief was subordinated to war minister by War Office Act of 1870; opposed such innovations as short service, formation of army reserve, and linking of battalions; commander-in-chief with sole control of supply, 1887; difficulties with secretary for war led to inquiry into naval and military administration (1888–90), and to his enforced resignation, 1895; as chief personal ADC to Queen Victoria he undertook for her many social duties; opened London International Exhibition, 1862; president of Christ's Hospital and London Hospital for over fifty years; ranger of Hyde Park, 1852, and of Richmond Park, 1857; KT, 1881; elder brother of Trinity House, 1885; received freedom of City of London, 1857; paid last visit to Germany, 1903.

GERALD, Saint and Bishop (d. 731), according to the Bollandist *Life*, a monk who left Winchester for Ireland to lead a solitary life; built a church in Mayo called Cill n-ailither ('Church of the Pilgrims'), where he was buried; termed in *Annals of the Four Masters* the 'Pontifex of Mayo of the Saxons', and 'Episcopus' in the Litany of Oengus.

GERALD, Joseph (1763–1796), political reformer. See GERRALD.

GERALDO (pseudonym) (1904–1974), dance-band leader and musician. See WALCAN-BRIGHT, GERALD.

GERARD (or GIRARD) (d. 1108), archbishop of York; when clerk of the chapel and Chancery sent by William II on a secret mission to Pope Urban, from whom he obtained the despatch of a legate and pallium, 1095; rewarded with see of Hereford, being ordained only a day before consecration, 1096; witnessed Henry I's charter, 1100; archbishop of York, 1100–8; opposed Archbishop *Anselm, and successfully represented Henry I against him at Rome in the investiture dispute; eventually repudiated by Pope Paschal and compelled to profess obedience to Anselm; attempted to consecrate bishops; 'invested' by the king and was rebuked by Paschal; reconciled to Anselm, 1107; refused burial in the minster, but transferred thither by Archbishop Thomas II.

GERARD, Alexander (1728–1795), philosophical writer; professor of philosophy at Marischal College, Aberdeen, 1750, and of divinity, 1760–71; professor of divinity at King's College, 1771; DD; moderator of general assembly, 1764; published prize *Essay on Taste* (1759), *Essay on Genius* (1774), and apologetic works.

GERARD, Alexander (1792–1839), Himalayan explorer; son of Gilbert *Gerard; served with 13th Bengal Native Infantry, 1808–36; while engaged in surveying, 1812–17 and 1825–6, ascended peaks hitherto unscaled and penetrated into Tibet; ascended in 1821 the Charang Pass and Mount Tahigung (22,000 feet); his travels described in Indian scientific journals and in Edinburgh *Journal of Science*, and noticed in Reginald *Heber's *Journal*.

GERARD, Charles, first Baron Gerard of Brandon and earl of Macclesfield (d. 1694), great-grandson of Sir Gilbert *Gerard; educated abroad; commanded infantry brigade at Edgehill, 1642; wounded there and at Lichfield, 1643; arranged capitulation of Bristol, 1643; distinguished at first Battle of Newbury, 1643; again wounded at relief of Newark, 1644; conducted successful operations in South Wales, 1645; removed for rigorous treatment of Welsh, but created a peer, 1645; commander of Charles I's bodyguard, escorting him from Wales to Oxford, thence to Hereford, and afterwards to Chester, 1645; desperately wounded at Rowton Heath, 1645; retired with the king to Newark, but was dismissed his service for a disorderly protest against the supersession of Sir Richard Willis, 1645; rejoined Charles at Oxford, 1646, and raised a troop of horse; went abroad after the capitulation; vice-admiral of the fleet at Helvoetsluys, 1648; gentleman of the bedchamber to Charles II, 1649; served under Turenne at Arras, 1654; intrigued at Paris on behalf of *Henrietta Maria, and encouraged designs of his cousin, John *Gerard (1632–1654); returned with Charles II from Breda, 1660, at the head of the Life Guards; regained his estates and received a pension; envoy-extraordinary to Paris, 1662; supervised defences of Isle of Wight and Portsmouth against Dutch, 1666–7; created earl of Macclesfield, 1679; dismissed from the bedchamber as an adherent of *Monmouth, 1681; presented by Cheshire grand jury as disaffected, 1684; fled to the continent, 1685; commanded William III's bodyguard, 1688; privy councillor and president of Council of Welsh Marches, 1689; member of commission to inquire into conduct of Fleet, 1690.

GERARD, Charles, second earl of Macclesfield (1659?–1701), son of Charles *Gerard, first earl of Macclesfield; MP, Lancashire, 1679, 1680–1, and 1688–94; committed to the Tower on suspicion of treason, 1683, but acquitted; again arrested as adherent of *Monmouth, convicted of complicity in Rye House Plot, and sentenced to death, 1685; pardoned, 1687; lord-lieutenant of Lancashire, 1690, of North Wales, 1696; bail for Lord *Mohun, 1692; as major-general, 1694, succeeded Talmash after his death before Brest; envoy-extraordinary to Hanover, 1701; buried in Westminster Abbey.

GERARD, Sir Gilbert (d. 1593), judge; barrister, Gray's Inn, 1539; joint treasurer of Gray's Inn, 1556; MP, Liverpool, 1545, Wigan, 1552 and 1555, and Steyning, 1554; attorney-general, 1559; drew up reforms for Irish Exchequer court, 1560; counsel to Cambridge University, 1561; commissioner for sale of crown lands, 1563; member of Ecclesiastical Commission, 1567; member of commission for trial of northern rebels, 1570; took part in prosecution of Norfolk, Northumberland, and others, 1571–2; knighted, 1579; master of the Rolls, 1581; MP, Lancaster, 1584; took part in trials of *Somerville, 1583, *Parry, 1585, and Shelley, 1586, for conspiracy, and of *Arundel, 1589, and *Perrot, 1592; chief commissioner of the great seal, 1591–2.

GERARD, Gilbert (1760–1815), theological writer; son of Alexander *Gerard (1728–1795); minister of Scots Church, Amsterdam; professor of Greek at King's College, Aberdeen, 1791, of divinity, 1795; moderator of general assembly, 1803; *Compendious View of the Evidences of Natural and Revealed Religion*, the joint work of himself and his father (published 1828).

GERARD, James Gilbert (1795–1835), Bengal surgeon; son of Gilbert *Gerard; surgeon, 1826; accompanied his brother Alexander *Gerard (1792–1839) in Himalayan journeys; gave great scientific assistance to expedition of Sir Alexander *Burnes to Bokhara, 1831, but died at Subathoo from exhaustion.

GERARD, (Jane) Emily (1849–1905), novelist; sister of Sir Montagu Gilbert *Gerard; married Chevalier Miecislas de Laszowski, 1869; lived in Galicia; with sister Dorothea collaborated in four novels; wrote independently six novels, including *The Voice of a Flower* (1893).

GERARD, John (1545–1612), herbalist; member of court of assistants of Barber-Surgeons, 1595; master, 1607; superintendent of *Burgh-ley's gardens; the list of plants in his own garden (Holborn), first published catalogue, 1596 (ed. B. D. Jackson, 1876); his *Herball* (1597) edited by T. *Johnson, 1633.

GERARD, John (1564–1637), Jesuit; imprisoned for attempt to leave England without licence, 1585; joined Jesuits at Rome, 1588; active on the English mission; betrayed by a servant, imprisoned, and tortured; escaped from the Tower, 1597; gave information of William *Watson's plot, 1603; suspected of complicity in Gunpowder Plot; escaped to Rome, 1606; rector at Louvain, 1609; first rector at Liège, 1614–22; director of English College, Rome, 1627–37; his narrative of the Gunpowder Plot printed in John *Morris's *Condition of the Catholics* (1871), and Latin autobiography translated by G. Kingdon, SJ, 1881.

GERARD, John (1632–1654), Royalist colonel; cousin of Charles *Gerard, first earl of Macclesfield; beheaded for plot to kill *Cromwell and proclaim Charles II.

GERARD, Sir Montagu Gilbert (1842–1905), general; of Catholic parentage; joined army, 1864; served in Second Afghan War, 1878–80; present at Kassassin and Tel-el-Kebir and CB, 1882; sent on secret missions to Persia, 1881 and 1885; British military attaché at St Petersburg, 1892; negotiated in Pamirs boundary dispute, 1895; commanded first-class district, Bengal, 1899; KCSI, 1897; KCB, 1902; general, 1904; chief British attaché in Manchuria in Russo-Japanese War, 1904; died at Irkutsk on way home; published *Diaries of a Soldier and a Sportsman* (1903).

GERARD, Patrick (1794–1848), geographical writer; son of Gilbert *Gerard; served in Bengal army; captain, 1828; invalided, 1832; died at Simla; contributed meteorological observations to *Asiatic Researches*, and left in manuscript (British Museum) meteorological journal, 1817–29.

GERARD, Richard (1613–1686), Royalist; served in the Netherlands, 1638–42; escorted Queen *Henrietta Maria from The Hague to England; lieutenant-colonel in royal army, 1643; at second Battle of Newbury, 1644; attended Charles I at Hurst Castle, and carried letters between him and the queen in France.

GERARD (GARRET or GARRARD), Thomas (1500?–1540), divine; MA, Corpus Christi College, Oxford, 1524; entered Christ Church, Oxford; DD, Cambridge; distributed Lutheran books and *Tyndale's translation of the New Testament; examined and forced to recant before the bishops of London and Bath, 1528; pardoned and employed by *Wolsey; rector of All

Hallows, Honey Lane, and chaplain to *Cranmer, 1537; having preached at Paul's Cross, 1540, in answer to *Gardiner, was burnt at Smithfield for heresy.

GERARD, Sir William (d. 1581), lord chancellor of Ireland; cousin of Sir Gilbert *Gerard; barrister, Gray's Inn, 1546; MP, Preston, 1553, and Chester, 1555–72; recorder of Chester, 1565–72; vice-president of Council of Wales, 1562; lord chancellor of Ireland, 1576; knighted, 1577; returned to England and became master of requests, 1577; active member of Irish Ecclesiastical Commission; forwarded to *Walsingham an historical treatise on Wales, with suggestions for reform.

GERARDS, Marcus, (1561–1635), painter. See GHEERAERTS.

GERBIER, Sir Balthazar (1591?–1667), painter, architect, and courtier; native of Middelburg; came to England, 1616, becoming keeper of York House and collector for *Buckingham; accompanied Buckingham to Spain, 1623, and Paris, 1625; negotiated with Rubens for a peace with Spain, 1625–7; entered service of Charles I and was knighted, 1628; trusted agent of the king at Brussels, 1631, but betrayed for money his negotiations with the Flemish nobles, 1633; became master of the ceremonies, 1641; his house at Bethnal Green attacked by mob as supposed asylum for papists, 1642; retired to France, 1643; returned to England after the king's execution; engaged in mining projects at Cayenne, 1659–60; returned to England, but, being unable to regain his position at court, turned his attention to architecture; a miniature by him of Charles I preserved at South Kensington.

GERE, Charles March (1869–1957), artist; studied at Gloucester and Birmingham art schools; illustrated books for William *Morris and St John *Hornby; settled in Painswick, 1904; painted landscapes with figures in oil, tempera, and water-colour; most successful with small landscapes of Cotswold countryside and watercolour portraits of children; ARA, 1934; RA, 1939; paintings to be seen in Tate and galleries at Birmingham and Liverpool.

GEREDIGION, Daniel du o (1792–1846), Welsh poet. See EVANS, DANIEL.

GEREE, John (1601?–1649), Puritan divine; MA, Magdalen Hall, Oxford, 1621; as incumbent of Tewkesbury 'silenced' for nonconformity (after 1624), but restored, 1641; rector of St Albans, 1646–7; preacher at St Faith's, London, 1647; advocated right of the king to abolish episcopacy in *A Case of Conscience Resolved*, 1646.

GEREE, Stephen (1594–1656?), Puritan; elder brother of John *Geree; BA, Magdalen Hall, Oxford, 1615; vicar of Wonersh, and, c.1641, rector of Abinger; published theological pamphlets.

GERHARDIE, William Alexander (1895–1977), novelist and critic; born in St Petersburg (Leningrad), the youngest son of a British industrialist settled in Russia, and educated there; sent to London to train for a commercial career; posted to staff of British Embassy in Petrograd (Leningrad), 1916–18; attached to Scots Guards and sent to British Military Mission in Siberia, 1918; OBE and Russian and Czechoslovakian decorations, 1920; obtained BA in Russian at Worcester College, Oxford, 1922; published first novel, *Futility* (1922), followed by *The Polyglots* (1925); a prolific author, publishing collections of short stories, including *Pretty Creatures* (1927) and *Pending Heaven* (1930), and further novels such as *Resurrection* (1934) and *Of Mortal Love* (1936); travelled extensively in Europe, India, and America; published autobiography, *Memoirs of a Polyglot* (1931), and a study of the Russian dynasty *The Romanovs* (1940); worked with BBC during 1939–45 war; first editor of 'English by Radio', 1943–5; changed his name from Gerhardi to Gerhardie on second Collected Edition of his work, published 1970–74 (ten vols.); his *God's Fifth Column*, edited by Michael Holroyd and Robert Skidelsky, published posthumously (1981).

GÉRIN, Winifred Eveleen (1901–1981), biographer; daughter of Frederick Charles Bourne; educated at Sydenham High School for Girls, and Newnham College, Cambridge; married Eugéne Gérin, a Belgian professional cellist, 1932; in Vichy France, 1939–40; worked together in political intelligence, Foreign Office, 1941–5; published *Anne Brontë* (1959), *Branwell Brontë* (1961), *Charlotte Brontë, the Evolution of Genius* (1967, awarded James Tait Black Memorial Prize), *Emily Brontë* (1971), *Elizabeth Gaskell* (1976), and *Anne Thackeray* (1981); OBE, 1975; fellow and member of council of Royal Society of Literature.

GERMAIN, Lady Elizabeth ('Betty') (1680–1769), daughter of Charles, second earl of Berkeley, and second wife of Sir John *Germain, who left her a large fortune, including the Arundel cameos; friend of *Swift. Edward *Young dedicated to her his sixth satire on woman.

GERMAIN, George Sackville, first Viscount Sackville (1716–1785), soldier and statesman (known as Lord George Sackville till 1770); third son of Lionel *Sackville, first duke of Dorset; educated at Westminster and Trinity

Germain

College, Dublin; MA, 1734; as lieutenant-colonel of the 28th Foot (1st Gloucester) distinguished himself at Fontenoy, 1745, where he was wounded and captured; colonel of 20th Foot (1st Lancashire Fusiliers), 1746, of 12th Dragoons (Lancers), 1749, and of 6th Carabineers, 1750; major-general, 1755; member of the court of inquiry into conduct of Sir John *Mordaunt at Rochefort, 1757; lieutenant-general of the ordnance, and colonel, 2nd Dragoon Guards, 1757; second-in-command of St Malo expedition, 1758; as commander of British contingent with Prince Ferdinand neglected to lead British cavalry in pursuit of the French at Minden, 1759, for which he was dismissed the service, declared by a court martial unfit to serve in any military capacity, and his name erased from the Privy Council, 1760; MP, Dover, 1741–61, Hythe, 1761–8, East Grinstead, 1768–82; chief secretary to the viceroy of Ireland (Dorset), 1751–6; his name restored to Privy Council by George III; assumed name of Germain, 1770; fought duel with Captain Johnstone, late governor of Pensacola; commissioner of trade and plantations, and secretary of state for colonies, 1775–82; created Viscount Sackville, 1782; absurdly credited by some with authorship of 'Junius'.

GERMAIN, Sir John (1650–1718), soldier of fortune; reputed son of William II, prince of Orange; accompanied William III to England, and served under him in Ireland and Flanders; created baronet, 1698; married Lady Mary Mordaunt, 1701; inherited from her Drayton and other property; his second wife was Lady 'Betty' Berkeley (see GERMAIN, Lady ELIZABETH).

GERMAN, Sir Edward (1862–1936), composer (originally Edward German Jones); studied at Royal Academy of Music; works include incidental music for Shakespearian productions, *Merrie England* (1902), *A Princess of Kensington* (1903), and *Tom Jones* (1907); wrote march and hymn for coronation, 1911; knighted, 1928; combined artistic achievement with popular appeal.

GERMANUS (378?–448), bishop of Auxerre and missionary to Britain; one of the six dukes of Gaul; was forcibly made a cleric by Amator of Auxerre; succeeded Amator as bishop, 418; founded monastery on the Yonne; with St Lupus went to Britain, 429, and overcame Pelagians in disputation at Verulamium (St Albans); said to have aided the Britons to overcome the Picts by causing them to cry Alleluia, 430; built church at Auxerre in honour of St Alban; overcame the Pelagians in a second visit to Britain, 447; went to Ravenna to intercede with the empress-mother for the Alans against the Armoricans; died there, but was buried near Auxerre.

GERRALD, Joseph (1763–1796), political reformer; native of St Christopher, West Indies; pupil of Samuel *Parr at Stanmore, and his lifelong friend; went to Edinburgh Convention as a delegate of the London Corresponding Society, 1793; was sentenced by *Braxfield to fourteen years' transportation for sedition, 1794; died five months after his arrival at Botany Bay.

GERTLER, Mark (1891–1939), painter; born in Spitalfields of Austro-Jewish parents; studied at Slade School; by his talents, vivacity, and exotic beauty gained early entry into artistic and intellectual circles; work profoundly original, of masterly craftsmanship, large and firm design, in rich and harmonious colour; committed suicide.

GERVASE OF CANTERBURY (GERVASIUS DOROBORNENSIS) (fl. 1188), chronicler; became a monk of Christ Church, Canterbury, 1163, and sacrist, 1193; engaged in disputes between the archbishop of Canterbury and the abbot of St Augustine's, 1179–83, and with his own monastery, 1185–91. His works, edited by Bishop Stubbs (Rolls Series, 1879, 1880), include an account of the burning and rebuilding of the cathedral (1174), a history of the archbishops of Canterbury from *Augustine to *Hubert, *Mappa Mundi*, a Canterbury Chronicle (1100–99), and *Gesta Regum*, which after his death was continued to 1328, and is of value for the early years of John's reign.

GERVASE OF CHICHESTER (fl. 1170), author of an extant commentary on Malachi; disciple of Thomas *Becket.

GERVASE OF TILBURY (fl. 1211), author of *Otia Imperialia*; brought up at Rome; taught law at Bologna, among his pupils being Pignatelli; present at meeting of the emperor Frederick I and Pope Alexander III, 1177; attached to Henry, son of Henry II of England; high in favour of William II in Sicily; made marshal of Arles by the emperor Otto IV, to whom he dedicated his *Otia Imperialia*; probably died in England.

GERVAYS, John (d. 1268), bishop of Winchester. See JOHN.

GETHIN, Grace, Lady (1676–1697), learned lady; daughter of Sir George Norton; married Sir Richard Gethin; buried in Westminster Abbey.

GETHING, Richard (1585?–1652?), calligrapher; pupil of John *Davies of Hereford; native of Herefordshire; published at the 'Hand and Pen', Fetter Lane, a copybook (1616) and *Chirographia* (1645).

GETSIUS, John Daniel (1592–1672), divine and tutor; native of the Palatinate; doctor of philosophy, Marburg, 1618; BA, Cambridge; taught Hebrew at Exeter College, Oxford, and was incorporated BA, 1628; vicar of Stoke Gabriel, 1636, where he took pupils; imprisoned, 1643, for a Royalist sermon; published a Greek Testament lexicon, with other works.

GHEERAERTS (GEERAERTS or GARRARD), Marcus, the elder (1510?–1590?), painter and engraver; native of Bruges, where he designed the tomb of Charles the Bold; engraved view of the town, now among the archives, and painted the *Descent from the Cross*; came to England as a Protestant refugee, 1568; said to have died in England.

GHEERAERTS (GHEERAEDTS, GEERAERTS, GERARDS, or GARRARD), Marcus, the younger (1561–1635), painter; son of Marcus *Gheeraerts the elder; accompanied his father to England; among his portraits were several of Elizabeth and *Camden; his *Conference of English and Spanish Plenipotentiaries* bought for National Portrait Gallery, 1882; published *Handbook to Art of Drawing*.

GHENT (or GAUNT), John of, duke of Lancaster (1340–1399). See JOHN OF GAUNT.

GHENT, Simon de (d. 1315), bishop of Salisbury; archdeacon of Oxford, 1284; chancellor of the university, 1291–3; bishop of Salisbury, 1297–1315; one of the lords ordainers, 1310; ardent ecclesiastical reformer; resisted admission of papal nominee to deanery of Salisbury; preserved his right of tallage against the citizens; wrote *Regula Anchoritarum* and drew up *Statuta ecclesiastica*.

GIB, Adam (1714–1788), Scots anti-burgher divine; educated at Edinburgh; joined the 'Associate Presbytery' of 1735; minister of Secession Congregation, Bristo Street, Edinburgh, 1741; captured a rebel spy, 1745; leader of the Anti-Burgher Synod, 1747; when dispossessed of Bristo Street Church ministered in one built for him in Nicholson Street; called 'Pope Gib'; published *Proceedings of the Associate Synod* (1748).

GIBB, Sir Alexander (1872–1958), engineer; educated at Rugby; worked with (Sir) John *Wolfe-Barry; then joined family firm; constructed Rosyth Naval Base; chief engineer, ports construction, France and Belgium, 1916–18; director-general, civil engineering, Ministry of Transport, 1919–21; established consulting firm, 1922; designs included London Zoo aquarium, Singapore Naval Base, Cook Graving Dock, Sydney; collaboration in Galloway hydro-electric scheme and Mulberry harbour; CB and KBE, 1918; GBE, 1920; FRS, 1936; hon. LL D, Edinburgh.

GIBB, Sir Claude Dixon (1898–1959), engineer; born in South Australia; studied at South Australian School of Mines and Adelaide University; graduated in engineering, 1923; joined firm of Sir C. A. *Parsons in England, 1924; chief engineer, 1929; general manager, 1937; joint managing director, 1943; with Ministry of Supply, 1940–5; as chairman and managing director from 1945 re-equipped and expanded Parsons; collaborated in first designs for gas-cooled nuclear power plants; formed Nuclear Power Plant Company; FRS, 1946; knighted, 1945; KBE, 1956; honorary degrees, London and Durham.

GIBB, Elias John Wilkinson (1857–1901), orientalist; educated at Glasgow University; early studied Arabic, Persian, and Turkish languages and literatures; translated Ottoman prose and verse, 1879–84; published a detailed *History of Ottoman Poetry* (vol. i, 1900; vols. ii–vi edited by E. G. *Browne after Gibb's death, 1902–9); fine oriental library divided among British Museum, Cambridge University, and British Embassy at Constantinople.

GIBB, Frederick (d. 1681), miscellaneous writer; MD, Valence, 1651; wrote occasionally under the name of Philalethes; contributed verses to a volume of De Thou 1678.

GIBB, Sir Hamilton Alexander Rosskeen (1895–1971), Arabic scholar; educated at the Royal High School, Edinburgh, and Edinburgh University, 1912–14; served with Royal Field Artillery in France and Italy, 1914–18; studied Arabic at School of Oriental Studies, London University; MA, 1922; lecturer at School of Oriental Studies, 1921; reader, 1929; professor, 1930–7; one of the editors of *Encyclopaedia of Islam*; published an introductory book on *Arabic Literature* (1926), and translations of Arabic historical works and articles on contemporary Arabic literature; Laudian professor of Arabic, Oxford, and fellow of St John's College, 1937–55; FBA, 1944; produced, with Harold Bowen, *Islamic Society and the West* (vol. i, part 1, 1950, part 2, 1957); other publications include *Modern Trends in Islam* (1947) and *Mohammedanism* (1949); James Richard Jewett professor of Arabic, Harvard University, 1955–64; director of Harvard's Center for Middle Eastern Studies; hon. fellow, St John's College, Oxford, 1955; number of honorary doctorates; knighted, 1954.

GIBB, John (1776–1850), civil engineer and contractor; assisted *Rennie in construction of Greenock Harbour; repaired Crinan Canal, 1817; completed *Telford's Glasgow Bridge.

GIBB, Robert (d. 1837), landscape painter; an original ARSA; RSA, 1829.

GIBBERD, Sir Frederick Ernest (1908–1984), architect; educated at King Henry VIII School, Coventry, and Birmingham School of Architecture; shared office in London with F. R. S. *Yorke, 1930; having set up on his own, first substantial building, Pullman Court flats at Streatham; works executed between 1930 and 1970 include first terminal buildings at Heathrow airport, civic buildings at Doncaster, St Albans, and Hull, power stations at Hinckley Point and Didcot, controversial reconstruction of Coutts Bank in the Strand, London, London mosque in Regent's Park, and Roman Catholic cathedral, Liverpool; his most considerable achievement, Harlow New Town, of which he was planner and chief architect, 1946–72; expert and imaginative gardener; vice-president, Royal Institute of British Architects; president, Building Centre; principal, Architectural Association School of Architecture, London, 1942–4; fellow, Royal Institute of British Architects (1939), Royal Town Planning Institute, and Institute of Landscape Architects; ARA, 1961; RA, 1969; CBE, 1954; knighted, 1967; hon. LL D, Liverpool, 1969; publications include *Town Design* (1953).

GIBBES, Charles (1604–1681), divine; MA, Magdalen Hall, Oxford, 1628; DD, 1662; fellow of Merton College, Oxford, 1624; prebendary of Wells; prebendary of Westminister, 1662.

GIBBES, Sir George Smith (1771–1851), physician to Bath Hospital; fellow of Magdalen College, Oxford; BA, 1792; MD, 1799; FRCP, 1804; Harveian orator, 1817; physician to Bath Hospital, 1804; knighted, 1820; FRS and FLS. His works include treatises on the Bath waters.

GIBBES (or GHIBBES), James Alban (1611–1677), Latin poet; studied under Vesling at Padua; from 1644 practised as a physician at Rome; enjoyed favour of four successive popes; dedicated to Clement IX his *Carminum Pars Lyrica ad exemplum Q. Horatii Flacci* (1668); sent to Oxford a gold chain and medal attached to his diploma of poet laureate from the emperor Leopold I, 1667; created MD, Oxford, 1671, as 'the Horace of his age'.

GIBBINGS, Robert John (1889–1958), wood-engraver, author, and book designer; studied at Slade School and Central School of Arts and Crafts; first honorary secretary of and exhibited with Society of Wood Engravers, 1920; owned Golden Cockerel Press, 1924–33; employed engravers such as Eric *Ravilious and Eric *Gill; himself illustrated nineteen out of the seventy-two books produced; lecturer in book production, Reading University, 1936–42; wrote and illustrated *Sweet Thames Run Softly* (1940) and other 'river books'.

GIBBINS, Henry De Beltgens (1865–1907), writer on economic history; born in Cape Colony; Cobden prizeman at Oxford, 1890; D.Litt., Dublin, 1896; wrote works on industrial and commercial history; edited Methuen's 'Social Questions of the Day' series, 1891.

GIBBON, Benjamin Phelps (1802–1851), line-engraver; executed engravings after *Landseer and *Mulready's *Wolf and Lamb*.

GIBBON, Charles (*fl.* 1589–1604), author; published six works, including *The Order of Equalitie* (1604), an appeal for proportional equalization of the incidence of taxation.

GIBBON, Charles (1843–1890), novelist; journalist at Glasgow, *c*.1860; published about thirty novels; edited *Casquet of Literature* (1873–4).

GIBBON, Edward (1737–1794), historian; educated at Westminster; owed his taste for books to his aunt, Catherine Porten; spent fourteen 'unprofitable' months at Magdalen College, Oxford, 1752–3; became a Romanist after reading Conyers *Middleton's *Free Inquiry* and works by Bossuet and Robert *Parsons, 1753; at Lausanne (1753–8), where his tutor, Pavillard, drew him back to Protestantism, and where he made friends with Deyverdun and read widely; became attached to Susanne Curchod (afterwards Madame Necker), but in deference to his father broke off the engagement, 1757; published *Essai sur l'Etude de la Littérature* (1761, English version, 1764); served in Hampshire Militia, 1759–70, and studied military literature; at Lausanne met *Holroyd (afterwards Lord Sheffield); during a tour in Italy, 1764–5, formed plan of his *History* amid the ruins of the Capitol; with Deyverdun published *Mémoires Littéraires de la Grande-Bretagne* (1767–8), contributing a review of *Lyttelton's *Henry II*; issued *Critical Observations on the Sixth Book of the Aeneid*, attacking William *Warburton (1770); settled in London, 1772; joined Dr *Johnson's Club, 1774; became professor in ancient history at the Royal Academy in succession to *Goldsmith; MP, Liskeard, 1774–80, Lymington, 1781–3; drew up a state paper against France, and was commissioner of trade and plantations, 1779–82; issued in 1776 the first volume of his *Decline and Fall of the Roman Empire*, which passed into three editions, and obtained the favourable verdict of *Hume, Robertson, *Warton, and *Walpole; defended the chapters on growth of Christianity in his *Vindication* (1779); issued the second and third volumes, 1781, after a visit to Paris, where he met Buffon and disputed with De Mably; retired with

Deyverdun to Lausanne, 1783, where he finished the work, 1787 (published, 1788); returned to England, 1793; died suddenly in London; a Latin epitaph written for his monument at Fletching, Sussex, by Dr Samuel *Parr. His *Miscellaneous Works* (edited by his friend Lord Sheffield, 1796) contained an autobiographical memoir, and *Antiquities of the House of Brunswick* (1814).

GIBBON, Sir (Ioan) Gwilym (1874–1948), civil servant; served in Local Government Board, 1903–19; assistant secretary, Ministry of Health, 1919; director, Local Government Division, 1934–5; leader in framing Rating and Valuation (1925) and Local Government (1929) Acts; fostered expansion of social services and town planning; knighted, 1936; left about £50,000 to Nuffield College, Oxford.

GIBBON, John (1629–1718), writer on heraldry; educated at Merchant Taylors' and Jesus College, Cambridge; travelled in Europe and America, where he saw Indian aborigines, whose war-paint he took as a proof of the universality of heraldry; created Blue Mantle, 1671; chief work *Introductio ad Latinam Blasoniam* (1682); his 'Heraldo-Memoriale' published in *Strype's edition of *Stow's *Survey* (1720).

GIBBON (or GIBBONS), Nicholas, the elder (*fl.* 1600), theological writer; MA, Clare College, Cambridge, 1592; incorporated at Oxford, 1592; published *Questions and Disputations concerning the Holy Scripture* (1601).

GIBBON, Nicholas, the younger (1605–1697), divine; son of Nicholas *Gibbon the elder; MA, St Edmund Hall, Oxford, 1629; DD, 1639; rector of Sevenoaks, 1632–50; consulted by Charles I at Carisbrooke, 1647; worked as farm labourer during the Commonwealth; rector of Corfe Castle, 1660–97; published *A Summe or Body of Divinity Real* (1653), with a key.

GIBBONS. See also GIBBON.

GIBBONS, Christopher (1615–1676), organist; elder son of Orlando *Gibbons; educated in Exeter choir; organist of Winchester Cathedral, 1638–61; at Restoration appointed to Chapel Royal, to Westminster Abbey, and court organist; Mus.Doc., Oxford, 1663; contributed to *Cantica Sacra* (1674); collaborated with *Locke in music to *Shirley's 'Cupid and Death', 1653.

GIBBONS, Edward (1570?–1653?), organist; brother of Orlando *Gibbons; Mus.Bac., Cambridge and Oxford; organist at King's College, Cambridge, 1592–9; afterwards at Bristol Cathedral, and (1611–44) at Exeter Cathedral; his manuscript compositions preserved in Music School, Oxford.

GIBBONS, Ellis (*fl.* 1600), musical composer; brother of Edward *Gibbons; probably organist at Salisbury; composed madrigals in *Triumphs of Oriana* (1603).

GIBBONS, Grinling (1648–1720), wood-carver and statuary; born at Rotterdam; discovered by John *Evelyn in 1671 working at Deptford at his carving of Tintoretto's *Crucifixion*, which was shown to *Wren and *Pepys, and afterwards to the royal family; employed by Wren to carve stalls in St Paul's and new London churches; employed in library of Trinity College, Cambridge, and by the king at Windsor, Whitehall, and Kensington; carved the throne in Canterbury Cathedral; executed statues of Charles II at the Royal Exchange and Chelsea, and of James II at Whitehall; buried in St Paul's, Covent Garden; his portrait painted by *Kneller.

GIBBONS, John (1544–1589), Jesuit; doctor of philosophy and divinity at German College, Rome, 1576; rector of Jesuit College, Trèves; died at Himmelrode; his *Concertatio Ecclesiae Catholicae in Anglia, adversus Calvino-Papistas et Puritanos* (1583), enlarged by John *Bridgewater.

GIBBONS, Orlando (1583–1625), musical composer; entered choir of King's College, Cambridge, 1596, for which he composed music; Mus.Bac., Cambridge, 1606; Mus.Doc., Oxford, 1622; organist of Chapel Royal, 1604; composed music for the reception of Queen *Henrietta Maria at Canterbury; buried in Canterbury Cathedral; contributed the remarkable fantasia 'The Lord of Salisbury his Pavin', to *Byrd and *Bull's *Parthenia* (1611); published *First Set of Madrigals and Mottets* (1612), containing 'The Silver Swan', and other masterpieces; composed also settings of George *Wither's *Hymns and Songs of the Church* (1623) and instrumental *Fantasies of Three Parts*. His sacred compositions, including services in F and D minor, 'preces', and many anthems for special occasions, were edited by Sir F. A. Gore *Ouseley, 1873.

GIBBONS, Richard (1550?–1632), Jesuit; younger brother of John *Gibbons; taught mathematics, philosophy, Hebrew, and canon law in several continental countries; died at Douai; edited *Harpsfield's *Historia Anglicana Ecclesiastica* (1622), and translated Bellarmine's *Christian Doctrine*, and other works from Italian, Spanish, and Portuguese.

GIBBONS, Thomas (1720–1785), Dissenting minister and author; Independent minister of Haberdashers' Hall, 1743; tutor of Mile End Academy, 1754; DD, Aberdeen, 1764; MA, New Jersey, 1760; published *Memoirs of Rev. J. Watts, D.D.* (1780), also hymns and devotional verses.

Gibbons

GIBBONS, William (1649–1728), physician; of Merchant Taylors' School; BA, St John's College, Oxford, 1672; MD, 1683; FRCP, 1692, and censor, 1716; ridiculed by *Garth as Mirmillo; benefactor of Wolverhampton; said to have made mahogany fashionable.

GIBBS, Mrs (*fl.* 1783–1844), actress; appeared at the Haymarket as Sally in Colman's *Man and Wife*, 1783; married the younger George *Colman, in whose plays she acted, 1797–1803. Her other parts included Katherine, Miss Hardcastle, and Mrs Candour.

GIBBS, Mrs (1804–1854), vocalist. See GRADDON, Miss.

GIBBS, Henry Hucks, first Baron Aldenham (1819–1907), merchant and scholar; MA, Exeter College, Oxford, 1844; joined family firm of bankers, 1843; head of firm, 1875; director of Bank of England, 1853–1901; governor, 1875–7; wrote many pamphlets advocating bimetallism; published *A Colloquy on Currency* (1893); helped to found *St. James's Gazette*, 1880; Conservative MP for City of London, 1891–2; served on Royal Commission on Stock Exchange, 1877–8; baron, 1896; benefactor to Keble College, Oxford; leading member of English Church Union from 1862; bought advowson of and restored church at Aldenham; helped to restore St Albans Abbey; fond of shooting, he lost right hand in gun accident, 1864; helped in preparation of *New English Dictionary*; edited works for Early English Text Society and Roxburgh Club; Spanish scholar and bibliophile; trustee of National Portrait Gallery; FSA, 1885.

GIBBS, James (d. 1724), physician and poet; published metrical version of Psalms i–xv (1701), and essay on cure of scrofula.

GIBBS, James (1682–1754), architect; MA, Marischal College, Aberdeen; studied under Fontana at Rome; designed St Mary-le-Strand, St Peter's, Vere Street, and St Martin-in-the-Fields, part of the Senate House and of King's College, Cambridge; the monuments of Ben *Jonson, Matthew *Prior, and John *Holles, duke of Newcastle in Westminster Abbey; the quadrangle of St Bartholomew's Hospital, and the Radcliffe Library, Oxford; published *A Book of Architecture* (1728) and *Rules for Drawing the several Parts of Architecture* (1732), and translated Fonseca's *De Rebus Emanuelis* (1752).

GIBBS, Joseph (1700?–1788), organist of St Mary-at-Tower, Ipswich; composed *Eight Solos for a Violin, with a Thorough Bass for the Harpsichord* (1740?).

GIBBS, Philip (*fl.* 1740), Dissenting minister and stenographer; joint pastor at Hackney, 1729;

Unitarian, 1737; published *An Historical Account of Compendious and Swift Writing* (1736) and *Essay towards a further Improvement of Short-Hand* (1736).

GIBBS, Sir Philip Armand Hamilton (1877–1962), writer; educated at home; worked for publishing house of Cassell; editor of Tillotson's literary syndicate; literary editor, *Daily Mail*, 1902; moved to *Daily Express*, and then to *Daily Chronicle*, 1908; also worked with *Daily Graphic*; war correspondent during 1914–18 war; KBE, 1920; chevalier of the Legion of Honour; toured United States lecturing, 1919; resigned from *Daily Chronicle*, 1920; edited *Review of Reviews*, 1921–2; war correspondent with *Daily Sketch*, 1939; publications include *Founders of the Empire* (1899), *The Street of Adventure* (1909), *The Soul of War* (1915), *Realities of War* (1920), *The Middle of the Road* (1922), *Adventures in Journalism* (1923), *Since Then* (1930), *Across the Frontiers* (1938), *America Speaks* (1942), *The Pageant of the Years* (1946), and *Life's Adventure* (1957).

GIBBS, Sir Samuel (d. 1815), major-general; ensign, 102nd Foot, 1783; commanded the 11th in West Indies, 1799, and 59th Foot at Cape, 1805–6, and in Travancore, 1808–9; distinguished himself in the Java expedition, 1811; major-general, 1812, in Holland; mortally wounded at New Orleans, 1815; KCB, 1815.

GIBBS, Sir Vicary (1751–1820), judge; educated at Eton; contributed to *Musae Etonenses*; fellow; MA, King's College, Cambridge, 1778; Craven scholar, 1772; barrister, Lincoln's Inn, 1783; recorder of Bristol, 1794; assisted Erskine in defence of Thomas *Hardy and Horne *Tooke, 1794, and was highly complimented by the attorney-general, Sir John *Scott, 1794; MP, Totnes, and chief justice of Chester, 1804; solicitor-general, 1805–6; knighted, 1805; MP, Great Bedwin, 1807; MP for Cambridge University, 1807; attorney-general, 1807–12; serjeant-at-law and judge of common pleas, 1812; lord chief baron and privy councillor, 1813; chief justice of common pleas, 1814–18; called 'Vinegar Gibbs'; his numerous *ex officio* informations noticed in parliament, 1811.

GIBBS, Vicary (1853–1932), genealogist and gardener; son of first Lord *Aldenham; educated at Eton and Christ Church, Oxford; Conservative MP, St Albans, 1892–1904; developed famous gardens at Aldenham House; edited (1910–20) and financed first five volumes of new and scholarly edition of *Complete Peerage*.

GIBSON, Sir Alexander, Lord Durie (d. 1644), Scottish judge; MA, Edinburgh, 1588; third clerk of session, 1594; lord of session as Lord Durie, 1621; created baronet of Nova Sco-

1136

tia, 1628; commissioner for reviewing the laws and customs, 1633; member of Committee of Estates, 1640; twice president of College of Justice; story of his being kidnapped by Traquair subject of *Scott's 'Christie's Will'; *Lord Durie's Practicks* (1690) the earliest collection of Scottish legal decisions.

GIBSON, Sir **Alexander,** Lord Durie (d. 1656), Scottish judge; son of Sir Alexander *Gibson (d. 1644); clerk of session, 1621; opposed ecclesiastical policy of Charles I; commissary-general of forces against Charles I, 1640; knighted, 1641; lord clerk register, 1641; commissioner of the Exchequer, 1645; lord of session as Lord Durie, 1646–9.

GIBSON, Sir **Alexander** (d. 1693), principal clerk of session and clerk to Scottish Privy Council; grandson of Sir Alexander *Gibson (d. 1644), whose *Practicks* he edited; knighted, 1682.

GIBSON, Alexander (1800–1867), botanist; MD, Edinburgh; surgeon to East India Company; superintendent of Dapuri Botanical Gardens, 1838–47; conservator of Bombay forests, 1847–60; FLS, 1853; published works, including *Forest Reports* (1849–55) and *Bombay Flora*.

GIBSON, Alexander Craig (1813–1874), Cumberland antiquary; MRCS, 1846; published *The Old Man, or Ravings and Ramblings round Coniston* (1849) and *The Folk-speech of Cumberland* (1869).

GIBSON, David Cooke (1827–1856), painter; studied in Edinburgh, London, Belgium, and Paris; painted portraits and wrote humorous verse; exhibited Spanish pictures at Royal Academy, 1855–6.

GIBSON, Edmund (1669–1748), bishop of London; nephew of Thomas *Gibson (1647–1722); fellow of The Queen's College, Oxford, 1694; MA, 1694; chaplain to Archbishop *Tenison and librarian at Lambeth, where he commenced catalogue of library; combated *Atterbury's views on Convocation; archdeacon of Surrey, 1710; bishop of Lincoln, 1716–23; bishop of London, 1723–48; used his influence with George I against masquerades; was Walpole's ecclesiastical adviser till his opposition to the Quaker's Relief Bill, 1736; declined primacy, 1747; published numerous works, including an edition of the Saxon Chronicle (1692), a translation of *Camden's *Britannia* (1695), *Reliquiae Spelmannianae* (1698), *Synodus Anglicana* (1702), *Codex Juris Ecclesiae Anglicanae* (1713).

GIBSON, Edward (1668–1701), portrait painter; nephew of William *Gibson (1644–1702); excelled in crayon work.

GIBSON, Edward, first Baron Ashbourne (1837–1913), lord chancellor of Ireland; BA, Trinity College, Dublin; called to Irish bar, 1860; QC, 1872; Conservative MP, Dublin University, 1875; Irish attorney-general, 1877–80; baron, 1885; lord chancellor of Ireland with seat in Cabinet, 1885, 1886–92, 1895–1905.

GIBSON, Francis (1753–1805), author; collector of customs at Whitby, 1787; published *Sailing Directions for the Baltic* (1791) and *Streanshall Abbey* (play, 1800).

GIBSON, George Stacey (1818–1883), botanist; Quaker banker and benefactor of Saffron Walden; FRS, 1847; published *Flora of Essex* (1862); contributed to *Phytologist*, 1842–51, adding six new species to British flora.

GIBSON, Guy Penrose (1918–1944), airman; educated at St Edward's School, Oxford; commissioned in Royal Air Force, 1936; took part in first attack (on Kiel Canal) of war; served in Fighter Command, 1940–2; wing commander, 1942; superb commander of No. 106 (bomber) squadron, 1942–3; DSO and bar; commanded special squadron for, and led successful attack on, Möhne Dam, May 1943; VC; operations officer, No. 55 base, 1944; crashed in Holland.

GIBSON, James (1799–1871), Free Church polemic; edited *Church of Scotland Magazine*, 1834–7; incumbent of Kingston, 1839–43; joined Free Church, 1843; professor of theology and church history at Glasgow Theological College, 1856; published theological treatises.

GIBSON, Sir **James Brown** (1805–1868), physician; MD, Edinburgh; served in Crimea; director-general of Army Medical Department, 1860–7; KCB, 1865; died at Rome.

GIBSON, James Young (1826–1886), translator from the Spanish; studied at Edinburgh and Halle; contributed some poetical renderings to *Duffield's version of *Don Quixote* (1881); translated also Cervantes's *Viage al Parnaso* (1883) and *Numantia* (1885).

GIBSON, Sir **John** (1637–1717), colonel; in Dutch service, 1675–88; lieutenant-colonel in English Army, 1689; colonel, 1694; lieutenant-governor of Portsmouth, 1689; MP, Portsmouth, 1701–2; commander of force sent to capture Newfoundland, 1697; knighted, 1705.

GIBSON, John (d. 1852), portrait painter; exhibited at West of Scotland Academy, where a fatal accident caused his death.

GIBSON, John (1790–1866), sculptor; of humble parentage; while at Liverpool attracted the attention of William *Roscoe; lived at Rome, and received instruction from Canova and Thorwaldsen, 1817; his first commission, the Chatsworth *Mars and Cupid*, followed by *Psyche and Zephyrs*, *Sleeping Shepherd Boy*, *Hylas and the Nymphs*, 1819–26, *Cupid disguised as a Shepherd*, 1837, and other works; RA, 1838; during visit to England (1844) publicly entertained at Glasgow, and received commission for bust of Queen Victoria, his first tinted work; modelled, statue of Queen Victoria for Houses of Parliament, 1850–5, which, with his *Tinted Venus, Pandora*, and *Cupid* (all coloured), were seen at the International Exhibition, 1862; executed three statues of Huskisson, and one of Sir Robert Peel in Westminster Abbey; the last of the purist or abstract school of sculptors; bequeathed his property to the Royal Academy.

GIBSON, John (1794–1854), glass-stainer; sheriff of Newcastle upon Tyne, 1854.

GIBSON, John (1817–1892), architect; articled to Joseph Aloysius *Hansom, and (Sir) Charles *Barry; successful in competition for National Bank of Scotland, Glasgow, 1844, and carried out work; ARIBA, 1849; FRIBA, 1853. His works—chiefly country houses and banks—include the head offices and numerous branches of the National Provincial Bank of England.

GIBSON, Sir John Watson (1885–1947), contracting engineer; worked for Lord *Cowdray in charge of construction of Sennar Dam and irrigation works in Sudan; founded own firm working for Sudan and Egyptian governments; directed construction of Mulberry harbours for invasion of Normandy; knighted, 1945.

GIBSON, Kennet (1730–1772), antiquary; educated at Eton; BA, Christ's College, Cambridge, 1752; rector of Marham, Northamptonshire; his *Comment on part of the Fifth Journey of Antoninus through Britain* printed by Nichols (1800).

GIBSON, Mathew (d. 1741?), antiquary; BA, The Queen's College, Oxford, 1700; rector of Abbey Dore, 1722–41; published *View of Ancient and Present State of the Churches of Dore, Home-Lacy, and Hempsted*, 1727, with memoirs of Scudamore family.

GIBSON, Matthew (1734–1790), Roman Catholic prelate; professor at Douai; vicar-general to Bishop Walton, 1776; vicar-apostolic of Northern England, 1780; joined in issuing 'Protestation oath' encyclical, 1789; with Thomas *Eyre (1748–1810) published *The London, or Little Catechism* (1784).

GIBSON, Patrick (1782?–1829), landscape painter and writer; exhibited at Royal Academy, 1805–7, and at several Edinburgh galleries; foundation member of Scottish Academy, 1826; professor of painting at Dollar Academy,

1824–9; his *Landscape Composition* preserved in Scottish National Gallery, and portrait of himself (water-colour) in the Portrait Gallery; published *Etchings of Select Views in Edinburgh* (1818); contributed to Brewster's *Edinburgh Encyclopaedia*.

GIBSON, Richard (1615–1690), dwarf and miniature painter; page to Charles I and *Henrietta Maria; executed several portraits of *Cromwell and many miniatures; his marriage to Anne Shepherd, also a dwarf, commemorated by *Waller; portrait of him and his wife painted by *Lely.

GIBSON, Solomon (d. 1866), sculptor; brother of John *Gibson (1790–1866); best known for his small *Mercury* modelled at 16; wrote papers on Welsh literature; died at Paris.

GIBSON, Susan Penelope (1652–1700), miniaturist; daughter of Richard *Gibson.

GIBSON, Thomas (d. 1562), printer, medical practitioner, and author; noted for extraordinary cures; recommended by *Latimer to *Cromwell, 1537; fled to Geneva in reign of Mary; licensed by Cambridge University to practise physic, 1559; printed in London his own books, including a New Testament concordance (1535), and several medical and anti-papal works.

GIBSON, Thomas (1647–1722), physician; MD, Leiden, 1675; physician-general to the army, 1719–22; published *Anatomy of Humane Bodies epitomized* (1682).

GIBSON, Thomas (1680?–1751), portrait painter; friend of *Vertue; painted portraits of Vertue, *Locke, *Flamsteed, and Archbishop *Wake.

GIBSON, Thomas Milner- (1806–1884), statesman; at school with Disraeli at Higham Hill, Essex, afterwards at Charterhouse; BA and thirty-sixth wrangler, Trinity College, Cambridge, 1830; Conservative MP for Ipswich, 1837–9; resigned on change of views; active member and speaker of Anti-Corn-Law League; Liberal MP, Manchester, 1841; vice-president of Board of Trade, 1846–8; privy councillor, 1846; seconded *Cobden's vote of censure on Palmerston's Chinese policy, 1857; MP for Ashton-under-Lyne, 1857–68; carried motion to amend law of conspiracy, which caused Palmerston's resignation, 1858; president of the Board of Trade in Palmerston's last ministry, 1859–65, and under Lord Russell, 1865–6; active promoter of the commercial treaty with France, and the abolition of the newspaper stamp, advertisement, and paper duties; received a pension of £2,000 on retirement; died on his yacht off Algiers.

GIBSON, Wilfrid Wilson (1878–1962), poet; educated at private schools; published *The Stone-folds* (1907); moved to London, 1912; contributed to the five volumes of *Georgian Poetry* (1912–22) of (Sir) Edward *Marsh; helped, with Rupert *Brooke and others, to produce *New Numbers*; legacy from Rupert Brooke enabled him to live as a poet; served in Army Service Corps, 1917–19; published *Collected Poems* (1926), and fourteen other books including *The Alert* (1941) and *Within Four Walls* (1950).

GIBSON, William (*fl.* 1540), lord of session; graduated at Glasgow, 1507; dean of Restalrig; lord of session, 1532; employed on embassies to the pope, who bestowed on him armorial bearings; suffragan to Cardinal Beaton and *Custos Ecclesiae Scotiae* (1540).

GIBSON, William (1629–1684), Quaker; served at one time in Parliamentarian army; frequently imprisoned for preaching and refusing oaths, 1654–61; his goods distrained for non-payment of tithe, 1676–7; published theological treatises.

GIBSON, William (1644–1702), miniature painter; nephew of Richard *Gibson; pupil and copyist of Lely.

GIBSON, William (1720–1791), mathematician; while working as a farmer taught himself reading, writing, geometry, algebra, and trigonometry, and acquired a knowledge of higher mathematics; land-surveyor.

GIBSON, William (1738–1821), Roman Catholic prelate; brother of Matthew *Gibson (1734–1790); president of Douai College, 1781–90; vicar-apostolic of northern England, 1790; founded Ushaw College.

GIBSON, William (1808–1867), Presbyterian divine; established 'Banner of Ulster', 1842; moderator of general assembly, 1859; author of *The Year of Grace, a History of the Ulster Revival of 1859*.

GIBSON, William Pettigrew (1902–1960), keeper of the National Gallery; educated at Westminster and Christ Church, Oxford; abandoned medicine for history of art; lecturer and assistant keeper, Wallace Collection, 1927–36; reader, history of art, London University, and deputy director, Courtauld Institute, 1936–9; keeper of National Gallery, 1939–60.

GIBSON, William Sidney (1814–1871), author; barrister, Lincoln's Inn, 1843; registrar of the Newcastle upon Tyne district court of bankruptcy, 1843–69; published works, including *History of Tynemouth Monastery* (1846–7), *Descriptive and Historical Notices of Northumbrian*

Antiquities (1848–54), *Memoir of Northumberland* (1860), and *Memoir of Lord Lyndhurst* (1866).

GIDDY, Davies (1767–1839), president of the Royal Society. See GILBERT.

GIDEON, Sampson (1699–1762), Jewish financier; of Portuguese extraction; consulted by Walpole and Pelham; raised £1,700,000 for government, 1745; advised and executed consolidation of National Debt, 1749; paid bounties for recruiting, 1756, and raised several government loans during Seven Years' War; his son created a baronet and Baron Eardley in peerage of Ireland.

GIELGUD, Val Henry (1900–1981), novelist, playwright, and head of radio drama at BBC; older brother of (Sir) John Gielgud; educated at Rugby and Trinity College, Oxford; served in Household Brigade Officers' Cadet battalion, 1918; worked in various jobs and became an actor, 1921–8; as author wrote twenty novels, seven volumes of autobiography, and eighteen plays; assistant to editor of *Radio Times*, 1928; director of productions, BBC, 1929–63; responsible for serialization of classic novels and series of popular plays; produced *The Man Born to be King* by Dorothy L. *Sayers, 1941; moved into television drama without success, 1949–51, and returned to radio; OBE, 1942; CBE, 1958; autobiographical works include *Years of the Locust* (1947), *One Year of Grace* (1950), and *Years in a Mirror* (1965); plays include *Party Manners* (1951).

GIFFARD. See also GIFFORD.

GIFFARD, Sir Ambrose Hardinge (1771–1827), chief justice of Ceylon, 1819–27; barrister, Inner Temple.

GIFFARD, Bonaventure (1642–1734), Roman Catholic bishop; DD from the Sorbonne, 1677; chaplain to James II; first vicar-apostolic of midland district, 1688; bishop of Madaura, *in partibus*, 1688; made by James II president of Magdalen College, Oxford; installed by proxy, 31 Mar. 1688; ejected, on the restoration of his predecessor, John *Hough, 25 Oct. 1688; imprisoned in Newgate at the Revolution; transferred to London district on liberation; had also western district, 1708–13; in constant danger; bequeathed his heart to Douai College.

GIFFARD, Sir George James (1886–1964), general; educated at Rugby and the Royal Military College, Sandhurst; commissioned into the Queen's Royal Regiment, 1906; seconded to King's African Rifles, 1911; served in East Africa, 1913–18; DSO; Croix de Guerre; selected for Staff College, Camberley, 1919; served in number of staff posts, 1920–33; aide-de-camp to the King, 1935–6; major-general; inspector-general, African Colonial Forces, 1936; CB, 1938; military secretary to secretary of state for war, Leslie (later Lord) *Hore-Belisha, 1939; commander-in-chief, West Africa, 1940; general, KCB, 1941; commanded Eastern Army, India, 1943; commander-in-chief, 11th Army Group, under Lord Louis (later Earl) *Mountbatten, 1943; gave firm support to William (later Viscount) *Slim and the 14th Army; disagreement with Mountbatten led to dismissal, 1944; GCB; aide-de-camp general to the King, 1945–6; president, Army Benevolent Fund; colonel, the Queen's Royal Regiment, 1945–54.

GIFFARD, Sir George Markham (1813–1870), lord justice of appeal; educated at Winchester and New College, Oxford; fellow, 1832; BCL, 1841; barrister, Inner Temple, 1840; leading Chancery junior; QC, 1859; lord justice of appeal, 1868–70; privy councillor, 1868.

GIFFARD, Godfrey (1235?–1302), chancellor of England and bishop of Worcester; younger brother of Walter *Giffard; archdeacon of Barnstaple, 1265, and York, 1267, though a deacon; chancellor of England, 1266–8; bishop of Worcester, 1268–1302; treated with *Llewelyn ab Gruffydd, 1272; went to meet Edward I on his return from the Holy Land, 1273; justice-itinerant, 1278; negotiated with the Scots, 1289; involved in constant disputes with chapter of Worcester; a benefactor of the cathedral.

GIFFARD, Hardinge Stanley, first earl of Halsbury (1823–1921), lord chancellor; son of Stanley Lees *Giffard; BA, Merton College, Oxford; called to bar (Inner Temple), 1850; joined South Wales circuit, 1851; practised at Old Bailey and at Middlesex sessions at Clerkenwell; junior prosecuting counsel at Central Criminal Court, 1859; QC, 1865; leading counsel for Governor E. J. *Eyre, 1867–8; second counsel for Tichborne claimant, Arthur *Orton, 1871–2; solicitor-general and knighted, 1875; led for crown in *Franconia* case, 1876; Conservative MP, Launceston, 1877; took active part in parliament and law courts over case of Charles *Bradlaugh; greatest forensic triumph, case of *Belt* v. *Lawes*, 1882; lord chancellor, 1885–6; 1886–92, 1895–1905; baron, 1885; earl, 1898; largely responsible for Land Transfer Act (1897) and Criminal Evidence Act (1898); presided over production of complete digest of *Laws of England* (1905–16); led 'diehards' among peers against Parliament Bill, 1911.

GIFFARD, Henry Wells (1810–1854), navy captain; present as midshipman at Navarino, 1827; present at capture of Chusan and Canton, 1839, and reduction of Amoy and Chingbae,

1841; mortally wounded and captured in the *Tiger* at Odessa.

GIFFARD, John, Baron Giffard of Bromsfield (1232–1299), fought for de Montfort in the west; captured Warwick Castle, 1264; taken at Lewes, but rescued, 1264; attached himself to Gilbert de Clare and fought for the royalists at Evesham, 1265; served Edward I in Wales, Gascony, and Scotland; summoned by writ to parliament of 1295; member of Council of Regency, 1297; founded Gloucester Hall (now Worcester College), Oxford, 1283.

GIFFARD, Roger (d. 1597), president of the College of Physicians; fellow of Merton College, Oxford, and of All Souls; MA, 1560; MD, 1566; physician to Queen Elizabeth; president, College of Physicians, 1581–4.

GIFFARD, Stanley Lees (1788–1858), first editor of the *Standard*; brother of Sir Ambrose Hardinge *Giffard; MA, Trinity College, Dublin, 1811; barrister, Middle Temple, 1811; LL D; editor of the *Standard* from 1827; editor of *St. James's Chronicle*; contributed to the *Quarterly* and *Blackwood*.

GIFFARD, Walter (d. 1279), archbishop of York; consecrated at Paris bishop of Bath and Wells, 1265; excommunicated the earl of *Leicester and his followers; chancellor after Evesham, 1265–6; one of the arbitrators of the award of Kenilworth, 1266; archbishop of York, 1266–79; tutor to Prince Edward's sons; one of the three regents, 1272–4, and 1275.

GIFFARD, William (d. 1129), bishop of Winchester; dean of Rouen and chancellor to William II; nominated to see of Winchester by Henry I on his accession, 1100; inducted by Anselm; refusing to receive consecration from *Gerard, the newly appointed archbishop of York, was banished by the king; maintained intimate relations with Anselm, whom he accompanied to Rome, 1103; consecrated, after settlement of the investiture dispute, 1107; as deputy for the primate married Henry I and Queen Adela, 1121; his disputes with the monks of Winchester ended by royal intervention, 1124; founded at Waverley, Surrey, 1128, the first English Cistercian house; benefactor of St Mary Overies, Southwark; built London residence for bishops of Winchester in Southwark.

GIFFEN, Sir Robert (1837–1910), economist and statistician; apprenticed to lawyer in Glasgow; took up journalism, 1860; sub-editor of *Globe*, 1862–6; assistant editor of *The Economist*, 1868–76; chief of statistical department to Board of Trade, 1876–97; the commercial (1882) and the labour (1892) departments were subsequently included in his control; served on many royal commissions; edited *Journal of Royal Statistical Society*, 1876–91; helped to found Economic Society, 1890; criticized Gladstone's home-rule finance, 1893; Liberal Unionist from 1886, and finally Unionist Free Trader; KCB, 1895; strong individualist; advocated 'free banking'; voluminous writings include *Essays in Finance* (2 series, 1880–6), *The Case against Bimetallism* (1892), and *Economic Enquiries and Studies* (2 vols., 1904).

GIFFORD. See also GIFFARD.

GIFFORD, countess of (1807–1867), songwriter. See SHERIDAN, HELEN SELINA.

GIFFORD, Adam, Lord Gifford (1820–1887), lord of session; called to Scottish bar, 1849; advocate-depute, 1861; sheriff of Orkney and Zetland, 1865; lord of session as Lord Gifford, 1870–81; founded Gifford lectureships in natural theology.

GIFFORD, Andrew (1700–1784), Baptist minister and numismatist; DD, Aberdeen, 1754; chaplain to Sir Richard *Ellys and Lady Ellys, 1731–45; minister at Eagle Street, London, 1730–84; assistant librarian at British Museum, 1757–84; his collection of coins purchased by George II; left valuable books, manuscripts, pictures, and curios to Baptist Academy, Bristol; edited *Folkes's Tables of English Silver and Gold Coins* (1763).

GIFFORD, Edwin Hamilton (1820–1905), schoolmaster and theologian; BA, St John's College, Cambridge (senior classic and fifteenth wrangler), 1843; fellow, 1843–4; hon. fellow, 1903; headmaster of King Edward's School, Birmingham, 1848–62; archdeacon of London and canon of St Paul's, 1884; wrote *Voices of the Past* (1874) and edited with translation Eusebius's *Praeparatio Evangelica* (5 vols., 1903).

GIFFORD, George (d. 1600), divine; student at Hart Hall, Oxford, before 1568; MA, Christ's College, Cambridge, 1573; incumbent of All Saints' with St Peter's, Maldon, 1582; deposed for nonconformity, 1584; carried on controversy with the Brownists, Henry *Barrow, and John *Greenwood; published theological works; his *Dialogue concerning Witches and Witchcrafts* (1593) reprinted by Percy Society.

GIFFORD, George (*fl.* 1635), engraver; chiefly known for the portrait of *Latimer prefixed to the 1635 edition of Latimer's sermons.

GIFFORD (or GIFFARD), Gilbert (1561?–1590), Roman Catholic spy; of the Chillington family; while at the English College, Rome, entered English secret service, 1583; visited *Mary Queen of Scots at Chartley, 1584, and was entrusted with her secret correspondence with the French embassy; treacherously copied

letters, sending originals to *Walsingham; intimate of Anthony *Babington, whose designs he encouraged and communicated to Walsingham; carried letters from Mary to Babington approving the conspiracy; accused by Romanists of concocting the whole plot; died in prison at Paris.

GIFFORD, Humphrey (*fl.* 1580), poet; author of *A Posie of Gilloflowers* (1580).

GIFFORD, James, the elder (1740?–1813), Unitarian writer; educated at Rugby; served in the 14th Foot during American War; published theological works, including *Elucidation of the Unity of God* (1783).

GIFFORD, James, the younger (1768–1853), rear-admiral; son of James *Gifford the elder; born at Halifax, Nova Scotia; lieutenant in the navy, 1793; rear-admiral, 1846; published *Remonstrance of a Unitarian . . . to Bishop of St. David's* (1818).

GIFFORD, John (*fl.* 1636–1642), DD, Christ Church, Oxford; rector of St Michael Bassishaw, 1636–42; expelled as a Royalist, 1642.

GIFFORD, John (1758–1818), author; of Westminster and St John's College, Oxford; abandoned his paternal name of Green, and assumed that of Gifford to deceive his creditors, *c.*1781; London police magistrate; edited, in imitation of the *Anti-Jacobin* of William *Gifford (1756–1826), the *Anti-Jacobin Review and Magazine*, published 1798–1821; also published *History of France* (1791–4) and *Political Life of Pitt* (1809).

GIFFORD, Richard (1725–1807), author; BA, Balliol College, Oxford, 1748; vicar of Duffield, 1759; rector of North Okendon, 1772; his *Contemplation, a Poem* (1753) quoted in *Johnson's Dictionary; published an answer to *Priestley's dissertation on matter and mind.

GIFFORD, Robert, first Baron Gifford (1779–1826), judge; special pleader; barrister, Middle Temple, 1808; recorder of Bristol, 1812; solicitor-general, 1817; attorney-general, 1819; prosecuted Cato Street conspirators, 1820; MP, Eye, 1817–1824; addressed House of Lords against Queen *Caroline, 1820; serjeant-at-law, 1824; chief justice of common pleas, privy councillor, and created peer, 1824; master of the Rolls and deputy-speaker of House of Lords.

GIFFORD, William (1554–1629), archbishop of Reims; studied at Lincoln College, Oxford; studied at Louvain under Bellarmine and at the Sorbonne and English colleges at Reims and Rome; MA, Louvain; almoner and chaplain to Cardinal *Allen at Rome, 1587; dean of Lille, 1596; rector of Reims University, 1608, where he became a Benedictine; famed as a preacher at Paris and throughout France; first president of

English Benedictines, 1617; coadjutor of cardinal of Guise, 1618, at Reims; archbishop of Reims, 1622; edited Dr W. Reynolds's *Calvino-Turcismus* (1597) and wrote several works in the interests of the duc de Guise.

GIFFORD, William (1756–1826), first editor of the *Quarterly Review*; son of a glazier at Ashburton; shoemaker's apprentice; sent by a surgeon named William Cookesley to Exeter College, Oxford; BA, 1782; afterwards patronized by Lord *Grosvenor; became known by his satires, the *Baviad* (1794) and *Maeviad* (1795), against the Della Cruscans and small dramatists; editor of and writer in *Anti-Jacobin* (1797–8); published *Epistle to Peter Pindar* (1800), attacking *Wolcot, who assaulted him at a bookshop in mistake for his namesake, John *Gifford, of the *Anti-Jacobin Review*; editor of the *Quarterly Review*, 1809–24; probably wrote the *Quarterly*'s attack on *Keats's *Endymion*, 1818; inspected *Byron's works before publication; founded exhibitions at Exeter College, Oxford; edited Juvenal, with autobiography (1802) and translated Persius (1821); edited the dramatic works of *Massinger (1805 and 1813), of Ben *Jonson (1816), and of *Ford (1827).

GIGLI, Giovanni (d. 1498), bishop of Worcester; came to England as collector for Pope Sixtus IV; commissioner for sale of indulgences, 1489; rewarded for his services for Henry VII at Rome by see of Worcester, 1497, but died at Rome before enthronement; wrote epithalamium on marriage of Henry VII.

GIGLI, Silvestro (1463–1521), bishop of Worcester; nephew of Giovanni *Gigli; bishop of Worcester, 1498; resident ambassador of Henry VII at Rome; envoy of Pope Julius II to England, 1504; stayed at court as master of ceremonies; envoy to the Lateran Council, 1512; confidential agent for *Wolsey at Rome; correspondent of Erasmus.

GIGLIUCCI, Countess (1818–1908), oratorio and operatic prima donna. See NOVELLO, CLARA ANASTASIA.

GILBART, James William (1794–1863), writer on banking; banker in London, Birmingham, and Ireland; manager of the London and Westminster Bank, 1833–59; FRS and member of Statistical Society; chief works, *Practical Treatise on Banking* (1827) and *History and Principles of Banking* (1834).

GILBERT, Sir Alfred (1854–1934), sculptor; studied at Heatherley's, Royal Academy Schools, under (Sir) Edgar *Boehm, at École des Beaux-Arts, and in Italy; founded reputation with works such as *Icarus*; settled in England, 1884; ARA, 1887; RA, 1892; lived in Bruges, 1901–26; works

include memorials to *Shaftesbury (the fountain and *Eros* in Piccadilly Circus), the duke of *Clarence (at St George's, Windsor), and Queen *Alexandra (at Marlborough Gate, St James's); knighted, 1932.

GILBERT, Mrs Ann (1782–1866), writer of children's poetry; better known under her maiden name, Ann Taylor; with her sister Jane wrote *Original Poems for Infant Minds* (1804–5), *Rhymes for the Nursery* (1806), and *Hymns* (1810); married Joseph *Gilbert, 1813; afterwards published *Seven Blessings for Little Children* (1844); contributed to *Leifchild's *Original Hymns*, and compiled memoir of her husband (1853); her *Autobiography* issued (1874).

GILBERT, Ashurst Turner (1786–1870), bishop of Chichester; fellow of Brasenose College, Oxford; MA, 1811; DD, 1822; principal of Brasenose College, Oxford, 1822–42; vice-chancellor, 1836–40; bishop of Chichester, 1842–70; interdicted the Revd John *Purchas, 1868; published sermons and charges.

GILBERT, Charles Sandoe (1760–1831), historian of Cornwall; itinerant vendor of medicines in Devon and Cornwall; published two volumes (1817 and 1820) of *Historical Survey of Cornwall*.

GILBERT, Claudius, the elder (d. 1696?), ecclesiastic; BA, St Catharine's College, Cambridge, 1647–8; minister under Commonwealth of the precinct of Limerick; active against the Quakers; settled at Belfast after the Restoration; published *The Libertine School'd, or a Vindication of the Magistrates' Power in Religious Matters* (1657) and other works.

GILBERT, Claudius, the younger (1670–1743), ecclesiastic; son of Claudius *Gilbert the elder; fellow of Trinity College, Dublin, 1693; DD and LL D, 1706; vice-provost, 1716; rector of Ardstraw, 1735; bequeathed many books to Trinity College, Dublin.

GILBERT (formerly GIDDY), Davies (1767–1839), president of the Royal Society; assumed wife's name of Gilbert, 1817; educated at Penzance and Pembroke College, Oxford; MA, 1789; DCL, 1832; high sheriff of Cornwall, 1792–3; MP, Helston, 1804, Bodmin, 1806–32; promoted cause of science and art in parliament, acquired large property in Sussex by marriage, 1808; published *Plain Statement of the Bullion Question* (1811); FSA, 1820; early encouraged Sir Humphry *Davy; treasurer of Royal Society, 1820, president, 1827–30; nominated writers of Bridgewater Treatises, and (1830) selected Brunel's design for Clifton Bridge; published *Parochial History of Cornwall* (1838); edited *Collection of Christmas Carols* and two Cornish mystery plays.

GILBERT, Elizabeth Margaretta Maria (1826–1885), philanthropist; second daughter of Ashurst Turner *Gilbert; rendered blind as a child by scarlet fever; with William Hanks Levy founded *Association for Promoting the General Welfare of the Blind*; assisted Levy in writing *Blindness and the Blind* (1872).

GILBERT, Sir Geoffrey (or Jeffray) (1674–1726), judge; barrister, Inner Temple, 1698; chief baron of Irish Exchequer, 1715–22; resisted claim to jurisdiction of the Irish parliament in case of *Annesley* v. *Sherlock*, 1718; English judge of Exchequer, 1722; knighted, 1725; a commissioner of great seal, 1725; his *Law of Uses and Trusts* (1734), edited by *Sugden (1811), and *Treatise of Tenures* (1754), by Charles *Watkins and Robert *Vidal (1824); his *History and Practice of Civil Actions in the Court of Common Pleas* (1737) praised by *Blackstone.

GILBERT, George (1555–1583), founder (with Thomas Pound of Belmont) of the Catholic Association, 1579; became a Jesuit; died at Rome.

GILBERT, Sir Humphrey (1539?–1583), navigator; stepbrother of *Ralegh; educated at Eton and Oxford; served under Sir Henry *Sidney in Ireland; given charge of Munster, 1569; knighted, 1570; MP, Plymouth, 1571; rebuked in parliament by Peter *Wentworth; unsuccessful against the Spaniards in Zeeland, 1572; composed in retirement his *Discourse of a Discouery for a New Passage to Cataia* (ed. G. *Gascoigne, 1576); obtained charter for discovery and plantation, 1578; failed in his first voyage, 1579; served under *Perrot against the Spanish ships off Munster, 1579; left Plymouth with five ships to colonize Newfoundland, 1583; landed at harbour of St John (5 Aug. 1583) and there founded the first British colony in North America; after a voyage of discovery along the south coast sailed for England (1 Sept.), but was lost in a storm off the Southern Azores; his scheme for the erection in London of an 'Achademy' to educate royal wards and others printed by Dr Furnivall (1869).

GILBERT, John (*fl.* 1680), theological writer; MA, Hart Hall, Oxford, 1680; published *Answer to the Bishop of Condom* [now of Meaux], *his Exposition of the Catholic Faith* (1686).

GILBERT, John (1693–1761), archbishop of York; BA, Trinity College, Oxford, 1713; MA, Merton College, 1718; prebendary (1723), subdean (1724–6) and dean (1726) of Exeter; LL D, Lambeth, 1724; bishop of Llandaff, 1740–9, of Salisbury, 1749; clerk of the closet, 1750; archbishop of York, 1757–61; began the practice of laying hands on each candidate at confirmation.

GILBERT, Sir John (1817–1897), historical painter and draughtsman on wood; entered estate agents' office in City of London, 1833; exhibited two drawings of historical subjects at Suffolk Street, 1836, and two oil-paintings at British Institution, 1837; exhibited at Royal Academy, 1838–51, and from 1867; worked at book illustration, illustrating most of the English poets and other works, including Howard *Staunton's edition of Shakespeare, 1856–60; joined staff of *Illustrated London News*, 1842, as draughtsman on wood, and contributed drawings regularly to *London Journal* from 1845; president of Old Water-colour Society, 1871–97; knighted, 1872; RA, 1876; made presents of collections of his pictures to municipal galleries of London, Birmingham, Liverpool, and Manchester, 1893.

GILBERT, John Graham- (1794–1866), painter. See GRAHAM-GILBERT.

GILBERT, Sir John Thomas (1829–1808), Irish historian and antiquary; joint honorary secretary to Irish Celtic and Archaeological Society, 1855; secretary of Public Record Office, Dublin, 1867–75; vice-president of Royal Irish Academy; LL D, Royal University, 1892; knighted, 1897. His works include *Historical Essays on Ireland* (1851), *History of the City of Dublin* (1854–9), *History of the Viceroys of Ireland* (1865), and *Contemporary History of Affairs in Ireland, 1641–1652* (1879–80).

GILBERT, Joseph (1779–1852), Congregational divine; classical tutor at Rotherham College; minister at Sheffield and Nottingham, 1828–51; published life of Dr Edward *Williams (1750–1813), (1825), a defence of Williams's hypothesis of origin of evil (1808), and a work on the atonement (1836).

GILBERT, Joseph Francis (1792–1855), painter; exhibited at the Royal Academy after 1813.

GILBERT, Sir Joseph Henry (1817–1901), agricultural chemist; son of Joseph and Ann *Gilbert; studied agricultural chemistry at Glasgow, London, and at Giessen under Liebig; co-worker with John Bennet *Lawes in Rothamsted agricultural experiments; president of Chemical Society, 1882–3; FRS, 1860; professor of rural economy at Oxford, 1884–90; knighted, 1893.

GILBERT, Marie Dolores Eliza Rosanna (1818–1861), adventuress; known by her stage name Lola Montez; daughter of military officer; married Captain Thomas James, 1837; divorced, 1842; appeared at Her Majesty's Theatre, London, as a dancer, 1843, pretending to be a native of Spain; highly successful at Dresden, Berlin, Warsaw, St Petersburg, and Paris; became mistress of Ludwig I of Bavaria, who created her Baronne de Rosenthal and Comtesse de Lansfeld, 1847; exercised full control over government of Bavaria, 1847–8; banished, owing to Austrian and Jesuit influence, 1848; married in England George Trafford Heald, 1849; fled with him to Spain to avoid bigamy proceedings; appeared at New York and Philadelphia, 1852, in Ware's *Lola Montez in Bavaria*; married P. P. Hull of the *San Francisco Whig* in California, 1853; played at Sydney and Melbourne, 1855; horsewhipped the editor of the *Ballarat Times*, 1856; played and lectured at New York, 1857–8, and published *The Art of Beauty*; devoted herself to helping fallen women; died at Asteria, New York.

GILBERT, Nicolas Alain (1762–1821), Roman Catholic divine; born at St Malo; established mission at Whitby; published theological works.

GILBERT, Richard (1794–1852), printer and compiler, of St John's Square, Clerkenwell.

GILBERT, Samuel (d. 1692?), floriculturist; son-in-law of John *Rea; rector of Quatt, Shropshire; published *Florist's Vade-mecum and Gardener's Almanack* (1683).

GILBERT, Thomas (1610–1673), ejected minister; rector of Cheadle; when ejected from vicarage of Ealing emigrated to New England; pastor of Topsfield, Massachusetts; buried at Charlestown.

GILBERT, Thomas (1613–1694), ejected minister; MA, St Edmund Hall, Oxford, 1638; vicar of Upper Winchendon, and c.1644, St Lawrence, Reading; rector of Edgmond; took the Covenant; nicknamed 'bishop of Shropshire'; lost Edgmond at Restoration; ejected from Winchendon, 1662; preached in family of Lord *Wharton; wrote Latin and English poems.

GILBERT, Thomas (1720–1798), poor-law reformer; barrister, Inner Temple, 1744; treasurer, 1789; advised Bridgewater to engage James *Brindley, whose canals he promoted; MP, Newcastle under Lyme, 1763–8, Lichfield, 1768–95; carried two poor-law measures, 1782; his Poor Law Bill of 1787 criticized by Sir Henry Bate *Dudley; chairman of committees, 1784; carried measures for reform of houses of correction and improvement of highways, and an act for facilitating clerical residence by loans from Queen Anne's Bounty ('Gilbert's Act'); his propositions for helping friendly societies by parochial grants embodied in act of 1793; edited *Collection of Pamphlets concerning the Poor* (1787).

GILBERT, Sir Walter Raleigh (1785–1853), lieutenant-general; lieutenant, 15th Bengal Native Infantry, 1803; served under (Sir) John *Macdonald at Ally Ghur, Delhi, Agra, Laswarrie, and siege of Bhurtpore; colonel, 1832; lieutenant-general, 1851; commanded division in Sikh Wars; captured remnant of enemy's force after Gujerat, 1849; GCB and member of Council of India, 1850; created baronet, 1851.

GILBERT, William (1540–1603), physician to Queen Elizabeth and James I; fellow of St John's College, Cambridge, 1561; MA, 1564; MD, 1569; president of College of Physicians, 1600; declared the earth to be a magnet in his *De Magnete, Magneticisque Corporibus* (1600), the first great scientific book published in England.

GILBERT, William (1760?–1825?), poet; born in Antigua; educated for the bar; in asylum at Bristol, 1787–8; friend of *Coleridge and *Southey; published *The Hurricane: a Theosophical and Western Eclogue* (1796).

GILBERT, William (1804–1890), author; midshipman in East India Company's service, 1818–21; studied at Guy's Hospital, 1825; for short period assistant surgeon in navy; published novels, many of which dealt with the contrast between the lots of rich and poor; some of his works illustrated by his son, William Schwenck Gilbert.

GILBERT, Sir William Schwenck (1836–1911), dramatist; son of William *Gilbert (1804–90); used his own pet name 'Bab' as pseudonym in later life; BA, London, 1857; joined militia, 1857; retired as major, 1883; clerk in Privy Council office (education department), 1857–61; called to bar, 1863; commenced author and artist as regular contributor to *Fun* from 1861; illustrated books by father, 1863 and 1869; his 'Yarn of the Nancy Bell' refused by *Punch* as 'too cannibalistic', 1866; this and other 'Bab' ballads appeared in *Fun* from 1866 to 1871 and were published in volume form as *Bab Ballads* (1869) and *More Bab Ballads* (1873); commenced playwright with *Dulcamara*, a successful burlesque, 1866; wrote many other extravaganzas; collaborated with Frederick *Clay in musical sketches for the German *Reeds, 1869–72; introduced by Clay to (Sir) Arthur *Sullivan, 1871; first collaborated with Sullivan in a burlesque, *Thespis*, 1871; wrote blank-verse fairy comedy, *The Palace of Truth* (1870), *Pygmalion and Galatea* (1871), *The Wicked World* (1873); wrote series of comedies (some under pseudonym of F. L. Tomline) for Marie *Litton at Court Theatre; *The Happy Land* (1873) roused much enthusiasm and public excitement; produced also serious plays, including *Charity* (1874), *Broken Hearts* (1875), and *Dan'l Druce* (1876); collaborated with Sullivan for D'Oyly *Carte's Opera Company in long series of comic operas, viz. *Trial by Jury* (1875), *The Sorcerer* (1877), *H.M.S. Pinafore* (1878), *The Pirates of Penzance* (produced in New York, 1879), *Patience* (1881); operas transferred to Savoy Theatre, 1881; later 'Savoy' operas were *Iolanthe* (1882), *Princess Ida* (1884), *The Mikado* (1885)—the most popular work—*Ruddigore* (1887), *The Yeomen of the Guard* (1888), *The Gondoliers* (1889); separated from Sullivan and Carte owing to financial disagreement, 1890–3; collaborated with Alfred *Cellier in *The Mountebanks*, 1892; resumed collaboration with Sullivan in *Utopia, Limited* (1893) and *The Grand Duke* (1896); produced *Fallen Fairies* with (Sir) Edward *German, 1909, and *The Hooligan*, a serious sketch, 1911; built and owned Garrick Theatre, 1889; interested in astronomy, bee-keeping, and horticulture; knighted, 1907; plays show literary grace, whimsical humour (known as 'Gilbertian' humour), urbane satire, good taste, and lyric excellence; master of stage management; fond of epigram and repartee; a kindly cynic; dramatic works collected in *Original Plays* (4 series, 1876–1911) and in *Original Comic Operas* (8 parts, 1890).

GILBERT OF HOYLAND (d. 1172), theological writer; an English Cistercian, often confused with *Gilbert the Great; disciple of St Bernard of Clairvaux; abbot of Swineshead, Lincolnshire, 1163; said to have died at Rivour, near Troyes; his sermons and *Tractatus Ascetici* printed in Migne's *Patrologia* and Mabillon's works of St Bernard.

GILBERT OF LOUTH (d. 1153?), abbot of Basingwerk, Flintshire; sent from Louth by Gervase, *c.*1140, to obtain grant for an Irish monastery; the *Purgatorium Sancti Patricii* wrongly ascribed to him.

GILBERT OF MORAY (d. 1245), bishop of Caithness, 1223; archdeacon of Moray, 1203; built Dornoch Cathedral; last Scotsman enrolled in calendar of saints.

GILBERT OF ST LIFARD (d. 1305), bishop of Chichester; a foreigner, probably named from church of St Lifard (Leofard), near Meung-sur-Loire; practised as ecclesiastical lawyer chiefly in the north of England; treasurer of Chichester by 1282; employed by Archbishop *Peckham on commission to define rights of metropolitical jurisdiction, 1282, and in disputes with monks; bishop of Chichester, 1288–1305; his constitutions of reform (1289) re-enacted by Archbishop *William of Greenfield; rebuilt east end of his cathedral.

GILBERT OF SEMPRINGHAM (1083?–1189), founder of the Gilbertine order, the head of the thirteen houses being at Sempringham, Lincoln-

shire, *c.*1135; met Pope Eugenius III at Cîteaux; received abbot's staves from St Bernard and St Malachy; supported *Becket against Henry II; held in great regard by Henry II and Queen *Eleanor, who protected him against the enemies made by the rapacity of his servants; lived to be over 100, but retired from his abbacy long before death; canonized by Innocent III, 1202.

GILBERT THE ENGLISHMAN (or DE AQUILA) (*fl.* 1205), medical writer; studied and practised abroad, and is said to have been chancellor of Montpellier; his *Compendium Medicinae* or *Laurea Anglicana*, largely a compilation from Greek and Arab writers, first printed at Lyons (1510).

GILBERT THE GREAT (or THE THEOLOGIAN) (d. 1167?), eighth abbot of Cîteaux; an Englishman; abbot of Cistercians at Ourcamp, 1143, at Cîteaux, 1163; supported Geoffrey of Clairvaux against the pope and king of France; author of *Commentaries on the Psalms* and other works.

GILBERT THE UNIVERSAL (d. 1134?), bishop of London; 'magister' at Auxerre, *c.*1120; bishop of London, 1128; took part in Council of London, 1129, which condemned marriage of priests; his 'infinite' wealth confiscated by Henry I; accused by the chronicler, *Henry of Huntingdon, of avarice, but highly commended by St Bernard; benefactor of sees of London and Auxerre; owed his title 'Universal' to his encyclopaedic learning; his only extant work, a treatise on Lamentations; many of his works confused with those of Gilbert of Auxerre and Gilbert *Foliot.

GILBURNE (or GILBORNE), Samuel (*fl.* 1605), actor; mentioned as one of Shakespeare's fellow actors in the Shakespeare first folio, 1623.

GILBY, Anthony (*c.*1510–1585), Puritan divine; MA, Christ's College, Cambridge, 1535; entertained *Foxe at Frankfurt; a pastor of the English congregation at Geneva, 1555; assisted in Geneva translation of the Bible; presented by *Huntingdon to living of Ashby-de-la-Zouch before 1564; his prosecution for nonconformity ordered by Matthew *Parker, 1571; translated commentaries of Calvin and Beza, and published commentaries on Micah and Malachi and controversial works.

GILBY, Goddard (*fl.* 1561), translator; son of Anthony *Gilby; translated Cicero's *Epistle to Quintus* (1561) and Calvin's *Admonition against Judicial Astrology*.

GILBY, William Hall (d. 1821?), geologist; MD, Edinburgh, 1815; president of Royal Society of

Medicine; contributed geological papers to *Edinburgh Philosophical Journal*.

GILCHRIST, Alexander (1828–1861), biographer; his *Life of Etty* published (1855), and that of *Blake (1863).

GILCHRIST, Anne (1828–1885), author; wife of Alexander *Gilchrist; finished Alexander Gilchrist's *Life of Blake*, prefixing a memoir of the author; published *Life of Mary Lamb* (1883), essays on Walt Whitman's poetry, and a translation of Hugo's *Légende des Siècles* (1884).

GILCHRIST, Ebenezer (1707–1774), physician; graduated at Reims; practised at Dumfries; published *Use of Sea Voyages in Medicine* (1756), and *Essays, Physical and Literary* (1770).

GILCHRIST, James (d. 1777), naval captain; was serving on the *Namur* when lost, 1749; in command of the *Experiment* captured sixteen French ships, 1755; fought off Minorca, 1756; captured the *Emeraude* and two privateers, 1757; severely wounded in taking the *Danae*, 1759.

GILCHRIST, John Borthwick (1759–1841), orientalist; educated at Heriot's Hospital, Edinburgh; LL D, Edinburgh, 1804; surgeon under East India Company at Calcutta, 1794; acquired knowledge of Hindustani, Sanskrit, and Persian; as principal of Fort William College, 1800–4, superintended the production by vernacular scholars of Urdu and Hindi textbooks for Europeans; retired from service, 1809; professor of Hindustani at Oriental Institution, Leicester Square, 1818–26; published *Hindustani Dictionary* (1787–90), *Hindustani Grammar* (1796), *Dialogues, English and Hindustani* (1804), and *British Indian Monitor* (1806–8), also Persian textbooks.

GILCHRIST, Octavius Graham (1779–1823), antiquary; FSA, 1803; edited poems of Richard *Corbet, 1807; published (1808) *Examination of the Charges maintained by Malone, Chalmers, and others of Ben Jonson's Enmity towards Shakespeare*; had controversies with Stephen *Jones, editor of *Biographia Dramatica*, and with William Lisle *Bowles.

GILDAS minor (or **NENNIUS**) (*fl.* 796), historian. See NENNIUS.

GILDAS (516?–570?), British historian; went to Brittany, *c.*550, and is said to have founded monastery of Ruys, near Vannes; a popular Breton saint; called by Alcuin 'the wisest of the Bretons'; his *De Excidio Britanniae* first printed by Polydore Vergil (1525), the first English version being that of Habington (1638).

GILDERDALE, John (1802–1864), divine; MA, St Catharine's Hall, Cambridge, 1830; DD, 1853; incumbent of Walthamstow and principal of Forest School; published *Essay on Natural Religion and Revelation* (1837).

GILDON, Charles (1665–1724), author; advocated deism in an edition of the works of Charles *Blount (1654–93); defended orthodoxy in *Deist's Manual* (1705); attacked Pope as 'Sawney Dapper', and was included by him in *The Dunciad*; published *Life and Adventures of Defoe*, five plays, and an edition, with continuation, of *Langbaine's *Dramatic Poets* (1699).

GILES, Francis (1787–1847), civil engineer; engaged in surveying under *Rennie; constructed works on South-Western Railway and Newcastle and Carlisle Railway; constructed the Warwick Bridge, Cumberland; long opposed as expert railway enterprises of George *Stephenson.

GILES, Herbert Allen (1845–1935), Chinese scholar and author; son of J. A. *Giles; educated at Charterhouse; served in China Consular Service, 1867–93; professor of Chinese, Cambridge, 1897–1932; fostered intelligent understanding of Chinese culture by a stream of books ranging from technical to popular.

GILES, James (1801–1870), landscape painter; at 13 maintained mother and sister by painting; RSA, 1829; his best works angling pictures.

GILES, John Allen (1808–1884), editor and translator; educated at Charterhouse; MA, Corpus Christi College, Oxford, 1831; fellow, 1832; double first and Vinerian scholar; DCL, 1838; headmaster of the City of London School, 1836–40; obliged by Bishop *Wilberforce to suppress his *Christian Records* (1854); imprisoned for making a false entry in Bampton marriage register to shield one of his servants, 1855; vicar of Sutton, 1867–84; published *Patres Ecclesiae Anglicanae* (1837–43), edited works for Caxton Society (1845–54); translated for *Bohn, Matthew *Paris, *Bede's *Ecclesiastical History*, and the *Saxon Chronicle*; published also life of *Becket (1845) and of King *Alfred (1848), and histories of Bampton and Witney.

GILES, Nathaniel (d. 1634), musical composer; organist of St George's, Windsor, 1595; master of the Children of the Chapel Royal, 1597; Mus.Doc., Oxford, 1622; published *Lesson of Descant of thirtie-eighte Proportions* on the plainsong, Miserere; his Service in C and anthem, 'O give thanks', printed in *Barnard's collection.

GILES, Peter (1860–1935), philologist and master of Emmanuel College, Cambridge; educated at Aberdeen University and Gonville and Caius College, Cambridge; first classes, classics, 1884–7; fellow of Emmanuel, 1890; master, 1911–35; vice-chancellor, Cambridge, 1919–21;

university reader in comparative philology, 1891–1935; published *Short Manual of Comparative Philology* (1895).

GILFILLAN, George (1813–1878), author; son of Samuel *Gilfillan; friend of Thomas *Aird, *De Quincey, and *Carlyle; educated at Glasgow College; United Presbyterian minister of the School-Wynd Church, Dundee, 1836–78; twice accused of heresy; helped Sydney *Dobell and Alexander *Smith; published works, including *Hades*, a sermon (1843), *Gallery of Literary Portraits, Alpha and Omega* (1850), *Bards of the Bible, History of a Man* (1856), editions of poets, with lives (1853–60); the Gilfillan Testimonial Trust formed for founding scholarships from a subscription raised in his honour, 1877–8.

GILFILLAN, James (1797–1874), Scottish divine; brother of George *Gilfillan; ordained in Stirling Secession congregation, 1822; LL D, Glasgow, 1866; published *The Sabbath, viewed in the Light of Reason, Revelation, and History* (1861).

GILFILLAN, Robert (1798–1850), poet; his 'Peter M'Craw' praised in *Noctes Ambrosianae*; published (1831) *Original Songs* (set by Peter M'Leod).

GILFILLAN, Samuel (1762–1826), Secession minister of Comrie, Strathearn, Perthshire; educated at Glasgow; his wife, Rachel Barlas, known as 'the star of the north'; published *Discourses on the Dignity, Grace, and Operations of the Holy Spirit* (1826).

GILL, Alexander, the elder (1565–1635), high master of St Paul's School; MA, Corpus Christi College, Oxford, 1589; high master of St Paul's School, 1608–35, Milton being one of his pupils; published *Logonomia Anglica* (1619).

GILL, Alexander, the younger (1597–1642), high master of St Paul's, 1635–9; son of Alexander *Gill the elder; MA, Wadham College, Oxford, 1619; DD, Trinity College, Oxford, 1637; his Latin verses praised by *Milton; sentenced to imprisonment, fine, and loss of his ears for speaking disrespectfully of Charles I and drinking a health to *Buckingham's assassin, 1628; pardoned, 1630; dismissed for severity from St Paul's; attacked Ben *Jonson's *Magnetick Lady*.

GILL, (Arthur) Eric (Rowton) (1882–1940), stone-carver, engraver, typographer, and author; attended Chichester Art School; in London studied lettering under Edward *Johnston, architecture, and masonry; became a letter-cutter; carved first figure direct from stone, 1909; became Roman Catholic (1913) and carved Stations of the Cross, Westminster Cathedral (1913–18); sculptures include *Mankind* (Tate Gallery), work

at Broadcasting House, and *Creation of Adam* at Geneva; designed ten printing types including 'Perpetua' and 'Gill Sans-serif'; illustrations include the *Canterbury Tales* and the *Four Gospels*; books include *The Necessity of Belief* (1936) and *Autobiography* (1940); ARA, 1937.

GILL, Sir **David** (1843–1914), astronomer; educated at Dollar Academy, Marischal College, and the university, Aberdeen; established in Aberdeen time service similar to that installed in Edinburgh by Charles Piazzi *Smyth, 1863; in charge of private observatory erected at Dunecht by Lord *Lindsay (afterwards twenty-sixth earl of Crawford), 1872–6; took part in observations of transit of Venus at Mauritius, 1874; chief result of expedition revelation of possibilities of heliometer for astronomical measurements; made successful expedition to island of Ascension in order to measure with heliometer distance of Mars from Earth and thus derive sun's distance, 1877; HM astronomer at Cape of Good Hope, 1879–1907; obtained larger heliometer with which he redetermined sun's distance and determined mass of Jupiter; pioneer in application of photography to astronomy, and carried out photographic survey of Southern heavens, 1885–98; organized geodetic survey of South Africa; KCB, 1900.

GILL, John (1697–1771), Baptist minister; Wednesday-evening lecturer in Great Eastcheap, 1729–56; DD, Aberdeen, 1748; published works, including *Exposition of the Holy Scriptures* (1746–8, 1766) and *Dissertation on the Antiquity of the Hebrew Language* (1767).

GILL, William John (1843–1882), captain of Royal Engineers; served in India, 1869–71; travelled with Valentine Baker in Persia, 1873, making a valuable survey; with E. Colborne Baker in Szechuan, China, and with Mesny in Eastern Tibet, making a large map and valuable observations, for which the Geographical Society's Gold Medal was awarded; assistant commissioner for delimiting Asiatic boundary of Russia and Turkey, 1879; travelled in country between Tunis and Egypt, 1881; with Professor *Palmer and Lieutenant Charrington murdered by Bedouin in the desert when on his way as intelligence officer to cut the telegraph wire from Cairo to Constantinople to prevent its use by Arabi Pasha.

GILLAN, Robert (1800–1879), Scottish divine; studied at Edinburgh High School and University; minister of St John's, Glasgow, 1847–61, and of Inchinnan, Renfrewshire, 1861–79; DD, Glasgow, 1853; moderator of the general assembly, 1873; lectured on pastoral theology at four Scottish universities.

GILLE (or GILLEBERT) (*fl.* 1105–1145), bishop of Limerick; termed by Keating Giolla Easbog; friend and correspondent of *Anselm, who induced him to attempt the introduction into Ireland of the Roman liturgy; presided over the Synod of Rathbreasail as papal legate, about 1111.

GILLESPIE, George (1613–1648), Scottish divine; *Milton's 'Galasp'; MA, St Andrews, 1629; issued anonymously *Dispute against the English Popish Ceremonies obtruded upon the Church of Scotland* (1637); presented to Wemyss, Fifeshire, 1638, and ordained non-episcopally; preached before Charles I at Holyrood, 1641; pensioned, 1641; translated to Greyfriars, Edinburgh, 1642; the youngest member of the Westminster Assembly, 1643, where he opposed *Selden's views on church government; introduced the directory to Edinburgh Assembly, 1645; presented confession of faith to general assembly, 1647; moderator, 1648; elected to the High Church of Edinburgh, 1648; his tombstone at Kirkcaldy broken by the hangman by order of the committee of estates, 1661; published theological works.

GILLESPIE, James (1726–1797), founder of hospital at Edinburgh; owned a snuff-mill at Colinton; with his younger brother carried on business in High Street, Edinburgh; left bequests for foundation of a hospital for old people and a school.

GILLESPIE, Patrick (1617–1675), principal of Glasgow University; brother of George *Gillespie; graduated at St Andrews, 1635; minister at Kirkcaldy, 1642, of the High Church, Glasgow, 1648; opposed the 'engagement' to rescue Charles I; after Dunbar, raised the 'Westland Force' and drew up its 'Remonstrance' condemning the treaty with Charles II, and making grave charges against the Scottish authorities, 1650; deposed from ministry for protesting against legality of the resolutions making terms with 'malignants', 1651; leader of the 'protesters', 1651; made principal of Glasgow University by *Cromwell, 1652; granted 'Gillespie's Charter', 1653, empowering 'protesters' to remodel the church in their own interest; again visited London; became an intimate of *Lambert and *Fleetwood; obtained revenues for his university from church property; deprived and (1661) imprisoned.

GILLESPIE, Sir Robert Rollo (1766–1814), major-general; as adjutant-general in San Domingo, 1796, was attacked by eight assassins and killed six; left Jamaica in command of his regiment, 1801; rescued the 69th at Vellore, 1806; commanded cavalry against Runjeet Singh, 1809; as brigadier headed advance of Auchmuty's Java expedition, directing attack on Cornelis, 1811; deposed sultan of Palembang, Sumatra, 1812; defended Javanese confederacy at Yodhyakarta; major-general, 1812; killed in attack on Kalunga, Nepaul; buried at Meerut; named KCB, 1815.

GILLESPIE, Thomas (1708–1774), founder of the Relief Church; studied at Edinburgh University; minister of Carnock, near Dunfermline, 1741; deposed by general assembly for refusing to ordain Andrew Richardson, 1752; for six-and-a-half years stood alone preaching on the highway and at Dunfermline; joined by Thomas *Boston the younger, and by the congregation of Colinsburgh; formed a Presbytery, 1761; published *Practical Treatise on Temptation* (1774).

GILLESPIE, Thomas (1777–1844), professor at St Andrews; distinguished at Edinburgh University; LL D, Glasgow, 1824; professor of humanity at St Andrews, 1836; contributed to *Blackwood, Constable's Miscellany*, and *Tales of the Borders*.

GILLESPIE, William (1776–1825), poet; minister of Kells, 1800; confined to Kirkcudbrightshire for praying for Queen *Caroline, 1820; published *The Progress of Refinement and other Poems* (1805) and *Consolation, and other Poems* (1815).

GILLIATT, Sir William (1884–1956), obstetrician; educated at Wellingborough College; qualified from Middlesex Hospital, 1908; MD, 1910; FRCS, 1912; appointed assistant obstetric and gynaecological surgeon, King's College Hospital, 1916; senior surgeon, 1925–46; on honorary staff, Samaritan Hospital, 1926–46; attended Princess *Marina, Duchess of Kent, for birth of her children and Princess Elizabeth for birth of Prince Charles (1948) and Princess Anne (1950); surgeon-gynaecologist to the queen, 1952–6; CVO, 1936; knighted, 1948; KCVO, 1949; FRCP, 1947; president, Royal Society of Medicine, 1954–6.

GILLIE, Dame Annis Calder (1900–1985), general practitioner and medical politician; educated at Wycombe Abbey School, University College, London, and University College Hospital; MB, BS, 1925; MRCP, 1927; entered general practice in London; played prominent part in renaissance of general practice after 1939–45 war; member of General Medical Council, 1946–8; president, Medical Women's Federation, 1954–5; member of number of statutory bodies concerned with general practice; member BMA council, 1950–64; founder member of College of General Practitioners; chairman, 1959–62; president, 1964–7; OBE, 1961;

DBE, 1968; FRCP, 1964; hon. MD, Edinburgh, 1968; fellow of BMA, 1960; first woman to be vice-president, 1968.

GILLIES, Adam, Lord Gillies (1760–1842), Scottish judge; sheriff-depute of Kincardineshire, 1806; judge, 1811; lord of justiciary, 1812–37; lord commissioner of the jury court, 1816; judge of Exchequer, 1837.

GILLIES, Duncan (1834–1903), premier of Victoria; emigrated from Glasgow to Ballarat goldfields, 1852; led miners in resistance to government, 1853–4; member of Ballarat Mining Boards, 1858; member of Legislative Assembly, 1859; president of Board of Land and Works, 1868; commissioner of railways and roads, 1872–5; minister of agriculture, 1875–7; commissioner of railways in Service government, 1880, and in Service–Berry coalition, 1883–6; premier and treasurer, 1886–90; extended revenue, expenditure, and railways; passed Irrigation Act, 1886; supported Australian federation; agent-general for Victoria in London, 1894–7; speaker of Victoria House of Assembly, 1902–3.

GILLIES, Sir Harold Delf (1882–1960), plastic surgeon; born in New Zealand; educated at Wanganui College and Gonville and Caius College, Cambridge; qualified from St Bartholomew's Hospital, 1908; FRCS, 1910; in charge of pioneer centres for plastic surgery in both wars; plastic surgeon to St Bartholomew's, LCC, and RAF; first president of British Association of Plastic Surgeons, 1946; published *Plastic Surgery of the Face* (1920) and *The Principles and Art of Plastic Surgery* (with D. R. Millard, 2 vols., 1975); knighted, 1930; played golf for England, and was a proficient painter in oils.

GILLIES, John (1712–1796), theological writer; minister of the College Church, Glasgow, from 1742; published *Historical Collections relating to the Success of the Gospel* (1754, supplemented, 1761 and 1780), and *Life of George Whitefield* (1772).

GILLIES, John (1747–1836), historian and classic; brother of Adam, Lord *Gillies; educated at Brechin and Glasgow University; LL D, 1784; FRS and FSA; historiographer royal of Scotland, 1793; published *History of Greece* (1786), *History of the World from Alexander to Augustus* (1807), *View of the Reign of Frederick II of Prussia* (1789), and translations from Aristotle, Lysias, and Isocrates.

GILLIES, Margaret (1803–1887), painter; educated by her uncle Adam, Lord *Gillies; painted miniatures of *Wordsworth and *Dickens, and exhibited portraits at Royal Academy; studied at Paris under Hendrik and Ary Scheffer;

associate of the Old Society of Painters in Watercolours, 1852–87.

GILLIES, Robert Pearse (1788–1858), autobiographer; a member of the *Ballantyne circle; the Kemperhausen of Christopher *North's *Noctes Ambrosianae*; friend of *Scott and *Wordsworth; contributed to *Blackwood* translations from German; in constant pecuniary distress; edited *Foreign Quarterly*, to which Scott, *Southey, and *Maginn contributed; published, besides *Memoirs of a Literary Veteran* (1851, 3 vols.), several volumes of poems, prose romance, and translations from the German.

GILLIES, Sir William George (1898–1973), painter and art teacher; educated at Knox Academy and Edinburgh College of Art; served with Scottish Rifles, 1917–19; returned to College of Art, 1919–23; worked with André Lhote in Paris, 1923–4; returned to Edinburgh and became active with 1922 Group; art master, Inverness Academy, 1925; part-time assistant, School of Drawing and Painting, Edinburgh, 1926; elected member of Society of Eight, 1932; moved to village of Temple, Midlothian, 1939; leading figure in contemporary Scottish painting; appointed head of Edinburgh School of Drawing and Painting, 1946–61; principal, College of Art, Edinburgh, 1961–6; large retrospective exhibition of portraits, still lifes, and landscapes mounted by Scottish Arts Council, 1970; ARSA, 1940; RSA, 1947; president, Royal Scottish Society of Painters in Watercolour, 1963; ARA, 1964; hon. D.Litt., Edinburgh, 1966; CBE, 1957; knighted, 1970; RA, 1971.

GILLILAND, Thomas (*fl.* 1804–1816), author; said to have haunted the green room of Drury Lane as 'a spy upon the private conduct of public men'; published *The Dramatic Mirror* (1808) and satirical pamphlets.

GILLING, Isaac (1662?–1725), Presbyterian minister; relative of John *Fox (1693–1763), his biographer; received Presbyterian ordination, 1687; ministered at Axminster, Silverton, and Newton Abbot; active member of Exeter Assembly for union of Presbyterians and Independents, 1691; excluded for siding against subscription; published *Qualifications and Duties of Ministers* (1708) and *Life of George Trosse* (1715).

GILLINGWATER, Edmund (1735?–1813), topographer; published *Essay on Parish Workhouses* (1786), *Historical Account of Lowestoft* (1790), and *Historical Account of St. Edmund's Bury* (1804).

GILLIS, James (1802–1864), Roman Catholic prelate; born at Montreal; ordained at Aquhorties, 1827; founded St Margaret's Convent, Edinburgh, the first Scottish post-Reformation religious house, 1835; bishop of Limyra *in partibus*, 1838; vicar-apostolic of eastern Scotland, 1852; pronounced panegyric on Joan of Arc at Orleans, 1857, and was presented with the heart of Henry II of England; published pamphlets.

GILLOTT, Joseph (1799–1873), steel-pen maker of Birmingham; for some time made pens at Birmingham with aid only of a woman, selling them at a shilling each to a stationer; finally employed 450 hands; his collection of pictures, rich in Turners and Ettys, sold for £170,000, and his violins for £4,000.

GILLOW, John (1753–1828), president of Ushaw College, 1811–28; professor at Douai; for twenty years in charge of the York mission.

GILLOW, Thomas (1769–1857), Roman Catholic divine; at the Revolution escaped from Douai to Crook Hall, Durham; chaplain at Callaly Castle, Northumberland; missioner at North Shields, 1821–57.

GILLRAY, James (1757–1815), caricaturist; apprenticed to a letter-engraver; studied at Royal Academy; said to have etched a caricature at 12; treated at first anonymously social subjects, turning to political themes after 1780; executed 1,500 pieces, mostly issued by Miss Humphrey at 29 St James's Street, Piccadilly, London, where he lived; imbecile after 1811. Among his caricatures were many ridiculing the habits of the royal family, such as *Wife or no Wife* (1788), *Ancient Music* (1787), *Anti-Saccharites* (1792), *Temperance Enjoying a Frugal Meal* (1792), *A Voluptuary under the Horrors of Digestion* (1792), and *Sin, Death, and the Devil* (1792). He depicted Pitt in *The Vulture of the Constitution* (1789), *God save the King* (1795), and *Disciples Catching the Mantle* (1808); *Fox in *Spouting* (1792), *Blue and Buff Charity* (1793), and *The Worn-out Patriot* (1800); *Sheridan and *Burke in *The Dagger Scene* (1792), and Fox, Sheridan, and leading radicals in *Doublures of Characters* for *Anti-Jacobin* (1798?). Other caricatures dealt with Napoleon, Nelson, and the Revolution. His serious work included a profile of *Arne after *Bartolozzi, two portraits of Pitt, and the miniature of himself in the National Portrait Gallery.

GILLY, William Stephen (1789–1855), divine; educated at Christ's Hospital, Caius College, and St Catharine Hall, Cambridge; MA, 1817; DD, 1833; vicar of North Fambridge, Essex, 1817; perpetual curate of St Margaret, Durham, 1827; vicar of Norham, 1831; canon of Durham, 1853; published works describing his visits to the Vaudois, *The Peasantry of the Border; an appeal* (1841), *Our Protestant Forefathers* (1835), and other writings.

GILMOUR, Sir John (d. 1671), Scottish judge; counsel for Montrose, 1641; lord president of the court of session, 1661; privy councillor and lord of the articles; defended *Argyll and helped to overthrow John *Middleton, 1663.

GILMOUR, Sir John, second baronet, of Lundin and Montrave (1876–1940), politician; Unionist MP, East Renfrewshire (1910–18), Pollok division of Glasgow, 1918–40; PC, 1922; secretary for Scotland, 1924–9; minister of agriculture, 1931–2; home secretary, 1932–5; minister of shipping, 1939–40; succeeded father, 1920; GCVO, 1935.

GILPIN, Bernard (1517–1583), the 'Apostle of the North'; fellow of The Queen's College, Oxford; MA, 1542; BD, 1549; one of the first elected to Wolsey's foundation; disputed on the Romanist side with John *Hooper and *Peter Martyr; denounced spoliation of church property in a sermon before Edward VI, 1552; rector of Easington and (1556) archdeacon of Durham; denounced for heresy, but defended by Bishop *Tunstall, and promoted to benefice of Houghton-le-Spring; on his way to answer a second charge of heresy when Queen Mary died; refused see of Carlisle, 1559, and provostship of The Queen's College, Oxford, 1560; made annual progresses through neglected parts of Northumberland and Yorkshire, preaching and relieving the inhabitants; founded grammar school at Houghton, and supported some of the scholars at his own cost; interceded for rebels of 1569.

GILPIN, George (1514?–1602), 'the Elder'; diplomat and translator; elder brother of Bernard *Gilpin; agent of English government in Zeeland, and secretary to Gresham; published *The Beehive of the Romish Church* (translation of St Aldegonde's *Apiarium Romanum*, 1571).

GILPIN, Randolph (d. 1661), divine; educated at Eton; MA, King's College, Cambridge, 1618; chaplain to the Rochelle expedition and rector of Barningham, Suffolk, 1628; DD *per lit. reg.*, 1661; rector of Worlingham, 1661; published *Liturgica Sacra* (1657).

GILPIN, Richard (1625–1700), Nonconformist divine and physician; MA, Edinburgh, 1646; as rector of Greystoke, 1653–61, organized his parish on the Congregational model, and formed voluntary association of Cumberland and Westmoreland churches; refused see of Carlisle, 1660; removed to Newcastle upon Tyne, 1662, where he preached in defiance of the statutes against Dissenters, and practised as a physician; MD, Leiden, 1676; published *Daemonologia sacra; a Treatise of Satan's Temptations* (1677).

GILPIN, Sawrey (1733–1807), animal painter; worked under Samuel *Scott (1710?–1772);

employed by the duke of Cumberland to draw from his stud; exhibited at Incorporated Society of Artists, 1762–83, becoming president, 1774; exhibited at Royal Academy from 1786; RA, 1797; excelled as a painter of horses.

GILPIN, William (1724–1804), author; descendant of Bernard *Gilpin, and brother of Sawrey *Gilpin; MA, The Queen's College, Oxford, 1748; kept school at Cheam, Surrey, *Sidmouth, *Redesdale, and the historian *Mitford being among his pupils; an advanced educationalist; vicar of Boldre, 1777; built a new poorhouse and endowed school at Boldre; published lives of Bernard Gilpin (1753), *Latimer (1755), *Wycliffe (1765), *Cranmer (1784), and other reformers, *Essay on Prints* (1768), *Lectures on the Church Catechism* (1779), *Exposition of the New Testament* (1790), and five works illustrated by aquatint drawings, describing his summer tours.

GILPIN, William Sawrey (1762–1843), water-colour painter and landscape gardener; son of Sawrey *Gilpin; first president of the Old Water-Colour Society, 1804–6; seceded, 1813; laid out gardens at Danesfield, Enniskillen Castle, and other seats; published *Practical Hints for Landscape Gardening* (1832).

GILSON, Julius Parnell (1868–1929), palaeographer and scholar; BA, Trinity College, Cambridge; assistant, department of manuscripts, British Museum, 1894; assistant keeper, 1909; keeper and Egerton librarian, 1911; largest work *A Catalogue of Western Manuscripts in the Old Royal and King's Collection* (with Sir G. F. *Warner, 1921).

GINKEL, Frederick Christian, second earl of Athlone (1668–1719), general; served under William III and Anne; lieutenant-general of Dutch cavalry; taken prisoner, 1710.

GINKEL, Godert de, first earl of Athlone (1644–1703), general; native of Amerongen; present at Senef, 1674; accompanied William of Orange to England, 1688; distinguished at the Boyne and first siege of Limerick, 1690; left in command in Ireland on departure of William III; captured Athlone, won the victory of Aughrim, and took Limerick, 1691; created baron of Aughrim and earl of Athlone and thanked by the speaker, 1692; fought at Steinkirk, 1692, and Landen, 1693; commanded Dutch horse at recapture of Namur, 1695, and assisted in surprise of Givet, 1696; second-in-command to *Marlborough, 1702; died at Utrecht.

GINNER, Isaac Charles (1878–1952), artist; born in Cannes of British parentage; inspired by Van Gogh, whose ideals and the continental movements in art he introduced to British painters after settling in London, 1910; exhibited

with Camden Town and London groups; founder-member, Cumberland Market Group and member of New English Art Club; sought complete transposition of nature, working *en plein air*; ARA, 1942; CBE, 1950.

GINSBERG, Morris (1889–1970), sociologist and moral philosopher; born in Lithuania; migrated to England, 1910; read philosophy at University College, London; BA, first class, 1913; MA, 1915; part-time assistant to L. T. *Hobhouse at London School of Economics, 1914; reader, 1924; professor of sociology, 1929; emeritus professor, 1954; collaborated with L. T. Hobhouse and G. C. Wheeler on *The Material Culture and Social Institutions of the Simpler Peoples* (1915); other publications include *Moral Progress* (1944), *The Idea of Progress: A Revaluation* (1953), *Reason and Unreason in Society* (1947), and *On Justice in Society* (1965); FBA, 1953; honorary degrees, London, Glasgow, and Nottingham; hon. fellow, LSE; president, Aristotelian Society, 1942–3; Huxley Medal, 1953; Herbert Spencer lecturer, 1958.

GINSBURG, Christian David (1831–1914), Old Testament scholar; born at Warsaw of Jewish parentage; educated at rabbinic school at Warsaw; became Christian, c.1847; came to England; naturalized, 1858; original member of Old Testament Revision Company, 1870; published first volume of his principal work, edition of *The Massorah* (1880).

GIPPS, Sir George (1791–1847), colonial governor; entered Royal Engineers, 1809; wounded in assault on Badajoz, 1812; superintended fortifications of Ostend, 1815; while in West Indies, 1824–9, sent home elaborate reports; private secretary to Lord *Auckland, 1834; joint commissioner in Canada, 1835–7; governor of New South Wales, 1838–46; opened up the country and protected the aborigines, but became unpopular, owing to his arbitrary policy and insistence on the right of the crown to territorial revenue.

GIPPS, Sir Richard (1659–1708), master of the revels at Gray's Inn, 1682; matriculated from Caius College, Cambridge, 1675; student, 1676; knighted by Charles II; made collections for history of Suffolk.

GIPPS, Thomas (d. 1709), rector of Bury, Lancashire, 1674–1709; educated at St Paul's School; fellow of Trinity College, Cambridge; MA, 1662; carried on a controversy with James *Owen of Oswestry regarding the Presbyterian interpretation of Acts 6: 3.

GIRALDUS DE BARRI (1146?–1220?), topographer called Cambrensis; native of Pembrokeshire and grandson of *Nesta, a Welsh princess; lectured on the Trivium at Paris; as archdeacon of Brecknock, 1172, procured excommunication of bishop of St Asaph for trespassing on rights of St David's; nominated to see of St David's, 1176, but rejected by Henry II as a Welshman of royal blood; commissary to the bishop of St David's, 1180; accompanied Prince John to Ireland, 1184, where he refused several sees; assisted Archbishop *Baldwin to preach the crusade in Wales, 1188; sent to keep the peace there on death of Henry II; refused sees of Bangor and Llandaff, 1190–1; led a student's life at Lincoln, 1192–8; elected to see of St David's, 1198; went to Rome, but failed to obtain metropolitan dignity; received support from the Welsh princes, but was outlawed and disowned by the chapter, 1202; fled abroad and again reached Rome; imprisoned at Châtillon; gave way to Henlaw, the newly elected bishop of St David's, and was reconciled to the king and archbishop, receiving a pension and the expenses of his suit; buried at St David's. His works (edited by J. S. *Brewer and J. F. *Dimock, 1861–77) include *Topographia Hibernica, Expugnatio Hibernica, Itinerarium Cambriae, Gemma Ecclesiastica, De Rebus a se gestis*, and lives of St *Hugh of Lincoln, St *David, and others.

GIRARDUS CORNUBIENSIS (*fl.* 1350?), author of *De gestis Britonum* and *De gestis Regum West-Saxonum*.

GIRAUD, Herbert John (1817–1888), physician; chemist and botanist; MD, Edinburgh, 1840; principal of Grant Medical College, Bombay; chief medical officer of Sir Jamsetjee Jeejeebhoy's Hospital, deputy inspector-general and (1863) dean of faculty of medicine, Bombay University; author of botanical and chemical papers.

GIRDLESTONE, Charles (1797–1881), biblical commentator; BA, Wadham College, Oxford, 1818; fellow of Balliol, 1818; MA, 1821; vicar of Sedgley, Staffordshire, 1826, working there during the cholera epidemic of 1832; incumbent of Alderley, 1837; rector of Kingswinford, 1846–77, where he faced a second cholera epidemic; published commentary on New Testament (1832–5) and Old Testament (1842).

GIRDLESTONE, Edward (1805–1884), canon of Bristol; brother of Charles *Girdlestone; scholar of Balliol College, Oxford, 1823; MA, 1829; vicar of Deane, 1830; canon of Bristol, 1854; vicar of Wapley, Gloucestershire, 1858, of Halberton, Devonshire, 1862, of Olveston, Gloucestershire, 1872; called 'the Agricultural Labourers' Friend'; published controversial works.

GIRDLESTONE, Gathorne Robert (1881–1950), orthopaedic surgeon; qualified at St Thomas's Hospital, 1908; worked with Sir Robert *Jones; with him formed Central Council for Care of Cripples, 1920; from 1915 in charge of Military Orthopaedic Centre, Oxford, which became (1922) Wingfield (rebuilt 1933 as Wingfield-Morris) Orthopaedic Hospital; professor of orthopaedic surgery, Oxford, 1937–9; also responsible for establishment of Churchill Hospital, Oxford.

GIRDLESTONE, John Lang (1763–1825), classical translator; fellow of Caius College, Cambridge; MA, 1789; master of Beccles School; translator of Pindar, 1810.

GIRDLESTONE, Thomas (1758–1822), translator of Anacreon; army surgeon at Minorca and in India; practised thirty-seven years at Great Yarmouth; translated Anacreon, 1803; published medical essays and a work to prove that Arthur Lee wrote 'Junius' (1813).

GIRLING, Mary Anne (1827–1886), founder of 'The People of God' sect; daughter of one Clouting, a Suffolk farmer; married George Stanton Girling; proclaimed herself to be a new incarnation of the Deity, 1864; held meetings in Battersea, 1870; her community transferred to New Forest Lodge, purchased for them by Miss Wood, 1872; ejected with her followers, 1873; obtained Tiptoe Farm, Hordle, Hampshire, 1879, whence she issued *The Close of the Dispensation* (1883), signed 'Jesus First and Last'.

GIROUARD, Désiré (1836–1911), Canadian judge; born in Quebec province; DCL, McGill University, 1874; called to bar of Lower Canada, 1860; QC, 1880; published treatise on bills of exchange, 1860; Conservative MP for Jacques Cartier constituency, 1878–95; opposed execution of Louis *Riel, 1885; judge of the Supreme Court of Canada, 1895–1911.

GIROUARD, Sir (Edouard) Percy (Cranwill) (1867–1932), railway engineer and colonial administrator; born at Montreal; son of Désiré *Girouard; commissioned in Royal Engineers, 1888; director of railways in Sudan (1896–8) and South Africa (1899–1902); KCMG, 1900; high commissioner (1907), governor (1908–9), Northern Nigeria; constructed first railway; governor, British East Africa Protectorate, 1909–12; director-general, munitions supply, 1915–17.

GIRTIN, Thomas (1775–1802), water-colour painter; imprisoned for refusing to serve out his indentures under Edward *Dayes; made a sketching tour with *Turner, 1793; first exhibited at Royal Academy, 1794; sent to the Royal Academy ten drawings, including views of York and St Cuthbert's, Holy Island, 1797; contributed fifteen topographical sketches to J. Walker's *Itinerant*; member of the first London sketching society; exhibited *Bolton Bridge*, an oil-painting, 1801; drew and etched for Lord Essex twenty sketches of Paris, 1802 and panorama of London from south side of Blackfriar's Bridge; founder of modern water-colour painting as distinct from 'tinting'; examples of his work preserved in the British Museum and at South Kensington.

GISA (or GISO, sometimes GILA) (d. 1088), bishop of Wells; native of diocese of Liège; chaplain of *Edward the Confessor; bishop of Wells, 1060; on return from Rome with *Tostig and Archbishop *Aldred, robbed by brigands; complained in his *Historiola* of *Harold's treatment; recovered manor of Winsham from William I; made his canons conform to Metz rule and live together in Lotharingian fashion.

GISBORNE, John (1770–1851), poet; educated at Harrow; BA, St John's College, Cambridge, 1792; called the 'Man of Prayer'; published *The Vales of Wever* (1797) and *Reflections*.

GISBORNE, Maria (1770–1836), friend of *Shelley; née James; brought up at Constantinople by her father; refused William *Godwin; married John *Gisborne, 1800; lived in Italy; Shelley's 'Letter to Maria Gisborne' written during her visit to England, 1820; introduced Shelley to the study of Calderon.

GISBORNE, Thomas (d. 1806), president of College of Physicians; fellow of St John's College, Cambridge; MA, 1751; MD, 1758; FRS, 1758; physician to St George's Hospital, 1757–81; Gulstonian lecturer, 1760; president, College of Physicians, 1791, 1794, 1796–1803; physician-in-ordinary to the king.

GISBORNE, Thomas, the elder (1758–1846), divine; brother of John *Gisborne; of Harrow and St John's College, Cambridge; BA, 1780; first chancellor's medallist, 1780; perpetual curate of Barton-under-Needwood, 1783; prebendary of Durham, 1823 and 1826; friend of William *Wilberforce; published *Principles of Moral Philosophy* (1789), *Walks in a Forest* (1794), and other works.

GISBORNE, Thomas, the younger (*c.*1790–1852), politician; son of Thomas *Gisborne the elder; BA, Trinity College, Cambridge, 1810; Whig MP for Stafford, 1830–1; north Derbyshire, 1832–7; Carlow, 1839–41, and Nottingham, 1843–52; published *Essays on Agriculture* (1854).

GISBURNE, Walter of (*fl.* 1300), chronicler. See HEMINGFORD.

GISSING, George Robert (1857–1903), novelist; left Owens College, Manchester, in disgrace for America, where he wandered penniless until 1877; studied literature and philosophy at Jena; returned to England, 1878; published *Workers in the Dawn* (1880); found an appreciative reader in Frederic *Harrison, to whose sons he became tutor, 1882; gained precarious livelihood by occasional journalism; published *The Unclassed* (1884), *Demos* (1886), and other novels illustrating degrading effects of poverty on character; visited Naples, Rome, and Athens; published *A Life's Morning* (1888), *The Nether World* (1889), *The Emancipated* (1890), *New Grub Street* (1891), *Born in Exile* (1892), and *The Odd Women* (1893); revisited Italy with H. G. *Wells, 1897, recording some experiences and impressions in *By the Ionian Sea* (1901); in Rome he found material for historical romance *Veranilda* (published posthumously, 1907); on return to England wrote *The Town Traveller* (1898) and *Our Friend the Charlatan* (1901); died of pneumonia at St Jean-de-Luz; other works include critical study of *Charles Dickens* (1898), *The Private Papers of Henry Ryecroft* (1903), and *The House of Cobwebs* (1906).

GLADSTANES, George (d. 1615), archbishop of St Andrews; MA, St Andrews, 1580; minister successively of St Cyrus, Arbirlot, and (1597) St Andrews; member of general assembly; one of the three clerical representatives in parliament, 1598; vice-chancellor of St Andrews, 1599; bishop of Caithness, 1600; privy councillor of Scotland, 1602; consecrated archbishop of St Andrews, 1611; attended Hampton Court Conference; obtained removal of Andrew *Melville, principal of St Andrews University, 1606; permanent moderator, 1607.

GLADSTANES, John (d. 1574), Scottish judge; 'Advocatus Pauperum', 1534; lord of session, 1546; LL D.

GLADSTONE, Herbert John, Viscount Gladstone (1854–1930), statesman; youngest son of W. E. Gladstone, prime minister; educated at Eton; BA, University College, Oxford, 1876; Liberal MP, Leeds, 1880–5, West Leeds, 1885–1910; a Liberal whip and junior lord of Treasury, 1881–5; financial secretary at War Office, 1886; under-secretary, Home Office, 1892–4; first commissioner of works, 1894–5; chief Liberal whip, 1899; preserved neutrality within party during South African War, 1899–1902; secretary of state for home affairs, 1905–10; carried through parliament twenty-two bills, which showed growing tendency towards bureaucracy; Court of Criminal Appeal established, 1907; deeply interested in problem of young offender; instituted Borstal system and children's courts; first governor-general and high commissioner of Union of South Africa, 1910–14; worked in full harmony with Louis *Botha; viscount, 1910; manifested pious pugnacity on behalf of father's reputation; published *After Thirty Years* (1928).

GLADSTONE, Sir **John,** first baronet (1764–1851), Liverpool merchant; partner in Corrie & Co.; despatched first vessel to Calcutta on the opening up of the trade with India; became sole proprietor of his firm and took six brothers into the business; acquired large East Indian trade; became also West Indian merchant, defending (1823) the slave trade against James *Cropper; issued (1830) *Statement of Facts connected with the present state of Slavery*; chief supporter of Canning at Liverpool, 1812; Canningite MP, Lancaster, 1818, Woodstock, 1820, and Berwick, 1826–7; wrote against repeal of the corn laws, but was ultimately convinced by Peel; created baronet, 1846; benefactor of religious and charitable institutions at Leith and Liverpool.

GLADSTONE, John Hall (1827–1902), chemist; studied chemistry in London and Giessen; FRS, 1853; Fullerian professor of chemistry at Royal Institution, 1874–7; president of Physical (1874) and Chemical (1877–9) societies; hon. D.Sc., Trinity College, Dublin, 1892; made pioneer researches into chemistry in relation to optics; early student of spectroscopy; discovered copper–zinc union for decomposition of water; member of London school board, 1873–94; advocate of technical education, manual instruction, and spelling reform; works include *Theology and Natural Science* (1867), *Michael Faraday* (1872), *Miracles* (1880), and hymns.

GLADSTONE, William Ewart (1809–1898), statesman and author; son of (Sir) John *Gladstone; educated at Eton and Christ Church, Oxford; president of the Oxford Union Society, 1830; double first in classics and mathematics, 1831; Conservative MP for Newark, 1832, 1835, and 1837, and again 1841–5; entered Lincoln's Inn, 1833; made first important speech, 1833, favouring 'gradual' emancipation of slaves; successfully opposed appropriation clause in Irish Church Temporalities Bill, 1833; junior lord of Treasury in Sir Robert Peel's first administration, 1834; under-secretary for war and colonies in the same government, 1835; published *The State in its Relations with the Church* (1838) and *Church Principles considered in their Results* (1840); took part in founding Trinity College, Glenalmond, 1840; opposed first Opium War with China, 1840; vice-president of Board of Trade and master of Mint in Sir Robert Peel's second administration, 1841; privy councillor, 1841; took charge of Customs Bill, 1842; became pres-

ident of Board of Trade and entered Sir Robert Peel's Cabinet, 1843; introduced and carried first General Railway Bill providing 'parliamentary' trains, 1844; resigned office owing to his disapproval of proposed increase of Maynooth College grant, 1845; published *Remarks on Recent Commercial Legislation* (1845); accepted Peel's policy of repealing the corn laws; became secretary of state for colonies in succession to Lord *Stanley, who seceded from ministry as a protectionist, 1845–6; vacated seat for Newark on taking office, and did not seek re-election; remained out of parliament through 1846; 'Peelite' MP for Oxford University, 1847–65; opposed Palmerston's Greek policy, 1850; visited Naples and published letters condemning the atrocities perpetrated by Ferdinand, king of the Two Sicilies, 1851; opposed Ecclesiastical Titles Bill, 1851; chancellor of Exchequer in Aberdeen's coalition ministry, 1852–5; introduced and passed his first budget, suggesting progressive reduction of income tax and extension of legacy duty, under name of succession duty, to real property, 1853; brought in second budget, 1854; resigned office on Palmerston becoming prime minister, 1855; supported *Cobden in condemning bombardment of Canton, 1856; vigorously opposed bill for establishing divorce court, 1857; published *Studies on Homer and the Homeric Age* (1858); entrusted by Sir Edward Bulwer *Lytton, secretary for colonies, with special mission to Ionian islands, and failed to quell agitation for their incorporation with Greek kingdom instead of remaining under British protectorate, 1858–9; spoke in favour of Disraeli's first Reform Bill, 1859; chancellor of Exchequer under Lord Palmerston, 1859–66; introduced budget, and was successful in upholding commercial treaty with France (1859), reducing taxes on articles of food, and granting excise licenses to keepers of eating-houses, but failed to induce House of Lords to repeal paper duty, 1860; lord rector of Edinburgh University, 1860; introduced and passed Post Office Savings Bank Bill, 1861; succeeded in repealing paper duty by including all taxation proposals in one Money Bill which had to be accepted or rejected in its entirety by House of Lords, 1861; published, with Lord *Lyttelton, joint volume of *Translations* (1863); supported Reform Bill moved by (Sir) Edward *Baines, 1864; opposed bill for removing theological tests for university degrees, 1865; MP, South Lancashire, 1865–8; chancellor of Exchequer and leader of House of Commons on Palmerston's death, 1865; introduced government's Reform Bill, which failed to pass in committee, and occasioned resignation of government, 1866; introduced budget, pointing out importance of paying off national debt, 1866; proposed successful amendments to Disraeli's Reform Bill, 1866; leader of Liberal party in succession to Lord Russell, 1867; supported bill to abolish compulsory church rates, 1868; successfully moved resolutions embodying principle of Irish Church disestablishment, 1868; MP for Greenwich, 1868–74 and 1874–80; prime minister for the first time, 1868, the ministry including Robert *Lowe (afterwards Viscount Sherbrooke) as chancellor of Exchequer, John *Bright as president of Board of Trade, Sir William Page *Wood (afterwards Baron Hatherley) as chancellor, and Edward (afterwards Baron) *Cardwell as secretary for war; introduced and passed Irish Church Disestablishment Bill, 1869; published *Juventus Mundi* (1869); passed first Irish Land Bill, 1870; procured by royal warrant abolition of purchase in the army, 1871; passed University Test Bill, 1871; appointed commission to discuss claims of American government for damages caused by cruisers fitted out at British ports during Civil War, 1871; passed Ballot Bill, 1872; introduced Irish University Bill proposing foundation of an undenominational university in Ireland, 1873, and resigned on its rejection at second reading; resumed office on Disraeli's refusal to form ministry, 1873, and, while retaining first lordship of Treasury, took chancellorship of the Exchequer without resigning seat as member for Greenwich; resigned office on defeat of his party at the general election, 1874, and was succeeded by Disraeli (afterwards Lord Beaconsfield); resigned leadership of Liberal party, 1875; vehemently denounced Turkish outrages in Bulgaria and advocated alliance of England and Russia to secure independence of the sultan's Christian provinces, 1875; published *Homeric Synchronism* (1876); advocated, unsuccessfully, coercion of the Porte by united Europe, 1877–8; lord rector of Glasgow, 1877; spoke vehemently against Afghan policy of the government, 1878; conducted political campaign in Midlothian, condemning the aggressive imperialism of the prime minister, but dissociating himself from the doctrines of the Manchester school and of peace at any price, 1879–80; MP for Midlothian, 1880–95; prime minister for the second time after Beaconsfield's defeat at the general election, 1880; also held office of chancellor of the Exchequer, 1880–2; supported Irish Compensation for Disturbance Bill, 1880; succeeded in passing Irish Coercion Bill, 1881; announced, after defeat of British Army at Majuba Hill, conditions of peace with Transvaal, which provided for the maintenance of British suzerainty, self-government for burghers, and British control of foreign relations, 1881; introduced and passed second Irish Land Bill, proposing to institute a land court for fixing judicial

rents, 1881; introduced and passed Irish Arrears Bill, proposing to wipe out arrears of rent in Ireland altogether where tenants were unable to pay them, 1882; adopted policy that it was duty of British government to relieve Egyptian people from military tyranny of Arabi Pasha, 1882; supported military campaign in Egypt; gave up chancellorship of Exchequer to Hugh C. E. *Childers, 1882; successfully combated two votes of censure in House of Commons on Egyptian policy, 1883; introduced bill for extension of franchise to agricultural labourers and others, which passed Commons, but was only accepted by Lords after much hesitation, on condition that Gladstone passed simultaneously a bill for redistribution of seats, 1884; adversely criticized for his failure to rescue *Gordon, and for his policy of abandonment of Sudan to the Mahdi, 1884; resigned office on passing of amendment opposing points in Budget Bill, 1885; declined offer of earldom, 1885; was succeeded as prime minister by Lord Salisbury who, however, failed to obtain a majority for his party at general election at the end of 1885; on defeat of Conservatives in House of Commons early in 1886, and the resignation of Lord Salisbury, Gladstone formed ministry for the third time, which included Lord Rosebery in foreign office, Lord *Granville as colonial secretary, John Morley as chief secretary for Ireland, and *Chamberlain (who resigned on introduction of Home Rule Bill) as president of Local Government Board; brought in Home Rule Bill, 8 Apr. 1886, proposing to create legislative body to sit at Dublin for dealing with affairs exclusively Irish, but reserving to British government certain powers affecting the crown, army, navy, and foreign or colonial relations; introduced Irish Land Purchase Bill, which passed only first reading, 16 Apr. 1886; appealed to country on rejection of Home Rule Bill on second reading, 7 June 1886; resigned office with rest of Cabinet after general election declared against home rule, 20 July 1886; continued to advocate his Irish policy in session, 1887–92; member of select committee appointed by House of Commons to consider Queen Victoria's message asking for additional grants for maintenance of royal family, 1889; advocated Newcastle programme of radical reforms, 1891; on the defeat of Lord Salisbury's government at general election of 1892, became prime minister for the fourth and last time; also held office of lord privy seal, 1892, his ministry including Lord Rosebery, Asquith as home secretary, and Sir Edward *Grey, under-secretary for foreign affairs; introduced, 13 Feb. 1893, second Home Rule Bill, which, after passing the Commons, was rejected by 419 to 41 in House of Lords, 8 Sept. 1893; made, in support of Parish Councils Bill, his last speech in House of Commons, 1 Mar. 1894; resigned office of prime minister, 3 Mar. 1894; founded St Deiniol's Library for theological students at Hawarden, 1895; urged right and necessity of British intervention in Armenia, 1895–6; published editions of Butler's *Analogy, Sermons*, and *Studies Subsidiary to Works of Bishop Butler* (1896); delivered his last speech at opening of Victoria Jubilee Bridge over Dee, 2 June 1897; died at Hawarden, 19 May 1898; buried in Westminster Abbey.

Gladstone's contributions to magazines were collected, under title *Gleanings from Past Years* (1879–90, 8 vols.). His portrait by *Millais, 1879, is in the National Portrait Gallery. As an orator Gladstone's only contemporary rival was John Bright. As a financier he can only be compared with Walpole, Pitt, and Peel.

GLADWIN, Francis (d. 1813?), orientalist; of the Bengal Army; commissary resident at Patna, 1808; under patronage of Warren *Hastings, issued translation of *Institutes of the Emperor Akbar* (1783–6) and a Persian–Hindustani–English dictionary (1809).

GLAISHER, James (1809–1903), astronomer and meteorologist; assistant at Cambridge University Observatory, 1833–5, and at Greenwich, 1835–8; chief of magnetic and meteorological department there, 1838–74; improved instruments; published *Hydrometrical Tables* (1847); organized voluntary system of precise meteorological observation throughout England, 1847; prepared meteorological reports for registrar-general, 1847–1902; helped to establish daily weather report for *Daily News*, 1849; FRS, 1849; secretary of Royal Meteorological Society, 1850–72; defined relations between weather and cholera epidemics and water supply; made balloon ascents for meteorological observations with Henry *Coxwell, 1862–6; published observations in *British Association Reports*, 1862–6, and account of his ascents in *Voyages Aériens* (1869, translated into English as *Travels in the Air*, 1871); was also interested in astronomy and mathematical science; completed and published *Factor Tables* (3 vols., 1879–83); on committee of Palestine Exploration Fund; translated Flammarion's *Atmosphere* and Guillemin's *World of Comets* (1876).

GLAISHER, James Whitbread Lee (1848–1928), mathematician, astronomer, and collector; son of James *Glaisher; BA, Trinity College, Cambridge (second wrangler), 1871; fellow, 1871–1928; lecturer, 1871–1901; member of council of Royal Astronomical Society, 1874–1928; president, 1886–8, 1901–3; FRS, 1875; maintained lifelong connection with London Mathematical Society; member of council, 1872–1906; president, 1884–6; worked hard on behalf of British Association; published nearly four hundred papers on pure mathematics and astronomy; in middle life took up study of pottery, on which he became recognized authority; bequeathed his collection to Fitzwilliam Museum, Cambridge.

GLAMMIS, Barons. See LYON, JOHN, seventh baron, 1510?–1558; LYON, JOHN, eighth baron, d. 1578.

GLAMMIS, Lady (d. 1537). See DOUGLAS, JANET.

GLAMMIS, master of (d. 1608). See LYON, Sir THOMAS.

GLAMORGAN, titular earl of (1601–1667). See SOMERSET, EDWARD, second marquis of Worcester.

GLANVILL, John (1664?–1735), poet and translator; grandson of Sir John *Glanville the younger; MA, Trinity College, Oxford, 1685; barrister, Lincoln's Inn; translated, among other works, Fontenelle's *Plurality of Worlds* (1688).

GLANVILL, Joseph (1636–1680), divine; BA, Exeter College, Oxford, 1655; MA, Lincoln College, 1658; rector of the Abbey Church, Bath, 1666–80, and other benefices; an admirer of Baxter, whom he excepted from his attacks on Nonconformists in *The Zealous and Impartial Protestant* (1681); an original FRS, 1664; attacked the scholastic philosophy in *The Vanity of Dogmatizing* (1661), a work containing the story of the 'Scholar Gipsy'; defended the pre-existence of souls in *Lux Orientalis* (1662), and the belief in witchcraft in *Philosophical considerations touching Witches and Witchcraft* (1666), generally known as *Sadducismus Triumphatus*.

GLANVILLE, Bartholomew de (*fl.* 1230–1250), minorite friar; properly known as Bartholomew Anglicus, the addition de Glanville being most uncertain; professor of theology at Paris; went to Saxony, 1231, in the interests of his order; author of *De Proprietatibus Rerum*, the encyclopaedia of the middle ages, first printed (*c.*1470) at Basle; an English version by John of *Trevisa was issued by Wynkyn de *Worde (*c.*1495).

GLANVILLE, Gilbert de (d. 1214), bishop of Rochester, 1185; one of Becket's scholars; archdeacon of Lisieux, 1184; bishop of Rochester, 1185; one of the embassy to Philip Augustus of France, 1186; preached the crusade at Geddington, 1188; supported *Longchamp against Prince John; summoned by Richard I to Germany, 1193; excommunicated Prince John on returning, 1194; fled from King John, 1207; absolved Scots from homage to him, 1212.

GLANVILLE, Sir John, the elder (1542–1600), judge; the first attorney who reached the bench; barrister, Lincoln's Inn, 1574; serjeant-at-law, 1589; MP, Launceston, 1585, Tavistock, 1586, and St Germans, 1592; judge of common pleas, 1598.

GLANVILLE, Sir John, the younger (1586–1661), serjeant; son of Sir John *Glanville the elder; barrister, Lincoln's Inn, c.1610; MP, Plymouth, 1614, 1620, 1623, 1625, 1626, and 1628; opposed the crown; prepared protest against dissolution, 1625; secretary to the Council of War at Cadiz, 1625; took leading part in *Buckingham's impeachment, 1626–8; eminent as counsel; recorder of Plymouth, 1614; of Bristol, 1638; serjeant, 1637; MP, Bristol; speaker of the Short Parliament, 1640; knighted, 1641; DCL, Oxford, 1643; tried *Northumberland and other peers; disabled and imprisoned by parliament, 1645–8; MP for Oxford University under Commonwealth.

GLANVILLE, Ranulf de (d. 1190), chief justiciar of England; sheriff of Yorkshire, 1163–70, and 1174–89; as sheriff of Lancashire, defeated Scots at Alnwick, and captured *William the Lion, 1174; ambassador to Flanders, 1177; justice-in-eyre and a member of the permanent royal court, 1179; as justiciar of England, 1180–9, was Henry II's 'eye', fighting and negotiating with the Welsh and French, and helping the king against his sons; went with Richard I on crusade, 1190, and died at Acre. The authorship of *Treatise on the Laws and Customs of England* has been doubtfully ascribed to him on the evidence of *Roger of Hoveden.

GLANVILLE, Sir William Henry (1900–1976), civil engineer; educated at Kilburn Grammar School, and East London (Queen Mary) College, University of London; first class, civil engineering, 1922; Ph.D., 1925; D.Sc., 1930; engineering assistant, Building Research Station, Department of Scientific and Industrial Research, 1922; deputy director, Road Research Laboratory, 1936, director, 1939–65; published research results in 'Studies in Reinforced Concrete' (1930); turned over laboratory to war work, 1939; carried out research on bomb blast and road-making materials suitable for airfields; set up traffic and safety division of laboratory, 1947, and tropical section, 1955; under his direction laboratory acquired international reputation in road research; president, Institution of Civil Engineers, 1950–1; received Ewing Gold Medal and other awards; almoner and governor, Christ's Hospital; fellow and governor, Queen Mary College, London University; FRS, 1958; CBE, 1944; CB, 1953; knighted, 1960.

GLAPTHORNE, Henry (1610–1643?), dramatist; matriculated at Corpus Christi College, Cambridge, 1624; published *Argalus and Parthenia* (1639) and *Albertus Wallenstein* (1639), tragedies, *The Hollander* (1640), *Wit in a Constable* (1640), and *The Ladies Priviledge* (1640), comedies, and *Poems* (1639); dedicated 'Whitehall' to *Lovelace, 1642; his works collected, 1874.

GLAS, George (1725–1765), mariner; son of John *Glas; discovered between Cape Verde and Senegal a river, which he thought suitable for a settlement; obtained promise of a government grant in exchange for a free cession to the British crown; founded the settlement, naming it Port Hillsborough, 1764; imprisoned by Spaniards at Teneriffe for contraband trading; murdered on his way home; translated from the Spanish *Account of the Discovery and History of the Canaries* (1764).

GLAS, John (1695–1773), founder of the Glasites; MA, St Andrews, 1713; minister of Tealing, Forfarshire, 1719–28, when he was deposed by the general assembly for his *Testimony of the King of Martyrs* (1727); formed, at Dundee, a sect of Independent Presbyterians; removed to Perth, 1773, where he was joined by Robert *Sandeman, afterwards his son-in-law; published an edition (with translation) of the *True Discourse* of Celsus (1753) and many other works.

GLASCOCK, William Nugent (1787?–1847), captain in the navy; present at the action off Finisterre, 1805, and reduction of Flushing, 1809; promoted to post-rank and specially thanked for his services in the *Douro*, 1832–3; chief work *Naval Service, or Officers' Manual* (1836).

GLASS, David Victor (1911–1978), sociologist and demographer; educated at Raine's Grammar School and the London School of Economics, 1928–31; research assistant to Sir William (later Lord) *Beveridge, director of LSE; first research secretary of the (Sir) A. M. *Carr-Saunders Committee on Population Investigation, 1936; engaged on demographic research and published *Population, Policies and Movements in Europe* (1940); during 1939–45 war, assistant director of British Petroleum Mission in Washington and worked in Ministry of Supply; reader in demography, LSE, 1945; professor of sociology, 1948; Martin White professor, 1961; actively associated with Royal Commission on Population, 1944–9; also with the National Survey of Health and Development of Children; UK delegate to Population Commission of the United Nations; published *Social Mobility in Britain* (1954); FBA, 1964; FRS, 1971; many honorary degrees; president, International Union for the Scientific Study of Population.

GLASS, Joseph (1791?–1867), philanthropist; received silver medal and £200 for his invention a chimney-sweeping machine.

GLASS, Sir Richard Atwood (1820–1873), manufacturer of telegraph cables; educated at King's College, London; adapted Elliot's wire-rope covering to submarine cables, 1852; superintended making of Atlantic cables of 1865–6; knighted, 1866; chairman of Anglo-American Telegraph Company; MP, Bewdley, 1868–9.

GLASS, Thomas (d. 1786), physician; MD, Leiden, 1731; practised at Exeter; imparted to his brother Samuel (of Oxford) the process for preparing magnesia alba, afterwards perfected and applied by him; authority on inoculation for smallpox; published medical works.

GLASSE, George Henry (1761–1809), classic and divine; son of Samuel *Glasse; MA, Christ Church, Oxford, 1782; rector of Hanwell, 1785; chaplain successively of the earl of *Radnor, duke of *Cambridge, and earl of Sefton; rendered *Samson Agonistes* into Greek, 1788; translated *L'Inconnue, Histoire Véritable* as *Louisa*, dealing with the lady of the Haystack problem, 1801; spent a fortune; committed suicide.

GLASSE, Hannah (1708–1770), author of *The Art of Cookery made Plain and Easy* (1747), *The Compleat Confectioner* (1770) and *The Servant's Directory, or Housekeeper's Companion* (1770); habit-maker to the prince of Wales, 1757.

GLASSE, Samuel (1735–1812), theologian; educated at Westminster; MA, Christ Church, Oxford, 1759; DD, 1769; FRS, 1764; chaplain-in-ordinary to the king, 1772; rector of Hanwell; vicar of Epsom, 1782; Wanstead, 1786; prebendary of St Paul's, 1798; friend of Bishop Horne; author of a work advocating Sunday schools, 1786.

GLASSFORD, James (d. 1845), legal writer and translator; son of John *Glassford; sheriff-depute of Dumbartonshire; a commissioner to inquire into Irish education, 1824–6; published *Remarks on the Constitution and Procedure of the Scottish Courts* (1812), *Essay on Principles of Evidence* (1812), translations from *Bacon and the Italian poets.

GLASSFORD, John (1715–1783), tobacco merchant and shipowner; bailie of Glasgow, 1751; purchased Dougalston, Dumbartonshire.

GLASTONBURY, John of (*fl.* 1400), historian. See JOHN.

GLAZEBROOK, James (1744–1803), divine; a Madeley collier, who came under the influence of John *Fletcher of Madeley; incumbent of St James's, Latchford; vicar of Bolton, Lancashire, 1796–1803; published *Defence of Infant Baptism* (1781).

GLAZEBROOK, Michael George (1853–1926), schoolmaster; BA, Balliol College, Oxford, 1877; high master of Manchester Grammar School, 1888; ordained, 1890; headmaster of Clifton College, where he encouraged music, 1891–1905; canon of Ely, 1905; leader of 'Modern Churchmen' movement; works include *Lessons from the Old Testament* (1890), *The End of the Law* (1911), and *Faith of a Modern Churchman* (1918).

GLAZEBROOK, Sir Richard Tetley (1854–1935), physicist; fifth wrangler (1876), fellow (1877), senior bursar (1895), Trinity College, Cambridge; assistant director, Cavendish Laboratory, 1891; principal, University College, Liverpool, 1898–9; first director, National Physical Laboratory, 1899–1919; gave priority to construction of units and standards and after 1909 carried out important research in aeronautics, notably on conditions of stability; Zaharoff professor of aviation, Imperial College of Science, 1920–3; fellow (1882), foreign secretary (1926–9), Royal Society; knighted, 1917; KCB, 1920; KCVO, 1934.

GLAZEBROOK, Thomas Kirkland (1780–1855), author; son of James *Glazebrook; translated Virgil's first eclogue, 1807, and published poetical works.

GLEICHEN, Count (1833–1891). See VICTOR.

GLEICHEN, Lady Feodora Georgina Maud (1861–1922), sculptor; daughter of Prince *Victor of Hohenlohe-Langenburg; pupil of Alphonse *Legros; exhibited regularly at Royal Academy; works include public memorials and portrait busts; first woman member (posthumous) of Royal Society of British Sculptors.

GLEIG, George (1753–1840), bishop of Brechin; educated at King's College, Aberdeen; thrice elected bishop of Dunkeld, 1786, 1792, and 1808, but his election made ineffectual by hostility of Bishop *Skinner; LL D, Aberdeen; bishop of Brechin, 1808–40; as primus, 1816–37, endeavoured to secure *regium donum*; contributed important articles to the *Encyclopaedia Britannica* (3rd edition) and edited the last six volumes, and (1801) wrote most of the 'Supplement'; published life of Principal William Robertson, 1812, and edited Thomas *Stackhouse's *History of the Bible* (1817).

GLEIG, George Robert (1796–1888), chaplain-general of the forces; son of George *Gleig; at Glasgow and Balliol College, Oxford; served with the 85th in the Peninsula, 1813–14; wounded at Nivelle and the Nive, and in the American War of 1814; BA, Magdalen Hall, Oxford, 1818; took orders, 1820; MA, 1821; perpetual curate of Ash, and rector of Ivy Church, 1822; chaplain of Chelsea Hospital, 1834; chaplain-general of the forces, 1844–75; contributed to the *Quarterly, Edinburgh, Blackwood*, and *Fraser* magazines; wrote 'The Subaltern' for *Blackwood*, 1826; published *The Story of Waterloo* (1847), *Lives of Military Commanders* (1831), biographies of Warren *Hastings (1841), *Clive (1848), and Wellington (1862), and *Chelsea Pensioners* (1829), with other works.

GLEMHAM, Edward (*fl.* 1590–1594), voyager; of Benhall, Suffolk; in his ship the *Edward and Constance* destroyed two Spanish vessels, repulsed four galleys, and captured a rich Venetian merchant ship, 1590; made second voyage; his adventures described in black-letter pamphlets (reprinted, 1829 and 1866).

GLEMHAM, Sir Thomas (d. 1649?), Royalist; knighted, 1617; MP, Aldeburgh, in the first two parliaments of Charles I; served on the continent and in first Scottish War; commandant of York, 1642 and 1644; capitulated, 1644; tried to hold Carlisle against the Scots, 1645, and to defend Oxford; took part in the second Civil War till Musgrave's seizure of Carlisle, 1648.

GLEN, Andrew (1665–1732), botanist; MA, Jesus College, Cambridge, 1687; rector of Hathern, Leicestershire; formed an herbarium, 1685, including two hundred foreign plants, to which he made additions at Turin, 1692.

GLEN, William (1789–1826), Scottish poet; published *Poems, chiefly Lyrical* (1815), including 'Wae's me for Prince Charlie' and other love and war songs.

GLENAVY, Barons. See CAMPBELL, JAMES HENRY MUSSEN, first baron, 1851–1931; CAMPBELL, PATRICK GORDON, third baron, 1913–1980.

GLENBERVIE, Baron (1743–1823). See DOUGLAS, SYLVESTER.

GLENCAIRN, earls of. See CUNNINGHAM, ALEXANDER, first earl, d. 1488; CUNNINGHAM, WILLIAM, fourth earl, d. 1547; CUNNINGHAM, ALEXANDER, fifth earl, d. 1574; CUNNINGHAM, WILLIAM, ninth earl, 1610?–1664.

GLENCORSE, Lord (1810–1891). See INGLIS, JOHN.

GLENDOWER, Owen (1359?–1416?), (Owain ab Gruffydd), Welsh rebel; lord of Glyndwr and Sycharth; claimed descent from Bleddyn ab Cynvyn and from *Llywelyn; studied law at Westminster; served with Richard II against the Scots, 1385; witness in suit of *Scrope* v. *Grosvenor*, 1386; as squire to earl of *Arundel served Henry of Lancaster, but headed Welsh rebellion against him on his accession as Henry IV; assumed title of 'prince of Wales'; his estates granted by Henry IV to John *Beaufort, earl of Somerset; invaded South Wales, and harassed the royal army in the north; repulsed before Caernarfon, 1401; negotiated with *Northumberland for peace, but at the same time appealed for help to Scotland and the Irish lords; captured Reginald de *Grey and Sir Edmund *Mortimer at Pilleth, 1402; baffled the English army and released Mortimer after marrying him to his daughter, Nov. 1402; his chief residences burnt by Prince Henry, 1403; took Carmarthen, Usk, Caerleon, and Newport, failed to join the Percies at Shrewsbury, 1403; ravaged English border; aided by French and Bretons captured Harlech and Cardiff, 1404; concluded an alliance with France, 1405; recognized Benedict XIII as pope, 1405; summoned a Welsh parliament, 1405; probably formed his alliance with Mortimer and Northumberland, *c.*1405; his sons captured by Prince Henry; retook Carmarthen with help of a French force, 1406; again defeated, 1406; deserted by Northumberland; lost Aberystwith, 1407, and South Wales, 1408; his wife and relations captured, 1413; admitted to the king's grace and obedience, 1415; his end unknown.

GLENELG, Baron (1778–1866). See GRANT, CHARLES.

GLENESK, Baron (1830–1908), proprietor of the *Morning Post*. See BORTHWICK, ALGERNON.

GLENHAM, Edward (*fl.* 1590–1594), Royalist. See GLEMHAM.

GLENIE, James (1750–1817), mathematician; MA St Andrews; served in the artillery and engineers during the American War; elected FRS, 1779, for papers written while on service; lieutenant, 1787; retired, 1787; emigrated to New Brunswick, and became member of House of Assembly; on return to England appointed engineer-extraordinary and (1806) instructor to East India Company's artillery officers; dismissed in consequence of evidence in Wardle case, 1809; died in poverty; published, among other works, *History of Gunnery* (1776), *Doctrine of Universal Comparison* (1789), *The Antecedental Calculus* (1793), and *Observations on Defence of Great Britain* (1807).

GLENLEE, Barons. See MILLER, Sir THOMAS, 1717–1789; MILLER, Sir WILLIAM, 1755–1846.

GLENNY, Alexander Thomas (1882–1965), immunologist; educated at Alleyn's School and Chelsea Polytechnic; B.Sc., London; joined Wellcome Physiological Research Laboratories,

1899; head of Immunology Department, 1906; responsible for production of antitoxins; made important contributions to schedules of immunization of man and animals, including immunization against diphtheria and tetanus; FRS, 1944; retired from Wellcome Laboratories, 1947.

GLENNY, George (1793–1874), horticultural writer; edited the *Royal Lady's Magazine*; started the *Horticultural Journal*, 1832, in which his 'Properties of Flowers' first appeared; edited many other horticultural papers, including *Glenny's Almanac*; a successful grower of auriculas, dahlias, and tulips; originated Metropolitan Society of Florists, 1832.

GLENORCHY, Viscountess (1741–1786). See CAMPBELL, WILLIELMA.

GLENVIL HALL, William George (1887–1962), politician. See HALL.

GLISSON, Francis (1597–1677), physician; MA, Caius College, Cambridge, 1624; incorporated at Oxford, 1627; MD, Cambridge, 1634; regius professor of physic, Cambridge, 1636–77; Gulstonian lecturer, 1640; sent out of Colchester to ask for better terms during the siege, 1648; an original FRS; president, College of Physicians, 1667–9; published (1650) *Tractatus de Rachitide* (the Rickets), almost the first English medical monograph; published also *Anatomia Hepatis* (1654), from which the name 'Glisson's capsule' was applied to the sheath of the liver.

GLOAG, Paton James (1823–1906), theological writer; student of Edinburgh and St Andrews universities; thrice visited Germany (1857–67) and studied German theological literature; Church of Scotland minister of Galashiels, 1871–92; Baird lecturer, 1879; moderator of General Assembly, 1889; professor of biblical criticism in Aberdeen University, 1896–9; hon. DD, St Andrews, 1867, and LL D, Aberdeen, 1899; wrote much on New Testament exegesis.

GLOAG, William Ellis, Lord Kincairney (1828–1909), Scottish judge; called to Scottish bar, 1853; advocate depute, 1874; sheriff of Perthshire, 1885; raised to bench as Lord Kincairney, 1889.

GLOUCESTER, duchess of (d. 1446?). See COBHAM, ELEANOR.

GLOUCESTER, dukes of. See THOMAS OF WOODSTOCK, 1355–1397; HUMPHREY, 1391–1447; RICHARD III, 1452–1485; HENRY, 1640–1660; WILLIAM, 1689–1700; WILLIAM HENRY, 1743–1805; WILLIAM FREDERICK, 1776–1834; HENRY WILLIAM FREDERICK ALBERT, 1900–1974.

GLOUCESTER, earls of. See ROBERT, d. 1147; CLARE, GILBERT DE, sixth earl, d. 1230; CLARE, RICHARD DE, seventh earl, 1222–1262; CLARE, GILBERT DE, eighth earl, 1243–1295; CLARE, GILBERT DE, ninth earl, 1291–1314; MONTHERMER, RALPH DE, d. 1325?; DESPENSER, THOMAS LE, 1373–1400.

GLOUCESTER, Miles de, earl of Hereford (d. 1143), sheriff of Gloucestershire and Staffordshire from 1128; justice-itinerant, a justice of the forest, and royal constable from 1128; adhered to Stephen till 1139, when he joined Gloucester in inviting the empress *Maud to England; relieved Brian *Fitzcount at Wallingford, 1139; burnt Worcester, 1139; took Hereford Castle, 1139; present at Lincoln, 1141; accompanied the empress to Winchester as one of her three chief supporters, 1141; fled with her from London, and persuaded her to return to Oxford from Gloucester, 1141; received as a reward the earldom and castle of Hereford, 1141; excommunicated by the bishop of Hereford for demands on church lands, 1143; slain by an arrow shot at a deer.

GLOUCESTER, Robert of (*fl.* 1260–1300), historian. See ROBERT.

GLOVER, Boyer (*fl.* 1758–1771), Muggletonian; watchmaker; contributed to *Songs of Gratefull Praise* (1794), and *Divine Songs of the Muggletonians* (1829).

GLOVER, Charles William (1806–1863), violinist and composer of popular songs; musical director at Queen's Theatre, 1832.

GLOVER, Edmund (1813?–1860), actor and manager; son of Julia *Glover; took 'leading business' under William *Murray at Edinburgh, 1841–8; manager for Jenny *Lind in Scotland; leased theatres at Glasgow, Paisley, and Greenock; played Othello at Edinburgh, 1850, and Falkland, 1851; alternated Macbeth and Macduff with Thomas Powrie, 1856.

GLOVER, George (*fl.* 1625–1650), early English engraver; engraved from life portraits of eminent contemporaries; engraved broadside representing Evans the giant porter, Jeffery *Hudson the dwarf, and old Thomas *Parr.

GLOVER, Jean (1758–1801), Scottish poetess; daughter of a Kilmarnock weaver and wife of a strolling player; her song 'Ower the Muir among the Heather' taken down by *Burns from her singing.

GLOVER, John (1714–1774), preacher; author of religious pamphlets.

GLOVER, John (1767–1849), landscape painter; president of the Water-Colour Society, 1815; exhibited at Paris *Landscape Composition*; sketched in Switzerland and Italy; held exhibition of water-colours and oils in Old Bond Street, 1821; a founder of Society of British Artists, with whom he exhibited, 1824–30; emigrated to Western Australia, 1831; died in Tasmania.

GLOVER, Sir John Hawley (1829–1885), colonial governor; served in navy, 1841–77; joined *Baikie's Niger expedition, 1857; captain, 1877; administrator of Lagos, 1863–4 and 1866–72; commanded Houssas in Ashanti campaign, 1873–4; GCMG, 1874; governor of Newfoundland, 1875–81 and 1883–4, of the Leeward Islands, 1881–3.

GLOVER, Mrs Julia (1779–1850), actress, née Betterton; played on the York circuit, 1789; performed at Covent Garden, 1797–1801; married Samuel Glover, 1800; played the Queen to Kean's Richard III and Emilia to Othello, 1814; acted Andromache at *Macready's first appearance at Covent Garden, 1816; with Benjamin *Webster at Haymarket, James *Anderson at Drury Lane, and William *Farren at the Strand; played Mrs Malaprop at her farewell (Drury Lane), 1850; first comic actress of the period of her middle life.

GLOVER, Moses (*fl.* 1620–1640), painter and architect; chiefly known by his large survey vellum of Syon House and Isleworth hundred, 1635.

GLOVER, Richard (1712–1785), poet; several times addressed the House of Commons as the merchants' representative; as opponent of Walpole received legacy from the duchess of *Marlborough; MP, Weymouth, 1761–8; published *Leonidas* (1737); his ballad, 'Hosier's Ghost', included in Thomas *Percy's *Reliques*; his *Boadicea* (1753) and *Medea* (1763) acted at Drury Lane; his *Athenaid* published 1787, and *Memoirs* (1742–57), 1813.

GLOVER, Robert (d. 1555), Protestant martyr; of Eton and King's College, Cambridge; MA, 1541; burnt for heresy at Coventry.

GLOVER, Robert (1544–1588), Somerset herald; Portcullis pursuivant of the College of Arms, 1567; Somerset herald, 1571; conducted visitations of Durham (1575), Cheshire (1580), and Yorkshire (1584–5); assisted *Camden in his *Britannia*; *The Catalogue of Honor* (1610) compiled from his collections.

GLOVER, Stephen (d. 1869), author of *History and Gazetteer of Derbyshire* (1831–3, unfinished) and compiler of the *Peak Guide* (1830).

GLOVER, Stephen (1812–1870), composer of songs, ballads, and duets; brother of Charles William *Glover.

GLOVER, Terrot Reaveley (1869–1943), classical scholar and historian; educated at Bristol Grammar School and St John's College, Cambridge; first classes, classical tripos, 1891–2; fellow, 1892; teaching fellow, 1901; professor of Latin, Queen's University, Kingston, Ontario, 1896–1901; university lecturer in ancient history, Cambridge, 1911–39; orator, 1920–39; president, Baptist Union, 1924, Classical Association, 1938; works include *Studies in Virgil* (1904), *The Conflict of Religions in the Early Roman Empire* (1909), *The Jesus of History* (1917), and *Democracy in the Ancient World* (1927).

GLOVER, William Howard (1819–1875), musical composer and writer; second son of Julia *Glover; gave operatic performances at Manchester and annual concerts at St James's Hall and Drury Lane; musical critic to *Morning Post*, 1849–65; died at New York; composed *Tam o' Shanter* (produced at the New Philharmonic, 1855), *Ruy Blas* (Covent Garden, 1861), and *Manfred*, an overture, and many songs.

GLUCKMAN, (Herman) Max (1911–1975), social anthropologist; born in Johannesburg of parents with Russian-Jewish background; educated at King Edward VII School, Johannesburg, and University of the Witwatersrand, 1928–33; Transvaal Rhodes scholar, 1934; studied social anthropology at Exeter College, Oxford; D.Phil., 1936; spent two years of field research in Zululand; returned to Oxford, 1938; appointed to staff of Rhodes–Livingstone Institute, Northern Rhodesia, 1939; temporary director, 1941; director, 1942–7; lecturer, Oxford University, 1947; professor at Manchester, 1949; became naturalized British citizen, 1950; established celebrated research seminar; visited Zambia (Northern Rhodesia) at invitation of government, 1965; published *Custom and Conflict in Africa* (1955), *Politics, Law and Ritual in Tribal Society* (1965), *The Judicial Process among the Barotse* (1955, 1967), and *The Ideas in Barotse Jurisprudence* (1965, 1972); FBA, 1968; received many academic honours and awards; vice-chairman, International African Institute, 1974; chairman, Association of Social Anthropologists of the British Commonwealth, 1962–6; held number of academic and non-academic public positions, including membership of advisory committee to Her Majesty's Sports Council, 1974.

GLYN, Elinor (1864–1943), novelist; born Sutherland; educated privately and read widely; made successful entry into society; married (1892) Clayton Glyn, landowner; wrote *The Visits of Elizabeth* (1900) and other 'society' novels; passionate romances, notably *Three Weeks* (1907) and *His Hour* (1910); and more serious character studies, including *Halcyone* (1912) containing recognizable portraits of her friends Lord *Curzon and F. H. *Bradley; *It* (1927) made word synonymous with personal magnetism; scriptwriter in Hollywood, 1920–9.

GLYN, George Grenfell, second Baron Wolverton (1824–1887), grandson of Sir Richard Carr *Glyn; educated at Rugby and University College, Oxford; of banking firm, Glyn, Mills, Currie & Co.; MP, Shaftesbury, 1857–73; secretary to the Treasury, 1868–73; paymaster-general, 1880–5; postmaster-general in home-rule ministry, 1886; personal friend of William Ewart Gladstone.

GLYN, Isabella Dallas (1823–1889), actress; née Gearns; played under her mother's name of Glyn; made début at Manchester as Constance in *King John*, 1847; appeared in Shakespearean parts on York circuit and at Sadler's Wells, 1848–51 and 1859; first appeared at Drury Lane, 1851; played Cleopatra at the Princess's, 1867; gave Shakespearean readings and lessons in England and America; obtained divorce from Eneas Sweetland *Dallas, 1874.

GLYN, Sir **Richard Carr,** first baronet (1755–1838), lord mayor of London; partner in Hallifax, Mills, Glyn & Mitton, bankers; sheriff of London, 1790; lord mayor, 1798–9; MP, St Ives, 1796–1802; created baronet, 1800.

GLYN, William (1504?–1558), bishop of Bangor; fellow of Queens' College, Cambridge, 1530; dean, 1540; MA, 1530; DD, 1544; Lady Margaret professor of divinity, 1544–9; original fellow of Trinity, 1546; rector of St Martin's, Ludgate, 1551; president of Queens' College, 1553; one of the six delegates who disputed with *Cranmer, *Latimer, and *Ridley, 1554; bishop of Bangor, 1555; Welsh scholar.

GLYNN, John (1722–1779), politician and lawyer; matriculated at Exeter College, Oxford, 1738; barrister, Inner Temple, 1748; serjeant-at-law, 1763; recorder of Exeter, 1764; counsel for *Wilkes; Wilkes's colleague as MP for Middlesex, 1768–79; leading member of Society of Bill of Rights; recorder of London, 1772.

GLYNN (afterwards **CLOBERY**), **Robert** (1719–1800), physician; educated at Eton and King's College, Cambridge; MA, 1745; MD, 1752; Seatonian prizeman, 1757; attended *Gray and Bishop *Watson; supported authenticity of *Chatterton forgeries against George *Steevens, and bequeathed the manuscripts to the British Museum; said to have assisted *Mathias in *Pursuits of Literature*; left legacy to King's College.

GLYNNE, Sir **John** (1603–1666), judge; educated at Westminster and Hart Hall, Oxford; barrister, Lincoln's Inn, 1628; MP, Westminster, 1640; sat on important committees in the Long Parliament; managed conference with the Lords in the *Goodman case, 1641; conducted several articles of *Strafford's impeachment, and replied to his defence, 1642; chosen to impeach the bishops, 1641; one of committee to consider the attempted arrest of the five members, 1642; recorder of London, 1643; took the Covenant; one of the eleven excluded members, 1647; sent to the Tower, but released and readmitted to parliament, 1648; one of the commissioners to treat with the king at Carisbrooke, 1648; again excluded before 'Pride's Purge'; MP, Caernarfonshire, 1654 and 1660, Flint, 1655; serjeant to the Protector and justice of assize, c.1654; prosecuted John *Gerard (1632–1654) and other conspirators, 1654; tried the conspirator, Miles *Sindercombe, 1656; chief justice of the upper bench, 1655–9; supported the 'petition and advice', 1656; as king's serjeant prosecuted Sir Henry *Vane, 1662; his speech before *Cromwell (1658) in favour of monarchy printed, 1660; knighted, 1660.

GLYNNE, Sir **Stephen Richard,** ninth and last baronet (1807–1874), antiquary; brother-in-law of William Ewart Gladstone; succeeded as baronet, 1815; educated at Eton; MA, Christ Church, Oxford, 1831; MP, Flint burghs, 1832–7, and Flintshire, 1837–47; surveyed and made notes on 5,530 English churches; his notes concerning Kent published by his nephew, W. H. Gladstone, 1877.

GOAD, George (d. 1671), master at Eton; MA, King's College, Cambridge, 1627; senior proctor, 1637; rector of Horstead and Coltishall, 1646; fellow of Eton, 1648; continued Eton catalogues.

GOAD, John (1616–1689), headmaster of Merchant Taylors' School; fellow of St John's College, Oxford; MA, 1640; BD, 1647; vicar of St Giles's, Oxford, 1643, of Yarnton, 1646–60; headmaster of Tunbridge, 1660, of Merchant Taylors' School, 1661–81; dismissed from Merchant Taylors' as a papist, 1681; declared himself a Romanist, 1686; afterwards kept private school at Piccadilly, London; wrote *Astro-Meteorologia sana* (1686) and a similar work, published 1690.

GOAD, Roger (1538–1610), provost of King's College, Cambridge, 1570; educated at Eton and King's College, Cambridge; fellow, 1558; MA, 1563; master of Guildford School; DD, 1576; thrice vice-chancellor; chancellor of Wells, 1577; with Dr *Fulke had conferences in the Tower with Edmund *Campion, 1581; re-established college library.

GOAD, Thomas (1576–1638), rector of Hadleigh, 1618–38; second son of Roger *Goad; educated at Eton and King's College, Cambridge; fellow, 1595; BA, 1596; DD, 1615; domestic chaplain to Archbishop Abbot; prebendary of Winchester, 1621; succeeded Joseph *Hall at synod of Dort, 1619, where he became an Arminian; disputed with the Jesuits; prolocutor of lower House of Convocation, 1625; dean of Bocking, 1633; embellished Hadleigh Church and rectory with paintings; published theological tracts.

GOAD, Thomas (d. 1666), regius professor of laws at Cambridge; brother of George *Goad; of Eton, King's College, Cambridge, and Gray's Inn; MA and LL D; reader of logic at Cambridge, 1620; regius professor, 1635.

GOADBY, Robert (1721–1778), printer and compiler; left endowment to Sherborne Church; chief production, *Illustration of the Holy Scriptures* (1759).

GOBBAN SAER (*fl.* 7th cent.), 'the Artificer'; builder of churches and fortresses in north and east of Ireland.

GOBION, Ralph (d. 1151), abbot of St Albans. See RALPH.

GODBER, Frederick, first Baron Godber (1888–1976), international industrialist; left school at 15 and joined Asiatic (later Shell) Petroleum Company as office boy, 1904; member of group concerned with merger of Shell Transport and Trading Company and Royal Dutch Petroleum, 1906–7; head of newly formed American department, 1912–19; president, Rhoxana Petroleum, St Louis, USA, 1919–29; managing director, Royal Dutch / Shell Group, 1929; travelled widely, visiting Shell's expanding empire; during 1939–45 war, chairman of Overseas Supply Committee, Petroleum Board, co-ordinating supplies of petroleum; knighted, 1942; chairman, Shell Transport and Trading Co., and chairman, Shell Petroleum Co. Ltd., 1946–61; chairman, Help Holland Fund; created grand officer of Order of Orange Nassau, 1947; chairman, Commonwealth Development Finance Corporation, 1953–68; raised to peerage, 1956; hon. bencher, Middle Temple, 1954; trustee, Churchill College, Cambridge, 1958; hon. liveryman, Leathersellers' Company, 1962; barony became extinct when he died, 1976.

GODBOLT, John (d. 1648), judge; admitted at Caius College, Cambridge, 1599; barrister, Gray's Inn, 1611; serjeant-at-law, 1636; MP, Bury St Edmunds, 1640; judge of common pleas by vote of parliament, 1647; reports revised by him published, 1653.

GODBY, James (*fl.* 1790–1815), stipple-engraver.

GODDAM (or WOODHAM), Adam (d. 1358), Franciscan; attended Ockham's lectures on Peter Lombard's *Sentences* at Oxford; his *Commentary on Four Books of the 'Sentences'*, as edited (1512) by John *Major (1469–1550), probably only an abridgment of *Goddam's work.

GODDARD, George Bouverie (1832–1886), animal painter; exhibited at the Academy, 1856–85.

GODDARD, John (*fl.* 1645–1671), engraver; his *Seven Deadly Sins* in British Museum.

GODDARD, Jonathan (1617–1675), Gresham professor of physic; MB, Christ's College, Cambridge, 1638; MD Catharine Hall, 1643; FRCP, 1646; Gulstonian lecturer, 1648; as physician-in-chief accompanied *Cromwell to Ireland, 1649, and Scotland, 1650; warden of Merton College, Oxford, 1651–60; member of Little Parliament and Council of State, 1653; on council of Royal Society; appointed Gresham professor of physic, 1655; wrote two *Discourses* against the apothecaries; according to Seth *Ward, the first Englishman to make telescopes.

GODDARD, Rayner, Baron Goddard (1877–1971), lord chief justice; educated at Marlborough and Trinity College, Oxford; athletics blue; called to bar (Inner Temple), 1899; joined western circuit; specialized in banking and other commercial cases; recorder of Poole (1917), Bath (1925), and Plymouth (1928); legal adviser to Board of Trade during 1914–18 war; KC, 1923; bencher of Inner Temple, 1929; judge of King's Bench, 1932; knighted; appellate judge, and PC, 1938; lord of appeal in ordinary and life peer, 1944; succeeded Viscount *Caldecote as lord chief justice, 1946, first non-political holder of the office; refused hereditary peerage as he had no son; responsible for improvements in administration and speeding-up of trials; tried number of notable murder cases including the Craig–Bentley trial; strong supporter of corporal and capital punishment; resigned because of failing eyesight and hearing, 1958; GCB; hon. fellow, Trinity College, Oxford, 1940; honorary degrees from number of universities in England and USA.

GODDARD, Thomas (d. 1783), Indian general; lieutenant, 1758; served at Madras, 1759–61, and in Bengal, 1763; raised sepoy battalion for East India Company, 1764; lieutenant-colonel, 1768; served at capture of Burrareah, 1770, and against Mahrattas, 1772; much trusted by Warren *Hastings; commanded Bengal contingent with Bombay Army against Mahrattas, 1778–81; brigadier-general; died at sea.

GODDARD, William (*fl.* 1615), satirist; resided in Holland; his three works first printed under Dr Furnivall's editorship (1878).

GODDARD, William Stanley (1757–1845), headmaster of Winchester; MA, Merton College, Oxford, 1783; DD, 1795; second master at Winchester, 1784–96; as headmaster (1806–9) raised the school from 60 to 144, among his pupils being Dr *Arnold; prebendary of St Paul's, 1814; canon of Salisbury, 1829; presented £25,000 to Winchester for masters' salaries; scholarship founded in memory of him, 1846.

GODDEN (properly **TYLDEN**), **Thomas** (1624–1688), controversialist; BA, St John's College, Cambridge, 1642; converted to Romanism by John *Sergeant; president of the English College, Lisbon, 1655, and DD, 1660; chaplain to Queen *Catharine of Braganza, 1661; accused of complicity in murder of Sir Edmund Berry *Godfrey, 1678; escaped to Paris, but returned under James II; carried on theological controversy with *Stillingfleet.

GODEL, William (fl. 1173), historian; probably a Cistercian in diocese of Sens or Bourges, although of English birth; his chronicle reaching to 1173 (with continuation to 1320), printed in *Recueil des Historiens de la France*.

GODERICH, Viscount (1782–1859). See ROBINSON, FREDERICK JOHN, earl of Ripon.

GODFREY (or **GODFREY-HANCKWITZ**), **Ambrose,** the elder (d. 1741), chemist; employed by Robert *Boyle; FRS, 1730; patented machine for extinguishing fires 'by explosion and suffocation', 1724.

GODFREY, Ambrose, the younger (d. 1756), chemist; son of Ambrose *Godfrey the elder; carried on his father's laboratory in Southampton Street, London; published, with his brother John *Godfrey, *A Curious Research into the Element of Water* (1747).

GODFREY, Arabella (1648–1730). See CHURCHILL, ARABELLA.

GODFREY, Boyle (d. 1756?), alchemist; brother of Ambrose *Godfrey the younger; ruined himself by his passion for alchemy.

GODFREY, Daniel (1831–1903), bandmaster of Grenadier Guards, 1856–96; composed famous 'Guards' waltz, 1863, and much popular military music; toured with band in America, 1876; promoted second lieutenant, 1887.

GODFREY, Sir Edmund Berry (1621–1678), justice of the peace for Westminster; educated at Westminster and Christ Church, Oxford; entered Gray's Inn, 1640; knighted for services during plague, 1665, 1666; offended the court by causing arrest of Sir Alexander *Fraizer, 1669; reputed best justice of the peace in England; a zealous Protestant; received first depositions of Titus *Oates, 1678; found dead on south side of Primrose Hill a month later; believed murdered

by Roman Catholics; two Romanists and a Protestant were hanged at Tyburn in consequence of the confession (made under torture and once repudiated) of Miles *Prance, a Catholic silversmith, avowing himself to have been an accomplice in the murder. Prance was punished for perjury, 1686. The crime was perhaps perpetrated at the instigation of Oates himself.

GODFREY, John (fl. 1747), chemist: with his brother Ambrose *Godfrey the younger carried on the business of his father Ambrose *Godfrey the elder; published, also with his brother, *A Curious Research into the Element of Water* (1747).

GODFREY, John Henry (1888–1971), admiral; educated at King Edward's Grammar School, Birmingham; entered *Britannia*, 1903; served on destroyers, gunboats, and cruisers, and specialized in navigation, 1909–13; served in Gallipoli campaign, and as staff officer, 1917–19; Legion of Honour (chevalier); served in plans division, 1921–3, and on directing staff of Staff College, Greenwich; deputy director, Staff College, 1929–31; commanded battle cruiser, *Repulse*, 1936–8; CB; director of naval intelligence, rear-admiral, 1939–42; responsible for important increase in efficiency of the division, but his uncompromising attitude led to clashes with (Sir) Winston Churchill and hostility of colleagues on Joint Intelligence Committee; promoted to vice-admiral and transferred to post of flag officer commanding Royal Indian Navy, 1943–6; suppressed mutiny; placed on retired list and promoted to admiral, 1945; finally retired, 1946; chairman of Chelsea Group of hospitals, 1946–61; helped to create Cheyne Centre for spastic children; only officer of his rank to receive no official recognition for his war services, a palpable injustice.

GODFREY, Michael (d. 1695), financier; nephew of Sir Edmund Berry *Godfrey; first deputy-governor of the Bank of England; killed in the trenches at Namur while on his way to establish branch at Antwerp; wrote 'short account' of the Bank of England.

GODFREY, Richard Bernard (b. 1728), engraver of views and antiquities for *Grose's *Antiquarian Repertory* (1775).

GODFREY, Thomas (1736–1763), poet and dramatist; born at Philadelphia; served in expedition against Fort Duquesne, 1758; while a factor in North Carolina composed *The Prince of Parthia*, the first play written in America (published 1765).

GODFREY, Walter Hindes (1881–1961), architect and antiquary; educated at Whitgift Grammar School, Croydon, and Central School of Arts and Crafts; joined architectural section of

London County Council, 1900; member of Committee for the Survey of London, 1901; prepared four volumes of Surrey, 1909–27; left LCC for private practice, 1903; formed partnership of Wratten and Godfrey, 1905; prepared illustrations and architectural studies in Survey of London series; employed in Accounts Division, Ministry of Munitions, 1915–19; resumed private practice; FRIBA, 1926; retired from practice but undertook restoration of Herstmonceaux Castle and other buildings, 1932–9; director, National Buildings Record (later the National Monuments Record), 1941–60; published many books, including *A History of Architecture in London* (1911), *The Story of Architecture in England* (2 vols., 1928 and 1931), and *The English Almshouse* (1955); member of Royal Commission on Historical Monuments, 1944, and other committees; CBE, 1950.

GODFREY, William (1889–1963), cardinal, seventh archbishop of Westminster; educated at St John's, Kirkdale, Ushaw College, Durham, and the Venerable English College, Rome; doctorates in philosophy and theology at the Gregorian University, 1913 and 1917; ordained priest, 1916; curate, St Michael's, Liverpool, 1917; classics master, Ushaw College, 1919; professor of philosophy and, in 1928, of dogmatic theology; published *The Young Apostle* (1924) and *God and Ourselves* (1927); contributed to *Ushaw Magazine*, 1921–30; succeeded Archbishop *Hinsley as rector, English College, Rome, 1930; domestic prelate to Pope Pius XI; member of the Supreme Council for the Propagation of the Faith; counsellor in the papal mission for George VI's coronation, 1937; apostolic visitor of all seminaries in Great Britain, 1938; archbishop of Liverpool, 1953; succeeded Cardinal *Griffin as seventh archbishop of Westminster, 1956; created cardinal, 1958; member of Central Preparatory Commission to examine and recast the *schemata* for discussion in the Second Vatican Council, 1961.

GODFREY OF MALMESBURY (*fl.* 1081), supposed author of a chronicle extending from the coming of the Saxons to 1129; wrongly identified by *Tanner with Godfrey, abbot of Malmesbury.

GODFREY OF WINCHESTER (d. 1107), Latin poet; native of Cambrai; prior of St Swithin's, Winchester, 1081–1107; his epigrams in imitation of Martial, and *De Primatum Angliae Laudibus*, printed in Thomas *Wright's (1810–1877) *Latin Satirical Poets of the Twelfth Century*.

GODFREYSON, Reginald (d. 944?), king of the Danes. See REGINALD.

GODHAM, Adam (d. 1358). See GODDAM.

GODIVA (or GODGIFU) (d. 1067), benefactress; wife of *Leofric, earl of Mercia; built and endowed monasteries at Stow and Coventry; benefactress of houses at other places. The oldest form of the legend of her riding naked through Coventry to obtain the release of the 'villa' from toll is given by Roger of *Wendover (*Flores Historiarum*); the current story originates with *Rapin (1732); the procession at Coventry (last held, 1887) was instituted in 1678.

GODKIN, Edwin Lawrence (1831–1902), editor and author; son of James *Godkin; BA, London, 1851; left law for authorship; published *The History of Hungary* (1853); *Daily News* correspondent in Crimea; settled in United States, 1856; called to New York bar, 1858; supported North in Civil War, 1862; edited New York *Nation*, which by its independence and literary power influenced American public opinion, 1865–99; the paper was recognized organ of independent 'Mugwumps', 1884–94; Godkin denounced system of Tammany Hall and caused defeat of Tammany, 1894; opposed American annexation of Hawaii and Philippines, high tariffs, and bimetallism; revisited England, 1889; his philosophical radical views expounded in *Reflections and Comments* (1895), *Problems of Modern Democracy* (1896), and *Unforeseen Tendencies of Democracy* (1897); hon. DCL, Oxford, 1897; Godkin memorial lectures on citizenship founded at Harvard University.

GODKIN, James (1806–1879), writer on Ireland; established *Christian Patriot* at Belfast, 1849; edited *Derry Standard* and Dublin *Daily Express*; active member of the Tenant League, 1850; received civil list pension, 1873; published works, including *The Land War in Ireland* (1870) and *Religious History of Ireland* (1873).

GODLEE, Sir Rickman John, baronet (1849–1925), surgeon; nephew of Lord *Lister; studied medicine at London University; MB, 1872; MS, 1873; assistant surgeon, University College Hospital, 1877; full surgeon, 1885; professor of clinical surgery, 1892; Holme professor of clinical surgery, 1900; emeritus professor, 1914; performed first operation for removal of tumour from the brain, 1884; stimulated development of thoracic surgery; FRCS, 1876; president, Royal Society of Medicine, 1916–18; baronet, 1912; KCVO, 1914; works include *Atlas of Human Anatomy* (1880) and life of Lister (of whom he had intimate personal knowledge, 1917).

GODLEY, Sir Alexander John (1867–1957), general; cousin of A. D. *Godley and Lord *Kilbracken; educated at Haileybury, United Services College, and Sandhurst; gazetted to Royal Dublin Fusiliers, 1886; served in South Africa, 1896–7 and 1899–1901; appointed to command

New Zealand military forces and major-general, 1910; commanded New Zealand Expeditionary Force, 1914–18; commanded New Zealand and Australian division at Gallipoli, II Anzac Corps in France, 1916–18, XXII Corps, 1918–19; military secretary to Churchill, 1920–2; commander-in-chief, British Army of Rhine, 1922–4; GOC, Southern Command, 1924–8; governor of Gibraltar, 1928–33; general, 1923; KCMG, 1914; KCB, 1916; GCB, 1928.

GODLEY, Alfred Denis (1856–1925), classical scholar and man of letters; BA, Balliol College, Oxford, 1878; tutor and fellow of Magdalen College, 1883–1912; public orator, 1910–25; writer of light humorous or satiric verse and prose; commentator on and translator of Herodotus, Tacitus, and Horace; 'an almost perfect writer of elegant Latin' in his Creweian orations.

GODLEY, (John) Arthur, first Baron Kilbracken (1847–1932), civil servant; son of J. R. *Godley; educated at Rugby and Balliol College, Oxford; assistant (1872–4) and principal (1880–2) private secretary to Gladstone; fellow of Hertford, 1874–81; permanent under-secretary of state for India, 1883–1909; established efficiency of India Office on firm basis; KCB, 1893; baron, 1909.

GODLEY, John Robert (1814–1861), politician; educated at Harrow; BA, Christ Church, Oxford, 1836; propounded plan for relief of Irish distress by emigration to Canada; friend of Edward Gibbon *Wakefield; lived at Canterbury, New Zealand, 1850–2, a settlement founded on his own plan; afterwards income-tax commissioner in Ireland; under-secretary-at-war; selection from his writings and speeches published in New Zealand (1863).

GODMOND, Christopher (*fl.* 1840), author of *The Campaign of 1346* (1836) and *Vincenzo, Prince of Mantua* (1840), two dramas; FSA, 1837.

GODOLPHIN, Francis, second earl of Godolphin (1678–1766), son of Sidney *Godolphin, first earl; his education superintended by John *Evelyn (1620–1706); of Eton and King's College, Cambridge; MA, 1705; MP for East Looe, 1701, Helston, 1702–10, for Oxfordshire, 1708–10, and Tregony, 1710–12; Viscount Rialton, 1706–12; cofferer of the household, 1704–11 and 1714–23; privy councillor, 1723; groom of the stole and first lord of the bedchamber, 1727–35; acted as lord justice, 1723, 1725, and 1727; lord privy seal, 1735–40.

GODOLPHIN, Henry (1648–1733), provost of Eton and dean of St Paul's, younger brother of Sidney, earl of *Godolphin; educated at Eton and Wadham College, Oxford; BA, 1668; fellow of All Souls, 1668; MA, 1672; DD, 1685; fellow of Eton, 1677; provost, 1695–1707 and 1726–33; dean of St Paul's, 1707–26; benefactor of Eton and Salisbury.

GODOLPHIN, John (1617–1678), civilian; DCL, Gloucester Hall, Oxford, 1643; judge of the Admiralty, 1653; king's advocate, 1660; published, among other works, *The Holy Limbec* (1650) and *Repertorium Canonicum* (1678).

GODOLPHIN, Mrs Margaret (1652–1678), friend of John *Evelyn; née Blagge; maid of honour to duchess of *York and to Queen *Catharine; privately married Sidney (afterwards earl of) *Godolphin, 1675; Evelyn's account of her published (1847).

GODOLPHIN, Sidney (1610–1643), poet; educated at Exeter College, Oxford; MP, Helston, 1628–43; joined Sir Ralph *Hopton's force and fell in skirmish at Chagford; friend of *Falkland, *Hobbes, and *Clarendon; *Suckling's 'Little Sid'; his *Passion of Dido* (finished by *Waller) contained in *Dryden's *Miscellany*, and songs by him in George *Ellis's *Specimens* and the *Tixall Poetry*.

GODOLPHIN, Sidney, first earl of Godolphin (1645–1712), statesman; page of honour to the king, 1662; master of the robes, 1678; MP, Helston, 1668–79, St Mawes, 1679–81; a lord of the Treasury, 1679; allied with *Sunderland and the duchess of *Portsmouth; corresponded with the prince of Orange; secretary of state, 1684; created Baron Godolphin, 1684; chamberlain to Queen *Mary of Modena, 1685, with whom he attended mass; a commissioner of the Treasury, 1687; one of James II's last adherents; advocated regency on James II's flight; constantly corresponded with St Germain, sending warning of the projected attack on Brest, 1694; head of the Treasury, 1690–6; the only Tory lord justice, 1695; implicated in confession of Sir John *Fenwick, 1696; resigned; again first lord, 1700–1; lord high treasurer and *Marlborough's confidential ally, 1702–10; induced by the duchess to force the queen to replace Tory by Whig ministers; took part in promoting union with Scotland and in Portuguese and Spanish affairs; supported Whigs in insisting on barrier treaty with Dutch; attacked by *Sacheverell as 'Volpone', vehemently urged his impeachment, 1709; dismissed by Anne with a pension, 1710; his financial administration defended by Walpole.

GODOLPHIN, Sir William (1634?–1696), ambassador; educated at Westminster and Christ Church, Oxford; student, 1651; MA, 1661; DCL, Oxford, 1663; MP, Camelford, 1665; knighted, 1668; envoy-extraordinary to Spain, 1669; ambassador at Madrid, 1671–8; recalled under suspicion of Roman Catholicism (1678), which he soon openly professed; died at Madrid; his notarial act providing for a posthumous will declared invalid by parliament, 1698.

GODRIC (1065?–1170), founder of Finchale; for sixteen years merchant and shipowner; probably the 'Gudericus, pirata de regno Angliae', with whom Baldwin I of Jerusalem sailed from Arsuf to Jaffa, 1102; made pilgrimages to Rome, St James of Compostella, and St Gilles in Provence; for sixty years lived as a hermit under Rannulf *Flambard's protection at Finchale on the Wear, where he built a wooden chapel dedicated to the Virgin.

GODSALVE, Edward (d. 1568?), Roman Catholic divine, original fellow of Trinity College, Cambridge, 1546; BD, 1554; prebendary of Chichester; rector of Fulbourn, 1554; retired to Antwerp, c.1560, as professor of divinity in St Michael's Monastery; edited Christopherson's version of Eusebius (part i) and translated part iii.

GODSALVE, Sir John (d. 1556), clerk of the signet to Henry VIII, and comptroller of the Mint under Edward VI; knight of the carpet, 1547.

GODWIN (or **GODWINE**) (d. 1053), earl of the West Saxons; described as 'dux' in 1018; accompanied *Canute to Denmark, 1019; appointed by Canute earl of the West Saxons, and married to Gytha, sister of Ulf; acquired great influence by his wealth and talent for oratory; supported claims of Harthacnut to the crown, 1035, but afterwards accepted *Harold (Harefoot); accused by many writers of causing death (1036) of *Ælfred the ætheling; compelled to clear himself by oath on accession of Harthacnut, 1040; procured the peaceful accession of *Edward the Confessor, 1042; headed the national party against the Norman favourites; married his daughter *Eadgyth (Edith) to King Edward; obtained for his second son *Harold earldom of East Anglia and for his eldest son Swegen earldom of some Mercian shires; weakened by the accession of *Robert of Jumièges to the sees of London (1044) and Canterbury (1050), who revived the old charge against him; outlawed with his sons, 1051; took refuge with Baldwin, count of Flanders, his son *Tostig's father-in-law; made descents on the Isle of Wight and Portland, 1052; with the support of Kent, Surrey, Sussex, and London sailed up the Thames; restored with his family to favour; died at Winchester of apoplexy while supping with Edward.

GODWIN, Mrs Catherine Grace (1798–1845), poet; daughter of Thomas *Garnett (1766–1802); married Thomas Godwin, 1824; published *The Night before the Bridal* and *The Wanderer's Legacy* (1829).

GODWIN, Edward William (1833–1886), architect; practised in Bristol and London; assisted Burgess in designs for new law courts, and Edis in those for the Berlin parliament house; restored Dromore Castle and Castle Ashby; designed theatrical costumes and scenery; published *Temple Bar Illustrated* (1877) and an adaptation of *The Faithfull Shepherdesse*, and other works.

GODWIN, Francis (1562–1633), bishop of Llandaff and Hereford; son of Thomas *Godwin (1517–1590); MA, Christ Church, Oxford, 1584; DD, 1596; sub-dean of Exeter, 1587; bishop of Llandaff, 1601, of Hereford, 1617; his *Catalogue of the Bishops of England*, with lives (1601), edited and continued by William Richardson, 1643; his Latin *Annals* (Henry VIII–Mary), translated by his son Morgan. From Godwin's *Man in the Moone* (published posthumously, 1638), John *Wilkins, bishop of Chester, and Cyrano de Bergerac are supposed to have borrowed their imaginary sketches of life in the moon.

GODWIN, George (1815–1888), architect; won British Architects' Prize for essay on 'Concrete', 1835; honorary secretary, Art Union of London, 1836–7; became editor of the *Builder*, 1844; restored St Mary Redcliffe, and erected many buildings in Bristol; treasurer of Royal Literary Fund; FRS and FSA; gold medallist of Institute of Architects, 1881; founded Godwin bursary; active member of Royal Commission on Housing of Working Classes, 1884; noted collector of chairs of celebrities. His works include *The Churches of London* (1838) and architectural monographs.

GODWIN, George Nelson (1846–1907), Hampshire antiquary; chaplain of the forces, 1877–90; antiquary and historian of Hampshire and neighbouring counties; published *Civil War in Hampshire, 1642–5* (1882), *Bibliotheca Hantoniensis* (1891), and other works.

GODWIN, Sir Harry (1901–1985), botanist; educated at Long Eaton County Secondary School and Clare College, Cambridge; scholar; first class, parts i and ii, natural sciences tripos, 1921 and 1922; research student in plant physiology; Ph.D., 1926; university demonstrator in botany, 1923; university lecturer, 1934; fellow, Clare College, 1934–68; professor of botany, 1960–8; made systematic studies of Wicken Fen; published *Vegetation of Wicken Fen* (part V of *The Natural History of Wicken Fen*, with (Sir) A. G. *Tansley, 1929; also *The History of British Flora* (1956, 2nd edn., 1975); president, British Ecological Society, 1942–3; editor, *Journal of Ecology*, 1948–56; joint editor, *New Phytologist*, 1931–61;

director, sub-department of quaternary research, Cambridge botany school, 1948–66; FRS, 1945; member of Royal Society council (1957–9); Croonian lecturer, 1960; knighted, 1970; received number of medals and other academic awards; Sc.D. (Cantab.), 1942; honorary doctorates from Trinity College, Dublin, and Lancaster and Durham universities.

GODWIN, Sir Henry Thomas (1784–1853), major-general; ensign, 9th Foot, 1799; served in Hanover, 1805, and in the Peninsula; severely wounded at Barossa, 1811; CB; lieutenant-colonel, 41st Foot, 1815; commanded it in first Burmese War, 1824–6; major-general, 1846; commander-in-chief in second Burmese War, 1852–3; KCB; died at Simla.

GODWIN, Mrs Mary Wollstonecraft (1759–1797), author; née Wollstonecraft; kept school at Newington Green with her sister Eliza; governess to Lord Kingsborough's children, 1787–8; employed for five years by Johnson, a London publisher; at Paris formed connection with Gilbert *Imlay, 1793–5; attempted to drown herself in despair at his unfaithfulness; married William *Godwin the elder, 1797; died at the birth of her daughter Mary; *Opie's portraits of her engraved in her life by C. Kegan Paul. She published *Thoughts on the Education of Daughters* (1787), *Original Stories from Real Life* (1788), *Vindication of the Rights of Woman* (1792), and other works; her *Letters to Imlay* edited by C. K. Paul (1879).

GODWIN, Morgan (*fl.* 1685), minister in Virginia; grandson of Bishop Francis *Godwin; BA, Christ Church, Oxford, 1664; minister in Virginia; died in England; published *The Negro's and Indian's Advocate suing for their Admission into the Church* (1680).

GODWIN, Thomas (1517–1590), bishop of Bath and Wells; fellow of Magdalen College, Oxford, 1545; MA, 1548; first headmaster of Brackley school, 1549; licensed medical practitioner, 1555; chaplain to Bishop Nicholas *Bullingham; DD, 1565; dean of Christ Church, 1565, of Canterbury, 1567; bishop of Bath and Wells, 1584–90; offended Elizabeth by making a second marriage.

GODWIN, Thomas (d. 1642), master of Abingdon school; MA, Magdalen Hall, Oxford, 1609; DD; rector of Brightwell, Berkshire; published *Romanae Historiae Anthologia* (16th edn., 1696), *Moses and Aaron* (12th edn., 1685), and other works.

GODWIN, William, the elder (1756–1836), philosopher and novelist; began philosophical studies at Hoxton Academy under Dr *Rees; Dissenting minister for four years; became connected with extreme Whigs, and an atheist, under influence of Thomas *Holcroft; married Mary Wollstonecraft (see GODWIN, Mrs MARY WOLLSTONECRAFT), 1797; after refusals from Harriet *Lee and Mrs Reveley (Maria *Gisborne), married (1801) Mrs Clairmont, mother of Clara Mary Jane *Clairmont; quarrelled with Dr *Parr and Sir J. *Mackintosh, who had criticised his ethics; converted by *Coleridge to theism; his *Tragedy of Antonio* unsuccessful at Drury Lane, 1800; started (1805) a publishing business, which failed in 1822, though at first successful with *Lamb's *Tales from Shakespeare*, and some children's books written by Godwin under the name Baldwin; derived pecuniary assistance from his acquaintance with *Wedgwood and *Shelley; obtained the sinecure office of yeoman usher of the Exchequer from Earl Grey, 1833; published *Enquiry concerning Political Justice* (1793), which made him known as the philosophical representative of English radicalism, a memoir of Mary Wollstonecraft (1798), the novels *Adventures of Caleb Williams* (1794, dramatised as *The Iron Chest*), *St. Leon* (1799), and others; produced *Life of Chaucer* (1803), *Of Population*, answer to *Malthus (1820), and *History of the Commonwealth* (1824–8); posthumous essays by him issued (1873).

GODWIN, William, the younger (1803–1832), reporter to the *Morning Chronicle*, 1823–32; son of William *Godwin the elder; his novel, *Transfusion*, published by his father (1835).

GODWIN-AUSTEN, Henry Haversham (1834–1923), explorer and geologist; son of R. A. C. *Godwin-Austen; educated at Royal Military Academy, Sandhurst; joined 24th Foot, 1851; served in Second Burmese War, 1852; attached to Great Trigonometrical Survey of India to assist with first survey of Kashmir, 1856; permanent topographical assistant to survey, 1860; discovered and surveyed great Karakoram glaciers, etc., 1861; served on political mission of (Sir) Ashley *Eden to Bhutan in eastern Himalaya, 1863; explored Naga hills, 1873–4; accompanied first Dafla expedition, 1875; carried out important geological investigations; retired, owing to ill health, 1877; FRS, 1880.

GODWIN-AUSTEN, Robert Alfred Cloyne (1808–1884), geologist; fellow of Oriel College, Oxford, 1830; BA, 1830; pupil of *Buckland; FGS, 1830; FRS, 1849; took additional surname of Godwin, 1853; published essay 'on the possible extension of the coal-measures beneath the south-eastern parts of England', 1854; Wollaston medallist, 1862; foreign secretary of Geological Society, 1865–7; wrote important papers on the geological formation of Devonshire, southern

England, and parts of France; completed works by Edward *Forbes.

GOETZ, John Daniel (1592–1672), divine and tutor. See GETSIUS.

GOFFE. See also GOUGH.

GOFFE (or GOUGH), John (1610?–1661), divine; perpetual fellow of Magdalen College, Oxford, 1630; MA, 1631; DD, 1660; ejected from living of Hackington, and imprisoned for refusing the Covenant, 1643; restored, 1660, having meanwhile held the living of Norton; published *Ecclesiae Anglicanae Threnodia* (1661).

GOFFE (or GOUGH), Stephen (1605–1681), Royalist divine; brother of John *Goffe; MA, Merton College, Oxford, 1627; DD, 1636; chaplain in the Low Countries and to Charles I; employed by the king abroad and in negotiating with the Scots; became a Romanist; superior of French Oratorians, 1655; chaplain to *Henrietta Maria and tutor to *Crofts (Monmouth); befriended English exiles; friend and correspondent of *Vossius; died at Paris.

GOFFE (or GOUGH), Thomas (1591–1629), divine and poet; educated at Westminster and Christ Church, Oxford; MA, 1616; MA, Cambridge, 1617; BD, 1623; incumbent of East Clandon, 1620–9; three of his tragedies acted at Christ Church; said to have died from his wife's persecution; *Three Excellent Tragedies* by him published posthumously.

GOFFE (or GOUGH), William (d. 1679?), regicide; brother of Stephen *Goffe; captain in *Harley's new model regiment, 1645; member of deputation which presented charge against the eleven members, 1647; one of the king's judges, 1648; commanded *Cromwell's regiment at Dunbar, 1650, and led another at Worcester, 1651; helped to eject Barebones Parliament, 1653; active against *Penruddock; major-general for Berkshire, Sussex, and Hampshire, 1655; one of the Protector's lords; member of Committee of Nine, 1658; one of four sent by the army to mediate with *Monck, 1659; on the Restoration fled with *Whalley to Massachusetts, lived concealed for three years; traditionally supposed to have repelled an attack of Indians at Hadley, Massachusetts, 1675; buried at Hadley.

GOGARTY, Oliver Joseph St John (1878–1957), surgeon, man of letters, and wit; born in Dublin; educated at Stonyhurst and Clongoweswood; qualified in Dublin, 1907; practised as nose and throat surgeon; moved into literary and political circles, gaining reputation as great Irish wit; member of first Senate of Irish Free State; moved to London, 1937, to United States, 1939; published *As I was Going Down Sackville Street*

(1937) and other volumes of reminiscences, novels, and *Collected Poems* (1951).

GOLD, Ernest (1881–1976), meteorologist; educated at Coleshill Grammar School, Mason's College, Birmingham, and St John's College, Cambridge; third wrangler, mathematics tripos, 1903; fellow of St John's College, 1906; first Schuster reader in meteorology, 1907–10; on staff of Meteorological Office, 1910; research provided an explanation of the stratosphere, 1909; FRS, 1918; commissioned in Royal Engineers, 1915; gradually created military meteorological service; DSO, 1916; OBE (military), 1919; returned to Meteorological Office, 1919; president, Commission for Synoptic Weather, 1919–47; during 1939–45 war organized comprehensive meteorological military service; CB, 1942; American Medal of Freedom with silver palms, 1946; influential in reorganizing peacetime Meteorological Office under Sir Nelson *Johnson; president, Royal Meteorological Society, 1934–5; hon. member, American Meteorological Society.

GOLD, Sir Harcourt Gilbey (1876–1952), oarsman; educated at Eton and Magdalen College, Oxford; stroked Eton to victory in Ladies' Plate (1893–5), Oxford (1896–8), and Leander thrice in Grand Challenge Cup; coached two winning Olympic eights (1908, 1912); appointed steward of Henley Regatta, 1909, committee member, 1919, chairman, 1945, president, 1952; OBE, 1918; knighted, 1949.

GOLDAR, John (1729–1795), engraver.

GOLDESBURG (GOLDESBOROUGH or GOULDSBOROUGH), John (1568–1618), law reporter; barrister, Middle Temple; protonotary of common pleas.

GOLDICUTT, John (1793–1842), architect; received gold medallion from the pope for coloured drawing of the transverse section of St Peter's, 1818; exhibited at the Academy, 1810–42; honorary secretary of Institute of Architects, 1834–6; published *Antiquities of Sicily* (1819), *Specimens of Ancient Decorations from Pompeii* (1825), and *Ancient Wells and Reservoirs* (1836).

GOLDIE, Sir George Dashwood Taubman (1846–1925), founder of Nigeria; commissioned in Royal Engineers, 1865–7; first visited West Africa, 1877; discovered some British firms in Niger delta engaged in competition and not attempting to open up trade with rich interior; formed United African Company, 1879; launched National African Company, 1881; French companies, which shortly appeared on scene, amalgamated with it, 1884; situation further complicated by summoning of West African Conference in Berlin, 1884–5; race between England, France, and Germany for Africa inaugurated; secured grant of royal charter to company under title of Royal Niger Company Chartered and Limited, which remained trading company while charged with administrative duties, 1886; appointed political administrator and deputy-governor; governor, 1895; concluded numerous treaties with native rulers of interior; secured end of struggle with Germany (1893) and France (1898) and final definition of respective spheres; although British sphere smaller than originally projected, secured half a million square miles of most fertile, highly mineralized, and thickly populated portion of West Africa; territory known as Nigeria, 1897; carried out successful campaigns against slave-raiding Mohammedan states of Nupé and Ilorin, 1897; legal status of slavery thereupon abolished in company's territory; company's charter surrendered to British crown, 1900; KCMG, 1887; FRS, 1902.

GOLDIE (or GOUDIE), John (1717–1809), author of *Essay on various important subjects, Moral and Divine* (1779), known as 'Goudie's Bible'.

GOLDING, Arthur (1536?–1605?), translator from Latin and French; matriculated from Jesus College, Cambridge, 1552; employed by *Somerset; half-brother of Margaret, wife of John De *Vere, sixteenth earl of Oxford; friend of Sir Philip *Sidney, whose translation of De Mornay's *Truth of Christianity* he completed, 1589; member of Archbishop Matthew *Parker's Society of Antiquaries; his version of Ovid's *Metamorphoses*, 1565–7 (dedicated to *Leicester and praised by *Meres), known to Shakespeare; dedicated to *Burghley his translation of Caesar's *Commentaries* (1565), of Mela (1585).

GOLDING, Benjamin (1793–1863), physician; MD, St Andrews, 1823; LRCP, 1825; the extension of the West London Infirmary into the Charing Cross Hospital mainly his work; published *Historical Account of St. Thomas's Hospital* (1819) and an account of his own hospital (posthumous).

GOLDING, John (d. 1719), musical composer. See GOLDWIN.

GOLDING, Richard (1785–1865), line-engraver; engraved *West's *Death of Nelson*, *Smirke's designs for *Don Quixote* and *Gil Blas*, and portraits.

GOLDMAN, Francis (d. 1688?), lexicographer. See GOULDMAN.

GOLDNEY, Philip (1802–1857), Indian officer; interpreter in the Truckee Hills' expedition; commanded brigade sent to subdue Oudh; in charge of Fyzabad at the outbreak of the Mutiny; shot at Begumjee.

GOLDSBOROUGH, Godfrey (1548–1604), bishop of Gloucester; major fellow, Trinity College, Cambridge, 1569; MA, 1569; DD, 1583; archdeacon of Worcester, 1579, of Shropshire, 1589; canon of Worcester, 1581; bishop of Gloucester, 1598–1604.

GOLDSBOROUGH, Sir John (d. 1693), captain in East Indian Navy; captured by Dutch in 1673; named chief governor of the East India Company, 1692; knighted, 1692; died of fever at Chatanati (Calcutta).

GOLDSBOROUGH, Richard (1821–1886), colonial wool-trader; emigrated from Bradford to Australia; settled at Melbourne, 1848; his wool business amalgamated in 1881 with Australian Agency and Banking Corporation, became a limited company, with Goldsborough as chief director.

GOLDSCHMIDT, Jenny Lind (1820–1887). See LIND, JOHANNA MARIA.

GOLDSCHMIDT, Otto (1829–1907), pianist and composer; born of Jewish parents at Hamburg; studied pianoforte at Leipzig under Mendelssohn, who greatly influenced him; in London, 1848; toured in America with Jenny *Lind, 1851; married her, 1852; settled in England, 1856; pianoforte professor at Royal Academy of Music, 1863; vice-principal, 1866–8; produced *Ruth* at Hereford Musical Festival, 1867; became conductor of newly founded 'Bach Choir', 1876; composed *Music, an Ode*, 1898, and works for pianoforte.

GOLDSMID, Abraham (1756?–1810), Jewish financier; with his brother Benjamin *Goldsmid started as bill-broker, *c.*1777; after 1792 largely engaged in government business; committed suicide in consequence of the failure of the government loan of 1810.

GOLDSMID, Anna Maria (1805–1889), philanthropist; daughter of Sir Isaac Lyon *Goldsmid; educated under *Campbell the poet, some of whose manuscripts she left to the British Museum.

GOLDSMID, Benjamin (1753?–1808), financier; brother of Abraham *Goldsmid; founder of the Royal Naval Asylum.

GOLDSMID, Sir Francis Henry (1808–1878), lawyer and politician; son of Sir Isaac Lyon *Goldsmid; first Jewish barrister (Lincoln's Inn); QC, 1858; wrote in favour of the abolition of Jewish disabilities; MP for Reading from 1860; spokesman of the Jewish community in parliament; established Jews' Infant School,

1841, and Anglo-Jewish Association, 1871; died from an accident at Waterloo Station.

GOLDSMID, Sir Frederic John (1818–1908), major-general; born at Milan; joined 37th Madras Native Infantry, 1839; served in China (1840), in Crimea, and in Indian Mutiny; arranged for telegraph construction along coast of Gwadar, 1861; superintended carrying of wires from Europe across Persia to India, 1864; director-general of Indo-European telegraph; negotiated Anglo-Persian Telegraph Treaty, 1865; CB, 1866; constructed telegraph line across whole of Persia; described the experience in *Travel and Telegraph* (1874); commissioner for delimitation of Persian and Baluchistan boundary, 1871; investigated Persian and Afghan claims to Seistan; recorded proceedings in *Eastern Persia, 1870–2* (2 vols., 1876); KCSI, 1871; controller of crown lands in Egypt, 1880–3; organized intelligence department in campaign of 1882; established administrative system in Congo, 1883; published *Life of Sir James Outram* (2 vols., 1880); accomplished oriental linguist; vice-president of Royal Asiatic Society, 1890–1905.

GOLDSMID, Henry Edward (1812–1855), Bombay civilian; educated at Haileybury; assistant to the revenue commissioner, Bombay, 1835; devised the revenue survey and assessment system of Western India; financial secretary to Bombay Government, 1848; chief secretary, 1854; died at Cairo.

GOLDSMID, Sir Henry Joseph D'Avigdor-, second baronet (1909–1976), politician and bullion broker. See D'AVIGDOR-GOLDSMID.

GOLDSMID, Sir Isaac Lyon (1778–1859), financier and philanthropist; nephew of Abraham *Goldsmid; made a large fortune in monetary operations with Portugal, Brazil, and Turkey; created baron da Palmeira of Portugal, 1846; prominent in foundation of University College, London, 1825, and of the North London Hospital, 1834; interested in prison reform and Robert *Owen's system; first Jewish baronet, 1841.

GOLDSMID-MONTEFIORE, Claude Joseph (1858–1938), Jewish biblical scholar and philanthropist. See MONTEFIORE.

GOLDSMITH, Francis (1613–1655), translator of Grotius's *Baptizatorum Puerorum Institutio* (1647) and *Sophompaneas* (1652); of Merchant Taylors' and Pembroke and St John's colleges, Oxford; BA.

GOLDSMITH, Hugh Colvill (1789–1841), lieutenant in the navy; grandson of Henry,

brother of Oliver *Goldsmith; moved and replaced the Logan Rock, Cornwall, 1824; died at sea in the West Indies.

GOLDSMITH, Lewis (1763?–1846), political writer and journalist; in Poland during War of Independence; attacked the powers who repressed the Revolution in *The Crimes of Cabinets* (1801); established in Paris, by arrangement with Bonaparte, *The Argus, or London reviewed in Paris*, 1802; imprisoned for refusing to print articles against English royal family, 1803; entrusted by Napoleon with offer of the Polish crown to the future Louis XVIII in exchange for renunciation of claims in France; escaped to England, 1809; conducted (1811–25) an anti-French weekly (*Anti-Gallican*, afterwards *British Monitor*) which advocated tyrannicide; published brochures against Napoleon; returning to Paris, 1825, became interpreter to Tribunal of Commerce, and published *Statistics of France* (1832); died in Paris.

GOLDSMITH, Oliver (1730?–1774), author; second son of an Irish clergyman; entered Trinity College, Dublin, as a sizar, 1744; sold his books and ran away to Cork on account of 'personal chastisement' received from his tutor at a supper, 1747; returned and graduated BA, 1749; led an unsettled life in Ireland till 1752, when he went to Edinburgh to study medicine; while on his way to the continent imprisoned at Newcastle on suspicion of recruiting for the French; thence went to Leiden; wandered about for a year in France, Switzerland, and Italy, 1755–6; said to have visited Voltaire at his house near Lausanne; reached London in destitution, 1756; physician in Southwark; usher at Peckham; met *Griffiths, for whose *Monthly Review* he wrote, 1757; failed to qualify for medical appointment in India, 1758; through his *Enquiry into the Present State of Polite Learning* (1759) became acquainted with Thomas *Percy, afterwards bishop of Dromore; contributed to *Critical Review* and other magazines; employed by John *Newbery, in whose *Public Ledger* his *Citizen of the World* (1762) appeared as 'Chinese Letters'; made acquaintance of Dr *Johnson, 1761, and afterwards became a member of his club; his *Traveller* (1764) highly praised by Johnson; introduced by the *Traveller* to his only patron, Lord *Clare; set up for the last time as a physician on the strength of his collected essays, 1765; *The Vicar of Wakefield* sold by Johnson for him, 1766 (96th edn., 1886); saved by the proceeds from arrest for debt; left Islington for the Temple; wrote for the booksellers a *History of Rome* (1769), lives of Thomas *Parnell and Henry *St John, Viscount Bolingbroke (1770), and an English history (1771); his *Goodnatured Man* rejected by *Garrick, but produced by *Colman at Covent Garden, 1768; his comedy *She stoops to Conquer* played at Covent Garden, 1773; went to Paris with the Hornecks, 1770; had altercation (1771) with Evans, the publisher of the *London Packet*, in which the insulting letter of 'Tom Tickle' appeared; *The Deserted Village* (1770), *The Retaliation* (1774), *The History of Greece* (1774), and *Animated Nature* (1774), were his last works. He was buried in the Temple Church, a monument at the expense of 'the Club' being placed in Westminster Abbey. Dublin editions of poems and plays appeared, (1777 and 1780), English (1831 and 1846); *Miscellaneous Works*, with memoir from Bishop Percy's materials (1831).

GOLDSTUECKER, Theodor (1821–1872), orientalist; of Jewish parentage; graduated at his native Königsberg, 1840; studied at Bonn; while at Paris assisted Burnouf in *L'Introduction à l'Histoire du Bouddhisme indien*; at Berlin helped A. von Humboldt with his *Kosmos*; came to England, 1850, to assist Professor H. H. *Wilson with new edition of his *Sanskrit Dictionary*; professor of Sanskrit at University College, London, 1852; member of Royal Asiatic Society; founded Sanskrit Text Society, 1866; attacked Böhtlingk, Roth, and Weber in a work on Panini, 1861; his *Literary Remains* issued (1879).

GOLDWELL, James (d. 1499), bishop of Norwich; DCL, All Souls College, Oxford, 1441; dean of Salisbury, 1463; secretary of state under Edward IV; negotiated peace with France, 1471; proctor at Rome, 1472; bishop of Norwich, 1472–99; completed the tower of his cathedral, and fitted up the choir and chapels; benefactor of All Souls.

GOLDWELL, Thomas (d. 1585), bishop of St Asaph; MA, All Souls College, Oxford, 1531; vicar of Cheriton, 1531; chaplain to Reginald *Pole, with whom he lived at Rome; attainted, 1539; returned to England, 1553; bishop of St Asaph, 1555–8; Romanized his diocese; attended Pole on his deathbed, 1558; escaped to the continent, 1559; superior of Theatines at Naples, 1561; the only English bishop at Council of Trent, 1562; attainted, 1562; vicar-general to Archbishop Borromeo, 1563; vicegerent for the cardinal-vicar at Rome, 1574; prevented by illness from heading the English mission; died in Rome; last of the English Romanist bishops.

GOLDWIN (or GOLDING), John (d. 1719), musical composer; organist of St George's Chapel, Windsor, 1697; master of the choristers, 1703; some of his sacred compositions published in *Boyce and *Arnold's *Cathedral Music* and John *Page's *Harmonia Sacra*.

GOLIGHTLY, Charles Pourtales (1807–1885), divine; educated at Eton and Oriel College, Oxford; MA, 1830; a subscriber to *Tracts for the Times*; disagreed with *Newman, and afterwards wrote largely against the Ritualists, especially attacking Cuddesdon College.

GOLLAN, John (1911–1977), general secretary of the Communist party of Great Britain; educated at James Clark School, Edinburgh; left before he was 14 and was soon involved in political activity; sentenced to six months' solitary confinement for selling socialist papers to soldiers, 1931, having joined the Communist party in the previous year; editor of Young Communist League's paper, *Challenge*, 1932; general secretary of the League, 1935; active in support of republican Spain; his book, *Youth in British Industry*, published by the Left Book Club, 1937; secretary, Communist party's North-East District Committee, 1939, and of Scottish Committee, 1941; published *Scottish Prospect* (1948); assistant general secretary of the party, 1947–9; assistant editor, *Daily Worker*, 1949–54; succeeded Harry *Pollitt as general secretary, 1956; involved in the party's programme, *The British Road to Socialism* (1950), and subsequent editions up to 1978; other publications include *The British Political System* (1954) and political pamphlets; firm upholder of the internationalist traditions of the party; published article, 'Socialist Democracy—Some Problems', in *Marxism Today* (1976), dealing with Stalinism and the development of socialist democracy.

GOLLANCZ, Sir Hermann (1852–1930), rabbi, Semitic scholar; born at Bremen; brother of Sir Israel *Gollancz; BA, University College, London, 1873; preacher at various synagogues in London, Manchester, and Dalston, 1876–92; first minister at Bayswater Synagogue, Harrow Road, 1892–1923; obtained rabbinic degree in Galicia, which caused great controversy, 1897; his degree finally recognized and the requirements for obtaining rabbinical diploma in Great Britain defined; Goldsmid professor of Hebrew, University College, London, 1902–23; knighted, 1923; undertook much public work outside interests of Jewish community.

GOLLANCZ, Sir Israel (1863–1930), scholar and man of letters; brother of Sir Hermann *Gollancz; BA, Christ's College, Cambridge, 1887; lecturer in English at Cambridge, 1896–1906; professor of English language and literature, King's College, London, 1903–30; a founder, original fellow, and secretary of British Academy, 1902–30; knighted, 1919; in the first rank as English and Shakespearian scholar.

GOLLANCZ, Sir **Victor** (1893–1967), publisher; nephew of Sir *Hermann and Sir Israel *Gollancz; educated at St Paul's School and New College, Oxford; commissioned in Northumberland Fusiliers, 1914; seconded to Repton School as master, 1916–18; began publishing with Benn Brothers, 1920; joined by Douglas *Jerrold, 1923; founded own firm, with Stanley *Morison as typographer, 1928; first success, R. C. *Sherriff's *Journey's End*; list included Daphne du Maurier, Elizabeth *Bowen, and Dorothy *Sayers; founded Left Book Club, 1936; good public speaker in support of nuclear disarmament and other causes; started Save Europe Now movement, 1945; published *A Year of Grace* (1950), *From Darkness to Light* (1956), and *Reminiscences of Affection* (1968); awarded Peace Prize of German Book Trade, 1960; knighted, 1965.

GOMERSALL, Robert (1602–1646?), dramatist and divine; MA, Christ Church, Oxford, 1621; BD, 1628; vicar of Thorncombe; published *The Tragedie of Lodovick Sforza* and *The Levites Revenge*, a poem (together, 1633).

GOMM, Sir **William Maynard** (1784–1875), field marshal; ensign, 1794; served with the 9th Foot in Holland, 1799; at Ferrol, 1800, and Hanover, 1805; captain, 1803; assistant quartermaster-general in Copenhagen expedition of 1807, and in Portugal, 1808; at Corunna with *Moore; on staff of Walcheren expedition, 1809; served in the Peninsula, 1810–14; lieutenant-colonel, 1812, having greatly distinguished himself at Salamanca, 1812; led his division in subsequent retreat on Portugal and advance to the Ebro; created KCB and transferred to Coldstream Guards; on staff at Quatre Bras and Waterloo, 1815; major-general, 1837; commander in Jamaica, 1839–42; governor of Mauritius, 1842–9; commander-in-chief in India, 1850–5; general, 1854; field marshal, 1868; constable of the Tower, 1872–5; hon. DCL, Oxford; hon. LL D, Cambridge; GCB; his letters from the Peninsula published (1881).

GOMME, Sir **Bernard de** (1620–1685), military engineer; served under Frederick Henry, prince of Orange; knighted by Charles I; engineer and quartermaster-general in royalist army, 1642–6; his plans of Marston Moor, Naseby, and second fight at Newbury in British Museum; as engineer-in-chief (1661) erected fortifications at Dunkirk, Portsmouth, and Plymouth, and made plans for works at Harwich and Dublin; surveyor-general of ordnance, 1685.

GOMPERTZ, Benjamin (1779–1865), mathematician and actuary; of Jewish extraction; president of the old Mathematical Society of Spitalfields; FRS, 1819; member of council of Astronomical Society, 1821–31; with Francis *Baily began catalogue of stars, 1822; last of the Newtonian school; published tracts on imaginary quantities and porisms, 1817–18; as actuary of Alliance Assurance Company (1824–48) propounded his law of human mortality, 1825.

GOMPERTZ, Lewis (d. 1861), lover of animals and inventor; brother of Benjamin *Gompertz; for some years honorary secretary of Society for Prevention of Cruelty to Animals, which he left when charged with Pythagoreanism; founded Animals' Friend Society, 1832, for which he edited *The Animals' Friend*; published *Mechanical Inventions and Suggestions on Land and Water Locomotion* (1850). His thirty-eight inventions included the expanding chuck still in use.

GONDIBOUR (or GOUDIBOUR), Thomas (fl. 1484), prior of Carlisle, 1484–1507.

GONELL, William (d. 1546?), friend of Erasmus; MA, Cambridge, 1488; 'public professor' at Cambridge; tutor to Sir Thomas *More's children; rector of Conington, 1517; possibly author of *Ad Erasmum Roterodamensem Epistolarum Liber*.

GONVILE, Edmund (d. 1351), founder of Gonville Hall (now Gonville and Caius College), Cambridge; steward of William, Earl Warren, and of the earl of Lancaster; rector of Thelnetham, Suffolk; rector of Rushworth, 1326, and Terrington St John, 1343; his foundation at Rushworth (1342) for a master and four priests suppressed, 1541. Gonville Hall, originally (1348) a purely theological foundation on the present site of Corpus Christi College, was removed by Bishop *Bateman and its statutes remodelled. It was enlarged by Dr John *Caius, 1558.

GOOCH, Benjamin (fl. 1775), surgeon to Shotesham Infirmary and (1771) consulting surgeon to Norwich Hospital; his works issued (1792).

GOOCH, Sir **Daniel,** first baronet (1816–1889), railway pioneer and inventor; trained in George *Stephenson & Edward *Pease's works at Newcastle upon Tyne; twenty-seven years locomotive superintendent of Great Western Railway; designed the best broad-gauge engines; invented 'the suspended link motion with the shifting radius link', 1843, and experimented with a dynamometer carriage; created baronet, 1866, for inauguration of telegraphic communication with America; as chairman, 1865–87, reorganized the Great Western Railway; MP, Cricklade, 1865–85.

GOOCH, George Peabody (1873–1968), historian; educated at Eton, King's College, London, and Trinity College, Cambridge; first class, historical tripos, 1894; Lightfoot scholar, 1895; studied in Berlin and Paris, 1895–6; taught at Mansfield House, the Working Men's College, and Toynbee Hall; distressed by South African War; Liberal MP, Bath, 1906–10; joint editor with J. Scott *Lidgett of *Contemporary Review*, 1911–60; assisted by Lord *Acton in preparation of *English Democratic Ideas in the Seventeenth Century* (1898); published *History and Historians in the Nineteenth Century* (1913) and *Germany and the French Revolution* (1920); criticized policy of Sir Edward *Grey (later Viscount Grey of Fallodon), leading to 1914–18 war; joined Sir Adolphus *Ward in editing the *Cambridge History of British Foreign Policy* (3 vols., 1922–3), and with H. W. V. *Temperley edited *British Documents on the Origins of the War* (13 vols., 1926–38); other publications include *Before the War: Studies in Diplomacy* (1936–8) and *Frederick the Great* (1947); honorary doctorates, Durham and Oxford; FBA, 1926; hon. fellow, Trinity College, Cambridge, 1935; CH, 1939; OM, 1963.

GOOCH, Robert (1784–1830), physician; descendant of Sir Thomas *Gooch; MD, Edinburgh, 1807; LRCP, 1812; practised in Berners Street as a gynaecologist; librarian to the king, 1826; contributed to the *Quarterly*; his 'Beguines and Nursing' appended to Southey's *Colloquies*; wrote on the diseases of women, 1829.

GOOCH, Sir Thomas, second baronet (1674–1754), bishop of Ely; MA and fellow, Caius College, Cambridge, 1698; chaplain to Queen Anne; archdeacon of Essex, 1714–37; master of Caius College, Cambridge, 1716–54; vice-chancellor of Cambridge, 1717; bishop of Bristol, 1737–8, of Norwich, 1738–48, Ely, 1748–54; succeeded as baronet, 1751.

GOOD, John Mason (1764–1827), physician and author; active member of Guy's Hospital Physical Society; practised at Sudbury; came to London, 1793; MRCS; published a *History of Medicine* (1795); edited *Critical Review*, and studied Spanish, Portuguese, and Russian, besides Sanskrit and oriental languages; left Unitarianism for the Anglican Church, 1807; FRS, 1808. Among his numerous works the chief are annotated translations of *The Song of Songs* (1803), *Lucretius* (1805–7, reissued by *Bohn), *Pantologia* (1802–13, in conjunction with Olinthus Gilbert *Gregory), and *The Book of Nature* (1826).

GOOD, Joseph Henry (1775–1857), architect; designed Vestry Hall and National School, Holborn, and the new hall of the Armourers' Company, Coleman Street; architect to the Pavilion, Brighton, and to the commission for building new churches; clerk of works to the Tower, 1830,

and Kensington Palace, 1831; an original fellow of the Institute of Architects.

GOOD, Thomas (1609–1678), master of Balliol College, Oxford; fellow of Balliol, 1630–58; MA, 1631; rector of Coreley, Shropshire; DD; prebendary of Hereford, 1660; master of Balliol, 1672–8; published *Firmianus and Dubitantius* (1674).

GOOD, Thomas Sword (1789–1872), painter, of the school of *Wilkie; excelled in pictures of boys, fishermen, and smugglers; exhibited at the principal London exhibitions, 1820–34.

GOOD, William (1527–1586), Jesuit; fellow of Corpus Christi College, Oxford, 1548; MA, 1552; headmaster and prebendary of Wells in Queen Mary's reign; professed Jesuit, 1577; missioner to Ireland, Sweden, and Poland; confessor to English College, Rome; published (1584), engraved pictures of English martyrs (formerly in the English College); reproduced, under supervision of Revd John *Morris, 1888; died at Naples.

GOODACRE, Hugh (d. 1553), primate of Ireland, 1553; previously vicar of Shalfleet and chaplain to Bishop *Poynet of Winchester.

GOODAL, Walter (1706?–1766), Scottish historical writer. See GOODALL.

GOODALL, Charles, the elder (1642–1712), physician; MD, Cambridge, 1670 incorporated from Leiden; admitted at Emmanuel College, Cambridge, 1658–9; FRCP, 1680; Gulstonian lecturer, 1685; twice Harveian orator; four times censor; president, 1708–12; physician to the Charterhouse, 1691; friend of Sydenham and Sloane; published treatises relating to the College of Physicians, 1684.

GOODALL, Charles, the younger (1671–1689), poet; son of Charles *Goodall the elder; of Eton and Merton College, Oxford; published *Poems and Translations* (1689).

GOODALL, Charlotte (d. 1830), actress; made a successful début at Bath (as Miss Stanton) in Rosalind, 1784; married Thomas *Goodall, 1787; first appeared at Drury Lane, 1788; acted there till 1798–9; Sir Harry Wildair and Katharine among her chief parts; divorced by her husband, 1813.

GOODALL, Edward (1795–1870), line-engraver; engraved many of *Turner's pictures and the vignettes for his illustrations of Samuel *Rogers's *Italy* and *Poems*; executed several of the *Engravings from Pictures in the National Gallery*; engraved figure-subjects after paintings by his son Frederick Goodall, RA, and plates for the *Art Journal* and other works.

GOODALL, Frederick (1822–1904), artist; taught by father, Edward *Goodall; exhibited at Royal Academy, 1839–1902; ARA, 1852; RA, 1862; early works show influence of Sir David *Wilkie, e.g. *The Tired Soldier* (1842) and *The Village Holiday* (1847); visits to Egypt (1858–9 and 1870) determined subject of later pictures, as *The Nubian Slave* (1864), *The Flight into Egypt* (1884), *Sheep Shearing in Egypt* (1892); also painted English landscape and portraits; showed technical ability but little inspiration; published gossiping *Reminiscences* (1902).

GOODALL, Frederick Trevelyan (1848–1871), painter; grandson of Edward *Goodall; Academy gold medallist with *Return of Ulysses*, 1869; died from an accident at Capri.

GOODALL, Howard (1850–1874), painter; brother of Frederick Trevelyan *Goodall; exhibited at the Royal Academy, 1870–3; died at Cairo.

GOODALL, Joseph (1760–1840), provost of Eton; fellow of King's College, Cambridge, 1782–8; Craven scholar, 1782; MA, 1786; headmaster of Eton, 1802–9; provost, 1809; canon of Windsor, 1808; founded scholarship at Eton.

GOODALL, Norman (1896–1985), missionary, statesman, and pioneer in ecumenism; educated in Birmingham and left school at 14 to work as office boy; clerk in Birmingham city treasurer's department; enlisted in RAMC, 1915; seconded to Ministry of Munitions; on staff of Department of National Service; admitted to Mansfield College, Oxford, 1919; honours degree in theology, 1922; ordained and appointed minister of Trinity Congregational church, Walthamstow, 1922–8; moved to church in New Barnet, 1928; on staff of London Missionary Society, 1936; travelled extensively in India and South Pacific; London secretary, International Missionary Council, 1944; worked for union with World Council of Churches up to 1961 when this was achieved; moderator, International Congregational Council, 1962–6; moderator, Free Church Federal Council, 1967; played influential part in establishment of United Reform Church; author of standard works on history of the ecumenical movement; visiting lecturer at colleges at home and overseas; D.Phil., Oxford, 1950; published autobiography, *Second Fiddle* (1979).

GOODALL, Samuel Granston (d. 1801), admiral; captured French privateer on the coast of Norway, 1760; present at reduction of Havana, 1762; commanded the *Defiance* at Ushant, 1778; in the *Valiant* at relief of Gibraltar, 1781, and in the actions off Dominica, 1782; commander-in-chief in Newfoundland, 1792; admiral, 1799.

GOODALL, Thomas (1767–1832?), 'admiral of Haiti'; ran away to sea and was wrecked on St Kitts, 1780; midshipman in Dominica action, 1782; married Charlotte Stanton (see GOODALL, CHARLOTTE), 1787; obtained divorce, 1813; took command of merchant ship bound for West Indies; captured by French, but allowed to escape; made numerous captures with a privateer before 1801; again captured by the French, 1803; escaped through Germany; assisted Christophe in Haiti.

GOODALL, Walter (1706?–1766), Scottish historical writer; sub-librarian of the Advocates' Library, Edinburgh, 1735; his examination (1754) of the letters of *Mary Stewart to *Bothwell, the first apology for the queen; assisted Keith in *Catalogue of Scots Bishops*; edited, among other works, *Fordun's *Scotichronicon* (1759).

GOODALL, Walter (1830–1889), water-colour painter; youngest son of Edward *Goodall; member of the Old Water-colour Society, 1862; some of his best work exhibited at Manchester, 1861; and his *Lottery Ticket* at Philadelphia Exhibition, 1876.

GOODCOLE, Henry (1586–1641), divine; attended prisoners in Newgate, and published their confessions.

GOODE, Francis (1797?–1842), divine; son of William *Goode the elder; of St Paul's School and Trinity College, Cambridge; seventh wrangler, 1820; fellow, 1822; MA, 1823; Bell university scholar, 1817; CMS missionary in India; published *The Better Covenant*.

GOODE, William, the elder (1762–1816), divine; MA, Magdalen Hall, Oxford, 1787; rector of St Andrew by the Wardrobe and St Anne, Blackfriars, 1795; president of Sion College, 1813; his *Essays on all the Scriptural Names and Titles of Christ* published by his son William (1822).

GOODE, William, the younger (1801–1868), divine; son of William *Goode the elder; of St Paul's School and Trinity College, Cambridge; BA, 1825; MA, 1828; rector of St Antholin, Watling Street, 1835–49; of All Hallows the Great, Thames Street, 1849–56; St Margaret's, Lothbury, 1856–60; dean of Ripon, 1860; edited *Christian Observer*; published, besides life of his father (1828), many evangelical tracts and pamphlets, and *The Divine Rule of Faith and Practice* (1842).

GOODE, Sir William Athelstane Meredith (1875–1944), journalist and financial adviser; represented Associated Press with Admiral Sampson throughout Spanish-American War, and in London, 1898–1904; managing editor, *Standard*, 1904–10; joint news editor, *Daily Mail*,

1911; director, cables department, Ministry of Food, 1917–19; British director, relief in Europe, 1919–20; reported on economic conditions in Central Europe, 1920; president, Austrian section, Reparation Commission, 1920–1; financial agent in London to Hungary, 1923–41; chief security officer, Ministry of Food, 1939–42; KBE, 1918.

GOODEN, James (1670–1730), Jesuit; rector of St Omer, 1722–8; superior of the house of probation, Ghent, 1728–30; issued at Liège *Trigonometria Plana et Sphaerica* (1704).

GOODEN, Peter (d. 1695), Roman Catholic controversialist; sent from Lisbon on the English mission; chaplain to duke of Berwick's regiment; disputed with Thomas Birch on the temporal power of the pope, and with *Stillingfleet and with William *Clagett on transubstantiation.

GOODEN, Stephen Frederick (1892–1955), engraver; educated at Rugby and Slade School; illustrated books in line-engraving, notably the Nonesuch *Bible* (5 vols., 1925–7); ARA, 1937; RA, 1946; CBE, 1942.

GOODENOUGH, Edmund (1785–1845), dean of Wells; son of Samuel *Goodenough; of Westminster School and Christ Church, Oxford; MA, 1807; DD, 1820; vicar of Warkworth, 1818; headmaster of Westminster, 1819–28; prebendary of York, Carlisle, and Westminster; prolocutor of lower house; dean of Wells, 1831–45; member of council of Royal Society, 1828; published sermons.

GOODENOUGH, Frederick Craufurd (1866–1934), banker; born in Calcutta; educated at Charterhouse and Zurich University; admitted solicitor; secretary of Barclay & Co. Ltd. (1896), general manager (1903), director (1913), chairman (1917); a convinced imperialist; formed Barclays Bank (Dominion, Colonial, and Overseas); founded London House as hall of residence in London chiefly for dominion students, 1930; member of Council of India, 1918–30; hon. DCL, Oxford, 1933.

GOODENOUGH, James Graham (1830–1875), commodore; son of Edmund *Goodenough; in the *Royal William* at siege of Bomarsund, 1854; gunnery lieutenant of *Hastings* at bombardment of Sveaborg, 1855; served in Chinese wars, 1857–8, and 1860–1; went to North America to report on naval gunnery, 1862; served on French Peasant Relief Fund, as naval attaché, and on Admiralty Designs Committee, 1870–2; commodore of the Australian Station, 1873–5; died at sea of tetanus from wound caused by a poisoned arrow at Santa Cruz.

GOODENOUGH, Richard (*fl.* 1686), Whig conspirator; under-sheriff of London, 1682; fined for riot and assault on the lord mayor, 1683; outlawed in connection with Rye House Plot, 1683; *Monmouth's 'secretary of state'; when taken after Sedgemoor turned king's evidence, 1685; afterwards lived in Ireland.

GOODENOUGH, Samuel (1743–1827), bishop of Carlisle; of Westminster and Christ Church, Oxford; MA, 1767; DCL, 1772; under-master at Westminster; conducted high-class school at Ealing; canon of Windsor, 1798; dean of Rochester, 1802; bishop of Carlisle, 1808–27; vice-president of Royal Linnean societies; wrote papers on the genus *Carex* and British *Fuci*; genus *Goodenia* named after him.

GOODENOUGH, Sir William Edmund (1867–1945), admiral; son of J. G. *Goodenough; entered navy, 1880; first captain of Dartmouth, 1905–7; appointed to *Southampton* as commodore, First (later Second) Light Cruiser Squadron, 1913–16; trained his captains to know his mind enabling them to act without instructions; fought at Heligoland Bight (1914), Dogger Bank (1915), and Jutland (1916); rear-admiral, Second Battle Squadron, 1916–18; superintendent, Chatham Dockyard, 1919–20; KCB, 1919; vice-admiral, 1920; commander-in-chief, Africa Station, 1920–2; the Nore, 1924–7; admiral, 1925; criticized Admiralty administration but declined post of second sea lord, 1925; GCB, 1930; president, Royal Geographical Society, 1930–3; chairman, British Sailors' Society.

GOODENOUGH, Sir William Macnamara, first baronet (1899–1951), banker; son of F. C. *Goodenough; educated at Wellington College and Christ Church, Oxford; joined Barclays Bank; local director, Oxford, 1923; director of bank, 1929; vice-chairman, 1934; deputy chairman, 1936; chairman, 1947–51; director, Barclays DCO, 1933; deputy chairman, 1937; chairman, 1943–7; chairman of Nuffield trusts for developing Oxford Medical School and founding (1937) Nuffield College, of Nuffield Provincial Hospitals Trust, and (1943) of Nuffield Foundation; chairman, Inter-Departmental Committee on Medical Schools, 1942–4; baronet, 1943; a founder of the Oxford Society and curator of University Chest; hon. LL D, Manchester.

GOODERE, Samuel (1687–1741), murderer; dismissed for misconduct in attack on San Sebastian, 1719; quarrelled with his elder brother, Sir John Dineley-Goodere, uncle of Sir J. *Dineley-Goodere, and having kidnapped him caused him to be strangled on board his vessel, the *Ruby*, in King's Road, Bristol, 1741; hanged with his accomplices.

GOODEVE, Sir Charles Frederick (1904–1980), industrial scientist; born in Neepawa, Canada; educated at Kelvin High School, Winnipeg, and Manitoba University; B.Sc. (honours in chemistry and physics), 1925; joined Royal Canadian Naval Volunteer Reserve; awarded 1851 Exhibition scholarship at University College, London, 1927; M.Sc., 1927; assistant lecturer, 1928; lecturer in physical chemistry, 1930; reader, 1937; D.Sc., 1936; FRS, 1940; continued in RNVR and appointed to HMS *Vernon*, 1939; wartime work, including conquest of magnetic mine by degaussing, described in *The Secret War* (1956) by Gerald Pawle; attached to new department of miscellaneous weapon development, 1940–2; OBE, 1941; deputy controller, research and development, Admiralty; set up Royal Naval Scientific Service; knighted, 1946; US Medal of Freedom with silver palm; director, British Iron and Steel Research Association, 1945; founded Operational Research Club and *Operational Research Quarterly*; president, Iron and Steel Institute, 1961–2 and Faraday Society, 1950–2; vice-president, Royal Society, 1968–70; held similar posts and directorships of three industrial companies and number of honorary doctorates.

GOODEY, Tom (1885–1953), nematologist; educated at Northampton Grammar School and Birmingham University; B.Sc., 1908; worked at Rothamsted Experimental Station and zoology department, Birmingham; at London School of Tropical Medicine, 1921–6; at Institute of Agricultural Parasitology, 1926–47; head of nematology department, Rothamsted, 1947–52; published *Plant Parasitic Nematodes and the Diseases They Cause* (1933) and *Soil and Freshwater Nematodes* (1951); sang professionally under name of Roger Clayson; FRS, 1947; OBE, 1950.

GOODFORD, Charles Old (1812–1884), provost of Eton; fellow of King's College, Cambridge; MA, 1839; DD, 1853; headmaster of Eton, 1853–62; provost, 1862–84; edited Terence, 1854.

GOODGROOME, John (1630?–1704?), composer, lutenist, singer, and teacher; gentleman of the Chapel Royal in three reigns; four airs by him published in *Playford's Select Airs* (1669), and three in *Musical Companion* (1673).

GOODHART, Arthur Lehman (1891–1978), academic lawyer and Anglophile; born in New York of wealthy Jewish parents; educated at Hotchkiss School, Yale University, and Trinity College, Cambridge; rejected for service with British forces, 1914; became member of American forces when USA joined the war; counsel to American mission to Poland, 1919; published *Poland and the Minority Races* (1920); called to bar (Inner Temple), 1919; fellow of Corpus Christi College, Cambridge, and lecturer in jurisprudence; edited *Cambridge Law Journal*, 1921–5; editor, *Law Quarterly Review*, 1926; as member, Law Revision Committee, helped to promote improvements in various branches of the law; professor of jurisprudence, Oxford, 1931–51; publications include *Essays in Jurisprudence and the Common Law* (1931); chairman, Southern Price Regulations Committee, 1940–51; master, University College, Oxford, 1951–63; generously endowed the college; honorary degrees from twenty universities; KC, 1943; FBA, 1952; hon. fellow, Trinity College, Cambridge; hon. bencher, Lincoln's Inn, 1938; made lecture tours in USA during 1939–45 war; hon. KBE, 1948; never took naturalization as British citizen though almost the whole of his working life was spent in Britain.

GOODHART-RENDEL, Harry Stuart (1887–1959), architect; grandson of Lord Rendel who left him the life interest of his fortune, 1913; educated at Eton and Mulgrave Castle, Yorkshire; Mus.B., Trinity College, Cambridge, 1909; began architectural practice, 1909; had comprehensive knowledge of Victorian architecture from which his own work was a vigorous and original development; became Roman Catholic in middle life; later work mainly concerned with churches; his buildings less important than his devoted services to the profession as a scholarly personality of eloquence and wit; president, Architectural Association, 1924–5; of Royal Institute of British Architects, 1937–9, of Design and Industries Association, 1948–50; Slade professor of fine art, Oxford, 1933–6; director, Architectural Association School of Architecture, 1936–8; CBE, 1955; publications include *Nicholas Hawksmoor* (1924); governor, Sadler's Wells.

GOODHUGH, William (1799?–1842), compiler of part of a Bible cyclopaedia, and several linguistic handbooks.

GOODINGE, Thomas (1746–1816), divine; BA, Trinity College, Oxford, 1766; DCL, 1778; MA, Cambridge, 1778; headmaster of the King's School, Worcester, 1768–76; headmaster of Leeds Grammar School, 1779; rector of Cound, Shropshire, 1789.

GOODMAN, Cardell (or **Cardonnell**) (1649?–1699), adventurer; BA, St John's College, Cambridge, 1670; page of the backstairs to Charles II; afterwards an actor, winning his chief success as Julius Caesar and Alexander; pardoned by James II for a highway robbery; paramour of the duchess of *Cleveland, but fined for attempt to poison her children; expert at ombre; bribed by friends of *Fenwick not to turn evidence against him, 1697; died in France.

GOODMAN, Christopher (1520?–1603), Puritan divine; BA, Brasenose College, Oxford, 1541; senior student, Christ Church, 1547; MA, 1544; BD, 1551; Margaret professor of divinity; friend and colleague of *Knox at Geneva, 1555; issued violent tract against female government, 1558; at Edinburgh, 1559, one of the council concerning religion; minister of Ayr and St Andrews; chaplain to Sir Henry *Sidney in Ireland, 1566; deprived of the benefice of Alford for nonconformity, and obliged to recant his published opinions, 1571; afterwards forbidden to preach; refused subscription to the articles and service-book, 1584; visited on his deathbed at Chester by Archbishop *Ussher.

GOODMAN, Gabriel (1529?–1601), dean of Westminster; MA, Christ's College, Cambridge, 1553; DD, St John's, 1564; fellow of Christ's, 1552–4, of Jesus, c.1554–5; chaplain to Sir William *Cecil (Lord Burghley); dean of Westminster, 1561–1601; member of Ecclesiastical Commission; one of Burghley's executors; founded Christ's Hospital and the Grammar School, Ruthin, and left benefactions to various Cambridge colleges; translated 1 Corinthians in 'Bishops' Bible', and assisted in William *Morgan's Welsh version and in *Camden's *Britannia*.

GOODMAN, Godfrey (1583–1656), bishop of Gloucester; nephew of Gabriel *Goodman; of Westminster and Trinity College, Cambridge; MA and BD; vicar of Stapleford Abbots, Essex, 1606–20; chaplain to the queen-consort, *Anne of Denmark, 1616; dean of Rochester, 1621; bishop of Gloucester, 1625–43; reprimanded by convocation for a sermon on the real presence, 1626; charged with ritualistic practices; his election to the see of Hereford nullified by the advice of *Laud, 1633, on account of his negligence; refused to sign the new canons (1640), until deprived by convocation and imprisoned; imprisoned by the House of Commons, 1642–3, for signing the canons; compelled to retire from Gloucester, 1643; Laud's treatment of him in the matter of the canons the ninth article of his impeachment; shown by his will to have been a Roman Catholic; his *Court of James I* (a defence of the king) printed by J. S. *Brewer (1839); his *Fall of Man proved by the Light of his Naturall Reason* (1616) quoted by *Southey.

GOODMAN, Julia (1812–1906), portrait painter; born Salaman; exhibited at Royal Academy, 1838–1901; painted over 1,000 portraits in oils or pastels.

GOODMAN, Sir Stephen Arthur (d. 1844), major-general; served with 48th Foot at reduction of Malta and in the Peninsula, 1809–14, being some time acting adjutant-general; deputy judge-advocate in the Netherlands and at Paris, 1814–15; created CB and KH; colonial secretary of Berbice, 1819–44, and vendue-master, 1821–44.

GOODRICH, Edwin Stephen (1868–1946), zoologist; educated in Pau; entered Slade School, 1888; assistant to (Sir) E. R. *Lankester and commoner of Merton College, Oxford, 1892; first class, natural science, 1895; fellow, 1900; Aldrichian demonstrator in comparative anatomy, 1898; Linacre professor, 1921–45; researched and travelled widely; distinguished between the nephridium and coelomoduct; established true nature of differences between various types of fish-scales; publications include *Cyclostomes and Fishes* (1909), *Living Organisms* (1924), and *Studies on the Structure and Development of Vertebrates* (1930); FRS, 1905.

GOODRICH, Richard (d. 1562), ecclesiastical commissioner under Edward VI and Elizabeth; nephew of Thomas *Goodrich, bishop of Ely; ancient of Gray's Inn, 1542; attorney of the courts of augmentations and of ward and liveries; MP, Grimsby, 1545.

GOODRICH (or GOODRICKE), Thomas (d. 1554), bishop of Ely and lord chancellor; fellow of Jesus College, Cambridge, 1510; MA, 1514; rector of St Peter Cheap, London, 1529; DD; chaplain of Henry VIII; bishop of Ely, 1534–54; ecclesiastical commissioner under Henry VIII and Edward VI; a compiler of the 'Bishops' Book', 1537, and the first Book of Common Prayer; privy councillor, 1547; joined opposition to *Somerset; commissioner for trial of *Gardiner, 1550; ambassador to Henry II of France, 1551; lord chancellor, 1552–3.

GOODRICKE, Sir Henry, second baronet (1642–1705), MP, Boroughbridge, 1673–9 and 1689–1705; envoy-extraordinary to Madrid, 1678–82; lieutenant-general of ordnance, 1689–1702; privy councillor, 1680.

GOODRICKE, John (1764–1786), astronomer; Copley medallist, 1783, for discovery of the period and law of Algol's changes; discovered variability of β Lyrae and of δ Cephei, 1784; FRS, 1786.

GOODSIR, John (1814–1867), anatomist; studied at St Andrews and Edinburgh; practised with his father at Anstruther; lived at Edinburgh, 1840, with Edward *Forbes; curator of College of Surgeons, 1841; curator of university museum and demonstrator in anatomy, 1843–6; professor of anatomy, 1846–67; ruined his health by careless living; wrote thirty scientific papers, 1838–46, including those on the growth of teeth (1839) and on 'Centres of Nutrition'; his *Anatomical Memoirs* issued 1868; Virchow dedicated to him his *Cellular-Pathologie* (1859).

GOODSON, Richard, the elder (d. 1718), organist of Christ Church and New College, Oxford; Oxford professor of music, 1682; Mus.-Bac., Oxford.

GOODSON, Richard, the younger (d. 1741), organist of New College and Christ Church, Oxford; professor of music, 1718; Mus.Bac., Oxford, 1716; son of Richard *Goodson the elder.

GOODSONN, William (*fl.* 1634–1662), vice-admiral; captain of the *Entrance* in the fight off Portland, 25 Jan. 1653; rear-admiral of the blue in the battles of June and July 1653; vice-admiral under *Penn, 1654, with him at attempt on Hispaniola, and capture of Jamaica, 1655; took part in siege of Dunkirk, 1658.

GOODWIN, Arthur (1593?–1643), friend of *Hampden at Oxford; BA, Magdalen College, Oxford, 1614; member of the Inner Temple, 1613; MP, Chipping Wycombe, 1620–4, Aylesbury, 1625–6; colleague of Hampden as MP for Buckinghamshire in Long Parliament, 1640; Parliamentary commander-in-chief in Buckinghamshire, 1643; present at Hampden's death.

GOODWIN, Charles Wycliffe (1817–1878), Egyptologist; brother of Harvey *Goodwin, bishop of Carlisle; fellow of St Catharine Hall, Cambridge; MA, 1842; barrister, Lincoln's Inn, 1848; last editor of *Literary Gazette* and *Parthenon*; assistant-judge in Supreme Court of China and Japan, 1865; acting judge, 1868–78; died at Shanghai. His 'Mosaic Cosmogony' was the only lay contribution to *Essays and Reviews* (1860). He collaborated with Chabas in *Voyage d'un Egyptien en Phénicie . . . etc., au XIVe Siècle avant notre ère* (1866), and contributed to his *Mélanges Egyptologiques* (1864), besides editing *Story of Saneha* (1866) and Anglo-Saxon texts.

GOODWIN, Christopher (*fl.* 1542), author of *The Chaunce of the Dolorous Lover*, printed by Wynkyn de *Worde (1520) and *The Maydens Dreme* (1542), two poems.

GOODWIN, Francis (1784–1835), architect; exhibited drawings at Royal Academy, 1822–34; designed Town Hall and Assembly Rooms, Manchester (now Free Reference Library), Derby Gaol, Bradford Exchange, and Leeds and Salford markets; built churches in the Midlands;

published *Plans of the new House of Commons*, pronounced the best sent in (1833); his *Domestic Architecture* (1833–4) republished as *Rural Architecture* (1835).

GOODWIN, George (*fl.* 1620), Latin verse-writer.

GOODWIN, Harvey (1818–1891), bishop of Carlisle; educated at Gonville and Caius College, Cambridge; second wrangler and second Smith's prizeman, 1840; MA, 1843; DD, 1859; mathematical lecturer, 1840; fellow, 1841; honorary fellow, 1880; ordained deacon, 1842; priest, 1844; assisted in founding Ecclesiological Society, 1848; dean of Ely, 1858; bishop of Carlisle, 1869 till death; hon. DCL, Oxford, 1885; published mathematical and religious treatises.

GOODWIN, James Ignatius (1603?–1667), Jesuit missioner; professor of moral theology and controversy at Liège.

GOODWIN, John (1594?–1665), republican divine; fellow of Queens' College, Cambridge, 1617; MA, 1619; vicar of St Stephen's, Coleman Street, 1633–45; after his ejection set up an Independent congregation there; assisted in drafting London petition against the canons of 1640; held controversies with London ministers on justification, 1638–42, maintaining an Arminian position; published *Anti-Cavalierisme* (1642); attacked divine right in *Os Ossorianum* (1643), written against the bishop of Ossory, and militant Presbyterianism in Θεομαχία (1644) and *Hagiomastix* (1646); translated and edited (1648 and 1651) part of the *Stratagemata Satanae* of Jacobus *Acontius, an early advocate of toleration; applauded *Pride's Purge in *Might and Right well met* (1648); offered spiritual advice to Charles I; in Υβριστοδίκαι (1649, publicly burnt, 1660), defended the proceedings against Charles I; ordered into custody at the Restoration, but finally indemnified; published work in favour of general redemption, 1651 (reprinted 1840), and tracts against the Baptists, Fifth-Monarchy men, and *Cromwell's 'Triers'.

GOODWIN, Philip (d. 1699), divine; MA, St John's College, Cambridge, 1630; one of Cromwell's 'Triers'; vicar of Watford, 1645–61; rector of Liston, 1673; published *The Mystery of Dreames* (1658) and theological works.

GOODWIN, Thomas, the elder (1600–1680), Independent divine; BA, Christ's College, Cambridge, 1616; MA, Catharine Hall, 1620; fellow; DD, Oxford, 1653; pastor of English Church at Arnheim, 1639–40; member of Westminster Assembly, 1643, but (1644) joined the 'dissenting brethren', and became their leader; chaplain to Council of State, 1649; president of Magdalen College, Oxford, 1650; a commissioner for inventory of Westminster Assembly, 1650, and approbation of preachers, 1653; attended *Cromwell on his deathbed; with John *Owen drew up amended Westminster Confession, 1658; founded Independent congregation in London, 1660; his works issued posthumously (reprinted, 1861, and condensed, 1847–50).

GOODWIN, Thomas, the younger (1650?–1716?), son of Thomas *Goodwin the elder; Independent minister in London and Pinner; edited his father's works, and published *History of Reign of Henry V* (1704).

GOODWIN (or GODWIN), Timothy (1670?–1729), archbishop of Cashel; MA, St Edmund Hall, Oxford, 1697; chaplain to duke of *Shrewsbury; archdeacon of Oxford, 1707–14; bishop of Kilmore, 1714–27; archbishop of Cashel, 1727–9.

GOODWIN, William (d. 1620), dean of Christ Church, Oxford; scholar of Westminster; DD, 1602; chancellor of York, 1605–11; dean of Christ Church, 1611–20; archdeacon of Middlesex, 1616; chaplain to James I; vice-chancellor of Oxford, 1614, 1615, 1617, and 1618.

GOODWYN, Edmund (1756–1829), medical writer; MD, Edinburgh; published two medical works.

GOODYEAR, Joseph (1799–1839), engraver; engraved *Eastlake's *Greek Fugitives* for *Finden's *Gallery*.

GOODYER (or GOODIER), Sir Henry (1534–1595), colonel; imprisoned in Tower, 1571–2, for complicity in *Norfolk's intrigue on behalf of *Mary Queen of Scots; served in Low Countries, 1585–6; knighted, 1586; colonel; patron of Michael *Drayton.

GOODYER (or GOODIER), Sir Henry (1571–1627), literary patron; son of Sir Henry *Goodyer (1534–1595); friend of John *Donne; probably knighted in Ireland, 1599; gentleman of privy chamber, 1605; famous for his hospitality to literary men. Verses by him appear in several contemporary publications.

GOOGE, Barnabe (1540–1594), poet; kinsman of Sir William *Cecil, who employed him in Ireland, 1574–85; published *Eglogs, Epytaphes, and Sonnetes* (1563, reprinted, 1871), and translations, including Heresbachius's *Foure Bookes of Husbandrie* (1577).

GOOKIN, Daniel (1612?–1687), writer on the American Indians; nephew of Sir Vincent *Gookin; went to Virginia with his father; obtained grants of land, 1637 and 1642; settled at Boston (Massachusetts), 1644; founded Roxbury School, 1646; removed to Cambridge, Massachusetts, and became speaker of the house, 1651;

sent by *Cromwell to settle Jamaica, 1655; employed financially at Dunkirk, 1659; returned to America, 1660, with the regicides, Edward *Whalley and William *Goffe, whom he protected; superintendent of Massachusetts Indians, 1661–87; major-general of the colony, 1681; buried at Cambridge; his *Historical Collections of the Indians in New England* printed by Massachusetts Historical Society (1792).

GOOKIN, Captain Robert (d. 1667), Parliamentarian; brother of Vincent *Gookin; served parliament in Ireland, and received grants of land.

GOOKIN, Sir Vincent (1590?–1638), anti-Irish writer; knighted, 1631; created disturbance in Munster by publishing letter to Lord Deputy *Wentworth attacking the Irish nation, 1634; fled to England on issue of warrant for his arrest. His case raised the question of the judicial powers of the Irish parliament.

GOOKIN, Vincent (1616?–1659), surveyor-general of Ireland; son of Sir Vincent *Gookin; represented Irish constituencies in *Cromwell's parliaments; published pamphlets (1655) deprecating enforcement of orders for transplantation of Irish to Connaught.

GOOLD, Thomas (1766?–1846), Irish master in Chancery; barrister, 1791; had large *nisi prius* practice; king's serjeant, 1830; master in Chancery, 1832; opposed the Union.

GOOSSENS, Sir Eugene (1893–1962), conductor and composer of music; educated at the Muzick-Conservatorium, Bruges, the Liverpool College of Music, and the Royal College of Music, London, 1907; began professional career as violinist in Queen's Hall Orchestra under Sir Henry J. *Wood, 1912; began conducting career with various opera companies, 1916; conducted for Diaghilev Ballet; choral work, *Silence*, performed at Gloucester Three Choirs' Festival, 1922; conductor, Rochester Philharmonic Orchestra, New York State, 1923–31; conductor, Cincinnati Symphony Orchestra, 1931–47; chevalier of Legion of Honour, 1934; conducted first performance of his own opera, *Don Juan de Mañara*, at Covent Garden, 1937; conductor, Sydney Symphony Orchestra, 1947–56; knighted, 1955; other compositions include *The Apocalypse*, a choral work, and *Judith*, another opera; published autobiography, *Overture and Beginners* (1951).

GOOSTRY, Mrs Amy (1830–1897), actress. See SEDGWICK.

GORANUS, Gabhran (*fl.* 538–560?), king of Scotland; being fourth king of Dalriada; succeeded his brother, *Congallus I, 538.

GORDON, Lord **Adam** (1726?–1801), general; son of Alexander, second duke of *Gordon; MP, Aberdeenshire, 1754–68, Kincardineshire, 1774–88; served with Guards in *Bligh's expedition, 1758; colonel of 66th in Jamaica, 1762–6; commander of forces in Scotland, 1782–98; general, 1796.

GORDON, Sir **Adam de** (d. 1305), warrior. See GURDON.

GORDON, Sir **Adam de** (d. 1333), statesman and warrior; accompanied Edward I to England to arrange for pacification of Scotland, 1304; justiciar of Scotland, 1310–14; granted barony of Stitchel by Robert *Bruce, 1315; with Mabinson carried to Avignon letter asserting Scottish independence, 1320; obtained lordship of Strathbogie, which he named Huntly; killed at Halidon Hill.

GORDON, Sir **Adam de** (d. 1402), warrior; prominent in raid of Roxburgh, 1377, and subsequent raids; present at Otterburn, 1388; fell at Homildon Hill. His daughter Elizabeth was ancestress of the earls of Huntly and the dukes of Gordon and Sutherland.

GORDON, Adam Lindsay (1833–1870), Australian poet; joined Australian Mounted Police, 1853; member for Victoria in House of Assembly, 1865; noted steeplechaser; committed suicide; his three volumes of verse edited by Marcus *Clarke, 1880.

GORDON, Alexander, third earl of Huntly (d. 1524), rendered valuable assistance in reduction of the Western Isles, 1504; sheriff and castellan of Inverness, 1509, with jurisdiction over Ross and Caithness; led Scots vanguard at Flodden, 1513; member of the queen-mother's council; adherent of Albany; lieutenant of Scotland, 1518, and twice member of the Council of Regency.

GORDON, Alexander (1516?–1575), bishop-elect of Galloway and titular archbishop of Athens; brother of George *Gordon, fourth earl of Huntly; favourite of his half-brother, King James V; administrator of Caithness, 1544; his election as archbishop of Glasgow overruled in favour of James *Beaton, 1551; bishop of the Isles, 1553; abbot of Inchaffray and Icolmkill; elected to see of Galloway, 1558; joined the reformers, 1560; demanding title of superintendent of Galloway; privy councillor and extraordinary lord of session, 1566; resumed title of bishop; temporized between *Mary Queen of Scots and the lords; resigned his see in favour of his son John, 1568, but retained 'supervision'; inhibited for signing bond for restoration of Mary, 1569; her commissioner in England, 1570–1; attended *Kirk-caldy of Grange's parliament, 1571; ordered to do penance, 1573.

GORDON, Alexander, eleventh or twelfth earl of Sutherland (1552–1594), succeeded John *Gordon, tenth or eleventh earl, 1567; engaged in struggle with earls of Caithness to secure possession of his earldom; married (1573), as his second wife, Jean Gordon, *Bothwell's divorced wife.

GORDON, Alexander (1587–1654), of Earlston, Covenanter; friend of Samuel *Rutherford; fined for refusing to present Episcopalian curate; MP for Galloway, 1641–9; opposed ecclesiastical policy of Charles I, who called him 'Earl of Earlston'.

GORDON, Sir **Alexander** (1650–1726), of Earlston, Covenanter, grandson of Alexander *Gordon (1587–1654); after Bothwell Brigg (1680) escaped to Holland; arrested at Newcastle upon Tyne, 1683, and examined at Edinburgh concerning the Rye House Plot; imprisoned till 1689; his estates restored at the Revolution.

GORDON, Alexander, second duke of Gordon (1678?–1728), Jacobite; when marquis of Huntly brought 2,300 men to *James Edward, the Old Pretender, at Perth; at Sheriffmuir, 1715; submitted and received pardon; succeeded to dukedom, 1716; visited and corresponded with king of Prussia and grand duke of Tuscany; received presents from Pope Clement XII.

GORDON, Alexander (1692?–1754?), antiquary; MA, Aberdeen; studied music in Italy, and became known as 'Singing Sandie'; travelled in Scotland and northern England; published *Itinerarium Septentrionale* (1726), with supplement (1732); also *Lives of Alexander VI and Cæsar Borgia* (1729) and translation of *De Amphitheatro* of Maffei (1730); secretary to Society for the Encouragement of Learning, Society of Antiquaries (1736), and the Egyptian Society; went to South Carolina, 1741, as secretary to the governor; died there.

GORDON, Alexander, fourth duke of Gordon (1743–1827), described by Kaimes as the greatest subject in Britain; Scottish representative peer, 1767; created a British peer, 1784; lord keeper of Scotland; raised regiments for American and Revolutionary wars; wrote, 'There is Cauld Kail in Aberdeen'.

GORDON, Sir **Alexander** (1786–1815), lieutenant-colonel; brother of George Hamilton-*Gordon, fourth earl of Aberdeen; aide-de-camp to his uncle, Sir David *Baird, at the Cape, 1806, at Copenhagen, 1807, and in Spain, 1808–9; employed by Beresford in negotiations at Buenos Aires; lieutenant-colonel, 1813; aide-de-camp to Wellington in the Peninsula and in Belgium; KCB; mortally wounded at Waterloo.

GORDON, Andrew (1712–1751), natural philosopher; professor of philosophy at Erfurt, 1737; gained great reputation as an electrician; the first to use a cylinder; published, among other works, *Phaenomena Electricitatis exposita* (1744).

GORDON, Archibald (1812–1886), inspector-general of hospitals; MD, Edinburgh, 1834; surgeon in Sutlej and Punjab campaigns; principal medical officer of second division at Sebastopol; chief medical officer in China, 1857, and Oudh, 1858–9; CB; inspector-general, 1867–70; knight of the Legion of Honour.

GORDON, Arthur Charles Hamilton-, first Baron Stanmore (1829–1912), colonial governor; son of fourth earl of *Aberdeen; MA, Trinity College, Cambridge; lieutenant-governor of New Brunswick, 1861; governor of Trinidad, 1866–70; Mauritius, 1871–4; Fiji, 1875–80; New Zealand, 1880–3; Ceylon, 1883–90; KCMG, 1871; GCMG, 1878; baron, 1893.

GORDON, Charles, first earl of Aboyne (d. 1681), fourth son of George *Gordon, second marquis of Huntly; created Baron Gordon of Strathavon and Glenlivat, and earl of Aboyne, 1660; built Aboyne Castle.

GORDON, Charles, second earl of Aboyne (d. 1702), allowed to sit in Scottish parliament on declaring himself a Protestant, 1698.

GORDON, Sir Charles (1756–1835), governor of St Lucia; served in the American War; assisted Brunswick in capture of Amsterdam, 1787, and as British commissioner, 1791–2; lieutenant-colonel of 41st, 1787; knight of Prussian Order of Military Merit, 1790; took part in capture of Martinique and St Lucia, 1793; governor of St Lucia; dismissed from governorship for extortion, 1794.

GORDON, Charles George (1833–1885), 'Chinese Gordon'; entered Royal Engineers, 1852; wounded in trenches before Sebastopol, 1855; took part in attack on the Redan, 1855; received Legion of Honour and Turkish Medal; assisted in delimitation of Russo-Turkish boundaries in Europe and Asia, 1856–8; promoted for services in Chinese War, 1860–2; explored section of Great Wall of China; appointed to command Chinese forces against the Taipings in the Kiangsoo district, 1863; captured Soochow, but retired on account of Li Hung Chang's breach of faith in putting to death rebel leaders (Wangs); refused the honours and gifts offered by the emperor, 1864; induced to resume the command; in four months completed reduction of the rebels by storming of Chanchu-fu, 27 Apr. 1864; made mandarin of the first class, but again refused money present; lieutenant-colonel and CB, 1865; British member of commission for improving navigation of Sulina mouth of the Danube, 1871; governor of equatorial provinces of Africa (Egyptian), 1874–6, organizing a letter-post between Cairo and the Albert Nyanza, and establishing by personal observation the course of the Victoria Nile into Lake Albert; thwarted by Ismail Pasha in his efforts to suppress the slave trade, resigning in consequence, 1876; returned, 1877, as governor-general of the Sudan and of the equatorial provinces and the Red Sea littoral; conquered and pacified Darfour; overawed Suleiman, the slave-trader, in personal interview, 1877, and completely suppressed the slave trade, 1878; failed to come to an understanding with Abyssinia, where he was for a time a prisoner; returned to England, 1880; went to India as secretary to the marquis of Ripon, 1880; resigned, 1880; induced Chinese government to resume friendly relations with Russia, 1880; commanding Royal Engineer and head of the troops in Mauritius, 1881–2; major-general, 1882; accepted command of colonial forces in South Africa, 1882; resigned when his negotiations with Masupha, the Basuto chief, were interrupted by the treacherous attack instigated by Sauer, secretary for native affairs, 1882; in Palestine, 1883; had agreed to go to the Congo for the king of Belgium, but was despatched by the British government (1884) to rescue Egyptian garrisons in the Sudan previous to its abandonment; was appointed at Cairo governor-general of the Sudan, with orders to organize an independent government; his requests for the co-operation of Zebehr and the assistance of Turkish troops refused; hemmed in by the Mahdi at Khartoum, was the only Englishman there after the murder of his companions Colonel Stewart and Frank Power; killed, after having sustained a siege of 317 days, succour being sent from England too late. His memory is perpetuated by statues in London, Chatham, and Khartoum, and by the Gordon Boys' Homes. His Chinese diaries, Khartoum journals, and several volumes of letters have been published.

GORDON, Charles William (1860–1937), divine, and author under the pseudonym of Ralph Connor; born and educated in Ontario; ordained Presbyterian minister, 1890; minister of St Stephen's Church, Winnipeg, 1894–1936; CMG, 1935; his romantic novels with religious motif such as *The Sky Pilot* (1899) and *The Man from Glengarry* (1901) were Canadian best-sellers.

GORDON, Duke (1739–1800), assistant librarian to Edinburgh University, 1763–1800; MA, Edinburgh, 1800.

GORDON, Edward Strathearn, Baron Gordon (1814–1879), lord of appeal; LL B, Glasgow and Edinburgh; called to Scottish bar, 1835; solicitor-general for Scotland, 1866–7; QC, 1868; lord-advocate, 1867–8 and 1874–6; dean of faculty, 1868–74; MP, Thetford, 1867–8, Glasgow and Aberdeen universities, 1869–76; privy councillor, 1874; lord of appeal, 1876–9.

GORDON, Elizabeth, duchess of Gordon (1794–1864), daughter of Alexander Brodie; married, 1813, George *Gordon, marquis of Huntly, afterwards fifth duke of Gordon; joined Free Church of Scotland, 1846.

GORDON, George, second earl of Huntly (d. 1502?), lord high chancellor of Scotland; succeeded to earldom, 1470; commissioner for peace with England, 1484; supported *James III against the nobles, 1487; lord justiciary north of Forth, 1488; made privy councillor by *James IV, and lieutenant, north of Esk, 1491; married Princess Annabella, daughter of *James I; divorced, as being, by a prior marriage, within the forbidden degrees of affinity, 1471; chancellor of Scotland, 1498–1501.

GORDON, George, fourth earl of Huntly (1514–1562), grandson of Alexander *Gordon, third earl of Huntly; succeeded as earl, 1524; brought up with *James V by Angus; privy councillor, 1535; one of the regents, 1536–7; defeated English at Hadden Rig, 1542; supported Cardinal *Beaton against *Arran, and concerted with him carrying off the young queen, 1543; as lieutenant of the north crushed the Camerons and Macdonalds, 1544; lord chancellor, 1546; defeated and captured by *Somerset at Pinkie, 1547, after offering single combat; temporarily supported English in Scotland, but afterwards (1548) favoured French alliance; disgraced and imprisoned, 1554, owing to the queen regent's jealousy of his power over the north; joined lords of the congregation against her, 1560; made privy councillor on the arrival of *Mary Queen of Scots, but his earldom of Moray given to her half-brother; died at Corrichie in arms against the royal authority. His body was set at the bar of parliament while an act of attainder was passed, 1563, and lay unburied for three years.

GORDON, George, fifth earl of Huntly (d. 1576), second son of George *Gordon, fourth earl of Huntly; sheriff of Inverness, 1556; imprisoned at Dunbar till the marriage of *Mary Queen of Scots with *Darnley, 1565, when his lands and dignities were nominally restored; allied himself with *Bothwell, 1566; joined Queen Mary at Dunbar, after *Rizzio's murder, 1566; became lord chancellor; joined Bothwell in plot to murder *Moray at Jedburgh; signed the bond at Craigmillar for Darnley's murder; accompanied Bothwell and Mary on a visit to Darnley the night before his murder; his estates actually restored after Bothwell's acquittal, 1567; Bothwell's divorce from his sister facilitated by his influence over her; witnessed marriage contract between Mary and Bothwell, 1567; connived at capture of the queen, and accompanied her to Edinburgh; escaped to the north after her flight; joined her partisans at Dumbarton; after a temporary agreement with Moray, conspired for her deliverance from Lochleven, 1567; after Mary's escape to England (1568) held all the north in alliance with Argyll, but received Mary's order to disperse; after a temporary submission gained possession of Edinburgh Castle, held a parliament, captured the regent *Lennox at Stirling, and (1572) came to terms with the regent *Morton.

GORDON, George, first marquis and sixth earl of Huntly (1562–1636), educated in France; allied himself with the duke of *Lennox against *Morton, and was prominent in the counter-revolution of 1583; secretly corresponded with Spain for the restoration of Catholicism; frequently compelled by the kirk to subscribe the confession of faith; captain of the guard at Holyrood, 1588; raised, with Erroll, a rebellion in the north, 1589, but submitted to James VI; protected by the king after his murder of the 'bonnie Earl' of *Moray, 1592, as also after his rebellion and excommunication, 1593; joined in a rebellion against James VI's government, 1594; his castle of Strathbogie blown up by the king, 1594; compelled (1595) to leave Scotland on his refusal to give up his confederate, *Bothwell (the fifth earl); pardoned and received into the kirk, 1597, and created marquis and joint lieutenant of the north, 1599; again excommunicated and compelled to subscribe, 1608; imprisoned on refusing a fresh demand for subscription; on his release went to England and obtained absolution from the archbishop of Canterbury, 1616; deprived by Charles I of his family jurisdiction in the north, 1630; subsequently twice summoned before the Privy Council and imprisoned.

GORDON, George, second marquis of Huntly (d. 1649), eldest son of George *Gordon, sixth earl and first marquis; educated in England, and created earl of Enzie; commanded company of *gens d'armes* in France; created viscount of Aboyne, 1632; succeeded his father, 1636; refused to subscribe the Covenant, 1638;

driven, when lieutenant of the north, from Strathbogie by *Montrose; refusing the Covenanters' demands was taken to Edinburgh under guard, 1639; joined Charles I; outlawed by the Scots, 1643; excommunicated, 1644; retired before *Argyll to Caithness; subsequently stormed Aberdeen, 1645; raised forces for Charles I; captured by Colonel Menzies at Dalnabo, 1647; beheaded at Edinburgh, 1649.

GORDON, George, first earl of Aberdeen (1637–1720), statesman; second son of Sir John *Gordon (d. 1644); MA, King's College, Aberdeen, 1658; four years professor at Aberdeen; succeeded to baronetcy, 1667; practised at Edinburgh bar; represented Aberdeenshire in Scots parliament; raised to the bench as Lord Haddo, 1680; a lord of the articles and president of session, 1681; chancellor of Scotland under James, duke of York, 1682–4; created earl of Aberdeen, 1682; dismissed from chancellorship for leniency to Nonconformists, 1684; supported Treaty of Union, 1705–6.

GORDON, George, first duke of Gordon and fourth marquis of Huntly (1643–1716), succeeded as fourth marquis of Huntly, 1653; educated abroad; saw military service with the French and the prince of Orange, 1672–5; created duke of Gordon at instigation of Claverhouse, 1684; appointed by James II privy councillor and captain of Edinburgh Castle, 1686; surrendered the castle to the Convention of Estates, 1689; several times afterwards imprisoned.

GORDON, Lord George (1751–1793), agitator; served in the navy; MP for Ludgershall, 1774–81; as president of the Protestant Association for repeal of Relieving Act of 1778, presented petition which led to the No-Popery riots of 1780; acquitted of treason, 1781; again appeared as Protestant champion, 1784, in the quarrel between the Dutch and the emperor Joseph; became a Jew; imprisoned for libels on the British government and Marie Antoinette, 1788 till death; died in Newgate.

GORDON, George, ninth marquis of Huntly (1761–1853), served in the army as Lord Strathaven; succeeded as fifth earl of Aboyne, 1794; Scottish representative peer, 1796–1815; created peer of United Kingdom, 1815; KT, 1827; succeeded as marquis of Huntly, 1836.

GORDON, George, fifth duke of Gordon (1770–1836), general; as marquis of Huntly served with Guards in Flanders, 1793–4; raised regiment now known as Gordon Highlanders; commanded it (1795–9) in Spain, Corsica, Ireland, and Holland, where he was badly wounded; lieutenant-general, 1808; general, 1819; commanded division in Walcheren expedition, 1809; MP, Eye, 1806; created Baron Gordon, 1807; GCB, 1820; succeeded to dukedom, 1827.

GORDON, George (1806–1879), horticultural writer; with Robert Glendinning published *Pinetum* (1858), with supplement (1862).

GORDON, George Hamilton-, fourth earl of Aberdeen (1784–1860), statesman; at Harrow with *Althorp and Palmerston; MA, St John's College, Cambridge, 1804; travelled in Greece and founded the Athenian Society; 'the travell'd thane' of *English Bards and Scotch Reviewers*; Scottish representative peer, 1806–14; ambassador extraordinary at Vienna, 1813, and representative at the Congress of Châtillon, 1814; privy councillor and Viscount Gordon of the United Kingdom, 1814; president of Society of Antiquaries, 1812–46; chancellor of the duchy of Lancaster in Wellington's Cabinet, and afterwards foreign secretary, 1828–30; secretary for war and the colonies under Peel, 1834–5; endeavoured to prevent schism in the Scottish Church by his Non-Intrusion Bill and the Act of 1843; foreign secretary, 1841–6, preserving peace with France through his friendship with Guizot; improved relations with America by the Oregon Treaty, 1846; followed Peel out of office, and on his death led his adherents; spoke ably against Russell's Ecclesiastical Titles Bill, 1851; brought about the defeat of Lord Derby by joining the Whigs on the house-tax resolution, 1852; formed a coalition ministry of Whigs and Peelites, 1852; forced into the Crimean War by Palmerston and Stratford *Canning, 1854; resigned after the carrying of Roebuck's vote of censure of the ministry's conduct of the war, 1855; naturally inclined to policy of non-intervention; KG, 1855; published a few miscellaneous works. His bust, by *Noble, is in Westminster Abbey. His correspondence was privately printed by his son, Sir A. H. Gordon, afterwards Lord Stanmore.

GORDON, George Ross (*fl.* 1832), Gaelic poet; brother of William *Gordon (1770–1820); published poems by himself and brothers, 1804–5.

GORDON, George Stuart (1881–1942), president of Magdalen College, Oxford, and professor of poetry; educated at Glasgow University and Oriel College, Oxford; first class, Lit. Hum., 1906; prize fellow in English literature, Magdalen College, 1907; professor at Leeds, 1913–22; Merton professor of English literature, Oxford, 1922–8; president of Magdalen, 1928–42; professor of poetry, 1933–8; vice-chancellor, 1938–41; publications include notable articles in the *Times Literary Supplement*; school editions of Shakespeare; and posthumously *Anglo-American*

Literary Relations (1942), *Shakespearian Comedy* (1944), and *Lives of Authors* (1950).

GORDON, Henrietta, 'Lady Henrietta' (*fl.* 1658), maid of honour to Princess Henrietta, duchess of Orleans; daughter of John Gordon, Viscount Melgum; educated in Parisian convents; entered the service of Anne of Austria, 1649; a favourite of the Duc d'Orléans, and attendant on both his wives.

GORDON, Sir Henry William (1818–1887), commissary-general; brother of Charles George *Gordon; served in the army, 1835–55; CB for services in Crimea, 1857; commissary-general, 1875; KCB, 1877; published *Events in the Life of Charles George Gordon* (1886).

GORDON, Ishbel Maria, marchioness of Aberdeen and Temair (1857–1939); born Marjoribanks; married future first marquess, John *Campbell, 1877; devoted to religious and humanitarian pursuits and to liberalism; initiated Onward and Upward Association; in Canada founded Victorian Order of Nurses, 1898; president for many years of International Council of Women; GBE, 1931.

GORDON, James (1541–1620), Jesuit; fifth son of George *Gordon, fourth earl of Huntly; while on mission with Father William *Crichton to Scotland, 1584, disputed with George *Hay (d. 1588), and converted Francis, earl of Erroll; held conference with Protestants at Holyrood in presence of James VI, 1588; sent by James VI to Rome to arrange for restoration of Romanism, 1592; exiled after his return; author of controversial works; died at Paris.

GORDON, James (1553–1641), Jesuit; rector of the colleges at Toulouse and Bordeaux; DD; confessor to Louis XIII; died at Paris. His works include biblical commentaries (1632) and *Opus Chronologicum* (1613).

GORDON, James, second Viscount Aboyne (d. 1649), second son of George *Gordon, second marquis of Huntly; succeeded as viscount, 1636; defeated by *Montrose at Bridge of Dee, 1639; outlawed by Scottish Council, 1643; joined Montrose against Covenanters, and was made lieutenant of the north; excommunicated, 1644, and exempted from pardon, 1648; died of grief in Paris on hearing of Charles I's execution.

GORDON, James (1615?–1686), topographer; son of Robert *Gordon (1580–1661); graduated at King's College, Aberdeen, 1636; pastor of Rothiemay, 1641–86; executed survey of Edinburgh, 1646–7, and views and plan of Aberdeen, 1661. His *History of Scots Affairs* (wrongly attributed to his father, Robert) was printed (1841); his *Aberdoniae utriusque Descriptio* (1842).

GORDON, James (1664–1746), Scottish Roman Catholic prelate; educated at Scots College, Paris; elected coadjutor of Bishop Thomas Joseph *Nicholson, and consecrated secretly to see of Nicopolis *in partibus*, 1706; vicar-apostolic in Scotland, 1718; first vicar-apostolic of lowland district, 1731–46.

GORDON, James (1762–1825), eccentric; solicitor at Cambridge; made a living in London by waiting at coach offices; his portrait and some of his jests preserved in *Hone's Everyday Book.

GORDON, Sir James Alexander (1782–1869), admiral of the fleet; entered navy, 1793; saw service at L'Orient, 1795, and in the *Goliath* at St Vincent and the Nile; in the *Racoon* at capture of the *Lodi* and the *Mutine*, 1803; distinguished himself at capture of the Spanish convoy off Rota, 1808; while in command of the *Active* received gold medal for conduct at Lissa, 1811; lost a leg in the capture of the *Pomone*, 1812; commanded squadron in American War, which reduced Fort Washington and took city of Alexandria and twenty-one ships, 1814; lieutenant-governor of Greenwich, 1840; governor, 1853; admiral, 1854; GCB, 1855; admiral of the fleet, 1868.

GORDON, James Alexander (1793–1872), physician; MD, Edinburgh, 1814; FRCP, 1836; censor, 1838; physician to the London Hospital, 1828–44; with Dr Mackenzie established *Quarterly Journal of Foreign Medicine and Surgery*, 1819.

GORDON, James Bentley (1750–1819), historian; BA, Trinity College, Dublin, 1773; incumbent of Cannaway, Cork, and Killegney, Wexford; published works, including *History of the Rebellion in Ireland in 1798* (1801) and *History of Ireland* (1805), etc.

GORDON, James Edward Henry (1852–1893), electrical engineer; son of James Alexander *Gordon (1793–1872); BA, Caius College, Cambridge, 1875; manager of electric lighting department of Telegraph Construction and Maintenance Company, 1883; engineer to Metropolitan Electric Supply Company, 1888–9; started practice with W. J. Rivington, 1889; MICE, 1890; published works on electricity.

GORDON, James Frederick Skinner (1821–1904), Scottish antiquary; MA, St Andrews, 1842; in charge of St Andrew's Episcopal Church, Glasgow, 1844–90; pioneer in abolition of ruinous tenements in Glasgow; published *The Ecclesiastical Chronicle for Scotland* (4 vols., 1867), *A History of Glasgow* (1872), and topographical works; enthusiastic freemason.

GORDON, Sir James Willoughby, first baronet (1773–1851), general; served with the 66th in Ireland, the West Indies, Gibraltar, and North America, 1783–1800; lieutenant-colonel of the 85th, 1801, of the 92nd, 1804; military secretary to the duke of *York when commander-in-chief; quartermaster-general in Peninsula, 1811–12, and afterwards at Horse Guards; lieutenant-general, 1825; general, 1841; created baronet, 1818; privy councillor, 1830; GCB, 1831; published (1809) *Military Transactions of the British Empire* (1803–7).

GORDON, Jane, duchess of Gordon (1749?–1812), wife of Alexander *Gordon, fourth duke of Gordon; daughter of Sir William Maxwell of Monreith; married, 1767; head of Tory salon at her house in Pall Mall, 1787–1801; married three of her daughters to dukes and another to a marquis; her portrait painted by *Reynolds, 1775.

GORDON, John, tenth or eleventh earl of Sutherland (1526?–1567), succeeded his grandfather, Adam, earl of Sutherland, 1537; lieutenant of Moray, 1547–8; accompanied queen mother of Scotland to France, 1550; received earldom of Ross, 1555; employed by his relative, *Huntly, in diplomatic negotiations, 1560; said to have been concerned in plot for carrying off the young Queen *Mary; attainted while in Flanders, 1563; captured (1565) and detained in England; restored to his estates with Huntly; poisoned at Helmsdale, probably at instigation of George, fourth earl of *Caithness.

GORDON, John (1544–1619), dean of Salisbury; probably eldest son of Alexander *Gordon (1516?–1575), bishop-elect of Galloway; served Louis, prince of Condé; attended Thomas, duke of *Norfolk, 1568, and *Mary Queen of Scots, 1569–72; gentleman of the privy chamber to Charles IX, Henri III, and Henri IV; saved lives of several countrymen during massacre of St Bartholomew, 1572; held public disputations with Benetrius, the chief rabbi at Avignon, 1574, and against Du Perron, 1601; invited to England in consequence of his eulogies of James I; dean of Salisbury, 1604–19; took part in the Hampton Court Conference, 1604; DD, Oxford, 1605; received barony of Glenluce, 1611; benefactor of Salisbury Cathedral; published theological works, some of them in answer to Bellarmine.

GORDON, Sir John, first Viscount Kenmure and Baron Lochinvar (1599?–1634), of Lochinvar, brother-in-law of the marquis of Argyll and friend of Samuel *Rutherford; created Scottish peer, 1633.

GORDON, Sir John, first baronet (d. 1644), Royalist; distinguished himself against the Covenanters at Turriff, 1639, and joined Charles I in England; created baronet, 1642; excommunicated and taken at Kellie by *Argyll; beheaded at Edinburgh.

GORDON, John, thirteenth or fourteenth earl of Sutherland (1609–1663), sheriff and coroner of Sutherland; nephew of Sir Robert *Gordon (1580–1656); obtained many subscriptions to the Covenant in the north; one of the leaders at Battle of Auldearn, 1645; lord privy seal in Scotland, 1649; raised forces against *Cromwell, 1650; his piety commemorated by *Wodrow.

GORDON, John (1644–1726), bishop of Galloway, 1688; followed James II to Ireland and France; DD; converted to Romanism by Bossuet; appointed by Clement XI to abbey of St Clement; died at Rome.

GORDON, John, fifteenth or sixteenth earl of Sutherland (1660?–1733), offered to mediate with William III on behalf of his connection, Dundee, 1689; served under William III in Flanders; succeeded to earldom, 1703; privy councillor to Queen Anne, 1704; a commissioner for the Union; Scottish representative peer, 1706, 1715, 1722, and 1727; president of the Board of Trade, 1715; received pension for services as lieutenant of the north in 1715; KT.

GORDON, John (1702–1739), Gresham professor of music; educated at Westminster and Trinity College, Cambridge; barrister, Gray's Inn, 1725; Gresham professor, 1723–39.

GORDON, John Campbell, seventh earl of Aberdeen and first marquess of Aberdeen and Temair (1847–1934), statesman; third son of fifth earl; educated at St Andrews University and University College, Oxford; succeeded to title, 1872; became a constant Liberal; lord-lieutenant of Ireland, 1886, 1906–15; governor-general of Canada, 1893–8; PC, 1886; KT, 1906; marquess, 1916; lord rector of St Andrews, 1913–16; much occupied in social welfare.

GORDON, Sir John James Hood (1832–1908), general; entered army, 1849; served in Indian Mutiny and in Afridi expedition, 1877–8; prominent in Afghan War, 1878–9; CB, 1879; commanded troops in expeditions to Karmana and against Malikshahi Waziris, 1880, and in Mahsud Waziris expedition, 1881; commanded brigade in Burmese expedition, 1886–7; assistant military secretary at headquarters, 1890–6; general, 1894; member of India Council, 1897–1907; KCB, 1898; GCB, 1908; published history of Sikhs, 1904.

GORDON, John Rutherford (1890–1974), newspaper editor; educated at Morgan Academy, Dundee; left school at 14 to work as junior reporter on Dundee *Advertiser*; at age of 19 in charge of Perthshire and Dundee editions of the *People's Journal*; left Dundee for London, 1911, and worked for the *Advertiser* and then the *Glasgow Herald*; during 1914–18 war served in the Rifle Brigade and King's Royal Rifle Corps; joined London *Evening News* after the war; chief sub-editor, 1922; joined *Daily Express*, 1924; editor, *Sunday Express* (jointly with James Douglas for three years), 1928–52; turned an ailing newspaper into one of most successful and profitable in the world; introduced the crossword puzzle and astrological forecasts; also captured Carl Giles, the cartoonist, and Nathaniel Gubbins, the humorist; during 1939–45 war, writer and commentator of considerable force; never an intimate of *Beaverbrook; wanting younger man in charge, Beaverbrook promoted Gordon to editor-in-chief, a sinecure appointment, 1952; Gordon achieved new renown as columnist until his death, 1952–74.

GORDON, Sir John Watson- (1788–1864), portrait painter; assumed name of Gordon, 1826; the leading portrait painter after *Raeburn's death, 1823; exhibited at Scottish Academy, 1830–64; president, 1850; exhibited at Royal Academy from 1827; RA, 1851; knighted, 1850; the Watson-Gordon professorship at Edinburgh endowed in his memory, 1879.

GORDON, Sir John William (1814–1870), major-general; entered engineers, 1833; present at Alma and Inkerman, and prominent in siege of Sebastopol; severely wounded at the great sortie, but commanded engineers in Kertch expedition; deputy adjutant-general at the Horse Guards, 1856–61; KCB and major-general; commanded in the Trent affair, 1861; inspector-general of fortifications; killed himself in a fit of insanity resulting from wound.

GORDON, Lord Lewis (d. 1754), Jacobite; third son of Alexander *Gordon, second duke of Gordon; one of Prince *Charles Edward's council, 1745; defeated Macleod near Inverury, 1745; died at Montreuil.

GORDON, Lucy, Lady Duff- (1821–1869). See DUFF-GORDON, LUCIE or LUCY.

GORDON, Mervyn Henry (1872–1953), medical bacteriologist; grandson of William *Buckland; educated at Marlborough, Keble College, Oxford, and St Bartholomew's Hospital; BM, 1898; DM, 1903; on staff of pathology department, St Bartholomew's, 1898–1923; thereafter remained in department as staff member of Medical Research Council; studied streptococci, transmission of bacteria through the air, cerebro-spinal fever, filtrable viruses; directed a team studying Hodgkin's disease; member, Army Pathological Advisory Committee from 1909;

served in RAMC, 1914–18; CMG, 1917; CBE, 1919; FRS, 1924; hon. LL D, Edinburgh.

GORDON, Osborne (1813–1883), divine; of Christ Church, Oxford; censor, 1846; Ireland scholar, 1835; MA, 1839; BD, 1847; reader in Greek, Christ Church, Oxford, 1846; active against 'papal aggression', 1850; prominent in the university till presented (1860) to living of Easthampstead, Berkshire; chairman of Commission of Inquiry into Queen's Colleges in Ireland, 1876; member of the Oxford Commission; his epitaph at Easthampstead written by *Ruskin; edited Eusebius (1842).

GORDON, Patrick (*fl.* 1615–1650), poet; perhaps author of *A Shorte Abridgment of Britenes Distemper* (printed, 1844); published *Neptunus Britannicus Corydonis* (1614), as well as a poem on *Bruce, and *First Booke . . . of Penardo and Laissa* (1615).

GORDON, Patrick (1635–1699), general and friend of Peter the Great; left Scotland, 1651; served alternately the Swedes and the Poles; attempted assassination at Wender, 1658, of Richard *Bradshaw, mistaking him for the president at the trial of Charles I; entered the Russian service, 1661; suppressed a revolt, 1662; on mission to England, 1664; drove Turks from the Ukraine; lieutenant-general and governor of Kiev, 1679; not allowed to retire from Russian service; general for services against the Crimean Tartars, 1687; assisted Peter in his *coup d'état*; suppressed the Strelitzes, 1697; buried at Moscow; extracts from his autobiography (in the St Petersburgh archives) edited by Joseph *Robertson (1859).

GORDON, Pryse Lockhart (*fl.* 1834), author of *Personal Memoirs* (1830) and of *Holland and Belgium* (1834); from 1815 lived at Brussels.

GORDON, Sir Robert (1580–1656), historian of house of Sutherland; fourth son of Alexander *Gordon, eleventh or twelfth earl of Sutherland; gentleman of the privy chamber to James I and Charles I; married heiress of John *Gordon (1544–1619), dean of Salisbury and lord of Glenluce, 1613; created premier baronet of Nova Scotia, 1625; confidential messenger between Charles I and his queen; sheriff of Inverness-shire, 1629; vice-chamberlain of Scotland, 1630; privy councillor of Scotland, 1634; mediator during the Civil War; founder of family of Gordonstoun; his *Genealogical History of the Earldom of Sutherland* edited by Henry *Weber (1813).

GORDON, Robert (1580–1661), of Straloch, geographer; first graduate of Marischal College, Aberdeen; mediated between *Huntly and *Montrose; corrected and completed *Pont's maps for Scottish section of Bleau's *Atlas* (vol. vi of 1662 edition) and contributed 'Remarks on the Charts of the Ancient Scots'; wrote family history, which William Gordon utilized; supplied materials for the *Scots Affairs* of his son James *Gordon (1615?–1686) of Rothiemay.

GORDON, Sir **Robert** (1647–1704), 'Sir Robert the warlock', of Gordonstoun; grandson of Sir Robert *Gordon (1580–1656); knighted, 1673; succeeded as baronet, 1685; gentleman of James II's household; member of Scots parliament of 1672–4, and of conventions of 1678, 1681–2, 1685–6; correspondent of *Boyle; invented a pump; FRS, 1686.

GORDON, **Robert** (1665–1732), founder of Gordon's College (formerly Hospital), Aberdeen; grandson of Robert *Gordon (1580–1661) of Straloch; acquired fortune as a merchant at Danzig; his hospital for thirty boys opened 1750, increased by bequest of Alexander Simpson, 1834, converted into a college, 1881.

GORDON, **Robert** (1687–1764), biblical scholar; prefect of studies at Paris, 1712–18; chaplain to duke of Gordon, 1718–28; procurator at Edinburgh, 1728–40; arrested in London, 1745, and banished; died at Lens; his manuscript translation of the New Testament not approved at Rome.

GORDON, **Robert** (1786–1853), Free Church minister; DD, Marischal College, Aberdeen, 1823; minister of the High Church, Edinburgh, 1830; supported non-intrusionists; as moderator of the general assembly, 1841, had to pronounce deposition of the Strathbogie ministers; seconded Thomas *Chalmers, 1842; left Established Church, 1843, followed by his congregation; contributed to the *Edinburgh Encyclopaedia*.

GORDON, Sir **Robert** (1791–1847), diplomat; brother of Sir Alexander *Gordon (1786–1815); matriculated from St John's College, Cambridge, 1809; plenipotentiary at Vienna, 1815, 1817, 1821; privy councillor; envoy-extraordinary to Brazil, 1826; at Constantinople, 1828–31; at Vienna, 1841–6; GCB, 1829.

GORDON, **Theodore** (1786–1845), inspector of army hospitals; MD, Edinburgh, 1802; army surgeon in Germany and the Peninsula; wounded in crossing Pyrenees; physician to the forces, 1815; professional assistant at medical board of War Office; deputy-inspector-general of hospitals, 1836.

GORDON, **Thomas** (1691?–1750), author; reputed the Silenus of the *Dunciad*; with his patron John *Trenchard issued a weekly paper called *Independent Whig*, collected in volume, 1721 (reissued later as *A Defence of Primitive Christianity*); employed by Walpole; published translation of Tacitus (1728) and Sallust (1744), and miscellaneous works.

GORDON, **Thomas** (1788–1841), major-general in the Greek Army; educated at Eton and Brasenose College, Oxford; cornet, 2nd Dragoons, 1808; served in Scots Greys; captain in Russian Army, 1813; served under Ipsilanti against the Turks, but retired after massacre at Tripolizza, 1821; member of Greek committee in London, 1823; returned to Greece, 1826; commanded expedition for relief of Athens, 1827; lived at Argos, 1828–31; served in Greek Army, 1833–9; published *History of the Greek Revolution* (1832) and translations from the Turkish.

GORDON, Sir **Thomas Edward** (1832–1914), general; joined army, 1849; served in Indian Mutiny, 1857–9, and Afghan War, 1879–80; CB, 1881; attached to legation at Tehran, 1889–93; full general, 1894; KCB, 1900.

GORDON, **William** (d. 1577), last pre-Reformation bishop of Aberdeen; fourth son of Alexander *Gordon, third earl of Huntly; bishop of Aberdeen, 1546–77.

GORDON, **William** (1614–1679), of Earlston, Convenanter; second son of Alexander *Gordon of Earlston (1587–1654); shared in *Glencairn's rising against *Cromwell, 1653, but submitted; banished from Scotland for refusing to present an episcopal curate, 1663; shot after Bothwell Brigg.

GORDON, William, sixth Viscount Kenmure (d. 1716), Jacobite; induced by his wife, sister of Sir Robert *Dalyell, to join rising of 1715; appointed by *Mar to command in southern Scotland; failed to surprise Dumfries and marched into England; captured at Preston, 1715; pleaded guilty and made strong appeal to the peers, but was beheaded.

GORDON, **William** (1728–1807), Independent minister, at Ipswich and Gravel Lane, Southwark; in America, 1770–85, at Roxbury, Massachusetts, and Jamaica Plain; private secretary to Washington, and chaplain to Provincial Congress of Massachusetts; DD, New Jersey; pastor of St Neots, 1789–1802; published *History of the Rise and Independence of the United States* (1788).

GORDON, **William** (1770–1820), Gaelic poet; brother of George Ross *Gordon; while serving with Reay fencibles in Ireland wrote Gaelic hymns and songs, published as *Dantadh Spioradal* (1802).

GORDON, **William** (1800–1849), philanthropist; MD, Edinburgh, 1841; physician at Hull; subject of Newman Hall's *Christian Philanthropist triumphing over Death* (1849).

GORDON-CUMMING, Roualeyn George (1820–1866), African lion-hunter. See CUMMING.

GORDON-LENNOX, Charles Henry, sixth duke of Richmond and first duke of Gordon (1818–1903), lord president of the Council; son of fifth duke of *Richmond; ADC to duke of Wellington, 1842–52; Conservative MP for West Sussex, 1841–60; president of Poor Law Board and PC, 1859; succeeded father, 1860; KG, 1867; president of Board of Trade, 1867–9; leader of Conservative party in House of Lords, 1868; lord president of Council, 1874–80; introduced the agricultural holdings (1875) and elementary schools (1876) bills; created first duke of Gordon, 1876; carried Contagious Diseases (animals) Bill, 1877; reorganized veterinary department of Privy Council; chairman of Royal Commission on Agriculture (1879–82), whose report led to Agricultural Holdings Act, 1883, and creation of Board of Agriculture; a mediator between Liberal government and House of Lords in Franchise Bill crisis of 1884; secretary for Scotland, 1885–6; chancellor of Aberdeen University, 1861; hon. LL D, 1895; DCL, Oxford, 1870; LL D, Cambridge, 1894; member (1838) and president (1868 and 1883) of Royal Agricultural Society; improved famous Southdown sheep at Goodwood, and shorthorns at Gordon Castle.

GORDON-TAYLOR, Sir **Gordon** (1878–1960), surgeon; educated at Robert Gordon's College and the University, Aberdeen; qualified from Middlesex Hospital, 1903; B.Sc., London, 1904; FRCS, 1906, council member, 1932–48; appointed assistant surgeon, Middlesex Hospital, 1907; surgeon, 1920; surgeon to Fourth Army in France in 1914–18 war and surgeon rear-admiral, 1939–45; published *The Dramatic in Surgery* (1930) and *The Abdominal Injuries of Warfare* (1939); CB, 1942; KBE, 1946.

GORDON WALKER, Patrick Chrestien, Baron Gordon-Walker (1907–1980), politician, author, and broadcaster; educated at Wellington College, and Christ Church, Oxford, where he was a scholar; B.Litt.; student and history tutor, Christ Church, 1931; spent year at German universities; his knowledge of German valuable in BBC's broadcasting to Europe during 1939–45 war; chief editor, Radio Luxemburg, 1944; Labour MP for Smethwick, 1945; parliamentary private secretary to Herbert *Morrison (later Lord Morrison of Lambeth), 1946; under-secretary of state, Commonwealth Relations Office, 1947; secretary of state and PC, 1950; defended decision to refuse recognition as head of Bamangwato tribe to (Sir) Seretse *Khama, and supported plans for establishing a Central

African Federation; in opposition, principal Labour spokesman on foreign affairs, 1951–64; loyal supporter of Hugh *Gaitskell; shadow foreign secretary, 1963; defeated in general elections of 1964 and 1965; returned as MP for Leyton, 1966; chairman, Book Development Council; rejoined Cabinet as minister without portfolio, 1966; secretary of state for education and science, 1967–8; CH, 1968; became life peer, 1974; British member of European Parliament 1975–6.

GORE, Albert Augustus (1840–1901), surgeon-general; MD, Queen's University, Ireland, 1858; LRCS, Ireland, 1860; served with army medical staff in West Africa (1861), Ashanti War (1873), and Egypt (1882); principal medical officer to forces in India; CB, 1899; wrote account of his campaigns.

GORE, Mrs Catherine Grace Frances (1799–1861), novelist and dramatist; née Moody; married, 1823, to Captain Charles Arthur Gore; published about seventy works between 1824 and 1862, including the novels *Manners of the Day* (1830), *Mrs. Armytage* (1836), *Cecil, or the Adventures of a Coxcomb* (1841), and *The Banker's Wife* (1843); her *School for Coquettes* acted at the Haymarket, 1831, *Lords and Commons* at Drury Lane, and *Quid pro Quo* at the Haymarket, 1844; parodied by *Thackeray in *Novels by Eminent Hands*; composed music for 'And ye shall walk in silk attire', and other favourite songs.

GORE, Charles (1853–1932), bishop successively of Worcester, Birmingham, and Oxford; educated at Harrow and Balliol College, Oxford; first class, Lit. Hum., and fellow of Trinity, 1875; deacon, 1876; priest, 1878; a lifelong Anglo-Catholic; vice-principal of Cuddesdon College, 1880–3; 'principal librarian', Pusey House, 1884–93; mainly through personal relations exercised very strong influence on the religious life of the university; active on behalf of Christian Social Union; formed (1892), and until 1901 was superior of, the Community of the Resurrection, a brotherhood of celibate priests 'having all things in common'; established it at Mirfield, 1898; in his essay 'The Holy Spirit and Inspiration' in *Lux Mundi* (1889) to the distress of his friends concluded that the humanity of Christ entailed certain limitations of consciousness; canon of Westminster, 1894; bishop of Worcester, 1902; of the new diocese of Birmingham to the creation of which he contributed almost all his private fortune, 1905; established excellent relations with civic authorities, Free Churchmen, and Evangelicals; unfailingly interested in Workers' Educational Association; supported the budget of 1909; a strong and generally successful disciplinarian; translated (1911) to Oxford which was less responsive to his masterful personal influence; his decisive temper drew him into constant controversy; led protest against consecration of Hensley *Henson, 1917–18; resigned (1919) and moved to London; dean of theological faculty, King's College, 1924–8; attended Malines conversations; supported revision of the Prayer Book, 1927–8; works include *The Ministry of the Christian Church* (1888), *The Body of Christ* (1901), *The Basis of Anglican Fellowship* (1914), *The Reconstruction of Belief* (1926), *Christ and Society* (1928); through a mind and character of singular force exercised upon his Church an influence unequalled in his generation.

GORE, Sir Charles Stephen (1793–1869), general; served with 43rd in the Peninsula; took part in storming of Ciudad Rodrigo, 1812, and Badajoz, 1812; aide-de-camp to Sir A. *Barnard at Salamanca, 1812; to Sir J. *Kempt at Vittoria, 1813, and in Canada, 1814; at Quatre Bras and Waterloo; deputy quartermaster-general in Canada, 1838–9; lieutenant-general, 1854; general, 1863; GCB and governor of Chelsea Hospital.

GORE, George (1826–1908), electrochemist; head of Institute of Scientific Research, Birmingham, 1880; discovered amorphous antimony and electrolytic sounds; FRS, 1865; improved methods of electroplating; wrote *The Art of Electrometallurgy* (1877) and philosophic works; hon. LL D, Edinburgh, 1877; awarded Civil List pension, 1891; left estate of £5,000 to Royal Society and Royal Institution.

GORE, John, Baron Annaly (1718–1784), Irish judge; BA, Dublin, 1737; MP, Jamestown, 1745; solicitor-general for Ireland, 1760; chief justice of King's Bench, 1764; privy councillor; created an Irish peer, 1766.

GORE, Sir John (1772–1836), vice-admiral; entered navy, 1781; distinguished himself at Corsica and Toulon, 1794–5; captured by the French; while in command of the *Triton* in the Channel, 1796–1801, took many prizes; received £40,000 prize-money after capture of *Santa Brigida* and *Thetis*, 1799; with the *Medusa* assisted in capture of Spanish ships off Cadiz, 1804; knighted, 1805; KCB, 1815; vice-admiral, 1825; commander of the Nore, 1818–21; in the East Indies, 1831–5.

GORE, John Ellard (1845–1910), astronomical writer; engineer in Indian Works Department, 1868–79; published *Catalogue of Known Variable Stars* (1884), *The Worlds of Space* (1894), and *The Stellar Heavens* (1903); FRAS, 1878; member of Royal Irish Academy.

GORE, Montagu (1800–1864), politician; Whig MP for Devizes, 1832–4; Conservative MP for Barnstaple, 1841–7; supported Peel on corn-law question; published political pamphlets.

GORE, Thomas (1632–1684), writer on heraldry; BA, Magdalen College, Oxford; member of Lincoln's Inn; gentleman of the privy chamber, 1667; high sheriff of Wiltshire, 1681; chief work *Nomenclator Geographicus Latino-Anglicus et Anglico-Latinus* (1667); two valuable manuscripts by him in British Museum.

GORE, (William) David Ormsby, fifth Baron Harlech (1918–1985), politician and ambassador. See ORMSBY GORE.

GORE, William George Arthur Ormsby-, fourth Baron Harlech (1885–1964), statesman and banker. See ORMSBY-GORE.

GORE-BOOTH, Paul Henry, Baron Gore-Booth (1909–1984), diplomat; educated at Eton (King's scholar), and Balliol College, Oxford; entered Diplomatic Service, 1933; served in Foreign Office and Vienna, 1933–8, and in Japan, 1938–42; at British embassy in Washington, 1942–5, dealing with post-war reconstruction; engaged in political and economic work in Foreign Office, 1945–9; director, British Information Services in USA, 1949–53; ambassador to Burma, 1953–6; deputy under-secretary in charge of economic affairs, Foreign Office, 1956–60; high commissioner, Delhi, 1960–5; permanent under-secretary, Foreign Office, 1965–9; CMG, 1949; KCMG, 1957; KCVO, 1961; GCMG, 1965; life peer, 1969; chairman, Save the Children Fund, 1970–6, and board of governors of School of Oriental and African Studies, 1975–80, and Disasters Emergency Committee, 1974–7; president, Sherlock Holmes Society, 1967–79; published autobiography, *With Great Truth and Respect* (1974), and edited fifth edition of *Satow's Guide to Diplomatic Practice* (1979).

GORE-BROWNE, Sir Stewart (1883–1967), soldier, and settler and politician in Northern Rhodesia (Zambia); educated at Harrow and Royal Military Academy, Woolwich; commissioned to Royal Field Artillery; served in South Africa; appointed to Anglo-Belgian Boundary Commission to determine boundary between Northern Rhodesia and Belgian Congo, 1911–14; served in France during 1914–18 war; DSO, 1917; returned with rank of lieutenant-colonel, 1921; settled in Northern Rhodesia; elected to Legislative Council, 1935; leader of unofficial members; nominated to represent African interests, 1938; knighted, 1945; lost support of Europeans and resigned unofficial leadership, 1946; supported (Sir) Roy Welensky in opposing rule of Colonial Civil Service; resigned from Legislative Council, 1951; failed to make come-back with United National Independence party, founded by Kenneth Kaunda, 1962.

GORELL, first Baron (1848–1913), judge. See BARNES, JOHN GORELL.

GORER, Peter Alfred Isaac (1907–1961), biologist and geneticist; educated at Charterhouse and Guy's Hospital, London; B.Sc., 1929; MRCS, LRCP, 1932; studied genetics with J. B. S. *Haldane at University College, London; joined Lister Institute, 1934; colleague of D. W. W. *Henderson; studied genetics of individuality by investigating marker substances (antigens) on the surface of red cells and tissues; returned to Guy's Hospital, 1940–6; collaborated on immunogenetics with George D. Snell and Sally Lyman Allen at Bar Harbor, Maine, 1946–7; reader in experimental pathology, Guy's Hospital, 1947; published many papers; one of the most important contributors to the study of organ- and tissue-graft rejection, tumour immunity, and the genetics of immune responsiveness; FRS, 1960.

GORGES, Sir **Arthur** (d. 1625), poet and translator; commanded the *Wast Spite*, *Ralegh's flagship, on the Islands voyage, 1597; knighted; his account of the voyage published by Samuel *Purchas in *Pilgrimes* (1625–6); MP, Yarmouth, 1584, Camelford, 1588, Dorsetshire, 1592, and Rye, 1601; translated Lucan's *Pharsalia* (1614) and *Bacon's *De Sapientia Veterum* (1619), and made French version of the *Essays*; the 'Alcyon' of *Spenser's *Daphnaida* and *Colin Clout's come home again*.

GORGES, Sir **Ferdinando** (1566?–1647), military and naval commander and colonizer; cousin of Sir Arthur *Gorges; knighted by *Essex for gallantry at siege of Rouen, 1591; with him in the Island voyage, 1597, and in Ireland, 1599; joined his conspiracy, but gave evidence against him, 1601; governor of Plymouth; became interested in colonization, and formed two companies which received grants of land in North America, and formed settlement of New Plymouth, 1628; lord proprietary of Maine, 1639.

GORHAM, Geoffrey of (d. 1146), abbot of St Albans. See GEOFFREY.

GORHAM, George Cornelius (1787–1857), divine and antiquary; fellow of Queens' College, Cambridge, 1810; third wrangler and second Smith's prizeman, 1809; MA, 1812; BD, 1821; vicar of St Just in Penwith, Cornwall, 1846, of Brampford Speke, Devonshire, 1847–57; refused institution (1847) on account of Calvinistic views on baptismal regeneration by Bishop Henry *Phillpotts of Exeter, who was supported by court of arches, but obtained institution soon after the decision had been reversed by the judicial committee of Privy Council, 1850. Besides his own account of the case, Gorham published books on the two St Neots (1820), and on the chapel, chauntry, and guild of Maidenhead, and the *Book of Enoch* (1829), besides genealogical works.

GORING, George, earl of Norwich (1583?–1663), Royalist; educated at Sidney Sussex College, Cambridge; gentleman of the privy chamber to *Henry, prince of Wales, 1610; one of James I's three 'chief and master fools'; accompanied Prince Charles to Spain, 1623; negotiated his marriage with *Henrietta Maria of France; became her master of the horse and Baron Goring, 1628; received numerous offices and grants; 'the leader of the monopolists'; privy councillor, 1639; spent money freely for Charles I during the Civil War; accompanied the queen to and from Holland, 1642–3; as envoy to France obtained from Mazarin promise of arms and money, 1643; impeached for high treason by parliament, 1644; created earl of Norwich, 1644; subsequently commanded in Kent and Essex; after capitulation at Colchester (1648) sentenced to death, but respited by casting vote of Speaker *Lenthall; with Charles II on the continent, 1649; employed in negotiations with *Sexby and the Levellers; captain of the guard and pensioned, 1661.

GORING, George, Baron Goring (1608–1657), Royalist; son of George *Goring, earl of Norwich; wounded in Dutch service at siege of Breda, 1637; held commands in Scottish wars; revealed 'first army plot' to parliament, 1641, but when governor of Portsmouth declared for the king, 1642; raised reinforcements for Royalists in Holland; as general of the horse routed *Fairfax at Seacroft Moor, 1643, but was captured by him at Wakefield and sent to the Tower; exchanged for the earl of *Lothian, 1644; commanded left wing at Marston Moor, 1644; lieutenant-general of the main army in the south; made successful charge at second Battle of Newbury, 1644; conducted unsuccessful operations in the south and west, and injured the royal cause by ambitious intrigues; received command in the west, 1645; defeated at Langport; went abroad and obtained command of English regiments in Spanish service; thenceforth lived in Spain.

GORRIE, Sir **John** (1829–1892), colonial judge; educated at Edinburgh; advocate, 1856; honorary advocate-deputy for Scotland, 1860; began practice at English bar, 1862; substitute procureur-général of Mauritius, 1869; second puisne judge, 1870; chief justice and member of legislative council of Fiji Islands, 1876; chief justice of Leeward Islands, and knighted, 1882; chief justice of Trinidad, 1886; suspended on report of commission to investigate his methods of administering justice, 1892.

GORST, Sir **John Eldon** (1835–1916), lawyer and politician; BA, St John's College, Cambridge (third wrangler); went to New Zealand, 1860; returned to England and called to bar, 1865; Conservative MP, borough of Cambridge, 1866; MP, Chatham, and QC, 1875; member of 'fourth party', 1880–4; solicitor-general and knighted, 1885; under-secretary of state for India, 1886; MP, Cambridge University, 1892–1906; last vice-president of committee of Privy Council on education, 1895–1902; left Conservative party over Chamberlain's fiscal campaign.

GORST, Sir **(John) Eldon** (1861–1911), consul-general in Egypt; son of Sir J. E. *Gorst; born in New Zealand; called to bar, 1885; attaché to British agency at Cairo, 1886; controller of direct revenues, 1890–2; adviser to ministry of the interior, 1894; financial adviser, 1898–1904; CB, 1900; KCB, 1902; assistant under-secretary of state to Foreign Office, 1904–7; consul-general in Egypt, 1907–11; promoted municipal and local self-government there; passed law for enlarging powers of provincial councils, 1910; broad-minded administrator, with financial and linguistic ability; GCMG, 1911.

GORT, Viscounts. See VEREKER, CHARLES, 1768–1842; VEREKER, JOHN STANDISH SURTEES PRENDERGAST, 1886–1946.

GORTON, John (d. 1835), compiler; published *A General Biographical Dictionary* (1828) and, with G. N. *Wright, *A Topographical Dictionary of Great Britain and Ireland* (1831–3).

GORTON, Samuel (d. 1677), founder of the Gortonites; of Gorton, Lancashire; went to New England, 1636; lived at Boston and New Plymouth; obliged to remove to Rhode Island; made himself obnoxious to the authorities by his aggressive spirit; purchased land from the Narragansett Indians at Shawomet, 1643; ejected by Massachusetts government and imprisoned for heresy at Charlestown, 1643; came to England, 1644; published *Simplicities Defence against Seven-Headed Policy* (1646, reprinted 1835); having obtained protection against Massachusetts government, returned to Shawomet, 1648, renaming it Warwick in honour of his protector; published religious tracts with an eccentric phraseology.

GOSCELIN (or **GOTSELIN)** (*fl.* 1099), biographer; came to England with Bishop *Hermann of Salisbury; lived in monastery of Canterbury and other houses; wrote lives of St *Augustine (dedi-

cated to *Anselm), and St *Swithun and other saints, and *Historia Translationis S. Augustini*; highly commended by *William of Malmesbury.

GOSCHEN, George Joachim, first Viscount Goschen (1831–1907), statesman; grandson of Georg Joachim Göschen, a Leipzig publisher, and son of a London banker; educated in London and Saxe Meiningen, at Rugby and Oriel College, Oxford; first class in Lit. Hum. and president of the Union, 1853; founded 'Essay Club' at Oxford, 1852; entered father's banking firm; in South America on business, 1854–6; director of Bank of England, 1858; published *Theory of the Foreign Exchanges* (1861) which attracted wide attention; Liberal MP for City of London, 1863–80; made a good position in House of Commons; joined Lord Russell's ministry as vice-president of Board of Trade, 1865, and entered the Cabinet as chancellor of the duchy of Lancaster, 1866; president of Poor Law Board in Gladstone's first administration, 1868–71; reformed local government system; first lord of the Admiralty, 1871–4; his refusal to reduce estimates largely responsible for dissolution of government in 1874; investigated financial position of Egypt at viceroy's invitation, 1876; opposed to his party's plan of equalization of borough and county franchise, 1877; MP for Ripon, 1880–5; declined viceroyalty of India, 1880; went on special embassy to sultan, to compel Turks to carry out Treaty of Berlin as regards Greece, Montenegro, and Bulgaria, 1880–1; refused secretaryship for war, 1882, and speakership of Commons, 1883; opposed to radicalism of Joseph *Chamberlain and Sir Charles *Dilke; out of sympathy with Gladstone's foreign policy, and *Parnell's policy of home rule; elected for East Edinburgh, defeating extreme Radical candidate, 1885; joined Lord *Hartington in forming Liberal Unionist party, and helped to defeat Gladstone's Home Rule Bill, 1886; chancellor of Exchequer in succession to Lord Randolph *Churchill in Lord Salisbury's government, 1886–92; MP for St George's. Hanover Square, 1887–1900; converted national debt from 3 per cent to 2½ per cent stock, 1888; his firmness prevented financial panic in Baring crisis, 1890; strenuous in opposition to Gladstone's Home Rule Bill of 1893; first lord of the Admiralty in Salisbury's third administration, 1895–1900; made vast increases in naval strength and naval estimates; created viscount, 1900; published life of grandfather (1903) and *Essays on Economic Questions* (1905); opposed Chamberlain's fiscal policy, 1903; showed remarkable consistency of character as statesman; powerful speaker; busy in non-political affairs; ecclesiastical commissioner, 1882; strong supporter of extension of university teaching in London from 1879; hon. DCL, Oxford, 1881; hon. LL D of Aberdeen and Cambridge, 1888, and Edinburgh, 1890; made chancellor of Oxford University, 1903.

GOSFORD, Baron (1616?–1679). See WEDDER-BURN, Sir PETER.

GOSFORD, second earl of, in the Irish peerage (1776–1849). See ACHESON, Sir ARCHIBALD.

GOSLING, Harry (1861–1930), trade-union leader; apprenticed as Thames waterman, 1875; took leading part in struggle to improve working conditions of dock and river labour throughout country; ardent trade-unionist; alderman of London County Council, 1898–1925; Labour MP, Whitechapel and St George's, 1923–30; minister of transport and paymaster-general, 1924.

GOSLING, Jane (d. 1804), author; published *Moral Essays* (1789) and *Ashdale Village*.

GOSLING, Ralph (1693–1758), topographer; writing-master and schoolmaster at Sheffield; published earliest known map of Sheffield (1732).

GOSNOLD, Bartholomew (d. 1607), navigator; sailed from Falmouth in the *Concord*, 1602; discovered Cape Cod and adjoining islands, 1602; a leader of the expedition which, under the auspices of Sir Ferdinando *Gorges, discovered the Capes of Virginia, and founded Jamestown, 1606; died at Jamestown.

GOSNOLD, John (1625?–1678), Anabaptist; of Charterhouse and Pembroke Hall, Cambridge; during the Civil War founded Baptist congregation in Paul's Alley, Barbican, London, and attracted large audiences; published tracts against infant baptism.

GOSPATRIC (or COSPATRIC), earl of Northumberland (*fl.* 1067), probably the 'Gaius patricius' who accompanied *Tostig to Rome, 1061; bought from William I earldom of Northumbria, 1067, but joined rising against the king, 1068; took part in Danes' sack of York, 1069; his earldom restored on submission, but again forfeited, 1072; fled to Scotland and Flanders; received Dunbar from *Malcolm III of Scotland.

GOSS, Alexander (1814–1872), Roman Catholic bishop of Liverpool; vice-president of St Edward's College, Everton, 1843–53; coadjutor bishop of Liverpool, 1853; bishop, 1856–72; contributor to Chetham, Holbein, and Manx societies.

GOSS, Sir **John** (1800–1880), musical composer; Chapel Royal chorister and pupil of Thomas *Attwood; organist of St Luke's, Chelsea,

1825; of St Paul's Cathedral, 1838–72; won Gresham Prize, 1833; knighted, 1872; Mus.-Doc., Cambridge, 1876; published *Introduction to Harmony* (1833), and (with Turle) *Cathedral Services* (1841) and *Chants, Ancient and Modern* (1841); composed many anthems (including one for Wellington's funeral), orchestral works and glees.

GOSSAGE, Sir **(Ernest) Leslie** (1891–1949), air marshal; educated at Rugby and Trinity College, Cambridge; served in Royal Flying Corps, 1915–18; DSO, 1919; commanded No. 11 (fighter) group, 1936–40; Balloon Command, 1940–4; Air Training Corps, 1944–6; KCB, 1941.

GOSSE, Sir **Edmund William** (1849–1928), poet and man of letters; son of P. H. *Gosse; worked in catalogue section of British Museum, 1865–75; began to study literature, from which he had been debarred by rigid upbringing; first writer to introduce Ibsen to English public; as writer for reviews earned reputation of sound critic; translator to Board of Trade, attached to commercial department, 1875; Clark lecturer in English literature, Trinity College, Cambridge, 1885–90; attacked for inaccuracy by J. Churton *Collins, 1886; librarian to House of Lords, 1904–14; contributed weekly literary articles to *Sunday Times*, 1918–28; knighted, 1925; his numerous volumes of poetry, criticism, and biography include *Collected Poems* (1911), *Seventeenth Century Studies* (1883), and *Father and Son* (1907).

GOSSE, Emily (1806–1857), religious writer; first wife of Philip Henry *Gosse; published devotional verse and religious and educational tracts.

GOSSE, Philip Henry (1810–1888), zoologist; while in a whaler's office at Carbonear, Newfoundland, devoted himself to study of insects; after farming in Canada and the United States returned to England, 1839, and published *The Canadian Naturalist* (1840) and *Introduction to Zoology* (1843); collected birds and insects in Jamaica for British Museum, 1844–6; issued *Birds of Jamaica* (1847, with plates, 1849) and *A Naturalist's Sojourn in Jamaica* (1851); suggested a marine aquarium in *Rambles on the Devonshire Coast* (1853), a work followed by *The Aquarium* (1854) and *Manual of Marine Zoology* (1855–6); FRS, 1856; published *Actinologia Britannica* (1858–60) and *Romance of Natural History* (1860, 1862); devoted last years to *rotifera* and orchids.

GOSSELIN, Sir **Martin Le Marchant Hadsley** (1847–1905), diplomat; secretary of embassy at Brussels, Madrid, Berlin, and Paris, 1885–98; joint British delegate in Customs Tariffs Conferences at Brussels, 1889–90; secretary of International Conference for Suppression of African Slave Trade, 1889–90; CB, 1890; member of commission for delimitation of French and English possessions about River Niger, 1898; KCMG, 1898; British envoy at Lisbon, 1902–5; GCVO, 1904; joined Roman Church, 1878.

GOSSELIN, Thomas le Marchant (1765–1857), admiral; entered navy, 1778; captured in the *Ardent* off Plymouth, 1779; assisted in reduction of Surinam, 1799; convoyed troops to the Tagus, 1808, and covered embarkation at Corunna, 1809; vice-admiral, 1825; admiral, 1841.

GOSSET, Isaac, the elder (1713–1799), modeller of portraits in wax; exhibited with the Incorporated Society of Artists, 1760–78.

GOSSET, Isaac, the younger (1735?–1812), bibliographer; son of Isaac *Gosset the elder; MA, Exeter College, Oxford, 1770; the 'Lepidus' of *Dibdin's *Bibliomania*; assisted in Dibdin's *Introduction to the Classics* (1802) and John *Nichols's edition of *Bowyer's *Critical Conjectures and Observations on the New Testament* (1782); FRS, 1772.

GOSSET, Matthew (1683–1744), wax modeller and member of Spalding Society; uncle of Isaac *Gosset the elder.

GOSSET, Montague (1792–1854), surgeon; a favourite pupil of Sir Astley *Cooper; practised in the City thirty-four years; hon. FRCS, 1843; introduced improved tonsil iron for enlarged tonsils and nitric acid for the destruction of naevi.

GOSSET, William Sealy ('Student') (1876–1937), statistician and industrial research scientist; scholar of Winchester and New College, Oxford; first class, natural science, 1899; joined Arthur Guinness, Son & Co. (1899) and became head brewer (1937); applied statistical methods to problems of the chemist and biologist and did pioneer work in agricultural experimentation.

GOSSON, Stephen (1554–1624), author; BA, Corpus Christi College, Oxford, 1576; ranked by *Meres among 'the best for pastoral'; his plays not now extant; attacked poets and players in his *Schoole of Abuse* (1579, often reprinted); defended it in *Ephemerides of Phialo* (1579); replied to Lodge and *The Play of Playes* in *Playes confuted in Fiue Actions* (1582); evoked by his unauthorized dedications of his works to Sir Philip *Sidney, Sidney's *Apologie for Poetrie* (published, 1595); rector of Great Wigborough, 1581, and St Botolph's, Bishopsgate, 1600.

GOSSON, Thomas (*fl.* 1598), publisher of *Playes Confuted* (1582); probably brother of Stephen *Gosson.

GOSTLIN, John (1566?–1626), master of Gonville and Caius College, Cambridge; MA, Gonville and Caius College, Cambridge, 1590; fellow, 1592–1619; MD, 1602; MP, Barnstaple, 1614; twice vice-chancellor; Cambridge regius professor of physic, 1623; master of Gonville and Caius College, Cambridge, 1619–26; benefactor of Caius and St Catharine's colleges, Cambridge.

GOSTLIN, John (1632–1704), benefactor of Gonville and Caius College, Cambridge; related to John *Gostlin (1566?–1626); fellow of Peterhouse and (1661) Caius College, Cambridge; MD, Cambridge, 1661; vice-master of Caius College, 1679.

GOSTLING, John (d. 1733), chorister; BA, St John's College, Cambridge, 1672; famous bass in the Chapel Royal, for whom *Purcell wrote the anthem *They that go down to the sea in ships*; vicar of Littlebourne, sub-dean of St Paul's, and prebendary of Lincoln.

GOSTLING, William (1696–1777), antiquary; son of John *Gostling; MA, St John's College, Cambridge, 1719; minor canon of Canterbury, 1727–77; vicar of Littlebourne, 1733–53, of Stone in Oxney, 1753–77; published *Walk in and about the City of Canterbury* (1774); his rendering into verse of *Hogarth's expedition to Canterbury (1732) inserted in *Hone's *Table-book* (reprinted, 1872).

GOSYNHYLL, Edward (*fl.* 1560), poet; author of *Scole House of Women* (1541, anon.), reprinted by E. V. *Utterson (*Select Pieces*, 1817).

GOTAFRIDUS (*fl.* 1290), translator. See JOFROI.

GOTCH, John Alfred (1852–1942), architect and author; educated at Kettering Grammar School, Zurich, and King's College, London; in partnership with Charles Saunders in Kettering; built houses, schools, banks, war memorials, etc.; admirer of the old building crafts; no sympathy with modern trends; PRIBA, 1923–5; authoritative publications include *Architecture of the Renaissance in England* (2 vols., 1891), *The Growth of the English House* (1909), *Inigo Jones* (1928).

GOTER (or GOTHER), John (d. 1704), Roman Catholic divine; educated as a Presbyterian; at Lisbon, 1668–82; his *Papist Misrepresented and Represented* (1685, parts ii and iii, 1687), answered by *Stillingfleet, *Sherlock, and *Clagett; commended by *Dryden for his English; died at sea; published *Pope Pius [IV] his Profession of Faith vindicated* (1687) and other controversial works; his *Spiritual Works* (ed. Revd W. *Crathorne, 16 vols., 1718) often reprinted.

GOTSELIN (*fl.* 1099), biographer. See GOSCELIN.

GOTT, John (1830–1906), bishop of Truro; MA, Brasenose College, Oxford, 1854; DD, 1873; vicar of Leeds, 1873–85; founded Leeds Clergy School, 1875; dean of Worcester, 1886; bishop of Truro, 1891–1906; inherited valuable library, which included the four Shakespeare folios; published *The Parish Priest of the Town* (1887).

GOTT, Joseph (1785–1860), sculptor; patronized by Benjamin Gott, for whom at Armley his chief work was done; exhibited at Royal Academy, 1830–48; died at Rome.

GOTT, William Henry Ewart (1897–1942), lieutenant-general; educated at Harrow and Sandhurst; commissioned in King's Royal Rifle Corps, 1915; nicknamed 'Strafer'; taken prisoner, 1917; commanded 1st battalion in Egypt, 1938–9; GSO 1, 7th Armoured division, 1939; commanded its support group in successful campaign against Italians, 1940–1; 7th Armoured division in autumn offensive, 1941; XIII Corps, 1942; outstanding desert leader; selected by (Sir) Winston Churchill to command Eighth Army but shot down returning to Cairo, Aug. 1942; DSO and bar, 1941; CB, 1942.

GOUDGE, Elizabeth de Beauchamp (1900–1984), author; educated at Grassendale School, Southbourne, and the Art School at Reading College; worked as handicraft teacher at Oxford when her father, the Revd Henry Leighton Goudge, DD became regius professor of divinity, 1923; first novel *Island Magic* (1934) followed by fifteen other novels, including *City of Bells* (1936), *Towers in the Mist* (1938), *Green Dolphin Country* (1944, made into successful film in 1947), trilogy *The Eliots of Damerosehay* made up of *The Bird in the Tree* (1940), *The Herb of Grace* (1948), and *The Heart of the Family* (1953); also published *The Dean's Watch* (1960), *The Scent of Water* (1963), and *The Child from the Sea* (1970); and six children's books including *God so loved the World* (1951) and *St Francis of Assisi* (1959), and autobiography *The Joy of the Snow* (1974); FRSL, 1945; Literary Guild Award; MGM Film Prize for *Green Dolphin Street*, and Carnegie Medal for children's book, *The Little White Horse* (1946).

GOUDIE, John (1717–1809), author. See GOLDIE.

GOUDY, Alexander Porter (1809–1858), Presbyterian; minister of Strabane, 1833–58; DD, Jefferson College, USA, 1851; moderator of general assembly, 1857; took part in controversy with Archibald (afterwards Dean) *Boyd, publishing *Presbyterianism Defended* (1839), *The Plea of Presbytery*, and other works.

GOUGE, Robert (1630–1705), Independent divine; pupil of Henry *More at Christ's College, Cambridge; rector of St Helen's, Ipswich, 1652–62; afterwards had Independent congregations there and at Coggeshall.

GOUGE, Thomas (1605–1681), Nonconformist divine and philanthropist; son of William *Gouge; of Eton and King's College, Cambridge; fellow, 1628; MA; vicar of St Sepulchre's, London, 1638–62; provided work for the poor in flax-and hemp-spinning; friend of Thomas *Firmin; organized religious instruction in South Wales, and assisted in forming trust for printing and circulating religious works in the vernacular, 1674; works collected (1706).

GOUGE, Thomas (1665?–1700), Independent divine; son of Robert *Gouge; pastor of English Church at Amsterdam and of Independent congregation in Fruiterers' Alley, Thames Street, 1689; merchant lecturer at Pinners' Hall, 1694; praised by Isaac *Watts in *Elegiac Essay* (published 1700).

GOUGE, William (1578–1653), Puritan divine; of St Paul's School and Eton; fellow of King's College, Cambridge, 1598; MA, 1602; DD, 1628; rector of St Anne's, Blackfriars, 1621–53; imprisoned for his edition of Finch's *World's Great Restauration* (1621); joined scheme for buying up impropriations for Puritans, 1626; refused to read 'Book of Sports', 1618 and 1633; an assessor of the Westminster Assembly, 1647; took the Covenant, but denounced the king's trial; his commentary on Hebrews reprinted (1866).

GOUGH. See also GOFFE.

GOUGH, Alexander Dick (1804–1871), architect and engineer; pupil of B. *Wyatt; with R. L. Roumieu exhibited at the Academy, 1837–47; built or restored churches in Islington, North London, and elsewhere; occupied in railway surveying.

GOUGH, Sir Charles John Stanley (1832–1912), general; born in India; joined army, 1848; VC for gallantry during Indian Mutiny; KCB for services in Afghan War, 1881; general, 1891; retired, with GCB, 1895.

GOUGH, Herbert John (1890–1965), engineer and expert on metal fatigue; educated at Regent Street Polytechnic Technical School, London, and University College School; apprenticed to Messrs Vickers, Sons & Maxim, 1909–13; designer draughtsman; B.Sc., London (and later, D.Sc. and Ph.D.); joined staff of National Physical Laboratory, 1914–38; superintendent, engineering department, 1930; served with Royal Engineers, 1914–19; MBE (military), 1919; at NPL established causes of metal fatigue and developed new methods of design; published

The Fatigue of Metals (1924); first director of scientific research, War Office, 1938; director-general of scientific research and development, Ministry of Supply, 1942–5; engineer-in-chief, Lever Brothers and Unilever Ltd., 1945–55; CB, 1942; FRS, 1933, council member, 1939–40.

GOUGH, Sir **Hubert De La Poer** (1870–1963), general; elder son of (General Sir) Charles John Stanley *Gough, GCB, VC; educated at Eton and Sandhurst; commissioned in 16th Lancers, 1889; served in India and in the South African War; instructor, Staff College, 1903–6; commanded 16th Lancers; brigadier-general commanding 3rd Cavalry brigade at the Curragh, 1911; prepared to resign rather than initiate military operations against Ulster, 1914; major-general; lieutenant-general; commanded 7th division and 1st Corps in France, 1915; commanded Fifth Army in third Ypres campaign, 1917; replaced by Sir Henry *Rawlinson, 1918; retired with rank of full general, 1922; KCB, 1916; KCVO, 1917; GCMG, 1919; published his account of 1918 campaign in *Fifth Army* (1931); amends made by Lloyd George in his *War Memoirs* (1936); GCB, 1937; commanded a London zone Home Guard, 1940–2; published memoirs, *Soldiering On* (1954).

GOUGH, Sir **Hugh,** first Viscount Gough (1779–1869), field marshal; adjutant of Colonel Rochford's Foot (119th) at 15; with 78th Highlanders at capture of the Cape, 1795; commanded 2nd battalion at Talavera, 1809, being severely wounded, and promoted lieutenant-colonel; distinguished at Barossa and Tarifa, 1811; again wounded at Nivelle, 1813; knighted and given freedom of Dublin, 1815; major-general, 1830; KCB, 1831; GCB for capture of Canton forts, 1841, and a baronet for further services in China, 1842; commander-in-chief in India, 1843, when he defeated the Mahrattas; created Baron Gough at conclusion of first Sikh War, 1845, having won the battles of Mudki, 1845, Ferozeshah, 1845, and Sobraon, 1846; created viscount after the second war, 1848–9, which he brought to a close with Battle of Gujerat; received freedom of the City of London and a pension; general, 1854; KP, 1857; privy councillor, 1859; GCSI, 1861; field marshal, 1862.

GOUGH, Sir **Hugh Henry** (1833–1909), general; brother of Sir C. J. S. *Gough; born at Calcutta; joined Bengal Army, 1853; served in Indian Mutiny; at siege of Delhi and relief of Cawnpore; won VC for gallantry at Alambagh, 1857; conspicuous for bravery at Lucknow, 1858; commanded 12th Bengal Cavalry in Abyssinia campaign, 1868; CB, 1868; commanded cavalry of Kuram Field Force, 1878–9; brigadier-general of communications with Kabul Field Force; commanded cavalry brigade in march to Kandahar, 1880; KCB, 1881; general, 1894; GCB, 1896; keeper of crown jewels in London, 1898; published *Old Memories* (1897).

GOUGH (GOWGHE, GOWGH, or **GOUGE), John** (*fl.* 1528–1556), printer, stationer, and translator; of the Mermaid, Fleet Street, and Lombard Street; imprisoned for uttering seditious works, 1541; published first English treatise on bookkeeping (1543).

GOUGH, John (*fl.* 1570), divine; rector of St Peter's, Cornhill, 1560–7; deprived for nonconformity; published a religious work.

GOUGH, John (1610?–1661), divine. See GOFFE.

GOUGH, John (1721–1791), master of the Friends' School, Dublin, 1752–74; afterwards at Lisburn; published *History of the People called Quakers* (1789–90) and a popular tract giving reasons for non-payment of tithes.

GOUGH, John (1757–1825), scientific writer; lost his sight from smallpox when a child, but so trained his sense of touch that he became an accomplished botanist; taught mathematics to John *Dalton, the chemist, and William *Whewell; contributed to Manchester Philosophical Society and *Nicholson's *Philosophical Magazine*; alluded to in *Wordsworth's *Excursion* and *Coleridge's 'Soul and its Organ of Sense'.

GOUGH, John Ballantine (1817–1886), temperance orator; born at Sandgate, Kent; went to the United States at 12, and was a bookbinder till 1843; the foremost temperance lecturer in America, he thrice visited England and addressed immense audiences; died at Philadelphia; published *Autobiography* (1846 and 1871), *Orations* (1877), and other works.

GOUGH, John Edmond (1871–1915), brigadier-general; son of Sir C. J. S. *Gough; born in India; joined army, 1892; VC, 1903; served on staff of (Lord) *Haig, 1914–15; killed in France; posthumous KCB, 1915.

GOUGH, Richard (1735–1809), antiquary; educated at Corpus Christi College, Cambridge; FSA, 1767, and director of the society, 1771–97; FRS, 1775; contributor to *Gentleman's Magazine* as 'D.H.'; made excursions through England for twenty years, often accompanied by John *Nichols; published about twenty works, including *British Topography* (1768 and 1780), *Sepulchral Monuments of Great Britain* (1786, 1796, 1799), an edition of *Camden's *Britannia*, translated and enlarged (1789), a translation of the *Arabian Nights* (1798), and several topographical and numismatic monographs.

GOUGH, Stephen (1605–1681), Royalist divine. See GOFFE.

GOUGH, Strickland (d. 1752), controversial writer; rector of Swayfield and vicar of Swinstead, Lincolnshire; published *Enquiry into the Causes of the Decay of the Dissenting Interest* (1730, anon.).

GOUGH, Thomas (1591–1629), divine and poet. See GOFFE.

GOUGH, William (d. 1679?), regicide. See GOFFE.

GOUGH, William (1654?–1682), antiquary; BA, St Alban Hall, Oxford, 1675; published *Londinum Triumphans* (1682).

GOUGH-CALTHORPE, Augustus Cholmondeley, sixth Baron Calthorpe (1829–1910), agriculturist; educated at Eton and Merton College, Oxford; MA, 1855; succeeded brother in peerage, 1893; started at Elvetham famous herd of shorthorn cattle, Southdown sheep, and Berkshire pigs; generous donor of land to Birmingham city (1894) and university (1900).

GOUGH-CALTHORPE, Sir **Somerset Arthur** (1864–1937), admiral of the fleet. See CALTHORPE.

GOUGHE (or GOFFE), Robert (d. 1624), actor in Shakespeare's plays.

GOULBURN, Edward (1787–1868), serjeant-at-law; barrister, Middle Temple, 1815; previously served in Horse Guards; Welsh judge; recorder of Leicester, Lincoln, and Boston; MP, Leicester, 1835–7; bankruptcy commissioner, 1842; published two satirical poems and a novel.

GOULBURN, Edward Meyrick (1818–1897), dean of Norwich; educated at Eton and Balliol College, Oxford; MA, 1842; DCL, 1850; DD, 1856; fellow, 1841–6; tutor and dean of Merton College, 1843–5; ordained priest, 1843; chaplain to Samuel *Wilberforce bishop of Oxford, 1847; headmaster of Rugby, 1849–57; accepted ministry of Quebec Chapel, St Marylebone, 1857; dean of Norwich, 1866–89. His works include *Life of Burgon* (1892) and theological manuals.

GOULBURN, Henry (1784–1856), statesman; brother of Edward *Goulburn; MA, Trinity College, Cambridge, 1808; MP, successively, for Horsham, 1808, St Germans, West Looe, Armagh city, and Cambridge University (1831–56); under-secretary for Home Department, 1810, for war and the colonies, 1812–21; commissioner for peace with United States, 1814; privy councillor, 1821; as chief secretary for Ireland, 1821–7, carried Tithe Composition Bill and measure for the suppression of unlawful societies; as chancellor of the Exchequer under Wellington reduced interest of 4 per cent to $3\frac{1}{2}$;

home secretary under Peel, 1834–5, chancellor of the Exchequer, 1841–6; by conversion of stock in budget of 1844 effected an ultimate saving of a million and a quarter; friend and executor of Peel; DCL, Oxford, 1834.

GOULBURN, Henry (1813–1843), senior classic and second wrangler, Cambridge, 1835; barrister, Middle Temple, 1840; son of Henry *Goulburn (1784–1856).

GOULD (afterwards MORGAN), Sir Charles (1726–1806), judge advocate-general; educated at Westminster and Christ Church, Oxford; MA, 1750; hon. DCL, 1773; admitted to Lincoln's Inn, 1742/3; judge advocate-general, 1768; chancellor of Salisbury, 1772; MP, Brecon, 1778–87, Brecon county, 1787–1806; knighted 1779; created baronet, 1792; privy councillor, 1802; assumed name of Morgan, 1792.

GOULD, Sir Francis Carruthers (1844–1925), cartoonist; drew caricatures for amusement while broker and jobber on Stock Exchange; member of *Pall Mall Gazette* staff, 1890; of *Westminster Gazette*, 1893–1914; assistant editor, 1896; a keen radical; knighted, 1906; edited his own paper, *Picture Politics*, 1894–1914; his political cartoons show wit, wealth of ideas, faculty for seizing a likeness, and urbanity; his favourite subject Joseph *Chamberlain.

GOULD, George (1818–1882), Baptist minister in Dublin, Exeter, and (1849–82) St Mary's Chapel, Norwich; president of Baptist Union, 1879; a founder of the 'anti-state-church association', 1844; edited (1862) *Documents relating to the Settlement of the Church of England . . . by the Act of Uniformity, 1662.*

GOULD, Sir Henry, the elder (1644–1710), judge; barrister, Middle Temple, 1667; king's serjeant, 1693; counsel against Sir John *Fenwick, 1696; judge of the King's Bench, 1699–1710.

GOULD, Sir Henry, the younger (1710–1794), judge; grandson of Sir Henry *Gould the elder; barrister, Middle Temple, 1734; KC, 1754; baron of the Exchequer, 1761; transferred to common pleas, 1763.

GOULD, James Alipius (1812–1886), first Roman Catholic archbishop of Melbourne; first bishop of Port Phillip (Victoria), 1848; archbishop of Melbourne, 1876–86.

GOULD, John (1804–1881), ornithologist; taxidermist to the Zoological Society, 1827; travelled in Australasia, 1838–40, making valuable observations and collections; FRS, 1843; exhibited collection of humming-birds, 1851, now with his Australian mammals at South Kensington; published forty-one folios on birds, with 2,999 illustrations, including *A Century of Birds, from the Himalayan Mountains* (1832), *Birds of Europe* (1832–7), *Birds of Australia* (1840–8), and supplement (1851–69), *Birds of Asia* (1850–80), *Birds of Great Britain* (1862–73), and numerous monographs.

GOULD, Nathaniel ('Nat') (1857–1919), novelist; journalist in Australia, 1884–95; first book, *The Double Event* (1891), great success; wrote about 132 books all concerned with horse-racing.

GOULD, Robert (d. 1709?), poet; servant of Charles, earl of *Dorset; published *Poems chiefly consisting of Satyrs and Satyrical Epistles* (1689) and *The Rival Sisters*, tragedy (1696), acted at Drury Lane; works collected (1709).

GOULD, Thomas (1657–1734), controversialist; obtained from Louis XIV abbey of St-Laon de Thouars for missionary work in Poitou; published several anti-Protestant treatises, including *Lettre à un Gentilhomme du Bas-Poitou.*

GOULDING, Frederick (1842–1909), master printer of copper plates; 'devil' to J. A. M. *Whistler in printing some of his etchings, 1859; friend of Sir F. S. *Haden from 1862; printed works by Whistler, Haden, Alphonse *Legros, Rodin, and others; assistant to Legros in etching class at National Art Training School, 1876–82; succeeded Legros, 1882–91; first master printer to Royal Society of Painter-Etchers, 1890.

GOULDMAN, Francis (d. 1688?), lexicographer; MA, Christ's College, Cambridge, 1630; rector of South Ockendon, Essex, 1634–44, and after Restoration; compiled an English–Latin and Latin–English dictionary with proper names, 1664.

GOULSTON (or GULSTON), Theodore (*c.*1575–1632), founder of Gulstonian lecture; BA, Peterhouse, Cambridge, 1594–5; fellow of Merton College, Oxford, 1596; MA, 1600; MD, 1610; FRCP, 1611; four times censor; practised in St Martin-extra-Ludgate; published Latin versions of Aristotle's *Rhetoric* (1619) and *Poetics* (1623), and a critical edition of Galen (posthumous, 1640).

GOUPY, Joseph (d. 1763), water-colour painter and etcher; nephew of Lewis *Goupy; 'cabinet-painter' to *Frederick, prince of Wales, 1736; pensioned by George III on his accession; executed water-colour copies of Raphael's cartoons; nine etchings by him after Salvator Rosa in the British Museum.

GOUPY, Lewis (d. 1747), painter; of French extraction; seceded from *Kneller's academy to that of Louis *Chéron, 1720; accompanied Lord

*Burlington to Italy; painted portraits and miniatures, and drew in crayons and tempera.

GOURDON, William (*fl.* 1611), traveller; master pilot on two expeditions to north of Russia, described in his 'Voyage made to Pechora' and 'Later Observations' (in *Purchas's Pilgrimes*, iii.)

GOURLIE, William (1815–1856), botanist; FLS, 1855; studied under *Hooker and *Balfour; collected mosses, shells, and fossil plants.

GOURNEY, Sir Matthew (1310?–1406), soldier of fortune; present at Sluys, 1340, Algeciras, 1342–4, Crécy, 1346, and Poitiers, 1356; governor of Brest, 1357; a jurat of peace of Bretigni, 1360; imprisoned in the Tower, 1362; present at Auray, 1364; ambassador of Henry, king of Castile, to Portugal; took service with Black Prince, and assisted in Henry's defeat at Najara, 1367; created a baron of Guienne; served again in France and fell into ambush near Soissons; defended Bayonne against Anjou and Henry of Castile, 1378; seneschal of the Landes, 1379; constable of the forces in Portuguese expedition, 1388; sat in upper house in first parliament of Henry IV.

GOUTER (or GAULTIER), James (*fl.* 1636), French lutenist; in service of Charles I of England; referred to by *Herrick.

GOUZENKO, Igor Sergeivich (1919–1982), Soviet Russian defector and author; born at Rogachovo, near Moscow; educated at Maxim Gorky School, Moscow, Art Studio Chemko, and the Architectural Institute, Moscow University; nominated for Stalin fellowship, 1941, but war ended his training as architect; posted to Kuibishev Engineering Academy; studied ciphering and assigned to Moscow headquarters of GRU military intelligence as cipher clerk, 1942; transferred to office of military attaché, Ottawa legation, 1943; defected and testified before royal commission on Russian espionage in Canada, 1945; his information led to arrest of number of Russian agents, including the British atomic physicist Allan Nunn May; given Canadian citizenship and new identity; published memoirs *This Was My Choice* (1948) and best-selling novel *The Fall of a Titan* (1954), and wrote several unpublished works including another novel, *Ocean of Time.*

GOVE, Richard (1587–1668), Puritan divine; MA, Magdalen Hall, Oxford, 1611; incumbent of Hinton St George, 1618; afterwards rector of East Coker, Somerset; published *The Saints' Honeycomb* (1652), *Pious Thoughts vented in Pithy Ejaculations* (1658), and other works.

GOVER, Charles E. (d. 1872), folklorist; principal of Madras Military Male Orphan Asylum,

1864–72; member of Royal Asiatic Society, 1868–72; his essays collected in *Folk-Songs of Southern India* (1872).

GOW, Nathaniel (1766–1831), Scottish violinist and composer; son of Niel *Gow (1727–1807); as leader of M'Glashan's band, 1791, frequently played before George, prince of Wales; published two hundred original melodies, and assisted in and continued his father's volumes.

GOW, Niel (1727–1807), violinist and composer; patronized by duke of *Atholl; was much in request at fashionable gatherings in Scotland and England; his portrait four times painted by *Raeburn; renowned as composer and player of reels and strathspeys, for some of which *Burns wrote words.

GOW, Niel (d. 1823), composer of 'Bonnie Prince Charlie' ('Cam' ye by Athol?'); son of Nathaniel *Gow.

GOWAN, Thomas (1631–1683), writer on logic; minister of Glasslough, Monaghan, 1658; ejected, 1661; with John *Howe carried on school of philosophy and divinity at Antrim; published *Ars Sciendi* (1681) and *Logica Elenctica* (1683).

GOWARD, Mary Ann (1805?–1899), actress. See KEELEY.

GOWER, first Baron (1675–1709). See LEVESON-GOWER, JOHN.

GOWER, first Earl (d. 1754). See LEVESON-GOWER, JOHN.

GOWER. See also LEVESON-GOWER.

GOWER, (Edward) Frederick Leveson- (1819–1907), politician. See LEVESON-GOWER.

GOWER, Sir Erasmus (1742–1814), admiral; in the *Medea* captured the Dutch *Vryheid* and retook the *Chaser* with despatches in East Indies, 1783; knighted after convoying Lord *Macartney to China, 1794; commanded the *Triumph* with Sir William *Cornwallis (1744–1819), 1795; vice-admiral, 1804; admiral, 1809.

GOWER, Foote (1726?–1780), antiquary; MA, Brasenose College, Oxford, 1750; MD, 1757; rector of Chignall St James, Essex, 1761–77; published *Sketch of the Materials for a new History of Cheshire* (1771).

GOWER, George (*fl.* 1575–1585), sergeant-painter to Queen Elizabeth, 1584.

GOWER, Henry (d. 1347), bishop of St David's; fellow of Merton College, Oxford, and DCL; chancellor of Oxford, 1322–5; archdeacon of St David's, 1320; employed by Edward III; bishop of St David's, 1328–47; made 'decorated' additions to his cathedral, and built the rood-screen; built the episcopal palace (now in ruins) and the wall round the close; founded and endowed Swansea Hospital.

GOWER, Sir Henry Dudley Gresham Leveson (1873–1954), cricketer; grandson of first Baron *Leigh; captain of cricket at Winchester (1892) and Oxford (1896); of MCC team in South Africa, 1909–10; of Surrey, 1908–10; president, Surrey County Cricket Club, 1929–40; test-match selector; associated with Scarborough Cricket Festival for fifty years; knighted, 1953.

GOWER, Humphrey (1638–1711), master of St John's College, Cambridge; fellow of St John's College, Cambridge, 1659; MA, 1662; incumbent successively of Hammoon, Dorsetshire, Packlesham, 1667–75, Newton, Isle of Ely, and Fen Ditton; prebendary of Ely, 1679; when vice-chancellor entertained Charles II at St John's, 1681; master of St John's, 1679–1711; Margaret professor of divinity, 1688; benefactor of his college.

GOWER, John (1325?–1408), poet; probably travelled in France in early life, afterwards settling down as a country gentleman; well known at court in his last years; became blind, 1400; died at the priory of St Mary Overies, Southwark, and was buried in the church (now St Saviour's); his will extant at Lambeth; friend of *Chaucer, who called him 'moral Gower', but probably quarrelled with him later. Of his chief works, the *Speculum Meditantis* is a poem written in French, which was discovered by G. C. Macaulay, and published in his edition of Gower. The *Vox Clamantis* (in Latin elegiacs), dedicated to Archbishop *Arundel, contains an account of the Peasants' Revolt of 1381, and an indictment of government and society under Richard II. Attached to it in Coxe's collation is Gower's *Chronica Tripartita*, a Latin poem dealing with events as far as the abdication of Richard II, in which the victims of his *coup d'état* are eulogized (the whole first printed by the Roxburghe Club, ed. H. O. *Coxe, 1850). The *Confessio Amantis* (Gower's only English poem), extant in two versions, the first dedicated to Richard II, the second to Henry IV, contains many stories drawn from Ovid and later sources, with learned digressions, and is preceded by a prologue. *Caxton's edition (1483) follows the second version, as does Berthelet's (1532), the latter being the basis of Pauli's text (1857), reprinted by Professor H. *Morley (1888). Extracts from a manuscript volume of other poems presented by Gower to Henry IV were printed (1818).

GOWER, Richard Hall (1767–1833), naval architect; son of Foote *Gower; educated at

Winchester; midshipman in East India Company's service, 1780; built sailing yachts on an improved plan; chief work, *A Treatise on the Theory and Practice of Seamanship* (1793).

GOWER, Sir **Thomas** (*fl.* 1543–1577), marshal of Berwick and surveyor of royal estates in Northumberland; captured by Scots at Pinkie, 1547; as master of the ordnance in the north directed siege of Leith, 1560.

GOWERS, Sir **Ernest Arthur** (1880–1966), public servant; son of (Sir) William Richard *Gowers; educated at Rugby and Clare College, Cambridge; first class, classical tripos, 1902; entered Civil Service; posted to Inland Revenue Department and transferred to India Office; called to the bar (Inner Temple), 1906; private secretary to several ministers; principal private secretary to David Lloyd George, chancellor of the Exchequer, 1911; chief inspector, National Health Insurance Commission (England), 1912–17; secretary to Conciliation and Arbitration Board for Government Employees, 1917; director of production, Mines Department (Board of Trade), 1919; permanent under-secretary for mines, 1920; chairman, Board of Inland Revenue, 1927–30; chairman, Coal Commission, 1938; chairman, manpower subcommittee of Committee of Imperial Defence; regional commissioner for civil defence, London region, 1939; senior regional commissioner, 1941; chairman of number of other commissions and committees; chairman, National Hospitals for Nervous Diseases, London, 1948–57; one of greatest public servants of his day; published *Plain Words: a Guide to the Use of English* (1948), written at invitation of Sir Edward (later Lord) *Bridges; other publications include *ABC of Plain Words* (1951) and a revision of *Modern English Usage* (1965), by H. W. *Fowler; hon. D.Litt., Manchester; hon. associate, Royal Institute of British Architects; CB, 1917; KBE, 1926; KCB, 1928; GBE, 1945; GCB, 1953.

GOWERS, Sir **William Richard** (1845–1915), physician; educated at University College, London; MRCS, 1867; on staff of hospital for paralysed and epileptic, Queen Square, London, 1870; and on that of University College Hospital, 1872; FRS, 1887; specialized in neurology; chief work, *A Manual of Diseases of the Nervous System* (1886).

GOWRAN, first Baron (d. 1727). See FITZ-PATRICK, RICHARD.

GOWRIE, earls of. See RUTHVEN, WILLIAM, first earl, 1541?–1584; RUTHVEN, JOHN, third earl, 1578?–1600; HORE-RUTHVEN, ALEXANDER GORE ARKWRIGHT, 1872–1955.

GRABE, John Ernest (1666–1711), divine; came to England from Königsberg and received a pension from William III; chaplain of Christ Church, Oxford, 1700; DD, Oxford, 1706; published *Spicilegium SS. Patrum* (1698–9), also editions of Justin Martyr (1700) and Irenaeus (1702), and of Bishop *Bull's works, and a transcript of the *Codex Alexandrinus* (Septuagint) with numerous emendations (vol. i, 1707, vol. ii, 1709).

GRACE, Edward Mills (1841–1911), cricketer; studied medicine at Bristol; MRCS, 1865; practised at Thornbury from 1869 till death; coroner for West Gloucestershire, 1875–1909; played cricket for Gentlemen v. Players between 1862 and 1869; visited Australia with George *Parr's team, 1863; with brother W. G. *Grace raised Gloucestershire to first-class cricketing county and played for England v. Australia, 1880; unorthodox and forcible batsman; pioneer of 'pull' stroke; unrivalled as fielder at point; played till age of 70.

GRACE, Mrs **Mary** (d. 1786?), painter; exhibited with Incorporated Society of Artists.

GRACE, Richard (1620?–1691), Irish soldier; carried on guerilla warfare against the Commonwealth; captured at Portumna, and allowed to transport himself and followers to Spain, 1652; joined French service with his regiment, but in 1655 returned to Spanish service, in which he fought at Battle of the Dunes, 1658; at the Restoration regained his estates, and received others with a pension; when governor of Athlone joined James II, and compelled *Douglas to raise the siege, 1690; killed in second siege.

GRACE, Sheffield (1788?–1850), historical writer; patron of *Banim; FRS and FSA; published *Memoirs of the Family of Grace* (1823) and other works relating to the family; also (1827) Lady *Nithsdale's account of the escape (1717) of her husband from the Tower.

GRACE, William Gilbert (1848–1915), cricketer; brother of Edward Mills *Grace; studied medicine in Bristol and London; MRCS, 1879; surgeon in Bristol, 1879–99; played cricket for Gentlemen v. Players between 1865 and 1906; supreme as batsman in England, 1866–76; long series of extraordinary scores reached its zenith in 1876 with 400 not out; with brothers started, and made first-class, Gloucestershire county eleven, 1870; visited Australia, 1873 and 1891; played for England v. Australia, 1880 and 1882; presented with £5,000 by *Daily Telegraph* fund, 1895; in 43 years' career made 126 centuries, scored 54,896 runs, and took 2,876 wickets; first-rate as bowler and fielder as well as batsman; his powerful physique capable of great endurance; known to public as 'W. G.' and widely recognized by his thick black beard.

GRADDON, Miss (afterwards Mrs **GIBBS)** (1804–1854?), vocalist; sang at Drury Lane as Susanna in *Marriage of Figaro*, 1824, and as Linda in *Der Freischütz*.

GRADWELL, Robert (1777–1833), Roman Catholic prelate; imprisoned with other students of Douai on the suppression of Douai College; rector of English College of St Thomas at Rome, 1818; created DD by the pope, 1821; coadjutor (bishop of Lydda *in partibus*) to Bishop *Bramston, vicar-apostolic of London district, 1828; published *Winter Evening Dialogue between John Hardman and John Cardwell* (1817).

GRAEME, James (1749–1772), poet; his verses published by Robert *Anderson (1750–1830), 1773.

GRAFTON, dukes of. See FITZROY, HENRY, first duke, 1663–1690; FITZROY, AUGUSTUS HENRY, third duke, 1735–1811; FITZROY, GEORGE HENRY, fourth duke, 1760–1844.

GRAFTON, Richard (d. 1572?), chronicler and printer; with Edward *Whitchurch had *Coverdale's Bible reprinted at Antwerp (Matthews's Bible), 1537, and Paris, 1538; their 'Great Bible' suppressed at Paris, but printed in England, 1539; ordered to be purchased by every parish, and frequently reissued; with Whitchurch received exclusive patents for church service-books and primers; as 'king's printer' issued Prayer-Book of 1549, acts of parliament (1552–3), and Lady Jane *Grey's proclamation; chief master of Christ's Hospital, 1560; MP, London, 1553–4 and 1556–7, and Coventry, 1562–3; warden of the Grocers' Company, 1555–6; master of Bridewell, 1559–60; charged by Stow with garbling the editions issued by him of *Hardyng's *Chronicle* (1543) and Edward *Hall's *Union* (1548); himself compiled *Abridgement of the Chronicles of England* (1562) and a *Chronicle at Large* (1568). An 'augmented' edition of the latter (1611) was reprinted by Sir H. *Ellis (1809).

GRAHAM, Mrs Catherine (1731–1791). See MACAULAY, Mrs CATHERINE.

GRAHAM, Clementina Stirling (1782–1877), authoress of *Mystifications* (ed. Dr John *Brown, 1865); translated Jonas de Gelieu's *Bee Preserver* (1829), and wrote songs.

GRAHAM, Dougal (1724–1779), chapbook writer and bellman of Glasgow; took part in the Jacobite rising of 1745 as a camp follower, and published an account of the Rebellion in doggerel, 1746; his chapbooks valuable for folklore;

collected writings edited by G. MacGregor (1883).

GRAHAM, Sir **Fortescue** (1794–1880), general; entered Royal Marine Artillery, 1808; served at Walcheren, 1809, in the Peninsula, America, and Canada; commanded marine battalion at Nanking in first Chinese War, and (1855) a brigade of marines at Bomarsund; CB, 1855; lieutenant-general, 1865; KCB, 1865; general, 1866.

GRAHAM, George (1673–1751), mechanician; invented the mercurial pendulum, the 'dead-beat escapement', and astronomical instruments for *Halley, Bradley, and the French Academy; FRS; buried in Westminster Abbey with Tompion.

GRAHAM, George (1728–1767), dramatist; assistant master at Eton and fellow of King's College, Cambridge; MA, 1754; published a masque, *Telemachus* (1763).

GRAHAM, George Farquhar (1789–1867), musical amateur; secretary to first Edinburgh festival, 1815; composed 'County Guy' and other songs; republished from seventh edition of *Encyclopaedia Britannica, Essay on Theory and Practice of Musical Composition* (1838); contributed to J. M. *Wood's *Songs of Scotland*, and other works.

GRAHAM, Sir **Gerald** (1831–1899), lieutenant-general; educated at Royal Military Academy, Woolwich; lieutenant, Royal Engineers, 1854; major, 1872; major-general, 1881; lieutenant-general, 1884; colonel-commandant, Royal Engineers, 1899; served in Crimea, 1854–6, and received Victoria Cross, 1857; brevet-major, 1859; served in Anglo-French expedition against China, 1860–1; brevet-lieutenant-colonel; commanding Royal Engineer in Montreal, 1866–9; CB and brevet-colonel; commanded second infantry brigade of first division in expedition to Egypt, 1882; won victory at Kassassin; led assault on Tel-el-Kebir; commanded brigade of British Army of Occupation in Egypt; KCB, 1882; commanded expedition against Osman Digna, 1884; won battles of El Teb and Tamai; urged unsuccessfully importance of opening up Suakin-Berber route to assist General Charles George *Gordon; advanced from Suakin, 1885, against Osman Digna; repulsed enemy at Hashin and Tamai; GCMG, 1885; published writings on professional and other subjects.

GRAHAM, Henry Grey (1842–1906), writer on Scottish history; educated at Edinburgh University; Church of Scotland minister in Glasgow, 1884–1906; published life of *Rousseau* (1882), *Social Life of Scotland in the 18th Century*

(2 vols., 1899), and *Scottish Men of Letters of the 18th Century* (1901).

GRAHAM, Hugh, Baron Atholstan (1848–1938), newspaper proprietor; born in Quebec; founded *Montreal Star* (1869), *Family Herald, Weekly Star,* and *Montreal Standard*; acquired *Montreal Herald*; uncannily skilful in assessing news values and public taste; strong protectionist and imperialist; gave generously to hospitals and medical research, etc.; knighted, 1908; baron, 1917.

GRAHAM, James, first marquis and fifth earl of Montrose (1612–1650), succeeded as fifth earl, 1626; on return from three years' travel coldly received by Charles I, 1636; joined Covenanters, 1637; occupied Aberdeen, carried off *Huntly, and defeated his son at the Bridge of Dee, 1639; invaded England with Covenanters, 1640; joined Charles I, 1641; imprisoned by *Argyll, but liberated on the king's arrival; his advice long rejected for that of *Hamilton; created marquis and lieutenant-general in Scotland, 1644; won six battles with mixed Irish and Highland force, 1644–5; after Kilsyth entered Glasgow and summoned a parliament; deserted by the Highlanders; defeated at Philiphaugh, 1645; escaped to the continent; made field marshal by the emperor Ferdinand III, with leave to levy troops for Charles I, 1648; advised Charles II against accepting throne of Scotland from Covenanters, and became his lieutenant-governor, 1649; raised money in Denmark and Sweden, but lost many men by shipwreck; defeated at Invercarron, 1650; betrayed by *Macleod of Assynt, and hanged in the Grassmarket, Edinburgh; wrote vigorous verse.

GRAHAM, James, second marquis of Montrose (1631?–1669), 'the good Marquis'; second son of James *Graham, first marquis; imprisoned as a youth in Edinburgh; received back his estates, but joined *Glencairn's rising, 1653; declined to vote at marquis of *Argyll's trial, 1661; established claim of £100,664 Scots against earl of *Argyll, 1667; extraordinary lord of session, 1668.

GRAHAM, James (1649–1730), colonel; of Westminster and Christ Church, Oxford; captain of Scottish infantry in French service, 1671; entered English service, 1675; lieutenant-colonel of Morpeth's Foot, 1678; keeper of privy purse to duke of York, 1679, and James II, 1685; MP, Carlisle, 1685; corresponded with James II at St Germain; outlawed; pardoned, 1692; imprisoned in connection with the 'assassination plot', 1696; took the oaths, 1701; MP, Appleby, 1705–7, and Westmoreland, 1708–27; intimate of the third earl of *Sunderland.

GRAHAM, James, fourth marquis and first duke of Montrose (d. 1742), succeeded as fourth marquis, 1684; acquired property of the duke of Lennox, 1702; high admiral of Scotland, 1705; president of the council, 1706; created duke for promoting the Union, 1707; representative peer; keeper of privy seal (Scotland), 1709–13 and 1716–33; named by George I a lord of the regency and one of the secretaries of state, 1714; privy councillor, 1717.

GRAHAM, James (1676–1746), dean of the Faculty of Advocates; judge of the Scottish Admiralty court, 1739; founded family of Graham of Airth Castle.

GRAHAM, James (1745–1794), quack doctor; studied medicine at Edinburgh under *Monro primus; practised as oculist and aurist in America; settled at Bristol, 1774, and began to advertise wonderful cures; removed to Bath, 1777; used electricity, milk baths, and friction; treated the duchess of Devonshire at Aix, 1779; set up his 'Temple of Health' in the Adelphi, where he lectured, sold medicines, and opened a show; caricatured by *Colman in *The Genius of Nonsense* (1780); Emma Lyon (Lady *Hamilton) said to have represented the Goddess of Health in his show, which was removed to Pall Mall, 1781; his property seized for debt, 1782; lectured in Edinburgh, 1783; imprisoned for libelling Edinburgh magistrates; lectured in Paris, 1786, the Isle of Man, 1788, and Bath, 1789; afterwards became a religious enthusiast and was confined as a lunatic at Edinburgh; author of twenty publications.

GRAHAM, James, third duke of Montrose (1755–1836), statesman; educated at Eton and Trinity College, Cambridge; MP, Richmond, 1780, Great Bedwin, 1784–90; a lord of the Treasury, 1783–9; co-paymaster-general, 1789–91; privy councillor and vice-president of the Board of Trade, 1789; master of the horse, 1790–5 and 1807–21; commissioner for India, 1791–1803; lord justice general, 1795–1836; president of the Board of Trade, 1804–6; lord chamberlain, 1821–7 and 1828–30; KG, 1812; chancellor of Glasgow University, 1780–1836.

GRAHAM, James (1765–1811), Scottish poet. See GRAHAME.

GRAHAM, James (1791–1845), army pensioner; distinguished himself in Coldstream Guards at Waterloo, and was one of the two Norcross pensioners; said to have saved *Fitzclarence's life at seizure of the Cato Street conspirators, 1820; died in Kilmainham Hospital.

GRAHAM, James, seventh marquis and fourth duke of Montrose (1799–1874), statesman; MP, Cambridge University, 1825–32; a commissioner of India board, 1828–30; succeeded to dukedom, 1836; lord steward, 1852–3; chancellor of the duchy of Lancaster, 1858; postmaster-general, 1866–8; died at Cannes.

GRAHAM, James Gillespie (1777?–1855), architect; on his marriage assumed name of Graham or Græme; his *chef-d'œuvre* the Convent, with Saxon chapel, White Horse Lane, Edinburgh, 1835; introduced purer Gothic into Scotland; with A. W. *Pugin designed Victoria Hall, Edinburgh, 1842–4.

GRAHAM, Sir **James Robert George** (1792–1861), statesman; educated at Westminster and Christ Church, Oxford; as secretary to Lord Montgomerie had chief conduct of negotiations with King Joachim (Murat) of Naples, 1813–14; Whig MP for Hull, 1818, for St Ives, 1820; resigned on petition next year, 1821; during five years' retirement paid attention to agriculture, and published *Corn and Currency* (1826); succeeded to baronetcy, 1824; MP, Carlisle, 1826–9, Cumberland, 1829–32, East Cumberland, 1832–7; moved reduction of official salaries, 1830; first lord of the Admiralty under Earl Grey, and one of committee of four which prepared first Reform Bill; resigned with Lord Stanley on Irish Church question, 1834, becoming one of the 'Derby Dilly'; MP, Pembroke, 1838, Dorchester, 1841; as home secretary under Peel, 1841–6, dealt with Scottish Church question and trial of *O'Connell; became highly unpopular, especially after his admissions of tampering with foreign refugees' letters, 1844; fall of the ministry occasioned by the defeat of his bill for the protection of life in Ireland, 1846; acted with Peelites; elected for Ripon; refused Lord John Russell's offer of governor-generalship of India, 1847, the Admiralty, 1848, and the Board of Control, but supported him against protectionists; again returned for Carlisle, 1852; first lord of the Admiralty in Aberdeen's coalition ministry, 1852–5; retained office under Palmerston, but resigned with Gladstone and Sidney *Herbert.

GRAHAM, Janet (1723–1805), poet; author of *The Wayward Wife*.

GRAHAM, Sir **John** (d. 1298), warrior; rescued *Wallace at Queensberry; killed at Falkirk, where a monument was afterwards erected to him.

GRAHAM, John, third earl of Montrose (1547?–1608), received renunciation of Scottish crown by Queen *Mary, 1567; fought for the regent at Langside, 1568; succeeded his grandfather in the earldom, 1571; privy councillor under the regent *Mar; a commissioner for *Morton at the pacification of Perth, 1572; one of James VI's council from 1578; prominent member of opposition to Morton and chancellor of assize held on him, 1581; joined in raid of Ruthven, but rallied to the king on his escape, 1583; lord chancellor, 1584–5; planned death of *Angus, 1584; reconciled to Angus, 1587; extraordinary lord of session, 1591; president of the council, 1598; lord chancellor, 1599; king's commissioner at Union Conference, and viceroy of Scotland, 1604.

GRAHAM, John, of Claverhouse, first Viscount Dundee (1649?–1689), studied at St Andrews; served under William of Orange; said to have saved William's life at Seneff, 1674; recommended by him to James, duke of York; captain under *Montrose; sent to repress conventicles in Dumfries and Annandale, 1678; named sheriff-depute of those districts, 1679; defeated at Drumclog, 1679; held Glasgow; present at Bothwell Brigg, 1679; procured supersession of *Monmouth as commander-in-chief by Thomas *Dalyell and adoption of a severer policy towards Covenanters, 1679; failed in his scheme of marriage with heiress of Menteith; carried out new policy in Galloway, 1681, being implacable to ringleaders, but not wantonly cruel to the people; supported by the council against Sir John *Dalrymple, and appointed colonel of newly raised regiment, 1682; visited Charles II at Newmarket, and obtained money grant and estate of Dudhope, 1683; made privy councillor of Scotland; sent into Ayr and Clydesdale with civil as well as military powers, 1684, soon after which the Covenanter *Renwick's manifesto was followed by the 'killing time'; lost influence through quarrel with *Queensberry, and was partially superseded by Colonel Douglas, 1685; temporarily excluded from Privy Council, 1685; not clearly responsible for deaths of the 'Wigtown martyrs', but directly concerned in execution of John *Brown (1627?–1685) of Priestfield; brigadier-general of horse, 1685; supported James II's Romanizing policy; appointed major-general, 1686; examined Renwick, the last of the martyrs (1688), before the council; provost of Dundee, 1688; joined James II at Salisbury as second-in-command of the force from Scotland, 1688; created Viscount Dundee, 1688; with *Balcarres, the only Scots noble in London who remained faithful; allowed by William III to return to Scotland with fifty troopers; found Edinburgh in possession of the Covenanters, and escaped through Stirling to Dudhope, 1689; outlawed on refusal to return to Edinburgh; having received James's commission to command for him in Scotland, made his way to the clans at Lochaber; collected three thousand men, and by Lochiel's advice selected Killiecrankie to await *Mackay's attack; defeated Mackay, but fell mortally wounded.

GRAHAM, John (*fl.* 1720–1775), history painter; settled at The Hague.

GRAHAM, John (1754–1817), painter; director of Trustees' Academy for Scottish manufactures, 1800–17, having *Wilkie, *Allan, and Watson-Gordon as pupils; exhibited at Royal Academy, 1780–97.

GRAHAM, John (1776–1844), historian; MA, Trinity College, Dublin, 1815; rector of Magilligan, 1824–44; published *Annals of Ireland* (1819), *Derriana* (1823), and *History of Ireland, 1689–91* (1839).

GRAHAM, John (1794–1865), bishop of Chester; fourth wrangler and chancellor's medallist, Christ's College, Cambridge; fellow, 1816; MA, 1819; DD, 1831; master of Christ's College, 1830–48; twice vice-chancellor; chaplain to Prince *Albert, 1841; clerk of the closet, 1849; active member of Universities' Commission; bishop of Chester, 1848–65; published sermons.

GRAHAM, John (1805–1839), superintendent of Botanic Garden, Bombay; deputy postmaster-general of Bombay, 1826–39; compiled catalogue of Bombay plants; died at Khandalla.

GRAHAM, John Anderson (1861–1942), missionary; educated at Glasgow High School and Edinburgh University; ordained and appointed missionary of Church of Scotland Young Men's Guild in Kalimpong, 1889; made it centre of educational, welfare, and religious advance; founded children's (Dr Graham's) homes, 1900; first missionary moderator, General Assembly, Church of Scotland, 1931; died in Kalimpong.

GRAHAM, John Murray (1809–1881), historian; MA, Edinburgh, 1828; adopted name Graham on succession to part of the estates of Thomas, Baron *Lynedoch, 1859, a memoir of whom he compiled (1869); published also *Annals and Correspondence of the Viscount and first and second Earls of Stair* (1875).

GRAHAM, Mrs Maria (1785–1842). See CALLCOTT, MARIA, Lady.

GRAHAM, Patrick (d. 1478), archbishop of St Andrews; dean of arts at St Andrews, 1457; bishop of Brechin, 1463–6; succeeded his half-brother, James *Kennedy, as primate, 1466, but went to Rome till fall of the Boyds, 1469; obtained from Sixtus IV the bulls of 1472, constituting St Andrews a metropolitan see; his deposition from the archbishopric of St Andrews by the papal nuncio on charges of heresy and simony procured by William *Schevez, archdeacon of St Andrews, and John Lock (Lok), rector of the university, with the assistance of the king, James III, 1478; died in prison in Lochleven Castle.

GRAHAM, Richard, Viscount Preston (1648–1695), Jacobite; educated at Westminster and Christ Church, Oxford; MA, 1666; created baronet, 1662; MP, Cockermouth, 1675–81 and 1685–8; created a Scottish peer for parliamentary services to James, duke of York, 1680; as envoy-extraordinary to France (1682–5), protested against the seizure of Orange; with Middleton managed the House of Commons for James II; secretary of state, 1688, and one of the council of five left by James in London; created British peer at St Germain, 1689; arrested and sent to the Tower, 1689; his claim of the privilege of a peer disallowed and withdrawn, 1689; released on apologizing, but arrested next year while carrying treasonable papers on board a smack bound for France; tried and sentenced for treason, but pardoned after making confessions implicating *Penn and others, 1691; in retirement revised the translation of Boethius (published, 1695–6), with preface containing allusions to his political conduct.

GRAHAM, Richard (*fl.* 1680–1720), author of *Short Account of the most Eminent Painters*, originally supplement to *Dryden's version of Du Fresnoy's *Art of Painting* (1695).

GRAHAM, Sir Robert (d. 1437), conspirator; banished for language derogatory to the king, 1435; chief agent in conspiracy of Walter, earl of *Atholl, in which *James I was murdered at Perth, 1437; captured in Highlands and tortured to death at Stirling.

GRAHAM (or GRAEME), Robert (1679?–1701), Trappist monk; after a restless life entered monastery of La Trappe, 1699.

GRAHAM (afterwards CUNNINGHAME-GRAHAM), Robert (d. 1797?), composer of 'If doughty deeds my lady please'; some time receiver-general of Jamaica; Radical MP for Stirlingshire, 1794–6; rector of Glasgow University, 1785.

GRAHAM, Sir Robert (1744–1836), judge; fellow of Trinity College, Cambridge, 1767, and third wrangler, 1766; MA, 1769; barrister, Inner Temple; attorney-general to prince of Wales, 1793; KC, 1793; baron of the Exchequer, 1799; knighted, 1800.

GRAHAM, Robert (1786–1845), MD and botanist; professor of botany at Glasgow, 1818–20; regius professor at Edinburgh, 1820–45; contributed to Edinburgh botanical periodicals and *Hooker's *Companion*.

GRAHAM, Robert Bontine Cunninghame (1852–1936), traveller, scholar, Scottish nationalist, socialist, etc.; educated at Harrow and in Brussels; rode with 'gauchos' in Spanish

America; became friend of 'Buffalo Bill' in Mexico; equally at home in Spain, Morocco, or Scotland; Liberal MP, North-West Lanarkshire, 1886–92; became ardent socialist, devoted to William *Morris; imprisoned (1887) after Trafalgar Square riot; first president, national party of Scotland, 1928; works include studies of old Spanish life and the *conquistadores*, and volumes of stories, essays, and sketches; died at Buenos Aires; new city of Don Roberto (Argentina) named after him.

GRAHAM, Sir **Ronald William** (1870–1949), diplomat; educated at Eton and abroad; entered Diplomatic Service, 1892; first secretary, 1904; counsellor of embassy, Cairo, 1907; adviser, Egyptian Ministry of Interior, 1910–16; represented British commanding officer with Egyptian administration, 1914–16; assistant under-secretary, Foreign Office, 1916–19; minister to Holland, 1919–21; ambassador to Italy in an increasingly difficult period, 1921–33; signed Four-Power Pact on behalf of Britain, 1933; KCMG, 1915; PC, 1921; GCVO, 1923.

GRAHAM, Simion (1570?–1614), Franciscan. See GRAHAME.

GRAHAM, Thomas, Baron Lynedoch (1748–1843), general; entered Christ Church, Oxford, 1766; played in first Scottish cricket match, 1785; introduced Cleveland horses and Devon cattle into Scotland; aide-de-camp to Lord *Mulgrave at Toulon, 1793; raised 'Perthshire volunteers' (2nd Scottish Rifles) and received temporary rank of lieutenant-colonel commandant, 1794; Whig MP for Perthshire, 1794–1807; when British commissioner with Austrian Army in Mantua made his way, disguised as a peasant, to Austrian headquarters, 1796–7; distinguished at capture of Minorca, 1798; reorganized defences of Messina and commanded troops blockading Malta, 1799–1800; obtained permanent military rank by influence of Sir John *Moore; Sir John Moore's aide-de-camp in Corunna campaign; commanded brigade in Walcheren expedition, 1809; lieutenant-general, 1810; won victory of Barossa, 1811, but resigned his command on the Spanish generals unfairly claiming the whole credit of the victory; led division under Wellington and assisted at capture of Ciudad Rodrigo, 1812, and Badajos, 1812; commanded left wing at Vittoria, 1813; wounded at Tolosa, 1813; repulsed before San Sebastian, but afterwards reduced the place, 1813; invalided after crossing Bidassoa; commanded British contingent in Holland, 1814; created a peer, 1814, refusing pension; general, 1821; chief founder of United Service Club, where is his portrait by Sir Thomas *Lawrence; GCB and GCMG.

GRAHAM, Thomas (1805–1869), chemist; MA, Glasgow, 1824; subsequently studied at Edinburgh; professor of chemistry at Andersonian University, Glasgow, 1830–7, at University College, London, 1837–55; master of the Mint, 1855–69; vice-president of chemical jury of exhibition of 1851; awarded Keith Prize for discovery of law of diffusion of gases, 1834, and gold medals of Royal Society, 1840 and 1850; first president of Chemical (1840) and Cavendish (1846) societies; edited *Chemical Reports and Memoirs* (1848); FRS, 1836; twice vice-president; Bakerian lecturer, 1850 and 1854; DCL, Oxford, 1853; discovered the polybasic character of phosphoric acid, and made valuable researches on the compounds of alcohol with salts; introduced the 'Graham tube'; published *Elements of Chemistry* (1842).

GRAHAM, Thomas Alexander Ferguson (1840–1906), artist; studied at Edinburgh under Scott *Lauder; in Paris (1860), Brittany (1862), Venice (1864), Morocco (1885); painted much in Fifeshire fishing villages; in *The Passing Salute* and *The Siren* showed command of colour and sense of atmosphere; hon. RSA, 1883; friend of *Orchardson and *Pettie.

GRAHAM, William, seventh earl of Menteith and first earl of Airth (1591–1661), member of the Scottish Privy Council, 1626; president, 1628; justice general of Scotland, 1628; in great favour with Charles I, who made him privy councillor of England; created earl of Strathearn, 1631, but, the patent being withdrawn in 1633, was made earl of Airth instead; disgraced soon afterwards, being charged with boasting of his descent from Robert II; restored to favour, 1637; served against Covenanters.

GRAHAM, William (1737–1801), Secession minister at Whitehaven, 1759; at Newcastle, 1770–1801; published, among other works, *Candid Vindication of the Secession Church* (1790) and *Review of Ecclesiastical Establishments in Europe* (1792).

GRAHAM, William (1810–1883), Irish Presbyterian divine; missionary (1842–83) to Jews at Damascus, Hamburg, and Bonn; wrote commentaries on Ephesians, 1 John, and Titus, and *An Appeal to Israel* (in four languages).

GRAHAM, William (1839–1911), philosopher and political economist; BA, Trinity College, Dublin, 1867; MA, 1870; vindicated *Berkeley's philosophy in *Idealism* (1872); lecturer in mathematics at St Bartholomew's Hospital, 1877; his *The Creed of Science* (1881) praised by *Darwin and Gladstone; professor of jurisprudence and political economy in Queen's College, Belfast, 1882–1909; hon. Litt.D., Dublin, 1905; other works include *Socialism New and Old* (1890) and *English Political Philosophy from Hobbes to Maine* (1899).

GRAHAM, William (1887–1932), labour leader; educated at George Heriot's School, Edinburgh; became journalist; joined Independent Labour party, 1906; elected to Edinburgh Town Council, 1913; MA, Edinburgh, 1915; Labour MP, Central Edinburgh, 1918–31; served on royal commissions on income-tax and Oxford and Cambridge, and many committees; financial secretary to Treasury, 1924; president of Board of Trade, 1929–31; responsible for Coal-Mines Bill, several overseas missions, and industrial inquiries; PC, 1924.

GRAHAM BROWN, Thomas (1882–1965), neurophysiologist and mountaineer. See BROWN.

GRAHAME, James (1765–1811), Scottish poet; educated at Glasgow; successively writer to the signet, advocate, and episcopal clergyman; published (at first anonymously), *The Sabbath* (1804), *Birds of Scotland* (1806), and *British Georgics* (1809), and other verse; praised by 'Christopher *North', but satirized by *Byron.

GRAHAME, Kenneth (1859–1932), author; educated at St Edward's School, Oxford; clerk in Bank of England, 1879; secretary of Bank of England, 1898–1908; publications include *The Golden Age* (1895), *Dream Days* (1898), and *The Wind in the Willows* (1908).

GRAHAME, Simion (1570?–1614), Franciscan; made prebendary of Brodderstanis by James VI; led licentious life as traveller, soldier, and courtier; died a Franciscan at Carpentras; his *Passionate Sparke of a Relenting Minde* and *Anatomie of Hvmors* reprinted (1830).

GRAHAME-WHITE, Claude (1879–1959), pioneer aviator and aircraft manufacturer; educated at Bedford Grammar School; trained as engineer; obtained pilot's certificate from French Aero Club and made notable flights in England and America, 1910; set up London Aerodrome and aviation company at Hendon, 1911; trained pilots and made advances in design and manufacture; his factories and aerodrome purchased by Government after 1914–18 war; wrote many books on flying.

GRAHAM-GILBERT, John (1794–1866), painter; assumed additional name of Gilbert on marriage, 1834; exhibited at Royal Academy, 1820–3; RSA, 1829; exhibited constantly at the Scottish and occasionally at the Royal Academy; painted mainly portraits.

GRAHAM-HARRISON, Sir William Montagu (1871–1949), parliamentary draftsman; born Harrison; changed name on marriage, 1900; educated at Wellington and Magdalen College, Oxford; first class, jurisprudence, 1894; fellow of All Souls, 1895; called to bar (Lincoln's Inn), 1897; member, London School Board, 1900–3; entered Parliamentary Counsel Office, 1903; solicitor for HM Customs and Excise, 1913; second parliamentary counsel, 1917; first, 1928–33; KC, 1930; KCB, 1926.

GRAHAM-LITTLE, Sir Ernest Gordon Graham (1867–1950), physician, and member of parliament for London University; born in India; educated in South Africa; BA, Cape University, 1887; graduated in medicine, London, 1893; physician, skin department, and lecturer in dermatology, St Mary's Hospital, 1902; consulting physician, 1934; member, London University Senate, 1906–50; Independent MP, London University, 1924–50; first elected to oppose *Haldane's proposed reforms; sturdy progressive individualist; implacable opponent of National Health Service; knighted, 1931.

GRAILE, Edmund (*fl.* 1611), poet; entered Magdalen College, Oxford, 1593; MA, 1600; physician of St Bartholomew's Hospital, Gloucester; published *Little Timothie, his Lesson* (1611).

GRAIN, Richard Corney (1844–1895), public entertainer; barrister, Inner Temple, 1866; member of German Reed entertainment, 1870–95; wrote songs and musical sketches.

GRAINGER, Edward (1797–1824), anatomical teacher; dresser to Sir Astley *Cooper; opened an anatomical school in Southwark, 1819.

GRAINGER, James (1721?–1766), physician and poet; army surgeon, 1745–8; MD, Edinburgh, 1753; friend of Dr *Johnson, *Shenstone, and Bishop Thomas *Percy; contributed to *Monthly Review*, 1756–8; LRCP, 1758; his version of Tibullus attacked by *Smollett, 1759; practised in St Christopher, 1759–63; published *The Sugar Cane* (1764) and *Essay on the more common West India Diseases* (1764); died in St Christopher; contributed a West Indian ballad to Percy's *Reliques*; his *Poetical Works* edited by Robert *Anderson (1836).

GRAINGER, Richard (1798–1861), architect; of Newcastle upon Tyne.

GRAINGER, Richard Dugard (1801–1865), anatomist and physiologist; brother of Edward *Grainger, whose anatomical school he carried on; lecturer at St Thomas's Hospital, 1842–60; declined to receive a money testimonial, 1860, on which the Grainger Testimonial Prize was founded with the money collected; as Board of Health inspector wrote valuable report on chol-

era, 1850; inspector under Burials Act, 1853; FRS; member of council of College of Surgeons; Hunterian orator, 1848; published *Elements of General Anatomy* (1829) and *Observations on . . . the Spinal Cord* (1837).

GRAINGER, Thomas (1794–1852), civil engineer; laid down many railways in Scotland and northern England; fatally injured in railway accident.

GRAMMONT, Elizabeth, comtesse de (1641–1708). See HAMILTON, ELIZABETH.

GRANARD, earls of. See FORBES, Sir ARTHUR, first earl, 1623–1696; FORBES, GEORGE, third earl, 1685–1765; FORBES, GEORGE, sixth earl, 1760–1837.

GRANBY, marquis of (1721–1770). See MANNERS, JOHN.

GRANDISON, Viscounts. See ST JOHN, OLIVER, first viscount, 1559–1630; VILLIERS, GEORGE BUSSY, seventh viscount, 1735–1805; VILLIERS, GEORGE CHILD-, eighth viscount, 1773–1859.

GRANDISON, John (1292?–1369), bishop of Exeter; prebendary of York, 1309, of Lincoln, 1317; archdeacon of Nottingham, 1310; chaplain to Pope John XXII, and papal legate, 1327; appointed bishop of Exeter by provision, and consecrated at Avignon, 1327; successfully resisted visitation of Archbishop *Mepeham, 1332; completed nave of his cathedral and erected episcopal throne; his tomb in St Radegunde's Chapel ransacked in sixteenth century; his *Lessons from the Bible* and *Legends of the Saints* still extant.

GRANE, Viscount (d. 1541). See GREY, Lord LEONARD.

GRANET, Sir (William) Guy (1867–1943), barrister, railway administrator and chairman; educated at Rugby and Balliol College, Oxford; called to bar (Lincoln's Inn), 1893; secretary, Railway Companies' Association, 1900; general manager, Midland Railway Company, 1906; director, 1918; chairman, 1922; chairman, London, Midland, and Scottish Railway, 1924–7; on Royal Commission on Civil Service, 1912–14; National Economy Committee, 1921–2; director-general, Movements and Railways, 1917; chairman, British and Allied Provisions Commission, 1918; knighted, 1911; GBE, 1923.

GRANGE, Lord (1679–1754). See ERSKINE, JAMES.

GRANGE, John (*fl.* 1577), poet; author of *The Golden Aphroditis* (1577).

GRANGER, James (1723–1776), biographer and print collector; entered Christ Church, Oxford, 1743; vicar of Shiplake, Oxfordshire;

collected fourteen thousand engraved portraits; published *Biographical History of England, from Egbert the Great to the Revolution . . . adapted to a Methodical Catalogue of Engraved British Heads* (1769, with supplement, 1774); a continuation of the work from Granger's manuscripts, by Mark *Noble, bringing the history down to 1727, was published (1806).

GRANT, Albert, known as Baron Grant (1830–1899), company promoter; son of W. Gottheimer; assumed name of Grant; achieved extraordinary success as company promoter; gained £100,000 as promotion money for the Emma Silver Mine, which paid investors a shilling for each £20 share; MP, Kidderminster, 1865–8 and 1874–80; purchased Leicester Square, London, which he converted into a public garden and handed over to Metropolitan Board of Works, 1874; died comparatively poor owing to series of actions in bankruptcy court.

GRANT, Alexander (1679–1720), laird of Grant; brigadier-general; son of Ludovick *Grant; MP for Inverness-shire in Scottish parliament, 1703–7; a commissioner for the Union; served in Flanders; brigadier-general, 1711; constable of Edinburgh Castle, 1715; MP for Inverness-shire and Elgin and Forres in British parliament.

GRANT, Sir Alexander, tenth baronet, 'of Dalvey' (1826–1884), principal of Edinburgh University; educated at Harrow; scholar of Balliol College, Oxford; fellow of Oriel College, 1849; succeeded as baronet, 1856; professor of history at the Elphinstone Institution, Madras, 1860, and principal, 1862; vice-chancellor of Bombay University, 1863–8, and director of public instruction; member of Legislative Council, 1868; as principal at Edinburgh University (1868–84) closed the disagreement with civic authorities, obtained new buildings for the medical department, and (1884) organized tercentenary celebration; hon. DCL, Oxford, and LL D, Cambridge, Edinburgh, and Glasgow; prepared first Scottish education code; edited Aristotle's *Ethics* (1857); published lives of Aristotle and Xenophon, and *The Story of the University of Edinburgh* (1884).

GRANT, Sir Alexander Cray, eighth baronet, 'of Dalvey' (1782–1854), civil servant; MA, St John's College, Cambridge, 1806; MP, Tregony, 1812, Lostwithiel, 1818–26, Aldborough, 1826–30, Westbury, 1830–2, and Cambridge, 1840–3, representing interests of West Indian planters; chairman of committees, 1826–32; member of Board of Control, 1834–5; commissioner of accounts, 1843–54.

GRANT, Sir **(Alfred) Hamilton,** twelfth baronet, of Dalvey (1872–1937), Indian civil servant; son of Sir Alexander *Grant; educated at Fettes and Balliol College, Oxford; served in foreign and political department, North-West Frontier Province; deputy secretary, Indian Foreign Department, 1912; foreign secretary, 1914–19; successfully conducted preliminary negotiations (1919) for treaty with Afghanistan (1921); chief commissioner, North-West Frontier Province, 1919–22; KCIE, 1918; KCSI, 1922; succeeded brother, 1936.

GRANT, Andrew (*fl.* 1809), physician; author of *History of Brazil* (1809).

GRANT, Mrs Anne (1755–1838), authoress; née Macvicar; wife of minister of Laggan, Inverness-shire; from 1810 lived at Edinburgh and was admitted to the best literary society, who procured her (1826) a pension; her *Letters from the Mountains* (1806) highly popular; published also *Memoirs of an American Lady* (1808) and *Essays on the Superstitions of the Highlands* (1811).

GRANT, Anthony (1806–1883), divine; of Winchester and New College, Oxford; fellow, 1827; Ellerton prizeman, 1832; DCL, 1842; vicar of Romford, 1838–62, of Aylesford, 1862–77; archdeacon of St Albans, 1846; canon of Rochester, 1860; published (1844) *Past and Prospective Extension of the Gospel by Missions* (Bampton Lecture, 1843) and other works.

GRANT, Charles (1746–1823), statesman and philanthropist; made large fortune in service of East India Company; senior merchant, 1784; fourth member of Board of Trade at Calcutta, 1787; his pamphlet (1792) advocating toleration of missionary and educational work in the East printed (1813) by order of House of Commons; MP, Inverness-shire, 1804–18; chairman of court of directors of East India Company from 1805; opposed policy of Wellesley, and supported (1808) motion for his impeachment; procured the assignment of a grant towards education under charter of 1813; promoted building of churches in India and elsewhere; introduced Sunday schools into Scotland; originated scheme for foundation of Haileybury College.

GRANT, Charles, Baron Glenelg (1778–1866), statesman; eldest son of Charles *Grant (1746–1823); fellow of Magdalene College, Cambridge, 1802; fourth wrangler and chancellor's medallist; MA, 1804; hon. LL D, 1819; member of Speculative Society, Edinburgh; MP for Inverness and Fortrose, 1811–18, for Inverness-shire, 1818–35; a lord of the Treasury, 1813; privy councillor and Irish secretary, 1819–23; vice-president of Board of Trade, 1823–7; president of Board of Trade and treasurer of Navy, 1827–8; as president of Board of Control (1830–5) carried charter (1833) vesting the East India Company's property in the crown; as colonial secretary under Melbourne, 1835–9, introduced bill abolishing West Indian slavery; created Baron Glenelg, 1835; refused to sanction action of Sir Benjamin *D'Urban after Kaffir invasion of Cape Colony, 1835; offended both Tories and Radicals by his irresolute Canadian policy; resigned, 1839, receiving a pension and commissionership of the land tax; died at Cannes.

GRANT, Sir **Charles** (1836–1903), Anglo-Indian administrator; brother of Sir Robert *Grant; entered Bengal Civil Service, 1858; foreign secretary to Indian government, 1881; KCSI, 1885; edited *Central Provinces Gazetteer*, 1870.

GRANT, Colquhoun (d. 1792), Jacobite; distinguished at Prestonpans, 1745, and one of Charles *Edward's life guards at Culloden, 1746; afterwards practised in Edinburgh as writer to the signet.

GRANT, Sir **Colquhoun** (1764?–1835), lieutenant-general; with 25th dragoons at Seringapatam, 1799; lieutenant-colonel of 72nd Highlanders, 1802; wounded at recapture of the Cape, 1806; commanded 15th hussars in *Moore's retreat and (1813) at Vittoria; KCB, 1814; led hussar brigade at Waterloo; lieutenant-general, 1830; MP, Queensborough, 1831–2.

GRANT, Colquhoun (1780–1829), lieutenant-colonel; captured at Ostend with 11th Foot, 1798; deputy-assistant adjutant-general and secret intelligence officer in the Peninsula; captured near the Coa, 1812; escaped from Bayonne to Paris, whence he sent intelligence to Wellington; disguised as a sailor reached England, and having arranged for his exchange, rejoined Wellington in Spain; as intelligence officer in 1815 sent news from Condé of Napoleon's intentions; lieutenant-colonel of the 54th, 1821; commanded brigade in first Burmese War; CB; died at Aix-la-Chapelle.

GRANT, David (1823–1886), author of *Metrical Tales* (1880) and *Lays and Legends of the North* (1884); his *Book of Ten Songs* published posthumously.

GRANT, Duncan James Corrowr (1885–1978), painter; educated at St Paul's School; during parents' absence abroad stayed with Strachey relations; studied at Westminster School of Art; visited Italy, 1902–3; studied in Paris, 1906–7; met Picasso and Matisse, 1909; friends in London included Virginia and Vanessa Stephen (later Virginia *Woolf and Vanessa *Bell), and Roger *Fry; after 1910 recognized as one of the proponents of 'modernism'; although a homosexual, became intimate with Vanessa Bell, 1913–14; during 1914–18 war found non-combatant work and lived with the Bells; his and Vanessa's daughter, Angelica, born 1918; joined Roger Fry as decorator in Omega Workshops, 1913–19; commissioned with Vanessa Bell to execute decorations for the *Queen Mary* but the murals rejected by Cunard Co., 1935; decorated (with Vanessa Bell) interior of church at Upper Berwick, Sussex, 1941–3; became Royal Designer for Industry for work on printed textiles, 1941; after 1945 his work out of fashion; lived alone after death of Vanessa Bell in 1961; an accomplished decorator, valued for his landscapes and still lifes.

GRANT (or GRAUNT), Edward (1540?–1601), headmaster of Westminster; BA, St John's College, Cambridge, 1567; BA, Oxford, 1572; MA, Oxford, 1572; MA, Cambridge, 1573; DD, Cambridge, 1589; canon of Westminster, 1577, of Ely, 1589; friend of Ascham; headmaster of Westminster, 1572–93; author of *Graecae Linguae Spicilegium* (1575) and a revised edition of Crispin's Greek–Latin lexicon, and Greek, Latin, and English verses.

GRANT (afterwards MURRAY), Mrs Elizabeth (1745?–1814?), author of the song, 'Roy's Wife'.

GRANT, Sir Francis, Lord Cullen (1658–1726), Scottish judge; educated at Aberdeen and Leiden; admitted advocate, 1691; defended power of the estates to settle succession to the crown; created baronet of Nova Scotia, 1705; lord of session, 1709; wrote on societies for the reformation of manners and patronage question in Scottish church.

GRANT, Sir Francis (1803–1878), portrait painter; brother of Sir James Hope *Grant; made reputation as a painter of sporting-scenes; fashionable as a portrait painter after exhibition at the Academy of his equestrian group of the queen, Lord Melbourne, and company, 1840; RA, 1851; president, RA, 1866–78; knighted, 1866; painted portraits of contemporary celebrities, including *Macaulay, Lord-Chancellor John *Campbell, Viscount *Hardinge, and *Landseer.

GRANT, George Monro (1835–1902), principal of Queen's University, Kingston, Canada, from 1877; born in Nova Scotia; educated at Glasgow University; hon. DD, 1877; Presbyterian missionary in Nova Scotia, 1860–3; united the Presbyterian Church throughout Canada, and inaugurated first General Assembly, 1875; moderator, 1889; secured state endowment of School of Mines in Queen's University, 1893;

twice (1872 and 1883) travelled through Canada, describing his experiences in *Ocean to Ocean* (1873) and *Picturesque Canada* (1884); strong imperialist; wrote *Religions of the World*, 1894; president of Royal Society of Canada, 1891; CMG, 1901.

GRANT, James (1485?–1553), laird of Freuchie ('the Bold'); son of John *Grant (d. 1528) of Freuchie; fined for protecting members of the clan Chattan, 1528; took part in expedition against the Clanranald and Mackenzies of Kintail, 1544; exempted by *James V from jurisdiction of inferior courts.

GRANT, James (1706–1778), Scottish Catholic prelate; admitted into the Scots College, Rome, 1726; priest, 1733; missioner in Scotland, 1734; surrendered himself (1746) to some men who threatened to desolate the Isle of Barra, in which he was residing, unless the priest were delivered up to them; imprisoned at Inverness; consecrated bishop of Sinita *in partibus*, 1755.

GRANT, James (1720–1806), of Ballindalloch, general; served with 1st Royal Scots in Flanders, 1746–8, and at Culloden, 1746; surprised and captured at Fort Duquesne, 1758; lieutenant-colonel of the 40th and governor of East Florida, 1760; defeated Cherokees at Etchoe, 1761; MP, Wick, 1773, and Sutherlandshire, 1774 and 1787–1806; commanded brigades at Long Island, Brandywine, and Germanstown; captured St Lucia and held it against d'Estaing, 1778; major-general, 1777; general, 1796.

GRANT, Sir James (1738–1811), eighth baronet of Grant, 1773; chief of the clan Grant; MP, Elgin and Forres, 1761–8, Banff, 1790–5; lord-lieutenant of Inverness-shire, 1794–1809; raised two Highland regiments; colonel, 1793.

GRANT, James (1743?–1835), advocate; died senior of Scottish bar; friend of *Jeffrey, Henry *Erskine (1746–1817), and Scottish Whigs; published *Essays on the Origin of Society*, etc. (1785), and *Thoughts on the Origin and Descent of the Gael*, containing discussion of the Ossian question (1814).

GRANT, James (1802–1879), journalist; edited *Elgin Courier, Morning Advertiser* (1850–71), and Grant's *London Journal*; published *Random Recollections of the House of Commons and . . . Lords* (1836), *Sketches in London* (1838), and *The Newspaper Press* (1871–2), and other works.

GRANT, James (1822–1887), novelist and historical writer; grandson of James *Grant (1743?–1835); served in the 62nd three years; founded National Association for the Vindication of Scottish Rights, 1852; a military expert. Of his fifty-six novels the best are *The Romance of War* (1845) and *Adventures of an Aide-de-Camp*. His other works include memoirs of *Kirkcaldy of Grange, Sir J. *Hepburn, and Montrose, *British Battles on Land and Sea* (1873, with continuation, 1884), and *Old and New Edinburgh* (1880).

GRANT, James (1840–1885), Scottish antiquary; MA, Aberdeen; assisted in editing Scots Privy Council records, and published *History of the Burgh and Parish Schools of Scotland*, (vol. i, 1876).

GRANT, James Augustus (1827–1892), lieutenant-colonel; African traveller; educated at Marischal College, Aberdeen; received commission in 8th Native Bengal Infantry, 1846; adjutant, 1853–7; attached to 78th Highlanders at relief of Lucknow; accompanied John Hanning *Speke in African exploring expedition from Ukuni to Karague, 1861, and from Uganda to falls of Karuma, Faloro, and Gondokoro, 1862–3; made elaborate botanical and meteorological notes, and published *A Walk across Africa* (1864); received Gold Medal of Royal Geographical Society, 1864; CB, 1866; in Intelligence Department in Abyssinian expedition, 1868; CSI, 1868; lieutenant-colonel, 1868.

GRANT, Sir James Hope (1808–1875), general; served with the 9th Lancers, 1826–58; lieutenant-colonel, 1849; brigade-major to Lord Saltoun in first Chinese War, 1840–2; distinguished himself in the Sikh wars, 1845–6 and 1848–9; during the Mutiny did good service with movable columns; commanded the Trans-Ghogra force; KCB, 1858; commanded successfully in the second Chinese War (1860–1); GCB; commander-in-chief at Madras, 1862–3; quartermaster-general at the Horse Guards, 1865; at Aldershot initiated in 1871 the annual autumn manœuvres, and introduced the war game and military lectures.

GRANT, James Macpherson (1822–1885), Australian statesman; emigrated to Sydney when 14; solictor at Sydney and Melbourne; successful gold-digger at Bendigo; acted for Ballarat miners after riots of 1854; member for Bendigo, 1855, Sandhurst, 1856, and Avoca, 1859, in Victoria legislative council; vice-president of lands, 1860–1; president, 1864, 1868–9, and 1871–2; carried Land Act of 1865; minister of justice under Berry, 1875 and 1877–80; chief secretary under Sir Bryan O'Loghlen, 1881–3.

GRANT, James William (1788–1865), astronomer, in East India Company's service, 1805–49; erected at Elchies, Morayshire, a granite observatory, where was the 'Trophy Telescope' seen at exhibition of 1851; FRAS, 1854; discovered companion of Antares, 1844.

GRANT, John (d. 1528), second laird of Freuchie ('The Bard'); fought for *James III against his son; rewarded by *James IV for his support of *Huntly in the northern counties with lands of Glencarny and Ballindalloch, 1489, and barony of Urquhart, 1509.

GRANT, John (1568?–1622), fifth laird of Freuchie; took part with James VI against George *Gordon, first marquis of Huntly, in 1589 and 1592; commissioned to suppress witchcraft in Highlands, 1602; fined for relations with Macgregors; commissioned to deal with gypsies, 1620; a juror at Orkney's trial, 1615; acquired estates in Strathspey.

GRANT, John (1782–1842), lieutenant-colonel, Portuguese service; served with the Lusitanian Legion in 1808–9, and afterwards under *Beresford; a famous spy in the Peninsula War; lieutenant, 2nd Royal Veteran Battalion; secretary to London committee following Beresford's dismissal from Portuguese service, 1820.

GRANT, Sir John Peter (1774–1848), chief justice of Calcutta; barrister, Lincoln's Inn, 1802; MP, Grimsby and Tavistock; knighted; puisne judge of Bombay, 1827, afterwards of Calcutta; chief works, *Essays towards illustrating some elementary principles relating to Wealth and Currency* (1812) and *Summary of the Law relating to granting New Trials in Civil Suits* (1817).

GRANT, Sir John Peter (1807–1893), Indian and colonial governor; son of Sir John Peter *Grant (1774–1848); educated at Eton, Haileybury, and Edinburgh University; joined Bengal Civil Service, 1828; assistant in Board of Revenue, Calcutta, 1832; secretary to government of Bengal, 1848, and virtually ruled province, 1848–52; foreign secretary, 1853; permanent secretary in home department of Government of India, 1853; member of Council of Governor-General of Bengal, 1854–9; governor-general of Central Provinces, 1857–9; lieutenant-governor of Bengal, 1859–62; KCB, 1862; governor of Jamaica, 1866–73, and completely reorganized political and legal status of the island.

GRANT, Johnson (1773–1844), divine; grandson of Sir Francis *Grant, Lord Cullen; MA, St John's College, Oxford, 1805; incumbent of Kentish Town, 1822–44; published, among other works, *Summary of the History of the English Church* (1811–26).

GRANT, Joseph (1805–1835), Scottish poet; author of *Juvenile Lays* (1828), *Kincardineshire Traditions* (1830), and *Tales of the Glens* (posthumous).

GRANT, Lilias (d. 1643), poetess; née Murray; wife of John *Grant, fifth laird of Freuchie.

GRANT, Ludovick (1650?–1716), of Grant; eighth laird of Freuchie, 1663; fined for protecting Covenanters, 1685; sat for Elgin and Inverness-shire in Scottish parliament; as sheriff of Inverness-shire assisted General *Mackay against Dundee, 1689; obtained (1694) charter converting Freuchie into regality of Grant, Castleton becoming Grantown.

GRANT, Malcolm (1762–1831), lieutenant-general in East India Company's service; served against Mahrattas, 1779, and in Malabar, 1792–8; held chief command in Malabar and Canara, 1804, and reduced Savendroog; lieutenant-general, 1825.

GRANT, Patrick, Lord Elchies (1690–1754), Scottish judge; admitted advocate, 1712; raised to the bench, 1732; lord of justiciary, 1737; collected decisions (1733–54) of session (printed, 1813).

GRANT, Sir Patrick (1804–1895), field marshal; ensign, 11th Bengal Native Infantry, 1820; lieutenant, 1823; major, 1845; lieutenant-colonel, 1851; major-general, 1854; colonel, 104th Foot, 1862; lieutenant-general, 1862; colonel, Seaforth Highlanders, 1863; general, 1870; field marshal, 1883; colonel, Royal Horse Guards, and gold-stick-in-waiting to Queen Victoria, 1885; served in Gwalior campaign, 1843, first Sikh War, 1845–6; CB, 1846; adjutant-general of Bengal Army, 1846; served in second Sikh War, 1849; brevet-colonel and aide-de-camp to Queen Victoria, 1849; commander-in-chief of Madras Army, 1856–61; temporarily commander-in-chief in India, 1857; KCB, 1857; GCB, 1861; governor and commander-in-chief of Malta, 1867–72; GCMG, 1868; governor of Chelsea Hospital, 1874–95.

GRANT, Peter (d. 1784), Scottish abbé and favourite of the pope; as agent at Rome rendered great services to British travellers; died at Rome.

GRANT, Richard (d. 1231), also called Richard of Wethershed; archbishop of Canterbury; chancellor of Lincoln, 1221–7; appointed primate at request of Henry III and the bishops, 1227; opposed king's demand for scutage, 1228; claimed custody of Tunbridge Castle from Hubert de *Burgh, and excommunicated those in possession; went to Rome and brought complaints against Hubert de Burgh; won his cause, but died on the way home at St Gemini.

GRANT, Sir Robert (1779–1838), governor of Bombay; second son of Charles *Grant (1746–1823); fellow of Magdalene College, Cambridge, 1802; third wrangler, 1801; MA, 1804; barrister,

Lincoln's Inn, 1807; MP, Elgin 1818–26, Inverness, 1826–30, Norwich, 1830–2, Finsbury, 1832–4; commissioner of Board of Control, 1830; judge advocate-general, 1832; carried Jewish emancipation resolution, and two bills in the Commons, 1833–4; governor of Bombay, 1834–8; KCH, 1834; published *Sketch of the History of the East India Company to 1773*; died at Dalpoorie; sacred poems by him edited by Lord *Glenelg (1839).

GRANT, Robert (1814–1892), astronomer; studied at King's College, Aberdeen; published *History of Physical Astronomy* (1852), and received Royal Astronomical Society's Gold Medal, 1856; FRAS, 1850, edited *Monthly Notices*, 1852–60; MA, 1855, and LL D, 1865, Aberdeen; joined Royal Society, 1865; professor of astronomy and director of observatory, Glasgow University, 1859; published scientific writings.

GRANT, Sir Robert (1837–1904), lieutenant-general; born at Bombay; son of Sir Robert *Grant; joined Royal Engineers, 1854; served in West Indies and North America, 1857–65; in command of Royal Engineers at Aldershot (1877–80), Plymouth (1880), Woolwich (1881), and in Scotland (1884); and with Nile Expeditionary Force, 1885; CB, 1889; inspector-general of fortifications and major-general, 1891; lieutenant-general, 1897; carried out works of defence and barrack construction; KCB, 1896; GCB, 1902.

GRANT, Robert Edmond (1793–1874), comparative anatomist; MD, Edinburgh, 1814; contributed important papers on sponges to *Edinburgh Philosophical Journal*, 1825–6; professor of comparative anatomy and zoology at London University, 1827–74; FRS, 1836; Fullerian professor of physiology, 1837–40; Swiney lecturer on geology at British Museum; friend of *Darwin and correspondent of Cuvier and Saint-Hilaire; left property and collections to University College.

GRANT, Roger (d. 1724), oculist to Anne and George I; alluded to in *Spectator* as a quack.

GRANT, Thomas (1816–1870), Roman Catholic bishop of Southwark; DD; rector of the English College, Rome, 1844; active promoter of re-establishment of English hierarchy and bishop of Southwark, 1851–70; Latinist to Vatican Council, 1869; died at Rome.

GRANT, Sir Thomas Tassell (1795–1859), inventor; comptroller of victualling and transport service, 1850–8; KCB on retirement; FRS; awarded grant of £2,000 for his steam biscuit machine, 1829; his 'patent fuel' and apparatus for distillation of sea-water adopted c.1848.

GRANT, William, Lord Prestongrange (1701?–1764), Scottish judge; second son of Sir Francis *Grant, Lord Cullen; admitted advocate, 1722; procurator for Scottish Church and clerk to general assembly, 1731; solicitor-general for Scotland, 1737; lord advocate, 1746; MP, Elgin, 1747–54; carried bills for abolition of heritable jurisdictions and ward-holding and for annexation of forfeited estates to the crown; lord of session and of justiciary, 1754; commissioner of annexed estates, 1755; published pamphlet against patronage in the Scottish Church, 1736.

GRANT, William (d. 1786), physician; MD, Aberdeen, 1755; LRCP, 1763; physician to Misericordia Hospital, Goodman's Fields; published treatises on London fevers and (1783) *Observations on the Influenza of 1775 and 1782*.

GRANT, Sir **William** (1752–1832), master of the Rolls; barrister, Lincoln's Inn, 1774; treasurer, 1798; commanded volunteers at siege of Quebec, 1775; attorney-general of Canada, 1776; MP, Shaftesbury, 1790, Windsor, 1794, Banffshire, 1796–1812; joint commissioner on laws of Jersey, 1791; chief justice of Chester, 1798; solicitor-general, 1799–1801; knighted, 1799; privy councillor, 1801; master of the Rolls, 1801–17; a highly successful speaker in parliament; supported reform of criminal law; lord rector of Aberdeen, 1809; DCL, Oxford, 1820.

GRANT, William James (1829–1866), painter; exhibited at Royal Academy, 1847–66; also drew in red and black chalk.

GRANT, Sir **William Keir** (1772–1852), previously Keir and Grant-Keir; general; distinguished himself in Flanders and at Villiers-en-Couche, 1794; helped to save the emperor Francis II from capture, 1794; received gold medals and the order of Maria Theresa; served with Russian and Austrian armies in Italy, 1799–1801, being present at Rivoli, 1797, and Marengo, 1800, and siege of Genoa, 1800; adjutant-general in Bengal, 1806; commander-in-chief in Java, 1815; commanded Guzerat Field Force against the Pindaris, 1817; took hill fort of Raree, and defeated the rajah of Kutch, 1819; suppressed piracy in the Persian Gulf, 1819–20; KCB, 1822; general, 1841.

GRANT-DUFF. See DUFF.

GRANT DUFF, Sir **Mountstuart Elphinstone** (1829–1906), statesman and author; son of James Grant *Duff; MA, Balliol College, Oxford, 1853; LL B, London, and called to bar, 1854; Liberal MP for Elgin Boroughs, 1857–81; became authority on questions of foreign policy; under-secretary of state for India, 1868–74, and for colonies, 1880; PC, 1880; governor of Madras, 1881–6; CIE, 1881; GCSI, 1887; on return to England (1887) devoted himself to literature; published *Notes from a Diary* (14 vols., 1897–1905), a valuable contribution to social history; travelled much in Europe and Asia; lord rector of Aberdeen University, 1866–72; president of Royal Geographical and Historical societies; FRS, 1901; trustee of British Museum, 1903; wrote also *Studies of European Politics* (1866) and *A Victorian Anthology* (1902).

GRANTHAM, Barons. See ROBINSON, THOMAS, first baron, 1695–1770; ROBINSON, THOMAS, second baron, 1738–1786.

GRANTHAM (or GRANTHAN), Henry (*fl.* 1571–1587), translator; published *Italian Grammar written in Latin by Scipio Lentulo* (1571).

GRANTHAM, Thomas (d. 1664), schoolmaster; BA, Hart Hall, Oxford, 1630; MA, Peterhouse, Cambridge, 1634; rector of Waddington, Lincolnshire, till 1656; taught school in London, where he made a point of doing without corporal punishment; published pamphlets against free schools (1644) and imprisonment for debt (1642), also a curious *Marriage Sermon* (1641).

GRANTHAM, Sir **Thomas** (*fl.* 1684), naval commander; convoyed twenty-five sail from Virginia to England during Dutch War, 1673; assisted in pacifying the colony, 1676; knighted and given command of the East India Company's ship *Charles II*, 1683; suppressed *Keigwin's mutiny at Bombay, 1684; gentleman of the privy chamber to William III and Anne.

GRANTHAM, Thomas (1634–1692), General Baptist divine; pastor of a small congregation of Baptists in south Lincolnshire, 1656; drew up and presented to Charles II 'narrative and complaint' of the General Baptists, with a petition for toleration, 1660; imprisoned at Lincoln for preaching, 1662–3, and at Louth, 1670; had another interview with the king, 1672; founded congregations at Norwich, Yarmouth, and King's Lynn, 1685–6; published *Christianismus Primitivus* (1678) and many controversial tracts, of which *A Dialogue between the Baptist and the Presbyterian* (1691) contains remarkable verses on Servetus.

GRANTHAM, Sir **William** (1835–1911), judge; called to bar, 1863; QC, 1877; treasurer of Inner Temple, 1904; successful in circuit work; Conservative MP for East Surrey, 1874–85, and for Croydon, 1885–6; made judge of Queen's Bench division and knighted, 1886; industrious, energetic, but garrulous judge; his decisions as judge in election petition cases (1906) were severely criticized; rebuked by prime minister for indiscreet speech from bench, 1911; model country gentleman, and good judge of horses.

GRANTLEY, first Baron (1716–1789). See NORTON, FLETCHER.

GRANTMESNIL, Hugh of (d. 1094), baron and sheriff of Leicestershire. See HUGH.

GRANTON, Lord (1763–1851). See HOPE, CHARLES.

GRANVILLE. See also GRENVILLE.

GRANVILLE, Earls. See CARTERET, JOHN, first earl, 1690–1763; LEVESON-GOWER, GRANVILLE, first earl, 1773–1846; LEVESON-GOWER, GRANVILLE GEORGE, second earl, 1815–1891.

GRANVILLE, Augustus Bozzi (1783–1872), physician and Italian patriot; son of postmaster-general at Milan; assumed name of Granville by his mother's wish; MD, Pavia, 1802; physician to the Turkish Fleet and in Spain; in the English Fleet, 1806–12; settled in London as tutor to the sons of William Richard *Hamilton, 1813; MRCS, 1813; LRCP, 1817; brought warning of Napoleon's expected escape, and introduced iodine, 1814; headed Milan deputation offering duke of Sussex the crown, 1815; assisted Canova in obtaining restoration of Italian art treasures; FRS, 1817; physician-accoucheur to Westminster Dispensary, 1818; established West-End Infirmary for Children; introduced use of prussic acid for chest affections; president of Westminster Medical Society, 1829; secretary of the visitors of the Royal Institution, 1832–52; published *Catechism of Health* (1831) and books on the spas of Germany (1837) and England (1841); also *Counter-irritation* (1838); practised at Kissingen, 1861–8; published pamphlets advocating the reform of the Royal Society (1830, 1836), the formation of a kingdom of Italy (1848), a work on Thames sewage (1835, 1865) and an *Autobiography* (posthumous).

GRANVILLE (or GRENVILLE), Sir Bevil (d. 1706), governor of Barbados; grandson of Sir Bevil *Grenville; MA, Trinity College, Cambridge, 1679; knighted by James II; favourite of William III; colonel of Lord *Bath's regiment in Flanders, 1694–8; governor of Barbados, 1702–6; acquitted of tyranny and extortion, but recalled from Barbados; died on his way home.

GRANVILLE (or GRENVILLE), George, Baron Lansdowne (1666–1735), poet and dramatist; brother of Sir Bevil *Granville; educated in France and at Trinity College, Cambridge; MA, 1679; MP, Fowey, 1702, Cornwall, 1710–11; secretary-at-war, 1710; one of the twelve peers created for the peace, 1711; privy councillor and comptroller of the household, 1712; treasurer of the household, 1713; imprisoned in the Tower on suspicion of Jacobitism, 1715–17; published plays acted at Lincoln's

Inn Fields and Drury Lane, including *Heroick Love* (1698), and an opera, with epilogue by *Addison. His complete works (1732) include *Vindication* of *Monck and Sir Richard Granville. His poems were praised by *Pope (of whom he was an early patron), but declared by *Johnson mere imitations of *Waller.

GRANVILLE-BARKER, Harley Granville (1877–1946), actor, producer, dramatist, and critic; first London stage appearance, 1892; acted and produced for Stage Society; great friend of G. B. *Shaw; made Shaw's name as dramatist and his own as director, in partnership with J. E. Vedrenne at Court Theatre, 1904–7; produced repertory for Charles Frohman including *Galsworthy's *Justice*, 1910; his productions of *The Winter's Tale* and *Twelfth Night* (1912) and *Midsummer Night's Dream* (1914) set completely new standard and proved profoundly influential; made great success with Shaw's *Fanny's First Play* (1911) and Arnold *Bennett's *The Great Adventure* (1913); opened season at St James's with *Androcles and the Lion*, 1913; war interrupted his career, which he virtually abandoned after his second marriage, 1918; chairman, British Drama League, 1919–32; wrote valuable prefaces for edition of Shakespeare, 1923–46; director, British Institute, Paris, 1937–9; his own plays included *Weather Hen, The Marrying of Ann Leete, Waste, The Voysey Inheritance,* and *The Madras House.*

GRASCOME, Samuel (1641–1708), nonjuror; MA, Magdalene College, Cambridge, 1674; rector of Stourmouth, Kent, 1680–90; his *Account of Proceedings in House of Commons in relation to Recoining Clipt Money* (1696) ordered to be burned by the hangman; published numerous controversial tracts.

GRATTAN, Henry (1746–1820), statesman; graduated at Trinity College, Dublin, 1767; with *Flood contributed nationalist articles to the *Freeman's Journal*; called to Irish bar, 1772; elected to Irish parliament for Charlemont, 1775; carried amendment to the address in favour of free trade, and resolution affirming inexpediency of granting new taxes, 1779; moved in brilliant speeches, but without success, resolutions in favour of legislative independence, and amendments to limit duration of Perpetual Mutiny Bill, 1780–1; after the meeting of the Volunteers at Dungannon moved address to the crown demanding legislative independence, and a few months later carried it, 1782; declined office; granted £50,000 by Irish parliament after consent of British government to his claims; opposed Flood's demand for 'simple repeal', and favoured disbandment of the Volunteers, 1783; successfully opposed *Orde's commercial propositions,

1785; brought forward question of tithe commutation, 1788–9; on refusal of the lord-lieutenant to transmit his regency resolutions, formed deputation to present them in person to prince of Wales, 1789; founded Dublin Whig Club; elected for Dublin, 1790; attacked parliamentary corruption, and supported Catholic emancipation, 1791–3; interviewed Pitt, 1794; declined office from *Fitzwilliam, on whose recall he renewed opposition; after rejection of *Ponsonby's reform resolutions seceded from the house, 1797; in England during the Rebellion of '98, but struck off the Irish Privy Council; during last session of Irish parliament represented Wicklow; spoke for two hours, sitting, against the Union, 1800; fought duel with Isaac *Corry; in last speech had altercation with *Castlereagh; as MP for Malton, 1805–6, in the imperial parliament made impressive maiden speech; MP for Dublin, 1806–20; declined office; frequently raised Catholic emancipation question; carried motion for committee of inquiry, and second reading of Relief Bill, 1813; supported continuance of the war, 1815; died in London, and was buried in Westminster Abbey. The best collection of his speeches is that edited by his son (1822).

GRATTAN, Thomas Colley (1792–1864), author; described his French tours in *Highways and Byways* (three series, 1823–9); at Brussels, 1828–39, issued *Traits of Travel* (1829) and *History of the Netherlands* (1830), and described the riots of 1834 for *The Times*; as British consul at Boston, 1839–46, assisted at settlement of northeast boundary question by the Ashburton Treaty; published also *Legends of the Rhine* (1832), several historical novels, two works on America, and *Beaten Paths* (1862, autobiographical).

GRATTON, John (1641–1712), Quaker; joined the Friends, c.1672; imprisoned at Derby; afterwards travelled ministerially throughout the United Kingdom; his *Journal* (1720) often reprinted.

GRAUNT, Edward. See GRANT.

GRAUNT, John (1620–1674), statistician; was appointed original member of Royal Society, after his publication of *Natural and Political Observations . . . made upon the Bills of Mortality* (1661); falsely charged with being privy to the great fire of 1666.

GRAVELOT (properly **BOURGUIGNON**), **Hubert François** (1699–1773), draughtsman and book-illustrator; came to England, 1732, on the invitation of Claude *du Bosc; friend of *Garrick; executed illustrations for *Theobald's and *Hanmer's Shakespeares, *Gay's *Fables, The Dunciad*, and *Tom Jones*, and (in France) of the works of Voltaire and Racine and Marmontel's *Contes*.

GRAVES, Alfred Perceval (1846–1931), author and educationist; son of Charles *Graves; educated at Trinity College, Dublin; Home Office clerk, 1869–75; inspector of schools (1875–1910), for many years in Taunton, from 1895 in Southwark; with (Sir) C. V. *Stanford published *Songs of Old Ireland* (1882) and *Songs of Erin* (1892); poet, essayist, and anthologist on Irish subjects.

GRAVES, Charles (1812–1899), bishop of Limerick and mathematician; educated at Trinity College, Dublin; graduated, 1834; fellow, 1836; professor of mathematics, Dublin University, 1843; dean of the Castle Chapel, Dublin, 1860; dean of Clonfert, 1864; bishop of Limerick, Ardfert, and Aghadoe, 1866 till death; member of Royal Irish Academy, 1837, and president, 1861; FRS, 1880; hon. DCL, Oxford, 1881; published translation, with many original notes, of Chasles's *General Properties of Cones of Second Degree and of Spherical Conics* (1841), and wrote on Irish antiquarian subjects.

GRAVES, George Windsor (1873?–1949), comedian; gave unique presentation of comic elderly men; memorable performances in *The Merry Widow* (1907) as Baron Popoff and in *Me and My Girl* (1937); played comedy lead in Drury Lane pantomimes, 1909–15; successful also on music-halls and films.

GRAVES, Henry (1806–1892), printseller; brother of Robert *Graves; sole proprietor of firm of Henry Graves & Co., 1844; published numerous engravings after *Landseer and other eminent painters; one of founders of *Art Journal* and *Illustrated London News*.

GRAVES, James (1815–1886), archaeologist; BA, Trinity College, Dublin; incumbent of Inisnag, 1863–86; with J. G. Prim established Kilkenny Archaeological Society (Royal Historical Association of Ireland); published work on St Canice Cathedral, Kilkenny, 1857.

GRAVES, John Thomas (1806–1870), jurist and mathematician; great-nephew of Richard *Graves (1763–1829), dean of Ardagh; graduate of Dublin and Oxford; barrister, Inner Temple, 1831; professor of jurisprudence at University College, London, 1839; FRS, 1839; poor-law inspector, 1847–70; contributed articles on jurists to Smith's *Dictionary of Greek and Roman Biography*; friend and correspondent of Sir William Rowan *Hamilton, towards whose discovery of quaternions he did much by researches concerning imaginary logarithms; his mathematical library bequeathed to University College.

GRAVES, Richard, the elder (1677–1729), antiquary; educated at Pembroke College, Oxford; said to have been original of Mr Townsend in the *Spiritual Quixote*.

GRAVES, Richard, the younger (1715–1804), poet and novelist; with *Whitefield graduated BA, Pembroke College, Oxford, 1736; fellow of All Souls, 1736; intimate of *Shenstone; offended his relations by marrying a farmer's daughter; rector of Claverton, 1749–1804; by influence of Ralph *Allen obtained also vicarage of Kilmersdon and chaplaincy to countess of Chatham; among his pupils, *Malthus and Prince *Hoare; published *The Spiritual Quixote* (1773), ridiculing the Methodists, *Recollections of Shenstone* (1788), a translation of Marcus Aurelius (1792), and *The Reveries of Solitude* (1793), besides verses and essays.

GRAVES, Richard (1763–1829), dean of Ardagh; senior fellow of Trinity College, Dublin, 1799; Donnellan lecturer, 1797 and 1801; DD, 1799; professor of oratory, 1799; regius professor of Greek, 1810, of divinity, 1819; prebendary of St Michael's, Dublin, 1801; rector of Raheny, 1809; dean of Ardagh, 1813–29; his works collected (1840).

GRAVES, Richard Hastings (1791–1877), theological writer; son of Richard *Graves (1763–1829); MA, Trinity College, Dublin, 1818; DD, 1828; rector of Brigown and prebendary of Cloyne.

GRAVES, Robert (1798–1873), line-engraver; pupil of John *Romney the engraver, executed pen-and-ink facsimiles of rare prints; engraved plates for James *Caulfield's *Portraits*, Dove's *English Classics*, John *Neale's *Westminster Abbey*, and Gilbert *Burnet's *Reformation*; exhibited with Society of British Artists, 1824–30, and Royal Academy; associate engraver to Royal Academy, 1836, engraving works after *Wilkie, *Landseer, and *Gainsborough.

GRAVES, Robert James (1796–1853), physician; third son of Richard *Graves (1763–1829), dean of Ardagh; MB, Dublin, 1818; travelled with *Turner in the Alps and in Italy; physician to Meath Hospital and a founder of the Park Street School of Medicine; professor of medicine to the Irish College of Physicians; president, Irish College of Physicians, 1843–4; FRS, 1849; gained a European reputation by his *Clinical Lectures on the Practice of Medicine* (1848, reprinted, 1884).

GRAVES, Robert Ranke (1895–1985), writer and poet; educated at Charterhouse and St John's College, Oxford; B.Litt., 1925; during 1914–18 war served in Royal Welch Fusiliers; published autobiographical *Goodbye to All That* (1929, revised 1957); lived in Majorca, 1929–36; published novels include *I, Claudius* (1934, awarded Hawthornden and James Tait Black Memorial prizes), *Claudius the God* (1934), *Count Belisarius* (1938), *Sergeant Lamb of the Ninth* (1940), *King Jesus* (1946), and *Homer's Daughter* (1955); returned to Majorca from Devon, 1946; Clark lecturer at Cambridge, 1954; lectures published as *The Crowning Privilege* (1955); professor of poetry, Oxford, 1961–6; published many volumes of poetry including *Poems 1938–45* (1948); also published *The White Goddess* (1948, revised 1952), *Oxford Addresses on Poetry* (1961), and *Wife to Mr Milton* (1943); hon. fellow, St John's College, Oxford, 1971.

GRAVES, Samuel (1713–1787), admiral; served under his uncle at Cartagena, 1741; commanded the *Barfleur* in the Basque Roads, 1757, and the *Duke* at Quiberon Bay, 1759; vice-admiral, 1770; as commander on North American Station attempted to carry out Boston Port Act, 1774; admiral, 1778.

GRAVES, Thomas, first Baron Graves (1725?–1802), admiral; cousin of Samuel *Graves; commanded the *Unicorn* at bombardment of Havre, 1758; present in *Arbuthnot's action off the Chesapeake, 1781, and commanded at an indecisive action with De Grasse a few months later; despatched by *Rodney in charge of prizes to England, losing all but two ships, 1782; vice-admiral, 1787; admiral, 1794; received an Irish peerage and a pension for his conduct as second-in-command in *Howe's action of 1 June 1794, when he was badly wounded.

GRAVES, Sir Thomas (1747?–1814), admiral; nephew of Samuel *Graves, under whom he served in the Seven Years' War; severely wounded when in command of the *Diana*, 1775, in the Charles river; commanded the *Bedford* in his cousin's action off the Chesapeake, 1781, and in the battles off St Kitts and Dominica, 1782; with the *Magicienne* fought the *Sybille*, 1783; created KCB for conduct as *Nelson's second-in-command at Copenhagen; vice-admiral, 1805; admiral, 1812.

GRAVESEND, Richard de (d. 1279), bishop of Lincoln; dean of Lincoln, 1254; associated with dean of London in carrying out papal excommunication of violators of Magna Charta, 1254; bishop of Lincoln, 1258–79; assisted in negotiations for peace with France, 1258–9, and for a pacification between Henry III and the barons, 1263; suspended by the legate as an adherent of De *Montfort, 1266; lived abroad till 1269; granted a coadjutor, 1275.

GRAVESEND, Richard de (d. 1303), bishop of London; archdeacon of Northampton,

1272–80; prebendary of Lincoln; bishop of London, 1280–1303; sent on mission to France, 1293; one of Prince Edward's councillors, 1297; instituted office of sub-dean; benefactor of St Paul's, the poor of London, and Cambridge University; his executors' accounts printed by Camden Society (1874).

GRAVESEND, Stephen de (d. 1338), bishop of London; nephew of Richard de *Gravesend (d. 1303); rector of Stepney, 1306; canon of St Paul's 1313; bishop of London, 1318–30; tried to mediate between Edward II and *Isabella, 1326; his life menaced by the Londoners; took part with *Lancaster and *Kent against Edward III, 1328; imprisoned for complicity in Kent's plot, 1330; excommunicated Lewis of Bavaria and the anti-pope Nicholas, 1329; king's deputy at councils of 1335 and 1336.

GRAVET, William (d. 1599), divine; BA, Peterhouse, Cambridge, 1558; fellow of Pembroke Hall, Cambridge, 1558; MA, 1561; vicar of St Sepulchre, 1566; rector of Little Laver and of Bradfield, and prebendary of St Paul's; accused by 'Martin Mar-Prelate' of drunkenness.

GRAY. See also GREY.

GRAY, Sir Alexander (1882–1968), economist and poet; educated at Dundee High School and Edinburgh University; first class, mathematics, 1902, and economic science, 1905; placed second in Civil Service examination to John *Anderson (later Viscount Waverley), a lifelong friend; posted to Local Government Board, 1905–9; transferred to Colonial Office, 1909–12; National Health Insurance Commission, 1912–19; Ministry of Health, 1919–21; Jeffrey professor of political economy, Aberdeen, 1921–35; Edinburgh, 1935–56; publications include *The Scottish Staple at Veere* (1909), *Development of Economic Doctrine* (1931), and *Socialist Tradition, Moses to Lenin* (1946); produced volumes of translations of songs and ballads from German, Dutch, and Danish, including *Songs and Ballads Chiefly from Heine* (1920), *Arrows* (1932), and *Four and Forty* (1954); also published his own verse in English or in Scottish dialect, including *Any Man's Life* (1924) and *Gossip* (1928); served on number of government committees; chairman, Scottish Schools Broadcasting Council; member, Fulbright Commission; president, Scottish Economic Society, 1960–3; CBE, 1939; knighted, 1947; honorary degrees from four universities, including Aberdeen and Edinburgh.

GRAY, Andrew, first Baron Gray (1380?–1469), hostage in England for payment of ransom of *James I of Scotland, 1424–7; created Baron Gray of Fowlis (Scotland), 1445; master of the household to *James II of Scotland, 1452; a lord auditor, 1464.

GRAY, Andrew (1633–1656), Scottish divine; graduated at St Andrews, 1651; minister of Outer High Church, Glasgow, 1653–6; famous preacher; last edition of *Works*, 1839.

GRAY, Andrew, seventh Baron Gray (d. 1663), son of Patrick *Gray, sixth baron; succeeded, 1612; lieutenant of Scots *gens d'armes* in France, 1624; member of Scottish Council of War, 1628; commissioner for Fisheries Treaty, 1630; supported Charles I against Covenanters; excommunicated by general assembly as papist, 1649; fined by *Cromwell, 1654.

GRAY, Andrew (d. 1728), divine; vicar of Mottram, Cheshire; his *Door opening into Everlasting Life* (1706, reprinted, 1810).

GRAY, Andrew (1805–1861), Presbyterian divine; MA, Aberdeen, 1824; minister of the West Church, Perth, 1836–61; joined Free Church and drew up *Catechism of Principles of the Free Church* (1845); his *Gospel Contrasts and Parallels* edited by *Candlish (1862).

GRAY, Sir Archibald Montague Henry (1880–1967), dermatologist; educated at Cheltenham College and University College and Hospital, London; MRCS, LRCP, MB, London, 1903; BS, 1904; resident and junior appointments at University College Hospital and Hospital for Women, Soho Square, 1904–9; MD, 1905; MRCP, 1907; FRCS, 1908; fellow, University College; first obstetric registrar, University College Hospital; physician for diseases of the skin, University College Hospital, 1909–46; served at War Office in RAMC, 1914–18; consulting dermatologist with army in France, 1918–19; CBE; consulting dermatologist to RAF; in charge of skin department, Hospital for Sick Children, Great Ormond Street, 1920–34; made important observations on rare disease, sclerema neonatorum, 1926; editor, the *British Journal of Dermatology*, 1916–29; president, British Association of Dermatology, 1938–9; represented London University on governing body of Postgraduate Medical School, Hammersmith, 1935–60; contributed to sections on skin diseases in official publications; president, Royal Society of Medicine, 1940–2; adviser in dermatology to Ministry of Health, 1948–62; chairman, medical committee, University College Hospital, 1926–35; member, London University Senate, 1929–50; dean of faculty of medicine, 1932–6; member, General Medical Council, 1950–2; hon. LL D, London, 1958; knighted, 1946; KCVO, 1959.

GRAY, Benjamin Kirkman (1862–1907), economist; son of Congregational minister;

Unitarian minister, 1894–7; engaged in social work in London, 1898–1902; developed strong socialistic views; published *History of English Philanthropy* (1905) and *Philanthropy and the State* (1910).

GRAY, Charles (1782–1851), captain in the Marines and song-writer; published *Poems and Songs* (1811) and *Lays and Lyrics* (1841); also contributions to John Muir *Wood's *Book of Scottish Song* and *Whistle-Binkie*, and *Notes on Scottish Song* (1845).

GRAY, David (1838–1861), Scottish poet; friend of Sydney T. *Dobell; his *Luggie and other Poems* published (1862), with preface by Lord *Houghton, who had befriended him.

GRAY, Edmund Dwyer (1845–1888), journalist and politician; son of Sir John *Gray; proprietor of *Freeman's Journal* and *Belfast Morning News*; saved lives of five persons in Dublin Bay, 1866; lord mayor of Dublin, 1880; MP, Tipperary, 1877–80, Carlow, 1880–5, and Dublin, 1885–8; imprisoned, when high sheriff of Dublin, for comments on Hynes case in *Freeman's Journal*; member of Housing of the Poor Commission, 1884.

GRAY, Edward Whitaker (1748–1806), botanist; librarian to College of Physicians before 1773; LCP, 1773; MD; keeper of natural history and antiquities at British Museum; secretary to Royal Society, 1797; original associate of Linnean Society.

GRAY, Edward William (1787?–1860), editor of *History and Antiquities of Newbury* (1839).

GRAY, Sir George (d. 1773), baronet; colonel of 17th Foot and major-general in army; younger brother of Sir James *Gray (d. 1773), with whom he founded Society of Dilettanti, 1732; secretary and treasurer to society, 1738–1771.

GRAY, George (1758–1819), painter; went to North America on botanical expedition, 1787, and to Poland on geological expedition, 1791.

GRAY, George Buchanan (1865–1922), Congregational minister; BA, University College, London, 1886; first class, school of oriental studies, Oxford, 1891; tutor, Mansfield College, Oxford, 1891; ordained Congregational minister, 1893; professor of Hebrew and exegesis of Old Testament, Mansfield, 1900–22; a stimulating teacher and original investigator; interested in problems of social welfare; works include *Hebrew Proper Names* (1896), *Commentary on Numbers* (1903), *Commentary on Isaiah I–XXVII* (1912), *Forms of Hebrew Poetry* (1915), *Commentary on Job* (completing work of S. R. *Driver, 1921), and *Sacrifice in the Old Testament* (1925).

GRAY, George Edward Kruger (1880–1943), designer; born Kruger; added Gray, 1918; diploma in design, Royal College of Art; work includes King George V and VI silver coinage; great seals of King George VI and Canada; stained-glass windows, Eltham Palace; and heraldic designs.

GRAY, George Robert (1808–1872), zoologist; youngest son of Samuel Frederick *Gray; educated at Merchant Taylors' School; zoological assistant in British Museum, 1831; FRS, 1865; published ornithological works; assisted Agassiz in *Nomenclator Zoologicus* (1842).

GRAY, Gilbert (d. 1614), second principal of Marischal College, Aberdeen, 1598; delivered a Latin oration, 'Oratio de Illustribus Scotiae Scriptoribus', 1611.

GRAY, Herbert Branston (1851–1929), schoolmaster; BA, The Queen's College, Oxford; assistant master, Westminster, 1875; ordained, 1877; headmaster of Louth Grammar School, 1879; of St Andrew's College, Bradfield, 1880–1910; saved college from extinction, supplying new constitution and buildings and raising numbers from 50 to 300; founded Bradfield Greek Play; on retirement travelled, wrote, and held two livings.

GRAY, Hugh (d. 1604), Gresham professor of divinity; fellow of Trinity College, Cambridge, 1581; MA, 1582; DD, 1595; prebendary of Lincoln, 1600.

GRAY, Sir James (d. 1773), diplomat and antiquary; baronet by succession; brother of Sir George *Gray; British resident at Venice, 1744–53; envoy-extraordinary to king of Naples and Two Sicilies, 1753–61; KB and minister plenipotentiary to king of Spain, 1761; privy councillor, 1769.

GRAY, James (d. 1830), poet; intimate of *Burns at Dumfries; master in High School, Edinburgh, 1801–22; rector of Belfast Academy, 1822; went to Bombay as chaplain, 1826; died at Bhuj in Kutch. He published *Cona and other Poems* (1814), edited Robert *Fergusson's *Poems* (1821), and translated St Matthew into Kutchee (printed 1834).

GRAY, Sir James (1891–1975), zoologist; educated at Merchant Taylors' School and King's College, Cambridge, of which he was a scholar; first class, parts i and ii, natural sciences tripos, 1911–13; fellow of King's, 1914; served in France and Palestine with Queen's Royal West Surrey Regiment, 1914–18; MC and Croix de Guerre with palm; resumed fellowship at King's College, 1919; university demonstrator, 1924; university lecturer, 1926; FRS, 1929; reader in experimental zoology, 1931; published *A Text-book of Experimental Cytology* (1931); professor of zoology, 1937; also Fullerian professor of physiology at Royal Institution, 1943–7; editor, *Journal of Experimental Biology*; chairman, Advisory Committee on Fishery Research, 1945–65; president, Marine Biological Association, 1945–55 and British Association, 1959; honorary degrees from Aberdeen, Edinburgh, Durham, Manchester, and Wales; CBE, 1946; knighted, 1954.

GRAY, John (1807–1875), legal author; as solicitor to Treasury conducted prosecution of Tichborne claimant, 1873; published *Country Attorney's Practice* (1836), *Country Solicitor's Practice* (1837), and *Law of Costs* (1853).

GRAY, Sir John (1816–1875), journalist; MD and master in surgery, Glasgow, 1839; political editor of *Freeman's Journal*, 1841; sole proprietor, 1852; indicted for conspiracy, 1843; knighted, 1863; MP, Kilkenny, 1865–75; advocated disestablishment and land reform; published *The Church Establishment in Ireland* (1866).

GRAY, John Edward (1800–1875), naturalist; second son of Samuel Frederick *Gray; assistant zoological keeper at British Museum, 1824; keeper, 1840–74; FRS, 1832; vice-president, Zoological Society; president of Botanical and Entomological societies; formed largest zoological collection in Europe, 1852; doctor of philosophy, Munich, 1852; published numerous zoological papers and other works, including *Handbook of British Waterweeds* (1864).

GRAY, John Miller (1850–1894), curator of Scottish National Portrait Gallery, 1884–94; entered commercial Bank, Edinburgh; worked at art criticism and contributed to various periodicals and other publications, including this Dictionary; published monograph on George *Monson, and other works.

GRAY, (Kathleen) Eileen (Moray) (1879–1976), designer and architect; youngest child of James Maclaren Smith; mother became Baroness Gray, 1895; children took surname Gray; enrolled at Slade School of Art, 1898; learnt technique of lacquer-making in London and Paris; settled in Paris, 1907; designed highly original abstract rugs and carpets and opened furniture gallery, 1922; contacts with avant-garde Dutch architects led to interest in architecture; collaborated with Jean Badovici, Romanian architect and editor of *L'Architecture Vivante*, on design of house at Roquebrune, South of France, for which Le Corbusier painted mural; similar innovative design used for house at Castellan (later acquired by Graham *Sutherland), 1932–4; interned during 1939–45 war and suffered period of decline; article on her work in

Domus by architectural historian, Joseph Rykwert, revived interest, 1968; retrospective exhibition at RIBA Heinz Gallery, London, 1971; other exhibitions at Victoria and Albert Museum and Museum of Modern Art, New York; appointed at age of 93 Royal Designer for Industry, 1972.

GRAY, Louis Harold (1905–1965), physicist and radiobiologist; educated at Latimer School, Christ's Hospital, and Trinity College, Cambridge; first class, parts i and ii, natural sciences tripos, 1926–7; admitted to Cavendish Laboratory under Sir Ernest (later Lord) *Rutherford, 1928; Ph.D., fellow of Trinity, 1930; senior physicist and Prophit scholar of Royal College of Surgeons at Mount Vernon Hospital, Middlesex, 1933–46; set up physics laboratory to measure radiation in treatment of cancer; planned and built 400 kV neutron generator; recruited by Sir Edward *Mellanby to head laboratory side of the radiotherapeutic unit, Hammersmith Hospital, 1946; research in basic science of radiobiology; director, British Empire Cancer Research Campaign Research Unit, Mount Vernon Hospital, 1953–65; FRS, 1961; hon. D.Sc., Leeds, 1962; president, British Institute of Radiology, 1950; founder and first chairman, Association for Radiation Research.

GRAY, Maria Emma (1787–1876), conchologist; née Smith; wife of John Edward *Gray; published etchings of molluscans for use of students, and arranged the Cuming collection in British Museum; her collection of algae bequeathed to Cambridge University.

GRAY, Patrick, fourth Baron Gray (d. 1582), of Buttergask; captured at Solway Moss, 1542; joined Cardinal *Beaton's party; after Beaton's murder went over to English alliance; again imprisoned in England, 1561–2; joined Queen *Mary's lords, 1570; one of *James VI's council, 1577.

GRAY, Patrick, sixth Baron Gray (d. 1612), master of Gray till 1609; while resident in France intimately connected with the Guises and French friends of *Mary Queen of Scots; betrayed Mary's secrets to *James VI and *Arran; concluded an agreement between Elizabeth and James to the exclusion of Mary, but at the same time arranged for deposition of Arran by recall of the banished lords, 1584; carried out the scheme with the help of English ambassador, 1585; formally remonstrated against condemnation of Mary, but secretly advised her assassination, 1586; exiled from Scotland on charge of sedition and of impeding the king's marriage with *Anne of Denmark, 1587; returned, 1589; attempted, with Francis Stewart *Hepburn, fifth earl of Bothwell, to capture the king at Falkland, 1592.

GRAY, Peter (1807?–1887), writer on life contingencies; published works on logarithms and computation of life contingencies.

GRAY, Robert (1762–1834), bishop of Bristol; MA, St Mary Hall, Oxford; Bampton lecturer, 1796; canon of Durham, 1804; bishop of Bristol, 1827–34; published *Religious Union* (1800) and other works.

GRAY, Robert (1809–1872), bishop of Cape Town; son of Robert *Gray (1762–1834); BA, University College, Oxford, 1831; incumbent of Stockton, 1845–7; bishop of Cape Town, 1847–72; appointed metropolitan of Africa by letters patent, 1853, but his power as such held invalid by Privy Council in cases of Long and John William *Colenso, 1863; supported by convocation in appointing new bishop in place of Colenso (excommunicated, 1863); suggested formation of universities mission in Central Africa, and added five new sees to South African Church.

GRAY, Robert (1825–1887), ornithologist; cashier of Bank of Scotland; a chief founder of Glasgow Natural History Society, 1851; secretary of Royal Physical Society, Edinburgh, 1877; vice-president of Royal Society of Edinburgh, 1882; published *Birds of the West of Scotland* (1871).

GRAY, Samuel Frederick (*fl.* 1780–1836), naturalist and pharmacologist; published *Supplement to the Pharmacopoeia* (1818); published with his son, John Edward *Gray, *Natural Arrangement of British Plants*, according to Jussieu's method (1821); published *Elements of Pharmacy* (1823) and *The Operative Chemist* (1828).

GRAY, Stephen (d. 1736), electrician; pensioner of the Charterhouse; FRS, 1732; first to divide substances into electrics and non-electrics, discovering means of their mutual transformation.

GRAY, Sir Thomas (d. 1369?), author of the *Scala-chronica*; served in France, 1338–44; fought at Neville's Cross, 1346; warden of Norham Castle; captured by Scots at Norham, 1355; warden of east marches, 1367; his *Scala-chronica* especially valuable for Scottish and French wars; prologue and latter half printed (1836), with *Leland's abstract of the complete work.

GRAY, Thomas (1716–1771), poet; educated at Eton with Horace *Walpole and Richard *West, whom he joined in 'Hymeneals' on marriage of *Frederick, prince of Wales, 1736; at Peterhouse, Cambridge, 1734–8; travelled on continent with Walpole, 1739–40, but quarrelled with him; made elaborate notes and wrote Latin ode on the Grande Chartreuse; resided at Cambridge; LL B, Cambridge, 1743; renewed friendship with Walpole; became intimate of William *Mason the poet; removed from Peterhouse to Pembroke College, Cambridge, on account of a practical joke, 1756; refused poet-laureateship, 1757; in London, 1759–61; appointed professor of history and modern languages at Cambridge through the influence of Richard *Stonehewer, 1768; formed friendship with Norton *Nicholls and Charles Victor de Bonstetten; toured in Scotland and various parts of England; gave plan of a history of English poetry to *Warton; classical scholar, linguist, and student of science; buried at Stoke Poges. His letters are among the best of his period. His poems include imitations from the Norse and Welsh, an *Ode on a distant prospect of Eton College* (at Walpole's suggestion issued anonymously, 1747, and included with those to spring and on the death of his cat in vol. ii of *Dodsley's collection, 1748), *Elegy in a Country Churchyard* (1751), the *Progress of Poesy* and *The Bard* (1758). The collections of Dodsley and *Foulis (1768) contained his poem 'The Fatal Sisters', and other new works. His complete works were edited by T. J. *Mathias (1814), by *Mitford (Aldine edn., 1835–43), and by Edmund *Gosse (1882). Pembroke College was largely rebuilt (1870–9) from the proceeds of a commemoration fund formed by friends of Gray, whose bust by Hamo *Thornycroft was placed there in 1885; *Bacon's bust on the Westminster Abbey monument is from Mason's portrait.

GRAY, Thomas (1787–1848), railway pioneer; published *Observations on a General Railway, with Plates and Maps* (1820).

GRAY, William (1802?–1835), author; MA, Magdalen College, Oxford, 1831; edited Sir Philip *Sidney's works (1829); barrister, Inner Temple, 1831; published *Historical Sketch of Origin of English Prose Literature* (1835).

GRAYDON, John (d. 1726), vice-admiral; commanded the *Defiance* at Beachy Head, 1690, and the *Hampton Court* off Cape Barfleur, 1692; rear-admiral with *Rooke at Cadiz and Vigo, 1702; vice-admiral in command of fleet to attack French settlement of Placentia, 1703; irregularly cashiered on report of House of Lords committee, 1703.

GRAYLE (or GRAILE), John (1614–1654), Puritan minister; MA, Magdalen Hall, Oxford, 1637; rector of Tidworth; published work defending himself from charge of Arminianism (1655).

GRAYSTANES, Robert de (d. 1336?), chronicler of the church of Durham; sub-prior of St Mary's, Durham; elected bishop and consecrated, 1333, but refused the temporalities and ousted by Richard de *Bury; continued Geoffrey de *Coldingham's chronicle from 1213; his work first printed (1691).

GREAME, Philip Lloyd-, first earl of Swinton (1884–1972), politician. See CUNLIFFE-LISTER.

GREATHEAD, Henry (1757–1816), lifeboat inventor; received grant of £1,200 for his boat.

GREATHED, William Wilberforce Harris (1826–1878), major-general; entered Bengal Engineers, 1844; first officer in the breach at storming of Mooltan, 1849; consulting engineer at Allahabad, 1855–7; twice carried despatches from Agra to Meerut through mutineers, 1857; as director of left attack on Delhi severely wounded; field-engineer of Doab force, 1857; directing engineer in *Napier's attack on Lucknow; CB and brevet-major; brevet-lieutenant-colonel for services in China, 1860; assistant military secretary at Horse Guards, 1861–5; chief of irrigation department in North-West Provinces, 1867–75; constructed Agra and Lower Ganges canals; major-general, 1877.

GREATHEED, Bertie (1759–1826), dramatist; the Reuben of *Gifford's *Baviad* and *Maeviad*; his tragedy, *The Regent*, acted at Drury Lane, 1788.

GREATOREX, Ralph (d. 1712?), mathematical-instrument maker; friend of *Oughtred and acquaintance of *Evelyn and *Pepys.

GREATOREX, Thomas (1758–1831), organist and conductor; musical director to Lord *Sandwich at Hinchinbrook; sang in Concerts of Ancient Music; organist of Carlisle Cathedral, 1780–4, Westminster Abbey, 1819; became conductor of Ancient Concerts, 1793; revived Vocal Concerts, 1801; first organ and pianoforte professor at Royal Academy of Music, 1822; FRS for discovery of method of measuring altitude of mountains; published *Parochial Psalmody* (1825) and *Twelve Glees from English, Irish, and Scotch Melodies* (1833).

GREATRAKES, Valentine (1629–1683), 'the stroker'; of Affane, Co. Waterford; served in the Cromwellian army in Ireland under Robert *Phaire; received offices in Co. Cork, 1656; began to cure scrofula and other diseases by laying on of hands, 1662; performed gratuitously cures at Ragley, Worcester, and Lincoln's Inn, 1666; answered attack by David *Lloyd (1625–1691) with a *Brief Account* (1666) of himself and of his cures addressed to Robert *Boyle, as well as testimonials from Andrew *Marvell, *Cudworth, Bishop *Wilkins, and *Whichcote.

GREATRAKES, William (1723?–1781), barrister; of Trinity College, Dublin; called to Irish bar, 1761; authorship of 'Junius' letters attributed to him, 1799.

GREAVES, Sir Edward (1608–1680), physician to Charles II; fellow of All Souls, Oxford, 1634; studied at Padua and Leiden; MD, Oxford, 1641; Linacre reader of physic, 1643; perhaps created baronet by Charles I, 1645; FRCP, 1657; Harveian orator, 1661.

GREAVES, James Pierrepont (1777–1842), mystic; joined Pestalozzi, 1817, at Yverdun; secretary of London Infant School Society, 1825; follower of Jacob Boehme; founded educational institution at Ham, Surrey.

GREAVES, John (1602–1652), mathematician and traveller; brother of Sir Edward *Greaves; BA, St Mary's Hall, Oxford, 1621; fellow of Merton College, Oxford, 1624; MA, 1628; Gresham professor of geometry, London, 1630; visited Paris, Leiden, Italy, Constantinople, and Egypt, measuring the Pyramids and collecting coins, gems, and oriental manuscripts, 1637–40; Savilian professor of astronomy on death (1643) of John *Bainbridge; ejected from chair and fellowship by parliament, 1648; published scientific works; his miscellaneous works edited by Thomas *Birch (1737).

GREAVES, Thomas (*fl.* 1604), composer and lutenist to Sir H. *Pierrepont; published *Songes of sundrie kinds* (1604); three madrigals by him edited by G. W. Budd (1843 and 1857).

GREAVES, Thomas (1612–1676), orientalist; brother of John *Greaves; of Charterhouse and Corpus Christi College, Oxford; fellow, 1636; DD, 1661; deputy-reader of Arabic, 1637; held livings in Northamptonshire; published *De linguae Arabicae utilitate* (1637) and treatises on Persian versions of the scriptures.

GREAVES, Walter (1846–1930), painter; son of a Chelsea waterman; pupil of J. A. M. *Whistler; painted portraits and landscape subjects, largely of Chelsea district, in oil and water-colour; later works show influence of Whistler; work not 'discovered' and exhibited until 1911.

GREEN, Alexander Henry (1832–1896), geologist; BA and fellow, Gonville and Caius College, Cambridge, 1855; MA, 1858; hon. fellow, 1892; worked on Geological Survey, 1861–74; professor of geology, Yorkshire College, Leeds, 1874, and also professor of mathematics, 1885; professor of geology at Oxford, 1888; hon. MA, Oxford, 1888; FGS, 1862; FRS,

1886; chief work, *Manual of Physical Geology* (1876).

GREEN, Alice Sophia Amelia (1847–1929), better known as Mrs Stopford Green, historian; born Stopford; came from Ireland to England, 1874; married J. R. *Green, the historian, 1877; became ardent radical and home ruler; took up study of early Irish history; settled in Dublin, *c.*1917; works include *Henry the Second* (1888), *Town Life in the Fifteenth Century* (1894), *The Making of Ireland and its Undoing* (1908), and *A History of the Irish State to 1014* (1925).

GREEN, Amos (1735–1807), flower, fruit, and landscape painter; friend of *Shenstone.

GREEN, Bartholomew (or Bartlet) (1530–1556), Protestant martyr; burnt at Smithfield.

GREEN, Benjamin (1736?–1800?), mezzotint engraver; probably brother of Amos *Green; drawing-master at Christ's Hospital; exhibited with Incorporated Society of Artists, 1765–74; engraved illustrations for *Morant's *Essex* (1768); drew and etched plates of antiquities.

GREEN, Benjamin Richard (1808–1876), water-colour painter; son of James *Green, portrait-painter; exhibited at Royal Academy and Suffolk Street from 1832.

GREEN, Charles (1785–1870), aeronaut; made the first ascent with carburetted hydrogen gas, 1821; constructed great Nassau balloon and went up from Vauxhall to Weilburg, Nassau, 1836; invented the guide-rope; made 526 ascents, 1821–52.

GREEN, Charles Alfred Howell (1864–1944), archbishop; scholar of Charterhouse and Keble College, Oxford; deacon, 1888; priest, 1889; vicar of Aberdare, 1893–1914; archdeacon of Monmouth and canon of Llandaff, 1914–21; bishop of Monmouth, 1921; of Bangor, 1928–44; archbishop of Wales, 1934–44; published *The Setting of the Constitution of the Church in Wales* (1937).

GREEN, Mrs Eliza S. Craven (1803–1866), poet; née Craven; published *A Legend of Mona* (1825) and *Sea Weeds and Heath Flowers* (1858).

GREEN, Frederick William Edridge- (1863–1953), authority on colour perception. See EDRIDGE-GREEN.

GREEN, George (1793–1841), mathematician; fellow of Caius College, Cambridge, 1839–41; fourth wrangler, 1837; published *Essay on the Application of Mathematical Analysis to the Theories of Electricity and Magnetism* (1828); read before Cambridge Philosophical Society papers on 'Reflection and Refraction of Sound' and 'Reflection and Refraction of Light at the common surface of two non-crystallised Media'.

GREEN, George Smith (d. 1762), author; Oxford watchmaker, published *The Life of Mr. J. Van* (1750), poems, and plays.

GREEN, Gustavus (1865–1964), aero-engine designer; established cycle business at Bexhill, 1897; took out first patent for internal combustion engine, 1900; founded Green Motor Patents Syndicate, manufacturing small stationary engines and motor cycles, 1906–14; Green water-cooled V.8 engine used in airship *Gamma*, 1910; produced most successful British aero-engines, 1909–14; international prizes won by aeroplanes and motor boats equipped with Green engines; technical director, Green Engine Co. Ltd., 1912–25; a gifted mechanic rather than a trained engineer; hon. companion, Royal Aeronautical Society, 1958.

GREEN, Sir Henry (d. 1369), judge; king's serjeant, 1345; knighted and judge of common pleas, 1354; excommunicated by the pope for sentencing the bishop of Ely, 1358; chief justice of King's Bench, 1361–5.

GREEN, Henry (1801–1873), author; MA, Glasgow, 1825; Presbyterian minister of Knutsford, 1827–72; edited six works for the Holbein Society, and published works, including *Sir Isaac Newton's Views on Points of Trinitarian Doctrine* (1856), *The Cat in Chancery* (1858, anon.), and *Shakespeare and the Emblem Writers* (1870).

GREEN, Henry (pseudonym) (1905–1973), writer. See YORKE, HENRY VINCENT.

GREEN, Hugh (1586–1642), alias Ferdinand Brooks, Roman Catholic martyr; BA, Peterhouse, Cambridge, 1605–6; studied at Douai; executed at Dorchester under proclamation of 1642.

GREEN, James (*fl.* 1743), organist at Hull; published *Book of Psalmody* (1724).

GREEN, James (1771–1834), portrait painter; copied *Reynolds's pictures; exhibited at Royal Academy after 1792, and at British Institution.

GREEN, Mrs Jane (d. 1791), actress. See HIPPISLEY, JANE.

GREEN, John (1706?–1779), bishop of Lincoln; fellow of St John's College, Cambridge, 1730; MA, 1731; DD, 1749; as master at Lichfield knew *Johnson and *Garrick; regius professor of divinity at Cambridge, 1748–56; master of Corpus Christi College, Cambridge, 1750–63; dean of Lincoln and vice-chancellor of Cambridge, 1756; bishop of Lincoln, 1761–79; published anonymously pamphlets on university reform and against Methodists; contributed to *Athenian Letters* (published 1781).

GREEN, John (*fl.* 1758), line-engraver; brother of Benjamin *Green.

GREEN, John (or **'Paddy'**) (1801–1874), singer and actor; was successively manager and conductor of entertainments at the Cider Cellars and Evans's Hall in Covent Garden; of latter he was proprietor, 1845–65.

GREEN, John Richard (1837–1883), historian; of Magdalen College School and Jesus College, Oxford; BA, 1860; in sole charge of Holy Trinity, Hoxton, 1863; incumbent of St Philip's, Stepney, 1866; librarian at Lambeth, 1869; published *Short History of the English People* (1874), *The Making of England* (1881), and *Conquest of England* (1883); suggested Oxford Historical Society and *English Historical Review*.

GREEN, John Richards (1758–1818), author. See GIFFORD, JOHN.

GREEN, Jonathan (1788?–1864), medical writer; MD, Heidelberg, 1834; MRCS, 1810; patented vapour-bath; died in the Charterhouse; published tracts on fumigating baths and skin diseases.

GREEN, Joseph Henry (1791–1863), surgeon; educated in Germany and St Thomas's Hospital; surgeon at St Thomas's, 1820; professor of anatomy at College of Surgeons, 1824; FRS, 1825; anatomical professor at Royal Academy, 1825–52; professor of surgery at King's College, London, 1832–7; president of College of Surgeons, 1849–50 and 1858–9; Hunterian orator, 1841 and 1847; president of General Medical Council, 1860; friend and literary executor of S. T. *Coleridge; published *The Dissector's Manual* (1820) and *Spiritual Philosophy* (1865).

GREEN, Sir Justly Watson (d. 1862), second baronet; son of Sir William *Green; officer, 1st Royals; selected to attend Prince Edward (afterwards duke of Kent) in his travels.

GREEN, Mrs Mary Anne Everett (1818–1895), historian; née Wood; of Wesleyan parentage; married, 1846, George Pycock Green (d. 1893); published *Letters of Royal Ladies down to Mary's reign* (1846), *Lives of Princesses of England* (1849–55, 6 vols.), and *Life and Letters of Henrietta Maria* (1857). She edited at the Public Record Office forty-one volumes of Calendars of Domestic State Papers (1857–95).

GREEN, Matthew (1696–1737), poet; friend of Richard *Glover; his poem *The Spleen* (1737) admired by Pope and Gray.

GREEN, Richard (1716–1793), Lichfield antiquary and surgeon. See GREENE, RICHARD.

GREEN, Richard (1803–1863), shipowner and philanthropist; helped to establish firm of Green, Wigram & Green, shipowners; built East Indiamen and ships for the voyage to Australia; established Sailors' Home at Poplar; benefactor of many institutions in East London.

GREEN, Rupert (1768–1804), print publisher and artist; son of Valentine *Green.

GREEN, Samuel (1740–1796), organ-builder.

GREEN, Samuel Gosnell (1822–1905), Baptist minister and bibliophile; joined Baptist ministry, 1844; classical tutor (from 1851) and president (1863–76) of Horton College, Bradford; editor (1876), editorial secretary (1881), and historian (1899) of the Religious Tract Society; published *Handbook to Grammar of Greek Testament* (1870), *Christian Ministry to the Young* (1883), and other theological works; president of Baptist Union, 1895; chairman of editorial committee of *Baptist Hymnal*; assisted Mrs Rylands in forming John Rylands Library, Manchester, 1899; hon. DD, St Andrews, 1900.

GREEN, Thomas (d. 1705), captain of the East Indiaman *Worcester*, hanged at Edinburgh on charge (apparently baseless) of piracy and murder.

GREEN, Thomas (1658–1738), bishop; fellow of Corpus Christi College, Cambridge, 1680; MA, 1682; DD, 1695; master of Corpus, 1698–1716; vice-chancellor, 1699 and 1713; archdeacon of Canterbury, 1708; incumbent of St Martin's-in-the-Fields, 1716; bishop of Norwich, 1721–3, of Ely, 1723–38; directed proceedings against Richard *Bentley, the classical scholar.

GREEN, Thomas, the elder (1722–1794), political pamphleteer.

GREEN, Thomas, the younger (1769–1825), author; son of Thomas *Green the elder; extracts from his 'Diary of a Lover of Literature', published (1810 and 1834–43); published poems and political pamphlets.

GREEN, Thomas Hill (1836–1882), idealist philosopher; educated at Rugby and Balliol College, Oxford; fellow and tutor, 1860; Whyte professor of moral philosophy, 1878–82; assistant-commissioner on middle-class schools, 1865; benefactor of Balliol College and the Oxford High School, and founder of a university prize; the 'Mr Gray' of 'Robert Elsmere'; his *Prolegomena to Ethics* published (1883); his works edited by Richard Lewis *Nettleship, 1885–8.

GREEN, Valentine (1739–1813), mezzotint engraver and author; keeper of British Institution, 1805–13; associate engraver, 1775; FRS and FSA; engraved twenty-two plates from Düsseldorf Gallery, 1789–95; engraved four hundred plates; published *Review of the Polite Arts in France* (1782), and other works.

GREEN, William (1714?–1794), Hebraist; scholar and fellow of Clare Hall, Cambridge; MA, 1741; rector of Hardingham, Norfolk, 1759–94; chief work, *Poetical Parts of the Old Testament... translated... with Notes* (1781).

GREEN, Sir William, first baronet (1725–1811), general; served with engineers in Flanders and Brittany, 1745–8; wounded and captured at Val, 1747; chief engineer of Newfoundland, 1755; took part in capture of Louisberg, 1758; wounded at Quebec, 1759; present at Sillery, 1760, and defence of Quebec; during twenty-two years' service at Gibraltar (1761–83) designed chief fortifications (being promoted director, 1778), general hospital, and subterranean galleries; during the siege (1779–83) made kilns for heating shot, and rebuilt Orange bastion under fire; thanked by parliament; created baronet and chief engineer of Great Britain, 1786; president of Defence Committee, 1788–97; general, 1798.

GREEN, William (1761–1823), water-colour painter and engraver; published prints and etchings of English Lake scenery, 1808–14, and *Tourist's New Guide* (of the Lake district), with forty etchings (1822).

GREEN, William Curtis (1875–1960), architect; educated at Newton College; articled to John *Belcher and trained at Royal Academy Schools under Phené *Spiers; commenced practice, 1898; FRIBA, 1909, and Royal medallist, 1942; works include Wolseley House (later Barclays Bank), Westminster Bank, and Stratton House, Piccadilly; London Life Association, King William Street; Scotland Yard, Embankment; Cambridge University Press, Euston Road; Dorchester Hotel, Park Lane; Queen's Hotel, Leeds; Stockgrove Park near Leighton Buzzard; a scholarly architect who produced work of lasting English quality; ARA, 1923; RA, 1933; president, Architectural Association.

GREEN, Sir William Kirby Mackenzie (1836–1891), diplomat; entered Consular Service, c.1854; vice-consul at Tetuan and acting consul at Tangier, 1859–69; acting agent and consul-general at Tunis, 1869–71, Damascus, 1871–3, Beirut, 1873–6; consul at Scutari, 1876–9; consul-general for Montenegro, 1879–86; envoy to Morocco and consul-general at Tangier, 1886–91; KCMG, 1887.

GREEN, William Pringle (1785–1846), inventor; entered navy, 1797; promoted lieutenant for services at Trafalgar, 1805; appointed to the *Victory*, 1842; took out patents, 1836–7, for improvements in capstans and levers; received silver medals from Society of Arts for various naval inventions, 1823; published *Fragments from remarks of twenty-five years ... on Electricity, Magnetism, Aerolites*, etc. (1833).

GREENACRE, James (1785–1837), murderer; manufactured 'amalgamated candy' for medical purposes in Camberwell; prepared to marry Hannah Brown, a washerwoman, as his fifth wife, but murdered her, 24 Dec. 1836; hanged.

GREENAWAY, Catherine ('Kate') (1846–1901), artist; studied art at South Kensington, at Heatherley's, and under Alphonse *Legros in Slade School, London; exhibited at Royal Academy, 1877; won fame as exponent of child life and inventor of original children's books; published *Under the Window* (1879), *Kate Greenaway's Birthday Book* (1880), *Mother Goose* (1881), *Little Ann and other Poems* (1883); also *Language of Flowers* (1884), *Marigold Garden* (1885), and an annual *Almanack* from 1883 to 1895; work much admired by John *Ruskin; created a gallery of children with quaint costumes and unhackneyed accessories; designed beautiful book-plates.

GREENBURY, Robert (*fl.* 1616–1650), painter; executed portraits of William *Waynflete and Bishop Arthur *Lake, and a picture of Dutch cruelties at Amboyna.

GREENE, Anne (*fl.* 1650), criminal; revived, and was pardoned, after being hanged for murder of her illegitimate child, 1650.

GREENE, Edward Burnaby (d. 1788), poet and translator; originally Burnaby, assumed additional name of Greene, 1741; published translations from classical poets and from *Gray's Latin verse.

GREENE, George (*fl.* 1813), traveller; with wife and children imprisoned, when land steward to prince of Monaco, at Torigny, Normandy, by French revolutionists, 1793–5 and 1799–1800; published account of the Revolution in that district (1802) and *Journal from London to St. Petersburg by way of Sweden* (1813).

GREENE, Harry Plunket (1865–1936), singer; born in Ireland; educated at Clifton; professor of singing, Royal Academy (1911–19) and Royal College (1912–19) of Music; first appeared as bass-baritone, 1888; established reputation in *Lieder* and Brahms songs, and as interpreter of (his father-in-law) Sir Charles *Parry's cantatas and oratorios and of Sir Charles *Stanford's Irish song-cycles.

GREENE, Maurice (1696?–1755), musical composer; organist of St Dunstan's-in-the-West, 1716, and St Andrew's, Holborn, 1717; organist of St Paul's Cathedral, 1718, of Chapel Royal, 1727; Mus.Doc. and professor of music, Cambridge, 1730; master of George II's band, 1735; sided with Buononcini against *Handel; assisted in founding Royal Society of Musicians, 1738; the only English organist named by Mattheson; composed music to *Pope's *Ode on St. Cecilia's Day*, *Addison's *Spacious Firmament*, and *Spenser's *Amoretti*, also two oratorios and songs, including 'Go, Rose', and 'The Bonny Sailor', with other works.

GREENE, Richard (1716–1793), Lichfield antiquary and surgeon; related to Dr *Johnson; established printing press and collection of curiosities, to which Johnson, *Pennant, and Erasmus *Darwin contributed.

GREENE, Robert (1560?–1592), pamphleteer and poet; BA, St John's College, Cambridge, 1579; MA, Clare Hall, 1583; incorporated at Oxford, 1588; led a dissolute life on the continent and in London; assailed by Gabriel *Harvey in *Foure Letters* as 'The Ape of Euphues'; defended by *Nashe in *Strange Newes*. He probably had some share in the authorship of the original *Henry VI* plays, which Shakespeare revised or rewrote. Among his thirty-eight publications were pamphlets, romances, and five (posthumous) plays, including *The Honorable Historie of frier Bacon and frier Bongay* (acted 1594). Of the romances, *Menaphon* (1589), reprinted as *Greene's Arcadia* (1599, etc.) and *Perimedes the Blacke-Smith* (1588) contain passages in verse which are his best efforts in poetry. His numerous pamphlets include *Euphues, his Censure to Philautus* (continuation of *Lyly's work, 1587), *Greene's Mourning Garment* (1590), *Never Too Late* (1590), and *Farewell to Folly* (1591), and the autobiographical *Groatsworth of Wit bought with a Million of Repentance* (ed. Chettle), which attacks *Marlowe and *Peele and contains the famous reference to Shakespeare as an 'upstart crow'. His plays and poems were edited by *Dyce (1831), his *Complete Works* by *Grosart, 1881–6.

GREENE, Robert (1678?–1730), philosopher; fellow and tutor of Clare Hall, Cambridge; MA, 1703; DD, 1728; published philosophical works, 1712 and 1727.

GREENE, Thomas (d. 1780), chancellor of Lichfield (1751) and dean of Salisbury (1757); son of Thomas *Green (1658–1738).

GREENE, Wilfrid Arthur, Baron Greene (1883–1952), judge; educated at Westminster and Christ Church, Oxford; first class, Lit. Hum., 1906; fellow, All Souls, 1907; Vinerian scholar and called to bar (Inner Temple), 1908; bencher, 1925; KC, 1922; lord justice of appeal, knighted, and PC, 1935; master of Rolls, 1937–49; baron, 1941; lord of appeal in ordinary, 1949–50; chairman of committees on company law (1925), trade practices (1930), international communications (1931), and beet-sugar industry (1935); principal, Working Men's College, 1936–44; chairman, National Buildings Record Office, 1941–5; DCL, Oxford, and number of honorary degrees.

GREENE, William Friese- (1855–1921), pioneer of cinematography; began life as travelling photographer; experimented with J. A. R. Rudge, of Bath, on reproduction, by camera and projecting lantern, of synthesis of motion, 1882–4; established photographic business in London; after many experiments produced sensitized celluloid ribbon-film, 1889; film patented, and projected scene exhibited, 1890.

GREENE, Sir (William) Graham (1857–1950), civil servant; educated at Cheltenham College; entered Admiralty, 1881; assistant private secretary and head of private office to successive first lords, 1887–1902; principal clerk, in charge of personnel branch and carrying educational reforms into effect, 1902; assistant secretary, Admiralty, 1907; permanent secretary, 1911; retired by Lloyd George (1917); appointed by (Sir) Winston Churchill as secretary, Ministry of Munitions, 1917–20; KCB, 1911.

GREENFIELD, John (1647?–1710?), physician. See GROENVELDT.

GREENFIELD, William (1799–1831), philologist; published *The Comprehensive Bible* (1827), *The Polymicrian Greek Lexicon to the New Testament* (1829), and publications for British and Foreign Bible Society.

GREENFIELD, William of (d. 1315), archbishop of York; studied at Oxford and Paris; doctor of civil and canon law; prebendary of Southwell, 1269, Ripon, 1272, and York, 1287; rector of Stratford-upon-Avon, 1294; member of royal embassy to Rome, 1290; present at Treaty of Tarascon, 1291, dean of Chichester, c.1301; of Norham, 1292; summoned to parliaments, 1295–1302; a royal proctor for peace with France, 1302; chancellor, 1302–4; joint regent, 1307; defended the marches against Robert *Bruce; lenient to the Templars; promulgated constitutions, 1306.

GREENHALGH, John (d. 1651), Royalist; governor of the Isle of Man, 1640; distinguished himself at Worcester; died of wounds.

GREENHAM (or GRENHAM), Richard (1535?–1594?), Puritan divine; fellow of Pembroke Hall, Cambridge, c.1566; MA, 1567; rector of Dry Drayton, Cambridgeshire, 1570–91; cited by Bishop *Cox for nonconformity; preached against the Mar-Prelate tracts, 1589; preacher at Christ Church, Newgate; his works edited by Henry *Holland, 1599.

GREENHILL, Henry (1646–1708), governor of the Gold Coast; principal commissioner of the Navy, 1691; directed completion of Plymouth Dockyard.

GREENHILL, John (1644?–1676), portrait painter; brother of Henry *Greenhill; pupil of *Lely; executed portraits of *Cowley, *Locke, Bishop Seth *Ward, Anthony *Ashley, earl of Shaftesbury, and Charles II.

GREENHILL, Joseph (1704–1788), theological writer; nephew of Thomas *Greenhill; MA, Sidney Sussex College, Cambridge, 1728; rector of East Horsley, 1727, and East Clandon, Surrey, 1732; published *Essay on the Prophecies of the New Testament* (7th edn., 1776).

GREENHILL, Thomas (1681–1740?), author of Νεκροκηδεία, *or the Art of Embalming* (1705).

GREENHILL, William (1591–1671), Nonconformist divine; demy of Magdalen College, Oxford, 1605–12; MA, 1612; incumbent of New Shoreham, Sussex, 1615–33; first pastor of Stepney Congregational Church, 1644–71; member of Westminster Assembly, 1643; Parliamentarian chaplain to royal children, 1649; a 'trier', 1654; vicar of St Dunstan-in-the-East, 1653–60; published *Exposition of Ezekiel* (1645–62).

GREENHILL, William Alexander (1814–1894), physician; educated at Rugby and Trinity College, Oxford; studied medicine at Radcliffe Infirmary, Oxford, and in Paris; MD, 1840; physician to Radcliffe Infirmary, Oxford, 1839–51; practised at Hastings from 1851; founder, 1857, and secretary, 1857–91, of Hastings Cottage Improvement Society; published editions of works by Sir Thomas *Browne, including *Religio Medici, Christian Morals*, and other writings, including contributions to this Dictionary.

GREENHOW, Edward Headlam (1814–1888), physician; MD, Aberdeen, 1852; studied at Edinburgh and Montpellier; practised at North Shields and Tynemouth; lecturer on public health at St Thomas's Hospital, 1855; consulting physician to Middlesex Hospital, 1870; chief founder of Clinical Society; president, 1879; Croonian lecturer of College of Physicians, 1875; published medical works.

GREENIDGE, Abel Hendy Jones (1865–1906), writer on ancient history and law; born at Barbados; BA, Balliol College, Oxford, 1888; MA, 1891; D.Litt., 1904; fellow (1889) and tutor (1902) of Hertford College; fellow of St John's College, Oxford, 1905; published *Infamia* (1894), *Handbook on Greek Constitutional History* (1896); edited William Smith's and *Gibbon's histories of Rome; commenced a new *History of Rome* (vol. i, 1904); accurate and critical historian.

GREENOUGH, George Bellas (1778–1855), geographer and geologist; assumed additional name of Greenough at Eton; studied at Pembroke College, Cambridge, and Göttingen and Freiburg; secretary to Royal Institution; MP, Gatton, 1807–12; first president of Geological Society, 1811; of Geographical Society, 1839–40; published *Critical Examination of the first Principles of Geology* (1819) and geological maps of the United Kingdom (1820) and of Hindustan; died at Naples.

GREENWAY, Oswald (1563–1635), Jesuit. See TESIMOND.

GREENWELL, Dora (1821–1882), poet and essayist; published books of poems, including (1869) *Carmina Crucis*, and prose works, comprising *The Patience of Hope* (1860) and lives of Lacordaire and John *Woolman.

GREENWELL, Sir Leonard (1781–1844), major-general; with 45th Foot at Buenos Aires and in Peninsular War; frequently wounded; succeeded to the command after Toulouse, 1814; major-general, 1837; KCB and KCH.

GREENWELL, William (1820–1918), archaeologist; brother of Dora *Greenwell; BA, Durham; minor canon of Durham, 1854–1907; librarian to dean and chapter, 1862–1907; rector of St Mary-the-Less, Durham, 1865–1918; documents edited include *Feodarium Prioratus Dunelmensis* (1872); FRS, 1878.

GREENWICH, duke of (1678–1743). See CAMPBELL, JOHN, second duke of Argyll.

GREENWOOD, Arthur (1880–1954), politician; educated at higher grade school and Yorkshire College; B.Sc., Leeds, 1905; lecturer in economics, 1913; moved to London, 1914; civil servant, 1916–20; secretary, Labour Party Research Department, 1920–43; responsible for much of the party's constructive thought after 1931 and united intellectual and trade-union wings of party; MP, Nelson and Colne, 1922–31, Wakefield, 1932–54; parliamentary secretary, Ministry of Health, 1924; minister of health, 1929–31; responsible for Widows', Orphans', and Old Age Contributory Pensions Act, 1929; elected deputy leader of Labour party, 1935; treasurer, 1943–54; member, War Cabinet,

1940–2, without portfolio; responsible for economic affairs (1940) and reconstruction (1941–2); appointed Beveridge Committee; lord privy seal, 1945–7; paymaster-general, 1946–7; minister without portfolio, 1947; PC, 1929; CH, 1945; hon. LL D, Leeds.

GREENWOOD, Arthur William James ('Anthony'), Baron Greenwood of Rossendale (1911–1982), politician; educated at Merchant Taylors' School and Balliol College, Oxford; president of the Union (1933); worked with National Fitness Council, 1938–9; joined Ministry of Information, 1939; intelligence officer, RAF, 1942; worked with Allied reparations commission; led Labour group, Hampstead Borough Council, 1945–9; JP, 1950; Labour MP for Heywood and Radcliffe, 1946–50; MP for Rossendale, 1950–70; parliamentary private secretary to postmaster-general, 1949; vice-chairman, Parliamentary Labour party, 1950–1; strong supporter of Aneurin *Bevan and Harold Wilson (later Lord Wilson of Rievaulx); served on national executive committee, 1954–70; member Labour shadow Cabinet; staunch supporter of Campaign for Nuclear Disarmament; party chairman, 1963–4; colonial secretary, 1964–5; PC, 1964; moved to Ministry of Overseas Development, 1965–6; minister of housing and local government, 1966–9; housing department placed under Department of Local Government and Regional Planning, and Greenwood dropped from Cabinet, 1969; life peer, 1970; held number of business directorships; active in charitable causes, including Greenwood Development Housing Company; deputy-lieutenant of Essex, 1974; pro-chancellor, Lancaster University, 1972–8; hon. LL D, Lancaster, 1979.

GREENWOOD, Frederick (1830–1909), journalist; at first a printer's reader; published novels, 1854–60; first editor of *Queen* illustrated paper, 1861–3; contributed his novel *Margaret Denzil's History* serially to *Cornhill Magazine*, 1863; succeeded W. M. *Thackeray as editor of *Cornhill*, 1862–8; founded with George *Smith, and edited, *Pall Mall Gazette*, 1865; secured its triumph in 1866 by three papers by his brother James, 'A Night in a Casual Ward'; an independent Conservative and vigilant student of foreign affairs; suggested to Lord Beaconsfield purchase of Suez Canal shares, 1875; attacked Gladstone's anti-Turkish attitude, 1876–8; left *Pall Mall Gazette*, on its conversion by a new owner into a radical organ, for newly founded Conservative *St James's Gazette*, 1880; advocated occupation of Egypt, 1882; retired from *St James's*, 1888; founded and edited weekly *Anti-Jacobin*, 1891–2; opposed South African War,

1899; friend of George *Meredith; published *The Lover's Lexicon* (1893), *Imagination in Dreams* (1894).

GREENWOOD, Hamar, first Viscount Greenwood (1870–1948), politician; born in Canada; officer in militia; BA, Toronto, and moved to England, 1895; called to bar (Gray's Inn), 1906; KC, 1919; Liberal MP, York (1906–10), Sunderland (1910–22); 'anti-socialist', East Walthamstow (1924–9); served in France, 1914–16; secretary, Overseas Trade Department, 1919–20; chief secretary for Ireland, 1920–2; reinforced Royal Irish Constabulary with undisciplined recruits ('Black and Tans') whose violence he defended; took little part in discussions preceding Irish Treaty; honorary treasurer, Conservative party, 1933–8; baronet, 1915; baron, 1929; viscount, 1937.

GREENWOOD, James (d. 1737), grammarian; sur-master of St Paul's School, 1721–37; published *Essay towards a Practical English Grammar* (1711, abridged as *Royal English Grammar*), and *The London Vocabulary, English and Latin* (3rd edn., 1713).

GREENWOOD, John (d. 1593), Independent divine; BA, Corpus Christi College, Cambridge, 1581; imprisoned with Henry *Barrow for holding a conventicle; collaborated with him, 1592; assisted in forming private congregation in Nicholas Lane (possibly the beginning of Congregationalism); hanged with Barrow at Tyburn for publishing seditious books.

GREENWOOD, John (d. 1609), schoolmaster; fellow of Catharine Hall, Cambridge; MA, 1565; master of Brentwood Grammar School; published *Syntaxis et Prosodia*, in verse (1590).

GREENWOOD, John (1727–1792), portrait painter; born at Boston, Massachusetts; lived five years at Surinam, and (1758–63) at Amsterdam; settled in London, 1763; original fellow of the Incorporated Society of Artists; his *Amelia Hone* (1771) perhaps his best work.

GREENWOOD, Joseph Gouge (1821–1894), principal of the Owens College, Manchester; educated at University College School, and University College, London; BA, London, 1840; private tutor and assistant-master at his old school; first professor of classics and history, Owens College, Manchester, 1850; principal, 1857–89, and vice-chancellor, 1880–6; hon. LL D, Cambridge, 1874, and Edinburgh, 1884; did much to promote public interest in the college.

GREENWOOD, Thomas (1790–1871), historian; MA, St John's College, Cambridge, 1831; barrister, Gray's Inn, 1817, bencher, 1837, and treasurer, 1841–2; fellow and reader in history and polite literature, Durham University; published *History of Germans* down to AD 772 (1836) and *History of Great Latin Patriarchate* (1856–65).

GREENWOOD, Thomas (1851–1908), promoter of public libraries; library assistant at Sheffield; founded in London (1871) firm of printers of trade journals, which he edited; advocated rate-supported libraries; published *Public Libraries* (1886), *Museums and Art Galleries* (1888), and *Greenwood's Library Year Book* (1897); presented library of Edward *Edwards (1812–86), as well as his own 'Library for Librarians' (1906), to Manchester Public Library; wrote life of Edwards, 1902.

GREENWOOD, Walter (1903–1974), novelist and playwright; educated to age of 13 at Langworthy Road Council School, Salford; employed in numerous jobs from stable-boy to salesman, 1916–33; recorded impressions of working-class life, leading to his first book, *Love on the Dole* (1933), redrafted for the stage in collaboration with Ronald Gow (1934), filmed (1941), and produced as a musical (1970); published nine other novels and a book of short stories; also plays, including *My Son My Son* (1935), *The Cure for Love* (1951), and *Saturday Night at the Crown* (1953); wrote *No Limit*, a film script for George *Formby; also scripts for BBC TV, including the serial 'The Secret Kingdom' (1960); published his autobiography, *There was a Time* (1967); hon. D.Litt., Salford University, 1971.

GREER, (Frederick) Arthur, Baron Fairfield (1863–1945), judge; educated at Old Aberdeen Grammar School and the university; called to bar (Gray's Inn), 1886; practised in Liverpool and London; KC, 1910; judge of King's Bench division and knighted, 1919; presided over trial for murder of F. R. Holt, 1920; lord justice of appeal, 1927–38; his dissenting judgements several times approved in the Lords; member (1917), chairman (1934–6), Council of Legal Education; PC, 1927; baron, 1939.

GREER, Samuel MacCurdy (1810–1880), Irish politician; educated at Belfast Academy and Glasgow; an originator of the Tenant League, 1850; Liberal MP for Londonderry, 1857; recorder, 1870–8; county-court judge of Cavan and Leitrim, 1878–80.

GREER, William Derrick Lindsay (1902–1972), bishop of Manchester; educated at Campbell College, Belfast, St Columba's College, Rathfarnham, Dublin, and Trinity College, Dublin, where he was a scholar; senior moderator in mental and moral philosophy, 1924; served in Northern Ireland Civil Service, 1925–9; trained at Westcott House, Cambridge, and ordained to curacy in Newcastle upon Tyne, 1925; general secretary, Student Christian Movement, 1935–44; involved in formation of World Council of Churches; principal, Westcott House, 1944–7; bishop of Manchester, 1947–70; established close relations with business community and played leading part in founding William House at Withington (1963), a hostel for discharged prisoners, and St Ann's Hospice, Cheadle (1971) for terminal cancer patients; honorary doctorates from Trinity College, Dublin, 1947, and Edinburgh (1951) and Manchester (1971), universities; published *John Bainbridge Gregg* (1931), his only book.

GREET, Sir Phillip Barling Ben (1857–1936), actor-manager; first London appearance, 1883; entered (1886) upon lifework with series of open-air ('pastoral') performances of Shakespeare; revived *Everyman*, 1902; with Lilian *Baylis at Old Vic, 1914–18; gave Shakespearian performances for London County Council schools, etc., 1918–22; with Regent's Park Open-Air Theatre, 1933–5; knighted, 1929.

GREETING, Thomas (*fl.* 1675), musician; published lessons and instructions for the flageolet (1675); taught Mrs Pepys, 1667.

GREG, Percy (1836–1889), author; son of William Rathbone *Greg; published political and religious essays, novels, and poems.

GREG, Robert Hyde (1795–1875), economist and antiquary; brother of William Rathbone *Greg and of Samuel *Greg; contributed archaeological memoirs, suggested by his travels, to Manchester Literary Society, 1823–38; MP, Manchester, 1839–41; president of Chamber of Commerce; published pamphlets on factory question, corn laws, and agriculture.

GREG, Samuel (1804–1876), philanthropist; brother of Robert Hyde *Greg and of William Rathbone *Greg; friend of Dean *Stanley; established schools, classes, baths, and libraries for his mill-hands at Bollington, 1832–47; compelled to retire from business by a strike against cloth-stretching machinery; entertained Kossuth, 1857; gave scientific lectures, and published religious works.

GREG, Sir Walter Wilson (1875–1959), scholar and bibliographer; son of William Rathbone *Greg and grandson of James *Wilson; educated at Harrow and Trinity College, Cambridge; graduated, 1897; librarian, 1907–13; honorary fellow, 1941; joined Bibliographical Society, 1898; spent sixty years working on descriptive bibliography of English drama in four volumes (1939–59); general editor (1906–39), president (1939–59), Malone Society; close friend of R. B. *McKerrow and A. W. *Pollard; edited the

*Henslowe *Diary* and *Papers* (1904–8) and wrote *Pastoral Poetry and Pastoral Drama* (1906) for A. H. *Bullen; his editions of manuscript plays include *Sir Thomas More* (1911); other publications include *Dramatic Documents from the Elizabethan Playhouses* (1931), *English Literary Autographs, 1550–1650* (1925–32), *Marlowe's 'Doctor Faustus' 1604–1616* (1950), and *The Editorial Problem in Shakespeare* (3rd edn., 1954); FBA, 1928; knighted, 1950; hon. D.Litt., Oxford, and LL D, Edinburgh; hon. fellow, Trinity College, Cambridge.

GREG, William Rathbone (1809–1881), essayist; brother of Robert Hyde *Greg and of Samuel *Greg; educated at Edinburgh University; eighteen years a mill-owner; commissioner of customs, 1856; comptroller of the Stationery Office, 1864–77; published works, including *The Creed of Christendom* (1851), *Mistaken Aims and Attainable Ideals of the Working Classes* (1876), and political and social essays (1853).

GREGAN, John Edgar (1813–1855), architect; designed buildings at Manchester.

GREGG, John (1798–1878), Irish bishop; graduated at Trinity College, Dublin, 1824; incumbent of Bethesda Chapel, Dublin, 1836, of Trinity Church, 1839–62; archdeacon of Kildare, 1857; bishop of Cork, Cloyne, and Ross, 1862; built new cathedral of St Finn Barre, Cork.

GREGG, Robert Samuel (1834–1896), archbishop of Armagh; son of John *Gregg; MA, Trinity College, Dublin, 1860; incumbent of Christ Church, Belfast; rector of Frankland and chaplain to his father, then bishop of Cork, 1862; rector of Carrigrohane and preceptor of St Finn Barre's Cathedral, Cork, 1865; dean of Cork, 1874; bishop of Ossory, Ferns, and Leighlin, 1875, and of Cork, 1878; archbishop of Armagh, 1893, till death; DD, Dublin, 1873.

GREGG, William (d. 1708), conspirator; of Scottish origin; under-clerk in office of Robert *Harley, secretary of state, 1706; hanged at Tyburn for sending to the French minister, Chamillart, copies of important state documents.

GREGO, Joseph (1843–1908), writer on art; collected works by *Rowlandson, *Morland, and *Cruikshank; published *Rowlandson the Caricaturist* (2 vols., 1880), *Cruikshank's Water Colours* (1904), *Thackerayana* (1875), *History of Parliamentary Elections* (1886), and *Pictorial Pickwickiana* (2 vols., 1899); organized picture exhibitions; invented a system of reproducing eighteenth-century colour prints.

GREGOR, cacique of Poyais (*fl.* 1817), South American adventurer. See MACGREGOR, Sir GREGOR.

GREGOR, William (1761–1817), chemist and mineralogist; fellow of St John's College, Cambridge, 1783–7; MA, 1787; rector of Diptford, Devonshire, 1787–93; of Creed, Cornwall, 1794–1817; discovered Menacchanite, sometimes called after him Gregorite; experimented on zeolite, wavellite, and other substances; published pamphlets.

GREGORY, Lady (1815–1895), actress. See STIRLING, Mrs MARY ANNE.

GREGORY, Mrs (d. 1790?), actress. See Mrs FITZHENRY.

GREGORY, Sir Augustus Charles (1819–1905), Australian explorer and politician; born at Farnsfield, Nottinghamshire; joined survey department of West Australia, 1841; explored interior of continent; discovered pastoral and mineral wealth of Murchison district; undertook unsuccessful expeditions in search of F. W. L. *Leichhardt, 1855, 1858; explored rivers of east coast of Australia, 1855–6; surveyor for Queensland, 1859–75; member of Legislative Council, 1882; first mayor of Toowong, 1902; sat on Commission of Inquiry into Condition of Aborigines, 1876–83; CMG, 1875; KCMG, 1903; joint-author with brother Francis of *Journals of Australian Exploration* (1884).

GREGORY, Barnard (1796–1852), journalist; owned and edited, 1831–49, *The Satirist, or Censor of the Times*; condemned for libel on Duke Charles of Brunswick after seven years' litigation, 1843–50.

GREGORY, David (1627–1720), inventor of an improved cannon; practised medicine in Aberdeenshire.

GREGORY, David (1661–1708), astronomer; son of David *Gregory (1627–1720); professor of mathematics at Edinburgh, 1683–91; appointed Savilian professor of astronomy at Oxford, 1691; MA, and MD, Oxford, 1692; master commoner of Balliol College; FRS, 1692; published *Astronomiae Physicae et Geometricae Elementa* (1702), being the first textbook on gravitational principles, and an edition of Euclid (1703); observed partial solar eclipse, 13 Sept. 1699.

GREGORY, David (1696–1767), dean of Christ Church, Oxford; son of David *Gregory (1661–1708); educated at Westminster and Christ Church, Oxford; MA, 1721; DD, 1732; first Oxford professor of modern history and languages, 1724–36; dean of Christ Church, 1756–67; master of Sherborne Hospital, 1759; prolocutor of lower house, 1761; benefactor of Christ Church and Sherborne Hospital.

GREGORY, Donald (d. 1836), antiquary; secretary to Scottish Antiquaries' Society and the

Iona Club; published *History of the Western Highlands and the Isles of Scotland, 1493–1625* (1836).

GREGORY, Duncan Farquharson (1813–1844), mathematician; youngest son of James *Gregory (1753–1821); educated at Edinburgh, Geneva, and Trinity College, Cambridge; fellow, 1840; fifth wrangler, 1837; MA, 1841; first editor of *Cambridge Mathematical Journal*; assistant to chemistry professor; his *Mathematical Writings* edited by W. Walton (1865).

GREGORY, Edmund (*fl.* 1646), author of *Historical Anatomy of Christian Melancholy* (1646); BA, Trinity College, Oxford, 1636.

GREGORY, Edward John (1850–1909), painter; studied at Royal Academy, 1869; contributed sketches to *Graphic* till 1875; best work exhibited at Royal Institute of Painters in Water Colours, of which he became president in 1898; exhibited mainly portraits at Royal Academy; ARA, 1883; RA, 1898; best-known pictures in oil are *Marooning* (1887), *Boulter's Lock—Sunday Afternoon* (1898); in water-colours, *A Look at the Model* and *Souvenir of the Institute*.

GREGORY, Francis (1625?–1707), schoolmaster; of Westminster and Trinity College, Cambridge; MA, 1648; successively headmaster of Woodstock and Witney grammar schools; incumbent of Hambleden, Buckinghamshire, 1671–1707; published lexicons and theological treatises.

GREGORY, Frederick Gugenheim (1893–1961), plant physiologist; born Fritz Gugenheim, son of Jewish expatriate from Germany; educated at Owen's School, Islington, and Imperial College, London; first class, botany; ARCS, 1914; B.Sc., 1915; DIC, 1917; M.Sc., 1920; D.Sc., 1921; worked on physiology of greenhouse crops, Cheshunt Experimental Station, 1914–17; victim of abuse for people with German names; changed name by deed poll, 1916; appointed to post in Research Institute of Plant Physiology, Imperial College, 1917; interested in analysis of plant growth; studied growth of barley crop, 1919; experimented with effects of major plant nutrients in controlling growth; collaborated with F. J. *Richards, 1926–58; visited Sudan to advise on cotton-growing by irrigation, 1928; assistant professor of plant physiology, Imperial College,. under V. H. *Blackman, 1929–37; succeeded Blackman as professor, 1937; director, Research Institute, 1947–58; FRS, 1940, served on council, 1949–51; left legacy to create Frederick Gregory Fund for benefit of Botany Department, Imperial College.

GREGORY, George (1754–1808), divine and author; DD, Edinburgh, 1792; prebendary of St Paul's, 1806; edited *Biographia Britannica* (1795)

and *New Annual Register*. His works include a *History of the Christian Church* (1790) and a *Dictionary of the Arts and Sciences* (1808).

GREGORY, George (1790–1853), physician; grandson of John *Gregory (1724–1773); MD, Edinburgh, 1811; MRCS, 1812; assistant-surgeon to forces in Mediterranean, 1813–15; physician to Smallpox Hospital, 1824; FRS; FRCP, 1839; published *Elements of the Theory and Practice of Physic* (1820).

GREGORY, Isabella Augusta, Lady (1852–1932), playwright and poet; born Persse; married Sir W. H. *Gregory, 1880; a founder with W. B. *Yeats and G. A. *Moore (1899) of Irish Literary Theatre; and with Yeats and J. M. *Synge (1904–32) of Abbey Theatre, Dublin; director, 1904–32; wrote twenty-seven plays, including *The Image* (1910), *The Golden Apple* (1916), *The Dragon* (1920), and *Sancho's Master* (1928); translated Gaelic sagas.

GREGORY, James (1638–1675), mathematician; brother of David *Gregory (1627–1720); educated at Aberdeen; published *Optica Promota* (1663), describing his reflecting telescope; printed at Padua, *Vera Circuli et Hyperbolae Quadratura* (1667), which provoked controversy with Huygens; FRS, 1668; mathematical professor at St Andrews, 1668; first professor of mathematics at Edinburgh, 1674; struck blind with amaurosis; corresponded with *Newton on their respective telescopes; original discoverer in mathematics and astronomy.

GREGORY, James (1753–1821), professor of medicine at Edinburgh; son of John *Gregory (1724–1773); educated at Aberdeen, Edinburgh, and Oxford; MD, Edinburgh, 1774; professor of institutes of medicine at Edinburgh, 1776, of practice of medicine, 1790; had violent controversies with Dr Alexander and James *Hamilton (managers of Edinburgh Royal Infirmary and College of Physicians); suspended from fellowship, Edinburgh College of Physicians, 1808; published *Conspectus Medicinae Theoreticae* (1780–2) and miscellaneous works.

GREGORY, John (1607–1646), orientalist; MA, Christ Church, Oxford, 1631; chaplain to Brian *Duppa; collective editions of his writings issued as *Gregorii Posthuma* (1649) and *Opuscula* (1650); translated works on the Brahmans from Greek into Latin.

GREGORY, John (1724–1773), professor of medicine at Edinburgh; grandson of James *Gregory (1638–1675); studied at Edinburgh and Leiden; MD, Aberdeen; professor of philosophy, Aberdeen, 1746–9; removed to London, 1754; FRS; professor of medicine, Edinburgh, 1766–73; intimate of *Akenside, *Hume,

*Beattie, and other literary celebrities. His works (collected, 1788) include a *Comparative View of the State and Faculties of Man with those of the Animal World* (1766).

GREGORY, John Walter (1864–1932), geologist and explorer; graduate of London University; assistant in geological department, British Museum, 1887–1900; professor of geology, Melbourne, 1900–4, Glasgow, 1904–29; made world-wide expeditions; drowned in Peru; publications include *The Great Rift Valley* (1896), *Geography, Structural, Physical, and Comparative* (1909), and works on bryozoa; FRS, 1901.

GREGORY, Olinthus Gilbert (1774–1841), mathematician; of humble birth; taught mathematics at Cambridge; mathematical master at Woolwich, 1802; MA, Aberdeen, 1805, and LL D, 1808; *Hutton's successor at Woolwich, 1807–38; one of the projectors of London University; published treatises on astronomy (1802) and mechanics (1806), besides *Letters on Christian evidences* (1811), and lives of John Mason *Good and Revd Robert *Hall.

GREGORY, Sir Richard Arman, baronet (1864–1952), author, scientific journalist, and editor of *Nature*; received elementary school education; obtained scholarship to Normal School of Science; fellow student and lifelong friend of H. G. *Wells; first classes, astronomy and physics, 1887; computer, Solar Physics Committee, and assistant to (Sir) Norman *Lockyer, 1889–92; his assistant editor on *Nature*, 1893; editor, 1919–38; scientific editor, Macmillans, 1905–39; joint founder and editor, *School World* (incorporated in *Journal of Education*, 1918), 1899–1939; joined British Association, 1896; president, 1939–46; a founder and first secretary (1901) of Association's educational science section; active in British Science Guild and obtained its merger with British Association, 1936; publications include *Honours Physiography* (with H. G. Wells, 1893) and *Discovery or the Spirit and Service of Science* (1916; revised as Penguin, 1949); knighted, 1919; baronet, 1931; FRS, 1933.

GREGORY, Robert (1819–1911), dean of St Paul's; MA, Corpus Christi College, Oxford, 1846; DD, 1891; vicar of St Mary-the-Less, Lambeth, 1853–73; served on Royal Commission on Ritual, 1867; canon of St Paul's, 1868; helped to improve cathedral fabric and finances; a zealous member of Lower House of Canterbury Convocation from 1868; defended Athanasian Creed and ritual; member of education commission, 1886; dean of St Paul's, 1890; able administrator; published *Elementary Education* (1895) and sermons; autobiography edited by W. H. *Hutton, 1912.

GREGORY, William (*fl.* 1520), Scottish Carmelite; prior successively at Melun, Albi, and Toulouse; doctor of the Sorbonne and confessor to Francis I.

GREGORY, William (d. 1467), chronicler; lord mayor of London, 1451–2; benefactor of St Anne's, Aldersgate, and other churches and hospitals; his chronicle printed in *Collections of a London Citizen*.

GREGORY, William (d. 1663), composer; violinist to Charles I and Charles II; his compositions contained in *Playford's *Court Ayres* and in the *Treasury of Musick* and *Ayres and Dialogues*.

GREGORY, Sir William (1624–1696), judge; barrister, Gray's Inn, 1650; recorder of Gloucester, 1672; serjeant-at-law, 1677; MP, Weobly, 1678; speaker, 1679; baron of the Exchequer and knighted, 1679; removed for giving judgment against royal dispensing power, 1685; judge of King's Bench, 1689; rebuilt church at How Capel, Herefordshire.

GREGORY, William (1766–1840), Irish under-secretary; educated at Harrow and Trinity College, Cambridge; MA, 1787; studied at Inner Temple; member for Portarlington in Irish parliament, 1798–1800; under-secretary to lord-lieutenant of Ireland, 1812–31, and was confidential adviser of successive viceroys and chief secretaries; retired from public life, 1831; ranger of Phoenix Park from 1812.

GREGORY, William (1803–1858), chemist; fourth son of James *Gregory (1753–1821); MD, Edinburgh, 1828; professor of medicine and chemistry at King's College, Aberdeen, 1839, of chemistry at Edinburgh, 1844–58; edited English editions of Liebig's works; published *Outlines of Chemistry* (1845).

GREGORY, Sir William Henry (1817–1892), governor of Ceylon; grandson of William *Gregory (1766–1840); educated at Harrow and Christ Church, Oxford; Conservative MP for Dublin, 1842–7; actively supported Poor Relief Act, 1847; high sheriff of Galway, 1849; devoted himself to the turf; Liberal-Conservative MP for Co. Galway, 1857, and retained seat till 1871; formally joined Liberal party on death of Palmerston, 1865; took interest in Irish agrarian legislation; chairman of House of Commons inquiry into accommodation at British Museum, 1860; trustee of National Gallery, 1867–92; Irish privy councillor, 1871; governor of Ceylon, 1871–7; KCMG, 1876. His autobiography was published (1894).

GREGORY OF CAERGWENT (*fl.* 1270), historian; monk of Gloucester, 1237; wrote annals

(682–1290) of monastery of St Peter's, Gloucester.

GREGORY OF HUNTINGDON (*fl.* 1290), prior of Ramsey and author.

GREGORY THE GREAT (d. 889), Grig, king of Scotland; according to William *Skene fifth king of the united kingdom of Scone; succeeded Aed, 878, being associated with Eocha; said to have subjected Bernicia and the greater part of Anglia (probably Northumbria only), and to have been 'the first to give liberty to the Scottish churches'; expelled with Eocha.

GREGSON, Matthew (1749–1824), antiquary; made a fortune at Liverpool as an upholsterer; elected FSA for his *Portfolio of Fragments relative to the History and Antiquities of the County Palatine and Duchy of Lancaster* (1817).

GREIFFENHAGEN, Maurice William (1862–1931), painter; studied at Royal Academy Schools and exhibited at Academy from 1884; ARA, 1916; RA, 1922; executed striking portraits of men and large-scale decorative work; headmaster, life department, Glasgow School of Art, 1906–29.

GREIG, Alexis Samuilovich (1775–1845), admiral in Russian service; son of Sir Samuel *Greig; distinguished himself in Russo-Turkish wars of 1807 and 1828–9; reorganized Russian Navy and created Black Sea Fleet.

GREIG, John (1759–1819), mathematician.

GREIG, Sir Samuel (1735–1788), admiral of the Russian Navy; in British service till 1763; present at Quiberon Bay, 1759, and reduction of Havanna, 1762; entered Russian service, 1764; commanded division under Orloff in Chesme Bay, 1770; appointed grand admiral, governor of Kronstadt and knight of several orders by Tsarina Catherine; commanded against Sweden at action off Hogland, 1788; created the modern Russian Navy, manning it largely with Scottish officers.

GREISLEY, Henry (1615?–1678), translator; of Westminster and Christ Church, Oxford; student, 1634; MA, 1641; ejected from studentship, 1651; prebendary of Worcester, 1672; translated Balzac's *Prince* (1648) and Senault's *Christian Man* (1650).

GREISLEY, Sir Roger (1779–1837). See GRESLEY.

GRELLAN, Saint (*fl.* 500), of Craebh-Grellain, Roscommon; renounced succession to throne of Leinster, and accompanied St *Patrick to Dublin; granted Craebh-Grellain by queen of Connaught for restoring her dead child; intervened in war between Cian and Maine the Great; his cro-

zier said to have been in possession of John Cronelly, 1836.

GRENE, Christopher (1629–1697), Jesuit; professed, 1669; director at English College, Rome, 1692; collected records of Romanist martyrs.

GRENE, Martin (1616–1667), Jesuit; brother of Christopher *Grene; professed, 1654; professor at Liège, 1642; died at St Omer; published *Account of the Jesuites Life and Doctrine* (1661).

GRENFELL, Bernard Pyne (1869–1926), papyrologist; BA, The Queen's College, Oxford, 1892; researched in Egypt, 1893–4–5; carried out excavations at the Fayum and Behneseh, 1895–6–7, 1898–1902, 1903–6; made important discoveries for Graeco-Roman period; found quantities of papyri; professor of papyrology at Oxford, 1908; FBA, 1905; works, mostly in collaboration with his friend A. S. *Hunt, include *Revenue Laws of Ptolemy Philadelphus* (1896); *An Alexandrian Erotic Fragment* (1896); *The Oxyrhynchus Papyri* (17 vols., 1898–1927); *The Amherst Papyri* (1900–1); *The Tebtunis Papyri* (1902–7); an exemplary editor.

GRENFELL, Edward Charles, first Baron St Just (1870–1941), banker and politician; cousin of W. H. Grenfell, Lord *Desborough; educated at Harrow and Trinity College, Cambridge; manager, J. S. Morgan & Co. (from 1909 Morgan, Grenfell & Co.), London, 1900; partner, 1904–41; a director of Bank of England, 1905–40; Conservative MP, City of London, 1922–35; baron, 1935.

GRENFELL, Francis Wallace, first Baron Grenfell (1841–1925), field marshal; joined army, 1859; went on service to South Africa, 1874; staff officer during last Kaffir War, 1878; took part in final defeat of Zulus at Ulundi, 1879; assistant-adjutant-general to Sir Garnet *Wolseley in Egyptian expedition, 1882; sirdar of Egyptian Army, 1885–92; consolidated Egyptian hold on Suakin, 1891; reorganized Egyptian forces; inspector-general, reserve forces, War Office, 1894; commanded British garrison in Egypt, 1897; governor and commander-in-chief, Malta, 1899; created baron, 1902; full general, 1904; commander-in-chief, Ireland, 1904–8; field marshal, 1908.

GRENFELL, George (1849–1906), Baptist missionary and explorer of the Congo; did pioneering work up Lower Congo River; reached Stanley Pool, 1881; surveyed Congo as far as equator, 1884; discovered Ruki River; navigated the Ikelemba; met cannibals in Bangala region; reached 'Grenfell' Falls, the most northerly point yet achieved in Congo basin, 1884; explored affluents of Congo from east and south, and discovered the Batwa dwarf tribes, 1885; went up main stream of the Kasai, and Kwa and Mfini to Lake Leopold II, and the Kwango to the Kingunji Rapids, 1886; received by King Leopold at Brussels, 1887; made chevalier and Belgian plenipotentiary for settlement with Portugal of the Lunda frontier, 1891–3; at Bolobo, 1893–1900; explored Aruwimi River (1900–2) and established missionary station at Yalemba, 1903; died of blackwater fever at Basoko.

GRENFELL, Hubert Henry (1845–1906), expert in naval gunnery; joined navy, 1859; made first designs of hydraulic mountings for naval ordnance, 1869; naval adviser at Berlin Congress, 1878; invented self-illuminating night sights for naval ordnance, 1891; helped to found Navy League.

GRENFELL, John Pascoe (1800–1869), admiral in Brazilian Navy; served under Cochrane in Chilian Navy; wounded in cutting out of the *Esmeralda*; in Brazilian Navy; lost arm in action off Buenos Aires, 1826; compelled surrender of rebel flotillas in Rio Grande do Sul, 1836; commanded against Argentina, 1851–2; consul-general in England, 1846–50 and 1852–69.

GRENFELL, Joyce Irene (1910–1979), actress and broadcaster; elder child of Paul Phipps, an architect, and his wife, Nora Langhorne, from Virginia, USA, the sister of Nancy (later Viscountess) *Astor; educated at Francis Holland School, London, and the Christian Science School, Clear View, South Norwood; 'finished' in Paris; studied at the Royal Academy of Dramatic Art; married Reginald Pascoe Grenfell, 1929; appointed radio critic of the *Observer* by J. L. *Garvin, 1936–9; gave entertainment with 'Useful and Acceptable Gifts' in Herbert Farjeon's *The Little Revue*, 1939; this the first of a series of classic monologues with characters from all walks of life, an instant success; during 1939–45 war toured with ENSA; OBE, 1946; appeared in revues by Noël *Coward, *Sigh No More* (1945), *Tuppence Coloured* (1947), and *Penny Plain* (1951); acted in variety of films, including *Genevieve*, *The Happiest Days of Your Life*, *The Million Pound Note*, and the *Yellow Rolls-Royce*; won fame as the games mistress in the St Trinian series; had her own show, *Joyce Grenfell Requests the Pleasure* (1954); toured the world with it; broadcast with Stephen *Potter and made television appearances, notably in 'Face the Music'; president, Society of Women Writers and Journalists, 1957; member of Pilkington Committee on 'the future of broadcasting in the UK', 1960–2; a lifelong Christian Scientist; lectured on 'communication'; honorary fellow, Lucy Cavendish College, Cambridge, and Manchester

Polytechnic; contributed to BBC's 'Thought for the Day'; published autobiography, *Joyce Grenfell Requests the Pleasure* (1976) and *In Pleasant Places* (1979); a unique talent with a huge following; but for her death in 1979 would have been appointed DBE in 1980.

GRENFELL, Julian Henry Francis (1888–1915), soldier and poet; son of W. H. *Grenfell, Lord *Desborough; educated at Eton and Balliol College, Oxford; entered army (1st Dragoons), 1910; accompanied regiment to France and DSO, 1914; died of wounds at Boulogne; best-known poem 'Into Battle' (1915).

GRENFELL, Pascoe (1761–1838), politician; engaged with Thomas Williams of Temple House, Great Marlow, in developing mining industries of Anglesey and Cornwall; purchased Taplow House; MP, Great Marlow, 1802–20; Penryn, 1820–6; abolitionist; authority on finance.

GRENFELL, Sir Wilfred Thomason (1865–1940), medical missionary and author; educated at Marlborough and London Hospital; qualified, 1886; joined Royal National Mission to Deep-Sea Fishermen, 1887; founded and developed (1893–1935) Labrador Medical Mission; raised most of the funds himself, after 1912 by means of the International Grenfell Association for which he lectured and wrote; first honorary DM, Oxford, 1907; KCMG, 1927.

GRENFELL, William Henry, Baron Desborough (1855–1945), athlete, sportsman, and public servant; educated at Harrow and Balliol College, Oxford; president, University Boat and Athletic clubs; master, draghounds; Liberal MP, Salisbury (1880–2, 1885–6), Hereford City (1892–3, resigned); Conservative MP, Wycombe division, 1900–5; baron, 1905; active in local government; for thirty-two years chairman, Thames Conservancy Board; president, London Chamber of Commerce; won Thames punting championship, 1888–90; twice swam Niagara; climbed in Alps; shot in Rockies, India, and Africa; president, Olympic Games, 1908; of Bath Club (1894–1942), Marylebone Cricket Club, Lawn Tennis and Amateur Fencing associations, Coaching and Four-in-Hand clubs; chairman, Pilgrims of Great Britain, 1919–29; GCVO, 1925; KG, 1928.

GRENVILLE. See also GRANVILLE.

GRENVILLE, Sir Bevil (1596–1643), Royalist; BA, Exeter College, Oxford, 1614; MP, Cornwall, 1621–4 and 1640–2, Launceston, 1625–40; served against Scots, 1639; defeated Parliamentarians at Bradock Down, 1643; killed at Lansdowne.

GRENVILLE, Denis (1637–1703), Jacobite divine; son of Sir Bevil *Grenville; MA, Exeter College, Oxford, 1660; DD, 1671; incumbent of Kilkhampton, 1661; archdeacon of Durham, 1662; rector of Sedgefield, 1667; dean of Durham, 1684; raised money for James II and fled the kingdom, 1691; named by James II in exile archbishop of York; died at Paris; two collections of his remains issued by Surtees Society.

GRENVILLE, George (1712–1770), statesman; educated at Eton and Christ Church, Oxford; barrister, Inner Temple, 1735, bencher, 1763; MP, Buckingham, 1740–70; joined the 'Boy Patriots', and long acted with Pitt, even when holding subordinate office under Pelham and Newcastle; resigned treasurership of the Navy on dismissal of Pitt and Temple, 1756, but held it again in Newcastle-Pitt ministry, 1757–62; admitted to Cabinet, 1761; secretary for the northern department and first lord of the Admiralty under Bute, 1762–3; as first lord of the Treasury and chancellor of the Exchequer, 1763–5, successfully resisted Bute's influence with George III; his ministry chiefly remarkable for the enactment of the Stamp Act (1765) and the early proceedings against *Wilkes (1763); alienated the king by omission of the princess-dowager's name from the Regency Bill; while in opposition defeated the budget of 1767, spoke against the expulsion of Wilkes, 1769, and carried a measure transferring the trial of election petitions from the whole house to a select committee, 1770. He was nicknamed 'the Gentle Shepherd' in allusion to Pitt's mocking quotation 'Gentle shepherd, tell me where', in the course of Grenville's speech in defence of the cider-tax, 1763.

GRENVILLE, George Nugent, Baron Nugent of Carlanstown, Ireland (1788–1850), author; younger son of George Nugent-Temple-*Grenville, first marquis of Buckingham; succeeded to his mother's Irish peerage, 1813; MP, Aylesbury, 1812–32 and 1847–8; a lord of the Treasury, 1830–2; high commissioner of the Ionian Islands, 1832–5; published works, including *Memorials of John Hampden* (1832) and *Legends of the Library at Lillies* (1832).

GRENVILLE, George Nugent-Temple-, first marquis of Buckingham (1753–1813), statesman; second son of George *Grenville; MP, Buckinghamshire, 1774–9; succeeded as second Earl Temple, 1779; privy councillor and lord-lieutenant of Ireland, 1782–3 and 1787–9; advised enactment of Irish Judicature Act, 1783; instituted order of St Patrick, 1783; George III's instrument in procuring defeat of *Fox's India Bill in House of Lords, 1783, and secretary of state for three days (Dec.); created marquis of Buckingham, 1784; refused to transmit address of Irish parliament to prince of Wales, 1789.

GRENVILLE, John, earl of Bath (1628–1701), eldest surviving son of Sir Bevil *Grenville; knighted at Bristol, 1643; wounded at Newbury, 1644; held Scilly Islands for Charles II, 1649–51; lord warden of the stannaries, 1660; groom of the stole, 1660; created earl of Bath, 1661; governor of Plymouth, 1661; ultimately joined William III; lord-lieutenant of Cornwall and Devon and privy councillor, 1689.

GRENVILLE (or GREYNVILE), Sir Richard (1541?–1591), naval commander; student of the Inner Temple, 1559; knighted; MP, Cornwall, 1571 and 1584, and sheriff, 1577; commanded, for his cousin, Sir Walter *Ralegh, fleet for colonization of Virginia, and on return voyage captured a Spanish ship, 1585; pillaged the Azores, 1586; engaged in organizing defences of the west of England, 1586–8; second-in-command under Lord Thomas *Howard of the Azores Fleet, 1591; his ship, the *Revenge*, being isolated off Flores, he was mortally wounded, after fighting during fifteen hours fifteen Spanish ships.

GRENVILLE, Sir Richard (1600–1658), first baronet; grandson of Sir Richard *Grenville (1541?–1591); served in expeditions to Cadiz and the Isle of Ré, writing narrative of the latter; knighted, 1627; created baronet, 1630; fought as Royalist in Ireland, 1642–3; arrested by parliament at Liverpool, but released and given a command, 1643; joined Charles I at Oxford, 1644; assisted in defeat of *Essex in Cornwall, 1644; failed before Plymouth, 1645; quarrelled with Sir John *Berkeley, *Goring, and *Hopton; imprisoned in Cornwall, 1646; passed last years in Brittany and Holland; published an autobiographical pamphlet; buried at Ghent.

GRENVILLE, Richard Plantagenet Campbell Temple Nugent Brydges Chandos, third duke of Buckingham and Chandos (1823–1889), statesman; son of Richard Plantagenet T. N. B. C. *Grenville, second duke of Buckingham; Earl Temple till 1839; marquis of Chandos, 1839–61; at Eton and Christ Church, Oxford; DCL, 1852; MP, Buckingham, 1846–57; a lord of the Treasury, 1852; chairman of London and North-Western Railway, 1853–61; chairman of executive committee of Exhibition Commission of 1862; privy councillor, 1866; president of the council, 1866–7, and colonial secretary, 1867–8; governor of Madras, 1875–80; chairman of committees in House of Lords, 1886–9.

GRENVILLE, Richard Plantagenet Temple Nugent Brydges Chandos, second duke of Buckingham and Chandos (1797–

1861), historical writer; son of Richard T. N. B. C. *Grenville; Earl Temple, 1813–1822; matriculated from Oriel College, Oxford, 1815; marquis of Chandos, 1822–39; MP, Buckinghamshire, 1818–39; introduced into Reform Bill tenant-at-will clause (Chandos clause), 1832; lord privy seal, 1841–2; protectionist; obliged to sell much of his property, 1847; published court memoirs.

GRENVILLE (afterwards GRENVILLE-TEMPLE), Richard Temple, Earl Temple (1711–1779), statesman; brother of George *Grenville; MP, Buckingham, 1734–41 and 1747–52, Buckinghamshire, 1741–7; succeeded to his mother's peerage, 1752; first lord of the Admiralty, 1756–7; greatly disliked by George II, who dismissed him, 1757; lord privy seal, 1757–61; dismissed from the lord-lieutenancy of Buckinghamshire for his patronage of *Wilkes, 1763; dissuaded Pitt from forming a ministry on the basis of a reconciliation with George Grenville, 1765; twice refused the Treasury, 1765; intrigued against Rockingham, 1766; again refused the Treasury and quarrelled with Chatham, 1766; strongly opposed to conciliating the Americans; DCL, Oxford, 1771; paid Wilkes's law expenses, and assisted Pitt financially; known to contemporaries as 'Squire Gawkey'; died of an accident. The authorship of Junius's *Letters* has been ascribed to him.

GRENVILLE, Richard Temple Nugent Brydges Chandos, first duke of Buckingham and Chandos (1776–1839), statesman; son of George Nugent-Temple-*Grenville, first marquis of Buckingham; of Brasenose College, Oxford, 1791; MP (as Earl Temple) for Buckinghamshire, 1797–1813; Indian commissioner, 1800–1; privy councillor, 1806; joint paymaster-general and deputy-president of the Board of Trade, 1806–7; DCL, Oxford, 1810; LL D, Cambridge, 1811; lord-lieutenant of Buckinghamshire, 1813; KG, 1820; created duke, 1822; collected rare prints; his *Private Diary* published (1862).

GRENVILLE, Thomas (1719–1747), navy captain; younger brother of George *Grenville (1712–1770); while commanding the *Romney* captured off Cape St Vincent a valuable French ship, 1743; mortally wounded under Anson off Finisterre.

GRENVILLE, Thomas (1755–1846), bookcollector; third son of George *Grenville; educated at Christ Church, Oxford; lieutenant in Rutland regiment, 1779; MP, Buckinghamshire, 1780–4, Aldborough, 1790–6, Buckingham, 1796–1818; adherent of *Fox, subsequently joining the old Whigs; began negotiations with America, 1782; envoy-extraordinary to Vienna, 1794, to Berlin, 1799; privy councillor, 1798; president of Board of Control and first lord of the Admiralty, 1806–7. His bequest of books to British Museum (including first-folio Shakespeare) forms the Grenville Library.

GRENVILLE, William Wyndham, Baron Grenville (1759–1834), statesman; youngest son of George *Grenville; educated at Eton; BA, Christ Church, Oxford, 1780; student of Lincoln's Inn, 1780; MP, Buckingham, 1782–4, Buckinghamshire, 1784–90; created a peer, 1790; chief secretary for Ireland, 1782–3; privy councillor, 1783; joint paymaster-general, 1784; vice-president of Board of Trade, 1786–9; speaker, 1789; home secretary, 1789–90; president of Board of Control, 1790–3; foreign secretary, 1791–1801; headed war party in ministry; led for ministry in the House of Lords; resigned with Pitt on the Catholic question, 1801; refused office without *Fox in Pitt's second ministry, 1804; head of the ministry of 'All the Talents', 1806–7, which abolished the slave trade, 1807, and resigned on the Catholic question, 1807; chancellor of Oxford, 1809; refused several offers to enter a mixed ministry, 1809–12; supported continuance of the war, 1815; allowed his adherents to join Liverpool, 1821; supported repressive measures of 1816, and bill of pains and penalties against Queen *Caroline, 1820.

GRESHAM, James (*fl.* 1626), poet; his *Picture of Incest* (1626) reprinted by *Grosart, 1876.

GRESHAM, Sir John (d. 1556), lord mayor of London, member of the Mercers', and a founder of the Russia Company; partner of his brother Richard; sheriff of London, 1537, lord mayor, 1547; founded Holt Grammar School, Norfolk.

GRESHAM, Sir Richard (1485?–1549), lord mayor of London; gentleman usher-extraordinary in royal household, 1516; had financial dealings with the king, and lent money to the nobility; confidential correspondent of *Wolsey (whose benevolence of 1525 he supported in the Common Council) and *Cromwell; warden of Mercers' Company, 1525, and thrice master; sheriff of London and Middlesex, 1531; a commissioner, 1534, to inquire into value of benefices previous to suppression of the abbeys; alderman; lord mayor of London, 1537; knighted, 1537; suggested appropriation for poor and sick of St Mary's, St Bartholomew's, and St Thomas's hospitals; initiated design of a Royal Exchange; member of Six Articles' Commission; bought Fountains Abbey, 1540, and had other grants of monastic lands.

GRESHAM, Sir Thomas (1519?–1579), founder of the Royal Exchange; second son of Sir

Richard *Gresham; learnt business under his uncle, Sir John *Gresham; assisted his father, on whose death he removed to Lombard Street; appointed royal agent or king's merchant at Antwerp, 1552, by influence of *Northumberland; raised rate of exchange from 16 to 22 shillings for the pound; raised loan in Spain, 1554; received grants in Norfolk from Edward VI and Mary; present at Elizabeth's first council, 1558; intimate friend of *Cecil; advised restoration of purity of the coinage; as ambassador to regent of the Netherlands (1559–61) sent important political information to Cecil, besides shipping secretly munitions of war; established at Osterley the first English paper-mills, 1565; finally left Antwerp, 1567; arranged for raising of loans from English merchants instead of foreigners, 1569, and for the settlement of dispute about seizure of Spanish treasure; ceased to be crown financial agent, 1574; the Royal Exchange built at his expense on a site provided by the City, 1566–8 (visited and named by the queen, 1570, destroyed in great fire, 1666); founded also Gresham College, for which he bequeathed (1575) his house in Bishopsgate Street to the corporation and the Mercers' Company; the building sold to the government, 1767, and converted into an excise office; present college built, 1841.

GRESLEY (or GREISLEY), Sir Roger (1799–1837), baronet by succession; MP, Durham, 1830, New Romney, 1831, South Derbyshire, 1835–7; published pamphlets.

GRESLEY, William (1801–1876), divine; educated at Westminster and Christ Church, Oxford; MA, 1825; perpetual curate of All Saints', Boyne Hill, 1857–76; published *Portrait of an English Churchman* (1838) and religious and social tales, besides *The Ordinance of Confession* (1851) and works against scepticism and Evangelical doctrines.

GRESSE, John Alexander (1741–1794), painter and royal drawing-master; of Swiss parentage; exhibited miniatures with Free Society and Incorporated Society of Artists.

GRESSWELL, Dan (1819–1883), veterinary surgeon; mayor of Louth, Lincolnshire, 1871–2.

GRESWELL, Edward (1797–1869), chronologist; son of William Parr *Greswell; MA, Corpus Christi College, Oxford, 1822; fellow, 1823–69; vice-president from 1840; BD, 1830; published works, including *Harmonia Evangelica* (1830), *Fasti Temporis Catholici and Origines Kalendariae* (1852), *Origines Kalendariae Italicae* (1854), and *Origines Kalendariae Hellenicae* (1861).

GRESWELL, Richard (1800–1881), 're-founder of the National Society'; brother of Edward *Greswell; thirty years fellow and tutor of Worcester College, Oxford; MA, 1825; BD, 1836; opened subscription on behalf of national education with a donation of £1,000, 1843; one of the founders of the Museum and the Ashmolean Society, Oxford; chairman of Gladstone's Oxford Election Committee, 1847–65.

GRESWELL, William Parr (1765–1854), bibliographer; incumbent of Denton, Lancashire, 1791–1853; published *Annals of Parisian Typography* (1818) and *View of the Early Parisian Greek Press* (1833, 1840); edited vol. iii of Chetham Catalogue.

GRETTON, William (1736–1813), master of Magdalene College, Cambridge; educated at St Paul's School and Peterhouse, Cambridge; MA, 1761; vice-chancellor, 1800–1; master of Magdalene, 1797–1813; archdeacon of Essex, 1795.

GREVILLE, Algernon Frederick (1789–1864), private secretary to duke of Wellington, 1827–42, having been his aide-de-camp and ensign in Grenadier Guards at Waterloo; Bath king-of-arms.

GREVILLE, Charles Cavendish Fulke (1794–1865), clerk to the council; brother of Algernon Frederick *Greville; manager of duke of York's stud, and racing partner of Lord George *Bentinck, his cousin; clerk to the council, 1821–59; intimate of statesmen of both parties, especially Wellington and Palmerston; his diary (mainly political) published, 1st series: 1817–37 (1875), 2nd and 3rd: to 1860 (1885 and 1887, ed. H. *Reeve); edited Raikes's *Memoirs* and part of Moore's correspondence.

GREVILLE, Frances Evelyn, countess of Warwick (1861–1938), born Maynard; married (1881) Lord Brooke (fifth earl of Warwick, 1893); celebrated beauty and member of the prince of Wales's circle; converted to socialism by Robert *Blatchford; thereafter used her position, fortune, and energies in charitable and social interests.

GREVILLE, Sir Fulke, first Baron Brooke (1554–1628), poet and statesman; intimate of Philip *Sidney at Shrewsbury; fellow-commoner, Jesus College, Cambridge, 1568; came to court with Sidney, and became favourite of Elizabeth; accompanied Sidney to Heidelberg, 1577; joined Gabriel *Harvey's 'Areopagus'; entertained Giordano Bruno at his London house, 1583; pallbearer at Sidney's funeral at St Paul's, 1587; secretary for principality of Wales, 1583 till death; MP, Southampton, 1580, Heydon, Yorkshire, 1584, Warwickshire, 1586, 1588, 1593, 1597, 1601, and 1621; 'treasurer of the wars' and the navy, 1598; KB, 1603; chancellor of the Exchequer, 1614–21; created peer, 1621; granted Warwick Castle and Knowle Park by

James I; befriended *Bacon, *Camden, *Coke, *Daniel, and *D'Avenant; stabbed by a servant. A collection of works 'written in his youth' (including tragedies and sonnets) was printed (1633), his *Life of Sidney* (1652, reprinted by *Brydges, 1816), and his *Remains* (1670). His complete works were reprinted by *Grosart (1870).

GREVILLE, Henry William (1801–1872), diarist; brother of Charles Cavendish Fulke *Greville; attaché to Paris embassy, 1834–44; gentleman usher at court; his *Leaves from a Diary* published (1883–4).

GREVILLE, Robert, second Baron Brooke (1607–1643), Parliamentarian general; adopted by his cousin, Sir Fulke *Greville, first Baron Brooke; MA, Cambridge, 1629; MP, Warwick, 1628–9; member of company for plantation of Providence and Henrietta islands (incorporated, 1630); commissioner for Treaty of Ripon, 1640; speaker, House of Lords, 1642; defeated Northampton at Kineton, 1642; served under *Essex in Midlands; took Stratford-upon-Avon, 1643, but was killed in attack on Lichfield; published *The Nature of Truth* (1640).

GREVILLE, Robert Kaye (1794–1866), botanist; settled at Edinburgh, 1816; joined the Wernerian Society, 1819; FRSE, 1821; LL D, Glasgow, 1824; made botanical tours in the Highlands; vice-president, Anti-Slavery Convention, 1840; MP, Edinburgh, 1856; published *Scottish Cryptogamic Flora, Flora Edinensis* (1824), *Icones Filicum*, with *Hooker (1829–31), and *Algae Britannicae* (1830); edited (with Dr R. Huie), *The Amethyst* (poems), 1832–4, and (with T. K. Drummond) *The Church of England Hymnbook* (1838); his collection of algae acquired by British Museum, insects by Edinburgh University, flowering plants by Glasgow, and other cryptogamia by Edinburgh Botanic Garden.

GREW, Jonathan (1626–1711), first Presbyterian minister of Dagnal Lane, St Albans, 1698–1711; nephew of Obadiah *Grew.

GREW, Nehemiah (1641–1712), vegetable-physiologist; son of Obadiah *Grew; BA, Pembroke Hall, Cambridge, 1661; MD, Leiden, 1671; FRS, 1671; secretary to Royal Society, 1677–9; probably first to observe sex in plants; published *The Anatomy of Plants* (1682, 4 vols.), embodying previous publications, and *Cosmologia Sacra* (1701), against Spinoza, besides scientific pamphlets; genus named *Grewia* after him by Linnaeus.

GREW, Obadiah (1607–1689), ejected minister; MA, Balliol College, Oxford, 1632; DD, 1651; master of Atherstone Grammar School, 1632; appointed vicar of St Michael's, Coventry,

1645; pleaded with *Cromwell for the king's life, 1648; favoured Royalist rising, 1659; obliged to resign living, 1662, and leave Coventry, 1666; returned, 1672, and with John *Bryan (d. 1676) founded Presbyterian congregation; imprisoned under Five Mile Act, 1682; his *Sinner's Justification* (1670) translated into Welsh (1785).

GREY. See also GRAY.

GREY, Albert Henry George, fourth Earl Grey (1851–1917), statesman; son of Charles *Grey; educated at Harrow and Trinity College, Cambridge; Liberal MP, South Northumberland, 1880–5, and for Tyneside division of county, 1885–6; concentrated his energies on promotion of imperial unity; joined board of directors of British South Africa Company, 1889; administrator of Rhodesia, 1896–7; very successful governor-general of Canada, 1904–11; succeeded uncle, Sir Henry *Grey, 1894.

GREY, Anchitell (d. 1702), compiler of debates; second son of Henry *Grey, first earl of Stamford; MP, Derby, 1665–85, in convention of 1689 and parliament of 1690–4; his notes printed (1769) as *Debates of the House of Commons, 1667–94*.

GREY, Arthur, fourteenth Baron Grey de Wilton (1536–1593), son of Sir William *Grey, thirteenth Baron Grey de Wilton; served at St Quentin, 1557; wounded during siege of Leith, 1560; succeeded to title, 1562; commissioner at trials of duke of Norfolk, 1574, *Mary Queen of Scots, and William *Davison (1541?–1608), whom he defended; as lord-deputy of Ireland, 1580–2, had *Spenser as secretary; overcame rebels of the pale, and pacified Munster; member of Committee of Defence of the Kingdom, 1587–8.

GREY, Lady **Catherine** (1538?–1568). See SEYMOUR.

GREY, Charles, first Earl Grey (1729–1807), general; with *Wolfe's regiment at Rochefort, 1757, and in Germany; aide-de-camp to Prince Ferdinand at Minden, 1759, being wounded there and at Campen, 1760; lieutenant-colonel of 98th at Belle Isle, 1761, and Havana, 1762; while in America defeated Wayne; commanded third brigade at Germanstown, 1777; annihilated Bayler's Virginian Dragoons, 1778; major-general, 1778; KB, 1782; relieved Nieuport, 1793; co-operated with *Jervis in capture of French West Indies, 1794; general and privy councillor, 1795; created baron, 1801, and earl, 1806.

GREY, Charles, second Earl Grey, Viscount Howick, and Baron Grey (1764–1845), statesman; son of Charles *Grey, first earl; educated at Eton and Trinity College, Cambridge; MP, Northumberland, 1786–1807, Appleby (Viscount Howick), 1807, Tavistock, 1807–8; acted with *Fox, except on the regency question, during Pitt's first ministry; one of the managers of Warren *Hastings's impeachment, 1787; took up reform question for Society of Friends of the People, 1793, and in 1797 brought forward his first bill; attacked Pitt's foreign policy and repressive legislation; seceded from House of Commons with Whig party, 1797; returned to resist Irish union, 1800; refused to join *Addington, favoured renewal of the war, and acted with Grenville during Pitt's second ministry; first lord of the Admiralty, 1806; foreign secretary, 1806–7, resigning when George III required a pledge not to reintroduce Catholic emancipation; acted with Grenville as joint adviser to the prince regent, 1811; with Grenville refused either to form a Whig ministry without control of the household, or to join coalition with Tories, but maintained, in opposition to Grenville, the principle of supporting independence of nationalities in foreign affairs, and differed from him in opposing all repressive legislation; opposed the king's Divorce Bill of 1820, and refused to co-operate with Canning; again took up parliamentary reform, 1830; prime minister of Whig administration, 1831; introduced a Reform Bill, 1831; defeated in committee; dissolved, 1831; carried new bill in Commons, but lost it on second reading in Lords; reintroduced it in Lords, but was defeated on motion to postpone disfranchising clauses, 1832; resigned, but returned in a few days (May 1832) with promise of power to create peers, and finally carried the bill; retired, 1834, in consequence of a disagreement in the Cabinet on the renewal of the Irish Coercion Act of 1833, he himself favouring severity; KG.

GREY, Charles (1804–1870), general; second surviving son of Charles *Grey, second Earl Grey; lieutenant-colonel, 71st Highlanders, 1833–42; general, 1865; private secretary to his father, 1830–4, to Prince *Albert, 1849–61, and afterwards to Queen Victoria, 1861–70; MP, High Wycombe, 1831–7; published biography of his father (1861) and *Early Years of The Prince Consort* (1867).

GREY, Sir Charles Edward (1785–1865), Indian judge and colonial governor; BA, University College, Oxford, 1806; fellow of Oriel College, Oxford, 1808; barrister, 1811; bankruptcy commissioner, 1817; judge of Madras Supreme Court, 1820; knighted, 1820; chief justice of Bengal, 1825; special commissioner to Canada, 1835; MP, Tynemouth, 1838–41; governor of

Barbados and other islands, 1841–6, of Jamaica, 1847–53.

GREY, Charles Grey (1875–1953), writer on aviation; grandson of John *Grey, nephew of Josephine *Butler; educated at Erasmus Smith School, Dublin, and Crystal Palace School of Engineering; joined *Autocar*, 1905; joint editor, *Aero*, 1909; founded (1911) and edited (1911–39) *Aeroplane*, the most widely read aviation newspaper; campaigned for preservation of Royal Air Force, for British aircraft industry, and for Imperial Airways; edited *Jane's All the World's Aircraft*, 1916–41.

GREY, Edmund, first earl of Kent (1420?–1489), lord high treasurer; grandson of Reginald de *Grey, third Baron Grey of Ruthin, whom he succeeded, 1440; supported Henry VI; deserted to Yorkists at Battle of Northampton, 1460; privy councillor, 1463; lord treasurer, 1463; created earl of Kent, 1465; commissioner of oyer and terminer in London and home counties, 1483.

GREY, Sir Edward, third baronet, and Viscount Grey of Fallodon (1862–1933), statesman and bird-lover; brought up at Fallodon, Northumberland, where from boyhood he watched birds and fished; inherited estate and title from grandfather, Sir George *Grey, 1882; educated at Winchester and Balliol College, Oxford; sent down for incorrigible idleness, 1884; from Mandell *Creighton learnt moderate democratic liberalism and a sense of public duty which was to keep him in politics despite strong preference for country life; at Fallodon enlarged the famous ponds and tamed many varieties of duck; private secretary to Sir Evelyn *Baring (later earl of Cromer) and H. C. E. *Childers, 1884; Liberal MP, Berwick-on-Tweed, 1885–1916; parliamentary under-secretary, Foreign Office, 1892–5; made declaration on French encroachment on Nile, 1895; member, West Indian Royal Commission, 1897; his support of South African War sowed seeds of distrust in him as foreign secretary felt by more radical members of his party; director (1898), chairman (1904), North Eastern Railway; foreign secretary, 1905–16; established cordial relations with Campbell-Bannerman who supported his policy of friendship with France; let France and Germany know that in his opinion England would fight in event of German aggression; continued 'military conversations' with France initiated by Lord *Lansdowne; Algeciras Conference (1906) on Morocco resulted in Germany accepting compromise because England had rallied to France; determined to secure friendship of United States and began intimate correspondence with Theodore Roosevelt; principal author of Anglo-Russian Agreement (1907) as only means of avoiding clashes in Tibet, Afghanistan, or Persia and of preventing Russia entering German orbit; his ententes with France and Russia disliked by many Liberals although later he was criticized for not having turned them into alliances; this he would not have done, even had public opinion permitted, lest France or Russia should thereby feel encouraged to provoke unjustified war; renewed alliance with Japan, 1911; by his firmness and tact over Congo atrocities secured reform and retained Belgian friendship; published (1912) Putumayo Blue Book based on reports of Roger *Casement; during Agadir crisis (1911) strongly supported by Lloyd George whose speech made Germany realize that Britain would fight if she attacked France; agreed to unsuccessful attempt (1912) by Lord *Haldane to persuade Germany to limit growth of navy; concessions to remove German complaint of encirclement included Baghdad Railway Agreement (1913) and willingness to allow her a large share of Portuguese colonies in Africa should they be sold; refused to make a secret agreement on this or any other matter except as wartime measure; supported by France and Germany (1913) in averting European war after Serbian defeat of Turkey; unsuccessful after murder of Archduke Francis Ferdinand (1914) because Germany refused a conference and backed Austria; his handling of crisis kept country united and gained American support; despite difficulties arising from blockade maintained excellent relations with America; concluded secret treaty of London (Apr. 1915) with Italy whose extortionate terms he accepted, since the Allies might have lost the war had Italy joined the Central Powers; deliberately sacrificed chance of preserving eyesight to continuance of duty; created viscount, July 1916; resigned, Dec. 1916; president of League of Nations Union from 1918; became increasingly blind; chancellor of Oxford University, 1928–33; wrote *Twenty-five Years, 1892–1916* (2 vols., 1925); his *Fly Fishing* (1899), *Fallodon Papers* (1926), and *The Charm of Birds* (1927) place him in front rank of English nature writers; PC, 1902; KG, 1912; FRS, 1914.

GREY, Elizabeth, countess of Kent (1581–1651), authoress; née Talbot; married Henry, seventh earl of Kent; said to have been afterwards secretly married to *Selden; published *A Choice Manuall, or Rare and Select Secrets in Physick and Chyrurgery* (2nd edn., 1653), and a book of culinary recipes (19th edn., 1687).

GREY, Forde, earl of Tankerville (d. 1701), Whig politician; succeeded as third Baron Grey of Werk, 1675; a zealous exclusionist, 1681; convicted of conspiracy to carry off his sister-in-law, Lady Henrietta Berkeley, 1682; fled to Holland

on discovery of Rye House Plot, 1683; commanded *Monmouth's horse at Sedgemoor, 1685; gave evidence against his associates, and was restored to title, 1685; joined William of Orange; created earl of Tankerville, 1695; privy councillor, 1695; commissioner of trade, 1696; first commissioner of the Treasury, 1699; lord privy seal, 1700.

GREY, George, second earl of Kent (d. 1503), soldier; styled Lord Grey of Ruthin till 1489; saw military service in France under Edward IV and Henry VII; commanded against Cornish rebels at Blackheath, 1497.

GREY, Sir George, second baronet (1799–1882), statesman; grandson of Charles *Grey, first Earl Grey; graduated at Oriel College, Oxford, 1821; barrister, 1826; practised as barrister; succeeded as baronet, 1828; MP, Devonport, 1832–47, North Northumberland, 1847–52, and Morpeth, 1853–74; under-secretary for colonies, 1834 and 1835–9; judge advocate-general, 1839–41; chancellor of duchy of Lancaster, 1841; home secretary under Russell, 1846–52, and under Palmerston, 1855–8 and 1861–6; colonial secretary in Lord Aberdeen's coalition ministry, 1854–5; chancellor of duchy of Lancaster, 1859–61; carried Convict Discipline Bill, which abolished transportation.

GREY, Sir George (1812–1898), colonial governor; educated at Sandhurst; received commission in 83rd Foot, 1829; captain, 1839; left army, 1839; made exploring expeditions for Royal Geographical Society, north-western coast of Western Australia; governor of South Australia, 1841–5, New Zealand, 1845–53 (both of which colonies he raised from state of disorder to that of peace and comparative prosperity), and Cape Colony, 1855; recalled, 1859, for encouraging, without official permission, a policy of South African federation; restored to office, 1859; again governor of New Zealand, 1861–7, during which period he came into frequent conflict with his ministers and the Colonial Office; chosen (1874) superintendent of province of Auckland; member of House of Representatives for Auckland city (1875–94), led opposition to centralist party; prime minister, 1877–9; successfully advocated adult franchise, triennial parliaments, taxation of land values, leasing instead of sale of crown lands, and compulsory repurchase of private estates; returned to England, 1894; privy councillor, 1894; buried publicly in St Paul's Cathedral; published works relating to language, topography, and history of Australia and New Zealand.

GREY, Henry, duke of Suffolk, third marquis of Dorset (d. 1554), father of Lady Jane

*Grey; succeeded as third marquis of Dorset, 1530; KG, 1547; prominent during Edward VI's minority; privy councillor, 1549; attached himself first to Seymour of Sudeley, and from 1548 to Dudley (Northumberland); created duke on death of wife's male relations, 1551; gave up Lady Jane Grey's cause, 1553, and was pardoned by Mary; joined rising against Spanish marriage; executed for treason.

GREY, Henry, ninth earl of Kent (1594–1651), Parliamentarian; MP (as Lord Ruthin) for Leicestershire, 1640–3; commissioner of great seal, 1643–4, 1645–6, and 1648–9; speaker of House of Lords, 1645 and 1647.

GREY, Henry, first earl of Stamford (1599?–1673), Parliamentarian general; succeeded as second Baron Grey of Groby, 1614; MA, Trinity College, Cambridge, 1615; created earl of Stamford, 1628; commanded under *Essex in the west, 1642–3; defeated at Stratton, 1643; besieged and compelled to surrender to Prince *Maurice at Exeter, 1643; impeached for assaulting Sir Arthur *Heselrige, 1645; declared for Charles II, 1659; committed to the Tower, 1659.

GREY, Henry, duke of Kent, eleventh earl of Kent (1664?–1740), grandson of Henry *Grey, ninth earl of Kent, created duke, 1710; a lord justice, 1714.

GREY, Henry (1778–1859), Free Church minister; at Stenton, St Cuthbert's Chapel, Edinburgh, 1813–21, the New North Church, 1821–5, and St Mary's, 1829; seceded, 1843; chairman of General Assembly, 1844; the Grey scholarships at New College, Edinburgh, founded in his honour.

GREY, Sir Henry George, Viscount Howick, and afterwards third Earl Grey (1802–1894), statesman; son of Charles *Grey, second Earl Grey; MA, Trinity College, Cambridge, 1823; Whig MP, Winchelsea, 1826–30, Higham Ferrers, 1830; under-secretary for colonies in his father's administration, 1830–3, and for home affairs, 1834; MP, Northumberland, 1831, and for northern division of Northumberland, 1832–41; privy councillor and secretary-at-war, 1835–9; proposed amendment to Irish Franchise Bill which resulted in defeat of government, 1841, and abandonment of bill; MP, Sunderland, 1841; succeeded to earldom, 1845, and became active leader of his party in House of Lords; secretary for colonies, 1846–52; instituted ticket-of-leave system, 1848; strongly advocated transportation of convicts; revived committee of Privy Council for trade and foreign plantations as a deliberative and advisory body, 1849; published *Colonial Policy of Lord John Russell's Adminis-*

tration (1853); maintained a critical and independent attitude after 1852; strongly opposed Gladstone's home-rule policy, 1885–6; published political writings.

GREY, Lady **Jane** (1537–1554). See DUDLEY.

GREY (or GRAY), John, earl of Tankerville (d. 1421), soldier; grandson of Thomas *Gray (d. 1369?); took part in siege of Harfleur and Battle of Agincourt, 1415; received executed brother's lands at Heton; served in Henry V's second expedition, 1417, and assisted in conquest of the Cotentin, 1418; created earl of Tankerville, chamberlain of Normandy, and KG, 1419; one of the commissioners to negotiate for king's marriage; served at siege of Rouen, 1419; killed at Battle of Beaugé.

GREY, John, eighth Baron Ferrers of Groby (1432–1461), Lancastrian; not summoned to parliament, and usually styled Sir John; first husband of *Elizabeth Woodville (queen of Edward IV); killed at second Battle of St Albans.

GREY, Lord **John** (d. 1569), youngest son of Thomas *Grey, second marquis of Dorset; deputy of Newhaven under Edward VI; received grants of land from Edward VI and Mary; joined *Wyatt's rising, 1554, and only obtained his life at intercession of his wife; granted Pyrgo, Essex, and other estates by Elizabeth; one of the four nobles who superintended alterations in Prayer-Book, 1558; lost favour by espousing cause of Catherine *Seymour, his niece.

GREY, Sir **John** (1780?–1856), lieutenant-general; served with 75th against Tippoo Sahib; with 5th in Peninsula, being wounded at storming of Ciudad Rodrigo, 1812; lieutenant-colonel, 2nd battalion, 1812–16; commanded left wing at Punniar, Gwalior, 1843; created KCB; commander-in-chief and member of Bombay Council, 1850–2; lieutenant-general, 1851.

GREY, John (1785–1868), of Dilston, agriculturist; managed Greenwich Hospital mining estates, 1833–63, and by applying Liebig's discoveries increased their value; assisted *Clarkson and *Brougham in anti-slavery agitation; intimate of Earl Grey, *Althorpe, and *Jeffrey.

GREY (or GRAY), John de (d. 1214), bishop of Norwich, 1200–14; elected by King John's influence to the primacy, 1205, but his election quashed in favour of *Langton by Innocent III, 1207; justice-itinerant; lent money to John; named by Matthew *Paris among the king's evil counsellors; excluded from the general absolution of 1213; as justiciar of Ireland (1210–13) remodelled the coinage on the English pattern; bishop-elect of Durham; died at St Jean d'Audely while returning from Rome.

GREY, Sir **John de** (d. 1266), judge; fined and deprived of justiceship of Chester for marrying without royal license, 1251; forgiven after taking the cross, 1253; steward of Gascony, 1253; one of the twelve representatives of the commonalty, 1258; justice in eyre in Somerset, Dorset, and Devon, 1260; fought in Wales against the barons; sheriff of Nottinghamshire and Derbyshire, 1265.

GREY, John de, second Baron Grey of Wilton (1268–1323), grandson of Sir John de *Grey; summoned to parliament, 1309; a lord ordainer, 1310, and member of Barons' Council, 1318; justice of North Wales, 1315; joined Edward II, 1322.

GREY, John de, second Baron Grey of Rotherfield (1300–1359), soldier; constantly employed in wars of Edward III; one of the original KGs, 1344; steward of the household, 1350.

GREY, John de, third Baron (sixth by tenure) Grey of Codnor (1305–1392), soldier; served Edward III in Scotland, Flanders, and France; governor of Rochester Castle, 1360.

GREY (or GRAY), Lord **Leonard,** Viscount Grane of Ireland (d. 1541), statesman; sixth son of Thomas *Grey, first marquis of Dorset; when marshal of the English Army in Ireland, 1535, obtained surrender of Thomas *Fitzgerald, tenth earl of Kildare, his connection; as deputy-governor of Ireland presided over the important parliament of 1536–7, allied himself with *Desmond against *Ormonde; defeated Desmond, 1539; beheaded on Tower Hill on charge of supporting native Irish and favouring Geraldines.

GREY, Maria Georgina (1816–1906), promoter of women's education; born Shirreff; sister of Emily *Shirreff; married William Thomas Grey, 1841; initiated Girls' Public Day School Company, 1872, which in 1929 had twenty-five schools; founded Maria Grey Training College for women teachers, 1878; published a novel, and works on women's enfranchisement and education.

GREY, Lady **Mary** (1540?–1578). See KEYS.

GREY, Nicholas (1590?–1660), headmaster of Eton; educated at Westminster and Christ Church, Oxford; MA, 1613; MA, Cambridge, 1614; headmaster of Charterhouse, 1614, of Merchant Taylors', 1625–32, and of Tonbridge during Commonwealth; headmaster of Eton and fellow, 1632; ejected during the Civil War; restored, 1660.

GREY, Reginald de, third Baron Grey of Ruthin (1362?–1440), succeeded to title, 1388; successful in a suit (1401–10) against Edward *Hastings for right to bear Hastings arms and title earl of Pembroke; governor of Ireland, 1398; as member of Henry IV's council advised recourse to parliament on question of war with France, 1401; carried on war with Owen *Glendower, by whom he was captured, 1402, and kept prisoner near Snowdon; continued Welsh War, 1409; member of Council of Regency, 1415.

GREY, Lord **Richard** (d. 1483), brother of Thomas *Grey, first marquis of Dorset; KB, 1475; accused by Richard, duke of Gloucester, of estranging Edward V from him; beheaded.

GREY, Richard (1694–1771), author; MA, Lincoln College, Oxford, 1719; chaplain and secretary to Bishop *Crew of Durham; rector of Hinton, Northamptonshire, 1720, and Kimcote, Leicestershire, 1725; friend of *Doddridge and Dr *Johnson; his *Memoria Technica* (1730) reprinted as late as 1861; for *System of English Ecclesiastical Law* created DD, Oxford, 1731.

GREY, Richard de, second Baron Grey of Codnor (*fl.* 1250), baronial leader; governor of Channel Islands, 1226; sheriff of Northumberland, 1236, of Essex and Hertford, 1239; took the cross, 1252; one of the twenty-four and the fifteen perpetual councillors, 1258; custos of Dover and warden of Cinque Ports and Rochester for barons; captured by Prince Edward at Kenilworth, 1265; surrendered again, 1266.

GREY, Richard de, Baron Grey of Codnor (d. 1335), served in Scotland under Edward II and Edward III; steward of Aquitaine, 1324; constable of Nottingham, 1326–7.

GREY, Richard de, fourth Baron (seventh by tenure) Grey of Codnor (d. 1419), succeeded his grandfather, John *Grey, third baron (1305–1392), 1392; admiral of the fleet and governor of Roxburgh, 1400; justice of South Wales, 1404; lieutenant, 1405–6, constable of Nottingham, 1407; much employed on diplomatic missions.

GREY, Roger, first Baron Grey of Ruthin (d. 1353), younger son of John de *Grey, second baron Grey of Wilton; summoned to parliament as Roger de Grey, 1324; served in Scotland, 1318, 1322, and 1341; custos of Abergavenny Castle, 1331.

GREY, Thomas, first marquis of Dorset (1451–1501), succeeded his father, John *Grey, eighth Baron Ferrers of Groby as ninth baron, 1461; created earl of Huntingdon, 1471, having fought for Edward IV at Tewkesbury; KB and marquis of Dorset, 1475; KG, 1476; privy councillor, 1476; took arms against Richard III and joined Richmond (see HENRY VII) in Brittany, but did not accompany him to England; his titles confirmed, 1486; imprisoned on suspicion, 1487;

served with the expedition to aid the emperor Maximilian, 1492, and against the Cornish rebels, 1497; early patron of *Wolsey.

GREY, Thomas, second marquis of Dorset (1477–1530), third son of Thomas *Grey, first marquis of Dorset; educated at Magdalen College School; styled Lord Harington till 1501; KG, 1501; imprisoned during last years of Henry VII's reign; won favour of Henry VIII by skill in tournaments; commanded unsuccessful expedition for recovery of Guienne, 1512; took part in French war, 1513; present at meetings of Henry VIII with Francis I and Emperor Charles V, 1520; warden of Scottish marches; witness against Queen *Catherine and signer of articles against *Wolsey, 1529; pensioner of the emperor and the French king.

GREY, Thomas, fifteenth and last Baron Grey of Wilton (d. 1614), succeeded his father, Arthur *Grey, fourteenth baron, 1593; served against the Armada; a volunteer in the Islands' voyage, 1597; colonel of horse in Ireland, 1599; in Netherlands Army at Nieuport, 1600; general of the horse against *Essex and *Southampton, and a commissioner at their trial, 1601; involved in 'Bye' plot against James I; reprieved on the scaffold, 1603; detained in the Tower till his death.

GREY, Thomas, Baron Grey of Groby (1623?–1657), regicide; son of Henry *Grey, first earl of Stamford; MP for Leicester in Long Parliament and that of 1654; commander of Midland counties association, 1643; present at first Battle of Newbury, 1643; thanked by parliament for capture of duke of *Hamilton, 1648; active in '*Pride's Purge', 1648; one of Charles I's judges; member of Council of State, 1649–54; received surrender of *Massey after Worcester, 1651; imprisoned as a Fifth-Monarchy man, 1655.

GREY, Thomas, second earl of Stamford (1654–1720), statesman; son of Thomas *Grey, Baron Grey of Groby; MA, Christ Church, Oxford, 1668; succeeded his grandfather, Henry *Grey, first earl, as second earl, 1673; member of *Shaftesbury's party; imprisoned as connected with Rye House Plot, 1683; pardoned, 1686; member of committee for investigating deaths of *Russell and *Sydney, 1689; privy councillor, 1694; commissioner of trade, 1695; chancellor of the duchy of Lancaster, 1697; president of Board of Trade and Foreign Plantations, 1699–1702 and 1707–11; FRS, 1708.

GREY, Thomas Philip de, earl de Grey (1781–1859), statesman; descendant of Henry *Grey, ninth earl of Kent; succeeded his father as third Baron Grantham, 1786; assumed name of Weddell, 1803, of de Grey on death of the

countess de Grey, his aunt, 1833; first lord of the Admiralty, 1834–5; viceroy of Ireland, 1841–4; FRS, 1841; first president, Society of British Architects, 1834–59; published *Memoir of the Life of Sir Charles Lucas* (1845) and *Characteristics of the Duke of Wellington* (1853).

GREY (or GRAY), Walter de (d. 1255), archbishop of York; as chancellor of England, 1205–14, one of King John's chief instruments and recipient of numerous benefices from him; his election to see of Lichfield, 1210, quashed by papal legate; bishop of Worcester, 1214; one of John's supporters at Runnymead, 1215; obtained at Rome the quashing of Simon *Langton's election to see of York; archbishop of York, 1215–55; acted against French party during minority of Henry III; married *Alexander II of Scotland to *Joanna, sister of Henry III of England, 1221; received profession of obedience from bishop-elect of Durham; employed diplomatically by Henry III; chief justiciar during Henry III's absence, 1242–3; entertained *Alexander III of Scotland on his marriage at York with *Margaret, daughter of Henry III, 1252; ranked among the patriotic prelates in later years; built south transept of York Minster; benefactor of Ripon and Oxford University.

GREY, William (*fl.* 1649), author of *Chorographia, or a Survey of Newcastle upon Tine* (1649).

GREY, William (d. 1478), bishop of Ely; DD, Balliol College, Oxford; prebendary of St Paul's, Lincoln, Lichfield, and York; chancellor of Oxford, *c.*1441–2; lived much in Italy, and was patron of scholars; proctor of Henry VI at Rome, 1445–54; bishop of Ely, 1454–78; acted as mediator, 1455 and 1460; lord high treasurer, 1469–70; head of commission to negotiate with Scotland, 1471–2; benefactor of Ely Cathedral and Balliol College library.

GREY, Sir William, thirteenth Baron Grey de Wilton (d. 1562), succeeded, 1529; distinguished in French War, 1545–6, and as commander at Pinkie, 1547; captured and fortified Haddington, 1548; pacified west of England, 1549; imprisoned on fall of *Somerset, 1551; governor of Guisnes; attainted for supporting *Northumberland, but pardoned, 1553; obliged to surrender Guisnes to the French, 1558; restored to his honours by Queen Elizabeth; governor of Berwick, 1559; failed in assault on Leith, 1560.

GREY, William, first Baron Grey of Werke (d. 1674), Parliamentarian; created baronet, 1619; created Baron Grey, 1624; commander of Parliamentarian forces in the east, 1642; imprisoned for refusing to go as commissioner to Scotland, 1643; speaker of House of Lords, 1643; a commissioner of great seal, 1648; refused the engagement, 1649; pardoned at Restoration.

GREY, Sir William (1818–1878), Indian and colonial governor; educated at Haileybury; secretary to Bank of Bengal, 1851–4, to the government, 1854–7; director-general of the Post-Office during the Mutiny; secretary to Government of India, 1859; member of Governor-General's Council, 1862–7; lieutenant-governor of Bengal, 1867–71; governor of Jamaica, 1874–7.

GREY, William de, first Baron Walsingham (1719–1781), judge; educated at Trinity Hall, Cambridge; barrister, Middle Temple, 1742; KC, 1758; MP, Newport (Cornwall), 1761–70, Cambridge University, 1770–1; attorney-general, 1766–71; chief justice of common pleas, 1771–80; created Baron Walsingham, 1780.

GREY, Zachary (1688–1766), antiquary; scholar of Trinity Hall, Cambridge, 1707; LL D, 1720; rector of Houghton Conquest, 1725, and vicar of St Giles and St Peter's, Cambridge; published *Hudibras . . . corrected and amended, with large annotations and a preface,* and cuts by *Hogarth (1744, supplement, 1752); also controversial pamphlets against Dissenting writers, and attacks on *Warburton's critical and controversial methods.

GRIBELIN, Simon (1661–1733), line-engraver; came to England, c.1680; engraved seven small plates of Raphael's cartoons, 1707; engraved portraits and, among other pictures, Rubens's *Apotheosis of James I,* 1730.

GRIERSON, Mrs Constantia (1706?–1733), classical scholar; intimate of *Swift; edited Terence (1727) and Tacitus (1730) for her husband, George Grierson, George II's printer in Ireland; wrote English verse.

GRIERSON, Sir George Abraham (1851–1941), Indian civil servant and philologist; educated at St Bees, Shrewsbury, and Trinity College, Dublin; served in Bengal presidency, 1873–98; completed *Linguistic Survey of India* (1898–1928) describing 179 separate languages and 544 dialects belonging to five distinct families; retired from India, 1903; publications include *Seven Grammars of the Dialects and Subdialects of the Bihārī Language* (8 parts, 1883–7) and *Bihār Peasant Life* (1885); *The Modern Vernacular Literature of Hindustan* (1889); series of articles and books on Kashmīrī culminating in *A Dictionary of the Kashmīrī Language* (1916–32); *The Pisāca Languages of North-Western India* (1906) and *Torwālī* (1929); and studies of Prakrit, Ahom, and the Kuki-Chin languages; KCIE, 1912; FBA, 1917; OM, 1928.

GRIERSON, Sir Herbert John Clifford (1866–1960), scholar; educated at the Gymnasium and University, Aberdeen (graduated, 1887), and Christ Church, Oxford; first class, Lit. Hum., 1893; first professor of English, Aberdeen, 1894; regius professor of rhetoric and English literature, Edinburgh, 1915–35; rector, 1936–9; edited the poems of *Donne (2 vols., 1912), *Byron (1923), *Milton (1925), *Scott's letters (in collaboration, 12 vols., 1932–7), *The Oxford Book of Seventeenth Century Verse* (with G. Bullough, 1934); other works include *Cross Currents in English Literature of the XVII Century* (1929) and biography of Scott (1938); FBA, 1923; knighted, 1936; honorary degrees from many universities.

GRIERSON, Sir James Moncrieff (1859–1914), lieutenant-general; joined Royal Artillery from Woolwich, 1878; employed on intelligence work in India; passed first into Staff College, 1883; head of Russian section of Intelligence Division, 1889; military attaché at Berlin, 1896; served in South African War and China, 1900; CB, 1901; director of military operations at War Office and major-general, 1904; largely helped to lay foundations of military co-operation between Great Britain and France; held home commands, 1906–14; KCB, 1911; author of military works; died in France on way to Front.

GRIERSON (or GRISSON), John (d. 1564?), Dominican; principal of King's College, Aberdeen, 1500; afterwards prior of St Andrews and provincial in Scotland.

GRIERSON, John (1898–1972), founder of the British documentary-film movement; educated at Stirling High School; worked in munitions factory, 1915–17; served in Royal Naval Volunteer Reserve, 1917–19; MA, Glasgow University, 1923; awarded Rockefeller fellowship and studied social significance of the cinema at Chicago University; employed as assistant film officer by (Sir) Stephen *Tallents, secretary of Empire Marketing Board; made first documentary film, *Drifters* (1929); built up group of young directors to make 'documentary films'; went with Tallents to General Post Office, 1933; produced more films, including *Industrial Britain* (1933), *The Song of Ceylon* (1934–5), *Coal Face* (1935), and *Night Mail* (1936); established advisory service, the Film Centre, 1937; became head of National Film Board of Canada, 1939–45; worked for number of organizations, including Unesco and Central Office of Information, 1945–57; produced television programme 'This Wonderful World' for Scottish Television Company; part-time professor of mass communication, McGill University, 1968–72; CBE, 1961; honorary degrees, Glasgow (1948) and Heriot

Watt (1969) universities; published *Grierson on Documentary* (1946, new edns., 1966 and 1979).

GRIERSON, Sir **Robert** (1655?–1733), laird of Lag; notorious for severity towards Covenanters; created a Nova Scotia baronet, 1685; presided at trial and execution of 'Wigtown martyrs'; fined and imprisoned after the Revolution; the 'Sir Robert Redgauntlet' of *Scott.

GRIEVE, Christopher Murray (1892–1978), poet and prose-writer under pseudonym Hugh MacDiarmid; educated at Langholm Academy, Dumfriesshire; became member of Independent Labour party and Fabian Society and worked as journalist; served in army during 1914–18 war; published *Annals of the Five Senses* (1923), poems written during the war; journalist on *Montrose Review*; edited anthologies, *Northern Numbers* (1920, 1921, and 1922); joined movement to revive Scots language as literary medium, assuming pen-name, Hugh MacDiarmid; in this medium wrote *Sangschaw* (1925), *Penny Wheep* (1926), and *A Drunk Man Looks at the Thistle* (1926); active in encouraging the National party of Scotland, 1928–33; editor of radio journal, 'Vox', 1928; joined Communist party, 1934–8; composed two 'Hymns to Lenin', 1931 and 1935; rejoined Communist party, 1957; visited Russia and China; granted Civil List pension, 1956; hon. LL D, Edinburgh, 1957; hon. RSA; president, Poetry Society of Great Britain, 1976; published *Lucky Poet: a Self-study in Literature and Political Ideas, Being the Autobiography of Hugh MacDiarmid (Christopher Murray Grieve)* (1943), and *The Company I've Kept* (1966).

GRIEVE (or GREIVE), George (1748–1809), persecutor of Madame Du Barry; emigrated to America from Alnwick, *c.*1780; came to Paris, 1783; on Madame Du Barry's return from London, Mar. 1793, caused her name to be placed on list of suspects, published a pamphlet against her, and thrice obtained her arrest; died at Brussels.

GRIEVE, James (d. 1773), translator of Celsus; MD, Edinburgh, 1752; physician to St Thomas's, 1764, and the Charterhouse, 1765; FRS, 1769; FRCP, 1771; translated Celsus *De Medicina* (1756).

GRIEVE, John (1781–1836), Scottish poet and friend of *Hogg; contributed to *Forest Minstrel*.

GRIEVE, Thomas (1799–1882), scene-painter at Covent Garden and Drury Lane; designed the diorama, *Overland Mail* (1850), and assisted Telbin and Absolon in panoramas; illustrated *Goody Two Shoes* (1862).

GRIEVE, William (1800–1844), scene-painter; brother of Thomas *Grieve; at Drury Lane and Her Majesty's.

GRIFFIER, Jan, the elder (1656–1718), painter and etcher; intimate of Rembrandt and Ruysdael at Amsterdam; followed *Looten to England; made a drawing during the great fire, 1666; lived on a yacht on the Thames, and took views of London and the environs; etched plates of *Barlow's birds and animals.

GRIFFIER, Jan, the younger (d. 1750?), landscape painter; son of Jan *Griffier the elder.

GRIFFIER, Robert (1688–1760?), landscape painter; son of Jan *Griffier the elder.

GRIFFIN, B. (*fl.* 1596), poet (probably Bartholomew Griffin of Coventry), author of *Fidessa, more chaste than kinde* (1596), the third sonnet of which was reproduced in *The Passionate Pilgrime* (1599).

GRIFFIN, Benjamin (1680–1740), actor and dramatist; at Lincoln's Inn Fields, 1715–21, and at Drury Lane, 1721–40; played Lovegold in *Fielding's *Miser*, Sir Hugh Evans, and Sir Paul Pliant; wrote farces and *Whig and Tory*, comedy (1720).

GRIFFIN, Bernard William (1899–1956), cardinal; studied at Cotton and Oscott colleges and English College, Rome; ordained, 1924; obtained doctorates in theology and canon law; secretary to successive archbishops of Birmingham, 1927–37; appointed auxiliary bishop, Birmingham, 1938, and vicar-general of diocese; archbishop of Westminster, 1943; cardinal, 1946; travelled widely in cause of international understanding; deplored financial burden to Catholics of 1944 Education Act and kept Catholic hospitals outside National Health Service.

GRIFFIN, Gerald (1803–1840), dramatist, novelist, and poet; came to London from Ireland, 1823; assisted by Banim; returned to Limerick, 1838, and joined the Christian Brothers; published stories illustrative of Munster life and *The Collegians* (1829); his play, *Gisippus*, produced by *Macready at Drury Lane, 1842. His novels and poems were edited by his brother (1842–3), his poetical and dramatic works (1857–9).

GRIFFIN (originally WHITWELL), John, fourth Baron Howard de Walden (1719–1797), field marshal; served in Netherlands and Germany during Austrian Succession and Seven Years' wars; major-general, 1759; KB, 1761; general, 1778; field marshal, 1796; MP, Andover, 1749–84; succeeded to barony of Howard de Walden, 1784; created Baron Braybrooke, 1788.

GRIFFIN, John Joseph (1802–1877), chemist; a publisher till 1852; assisted in foundation of Chemical Society, 1840; did much to popularize chemistry by *Chemical Recreations* (1834) and other works.

GRIFFIN, Sir **Lepel Henry** (1838–1908), Indian civil servant; joined Indian Civil Service in Punjab, 1860; compiled standard accounts of Punjab families in *Punjab Chiefs* (1865), *The Law of Inheritance to Sikh Chiefships* (1869), and *The Rajas of the Punjab* (1870); superintendent of Kapurthala state from 1875; helped to establish Abdur Rahman on Afghan throne and reconciled him to English policy, 1880; CSI, 1878; KCSI, 1881; agent-general to governor-general in central India, 1881–9; advocated use of Indian vernaculars in teaching in India; joint founder of *Asiatic Quarterly Review*, 1885; settled in England, 1889; chairman of Imperial Bank of Persia; works include *Ranjit Singh* (in 'Rulers of India' series, 1892).

GRIFFIN, Thomas (d. 1771), admiral; incurred much obloquy for not engaging two French ships off Ushant, 1745; vice-admiral, 1748; suspended for negligence while commanding in West Indies, 1750; reinstated, 1752; admiral, 1771; not employed again; MP, Arundel, 1754–61.

GRIFFIN, Thomas (1706?–1771), organbuilder; Gresham professor of music, 1763.

GRIFFITH. See also GRIFFIN, GRIFFITHS, and GRUFFYDD.

GRIFFITH, Alan Arnold (1893–1963), aeroengineer; educated at Douglas Secondary School and Liverpool University; B.Eng., first class, mechanical engineering, 1914; M.Eng., 1917; D.Eng., 1921; joined Royal Aircraft Factory (later Royal Aircraft Establishment), Farnborough, 1915; published important paper 'The Theory of Rupture' (*Phil. Trans. A*, 1920) on behaviour of materials; investigated propeller problems and turbine blading; demonstrated that gas turbine was a feasible aircraft engine, 1926; principal scientific officer, Air Ministry Laboratory, South Kensington, 1928–31; head of Engine Department, Farnborough, 1931; conducted axial compressor experiments with Hayne *Constant; research engineer, Rolls-Royce, Derby, 1939–60, directly responsible to E. W. (later Lord) *Hives for aero-engine research; research led directly to production of Rolls-Royce RB 108 engines, designed specifically for jet lift and vertical take-off; FRS, 1941; CBE, 1948.

GRIFFITH, Alexander (d. 1690), divine; MA, Hart Hall, Oxford, 1631; deprived of Welsh livings for loyalty; vicar of Glasbury, 1661; wrote against parliamentary itinerant preachers, 1654.

GRIFFITH, Arthur (1872–1922), Irish political leader; at an early age associated himself with Irish nationalist movement; employed in Transvaal, 1896–9; returned to Ireland to take part in founding weekly newspaper which was to be organ of ''98 clubs' separatist movement; edited *The United Irishman*, 1899–1906; preached doctrine that Irish self-government could never be attained through parliamentary action at Westminster, a doctrine which did not then appeal to most Irishmen; at convention of 'National Council' advocated adaptation to Irish conditions of 'Hungarian' method of passive resistance under title of 'Sinn Fein' policy, 1905; Sinn Fein ('Ourselves Alone') enunciated doctrine of national self-help and self-reliance; aimed at independent self-government for Ireland; believer in use of physical force; president of Sinn Fein party, 1910; associated himself with Irish National Volunteers, 1913; opposed any Irishman joining British Army during European war; his papers suppressed, 1914–15; took no part in Easter Rebellion, 1916; support for Sinn Fein increased after 1916; several times imprisoned, 1916–21; resigned presidency of party in favour of Mr *de Valera, 1917; MP, East Cavan, 1918; minister for home affairs on formation of Dail Eireann, 1919; acting-president, 1919–20; carried out 'Hungarian' policy against British government; with Michael *Collins and three other plenipotentiaries negotiated with British government and finally secured treaty, 1921; president of Dail Eireann, 1922; the real creator of autonomous Irish state.

GRIFFITH, Edmund (1570–1637), bishop of Bangor; MA, Brasenose College, Oxford, 1592; canon of Bangor, 1600, dean, 1613, and bishop, 1634–7; DD.

GRIFFITH, Edward (1790–1858), naturalist; educated at St Paul's School; master in court of common pleas; FRS; original member of Zoological Society; edited translation of Cuvier's *Animal Kingdom* (1827–34); published collection of Huntingdon records (1827).

GRIFFITH, Mrs **Elizabeth** (1720?–1793), playwright and novelist; married, *c*.1752, Richard *Griffith (d. 1788); published *Genuine Letters between Henry and Frances* (1757) and novels, translations, and plays.

GRIFFITH, Francis Llewellyn (1862–1934), Egyptologist; educated at Sedbergh, Highgate, and The Queen's College, Oxford; official student of Egypt Exploration Fund, 1884; assistant in department of British and medieval antiquities and ethnography, British Museum, 1888–96; assistant professor of Egyptology, University College, London, 1892–1901; honorary lecturer, Manchester, 1896–1908; reader (1901), honorary professor (1924–32), Oxford; created Griffith Egyptological Fund at Oxford, 1907; in charge of Oxford excavations in Nubia; prolific and accurate scholar with genius for decipherment; his *Stories of the High Priests of Memphis* (1900) first established demotic on firm scientific basis; bequeathed his papers, estate, and Egyptological library to found Griffith Institute at Oxford; FBA, 1924.

GRIFFITH, George (1601–1666), bishop of St Asaph; of Westminster and Christ Church, Oxford; MA, 1626; DD, 1635; chaplain to Bishop John *Owen; rector of Llanymynech, 1633; disputed with Vavasor *Powell, 1652–3; bishop of St Asaph, 1660–6; helped to draw up form of baptisms for adults.

GRIFFITH (or GRIFFIN), John (*fl.* 1553), premonstratensian, of Halesowen; published *Conciones Aestivales* and *Conciones Hyemales*.

GRIFFITH, John (1622?–1700), General Baptist minister of Dunning's Alley, Bishopsgate Street Without; frequently imprisoned.

GRIFFITH, John (1714–1798), Independent minister; published *A Brand Plucked out of the Fire* (1759).

GRIFFITH, Matthew (1599?–1665), master of the Temple; BA, Gloucester Hall, Oxford, 1618; rector of St Mary Magdalen, Old Fish Street, and (1640) St Benet Sherehog; sequestered, 1642; DD, Oxford, 1643; royal chaplain, 1643; helped to defend Basing House, 1645; his royalist sermon (1660) answered by *Milton, 1660; master of the Temple and rector of Bladon, Oxfordshire, *c.*1661–5.

GRIFFITH (GRIFFYTH or GRIFFYN), Maurice (d. 1558), bishop of Rochester; BD, Oxford, 1582; archdeacon of Rochester, 1537; bishop, 1554–8.

GRIFFITH, Moses (1698/9–1785), physician; of Melbourne, Cambridgeshire, and St John's College, Cambridge; MD, Leiden, 1744; said to have invented Pharmacopoeia iron mixture.

GRIFFITH, Moses (*fl.* 1769–1809), draughtsman and engraver; employed by Thomas *Pennant and Francis *Grose.

GRIFFITH, Piers (d. 1628), naval adventurer; according to tradition commanded a ship against the Armada, and was disgraced for attacks on Spanish after the war; possibly identical with 'Welsh pirate' taken at Cork in 1603.

GRIFFITH, Ralph Thomas Hotchkin (1826–1906), Sanskrit scholar; BA, The Queen's College, Oxford, 1846; Boden Sanskrit scholar, 1849; professor of English literature (1853) and headmaster (1854) of Benares Government College; inspector of schools, 1856; principal of Benares College, 1861–78; founded *Pandit*, college monthly journal, 1866; director of public instruction in North-West Provinces,

1878–85; CIE, 1885; retired to Kotagiri; published verse translations, embodying spirit of originals, of Sanskrit classics, including Kālidāsa's *Kumárasambhava* (1853), the *Rámáyan of Válmíki* (5 vols., 1870–3), hymns of the *Rigveda* (4 vols., 1889–92), *Sámaveda* (1893), and *Atharvaveda* (2 vols., 1895–6).

GRIFFITH, Richard (1635?–1691), physician; fellow of University College, Oxford, 1654; MA, 1660; MD, Caen, 1664; FRCP, 1687, and twice censor; published *A-la-Mode Phlebotomy no good fashion* (1681).

GRIFFITH, Richard (d. 1719), navy captain; for recapturing with the aid of a boy a merchantman taken by the French, 1691, given command of the *Mary* galley, tender to the admiral at La Hogue, 1692; suspended for not maintaining discipline, but after 1702 reappointed commander.

GRIFFITH, Richard (d. 1788), author; collaborated with his wife, Elizabeth *Griffith; published *The Triumvirate . . . by Biograph Triglyph*, novel (1764) and *Variety*, comedy, acted 1782.

GRIFFITH, Richard (1752–1820), son of Richard *Griffith (d. 1788); deputy-governor, Co. Kildare; sat for Askeaton in Irish parliament, 1783–90.

GRIFFITH, Sir Richard John, first baronet (1784–1878), geologist and civil engineer; son of Richard *Griffith (1752–1820); surveyed coalfields of Leinster, 1808; reported on Irish bogs; professor of geology and mining engineer to Royal Dublin Society, 1812; inspector of Irish mines; Wollaston medallist for geological map, 1815; superintended road construction in the south, 1822–30; commissioner of valuation, 1828–68; chairman of Irish Board of Works, 1850–64; hon. LL D, Dublin, 1851; created baronet, 1858.

GRIFFITH, Walter (d. 1779), captain in the Navy; gave *Hawke important intelligence of French fleet off Brest, Nov. 1759; took part in defence of Sandy Hook, 1778; present at actions off St Lucia and Grenada, 1778–9; killed in Fort Royal Bay.

GRIFFITH, William (1810–1845), botanist; studied at London University under *Lindley; entered East India Company's medical service, 1832; accompanied a botanical expedition to Assam and Burma (1835–6), Bhutan, Khorassan, and Afghanistan; died at Malacca; works published posthumously by Dr MacClelland.

GRIFFITH, William Pettit (1815–1884), architect and archaeologist; FRIBA, 1842; superintended reparations at St John's and St James's churches, and St John's Gate, Clerkenwell, 1845–51. His works include *Ancient Gothic*

Churches (1847–52), *Suggestions for a more Perfect and Beautiful Period of Gothic Architecture* (1855), and papers on ornamental architecture.

GRIFFITHS, Ann (1780–1805), Welsh hymnwriter.

GRIFFITHS, Arthur George Frederick (1838–1908), inspector of prisons and author; born at Poona; joined 63rd Regiment, 1855; served in Crimea; brigade major at Gibraltar, 1864–70; inspector of prisons in England, 1878–96; historian of Millbank Jail, 1875, and of Newgate, 1884; editor of *Army and Navy Gazette*, 1901–4; best known as writer of some thirty novels of prison life and detective stories; wrote also *Fifty Years of Public Service* (1904).

GRIFFITHS, David (1792–1863), missionary in Madagascar, 1821–35; published New Testament in language of Madagascar; expelled, 1835; allowed to return as merchant, 1838; finally expelled, 1842; published *History of Madagascar* in Welsh, and Malagasy grammar and textbooks.

GRIFFITHS, Ernest Howard (1851–1932), physicist; educated at Owens College, Manchester, and Sidney Sussex College, Cambridge; fellow, 1897; a university coach; principal and professor of experimental philosophy, University College of South Wales, Cardiff, 1901–18; deeply interested in completion (1909) of Viriamu Jones Memorial Research Laboratory; his researches included the boiling-point of sulphur, the latent heat of evaporation of water, freezing-points of dilute aqueous solutions, and other accurate measurements of heat; FRS, 1895.

GRIFFITHS, Evan (1795–1873), Welsh Independent minister. His works include a Welsh–English dictionary (1847) and Welsh versions of Matthew *Henry's Commentary*.

GRIFFITHS, Ezer (1888–1962), physicist; educated at Aberdare Intermediate School and University College, Cardiff; first class, physics; fellow, University of Wales; D.Sc.; joined heat section of National Physical Laboratory, Teddington, 1915–53; one of leading world authorities on heat insulation, heat transfer, evaporation, and related matters, such as refrigeration; visited Australia to examine problems of transportation of apples, 1923; worked on such problems as vapour trails made by modern aircraft, 1939–45; carried out experiments for Medical Research Council and the Admiralty on effects of radiation on man; vice-president, Physical Society; chairman, Research Committee, Institute of Refrigeration, 1936–8; chairman, governing body of Twickenham Technical College; member of many scientific committees; FRS, 1926; OBE, 1950; published *Methods of Measuring Temperature* (1918), *Pyrometers* (1926), and

Refrigeration, Principles and Practice (1951); also responsible for articles in Sir R. T. *Glazebrook's *Dictionary of Applied Physics* and in Sir T. E. *Thorpe's *Dictionary of Applied Chemistry*.

GRIFFITHS, Frederick Augustus (1795–1869), major, RA; published *Artillerist's Manual* (1840).

GRIFFITHS, George-Edward (d. 1829), editor of the *Monthly Review* till 1825, and verse-writer; son of Ralph *Griffiths.

GRIFFITHS, James (1890–1975), trade unionist and politician; son of a Welsh blacksmith; left Betws Board School at 13 to work in the local coal-pit; founder member and secretary of Ammanford branch of Independent Labour party, 1908; campaigned against Britain's involvement in 1914–18 war; secretary, Ammanford Trades and Labour Council, 1916; student at Central Labour College, London, 1919–21; involved in miners' Strike and General Strike, 1926; vice-president, South Wales Miners, 1932, president, 1934; Labour MP for Llanelli, 1936–70; played leading part in Welsh Advisory Committee on Post-war Reconstruction; minister of national insurance, 1945; PC; responsible for National Insurance Act (1946) and Industrial Injuries Act (1948); chairman of Labour party, 1948–9; secretary of state for the colonies, 1950–1; in opposition, 1951–64; deputy leader, under Hugh *Gaitskell, 1956; attempted to deflect Labour away from further nationalization; closely identified with his native Wales; first secretary of state for Wales, 1964–6; published memoirs, *Pages from Memory* (1969); in favour of Britain joining the European community; hon. LL D, University of Wales, 1946; governor of the BBC; CH, 1966.

GRIFFITHS, John (1731–1811), Congregationalist; pastor of Glandwr, Pembrokeshire, and founder of expository classes; translated English hymns into Welsh; published works, including Welsh versions of the *Shorter Catechism*.

GRIFFITHS, John (1806–1885), keeper of the archives at Oxford; educated at Winchester and Wadham College, Oxford; BA, 1827; fellow, 1830; sub-warden of Wadham College, 1837–54; one of the 'four tutors' who protested against 'Tract XC', 1841; keeper of the archives at Oxford, 1857; warden of Wadham College, 1871–81; edited *Inett's *Origines Anglicanae* (1855), the *Homilies* (1859), two plays of Aeschylus, and the Laudian *Statutes* (1888); published also work on Greek accents (1831).

GRIFFITHS, Sir John Norton-, first baronet (1871–1930), engineer. See NORTON-GRIFFITHS.

GRIFFITHS (alias ALFORD), Michael (1587–1652), Jesuit. See ALFORD.

GRIFFITHS, Ralph (1720–1803), founder, proprietor and publisher of the *Monthly Review*; previously partner with Thomas (Tom) *Davies (1712?–1785) in an evening paper; started the *Monthly Review*, 1749; assisted by *Goldsmith, 1757–8, and his first wife.

GRIFFITHS, Robert (1805–1883), inventor; patented mechanical contrivances, including rivet-machine, 1835, and (with John Gold) glass-grinding and polishing machine, 1836; carried on engineering works at Havre with M Labruère, 1845–8; his first screw propeller patented, 1849, improvements, 1853, 1858, 1878.

GRIFFITHS, Thomas (1791–1847), Roman Catholic prelate; president of St Edmund's (new) College, 1818–33; bishop of Olena *in partibus*, 1833; vicar-apostolic of London district, 1836–47.

GRIGG, Edward William Macleay, first Baron Altrincham (1879–1955), administrator and politician; born in Madras; grandson of Sir Edward Deas *Thomson; scholar of Winchester and New College, Oxford; on staff of *The Times*, 1903–5 and as head of colonial department) 1908–13; joint editor, *Round Table*, 1913; in France with Guards division, 1914–18; MC; DSO; military secretary to prince of Wales, 1919–20; CMG; CVO, 1919; KCVO, 1920; a private secretary to Lloyd George, 1920–2; Liberal MP, Oldham, 1922–5; secretary, Rhodes Trust, 1923–5; governor of Kenya, 1925–30; KCMG, 1928; Conservative MP, Altrincham, 1933–45; parliamentary secretary, Ministry of Information, 1939–40; joint parliamentary under-secretary, War Office, 1940–2; minister resident, Middle East, 1944–5; PC, 1944; baron, 1945; editor, *National Review*, 1948–55; publications include *The Faith of an Englishman* (1936) and *Kenya's Opportunity* (1955).

GRIGG, Sir (Percy) James (1890–1964), public servant; educated at Bournemouth (secondary) School and St John's College, Cambridge; first class, parts i and ii, mathematical tripos, 1910–12; headed list of entrants to administrative class of Civil Service, and appointed to Treasury, 1913; served in Eastern Europe and Office of External Ballistics, 1915–18; principal private secretary to five chancellors of the Exchequer, 1921–30; chairman, Board of Customs and Excise; chairman, Board of Inland Revenue; finance member, Viceroy's Executive Council, India, 1933–9; permanent secretary, War Office, 1939; collaborated closely with Sir Alan *Brooke (later Viscount Alanbrooke), chief of Imperial General Staff; appointed by Churchill as sec-

retary of state for war, 1942–5; Nationalist MP, East Cardiff, 1942–5; first British executive director, International Bank for Reconstruction and Development, 1946; director of companies; published autobiography, *Prejudice and Judgment* (1948); KCB, 1932; KCSI, 1936; PC, 1942; hon. fellow, St John's College, Cambridge, 1943; hon. LL D, Bristol, 1946; hon. bencher, Middle Temple, 1954.

GRIGGS, William (1832–1911), inventor of photo-chromolithography; technical assistant to director of Indian Museum, 1855; photo-lithographer in India Office till 1885; invented photo-chromolithographic process; set up works at Peckham, 1868; published plates for Forbes Watson's *Textile Manufactures . . . of India* (1866); reproduced facsimile editions of *Mahābhāsya* (1871), Shakespeare quartos (43 vols., 1881–91), and Ashbee reprints; issued from 1881 some 200 *Portfolios of Industrial Art* of all countries, and from 1884 *Journal of Indian Art and Industry*.

GRIGNION (or GRIGNON), Charles, the elder (1717–1810), line-engraver; uncle of Charles *Grignion; studied under Gravelot and Le Bas; employed by Hogarth on his *Canvassing for Votes* and *Garrick as Richard III*; executed plates for *Walpole's *Anecdotes of Painting* and other publications.

GRIGNION (or GRIGNON), Charles, the younger (1754–1804), painter; pupil of Cipriani; exhibited at Royal Academy, 1770–81; afterwards at Rome as history and portrait painter; painted portrait of *Nelson, 1798; died at Leghorn.

GRIGNION, Reynolds (d. 1787), engraver for the booksellers.

GRIGOR, James (1811?–1848), botanist; published *Eastern Arboretum, or Register of Remarkable Trees, Seats, &c., in Norfolk* (1840–1).

GRIGSON, Geoffrey Edward Harvey (1905–1985), poet, critic, anthologist, and man of letters; educated at a Leatherhead school and St Edmund Hall, Oxford; worked on *Yorkshire Post* and as literary editor, *Morning Post*; founded *New Verse*, 1933–9; reviews for *Observer*, *Guardian*, and *New Statesman* collected in *The Contrary View* (1974) and *Blessings, Kicks and Curses* (1982); wrote numerous books including essays on art *The Harp of Aeolus* (1947), and *Samuel Palmer, the Visionary Years* (1947), and anthologies, *The Romantics* (1943) and *Before the Romantics* (1948), and works about the English countryside such as *The Englishman's Flora* (1955) and *The Shell Country Book* (1962); published poems including *Several Observations* (1939), *Collected Poems* (1963), and *The Private Art* (1963); received Duff Cooper Memorial

Prize, 1972; published autobiography, *The Crest on the Silver* (1950).

GRIM, Edward (*fl.* 1170–1177), author of biography of Thomas *Becket, *c.*1175; eyewitness of Becket's murder.

GRIMALD (GRIMALDE or **GRIMOALD), Nicholas** (1519–1562), poet; BA, Christ's College, Cambridge, 1540; MA, Oxford, 1544; chaplain to Bishop *Ridley; imprisoned as a Protestant, 1555, but recanted; contributed verses to *Tottel's *Songs and Sonettes* (1557); published translations from Virgil and Cicero, and two Latin dramas, *Archi-propheta* (printed 1548) and *Christus Redivivus* (1543).

GRIMALDI, Joseph (1779–1837), actor and pantomimist; appeared as an infant dancer at Sadler's Wells; acted there and at Drury Lane for many years; played also at Dublin and in the provinces; his greatest successes as Squire Bugle and clown in *Mother Goose* at Covent Garden.

GRIMALDI, Joseph S. (d. 1863), pantomimist, son and successor of Joseph *Grimaldi.

GRIMALDI, Stacey (1790–1863), antiquary; Marquis Grimaldi of Genoa; second son of William *Grimaldi; eminent 'record lawyer' in London; FSA, 1824; frequent contributor to *Gentleman's Magazine*; published *Origines Genealogicae* (1828) and *Genealogy of the Family of Grimaldi* (1834); his *Miscellaneous Writings* edited (1874–81).

GRIMALDI, William (1751–1830), miniature painter; apprenticed to his uncle Thomas *Worlidge, whose *Antique Gems* he published (1768); copied in miniature pictures by *Reynolds; exhibited at the Royal Academy, 1786–1824; enamel painter to George IV and the duke of *York.

GRIMBALD (GRIMBOLD or **GRYMBOLD),** Saint (820?–903), abbot of new minster at Winchester; previously prior of St Bertin in Flanders; came to England at *Alfred's invitation, *c.*893; one of Alfred's mass priests and educational assistants; the new minster built for him by *Edward the Elder, 903; prominent in mythical story of Oxford.

GRIMBLE, Sir Arthur Francis (1888–1956), colonial administrator, broadcaster, and writer; born in Hong Kong; educated at Chigwell School and Magdalene College, Cambridge; entered Colonial Service, 1914; posted to Gilbert and Ellice Islands; resident commissioner, 1926; administrator and colonial secretary, St Vincent, 1933–6; governor, Seychelles, 1936–42, Windward Isles, 1942–8; obtained popular success recounting his Pacific experiences for BBC, subsequently published as *A Pattern of Islands* (1952)

and *Return to the Islands* (1957); CMG, 1930; KCMG, 1938.

GRIMES, Robert (d. 1701), colonel and Trappist. See GRAHAM, ROBERT.

GRIMESTONE, Elizabeth (d. 1603), author. See GRIMSTON.

GRIMM, Samuel Hieronymus (1734–1794), water-colour painter; born at Burgdorf, Switzerland; came to London; exhibited at first exhibition of Royal Academy.

GRIMSHAW, William (1708–1763), incumbent of Haworth, Yorkshire, 1742–63; of Christ's College, Cambridge; BA, 1729–30; acted with the Methodists and John *Wesley; preached throughout the north of England with great success.

GRIMSHAWE, Thomas Shuttleworth (1778–1850), biographer; MA, Brasenose College, Oxford, 1800; vicar of Biddenham and rector of Burton Latimer; chief work, *Life and Works of William Cowper* (1835).

GRIMSTON, Edward (1528?–1599), comptroller of Calais, 1552–8; studied at Gonville Hall, Cambridge; after capture of Calais by Guise escaped from Bastille to London, 1559; muster-master of the north, 1560; MP, Ipswich, 1563, 1571 and 1572, Orford, 1593; employed as a spy in France.

GRIMSTON (or GRYMESTON), Elizabeth (d. 1603), author of *Miscelanea: Meditations: Memoratives*, in verse (published 1604).

GRIMSTON, Sir Harbottle, second baronet (1603–1685), speaker and judge; educated at Emmanuel College, Cambridge; barrister, Lincoln's Inn; recorder of Harwich, 1634, of Colchester, 1638–49; MP, Harwich, 1628; sat for Colchester, 1640, and in Long Parliament; prominent in debates of 1640–2, particularly on ecclesiastical questions; president of committee which inquired into escape of Charles I from Hampton Court, 1647; took leading part in negotiations with Charles I in the Isle of Wight; succeeded to baronetcy, 1648; excluded by *Pride, 1648, and prevented from resuming his seat in 1656; appointed to Council of State on abdication of Richard *Cromwell, 1659; speaker of the Convention Parliament, 1660; member of commission which tried regicides, 1660; master of the Rolls, 1660–85; published *Strena Christiana* (1644, Eng. trans., 1872), and law reports.

GRIMSTON, Robert (1816–1884), sportsman; of Harrow and Christ Church, Oxford; BA, 1838; barrister, Lincoln's Inn, 1843; chairman, International Telegraph Company; chairman, Indo-European Telegraph Company, 1868; boxer, swimmer, rider, and cricketer.

GRIMSTON, Sir **Samuel,** third baronet (1643–1700), son of Sir Harbottle *Grimston; MP, St Albans, 1668, 1679, 1680, and 1689–99; much disliked by James II.

GRIMSTON, William Luckyn, first Viscount Grimston (1683–1756), succeeded to the Grimston estates, and assumed the name, on death of uncle, Sir Samuel *Grimston, 1700; succeeded his brother, Sir Harbottle Luckyn, 1737; MP, St Albans, 1710; created Baron Dunboyne and Viscount Grimston in peerage of Ireland, 1719; published *The Lawyer's Fortune, or Love in a Hollow Tree* (1705), a play ridiculed by *Swift and *Pope.

GRIMTHORPE, first Baron (1816–1905), lawyer, mechanician, and controversialist. See BECKETT, Sir EDMUND.

GRINDAL, Edmund (1519?–1583), archbishop of Canterbury; fellow of Pembroke Hall, Cambridge, 1538; MA, 1541; DD, 1564; proctor, 1548–9; chosen by *Ridley as a Protestant disputant at Cambridge; one of Ridley's chaplains; precentor of St Paul's, 1551; one of the royal chaplains; at Strasburg and in Germany during Mary's reign; commissioner for revision of the liturgy, and bishop of London, 1558; master of Pembroke Hall, 1558–61; member of the High Commission court; when bishop of London sympathized with Puritans; as archbishop of York (1570–5) enforced uniformity on the Romish party; elected archbishop of Canterbury by Cecil's influence, 1576; undertook to reform the ecclesiastical courts; under sentence of suspension (1577–82) for refusing to carry out Elizabeth's mandate suppressing 'prophesyings'; eulogized in *Spenser's *Shepherd's Calendar*.

GRINDAL, William (d. 1548), tutor to Queen Elizabeth; fellow of St John's College, Cambridge, 1543; BA, 1541–2; a favourite pupil of *Ascham; died of the plague.

GRINFIELD, Edward William (1785–1864), biblical scholar; schoolfellow of *De Quincey; MA, Lincoln College, Oxford, 1808; minister of Laura Chapel, Bath; founded and endowed Oxford lectureship on Septuagint, 1859; published Hellenistic edition of New Testament, *Apology for the Septuagint*, and theological pamphlets.

GRINFIELD, Thomas (1788–1870), divine and hymn-writer; brother of Edward William *Grinfield; BA, Trinity College, Cambridge, 1812; curate in charge of St Mary-le-Port, Bristol; published religious verse, *History of Preaching* (edited by Canon Eden, 1880), and other works.

GRISAUNT, William (or William English) (*fl.* 1350), physician; in youth taught philosophy at Oxford; physician at Marseilles; long reputed the father of Pope Urban V.

GRISEWOOD, Frederick Henry (1888–1972), broadcaster; educated at Radley and Magdalen College, Oxford; studied singing in London, Paris, and Munich; during 1914–18 war served with Oxford and Buckinghamshire Light Infantry; joined staff of BBC, 1929; worked as announcer and took part in 'Children's Hour'; moved into outside broadcasting, 1937; commentator at coronation of George VI; during 1939–45 war, announcer in Overseas Service and regular speaker on 'The Kitchen Front'; became well-known as question-master on 'Any Questions'; published *My Story of the BBC* (1959) and autobiography, *The World Goes By* (1952).

GRISONI, Giuseppe (1692–1769), portrait painter; born at Florence; brought to England by John Talman, 1715; died at Rome.

GROCYN, William (*c.*1450–1519), Greek scholar; educated at Winchester and New College, Oxford; fellow, 1467; incumbent of Newton Longueville, 1480; divinity reader at Magdalen College, Oxford, 1483; prebendary of Lincoln, 1485; in Italy, 1488–90, with *Linacre, studying under Politian and Chalcondyles; became acquainted with Aldus the printer; lectured in Greek at Oxford; became rector of St Lawrence Jewry, 1496, but did not reside in London till three years later; criticised Dean *Colet's lectures on 'The Ecclesiastical Hierarchy of Dionysius'; intimate in London with Linacre, *More, and Erasmus; master of All Hallows, Maidstone, 1506, and rector of Shepperton and East Peckham; catalogue of his library printed, 1889.

GROENVELDT, John (1647?–1710?), physician; born at Deventer; MD, Utrecht, 1670; came to London, 1683; twice summoned before College of Physicians for internal use of cantharides; published medical treatises.

GROGAN, Cornelius (1738?–1798), United Irishman; high sheriff of Wexford and MP for Enniscorthy, 1783–90; commissary-general in insurgent army, 1798; beheaded on Wexford Bridge.

GROGAN, Nathaniel (d. 1807?), painter of Irish life; served in American War.

GRONOW, Rees Howell (1794–1865), writer of reminiscences; intimate with Shelley at Eton; served in 1st Foot Guards in the Peninsula, 1813–14; at Quatre Bras and Waterloo; witnessed *coup d'état* of 1851; died in Paris. His *Reminiscences* appeared, 1861, 1863, 1865, 1866 (collected, 1888).

GROOMBRIDGE, Stephen (1755–1832), astronomer and West India merchant; published

(1838) *Catalogue of Circumpolar Stars . . . reduced to Jan. 1, 1810*, containing 4,243 star-places, among them No. 1,830, first observed by himself; FRS, 1812; a founder of the Astronomical Society; observed eclipses of the sun in 1816 and 1820.

GROOMBRIDGE, William (*fl.* 1770–1790), water-colour painter; published *Sonnets* (1789).

GROOME, Francis Hindes (1851–1902), Romany scholar and miscellaneous writer; son of Robert Hindes *Groome; interested in gypsy life from boyhood; lived with gypsies at home and abroad; settled down to literary work in Edinburgh, 1876; joined staff of Messrs Chambers, 1885; sub-editor of *Chambers's Encyclopaedia* (10 vols., 1888–92); published *In Gipsy Tents* (1880), *Kriegspiel* (a Romany novel, 1896), and *Gypsy Folk Tales* (1899); had wide knowledge of Jacobite literature.

GROOME, John (1678?–1760), divine; BA, Magdalene College, Cambridge, 1699, where he founded exhibitions; vicar of Childerditch, Essex, 1709; published *The Dignity and Honour of the Clergy* (1710).

GROOME, Robert Hindes (1810–1889), archdeacon of Suffolk; MA, Caius College, Cambridge, 1835; archdeacon of Suffolk, 1869–87; intimate of Edward *Fitzgerald; edited *Christian Advocate and Review*, 1861–6; his Suffolk stories published posthumously.

GROSART, Alexander Balloch (1827–1899), author and editor; studied at Edinburgh University; licensed by Edinburgh Presbytery, 1856; minister at Kinross, Loch Leven, 1856–65; Princes Park, Liverpool, 1865–8, and Blackburn, 1868–92; edited reprints of rare Elizabethan and Jacobean literature, besides the works of several Puritan divines. His publications include *Fuller Worthies Library* (39 vols., 1868–76), *Occasional Issues of Unique and very Rare Books* (38 vols., 1875–81), *Chertsey Worthies Library* (14 vols., 1876–81), *Huth Library* (33 vols., 1886), *Spenser's Works* (10 vols., 1880–8), *Daniel's Works* (5 vols., finished 1896). He also published several original devotional works.

GROSE, Francis (1731?–1791), antiquary and draughtsman; Richmond herald, 1755–63; FSA, 1757; met *Burns during tour in Scotland; in early life exhibited tinted drawings of architecture at the Academy; died suddenly at Dublin; published *Antiquities of England and Wales* (1773–87), with many drawings by himself, *Antiquities of Scotland* (1789–91), *Classical Dictionary of the Vulgar Tongue* (1785, reissued as *Lexicon Balatronicum*, 1811), and other works.

GROSE, John (1758–1821), divine; son of John Henry *Grose; MA, St Mary Hall, Oxford; minister of the Tower of London; rector of Netteswell, Essex; published *Ethics, Rational and Theological* (1782).

GROSE, John Henry (*fl.* 1750–1783), writer to East India Company; brother of Francis *Grose; his *Voyage to the East Indies* (1757), said to have been compiled from his notes by John *Cleland.

GROSE, Sir Nash (1740–1814), judge; fellow of Trinity Hall, Cambridge; LL B, 1768; barrister, Lincoln's Inn, 1766; serjeant-at-law, 1774; judge of King's Bench, 1787–1813; knighted, 1787.

GROSE, Thomas Hodge (1845–1906), registrar of Oxford University, 1877–1906; scholar of Balliol College, Oxford; BA, with first classes in classics and mathematics, 1868; president of the Union, 1871; fellow and tutor of The Queen's College, Oxford, from 1871; helped T. H. *Green in editing *Hume's works, 1874–5; ardent alpinist.

GROSS, (Imre) Anthony (Sandor) (1905–1984), painter and etcher; educated at Repton; studied at Slade School of Fine Art and Central School of Arts and Crafts, London, and Académie Julian and École des Beaux Arts, Paris; first one-man exhibition in London, 1925; travelled in Spain and other countries on the Continent and in North Africa; produced series of paintings and prints *Sortie d'Usine* (1930–1) and *La Zone*; collaborated with American, Hector Hoppin, on drawings for cartoon films *La Joie de Vivre* (1933) and *Fox Hunt* (1936); illustrated Jean Cocteau's *Les Enfants Terribles* (1936); during 1939–45 official war artist, producing over 300 sketches now in Imperial War Museum; illustrated Emily *Brontë's *Wuthering Heights* (1947) and John *Galsworthy's *Forsyte Saga* (1950); taught at Central School, 1948–54; produced etchings, *Le Boulvés Suite* (1956); head of etching and engraving department, Slade School, 1955–71; published *Etching, Engraving and Intaglio Printing* (1970) and *The Very Rich Hours of Le Boulvé* (1980); member of London Group, 1948–71; hon. RE and ARA, 1979; RA, 1980; CBE, 1982.

GROSSE, Alexander (1596?–1654), Presbyterian divine; MA, Gonville and Caius College, Cambridge; MA, Exeter College, Oxford; BD, Oxford, 1632; rector of Bridford, and Ashburton, Devonshire; published devotional works.

GROSSETESTE, Robert (d. 1253), bishop of Lincoln; of humble birth; educated at Oxford and (probably) Paris; first rector of Franciscans at Oxford, 1224; chancellor of Oxford; archdeacon successively of Wilts, Northampton, and Leicester; prebendary of Lincoln, 1221; bishop, 1235–53; maintained his right of visitation against the Lincoln chapter after a six years' dispute (1239–45) and a journey to Rome; had disputes also with the Canterbury monks and Henry III; resisted Archbishop *Boniface's visitation, 1250; failed in an appeal to the pope against the appropriation by monks of parochial revenues; preached at Lyons against papal abuses; suspended by the pope for refusing to appoint an Italian to a benefice, 1251; chief opponent of Henry III's demand for a tenth of church revenues, 1252; wrote letter refusing to induct pope's nephew to a Lincoln canonry, 1253; translated Greek books; wrote works on theology, philosophy, and husbandry, and commentaries on Aristotle and Boethius, besides French poems. Grosseteste's *Le Chasteau d'Amour* was edited by R. F. Weymouth (1864), *Carmina Anglo-Normannica*, printed (1844).

GROSSMITH, George (1847–1912), entertainer and singer in light opera; gave 'humorous and musical recitals'; employed in *Gilbert and *Sullivan's series of comic operas, first at Opera Comique and then at Savoy Theatre, 1877–89; 'created' many of the chief parts; with brother, Walter *Grossmith, wrote *Diary of a Nobody* (1894).

GROSSMITH, George, the younger (1874–1935), actor-manager and playwright; son of George *Grossmith; originated the 'dude' in musical comedy; at Gaiety Theatre, 1901–13; later notable performances included *Kissing Time* (1919) and *No, No, Nanette* (1925); in management after 1914; wrote musical plays including *The Spring Chicken, Rogues and Vagabonds* (first modern-type revue in London, 1905), and *The Bing Boys are Here*; introduced cabaret entertainment, 1922.

GROSSMITH, Walter Weedon (1854–1919), comedian; brother of George *Grossmith, the elder; excelled in part of 'dudes' and small, underbred, unhappy men.

GROSVENOR (GRAVENOR or GRAVENER), Benjamin (1676–1758), Dissenting divine; Presbyterian pastor at Crosby Square, 1704–49; 'merchants' lecturer' at Salters' Hall, 1716; contributed to *Bagwell Papers* (1716); said to have drawn up *Authentick Account* (1719) of the Salters' Hall proceedings; Williams trustee, 1723; his sermons collected (1809).

GROSVENOR, Hugh Lupus, first duke of Westminster (1825–1899), son of Richard *Grosvenor, second marquis of Westminster; educated at Balliol College, Oxford; Liberal MP for Chester, 1847–69; opposed government on franchise question, 1866; succeeded as third

marquis of Westminster, 1870; created duke of Westminster, 1874; master of horse, 1880–5; opposed home rule, 1886; KG, 1870; privy councillor, 1880; aide-de-camp to queen, 1881; lord-lieutenant of Cheshire, 1883, and of county of London, 1888; breeder of racehorses.

GROSVENOR, John (1742–1823), surgeon; successful in friction treatment; proprietor and editor of *Oxford Journal*, 1795.

GROSVENOR, Richard, first Earl Grosvenor (1731–1802), horse-breeder; grandson of Sir Thomas *Grosvenor; MA, Oriel College, Oxford, 1751; DCL, 1754; succeeded as seventh baronet, 1755; mayor of Chester, 1759; MP, Chester, 1754–61; created baron, 1761, earl, 1784; patron of William *Gifford (1756–1826).

GROSVENOR, Richard, second marquis of Westminster (1795–1869), MP (Viscount Belgrave) for Chester, 1818–20, and 1826–30, Cheshire, 1831–2, South Cheshire, 1832–5; succeeded to marquisate, 1845; lord-lieutenant, Cheshire, 1845–67; lord steward under Russell, 1850–2.

GROSVENOR, Richard De Aquila, first Baron Stalbridge (1837–1912), railway administrator and politician; son of second marquess of *Westminster; Liberal MP, Flintshire, 1861–86; PC, 1872; created baron and became Liberal Unionist, 1886; director of North Western Railway Company, 1870; chairman, 1891–1911.

GROSVENOR, Sir Robert (d. 1396), defendant in *Scrope* v. *Grosvenor*; saw military service at Poitiers, 1356, Najara, 1367, La Roche-sur-Yon, 1369, and siege of Limoges, 1370; challenged by Sir Richard *Scrope for wearing the arms, 'azure, a bend or', 1385; judgment given against him by the constable, 1389, and confirmed by the king, 1390; sheriff of Cheshire, 1394.

GROSVENOR, Robert, second Earl Grosvenor and first marquis of Westminster (1767–1845), son of Richard, first Earl *Grosvenor; MA, Trinity College, Cambridge, 1786; MP (Viscount Belgrave) for St Looe, 1788–90, Chester, 1790–1802; a lord of the Admiralty, 1789–91; commissioner of the Board of Control, 1793–1801; succeeded as Earl Grosvenor, 1802; created marquis, 1831; KG, 1841; joined Whigs after Pitt's death; laid out Belgravia, 1826, and rebuilt Eaton Hall, Cheshire, 1803; great picture collector and racer; acquired by marriage Egerton estates, 1794.

GROSVENOR, Lord Robert, first Baron Ebury (1801–1893), son of Robert *Grosvenor, first marquis of Westminster; educated at Westminster and Christ Church, Oxford; BA, 1821; entered Lincoln's Inn, 1821; Whig MP for

Shaftesbury, 1822–6, Chester, 1826–47, and Middlesex, 1847–57; privy councillor, 1830; treasurer of household, 1846; created Baron Ebury, 1857; devoted himself to cause of Protestantism in Church of England; opposed home rule; published personal journals, and pamphlets advocating liturgical reform.

GROSVENOR, Sir Thomas, third baronet (1656–1700), succeeded his grandfather, 1664; many years MP for Chester; sheriff of the county, 1688; by his marriage with Mary Davies, daughter of a London scrivener, obtained the bulk of the present Westminster estates.

GROSVENOR, Thomas (1764–1851), field marshal; nephew of Richard *Grosvenor, first Earl Grosvenor; with 1st Foot Guards in Flanders, Holland, and (1799), the Helder expedition; commanded brigades in Copenhagen (1807) and Walcheren (1809) expeditions; general, 1819; field marshal, 1846; MP, Chester, 1795–1825, Stockbridge, 1825–30.

GROTE, Arthur (1814–1886), Bengal civilian; president of Asiatic Society of Bengal, 1859–62 and 1865; brother of George *Grote.

GROTE, George (1794–1871), historian; brother of Arthur *Grote; educated at Charterhouse; a banker till 1843; became acquainted through *Ricardo with James *Mill and *Bentham; compiled for Bentham *Analysis of the Influence of Natural Religion on Temporal Happiness . . . by Philip Beauchamp* (1822); joined J. S. Mill's reading society; reviewed *Mitford's *Greece* in the *Westminster*, 1826; an original founder of the first London University, 1828–30; visited Paris, 1830, and began relations with French liberals; took active part in Reform agitation; MP for City of London, 1832–41; brought forward four resolutions (1833, 1835, 1838, 1839) and two bills (1836, 1837) in favour of the ballot; retired to devote himself to his history, completing the first two volumes, 1845; re-elected to council of University College, London, 1849; treasurer, 1860, and president, 1868; procured the rejection of Dr *Martineau for the chair of logic on the ground of sectarianism, 1866; guarded the endowment which (dated 1869) he left for a similar professorship by a provision against payment to any minister of religion; advocated examinations and the admission of women to them; trustee of the British Museum, 1859; hon. DCL, Oxford, 1853; hon. LL D, Cambridge, 1861; FRS, 1857; vice-chancellor, London University, 1862; foreign associate of the Académie des Sciences, 1864; declined a peerage, 1869; buried in Westminster Abbey. *The History of Greece* (1846–56, 8 vols.) has been four times reissued (lastly, 1888, 10 vols.), and translated into French

and German. His *Minor Works* were edited by Professor Bain (1873).

GROTE, Harriet (1792–1878), biographer; née Lewin; married George *Grote, 1820; intimate of *Mendelssohn and Jenny *Lind; published *Memoir of Ary Scheffer* (1860) and *Personal Life of George Grote* (1873), besides the privately printed *Philosophic Radicals of 1832*.

GROTE, John (1813–1866), philosopher; brother of George *Grote; fellow of Trinity College, Cambridge, 1837–66; BA, 1835; incumbent of Trumpington, 1847–66; Knightsbridge professor of moral philosophy, 1855–66; published *Exploratio Philosophica* (1865); his *Examination of Utilitarian Philosophy* (1870) and *Treatise on Moral Ideals* (1876) edited by the Revd J. B. Mayor.

GROVE, Sir George (1820–1900), writer on music; articled as civil engineer; MICE, 1839; superintended erection of lighthouses at Morant Point, Jamaica, 1842, and on Gibbs' Hill, Bermuda, 1846; secretary to Society of Arts, 1849; secretary at Crystal Palace, where he paid special attention to development of music; compiled weekly, from 1856, analytical programmes of music, of which the more important were published in volume, 1884; editor of *Macmillan's Magazine*, 1873; contributed to Sir William *Smith's (1813–1893) *Dictionary of the Bible*; founder of Palestine Exploration Fund, 1865; projected and edited *Dictionary of Music and Musicians* (4 vols., 1878–89); first director of Royal College of Music at Kensington, 1883–94; knighted, 1883; CB, 1894; hon. DCL, Durham, and LL D, Glasgow; published writings on a great variety of subjects.

GROVE, Henry (1684–1738), Dissenting tutor; educated at Taunton Grammar School and Academy; intimate of Isaac Watts; from 1706 taught at Taunton Academy; contributed to revived *Spectator*, 1714; published *System of Moral Philosophy* (ed. *Amory, 1749) and treatises, including demonstration of the soul's immateriality (1718).

GROVE, Joseph (d. 1764), biographer. His works include *Life and Times of Cardinal Wolsey* (1742–4) and *Lives of all the* [Cavendish] *Earls and Dukes of Devonshire* (1764).

GROVE, Mathew (fl. 1587), poet; author of *The most famous and tragicall historie of Pelops and Hippodamia*, ballad (1587).

GROVE, Robert (1634–1696), bishop of Chichester; of Winchester and St John's College, Cambridge; fellow, 1658; MA, 1660; DD, 1681; chaplain to Bishop *Henchman, 1667; rector of St Andrew Undershaft, 1670; prebendary of St

Paul's, 1679; chaplain-in-ordinary, 1690; helped to draw up petition against Declaration of Indulgence, 1688; bishop of Chichester, 1691–6; published pamphlets against William *Jenkyn.

GROVE, Sir **William Robert** (1811–1896), man of science and judge; MA, Brasenose College, Oxford, 1835; hon. DCL, 1875; hon. LL D, Cambridge, 1879; barrister, Lincoln's Inn, 1835; member of Royal Institution, 1835, and vice-president, 1844; invented Grove gas voltaic battery, 1839; FRS, 1840, and royal medallist, 1847; professor of experimental philosophy, London Institution, 1847; published *Correlation of Physical Forces* (1846), establishing theory of mutual convertibility of forces; QC, 1853; member of Royal Commission on Law of Patents, 1864; judge of court of common pleas, 1871; invested with coif and knighted, 1872; judge of Queen's Bench, 1880; privy councillor, 1887.

GROVER, Henry Montague (1791–1866), author; LL B, Peterhouse, Cambridge, 1830; rector of Hitcham, Buckinghamshire, 1833–66; published works, including two dramatic poems and *History of the Resurrection authenticated* (1841).

GROVER, John William (1836–1892), civil engineer; educated at Marlborough College; pupil of Sir Charles *Fox; employed in office of works of science and art department; set up as consulting engineer at Westminster, 1862; MICE, 1867; FSA; vice-president of British Archaeological Association; carried out several important engineering works, mainly in connection with railways and waterworks; assisted Major-General Walter Scott in design of Albert Hall; published engineering treatises and pamphlets.

GROVES, Anthony Norris (1795–1853), missionary; friend of John *Kitto; a founder of the Plymouth Brethren; unsectarian missionary at Baghdad, 1830–3, and afterwards in India till 1852; died at George *Müller's house at Bristol; his journals from 1829 to 1831 published posthumously.

GROVES, John Thomas (d. 1811), architect; clerk of the works at St James's, Whitehall, and Westminster, 1794; architect to the General Post Office, 1807; lived in Italy, 1780–90; exhibited Italian subjects at Royal Academy, 1791–2.

GROZER, Joseph (*fl.* 1784–1798), mezzotint engraver.

GRUB, George (1812–1893), Scottish ecclesiastical historian; educated at King's College, Aberdeen; apprenticed as advocate; admitted advocate, 1836, and was librarian to Society of Advocates, Aberdeen, 1841 till death; lecturer on

Scots law, Marischal College, Aberdeen, 1843; professor of law, Aberdeen University, 1881–91; AM, Aberdeen, 1856; LL D, 1864; assisted in formation of Spalding Club, for which he edited several works; published *Ecclesiastical History of Scotland* (1861).

GRUBB, Sir **Kenneth George** (1900–1980), churchman, explorer, missionary, and public servant; educated as foundation scholar of Marlborough College; absconded from school to join the Royal Navy; after the 1914–18 war enlisted with Worldwide Evangelization Crusade to study Indian dialects of the Amazon basin; mastered 200 dialects and published linguistic survey, 1927; joined the Survey Application Trust and spent ten years producing surveys of the missionary situation in Latin America and other parts of the world; joined group planning the Ministry of Information; appointed head of Latin American section; promoted to be overseas controller of publicity, 1941; CMG, 1942; president, Church Missionary Society, 1944; chairman, Commission of the Churches on International Affairs, jointly sponsored by the World Council of Churches and the International Missionary Council; organized the Hispanic Council and Luzo-Brazilian Council, 1946; member of Royal Institute of International Affairs and first chairman of the Institute for Strategic Studies; edited successive editions of the *World Christian Handbook* for twenty years; knighted, 1953; published *Amazon and Andes* (1930), *Parables from South America* (1932), and his autobiography, *Crypts of Power* (1971); KCMG, 1970.

GRUBB, Thomas (1800–1878), optician; constructed reflectors, including the Armagh fifteen-inch, 1835, the Glasgow Observatory reflector (twenty inch), and the great Melbourne reflector (four feet), 1867; FRS, 1864; FRAS, 1870.

GRUFFYDD, Thomas (1815–1887), harper; played at Buckingham Palace and Marlborough House, 1843; won many prizes at the Eisteddfodau; visited the Comte de la Villemarqué in Brittany, 1867; harper to Edward VII when prince of Wales.

GRUFFYDD AB CYNAN (1055?–1137), king of Gwynedd or North Wales; said to have been born at Dublin; defeated *Trahaearn and made himself master of Gwynedd, 1081; betrayed to *Hugh of Chester and imprisoned before 1087; retaliated on the Normans with help of *Rhys ab Tewdwr and a Norse fleet; again compelled to retire to Ireland, 1098; ruled Anglesey after 1099; compelled to pay tribute to Henry I, to whom he is said to have given up *Gruffydd ab Rhys, 1115; supported Henry I in invasion of

Powys, 1121; patron of the clergy and of litera-ture; introduced bagpipes and the Irish element into Welsh music.

GRUFFYDD AB GWENWYNWYN (d. 1286?), lord of Cyveiliog or Upper Powys; son of *Gwen-wynwyn; brought up in England; did homage for his father's estate to Henry III, 1241; faithful to Henry III during the revolt of *Davydd II; deprived by *Llywelyn ab Gruffydd of his do-minions, fled to England, 1256–7; revolted and did homage to Llywelyn, 1263; plotted with his brother Davydd against Llywelyn, 1276, and thenceforth returned permanently to English allegiance.

GRUFFYDD AB LLYWELYN (d. 1063), king of the Welsh; slew *Iago and made himself king over Gwynedd, 1039, and defeated English at Crossford; defeated *Howel and his Norse allies, and secured possession of Deheubarth, 1044; in alliance with the outlawed *Ælfgar of Mercia, ravaged Herefordshire and burnt Hereford; compelled by *Harold to make peace, with the loss of his lands beyond the Dee, 1052; slew *Gruffydd ab Rhydderch and became king of the Britons, 1055; renewed his ravages, 1056; again defeated the English, married *Aldgyth (after-wards wife of Harold), and restored the outlawed Ælfgar, 1058; was finally crushed and treacher-ously slain in combined attack of Harold and *Tostig.

GRUFFYDD AB LLYWELYN (d. 1244), Welsh prince; rebelled against his father, *Llywelyn ab Iorwerth; headed army against William *Mar-shal, earl of Pembroke, 1223–4; seized and imprisoned by his brother *Davydd, 1239; handed over to Henry III, 1241; broke his neck in attempted escape from Tower of London.

GRUFFYDD AB MADOG (d. 1269), called Gruffydd of Bromfield, lord of Lower Powys; refused to fight against the English, 1244; driven out by *Llywelyn ab Gruffydd, 1256, but in alliance with him next year; joined Scottish-Welsh confederacy, 1258.

GRUFFYDD AB RHYDDERCH (d. 1055), king of the South Welsh; headed opposition of the south to *Gruffydd ab Llywelyn, by whom he was at length slain.

GRUFFYDD AB RHYS (d. 1137), king or prince of South Wales (Deheubarth); returned from Ireland, c.1113; took refuge with *Gruffydd ab Cynan, but fled from sanctuary to the south, to avoid being given up to the English; ravaged French and Flemish settlements; driven from his territories to Ireland, 1127; allied himself with king of North Wales; won Battle of Aberteivi (Cardigan), 1136; recovered great part of his ter-ritory; slain by his wife's treachery.

GRUFFYDD AB RHYS (d. 1201), South Welsh prince; grandson of *Gruffydd ab Rhys (d. 1137); at feud with his brother Maelgwyn; obtained recognition from England, 1197, but fell into his brother's hands and was imprisoned by the English in Corfe Castle; died a monk at Strata Florida.

GRUFFYDD RHISIART (1810–1883), author. See ROBERTS, RICHARD.

GRUNDY, John (1782–1843), Unitarian; min-ister at Nottingham, 1806–18, Cross Street, Manchester, 1818–24, and Paradise Street, Liverpool, 1824–35; published religious works.

GRUNDY, John Clowes (1806–1867), print-seller and art patron.

GRUNDY, Thomas Leeming (1808–1841), engraver; brother of John Clowes *Grundy; his best work *The Lancashire Witch*, after W. Bradley.

GRUNEISEN, Charles Lewis (1806–1879), journalist and musical critic; sub-editor of the *Guardian*, 1832, of the *Morning Post*, 1833; special correspondent with the Carlist army, 1837; captured by Christinists and saved only by intervention of Palmerston; Paris correspondent, 1839–44; organized an express system between Paris and London and sent despatches by pigeons; afterwards musical critic to *Illustrated News* and *Morning Chronicle*, and, from 1868, of the *Athenaeum*; initiated revival of Italian opera at Covent Garden, 1846, and superintended pro-duction of *Le Prophète*, 1849.

GRYG, Gruffydd (*fl.* 1330–1370), Welsh poet; chiefly noted for his poetical contention with *David ab Gwilym.

GRYMESTON, Elizabeth (d. 1603), author. See GRIMSTON.

GUADER (or WADER), Ralph, earl of Nor-folk (*fl.* 1070); outlawed by Harold; retired to Brittany; at Hastings, the only British traitor, 1066; created earl by William I; married, against his own wish, to Emma, daughter of William *Fitzosbern; at the bridal conspired with Roger, earl of *Hereford, against the king, 1075; fled and was outlawed; crusader with *Robert of Nor-mandy; at the siege of Nicaea, 1097; died 'in via Dei'.

GUALDRIC (d. 1112), bishop of Laon. See GAL-DRIC.

GUALENSIS, Thomas (d. 1255), bishop of St David's. See WALLENSIS.

GUARO, William (*fl.* 1300?), philosopher. See WILLIAM OF WARE.

GUBBINS, Sir Colin McVean (1896–1976), major-general and leader of Special Operations

Executive (SOE); educated at Cheltenham College and the Royal Military Academy, Woolwich; commissioned in Royal Field Artillery, 1914; served on Western Front in 1914–18 war, wounded, and awarded MC; joined staff of W. E. (later Lord) *Ironside in north Russia, 1919; experiences there and in Ireland in 1920–2 stimulated interest in irregular warfare; graduated at Staff College, Quetta, 1928; served in Russian section of War Office, 1931; joined MT 1, policy-making branch of Military Training Directorate, 1935; sent to Sudetenland as member of international commission, 1938; joined G(R), later MI(R), 1939; prepared training manuals on irregular warfare; chief of staff to military mission to Poland, 1939; sent to Paris as head of military mission to Czech and Polish forces under French command, 1939–40; recalled to raise 'independent companies', forerunners of the commandos, which he later commanded in Norway; DSO, 1940; seconded to SOE, 1940; responsible for training and dispatch of operators to the field; succeeded Sir Charles *Hambro as executive head of SOE, 1943; major-general; survived attempts to dismantle SOE and took blame for débâcle in Holland, where operations were penetrated by German intelligence; retired from army when SOE was wound up, 1946; managing director of large firm of carpet and textile manufacturers; CMG, 1944; KCMG, 1946; co-founder of Special Forces Club; deputy lieutenant, Islands Area of the Western Isles, 1976; fourteen foreign decorations.

GUBBINS, John (1838–1906), breeder and owner of racehorses; settled at Bruree, Co. Limerick, 1886, and bred horses and hounds; bred Galtee More (winner of Two Thousand Guineas, St Leger, and Derby, 1897), and Ard Patrick (Eclipse Stakes, 1903); headed list of winning owners, 1897.

GUBBINS, Martin Richard (1812–1863), Anglo-Indian official; financial commissioner in Oudh, 1856–7; prominent at Lucknow during the Mutiny; accompanied Sir Colin *Campbell to Cawnpore; judge of the Agra Supreme Court, 1858–62; published *The Mutinies in Oudh* (1858); committed suicide at Leamington.

GUBIUN, Ralph (d. 1151), abbot of St Albans. See RALPH.

GUDWAL, Saint (*fl.* 650), bishop and confessor; founded monastery in Devonshire (according to the Bollandists), at Cormon (according to Surius and Malebrancq).

GUDWAL (or **GURVAL**) (7th cent.), second bishop of St Malo; disciple of St *Brendan.

GUEDALLA, Philip (1889–1944), historian and essayist; educated at Rugby and Balliol College,

Oxford; president of Union; first class, modern history, 1912; called to bar (Inner Temple), 1913; five times defeated as Liberal candidate, 1922–31; publications include *Palmerston* (1926), *Gladstone and Palmerston* (1928), *The Duke* (1931), *The Queen and Mr. Gladstone* (2 vols., 1933), *The Hundred Days* (1934), *The Hundred Years* (1936), *Mr. Churchill* (1941), and *The Two Marshals* (1943).

GUERIN, Thomas, reputed centenarian. See GEERAN.

GUERSYE, Balthasar (d. 1557), Italian physician; surgeon to *Catherine of Aragon and Henry VIII; MD, Cambridge, 1546; FRCP, 1556.

GUEST, Lady **Charlotte** (1812–1895), Welsh scholar. See SCHREIBER.

GUEST (GHEAST or **GESTE), Edmund** (1518–1577), bishop of Salisbury; MA, King's College, Cambridge, 1544; while vice-provost of King's College, Cambridge, disputed on the Protestant side, 1549; domestic chaplain to *Parker and archdeacon of Canterbury, 1559; a reviser of the liturgy; bishop of Rochester, 1560–71; chancellor of the Garter, *c.*1560, and chief almoner to Queen Elizabeth, 1560–72; DD, 1571; bishop of Salisbury, 1571–7; friend of *Cecil, *Hatton, and *Bacon; left his library to Salisbury Cathedral; maintained the real presence, 1564; translated psalms in 'Bishops' Bible'.

GUEST, Edwin (1800–1880), historical writer, philologist, and historian; eleventh wrangler, Caius College, Cambridge, 1824; MA, 1827; LL D, 1853; DCL, Oxford, 1853; fellow, Caius College, 1824; master, 1852–80; barrister, 1828; chief founder of the Philological Society, 1842; FRS, 1839; hon. sec., SA, 1852; wrote *History of English Rhythms* (1838), papers on philology and Roman-British history, and *Origines Celticae*, ed. Stubbs and Deedes (1883).

GUEST, Frederick Edward (1875–1937), politician and promoter of aviation; brother of first Viscount *Wimborne; educated at Winchester; private secretary to his cousin (Sir) Winston Churchill; Liberal MP, 1910–22, 1923–9; Conservative MP, 1931–7; PC, 1920; secretary of state for air, 1921–2; master, Guild of Air Pilots and Air Navigators, 1932.

GUEST, George (1771–1831), organist at St Peter's, Wisbech, 1789–1831; son of Ralph *Guest; composed cantatas, organ pieces, quartets, and glees.

GUEST, Sir Ivor Churchill, third baronet, and first Viscount Wimborne (1873–1939), politician; son of first Lord Wimborne; brother of F. E. *Guest; educated at Eton and Trinity College, Cambridge; Conservative MP, Plymouth, 1900–6; Liberal MP, Cardiff Boroughs, 1906–10; PC and baron (as Ashby St Ledgers), 1910; paymaster-general, 1910–12; succeeded father, 1914; lord-lieutenant of Ireland, 1915–18; viscount, 1918.

GUEST, Joshua (1660–1747), lieutenant-general; enlisted in the Dragoons, 1685; served in Ireland, Flanders, and Spain; brevet-colonel, 1713; lieutenant-general, 1745; defended Edinburgh Castle against Prince *Charles Edward, though, according to Robert *Chambers, a Jacobite; buried in Westminster Abbey.

GUEST, Sir Josiah John, baronet (1785–1852), ironmaster; as sole manager of Dowlais Ironworks introduced chemical and engineering improvements; proprietor, 1849; MP, Honiton, 1822–31, Merthyr Tydvil, 1832–52; mediator in Merthyr riots of 1831; FRS, 1830; created baronet, 1838.

GUEST, Ralph (1742–1830), organist at St Mary's, Bury St Edmunds, 1805–22.

GUEST, Thomas Douglas (*fl.* 1803–1839), historical and portrait painter; exhibited at Academy (1803–38) and British Institution; published *Inquiry into Causes of the Decline of Historical Painting* (1829).

GUGGENHEIM, Edward Armand (1901–1970), authority on thermodynamics; educated at Charterhouse and Gonville and Caius College, Cambridge; first class, part i, mathematical tripos, and part ii, natural sciences (chemistry) tripos, 1921–3; research under (Professor Sir) Ralph H. *Fowler, 1923–5; continued scientific studies in Denmark, 1925–31; worked under Professor F. G. *Donnan at University College, London; wrote first book *Modern Thermodynamics by the methods of W. Gibbs* (1933); held number of lecturing posts in the United States and England, 1932–9; Sc.D., Cambridge; worked for Royal Navy and Montreal Laboratory of Atomic Energy, 1939–46; suggested successful means of neutralizing German magnetic mines; FRS, 1946; professor of chemistry, Reading University, 1946–66; hon. life member, Faraday Society, 1967; member of number of scientific committees; published many scientific papers and books.

GUGGISBERG, Sir Frederick Gordon (1869–1930), soldier and administrator; born at Toronto; commissioned in Royal Engineers, 1889; employed by Colonial Office on special survey of Gold Coast Colony and Ashanti, 1902; director of surveys there, 1905; in Southern Nigeria, 1910; served in France, 1914–18; governor of Gold Coast, 1919; his policy directed to government by and for Africans; governor of British Guiana, 1928–9; KCMG, 1922; his writings include *Handbook of the Southern Nigeria Survey* (1911).

GUIDOTT, Thomas (*fl.* 1698), physician; MA, Wadham College, Oxford, 1662; MB, 1666; practised about Oxford, subsequently at Bath and in London; edited *Jorden's Discourse of Natural Bathes* (3rd edn., 1669), Theophilus περὶ οὔρων (1703), and *Maplet's De Thermarum Bathoniensium Effectis* (1694); published medical works on English spas.

GUILD, William (1586–1657), Scottish divine; member of the 'mutinous assembly' which in Edinburgh protested for the liberties of the kirk, 1617; DD and chaplain to Charles I; supported Episcopacy, but took the Covenant with reservations; principal of King's College, Aberdeen, 1640–51; deprived for lukewarmness, 1651; his *Moses Unvailed* (1620) dedicated to Bishop *Andrewes; purchased the Trinity Friars' convent at Aberdeen and endowed it as a hospital.

GUILDFORD, Sir Henry (1489–1532), master of the horse and comptroller of the household; son of Sir Richard *Guildford; served against the Moors and was knighted by Ferdinand, 1511; king's standard-bearer in French campaign of 1513; accompanied Henry VIII to Field of Cloth of Gold (1520) and to Gravelines, and *Wolsey to Calais; master of the horse, 1515–22; comptroller of the household; knight of the shire for Kent, 1529; signed articles against Wolsey, 1529, but remained his friend, though retaining Henry VIII's favour.

GUILDFORD, Nicholas de (*fl.* 1250), poet; supposed author of *The Owl and the Nightingale* (first printed, 1838) and *La Passyun Jhu Crist, en Engleys*, printed in Morris's *Old English Miscellany*.

GUILDFORD, Sir Richard (1455?–1506), master of the ordnance under Henry VII; attainted by Richard III; reclaimed land in Sussex (Guildford Level); built ships; attended Henry VII at Boulogne, 1492; sheriff of Kent; comptroller of the household; created banneret for services against Cornish rebels, 1497; KG, 1500; died at Jerusalem on pilgrimage; his account printed by *Pynson, 1511.

GUILFORD, Barons. See NORTH, FRANCIS, first baron, 1637–1685; NORTH, FRANCIS, third baron, 1704–1790.

GUILFORD, earls of. See NORTH, FRANCIS, first earl, 1704–1790; NORTH, FREDERICK, second earl, 1732–1792; NORTH, GEORGE AUGUSTUS, third earl, 1757–1802; NORTH, FRANCIS, fourth earl, 1761–1817; NORTH, FREDERICK, fifth earl, 1766–1827.

GUILLAMORE, Viscounts. See O'GRADY, STANDISH, first viscount, 1766–1840; O'GRADY, STANDISH, second viscount, 1792–1848.

GUILLEMARD, William Henry (1815–1887), divine; of Christ's Hospital and Pembroke College, Cambridge; fellow, 1839; MA, 1841; DD, 1870; headmaster of Royal College, Armagh, 1848–69; vicar of St Mary-the-Less, Cambridge, 1869–87; introduced Oxford Movement at Cambridge; published *Hebraisms of the Greek Testament* (1879).

GUILLIM, John (1565–1621), herald; entered Brasenose College, Oxford, 1581; Rouge Croix pursuivant, 1619; systematized science of heraldry; published *A Display of Heraldrie* (1610).

GUILLUM SCOTT, Sir John Arthur (1910–1983), secretary of the Church Assembly and first secretary-general of the General Synod of the Church of England. See SCOTT.

GUINNESS, Sir Arthur Edward, second baronet, and first Baron Ardilaun (1840–1915), philanthropist; son of Sir Benjamin *Guinness, first baronet; BA, Trinity College, Dublin; succeeded father, 1868; head of Guinness Brewery, Dublin, 1868–77; Conservative MP, Dublin City, 1868–9, 1874–80; baron, 1880; munificent benefactor to Dublin and to Irish Church.

GUINNESS, Sir Benjamin Lee, first baronet (1798–1868), brewer; succeeded his father as sole proprietor, 1855, and developed export side of the business; lord mayor of Dublin, 1851; restored St Patrick's Cathedral at cost of £150,000, 1860–5; LL D, Dublin, 1863; created baronet, 1867; MP, Dublin, 1865–8.

GUINNESS, Edward Cecil, first earl of Iveagh (1847–1927), philanthropist; son of Sir B. L. *Guinness; shared in management of Guinness's Brewery; chairman of company, 1886; baronet, 1885; baron, 1891; viscount, 1905; earl, 1919; FRS, 1906; benefactions include: £250,000 to erect workmen's dwellings in London and Dublin; £250,000 for destroying Dublin slum property; £250,000 to Lister Institute of Preventive Medicine, London; bequeathed to the nation portion of Kenwood estate and art collection for Kenwood house.

GUINNESS, Henry Grattan (1835–1910), divine and author; ordained as evangelist, 1857; preached in England, Ireland, America, and on the Continent, 1857–72; at Dublin helped in 'conversion' of Dr *Barnardo, 1866; founded East London Institute for training missionaries, 1873; 'Livingstone Inland Mission' in Congo, 1878, and other missions in South America and India, all of which were amalgamated into 'Regions Beyond Missionary Union', 1899; made missionary tour of the world, 1903; collaborated with wife in *The Approaching End of the Age* (1878) and *The Divine Programme of the World's History* (1888); he also published grammars of the Congo language.

GUINNESS, Sir Rupert Edward Cecil Lee, second earl of Iveagh (1874–1967), philanthropist; chairman, Guinness Company, brewers, 1927–62; educated at Eton and Trinity College, Cambridge; won diamond sculls, 1895–6; won King's Cup at Cowes, 1903; director, Arthur Guinness, Son. & Co. Ltd., 1899; worked with Irish hospital in South Africa, 1900; CMG, 1901; member, London County Council; Conservative MP, Haggerston, Shoreditch, 1908–10; set up Woking Park Farm, training establishment for emigrants to Canada; MP, SE Essex (later Southend), 1912–27; governor, Lister Institute of Preventive Medicine; chairman, Wright–Fleming Institute of Microbiology; financed research into production of clean milk at Rothamsted Institute; commanded London division, RNVR, 1914; ADC to the king, 1916; first chairman, Tuberculin Tested Milk Producers Association, 1920; assisted in development of Research Institute in Dairying, University College, Reading; hon. D.Sc., Reading; chancellor; chairman, Chadacre Agricultural Institute; became earl of Iveagh and inherited Elveden estate, 1927; converted Elveden into efficient, economic farming unit; lieutenant of the City of London; deputy lieutenant, Surrey and Essex; chairman, Guinness Trust and Iveagh Trust; presented Iveagh House, Dublin, to Republic of Ireland, 1939; CB, 1911; KG, 1955; FRS, 1964; chancellor, Trinity College, Dublin; married (1903) **Gwendolen Florence Mary Onslow** (1881–1966), philanthropist; elder daughter of fourth earl of *Onslow; Conservative MP, Southend (succeeding husband), 1927–35; member, National Prisoners of War Fund; CBE, 1920; chairman, National Union of Conservative and Unionist Associations.

GUINNESS, Walter Edward, first Baron Moyne (1880–1944), statesman; son of E. C. Guinness, first earl of *Iveagh; educated at Eton; served in South African and 1914–18 wars; DSO and bar, 1917–18; Conservative MP, Bury St Edmunds, 1907–31; under-secretary for war, 1922–3; financial secretary to Treasury, 1923–4, 1924–5; PC, 1924; minister of agriculture, 1925–9; baron, 1932; chairman, royal commissions on Durham University (1934) and West Indies (1938–9); colonial secretary, 1941–2; deputy minister of state, Cairo, 1942; minister, Jan. 1944; assassinated, Nov. 1944.

GUISE, John (1680–1761), independent minister. See GUYSE.

GUISE, John (d. 1765), general; served with the 1st Foot Guards under *Marlborough in Flanders; commanded the battalion in Vigo expedition, 1719; brigadier and colonel commanding 6th Foot at Carthagena, 1739; major-general, 1742; general, 1762.

GUISE, Sir John Wright, third baronet (1777–1865), general; served with 3rd Foot Guards at Ferrol, Vigo, and Cadiz, 1800, in Egypt, 1801, and Hanover, 1805–6; commanded light companies at Fuentes d'Onoro, and the first battalion in Spain, 1812–14; general, 1851; GCB, 1863; succeeded to baronetcy, 1834.

GUISE, William (1653?–1683), orientalist; fellow of All Souls, Oxford, 1674–80; MA, 1677; his *Misnae Pars* (Mishnah), edited by Professor Edward *Bernard, 1690.

GULL, Sir William Withey, first baronet (1815–1890), physician to Queen Victoria; MD, London, 1846; medical tutor and lecturer at Guy's Hospital, and (1856) physician; FRCP, 1848 (councillor, 1863–4); Fullerian professor of physiology, 1847–9; FRS, 1869; hon. DCL, Oxford, 1868; hon. LL D, Cambridge, 1881, and Edinburgh, 1884; member of General Medical Council, 1871–83; attended Edward VII, when prince of Wales, during his severe illness, 1871; created baronet, 1872; physician-in-ordinary to Queen Victoria, 1887–90; Gulstonian lecturer, 1849; Hunterian orator, 1861, and Harveian orator, 1870; pre-eminent as clinical physician.

GULLIVER, George (1804–1882), anatomist and physiologist; prosector to *Abernethy and dresser to Sir William *Lawrence at St Bartholomew's Hospital; FRS, 1838; FRCS, 1843; Hunterian professor of comparative anatomy and physiology, 1861; surgeon to Royal Horse Guards; edited medical works.

GULLY, James Manby (1808–1883), physician; studied at Paris; MD, Edinburgh, 1829; practised in London and afterwards at Malvern, where he and his friend James Wilson introduced the hydropathic treatment of disease; the 'Dr Gullson' of Charles *Reade's *It is never too late to mend*; his reputation damaged by the Bravo case, 1876; published works, including *The Water Cure in Chronic Disease* (1846).

GULLY, John (1783–1863), prize-fighter and horse-racer; fought Henry Pearce, the 'Game Chicken', at Hailsham, 1805; leading boxer till 1808; won the Derby and the St Leger, 1832, the Derby and Oaks, 1846, the Two Thousand Guineas, 1844, and the Derby and Two Thousand Guineas, 1854; MP, Pontefract, 1832–7.

GULLY, William Court, first Viscount Selby (1835–1909), speaker of the House of Commons; son of James Manby *Gully; BA, Trinity College, Cambridge, 1856; president of Union; called to bar, 1860; QC, 1877; established good practice in commercial cases; Liberal MP for Carlisle, 1892; recorder of Wigan, 1892; elected speaker of the House of Commons, 1895; distinguished for dignity, courtesy, and impartiality; ordered forcible removal of Irish members from the House, Mar. 1901; resigned speakership and raised to peerage, 1905; hon. LL D, Cambridge, 1900, DCL, Oxford, 1904.

GULSTON, Joseph (1745–1786), collector and connoisseur; born at Greenwich in romantic circumstances; spent a large fortune chiefly in collecting books and prints, the sale of the latter (1786) lasting forty days; MP, Poole, 1780–4.

GULSTON, Theodore (1572–1632), founder of Gulstonian lecture. See GOULSTON.

GUMBLE, Thomas (*c.*1627–1676), biographer; MA, Caius College, Cambridge, 1650; chaplain to *Monck in Scotland, 1655; entrusted by him with letters to the parliament and city, 1660; DD, Cambridge and prebendary of Winchester, 1661; rector of East Lavant, Sussex, 1663; published *Life of General Monck, Duke of Albemarle* (1671).

GUNDLEUS, Saint (6th cent.). See GWYNLLYW.

GUNDRADA, de Warenne (d. 1085), wife of William de *Warenne, first earl of Surrey, and co-founder with him of Lewes Priory, 1077; her tombstone placed in St John's Church, Southover, Lewes, at end of eighteenth century.

GUNDRY, Sir Nathaniel (1701?–1754), judge; barrister, Middle Temple, 1725; MP, Dorchester, 1741–50; KC, 1742; judge of common pleas, 1750–4; died of gaol fever.

GUNDULF (1024?–1108), bishop of Rochester; made a pilgrimage with William, archdeacon of Rouen, to Jerusalem; monk of Bec; followed *Lanfranc to Caen and to England, and became his proctor; as bishop of Rochester (1077–1108) remodelled chapter on monastic basis and rebuilt cathedral; architect of the Tower of London, St Leonard's Tower, West Malling, and other buildings; had charge of see of Canterbury during vacancy, 1089; exercised influence over William II; was attended on his deathbed by *Anselm.

GUNN, Barnabas (d. 1753), musical composer; organist at Gloucester Cathedral, 1732–40, at St Philip's and St Martin's, Birmingham, 1740–53, and Chelsea Hospital, 1750–3; published *Six

Solos for Violin and Violoncello (1745) and songs and cantatas.

GUNN, Battiscombe George (1883–1950), Egyptologist; educated at Bedales, Westminster, and Allhallows; published *The Instruction of Ptah-hotep* (1906); worked at Harageh (1913–14), El-Amarna (1921–2), and Saqqara (1924–7); published *Studies in Egyptian Syntax* (1924); assistant keeper, Egyptian Museum, Cairo, 1928–31; curator, Egyptian section, University Museum, Philadelphia, 1931–4; professor of Egyptology, Oxford, 1934–50; edited *Journal of Egyptian Archaeology*, 1935–9; FBA, 1943.

GUNN, Daniel (1774–1848), Congregational minister; celebrated for his unemotional preaching and his schools at Christchurch, Hampshire.

GUNN, Sir James (1893–1964), painter; educated at Glasgow High School, Glasgow School of Art, Edinburgh College of Art, and the Académie Julien, Paris; commissioned with 10th Scottish Rifles, 1914–18; painted portraits of prime ministers, field marshals, judges, dons, bankers, and writers and artists, including *Belloc, *Chesterton, and Maurice *Baring (1932), and *Delius (1933); painted George VI and family at Windsor, and state portrait of Queen Elizabeth II (1956); followed Augustus *John as president, Royal Portrait Society, 1953; ARA, 1953; RA, 1961; knighted, 1963; honorary degrees, Manchester and Glasgow.

GUNN, John (*fl.* 1790), musical writer; published *Treatise on the Origin of Stringed Instruments* (1789) and a supplemental *Forty favourite Scotch Airs adapted for Violin, Violoncello, or Flute*, also *Historical Enquiry respecting the performances of the Harp in the Highlands* (1807) and works on the flute.

GUNN, Ronald Campbell (1808–1881), naturalist; superintendent of convict prisons in Tasmania, whence he sent home plants and animals; FLS, 1850; FRS, 1854; died at Hobart Town.

GUNN, William (1750–1841), antiquarian writer; BD, Caius College, Cambridge, 1795; rector of Barton Turf and Irstead, Norfolk, 1786–1829, and afterwards of Gorleston; published *Extracts* from state papers in the Vatican and other libraries (1803), a tenth-century manuscript of *Historia Britonum* (1819), and an account of the Vatican tapestries (1831).

GUNNING, Elizabeth, afterwards duchess of Hamilton and of Argyll (1734–1790), famous beauty; youngest daughter of James Gunning, of Castlecoote, Roscommon; secretly married James, sixth duke of Hamilton, at midnight in Mayfair Chapel, 14 Feb. 1752, and in 1759 John Campbell, afterwards duke of Argyll; lady of the bedchamber to Queen *Charlotte; created Baroness Hamilton, 1776.

GUNNING, Elizabeth (1769–1823), afterwards Mrs Plunkett; novelist; daughter of Susannah *Gunning.

GUNNING, Henry (1768–1854), senior esquire bedell of Cambridge University; scholar of Christ's College, Cambridge; fifth wrangler, 1788; MA, 1791; esquire bedell, 1789 (senior, 1827–54); published *Reminiscences of the University, Town, and County of Cambridge* (1854) and new edition of Wall's *Ceremonies observed in the Senate House*.

GUNNING, John (d. 1798), surgeon to St George's Hospital, 1765–98; as master of the Surgeons' Company (1789–90) effected many reforms; had violent controversies with John *Hunter, whom he succeeded as surgeon-general, 1793.

GUNNING, Maria, afterwards countess of Coventry (1733–1760). See COVENTRY.

GUNNING, Peter (1614–1684), bishop of Ely; ancestor of the famous beauties; MA, Clare Hall, Cambridge, 1635; fellow of Corpus Christi College, 1633–44; master, 1661; famous as Royalist preacher when incumbent of Little St Mary's; retired to Oxford, 1646; during the Commonwealth celebrated Episcopalian service at Exeter Chapel, Strand; DD, *per literas regias* 1660; Lady Margaret professor of divinity, 1660; master of St John's and regius professor, 1661; proctor for Canterbury and Peterborough in the Lower House of Convocation; prominent in Savoy Conference; bishop of Chichester, 1669–75, of Ely, 1675–84; his *Paschal or Lent Fast* (1662) republished (1845).

GUNNING, Sir Robert, baronet (1731–1816), diplomat; plenipotentiary at Copenhagen, 1768; transferred to Berlin, 1771; ambassador at St Petersburg, 1772–5; negotiated for employment of Russian troops in America, 1775; KB, 1778; created baronet, 1778.

GUNNING, Mrs Susannah (1740?–1800), novelist; née Minifie; married John Gunning (afterwards lieutenant-general), brother of the famous beauties, 1768; joined her daughter, Elizabeth *Gunning, when her husband turned the girl out of the house, both being received by the duchess of Bedford; published several novels; her *Memoirs of Mary* (1793) supposed to mention family scandals.

GUNTER, Edmund (1581–1626), mathematician; educated at Westminster and Christ Church, Oxford; MA, 1606; BD, 1615; incumbent of St George's, Southwark, 1615; Gresham professor of astronomy, 1619–26; discovered by experiments at Deptford variation of the magnetic needle, 1622; introduced 'Gunter's chain' and the decimal separator; 'Gunter's line' or rule of proportion described in his *Book of the Sector*; published *Canon Triangulorum; or, Table of Artificial Sines and Tangents* (1620); complete works edited by Samuel *Foster (1636) and William *Leybourn (1673).

GÜNTHER, Albert Charles Lewis Gotthilf (1830–1914), zoologist; born in Württemberg; took medical degree at Tübingen, 1858; appointed to staff of British Museum and naturalized, 1862; keeper of zoological department, 1875–95; vice-president of Royal Society, 1875–6; gold medallist of Royal and Linnean societies; works include *Catalogue of Fishes in the British Museum* (1859–70) and *Introduction to the Study of Fishes* (1880).

GUNTHER, Robert William Theodore (1869–1940), zoologist and antiquary; son of A. C. L. G. *Günther; educated at Magdalen College, Oxford; lecturer (1894), tutor (1896), in natural science, fellow (1897–1928); university reader in history of science, 1934–9; created Museum of the History of Science, Oxford, 1935; publications include 'Early Science in Oxford' series (1920–45).

GUNTHORPE (or GUNDORP), John (d. 1498), dean of Wells; chaplain to Edward IV; warden of the King's Hall at Cambridge, 1467–75; prebendary of Lincoln, 1471–98; dean of Wells, 1472–98; clerk of the parliaments, 1471; keeper of the privy seal, 1483; employed to treat with the emperor Maximilian, 1486, Ferdinand and Isabella, 1488, and other European princes; built deanery at Wells.

GUNTON, Simon (1609–1676), divine and antiquary; MA, Magdalene College, Cambridge, 1634; vicar of Pytchley, 1637, of Peterborough, 1660–6, and of Fiskerton, Lincolnshire, 1666–76; history of Peterborough Cathedral compiled from his collection issued (1686).

GURDON (or GORDON), Sir Adam de (d. 1305), warrior; fought against Henry III in Barons' War; repulsed Welsh, 1265; defeated in single combat by Prince Edward, 1266, who restored his estates; a justice of the forest and commissioner of array in Hampshire, Dorset, and Wiltshire under Edward I.

GURDON, Brampton (d. 1741), Boyle lecturer; fellow of Caius College, Cambridge; MA, 1695; chaplain to Lord *Macclesfield; archdeacon of Sudbury, 1727; rector of Denham, 1730, of St Edmund the King, Lombard Street, 1724–41; his Boyle lectures (1721–2), *The Pretended Difficulties in Natural or Reveal'd Religion no Excuse for Infidelity* printed (1723).

GURDON, John (1595?–1679), Parliamentarian; MP for Ipswich in Long Parliament; MP, Suffolk, 1654, and Sudbury, 1660; member of Eastern Counties Association; member of Council of State, 1650; refused to attend when commissioner for Charles I's trial.

GURDON, Thornhagh (1663–1733), antiquary; brother of Brampton *Gurdon; MA, Caius College, Cambridge, 1682; FSA, 1718; receiver-general of Norfolk; published *Essay on the Antiquity of the Castel of Norwich* (1728) and a history of parliament (1731).

GURNALL, William (1617–1679), divine; MA, Emmanuel College, Cambridge, 1639; rector of Lavenham, Suffolk, 1644–79; published *The Christian in Complete Armour* (1655, 1658, 1662).

GURNEY, Anna (1795–1857), Anglo-Saxon scholar; though paralysed throughout life visited Rome, Athens, and Argos; first female member (1845) of British Archaeological Association; published privately *Literal Translation of the Saxon Chronicle. By a Lady in the Country* (1819).

GURNEY, Archer Thompson (1820–1887), divine and author; son of Richard *Gurney; chaplain to the Court Chapel, Paris, 1858–71; published books of verse, including *Songs of the Present* (1854), and *Iphigenia at Delphi*, tragedy (1855); also translations from the German and prose treatises.

GURNEY, Daniel (1791–1880), banker and antiquary; FSA; printed privately essays on banking and *Record of the House of Gournay* (1858).

GURNEY (or GURNAY), Edmund (1577–1648), divine; BA, Queens' College, Cambridge, 1600; Norfolk fellow of Corpus Christi College, Cambridge, 1601; BD, 1609; rector of Edgefield, Norfolk, 1614, of Harpley, 1620; published anti-Romanist treatises.

GURNEY, Edmund (1847–1888), philosophical writer; third son of John Hampden *Gurney; fourth classic, 1871; fellow of Trinity College, Cambridge, 1872; studied successively music, medicine, and law; afterwards devoted himself to experimental psychology, and was one of the chief founders of the Society for Psychical Research, 1882, in whose *Proceedings* and *Journal* he wrote on hallucination and hypnotism; published *The Power of Sound* (1880), *Phantasms of the Living* (1886, with Frederic William Henry *Myers and F. Podmore), and *Tertium Quid* (1887).

GURNEY, Sir Goldsworthy (1793–1875), inventor; in a course of chemistry lectures at the Surrey Institution anticipated principle of electric telegraph; invented oxy-hydrogen blowpipe; and discovered the so-called 'Drummond light';

his steam-jet first applied to steamboats, 1824; with his steam carriage went from London to Bath and back at rate of fifteen miles an hour, 1829; extinguished mine fires by his steam-jet; principle of 'Gurney stove' applied in warming and ventilation of old House of Commons; superintended lighting and ventilation in new Houses of Parliament, 1854–63; knighted, 1863; published descriptions of his inventions and *Observations pointing out a means by which a Seaman may identify Lighthouses* (1864).

GURNEY, Sir Henry Lovell Goldsworthy (1898–1951), colonial civil servant; educated at Winchester and University College, Oxford; played golf for university; served in Kenya, 1921–35, 1936–44; secretary, East African Governors Conference co-ordinating defence and supply problems of the territories, 1938–44; chief secretary, 1941; colonial secretary, Gold Coast, 1944–6; as chief secretary, Palestine (1946–8), and high commissioner, Malaya (1948–51), worked closely with military authorities at time of great terrorist activity; CMG, 1942; knighted, 1947; KCMG, 1948; ambushed and killed, 1951.

GURNEY, Henry Palin (1847–1904), scientist; scholar of Clare College, Cambridge; fourteenth wrangler, 1870; fellow, 1870–83; partner of firm of Wren & Gurney, examination coaches, 1877; published book on crystallography, 1875; from 1894 to death principal of Durham College of Science (renamed Armstrong College, 1901), Newcastle upon Tyne; founded department of mineralogy and crystallography there, 1895; hon. DCL, Durham, 1896; killed in alpine accident near Arolla.

GURNEY, Hudson (1775–1864), antiquary and verse-writer; half-brother of Anna *Gurney; friend of Lord Aberdeen; MP, Newtown, Isle of Wight, from 1816; FRS, 1818; vice-president, Society of Antiquaries, 1822–46; published *Cupid and Psyche* (1799), *Heads of Ancient History* (1814), a verse translation of *Orlando Furioso* (1843), and *Norfolk Topographer's Manual* and *History of Norwich Castle.*

GURNEY, John (1688–1741), Quaker; friend of Sir Robert Walpole; ably defended Norwich wool-trade before parliamentary committee, 1720.

GURNEY, Sir John (1768–1845), judge; son of Joseph *Gurney (1744–1815); educated at St Paul's School; barrister, Inner Temple, 1793; junior counsel for Hardy, Horne *Tooke, and *Thelwall, 1794; defended Crossfield, 1796, and Arthur *O'Connor, 1798; KC after prosecuting Cochrane, 1816; procured conviction of two

Cato Street conspirators, 1820; baron of the Exchequer, 1832–45, and knighted, 1832.

GURNEY, John Hampden (1802–1862), author; eldest son of Sir John *Gurney; MA, Trinity College, Cambridge, 1827; rector of St Mary's, Bryanstone Square, 1847–62; prebendary of St Paul's, 1857. His works include *Psalms and Hymns for Public Worship* (1852) and three series of *Historical Sketches.*

GURNEY, Joseph (1744–1815), shorthand writer; son of Thomas *Gurney; employed on official reports of civil cases from 1790; ordered to read from his notes of the Warren *Hastings trial words of *Burke accusing Impey of murder, 1789; reported election petition committees, 1791; published thirteen reports, 1775–96; edited ninth edition of *Brachygraphy* (1778).

GURNEY, Joseph (1804–1879), shorthand writer and biblical scholar; son of William Brodie *Gurney; reporter to Houses of Parliament, 1849–72; published *The Annotated Paragraph Bible* (1850–60) and *The Revised English Bible* (1877).

GURNEY, Joseph John (1788–1847), Quaker philanthropist and writer; brother of Daniel *Gurney and Mrs Elizabeth *Fry; studied classics at Oxford; Quaker minister, 1818; interested in prison reform, negro emancipation, and the abolition of capital punishment; visited the chief European countries, and in 1837–40 the United States, Canada, and the West Indies; published *Essays on the Evidences, Doctrines, and Practical Operation of Christianity* (1825) and *Biblical Notes and Dissertations* (1830); his *Letters to Mrs. Opie* and *Autobiography* printed privately; his *Chalmeriana* published posthumously.

GURNEY (or GURNARD), Sir Richard, baronet (1577–1647), lord mayor of London, 1641–2; created baronet by Charles I; refused to call out the trained bands to keep the peace when the arrest of the five members was contemplated, 1642; imprisoned in the Tower, 1642–7, for causing to be read the king's proclamation against parliament's militia ordinance, 1642.

GURNEY, Richard (1790–1843), vice-warden of the stannaries of Devon, and author of *Fables on Men and Manners* (1809), *The Maid of Prague* (1841), and other works; died at Bonn.

GURNEY, Russell (1804–1878), recorder of London; son of Sir John *Gurney; BA, Trinity College, Cambridge, 1826; barrister, Inner Temple, 1828; common pleader in city of London, 1830; QC, 1845; judge of sheriff's court, 1850; common serjeant, 1856; recorder, 1857–78; MP, Southampton, 1865; took charge of Married Women's Property Bill (1870) and other important measures; commissioner in Jamaica, 1865, and for Treaty of Washington, 1871; privy councillor, 1866; FRS, 1875; served on many royal commissions.

GURNEY, Samuel (1786–1856), bill-discounter and philanthropist; brother of Joseph John *Gurney; entered firm of Richardson & Overend (afterwards Overend, Gurney & Co.), 1807; became known as 'the bankers' banker'; worked for reform of criminal code; interested in the Niger expedition of 1841, and the colony of Liberia; treasurer of British and Foreign School Society from 1843.

GURNEY, Thomas (1705–1770), shorthand writer; clockmaker near Blackfriars Road; shorthand teacher; his engagement at the Old Bailey the first official appointment of a shorthand writer; afterwards practised in other courts and in the House of Commons; his *Brachygraphy* (1750) originally an improvement on William *Mason's *Shorthand*, frequently reissued and improved. Gurney's 'System' was employed by Sir Henry *Cavendish, and later for most government and parliamentary work.

GURNEY, William Brodie (1777–1855), shorthand writer and philanthropist; brother of Sir John *Gurney; reported trials, speeches, etc., throughout the United Kingdom, 1803–44; official reporter to parliament from 1813; mentioned in *Don Juan*; edited fifteenth and sixteenth editions of *Brachygraphy* (1824–35), and the *Youth's Magazine* (commenced 1805); president of Sunday School Union; treasurer of Stepney College and the Baptist foreign missions.

GURWOOD, John (1790–1845), editor of the *Wellington Despatches*; served in Peninsula as subaltern of 52nd till storming of Ciudad Rodrigo, 1812, where he was severely wounded; exchanged into cavalry; aide-de-camp to Sir Henry *Clinton in the Netherlands; severely wounded at Waterloo; brevet-colonel, 1841; as private secretary to Wellington edited his despatches, 1837–44; CB and deputy-lieutenant of the Tower; committed suicide.

GUSTUN (or GUNSTUM), Roger of (*fl.* 1170), Cistercian monk. See ROGER OF FORD.

GUTCH, John (1746–1831), antiquary and divine; MA, All Souls College, Oxford, 1771; chaplain of All Souls, 1770, of Corpus Christi College, Oxford, 1778; registrar of the university, 1797–1824; rector of St Clement's, 1795–1831; published *Collectanea Curiosa* (1781) and, from Wood's manuscripts, *History and Antiquities of the Colleges and Halls in the University of Oxford* (1786), *Fasti Oxonienses* (1790), and *History of the University of Oxford* (1792–6).

GUTCH, John Mathew (1776–1861), journalist; eldest son of John *Gutch; at Christ's Hospital with *Coleridge and *Lamb; lodged with Lamb, 1800; removed to Bristol, 1803, and conducted *Felix Farley's Bristol Journal* till 1844; prosecuted for libels on George IV and Lord Lyndhurst in London *Morning Journal*, 1829; edited George *Wither's *Poems* (1820) and Robin Hood *Ballads* (1850 and 1867); called the 'Bristol Junius' from his *Letters of Cosmo*.

GUTCH, John Wheeley Gough (1809–1862), queen's messenger; son of John Mathew *Gutch; edited *Literary and Scientific Register*, 1842–56.

GUTCH, Robert (1777–1851), divine; second son of John *Gutch; fellow of Queens' College, Cambridge, 1802; MA, 1804; rector of Seagrave, Leicestershire, 1809–51; published anonymously satirical tract on a Roman Catholic miracle (1836).

GUTHLAC, Saint (663?–714), of the Mercian royal race; after a youth spent in war entered monastic community at Repton; hermit in the Isle of Crowland for fifteen years; visited by *Ethelbald, who, on becoming king of Mercia, built over his shrine Crowland Abbey.

GUTHRIE, Sir David (*fl.* 1479), lord treasurer of Scotland; sheriff of Forfarshire, 1457, and armour-bearer to *James II; lord treasurer of Scotland, 1461 and 1467; comptroller of the household, 1466; clerk of the register, 1468; master of the Rolls, 1469; lord chief justice, 1473; founded collegiate church at Guthrie.

GUTHRIE, Frederick (1833–1886), scientific writer; BA, London, 1855; Ph.D., Marburg, 1854; studied under Bunsen at Heidelberg; assisted *Frankland at Owens College and Playfair at Edinburgh; professor of chemistry and physics in Royal College, Mauritius, 1861–7; afterwards professor in the Normal School of Science, South Kensington; founded Physical Society of London, 1873; discovered 'approach caused by vibration', 1870, and 'cryohydrates'; published *Elements of Heat* (1868) and *Magnetism and Electricity* (1873), and under the pseudonym Frederick Cerny, poems, *The Jew* (1863) and *Logroño* (1877).

GUTHRIE, George James (1785–1856), surgeon; with the 29th in Canada as assistant-surgeon; in the Peninsula, 1808–14; at Waterloo performed several novel operations; declined knighthood; founded Eye Infirmary (afterwards Westminster Ophthalmic Hospital), 1816; surgeon to Westminster Hospital, 1827–43; professor of anatomy and surgery, 1828–31, and president of College of Surgeons, 1833, 1841, and 1854; gave Hunterian oration without note, 1830; published *Commentaries on the Surgery of the*

War (1808–15), 1853, with supplement, including the Crimean War (1855), and separate treatises on gunshot wounds, on operative surgery of the eye, and arterial affections.

GUTHRIE (or GUTHRY), Henry (1600?–1676), bishop of Dunkeld; MA, St Andrews, 1620; minister of Stirling, 1632–48; member of the High Commission, 1634; opposed Laudian policy and took the Covenant, but as a member of the general assembly opposed the 'root and branch' abolition of Episcopacy, and favoured the 'engagement' of 1647; dismissed as a malignant, but admitted minister of Kilspindie, 1656, and restored at Stirling, 1661; bishop of Dunkeld, 1665–76; his *Memoirs of Scottish Affairs, 1637 to Death of Charles I* published (1702).

GUTHRIE, James (1612?–1661), Presbyterian divine; MA and regent, St Andrews; became Presbyterian under influence of *Rutherford; minister of Lauder, 1642–9; member of general assembly, 1644–51; commissioner to Charles I at Newcastle, 1646; minister of Stirling, 1649–61; excommunicated *Middleton, 1650; deposed as an extreme 'protester', 1651; named a 'trier' by the English Privy Council, 1654; refused reparation for insults from 'resolutions' by *Cromwell, 1656; hanged at Edinburgh for contriving the 'western remonstrance' and rejecting the king's ecclesiastical authority, 1661; his attainder reversed, 1690.

GUTHRIE, Sir James (1859–1930), portrait painter and president of the Royal Scottish Academy; almost entirely self-trained; associated with 'Glasgow School'; portrait painter in Glasgow, 1885; president of Royal Scottish Academy, 1902–19; removed to Edinburgh; RSA, 1892; knighted, 1903; painted 'War Statesmen' group for National Portrait Gallery, London.

GUTHRIE, John (d. 1649), bishop of Moray; MA, St Andrews, 1597; minister successively of Kinnel, Arbirlot, Perth (1617) and St Giles's, Edinburgh (1621); bishop of Moray, 1623–38; preached before Charles I in his rochet, 1633; deposed and brought by Monro to the estates, who imprisoned him in the Tolbooth, 1639; allowed to retire to Guthrie.

GUTHRIE, Thomas (1803–1873), preacher and philanthropist; studied at Edinburgh, subsequently in Paris; minister of Arbirlot, 1830–7, Old Greyfriars, Edinburgh, 1837–40, St John's, 1840–64; joined Free Church, 1843, followed by most of his congregation; moderator, 1862; DD, Edinburgh, 1849; the apostle of ragged schools; platform speaker in cause of temperance; first editor of *Sunday Magazine*, 1864–73; published *Plea for Ragged Schools* (1847–9), *Plea on behalf of Drunkards* (1851), and devotional works.

GUTHRIE, Thomas Anstey (1856–1934), humorous writer under pseudonym of F. Anstey; educated at King's College School and Trinity Hall, Cambridge; *Vice-Versa* (1882), *The Brass Bottle* (1900), and *Only Toys!* (1903) the most successful of his fantastic novels based on magic; in contributions to *Punch* developed talent for burlesque and parody.

GUTHRIE, William (1620–1665), Presbyterian divine; cousin of James *Guthrie; MA, St Andrews, 1638; minister of Fenwick, Ayrshire ('the fool of Fenwick'), 1644–64; army chaplain at Mauchline Moor, 1648; joined 'protesters', 1651; a 'trier', 1654; struggled against Episcopacy after the Restoration; his *The Christian's Great Interest* frequently reprinted and translated.

GUTHRIE, William (1708–1770), author; educated at Aberdeen; wrote reports for the *Gentleman's Magazine*, c.1730; obtained pension from Pelham ministry, 1745; published works, including *A General History of the World* (1764–7) and *Geographical, Historical, and Commercial Grammar* (1770); referred to with respect by Dr *Johnson.

GUTHRIE, William (1835–1908), legal writer; educated at Glasgow and Edinburgh universities; called to Scottish bar, 1861; registrar of friendly societies for Scotland, 1872; hon. LL D, Edinburgh, 1881; sheriff-principal at Glasgow, 1903; edited many legal works.

GUTHRIE, (William) Keith (Chambers) (1906–1981), classical scholar; educated at Dulwich College and Trinity College, Cambridge; first class, classical tripos, parts i and ii, 1926 and 1928; Browne university scholar, 1927; Craven student, 1928; Chancellor's Medal, 1929; took part in archaeological expeditions to Asia Minor, 1929–32; mainly interested in Greek religion and philosophy; bye-fellow (1930) and full fellow, Peterhouse (1932); university lecturer, 1935; during 1939–45 war served in Intelligence Corps; Laurence reader, Cambridge, 1947; Laurence professor of ancient philosophy, 1952–73; public orator, 1939–57; master, Downing College, 1957–72; publications include *Orpheus and Greek Religion* (1935), *The Greeks and their Gods* (1950), *The Greek Philosophers* (1950) and his Messenger lectures at Cornell, *In the Beginning* (1957); invited by Cambridge University Press to undertake *History of Greek Philosophy*, 1956; completed volume on Aristotle, 1981; FBA, 1952; hon. fellow, Downing and Peterhouse; president, Classical Association, 1967–8; Litt.D., Cambridge, 1959; hon. D.Litt., Melbourne, 1957 and Sheffield, 1967.

GUTHRIE, Sir (William) Tyrone (1900–1971), director, and theatre designer; cousin of Tyrone Power, film actor; educated at Wellington College, and St John's College, Oxford, of which he was a scholar; joined company of J. B. *Fagan at the Playhouse, Oxford, but gave up acting to become a director; directed *The Anatomist* by James *Bridie at Westminster Theatre, with Henry *Ainley and Flora *Robson, 1931; appointed by Lilian *Baylis director of plays at the Old Vic and Sadler's Wells, 1933; appointed administrator after Lilian Baylis's death, 1937; resigned, 1947; directed *Ane Satyre of the Three Estaits* in the Assembly Hall of the Church of Scotland at second Edinburgh Festival, 1948; the audience on three sides of the stage gave Guthrie a new enthusiasm; established Stratford Ontario Festival in second largest theatrical tent in the western hemisphere, 1952; theatre in Minneapolis based on principles worked out at Edinburgh, 1963; influenced building of new theatres, including Chichester Festival Theatre (1962) and the Olivier (1976); knighted, 1961; chancellor of Queen's University, Belfast, 1963–70; hon. fellow, St John's College, Oxford, 1964; received number of honorary degrees; published *A Life in the Theatre* (1960).

GUTHRUM (or GUTHORM) (d. 890), king of East Anglia; one of the Danish invaders who conquered Mercia, 871, and waged war with *Alfred; became a Christian after the Battle of Ethandun, and by the Treaty of Wedmore, 878, was given East Anglia (including Essex and London) as his share of the Danish kingdom; broke the treaty by aiding the foreign Norsemen to attack Wessex, and lost London and Western Essex, 886.

GUTHRY, Henry (1600?–1676), bishop of Dunkeld. See GUTHRIE.

GUTO Y GLYN (*fl.* 1430–1468), Welsh poet; domestic bard to abbot of Valle Crucis (Glyn Egwestl); made triennial circuits of Wales; 119 of his poems said to be extant.

GUTTERIDGE, Harold Cooke (1876–1953), barrister and professor; born in Naples; educated there, at Leys School, and King's College, Cambridge; first class, history (1898), law (1899); called to bar (Middle Temple), 1900; KC, 1930; Sir Ernest Cassel professor of industrial and commercial law, London, 1919–30; reader, later professor, in comparative law, Cambridge, 1930–41; publications include *Smith's Mercantile Law*, 13th edn. (1931), *Bankers' Commercial Credits* (1932), and *Comparative Law* (1946).

GUTTERIDGE, William (1798–1872), violinist and organist; led band of Brussels theatre, 1815, and afterwards at Birmingham; member of George IV's and William IV's bands; organist of St Peter's, Brighton, from 1828; conductor and leader of New Harmonic Society; formed one of a quartet with King George and the future kings of the Belgians and Hanover, and accompanied Queen Victoria in 1837.

GUTTERIDGE, William (*fl.* 1813), bandmaster of the 62nd; published *The Art of playing Gutteridge's Clarinet* (1824).

GUTTMANN, Sir Ludwig (1899–1980), neurosurgeon; born of Jewish parents in Tost, Upper Silesia, then in Poland; educated in Königshütte, Breslau, Würzburg, and Freiburg; MD, Freiburg, 1924; worked with Professor Otfrid Foerster in Breslau; forced by Nazis to leave Aryan hospital 1933; became neurologist and neurosurgeon to Jewish hospital, Breslau; medical director, 1937; allowed to visit England, 1928; emigrated from Germany, 1939; worked in Oxford under (Sir) Hugh *Cairns; started centre for paraplegics at Stoke Mandeville, 1944; encouraged patients to take part in sports, 1947; started Olympic Games for Paralysed; medical staff from many countries visited Stoke Mandeville for training; centres named after Guttmann in Spain, West Germany, and Israel; published *Spinal Cord Injuries* (1973, 2nd edn., 1976) and *Textbook of Sport for the Disabled* (1976); founded *Paraplegia* and the International Society for Paraplegia; naturalized, 1945; OBE, 1950; CBE, 1960; knighted, 1966; FRCS, 1961; FRCP, 1962; FRS and hon. FRCP(C), 1976; received number of honorary degrees and many foreign honours.

GUY, Henry (1631–1710), politician; admitted at the Inner Temple, 1652; MA, Christ Church, Oxford, 1663; MP, Hedon (Yorkshire), 1670–95 and 1702–5, where he erected a town hall, 1693; boon companion of Charles II; secretary to the Treasury, 1679–88 and 1691–5; sent to the Tower for receiving a bribe; granted the manor of Great Tring and other property; left money to William *Pulteney.

GUY, Sir Henry Lewis (1887–1956), chartered mechanical engineer; educated at Penarth County School; diploma in mechanical and electrical engineering, University College, South Wales, 1909; joined British Westinghouse; chief engineer, mechanical department, Metropolitan-Vickers Electrical Company, 1918–41; secretary, Institution of Mechanical Engineers, 1941–51; member, advisory councils of Ministry of Supply and Department of Scientific and Industrial Research, committee of National Physical Laboratory, and many other technical bodies; FRS, 1936; CBE, 1943; knighted, 1949.

GUY, John (d. 1628?), governor of Newfoundland; sheriff, 1605–6, mayor, 1618–19; MP, Bristol, 1620–8; published (1609) appeal for colonization of Newfoundland; led out a body of planters, 1610; wrote (1612) account of voyage to Trinity Bay; returned to Bristol.

GUY, Thomas (1645?–1724), founder of Guy's Hospital; educated at Tamworth; admitted to Stationers' Company, 1668; set up as bookseller in London, 1668; one of the Oxford University printers, 1679–92; imported Dutch type and sold bibles; MP, Tamworth, 1695–1707; built Tamworth Town Hall (1701) and founded an almshouse; lived penurious life, but was liberal; from 1704 an active governor of St Thomas's Hospital; greatly increased his fortune by selling his South Sea stock; erected at a cost of £18,793 a new hospital (leaving £200,000 for its endowment), which was to receive incurables and lunatics, though discretion was left to the governors. By his will (reprinted 1732) Guy also left benefactions to Christ's Hospital and the debtors of London, Middlesex, and Surrey.

GUY, William Augustus (1810–1885), medical statistician; educated at Christ's Hospital and Guy's Hospital; studied at Heidelberg and Paris; MB, Cambridge, 1837; professor of forensic medicine at King's College, London, 1842; assistant physician at King's College Hospital, 1842, dean of the faculty of medicine, 1846–58; edited *Journal* of Statistical Society, 1852–6; president of Statistical Society, 1873–5; vice-president of Royal Society, 1876–7; Croonian (1861), Lumleian (1868), and Harveian (1875) lecturer at College of Physicians; a founder of the Health of Towns Association; member of commission on penal servitude and criminal lunacy; published *Principles of Forensic Medicine* (1844), *Public Health* (1870–4), and statistical papers.

GUYLDFORDE, Sir **Richard** (1455?–1506). See GUILDFORD.

GUY OF WARWICK, hero of romance; reputed son of Siward of Wallingford; when page of Roalt or Rohand, earl of Warwick, falls in love with his daughter Felice; wins her after fighting against the Saracens and slaying the Northumbrian dragon; journeys as a palmer to the Holy Land, and on his return slays in single combat, before Winchester, the Danish giant Colbrand; leads ascetic life at Warwick until death. The story, current in Winchester in the fourteenth century, was accepted as authentic by the chroniclers and was versified by *Lydgate, c.1450. At Warwick the Beauchamp earls assumed descent from Guy, Earl Richard erecting a chantry for the repose of his soul, 1423, one of the priests of which, John *Rous, treated the legends as authentic, and was followed by *Dugdale in his *Warwickshire*. Samuel *Pegge (1781) first showed their unhistorical character. The thirteenth-century French poem was first printed 1525, the English version some years later.

GUYON, Richard Debaufre (1803–1856), general in the Hungarian Army; some time in the Austrian service; received command of the landsturm and the honveds in 1848 and won for the Hungarians the battles of Sukoro (1848), Schewechat (1848), and the pass of Branitzko; raised the siege of Komorn (1849) and defeated the ban of Croatia at Hegyes, 1849; after the surrender of Görgey (1849), took service with the sultan; as lieutenant-general (1852) with title of Khourschid Pasha, the first Christian to be given a command; did good service against the Russians in Anatolia, 1853–5; removed after Kurekdere, 1855; died of cholera at Scutari.

GUYSE, John (1680–1761), Independent minister at Hertford and in New Broad Street; had controversy with Samuel *Chandler, 1729–31; DD, Aberdeen, 1733; published *Exposition of the New Testament in form of paraphrase* (1739–52).

GUYTON, Mrs **Emma Jane** (1825–1887), author. See WORBOISE.

GWATKIN, Henry Melvill (1844–1916), historian, theologian, and conchologist; BA, St John's College, Cambridge; Dixie professor of ecclesiastical history, Cambridge, 1891–1916; Gifford lecturer, Edinburgh, 1903; works include *Studies of Arianism* (1882), *The Knowledge of God* (1906), and *Early Church History* (1909); a distinguished teacher.

GWAVAS, William (1676–1741), writer in Cornish; corresponded with Thomas *Tonkin, Edward *Lhuyd, and John *Keigwin on the old Cornish language; his writings among British Museum manuscripts.

GWENFREWI. See WINEFRIDE.

GWENT, Richard (d. 1543), archdeacon of London; fellow of All Souls College, Oxford, 1515; DCL, 1525; advocate for Queen *Catherine, 1529; rector of two London parishes; dean of arches, 1532; archdeacon of London, 1534–43; prolocutor of Convocation, 1536, 1540, 1541; archdeacon of Huntingdon, 1542; prebendary of St Paul's, 1542; eulogized by Leland.

GWENWYNWYN (d. 1218?), prince of Upper Powys; succeeded Owain Cyveiliog, 1197; fought against the English and *Llywelyn ab Iorwerth; granted lands in Derbyshire by King John; joined Llewelyn against King John, 1215; having made peace with the English was driven into Cheshire and lost his territory, 1216; Powys Gwenwynwyn named after him.

GWILT, Charles Perkins (d. 1835), antiquarian writer; eldest son of Joseph *Gwilt.

GWILT, George, the elder (1746–1807), architect; surveyor of Surrey, c.1770, district surveyor of St George's, Southwark, 1774, and surveyor to Surrey Sewers Commission, c.1777; patronized by Henry Thrale the brewer; architect to West India Dock Company.

GWILT, George, the younger (1775–1856), architect; son of George *Gwilt the elder; superintended rebuilding of tower of St Mary-le-Bow, 1820, and (gratuitously) restoration of St Mary Overy, Southwark, 1822–5; FSA, 1815.

GWILT, John Sebastian (1811–1890), architect; second son of Joseph *Gwilt; made drawings for the *Encyclopaedia of Architecture.*

GWILT, Joseph (1784–1863), architect and archaeologist; son of George *Gwilt the elder; educated at St Paul's School; surveyor of Surrey, 1807–46; designed Markree Castle, Sligo, the approaches to Southwark Bridge, and St Thomas's Church, Charlton; FSA, 1815; MRAS, 1838; published works, including *Treatise on the Equilibrium of Arches* (1811), *Sciography* (1822), a translation of Vitruvius (1826), and *Encyclopaedia of Architecture* (1842).

GWILYM, David ap (14th cent.). See DAVID.

GWILYM LLEYN (1802–1865), Welsh bibliographer. See ROWLANDS, WILLIAM.

GWIN, Robert (*fl.* 1591), Roman Catholic divine; BA, Corpus Christi College, Oxford, 1568; BD, Douai, 1575; preacher in Wales; translated *The Resolution* of Robert Parsons into Welsh.

GWINNE, Matthew (1558?–1627), physician; of Merchant Taylors' School and St John's College, Oxford; fellow; MA, 1582; junior proctor, 1588; MD, 1593; first Gresham professor of physic, 1598–1607; FRCP, 1605; disputed before Queen Elizabeth (1592) and James I (1605) at Oxford; friend of *Florio, to whose works he contributed sonnets, as 'Il Candido'; refuted Francis *Anthony's view of 'aurum potabile', 1611; published also two Latin plays, *Nero*, acted at St John's College (1603), *Vertumnus* at Magdalen College (1605).

GWINNET, Richard (d. 1717), dramatist; corresponded as 'Pylades' with Elizabeth *Thomas (*Dryden's 'Corinna'); with their published correspondence (1732) appeared his play *The Country Squire.*

GWYER, Sir Maurice Linford (1878–1952), lawyer and civil servant; educated at Highgate, Westminster, and Christ Church, Oxford; fellow, All Souls, 1902; called to bar (Inner Temple), 1903; KC, 1930; on legal staff, National Health Insurance Commission, 1912, Ministry of Shipping, 1917; legal adviser, Ministry of Health, 1919–26; Treasury solicitor and King's proctor, 1926–34; first parliamentary counsel to Treasury, 1934–7; drafted Government of India Bill; chief justice of India, 1937–43; vice-chancellor, Delhi University, 1938–50; CB, 1921; KCB, 1928; KCSI, 1935; GCIE, 1948; honorary degrees from Oxford and Indian universities.

GWYN, David (*fl.* 1588), poet; published a metrical narrative of his imprisonment in Spain (1588).

GWYN, Eleanor ('Nell') (1650–1687), actress and mistress of Charles II; sold oranges in Theatre Royal, Drury Lane; first appeared at Drury Lane as Cydaria in *Dryden's *Indian Emperor*, 1665; continued to play there till 1670; appeared at Dorset Garden, 1677–8, and again at Drury Lane, 1682; illiterate, but good in comedy, prologues, and epilogues; rival of the duchess of Portsmouth with Charles II, retaining his favour till death; one of her sons by the king created duke of St Albans, 1684; her portrait painted by *Lely.

GWYN, Francis (1648?–1734), politician; friend of Rochester; MP, Chippenham, 1673–9, Cardiff, 1685, Christchurch, 1689–95, Callington, 1695–8, Totnes, 1699–1701 and 1710–15, Wells, 1673–1727; under-secretary of state, 1681–3 and 1688–9; privy councillor, 1701; Irish secretary, 1701; commissioner of trade, 1711–13; secretary-at-war, 1713–14; his diary of James II's expedition to the west (1688) printed, 1886.

GWYNLLYW (or GUNLYU) (6th cent.), called Gwynllyw Filwr, 'the Warrior' Welsh saint (Gundleus); reputed eldest of six sons of Glywys, a South Welsh king and hermit; Gunlyu's tomb, where miracles were worked, supposed site of St Woolos Church, Newport-on-Usk.

GWYNN (GWYN or GWYNNE), John (d. 1786), architect; with S. Wale published (1749) Wren's *Plan for rebuilding the City of London after the great fire in 1666*, and a plan of St Paul's and other works; member of committee for creating Royal Academy, 1755; an original member, 1768; as surveyor at Oxford designed Magdalen Bridge, 1772; built also the 'English' Bridge at Shrewsbury (finished, 1774), and Worcester Bridge (finished, 1780); friend of Dr *Johnson, who assisted in several of his writings; proposal for establishing an academy of art contained in his *Essay on Design* (1749).

GWYNN, John (1827–1917), scholar and divine; BA and fellow, Trinity College, Dublin; country parson in County Donegal, 1864–82; regius professor of divinity, Trinity College, Dublin, 1888–1917; published numerous Syriac studies and edition of *Book of Armagh* (1913).

GWYNN, Stephen Lucius (1864–1950), author and Irish nationalist; son of John *Gwynn and grandson of W. S. *O'Brien; educated at St Columba's College, Dublin, and Brasenose College, Oxford; first class, Lit. Hum., 1886; Nationalist MP, Galway City, 1906–18; on Irish Convention, 1917; published *The Queen's Chronicler and Other Poems* (1901), lives of *Scott (1930), *Swift (1933), *Goldsmith (1935), and R. L. *Stevenson (1939), and many books on Ireland.

GWYNNE, Howell Arthur (1865–1950), journalist; educated at Swansea Grammar School; special and war correspondent, Reuter's, 1893–1904; organized its South African War service, 1899–1902; editor, *Standard*, 1904–11; *Morning Post*, 1911–37; supported tariff reform and by his intimacy with all those of note who shared his convictions maintained prestige (but not circulation) of the paper; CH, 1938.

GWYNNE, John (*fl.* 1660), captain in Charles I's guards; distinguished himself in first Civil War; with *Montrose, 1650, *Middleton, 1654, and the duke of York at Dunkirk, 1658; his statement of services published (1822) by Sir Walter *Scott as *Military Memoirs of the Great Civil War*.

GWYNNE, Nell (1650–1687), actress and mistress of Charles II. See GWYN, ELEANOR.

GWYNNE, Robert (*fl.* 1591), Roman Catholic divine. See GWIN.

GWYNNE-JONES, Allen (1892–1982), artist; educated at Bedales School; qualified as solicitor but never practised; painted East Anglian subjects and fairs including large oil in Tate Gallery, 1937–8; student at Slade School of Fine Art, 1914, but joined 1st Cheshire Regiment at outbreak of 1914–18 war; DSO, 1916; transferred to Welsh Guards until 1919; rejoined Slade, encouraged by Henry *Tonks; won several prizes, 1920–2; joined staff of Royal College of Art, 1923; studied etching; senior lecturer at Slade, 1930–59; painted portraits of many distinguished sitters; also made countless flower paintings; ARA, 1955; RA, 1965; CBE, 1980; trustee, Tate Gallery, 1939–46; published *Portrait Painters* (1950) and *Introduction to Still-Life* (1954).

GWYNNETH, John (*fl.* 1557), Roman Catholic divine and musician; Mus.Doc., Oxford, 1531; rector of Clynog, St Peter, Westcheap (1543), and vicar of Luton, 1554; published treatises against John *Frith's works and 'My love mourneth' (1530), with other musical compositions.

GWYNNE-VAUGHAN, Dame Helen Charlotte Isabella (1879–1967), botanist and leader of women's services in both world wars; educated at Cheltenham Ladies' College and King's College, London; B.Sc. in botany, 1904; D.Sc., for thesis on fungi, 1907; demonstrator for V. H. *Blackman, University College, London, 1904; assistant lecturer, Royal Holloway College, 1905; lecturer, University College of Nottingham, 1907; head of department of botany, Birkbeck College, London, 1909; fellow of Linnean Society; founded, with Dr Louisa Garrett Anderson, University of London Suffrage Society, 1907; joint chief controller, Women's Army Auxiliary Corps in France, 1917; CBE, 1918; commandant, Women's Royal Air Force, 1918–19; DBE, 1919; professor of botany, Birkbeck College, 1921; member, Royal Commission on Food Prices, 1924; president, Mycological Society, 1928; GBE, 1929; first director, Auxiliary Territorial Service, 1939–41; disagreements with senior officers brought about enforced resignation; returned to Birkbeck College, 1941–4; hon. LL D, Glasgow, 1920; published many scientific studies and two textbooks on fungi; also her autobiographical *Service with the Army* (1942).

GYBSON. See GIBSON.

GYE, Frederick, the elder (1781–1869), entertainment manager; with £30,000 won in a lottery established wine and tea companies; bought and conducted Vauxhall Gardens, 1821–40; MP, Chippenham, 1826–30.

GYE, Frederick, the younger (1810–1878), director of Italian opera; son of Frederick *Gye the elder; assisted Jullien in promenade concerts of 1846, and as acting manager at Drury Lane, 1847; leased Covent Garden for opera, 1849, and as manager produced *Le Prophète, Rigoletto* (1853), and other pieces; carried on opera at the Lyceum till the opening of new Covent Garden Theatre, 1858, where Patti (1861), Lucca (1863), and Albani (1873) made their débuts, and the first Wagner operas were given, 1875–6; with Mapleson carried on Covent Garden and Her Majesty's in conjunction, 1869–70; accidentally shot.

GYLBY, Goddred (*fl.* 1561), translator. See GILBY.

GYLES (or GILES), Henry (1640?–1709), glass-painter; friend of Ralph *Thoresby; revived pictorial glass-work in England, *c.*1682; his best-known work the east window of University College, Oxford.

GYLES, Mascal (d. 1652), divine; BA, Pembroke College, Cambridge, 1618–19; vicar of Ditchling, Sussex, 1621–44, and Wartling, 1648–52; published against Thomas *Barton; his *Treatise against Superstitious Jesu-Worship* (1642) and *Defense* (1643).

Gyrth

GYRTH (d. 1066), earl of East Anglia, 1057–66; fourth son of *Godwine; accompanied *Tostig to Rome, 1061; probably with *Harold at Stamford Bridge, 1066; according to the *Roman de Rou* advised Harold to leave him (Gyrth) to lead the army against William the Norman; said to have slain William's horse at Hastings before being struck down by him.

H

HAAK, Theodore (1605–1690), translator; born at Neuhausen; came to England, 1625; studied at Oxford; employed by parliament to translate *Dutch Annotations upon the whole Bible* (1657); suggested idea of Royal Society, *c.*1645, and became an original member, 1663; translated into High Dutch blank verse half of *Paradise Lost*.

HAAST, Sir John Francis Julius von (1824–1887), geologist and explorer; discovered coal- and gold-fields south-west of Nelson, New Zealand, 1859; as surveyor-general of Canterbury carried on ten years' exploration, 1861–71, discovering the Southern Alps; professor of geology in New Zealand university and (1866) founder of Canterbury Museum; FRS, 1867; knighted in connection with Colonial Exhibition of 1885; published *Geology of . . . Canterbury and Westland* (1879); died at Wellington.

HABERSHON, Matthew (1789–1852), architect; exhibited at Royal Academy, 1807–27; visited Jerusalem (1852) to arrange for erection of Anglican cathedral; received from king of Prussia Gold Medal for his *Ancient half-timbered Houses of England* (1836); published works on prophecy.

HABERSHON, Samuel Osborne (1825–1889), physician; studied at Guy's Hospital; MD, London, 1851; physician to Guy's Hospital, 1866–80; lecturer on materia medica, 1856–73, and medicine, 1873–7; FRCP, 1856; Lumleian lecturer, 1876, Harveian orator, 1883, and vice-president of College of Physicians, 1887; president of London Medical Society, 1873; published works on diseases of the abdomen, stomach, and liver.

HABINGTON (ABINGTON or ABINGDON), Edward (1553?–1586), conspirator in *Babington's plot; BA, Exeter College, Oxford, 1574; a leading conspirator in Babington's plot, 1586; hanged and quartered, denying his guilt.

HABINGTON (or ABINGTON), Thomas (1560–1647), antiquary; brother of Edward *Habington; studied at Lincoln College, Oxford, Paris, and Reims; imprisoned for complicity in *Babington's plot, 1586; constructed in his house secret chambers and hid Jesuits; the letter warning *Monteagle of Gunpowder Plot said to have been written by his wife; published translation of *Gildas (1638 and 1641); his collections

for history of Worcestershire issued (1717 and 1723).

HABINGTON, William (1605–1654), poet; son of Thomas *Habington; educated in France; married Lucy Herbert, daughter of William, first Baron Powis, whom he celebrated as *Castara* (1634); published also *The Queene of Arragon*, tragicomedy (1640) and two historical works. *Castara* was reprinted by Arber (1870); *The Queene of Arragon* is in *Dodsley's collection.

HACK, Maria (1777–1844), writer of children's books, including *Grecian Stories* (1819) and *English Stories* (1820, 1825).

HACKER, Arthur (1858–1919), painter; studied at Royal Academy Schools and in Paris; painted subject pictures, chief being *The Annunciation* (1892), London street scenes, and portraits; ARA, 1894; RA, 1910.

HACKER, Francis (d. 1660), regicide; captured at Melton Mowbray, 1643, and again at fall of Leicester, 1645; commanded Parliamentarian left wing at Royalist defeat at Willoughby Field, 1648; commanded regiment in Scottish War under *Cromwell; charged with custody of Charles I at Westminster Hall; supervised Charles I's execution; supported protectorate; followed Haslerig in opposition to the army, 1659; hanged as regicide.

HACKET, George (d. 1756). See HALKET.

HACKET, James Thomas (1805?–1876), astrologer; author of *Student's Assistant in Astronomy and Astrology* (1836); contributed statistical tables to *Herapath's *Railway and Commercial Journal*.

HACKET, John (1590–1670), bishop of Coventry and Lichfield; educated at Westminster and Trinity College, Cambridge; chaplain to Lord-Keeper Williams; incumbent of St Andrew's, Holborn, 1624–45, and Cheam, Surrey, 1624; chaplain to Charles I and II; prebendary of Lincoln, 1623; archdeacon of Bedford, 1631; attempted to moderate *Laud's zeal; as member of Committee of Religion made able speech before Commons in defence of deans and chapters, 1641; after the Restoration resumed preaching at St Paul's as canon residentiary; bishop of Coventry and Lichfield, 1661–70; restored Lichfield Cathedral, partly at his own expense; bequeathed money to Trinity College, Cambridge, and his books to the university; chief work, *Scrinia Reserata* (first published, 1693), a life of Archbishop Williams.

HACKET (HACQUET or HECQUET), John-Baptist (d. 1676), theologian; originally a Dominican of Cashel; teacher at Milan, Naples, and Rome, where he died; published theological works.

HACKET, Roger (1559–1621), divine; of Winchester and New College, Oxford; fellow, 1577; MA, 1583; DD, 1596; rector of North Crawley, Buckinghamshire, 1590–1621.

HACKET, William (d. 1591), fanatic; announced mission to prepare the way for the Messiah; imprisoned for reviling Queen Elizabeth; with Edmund *Coppinger proposed to dethrone the queen and abolish Episcopacy; after riot in Cheapside was tried and executed.

HACKING, Sir John (1888–1969), chartered electrical engineer; educated at Burnley Grammar School and Leeds Technical Institute; engineering experience with Newcastle upon Tyne Electric Supply Co., 1908–13; joined Merz & McLellan, electrical consultants, and engaged on electrification of railways in Argentina and India and other projects in South Africa, 1915–33; deputy chief engineer, Central Electricity Board, 1933–44; chief engineer, 1944–7; maintained electricity supply in difficult wartime conditions; deputy chairman (operations), British Electricity Authority, 1947–53; returned to Merz & McLellan as consultant, 1953–66; knighted, 1949; president, Electrical Research Association, British Electrical Power Convention, and Institution of Electrical Engineers, 1951–2.

HACKMAN, Alfred (1811–1874), sub-librarian at the Bodleian, 1862–73; precentor of Christ Church, Oxford, 1841–73; vicar of St Paul's, 1844–71; published *Catalogue of Tanner MSS.* in the Bodleian (1860).

HACKMAN, James (1752–1779), murderer; lieutenant in army, 1776; incumbent of Wiveton, Norfolk, 1779; fell in love with Martha *Ray, mistress of Lord *Sandwich, and on her refusal to marry him shot her outside Covent Garden Theatre.

HACKSTON (or HALKERSTONE), David (d. 1680), Covenanter; present at Archbishop *Sharp's murder, 1679; fled to the west and helped to draw up the *Declaration and Testimony* (1679); one of the leaders at Drumclog and Bothwell Brigg, 1679; captured at Aird's Moss and executed at Edinburgh.

HACOMBLEN, Robert (d. 1528), provost of King's College, Cambridge; educated at Eton

and King's College, Cambridge; DD, Cambridge, 1507; vicar of Prescot, Lancashire, 1492; provost of King's College, Cambridge, 1509–28; gave the brass lectern still in use, and fitted up chantry on south side, where he is buried.

HADDAN, Arthur West (1816–1873), ecclesiastical historian; BA, Trinity College, Oxford, 1837; fellow, 1839; MA; Johnson theological scholar, 1839; curate to Newman at St Mary's, 1841–2; one of the secretaries of Gladstone's election committee, 1847; vice-president, Trinity College, Oxford; incumbent of Barton-on-the-Heath, Warwickshire, 1857–73; published editions of the works of Archbishop *Bramhall and of H. *Thorndike in Anglo-Catholic Library, *Rationalism*, reply to Mark *Pattison (1862), *Apostolical Succession in the Church of England* (1869), and with Bishop Stubbs *Councils and Ecclesiastical Documents* (1869–73); his *Remains* edited (1876).

HADDAN, Thomas Henry (1814–1873), barrister and first editor of the *Guardian*; brother of Arthur West *Haddan; MA, Brasenose College, Oxford, 1840; fellow of Exeter College, Oxford, 1837–43; Vinerian fellow, 1847; BCL, 1844; barrister, Inner Temple, 1841; equity draughtsman; projected and first edited *Guardian*, 1846; published works, including *Outlines of Administrative Jurisdiction of the Court of Chancery* (1862); died at Vichy.

HADDEN, James Murray (d. 1817), surveyor-general of the ordnance; distinguished himself as an artillery officer with *Burgoyne in Canada; captured at Saratoga, 1777; adjutant-general in Portugal, 1797; secretary to *Richmond when master-general of ordnance, 1794–5; surveyor-general of ordnance, 1804–10; colonel, 1806; major-general, 1811; his *Journal* of 1776 printed at Albany, New York (1884).

HADDENSTON, James (d. 1443). See HALDENSTOUN.

HADDINGTON, earls of. See HAMILTON, Sir THOMAS, first earl, 1563–1637; HAMILTON, THOMAS, second earl, 1600–1640; HAMILTON, THOMAS, sixth earl, 1680–1735; HAMILTON, THOMAS, ninth earl, 1780–1858.

HADDINGTON, Viscount (1580?–1626). See RAMSAY, Sir JOHN.

HADDOCK. See also HAYDOCK.

HADDOCK, Nicholas (1686–1746), admiral; second son of Sir Richard *Haddock; distinguished himself as midshipman at destruction of Franco-Spanish Fleet at Vigo, 1702; lieutenant at relief of Barcelona, 1706; as captain of the *Ludlow Castle*, 1707, recaptured the *Nightingale* in North Sea; led attack at Cape Passaro, 1718;

commander at the Nore, 1732; as commander-in-chief in Mediterranean, 1738–42, blockaded Spanish coast and took valuable prizes; vice-admiral, 1741; admiral of the blue, 1744; MP, Rochester, 1734–46.

HADDOCK, Sir Richard (1629–1715), admiral; took part in attack on Vlie and Schelling, 1666; commanded *Sandwich's flagship, the *Royal James*, in Battle of Solebay, 1672, afterwards Prince *Rupert's flagship, the *Royal Charles*; knighted, 1675; commander at the Nore, 1682; commissioner of victualling, 1683–90; admiral and joint commander-in-chief, 1690; afterwards comptroller of the navy.

HADDON, Alfred Cort (1855–1940), anthropologist; educated at Christ's College, Cambridge (fellow, 1901); first class, natural sciences tripos (comparative anatomy), 1878; professor of zoology, Royal College of Science, Dublin, 1880–1901; studied marine biology in Torres Strait (1888–9) and determined to save vanishing ethnological data; lecturer in physical anthropology, Cambridge, 1894–8; in ethnology, 1900–9; reader, 1909–25; planned Cambridge anthropological expedition (1898–9) to Torres Strait, New Guinea, and Sarawak (6-vol. report published, 1901–35); helped to make University Museum of Archaeology and Ethnology a primary centre for research; FRS, 1899.

HADDON, James (*fl.* 1556), divine; MA, Cambridge, 1544; original fellow of Trinity College, Cambridge, 1546; chaplain to duke of Suffolk and tutor to Lady Jane Grey (*Dudley), *c.*1551; dean of Exeter, 1553; one of the Protestant disputants on the real presence, 1553; went to Strasburg, 1554.

HADDON, Walter (1516–1572), civilian; brother of James *Haddon; educated at Eton and King's College, Cambridge; BA, 1537; LL D, 1549; vice-chancellor, 1549–50; regius professor of civil law, 1551; master of Trinity Hall, 1552; engaged with Cheke in reform of ecclesiastical laws; president, Magdalen College, Oxford, 1552–3; MP, Reigate, 1555, Thetford, 1558, Poole, 1559, and Warwick, 1563; on accession of Elizabeth named master of requests, commissioner for visitation of Cambridge and Eton, ecclesiastical commissioner, and judge of prerogative court; employed in commercial negotiations with Flanders, 1565–6; member of parliamentary committee to petition Queen Elizabeth to marry, 1566; defended the Reformation against Osorio da Fonseca; published, with *Cheke, *Reformatio Legum Ecclesiasticarum* (1571). His *Lucubrationes* (ed. T. *Hatcher, 1567) contains Latin letters and orations.

HADDOW, Sir Alexander (1907–1976), experimental pathologist (oncology); educated at Broxburn High School, Broxburn Academy, and Edinburgh University; graduated MB, Ch.B., 1929; assistant lecturer in bacteriological department, 1929; lecturer, 1932; Ph.D. and MD, 1937; D.Sc., 1938; moved from Edinburgh to research institute of Royal Cancer Hospital, London, 1936–46; succeeded Sir Ernest L. *Kennaway as director, Chester Beatty Research Institute, 1946–69; professor of experimental pathology, London University; one of the founders of carcino-chemotherapy; studied derivatives of cholic acids and steroids and use of other carcinotherapeutic agents such as melphalan; FRS, 1958; FRSE and hon. FRCP, 1968; president, International Union against Cancer, 1962–6.

HADEN, Sir Francis Seymour (1818–1910), etcher and surgeon; studied medicine at the Sorbonne and at Grenoble; FRCS, 1857; formed large private practice in London and did much public work; published pamphlets strongly opposed to cremation; devoted leisure to etching, mainly of landscape, from 1843 onwards; influenced by J. A. M. *Whistler, whose half-sister he married; chief works include *Thames Fishermen, Shere Mill Pond, Breaking up of the* Agamemnon; his drypoints executed in 1877, *Windmill Hill, Sawley Abbey, Essex Farm, Boat House*, show vigorous style; founder and president of Society of Painter-Etchers, 1880; knighted, 1894; member of several French artistic societies; exhibited at Royal Academy, 1860–85; worked also in water-colour and black chalk; chief collections of work are in British Museum and New York Public Library; pioneer of scientific criticism of Rembrandt's etchings; published *The Etched Work of Rembrandt* (1879), *About Etching* (1879), and kindred works.

HADENHAM, Edmund of (*fl.* 1307), chronicler; monk of Rochester; work ascribed to him by *Lambarde printed in *Wharton's *Anglia Sacra* (1691).

HADFIELD, Charles (1821–1884), journalist; edited *Manchester City News*, 1865–7, *Warrington Examiner*, and *Salford Weekly News*, 1880–3.

HADFIELD, George (d. 1826), architect; brother of Mrs Maria Cecilia Louisa *Cosway; travelling student of Royal Academy; at Rome, 1790; exhibited in 1795 drawing for a restoration of the temple at Palestrina, and drawings of the temples of Mars and Jupiter Tonans, and an interior of St Peter's; designed buildings in Washington; died in America.

HADFIELD, George (1787–1879), politician; Radical MP for Sheffield, 1852–74; introduced measures for registration of judgments and for abolition of qualifications for offices, 1866; took part in formation of Anti-Corn-Law League and (1840) establishment of the Lancashire Independent College; edited Charity Commission reports (1829) and other works.

HADFIELD, Matthew Ellison (1812–1885), architect; with his son Charles designed St Mary's, Sheffield, the Roman Catholic Cathedral at Salford; employed by four dukes of Norfolk.

HADFIELD, Sir **Robert Abbott,** baronet (1858–1940), metallurgist and industrialist; educated at Collegiate School, Sheffield; entered father's steelworks; chairman and managing director, 1888; an enlightened employer; established laboratory and built up strong experimental organization; discovered manganese steel, 1882; other investigations included silicon and alloy steels, production of sound steel ingots, deformation of steel at high velocities, and corrosion; studied history of metallurgy; publications include *Metallurgy and its Influence on Modern Progress* (1925) and *Faraday and his Metallurgical Researches . . .* (1931); knighted, 1908; baronet, 1917; FRS, 1909.

HADFIELD, William (1806–1887), writer on Brazil; secretary to Buenos Aires Great Southern Railway and South American Steam Navigation Company; editor (1863–87) of *South American Journal*; published works on Brazil and the River Plate (1854 and 1869).

HADHAM, Edmund of, earl of Richmond (1430?–1456). See TUDOR.

HADLEY, George (1685–1768), scientific writer; brother of John *Hadley (1682–1744); of Pembroke College, Oxford, and Lincoln's Inn; barrister, 1709; FRS, 1735; formulated present theory of trade winds; published also *Account and Abstract of the Meteorological Diaries communicated for 1729 and 1730* to Royal Society.

HADLEY, George (d. 1798), orientalist; served in East India Company's army, 1763–71; published *Grammatical Remarks* on Moors (dialect of Hindustani), with vocabulary (4th edn., 1796), and on Persian, with vocabulary (1776).

HADLEY, John (1682–1744), mathematician and scientific mechanist; wrote advanced mathematical papers for Royal Society; FRS, 1717; vice-president, Royal Society, 1728; invented first serviceable reflecting telescope, 1719–20; his reflecting quadrant tested by Admiralty, and further improved, 1734.

HADLEY, John (1731–1764), professor of chemistry at Cambridge; nephew of John *Hadley (1682–1744); fifth wrangler; fellow of Queens' College, Cambridge, 1756–64; MA, 1756; professor of chemistry, 1756; MD, 1763; FRS, 1758; FRCP, 1764; physician to Charterhouse, 1763; intimate with Thomas *Gray (1716–1771).

HADLEY, Patrick Arthur Sheldon (1899–1973), music composer and teacher; educated at King's College School, Cambridge, and Winchester, 1912–17; commissioned in Royal Field Artillery, 1918; wounded and lost a leg; studied at Pembroke College, Cambridge, of which his father had been master, 1919–22; Mus.B., 1922; MA, 1925; studied at Royal College of Music, 1922–5; FRCM; won Sullivan Prize for composition; composition pupil of Ralph *Vaughan Williams, with whom he shared enthusiasm for folk-song; appointed to staff of RCM, 1925; influenced by music of Frederick *Delius; composed symphonic ballad, *The Trees so High* (1931); Mus.D., 1938; elected fellow of Gonville and Caius College, Cambridge, 1938 and lecturer in university music faculty; official university lecturer, 1945; professor of music, 1946–62; reorganized choir and secular chorus of his college; number of major compositions included music for *Antigone* (Sophocles), 1939 and *Agamemnon* (Aeschylus), 1953; conducted Cambridge University Musical Society's chorus and orchestra, 1941–5; produced choral symphony, *The Hills* (1946); trustee, Cambridge Arts Theatre; co-founder, King's Lynn Festival and Noise Abatement Society.

HADLEY, William Waite (1866–1960), editor of the *Sunday Times*; educated at village and night schools; apprenticed to *Northampton Mercury*; joined *Rochdale Observer*, 1887; editor, 1893–1908; managing editor, *Northampton Mercury* group, 1908–23; parliamentary correspondent, *Daily Chronicle*, 1924–30; assistant editor, 1931, editor, 1932–50, *Sunday Times*; maintained notable team of regular contributors, including Ernest *Newman, James *Agate, (Sir) Desmond *MacCarthy, and (Sir) R. C. K. *Ensor; published *Munich: Before and After* (1944).

HADOW, Grace Eleanor (1875–1940), principal of the Society of Oxford Home-Students (now St Anne's College) and pioneer in social work; sister of Sir W. H. *Hadow; first class, English, Somerville College, Oxford, 1903; tutor in English, Lady Margaret Hall (1906), lecturer (1909–17); secretary, Barnett House, Oxford, 1920–9; principal, Society of Home-Students, 1929–40; vice-chairman, National Federation of Women's Institutes, 1916–40.

HADOW, James (1670?–1747), 'the Detector'; professor of divinity at St Mary's College, St Andrews, 1699, principal, 1707; published theological treatises, including *Antinomianism of the Marrow of Modern Divinity detected* (1721).

HADOW, Sir (William) Henry (1859–1937), scholar, educationist, and critic and historian of music; educated at Malvern and Worcester College, Oxford; first class, Lit. Hum., 1882; lecturer (1884), fellow, tutor, and dean (1889); B.Mus., 1890; principal, Armstrong College, Newcastle, 1909–19; vice-chancellor, Sheffield University, 1919–30; chairman, consultative committee, Board of Education, 1920–34; established music as part of a liberal education; works include *Sonata Form* (1896) and *English Music* (1931); edited Oxford History of Music and contributed *The Viennese Period* (vol. v, 1904); knighted, 1918.

HADRIAN IV (d. 1159). See ADRIAN IV.

HADRIAN, de Castello (1460?–1521?). See ADRIAN DE CASTELLO.

HADRILL, (John) Michael Wallace- (1916–1985), historian. See WALLACE-HADRILL.

HAGGARD, Sir Henry Rider (1856–1925), novelist; went to South Africa as secretary to Sir H. E. G. Bulwer, governor of Natal, 1875; master and registrar of Transvaal High Court, 1878; returned to England and settled in Norfolk, 1879; travelled round world as member of Dominions Royal Commission, 1912–17; knighted, 1912; KBE, 1919; had two interests, agriculture and romantic writing; works include *Rural England* (1902), *King Solomon's Mines* (1885), *She* (1887), and *Ayesha* (1905).

HAGGARD, John (1794–1856), civilian; of Westminster and Trinity Hall, Cambridge; fellow, 1815–20; LL D, 1818; chancellor of Lincoln, 1836, of Winchester, 1845, of Manchester, 1847; edited reports of cases in consistory court of London, Admiralty court, and Doctors' Commons.

HAGGART, David (1801–1821), criminal; frequented fairs and race-meetings in Scotland and the north of England; six times imprisoned for theft; four times broke gaol; killed a turnkey at Dumfries, 1820; arrested in Ireland; hanged at Edinburgh; compiled an autobiography in Scottish thieves' cant, published, with notes by George *Combe.

HAGHE, Charles (d. 1888), lithographer; brother of Louis *Haghe.

HAGHE, Louis (1806–1885), lithographer and water-colour painter; born at Tournai; worked only with his left hand; in his youth left Belgium for England; in partnership with William Day lithographed David *Roberts's *Holy Land and Egypt* and his own *Sketches in Belgium and Germany*; president of the New Water-colour

Society, 1873–84; exhibited regularly from 1854, chiefly Flemish interiors.

HAGTHORPE, John (*fl.* 1627), poet; probably identical with the Captain John Hagthorpe who took part in Cadiz expedition, 1625; published *Divine Meditations and Elegies* (1622, selection edited by *Brydges, 1817), *Visiones Rerum* (1623), and *Englands-Exchequer*, in prose and verse (1625).

HAGUE, Charles (1769–1821), professor of music at Cambridge; gained repute as a violinist; professor of music, Cambridge, 1799–1821; Mus.Doc., Cambridge, 1801; published glees, Haydn's symphonies arranged as quintets, and setting of William *Smyth's ode at the installation of the duke of *Gloucester.

HAHN, Kurt Matthias Robert Martin (1886–1974), founder and headmaster of Gordonstoun School; born in Berlin of Jewish parents; educated at the Wilhelmsgymnasium, Berlin, Christ Church, Oxford, and Berlin, Heidelberg, Freiburg, and Göttingen universities; during 1914–18 war worked in German Foreign Office and in the Supreme Command as a lector of British newspapers; secretary to Prince Max von Baden, last imperial chancellor of Germany; attended Versailles Conference, 1919; with Prince Max founded Salem, a coeducational boarding school by Lake Constance, 1920; anti-Nazi; imprisoned by Hitler, 1933; emigrated to Britain and founded Gordonstoun School in Moray, 1934; the school aimed at producing the whole person; became naturalized British citizen, 1938; founded first Outward Bound School at Aberdovey, Wales, 1941; Outward Bound Trust formed, 1945; instigated Greek Gordonstoun at Anavryta, 1949; retired from Gordonstoun, 1953; Moray Badge launched as Duke of Edinburgh's Award Scheme, 1956; opened St Donat's Castle, the first United World College, 1962; CBE, 1964; impetus behind the Trevelyan scholarships at Oxford and Cambridge; honorary doctorates from Scottish and German universities; awarded the Freiherr-vom-Stein Prize for pioneering work in education, 1962.

HAIG, Douglas, first Earl Haig (1861–1928), field marshal; educated at Clifton, Oxford, and Sandhurst; gazetted to 7th Hussars, 1885; entered Staff College, 1896; special service officer employed in Sudan campaign, 1898; accompanied Major-General *French (afterwards earl of Ypres) to South Africa as staff officer, 1899; conspicuous for ingenuity, enterprise, and brilliant staff work; column commander, 1900–2; inspector-general of cavalry to Lord *Kitchener in India, 1903–6; major-general, 1904; a director on General Staff at War Office, 1906; responsible for scheme of Imperial General Staff and drafting of first British field-service regulations; chief of staff to Sir O'Moore *Creagh in India, 1909–11; commanded at Aldershot, 1911; aide-de-camp general, 1914; took to France I Army Corps on outbreak of European war, Aug. 1914; urged on Lord Kitchener necessity of creating great national army; conducted orderly retreat of I Corps after Battle of Mons, Aug.–Sept.; won confidence of his men and of commander-in-chief; at first Battle of Ypres (19 Oct.–22 Nov.) his magnificent defence, imperturbable calm, and tactical skill made him national figure; commanded First Army, 1915; planned successful attack on Neuve Chapelle, which marked beginning of new epoch in war, Mar.; entrusted with attack on Loos, Sept.; succeeded French as commander-in-chief, Dec.; at Joffre's request prepared counter-offensive to relieve Verdun which resulted in Battle of Somme, July–Nov. 1916; directed to conform to instructions of General Nivelle, new French commander-in-chief, at Allied conference at Calais, 1917; Vimy Ridge captured by British, but failure of French attacks produced breakdown of French morale, to cover which British continued attacks, capturing Messines Ridge (June) and attacking Ypres Front (July); after exhausting effort Passchendaele captured, Nov.; situation critical for Allies in winter of 1917–18; expected German blow fell upon British Third and Fifth Armies, Mar. 1918; secured appointment of Foch to control operations on Western Front, Mar.; his courage and resolution inspired his men to resist second great German attack in Flanders, Apr.; loyally supported Foch; his conviction that time had come for supreme effort, issuing in decision to make general advance against enemy, secured victory in 1918; led armies to Rhine; commander-in-chief, Home Forces, 1919–21; received thanks of parliament, £100,000, and created earl, 1919; devoted himself to cause of ex-servicemen; president of British Legion and chairman of United Services Fund.

HAIG BROWN, William (1823–1907), master of Charterhouse; educated at Christ's Hospital and Pembroke College, Cambridge; second classic, 1846; MA, 1849; LL D, 1864; fellow, 1848; hon. fellow, 1899; appointed headmaster of Charterhouse School, 1863; active in advocating removal of school from London to Godalming, 1864; school opened at Godalming, 1872; numbers rose from 150 in 1872 to 500 in 1876; made many additions and improvements; known as 'our second founder'; appointed master of the Charterhouse, 1897; honorary canon of Winchester, 1891; published *Charterhouse, Past and Present* (1879), *Carthusian Memories* (verse, 1905), and other works.

HAIGH, Arthur Elam (1855–1905), classical scholar; BA, Corpus Christi College, Oxford (first class, classics), 1878; fellow of Hertford College, 1878–86; fellow and tutor of Corpus, 1901; author of *The Attic Theatre* (1889) and *The Tragic Drama of the Greeks* (1896).

HAIGH, Daniel Henry (1819–1879), priest and antiquary; converted to Romanism, 1847; became priest, 1840; built St Augustine's, Erdington, near Birmingham, chiefly at his own expense; the chief English authority on runic literature; assisted Professor *Stephens in his *Runic Monuments*, and published works on early numismatics, the Saxon conquest, and the Anglo-Saxon sagas.

HAIGH, Thomas (1769–1808), violinist, pianist, and composer; studied under Haydn; composed sonatas (chiefly for pianoforte), and ballads.

HAIGHTON, John (1755–1823), physician and physiologist; MD; demonstrator under Henry *Cline at St Thomas's Hospital; lectured for St Thomas's and Guy's on physiology and midwifery, 1789; called 'the merciless doctor'; joint editor of *Medical Records and Researches*, 1798; silver medallist of London Medical Society for paper on 'Deafness', 1790.

HAILES, Barons. See HEPBURN, PATRICK, third baron, d. 1508; BUCHAN-HEPBURN, PATRICK GEORGE THOMAS, 1901–1974.

HAILES, Lord (1726–1792). See DALRYMPLE, Sir DAVID.

HAILEY, (William) Malcolm, Baron Hailey (1872–1969), public servant; educated at Merchant Taylors' School and Corpus Christi College, Oxford; first class, classical hon. mods. and Lit. Hum., 1892–4; entered Indian Civil Service; posted to Punjab 1896; colonization officer, Jhelum Canal Colony, 1901; served in secretariat of Punjab and Government of India, 1907–12; first chief commissioner, Delhi, 1912–18; finance member, Viceroy's Executive Council, 1919–22; home member and leader of government bloc in Legislative Assembly, 1922; attached great importance to principle of dyarchy; governor, Punjab, 1924–8; governor, United Provinces, 1928–34; attended Round Table Conference, 1930–1; baron, 1936; director, survey of Africa, proposed by J. C. *Smuts; published *An African Survey* (1938); employed on missions to African colonies and Belgian Congo, 1939–40; chairman of committees concerned with research in Africa; wrote books on Africa, last of which, *The Republic of South Africa and the High Commission Territories*, was published in 1963; KCSI, 1922; GCSI, 1932; GCIE, 1928; GCMG, 1939; PC, 1949; OM, 1956; hon. fellow, Corpus Christi College, Oxford, and many other academic honours; Rhodes trustee, 1946–66; few men contributed so much to the transition from bureaucratic rule to democracy in India; few so much to the peaceful transfer of power in Africa.

HAILS (or HAILES), William Anthony (1766–1845), author; while working as a shipwright acquired knowledge of classics and Hebrew; published *Nugae Poeticae* (1806) and controversial tracts against Socinianism and Unitarianism.

HAILSHAM, first Viscount (1872–1950), statesman and lord chancellor. See HOGG, DOUGLAS MCGAREL.

HAILSTONE, Edward (1818–1890), author of *Portraits of Yorkshire Worthies* (1869); son of Samuel *Hailstone.

HAILSTONE, John (1759–1847), geologist; second wrangler, Trinity College, Cambridge, 1782; fellow, 1783; Woodwardian professor of geology, Cambridge, 1788–1818; vicar of Trumpington, 1817–47; FRS, 1801; original member of Geological Society; made additions to Woodwardian Museum.

HAILSTONE, Samuel (1768–1851), botanist; brother of John *Hailstone; solicitor at Bradford; leading authority on Yorkshire flora.

HAILWOOD, (Stanley) Michael (Bailey) (1940–1981), world champion motor-cycle rider and car driver; educated at Pangbourne Nautical College; worked at Triumph Motorcycles near Coventry; had first motor-cycle race, 1957, and won for first time two months later; came third in his first 250cc event in Isle of Man TT race, 1958; finished 1958 as British champion in 125, 250, and 350cc classes; won first of seventy-six Grands Prix victories, 1959; won first of nine world titles, 1961; first rider to win three TT races in one week, 1961; switched to car racing, 1968, but with less success than in his motor-cycle career; ended career as car driver as result of injury, 1974; retired to New Zealand, but returned to motor-cycle racing, 1978, and won his fourteenth TT race in Isle of Man, 1979; MBE, 1968; George Medal, 1973; awarded Segrave Trophy, 1979.

HAIMO (d. 1054). See HAYMO.

HAINES, Sir Frederick Paul (1819–1909), field marshal; joined 4th (King's Own) Regiment, 1839; served in First Sikh War; military secretary to Lord *Gough, 1846–9; served at Alma and Balaclava; prominent at Inkerman; military secretary to Sir Patrick *Grant at Mad-

ras, 1856–60; commanded Mysore division, 1865–70; commander-in-chief at Madras, 1871–5; KCB, 1871; lieutenant-general, 1873; commander-in-chief in India, 1876–81; superintended Afghan War, 1878–9; general and GCB, 1877; CIE, 1878; GCSI, 1879; differed from the viceroy, Lord *Lytton, in regard to the plans of attack on Afghanistan, 1878–9; suggested the relief of Kandahar by Lord *Roberts's (1832–1914) force from Kabul, 1880; declined baronetcy; field marshal, 1890.

HAINES, Herbert (1826–1872), archaeologist; MA, Exeter College, Oxford, 1851; as undergraduate, published *Manual for the Study of Monumental Brasses* (1848); second master, College School, Gloucester, 1850–72; published guide to Gloucester Cathedral (1867).

HAINES, John Thomas (1799?–1843), actor and dramatist; author of many popular melodramas, in some of which he acted, including *My Poll and my Partner Joe* (1835) and several nautical dramas.

HAINES (or HAYNES), Joseph (d. 1701), actor; known as 'Count Haines'; educated at The Queen's College, Oxford; Latin secretary to Sir Joseph *Williamson; dancer and afterwards actor at Theatre Royal; Benito in *Dryden's *Assignation*, written expressly for him, 1672; the original Sparkish in *The Country Wife*, 1673, and Lord Plausible in *The Plain Dealer*, 1674; his best parts, Noll Bluff in *Congreve's *Old Batchelor*, and Roger in *Aesop*; recited prologues and epilogues.

HAINES, William (1778–1848), engraver and painter; worked on *Boydell-Shakespeare plates; made drawings at the Cape, and engravings at Philadelphia, 1800–5; painted miniatures in London.

HAITE, John James (d. 1874), musical composer; published *Favourite Melodies as Quintets* (1865), *Principles of Natural Harmony* (1855), and other musical compositions.

HAKE, Edward (*fl.* 1579), satirist; mayor of Windsor, 1586; MP, Windsor, 1588–9; satirized clerical and other abuses in pieces, including *Newes out of Powles Churchyarde* (1567, 1579, reprinted in *Isham Reprints*, 1872), and *A Touchstone for this Time Present* (1574); translated the *Imitatio Christi* (1567).

HAKE, Thomas Gordon (1809–1895), physician and poet; educated at Christ's Hospital; studied medicine at St George's Hospital and at Glasgow and Edinburgh; practised successively at Brighton, Bury St Edmund's, and Roehampton (filling post of physician to West London Hospital), and finally settled at St John's Wood, London. He published, between 1839 and 1890, several volumes of poems, the earlier of which were highly appreciated by Dante Rossetti, whom Hake attended during his last days (1872). His *Memoirs of Eighty Years* appeared (1892).

HAKEWILL, Arthur William (1808–1856), architect; elder son of James *Hakewill; published *Apology for the Architectural Monstrosities of London* (1835) and other architectural works.

HAKEWILL, Edward Charles (1812–1872), architect, younger son of Henry *Hakewill; designed churches in Suffolk and East London; published *The Temple* (1851).

HAKEWILL, George (1578–1649), divine; fellow of Exeter College, Oxford, 1596–1611; MA, 1602; DD, 1611; rector of Exeter College, 1642–9; chaplain to Prince Charles, 1612, but dismissed on account of manuscript treatise against the Spanish match; archdeacon of Surrey, 1617; rector of Heanton Purchardon during Civil War; built chapel for Exeter College (consecrated 1624); one of the writers on whom *Johnson formed his style. His works include *The Vanitie of the Eie* (last edn., 1633), a Latin treatise against regicides (1612), and *Apologie . . . of the Power and Providence of God* (1627).

HAKEWILL, Henry (1771–1830), architect; eldest son of John *Hakewill; designed Gothic buildings and chapel at Rugby, Rendlesham House, and Cave Castle.

HAKEWILL, Henry James (1813–1834), sculptor; son of James *Hakewill; exhibited at Royal Academy, 1832.

HAKEWILL, James (1778–1843), architect; son of John *Hakewill; published *Views of the Neighbourhood of Windsor* (1813), *Picturesque Tour of Italy* (1817), with drawings finished by *Turner, and *Picturesque Tour in the Island of Jamaica* (1821).

HAKEWILL, John (1742–1791), painter and decorator; employed on decorative work at Blenheim and other mansions; exhibited at Society of Artists, mainly portraits.

HAKEWILL, John Henry (1811–1880), architect; elder son of Henry *Hakewill.

HAKEWILL, William (1574–1655), legal antiquary; brother of George *Hakewill; MP, Bossiney, 1601, Michell, 1604–11, Tregony, 1614–28, and Amersham, 1628–9; kinsman and executor of Sir Thomas *Bodley; MA, Oxford, 1613; member of commission to revise the laws, 1614; solicitor-general to James I's queen, 1617; bencher of Lincoln's Inn; master of Chancery, 1647; chief works, *Libertie of the Subject against the pretended Power of Imposition* (1641) and *The Manner how Statutes are enacted in Parliament* (1641).

HAKING, Sir **Richard Cyril Byrne** (1862–1945), general; commanded 5th brigade, 1911–14; 1st division, 1914–15; XI Corps, 1915–18, in France and Italy; chief British representative, Allied Armistice Commission, 1918–19; headed British Military Mission to Russia and Baltic, 1919; commanded allied troops, East Prussia plebiscite area, 1920; League of Nations high commissioner, Danzig, 1921–3; commanded British troops in Egypt, 1923–7; general, 1925; KCB, 1916.

HAKLUYT, Richard (1552?–1616), geographer; of Westminster and Christ Church, Oxford; MA, 1577; published *Divers Voyages touching the Discovery of America* (1582); chaplain to Sir Edward *Stafford, ambassador at Paris, 1583–8; prebendary of Bristol, 1586; rector of Wetheringsett, 1590; archdeacon of Westminster, 1603; a chief adventurer in the South Virginian Company; buried in Westminster Abbey; his *Principall Navigations, Voiages, and Discoveries of the English Nation* issued (1589, and, much enlarged, 3 vols., 1598–1600); published also *A notable History, containing four Voyages made by certain French Captains into Florida* (1587) and translations.

HALCOMB, John (1790–1852), serjeant-at-law; barrister, Inner Temple; MP, Dover, 1831–5; published *Practical Treatise on passing Private Bills* (1836).

HALCROW, Sir **William Thomson** (1883–1958), civil engineer; educated at George Watson's College and University of Edinburgh; trained with Thomas Meik & Sons; chief engineer, contracting firm, Topham, Jones, and Railton, 1910; consultant in partnership with C. S. Meik from 1921; designed and constructed ordnance factories, deep-level shelters, Phoenix units of Mulberry harbours; chairman, engineers' panels reporting on Severn Barrage (1944) and hydroelectric projects in Rhodesia (1951); knighted, 1944; president, Institute of Civil Engineers, 1946–7.

HALDANE, Daniel Rutherford (1824–1887), physician; son of James Alexander *Haldane; MD, Edinburgh, 1848; president, Edinburgh College of Physicians; LL D at tercentenary of Edinburgh University.

HALDANE, Elizabeth Sanderson (1862–1937), sister of J. S. and R. B. (Viscount) *Haldane; a lifelong Liberal; worked under Octavia *Hill; helped to establish similar organization in Edinburgh, 1884; first woman member, Scottish Savings Committee, 1916; first woman JP in Scotland, 1920; member of Scottish Universities' Committee (1909), Royal Commission on Civil Service (1912), General Nursing Council (1928); vice-chairman, Territorial Forces Nursing Service; a governor, Birkbeck College; Carnegie trustee, 1914–37; publications include translations of Descartes and Hegel; CH, 1918.

HALDANE, James Alexander (1768–1851), religious writer; made voyages to India and China as midshipman on an East Indiaman; first Congregational minister in Scotland, 1799; founded Society for Propagating the Gospel at Home, 1797; Baptist, 1808; took part in most contemporary religious controversies; published journal of his first evangelistic tour, and devotional works.

HALDANE, John Burdon Sanderson (1892–1964), geneticist; son of John Scott *Haldane, and nephew of both Richard Burdon *Haldane (later Viscount Haldane) and Elizabeth Sanderson *Haldane; educated at Dragon School, Oxford, Eton, and New College, Oxford; first class, mathematical mods. and Lit. Hum., 1912–14; served in Black Watch in France, Mesopotamia, and India, 1914–18; fellow, New College, 1919; reader in biochemistry, Cambridge, under (Sir) F. Gowland *Hopkins; dismissed because cited in divorce case, 1925; appealed and reinstated, 1926; also 'officer in charge of genetical investigations', John Innes Horticultural Research Station, 1927–36; FRS, 1932; Fullerian professor of physiology, Royal Institution, 1930–2; professor of genetics, and then of biometry, University College, London, 1933–57; member, Biometry Research Unit, Indian Statistical Institute, Calcutta, 1957; became Indian citizen, 1961; head of Laboratory of Genetics and Biometry, Bhubaneswar, 1962; major contribution to science, the re-establishment of Darwinian natural selection as accepted mechanism of evolutionary change; investigated disaster in submarine *Thetis* and did other work for Royal Navy and Royal Air Force, 1939–45; publications include *Daedalus* (1924), *Possible Worlds* (1927), *The Inequality of Man* (1932), and *My Friend Mr. Leakey* (1937), a collection of children's stories; chairman, editorial board, the *Daily Worker*, 1940–50; hon. D.Sc. (Oxford), 1961; hon. fellow, New College, 1961; doctorate of Paris University, and many other academic honours.

HALDANE, John Scott (1860–1936), physiologist and philosopher; brother of R. B. (Viscount) *Haldane and Elizabeth *Haldane; educated at Edinburgh Academy and University and at Jena; graduated in medicine (Edinburgh), 1884; demonstrator in physiology, Oxford, 1887; reader, 1907–13; investigated suffocative gases in coal-mines and wells; reported (1896) to home secretary on causes of death in colliery explosions and fires; introduced new methods for gas analysis and for investigating physiology of the respi-ration and blood; investigated physiology of lung respiration, cardiac output, and function of kidney in relation to body's physiological requirements; developed (1907) 'stage decompression' for bringing deep-divers to surface; worked (1914–18) on identification of war-gases and pathology and treatment of their effects; director (1912–36), Mining Research Laboratory, supported by colliery owners; investigated ventilation, rescue apparatus, underground fires, and pulmonary disease; publications include *Respiration* (1922) and *The Sciences and Philosophy* (1929); FRS, 1897; CH, 1928.

HALDANE, Richard Burdon, Viscount Haldane (1856–1928), statesman, lawyer, and philosopher; grandson of James Alexander *Haldane; educated at Edinburgh Academy and universities of Göttingen and Edinburgh (MA, with first-class honours in philosophy); called to bar (Lincoln's Inn), 1879; most successful in type of legal work involving consideration of legal principles rather than mere interpretation of facts; junior to Horace (afterwards Lord) *Davey, 1882; Liberal MP, East Lothian, 1885–1911; QC, 1890; 'went special', 1897; employed in Canadian and Indian cases and other appeals before Privy Council; also dealt with considerable number of appeals before House of Lords, including important United Free Church of Scotland case (1904); lord chancellor, 1912–15; secured increase in number of lords of appeal and raised judicial committee of Privy Council to position in which it commanded increasing confidence at home and in dominions; secretary of state for war, 1905–12; took office in difficult conditions, chief of which was indifference of Liberal party to army; made extensive study of whole problem of army organization; Imperial General Staff created, 1909; carried through House of Commons legislation necessary to give effect to schemes of army reform; these included formation of militia into special reserve, creation of Officers' Training Corps, and improvement of medical and nursing services under Territorial system; created viscount, 1911; sent by Cabinet on abortive mission to Germany, 1912; owing to this later groundlessly accused of pro-German sympathies; interested in higher education and administration, one of his principal efforts on behalf of university organization being directed towards establishment of provincial or 'civic' universities; chairman (1904) of small committee whose recommendations resulted in creation of University Grants Committee; chairman of Royal Commission on University Education in London, 1909; worked towards increasing efficiency of public administration; after leaving office (1915) became progressively estranged from official Liberal party; lord chancellor in Labour administration, 1924; led small number of Labour peers who formed official opposition in House of Lords, 1925–8; FRS, 1906; FBA, 1914; his works include *The Pathway to Reality* (1903), *The Reign of Relativity* (1921), *The Philosophy of Humanism* (1922), and *Human Experience* (1926).

HALDANE, Robert (1764–1842), religious writer; brother of James Alexander *Haldane; spent largely in founding and endowing tabernacles and seminaries; co-operated with his brother at Edinburgh; carried on evangelistic work in Geneva and southern France, 1816–19; from 1824 attacked British and Foreign Bible Society for circulating the Apocrypha; published *Evidences and Authority of Divine Revelation* (1816) and *Exposition of the Epistle to the Romans* (1835–9).

HALDANE, Robert (1772–1854), divine; named after Robert *Haldane (1764–1842); professor of mathematics at St Andrews, 1807–20; principal of St Mary's, and primarius of divinity, 1820–54; moderator of general assembly, 1827, and at the disruption.

HALDENSTOUN (or HADDENSTON), James (d. 1443), prior of St Andrews, 1418; member of James I's embassy to Rome, 1425.

HALDIMAND, Sir Frederick (1718–1791), lieutenant-general; of Swiss birth; some years in Dutch service; lieutenant-colonel, 62nd Royal Americans (King's Royal Rifle Corps), 1756; afterwards commanding it as 60th Foot; distinguished at Ticonderoga, 1758, and Oswego, 1759; with *Amherst's expedition against Montreal, 1760; commanded in Florida, 1766–78; governor and commander-in-chief of Canada, 1778–85; died at Yverdun; his correspondence (1758–85) in British Museum.

HALDIMAND, William (1784–1862), philanthropist; grandnephew of Sir Frederick *Haldimand; a director of the Bank of England; MP, Ipswich, 1820–6; gave pecuniary support to cause of Greek independence; founded Hortense Hospital, Aix-les-Bains, and a blind asylum at Lausanne; died at Denantou.

HALE, Sir Bernard (1677–1729), judge; MA, Peterhouse, Cambridge, 1702; fellow, 1700–15; barrister, Gray's Inn, 1704; lord chief baron, Irish Exchequer, 1722; puisne baron of English Exchequer and knighted, 1725.

HALE, Bernard (*fl.* 1773), general; son of Sir Bernard *Hale; governor of Chelsea Hospital, 1773; lieutenant-general of the ordnance.

HALE, Horatio (1817–1896), anthropologist; born at Newport, New Hampshire, United States; MA, Harvard; ethnologist and philologist to exploring expedition under Captain Wilkes, 1838–42; admitted to Chicago bar, 1855; resided at Clinton, Ontario, 1856–96; supervised anthropological work of British Association in Canadian north-west and British Columbia; published (1883), with translation and introduction, *Iroquois Book of Rites (1714–35)*, the only literary American-Indian work extant, and anthropological writings.

HALE, John (d. 1806), general; son of Sir Bernard *Hale.

HALE, Sir Matthew (1609–1676), judge; of Magdalen Hall, Oxford, and Lincoln's Inn; counsel for Sir John *Bramston (1641) and Archbishop *Laud (1643) on impeachment; counsel for Lord *Maguire, 1645, and the eleven members accused by *Fairfax, 1646; defended James, duke of *Hamilton, 1649; said to have tendered his services to Charles I; took the oath to the Commonwealth, but defended Christopher *Love, 1651; member of committee for law reform, 1652; serjeant-at-law, 1654; justice of common pleas, 1654; MP, Gloucestershire, 1654, and in Convention Parliament (1660), for Oxford University, 1659; prominent in the Convention; lord chief baron of the Exchequer, 1660; knighted, 1662; member of special court to adjudicate on questions of property arising out of the fire of 1666; presided at conviction of two women for witchcraft, 1662; endeavoured to mitigate severity of conventicle acts, and to forward 'comprehension'; lord chief justice of King's Bench, 1671; friend of *Baxter and *Selden and of the latitudinarian bishops; published two scientific works answered by Henry *More. His posthumous works include *Contemplations, Moral and Divine, Pleas of the Crown* (1678), *The Primitive Origination of Mankind Considered, Historia Placitorum Coronae* (ordered by parliament to be printed), and *The Judgment of the late Lord Chief Justice of the Nature of True Religion*, edited by Baxter (1684); *Works Moral and Religious*, edited by Revd T. *Thirlwall (1805).

HALE, Richard (1670–1728), physician; MA, Trinity College, Oxford, 1695; FRCP, 1716; gave £500 to the Royal College of Physicians library; his Harveian oration on English medieval physicians published (1735).

HALE, Warren Stormes (1791–1872), lord mayor of London; master of Tallow Chandlers' Company, 1849 and 1861; alderman of London, 1856; sheriff, 1858–9; lord mayor, 1864–5; chief founder of City of London School on the old foundation of John *Carpenter (1370?–1441?).

HALE, William Hale (1795–1870), divine and antiquary; educated at Charterhouse and Oriel

College, Oxford; MA, 1820; domestic chaplain to Bishop *Blomfield, 1824; prebendary of St Paul's, 1829–40; archdeacon of St Albans, 1839–40, and of London, 1842; master of the Charterhouse, 1842–70; edited (1858) *The Domesday of St. Paul's of 1222*, etc., the *Epistles of Bishop Hall* (1840), and *Institutiones piae*, ascribed to Bishop *Andrewes; published also accounts of Charterhouse and Christ's Hospital.

HALES, Alexander of (d. 1245). See ALEXANDER.

HALES, Sir Christopher (d. 1541), master of the Rolls; ancient of Gray's Inn, 1516; MP, Canterbury, 1523; solicitor-general, 1525; attorney-general, 1529; preferred indictment against *Wolsey, 1529; justice of assize, 1532; conducted proceedings against *More, *Fisher, and *Anne Boleyn, 1535; granted church lands in Kent.

HALES, Sir Edward, baronet, titular earl of Tenterden (1645–1695); at University College, Oxford, under Obadiah *Walker; professed himself a papist, 1685; convicted for having acted as colonel of foot without taking the statutory oaths and the sacrament, but his plea of the king's dispensation allowed by King's Bench, 1686; lieutenant of the Tower; dismissed, 1688; arrested while with James II at Faversham and imprisoned; went to St Germain, 1690; received a Jacobite title, 1692.

HALES, Sir James (d. 1554), judge; son of John *Hales (d. 1539); ancient of Gray's Inn, 1528; serjeant-at-law, 1540; king's serjeant, 1544; KB, 1547; judge of common pleas, 1549; member of courts which tried *Bonner and *Gardiner, and of commission for reforming ecclesiastical laws, 1551; refused to affix his seal to act of council settling the crown on Lady Jane Grey (*Dudley), 1553; imprisoned at instance of Gardiner, 1553–4; drowned himself after release.

HALES, John (d. 1539), baron of the Exchequer, 1522–39.

HALES (or HAYLES), John (d. 1571), author; clerk of the hanaper to Henry VIII, Edward VI, and Elizabeth; converted his grant of St John's Hospital, Coventry, into free school, 1545; as MP for Preston introduced measures for benefiting the poor, 1548; at Frankfurt in Mary's reign; his property confiscated, 1557; imprisoned by Elizabeth for pamphlet affirming legality of marriage of Lord Hertford and Lady Catherine *Grey, 1564; published *Highway to Nobility* (1543) and *Introductiones ad Grammaticam*; translated Plutarch's *Precepts for the Preservation of Health* (c.1543).

HALES, John (1584–1656), 'the ever-memorable'; educated at Bath Grammar School and Corpus Christi, Oxford; fellow of Merton, 1605; MA, 1609; public lecturer in Greek, 1612; fellow of Eton, 1613–49; as chaplain to Sir Dudley *Carleton attended synod of Dort, 1618–19; canon of Windsor and chaplain to *Laud, 1639; his tract on *Schism and Schismaticks* printed anonymously and unsanctioned (1642); during the Commonwealth lived in retirement; published oration on Sir Thomas *Bodley, also several remarkable sermons (1613); his *Golden Remains* first issued 1659; his works printed by *Foulis (Glasgow, 1765), edited by Lord *Hailes.

HALES, John (d. 1679). See HAYLS.

HALES, Stephen (1677–1761), physiologist and inventor; fellow of Corpus Christi College, Cambridge, 1703; MA, 1703; BD, 1711; DD, Oxford, 1733; perpetual curate of Teddington, 1709 until death; also incumbent of Farringdon, Hampshire, during same period, but resided chiefly at Teddington; FRS, 1718; Copley medallist, 1739; a founder and (1755) vice-president of Society of Arts; clerk of the closet to the princess-dowager, and chaplain to her son (afterwards George III), 1751; trustee of colony of Georgia; invented artificial ventilators and numerous other mechanical contrivances; his *Vegetable Staticks* (1727) the most important contribution of the eighteenth century to plant-physiology; his contributions to animal physiology in *Statical Essays* (1733) second only to those of *Harvey in the inauguration of modern physiology. His monument was placed in Westminster Abbey by the princess-dowager of Wales. His works include two pamphlets against spirit-drinking as well as *Philosophical Experiments* (1739), containing *inter alia* suggestions for distilling water and preserving provisions at sea, proposals for cleaning harbours, and *A Description of Ventilators* (1743).

HALES, Thomas (*fl.* 1250), Franciscan; famous for his learning; his poem 'A Luve Ron' printed in Morris's *Old English Miscellany*.

HALES, Thomas (1740?–1780), French dramatist; known as d'Hele, d'Hell, or Dell; of English birth; served in the English Navy; went to Paris, c.1770; contributed to Grimm's *Correspondance Littéraire* 'Le Roman de Mon Oncle' (1777); published comedies, with music by Grétry, of which *Le Jugement de Midas* was acted and printed (1778), *Les Fausses Apparences*, acted 1778 (revived 1850), *Les Evènemens Imprévus* (acted 1779), translated by *Holcroft, 1806, and *Gilles Ravisseur* (acted 1781).

HALES, William (1747–1831), chronologist; fellow of Trinity College, Dublin, 1768; BA and

DD; professor of oriental languages, Trinity College, Dublin; rector of Killeshandra, Cavan, 1788–1831. His twenty-two works include *A New Analysis of Chronology* (1809–12), also mathematical papers in *Maseres's *Scriptores Logarithmici*, and theological treatises.

HALE-WHITE, Sir **William** (1857–1949), physician; son of William Hale *White (Mark Rutherford); qualified at Guy's Hospital, 1879; demonstrator of anatomy, 1881; assistant physician, 1885; full physician, 1890–1918; developed large consulting practice; retired, 1927; an editor of *Guy's Hospital Reports* (1886–93) and of *Quarterly Journal of Medicine*; wrote on many branches of medicine and on medical history; publications include *Materia Medica, Pharmacology and Therapeutics* (1892); medical biographies published in *Guy's Hospital Reports*; *Great Doctors of the Nineteenth Century* (1935); and *Keats as Doctor and Patient* (1938); KBE, 1919.

HALFORD, Frank Bernard (1894–1955), aircraft-engine designer; educated at Felsted and Nottingham University College; joined Royal Flying Corps, 1914; redesigned Austro-Daimler engine for DH4; worked with Sir Harry *Ricardo, 1919–23, for Aircraft Disposal Company, 1924–7; technical director, Napier Engine Company, 1935–44, de Havilland Engine Company, 1944–55; designed Cirrus (1925) and Gipsy (1928) engines; Rapier and Sabre for Napier; and for jet propulsion the Goblin, Ghost, Gyron, Sprite, and Spectre engines; CBE, 1948; president, Royal Aeronautical Society, 1951–2.

HALFORD, Sir **Henry,** first baronet (1766–1844), physician; son of Dr James Vaughan; BA, Christ Church, Oxford, 1788; MD, 1791; physician to Middlesex Hospital, 1793–1800; FRCP, 1794; created baronet, 1809; changed his name, 1814, attended George IV, William IV, and Queen Victoria; president, College of Physicians, 1820–44; published *Account of what appeared on opening the Coffin of King Charles I* (1813) and *Essays and Orations delivered at the Royal College of Physicians* (1831).

HALFORD, Sir **Henry St John,** third baronet (1828–1897), rifleman; educated at Eton and Merton College, Oxford; BA, 1849; succeeded to baronetcy, 1868; CB, 1886; shot for England in first match for Elcho Shield, 1862, and in many subsequent years till 1893; made highest scores in 1862 and 1872; won Albert Prize, 1862 and 1893, Duke of Cambridge Prize and Association Cup, 1871, and Dudley, 1893; member of government small arms committee, 1880; published *Art of Shooting with the Rifle* (1888).

HALFPENNY, Joseph (1748–1811), topographical draughtsman and engraver; clerk of the works to John *Carr (1723–1807) at restoration of York Cathedral; published *Gothic Ornaments in the Cathedral Church of York* (1795–1800) and *Fragmenta Vetusta* (1807).

HALFPENNY, William (*fl.* 1752), alias Michael Hoare; credited with invention of drawing arches by intersection of straight lines; published *Practical Architecture, Useful Architecture* (1751), *Geometry, Theoretical and Practical* (1752), and handbooks on rural architecture.

HALGHTON, John of (d. 1324). See HALTON.

HALHED, Nathaniel Brassey (1751–1830), orientalist; at Harrow with Richard Brinsley *Sheridan; knew Sir William *Jones while at Christ Church, Oxford; entered East India Company's service; translated the Gentoo Code from the Persian, 1776; issued from first press set up in India Bengali grammar (1778); first called attention to affinity between Sanskrit words and 'those of Persian, Arabic, and even of Latin and Greek'; returned to England; MP, Lymington, 1790–5; became a believer in Richard *Brothers; moved that Brothers's *Revealed Knowledge* be laid before the House of Commons, 1795; entered East India House, 1809; published (1771) verse translation (with Sheridan) of *The Love Epistles of Aristaenetus* and *Imitations of some of the Epigrams of Martial* (1793).

HALIBURTON, Arthur Lawrence, first Baron Haliburton (1832–1907), civil servant; son of Thomas Chandler *Haliburton; born and educated at Windsor, Nova Scotia; called to bar there, 1855; joined commissariat department of British Army, 1855; served in Crimea and in Canada; civilian assistant director of supplies and transports, 1869; director, 1879; supervised victualling of eight campaigns; KCB, 1885; permanent under-secretary for war, 1895–7; GCB, 1897; baron, 1898; vigorously defended short military service in *The Times*, 1897; in later years advocated universal military training.

HALIBURTON, George (1616–1665), bishop of Dunkeld; graduated at King's College, Aberdeen, 1636; attended Scots army at Newcastle, 1643; deposed from ministry for holding communication with *Montrose, 1644; restored, 1645; silenced for preaching in the king's interest, 1651; parliamentary commissioner for visiting Aberdeen University, 1661; bishop of Dunkeld, 1662–5.

HALIBURTON, George (1628–1715), bishop of Aberdeen; MA, St Andrews, 1646; DD, 1673; minister of Coupar-Angus, 1648; bishop of Brechin, 1678–82, of Aberdeen, 1682–9; conducted episcopal services at Newtyle, 1698–1710.

HALIBURTON (formerly **BURTON**), **James** (1788–1862), Egyptologist; MA, Trinity College, Cambridge, 1815; resumed his father's first name of Haliburton, 1838; while engaged on geological survey of Egypt for Mehemet Ali decided position of Myos Hormos or Aphrodite; travelled with Edward W. *Lane; published *Excerpta Hieroglyphica* (1822–8); again in the eastern desert, 1830–2; worked with Joseph *Bonomi the younger and Sir John Gardner *Wilkinson; his *Collectanea Egyptiaca* presented to British Museum, 1864.

HALIBURTON, Thomas (1674–1712). See HALYBURTON.

HALIBURTON, Thomas Chandler (1796–1865), author of 'Sam Slick'; born and educated in Nova Scotia; chief justice in Nova Scotia of common pleas, 1828–40, and judge of Supreme Court, 1842–56; afterwards lived in England; MP, Launceston, 1859–65; DCL, Oxford, 1858. In his *Clockmaker, or Sayings and Doings of Sam Slick* (1837, 1838, and 1840) he founded American school of humour. His other works include *The Attaché, or Sam Slick in England* (1843–4), besides two books on Nova Scotia, and *The Old Judge, or Life in a Colony* (1843).

HALIDAY, Alexander Henry (1728?–1802), physician and politician; son of Samuel *Haliday; physician at Belfast; saved Belfast from destruction by 'Hearts of Steel' rioters, 1770; corresponded with *Charlemont.

HALIDAY, Charles (1789–1866), antiquary; brother of William *Haliday; secretary of Dublin Chamber of Commerce, director of Bank of Ireland, and consul for Greece; published pamphlets on social subjects, harbour and lighthouse reform, etc.; his *Scandinavian Kingdom of Dublin* edited by J. P. *Prendergast (1881).

HALIDAY (or **HOLLYDAY**), **Samuel** (1685–1739), Irish non-subscribing divine; graduated at Glasgow; ordained at Geneva, 1708; chaplain to Scots Cameronians in Flanders; when minister at Belfast refused to subscribe Westminster Confession, 1720, defending his conduct in *Reasons against Imposition of Subscription . . .*, etc. (1724).

HALIDAY, William (1788–1812), Irish grammarian; learnt Irish from three Munstermen in Dublin; a founder of the Gaelic Society of Dublin, 1807; published, as 'Edmond O'Connell', *Uraicecht na Gaedhilge* (Irish grammar, 1808) and vol. i of a translation of *Keating's *History of Ireland* (1811).

HALIFAX, earls of. See MONTAGU, CHARLES, first earl of second creation, 1661–1715; DUNK, GEORGE MONTAGU, first earl of third creation, 1716–1771; WOOD, EDWARD FREDERICK LINDLEY, first earl, 1881–1959.

HALIFAX, marquises of. See SAVILE, Sir GEORGE, 1633–1695; SAVILE, WILLIAM, second marquis, 1665–1700.

HALIFAX, Viscounts. See WOOD, Sir CHARLES, first viscount, 1800–1885; WOOD, Sir CHARLES LINDLEY, second viscount, 1839–1934.

HALIFAX, John (*fl.* 1230). See HOLYWOOD.

HALKERSTON, Peter (d. 1833?), Scottish lawyer; hon. LL D; bailie of Holyrood Abbey; published *Treatise on the History, Law, and Privileges of Holyrood House* (1831) and several legal works.

HALKERSTONE, David (d. 1680). See HACKSTON.

HALKET, Elizabeth, afterwards Lady Wardlaw (1677–1727). See WARDLAW.

HALKET, George (d. 1756), Scottish songwriter; schoolmaster and session-clerk of Rathen, 1714–25, and Cairnbulg, 1725–50; published works, including *Occasional Poems upon several Subjects* (1727) and two ballads, entitled 'Logie o' Buchan' and 'Whirry Whigs, Awa' Man'; *Dialogue between the Devil and George II* also ascribed to him.

HALKETT, Anne (or **Anna**), **Lady** (1622–1699), Royalist and author; née Murray; skilled in surgery; with her lover, Joseph *Bampfield, contrived escape of James, duke of York, 1647; attended soldiers wounded at Dunbar, 1650, and was thanked by Charles II; married Sir James Halkett, 1656; left manuscript devotional works; her autobiography printed (1875).

HALKETT, Sir **Colin** (1774–1856), general; son of Frederick Godar *Halkett; served in the Dutch Foot Guards, 1792–5, and Light Infantry (in British pay); commanded 2nd light battalion of the German Legion in Germany, 1805–6, Ireland, 1806, the Peninsula and the Walcheren expedition, 1809; led the German light brigade at Albuera, 1811, during Burgos retreat, 1812, and Vittoria, 1813, and succeeding battles; commanded British brigade at Quatre Bras and Waterloo; lieutenant-general, 1830; general, 1841; commander at Bombay, 1831–2; governor of Chelsea Hospital, 1849; GCB and GCH.

HALKETT, Frederick Godar (1728–1803), major-general; lieutenant-colonel, 2nd battalion of the Dundas Regiment, in Holland, 1777; retired, 1782; raised a Scots battalion for English Army; major-general, 1802.

HALKETT, Hugh, Baron von Halkett (1783–1863), Hanoverian general and British colonel; son of Frederick Godar *Halkett; served in India in Scots brigade, 1798–1801; distinguished himself at Copenhagen, 1807; led battalion at Albuera, 1811, Salamanca, 1812, the Burgos retreat and Venta de Pozo, 1812; organized Hanoverian levies, 1813; commanded brigade at Göhrde, 1813, and Schestedt, 1813; led the 3rd and 4th brigades of Hanoverian militia at Waterloo, 1815, and captured Cambronne (chief of the Imperial Guard) with his own hand; commanded 10th Army Corps of German confederation in Schleswig-Holstein, 1848; created baron with full pension, 1858; CB and GCH; died at Hanover.

HALKETT, Samuel (1814–1871), keeper of Advocates' Library, Edinburgh, 1848–71; began *Dictionary of Anonymous and Pseudonymous Literature of Great Britain* (published 1882–8).

HALL, Mrs Agnes C. (1777–1846), author; wife of Robert *Hall (1763–1824); contributed to various cyclopaedias; translated Alfieri's *Autobiography* (1810) and works by Madame de Genlis; published novels.

HALL, Sir (Alfred) Daniel (1864–1942), educationist, administrator, and scientific research worker; scholar of Manchester Grammar School and Balliol College, Oxford; first class, natural science, 1884; first principal, South Eastern Agricultural College, Wye, Kent, 1894–1902; director, Rothamsted Experimental Station, 1902–12; member of Development Commission, 1910–17; secretary, Board of Agriculture, 1917–20; chief scientific adviser, Ministry of Agriculture, 1920–7; director, John Innes Horticultural Institution, 1927–39; publications include *The Soil* (1903), *The Book of the Rothamsted Experiments* (1905), *A Pilgrimage of British Farming* (1913), *The Apple* (1933, with M. B. Crane), *The Genus Tulipa* (1940), and *Reconstruction and the Land* (1941); FRS, 1909; KCB, 1918.

HALL, Mrs Anna Maria (1800–1881), author; née Fielding; married Samuel Carter *Hall, 1824; edited *St. James's Magazine*, 1862–3; received civil list pension, 1868; assisted in foundation of Brompton Consumption Hospital and other benevolent institutions; published nine novels, including *Marian, or a Young Maid's Fortunes* (1840) and *Lights and Shadows of Irish Life* (1838); published two plays and *Tales of the Irish Peasantry* (1840) and *Midsummer Eve, a Fairy Tale of Love* (1848); collaborated with her husband.

HALL, Anthony (1679–1723), antiquary; fellow of The Queen's College, Oxford, 1706; MA, 1704; DD, 1721; rector of Hampton Poyle, 1720; edited *Leland's Commentaries* (1709) and works of Nicholas *Trivet (1719); superintended publication of *Hudson's Josephus (1720).

HALL, Archibald (1736–1778), divine; studied at Edinburgh and Glasgow universities; minister

of Torphicen, West Lothian, and from 1765 of the Secession church, Well Street, London; published religious works.

HALL, Arthur (*fl.* 1563–1604), translator and politician; ward of Sir William *Cecil (Lord Burghley); MP, Grantham, 1571–81 and 1585; reprimanded by speaker for lewd speaking, 1572; expelled the house, 1581, for offensive pamphlet impugning action of speaker and members in the case of his servant, who, being freed from ordinary arrest as privileged, was sent to the Tower by the House of Commons for assault; confined in the Tower two years, 1581–3; offered political advice to Burghley (1591) and to James I (1604); his *Ten Books of Homer's Iliades, translated out of French* (1581) the first English version of Homer's *Iliad*.

HALL, Arthur Henry (1876–1949), engineer; educated at Clifton and Trinity Hall, Cambridge; first class, mechanical sciences, 1898; served engineering apprenticeship; assistant mechanical engineer, Woolwich Arsenal, 1905; assistant superintendent, 1914–17; director, torpedoes and mines production, Admiralty, 1917–19; superintendent, airship construction, Cardington, 1926–8; chief superintendent, Royal Aircraft Establishment, Farnborough, 1928–41; CB, 1937.

HALL, Sir Arthur John (1866–1951), physician; educated at Rugby, Caius College, Cambridge, and St Bartholomew's Hospital; qualified, 1889; FRCP, 1904; on staff of Sheffield Royal Hospital, 1890–1931; taught physiology and pathology in and built up Sheffield Medical School into faculty of medicine, Sheffield University (1905); dean, 1911–16; professor of medicine, 1915–31; authority on encephalitis lethargica; knighted, 1935; hon. D.Sc., Sheffield, 1928; president, Association of Physicians of Great Britain and Ireland, 1931.

HALL, Basil (1788–1844), captain in the navy and author; son of Sir James *Hall; witnessed Battle of Corunna, 1809; accompanied Lord *Amherst's Chinese embassy; carried out pendulum observations off South America; interviewed Napoleon; FRS, 1816; travelled in North America, 1827–8; died insane in Haslar Hospital; his *Fragments of Voyages and Travels* (1831–3) often reprinted.

HALL, Sir Benjamin, first Baron Llanover (1802–1867), politician; of Westminster and Christ Church, Oxford; MP, Monmouth, 1831–7, Marylebone, 1837–59; created baronet, 1838; active in cause of ecclesiastical reform; privy councillor, 1854; president of Board of Health, 1854; as chief commissioner of works,

1855–8, established Metropolitan Board of Works; created Baron Llanover, 1859.

HALL, Chambers (1786–1855), virtuoso; presented to British Museum drawings by *Girtin and antiquities, and to Oxford University antiquities and pictures.

HALL, Charles (1720?–1783), line-engraver.

HALL, Charles (1745?–1825?), writer on economics; MD, Leiden; published *Effects of Civilisation on the People in European States* (1805); died in the Fleet.

HALL, Sir Charles (1814–1883), vice-chancellor; barrister, Middle Temple, 1838; assisted and subsequently succeeded Lewis *Duval in conveyancing practice; conveyancer to court of Chancery, 1864; authority on real property law; vice-chancellor, 1873; knighted, 1873; twice refused silk.

HALL, Sir Charles (1843–1900), recorder of London; son of Sir Charles *Hall (1814–1883); educated at Harrow and Trinity College, Cambridge; MA, 1870; barrister, Lincoln's Inn, 1866; attorney-general to prince of Wales, 1877–92; QC, 1881; KCMG, 1890; recorder of London, 1892; privy councillor, 1899; MP for the Chesterton division of Cambridgeshire, 1885–6 and 1886–92, and for Holborn division of Finsbury, 1892.

HALL, Charles Henry (1763–1827), dean of Durham; educated at Westminster and Christ Church, Oxford; MA, 1786; DD, 1800; won university prizes for Latin and English essays; dean of Christ Church, 1809–24; Bampton lecturer and prebendary of Exeter, 1798; regius professor of divinity and vicar of Luton, 1807; dean of Durham, 1824–7.

HALL, Chester Moor (1703–1771), inventor of the achromatic telescope, 1733; bencher, Inner Temple, 1763.

HALL, Christopher Newman (1816–1902), Congregationalist divine; son of John Vine *Hall; ordained, 1842; accomplished preacher of evangelical fervour; minister of Surrey Chapel, 1854; LL B, London, 1856; chairman of Congregational Union, 1866; built Christ Church, Westminster Bridge Road, 1876; resigned pastorate, 1892; hon. DD, Edinburgh, 1902; wrote many devotional works and hymns; autobiography published, 1898.

HALL, Edmund (1620?–1686), divine; left Oxford to fight for parliament; fellow of Pembroke, 1647; MA, 1650; imprisoned for attacking *Cromwell, 1651–2; rector of Chipping Norton and (1680–6) of Great Risington; published *Scriptural Discourse of the Apostacy and the Anti-*

christ (1653) and anonymous monarchical pamphlets.

HALL, Edward (d. 1547), historian; educated at Eton and King's College, Cambridge; fellow, 1517–18; reader at Gray's Inn, 1534; common serjeant, 1532; MP, Bridgnorth, 1542; commissioner to inquire into transgressions of Six Articles, 1541–4; his *Union of the Noble and Illustre Famelies of Lancastre and York* (1542, completed by *Grafton, 1550), followed by Shakespeare, prohibited by Queen Mary, and not reprinted till 1809.

HALL, Sir Edward Marshall (1858–1927), lawyer; called to bar (Inner Temple), 1883; first real opportunity, murder case (*Rex.* v. *Hermann*), when he obtained verdict of manslaughter, 1894; QC, 1898; Conservative MP, Southport division, Lancashire, 1900–6, East Toxteth division, Liverpool, 1910–16; practice temporarily affected by Court of Appeal's criticism of his conduct in libel case against *Daily Mail*, 1901; greatest triumph, *Russell (1896–1973) divorce case, 1923; recorder of Guildford, 1916; knighted, 1917; at his best, a powerful advocate.

HALL, Elisha (*fl.* 1562), fanatic; examined by Bishop *Grindal, 1562.

HALL, Fitzedward (1825–1901), philologist; born at Troy, New York; went to India, 1846; tutor (1850) and professor of Sanskrit (1853) at Benares Government College; served in Sepoy mutiny; settled in London, 1862; professor of Sanskrit at King's College, and librarian to India Office; while in India discovered many Sanskrit MSS, and edited many Sanskrit and Hindi literary works and treatises of Hindu philosophy; edited works for Early English Text Society, 1864–9, published many philological researches, and from 1878 helped in preparation of *New English Dictionary* and Joseph *Wright's *Dialect Dictionary*; hon. DCL, Oxford, 1860; hon. LL D, Harvard, 1895.

HALL, Francis (1595–1675). See LINE.

HALL, Francis Russell (1788–1866), theological writer; educated at Manchester and St John's College, Cambridge; fellow; MA, 1813; DD, 1839; rector of Fulbourn, 1826–66; published theological pamphlets, including *Reasons for not contributing to circulate the Apocrypha* (1825).

HALL, George (1612?–1668), bishop of Chester; son of Joseph *Hall; fellow of Exeter College, Oxford, 1632; MA, 1634; DD, 1660; deprived by parliament of vicarage of Menheniot and archdeaconry of Cornwall, but allowed to officiate in London; canon of Windsor and archdeacon of Canterbury, 1660; bishop of Chester, 1662–8; held with his see rectory of Wigan.

HALL, George (1753–1811), bishop of Dromore; scholar, fellow, senior fellow (1790–1800), professor of Greek, modern history, and mathematics, and provost (1806–11) of Trinity College, Dublin; MA, 1778; DD, 1790; bishop of Dromore, 1811.

HALL, Harry Reginald Holland (1873–1930), archaeologist; BA, St John's College, Oxford, 1895; assistant, department of Egyptian and Assyrian antiquities, British Museum, 1896; took part in Egypt Exploration Fund excavations in winters of 1903–6; deputy keeper, department of Egyptian and Assyrian antiquities, 1919; keeper, 1924; FBA, 1926; works include *The Oldest Civilisation of Greece* (1901) and *The Ancient History of the Near East* (1913).

HALL, Henry (d. 1680), Covenanter; joined Covenanters on Pentland Hills, 1676; imprisoned; after his release wandered about with *Cargill and others; assisted in drawing up Covenanting manifesto, 1679; one of the leaders at Drumclog and Bothwell Brigg, 1679; fled to Holland; captured on his return by Thomas *Dalyell; died of a wound; 'Queensferry Paper' found on him.

HALL, Henry, the elder (1655?–1707), organist; chorister of the Chapel Royal; studied with *Purcell under *Blow; organist of Exeter (1674) and Hereford (1688) Cathedrals; services and anthems by him in Tudway's collection.

HALL, Henry, the younger (d. 1713), organist; son of Henry *Hall the elder; organist of Hereford Cathedral, 1707; admired by contemporaries as composer of light verse.

HALL, Hubert (1857–1944), archivist; educated at Shrewsbury; entered Public Record Office, 1879; senior clerk, 1892; assistant keeper, 1912–21; secretary, Royal Commission on Public Records, 1910–18; reader in palaeography and economic history, London, 1896–1926; publications include *Studies in English Official Historical Documents* (1908).

HALL, Jacob (*fl.* 1668), rope-dancer; seen by *Pepys at Bartholomew Fair, Smithfield, 1668; much favoured by Lady *Castlemaine.

HALL, James (d. 1612), navigator; made two voyages (1605, 1606) to Greenland as pilot of Danish expeditions, described by *Purchas; commanded English expedition to Greenland, 1612; mortally wounded by an Eskimo.

HALL, James (1755–1826), Presbyterian divine; educated at Glasgow University; pastor of associate congregations at Cumnock, 1777, and Edinburgh, 1786; chairman of Reunion Committee, 1820.

HALL, Sir James, fourth baronet (1761–1832), geologist and chemist; intimate with *Hutton and *Playfair; tested Huttonian system by study of continental and Scottish formations; refuted Wernerian views by laboratory experiments; president of Royal Society of Edinburgh; MP, Mitchell or Michael, Cornwall, 1807–12; published *Essay on Gothic Architecture* (1813).

HALL, James (1800?–1854), amateur painter; son of Sir James *Hall; friend of *Wilkie and Watson Gordon; exhibited Scottish landscapes and portraits, including *Wellington (1838) and *Scott, at Royal Academy, 1835–54; presented manuscript of *Waverley* to Advocates' Library.

HALL (or HALLE), John (1529?–1566?), poet and medical writer; member of Worshipful Company of Chirurgeons; published metrical versions of Proverbs, Ecclesiastes, and some Psalms, 1549; translated Lanfranc's *Chirurgia Parva* (1565); published other medical tracts, of which one was reprinted (1844).

HALL, John (1575–1635), physician, of Stratford-upon-Avon; educated Queens' College, Cambridge, BA, 1593–4; married Susanna, Shakespeare's eldest daughter, 1607; with her acted as Shakespeare's executor, and inherited New Place; their daughter Elizabeth (d. 1670), Shakespeare's last direct descendant; his *Select Observations on English Bodies, and Cures both Empericall and Historicall* issued by James Cooke (1657).

HALL, John (1627–1656), poet and pamphleteer; of Durham and St John's College, Cambridge; friend of *Hobbes and Samuel *Hartlib; accompanied *Cromwell to Scotland, 1650 and wrote *The Grounds and Reasons of Monarchy* and other political pamphlets. His works include *Horae Vacivae, or Essays* (1646), *Poems* (1647, reprinted, 1816), and *Satire against Presbytery* (1648).

HALL, John (d. 1707), criminal; sentenced to death for housebreaking, 1700; pardoned on condition of removing to America; deserted the ship and returned, 1704; executed at Tyburn; credited with *Memoirs of the Right Villanous John Hall* (published, 1708).

HALL, John (d. 1707), author of *Jacobs Ladder* (1676); fellow of Trinity College, Cambridge, 1658; MA, 1659; BD, 1666; prebendary of St Paul's, 1664; president of Sion College; rector of Finchley, 1666.

HALL, John (1633–1710), bishop of Bristol; nephew of Edmund and Thomas *Hall (1610–1665); of Merchant Taylors' School and Pembroke College, Oxford; scholar, fellow (1653), and master (1664–1710); MA, 1653; DD, 1669;

Margaret professor of divinity, 1676; bishop of Bristol, 1691–1710; the last Puritan bishop; benefactor of his college and Bromsgrove.

HALL, John (1739–1797), line-engraver; executed plates in *Bell's *Shakespeare* and *British Theatre*; exhibited with Incorporated Society of Artists, 1766–76; historical engraver to George III, 1785; engraved Benjamin *West's works and portraits after *Reynolds, *Gainsborough, and others.

HALL, Sir John (1795–1866), army surgeon; MD, St Andrews, 1845; principal medical officer in Kaffraria, 1847 and 1851, in Crimea, 1854–6; KCB and inspector-general of hospitals; defended Crimean medical service, 1857 and 1858; died at Pisa.

HALL, Sir John (1824–1907), premier of New Zealand; born at Hull; employed at London General Post Office, 1843–52; emigrated to Lyttelton, New Zealand, for sheep-farming, 1852; first mayor of Christchurch, 1862–3; elected for Christchurch to first House of Representatives, 1855; colonial secretary, 1856; postmaster-general and electric telegraph commissioner, 1866–9; called to Legislative Council, 1872; Colonial Secretary, 1872–3; opposed (secular) Education Act of 1877; premier, 1879–82; KCMG, 1882; his ministry repealed Sir George *Grey's land-tax, passed Triennial Parliaments Bill and Universal Suffrage Bill; Hall introduced woman's suffrage amendment into Electoral Bill, 1893.

HALL, John Vine (1774–1860), author of *The Sinner's Friend*; bookseller at Maidstone, 1814–50; his *Sinner's Friend* originally composed of extracts from Bogatzky, but completely rewritten in later editions, and translated into thirty languages.

HALL, Joseph (1574–1656), bishop of Exeter and Norwich; educated at Ashby-de-la-Zouch and Emmanuel College, Cambridge; fellow, 1595; MA, 1596; DD, 1610; published *Virgidemiarum* (vol. i, 1597, vol. ii, 1598, satires, ed. Grosart, 1879); attacked by *Marston, 1598; incumbent of Hawstead, Suffolk, 1601; accompanied Sir Edmund Bacon to Spa, 1605; chaplain to *Henry, prince of Wales, 1608; incumbent of Waltham, Essex, 1608; chaplain to Lord *Doncaster in France, 1616; dean of Worcester, 1616; accompanied James I to Scotland, 1617; deputy at synod of Dort, 1618; bishop of Exeter, 1627–41; conciliatory towards Puritans; issued (with Laud's alteration) *Divine Right of Episcopacy* (1640); defended the liturgy both in the House of Lords and in controversy; member of the Lords' committee on religion, 1641; bishop of Norwich, 1641–7; defended canons of 1640, and was

impeached and imprisoned, 1642; his episcopal revenues were sequestrated, 1643, and his cathedral desecrated; expelled from his palace, *c.*1647. Besides satires and controversial works against Brownists and Presbyterians, he published poems (ed. *Singer, 1824, *Grosart, 1879), meditations, devotional works, and autobiographical tracts, also *Observations of some Specialities of Divine Providence, Hard Measure* (1647), and *The Shaking of the Olive Tree* (posthumous, 1660); collective editions issued (1808, 1837, and 1863).

HALL, Marshall (1790–1857), physiologist, son of Robert *Hall (1755–1827); MD, Edinburgh, 1812; visited medical schools at Paris, Göttingen, and Berlin, 1814–15; practised in Nottingham, 1817–25; FRGS, 1818; FRS, 1832; practised in London, 1826–53, making his speciality nervous diseases; FRCP, 1841; Gulstonian lecturer, 1842, Croonian, 1850–2; prominent in foundation of British Association. During his investigations into the circulation of the blood he made his important discovery of reflex action, 1832, which he applied to the explanation of convulsive paroxysms. He rationalized the treatment of epilepsy, and introduced the ready method in asphyxia. Besides numerous scientific and medical works, he published *Twofold Slavery of the United States* (1854). He devised the system now in use for restoring animation to the partially drowned.

HALL, Peter (1802–1849), divine and topographer; of Winchester and Brasenose College, Oxford; MA, 1830; successively minister of Tavistock Chapel, Drury Lane, Long Acre Chapel, St Martin's, and St Thomas's, Walcot, Bath; edited Bishop Joseph *Hall's works, 1837–9, and *Satires* (1838), also Bishop *Andrewes's *Preces privatae* (1848), some *Remains* of Bishop *Lowth of disputed authenticity; published topographical works on Winchester, Salisbury, Wimborne Minster, and the New Forest.

HALL, Philip (1904–1982), mathematician; educated at Christ's Hospital and King's College, Cambridge; senior scholar; first class, part i, 1923, and wrangler, part ii, 1925, mathematical tripos; fellow of King's, 1927; university lecturer, 1933; worked at Government Code and Cipher School, Bletchley, 1941–5; reader in algebra, Cambridge, 1949; Sadleirian professor of pure mathematics, 1953–67; published papers on group theory including 'A Contribution to the Theory of Groups of Prime-power Order' (1934); FRS, 1942; Sylvester medallist, 1961; president, London Mathematical Society, 1955–7; awarded other prizes and honorary doctorates; hon. fellow, Jesus College, Cambridge, 1976.

HALL, Richard (d. 1604), Roman Catholic divine; fellow of Pembroke Hall, Cambridge, 1556; MA, 1559; DD, Rome; professor of holy scripture at Douai, and canon of St Omer, where he died; his *Life of John Fisher, bishop of Rochester* printed surreptitiously and incorrectly, 1655; published Latin writings on the revolt of the Netherlands and other works.

HALL, Robert (1753–1836), raised Devon and Cornwall Fencibles, 1794.

HALL, Robert (1755–1827), first user of chlorine for bleaching, and inventor of a new crane.

HALL, Robert (1763–1824), medical writer; great-grandson of Henry *Hall (d. 1680) the Covenanter; MD, Edinburgh; naval surgeon on Jamaica Station and medical officer to a Niger expedition; works include translation of Spallanzani on the circulation (1801) and Guyton de Morveau's *Means of Purifying Infected Air* (1802).

HALL, Robert (1764–1831), Baptist divine; said to have preached when 11; educated at Baptist Academy, Bristol, and King's College, Aberdeen; MA, Aberdeen, 1784; assistant to Caleb *Evans at Broadmead Chapel, 1785–90; succeeded Robert *Robinson at Cambridge, 1791–1806; temporarily insane, 1804–5 and 1805–6; at Harvey Lane, Leicester, 1807–25; preached celebrated sermon on death of Princess *Charlotte, 1817; DD, Aberdeen, 1817; created much sensation by his *Modern Infidelity considered with respect to its Influence on Society* (1800); returned to Bristol, 1826; *Fifty Sermons* by him issued (1843), *Miscellaneous Works and Remains* (Bohn, 1846).

HALL, Robert (1817–1882), vice-admiral; entered navy, 1833; commanded the *Stromboli* in Baltic and Black seas, 1854–5; took part in Kertch expedition, 1855; naval secretary to Admiralty, 1872–82.

HALL, Samuel (1769?–1852), 'the Sherwood Forest Patriarch'; cobbler at Sutton-in-Ashfield; invented machine for simultaneous sowing, manuring, and pressing of turnip-seed.

HALL, Samuel (1781–1863), engineer and inventor; son of Robert *Hall (1755–1827); took out patent for 'gassing' lace and net, 1817 and 1823, and for a 'surface condenser' for use at sea, 1838.

HALL, Samuel Carter (1800–1889), author and editor; son of Robert *Hall (1753–1836); left Cork for London, 1821; literary secretary to Ugo Foscolo, 1822, and a reporter in House of Lords, 1823; founded and edited *The Amulet*, 1826–37; connected with *New Monthly Magazine*, 1830–6; edited *Art Union Monthly* (afterwards *Art Jour-*

nal), 1839–80; received civil list pension, 1880; published works, including *Book of British Ballads* (1842), *Gallery of Modern Sculpture* (1849–54), and *Memoirs of Great Men and Women . . . from personal acquaintance* (1871).

HALL, Spencer (1806–1875), librarian of the Athenaeum Club, 1833–75; FSA, 1858; among other works translated and edited *Documents from Simancas relating to Reign of Elizabeth* (1865).

HALL, Spencer Timothy (1812–1885), 'the Sherwood Forester'; son of Samuel *Hall (1769?–1852); gained the co-editorship of the *Iris* and governorship of Hollis Hospital, Sheffield, by his *Forester's Offering* (1841), set up in type by himself; lectured on phrenology and mesmerism; published *Mesmeric Experiences* (1845); cured Harriet *Martineau, 1844; issued *Homoeopathy, a Testimony* (1852); received degrees from Tübingen; published miscellaneous works.

HALL, Thomas (1610–1665), ejected minister; uncle of John *Hall (1633–1710); BA, Pembroke College, Oxford, 1629; BD, 1652; perpetual curate and master of the Grammar School, King's Norton; signed *Baxter's Worcestershire petition; ejected, 1662; wrote against unlicensed preachers, indiscriminate baptism, Fifth-Monarchy men, and cavalier customs.

HALL, Thomas (1660?–1719?), Roman Catholic divine; brother of William *Hall (d. 1718?); DD, Paris; philosophy professor at Douai, 1688–90; died at Paris.

HALL, Timothy (1637?–1690), titular bishop of Oxford; BA, Pembroke College, Oxford; ejected from Norwood and Southam, 1662; afterwards conformed; incumbent of Allhallows Staining, 1677; denied installation to bishopric of Oxford by canons of Christ Church, 1688; read the Declaration of Indulgence at Staining, 1687.

HALL, Westley (1711–1776), eccentric divine; pupil of John *Wesley at Lincoln College, Oxford; married Wesley's sister Martha after engaging himself to Keziah; active in management of Methodist Society, but adopted Moravian views and (1743) formed new society at Salisbury; afterwards preached deism and polygamy; disturbed Charles *Wesley's meetings at Bristol, 1750–1.

HALL, William (d. 1700), violinist; son of Henry *Hall the elder.

HALL, William (d. 1718?), Carthusian; chaplain and preacher in ordinary to James II; afterwards prior of Nieuwpoort, in Flanders.

HALL, William (1748–1825), poet and antiquary; gozzard and cow-leech in the fens; afterwards bookseller at Lynn; published *Sketch of*

Local History (1812) and *Reflections upon Times, and Times, and Times!* (1816–18).

HALL, William Edward (1835–1894), legal writer; MA, University College, Oxford, 1859; barrister, Lincoln's Inn, 1861; travelled widely, making valuable collection illustrative of the archaeology of art; published *International Law* (1880) and other writings; elected member of Institut de Droit International, 1882.

HALL, William George Glenvil (1887–1962), politician; educated at Friends' School, Saffron Walden; clerk in Barclay's Bank, London; did social work in East End; joined Independent Labour party, 1905; although a Quaker, enlisted and served in army, 1914–18; financial officer, Labour party, 1919–39; unsuccessful candidate in 1922–4 elections; Labour MP, Portsmouth Central, 1929–31; MP, Colne Valley, Yorkshire, 1939–62; called to bar (Gray's Inn), 1933; financial secretary to Treasury, 1945–50; PC, 1947; British representative, United Nations Assembly, 1945–6, and 1948; chairman, Parliamentary Labour party, 1950–2; attended Consultative Assembly, Strasburg, 1950–2; member, BBC Advisory Council, 1952; president, United Kingdom Alliance, 1959.

HALL, Sir William Hutcheon (1797?–1878), admiral; with Basil *Hall in China, 1815–17; employed in steamboats on the Hudson and Delaware, 1836–9; in command of the *Nemesis* (paddle-steamer); rendered valuable service in Chinese War, 1840–3, and was given naval rank; FRS, 1847; commanded the *Hecla* and the *Blenheim* in the Baltic, 1854–5; KCB, 1867; vice-admiral, 1869; admiral, 1875; published pamphlets on Sailors' Homes and National Defences.

HALL, Sir William King (1816–1886), admiral; mate of the *Benbow* under Houston *Stewart at bombardment of Acre, 1840; flag-captain to *Napier and Sir M. *Seymour in the Baltic, 1854–5; distinguished himself during second Chinese War, 1856–8; KCB, 1871; admiral, 1879; commander at the Nore, 1877–9.

HALL, Sir (William) Reginald (1870–1943), admiral; entered navy, 1884; commanded battle cruiser *Queen Mary*, 1913–14; introduced many reforms including three-watch system; director, intelligence division, Admiralty, 1914–18; recruited large staff whose deciphering of German naval signals became a principal factor in naval warfare; intercepted German messages to other countries including Zimmermann telegram proposing German–Mexican offensive alliance; its publication influential on American entry into war; instrumental in capturing Sir Roger *Casement; employed counter-agents and devised many ruses to deceive Germans; rear-admiral,

1917; vice-admiral, 1922; admiral, 1926; Conservative MP, West Derby division of Liverpool (1918–23), Eastbourne (1925–9); KCMG, 1918.

HALL, (William) Stephen (Richard) King-, Baron King-Hall (1893–1966), writer, and broadcaster on politics and international affairs. See KING-HALL.

HALLAHAN, Margaret Mary (1803–1868), foundress of the English congregations of St Catherine of Siena; founded five convents in England, besides schools, churches, and orphanages.

HALLAM, Arthur Henry (1811–1833), subject of Tennyson's *In Memoriam*; elder son of Henry *Hallam; educated at Eton and Trinity College, Cambridge, where he met *Tennyson; studied at the Inner Temple; died suddenly at Vienna (buried at Clevedon). His *Remains* issued (1834).

HALLAM, Henry (1777–1859), historian; educated at Eton and Christ Church, Oxford; BA, 1799; barrister; commissioner of stamps; treasurer of the Statistical Society; vice-president of the Society of Antiquaries; occasionally contributed to *Edinburgh Review*; published *State of Europe during the Middle Ages* (1818), *Constitutional History of England from Henry VII's Accession to the death of George II* (1827), and *Introduction to Literature of Europe* (1837–9), besides a privately printed memoir of his son Arthur.

HALLAM, Henry Fitzmaurice (1824–1850), younger son of Henry *Hallam; of Eton and Trinity College, Cambridge; second chancellor's medallist; founder of the 'Historical' debating club, and one of the 'Apostles'; friend of *Maine and Franklin Lushington; died suddenly at Siena; buried at Clevedon.

HALLAM, John (d. 1537), conspirator; took part in Pilgrimage of Grace, 1536; rebel governor of Hull; hanged for participation in the second 'pilgrimage'.

HALLAM (or HALLUM), Robert (d. 1417), bishop of Salisbury; prebendary of Salisbury, 1395, of York, 1400; archdeacon of Canterbury, 1400; chancellor of Oxford University, 1403; his nomination by the pope as archbishop of York disallowed by the king, 1405; bishop of Salisbury, 1407–17; one of the English representatives at Council of Pisa, 1409; took lead of English 'nation' at Council of Constance, 1414, opposing John XXIII and urging consideration of ecclesiastical reform before election of a new pope; died at Gottlieben Castle, and was buried in Constance Cathedral.

HALLÉ, Sir Charles (Carl Hallé) (1819–1895), pianist and conductor; born at Hagen,

Westphalia; studied under Rinck and Gottfried Weber at Darmstadt; performed with Alard and Franchomme in Paris; visited England, 1843, and made it his home, 1848, settling at Manchester; fulfilled numerous engagements as conductor, Hallé's orchestra, instituted 1857, at Manchester, becoming celebrated in north of England; began series of pianoforte recitals, 1850; first principal, Royal College of Music, Manchester, 1893; hon. LL D, Edinburgh, 1880; knighted, 1888.

HALLE, John (d. 1479), merchant of Salisbury; mayor of Salisbury, 1451, 1458, 1464, and 1465; MP, Salisbury, 1453, 1460, and 1461; the hall of his house in New Canal, Salisbury, still remains with its stained glass.

HALLÉ (formerly **NORMAN-NERUDA), Wilma Maria Francisca,** Lady (1839–1911), violinist; daughter of Josef Neruda; born in Moravia; appeared in London, 1849; married Ludwig Norman, 1864, and secondly Sir Charles *Hallé, 1888; teacher in Berlin, 1898; violinist to Queen *Alexandra, 1901.

HALLETT, John Hughes- (1901–1972), vice-admiral. See HUGHES-HALLETT.

HALLETT (or HALLET), Joseph, I (1628?–1689), ejected minister; held the sequestered living of West Chinnock, Somerset, 1656–63; fined and imprisoned under Conventicle Act, 1673; first Presbyterian minister at Exeter.

HALLETT (or HALLET), Joseph, II (1656–1722), Nonconformist minister of Exeter; son of Joseph *Hallett or Hallet (1628?–1689); pastor of James's meeting, 1713; his academy reputed Unitarian; James *Foster and Peter *King (afterwards lord chancellor) among his pupils.

HALLETT (or HALLET), Joseph, III (1691?–1744), Nonconformist; son of Joseph *Hallett or Hallet (1656–1722); corresponded with *Whiston and adopted his form of Unitarianism; from 1722 pastor at Exeter; published *Free and Impartial Study of the Holy Scriptures* (1729–36) and controversial tracts.

HALLEY, Edmund (1656–1742), astronomer; educated at St Paul's School and The Queen's College, Oxford; laid the foundation of southern astronomy during residence in St Helena, 1676–8, and made the first complete observation of a transit of Mercury, 1677; published on his return *Catalogus Stellarum Australium* (1678); MA, Oxford, 1678; FRS, 1678; arbitrated at Danzig between *Hooke and Hevelius, 1679; made observations of the comet of 1680; travelled in Italy, 1681; originated (by his suggestions) Newton's *Principia*, which he introduced to the Royal Society, and published (1687) at his

own expense, correcting all the proofs; assistant-secretary to the Royal Society and editor of its *Transactions*, 1685–93, contributing first detailed description of trade winds; while deputy-controller of the Mint at Chester, 1696–8, ascended Snowdon to test his method of determining heights by the barometer; in command of the *Paramour Pink* explored Atlantic, and prepared 'General Chart' of variation of compass with the 'Halleyan lines', 1699–1701; surveyed coasts and tides of British Channel and published map, 1702; inspected harbours of Adriatic for Emperor Leopold; Savilian professor of geometry at Oxford, 1703; DCL, Oxford, 1710; a leading member of committee which prepared *Flamsteed's observations for the press, and editor of first (1712) version of Flamsteed's *Historia Coelestis*; predicted accurately total solar eclipse of 1715; observed eclipse and great aurora, 1715; secretary to Royal Society, 1713; astronomer royal, 1721; foreign member of Académie des Sciences, 1729. His lunar and planetary tables appeared posthumously (1749), *Astronomiae Cometicae Synopsis* (1705) being reprinted with them. He accurately predicted the return in 1758 of the comet of 1531, 1607, and 1682, first recommended employment of transits of Venus for ascertaining the sun's distance, and demonstrated (1686) law connecting atmospheric elevation with density. In addition he originated the science of life statistics by 'Breslau Table of Mortality', and that of physical geography by his scientific voyages.

HALLEY, Robert (1796–1876), Nonconformist divine and historian; classical tutor at Highbury College, 1826–39; DD, 1834; minister of Mosley Street Chapel, Manchester, 1839 (Cavendish Street, 1848); chairman of Congregational Union, 1855; principal of New College, St John's Wood, 1857–72; published *Lancashire: its Puritanism and Nonconformity* (1869).

HALL-HOUGHTON, Henry (1823–1889). See HOUGHTON.

HALLIBURTON, William Dobinson (1860–1931), physiologist and biochemist; educated at University College School and University College, London; B.Sc., 1879; MD, 1884; professor of physiology, King's College, 1890–1923; FRS, 1891; pioneer in biochemistry; publications include *Chemical Physiology and Pathology* (1891), *Essentials of Chemical Physiology* (1893), 'Halliburton's' *Physiology* (1896; 19 editions); edited first seven volumes of *Physiological Abstracts*.

HALLIDAY. See also HALIDAY.

HALLIDAY, Sir Andrew (1781–1839), physician; MD, Edinburgh, 1806; served with Portuguese in the Peninsula and with British at

Waterloo; LRCP, 1819; knighted, 1821; domestic physician to duke of Clarence; inspector of West Indian hospitals, 1823; wrote on lunatic asylums (1808 and 1828), the campaign of 1815, and the West Indies (1837).

HALLIDAY, Andrew (1830–1877), essayist and dramatist; son of William Duff, but dropped his surname; educated at Aberdeen; contributed to the magazines; president of Savage Club, 1857, and editor of *Savage Club Papers*, 1868–9; collaborated with William *Brough in *The Area Belle* and other farces; produced also *The Great City* (1867), domestic dramas, and adaptations from *Dickens and *Scott.

HALLIDAY, Edward Irvine (1902–1984), artist; educated at Liverpool Institute and Liverpool College; studied at Liverpool City School of Art, Académie Colarossi, Paris, and Royal College of Art, London; won scholarship to British School, Rome, 1925–8; painted murals for Athenaeum Club, Liverpool and London restaurants; exhibited regularly at Royal Academy from 1929, portraits and conversation pieces; during 1939–45 war served with Royal Air Force and with 'black propaganda' team led by D. Sefton *Delmer; worked in broadcasting for BBC, 1949–54; became royal portrait painter with portrait of Princess Elizabeth, 1948; subsequently painted number of portraits of royal family, including that of the Queen Mother, and portraits of other personages including Jawaharlal Nehru; helped to found Federation of British Artists; president, Royal Society of Portrait Painters, 1970–5, and of Royal Society of British Artists, 1958–75; chairman Artists' General Benevolent Institution, 1965–81; ARCA, 1925; RBA, 1942; RP, 1952; FRSA, 1970; CBE, 1973.

HALLIDAY, Sir Frederick James (1806–1901), first lieutenant-governor of Bengal; joined Bengal Civil Service, 1825; judicial and revenue secretary in Bengal, 1838; secretary in the Home Department, 1849–53; lieutenant-governor of Bengal, 1854–9; reorganized police, improved roads, and advanced education; initiated Calcutta University, 1856; suppressed rising of Santal tribes, 1855; helped to check Sepoy mutiny in Bengal, 1858; KCB, 1860; involved in long controversy—from 1857 to 1888—with a subordinate, William *Tayler, commissioner of Patna, whom he removed from his office, 1857; member of Council of India, 1868–86; an accomplished musician, he frequently performed in concerts in Bengal, London, and elsewhere.

HALLIDAY, Michael Frederick (1822–1869), amateur artist; one of the first English eight in the rifle-shooting competition at Wim-bledon for the Elcho Shield, 1862; an early Pre-Raphaelite; exhibited at the Royal Academy.

HALLIFAX, Samuel (1733–1790), bishop of Gloucester and St Asaph; third wrangler and chancellor's medallist at Cambridge, 1754; fellow of Jesus College, Cambridge, 1756–60, of Trinity Hall, Cambridge, 1760–75; MA, 1757; LL D, 1764; DD, 1775; held both professorships of Arabic, 1768–70, and chair of civil law, 1770–82; letters of 'Erasmus' in favour of continued subscription to Thirty-Nine Articles attributed to him, 1772; chaplain to the king, 1774; rector of Warsop, 1778; bishop of Gloucester, 1781–9, of St Asaph, 1789–90; his *Analysis of the Roman Civil Law* (1774) reissued with additions.

HALLIFAX, Sir Thomas (1721–1789), lord mayor of London; prime warden of Goldsmiths' Company, 1768–9; knighted, 1773; as sheriff of London acted as returning officer when *Wilkes was elected for Middlesex, 1769; one of the court nominees for the mayoralty against him, 1772; lord mayor, 1776–7; opposed press-gang system; MP, Aylesbury, 1784–9.

HALLIFAX, William (1655?–1722), divine; fellow of Corpus Christi College, Oxford, 1682; MA, 1678; DD, 1695; chaplain at Aleppo, 1688–95; rector of Old Swinford, 1699, and vicar of Salwarpe; his account of Palmyra printed in *Philosophical Transactions* (1695); bequeathed books and collections to Corpus Christi College.

HALLILEY, John Elton (1912–1983), actor. See LE MESURIER, JOHN.

HALLIWELL, Henry (1765–1835), classical scholar; MA, Brasenose College, Oxford, 1789; fellow, 1790; rector of Clayton-cum-Keymer, 1803; assisted the Falconers with their edition of Strabo (1807) (see FALCONER, THOMAS, 1772–1839); satirized by *Heber in the *Whippiad* (1843).

HALLIWELL (afterwards **HALLIWELL-PHILLIPPS), James Orchard** (1820–1889), biographer of Shakespeare; scholar and librarian of Jesus College, Cambridge; published *Life and Inventions of Sir Samuel Morland* (1838) and an edition of *Mandeville's *Travels* (1839); FSA and FRS, 1839; in 1840–1 prepared for press twenty-three works, including three tracts on Cambridge manuscripts, *Rara Mathematica*, and his earliest Shakespearean works; edited works for Camden Society, 1839–44, Percy Society, 1842–50 (including *Nursery Rhymes of England*), and Shakespeare Society; catalogued Chetham Library manuscripts, 1841–2; married Henrietta, daughter of Sir Thomas *Phillipps, 1842, whose surname he assumed thirty years later; LL D, Edinburgh, 1883. His *Dictionary of Archaic and Provincial Words* appeared (1847), *Life of Shakespeare (1848) *New Boke about Shakespeare and Stratford-on-Avon* (1850), folio edition of Shakespeare (1853–65), lithograph facsimiles of the Shakespeare quartos (1862–71), *Dictionary of Old English Plays* (1860), *Illustrations of the Life of Shakespeare* (pt. i, 1874), and *Outlines of the Life* (private issue, 1881, published, 1882, 1883, 1884, 1887). He arranged and described the Stratford-upon-Avon archives, and wrote much on the history of the town, besides initiating the movement (1863) for purchase of the site of New Place, Shakespeare's residence there.

HALLORAN (or O'HALLORAN), Lawrence Hynes (1766–1831), author; published poems, 1790–1, and 1801; chaplain to earl of *Northesk at Trafalgar, 1805; dismissed from chaplaincy to forces at Cape Town for his *Cap-Abilities, or South African Characteristics* (1811); transported for forging a frank, 1818.

HALLOWELL, Benjamin (1760–1834). See CAREW, Sir BENJAMIN HALLOWELL.

HALL-PATCH, Sir Edmund Leo (1896–1975), civil servant; brought up in France as a Roman Catholic; trained in Paris as professional musician; commissioned in Royal Artillery, 1914; won Croix de Guerre with palms; worked in band of a Paris cabaret, 1919; met (Sir) Frederick *Leith-Ross, who found him post with Supreme Allied Economic Council and then with Reparations Commission, 1920; head of finance section, 1925–9; financial adviser to government of Siam (Thailand), 1930–2; financial adviser to British group in Turkey, 1933; British member of League of Nations commission of economic experts in Romania, 1934; joined Treasury as assistant secretary and accompanied Leith-Ross to China, 1935; financial adviser to British Embassy in China and Japan, 1936; CMG, 1938; government's financial adviser throughout Far East, 1940; returned to Treasury, 1941; involved in Lend-Lease negotiations; transferred to Foreign Office; promoted to deputy under-secretary, 1946; KCMG, 1947; as principal economic adviser to Ernest *Bevin played important part in British response to the Marshall Plan; ambassador and leader of British delegation to the Organization for European Economic Co-operation (OEEC), 1948; GCMG, 1951; British executive director, International Monetary Fund and International Bank for Reconstruction and Development, Washington, 1952–4; retired from Civil Service and joined Leith-Ross on board of Standard Bank of South Africa, 1954; succeeded Leith-Ross as chairman, 1957–62; on board of Lambert International in New York; an enigmatic character with unusual friends such as Chou En Lai, Syngman Rhee, Yvonne Printemps, and Sacha Guitry.

HALLS, John James (*fl.* 1791–1834), painter; his *Witch* and full-length of Charles *Kean in Richard III engraved by Charles *Turner; published lives of Henry *Salt, FRS (1834) and Nathaniel *Pearce (1831).

HALL-STEVENSON, John (1718–1785). See STEVENSON, JOHN HALL-.

HALPEN (or HALPIN), John Edmond (*fl.* 1780), painter; son of Patrick *Halpen.

HALPEN (or HALPIN), Patrick (*fl.* 1750–1790), line-engraver.

HALPIN (or HALPINE), Charles Graham (1829–1868), writer under name of 'Miles O'Reilly'; son of Nicholas John *Halpin; emigrated from Ireland, 1851; journalist at Boston, Washington, and New York, where he edited the *Times*, and from 1851 the *Leader*; enlisted in Federal Army, 1861; assistant adjutant-general to General David Hunter and General Henry W. Halleck; published *Life and Adventures, &c., of Private Miles O'Reilly* (1864) and *Baked Meats of the Funeral . . . by Private M. O'Reilly* (1866); registrar of New York county, 1867–8; died from an overdose of chloroform.

HALPIN, Nicholas John (1790–1850), author; BA, Dublin, 1815; edited *Dublin Evening Mail*; published three works of Shakespearean criticism and *Observations on certain Passages in the Life of Edmund Spenser* (1850).

HALS, William (1655–1737?), Cornish writer; grandson of Sir Nicholas *Halse; made collections for *History of Cornwall* (part ii published about 1750).

HALSBURY, first earl of (1823–1921), lord chancellor. See GIFFARD, HARDINGE STANLEY.

HALSE, Sir Nicholas (d. 1636), inventor of new mode of drying malt and hops by iron plates; knighted, 1605; governor of Pendennis Castle, 1608; left in manuscript 'Great Britain's Treasure'.

HALSEY, Sir Lionel (1872–1949), admiral; entered navy, 1885; commanded *New Zealand*, 1912–15; captain of fleet to (Lord) *Jellicoe, 1915–16; fourth sea lord, 1916; third sea lord, 1917–18; rear-admiral, 1917; commanded Second Battle Cruiser Squadron in *Australia*, 1918–19; commanded *Renown* as chief of staff to prince of Wales visiting Canada and United States (1919), Australia, New Zealand, West Indies, etc. (1920); comptroller and treasurer to prince of Wales, 1920–36; vice-admiral, 1921; admiral, 1926; KCMG, 1918.

HALSTEAD, Robert (pseudonym) (1624?–1697), Cavalier. See MORDAUNT, HENRY.

HALSWELLE, Keeley (1832–1891), artist; engaged as book illustrator; exhibited at Royal Scottish Academy from 1857; ARSA, 1866; subsequently exhibited many landscapes at Royal Academy; member of Institute of Painters in Oils, 1882.

HALSWORTH (or HOLDSWORTH), Daniel (1558?–1595?), classical scholar; of the English colleges of Douai and Rome; theologian to St Charles Borromeo; made Greek translation of Virgil's *Bucolics* (1591) and Latin version of epigrams of Archias (1596); died at Rome.

HALTON, Immanuel (1628–1699), astronomer; auditor to the household of Thomas, earl of *Arundel; friend of *Flamsteed, who communicated to Royal Society Halton's observations of a solar eclipse, 1675.

HALTON (or HALGHTON), John of (d. 1324), bishop; canon of St Mary's, Carlisle; bishop of Carlisle, 1292–1324; ambassador to King John of Scotland, 1295; excommunicated *Bruce for murder of Comyn, 1309; sat in *Lancaster's council, 1318; envoy to Scotland, 1320; his register still preserved.

HALTON, Timothy (1632?–1704), provost of The Queen's College, Oxford; probably brother of Immanuel *Halton; fellow of The Queen's College, Oxford, 1657; DD, 1674; archdeacon of Brecknock, 1672, of Oxford, 1675; provost of The Queen's College, Oxford, 1677–1704; vice-chancellor of Oxford, 1679–81 and 1685.

HALYBURTON, George (d. 1682), Scots Nonconformist minister; ejected, 1662.

HALYBURTON (or HALIBURTON), James (1518–1589), provost of Dundee; MA, St Andrews, 1538; distinguished at capture of Broughty Castle, 1549; provost of Dundee, 1553–86; captured by the Grahams in Liddesdale, 1556, but soon rescued; a lord of the congregation; commander of musters of Fife and Forfar against the queen regent, 1559; took part in defence of Edinburgh, and signed 'last band at Leith' and (1561) first Book of Discipline; commissioner to administer Act of Oblivion, 1563; joined *Moray's movement against *Darnley marriage; present at Langside, 1568, and at Restalrig, 1571; afterwards captured by queen's forces and barely escaped execution, 1571; *Morton's representative at conference of 1578; privy councillor, 1582; one of the king's commissioners to General Assembly, 1582 and 1588.

HALYBURTON, Thomas (1674–1712), theologian; son of George *Halyburton; educated at Rotterdam and St Andrews; professor of divinity at St Mary's College, 1710–12; his writings against deists reissued (1865) as *Essay on the Ground or formal Reason of a saving Faith*; his *Memoirs* (2nd edn., 1715) frequently reprinted; works collected (1835).

HAMBLEDEN, second Viscount (1868–1928), philanthropist. See SMITH, WILLIAM FREDERICK DANVERS.

HAMBLIN SMITH, James (1829–1901), mathematician. See SMITH.

HAMBOURG, Mark (1879–1960), pianist; born in Southern Russia; brought to London, 1889, and played as infant prodigy; studied in Vienna and made début at Vienna Philharmonic symphony concert as adult pianist, 1895; naturalized, 1896; began recording for HMV with the 'Moonlight Sonata', 1909; made worldwide tours playing chamber music and concertos, but especially remembered as recitalist in grand virtuoso manner; last public performance, 1955.

HAMBOYS, John (*fl.* 1470). See HANBOYS.

HAMBRO, Sir **Charles Jocelyn** (1897–1963), merchant banker; educated at Eton and Sandhurst; served in Coldstream Guards in France, 1916–18; MC; secretary, C. J. Hambro & Son, family firm; played important part in merger with British Bank of Northern Commerce and establishment of Hambros Bank, 1921; director, Bank of England, 1928; established, under (Lord) Montagu C. *Norman's direction, the exchange control division, 1932–3; chairman, Great Western Railway, 1940–5; joined Ministry of Economic Warfare, 1939; worked in Special Operations Executive (SOE); visited Sweden, 1940; KBE, 1941; deputy head, SOE, 1941–2; executive chief, succeeding (Sir) Frank *Nelson, 1942–3; head of British raw materials mission, Washington, 1943–5; chairman, Hambros Bank, 1961–3.

HAMBURY, Henry de (*fl.* 1330), justice of common pleas in Ireland, *c.*1324; chief justice, 1327; judge of the King's Bench (England), 1328.

HAMERTON, Philip Gilbert (1834–1894), artist and essayist; studied art in London; resided on isle of Innistrynich, Loch Awe, 1858; published *A Painter's Camp in the Highlands* (1862); art critic to *Saturday Review*; established with Richmond Seeley, the publisher, *The Portfolio* periodical, 1869; directed *Portfolio* till his death; LL D, Aberdeen, 1894. He published two novels, besides numerous valuable contributions to art literature. His autobiography was completed and published by his widow (1897).

HAMEY, Baldwin, the elder (1568–1640), physician to the tsar of Muscovy, 1592–8; MD, Leiden; LRCP, 1610.

HAMEY, Baldwin, the younger (1600–1676), physician; son of Baldwin *Hamey the elder; MD, Leiden, 1626, Oxford, 1629; visited Paris, Montpelier, and Padua; FRCP, 1633; eight times censor; treasurer, 1664–6; Gulstonian lecturer, 1647; benefactor of the Royal College of Physicians; left manuscript account of contemporary physicians; his dissertation on the ὅρκος Ἱπποκράτους edited (1693).

HAMIDULLAH, nawab of Bhopal (1894–1960). See BHOPAL.

HAMILTON, dukes of. See HAMILTON, JAMES, first duke, 1606–1649; HAMILTON, WILLIAM, second duke, 1616–1651; DOUGLAS, WILLIAM, third duke, 1635–1694; DOUGLAS, JAMES, fourth duke, 1658–1712; DOUGLAS, ALEXANDER HAMILTON, tenth duke, 1767–1852; DOUGLAS, WILLIAM ALEXANDER ANTHONY ARCHIBALD, eleventh duke, 1811–63.

HAMILTON, Mrs (fl. 1745–1772), actress; appeared for some years as Mrs Bland, playing with Garrick at Covent Garden in Shakespearean parts, 1746; reappeared at Covent Garden, 1752–62; afterwards went to Ireland; her distresses the cause of the establishment of the Theatrical Fund.

HAMILTON, Alexander (d. 1732?), merchant and author; published New Account of the East Indies (1727).

HAMILTON, Alexander (1739–1802), professor of midwifery at Edinburgh University; deacon of the Edinburgh College of Surgeons; professor of midwifery, Edinburgh, 1780–1800; chief founder of Lying-in Hospital, 1791; published treatises on midwifery.

HAMILTON, Alexander (1762–1824), orientalist; while hostage in France drew up for Paris Library analytical catalogue of Sanskrit manuscripts, and taught the language to Schlegel and Fauriel; FRS, 1808; professor of Sanskrit and Hindu literature at Haileybury; published works on Sanskrit.

HAMILTON, Andrew (d. 1691), rector and prebendary of Kilskerry, 1666; raised troops against James II; published True Relation of the Actions of the Inniskilling Men (1690).

HAMILTON, Anne, duchess of Hamilton (1636–1716), daughter of the first duke of Hamilton; married William *Douglas (1635–1694), who became on her petition duke of Hamilton.

HAMILTON, Lady Anne (1766–1846), lady-in-waiting to Queen *Caroline; daughter of Archibald, ninth duke of Hamilton; accompanied Queen Caroline to England, 1820; her Secret History of the Court (1832), published in her name, but without her sanction.

HAMILTON, Anthony (1646?–1720), author of Mémoires du Comte de Grammont; third son of Sir George *Hamilton; as governor of Limerick, 1685, openly went to mass; privy councillor, 1686; commanded Jacobite dragoons at Enniskillen and Newtown Butler, 1689; present at the Boyne, 1690; spent the rest of his life at St Germain-en-Laye, being an intimate of *Berwick; addressed letters and verses to the duchess of Berwick and Laura Bulkeley, and wrote for Henrietta Bulkeley four satirical Contes in French. His Epistle to the Comte de Grammont (his brother-in-law) announcing intention of writing his memoirs was approved by Boileau, 1705. The Mémoires appeared anonymously (1713), and were edited by Horace *Walpole (1772), Sir Walter *Scott (1811), and M de Lescure (1876); Œuvres Complètes were issued (1749–76).

HAMILTON, Archibald (d. 1593), Roman Catholic controversialist; disputed publicly with *Knox; published Latin works against Scottish Calvinists and a treatise on Aristotle; died at Rome.

HAMILTON, Archibald (1580?–1659), archbishop of Cashel and Emly; DD, Glasgow; bishop of Killala and Achonry, 1623; archbishop of Cashel and Emly, 1630; after rebellion of 1641 fled to Sweden, where he died.

HAMILTON, Lord Archibald (1770–1827), politician; brother of Lady Anne *Hamilton; MA, Christ Church, Oxford, 1795; barrister, Lincoln's Inn, 1799; MP, Lanarkshire, 1802–27; published pamphlet (1804) condemning Pitt's second ministry and that of *Addington; moved vote of censure on *Castlereagh as president of Board of Control, 1809; carried resolution for referring petition from Scottish royal burghs to select committee, 1819; moved insertion of Queen *Caroline's name in the liturgy, 1820.

HAMILTON, Charles (1691–1754), historian; natural son of James *Douglas, fourth duke of Hamilton, and Lady Barbara Fitzroy; styled Count Arran; accompanied his father in duel with *Mohun, 1707, and himself fought General *Macartney; settled in Switzerland; died at Paris; Transactions during the Reign of Anne (1790) attributed to him, but written by his son.

HAMILTON, Charles, by courtesy Lord Binning (1697–1733), poet; son of Thomas *Hamilton, sixth earl of Haddington; fought for government at Sheriffmuir, 1715; MP, St Germans, 1722; died at Naples; his pastoral 'Ungrateful Nanny' in *Ritson's Scottish Songs (1794).

HAMILTON, Charles (1753?–1792), orientalist; in military service of East India Company; published historical work on the Rohilla Afghans (1787), and translation of the Persian *Hedaya* (1791).

HAMILTON, Sir Charles, second baronet (1767–1849), admiral; commanded the *Dido* at sieges of Bastia, Calvi, and San Fiorenzo (1793), the *Melpomene* on Dutch coast, and at capture of Goree and in West Indies, 1799–1802; vice-admiral, 1814; admiral, 1830; MP, Dungannon, 1801–7, Honiton, 1807–12; governor of Newfoundland, 1818–24.

HAMILTON, Charles Harold St John (1876–1961), writer, better known as Frank Richards; educated at schools in West London; received first cheque for a short story at age of 17; wrote (under pseudonyms) for the *Gem* and the *Magnet*, boys' papers, in particular about Greyfriars School and its 'Famous Five', including Billy Bunter, 1907–40; wrote Bunter scripts for television, 1952; created other schools, including Rookwood in the *Boys' Friend* and Cliff House School, with Bessie Bunter, in the *School Friend*.

HAMILTON, Charles William (1670–1754), painter at Augsburg; son of James *Hamilton (*fl.* 1640–1680) of Murdieston.

HAMILTON, Claud, Baron Paisley (1543?–1622), known as Lord Claud Hamilton; fourth son of James *Hamilton, duke of Châtelherault; convoyed *Mary Queen of Scots from Lochleven to Niddry and Hamilton, 1568, and (probably) led the van for her at Langside, 1568; concerned in plot by which *Moray was assassinated, 1570; led attempt to capture *Lennox and king's lords at Stirling, 1571; recovered his estates by pacification of Perth, 1573; privy to plot against *Morton, 1578; denounced by council for murder of the regents; fled to England, 1579; took part in *Gowrie conspiracy, 1584; recalled from Paris by James VI, 1586; with *Huntly shared leadership of Scottish Catholics, and was commissioned by the Guises to reconcile Mary and her son James, 1586; entered into communication with Spain, and urged on Armada project; created Baron Paisley, 1587; became insane.

HAMILTON, Sir David (1663–1721), physician to Queen Anne; MD, Reims, 1686; FRCP, 1703; FRS, 1708; knighted; published religious and medical tracts.

HAMILTON, David (1768–1843), architect; designed many buildings in western Scotland, including Hamilton Palace, Lennox Castle, and the Glasgow Exchange.

HAMILTON, David James (1849–1909), pathologist; studied medicine at Edinburgh; worked at pathology at Vienna and Paris, 1874–6; professor of pathology at Aberdeen, 1882–1908; pioneer of bacteriological diagnosis of diphtheria and typhoid; investigated 'braxy' and 'louping ill' in sheep; published standard textbook on pathology (2 vols., 1889–94); FRS, 1908; hon. LL D, Edinburgh, 1907.

HAMILTON, Sir Edward, first baronet (1772–1851), admiral; MA, Emmanuel College, Cambridge, 1803; brother of Sir Charles *Hamilton; while in command of *Surprise* said to have taken or destroyed eighty privateers and merchantmen, 1797–9; knighted and awarded the freedom of the city for cutting out the *Hermione* at Puerto Cabello, 1799; captured by French, but exchanged; engaged in blockading northern French coast, 1801; dismissed the service for inflicting excessive punishment, 1802, but specially reinstated, 1802; commanded royal yacht and *Prince Regent*, 1806–19; KCB, 1815; created baronet, 1818; vice-admiral, 1837; admiral, 1846.

HAMILTON, Sir Edward Walter (1847–1908), Treasury official; son of Walter Kerr *Hamilton; educated at Eton and Christ Church, Oxford; private secretary successively to Robert *Lowe and Gladstone, 1872–85; Treasury official, 1885–1907; permanent secretary to the Treasury (with Sir George *Murray), 1902–7; KCB, 1894; GCB, 1906; PC, 1908; specially connected with *Goschen's financial measures, of which he wrote an account, 1889; published monograph on Gladstone, 1898.

HAMILTON, Elizabeth, comtesse de Grammont (1641–1708), 'la belle Hamilton'; sister of Anthony *Hamilton, who brought about her marriage with Philibert, comte de Grammont, 1663; lived in France from 1664.

HAMILTON, Elizabeth, duchess of Hamilton, afterwards of Argyll (1734–1790). See GUNNING.

HAMILTON, Elizabeth (1758–1816), author; sister of Charles *Hamilton (1753?–1792); published *The Hindoo Rajah* (1796), *Memoirs of Modern Philosophers* (1800), and several educational works, besides *The Cottagers of Glenburnie* (1808) and 'My ain Fireside' (song).

HAMILTON, Emma, Lady (1761?–1815), wife of Sir William *Hamilton (1730–1803) the ambassador; née Lyon; went to London, 1778, probably as a nursemaid to family of Dr Richard *Budd; said to have been the 'Goddess of Health' in exhibition of James *Graham (1745–1794); lived under protection of Sir Harry Fetherstonhaugh and Hon. Charles Greville as Emily Hart, 1780–4; refined by friendship with *Romney, 1782; became mistress of Sir William

Hamilton at Naples, 1786, and was married to him in England, 1791; an intimate of Queen Maria Carolina at Naples; first saw *Nelson, 1793; became acquainted with Nelson on his return from the Nile, 1798; together with her husband accompanied Nelson to Palermo, 1800, and afterwards to England, giving birth to Horatia, 30 Jan. 1801; received the Cross of Malta from the tsar for supposed services to the Maltese, 1799; claimed to have rendered important political services while at Naples, but these claims, although endorsed by Nelson, were ignored by British ministry; involved in debt by her extravagances, in spite of legacies from Nelson and Hamilton; assisted by Alderman Joshua J. Smith to escape from king's bench to Calais, where she died in obscurity.

HAMILTON, Eugene Jacob Lee- (1845–1907), poet and novelist. See LEE-HAMILTON.

HAMILTON, Ferdinand Philip (1664–1750), painter to Charles V at Vienna; eldest son of James *Hamilton (*fl.* 1640–1680) of Murdieston.

HAMILTON, Francis (1762–1829). See BUCHANAN.

HAMILTON, Sir Frederick Hew George Dalrymple- (1890–1974), admiral. See DALRYMPLE-HAMILTON.

HAMILTON, Gavin (1561?–1612), bishop of Galloway; graduated at St Andrews, 1584; minister of Hamilton; bishop of Galloway, 1605 (consecrated, 1610); dean of Chapel Royal, Holyrood, 1606.

HAMILTON, Gavin (1730–1797), painter and excavator; lived principally at Rome; during short residence in London member of committee for forming Royal Academy, 1755; occasionally exhibited at the Royal Academy; his *Apollo* seen at International Exhibition of 1862; published *Schola Italica Picturae* (1773); carried on excavations at Hadrian's villa below Tivoli, Monte Cagnuolo, the district of the Alban hills and the territory of ancient Gabii, selling his 'finds' to the Museo Pio-Clementino, the Townley collection, Lord Lansdowne, and other collectors; his marbles now in the Louvre.

HAMILTON, Gavin (1753–1805), friend of *Burns; prominent in 'New Light' dispute in Mauchline; defended in Burns's theological satires.

HAMILTON, Sir George, first baronet (d. 1679), Royalist; fourth son of James *Hamilton, first earl of Abercorn; created an Irish baronet, 1660, for services during the rebellion.

HAMILTON, Lord George, earl of Orkney (1666–1737), general; fifth son of William *Douglas, third duke of Hamilton; distinguished

under William III in Ireland and Flanders; severely wounded at Namur, 1695, and promoted brigadier; married (1695) Elizabeth *Villiers, William's mistress; created a Scottish peer, 1696; lieutenant-general, 1704; KT, 1704; captured 12,000 men and 1,300 officers at Blenheim, 1704; saved citadel of Liège, 1705; led pursuit after Ramillies, 1706; prominent at Oudenarde, 1706, favouring immediate advance on Paris; commanded the van at passage of Scheldt, 1708; opened attack at Malplaquet, 1709; elected a Scottish representative peer, 1707; privy councillor, 1710; lord of the bedchamber, 1714; governor of Virginia, 1714; field marshal, 1736.

HAMILTON, George (1783–1830), biblical scholar; fourth son of Hugh *Hamilton (1729–1805); MA, Trinity College, Dublin, 1821; rector of Killermogh, 1809–30; published *Introduction to Study of the Hebrew Scriptures* (1813), *Codex Criticus of the Hebrew Bible* (1821), and controversial tracts.

HAMILTON, George Alexander (1802–1871), politician; of Rugby and Trinity College, Oxford; BA, 1821; DCL, 1853; elected on petition for Dublin, 1836; sat for Dublin University, 1843–59; formed Conservative Society for Ireland; presented Protestant petition of 1837; financial secretary to Treasury, 1852, and 1858–9; permanent secretary, 1859; privy councillor, 1869.

HAMILTON, Lord George Francis (1845–1927), statesman; son of first duke of *Abercorn; Conservative MP, Middlesex, 1868–84; for Ealing division of county, 1885–1906; undersecretary for India, 1874–80; introduced Indian Loans Bill, 1874; first lord of Admiralty, 1885–6, 1886–92; his administration period of extensive naval reform and construction; secretary of state for India, 1895–1903; decided not to evacuate Chitral, 1895; faced with revolt of Waziris and Afridis, 1897; had to deal with problems of famine and plague; his suggestion of dispatch of troops to Cape in South African War accepted, 1899; resigned as free trader, 1903; chairman of royal commissions on poor law and unemployment, 1905–9, and on Mesopotamian campaign, 1916–17.

HAMILTON, Gustavus, Viscount Boyne (1639–1723), grandson of Claud *Hamilton, Baron Paisley; commanded a regiment at the Boyne, 1690, Athlone, 1691, and Vigo, 1707; major-general, 1703; privy councillor under William III, Anne, and George I; created Irish baron, 1715; created Viscount Boyne in Irish peerage, 1717.

HAMILTON, Henry Parr (1794–1880), dean of Salisbury; son of Alexander *Hamilton (1739–1802); fellow of Trinity College, Cambridge; ninth wrangler, 1816; MA, 1819; rector of Wath, Yorkshire, and incumbent (1833–44) of St Mary the Great, Cambridge; FRS, 1828; contributed largely to restoration of his cathedral; published educational pamphlets and works on analytical geometry and conic sections.

HAMILTON, Hugh (or Hugo), first Baron Hamilton of Glenawley (d. 1679), soldier; having served in Swedish Army was naturalized and ennobled; created an Irish peer, 1660; settled in Ireland.

HAMILTON, Hugh, Baron Hamilton in Sweden (d. 1724), Swedish general; nephew of Hugh *Hamilton (d. 1679); distinguished himself against the Danes, 1710, and Russians, 1719; ancestor of Swedish counts.

HAMILTON, Hugh (1729–1805), bishop of Clonfert and Ossory; MA, Dublin, 1750; DD, 1762; fellow of Trinity College, Dublin, 1751–64; professor of natural philosophy, 1759; dean of Armagh, 1768–96; FRS; bishop of Clonfert, 1796–9, of Ossory, 1799; collected works issued, 1809.

HAMILTON, Hugh Douglas (1734?–1806), portrait painter; exhibited with Incorporated Society (1771, and 1773–5) and Free Society of Artists, 1772; went to Rome, 1778; returned to Dublin, 1791.

HAMILTON, Sir Ian Standish Monteith (1853–1947), general; educated at Wellington College and Sandhurst; posted to 92nd Highlanders, India, 1873; wounded at Majuba Hill, Natal, 1881; aide-de-camp to (Lord) *Roberts, 1882–90; assistant adjutant-general, musketry, Bengal, 1890–3; military secretary to Sir George *White, 1893–5; deputy quartermaster-general, Simla, 1895–7; commandant, Musketry School, Hythe, 1898; in South Africa (1899–1902) showed conspicuous gallantry at Elandslaagte; present at siege of Ladysmith; commanded mounted infantry division in advance on Pretoria; KCB, 1900; chief of staff to Lord *Kitchener; commanded four columns in final drive in Western Transvaal; military secretary, War Office, 1900–3; quartermaster-general, 1903–4; headed military mission with Japanese, 1904–5; published *A Staff Officer's Scrap Book* (2 vols., 1905–7); held Southern Command, 1905–9; general, 1907; adjutant-general, 1909–10; GCB, 1910; his memorandum favouring voluntary enlistment published as *Compulsory Service* (1910); GOC-in-C, Mediterranean Command, and inspector-general of overseas forces, 1910–14; commanded Central Force, 1914–15;

appointed to command Anglo-French army to assist navy in forcing Dardanelles, March 1915; first attack (25 April) within ace of success; three further attacks failed for lack of men or ammunition; made final attempt with landing at Suvla, 6 Aug.; recalled Oct. 1915; GCMG, 1919; published *Gallipoli Diary* (2 vols., 1920); lord rector, Edinburgh University, 1932–5.

HAMILTON, Sir James, of Cadzow, first Baron Hamilton (d. 1479), connected with house of Douglas by his marriage with widow of fifth earl and that of her daughter (Fair Maid of Galloway) with William, eighth earl; lord of parliament, 1445; accompanied the eighth earl of Douglas to Rome, 1450, and attended him to his fatal meeting with *James II at Stirling, 1452; joined James, ninth earl of Douglas, in renunciation of allegiance and subsequent submission, 1453; advised another rebellion, but went over to the king owing to Douglas's weakness; commissioner for peace with England and sheriff of Lanarkshire, 1455; married Mary Stewart, sister of James III, 1469.

HAMILTON, James, second Baron Hamilton and first earl of Arran (1477?–1529), son of Sir James *Hamilton, first Baron Hamilton; made privy councillor by *James IV, whose marriage with *Margaret Tudor he negotiated, 1503; created earl of Arran for skill in tournament, 1503; when lieutenant-general of Scotland helped to reduce Western Isles (1504) and to re-establish king of Denmark; detained in England by Henry VII after embassy to France, 1507; during minority of *James V opposed *Angus and the English party; plotted against the regent *Albany; president of Council of Regency during Albany's absence in France, 1517–20; defeated in attempt to overpower Angus in Edinburgh, 1520; again member of Council of Regency, 1522, and lieutenant of the south; joined queen-dowager in ousting Albany and proclaiming James V, 1524; compelled by Henry VIII to readmit Angus to council; supported Angus against *Lennox, 1526, but on escape of James V from the Douglases received *Bothwell from Angus's forfeited estates.

HAMILTON, Sir James, of Finnart (d. 1540), royal architect; natural son of James *Hamilton, second Baron Hamilton; prominent as the 'Bastard of Arran' in his father's feuds with the Douglases, especially at 'Cleanse the Causeway', 1520; assassinated *Lennox when a prisoner after Linlithgow, 1526; legitimated by *James V, as designer of Craignethan and restorer of Linlithgow and Falkland; executed for alleged plot to murder the king.

HAMILTON, James, second earl of Arran and duke of Châtelherault (d. 1575), governor of Scotland; eldest son of James *Hamilton, second Baron Hamilton; chosen governor of Scotland (as 'second person in the realm'), 1542; for a short time head of the English party, but came to terms with Cardinal David *Beaton, 1543; successfully resisted transference of power to queen-dowager, 1545; created duke of Châtelherault, 1548; obliged to abdicate regency, 1554; returned to English alliance on capture of Edinburgh by lords of congregation, 1559; revived his project for marriage of his son with Queen *Mary on her arrival in Scotland; for his opposition to *Darnley marriage banished to France, 1566; returned to Scotland, 1569, as supporter of the queen and was imprisoned with *Moray.

HAMILTON, James, third earl of Arran (1530–1609), eldest son of James *Hamilton, second earl of Arran; proposed by Henry VIII as husband for Princess Elizabeth, 1543, but destined by his father for *Mary Queen of Scots; served in Scots Guards in France, 1550–8; distinguished at St Quentin, 1557; styled earl of Arran after 1553; became a Protestant while in France, and by *Knox's advice was brought to England to confer with the government, 1558; despatched secretly to Scotland, 1559; strengthened his father in Protestant policy; with Lord James *Stuart (Moray) attempted to capture *Bothwell, and by defending Dysart saved Fife from the French; took part in siege of Leith, and signed the 'last band' and the first Book of Discipline; again made proposals for hand of Elizabeth, 1560–1; on Knox's advice renewed also his suit to Mary; reconciled with Bothwell by Knox, 1562; revealed to latter alleged advice of Bothwell to him to carry off Mary, marry her, and murder Moray and *Maitland, 1562; imprisoned till 1566, now almost insane; afterwards lived in retirement at Craignethan till brought to Linlithgow by James VI, 1579.

HAMILTON, James, first earl of Abercorn (d. 1617), son of Claud *Hamilton, Baron Paisley; gentleman of the bedchamber to James VI; privy councillor (as master of Paisley), 1598; sheriff of Linlithgow, 1600; created Baron Abercorn (Scotland), 1603; created earl for services as commissioner for union with England, 1606.

HAMILTON, James, first Viscount Claneboye in Irish peerage (1559–1643), Ulster planter; educated at St Andrews University; despatched by James VI on secret mission to Ireland, 1587; carried on Latin school in Dublin, which Ussher attended: original fellow of Trinity College, Dublin, 1592; James VI's agent in London, 1600; knighted and given large grants in Ulster,

1605; MP, Co. Down, 1613; commissioner for plantation of Longford, 1619; created Irish peer, 1622; granted dissolved monastery of Bangor, 1630; privy councillor, 1634; armed Scots in Ulster, 1641.

HAMILTON, James, of Bothwellhaugh (fl. 1566–1580), assassin of the regent *Moray; captured at Langside 1568, but pardoned at *Knox's intercession; shot the regent Moray at Linlithgow, 1570 (see STEWART, Lord JAMES, 1531?–1570); escaped to France and tried to obtain aid for *Mary; excepted from pacification of Perth; refused to assist in murder of Coligny, but acted as agent for the Spanish king in attempts on life of William the Silent, 1573 and 1575; disinherited; probably died abroad.

HAMILTON, James, second marquis of Hamilton (1589–1625), succeeded his father, Lord John *Hamilton, as marquis, 1604, and his uncle as earl of Arran, 1609; privy councillor of Scotland, 1613, of England, 1617; created an English peer (earl of Cambridge), 1619; advocated leniency to *Bacon, 1621; as high commissioner to Scottish parliament, 1621, carried Five Articles of Perth; a commissioner for marriage of Prince Charles to the Spanish Infanta, 1623; lord-steward, 1624; opposed *Buckingham's French policy, 1624; said to have been poisoned by Buckingham.

HAMILTON, James, third marquis and first duke of Hamilton in the Scottish peerage, second earl of Cambridge in the English peerage (1606–1649), succeeded as third marquis, 1625; master of the horse, 1628; privy councillor, 1628; commanded British force under Gustavus Adolphus, 1630–4; as Charles I's adviser on Scottish affairs, persuaded him to revoke the Prayer-Book, canons, and High Commission, and to call a parliament, 1638; commanded against Covenanters, but resigned commissionership, 1639; carried on intrigues between Charles and Covenanters, and opposed *Strafford and *Montrose; allied himself (1641) for a time with *Argyll, but (1642) endeavoured to prevent Scots from supporting English parliament; refused to take the Covenant, 1643, and joined the king at Oxford, but was imprisoned, 1644; liberated by *Fairfax, 1646; again attempted to mediate between Charles and the Scots, 1646; led Scottish army into England, but was defeated at Preston, 1648; condemned and executed, 1649.

HAMILTON, James (d. 1666), divine; educated at Glasgow University; incumbent of Ballywalter, 1626–36; deposed for heresy after public disputation, 1636; afterwards minister at Dumfries and Edinburgh.

HAMILTON, James (1610–1674), bishop of Galloway; graduated at Glasgow, 1628; minister of Cambusnethan, 1634; deposed, 1638, but restored, 1639; supported the 'Engagement', 1648; bishop of Galloway, 1661–74.

HAMILTON, James, of Murdieston (*fl.* 1640–1680), painter of animals and still life at Brussels.

HAMILTON, James, sixth earl of Abercorn (1656–1734), grandson of Sir George *Hamilton; assisted in defence of Derry, 1689; succeeded as earl of Abercorn, 1701; created Viscount Strabane (Irish peerage), 1701; privy councillor.

HAMILTON, James, seventh earl of Abercorn (d. 1744), second son of James *Hamilton, sixth earl of Abercorn; privy councillor of England (1738) and Ireland (1739); FRS; published *Calculations and Tables relating to Attractive Power of Loadstones* (1729).

HAMILTON, James, eighth earl of Abercorn (1712–1789), eldest son of James *Hamilton, seventh earl of Abercorn; summoned to Irish House of Peers as Baron Mountcastle, 1736; representative peer of Scotland, 1761–86; created British peer as Viscount Hamilton, 1786.

HAMILTON, James, the elder (1749–1835), Edinburgh physician; noted for old-fashioned dress and manners and his works on purgative treatment.

HAMILTON, James (1769–1829), author of Hamiltonian linguistic system; derived rudiments of his system from D'Angeli, an *émigré*; detained in Paris at rupture of Peace of Amiens; began to teach his system at Philadelphia, 1816, and to print texts for use of pupils; very successful at Boston, the American universities, and in Canada; came to London, 1823, and taught in chief cities of United Kingdom; was defended in *Edinburgh Review*, 1826, by Sydney *Smith, and in *Westminster Review*.

HAMILTON, James, the younger (d. 1839), professor of midwifery at Edinburgh, 1800, succeeding his father, Alexander *Hamilton (1739–1802); recovered damages from Dr James *Gregory, 1753–1821 for assault, 1793; succeeded in getting obstetrics made compulsory in medical course of Edinburgh University, 1830; published medical works.

HAMILTON, James, first duke of Abercorn (1811–1885), succeeded his grandfather as second marquis of Abercorn, 1818; groom of the stole to Prince Albert, 1846–59; lord-lieutenant of Ireland, 1866–8 and 1874–6; created duke, 1868.

HAMILTON, James (1814–1867), Presbyterian minister; graduated at Glasgow, 1835; Candlish's assistant at St George's, Edinburgh, 1838; minister of National Scottish Church, Regent Square, London, 1841–67; published devotional and biographical works; his *Book of Psalms and Hymns* adopted by Presbyterian churches.

HAMILTON, James, second duke of Abercorn (1838–1913), son of James *Hamilton, first duke; Conservative MP, Co. Donegal, 1860–80; succeeded father, 1885; KG, 1892; official figurehead of Irish landlords in land war; resisted home rule.

HAMILTON, James Alexander (1785–1845), compiler of musical handbooks, including the *Pianoforte Tutor* (1,728th edn., 1890).

HAMILTON, James Archibald (1747–1815), astronomer; educated at Armagh and Trinity College, Dublin; BA; DD, 1784; made observations on transit of Mercury from private observatory in Cookstown; archdeacon of Ross, 1790; dean of Cloyne, 1804; first astronomer at Armagh Observatory, 1790.

HAMILTON, Janet (1795–1873), Scottish poetess; daughter of a Lancashire shoemaker; her *Poems and Prose Works* collected by her son (1880).

HAMILTON, John (1511?–1571), archbishop of St Andrews; natural son of James *Hamilton, first earl of Arran; keeper of the privy seal, 1543; bishop of Dunkeld, 1545; archbishop of St Andrews, 1546; reconciled Arran with *Beaton; promulgated Hamilton's catechism at synod of 1552; endowed St Mary's College, St Andrews; persecuted Protestants; accepted new confession, 1560; imprisoned for popish practices, 1563; member of councils of *Mary Queen of Scots, 1566; divorced *Bothwell from Lady Jane Gordon, 1567; present at Langside, 1568; hanged at Stirling on charge of being accessory to *Darnley's murder and of complicity in that of *Moray.

HAMILTON, John, first marquis of Hamilton (1532–1604), second son of James *Hamilton, duke of Châtelherault; assisted *Bothwell and negotiated with England for deliverance of *Mary; furthered assassination of *Moray (1570) in revenge for forfeiture; represented his family at pacification of Perth, 1573; head of his family after death of Châtelherault, 1575; in constant danger of his life from Sir William *Douglas (d. 1606); escaped to France, 1579; joined his brother, Lord Claud *Hamilton, in England, and thence went to Scotland, 1584; recovered his estates; in favour with James VI; went on embassy to Denmark, 1588; a lord of the articles, 1594; accompanied James VI against Huntly; sat on Huntly's trial; created marquis, 1599.

HAMILTON, John (*fl.* 1568–1609), anti-Protestant writer; described himself as the queen's 'daily orator'; probably *Mary Stuart's messenger to Alva, 1568–9; tutor to Cardinal de Bourbon, 1576; rector of Paris University, 1584; prominent member of French Catholic League; adjutant of 1,300 armed ecclesiastics, 1590; on the entry of Henri Quatre (1594) escaped to Brussels; executed in effigy for murder of Tardif; returned to Scotland, 1600, with Edmund *Hay, and secretly celebrated mass; captured, 1608; died in prison. He published at Paris (1581) tract in favour of transubstantiation, with appendix dedicated to James VI, and at Louvain (1600) a treatise, with prayers, also dedicated to the king.

HAMILTON, Sir John, first Baron Bargeny (d. 1658), Royalist; grandson of John, first marquis of *Hamilton; created a Scottish peer, 1639.

HAMILTON, John, second Baron Bargeny (d. 1693), son of Sir John *Hamilton, first Baron Bargeny; imprisoned as disaffected, 1679–80; raised regiment for William of Orange, 1689.

HAMILTON, John, second Baron Belhaven (1656–1708), imprisoned and compelled to apologize for remarks on duke of York, 1681; contributed to settlement of Scottish crown on William III, 1689, and became privy councillor; strong supporter of Darien scheme; advocated Act of Security, 1703, and strongly opposed the Union, his speech of 1706 becoming famous as 'Belhaven's Vision'; imprisoned (1708) on suspicion of favouring French invasion.

HAMILTON, John (d. 1755), captain in the navy; second son of James *Hamilton, seventh earl of Abercorn; distinguished at wreck of the *Louisa*, 1736; had the *Kinsale* fitted with nine-pounders and canvas screens, 1742; drowned near Spithead.

HAMILTON, Sir John, first baronet (1755–1835), lieutenant-general; served in East Indian army in Cutch Behar and against Mahrattas (1778), and in British against Tippoo Sahib, 1790–1; lieutenant-colonel of the 81st in San Domingo and Kaffir War of 1800; inspector-general of Portuguese Army, 1809; commanded divisions at Albuera, 1811, and the Nivelle, 1813; lieutenant-general, 1814; created baronet, 1815.

HAMILTON, John (1761–1814), Scottish song-writer; contributed to *Johnson's *Museum* and helped *Scott with *Border Minstrelsy*; composed songs, including 'Up in the Mornin' Early' and 'The Ploughman'.

HAMILTON, John (*fl.* 1765–1786), painter; director of Incorporated Society of Artists, 1773.

HAMILTON, John Andrew, Viscount Sumner (1859–1934), judge; educated at Manchester Grammar School and Balliol College, Oxford; first class, Lit. Hum., 1881; president of Union, 1882; prize fellow of Magdalen, 1882–9; called to bar (Inner Temple), 1883; bencher, 1909; joined northern circuit; voluminous contributor to this Dictionary; developed large commercial-court practice; KC, 1901; judge of King's Bench division, 1909; never reserved a judgement; promoted to Court of Appeal and PC, 1912; lord of appeal in ordinary, 1913–30; life peerage, 1913; viscount, 1927; took leading part in appeals from prize court; judgements remarkable for style and wit as well as legal merits; a British delegate to Reparation Commission, 1919; GCB, 1920; chairman, Royal Commission on Compensation for War Damage, 1921.

HAMILTON, John George (1662–1736?), painter at Vienna; son of James *Hamilton (*fl.* 1640–1680).

HAMILTON, Malcolm (1635–1699), Swedish general; naturalized as Swedish noble, 1664; created Baron Hamilton de Hageby, 1693.

HAMILTON, Mary, duchess of Hamilton (1613–1638), lady of the bedchamber to *Henrietta Maria; *Waller wrote 'Thyrsis Galatea' in her praise.

HAMILTON, Lady Mary (1739–1816), novelist; née Leslie; lived with her second husband in France, and was a friend of Sir Herbert *Croft (1751–1816) and Charles Nodier; published four novels.

HAMILTON, Patrick (1504?–1528), Scottish martyr; grandson of Sir James *Hamilton of Cadzow, Lord Hamilton; MA, Paris, 1520; MA, St Andrews, 1524; saw Luther and Melanchthon at Wittenberg; at Marburg, 1527, composed his *Loci Communes* ('Patrick's Pleas'); after return to Scotland charged with seven articles of heresy; sentenced by Archbishop *Beaton and burnt at St Andrews; had previously converted Alexander *Alesius.

HAMILTON, Richard (*fl.* 1688), Jacobite lieutenant-general; brother of Anthony *Hamilton; served with distinction in French Army; banished French court for seeking Princess de Conti in marriage; despatched by *Tyrconnel with troops to help James II in England, 1688; sent by William III with offers to Irish Catholics; deserted to Tyrconnel, 1689; commanded at siege of Derry, 1689; captured at the Boyne; sent to the Tower, 1690; rejoined James in France.

HAMILTON, Sir Richard Vesey (1829–1912), admiral; entered navy, 1843; served on Arctic voyages, 1850–4; in Crimean and second Chinese wars, 1855–7; attained flag rank, 1877;

vice-admiral, 1884; commander-in-chief, China Station, 1885–8; admiral and KCB, 1887; first sea lord, 1889–91; GCB, 1895.

HAMILTON, Richard Winter (1794–1848), Independent minister; minister of Albion (afterwards of Belgrave) Chapel, Leeds; LL D, Glasgow, 1844; chairman of Congregational Union, 1847; published *Horae et Vindiciae Sabbaticae* (1847).

HAMILTON, Sir **Robert,** second baronet (1650–1701), Covenanting leader; educated under Burnet at Glasgow; one of the composers of Rutherglen Declaration, 1679; showed cowardice in command at Drumclog and at Bothwell Brigg, 1679; fled to Holland; visited Germany and Switzerland as commissioner for Scottish Presbyterian Church; returned and succeeded as baronet, 1688; imprisoned on suspicion of having drawn up Sanquhar Declaration, 1692–3.

HAMILTON, Robert (1721–1793), physician; published work on scrofula (1791).

HAMILTON, Robert (1743–1829), professor of natural philosophy and mathematics at Aberdeen, 1779–1829; published *Inquiry concerning the Rise and Progress, Reduction and Present State, and the Management of the National Debt* (1813).

HAMILTON, Robert (1749–1830), physician; MD, Edinburgh, 1780; served in the army; practised at Ipswich; published *Duties of a Regimental Surgeon* (1788) and a book on the cure of hydrophobia.

HAMILTON, Robert (1750?–1831), legal writer and genealogist; served in American War; sheriff of Lanarkshire; clerk of session; accompanied Scott on voyage (1814) as commissioner of northern lights; edited (1803) *Decisions of Court of Session, from November 1769 to January 1772.*

HAMILTON, Sir **Robert George Crookshank** (1836–1895), governor of Tasmania; educated at University and King's College, Aberdeen; MA, 1854; hon. LL D, 1885; clerk in Commissariat Department in Crimea, 1855; in charge of finance of Education Department, 1861; accountant, 1869, and assistant-secretary, 1872–8, to Board of Trade; accountant-general of navy 1878; permanent secretary to Admiralty, 1882; permanent under-secretary for Ireland, 1883–6; KCB, 1884; governor of Tasmania, 1886–93.

HAMILTON, Sir **Robert North Collie,** sixth baronet (1802–1887), Indian official; educated at Haileybury; acting secretary in political department, Benares, 1830; resident with Holkar of Indore, 1844–57; succeeded to baronetcy, 1853; viceroy's agent for Central India, 1854–9; his plan for pacification of Central India adopted;

KCB; member of supreme council of India, 1859–60.

HAMILTON, Sir **Thomas,** Lord Drumcairn, earl of Melrose, and afterwards first earl of Haddington (1563–1637), educated under his uncle, John *Hamilton (*fl.* 1568–1609) at Paris; admitted advocate, 1587; lord of session as Lord Drumcairn, 1592; probably suggester and was a member of the 'Octavians'; favourite of James VI; king's advocate, 1596; knighted soon after James VI's accession as James I of England; a commissioner for union, 1604; procured imprisonment of Andrew *Melville and execution of *Sprott for connection with *Gowrie conspiracy of 1600; one of the new Octavians, 1611; secretary of state, 1612–26; created Baron Binning and Byres, 1613; president of court of session, 1616–26; created earl of Melrose, 1619, for obtaining adoption of episcopalianism by six articles of Perth, 1618; lord privy seal, 1626; his title changed to earl of Haddington, 1626. *Notes of the Charters, &c., by the Earl of Melrose* was issued (1830), his *State Papers* (1837).

HAMILTON, Thomas, second earl of Haddington (1600–1640), Covenanter; son of Sir Thomas *Hamilton, first earl of Haddington; privy councillor, 1637; signed 'king's covenant', 1638; drew up Glasgow Proclamation, 1638; defended borders, 1640; perished in explosion at Dunglass Castle.

HAMILTON, Thomas, sixth earl of Haddington (1680–1735), member of the *squadrone volante*; wounded at Sheriffmuir, 1715; elected a representative peer, 1716; caricatured as 'Simon the Skipper'; his treatise on forest trees printed (1761).

HAMILTON, Thomas, ninth earl of Haddington (1780–1858); educated at Edinburgh and Christ Church, Oxford; MA, Oxford, 1815; Tory MP for St Germans, 1802–6, Callington, 1807–14, Michael-Borough, 1814–18, Rochester, 1818–26, and Yarmouth (Isle of Wight), 1826; Indian commissioner, 1814–22; created Baron Melros of Tynninghame, 1827; succeeded to Scottish peerage, 1828; lord-lieutenant of Ireland, 1834–5; first lord of the Admiralty, 1841–6; lord privy seal, 1846.

HAMILTON, Thomas (1784–1858), architect; designed Burns monuments at Alloway, 1818, and Edinburgh, 1830, Knox Column at Glasgow, 1825, Edinburgh High School (opened 1829), and town buildings and spire at Ayr, 1828; a founder and first treasurer of RSA; FRIBA, 1836–46.

HAMILTON, Thomas (1789–1842), author; second son of William *Hamilton (1758–1790); wounded at Albuera, 1811; settled in Edinburgh, *c.*1818; one of the *Blackwood* writers praised in *Noctes Ambrosianae* (1826); an intimate of *Scott at Chiefswood and *Wordsworth at Elleray; published *Cyril Thornton* (1827), *Annals of the Peninsular Campaign* (1829), *Men and Manners in America* (1833); died at Pisa and was buried at Florence.

HAMILTON, Walter Kerr (1808–1869), bishop of Salisbury; nephew of William Richard *Hamilton; at Eton and as private pupil of Dr *Arnold of Rugby at Laleham; student of Christ Church, Oxford, 1827; BA, 1830; fellow of Merton College, 1832; vicar of St Peter's-in-the-East, Oxford, 1837–41; canon of Salisbury, 1841; bishop of Salisbury, 1854–69, establishing theological college, 1861; published pamphlet on *Cathedral Reform* (1853).

HAMILTON, William, second duke of Hamilton (1616–1651), brother of James *Hamilton, first duke; created earl of Lanark, 1639 (so styled till 1649); secretary of state for Scotland, 1640–3 and 1646; fled with his brother (1641) after the Incident, but was at peace with the king till arrest at Oxford, 1643; escaped and made his peace with Scottish estates, 1644; one of commissioners at Newcastle, 1646; again reconciled to Charles I, 1646; protested against his surrender to English Army; concluded treaty with the king at Carisbrooke on basis of introduction of Presbyterianism into England, 1647; commanded force against Westland Whigs, but had to submit to *Argyll; succeeded to dukedom while in Holland; made KG and privy councillor by Charles II, whom he accompanied to Scotland, 1650; mortally wounded at Worcester.

HAMILTON, William (d. 1724), of Wishaw; antiquary; his *Account of the Shyres of Renfrew and Lanark* edited by William *Motherwell (1832).

HAMILTON, William (d. 1729), archdeacon of Armagh; MA, Trinity College, Dublin, 1696; LL B, 1700; archdeacon of Armagh, 1700–29; published life of James *Bonnell (1703).

HAMILTON, William (1665?–1751), of Gilbertfield; poet; corresponded in verse with Allan *Ramsay in *Seven Familiar Epistles which passed between Lieutenant Hamilton and the Author* (1719); wrote elegy on his dog, 'Bonny Heck', and 'Willie was a Wanton Wag'; abridged and modernized Blind Harry's *Wallace* (1722).

HAMILTON, William (1704–1754), of Bangour; poet; contributed lyrics to Allan *Ramsay's *Tea-Table Miscellany*, between 1724 and 1727; celebrated victory of Prestonpans in *Gladsmuir*, and while hiding after Culloden wrote 'Soliloquy . . . in June 1746'; composed ballads and *Episode of the Thistle*; made the earliest Homeric transla-

tion into English blank verse; his poems issued by Foulis (1749), and posthumously; died at Lyons.

HAMILTON, Sir William (1730–1803), diplomat and archaeologist; grandson of William *Douglas, third duke of Hamilton; MP, Midhurst, 1761–4; plenipotentiary at Naples, 1764–1800; KB, 1772; made twenty-two ascents of Vesuvius, witnessing 1776 and 1777 eruptions; visited Etna; FRS, 1766; published *Campi Phlegraei* (1776, also a supplement, 1779) and other works describing observations of volcanoes and Calabrian earthquakes; sent account of Pompeian discoveries to Society of Antiquaries; sold collections of Greek vases and antiquities to British Museum, 1772; and to Thomas *Hope, 1801; purchased from Gavin *Hamilton (1730–1797) 'Warwick Vase', and from Byres, the architect, 'Portland Vase'; privy councillor, 1791; married Emma Hart (see HAMILTON, EMMA), 1791; entertained *Nelson at Naples, 1798; accompanied Neapolitan court to Palermo, 1798; travelled to England with Nelson; DCL, Oxford, 1802.

HAMILTON, William (1751–1801), painter; studied under Zucchi in Italy; RA, 1789; exhibited from 1774 historical pictures, arabesques and ornaments, scriptural and Shakespearean pictures, and portraits, including full-lengths of Mrs *Siddons and John *Wesley.

HAMILTON, William (1755–1797), naturalist and antiquary; fellow of Trinity College, Dublin, 1779; MA, 1779; rector of Clondavaddog or Fannet, Donegal, 1790; published *Letters concerning the Northern Coast of Antrim* (1786); murdered by banditti at Sharon, 1797.

HAMILTON, William (1758–1790), surgeon; MA, Glasgow, 1775; professor of anatomy and botany at Glasgow, 1781.

HAMILTON, William (1780–1835), theological writer; minister of Strathblane, Stirlingshire, 1809–35; moved resolution against lay patronage in general assembly, 1834; published theological works, 1820–35.

HAMILTON, Sir William, baronet (1788–1856), metaphysician; educated at Glasgow and Balliol College, Oxford, where he was a friend of J. G. *Lockhart; MA, 1814; established claim to baronetcy, 1816; introduced by 'Christopher North' to *De Quincey at Edinburgh, 1814; visited Germany, 1817 and 1820; elected professor of civil history at Edinburgh, 1821; had controversy with *Combe on phrenology; solicitor of teinds, 1832; his philosophical reputation made by articles in *Edinburgh Review*, 1829–36; elected to chair of logic and metaphysics at Edinburgh, 1836; made great impression by lectures (ed. *Mansel and *Veitch, 1859); attacked 'non-intrusion' principle in ecclesiastical controversy of 1843; partially paralysed after 1844; edited Reid's works, 1846 (completed by Mansel); Hamilton philosophical examination founded in his honour, 1865. His doctrine of the 'quantification of the predicate' was assailed by *De Morgan, and that of the unknowability of the infinite by *Calderwood. He contributed to psychology and logic the theories of the association of ideas, of unconscious mental modifications, and the inverse relation of perception and sensation. Posthumous criticism was led by *Mill and Hutchison Stirling.

HAMILTON, William de (d. 1307), chancellor of England; vice-chancellor to the king, 1286; dean of York, 1298; chancellor of England, 1305–7.

HAMILTON, William Gerard (1729–1796), 'Single-speech Hamilton'; grandson of William *Hamilton (d. 1724); educated at Winchester and Oriel College, Oxford; student of Lincoln's Inn, 1744; as MP for Petersfield made celebrated maiden speech, 1755 (the so-called 'single speech'); a commissioner of trade, 1756; MP, Pontefract, 1761, Killebegs (Irish parliament), 1761–8; chief secretary for Ireland, 1761–4, and chancellor of Irish Exchequer, 1763–84; spoke ably in Irish parliament, 1761–2; obtained, 1763, but subsequently appropriated, pension for *Burke, who was for a time his private secretary; MP, Old Sarum, 1768, Wareham, 1774, Wilton, 1780, and Haslemere, 1790; his conversational powers highly praised by Dr *Johnson; *Letters of Junius* attributed to him by some of his contemporaries; his works published after his death by *Malone under title of *Parliamentary Logick*.

HAMILTON, William John (1805–1867), geologist; son of William Richard *Hamilton; educated at Charterhouse and Göttingen; pupil of *Murchison; FGS, 1831; secretary of Geological Society, 1832–54, president, 1854 and 1865; MP, Newport (Isle of Wight), 1841–7; his tour in the Levant, 1835–7, described in *Researches in Asia Minor, Pontus, and Armenia* (1842); president of Royal Geographical Society, 1837, 1841, 1842, and 1847; made excursions in France and Belgium, and wrote papers on rocks of Tuscany and geology of the Mayence basin and Hesse-Cassel.

HAMILTON, William Richard (1777–1859), antiquary and diplomat; cousin of William Gerard *Hamilton; lamed for life at Harrow; as secretary to Lord *Elgin prevented France carrying off Rosetta stone; superintended safe transportation to England of Grecian marbles, 1802; under-secretary for foreign affairs, 1809–22; minister at Naples, 1822–5; obtained restoration

by France of works of art taken from Italy, 1815; trustee of British Museum, 1838–58; published *Aegyptiaca* (1809), containing first translations of Rosetta inscriptions.

HAMILTON, Sir William Rowan (1805–1865), mathematician; discoverer of science of quaternions; as a child competed with Zerah Colburn, the 'calculating boy'; at sixteen detected an error of reasoning in Laplace's *Mécanique Céleste*; at Trinity College, Dublin, obtained the 'double optime' and twice won vice-chancellor's prize for English verse; while an undergraduate predicted 'conical refraction'; appointed Andrews professor of astronomy, 1827; astronomer royal of Ireland; gold medallist of Royal Society for optical discovery and for (1834) theory of a general method of dynamics; knighted, 1835; president of Royal Irish Academy, 1837; published *Lectures on Quaternions* (1853). His *Elements of Quaternions* appeared posthumously (1866).

HAMILTON DE HAGEBY, Baron (1635–1699). See HAMILTON, MALCOLM.

HAMILTON FAIRLEY, Sir Neil (1891–1966), physician. See FAIRLEY.

HAMILTON FYFE, Sir William (1878–1965), headmaster and university vice-chancellor. See FYFE.

HAMILTON OF GLENAWLEY, Baron (d. 1679). See HAMILTON, HUGH.

HAMILTON-ROWAN, Archibald (1751–1834). See ROWAN.

HAMLEY, Edward (1764–1834), poet; fellow of New College, Oxford, 1785; BCL, 1791; rector of Cusop, 1805–34, and Stanton St John, 1806–34; published poems (1795), translations from Petrarch and Metastasio (1795), and sonnets (1795).

HAMLEY, Sir Edward Bruce (1824–1893), general; studied at Royal Military Academy, Woolwich; lieutenant, Royal Artillery, 1843; stationed at Gibraltar; adjutant to Colonel (Sir) Richard James *Dacres in Crimea; brevet lieutenant-colonel, 1855; contributed to Fraser's and Blackwood's magazines; edited first series of *Tales from Blackwood*, 1858; professor of military history, Sandhurst, 1859–64; published *Operations of War* (1866); lieutenant-colonel, 1864; member of Council of Military Education, 1866–70; commandant of staff college, 1870–7; major-general, 1877; British commissioner for delimitation of Bulgaria, 1879, Armenian frontier, 1880, and Greek frontier, 1881; KCMG, 1880; lieutenant-general, 1882; commanded division in Egypt, 1882; fought at Tel-el-Kebir; KCB, 1882; MP for Birkenhead, 1885, and

1886–92; colonel-commandant, Royal Artillery, 1886; general, 1890; published novels, *Shakespeare's Funeral* (1869), and military works.

HAMMERSLEY, James Astbury (1815–1869), painter; master of Manchester School of Design, 1849–62; first president, Manchester Academy of Fine Arts, 1857–61.

HAMMICK, Sir **Stephen Love,** first baronet (1777–1867), surgeon extraordinary to George IV and William IV; surgeon to Naval Hospital, Plymouth, 1803; created baronet, 1834; an original member of London University senate; published *Practical Remarks on . . . Strictures of the Urethra* (1830).

HAMMOND. See also HAMOND.

HAMMOND, Anthony (1668–1738), poet and pamphleteer; grand-nephew of William *Hammond; MP, Huntingdonshire, 1695–8, Cambridge University, 1698–1701, Huntingdon, 1702–8; MA St John's College, Cambridge, 1698; commissioner of public accounts, 1701; commissioner of the navy, 1702; declared incapable of sitting in parliament as holding the latter office, 1708; treasurer of forces in Spain, 1711; published pamphlets on finance and parliamentary practice; edited *New Miscellany of Original Poems* (1720); died debtor in the Fleet.

HAMMOND, Anthony (1758–1838), legal writer; prepared draft of act of 1827 consolidating and amending the criminal law.

HAMMOND, Edmund, Baron Hammond (1802–1890), diplomat; son of George *Hammond; of Harrow and University College, Oxford; fellow, 1828–46; MA, 1826; accompanied Stratford *Canning to Constantinople, 1831, Madrid, and Lisbon, 1832; chief of the oriental department of Foreign Office; permanent under-secretary, 1854–73; privy councillor, 1866; created a peer, 1874; died at Mentone.

HAMMOND, George (1763–1853), diplomat; educated at Merton College, Oxford; fellow, 1787; MA, 1788; secretary to David *Hartley the younger at Paris, 1783; chargé d'affaires at Vienna, 1788–90; first British minister at Washington, 1791–5; as under-secretary for foreign affairs (1795–1806 and 1807–9) intimate with Grenville and Canning; joint editor of *Anti-Jacobin*; DCL Oxford, 1810.

HAMMOND, Henry (1605–1660), chaplain to Charles I; son of John *Hammond (d. 1617); of Eton and Magdalen College, Oxford; fellow, 1625, MA, 1625, DD, 1639; incumbent of Penshurst, 1633; archdeacon of Chichester, 1643; became known to Charles I by *Practical Catechism*, 1644; canon of Christ Church and public orator at Oxford, 1645; chaplain to royal commissioners at Uxbridge, and to Charles I, 1645; deprived and imprisoned, but afterwards allowed to live with Sir Philip *Warwick and Sir John *Pakington; published *Paraphrase and Annotations on the New Testament* (1653); his collected works edited by William *Fulman, 1674–84, *Miscellaneous Theological Works*, by Nicholas *Pocock, 1847–50.

HAMMOND, James (1710–1742), poet; son of Anthony *Hammond (1668–1738); educated at Westminster; equerry to *Frederick, prince of Wales, 1733; MP, Truro, 1741–2; said to have died for love of Kitty Dashwood; his *Love Elegies* (1743) (with preface by Chesterfield) condemned by Dr *Johnson for 'frigid pedantry'.

HAMMOND, John (1542–1589), civilian; fellow of Trinity Hall, Cambridge; LL D, 1569; commissary of deanery of St Paul's, 1573; master of Chancery, 1574; chancellor of London, 1575; delegate to diet of Smalkald, 1578; MP, Rye, 1584, West Looe, 1586; as member of High Commission examined *Campion (1581) and other Jesuits under torture.

HAMMOND, John (d. 1617), physician to James I; son of John *Hammond (1542–1589); MA Trinity College, Cambridge, 1586; MD, 1597, incorporated at Oxford, 1605; FRCP, 1608; made post-mortem examination of *Henry, prince of Wales.

HAMMOND, Sir **John** (1889–1964), animal scientist; educated at Gresham's School, Holt, Edward VI Middle School, Norwich, and Downing College, Cambridge; diploma in agriculture, 1910; served in France in Royal Norfolk Regiment, 1914–16; physiologist, Animal Nutrition Institute, Cambridge, 1920; superintendent, Animal Research Station, 1931–54; interested in artificial insemination; supervised Downing College estate farms, 1939–45; first president, British Society of Animal Production; CBE, 1949; knighted, 1960; FRS, 1933; fellow, Downing College, 1936; many honorary doctorates and other distinctions; publications include *The Physiology of Reproduction in the Cow* (1927) and *Growth and Development of Mutton Qualities in the Sheep* (1932); on editorial boards of *Journal of Agricultural Science, Empire Journal of Experimental Agriculture*, and *Journal of Dairy Research*.

HAMMOND, John Lawrence Le Breton (1872–1949), journalist and historian; educated at Bradford Grammar School and St John's College, Oxford; second class, Lit. Hum., 1895; edited Liberal *Speaker*, 1899–1907; secretary, Civil Service Commission, 1907–13; special correspondent, *Manchester Guardian*, 1919–49; married (1901) Lucy Barbara Bradby; with her wrote *The Village Labourer, 1760–1832* (1911),

The Town Labourer, 1760–1832 (1917), *The Skilled Labourer, 1760–1832* (1919), *Lord Shaftesbury* (1923), *The Rise of Modern Industry* (1925), *The Age of the Chartists* (1930), *James Stansfeld* (1932), and *The Bleak Age* (1934); wrote also *Charles James Fox* (1903), *C. P. Scott* (1934), and *Gladstone and the Irish Nation* (1938); FBA, 1942.

HAMMOND, Robert (1621–1654), Parliamentarian; grandson of John *Hammond (d. 1617); member of Magdalen Hall, Oxford, 1636; captain in Parliamentary Army, 1642; distinguished himself at Tewkesbury, 1644; as colonel of foot in the New Model Army, 1645, captured Powderham Castle and St Michael's Mount; taken by Royalists at Basing House, 1645; governor of Isle of Wight, 1647; custodian of Charles I, who had mistakenly taken refuge with him in the Isle of Wight, Nov. 1647 to Nov. 1648; member of the Irish council, 1654.

HAMMOND, Samuel (d. 1665), Nonconformist divine; fellow of Magdalene College, Cambridge; chaplain to Sir Arthur *Hesilrige; while minister at Newcastle (1652–60) assisted in exposing the impostor, Thomas *Ramsay; assisted in writing a tract against Quakers, 1654.

HAMMOND, Walter Reginald (1903–1965), cricketer; educated at Cirencester Grammar School; played for Gloucestershire at age of 17; established as fine all-rounder, 1925; in MCC side in West Indies; made 238 not out at Bridgetown; first player since W. G. *Grace to score 1,000 runs in May (1927); played in all five tests in South Africa, 1927–8; first encounter with Australians, 1928–9; made 905 runs in victorious series in Australia; headed English averages with 3,323 runs, 1933, and in every season but one for the rest of his career; played finest test-match innings at Lords, 240 in 6 hours, 1938; captained Gloucestershire and England; served in Royal Air Force, 1939–45; retired at end of 1946–7 tour to Australia; made over 50,000 runs in his career, took over 700 wickets, and over 800 catches; in 140 test innings, scored 7,249 runs, with 22 centuries, took 83 wickets, and made 110 catches; published *Cricket My Destiny* (1946).

HAMMOND, William (*fl.* 1655), poet; his *Poems* (1655) reprinted (1816).

HAMOND. See also HAMMOND and HAMONT.

HAMOND, Sir Andrew Snape, first baronet (1738–1828), comptroller of the navy; present at Quiberon Bay, 1759; captain, 1770; knighted for services in Chesapeake expedition and defence of Sandy Hook, 1778; governor of Nova Scotia, 1780–2; created baronet, 1783; commander at the Nore, 1785–8; commissioner of the navy,

1793; MP, Ipswich, 1796–1806; comptroller of the navy, 1794–1806.

HAMOND, George (1620–1705), ejected divine; MA Exeter College, Oxford; studied at Trinity College, Dublin; ejected from St Peter's and Trinity, Dorchester, 1662; Presbyterian minister and schoolmaster at Taunton, 1672–85; pastor of Armourers' Hall, London, and lecturer at Salters' Hall.

HAMOND, Sir Graham Eden, second baronet (1779–1862), admiral; son of Sir Andrew Snape *Hamond; midshipman on *Howe's flagship at victory of 1794; commanded the *Blanche* at Copenhagen, 1801; captured Spanish treasure ships, 1804; at reduction of Flushing, 1809; commander on South American station, 1834–8; admiral, 1847; admiral of the fleet, 1862; GCB, 1855.

HAMOND, Walter (*fl.* 1643), author of tracts on Madagascar (1640 and 1643).

HAMONT, Matthew (d. 1579), heretic; burnt at Norwich. On his case Philip van Limborch corresponded with *Locke, 1699.

HAMPDEN, Viscounts. See TREVOR, ROBERT HAMPDEN-, first viscount, 1706–1783; TREVOR, JOHN HAMPDEN-, third viscount, 1749–1824; BRAND, Sir HENRY BOUVERIE WILLIAM, first viscount of new creation, 1814–1892; BRAND, HENRY ROBERT, second viscount, 1841–1906.

HAMPDEN, John (1594–1643), statesman; educated at Thame School and Magdalen College, Oxford; also studied at Inner Temple; MP for Grampound, 1621–5, and for Wendover in first three parliaments of Charles I; afterwards represented Buckinghamshire; imprisoned (1627) for refusing to pay forced loan of 1626; prominent in Charles I's third parliament; closely associated with Sir John *Eliot, corresponding with him when Eliot was in prison; one of the twelve grantees of land in Connecticut, 1632; by resisting second ship-money writ, 1635 (declared legal by Exchequer Court, 1638), caused it to be paid with increasing reluctance; most popular member in the Short Parliament, 1640; led the opposition to the king's demand for twelve subsidies in exchange for the abandonment of ship-money, 1640; exercised great influence over *Pym in the Long Parliament, and proved a powerful debater and strategist; as one of the managers of *Strafford's impeachment opposed the resolution for a bill of attainder, and (1641) obtained leave for Strafford's counsel to be heard; supported the Root-and-Branch Bill; attended the king to Scotland, 1641; calmed House of Commons after the carrying of the Grand Remonstrance, 1641; impeached by the attorney-general, 1642 (3 Jan.), but escaped the attempted arrest by the king next day; returned to move (20 Jan. 1642) the resolution giving control of the militia and the Tower to parliament; leading member of the Committee of Safety; raised regiment of foot and executed the militia ordinance in his own county after Edgehill, joining the main army (1642) under Essex, whose retreat after Edgehill he condemned; resisted acceptance of Charles I's overtures for peace, 1642–3, and urged an immediate attack on Oxford; mortally wounded in a skirmish with Prince *Rupert at Chalgrove Field; died at Thame, and was buried in Great Hampden Church.

HAMPDEN, John, the younger (1656?–1696), politician; son of Richard *Hampden; MP, Buckinghamshire, 1679, Wendover, 1681–90; imprisoned and fined on charge of plotting an insurrection, 1684; condemned to death for high treason after *Monmouth's rising, 1685, but bribed *Jefferies and *Petre, and was pardoned; prominent in Convention Parliament (1689) as an extreme Whig; opposed employment by William III of *Halifax and other ex-ministers; committed suicide.

HAMPDEN, Renn Dickson (1793–1868), bishop of Hereford; fellow of Oriel College, Oxford, 1814; double first, 1814; MA, 1816; DD, 1833; intimate of *Arnold and *Whately; Bampton lecturer, 1832; principal of St Mary Hall, 1833; professor of moral philosophy, 1834; canon of Christ Church, Oxford, 1836–48; his appointment by Melbourne to the regius professorship of divinity (1836) opposed on ground of his unorthodoxy, as also his nomination to bishopric (1848); bishop of Hereford, 1848–68; published *The Scholastic Philosophy considered in its Relation to Christian Theology* (Bampton lectures, 1833).

HAMPDEN, Richard (1631–1695), chancellor of the Exchequer; son of John *Hampden (1594–1643); MP, Buckinghamshire, 1656, and 1681–90, Wendover, 1660–79, and 1690–5; member of Protector's House of Lords; entertained *Baxter during the plague, 1665; moved Exclusion Bill of 1679; chairman of Commons' committee that declared the throne vacant, 1689; privy councillor, 1689; commissioner of the Treasury, 1689; chancellor of the Exchequer, 1690–4; refused emoluments from William III.

HAMPDEN-TREVOR. See TREVOR.

HAMPER, William (1776–1831), antiquary; FSA, 1821; contributed to *Gentleman's Magazine*; assisted John *Britton and other topographical writers; published *Observations on certain Ancient Pillars of Memorial called Hoar-Stones* (1820), and *Life, Diary, and Correspondence of Sir W. Dugdale* (1827).

HAMPOLE, Richard (1290?–1349). See ROLLE, RICHARD.

HAMPSON, Frank (1918–1985), strip cartoonist; educated at King George V Grammar School, Southport; left at 14 and became telegraph boy; served in Royal Army Service Corps during 1939–45 war; studied at Southport School of Arts and Crafts; engaged by local vicar, the Revd Marcus Morris, to illustrate parish magazine, 1948; artist for 'Interim', a Society for Christian Publicity; created cartoon character, Dan Dare, Space Pilot; employed by *Eagle* magazine, launched by Hulton Press with Marcus Morris as editor, 1950; left *Eagle* in 1961 after Odham's Press had bought the magazine, wished to alter Dan Dare, and Morris had resigned; undertook small advertising commissions and illustrations for magazines; developed cancer of trachea, 1970; graphics technician at Ewell Technical College; received Open University degree, 1979; received awards as best writer and illustrator of strip cartoons.

HAMPSON, John (1760–1817?), author; MA, St Edmund Hall, Oxford, 1792; rector of Sunderland, 1801; published works including *Memoirs of Rev. John Wesley* (1791); translated *The Poetics of Marcus Hieronymus Vida* (1793).

HAMPTON, first Baron (1799–1880). See PAKINGTON, Sir JOHN SOMERSET.

HAMPTON, Christopher (1552–1625), archbishop of Armagh; MA, Trinity College, Cambridge, 1575; DD, 1598; fellow, 1574; nominated to see of Derry, 1611, but not consecrated; archbishop of Armagh, 1613–25; restored Armagh Cathedral; maintained primacy of Armagh.

HAMPTON, James (1721–1778), translator of Polybius; of Winchester and Corpus Christi College, Oxford; MA, 1747; rector of Monkton Moor, 1762, and Folkton, Yorkshire, 1775; translated Polybius, first five books (1756–61); issued extracts from sixth book of Polybius (1764).

HAMSHAW THOMAS, Hugh (1885–1962), palaeobotanist. See THOMAS, HUGH HAMSHAW.

HANBOYS (or HAMBOYS), John (fl. 1470), doctor of music; his commentary on works of the two Francos printed by Coussemaker.

HANBURY, Benjamin (1778–1864), Nonconformist historian; first treasurer of Congregational Union, 1831–64; published *Historical Memorials relating to the Independents ... from their Rise to the Restoration* (1839–44), and an edition of *Hooker (1830).

HANBURY, Daniel (1825–1875), pharmacist; treasurer of Linnean Society; FRS, 1867; visited

Palestine with Sir Joseph Hooker, 1860; published *Pharmacographia* (with Professor Flückiger, 1874).

HANBURY, Elizabeth (1793–1901), centenarian and philanthropist; of Quaker parentage; visited prisons with Elizabeth *Fry; married Cornelius Hanbury, 1826; active in anti-slavery movement and prison reform; aided in her work by her daughter Charlotte (1830–1900), who established mission at Tangier for ameliorating lot of Moorish prisoners; autobiography published, 1901.

HANBURY, Sir James (1782–1863), lieutenant-general; served with the 58th in Egypt, 1801; present at operations of Corunna, 1808–9; with the Guards at Walcheren (1809) and in the Peninsular War; major-general, 1830; KB, 1830; lieutenant- general, 1841.

HANBURY, Sir James Arthur (1832–1908), surgeon-general; MB, Trinity College, Dublin, 1853; entered army medical service; FRCS England, 1887; served in Afghan War, 1878–9; at Battle of Tel-el-Kebir, 1882; KCB, 1882; surgeon-general of forces in Madras, 1888–92; surgeon-general, 1892.

HANBURY, John (1664–1734), politician; developed his estate and ironworks at Pontypool; MP, Gloucester, 1701–15, Monmouthshire, 1721–34; director of the New South Sea Company, 1721; one of *Marlborough's executors, 1722.

HANBURY, Robert William (1845–1903), politician; educated at Rugby and Corpus Christi College, Oxford; Conservative MP for Tamworth, 1872–8, for North Staffordshire, 1878–80, and for Preston, 1885–1903; ceaselessly attacked policy of Gladstone's government, 1892–5; PC and financial secretary of the Treasury, 1895–1900; joined Cabinet as president of Board of Agriculture, 1900.

HANBURY, William (1725–1778), clergyman; BA, St Edmund Hall, Oxford, 1748; rector of Church Langton, Leicestershire, 1753–78; MA, St Andrews, 1769; issued (1758) *Essay on Planting, and a Scheme for making it conducive to the Glory of God and the advantage of Society*; his scheme carried out by court of Chancery, 1864; published *Complete Body of Planting and Gardening* (1770–1).

HANBURY-WILLIAMS, Sir John Coldbrook (1892–1965), industrialist; educated at Wellington College; served in France with 10th Royal Hussars, 1914–18; travelled in China and Japan on family business; joined Courtaulds Ltd., 1926; director, Snia Viscosa, Italian associate company, 1928–65; initiated developments leading to manufacture of 'cellophane' and (with Imperial Chemical Industries) nylon; managing director, Courtaulds, 1935; deputy chairman, 1943; succeeded Samuel *Courtauld as chairman, 1946–62; made the firm one of largest industrial concerns in Britain; gentleman usher, 1931–46; knighted, 1950; CVO, 1956; director, Bank of England, 1936–63; in charge of foreign-exchange control, 1940–1; refused to succeed Lord *Catto as governor, 1949; served at Ministry of Economic Warfare, 1942; high sheriff, County of London, 1943 and 1958; actively associated with charitable causes and member of number of committees and missions.

HANCE, Henry Fletcher (1827–1886), botanist; vice-consul at Whampoa, 1861–78; consul at Canton, 1878–81 and 1883; acting consul at Amoy at his death; contributed papers on Chinese plants to *Hooker's *Journal of Botany*, and supplement to *Bentham's *Flora Hongkongensis*.

HANCKWITZ, Ambrose Godfrey (d. 1741). See GODFREY, AMBROSE.

HANCOCK, Albany (1806–1873), zoologist; received the Royal Medal of Royal Society for paper on 'The Organisation of Brachiopoda' (1857); FLS, 1862; collaborated with Joshua *Alder in *Monograph of British Nudibranchiate Mollusca* (1845–55); with Dr D. Embleton investigated structure of genera *oeolis* and *doris*.

HANCOCK, Anthony John ('Tony') (1924–1968), comedian; educated at Durlston Court, Swanage, and Bradfield College; enlisted in Royal Air Force, 1942; toured with ENSA and Ralph Reader 'Gang Shows'; appeared at Windmill Theatre, London, 1948; met immediate success with 'Hancock's Half-Hour' on BBC radio, 1954; owed much to Bill Kerr, Kenneth Williams, and particularly, Sid *James, as well as his script-writers, Alan Simpson and Ray Galton; transferred to television, 1956; success ended when Sid James and the script-writers were abandoned; last of cherished line of English comedians, but success brought boredom and disaster; died by his own hand.

HANCOCK, Dame Florence May (1893–1974), president of the Trades Union Congress; left Chippenham Elementary School at 12 to work in café and later moved to work in condensed milk factory; helped to organize strike, 1913; joined Independent Labour party, 1915; appointed full-time organizer of Workers' Union in Wiltshire, 1917; when her union merged in Transport and General Workers' Union, she became woman officer for Area 3 based in Bristol, 1929; elected one of two women members of General Council of the TUC, 1935; chief woman officer of TGWU, 1942–58; remained member of General Council till 1958; president, 1947–8; member of National Advisory Council for Juvenile Employment, 1936; trade-union adviser to wartime south-west regional commissioner; member of *Piercy Committee on review of provision for disabled, 1953; member of committee on adminstrative tribunals chaired by Sir Oliver (later Lord) Franks, 1955; governor of BBC, 1956–62; director of *Daily Herald*, 1955–7, and Remploy, 1958–66; regular TUC representative at International Labour Organization; OBE, 1942; CBE, 1947; DBE, 1951; married John Donovan, CBE, a colleague in the TGWU, 1964.

HANCOCK, Sir Henry Drummond (1895–1965), civil servant; educated at Haileybury and Exeter College, Oxford; served in Sherwood Foresters and Intelligence Corps, 1914–18; entered administrative class, Civil Service, 1920; appointed to Ministry of Labour; private secretary to Sir Horace *Wilson, permanent secretary; deeply involved in unemployment problems, 1928–38; private secretary to J. H. *Thomas, lord privy seal; member of staff of National Assistance Board; transferred to Home Office, 1938; organized financing of Civil Defence; secretary-general, British Purchasing Commission, Washington, 1941; CMG, 1942; deputy secretary, Ministry of Supply, 1942–5; deputy secretary Ministry of National Insurance, 1945; KBE, 1947; succeeded Sir Thomas Phillips as permanent secretary, 1949; KCB, 1950; permanent secretary, Ministry of Food, 1951; chairman, Board of Inland Revenue, 1955–8; chairman, Local Government Commission for England; member of boards of Booker Bros., McConnell & Co., and Yorkshire Insurance Co.; GCB, 1962.

HANCOCK, John (d. 1869), sculptor; exhibited at Royal Academy from 1843.

HANCOCK, Robert (1730–1817), mezzotint engraver and draughtsman; engraver to Worcester Porcelain Works, 1757–74; executed small crayon portraits of *Lamb, *Wordsworth, *Coleridge, and *Southey.

HANCOCK, Thomas (1783–1849), Quaker physician; MD, Edinburgh, 1809; practised in London and Liverpool; published (1825) *Principles of Peace exemplified in conduct of Society of Friends in Ireland during the Rebellion of 1798*, and treatises on epidemics; edited 'Discourses' from Nicole's *Essays by John Locke* (1828).

HANCOCK, Thomas (1786–1865), founder of the india-rubber trade in England; took out patent for applying india-rubber springs to articles of dress, 1820; first made 'vulcanized' india-rubber, 1843; published *Personal Narrative of the Origin and Progress of the Caoutchouc or Indiarubber Manufacture in England* (1857).

HANCOCK, Walter (1799–1852), engineer; brother of Thomas *Hancock (1786–1865); invented steam-engines for road traffic, 1824–36; described experiments in *Narrative* (1838); obtained patent for cutting india-rubber into sheets, and for a method of preparing solutions of india-rubber, 1843.

HAND, Thomas (d. 1804), painter; friend and imitator of *Morland; exhibited at Royal Academy.

HANDASYDE, Charles (*fl.* 1760–1780), miniature painter.

HANDEL (HAENDEL), George Frederick (Georg Friedrich) (1685–1759), musical composer; son of the town surgeon of Giebichenstein, Saxony; studied music under Zachau at Halle; presented to elector of Brandenburg at Berlin, *c*.1696; went to Hamburg, 1703, and became conductor of the opera; fought a duel with Matheson (first tenor); composed his first opera, *Almira*, 1705; went to Italy, 1707; produced the operas *Rodrigo* at Florence and *Agrippina* at Venice, 1708; at Rome composed the oratorios *Il Trionfo del Tempo* and *La Resurrezione*; visited Naples, 1708–9, composing songs and cantatas; went to Hanover and became kapellmeister, 1710; came to England, 1710; his opera *Rinaldo* produced with great success at the Queen's Theatre, Haymarket, 1711; returned to Hanover, but was again in England in 1712, where, breaking his pledge to the elector of Hanover (afterwards George I) to return to Hanover, he thenceforth remained; his operas *Pastor Fido* and *Teseo* and the Utrecht Te Deum and Jubilate, performed before the death of Anne, the composer receiving for the last an annuity of £200, increased by George I after Handel's reconciliation with him, effected through *Burlington and Kielmannsegge by means of the *Water Music*, 1715; as director for the duke of *Chandos at Canons (1718–20) composed twelve anthems, *Esther* (his first English oratorio, performed 1720), and *Acis and Galatea* (performed 1720 or 1721); director of the Royal Academy of Music, 1720–8, composing thirteen operas, besides collaborating in *Muzio Scevola* with Buononcini, thenceforth his rival in popular favour; naturalized, 1726; appointed court composer; produced coronation anthems on the accession of George II, 1727; carried on (1729–35) a second operatic undertaking at the King's Theatre, Covent Garden, producing several new operas, and giving performances of *Esther* and *Acis and Galatea*, 1732, and *Deborah*, 1733; *Athaliah* first heard at Oxford, 1733; ousted from the King's Theatre by his rivals, 1735; gave more operas, and repeated his oratorios in Lent at *Rich's new theatre, Covent Garden, 1735–7, when he became bankrupt and partially paralysed; composed a fine anthem for the funeral of Queen *Caroline, 1737, and two new operas, 1738, when his debts were paid by a benefit concert; his statue by *Roubilliac set up at Vauxhall, 1738; his last operas given at Lincoln's Inn Fields, 1740–1, also setting of *Dryden's shorter *Ode on St. Cecilia's Day*, 1739; the first annual performance of *Alexander's Feast* for the Society of Musicians, with himself at the organ, given 1739; his *Saul* and *Israel in Egypt* produced at the King's Theatre, 1739; his oratorio the *Messiah* (composed in twenty-three days) first heard at Dublin, 1741, in London, 1743 (Covent Garden), and in Germany (Hamburg), 1772; his *Samson* given at a subscription concert at Covent Garden, and the Dettingen Te Deum at St James's Palace, 1743; *Joseph and his Brethren* and *Semele*, 1744 (Covent Garden); *Hercules* and *Belshazzar* (King's Theatre), 1744–5; *Judas Maccabaeus*, 1747; *Alexander Balus* and *Joshua*, 1748 (Covent Garden); his oratorios *Susanna* and *Solomon*, produced, 1749; his *Music for the Fireworks* performed at Vauxhall and the Green Park to celebrate the peace of Aix-la-Chapelle, 1749; his *Theodora*, 1750, a failure; conducted a performance of the *Messiah* (with the organ presented by himself) at the Foundling Hospital, 1750; his last oratorio, *Jephthah*, produced at Covent Garden, 1752; his last composition, *The Triumph of Time and Truth*, 1757; buried in Westminster Abbey. His manuscript scores passed from John Christopher *Smith to George III. He carried choral music to its highest point, but in instrumental did not advance beyond his contemporaries. His almost certain appropriation (notably in *Israel in Egypt*) of the work of others is in strong contradiction with his known character. A collection of his works, begun in Germany, 1856, with the help of the king of Hanover, was continued under the auspices of the Prussian government. Roubilliac executed his monument in Westminster Abbey and three busts.

HANDLEY, Thomas Reginald ('Tommy') (1892–1949), radio comedian; produced own radio revues from 1925; presented brilliantly absurd weekly cartoon of daily life in ITMA ('It's That Man Again!'), 1939–49; introduced 'Office of Twerps', seaside resort 'Foaming-at-the-Mouth', post-war 'Island of Tomtopia', and notable characters including Mrs Mopp and Funf; first radio show Royal Command Performance, 1942.

HANDLEY PAGE, Sir **Frederick** (1885–1962), aircraft designer. See PAGE.

HANDLO, Robert de (*fl.* 1326), writer on music; author of *Regulae* (printed by Coussemaker).

HANDYSIDE, William (1793–1850), engineer; employed by the Russian government.

HANGER, George, fourth Baron Coleraine (1751?–1824), eccentric; educated at Eton and Göttingen; served during American War in Hessian Jäger Corps and in *Tarleton's Light Dragoons; aide-de-camp to Sir Henry *Clinton at Charlestown, 1779; his *Life, Adventures, and Opinions* issued by William *Combe (1801); succeeded his brother in peerage, 1814, but did not assume title; caricatured by *Gillray and George *Cruikshank; published *Lives and Adventures . . . of Eminent Gamesters* (1804) and military pamphlets.

HANKEFORD, Sir **William** (d. 1422), judge; king's serjeant, 1390; justice of common pleas, 1398; KB, 1399; chief justice of King's Bench, 1413–22.

HANKEY, Maurice Pascal Alers, first Baron Hankey (1877–1963), secretary to the Cabinet; educated at Rugby School; joined Royal Marine Artillery, 1895; sword of honour, Royal Naval College; served in *Ramillies*, 1899–1902; transferred to Naval Intelligence, Admiralty, 1905–7; returned to sea as intelligence officer, 1907; assistant secretary, Committee of Imperial Defence, 1908; secretary, 1912; chief of War Cabinet secretariat, 1916; secretary to the Cabinet, secretary, Committee of Imperial Defence, and clerk to the Privy Council, 1923–38; secretary on British side, Paris Peace Conference, 1919, and conferences at Washington, 1921, Genoa, 1922, Lausanne, 1932, and The Hague, 1929 and 1930; secretary of imperial conferences, 1921, 1923, 1926, 1930, and 1937, and the London Naval Conference, 1930; created the Cabinet secretariat, 1916, and laid down principles which have since guided its performance; baron, 1939; joined Neville Chamberlain's War Cabinet, as minister without portfolio; chancellor, duchy of Lancaster and paymaster-general in Churchill's government, 1940–2; chairman, Cabinet's Scientific Advisory Committee; FRS, 1942; publications include *The Supreme Command 1914–18* (2 vols., 1961), *Government Control in War* (1945), *Diplomacy by Conference* (1946), and *The Science and Art of Government* (1951); CB, 1912; KCB, 1916; GCB, 1919; GCMG, 1929; GCVO, 1934; PC, 1939; honorary degrees from Oxford, Cambridge, Edinburgh, and Birmingham.

HANKEY, Thomson (1805–1893), politician; senior partner in his father's West Indian mercantile firm; elected a director of Bank of England, 1835; governor, 1851–2; Liberal MP for Peterborough, 1853–68, and 1874–80; published works on questions of political economy.

HANKIN, Edward (1747–1835), author; rector of West Chiltington, Sussex; published pamphlets on clerical grievances and political subjects.

HANKIN, St John Emile Clavering (1869–1909), playwright; educated at Malvern and Merton College, Oxford; wrote plays of realistic frankness; his *The Return of the Prodigal* (1905), *The Charity that began at Home* (1906), *The Cassilis Engagement* (the most popular of his plays, 1907), were published in 1907 as *Three Plays with Happy Endings*; pushed realism further in *The Last of the De Mullins* (1908); cynically satirized middle-class convention and sentiment.

HANKINSON, Thomas Edwards (1805–1843), poet; MA, Corpus Christi College, Cambridge, 1831; incumbent of St Matthew's Chapel, Denmark Hill; won Seatonian Prize at Cambridge nine times; his *Poems* collected (1844).

HANLAN (properly **HANLON**), **Edward** (1855–1908), Canadian oarsman; born at Toronto; rowing champion of Canada, 1877, of America, 1878, of England, 1879, and of the world, 1880; retained the last title, 1881–4.

HANMER, John (1574–1629), bishop of St Asaph; matriculated at Oriel College, Oxford, 1592; fellow of All Souls College, Oxford, 1596; MA, 1600; DD, 1616; chaplain to James I; prebendary of Worcester, 1614; bishop of St Asaph, 1624–9.

HANMER, John (1642–1707), Nonconformist minister; son of Jonathan *Hanmer; graduated at St John's College, Cambridge, 1662; pastor at Barnstaple, 1692–1705.

HANMER, Sir John, Baron Hanmer (1809–1881), poet; succeeded as third baronet, 1828; educated at Eton and Christ Church, Oxford; Whig MP for Shrewsbury, 1832–7, Hull, 1841–7, and Flint, 1847–72; created a peer, 1872; published *Fra Cipolla and other poems* (1839), *Sonnets* (1840), and *Memorials of Family and Parish of Hanmer* (1877).

HANMER, Jonathan (1606–1687), divine; MA, Emmanuel College, Cambridge, 1631; ejected from vicarage of Bishop's Tawton and lectureship of Barnstaple, 1662, where he founded, with Oliver Peard, the first Nonconformist congregation; published *An Exercitation upon Confirmation* (1657) and *A View of Antiquity* (1677).

HANMER, Meredith (1543–1604), historian; chaplain of Corpus Christi College, Oxford, 1567; MA, 1572; DD, 1582; vicar of St Leonard's, Shoreditch, 1581–92; vicar of Islington, 1583–90; accused of celebrating an illegal marriage; went to Ireland, becoming archdeacon of Ross (1591), treasurer of Waterford (1593), vicar choral and prebendary of Christ Church, Dublin (1594–5), chancellor of Kilkenny (1603); published a translation of the histories of Eusebius, Socrates, and Evagrius (1577); his *Chronicle of Ireland* printed by Sir James *Ware (1633).

HANMER, Sir Thomas, fourth baronet (1677–1746), speaker; of Westminster and Christ Church, Oxford; succeeded his uncle as baronet, 1701; Tory MP for Thetford, 1701 and 1705–8, Flintshire, 1702–5, and Suffolk, 1708–27; chairman of the committee which made the 'representation' of 1712; received in great state by Louis XIV at Paris, 1712; refused office from Harley and procured rejection of two articles of the commercial treaty of 1713; speaker, 1714–15; chief of the Hanoverian Tories; while in retirement, prepared sumptuous, but not critically very valuable, edition of Shakespeare, 1743–4; alluded to in the *Dunciad* as Montalto.

HANN, James (1799–1856), mathematician; calculator in Nautical Almanack office; mathematical master at King's College School, London, till death; published works on mechanics and pure mathematics, including *Principles and Practice of the Machinery of Locomotive Engines* (1850), and, with Olinthus Gilbert *Gregory, *Tables for the Use of Nautical Men* (1841).

HANNA, Samuel (1772?–1852), Presbyterian divine; MA, Glasgow, 1789; DD, 1818; minister of Rosemary Street, Belfast, 1799; professor of divinity, Belfast Presbyterian College, 1817; first moderator of general assembly, 1840.

HANNA, William (1808–1882), theological writer; son of Samuel *Hanna; colleague of Thomas *Guthrie at Edinburgh, 1850–66; LL D, Glasgow, 1852; DD, Edinburgh, 1864; son-in-law of *Chalmers, whose life he issued in 1849–52, afterwards editing his posthumous works; edited also *Essays by Ministers of the Free Church of Scotland* (1858) and *Letters of Thomas Erskine of Linlathen* (1877).

HANNAH, John, the elder (1792–1867), Wesleyan minister; delegate to United States of Wesleyan Conference, 1824 and 1856; secretary to Conference, 1840–2, and 1854–8, president, 1842 and 1851; tutor of Didsbury, 1843–67; published works, including a defence of infant baptism (1866).

HANNAH, John, the younger (1818–1888), archdeacon of Lewes; son of John *Hannah the elder; scholar of Corpus Christi College, Oxford, 1837; fellow of Lincoln, 1840; BA, 1840; DCL, 1853; rector of the Edinburgh Academy, 1847–54; principal of Glenalmond, 1854–70; Bampton lecturer, 1862; vicar of Brighton, 1870–87; archdeacon of Lewes, 1876–88; published, besides Bampton lectures (1863), *Courtly Poets from Raleigh to Montrose* (1870).

HANNAM, Richard (d. 1656), robber; imprisoned for burglary; escaped from England, robbed the Danish treasury and the queen of Sweden; returned to England with money entrusted to him by Rotterdam broker merchants; broke prison at Paris and in London after being sentenced to death; hanged for murder at Smithfield.

HANNAN, William (d. 1775?), draughtsman and decorative painter.

HANNAY, James (1827–1873), author and journalist; dismissed the navy for insubordination, 1845; edited *Edinburgh Evening Courant*, 1860–4; consul at Barcelona, 1868–73; published *Singleton Fontenoy* (1850) and *Eustace Conyers* (1855), naval novels; published *Satire and Satirist* (1854) and *Studies on Thackeray* (1869).

HANNAY, James Owen (1865–1950), novelist under pseudonym George A. Birmingham; educated at Haileybury and Trinity College, Dublin; deacon, 1888; priest, 1889; rector of Westport, Co. Mayo, 1892–1913; Mells, Somerset, 1924–34; canon of St Patrick's, 1912–22; vicar, Holy Trinity, Kensington, 1934–50; many humorous novels include *General John Regan* (1913) and *Send for Dr. O'Grady* (1923).

HANNAY, Patrick (d. 1629?), poet; master of Chancery in Ireland, 1627; said to have died at sea; his 'Happy Husband' (1618–19) and *Brathwait's 'Good Wife' (1619) reissued with 'The Nightingale' and other poems, 1622; facsimile of 1622 collection printed (1875).

HANNAY, Robert Kerr (1867–1940), Scottish historian; educated at Glasgow and Oxford; curator, historical department, Register House, Edinburgh, 1911–19; professor of ancient (Scottish) history and palaeography, Edinburgh, 1919–40; historiographer-royal for Scotland, 1930–40; works include *The Archbishops of St. Andrews* (with Sir John Herkless, 5 vols., 1907–15).

HANNEMAN, Adriaen (1601?–1668?), portrait painter; resided in England, *c.*1625–40; returned to The Hague and became first director of the new guild of St Luke, 1656; executed portraits of Charles II, the duke of *Hamilton, *Van Dyck, and William III and Mary.

HANNEN, Sir James, Baron Hannen (1821–1894), judge; educated at St Paul's School and Heidelberg University; barrister, Middle Temple, 1848; bencher, 1878; joined home circuit; junior counsel to Treasury, 1863; judge of court of Queen's Bench, 1868; knighted, 1868; appointed serjeant-at-law, 1868; privy councillor, 1872; judge of courts of probate and divorce, 1872; president of probate, divorce, and Admiralty division of High Court, 1875–91; life baron and lord of appeal in ordinary, 1891; DCL, Oxford, 1888; president of *Parnell commission, 1888; arbitrator in question of Bering Sea seal fisheries, 1892.

HANNES, Sir Edward (d. 1710), physician; of Westminster and Christ Church, Oxford; MA, 1689; MD, 1695; attended *William, duke of Gloucester, 1700; physician to Queen Anne, 1702; knighted, 1705.

HANNEY (or DE HANNEYA), Thomas (*fl.* 1313), author of Bodleian manuscript 'Memoriale Juniorum' (a work on grammar).

HANNIBAL, Thomas (d. 1531), master of the Rolls; D.Civ.L., Cambridge, 1502; D.Can.L., 1504; incorporated at Oxford, 1513; ambassador at Rome, 1522–4; master of the Rolls, 1523–7; frequently employed as diplomat.

HANNINGTON, James (1847–1885), bishop of Eastern Equatorial Africa; MA, St Mary Hall, Oxford, 1875; DD, 1884; curate in charge of St George's, Hurstpierpoint, 1875–82; went out for the Church Missionary Society to Uganda, 1882; visited Palestine on way to Africa as bishop (1884–5); led expedition which reached Lake Victoria Nyanza, 1885; murdered by order of king of Uganda, 1885.

HANOVER, king of. See ERNEST AUGUSTUS, 1771–1851.

HANSARD, Luke (1752–1828), printer; printed for the Dodsleys; printed House of Commons' *Journals* from 1774.

HANSARD, Thomas Curson (1776–1833), printer; eldest son of Luke *Hansard; began to print parliamentary debates in 1803; imprisoned for libel as *Cobbett's printer, 1810; patented improved hand-press; published *Typographia* (1825).

HANSBIE, Morgan Joseph (1673–1750), Dominican; rector at Louvain, 1717; provincial, 1721; prior of Bornhem and vicar-provincial of Belgium; vicar-provincial in England, 1738–42; vicar-general, 1747; an ardent Jacobite; published theological treatises.

HANSELL, Edward Halifax (1814–1884), biblical scholar; educated at Norwich and Oxford; fellow of Magdalen College, Oxford, 1847–53; MA, 1838; BD, 1847; afterwards divinity lecturer; Grinfield lecturer, 1861–2; vicar of East Ilsley, 1865–84; edited *Nov. Test. Graec. . . . Acc. Collatio Cod. Sinaitici* (1864).

HANSFORD JOHNSON, Pamela, Lady Snow (1912–1981), novelist, dramatist, and critic. See JOHNSON.

HANSOM, Joseph Aloysius (1803–1882), architect and inventor; erected the Birmingham Town Hall, 1833; registered 'Patent Safety Cab', 1834, differing in many respects from later hansom; established *The Builder*, 1842.

HANSON, (Emmeline) Jean (1919–1973), biophysicist and zoologist; educated at Burton-upon-Trent High School for Girls, and Bedford College, London; first class, zoology, 1941; during 1939–45 war worked at Strangeways Laboratory; demonstrator in zoology, Bedford College, 1944–8; joined the Biophysics Research Unit, King's College, London, 1948; Ph.D., 1951; worked on muscular contraction and other problems at Massachusetts Institute of Technology, studying electron microscopy, 1953–4; returned to Biophysics Research Unit, 1954, and continued study of molecular aspects of contraction mechanism of muscle; professor of biology, London University, 1966; FRS, 1967; director of Muscle Biophysics Unit, King's College, London, 1970–3.

HANSON, John (*fl.* 1604), poet; BA, Peterhouse, Cambridge, 1604; author of *Time is a Turn-coate, or England's Threefold Metamorphosis* (1604).

HANSON, John (*fl.* 1658?), author of *The Sabbatarians confuted by the New Covenant* (1658); of Pembroke College, Oxford.

HANSON, 'Sir' Levett (1754–1814), author; schoolfellow of *Nelson and friend of Warren *Hastings; of Trinity and Emmanuel Colleges, Cambridge; councillor to the grand duke of Holstein and knight of St Philip, 1780; knight vice-chancellor of St Joachim, 1800; lived in many European states; imprisoned in Austria, 1794; published account of European orders of knighthood (1803), and poems (1811); died at Copenhagen.

HANSON, Sir Richard Davies (1805–1876), chief justice of South Australia; edited the *Globe* in London; supported Edward Gibbon *Wakefield's colonization schemes; one of the founders of South Australia; accompanied Lord *Durham to Canada, 1838; crown prosecutor in New Zealand, 1840–6; drafted constitution of South Aus-

tralia, 1851–6; attorney-general, 1857–60; chief justice of South Australia, 1861–74; knighted, 1869; sometime acting-governor; published works, including *The Jesus of History* (1869).

HANWAY, Jonas (1712–1786), traveller and philanthropist; as partner of a St Petersburg merchant made journey (1743–5) down the Volga and by the Caspian to Persia with a caravan of woollen goods, and returned after perilous adventures by the same route, 1745; left Russia and lived in London after 1750; published an account of his travels (1753), an essay attacking tea-drinking (severely criticized by *Johnson and *Goldsmith), and other works mostly connected with his philanthropic undertakings; appointed commissioner of Victualling Office, 1762, as reward for public services. He is best known as one of the chief founders of the Marine Society (1756) and the Magdalen charity (1758), the reformer of the Foundling Hospital, and the pioneer of the umbrella; a monument was erected to him in Westminster Abbey, 1788.

HANWORTH, first Viscount (1861–1936), judge. See POLLOCK, ERNEST MURRAY.

HARARI, Manya (1905–1969), publisher and translator; born at Baku, daughter of Grigori Benenson, a Jewish financier; family emigrated to London, 1914; educated at Malvern Girls' College and Bedford College, London; BA, 1924; visited Palestine and married Ralph Andrew *Harari, 1925; became Roman Catholic, 1932; worked on *Dublin Review*; edited her own periodical, the *Changing World*, 1940–2; joined Political Warfare Department as translator; founded Harvill Press with Marjorie Villiers, 1946; continued as director when the Press became subsidiary of Collins, 1954; publisher and joint translator, with Max Hayward, of Boris Pasternak's *Dr. Zhivago*, 1958; also published other Russian authors such as Alexander Solzhenitsyn and Ilya Ehrenburg; visited Palestine and Russia, 1948–61; working on her memoirs when she died; *Memoirs* published in 1972.

HARARI, Ralph Andrew (1892–1969), merchant banker, art scholar, and collector; born in Cairo; son of (Sir) Victor Harari Pasha; leading member of Egypt's Anglo-Jewish community; educated at Lausanne and Pembroke College, Cambridge; first class, parts i and ii, economics tripos, 1912–13; boxing blue; served under Sir Edmund (later Viscount) *Allenby in Palestine, 1914; finance officer to (Sir) Ronald *Storrs, military governor of Jerusalem; director, trade and commerce, under Sir Herbert (later Viscount) *Samuel, 1920–5; economic adviser, GHQ Middle East, 1939; worked in Department of Political Warfare; OBE; managing director, S.

Japhet & Co., London merchant bankers, 1945; collector and authority on Islamic metalwork, and collector of *Beardsley drawings; also collected an important album of Hokusai (1760–1849) sketches, and other Japanese art; with his wife *Manya noted for hospitality in their London home.

HARBEN, Sir **Henry** (1823–1911), pioneer of industrial life assurance; accountant of Prudential Mutual Assurance Association, 1852; started scheme of life assurance for working classes and proved its practicability, 1854; secretary, 1856; actuary, 1870; resident director, 1873; chairman, 1905; president, 1907; knighted, 1897; master of Carpenters' Company, 1893; founded working men's convalescent home at Rustington, 1895; represented Hampstead on London County Council, 1889–94; first mayor of Hampstead, 1900; generously supported local charities; published *Mortality Experience of the Prudential Assurance Company* (1871).

HARBERT. See HERBERT.

HARBIN, George (*fl.* 1713), nonjuror; BA, Emmanuel College, Cambridge, 1686; chaplain to Bishop *Turner of Ely and Viscount *Weymouth; friend of *Ken.

HARBORD, Edward, third Baron Suffield (1781–1835), philanthropist; MP, Great Yarmouth, 1806–12, Shaftesbury, 1820–1; succeeded as peer, 1821; carried reforms concerning prison discipline and game laws; abolitionist.

HARBORD, William (1635?–1692), politician; secretary to earl of *Essex, 1672; took active part in attack on *Danby in connection with Popish Plot; MP, Thetford, 1679, Launceston, 1680 and 1681; volunteered in Imperial Army at Buda, 1686; accompanied William of Orange to England, 1688; privy councillor and paymaster-general, 1688–90; vice-treasurer of Ireland, 1690; sent as ambassador to Turkey to mediate between sultan and the emperor Leopold, 1691; died on his way at Belgrade.

HARBORNE, William (d. 1617), first English ambassador in Turkey, 1582–8; concluded treaty for the establishment of Turkey company, 1581; account of his return journey (1588) printed in *Hakluyt's *Voyages;* manuscript account of his proceedings in Turkey in British Museum.

HARCLAY (HARCLA or **HARTCLA), Andrew,** earl of Carlisle (d. 1323), sheriff of Cumberland, warden of the west marches and of Carlisle Castle; summoned as a baron to parliament, 1321; defeated and captured Earl *Thomas of Lancaster at Boroughbridge, and executed him at Pontefract, 1322; created earl by Edward II, with patent specifying his services; executed at Carlisle for making compact with *Bruce.

HARCOURT, Viscounts. See HARCOURT, SIMON, first viscount, of the first creation, 1661?–1727; HARCOURT, LEWIS, first viscount, 1863–1922; HARCOURT, WILLIAM EDWARD, second viscount, 1908–1979.

HARCOURT, Augustus George Vernon (1834–1919), chemist; BA, Balliol College, Oxford; assistant to (Sir) B. C. *Brodie; Lee's reader in chemistry and a senior student of Christ Church, Oxford, 1859; tutor, 1864–1902; FRS, 1863; researched on rate of chemical change, on coal-gas, and chloroform as anaesthetic.

HARCOURT, Charles (1838–1880), actor; real name Charles Parker Hillier; first appeared at St James's Theatre, 1863; lessee of Marylebone Theatre, 1871–2; best exponent of Mercutio after Vining's death.

HARCOURT, Edward (1757–1847), archbishop of York; took name Harcourt on succession to family estates, 1831, being previously known as Vernon; educated at Westminster and Oxford; fellow of All Souls College, Oxford, 1777; DCL, 1786; canon of Christ Church, 1785, and vicar of Sudbury; prebendary of Gloucester, 1785–91; bishop of Carlisle, 1791–1807; archbishop of York, 1807–47; privy councillor, 1808; member of Queen *Charlotte's council; member of Ecclesiastical Commission, 1835.

HARCOURT, Henry (1612–1673), Jesuit; real name Beaumont; spiritual coadjutor, 1643; published *England's Old Religion faithfully gathered out of the Church of England* (1650).

HARCOURT (alias **PERSALL), John** (1633–1702). See PERSALL.

HARCOURT, Leveson Francis Vernon- (1839–1907), civil engineer. See VERNON-HARCOURT.

HARCOURT, Leveson Venables Vernon (1788–1860), chancellor of York; MA, Christ Church, Oxford, 1813; author of *Doctrine of the Deluge* (1838); son of Edward *Harcourt.

HARCOURT, Lewis, first Viscount Harcourt (1863–1922), politician; son of Sir William *Harcourt; private secretary to father, 1881–6, 1892–5, 1895–1904; Liberal MP, Rossendale division of Lancashire, 1904–16; helped to found Free Trade Union; first commissioner of works, 1905–10; with Viscount *Esher founded London Museum, 1911; secretary of state for colonies, 1910–15; his main interest economic and scientific development; returned to Office of Works, 1915–16; viscount, 1917.

HARCOURT, Octavius Henry Cyril Vernon (1793–1863), admiral; son of Edward *Harcourt; saw active service in Egypt and at Toulon and Tarragona; captured martello tower and convoy at Piombo, 1814; surveyed coast of Central America, 1834–6; vice-admiral, 1861; built several churches and Masham almshouses.

HARCOURT, Robert (1574?–1631), traveller; gentleman-commoner, St Alban Hall, Oxford, 1590; went to Guiana and took possession of land for the crown, 1609; obtained letters patent for colonization of Guiana; his company incorporated with *Roger North's, 1626; his *Relation of a Voyage to Guiana* (1613) reprinted in *Purchas.

HARCOURT, Sir Simon (1603?–1642), soldier of fortune; son of Robert *Harcourt; knighted, 1627; served prince of Orange against Spaniards; commanded regiment against Scots, 1639–40; governor of Dublin, 1641; mortally wounded by rebels at Kilgobbin Castle.

HARCOURT, Simon, first Viscount Harcourt (1661?–1727), of Stanton Harcourt, Oxfordshire; BA, Pembroke College, Oxford, 1678; DCL, 1702; barrister, Inner Temple, 1683; recorder of Abingdon, 1683; Tory MP for Abingdon, 1690–1705, Bossiney, 1705–8, Cardigan, 1710; directed impeachment of *Somers, 1701; as solicitor-general (1702–7) took part in prosecuting *Defoe (1703) and asserting jurisdiction of the Commons in election petitions, 1704; as commissioner for the union drafted Ratification Bill, 1707; attorney-general, 1707–8; ably defended Sacheverell, 1710; privy councillor, 1710; lord keeper, 1710; created Baron Harcourt, 1711; lord chancellor, 1713–14; obtained acquittal of *Oxford and pardon of *Bolingbroke; created viscount, 1721; readmitted privy councillor, 1722; several times a lord justice; best speaker of his day; friend of Bolingbroke, *Pope, and *Swift.

HARCOURT, Simon (1684–1720), second son of Simon *Harcourt, first Viscount Harcourt; MA, Christ Church, Oxford, 1712; secretary to the society of 'Brothers'; MP, Wallingford and Abingdon; wrote verses in preface to *Pope's *Works* (1717); his epitaph composed by Pope.

HARCOURT, Simon, first Earl Harcourt (1714–1777), son of Simon *Harcourt (1684–1720); educated at Westminster; attended George II at Dettingen, 1743; created Viscount Harcourt of Nuneham-Courtney and Earl Harcourt of Stanton Harcourt, 1749; privy councillor, 1751; governor to prince of Wales, 1751–2; envoy to Mecklenburg-Strelitz for the prince of Wales's marriage with Princess *Charlotte, 1761; ambassador at Paris, 1768–72; viceroy of Ireland, 1772–7; recommended tax on absen-

tees, and created numerous peers; drowned in attempt to extricate his dog from a well at Nuneham.

HARCOURT, Thomas (1618–1679), Jesuit; real name Whitbread; professed, 1652; on English mission thirty-two years; while provincial refused Titus *Oates admission to the Jesuit order; was convicted of complicity in the 'Popish Plot' on Oates's evidence, and was executed.

HARCOURT, alias **WARING, William** (1610–1679). See WARING.

HARCOURT, William (1625–1679), Jesuit; real name Aylworth; missioner in England and Holland; died at Haarlem; manuscript account at Brussels of his escape during 'Popish Plot'.

HARCOURT, William, third Earl Harcourt (1743–1830), field marshal; son of Simon *Harcourt, first earl; succeeded his brother in peerage, 1809; aide-de-camp to Lord *Albemarle at Havannah, 1762; MP, Oxford, 1768–74; commanded 16th Light Dragoons in America, and captured General Charles *Lee, 1776; lieutenant-general, 1793; commanded cavalry in Flanders under duke of *York, 1793–4, whom he succeeded in chief command; general, 1796; field marshal and GCB at coronation of George IV.

HARCOURT, William Edward, second Viscount Harcourt (1908–1979), merchant banker; educated at West Downs, Eton, and Christ Church, Oxford; succeeded his father, 1922; through his mother, granddaughter of J. S. Morgan, American banker, joined Morgan Grenfell & Co. Ltd., 1931; became a managing director, 1938; during 1939–45 war served with 63rd (Oxford Yeomanry) Anti-Tank Regiment, Royal Artillery; MBE, 1943; OBE, 1945; economic minister, British Embassy, Washington, and head of UK Treasury delegation in USA, 1954; UK executive director, International Bank for Reconstruction and Development and International Monetary Fund; KCMG, 1957; member of Radcliffe Committee on working of the monetary system, 1957–9; chairman, Legal and General Assurance Society; member of Plowden Committee on overseas representational services, 1962–4; chairman of governors of Museum of London, 1965; chairman, Oxford Preservation Trust; chairman, Rhodes trustees; hon. fellow, St Antony's College; vice-lord lieutenant of Oxfordshire; DCL, Oxford, 1978; chairman, Morgan Grenfell, 1968–73; viscountcy became extinct on death.

HARCOURT, Sir William George Granville Venables Vernon (1827–1904), statesman; born at York; son of William Vernon *Harcourt and grandson of Edward *Harcourt; of Plantagenet descent; educated privately and at Trinity College, Cambridge; member of 'Society of Apostles', and president of Union Debating Society, 1849; contributed to *Morning Chronicle* while an undergraduate; called to bar, 1854; acquired large practice at the parliamentary bar; wrote regularly for newly founded *Saturday Review*, 1855–9; contributed to *The Times* under signature of 'Historicus' many letters on international law in regard to American war from 1861 onwards; letters were published separately as *Letters by Historicus on . . . International Law* (1863) and *American Neutrality* (1865); QC, 1866; member of Neutrality Laws Commission, 1869; served also on royal commissions on naturalization laws, 1870, and on extradition, 1878; Whewell professor of international law at Cambridge, 1869–87; contributed further letters to *The Times* on parliamentary reform, redistribution of seats, and Irish Church disestablishment, 1866–9; engaged in party politics, 1867; returned Liberal MP for Oxford, 1868; declined post of judge-advocate-general; active in discussion on Irish Church Bill; candid critic of Liberal government; chairman of committee whose deliberations resulted in Registration of Parliamentary Voters Bill, 1871; championed religious equality in debates on Elementary Education Bill and on University Tests Bill, 1870; advocated abolition of purchase of commissions in army, 1871; opposed payment of election expenses by constituencies: urged law reform, and helped to pass the Judicature Act of 1873; member of Select Committee on Civil-Service Expenditure, 1873; succeeded Sir Henry *James as solicitor-general and knighted, 1873; while in opposition, he supported Public Worship Regulation Bill, 1874; opposed Royal Titles Bill and Merchant Shipping Bill, 1876; vigorously denounced Turkey, 1876–8; severely criticized Conservative government's policy in Afghanistan and South Africa, 1878–9; by speeches and letters to *The Times* greatly influenced political opinion; made home secretary and PC in Gladstone's administration, Apr. 1880; on defeat at Oxford, was returned MP for Derby, May 1880; introduced Ground Game Act, giving occupier equal right with landlord to kill ground game; recommended central control of London water supply, 1880; advocated birch instead of detention for juvenile offenders, and proposed commission of inquiry into industrial schools, 1881; during troubles in Ireland he carried Peace Preservation (Ireland) Bill (1881), Prevention of Crimes (Ireland) Bill (1882), and Explosive Substances Bill (1883); by his firmness stamped out the dynamite conspiracy in London, 1883; improved labour conditions in coal-mining; introduced Local Government Board (Scotland) Bill, which was rejected by the Lords, 1883; introduced but abandoned London Government Bill, 1884; active in franchise agitation, 1884; replaced clause in Registration Bill abolishing electoral disqualification on receipt of medical relief, 1885; dissociated himself from Joseph *Chamberlain's radicalism, 1885; joined Gladstone's Cabinet as chancellor of the Exchequer on Gladstone's acceptance of home rule, Feb.–July 1886; criticized new Conservative government, and attempted to reunite Liberal party; attacked Irish coercion policy of Lord Salisbury's government; censured government's treatment of *The Times*' attacks on *Parnell; supported Irish Land Bill and Allotments Act, 1887; opposed cession of Heligoland to Germany, 1890; persuaded Gladstone to repudiate Parnell's leadership of Irish party after divorce proceedings, Nov. 1890; in his speeches which won him popularity through the country he urged much domestic reform; opposed A. J. Balfour's Irish Local Government Bill, 1892; again chancellor of the Exchequer in Gladstone's fourth administration, 1892; had charge of Local Veto Bill, which was abandoned; passed Home Rule Bill through Commons; carried Parish Councils Bill, which was greatly amended by the Lords, 1894; bitterly denounced upper house; served under new prime minister, Lord Rosebery, as leader of the House of Commons, 1894; introduced death-duties budget which imposed a single graduated tax on real and personal property and revolutionized existing system of taxation; raised income-tax and duties on beer and spirits; this budget established his financial reputation; he passed Local Government Bill for Scotland; introduced Local Liquor Control Bill, 1895; passed fourth budget (May 1895); resigned on defeat of government on motion dealing with cordite supply (June); was defeated at Derby (July) and elected for West Monmouth; denounced advance of Anglo-Egyptian Army in Sudan, and urged inquiry into Jameson Raid; as member of committee he made searching examination of Cecil *Rhodes, but defended committee's report from radical attack, 1897; opposed Unionist Education Bill (1896) and Agricultural Rating Bill; supported Gladstone's censure of Armenian massacres in opposition to Lord Rosebery, 1896; urged annexation of Crete by Greece; championed Protestantism and attacked ritualism in his letters to *The Times* on 'Lawlessness in the Church', which led to certain reforms, 1898; resigned leadership of Liberal party, Dec. 1898; was opposed to extreme imperialist policy; censured English conduct of South African War, Jan. 1900; denounced the war as 'unjust and engineered', 1901; protested against introduction of forced Chinese labour into South Africa,

1903; resisted proposed tax on imported corn and Balfour's Education Bill, 1902; reiterated faith in free trade in opposition to Chamberlain's fiscal reform proposals, 1903; declined peerage, 1902; hon. fellow, Trinity College, Cambridge, 1904; succeeded to family estates at Nuneham, Oxfordshire, 1904; last of the old school of parliamentarians; speeches abound in argument and irony; an aristocrat by instinct; fond of gardening and dairy-farming.

HARCOURT, William Venables Vernon (1789–1871), general secretary to first meeting of British Association (York, 1831); son of Edward *Harcourt; MA, Christ Church, Oxford, 1814; student of Christ Church; canon of York, 1821–71; rector of Wheldrake and Bolton Percy; FRS, 1824; carried on chemical experiments with *Davy and *Wollaston; president of British Association at Birmingham, 1839.

HARCOURT-SMITH, Sir Cecil (1859–1944), archaeologist and director of the Victoria and Albert Museum; scholar of Winchester; entered department of Greek and Roman antiquities, British Museum, 1879; assistant keeper, 1896; keeper, 1904–9; chairman, reorganization commission, South Kensington Exhibits, 1908; director and secretary, Victoria and Albert Museum, 1909–24; adviser, royal art collections, 1925; surveyor, royal works of art, 1928–36; knighted, 1909; KCVO, 1934.

HARDCASTLE, Ephraim (pseudonym), (1769–1843). See PYNE, WILLIAM HENRY.

HARDCASTLE, Thomas (d. 1678?), ejected minister; BA, St John's College, Cambridge, 1655; ejected from Bramley, Yorkshire, 1662; frequently imprisoned for nonconformity; Baptist minister at Broadmead, Bristol, 1670–8.

HARDEBY, Geoffrey (fl. 1360?), Austin friar; provincial of his order; confessor (and perhaps councillor) to Richard II; wrote treatise in answer to Archbishop *Fitzralph's attack upon 'evangelical poverty'.

HARDECANUTE (HARDACNUT or **HARTHACNUT)** (1019?–1042), king; younger son of *Canute or Cnut and *Emma; succeeded his father on throne of Denmark, 1035; chosen king of Wessex in absence, 1037; concerted measures for invasion of England at Bruges with Emma, 1039; chosen king of England on death of *Harold, his reputed half-brother, 1040; disinterred and insulted the body of King Harold; levied heavy danegelds, 1041; invited his half-brother *Edward (the Confessor) to court, 1041; died suddenly at a bridal feast.

HARDEN, Sir Arthur (1865–1940), chemist; first class, chemistry, Owens College, Manches-

ter, 1885; lecturer in chemistry, Manchester University, 1888; chemist to Lister Institute (1897), head of department of biochemistry, 1907–30; investigated fermentation of sugar by various bacteria; discovered essential part played by phosphorylation and dephosphorylation in breakdown of sugar by yeast and in fermentation by other micro-organisms; joint editor, *Biochemical Journal*, 1913–37; FRS, 1909; shared Nobel Prize, 1929; knighted, 1936.

HARDHAM, John (d. 1772), tobacconist; employed by *Garrick at Drury Lane; at his shop in Fleet Street sold the celebrated '37' snuff, which *Reynolds used to take; left money to pay poor rates at his native place, Chichester.

HARDIE, (James) Keir (1856–1915), socialist and labour leader; miner in Lanarkshire, 1866; dismissed as agitator, 1878; took up journalism and began to work for organization of miners; successively miners' county agent for Lanarkshire and secretary for Ayrshire; secretary of Scottish Miners' Federation, 1886; left Liberals and became chairman of newly formed Scottish Labour party, 1888; founded *Labour Leader*, 1889; Independent Labour MP, South West Ham, 1892–5; chairman of newly formed Independent Labour party, 1893–1900, and 1913–15; MP, Merthyr Burghs, 1900–15; first leader of Labour party in parliament, 1906–7; excellent speaker; did more than any man to create British political labour movement.

HARDIE, Martin (1875–1952), artist and museum official; nephew of John *Pettie; educated at St Paul's School and Trinity College, Cambridge; entered Victoria and Albert Museum, 1898; keeper, departments of painting and of engraving, illustration, and design, 1921–35; talented etcher and water-colourist; publications include *The British School of Etching* (1921), book on Samuel *Palmer (1928) whose work he rediscovered, and history of British water-colour painting (3 vols., 1966–8); CBE, 1935.

HARDIE, William Ross (1862–1916), classical scholar; MA, Edinburgh; scholar, BA, and fellow, Balliol College, Oxford; tutor, 1885–95; professor of humanity, Edinburgh, 1895–1916; brilliant composer and teacher; wrote *Lectures on Classical Subjects* (1903), *Latin Prose Composition* (1908), *Silvulae Academicae* (1911), *Res Metrica* (1920).

HARDIMAN, Alfred Frank (1891–1949), sculptor; scholar, British School, Rome, 1920–2; style strongly decorative tending to hardness, based on Roman, early fifth-century Greek, and Etruscan work; executed statue of *Haig, Whitehall, and statues on eastern half of County Hall; ARA, 1936; RA, 1944.

HARDIMAN, James (1790?–1855), Irish writer; sub-commissioner of the records at Dublin, afterwards librarian of Queen's College, Galway; published works, including *History of County and Town of Galway* (1820) and *Irish Minstrelsy ... with English Poetical Translations* (1831).

HARDIME, Simon (1672–1737), flower painter, of Antwerp; lived in London, 1720–37.

HARDING (or Saint STEPHEN) (d. 1134), abbot of Cîteaux; born and educated at Sherborne; visited Scotland, Paris, and Rome; received tonsure at Molême in Burgundy; left it in order to observe a stricter rule; founded with Robert, abbot of Molême, house at Cîteaux, from which the Cistercian order derived its name; abbot, 1110–33; founded thirteen other abbeys (including Clairvaux, 1115, of which he made Bernard abbot) under the severe Cistercian rule; by his 'charter of charity' (confirmed by Calixtus II, 1119) exempt from episcopal visitation; his constitutions approved at Council of Troyes (1127), and the white habit adopted; canonized; Cistercian houses exempted from episcopal jurisdiction and payment of tithe by Innocent II, 1132.

HARDING, Mrs Anne Raikes (1780–1858), novelist and miscellaneous writer.

HARDING, Edward (1755–1840), librarian to Queen *Charlotte, 1803–18, and to the duke of *Cumberland, 1818–40; brother of Silvester *Harding.

HARDING, Sir Edward John (1880–1954), civil servant; educated at Dulwich College and Hertford College, Oxford; joined Colonial Office, 1904; called to bar (Lincoln's Inn), 1912; secretary, Dominions Royal Commission, 1912–17; deputy secretary, imperial conferences, 1923, 1926; assistant under-secretary, Dominions Office, 1925; permanent under-secretary, 1930–9; high commissioner in South Africa, 1940–1; CMG, 1917; CB, 1926; KCMG, 1928; KCB, 1935; GCMG, 1939.

HARDING, George Perfect (d. 1853), portrait painter and copyist; son of Silvester *Harding; made water-colour copies of old portraits; exhibited at Royal Academy; helped to establish Granger Society, 1840; published portraits of deans of Westminster (1822–3), and supplied plates to J. H. *Jesse (1840) and other writers.

HARDING, Gilbert Charles (1907–1960), broadcasting and television star; educated at Royal Orphanage, Wolverhampton, and Queens' College, Cambridge; became Roman Catholic, 1929, and schoolmaster; joined BBC, 1939;

served in Canada, 1944–7; thereafter conducted popular programmes ('Brains Trust', 'What's My Line?', etc.) with refreshing but stormy spontaneity; a humane and learned individual at odds with the Establishment and himself; published autobiography, *Along My Line* (1953).

HARDING, James Duffield (1798–1863), landscape painter and lithographer; exhibited with Water-Colour Society from 1818 (member, 1821); unsuccessfully tried oil-painting; abandoned exclusive use of transparent colours. He brought lithography to perfection, invented lithotint, and introduced tinted paper for sketches; published *Principles and Practice of Art* and other manuals; *Picturesque Selections* (1861) his first achievement in lithography.

HARDING, John (1378–1465?). See HARDYNG.

HARDING, John (1805–1874), bishop of Bombay; of Westminster and Worcester College, Oxford; BA, 1826; DD, 1851; rector of St Andrew's and St Anne's, Blackfriars, 1836–51; bishop of Bombay, 1851–69; secretary of Pastoral Aid Society.

HARDING, Samuel (*fl.* 1641), dramatist; BA, Exeter College, Oxford, 1638; his tragedy, *Sicily and Naples*, issued (1640).

HARDING, Silvester (1745–1809), artist and publisher; established with his brother, Edward *Harding, a book-and print-shop, 1786, and issued works illustrated by himself, including *The Biographical Mirrour* (1795).

HARDING, Thomas (1516–1572), divine; educated at Winchester and New College, Oxford; fellow of New College, 1536; MA, 1542; Hebrew professor and chaplain to Henry *Grey, marquis of Dorchester (afterwards duke of Suffolk); named warden of New College by Edward VI; abandoned Protestantism and became chaplain to *Gardiner and (1555) treasurer of Salisbury; in reign of Elizabeth retired to Louvain; carried on a long controversy with John *Jewel, 1564–8; died at Louvain.

HARDING, Thomas (d. 1648), historian; BD, Oxford; second master of Westminster, 1610; rector of Souldern, 1622–48; his history of England to 1626 recommended for publication by parliament, 1641, but never issued.

HARDING, William (1792–1886), author of *History of Tiverton* (1847); served in the Peninsular campaign from 1812; retired as lieutenant-colonel, 1841.

HARDINGE, Alexander Henry Louis, second Baron Hardinge of Penshurst (1894–1960), private secretary to King Edward VIII and King George VI; succeeded father, first Lord *Hardinge of Penshurst, 1944; educated at Harrow and Trinity College, Cambridge; appointed assistant private secretary to King George V, 1920; principal private secretary to King Edward VIII, 1936, to King George VI, 1936–43; PC, 1936; MVO, 1925; CVO, 1931; CB, 1934; GCVO and KCB, 1937; GCB, 1943.

HARDINGE, Sir **Arthur Edward** (1828–1892), general; second son of Sir Henry *Hardinge, first Viscount Hardinge; educated at Eton; ensign, 1844; served in first Sikh War; lieutenant, 1845; lieutenant and captain, 1849; served in Crimea on quartermaster-general's staff, 1854–6; lieutenant-colonel, 1855; CB, 1857; brevet-colonel, 1858; equerry successively to Prince *Albert and Queen Victoria; major-general, 1871; general, 1883; commanded Bombay Army, 1881–5; governor of Gibraltar, 1886–90; KCB and CIE, 1886.

HARDINGE, Charles, Baron Hardinge of Penshurst (1858–1944), statesman; grandson of first Viscount *Hardinge; educated at Harrow and Trinity College, Cambridge; entered Foreign Office, 1880; served successively in Constantinople, Berlin, Washington, Sofia, Bucharest, Paris, Tehran, and St Petersburg; assistant under-secretary of state, 1903–4; accompanied King Edward VII on tour of western European capitals; PC, KCMG, KCVO, 1904; ambassador to Russia, 1904–6; permanent under-secretary of state, 1906–10, 1916–20; attended King on visits to Europe and (1908) Russia; viceroy of India, 1910–16; work for social betterment included establishment of Moslem (Aligarh) and Hindu (Benares) universities; seriously wounded by bomb thrown during state entry into Delhi, 1912; censured by Commission of Inquiry into Mesopotamia expedition, 1917; ambassador in Paris, 1920–2; baron, 1910; KG, 1916.

HARDINGE, Charles Stewart, second Viscount Hardinge (1822–1894), son of Sir Henry *Hardinge, first Viscount Hardinge; educated at Eton and Christ Church, Oxford; BA, 1844; private secretary to his father in India from 1844; Conservative MP for Downpatrick, 1851–6; under-secretary for war, 1858–9; trustee of National Portrait Gallery, 1868–94, and chairman of board from 1876.

HARDINGE, George (1743–1816), author; the Jefferies Hardsman of Byron's *Don Juan*; son of Nicholas *Hardinge; of Eton and Trinity College, Cambridge; MA by royal mandate, 1769; barrister, Middle Temple, 1769; solicitor-general (1782) and attorney-general to Queen *Charlotte, 1794; senior justice of Brecon, Glamorgan, and Radnor, 1787–1816; counsel for East India Company against Fox's India Bill, 1783; Tory MP for Old Sarum, 1784–1802; friend of Horace *Walpole; FSA, 1769; FRS, 1788; published *Letters to Rt. Hon. E. Burke*, an impeachment of *Hastings (1791), *Essence of Malone* (1800 and 1801), and *Rowley and Chatterton in the Shades* (1782). His *Miscellaneous Works* edited (1818).

HARDINGE, George Nicholas (1781–1808), captain in the navy; nephew and adopted son of George *Hardinge; received post-rank for cutting out the Dutch *Atalante* in Vlie Roads, Texel, 1804; took part in capture of the Cape; killed at capture of French cruiser *Piedmontaise* off Ceylon; voted public monument in St Paul's Cathedral.

HARDINGE, Sir **Henry,** first Viscount Hardinge of Lahore (1785–1856), field marshal; brother of George Nicholas *Hardinge; deputy assistant quartermaster-general of force under Brent *Spencer, which joined *Wellesley and fought at Roliça and Vimeira; with *Moore in last moments at Corunna, 1809; deputy quartermaster-general of Portuguese Army; urged final advance of Sir Galbraith Lowry *Cole at Albuera, 1811; wounded at Vittoria, 1813; commanded Portuguese brigade at storming of Palais, 1814; KCB, 1815; watched Napoleon's movements for Wellington on escape from Elba, 1815; British commissioner with Blücher at Battle of Quatre Bras; commissioner with Prussians in France till 1818; Tory MP for Durham, 1820–30, Newport (Cornwall), 1830–4, Launceston, 1834–44; secretary at war, 1828–30 and 1841–4; Irish secretary, 1830 and 1834–5; lieutenant-general, 1841; GCB, 1844; governor-general of India, 1844–8; served as second in command to Sir Hugh *Gough in first Sikh War, 1845; created a peer, with pension for three lives, 1846; annulled *Bentinck's order abolishing corporal punishment in native regiments; endeavoured to abolish suttee in native states; originated carrying of soldiers' kits at public expense. Though not a general till 1854, he was commander-in-chief, 1852–5; field marshal, 1855.

HARDINGE, Nicholas (1699–1758), clerk to the House of Commons; of Eton and King's College, Cambridge; fellow; MA, 1726; clerk to House of Commons, 1731–48; MP, Eye, 1748–58; joint secretary to the Treasury, 1752; his *Poems, Latin, Greek, and English* published (1818).

HARDMAN, Edward Townley (1845–1887), geologist; accompanied Hon. J. Forrest's expedition to report on mineral resources of Kimberley, West Australia, and discovered goldfield near the Napier Range, 1883–5; a range of Australian mountains named after him.

HARDMAN, Frederick (1814–1874), novelist and journalist; joined British legion in Spain, 1834; foreign correspondent of *The Times* at Madrid, Constantinople, in the Crimea and Danubian provinces, Italy, France, and Paris; published stories, contributed to *Blackwood*; died at Paris.

HARDRES, Sir **Thomas** (1610–1681), serjeant-at-law; barrister, Gray's Inn, 1636; king's serjeant, 1675; MP, Canterbury, 1664–79 and 1679–81; knighted; his *Reports of Cases in the Exchequer, 1655–70* issued, 1693.

HARDWICK, Charles (1817–1889), antiquary; published works, including *History . . . of Friendly Societies* (1859 and 1869), *Traditions, Superstitions, and Folk-Lore* (1872), and *On Some Ancient Battlefields in Lancashire* (1882).

HARDWICK, Charles (1821–1859), archdeacon of Ely; fellow of St Catharine's Hall, Cambridge, 1845; MA, 1847; professor of divinity, Queen's College, Birmingham, 1853; divinity lecturer at King's College, Cambridge, 1855; archdeacon of Ely, 1857; edited catalogue of Cambridge University MSS (vols. i–iii, 1856–8) and works for Percy Society and Rolls Series; published also history of the Articles of Religion (1851) and of the Christian Church (ed. Stubbs, 1872); killed by falling over a precipice in the Pyrenees.

HARDWICK, John (1791–1875), magistrate at Lambeth (1821) and Marlborough Street, 1841–56; eldest son of Thomas *Hardwick; fellow of Balliol College, Oxford, 1808–22; barrister, Lincoln's Inn, 1816; DCL, 1830.

HARDWICK, Philip (1792–1870), architect; youngest son of Thomas *Hardwick; exhibited drawings at Academy, including his buildings at St Katharine's Docks and Euston Railway Station, and designs for Lincoln's Inn; FSA, 1824; FRS, 1831; RA, 1841; vice-president of Institute of British Architects, 1839 and 1841; treasurer of Royal Academy, 1850–61.

HARDWICK, Thomas (1752–1829), architect; pupil and biographer of Sir W. *Chambers; exhibited at Academy, 1772–1805; designed Galway Gaol, Marylebone Church, and other London buildings; FSA, 1781; advised J. M. W. *Turner to abandon architecture.

HARDWICKE, earls of. See YORKE, PHILIP, first earl, 1690–1764; YORKE, PHILIP, second earl, 1720–1790; YORKE, PHILIP, third earl, 1757–1834; YORKE, CHARLES PHILIP, fourth earl, 1799–1873; YORKE, ALBERT EDWARD PHILIP HENRY, sixth earl, 1867–1904.

HARDWICKE, Sir **Cedric Webster** (1893–1964), actor; educated at King Edward VI Grammar School, Stourbridge, and Bridgnorth School; studied at the (Royal) Academy of Dramatic Art, 1912; joined the Shakespeare Company of (Sir) Frank *Benson, 1913; with Old Vic Company, 1914; served in army, 1914–21; joined company of (Sir) Barry *Jackson at Birmingham Repertory Theatre, 1922; went with Jackson to Court Theatre, London, 1924; made success in long running *The Farmer's Wife* (1925), followed by *Yellow Sands* (1926), *Show Boat* (1928), *The Apple Cart* (1929), and *The Barretts of Wimpole Street* (1930–1); further successes included Abel Drugger in *The Alchemist* (1932), and the doctor in *The Late Christopher Bean* (1933); knighted, 1934; made first appearance on New York stage in *Shadow and Substance* (1938); played in films in Hollywood, 1939–45; returned to London, 1944; joined Old Vic Company, 1948, but later returned to New York and died there; published *Let's Pretend* (1932) and *A Victorian in Orbit* (1961).

HARDY, Sir **Alister Clavering** (1896–1985), zoologist and investigator of religious experience; educated at Oundle and Exeter College, Oxford (Christopher Welsh scholar); served in the army, 1915–19; assistant naturalist, Ministry of Agriculture and Fisheries laboratory, Lowestoft, working on herring and plankton, 1921–4; chief zoologist, Colonial Office *Discovery* Expedition to Antarctic, 1924–7; professor of zoology and oceanography, Hull University, 1928–42; regius professor of natural history, Aberdeen, 1942–5; Linacre professor of zoology, Oxford, 1945–61; professor of field studies, 1961–3; director (and founder) of Religious Experience Research Unit, Manchester College, Oxford, 1963, (later renamed the Alister Hardy Research Centre); D.Sc. (Oxford), 1938; Scientific medallist of Zoological Society, 1939; FRS, 1940; knighted, 1957; fellow and hon. fellow, Merton and Exeter Colleges, Oxford; honorary degrees from Southampton, Hull, and Aberdeen; publications include *The Open Sea*: Pt. I, *The World of Plankton* (1956) and Pt. II, *Fish and Fisheries* (1959), and *Great Waters* (1967); also *The Living Stream* (Gifford lectures, 1965), *The Divine Flame* (1966), *The Biology of God* (1975), and *Darwin and the Spirit of Man* (1984).

HARDY, Sir **Charles,** the elder (1680?–1744), vice-admiral; entered navy as volunteer, 1695; served under *Norris and *Wager in the Baltic and at Gibraltar; commanded royal yacht *Carolina*, 1730–42; knighted, 1742; vice-admiral and a lord of the Admiralty, 1743.

HARDY, Sir **Charles,** the younger (1716?–1780), admiral; son of Sir Charles *Hardy the elder; entered navy as volunteer, 1731; tried for loss of convoy to Newfoundland, 1744, but acquitted, 1745; governor of New York, 1755–7; knighted, 1755; rear-admiral, 1756; second-in-command under *Hawke at Brest and Quiberon Bay, 1759; admiral, 1770; governor of Greenwich, 1771; MP, Portsmouth, 1774; commander, Channel Fleet, 1779.

HARDY, Elizabeth (1794–1854), novelist (anonymous); died in Queen's Bench Prison.

HARDY, Francis (1751–1812), biographer; BA, Trinity College, Dublin, 1771; barrister, 1777; MP, Mullingar, in Irish parliament, 1782–1800; commissioner of appeals, 1806; friend of *Grattan; published *Memoirs . . . of James Caulfield, Earl of Charlemont* (1810).

HARDY, Frederic Daniel (1827–1911), painter of domestic subjects and portraits; exhibited at Royal Academy, 1851–98; pictures fetched high prices; represented in public galleries in London, Leicester, Wolverhampton, and Leeds.

HARDY, Gathorne Gathorne-, first earl of Cranbrook (1814–1906), statesman. See GATHORNE-HARDY.

HARDY, Godfrey Harold (1877–1947), mathematician; educated at Cranleigh, Winchester, and Trinity College, Cambridge; fourth wrangler, 1898; fellow, 1900; Cayley lecturer in mathematics, 1914; Savilian professor of geometry, Oxford, 1920; Sadleirian professor of pure mathematics, Cambridge, 1931–42; published *A Course of Pure Mathematics* (1908), four volumes in 'Cambridge Mathematical Tracts', *An Introduction to the Theory of Numbers* (1938, with E. M. Wright), *Divergent Series* (1949), and over 350 original papers; much of best work done in collaboration, notably with Professor J. E. *Littlewood; with him and Professor George Pólya published *Inequalities* (1934); worked also (1914–20) with Srinivasa Ramanujan; edited his collected works and published *Ramanujan* (1940); contributed to genetics 'Hardy's law' on transmission of dominant and recessive Mendelian characters; FRS, 1910.

HARDY, Herbert Hardy Cozens-, first Baron Cozens-Hardy (1838–1920), judge. See COZENS-HARDY.

HARDY, John Stockdale (1793–1849), antiquary and ecclesiastical lawyer; FSA, 1826; his *Literary Remains* published by John Gough *Nichols (1852).

HARDY, Mary Anne, Lady (1825?–1891), novelist and traveller; daughter of Charles MacDowell; married Sir Thomas Duffus *Hardy; travelled in America and other countries; published novels and books of travel.

HARDY, Nathaniel (1618–1670), dean of Rochester; BA, Magdalen Hall, Oxford, 1635; MA, Hart Hall, Oxford, 1638; DD, 1660; rector of St Dionis Backchurch, Fenchurch Street, 1660; dean of Rochester, 1660; vicar of St Martin's-in-the-Fields, 1661; archdeacon of Lewes, 1667; active in restoring churches; his lectures on first Epistle of St John (1656 and 1659) republished (1865).

HARDY, Sam (1882–1966), footballer; attended Newbold Church School, Chesterfield; joined Chesterfield Football Club, as goalkeeper, 1903; transferred to Liverpool, 1905; began international career, 1907; capped twenty-one times for England, 1907–20; in 1908–9 England defeated Wales, Ireland, and Scotland without conceding a goal; moved to Aston Villa, 1912; won two FA cup medals; moved to Nottingham Forest, 1921; retired after 552 League appearances, 1925; a model professional; licensee of the 'Gardener's Arms', Chesterfield.

HARDY, Samuel (1636–1691), Nonconformist minister; BA, Wadham College, Oxford, 1659; minister of 'peculiars' at Charminster, 1660–7, and Poole, 1667–82; ejected by Royal Commission for Nonconformity, 1682; *Guide to Heaven* attributed to him by *Calamy.

HARDY, Sir Thomas (1666–1732), vice-admiral; cousin of Sir Charles *Hardy the elder; first lieutenant under George *Churchill at Barfleur; knighted for services under *Rooke at Vigo, 1702; present at Malaga, 1704; commander at the Nore, 1711; MP, Weymouth, 1711; captured convoy in North Sea, 1712; second-in-command under *Norris in Baltic, 1715; said to have been dismissed for Jacobitism, but reinstated; vice-admiral; buried in Westminster Abbey.

HARDY (or HARDIE), Thomas (1748–1798), Scottish divine; published *Principles of Moderation* (1782), advocating repeal of Queen Anne's acts (1712) and substitution of parochial committee for single patron; colleague of Hugh *Blair in High Church, Edinburgh, 1783–6; minister of New North Church (now West St Giles), 1786, and professor of church history at Edinburgh; moderator, 1793; dean of Chapel Royal, 1794.

HARDY, Thomas (1752–1832), radical politician and boot-maker; founded 'London Corresponding Society' to promote parliamentary reform, 1792; charged with high treason with Horne *Tooke and others, but defended by *Erskine, and acquitted, 1794; pensioned by Sir Francis *Burdett; autobiographical memoir issued posthumously (1832).

HARDY, Thomas (1840–1928), poet and novelist; came of native Dorset stock on both sides;

inherited tradition of rural music, sacred and profane; his experiences of rural life supplied many years later rich material for his art; educated at private school at Dorchester; pupil of ecclesiastical architect at Dorchester, 1856; continued to study Latin and Greek; became acquainted with William *Barnes, the Dorset poet; carried out architectural work in London, 1862–7; employed by (Sir) A. W. *Blomfield; his interest at this time centred almost entirely on poetry; his first novel, *The Poor Man and the Lady*, accepted for publication, 1869, but he destroyed the manuscript on being advised by George *Meredith not to publish; gradually abandoned architecture for fiction; published *Desperate Remedies* (1871), *Under the Greenwood Tree* (1872), *A Pair of Blue Eyes* (1873), *Far from the Madding Crowd* (1874), *The Hand of Ethelberta* (1875), and *The Return of the Native* (1878); thenceforth for nearly twenty years his fiction was not only his profession (a fact which he somewhat regretted as he wished to devote himself to poetry), but an art of noble form, amazing wealth of substance, and profound significance; his later novels include *The Trumpet Major* (1880), *Two on a Tower* (1882), *The Mayor of Casterbridge* (1886), *The Woodlanders* (1887), *Tess of the D'Urbervilles* (1891), and *Jude the Obscure* (1895); abandoned fiction, which had now served his turn, practically and artistically, for poetry; published two collections of lyrics, *Wessex Poems* (1898) and *Poems of Past and Present* (1901); published his greatest single achievement, dramatic epic on the Napoleonic theme, *The Dynasts*, in three parts, 1903, 1906, 1908, a grand exhibition of absolute determinism; published *Time's Laughingstocks* (a collection of lyrics), 1909; this inaugurated period of wholly lyrical activity and one of daring development, only exception being *The Famous Tragedy of the Queen of Cornwall* (1923).

HARDY, Sir **Thomas Duffus** (1804–1878), archivist; trained under *Petrie; edited *Modus tenendi Parliamentum* (1846); as deputy-keeper of Record Office from 1861 to 1876 edited documents for Rolls Series; member of Historical MSS Commission, 1869; knighted, 1869; DCL and LL D.

HARDY, Sir **Thomas Masterman,** first baronet (1769–1839), vice-admiral; lieutenant in the *Minerve* at her capture of the *Sabina*, defending which prize he was made prisoner, 1796; exchanged in time to be present at St Vincent, 1797; at Santa Cruz directed cutting out of the *Mutine*, which he commanded at the Nile, 1798; flag-captain of *Nelson in the *Vanguard* and *Foudroyant*, 1799, in the *San Josef* and the *St George*, 1801, in the *Amphion* and the *Victory*, 1803–5; created baronet, 1806; commodore and commander on South American Station, 1819–24; first sea lord at Admiralty, 1830; GCB, 1831; governor of Greenwich Hospital, 1834; vice-admiral, 1837.

HARDY, Sir **William** (1807–1887), archivist; brother of Sir Thomas Duffus *Hardy; keeper of duchy of Lancaster records, 1830–68; deputy-keeper of public records, 1878–86; on Historical MSS Commission, 1878; knighted, 1883; calendared Lancaster records; edited *Charters of Duchy of Lancaster* (1845) and Jehan de Waurin's *Recueil des Croniques* (Rolls Series).

HARDY, Sir **William Bate** (1864–1934), biologist; educated at Framlingham and Gonville and Caius College, Cambridge; first class, natural sciences tripos (zoology), 1888; fellow, 1892; tutor, 1900–18; university lecturer in physiology, 1913; first chairman of Food Investigation Board, 1917–28; director of food investigation, 1917–34; superintendent, Low Temperature Research Station, Cambridge, 1922–34; FRS, 1902; knighted, 1925; pioneer in colloid chemistry, the molecular physics of films, surfaces, and boundary conditions, static friction, and lubricants.

HARDYMAN, Lucius Ferdinand (1771–1834), rear-admiral; midshipman at Dominica, 1782; first lieutenant of the *Sibylle* at her capture of the *Forte*, 1799; commanded the *Unicorn* at Montevideo, 1807, and at the Basque Roads, 1809; CB, 1815; rear-admiral, 1830.

HARDYNG, John (1378–1465?), chronicler; in the service first of Hotspur (Sir Henry *Percy), afterwards of Sir Robert *Umfraville; present at Battle of Homildon, 1402, and of Agincourt, 1415; constable of Kyme Castle, Lincolnshire; received grants of land for documents which he pretended to have procured in Scotland containing admissions of the feudal subordination of Scottish kings to English crown. His chronicle in its original form (Lancastrian) ended 1436; the version (Yorkist) presented to Edward IV reached 1461. *Grafton printed two versions varying from these original forms and each other (1543).

HARE, Augustus John Cuthbert (1834–1903), author; born in Rome; nephew of Augustus *Hare and Julius *Hare; BA, University College, Oxford, 1857; lived mostly in Italy and on Riviera, 1863–70; published *Memorials of a Quiet Life* (i.e. of Mrs Augustus Hare, his aunt), 3 vols., 1872–6; accomplished water-colour artist; book and art collector; compiled numerous guide books—to Rome (2 vols., 1871), London (1878), Italy (5 vols., 1883–4), and France (4 vols., 1890–5); also published *The Story of My Life* (6 vols., 1896–1900) and *Life of Baroness Bunsen* (2 vols., 1878).

HARE, Augustus William (1792–1834), divine; son of Francis *Hare-Naylor; adopted by his aunt, widow of Sir William *Jones, 1797; of Winchester and New College, Oxford; tutor of New College, 1818; incumbent of Alton-Barnes, 1829–34; joint author of *Guesses at Truth* (1827); died at Rome.

HARE, Francis (1671–1740), bishop of Chichester; of Eton and King's College, Cambridge, where he was tutor of (Sir) Robert Walpole; MA, 1696; DD, 1708; chaplain-general in Flanders, 1704; a royal chaplain; defended *Marlborough and answered *Swift's *Conduct of the Allies*, 1711; fellow of Eton, 1712; rector of Barnes, 1713–23; dean of Worcester, 1715–26; took part against *Hoadly in Bangorian controversy, *c*.1718; dean of St Paul's, 1726–40; bishop of St Asaph, 1727–31; bishop of Chichester, 1731–40; his preaching complimented in the *Dunciad* (iii. 204); rival of *Bentley in Latin scholarship; patron of *Warburton and *Markland; his Hebrew edition of Psalms attacked by *Lowth, 1736; his *Difficulties and Discouragements . . . in the way of Private Judgement* (1714) censured by Convocation, but often reprinted; published edition of Terence, forestalling Bentley (1724).

HARE, Henry, second Baron Coleraine (1636–1708), antiquary; succeeded his father, Hugh *Hare, first Baron Coleraine, 1667; built vestry and family vault at Tottenham, of which he left manuscript account.

HARE, Henry, third Baron Coleraine (1693–1749), antiquary; grandson of Henry *Hare, second Baron Coleraine; of Corpus Christi College, Oxford; FSA, 1725 (frequently vice-president); FRS, 1730; member of Spalding Society; patron of Vertue; MP, Boston, 1730–4; visited Italy with Conyers *Middleton, collecting prints and drawings of antiquities.

HARE, Hugh, first Baron Coleraine in Irish peerage (1606?–1667), eccentric Royalist; created Irish peer, 1625; supplied Charles I with money in the Civil War, during which he lost £40,000; declined an English peerage; his translation of Loredano's paraphrases on *The Fifteen Psalms of Degrees* issued (1681), and *The Situation of Paradise found out* (spiritual romance, 1683).

HARE, Hugh (1668–1707), translator; son of Henry *Hare, second Baron Coleraine; took part in translation of Lucian (published 1710) and rendered from Italian Mascardi's account of the conspiracy of Count de Fieschi against Genoa, 1693.

HARE, James (1749–1804), wit and friend of Charles James *Fox; educated at Eton and Balliol College, Oxford; MA, St Edmund Hall, Oxford, 1791; MP, Stockbridge, 1772–4, Knaresborough, 1781–1804; ambassador at Warsaw, 1779–82; ruined by losses at cards.

HARE, Sir John (Fairs) (1844–1921), actor, whose original name was John Fairs; made first professional appearance at Liverpool, 1864; acted, chiefly in plays by T. W. *Robertson, with Prince of Wales's Company, London, 1865–74; actor-manager, with W. H. *Kendal, of Court Theatre, 1874–9, and St James's Theatre, 1879–88; manager of Garrick Theatre, 1889–95; toured in America and provinces; knighted, 1907; helped considerably to mould and develop modern English acting tradition which avoids both formality and rhetoric.

HARE, John Hugh, first Viscount Blakenham (1911–1982), politician and farmer; educated at Eton; alderman of London County Council, 1937–52; chairman, London Municipal Society, 1947–52; served with Suffolk Yeomanry in 1939–45 war; MBE, 1943; OBE, 1945; US Legion of Merit, 1944; Conservative MP for Woodbridge (later Sudbury and Woodbridge), 1945–63; vice-chairman Conservative party, 1951; minister of state for colonial affairs, 1955–6; secretary of state for war, 1956–8; minister of agriculture, fisheries, and food, 1958–60; minister of labour, 1960–3; PC, 1955; first Viscount Blakenham, 1963; chancellor, Duchy of Lancaster; chairman, Conservative party and deputy leader of House of Lords; on retirement gave much time to charities; member of council, Toynbee Hall, 1966 and governing body, Peabody Trust, 1967; treasurer, Royal Horticultural Society, 1971; Victoria Medal of Honour, 1974; developed farming activities in Suffolk; deputy lieutenant for Suffolk, 1968.

HARE, (John) Robertson (1891–1979), actor; educated at Margate College; coached for stage by Lewis Cairns James; first professional appearance, 1911; after appearances in small parts in West End, toured for some years in title role of *Grumpy*; served with army in France, 1917–18; played in *Tons of Money*, 1922; appeared for ten years in famous Aldwych farces of Ben *Travers with Tom *Walls and Ralph Lynn, including *A Cuckoo in the Nest* (1925), *Rookery Nook* (1926), *Thark* (1927), and *A Cup of Kindness* (1929); played in twelve consecutive plays between 1924 and 1933, always the fussy, nervous little man continually trapped in awkward situations, remembered for his cry of despair 'Oh, calamity'; appeared in over twenty more farces between 1933 and 1960; toured in *Arsenic and Old Lace* (1968) and *Oh, Clarence* (1970); also appeared in films produced by Herbert *Wilcox, and in television, including playing the archdeacon in the comedy series 'All Gas and Gaiters' with Derek Nimmo; published autobiography, *Yours Indubitably* (1957); OBE, 1979.

HARE, Julius Charles (1795–1855), archdeacon of Lewes; son of Francis *Hare-Naylor; educated at Charterhouse and Trinity College, Cambridge; intimate of *Whewell and Kenelm *Digby; fellow of Trinity College, 1818; classical lecturer, 1822; incumbent of Hurstmonceaux, 1832, where John *Sterling was his curate and Bunsen his neighbour; joint author of *Guesses at Truth* (1827); published translations (with notes) of Niebuhr's *History of Rome* (with *Thirlwall), 1828–32, and other German works, also *The Victory of Faith* (1840), *The Mission of the Comforter* (1846), vindications of Niebuhr, Luther, and others, and *Miscellaneous Pamphlets on Church Questions* (1855); edited *Philological Museum* (1833).

HARE, Sir Nicholas (d. 1557), judge; educated at Gonville Hall, Cambridge; autumn reader of Inner Temple, 1532; MP, Downton, 1529, Norfolk, 1539–40, Lancaster, 1544–5; defended Wolsey, 1530; recorder of Norwich, 1536; knighted, 1537; master of requests, 1537 (again, 1552); when speaker imprisoned for advising Sir John Skelton how to evade Statute of Uses in his will, 1540; chief justice of Chester and Flint, 1540–5; instrumental in passing Treason Act of 1551–2; master of the Rolls, 1553; commissioner during vacancy of great seal, 1555.

HARE, Robert (d. 1611), antiquary; son of Sir Nicholas *Hare; clerk of the pells, 1560–71; MP, Dunwich, 1563; presented manuscripts and books to Caius College and Trinity Hall, Cambridge, and to the university's collections relating to their history and privileges.

HARE, Thomas (1806–1891), political reformer; barrister, Inner Temple, 1833; bencher, 1872; reported in Vice-Chancellor *Wigram's court from 1841; inspector of charities, 1853, and assistant-commissioner, with seat on board, 1872; published works relating to a scheme to secure proportional representation in electoral assemblies of all classes in the kingdom, and other political questions.

HARE, William (fl. 1829), criminal; accomplice of the murderer William *Burke (1792–1829); indicted for the murder of James Wilson, one of the victims; set at liberty, 1829, from the Tolbooth, the law officers having decided that he could not legally be put on his trial.

HARE-NAYLOR, Francis (1753–1815), author; grandson of Francis *Hare; an intimate of *Fox and the duchess of *Devonshire, who gave him an annuity to enable him to marry her cousin; lived many years at Bologna in friendship with Clotilda Tambroni (female professor) and Mezzofanti, and afterwards at Weimar; published works, including *History of Germany from the landing of Gustavus to Treaty of Westphalia* issued (1816); died at Tours.

HAREWOOD, earls of. See LASCELLES, HENRY, second earl, 1767–1841; LASCELLES, HENRY GEORGE CHARLES, sixth earl, 1882–1947.

HARFLETE, Henry (fl. 1653), author; member of Gray's Inn, 1630; published *The Hunting of the Fox, or Flattery Displayed* (1632), *Vox Coelorum* (a defence of William *Lilly), and *A Banquet of Essayes, fetcht out of Famous Owens Confectionary* (1653).

HARFORD, John Scandrett (1787–1866), biographer; educated at Christ's College, Cambridge; one of the founders of Lampeter College; DCL, Oxford, 1822; FRS, 1823; the 'Coelebs' of Hannah *More, of whom he published reminiscences in *Recollections of W. Wilberforce during nearly thirty years* (1864); published also lives of Michelangelo (1857, 2 vols.) and of Bishop *Burgess (1840).

HARGOOD, Sir William (1762–1839), admiral; served under Sir Peter *Parker (1721–1811) in attack on Sullivan's Island, 1776; captured by Spaniards at Pensacola, 1781; with *Rodney at Dominica, 1782; captain, 1790; captured by the *Concorde*, 1792; commanded the *Belleisle* under *Nelson at Toulon and Trafalgar, 1804–5; vice-admiral, 1814; admiral and GCB, 1831; corresponded with William IV.

HARGRAVE, Francis (1741?–1821), legal antiquary; treasurer of Lincoln's Inn; prominent in the Sommersett habeas corpus case, 1772; recorder of Liverpool, 1797; edited *State Trials, Henry IV to 19 George III* (1776), *Hale's Jurisdiction of the Lords' House* (1796), and (with Charles *Butler) *Coke upon Lyttleton* (1775); published also *Collection of Tracts relative to the Law of England* (1787), *Collectanea Juridica* (1791–2), and other works.

HARGRAVE, John Gordon (1894–1982), artist and writer; educated at Hawkshead Grammar School; at age of 15 illustrated *Gulliver's Travels* and *The Rose and the Ring*; chief cartoonist, *London Evening Times* at 17; served with RAMC and 10th (Irish) division, 1914–16; art manager, C. Arthur Pearson Ltd., 1917–20; worked as cartoonist for over thirty years; created character 'Bushy' for *Sketch*, 1952; commissioner for woodcraft and camping in Boy Scout movement, 1921; inaugurated Kindred of the Kibbo Kift (test of strength) movement, 1920, supported by number of eminent personalities;

movement developed into Green Shirts, 1931, opposed to Black Shirts of Sir Oswald *Mosley; both movements affected by Public Order Act of 1937; under influence of Clifford Hugh *Douglas adopted theory of Social Credit; advised Alberta government of Canada on this system, 1936–7; indefatigable writer; published number of books on woodcraft, Social Credit, and the Kibbo Kift, and novels including *Summer Time Ends* (1935); also published *The 'Paragon' Dictionary* (1953), a life of Paracelsus (1951), and wartime experiences, *The Suvla Bay Landing* (1964); invented automatic navigator for aircraft, but failed to substantiate claim that this was basis for equipment in Concorde, 1976.

HARGRAVES, Edward Hammond (1816–1891), pioneer of gold-mining in Australia; sheep-farmer in Sydney, 1834–49; began gold-mining at Lewis Ponds Creek, near Bathurst, 1851; temporary commissioner of crown lands, 1851; published *Australia and its Goldfields* (1855).

HARGREAVE, Charles James (1820–1866), lawyer and mathematician; LL D, London; hon. LL D, Dublin, 1852; barrister, Inner Temple, 1844; bencher, 1851; reader, 1866; professor of jurisprudence at University College, London, 1843–9; FRS, 1844; commissioner of incumbered estates, 1849–58; judge of landed estate court, 1858–66; drew Record of Title Bill; gold medallist, Royal Society, for paper 'On the Solution of Linear Differential Equations'; wrote other important mathematical essays.

HARGREAVES, James (d. 1778), inventor of the spinning-jenny; employed by Robert Peel (grandfather of the statesman) to construct improved carding-machine, *c.*1760; supposed to have invented spinning-jenny, *c.*1764 (patented, 1770); his house and machinery destroyed by mob, 1768; appropriated *Arkwright's improved carding-machine.

HARGREAVES, James (1768–1845), Baptist minister; at Bolton, Ogden (1798–1822), Wild Street, London, and Waltham Abbey Cross (1828–45); secretary to Peace Society; published *Life and Memoir of the Rev. John Hirst of Bacup* (1816) and *Essays and Letters on important Theological Subjects* (1833).

HARGREAVES, Thomas (1775–1846), miniature painter; apprenticed to Sir Thomas *Lawrence; original member of Society of British Artists; executed miniatures of Gladstone and his sister as children, of Mrs Gladstone, and Sir Thomas Lawrence.

HARGROVE, Ely (1741–1818), author of *History of . . . Knaresborough* (1769), *Anecdotes of Archery*, with life of Robin *Hood (1792) and *Yorkshire Gazetteer* (1806).

HARGROVE, William (1788–1862), topographer and journalist; son of Ely *Hargrove; thirty-five years editor of the *York Herald*; sheriff of York, 1831; published *History and Description of the ancient city of York* (1818) and *New Guide to York* (1842), and other works.

HARINGTON, Sir Charles ('Tim') (1872–1940), general; educated at Cheltenham and Sandhurst; posted to 2nd battalion, Liverpool (later King's) Regiment, 1892; major-general, General Staff, under General *Plumer, 1916–18; deputy chief, Imperial General Staff, 1918–20; GOC-in-C, Army of Black Sea (1920–1), allied forces of occupation in Turkey (1921–3); handled Chanak crisis (1922) with tact and skill; held Northern Command (1923–7), Western Command, India (1927–31), Aldershot (1931–3); general, 1927; governor of Gibraltar, 1933–7; KCB, 1919; GCB, 1933.

HARINGTON, Sir Charles Robert (1897–1972), biochemist; educated at Malvern College and Magdalene College, Cambridge; first class, part i, natural sciences tripos, 1919; worked in department of medical chemistry under Professor George *Barger and in department of therapeutics; Ph.D., 1922; lecturer in charge of department of chemical pathology, University College Hospital Medical School, London, 1923; established the chemical constitution of thyroxine and effected its synthesis, 1929; appointed reader, 1928; FRS and professor, 1931; edited the *Biochemical Journal*, 1930–42; published *The Thyroid Gland; its Chemistry and Physiology* (1933); member of Medical Research Council, 1938; succeeded Sir Henry *Dale as director, National Institute for Medical Research, 1942–62; abandoned research for administration; Croonian lecturer, 1944; FRSE, 1951; hon. FRSM, 1959; knighted, 1948; KBE, 1962; hon. FRCP, 1963; awarded honorary doctorates by Paris, Cambridge, and London.

HARINGTON, Sir Edward (1753?–1807), author; son of Henry *Harington (1727–1816); knighted as mayor of Bath, 1795; published *Excursion from Paris to Fontainebleau* (1786), *A Schizzo on the Genius of Man* (1793), and other works.

HARINGTON, Edward Charles (1804–1881), chancellor and sub-dean of Exeter; grandson of Sir Edward *Harington; MA, Worcester College, Oxford, 1833; chancellor of Exeter, 1847, and canon residentiary, 1856; gave money for repair of Exeter Cathedral; left bequests to the chapter; published theological works.

HARINGTON, Henry (1727–1816), musician and author; MA, The Queen's College, Oxford, 1752; MD, 1762; physician at Wells and Bath; mayor of Bath; founded Bath Harmonic Society; published collections of songs, glees, trios, and duets, and separate compositions. His other works include *Geometrical Analogy of the Doctrine of the Trinity* (1806).

HARINGTON, Henry (1755–1791), compiler of *Nugae Antiquae* (family papers belonging to his father, Henry *Harington, 1727–1816); MA, The Queen's College, Oxford, 1777; DD, 1788; minor canon of Norwich; second enlarged edition of his *Nugae Antiquae* (1779).

HARINGTON, John (*fl.* 1550), treasurer to Henry VIII's camps and buildings; married the king's natural daughter, Etheldreda, 1546, and inherited monastic forfeitures in Somerset; imprisoned in the Tower with his second wife, in company with Princess Elizabeth, 1554.

HARINGTON, Sir John (1561–1612), wit and author; son of John *Harington (*fl.* 1550); godson of Queen Elizabeth; educated at Eton and King's College, Cambridge; studied at Lincoln's Inn; compelled by Queen Elizabeth to translate *Orlando Furioso* (issued, 1591, with preface, 'An Apologie of Poetrie'); as high sheriff of Somerset, 1592, entertained Elizabeth at Kelston; for *Metamorphosis of Ajax* and other satires (1596) banished from court; accompanied *Essex to Ireland, 1598; knighted by Essex, 1599; deputed by Essex to appease the queen's anger against him, but sent out of her presence; wrote and handed to the queen a journal of the proceedings of Essex; wrote an account of Elizabeth's last days, and a *Tract on the Succession to the Crown* in the interest of James VI (printed, 1880); offered to go to Ireland as chancellor and archbishop, 1605; for instruction of *Henry, prince of Wales, wrote appendix to *Godwin's *De Praesulibus Angliae* ('Briefe View of Church of England in Q. Elizabeth's and K. James his Reigne', 1653); his collected *Epigrams* issued (1618); letters and miscellaneous writings in *Nugae Antiquae* (first published 1769).

HARINGTON, John, first Baron Harington of Exton (d. 1613), cousin of Sir John *Harington; created a peer at coronation of James I, 1603; guardian of Princess *Elizabeth at Combe Abbey; prevented her abduction by gunpowder plotters, 1605; escorted her to Germany on her marriage to the elector palatine, 1613; died at Worms on return journey; given (1613) three years' patent for coining brass farthings ('Haringtons').

HARINGTON, John, second Baron Harington of Exton (1592–1614), son of John

*Harington, first baron; friend and correspondent of *Henry, prince of Wales; benefactor of Sidney Sussex College, Cambridge; funeral ode on him written by *Donne.

HARINGTON, John Herbert (d. 1828), orientalist; chief judge of the Sudder Dewanny and Nizamut Adawlut, 1811; governor-general's agent at Delhi, 1823; member of supreme council and president of Board of Trade, 1825; edited *Persian and Arabic Works of Sâ'dee* (1791–5).

HARIOT, Thomas (1560–1621). See HARRIOT.

HARKELEY, Henry (*fl.* 1316), chancellor of Oxford University, 1313–16; author of theological works.

HARKER, Alfred (1859–1939), petrologist; educated at St John's College, Cambridge; fellow, 1885; demonstrator in geology, 1884; university lecturer, 1904; reader in petrology, 1918–31; surveyed Western Isles for Geological Survey of Scotland, 1895–1905; works include *Natural History of Igneous Rocks* (1909) and *Metamorphism* (1932); FRS, 1902.

HARKNESS, Robert (1816–1878), geologist; educated at Dumfries and Edinburgh University; professor of geology, Queen's College, Cork, 1853–78; FRSE, 1854; FRS, 1856; wrote papers on geology of south-western Scotland and English Lake District.

HARLAND, Henry (1861–1905), novelist; born at St Petersburg of American parents; commenced literary career under pseudonym Sidney Luska; showed mastery of short story in *Grey Roses* (1895) and *Comedies and Errors* (1898); literary editor of *Yellow Book*, 1894–7; chief works were *The Cardinal's Snuff Box* (1900) and *My Friend Prospero* (1904).

HARLAND, John (1806–1868), reporter and antiquary; introduced improvements in stenography; edited works for Chetham Society; published *Lancashire Lyrics, Lancashire Ballads,* and *Lancashire Folk-lore.*

HARLAND, Sir Robert, baronet (1715?–1784), admiral; prominent in capture of *Magnanime*, 1748; second-in-command under *Keppel at Ushant, 1778; a lord of the Admiralty, 1782–3; admiral, 1782.

HARLAND, Sydney Cross (1891–1982), agricultural botanist and geneticist; educated at Scarborough Municipal Secondary School and King's College, London; honours in geology, 1912; assistant to director of agricultural experiment station on St Croix (now part of US Virgin Islands), 1913–14; studied genetics of cotton; assistant agricultural superintendent, St Vincent, 1915; D.Sc. London; head of botany, British Cotton Industry Research Association, Shirley

Institute, Manchester, 1920; professor of botany and genetics, Imperial College of Tropical Agriculture, Trinidad, 1923; in charge of cotton genetics at new research station of Empire Cotton Growing Corporation, Trinidad, 1926–35; published *The Genetics of Cotton* (1939); general adviser to state cotton industry, Brazil, 1935–40; director, Institute of Genetics, Lima, Peru, 1940–9; reader in genetics, Manchester University, 1949; professor of botany, 1950–8; FRS, 1943; FRSE, 1951; hon. fellow, Textile Institute, 1954; hon. D.Sc., University of West Indies, 1973; president, Genetical Society, 1952–5.

HARLECH, Barons. See ORMSBY-GORE, WILLIAM GEORGE ARTHUR, fourth baron, 1885–1964; ORMSBY GORE, (WILLIAM) DAVID, fifth baron, 1918–1985.

HARLEY, Brilliana, Lady (1600?–1643), letter-writer; daughter of Edward, afterwards Viscount, *Conway; third wife of Sir Robert *Harley, 1623; died while besieged at Brampton Bryan Castle, 1643; her letters, 1625–43, printed (1854).

HARLEY, Sir **Edward** (1624–1700), governor of Dunkirk; eldest son of Sir Robert *Harley; distinguished as Parliamentarian officer at Red Marley, 1644; general of horse for Herefordshire and Radnor, 1645; MP, Herefordshire, 1646 and 1656; impeached for supporting the disbanding ordinance, 1648; member of Council of State, 1659; governor of Dunkirk, 1660–1; opposed sale of Dunkirk, 1661; KB; during reign of Charles II opposed in parliament legislation against Nonconformists; sat also in first, third, and fourth parliaments of William III; published theological tracts.

HARLEY, Edward (1664–1735), auditor of the imprest; son of Sir Edward *Harley; educated at Westminster; barrister, Middle Temple; acted in Revolution of 1688; recorder of Leominster, 1692; MP, Leominster, 1698–1722; published *Harmony of the Four Gospels* (1733, anon.).

HARLEY, Edward, second earl of Oxford (1689–1741), collector; son of Robert *Harley, first earl, whom he succeeded, 1724; friend and correspondent of *Pope and *Swift; patron of *Vertue and *Oldys; circulated second edition of the *Dunciad*, 1729; an assignee of the copyright of third edition; added to his father's collection of books and manuscripts; his books, prints, and pamphlets sold to Thomas *Osborne, 1742, and manuscripts to the British Museum.

HARLEY, George (1791–1871), water-colour painter and drawing master.

HARLEY, George (1829–1896), physician; MD, Edinburgh, 1850; house surgeon and phys-

ician to Edinburgh Royal Infirmary; studied physiology and chemistry at Paris; president of Parisian Medical Society, 1853; lecturer on practical physiology and histology at University College, London, 1855; fellow of Chemical Society and FCP, Edinburgh, 1858; professor of medical jurisprudence at University College, 1859, and physician to the hospital, 1860; FRS, 1865; published medical works.

HARLEY, George Davies (d. 1811?), actor and author; known as the 'Norwich Roscius'; real name Davies; played Richard III and other Shakespearian parts at Covent Garden, 1789–91, and old men in the country; supported Mrs *Siddons at Dublin, 1802; published verse and biographical sketch of William Henry West *Betty, 'the celebrated young Roscius', 1802.

HARLEY, John (d. 1558), bishop of Hereford; MA, Magdalen College, Oxford, 1540; probationer-fellow, 1537–42; master of Magdalen School, 1542–8; chaplain to John *Dudley, earl of Warwick, 1548, to Edward VI, 1551; prebendary of Worcester, 1552; bishop of Hereford, 1553–4.

HARLEY, John Pritt (1786–1858), actor and singer; succeeded to John *Bannister's parts; appeared at Drury Lane and the Lyceum, 1815–35, and under *Bunn's management, 1841–8; at Covent Garden with *Macready and Madame *Vestris, 1838 and 1840; excelled in role of Shakespearian clowns; played Bobadil to Edmund *Kean's Kitely, 1816; seized with paralysis while playing Lancelot Gobbo at the Princess's.

HARLEY, Sir **Robert** (1579–1656), master of the Mint; BA, Oriel College, Oxford; KB, 1603; MP, Radnor and Herefordshire; master of the Mint, 1626–35 and 1643–9; active in Long Parliament against 'idolatrous monuments', against *Strafford, and in Scottish and Irish affairs; lent plate and money to parliament; organized the militia; his castle at Brampton Bryan captured by Royalists, 1644; imprisoned, 1648–9, for voting to treat with the king.

HARLEY, Robert, first earl of Oxford (1661–1724), statesman; eldest son of Sir Edward *Harley; member of the Inner Temple, 1682; high sheriff of Herefordshire, 1689; MP, Tregony, 1689–90, New Radnor, 1690–1711; a moderate Tory, but always on terms with the Whigs; brought in Triennial Bill, 1694; established National Land Bank, 1696; carried reductions in the army, 1697, 1698; speaker, 1701–5; secretary of state for northern department, 1704; commissioner for union, 1706; intrigued against colleagues through Abigail *Hill's influence with the queen; resigned, 1708; chancellor of the

Exchequer and head of solid Tory ministry, 1710; his life attempted by Guiscard, 1711; initiated scheme for funding national debt through South Sea Company, 1711; created Baron Harley, earl of Oxford and Mortimer, and named lord treasurer, 1711; obtained dismissal of *Marlborough and creation of twelve peers to carry Peace of Utrecht; KG, 1712; ousted by *Bolingbroke from favour of queen and Tory party; dismissed for neglect of business and disrespect to queen, 1714; his impeachment (1717) on charges of making the peace, secretly favouring *James Stuart, the Old Pretender, and advising dangerous exercise of prerogative dismissed mainly on account of differences on the question of procedure between the two houses, 1717; excepted from the Act of Grace; forbidden the court; continued to appear in the House of Lords, and to correspond with the Old Pretender, though refusing to lead the Jacobite Tories. High characters of him are given by *Pope and *Swift, but he corresponded simultaneously with Hanoverians and Jacobites, and though a skilful party leader was an incapable statesman. He formed a great library, purchasing the manuscript collections of *Foxe, *Stow, and *D'Ewes.

HARLEY, Robert (1828–1910), mathematician; Congregational minister at Brighouse and Leicester, 1854–72, and subsequently at Oxford and in Australia; vice-principal of Mill Hill School, 1872–81; principal of Huddersfield College, 1882–5; made researches in higher algebra, especially in the theory of quintics; FRS, 1863.

HARLEY, Thomas (1730–1804), lord mayor of London; grandson of Edward *Harley, second earl of Oxford; prime warden of Goldsmiths' Company, 1762–3; MP, City of London, 1761; re-elected against *Wilkes, 1768; MP, Herefordshire, 1776–1802; as sheriff of London and Middlesex caused No. 45 of the *North Briton* to be burnt, 1763; lord mayor of London, 1767–8; privy councillor for services during Wilkite riots, 1768; mobbed, 1770; senior alderman, 1785; lord-lieutenant of Radnorshire.

HARLISTON, Sir Richard (*fl.* 1480), governor of Jersey; captured Mont-Orgueil from the French, 1460 or 1467; captain-in-chief of Jersey, 1473; attainted for participating in *Simnel's rising, 1486, and in that of Perkin *Warbeck, 1495; in service of duchess of *Burgundy.

HARLOW, George Henry (1787–1819), painter; eighteen months in *Lawrence's studio; a declared opponent of the Academy; exhibited portraits and historical pieces at the Academy from 1804; attracted notice by group of portraits of Charles *Mathews (1814) and *Trial Scene* from *Henry VIII*, containing portraits of Mrs *Siddons

and the *Kembles, 1817; while in Italy, 1818, made acquaintance with Canova; member of Academy of St Luke, Rome; painted portraits of various artists; painted, by invitation, his own portrait for Uffizi Gallery, Florence.

HARLOWE, Sarah (1765–1852), actress; wife of Francis *Waldron; after making a name at Sadler's Wells, appeared at Covent Garden, 1790, Haymarket, Drury Lane, English Opera House, and Royalty; retired, 1826; her best parts, Lucy (*Rivals*), Widow Warren (*Road to Ruin*), Miss MacTab (*Poor Gentleman*), and old Lady Lambert (*Hypocrite*).

HARLOWE, Thomas (d. 1741), captain in the navy; commanded the *Burford* at Barfleur, 1692; engaged unsuccessfully French squadron carrying spoils from Carthagena, 1697; acquitted by court martial under *Rooke; engaged at Vigo in the *Grafton*, 1702; died senior captain.

HARMAN, Sir Charles Eustace (1894–1970), judge; educated at Eton and King's College, Cambridge; commissioned in Middlesex Regiment; prisoner of war, 1915–18; returned to Cambridge; first class, parts i and ii, classical tripos; BA, 1920; called to bar (Lincoln's Inn) 1921; KC, 1935; judge, Chancery division, 1947; knighted; Appeal Court judge and PC, 1959; bencher, Lincoln's Inn, 1939; treasurer, 1959; retired, 1970.

HARMAN, Sir George Byng (1830–1892), lieutenant-general; educated at Marlborough; ensign, 1849; captain, 1855; served in Crimea, 1854; brevet-major, 1855; served in Indian Mutiny, 1857; on staff in West Indies, 1866–72; brevet-colonel, 1871; on staff in expeditionary force in Egypt, 1882; deputy adjutant-general at headquarters, 1883; military secretary, 1885; KCB, 1887; lieutenant-general, 1890.

HARMAN (alias **VEYSEY** or **VOYSEY**), **John** (1465?–1554). See VEYSEY.

HARMAN, Sir John (d. 1673), admiral; commanded the *Welcome* at Battle of Portland, 1653, and in action off the Thames, 1653; in *Worcester* under *Blake at Santa Cruz; flag-captain to duke of York in *Royal Charles* in action with Dutch, 1665; knighted, 1665; rear-admiral, 1665; prominent in four days' fight off North Foreland, 1666; as commander-in-chief in West Indies destroyed French fleet at Martinique and seized Cayenne and Surinam, 1667; rear-admiral of the blue at Solebay, 1672; vice-admiral in second action with De Ruyter, 1673; admiral, 1673.

HARMAN, Thomas (*fl.* 1567), writer on beggars; his *A Caueat, or Warening for commen cvrsetors Vvlgarely called Vagabones* (first edn., 1566, reprinted, 1869), plagiarized by *Dekker.

HARMAR (or HARMER), John (1555?–1613), professor of Greek at Oxford; educated at Winchester and New College, Oxford; fellow of New College; MA, 1582; BD, 1605; disputed at Paris with Romanists; patronized by *Leicester; regius professor of Greek, Oxford, 1585; headmaster of Winchester, 1588–95; warden of St Mary's College, 1596; a translator of the New Testament, 1604; edited Chrysostom's *Homilies* (1586 and 1590).

HARMAR (or HARMER), John (1594?–1670), professor of Greek at Oxford; nephew of John *Harmar or Harmer (1555?–1613); educated at Winchester and Magdalen College, Oxford; MA, 1617; MB, 1632; master of Free School, St Albans, 1626; professor of Greek, Oxford, 1650–c.1660; translated Heinsius's *Mirrour of Humility* (1618) and published *Life of Cicero* (1662), with other works.

HARMER, Anthony (pseudonym). See WHARTON, HENRY, 1664–1695.

HARMER, James (1777–1853), alderman of London, 1833–40; sheriff, 1834–5; gave important evidence before the Committee for Reform of Criminal Law; a founder of Royal Free Hospital.

HARMER, Thomas (1714–1788), Independent minister of Wattisfield, Suffolk, 1734–88; left manuscript accounts of Norfolk and Suffolk Dissenting churches; published *Observations on Divers Passages of Scripture . . . from . . . Books of Voyages and Travels* (1764) and *Outlines of New Commentary on Solomon's Song* (1768); *Miscellaneous Works* issued (1823).

HARMSWORTH, Alfred Charles William, Viscount Northcliffe (1865–1922), journalist and newspaper proprietor; largely self-educated; helped to give his younger brothers start in life; took up freelance journalism, 1882; gained practical experience with publishing firm in Coventry, 1885–7; with his brother Harold (afterwards Viscount *Rothermere) formed general publishing business in London (Amalgamated Press), 1887; issued from it growing number of periodicals, including *Answers* (1888); acquired *Evening News*, 1894; founded *Daily Mail*, an elaborately planned halfpenny morning newspaper, which was his greatest achievement in creative journalism and opened new epoch in Fleet Street, 1896; enlisted services of number of skilled writers; advertised and stimulated inventions of day, financed exploration schemes, and offered prizes for various kinds of skill, including aviation feats later on; founded *Daily Mirror*, 1903; first decade of twentieth century zenith of his career; won remarkable position in English life and amassed huge fortune; leased famous Tudor mansion, Sutton Place, Surrey, where he entertained stream of British and foreign visitors, 1899–1917; created baronet, 1903; baron, 1905; chief proprietor of *The Times* on formation of company, 1908; never had more difficult task than in struggle to put *The Times* on its feet; question of price, which he changed seven times in little more than seven years, constant anxiety; at critical moment wholly responsible for saving it from extinction, but when he died it needed steadiness added to vitality; the European war made him a public figure; placed himself at head of all popular movements of moment; initiated *The Times* fund for sick and wounded which reached nearly £17 million; paid several visits to armies in France and Italy; on invitation of Lloyd George undertook British war mission in USA, 1917; created viscount, 1917; director of propaganda in enemy countries, 1918; after the Armistice became estranged from and bitterly attacked Lloyd George; influence of *The Times* potent in bringing about Irish settlement, 1921; celebrated twenty-fifth birthday of *Daily Mail* at Olympia with great magnificence, 1921; made world tour, 1921–2; a consummate journalist, who changed whole course of British journalism by making it both lively and prosperous.

HARMSWORTH, Esmond Cecil, second Viscount Rothermere (1898–1978), newspaper proprietor; educated at Eton; commissioned into Royal Marine Artillery, 1917; accompanied Lloyd George as aide-de-camp at Paris Peace Conference, 1919; Conservative MP for Isle of Thanet, 1919–29; chairman, Associated Newspapers, 1932; succeeded Lord *Riddell as chairman, Newspaper Proprietors Association, 1934–61; chairman, Newsprint Supply Company, 1940–59; friend of prince of Wales and Mrs Simpson; suggested Abdication crisis should be solved by morganatic marriage, 1936; succeeded his father, 1940; with Lord *Beaverbrook, rival owner of British mass-circulation press; interests in Canadian paper-making industry; first chancellor, Memorial University of Newfoundland, 1952–61; took over *Daily Sketch* (1950) and *News Chronicle* and *Star* (1960); retired, 1971; owned Daylesford, near Chipping Norton, former home of Warren *Hastings, 1946–77.

HARMSWORTH, Harold Sidney, first Viscount Rothermere (1868–1940), newspaper proprietor; younger brother of Alfred *Harmsworth, Viscount Northcliffe, whose firm (later the Amalgamated Press) he entered, 1888; developed rare financial ability; with brother acquired *Evening News*, 1894; founded *Daily Mail*, 1896; baronet, 1910; baron, 1914; took over *Daily Mirror*, 1914; founded *Sunday Pictorial* (1915) and Glasgow *Record*; air minister, 1917–18; viscount,

1919; controlled Associated Newspapers (*Daily Mail, Evening News, Sunday Dispatch*), 1922–32; founded a professorship at Oxford, two at Cambridge; other benefactions included gifts to Middle Temple, Foundling Hospital, municipal art galleries.

HARNESS, Sir Henry Drury (1804–1883), general; brother of William *Harness; studied mining engineering in Mexico; instructor in fortification at Woolwich, 1834–40, professor, 1844–6; secretary to Railway Commission, 1846–50; deputy-master of the Mint, 1850–2; commissioner of Irish Works, 1852–4; lieutenant-colonel, 1855; chief engineer under Lord *Clyde in the Mutiny; director at Chatham, 1860; KCB, 1873; general, 1878.

HARNESS, William (1790–1869), divine and author; brother of Sir Henry Drury *Harness; of Harrow and Christ's College, Cambridge; MA, 1816; friend and correspondent of *Byron; Boyle lecturer at Cambridge, 1822; incumbent of Regent Square Chapel, 1826–14; perpetual curate of All Saints', Knightsbridge, 1849–69; published an edition of Shakespeare with life (1825), plays of *Massinger and *Ford, *Life of Mary Russell Mitford* (1870); the Harness Prize for a Shakespearian essay founded at Cambridge in his memory.

HAROLD (called **HAREFOOT)** (d. 1040), king of the English; reputed son of *Canute and *Ælfgifu of Northampton; elected by the witan through Danish support king north of the Thames, and (apparently) over-king of all England, 1035; said to have lured to England by forged letter his half-brothers, and to have slain *Ælfred, 1036; chosen king of all England, 1037; banished his stepmother *Emma from Wessex; buried in St Clement Danes after disinterment by *Hardecanute.

HAROLD (1022?–1066), king of the English; second son of *Godwin or Godwine and Gytha; earl of East Anglia, 1045; received half of Swegen's earldom (1046), and opposed his restoration; raised forces in Ireland, ravaged Somerset coast, and sailed with Godwin from Portland to London, 1052; succeeded his father in Wessex, 1053, and as head of the national party probably caused unjust banishment of *Ælfgar, earl of the East Angles, 1055; arranged peace between *Gruffydd ab Llywelyn and the English king, 1056; probably prevented meeting between *Edward the Confessor and his intended heir, the ætheling Edward, 1057; received earldom of Hereford, 1058; went on pilgrimage to Rome, and visited France, *c.*1058; his church at Waltham dedicated by Cynesige of York, 1060; sailed round the Welsh coast, 1062–3, and, aided by

*Tostig, subdued and dethroned Gruffydd, ravaged the land, and exacted tribute; wrecked on the coast of Ponthieu, and delivered by Count Guy to William of Normandy; after serving William against the Bretons, swore on the relics to be his man in England and to marry his daughter, *c.*1064; on his return married *Aldgyth and advised the outlawing of Tostig and his supersession in Northumbria by Morkere to gain Mercian support for his own succession to the English throne; chosen king, January 1066, by the nobles, as Edward the Confessor enjoined on his deathbed, and crowned; obtained recognition from the Northumbrians; sailed to the Isle of Wight, and for four months kept together an army for defence against Normandy; defeated Harold Hardrada of Norway and Tostig at Stamford Bridge (25 Sept. 1066); left York for London, and thence marched to Senlac or Battle near Hastings with men of the east and south; fortified a position on the hill, where he was attacked (14 Oct. 1066) by the Normans, and, after repelling one attack, was defeated and slain owing to the enemy's stratagem of pretended flight. His body is supposed first to have been buried by William's order on the sea-coast, and afterwards transferred to Waltham.

HAROLD, Francis (d. 1685), chronographer of the order of St Francis; nephew of Luke *Wadding; chief works: epitome (1662) of Wadding's 'Franciscan Annals,' with 'life,' and (1683) 'life' of Mogrobeio, archbishop of Lima; died at Rome.

HARPER, Sir George Montague (1865–1922), lieutenant-general; entered Royal Engineers, 1884; served in South African War, 1899–1900; deputy-director, military operations, War Office, 1911; went to France on outbreak of European war, 1914; commanded 51st (Highland) division, Territorial Force, 1915–18; took part in battles of Somme (1916), Arras, Ypres, and Cambrai (1917); commanded IV Army Corps, 1918; lieutenant-general, 1919; commander-in-chief, Southern Command, 1919; KCB, 1918.

HARPER, James (1795–1879), theologian; educated at Edinburgh; sixty years Secession minister of North Leith; chairman of the synod, 1840; Secession Church professor of pastoral theology, 1843, of systematic theology, 1848; hon. DD, Jefferson College, America, 1843; effected union of Secession and Relief bodies; moderator of United Presbyterian synod, 1860; hon. DD, Glasgow, 1877.

HARPER, John (d. 1742), actor; played at Lincoln's Inn Fields, 1719–21, Dr Caius and Ajax, and several original parts; at Drury Lane, Falstaff, Sir Epicure Mammon, Jobson the Cobbler (*The Devil to Pay*), Sir Wilful Witwould (*Way of the World*), Cacafogo (*Rule a Wife and have a Wife*); prosecuted in a test action for vagrancy, and discharged, 1733.

HARPER, John (1809–1842), architect; friend of *Etty and *Stanfield; with the Wyatts prepared designs for Apsley House and York House; died at Naples.

HARPER, Thomas (1787–1853), inspector of musical instruments to the East India Company; trumpet-player; engaged at Drury Lane and Lyceum English opera, 1806, at Ancient Concerts and Italian Opera, 1821, and at Philharmonic Concerts.

HARPER, Sir William (1496?–1573), lord mayor of London; master of Merchant Taylors' Company, 1553; sheriff of London, 1557–8; lord mayor, 1561–2; knighted, 1562; helped to found Merchant Taylors' School; founded school at Bedford, 1566.

HARPER, William (1806–1857), author and journalist; published two volumes of religious verse and *Memoir of Benjamin Braidley* (1845).

HARPSFIELD (or HARPESFELD), John (1516–1578), chaplain to Bishop *Bonner; of Winchester and New College, Oxford; fellow of New College, 1534–c.1551; MA, 1538; DD, 1554; archdeacon of London, 1554; dean of Norwich, 1558; zealous persecutor of Protestants; disputed with *Cranmer, *Ridley, and *Latimer, at Oxford; active in convocation against Reformation, 1559; deprived and imprisoned in the Fleet; published homilies.

HARPSFIELD (or HARPESFELD), Nicholas (1519?–1575), theologian; brother of John *Harpsfield or Harpesfeld; educated at Winchester and New College, Oxford; fellow, 1535; principal of White Hall Hostel, 1544; lived at Louvain during reign of Edward VI; DCL, Oxford, 1554; proctor in court of arches, 1554; vicar of Laindon, Essex, 1554; archdeacon of Canterbury and official of court of arches; one of the eight Romanist disputants, 1559; imprisoned in the Tower, 1559–74; his *Historia Anglicana Ecclesiastica* edited by Richard *Gibbons (1622), *Treatise on the pretended Divorce between Henry VIII and Catherine of Arragon* by Nicholas *Pocock (1878), and six Latin dialogues attacking 'pseudo-martyrs' by Alan *Cope (1566, Antwerp); left manuscript lives of *Cranmer and *More.

HARPUR, Joseph (1773–1821), critic; matriculated at Trinity College, Oxford, 1790; deputy professor of civil law at Oxford, 1806 (DCL, 1813); published *Essay on the Principles of Philosophical Criticism applied to Poetry* (1810).

HARRADEN, Beatrice (1864–1936), novelist; educated at Cheltenham, Queen's, and Bedford colleges; BA, London; worked for female suffrage and emancipation; wrote *Ships That Pass in the Night* (1893) and less successful novels on similar theme.

HARRADEN, Richard (1756–1838), artist and engraver; published views of Cambridge (1797–8, and 1800), *Costume of the various orders in the University* (1803), and *Cantabrigia Depicta* (1811).

HARRADEN, Richard Bankes (1778–1862), artist; son of Richard *Harraden; made drawings for *Cantabrigia Depicta*, 1811, and published further *Illustrations* (1830).

HARREL, Sir David (1841–1939), Irish administrator and public servant; entered Royal Irish Constabulary, 1859; resident magistrate, 1879; chief commissioner, Dublin Metropolitan Police, 1883–93; under-secretary for Ireland, 1893–1902; later served on trade-disputes boards in England; Irish PC, 1900; knighted, 1893; GCB, 1920.

HARRIES, Margaret (1797–1846). See WILSON, Mrs CORNWELL BARON.

HARRILD, Robert (1780–1853), inventor of 'composition rollers' for inking types, 1810; preserved Benjamin Franklin's press, and left money for a 'Franklin pension' for printers.

HARRIMAN, John (1760–1831), botanist; clergyman in Northumberland and Durham; FLS; furnished plants for *Smith's *English Botany* and discovered many species of lichens; the microscopic dot lichen named after him.

HARRINGTON, earls of. See STANHOPE, WILLIAM, first earl, 1690?–1756; STANHOPE, WILLIAM, second earl, 1719–1779; STANHOPE, CHARLES, third earl, 1753–1829; STANHOPE, CHARLES, fourth earl, 1780–1851; STANHOPE, LEICESTER FITZGERALD CHARLES, fifth earl, 1784–1862.

HARRINGTON (or HARINGTON), James (1611–1677), political theorist; great-nephew of John *Harington, first Baron Harington of Exton; studied at Trinity College, Oxford; some time in service of elector palatine; visited Rome and Venice; groom of the bedchamber to Charles I at Holmby and in the Isle of Wight; published *The Commonwealth of Oceana* (1656), the *Art of Lawgiving* (abridgment of *Oceana*, 1659), and several tracts in defence of it; formed the 'Rota' club for political discussion, 1659–60; imprisoned in the Tower, 1661, and afterwards at Plymouth; works edited by *Toland (1700).

HARRINGTON, James (1664–1693), lawyer and poet; educated at Westminster and Christ Church, Oxford; MA, 1690; barrister, Inner Temple; published Latin hexameter poem on the death of Charles II, *Defence of the Rights and Privileges of the University of Oxford* (1690), and other pamphlets; contributed preface and introduction to first edition of *Athenae Oxonienses*.

HARRINGTON, Sir John (1561–1612). See HARINGTON.

HARRINGTON, Maria, fourth countess of. See FOOTE, MARIA, 1797?–1867.

HARRINGTON, Robert (d. 1837), writer on natural philosophy; published, as 'Richard Bewley, M.D.', a *Treatise on Air* (1791), and other works against Lavoisier's theory of combustion and in favour of phlogiston, *Chemical Essay* (against *Priestley, 1794), and other works.

HARRINGTON, Timothy Charles (1851–1910), Irish politician; founded *Kerry Sentinel*, 1877; imprisoned under Coercion Acts, 1881 and 1883; as secretary of National League, devised 'Plan of Campaign' for land war, 1886; Nationalist MP for Co. Westmeath, 1883–5, and for Dublin (harbour) division, 1885–1910; called to Irish bar, 1887; counsel for C. S. *Parnell in Parnell Commission, 1888–9; remained faithful to Parnell after Parnell's divorce action; helped to reunite Irish party, 1900; lord mayor of Dublin, 1901–4.

HARRINGTON, William (d. 1523), divine; B.Civ.L., Cambridge, 1492–3; incorporated at Cambridge as Heryngton; LL D from Bologna, 1500; prebendary of St Paul's, 1497; rector of St Anne's, Aldersgate, 1505–10; published a work in commendation of matrimony.

HARRIOT, Thomas (1560–1621), mathematician and astronomer; BA, St Mary Hall, Oxford, 1580; mathematical tutor to Sir W. *Ralegh, who sent him, 1585, to survey Virginia; his *Brief and True Report* (1588) reproduced in De Bry's *Americae Descriptio* and in *Hakluyt; pensioned by Henry, earl of *Northumberland, one of whose 'three magi' he became. His *Artis Analyticae Praxis ad Aequationes Algebraicas resolvendas* edited (1631) by Walter Warner, embodies inventions which gave algebra its modern form. He used telescopes simultaneously with Galileo; he observed sun-spots and the comets of 1607 and 1618. Collections of his papers are at the British Museum and Sion House.

HARRIOTT, John (1745–1817), projector of the London Thames Police; served in the navy and in the merchant service; also in military employ of East India Company; received Gold Medal from Society of Arts for reclaiming from the sea (1781–2) Rushley Isle, Essex; lived in America, 1790–5; patented improved ship's pump (1797) and other inventions; resident magistrate at Thames Police Court, 1798–1816; addressed (1797) letter to the duke of Portland, secretary of state, broaching his scheme of Thames police (marine police established, 1798); published *Struggles through Life* (1815).

HARRIS, Sir Arthur Travers, first baronet (1892–1984), marshal of the Royal Air Force; educated at Gore Court, Sittingbourne, and All Hallows, Honiton; at 17 went to farm in Rhodesia; joined 1st Rhodesian Regiment as bugler, 1914; fought in South-West Africa; returned to England and joined Royal Flying Corps, 1915; did fighter work with No. 45 Squadron and commanded No. 44 Squadron for training in night-fighting, 1918; AFC; squadron leader in RAF, 1919; served in India and Iraq, 1919–25; commanded No. 58 Squadron, 1925–7; OBE, 1927; passed through Army Staff College, 1928–9; served on air staff in Middle East, 1930–2; commanded No. 210 (Flying-boat) Squadron, 1933; deputy director of plans, Air Ministry, 1934–7; air commodore, 1937; commanded No. 4 (Bomber) Group; air officer commanding Palestine and Transjordan, 1938–9; air vice-marshal, 1939; commanded No. 5 (Bomber) Group, 1939; CB, 1940; deputy CAS under Sir Charles *Portal (later Viscount Portal of Hungerford), 1940; head of RAF delegation in Washington, 1941; AOC-in-C, Bomber Command, 1942–6; under directive from Air Ministry organized area bombing of German industrial targets and cities, 1942–4; continued saturation bombing of German oil plants and communications after precision bombing by night became possible; air chief marshal, 1943; subsequently criticized for his continued advocacy of saturation-bombing policy; contribution of Bomber Command to Allied victory of outstanding importance; KCB, 1942; many foreign honours including US DSM, 1946; marshal of the RAF, 1946; hon. LL D, Liverpool, 1946; refused peerage, but accepted baronetcy, 1953; published *Bomber Offensive* (1947); retired to South Africa, aggrieved at what he regarded as lack of appreciation of Bomber Command's achievements.

HARRIS, Augustus Glossop (1825–1873), actor and manager; appeared on American stage when 8 years old; managed Princess's Theatre, London, 1859–62; manager of Covent Garden; introduced *Fechter to London.

HARRIS, Sir Augustus Henry Glossop (1852–1896), actor, impresario, and dramatist; son of Augustus Glossop *Harris; manager at Covent Garden, c.1875; became lessee of Drury Lane, 1879, and produced, in collaboration with various authors, a succession of highly popular melodramas and pantomimes, besides operas; sheriff of London and knighted, 1891.

HARRIS, Charles Amyand (1813–1874), bishop of Gibraltar; MA, Oriel College, Oxford, 1837; fellow of All Souls College, Oxford, 1835–7; rector of Wilton, 1840–8; prebendary of Salisbury, 1841; archdeacon of Wilts, 1863; vicar of Bremhill-with-Highway, 1863–8; bishop of Gibraltar, 1868–73.

HARRIS, Sir Edward Alfred John (1808–1888), admiral; brother of James Howard *Harris, third earl of Malmesbury; MP, Chippenham, 1844–52; consul-general in Denmark, 1852; Peru, 1852, Chile, 1853, and Austrian coasts of the Adriatic, 1858; minister at Berne and (1867) The Hague; KCB, 1872; admiral, 1877.

HARRIS, Francis (1829–1885), physician; BA, Caius College, Cambridge, 1852; MD, 1859; studied at St Bartholomew's Hospital, and in Paris and Berlin; assistant physician at St Bartholomew's Hospital, 1861; published thesis on amyloid degeneration (1859).

HARRIS, Frederick Leverton (1864–1926), politician and art collector; shipowner; Conservative MP, Tynemouth, 1900–6; Unionist MP, Stepney, 1907–10, East Worcestershire, 1914–18; largely contributed to defeat of bill embodying Declaration of London, 1911; joined trade division of Admiralty, 1914; largely devised and directed blockade of Germany, 1915–19; PC, 1916; bequests include 'grangerized' life of Fanny Burney (see Madame d'ARBLAY) to National Portrait Gallery and majolica collection to Fitzwilliam Museum, Cambridge.

HARRIS, George (1722–1796), civilian; DCL, Oriel College, Oxford, 1750; chancellor of Durham, Hereford, and Llandaff; bequeathed £40,000 to St George's and £15,000 to Westminster Lying-in hospitals; edited Justinian's 'Institutes', with translation, 1756.

HARRIS, George, first Baron Harris (1746–1829), general; served with 5th Fusiliers in America; wounded at Bunkers Hill, 1775; commanded Grenadier battalion at capture of St Lucia, 1778; second-in-command at defence of La Vigie; served against Tippoo Sahib, 1790–2; commanded troops in Madras, 1796–1800; captured Seringapatam and subdued Mysore, 1799; lieutenant-general, 1801; general, 1812; created a peer, 1815; GCB, 1820.

HARRIS, George (1794–1859), Unitarian minister; studied at Glasgow University; secretary of Scottish Unitarian Association; minister at Liverpool, 1817–22, Bolton, 1822–5, Glasgow, 1825–41, Edinburgh, 1841–5, and New-

castle, 1845–59; eager controversialist and successful preacher.

HARRIS, George (1809–1890), author; educated at Rugby; barrister, Middle Temple, 1843; deputy county-court judge of Bristol district, 1853; acting judge of county court, Birmingham, 1861; registrar of court of bankruptcy, Manchester, 1862–8; headed deputation to Palmerston suggesting formation of Historical Manuscripts Commission, 1859; vice-president of Anthropological Society of London, 1871; joint founder and vice-president of Psychological Society, 1875. His works include *Life of Lord-chancellor Hardwicke* (1847), *Civilization considered as a Science* (1861), and an *Autobiography* (1888).

HARRIS, George Francis Robert, third Baron Harris (1810–1872), governor of Madras; grandson of George *Harris, first baron; educated at Eton and Merton and Christ Church colleges, Oxford; BA, 1832; hon. DCL, 1863; governor of Trinidad, 1846; governor of Madras, 1854–9; reinforced Earl Canning during the Mutiny; GCSI, 1859; chamberlain to princess of Wales.

HARRIS, George Robert Canning, fourth Baron Harris (1851–1932), cricketer and administrator; born in Trinidad; son of third Baron *Harris; succeeded father, 1872; played in Eton (1868–70) and Oxford (1871, 1872, 1874) elevens; captained Kent, 1875–89; prominent in early matches with Australia; English captain, 1880, 1884; under-secretary for India, 1885–6, for war, 1886–9; governor of Bombay, 1890–5; popularized cricket among Indians; president, MCC, 1895; GCIE, 1890; GCSI, 1895; CB, 1918.

HARRIS, Henry (d. 1704?), chief engraver to the Mint, 1690–1704; engraver of public seals.

HARRIS, (Henry) Wilson (1883–1955), journalist and author; nephew of James Rendel *Harris; a Quaker; educated at Plymouth College and St John's College, Cambridge; president of Union, 1905; joined *Daily News*, 1908; League of Nations Union, 1923, editing *Headway*; editor, *Spectator*, 1932–53; Independent MP, Cambridge University, 1945–50; publications include autobiography, *Life So Far* (1954); hon. LL D, St Andrews.

HARRIS, Howel (1714–1773), Welsh Methodist pioneer; worked with Daniel *Rowlands till Methodist disruption, 1751; founded 'family' or community at Trevecca, 1752; served in Brecknockshire Militia, 1759; visited and corresponded with countess of Huntingdon (see HASTINGS, SELINA); preached at *Whitefield's tabernacle.

HARRIS, James (1709–1780), author of *Hermes, or a Philosophical Inquiry concerning Universal Grammar* (1751) and other works (collected, 1801); MP, Christchurch, 1761–80; a lord of the Treasury, 1763–5; secretary to George III's queen, 1774.

HARRIS, James, first earl of Malmesbury (1746–1820), diplomat; son of James *Harris; educated at Winchester, Merton College, Oxford, and Leiden; when chargé d'affaires at Madrid prevented Spanish expedition against Falkland Isles, 1770; minister at Berlin, 1772–6; ambassador at St Petersburg, 1777–82; named minister at The Hague by Pitt, 1784; promoted counter-revolution in favour of house of Orange; negotiated alliance with Prussia and Holland, 1788; created Baron Malmesbury, 1788; supported *Fox on regency question, but (1793) left him with 'old Whigs'; negotiated fresh alliance with Prussia, 1794, and match between the prince of Wales and Princess *Caroline of Brunswick; engaged in fruitless negotiations at Paris and Lille, 1796–7; incapacitated by deafness, but much consulted by Pitt and Canning on foreign affairs; created earl of Malmesbury and Viscount Fitzharris, 1800; *Diaries* edited by grandson (1844), family letters issued (1870).

HARRIS, James Howard, third earl of Malmesbury (1807–1889), statesman; grandson of James *Harris, first earl of Malmesbury; educated at Eton and Oriel College, Oxford; BA, 1827; during continental trips became acquainted with Louis Napoleon; MP, Wilton, 1841; succeeded to peerage, 1841; protectionist whip in the Upper House; joined Disraeli in urging reform on Lord Derby; as foreign secretary (Feb.–Dec. 1852) recognized Napoleon III, whom he interviewed in Paris, 1853; during second tenure of office (1858–9) re-established good relations with him, helped to compose dispute between France and Portugal, exacted reparation from Naples for 'Cagliari' affair, 1858, delayed war between Austria and Sardinia, and strove to localize it when declared (1859), adopting policy of strict neutrality; created GCB on retirement; offered support to Palmerston against Russell, 1860; attempted to remove Napoleon's prejudices against the conservatives, 1861; carried vote of censure on Palmerston for policy on Danish question, 1864; lord privy seal in Lord Derby's last ministry, 1866–8, and under Disraeli, 1874–6; published *Memoirs of an Ex-minister* (1884).

HARRIS, James Rendel (1852–1941), biblical scholar, archaeologist, and orientalist; educated at Plymouth Grammar School and Clare College, Cambridge; third wrangler, 1874; fellow, 1875; professor, Johns Hopkins University, 1882–5; Haverford College, 1885–92; lecturer in palaeography, Cambridge, 1893–1903; director of studies, Woodbrooke Quaker settlement, 1903–18; curator, eastern manuscripts, John Rylands Library, Manchester, 1918–25; found Syriac versions of *Apology of Aristides* (1889) and *Odes of Solomon* (1909); published specialist studies and devotional writings; FBA, 1927.

HARRIS, James Thomas ('Frank') (1856–1931), author, editor, and adventurer; spent early years in Ireland and America; became lifelong systematic amorist; used editorship of *Fortnightly Review* (1886–94) for own social advancement; aimed unsuccessfully at socialist premiership; made *Saturday Review* (1894–8) most brilliant weekly of the time; ruined reputation with later journalistic ventures; his biographies of *Wilde (1916) and *Shaw (1931), and *My Life* (1925–30) reveal delusions of greatness and reckless unreliability but contain valuable sidelights.

HARRIS, John (1588?–1658), warden of Winchester College; MA, New College, Oxford, 1611; DD; fellow, 1606–22; regius professor of Greek, 1619–22; prebendary of Wells, 1622; member of Westminster Assembly; warden of Winchester College, 1630–58; published life of Bishop Arthur *Lake.

HARRIS, John (1667?–1719), divine and author; MA, St John's College, Cambridge, 1691; DD, Lambeth, 1706; prebendary of Rochester, 1708; incumbent of St Mildred, Bread Street, London, with St Margaret Moses; rector of East Barming, 1715; ridiculed in *Picture of a High-flying Clergyman* (1716); FRS, 1696 (secretary, 1709); lectured on mathematics in Birchin Lane, London; died a pauper. His works include defence of the Woodwardian system (1697), Boyle lectures (1698), *Lexicon Technicum* (1704) and *Navigantium atque Itinerantium Bibliotheca* (1705).

HARRIS, John (*fl.* 1680–1740), architectural and topographical engraver.

HARRIS, John (*fl.* 1737), organ-builder; son of Renatus *Harris.

HARRIS, John (1756–1846), publisher; assisted John *Murray and F. *Newbery, and succeeded to latter's business.

HARRIS, John (1767–1832), water-colour painter; exhibited at Royal Academy, 1802–15.

HARRIS, John (1802–1856), principal of New College, London; 'boy preacher' near Bristol; theological professor at Cheshunt College, 1837; DD, Brown University, Rhode Island, USA, 1838; principal of New College, London, and its professor of theology, 1851; chairman of Congregational Union, 1852; published *The Great Teacher* (1835) and theological prize essays.

HARRIS, John (1820–1884), Cornish poet; worked in Dolcoath mine; won first prize for Shakespeare tercentenary poem, 1864; received grants from Royal Literary Fund and Royal Bounty Fund; published *Lays from the Mine, the Moor, and the Mountain* (1853) and other verse.

HARRIS, John Ryland (Ieuan Ddu o Lan Tawy) (1802–1823), writer in Welsh; son of Joseph *Harris (Gomer); contributed to *Seren Gomer* newspaper, 1818–23; made Welsh version of *Paradise Regained*; published Welsh guide to reading of music.

HARRIS, John Wyndham Parkes Lucas Beynon (1903–1969), writer, best known as John Wyndham; educated at Bedales, 1918–21; wrote science fiction for American magazines, 1930; published as serial in *The Passing Show* 'The Secret People', under name John Beynon, 1935; this and *Stowaway to Mars* published in book form, 1936; worked as civil servant and served in Royal Corps of Signals, 1939–45; published *The Day of the Triffids*, under name John Wyndham (1951); made into film (1963); other published novels include *The Kraken Wakes* (1953), *The Chrysalids* (1955), *The Midwich Cuckoos* (1957), filmed as 'Village of the Damned' (1960), and *The Outward Urge* (1959); also published collections of short stories, including *The Seeds of Time* (1956) and *Consider her Ways* (1961); a notable writer of science fiction.

HARRIS, Joseph(?) (*fl.* 1661–1681), actor; played in Sir William *D'Avenant's company at Lincoln's Inn Fields and Dorset Garden; Romeo to *Betterton's Mercutio, 1662; took original roles in plays by D'Avenant, *Dryden, *Etherege, and *Otway; intimate with *Pepys.

HARRIS, Joseph (*fl.* 1661–1702), actor and dramatist; member of king's company at Theatre Royal; engraver to the Mint on accession of Anne; four plays ascribed to him.

HARRIS, Joseph (1702–1764), assay master of the Mint, 1748; author of monometallist *Essay on Money and Coins* (two parts, 1756 and 1758), cited by Lord *Liverpool, 1805, and praised by *McCulloch, and posthumous (1775) treatise on optics.

HARRIS, Joseph (d. 1814), organist of St Martin's, Birmingham (1787); composed songs and harpsichord quartets.

HARRIS, Joseph (Gomer) (1773–1825), Welsh author; Baptist pastor at Swansea; edited *Seren Gomer* (first newspaper in Welsh), 1814–15, and afterwards as monthly magazine; published selection of Welsh hymns (*Ychydig o hymnau*, 1796), the Bible in Welsh and English (1825), *Cofiant Ieuan Ddu* (memoir of his son, 1823), and other works.

HARRIS, Joseph John (1799–1869), organist at Manchester, 1848–69; published *The Cathedral Daily Service* (1844), *The Musical Expression* (1845).

HARRIS, Joseph Macdonald (1789–1860), musician; arranged Burgoyne's *Collection of Psalms* (1827); published musical compositions.

HARRIS, Joseph Thorne (1828–1869), pianist and composer; son of Joseph John *Harris.

HARRIS, Moses (*fl.* 1766–1785), entomologist and artist; published, with plates by himself *The Aurelian or Natural History of English Insects* (1766), *English Lepidoptera* (1775), *Exposition of English Insects* (1776), and other works; his *Natural System of Colours* edited by Thomas *Martyn (1811).

HARRIS, Paul (1573–1635?), Roman Catholic divine; banished from Dublin for attacking Franciscans; published tracts against Archbishop Thomas *Fleming and against Francis Matthews.

HARRIS, Sir Percy Alfred, first baronet (1876–1952), politician; educated at Harrow and Trinity Hall, Cambridge; called to bar (Middle Temple), 1899; joined family firm, Bing, Harris; Liberal member for South-West Bethnal Green of LCC (1907–34, 1946–52) and of parliament, 1922–45; MP, Market Harborough, 1916–18; chief Liberal whip, 1935–45; publications include *London and its Government* (1913, rewritten 1931); baronet, 1932; PC, 1940.

HARRIS, Sir Percy Wyn- (1903–1979), colonial governor. See WYN-HARRIS.

HARRIS, Renatus (or René) (1640?–1715?), organ-builder; defeated by 'Father Smith' (Bernard *Smith) in contest for building organ in Temple Church, 1684; afterwards built thirty-nine organs, including those in King's College Chapel, Cambridge (1686), and in cathedrals of Chichester (1678), Winchester (1681), Ely, Bristol (1685), Gloucester, Worcester, Hereford (1686), St Patrick (1697), and Salisbury (1710).

HARRIS, Richard (*fl.* 1613), theologian; fellow of St John's College, Cambridge, 1580; senior fellow, 1593; MA, 1583; DD, 1595; rector of Gestingthorp, 1597, and Bradwell-juxta-Mare, 1613; published *Concordia Anglicana* (1612) in reply to Becane *De dissidio Anglicano.

HARRIS, Robert (1581–1658), president of Trinity College, Oxford; BA, Worcester College, Oxford, 1600; DD, 1648; incumbent of Hanwell, Oxfordshire, 1614–42; member of assembly of divines; visitor to the university, 1647–52 and

1654–8; president of Trinity College, Oxford, 1648–58; an eminent preacher; sometime incumbent of St Botolph's, Bishopsgate.

HARRIS, Robert (1809–1865), captain in the navy; brother of Sir William Cornwallis *Harris; midshipman at Algiers, 1824, and at Navarino, 1827; promoted commander for services at capture of Bogue forts, 1841; captain, 1849; commanded *Illustrious* training-ship, 1854–9, and *Britannia* till 1862.

HARRIS, Samuel (1682–1733), first regius professor of modern history at Cambridge; MA, Peterhouse, Cambridge, 1707; Craven scholar, 1701; fellow of Peterhouse; professor of modern history, 1724–33.

HARRIS, Thomas (1705–1782), clothing contractor to the army; brother of Howel *Harris.

HARRIS, Thomas (d. 1820), proprietor and manager of Covent Garden; had violent dispute with *Colman the elder as to management, 1769–70; stage-manager, 1774.

HARRIS, Thomas Lake (1823–1906), mystic; emigrated with parents from Buckinghamshire to America, 1828; organized 'independent Christian congregation' on Swedenborgian principles in New York, 1848; claimed to be a medium; published, from 1850 onwards, lengthy poems which were (he claimed) revealed to him in trances; edited *Herald of Light*, 1857–61; paid visits to England, 1859–61, 1865–6; set up a community near Wassaic, 1861; joined in America by Laurence *Oliphant, with whose money Harris purchased farms at Brocton, Lake Erie, 1886, and engaged in vine-growing; exerted complete sway over Oliphant until legally compelled to restore Oliphant's property, 1881; removed to Santa Rosa, 1875; advocated theory of celestial marriages, 1876; proclaimed his attainment of immortality, 1891; depicted by Oliphant as David Masollam in *Masollam* (1886); published much mystical prose and verse.

HARRIS, Tomás (1908–1964), artist, art dealer, and intelligence officer; educated at University College School, London; won scholarship to Slade School of Art, 1923–6; studied at British Academy, Rome; decided to become art dealer, 1928; joined his father at Spanish Art Gallery, Bruton Street, London; continued to own gallery after father's death, 1943; brought to England great variety of valuable Spanish *objets d'art*; joined Security Service, 1940; one of principal organizers of 'Operation Garbo', which seriously misled Germans about Allied invasion plans, 1944; OBE, 1945; after 1939–45, spent much time in Spain, painting and designing tapestries; made magnificent collection of etchings and lithographs by Goya (now in British Museum);

wrote standard work on etchings of Goya (2 vols., 1964).

HARRIS, Walter (1647–1732), physician; MD, Bourges and Cambridge; scholar of Winchester and (1666) fellow of New College, Oxford; BA, 1670; FRCP, 1682, five times censor and treasurer, 1714–17; physician to Charles II, 1683; physician to William III; Lumleian lecturer, 1710–32; Harveian orator; attended Queen Mary on her deathbed, 1694; published medical works; admirer of *Sydenham.

HARRIS, Walter (1686–1761), Irish historiographer; scholar of Trinity College, Dublin, 1707; hon. LL D, Dublin, 1753; vicar-general of the Protestant bishop of Meath, 1753; published translation with continuation of Sir James *Ware's *Works concerning Ireland* (1739–46); also history of Irish writers (1736), *Hibernica* (1747–50), and *History of William III* (1749).

HARRIS, William (1546?–1602), Roman Catholic divine; fellow of Lincoln College, Oxford; MA, 1570; left England and was ordained priest at Louvain; missioner in England, 1575; wrote *Theatrum, seu Speculum verissimae et antiquissimae Ecclesiae Magnae Britanniae.*

HARRIS, William (1675?–1740), Presbyterian divine; hon. DD, Edinburgh, 1728, and Aberdeen; minister of Crutched Friars from 1698; Friday evening lecturer at Weighhouse, Eastcheap, 1708; merchants' lecturer at Salters' Hall, 1727; a non-subscriber; original Williams trustee; published *Exposition of Philippians and Colossians* (1710) and other works.

HARRIS, William (1720–1770), biographical writer; hon. DD, Glasgow, 1765. His collected works (1814) contain lives of Hugh *Peters, James I, Charles I, *Cromwell, and Charles II.

HARRIS, William (1776?–1830), Independent minister at Cambridge and Stoke Newington, tutor at Hoxton and Highbury; author of *Grounds of Hope for salvation of all dying in Infancy* (1821).

HARRIS, Sir William Cornwallis (1807–1848), engineer and traveller; superintending engineer of northern provinces of India, 1848; with William Richardson made a big-game expedition to country between Orange River and the Matabele chief Moselikatze's kraal, 1836–7 (narratives published, 1839 and 1841); knighted, 1844, for negotiating treaty with Shoa; published *Portraits of the Game Animals of South Africa* (1840), and account of his Abyssinian expedition; died at Surwur.

HARRIS, William George, second Baron Harris (1782–1845), lieutenant-general; son of George, first Baron *Harris; served against Tippoo Sahib 1799, in the Copenhagen expedition

(1801), and in Canada, 1802; volunteer at recapture of the Cape, 1805; commanded 2nd battalion of 73rd in North Germany and the Netherlands, 1813–14; wounded at Waterloo, 1815; lieutenant-general, 1837; commanded northern district, 1825–8; succeeded to peerage, 1829.

HARRIS, Sir William Henry (1883–1973), organist, choral conductor, and composer; articled at age of 14 to Herbert Morris, organist of St David's Cathedral; fellow of Royal College of Organists; won open scholarship to Royal College of Music; assistant organist, Lichfield Cathedral, 1911–19; teacher at Birmingham and Midland Institute; served in Artists' Rifles during 1914–18 war; succeeded (Sir) Hugh *Allen as organist of New College, Oxford, 1919–28; D.Mus.; conducted Oxford Bach Choir, 1926–33; helped to form University Opera Club; conducted production by (Sir) Jack *Westrup of Monteverdi's *Orfeo*, 1925; directed Balliol Concerts, 1925–33; organist of Christ Church, 1928–33; organist at St George's Chapel, Windsor, 1933–61; president, Royal College of Organists, 1946–8; director of musical studies at Royal School of Church Music, 1956–61; skilful composer, a number of whose motets and anthems passed into repertory of cathedral choirs and choral groups; largest choral work, a setting of *The Hound of Heaven* (1919); professor of organ and harmony, RCM, 1921–53; CVO, 1942; KCVO, 1954; hon. RAM.

HARRIS, Sir William Snow (1791–1867), electrician; knighted in 1847 for his improved lightning-conductor; FRS, 1831; Copley medalist, 1835; gave Bakerian lecture, 1839, on elementary laws of electricity; received government grant of £5,000; appointed scientific referee, 1860.

HARRISON, Benjamin, the elder (1771–1856), treasurer of Guy's Hospital, 1797–1856; FRS and FSA; deputy-governor of Hudson's Bay and South Sea companies; chairman, Exchequer Loan Board.

HARRISON, Benjamin, the younger (1808–1887), archdeacon of Maidstone; son of Benjamin *Harrison the elder; student of Christ Church, Oxford, 1828; MA, 1833; Ellerton, Kennicott, and chancellor's prizeman; Ellerton Hebrew scholar; chaplain to Archbishop *Howley, 1843–8; archdeacon of Maidstone, 1845–87; a reviser of the Old Testament, 1885; presented his library to Canterbury Cathedral; edited Bishop *Broughton's sermons (1857) and *Christianity in Egypt* (1883).

HARRISON, Frederic (1831–1923), author and positivist; BA, Wadham College, Oxford; fellow, 1854–6; called to bar (Lincoln's Inn), 1858; at Oxford adopted Liberal tenets and positivist doctrines, the latter owing to influence of Richard *Congreve; president of English Positivist Committee, 1880–1905; influenced life and thought of his time by vigour as man of practical experience; served on Royal Commission on Trade Unions, 1867–9; secretary, Royal Commission for Digesting the Law, 1869–70; professor of jurisprudence, constitutional and international law for Council of Legal Education, 1877–89; travelled widely; a prolific writer on historical and literary subjects; his works include *Cromwell* (1888) and *Chatham* (1905), both in 'Twelve English Statesmen' series; *William the Silent* (1897), *Ruskin* (1902), and *Theophano: the Crusade of the Tenth Century*, a romance (1904).

HARRISON, Sir George (d. 1841), legal writer; auditor for life of the duchy of Cornwall, 1823; of Lancaster, 1826; GCH, 1831; published *Memoir respecting the hereditary revenues of the crown* (1838) and other works.

HARRISON, George Henry (1816–1846), water-colour painter; son of Mary *Harrison; exhibited at Royal Academy and elsewhere, 1840–6; associate of Old Water-Colour Society, 1845.

HARRISON, Henry (1867–1954), Irish nationalist and writer; educated at Westminster School and Balliol College, Oxford; MP for mid-Tipperary, 1890–2; strong supporter of C. S. *Parnell and his widow; commissioned, Royal Irish Regiment, 1915; MC, OBE; Irish correspondent, *The Economist*, 1922–7; edited *Irish Truth*, 1924–7; supplied corrections to *History of 'The Times'* (vol. iv, 1952) over Richard *Pigott forgeries; publications include *Parnell Vindicated* (1931) and *Parnell, Joseph Chamberlain and Mr. Garvin* (1938); hon. LL D, Dublin.

HARRISON, Jane Ellen (1850–1928), classical scholar; educated at Cheltenham College; student at Newnham College, Cambridge, 1874–9; obtained second class in classical tripos, 1879; studied archaeology in London and paid three visits to Greece, 1880–98; lecturer in classical archaeology at Newnham College (her home until 1922), 1898; took up study of Russian during European war; works include *The Mythology and Monuments of Ancient Greece* (1890), *Prolegomena to the Study of Greek Religion* (1903), and *Themis, a Study of the Social Origins of Greek Religion* (1912).

HARRISON, John (1579–1656), philanthropist; first chief magistrate of Leeds, 1626, and again, 1634; built New Street or Kirkgate with St John's Church and almshouses and the market-cross, Leeds.

HARRISON, John (1613?–1670), Presbyterian divine; rector of Ashton-under-Lyne, 1642–62; active member of Manchester classis, 1646–60; imprisoned as Royalist, 1651 and 1659–60.

HARRISON, John (*fl.* 1630), envoy to Barbary and author; groom of the privy chamber to Prince *Henry; afterwards in service of electress palatine; sheriff of Bermuda, 1622; after several visits to Barbary obtained release of 260 British subjects, 1625–30; published work against Jews (3rd edn., 1656), and books relating to the elector palatine and Bohemia, and *Mvley Abdala Melek, the late king of Barbarie* (1633).

HARRISON, John (1693–1776), horologist; son of a carpenter; devised gridiron pendulum (1726), recoil escapement, 'going ratchet' (secondary spring), and 'new musical scale'; competed for Board of Longitude's prizes for determining longitude at sea within sixty, forty, and thirty geographical miles respectively with his first chronometer, 1736; Copley medallist for third chronometer, 1749; awarded £5,000 (part of the Board of Longitude's prize) by parliament for fourth chronometer, 1763; after the construction of fifth and interposition of George III received the whole reward, 1773; published narrative relating to his discovery of longitude at sea and other inventions; his tomb in Hampstead Churchyard reconstructed by Clockmakers' Company, 1879.

HARRISON, Joseph (d. 1858?), horticulturist; edited *Floricultural Cabinet* (later *Gardener's Magazine*), 1833–55, and similar publications.

HARRISON, Mary (1788–1875), flower painter; née Rossiter; married William Harrison, 1814; an original member and exhibitor of New Water-colour Society, 1831.

HARRISON, Mary St Leger (1852–1931), novelist under pseudonym of Lucas Malet; daughter of Charles *Kingsley; married Revd William Harrison, 1876; successful novelist in romantic tradition although considered extremely outspoken; publications include *Colonel Enderby's Wife* (1885) and *The Wages of Sin* (1891).

HARRISON, Ralph (1748–1810), Nonconformist divine and tutor; minister at Cross Street, Manchester, 1771; professor of classics and belles lettres at Manchester Academy, 1786–9; published educational manuals.

HARRISON, Reginald (1837–1908), surgeon; MRCS, 1859; FRCS, 1866; surgeon at Royal Infirmary, Liverpool (1867–89), and lecturer on anatomy (1865) and on surgery (1872) at medical school there; helped to convert school into medical faculty of Liverpool University; vice-president (1894–5) of Royal College of Surgeons; Hunterian professor of surgery, 1890–1, and Bradshaw lecturer, 1896; president of Medical Society of London, 1890; established system of street ambulances in Liverpool.

HARRISON, Robert (d. 1585?), Brownist; MA, Corpus Christi College, Cambridge, 1572; removed from mastership of Aylsham School for objections to the Prayer-Book, 1574; when master of a hospital at Norwich, helped Robert *Browne to form a Nonconformist congregation; migrated to Middelburg, 1581; published theological tracts; corresponded with *Cartwright.

HARRISON, Robert (1715–1802), mathematician and linguist; master of Trinity House School, Newcastle, 1757; published (with Isaac Thomson) *Short Account of a Course of Natural and Experimental Philosophy* (1757).

HARRISON, Samuel (1760–1812), vocalist; soprano at Ancient Concerts and Society of Sacred Music, 1776; principal tenor at Gloucester Festival, 1781; engaged for Handel Commemoration, 1784, at instance of George III; sang at Hereford, 1786–1808, and at Gloucester and Worcester, 1801–8, at the Ancient Concerts, 1785–91, and afterwards at the Vocal Concerts.

HARRISON, Stephen (*fl.* 1603), joiner and architect; designed arches for entry of James I into London, 1604, described in rare work issued that year.

HARRISON, Susannah (1752–1784), religious poet; sometime a domestic servant; published *Songs in the Night* (1780).

HARRISON, Thomas (1555–1631), biblical scholar; BA, Trinity College, Cambridge, 1578; BD, 1588; fellow, 1579–1631; vice-master, 1611–31; fellow and vice-prefect of Trinity College; a reviser of James I's Bible.

HARRISON, Thomas (1606–1660), regicide; when a member of Inns of Court enlisted in *Essex's bodyguard, 1642; major in *Fleetwood's Horse at Marston Moor, 1644; entered the 'new model'; present at Naseby, 1645, Langport, and captures of Winchester and Basing; MP, Wendover, 1646; colonel of horse, 1647; opposed further negotiation with Charles I, 1647; distinguished himself under *Lambert at Appleby, and was wounded, 1648; negotiated with Levellers, 1648; zealous for trial of Charles I, whom he escorted from Hurst to London; regularly attended meetings of High Court of Justice; held chief command in England during *Cromwell's absence, 1650–1; directed pursuit after Worcester, 1651; elected to Council of State, 1651; a promoter of army petition of 12 Aug. 1652; assisted in expelling Long Parliament, 1653; member of Council of Thirteen, and a leading spirit in Barebones Parliament, 1653; deprived of his commission under the instrument of government, 1653; reprimanded by Cromwell for relations with Anabaptists, 1654; imprisoned, 1655–6 and 1658–9; refused flight or compromise at the Restoration; exempted from Act of Indemnity, 1660; justified his action against Charles I by the authority of parliament; showed great courage at his execution.

HARRISON, Thomas (1619–1682), Nonconformist divine; chaplain to governor of Virginia; succeeded Dr Godwin at St Dunstan's-in-the-East, c.1650; accompanied Henry *Cromwell to Ireland, 1657; BA, Sidney Sussex College, Cambridge, 1637–8; founded Dissenting church at Dublin; published *Topica Sacra: Spiritual Logick* (1658, second part added by John Hunter of Ayr, 1712).

HARRISON, Thomas (1693–1745), divine and poet; pastor of particular baptists in Little Wild Street, 1715–29; conformed and was vicar of Radcliffe-on-the-Wreke, 1729–45; published *Poems on Divine Subjects* (1719).

HARRISON, Thomas (1744–1829), architect; studied at Rome; admitted to Academy of St Luke, and awarded medals by Clement XIV; rebuilt Chester Castle, and (1829) erected the Grosvenor Bridge; built Broomhall, Fifeshire, 1796; suggested to Lord *Elgin collection of Greek works of art.

HARRISON, Thomas Elliott (1808–1888), civil engineer; worked with Robert *Stephenson, and succeeded as chief engineer of York, Newcastle, and Berwick line; designed Jarrow (1858) and Hartlepool Docks; president of Institute of Civil Engineers, 1874.

HARRISON, William (1534–1593), topographer and chronologist; educated at St Paul's School and Westminster, Cambridge, and Christ Church, Oxford; MA, 1560; rector of Radwinter, 1559–93; canon of Windsor, 1586; his *Description of England* (1577) printed with *Holinshed, as also his version of *Bellenden's translation of Boece's *Description of Scotland*; extracts from his 'Great Chronologie' (unprinted) in Furnivall's edition of *Description of England* (1877).

HARRISON, William (1553–1621), last arch-priest of England; DD, Douai; professor of theology at Douai, 1597–1603; arch-priest of England, Scotland, and Ireland, 1615; obtained freedom of clergy from Jesuit control and restoration of episcopal government.

HARRISON, William (1685–1713), poet; educated at Winchester and New College, Oxford; fellow of New College, 1706; protégé of

*Addison and *Swift; secretary to Lord *Raby at The Hague, 1711, afterwards to Utrecht embassy; continued the *Tatler* (Jan. to May 1711), with assistance of Swift and St John; his 'Woodstock Park' in *Dodsley's collection.

HARRISON, William (1802–1884), antiquary; established Manx Society, 1858; published *Bibliotheca Monensis* (1861) and other works.

HARRISON, William (1812–1860), commander of the *Great Eastern* steamship; selected in 1856 to command the *Great Leviathan*, afterwards called the *Great Eastern*; brought her into Portland after trial trip, 1859; capsized in ship's boat near Southampton dock.

HARRISON, William (1813–1868), opera singer and manager; appeared at Covent Garden, 1839; sang at Drury Lane in English operas; accompanied Louisa Pyne to America, 1854; with her directed English opera at Lyceum, 1857, and Covent Garden, 1858–64; sole manager of Her Majesty's, 1864–5, when he played Charles Surface.

HARRISON, William Frederick (1815–1880), water-colour painter; eldest son of Mary *Harrison.

HARRISON, William George (1827–1883), lawyer; BA, St John's College, Cambridge, 1850; barrister, Middle Temple, 1853; QC, 1877; part author of 'Joint-Stock Companies' Act', 1856.

HARRISON, Sir William Montagu Graham- (1871–1949), parliamentary draftsman. See GRAHAM-HARRISON.

HARRISSON, Thomas Harnett (Tom) (1911–1976), traveller, explorer, and scholar; educated at Harrow and Pembroke College, Cambridge; published *Birds of the Harrow District* (1931); joined Oxford University expedition to the Arctic, 1930, and went with Oxford University expedition to Borneo, 1932, and to the New Hebrides, where he studied cannibal tribes; founded Mass-Observation, 1937, which, in 1939, was employed by the Ministry of Information for detailed studies on civilian morale during the war; joined King's Royal Rifle Corps, 1942; led Special Operations Executive (SOE) team behind Japanese lines in Borneo, 1944–5; DSO, 1946; directed Kuching Museum, Sarawak, 1947–66; reorganized museum and made significant archaeological discoveries; visiting professor, Cornell University, 1967–8; wrote many books and articles; with Hugh Gibb, won Grand Prix at Cannes for film, *Birds' Nest Soup*; received Speleological Society Award, USA, 1960, Royal Geographical Society Founder's Medal, 1962, and Medal of Royal Society of Arts, 1964; OBE, 1959.

HARROD, Henry (1817–1871), professional antiquary; secretary to Norfolk Archaeological Society; FSA, 1854; published *Gleanings among Castles and Convents of Norfolk* (1857); arranged records of Norwich, Lynn, and other boroughs.

HARROD, Sir (Henry) Roy (Forbes) (1900–1978), economist; educated as a scholar at St Paul's Westminster, and New College, Oxford; first class, Lit. Hum., 1921, and modern history, 1922; lectureship of Christ Church, 1922, studentship (fellowship), in modern history and economics, 1924–67; fellow of Nuffield College, Oxford, 1938–47 and 1954–8; joint editor, *Economic Journal*, 1945–61; published papers on economic problems in *Economic Essays* (2nd edn., 1972), *International Economics* (1933, 4th edn., 1957), and *The Trade Cycle* (1936); also contributed 'An Essay in Dynamic Theory' to the *Economic Journal* (1939), later incorporated in *Towards a Dynamic Economics* (1948, 2nd revised edn., 1973); following J. M. (later Lord) *Keynes, Harrod persistent advocate of fiscal and monetary expansion, publishing *Are These Hardships Necessary?* (1947), *Topical Comment: Essays in Dynamic Economics Applied* (1961), *Towards a New Economic Policy* (1967), and *Reforming the World's Money* (1965); also published books on biography and philosophy, including *Life of John Maynard Keynes* (1951), and *The Prof* (1959), a memoir of F. A. *Lindemann, Viscount Cherwell; also *Foundations of Inductive Logic* (1956) and a paper in *Mind* (1936) entitled 'Utilitarianism Revised'; FBA, 1947; knighted, 1969; honorary degrees from British, American, and European universities; hon. student, Christ Church, 1967; hon. fellow, Nuffield College, 1958 and New College, 1975.

HARROD, William (d. 1819), compiler of histories of Stamford (1785), Mansfield (pt. i, 1786, pt. ii, 1801), and Market Harborough (1808).

HARROWBY, Barons. See RYDER, NATHANIEL, first baron, 1735–1803; RYDER, DUDLEY, second baron, 1762–1847.

HARROWBY, earls of. See RYDER, DUDLEY, first earl, 1762–1847; RYDER, DUDLEY, second earl, 1798–1882; RYDER, DUDLEY FRANCIS STUART, 1831–1900.

HARRY, Blind (*fl.* 1470–1492). See HENRY THE MINSTREL.

HARRY, George Owen (*fl.* 1604), Welsh antiquary; rector of Whitchurch, Pembrokeshire; assisted *Camden in his *Britannia* and published a genealogy of King James (1604) and *The Wellsprynge of True Nobility*.

HARRY, Nun Morgan (1800–1842), Congregational minister at Banbury, and (1832–42) New Broad Street; honorary secretary of Peace Society, 1837; editor of *Herald of Peace*.

HARSNETT, Adam (d. 1639), divine; BA, Pembroke Hall, Cambridge, 1601; MA, St John's College, 1604; BD, Pembroke College, 1612; vicar of Hutton, 1609–39; rector of Cranham, 1612–39; published religious works.

HARSNETT, Samuel (1561–1631), archbishop of York; scholar and fellow (1583) of Pembroke Hall, Cambridge; MA, 1584; DD, 1606; master of Pembroke Hall, 1605–16; censured by *Whitgift for sermon against predestination, 1584; vicar of Chigwell, 1597–1605; chaplain to *Bancroft when bishop of London; archdeacon of Essex, 1603–9; rector of Stisted, 1609–19; vice-chancellor of Cambridge, 1606 and 1614; bishop of Chichester, 1609–19, of Norwich, 1619–28; archbishop of York, 1629–31; unpopular with Puritans; published an exposure (1599) of the exorcist, John *Darrel, and *A Declaration of egregious Popish impostures* (1603), from which Shakespeare took the names of the spirits in *Lear*; his *Considerations for the better settling of Church government* ordered by Charles I to be circulated among bishops, 1629; founded schools at Chigwell; bequeathed his library to corporation of Colchester.

HART, Aaron (1670–1756), chief rabbi; rabbi of first synagogue of German and Polish Jews, Mitre Square, 1692, at Duke's Place, Aldgate, 1721–56; published *Urim ve-Thumim*, the first Hebrew book printed in London (1707).

HART, Aaron (1722–1800), first British merchant in Lower Canada.

HART, Adolphus M. (1813–1879), Canadian writer ('Hampden'); son of Ezekiel *Hart; published *History of Discovery of Valley of the Mississippi* (1852).

HART, Andrew (or **Andro)** (d. 1621), Edinburgh printer and publisher; issued works of Sir William *Alexander and *Drummond of Hawthornden; published editions of the Bible (1610) and *Barbour's *Brus*; imported many works; imprisoned as a leader of tumult of 17 Dec. 1596.

HART, Sir Andrew Searle (1811–1890), vice-provost of Trinity College, Dublin; fellow of Trinity College, Dublin, 1835; MA, 1839; LL D, 1840; senior fellow, 1858; vice-provost, 1876–90; knighted, 1886; contributed to mathematical journals, and published elementary treatises on mechanics (1844), hydrostatics, and hydrodynamics (1846).

HART, Sir Anthony (1754?–1831), lord chancellor of Ireland; barrister, Middle Temple, 1781; KC, 1807; solicitor-general to Queen *Charlotte, 1816; vice-chancellor of England,

1827; privy councillor and knighted, 1827; lord chancellor of Ireland, 1827–30.

HART, Sir Basil Henry Liddell (1895–1970), military historian and strategist; educated at St Paul's School and Corpus Christi College, Cambridge; commissioned in King's Own Yorkshire Light Infantry, 1914–16; as adjutant, training units, Volunteer Force, evolved new methods of instruction and battle drill, 1917–21; helped to compile post-war *Infantry Training* manual; transferred to Army Education Corps, 1921–7; published views on new approach to warfare in *Strategy—The Indirect Approach* (1929); military correspondent, the *Daily Telegraph*, 1925–35; correspondent and defence adviser, *The Times*, 1935–9; published over thirty books on military leaders, and *The Real War* (1930) and *The Ghost of Napoleon* (1933); unofficial adviser to minister of war, Leslie (later Lord) *Hore-Belisha, 1937–8; suggested reforms distrusted by military establishment; consistently opposed to 'total war', 1939–45; published *The Other Side of the Hill* (1948), *The Rommel Papers* (1953), *The Tanks* (2 vols., 1959), *Memoirs* (2 vols., 1965), and *History of the Second World War* (1970); denied that nuclear weapons would preclude non-nuclear warfare; hon. D.Litt., Oxford, 1964; hon. fellow, Corpus Christi College, Cambridge, 1965; knighted, 1966.

HART, Charles (d. 1683), actor; grandnephew of Shakespeare; played the duchess in *Shirley's Cardinal*, 1641; lieutenant in Prince *Rupert's regiment during rebellion; arrested while playing *Beaumont and *Fletcher's *Bloody Brother*, 1646; after Restoration played at Vere Street House, and with *Killigrew at Theatre Royal; his best tragic parts, Arbaces (*King and No King*), Amintor (*Maid's Tragedy*), Alexander, Othello, and Brutus; his best comic parts, Mosca (*Volpone*), Don John (*The Chances*), Wildblood (*Mock Astrologer*); said to have introduced Nell *Gwyn to the stage.

HART, Charles (1797–1859), organist and composer; gained Gresham Prize with Te Deum, 1831; published hymns, anthems, an oratorio, and other musical compositions.

HART, Ernest Abraham (1835–1898), medical journalist and reformer; educated at City of London School; Lambert Jones scholar, 1848; studied medicine at St George's Hospital, and was surgical registrar and demonstrator of anatomy; MRCS, 1856; surgeon, West London Hospital, 1860–3; ophthalmic surgeon at St Mary's Hospital, 1863–8; dean of medical school, 1863–8; edited *British Medical Journal*, 1886–98; adviser on medical publications to George *Smith, head of firm of Smith, Elder & Co., to whom he suggested possibilities of devel-oping the Apollinaris spring; president of Harveian Society, 1868; hon. DCL, Durham, 1893; organized numerous medical and sanitary reforms; published addresses, pamphlets, and other works.

HART, Ezekiel (1770–1843), Canadian Jew; son of Aaron *Hart (1722–1800); established political rights of Jews in Lower Canada, 1831.

HART, George Vaughan (1752–1832), general; served with the 46th in American War; present at Long Island, Brandywine, 1777, and Monmouth; afterwards served in India (Bangalore, Seringapatam, Mullavelly); lieutenant-general, 1811; MP, Co. Donegal, 1812–31.

HART, Henry (*fl.* 1549), author of devotional treatises.

HART, Henry George (1808–1878), lieutenant-general; editor and proprietor of *Hart's Army List*; lieutenant-colonel of the 49th Foot, 1856; colonel, 1860; lieutenant-general, 1877; published first quarterly army list (1839), first annual (1840).

HART, James (*fl.* 1633), physician; studied at Paris and in Germany; graduated abroad; practised at Northampton; published *Anatomie of Urines* (1625) and Κλινική, *or Diet of the Diseased* (1633).

HART, James (1663–1729), minister of Greyfriars, Edinburgh; MA, Edinburgh, 1687; minister of Ratho, 1692–1702, of Greyfriars, Edinburgh, 1702–29; opposed the Union; called by Steele 'the hangman of the Gospel'; his *Journal in 1714* edited (1832).

HART, John (d. 1574), orthographer; Chester herald, 1566; his *Orthographie*, on the phonetic system (1569), reprinted by *Pitman (1850).

HART, John (d. 1586), Jesuit; BD, Douai, 1577; priest, 1578; condemned to death as a priest; recanted on the hurdle; withdrew recantation and disputed with John *Rainoldes at Oxford; sent back to the Tower, where (1582) he became a Jesuit; banished, 1585; landed in Normandy, 1585; died in Poland.

HART, John (1809–1873), pioneer colonist and premier of South Australia; engaged in mercantile service to Tasmania; director of Adelaide Auction Company, 1840; member for Victoria district in old legislative council, 1851; member for Port Adelaide in first House of Assembly, 1857; treasurer, 1857; colonial secretary, 1863 and 1864–5; premier, 1865–6, 1868, and 1870–1; CMG, 1870.

HART, Joseph (1712?–1768), Independent preacher at Jewin Street Chapel, London, 1760–8; author of hymns, 1759.

HART, Joseph Binns (1794–1844), organist and composer; wrote songs when chorus-master and pianist at the English opera, 1818–21; composed dance music.

HART, Moses (1676?–1756), builder of the Great Synagogue, Aldgate, 1721; brother of Aaron *Hart (1670–1756).

HART, Philip (d. 1749), organist and composer; played at *Britton's with *Handel and Pepusch; set *Hughes's *Ode in Praise of Music* (1703), and *Milton's *Morning Hymn* (1729); composed fugues, songs, and anthems.

HART, Sir Raymund George (1899–1960), air marshal; educated at Simon Langton School, Canterbury; commissioned in Royal Flying Corps, 1917; ARCS, Imperial College of Science, 1921; joined Royal Air Force, 1924; worked on radar from 1936; deputy director of radar, 1941–3; chief signals officer, Allied Expeditionary Air Force, 1943–5, British Air Force, 1945–6; at Air Ministry: in charge of technical service plans (1947–9), director-general of engineering (1951–5), controller, engineering and equipment, 1956–9; OBE, 1940; CBE, 1944; CB, 1946; air marshal and KBE, 1957.

HART, Sir Robert, first baronet (1835–1911), inspector-general of customs in China; BA, Queen's College, Belfast, 1853; MA, 1871; hon. LL D, 1882; entered Chinese Consular Service, 1854; assistant at Ningpo, 1855–8, and at Canton, 1858; secretary to allied Anglo-French commissioners at Canton; joined Chinese Imperial Maritime Customs Service as deputy commissioner at Canton, 1859; organized customs service at Foochow and other ports, 1861–3; commissioner of customs at Shanghai, 1863; inspector-general, 1863–1906; met C. G. *Gordon after Taiping rebellion, 1864; reconciled Gordon and Li Hung Chang; remained in Peking from 1864 till 1908; revisited Europe only twice, in 1866 and 1878; practical creator of Chinese Imperial Customs; controlled also imperial posts from 1896; helped to settle difficulties between Great Britain and China, 1875, which resulted in Chefoo Convention, 1876, and those in Formosa between China and France, 1885; advocated necessary reforms in China, 1894–5; besieged in British Legation at Peking during Boxer outbreak, 1900; organized native customs service, 1901; helped in re-establishment of Manchu dynasty; published experiences in *These from the Land of Sinim* (1901); authority terminated by Chinese government, which subordinated his service to a board of Chinese officials, 1906; KCMG, 1882; GCMG, 1889; baronet, 1893.

HART, Solomon Alexander (1806–1881), painter; exhibited in Suffolk Street his *Elevation of the Law*, 1830; RA, 1840; professor of painting, Royal Academy, 1854–63; librarian from 1865; exhibited, 1826–80; his *Reminiscences* edited (1882).

HARTCLIFFE, John (1651–1712), schoolmaster; of Eton, Magdalen College, Oxford, and King's College, Cambridge; MA, King's College, Cambridge, 1676; fellow; BD, 1689; head-master of Merchant Taylors' School, 1681–6; canon of Windsor, 1691–1712; chief work, *Treatise on Moral and Intellectual Virtues* (1691).

HARTE, Henry Hickman (1790–1848), mathematician; fellow of Trinity College, Dublin, 1819; incumbent of Cappagh, 1831–48; translated and added to Laplace's *Système du Monde* and Poisson's *Mécanique Céleste*.

HARTE, Walter (1709–1774), author; MA, St Mary Hall, Oxford, 1731; friend of *Pope and Arthur *Young; travelling tutor to *Chesterfield's natural son; vice-principal of St Mary Hall, Oxford, 1740; canon of Windsor, 1750; published *History of the Life of Gustavus Adolphus* (1759), *Essays on Husbandry* (1764), and religious poems.

HARTGILL (or HARTGYLL), George (fl. 1594), author of *Generall Calenders, or Most Easie Astronomicall Tables* (1594).

HARTINGTON, marquess of (1833–1908), statesman. See CAVENDISH, SPENCER COMPTON.

HARTLEY, Arthur Clifford (1889–1960), engineer and inventor; educated at Hymers College, Hull, and City and Guilds College, London; B.Sc. (Eng.), London, 1910; qualified as pilot and worked on armaments with Royal Flying Corps, 1914–18; joined engineering division, Anglo-Persian Oil Company, 1924; chief engineer, 1934–51; at Ministry of Aircraft Production (1939–45) with others produced FIDO (fog dispersal) and HAIS and HAMEL pipelines for PLUTO; in private practice invented hoister for loading tankers at sea; CBE, 1944; president, Institution of Civil Engineers, 1959.

HARTLEY, Sir Charles Augustus (1825–1915), civil engineer; served in Crimean War; chief engineer to European Commission of Danube, 1856–1907; earned sobriquet 'father of the Danube' for work in clearing and making navigable Sulina and St George estuaries; knighted, 1862; left Romania, 1872; KCMG, 1884; member of international technical commission of Suez Canal, 1884–1906; advice sought by Indian, Russian, and American governments.

HARTLEY, David, the elder (1705–1757), philosopher; educated at Bradford Grammar School and Jesus College, Cambridge; fellow, 1727–30; MA, 1729; physician in Newark, Bury St Edmunds, and London; supporter of *Byrom's shorthand and Mrs Stephens's medicine for the stone; friend of Bishops *Butler and *Warburton; FRS; acquaintance of *Hales. His *Observations on Man* (1749, abridged by *Priestley, 1775), containing the doctrine of association, influenced *Coleridge.

HARTLEY, David, the younger (1732–1813), statesman and inventor; son of David *Hartley the elder; BA, Corpus Christi College, Oxford, 1750; fellow of Merton College, Oxford; MP, Hull, 1774–80 and 1782–4; opposed American War and slave trade; with Franklin drew up and signed treaty between Great Britain and the United States, 1783; published *Letters on the American War* (1778–9), editions of his father's *Observations on Man* (1791, 1801), and *Account of a Method of Securing Buildings and Ships against Fire* (1785).

HARTLEY, Mrs **Elizabeth** (1751–1824), actress; née White; appeared at Haymarket in *Oroonoko,* 1769; played at Covent Garden, 1772–80, in *Mason's *Elfrida* and *Caractacus*; played Lady Frances Touchwood (*Belle's Stratagem*), Cleopatra (*All for Love*), and Shakespearian parts; painted by *Reynolds as Jane Shore, Calista, and a Bacchante.

HARTLEY, Sir **Harold Brewer** (1878–1972), physical chemist; educated at Dulwich College, and Balliol College, Oxford; Brackenbury scholar; first class, natural science (chemistry and mineralogy), 1900; tutorial fellow, Balliol College, 1901; developed new university course in physical chemistry, 1904; during 1914–18 war served in 7th Leicestershire Regiment and became chemical adviser to Third Army, 1915; assistant director of Gas Services, GHQ; MC, 1916; OBE; head of Chemical Warfare Department, Ministry of Munitions; CBE, 1919; returned to Oxford and (Sir) Cyril *Hinshelwood one of his pupils; helped to raise teaching standards in schools by organizing summer schools in physical chemistry at Balliol College; carried out research into the electrical conductivity of solutions; FRS, 1926; investigated chemical side of German wartime activities; member of Chemical Warfare Board; joined Society of Chemical Engineers, 1922, and Fuel Research Board of DSIR, 1929, chairman, 1932–47; deputy governor, Gas Light and Coke Company during 1939–45 war; resigned tutorial fellowship and became vice-president and director of research of LMS railway system, 1930; chairman, Railway Air Services, 1934; chairman, British European Airways, 1946–7, and British Overseas Airways Corporation, 1947–9; first chairman, Electricity Supply Council, 1949–52; president, Institution of Chemical Engineers, 1951–2 and 1954–5; president, Society of Instrument Technology, 1957–61; adviser, John Brown Co., 1954–61; freeman, Goldsmiths' Company, 1929; prime warden, 1941–2; editor, *Notes and Records of the Royal Society,* 1952–70; president, British Association; chairman, Duke of Edinburgh's Study Conference, 1954–6; knighted, 1928; KCVO, 1944; GCVO, 1957; CH, 1967; Romanes lecturer, 1964.

HARTLEY, James (1745–1799), Indian officer; aide-de-camp to governor of Bombay, 1770; saved expeditionary force against the Konkan, 1779; repulsed Mahrattas at Doogaur, 1780; his promotion overruled by directors; appointed lieutenant-colonel, 75th Regiment; quartermaster-general of Bombay Army, 1788; defeated Hussein Ali at Calicut, 1790; captured French settlement of Mahé, 1793; major-general, 1796; supervisor and magistrate for province of Malabar; second-in-command of Bombay Army against Tippoo Sahib, 1799; died at Cannanore.

HARTLEY, Jesse (1780–1860), engineer for Bolton and Manchester Railway and canal.

HARTLEY, Leslie Poles (1895–1972), novelist and critic; educated at Harrow and Balliol College, Oxford; served in Norfolk Regiment, 1916–18; published stories in *Oxford Outlook,* of which he was an editor; friend of Lady Ottoline *Morrell and Margot, countess of Oxford and *Asquith; reviewer, mainly of fiction, in *Saturday Review* and the *Sketch*; published short stories, *Night Fears* (1924) and *The Killing Bottle* (1932); also a trilogy of novels, *The Shrimp and the Anemone* (1944), *The Sixth Heaven* (1946), and *Eustace and Hilda* (1947); also *The Go-Between* (1953), which was made into a film; Clark lecturer on Nathaniel Hawthorne, 1964; CBE, 1956; C.Lit., 1972; president of English section of PEN Club.

HARTLEY, Thomas (1709?–1784), translator of Swedenborg; MA, St John's College, Cambridge, 1745; rector of Winwick, 1744–84; paid frequent visits to Swedenborg; translated Swedenborg's *De Commercio Animae et Corporis* (1769); author of *Nine Queries* concerning Swedenborg's doctrine of the Trinity (published 1785), and *Paradise Restored,* against *Warburton (1764).

HARTLIB, Samuel (d. 1670?), friend of *Milton; came to England from Poland, c.1628; introduced writings of Comenius; praised by Milton in treatise on education, 1644; received pension from parliament for works on husbandry, 1646;

published pamphlets on education and husbandry, including *Description of the famous Kingdom of Macaria* (1641) and *Discours of Husbandrie used in Brabant and Flanders* (1652).

HARTNELL, Sir **Norman Bishop** (1901–1979), dress designer; educated at Mill Hill School and Magdalene College, Cambridge, 1921–2; acted and designed costumes and sets for Footlights dramatic club; with his sister opened couture establishment in London's West End, 1923; designed dresses for shows produced by (Sir) Charles *Cochran and André *Charlot and plays of (Sir) Noël *Coward; designed wedding gown for Lady Alice Montagu-Douglas-Scott for her marriage to duke of *Gloucester, 1935; designed clothes for queen's state visit to Paris, 1938; received first royal warrant of appointment to the queen, 1940; during 1939–45 war designed 'utility' dresses for the mass market; founder member of Incorporated Society of London Fashion Designers, 1944; chairman, 1947–56; designed wedding dress for Princess Elizabeth and dresses for bridesmaids, 1947; produced coronation robe for Queen Elizabeth II, 1953; MVO; designed dresses for queen's royal tours and state visits; KCVO, 1977; published autobiography, *Silver and Gold* (1955).

HARTOG, Numa Edward (1846–1871), senior wrangler and second Smith's prizeman, 1869; BA and B.Sc., London, 1864; scholar of Trinity College, Cambridge, 1866; admitted BA by special grace as a Jew, 1869; gave evidence before select committee of House of Lords on university tests, 1871.

HARTOG, Sir **Philip(pe) Joseph** (1864–1947), educationist; brother of N. E. *Hartog; educated at University College School and Owens College, Manchester; B.Sc., 1882; assistant chemistry lecturer, 1891; academic registrar, London University, 1903–20; enthusiastic promoter of School of Oriental Studies; on Calcutta University Commission, 1917; vice-chancellor, Dacca, 1920–5; on Indian Public Service Commission, 1926–30; chairman, Indian Education Committee, 1928–9; published *The Writing of English* (1907), *Words in Action* (1947); and with E. C. Rhodes *An Examination of Examinations* (1935) and *The Marks of Examiners* (1936); knighted, 1926; KBE, 1930.

HARTOPP, Sir **John,** third baronet (1637?–1722), Nonconformist; succeeded to baronetcy, 1658; MP, Leicestershire, 1678–81; heavily fined for nonconformity, 1682; alderman of London; member of Dr John *Owen's congregation and friend of Isaac *Watts; left endowment for education of Dissenting ministers.

HARTREE, Douglas Rayner (1897–1958), scientist; educated at Bedales and St John's College, Cambridge; Ph.D., 1926; professor of applied mathematics (1929–37), of theoretical physics (1937–45), Manchester; Plummer professor of mathematical physics, Cambridge, 1946–58; improved calculation of trajectories and became a leader in science of computation; invented 'self-consistent field' method for solution of atomic problems; developed methods of automatic control; published *Numerical Analysis* (1952); FRS, 1932.

HARTRY, Malachy (alias **John)** (*fl.* 1640), compiler of Latin works on Irish Cistercian houses (unpublished); died in Flanders.

HARTSHORN, Vernon (1872–1931), miners' leader and politician; miners' agent for Maesteg, 1905; elected to national executive, Miners' Federation, 1911; Labour MP, Ogmore division of Glamorganshire, 1918–31; postmaster-general and PC, 1924; member of Indian Statutory Commission, 1927–30; lord privy seal, 1930–1.

HARTSHORNE, Albert (1839–1910), archaeologist; son of Charles Henry *Hartshorne; secretary of Archaeological Institute of Great Britain, 1876–83, 1886–94; edited *Archaeological Journal*, 1878–92; FSA, 1882; published *Old English Glasses* (1897), *Oxford, 1691–1712* (1910); and works on monumental effigies and English churches.

HARTSHORNE, Charles Henry (1802–1865), antiquary; MA, St John's College, Cambridge, 1828; incumbent of Cogenhoe, 1838–50; rector of Holdenby, 1850–65; published *Book Rarities of the University of Cambridge* (1829), *Ancient Metrical Tales* (1829), and archaeological works.

HARTSTONGE, John (1654–1717), bishop of Derry; MA, Trinity College, Dublin, 1680; fellow of Caius College, Cambridge, 1681; chaplain to first and second dukes of *Ormonde; bishop of Ossory, 1693; DD, Oxford, 1693; bishop of Derry, 1714.

HARTWELL, Abraham, the elder (*fl.* 1565), Latin poet; educated at Eton and King's College, Cambridge; fellow, 1562–7; MA, 1567.

HARTWELL, Abraham, the younger (*fl.* 1600), translator and antiquary; MA, Trinity College, Cambridge, 1575; incorporated at Oxford, 1588; secretary to Archbishop *Whitgift; rector of Toddington; member of old Society of Antiquaries; published translations of Italian works by Minadoi and Pigafetta, and the *Ottoman of Lazaro Soranzo* (1603).

HARTY, Sir (Herbert) Hamilton (1879–1941), musician; held organ appointments, Belfast and Dublin; established himself in London as accompanist, 1900; conducted Hallé Orchestra, Manchester, 1920–33; composer in romantic tradition; works include songs, Violin Concerto (1909), tone-poem *With the Wild Geese* (1910), cantata *The Mystic Trumpeter* (1913), 'Irish' Symphony (1924), arrangements of Handel's 'Water Music' and 'Music for Royal Fireworks', and suite from works of John *Field; knighted, 1925; commemorated by chair of music, Queen's University, Belfast.

HARTY, William (1781–1854), physician; MA, Trinity College, Dublin, 1804; MD, 1830; FRCP, 1824–7; physician to Dublin prisons; published *Dysentery and its Combinations* (1805) and *Historic Sketch of Contagious Fever Epidemic in Ireland in 1817–19*.

HARVARD, John (1607–1638), principal founder of Harvard College, Massachusetts; of humble origin; MA, Emmanuel College, Cambridge, 1635; settled in Charlestown, Massachusetts, 1637; bequeathed half his estate and library for new college at Cambridge, Massachusetts.

HARVEY, Beauchamp Bagenal (1762–1798), politician; of Trinity College, Dublin; Irish barrister, 1782; presided at meetings of United Irishmen, 1793; appointed to command Wexford rebels, May 1798; deposed after repulse at Ross; arrested on island near Wexford; court-martialled and hanged.

HARVEY, Christopher (1597–1663), poet and friend of Isaak *Walton; MA, Brasenose College, Oxford, 1620; rector of Whitney, 1630; vicar of Clifton, Warwickshire, 1639–63; chief work *The Synagogue* (devotional poems appended anonymously to 1640 edition of George *Herbert's *Temple*).

HARVEY, Daniel Whittle (1786–1863), radical politician; fellow of the Inner Temple, 1818; attorney at Colchester; twice refused admission to bar; MP, Colchester, 1818–20 and 1826–34, Southwark, 1835–40; founded *Sunday Times*, 1822; commissioner of London Police, 1840–63.

HARVEY, Edmond (*fl.* 1661), regicide; colonel of horse under *Essex, 1642; commissioner for trial of Charles I; refused to sign warrant, 1649; imprisoned for fraud as first commissioner of customs, 1655; sentenced to death, 1660; imprisoned in Pendennis Castle, 1661.

HARVEY, Edmund George (1828–1884), musical composer and author; son of William Woodis *Harvey; BA, Queens' College, Cambridge, 1850; rector of St Mary's, Truro, 1860; vicar of Mullyon, 1865; composed Gregorian chants, hymn-tunes, and waltzes; edited *The Truro Use* (1877); published *History of Mullyon* (1875).

HARVEY, Sir Edward (1783–1865), admiral; third son of Captain John *Harvey (1740–1794), with whom he served in action of 1 June 1794; present at Camperdown, 1797, and bombardment of Acre, 1840; rear-admiral, 1847; commander at the Nore, 1857–60; admiral, 1860; GCB, 1865.

HARVEY, Sir Eliab (1758–1830), admiral; MP, Maldon, 1780, Essex, 1803–12 and 1820–6; a reckless gambler; commanded the *Téméraire* at blockade of Brest and at Trafalgar, after which he was promoted rear-admiral, 1805; with *Gambier in Basque Roads, 1809; dismissed for abuse of Lord Gambier, 1809; reinstated, 1810; KCB, 1815; admiral, 1819.

HARVEY, Gabriel (*c.*1550–1630), poet; BA, Christ's College, Cambridge, 1570; MA, Pembroke, 1573; as fellow of Pembroke Hall became acquainted with *Spenser; the Hobbinol of *The Shepheards Calender*; claimed to be father of English hexameter; lectured on rhetoric; fellow of Trinity Hall, 1578; junior proctor, 1583; DCL, Oxford, 1585; published satirical verses which gave offence at court, 1579; attacked Robert *Greene in *Foure Letters* (1592); wrote *Pierce's Supererogation* (1593) and *Trimming of Thomas Nashe* (1597), against *Nashe, both Nashe and Harvey being silenced by authority, 1599; published Latin works on rhetoric (1577); English works, including correspondence with Spenser (1579–80), edited by Dr *Grosart.

HARVEY, Sir George (1806–1876), painter; an original associate, Royal Scottish Academy, and contributor (1827) to first exhibition; full member, 1829; president, 1864–76; knighted, 1864; became known by figure-pictures; excelled later as landscape painter; published *Notes on Early History of the Royal Scottish Academy* (1870).

HARVEY, Gideon, the elder (1640?–1700?), physician; studied at Oxford, Leiden, and Paris; FCP, Hague; MD; doctor-general to king's army in Flanders after the Restoration; physician to Charles II, *c.*1675; attacked College of Physicians in his *Conclave of Physicians* (1683); physician to the Tower, 1689; his *Art of Curing Disease by Expectation* (1689) translated into Latin by George Ernest Stahl (1730); published also *Discourse of the Plague* (1665) and *Vanities of Philosophy and Physick* (1699).

HARVEY, Gideon, the younger (1669?–1755?), physician; son of Gideon *Harvey the elder; MD, Leiden, 1690, Cambridge, 1698; FRCP, 1703; king's physician to the Tower, *c.*1702.

HARVEY (or HERVEY), Henry (d. 1585), master of Trinity Hall, Cambridge; LL D, Trinity Hall, Cambridge, 1542; vicar-general of London and Canterbury; commissioner for detection of heretical books at Cambridge, 1556; prebendary of Southwell, 1558, Salisbury, 1558; master of Trinity Hall on Elizabeth's accession; vice-chancellor, 1560; canon of Ely, 1567; master in Chancery, 1568; founded scholarships at Trinity Hall.

HARVEY, Sir Henry (1737–1810), admiral; wrecked off Cape François in the *Hussar*, 1762; in sloop *Martin* at relief of Quebec; commanded the *Convert* at Dominica, 1782; in the *Ramillies* under Howe at action of 1 June 1794; rear-admiral, 1794; took part in action off Lorient, 1795; captured Trinidad, 1796; KB, 1800; admiral, 1804.

HARVEY, Hildebrand Wolfe (1887–1970), marine biologist; educated at Gresham's School, Holt, and Downing College, Cambridge, 1906–10; served in RNVR, 1914–18; on staff of Marine Biological Association, Plymouth, 1921–58; worked on physical oceanography of western English Channel; produced number of papers on biological chemistry and physics of sea water, plankton production, and the rate of diatom growth, 1928–33; FRS, 1945; CBE, 1958; one of the founders of systematic research on the biological productivity of the sea.

HARVEY, John (1563?–1592), astrologer; brother of Gabriel *Harvey; MA, Queens' College, Cambridge, 1584; MD; physician at King's Lynn; published astrological works.

HARVEY, John (1740–1794), captain in the navy; brother of Sir Henry *Harvey; took part in defence of Gibraltar, 1779–82; mortally wounded as captain of the *Brunswick* in *Howe's victory, 1 June 1794; his monument in Westminster Abbey.

HARVEY, Sir John (1772–1837), admiral; second son of John *Harvey (1740–1794); flag-captain to his uncle, Sir Henry, at Lorient, 1795; commanded the *Agamemnon* under Calder at Finisterre; rear-admiral, 1813; commander in West Indies, 1816–19; KCB, 1833; admiral, 1837.

HARVEY, Sir John Martin Martin- (1863–1944), actor-manager. See MARTIN-HARVEY.

HARVEY, Margaret (1768–1858), poet; published *Lay of the Minstrel's Daughter* (1814) and *Raymond de Percy* (1822).

HARVEY, Oliver Charles, fourth baronet, and first Baron Harvey of Tasburgh (1893–1968), diplomat; educated at Malvern College and Trinity College, Cambridge; first class, part i, historical tripos, 1914; served in France, Egypt, and Palestine, 1914–18; entered Diplomatic Service, 1919; head of Chancery, Paris, 1931; private secretary to Anthony Eden (later earl of Avon), 1936; and to Lord *Halifax, 1938; minister in Paris, 1939; reappointed as Eden's private secretary, 1941–3; assistant under-secretary, Foreign Office, 1943; succeeded Sir Orme *Sargent as deputy under-secretary, 1946; worked closely with Ernest *Bevin as he had done with Eden; ambassador, Paris, following Duff *Cooper (later Viscount Norwich), 1948–54; baron, 1954; succeeded as fourth baronet, 1954; trustee, Wallace Collection; chairman, Franco-British Society; CMG, 1937; CB, 1944; KCMG, 1946; GCMG, 1948; GCVO, 1950; published *Diplomatic Diaries, 1937–1940* (ed. John Harvey, 1970) and *War Diaries, 1941–1945* (ed. John Harvey, 1978).

HARVEY, Richard (1560?–1631), astrologer; brother of Gabriel *Harvey; fellow of Pembroke Hall, Cambridge; MA, 1581; incurred much ridicule for his predictions, 1583; with his *Plaine Percevall, the Peacemaker of England* (c.1590), in Martin Mar-Prelate controversy, provoked *Greene's *Quippe for an Upstart Courtier* (1592); his *Astrological Discourse* (1583) parodied (1592) by *Nashe, who also ridiculed his *Theologicall Discourse of the Lamb of God and his Enemies* (1590).

HARVEY, Sir Thomas (1775–1841), vice-admiral; fourth son of Sir Henry *Harvey, under whom he served, 1794–5; captain, 1797; took part in destruction of Turkish squadron in Dardanelles, 1807; KCB, 1833; vice-admiral, 1837; died at Bermuda as commander-in-chief in West Indies.

HARVEY, Thomas (1812–1884), Quaker; accompanied Joseph *Sturge to West Indies to inquire into condition of negroes, 1836; to Finland, 1856; visited Jamaica, 1866, and relieved sufferers from 'Gordon' riots; removed Mennonites from South Russia to Canada; published theological works.

HARVEY (or HERVEY), William (d. 1567), Clarenceux king-of-arms, 1557; as Norroy paid seven official visits to Germany and declared war on France, 1557; many of his visitations of English counties printed.

HARVEY, William (1578–1657), discoverer of circulation of the blood; educated at King's School, Canterbury, and Caius College, Cambridge; BA, 1597; MD, Padua and Cambridge, 1602 (Oxford, 1642); FRCP, 1607; physician to St Bartholomew's Hospital, 1609; Lumleian lecturer from 1615, when he first publicly stated his theory of circulation; named physician-extraordinary to James I, 1618; published at Frankfurt *Exercitatio Anatomica de Motu Cordis et Sanguinis in Animalibus* (1628), describing his great discovery; with Charles I in Scotland, 1633; superintended physical examination of women accused of witchcraft, 1634; attended Lord *Arundel in Germany and Italy, 1636; with Charles I at Edgehill, 1642, and at Oxford, where he was made warden of Merton College, 1645; published at Cambridge *Exercitatio Anatomica de Circulatione Sanguinis* (1649, English version 1653), in reply to Riolanus; his last work, *Exercitationes de Generatione Animalium* (1651); his statue erected at Royal College of Physicians in London, 1652, for whom he built a library; his collected works (Latin) edited by Dr *Lawrence (1766); English edition (Sydenham Society, 1847).

HARVEY, William (1796–1866), woodengraver and designer; pupil of *Bewick and *Haydon; designed for Charles *Knight; illustrations to *Northcote's Fables* (1828–33) and *Lane's *Thousand and One Nights* (1838–40) his masterpieces.

HARVEY, William Henry (1811–1866), botanist; discovered *Hookeria laete virens* at Killarney, 1831; colonial treasurer at Cape Town, 1836–42; hon. MD, Dublin, 1844, and professor of botany, 1856; lectured in America, 1849; visited India, Australia, and the South Seas, 1853–6; published *Genera of S. African Plants* (1838) and works on British and Australasian algae.

HARVEY, William Wigan (1810–1883), divine; of Eton and King's College, Cambridge; fellow of King's, 1831; MA, 1836; BD, 1855; the equity of his appointment by Gladstone to rectory of Ewelme shortly after incorporation as MA at Oxford (1871) warmly discussed in parliament, 1872; published an edition of Irenaeus (1857), and theological works.

HARVEY, William Woodis (1798–1864), author; MA, Queens' College, Cambridge, 1835; vicar of Truro, 1839–60; edited *Wesley's minor works, and published *Sketches of Hayti* (1827), with other writings.

HARWARD, Simon (*fl.* 1572–1614), divine and author; BA, Christ's College, Cambridge, 1574–5; MA, Oxford, 1578; rector of Warrington, 1579–81; vicar of Banstead, 1604; published miscellaneous works.

HARWOOD, Basil (1859–1949), musician and composer; educated at Charterhouse and Trinity College, Oxford; organist, St Barnabas, Pimlico, 1883; Ely Cathedral, 1887; Christ Church, Oxford, 1892–1909; church and organ compositions include Services in A flat and E minor and Sonata in C sharp minor; edited *Oxford Hymn Book*.

HARWOOD, Sir Busick (1745?–1814), professor of anatomy at Cambridge; after having practised as a surgeon in India graduated at Christ's College, Cambridge; MB, 1785; MD, Emmanuel, 1790; FSA, 1783; FRS, 1784; knighted, 1806; professor of anatomy (1785) and Downing professor of medicine (1800) at Cambridge; celebrated for his experiments on transfusion of blood.

HARWOOD, Sir Edward (1586?–1632), colonel; killed at Maastricht; *Advice of Sir Edward Harwood* issued with life by Hugh *Peters (1642).

HARWOOD, Edward (1729–1794), scholar and biblical critic; educated at Blackburn Grammar School; Presbyterian minister at Bristol, 1765; DD, Edinburgh, 1768, for *Introduction to New Testament Studies*. His works include *Liberal Translation of New Testament, with select Notes* (1768), a reconstructed text of the Greek Testament (1776), editions of Tibullus, Propertius, and Catullus (1774), *Biographia Classica* (2nd edn., 1778), and theological and devotional writings.

HARWOOD, Edward (d. 1814), numismatist; son of Edward *Harwood (1729–1794); published *Populorum et Urbium selecta numismata Graeca ex aere descripta* (1812).

HARWOOD, Sir Henry Harwood (1888–1950), admiral; entered navy, 1903; specialized in torpedo; captain, 1928; commanded South American division, 1936–40; fought Battle of River Plate resulting in scuttling of *Admiral Graf Spee*, Dec. 1939; rear-admiral and KCB, 1939; assistant chief of naval staff, Admiralty, 1940–2; commander-in-chief, Mediterranean (later Levant), 1942–3; engaged in flank support and seaborne supply of Eighth Army; commander-in-chief, Orkneys and Shetlands, 1944–5; admiral and invalided out, 1945.

HARWOOD, Isabella (1840?–1888), novelist and dramatist; daughter of Philip *Harwood; published successful novels, 1864–70, and, as 'Ross Neil', dramas, including *Inez* (1871) and *Pandora* (1883).

HARWOOD, Philip (1809–1887), journalist; in early life a Unitarian minister; when assistant to William Johnson *Fox introduced to John *Forster; sub-editor successively of the *Examiner, Spectator, Morning Chronicle*, 1849–54, and *Saturday Review*, 1855–68; editor of *Saturday Review*, 1868–83; published *Materialism in Religion* (1840), *German Anti-Supernaturalism* (1841), and other works.

HARWOOD, Thomas (1767–1842), author; educated at Eton, University College, Oxford, and Emmanuel College, Cambridge; DD, Cambridge, 1822; headmaster of Lichfield Grammar School, 1791–1813; incumbent of Hammerwich and Burntwood; FSA; published *Alumni Etonenses* (1797), *History of Lichfield* (1806), and other works.

HASELDEN, Thomas (d. 1740), mathematician; published *Description and Use of . . . Mercator's Chart* (1722).

HASELEY, William de (*fl.* 1266), sub-prior of Westminster; compiler of 'Consuetudinarium Monachorum Westmonasteriensium' (Cotton. MSS Otho C. xi).

HASELL, Elizabeth Julia (1830–1887), author; published books on Calderón and Tasso (1877), and devotional works.

HASELRIG, Sir Arthur (d. 1661). See HESILRIGE.

HASELWOOD, Thomas (*fl.* 1380), author of *Chronicon Compendiarium Cantuariense*; canon regular of Leeds, Kent.

HASKELL, Arnold Lionel David (1903–1980), balletomane; educated at Westminster School and Trinity Hall, Cambridge; reader for William Heinemann Ltd., 1927–32; close friend of (Dame) Alicia Markova and from 1925 had entrée to the Diaghilev Ballet; joint founder of Camargo Society, 1930; administrative assistant to Colonel de Basil's Russian Ballet on American tour, 1933–4; published widely successful book, *Balletomania* (1934); dance critic to *Daily Telegraph*, 1935–8; worked with Russian ballet on Australian tour, 1938–9; during 1939–45 war assisted Air Raid Precautions and lectured to the forces; director of new Royal Ballet School, 1946–65; established a style that influenced succeeding generations of dancers; wrote many books and articles on ballet, and *The Sculptor Speaks* (1931), a defence of (Sir) Jacob *Epstein, and books on Australia, *Waltzing Matilda* (1940), *Australia* (1941), and *The Australians* (1943); also wrote autobiographical books, *In His True Centre* (1951) and *Balletomane at Large* (1972); chevalier of Legion of Honour (1950); CBE, 1954; hon. D.Litt., Bath, 1974; FRSL, 1977; Queen Elizabeth Coronation Award of Royal Academy of Dancing, 1979.

HASLAM, John (1764–1844), medical writer; apothecary to Bethlehem Hospital; hon. MD, Aberdeen, 1816; LRCP, 1824; published *Observations on Insanity* (1798) and similar works.

HASLEM, John (1808–1884), china and enamel painter; exhibited at the Academy, 1836–65; published *The Old Derby China Factory* (1876).

HASLETON, Richard (*fl.* 1595), traveller; published *Strange and Wonderful Things*, narrative of travel (1595).

HASLETT, Dame Caroline Harriet (1895–1957), electrical engineer; educated at Haywards Heath High School; qualified in general and electrical engineering; first secretary, Women's Engineering Society, 1919, and editor of its journal, *Woman Engineer*; founded (1924) and directed until 1956 Electrical Association for Women and edited its organ *Electrical Age*; encouraged domestic use of electricity; served on British Electricity Authority and its successors, 1947–57; CBE, 1931; DBE, 1947.

HASLEWOOD, Joseph (1769–1833), antiquary; a founder of the Roxburghe Club, of which he left a manuscript account; FSA; edited *Tusser's Five Hundred Points* (1810), the *Mirror for Magistrates* (1815), and other works; published *Green-Room Gossip* (1809) and an account of Joseph *Ritson (1824).

HASSALL, Christopher Vernon (1912–1963), poet, biographer, playwright, and librettist; son of John *Hassall, painter; educated at Brighton College and Wadham College, Oxford; spent some years as actor; won Hawthornden Prize with *Penthesperon* (poems), 1938; commissioned, 1941; joined Army Education Corps, 1942; published *The Slow Night* (1949), *The Red Leaf* (1957), and *Bell Harry, and Other Poems* (posthumously, 1963); plays include *Christ's Comet*, *The Player King*, and *Out of the Whirlwind*; wrote libretti for many composers, including *Walton's *Troilus and Cressida* (1954); also published biographies, including *Edward Marsh: Patron of the Arts* (1959, awarded the James Tait Black Memorial Prize) and *Rupert Brooke* (1964); collaborated with Ivor *Novello on lyrics for *Glamorous Night* (1935); fellow, Royal Society of Literature; governor, London Academy of Music and Dramatic Art.

HASSALL (or HALSALL), Edward (*fl.* 1663), Royalist; supposed author of diary of defence of Lathom House, 1644 (Draper's 'House of Stanley'); one of the assassins of Antony *Ascham at Madrid, 1650; engaged in plot against *Cromwell, 1655; equerry to Charles II's queen, 1663.

HASSALL, James (*fl.* 1667), Royalist; brother of Edward *Hassall or Halsall; imprisoned in Tower for plot to murder *Cromwell, 1655–60; corresponded with Aphra *Behn; captain of foot at Portsmouth, 1667.

HASSALL, John (1868–1948), poster artist; educated at Newton Abbot College and Neuenheim College, Heidelberg; studied farming in Canada and art in Antwerp and Paris; began poster designing, 1895; work humorous, robust, and simple, with direct advertising message and high decorative standard; also illustrated children's books.

HASSÉ, Christian Frederick (1771–1831), musical composer; native of Russia; organist at Fulneck (Moravian settlement near Leeds); arranged music for *Polyhymnia* (words by James *Montgomery), 1822; compiled *Sacred Music*.

HASSELL, Edward (d. 1852), water-colour painter; son of John *Hassell; secretary to Society of British Artists; exhibited at Royal Academy and British Institution.

HASSELL, John (d. 1825), water-colour painter and engraver; friend and biographer of George *Morland; published *Speculum, or Art of Drawing in Water-colours* (1809), *Art of multiplying Drawings* (1811), treatise on etching (posthumous, 1836), and other works.

HASSELLS, Warner (*fl.* 1680–1710), portrait painter of the school of *Kneller.

HASTED, Edward (1732–1812), historian of Kent; of Eton and Lincoln's Inn; FRS, 1766; FSA; occupied for forty years in compilation of *History and Topographical Survey of Kent* (4 vols., 1778–99; 2nd edn., 12 vols., 1797–1801); published also genealogical tables, 1797; died master of Corsham Hospital.

HASTIE, James (1786–1825), civil agent of Great Britain in Madagascar; served in the ranks during Mahratta War; as civil agent (1817–25) negotiated treaty with Radama I of Madagascar, whom he helped to conquer the eastern, northern, and western tribes.

HASTIE, William (1842–1903), professor of divinity at Glasgow; MA, Edinburgh, 1867; BD, 1869; Croall lecturer, 1892; hon. DD, Edinburgh, 1894; principal of Church of Scotland College, Calcutta, 1878; relieved of post, 1883; professor of divinity at Glasgow, 1895; translated many German theological works; wrote *Theology as Science* (1899), *The Theology of the Reformed Church* (1904), as well as *La Vita Mia*, a sonnet sequence (1896), *The Vision of God* (1898), and other verse.

HASTINGS, Anthea Esther (1924–1981), publisher (known professionally as the Hon Mrs Michael Joseph); only daughter of Lord Justice Hodson, PC, MC; educated at Queen's Gate School, London; worked at American Embassy in London during 1939–45 war; secretary to Michael Joseph, publisher, 1946; married him, 1950; after his death in 1958 took charge of the company; deputy chairman, Michael Joseph Ltd., 1962; chairman, 1978; sensitive judge of fiction, worked with and published work of many writers, including Dick Francis, James Baldwin,

James Herriot, H. E. *Bates, Alun Richards, and Julian Rathbone; married (Douglas) Macdonald Hastings, 1963.

HASTINGS, Sir Charles (1794–1866), founder of British Medical Association; MD, Edinburgh, 1818; physician to Worcester Infirmary; formed *Provincial Medical and Surgical Association* (1832, styled British Medical Association from 1856), and established its *Journal*, 1840; knighted, 1850; Hastings Medal and Prize in his memory awarded annually by British Medical Association; published *Illustrations of Natural History of Worcestershire* (1834).

HASTINGS, Edmund, Baron Hastings of Inchmahome (d. 1314?), younger son of Henry *Hastings, first Baron Hastings; served in Scotland, 1298–1300; summoned to parliament, 1299; signed 'letter of remonstrance' to the pope, 1301; warden between Forth and Orkney, 1308; of Berwick, 1312; last summoned, 1313.

HASTINGS, Sir Edward (1381–1437), claimant of the Hastings barony; descendant of John *Hastings, second Baron Hastings, through his second wife. The right to bear the family arms was contested by Reginald *Grey, third Baron Grey of Ruthin, and decided in favour of Grey, 1410. The barony was in abeyance till 1841.

HASTINGS, Sir Edward, first Baron Hastings of Loughborough (d. 1573), third son of George *Hastings, first earl of Huntingdon; knighted, 1546; MP, Leicestershire, 1547 and 1552; a strong Romanist; created privy councillor and master of the horse by Queen Mary; opposed Mary's marriage with *Philip of Spain; MP, Middlesex, 1554 and 1555; KG, 1555; accompanied *Clinton against French, and became lord chamberlain, 1557; created a peer, 1558; imprisoned for hearing mass, 1561, but released on taking oath of supremacy.

HASTINGS, Lady Elizabeth (1682–1739), philanthropist and beauty; eulogized as Aspasia in the *Tatler* by *Steele and *Congreve; friend of William *Law and Bishop Thomas *Wilson; founded scholarships at The Queen's College, Oxford, and endowed charities at Ledsham and in Isle of Man.

HASTINGS, Lady Flora Elizabeth (1806–1839), lady of the bedchamber to duchess of Kent; daughter of Francis Rawdon *Hastings, first marquis of Hastings; subject of a court scandal, 1839; her poems published (1841).

HASTINGS, Francis, second earl of Huntingdon (1514?–1561), eldest son of George *Hastings, first earl of Huntingdon; summoned to parliament as Baron Hastings, 1529; succeeded as earl, 1545; adherent of *Dudley; KG,

1549; chief captain of army and fleet abroad, 1549; privy councillor, 1550; attempted to save Boulogne, 1550; granted Leicestershire estates of John *Beaumont (*fl.* 1550), 1552; captured with Northumberland at Cambridge, 1553, but released; as lord-lieutenant of Leicestershire arrested Henry *Grey, duke of Suffolk, 1554.

HASTINGS, Sir Francis (d. 1610), Puritan politician; fifth son of Francis *Hastings, second earl of Huntingdon; sheriff of Leicestershire, 1572 and 1581; MP, Leicestershire, 1571, 1585, 1597, Somerset, 1592, 1604; knighted, *c.*1589; cited before Privy Council for promoting petition in favour of Nonconformists, 1605; issued anti-Catholic pamphlets.

HASTINGS, Francis Rawdon-, first marquis of Hastings and second earl of Moira (1754–1826), soldier and statesman; educated at Harrow and University College, Oxford; distinguished himself at Bunker's Hill, 1775; fought in battles of Brooklyn and White Plains, 1776; adjutant-general to forces in America, 1778; commanded left wing at Camden, 1780; defeated Greene at Hobkirk's Hill, 1781; captured by French on voyage home; created Baron Rawdon, 1783; joined the opposition, 1789; intimate of prince of Wales; championed his cause on regency question, 1789; assumed additional name of Hastings, 1790; succeeded as Irish earl of Moira, 1793; commanded expedition to Brittany, 1793, and reinforcements for duke of *York in Flanders, 1794; spoke against Irish union, 1799; general, 1803; commander-in-chief in Scotland, 1803; master of the ordnance, 1806–7; active in support of prince of Wales, 1810–11; attempted, with *Wellesley, to form a ministry, 1812; governor-general of Bengal, 1813–22; carried on a successful war against Nepal, 1814–16; created marquis of Hastings, 1817; extirpated Pindaris, and by defeating Mahrattas established British supremacy in Central India, 1817–18; secured cession of Singapore, 1819; opened relations with Siam, 1822; pursued liberal policy towards natives; granted £60,000 by the East India Company, but resigned on account of the annulling by court of directors of his permission to banking house of Palmer to lend money to Hyderabad; named governor of Malta, 1824; died at sea in Baia Bay; published a summary of his Indian administration (1824); his statue, by *Chantrey, is at Dalhousie Institute, Calcutta.

HASTINGS, Frank Abney (1794–1828), naval commander in Greek War of Independence; fought at Trafalgar, 1805; dismissed British Navy for sending a challenge; joined Greeks, 1822; raised fifty men and purchased the steamer *Karteria*; attacked Turkish camp near Athens, 1827; captured several ships, destroyed fleet in Bay of Salona (1827) and took Vasiladi, 1827; died of wounds after attack on Anatolikon.

HASTINGS, George, first earl of Huntingdon and third Baron Hastings of Hastings (1488?–1545), favourite of Henry VIII; grandson of William *Hastings, Baron Hastings; succeeded as Baron Hastings, 1508; joined *Suffolk's expedition against France, 1523; created earl of Huntingdon, 1529; leader against rebels in the Pilgrimage of Grace.

HASTINGS, George Fowler (1814–1876), vice-admiral; second son of Hans Francis *Hastings, eleventh earl of Huntingdon; served in the *Harlequin* in Chinese War and against Sumatra pirates, 1841–5; captain of the *Curaçoa* during Crimean War; CB, 1857; vice-admiral, 1869; commanded in Pacific, 1866–9, at the Nore, 1873–6.

HASTINGS, Hans Francis, eleventh earl of Huntingdon (1779–1828), sailor; wounded in Quiberon Bay expedition, 1795; first lieutenant of *Thisbe* in Egyptian expedition, 1800; tried for murder while superintending impressing of seamen in Weymouth Roads, 1803; right to peerage established, 1818; governor of Dominica, 1822–4; post-captain, 1824.

HASTINGS, Henry, first Baron Hastings by writ (d. 1268), baronial leader; supported *Montfort in parliament of 1263; excommunicated as rebel, 1263; commanded Londoners at Lewes, 1264; summoned to parliament of 1265; captured at Evesham, 1265; joined *Derby at Chesterfield and held Kenilworth against the king; leader of 'the disinherited' at Ely; submitted, 1267.

HASTINGS, Henry, third earl of Huntingdon (1535–1595), son of Francis *Hastings, second earl of Huntingdon; married the duke of *Northumberland's daughter Catherine, 1553; summoned to parliament as Baron Hastings, 1559; succeeded to earldom, 1560; heir-presumptive to crown through mother; supporter of Puritans; associated with *Shrewsbury in custody of *Mary Queen of Scots, 1569–70; KG, 1570; lord-lieutenant of Leicester and Rutland, 1572; president of the north, 1572; assisted at trial of Norfolk, 1572; raised force in north, 1581; active against threatened Spanish invasion, 1588; benefactor of Emmanuel College, Cambridge; compiled family history.

HASTINGS, Henry (1551–1650), sportsman; nephew of Henry *Hastings, third earl of Huntingdon, of Woodlands, Dorset; account of him written by his neighbour, Sir Anthony Ashley *Cooper, first earl of Shaftesbury.

HASTINGS, Henry, first Baron Loughborough (d. 1667), Royalist; second son of Henry Hastings, fifth earl of Huntingdon; raised and commanded troop of horse at Edgehill, 1642; held Ashby House against parliament till 1646; called 'Rob-carrier' for frequent interception of communications between London and the north; created Baron Loughborough, 1643; distinguished at relief of Newark, 1644; governor of Leicester, 1645; escaped to Holland, 1649; Royalist conspirator; received pension and lieutenancy of Leicester, 1661.

HASTINGS, Sir Hugh (1307?–1347), soldier; elder son of John *Hastings, second Baron Hastings; summoned to parliament, 1342; served in Flanders, 1343, and Gascony, 1345–6.

HASTINGS, James (1852–1922), editor and divine; engaged in pastoral work of Scottish Free Church, 1884–1911; founder and editor of *Expository Times*, 1889–1911; works include *Dictionary of the Bible* (1898–1904) and *Encyclopaedia of Religion and Ethics* (1908–21).

HASTINGS, John, second Baron Hastings (eighth by tenure) and Baron Bergavenny (1262–1313), claimant to Scottish throne; married Isabella de Valence, niece of Henry III, 1275; served against Scots, 1285, and Welsh, 1288; claimed (1290) Scottish succession through his grandmother, Ada, third daughter of *David, earl of Huntingdon; served in Ireland, 1294; first summoned to parliament, 1295; commanded Durham contingent at siege of Caerlaverock, 1300; at parliament of Lincoln, 1301, denied pope's right to adjudicate on dispute with Scotland; king's lieutenant in Aquitaine, 1302; seneschal, 1309; received grant of Menteith estates, 1306; signed baronial letter to the pope, 1306.

HASTINGS, John, third Baron Hastings (1287–1325); served in Scottish wars, 1311–19; sided first with barons, but afterwards joined Edward II; governor of Kenilworth, 1323.

HASTINGS, John, second earl of Pembroke (1347–1375), soldier and protector of Froissart; son of Laurence *Hastings, first earl of Pembroke; KG, 1369; served with earl of *Cambridge and Black Prince in France; when lieutenant of Aquitaine was defeated and captured by Spanish fleet at La Rochelle, 1372; imprisoned three years in Spain; died in France, having been handed over to Du Guesclin.

HASTINGS, Laurence, first earl of Pembroke (1318?–1348), warrior; son of John *Hastings, third Baron Hastings; succeeded as fourth Baron Hastings (by writ), 1325; created earl palatine as representative of Aymer de *Valence, 1339, when first summoned to parliament; present at Sluys, 1340; according to *Murimuth, a knight of Round Table, 1344; prominent in Gascon campaigns, 1345–6; with *Northampton defeated French fleet near Crotoy, 1347.

HASTINGS, Sir Patrick Gardiner (1880–1952), lawyer; educated at Charterhouse; called to bar (Middle Temple), 1904; succeeded to chambers of Sir Horace *Avory, 1910; KC, 1919; Labour MP, Wallsend, 1922–6; attorney-general and knighted, 1924; his withdrawal of prosecution of Campbell of *Workers' Weekly* for sedition precipitated government's downfall; became eminent leader of common-law bar until retirement in 1948; appeared in spectacular cases such as the actions between Dr *Stopes and Dr *Sutherland, for libel by H. J. *Laski, and the Savidge tribunal; his gift for simplification expedited hearing of commercial cases; brilliant in cross-examination and addressed jury with wit and incisive appeal to intelligence; publications include *Autobiography* (1948) and *Famous and Infamous Cases* (1950); also wrote plays, including *The Blind Goddess* (1947).

HASTINGS, Selina, countess of Huntingdon (1707–1791), founder of 'Lady Huntingdon's Connection'; wife of Theophilus Hastings, ninth earl of Huntingdon; 'converted' by her sister-in-law, Lady Margaret Hastings; intimate of the *Wesleys; member of first Methodist Society in Fetter Lane, 1739; first supporter of itinerant lay preaching; employed among her chaplains, *Whitefield, *Romaine, and *Venn; intimate also of *Toplady, *Doddridge, and Dr *Watts; established first regular chapel at Brighton, 1761; set up churches in London, Bath, Tunbridge, and other aristocratic centres; her chapels registered as Dissenting meeting-houses after 1779; her training college at Trevecca opened, 1768, removed to Cheshunt, 1792. She supported Whitefield against the Wesleys, but attempted a reconciliation, 1749, and took an active part in protest against the anti-Calvinistic minutes of Wesley's Conference, 1770, and against relaxation of subscription, 1772.

HASTINGS, Theophilus, seventh earl of Huntingdon (1650–1701); volunteer in French Army, 1672; privy councillor, 1683; ecclesiastical commissioner and lord-lieutenant of Leicester and Derby, 1687–8; imprisoned for attempt to seize Plymouth for James II, 1688; a manager of conference with Commons, 1689; imprisoned on suspicion of treason, 1692.

HASTINGS, Thomas (1740?–1801), itinerant bookseller; known as 'Dr Green'; author of political pamphlets.

HASTINGS, Sir Thomas (1790–1870), admiral; commanded gunboat in Walcheren expedition, 1809; first lieutenant of the *Undaunted* at Elba, 1814; captain of the *Excellent* (training ship), 1832–45, and superintendent of RN College, Portsmouth; knighted, 1839; KCB, 1859; admiral, 1866.

HASTINGS, Thomas (*fl.* 1813–1831), amateur etcher; published *Etchings from works of Richard Wilson* (1825) and other works.

HASTINGS, Warren (1732–1818), governor-general of India; first king's scholar at Westminster, 1747; went to India, 1750; when member of council at Kasim-Bazar imprisoned by nawab of Bengal, 1756; as resident of Moorshedabad, 1757–60, corresponded with *Clive; member of Calcutta Council, 1761; despatched on mission to Patna, 1762; returned to England, 1764; gave evidence on Indian affairs before parliamentary committee, 1766; sent out as second in council at Madras, 1769; governor of Bengal, 1772; reorganized the financial and judicial system of Bengal, Bihar, and Orissa; investigated conduct of native deputy-governors; assisted, in accordance with treaty of alliance of 1764, nawab of Oudh against the Rohillas, 1773; took measures against dacoity; created governor-general by the Regulating Act, 1773; opposed by a majority of his new council and accused by Nand Kumar (Macaulay's Nuncomar) of corruption; sent home a conditional resignation and brought a counter-charge of conspiracy against Nand Kumar, who was condemned and hanged for forgery (1775) on a private suit before the case came on; had the opium trade farmed for a term of years, the proceeds being credited in the public accounts; supported by Supreme Court, which ignored the acceptance of his resignation by the directors, 1777; checked confederacy between Mahrattas and Haidar; freed himself from the opposition in council of Sir Philip *Francis (1740–1818) by wounding him in a duel, 1780; drove Haidar Ali from the Carnatic; attacked the French settlements; deposed Chait Singh and appropriated (1781) his treasure; suspected of conniving at imprisonment of the Begums of Oudh and the seizure of their land and money; concluded Treaty of Salbai with Tippoo Sultan, 1783; obtained reversal of vote of censure by directors on his treatment of Chait Singh; founded Asiatic Society of Bengal and Calcutta Madrisa, 1784; left India, 1785. His impeachment on ground of corruption and cruelty in his Indian administration, begun, 1788, and concluded, 1795, resulted, after a trial of 145 days, in an acquittal, but cost him £70,000. The company gave him pecuniary assistance; he was created privy councillor and DCL of Oxford, was presented by the prince regent to the allied sovereigns in London,

and was enabled to repurchase the family estate of Daylesford.

HASTINGS, William, Baron Hastings (1430?–1483), sheriff of Leicestershire and Warwickshire; a devoted Yorkist; created a peer by Edward IV, 1461; master of the Mint, 1461; lieutenant of Calais, 1471; lord chamberlain, 1461–83; joint ambassador with *Warwick to Charles the Bold, 1465–6; assisted Edward IV's escape to Holland, 1470; acted for him in his absence and gained over *Clarence; prominent at Barnet, 1471, and Tewkesbury, 1471; commanded English force in France, 1475; on accession of Edward V opposed *Rivers, and, declining Gloucester's overtures, was beheaded.

HATCH, Edwin (1835–1889), theologian; BA, Pembroke College, Oxford, 1857; professor of classics at Toronto, 1859–62; rector of High School, Quebec, 1862–7; vice-principal of St Mary Hall, Oxford, 1867–85; first editor of university *Gazette*, 1870; published Bampton lectures (1880) on *Organisation of Early Christian Churches*, 1881; DD, Edinburgh, 1883; Grinfield lecturer, 1882–4; reader in ecclesiastical history, 1884; Herbert lecturer on 'Greek Influence on Christianity', 1888; published also *Growth of Church Institutions* (1887), *Essays in Biblical Greek* (1889), and *Towards Fields of Light*.

HATCHARD, John (1769–1849), publisher; issued *Christian Observer*, 1802–45, and publications of Society for Bettering the Condition of the Poor.

HATCHARD, Thomas Goodwin (1817–1870), bishop of Mauritius; grandson of John *Hatchard; MA, Brasenose College, Oxford, 1845; DD, 1869; rector of Havant, 1846–56, of St Nicholas, Guildford, 1856–69; bishop of Mauritius, 1869–70; died of fever in Mauritius.

HATCHER, Henry (1777–1846), Salisbury antiquary; published translation, with commentary, of *Richard of Cirencester's *Description of Britain* (1809), and *Historical Account of Old and New Sarum* (1834); contributed to *Hoare's *Modern Wiltshire* and *Britton's *Beauties of Wiltshire* (1825), and *Picturesque Antiquities* (1830).

HATCHER, Thomas (d. 1583), antiquary; of Eton and King's College, Cambridge; MA, 1563; admitted at Gray's Inn, 1565; friend and correspondent of *Stow and Dr John *Caius; began catalogue of King's College, Cambridge, and edited *Haddon's *Lucubrationes* (1567) and Carr's *De scriptorum Britannicorum paucitate* (1576).

HATCHER, Thomas (1589?–1677), Parliamentarian captain; grandson of Thomas *Hatcher (d. 1583); MP, Lincoln, Grantham, Stamford (in

Long Parliament), and Lincolnshire, 1654–9; commissioner to Scotland, 1643; present at Marston Moor, 1644, and siege of York, 1644.

HATCHETT, Charles (1765?–1847), chemist; FRS, 1797; treasurer of the Literary Club, 1814; chief works, treatise on *Spikenard of the Ancients* (1836) and *Analysis of the Magnetical Pyrites* (1804).

HATCLIFFE, Vincent (1601–1671). See SPENCER, JOHN.

HATFIELD, John (1758?–1803), forger; married and deserted a natural daughter of Lord Robert *Manners; twice released from a debtor's prison by duke of *Rutland; imprisoned seven years at Scarborough, from 1792; released and married Miss Nation, 1800; deserted her and lived in Cumberland as brother of Lord *Hopetoun; married Mary *Robinson, the 'Buttermere Beauty', 1802; tried at Carlisle for forgery and hanged.

HATFIELD, Martha (*fl.* 1652), cataleptic; her case described in *The Wise Virgin* (1653).

HATFIELD, Thomas of (d. 1381), bishop of Durham; keeper of the privy seal, 1338–44; accompanied Edward III to France, 1346 and 1355; bishop of Durham, 1345–81; commissioner to treat for peace with Scotland, 1350–7 and subsequently; resisted visitations of archbishops of York; at Durham built part of south side of cathedral choir and hall of castle; founded Carmelite house of Northallerton and college at Oxford for Durham monks; his survey of Durham edited by W. Greenwell, 1857.

HATHAWAY, Richard (*fl.* 1702), impostor; sentenced to fine, pillory, and hard labour for imposture, riot, and assault, 1702.

HATHERLEY, Baron (1801–1881). See WOOD, WILLIAM PAGE.

HATHERTON, first Baron (1791–1863). See LITTLETON, EDWARD JOHN.

HATHWAY, Richard (*fl.* 1602), dramatist; mentioned by *Meres (1598) among best contemporary writers of comedy; part author of *First Part of the True and Honorable Historie of the Life of Sir John Old-castle* (1599) and of unprinted plays.

HATRY, Clarence Charles (1888–1965), company promoter and financier; educated at St Paul's School, London; took over bankrupt business on death of his father, 1906; established as insurance broker, 1911; purchased and resold Leyland Motors with large profit; registered his Commercial Bank of London, 1920; a shrewd gambler who made large gains and large losses; registered the Austin Friars Trust group, 1927; firms taken over and reorganized as the Drapery Trust and Allied Ironfounders; with another of his companies, Corporation and General Securities, attempted to take over United Steel, 1929; failure of this project led to heavy losses by investors, prosecution, and admission of forgery; sentenced by Mr Justice *Avory to fourteen years penal servitude, 1930; released by home secretary, 1939; published *Light out of Darkness* (1939); continued his career as financier, with fluctuating fortunes, 1940–65.

HATSELL, Sir Henry (1641–1714), judge; BA, Exeter College, Oxford, 1659; barrister, Middle Temple, 1667; serjeant-at-law, 1689; knighted, 1697; baron of the Exchequer, 1697–1702 (removed).

HATSELL, John (1743–1820), clerk of House of Commons; of Queens' College, Cambridge, and Middle Temple; senior bencher; clerk of House of Commons, 1768–97; published *A Collection of Cases of Privilege of Parliament . . . to 1628* (1776) and *Precedents of Proceedings in House of Commons* (1781).

HATTECLYFFE, William (*fl.* 1500), under-treasurer of Ireland, 1495.

HATTECLYFFE, William (d. 1480), physician and secretary to Edward IV; original scholar of King's College, Cambridge, 1440; physician to Henry VI, 1454; captured by Lancastrians, 1470; afterwards master of requests and royal councillor.

HATTON. See also FINCH-HATTON.

HATTON, Sir Christopher (1540–1591), lord chancellor; gentleman-commoner, St Mary Hall, Oxford, *c.*1555; took part in masque at Inner Temple, 1561; became one of Elizabeth's gentlemen-pensioners, 1564; received grant of estates, court offices, and an annuity; MP, Higham Ferrers, 1571, Northamptonshire, 1572, 1584, and 1586; knighted, 1577; captain of the bodyguard, 1572; charged with being Elizabeth's paramour by *Mary Queen of Scots, 1584; the bishop of Ely ordered to surrender fee-simple of Ely Place, Holborn, for his benefit; made vice-chamberlain and knighted, 1578; the queen's mouthpiece in parliament; opposed the queen's match with the duke of Anjou, 1581; member of committees for trials of *Babington, 1586, and Mary Queen of Scots, 1586; spoke strongly in parliament against Mary, and advised *Davison to despatch warrant for her execution, 1587; high steward of Cambridge University, 1588; lord chancellor, 1587–91; assisted by Sir Richard *Swale, and had four masters in Chancery as assessors; KG, and chancellor of Oxford, 1588; friend and patron of *Spenser and *Churchyard; wrote act iv of *Tancred and Gismund*, acted at Inner Temple, 1568; buried in St Paul's Cathedral; his correspondence printed (1847).

HATTON, Christopher, first Baron Hatton (1605?–1670), Royalist; relative of Sir Christopher *Hatton; MA, Jesus College, Cambridge, 1622; KB, 1626; MP, Peterborough, 1625, Higham Ferrers, 1640; hon. DCL, Oxford, 1642; created Baron Hatton and privy councillor, 1643; comptroller of Charles I's household, 1643–6; royal commissioner at Uxbridge, 1645; retired to Paris, 1648; allowed to return, 1656; privy councillor and governor of Guernsey, 1662; FRS, 1663; published psalter with prayers (1644).

HATTON, Christopher, first Viscount Hatton (1632–1706), governor of Guernsey; elder son of Christopher, first Baron *Hatton; succeeded as second baron, 1670; his mother and first wife killed by explosion of powder magazine in Guernsey, 1672; presented to Bodleian Anglo-Saxon Homilies, 1675; created Viscount Hatton, 1683; *custos rotulorum* of Northampton, 1681–9; hon. DCL, Oxford, 1683; selection from correspondence edited (1878).

HATTON, Edward (1701–1783), Dominican; provincial, 1754 and 1770; his *Memoirs of the Reformation of England* appeared with pseudonym 'Constantius Archæophilus' (1826 and 1841).

HATTON, Frank (1861–1883), mineral explorer to British North Borneo Company, 1881–3; accidentally killed in jungle; left interesting letters and diaries.

HATTON, Harold Heneage Finch- (1856–1904), imperialist politician. See FINCH-HATTON.

HATTON, John Liptrot (1809–1886), musical composer; organist in three Lancashire churches at 16, afterwards at St Nicholas, Chapel Street, Liverpool; appeared in London as an actor, 1832–3; directed opera choruses at Drury Lane, 1842–3; produced his *Queen of the Thames*, 1843; his *Pascal Bruno* given at Vienna for Staudigl's benefit, 1844; on return published trios and eighteen songs, including 'To Anthea'; sang and played on tour and in America, 1848–50; conductor of Glee and Madrigal Union, c.1850; conductor for Charles *Kean at Princess's Theatre, London, 1853–9; his cantata *Robin Hood* produced at Bradford, 1856; his opera *Rose* at Covent Garden, 1864, and his oratorio *Hezekiah* at Crystal Palace, 1877; edited collections of old English songs; composed 300 songs and excellent part-songs.

HATTON, Joseph (1841–1907), novelist and journalist; editor successively of *Bristol Mirror* (1863–8), *Gentleman's Magazine* (1868), *Sunday Times*, and *People* (1892); published American experiences in *Today in America* (2 vols., 1881); accompanied (Sir) Henry *Irving to America, 1883; chronicled Irving's *Impressions of America* (2 vols., 1884), and *Reminiscences* of J. L. *Toole (2 vols., 1889); published novels *Clytie* (1874—which he dramatized) and *By Order of the Czar* (1890), *The New Ceylon* (1882), *Journalistic London* (1882), and other works.

HATTON, Sir Ronald George (1886–1965), horticultural scientist; educated at Brighton College, Exeter School, and Balliol College, Oxford; worked as farm labourer; published *Folk of the Furrow* under pen-name, Christopher Holdenby (1913); studied agriculture at Wye College, Kent, 1912; acting director, East Malling Research Station, 1914; director, 1918–49; developed East Malling into leading fruit-research institute in the world; classified and standardized root-stocks; collaborated effectively with John Innes Horticultural Institute and Institute of Plant Physiology, Imperial College of Science, London; instrumental in starting the *Journal of Pomology*, 1919, which became the *Journal of Horticultural Science*, 1948; joint editor, 1924–47; first director, Imperial (later Commonwealth) Bureau of Horticulture and Plantation Crops, 1929; vice-president, Royal Horticultural Society, 1952; CBE, 1934; knighted, 1949; FRS, 1944; fellow, Wye College, 1949.

HAUGHTON, Sir Graves Champney (1788–1849), orientalist; served in Indian Army and studied at Baraset and Fort William; professor of Sanskrit and Bengali at Haileybury, 1819–27; hon. MA, Oxford, 1819; FRS, 1821; foreign member of Paris Asiatic Society and Institute of France; honorary secretary of Royal Asiatic Society, 1831–2; KH, 1833; issued Bengali grammar, glossaries, and texts, an edition of *Institutes of Menu* (1825), Bengali–Sanskrit dictionary (1833), *Prodromus* (1839), and other metaphysical treatises; died of cholera at St Cloud.

HAUGHTON, James (1795–1873), philanthropist; friend and supporter of Father *Mathew and *O'Connell; prominent in anti-slavery, temperance, and other social movements; president of Vegetarian Society; published *Slavery Immoral* (1847), *Memoir of T. Clarkson* (1847), and *Plea for Teetotalism* (1855).

HAUGHTON, John Colpoys (1817–1887), lieutenant-general; nephew of Sir Graves Champney *Haughton; as adjutant of 4th Gurkhas distinguished himself in defence of Char-i-kar, 1841, publishing an account, 1867; escaped wounded to Kabul; commissioner at Cooch Behar, 1865–73; CSI, 1866; lieutenant-general, 1882.

HAUGHTON, Moses, the elder (1734–1804), still-life and enamel painter; exhibited at Academy, 1788–1804.

HAUGHTON, Moses, the younger (1772?–1848?), miniaturist and engraver; nephew of Moses *Haughton the elder; friend of *Fuseli; exhibited at Royal Academy, 1808–48.

HAUGHTON, Samuel (1821–1897), man of science; son of James *Haughton; BA and fellow, Trinity College, Dublin, 1844; MA, 1852; senior fellow, 1881; ordained priest, 1847; professor of geology, Dublin University, 1851–81; MD, Dublin, 1862; registrar of Medical School, subsequently chairman of Medical School Committee, and university representative on General Medical Council; member of council of Royal Zoological Society of Ireland, 1860 (president, 1883); FRS, 1858; hon. DCL, Oxford, 1868; hon. LL D, Cambridge, 1881; hon. LL D, Edinburgh, 1884; president of Royal Irish Academy, 1887; published scientific works and papers.

HAUGHTON, William (fl. 1598), dramatist; author of *English-Men for my Money* (1616); collaborator with *Dekker, *Chettle, John *Day, and others.

HAUKSBEE, Francis, the elder (d. 1713?), electrician; FRS, 1705; contrived first electrical machine, 1706; published *Physico-Mechanical Experiments* (1709); suggested an improved air-pump; determined relative weight of water and air.

HAUKSBEE, Francis, the younger (1687–1763), writer on science; perhaps son of Francis *Hauksbee the elder; clerk and housekeeper to Royal Society, 1723; published (with P. *Shaw) *Essay for introducing a Portable Laboratory* (1731), and syllabus for courses of experimental lectures (which he was the first to give, c.1714), also *Course of Mechanical, Optical, and Pneumatical Experiments* (with W. Whiston).

HAUSTED, Peter (d. 1645), dramatist; MA, Queens' College, Cambridge, 1627; rector of Hadham, vicar of Gretton; DD, Oxford, 1642; died at Banbury Castle during the siege; published, among other works, *The Rival Friends* (comedy, 1632), and *Senile Odium* (Latin play, 1633); his *Hymnus Tabaci*, by 'Raphael Thorius', appeared (1650).

HAUTEVILLE, John de (fl. 1184), Latin poet; his satire *Architrenius* first printed at Paris (1517).

HAVARD, William (1710?–1778), actor and dramatist; appeared at Goodman's Fields, 1730–7; at Drury Lane till retirement, 1769, playing generally secondary parts; depreciated in *Rosciad*; appeared also in his own plays, *King Charles I*, at Lincoln's Inn Fields (1737), *Regulus*,

Drury Lane (1744), and *The Elopement*, Drury Lane (1763).

HAVELL, Robert, the elder (fl. 1800–1840), engraver and art publisher; issued aquatint engravings from drawings by W. *Havell and others, 1812–28; published Audubon's *Birds of America*, Salt's *Views in Africa*, and other works.

HAVELL, Robert, the younger (fl. 1820–1850), painter; son of Robert *Havell the elder; settled in America as landscape painter.

HAVELL, William (1782–1857), landscape painter; original member of Old Water-Colour Society; visited China and India, 1816–25; after his return painted in oil, exhibiting (Italian subjects) at Royal Academy, British Institution, and Suffolk Street; died a Turner pensioner.

HAVELOCK, Sir Arthur Elibank (1844–1908), colonial governor; son of William *Havelock; joined army, 1862; retired, 1877; held administrative posts in West Indies, 1874–81; CMG, 1880; governor of West African Settlements, 1881; forcibly settled frontier dispute with Liberia, and occupied territories between rivers Sherbro and Mano, 1882–3; KCMG, 1884; governor of Natal (1886–9), of Ceylon (1890–5), where he extended railways and abolished levy on rice cultivation, of Madras (1895–1901), and of Tasmania (1901–4); GCMG, 1895; GCIE, 1896; GCSI, 1901.

HAVELOCK, Sir Henry, first baronet (1795–1857), major-general; intimate at Charterhouse of Julius *Hare; studied at Middle Temple under Joseph *Chitty; entered army, 1815; went to India as subaltern in 13th, 1823; deputy assistant adjutant-general in Burmese expedition, 1824–6, publishing narrative (1828); while stationed at Chinsurah became a Baptist; regimental adjutant, 1835–8; aide-de-camp to Sir Willoughby *Cotton in first Afghan campaign, 1839, of which he published an account; Persian interpreter to General William G. K. *Elphinstone in Afghanistan, 1840; accompanied Sir R. *Sale to the passes, and assisted him in holding Jellalabad, 1841; returned with *Pollock to Kabul, and accompanied Hindu Khush and Kohistan expedition; CB and brevet-major, 1842; interpreter to Sir Hugh *Gough in Gwalior campaign, 1843; present at Mudki, 1845, Ferozeshah, 1845, and Sobraon, 1846; deputy adjutant-general, Bombay, 1847; visited England for last time, 1849–51; planned the operations at Mohumra in Persian War of 1857; during the Indian Mutiny commanded a column which recaptured Cawnpore, after winning four victories and marching 120 miles in nine days, 17 July 1857; major-general, 1857; defeated the sepoys at Onao and thrice at Busseerutgunge, but owing to sickness and want of ammunition was compelled to fall back on Cawnpore, Aug. 1857; reinforced by *Outram; carried the Allumbagh and effected first relief of Lucknow, Sept. 1857; co-operated with Sir Colin *Campbell in second relief, Nov. 1857; died of diarrhoea on morning of withdrawal. He had been created KCB and a baronet, with a pension of £1,000, Nov. 1857.

HAVELOCK, Sir Thomas Henry (1877–1968), naval mathematician; educated at Durham College of Physical Science, Newcastle upon Tyne, and St John's College, Cambridge; B.Sc., 1895; first class, part ii, mathematics tripos, 1901; suffered serious injury in an accident, 1898; Gregson fellow, St John's College, 1903; lecturer in applied mathematics, Armstrong College (formerly Durham College of Science), 1906; D.Sc., 1907; FRS, 1914; professor of applied mathematics, 1915; his injury precluded active service, 1914–18; carried out research on optics and naval hydrodynamics; professor of pure and applied mathematics, 1928–45; hon. member, Royal Institution of Naval Architects, 1943; hon. DCL, Durham, 1958; hon. D.Sc., Hamburg, 1960; hon. fellow, St John's College, Cambridge, 1945; knighted, 1951; succeeded Sir Westcott *Abell as honorary acting head of Department of Naval Architecture, 1941–4; vice-principal, Armstrong College, 1933–7; sub-rector, King's College, Newcastle upon Tyne, 1937–42.

HAVELOCK, William (1793–1848), lieutenant-colonel; brother of Sir Henry *Havelock; aide-de-camp in Peninsula and at Waterloo to Count *Alten; distinguished at Vera, 1813; aide-de-camp to Sir Charles *Colville at Bombay; military secretary to Lord *Elphinstone at Madras; lieutenant-colonel, 14th Dragoons, 1841; mortally wounded at Ramnuggur in second Sikh War, 1848.

HAVELOCK-ALLAN, Sir Henry Marshman, first baronet (1830–1897), lieutenant-general; son of Sir Henry *Havelock; ensign, 1846; adjutant, 10th Foot, 1852; captain, 18th Foot (Royal Irish Regiment), 1857; brevet-lieutenant-colonel, 1859; unattached major, 1864; brevet-colonel, 1868; major-general, 1878; lieutenant-general, 1881; colonel of Royal Irish Regiment of Foot, 1878; in Persian War and Indian Mutiny, 1857–9; took part in defence of Lucknow; received Victoria Cross, 1858; created baronet on death of his father, 1858; in Maori War, 1863–4; CB, 1866; assistant quartermaster-general in Canada, 1867–9, and in Dublin, 1869; Liberal MP for Sunderland, 1874–81, and south-east Durham county, 1885; assumed additional name of Allan, 1880; Liberal-Unionist MP for south-east Durham county, 1886–92 and

1895; KCB, 1897; killed while visiting British troops on Afghan frontier.

HAVERFIELD, Francis John (1860–1919), Roman historian and archaeologist; scholar of Winchester and New College, Oxford; a senior student of Christ Church, 1892–1907; Camden professor of ancient history and fellow of Brasenose, 1907–19; created scientific study of Roman Britain; works include *Romanization of Roman Britain* (1905) and *Roman Occupation of Britain* (Ford's lectures, published 1924).

HAVERGAL, Frances Ridley (1836–1879), writer of religious verse; daughter of William Henry *Havergal; published *Ministry of Song* (1870) and other hymns and poems; *Poetical Works* issued (1884); autobiography in *Memorials* (2nd edn., 1880).

HAVERGAL, Francis Tebbs (1829–1890), author; son of William Henry *Havergal; MA, New College, Oxford, 1857; vicar-choral (1853–74) and prebendary of Hereford, 1877–90; published *Fasti Herefordenses* (1869), *Herefordshire Words and Phrases* (1887), and other works.

HAVERGAL, Henry East (1820–1875), musician; son of William Henry *Havergal; MA, Magdalen Hall, Oxford, 1846; chaplain at Christ Church and New College, Oxford; while vicar of Cople, Bedfordshire, 1847–75, constructed organ and chiming apparatus; vocalist and instrumentalist; author of musical publications.

HAVERGAL, William Henry (1793–1870), composer of sacred music; educated at Merchant Taylors' School and St Edmund Hall, Oxford; MA, 1819; rector of Astley, 1829, of St Nicholas, Worcester, 1845; vicar of Shareshill, 1860; gained Gresham Prize for Evening Service in A, 1836, and for anthem, *Give Thanks*, 1841; composed *A Hundred Psalm and Hymn Tunes* (1859); published *Old Church Psalmody* (1847) and other works.

HAVERS, Alice (1850–1890). See MORGAN, Mrs ALICE MARY.

HAVERS, Clopton (1657–1702), physician and anatomist; of Catharine Hall, Cambridge; MD, Utrecht, 1685; LRCP, 1687; FRS, 1686; his chief anatomical work, *Osteologia Nova*, giving the first minute account of the structure of bone, printed (1691); the 'Haversian canals' named after him.

HAVERSHAM, first Baron (1647–1710). See THOMPSON, Sir JOHN.

HAVERTY, Joseph Patrick (1794–1864), painter; executed portraits of *O'Connell and Bishop *Doyle.

HAVERTY, Martin (1809–1887), historian; brother of Joseph Patrick *Haverty; educated at Irish College, Paris; sub-librarian of King's Inns, Dublin; published *History of Ireland* (1860) and *Wanderings in Spain* (1844).

HAVILAND, John (1785–1851), professor of medicine at Cambridge; of Winchester and St John's College, Cambridge; twelfth wrangler, 1807; fellow; MA, 1810; professor of anatomy, Cambridge, 1814; regius professor of medicine, 1817–51; FRCP, 1818; MD, 1817; Harveian orator, 1837.

HAVILAND, William (1718–1784), general; aide-de-camp to *Blakeney, 1745–6; lieutenant-colonel of 27th, 1752; served in North America, 1757–60, under *Abercromby and *Amherst, rendering valuable assistance in capture of Montreal, 1760; invented a pontoon for rapids; second-in-command at reduction of Martinique; commanded brigade at capture of Havana, 1762; general, 1783; friend and connection of *Burke.

HAVILLAND, Sir Geoffrey de (1882–1965), aircraft designer and manufacturer. See DE HAVILLAND.

HAVILLAND, Thomas Fiott de (1775–1866), lieutenant-colonel in Madras Army; served at siege of Pondicherry, 1793, reduction of Ceylon, 1795–6, in operations against Tippoo Sahib, 1799, and in Egypt, 1801; as architect of Madras, 1814–25, built cathedral and St Andrew's Presbyterian Church; lieutenant-colonel, 1824; member of Guernsey Legislature.

HAWARD, Francis (1759–1797), engraver; exhibited at Academy engravings after *Reynolds and other artists; associate engraver, 1783.

HAWARD, Nicholas (fl. 1569), author; of Thavies Inn; published *The Line of Liberalitie dulie directinge the wel bestowing of Benefites*, etc. (1569).

HAWARD, Simon (fl. 1572–1614). See HARWARD.

HAWARDEN, Edward (1662–1735), Roman Catholic controversialist; vice-president of Douai College, 1690–1707; head of Romanist colony at Oxford, 1688–9; disputed with Samuel *Clarke on the Trinity before Queen *Caroline, 1719; published against *Leslie's *The Case Stated, The True Church of Christ* (1714–15), *Charity and Truth* (1728) against *Chillingworth's *Religion of Protestants*, and *Answer to Dr. Clarke and Mr. Whiston concerning the Divinity of the Son and of the Holy Spirit* (1729).

HAWEIS, Hugh Reginald (1838–1901), author and preacher; grandson of Thomas *Haweis; showed musical ability, especially as violinist, from boyhood; lame through hip disease; BA, Trinity College, Cambridge, 1859; started university magazine *Lion*; travelled for health in Italy, 1859–60; incumbent of St James's, Westmoreland Street, Marylebone, from 1866 till death; by means of somewhat sensational methods filled the church; organized 'Sunday evenings for the people'; pioneer of Sunday opening of museums; published *Music and Morals* (1871), *My Musical Life* (1884), *Old Violins* (1898); theological writings include *Thoughts for the Times* (1872), *Winged Words* (1885), and *Christ and Christianity* (5 vols., 1886–7); successful lecturer on music; Lowell lecturer at Boston, 1885; toured the colonies, 1893; described experiences in *Travel and Talk* (2 vols., 1896); visited Rome, 1897; married in 1867 **Mary** (d. 1898), daughter of Thomas Musgrave *Joy; she published *Chaucer for Children* (1877), *Chaucer for Schools* (1880), and other works; a capable artist, she exhibited at Royal Academy.

HAWEIS, Mary (d. 1898). See under HAWEIS, HUGH REGINALD.

HAWEIS, Thomas (1734–1820), divine; studied at Christ Church and Magdalen Hall, Oxford; assistant to Martin *Madan at Lock Chapel; rector of Aldwinkle, Northamptonshire, 1764–1820; LL B, Cambridge, 1772; manager of Trevecca College; trustee and executor of Selina *Hastings, countess of Huntingdon, 1791; published, among other works, *Life of William Romaine* (1797) and *History of Rise, Declension, and Revival of the Church* (1800); edited John *Newton's *Authentic Narrative* (1764).

HAWES, Sir Benjamin (1797–1862), under-secretary for war; Whig MP, Lambeth, 1832–47, Kinsale, 1848–52; caused appointment of Fine Arts Commission and opening of British Museum on holidays; advocate of penny postage and electric telegraph; under-secretary for colonies, 1846; KCB, 1856; under-secretary for war, 1857–62; published narrative of ascent of Mont Blanc (1827).

HAWES, Edward (fl. 1606), poet; author, while at Westminster School, of *Trayterous Percyes and Catesbyes Prosopopeia* (1606).

HAWES, Richard (1603?–1668), Puritan divine; MA, Corpus Christi College, Cambridge, 1627; when rector of Kentchurch tried by Royalists for supposed conspiracy; ejected from vicarage of Leintwardine, 1662, but occasionally allowed to preach.

HAWES, Robert (1665–1731), topographer; part of his manuscript history of Framlingham and Loes-Hundred printed by R. Loder (1798).

HAWES, Stephen (d. 1523?), poet; groom of the chamber to Henry VII; his *Passetyme of Pleasure, or History of Graunde Amoure and la Bel Pucel* first printed by Wynkyn de *Worde (1509, reprinted by *Southey, 1831); other works by him reprinted (ed. David *Laing, 1865).

HAWES, William (1736–1808), founder of Royal Humane Society; educated at St Paul's School; MP; physician to London Dispensary; founded Royal Humane Society, 1774; published account of *Goldsmith's illness (1774), examination of *John Wesley's Primitive Physic* (1776), and tracts on premature interment and suspended animation.

HAWES, William (1785–1846), singer and composer; chorister, gentleman, and master of children (1817) at Chapel Royal; original associate of Philharmonic Society; almoner and vicar-choral at St Paul's, 1814; lay vicar of Westminster, 1817–20; assisted Arnold in management of English opera at Lyceum; conducted Madrigal Society and directed oratorios; composed songs and glees and edited, among other works, *Triumphs of Oriana* (1818).

HAWFORD, Edward (d. 1582), master of Christ's College, Cambridge; BA, Jesus College, Cambridge, 1543; fellow of Christ's College; MA, 1545; master of Christ's College, 1559–82; DD, 1564; vice-chancellor, 1563–4; took part in framing of university statutes, 1570.

HAWKE, Edward, first Baron Hawke (1705–1781), admiral of the fleet; brought up by his uncle, Martin *Bladen; entered navy as volunteer, 1720; first saw fighting as commander of the *Berwick* in Battle of Toulon, 1744; promoted rear-admiral of the white by special interposition of George II, 1747; defeated and captured great part of French squadron protecting convoy from Rochelle, 1747; KB, 1747; MP, Portsmouth, 1747; commanded Home Fleet, 1748–52; presided over courts martial (1750) on admirals Sir Charles *Knowles and Thomas *Griffin; commanded Western Fleet, 1755–6, Mediterranean Fleet, 1756; admiral, 1757; co-operated with Sir John *Mordaunt in the Rochefort expedition, 1757; succeeded in delaying, but failed to destroy, French convoy for America, 1758; struck his flag owing to his treatment by Admiralty, but resuming his command blockaded Brest from May to Nov. 1759; in heavy weather defeated Conflans in Quiberon Bay, 20 Nov. 1759, capturing five ships and running others ashore; thanked by parliament and given a pension of £1,500 for two lives; after capturing Spanish treasure-ships finally struck his flag, 1762; first lord of the Admiralty, 1766–71; admiral of the fleet, 1768; created Baron Hawke of Great Britain, 1776.

HAWKE, Sir (Edward) Anthony (1895–1964), judge; son of (Sir) (John) Anthony

*Hawke, judge; educated at Charterhouse and Magdalen College, Oxford; called to bar (Middle Temple) 1920; joined western circuit and Devon sessions; junior prosecuting counsel, Central Criminal Court, 1932; third senior prosecuting counsel, 1937; second senior prosecuting counsel, 1942; senior prosecuting counsel, 1945–50; recorder, Bath, 1939–50; deputy chairman, Hertfordshire quarter-sessions, 1940–50; bencher, 1942; chairman, county of London quarter-sessions, 1950; knighted; common serjeant, City of London, 1954; recorder of London, 1959; treasurer, Middle Temple, 1962; edited fifteenth edition of Roscoe's *Criminal Evidence*.

HAWKE, Sir (John) Anthony (1869–1941), judge; first class, jurisprudence, St John's College, Oxford, 1891; called to bar (Inner Temple), 1892; KC, 1913; recorder of Plymouth, 1912–28; attorney-general to prince of Wales, 1923–8; judge, King's Bench division, 1928–41; Conservative MP, St Ives, 1922–3, 1924–8; knighted, 1928.

HAWKE, Martin Bladen, seventh Baron Hawke of Towton (1860–1938), cricketer; played in Eton (1878, 1879) and Cambridge (1882, 1883, 1885) elevens; captained Yorkshire, 1883–1910; took teams to India, West Indies, South Africa, etc.; president, MCC, 1914–18; succeeded father, 1887.

HAWKER, Edward (1782–1860), admiral; son of James *Hawker; entered navy, 1793; successful in cruising against privateers in Mediterranean; flag-captain to Sir Richard *Keats at Newfoundland, 1813–15, to earl of *Northesk at Plymouth, 1827–30; admiral, 1853; correspondent of *The Times* as 'A Flag Officer'.

HAWKER, James (d. 1787), captain in the navy; posted, 1768; with the *Iris* fought drawn battle with *La Touche Tréville* in the *Hermione* off New York, 1780; commanded the *Hero* in Porto Praya under Commodore G. *Johnstone, 1781.

HAWKER, Mary Elizabeth (1848–1908), novelist writing under the pseudonym of Lanoe Falconer; granddaughter of Peter *Hawker; gained success as novelist by *Mademoiselle Ixe* (1890), translated into many foreign languages, *Cecilia de Noel*, and *The Hôtel d'Angleterre* (both 1891).

HAWKER, Peter (1786–1853), soldier and author; served with 14th Light Dragoons in Peninsula; badly wounded at Talavera, 1809; retired, 1813; patented improvements in pianoforte, 1820; published military journal (1810), *Instructions to Young Sportsmen* (1814).

HAWKER, Robert (1753–1827), divine and author; member of Magdalen Hall, Oxford, 1778; curate of Charles, near Plymouth, 1778, vicar, 1784; DD, Edinburgh, 1792; highly popular as extempore preacher; published numerous devotional works, also *Concordance and Dictionary to Sacred Scriptures*; collected works edited (1831).

HAWKER, Robert Stephen (1803–1875), poet and antiquary; grandson of Robert *Hawker; matriculated at Pembroke College, Oxford, 1823; MA, Magdalen Hall, 1836; Newdigate prizeman, 1827; vicar of Morwenstow, 1834, with Wellcombe, 1851; became Romanist in last days; published *Quest of the Sangraal* (1864), *Cornish Ballads and other Poems* (1869), and other verse, including 'And shall Trelawny die', *Records of the Western Shore* (1832, 1836), and *Footprints of Former Men in Far Cornwall* (1870).

HAWKER, Thomas (d. 1723?), portrait painter.

HAWKESBURY, first Baron (1727–1808). See JENKINSON, CHARLES, first earl of Liverpool.

HAWKESWORTH, John (1715?–1773), author; said to have succeeded *Johnson as compiler of parliamentary debates for *Gentleman's Magazine*, 1744; with him and *Warton carried on the *Adventurer*, 1752–4; edited *Swift's works (1755); LL D, Lambeth, 1756; his *Edgar and Emmeline* produced at Drury Lane, 1761; published an account of voyages in the South Seas, 1773, when he became a director of the East India Company; early friend and imitator of Johnson.

HAWKESWORTH, Walter (d. 1606), dramatist; major fellow, Trinity College, Cambridge, 1595; MA, 1595; acted in his own comedies, *Leander* and *Pedantius*, 1603; secretary to Sir Charles *Cornwallis in Spain, c.1605; died of the plague in Spain.

HAWKEY, John (1703–1759), classical scholar; graduate of Trinity College, Dublin, 1725; edited Virgil, Horace, and Terence (1745), Juvenal and Persius (1746), Sallust (1747).

HAWKINS, Sir Anthony Hope (1863–1933), novelist under pseudonym of Anthony Hope; educated at Marlborough and Balliol College, Oxford; first class, Lit. Hum., 1885; president of Union, 1886; abandoned practice at bar after success (1894) of *The Prisoner of Zenda*, a modern romance of adventure, and the delicately witty *Dolly Dialogues*; later works included Ruritanian stories, analytical novels of character, and plays; knighted, 1918.

HAWKINS, Sir Caesar, baronet (1711–1786), surgeon; surgeon to St George's Hospital, 1735–74; sergeant-surgeon to George II and George III; created baronet, 1778; invented the cutting gorget.

HAWKINS, Caesar Henry (1798–1884), surgeon; grandson of Sir Caesar *Hawkins; educated at Christ's Hospital and St George's Hospital; surgeon to St George's Hospital, 1829–61; consulting surgeon, 1861; Hunterian orator, 1849; president of College of Surgeons, 1852 and 1861; sergeant-surgeon to Queen Victoria, 1862; FRS; first successful practiser of ovariotomy; collected works issued (1874).

HAWKINS, Edward (1780–1867), numismatist; keeper of antiquities at British Museum, 1826–60; FRS, 1821, FSA, 1826 (vice-president of both); president of London Numismatic Society; published *Silver Coins of England* (1841) and *Medallic Illustrations of the History of Great Britain and Ireland* (1885); his collection of medals and political caricatures purchased by British Museum, 1860.

HAWKINS, Edward (1789–1882), provost of Oriel College, Oxford; brother of Caesar Henry *Hawkins; educated at Merchant Taylors' School and St John's College, Oxford; MA, 1814; DD, 1828; fellow of Oriel, 1813; vicar of St Mary's, 1823–8; provost of Oriel, 1828–74; canon of Rochester, 1828–82; Bampton lecturer, 1840; first Ireland professor of exegesis, 1847–61; though a High Churchman opposed Tractarian movement and (1841) drew up condemnation of Tract XC; retired to Rochester, 1874; published an edition of *Milton's poetry with *Newton's life (1824), *A Manual for Christians* (1826), and sermons and pamphlets on university affairs.

HAWKINS, Ernest (1802–1868), canon of Westminster; MA, Balliol College, Oxford, 1827; BD, 1839; fellow of Exeter College, 1831; sub-librarian of Bodleian, 1831; secretary of the SPG, 1843–64, canon of Westminster, 1864–8; minister of Curzon Chapel, Mayfair, 1850; vice-president, Bishop's College, Cape Town, 1859; published works relating to history of missions.

HAWKINS, Francis (1628–1681), Jesuit; son of John *Hawkins (*fl.* 1635); professor of holy scripture at Liège College, 1675–81; translated, at age of 8, *Youth's Behaviour*, first printed (1641).

HAWKINS, Francis (1794–1877), physician; brother of Caesar Henry *Hawkins; educated at Merchant Taylors' School and St John's College, Oxford; fellow; Newdigate prizeman, 1813; BCL, 1819; MD, 1823; FRCP, 1824; first professor of medicine at King's College, London, 1831–6; physician to Middlesex Hospital, 1824–58, and to royal household; registrar of

College of Physicians, 1829–58, of Medical Council, 1858–76.

HAWKINS, George (1809–1852), lithographic artist.

HAWKINS, Henry (1571?–1646), Jesuit; studied at St Omer and Rome; exiled from England, 1618; published translations from Latin, French, and Italian, and *Partheneia Sacra* (1632); died at Ghent.

HAWKINS, Henry, Baron Brampton (1817–1907), judge; son of solicitor; called to bar, 1843; QC, 1858; obtained foremost place among leaders of bar; defended Simon Bernard (1852), Sir John Dean *Paul (1855), and Miss Sugden in Lord *St Leonards' will case (1875–6); appeared for defence against Arthur *Orton, claimant in Tichborne ejectment case; led for crown in criminal action against claimant for perjury, 1873–4; a master in cross-examination; largely employed in compensation and election-petition cases; appointed judge of Queen's Bench division and knighted, 1876; transferred to Exchequer division; tried the Stauntons for murder in the 'Penge case', 1877; tried other murder cases, and unjustly obtained the nickname of 'Hanging Hawkins'; an admirable criminal judge, patient and thorough; favoured leniency for first offences; as civil judge less successful, being verbose, tautological, and contradictory in judgments; resigned judgeship and sworn PC, 1898; baron, 1899; fond of horse-racing; joined Roman Catholic communion after retirement from bench; *Reminiscences* (2 vols.) published, 1904.

HAWKINS, Herbert Leader (1887–1968), geologist and palaeontologist; educated at Reading School, Kendal Grammar School, and Manchester University; first class, geology; M.Sc., 1910; lecturer, University College of Reading, 1909; professor of geology, 1920–52; D.Sc., Manchester; FRS, 1937; specialist on fossil echinoides; published 102 scientific papers between 1909 and 1965; also *Humanity in Geological Perspective* (1939); president, geological section, British Association for the Advancement of Science, 1936; president, Geological Society, 1941–2; president, Palaeontographical Society, 1943–66; consulting geologist, Thames Valley Water Board, 1961.

HAWKINS, James, the elder (1662–1729), organist; Mus.Bac., St John's College, Cambridge, 1719; organist of Ely Cathedral, 1682–1729; arranged Ely MS choir-books, of which vol. vii contains music by himself.

HAWKINS, James, the younger (*fl.* 1714–1750), organist of Peterborough Cathedral, 1714–50; son of James *Hawkins the elder.

HAWKINS (or HAWKYNS), Sir John (1532–1595), naval commander; second son of William *Hawkyns; freeman of Plymouth, 1556; made voyages to the Canaries before 1561; in three ships fitted out with assistance of his father-in-law and Sir William *Wynter sailed to Sierra Leone, kidnapped negroes, and exchanged them with Spaniards in San Domingo (Hispaniola) for hides and other commodities, 1562–3; in second voyage, 1564–5, having loan of the *Jesus* (queen's ship) and support of *Pembroke and *Leicester, forced his negroes on Spaniards at Rio de la Hacha, and relieved French colony in Florida; his third expedition, delayed by Spanish remonstrances with Elizabeth, left Plymouth, Oct. 1567, with six ships (two queen's), took money from the Portuguese and negroes from Sierra Leone; brought some of the slaves to Vera Cruz; most of his ships destroyed and treasure seized in the harbour of San Juan de Lua by a Spanish fleet; forced by famine to land some of his men in Mexico; reached Vigo; arrived in England Jan. 1569; pretended, with *Burghley's connivance, to favour a Spanish invasion of England, thereby obtaining from *Philip II the release of his captured sailors, £40,000, and the patent of grandee of Spain; MP, Plymouth, 1572; treasurer and comptroller of the navy; introduced many improvements in the construction of ships for the navy; member of Council of War at Plymouth during fight with Armada, 1588; commanded rear squadron during fighting in Channel, 1588; knighted after action off Isle of Wight; commanded centre of *Howard's division at Gravelines, 29 Nov. 1588; joint commander with *Frobisher of squadron sent to Portuguese coast, 1590; while serving with *Drake's expedition to West Indies died at sea off Puerto Rico. He founded the hospital called after him at Chatham, 1592, where is a genuine portrait.

HAWKINS, John (*fl.* 1635), translator; brother of Henry *Hawkins; MD, Padua; published *Briefe Introduction to Syntax* (1631) and translations of Andreas de Soto's *Ransome of Time* and an Italian *Paraphrase upon the seaven Penitential Psalms* (1635).

HAWKINS, Sir John (1719–1789), author; claimed descent from Sir John *Hawkins (1532–1595); Middlesex magistrate; knighted, 1772; became known to Dr *Johnson through connection with *Gentleman's Magazine*; member of the club at King's Head, Ivy Lane, and of famous club of 1763; drew up Johnson's will, 1784; published Johnson's *Life and Works* (1787–9); edited *Walton's *Compleat Angler* (1760); his *General History of Music* issued, 1776.

HAWKINS, John (1758?–1841), author; FRS; travelled in Greece and the east; contributed to

*Walpole's *Memoirs of European and Asiatic Turkey* (1818) and *Travels in . . . the East.*

HAWKINS, John Sidney (1758–1842), antiquary; son of Sir John *Hawkins (1719–1789); FSA; edited *Ruggle's *Ignoramus* (1787) and *Rigaud's version of Da Vinci *On Painting* (1802); published work on Gothic architecture (1813), *Inquiry into . . . Greek and Latin Poetry* (1817), and *Inquiry into . . . Thorough Bass on a new plan* (1817).

HAWKINS, Major Rohde (1820–1884), architect to the committee of Council on Education; third son of Edward *Hawkins (1780–1867); accompanied Sir Charles *Fellows's expedition to Asia Minor, 1841.

HAWKINS, Nicholas (d. 1534), bishop-designate of Ely; of Eton and King's College, Cambridge; LL D; in youth imprisoned for Lutheranism; as archdeacon of Ely attended convocation of 1529; resident ambassador at imperial court, 1532; had interview with Clement VII at Bologna about Henry VIII's divorce from *Catherine of Aragon, 1533; communicated to Charles V in Spain news of the divorce and Henry's private marriage with *Anne Boleyn; bishop-designate of Ely, 1533; died at Balbase, Aragon.

HAWKINS (or HAWKYNS), Sir **Richard** (1562?–1622), naval commander; son of Sir John *Hawkins or Hawkyns (1532–1595); captain of the *Duck* galliot in *Drake's West Indian expedition, 1585–6; commanded the *Swallow* against Armada, 1588, and the *Crane* in his father's Portuguese expedition, 1590; left Plymouth in the *Dainty* on roving commission against Spaniards, 1593; put in at Santos in Brazil, Oct. 1593; passed Straits of Magellan, plundered Valparaiso, and took prizes; had to surrender, severely wounded, in bay of San Mateo, 1594; taken to Lima and (1597) sent to Spain; imprisoned at Seville and Madrid till 1602; knighted, 1603; MP, Plymouth, 1604; vice-admiral of Devon, 1604; vice-admiral under Sir Robert *Mansell in expedition against Algerine corsairs, 1620–1; published *Observations in his Voiage into the South Sea, a.d. 1593* (1622); died suddenly in the council chamber.

HAWKINS, Susanna (1787–1868), Scottish poet; daughter of a Dumfriesshire blacksmith; published and herself sold local and occasional verse, 1838–61.

HAWKINS, Thomas (d. 1577). See FISHER.

HAWKINS, Sir **Thomas** (d. 1640), translator; brother of John *Hawkins (fl. 1635); knighted, 1618; friend of Edmund *Bolton and James *Howell; published *Odes and Epodes of Horace in Latin and English Verse* (1625), and translations of Caussin's *Holy Court* (1626) and *Christian Diurnal* (1632), and other French works.

HAWKINS, Thomas (1810–1889), geologist; FGS, 1831; his collection of Devon, Somerset, and Dorset fossils bought by the nation; published *Memoirs of Ichthyosauri and Plesiosauri* (1834), *My Life and Works* (1887), and poems.

HAWKINS (or HAWKYNS), William (d. 1554?), sea-captain; made voyages to Guinea and Brazil, 1528–30; twice mayor of Plymouth; MP, Plymouth, 1539, 1547, 1553.

HAWKINS (or HAWKYNS), William (d. 1589), sea-captain and merchant; son of William *Hawkins or Hawkyns (d. 1554?); mayor of Plymouth, 1567, 1578, and 1587–8; partner with his brother, Sir John *Hawkins (1532–1595) in ownership of privateers; with Sir Arthur Champernowne seized Spanish treasure at Plymouth, 1568; commanded West Indian expedition, 1582; fitted out ships against Armada.

HAWKINS (or HAWKYNS), William (fl. 1595), sea-captain and merchant; son of William *Hawkins or Hawkyns (d. 1589); served in *Drake's voyage, 1577; lieutenant to Edward *Fenton in his East Indian voyage, 1582; probably commander of the *Advice* on Irish coast, 1587, and of the *Griffin* against the Armada, 1588; not identical with the William Hawkyns who went to Surat and resided with great mogul.

HAWKINS, William (d. 1637), poet; MA, Christ's College, Cambridge, 1626; master of Hadleigh School; published *Apollo Shroving* (1627), *Corolla Varia* (1634), and Latin complimentary verses.

HAWKINS, William (1682–1750), serjeant-at-law; BA, Oxford, 1699; fellow of Oriel College, 1700–8; MA, 1702; member of the Inner Temple, 1707; serjeant-at-law, 1724; chief work, *Treatise of Pleas of the Crown* (1716).

HAWKINS, William (1722–1801), author; son of William *Hawkins (1682–1750); fellow of Pembroke College, Oxford, 1742; MA, 1744; professor of poetry, 1751–6; rector of Whitchurch, Dorset, 1764–1801; Bampton lecturer, 1787; published *The Thimble* (1743), *Henry and Rosamond* (1749), and *The Siege of Aleppo*, and other plays, *Poems* (1781), and theological works; collected works issued (1758).

HAWKSHAW, Benjamin (d. 1738), divine; BA, St John's College, Cambridge, 1691; BA, Dublin, 1693; MA, 1695; incumbent of St Nicholas-within-the-Walls, Dublin; published *Poems* (1693) and *Reasonableness of constant Communion with Church of England* (1709).

HAWKSHAW, Sir **John** (1811–1891), civil engineer; worked under Alexander *Nimmo, 1821; engaged in mining work in Venezuela, 1832–4; employed by Jesse *Hartley, 1834, engineer to Manchester and Leeds Railway, 1845; consulting engineer in London, 1850. His works include the railways at Cannon Street and Charing Cross, with bridges over Thames, East London Railway, Severn Tunnel, 1887, and completion, with W. H. Barlow, of Clifton Suspension Bridge; reported favourably on site of proposed Suez Canal, 1863; FRS, 1855; knighted, 1873; MICE, 1836, and president, 1862 and 1863; president of British Association, 1875; published professional papers.

HAWKSLEY, Thomas (1807–1893), civil engineer; architect and surveyor at Nottingham; engineer to water companies supplying Nottingham, 1845–80; engineer-in-chief to Water-Supply Works at Liverpool, 1874–85, and Sheffield, 1864–93; planned Thornton Park and Bradgate reservoirs, Leicester, and carried out numerous other waterworks; MICE, 1840; president, 1872–3; president of Institution of Mechanical Engineers, 1876–7; FRS, 1878; published professional reports.

HAWKSMOOR, Nicholas (1661–1736), architect; employed by *Wren as deputy-surveyor at Chelsea Hospital, 1682–90; clerk of the works at Greenwich Hospital, 1698, Kensington Palace, 1691–1715, and at Whitehall, St James's, and Westminster, 1715–18; secretary to Board of Works and deputy-surveyor; assisted Wren at St Paul's, 1678–1710, and *Vanbrugh at Castle Howard, 1702–14, and Blenheim, 1710–15; erected library, 1700–14, and south quadrangle, 1710–59, of The Queen's College, Oxford, and part of north quadrangle (including towers) of All Souls, c.1730; directed repairs at Beverley Minster, 1713; joint surveyor of Queen Anne's new churches, 1716; designed numerous London churches; surveyor-general of Westminster Abbey, 1723; published *Short Historical Account of London Bridge* (1736), with plates.

HAWKWOOD, Sir **John de** (d. 1394), general; Froissart's 'Haccoude'; said to have served under Edward III; with troop of free lances stormed Pau, 1359; with Bernard de la Salle levied contributions from Innocent VII, 1360; shared in English victory of Brignais, 1362; took service with Monferrato against Milan, his troops becoming known as the White Company; held to ransom the Count of Savoy; defeated Visconti's Hungarian mercenaries, 1363; served unsuccessfully Pisa against Florence, 1363–4, and assisted Agnello to make himself doge of Pisa, 1364; with Company of St George ravaged country between Genoa and Siena, 1365–6, pillaged the Perugino;

escorted Agnello to meet the pope at Viterbo, 1367; took service with Milan, 1368; captured by the pope's mercenaries at Arezzo, but ransomed by Pisa, 1369; defeated at Rubiera the army of Monferrato, 1372; won a great victory for Pope Gregory XI over Gian Galeazzo Visconti at Gavardo, 1374; levied contributions on Florence, Pisa, Siena, Lucca, and Arezzo, 1375; received pension from Florence, 1375; obtained Cotignola and other places in Romagna in default of papal pay, but joined anti-papal league, 1377, marrying a natural daughter of Bernabo Visconti; with Count Landau forced Verona to pay tribute to Milan, 1378; defeated by Stephen Laczsk, and proscribed by Visconti; generally served Florence from 1380, but won the victory of Castagnaro against Verona for Padua, 1386; joint ambassador for England at Rome, 1382, and at Florence and Naples, 1385; as commander-in-chief at Florence carried on successful war against Milan, 1390–2; died at Florence and was buried in the Duomo. At the request of Richard II leave was given his widow to transfer his body to England; it was probably buried at Hedingham Sibil.

HAWLES, Sir **John** (1645–1716), Whig lawyer; educated at Winchester and The Queen's College, Oxford; barrister, Lincoln's Inn; MP, Old Sarum, 1689, Wilton, 1695 and 1702–5, St Michael, 1698, Truro, 1700, St Ives, 1702, Stockbridge, 1705–10; knighted, 1695; solicitor-general, 1695–1702; a manager of the *Sacheverell impeachment, 1710; published *Remarks* on contemporary state trials (1689) and other works.

HAWLEY, Frederick (1827–1889), Shakespearian scholar; as Frederick Haywell appeared with *Wallack at Théâtre aux Italiens, Paris, with *Phelps at Sadler's Wells, and with Charles *Calvert at Manchester; produced two plays at the Gaiety; as librarian at Stratford-upon-Avon, 1886–9, completed (1889) catalogue of editions in all languages of Shakespeare's plays.

HAWLEY, Henry (or **Henry C.)** (1679?–1759), lieutenant-general; served with the 4th Hussars, 1706–17; present at Almanza, 1707; wounded at Dunblane, 1715, when lieutenant-colonel; colonel of 33rd Foot, 1717, of 13th Dragoons, 1730; lieutenant-general, 1744; present at Dettingen, 1743, and Fontenoy, 1745; when commander-in-chief in Scotland defeated at Falkirk, 1746; commanded cavalry at Culloden, 1746, and in Flanders; governor of Portsmouth, 1752; a severe disciplinarian, known as the 'chief justice'.

HAWLEY, Jack (pseudonym) (1828–1875), sportsman and eccentric. See PILKINGTON, LIONEL SCOTT.

HAWLEY, Sir **Joseph Henry,** third baronet (1813–1875), patron of the turf; succeeded as baronet, 1831; lieutenant, 9th Lancers, 1833; left army, 1834; raced in partnership with J. M. Stanley in Italy and England; won the Oaks, 1847; cleared about £43,000 by his win (with Beadsman) of the Derby, 1858; again won the Derby, 1859 and 1868, and the St Leger, 1869; advocated turf reform, 1870.

HAWLEY, Thomas (d. 1557), Clarenceux king-of-arms; last Roseblanche pursuivant; as Rougecroix negotiated with Scots before Flodden; when Carlisle herald accompanied Henry VIII to Ardres, 1520; Norroy, 1534; Clarenceux king-of-arms, 1536–57; employed to treat with northern rebels, 1536; accompanied *Northumberland to Cambridge, 1553; induced Sir Thomas *Wyatt to submit, 1554; made visitations of Kent, Surrey, Hampshire, and Essex (printed 1878).

HAWORTH, Adrian Hardy (1767–1833), entomologist and botanist; FLS, 1798; founded Aurelian Society and Entomological Society of London, 1806; made large collection of lepidoptera; subdivision of aloe named after him; published works, including *Lepidoptera Britannica* (pt. i, 1803, pt. ii, c.1810, pt. iii, 1812) and *Synopsis Plantarum Succulentarum* (1812).

HAWORTH, Samuel (*fl.* 1683), empiric; MD, Paris; author of *True Method of curing Consumptions* (1682).

HAWORTH, Sir (Walter) Norman (1883–1950), chemist; first class, chemistry, Manchester, 1906; researched on chemistry of terpenes; studied at Göttingen; lecturer, St Andrews, 1912–20; worked on carbohydrates; professor of chemistry, Newcastle, 1920–5; Birmingham, 1925–48; built up important school of carbohydrate chemistry; produced first chemical synthesis of a vitamin (vitamin C), 1932; FRS, 1928; shared Nobel Prize, 1937; knighted, 1947.

HAWTHORN, John Michael (1929–1959), racing motorist; only son of motor engineer and racing motor-cyclist; educated at Ardingly College; raced at Goodwood, 1952; won French Grand Prix for Ferrari, 1953 and 1958; Spanish Grand Prix, 1954; Le Mans for Jaguar, 1955; world champion and British Automobile Racing Club Gold Medal, 1958; died in road accident, as had his father in 1954.

HAWTREY, Sir Charles Henry (1858–1923), actor; joined the stage, 1881; rewrote a German farce which he entitled *The Private Secretary* and which ran 1884–6; altogether managed eighteen London theatres, including the Globe and the Comedy, and produced about one hundred plays; knighted, 1922; excelled in staging farce and light comedy; made capital out of his facial immobility.

HAWTREY, Edward Craven (1789–1862), provost of Eton; educated at Eton; scholar (1807) and fellow (1810) of King's College, Cambridge; BA; as assistant master at Eton under *Keate, 1814–34, encouraged early efforts of *Praed, George *Lewis, and Arthur *Hallam; as headmaster of Eton, 1834–52, nearly doubled the numbers in twelve years, opened new buildings for foundationers (1846) and the sanatorium, suppressed 'montem' (1847), introduced principle of competition for king's scholars, founded English Essay Prize; provost, 1852–62; last person buried in college chapel. He printed translations into Italian, German, and Greek verse (1839), and translations from Homer into English hexameters (1843); edited Goethe's lyrics (1833 and 1834).

HAWTREY, Sir Ralph George (1879–1975), Treasury economist; educated at Eton and Trinity College, Cambridge; graduated in mathematics as nineteenth wrangler, 1901; an Apostle and friend of the Bloomsbury group; married Emilia Sophia d'Aranyi, sister of Jelly *d'Aranyi and Adila *Fachiri, 1915; entered Home Civil Service, 1903; moved to Treasury, 1904; director of financial inquiries, 1919; visiting professor, Harvard University, 1928–9; retired from Treasury, 1947; Price professor of international economics, Royal Institute of International Affairs (Chatham House), 1947–52; prolific writer; works include *Good and Bad Trade* (1913), *Currency and Credit* (1919), *The Economic Problem* (1926), *The Gold Standard in Theory and Practice* (1927), *The Art of Central Banking* (1932), *Capital and Employment* (1937), *Economic Destiny* (1944), and *Incomes and Money* (1967); constructive critic of J. M. (later Lord) *Keynes; not in favour of reducing unemployment through public works; critical of Bretton Woods proposals; FBA, 1935; hon. D.Sc. (Econ.), London, 1939; president, Royal Economic Society, 1946–8; hon. fellow, Trinity College, Cambridge, 1959; CB, 1941; knighted, 1956.

HAXEY, Thomas (d. 1425), treasurer of York Minster; keeper of the rolls of the Common Bench, 1387; chief clerk and keeper of the writs of the Common Bench, 1392; prebendary of Lichfield, 1391, Lincoln, 1395, and Salisbury; attended parliament of 1397 (according to *Hallam as a member) and brought forward an article in bill of complaints directed against non-residence of bishops and a tax on clergy; tried and condemned to death, but claimed as a clergyman and pardoned, 1397; prebendary of York, 1405, of Southwell, 1405; treasurer of York Minster, 1418–25.

HAY, Alexander, Lord Easter Kennet (d. 1594), Scottish judge; clerk to Scots Privy Council, 1564; clerk-register and senator of College of Justice, 1579.

HAY, Alexander, Lord Newton (d. 1616), clerk-register, 1612; son of Alexander *Hay (d. 1594); author of *Manuscript Notes of Transactions of King James VI written for use of King Charles.*

HAY, Alexander (d. 1807?), topographer; MA, of a Scottish university; chaplain of St Mary's Chapel, Chichester; vicar of Wisborough Green; published *History of Chichester* (1804).

HAY, Alexander Leith (1758–1838), general; assumed name of Hay, 1789; raised regiment called by his name, 1789; general, 1813.

HAY, Andrew (1762–1814), major-general; raised Banffshire Fencible Infantry, 1798; lieutenant-colonel, 3rd battalion, 1st Royals, at Corunna; commanded a brigade at Walcheren, 1809, and in Peninsula; major-general, 1811; mortally wounded before Bayonne.

HAY, Sir Andrew Leith (1785–1862), soldier and author; son of Alexander Leith *Hay; served in Peninsula, 1808–14, as aide-de-camp to James *Leith (his uncle); MP, Elgin, 1832–8 and 1841–7; clerk of the ordnance, 1834; KH, 1834; published *Narrative of the Peninsular War* (1831) and *Castellated Architecture of Aberdeenshire* (1849).

HAY, Archibald (*fl.* 1543), Scottish monk of Paris and Latin writer.

HAY, Arthur, ninth marquis of Tweeddale (1824–1878), soldier and naturalist; son of George *Hay, eighth marquis of Tweeddale; entered Grenadier Guards, 1841; aide-de-camp to *Hardinge in Sutlej campaign, 1845; travelled in Europe and the Himalayas; served in Crimea; colonel, 1866; Viscount Walden, 1862–76; marquis, 1876; president of Zoological Society; FRS; FLS; his papers on natural history collected (1881).

HAY, Lord Charles (d. 1760), major-general; brother of John *Hay, fourth marquis of Tweeddale; present at siege of Gibraltar, 1727; volunteer with Prince Eugene on the Rhine, 1734; MP, Haddingtonshire, 1741; distinguished himself with 1st Foot Guards at Fontenoy, 1745, and was severely wounded; major-general, 1757; court-martialled for reflections on conduct of Lord *Loudoun in Nova Scotia.

HAY, David Ramsay (1798–1866), decorative artist and author; employed by *Scott at Abbotsford; decorated hall of Society of Arts, *c.*1846; 'Ninety Club' founded by his pupils; published, among other works, *Laws of Harmonious Colouring adapted to House Painting* (1828) and *Natural Principles of Beauty as developed in the Human Figure* (1852), etc.

HAY, Edmund (d. 1591), Scottish Jesuit; accompanied secret embassy from Pius IV to *Mary Queen of Scots, 1562; first rector of Pont-à-Mousson, and provincial of French Jesuits; assistant for Germany and France to Aquaviva, general of the Jesuits.

HAY, Edward (1761?–1826), Irish writer; active in the cause of Catholic emancipation; tried for treason but acquitted, 1798; published *History of the Insurrection of County of Wexford, 1798* (1803).

HAY, Francis, ninth earl of Errol (d. 1631); succeeded to earldom, 1585; joined Huntly (see GORDON, GEORGE, 1562–1636) in schemes for re-establishing Romanism in Scotland; his letter to duke of Parma intercepted in England and forwarded to James VI, 1589; joined in rebellion of Huntly and *Crawford, and did not submit till king's second visit (1589) to the north; imprisoned on suspicion of complicity with *Bothwell, 1591; again in rebellion after 'Spanish Blanks' affair, 1592; excommunicated, outlawed, and exiled, 1593; defeated king's troops, but was severely wounded, 1594; his castle at Slains destroyed by the king, 1594; persuaded by *Lennox to leave Scotland, 1594; detained at Middelburg; returned secretly, 1596; restored and absolved on abjuring popery, 1597; commissioner for union with England, 1602; excommunicated and imprisoned at Dumbarton, 1608; absolved, 1617.

HAY, George (d. 1588), controversialist; minister of Eddlestone and Rathven; preached with *Knox in Ayrshire, 1562; disputed with abbot of Crossraguel, 1562; moderator of the Assembly, 1571; published work against the Jesuit Tyrie, 1576; deputy to council at Magdeburg, 1577.

HAY, Sir George, first earl of Kinnoull (1572–1634), lord chancellor of Scotland; gentleman of the bedchamber, 1596; knighted, *c.*1609; clerk-register and a lord of session, 1616; supported five articles of Perth; lord high chancellor of Scotland, 1622–34; created Viscount Dupplin, 1627, earl of Kinnoull, 1633; resisted king's regulations for lords of session (1626), and upheld precedency over archbishop of St Andrews.

HAY, George, seventh earl of Kinnoull (d. 1758); as Viscount Dupplin MP, Fowey, 1710; created peer of United Kingdom, 1711; succeeded as earl, 1719; suspected of Jacobitism, 1715 and 1722; British ambassador at Constantinople, 1729–37; maintained right of presentation to parish of Madderty in ecclesiastical courts, 1739–40.

HAY, Sir George (1715–1778), lawyer and politician; of Merchant Taylors' School and St John's College, Oxford; DCL, 1742; chancellor of Worcester, 1751–64; dean of arches, judge of prerogative court of Canterbury, and chancellor of diocese of London, 1764–78; vicar-general of Canterbury and king's advocate, 1755–64; MP, Stockbridge, 1754, Calne, 1757, Sandwich, 1761, Newcastle-under-Lyme, 1768; a lord of the Admiralty, 1756–65; judge of Admiralty court, 1773–8; knighted, 1773; intimate of *Hogarth and *Garrick.

HAY, George (1729–1811), Roman Catholic bishop of Daulis and vicar-apostolic of the lowland district of Scotland; imprisoned for Jacobitism, 1746–7; became a Romanist, 1748; entered Scots College at Rome, 1751; despatched with John *Geddes on Scottish mission, 1759; bishop of Daulis *in partibus* and coadjutor to Bishop James *Grant, 1769; vicar-apostolic of lowland district, 1778; his furniture and library burnt in Protestant riots at Edinburgh, 1779; went to Rome to get plan for reorganizing Scots College sanctioned, 1781; had charge of Scalan Seminary, 1788–93, and founded that of Aquhorties, whither he retired, 1802; published theological works, edited by Bishop Strain, 1871–3.

HAY, George, eighth marquis of Tweeddale (1787–1876), field marshal; succeeded to title, 1804; served in Sicily, 1806, the Peninsula, 1807–13, and America, 1813; wounded at Busaco, 1810, and Vittoria, 1813, also at Niagara, 1813, where he was captured; governor of Madras and commander of troops, 1842–8; general, 1854; field marshal, 1875; KT, 1820; GCB, 1867; representative peer of Scotland and lord-lieutenant of Haddingtonshire; agricultural reformer and president of Highland Society.

HAY, Sir Gilbert (*fl.* 1456), poet and translator; knighted; sometime chamberlain to Charles VII of France; afterwards resided with earl of *Caithness, and translated from French Bonnet's *Buke of Battailes*, also *The Buke of the Order of Knyghthood*; translated the spurious Aristotelian *Secretum Secretorum* as *Buke of the Governaunce of Princes*; rendered into Scottish verse *Buke of the Conqueror Alexaunder the Great.*

HAY, Sir Harley Hugh Dalrymple- (1861–1940), civil engineer; joined London and South Western Railway; resident engineer, Waterloo and City Railway, 1894; his system of constructing tube railways became standard practice; consulting engineer, London Underground, 1902–40; constructed Bakerloo, Northern, and Piccadilly lines; other works include widening of Richmond Bridge, tunnel under river Hugli, Calcutta (1931), London Post Office railway (1928), and secret intercommunication tunnels between government offices; knighted, 1933.

HAY, Ian (pseudonym) (1876–1952), writer. See BEITH, JOHN HAY.

HAY, James, first earl of Carlisle, first Viscount Doncaster, and first Baron Hay (d. 1636), courtier; came from Scotland to England with James I; knighted, and became gentleman of the bedchamber; received numerous grants of land, and (1607) the hand of an heiress; KB, 1610; master of the wardrobe, 1613; created baron for life, though without a seat in the Lords, 1606, Baron Hay, 1615, Viscount Doncaster, 1618, and earl of Carlisle, 1622; married Lucy Percy (see HAY, LUCY, countess of Carlisle), 1617; sent on missions to Heidelberg and the imperial court, 1619–20; recommended war on behalf of king of Bohemia; envoy to Paris, 1623, to Lorraine, Piedmont, and Venice, 1628; advised rejection of Richelieu's terms for marriage of *Henrietta Maria; advocated war with Spain, 1624, and support of Huguenots, 1628; celebrated for splendid hospitality.

HAY, John (1546–1607), Scottish Jesuit; disputed with Protestants at Strasburg, 1576; ordered to leave Scotland, 1579; professor of theology and dean of arts at Tournon, 1581; rector of college at Pont-à-Mousson; published *Certaine Demandes concerning the Christian Religion and Discipline, proposed to the Ministers of the new pretended Kirk of Scotlande* (1580), also *De Rebus Japonicis, Indicis et Peruvianis Epistolae recentiores* (1605); edited Sisto da Siena's *Bibliotheca Sancta* (1591).

HAY, Sir John, Lord Barra (*c.*1578–1654), Scottish judge; town clerk of Edinburgh; knighted, 1632; lord clerk register, 1632; ordinary lord of session, 1634; as provost of Edinburgh, 1637, tried to present petitions against new Prayer-Book; obliged to take refuge in England, 1639; imprisoned on his return, 1641; tried by a parliamentary committee, 1642; captured at Philiphaugh; his life saved by intervention of Lanark, 1645.

HAY, John, second earl and first marquis of Tweeddale (1626–1697), lord chancellor of Scotland; joined Charles I at Nottingham, 1642, but fought for parliament at Marston Moor, 1644, on account of his attitude towards Covenanters; held command in army of 'the engagement' party, 1648; succeeded as second earl of Tweeddale, 1654; imprisoned for support of James *Guthrie, 1660; president of the council, 1663; extraordinary lord of session, 1664; used influence as church commissioner to moderate proceedings against Covenanters; dismissed from office and Privy Council by advice of *Lauderdale, 1674; readmitted to Treasury, 1680, and the council, 1682; chancellor of Scotland,

1692–6; supported revolution in Scotland; created marquis of Tweeddale, 1694; as high commissioner ordered inquiry into Glencoe massacre, 1695; dismissed from chancellorship for supporting Darien scheme, 1696.

HAY, Lord **John** (d. 1706), brigadier-general; second son of John *Hay, second marquis of Tweeddale; commanded Scots Dragoons (Scots Greys) under *Marlborough; died of fever at Courtrai.

HAY, John, second marquis of Tweeddale (1645–1713), eldest son of John *Hay, first marquis of Tweeddale; created privy councillor, 1689; succeeded to title, 1697; high commissioner to Scottish parliament, 1704; lord chancellor, 1704–5; led *squadrone volante*, but ultimately supported the Union; representative peer, 1707.

HAY, John, titular earl of Inverness (1691–1740), Jacobite; brother of George *Hay, seventh earl of Kinnoull; employed by his brother-in-law *Mar in preparing Jacobite outbreak of 1715; made governor of Perth; went to France to urge the Chevalier *James Edward's immediate sailing, 1715; master of the horse to the Chevalier James Edward; joined St Germains court; revealed Mar's perfidy, and succeeded him as secretary, 1724 (removed 1727); created earl of Inverness, 1725.

HAY, John, fourth marquis of Tweeddale (d. 1762); succeeded to title, 1715; extraordinary lord of session, 1721; representative peer, 1722; secretary of state for Scotland, 1742–6; lord justice-general, 1761.

HAY, Lord **John** (1793–1851), rear-admiral; lost his left arm in Hyères Roads, 1807; commanded squadron on north coast of Spain during Civil War; CB, 1837; rear-admiral, 1851; MP, Haddington, 1826–30, Windsor, 1847; a lord of the Admiralty, 1847–50.

HAY, Sir John (1816–1892), Australian statesman; MA, University and King's College, Aberdeen, 1834; emigrated to New South Wales, 1838; member of legislative assembly for Murrumbidgee, 1856; secretary of lands and public works, 1856–7; member for Murray division, 1858–64, and Central Cumberland, 1864–7; speaker of legislative assembly, 1862–5; member of legislative council, 1867, and president, 1873–92; KCMG, 1878.

HAY, Sir **John Hay Drummond-** (1816–1893). See DRUMMOND-HAY.

HAY, Lucy, countess of Carlisle (1599–1660), beauty and wit; daughter of Henry *Percy, ninth earl of Northumberland; married James *Hay, first earl of Carlisle, 1617; praised and addressed by *Carew, *Herrick, *Suckling, *Waller, and *D'Avenant; exercised great influence over Queen *Henrietta Maria, and was an intimate of *Strafford and *Pym; revealed intended arrest of the five members; during Civil Wars acted with Presbyterians; active in support of Holland's preparations for second Civil War; intermediary between Scottish and English leaders; imprisoned in the Tower, 1649–50.

HAY, Mary Cecil (1840?–1886), novelist; her works (published 1873–86) highly popular, especially in America and Australia; the best known being *Old Myddelton's Money* (1874).

HAY, Richard Augustine (1661–1736?), Scottish antiquary; grandson of Sir John *Hay of Barra; canon regular of Sainte-Geneviève's, Paris, 1678; attempted to establish the order in Great Britain; compelled to leave the kingdom, 1689; prior of Bernicourt, 1694, of St-Pierre-mont-en-Argonne, 1695; published *Origine of Royal Family of the Stewarts* (1722), *Genealogie of the Hayes of Tweeddale, including Memoirs of his own Times* (privately printed 1835), and other works; died in Scotland.

HAY, Robert (1799–1863), of Linplum, Egyptologist; leading member of Egyptian expedition, 1826–38; published *Illustrations of Cairo* (1840); presented drawings and antiquities to British Museum.

HAY, Thomas, eighth earl of Kinnoull (1710–1787), statesman; eldest son of George *Hay, seventh earl of Kinnoull; as Viscount Dupplin MP, Cambridge, 1741–58; commissioner of Irish revenue, 1741; a lord of trade, 1746, of the Treasury, 1754; joint paymaster, 1755; chancellor of the duchy of Lancaster, 1758; privy councillor, 1758; succeeded to earldom, 1758; ambassador-extraordinary to Portugal, 1759; chancellor of St Andrews, 1765.

HAY, William, fifth Baron Yester (d. 1576); succeeded as baron, 1559; subscribed 'Book of Discipline', 1561, but commanded the van in raid against *Moray, 1565; joined *Mary and *Bothwell on their flight to Dunbar; signed the band for Mary's deliverance from Lochleven; fought for Mary at Langside, 1568; after 1572 joined 'king's party'.

HAY, William (1695–1755), author; of Glyndebourne, Sussex; matriculated at Christ Church, Oxford, 1712; barrister, Middle Temple, 1723; MP, Seaford, 1734–55; commissioner for victualling the navy, 1738; introduced measures for poor relief; keeper of Tower records, 1753. His collected works (1794) include *Essay on Civil Government, Religio Philosophi* (reprinted 1831), and a translation of Martial.

HAYA, Sir **Gilbert de** (d. 1330), lord high constable of Scotland, and ancestor of the earls of Errol; at first faithful to Edward I; joined *Bruce in 1306, and was granted Slains, *c.*1309, and the hereditary constableship, 1309; his funeral inscription and effigy discovered at Cupar.

HAYDAY, James (1796–1872), bookbinder; introduced Turkey morocco.

HAYDEN, George (*fl.* 1723), musical composer.

HAYDN, Joseph (d. 1856), compiler of *Dictionary of Dates* (1841) and *Book of Dignities* (1851); received government pension, 1856.

HAYDOCK, George Leo (1774–1849), biblical scholar; of Douai and Crook Hall, Durham; interdicted from saying mass at Westby Hall, 1831; restored, 1839; editor of the Douay Bible and Reims Testament, 1812–14.

HAYDOCK (or HADDOCK), Richard (1552?–1605), Roman Catholic divine; assisted in foundation of English College at Rome, whither he returned as *maestro di camera* to Cardinal *Allen, 1590; friend of *Parsons; dean of Dublin; died at Rome; his 'Account of Revolution in English College at Rome' printed in *Dodd's *Church History*.

HAYDOCK, Richard (*fl.* 1605), physician; of Winchester and New College, Oxford; fellow, 1590; MA, 1595; MB, 1601; practised at Salisbury; translated from Jo. Paul Lomatius *Tracte containing the Artes of Curious Paintinge, Carvinge, and Buildinge* (1598).

HAYDOCK, Roger (1643–1696), Quaker; imprisoned and fined for preaching in Lancashire, 1667; disputed at Arley Hall with John *Cheyney, 1677; visited Scotland, Ireland, 1680, and Holland, 1681, and subsequently obtained protection for Quakers in Isle of Man; collected writings edited by J. Field (posthumous, 1700).

HAYDOCK, Thomas (1772–1859), printer and publisher; brother of George Leo *Haydock.

HAYDOCK, William (d. 1537), Cistercian, of Whalley; executed for participation in Pilgrimage of Grace; his body found at Cottam Hall early in nineteenth century.

HAYDON. See also HEYDON.

HAYDON, Benjamin Robert (1786–1846), historical painter; came to London, 1804; attended Academy schools and Charles *Bell's lectures on anatomy; his first picture, *Joseph and Mary*, well hung at the Academy, 1806; visited, with *Wilkie, the Elgin marbles in Park Lane, and drew studies from them for his *Dentatus*; offended by position of *Dentatus* in Academy exhibition of 1809; awarded premium for it by British Gallery, 1810; attacked Richard *Knight

and the Academy in *Examiner*, 1812; created sensation with *Judgment of Solomon* (Water-Colour Society), 1814; did much by his letters on the Elgin marbles (1815) towards determining the national purchase; his *Christ's Entry into Jerusalem* exhibited at Egyptian Hall, 1820, and in Edinburgh and Glasgow; *Lazarus* (National Gallery) finished 1822; imprisoned for debt in King's Bench, 1822–3, and again three times before 1837; his scheme for government school of design accepted, 1835; compelled introduction of models by starting rival school at Savile House; began lectures on art in northern towns, 1839; committed suicide after failure of exhibition of *Aristides* and *Nero*. His later pictures include *Punch, Meeting of Anti-Slavery Society*, and *Wellington musing at Waterloo.* *Wordsworth and *Keats addressed sonnets to him. Among his pupils were *Eastlake, the *Landseers, *Lance, and *Bewick. He published works on historical painting in England (1829), the pernicious effect of academies on art (1839), the relative value of oil and fresco (in connection with decoration of houses of parliament, 1842), and *Lectures on Painting and Design* (1844–6), and left part of an autobiography.

HAYDON, Frank Scott (1822–1887), editor of *Eulogium Historiarum* (1868); eldest son of Benjamin Robert *Haydon; committed suicide.

HAYDON, Frederick Wordsworth (1827–1886), inspector of factories (dismissed, 1867); son of Benjamin Robert *Haydon; published *Correspondence and Table-Talk* of his father (1876); died at Bethlehem Hospital.

HAYES, Mrs **Catherine** (1690–1726), murderess; executed for murder of her husband in Tyburn (Oxford Street); convicted of petty treason and sentenced to be burned alive.

HAYES, Catherine (1825–1861), afterwards Mrs Bushnell; vocalist; first sang at Sapio's concert, Dublin, 1839; studied under Garcia at Paris and Ronconi at Milan; sang at La Scala, Milan, at Vienna, and Venice; made her début at Covent Garden in *Linda di Chamouni*, 1849; sang in New York, California, South America, Australia, India, and the Sandwich Islands, 1851–6; at *Jullien's concerts, 1857.

HAYES, Charles (1678–1760), mathematician and chronologist; sub-governor of Royal African Company till 1752; published *Treatise on Fluxions* (1704), *Dissertation on Chronology of the Septuagint* (1751), and similar works.

HAYES, Edmund (1804–1867), Irish judge; BA, Trinity College, Dublin, 1825; LL D, 1832; Irish barrister, 1827; QC, 1852; law adviser to Lord Derby's first and second administrations; judge of Queen's Bench in Ireland, 1859–66;

published treatise on Irish criminal law (2nd edn., 1843) and reports of Exchequer cases.

HAYES, Edwin (1819–1904), marine painter; studied art in Dublin; exhibited at Royal Academy, 1845–1904; member of Royal Hibernian Academy, 1870; chief works were *Off Dover* (1891), *Crossing the Bar* (1895); represented in Tate and other public galleries.

HAYES, Sir George (1805–1869), justice of the Queen's Bench; barrister, Middle Temple, 1830; serjeant-at-law, 1856; recorder of Leicester, 1861; leader of Midland circuit; justice of Queen's Bench, 1868; knighted, 1868; author of humorous elegy and song on the 'Dog and the Cock'.

HAYES, John (1775–1838), rear-admiral; commanded the *Alfred* at Corunna, 1809, *Achille* in Walcheren expedition, 1809, and frigate *Freya* at reduction of Guadeloupe, 1810; called 'Magnificent Hayes' from his handling of the *Magnificent* in Basque Roads, 1812; CB, 1815; rear-admiral, 1837.

HAYES, John (1786?–1866), portrait painter; exhibited at Royal Academy, 1814–51.

HAYES, Sir John Macnamara, first baronet (1750?–1809), physician; MD, Reims, 1784; army surgeon in North America and West Indies; LRCP, 1786; physician-extraordinary to prince of Wales, 1791; physician to Westminster Hospital, 1792–4; created baronet, 1797; inspector-general at Woolwich.

HAYES, Michael Angelo (1820–1877), painter; secretary to Royal Hibernian Academy, 1856; marshal of Dublin; exhibited with new Water-Colour Society, London; painted military and equestrian pictures; accidentally drowned in a tank.

HAYES, Philip (1738–1797), professor of music at Oxford; son of William *Hayes the elder; Mus.Bac., Magdalen College, Oxford, 1763; member of Royal Society of Musicians, 1769; professor of music, Oxford, 1777–97; Mus.Doc. and organist of Magdalen, 1777, of St John's, 1790; composed six concertos, eight anthems, songs, glees, an oratorio, and odes; edited and continued Jenkin Lewis's memoirs of Prince *William Henry, duke of Gloucester (1789) and *Harmonia Wiccamica* (1780).

HAYES, William, the elder (1706–1777), professor of music at Oxford; organist at Worcester Cathedral, 1731, and Magdalen College, Oxford, 1734; professor of music, Oxford, 1742–77; created Mus.Doc., 1749; conducted Gloucester Festival, 1763; defended *Handel against *Avison; set *Collins's *Ode on the Passions*; composed popular glees and canons.

HAYES, William, the younger (1742–1790), musical writer; third son of William *Hayes the elder; BA, Magdalen Hall, Oxford, 1761; MA, New College, 1764; minor canon of Worcester, 1765, of St Paul's, 1766; musical contributor to *Gentleman's Magazine*, 1765.

HAYES, William (*fl.* 1794), ornithologist.

HAYGARTH, John (1740–1827), physician; FRS; MB, St John's College, Cambridge, 1766; as physician to Chester Infirmary, 1767–98, first carried out treatment of fever by isolation, 1783; afterwards practised at Bath; published *Plan to Exterminate Small-pox and introduce General Inoculation* (1793) and other medical works; his plan for self-supporting savings banks adopted at Bath, 1813.

HAYLEY, Robert (d. 1770?), Irish artist in black and white chalk.

HAYLEY, Thomas Alfonso (1780–1800), sculptor; natural son of William *Hayley; modelled busts of *Flaxman (his master) and *Thurlow, and a medallion of *Romney.

HAYLEY, William (1745–1820), poet; of Eton and Trinity Hall, Cambridge, and the Middle Temple; friend of *Cowper, *Romney, and *Southey; published successful volumes of verse; his *Triumphs of Temper* (1781) and *Triumphs of Music* (1804) ridiculed in *English Bards and Scotch Reviewers*; his *Ballads founded on Anecdotes of Animals* (1805) illustrated by *Blake; published also lives of Milton (1794), Cowper (1803), and Romney (1809); his *Memoirs* (1823) edited by Dr John *Johnson (d. 1833).

HAYLS (or HALES), John (d. 1679), portrait painter and miniaturist; rival of *Lely and Samuel *Cooper (1609–1672); painted portraits of *Pepys and Pepys's wife and father.

HAYMAN, Francis (1708–1776), painter; designed illustrations for *Hanmer's *Shakespeare* (1743–4) and *Smollett's *Don Quixote*; best known for ornamental paintings at Vauxhall; chairman of committee of exhibition of works by living British painters, 1760; president of Society of British Artists, 1766; an original academician, 1768, and librarian, 1771–6; friend of *Hogarth and *Garrick.

HAYMAN, Henry (1823–1904), honorary canon of Carlisle and headmaster of Rugby; educated at Merchant Taylors' School and St John's College, Oxford; BA, 1845; MA, 1849; DD, 1870; fellow, 1844–55; treasurer of the Union; headmaster of St Olave's, Southwark, 1855–9, of Cheltenham, 1859–68, and Bradfield, 1868–9; elected headmaster of Rugby, under protest from masters, 1869; instituted unsuccessful proceedings against governors for dismissal, 1874; nominated to crown living of Aldingham, Lancashire, 1874; honorary canon of Carlisle, 1884; published classical translations, an edition of Homer's *Odyssey* (3 vols., 1881–6), sermons, and essays.

HAYMAN, Robert (d. 1631?), epigrammatist; BA, Exeter College, Oxford; governor of Newfoundland, c.1625; published volume of ancient and modern epigrams (1628); died abroad.

HAYMAN, Samuel (1818–1886), antiquarian writer; BA, Trinity College, Dublin, 1839; rector of Carrigaline and Douglas, 1872–86; canon of Cork; assisted Sir Bernard Burke in genealogical works; edited *Unpublished Geraldine Documents* (1870–81); published works dealing with Youghal.

HAYMO (or HAIMO) (d. 1054), archdeacon of Canterbury; often confused with Haymo, bishop of Halberstadt.

HAYMO OF FAVERSHAM (d. 1244), fourth general of the Franciscans; one of the first Franciscans to come to England; envoy of Gregory IX for union with Greek church, 1233; general of Franciscans, 1240; called 'Speculum honestatis'; edited *Breviarium Romanum*; died at Anagnia.

HAYNE, Charles Hayne Seale- (1833–1903), Liberal politician. See SEALE-HAYNE.

HAYNE, Thomas (1582–1645), schoolmaster; MA, Lincoln College, Oxford, 1612; master at Merchant Taylors' School (1605–8) and Christ's Hospital, 1608; benefactor of Lincoln College, Oxford, and Thrussington, Leicestershire; published theological works.

HAYNE (or HAYNES), William (d. 1631?), schoolmaster; MA, Christ's College, Cambridge; headmaster of Merchant Taylors' School, 1599–1624; published grammatical treatises.

HAYNES. See also HAINES.

HAYNES, Hopton (1672?–1749), Unitarian writer; intimate of *Newton at the Mint; his posthumous *Scripture Account of . . . God and . . . Christ* first edited by John Blackburn (1750).

HAYNES, John (d. 1654), New England statesman; sailed in the *Griffin* for Boston with *Cotton; governor of Massachusetts, 1635–6; first governor of Connecticut, 1639, re-elected, 1641 and 1643; promoted confederation of the four colonies, 1643.

HAYNES, John (fl. 1730–1750), draughtsman and engraver.

HAYNES, Joseph (d. 1701). See HAINES.

HAYNES, Joseph (1760–1829), etcher and engraver.

HAYNES, Samuel (d. 1752), historical writer; son of Hopton *Haynes; MA, King's College, Cambridge, 1727, DD, 1748; rector of Hatfield, 1737–52, Clothall, 1747–52; canon of Windsor, 1743; edited Hatfield State Papers (1542–70).

HAYNESWORTH, William (fl. 1659), early engraver.

HAYTER, Charles (1761–1835), miniature painter; exhibited at Royal Academy, 1786–1832; published *Introduction to Perspective* (1813) and *Practical Treatise on the three Primitive Colours* (1826).

HAYTER, Sir George (1792–1871), portrait and historical painter; son of Charles *Hayter; studied at Rome; member of Academy of St Luke; painted for duke of *Bedford, *Trial of Lord William Russell*, 1825, portraits of Princess Victoria for King Leopold and the City of London; portrait and historical painter to the queen, 1837; painter-in-ordinary, 1841; knighted, 1842; exhibited, at British Institution, *Moving of the Address in first Reformed Parliament*, 1848.

HAYTER, Henry Heylyn (1821–1895), statistician; educated at Charterhouse; emigrated to Victoria, 1852; entered department of registrar-general, 1857, and became head of statistical branch; government statist, 1874–93; brought annual statistical returns of colony of Victoria into elaborate and perfect shape, which formed model for whole of Australian colonies; originated *Victorian Year-Book*; published educational and other works.

HAYTER, John (1756–1818), antiquary; of Eton and King's College, Cambridge; fellow; MA, 1788; incorporated at Oxford, 1812; chaplain-in-ordinary to the prince of Wales; superintended deciphering of Herculaneum papyri, 1802–6; his facsimiles with engravings of the *Carmen Latinum* and 'Περὶ Θανάτου' presented to Oxford University, 1810; died at Paris.

HAYTER, Richard (1611?–1684), theological writer; MA, Magdalen Hall, Oxford, 1634; published *The Meaning of Revelation* (1675).

HAYTER, Thomas (1702–1762), bishop of Norwich and of London; BA, Balliol College, Oxford, 1724; MA, Emmanuel College, Cambridge, 1727; DD, Cambridge, 1744; chaplain to Archbishop *Blackburne of York, 1724; sub-dean, 1730, and archdeacon of York, 1730–51; prebendary of Westminster, 1739–49, Southwell, 1728–49; bishop of Norwich, 1749–61; preceptor to prince of Wales (George III), 1751; supported Jews' Naturalization Bill, 1753; bishop of London, 1761–2; privy councillor, 1761; published pamphlets.

HAYTER, Sir William Goodenough, first baronet (1792–1878), Liberal whip; educated at Winchester and Trinity College, Oxford; BA, 1814; barrister, Lincoln's Inn, 1819, treasurer, 1853; QC, 1839; MP, Wells, 1837–65; judge-advocate-general, 1847–9; patronage secretary to the Treasury, 1850–8; privy councillor, 1843; created baronet, 1858; found drowned at South Hill Park, Berkshire.

HAYTHORNE, Sir Edmund (1818–1888), general; served with 98th under Colin *Campbell in China, 1841–3; his aide-de-camp in second Sikh War and in Momund expedition (1851); with *Napier at forcing of Kohat Pass, 1850; lieutenant-colonel, 1854; commanded 1st Royals in Crimea; chief of staff in north China, 1859; adjutant-general in Bengal, 1860–5; KCB, 1873; general, 1879.

HAYTLEY, Edward (d. 1762?), painter of full-length of Peg Woffington.

HAYWARD, Abraham (1801–1884), essayist; educated by Francis *Twiss and at Tiverton School; studied at Inner Temple, 1824; edited Law Magazine, 1828–44; visited Germany, 1831; published translation of Faust, with critical introduction (1833); gave literary assistance to Prince Louis Bonaparte; QC, 1845; not elected bencher; contributed to Quarterly, Edinburgh, and Fraser's; supported Aberdeen's government in Morning Chronicle; his reply to De Bazancourt's Expédition de Crimée circulated on the continent by Palmerston; contributed regularly to Quarterly, 1869–83, and occasionally to The Times; published The Art of Dining (1852) and Sketches of Eminent Statesmen and Writers (1880); edited Mrs *Piozzi's Autobiography (1861), and Diaries of a Lady of Quality from 1797 to 1844 (1864). His three series of Essays (1858, 1873, 1874) include a vigorous attack on the theory identifying 'Junius' with Sir Philip *Francis. Selections from his correspondence were issued (1886).

HAYWARD, Sir Isaac James (1884–1976), trade union general secretary and leader of the London County Council; left school at 12 to work in local coal-mine; entered engineering and became full-time official of National Union of Enginemen, Firemen, Mechanics, and Electrical Workers; general secretary, 1938; his work brought him into contact with Herbert *Morrison (later Lord Morrison of Lambeth) who encouraged him to seek election to the LCC; elected member for Rotherhithe, 1928–37, and Deptford, 1937–55; chairman, Public Assistance Committee, 1934–7; took leading part in improvements in administration of the Poor Law; chairman, Consultative Council of London Electricity Board, 1948–60; as chairman of LCC Education Committee (1945–7), supported scheme for comprehensive schools under 1944 Education Act; leader of the council, 1947–65; responsible for South Bank scheme; played leading part in birth of the National Theatre, and Crystal Palace Sports Centre; chairman, British section of International Union of Local Authorities; knighted, 1959; hon. LL D, London, 1952; freeman of Bermondsey, 1955 and Deptford, 1961; hon. FRIBA, 1970; member of court of University of London.

HAYWARD, Sir John (1564?–1627), historian; MA, Pembroke College, Cambridge, 1584; LL D; imprisoned for publishing First Part of the Life and Raigne of Henrie the IIII, dedicated to *Essex, 1599–1601; practised in court of arches under James I; historiographer of Chelsea College, 1610; knighted, 1619; published (1603) reply to *Parsons's Conference about the Next Succession of 1594, Lives of the III Normans, Kings of England (1613), and tract in favour of union between England and Scotland (1604), with devotional works; his Life and Raigne of King Edward the Sixt (posthumous, 1630), reprinted with Beginning of Reign of Elizabeth (1840).

HAYWARD, John Davy (1905–1965), anthologist and bibliophile; educated at Gresham's School, Holt, and King's College, Cambridge, 1923–7; afflicted with muscular dystrophy; confined to invalid chair; formed salon where T. S. *Eliot, (Sir) Geoffrey *Faber, and F. V. Morley met together; publications include Collected Works of *Rochester (1926), Complete Poetry and Selected Prose of *Donne (1929), *Swift's Gulliver's Travels (1934), and Swift's Selected Prose Works (1949); compiled anthologies, including Nineteenth Century Poetry (1932), T. S. Eliot: Points of View (1941), Seventeenth Century Poetry (1948), Dr. Johnson (1948), The Penguin Book of English Verse (1956), and The Oxford Book of Nineteenth Century English Verse (1964); CBE, 1953; editorial adviser to Cresset Press; editorial director, the Book Collector; vice-president, Bibliographical Society; he and T. S. Eliot lived together, 1946–57; left books and letters from authors, including T. S. Eliot, to the library of King's College, Cambridge, where there is now a Hayward Room.

HAYWARD, Robert Baldwin (1829–1903), mathematician; BA, St John's College, Cambridge (fourth wrangler), 1850; fellow, 1852–60; mathematical master at Harrow, 1859–93; published original researches; FRS, 1876; original member of Alpine Club, 1858.

HAYWARD, Thomas (d. 1779?), editor of the British Muse (1738), reprinted as Quintessence of English Poetry (1740); FSA, 1756.

HAYWARD, Thomas (1702–1781), barrister of Lincoln's Inn; MP, Ludgershall, 1741–7 and 1754–61.

HAYWARD, Sir Thomas (1743–1799), clerk of the cheque to corps of gentlemen-pensioners; knighted, 1799.

HAYWOOD, Mrs Eliza (1693?–1756), novelist; née Fowler; employed by *Rich to rewrite *The Fair Captive*, 1721; wrote and acted (at Drury Lane) *A Wife to be Lett*, 1723; published *Frederick, Duke of Brunswick-Lunenburgh* (tragedy, 1729); satirized in the *Dunciad* (1728) for her libellous *Memoirs of a certain Island adjacent to Utopia* (1725) and *Secret History of the Present Intrigues of the Court of Caramania* (1727); retaliated in contributions to *Curll's *Female Dunciad* (1729); issued *Female Spectator*, 1744–6; published *History of Jemmy and Jenny Jessamy* (1753); her *Secret Histories, Novels, and Poems* (1725) dedicated to *Steele; doubtfully identified with Steele's 'Sappho'.

HAYWOOD, Francis (1796–1858), translator; published translation of Kant's *Critick of Pure Reason* (1828) and other works.

HAYWOOD, William (1600?–1663), Royalist divine; fellow of St John's College, Oxford; MA, 1624; DD, 1636; chaplain to Charles I and *Laud; prebendary of Westminster, 1638; ejected from St Giles-in-the-Fields, 1641, and imprisoned.

HAYWOOD, William (1821–1894), architect and civil engineer; pupil of George Aitchison, RA; chief engineer to commissioners of sewers for City of London, 1846 till death; MICE, 1853; constructed Holborn Viaduct, 1863–9; published professional reports.

HAZELDINE, William (1763–1840), ironfounder; erected locks on Caledonian Canal (1804–12) and supplied ironwork for Menai (1819–25) and Conway (1822–6) bridges.

HAZLEHURST, Thomas (*fl.* 1760–1818), miniature painter, of Liverpool.

HAZLEWOOD, Colin Henry (1823–1875), dramatist and low comedian at City of London Theatre; author of popular dramas, farces, and burlesques.

HAZLITT, William (1778–1830), essayist; educated for Unitarian ministry; heard *Coleridge's last sermon and visited him at Stowey, 1798; studied painting; painted *Lamb as a Venetian senator, 1805; defended *Godwin against *Malthus, 1807; married Sarah Stoddart, 1808; lectured on modern philosophy at Russell Institution, and wrote parliamentary reports; dramatic critic to *Morning Chronicle*, 1814; contributed to *Hunt's *Examiner*; wrote for *Edinburgh Review* from Nov.

1814; lectured at Surrey Institution, 1818–20; assisted Leigh Hunt in the *Liberal*; attacked Coleridge, *Wordsworth, and *Southey in the *Chronicle* and *Shelley in *Table Talk*; obtained divorce from first wife, 1822; his *Liber Amoris* (1823) the outcome of amour with Miss Walker; married Mrs Bridgewater, 1824, who left him on his return from continental tour of 1824–5; contributed to *London Magazine* and (1826–7) *Colburn's New Monthly*, where appeared his 'Conversations with Northcote'; appears as 'an investigator' in *Haydon's *Christ's Entry*. His writings include *Essay on the Principles of Human Action* (1805), *The Round Table* (from *Examiner*, 1815–17), *The Characters of Shakespeare's Plays* (1817), *Review of English Stage* (1818), *Lectures on English Poets* (1818), *Lectures on the Dramatic Literature of the Reign of Queen Elizabeth* (1821), *Table Talk* (1821–2), *Spirit of the Age* (1825), *The Plain Speaker* (1826), and *Life of Napoleon Buonaparte* (four vols., 1828–30); his *Literary Remains* issued (1836).

HAZLITT, William Carew (1834–1913), bibliographer and man of letters; grandson of William *Hazlitt, the essayist; works include *History of . . . Republic of Venice* (1858, etc.) and *Handbook to Popular, Poetical, and Dramatic Literature of Great Britain* (1867).

HEAD, Anthony Henry, first Viscount Head (1906–1983), soldier and politician; educated at Eton and the Royal Military College, Sandhurst; commissioned in 15th/19th Hussars; transferred to Life Guards, 1924; rode as amateur in Grand National and other races; sailed in *Herzogin Cecilie* in annual grain-race to Australia, 1932; at Staff College, 1939; brigade-major, 20th Guards brigade, 1940; MC; assistant secretary, Committee of Imperial Defence, 1940–1; in Guards Armoured division, 1941–2; chief military planner at combined operations HQ, 1943–5; attended Casablanca, Tehran, Quebec, and Yalta conferences; Conservative MP, Carshalton, 1945–60; PC and secretary of state for war, 1951–6; minister of defence, 1956–7; created first Viscount Head, 1960; first high commissioner, Nigeria, 1960–3; first high commissioner, Malaysia, 1963–6; trustee, Thompson Foundation, 1967; colonel commandant, SAS regiment, 1968–76; chairman, Royal National Institute for the Blind; CBE, 1946; KCMG, 1961; GCMG, 1963.

HEAD, Barclay Vincent (1844–1914), Greek numismatist; entered coins department, British Museum, 1864; keeper, 1893–1906; produced important series of Greek coin catalogues; chief work, *Historia Numorum* (1887).

HEAD, Sir Edmund Walker, baronet (1805–1868), colonial governor; fellow of Merton College, Oxford, 1830–7; MA, 1830; succeeded as baronet, 1838; poor-law commissioner, 1841; governor of New Brunswick, 1847; governor-general of Canada, 1854–61; PC, 1857; DCL, Oxford, 1862; FRS and KCB; edited Sir G. C. *Lewis's Essays on the Administrations of Great Britain* and Kugler's *Handbook of Painting.*

HEAD, Sir Francis Bond, first baronet (1793–1875), colonial governor and author; brother of Sir George *Head; served in Royal Engineers, 1811–25, being present at Waterloo; travelled in South America as manager of Rio Plata Mining Association, 1825–6; as lieutenant-governor of Upper Canada, 1835–7, quelled a rising; KCH, 1835; created baronet, 1836; privy councillor, 1867; contributed to *Quarterly Review*; published, among other works, *Rough Notes of Journeys in the Pampas and Andes*, and lives of Bruce the traveller (1830) and Sir J. M. Burgoyne (1872).

HEAD, Sir George (1782–1855), assistant commissary-general; brother of Sir Francis Bond *Head; served in commissariat during Peninsular War; assistant commissary-general, 1814; served in North America; deputy marshal at coronations of William IV and Queen Victoria; knighted, 1831; published, among other works, *A Home Tour . . . with Memoirs of an Assistant Commissary-general* (1840), and translations of Apuleius and Cardinal Pacca's memoirs.

HEAD, Guy (d. 1800), painter; copyist of works of Titian, Correggio, and Rubens.

HEAD, Sir Henry (1861–1940), neurologist; educated at Charterhouse, and Halle, Cambridge, and Prague universities, and University College Hospital; MB (Camb.), 1890; successively registrar, assistant physician (1896), full physician, consulting physician, London Hospital; established 'Head's Areas' by his thesis 'On disturbances of sensation, with special reference to the pain of visceral disease' (*Brain*, 1893–6); FRS, 1899; FRCP, 1900; editor of *Brain*, 1905–21; underwent experimental operation in nerve division performed by James Sherren (described in *Brain*, 1908); publications include *Aphasia and Kindred Disorders of Speech* (2 vols., 1926); knighted, 1927.

HEAD, Richard (1637?–1686?), author of first part of *The English Rogue* (1665); studied at New Inn Hall, Oxford; ruined by gambling; published also *Proteus Redivivus, or the Art of Wheedling* (1675), *The Canting Academy* (1673), *Life and Death of Mother Shipton* (1677), and other works; drowned at sea.

HEADDA, Saint (d. 1705). See HEDDI.

HEADLAM, Arthur Cayley (1862–1947), bishop of Gloucester; brother of Sir J. W. *Headlam-Morley; scholar of Winchester and New College, Oxford; first class, Lit. Hum., and fellow of All Souls, 1885; deacon, 1888; priest, 1889; rector of Welwyn, 1896–1903; principal, King's College, London, 1903–12; divided theological department from secular faculties; regius professor of divinity, Oxford, 1918–23; bishop of Gloucester, 1923–45; closely interested in Christian reunion; chairman, Church of England council on foreign relations, 1933–45; editor, *Church Quarterly Review*, 1901–21; prolific, vigorous theological writer of enlightened conservatism; CH, 1921.

HEADLAM, Thomas Emerson (1813–1875), judge advocate-general; MA, Trinity College, Cambridge, 1839; barrister, Inner Temple, 1839; treasurer, 1867; QC, 1851; chancellor of Ripon and Durham, 1854; Liberal MP, Newcastle, 1847–74; judge advocate-general, 1859–66; privy councillor, 1859; carried Trustee Act, 1850.

HEADLAM, Walter George (1866–1908), scholar and poet; educated at Harrow and King's College, Cambridge; gained many university classical prizes, 1885–7; BA, 1887; MA, 1891; Litt.D., 1903; fellow, 1890; rarely surpassed in Greek versions of English poetry; translated poems by Meleager, 1890, and Aeschylus, 1900–8; his *Letters and Poems* (1900) edited with memoir by his brother.

HEADLAM-MORLEY, Sir James Wycliffe (1863–1929), political historian; BA, King's College, Cambridge, 1887; fellow, 1890–6; professor of Greek and ancient history, Queen's College, London, 1894–1900; staff inspector of secondary schools, Board of Education, 1902–14; historical adviser to propaganda department, Wellington House, 1914–17; to Foreign Office, 1920–8; knighted, 1929; works include *Bismarck and the German Empire* (1899) and *The History of Twelve Days* (1915), material for third edition of which formed vol. xi of G. P. *Gooch and H. W. V. *Temperley's *British Documents on the Origins of the War* (1926).

HEADLEY, Henry (1765–1788), poet and critic; educated under *Parr at Colchester and Norwich; friend of *Bowles at Trinity College, Oxford; BA, 1786; published *Select Beauties of Ancient English Poetry, with Remarks* (1787); his *Poems* (1786) included in *Davenport's and Parr's collections.

HEAL, Sir Ambrose (1872–1959), furniture designer and dealer; educated at Marlborough; joined family firm, 1893; chairman, 1913–53; introduced furniture combining functional utility with simplicity of line; extended scope of business to include antiques, carpets, curtains, etc.; co-founder, Design and Industries Association, 1915; knighted, 1933; Royal Designer for Industry, 1939; Albert medallist of Royal Society of Arts for services to industrial design, 1954; wrote number of books, including *The English Writing-Masters and their Copy-Books, 1570–1800* (1931).

HEALD, James (1796–1873), Wesleyan philanthropist; MP, Stockport, 1847–52; founder of Stockport Infirmary.

HEALD, William Margetson (1767–1837), surgeon and divine; MA, Catharine Hall, Cambridge, 1798; vicar of Birstal, 1801–36; published *The Brunoniad* (1789).

HEALDE, Thomas (1724?–1789), physician; MD, Trinity College, Cambridge, 1754; FRCP, 1760; Harveian orator, 1765; Gulstonian, 1763, Croonian, 1770 and 1784–6, and Lumleian, 1786–9, lecturer; FRS, 1770; physician to London Hospital, 1770; Gresham professor, 1771; translated *New Pharmacopoeia* (1788).

HEALE, William (1581?–1627), divine; chaplain-fellow of Exeter College, Oxford, 1608–10; MA, 1606; vicar of Bishop's Teignton, 1610–27; published *Apologie for Women* (1609).

HEALEY, John (d. 1610), translator; friend of Thomas *Thorpe (1570?–1635?); published *Philip Mornay, Lord of Plessis, his Teares* (1609), *Discovery of a Newe World* (version of Bishop Hall's *Mundus alter et idem, c.*1609), *Epictetus his Manuall And Cebes his Table* (1610), and *St. Augustine of the Citie of God*, with *Vives's commentary (1610).

HEALY, James (1824–1894), Roman Catholic divine and humorist; educated at Maynooth; curate in Dublin, 1852, and at Bray, Co. Wicklow, 1858; administrator of Little Bray, 1867–93; parish priest of Ballybrack and Killiney, Co. Dublin, 1893 till death.

HEALY, John Edward (1872–1934), journalist; educated at Trinity College, Dublin; joined Dublin *Daily Express*; became editor; Dublin correspondent of *The Times*, 1899–1907; editor, *Irish Times*, 1907–34; actively defended the union during home-rule controversy; opposed partition and any broadening of gap between Dublin and London.

HEALY, Timothy Michael (1855–1931), Irish political leader and first governor-general of Irish Free State; educated by the Christian Brothers; clerk in Newcastle (1871) and London (1878); contributed weekly parliamentary letter to the *Nation*; organized Canadian tour for C. S. *Parnell, 1880; arrested but acquitted during agrarian agitation, 1880; MP, Wexford, 1880–3; expert at obstruction; showed constructive ability in

debate on Land Act, 1881; imprisoned for six months (1883) during further agrarian agitation; called to Irish bar, 1884; QC, 1899; Parnellite MP, Co. Monaghan (1883–5), South Londonderry (1885–6), North Longford (1887–92); became increasingly distrustful of Parnell; recommended his temporary retirement from Irish leadership when Gladstone refused to co-operate further with him after the *O'Shea (1840–1905) divorce case, 1890; anti-Parnellite MP, North Louth, 1892–1910; accused John *Dillon and T. P. *O'Connor of subservience to English Liberalism; expelled from National League, 1895; supported choice of John *Redmond as chairman of Nationalists (1900) but expelled from party (1902); friendly with chief secretary, George *Wyndham; founded 'All for Ireland' League (1910) to promote Irish cause by conciliation; MP, North-East Cork, 1910–18; in general sympathy with Sinn Fein; fulfilled duties as governor-general (1922–8) with social tact.

HEAPHY, Charles (1821?–1881), New Zealand official; son of Thomas *Heaphy the elder; assisted in purchase of Chatham Islands, 1840–1; published *Residence in New Zealand* (1842); land surveyor of Auckland, 1858; chief surveyor of New Zealand, 1864; received Victoria Cross (1867) for conduct during third Maori War as guide at Mangapiko River, 1864; member of House of Representatives, 1867–70; commissioner of native reserves, 1869; judge of native land court, 1878; died at Brisbane.

HEAPHY, Thomas, the elder (1775–1835), water-colour painter; exhibited at Water-Colour Society, 1804–12 (member, 1807); painted, on the spot, *Wellington and his officers before an action in the Peninsula; established Society of British Artists, 1824.

HEAPHY, Thomas (Frank), the younger (1813–1873), painter; son of Thomas *Heaphy the elder; exhibited at Royal Academy portraits and subject-pictures from 1831; member of Society of British Artists, 1867; investigated origin of the traditional likeness of Christ; his *Likeness of Christ*, with illustrations, edited by Wyke Bayliss (1880); published *A Wonderful Ghost Story*.

HEARD, Sir Isaac (1730–1822), Garter king-of-arms; Blue-mantle pursuivant, 1759; Lancaster herald, 1761; Norroy, 1774; Clarenceux, 1780; Garter king-of-arms, 1784; knighted, 1794.

HEARD, William (*fl.* 1778), poet and dramatist.

HEARDER, Jonathan (1810–1876), electrician to South Devon Hospital; patented suboceanic cable and thermometer for lead-soundings at sea; assisted researches of Sir William Snow *Harris.

HEARN, Mary Anne (1834–1909), hymn writer and author, under the pseudonym of Marianne Farningham; edited *Sunday School Times* from 1885; published forty volumes of essays and hymns, which included 'Watching and Waiting for me'; autobiography published, 1907.

HEARN, William Edward (1826–1888), legal and sociological writer; of Trinity College, Dublin; professor of Greek, Queen's College, Galway, 1849–54; first professor of modern history and literature at Melbourne University, 1854–72, afterwards dean of the law faculty; as member of legislative council of Victoria devoted himself to codification; published *The Government of England, its Structure and its Development* (1867), *The Aryan Household* (1879), and other works.

HEARNE, Samuel (1745–1792), traveller; explored north-western America for Hudson's Bay Company, 1768–70; captured by La Perouse, 1782; his *Account of a Journey from Prince of Wales's Fort . . . to the North-West* issued (1795).

HEARNE, Thomas (1678–1735), historical antiquary; educated at expense of Francis *Cherry; MA, St Edmund Hall, Oxford, 1703; second keeper of Bodleian Library, 1712; deprived as a nonjuror, 1716; refused chief librarianship and other academic offices on political grounds; published *Reliquiae Bodleianae* (1703) and editions of Latin classics, of *Leland's *Itinerary* (1710) and *Collectanea* (1715), *Camden's *Annales* (1717), and many English chronicles; his diaries and correspondence printed by Oxford Historical Society; the Wormius of *Pope's *Dunciad*.

HEARNE, Thomas (1744–1817), water-colour painter; FSA; made drawings during residence in Leeward Islands, 1771–5; executed fifty-two illustrations for Byrne's *Antiquities of Great Britain* (1777–81); exhibited at Royal Academy, 1781–1802; his drawings copied by *Girtin and *Turner.

HEATH, Benjamin (1704–1766), book-collector and critic; town clerk of Exeter, 1752–66; hon. DCL, Oxford, 1762; prominent in agitation for repeal of cider duty, 1763–6; published notes on Aeschylus, Sophocles, and Euripides (1762), and *Revisal of Shakespear's Text* (1765, anon.); left manuscript notes on Latin poets and supplement to *Seward's edition of *Beaumont and *Fletcher.

HEATH, Charles (1761–1831), topographer and painter; twice mayor of Monmouth; pub-

lished histories of Monmouth (1804) and neighbouring places of interest.

HEATH, Charles (1785–1848), engraver and publisher of illustrated *Annuals*; natural son of James *Heath (1757–1834); executed small plates for popular English classics; engraved works after Benjamin *West and other painters.

HEATH, Christopher (1802–1876), minister of Catholic Apostolic Church, Gordon Square; succeeded Edward *Irving at Newman Street Hall, and caused erection of new church, Gordon Square (opened 1853).

HEATH, Christopher (1835–1905), surgeon; son of Christopher *Heath; studied medicine at King's College, London; MRCS, 1856; FRCS, 1860; became surgeon (1866) and Holme professor of clinical surgery (1875) at University College Hospital; at Royal College of Surgeons, Hunterian professor of surgery (1886–7), Bradshaw lecturer (1892), Hunterian orator (1897), and president (1895); visited America, 1897; great teacher of anatomy and surgery, but backward in new bacteriological science; published many works on anatomy and surgery.

HEATH, Douglas Denon (1811–1897), classical and mathematical scholar; senior wrangler, first Smith's prizeman, and fellow, Trinity College, Cambridge, 1832; barrister, Inner Temple, 1835; county clerk of Middlesex, 1838–46; county-court judge, Bloomsbury district, 1847–65; edited *Bacon's legal works for *Spedding's edition of Bacon's works (1859); published *Doctrine of Energy* (1874) and mathematical, legal, and classical writings.

HEATH, Dunbar Isidore (1816–1888), heterodox divine; fellow of Trinity College, Cambridge; fifth wrangler, 1838; MA, 1841; deprived of living of Brading, Isle of Wight, 1861, for *Sermons on Important Subjects*; edited *Journal of Anthropology*; translated Egyptian *Proverbs of Aphobis* (1858).

HEATH, Henry (1599–1643), Franciscan, of St Bonaventure, Douai; BA, Corpus Christi College, Cambridge, 1621; published *Soliloquia seu Documenta Christianae Perfectionis* (1651); executed at Tyburn as a recusant.

HEATH, Sir (Henry) Frank (1863–1946), academic and scientific administrator; educated at Westminster, University College, London, and Strasburg; professor of English, Bedford College, 1890–96; assistant registrar and librarian, London University, 1895; academic registrar, 1901–3; director of special inquiries and reports, Board of Education, 1903–16; in charge of universities branch, 1910–16; joint-secretary, Royal Commission on University Education in London, 1909–13; member, Treasury Advisory Committee on University College Grants, 1909–11; proposed formation and first secretary of Advisory Council (1915–27) and executive, Department of Scientific and Industrial Research (1916–27); KCB, 1917.

HEATH, James (1629–1664), Royalist historian; of Westminster and Christ Church, Oxford; deprived of studentship, 1648; published *Brief Chronicle of the late Intestine War* (1663), *Flagellum* (a book on *Cromwell), and poems.

HEATH, James (1757–1834), engraver; pupil of Joseph *Collyer the younger; associate engraver of Royal Academy, 1791; historical engraver to George III, George IV, and William IV, 1794–1834; engraved designs for illustrations by *Stothard and *Smirke; engraved *West's *Death of Nelson*, *Copley's *Death of Major Pierson*, and pictures by foreign masters; re-engraved *Hogarth's plates.

HEATH, John (*fl.* 1615), epigrammatist and translator; MA, New College, Oxford, 1613; fellow, 1609–16; published *Two Centuries of Epigrammes* (1610).

HEATH, John (1736–1816), judge; MA, Christ Church, Oxford, 1762; barrister, Inner Temple, 1762; serjeant-at-law and recorder of Exeter, 1775; judge of common pleas, 1780–1816.

HEATH, Sir Leopold George (1817–1907), admiral; entered Royal Naval College, Portsmouth, 1830; served in Mediterranean and East Indies; commander, 1847; employed at destruction of Lagos, 1850, and in Crimean War, 1853–4; principal agent of transports and CB, 1855; commodore in command in East Indies, 1867–70; KCB, 1870; vice-president of Ordnance Select Committee, 1870–1; rear-admiral, 1871; admiral, 1884; published *Letters from the Black Sea* (1897).

HEATH, Nicholas (1501?–1578), archbishop of York and lord chancellor; fellow, Christ's College, 1521, and Clare Hall, Cambridge, 1524; MA, 1522; DD, 1535; archdeacon of Stafford, 1534; accompanied Edward *Fox to Germany to negotiate with Smalcaldic League, 1535; king's almoner, 1537; bishop of Rochester, 1539, Worcester, 1543; imprisoned and deprived, 1551, but restored on accession of Mary, 1553; as archbishop of York (1555–9) procured restitution of Ripon, Southwell, and other manors to York, and built York House, Strand; as chancellor (1556–8) proclaimed Elizabeth in House of Lords; arranged preliminaries of disputation at Westminster; released from Tower on promise to abstain from public affairs.

HEATH, Richard (d. 1702), judge; barrister, Inner Temple, 1659; serjeant-at-law, 1683; judge of Exchequer court, 1686–8; excepted from indemnity at Revolution.

HEATH, Sir Robert (1575–1649), judge; of Tunbridge and St John's College, Cambridge; barrister, Inner Temple, 1603, treasurer, 1625; clerk of pleas in King's Bench, 1607; recorder of London, 1618–21, and MP for the city, 1620; solicitor-general, 1621; knighted, 1621; MP, East Grinstead, 1623 and 1625; as attorney-general (1625–31) was engaged with cases of Sir T. *Darnell, *Felton, *Eliot, and Star Chamber prosecutions of 1629–30; prepared answer to Petition of Right, 1628; chief justice of common pleas, 1631; dismissed for supposed Puritan sympathies, 1634; king's serjeant, 1636, puisne judge, 1641, and chief justice of King's Bench, 1642; tried *Lilburne at Oxford and other Parliamentarians at Salisbury, 1642; impeached by parliament and his place declared vacant, 1645; died at Calais; his *Maxims and Rules of Pleading* published (1694), and autobiography in *Philobiblon Society Miscellany*.

HEATH, Robert (*fl.* 1650), poet; author of *Clarastella* and other poems (1650).

HEATH, Robert (d. 1779), mathematician; edited *Ladies' Diary*, 1744–53; after supersession by Thomas *Simpson (1710–1761) carried on rival publications; helped to popularize mathematics in periodicals; his *History of the Islands of Scilly* (1750) reprinted in *Pinkerton.

HEATH, Thomas (*fl.* 1583), mathematician; friend of John *Dee; MA, All Souls College, Oxford, 1573.

HEATH, Sir Thomas Little (1861–1940), civil servant and authority on ancient mathematics; educated at Clifton and Trinity College, Cambridge; first classes, classical tripos, 1881–3; twelfth wrangler, 1882; passed first into Civil Service, 1884; entered Treasury; assistant secretary, 1907; joint permanent secretary, controlling administrative side, 1913; comptroller-general, National Debt Office, 1919–26; KCB, 1909; KCVO, 1916; a leading authority on Greek mathematics; made accessible in modern notation works of Diophantus (1885), Apollonius of Perga (1896), Archimedes (1897), and Euclid (1908); other publications include *A History of Greek Mathematics* (2 vols., 1921) and *Greek Astronomy* (1932); FRS, 1912; FBA, 1932.

HEATHCOAT, John (1783–1861), inventor of lace-making machines known as the horizontal pillow and the 'old Loughborough' (1808–9); after Luddite riots at Loughborough in 1816 removed to Tiverton, which he represented,

1832–59; patented rotary self-narrowing stocking-frame and other inventions.

HEATHCOAT AMORY, Derick, fourth baronet, and first Viscount Amory (1899–1981), industrialist and statesman. See AMORY.

HEATHCOTE, Sir Gilbert (1651?–1733), lord mayor of London; MA, Christ's College, Cambridge, 1673; chief founder of new East India Company, 1693; member of first board of directors of Bank of England, 1694; knighted, 1702; sheriff of London, 1703; lord mayor, 1710–11; senior alderman, 1724; president of St Thomas's Hospital; commissioner for Georgia, 1732; Whig MP for the city, 1700–10, Helston, 1714, New Lymington, 1722, St Germans, 1727; his parsimony ridiculed by *Pope.

HEATHCOTE, John Moyer (1834–1912), tennis player; BA, Trinity College, Cambridge; pupil of Edmund Tompkins, professional tennis champion; amateur tennis champion, 1859–81, 1883, 1886.

HEATHCOTE, Ralph (1721–1795), divine and author; MA, Jesus College, Cambridge, 1748; DD, 1759; Boyle lecturer, 1763–5; prebendary of Southwell, 1768–95; took part in Middletonian controversy, 1752, and that between *Hume and Rousseau; published *Historia Astronomiae* (1746) and *The Irenarch or Justice of the Peace's Manual* (1771).

HEATHER (or HEYTHER), William (1563?–1627), musician; friend and executor of *Camden; gentleman of the Chapel Royal, 1615; Mus.Doc., Oxford, 1622; founder of the music lecturership at Oxford, 1626.

HEATHERINGTON, Alexander (d. 1878), mining agent; opened at Halifax, Nova Scotia, International Mining Agency, 1867; compiled *The Gold Yield of Nova Scotia* (1860–9, reissued 1870–4 as *Mining Industries*).

HEATHFIELD, first Baron (1717–1790). See ELIOTT, GEORGE AUGUSTUS.

HEATH ROBINSON, William (1872–1944), cartoonist and book-illustrator. See ROBINSON.

HEATON, Clement (1824–1882), glass-painter and church decorator; founded firm of Heaton & Butler.

HEATON, Sir John Henniker, first baronet (1848–1914), postal reformer; went to Australia, 1864; journalist in Sydney; settled in London, 1884; Conservative MP, Canterbury, 1885–1910; by his postal reform campaign (opened 1886) won imperial penny postage (1898), Anglo-American (1908), Anglo-Australian (1905–11); baronet, 1911.

HEATON, Mrs Mary Margaret (1836–1883), writer on art; née Keymer; married Professor Charles William Heaton, 1863; contributed to Bryan's *Dictionary of Painters and Engravers*; published *Life of Dürer* (1870), *Masterpieces of Flemish Art* (1869), and *Concise History of Painting* (1873).

HEAVISIDE, Oliver (1850–1925), mathematical physicist and electrician; by self-training acquired remarkable skill in application of mathematics to electrodynamics; pursued his studies in Camden Town, 1876–89; subsequently worked at Paignton, Newton Abbot, and Torquay, in his latter days living in great seclusion; propounded theory of 'surface conduction'; enriched and clarified language of electrodynamics; introduced 'Expansion Theorem', or operational calculus; his 'distortionless' case of wide application in general dynamics; FRS, 1891.

HEBER, Reginald (1783–1826), bishop of Calcutta; of Brasenose College, Oxford; won prizes for the English essay, Latin poem, and English verse ('Palestine'); fellow of All Souls College, Oxford, 1805; incumbent of Hodnet, 1807; prebendary of St Asaph, 1812; Bampton lecturer, 1815; preacher at Lincoln's Inn, 1822; bishop of Calcutta, 1822–6; completed establishment of Bishop's College, Calcutta; travelled in all parts of India; his hymns appeared first in *Christian Observer*, 1811; published *Poetical Works* (1812), and also life and critical examination of works of Jeremy *Taylor and accounts of journeys through India; died at Trichinopoly.

HEBER, Richard (1773–1833), book-collector; half-brother of Reginald *Heber; MA, Brasenose College, Oxford, 1797; intimate of *Scott; candidate for Oxford University, 1806; MP, 1821–6; DCL, 1822; a founder of the Athenaeum Club, 1824; travelled widely to collect books, spending on them about £100,000; his library rich in choice English works, the English portion being ultimately sold for £56,774; edited Persius (1790), Silius Italicus (1792), and Claudian (1793–6), and *Cutwode's *Caltha Poetarum* (1815).

HEBERDEN, William, the elder (1710–1801), physician; BA, St John's College, Cambridge, 1728; senior fellow, 1749; MD, 1739; contributed to *Athenian Letters*, 1741; FRCP, 1746; Gulstonian (1749) and Croonian (1760) lecturer; Harveian orator (1750) and censor; FRS, 1749; practised in London from 1748; first described *angina pectoris*; attended *Johnson, *Cowper, and *Warburton; published at his own expense plays of Euripides edited by *Markland, and Middleton's *Appendix to his Dissertation on servile condition of Physicians among the Ancients*. His works (edited in Germany by Soemmering) include *Commentarii de Morborum Historia et Curatione* (transl., 1803), and contributions to *Transactions* of College of Physicians and Royal Society.

HEBERDEN, William, the younger (1767–1845), physician; son of William *Heberden the elder; fellow, St John's College, Cambridge, 1788–96; MA, 1791; incorporated MA, Oxford; MD, Oxford, 1795; physician at St George's Hospital, 1793–1803; FRCP, 1796; FRS; physician-in-ordinary to the queen, 1806, and the king, 1809; published miscellaneous works, including a dialogue on education (1818), translations of Cicero's *Letters to Atticus* (1825), and medical tracts.

HECHT, Eduard (1832–1887), musical composer; born at Dürkheim-on-the-Haardt; settled at Manchester, 1854; conducted musical societies at Manchester, Bradford, and Halifax.

HECTOR, Annie French (1825–1902), novelist writing as Mrs Alexander; daughter of Robert French, Dublin solicitor; settled with parents in London; friend of W. H. *Wills; married (1858) Alexander Hector (d. 1875), explorer, merchant, and archaeologist; lived in Germany and France, 1876–82, and St Andrews, 1882–5; published her best-known novel, *The Wooing o't*, 1873, and over forty others.

HECTOR, Sir James (1834–1907), Canadian geologist; MD, Edinburgh, 1856; surgeon and geologist on exploring expedition of John *Palliser to western North America, 1857–60; discovered Hector's Pass; director of geological survey of New Zealand, 1865; reported on fossiliferous formations of New Zealand; observed volcanic and glacial phenomena; CMG, 1875; KCMG, 1887; FRS, 1866; Lyell medallist of Geological Society, 1876; died at Wellington, NZ; published *Outlines of New Zealand Geology* (1886).

HEDDI (HÆDDI, HEADDA, or **ÆTLA)** (d. 705), bishop of Gewissas or West Saxons, 676; fixed his see at Winchester; friend of Archbishop *Theodore.

HEDDIUS, Stephen (*fl.* 669). See EDDI.

HEDENDON, baron of (d. 1182?). See BASSET, THOMAS.

HEDGES, Sir Charles (d. 1714), politician and lawyer; BA, Magdalen Hall, Oxford, 1670, MA, Magdalen College, 1673; DCL, 1675; chancellor of Rochester, 1686; judge of Admiralty court, 1689–1714; knighted, 1689; MP, Orford (1698–1700), Dover, 1701, Malmesbury, 1701 (Nov.), Calne, 1702, West Looe, 1705, 1708, and 1710, East Looe, 1713–14; secretary of state, 1700–1, 1702–6; judge of prerogative court of Canter-

bury, 1711–14; reputed author of *Reasons for Setling* [*sic*] *Admiralty Jurisdiction* (1690).

HEDGES, Sir William (1632–1701), governor of Bengal; cousin of Sir Charles *Hedges; head of Levant Company's factory at Constantinople; governor of Bengal, 1682–4; failed in effecting reforms in Bengal; knighted, 1688; sheriff of London, 1693; director of the Bank, 1694; his diary and other documents edited by Sir Henry *Yule, 1887–8.

HEDLEY, William (1779–1843), inventor; patented smooth wheel and rails for locomotives, 1813; discovered principle of blast-pipe; introduced at Callerton Colliery improved system of pumping water.

HEEMSKERK, Egbert van (1645–1704), painter of subject-pictures; came to London from Haarlem.

HEENAN, John Carmel (1905–1975), cardinal, eighth archbishop of Westminster; educated at St Ignatius' College, Stamford Hill, London; studied for priesthood at St Cuthbert's College, Ushaw, Durham; awarded bursary to Venerable English College, Rome, 1924; became doctor of philosophy and theology; ordained priest, 1930; appointed assistant priest at church of SS Mary and Ethelburga, Barking, 1931; visited Soviet Union, 1936; parish priest, St Stephen's, Manor Park, 1937; became popular broadcaster, 1939–45; superior of Catholic Missionary Society, 1947–51; bishop of Leeds, 1951–7; bishop of Liverpool, 1957–63; responsible for building of Liverpool Cathedral, designed by (Sir) Frederick *Gibberd; archbishop of Westminster, 1963; attended Second Vatican Council; appointed to Secretariat for Christian Unity; cardinal, 1965; accepted changes that came from Second Vatican Council, but remained at heart a traditional Catholic; published *Not the Whole Truth* (1973) and *A Crown of Thorns* (1974, autobiography).

HEERE, Lucas van (1534–1584). See DE HEERE.

HEETE, Robert (or ROBERT OF WOODSTOCK) (d. 1428), canonist and civilian; fellow of New College, Oxford, 1407, of Winchester College, 1421; BCL; lectured on first book of decretals, 1413; probably author of manuscript life of *William of Wykeham; benefactor of Winchester.

HEFFER, Reuben George (1908–1985), bookseller; grandson of founder of W. Heffer & Sons Ltd., Cambridge booksellers, publishers, stationers, and printers; educated at Perse School and Corpus Christi College, Cambridge; trained at London School of Printing before joining family firm; chairman of firm, 1959–75; member of Booksellers Association, 1948 Book Trade Committee, Society of Bookmen, and Sette of Odde Volumes; expanded Heffers to become international booksellers of high repute; served in RAF and at the Air Ministry, 1942–5; served as JP and with Marriage Guidance Council, Trustee Savings Bank and Cambridge Preservation Society; helped to found Bell School of Languages; hon. MA, Open University (1979).

HEGAT, William (*fl.* 1600), professor of philosophy at Bordeaux; MA, Glasgow; friend of Robert *Balfour (1550?–1625?); author of Latin poems and orations.

HEGGE, Robert (1599–1629), author; MA, Corpus Christi College, Oxford, 1620, probationer fellow, 1624; his treatises on St Cuthbert's churches printed (1777).

HEIDEGGER, John James (1659?–1749), operatic manager; the 'Swiss Count' of the *Tatler* and 'Count Ugly' of *Fielding's *Pleasures of the Town*; managed Italian opera at Haymarket, 1713, for Royal Academy of Music, 1720–8; at the Haymarket in partnership with *Handel, 1728–34, and alone, 1737–8; carried on masquerades and 'ridottos'; entertained George II at Barn Elms; caricatured by *Hogarth.

HEIGHAM, Sir Clement (d. 1570), judge; barrister, Lincoln's Inn, autumn reader, 1538 and 1547, and governor; privy councillor and speaker of House of Commons under Queen Mary; knighted, 1555; lord chief baron of the Exchequer, 1558–9.

HEIGHAM, John (*fl.* 1639), Roman Catholic printer, writer, and translator; his *Devout Exposition of the Holie Masse* (1614) edited by A. J. Rowley (1876); version of Luis de la Puente's *Meditations on the Mysteries of our holie Faith* reprinted (1852).

HEIGHINGTON, Musgrave (1690–1774?), musical composer; of The Queen's College, Oxford; organist at Yarmouth, Leicester, 1739, and the Episcopal Chapel, Dundee, before 1760; member of Spalding Society; composed *The Enchantress* and set odes of Anacreon and Horace.

HEILBRON, Sir Ian Morris (1886–1959), chemist; educated at Glasgow High School and Royal Technical College, and Leipzig; lecturer, Royal Technical College, 1909–14; served in army, 1914–18; DSO; professor of organic chemistry, Royal Technical College, 1919–20; Liverpool, 1920–33; Manchester, 1933–5, Sir Samuel Hall professor of chemistry, 1935–8; Imperial College of Science, 1938–49; director, Brewing Industry Research Foundation,

1949–58; pioneer of organic chemical research developed for therapeutic and industrial use (i.e. vitamins, steroids, acetylenic derivatives, penicillin, DDT); FRS, 1931; knighted, 1946.

HEINEMANN, William (1863–1920), publisher; set up business in London, 1890; published novels by R. L. *Stevenson, *Kipling, Sarah Grand, Flora Annie *Steel, John *Galsworthy, Joseph *Conrad, H. G. *Wells, etc.; plays by Sir Arthur *Pinero, W. Somerset *Maugham, Israel *Zangwill, etc.; produced International Library of translations of fiction; commissioned translations of Dostoevsky, Turgenev, Tolstoy, Ibsen, Björnson, Rolland; chief literary enterprise, Loeb Classical Library of translations.

HEINS, John Theodore (1732–1771), engraver, draughtsman, and painter; painted miniature of *Cowper's mother, which occasioned Cowper's poem 'On receipt of my mother's picture'.

HEITLER, Walter Heinrich (1904–1981), physicist; born in Karlsruhe; educated at universities of Berlin and Munich; doctor's degree, Munich, 1926; worked on new wave mechanics in Zurich; published with Fritz London *Theory of Chemical Bond* (1927); did similar work at Göttingen, 1929–33; because of Jewish ancestry emigrated to Bristol University; worked on theory of cosmic radiation with Cecil *Powell, 1933–40; interned temporarily, 1940; assistant professor, Dublin Institute of Advanced Studies, 1941–6; director, 1946–9; became Irish citizen, 1946; professor of theoretical physics, Zurich University, 1949–60; turned to philosophy and religion and published books such as *Man and Science* (1963); FRS, 1948; honorary doctorates from universities of Dublin, Göttingen, and Uppsala; Max Planck medallist, 1968.

HELE, Sir John (1565–1608), serjeant-at-law; Lent reader at Inner Temple; recorder of Exeter, 1592–1606, and MP, 1592–1601; serjeant-at-law, 1594; queen's serjeant, 1602; knighted, 1603; employed at *Ralegh's trial, 1603; founded boys' hospital at Plymouth.

HÈLE (or HELL), Thomas d' (1740?–1780). See HALES.

HELENA VICTORIA (1870–1948), princess of Great Britain, whose full names were Victoria Louise Sophia Augusta Amelia Helena; elder daughter of Prince and Princess Christian; her interests philanthropic, social, and musical.

HELE-SHAW, Henry Selby (1854–1941), engineer; apprenticed in Bristol; graduated from University College, Bristol, 1880; first professor of engineering, Bristol, 1881–5; Liverpool,

1885–1904; Transvaal Technical Institute, 1904–5; principal, 1905–6; returned to England as consulting engineer; many inventions included instruments for recording wind velocities; integrating machines; friction clutch widely used on motor vehicles; hydraulic transmission gear and steering gear for ships; automatic variable-pitch airscrew; demonstrated nature of streamline flow; organized Liverpool trials on commercial motor vehicles, 1897; influential in introduction (1920) of national certificate scheme of training engineers; FRS, 1899.

HELLIER, Henry (1662?–1697), divine; MA, Corpus Christi College, Oxford, 1682, DD, 1697, vice-president at his death; published *Treatise concerning Schism and Schismaticks* (1697); committed suicide.

HELLINS, John (d. 1827), mathematician and astronomer; assistant in Greenwich Observatory; vicar of Potterspury, 1790; BD, Trinity College, Cambridge, 1800; FRS, 1796; Copley medallist for solution of problem in physical astronomy, 1798; published *Mathematical Essays* (1788); made calculations for War Office, 1806.

HELLMUTH, Isaac (1817–1901), bishop of Huron; born near Warsaw of Hebrew parents; joined Church of England in Liverpool, 1841; emigrated to Canada, 1844; ordained and made professor of Hebrew at Bishop's College, Lennoxville, 1846; DD, Lambeth, 1853; DCL, Trinity College, Toronto, 1854; visited England (1861) and collected funds for new Huron Evangelical Theological College at London, Ontario; first principal, 1863; bishop of Huron, 1871–3; founded Western University, 1878; coadjutor to Robert *Bickersteth, bishop of Ripon, 1883–4.

HELLOWES, Edward (fl. 1574–1600), translator; groom of the chamber, 1597; translated works of Guevara.

HELMES, Thomas (d. 1616). See TUNSTALL, THOMAS.

HELMORE, Thomas (1811–1890), musical writer and composer; MA, Magdalen Hall, Oxford, 1845; vice-principal (1840) and precentor of St Mark's College, Chelsea, 1846–77; priest-ordinary of Chapel Royal, St James's, 1847; composed carols and hymn-tunes; translated Fétis on choral singing, 1855; published *Catechism of Music* and *Plain-Song* (1878), and other works.

HELPS, Sir Arthur (1813–1875), clerk of the Privy Council; of Eton and Trinity College, Cambridge; MA, 1839; clerk of Privy Council, 1860–75; hon. DCL, Oxford, 1864; private secretary to Spring *Rice and Lord Morpeth; KCB, 1872; revised works by Queen Victoria; published, among other works, *Friends in Council* (four series, 1847–59), *Conquerors of the New World* (1848), *Spanish Conquest in America* (1855–61).

HELSHAM, Richard (1682?–1738), friend of *Swift; BA, Trinity College, Dublin, 1702, fellow, 1704, lecturer in mathematics, 1723–30, Erasmus Smith professor, 1724–38; regius professor of physic (1733–8) of Dublin University; his *Lectures on Natural Philosophy* edited by Bryan *Robinson (1739).

HELWYS, Edward (fl. 1589), author of *A Marvell Deciphered* (1589); member of Gray's Inn, 1550; brother of Thomas *Helwys.

HELWYS, Sir Gervase (1561–1615), lieutenant of the Tower; nephew of Thomas *Helwys; of St John's College, Cambridge, and Lincoln's Inn; lieutenant of the Tower, 1613–15; conducted torture of Edmond *Peacham, 1615; hanged on Tower Hill for complicity in murder of Sir Thomas *Overbury (1581–1613).

HELWYS, Thomas (1550?–1616?), Puritan divine; uncle of Sir Gervase *Helwys; member of Brownist congregation at Amsterdam; formed at Pinners' Hall, London, first General Baptist congregation; published tract against *Persecution for Religion* (1615).

HELYAR, John (fl. 1535), classical scholar and friend of Erasmus; fellow of Corpus Christi College, Oxford; MA, 1525; BD, 1532; his 'Carmina in obitum Erasmi' (Greek and Latin) in *Epitaphs on Erasmus*.

HELY-HUTCHINSON, Christopher (1767–1826), soldier and politician; fifth son of John *Hely-Hutchinson (1724–1794); Irish barrister, 1792; MP, Taghmon (in Irish parliament), 1795; as a volunteer distinguished himself at Ballinamuck, 1798; on the Helder (1799) and Egyptian (1801) expeditions; lieutenant-colonel, 1801; MP, Cork, 1801–12 and 1819–26, and Co. Longford, 1812–19; served (1807) in Russian Army at Eylau and Friedland.

HELY-HUTCHINSON, John (1724–1794), lawyer and statesman; BA, Trinity College, Dublin, 1744; Irish barrister, 1748; assumed additional name of Hutchinson, 1751; MP (in Irish parliament) for Lanesborough, 1759, Cork, 1761–90, and Taghmon, 1790–4; privy councillor and prime serjeant, 1760; secretary of state, 1778; provost of Trinity College, 1774; attacked for abusing his powers; founded modern languages professorship; advocated free trade in *Commercial Restraints of Ireland* (1779, anon.), also home rule, Catholic emancipation, and parliamentary reform; supported commercial propositions of 1785, but joined opposition on regency question; friend of *Burke and William Gerard *Hamilton; his wife created Baroness Donoughmore, 1783.

HELY-HUTCHINSON, John, first Baron Hutchinson, afterwards second earl of Donoughmore (1757–1832), general; second son of John *Hely-Hutchinson (1724–1794); educated at Eton and Dublin; lieutenant-colonel of Athole Highlanders, 1783; served with duke of *York, 1793; major-general on Irish staff when troops at Castlebar fled from Humbert, 1798; represented Lanesborough, 1776–83, and Cork, 1790–1800, in Irish parliament; supported the Union; severely wounded at Alkmaar while in charge of Craven's brigade, 1799; commanded first division under *Abercromby in Egypt; succeeded to chief command, 1801; captured (1801) Cairo and Alexandria; created Baron Hutchinson, with a pension; general, 1813; GCB, 1814; undertook mission to Prussia and Russia, 1806–7; carried George IV's proposals to Queen *Caroline at St Omer, 1820; succeeded as earl of Donoughmore, 1825.

HELY-HUTCHINSON, John, third earl of Donoughmore (1787–1851), soldier; grandson of John *Hely-Hutchinson (1724–1794); served with Grenadiers in Peninsula and at Waterloo; captain, 1812; deprived of his commission for assisting escape (1815) of General Lavalette at Paris; subsequently reinstated; succeeded his uncle as third earl, 1832; KP, 1834.

HELY-HUTCHINSON, Richard, first earl of Donoughmore (1756–1825), advocate of Catholic emancipation; eldest son of John *Hely-Hutchinson (1724–1794); MP, Sligo and Taghmon in Irish parliament; created Viscount Suirdale, 1797; commanded Cork legion, 1798; supported the Union; created earl, 1800; Irish representative peer, 1800; postmaster-general in Ireland, 1805–9.

HELY-HUTCHINSON, Richard Walter John, sixth earl of Donoughmore (1875–1948), chairman of committees of House of Lords; educated at Eton and New College, Oxford; succeeded father, 1900; under-secretary for war, 1903–5; chairman of committees, 1911–31; of Ceylon Constitutional Commission, 1927–8; of committee on ministers' powers, 1929–31; PC, 1918.

HEMANS, Charles Isidore (1817–1876), antiquary; son of Felicia Dorothea *Hemans; hon. secretary and librarian of English Archaeological Society at Rome; published works on Roman history and archaeology; died at Lucca.

HEMANS, Felicia Dorothea (1793–1835), poet; née Browne; married Captain Alfred Hemans, 1812, but separated from him, 1818;

made acquaintance of *Scott and *Wordsworth, 1829; intimate at Dublin of Sir William Rowan *Hamilton, *Whately, and Blanco *White; her writings highly popular in America; the 'Egeria' of Maria Jane *Jewsbury's *Three Histories*. Her collected works (issued 1839) include *Translations from Camoens and other Poets, Lays of Many Lands, The Forest Sanctuary*, and *Songs of the Affections*.

HEMING, Edmund (*fl.* 1695), projector.

HEMING (or HEMMINGE), John (d. 1630), actor and co-editor of the first folio of Shakespeare; played in King Henry IV, Part I (said to have been the original Falstaff), and in plays of Ben *Jonson; before Elizabeth's death a chief proprietor of Globe Theatre and closely associated with Shakespeare; with Henry *Condell (d. 1627) issued first folio (1623).

HEMING (or HEMMINGE), William (*fl.* 1632), dramatist; son of John *Heming or Hemminge; of Westminster and Christ Church, Oxford; MA, 1628; his extant plays, *The Fatal Contract* (1653), revived as *Love and Revenge*, and reprinted as *The Eunuch* (1687), and *The Jewes Tragedy* (1662).

HEMINGFORD (or HEMINGBURGH), Walter de (also WALTER DE GISBURN) (*fl.* 1300), chronicler and sub-prior of St Mary's, Gisburn; his chronicle (1066–1346) printed in part by Gale and *Hearne; fully edited by H. C. Hamilton (1848).

HEMMING (*fl.* 1096), chronicler; sub-prior of Worcester; his Worcester chartulary edited by Hearne (1723).

HEMMING, George Wirgman (1821–1905), mathematician and law reporter; BA, St John's College, Cambridge (senior wrangler and first Smith's prizeman), and fellow, 1844; barrister of Lincoln's Inn, 1850; treasurer, 1897; QC, 1875; junior counsel to Treasury, 1871–5; published works on calculus (1848) and plane trigonometry (1851); edited *Equity Cases* and *Chancery Appeals*, subsequently merged in *Law Reports* of Chancery division.

HEMPEL, Charles (or Carl Frederick) (1811–1867), musical composer; son of Charles William *Hempel; Mus.Doc., Oxford, 1862; organist of St Mary's, Truro, and St John's Episcopal Church, Perth; published songs and part of *The Seventh Seal* (oratorio).

HEMPEL, Charles William (1777–1855), composer and poet; organist of St Mary's, Truro, 1804–44; composed, among other works, *Sacred Melodies* (1812) and a satirical poem; died in Lambeth Workhouse.

HEMPHILL, Barbara (d. 1858), novelist; née Hare; married John Hemphill; her *Lionel Deerhurst, or Fashionable Life under the Regency* (1846), edited by Lady *Blessington.

HEMPHILL, Charles Hare, first Baron Hemphill (1822–1908), lawyer and politician; son of Mrs Barbara *Hemphill; BA, Trinity College, Dublin, 1843; called to Irish bar, 1845; acquired large practice in Leinster circuit; QC, 1860; Irish county-court judge from 1863 till passing of County Courts (Ireland) Act, 1877; serjeant-at-law, 1882; supported Gladstone's home-rule policy (1886), but failed in efforts to enter parliament; Irish solicitor-general under Gladstone, 1892–5; Irish PC, 1895; Liberal MP for North Tyrone, 1895–1906; baron, 1906.

HEMPHILL, Samuel (d. 1741), Irish Presbyterian; MA, Glasgow, 1716, Edinburgh, 1726; minister of Castleblayney, Monaghan; published pamphlets in favour of subscription, 1722–6.

HENCHMAN, Humphrey (1592–1675), bishop of London; MA, Christ's College, Cambridge, 1616; DD, 1628; fellow of Clare Hall, 1616–23; canon and precentor of Salisbury, 1623, and rector of Isle of Portland; deprived during rebellion; assisted Charles II to escape after Worcester, 1651; bishop of Salisbury, 1660–3; FRS, 1665; took influential part in Savoy Conference, 1661; bishop of London, 1663–75; restored cathedral and palace at Salisbury, and contributed to rebuilding of St Paul's, Aldersgate Palace, and Clare Hall.

HENCHMAN, Humphrey (1669–1739), civilian; grandson of Humphrey *Henchman (1592–1675); MA, Christ Church, Oxford, 1694; DCL, 1702; friend of *Atterbury; chancellor of Rochester, 1714, London, 1715; counsel for *Sacheverell and against Whiston.

HENDERLAND, Lord (1736–1795). See MURRAY, ALEXANDER.

HENDERSON. See also HENRYSON.

HENDERSON, Alexander (1583?–1646), Presbyterian divine and diplomat; MA, St Andrews, 1603; minister of Leuchars, 1614, of the High Kirk, Edinburgh, 1639; opposed five articles of Perth, 1618; headed agitation against new Prayer-Book, 1637; promoted remonstrance against episcopacy, 1637; one of Presbyterian committee of four; prepared and read in Greyfriars, Edinburgh, the 'National Covenant', 1638; created burgess of Dundee for public services, 1638; moderator of Glasgow assembly (1638), which laid down lines of Presbyterian organization; commissioner at pacification of Berwick, 1639; ruling spirit at Edinburgh assembly which passed first 'Barrier Act', 1639; entered England with Covenanting army, 1640; negotiated treaty of 1641; as rector of Edinburgh University (1640–6), introduced teaching of Hebrew and 'circles'; as moderator of St Andrews Assembly (1641) proposed confession of faith, catechism, and directory of worship; chaplain to Charles I; at Oxford, 1643, urged him to call a Scottish parliament; drafted 'Solemn League and Covenant' taken by Westminster Assembly (Sept. 1643), and drew up the directory of worship; manager of proposed religious settlement at Uxbridge Conference, 1645; corresponded with Charles I on episcopacy and the coronation oath, 1646; his *Bishop's Doom* (1638) reprinted (1762); *Sermons, Prayers, and Addresses*, edited by R. T. Martin (1867); his deathbed *Declaration* of doubtful authenticity.

HENDERSON, Alexander (1780–1863), physician; MD, Edinburgh, 1803; published, among other works, *A Sketch of the Revolutions of Medical Science* (translated from Cabanis, 1806) and *History of Ancient and Modern Wines* (1824).

HENDERSON, (Alexander) Gavin, second Baron Faringdon (1902–1977), Labour politician; grandson of first Baron Faringdon; educated at Eton, McGill University, Montreal, and Christ Church, Oxford; joined the Labour party, 1934; succeeded grandfather, 1934; restored the family house, Buscot Park, Berkshire; helped to advance appreciation of Georgian architecture; strong pacifist, served in fire service during 1939–45; member of parliamentary goodwill mission to USSR, 1945; member of executive committee, Fabian Society, 1942–66, chairman, 1960–1; chairman, Fabian Colonial Bureau, 1952–8; London County Councillor, 1958–61; alderman, 1961–5; treasurer, National Council for Civil Liberties, 1940–5; member, Colonial Economic and Development Council, 1948–51; trustee, Wallace Collection, 1946–53 and 1966–73; president, Theatre Advisory Council, 1946; member, Historic Buildings Council, 1964–73; president, Friends of City Churches, 1943; chairman, Fire Service Association; Lords member of Parliamentary Labour party's executive, 1957–60; fellow, Royal Society of Arts, 1936; gave Buscot Park to National Trust.

HENDERSON, Andrew (fl. 1734–1775), author and bookseller; MA of a Scottish university; published *History of the Rebellion, 1745–6, by an impartial hand, who was an Eyewitness* (1748) and biographical works; published *Letters* (1775) attacking Dr *Johnson for *Tour in the Hebrides*.

HENDERSON, Andrew (1783–1835), Glasgow portrait painter; exhibited at Scottish Academy, 1828–30; published *Scottish Proverbs*, with etchings (1832); contributed to the *Laird of Logan*.

HENDERSON, Arthur (1863–1935), Labour leader and statesman; apprenticed as moulder; district delegate, Ironfounders' Union, and member of Newcastle City Council, 1892; Labour MP, Barnard Castle (1903–18), Widnes (1919–22), East Newcastle (1923), Burnley (1924–31), and Clay Cross division (1933–5); secretary, Labour party, 1911–34; PC, 1915; adviser on labour in Cabinet, 1915–17 (president, Board of Education, 1915, paymaster-general, 1916, minister without portfolio, 1916); visited Russia, 1917; resigned (1917) after recommending sending delegates to Stockholm International Socialist Conference; strengthened and broadened Labour party organization; chief whip, 1914, 1921–3, 1925–7; responsible for statement of aims 'Labour and the Nation', 1928; home secretary, 1924; foreign secretary, 1929–31; forced resignation of Lord *Lloyd in effort to reach Egyptian agreement; sent ambassador to Russia; established British leadership in seeking secure foundations for international peace; led Labour party opposition to MacDonald's 'National' government and lost his seat, 1931; presided over World Disarmament Conference, 1932–4; Nobel Peace Prize, 1934.

HENDERSON, Charles Cooper (1803–1877), equestrian painter and etcher; brother of John *Henderson (1797–1878).

HENDERSON, Sir David (1862–1921), lieutenant-general; entered army, 1883; served in South African War, 1899–1902; learned to fly, 1911; director of military training, War Office, 1912–13; director-general of military aeronautics, 1913; general officer commanding Royal Flying Corps, 1914–17; KCB, 1914; lieutenant-general, 1917; KCVO, 1919.

HENDERSON, David Willis Wilson (1903–1968), microbiologist; educated at Hamilton Academy, West of Scotland Agricultural College, and Glasgow University; B.Sc. (Agriculture), 1926; adviser in dairy bacteriology, Ministry of Agriculture and Fisheries; on staff of Armstrong College (then part of Durham University), 1927; M.Sc., 1930; Carnegie research fellow, Lister Institute of Preventive Medicine (London), 1931; Beit memorial research fellow, 1932–5; on bacteriological staff, Lister Institute, 1935–46; Ph.D. (London), 1934; D.Sc., 1941; dealt mainly with immunology of salmonella and clostridium species; member of biology group, Chemical Defence Experimental Establishment, Porton, 1940; played key role in Anglo-American liaison on microbiological defence; US Medal of Freedom,

bronze palm, 1946; chief superintendent (later director), Microbiological Research Establishment, 1946–64; continued interest in viral aerosols up to 1967; president, Society for General Microbiology, 1963–5; CB, 1957; FRS, 1959.

HENDERSON, Ebenezer, the elder (1784–1858), missionary; founded Bible societies in Denmark, Scandinavia, Russia, and Iceland, acquiring many languages; went to Iceland, 1814; Ph.D., Kiel, 1816; printed the Bible at St Petersburg in ten languages; lived several years in Russia; tutor of Highbury College, 1830–50; published translations from Hebrew and accounts of visits to Iceland, Russia, and Piedmont; edited *Buck's *Theological Dictionary* (1833) and other works.

HENDERSON, Ebenezer, the younger (1809–1879), mechanician and author; nephew of Ebenezer *Henderson the elder; constructed an orrery and astronomical clock, 1827, and wheels to show sidereal time, 1850; published treatises on horology and astronomy, also *Annals of Dunfermline* (1879).

HENDERSON, Sir Edmund Yeamans Walcott (1821–1896), lieutenant-colonel, Royal Engineers; educated at Woolwich; first lieutenant, Royal Engineers, 1841; lieutenant-colonel, 1862; engaged on boundary survey between Canada and New Brunswick, 1846–8; comptroller of convicts in western Australia, 1850–63; chairman of directors of prisons and inspector-general of military prisons, 1863; CB, 1868; chief commissioner of metropolitan police, 1869–86; instituted Criminal Investigation Department; KCB, 1878; resigned on fault being found with police arrangements at Trafalgar Square riots, 1886.

HENDERSON, George (1783–1855), lieutenant-colonel, Royal Engineers; distinguished in Peninsular War, 1812–14; lieutenant-colonel, RE, 1824; superintendent and director of London and South-Western Railway.

HENDERSON, George Francis Robert (1854–1903), colonel and military writer; son of William George *Henderson; scholar of St John's College, Oxford; entered Sandhurst, 1876; commanded a company at Tel-el-Kebir, 1882; served in ordnance store department, 1885–90; published *The Campaign of Fredericksburg* (1886); instructor at Sandhurst in military topography and tactics, 1890; exercised great influence as professor of military art and history at Staff College, 1892–9; published *Stonewall Jackson and the American Civil War* (2 vols., 1898); accompanied Lord *Roberts to the Cape, 1899; director of military intelligence and CB, 1900; died at Aswan.

HENDERSON, George Gerald (1862–1942), chemist; graduated in chemistry and arts, Glasgow; head of chemistry department, Queen Margaret College, 1889–92; Freeland professor, Royal Technical College, 1892–1919; built up close relations with manufacturing interests; obtained new laboratories; regius professor, Glasgow University, 1919–37; created new chemistry institute; FRS, 1916.

HENDERSON, Mrs Georgina Jane (1770–1850), painter. See KEATE.

HENDERSON, Sir Hubert Douglas (1890–1952), economist; educated at Aberdeen Grammar School, Rugby, and Emmanuel College, Cambridge; first class, part ii, economics tripos, and president of Union, 1912; acquired liberal and reforming views; secretary, Cotton Control Board, 1917–19; lecturer in economics, Cambridge, 1919–23; editor, *Nation and Athenaeum*, 1923–30; assistant, later joint secretary, Economic Advisory Council, 1930–4; fellow, All Souls, 1934–52; active in establishment of Institute of Statistics; member, West Indies Royal Commission, 1938–9; adviser at Treasury, 1940–4; Drummond professor of political economy, Oxford, 1945–51; member, Royal Commission on Population, 1944, chairman, 1946; chairman, Statutory Committee on Unemployment Insurance, 1945–8; warden, All Souls, 1951–2; his acute critical powers sought practical solutions to economic problems within political possibilities; FBA, 1948; knighted, 1942; president, Royal Economic Society, 1950.

HENDERSON, James (1783?–1848), geographical writer; consul-general for Colombia; FRS, 1831; published *History of the Brazil* (1822) and works on Spain; died at Madrid.

HENDERSON, John (1747–1785), 'the Bath Roscius'; appeared under name of Courtney at Bath as Hamlet, 1772; played Shylock at Haymarket, 1777; appeared at Drury Lane, 1777–9, and subsequently at Covent Garden, and chief provincial towns; considered second only to *Garrick; regarded with jealousy by him; among his best parts, Shylock, Sir Giles Overreach, Hamlet, and Falstaff; drew, etched, and wrote poems; with Thomas *Sheridan (1719–1788) published *Practical Method of Reading and Writing English Poetry* (1796); buried in Westminster Abbey.

HENDERSON, John (1757–1788), eccentric student; at 12 taught Greek and Latin at Trevecca; sent to Pembroke College, Oxford, at expense of Dean Tucker, 1781; a skilled linguist, with knowledge of medicine; accompanied *Johnson and Hannah *More over Pembroke College, 1782; BA, 1786; refused to adopt any profession, and abandoned himself to solitary study of Lavater and spiritualism.

HENDERSON, John (1780–1867), philanthropist; dry-salter and East India merchant; for twenty years contributed over £30,000 annually to religious and charitable schemes; founded Evangelical Alliance; active opponent of Sunday travelling.

HENDERSON, John (1797–1878), art collector and archaeologist; MA, Balliol College, Oxford, 1820; bequeathed antiquities to Oxford University, water-colour collections, porcelain, glass, and manuscripts to British Museum, and pictures to National Gallery.

HENDERSON, John (1804–1862), Scottish architect; designed Trinity College, Glenalmond, 1847.

HENDERSON, Joseph (1832–1908), portrait and marine painter; studied art at Trustees' Academy, Edinburgh; treated genre subjects till 1871, when he devoted himself to the sea; painted in oil and water-colour; exhibited at Royal Academy, 1871–86; best pictures shown at the Royal Glasgow Institute; *The Flowing Tide* is in the Glasgow Gallery.

HENDERSON, Sir Nevile Meyrick (1882–1942), diplomat; educated at Eton and abroad; entered Diplomatic Service, 1905; minister plenipotentiary, 1924; served at Cairo, 1924–8; Paris, 1928–9; minister plenipotentiary at Belgrade, 1929–35; formed close friendship with King Alexander; ambassador at Buenos Aires, 1935–7; Berlin, 1937–9; had mystical conception of role as mediator and no preconceived dislike of authoritarian government; sincerely believed in and encouraged British government's policy of appeasement until after occupation of Czechoslovakia, March 1939; published *Failure of a Mission* (1940); KCMG, 1932; PC, 1937; GCMG, 1939.

HENDERSON, Sir Reginald Guy Hannam (1881–1939), admiral; entered navy through *Britannia*; served in *Erin* at Jutland, 1916; on Admiralty war staff, 1916–19; his trial convoy led to adoption of system, 1917; captain, 1917; rear-admiral, 1929; rear-admiral, aircraft-carriers, 1931–3; vice-admiral, 1933; third sea lord and controller, 1934–9; responsible for great expansion of navy; KCB, 1936; GCB and admiral, 1939.

HENDERSON (or HENRYSON), Robert (1430?–1506?). See HENRYSON.

HENDERSON, Thomas (1798–1844), astronomer; secretary to earl of *Lauderdale and Lord *Jeffrey, 1819–31; as astronomer royal at the Cape (1832–3) observed Encke's and Biela's comets, and (1832) transit of Mercury; discovered first authentic case of annual parallax in a fixed star; FRAS, 1832; FRS, 1840; first Scottish astronomer royal and professor of practical astronomy at Edinburgh, 1834–44; Edinburgh observations published, 1838–43, and (edited by Piazzi Smyth), 1843–52.

HENDERSON, William (1810–1872), homoeopathist; MD, Edinburgh, 1831; studied also at Paris, Berlin, and Vienna; physician to Edinburgh Fever Hospital, 1832; pathologist to Royal Infirmary; professor of general pathology, 1842–69; adopted homoeopathy, 1845, and defended it against Sir John *Forbes (1787–1861) and others.

HENDERSON, William George (1819–1905), dean of Carlisle; BA, Magdalen College, Oxford (first-class classic), 1840; MA, 1843; DCL, 1853; DD, 1882; fellow, 1847–53; headmaster of Victoria College, Jersey, 1852–62, and of Leeds Grammar School, 1862–84; dean of Carlisle, 1884; edited for Surtees Society the Latin missals of York and Hereford.

HENDLEY, William (1691?–1724), divine; BA, Pembroke College, Cambridge, 1711; lecturer of St James's, Clerkenwell, 1716, at St Mary, Islington, 1718; his trial (1719) on charge of procuring unlawful gains under guise of collecting charities the subject of *Defoe's *Charity still a Christian Virtue*.

HENDY, Sir Philip Anstiss (1900–1980), director of the National Gallery; educated at Westminster where he was a King's scholar, and Christ Church, Oxford; assistant keeper and lecturer, Wallace Collection, London, 1923–7; worked on new edition of catalogue; invited to catalogue Gardner paintings (Isabella Stewart Gardner Museum, Boston, USA); spent three years in Italy preparing catalogue, published in 1931; appointed curator of paintings, Museum of Fine Arts, Boston, 1930–3; resigned after disagreement with trustees; director, Leeds City Art Gallery, 1934–46; paintings removed and rearranged in Temple Newsam House during 1939–45 war; Slade professor, Oxford University, 1036–46; succeeded Sir Kenneth (later Lord) *Clark as director of the National Gallery, 1946–67; knighted, 1950; president, International Council of Museums, 1959–65; adviser to Israel Museum, Jerusalem, 1968–71; rehabilitated pictures returned to National Gallery from air-conditioned storage in Wales during 1939–45 war; met some criticism regarding cleaning but supported by loyal friends; publications include essay on Spanish art (1946), monographs on Giovanni Bellini (1945), Masaccio (1957), and Piero della Francesca (1968), and

a small book on Matthew Smith (1944); Gardner catalogue republished, 1974.

HENEAGE, George (d. 1549), dean of Lincoln, 1528–44; archdeacon, 1542–9; B.Can.L., Cambridge, 1510; incorporated at Oxford, 1522.

HENEAGE, Michael (1540–1600), antiquary; brother of Sir Thomas *Heneage (d. 1595); fellow of St John's College, Cambridge, 1563; MA, 1566; MP, Arundel, 1571, East Grinstead, 1572, Tavistock, 1589, and Wigan, 1593; joint keeper of Tower records with his brother, c.1578; assisted Robert *Hare with Cambridge records.

HENEAGE, Sir Thomas, the elder (d. 1553), gentleman usher to *Wolsey, and of privy chamber; knighted, 1537.

HENEAGE, Sir Thomas (d. 1595), vice-chamberlain to Queen Elizabeth; nephew of George *Heneage; MP, Stamford, 1553, Boston, 1562, Lincolnshire, 1563, 1571, 1572, and Essex, 1584, 1586, 1588, and 1593; treasurer of queen's chamber, 1570; knighted, 1577; keeper of Tower records, c.1577; member of commissions to try *Lopez, 1594, and others; built Copthall, Essex; sent to Low Countries, 1586; paymaster of forces, 1588; vice-chamberlain, 1589; privy councillor, 1589; chancellor of Lancaster, 1590; friend of *Sidney, *Hatton, and John *Foxe.

HENFREY, Arthur (1819–1859), botanist; FLS, 1844; professor of botany at King's College, London, 1853; published *Elementary Course of Botany* (1857) and several translations; edited (with Huxley) *Scientific Memoirs* (1837), *Micrographic Dictionary* (1854, with J. W. Griffith) and *Francis's *Anatomy of British Ferns* (1855).

HENFREY, Henry William (1852–1881), numismatist; son of Arthur *Henfrey; principal work, *Numismata Cromwelliana* (1877).

HENGHAM (or HINGHAM), Ralph de (d. 1311), judge; chancellor of Exeter, 1275–9; justice of common pleas, 1273; chief justice of King's Bench, 1274–90; dismissed and heavily fined; the fine traditionally applied to building a tower in Palace Yard; chief justice of common pleas, 1301; reputed author of *Hengham Magna* and *Hengham Parva*, edited (1616) by *Selden.

HENGIST (d. 488), joint founder with his brother *Horsa of the kingdom of Kent; said to have arrived at Ebbsfleet from Jutland, 449 (according to *Nennius, 428), to have settled in Thanet, and, after defeat by Britons at Aylesford (455), to have founded Leiden; returned and established himself in Kent.

HENGLER, Frederick Charles (1820–1887), circus proprietor; purchased Palais Royal, Argyll Street, London, 1871 (rebuilt, 1884).

HENLEY, Barons. See EDEN, MORTON, first baron, 1752–1830; EDEN, ROBERT HENLEY, second baron, 1789–1841.

HENLEY, Anthony (d. 1711), wit; of Magdalen College, Oxford; Whig MP, Andover (1698–1700), Weymouth (1702–11); contributed to the *Tatler* and *Medley*; member of Kit-Cat Club; patron of musicians and men of letters.

HENLEY, John (1692–1756), 'Orator Henley'; MA, St John's College, Cambridge, 1716; contributed to the *Spectator* as 'Dr. Quir'; began his 'orations' at Newport, 1726; established himself in Lincoln's Inn Fields, 1729; employed by Walpole to write in Whig *Hyp Doctor*, 1730–9; his claims as restorer of church oratory ridiculed in the *Dunciad*; caricatured by *Hogarth; edited works of John *Sheffield, duke of Buckingham (1722); published works on oratory, theology, and grammar, and translations; his autograph lectures in British Museum.

HENLEY, Joseph Warner (1793–1884), conservative politician; MA, Magdalen College, Oxford, 1834; hon. DCL, 1854; MP, Oxfordshire, 1841–78; president of Board of Trade, 1852 and 1858–9; resigned on reform question, 1859; declined Home Office, 1866.

HENLEY, Phocion (1728–1764), musical composer; nephew of Robert *Henley, first earl of Northington; BA, Wadham College, Oxford, 1749; rector of St Andrew's and St Anne's, Blackfriars, 1759–64; some of his compositions are in T. *Sharp's *Divine Harmony* (psalms and hymns, 1798).

HENLEY, Robert, first earl of Northington (1708?–1772), lord chancellor; second son of Anthony *Henley; fellow of All Souls College, Oxford; MA, 1733; barrister, Inner Temple, 1732; practised on western circuit; MP, Bath, 1747–57; KC, 1751, and recorder of Bath; attorney-general, 1756; lord keeper (the last), 1757; speaker of House of Lords, 1757–60, though not a peer till 1760; lord chancellor, 1761; created an earl, 1764; procured dismissal of Rockingham; president of council under Grafton, 1766–7; intimate of George III.

HENLEY, Robert, second earl of Northington (1747–1786), lord-lieutenant of Ireland; of Westminster and Christ Church, Oxford; MA, 1766; MP, Hampshire, 1768; succeeded as earl, 1772; KT, 1773; viceroy of Ireland (1783–4) during Volunteer Convention; advocated annual parliaments and promoted Irish industries.

HENLEY, Samuel (1740–1815), commentator; professor of moral philosophy at Williamsburg, Virginia; afterwards assistant-master at Harrow; FSA, 1778; principal of East India College,

Hertford, 1805–15; published English translation, with notes, of *Vathek* (1784), and works of scriptural exegesis and classical scholarship.

HENLEY, Walter de (*fl.* 1250), author of *Hosebondrie* (13th cent.).

HENLEY (or HENLY), William (*fl.* 1775), electrician; FRS, 1773.

HENLEY, William Ernest (1849–1903), poet, critic, and dramatist; born at Gloucester; pupil there of T. E. *Brown; a cripple from boyhood; in Edinburgh infirmary, 1873–5; his *Hospital Verses*, some of which were published in *Cornhill Magazine* (July 1875), led the editor, (Sir) Leslie *Stephen, to visit him and introduce him to R. L. *Stevenson; worked in Edinburgh on staff of *Encyclopaedia Britannica*, 1875; settled in London (1877–8) as editor of weekly journal, *London*; while editor of *Magazine of Art* (1882–6) championed Rodin and J. A. M. *Whistler; became (1889) editor of *Scots Observer*, renamed in 1891 the *National Observer*, an imperialist weekly paper; encouraged young authors; edited *New Review*, 1894–8; obtained poetic fame by *Book of Verses* (1888); wrote *London Voluntaries* (1893), *For England's Sake* (patriotic songs, 1900), and *Hawthorn and Lavender* (lyrics, 1901); published literary *Views and Reviews* (1890) and a companion volume on art (1902); collaborated with R. L. Stevenson in the plays *Deacon Brodie, Beau Austin, Admiral Guinea*, and *Macaire*; initiated series of reprints of 'Tudor Translations', 1892; joint-compiler of *Slang Dictionary*, 1894–1904; contributed essay on *Burns's life to, and helped in, centenary edition of poetry of Robert Burns (4 vols., 1896–7); compiled *Lyra Heroica* (1891); hon. LL D, St Andrews, 1893; granted Civil List pension, 1898; portrayed as 'Burly' in R. L. Stevenson's essay, 'Talk and Talkers'; works collected in 6 vols. (1908).

HENLEY, William Thomas (1813?–1882), telegraphic engineer; self-taught; made apparatus for *Wheatstone and first Electric Telegraph Company; invented magnetic needle telegraph and formed company (1852) to take over patent; obtained medal at exhibition of 1851; made electric-light apparatus, and manufactured fourteen thousand miles of submarine cable.

HENN, Thomas Rice (1849–1880), lieutenant of Royal Engineers; fell at Maiwand.

HENNEDY, Roger (1809–1877), botanist; professor at Andersonian Institution, Glasgow, 1863–77; published *Clydesdale Flora* (1865).

HENNELL, Charles Christian (1809–1850), author of *Inquiry concerning the Origin of Christianity* (1838) and *Christian Theism* (1839); brother-in-law of Charles *Bray; with John Thomas

Barber *Beaumont established New Philosophical Institution, Mile End.

HENNELL, Mary (1802–1843), author of *Outline of the various Social Systems and Communities which have been founded on Principle of Co-operation* (published 1844); sister of Charles Christian *Hennell.

HENNELL, Sara. See under BRAY, CAROLINE.

HENNEN, John (1779–1828), army surgeon; served in Peninsula and at Waterloo; staff surgeon, 1812; principal medical officer for Scotland, 1817; MD, Edinburgh, 1819; died medical officer at Gibraltar; published, among other works, *Observations on . . . Military Surgery* (1818).

HENNESSEY, John Bobanau Nickerlieu (1829–1910), deputy surveyor-general of India, 1883–4; born at Fatehpur; worked on trigonometrical survey in jungle tracts of Bengal and in Punjab from 1844; studied mathematics at Jesus College, Cambridge, 1863–5; organized the reproduction of survey sheets in India by means of photo-zincographic process, 1865; superintendent of survey, 1874; FRS, 1875; hon. MA, Cambridge, 1876; CIE, 1885.

HENNESSY, Henry (1826–1901), physicist; brother of Sir John *Pope-Hennessy; professor of physics at Roman Catholic University, Dublin, 1855–74; at Royal College of Science, Dublin, 1874–90; vice-president of Royal Irish Academy, 1870–3; FRS, 1858; made valuable researches in meteorology and climatology.

HENNESSY, (Richard) James (Arthur) Pope- (1916–1974), writer. See POPE-HENNESSY.

HENNESSY, William Maunsell (1829–1889), Irish scholar; assistant deputy-keeper in Dublin Record Office; Todd professor at Royal Irish Academy, 1882–4; edited *Chronicon Scotorum* of Dubhaltach MacFirbisigh (1866), *Annals of Loch Cé* (1871), and other works; translated *Tripartite Life of St. Patrick* (1871); wrote on Ossian.

HENNIKER, Sir Frederick, baronet (1793–1825), traveller; of Eton and St John's College, Cambridge; BA, 1815; succeeded as baronet, 1816; published *Notes during a Visit to Egypt, Nubia, the Oasis, Mount Sinai, and Jerusalem* (1823).

HENNIKER-MAJOR, John, second Baron Henniker (1752–1821), antiquary; MA, St John's College, Cambridge, 1772; LL D, 1811; FSA, 1785; FRS, 1785; took additional name, 1792; succeeded to Irish peerage, 1803; MP, Dover, 1774–80, Romney, 1785–90, Steyning, 1794–1802, Rutland, 1805–12, Stamford,

1812–18; published *Account of Families of Major and Henniker* (1803) and antiquarian pamphlets.

HENNING, John (1771–1851), modeller and sculptor; a founder of Society of British Artists; modelled copies of Parthenon and Phigaleian friezes and Raphael's cartoons; executed busts of Mrs *Siddons and Princess *Charlotte.

HENRIETTA (or HENRIETTE ANNE), duchess of Orleans (1644–1670), fifth daughter of Charles I; born at Exeter; secretly carried off from St James's Palace to France, 1646; brought up as a Roman Catholic by her mother; came to England at Restoration and became popular at court; married Philippe, duc d'Orléans (brother of Louis XIV), 1661; patroness of Molière, Corneille, and Racine; intermediary between Louis XIV and Charles II; often consulted by former on state affairs; with Louise de *Kerouaille came to Dover, 1670, and negotiated the secret Treaty of Dover, 1670; died suddenly soon after her return to France, being poisoned, according to St Simon, with connivance of her jealous husband, by agents of his favourite, the Chevalier de Lorraine; her funeral oration delivered by Bossuet.

HENRIETTA MARIA (1609–1669), queen consort of Charles I; youngest daughter of Henri IV and Marie de Médicis; married by proxy and came to England, 1625; on indifferent terms with her husband during lifetime of *Buckingham; at first abstained from politics, but attracted courtiers and poets; evoked *Prynne's *Histriomastix* by taking part in rehearsal of *Shepherd's Pastoral,* 1632; under influence of George *Conn thwarted *Laud's proclamation against Catholic recusants, 1636; obtained money from the Catholics for Scottish War, 1639; after meeting of Long Parliament carried on intrigues with the papal court, but could obtain no help for the Royalists except on condition of Charles becoming a Romanist; after failure of overtures to Parliamentary leaders, authorized Henry *Jermyn and Sir John *Suckling to carry out the army plot, 1641; tried to save *Strafford; urged on attempted arrest of the five members, 1642; left England early in 1642, and bought munitions of war and obtained money in Holland; landed at Bridlington, Feb. 1643, under fire; impeached by parliament, 23 May 1643; failed to surprise Hull and Lincoln, 1643; entertained by Shakespeare's daughter at Stratford-upon-Avon; joined Charles at Edgehill and accompanied him to Oxford, 1643; advised bringing in of foreign or Irish army; escaped from Falmouth to France, 1644; pawned her jewels; negotiated with Mazarin and obtained promise of ten thousand men from duke of Lorraine, 1644–5; urged Charles to accept Scottish help on basis of Presbyterianism, 1646; active in negotiations with Irish Catholics and the anti-Parliamentarian English fleet, 1648; in state of destitution at the Louvre, 1648; retired into Carmelite nunnery; alienated Charles II's advisers by attempts to convert to Roman Catholicism her younger son, duke of *Gloucester; came to England, 1660, to get portion for her daughter *Henrietta Anne and to break off engagement between her second son duke of York and Anne *Hyde; lived at Somerset House; finally left England, 1665; died at Colombes and was buried in St Denis.

HENRIQUES, Sir **Basil Lucas Quixano** (1890–1961), club leader and magistrate; born into old, established Jewish family; educated at Harrow and University College, Oxford, 1909–13; under influence of Claude J. G. *Montefiore and (Sir) Alexander H. *Paterson, became active in liberal Jewish movement and in boys' clubs; opened the Oxford and St George's in the East Jewish Boys Club, 1914; served in the army and commanded first tank to be used in war, 1914–18; returned to Oxford and St George's Club (later, Bernhard Baron Settlement), 1918–47; magistrate, 1924–55; chairman, East London Juvenile Court, 1936–55; CBE, 1948; knighted, 1955; publications include *Club Leadership* (1933), *The Indiscretions of a Magistrate* (1950), and *Club Leadership Today* (1951).

HENRY I (1068–1135), king of England; younger son of William I and *Matilda; well educated in England; heir of his mother's possessions in England, 1083; bought the Avranchin and Côtentin from his elder brother *Robert, duke of Normandy; imprisoned by him at Bayeux, 1088–9; helped to put down revolt of Rouen, 1090; attacked by both William II and Robert, and obliged to evacuate Mont St Michel; became lord of Domfront, 1092, whence he carried on war against Robert and his vassals; visited William II in England, 1094, and returned to Normandy with money; received counties of Coutances and Bayeux, 1096; on the news of William II's death (1100) secured the treasure at Winchester; chosen king by the witan and crowned at Westminster, issuing at his coronation (1100) charter which formed the basis of Magna Charta; invited Archbishop *Anselm to return, 1100, and filled vacant sees; ruled by craft rather than force; agreed, on Anselm's refusal to do homage for his temporalities, to refer the question to the pope, but maintained his position till a compromise was agreed to (1105); married *Matilda (1080–1118), 1100, thereby introducing intermarriages between Normans and English, and becoming the re-founder of the English nation; chose his councillors and officials from lower ranks, and ennobled them as a counterpoise to the great bar-

ons; promised at Alton to give up all his Norman possessions (except Domfront) in return for a renunciation by Duke Robert of the English crown and a pension, 1101; defeated and banished *Robert of Bellême, 1101, and William of Mortain, 1104; compelled Robert to give up his pension and cede Evreux; with help of Anjou, Maine, and Brittany, conquered the whole of Normandy at Tinchebrai, 1106, capturing Robert and Mortain; returned to England and concluded the investiture agreement; developed the judicial and fiscal administration, sending out itinerant justices and organizing the Exchequer court; reformed the coinage, 1107, but levied heavy taxes; went to Normandy to seize William 'Clito' (Robert's son), 1108; began a war with Louis VI of France about the border fortress of Gisors, 1109; banished more barons, 1110; put down private war and restrained his mercenaries; captured Robert of Bellême, 1111; obtained acknowledgement of his right to Bellême, Maine, and Brittany; led an army into Wales, 1114; caused all barons to do homage to *William, his heir, in Normandy, 1115, and England, 1116; began fresh war with Louis VI, who was aided by Baldwin of Flanders and Fulk of Anjou; detached Fulk from the confederacy, 1120, by marrying to Fulk's daughter his son Prince William (lost in the White Ship the same year); defeated Louis in an encounter of knights at Brenneville; subdued rebel barons and made peace at Gisors with Louis and Baldwin by mediation of Pope Calixtus II, 1120; made a second marriage with Adela of Louvain, 1121; exacted tribute from Welsh by second invasion, 1121; upheld rights of Canterbury against both the pope and *Thurstan, archbishop of York; reduced fresh Norman rebellion, 1123–4; exacted from nobles (including Stephen of Boulogne) promise to support succession to crown of his daughter, the ex-empress *Matilda, 1126; married her to Geoffrey of Anjou, 1128; engaged again in war with France; exacted fines from clergy for keeping wives; supported Pope Innocent II against anti-pope Anaclete; exacted oaths to Matilda, 1131; went to Normandy, 1133; had fresh trouble with the Angevins and Normans; died at Angers; buried at Reading.

HENRY II (1133–1189), king of England; grandson of Henry I, and son of Geoffrey of Anjou and *Matilda (1102–1167); inherited Angevin territories, 1151; obtained Aquitaine by marriage with *Eleanor (1122?–1204), 1152; came to terms with Stephen, 1153; succeeded to crown, 1154; issued charter based on that of Henry I; expelled Flemish mercenaries and reduced rebellious barons, 1155; exacted homage and restoration of border counties from *Malcolm of Scotland; acquired county of Nantes and recognition of overlordship of Brittany, 1158; re-established Exchequer in England; developed curia regis; issued new coinage, 1158; extended in a 'great assize' the system of inquest by sworn recognitors to settlement of land disputes; broke down by the 'great scutage' military dependence of crown on feudal tenants, 1159; gained possession of the Vexin by French marriage of eldest surviving son *Henry, 1160; helped Pope Alexander III against the emperor, 1162; made *Thomas Becket archbishop, 1162, but was resisted by him, especially in his attempt to bring the clergy within civil jurisdiction, through the constitutions of Clarendon, 1164; caused Becket's condemnation at Northampton, 1164; on his flight enforced the constitutions; applied the principle of jury inquest to criminal matters by the assize of Clarendon, 1166, the first attempt in England to issue a new code of laws, and to break down feudalism by subordinating independent jurisdictions to a central court; allied himself, through his daughters' marriages, with the emperor Frederick Barbarossa and the kings of Castile, 1168-9, and Sicily, 1169; defeated the Bretons, 1166-9; by Treaty of Montmirail (1169) obtained sanction of France to establishment of his sons Henry, *Geoffrey, and Richard; had Prince Henry crowned by the archbishop of York, 1170; suspended, and, after inquiry into their conduct, replaced by Exchequer officials most of the sheriffs, 1170; made formal peace with Becket and his ally, Louis of France; after Becket's murder (1170) purged himself and abjured the 'customs', which had been the chief cause of quarrel; by an expedition to Ireland (1171-2) received the submission both of Normans in Ireland and natives, divided the land into fiefs, and left Hugh de Lacy as royal vicegerent; drove Louis from Normandy, 1173; crushed Breton revolt, 1173, and (after doing penance at Canterbury) the baronial rising in England; exacted homage from his prisoner, *William, king of Scots; checked by these successes combination headed by the young King Henry (crowned heir) and his mother (1173-4); issued assize of Northampton, 1176, including among its clauses the 'assize of mort d'ancester' and a provision requiring an oath of fealty from all Englishmen; obtained partial recognition of his constitutions from the pope; ordered a return of all crown tenements, 1177; constituted inner tribunal for higher work of curia regis, 1178; established judicial circuits, 1176-80; issued assize of arms, 1181, making defensive service obligatory, and personal property subject to taxation; received homage from king of Connaught, 1175; arbiter between Aragon and Toulouse, 1173, and Castile and Navarre, 1177; mediator in France, 1180-2; was asked to deliver the Holy Land,

1185, but was engaged in war with his sons Henry and Geoffrey on behalf of Richard, 1183, and afterwards with Richard and Philip Augustus of France, to whose claims he was reduced (1189) to submit at Colombières; died at Chinon; buried at Fontevraud, where is his tomb and effigy. He was a lover of learning and a great builder; his works of this kind including many palaces, the embankment of the Loire, and the Grand Pont at Angers.

HENRY, Saint (*fl.* 1150), apostle of Finland; of English birth; as bishop of Uppsala assisted (Saint) Eric IX of Sweden in his reforms, and accompanied him to Finland, remaining behind to found churches after its conquest; slain by one Lalli, whom he had reproved for homicide; his bones translated to St Henry's Cathedral, Abo, 1300.

HENRY, 'the Young King' (1155-1183), second son of Henry II of England; married while a child to Margaret, daughter of Louis VII of France, 1160; educated by *Becket; crowned at Westminster, 1170, and again with his queen at Winchester, 1172; on being refused lands by his father fled to the French court and joined his father's enemies; reconciled with his father, 1174; made war on his brother Richard in Aquitaine, 1182, and afterwards also on Henry II; struck down by fever, died penitent at Martel; buried at Rouen.

HENRY III (1207-1272), king of England; grandson of Henry II and son of John; crowned at Gloucester, 1216, and did homage to Gualo, the pope's legate; accompanied William *Marshal, the regent, to siege of London and to negotiate peace with Louis of France and his supporters, 1217; received homage from *Alexander II of Scotland; crowned again at Westminster, 1220, by direction of the pope; marched with the legate and the earl of *Chester to force William of Aumale to give up Biham Castle, 1221; agreed to confirm the Great Charter, 1223; compelled the Welsh to make peace; took Fulk de Breauté's castle at Bedford, 1224; declared himself of full age, 1227, having during his minority had a 'continual' council distinct from the court; lost most of his French possessions, 1224, but recovered Gascony, 1225; negotiated with Brittany, the emperor, and Bavaria; compelled by barons to restore the forest liberties; defeated by Welsh, 1228; secretly agreed to pope's demand for a tenth of all property, 1229; invaded Poitou and Gascony, 1230; obtained scutage in exchange for affirmation of liberties of church, 1231; refused aid for Welsh War; dismissed Hubert de *Burgh and made *Segrave justiciar, 1232; replaced English officers by Poitevin friends of Bishop *Peter des Roches; compelled after a contest by

Richard *Marshal and Archbishop *Edmund Rich to dismiss Poitevins and to be reconciled with De Burgh and the barons, 1234; thenceforth (1234) became his own minister; married his sister Isabella to the emperor Frederic II, 1235; wedded *Eleanor of Provence, 1236, in which year was passed the assize of Merton; depended on guidance of his wife's uncle, *William de Valence, and Provençal favourites; invited the legate Otho to England; favoured Simon de *Montfort (husband of his sister Eleanor), but quarrelled with him, 1239; opposed by *Richard, earl of Cornwall and citizens of London; made concessions; entertained Baldwin II, emperor of the East, 1238; his life attempted by a crazy clerk, 1238; kept see of Winchester vacant, the monks refusing (1238) to elect William of Valence; founded Netley Abbey, 1239; gave the archbishopric of Canterbury to *Boniface of Savoy, 1241, and see of Hereford to another foreigner; allowed the pope to take a fifth of the clergy's goods and many benefices, c.1240; made *Peter of Savoy earl of Richmond; joined the count of La Marche and others in an expedition to Gascony, 1242, but was deserted by him and forced by Louis IX to retreat, 1243; brought back more foreigners, detaching his brother Richard from the opposition by marrying him to Sanchia of Provence; compelled by Innocent IV to recall the banished bishop of Winchester; obliged, in order to get a scutage, to admit four 'guardians of liberties' to his council; made other concessions to the baronage; with money furnished by Richard of Cornwall undertook successful Welsh campaign, 1245; joined in remonstrance against the pope's exactions, but gave way, and laid a heavy tallage on London, 1246; enriched his foreign half-brothers from church revenues; refused an aid, 1249; exacted more money from Londoners and Jews; received homage for Lothian from *Alexander III of Scotland on his marriage, 1251; appointed Simon de Montfort governor of Gascony; insulted de Montfort with accusations, 1252; was refused money for a crusade, 1252; confirmed the charters in return for money, 1253, and made a second expedition into Gascony; visited Pontigny, Fontevraud, and Paris; agreed to bear cost of Pope Alexander II's war with Manfred in return for grant of Sicilian crown to his son *Edmund; unable to obtain regular grants; demanded from parliament at Westminster (1258) a third of all property, the barons attending in armour and led by *Roger Bigod, fourth earl of Norfolk; met barons in 'Mad Parliament' at Oxford (1258), which drew up 'Provisions', giving barons control of the executive and the nomination of half the council, a committee of twenty-four being appointed to carry out reforms; made peace with France by giving

up Normandy and his hereditary possessions; on his return from France to England brought accusation against Simon de Montfort, 1260; dismissed the barons' justiciar, 1261; seized Dover Castle, 1261; exhibited papal bull absolving him from keeping the provisions, 1261; ordered the knights of the shire to attend him at Windsor instead of the barons at St Albans, 1261; decision given in his favour by Louis IX of France in the 'Mise of Amiens', to whom the provisions had been referred for arbitration, 1264, the award being upheld by Pope Urban IV; captured the younger de Montfort at Northampton, Apr. 1264, the barons having refused to accept the award, and allied themselves with the Welsh; took Leicester, Nottingham, and Tonbridge; compelled to march into Sussex for provisions; routed at Lewes, 14 May 1264; compelled to summon a parliament (including four knights from each shire) and to forbid his queen to raise money for him, 1264; gave his assent to the constitution drawn up in the famous parliament of 1265; restored to power by his son Prince Edward's victory at Evesham, 1265, when he was wounded, being at the time detained in Montfort's army; revoked all his recent acts, declared the rebels' lands forfeited, fined the Londoners, reduced Kenilworth, and came to terms with *Gloucester in London and *Llywelyn in Wales; at the Marlborough parliament (1267) granted many reforms, but retained the executive; assented to statute forbidding the Jews to acquire debtors' land, 1269; completed (1269) and opened Westminster Abbey, the body of *Edward the Confessor being translated; buried in Westminster Abbey before the high altar, his heart being sent to Fontevraud. Most of the troubles of his reign were due to his foreign sympathies.

HENRY IV (1367–1413), king of England; son of *John of Gaunt; sometimes called Henry of Bolingbroke from his birthplace; styled earl of Derby in early life; KG, 1377; married Mary de Bohun, co-heiress of Hereford, 1380; praised by *Froissart; as one of the five lords appellant opposed Robert de *Vere, who, marching on London, compelled Richard II to grant their demands, 1387; took part in proceedings of 'Merciless Parliament', 1388, but gradually regained Richard's favour; joined 'crusade' of the Teutonic knights against Lithuania, 1390; went on pilgrimage to Jerusalem, 1392–3, being entertained by the kings of Bohemia and Hungary, the archduke of Austria, and the Venetians; one of the council during Richard's absence in Ireland, 1395; took a decided part for the king against his former allies, and was created duke of Hereford, 1397; appealed *Norfolk of treason, but was not allowed to fight with him, being banished the realm for ten years, 1398; exiled for life, his Lancaster estates also being confiscated during his stay at Paris; with the two Arundels and others, secretly left France and landed near Bridlington, 1399; joined by northern nobles; held council at Doncaster, and with a large army marched to Bristol, where some of the royal officers were executed, July 1399; met King Richard, who had been deserted by his army, at Flint; was promised restoration of his estates; took the king to London, where Richard resigned the crown, 29 Sept. 1399; obtained the throne by popular election; founded the Order of the Bath before his coronation, 1399; condemned Richard, who soon died, possibly starved, to perpetual imprisonment, 1399; crushed rising of Richard's dispossessed supporters, 1400; made expeditions against the Scots (1400) and Welsh (1400 and 1401) and entertained the Greek emperor, Manuel Palaiologos, 1400; married as his second wife *Joan, regent of Brittany, 1402; was attacked by the dukes of Orleans and Burgundy in France and by Franciscan conspirators in England, 1402; failed to subdue the Welsh, 1402; defeated the discontented Percies at Shrewsbury, 1403; received submission of *Northumberland, 1403; compelled to agree to expulsion of aliens; was strengthened by defeat of French at Dartmouth, 1404; received liberal supplies from 'Unlearned Parliament' at Coventry, 1404; escaped assassination at Eltham, 1404; suppressed revolt of Northumberland, Archbishop *Scrope, and the earl marshal, 1405; captured the heir to the Scottish throne, 1405; compelled by parliament to nominate a constitutional council, to submit to an audit of accounts, and reform his household, 1406; debarred the Beauforts from the succession, 1407; finally defeated Northumberland and *Bardolf at Bramham Moor, 1408; declined in health and energy, but interested himself in Archbishop *Arundel's attempt to heal the papal schism; supported the church party in preventing proposed confiscation of their temporalities, but was himself refused a revenue for life, 1410; defeated attempt to force him to abdicate in favour of Prince Henry, broke off Burgundian alliance, and undertook a progress, 1411–12; increased *Chaucer's pension and patron of *Gower; died in Jerusalem Chamber, Westminster; his tomb at Canterbury opened, 1832.

HENRY V (1387–1422), king of England; eldest son of Henry IV, by Mary de Bohun; born at Monmouth; said to have been educated by his uncle Henry *Beaufort (d. 1447) at The Queen's College, Oxford; attended Richard II, 1398–9; accompanied his father to Wales, 1400, where he represented him for the next three years,

recovering Conway, reducing Merioneth and Caernarfon, and checking *Glendower; assisted his father at Shrewsbury, 1403; returned to the Welsh marches and relieved Coyty Castle, 1405; after joining in petition against Lollards, 1406, captured Aberystwyth and invaded Scotland, 1407; warden of the Cinque Ports and constable of Dover, 1409; probably governed in his father's name during chancellorship of Thomas *Beaufort, 1410–12; sent an expedition to help Burgundy against the Armagnacs; withdrew from the council, 1412, his French policy being reversed; succeeded to the throne, 1413; the supposed wildness of his youth unsupported by contemporary authority, while his traditional conduct towards Gascoigne (taken by Shakespeare from Hall) is improbable, and is first mentioned in Sir T. *Elyot's *Governour* (1531); appointed Henry *Beaufort (d. 1447) chancellor, and the earl of *Arundel treasurer; gave the remains of Richard II honourable burial; had *Oldcastle arrested, and Lollardy repressed, 1414; demanded the restoration of French territories ceded at Brétigny, together with the Norman and Angevin lands, as a condition of his marriage with *Catherine of France; left Portsmouth to make war with France (Aug. 1415), just after a conspiracy to proclaim the earl of *March king had been discovered; took Harfleur and challenged the dauphin to single combat, 1415; sent back *Clarence in charge of many sick, and marched with the rest towards Calais; after futile negotiations attacked the greatly superior French army, himself commanding the centre, at Agincourt (25 Oct. 1415), where the French were routed with great slaughter; reached Calais a few days later, crossed the Channel within a fortnight, and after a triumphal entry into London was granted by parliament tonnage and poundage for life, the custom on wool, and other taxes, 1415; while in England restored the heirs of Mortimer, Percy, and Holland to their estates; made an alliance with Sigismund, king of the Romans, which led to the termination of the papal schism, 1416; came to an understanding with Burgundy, Oct. 1416; laid the foundations of a national navy and of military, international, and maritime law; took Caen, leading the assault in person, 1417; sent lieutenants against Cherbourg, Coutances, Avranches, and Evreux, subduing the greater part of Normandy; surrounded Rouen, cutting it off from the sea with the aid of a Portuguese fleet, and reduced it by famine after a long siege, 1419, while keeping open the feud between Armagnacs and Burgundians by alternate negotiations with each; after a short truce surprised Pontoise, 1419, and on the murder of John, duke of Burgundy, concluded an alliance with the new duke Philip; after more fighting and negotiation, accepted the Treaty of Troyes (1420), by which Henry was declared heir of Charles VI, regent of France, and lord of Normandy, the dauphin being excepted from the arrangement; married Catherine of France, 1420; personally directed capture of Melun, Nov. 1420, meeting the Sire de Barbazan in single combat; entered Paris in triumph, Dec. 1420; arranged for the government of Normandy; took his wife to England to be crowned; reformed the Benedictine monasteries; sent *James I back to Scotland; returned to France to reassert his sway, 1421; relieved Chartres, 1421; drove the dauphin across the Loire; took Meaux, 1422; while on his way to succour Burgundy at Cosne died at Bois de Vincennes. After a funeral procession through France his body was buried in Westminster Abbey, a chantry being endowed in his honour. The silver head of his effigy was stolen from the Confessor's Chapel in 1545. He was a patron of the poets *Lydgate and *Hoccleve. Inflexible justice, affability, and religious spirit were among his chief characteristics, and he was the first of contemporary generals and an able diplomat.

HENRY VI (1421–1471), king of England; son of Henry V; born at Windsor; ruled through a council during his minority, his uncle, *Humphrey of Gloucester, being protector, and Richard *Beauchamp, earl of Warwick, his 'master'; appeared in public functions in early childhood; crowned at Westminster, 1429, and at Paris, 1430; opened parliament in person, 1432; mediated at a great council between *Gloucester and *Bedford, 1434; his precocious interest in politics restrained by the council; admitted to share in government, 1437, but warned that he was exercising it unprofitably; identified himself with Cardinal *Beaufort's peace policy; greatly interested in scheme for his marriage with a daughter of the Comte d'Armagnac, 1441–3; attained legal majority, 1442; concluded two years' truce with France, 1443; married *Margaret of Anjou, daughter of the duke of Lorraine, 1445; under influence of Beaufort and *Suffolk, ordered *Gloucester's arrest, 1447; surrendered Maine for prolongation of truce with France, 1448; made constant progresses through England; secretly supported Suffolk, but was obliged to exile him, 1450; attempted to suppress *Cade's rising, but fled to Kenilworth, leaving the work to Archbishop *Kemp and *Waynflete, 1450; lost Normandy; obliged to make *Richard, duke of York, a councillor, and agree to arrest of Edmund *Beaufort, duke of Somerset; made Somerset captain of Calais, and refused to remove him from court, 1451; lost Guienne, 1451; deeply in debt; attempted a general pacification and pardon, 1452; won back part of Guienne, 1452, but

lost it all, 1453; temporarily lost his reason, 1453; on his recovery released Somerset and excluded York from the council, 1455; slightly wounded at first Battle of St Albans, 1455; again became ill; persuaded on recovery to remove York from office, 1456, but allowed him to remain in the council, and with the help of *Buckingham maintained peace for two years; after *Salisbury's victory (1459) at Bloreheath marched against Ludlow and drove York and the Nevilles from England, 1459, afterwards attainting them at Coventry; was defeated and captured by *Warwick at Northampton, and compelled to acknowledge York as heir to the crown, 1460; in spite of the defeat of the Yorkists by his queen (Margaret) at Wakefield (1460) and St Albans (1461), Henry fled northward after Edward, duke of York, was proclaimed king, 1461; at York while Towton Field was fought unsuccessfully by his friends, 1461; attainted by the Yorkists, 1461; took refuge with the Scots, 1461; granted charter to Edinburgh, 1464; narrowly escaped capture at Hexham, 1464; lurked disguised for a year on the Lancashire and Yorkshire border; was captured and imprisoned in the Tower for five years (1465–70); restored by Warwick, 1470; presided at a parliament, but (1471) fell into the hands of Edward IV, and was taken by him to Barnet; after Battle of Barnet (1471) was recommitted to the Tower; murdered on the night of Edward's return, Richard of Gloucester being held responsible; worshipped as a martyr by north countrymen; his canonization proposed by Henry VII. Henry VI was too weak to rule men, but was genuinely pious, and a liberal patron of learning. Besides taking great interest in the universities of Oxford and Caen, he founded Eton (1440) and King's College, Cambridge (1441), and suggested to his queen Margaret the foundation of Queens' College, Cambridge, 1448.

HENRY VII (1457–1509), king of England; son of Edmund *Tudor, earl of Richmond, and Margaret *Beaufort, heiress of *John of Gaunt; brought up in Wales by his uncle, Jasper *Tudor; captured at Harlech by the Yorkist *Herbert, 1468, but reclaimed by his uncle and presented to Henry VI, 1470; head of house of Lancaster on Henry VI's death, 1471; refugee in Brittany during reign of Edward IV; prevented by a storm from joining *Buckingham's rebellion against Richard III, 1483; at council of refugees held at Rennes promised to marry *Elizabeth of York on obtaining the English crown; after warning by *Morton of contemplated betrayal to Richard, escaped from Brittany to France; with *Oxford and some French troops landed at Milford Haven, 1485; joined by Welshmen and others; with the help of Sir William *Stanley (d. 1495) defeated and slew Richard at Bosworth, 1485; crowned, 1485; created peers and instituted a bodyguard; married Princess Elizabeth, 1486; defeated the conspirator *Simnel at Stoke-on-Trent, 1487; failed to mediate between France and Brittany, 1488; employed *Surrey to suppress discontent in the north, 1489; in alliance with Maximilian, king of the Romans, and Ferdinand and Isabella, besieged Boulogne (1492), but concluded the Treaty of Etaples with Charles VIII, 1492; took prompt action against Yorkists, and delayed for three years the invasion of England by Perkin *Warbeck; drove Warbeck from Ireland by the action of Sir Edward *Poynings, 1494, and through Spanish diplomacy procured Warbeck's dismissal from the Scottish court; lenient in suppressing Cornish insurrection, 1497; executed Warwick and Warbeck after their attempted escape from the Tower, 1499; concluded treaties with Scotland, 1499, Burgundy, 1500, and the emperor Maximilian, 1502; lost his queen, 1503; arranged marriages of his children with Spain and Scotland; entertained Philip and Joanna of Castile, and made commercial treaty with Flanders, 1506; died at Richmond in the palace named and built by himself. Through his agents *Empson and *Dudley he practised much extortion. He was considered one of the wisest princes of his time, and was a great promoter of commerce and learning. He built the chapel in Westminster Abbey called by his name.

HENRY VIII (1491–1547), king of England; second son of Henry VII; nominal lieutenant of Ireland, 1494; created prince of Wales, 1503, on the death of his elder brother *Arthur (1486–1502), to whose widow, *Catherine of Aragon, he was contracted, but marriage was delayed till his accession, 1509, owing to disputes about her dowry; had *Empson and *Dudley, the agents of his father's extortions, executed, 1510; helped his father-in-law against the Moors, 1511, and the regent of the Netherlands against Gueldres, 1511; joined the pope, Ferdinand, and Venice, in a league against France, 1511; some important naval victories won by his admirals, the Howards, one of whom captured Andrew *Barton, 1511; sent an unsuccessful expedition for the recovery of Guienne, 1512; built the *Henry Grace de Dieu* (largest ship hitherto floated); with the help of the emperor Maximilian won 'the Battle of Spurs', 1513 (the Scots being defeated at Flodden in his absence); deserted by his allies; made separate peace with France on the basis of a marriage between his sister *Mary and Louis XII, 1514; made Cardinal *Wolsey chancellor; followed Wolsey's advice in helping Maximilian with money to check the French in Italy, and in keeping on good terms with him, in securing Charles

in Castile, and (1518) in making peace with Francis I of France; became, against Wolsey's advice, a secret candidate for the empire, 1519; met Francis at the Field of the Cloth of Gold, 1520, but had previous and subsequent interviews with the emperor Charles V also; while pretending to mediate between them allied himself with Charles; next year at home had *Buckingham executed on a vague charge of treason; his demand for a forced loan, in consequence of the threatened hostilities with France, successfully resisted by London, 1525; helped by Wolsey's negotiations to a secret understanding with France; began negotiations with the pope for a divorce from Catherine of Aragon, 1527; given a commission to hear the case in England, 1528, which met (1529), but was revoked to Rome unfinished, 1529; dismissed Wolsey, Oct. 1529, and took *Cranmer as his adviser on the divorce; consulted English, French, and Italian universities, 1530, eight decisions against the validity of marriage with a brother's wife and against the pope's power to dispense being obtained by bribery; wrung from the clergy a qualified acknowledgement of his title as supreme head of the church in exchange for a pardon for having incurred the penalties of praemunire by recognizing Wolsey as papal legate, 1531; separated from Catherine on her refusal of arbitration, 1531; secretly married his second wife, *Anne Boleyn, and, Cranmer having decided against the validity of the marriage with Catherine, had Anne crowned publicly, 1533; secretly encouraged the Commons to present 'supplication against the ordinaries', 1532; took away independent powers of convocation; named Cranmer archbishop; provisionally withdrew first fruits of benefices (annates) and abolished appeals to Rome; was excommunicated, 1533; confirmed abolition of annates; caused Elizabeth *Barton to be attainted, 1533; abolished Roman jurisdiction and revenues in England, 1534; obtained act of succession (1534) compelling all subjects to acknowledge Anne Boleyn's issue as heirs to the crown; imprisoned *More and *Fisher; executed the Nun of Kent and her adherents, 1534; suppressed the observants, and imprisoned recusant friars; obtained severe treason law, parliamentary confirmation of headship of church, and transference of first fruits and tenths to crown (1534–5); executed Fisher, More, and some Charterhouse monks for refusing to accept the king's headship, 1535; opened negotiations with German Protestants; instituted visitations of monasteries and universities by royal officers under Thomas *Cromwell (1485?–1540), and appropriated the revenues of the smaller houses, 1535; beheaded Anne Boleyn and married his third wife, Jane *Seymour, 1536; had Succession

Act passed in interests of Jane Seymour, 1536; at first temporized with and then crushed rising in the north and east caused by religious changes and heavy taxation, 1536–7; lamented death of Jane Seymour, 1538; resumed dissolution of monasteries, but failed in negotiations with German Protestants; maintained old doctrines; procured statute of the Six Articles, 1539; executed last descendants of the Yorkist house; married his fourth wife, *Anne of Cleves, Jan. 1540; executed Cromwell and divorced Anne of Cleves, July 1540; at once married his fifth wife, *Catherine Howard; had *Barnes and other Protestants burned for heresy (1538–40); beheaded Queen Catherine Howard, 1542; proclaimed Ireland a kingdom, 1542; revived the feudal claim on Scotland, and defeated *James V, 1542; concluded alliance with Emperor Charles V, 1543; married his sixth and last wife, *Catherine Parr, 1543; debased the currency; sent an army into Scotland, which burned Leith and Edinburgh, 1544; captured Boulogne, 1545; was granted the endowments of many colleges, chantries, and hospitals, 1545; deserted by Charles V; made peace with France, 1546; gained possession of St Andrews by aiding the conspiracy against *Beaton, 1546; authorized many persecutions for heresy; caused the earl of *Surrey to be beheaded and the duke of *Norfolk attainted, 1547. Henry was technically constitutional, but practically absolute, and a consummate statesman. He completed Wolsey's college at Oxford, calling it Henry VIII's College (Christ Church), erected six new bishoprics from monastical endowments, and established suffragans. He wrote *Assertio Septem Sacramentorum* against Luther (1521) and preface to revised edition ('king's book') of *Institution of a Christian Man* ('bishops' book'). Many portraits of him by *Holbein are extant.

HENRY, duke of Gloucester (1640–1660), fourth son of Charles I; styled Henry of Oatlands; placed under care of earl of *Northumberland, and afterwards of countess of Leicester; while in France pressed by his mother, *Henrietta Maria, to become a Romanist, and disowned on his refusal; joined his brother Charles at Cologne; distinguished himself as a volunteer with the Spanish in Flanders, 1657–8; died of smallpox in London; buried in same vault as *Mary Queen of Scots at Westminster; highly praised by Clarendon.

HENRY, Sir **Edward Richard,** baronet, of Campden House Court (1850–1931), commissioner of Metropolitan Police; entered Indian Civil Service; inspector-general of police, Bengal, 1891; evolved system of classifying fingerprints which has been generally adopted;

assistant commissioner, Metropolitan Police, in charge of CID, 1901–3; commissioner (1903) at time of increasing public disorder due to unemployment, suffragettes, etc.; his determined efforts to improve police conditions could not prevent a strike, 1918; resigned and created baronet; KCVO, 1906; GCVO, 1911.

HENRY, James (1798–1876), physician and classic; gold medallist, Trinity College, Dublin; MA, 1822; MD, 1832; practised in Dublin till 1845, after which he travelled through Europe making Virgilian researches; published verse translation of *Aeneid* i and ii (1845), and poems; his *Aeneidea* appeared 1873–9.

HENRY, Matthew (1662–1714), commentator; son of Philip *Henry; studied law at Gray's Inn; Nonconformist minister at Chester, 1687–1712, afterwards at Mare Street, Hackney; his *Exposition of the Old and New Testament* (1708–10) completed by thirteen Nonconformist divines after his death, edited (1811) by George *Burder and John *Hughes, and often abridged; *Miscellaneous Writings* edited (1809 and 1830).

HENRY, Mitchell (1826–1910), Irish politician; studied medicine at Manchester; FRCS, 1854; MP for Co. Galway, 1871–85; supported Isaac *Butt; opposed Gladstone's Irish University Bill on question of sectarian education; persistently denounced over-taxation of Ireland, 1874–7; bought large estate of Kylemore, Co. Galway, and reclaimed bog land; disapproved of Land League operations; elected MP for Blackfriars division of Glasgow, 1885; voted against home rule, 1886; retired on defeat, 1886; chairman of firm of A. & S. Henry, merchants, of Manchester, 1889–93.

HENRY, Philip (1631–1696), Nonconformist divine; played with princes Charles and James as a child; favourite pupil of Richard *Busby at Westminster; student of Christ Church, Oxford, 1647; MA, 1652; witnessed execution of Charles I, 1649; minister of Worthenbury, and tutor in family of Mr Justice *Puleston, 1653–60; refused re-ordination; imprisoned on suspicion of conspiracy, 1663; preached as a Nonconformist, 1672–81; fined for keeping conventicles; disputed publicly with Quakers and with Bishop William *Lloyd and the elder *Dodwell, 1682; confined at Chester, 1685; ministered at Broad Oak, Flintshire, after Toleration Act; his *Life* written by his son; *Remains* edited by Sir J. B. *Williams (1848); *Diaries* published (1882).

HENRY, Robert (1718–1790), historian; studied at Edinburgh; DD, Edinburgh, 1771; Presbyterian minister successively at Carlisle, Berwick, New Grey Friars, Edinburgh (1768) and Old Grey Friars, 1776–90; moderator of general assembly, 1774; received pension in 1781 for his *History of England* (5 vols., 1771–85, 6th vol., 1793).

HENRY, Thomas (1734–1816), chemist; practised as a surgeon-apothecary in Manchester; secretary, Manchester Literary and Philosophical Society, 1781, and president, 1807; patented process for preparing calcined magnesia; issued *Experiments and Observations* (1773); FRS, 1775; member of American Philosophical Society; translated Lavoisier's chemical essays, 1776 and 1783; first observed use of carbonic acid to plants; published *Memoirs of Albert de Haller* (1783); assisted in foundation of College of Arts and Sciences at Manchester.

HENRY, Sir Thomas (1807–1876), police magistrate at Lambeth Street, Whitechapel, 1840–6, chief magistrate at Bow Street, 1864; knighted, 1864; barrister, Middle Temple, 1829; drew up Extradition Act and treaties connected therewith.

HENRY, William (d. 1768), dean of Killaloe; DD, Dublin, 1750; chaplain to Bishop Josiah *Hort; rector of Killesher, 1731, of Urney, 1734; dean of Killaloe, 1761–8; FRS, 1755; his *Description of Lough Erne* printed (1873).

HENRY, William (1774–1836), chemist; son of Thomas *Henry; MD, Edinburgh, 1807; published *General View of Nature and Objects of Chemistry* (1799), *Epitome of Chemistry* (1801); expanded into *Elements of Experimental Chemistry* (11th edn., 1829); FRS, 1808, and Copley medallist.

HENRY BENEDICT MARIA CLEMENT, Cardinal York (1725–1807), the Jacobite Henry IX; second son of Chevalier de St George, or 'James III'; came to England to support his brother *Charles Edward, 1745; on return to Italy became bishop of Ostia and prefect of St Peter's, Rome, cardinal (1747), archbishop of Corinth (1759), and bishop of Tusculum (1761); assumed title Henry IX, 1788; his residence at Frascati sacked by French, 1799; fled to Padua and Venice; relieved by gift of money from George III; died at Frascati, leaving crown jewels (carried off by James II) to George IV.

HENRY DE LEXINTON (d. 1258). See LEXINTON or LESSINGTON, HENRY DE.

HENRY DE LOUNDRES (d. 1228). See LOUNDRES.

HENRY DE NEWARK (or NEWERK) (d. 1299). See NEWARK.

HENRY DE NEWBURGH, earl of Warwick (d. 1123). See NEWBURGH.

HENRY FREDERICK, prince of Wales (1594–1612), eldest son of James VI of Scotland (James I of England); his guardianship by the earl of *Mar objected to by the queen but upheld by the king; came to England with *Anne of Denmark; matriculated at Magdalen College, Oxford, 1605; a Spanish marriage proposed for him; friend of *Raleigh; created prince of Wales, 1610; died of typhoid fever; buried in Westminster Abbey.

HENRY FREDERICK, duke of Cumberland and Strathearn (1745–1790), fourth son of *Frederick, prince of Wales; privy councillor and KG, 1767; £10,000 recovered against him for criminal conversation with Countess Grosvenor, 1770; alienated his brother, George III, by clandestine marriage with Mrs Horton, 1771; satirized by 'Junius'.

HENRY MAURICE OF BATTENBERG, Prince (1858–1896), third son of Prince Alexander of Hesse (1823–1888); married Princess *Beatrice, youngest daughter of Queen Victoria, 1885; volunteered with Ashanti expeditionary force, 1895, and died of fever.

HENRY OF ABENDON (d. 1437), warden of Merton College, Oxford; fellow of Merton College, 1390; as delegate from Oxford to Council of Constance defended priority of England over Spain, 1414; warden of Merton College, 1421; completed Merton Chapel and provided bells; attended Council of Basle, 1432; prebendary of Wells.

HENRY OF BLOIS (d. 1171), bishop of Winchester; son of Stephen, count of Blois, and younger brother of King Stephen of England; educated at Cluny; abbot of Glastonbury, 1126–71, where he built a palace and abbey buildings; bishop of Winchester, 1129–71; procured the crown for Stephen by guaranteeing liberty of the church, and supported him at siege of Exeter; said to have failed to secure the papal sanction for his translation to Canterbury (1138) through the king's influence; named legate in England, 1139; rebuked Stephen for imprisoning bishops of Salisbury and Ely; persuaded Stephen to allow the empress *Matilda to join *Gloucester at Bristol, 1139; negotiated for Stephen with Matilda at Bath, 1140; conferred with Louis VII on English affairs, 1140; his proposals rejected by Stephen; joined Matilda, and advocated her claim on the ground of Stephen's treachery to the church, 1141; offended by her and won over by the queen; besieged by the empress and *David of Scotland in Wolvesey Castle, Winchester, but receiving help from Stephen besieged her afterwards in Winchester; destroyed Hyde Abbey, and allowed the city to be sacked; formed scheme for making his see metropolitan; said to have received pall from Rome, 1142; held council to mitigate the evils of civil war, 1142; upheld election of his nephew, William *Fitzherbert, to see of York, but lost legateship after death (1143) of Innocent II; opposed at Rome by Bernard of Clairvaux; suspended from his bishopric for advising Stephen to forbid Archbishop *Theobald to attend papal council at Reims, 1148; obtained absolution at Rome, 1151; active in forwarding Treaty of Wallingford, 1153; left England (where Henry II destroyed three of his castles), 1155; stayed at Cluny, becoming its greatest benefactor; on his return consecrated *Becket as primate, 1162; gave Becket some support against Henry II, though pronouncing judgment against Becket at Northampton, 1164; disapproved Becket's conduct after his flight, but sent him assistance; gave away all his goods in charity, c.1168; on his deathbed rebuked the king for Becket's murder; probably buried before the high altar at Winchester, where he built a treasure-house, besides founding the hospital of St Cross.

HENRY OF CORNWALL (or OF ALMAINE) (1235–1271), son of *Richard, earl of Cornwall and king of the Romans, and Isabella Marshall; accompanied his father to France, 1247 and 1250, and witnessed his coronation at Aachen, 1257; one of the royal nominees to draw up constitution at Oxford, 1258; as partisan of Simon de *Montfort imprisoned at Boulogne, 1263; joined Prince Edward and fought for royalists at Lewes, 1264, when he gave himself up as a hostage; sent to France to treat with Louis IX, 1265; commanded expedition against Robert, Earl *Ferrers, 1266; co-opted referee under Dictum de Kenilworth, 1267; mediated between Henry III and *Gloucester, 1267; took the cross, 1268; followed Edward to Tunis and Sicily, 1270, but returned to settle the affairs of Gascony, where he had weight through his marriage with the daughter of Gaston, vicomte de Béarn; accompanied the kings of France and Sicily through Italy to Viterbo; murdered at church by de Montfort's sons and Count Rosso, though he had not even been present at Evesham; his heart deposited in Westminster Abbey.

HENRY OF EASTRY (d. 1331), prior of Christ Church, Canterbury, 1286–1331, of which he was a great benefactor; revived claim to exercise spiritual jurisdiction over Canterbury during vacancies; quarrelled with the citizens and abbot of St Augustine's; supported Archbishop Robert de *Winchelsea in resisting taxation, but was starved into submission by Edward I, 1297; completely reformed the financial administration of the priory; his letters to Archbishop *Reynolds

printed in *Letter Books of Christ Church* (ed. Dr Sheppard, 1887); corresponded with Archbishop *Meopham; died celebrating mass; earliest existing registers of the convent compiled by his direction; his MS 'Memoriale Henrici Prioris' in British Museum.

HENRY OF HUNTINGDON (1084?–1155), historian; archdeacon of Huntingdon from 1109; accompanied Archbishop *Theobald to Rome, 1139, meeting at Bec the Norman historian Robert de Torigny. His *Historia Anglorum*, compiled at request of Bishop *Alexander (d. 1148) of Lincoln, extends in latest form to 1154. It was first printed in *Scriptores post Bedam* (1596, reprinted by Migne, 1854); a complete edition (including biographical epistle 'De Contemptu Mundi') was published (1879).

HENRY OF LANCASTER, earl of Lancaster (1281?–1345), grandson of Henry III and second son of Edmund, earl of Lancaster (see LANCASTER, EDMUND, earl of); lord of Monmouth and Lancaster's Welsh estates, 1296; summoned as baron, 1299; served with Edward I in Flanders (1297–8) and Scotland, 1298; helped to subdue Llywelyn Bren, 1315; created earl of Lancaster and Leicester and steward of England on death of his brother *Thomas, earl of Lancaster (1277–1322), 1324; joined Queen *Isabella, 1326, and captured Edward II and the younger *Despenser, 1326; guardian and chief councillor of the young Edward III; formed confederacy against *Mortimer, but was obliged to submit, 1329; sent on embassy to France, 1330; became blind; devised overthrow of Mortimer; founded hospital near Leicester.

HENRY OF LANCASTER, first duke of Lancaster (1299?–1361), son of *Henry, earl of Lancaster (1281?–1345); a crusader in his youth; distinguished at capture of Dalkeith, 1333; summoned as Henry de Lancaster, 1334; created earl of Derby, 1337; sent with Sir Walter *Manny against Cadsant, 1337; with Edward III in Flanders, 1338–9, lending him money; distinguished himself at Sluys, 1340; captaingeneral against Scotland, 1341–2, overcoming Sir William *Douglas, knight of Liddesdale, in a tournament; went on missions to the pope and Alfonso XI of Castile; served against the Moors at Algeciras, 1343; lieutenant of Aquitaine, 1345–7; succeeded to his father's earldoms, 1347; took Bergerac, 1345, and defeated a much superior French force at Auberoche, and stormed Lusignan and Poitiers, 1346; reinforced Edward at Calais, 1347; an original KG; negotiated with French and Flemish, 1348–9; created earl of Lincoln and captain of Gascony and Poitou, 1349; prominent in sea fight called Espagnols-sur-mer, 1350; created duke of Lancaster, with palatine jurisdiction, and admiral of Western Fleet, 1351; attacked Boulogne, 1351; went to Prussia and Poland, 1351–2, and to Paris to fight Otto of Brunswick for an attempt to waylay him in Germany, 1352; head of embassy to king of Navarre, 1354; conducted campaigns in Normandy and Brittany, 1356–7; created earl of Moray by David II, 1359; co-operated with Edward in France, 1359–60; chief negotiator at Peace of Bretigny, 1360; died of the pestilence at Leicester, where he added to his father's foundation the collegiate church of St Mary-the-Greater. He was Edward III's most trusted counsellor, and esteemed throughout western Europe as a perfect knight. His daughter Blanche (wife of *John of Gaunt) was ancestress of the house of Lancaster.

HENRY OF MARLBOROUGH (or MARLE-BURGH) (*fl.* 1420), annalist; vicar of Balscaddan and Donabate, Co. Dublin; his Latin annals (1133–1421) of England and Ireland printed by *Ware (1633, reprinted 1809), as *Chronicle of Ireland*.

HENRY OF SALTREY (*fl.* 1150), Cistercian of Saltrey or Sawtrey, Huntingdonshire; obtained from his friend, *Gilbert of Louth, story of his 'Purgatorium Sancti Patricii', included in Matthew *Paris's *Chronica Majora*, and first printed in Massingham's *Florilegium insulae Sanctorum Hiberniae* (1624).

HENRY OF SCOTLAND (1114?–1152), son of *David I of Scotland; granted by Stephen the earldoms of Carlisle, Doncaster, and Huntingdon; fought at Battle of the Standard, 1138; created earl of Northumberland, 1139.

HENRYSON, Edward (1510?–1590?), Scottish judge; graduate of Bourges and professor of Roman law there, 1554; defended Equinar Baron's treatise on law of jurisdiction against Govea; published also *Commentatio in Tit. x. Libri Secundi Institutionum de Testamentis Ordinandis* (1555); commissary in Scotland, 1563; extraordinary lord of session, 1566; edited revision of Scottish laws (1424–1564).

HENRYSON (or HENDERSON), Robert (1430?–1506?), Scottish poet; original member of Glasgow University, 1462; probably a clerical schoolmaster attached to Dunfermline Abbey; his *Tale of Orpheus* first printed (1508); his *Testament of Cresseid* attributed to *Chaucer till 1721, though printed as his own (1593); his *Morall Fables of Esope the Phrygian* printed (1621); *Poems and Fables* collected and edited by Dr D. *Laing (1865).

HENRYSON (or HENDERSON), Sir Thomas, Lord Chesters (d. 1638), lord of session, 1622–37; knighted; son of Edward *Henryson.

HENRY THE MINSTREL (*fl.* 1470–1492), Scottish poet, also called Blind Harry or Hary; author of poem on *Wallace; mentioned in *Dunbar's 'Lament for the Makaris' (1508); probably a native of Lothian, writing under *James III; his work largely a translation from John *Blair; its chronology and general accuracy discredited by Hailes and others, but in some instances corroborated; complete manuscript (1488) in Advocates' Library. The best printed editions are those of *Jamieson and Moir (1885–6); William *Hamilton of Gilbertfield's modern version (1722) became more familiar than the original.

HENRY WILLIAM FREDERICK ALBERT, prince of York, and later duke of Gloucester (1900–1974); third son of Prince George, duke of York (later King George V) and Princess (Victoria) *Mary ('May') of Teck; educated at Eton, Sandhurst, and Trinity College, Cambridge; posted to 10th Royal Hussars, 1921; created duke of Gloucester, 1928; undertook official visits to Japan (1929), Abyssinia (1930), and Australia and New Zealand (1934–5); married Alice Christabel, third daughter of John Charles Montagu-Douglas-Scott, seventh duke of Buccleuch, 1935; chief liaison officer between British and French armies in Europe, 1939; slightly wounded, 1940; appointed second-in-command, 20th Armoured brigade 1941; visited troops in North Africa, Middle East, India, and Ceylon; governor-general of Australia, 1945–7; senior counsellor of state during royal visit to South Africa, 1947; represented queen at ceremonies in Iraq, Jordan, Malaysia, Ethiopia, and Nigeria, 1953–9; revisited Australia, 1965 and Malaysia, 1966; among many honours were KG, 1921; great master and knight Grand Cross of the Order of the Bath, 1942; PC, 1925; also many foreign decorations; colonel-in-chief of four regiments; succeeded by younger son, Prince Richard Alexander Walter George, 1974.

HENSCHEL, Sir George (1850–1934), musician; born at Breslau of Polish-Jewish parentage; studied in Leipzig and Berlin; a baritone singer of singular vitality and authority; his own accompanist; first conductor, Boston Symphony Orchestra (1881–4), Scottish Orchestra, Glasgow (1893–5); founder, organizer, and first conductor, London symphony concerts, 1886–97; gave remarkable duet recitals with first wife, 1881–1901; continued as conductor, concert singer, and composer, 1909–14; last broadcast, 1934; naturalized, 1890; knighted, 1914.

HENSEY, Florence (*fl.* 1758), spy; MD, Leiden; physician in Paris and London; supplied information to French Foreign Office during Seven Years' War, contributing to failure of

Rochefort expedition, 1757; convicted and condemned to death, 1758; pardoned, 1759.

HENSHALL, Samuel (1764?–1807), philologist; educated at Manchester and Brasenose College, Oxford (fellow); MA, 1789; rector of Bow, 1802–7; published *The Saxon and English Languages reciprocally illustrative* (1798), *The Gothic Gospel of St. Matthew* (1807), and some topographical works.

HENSHAW, Joseph (1603–1679), bishop of Peterborough; educated at Charterhouse and Magdalen Hall, Oxford; BA, 1624; DD, 1639; chaplain to the earl of *Bristol and duke of *Buckingham; held benefices in Sussex; as 'delinquent' had to compound for his estate, 1646; precentor and dean of Chichester, 1660; dean of Windsor, 1660; bishop of Peterborough, 1663–79; his *Horae Successivae* (1631) edited by W. *Turnbull, 1839, and *Meditations* (1637) reprinted at Oxford (1841).

HENSHAW, Nathaniel (1628–1673), physician; MD, Leiden and Dublin; FRS, 1663; practised in Dublin; published *Aero-Chalinos: or a Register for the Air* (1664, 2nd edn. 1677, printed by Royal Society).

HENSHAW, Thomas (1618–1700), author; brother of Nathaniel *Henshaw; of University College, Oxford, and Middle Temple; served in French Army, remaining abroad some years; barrister; gentleman of the Privy Council and French under-secretary to Charles II, James II, and William III; an original FRS, 1662; envoy-extraordinary in Denmark, 1672–5. His works include a translation of Samedo's history of China (1655) and an edition of Stephen *Skinner's *Etymologicon Linguae Anglicanae* (1671).

HENSLOW, John Stevens (1796–1861), botanist; educated at Rochester and St John's College, Cambridge; sixteenth wrangler, 1818; MA, 1821; FLS, 1818; assisted *Sedgwick in founding Cambridge Philosophical Society; Cambridge professor of mineralogy, 1822–5, of botany, 1825–61; recommended his pupil Charles Robert *Darwin as naturalist to the *Beagle*; vicar of Hitcham, Suffolk, 1837–61; published *Letters to the Farmers of Suffolk* on scientific agriculture (1843); discovered phosphatic nodules in Suffolk Crag, 1843; member of London University senate and examiner in botany; presided over discussion on *Origin of Species* at British Association, 1861; assisted Sir W. J. *Hooker at Kew; works include *Catalogue of British Plants* (1829), *Dictionary of Botanical Terms* (1857).

HENSLOWE, Philip (d. 1616), theatrical manager; settled in Southwark, 1577, where he became a dyer, pawnbroker, and money-lender; groom of royal chamber, 1593, and sewer, 1603; rebuilt and managed the Rose Playhouse on Bankside till 1603, and afterwards the Theatre at Newington Butts and the Swan on Bankside; associated with Edward *Alleyn in management of the Fortune in Golden Lane, Cripplegate Without, 1600–16, and in other enterprises; bought plays from *Dekker, *Drayton, *Chapman, and other dramatists, most of which are lost; extracts from his diary (preserved at Dulwich) printed by *Malone, and the whole (with forged interpolations) by J. P. *Collier (1845).

HENSMAN, John (1780–1864), divine; fellow of Corpus Christi, Cambridge; ninth wrangler, 1801; assistant to Charles *Simeon at Cambridge; brought about building of new parish church at Clifton, 1822; incumbent of Trinity, Hotwells, 1830–44; held living of Clifton, 1847–64; chapel of ease consecrated as a memorial of him, 1862.

HENSON, Gravener (1785–1852), author of a work on the framework knitting and lace trades (1831) and similar subjects; imprisoned for complicity in Luddite riots; expert in detection of smugglers.

HENSON, Herbert Hensley (1863–1947), bishop successively of Hereford and Durham; educated at private school, Broadstairs; non-collegiate student, Oxford; first class, modern history, and fellow of All Souls, 1884; deacon, 1887; priest, 1888; vicar of Barking, 1888–95; chaplain, Ilford Hospital, 1895–1900; canon of Westminster and rector of St Margaret's, 1900–12; proctor in convocation, 1903–12; dean of Durham, 1912–18; his orthodoxy suspect and consecration as bishop of Hereford (1918) strongly opposed by Anglo-Catholics; bishop of Durham, 1920–39; of increasingly liberal churchmanship, great eloquence, and independence of mind; took strenuous part in ecclesiastical conflicts; published sermons and addresses, *Ad Clerum* (1937), *Bishoprick Papers* (1946), and *Retrospect of an Unimportant Life* (3 vols., 1942–50).

HENSON, Leslie Lincoln (1891–1957), actor-manager; educated at Cliftonville College and Emanuel School, Wandsworth; joined concert party, 1910; gained immediate success as Henry in *To-Night's the Night* (Gaiety, 1915); organized entertainment for troops, 1916–18; appeared in series of musical comedies at Winter Garden and from 1935 at Gaiety; in management with Tom *Walls produced *Tons of Money* (1922) and series of Aldwych farces; worked for ENSA 1939–45; thereafter his brand of humour began to stale.

HENSTRIDGE, Daniel (d. 1736), organist at Rochester and (1700–36) Canterbury, and composer.

HENTON (or HEINTON), Simon (*fl.* 1360), Dominican provincial in England and commentator.

HENTY, Edward (1809–1878), pioneer of Victoria, forming Portland Bay settlement, 1834; member for Normanby in legislative assembly, 1856–61.

HENTY, George Alfred (1832–1902), writer for boys; educated at Westminster and Caius College, Cambridge; served in Crimea with hospital commissariat department; adopted journalism, 1865; correspondent to *Standard* during Austro-Italian War (1866), in Abyssinia (1867–8), Franco-German War (1870–1), in Ashanti (1873–4), and on prince of Wales's Indian tour (1875), and elsewhere; published his first boys' book, *Out in the Pampas* (1868), and from 1876 brought out some three volumes a year, dealing mainly with military history; edited *Union Jack*, 1880–3; keen yachtsman; also published some twelve orthodox novels.

HENWOOD, William Jory (1805–1875), mineralogist; supervisor of tin for Cornwall, 1832–8; FGS, 1828; FRS, 1840; took charge of Gongo-Soco mines, Brazil, 1843; reported to Indian government on metals of Kumaon and Gurhwal, 1855; president of Royal Institute of Cornwall, 1869; Murchison medallist, 1874; his name given to hydrous phosphate of aluminium and copper.

HEPBURN, Francis (or Francis Ker) (1779–1835), major-general; served with 3rd Foot (now Scots) Guards in Ireland, 1798, Holland, 1799, and Sicily; wounded at Barossa, 1811; present (1813) at Vittoria, Nivelle, and the Nive; commanded 2nd battalion in Netherlands, 1814–15; commanded at Hougoumont, 1815; CB; major-general, 1821.

HEPBURN, Francis Stewart, fifth earl of Bothwell (d. 1624), known by name of his mother (Lady Jane Hepburn), sister of James *Hepburn, fourth earl of Bothwell, whose title and offices he received on the report of his death, 1576; his father a natural son of *James V; supporter of the regent Morton; abroad at time of Morton's fall; on return posed as Protestant champion and successor of his uncle *Moray; a favourite with *James VI till discovery of his complicity in raid of Ruthven, 1582; joined Patrick *Gray's conspiracy against *Arran, 1585; with *Home fortified Kelso for the banished lords, 1585; killed Sir William *Stewart at Edinburgh, 1588; urged James to take advantage of the Spanish Armada to invade England; his influence

destroyed by rise of *Maitland; joined Catholic rebellion, but was pardoned by intercession of the kirk; during James's absence in Denmark assisted *Lennox as president of Privy Council; on his return accused of consulting witches and outlawed, 1591; attempted to capture the king and Maitland in Holyrood, 1591; denounced by James to parliament as a pretender to the throne, 1592; attempted to capture him in Falkland Palace, 1592; sentenced to forfeiture, but introduced by Maitland's enemies into James's presence disguised, 1593; temporarily pardoned, but soon denounced again; appeared with force at Leith and was unsuccessfully pursued by James, 1594; expelled from England; again joined the Catholic lords in the north, 1594; fled from Caithness to Normandy, 1595; died in poverty at Naples.

HEPBURN, Sir George Buchan, first baronet (1739–1819), baron of Scottish Exchequer; solicitor to lords of session, 1767–90; judge of Admiralty court, 1790–1; baron of Scottish Exchequer, 1791–1814; created baronet, 1815; published work on agriculture of East Lothian (1796).

HEPBURN, James, fourth earl of Bothwell (1536?–1578), husband of *Mary Queen of Scots; son of Patrick *Hepburn, third earl; succeeded to hereditary offices of his father, 1556; though nominally Protestant, was strong supporter of the queen-dowager and the French party; intercepted money sent by the English to lords of the congregation, 1559; his castle at Crichton seized by *Arran and Lord James Stuart after his escape with the treasure; sent on a foreign mission by the queen-dowager, 1560; visited Denmark; at Paris became gentleman of the royal chamber, 1560; returned to Scotland as a commissioner for Mary Queen of Scots, 1561; banished from Edinburgh for a brawl with the Hamiltons; reconciled to Arran by *Knox at Kirk-o'-Field; charged by Arran with design to carry off the queen to Dumbarton; escaped from ward, 1562; detained by the English while escaping to France and sent to the Tower, 1564; allowed to go to France on representations of Mary and *Maitland; on return to Scotland offered to meet his accusers, but failed to appear, 1565; by favour of Mary allowed to retire to France; recalled by the queen to help her against *Moray, 1565; escaped capture by the English, and obtained great influence with Mary; married Lady Jean Gordon, but remained Protestant, 1566; though in Holyrood, had no share in murder of *Rizzio, 1566; joined Mary and *Darnley on their escape to Dunbar, 1566; acquired increasing influence over the queen, who granted him lands and Dunbar Castle; temporarily reconciled with Moray and Maitland; wounded by an outlaw near the Hermitage, 1566; entertained Mary at Dunbar; at Craigmillar said to have favoured Mary's divorce from Darnley, and afterwards signed the bond for his removal, 1566; failed to obtain *Morton's help; superintended arrangements for Darnley's lodging at Kirk-o'-Field; escorted Darnley and Mary into Edinburgh (31 Jan. 1567); consulted subordinate plotters in apartments at Holyrood; had powder brought from Dunbar and placed in the queen's room below that of Darnley at Kirk-o'-Field (9 Feb.); went above before Mary set out for a ball; appeared there, but left at midnight and directed the firing of the train; attributed the explosion to lightning; was generally suspected of Darnley's murder, but still favoured by Mary and (with *Huntly) given charge of Prince James, 1567; accused by *Lennox, but prevented Lennox's appearance, and obtained formal acquittal (12 Apr. 1567); obtained written agreement of Protestant lords to support his marriage with the queen (19 Apr.); carried her off (perhaps by consent) to Dunbar (21 Apr.); obtained an irregular divorce from his wife (7 May); married to Mary at Holyrood (15 May 1567); created duke of Orkney and Shetland, 1567; threatened at Holyrood by the nobles; fled with the queen to Borthwick Castle; left her and fled to Dunbar; marched on Edinburgh, but when met by the lords at Carberry Hill was persuaded by Mary to leave her, 1567; rode to Dunbar and thence went north to join Huntly; escaped to Kirkwall; gathered together a pirate fleet, which was pursued by Kirkcaldy of Grange to the North Sea; landed in Norway, whence he was sent to Denmark, 1567; his surrender refused by the king of Denmark, who kept him in confinement; while at Copenhagen composed *Les Affaires du Conte de Boduel*; removed to Malmö; offered cession of Orkney and Shetland in exchange for release, 1568; his divorce from Mary passed by the pope, 1570; removed to closer prison at Drachsholm, 1573; became gradually insane; buried in Faareveile Church; deathbed confession not authentic.

HEPBURN, James (in religion **Bonaventure)** (1573–1620), linguist; travelled in Europe and the east; entered order of Minims at Avignon; six years oriental keeper in Vatican Library; published an Arabic grammar (1591), translation into Latin of *Kettar Malcuth*, and other works; died at Venice.

HEPBURN, Sir James (d. 1637), soldier; succeeded his cousin, Sir John *Hepburn, as commander of Scots brigade; killed at Damvillers.

HEPBURN, John (d. 1522), prior of St Andrews, 1482; brother of Patrick *Hepburn, first earl of Bothwell; founder of St Leonard's College, 1512; sometime keeper of the privy seal of Scotland; unsuccessful candidate for archbishopric of St Andrews, 1514.

HEPBURN, Sir John (1598?–1636), soldier of fortune; though a Roman Catholic, joined Scottish force in service of elector palatine, 1620; fought under Mansfeldt, 1622–3; colonel of Scottish regiment under Gustavus Adolphus, 1625; Swedish governor of Rügenwalde, 1630; commander of the Scots brigade, 1631; wounded at siege of Frankfurt-on-Oder, 1631; took decisive part in capture of Landsberg and Battle of Breitenfeld, 1631; publicly thanked by Gustavus after capture of Donauwörth, 1632; left the Swedish service and raised two thousand men in Scotland for that of France, 1633; his recruits incorporated with Scots archery guard nicknamed 'Pontius Pilate's guards'; took part as *maréchal-de-camp* in conquest of Lorraine, 1634–5; captured by imperialists, but released; assisted in relief of Hagenau, 1636; obtained precedence for his brigade, augmented by Scots in Swedish service, 1636; killed at siege of Saverne; his monument in Toul Cathedral destroyed at revolution.

HEPBURN, Patrick, third Baron Hailes and first earl of Bothwell (d. 1508); succeeded his father as third Baron Hailes; defended Berwick against English, 1482; fought against *James III at Sauchieburn, 1488; governor of Edinburgh, lord high admiral and master of the household, and created earl of Bothwell, 1488; received grants in Orkney and Shetland, 1489, and Liddesdale, 1492; took part in various embassies; a commissioner for marriage of *James IV and *Margaret Tudor, 1501.

HEPBURN, Patrick, third earl of Bothwell (1512?–1556), grandson of Patrick *Hepburn, first earl of Bothwell; succeeded on his father's death at Flodden, 1513; received share of Angus's forfeited estates, 1529; imprisoned (1529) for protecting border marauders; offered his services to Northumberland against Scotland, 1531; imprisoned at Edinburgh and banished from Scotland, 1533; returned, 1542, and resumed possession of Liddesdale and Hermitage Castle; acted with Cardinal *Beaton against English party, and brought queen-dowager and her daughter to Stirling, 1543; supported regency of *Mary of Guise and divorced his wife to become a suitor for her hand; arrested George *Wishart (1513?–1546), 1546, and was induced to hand him over to Beaton; imprisoned for intrigue with England, 1547–8; fled across the border; recalled by queen-dowager, 1553; lieutenant of the border, 1553.

HEPBURN, Patrick (d. 1573), bishop of Moray; prior of St Andrews, 1522; secretary to James V, 1524–7; one of those who condemned Patrick *Hamilton, 1527; bishop of Moray and abbot of Scone, 1535; member of Privy Council, 1546; border commissioner, 1553; his palace and church at Scone burnt by townsmen of Dundee in revenge for execution of Walter *Mylne, 1559; deprived of his rents for protecting *Bothwell, and tried as accessory to *Darnley's murder, 1567; notorious profligate.

HEPBURN, Patrick George Thomas Buchan-, Baron Hailes (1901–1974), politician. See BUCHAN-HEPBURN.

HEPBURN, Robert (1690?–1712), author; edited the *Tatler, by Donald MacStaff of the North* (1711); three posthumous works by him.

HEPWORTH, Dame **(Jocelyn) Barbara** (1903–1975), sculptor; educated at Wakefield Girls' High School; studied at Leeds School of Art, 1919 and Royal College of Art, London, 1920–3; went with scholarship to Italy, 1924; married John Rattenbury Skeaping, a fellow sculptor, 1925; lived in Florence and Rome and learned how to carve stone; moved to Hampstead and had first exhibition at Beaux Arts Gallery, London, 1928; creating totally abstract sculpture by 1934; marriage dissolved, 1933, and became associated with the painter, Ben *Nicholson; members of Paris-based group, Abstraction-Creation and in England of Unit One; close friend of Henry Moore and her home became centre of abstract-art movement in Britain; married Ben Nicholson, 1938; settled at St Ives, Cornwall; from 1944 onwards work influenced by Cornish landscape; important retrospective exhibitions at Venice Biennale (1950), Whitechapel Art Gallery (1954 and 1962), São Paolo Bienal, Brazil (1959), and Tate Gallery (1968); most important commission, *Single Form*, outside UN building, New York, memorial to her friend Dag Hammarskjöld, 1964; designed sets and costumes for (Sir) Michael Tippett's opera *The Midsummer Marriage* (1955); marriage to Ben Nicholson dissolved, 1951; CBE, 1958; DBE, 1965; honorary degrees from six universities; senior fellow, Royal College of Art, 1970; trustee, Tate Gallery, 1965–72; died in fire in her studio, 1975; studio presented to nation by her executors together with representative collection of her work, 1980.

HERAPATH, John (1790–1868), mathematician; contributed to the *Annals of Philosophy*; rejection of his paper offered to Royal Society, 1820, followed by controversy; his *Tables of Temperature* controverted by *Tredgold; corrected Brougham's mathematical works; proprietor and manager of *Railway Magazine* from 1836; published *Mathematical Physics* (1847).

HERAPATH, William (1796–1868), analytical chemist; cousin of John *Herapath; a founder of the London Chemical Society; professor of chemistry at Bristol Medical School, 1828; often called as an expert in poisoning cases; president of Bristol Political Union, 1831.

HERAUD, John Abraham (1799–1887), author and critic; assistant editor of *Fraser's Magazine*, 1830–3; contributed to *Quarterly*; friend of the *Carlyles, *Lockhart, and *Southey; dramatic critic of *Illustrated London News* (1849–79) and *Athenaeum*; Charterhouse brother, 1873; published *The Descent into Hell* (1830), *Judgment of the Flood* (1834), and other poems, as well as plays and miscellaneous works.

HERAULT, John (1566–1626), bailiff of Jersey; of All Souls College, Oxford; as bailiff, 1615, vindicated against Sir John *Peyton (1544–1630) right of crown to appoint and of bailiff to exercise civil and judicial power.

HERBERT, Sir Alan Patrick (1890–1971), author and wit; educated at Winchester and New College, Oxford; first class, jurisprudence, 1914; free-lance contributor to *Punch*; enlisted in RNVR; commissioned, 1915; on active service at Gallipoli and in France; wounded, 1917; published *The Secret Battle* (1919); called to bar (Inner Temple), 1918; joined staff of *Punch*, 1924; responsible for long-running 'Misleading Cases', published as book (1927); wrote revue, *Riverside Nights* (1926) and operettas, *La Vie Parisienne* (1929), *Tantivy Towers* (1931), and *Derby Day* (1932); frequently wrote amusing letters to *The Times*; published novels, *The Water Gipsies* (1930) and *Holy Deadlock* (1934), which exposed crudities of divorce laws; Independent junior burgess representing Oxford University in Parliament, 1935–50; as private member won acceptance of his Matrimonial Causes Act, 1936; joined River Emergency Service, 1939 and became petty officer, RN; gave account of wartime years on Thames in *A. P. H., his Life and Times* (1970); successfully opposed proposal for purchase tax on books; knighted, 1945; published *Independent Member* (1950); had conspicuous success with musical, *Bless the Bride* (1950); campaigned vigorously for causes such as a public lending right for authors and for a Thames barrage; trustee, National Maritime Museum; president, London Corinthian Sailing Club and Inland Waterways Association; president, Society of Authors; CH, 1970; DCL, Oxford, 1958.

HERBERT, Alfred (d. 1861), water-colour painter; son of a Thames waterman; exhibited at Royal Academy, 1847–60.

HERBERT, Algernon (1792–1855), antiquary; educated at Eton and Oxford; fellow of Merton College, 1814, dean, 1828; MA, 1825; published *Nimrod, a Discourse upon Certain Passages of History and Fable* (1828–30), edition of *Nennius* (1848), and other works.

HERBERT, Anne, countess of Dorset, Pembroke, and Montgomery (1590–1676). See CLIFFORD, ANNE.

HERBERT, Arthur, earl of Torrington (1647–1716), admiral of the fleet; second son of Sir Edward *Herbert (1591?–1657); entered navy, 1663; served against the Dutch, 1666, and against Algerine corsairs, 1669–71; commanded the *Dreadnought* at Solebay, 1672, and the *Cambridge*, 1673–5; lost an eye in capture of a corsair in Mediterranean, 1678; as admiral in the straits relieved Tangier, 1680, and continued to command against the Algerines till 1683; rear-admiral and master of the robes, 1684; MP, Dover, 1685; cashiered for refusing to support repeal of Test Act, 1687; commander of fleet which conveyed William of Orange to England, 1688; first lord of the Admiralty and commander of Channel Fleet, 1689; created earl of Torrington, 1689, after indecisive action with French in Bantry Bay; resigned the Admiralty, 1690; with insufficient squadron obliged by queen's order to engage whole French fleet off Beachy Head, 1690; his cautious tactics frustrated by Dutch contingent; charged before court martial with hanging back, 1690; acquitted, but never again held command; corresponded with William III.

HERBERT, Arthur John (1834–1856), historical painter; son of John Rogers *Herbert; died in Auvergne.

HERBERT, Auberon Edward William Molyneux (1838–1906), political philosopher and author; son of third earl of *Carnarvon; educated at Eton and St John's College, Oxford; fellow, 1855–69; joined army, 1858; resigned, 1862; president of Union at Oxford, 1862; DCL, 1865; present during Prusso-Danish War, 1864; in America during Civil War, and at Sedan in Franco-German War; private secretary to Sir Stafford *Northcote (later earl of Iddesleigh), 1866–8; abandoned Conservative views; Liberal MP for Nottingham, 1870–4; declared himself a republican, 1872; supported Joseph *Arch and Agricultural Labourers' Union, 1872; championed Charles *Bradlaugh, 1880; became ardent disciple of Herbert *Spencer and an agnostic; published *A Politician in Trouble about his Soul* (1884); issued a monthly *Organ of Voluntary Taxation*, 1890–1901, and *The Voluntaryist Creed* (1908); engaged in farming in the New Forest from 1874 till death; relinquished sport on becoming vegetarian; interested in prehistoric remains and in psychic research; also wrote verse.

HERBERT, Auberon Mark Yvo Henry Molyneux (1922–1974), Catholic champion of oppressed peoples; educated at Ampleforth and Balliol College, Oxford, 1940–2; rejected for service in British Army and Free French and Dutch forces but became only British-born officer in Polish Army; fought in Normandy campaign, 1944 and won Polish Order of Merit with swords; while on personal mission from (Sir) Winston Churchill, arrested as suspected spy by Canadian Military Police, 1944; passionately concerned with fate of Poland; organized Polish Resettlement Organization and Anglo-Polish Society; vice-president, Anglo-Ukrainian Society and founder president, Anglo-Byelorussian Society; made his home refuge for exiles, but had no success in British politics; like his brother-in-law, Evelyn *Waugh, was caused despair by Vatican II reforms, especially abandonment of the Latin mass.

HERBERT, Auberon Thomas, eighth Baron Lucas (1876–1916), politician and airman; son of A. E. W. M. *Herbert; BA, Balliol College, Oxford; succeeded maternal uncle, 1905; held office in Liberal government, 1908–15; PC, 1912; joined Royal Flying Corps, 1915; missing in France.

HERBERT, Cyril Wiseman (1847–1882), painter; son of John Rogers *Herbert; curator of antique school, Royal Academy, 1882; exhibited, 1870–5.

HERBERT, Edward, first Baron Herbert of Cherbury (1583–1648), philosopher, historian, and diplomat; while at University College, Oxford, taught himself the Romance languages and became a good musician, rider, and fencer; went to court, 1600; sheriff of Montgomeryshire, 1605; during a continental tour became intimate of *Casaubon and the Constable Montmorency, and fought several duels, 1608–10; volunteer at recapture of Juliers, 1610; joined prince of Orange's army, 1614; visited the elector palatine and the chief towns of Italy; offered help to the Savoyards, but was imprisoned by the French at Lyons, 1615; stayed with prince of Orange, 1616; on his return became intimate of *Donne, *Carew, and Ben *Jonson; named by *Buckingham ambassador at Paris, 1619; tried to obtain French support for elector palatine, and suggested marriage between *Henrietta Maria and

Prince Charles; recalled for quarrelling with the French king's favourite De Luynes, 1621, but reappointed on De Luynes's death, 1622; recalled, 1624, owing to his disagreement with James I about the French marriage negotiations; received in Irish peerage the barony of Cherbury, 1629, and seat in Council of War, 1632; attended Charles I on Scottish expedition, 1639–40; committed to the Tower for Royalist speech in House of Lords, 1642, but released on apologizing; aimed at neutrality during Civil War; compelled to admit Parliamentary force into Montgomery Castle, 1644; submitted to parliament and received a pension, 1645; steward of duchy of Cornwall and warden of the Stannaries, 1646; visited Gassendi, 1647; died in London, *Selden being one of his executors. His autobiography (to 1624), printed by Horace *Walpole (1764, thrice reissued) and edited by Sidney Lee (1886), scarcely mentions his serious pursuits. His *De Veritate* (Paris, 1624, London, 1633), the chief of his philosophical works, is the first purely metaphysical work by an Englishman. It was unfavourably criticized by *Baxter, *Locke, and others, but commended by Gassendi and Descartes. Though named the father of English deism, Herbert's real affinity was with the Cambridge Platonists. His poems were edited by Churton Collins (1881); his *Life of Henry VIII* (apologetic) first published (1649).

HERBERT, Sir Edward (1591?–1657), judge; cousin of Edward *Herbert, first Baron Herbert of Cherbury; barrister, Inner Temple, 1618, treasurer, 1638; MP, Montgomery, 1620, Downton, 1625–9, Old Sarum, 1641; a manager of *Buckingham's impeachment, 1626; one of *Selden's counsel, 1629; attorney-general to Charles I's queen, 1635; assisted in prosecution of *Prynne, *Burton, and *Bastwick, 1637; solicitor-general, 1640; attorney-general, 1641; knighted, 1641; impeached, imprisoned, and incapacitated, 1642, for his share in abortive impeachment of six members; joined Royalists; declined lord-keepership, 1645; sequestrated as 'delinquent', 1646; went to sea with Prince *Rupert, 1648; attorney-general to Charles II while abroad; lord keeper, 1653; died at Paris.

HERBERT, Edward, third Baron Herbert of Cherbury (d. 1678), grandson of Edward *Herbert, first Baron Herbert of Cherbury.

HERBERT, Sir Edward, titular earl of Portland (1648?–1698), judge; younger son of Sir Edward *Herbert (1591?–1657); educated at Winchester and New College, Oxford; BA, 1669; barrister, Middle Temple; KC in Ireland, 1677; chief justice of Chester, 1683; knighted, 1684; attorney-general to the queen of James II; MP for Ludlow, 1685; privy councillor, 1685; chief justice of King's Bench, 1685; gave judgment for dispensing power in case of *Godden* v. *Hales*, 1686; transferred to common pleas, 1687; as member of Ecclesiastical Commission opposed James II in Magdalen College case, 1687; followed James into exile, and was created lord chancellor, but offended James by his Protestantism; died at St Germain.

HERBERT, Edward, second earl of Powis (1785–1848), Tory politician; grandson of Robert *Clive, first Baron Clive of Plassey; assumed his mother's surname, 1807; educated at Eton and St John's College, Cambridge; MA, 1806; MP, Ludlow, 1806–39; as lord-lieutenant, Montgomeryshire, active in suppressing Chartist riots, 1839; KG, 1844; succeeded to peerage, 1839; his defeat of scheme for creation of see of Manchester by union of Bangor and St Asaph celebrated by foundation of Powis exhibitions, 1847; president of Roxburghe Club, 1835; candidate for chancellorship of Cambridge, 1847; accidentally killed.

HERBERT, Edwin Savory, Baron Tangley (1899–1973), solicitor, company director, and public servant; educated at Queen's College, Taunton; articled as solicitor's clerk, 1916; joined RNVR and served at sea, 1917–19; as London University law scholar studied at Law Society's School of Law; first class, LL B, 1919; qualified as solicitor, 1920; practised in Egham, 1921–4; joined City firm, Sydney Morse; eventually rose to be senior partner; member, Law Society Council, 1935, president, 1956; chairman, Regional Price Regulation Committee; director-general, Postal and Telegraph Censorship Department, 1940; in anticipation of American entry to war trained shadow organization to be ready when the time came; knighted for war services, 1943; US Medal for Merit and Norwegian Liberty Cross; after war acquired wide range of commercial interests; chairman, Ultramar oil company, 1946 and associated as director or chairman of number of other companies, including Rediffusion; served on number of interdepartmental committees; chairman of enquiry into electricity supply industry, 1954; KBE, 1956; chairman, Royal Commission on Local Government in Greater London, 1957–60; life peer, 1963; helped found Solicitors' European Group of Law Society, 1967; first president of Group; member, Royal Commission on Reform of Trade Unions and Employers' Associations, 1965–8; president, court of arbitration of International Chamber of Commerce, 1970; president, Alpine Club, 1953–5; chairman, Everest Committee, and chairman, finance committee, Commonwealth Trans-Antarctic Expedition; honorary degrees from Montreal,

1956 and Leeds, 1960; hon. fellow, Darwin College, Cambridge, and hon. LL D, 1969.

HERBERT, George (1593–1633), divine and poet; brother of Edward *Herbert, first Baron Herbert of Cherbury; of Westminster and Trinity College, Cambridge; major fellow, 1616; MA, 1616; public orator, 1619–27; induced to adopt religious life by Nicholas *Ferrar; prebendary of Lincoln, 1626; while deacon accepted benefice of Bemerton, Wiltshire, by *Laud's advice, 1630; ordained priest, 1630; *The Temple; Sacred Poems and Private Ejaculations* (prepared for press by Ferrar, 1633), read by Charles I in prison, and highly commended by *Crashaw, Henry *Vaughan, *Baxter, and *Coleridge; his chief prose work, *A Priest to the Temple*, first printed in his *Remains* (1652); complete works edited by Dr *Grosart (1874). His literary style was influenced by that of *Donne.

HERBERT, George Augustus, eleventh earl of Pembroke and eighth earl of Montgomery (1759–1827), general (son of Henry *Herbert, tenth earl of Pembroke); entered army, 1775; lieutenant-colonel, 2nd Dragoon Guards, 1783; vice-chamberlain, 1785; MP, Wilton, 1784–94; served in Flanders, 1793–4; major-general, 1795; KG, 1805; governor of Guernsey, 1807; ambassador-extraordinary to Vienna, 1807; general, 1812; said to have trebled value of his estates.

HERBERT, George Edward Stanhope Molyneux, fifth earl of Carnarvon (1866–1923), Egyptologist; son of Henry *Herbert, fourth earl; educated at Eton and Trinity College, Cambridge; succeeded father, 1890; wintered in Egypt from 1903; began sixteen years' collaboration in excavation with Howard *Carter, 1907; after European war obtained concession to excavate in valley of the Tombs of the Kings near Thebes; tomb of King Tutankhamun, of Dynasty XVIII, discovered, Nov. 1922; actual burial chamber and store-chamber unsealed, Feb. 1923; a wealth of treasures revealed; died at Cairo.

HERBERT, George Robert Charles, thirteenth earl of Pembroke and ninth earl of Montgomery (1850–1895), son of Sidney *Herbert, first Baron Herbert of Lea, whom he succeeded, 1861; succeeded his uncle in the earldoms, 1862; educated at Eton; travelled abroad with Dr George Henry *Kingsley, with whom he published *South Sea Bubbles* (1872); under-secretary for war, 1874–5. His *Letters and Speeches* were published (1896).

HERBERT, Henry, second earl of Pembroke (1534?–1601), elder son of Sir William *Herbert, first earl; educated at Peterhouse, Cambridge; styled Lord Herbert, 1551–70; KB, 1553; married Catherine Grey (*Seymour), sister of Lady Jane Grey (*Dudley), 1553; gentleman of the chamber to King Philip of Spain, 1554; succeeded as earl, 1570; prominent at trials of *Norfolk (1572), *Arundel (1589), and *Mary Queen of Scots (1586); president of Wales and admiral of South Wales, 1586.

HERBERT, Sir **Henry** (1595–1673), master of the revels; brother of George *Herbert (1593–1633); knighted, 1623; introduced *Baxter at court; as master of the revels claimed jurisdiction over all public entertainments, even licensing some books; his judgment in licensing *Middleton's *Game of Chesse* (1624) questioned; gentleman of privy chamber, attending Charles I in Scottish expedition, 1639; obliged to compound for his estates during rebellion; resumed his licensing functions at Restoration; his privileges confirmed, 1661, but his functions disputed by *D'Avenant and others; claimed to license plays, poems, and ballads, 1663; leased his office to deputies, 1663; MP, Bewdley, from 1661; friend of *Evelyn.

HERBERT, Henry, fourth Baron Herbert of Cherbury (d. 1691), cofferer of the household to William III and Mary; succeeded his brother Edward *Herbert, third Baron Herbert of Cherbury, 1678; served under *Monmouth in France, and supported him in England, afterwards promoting the revolution.

HERBERT, Henry, created Baron Herbert of Cherbury (1654–1709), son of Sir Henry *Herbert; of Trinity College, Oxford; MP, Bewdley, 1673–94; promoted revolution in Worcestershire; created Baron Herbert, 1694, and Castleisland (Ireland), 1695; commissioner of trade, 1707; chairman of committees in House of Lords; a zealous Whig.

HERBERT, Henry, second Baron Herbert of Cherbury of the second creation (d. 1738), son of Henry *Herbert, Baron Herbert of Cherbury (1654–1709); educated at Westminster; MP, Bewdley, 1708; committed suicide.

HERBERT, Henry, ninth earl of Pembroke and sixth earl of Montgomery (1693–1751), 'the architect earl'; groom of the stole, 1735; thrice a lord justice; FRS, 1743; lieutenant-general, 1742; promoted erection of first Westminster Bridge (1739–50); designed improvements at Wilton House and elsewhere.

HERBERT, Henry, tenth earl of Pembroke and seventh earl of Montgomery (1734–1794), general; commanded cavalry brigade in Germany, 1760–1; published *Method of Breaking Horses* (1762); lord of the bedchamber, 1769; deprived of lieutenancy of Wiltshire for voting against the court, 1780; restored, 1782; governor of Portsmouth, 1782; general, 1782.

HERBERT, Henry Howard Molyneux, fourth earl of Carnarvon (1831–1890), statesman; eldest son of Henry John George *Herbert, third earl; of Eton and Christ Church, Oxford; BA, 1852; succeeded to earldom, 1849; with Lord Sandon visited the Druses, 1853; moved address in House of Lords, 1854; under-secretary for colonies in Lord Derby's second administration, 1858–9; high steward of Oxford University, 1859; as colonial secretary in Lord Derby's and Disraeli's administration (1866–7) brought in British North America Confederation Bill, 1867; resigned on the reform question before the Confederation Bill became law (Mar. 1867); while in opposition, supported Irish disestablishment and the Land Bill of 1870; again colonial secretary in Disraeli's second administration, 1874–8; abolished slavery on the Gold Coast, 1874; sent Sir Garnet Wolseley as governor of Natal to report on the native and defence questions, 1875; attempted the confederation of South Africa; arranged for purchase of Boer claims in Griqualand West by Cape Colony, 1876; sent out Sir Theophilus *Shepstone and Sir Bartle *Frere to settle colonial and native differences, 1876; introduced a permissive Confederation Bill, 1877; sanctioned and upheld annexation of Transvaal, 1877; resigned (Jan. 1878), being opposed to breach of neutrality in Russo-Turkish affairs; chairman of Colonial Defence Commission, 1879–82; opposed Franchise Bill of 1884 till concurrent redistribution of seats conceded; joined Imperial Federation League, 1884; as lord-lieutenant of Ireland under Lord Salisbury (1885–6) attempted government by ordinary law, held conference with *Parnell, and personally favoured limited self-government; afterwards opposed Gladstone's Home Rule and Land Purchase bills; suggested (1887) appointment of special commission for investigating charges of *The Times* against Parnell; visited South Africa and Australia, 1887–8; interested in questions of colonial defence; president of Society of Antiquaries, 1878–85; published verse translations of the *Agamemnon* (1879) and the *Odyssey* (1886); edited (1869) his father's travels in Greece, *Mansel's Gnostic Heresies* (1875), and unpublished letters of Lord Chesterfield (1889).

HERBERT, Henry John George, third earl of Carnarvon (1800–1849), traveller; educated at Eton and Christ Church, Oxford; styled Viscount Porchester till his succession to earldom, 1833; travelled in Barbary, Spain, Portugal, and (later) in Greece; his tragedy, *Don Pedro*, acted by *Macready and Ellen *Tree at Drury Lane,

1828; published *Last Days of the Portuguese Constitution* (1830) and *Portugal and Galicia* (1830); Tory MP, Wootton Basset, 1831–2; his *Reminiscences of Athens and the Morea in 1839* issued (1869).

HERBERT, Henry William (1807–1858), author; son of William *Herbert (1778–1847); educated at Eton and Caius College, Cambridge; BA, 1830; became a classical tutor at New York, and established *American Monthly Magazine*, 1833; shot himself at New York; published as 'Frank Forester' *Field Sports of the United States and British Provinces* (1848) and similar works; published, under his own name, *The Roman Traitor* (1846) and other historical novels, translations from Dumas and Eugène Sue, and popular historical works.

HERBERT, John Rogers (1810–1890), portrait and historical painter; won his first success with Italian subject-pictures, 1834–40; became a Romanist, and thenceforth chiefly devoted himself to religious studies; a master of design at Somerset House, 1841; RA, 1846 (retired, 1886), his diploma work being *St. Gregory the Great teaching Roman Boys to sing*; painted for houses of parliament *King Lear disinheriting Cordelia*, in fresco, and *Human Justice* series.

HERBERT, Lady Lucy (1669–1744), devotional writer; daughter of William *Herbert, first marquis of Powis; prioress of English Convent, Bruges, 1709–44; her *Devotions* edited by Revd John *Morris, SJ (1873).

HERBERT, Mary, countess of Pembroke (1561–1621), sister of Sir Philip *Sidney; married Henry *Herbert, second earl of Pembroke, 1577; the Urania of *Spenser's *Colin Clout*; suggested composition of her brother Philip's *Arcadia* (first printed, 1590), which she revised and added to; collaborated with Philip in metrical psalms, first printed complete (1823); her elegy on him appended to Spenser's *Astrophel*; translated from Plessis du Mornay *A Discourse of Life and Death* (1593); patroness of Samuel *Daniel, Nicholas *Breton, Ben *Jonson, and other poets; fine epitaph on her by Ben *Jonson or William *Browne, first printed (1660).

HERBERT, Sir Percy Egerton (1822–1876), lieutenant-general; second son of Edward *Herbert, second Earl Powis; at Eton and Sandhurst; promoted brevet-lieutenant-colonel for services in the Kaffir War, 1851–3; assistant quartermaster-general of Sir George de Lacy *Evans's division in Crimea; wounded at the Alma, 1854; CB and aide-de-camp to the queen, 1855; commanded left wing in Rohilcund campaign, 1858; deputy quartermaster-general at Horse Guards, 1860–5; privy councillor, and treasurer of the household, 1867–8; major-general, 1868; KCB, 1869; MP, Ludlow, 1854–60, South Shropshire, 1865–76; lieutenant-general, 1875.

HERBERT, Philip, earl of Montgomery and fourth earl of Pembroke (1584–1650), Parliamentarian; younger son of Henry *Herbert, second earl of Pembroke; matriculated at New College, Oxford, 1593; favourite of James I, and gentleman of the bedchamber, 1605–25; created earl of Montgomery, 1605; KG, 1608; high steward of Oxford, 1615; privy councillor, 1624; lord-lieutenant of Kent, 1624; lord chamberlain, 1626–41; received grant of Trinidad, Tobago, and Barbados, 1628; succeeded his brother William *Herbert (1580–1630) as earl of Pembroke, and lord warden of the Stannaries, 1630; commissioner to negotiate with Scots, 1640; voted against *Strafford, 1641; member of Committee of Safety and Parliamentary governor of the Isle of Wight, 1642; Parliamentary commissioner at Oxford, 1643, and Uxbridge, 1645; received Charles I from the Scots, 1647; commissioner of the Admiralty, 1645; as vice-chancellor of Oxford (1641–50) superintended visitation of the colleges and ejection of Royalists; member of first Council of State and MP, Berkshire, 1649; a patron of *Massinger and *Van Dyck; addicted to sport; rebuilt front of Wilton House, and laid out gardens.

HERBERT, Philip, fifth earl of Pembroke (1619–1669), eldest surviving son of Philip *Herbert, fourth earl of Pembroke; MP, Glamorgan, in Long Parliament; succeeded to his father's seat for Berkshire, 1650; president of Council of State (June, July), 1652; councillor for trade and navigation, 1660; sold Wilton collections.

HERBERT, Philip, seventh earl of Pembroke (1653–1683), son of Philip *Herbert, fifth earl; convicted of manslaughter, 1678.

HERBERT, Richard, second Baron Herbert of Cherbury (1600?–1655), Royalist; son of Edward *Herbert, first Baron Herbert of Cherbury; conducted *Henrietta Maria from Bridlington to Oxford, 1643.

HERBERT, Sir Robert George Wyndham (1831–1905), colonial official; scholar of Eton and Balliol College, Oxford; fellow of All Souls from 1854 till death; DCL, 1862; private secretary to Gladstone, 1855; called to bar, 1858; went to Queensland as colonial secretary, 1859; member of Legislative Council and first premier, 1860–5; permanent under-secretary for the colonies in London, 1871–92; agent-general for Tasmania, 1893–6; KCB, 1882; GCB, 1902; hon. LL D, Cambridge, 1886.

HERBERT, Sidney, first Baron Herbert of Lea (1810–1861), statesman; second son of George Augustus *Herbert, eleventh earl of Pembroke; educated at Harrow and Oriel College, Oxford; BA, 1831; Conservative MP, South Wiltshire, 1832–60; secretary to Board of Control, 1834–5; secretary to Admiralty, 1841–5; war secretary under Peel, 1845–6, Aberdeen, 1852–5 (during the Crimean War), and Palmerston, 1859–60; primarily responsible for Florence *Nightingale going to the Crimea; freed by Roebuck Committee from suspicion of favouring Russia; led movement in favour of medical reform in the army and education of officers; encouraged Volunteer Movement; created peer, 1860; injured his health by administrative labour.

HERBERT, St Leger Algernon (1850–1885), war correspondent; scholar of Wadham College, Oxford, 1869; in Canadian Civil Service, 1875–8; private secretary to Sir Garnet Wolseley in Cyprus and South Africa; *The Times* correspondent, 1878–9; CMG; secretary to Transvaal Commission, 1881–2; correspondent of *Morning Post* in Egypt, 1883–4; wounded at Tamai; killed at Gubat during Sudan War while on the staff of Sir Herbert *Stewart.

HERBERT, Thomas (1597–1642?), seaman and author; brother of Edward *Herbert, first Baron Herbert of Cherbury; distinguished himself at Juliers, 1610; commanded East Indiaman against Portuguese, 1616; visited the great mogul at Mandow, 1617; served against Algerines, 1620–1; brought Prince Charles from Spain to England, 1623, and Count Mansfeldt to the Netherlands, 1625; published elegy on *Strafford (1641) and pasquinades, including *Newes out of Islington* (1641, reprinted by *Halliwell, 1849).

HERBERT, Sir Thomas, first baronet (1606–1682), traveller and author; studied at Oxford and Trinity College, Cambridge; went to Persia, 1628, with Sir Dodmore Cotton and Sir Robert *Shirley; travelled in Europe; commissioner with *Fairfax's army, 1644, and for surrender of Oxford, 1646; attended Charles I, 1647–9, and received presents from him, including the Shakespeare second folio now at Windsor; created baronet, 1660; published *Description of the Persian Monarchy* (1634), reprinted as *Some Yeares Travels into divers parts of Asia and Afrique* (1638, etc.); collaborated with *Dugdale; his reminiscences (1678) of Charles I's captivity reprinted as *Memoirs of the last two years of the Reign* etc. (1702 and 1813).

HERBERT, Thomas, eighth earl of Pembroke (1656–1733), lord high admiral; third son of Philip *Herbert, fifth earl; entered at Christ Church, Oxford, 1672; succeeded elder brothers in title, 1683; lieutenant of Wiltshire; dismissed, 1687; first lord of the Admiralty, 1690; one of Queen Mary's council, 1690; lord privy seal, 1692; opposed *Fenwick's execution, 1697, and Resumption Bill of 1700; first plenipotentiary at Treaty of Ryswick, 1697; KG, 1700; president of the council, 1702; lord high admiral, 1702 and 1708; a commissioner for the Union, 1706–7; lord-lieutenant of Ireland, 1707; a lord justice, 1714–15; lord-lieutenant of Wiltshire, Monmouth, and South Wales; PRS, 1689–90.

HERBERT, Sir **Thomas** (1793–1861), rear-admiral; promoted lieutenant for services at reduction of Danish West Indies, 1809; commander, 1814; as senior officer on Canton River commanded operations against Chuenpee and Bogue forts, and took part in capture of Amoy and Chusan and reduction of Chinghae, 1840; KCB, 1841; junior lord of the Admiralty, 1852; rear-admiral, 1852; MP, Dartmouth, 1852–7.

HERBERT, William (d. 1333?), Franciscan; preacher and philosopher at Oxford.

HERBERT, Sir **William,** earl of Pembroke of the first creation (d. 1469), Yorkist; knighted by Henry VI, 1449; taken prisoner at Formigny, 1450; during Wars of the Roses did good service against Jasper *Tudor; made privy councillor and chief justice of South Wales by Edward IV, 1461; created Baron Herbert, 1461; KG, 1462; chief justice of North Wales, 1467; after capture of Harlech Castle (1468) and attainder of Jasper Tudor (1468) was created earl of Pembroke and guardian to Henry (afterwards Henry VII), 1468; defeated and captured by Lancastrians at Hedgecote and executed.

HERBERT, William, second earl of Pembroke, afterwards earl of Huntingdon (1460–1491), son of Sir William *Herbert, earl of Pembroke of the first creation (d. 1469); English captain in France, 1475; exchanged earldom of Pembroke for that of Huntingdon, 1479; chief justice of South Wales, 1483.

HERBERT, Sir **William,** first earl of Pembroke of the second creation (1501?–1570), grandson of William *Herbert, earl of Pembroke of the first creation (d. 1469); esquire of the body to Henry VIII, 1526; married a sister of Catherine *Parr; granted the dissolved abbey of Wilton, where he built part of the present mansion; granted property in Wales, 1546; gentleman of the privy chamber, 1546; one of Henry VIII's executors; member of Edward VI's council; KG and master of the horse, 1548; helped to quell Cornish rising, 1549; supported *Warwick against *Somerset, and was made president of Wales, 1550; took part in Somerset's trial, 1551, and obtained Somerset's Wiltshire estates;

created earl of Pembroke, 1551; joined *Northumberland in proclaiming Lady Jane Grey (*Dudley), but (19 July 1553) declared for Mary; commanded against Sir Thomas *Wyatt, 1554; intimate of King *Philip; an envoy to France, 1555; governor of Calais, 1556; captain-general of English contingent at St Quentin, 1557; under Queen Elizabeth supported *Cecil and the Protestant party; lord steward, 1568; cleared himself when arrested for supporting scheme for duke of *Norfolk's marriage with *Mary Queen of Scots, 1569; buried in St Paul's.

HERBERT (or HARBERT), Sir **William** (d. 1593), Irish 'undertaker' and author; of St Julians, Monmouthshire; sole legitimate heir-male of William *Herbert, first earl of Pembroke (d. 1469); knighted, 1578; friend of John *Dee; an 'undertaker' for plantation of Munster, being subsequently allotted Desmond property in Kerry, 1587; vice-president of Munster in absence of Sir Thomas *Norris, c.1589; his *Croftus; siue de Hibernia Liber* (named in compliment to Sir James *Croft (d. 1591)) edited by W. E. Buckley (1887); his Irish tracts and letters to *Walsingham and *Burghley in *Calendars of Irish State Papers*.

HERBERT (or HARBERT), William (fl. 1604), poet; of Christ Church, Oxford; author of *A Prophesie of Cadwallader* (1604).

HERBERT, William, third earl of Pembroke of the second creation (1580–1630), eldest son of Henry *Herbert, second earl of the second creation; educated by Samuel *Daniel, of New College, Oxford; succeeded as earl, 1601; disgraced for an intrigue with Mary *Fitton; patron of Ben *Jonson, Philip *Massinger, Inigo *Jones, and William *Browne (1591–1643?); thrice entertained James I at Wilton; lord-warden of the Stannaries, 1604; member of the Council of New England, 1620; interested in the Virginia, Northwest Passage, Bermuda, and East India companies; lord chamberlain, 1615; opposed foreign policy of James I and *Buckingham; commissioner of the great seal, 1621; member of the Committee for Foreign Affairs and Council of War under Charles I, 1626; lord steward, 1626; chancellor of Oxford University from 1617, Pembroke College being named after him; presented Barocci library to Bodleian; wrote poems which were issued with those of Sir Benjamin *Rudyerd (1660). To him as lord chamberlain and to his brother Philip the first folio of Shakespeare's works was dedicated in 1623, but there is no good ground for identifying him with the subject of Shakespeare's sonnets, or with the 'Mr W. H.' noticed in the publisher *Thorpe's dedication of that volume (1609).

HERBERT, William (*fl.* 1634–1662), author of pious manuals and French conversation books.

HERBERT, William, first marquis and titular duke of Powis (1617–1696); succeeded as third Baron Powis, 1667; created earl of Powis, 1674; as chief of the Roman Catholic aristocracy imprisoned in connection with the 'Popish Plot', 1679–84; privy councillor, 1686; created marquis of Powis, 1687; commissioner to 'regulate' corporations, 1687; lord-lieutenant of Cheshire, 1688, and vice-lieutenant of Sussex, 1688; created by James II, in exile, a duke and chamberlain of his household; his estates in England confiscated; died at St Germain.

HERBERT, William, second marquis and titular duke of Powis (d. 1745), son of William *Herbert, first marquis of Powis; styled Viscount Montgomery till 1722, when his title as marquis and his estates were restored; imprisoned, 1689 and 1696–7, on suspicion of complicity in Sir J. *Fenwick's plot; again arrested, 1715.

HERBERT, William (1718–1795), bibliographer; went to India, *c.*1748, and drew plans of settlements for the East India Company; published *A new Directory for the East Indies* (1758); issued second edition of *Atkyns's *Ancient and Present State of Gloucestershire* (rare, 1768), and an enlarged edition of *Ames's *Typographical Antiquities* (1785–90).

HERBERT, William (1771–1851), antiquarian writer; librarian of the Guildhall, 1828–45; published *History of the Twelve great Livery Companies* (1836–7), *Antiquities of the Inns of Court* (1804), and similar works.

HERBERT, William (1778–1847), dean of Manchester; edited *Musae Etonenses* (1795); BA, Exeter College, Oxford, 1798; MA, Merton College, 1802, and DCL, 1808; MP, Hampshire, 1806, Cricklade, 1811; dean of Manchester, 1840–7; published *Select Icelandic Poetry* (1804–6) and translations, also *Attila, or the Triumph of Christianity,* an epic (1838), and other poems, English, Greek, and Latin; assisted in editions of *White's *Selborne* (1833 and 1837); published monographs on *Amaryllidaceae* (1837) and crocuses (edited by J. *Lindley, 1847); ferns named after him by *Sweet; collected works issued (1842).

HERBERT DE LOSINGA (1054?–1119). See LOSINGA.

HERBERT OF BOSHAM (*fl.* 1162–1186), biographer of *Becket; attended the archbishop as special monitor and master in study of holy writ at councils of Tours (1163), Clarendon (1164), and Northampton (1164), escaping with him from the last; brought him money and plate, and secured his reception abroad; shared his exile, encouraging him to hold his ground at Montmirail, 1169; returned with him to England, 1170, but was sent on a message to the French king and remained abroad till 1184; treated well by Henry II; his *Life of St. Thomas of Canterbury,* with letters and other works, printed in Dr *Giles's *Sanctus Thomas Cantuariensis* (1846), and edited by Canon J. C. *Robertson in *Materials for History of Archbishop Becket.*

HERBISON, David (1800–1880), Irish poet; known as 'The Bard of Dunclug'; chief work, *The Fate of McQuillan, and O'Neill's Daughter and . . . other Poems* (1841).

HERD, David (1732–1810), collector of *Ancient and Modern Scottish Songs, Heroic Ballads,* etc. (1776, reprinted 1869); president of the Cape Club, Edinburgh; literary adviser of Archibald *Constable.

HERD, John (1512?–1588), author of *Historia Anglicana* in Latin verse; of Eton and King's College, Cambridge; fellow, 1532; MA, 1546; MD, 1558; prebendary of Lincoln, 1557, and York, 1559.

HERDMAN, John (1762?–1842), medical writer; MD, Aberdeen, 1800; MA, Trinity College, Cambridge, 1817; physician to duke of *Sussex and city dispensary; ordained; published *Essay on the Causes and Phenomena of Animal Life* (1795) and other works.

HERDMAN, Robert (1829–1888), Scottish painter; studied at St Andrews, Edinburgh, and in Italy; exhibited at Royal Scottish Academy from 1850, and at Royal Academy from 1861; RSA, 1863; painted portraits of *Carlyle, Sir Noel Paton, principals *Shairp and *Tulloch, and others, and of many ladies. His other works comprise studies of female figures and figure-subjects from Scottish history.

HERDMAN, Sir William Abbott (1858–1924), marine naturalist; MA, Edinburgh University; assistant to Sir C. W. *Thomson in working on *Challenger* collections; first Derby professor of natural history, Liverpool University, 1881–1919; devoted attention to co-ordination of fishing industry with scientific research; his encouragement of plankton survey in Irish Sea especially noteworthy; FRS, 1892; CBE, 1920; knighted, 1922.

HERDMAN, William Gawin (1805–1882), artist and author; expelled from Liverpool Academy, 1857, for opposition to Pre-Raphaelite artists; exhibited at Royal Academy and Suffolk Street, 1834–61; published *Pictorial Relics of Ancient Liverpool* (1843, 1856), technical treatises on art, *Treatise on Skating,* and other works.

HERDSON, Henry (*fl.* 1651), author of *Ars Mnemonica* (1651) and *Ars Memoriae* (1651); BA, St John's College, Cambridge, 1629–30; 'professor of the art of memory' at Cambridge.

HEREBERT (or HERBERT), Saint (d. 687), hermit of Derwentwater and friend of St *Cuthbert.

HEREFERTH (d. 915). See WERFERTH.

HEREFORD, duke of (1367–1413). See HENRY IV.

HEREFORD, earls of. See RALPH THE TIMID, d. 1057; FITZOSBERN, WILLIAM, d. 1071; FITZWILLIAM, ROGER, alias ROGER DE BRETEUIL, *fl.* 1071–1075; GLOUCESTER, MILES DE, d. 1143; BOHUN, HENRY DE, first earl (of the Bohun line), 1176–1220; BOHUN, HUMPHREY V, DE, second earl, d. 1274; BOHUN, HUMPHREY VII, DE, third earl, d. 1298; BOHUN, HUMPHREY VIII, DE, fourth earl, 1276–1322.

HEREFORD, Viscounts. See DEVEREUX, WALTER, first viscount, d. 1558; DEVEREUX, WALTER, second viscount, 1541?–1576.

HEREFORD, Nicholas of (*fl.* 1390). See NICHOLAS.

HEREFORD, Roger of (*fl.* 1178). See ROGER.

HEREWALD (d. 1104), bishop of Llandaff; elected (1056) by *Gruffydd ab Llywelyn, Meurig ab Hywel, and Welsh magnates; confirmed by Archbishop *Kynsige of York, 1059; suspended by *Anselm.

HEREWARD (*fl.* 1070–1071), outlaw; first called 'the Wake' by *John of Peterborough; mentioned in Domesday as owner of lands in Lincolnshire; perhaps identical with owner of Marston Jabbett, Warwickshire, and Evenlode, Worcestershire; legendary account of his wanderings given by *Ingulf of Crowland and in *Gesta Herewardi*; headed rising of English at Ely, 1070; with assistance of Danish fleet plundered Peterborough, 1070; joined by *Morcar, Bishop Æthelwine of Durham, and other refugees; escaped when his allies surrendered to William the Conqueror; said to have been pardoned by William; slain by Normans in Maine, according to account of Geoffrey *Gaimar.

HERFAST (or ARFAST) (d. 1084?), first chancellor of England; chaplain to William I before the Conquest; chancellor of England, 1068–70; bishop of Elmham, 1070; bishop of Thetford, 1078; tried to defeat monastic claims to exemption from episcopal jurisdiction.

HERFORD, Brooke (1830–1903), Unitarian divine; brother of William Henry *Herford; Unitarian minister from 1851; founded and edited *Unitarian Herald*, 1861; minister at Strangeways, Manchester (1864–76), in Chicago (1876–82), and Boston (1882–92); preacher to Harvard University and DD, 1891; minister of Rosslyn Hill Chapel, Hampstead, 1892–1901; president of British and Foreign Unitarian Association, 1898–9; published *Brief Account of Unitarianism* (1903), sermons, tracts, and hymns.

HERFORD, Charles Harold (1853–1931), scholar and critic; nephew of B. and W. H. *Herford; eighth classic, Trinity College, Cambridge, 1879; professor of English, University College, Aberystwyth (1887–1901); Manchester (1901–21); the most accomplished English literary scholar of his age; publications embrace also the literature of Germany, Italy, Norway, and Russia; concentrated on ideas and characters of authors; FBA, 1926.

HERFORD, William Henry (1820–1908), writer on education; studied for Unitarian ministry at York and Manchester; spent three years in Bonn and Berlin; imbibed Pestalozzi's and Froebel's educational ideas on visit to Pestalozzian school at Hofwyl, near Berne, 1847; managed Pestalozzian school at Lancaster, 1850–61; inspiring preacher, teacher, and lecturer in Manchester from 1863; directed coeducational school for younger children at Fallowfield, Manchester, 1873–86; published *The School: an Essay towards Humane Education* (1889), *The Student's Froebel* (1893), and translated works on education.

HERICKE. See also HERRICK and HEYRICK.

HERICKE (or HERRICK), Sir **William** (1562–1653), goldsmith and money-lender; uncle of Robert *Herrick; went on mission from Elizabeth to the Grand Turk, 1580–1; MP, Leicester, 1601; principal jeweller to James I; knighted, 1605; exempted from liability to serve as sheriff, 1605; refused to pay ship money.

HERING, George Edwards (1805–1879), landscape painter; of German parentage; published *Sketches on the Danube, in Hungary, and Transylvania* (1838); exhibited at Royal Academy from 1836; his *Amalfi* and *Capri* purchased by prince consort.

HERIOT, George (1563–1624), founder of Heriot's Hospital, Edinburgh (opened 1659); jeweller to James VI, 1601, to his queen, 1597, and to James VI on his accession as James I of England, 1603; was granted imposition on sugar for three years, 1620; the 'Jingling Geordie' of *Scott's *Fortunes of Nigel*.

HERIOT, John (1760–1833), author and journalist; present as a marine in *Rodney's action of 17 Apr. 1780; published two novels (1787 and 1789) and *Historical Sketch of Gibraltar*

(1792); edited the *Sun* and the *True Briton*, 1793–1806; deputy paymaster-general in West Indies, 1810–16; comptroller of Chelsea Hospital, 1816–33.

HERKOMER, Sir Hubert Von (1849–1914), painter; born in Bavaria; brought to England, 1857; naturalized; studied at South Kensington Art Schools; achieved great success with picture, *The Last Muster—Sunday at the Royal Hospital, Chelsea*, 1875; ARA, 1879; portraits include those of Wagner, *Ruskin, Lord *Kelvin, and marquess of Salisbury; subject-pictures include *Found* (1885) and *On Strike* (1890); RA, 1890; founded and directed school of art at Bushey, 1883–1904; Slade professor of fine art at Oxford, 1885–94; knighted, 1907; wrote on etching, etc.

HERKS, Garbrand (*fl.* 1556). See GARBRAND, HERKS.

HERKS (alias **GARBRAND**), **John** (1542–1589). See GARBRAND.

HERLE, Charles (1598–1659), Puritan divine; MA, Exeter College, Oxford, 1618; presented by Stanley family to rectory of Winwick, Lancashire, 1626; represented Lancashire in Westminster Assembly of Divines, 1643, and was appointed prolocutor, 1646; refused to pray for Commonwealth; his chief work, *The Independency on Scriptures of the Independency of Churches* (1643); friend of *Fuller.

HERLE, William de (d. 1347), judge; as serjeant-at-law summoned to assist parliaments of Edward II; judge of common pleas, 1320; chief justice of common pleas, 1327–9 and 1331–7.

HERLEWIN (d. 1137). See ETHELMÆR.

HERMAN, Henry (1832–1894), dramatist and novelist; fought in Confederate ranks in American Civil War; produced independently and in collaboration with Henry Arthur Jones and other authors plays at London theatres from 1875.

HERMAND, Lord (d. 1827). See FERGUSSON, GEORGE.

HERMANN (*fl.* 1070), hagiographer; archdeacon of Thetford under *Herfast; afterwards monk of Bury; wrote *De Miraculis S. Ædmundi*, printed in *Memorials of St. Edmund's Abbey* (ed. T. *Arnold, 1890).

HERMANN (d. 1078), first bishop of Old Sarum (Salisbury); native of Lorraine; bishop of Ramsbury or Wilton, 1045; went to Rome for *Edward the Confessor, 1050; monk of St Bertin's Abbey at St Omer, 1055–8; bishop of Sherborne with Ramsbury, 1058; removed his see to Old Sarum, 1075; assisted at *Lanfranc's consecration and several councils.

HERMES, Gertrude Anna Bertha (1901–1983), engraver and sculptor; educated at Belmont School for Girls, Bickley; studied at Beckenham School of Art and Leon Underwood School of Painting and Sculpture, Hammersmith, 1919–25; qualified as finalist in Prix de Rome (engraving), 1925; married in 1926 and employed with her husband, Blair Rowlands Hughes-Stanton, as engraver for Gregynog Press in Central Wales, 1931; divorced, 1932; moved to London; member of Society of Wood Engravers, 1933; exhibited at Royal Academy, 1933; elected to London Group, 1934; entered in register of Industrial Art Designers, 1938; chosen to represent Great Britain at Venice International Exhibition, 1939; produced variety of sculptures and decorative pieces, including mosaic pool floor and stone foundation for Shakespeare Memorial Theatre, Stratford, 1933; in New York and Montreal making working-drawings in tank factories and shipyards, 1940–5; in London from 1945 worked mainly in print-making and sculpture; linocuts passed to national museums through Giles Bequest; also produced bronze portrait heads; fellow, Royal Society of Painters, Etchers, and Engravers, 1951; awarded Jean Masson Davidson Prize for portrait sculpture, 1967; ARA, 1963; RA, 1971; taught at London art schools and Royal Academy Schools; to honour her eightieth birthday Royal Academy held retrospective exhibition, 1981; OBE, 1982; work to be found in most major collections in Europe and North America.

HERNE, John (*fl.* 1644), lawyer; barrister, Lincoln's Inn; bencher, 1637; defended, among others, *Prynne, 1634, and Archbishop *Laud, 1644.

HERNE, John (*fl.* 1660), son of John *Herne (*fl.* 1644); author, among other works, of *The Pleader* (collection of precedents, 1657); translated *The Learned Reading of John Herne, Esq.*, his father (1659).

HERNE, Thomas (d. 1722), controversialist; scholar of Corpus Christi College, Cambridge, 1712; BA, 1715; incorporated at Oxford, 1716; fellow of Merton College, 1716; tutor to third and fourth dukes of *Bedford; as 'Phileleutherus Cantabrigiensis', published *False Notion of a Christian Priesthood*, against William *Law (1717–18) and some tracts; issued account of the Bangorian controversy (1720).

HERON, Haly (*fl.* 1565–1585), author of *A new Discourse of Morall Philosophie entituled the Kayes of Counsaile* (1579); BA, Queens' College, Cambridge, 1570.

HERON, Sir Richard, baronet (1726–1805), chief secretary to lord-lieutenant of Ireland,

1776–80; created baronet, 1778; published genealogical table of Herons of Newark (1798).

HERON, Robert (1764–1807), author; son of a Kirkcudbrightshire weaver; edited *Thomson's Seasons* (1789 and 1793); wrote part of a *History of Scotland* (1794) while imprisoned for debt; ruling elder for New Galloway; edited the *Globe* and other London papers; published, among other works, translations from the French, a life of *Burns (1797), and an edition of Junius (1802).

HERON, Sir **Robert,** baronet (1765–1854), Whig politician; of St John's College, Cambridge; succeeded his uncle, Sir Richard *Heron, in the baronetcy, 1805; MP, Grimsby, 1812–18, Peterborough, 1819–47; published political and social *Notes* (1851).

HERRICK. See also HERICKE and HEYRICK.

HERRICK, Robert (1591–1674), poet; apprenticed to his uncle, Sir William *Hericke, for ten years; afterwards went to St John's College, Cambridge, but graduated from Trinity Hall, 1617; MA, 1620; incumbent of Dean Prior, Devonshire, 1629; ejected, 1647; lived in Westminster; restored, 1662; many of his poems published anonymously in *Witts Recreations* (1650); several of his pieces set to music by Henry *Lawes and other composers; his *Hesperides* with *Noble Numbers* first issued, 1648; complete editions edited by Thomas Maitland (1823), Edward *Walford (1859), W. Carew Hazlitt (1869), and Dr *Grosart (1876).

HERRIES, Barons. See MAXWELL, Sir JOHN, fourth baron, 1512?–1583; MAXWELL, WILLIAM, fifth baron, d. 1603.

HERRIES, Sir **Charles John** (1815–1883), financier; son of John Charles *Herries; of Eton and Trinity College, Cambridge; MA, 1840; commissioner of excise, 1842; deputy-chairman of Inland Revenue, 1856; chairman of the Board of Inland Revenue, 1877–81; KCB, 1880.

HERRIES, John Charles (1778–1855), statesman and financier; educated at Leipzig; drew up for Pitt his counter-resolutions against *Tierney's financial proposals, 1800; private secretary to *Vansittart, 1801, and Perceval, 1807; translated Gentz's treatise *On the State of Europe before and after the French Revolution* (1802); defended financial policy of government, 1803; secretary and registrar of the Order of the Bath, 1809–22; commissary-in-chief, 1811–16; auditor of civil list, 1816; drew up second report of Irish Revenue Commission, 1822; MP, Harwich, 1823–41; financial secretary to Treasury, 1823–7; privy councillor, 1827; chancellor of the Exchequer in Goderich's ministry from 8 Aug. 1827 to 8 Jan. 1828; wrote a statement of events which led to dissolution of Goderich ministry; master of the Mint, 1828–30; drew up fourth report of Sir Henry *Parnell's finance committee, 1828, first making public accounts intelligible; president of Board of Trade, 1830; moved resolution against Russian–Dutch loan, 1832; secretary-at-war under Peel, 1834–5; his motion for return of public accounts carried against Whig government, 1840; MP, Stamford, 1847–53; protectionist; president of Board of Control in Lord Derby's first government, 1852 (Feb.–Dec.).

HERRING, Francis (d. 1628), physician; MD, Christ's College, Cambridge; MA, 1589; FRCP, 1599, and seven times censor; published treatises on the plague and Latin poem on the Gunpowder Plot (*Pietas Pontificia*, 1609).

HERRING, George (1832–1906), philanthropist; at first a turf-commission agent and owner of racehorses; subsequently made fortune as financial commission agent in City of London; chairman of City of London Electric Lighting Company; devoted wealth to London Sunday Hospital Fund from 1899, to Salvation Army land scheme at Boxted, Essex, and to North-West London Hospital, Camden Town; bequests to charities under will totalled £900,000.

HERRING, John Frederick (1795–1865), animal painter; drove coaches between Wakefield and Lincoln, Doncaster and Halifax, and London and York; painted winners of the St Leger for thirty-two years, and many other sporting subjects; member of Society of British Artists, 1841; exhibited at Royal Academy and Society of British Artists.

HERRING, Julines (1582–1644), Puritan divine; BA, Sidney Sussex College, Cambridge, 1603–4; ordained by an Irish bishop; incumbent of Calke, Derbyshire, c.1610–c.1618; afterwards preached at Shrewsbury from 1618; suspended for nonconformity; co-pastor of English church at Amsterdam, 1637–44.

HERRING, Thomas (1693–1757), archbishop of Canterbury; BA, Jesus College, Cambridge, 1713; fellow of Corpus Christi, 1716; MA, 1717; DD, 1728; preacher at Lincoln's Inn, 1727–33, and chaplain to George I, 1727–32; rector of Bletchingley, 1731; dean of Rochester, 1732; bishop of Bangor, 1737–43; as archbishop of York (1743–7) raised a large sum for government during the rebellion; archbishop of Canterbury, 1747–57; repaired Lambeth and Croydon palaces, and left benefactions to the sons of the clergy and Corpus Christi College; his letters (1728–57) to William *Duncombe edited by John *Duncombe (1777).

HERRING, William (d. 1774), dean of St Asaph, 1751–74; brother of Thomas *Herring.

HERRINGHAM, Sir Wilmot Parker (1855–1936), physician; educated at Winchester, Keble College, Oxford, and St Bartholomew's Hospital; assistant physician, 1895; full physician, 1904–19; especially interested in kidney diseases; honorary general secretary to Association of Physicians on its foundation (1907) and to International Medical Congress (1913); knighted, 1914; vice-chancellor, London University, 1912–15; consulting physician in France, 1914–18; KCMG, 1919; chairman of General Nursing Council (1922–6), governors of Old Vic (1921–9), and council of Bedford College.

HERSCHEL, Alexander Stewart (1836–1907), astronomer; son of Sir John *Herschel; born in South Africa; BA, Trinity College, Cambridge (twentieth wrangler), 1859; studied meteorology at Royal School of Mines, London, 1861; professor of physics at Glasgow, 1866–71, and at Durham College, Newcastle, 1871–86; reported on observations of meteors to British Association, 1862–81; experimented in photography; FRAS, 1867; FRS, 1884; DCL, Durham, 1886; observed solar eclipse in Spain, 1905.

HERSCHEL, Caroline Lucretia (1750–1848), astronomer; sister of Sir William *Herschel; came to live with her brother at Bath, 1772, and became his assistant; discovered eight comets (five undisputed) between 1786 and 1797; received a salary from George III, 1787; her *Index to Flamsteed's Observations of the Fixed Stars*, with list of Flamsteed's errata, published by Royal Society (1798); on Sir William's death went to Hanover, 1822; gold medallist of Astronomical Society for her catalogue in zones of Sir W. Herschel's star-clusters and nebulae, 1828, and was created honorary member, 1835; awarded Prussian Gold Medal for science on ninety-sixth birthday; entertained crown prince and princess next year; minor planet Lucretia named after her by Palisa, 1889.

HERSCHEL, Sir John Frederick William, first baronet (1792–1871), astronomer; son of Sir William *Herschel; senior wrangler and first Smith's prizeman, 1813; subsequently fellow of St John's College, Cambridge; MA, 1816; helped to found Analytical Society, Cambridge, 1813; with George *Peacock (1791–1858) translated Lacroix's *Elementary Treatise on the Differential Calculus*, with appendix on finite differences (1816); FRS, 1813; Copley medallist, 1821; first foreign secretary of Royal Astronomical Society; Lalande prizeman, Royal Astronomical Society, 1825, and gold medallist for revision of his father's double stars; secretary to Royal Society, 1824–7; received medals for catalogue of northern nebulae, 1836; president of Astronomical Society, 1827–32; discovered and catalogued many double stars; described new graphical method of investigating stellar orbits, 1832; wrote article on 'Light' in *Encyclopaedia Metropolitana* (1827), which gave European currency to undulatory theory; his *Preliminary Discourse on Study of Natural Philosophy* (1830) translated into French, German, and Italian, his *Outlines of Astronomy* (1849, 12th edn. 1873), into Russian, Chinese, and Arabic; during residence (1834–8) at Feldhausen, near Cape Town, discovered 1,202 pairs of close double stars and 1,708 nebulae and clusters, 'monographed' the Orion nebula, prepared a chart of the Argo, made first satisfactory measure of direct solar radiation, and suggested (1836–7) relation between solar and auroral activity; initiated while at the Cape system of national education, and sent tidal observations to *Whewell; created baronet, 1838; assisted in Royal Commission on Standards (1838–43); DCL, Oxford, 1839; lord rector of Aberdeen 1842, and president of British Association, 1845; received many foreign orders; prepared charts of all the lucid stars; invented photographic use of sensitized paper, 1839; introduced use of hyposulphite of soda as a fixing agent; discovered 'epipolic dispersion' of light, 1845; the results of his Cape observations printed, 1847, at expense of duke of *Northumberland; received the Copley Medal, 1847, and a special testimonial from the Astronomical Society, 1848; master of the Mint, 1850–5; assisted at the Great Exhibition and in the Universities Commission of 1850; his last great undertaking, a general and descriptive catalogue of double stars; buried in Westminster Abbey near the grave of *Newton. His miscellaneous writings were collected in *Essays* (1857) and *Familiar Lectures on Scientific Subjects* (1867).

HERSCHEL, Sir William (1738–1822), astronomer; born at Hanover; as a boy played the oboe and violin in Hanoverian guards; secretly sent to England by his parents, 1757; patronized by Dr Edward *Miller; organist at Halifax, 1765, at Octagon Chapel, Bath, 1766; began to construct optical instruments, 1773, and to observe stars, 1774; discovered Uranus (Georgium Sidus), 1781; Copley medallist and FRS, 1781; exhibited his telescope to George III, and was appointed court astronomer, 1782; removed to Slough, 1786; his polishing machine perfected, 1788; visited by distinguished men of science; his great forty-foot mirror begun (aided by a royal grant), 1785, first used, 1789 (a sixth satellite of Saturn being discovered), finished (with further aid), 1811, and used till 1839; discovered 'Enceladus' and 'Mimas', 1789; received numerous degrees and decorations; first president of the Astronomical Society; had interviews with Bonaparte and Laplace, 1802; sent sixty-nine memoirs to Royal Society; discovered more than 2,000 nebulae, and suggested their true nature; discovered mutually revolving stars, over 800 double stars (measuring them with the revolving wire and lamp micrometers), and (1783) the translation of the solar system towards a point in Hercules; invented 'method of sequences'; published six memoirs relative to Saturn, 1790–1808; suggested 'trade wind' explanation of Jupiter's belts, 1781; investigated rotation of Mars; made physical observations on comets of 1807 and 1811; discovered infra-red solar rays, 1800; KH, 1816.

HERSCHELL, Farrer, first Baron Herschell (1837–1899), lord chancellor; son of Ridley Haim *Herschell; educated at University College, London; BA, London, 1857; barrister, Lincoln's Inn, 1860, bencher, 1872; took silk, 1872; Liberal MP, Durham, 1874–85; knighted and appointed solicitor-general, 1880; created lord chancellor, with title of Baron Herschell of city of Durham, 1886; again lord chancellor, 1892–5; hon. DCL, Durham and Oxford; hon. LL D, Cambridge; GCB, 1893; died at Washington while at work on Anglo-American Commission.

HERSCHELL, Ridley Haim (1807–1864), Dissenting minister; born in Prussian Poland of Jewish parents; settled in England, 1830; took charge of Lady Olivia Sparrow's missions; opened a chapel in London, 1838; one of the founders of mission to Jews and of evangelical alliance; published works concerning relation of Judaism to Christianity.

HERSCHELL, Solomon (1761–1842). See HIRSCHEL.

HERSHON, Paul Isaac (1817–1888), Hebraist; born in Galicia; director of House of Industry for Jews at Jerusalem and the model farm at Jaffa; published *Talmudic Miscellany* (1880).

HERT, Henry (*fl.* 1549). See HART.

HERTELPOLL (or HARTLEPOOL), Hugh of (d. 1302?). See HUGH.

HERTFORD, countess of. See SEYMOUR, CATHERINE, 1538?–1568.

HERTFORD, earls of. See CLARE, RICHARD DE, said to be first earl, d. 1136?; CLARE, ROGER DE, third earl, d. 1173; CLARE, GILBERT DE, fifth earl, d. 1230; CLARE, RICHARD DE, sixth earl, 1222–1262; CLARE, GILBERT DE, seventh earl, 1243–1295; CLARE, GILBERT DE, eighth earl, 1291–1314; MONTHERMER, RALPH DE, d. 1325?; SEY-MOUR, EDWARD, first earl of the second creation, 1506?–1552; SEYMOUR, EDWARD, earl of the third creation, 1539?–1621.

HERTFORD, marquises of. See SEYMOUR, WILLIAM, first marquis, 1588–1660; CONWAY, FRANCIS SEYMOUR, first marquis of the second creation, 1719–1794; SEYMOUR, FRANCIS (INGRAM), second marquis, 1743–1822; SEY-MOUR-CONWAY, FRANCIS CHARLES, third marquis, 1777–1842.

HERTSLET, Sir Edward (1824–1902), librarian of the Foreign Office; assistant to father, Lewis *Hertslet, at Foreign Office Library, 1840; sub-librarian, 1855; librarian, 1857; attached to mission to Berlin Congress and knighted, 1878; CB, 1874; KCB, 1892; compiled *Hertslet's Commercial Treaties* (vols. xii–xix, 1871–95), *Recollections of the Foreign Office* (1901), and other works.

HERTSLET, Lewis (1787–1870), librarian to the Foreign Office, 1810–57; published collections of treaties between Great Britain and Foreign Powers (1820, continued by his son Edward), and between Turkey and Foreign Powers, 1835–55 (1855).

HERTZ, Joseph Herman (1872–1946), chief rabbi of the United Hebrew Congregations of the British Empire; migrated to America from Slovakia, 1884; Ph.D., Columbia University, graduated as rabbi, and appointed to Syracuse, 1894; Johannesburg, 1898; Orach Chayim Congregation, New York, 1911; chief rabbi, United Hebrew Congregations of British Empire, 1913–46; combative Conservative; strong Zionist; CH, 1943.

HERTZOG, James Barry Munnik (1866–1942), prime minister of South Africa; graduated from Victoria College, Stellenbosch (1888), and Amsterdam University (1892); judge, Orange Free State, 1895–9; commanded Boer southern forces, 1899–1902; attorney-general and minister of education, Orange River Colony, 1907–10; represented Smithfield in Union parliament, 1910–40; minister of justice, 1910–12; formed National party, 1913; prime minister, 1924–39; of native affairs, 1924–9; external affairs, 1929–39; gave Union its own flag, citizenship, and ministers plenipotentiary; substituted Afrikaans for Dutch; formed coalition with *Smuts, 1932; united party, 1933; carried through segregation policy, notably disfranchisement of Cape Bantu, 1936; defeated on proposal of neutrality, 5 Sept. 1939.

HERVEY (or HERVAEUS) (d. 1131), first bishop of Ely; made bishop of Bangor by William II, 1092, but driven from his diocese by the Welsh; confessor to Henry I; made administrator of the abbey of Ely, 1107; bishop of Ely, 1109–31; attended council on clerical marriages, 1129.

HERVEY, Lord Arthur Charles (1808–1894), bishop of Bath and Wells; fourth son of Frederick William Hervey, first marquis of Bristol; educated at Eton and Trinity College, Cambridge; BA, 1830; ordained priest, 1832; rector of Horringer and Ickworth, 1832–69; archdeacon of Sudbury, 1862; bishop of Bath and Wells, 1869–94; on committee of revisers of Authorized Version of Old Testament, 1870–84; published *Genealogies of our Lord* (1853).

HERVEY, Augustus John, third earl of Bristol (1724–1779), admiral; grandson of John *Hervey, first earl of Bristol; married Elizabeth *Chudleigh, 1744, divorced by collusion, 1769; post-captain, 1747; served under *Byng in Mediterranean; gave evidence at Byng's trial, 1757; of great service to *Hawke in the Channel, 1759; served under *Keppel at Belleisle, 1760; took part in capture of Martinique, St Lucia, and the Havannah, 1762; MP, Bury St Edmunds, 1757–63 and 1768–75, Saltash, 1763–8; groom of the bedchamber, 1763; chief secretary for Ireland, 1766–7; a lord of the Admiralty, 1771–5; succeeded to earldom, 1775; rear-admiral, 1775; vice-admiral, 1778; supported Keppel and opposed *Sandwich, 1778–9; his correspondence with Lord Hawke in Record Office, other journals in British Museum.

HERVEY, Carr, Lord Hervey (1691–1723), reputed father of Horace *Walpole; elder son of John *Hervey, first earl of Bristol; MA, Clare Hall, Cambridge, 1710; MP, Bury St Edmunds, 1713–22.

HERVEY, Frederick Augustus, fourth earl of Bristol and fifth Baron Howard de Walden (1730–1803), bishop of Derry; third son of John *Hervey, Baron Hervey of Ickworth; educated at Westminster and Corpus Christi College, Cambridge; MA, 1754; DD, 1770; principal clerk of privy seal, 1761; travelled in Italy and Dalmatia and studied volcanic phenomena; bishop of Cloyne, 1767–8, where he offered Philip *Skelton a chaplaincy, and reclaimed the great bog; as bishop of Derry (1768–1803) spent much money on public works and the see; succeeded his brother Augustus John *Hervey in earldom, 1779; advocated relaxation of Catholic penal laws and abolition of tithe; took prominent part at Volunteers' Convention, 1783; favoured parliamentary reform and the admission of Roman Catholics to House of Commons; travelled on the continent; imprisoned by the French at Milan; succeeded to barony of

Howard de Walden through his grandmother, 1799; died at Albano; buried at Ickworth.

HERVEY, George William, second earl of Bristol (1721–1775), eldest son of John *Hervey, Baron Hervey of Ickworth; succeeded his father as third baron, 1743, and his grandfather as second earl of Bristol, 1751; envoy-extraordinary to Turin, 1755–8; ambassador at Madrid, 1758–61; nominated lord-lieutenant of Ireland, but did not go, 1766; privy councillor, 1766; lord privy seal, 1768–70; groom of the stole, 1770.

HERVEY, James (1714–1758), devotional writer; at Lincoln College, Oxford, while John *Wesley was fellow; BA; MA, Clare Hall, Cambridge, 1752; incumbent of Weston Favell and Collingtree, 1752; his *Meditations and Contemplations* brought out in two parts (1746–7); published also *Dialogues between Theron and Aspasio* (1755), attacked by Wesley, his reply being issued posthumously (1766); collected works published (1769, 6 vols.).

HERVEY, James (1751?–1824), physician; MA, The Queen's College, Oxford, 1774; MD, 1781; physician to Guy's Hospital, 1779; FRCP, 1782; Gulstonian lecturer, 1783; six times censor, 1783–1809; Harveian orator, 1785, Lumleian lecturer, 1789–1811.

HERVEY, John (1616–1679), treasurer to *Catherine of Braganza; MP, Hythe, 1661–79; patron of *Cowley.

HERVEY, John, first earl of Bristol (1665–1751), Whig politician; LL D, Clare Hall, Cambridge, 1705; MP, Bury St Edmunds, 1694–1703; created Baron Hervey of Ickworth, 1703, by influence of the Marlboroughs; created earl of Bristol, 1714; his portrait by *Kneller at Guildhall, Bury.

HERVEY, John, Baron Hervey of Ickworth (1696–1743), pamphleteer and memoir writer; younger son of John *Hervey, first earl of Bristol; of Westminster and Clare Hall, Cambridge; MA, 1715; styled Lord Hervey after death of elder brother Carr *Hervey, 1723; MP, Bury St Edmunds, 1725; granted pension by George II on his desertion of *Frederick, prince of Wales; vice-chamberlain and privy councillor, 1730; fought a duel with William *Pulteney, 1731; summoned to House of Lords in his father's barony, 1733; exercised great influence over Queen *Caroline; lord privy seal, 1740–2; afterwards joined opposition; friend of Lady Mary Wortley *Montagu; attacked by *Pope as 'Lord Fanny', 1733; replied in 'Verses addressed to the Imitator of Horace' and 'Epistle to a Doctor of Divinity' (1733); the 'Sporus' of Pope's *Epistle to Arbuthnot*; wrote pamphlets on behalf of Sir Robert Walpole; *Letters between Lord Hervey and Dr. Mid-*

dleton concerning the Roman Senate, edited by T. Knowles (1778); Hervey's *Memoirs of Reign of George II*, edited by J. W. *Croker (1848, reprinted 1884).

HERVEY, Mary, Lady (1700–1768), daughter of Brigadier-General Lepell; eulogized by *Pope, *Gay, *Chesterfield, and Voltaire; married to John *Hervey, Baron Hervey of Ickworth, 1720; her letters to Revd Edmund Morris, 1742–68, published (1821), and others in Lady Suffolk's *Letters* (1824); epitaph composed by Horace *Walpole.

HERVEY, Thomas (1699–1775), eccentric pamphleteer; second son of John *Hervey, first earl of Bristol; MP, Bury, 1733–47; equerry to Queen *Caroline, 1728–37, and vice-chamberlain to her, 1733; eloped with wife of Sir Thomas *Hanmer; published pamphlets, including *Answer to a Letter he received from Dr. Samuel Johnson to dissuade him from parting with his Supposed* [second] *Wife* (1763).

HERVEY, Thomas Kibble (1799–1859), poet and critic; entered at Caius College, Cambridge, 1822, and Trinity, 1823; while at Cambridge published *Australia*, a poem (3rd edn. 1829), edited *Friendship's Offering*, 1826–7, and the *Amaranth*, 1839; contributed to annuals; edited *Athenaeum*, 1846–53.

HERVEY, William (d. 1567). See HARVEY.

HERVEY, William, Baron Hervey of Kidbrooke (d. 1642); distinguished himself against the Spanish Armada, 1588; knighted for services at capture of Cadiz, 1596; created Irish peer for services in Ireland, 1620; promoted to English barony, 1628.

HESELTINE, James (1690–1763), organist of Durham Cathedral, 1710–63, and composer.

HESELTINE, Philip Arnold (1894–1930), writer on music, and musical composer under the pseudonym of Peter Warlock; influenced by Frederick *Delius, D. H. *Lawrence, and Bernard van Dieren; compositions include songs and part songs, instrumental and choral works; his music that of a belated Elizabethan.

HESILRIGE (or HASELRIG), Sir Arthur, second baronet (d. 1661), Parliamentarian; as MP for Leicestershire opposed *Laud's religious policy; introduced Bill of Attainder against *Strafford; promoted 'Root-and-Branch Bill' and (1641) proposed Militia Bill; one of the five members impeached by Charles I, 1642; raised a troop of horse and fought at Edgehill, 1642; as *Waller's second-in-command distinguished himself at Lansdowne, 1643; wounded at Lansdowne and Roundway Down, 1643; present at Cheriton, 1644; a leader of the Independents

after the self-denying ordinance; while governor of Newcastle recaptured Tynemouth, 1648; refused nomination as one of the king's judges; accompanied *Cromwell to Scotland, 1648, and supported him with a reserve army, 1650; *Lilburne's charges against him declared false by the House of Commons, 1652; purchased confiscated lands of see of Durham; member of every Council of State during the Commonwealth; opposed Cromwell's government after dissolution of Long Parliament, 1653; MP, Leicestershire, 1640, and Newcastle-upon-Tyne, 1654, 1656, and 1659; refused to pay taxes and to enter or recognize the new upper chamber, 1657; opposed in Commons recognition of Richard *Cromwell, and intrigued with army leaders against him; became recognized leader of parliament; obtained cashiering of *Lambert and others, 1659; gained over Portsmouth and raised troops against Lambert, 1659; was outwitted by *Monck; arrested at the Restoration, but Monck interposed to save his life; died in the Tower.

HESKETH, Harriet, Lady (1733–1807), cousin and friend of the poet *Cowper; married Thomas Hesketh (created baronet, 1761).

HESKETH, Henry (1637?–1710), divine; BA, Brasenose College, Oxford, 1656; vicar of St Helen, Bishopsgate, 1678–94; chaplain to Charles II and William III; published religious works.

HESKETH, Sir Peter (1801–1866). See FLEETWOOD, Sir PETER HESKETH.

HESKETH, Richard (1562–1593), Roman Catholic exile; incited Ferdinando *Stanley, fifth earl of Derby, to claim the crown; executed at St Albans on the earl's information.

HESKETH, Roger (1643–1715), Roman Catholic controversialist; vice-president of English College, Lisbon, 1678–86; came to England; wrote a treatise on transubstantiation.

HESKETH (or HASKET), Thomas (1561–1613), botanist; brother of Richard *Hesketh.

HESKYNS (or HESKIN), Thomas (*fl.* 1566), Roman Catholic divine; fellow of Clare Hall, Cambridge; MA, 1540; DD, 1557; rector of Hildersham, 1551–6; chancellor of Sarum, 1558–9; and vicar of Brixworth, 1558–9; retired to Flanders and became a Dominican, but returned to England secretly; published *The Parliament of Chryste* (1565, Brussels).

HESLOP, Luke (1738–1825), archdeacon of Buckingham; fellow (1769) of Corpus Christi College, Cambridge; senior wrangler, 1764; MA, 1767; BD, 1775; prebendary of St Paul's, 1776; archdeacon of Buckingham, 1778; prebendary of Lincoln, 1778; rector of Adstock, Buckinghamshire, for twenty-five years; rector of Maryle-bone, London, 1809; published economic pamphlets.

HESLOP, Richard Henry (1907–1973), liaison officer with French Resistance, known as 'Xavier'; born in France; educated at Shrewsbury; played football for Corinthian Casuals; spent two years in Siam (Thailand) and two years in Spain and Portugal; spoke several languages; joined Devonshire Regiment, 1939; recruited to Special Operations Executive (SOE); landed near Cannes, 1942; arrested at Limoges but able to escape from prison, 1942; selected to organize scattered Resistance groups in Ain, Isère, Savoie, and Haute Savoie, 1943; by January 1944 had 3,500 armed and trained men under his orders; carried out important sabotage work on factories and railways; by 1944 parts of countryside under Maquis control; guerrillas fought Germans after D-Day landings until their area liberated by the US forces; mission accomplished, Xavier returned to England, 1944; DSO; Croix de Guerre with palm and chevalier of Legion of Honour; American Medal of Freedom with bronze palm; after the war joined Colonial Service; served in Tanganyika and Malaya, where he was valuable in jungle battles against Chinese infiltrators; also served in British Cameroons; published account of wartime missions, *Xavier* (1970).

HESLOP, Thomas Pretious (1823–1885), physician; MD, Edinburgh, 1848; lecturer on physiology at Queen's College, Birmingham, 1853–8; physician to Queen's Hospital, 1853–60 and 1870–82; chairman of Mason's College.

HESS, Dame (Julia) Myra (1890–1965), pianist; studied at Guildhall School of Music and the Royal Academy of Music, 1903–8; gave first concert, conducted by (Sir) Thomas *Beecham, at Queen's Hall, London, 1907; first great success in Holland with Concertgebouw Orchestra, 1912; made American début at Aeolian Hall, New York, 1922; played regularly with London String Quartet, and partnered Hungarian violinist, Jelly *d'Aranyi; organized daily chamber-music concerts at National Gallery, London, 1939–45; last concert appearance, Royal Festival Hall, London, 1961; increasingly troubled by arthritis of the hands and severe circulatory problems; disliked recording, but best recording probably Beethoven's Sonata in E major, Op. 109 (1954); piano transcription (1926) of chorale-setting from Bach's Cantata No. 147 ('Jesu, Joy of Man's Desiring') achieved immense popularity; CBE, 1936; DBE, 1941; honorary degrees from number of universities.

HESSE, princess of (1723–1772). See MARY.

HESSE-DARMSTADT, grand duchess of (1843–1878). See ALICE MAUD MARY.

HESSE-HOMBURG, Landgravine of (1770–1840). See ELIZABETH, princess.

HESSEL, Phoebe (1713?–1821), reputed female soldier and centenarian; a Brighton 'character'.

HESSEY, James Augustus (1814–1892), divine; educated at Merchant Taylors' School and St John's College, Oxford; MA, 1840; BD, 1845; DCL, 1846; vicar of Helidon, Northamptonshire, 1839; headmaster of Merchant Taylors' School, 1845–70; prebendary of St Paul's Cathedral, 1860–75; examining chaplain to John *Jackson (1811–1885), bishop of London, 1870; archdeacon of Middlesex, 1875–92; published theological writings.

HESTER, John (d. 1593), distiller, of St Paul's Wharf; author and translator of medical works; mentioned in Gabriel Harvey's *Pierces Supererogation* (1593).

HESTON, Walter (*fl.* 1350), Carmelite of Stamford; Cambridge scholar and DD.

HETHERINGTON, Sir **Hector James Wright** (1888–1965), university vice-chancellor; educated at Dollar Academy and Glasgow University, 1905–10; lecturer in moral philosophy under Sir Henry *Jones, 1910–14; warden, Glasgow University Settlement; professor of logic and philosophy, University College, Cardiff, 1915–20; principal and professor of philosophy, University College, Exeter, 1920–4; professor, moral philosophy, Glasgow, 1924–7; vice-chancellor, Liverpool University, 1927–36; principal, Glasgow University, 1936–61; hon. ARIBA; chairman, Committee of Vice-Chancellors and Principals, 1943–7 and 1949–52; associated with many charitable trusts; chairman of number of committees, including the Colonial Universities Grants Committee, 1942–8; recognized as doyen of vice-chancellors throughout the Commonwealth; chairman or president of over fifty educational and charitable bodies; publications include *Social Purpose* (with J. H. *Muirhead, 1918), *International Labour Legislation* (1920), and *Life and Letters of Sir Henry Jones* (1924); knighted, 1936; KBE, 1948; GBE, 1962; honorary degrees from many universities and professional bodies.

HETHERINGTON, Henry (1792–1849), printer and publisher of unstamped newspapers; drew up *Circular for the Formation of Trades Unions* (1830); began to issue the weekly *Poor Man's Guardian,* unstamped, July 1831; twice imprisoned for defying the law; indicted for publication of *Poor Man's Guardian* and trade-union *Poor Man's Conservative,* 1834, when the *Guard-*

ian was declared legal; imprisoned for publishing *Haslam's Letters to the Clergy of all Denominations* (1840); obtained conviction against Edward *Moxon for publishing *Shelley's works, 1841; died of cholera.

HETHERINGTON, William Maxwell (1803–1865), divine and poet; studied at Edinburgh; joined Free Church; became minister of Free St Paul's, Edinburgh, 1848; professor of apologetics in New College, Glasgow, 1857; published, among other works, histories of the Church of Scotland (1843) and the Westminster Assembly (1863, ed. R. Williamson, 1878).

HETON, Martin (1552–1609), bishop of Ely; of Westminster and Christ Church, Oxford; MA, 1578; DD, 1585; canon, 1582; vice-chancellor, 1588; dean of Winchester, 1589; bishop of Ely, 1599–1609; agreed to alienate to the crown richest manors of Ely.

HETON, Thomas (*fl.* 1573), London cloth-merchant and receiver of Protestant refugees.

HEUGH, Hugh (1782–1846), Presbyterian divine; moderator of general associate synod, 1819; minister of Regent Place, Glasgow, 1821–46; DD, Pittsburg, 1831; his life and works issued by Hamilton *Macgill (1850).

HEURTLEY, Charles Abel (1806–1895), Lady Margaret professor of divinity at Oxford; worked in timber merchant's office at Liverpool, 1822; scholar of Corpus Christi College, Oxford, 1823; MA, 1831; fellow, 1832; DD, 1853; vicar of Fenny Compton, 1840–72; Bampton lecturer, 1845; Lady Margaret professor, 1853–95.

HEVENINGHAM, William (1604–1678), regicide; sheriff of Norfolk, 1633; MP, Stockbridge, 1640; served on committee of Eastern Association, 1646; member of High Court, but refused to sign death-warrant of Charles I, 1649; member of Council of State, 1649; vice-admiral of Suffolk, 1651; at the Restoration his life saved by the exertions of his wife's relations, 1661; imprisoned at Windsor, 1664.

HEWART, Gordon, first Viscount Hewart (1870–1943), lord chief justice of England; educated at Bury and Manchester grammar schools and University College, Oxford; second class, Lit. Hum., 1891; called to bar (Inner Temple), 1902; KC, 1912; bencher, 1917; Liberal MP, Leicester, 1913–22; solicitor-general, 1916–19; attorney-general, 1919–22; lord chief justice, 1922–40; brilliant advocate; less successful as judge through tendency to forget he was no longer an advocate; president, Classical Association, 1926, English Association, 1929; knighted, 1916; PC, 1918; baron, 1922; viscount, 1940.

HEWETT, Sir George, first baronet (1750–1840), general; with 70th Foot in West Indies, 1764–74, and at siege of Charleston; exchanged with 43rd, and was deputy quartermaster-general to *O'Hara; adjutant-general in Ireland, 1793–9; raised regiment in Ireland; major-general, 1796; chief of Recruiting Department, 1799; inspector-general of Royal Reserve, 1803; commander-in-chief in East Indies, 1807–11, in Ireland, 1813–16; created baronet, 1818; colonel of 61st; general.

HEWETT, Sir John Prescott (1854–1941), Indian civil servant; educated at Winchester and Balliol College, Oxford; posted to North-Western Provinces and Oudh, 1877; under-secretary, Indian Home Department, 1886; deputy secretary, 1890; secretary, 1895–1902; secretary, Royal Commission on Opium, 1893; chief commissioner, Central Provinces, 1902–4; in charge of Indian Commerce and Industry Department, 1904–7; encouraged economic activities of Geological Survey and establishment of steel industry at Jamshedpur; lieutenant-governor, United Provinces, 1907–12; organized Naini Tal Industrial Conference and Allahabad Exhibition; presided over durbar committee, 1911; Conservative MP, Luton, 1922–3; KCSI, 1907; GCSI, 1911; KBE, 1917.

HEWETT, Sir Prescott Gardner, first baronet (1812–1891), surgeon; studied in Paris; MRCS, 1836; lecturer on anatomy at St George's Hospital, 1845; full surgeon, 1861, and consulting surgeon, 1875; FRCS, 1843, and president, 1876; FRS, 1874; surgeon-extraordinary to Queen Victoria, 1867; sergeant-surgeon, 1884; surgeon to prince of Wales, 1875; created baronet, 1883; published surgical papers.

HEWETT, Sir William (d. 1567), lord mayor of London; master of Clothworkers' Company, 1543; alderman of Vintry, 1550–4, afterwards of Candlewick; sheriff of London, 1553; lord mayor, 1559–60; knighted, 1560; a governor of Highgate School.

HEWETT, Sir William Nathan Wrighte (1834–1888), vice-admiral; midshipman during Burmese War, 1851; promoted for gallantry in the Crimea, 1854; one of the first recipients of Victoria Cross, 1857; commanded on royal yacht, 1858; captain, 1862; served on China Station, 1865–72; as commander-in-chief in West Africa had charge of naval operations in Ashanti War, 1873–4; KCB, 1874; rear-admiral, 1878; commander-in-chief in East Indies, 1882, conducting naval operations in Red Sea; assisted in defence of Suakin, 1884; undertook successful mission to Abyssinia, 1884; vice-admiral, 1884; commanded Channel Fleet, 1886–8.

HEWINS, William Albert Samuel (1865–1931), political economist, historian, and politician; second class, mathematics, Pembroke College, Oxford; organizer and first director, London School of Economics, 1895–1903; secretary, Tariff Commission (1903–17), chairman (1920–2); Conservative MP, Hereford City, 1912–18; fought six unsuccessful elections; prolific writer on economic and imperial matters.

HEWIT (or HEWETT), John (1614–1658), Royalist divine; of Pembroke College, Cambridge; DD, Oxford, 1643; minister of St Gregory's by St Paul's, London; said to have harboured *Ormonde, 1658; beheaded for Royalist plot, though interceded for by Mrs *Claypoole; published devotional works.

HEWITSON, William Chapman (1806–1878), naturalist; left to British Museum fine collection of diurnal lepidoptera, some birds and pictures; published *British Oology* (1833–42) and works on lepidoptera.

HEWITT, Sir **Edgar Rainey Ludlow-** (1886–1973), air chief marshal. See LUDLOW-HEWITT.

HEWITT, James, Viscount Lifford (1709–1789), lord chancellor of Ireland; barrister, Middle Temple, 1742; MP, Coventry, 1761; king's serjeant, 1760; judge of the King's Bench, 1766; lord chancellor of Ireland, 1768–89; created Baron Lifford in Irish peerage, 1768, and viscount, 1781; his decisions as chancellor printed (1839).

HEWITT, John (1719–1802), mayor of Coventry, 1755, 1758, and 1760; published *Journal* (1779–90), *Memoirs of Lady Wilbrihammon* (c.1778), and *Guide for Constables* (1779).

HEWITT, John (1807–1878), antiquary; wrote under name 'Sylvanus Swanquill'; published *Ancient Armour and Weapons* (1855–60), *Old Woolwich* (1860), handbooks on Lichfield, and other works.

HEWLETT, Ebenezer (*fl.* 1747), writer against the deists.

HEWLETT, James (1789–1836), flower painter.

HEWLETT, John (1762–1844), biblical scholar; BD, Magdalene College, Cambridge, 1796; rector of Hilgay, Norfolk, 1819; published *Vindication of the Authenticity of the Parian Chronicle* (1789), *The Holy Bible . . . with Critical, Philosophical, and Explanatory Notes* (1812), and other works.

HEWLETT, Joseph Thomas James (1800–1847), novelist; educated at Charterhouse and Worcester College, Oxford; MA, 1826; published *Peter Priggins, the College Scout* (1841), illustrated by *Phiz and edited by Theodore Hook, *Parsons and Widows* (1844), and other works.

HEWLETT, Maurice Henry (1861–1923), novelist, poet, and essayist; made his name by romantic fiction, but regarded himself as a poet; works include *The Forest Lovers* (1898), *The Life of Richard Yea-and-Nay* (1900), *The Queen's Quair* (1904), *Rest Harrow* (1910), and *The Song of the Plow* (1916).

HEWLEY, Sarah, Lady (1627–1710), founder of the Hewley Trust; heiress of Robert Wolrych and wife of Sir John Hewley; left land for support of Dissenting ministers.

HEWSON, John (d. 1662), regicide; sometime shoemaker; led forlorn hope at Bridgwater, 1647; one of the commissioners to represent soldiers' grievances, 1647; signed Charles I's death-warrant, 1649; commander of foot under *Cromwell in Ireland, and governor of Dublin; MA, Oxford, 1649; favoured Anabaptists, and headed faction against Henry *Cromwell; represented Ireland, 1653, Dublin, 1654, and Guildford, 1656; member of Cromwell's House of Lords, 1657, of Committee of Safety, 1659; much satirized after suppression of London 'prentice riot, 1659; escaped at Restoration, and died abroad.

HEWSON, William (1739–1774), surgeon and anatomist; partner of Dr William *Hunter, 1762–1771; Copley medallist, 1769; FRS, 1770; published *Experimental Inquiry into the Properties of the Blood*, in three parts (1771, 1774, and 1777, ed. Falconar); fatally wounded himself while dissecting; works edited for Sydenham Society, 1846.

HEWSON, William (1806–1870), theological writer; educated at St Paul's and St John's College, Cambridge; MA, 1833; headmaster of St Peter's School, York, 1838–47; perpetual curate of Goatland, 1848–70; published works, including *The Key of David* (1855).

HEXHAM, Henry (1585?–1650?), military writer; page in service of Sir Francis *Vere at siege of Ostend, 1601, and till 1606; quartermaster under Sir Horace (afterwards Baron) *Vere in expedition to relieve Breda, 1625, and subsequently under George (afterwards Baron) *Goring (1608–1657); in Dutch service, c.1642, till death. His works include an edition of Mercator's *Atlas* (1637), *English–Dutch Dictionary* (1648), and accounts of various military operations in which he took part.

HEXHAM, John of (*fl.* 1180). See JOHN.

HEXHAM, Richard of (*fl.* 1138–1154). See RICHARD.

HEY, John (1734–1815), divine; brother of William *Hey (1736–1819); BA, Catharine Hall, Cambridge, 1755; fellow of Sidney Sussex College, 1758–79; Seatonian prizeman, 1763; Norrisian professor of divinity, 1780–95; his lectures (1796) edited by *Turton (1841).

HEY, Richard (1745–1835), essayist; brother of John *Hey; third wrangler and chancellor's medallist, Cambridge, 1768; fellow of Sidney Sussex College, 1768–78, of Magdalene, 1782–96; published, among other works, dissertation on gaming (1783), on duelling (1784), and on suicide (1785).

HEY, William (1736–1819), surgeon; brother of John *Hey; senior surgeon to Leeds Infirmary, 1773–1812; FRS, 1775; friend of *Priestley; mayor of Leeds, 1787–8 and 1801–2; president of Leeds Literary and Philosophical Society, 1783; devised operation of partial amputation of the foot; published medical works.

HEY, William (1772–1844), author of *Treatise on Puerperal Fever* (1815); son of William *Hey (1736–1819).

HEY, William (1796–1875), surgeon to Leeds Infirmary, 1830–51; son of William *Hey (1772–1844).

HEYDON, Sir Christopher (d. 1623), writer on astrology; BA, Peterhouse, Cambridge, 1578–9; MP, Norfolk, 1588; knighted at capture of Cadiz, 1596; suspected of complicity in *Essex rising, 1601; chief work *Defence of Judiciall Astrologie* (1602).

HEYDON, Sir Henry (d. 1503), steward of the household of Cecilia, duchess of York; knighted, 1485.

HEYDON, John (fl. 1667), astrologer; imprisoned for two years by *Cromwell for foretelling his death by hanging, and for treasonable practices, 1663 and 1667; wrote many works on Rosicrucian mysticism, borrowing largely from anterior writers.

HEYDON, Sir John (d. 1653), lieutenant of the ordnance; son of Sir Christopher *Heydon; knighted, 1620; lieutenant-general of the ordnance to Charles I during Civil War; DCL, Oxford, 1642.

HEYER, Georgette (1902–1974), novelist; educated at schools in Paris and London; began her first historical novel, *The Black Moth* (1921), at age of 17; this was followed by *The Great Roxhythe* (1922), *Powder and Patch* (1923), and *These Old Shades* (1926), the latter two set in the period in which she came to excel, the Georgian; married George Ronald Rougier, 1925; went with him to Tanganyika; published *The Masqueraders* (1928); settled in England and husband called to bar (Inner Temple), 1939, eventually to become QC, 1959; their only child, a son, born, 1932; between 1930s and 1950s wrote modern detective novels including *Death in the Stocks* (1935), but her reputation made by her historical novels, particularly those of the Regency period; two other novels outstanding—*An Infamous Army* (1937), an account of the Battle of Waterloo, and *The Spanish Bride* (1940) about the Peninsular War; her final book, *My Lord John*, concerned with the duke of Bedford, brother of Henry V, prepared for publication after her death and appeared in 1975; much concerned to keep her private life private, impatient with intrusive journalists and admirers.

HEYLYN, John (1685?–1759), divine; 'the Mystic Doctor'; educated at Westminster and Trinity College, Cambridge; MA, 1714; DD, 1728; first rector of St Mary-le-Strand, 1724–59; prebendary of St Paul's and Westminster, and chaplain to George II; published *Theological Lectures at Westminster Abbey* (1749).

HEYLYN, Peter (1599–1662), ecclesiastical writer; first cousin (once removed) of Rowland *Heylyn; demy and fellow of Magdalen College, Oxford; MA, 1620; DD, 1633; published *Geography* (1621) and *Survey of France* (1656); royal chaplain, 1630; prebendary of Westminster, 1631; incumbent of Alresford, Hants, 1633; controverted Puritan views; assisted *Noye (1633) in preparation of case against *Prynne; proposed conference between Convocation and Commons, 1640; obtained money grant from Convocation for Charles I, 1640; asserted right of bishops to share in all proceedings of upper house; joined Charles I at Oxford and chronicled Civil War in *Mercurius Aulicus*; obliged to compound for his estate; attacked *L'Estrange's *Life of Charles I*, 1656, and, in *Examen Historicum* (1658–9), *Fuller and William *Sanderson; issued *Certamen Epistolare* (1659) against *Baxter, Nicholas *Bernard, and others; subdean of Westminster at coronation of Charles II, 1661; disabled by infirmities from promotion; chief works *Ecclesia Restaurata, or History of the Reformation* (1661, edited by J. C. *Robertson, 1849), *Cyprianus Anglicus* (i.e. Archbishop *Laud, published 1668) in answer to *Canterburies Doom*, and *Aerius Redivivus, or History of Presbyterianism* (published 1670).

HEYLYN (or HEYLIN), Rowland (1562?–1631), sheriff of London; master of Ironmongers' Company, 1614 and 1625; alderman of Cripplegate, 1624; sheriff of London, 1624–5; published Welsh Bible (1630); left bequests to Shrewsbury, the Ironmongers' Company, and London charities.

HEYMAN, Sir **Peter** (1580–1641), politician; knighted by James I for services in Ireland; MP, Hythe, 1620–1, and subsequently; ordered to serve abroad at his own expense on account of opposition to the government, c.1622; imprisoned, 1629; elected to Long Parliament for Dover, 1640; money voted to his heirs, 1646, for his service to Commonwealth.

HEYNES, Simon (d. 1552), dean of Exeter; fellow of Queens' College, Cambridge, 1516; MA, 1519; president, 1528; DD, 1531; vice-chancellor of Cambridge, 1533–4; vicar of Stepney, 1534; ambassador to France, 1535; dean of Exeter, 1537; joint envoy to Spain, 1538; prebendary of Westminster, 1540; assisted in compilation of first liturgy.

HEYRICK, Richard (1600–1667), warden of Manchester Collegiate Church; son of Sir William *Hericke; of Merchant Taylors' School and St John's College, Oxford; MA, 1622; fellow of All Souls, Oxford, 1625; warden of Manchester Collegiate Church, 1635; attacked Romanists and High Churchmen, 1641; member of Westminster Assembly; main establisher of Presbyterianism in Lancashire; published *Harmonious Consent of the Ministers within the County Palatine of Lancaster* (1648); obtained restoration of church revenues; imprisoned for implication in movement of Christopher *Love, 1651; conformed at Restoration.

HEYRICK, Thomas (d. 1694), poet; grandnephew of Robert *Herrick; MA, Peterhouse, Cambridge, 1675; curate of Market Harborough; published *Miscellany Poems* (1691).

HEYSHAM, John (1753–1834), physician; MD, Edinburgh, 1777; practised at Carlisle; his statistics (published 1797) used for Carlisle Table (1816); said to have assisted *Paley on question of structural design in nature.

HEYTESBURY, Baron (1779–1860). See A'COURT, WILLIAM.

HEYTESBURY, William (*fl.* 1340), logician; fellow of Merton College, Oxford, 1330; original fellow (Heightilbury) of The Queen's College, 1341; chancellor of university, 1370; works printed under name of 'Hentisberus' or 'Tisberius' at Pavia and Venice.

HEYTHER, William (1563?–1627). See HEATHER.

HEYWOOD, Sir **Benjamin,** first baronet (1793–1865), banker; founder and president (1825–40) of Manchester Mechanics' Institution; created baronet, 1838; FRS, 1843.

HEYWOOD, Eliza (1693?–1756). See HAYWOOD.

HEYWOOD, Ellis (or **Elizaeus**) (1530–1578), Jesuit; brother of Jasper *Heywood; fellow of All Souls, Oxford, 1548; BCL, 1552; secretary to Cardinal *Pole; Jesuit father at Antwerp; published (in Italian) fictitious conversations of Sir Thomas *More (Florence, 1556); died at Louvain.

HEYWOOD, James (1687–1776), author; published *Letters and Poems on several Occasions* (1722).

HEYWOOD, Jasper (1535–1598), Jesuit; son of John *Heywood; page of honour to Princess Elizabeth; probationer-fellow of Merton College, Oxford, 1554; fellow of All Souls, 1558; MA, 1558; became a Jesuit at Rome, 1562; professor at Dillingen seventeen years; superior of English Jesuit mission, 1581; deported to France, 1585; died at Naples; his translations from Seneca's tragedies reprinted in Thomas *Newton's *Seneca* (1581); contributed poems to *Paradyse of Daynty Deuises* (1576).

HEYWOOD, John (1497?–1580?), 'the old English epigrammatist'; under Henry VIII a singer and player on the virginals; wrote *Description of a most noble Ladye* (on Princess Mary); publicly recanted his denial of the royal supremacy, 1544; in great favour with Queen Mary as a kind of superior jester; on accession of Elizabeth (1558) retired to Malines, where he probably died. He published interludes, including *The Four P's* (first printed 1569, in Hazlitt's *Dodsley*, 1874), *The Play of the Wether* (1533), and *The Play of Love*; published also *Dialogue on Wit and Folly* (reprinted 1846), and another dialogue containing proverbs and epigrams (1562, reprinted 1867), besides ballads, and *The Spider and the Flie* (1556).

HEYWOOD, Nathaniel, the elder (1633–1677), ejected minister; BA, Trinity College, Cambridge, 1650; minister of Ormskirk, Lancashire, 1656–62; compelled to desist from preaching, 1674.

HEYWOOD, Nathaniel, the younger (1659–1704), Nonconformist minister at Ormskirk; son of Nathaniel *Heywood the elder.

HEYWOOD, Oliver (1630–1702), Nonconformist divine; brother of Nathaniel *Heywood the elder; BA, Trinity College, Cambridge, 1650; minister of Coley Chapel, Halifax, 1650; excommunicated for not using the Prayer-Book, 1662; licensed Presbyterian teacher, 1672–5; imprisoned at York for 'riotous assembly', 1685; his Northowram meeting-house licensed under Toleration Act; introduced into Yorkshire the 'happy union' between Presbyterians and Congregationalists, 1691; his works collected by R. *Slate (1825–7); *Diaries* edited by J. Horsfall

Turner (1881–5, 4 vols.), as well as his *Nonconformist Register*.

HEYWOOD, Peter (1773–1831), navy captain; sailed in the *Bounty*, 1786; confined by mutineers, 1789; remained with the party at Tahiti and joined the *Pandora*, 1791; treated as a mutineer; though in irons escaped when the *Pandora* went down in Endeavour Straits, 1791; convicted at Spithead with mutineers, 1792; obtained pardon by interposition of Lord *Chatham, 1792; promoted lieutenant by *Howe, 1794; attained postrank, 1803; surveyed part of east coast of Ceylon.

HEYWOOD, Robert (1574?–1645), poet; of Heywood Hall, Lancashire; his *Observations and Instructions, Divine and Morall* first edited by James *Crossley (1869).

HEYWOOD, Samuel (1753–1828), chief justice of Carmarthen circuit; of Trinity Hall, Cambridge; barrister, Inner Temple, 1772; serjeant-at-law, 1794; chief justice, Carmarthen circuit, 1807–28; friend of Charles James *Fox; published *Right of Protestant Dissenters to a Compleat Toleration asserted* (1787), digests of election law, and other works.

HEYWOOD, Thomas (d. 1641), dramatist; said to have been a fellow of Peterhouse, Cambridge; member of the Lord Admiral's Company, 1598; afterwards retainer of Henry *Wriothesley, earl of Southampton, and Edward *Somerset, earl of Worcester; one of the queen's players, 1619; composed lord mayor's pageants for many years; many of his plays lost; an ardent Protestant. His chief plays were *The Four Prentices of London* (produced *c.*1600, published 1615), ridiculed in *Fletcher's *Knight of the Burning Pestle, Edward IV* (two parts, 1600, 1605; ed. Barron *Field, 1842), *The Royal King and the Loyal Subject* (1637, ed. J. P. *Collier, 1850), *A Woman Killed with Kindness* (acted 1603, printed 1607, ed. Collier, 1850; revived 1887), *The Rape of Lucrece* (1608), *The Captives* (ed. *Bullen, 1885), and *The Wise Woman of Hogsdon* (1638). He also published *An Apology for Actors* (1612, reprinted 1841), and poems (including 'Hierarchy of the Blessed Angels', 1635), translations, and compilations.

HEYWOOD, Thomas (1797–1866), antiquary; brother of Sir Benjamin *Heywood; of Hope End, Herefordshire; edited for Chetham Society, *Norris Papers* (1846), *Diary of the Rev. Henry Newcome* (1849), and other works; his library sold at Manchester, 1868.

HEYWORTH, Geoffrey, first Baron Heyworth (1894–1974), industrialist; educated at Dollar Academy, Clackmannanshire; joined Lever Brothers as clerk, 1912; sent to Canada to work for Lever Brothers' subsidiary; served with 48th Highlanders in Canadian army, 1915–18; wounded in leg; returned to London to take over firm's export trade, 1924; later, headed the UK soap company at Port Sunlight; director, Lever Brothers and Unilever Ltd., 1931; reorganized Lever soap interests in British market; succeeded (Sir) F. D'Arcy *Cooper as chairman, Lever Brothers, 1942–60; established international reputation as expert in professional management; first chairman, court of governors of Administrative Staff College, Henley; member, Royal Commission on Taxation of Profits and Income, 1951–4, and company law amendment committee of Board of Trade, 1943; part-time member, Coal Board, 1950–3 and London Passenger Transport Board, 1942–7; president, National Council of Social Service, 1961–70; chairman, Leverhulme Trust; member, University Grants Committee, 1954–8; visiting fellow, Nuffield College, 1947; hon. fellow, 1961; received number of honorary doctorates; knighted, 1948; created baron, 1955; grand officer in Order of Orange Nassau, 1947.

HIBBART (or HIBBERT), William (*fl.* 1760–1800), etcher.

HIBBERD, (Andrew) Stuart (1893–1983), BBC announcer; educated at Weymouth College, and St John's College, Cambridge; choral scholar; served in Dorset Regiment at Gallipoli and in Mesopotamia, and in Punjabi Regiment of Indian Army, 1914–22; joined British Broadcasting Company Ltd. at Savoy Hill as announcer, 1924; served for twenty-six years, and recognized as chief announcer, though never officially appointed to such a post; also presented musical programmes and 'The Silver Lining', 1949–64; retired as announcer, 1951; published *This—is London . . .* (1950); MBE, 1935.

HIBBERD, Shirley (1825–1890), journalist and horticultural writer; edited *Floral World*, 1858–75, and *Gardener's Magazine*, 1861–90; published horticultural works.

HIBBERT, George (1757–1837), West Indian merchant and collector; alderman of London, 1798–1803; MP, Seaford, 1806–12; FRS, 1811; active in establishment of West India Docks and (1805) London Institution; edited for Roxburghe Club *Caxton's version of Ovid's *Metamorphoses* (1819); his collections sold, 1829.

HIBBERT, Henry (1600?–1678), divine; BA, Brasenose College, Oxford, 1622; DD, St John's, Cambridge, 1665; vicar of Holy Trinity, Hull, 1651–60, of All Hallows-the-Less and St Olave's Jewry, 1662; prebendary of St Paul's, 1669; published *Syntagma Theologicum* (1662).

HIBBERT, Sir John Tomlinson (1824–1908), politician; BA, St John's College, Cambridge, 1847; MA, 1851; called to bar, 1849;

Liberal MP for Oldham, 1862–74, 1877–85, 1892–5; held subordinate offices in Gladstone's four administrations; served on various commissions, and was interested in poor-law reform; PC, 1886; KCB, 1893; constable of Lancaster Castle, 1907–8.

HIBBERT, Robert (1769–1849), founder of the Hibbert Trust; BA, Emmanuel College, Cambridge, 1791; Jamaica merchant and slave owner, 1791–1836; author of radical pamphlets; his trust (designed for elevation of Unitarian ministry) widened in scope by efforts of Edwin Wilkins *Field.

HIBBERT-WARE, Samuel (1782–1848), antiquary and geologist; MD, Edinburgh; secretary, Scottish Society of Antiquaries, 1823–7; awarded Gold Medal by Society of Arts for discovery of chromate of iron in Shetland, 1820; assumed name of Ware, 1837; published, among other works, *Description of the Shetland Islands* and an account of Ashton-under-Lyne in the fifteenth century (1822), *Sketches of the Philosophy of Apparitions* (1824), *Lancashire Memorials of the Rebellion in 1715* (1845), and geological memoirs.

HIBBS, Richard (1812?–1886), author; MA, St John's College, Cambridge, 1844; established New Church of England Chapel, St Vincent Street, Edinburgh, 1855; afterwards chaplain at Lisbon, Rotterdam, and Utrecht; published *Prussia and the Poor; or Observations upon the Systematised Relief of the Poor at Elberfield* (1876).

HIBERNIA, Thomas de (d. 1270), Franciscan; to be distinguished from Thomas *Hibernicus; wrote the *Promptuarium Morale*.

HIBERNICUS, Peter (*fl.* 1224). See PETER.

HIBERNICUS, Thomas (1306–1316). See THOMAS.

HICHENS, Robert Smythe (1864–1950), novelist; educated at Clifton; studied music and journalism; published *The Green Carnation* (1894, a satire on Oscar *Wilde), many romances, frequently in desert settings, notably *The Garden of Allah* (1904), macabre stories, and several plays.

HICHENS, (William) Lionel (1874–1940), man of business; educated at Winchester and New College, Oxford; a dispatch rider in South Africa, 1899–1900; joined *Milner's 'kindergarten' as treasurer, Johannesburg (1901), Transvaal (1902–7), and Inter-Colonial Council; rebuilt and rehabilitated Cammell Laird & Co. as chairman, 1910–40; showed remarkable understanding of labour; pioneer in seeing industrial problem as a moral question.

HICKERINGILL (or HICKHORNGILL), Edmund (1631–1708), divine and pamphleteer; junior fellow of Caius College, Cambridge, 1651–2; chaplain to *Lilburne's regiment, 1653; successively Baptist, Quaker, and deist; afterwards a soldier in Scotland and in Swedish service, and captain in *Fleetwood's regiment; after residence in Jamaica published an account of it (1661); ordained by Bishop Robert *Sanderson, 1661; vicar of All Saints', Colchester, 1662–1708, and Boxted, 1662–4; quarrelled with *Compton, bishop of London, and was condemned to pay damages for slander, *Jeffreys being counsel against him, 1682; publicly recanted, 1684; excluded, 1685–8; convicted of forgery, 1707.

HICKES, Francis (1566–1631), translator of Lucian; BA, St Mary Hall, Oxford, 1583; his translation of Lucian published (1634).

HICKES, Gaspar (1605–1677), Puritan divine; MA, Trinity College, Oxford, 1628; held Cornish livings and was consulted by parliament; member of the Westminster Assembly, 1643; ejected from Landrake, 1662; fined under Conventicle Act, 1670.

HICKES, George (1642–1715), nonjuror; BA, Magdalen College, Oxford, 1663; fellow of Lincoln College, 1664; MA, 1665; chaplain to duke of *Lauderdale, 1676; prebendary of Worcester, 1680; vicar of All Hallows, Barking, 1680; chaplain to the king, 1681; dean of Worcester, 1683; rector of Alvechurch, 1686; opposed Declaration of Indulgence; deprived for refusing to take oath of allegiance to William and Mary, 1690; in hiding till proceedings against him stopped, 1699; went to St Germain, 1693, and was named suffragan of Sancroft, with title 'Bishop of Thetford'; was consecrated in a private chapel by Bishops *Turner, *Lloyd, and *White, 1694; his house on Bagshot Heath searched, 1696; with two Scottish bishops consecrated, in St Andrew's, Holborn, Samuel Hawes, Nathaniel *Spinckes, and Jeremy *Collier, 1713. His chief works were *Case of Infant Baptism* (1683), *Records of the New Consecrations*, editions of the *Imitatio Christi* and of Fénelon's *Instructions for the Education of a Daughter*, and *Linguarum veterum septentrionalium thesaurus grammatico-criticus et archaeologicus* (1703–5).

HICKES (or HICKS), John (1633–1685), Nonconformist divine; brother of George *Hickes; fellow of Trinity College, Dublin; ejected from Saltash, Cornwall, 1662; presented petition to Charles II in favour of Nonconformists; joined *Monmouth (1685) and was sheltered by Alice *Lisle; tried and executed at Taunton.

HICKES, Thomas (1599–1634), son of Francis *Hickes; MA, Balliol College, Oxford, 1623; chaplain of Christ Church, Oxford.

HICKEY, Antony (d. 1641), Irish Franciscan; professor of theology and philosophy at Louvain and Cologne; definitor of the order at Rome, 1639; published (under pseudonym 'Dermitius Thadaeus') *Nitela Franciscanae religionis* (1627), and an edition, with commentary, of the works of Duns *Scotus (1639); died at Rome.

HICKEY, John (1756–1795), Irish sculptor.

HICKEY, Thomas (*fl.* 1760–1790), portrait painter; brother of John *Hickey; accompanied *Macartney to China, 1792; probably visited India; published *History of Painting and Sculpture* (Calcutta, 1788).

HICKEY, William (1787?–1875), Irish philanthropist and author; BA, St John's College, Cambridge, 1809, and Trinity College, Dublin, 1809; MA, Dublin, 1832; incumbent of Bannow, Ferns, 1820; helped to found agricultural school at Bannow; with Thomas Boyce established South Wexford Agricultural Society; rector of Kilcormick, 1826, Wexford, 1831, Mulrankin, 1834; as 'Martin Doyle' published *Hints to Small Farmers* (1830) and similar works; edited *Illustrated Book of Domestic Poultry* (1854) and *Irish Farmer's and Gardener's Magazine*, 1834-42; gold medallist of Royal Dublin Society; received pension from Royal Literary Fund.

HICKMAN, Charles (1648–1713), bishop of Derry; educated at Westminster and Christ Church, Oxford; MA, 1674; DD, 1685; chaplain to William III, Anne, and Lawrence *Hyde, earl of Rochester; rector of Burnham, Buckinghamshire, 1698–1702; bishop of Derry, 1703–13.

HICKMAN, Francis (*fl.* 1690), scholar; of Westminster and Christ Church, Oxford; MA, 1688; nonjuror; Bodleian orator, 1693; contributed to *Musae Anglicanae*.

HICKMAN, Henry (d. 1692), controversialist; BA, St Catharine Hall, Cambridge; fellow of Magdalen College, Oxford, 1648; MA, 1649; ejected at the Restoration; retired to Holland; carried on controversies with Peter *Heylyn, John *Durel, and others; died at Leiden.

HICKMAN (subsequently **WINDSOR), Thomas,** seventh Baron Windsor of Stanwell and first earl of Plymouth (1627?–1687). See WINDSOR.

HICKS (or HICKES), Baptist, first Viscount Campden (1551–1629), mercer and moneylender; contractor for crown lands, 1609; created baronet, 1620; MP, Tavistock, 1620, Tewkesbury, 1624, 1625, 1626, and 1628; built Hicks's Hall, Clerkenwell; purchased manor of Campden, from which he took his title when created viscount, 1628.

HICKS, Edward Lee (1843–1919), bishop of Lincoln; BA, Brasenose College, Oxford; fellow of Corpus Christi College, Oxford, 1866; rector of Fenny Compton, Warwickshire, 1873; principal of Hulme Hall, Manchester, 1886; canon of Manchester and rector of St Philip's, Salford, 1892; bishop of Lincoln, 1910; writer on Greek epigraphy; a strong teetotaller.

HICKS, Sir (Edward) Seymour (George) (1871–1949), actor-manager and author; educated at Victoria College, Jersey; spent two years with the *Kendals; wrote and acted in *Bluebell in Fairyland*, 1901; *The Cherry Girl*, 1903; *The Catch of the Season*, 1904; *The Gay Gordons*, 1907; *The Dashing Little Duke*, 1909; built Aldwych Theatre, 1905; opened the Hicks, 1906; had memorable season at the Garrick, 1922; a versatile comedian; knighted, 1935.

HICKS, George Dawes (1862–1941), philosopher; educated at Royal Grammar School, Guildford, Owens College, Manchester, Manchester College, Oxford, and Leipzig; Ph.D., 1896; minister, Unity Church, Islington, 1897–1903; professor of moral philosophy, University College, London, 1904–28; leading authority on Kant and *Berkeley; set out his theory of knowledge in *Critical Realism* (1938); FBA, 1927.

HICKS, George Ernest (1879–1954), trade-unionist; educated at village school; national organizer, 1912, general secretary, 1919, Operative Bricklayers' Society; first general secretary, Amalgamated Union of Building Trade Workers, 1921–40; chairman, Trades Union Congress, 1926–7; Labour MP, East Woolwich, 1931–50; parliamentary secretary, Ministry of Works, 1940–5; CBE, 1946.

HICKS, Henry (1837–1899), geologist; studied at Guy's Hospital; LSA and MRCS, 1862; practised as surgeon at St David's and, from 1871, at Hendon; studied geology with John William *Salter; president of Geologists' Association, 1883–5; secretary of Geological Society, 1890–3, and president, 1896–8; FRS, 1885; published geological papers.

HICKS, Sir Michael (1543–1612), secretary to Lord *Burghley and Sir Robert *Cecil; brother of Baptist *Hicks or Hickes, first Viscount Campden; of Trinity College, Cambridge, and Lincoln's Inn; lent money to *Bacon and Fulke *Greville; knighted, 1604; ancestor of Sir Michael Hicks-Beach, baronet; MP, Truro, 1584, Shaftesbury, 1588, Gatton, 1597, Horsham, 1603.

HICKS, Robert Drew (1850–1929), classical scholar; BA, Trinity College, Cambridge; fellow, 1876–1929; became blind, 1900; among the most learned students of Greek philosophy in his generation; chief work, edition of Aristotle's *De Anima* (1907).

HICKS, William (1621–1660), Puritan; of Wadham College, Oxford; fought in Parliamentarian army; published an exposition of Revelation (1659).

HICKS, William, 'Captain Hicks' (*fl.* 1671), editor and part writer of *Oxford Drollery* (1671), *Grammatical Drollery* (1682), and similar publications.

HICKS, William (1830–1883), general in Egyptian Army ('Hicks Pasha'); saw service as British officer in India and Abyssinia, attaining rank of colonel, 1880; while in command of Egyptian Army for suppression of Mahdi was led into an ambuscade and slain in the 'Battle of Kashgil'.

HICKS, William Joynson-, first Viscount Brentford (1865–1932), statesman; educated at Merchant Taylors' School; admitted solicitor, 1887; Conservative MP, North-West Manchester (1908–10), Brentford (1911–18), Twickenham (1918–29); especially interested in road traffic and aviation; baronet, 1919; in 1923 successively postmaster- and paymaster-general, financial secretary to Treasury with Cabinet seat (PC), and minister of health; home secretary, 1924–9; dealt successfully with General Strike, 1926; passed Shops Act, 1928; president, National Church League, 1921; prominent in defeat of Prayer Book revision, 1927–8; viscount, 1929.

HICKS, William Robert (1808–1868), humorist; superintendent of Bodmin Asylum and auditor of metropolitan asylums; known as 'Yorick of the West'; wrote stories in western dialect, the most famous being 'The Jury'.

HICKS BEACH, Sir Michael Edward, ninth baronet, and first Earl St Aldwyn (1837–1916), statesman; educated at Eton and Christ Church, Oxford; succeeded to baronetcy, 1854; Conservative MP, East Gloucestershire, 1864–85, West Bristol, 1885–1906; parliamentary secretary of Poor Law Board, 1868; undersecretary for Home Department, 1868; in opposition, 1869–74; chief secretary for Ireland, and showed sympathy with reform, 1874–8; entered Cabinet, 1876; colonial secretary, 1878–80; chiefly preoccupied with South African affairs; followed general lines of policy of predecessor, the fourth earl of *Carnarvon; supported Sir Bartle *Frere until Oct. 1878; sympathized with Frere throughout, but after that date British policy in South Africa largely controlled by Disraeli; in opposition, 1880–5; attacked government for treatment of General *Gordon, 1884; chancellor of Exchequer and leader of House of Commons, 1885–6; as leader of opposition, conducted victorious anti-home-rule campaign, 1886; made way for Lord Randolph *Churchill as chancellor of Exchequer and leader of Commons, 1886; Irish secretary, 1886–7; president of Board of Trade, 1888–92; chancellor of Exchequer, 1895–1902; opponent of tariff reform; chairman, Royal Commission on Ecclesiastical Discipline, 1904–6; viscount, 1906; earl, 1915.

HICKSON, William Edward (1803–1870), educational writer; member of Royal Commission on Unemployed Hand-loom Weavers, 1837, presenting a separate report, 1841; studied German, Dutch, and Belgian school systems, and published results in *Westminster Review* (edited by him, 1840–52); wrote also music manuals.

HIEOVER, Harry (1795–1859). See BINDLEY, CHARLES.

HIERON, Samuel (*c.*1572–1617), Puritan divine; of Eton and King's College, Cambridge; incumbent of Modbury, Devonshire; published the *Preacher's Plea* (1604) and other works, collected 1614, reprinted 1624–5 by Robert Hill.

HIFFERNAN, Paul (1719–1777), author; MB, Montpellier; published in Dublin *The Tickler* in opposition to Charles *Lucas (1713–1771), 1750; issued in London *The Tuner*, 1753, and composed farces acted at Drury Lane and Covent Garden; published *Miscellanies in Prose and Verse* (1760) and *Dramatic Genius* (1770), dedicated to *Garrick, who raised a subscription for him.

HIGBERT (or HYGEBRYHT) (*fl.* 787), archbishop of Lichfield in 787, being bishop from 779. Lichfield was a Mercian see created by Pope Hadrian at request of *Offa, but was soon subordinated to Canterbury.

HIGDEN, Henry (*fl.* 1693), author of a comedy, *The Wary Widdow* (1693), and essays on *Satires* x and xiii of Juvenal (1686 and 1687); of the Middle Temple.

HIGDEN, Ranulf (d. 1364), chronicler; Benedictine of St Werburg's, Chester; his *Polychronicon* printed in English version (dated 1387) of John of *Trevisa by *Caxton (1482), Wynkyn de *Worde (1495), and Peter *Treveris (1527); another translation made in the fifteenth century; the original Latin was issued in Rolls Series, with both English versions and continuation.

HIGDEN, William (d. 1715), divine; MA, King's College, Cambridge, 1688; DD, 1710; prebendary of Canterbury, 1713; defended taking the oaths to the Revolution monarchy, 1709 and 1710; wrote also theological treatises.

HIGFORD, William (1581?–1657), Puritan; BA, Corpus Christi College, Oxford, 1599; his *Insti-

tutions, or Advice to his Grandson first printed (1658).

HIGGINS, Bryan (1737?–1820), physician and chemist; graduated at Leiden; established school of chemistry in Soho, 1774; invited to Russia by Tsarina Catherine, c.1785; assisted in improvement of Muscovado sugar and rum in Jamaica, 1797–9; published *Experiments and Observations relating to Acetous Acid, Fixable Air*, etc. (1786) and other works.

HIGGINS, Charles Longuet (1806–1885), benefactor of Turvey, Bedfordshire; of Trinity College, Cambridge (MA 1834), Lincoln's Inn, and St Bartholomew's Hospital.

HIGGINS, Edward John (1864–1947), third general of Salvation Army; helped to establish it in United States; subsequently dealt with its foreign affairs; British commissioner, 1911–18; chief of staff, 1918–29; played leading part in deposition of Bramwell *Booth; succeeded Booth, 1929; retired, 1934.

HIGGINS, Francis (1669–1728), archdeacon of Cashel; MA, Trinity College, Dublin, 1693; prebendary of Christ Church Cathedral, Dublin, 1705; 'the Irish Sacheverell'; prosecuted for seditious preaching, 1707 and 1712; archdeacon of Cashel, 1725–8.

HIGGINS, Francis (1746–1802), Irish adventurer; imprisoned for fraud in connection with his marriage, and became known as the 'Sham Squire'; as owner of *The Freeman's Journal* supported the government; magistrate, 1788–91; exposed by John *Magee; removed from the bench and law list; informed against Lord Edward *Fitzgerald and others.

HIGGINS, Godfrey (1773–1833), writer on the history of religion; of Trinity Hall, Cambridge; Yorkshire magistrate and reformer; wrote, besides political and social pamphlets, *Anacalypsis . . . Inquiry into the Origin of Languages, Nations, and Religions*, published (1836, reprinted 1878), and other works.

HIGGINS, John (*fl.* 1570–1602), poet and compiler; revised *Huloet's Dictionarie* (1572); published also *Flowers* (selections from Terence by himself and Nicholas *Udall, 1575), and supplements to the *Mirrour for Magistrates*, containing forty new poems (some of which were printed in 1574, and others in 1587), and other works.

HIGGINS, Sir John Frederick Andrews (1875–1948), air marshal; educated at Charterhouse and Woolwich; commissioned in Royal Artillery, 1895; seconded to Royal Flying Corps, 1912; commanded successively squadron, wing, and brigade in France, 1914–18; AOC, Iraq, 1924–6; air member, supply and research, Air Council, 1926–30; KBE, 1925; KCB, 1928; air marshal, 1929; AOC-in-C, India, 1939–40.

HIGGINS, Matthew James (1810–1868), journalist; of Eton and University College, Oxford; known as 'Jacob Omnium' from title of first published article (1845); twice visited British Guiana, where he owned an estate; active on behalf of sufferers from Irish famine, 1847; contributed to the Peelite *Morning Chronicle*, also to *The Times*, *Pall Mall Gazette*, and *Cornhill Magazine* (under Thackeray), exposing many abuses; his *Essays on Social Subjects* edited, 1875.

HIGGINS, William (d. 1825), chemist; nephew of Bryan *Higgins; librarian to Royal Dublin Society, 1795; in *Comparative View of Phlogistic and Antiphlogistic Theories* (1789) enunciated law of multiple proportions; claimed discovery of atomic theory against *Dalton in *Experiments and Observations* (1814).

HIGGINSON, Edward (1807–1880), Unitarian divine; minister successively at Hull (1828–46), Wakefield (1846–58), and Swansea (1858–76); president of the Royal Institute of South Wales, 1877–9; published theological works.

HIGGINSON, Francis (c.1586–1630), Puritan divine; of Jesus and St John's colleges, Cambridge; MA, 1613; deprived of preachership of St Nicholas, Leicester, for nonconformity, 1627; when threatened with prosecution by high commission became assistant minister at Salem, Massachusetts, 1629; published accounts of his voyage and of Massachusetts.

HIGGINSON, Francis (1617–1670), author of *Relation of Irreligion of Northern Quakers* (1653); son of Francis *Higginson (c.1586–1630); studied at Leiden; vicar of Kirkby Stephen.

HIGGINSON, John (1616–1708), minister at Saybrook, Guilford (USA), and Salem, where he died; brother of Francis *Higginson (1617–1670).

HIGGONS, Bevil (1670–1735), historian and poet; son of Sir Thomas *Higgons; of St John's College, Oxford, and Trinity Hall, Cambridge; student of Middle Temple; followed his family (Jacobites) into exile; arrested on charge of conspiracy against William III, 1696; published verses addressed to *Dryden and *Congreve, and a tragedy (acted 1702); his *Historical Works* (1736), consisted of *Short View of the English History* (1723) and a criticism of *Burnet's *Own Time* (1725).

HIGGONS, Theophilus (1578?–1659), divine; MA, Christ Church, Oxford, 1600; chaplain to bishop *Ravis and lecturer of St Dunstan's, Fleet Street; converted to Romanism; retired to

France; reconverted and given rectory of Hunton, Kent; published theological works.

HIGGONS, Sir Thomas (1624–1691), diplomat and author; of St Alban Hall, Oxford; MP, Malmesbury, 1661, St Germans, 1685; knighted, 1663; envoy-extraordinary to Saxony, 1669, to Vienna, 1673–9; published *History of Isuf Bassa* (1684); translated Busenello's *Prospective of the Naval Triumph of the Venetians over the Turk* (1658).

HIGGS, Griffin (or Griffith) (1589–1659), dean of Lichfield; BA, St John's College, Oxford, 1610; fellow of Merton, 1611; MA, 1615; senior proctor, 1622–3; chaplain to *Elizabeth, queen of Bohemia, 1627–38; DD, Leiden, 1630; dean of Lichfield, 1638; left bequests to South Stoke, the Bodleian, and Merton and St John's colleges; his *Account of the Christmas Prince exhibited in the University of Oxford in 1607*, printed by Bliss (1816).

HIGHAM, John (*fl.* 1639). See HEIGHAM.

HIGHAM, Thomas (1795–1844), line-engraver.

HIGHMORE, Anthony (1719–1799), draughtsman, son of Joseph *Highmore.

HIGHMORE, Anthony (1758–1829), legal writer; son of Anthony *Highmore (1719–1799); friend of Granville *Sharp; published *Digest of the Doctrine of Bail* (1783), *Succinct View of History of Mortmain* (1787), *Treatise on the Law of Idiotcy and Lunacy* (1807), and other works.

HIGHMORE, Joseph (1692–1780), painter; nephew of Thomas *Highmore; studied under *Kneller; executed portrait-drawings for *Installation of Knights of the Bath*, 1725; painted portraits of the prince and princess of Wales, the duke of *Cumberland, the Gunnings, Samuel *Richardson, General *Wolfe, and others, also conversation pieces and subject-pictures; published pamphlets on perspective.

HIGHMORE, Nathaniel (1613–1685), physician; MD, Trinity College, Oxford, 1642; practised at Sherborne, Dorset; endowed exhibition to Oxford from Sherborne School; friend of *Harvey; published *History of Generation* (1651) and other works; the cavity in the superior maxillary bone named after him.

HIGHMORE, Thomas (d. 1720), serjeant-painter to William III; cousin of Nathaniel *Highmore.

HIGHTON, Henry (1816–1874), author; under *Arnold at Rugby; MA, The Queen's College, Oxford, 1840, Michel fellow, 1841; principal of Cheltenham, 1859–62; published revised translation of the New Testament (1862), translation

of Victor Hugo's poems, and theological pamphlets; silver medallist, Society of Arts, for *Telegraphy without Insulation* (1872); patented artificial stone for building.

HIGINBOTHAM, George (1826–1892), chief justice of Victoria; BA, Trinity College, Dublin, 1848; MA, 1853; barrister, Lincoln's Inn, 1853; went to Victoria, and was admitted to the local bar, 1854; editor of the *Argus*, 1856–9; Independent Liberal member for Brighton in legislative assembly, 1861 and 1863; attorney-general, 1863–8; chairman of Education Commission, 1866; vice-president of Board of Works, 1868–9; member for East Bourke borough, 1874–6; puisne judge of Supreme Court of Victoria, 1880; chief justice, 1886.

HIGSON, John (1825–1871), topographer; compiled *Gorton Historical Recorder* (1852) and history of Droylsden.

HILARY (*fl.* 1125), Latin poet; supposed to have been an Englishman; disciple of Abelard and canon of Ronceray; his poems printed by M Champollion-Figeac (1838); extracts in Wright's *Biographia Britannica Literaria*.

HILARY (d. 1169), bishop of Chichester, 1147; elected archbishop of York, 1147, but not confirmed by the pope; reconciled King Stephen and Archbishop *Theobald, 1148; failed to enforce jurisdiction over the abbot of Battle, 1157; urged *Becket to accept the 'ancient customs'; included in embassy to the pope against Becket; granted absolution to those excommunicated by Becket.

HILBERY, Sir (George) Malcolm (1883–1965), judge; educated at University College School, London; called to bar (Gray's Inn), 1907; served in RNVR during 1914–18 war; bencher, Gray's Inn, 1927; recorder of Margate, 1927; KC, 1928; commissioner of assize, south-eastern circuit, 1935; judge, King's Bench division; knighted, 1935; chairman, Berkshire quarter-sessions, 1946–63; senior puisne judge, Queen's Bench division; PC, 1959–62; treasurer, Gray's Inn, 1941; collector of Dutch masters; published *Duty and Art in Advocacy* (1946); chairman, board of governors, Royal Masonic Hospital; prominent member of Thames Yacht Club.

HILDA (or, more properly, HILD), Saint (614–680), abbess of Whitby; baptized by *Paulinus at York, 627; abbess of Hartlepool, 649; Ælflæd, daughter of *Oswy of Northumbria, entrusted to her care, 655; founded monastery of Whitby (657), and ruled it with great wisdom; adopted Roman rule after Council of Whitby, 664.

HILDERSAM (or HILDERSHAM), Arthur (1563–1632), Puritan divine; entered at Christ's

College, Cambridge, 1576; disinherited for refusing to become a Romanist; MA, 1584; fellow of Trinity Hall, 1584; vicar of Ashby-de-la-Zouch, 1593; an active manager of 'millenary petition', 1604; silenced by his bishop, 1605, but licensed in diocese of Lichfield; restored, 1609, but suspended by high commission, 1613, and imprisoned for refusing the *ex officio* oath, 1615; sentenced to imprisonment and fine as schismatic, 1616; returned to Ashby, 1625, again suspended, 1630, but restored next year; published *Treatise on Ministry of the Church of England* (1595); his *CLII Lectures on Psalm LI* translated into Hungarian (1672).

HILDERSAM (or HILDERSHAM), Samuel (1594?–1674), divine; son of Arthur *Hildersam; fellow of Emmanuel College, Cambridge; BA and BD; member of Westminster Assembly; ejected from West Felton, Shropshire, 1662.

HILDESLEY, John (d. 1538). See HILSEY.

HILDESLEY, Mark (1698–1772), bishop of Sodor and Man; of Charterhouse and Trinity College, Cambridge; fellow, 1723; MA, 1724; rector of Holwell, Bedfordshire, 1735–67; prebendary of Lincoln, 1754; chaplain to Henry *Saint-John, Lord Bolingbroke, and John, Viscount Saint-John; DD, Lambeth, 1755; bishop of Sodor and Man, 1755–72; master of Christ's Hospital, Sherburn, Durham, 1767; promoted Manx translations of the Bible and the Book of Common Prayer.

HILDEYARD, Thomas (1690–1746), Jesuit; rector of the 'college' of St Francis Xavier, 1743; made astronomical clocks.

HILDILID, Saint (*fl.* 700), abbess of Barking.

HILDITCH, Sir Edward (1805–1876), inspector-general of hospitals; on West Indian Station, 1830–55; at Plymouth, 1855, Greenwich, 1861; inspector-general, 1854–65; first honorary physician to Queen Victoria, 1859; knighted, 1865.

HILDITCH, Thomas Percy (1886–1965), chemist; educated at Owen's School, North Islington, and University College, London; first class, B.Sc., 1907; associate of Institute of Chemistry, 1908; fellow, 1911; undertook research work in London, Jena, and Geneva, 1907–11; D.Sc. (London), 1911; technical research chemist, Joseph Crosfield & Sons, soap manufacturers, 1911–26; first Campbell Brown professor of industrial chemistry, Liverpool, 1926–51; carried out important research on natural fats; published *The Chemical Constitution of Natural Fats* (four editions, 1940–64); FRS, 1942; CBE, 1952.

HILDROP, John (d. 1756), divine; MA, St John's College, Oxford, 1705; DD, 1743; master

of Free Grammar School, Marlborough, 1703–33; rector of Maulden, Bedfordshire, and, 1734, of Wath-juxta-Ripon; friend of Zachary *Grey. His *Miscellaneous Works* (1754) include satires against the deists.

HILDYARD, James (1809–1887), classical scholar; educated at Shrewsbury; Tancred student, afterwards fellow of Christ's College, Cambridge; second classic and chancellor's medallist, 1833; MA, 1836; BD, 1846; senior proctor, 1843; preacher at Whitehall, 1843–4; incumbent of Ingoldsby, 1846–87; edited plays of Plautus; issued pamphlets advocating revision of liturgy and reform of university education.

HILES, Henry (1828–1904), musical composer; held many posts as organist; Mus.Bac., Oxford, 1862; Mus.Doc., 1867; lecturer on harmony and composition at Owens College, Manchester, 1876; professor at Royal Manchester College of Music; composed organ music, glees, cantatas, oratorios, anthems; published educational works on music; edited *Wesley Tune Book*.

HILL, Aaron (1685–1750), dramatist; educated at Westminster; travelled in the East; obtained patent for extracting oil from beechmast, 1713; proposed colonization of Georgia, 1718; addressed complimentary poems to Peterborough and Peter the Great; satirized by *Pope; attacked Pope in *Progress of Wit* (1730) and other publications, but afterwards corresponded amicably with him; corresponded with *Richardson; produced plays and operas, including words of *Handel's *Rinaldo* (1711), *Athelwold* (1732), *Zara, Merope*, and other translations from Voltaire; joint author with William *Bond (d. 1735) of the *Plaindealer* (1724).

HILL, Abigail (d. 1734). See MASHAM, ABIGAIL, Lady.

HILL, Abraham (1635–1721), treasurer of Royal Society, 1663–5 and 1679–1700; commissioner of trade, 1689; comptroller to Archbishop *Tillotson, 1691; published life of *Barrow, 1683; *Pepys and *Evelyn among his correspondents.

HILL, Adam (d. 1595), divine; fellow of Balliol College, Oxford, 1568–73; MA, 1572; DD, 1591; prebendary of Salisbury, 1586.

HILL (or HYLL), Alban (d. 1559), physician; graduated at Bologna; FRCP, 1552; censor, 1555–8.

HILL, Alexander (1785–1867), professor of divinity at Glasgow; son of George *Hill (1750–1819); graduated at St Andrews, 1804; DD, 1828; minister of Dailly, 1816; divinity professor, 1840–62; moderator of general assembly, 1845; published tracts.

HILL, Alexander Staveley (1825–1905), barrister and politician; BA, Exeter College, Oxford, 1852; DCL, 1855; fellow, 1854–64; called to bar, 1851; QC, 1868; treasurer of Inner Temple, 1886; acquired large parliamentary and probate practice; recorder of Banbury, 1866–1903; Conservative MP for Coventry and Staffordshire, 1868–1900; PC, 1892; early advocate of tariff reform; formed large cattle ranch in Canada, 1871; hon. LL D, Toronto, 1892; wrote *Practice of the Court of Probate* (1859).

HILL, Alsager Hay (1839–1906), social reformer; LL B, Trinity Hall, Cambridge, 1862; called to bar, 1864; urged more scientific classification of paupers and national system of labour registration for unemployed, 1867–8; established labour exchange in London (1871) and edited *Labour News*, organ of communication between masters and men seeking work; vice-president of National Sunday League, 1876–90; published *Rhymes with Good Reason* (1870–1) and other verse.

HILL, Archibald Vivian (1886–1977), physiologist; educated at Blundell's School and Trinity College, Cambridge, of which he was a scholar; third wrangler, mathematical tripos, 1907; first class, part ii, natural sciences tripos (physiology), 1909; research fellow, Trinity College, 1910–16; fellow, King's College, 1916–22; studied drug action in muscle tissue and other problems of muscle reactions; promoted 'biophysics'; with Hermann Helmholtz in Germany regarded as one of founding fathers of this science; during 1914–18 served in army doing research on anti-aircraft gunnery; OBE, 1918; FRS, 1918; returned to research on muscle at Cambridge, 1919; professor of physiology, Manchester, 1920–3; awarded Nobel Prize together with German physiologist, Otto Meyerhof, for research on muscular movement, 1922; succeeded E. H. *Starling as professor of physiology, University College, London, 1923; Foulerton research professor, Royal Society, 1926–51; continued research until 1966; published many important books including *Adventures in Biophysics* (1931), *Chemical Wave Transmission in Nerve* (1932), *Trails and Trials in Physiology* (1965), and *The Ethical Dilemma of Science* (1960); biological secretary, Royal Society, 1935–45, foreign secretary, 1945–6; secretary-general, International Council of Scientific Unions, 1952–6; Independent MP for Cambridge University, 1940–5; visited India to advise Indian government on post-war reconstruction, 1943–4; member of Tizard Committee, 1935.

HILL, Arthur (1601?–1663), Parliamentarian colonel; formed manor of Hillsborough from grants in Co. Down; MP, Cos. Down, Antrim, and Armagh, 1654; constable and Irish privy councillor, 1660.

HILL, Sir Arthur William (1875–1941), botanist; educated at Marlborough and King's College, Cambridge; first classes, natural sciences tripos, 1897–8; fellow, 1901; university demonstrator in botany, 1899; lecturer, 1904; assistant director, Royal Botanic Gardens, Kew, 1907; director, 1922–41; edited publications and extended activities and amenities of the Gardens; FRS, 1920; KCMG, 1931.

HILL, David Octavius (1802–1870), landscape and portrait painter; secretary to Scottish Society of Arts, 1830–8, and after its incorporation in the Royal Scottish Academy; his *Land of Burns* series of pictures issued, 1841; painted many other Scottish landscapes, and *Signing the Deed of Demission*, 1865; first artist to apply photography to portraiture; a commissioner of Scottish board of manufactures, 1850; originated Edinburgh Art Union.

HILL, Sir Dudley St Leger (1790–1851), major-general; served with 95th (Rifle Brigade) at Montevideo and Buenos Aires, 1807, being captured wounded; also in the Peninsula, 1808–10; held Portuguese commands at Busaco, 1810, and succeeding battles, being seven times wounded; continued in Portuguese service after the peace; lieutenant-governor of St Lucia, 1834–8; major-general, 1841; KCB, 1848; died at Umballa, holding a Bengal command.

HILL, Sir (Edward) Maurice (1862–1934), judge; son of G. B. N. *Hill; educated at Haileybury and Balliol College, Oxford; first class, Lit. Hum., 1884; called to bar (Inner Temple), 1888; bencher, 1917; KC, 1910; judge of Probate, Divorce, and Admiralty division (1917–30) trying mainly the many Admiralty cases resulting from war; his memorandum on freedom of seas the basis of Article 297 of Treaty of Versailles and embodied in Maritime Ports Convention, 1923.

HILL, Edwin (1793–1876), inventor and author; brother of Sir Rowland *Hill (1795–1879); supervisor of stamps at Somerset House, 1840–72; with Mr *De la Rue invented machine for folding envelopes, exhibited 1851; published *Principles of Currency* (1856).

HILL, Frank Harrison (1830–1910), journalist; studied for Unitarian ministry at Manchester under Dr James *Martineau, 1846–51; adopted profession of journalism; editor of *Northern Whig*, Belfast, 1861–5; alone of journalists in Ireland supported North in American war; friend of Harriet *Martineau, *Browning, and Crabb *Robinson; assistant editor of *Daily News*, 1865; editor, 1869–86; made paper an influential party organ; wrote with keen insight and caustic pen; retired owing to opposition to Gladstone's home-rule policy, 1886; leader-writer of the *World*, 1886–1906; published *Political Portraits* (1873) and *Life of George Canning* (1881).

HILL, George (1716–1808), king's serjeant, 1772 ('Serjeant Labyrinth'); of Lincoln's Inn.

HILL, George (1750–1819), principal of St Mary's College, St Andrews; graduated from St Andrews, 1764; joint professor of Greek, 1772–88; of divinity, 1788; DD, 1787; principal of St Mary's College, 1791–1819; dean of Chapel Royal, 1799; moderator of general assembly, 1789; his *Lectures on Divinity* published (1821).

HILL, George Birkbeck Norman (1835–1903), editor of *Boswell's *Life of Johnson*; grandson of Thomas Wright *Hill; BA, Pembroke College, Oxford, 1858; joined at the university Old Mortality Club, and came to know *Burne-Jones and *Rossetti; DCL, 1871; private schoolmaster, 1858–75; elaborately edited Boswell's *Life of Johnson* (6 vols., 1887), *Johnson's Letters* (2 vols., 1892), *Johnsonian Miscellanies* (2 vols., 1897), and *Johnson's Lives of the English Poets* (3 vols., 1905); described a tour in Scotland as *Footsteps of Samuel Johnson*, 1889; published also life of his uncle, Sir Rowland *Hill (2 vols., 1880), and *Letters of Rossetti to William Allingham* (1897); his *Letters* published, 1903 and 1906.

HILL, Sir George Francis (1867–1948), numismatist; educated at University College School, University College, London, and Merton College, Oxford; first class, Lit. Hum., 1891; entered department of coins and medals, British Museum, 1893; keeper, 1912; director and principal librarian of museum, 1931–6; launched successful campaign for purchase of *Codex Sinaiticus*; publications include *Corpus of Italian Medals before Cellini* (2 vols., 1930); FBA, 1917; KCB, 1933.

HILL, Sir Hugh (1802–1871), judge of the Queen's Bench; BA, Dublin, 1821; barrister, Middle Temple, 1841, after being a successful special pleader; QC, 1851; judge of Queen's Bench, 1858–61.

HILL, James (d. 1728?), antiquary; FSA, 1718; FRS, 1719; corresponded with William *Stukeley; made collections for history of Herefordshire.

HILL, James (d. 1817?), actor and vocalist; appeared at Bath and Covent Garden, 1796–1806; said to have died in Jamaica.

HILL, James John (1811–1882), painter; exhibited with Society of British Artists; best known by his rustic figure-pictures.

HILL, John? (d. 1697?), lieutenant-colonel and governor of Inverlochy (Fort William) at time of Glencoe massacre (1692), carried out by his second-in-command; both tried for murder and acquitted.

HILL, John (d. 1735), major-general; brother of Abigail, Lady *Masham; made page to Queen Anne and (1703) officer in army through *Marlborough influence; commanded brigade at Almanza, 1707; wounded at Mons, 1709; brigadier-general in command of Quebec expedition, 1711; major-general, 1712; afterwards in charge of Dunkirk.

HILL, John, calling himself Sir John (1714–1775), author; knight of Swedish order of Vasa; flourished as an apothecary and quack doctor in James Street, Covent Garden; patronized by *Bute; conducted the *British Magazine*, 1746–50; contributed to *London Advertiser* as 'The Inspector', 1751–3; attacked Royal Society, *Fielding, Christopher *Smart (who replied with the *Hilliad*), and *Garrick, who composed on him a celebrated epigram; published *The Vegetable System* (1759–75), for which he obtained his Swedish order, and translations and compilations dealing with medicine, botany, and horticulture, *Naval History of Britain* (1756), and other works; authorship of Mrs *Glasse's *Art of Cookery* (1747) erroneously ascribed to him.

HILL, Sir (John) Denis (Nelson) (1913–1982), psychiatrist; educated at Shrewsbury School and St Thomas's Hospital, London; MB, BS (Lond.), 1936; became expert in electroencephalography (EEG); assistant in department of psychiatry, St Thomas's, 1938–44; during 1939–45 war worked at Emergency Hospital, Belmont; MRCP and DPM, 1940; lecturer at Institute of Psychiatry, Maudsley Hospital, 1948–60, and at King's College Hospital, London, 1947–60; FRCP, 1949; with Geoffrey Parr published first comprehensive textbook on EEG (1950); professor of psychiatry, Institute of Psychiatry, London University, 1966–79; FRCPsych., 1971; member of number of important government committees dealing with prison medical services and mentally abnormal offenders; member, Medical Research Council, 1956–60, and General Medical Council, 1961–82; treasurer, GMC; knighted, 1966; lecturer in number of important named lectures on psychiatry such as the Ernest Jones lecture of the Institute of Psychoanalysis, 1970.

HILL, John Harwood (1809–1886), antiquary; FSA, 1871; BA, Peterhouse, Cambridge, 1834; librarian to Lord *Cardigan at Deene; rector of Cranoe, 1837, and vicar of Welham, 1841; published *History of Market Harborough* (1875).

HILL, Joseph (1625–1707), Nonconformist divine and lexicographer; fellow of Magdalene College, Cambridge; MA, 1651; his name removed for nonconformity, 1662; pastor of Scottish Church at Middelburg, Holland, 1667–73, where he published pamphlet advocating English alliance; English Presbyterian minister of Haringvliet, Rotterdam, 1678–1707; edited and enlarged Schrevelius's Greek–Latin lexicon (1663).

HILL, Joseph (1667–1729), Presbyterian minister at Rotterdam, 1699–1718, and Haberdashers' Hall, London, 1718–29.

HILL, Joseph Sidney (1851–1894), missionary bishop; studied at Church Missionary Society's College, Islington; deacon, 1876; joined mission at Lagos, 1876; appointed to New Zealand mission, 1878; priest, 1879; bishop in Western Equatorial Africa, 1893; died at Lagos.

HILL, Sir **Leonard Erskine** (1866–1952), physiologist; son of G. B. N. *Hill and brother of Sir Maurice *Hill; educated at Haileybury; qualified in medicine from University College Hospital, 1889; lecturer in physiology, London Hospital, 1895; professor, 1912–14; head, department of applied physiology, National Institute for Medical Research, 1914–30; researches covered the physiology of the circulatory and respiratory systems, including decompression of divers, measurement of efficiency of ventilation, significance of solar radiation for health; published *The Physiology and Pathology of the Cerebral Circulation* (1896); FRS, 1900; knighted, 1930; hon. LL D, Aberdeen; fellow, University College, London.

HILL, Leonard Raven- (1867–1942), artist, illustrator, and cartoonist. See RAVEN-HILL.

HILL, Matthew Davenport (1792–1872), reformer of criminal law; eldest son of Thomas Wright *Hill; barrister, Lincoln's Inn, 1819; defended John *Cartwright (1740–1824), the Nottingham rioters (1831), the Canadian prisoners (1839), and Rebecca rioters (1843); counsel for Daniel *O'Connell, 1844, and for Baron de Bode; took part in founding Society for the Diffusion of Useful Knowledge, 1826; as MP for Hull, 1832–5, had charge of colonization of South Australia bill (1834) and caused scene between Lord *Althorp and Richard Lalor *Sheil; QC, 1834; first recorder of Birmingham, 1839; advocated, in charges (collected in *Suggestions for Repression of Crime*, 1857), changes in treatment of criminals adopted in Penal Servitude Acts of 1853 and 1864; supported establishment of reformatories and industrial schools; commissioner of bankrupts (Bristol district), 1851–69.

HILL, Nicholas (1570?–1610), philosopher; of Merchant Taylors' School and St John's College, Oxford; fellow, 1592; BA, 1592; secretary to Edward de *Vere, earl of Oxford; published *Philosophia Epicurea, Democritiana, Theophrastica* (1601); died abroad.

HILL, (Norman) Graham (1929–1975), racing motorist; educated at a technical college, Hendon; left at 16 to be apprentice with Smiths, instrument makers; served in Royal Navy, 1950–2; started motor-racing as result of chance meeting with A. Colin B. *Chapman of Lotus Car Co.; joined Lotus as mechanic and became driver in 1957; left Lotus for BRM, 1960; won first Grand Prix in Holland and first in Germany and Italy, 1962; beat his great rival James ('Jim') *Clark in South Africa and became world champion, the first British driver to do so in an all-British car, 1962; rejoined Lotus in 1967 after four years of disappointments; Jim Clark killed in race at Hockenheim, and Hill became world champion for second time, 1968; won last Grand Prix at Monaco, 1969; shattered both legs in accident caused by puncture; continued to race during 1970–5, with moderate success; retired from racing, 1975; most experienced driver in Grand Prix history; OBE, 1968; freeman of City of London, 1974; published (with Neil Ewart), *Graham* (1976), and *Life at the Limit* (1969); killed in flying accident; £112,000 raised in his memory for National Orthopaedic Hospital at Stanmore, Middlesex.

HILL, Octavia (1838–1912), philanthropist; granddaughter of Dr Thomas Southwood *Smith; early influenced by Christian socialists, especially F. D. *Maurice; helped in artistic training by John *Ruskin; opened school with sisters in Marylebone; impressed by urgency of housing problem in which she interested Ruskin, 1864; first houses for improvement purchased through him, 1865; undertaking placed on business footing; through fund raised by friends, enabled to devote herself to housing reform, 1874; appointed manager of Southwark property by ecclesiastical commissioners, 1884; owed much to co-operation of sisters and workers trained by her; supporter of Charity Organization, Kyrle, and Commons Preservation societies; co-founder of National Trust; held aloof from political measures for social reform.

HILL, Pascoe Grenfell (1804–1882), author; BA, Trinity College, Dublin, 1836; chaplain in navy, 1836–45; to Westminster Hospital, 1852–7; rector of St Edmund the King and Martyr, 1863; published *Life of Napoleon* (1869) and other works.

HILL, Richard (1655–1727), diplomat; educated at Shrewsbury and St John's College, Cambridge, fellow and benefactor; BA, 1678–9; envoy-extraordinary to elector of Bavaria, 1696; ambassador at The Hague and a lord of the Treasury, 1699; member of Admiralty Council, 1702; as envoy to Savoy, 1703–6, gained adhesion of the duke to Grand Alliance and toleration of Vaudois (correspondence published 1845); fellow of Eton, 1714; FRS and hon. DCL of Oxford.

HILL, Sir Richard, second baronet (1732–1808), controversialist; grandnephew of Richard *Hill; educated at Westminster; MA, Magdalen College, Oxford, 1754; attacked university for expelling Methodist undergraduates, 1768; carried on controversies with *Wesley, Charles *Daubeny, and others; MP, Shropshire, 1780–1806; succeeded as baronet, 1783.

HILL (or HULL), Robert (d. 1425), judge; king's serjeant, 1399; judge of common pleas, 1408; chief justice of Isle of Ely, 1422.

HILL, Robert (d. 1623), divine; MA, Christ's College, Cambridge, 1588; fellow of St John's College, 1589; perpetual curate of St Andrew, Norwich, 1591–1602; rector of St Margaret Moyses, Friday Street, London, 1607; of St Bartholomew Exchange, London, 1613–23; published devotional works.

HILL, Robert (1699–1777), learned tailor, compared by Joseph *Spence with Magliabechi; acquired Greek and Hebrew, and wrote theological treatises.

HILL, Robert Gardiner (1811–1878), surgeon; brother of John Harwood *Hill; MRCS, 1834; as house-surgeon to Lincoln lunatic asylum (1835–40) dispensed with the restraint system; joint-proprietor of Eastgate House asylum, 1840–63; mayor of Lincoln, 1852; proprietor of Earl's Court House, Old Brompton, 1863–78; published works on treatment of lunatics.

HILL, Sir Roderic Maxwell (1894–1954), air chief marshal; nephew of Sir George Francis *Hill; educated at Bradfield College and University College, London; joined Royal Flying Corps, 1916; became highly skilled pilot; MC; in charge of experimental flying, Farnborough, 1917–23; served at Hinaidi (1924–6), Cairo (1926–7), Oxford (1930–2); deputy director, repair and maintenance, Air Ministry, 1932–6; commanded in Palestine and Trans-Jordan, 1936–8; director, technical development, Air Ministry, 1938–40; air vice-marshal, 1939; air marshal, 1940; director-general, research and development, Ministry of Aircraft Production, 1940–1; controller, technical services, British Air Commission, United States, 1941–2; commandant, RAF Staff College, 1942–3; air marshal commanding Air Defence of Great Britain, 1943–4, Fighter Command, 1944–5; planned defence against flying bombs and made courageous decision to redeploy forces more effectively after attack had begun, 1944; KCB, 1944; Air Council member for training, 1945–6, for technical services, 1947–8; air chief marshal, 1947; rector, Imperial College of Science and Technology, 1948–54.

HILL, Roger (1605–1667), judge; barrister, Inner Temple, 1632; bencher, 1649; junior counsel against *Laud, 1644; MP, 1640, for Taunton in the Short, and Bridport in the Long Parliament; assistant to Commonwealth attorney-general; judge of assize, 1656; baron of Exchequer, 1657; transferred to upper bench, 1660.

HILL, Rosamond Davenport- (1825–1902), educational administrator; daughter of Matthew Davenport *Hill; settled with parents at Bristol, 1851; assisted her father and Mary *Carpenter; visited Mettray Reformatory, 1855; founded on Mettray principles Girls' Industrial School at Bristol, 1866; visited prisons in Australia, 1872–4; published *What We Saw in Australia* (1874); member of London School Board, 1879–97; visited schools in United States and Canada, 1888; resisted provision of free meals in London schools; wrote *Elementary Education in England* (1893).

HILL, Sir Rowland (1492?–1561), lord mayor of London; warden of Mercers' Company, 1536, and four times master; sheriff, 1541; knighted; alderman, Castle Baynard ward, 1542, and Walbrook, 1545; first Protestant lord mayor, 1549–50; a commissioner against heretics, 1557; built Hodnet and Stoke churches, Shropshire; endowed school at Drayton and exhibitions to universities.

HILL, Rowland (1744–1833), preacher; brother of Sir Richard *Hill; educated at Shrewsbury, Eton, and St John's College, Cambridge; BA, 1769; was refused priest's orders owing to his itinerant preaching; from 1783 preached in Surrey Chapel, London, where he had Sunday schools; published hymns, *Village Dialogues* (1810), and a tract in favour of vaccination.

HILL, Rowland, first Viscount Hill (1772–1842), general; nephew of Rowland *Hill (1744–1833); studied at Strasburg Military School while subaltern; aide-de-camp at Toulon, 1793; lieutenant-colonel, 90th Foot (*Graham's Regiment), 1794; brevet-colonel, 1800; commanded regiment in Egypt, 1801 (wounded at Aboukir), and in Ireland, establishing regimental school and sergeants' mess; major-general, 1805; commanded brigades in Hanover, and at Roliça and

Corunna; led second division at Talavera, 1809; invalided after campaign of 1810; resumed command, May 1811, and defeated Gerard at Merida (Oct. 1811); lieutenant-general and KB, 1812; stormed Almaraz (May); commanded right at Vittoria, 1813; blockaded Pampeluna; distinguished at Nivelle and the Nive, 1813; won victories of Bayonne (13 Dec. 1813) and Toulouse (10, 11 Apr. 1814); created Baron Hill and given pension of £2,000, and the freedom of the City of London, 1814; sent on mission to prince of Orange, 1815; given command of army corps in Belgium; headed *Adam's brigade at Waterloo before the last charge, 1815; second-in-command of army of occupation in France, 1815–18; general, 1825; commander-in-chief in England, 1828–42; created viscount, 1842.

HILL, Sir **Rowland** (1795–1879), inventor of penny postage; son of Thomas Wright *Hill; educated in his father's school at Hill Top, Birmingham, where he afterwards taught; established school on his own plan and self-disciplined at Hazelwood (afterwards removed to Bruce Castle, Tottenham), as described in the *Public Education* (1822) of his brother, Matthew Davenport *Hill; invented rotatory printing-press and other machines; secretary to South Australian Commission, 1835; submitted to Lord Melbourne his *Post Office Reform: its Importance and Practicability* (1837); described his invention of adhesive stamp before commission, 1837; obtained parliamentary committee which recommended twopenny postage, 1838; secured adoption of penny postage in budget of 1839; was given appointment in the Post Office; his scheme of penny postage established, 1840; dismissed from Post Office, 1842; as chairman of Brighton Railway, 1843–6, introduced express and excursion trains; received public testimonial, 1846; secretary to postmaster-general, 1846; as secretary to the Post Office, 1854–64, established promotion by merit; FRS, 1857; KCB, 1860; hon. DCL of Oxford, 1864; received freedom of the City of London, 1879; as member of Railway Commission published separate report (1867) recommending state purchase and working by companies holding leases; buried in Westminster Abbey.

HILL, Rowley (1836–1887), bishop of Sodor and Man; of Christ's Hospital and Trinity College, Cambridge; MA, 1863; DD, 1877; vicar of St Michael's, Chester Square, London, 1871, of Sheffield, 1873; bishop of Sodor and Man, 1877–87.

HILL, Samuel (1648–1716), archdeacon of Wells; BA, St Mary Hall, Oxford, 1666; rector of Kilmington, 1687; archdeacon of Wells,

1705–16; published controversial works against Bishop *Burnet and the nonjurors.

HILL, Sir **Stephen John** (1809–1891), colonial governor; entered army, 1823; captain, 1842; served in West Africa; brevet-major, 1849; governor and commander-in-chief of Gold Coast, 1851; lieutenant-governor of Sierra Leone, 1854, and governor-in-chief, 1860–2; governor-in-chief of Leeward and Caribbee islands, 1863–9, and of Newfoundland, 1869–76; colonel of West India Regiment, 1854; KCMG, 1874.

HILL (alias **BUCKLAND), Thomas** (1564–1644), Benedictine; ordained at Rome, 1594, where he opposed the Jesuits; sent on English mission, 1597; condemned to death, 1612; reprieved; banished, 1613; published *A Quartron of Reasons of Catholike Religion* (1600); died at St Gregory's Monastery, Douai.

HILL, Thomas (*fl.* 1590), compiler and translator of horticultural and astrological works.

HILL, Thomas (d. 1653), master of Trinity College, Cambridge; scholar and fellow of Emmanuel College, Cambridge; MA, 1626; BD, 1633; original member of Westminster Assembly of Divines, 1643; master of Trinity College, Cambridge, 1645–53; vice-chancellor of Cambridge, 1645–7; Calvinist.

HILL, Thomas (1628?–1677?), Nonconformist minister; BA, Corpus Christi College, Cambridge; Presbyterian pastor at Orton, Leicestershire, 1653–60; perpetual curate of Shuttington, 1660–5.

HILL, Thomas (d. 1720), Nonconformist tutor; son of Thomas Hill (1628?–1677?).

HILL, Thomas (1661–1734), portrait painter.

HILL, Thomas (1760–1840), book-collector; patron of *Bloomfield and Kirke White; entertained literary and theatrical celebrities at Sydenham; the 'Hull' of *Hook's *Gilbert Gurney;* his collection, the basis of *Longmans' *Bibliotheca Anglo-Poetica* (1815).

HILL, Thomas (1808–1865), topographer; MA, Clare Hall, Cambridge, 1832; incumbent of Holy Trinity, Queenhithe, 1850–65; author of *History of Nunnery of St. Clare and Parish of Holy Trinity* (1851) and *The Harmony of the Greek and Latin Languages* (1841).

HILL, Thomas Ford (d. 1795), antiquary; FSA, 1792; travelled on continent; collected *Ancient Erse Songs* (1784); died at Ariano.

HILL, Sir **Thomas Noel** (1784–1832), colonel; brother of Rowland, Viscount *Hill; commanded Portuguese Regiment, 1810–14; lieutenant-colonel, 1st Foot Guards, 1814; assistant adjutant-general in Waterloo campaign; deputy adjutant-general in Canada, 1827–30; KCB.

HILL, Thomas Wright (1763–1851), schoolmaster and stenographer; a disciple of *Priestley; kept school at Hill Top, Birmingham, 1803–19; his *Remains* issued (1859) and *Selection from his Papers* (1860); they include his studies in letter-sounds, systems of shorthand and numerical nomenclature, and scheme of minority representation.

HILL, William (1619–1667), classical scholar; fellow of Merton College, Oxford, 1639; MA, 1641; DD, Dublin; master of Sutton Coldfield School, 1640; afterwards of St Patrick's, Dublin; edited *Dionysius Periegetes* (1658).

HILL, William (*fl.* 1662), informer; of Merton College, Oxford; gave information of plot to seize Charles II, 1662.

HILL, William Noel, third Baron Berwick (1773–1842), envoy-extraordinary and minister plenipotentiary to the king of Sardinia, 1807–24, and to the king of the Two Sicilies, 1824–32; succeeded his brother in title, 1832; FSA.

HILL, Wills, first marquis of Downshire (1718–1793), statesman; MP, Warwick, 1741–56; succeeded as second Viscount Hillsborough (Ireland), 1742; privy councillor of Ireland, 1746; created Irish earl, 1751; comptroller and treasurer to George II, 1754–6; created Baron Harwich (peerage of Great Britain), 1756; president of Board of Trade and Plantations, 1763–5, and 1766; joint postmaster-general, 1766–8; as secretary of state for colonies, 1768–72, and for southern department, 1779–82, pursued harsh policy towards America; attacked by 'Junius'; created Irish marquis, 1789; recommended union with Ireland.

HILLARY, William (d. 1763), physician; MD, Leiden, 1722, and pupil of Boerhaave; practised in Ripon, Bath, Barbados, and London; published *Observations on Changes of the Air, and the concomitant Epidemical Diseases in Barbadoes* (1759).

HILLARY, Sir **William,** first baronet (1771–1847), founder of Royal National Lifeboat Institution; equerry to duke of *Sussex; raised First Essex Legion of infantry and cavalry, 1803; created baronet, 1805; settled in Isle of Man, 1808; first proposed Royal National Lifeboat Institution, 1823, and became president of district association in Isle of Man; proposed schemes for public benefit in various pamphlets.

HILLGARTH, Alan Hugh (1899–1978), intelligence officer and captain in the Royal Navy; born Alan Hugh Evans; entered Osborne Naval College, 1907; proceeded to Dartmouth, 1913; on active service as midshipman; seriously wounded in Dardanelles, 1915; at end of war studied at King's College, Cambridge; continued to serve in navy until 1927; author of adventure novels, including *The Black Mountain* (1933); changed name to Hillgarth, 1928; British vice-consul, Palma, 1932; in Spanish Civil War, arranged peaceful surrender of Republican-held Minorca, 1939; considerable influence with Franco régime; OBE, 1937; naval attaché, Madrid, 1939; promoted to captain, RN, 1940; rendered valuable services to Britain during 1939–45 war, deterring Francoist authorities from assisting German submarines and alerting British government to danger of unnecessary provocation of Franco authorities; earned confidence of (Sir) Winston Churchill; in addition to competent espionage was able to bribe Spanish generals to prevent intervention in the war in support of Germany; CMG, 1943; appointed chief of intelligence, Eastern Fleet; chief of British naval intelligence, Eastern Theatre, 1944; developed high-grade intelligence organization of material assistance to British and US war efforts in the Pacific.

HILLIARD, Nicholas (1537–1619), first English miniature painter; as goldsmith, carver, and limner to Elizabeth engraved her second great seal, 1586; granted sole right to execute portraits of James I, 1617; praised by *Donne in 'The Storm'; painted miniature of himself at 13, and drew portrait of *Mary Queen of Scots at 18; executed miniatures of chief contemporaries, twenty-three of which were exhibited at the Royal Academy, 1879.

HILLIER, Charles Parker (1838–1880). See HARCOURT, CHARLES.

HILLIER, George (1815–1866), topographer; published works, including *Topography of the Isle of Wight* (1850) and a guide to Reading (1859).

HILLIER, Sir **Harold George Knight** (1905–1985), horticulturist; educated at King Edward VI Grammar School, Southampton; entered family firm Hillier Nurseries, 1921; partner, 1930; head of firm, 1944; assembled vast collection of trees and shrubs; visited Europe, Asia, Australasia, and the Americas collecting plants and seeds; presented collections to Ventnor Botanic Gardens, Wisley Gardens of Royal Horticultural Society, and Westonbirt Arboretum; created Hillier Arboretum at Ampfield, near Romsey and presented it to Hampshire County Council, 1977; prepared *Hillier's Manual of Trees and Shrubs* (first published 1972); hon. fellow, RHS, served on council for twenty-five years, vice-president, 1974; awarded Victoria Medal of Honour, 1957, and Veitch Memorial Medal,

1962; fellow, Linnean Society of London, 1954; hon. fellow, Japanese Horticultural Society; CBE, 1971; knighted, 1983.

HILLIER, Tristram Paul (1905–1983), painter; educated at Downside and Christ's College, Cambridge; studied under Henry *Tonks at Slade School, London, 1926, and as pupil of André Lhôte in Paris; influenced by Surrealist painters including Max Ernst; part of British Surrealist avant-garde in 1930s; member of Unit One Group led by Paul *Nash; served with Royal Navy during 1939–45 war; exhibited mainly at Tooth's and Lefevre Galleries; represented in Tate Gallery and many other collections; ARA, 1957; RA, 1967; exhibition 'A Timeless Journey' presented at Bradford Art Gallery, 1983.

HILLS, Arnold Frank (1857–1927), shipbuilder and philanthropist; BA, University College, Oxford; joined directorate of Thames Ironworks and Shipbuilding Company, Blackwall; lived in Canning Town giving much time and thought to improvement and recreation of firm's work-people, 1880–5; considerable prosperity enjoyed by firm, 1890–1900; after launching of the *Thunderer*, Thames Ironworks, unable to compete with northern shipyards, compelled to close down, 1911.

HILLS, Henry (d. 1713), printer to *Cromwell, Charles II, and James II; provision in statute (8 Anne) directing that fine-paper copies of all publications should be sent to public libraries occasioned by his piracies.

HILLS, Sir John (1834–1902), major-general; born in Bengal; joined Bombay Engineers, 1854; in Persian expedition, 1857; field engineer in Abyssinian expedition, 1867; commandant of Bombay Sappers at Kirkee, 1871–83; commanded division of Kandahar Field Force, 1879–80; at defence of Kandahar; CB, 1881; commanding royal engineer of Burma Expeditionary Force, 1886–7; major-general, 1887; KCB, 1900; published *The Bombay Field Force* (1880) and *Points of a Racehorse* (1903).

HILLS, Robert (1769–1844), water-colour painter and etcher; exhibited at Society of Painters in Water-Colours, being many years secretary.

HILLSBOROUGH, first Earl and second Viscount (1718–1793). See HILL, WILLS.

HILL-TREVOR, Arthur, third Viscount Dungannon of the second creation in peerage of Ireland (1798–1862). See TREVOR.

HILLYAR, Sir James (1769–1843), rear-admiral; midshipman under Lord *Hood, 1793; as lieutenant under Captain Robert *Stopford present in action of 1 June 1794; commanded armed boats at Barcelona and on Egyptian coast, 1800–1; commanded cruiser *Niger* in Mediterranean, 1800–7; recommended for post-rank by *Nelson, 1804; assisted in reduction of Mauritius (1810) and Java (1811); captured American ship *Essex*, 1813; KCH, 1834; rear-admiral, 1837; KCB, 1840.

HILSEY (or HILDESLEIGH), John (d. 1539), bishop of Rochester; BD, Oxford, 1527, DD, 1532; prior of Dominican house at Bristol, 1533; appointed by Thomas *Cromwell provincial and commissioner (with George *Browne (d. 1556)) to visit friaries, 1534; bishop of Rochester, 1535–8; censor of press, 1536; exposed the Boxley rood and other impostures, 1538; compiled *Manuall of Prayers, or the Prymer in Englyshe*, published (1539); assisted in compiling *Institution of a Christian Man*.

HILTON, James (1900–1954), novelist; educated at Sir George Monoux Grammar School, Walthamstow, Leys School, and Christ's College, Cambridge; first class, English tripos, 1921; obtained fame with *Lost Horizon* (1933) and *Goodbye Mr. Chips* (1934), a tender portrait of his schoolmaster father; became Hollywood scriptwriter; his later novels equally successful but less likely to endure; died at Long Beach, California.

HILTON, John (d. 1657), musical composer; Mus.Bac., Trinity College, Cambridge, 1626; parish clerk and organist of St Margaret's, Westminster, 1628; published *Ayres, or Fa La's for Three Voyces* (1627); wrote elegy on William *Lawes, 1645; contributed madrigals to *Triumphs of Oriana* (1601) and canons and catches to *Catch that catch can* (1652).

HILTON, John (1804–1878), surgeon at Guy's Hospital, 1849–70; professor of human anatomy and surgery at College of Surgeons, 1860–2; president, 1867; his treatise *On Rest and Pain* (1863) a surgical classic.

HILTON, Roger (1911–1975), painter; born Roger Hildesherm; family name changed to Hilton, 1916; educated at Bishop's Stortford College; studied at the Slade School of Fine Art, 1929–31 and 1935–6; awarded Orpen Prize, 1930 and Slade scholarship, 1931; studied in Paris; first one-man exhibition, Bloomsbury Gallery, London, 1936; joined army, 1939; transferred to commandos, 1940; taken prisoner in Dieppe raid, 1942; taught art at Bryanston School, 1947–8; began painting abstract pictures, 1950, mainly in black and white and a few earth colours; painted first of large-scale female nudes, overtly figurative, 1961; CBE, 1968; first prize at John Moores Exhibition, Liverpool, 1963; represented Britain at Venice Biennale, and awarded Unesco prize, 1964; exhibited at

Gimpel Fils, London, between 1952 and 1956, and at Waddington Galleries, London, from 1960; work represented at Tate Gallery and number of galleries in Europe and Canada.

HILTON, Walter (d. 1396), religious writer; Augustinian canon at Thurgarton, Nottinghamshire; his *Scala Perfectionis* (English) printed by Wynkyn de *Worde (1494) and *Pynson (1506), translated into Latin by Thomas Fyslawe and edited by Robert Guy (1869) and John Dobree *Dalgairns (1870).

HILTON, William (1786–1839), historical painter; exhibited at Royal Academy from 1803; RA, 1818, and keeper, 1827; his works exhibited at British Institution, 1840; his *Christ Crowned with Thorns* purchased for Chantrey bequest. His paintings include *Edith discovering dead body of Harold*, 1834, and *Sir Calepine rescuing Serena*, 1831.

HINCHINBROKE, first Viscount (1625–1672). See MONTAGU, EDWARD.

HINCHLIFF, John Elley (1777–1867), sculptor; assistant to *Flaxman, for whom he finished statues of *Hastings and John Philip *Kemble; chiefly known for mural tablets and sepulchral monuments.

HINCHLIFF, John James (1805–1875), engraver; son of John Elley *Hinchliff.

HINCHLIFF, Thomas Woodbine (1825–1882), president of Alpine Club; MA, Trinity College, Cambridge, 1852; barrister, Lincoln's Inn; took part in founding Alpine Club, 1857, and was first honorary secretary and president, 1874–7; published books relating to his travels.

HINCHLIFFE, John (1731–1794), bishop of Peterborough; educated at Westminster, where he was assistant master seven years and (1764) head for three months; scholar of Trinity, Cambridge, 1751; fellow, 1755; master, 1768–88; MA, 1757; DD, 1764; vice-chancellor, 1768; bishop of Peterborough, 1769–94; offended government by liberal speeches in House of Lords, and was made dean of Durham (1788) on condition of resigning the mastership of Trinity College.

HINCKLEY, John (1617?–1695), controversialist; MA, St Alban Hall, Oxford, 1640; DD, 1679; rector of Northfield, Worcestershire, 1661–95; prebendary of Lichfield, 1673; published, among other works, *Fasciculus Literarum* (1680), containing controversy with *Baxter.

HINCKS, Edward (1792–1866), orientalist; son of Thomas Dix *Hincks; gold medallist and BA, Trinity College, Dublin, 1811; rector of Killyleagh, 1825–66; according to Brugsch first employed true method of deciphering Egyptian hieroglyphics; simultaneously with *Rawlinson discovered Persian cuneiform vowel system; contributed to *Transactions* of Royal Irish Academy.

HINCKS, Sir Francis (1807–1885), Canadian statesman; brother of Edward *Hincks; emigrated to Canada, 1831; joined Liberals, 1837; entered parliament, 1841; inspector-general of public accounts in first *Baldwin–Lafontaine ministry, 1842–4; started *Montreal Pilot*, 1844; inspector-general in second Baldwin ministry, 1848–51; as premier, 1851–4, developed Canadian railway and commercial system, negotiated reciprocity treaty with United States and passed Parliamentary Representation Act; governor of Barbados and Windward isles, 1855–62, of British Guiana, 1862–9; KCMG, 1869; finance minister, 1869–73; wrote on Canadian politics.

HINCKS, Thomas (1818–1899), zoologist; BA, London, 1840; minister at Mill Hill Unitarian Chapel, Leeds, 1855–69; FRS, 1872; published *History of British Hydroid Zoophytes* (1868) and *History of British Marine Polyzoa* (1880).

HINCKS, Thomas Dix (1767–1857), Irish Presbyterian divine; left Trinity College, Dublin, for Hackney New College, 1788; ordained by Southern Presbytery, 1792; lecturer at Royal Cork Institution and Fermoy Academy; classical master of Belfast Academical Institution and professor of Hebrew, 1821–36; LL D, Glasgow, 1834; contributed Irish articles to *Rees's *Cyclopaedia*; wrote educational manuals.

HINCKS, William (1794–1871), professor of natural history at Queen's College, Cork, 1849–53, and University College, Toronto, 1853–71; son of Thomas Dix *Hincks.

HIND, Arthur Mayger (1880–1957), historian of engraving; educated at City of London School and Emmanuel College, Cambridge; first class, classics, 1902; entered prints and drawings department, British Museum, 1903; keeper, 1933–45; Slade professor of fine art, Oxford, 1921–7; catalogued fifteenth-century Italian engravings (7 vols., 1938 and 1948), Rembrandt's etchings (1912), and drawings by Dutch and Flemish artists in the British Museum (4 vols., 1915–31); published *History of Engraving and Etching* (1908), of *Woodcut* (1935), and *Engraving in England in the Sixteenth and Seventeenth Centuries* (3 vols., 1952–64); served in Army Service Corps, 1915–18; OBE; hon. LL D, Glasgow.

HIND, Henry Youle (1823–1908), geologist and explorer; went to Canada, 1846; professor of chemistry and geology in Trinity University, Toronto, 1853–64; conducted government explorations and geological surveys; explored Nova Scotia gold-fields, 1869–71; discovered extensive cod banks offshore above Belle Isle, 1876; published accounts of his explorations; arranged scientific evidence in fisheries controversy between America and Canada, 1877; DCL, King's College, Windsor, Nova Scotia.

HIND, James (d. 1652), Royalist and highwayman; escaped in woman's clothes from Colchester after its capture, 1648; served under *Ormonde in Ireland, 1649; fought in Charles II's army at Worcester, 1651; arrested in London, 1651; hanged for treason.

HIND, John (1796–1866), mathematician; second wrangler and Smith's prizeman, 1818; MA, Sidney Sussex College, Cambridge, 1821; fellow, 1823–4; published works on the differential calculus and other mathematical subjects.

HIND, John Russell (1823–1895), astronomer; entered magnetic and meteorological department of Royal Observatory, Greenwich, 1840; director of observatory founded by George *Bishop in Regent's Park, 1844–95; superintended *Nautical Almanack*, 1853–91; member of Royal Astronomical Society, 1844, president, 1880–1; FRS, 1863; hon. LL D, Glasgow, 1882; published astronomical works.

HIND, Richard Dacre Archer- (1849–1910), Greek scholar and Platonist. See ARCHER-HIND.

HINDE, William (1569?–1629), Puritan divine; of The Queen's College, Oxford; fellow; MA, 1594; perpetual curate of Bunbury, Cheshire, 1603–29; published devotional works; edited works by John *Rainolds, and Cleaver's *Bathshebaes Instructions* (1614).

HINDERWELL, Thomas (1744–1825), author of *History of Scarborough* (1798); mayor of Scarborough, 1781, 1784, 1790, and 1800; published *Authentic Narratives of Affecting Shipwrecks* (1799).

HINDLE, John (1761–1796), vocalist and composer; Mus.Bac., Magdalen College, Oxford; lay vicar of Westminster Abbey; sang at Worcester festival, 1788, and London Vocal Concerts, 1791 and 1792; composed glees for words of English poets, and songs.

HINDLEY, Sir Clement Daniel Maggs (1874–1944), railway engineer and public servant; educated at Dulwich and Trinity College, Cambridge; assistant engineer, East Indian Railway, 1897; secretary, 1914; deputy general manager, 1918; general manager, 1920–1; chief commissioner, Indian Railways, 1922–8; chairman, Racecourse Betting Control Board, 1928–44; knighted, 1925; KCIE, 1929.

HINDLEY, John Haddon (1765–1827), orientalist; MA, Brasenose College, Oxford, 1790; chaplain of Manchester Collegiate Church; Chetham librarian, 1792–1804; published *Persian Lyrics from the Diwan-i-Hafiz, with paraphrases* (1800); edited *Pendeh-i-Attar* (1807).

HINDLEY, John Scott, Viscount Hyndley (1883–1963), business man and administrator; educated at Weymouth College; engineering apprentice in Durham Colliery; changed over to commercial side of industry; made reputation in large-scale distribution of coal; member of Coal Controller's Export Advisory Committee, 1917; chairman, Stephenson, Clarke Ltd., coal exporters, 1938; on boards of several other companies; director, Bank of England, 1931; commercial adviser to Mines Department; controller-general, Ministry of Fuel and Power, 1942–3; first chairman, National Coal Board, 1946–51; knighted, 1921; baronet, 1927; baron, 1931; GBE, 1939; viscount, 1948.

HINDMARSH, Sir John (d. 1860), rear-admiral and colonial governor; saved the *Bellerophon* at Battle of the Nile (1798), where he lost an eye; lieutenant of the *Phoebe* at Trafalgar, 1805; with the *Beagle* in Basque road, 1809; KH, 1836; first governor of South Australia, 1836–7; lieutenant-governor of Heligoland, 1840–56; rear-admiral, 1856.

HINDMARSH, Robert (1759–1835), organizer of the 'New Church'; formed Swedenborgian Society, 1783, opened chapel in Eastcheap, 1788, built another in Cross Street, Hatton Garden; organized hierarchy, 1793; afterwards preached at Salford; *Rise and Progress of New Jerusalem Church* issued, 1861.

HINDS, Samuel (1793–1872), bishop of Norwich; MA, The Queen's College, Oxford, 1818; DD, 1831; principal of Codrington College, Barbados; vice-principal of St Alban Hall, Oxford, 1827–31; chaplain to Archbishop *Whately, and earls of *Bessborough and *Clarendon; dean of Carlisle, 1858; bishop of Norwich, 1849–57; published *Inquiry into Proofs, &c., of Inspiration and into the Authority of Scripture* (1831) and other works.

HINE, Henry George (1811–1895), landscape painter; apprenticed as draughtsman to Henry *Meyer; practised as wood-engraver at Brighton; on staff of *Punch*, 1841–4; subsequently contributed to *Illustrated London News* and other publications; exhibited landscapes at Royal Academy and Suffolk Street Gallery; member of Institute of Painters in Water-Colours, 1864.

HINE, William (1687–1730), organist of Gloucester Cathedral (1712–30), and composer.

HINGESTON-RANDOLPH (formerly **HINGSTON), Francis Charles** (1833–1910), antiquary; BA, Exeter College, Oxford, 1855; MA, 1859; rector of Ringmore, Devonshire, 1860–1910; early developed antiquarian tastes; edited *Capgrave's Chronicle and other works in Rolls Series, 1858–60; prebendary of Exeter Cathedral, 1885; edited *Episcopal Registers* of diocese (11 parts, 1886–1909); wrote also on church architecture.

HINGLEY, Sir Benjamin, first baronet (1830–1905), ironmaster; head of father's chain-making firm at Netherton, 1865; manufactured anchors; influential in Midlands in preservation of industrial peace; mayor of Dudley, 1890; Liberal MP for North Worcestershire, 1885; joined Liberal Unionists, 1886; returned to Liberalism, 1892; baronet, 1893.

HINGSTON, John (d. 1683), composer and organist; employed by Charles I, *Cromwell, and Charles II.

HINGSTON, Thomas (1799–1837), physician; of Queens' College, Cambridge; MD, Edinburgh, 1824; practised at Penzance and Truro; edited *Harvey's *De Motu Cordis* (1824), and contributed to D. *Gilbert's *Parochial History of Cornwall.*

HINGSTON, Sir William Hales (1829–1907), Canadian surgeon; born in province of Quebec; studied medicine at McGill University and Edinburgh; LRCS, 1852; hon. FRCS, 1900; practised in Montreal from 1854; joined staff of Hôtel Dieu, 1860; founded Women's Hospital; professor of clinical surgery at Laval University, 1878; first to remove the tongue and lower jaw in one operation, 1872; mayor of Montreal, 1875–6; knighted, 1895; senator, 1896; wrote on climate of Canada and on vaccination.

HINKS, Arthur Robert (1873–1945), astronomer and geographer; BA, Trinity College, and second assistant, Cambridge Observatory, 1895; chief assistant, 1903–13; worked on determination of solar parallax; lecturer in surveying and cartography, 1908–13; assistant secretary, Royal Geographical Society, 1913; secretary, 1915–45; published *Map Projections* (1912) and *Maps and Survey* (1913); FRS, 1913.

HINKSON, Katharine (1861–1931), better known as Katharine Tynan, poet and novelist; lived in Ireland until her marriage (1883) with Henry Albert Hinkson, barrister and novelist; published over 100 novels, collections of poems, and five volumes of autobiography valuable for personal accounts of such figures as *Parnell.

HINSHELWOOD, Sir Cyril Norman (1897–1967), physical chemist and biochemist; educated at Westminster City School and Balliol College, Oxford; worked as chemist in Explosives Supply Factory, Queensferry, 1916–19; assistant chief laboratory chemist; research fellow, Balliol College, 1920; tutorial fellow, Trinity College, 1921–37; first book, *Kinetics of Chemical Change in Gaseous Systems* (1926), a milestone in chemical literature; succeeded Frederick *Soddy as Dr Lee's professor, teaching physical and inorganic chemistry, 1937–64; moved to Exeter College; worked in new Physical Chemistry Laboratory, provided by Lord *Nuffield, 1941; took up study of chemical kinetics of living cells, 1936–67; senior research fellow, Imperial College, London, 1964; published *The Chemical Kinetics of the Bacterial Cell* (1946), *The Structure of Physical Chemistry* (1951), and *Growth, Function and Regulation in Bacterial Cells* (with A. C. R. Dean, 1966); FRS, 1929; president, Chemical Society, 1946–8; president, Royal Society, 1955–60; knighted, 1948; shared Nobel Prize with Semenov, 1956; OM, 1960; president, British Association, 1964–5; honorary fellow, Trinity, Balliol, Exeter, and St Catherine's colleges, Oxford; delegate, Oxford University Press, 1934; a clever linguist and a competent painter in oils; trustee, British Museum; chairman of number of advisory committees, including education committee of Goldsmiths' Company.

HINSLEY, Arthur (1865–1943), cardinal; studied at Ushaw and English College, Rome; DD, Gregorian University; ordained, 1893; founder and headmaster (1899–1904), St Bede's Grammar School, Bradford; taught at Wonersh and pastor of Sutton Park (1904–11) and Sydenham (1911–17); rector, English College, Rome, 1917–30; domestic prelate, 1917; titular bishop of Sebastopolis, 1926; visitor apostolic to Africa, 1927; delegate apostolic and titular archbishop of Sardis, 1930–4; archbishop of Westminster, 1935–43; cardinal, 1937; launched 'Sword of the Spirit' movement, 1940.

HINTON, Christopher, Baron Hinton of Bankside (1901–1983), engineer; educated at Chippenham Grammar School and Trinity College, Cambridge; engineering apprentice with Great Western Railway, 1917–23; engineering scholar, Trinity College, 1923–5; first class, mechanical sciences tripos, 1925; joined Brunner Mond (later Alkali Group, Imperial Chemical Industries), 1926–40; chief engineer, 1931–40; director, ordnance factory construction, Ministry of Supply, 1940; deputy director-general, explosive-filling factories, 1942–6; member of board for engineering and production and managing director, industrial group, UK Atomic Energy Authority, 1946–57; responsible for design and building of Calder Hall nuclear reactors and experimental fast-breeder reactor at Dounreay; chairman, Central Electricity Generating Board, 1956–64; knighted, 1951; KBE, 1957; life peer, 1965; OM, 1976; adviser to

World Bank; president, Institution of Mechanical Engineers; chancellor, Bath University; deputy chairman, Generating Industry Research Council; FRS, 1954; received many academic honours at home and abroad including honorary fellowship, Trinity College, Cambridge, 1957.

HINTON, James (1822–1875), surgeon and philosophical writer; son of John Howard *Hinton; made voyages to China, Sierra Leone, and Jamaica as medical officer; practised as aural surgeon in London, and became acquainted with Dr (Sir William Withey) *Gull; contributed to Holmes's *System of Surgery* (1862); edited *Year-Book of Medicine*, 1863, and published aural monographs; published *Mystery of Pain* (1866) and joined Metaphysical Society; died in the Azores. Hinton's *Chapters on the Art of Thinking and other Essays* were printed (1879), *Philosophy and Religion* (1881), *The Lawbreaker and the Coming of the Law* (1884).

HINTON, Sir John (1603?–1682), Royalist physician; studied at Leiden; present at Edgehill, 1642; MD, Oxford, 1642; attended *Henrietta Maria at Exeter, 1644; practised in London during Commonwealth; physician to Charles II and his queen; knighted, 1665; his *Memoires* printed (1814).

HINTON, John Howard (1791–1873), Baptist minister; MA, Edinburgh, 1816; minister of Devonshire Square Chapel, Bishopsgate, 1837–63; secretary of Baptist Union; edited *History and Topography of United States* and many theological, biographical, and educational works (collected 1864).

HIPKINS, Alfred James (1826–1903), musical antiquary; accomplished interpreter of Chopin on piano; studied history of keyboard instruments; published *Musical Instruments, Historic, Rare and Unique* (1881); FSA, 1886; left collection of musical instruments to Royal College of Music.

HIPPISLEY, E. (*fl.* 1741–1766), afterwards Mrs Fitzmaurice; actress; daughter of John *Hippisley (d. 1748).

HIPPISLEY, Jane (d. 1791), afterwards Mrs Green; actress; sister of E. *Hippisley; *Garrick's Ophelia at Goodman's Fields; original Mrs Malaprop, 1747–8.

HIPPISLEY, John (d. 1748), actor and dramatist; owned theatres at Bristol and Bath; at Lincoln's Inn Fields, 1722–33, played Fondlewife (*Old Bachelor*), Polonius, and Sir Hugh Evans, and 'created' Peachum; at Covent Garden played Shallow, Dogberry, Fluellen, and other characters; created Sir Simon Loveit (*Miss in her Teens*);

also played in his own *Journey to Bristol* (1731), and *Drunken Man* (1732).

HIPPISLEY, John (d. 1767), actor and author; probably governor of Cape Coast Castle; son of John *Hippisley (d. 1748).

HIPPISLEY, Sir John Coxe, first baronet (1748–1825), politician; DCL, Hertford College, Oxford, 1776; barrister, Inner Temple, 1771; treasurer, 1816; agent of British government in Italy, 1779–80 and 1792–6; employed by East India Company, 1786–9; negotiated marriage of princess royal with duke of Württemberg, and was created baronet, 1796; recorder of Sudbury and MP, 1790–6 and 1802–19; wrote pamphlets in favour of Catholic emancipation.

HIRAETHOG, Gruffydd (d. 1568?), Welsh poet, named from Denbighshire mountains; manuscript poems by him in British Museum and at Peniarth House.

HIRSCHEL, Solomon (1761–1842), chief rabbi of German and Polish Jews in London, 1802–42.

HIRST, Sir Edmund Langley (1898–1975), chemist; educated at schools in Burnley, Ipswich, and St Andrews, and at St Andrews University with Carnegie scholarship; called up and seconded to university for study of mustard gas, 1917; served in France with Royal Engineers, 1918; returned to St Andrews and graduated, 1919; awarded Carnegie research scholarship and studied carbohydrate chemistry under (Sir) W. N. *Haworth; Ph.D., 1921; lecturer in chemistry, Manchester University, 1923; rejoined Haworth at Armstrong College, Newcastle upon Tyne, 1924; went with Haworth to Birmingham University as lecturer and assistant director of research; concerned with molecular structures of simple sugars and complex polysaccharides culminating in determination of structure and synthesis of vitamin C; D.Sc. (Birmingham), 1929; reader and FRS, 1934; Alfred Capper Pass professor of organic chemistry, Bristol, 1936; involved in work on explosives, 1939–45; Samuel Hall professor of organic chemistry, Manchester, 1944; Forbes professor of organic chemistry, Edinburgh, 1947; continued research on carbohydrate chemistry; CBE, 1957; knighted, 1964; received number of honorary doctorates and medals; president, Chemical Society, 1956–8; president, Royal Society of Edinburgh, 1959–64; chairman, chemistry research board, Department of Scientific and Industrial Research, 1950–5.

HIRST, Francis Wrigley (1873–1953), economist and Liberal writer; educated at Clifton, Wadham College, Oxford (first class, Lit. Hum., and president of Union, 1896), and London School of Economics; joint editor, *Essays in*

Liberalism (1897); called to bar (Inner Temple), 1899; assisted Lord *Morley with biography of Gladstone; active in forming League against Imperialism and Militarism; wrote regularly for *Speaker* and *Nation*; editor, *The Economist*, 1907–16, supporting principles of peace, economy, and individual liberty; recruited competent staff and himself wrote the policy leaders; publications include biography of Adam *Smith (1904), *Early Life and Letters of John Morley* (2 vols., 1927), *Economic Freedom and Private Property* (1935); unsuccessful Liberal candidate for parliament, 1910 and 1929.

HIRST, George Herbert (1871–1954), cricketer; left village school at age of 10; obtained Yorkshire county trial, 1889; established himself with 99 wickets for 14·39, 1893; in 1906 made 2,385 runs (average 45·86) and took 208 wickets for 16·50; altogether took 2,727 wickets for 18·77 and made 36,203 runs, averaging 34·05; played without distinction in nine test matches; a dangerous left-arm bowler and right-handed batsman favouring the hook and the pull; chief coach at Eton, 1919–37; honorary member, MCC, 1949.

HIRST, Hugo, Baron Hirst (1863–1943), chairman of General Electric Company; born and educated in Munich; naturalized, 1883; managing director, General Electric Company, 1900–43; chairman, 1910–43; made it a leading firm manufacturing and supplying electric equipment; recognized expert on international trading; baronet, 1925; baron, 1934.

HIRST, Thomas Archer (1830–1892), mathematician; articled as land agent and surveyor at Halifax, Yorkshire; studied at Marburg and was Ph.D., 1852; lecturer in mathematics, Queenwood College, Hampshire, 1853–6; mathematical master of University College School, 1860; FRS, 1861; FRAS, 1866; professor of mathematical physics, University College, London, 1865, of pure and applied mathematics, 1867, and of pure mathematics only, 1868–70; director of naval studies, Royal Naval College, Greenwich, 1873–83; fellow of London University, 1882; published mathematical writings.

HIRST, William (d. 1769?), astronomer; MA, Peterhouse, Cambridge, 1754; FRS, 1755; naval chaplain at sieges of Pondicherry and Vellore; observed transit of Venus at Madras, 1761; while at Calcutta described two eclipses and an earthquake; described transit of Venus of 1769; lost at sea on a second voyage to India.

HISLOP, James (1798–1827). See HYSLOP.

HISLOP, Stephen (1817–1863), missionary and naturalist; studied at Edinburgh and Glasgow; joined Free Church of Scotland, 1843; went to India as missionary, 1844; founded school at Nagpore, near which he was drowned; his *Papers relating to Aboriginal Tribes of Central Provinces* edited by Sir R. Temple (1866).

HISLOP, Sir Thomas, first baronet (1764–1843), general; with 39th at siege of Gibraltar (1779–83), commanding it at capture of Demerara, Berbice, and Essequibo, 1796; headed first division at capture of Guadeloupe (1809); lieutenant-governor of Trinidad, 1803–11; captured on way to India by American frigate, 1812; created baronet and commander-in-chief at Madras, 1813; led army of Deccan in Mahratta War, 1817–18; won victory of Mahidpore, 1817; incurred blame for severity at Talner; GCB, 1818; left Madras, 1820.

HITCHAM, Sir Robert (1572?–1636), king's serjeant; of Pembroke Hall, Cambridge; barrister, Gray's Inn; MP, West Looe, 1597, Lynn, 1604, Cambridge, 1614, Orford, 1625, 1626; attorney-general to James I's queen, 1603; knighted, 1604; king's serjeant, 1616.

HITCHCOCK, Sir Alfred Joseph (1899–1980), film director; educated at St Ignatius's College, Stamford Hill, London; left at 14 and became draughtsman and advertising designer; obtained full-time job at Islington Studios, 1920; given opportunity to direct *The Pleasure Garden* by (Sir) Michael *Balcon, 1925; followed by *The Lodger* (1926), *Blackmail* (1929), *The Thirty Nine Steps* (1935), *Sabotage* (1936), and *The Lady Vanishes* (1938), all thrillers, for which he made his name; other films were adaptations of *The Manxman* (1928), *Juno and the Paycock* (1930), *The Skin Game* (1931), and *Jamaica Inn* (1939); went to Hollywood and made *Rebecca* (1940), which won an Academy Award; made two short films in French, 1944; other Hollywood films, made usually with British actors in key roles, include *Lifeboat* (1943), *Rope* (1948), *Dial M for Murder* (1954), and *Rear Window* (1954); psychological thrillers include *Strangers on a Train* (1951), *Psycho* (1960), *I Confess* (1952), and *The Wrong Man* (1957); for television he directed series 'Alfred Hitchcock Presents', 1955–61 and 'The Alfred Hitchcock Hour', 1961–5; became American citizen, 1955; made reputation as profound psychologist and Catholic moralist in France and the USA; received number of honorary doctorates and academic awards; KBE, 1980; after *The Birds* (1963) his skill declined, but in 1976 with *Family Plot* he showed himself still to be master of the comedy thriller.

HITCHCOCK, Sir Eldred Frederick (1887–1959), man of business; educated at Burford Grammar School; obtained Oxford diploma in economics, 1910; secretary, 1910, warden,

1917–19, Toynbee Hall; obtained interest in sisal company, Bird & Co. (Africa) Ltd., 1926; chairman, 1950–9; managing director of its Tanganyika estates, 1939–59; chairman or vice-chairman, Sisal Growers Association, 1946–59; established Sisal Marketing Association, 1949; obtained establishment of department of antiquities in Tanganyika; knighted, 1955; died in Tanga.

HITCHCOCK, Richard (1825–1856), Irish archaeologist.

HITCHCOCK, Robert (*fl.* 1580–1591), military writer; commissioned to raise volunteers in Buckinghamshire for service in Low Countries, 1586; published *A Politique Platt* (1580), expounding scheme for developing Newfoundland herring fisheries, and an edition of William Garrard's *Arte of Warre* (1591), and other works; left also military writings in manuscript.

HITCHCOCK, Robert (d. 1809), dramatic author; published *The Macaroni* (1773), *The Coquette* (1777), and *Historical View of the Irish Stage* (1788–94).

HITCHENS, (Sydney) Ivon (1893–1979), painter; educated at Bedales; studied at St John's Wood Art School, 1911 and the Royal Academy Schools, 1912–16 and 1918–19; exhibited at second Seven and Five show, 1921; first one-man exhibition at Mayor Gallery, 1925, followed by second at Tooth's, 1928; experiments with abstraction influenced by Ben *Nicholson; moved from London to Greenleaves, Lavington Common, near Petworth, 1940; showed regularly at Leicester Galleries, 1940–60; after 1960 showed at Waddington Galleries; became known principally for quasi-abstract landscapes inspired by Sussex downlands; also figure painter of distinction and excelled at mural painting, including that for the English Folk Song and Dance Society at Cecil Sharp House, Regent's Park; exhibited at Venice Biennale (1956), in major Arts Council retrospective exhibition at Tate (1963), and at Royal Academy (1979); CBE, 1958.

HITCHINS, Fortescue (1784–1814), Cornish poet and historian; son of Malachy *Hitchins.

HITCHINS, Malachy (1741–1809), astronomer; BA, Exeter College, Oxford, 1781; MA, St John's College, Cambridge, 1785; computer and comparer at Greenwich under Neville *Maskelyne; vicar of St Hilary and Gwinear, Cornwall; verified calculations for *Nautical Almanack*.

HIVES, Ernest Walter, first Baron Hives (1886–1965), educated at Redlands School, Reading; worked in Reading garage and other garage jobs, 1903–8; joined Rolls-Royce Company, 1908; test driver; directed development of notable aero-engines, including the Kestrel and the R engine, precursor of the Merlin, which powered the Hurricanes and Spitfires of World War II; general works manager, 1936; managing director, 1946; chairman, 1950–7; under his direction Rolls-Royce led the world in design, development, and manufacture of gas-turbine aero-engines; MBE, 1920; CH, 1943; baron, 1950; hon. D.Sc., Nottingham, 1949; hon. LL D, Cambridge, 1951; hon. D.Sc., London, 1958.

HOADLY, Benjamin (1676–1761), bishop successively of Bangor, Hereford, Salisbury, and Winchester; son of Samuel *Hoadly; fellow of Catharine Hall, Cambridge, 1697–1701; MA, 1699; lecturer of St Mildred's, Poultry, London, 1701–11, rector of St Peter-le-Poor, Broad Street, London, 1704–21, of Streatham, 1710–23; chaplain to George I, 1715; opposed Occasional Conformity Bill, but published against Calamy *Persuasive to Lay Conformity* (1704), *Defence of Reasonableness of Conformity* (1707), and similar treatises; upheld Whig doctrine of resistance against *Atterbury and Bishop *Blackall, 1709–10; wrote satirical 'Dedication to Pope Clement XI' for *Steele's *Account of state of Roman Catholic Religion* (1715); bishop of Bangor, 1715–21; by his *Preservative against Principles and Practices of the Nonjurors* (1716) and sermon on *Nature of the Kingdom or Church of Christ* (1717), caused Bangorian controversy (1717–20) and the silencing of Convocation; his *Reply to Representation of Convocation* *Hoadly's chief contribution; bishop of Hereford, 1721–3; as 'Britannicus' attacked Atterbury in *London Journal*, 1721; bishop of Salisbury, 1723–34; published pamphlets on foreign affairs (1725) and *Essay on Life and Writings of Dr. Samuel Clarke* (1732); bishop of Winchester, 1734–61; *Waterland's treatise on the eucharist elicited by his *Plain Account of the Nature and End of the Sacrament* (1735); advocated repeal of Corporation and Test Acts, 1736; eulogized by *Akenside, but derided by *Pope and *Swift.

HOADLY, Benjamin (1706–1757), physician; son of Benjamin *Hoadly (1676–1761); MD, Corpus Christi College, Cambridge, 1728; FRS, 1726; FRCP, 1736; Gulstonian lecturer, 1737; Harveian orator, 1742; physician to George II, 1742; his comedy, *The Suspicious Husband* (1747) acted at Covent Garden, *Garrick taking part.

HOADLY, John (1678–1746), archbishop successively of Dublin and Armagh; brother of Benjamin *Hoadly (1676–1761); BA, Catharine Hall, Cambridge, 1697; chaplain to Bishop *Burnet; prebendary (1706), archdeacon (1710), and chancellor (1713) of Salisbury; friend of

*Chubb the deist; rector of Ockham, Surrey, 1717; bishop of Leighlin and Ferns, 1727; archbishop of Dublin, 1730; primate of Ireland; archbishop of Armagh, 1742; shared with *Shannon chief direction of Irish politics.

HOADLY, John (1711–1776), poet and dramatist; son of Benjamin *Hoadly (1676–1761); LL B, Corpus Christi College, Cambridge, 1736; chancellor of Winchester, 1735; chaplain to *Frederick, prince of Wales, and princess dowager; LL D, Lambeth, 1748; master of St Cross, Winchester, 1760–76; friend of *Garrick and *Hogarth; had poems in *Dodsley's *Collection*; wrote words to oratorios and musical plays; assisted his brother, Benjamin *Hoadly (1706–1757) in *The Suspicious Husband*; edited his father's works.

HOADLY, Samuel (1643–1705), schoolmaster; studied at Edinburgh; headmaster of Norwich School, 1700–5; published *Natural Method of Teaching* (1683), and school editions of Phaedrus and Publius Syrus (1700).

HOADLY, Sarah (d. 1743), portrait painter; née Curtis; first wife of Bishop Benjamin *Hoadly.

HOAR, Leonard (1630?–1675), president of Harvard College; emigrated to America and graduated at Harvard, 1650; returned to England, 1653; ejected from Wanstead, Essex, 1662; returned to Harvard; MD, Cambridge, 1671; president of Harvard College, 1672–5; published *Index Biblicus* (1668) and *First Catalogue of Members of Harvard College* (printed 1864).

HOARD, Samuel (1599–1658), divine; MA, St Mary Hall, Oxford, 1621; BD, 1630; prebendary of St Paul's, 1637; published theological works.

HOARE, Charles James (1781–1865), archdeacon of Surrey; second wrangler and Smith's prizeman, St John's College, Cambridge, 1803; fellow, 1806; MA, 1806; Seatonian prizeman, 1807; vicar of Blandford, 1807–21, of Godstone, 1821–65; archdeacon of Winchester, 1829, and canon, 1831; archdeacon of Surrey, 1847–60; published religious works.

HOARE, Clement (1789–1849), vine-grower and writer on viticulture.

HOARE, Joseph Charles (1851–1906), bishop of Victoria, Hong Kong, from 1898; BA, Trinity College, Cambridge, 1874; DD, 1898; joined CMS Mid-China mission at Ningpo, 1875; founded there training college for native evangelists; drowned in Castle Peak Bay while on preaching tour; contributed much to vernacular literature.

HOARE, Michael (*fl.* 1752). See HALFPENNY, WILLIAM.

HOARE, Prince (1755–1834), artist and author; son of William *Hoare; exhibited at Royal Academy, 1781–5; made honorary foreign secretary of Academy, 1799; published *Academic Correspondence* (1804), and *Academic Annals of Painting* (1805); best known of his plays, *No Song, No Supper* (Drury Lane, 1790).

HOARE, Sir Reginald Hervey (1882–1954), diplomat; grandson of Lord Arthur *Hervey; educated at Eton; entered Diplomatic Service, 1905; counsellor in Turkey, 1924–8; in Egypt, 1928–31; minister to Persia, 1931, to Romania, 1935; protested against atrocities of Nazi-style regime; mission withdrawn on imposition of economic warfare on Romania, 1941; managing partner, family bank, 1944–54; CMG, 1926; KCMG, 1933.

HOARE, Sir Richard (1648–1718), lord mayor of London; founded bank and raised government loans; knighted, 1702; sheriff of London, 1709; Tory MP for the City, 1710–15; master of Goldsmiths' Company, 1712; lord mayor, 1712.

HOARE, Sir Richard (d. 1754), lord mayor of London; grandson of Sir Richard *Hoare (1648–1718); journal of his shrievalty (1741) printed by Sir Richard Colt *Hoare (1815).

HOARE, Sir Richard Colt, second baronet (1758–1838), historian of Wiltshire; grandson of Sir Richard *Hoare (d. 1754); published works, including *History of Modern Wiltshire* (1822–44), *Ancient History of North and South Wiltshire* (1812–21), journals of tours in Ireland (1807), Elba (1814), Italy and Sicily (1819), a topographical catalogue of the British Isles (1815), and monographs on Wiltshire genealogy, topography, and archaeology; FRS and FSA.

HOARE, Sir Samuel John Gurney, second baronet and Viscount Templewood (1880–1959), statesman; educated at Harrow and New College, Oxford; first class, history, 1903; played rackets and lawn tennis for Oxford; Conservative MP, Chelsea, 1910–44; succeeded father, 1915; lieutenant-colonel with military mission to Russia, 1916–17, to Italy, 1917–18; secretary of state for air, 1922–4, 1924–9; PC, 1922; went on first civil air flight to India, 1926–7; GBE, 1927; secretary of state for India, 1931–5; a principal witness before Joint Select Committee on Indian Constitution, 1933–4, and piloted Government of India Bill through Commons; GCSI, 1934; foreign secretary, 1935; made notable speech to League Assembly on collective security, Sept. 1935; resigned when his plan with Laval for solution of Italy's claims on Abyssinia seemingly belied his speech and was repudiated by the Cabinet, Dec. 1935; first lord of Admiralty, 1936–7; home secretary, 1937–9; defended

Munich agreement; recruited for ARP and WVS; lord privy seal and member of War Cabinet, 1939–40; secretary of state for air, 1940; ambassador to Spain, 1940–4; viscount, 1944; president, Lawn Tennis Association, 1932–56; of Howard League for Penal Reform, 1947–59; chancellor, Reading University, 1937–59; publications include *Ambassador on Special Mission* (1946), *Nine Troubled Years* (1954), and *Empire of the Air* (1957).

HOARE, William (1707?–1792), portrait painter; reputed the first English artist who visited Rome to study; lodged with *Scheemakers, and made acquaintance of Batoni; travelled in France and the Netherlands, 1749; one of those who attempted to form an academy in England, 1755; an original academician, 1768; exhibited till 1783, chiefly crayons; painted portraits of Chatham, Beau *Nash, and others; executed also a whole length of Grafton, and crayons of *Chesterfield and *Pope.

HOARE, William Henry (1809–1888), divine; fellow of St John's College, Cambridge, 1833; MA, 1834; took part in *Colenso controversy; published *Outlines of Ecclesiastical History before the Reformation* (1852).

HOBART, George, third earl of Buckinghamshire (1732–1804), son of John *Hobart, first earl; MP, St Ives, 1754–61, Beeralston, 1761–80; secretary of St Petersburg embassy, 1762; succeeded as third earl, 1793; manager of the opera.

HOBART, Sir **Henry,** first baronet (d. 1625), judge; great-grandson of Sir James *Hobart; barrister, Lincoln's Inn, 1584, governor, 1591; MP, St Ives, 1588, Yarmouth, 1597 and 1601, Norwich, 1604–10; serjeant-at-law, 1603; attorney-general, 1606–13; appeared for plaintiffs in 'post-nati' case; created baronet, 1611; chief justice of common pleas, 1613–25; chancellor to Prince Charles, 1617; successfully opposed *Coke in *Suffolk case, 1619; his reports published (1641).

HOBART, Sir **James** (d. 1507), attorney-general, 1486–1507; of Lincoln's Inn; knighted, 1503; friend of John *Paston.

HOBART, John, first earl of Buckinghamshire (1694?–1756), politician; of Clare Hall, Cambridge; MP, St Ives, 1715 and 1722–7, Norfolk, 1727–8; a commissioner of trade, 1721; treasurer of the chamber, 1727; created Baron Hobart, 1728, earl of Buckinghamshire, 1746; lord-lieutenant of Norfolk, 1740–56, and privy councillor, 1745.

HOBART, John, second earl of Buckinghamshire (1723–1793), lord-lieutenant of Ireland; son of John *Hobart, first earl of Buckinghamshire; of Westminster School and Christ's College, Cambridge; MP, Norwich, 1747–56; comptroller of the household, 1755; lord of the bedchamber, 1756–67; ambassador to Russia, 1762–5; as viceroy of Ireland (1777–80) had to concede free trade and measures for relief of Romanists and Dissenters.

HOBART, Sir **Miles** (d. 1632), politician; knighted, 1623; when MP for Great Marlow locked the door of the House during debate of 2 Mar. 1629; imprisoned for two years; died by carriage accident; monument voted to him by parliament, 1647.

HOBART, Sir **Percy Cleghorn Stanley** (1885–1957), major-general; born in India; educated at Clifton and Woolwich; joined Royal Engineers, 1904; served in India, 1906–15, 1921–7; in France, Mesopotamia, and Egypt, 1915–18; DSO; MC; OBE, 1919; joined Royal Tank Corps, 1923, and appointed its head, 1933; raised and commanded 1st Tank brigade, 1934–7; major-general and director of military training, 1937–8; raised 7th Armoured division, 1938–9; his advanced views unacceptable; re-employed at Churchill's behest; commanded 11th Armoured division, 1941–2; raised 79th Armoured division, 1942; trained it for and took part in invasion of Europe, 1944–5; CB, 1939; KBE, 1943.

HOBART, Robert, Baron Hobart, fourth earl of Buckinghamshire (1760–1816), statesman; eldest son of George *Hobart, third earl of Buckinghamshire; of Winchester College; served in American War; represented Bramber and Lincoln, 1788–94, and in Irish parliament Portarlington and Armagh; aide-de-camp to viceroy of Ireland, 1784–8; as chief secretary, 1789–93, acted with Protestant party; English privy councillor, 1793; as governor of Madras, 1794–8, conducted expedition against Malacca; took part in war against Tippoo Sahib; recalled owing to difference with Sir John *Shore (afterwards Lord Teignmouth), 1798; summoned as Baron Hobart, 1798; assisted *Auckland (1799) in arranging details of Irish union; secretary for war and the colonies, 1801–4; Hobart Town named after him; chancellor of the duchy of Lancaster, 1805 and 1812; postmaster-general under Grenville, 1807; president of Board of Control, 1812–16; killed by an accident while riding.

HOBART, Vere Henry, Baron Hobart (1818–1875), governor of Madras; BA, Trinity College, Oxford, 1840; clerk in Board of Trade, 1840–61; reported on Turkish finance, and became director-general of Ottoman Bank; governor of Madras, 1872–5, where he died of typhoid; his

Essays and Miscellaneous Writings edited by Lady Hobart (1885).

HOBART-HAMPDEN, Augustus Charles (1822–1886), known as Hobart Pasha; vice-admiral; brother of Vere Henry Hobart, Baron *Hobart; entered British Navy and distinguished himself on South American Station against slavers; during Russian War did good service in Baltic (1854–5), and was promoted; retired as captain, 1863; ran blockade off North Carolina during American Civil War; became naval adviser to sultan of Turkey, 1867; created pasha (1869) and mushir (1881) for services in reduction of Crete; commanded Black Sea Fleet in Russian War, 1877–8; reinstated in British Navy (as vice-admiral), 1885; died at Milan; *Sketches of My Life* issued (1887).

HOBBES, John Oliver (pseudonym) (1867–1906), novelist and dramatist. See CRAIGIE, PEARL MARY TERESA.

HOBBES, Robert (d. 1538), last abbot of Woburn, 1529–38; acknowledged royal supremacy, 1534, but proved recalcitrant and was executed.

HOBBES, Thomas (1588–1679), philosopher; educated at Malmesbury and Magdalen Hall, Oxford; BA, 1608; twenty years tutor and secretary to William *Cavendish, afterwards second earl of Devonshire, and his son; his translation of Thucydides published (1629); at Paris with Sir Gervase Clifton's son, 1629–31; visiting Italy and Paris, 1634, met Galileo, Gassendi, and Mersenne; said to have been *Bacon's amanuensis; intimate of *Harvey, Ben *Jonson, *Cowley, and Sidney *Godolphin (1610–1643); resided at Paris, 1641–52; transmitted anonymous objections to Descartes's positions, published his *Leviathan* (1651), and acted as mathematical tutor to Charles II; on his return to England submitted to Council of State; saw much of Harvey and *Selden; engaged in controversies with *Bramhall in defence of his religion and philosophy, and with Seth *Ward, *Boyle, and John *Wallis (1616–1703), on mathematical questions, the last exposing many of his blunders; received pension from Charles II, and was protected by him against *Clarendon and the church party; his *Behemoth* suppressed; left London, 1675; wrote autobiography in Latin verse at 84 and completed translation of Homer at 86; buried in Hault Hucknall Church. In metaphysics a thoroughgoing nominalist; his political philosophy (chiefly in *Leviathan*), arguing that the body politic has been formed as the only alternative to a natural state of war, was attacked by Sir Robert *Filmer, but mentioned with respect in *Harrington's *Oceana*. It influenced Spinoza, Leibniz, and Rousseau, and was revived in England by the utilitarians. The chief critics of his metaphysical and ethical writings were Clarendon, *Tenison, the Cambridge Platonists, and Samuel *Clarke. The standard edition of his works is that of Sir W. *Molesworth (1839–45). His works include, besides those mentioned, *De Cive* (1642; English, 1651), *Human Nature* (1650), *De Corpore Politico*, originally *Elements of Law* (1680), *De Homine* (1658), *Quadratura Circuli* and other geometrical treatises, and *Behemoth, or the Long Parliament* (edited by Dr Ferdinand Tönnies, 1889).

HOBBS, Sir John Berry ('Jack') (1882–1963), cricketer; son of groundsman at Jesus College, Cambridge; played cricket for Cambridgeshire, 1902; given trial for Surrey, 1903; awarded Surrey county cap, 1905; went with MCC side on Australian tour, 1907–8; played for England against South Africa, 1909–10, and against Australia, 1911–12; with Wilfred *Rhodes set up record of 323 for the first wicket at Melbourne; toured South Africa, and made 1,489 runs, 1913–14; made 11 centuries, and Surrey became champions, 1914; at retirement in 1934 had made 61,237 runs, including 197 centuries; made hundredth century, 1923; scored century in final test at the Oval when England recovered the Ashes, 1926; played his last test in Australia, 1928–9; final century in first-class cricket made at Old Trafford, 1934; played altogether in 61 test matches and made 5,410 runs; life member, Surrey Club, 1935; life member, MCC, 1949; knighthood, 1953, the first conferred on a professional cricketer; published *My Cricket Memories* (1924) and *My Life Story* (1935).

HOBDAY, Sir Frederick Thomas George (1869–1939), veterinary surgeon; MRCVS, 1892; FRCVS, 1897; began practice in Kensington, 1900; improved surgical methods; so successful in operating to relieve 'roaring' that horses so treated were termed 'hobdayed'; editor, *Veterinary Journal*, 1906–39; commanded a veterinary hospital in France and Italy, 1915–19; principal and professor of surgery, Royal Veterinary College, 1927; by 1936 had raised £285,000 for reconstruction, but alleged defects in college administration caused enforced retirement; knighted, 1933.

HOBDAY, William Armfield (1771–1831), portrait painter; exhibited many years at Academy; opened galleries in Pall Mall for sale of pictures on commission but failed; best work, picture of Carolus the hermit of Tong.

HOBHOUSE, Arthur, Baron Hobhouse (1819–1904), judge; son of Henry *Hobhouse; educated at Eton and Balliol College, Oxford;

BA (first-class classic), 1840; called to bar, 1845; acquired large Chancery practice; QC, 1862; treasurer of Lincoln's Inn, 1880–1; charity commissioner, 1866; one of three commissioners for reorganizing endowed schools, 1869–72; law member of Council of Governor-General of India, 1872–7; responsible for Specific Relief Act, 1877; opposed Lord *Lytton's Afghan policy; KCSI, 1877; member of judicial committee of Privy Council, 1881–1901; raised to peerage to try appeal cases in House of Lords, 1885; member of London School Board, 1882–4; alderman of London County Council, 1889; life by L. T. *Hobhouse and J. L. *Hammond, 1905.

HOBHOUSE, Sir Benjamin, first baronet (1757–1831), politician; MA, Brasenose College, Oxford, 1781; barrister, Middle Temple, 1781; MP, Bletchingley, 1797, Grampound, 1802, and Hindon, 1806–18; secretary to Board of Control under *Addington, 1803; chairman of committees, 1805; created baronet, 1812; published legal treatises.

HOBHOUSE, Edmund (1817–1904), bishop of Nelson, New Zealand, and antiquary; brother of Baron *Hobhouse; educated at Eton and Balliol College, Oxford; BA, 1838; DD, 1858; fellow of Merton, 1841–58; vicar of St Peter-in-the-East, Oxford, 1843–58; bishop of Nelson, 1858–65; assistant to bishops Selwyn and Maclagan at Lichfield, 1869–81; edited records for Somerset Record Society (1887–94), which he helped to found.

HOBHOUSE, Henry (1776–1854), archivist; of Eton and Brasenose College, Oxford; MA, 1799; DCL, 1827; barrister, Middle Temple, 1801; solicitor to the customs, 1806, to Treasury, 1812; permanent under-secretary for Home Department, 1817–27; privy councillor, 1828; keeper of state papers, 1826–54; superintended publication of *State Papers of Henry VIII*.

HOBHOUSE, Henry (1854–1937), pioneer in local government; nephew of Baron *Hobhouse; educated at Eton and Balliol College, Oxford; first class, Lit. Hum., 1875; called to bar (Lincoln's Inn) and county magistrate, 1880; with Sir Robert *Wright wrote *Outline of Local Government and Local Taxation . . .* (1884); Liberal (1885), Liberal Unionist (1886–1906) MP, East Somerset; chairman, Somerset County Council, 1904–24; a country squire, expert in county administration, especially interested in education and agriculture; PC, 1902.

HOBHOUSE, John Cam, Baron Broughton de Gyfford (1786–1869), statesman; son of Sir Benjamin *Hobhouse; of Westminster and Trinity College, Cambridge; won Hulsean Prize,

1808; MA, 1811; founded Cambridge Whig Club; travelled with *Byron in Spain, Portugal, Greece, and Turkey; wrote, from personal observation, Bonapartist account of the 'Hundred Days', 1816; visited Byron in Switzerland and Italy and wrote notes for Canto IV of *Childe Harold*; unsuccessfully contested Westminster as a Radical, 1819; sent to Newgate for breach of privilege, 1819; returned for Westminster, 1820; as Byron's executor advised destruction of his *Memoirs*, 1824; active member of Greek Committee in London; succeeded as baronet, 1831; secretary at war, 1832–3; chief secretary for Ireland, Mar.–Apr. 1833; resigned on house and window-tax, 1833; defeated when candidate for Westminster; elected for Nottingham, 1834; commissioner of woods and forests under Melbourne, 1834; president of Board of Control, 1835–41 and 1846–52; defeated at Nottingham, 1847; elected for Harwich, 1848; created peer, 1851; said to have invented phrase 'his majesty's opposition'; as Byron's 'best man' drew up reply (unpublished) to Lady Byron's *Remarks*; left manuscript 'Diaries, Correspondence, and Memoranda, &c., not to be opened till 1900'. His works include *Italy: Remarks made in several visits* (1859) and *Recollections of a Long Life* (1865).

HOBHOUSE, Sir John Richard (1893–1961), shipowner; son of Henry *Hobhouse; nephew of Beatrice *Webb; educated at Eton and New College, Oxford; served in Royal Garrison Artillery, 1914–18; MC, 1917; director, Ocean Steam Ship Company, Liverpool, 1920; chairman, 1953–7; director, Royal Insurance Company, 1933–61; chairman, 1954–7; chairman, Liverpool Steam Ship Owners' Association, 1941–2; chairman, National Association of Port Employers, 1948–50; magistrate, 1929–57; knighted, 1946; treasurer, council of Liverpool University, 1942–8; president, 1948–54; pro-chancellor, 1948–57; hon. LL D, 1958; chairman, council of Liverpool School of Tropical Medicine, 1949–55.

HOBHOUSE, Leonard Trelawny (1864–1929), philosopher and journalist; nephew of Baron *Hobhouse; BA, Corpus Christi College, Oxford, 1887; tutor of Corpus, 1890; fellow, 1894; on staff of *Manchester Guardian*, 1897–1902; first professor of sociology, London University, 1907–29; works include *The Labour Movement* (1893), *The Theory of Knowledge* (1896), *Mind in Evolution* (1901), *Morals in Evolution* (1906), *Development and Purpose* (1913), *The Metaphysical Theory of the State* (1918), *The Rational Good* (1921), *The Elements of Social Justice* (1922), *Social Development* (1924); died at Alençon, Normandy.

HOBLYN, Richard Dennis (1803–1886), educational writer; MA, Balliol College, Oxford, 1828; chief work, *Dictionary of Terms used in Medicine*.

HOBLYN, Robert (1710–1756), book collector; of Eton and Corpus Christi College, Oxford; BCL, 1734; MP, Bristol, 1742–54; FRS, 1745; twice speaker of Stannary parliament; his *Bibliotheca Hobliniana* printed (1768); library sold, 1778.

HOBSON, Edward (1782–1830), botanist and entomologist; first president of Banksian Society, 1829; published *Musci Britannici* (1818–24).

HOBSON, Ernest William (1856–1933), mathematician; brother of J. A. *Hobson; educated at Derby School, Imperial College of Science, and Christ's College, Cambridge; senior wrangler and fellow, 1878; private coach until 1903; university lecturer (1883), Stokes lecturer (1903), Sadleirian professor (1910–31); leader in reforming the tripos; his *Theory of Functions of a Real Variable* (1907, final form, 2 vols., 1926–7) of first importance to English mathematics; other works include *Treatise on Plane Trigonometry* (1891), *The Domain of Natural Science* (1923), and *Spherical and Ellipsoidal Harmonics* (1931); FRS, 1893.

HOBSON, Geoffrey Dudley (1882–1949), historian of bookbindings; educated at Harrow and University College, Oxford; first class, modern history, 1903; with others acquired auctioneering firm of Sotheby, 1909; leading authority on bookbindings; published *Maioli, Canevari and Others* (1926), *English Binding before 1500* (1929), and *Bindings in Cambridge Libraries* (1929).

HOBSON, John Atkinson (1858–1940), economist and publicist; brother of E. W. *Hobson; educated at Derby School and Lincoln College, Oxford; an original thinker on economics with approach of sociologist; developed theory of under-consumption in *The Physiology of Industry* (1889, with A. F. *Mummery) and later works; prescribed such remedies for inequality as steeply graduated taxation, extension of social services, and nationalization of monopolies in *The Industrial System: an Inquiry into Earned and Unearned Income* (1909) and subsequently; *The Evolution of Modern Capitalism: a Study of Machine Production* (1894) indispensable introduction to nineteenth-century economic history; studied search for new markets and opportunities for investment in *Imperialism* (1902); wrote frequently (1906–20) in the *Nation*.

HOBSON, Sir John Gardiner Sumner (1912–1967), attorney-general; educated at Harrow and Brasenose College, Oxford; called to bar (Inner Temple), 1938; served in Northamptonshire Yeomanry in France and North Africa, 1940–5; OBE, 1945; chairman, Rutland and Bedfordshire quarter-sessions; recorder, Northampton, 1958–62; KC, 1957; Conservative MP, Warwick and Leamington, 1957; solicitor-general, 1962; attorney-general, knighted, 1962; PC, 1963; prosecuted the spy, Vassall, 1962; involved in Enahoro case, 1963; returned to private practice, 1964–7.

HOBSON, Richard (1795–1868), physician; of St George's Hospital and Queens' College, Cambridge; MD, 1830; physician to Leeds Infirmary, 1833–43; attended Charles *Waterton and wrote a book on him (1866).

HOBSON, Thomas (1544?–1631), Cambridge carrier; referred to in *Spectator*; presented to Cambridge site of Spinning House, and provided for a conduit; refused always to let out any horse out of its proper turn ('Hobson's choice', this or none).

HOBY, Sir Edward (1560–1617), favourite of James I; son of Sir Thomas *Hoby; of Eton and Trinity College, Oxford; MA, 1576; knighted, 1582; accompanied his father-in-law, Lord *Hunsdon, to Scotland, 1584; MP for Queenborough, Berkshire, Kent, and Rochester; accompanied Cadiz expedition, 1596; constable of Queenborough, 1597; gentleman of privy chamber to James I; often entertained James I at Bisham; carried on controversies with Theophilus *Higgons and John *Floyd; translated from French and Spanish; friend and patron of *Camden.

HOBY, Elizabeth, Lady (1528–1609), linguist; wife of Sir Thomas *Hoby; afterwards married John, Lord Russell, 1574.

HOBY, Peregrine (1602–1678), natural son and heir of Sir Edward *Hoby; MP, Great Marlow, 1640, 1660, and 1661.

HOBY, Sir Philip (1505–1558), diplomat; knighted after capture of Boulogne, 1544; ambassador to the emperor Charles V, 1548; negotiated for marriage of Edward VI with a French princess, 1551; employed financially in Flanders; privy councillor, master of the ordnance, and grantee of Bisham, 1552; ambassador in Flanders, 1553; brought message from *Philip II to Queen Mary, 1556; friend of Titian and Aretino.

HOBY, Sir Thomas (1530–1566), diplomat and translator; half-brother of Sir Philip *Hoby; of St John's College, Cambridge; knighted, 1566; translated Martin Bucer's *Gratulation* to the Church of England (1549), and *The Courtyer of*

Count Baldessar Castilio (1561); died in Paris while ambassador to France.

HOCCLEVE (or OCCLEVE), Thomas (*c.*1369–*c.*1426), poet; clerk in Privy Seal Office; granted annuity by Henry IV; portrait of *Chaucer contained in his *De Regimine Principum*, written *c.*1411–12 (English), edited by Thomas *Wright (1860); his *Mother of God* and *La Male Regle* (autobiography), printed (1796); the former once attributed to Chaucer.

HOCKING, Joseph (1860–1937), novelist and preacher; ordained in United Methodist Free Church, 1884; minister, Woodford Green Union Church, 1887–1910; used fiction to convey religious ideas to popular public; his fifty-three books include *The Woman of Babylon* (1906) and *The God That Answers by Fire* (1930).

HOCKING, Silas Kitto (1850–1935), novelist and preacher; brother of J. *Hocking; ordained in United Methodist Free Church, 1870; minister, Duke Street, Southport, 1883–96; thereafter devoted himself to writing, lecturing, and Liberal politics; a best-selling author of healthy fiction.

HODDER, James (*fl.* 1661), arithmetician; author of *Arithmetick* (1661), *The Penman's Recreation* and *Decimal Arithmetick* (1668).

HODDESDON, Sir Christopher (1534–1611), master of Merchants Adventurers' Company; accompanied Richard *Chancellor on voyages to Russia; head of English factory at Moscow, 1557–62; sent to develop English trade in Baltic, 1567; chief of English factory at Narva, 1569; employed as financial agent to Queen Elizabeth in Germany from *c.*1574; master of Merchants Adventurers at Hamburg, 1578; MP, Cambridge, 1593; sheriff of Bedfordshire, 1591–2; master of Merchants Adventurers' Company before 1600; knighted, 1603.

HODDESDON, John (*fl.* 1650), religious writer; friend of *Dryden; published *Sion and Parnassus* (1650) and biographical compilation on Sir Thomas *More (1652).

HODGE, Arthur (d. 1811), West Indian planter; executed for causing death of negroes on his estate in Tortola.

HODGE, John (1855–1937), Labour leader; steel smelter at Motherwell; secretary to British Steel Smelters' Association on its foundation (1886); believed in conciliation and arbitration; president, Iron and Steel Trades Confederation, until 1931; served on National Committee of Labour party, 1900–15; MP, Gorton, 1906–23; first minister of labour, 1916–17; PC, 1917; minister of pensions, 1917–19; opposed to Association's participation in General Strike,

1926; a constitutionalist relying on education and legislation to achieve his socialist ideals.

HODGE, Sir William Vallance Douglas (1903–1975), mathematician; educated at George Watson's School, Edinburgh and Edinburgh University; first class, mathematics, 1923; exhibitioner of St John's College, Cambridge; wrangler, part ii, mathematical tripos, 1925; Ferguson scholar, 1926; assistant lecturer, Bristol, 1926–30; research fellow, St John's College, Cambridge, 1930; exhibition student, 1931; studied under Solomon Lefschetz at Princeton, 1931; university lecturer, Cambridge, 1933; fellow, Pembroke College, 1935; succeeded H. F. *Baker as Lowndean professor of astronomy and geometry, 1936; developed the theory of harmonic integrals; awarded Adams Prize, 1937; theory published, 1941; during 1939–45 took on additional post of steward of Pembroke; appointed master, 1958; retired from mastership and Lowndean chair, 1970; FRS, 1938; physical secretary, Royal Society, 1957–65; Royal medallist, 1957; Copley medallist, 1974; knighted, 1959; honorary degrees from many universities and honorary member of academic organizations abroad; hon. fellow, St John's and Pembroke colleges, Cambridge.

HODGES, Charles Howard (1764–1837), mezzotint-engraver and portrait painter; engraved portraits after *Reynolds, *Romney, C. G. Stuart, and *Hoppner, and subject-pictures after old masters; settled at Amsterdam, 1794, and painted portraits of William I of the Netherlands, Louis, king of Holland, himself, and his daughter.

HODGES, Edward (1796–1867), organist at Clifton, Bristol, and New York, 1839–63; Mus.Doc., Sidney Sussex College, Cambridge; composed and wrote works on church music, 1825.

HODGES, Edward Richmond (1826–1881), orientalist; missionary to Jews in Palestine and Algeria; assisted George *Smith (1840–1876) in cuneiform researches, and Gotch with *Paragraph Bible*; edited *Craik's *Principia Hebraica* (1863), *Cory's *Ancient Fragments* (1876), and revised *Mickle's *Lusiad* (1877).

HODGES, Nathaniel (1629–1688), physician; scholar of Westminster and Trinity College, Cambridge; student of Christ Church, Oxford; MA, 1654; MD, 1659; attended patients throughout plague of 1665; published an account (1672); FRCP, 1672; censor, 1682; died while in prison for debt.

HODGES, Sir William, first baronet (1645?–1714), Spanish merchant; created baronet, 1697, for financial assistance to government; published pamphlets advocating relief of British seamen from extortion.

HODGES, William (1744–1797), landscape painter; exhibited at Society of Artists, 1766–72; draughtsman in Captain *Cook's second expedition, 1772–5; exhibited at Academy view of Otaheite, 1776; painted views in India under patronage of Warren *Hastings, 1778–84; published *Travels in India* (1793); RA, 1789; visited St Petersburg, 1790.

HODGES, Sir William (1808–1868), chief justice of Cape of Good Hope; barrister, Inner Temple, 1833; published reports of common pleas, Queen's Bench cases, and treatises on railway law; recorder of Poole, 1846; drafted Public Health Act, 1848; knighted, 1857; chief justice of Cape of Good Hope, 1857–68.

HODGETTS, James Frederick (1828–1906), commander and archaeologist; in East India Company's fleet in Burmese War, 1851; commander in Indian Navy; professor of seamanship in Berlin, St Petersburg, and Moscow till 1881; published stories for boys and archaeological works.

HODGKIN, John (1766–1845), calligraphist; described in manuscript autobiography events during residence at Vincennes, 1792; tutor in London; works include *Calligraphia* and *Poecilographia Graeca* (1807), and *Introduction to Writing* (4th edn. 1811).

HODGKIN, John (1800–1875), barrister and Quaker; son of John *Hodgkin (1766–1845); friend of John Stuart *Mill; advocated register of titles; assisted in preparation of Encumbered Estates Act, 1849; visited Quakers in Ireland, France, and America.

HODGKIN, Thomas (1798–1866), physician; brother of John *Hodgkin (1800–1875); MD, Edinburgh, 1823; curator and pathologist at Guy's Hospital, 1825; member of London University senate; published *Essay on Medical Education* (1828), *Lectures on Morbid Anatomy of Serous and Mucous Membranes* (1836), and biographical works; glandular disease named after him; a founder of Aborigines Protection Society, 1838; died at Jaffa.

HODGKIN, Thomas (1831–1913), historian; BA, University College, London; partner in banking firm at Newcastle, 1859–1902; active Quaker; chief works, *Italy and her Invaders* (1879–99) and *History of England from the Earliest Times to the Norman Conquest* (1906).

HODGKINS, Frances Mary (1869–1947), painter; born, educated, and studied and practised art in Dunedin, New Zealand; visited Europe, 1901–3; returned and settled, 1906; in Paris, 1908–14; thereafter in England; maintained herself with difficulty; unsuccessfully attempted commercial designing; made contract with Alex. Reid and Lefevre, 1932; awarded civil list pension, 1942; a leading exponent of modern English painting, notable colourist, and one of the most gifted and original of women painters.

HODGKINSON, Eaton (1789–1861), writer on the strength of materials; made experiments resulting in 'Hodgkinson's beam', and gave theoretical expositions; FRS, with Royal Medal for paper on 'Strength of Pillars of Cast Iron and other Materials', 1840; royal commissioner on application of iron to railways, 1847–9; professor of mechanical engineering of University College, London, 1847; president of Manchester Literary and Philosophical Society, 1848–50; published *Experimental Researches on the Strength, etc. of Cast Iron* (1846).

HODGKINSON, George Christopher (1816–1880), meteorologist and educationalist; MA, Trinity College, Cambridge, 1842; principal of Royal Agricultural College, Cirencester, of Diocesan Training College, York; headmaster of Louth Grammar School, 1864–76; secretary of National Society; made astronomical observations on Mont Blanc.

HODGSON, Bernard (1745?–1805), principal of Hertford College, Oxford; captain of Westminster, 1764; student of Christ Church, Oxford; MA, 1771; DCL, 1776; principal of Hertford College, 1775–1805; translated Solomon's Song, Proverbs, and Ecclesiastes.

HODGSON, Brian Houghton (1800–1894), Indian civilian and orientalist; nominated to Bengal writership, 1816; studied at East India Company's College, Haileybury, and at college of Fort William; assistant commissioner of Kumaon, c.1818–20; assistant resident at Kathmandu, 1820–9, acting resident, 1829–31, and resident, 1833–43; came to England, 1843, but returned to India in private capacity to continue researches; studied ethnology at Darjeeling; finally left India, 1858; FRS, 1877; hon. DCL, Oxford, 1889; while in India made valuable collections of original Sanskrit and Tibetan manuscripts, which he distributed among public libraries. His works include *Illustrations of Literature and Religion of the Buddhists* (1841) and *Essays on Language, Literature, and Religion of Nepal and Tibet* (1874).

HODGSON, Christopher Pemberton (1821–1865), traveller; vice-consul at Pau, 1851–5, Caen, and in Japan, 1859–61; published *Reminiscences of Australia, El Udaivar* (1849), and other works; died at Pau.

HODGSON, Edward (1719–1794), flower painter; treasurer to Associated Artists of Great Britain.

HODGSON, Francis (1781–1852), provost of Eton; at Eton under *Keate; fellow of King's College, Cambridge, 1803–15, tutor, 1807; MA, 1807; BD, 1840; archdeacon of Derby, 1836; provost of Eton, 1840–52; friend of Lord *Byron; translated Juvenal (1807) and published English verse.

HODGSON, James (1672–1755), mathematician; master of Royal School of Mathematics, Christ's Hospital; FRS, 1703; helped to edit *Flamsteed's *Atlas Coelestis*; published also *Doctrine of Fluxions founded on Sir Isaac Newton's Method* (1736) and other works.

HODGSON, John (d. 1684), author of *Memoirs* (published 1806 with Sir Henry *Slingsby's *Original Memoirs*); served under *Fairfax in Yorkshire; taken by *Newcastle at Bradford, 1643; present at sieges of Pontefract, 1645 and 1648, and Battle of Preston, 1648; described Battle of Dunbar, 1650; refused to fight against *Lambert, 1659.

HODGSON, John (1757–1846), general; son of Studholme *Hodgson; served in North America; wounded in Holland, 1799; governor of Bermuda and Curaçoa; general, 1830.

HODGSON, John (1779–1845), antiquary; schoolmaster at Sedgefield, Lanchester, and other places; incumbent of Jarrow, 1808, Kirk Whelpington, 1823, and Hartburn, 1833; published part of a large history of Northumberland, guidebook to Newcastle upon Tyne (1812), *Account of the* [colliery] *Explosion at Felling* (1813), and other works; assisted *Davy in invention of safety lamp; built Heworth Church (consecrated 1822).

HODGSON, John Evan (1831–1895), painter; educated at Rugby; student at Royal Academy, 1853; exhibited at Royal Academy from 1856; RA, 1879; librarian and professor of painting at Royal Academy, 1882 till death; published lectures and other writings.

HODGSON, John Studholme (1805–1870), major-general in Bengal Army; second son of John *Hodgson (1757–1846); wounded at Sobraon, 1846; raised and commanded 1st Sikh Regiment, 1848–9; promoted for capture of Ukrot; organized Punjab irregular force, 1850; major-general, 1861.

HODGSON, Joseph (1756–1821), Roman Catholic divine; when vice-president of Douai College, imprisoned by revolutionaries; published an account; vicar-general to bishops Douglas and Poynter in England.

HODGSON, Joseph (1788–1869), surgeon; studied at St Bartholomew's Hospital; surgeon to Birmingham Dispensary, 1818–48; president of Medico-Chirurgical Society, 1851, of College of Surgeons, 1864; FRS; published treatise on diseases of arteries and veins (1815).

HODGSON, Ralph Edwin (1871–1962), poet; in his teens travelled to America and was employed in Thalia Theatre, New York; worked in London as black-and-white artist; edited *Fry's Magazine of Outdoor Life* for C. B. *Fry, 1912; founded 'The Sign of the Flying Fame', publishers, with Claud Lovat *Fraser and Holbrook Jackson, 1913; first published poem, 'The Storm Thrush', in *Saturday Review*, 1904; first collection of poems, *The Last Blackbird and Other Lines*, published, 1907; *Poems* followed (1917); served in forces, 1914–18; keen love of countryside; inspired campaign to end trade in birds' feathers for women's apparel, 1920; this led to the Plumage Act, 1921; lecturer at Sendai University, Japan, 1924–38; published *The Skylark and Other Poems* (1958); and *Collected Poems* (1961).

HODGSON, Richard Dacre (1849–1910), Greek scholar and Platonist. See ARCHER-HIND.

HODGSON, Sir Robert MacLeod (1874–1956), diplomat; educated at Radley and Trinity College, Oxford; hockey blue; BA, 1897; vice-consul, Marseilles, 1904–6; commercial agent, Vladivostock, 1906–19; commercial counsellor in Russia, 1919–21; official agent, British commercial mission to Russia, 1921–4; chargé d'affaires, 1924–7; minister to Albania, 1928–36; British agent to Franco's Burgos administration, 1937–9; chargé d'affaires, Spain, Feb.–Apr. 1939; CMG, 1920; KBE, 1925; KCMG, 1939.

HODGSON, Shadworth Hollway (1832–1912), philosopher; BA, Corpus Christi College, Oxford; chief works, *Time and Space* (1865), *Theory of Practice* (1870), *Philosophy of Reflection* (1878), and *Metaphysic of Experience* (1898).

HODGSON, Studholme (1708–1798), field marshal; aide-de-camp of duke of *Cumberland at Fontenoy, 1745, and Culloden, 1746; raised Royal West Kent Regiment (then 52nd), 1756; commanded brigade in Rochefort expedition, 1757; conducted siege of Belleisle, 1761; general, 1778; field marshal, 1796.

HODGSON, Studholme John (d. 1890), general; son of John *Hodgson (1757–1846); commanded forces in Ceylon and Straits Settlements.

HODGSON, William (1745–1851), politician and author; imprisoned and fined for revolutionary speech, 1793; MD; published educational manuals and other works.

HODGSON, William Ballantyne (1815–1880), educational reformer; studied at Edinburgh; principal of Liverpool Mechanics' Institute, 1844; LL D, Glasgow, 1846; principal of Chorlton High School, Manchester, 1847–51; assisted in inquiry into primary education, 1858; leading member of council of University College, London; first professor of political economy and mercantile law at Edinburgh, 1871–80; president of Educational Institute of Scotland, 1875; published, among other works, *Turgot* (1870) and lectures and treatises on girls' education and the study of economic science; joint editor of William Johnson *Fox's works; died at Brussels.

HODSOLL, Sir (Eric) John (1894–1971), civil servant; educated at Christ's Hospital; trained at Great Western Railway's works at Swindon; joined Royal Naval Air Service, 1914; transferred to Royal Air Force, 1918; served at Air Ministry, 1919–22; studied at Staff College, Camberley, 1923–4; posted to Delhi, 1925–9; assistant secretary (air) to Committee of Imperial Defence; at London Naval Conference, 1930, and Lausanne Conference, 1932; secretary of Air-Raid Precautions policy and official committees; in charge of ARP department, Home Office, 1934; assistant under-secretary, 1935–8; toured Britain to convince public of need for effective co-operation in ARP; inspector-general, ARP Services, 1938–45; director-general, Civil Defence Training, 1945–54; chief Civil Defence adviser to NATO, 1954–61; CB, 1934; knighted, 1944; awarded first Gold Medal of (British) Institute of Civil Defence and similar honours in Denmark, USA, and India.

HODSON, (Francis Lord) Charlton, Baron Hodson (1895–1984), lord of appeal in ordinary; educated at Cheltenham College, and Wadham College, Oxford, (scholar); served with 7th battalion, Gloucestershire Regiment, at Gallipoli and in Mesopotamia during 1914–18 war; MC; studied jurisprudence at Oxford, 1920; called to bar (Inner Temple), 1921; practised in divorce cases; junior counsel to Treasury (probate), 1935; KC, 1937; judge of High Court and knighted, 1937; bencher, Inner Temple, 1938; lord justice of appeal, 1951–60; PC, 1951; lord of appeal in ordinary, 1960–71; life peer, 1960; president, British branch of International Law Association, 1955; hon. fellow, Wadham College.

HODSON, Frodsham (1770–1822), principal of Brasenose College, Oxford; MA, Brasenose College, Oxford, 1793; DD, 1809; principal of Brasenose, 1809–22; vice-chancellor, 1818; regius professor of divinity, 1820; edited *Falconer's Chronological Tables* (1796).

HODSON, Henrietta (1841–1910), actress; went on stage, 1858; met (Sir) Henry *Irving (1860), and with him went to Manchester; popular burlesque actress; first appeared in London, 1866; joined Queen's Theatre Company, 1867; married as second husband (1868) Henry *Labouchere, who acquired sole control of Queen's Theatre, 1870; appeared there as Imogen in *Cymbeline*, 1871; assumed management of Royalty Theatre, Oct. 1871; inaugurated system of the unseen orchestra; revived *Wild Oats* (Dec. 1871), and won applause as Peg Woffington, 1875; introduced Mrs Langtry to stage, 1881; retired to Florence, 1903.

HODSON, Mrs Margaret (1778–1852), authoress; née Holford; married Septimus *Hodson, 1826; friend and correspondent of *Southey; works include *Wallace, Margaret of Anjou* (1815), and *Lives of Vasco Nuñez de Balboa and Francisco Pizarro* from the Spanish (1832).

HODSON, Septimus (1768–1833), rector of Thrapston and chaplain to prince of Wales; published *Address on High Price of Provisions* (1795).

HODSON, William (fl. 1640), theological writer; MA, Peterhouse, Cambridge, 1624; published theological works.

HODSON, William Stephen Raikes (1821–1858), cavalry leader; BA, Trinity College, Cambridge, 1844; entered Indian Army, 1845; served with 2nd Grenadiers in Sikh War; adjutant of the guides, 1847; assistant commissioner under Sir Henry *Lawrence in Punjab, 1849; commander of guides, 1852–4; removed on charge of dishonesty, 1855, but cleared by a second inquiry, 1856; served with 1st Fusiliers till given commission during Mutiny to raise 'Hodson's horse'; after capture of Delhi seized the king in Humayoon's tomb and shot the Shahzadas when rescue attempted; did good service at Cawnpore and Lucknow; was shot at Lucknow and buried there.

HODY, Humphrey (1659–1707), divine; scholar, 1677, fellow, 1685, dean, 1688, and bursar, 1691 and 1692, of Wadham College, Oxford; MA, 1682; DD, 1692; chaplain to Bishop *Stillingfleet, and afterwards to archbishops *Tillotson and *Tenison; regius professor of Greek at Oxford, 1698; archdeacon of Oxford, 1704; founded Greek and Hebrew exhibitions at Wadham; attacked the genuineness of Aristeas's account of the Septuagint, 1684; assisted in editing Aristeas's *History* (1692); conducted controversy with Henry *Dodwell the elder on nonjuring schism, 1691–9; published also *Resurrection of the Body asserted* (1694), *De Bibliorum Textibus Originalibus* (1705), and other works; his

De Graecis Illustribus edited by Samuel *Jebb (1742).

HODY, Sir John (d. 1441), judge; MP, Shaftesbury, 1423, 1425, 1428, and 1438, Somerset, 1434 and 1440; chief justice of the King's Bench, 1440; assisted *Lyttelton.

HODY, Sir William (d. 1522?), chief baron of the Exchequer, 1486; second son of Sir John *Hody; attorney-general and serjeant-at-law, 1485.

HOEY, Frances Sarah (known as Mrs **CASHEL HOEY**) (1830–1908), novelist; born Johnston; married John Cashel Hoey, CMG, 1858; contributed short stories to *Chambers's Journal*, 1865–94; wrote eleven novels dealing with fashionable society; helped Edmund *Yates in his novels; often visited Paris; translated many French and Italian works; received civil list pension, 1892.

HOFLAND, Barbara (1770–1844), authoress and friend of Miss *Mitford; married, first, T. Bradshaw Hoole, 1796, and secondly (1808) Thomas Christopher *Hofland; published novels, including *The Son of a Genius* (2nd edn. 1816).

HOFLAND, Thomas Christopher (1777–1843), landscape painter; exhibited at Academy, 1799–1805; gained British Institution Prize for *Storm off Scarborough*, 1814; held exhibition in Bond Street, 1821; foundation member of Society of British Artists; published *British Angler's Manual* (1839).

HOFMEYR, Jan Hendrik (1845–1909), South African politician; born and educated at Cape Town; edited *Ons Land* from 1871; formed Farmers' Association at Cape Town, 1878, amalgamated with the Afrikander Bond, 1883; chairman till 1895; member for Stellenbosch of Cape parliament, 1879–95; effective leader of constitutional Afrikanderdom; made the Dutch a political force; refused premiership, 1884; member of Executive Council of Cape Colony; as delegate in London (1887) proposed closer imperial union by means of imperial tariff of customs; negotiated for the British government with President Kruger the Swaziland Convention, 1890; supporter of Cecil *Rhodes till Jameson Raid of 1895; initiated Bloemfontein Conference between (Lord) *Milner and President Kruger, 1899; advocated conciliation after war, 1903; favoured federation in South Africa.

HOFMEYR, Jan Hendrik (1894–1948), South African statesman; nephew of J. H. *Hofmeyr; educated at South African College School; honours in classics (1909), mathematics (1910), Cape University; awarded Rhodes scholarship, 1910; first class, Lit. Hum., Balliol College, Oxford, 1916; professor of classics (1917–24), principal (1919–24), vice-chancellor (1926–30), and chancellor (1938–48), university of the Witwatersrand; administrator of Transvaal, 1924–9; MP, Johannesburg North, 1929–48; minister of interior public health, and education, 1933–6; mines, education, and labour and social welfare, 1936–8; finance and education, 1939–48; mines and education, and deputy prime minister, 1948; upheld Cape liberal tradition on native question; resigned from Cabinet (1938) over appointment of unsuitable representative of native affairs; from United party caucus (1939) over Asiatics Bill; PC, 1945.

HOG (or HOGG), James (1658?–1734), leader of 'Marrow men' in Church of Scotland; MA, Edinburgh, 1677; declined Oath of Allegiance, 1693; minister of Carnock, 1699–1734; republished *Marrow of Modern Divinity* (1718); denounced by general assembly, 1720; published controversial pamphlets.

HOG, Sir Roger, Lord Harcarse (1635?–1700), lord of session, 1677; knighted, 1677; lord of justiciary, 1678; removed, 1688; compiled *Dictionary of Decisions (1681–92)*, published (1757).

HOG, Thomas (1628–1692), Scottish divine; MA, Marischal College, Aberdeen; minister of Kiltearn, 1654–61 and 1691–2; deposed as protester, 1661; imprisoned for keeping conventicles; fined and banished, 1684; chaplain to William of Orange in Holland and when king.

HOGAN, John (1800–1858), Irish sculptor; during residence at Rome, 1824–49, executed his *Eve*, *Drunken Faun*, and *Dead Christ*; statues of *O'Connell and Thomas *Drummond by him at Dublin.

HOGARTH, David George (1862–1927), scholar and traveller; BA, Magdalen College, Oxford, 1885; Craven travelling fellow, 1886; travelled and excavated in Asia Minor, Cyprus, and Egypt, 1887–96; fellow of Magdalen, 1886; director of British School of Archaeology, Athens, 1897–1900; joined (Sir) Arthur *Evans in beginning of excavations at Knossos, 1900; keeper of Ashmolean Museum, Oxford, 1908–27; developed museum, especially in departments of Cretan and Hittite archaeology; commander, Royal Naval Volunteer Reserve, 1915–19; director of Arab Bureau, Cairo, 1916; FBA, 1905; CMG, 1918; works include *A Wandering Scholar in the Levant* (1896), *The Nearer East* (1902), *The Penetration of Arabia* (1904).

HOGARTH, George (1783–1870), music critic; inserted in *Evening Chronicle* sketches of London life by *Dickens, afterwards his son-in-law; music critic of *Daily News*, 1846–66, also of *Illustrated London News*; secretary of Philharmonic

Society, 1850–64; published *Musical History, Biography, and Criticism* (1835) and other works on music.

HOGARTH, William (1697–1764), painter and engraver; apprenticed to silver-plate engraver in Cranbourne Street, London; engraved and designed plates for booksellers and printsellers, including (1726) illustrations to *Hudibras*; painted conversation pieces, including scenes from *Beggar's Opera*, 1728–9; engraved *Large Masquerade Ticket*, 1727, and *Taste*, 1731; married clandestinely, at old Paddington Church, Jane Thornhill, 1729 ('Sigismunda'); assisted in decoration of Vauxhall and designed passtickets; his paintings of *The Harlot's Progress* engraved, 1732; took house in Leicester Square (then Fields) and made portrait of Sarah *Malcolm, murderess, 1733; his engraving of *Rake's Progress* and *Southwark Fair* issued complete, 1735, when 'Hogarth's Act', protecting designers from piracy, became operative; apostrophized by *Swift in the *Legion Club*; painted historical pictures at St Bartholomew's Hospital, 1736; issued the prints *The Distrest Poet, Company of Undertakers*, and *Sleeping Congregation*, 1736; his *Four Times of the Day, Strolling Actresses dressing in a Barn*, produced 1738; his *Enraged Musician* praised by *Fielding, 1741; his portraits of Captain Coram painted 1739, Martin *Folkes, 1741; his *Marriage-à-la-Mode*, 1745, engraved by French masters; etched Lord *Lovat, 1746; painted himself and dog, 1749; engraved *Industry and Idleness* and *Stage Coach*, 1747; visited France and revenged himself for arrest by his *Gate of Calais*, 1749; painted *The March to Finchley* and *Four Stages of Cruelty* (partly engraved on wood), 1750–1, *Moses and Pharaoh's Daughter* and *Paul before Felix*, 1752; published (with assistance) the *Analysis of Beauty*, with etched ticket, *Columbus breaking the egg*, 1753; issued the four *Election* prints, 1755–8, *England* and *France*, 1756, *The Bench*, 1758, *Cockpit*, 1759, and *Five Orders of Periwigs*, 1761; serjeant-painter, 1757; exhibited *Picquet, or the Lady's Last Stake* and *Sigismunda*, 1761; caricatured *Wilkes and *Churchill in *The Times*, 1762, and etched Fielding; his last plate, *The Bathos*, 1764. His epitaph was written by *Garrick. Many of his works are at the National Gallery, National Portrait Gallery, and Soane Museum. The *Apprentice* and *Cruelty* series, *France* and *England, Beer Street*, and *Gin Lane*, were probably never painted. A large collection of his engravings was acquired by the British Museum, 1828. Hogarth hated foreigners, and attacked art connoisseurs for neglect of native talent. He excelled as a pictorial satirist in depicting both tragic and humorous scenes, always with a sincerely ethical intention.

HOGARTH, William (1786–1866), Roman Catholic bishop; professor and general prefect at Ushaw; vicar-apostolic of northern district, 1848; first Roman Catholic bishop of Hexham and Newcastle, 1850–66.

HOGBEN, Lancelot Thomas (1895–1975), biologist; educated at Middlesex County Secondary School and Trinity College, Cambridge, where he was a scholar; first class, part i, natural sciences tripos, 1914; external B.Sc., London; joined Fabian Society; suffered from over-active thyroid; conscientious objector, 1914; imprisoned for three months; lecturer in zoology, Birkbeck College, London, 1917; moved to Royal College of Science, 1919; did research on chromosome cytology; deputy director, Institute of Animal Genetics, Edinburgh, 1922; assistant professor of medical zoology, McGill University, Montreal, 1925; published papers on blood of invertebrates; professor of zoology, Cape Town University, 1927; professor of social biology, London School of Economics, 1930; FRS, 1936; published *Mathematics for the Million* (1933) and *Science for the Citizen* (1938); regius professor of natural history, Aberdeen, 1937; Mason professor of zoology, Birmingham, 1941; acting director of medical statistics, War Office, 1944–6; professor of medical statistics, Birmingham, 1947–61; vice-chancellor, University of Guyana, 1963–5; hon. D.Sc., Wales and LL D, Birmingham.

HOGENBERG, Franz (d. 1590), engraver; brother of Remigius *Hogenberg.

HOGENBERG, Remigius (d. 1580?), engraver; came to England, c.1573; employed by Archbishop *Parker in constructing genealogies; his engraving of Parker's portrait by *Lyne said to be the first executed in England; engraved maps and portraits of Henri IV, Erasmus, and others.

HOGG, Douglas McGarel, first Viscount Hailsham (1872–1950), statesman and lord chancellor; son of Quintin *Hogg; educated at Eton; entered family sugar firm; interested himself in Polytechnic; called to bar (Lincoln's Inn), 1902; KC, 1917; bencher, 1920; attorney-general to prince of Wales, 1920–2; Conservative MP, St Marylebone, 1922–8; attorney-general, 1922–4, 1924–8; lord chancellor, 1928–9, 1935–8; leader of opposition in House of Lords, 1930–1; secretary of state for war and leader of House of Lords, 1931–5; a British delegate, Ottawa Conference (1932) and World Economic Conference (1933); lord president of the Council, 1938; knighted and PC, 1922; baron, 1928; viscount, 1929.

HOGG, Henry (1831–1874), Nottingham poet.

HOGG, Jabez (1817–1899), ophthalmic surgeon; apprenticed to medical practitioner, 1832–7; joined staff of *Illustrated London News*; editor and sub-editor in various publishing undertakings; studied at Hunterian School of Medicine and Charing Cross Hospital, 1845; MRCS, 1850; surgeon to Royal Westminster Ophthalmic Hospital, 1871–8, and to hospital for women and children; FLS, 1866; published scientific works.

HOGG, James (1770–1835), the Ettrick Shepherd; shepherd at Willanslee, *c.*1785; while employed by the father of William *Laidlaw began to write verse; printed *Donald M'Donald* (1800) and *Scottish Pastorals* (1801); made acquaintance of *Scott and gave material for *Border Minstrelsy*; his ballads published by *Constable as *The Mountain Bard* (1807); returned to Ettrick bankrupt, having failed as a farmer in Dumfriesshire; came to Edinburgh, 1810, and published the *Forest Minstrel*; obtained poetical reputation by *The Queen's Wake* (1813), and acquaintance, through *Byron, of John *Murray; formed friendships with Professor John *Wilson, *Wordsworth, and *Southey; issued *Pilgrims of the Sun* (1815), *The Poetic Mirror* (1816); settled at Eltrive Lake, 1816; assisted in the Chaldee MS for *Blackwood's Magazine*, 1817, and began prose tales; published *Jacobite Relics* and *Winter Evening Tales* (1820), *The Three Perils of Man* (1822), *Confessions of a Fanatic* (1824), *Queen Hynde* (1825), *Shepherd's Calendar* and *Songs* (1829); was entertained publicly in London, 1832, and at Peebles, 1833; issued *Domestic Manners and Private Life of Sir Walter Scott* (1834). A monument to him was erected on St Mary's Lake, 1860.

HOGG, James (1806–1888), Edinburgh publisher; edited *The Weekly Instructor* or *Titan*, 1845–59; published *De Quincey's and *Gilfillan's works, and *London Society*.

HOGG, Sir James Macnaghten Mcgarel, first Baron Magheramorne (1823–1890), son of Sir James Weir *Hogg; of Eton and Christ Church, Oxford; served in 1st Life Guards, 1843–59; Conservative MP, Bath, 1865–8, Truro, 1871–85, Hornsey, 1885–7; chairman of Metropolitan Board of Works, 1870–89; created peer, 1887.

HOGG, Sir James Weir, first baronet (1790–1876), East India director; scholar and gold medallist of Trinity College, Dublin; BA, 1810; registrar of Calcutta Supreme Court, 1822–33; a director of East India Company, 1839, chairman, 1846–7 and 1852–3; MP, Beverley, 1835–47, Honiton, 1847–57; created baronet, 1846; member of Indian Council, 1858–72; privy councillor, 1872.

HOGG, John (1800–1869), scholar and naturalist; brother of Thomas Jefferson *Hogg; fellow of Peterhouse, Cambridge, 1827; MA, 1827; foreign secretary and vice-president of Royal Society of Literature, 1866; FRS, 1839; published *Catalogue of Sicilian Plants* (1842) and other works of natural history.

HOGG, Quintin (1845–1903), philanthropist; son of Sir James Weir *Hogg; educated at Eton; partner in London firm of Hogg, Curtis, and Campbell, sugar merchants; started Ragged School for Boys at Charing Cross, 1864–5; purchased Royal Polytechnic Institution, Regent Street, and opened it for athletic, intellectual, spiritual, and social recreation, 1882; opened day school there and organized holiday tours (1886) and a labour bureau (1891); his success led to spread of polytechnic movement in London; alderman of London County Council, 1889–94; published *The Story of Peter* (religious addresses), 1900.

HOGG, Thomas Jefferson (1792–1862), friend and biographer of *Shelley; at University College, Oxford, with Shelley; sent down on the publication of Shelley's *Necessity of Atheism*; joined the poet and Harriet Shelley at Edinburgh; quarrel caused by his behaviour to Shelley's wife; published *Memoirs of Prince Alexy Haimatoff* (1813); called to bar, 1817; united himself to widow of Shelley's friend, Edward Ellerker *Williams; quarrelled with John Stuart *Mill; contributed reminiscences of Shelley at Oxford to *Bulwer's *New Monthly Magazine*, 1832; municipal corporation commissioner, 1833; afterwards revising barrister; published two volumes of life of Shelley (1858); contributed to *Edinburgh Review* and *Encyclopaedia Britannica*.

HOGGARDE, Miles (*fl.* 1557). See HUGGARDE.

HOGHTON, Daniel (1770–1811), major-general; major, 1794; served in Jamaica and India; brevet-lieutenant-colonel, 1796; lieutenant-colonel, 1804; brevet-colonel, 1805; brigadier at Cadiz, 1810; major-general, 1810; killed at Albuera. A public monument to him is in St Paul's Cathedral.

HOHENLOHE-LANGENBURG, Prince Victor of, Count Gleichen (1833–1891). See VICTOR.

HOLBEACH (or RANDS), Henry (d. 1551), bishop of Lincoln; assumed name of birthplace (Holbeach) on entering Crowland Monastery; DD, Cambridge, 1534; prior of Buckingham College, 1535, of Worcester, 1536; bishop suffragan (Bristol) to *Latimer, 1538; assisted in drawing up Prayer-Book (1548); first dean of Worcester, 1540; bishop of Rochester, 1544–7; bishop of Lincoln, 1547–51.

HOLBEACH, Henry (pseudonym) (1823–1882), 'the laureate of the nursery'. See RANDS, WILLIAM BRIGHTY.

HOLBEIN, Hans (1497–1543), painter; born at Augsburg; went to Lucerne; at Basle designed marginal illustrations in copy of Erasmus's *Encomium Moriae*, 1515, and painted portraits of Jacob Meyer and Hans Herbster, 1516, and mural paintings and religious works, 1521–2; executed paintings and designs at Lucerne, 1518; painted, *c*.1526, the Darmstadt *Madonna with Meyer family*; designed illustrations for Luther's German Testament and Pentateuch, 1522–3; painted three portraits of Erasmus, 1523; came to England, 1526, with introduction to Sir Thomas *More; painted portraits of More, 1527, *Warham, and others; designed large picture of More's household; during residence at Basle (1528–32) completed mural paintings at the town hall, and probably executed portraits of his wife and children and of Erasmus; many of his religious works destroyed in an iconoclastic outbreak; returned to England and executed portraits of merchant goldsmiths; drew *Queen of Sheba before Solomon*; painted *The Ambassadors*, 1533, and the *Morett* portrait; designed title-pages to *Coverdale's (1535) and *Cranmer's (1540) Bible and other Protestant publications; painted *Cromwell and *Jane Seymour, 1536; his *Henry VIII with Parents* destroyed, 1698, but a copy preserved at Hampton Court; took part (1538) in negotiations for marriage of Henry VIII to Christina of Denmark and painted her portrait; publicly entertained at Basle, and brought out designs to Old Testament and *The Dance of Death*, 1538; painted portraits of *Anne of Cleves, 1539, *Norfolk, *Surrey, Sir John Russell, and others; began large picture at Barber-Surgeons' Hall, 1542; died of the plague in London. He was one of the earliest miniaturists, painting in that manner *Catherine Howard and Anne of Cleves. Authentic pictures by Holbein are rare in England.

HOLBORNE, Anthony (*fl.* 1597), musical composer; published *Cittharn Schoole* (1597) and *Pavans, Galliards, Almains* etc., for wind instruments (1599).

HOLBORNE, Sir Robert (d. 1647), lawyer; of Furnival's and Lincoln's Inn (bencher and reader in English law); counsel for *Hampden in ship-money case; MP for Southwark in Short Parliament and for St Michael in Long Parliament; attorney-general to prince of Wales; knighted, 1643; published legal tracts.

HOLBROOK, Ann Catherine (1780–1837), actress; published *Memoirs of an Actress* (1807), *Memoirs of the Stage* (1809), and tales.

HOLBROOK, John (d. 1437), master of Peterhouse, Cambridge; fellow of Peterhouse, 1393, DD, 1418, master, 1421–36; chaplain to Henry V and Henry VI; chancellor of Cambridge, 1429–30; vicar of Hinton, 1430; reputed mathematician.

HOLBURNE, Francis (1704–1771), admiral; while commander in Leeward Islands obtained dismantling of Martinique fortifications; rear-admiral, 1755; served with Biscay Fleet, 1756; member of court martial on *Byng, 1757; his fleet almost destroyed before Louisbourg; admiral of the blue, 1767, of the white, 1770; eight years commander at Portsmouth; a lord of the Admiralty, 1770–1; died governor of Greenwich.

HOLCOMBE, Henry (1690?–1750?), musical composer; published collections of songs and instrumental pieces.

HOLCOT, Robert of (d. 1349), divine; Dominican and doctor in theology of Oxford; won repute for expositions of the Bible; said to have died of the plague; author of subsequently published commentaries, *Quaestiones* on Peter Lombard's *Sentences*, *Conferentiae*, and *Moralitates Historiarum*; in the service of Richard de *Bury, whose *Philobiblon sive de amore librorum* is attributed to Holcot by some manuscripts.

HOLCROFT, Francis (1629?–1693), Puritan divine; MA and fellow, Clare Hall, Cambridge; ejected from Bassingbourne, 1662; imprisoned at Cambridge, 1663–72, and in the Fleet; promoter of Independency in Cambridgeshire.

HOLCROFT, Thomas (1745–1809), dramatist and author; successively stable-boy, shoemaker, tutor in family of Granville *Sharp, and actor; his first comedy, *Duplicity*, produced at Covent Garden, 1781; correspondent of *Morning Herald* in Paris, 1783; translated *Mariage de Figaro* from memory, and produced adaptation at Covent Garden, himself playing Figaro, 1784; produced *The Road to Ruin*, 1792 (nine editions printed within the year); indicted for high treason, 1794, but discharged; his musical adaptation, *Tale of Mystery*, produced at Covent Garden, 1802, during his absence on continent; set up printing business in London, but failed; intimate of William *Godwin the elder, and spoken highly of by *Lamb; his *Memoirs* (published 1816) mainly compiled by *Hazlitt; published numerous comedies and comic operas, also *Human Happiness* (poem, 1783), some novels, including *Alwyn, or the Gentleman Comedian* (1780), translations, including *Life of Baron Trenck* (1788), Lavater's

Physiognomy (1793), and Goethe's *Hermann und Dorothea* (1801).

HOLDEN, Charles Henry (1875–1960), architect; apprenticed in Manchester and studied at art school and technical college; joined C. R. *Ashbee in London, 1897; assistant to Percy Adams, 1899, partner, 1907; works include buildings for Law Society, Chancery Lane; British Medical Association (Rhodesia House), Strand; Royal Northern Hospital; London University; Bristol Public Library and Royal Infirmary; for Frank *Pick designed 55 Broadway and many tube stations; his abstract architectural composition, austere and simple, provided for sculptures by Eric *Gill, Sir Jacob *Epstein, Henry Moore, etc.; prepared plan for Canterbury and, with (Lord) Holford, for City of London; ARIBA, 1906; FRIBA, 1921; royal medallist, 1936.

HOLDEN, George (1783–1865), theological writer; graduated at Glasgow; incumbent of Maghull, Liverpool, 1811–65; his library bequeathed to Ripon clergy; published theological works.

HOLDEN, Henry (1596–1662), Roman Catholic divine; DD and professor at the Sorbonne and vicar-general of Paris; petitioned for toleration of English Catholics, 1647; engaged in controversy with Arnault, 1656; criticized writings of Thomas *White (1593–1676); published *Divinae Fidei Analysis* (1652, English translation 1658); died at Paris, leaving bequests to English subjects in France.

HOLDEN, Henry Smith (1887–1963), academic botanist and forensic scientist; educated at Castleton School and Victoria University, Manchester; assistant lecturer, University College, Nottingham; M.Sc., Manchester, 1911; bacteriologist, Royal Naval Hospital, Plymouth, 1916–19; professor of botany, Nottingham, 1932–6; D.Sc., 1921; fellow, Linnean Society, 1910; FRS, Edinburgh, 1927; director, forensic science laboratory under Home Office, 1936–46; director, Metropolitan Police Laboratory, 1946–51; provided scientific evidence in number of notorious criminal cases; forensic science adviser to Home Office, 1951–8; CBE, 1958; published many papers on botanical subjects, mainly in *Annals of Botany* and the *Journal of the Linnean Society*.

HOLDEN, Hubert Ashton (1822–1896), classical scholar; BA, Trinity College, Cambridge, 1845; fellow, 1847–54; LL D, 1863; ordained priest, 1859; vice-principal of Cheltenham College, 1853–8; headmaster of Queen Elizabeth's School, Ipswich, 1858–83; fellow of London University, 1890; hon. Litt.D., Dublin, 1892; edited classical works for students.

HOLDEN, Sir Isaac, first baronet (1807–1897), inventor; worked in cotton mill; shawl weaver; assistant teacher successively at schools at Paisley, Leeds, Huddersfield, and Reading; bookkeeper in Townend Brothers' firm of worsted manufacturers, 1830–46; associated with Samuel Cunliffe Lister, afterwards first Baron Masham, with whom he obtained patent (1847) for new method of carding and combing and preparing genappe yarns; opened manufactory at St Denis, near Paris, 1848; concentrated business at Bradford, 1864; MP, Knaresborough, 1865–8, and Keighley division, 1882–95; created baronet, 1893.

HOLDEN, Lawrence, the elder (1710–1778), Dissenting divine; published *Paraphrase on . . . Job, Psalms, Proverbs, Ecclesiastes* (1763) and *A Paraphrase on . . . Isaiah* (1776).

HOLDEN, Lawrence, the younger (1752–1844), Dissenting divine at Tenterden, 1774–1844; son of Lawrence *Holden the elder.

HOLDEN, Luther (1815–1905), surgeon; studied at St Bartholomew's Hospital, Berlin, and Paris; MRCS, 1838; FRCS, 1844; president, 1878; Hunterian orator, 1881; demonstrator (1846), lecturer on surgical anatomy (1859–71), surgeon (1865) at St Bartholomew's Hospital; on retirement (1881) spent much time in foreign travel; good linguist, classicist, and sportsman; primarily interested in anatomical study of surgery; published *Human Osteology* (2 vols., 1855) and other medical works.

HOLDEN, Moses (1777–1864), Preston astronomer; constructed large orrery and magic lantern; published small celestial atlas (1818) and an almanac (1835).

HOLDER, Sir Frederick William (1850–1909), first speaker of the Australian Commonwealth House of Representatives, 1901–9; born in South Australia; editor and proprietor of *Burra Record*; mayor of Burra, 1886–90; member of Legislative Assembly of South Australia from 1887; treasurer of colony, 1889–90, 1894–9; premier, 1892 and 1899; commissioner of public works, 1893; KCMG, 1902.

HOLDER, William (1616–1698), divine; MA and fellow, Pembroke Hall, Cambridge, 1640; rector of Bletchington and Northwold; taught a deaf-mute to speak; FRS, 1663; canon of St Paul's; sub-dean of Chapel Royal, 1674–89; rector of Therfield, Hertfordshire, 1687; helped to educate Sir Christopher *Wren; published *Elements of Speech* (1669) and treatises on harmony and the Julian calendar.

HOLDERNESS, earls of. See RAMSAY, Sir JOHN, 1580?–1626; RUPERT, Prince, 1619–1682; D'ARCY, ROBERT, fourth earl of the third creation, 1718–1778.

HOLDERNESS, Sir **Thomas William,** first baronet (1849–1924), Indian civil servant; born in New Brunswick; passed into Indian Civil Service, 1870; proceeded to India, 1872; employed as secretary in Board of Revenue, etc., at Allahabad, 1876; under-secretary to government of India, revenue department, 1881–5; director of land records and agriculture, 1888; assisted in famine-relief operations, 1896–7; secretary to government of India, revenue and agricultural department, 1898–1901; secretary, revenue, statistics, and commerce department, India Office, 1901–12; permanent under-secretary of state, India Office, 1912–19; baronet, 1920.

HOLDICH, Sir **Thomas Hungerford** (1843–1929), Anglo-Indian frontier surveyor; entered Royal Engineers, 1862; sent to India, 1865; temporary assistant surveyor, Bhutan expedition, 1865–6; subsequently appointed permanently to survey department; began long connection with North-West Frontier as survey officer with Southern Afghanistan Field Force, 1878; served on Russo-Afghan Boundary Commission, 1884–6; superintendent of frontier surveys, 1892–8; member of Pamirs Commission, 1895; commissioner for Perso-Baluch boundary, 1896; for Argentine–Chile boundary, 1902–3; KCMG, 1902.

HOLDING, Frederick (1817–1874), Manchester water-colour painter.

HOLDING, Henry James (1833–1872), painter; brother of Frederick *Holding.

HOLDSWORTH, Daniel (1558?–1595?), classical scholar. See HALSWORTH.

HOLDSWORTH, Edward (1684–1746), classical scholar; of Winchester and Magdalen College, Oxford; MA, 1711; held Jacobite views; travelled in Italy and France; published *Muscipula sive Cambro-muo-machia* (1709), often reissued, and translated by Samuel *Cobb and others; *Remarks and Dissertations on Virgil*, with notes by *Spence, issued (1768).

HOLDSWORTH, Richard (1590–1649), master of Emmanuel College, Cambridge; scholar of St John's College, Cambridge, 1607; fellow, 1613; BA, 1610; incorporated MA, Oxford, 1617; rector of St Peter-le-Poor, London, 1624; Gresham professor of divinity, 1629; archdeacon of Huntingdon, 1634; master of Emmanuel College, Cambridge, 1637–43; president of Sion College, 1639; when vice-chancellor of Cambridge, 1640, resisted interference of parliament

with Emmanuel fellowships; sequestrated from mastership and rectory and imprisoned (1643) for withholding aid from parliament and publishing royal proclamation; visited Charles I at Holmby House, and was made dean of Worcester, 1647; his library bought by Cambridge University.

HOLDSWORTH, Sir **William Searle** (1871–1944), lawyer; educated at Dulwich and New College, Oxford; first class, history, 1893, jurisprudence, 1894; called to bar (Lincoln's Inn), 1896; bencher, 1924; fellow, St John's College, Oxford, 1897; All Souls reader in English law, 1910; Vinerian professor, 1922–44; member, Indian States Inquiry Committee (1928) and Committee on Ministers' Powers (1929–32); publications include *Sources and Literature of English Law* (1925), *Some Lessons from our Legal History* (1928), and *History of English Law* (13 vols., 1903–52); FBA, 1922; knighted, 1929; OM, 1943.

HOLE, Henry Fulke Plantagenet Woolicombe (d. 1820), wood-engraver.

HOLE, Matthew (d. 1730), rector of Exeter College, Oxford; MA, 1664; DD, 1716; vicar of Stogursey, 1688–1730; rector of Exeter College, 1716–30; made bequests to his college and to Oxford charities; tracts by him on the liturgy republished, 1837–8.

HOLE, Richard (1746–1803), poet; BCL, Exeter College, Oxford, 1771; vicar of Buckerell, 1777; rector of Faringdon, 1792, and of Inwardleigh; published *Poetical Translation of Fingal*, with *Ode to Imagination* (1772); his version of *Homer's Hymn to Ceres* (1781) in many collections; his *Essay on Character of Ulysses* edited, 1807; many poems by him in Richard *Polwhele's collection.

HOLE, Samuel Reynolds (1819–1904), dean of Rochester and author; BA, Brasenose College, Oxford, 1844; MA, 1878; published *Hints to Freshmen* (1847); vicar of Caunton, 1850–87; prebendary of Lincoln, 1875; enthusiastic huntsman, sportsman, and gardener; close friend of John *Leech from 1858, who introduced him to W. M. *Thackeray; contributed to *Punch*; a successful rose-grower and organizer of national show; his *Book about Roses* (1869) popularized rose-growing; a popular preacher and platform orator; dean of Rochester and DD, Lambeth, 1887; lectured in United States, 1894; a humorous and charming letter-writer; *Letters* edited with memoir by G. A. B. Dewar, 1907; published *Memories* (1892), *More Memories* (1894), and *Then and Now* (1901); wrote hymns, sermons, and addresses.

HOLE (or HOLLE), William (*fl.* 1600–1630), earliest English engraver of music on copper plates; also engraved portraits and title-pages of maps for *Camden's *Britannia* (1607).

HOLFORD, Margaret (1778–1852), authoress. See HODSON.

HOLFORD, William Graham, Baron Holford (1907–1975), architect; born in Johannesburg; educated at Diocesan College (Bishops), Rondebosch, near Capetown; studied at Liverpool University School of Architecture, 1925–30; B.Arch., with first-class honours; awarded Rome scholarship in architecture; spent three years in Italy; senior lecturer, Liverpool School of Architecture, 1933–6; succeeded (Sir) L. Patrick *Abercrombie as Lever professor of civic design, 1936; planning consultant to government industrial estate, Team Valley, near Newcastle upon Tyne, 1937; during 1939–45 war guided teams of architects in building ordnance factories and hostels and was principal adviser (1943–7) to new Ministry of Town and Country Planning; professor of town planning, University College, London, 1948; founded firm of Holford Associates; received many commissions, including City of London plan, work for Eton, King's College, Cambridge, City companies, five universities, surroundings of St Paul's and Piccadilly Circus, and much work in Scotland; president (Royal) Town Planning Institute, 1953–4 and Royal Institute of British Architects, 1960–2; awarded gold medals of both; ARA, 1961; RA, 1968; treasurer of Royal Academy, 1970; member, Royal Fine Art Commission, 1943–69 and Historic Buildings Council, 1953; member, Central Electricity Generating Board; trustee, British Museum (and Soane); honorary degrees from four universities; Romanes lecturer, Oxford, 1969; director, Leverhulme Trust; knighted, 1953; life peer, 1965.

HOLGATE (or HOLDEGATE), Robert (1481?–1556), archbishop of York; master of the order of St Gilbert of Sempringham, 1534, and prior of Watton, 1536; chaplain to Henry VIII; DD, Cambridge, 1537; bishop of Llandaff, 1537; assisted in composing *Institutes of a Christian Man*; president of the north, 1538–50; archbishop of York, 1545–54; impoverished his see; favoured reformed doctrines, and was deprived for being married, 1554; imprisoned, but released on submission; endowed hospital at Hemsworth.

HOLIDAY, Henry (1839–1927), painter and worker in stained glass; his best-known painting, *Dante and Beatrice*, exhibited 1883; worked for Powell Glass Works, Whitefriars, as designer of cartoons for stained glass, from 1863; examples of his work to be seen all over England, in Europe and in the United States.

HOLINSHED (or HOLLINGSHEAD), Raphael (d. 1580?), chronicler; came to London early in reign of Elizabeth; employed as translator by Reginald *Wolfe, and to continue a chronicle of universal history, which Wolfe had begun; his *Chronicles* of England (to 1575), Scotland (to 1571), and Ireland (to 1547) published (1578, expunged passages inserted in copy in Grenville Library, British Museum). The *Chronicle* was reissued, with continuation, edited by John *Hooker, alias Vowell, 1586, and politically offensive passages again taken out; it was utilized by Shakespeare and other dramatists.

HOLKER, Jean Louis (1770–1844), discoverer of the method of continuous combustion in vitriol manufacture; son of John *Holker (1745–1822).

HOLKER, John (1719–1786), Jacobite; captured with Manchester Volunteers at Carlisle, 1745; escaped from Newgate to France, 1746; in Irish brigade, 1747–51; accompanied Young Pretender on secret visit to England, 1750; engaged workmen from Manchester for Rouen cotton-mill, 1754; as inspector-general of manufactures established spinning schools and first French vitriol factory; knight of St Louis, 1770; ennobled, 1775; buried at Rouen.

HOLKER, John (1745–1822), French consul-general at Philadelphia from 1777; son of John *Holker (1719–1786).

HOLKER, Sir John (1828–1882), lord justice; barrister, Gray's Inn, 1854, and treasurer, 1875; QC, 1866; knighted, 1874; had large practice in patent cases; MP, Preston, 1872–82; solicitor-general, 1874; attorney-general, 1875–80; lord justice, 1882; carried Summary Procedure and Public Prosecution Acts, 1879.

HOLL, Francis (1815–1884), engraver; son of William *Holl the elder; engraved pictures for Queen Victoria, portraits by George *Richmond, Frith's *Railway Station*, and many chalk drawings; ARA, 1883.

HOLL, Francis Montague (1845–1888), painter, known as Frank Holl; son of Francis *Holl (1815–1884); educated at University College and Royal Academy schools; gold medallist, 1863; gained travelling studentship, 1868; exhibited at Academy from 1864; RA, 1883; exhibited *No Tidings from the Sea*, 1871, and *Leaving Home*, 1873; painted 198 portraits, 1879–88, including the duke of *Cambridge, Sir William *Jenner, Sir Henry *Rawlinson, John *Bright, Lord Roberts, and two of King Edward VII while prince of Wales.

HOLL, William, the elder (1771–1838), stipple-engraver; noted for portraits.

HOLL, William, the younger (1807–1871), stipple- and line-engraver; son of William *Holl the elder; executed portraits, subject pictures after Frith, and book illustrations.

HOLLAMS, Sir **John** (1820–1910), solicitor; admitted solicitor, 1844; president of Law Society, 1878–9; knighted, 1902; published *Jottings of an Old Solicitor* (1906).

HOLLAND, Barons. See FOX, HENRY, first baron, 1705–1774; FOX, HENRY RICHARD VASSALL, third baron, 1773–1840.

HOLLAND, first earl of (1590–1649). See RICH, HENRY.

HOLLAND, Lady (1770–1845). See FOX, ELIZABETH VASSALL.

HOLLAND, Abraham (d. 1626), poet; son of Philemon *Holland; BA, Trinity College, Cambridge, 1617; author of *Naumachia, or Hollands Sea-Fight* (1622), describing Lepanto; *Hollandi Posthuma* edited by his brother (1626).

HOLLAND, Charles (1733–1769), actor; appeared at Drury Lane, 1755–69; played Iago, Iachimo, Jaffier, Hamlet, Macbeth, Romeo, Chamont; praised by *Chatterton, but satirized by *Churchill for imitation of *Garrick; intimate of *Powell; inscription written by Garrick for his monument in Chiswick Church.

HOLLAND, Charles (1768–1849?), actor; nephew of Charles *Holland (1733–1769); appeared at Drury Lane, 1796–1820, at Haymarket, 1809–10; played Horatio to *Elliston's Hamlet at Lyceum, 1812, Mendizabel to *Kean's Manuel, 1817, Buckingham to his Richard III, 1819, Gloucester to his Lear, 1820.

HOLLAND, Cornelius (*fl.* 1649), regicide; of Merchant Taylors' School and Pembroke Hall, Cambridge; BA, 1618; clerk-comptroller to prince of Wales, 1635; MP, New Windsor, 1640; a commissioner for Scottish treaty, 1643; as member of Council of State, 1649, said to have drawn up charges against the king, but did not sign warrant; liberally rewarded by parliament; escaped to Holland, 1660; said to have died at Lausanne.

HOLLAND, Sir **Eardley Lancelot** (1879–1967), obstetrician; educated at Merchiston Castle, Edinburgh, and King's College Hospital, London; qualified, 1903; MB, BS, London, FRCS, 1905; held number of appointments in London hospitals and worked in Berlin; obstetric registrar and tutor, King's College Hospital, 1907; MD; MRCP, 1908; appointed obstetric and gynaecological surgeon, London Hospital,

1916–46, but only took up work in 1919; meanwhile, served in France with RAMC; researched into causes of still-birth, 1922; held number of public appointments concerned with gynaecology; adviser to Ministry of Health, 1937–40; president, Royal College of Obstetricians and Gynaecologists, 1943–6; author of a *Manual of Obstetrics*; edited (with Aleck Bourne) two volumes of *British Obstetric and Gynaecological Practice* (1955); edited the *Journal of Obstetrics and Gynaecology of the British Empire*; made special study of pregnancy of Princess *Charlotte who died in childbirth in 1817; honorary degrees and other academic honours; knighted, 1947.

HOLLAND, Edmund, fourth earl of Kent (d. 1408), second son of Sir Thomas *Holland, second earl; mortally wounded at Briant.

HOLLAND, Sir **(Edward) Milner** (1902–1969), lawyer; educated at Charterhouse and Hertford College, Oxford; BCL, 1927; called to bar (Inner Temple), 1927; substantial practice, mainly in Chancery division; assistant reader in equity, Council of Legal Education, 1931; reader, 1935; served in RASC, 1939–45; deputy director, Personal Services, War Office, 1943; CBE, 1945; KC, 1948; bencher, Lincoln's Inn, 1953; attorney-general, duchy of Lancaster, 1951; chairman, General Council of the bar, 1957–8 and 1962–3; member of Council on Tribunals, 1958–62; vice-chairman, Inns of Court Executive Council, 1962; chairman, London Rented Housing Survey, 1963; knighted, 1959; KCVO, 1965.

HOLLAND, George Calvert (1801–1865), physician; MD, Edinburgh, 1827; B.-ès-Lettres, Paris; practised at Manchester and Sheffield; defended the corn laws; abandoned practice to direct banks and railway companies, and failed; adopted homoeopathy, 1851; studied mesmerism; published *Experimental Enquiry into Laws of Animal Life* (1829), *Physiology of the Foetus* (1831), and other scientific works.

HOLLAND, Guy (1587?–1660), sometimes known as Guy Holt; Jesuit; BA, St John's College, Cambridge, 1605; entered English College, Valladolid, 1608; joined Jesuits in England, 1615; arrested in London, 1628; forty-five years on English mission; attacked Falkland's *Discourse of the Infallibility of the Church of Rome* (1645); defended immortality of the soul, 1653.

HOLLAND, Henry (*c.*1555–1603), divine; BA, Magdalene College, Cambridge, 1580; vicar of Orwell, 1580–92, of St Bride's, London, 1594–1604; works include *Treatise against Witchcraft* (1590) and *Spirituall Preseruatiues against the Pestilence* (1593).

HOLLAND, Henry (d. 1625), Roman Catholic divine; of Eton and St John's College, Oxford; BA, 1569; BD, Douai, 1578; on English mission, 1582; divinity reader at Marchiennes and Anchine; published *Urna Aurea* (1612) and Latin life of Thomas *Stapleton (1620); died at Anchine.

HOLLAND, Henry (1583–1650?), compiler and publisher; son of Philemon *Holland; free of Stationers' Company, 1608; issued his own *Monumenta Sepulchraria Sancti Pauli* (1614, continued and reissued, 1633), and *Baziliωlogia*, with engravings by *Elstracke, *Pass, and Francis *Delaram (1618), and *Herωologia Anglica* (with portraits, 1620); edited Philemon Holland's latin version of Bauderon's *Pharmacopoeia* (1639) and *Regimen Sanitatis Salerni* (1649); served in Parliamentary army, 1643.

HOLLAND, Henry (1746?–1806), architect; designed Claremont House, Esher, for *Clive, 1763–4, Battersea Bridge, 1771–2, Brooks's Club, 1777–8, and Brighton Pavilion, 1787; altered and enlarged Carlton House, 1788; designed Drury Lane for *Sheridan, 1791, and new East India House, demolished in 1862; laid out Sloane Street; member of committee to report on Houses of Parliament, 1789; FSA, 1797; drew up architects' report on fires, 1792.

HOLLAND, Sir Henry, first baronet (1788–1873), physician; MD, Edinburgh, 1811; studied at Guy's and St Thomas's hospitals; visited Iceland and contributed to Sir George S. *Mackenzie's account, 1810; medical attendant to princess of Wales (*Caroline) on the continent, 1814; gave evidence in her favour, 1820; FRS, 1816; FRCP, 1828; physician-in-ordinary to Prince *Albert, 1840, to Queen Victoria, 1852; created baronet, 1853; travelled much on continent; published *Travels* (1815), *Chapters on Mental Physiology* (1852), *Essays* (1862), and *Recollections* (1872).

HOLLAND, Henry Scott (1847–1918), theologian and preacher; BA, Balliol College, Oxford; a senior student of Christ Church, 1870–84; canon of St Paul's, 1884–1911; position became identified with social and economic questions; helped to found Christian Social Union, and edited *Commonwealth*, 1895–1912; contributed to *Lux Mundi*, 1889; regius professor of divinity at Oxford, 1911–18; raised standard required for divinity degrees; published little except sermons and articles, largely owing to indifferent health; liberal in politics and theology, but high churchman.

HOLLAND, Sir Henry Thurstan, second baronet, and first Viscount Knutsford (1825–1914), son of Sir Henry *Holland, first baronet; BA, Trinity College, Cambridge; called to bar (Inner Temple), 1849; assistant under-secretary for colonies, 1870–4; succeeded father, 1873; Conservative MP, Midhurst, 1874–85; PC, 1885; secretary of state for colonies, 1888–92; baron and GCMG, 1888; viscount, 1895.

HOLLAND, Sir Henry Tristram (1875–1965), eye surgeon, missionary, and philanthropist; grandson of Canon Henry Baker *Tristram; educated at Loretto School and Edinburgh University Medical School; MB; Ch.B., 1899; joined Punjab Mission of Church Missionary Society, 1900–48; worked in CMS Hospital, Quetta; established reputation for cataract surgery; FRCSE, 1907; performed over 60,000 operations for cataract; Quetta Hospital destroyed in earthquake, 1935; helped to raise funds for rebuilding; founder-member, Royal Commonwealth Society for the Blind; secretary, CMS Punjab Medical Executive Committee; Kaiser-i-Hind Silver Medal, 1910; Gold Medal, 1925; bar, 1931; CIE, 1929; knighted, 1936; hon. member, Ophthalmology Section, Royal Society of Medicine; vice-president, Pakistan Society; published *Frontier Doctor* (1958).

HOLLAND, Hezekiah (*fl.* 1638–1661), Puritan divine; rector of Sutton Valence, Kent; author of *Exposition or . . . Epitome of . . . Commentaries upon . . . Revelations* (1650).

HOLLAND, Hugh (d. 1633), poet; queen's scholar at Westminster and MA, 1597, Trinity College, Cambridge; converted to Romanism; travelled as far as Jerusalem; patronized by *Buckingham; a member of Mermaid Club; wrote sonnet prefixed to first folio Shakespeare; published *Pancharis* (1603) and *A Cypres Garland* (1625).

HOLLAND, James (1800–1870), water-colour painter; exhibited at Water-Colour Society, Royal Academy, Society of British Artists, and British Institution; drew for illustrated annuals, visiting France, Venice, Geneva, Portugal, and Italy.

HOLLAND, John, duke of Exeter and earl of Huntingdon (1352?–1400), third son of Sir Thomas *Holland, first earl of Kent, and half-brother to Richard II; KG, 1381; justice of Chester, 1381; murdered Ralph Stafford, 1385; married Elizabeth, daughter of *John of Gaunt, under whom he distinguished himself in Spain, 1386; created earl of Huntingdon, 1387; chamberlain of England, 1389; made pilgrimage to Palestine, 1394; commissary, west marches towards Scotland, 1393; rewarded by dukedom for activity against *Gloucester and *Arundel,

1397; accompanied Richard II to Ireland, 1399; conspired against Henry IV; executed.

HOLLAND, John, duke of Exeter and earl of Huntingdon (1395–1447), second son of John *Holland, duke of Exeter (1352?–1400); KB, 1413; distinguished at Agincourt, 1415; restored to earldom, 1416, and created KG; commanded fleet against Genoese off Harfleur, 1417; took part in sieges of Caen and Rouen; distinguished at surprise of Pontoise, 1419; won victory of Fresney, 1420; took part in capture of Melun, 1420; constable of Tower of London, 1420; captured by dauphinists, 1421; exchanged, 1425; English representative at Arras, 1435; commanded expedition for relief of Guisnes, 1438; governor of Aquitaine, 1440; restored to dukedom, 1443.

HOLLAND, John (d. 1722), founder of Bank of Scotland and first governor, 1695; with his son, Richard *Holland (1688–1730), projected Irish bank; published financial pamphlets.

HOLLAND, John (1766–1826), Nonconformist minister; nephew of Philip *Holland.

HOLLAND, John (1794–1872), poet and miscellaneous writer; edited *Sheffield Iris*, 1825–32; joint editor of *Sheffield Mercury*, 1835–48; published *Sheffield Park* (1820) and *Diurnal Sonnets* (1851); friend of James *Montgomery; joint editor of *Memoirs of Life and Writings of James Montgomery* (1854–6); completed Newsam's *Poets of Yorkshire* (1845); published also *History of Worksop* (1826), *Cruciana* (1835), and other works.

HOLLAND, Sir Nathaniel Dance-, first baronet (1735–1811), painter; third son of the elder George *Dance; original member of Royal Academy, to whose first exhibition he sent full lengths of George III and Queen *Charlotte; assumed additional name; MP, East Grinstead; created baronet, 1800.

HOLLAND, Philemon (1552–1637), translator; MA, Trinity College, Cambridge, 1574; major fellow, 1574; MD, 1597; master of Free School, Coventry, 1628; received pension from city, 1632; epitaph by himself in Holy Trinity Church; his chief translations those of Livy (1600), Pliny's *Natural History* (1601), Plutarch's *Morals* (1603), Suetonius (1606), Ammianus Marcellinus (1609), *Camden's *Britannia* (1610), and Xenophon's *Cyropaedia* (1632); praised by Fuller, *Hearne, and *Southey.

HOLLAND, Philip (1721–1789), Nonconformist divine; minister of Bank Street Chapel, Bolton, 1755–80; assisted *Seddon in establishment of Warrington Academy; active in agitation against subscription.

HOLLAND, Sir **Richard** (*fl.* 1450), Scottish poet and adherent of the Douglases; author of the *Buke of the Howlat*, edited by David *Laing (1823); praised by Blind *Harry, *Dunbar, and *Lyndsay.

HOLLAND, Richard (1596–1677), mathematician; educated at Oxford; author of astronomical manuals.

HOLLAND, Richard (1688–1730), medical writer; son of John *Holland (d. 1722); MA, Catharine Hall, Cambridge, 1712; MD, 1723; FRCP, 1725; FRS, 1726; published *Observations on Smallpox* (1728).

HOLLAND, Robert (1557–1622?), Welsh poet; MA, Jesus College, Cambridge, 1581; incumbent in Pembrokeshire and rector of Llanddowror, Carmarthen.

HOLLAND, Saba, Lady (d. 1866), second wife of Sir Henry *Holland; published memoir of her father, Sydney *Smith (1855).

HOLLAND, Seth (d. 1561), dean of Worcester; MA, All Souls College, Oxford, 1539; fellow; warden, 1555; dean of Worcester, 1557–9; chaplain to Cardinal *Pole; died in prison.

HOLLAND, Sir **Sidney George** (1893–1961), prime minister of New Zealand; educated at West Christchurch District High School; employed in hardware firm at age of 15; enlisted, 1915–17; formed Midland Engineering Co., with his brother; succeeded his father as Conservative MP, Christchurch North, 1935; leader of National party, 1940; prime minister, 1949–57; and minister of finance, 1949–54; middle-of-the-road Conservative government; joined Australia and United States in ANZUS treaty, 1951; joined Manila Pact, 1954; devoted to British Empire and the United States; PC, 1950; CH, 1951; GCB, 1957.

HOLLAND, Sir **Sydney George,** third baronet, and second Viscount Knutsford (1855–1931), hospital administrator and reformer; son of first Viscount *Knutsford; succeeded father, 1914; educated at Wellington and Trinity Hall, Cambridge; called to bar (Inner Temple), 1879; as a dock company director and chairman of Poplar Hospital (1891–6) put both concerns on their feet; chairman, London Hospital, 1896–1931; raised £5 million and transformed standard of nursing and administration.

HOLLAND, Sir **Thomas,** first earl of Kent of the Holland family (d. 1360), soldier; present at Sluys, 1340; an original KG, 1344; prominent at siege of Caen, and at Crécy, 1346; royal lieutenant in Brittany, 1354; governor of Channel Islands, 1356; summoned to parliament as Baron Holland, 1353–6; captain-general in France and

Normandy, 1359; earl of Kent in right of his wife Joan, daughter of *Edmund of Woodstock, earl of Kent.

HOLLAND, Sir Thomas, second earl of Kent of the Holland family (1350–1397), favourite and half-brother of Richard II; son of Thomas *Holland, first earl of Kent; succeeded as Baron Holland, 1360; knighted in Castile, 1366; KG, 1375; earl marshal, 1380–5; ambassador to the Emperor Wenceslaus, 1380; earl of Kent, 1381; constable of the Tower and privy councillor, 1389.

HOLLAND, Thomas, duke of Surrey and earl of Kent (1374–1400), eldest son of Sir Thomas *Holland, second earl of Kent; KG, 1397; active in arrest and execution of *Arundel; created duke of Surrey, 1397; marshal and lieutenant of Ireland, 1398; deprived of dukedom, 1399; conspired against Henry IV, holding Maidenhead Bridge three days; executed by men of Cirencester.

HOLLAND, Thomas (d. 1612), regius professor of divinity at Oxford; MA, Balliol College, Oxford, 1575; DD, 1584; chaplain to *Leicester in Netherlands, 1585; regius professor of divinity at Oxford, 1589–1612; rector of Exeter College, 1592; one of the six translators of the prophets in Authorized Version, 1611.

HOLLAND, Thomas (1600–1642), Jesuit; addressed Prince Charles at Madrid, 1623; prefect and confessor at St Omer; came to England, 1635; executed.

HOLLAND, Thomas (1659–1743). See ECCLESTON.

HOLLAND, Thomas Agar (1803–1888), poet; of Westminster and Worcester College, Oxford; MA, 1828; rector of Poynings, 1846–88; published *Dryburgh Abbey and other Poems* (1826).

HOLLAND, Sir Thomas Erskine (1835–1926), jurist; son of Revd T. A. *Holland; BA, Magdalen College, Oxford, 1858; called to bar (Lincoln's Inn), 1863; Chichele professor of international law and diplomacy, Oxford, 1874–1910; fellow of All Souls, 1875–1926; KC, 1901; FBA, 1902; knighted, 1917; works include edition of text of *De Jure Belli* of Alberico *Gentili (1917), *Letters to 'The Times' on War and Neutrality* (1909, 1921), *The Elements of Jurisprudence* (1880, 13th edn., 1924); this, his most important book, belongs to school of English analytical jurisprudence founded by John *Austin.

HOLLAND, Sir Thomas Henry (1868–1947), geologist and educational administrator; studied at South Kensington and Owens College, Manchester; assistant superintendent, Geological Survey of India, 1890; director, 1903–10; reorganized and extended its work; professor of geology, Manchester, 1910–18; president, Indian Industrial Commission, 1916, munitions board, 1917; member, Viceroy's Executive Council, 1920–1; rector, Imperial College of Science and Technology, 1922–9; principal and vice-chancellor, Edinburgh University, 1929–44; negotiated fusion of divinity faculty with New College of Church of Scotland; president, British Association, 1929; FRS, 1904; KCIE, 1908; KCSI, 1918.

HOLLAND-MARTIN, Sir Douglas Eric ('Deric') (1906–1977), admiral; son of Robert Martin Holland; family name changed to Holland-Martin, 1923; educated at Royal Naval College, Osborne, 1920–4; midshipman, 1924; held junior naval appointments, 1924–39; during 1939–45 war served in North Sea and Mediterranean; DSC, 1940; DSO, 1943; bar to DSC, 1943; naval attaché in Argentina, Paraguay, and Uruguay, 1947–9; captain D4 in *Agincourt*, 1949–50; director of plans, Admiralty, 1952–3; in command of *Eagle*, 1954; rear-admiral, 1955; trained and commanded assault forces in landings of Royal Marine Commandos at Port Said, 1956; deputy chief of naval personnel (officers), 1957; second sea lord and acting vice-admiral, 1957; CB, 1958; KCB, 1960; admiral, 1961; commander-in-chief, Mediterranean and commander-in-chief, allied forces, Mediterranean, 1961–4; GCB, 1964; commandant, Imperial Defence College, 1964–6; but for his opposition to independent nuclear deterrent at expense of conventional fleet, might have been appointed first sea lord in 1963; president and chairman (1967–77), Imperial War Museum; chairman, committee of enquiry into trawler safety, 1968; member, White Fish Authority and Herring Industry Board, 1969; vice-admiral of the UK and lieutenant of the Admiralty, 1973–6.

HOLLAR (HOLAR), Wenceslaus (Vaclav) (1607–1677), engraver; native of Prague; lived at Frankfurt, Cologne, and Antwerp; came to England with Thomas *Howard, second earl of Arundel, 1636; teacher of drawing to Prince Charles; engraved *Ornatus Muliebris Anglicanus* (1640), Charles I and his queen (after *Van Dyck, 1641), and *Theatrum Mulierum* (1643); captured by Parliamentarians at Basing; escaped to Antwerp; returned, 1652; illustrated *Dugdale's *St Paul*, *Ogilby's *Virgil*, and *Stapleton's *Juvenal*; as Hill's designer produced *Coronation of Charles II*; executed fine map of London after the fire of 1666; sent to Tangier, 1669; engraved picture of *Kempthorne's fight with Algerine pirates; illustrated *Thoroton's *Antiquities of Nottinghamshire*; 2,733 of his prints enumerated.

HOLLES, Denzil, first Baron Holles of Ifield (1599–1680), statesman; second son of John *Holles, first earl of Clare; MA, Christ's College, Cambridge, 1616; MP, St Michael, 1624, Dorchester, 1628, and in Long Parliament; opposed *Buckingham's foreign policy; held the speaker in his chair, 2 Mar. 1629; imprisoned and fined; escaped abroad; compensated by Long Parliament, 1641; tried to save his brother-in-law, *Strafford; carried up impeachment of *Laud; supported Grand Remonstrance and impeachment of *Digby and Bristol, 1641; impeached among the five members, 3 Jan. 1642; advocated Militia Bill and impeachment of Royalist peers; member of Committee of Safety, 4 July 1642; led regiment at Edgehill and Brentford; advocated peace, 1643; parliamentary representative at negotiations of 1644, 1645 (Uxbridge), and 1648 (Newport); headed Presbyterians against Independents and (1644) projected impeachment of *Cromwell; charged with intrigues with Charles I, 1645 and 1647; impeached by the army among the eleven members, 1647; disabled from sitting, but restored, 1648; escaped to France under threat of another impeachment; readmitted by *Monck and appointed to Council of State, 1660; commissioner to Charles II at The Hague; privy councillor and created peer, 1661; ambassador at Paris, 1663–6; a negotiator of Treaty of Breda, 1667; protested against the Test Act, 1675; supported impeachment of *Danby, 1678, and disbandment of army, 1678; opposed Exclusion Bill; one of the new privy councillors, 1679; his *Memoirs, 1641–8* printed (1699).

HOLLES, Sir Frescheville (1641–1672), captain in the navy; son of Gervase *Holles; volunteer in naval campaign, 1665; knighted, 1666; commanded the *Henrietta,* 1666; abused by *Pepys; MP, Grimsby, 1667; commanded the *Cambridge* under Sir Robert *Holmes, 1672; killed in Battle of Solebay; buried in Westminster Abbey.

HOLLES, Gervase (1607–1675), antiquary; comptroller of Middle Temple, 1635; Royalist mayor and MP for Grimsby; suspended and disabled from sitting for denunciation of Scots, 1641–2; fought at Edgehill, Banbury, Brentford, Newbury; captured at Colchester; allowed to retire to France, 1649; in Holland till 1660; master of the requests and MP, Grimsby, 1661–75; some of his Lincolnshire collections in British Museum.

HOLLES, Gilbert, third earl of Clare (1633–1689), member of the country party, 1660–88; son of John *Holles, second earl of Clare.

HOLLES, John, first earl of Clare (*c.*1566–1637), soldier and politician; served against Armada, 1588, and in Azores expedition, 1597; fought against Turks in Hungary; comptroller to *Henry, prince of Wales, 1610–12; friend of *Somerset and enemy of *Coke and Gervase *Markham; MP, Nottinghamshire, 1604, 1614; created Baron Holles, 1616, and earl of Clare, 1624; opposed *Buckingham; advocated compromise on Petition of Right; reprimanded for implication in proceedings of Sir Robert *Dudley, 1629.

HOLLES, John, second earl of Clare (1595–1666), son of John *Holles, first earl; represented East Retford as Lord Haughton, 1624–9; volunteer at Bois-le-Duc, 1629; succeeded to peerage, 1637; took part in negotiations with Scots, 1640; sided with five popular peers, 1641, but defended *Strafford, 1641; changed sides several times during the rebellion.

HOLLES, John, duke of Newcastle (1662–1711), son of Gilbert *Holles, third earl of Clare; known as Lord Haughton till father's death; MP for Nottinghamshire; gentleman of bedchamber to William III; married Margaret Cavendish, coheiress of duke of *Newcastle, 1690; created duke, 1694; KG, 1698; lord privy seal, 1705–11.

HOLLES, Thomas Pelham-, duke of Newcastle-upon-Tyne and Newcastle-under-Lyme (1693–1768). See PELHAM.

HOLLES (or HOLLIS), Sir William (1471?–1572), lord mayor of London; master of Mercers' Company, 1538; sheriff of London, 1527; knighted, 1533; lord mayor, 1539–40; left bequests to Coventry, the Mercers' Company, and St Helen's, Bishopsgate; ancestor of earls of *Clare and dukes of *Newcastle.

HOLLIDAY, John (1730?–1801), author; barrister, Lincoln's Inn, 1771; practised as conveyancer; FRS and FSA; published *Life of Lord Mansfield* (1797) and poems.

HOLLINGHURST, Sir **Leslie Norman** (1895–1971), air chief marshal; educated at schools in Essex; enlisted in Royal Engineers, 1914; wounded at Salonika; commissioned in 3rd battalion, Middlesex Regiment, 1916; seconded to Royal Flying Corps, 1916; DFC, 1918; permanently commissioned in RAF, 1919; served in India, 1919–22; attended RAF Staff College, 1925; served with Shanghai Defence Force, 1927–9; OBE, 1932; commanded No. 20 Squadron in India, 1933–4; on staff of RAF Staff College, 1935–7; air member for supply and organization, Air Ministry, 1939; director of organization, 1940; director-general of organization, 1941–3; acting air vice-marshal, 1942; commander, No. 9 Group, 1943; commander, No. 38 Group responsible for aircraft, gliders, and crews to airlift British airborne forces,

1943–4; made major contribution to D-Day landings and other airborne landings; air officer commanding, Base Air Forces, South-East Asia, 1944; air member for supply and organization, 1945–8; inspector-general of RAF, 1948–9; air member for personnel, 1949–52; air chief marshal, 1950; CB, 1942; CBE, 1944; KBE, 1945; KCB, 1948; GBE, 1952.

HOLLINGS, Edmund (1556?–1612), physician; BA, The Queen's College, Oxford, 1575; studied at Reims and Rome; intimate of *Pits; professor of medicine at Ingolstadt; published medical works; died at Ingolstadt.

HOLLINGS, John (1683?–1739), physician-general and physician-in-ordinary; MD, Magdalene College, Cambridge, 1710; FRS, 1726; FRCP, 1726; Harveian orator, 1734.

HOLLINGSHEAD, John (1827–1904), journalist and theatrical manager; after some commercial travelling, became joint editor with W. Moy *Thomas of *Weekly Mail*, 1856; joined staff of *Household Words*, 1857; wrote *The Birthplace of Podgers*, 1858; his contributions to press were republished in several volumes, 1859–62; one of first contributors to *Cornhill Magazine*, 1859; dramatic critic to *Daily News*, 1863–8; occasional contributor to *Punch*; took part in such public movements as reform of entertainment licensing regulations and of copyright law; stage director of Alhambra, 1865–8; first manager of Gaiety Theatre, 1868–88; inaugurated matinées; produced mainly burlesque, but also operas and serious drama; introduced Ibsen to English public in *Pillars of Society*, 1880; brought complete Comédie Française company, including Sarah Bernhardt and the Coquelins, to London, 1879; also managed for short time Opera Comique, London; lost fortune in theatrical speculation; published *My Lifetime* (2 vols., 1895) and *Gaiety Chronicles* (1898).

HOLLINGWORTH, Richard (1639?–1701), controversialist; MA, Emmanuel College, Cambridge, 1662; DD, 1684; vicar of West Ham, 1672–82, of Chigwell, 1690–1701; published pamphlets in defence of Charles I's authorship of Εἰκὼν Βασιλική, and reissued Edward Symmons's *Vindication* (1693).

HOLLINGWORTH, Sydney Ewart (1899–1966), geologist; educated at Northampton School and Clare College, Cambridge; first class, parts i and ii, natural sciences tripos, 1920–1; at Cambridge came under influence of J. E. *Marr and Alfred Hacker; joined staff of Geological Survey of Great Britain, 1921; assigned to unit in Cumberland; London D.Sc., 1931; transferred to West Midlands, 1935; with J. H. *Taylor, worked on Jurassic ironstones, chief domestic

source of iron ore for expansion of steel industry, 1939–45; succeeded W. B. R. *King as Yates-Goldsmid professor of geology, University College, London, 1945–66; became leading expert on 'porphyry'-type copper deposits in the Andes; fellow, Geological Society of London, 1922; secretary, 1949–56; president, 1960–2; hon. member, Geologists' Association, 1964; consultant to Metropolitan Water Board.

HOLLINS, John (1798–1855), painter; ARA, 1842; exhibited portraits and historical subjects, and, later, figure-pieces and landscapes.

HOLLINS, Peter (1800–1886), sculptor; son of William *Hollins; exhibited at Royal Academy. His works include statues of Peel and Sir Rowland *Hill for Birmingham.

HOLLINS, William (1754–1843), architect and sculptor; cousin of John *Hollins; designed public buildings at Birmingham and plans for St Petersburg Mint.

HOLLINWORTH (or HOLLINGWORTH), Richard (1607–1656), divine; educated at Manchester and Magdalene College, Cambridge; MA, 1630; minister of Trinity Chapel, Salford, 1636; fellow of Manchester Collegiate Church; assisted Richard *Heyrick in establishing Lancashire Presbyterianism, which he also defended controversially; imprisoned on charge of implication in *Love's plot, 1651; one of *Chetham's feoffees; his *Mancuniensis* printed (1839).

HOLLIS, Aiskew Paffard (1764–1844), vice-admiral; present in battle off Ushant, 1778; lieutenant, 1781; wounded in action of 1 June 1794; brought *Crescent* into Table Bay, 1797; commanded frigate *Thames* at action off Gibraltar, 1801; served in Baltic, 1809; vice-admiral, 1837.

HOLLIS, George (1793–1842), topographical engraver; pupil of George *Cooke.

HOLLIS, Sir Leslie Chasemore (1897–1963), general; educated at St Lawrence College, Ramsgate; commissioned in Royal Marine Light Infantry, 1915; posted to *Duke of Edinburgh* in First Cruiser Squadron, commanded by Sir Robert *Arbuthnot; at Battle of Jutland, 1916; served in various ships, 1921–7; passed naval staff course, 1928; intelligence officer on staff of commander-in-chief, Africa Station; attached to plans division, Admiralty, 1932–6; secretary, Joint Planning Subcommittee under Sir Maurice (later Lord) *Hankey, and Hastings (later Lord) *Ismay, 1936–46; secretary, Chiefs of Staffs Committee, 1938; deputy secretary, Committee of Imperial Defence, 1940–6; acting major-general, 1943; succeeded Ismay as deputy military secretary to the Cabinet, 1946–9; commandant general, Royal Marine Corps, 1949–52; CBE; CB; KBE, 1946; full general, and KCB, 1951; published biography of Prince Philip, Duke of Edinburgh, *The Captain General* (1961), *One Marine's Tale* (1956), and *War at the Top* (1959).

HOLLIS, (Maurice) Christopher (1902–1977), author, schoolmaster, and politician; elder brother of (Sir) Roger *Hollis; educated as scholar at Eton; Brackenbury scholar, Balliol College, Oxford; president of the Union, 1923; became Roman Catholic, 1924; history master, Stonyhurst College, 1925–35; visiting professor, Notre Dame University, Indiana, 1935; engaged in economic research there, 1935–9; during 1939–45 war served as intelligence officer, RAF; Conservative MP for Devizes division of Wiltshire, 1945–55; Parliamentary reporter, *Punch*; retired to Somerset, 1955, and wrote some thirty books on variety of subjects from the origins of Soviet Communism to St Ignatius Loyola and the foundation of the Jesuits, Erasmus, Thomas *More, *Dryden, Dr *Johnson, monetary reform, and foreign policy; published two autobiographical works, *Along the Road to Frome* (1958) and *The Seven Ages* (1974); also, *Oxford in the Twenties: Recollections of Five Friends* (1976).

HOLLIS, Sir Roger Henry (1905–1973), head of MI5; younger brother of M. Christopher *Hollis; educated at Leeds Grammar School, Clifton College, and Worcester College, Oxford; worked in DCO branch, Barclays Bank, and as journalist on Hong Kong newspaper; joined British American Tobacco Co., 1928–36; invalided with tuberculosis, 1936; joined the British security service, 1938; became one of key figures during 1939–45 war; deputy director-general, 1953; director-general, 1956–65; this the period of Cold War and number of spy cases including Vassall, George Blake, Gordon Lonsdale, and the Krogers; faced three major official enquiries into the service which he and the service survived with considerable credit; after retirement recalled to face further interrogation; Chapman Pincher's *Their Trade is Treachery* (1981), implied that Hollis had been a spy for the Soviets throughout his service; investigation by Lord Trend, secretary of the Cabinet (1963–73), cleared his name and reputation, and Margaret Thatcher confirmed this to House of Commons, 1981; OBE, 1946; CB, 1956; knighted, 1960; KBE, 1966.

HOLLIS, Thomas (1720–1774), 'republican'; entered at Lincoln's Inn, 1740; travelled much on continent; gave books to Harvard, Berne, and Zurich, and portraits of *Newton and *Cromwell to Trinity and Sidney Sussex colleges, Cam-

bridge; FRS, 1757; edited *Toland's *Milton* (1761), Algernon *Sidney's works (1772), and other publications.

HOLLIS, Thomas (1818–1843), son and assistant of George *Hollis.

HOLLOND, Ellen Julia (1822–1884), authoress and philanthropist; née Teed; as wife of Robert Hollond, MP, held liberal salon in Paris; published *Les Quakers* (1870) and a work on Channing (1857); established first crèche in London, 1844, and nurses' home at Paris and Nice.

HOLLOND (or HOLLAND), John (*fl.* 1638–1659), naval writer; paymaster of navy before 1635 till *c.*1642; one of commissioners for navy, 1642 till *c.*1645; member of 'committee of merchants for regulation of navy and customs', 1649; surveyor of the navy, 1649; member of parliament's Commission of Navy, 1649–52; wrote *First Discourse of the Navy* (1638) and *Second Discourse* (1659).

HOLLOWAY, Benjamin (1691?–1759), divine; of Westminster and St John's College, Cambridge; LL B, 1713; FRS, 1723; rector of Middleton Stoney, *c.*1730–59, and Bladon, 1736–9; translated Woodward's *Naturalis Historia Telluris* (1726); published works, including *Primaevity and Pre-eminence of Hebrew* (1754) and *Originals physical and theological* (1751).

HOLLOWAY, Sir Charles (1749–1827), major-general, Royal Engineers; second-lieutenant, Royal Engineers, 1776; lieutenant, 1783; captain-lieutenant, 1793; captain, 1795; lieutenant-colonel, 1804; colonel, 1811; major-general, 1814; at Gibraltar, 1779–83, during siege; brigade-major, 1781; assisted Major-General William *Roy in survey triangulations, 1784–7; commanding royal engineer in military mission to assist Turks in reorganization of army, 1798; commander of Turkish Army in Syria and Egypt against French, 1801–2; knighted, 1803; commanding royal engineer at Gibraltar, 1807–17.

HOLLOWAY, James (d. 1684), conspirator; formed scheme for improvement of linen manufacture; engaged in extensive plot against government, himself undertaking (1682) to secure Bristol; escaped by France to West Indies; betrayed by his factor in Nevis; while in Newgate wrote confession; refused trial and was executed at Tyburn.

HOLLOWAY, Sir Richard (d. 1695?), judge; barrister, Inner Temple, 1658; recorder of Wallingford, 1666; counsel against Stephen *College, 1681; knighted; judge of King's Bench, 1683; member of courts that tried *Sidney and condemned *Oates and *Devonshire for assaulting Thomas *Colepepper; dismissed by James II, 1688, for action in trial of seven bishops, excepted from indemnity after Revolution.

HOLLOWAY, Stanley Augustus (1890–1982), actor and singer; educated at Worshipful School of Carpenters, London; studied singing in Milan; served with Connaught Rangers during 1914–18 war; with Co-Optimists pierrot show in West End, 1921–7; introduced monologues into his work, 1927; starred on variety bills and in pantomime; successful as actor in comic parts in *Hamlet* (1951), *A Midsummer Night's Dream* (1954), *Candida* (1970), and *You Never Can Tell* (1973); toured Australia and Hong Kong, 1977; appeared in over thirty films including *This Happy Breed* (1944), *Brief Encounter* (1945), *The Way to the Stars* (1945), *The Lavender Hill Mob* (1951), *The Titfield Thunderbolt* (1952), and had resounding success as Alfred Doolittle in *My Fair Lady*, Loewe's musical version of *Pygmalion* by G. B. *Shaw, in Broadway première (1956–8), London production (1958–9), and film version (1964); OBE, 1960; Variety Club of Great Britain special award, 1978; published autobiography *Wiv a Little Bit o'Luck* (1967) and three anthologies of monologues (1979, 1980, and 1981).

HOLLOWAY, Thomas (1748–1827), engraver; exhibited seals at Academy; engraved gems and miniatures; executed plates for Lavater's *Physiognomy* (1789–98); engraved portraits after *Pine and *West and five of Raphael's cartoons.

HOLLOWAY, Thomas (1800–1883), patent medicine vendor; son of Penzance innkeeper; obtained idea of his ointment from Felix Albinolo; set up in the Strand as medicine vendor, 1839; advertised extensively in many languages, but failed to introduce medicines into France; made large fortune; bought pictures; endowed ladies' college at Egham and sanatorium at Virginia Water.

HOLLOWAY, William Cuthbert (1787–1850), colonel. See ELPHINSTONE-HOLLOWAY.

HOLLOWELL, James Hirst (1851–1909), advocate of unsectarian education; early became temperance agent and lecturer; joined Congregational ministry, 1875, serving in London, Nottingham, and Rochdale; founded Northern Counties Education League for unsectarian education; organized 'passive resistance movement', 1903; an untiring pamphleteer.

HOLLYDAY, Samuel (1685–1739). See HALIDAY.

HOLLYWOOD (or SACROBOSCO), Christopher (1562–1616), Jesuit. See HOLYWOOD.

HOLMAN, Francis (*fl.* 1760–1790), marine painter; exhibited with Free Society, 1767–72, and Royal Academy, 1774–84.

HOLMAN, James (1786–1857), blind traveller; travelled unattended in Europe, Siberia, Africa, America, and Australasia; published *Voyage round the World (1827–32)* (1834–5) and other narratives.

HOLMAN, Joseph George (1764–1817), actor and dramatist; of The Queen's College, Oxford; at Covent Garden, 1784–1800, played Romeo, Macbeth, Chamont (*The Orphan*), Hamlet; 'created' Harry Dornton in *Road to Ruin*, 1792; drew up statement of grievances of chief actors, 1800; acted in his own *What a Blunder* at Haymarket, 1800 (produced at Covent Garden, 1803); reappeared at Haymarket, 1812; with his daughter played at New York, Philadelphia, and Charleston in *The Provoked Husband*; died in Long Island; published comedies and comic operas.

HOLMAN, William (d. 1730), Essex antiquary; his collections used by *Morant; compiled catalogue of *Jekyll MSS.

HOLMAN HUNT, William (1827–1910), painter. See HUNT.

HOLME, Benjamin (1683–1749), Quaker; visited 'Friends' and preached in Ireland, Holland (1714), the West Indies (1719), Jersey, and America; published *Tender Invitation and Call* (1713) with other religious works, *A Serious Call in Christian Love* (1725), and an autobiography, published (1753).

HOLME, Charles (1848–1923), founder and editor of *The Studio* magazine; in woollen business, 1871–92; became interested in art; founded *The Studio*, a magazine of fine and applied art, 1893; primary aim not commercial, but illustration and furtherance of good design.

HOLME, Edward (1770–1847), physician; MD, Leiden, 1793; physician to Manchester Infirmary; president of Literary and Philosophical Society (1844), Natural History and Chetham societies; first president of medical section at British Association, 1831; left large bequest and library to University College, London.

HOLME, Randle (1571–1655), deputy to College of Arms for Cheshire, Shropshire, and North Wales; mayor of Chester, 1633–4.

HOLME, Randle (1601?–1659), genealogist; son of Randle *Holme (1571–1655); sheriff of Chester, 1633–4; mayor, 1643–4; added to Holme collection of MSS.

HOLME, Randle (1627–1699), principal contributor to Holme MSS; son of Randle *Holme

(1601?–1659); deputy Garter for Cheshire, Shropshire, Lancashire, and North Wales; published *The Academy of Armory* (1688).

HOLME, Randle (d. 1707), completer of family manuscripts; son of Randle *Holme (1627–1699); manuscripts acquired by British Museum, 1753.

HOLMES, Abraham (d. 1685), rebel; Anabaptist major in *Monck's army; arrested for conspiracy against Charles II, 1660; imprisoned at Windsor, 1664–7; engaged in *Argyll's plot, 1681–3; accompanied *Monmouth to England and commanded battalion at Sedgemoor, 1685; executed.

HOLMES, Alfred (1837–1876), violinist and composer; with his brother Henry played Kalliwoda's Double Concerto, 1853, and distinguished himself by rendering of Spohr's music during concert tours in Belgium, Germany (1856), Austria, Sweden, Denmark, Holland, and Paris, where he settled, 1864; produced at St Petersburg symphony *Jeanne d'Arc*, 1868, *Jeunesse de Shakespeare*, and other works given in Paris; died at Paris.

HOLMES, Arthur (1890–1965), geologist; educated at Gateshead High School and Imperial College, London; B.Sc., 1909; ARCS, 1910; DIC; contracted malaria and blackwater fever in East Africa; demonstrator in geology, Imperial College, 1912–20; research into radioactivity, petrogenesis, and physical geology; chief geologist, oil-prospecting company, Burma, 1921–4; reader in geology, Durham; professor, 1924; regius professor, Edinburgh, 1943–56; professor emeritus, 1956; made important contributions to geological implications of radioactivity and the origin of alkali-rich igneous rocks; FRS, 1942; hon. LL D, Edinburgh, 1960; many other academic honours; publications include *The Age of the Earth* (1913), *The Nomenclature of Petrology* (1920), *Petrographic Methods and Calculations* (1921), and *Principles of Physical Geology* (1944).

HOLMES, Augusta (Mary Anne) (1847–1903), composer; born in Paris; pupil of César Franck; published compositions from 1862 onwards; chief were *In Exitu Israel* (1874), *Irlande* (1882, a symphonic poem), *Ode Triomphale* (1889), *La Montagne noire* (opera); became Roman Catholic, 1902; died at Versailles.

HOLMES, Charles (1711–1761), rear-admiral; commanded *Stromboli* in Carthagena expedition, 1741; took part in action with Spanish in Gulf of Florida, 1748; member of court martial on *Byng, 1757; cut enemy's communications in the *Ems*, 1758; rear-admiral, 1758; third-in-command under Sir Charles *Saunders in *St Law-*rence, 1759; commander-in-chief at Jamaica, 1760–1; monument in Westminster Abbey.

HOLMES, Sir Charles John (1868–1936), landscape painter and art critic; educated at Eton and Brasenose College, Oxford; entered publishing; co-editor, *Burlington Magazine*, 1903–9; Slade professor, Oxford, 1904–10; director, National Portrait Gallery (1909–16), National Gallery (1916–28); organized photograph and publications departments; knighted, 1921; KCVO, 1928; a self-taught painter of mountain scenes and industrial subjects belonging to no school but his own; publications include *Constable and his Influence on Landscape Painting* (1902).

HOLMES, Edward (1797–1859), writer on music; friend of *Keats and Charles Cowden *Clarke; with Vincent *Novello raised subscription for Mozart's widow; published *Ramble among Musicians of Germany* (1828), and lives of Mozart (1845) and *Purcell; composed songs.

HOLMES, George (1662–1749), deputy-keeper of the Tower records; FRS and FSA; prepared first seventeen volumes of *Rymer's *Foedera*, 1727–35.

HOLMES, George (*fl.* 1673–1715), organist at Lincoln, 1704–15; grandson of John *Holmes (*fl.* 1602); contributed to *Musical Companion*, 1673; composed anthems and songs.

HOLMES, Sir Gordon Morgan (1876–1965), neurologist; born in Dublin; educated at Dundalk Educational Institute and Trinity College, Dublin; BA, 1897; qualified in medicine, 1898; studied neuro-anatomy at Frankfurt; housephysician, National Hospital for Nervous Diseases, Queen Square, London, 1901; MD, 1903; FRCP, 1914; pathologist and director of research, 1904; honorary physician, 1909; worked with (Sir) Henry *Head on clinical neurophysiology at London Hospital, 1911; consulting neurologist to British Army, 1914; CMG, 1917; CBE, 1919; succeeded Head as editor of *Brain*, 1922–37; FRS, 1933; made notable contributions to the physiology of the cerebral cortex, thalamus, and cerebellum; retired as consulting physician from National Hospital, 1941; knighted, 1951; received many academic honours; publications include *Introduction to Clinical Neurology* (1946).

HOLMES, James (1777–1860), water-colour painter and miniaturist; exhibited with Society of British Artists, 1829–59; his two miniatures of *Byron engraved.

HOLMES, John (*fl.* 1602), composer; organist of Winchester and Salisbury (1602–10).

HOLMES, Sir John (1640?–1683), admiral; brother of Sir Robert *Holmes; commanded the *Paul* at Lowestoft, 1665, and in fight of June 1666; commanded the *Bristol* in fight of 25 July 1666; served under Sir Edward *Spragge in Algerine War, 1670–1; wounded in fight with Dutch Smyrna fleet, 1672, and knighted; commanded the *Rupert* at Solebay, 1672, and in battles of 1673; commander in the Downs, 1677–9; MP, Newtown (Isle of Wight), 1677–83.

HOLMES, John (1800–1854), antiquary; adviser of Bertram, earl of Ashburnham, collector of manuscripts; compiled catalogue of manuscripts, maps, and plans in British Museum, 1844; edited Evelyn's *Life of Mrs. Godolphin* (1847), *Cavendish's *Wolsey* (1852), and *Wordsworth's *Ecclesiastical Biography* (1853).

HOLMES, John Beck (1767–1843), Moravian bishop of Fulneck; published historical works concerning his church.

HOLMES (or HOMES), Nathaniel (1599–1678), Puritan divine; BA, Exeter College, Oxford, 1620; MA, Magdalen Hall, 1623; DD, 1637; joined Henry *Burton in founding Independent congregation, 1643; published millenarian works.

HOLMES, Sir Richard Rivington (1835–1911), librarian of Windsor Castle, 1870–1906; son of John *Holmes; assistant at British Museum, 1854; archaeologist to Abyssinian expedition, 1868; purchased Abyssinian MSS for British Museum; rearranged and augmented the royal collections; KCVO, 1905; a delicate pen draughtsman, water-colour artist, stained-glass designer, and designer of bookbindings; FSA, 1860; compiled lives of Queen Victoria (1897), King Edward VII (1910), and works on Windsor.

HOLMES, Sir Robert (1622–1692), admiral; served under Prince *Rupert in Civil War; governor of Sandown Castle, 1660; seized Dutch possessions on Guinea coast and in North America, 1664; captain of the *Revenge* at Battle of Lowestoft, 1665; knighted, 1666; rear-admiral of the red, 1666; distinguished in fight of 1–4 June 1666; fought duel with Sir Jeremiah *Smith or Smyth arising out of his conduct in fight of 25 July 1666; destroyed shipping and stores at Vlie and Schelling; admiral at Portsmouth, 1667; one of *Buckingham's seconds in duel with Shrewsbury; governor of Isle of Wight, 1669; attacked Dutch Smyrna fleet in Channel, 1672; took part in Battle of Solebay, 1672; MP, Winchester, Yarmouth (Isle of Wight), and Newport.

HOLMES, Robert (1748–1805), biblical scholar; of Winchester and New College, Oxford; fellow; MA, 1774; DD, 1789; first winner of Chancellor's Prize for Latin Verse, 1769; rector of Stanton St John; Bampton lecturer, 1782; professor of poetry, 1783; collated Septuagint, 1788–1805; prebendary of Salisbury, Hereford, and Christ Church; dean of Winchester, 1804; FRS, 1797; published poems, theological works, and annual accounts of his collations.

HOLMES, Robert (1765–1859), Irish lawyer; brother-in-law of Robert *Emmet; BA, Trinity College, Dublin, 1787; imprisoned on suspicion of rebellion, 1803; defended John Mitchel, 1848; published anti-union pamphlets.

HOLMES, Thomas (d. 1638), musical composer; gentleman of the Chapel Royal, 1633.

HOLMES, Thomas (1846–1918), police-court missionary and philanthropist; iron-moulder, 1858–79; police-court missionary, Lambeth (1885–9), North London (1889–1905); founded Home Workers' Aid Association to redress conditions of sweated female labour, 1904; secretary to Howard Association for prison and criminal law reform, 1905–15; wrote on problems connected with crime.

HOLMES, Thomas Rice Edward (1855–1933), historian and classical scholar; educated at Merchant Taylors' School and Christ Church, Oxford; master, St Paul's School, 1886–1909; wrote *History of the Indian Mutiny* (1883) and many works on Julius Caesar.

HOLMES, Timothy (1825–1907), surgeon; BA, Pembroke College, Cambridge (forty-second wrangler and twelfth classic), 1847; hon. fellow, 1900; M.Ch., 1900; FRCS, 1853; house-surgeon at St George's Hospital; surgeon, 1867–87; Hunterian professor of surgery at Royal College of Surgeons, 1872; president of Royal Medical Society, 1900; edited *A System of Surgery* (4 vols., 1860–4); wrote life of Sir Benjamin *Brodie the elder (1898).

HOLMES, Sir Valentine (1888–1956), lawyer; educated at Charterhouse and Trinity College, Dublin; senior moderator, classics, 1911; called to bar (Inner Temple), 1913; bencher, 1935; joined (Sir) Leslie *Scott; moved to own chambers, 1929, specializing in libel suits; junior counsel to Treasury in common-law matters, 1935–45; KC, 1945; retired, 1949; legal consultant, Shell Oil group, 1950–6; knighted, 1946.

HOLMES, William (1689–1748), dean of Exeter; educated at Merchant Taylors' School; fellow of St John's College, Oxford, 1710; MA, 1715; proctor, 1721; BD; president of St John's College, Oxford, 1728; vice-chancellor, 1732–5; revived the act and invited *Handel to play at Oxford, 1733; regius professor of history,

1736–42; dean of Exeter, 1742–8; left estates to his college.

HOLMES, William (d. 1851), thirty years Tory whip; BA, Trinity College, Dublin, 1795; served in the army; MP, Grampound, 1808–12, Tregony, 1812–18, Totnes, 1819–20, Bishop's Castle, 1820–30, Haslemere, 1830–2, Berwick, 1837–41; treasurer of the ordnance, 1820–30.

HOLMES, William Anthony (1782–1843), chancellor of Cashel; scholar of Trinity College, Dublin; BA, 1803; DD, 1834; incumbent of Holywood, Down, 1810, of Ballyroan, 1818, and Core Abbey, 1822; chancellor of Cashel, 1832; helped to found Mendicity Institution, Belfast; published pamphlets.

HOLMYARD, Eric John (1891–1959), teacher, historian, and interpreter of science; educated at Sexey's School, Bruton, and Sidney Sussex College, Cambridge; first class, parts i and ii, natural sciences tripos (1910–12); head of science department, Clifton College, 1919–40; for ICI first editor, *Endeavour*, 1940–54, and editor (with C. *Singer), *History of Technology* (5 vols., 1954–8); contributed to study of alchemy.

HOLROYD, Sir Charles (1861–1917), painter-etcher and director of National Gallery, London; studied art under Alphonse *Legros at Slade School, London; fellow of Society of Painter-Etchers, 1885; travelled in Italy, 1889–91 and 1894–7; exhibited at Royal Academy, but chiefly excelled as etcher of figure subjects, landscapes (English and Italian), and portraits; first keeper of Tate Gallery, 1897–1906; knighted, 1903; director of National Gallery, 1906–16; wrote *Michael Angelo Buonarroti* (1903).

HOLROYD, Sir George Sowley (1758–1831), judge; educated at Harrow; special pleader, 1779–87; barrister, Gray's Inn, 1878; appeared for *Burdett against Speaker *Abbott, 1811; commissioner to Guernsey, 1815; judge of King's Bench, 1816–28.

HOLROYD, Henry North, third earl of Sheffield (1832–1909), patron of cricket; grandson of John *Holroyd, first earl; in Diplomatic Service, 1852–6; Conservative MP for East Sussex, 1857–65; president of Sussex County Cricket Club from 1879; arranged first-class cricket matches at Sheffield Park; took English team to Australia, 1891–2; sold his *Gibbon MSS to British Museum, 1895; died at Beaulieu.

HOLROYD, John Baker, first earl of Sheffield (1735–1821), statesman and friend of *Gibbon; purchased Sheffield Place, Sussex, 1769; raised and commanded dragoon regiment; MP, Coventry, 1780–3, Bristol, 1790–1802; active in suppressing Gordon riots, 1780; created

Irish baron, 1781; created earl of Sheffield and Viscount Pevensey in peerage of Ireland, 1816; British peer, 1802; president of Board of Agriculture, 1803; privy councillor, 1809; lord of Board of Trade, 1809; published pamphlets on social and commercial questions; edited Gibbon's *Miscellaneous Works* (1796) and *Memoirs* (1826).

HOLST, Gustav Theodore (1874–1934), composer, whose original name was Gustavus Theodore von Holst; born in Cheltenham of Swedish ancestry; educated at the grammar school; studied composition at Royal College of Music; influenced by Bach and Wagner, later by English folk-song and the Tudor composers; trombone player with Carl Rosa Company and Scottish Orchestra; director of music, St Paul's Girls' School (1905–34) and Morley College; professor of composition, Royal College of Music (1919–24), University College, Reading (1919–23); compositions of incomparable sureness of touch and clarity of texture; works include 'St Paul's' suite for strings (1913), *The Planets* (1914–17), *The Hymn of Jesus* (1917), *Ode to Death* (1919), operas *The Perfect Fool* (1922) and *At the Boar's Head* (1925), the 'Keats' Choral Symphony (1925), and *Egdon Heath* (1927).

HOLST, Imogen Clare (1907–1984), musician; daughter of Gustav Theodore *Holst; educated at St Paul's Girls' School; entered Royal College of Music, 1926; won open scholarship for composition, 1927, and scholarship for study abroad, 1930; turned to teaching and arranging music for plays when phlebitis prevented her becoming concert pianist; one of those appointed by Pilgrim Trust to organize amateur music in wartime Britain, 1940; director of music, Dartington Hall, 1943–51; amanuensis to Benjamin (later Lord) *Britten; artistic director, Aldeburgh Festival, 1956–7; founded and conducted Purcell Singers, 1953–67; wrote books for children on *Purcell, *Byrd, *Bach, and Britten; other publications include *Gustav Holst* (1938), *The Music of Gustav Holst* (1951, revised 1984), and *Thematic Catalogue of Gustav Holst's Music* (1974); CBE, 1975; fellow, Royal College of Music, 1966; hon. member, Royal Academy of Music, 1970; honorary degrees from Essex, Exeter, and Leeds universities.

HOLST, Theodore von (1810–1844), painter. See VON HOLST.

HOLT, Francis Ludlow (1780–1844), legal writer; of Westminster and Christ Church, Oxford; barrister, Middle Temple, 1809; KC, 1831; treasurer of Inner Temple, 1840; vice-chancellor of Lancaster, 1826–44; published *Law of Libel* (1812–16), *nisi prius* reports

(1815–17), shipping laws (1820), bankrupt laws (1829), and *The Land we Live in* (comedy, 1804).

HOLT, Guy (1587?–1660), Jesuit. See HOLLAND.

HOLT, John (d. 1418), judge; king's serjeant, 1377; judge of common pleas, 1383; knight-banneret, 1384; banished to Ireland, 1388, for decision against legality of permanent council; recalled, 1397.

HOLT, Sir John (1642–1710), judge; of Winchester and Oriel College, Oxford; barrister, Gray's Inn, 1663; counsel for *Danby and Lords *Powis and *Arundell, 1679; appeared for crown against Slingsby *Bethel, for Lord *Russell, and for East India Company against *Sandys, 1683; recorder of London, 1686–7; knighted, 1686; king's serjeant, 1686; MP, Beeralston; manager of conference with peers on vacancy of throne, 1689; lord chief justice of King's Bench, 1689–1710; pronounced dispensing power legal; decided in favour of bankers, 1700; against House of Commons in case of *Ashby* v. *White*, 1701; declined great seal, 1700; the Verus of the *Tatler*; his judgment in *Coggs* v. *Bernard* chief authority on law of bailments; edited reports of cases in pleas of the crown under Charles II, 1708. As judge he discouraged prosecutions for witchcraft, and put liberal construction on statute compelling attendance at church, but took serious view of treason and seditious libel.

HOLT, John (1743–1801), author; master of Walton Grammar School, near Liverpool; published *Characters of Kings and Queens of England* (1786–8) and a survey of Lancashire agriculture (1794).

HOLT, Joseph (1756–1826), Irish rebel; headed rebellion in Co. Wicklow, 1798; joined Edward Roche and won victory at Ballyellis, 1798; separated from him and was defeated at Castle Carberry; held out in Wicklow three months; transported to Botany Bay, 1799; successful farmer in New South Wales; banished to Norfolk Island on suspicion of rebellion, 1804; pardoned, 1809; wrecked on Eagle Island during voyage to England, 1813.

HOLT, Thomas (1578?–1624), architect; designed great quadrangle of the Examination Schools (now part of the Bodleian).

HOLT, William (1545–1599), Jesuit; BA, Brasenose College, Oxford, 1566; fellow of Oriel, 1568; MA, 1572; studied at Douai, 1574–6; Jesuit novice, 1578; intrigued with *Lennox in Scotland, 1581–2; arrested through English influence, 1583, but allowed to escape; rector of English College, Rome, 1586–7; Spanish agent at Brussels, 1588–98; died at Barcelona.

HOLTBY, Richard (1553–1640), Jesuit; of Cambridge and Hart Hall, Oxford; on English mission in north, 1579–81; joined Jesuits, 1583; superior of Scots College at Pont-à-Mousson, 1587–9; vice-prefect of English mission, 1606–9; though fifty years in England never imprisoned; his account of persecution in the north in *Morris's *Troubles of our Catholic Forefathers*.

HOLTE, John (*fl.* 1495), author of first Latin grammar in England (printed by Wynkyn de *Worde, c.1510, and *Pynson, 1520); fellow of Magdalen College, Oxford, 1491; MA, 1494.

HOLTE, John (d. 1540), bishop of Lydda, and suffragan to *Fitzjames, bishop of London, 1506–22.

HOLTE, Sir Thomas, first baronet (1571–1654), Royalist; sheriff of Warwickshire, 1599; created baronet, 1612; built Aston Hall; entertained Charles I before Edgehill.

HOLTZAPFFEL, Charles (1806–1847), mechanician; published *Turning and Mechanical Manipulation* (1843).

HOLWELL, John (1649–1686?), astrologer and mathematician; said to have surveyed New York, and been poisoned there; author of works, including *A Sure Guide to the Practical Surveyor* (1678) and *Trigonometry made easy* (1685).

HOLWELL, John Zephaniah (1711–1798), governor of Bengal; grandson of John *Holwell (1649–1686?); surgeon in East India Company, 1732–49; drew up scheme for reform of zemindar's court, Calcutta; zemindar of the Twenty-four Parganas, Calcutta, 1751; as member of council defended Calcutta against Suráj ud Dowlah, 1756, and was one of the survivors from the Black Hole; succeeded *Clive as temporary governor; dismissed from council for remonstrating against *Vansittart's appointment, 1761; first European who studied Hindu antiquities; published narrative of *Black Hole* (1758) and works on Indian politics and mythology.

HOLWELL, William (1726–1798), classical compiler; MA, Christ Church, Oxford, 1748; BD, 1760; vicar of Thornbury and chaplain to George III; compiled *Beauties of Homer* (1775).

HOLWORTHY, James (d. 1841), water-colour painter and friend of *Turner.

HOLYDAY (or HOLIDAY), Barten (1593–1661), divine and translator; MA, Christ Church, Oxford, 1615; chaplain to Sir Francis Steuart in Spain, 1618, and afterwards to Charles I; archdeacon of Oxford before 1626; DD, *per literas regias*, 1642; translated Persius, Juvenal (published 1673), and Horace.

HOLYMAN, John (1495–1558), bishop of Bristol; of Winchester and New College, Oxford; fellow of New College, 1512; BA, 1514; MA, 1518; DD, 1531; preached against Lutheranism and opposed divorce of Queen *Catherine; bishop of Bristol, 1554–8; helped to try the Oxford martyrs.

HOLYOAKE, Francis (1567–1653), lexicographer; studied at The Queen's College, Oxford; MA, Emmanuel College, Cambridge, 1599; rector of Southam, 1604; ejected by Parliamentarians, 1642; his *Dictionarium Etymologicum Latinum* (1633), enlarged by his son (1677).

HOLYOAKE, George Jacob (1817–1906), cooperator and secularist; at first a tinsmith and whitesmith of Birmingham; joined Birmingham Reform League, 1831; became a Chartist, 1832; joined Owenites, 1838; present at Birmingham Chartist riots, 1839; minister to Owenites at Worcester, 1840; became rationalist; edited *Oracle of Reason*, 1841; sentenced at Gloucester to six months' imprisonment for blasphemy, 1842; published account of trial, 1851; went to London, 1843, advocating freedom of thought and co-operation and co-partnership; edited *Reasoner*, 1846, and *Leader*, 1850; invented the term 'secularism', which he explained in pamphlet, 1854; advocated abolition of paper duties, extension of the franchise, and electoral reform; twice visited Canada and United States to study economic conditions; started *The Secular Review*, 1876; chief publications include *A History of Co-operation* (1875–7), *Self-help by the People* (1855), lives of Tom *Paine (1851), Robert *Owen (1859), and John Stuart *Mill (1873), besides his autobiographical books: *Sixty Years of an Agitator's Life* (2 vols., 1892) and *Bygones worth Remembering* (1905).

HOLYOAKE, Henry (1657–1731), headmaster of Rugby; son of Thomas *Holyoake; chaplain of Magdalen College, Oxford, 1681–90; MA, 1681; headmaster of Rugby, 1687–1731; held three Warwickshire livings; left money to poor of Rugby and to Magdalen College.

HOLYOAKE, Thomas (1616?–1675), divine; son of Francis *Holyoake; MA, 1639, and chaplain, The Queen's College, Oxford; captain of undergraduate Royalists; practised medicine till Restoration; prebendary of Wolverhampton.

HOLYWOOD, Christopher (1562–1616), Jesuit; joined Jesuits, 1582; professor of divinity at Dôle and Padua; imprisoned by English government, 1599; denounced by James I when superior of Jesuits' mission in Ireland, 1604–16; published controversial works.

HOLYWOOD (or HALIFAX), John (*fl.* 1230), in Latin Johannes de Sacro Bosco; mathematician; died at Paris; author of *Tractatus de Sphaera* (first printed at Ferrara, 1472, and frequently translated); his *Algorismus* edited by J. O. *Halliwell (1838).

HOME. See also HUME.

HOME (or HUME), Sir Alexander (d. 1456), of Home; warden of the marches, 1449; accompanied William, earl of Douglas, to Rome, 1450, and founded collegiate church of Dunglass.

HOME (or HUME), Sir Alexander, first Baron Home (d. 1491), eldest son of Sir Alexander *Home (d. 1456); created lord of parliament, 1473; joined the Hepburns in driving *Albany from Scotland; conspired against *James III, 1482 and 1484; in the van at Sauchieburn, 1480; had great influence under *James IV.

HOME (or HUME), Alexander, second Baron Home (d. 1506), lord chancellor of Scotland; grandson of Sir Alexander *Home or Hume, first Baron; joined conspiracy against *James III; privy councillor, 1488; lord chancellor of Scotland, 1488–1506; succeeded to barony, 1491; made pilgrimage to Canterbury, 1493; made raid in support of the pretender Perkin *Warbeck, 1496–7.

HOME, Alexander, third Baron Home (d. 1516), lord high chamberlain of Scotland; son of Alexander *Home or Hume, second Baron; lord high chamberlain, 1506; as warden of the borders invaded Northumberland, 1513; with *Huntly commanded van at Flodden, 1513; as chief justice south of Forth, 1514, proposed to recall *Albany; joined *Angus against him and intrigued with England and *Arran; pardoned, but arrested at Edinburgh, and beheaded by the regent Albany.

HOME, Alexander, fifth Baron Home (d. 1575); succeeded his father, George *Home, fourth Baron, 1547, while prisoner after Pinkie; recaptured his castle, 1548; assisted French at Haddington; warden of east marches, 1550; commissioner for Treaty of Upsettlington, 1559; made privy councillor by *Mary Queen of Scots, 1561; supported her till the *Bothwell marriage; tried to capture Bothwell at Borthwick, 1567; prominent at Carberry Hill, 1567; prevented Mary's escape at Edinburgh; member of regent's council on Mary's abdication; fought in van at Langside, 1568; saved *Moray from capture, 1569; rejoined queen's party after his death; *Kirkcaldy's lieutenant during siege of Edinburgh Castle; died in prison.

HOME (or HUME), Alexander, sixth Baron and first earl of Home (1566?–1619), son of Alexander, fifth Baron *Home; warden of the east marches, 1582–99; engaged in raid of Ruthven, 1582; imprisoned, 1583–4, for brawl with Francis Stewart *Hepburn, fifth earl of Bothwell; co-operated with Bothwell against *Arran and befriended him in disgrace; as captain of *James VI's bodyguard aided him against Bothwell; excommunicated as a papist, but absolved on subscribing confession of faith, 1593; lord of the articles, 1594; with James in the Tolbooth, 1596; accompanied James to England and became lieutenant of the marches, 1603; created earl of Home, 1605.

HOME, Cecil (pseudonym) (1837–1894). See WEBSTER, Mrs AUGUSTA.

HOME, Charles Cospatrick Douglas- (1937–1985), journalist. See DOUGLAS-HOME.

HOME, Daniel Dunglas (1833–1886), spiritualist medium; related to the earls of Home; while in Connecticut claimed to be warned by telepathy of his mother's death; turned out of the house by his aunt on account of alleged spiritualistic rappings; his seances attended by well-known Americans, including William Cullen Bryant and Judge Edmonds; said to have been 'levitated', 1852, at house of Ward Cheney; came to England, 1855; phenomena attested by Sir David *Brewster; seances attended by Sir Edward Bulwer and the *Brownings; while in Italy became a Roman Catholic; held seances before sovereigns of France, Prussia, and Holland, 1857–8; held seances in London at houses of Thomas Milner-*Gibson and other well-known persons, 1860–1; expelled from Rome as a sorcerer, 1864; secretary of Spiritual Athenaeum in London, 1866; his 'levitations' in England attested by Lord *Lindsay (earl of Crawford), Lord Adare (earl of Dunraven), and Mrs Samuel Carter Hall; followed German Army from Sedan to Versailles, 1870; convinced (Sir) William Crookes, FRS, by submitting to tests in full light, 1871; published *Incidents of My Life* (1863 and 1872) and, with William *Howitt, *Lights and Shadows of Spiritualism* (1877); died at Auteuil.

HOME, Sir Everard, first baronet (1756–1832), surgeon; king's scholar at Westminster, 1770; pupil of John *Hunter; FRS, 1785; lecturer on anatomy, 1792, and surgeon to St George's Hospital, 1793–1827; keeper of Hunterian collection; master (1813) and first president (1821) of Royal College of Surgeons; Hunterian orator, 1814 and 1822; created baronet, 1813; surgeon to Chelsea Hospital, 1821–32; destroyed Hunter's manuscripts after utilizing them; edited Hunter's *Treatise on the Blood*, prefixing short life (1794); published *Lectures on Comparative Anatomy* (1814) and other medical works.

HOME, Francis (1719–1813), professor of materia medica at Edinburgh; studied medicine at Edinburgh; surgeon of dragoons in Seven Years' War; MD, Edinburgh, 1750; professor of materia medica, 1768–98; published *Principia Medicinae* (1758) and other works.

HOME, George, fourth Baron Home (d. 1547), brother of Alexander *Home, third Baron; was restored to title and lands, 1522; frustrated Scott of Buccleugh's attempt on *James V, 1526; joined *Argyll against *Angus, 1528; helped to defeat English at Haddenrig, 1542; routed by Sir William *Grey, 1547.

HOME (or HUME), Sir George, earl of Dunbar (d. 1611), lord high treasurer of Scotland; of Primroknows, afterwards of Spott; accompanied *James VI to Denmark, 1589; master of the Wardrobe, 1590; ally of *Maitland and opponent of *Bothwell; special privy councillor, 1598; lord high treasurer, 1602; created an English baron, 1604, and Scottish earl, 1605; commissioner of the border for both kingdoms, 1606; managed for James the Linlithgow trial (1606), Glasgow Assembly (1610), and measures for introduction of episcopacy in Scotland; KG, 1608; obtained confession from George *Sprott, 1608, and James *Elphinstone, first Baron Balmerino.

HOME, Henry, Lord Kames (1696–1782), Scottish judge and author; called to Scots bar, 1724; published *Remarkable Decisions of Court of Session (1716–28)* (1728); lord of session as Lord Kames, 1752; lord of Justiciary, 1763–82; charged with heresy on account of his *Essays on the Principles of Morality and Natural Religion* (1751), written against *Hume; his *Elements of Criticism* (1762) praised by Dugald *Stewart; published also *Sketches of History of Man* (1774), *The Gentleman Farmer* (1776), and many legal and historical works.

HOME, Sir James, of Coldingknows, third earl of Home (d. 1666); succeeded as earl, 1633; at first a Covenanter; signed band at Cumbernauld, 1641, and thenceforth supported the king; served under *Hamilton at Preston, 1648; his estates seized by *Cromwell; reinstated, 1661, and named privy councillor of Scotland; member of High Commission, 1664.

HOME, James (1760–1844), professor of materia medica, Edinburgh, 1798, in succession to his father, Francis *Home; professor of medicine at Edinburgh, 1821–44.

HOME, John (1722–1808), author of *Douglas*; educated at Leith Grammar School and Edinburgh University; volunteer, 1745; captured at Falkirk, 1746; minister of Athelstaneford, 1747; intimate of *Hume, *Robertson, and the poet *Collins; his *Douglas* (rejected by *Garrick) performed in Edinburgh, 1756, and produced by *Rich at Covent Garden, 1757; resigned his ministerial charge, owing to proceedings of Presbytery, 1757; private secretary to *Bute and tutor to prince of Wales; his *Agis* (previously rejected) produced by Garrick at Drury Lane, 1758; his *Siege of Aquileia* (1760) and *Fatal Discovery* (1769) failures; received pension from George III and sinecure from Bute; his *Alonzo* played successfully by Mrs *Barry, 1773, but *Alfred* (1778) a failure; settled at Edinburgh, 1779, and was visited by *Scott; published *History of Rebellion of 1745* (1802); works edited by Henry *Mackenzie (1822).

HOME, Robert (d. 1836?), painter; brother of Sir Everard *Home; exhibited at the Academy and at Dublin; chief painter to king of Oudh; died at Calcutta.

HOME, Robert (1837–1879), colonel of Royal Engineers; ably reported on defence of Canadian frontier, 1864; deputy-assistant quartermaster-general at Aldershot, 1865; secretary to Royal Engineers' Committee, 1870; commanded Royal Engineers in Ashanti War, 1873; assistant quartermaster-general at headquarters, 1876; reported on defence of Constantinople; published *Précis of Modern Tactics* (1873).

HOME, William, eighth earl of Home (d. 1761), soldier; served under *Cope (1745) and commanded Glasgow Volunteer Regiment, 1745; lieutenant-general; governor of Gibraltar, 1757–61; Scottish representative peer.

HOMER, Arthur (1758–1806), author of *Bibliographia Americana* (1789); son of Henry *Homer the elder; fellow of Magdalen College, Oxford, 1782–1802; MA, 1781; DD, 1797.

HOMER, Henry, the elder (1719–1791), author of works on enclosures; MA, Magdalen College, Oxford, 1743; rector of Birdingbury.

HOMER, Henry, the younger (1753–1791), classical scholar and friend of Dr Parr; eldest son of Henry *Homer the elder; fellow of Emmanuel College, Cambridge, 1778–88; MA, 1776; BD, 1783; edited Tacitus (1790), Livy (1794), Ovid's *Heroides* (1789), Persius (1789), Sallust (1789), and Caesar (1790).

HOMER, Philip Bracebridge (1765–1838), assistant master at Rugby; brother of Henry *Homer the younger; fellow of Magdalen College, Oxford, 1802–6, of Rugby, 1825; MA, 1788; BD, 1804; published original poems, translations from Metastasio, and the Eton Greek grammar, with notes (1825); completed his brother Henry's classics.

HONDIUS (DE HONDT), Abraham (1638?–1691), painter of animals and hunting scenes; in England, 1665–91.

HONDIUS (DE HONDT), Jodocus (Joos or Josse) (1563–1611), engraver; came to England from Ghent; made large globes, illustrated voyages of *Drake and *Cavendish, and engraved portraits; at Amsterdam, 1594–1611.

HONE, Evie (1894–1955), artist; born and died in Dublin; descended from brother of Nathaniel *Hone; studied in London and France; worked with Albert Gleizes, 1921–31; exhibited abstract painting in Paris, London, and Dublin; turned to stained glass through interest in Rouault; became known for unique, richly colourful work in churches and public places, including large window for Eton College Chapel.

HONE, Horace (1756–1825), miniature painter; son of Nathaniel *Hone; exhibited at Academy, 1772–82, and in Dublin; ARA, 1799.

HONE, John Camillus (d. 1837), miniature painter in London and the East Indies; brother of Horace *Hone.

HONE, Nathaniel (1718–1784), portrait painter; studied in Italy; excelled in enamel painting; exhibited with Society of Artists; an original RA; caricatured *Reynolds in *The Conjuror*, 1775; painted also *Whitefield, John *Wesley, Sir John *Fielding, and his son, John Camillus *Hone, as *David* and *Spartan Boy*.

HONE, William (1780–1842), author and bookseller; commenced publishing (1817) political satires on the government (including *John Wilkes's Catechism* and *The Sinecurist's Creed*), illustrated by *Cruikshank; prosecuted for his *Political Litany*, but acquitted, 1817; aided by public subscription, set up shop in Ludgate Hill, where Cruikshank illustrated his *Political House that Jack Built* (1819), *Man in the Moon* (1820), *Bank-Restriction Barometer* (1820), *Political Showman* (1821), *Facetiae and Miscellanies* (1827); his *Apocryphal New Testament* (1820) attacked in *Quarterly Review*; published sixpenny reprints, *Ancient Mysteries* (1823), *Every Day Book* (1826–7), dedicated to *Lamb and praised by *Scott and *Southey, and *Table Book* (1827–8); edited *Strutt's *Sports and Pastimes* (1830); *Early Life and Conversion of William Hone, by Himself* edited by his son (1841).

HONEY, George (1822–1880), actor and vocalist; played in opera till 1863; afterwards took eccentric roles, such as Eccles in *Robertson's *Caste*, and Cheviot Hill in W. S. Gilbert's *Engaged*.

HONEY, Laura (1816?–1843), actress; very successful as Psyche in *Cupid* and as Lurline (Adelphi); at the City of London played in *The Waterman* and *Riquet with the Tuft*, and sang 'My beautiful Rhine'.

HONNER, Mrs Maria (1812–1870), actress; née Macarthy; excelled in pathetic parts; played Rosalie Somers with Edmund *Kean; played Julia in *The Hunchback* (1835); married Robert William *Honner, 1836; filled place of Mrs *Yates.

HONNER, Robert William (1809–1852), actor and manager; played under Andrew *Ducrow, *Grimaldi, *Elliston, Benjamin *Webster, and Davidge; lessee of Sadler's Wells, 1835–40; manager of the Surrey, 1835–8 and 1842–6.

HONORIUS, Saint (d. 653), fifth archbishop of Canterbury; consecrated by *Paulinus at Lincoln, 628; exercised jurisdiction over Kent and East Anglia.

HONYMAN, Sir **George Essex,** fourth baronet (1819–1875), judge; barrister, Middle Temple, 1849; QC, 1866; serjeant-at-law, 1873; justice of common pleas, 1873–5.

HONYWOOD, Mrs **Mary** (1527–1620), daughter of Robert Waters of Lenham; celebrated for longevity, piety, and number of lineal descendants (367).

HONYWOOD, Michael (1597–1681), dean of Lincoln; grandson of Mrs Mary *Honywood; fellow of Christ's College, Cambridge; MA, 1618; DD, 1661; with Henry *More and Edward *King ('Lycidas') as fellows and *Milton when student; rector of Kegworth; during Protectorate lived at Utrecht; dean of Lincoln, 1660–81; at Lincoln built cathedral library and gave books.

HONYWOOD, Sir **Robert** (1601–1686), of Charing; translator of Battista Nani's *History of the Affairs of Europe* (1673); served in Palatinate; knighted as steward to queen of Bohemia, 1625; member of Council of State, 1659; went on embassy to Sweden.

HONYWOOD, Sir **Thomas** (1586–1666), Parliamentarian; of Marks Hall, Essex; knighted, 1632; joined *Fairfax before Colchester, 1648; commanded regiment at Worcester, 1651; knight of the shire for Essex, 1654, 1656; sat in *Cromwell's House of Lords, 1657.

HOOD, Lady (1783–1862). See STEWART-MACKENZIE, MARIA ELIZABETH FREDERICA.

HOOD, Alexander, first Viscount Bridport (1727–1814), admiral; brother of Samuel *Hood, first Viscount Hood; flag-captain to Sir Charles *Saunders in Mediterranean, 1756–9; took part in *Hawke's victory of 20 Nov. 1759; captured the *Warwick* in Bay of Biscay, 1761; treasurer of Greenwich, 1766; commanded the

Robust at Ushant, 1777, and gave evidence in favour of *Palliser against *Keppel; assisted in relief of Gibraltar, 1782; entered parliament, 1784; KB, 1787; admiral of the blue, 1794; second-in-command to Lord *Howe on 1 June 1794, and was created Baron Bridport (Irish peerage); defeated Villaret-Joyeuse and captured three French ships, 1795; vice-admiral of England, 1796; created a British baron, 1796; as commander of Channel Fleet blockaded Brest almost continuously, 1797–1800; created viscount, 1801; often confused with his brother; portraits of him by *Reynolds at Greenwich.

HOOD, Alexander (1758–1798), navy captain; brother of Sir Samuel *Hood (1762–1814); served on the *Resolution* in Captain *Cook's second voyage, 1772; captain of the *Barfleur* off Cape Henry, 1781, and St Kitts, 1782; fought at Battle of Dominica, 1782; captured the *Cérès*; put ashore by Spithead mutineers, 1797; captured the *Hercule* off the Bec du Raz, but was killed; epitaph by *Southey on monument at Butleigh.

HOOD, Arthur William Acland, first Baron Hood (1824–1901), admiral; entered navy, 1836; commander, 1854; served in China, 1857–8, and in North America Station, 1862–6; in charge of Royal Naval College, Portsmouth, 1866; director of naval ordnance, 1869–74; CB, 1871; commanded Channel Fleet, 1878–82; first sea lord of Admiralty, 1885; admiral and KCB, 1885; GCB, 1889; baron, 1892.

HOOD, Charles (1826–1883), major-general; led attack on Redan, 1855; commanded the buffs on entry into Sebastopol, and 58th in Bengal, 1860; major-general, 1870.

HOOD, Edwin Paxton (1820–1885), Congregational divine and author; minister in London, Brighton, and Manchester; benefactor of Hospital for Incurables; published *Self-Education* (1851) and *The Peerage of Poverty* (1st ser., 3rd edn., 1859); published also popular works on great writers, statesmen, and preachers; died in Paris.

HOOD, Francis Grosvenor (1809–1855), lieutenant-colonel of Grenadier Guards, 1841; grandson of Samuel *Hood, first Viscount Hood; led (as major, 3rd battalion) 3rd battalion of Grenadiers at the Alma, 1854; shot in trenches before Sebastopol.

HOOD, Sir **Horace Lambert Alexander** (1870–1916), rear-admiral; entered navy, 1882; served in Nile campaign, 1897–8; DSO for attack on dervishes at Illig, Somaliland, 1904; commanded Naval College, Osborne, 1910–13; rear-admiral, 1913; naval secretary to first lord of Admiralty, 1914; commanded Third Battle Squadron of Grand Fleet, with flag on board

Invincible, 1915; blown up at Battle of Jutland, 1916; posthumous KCB.

HOOD, John (1720–1783?), surveyor; invented Hood's compass theodolite; said to have anticipated *Hadley's quadrant.

HOOD, Robin, legendary outlaw; the name, which originally represented a mythical forest-elf, 'Hodeken', is part of the designation of places and plants in every part of England. His historical authenticity is ill supported. As an historical character Robin Hood appears in *Wyntoun's *Chronicle of Scotland* (*c.*1420), and is referred to as a ballad hero by *Bower, *Major, and *Stow. The first detailed history, *Lytell Geste of Robyn Hoode* (printed *c.*1495), locates him in south-west Yorkshire, later writers placing him in Sherwood and Plumpton Park (Cumberland), and finally making him earl of Huntingdon. Plays dealing with his exploits were written by *Munday, *Chettle, and others (1600–1784). The *True Tale of Robin Hood* (verse) was issued (1632), *Robin Hood's Garland* (1670), and prose narrative (1678). Major first assigned him to the reign of Richard I. A date (18 Nov. 1247) was given for his death by Martin *Parker (*True Tale*, *c.*1632) and by *Thoresby, and his pedigree was supplied by *Stukeley. According to Joseph *Hunter he was a contemporary of Edward II and adherent of *Thomas of Lancaster.

HOOD, Samuel, first Viscount Hood (1724–1816), admiral; entered navy, 1741; saw junior service under captains Thomas *Smith (d. 1762), Thomas *Grenville (1719–1747), and *Rodney; while in temporary command of the *Antelope* captured French privateers, 1757; commanded the *Vestal* in Basque roads, 1758; captured the *Bellona* off Finisterre, 1759; commander on North American Station, 1767–70; created baronet, 1778; joined Rodney in expedition against St Eustatius, 1781; while blockading Martinique engaged by superior French force; commanded rear in *Graves's action off the Chesapeake, September 1781; repulsed De Grasse off Basseterre, 1782; second-in-command under Rodney at Dominica (12 Apr.); created Baron Hood of Catherington (Irish peerage), and given freedom of the city, 1782; MP, Westminster, 1784; vice-admiral, 1787; a lord of the Admiralty, 1788–93; as commander in the Mediterranean occupied Toulon, and when abandoning it took away anti-revolutionary refugees; captured Corsica, 1794; recalled for political reasons; admiral, 1794; created Viscount Hood and governor of Greenwich, 1796; GCB, 1815.

HOOD, Sir **Samuel,** first baronet (1762–1814), vice-admiral; brother of Alexander *Hood (1758–1798); on the *Courageux*, 1776; fought off Ushant, 1778; lieutenant at actions off Martinique, 1781, Cape Henry, 1781, and St Kitts, 1782, Dominica, 1782, and Mona Passage, 1782; commanded *Juno* in Mediterranean, 1793–5; with the *Zealous* under *Nelson at Santa Cruz, 1797; distinguished at the Nile, 1798; as commander-in-chief on Leeward Station captured St Lucia and Tobago and Dutch South American settlements, 1803–4; took French ships off Rochefort, but lost an arm, 1805; under *Gambier at Copenhagen, 1807; reduced Madeira, 1807; second-in-command under *Saumarez in Baltic, 1808; created baronet after Corunna, 1809; vice-admiral, 1811; commanded in East Indies, 1812–14; died at Madras.

HOOD, Samuel (1800?–1875), author of treatise *On the Law of Decedents* (1847); member of Philadelphia bar, 1836–75; grandson of John *Hood.

HOOD, Thomas (*fl.* 1582–1598), mathematician; fellow of Trinity College, Cambridge, 1579; MA, 1581; first Thomas Smith lecturer in mathematics in London, 1582; translated Ramus's *Elements of Geometry* (1590); published works on mathematical appliances.

HOOD, Thomas (1799–1845), poet; contributed to *London Magazine*, 1821–3, becoming acquainted with *Lamb, *Hazlitt, and *De Quincey; collaborated with John Hamilton *Reynolds in *Odes and Addresses to Great People* (1825); issued *Whims and Oddities* (1826–7); became editor of the *Gem*, 1829 (in which 'Eugene Aram's Dream' appeared); began *Comic Annual*, 1830; lived at Koblenz, 1835–7, and Ostend, 1837–40; published *Hood's Own* (1838) and *Up the Rhine* (1839); returned, 1840, and edited *New Monthly Magazine*, 1841–3, writing for it 'Miss Kilmansegg'; his 'Song of the Shirt' published anonymously in *Punch* (1843); established *Hood's Magazine*, 1844; issued *Whimsicalities* (1844); received pension; collected works issued (1882–4).

HOOD, Thomas, the younger (1835–1874), known as Tom Hood; humorist; son of Thomas *Hood (1799–1845); of Pembroke College, Oxford; became editor of *Fun*, 1865; began *Tom Hood's Comic Annual*, 1867; works include *Pen and Pencil Pictures* (1857) and *Captain Masters's Children* (1865).

HOOK, James (1746–1827), organist at Vauxhall Gardens, 1774–1820, and composer; composed over 2,000 songs, including 'Within a Mile' and 'The Lass of Richmond Hill', also dramatic and concerted pieces; died at Boulogne.

HOOK, James (1772?–1828), dean of Worcester; son of James *Hook (1746–1827); while at Westminster edited *The Trifler*; graduated from St Mary Hall, Oxford, 1796; private chaplain to prince of Wales; archdeacon of Huntingdon, 1814; rector of Whippingham, 1817; dean of Worcester, 1825–8; published novels and other works.

HOOK, James Clarke (1819–1907), painter; studied at Royal Academy Schools; exhibited at Academy from 1839; ARA, 1850; RA, 1860; subjects mainly old-fashioned genre of historical anecdote until 1854, when he visited Clovelly; thenceforth treated English coast scenery; praised by John *Ruskin; best-known works were *Pamphilus Relating his Story* (1844), *Luff, Boy!* (1859), *The Samphire Gatherer* (1875), *The Stream* (1885, now in Tate Gallery); also painted portraits.

HOOK, John (1634–1710), master of Savoy Hospital, 1699–1702; son of William *Hook.

HOOK, Theodore Edward (1788–1841), novelist and wit; son of James *Hook (1746–1827); educated at Harrow; as a boy wrote words for his father's comic operas and melodramas; early entered prince of Wales's set and became known as an improviser and practical joker; went to Mauritius as accountant-general, 1813; dismissed for deficiencies in accounts, 1817; imprisoned, 1823–5, and his property confiscated; published, as 'Richard Jones', *Exchange no Robbery* (farce) and *Tentamen* (satire on Queen *Caroline), 1819–20; began to edit the Tory *John Bull*, 1820; published *Sayings and Doings* (nine novels, 1826–9), *Maxwell* (1830), *Gilbert Gurney* (1836), *Gurney Married* (1838), *Jack Brag* (1836), and *Births, Marriages, and Deaths* (1839); edited *New Monthly Magazine*, 1836–41; his effects seized by the crown; the Lucian Gay of *Coningsby* and Mr Wagg of *Vanity Fair*.

HOOK, Walter Farquhar (1798–1875), dean of Chichester; son of James *Hook (1772?–1828); educated at Winchester and Christ Church, Oxford; MA, 1824; DD, 1837; curate at Whippingham; incumbent of Holy Trinity, Coventry, 1828–37; preached at Chapel Royal his sermon 'Hear the Church', 1838, affirming apostolical succession of English bishops; as vicar of Leeds, 1837–59, built new parish church (1841) and many others, with schools and parsonage houses; obtained act of parliament for subdivision of parish (1844); propounded in letter to Bishop *Thirlwall (1846) scheme of rate-paid schools with separate religious instruction; dean of Chichester, 1859–75. His works include *Church Dictionary* (1842), *Dictionary of Ecclesiastical Biography* (1845–52), and *Lives of Archbishops of Canterbury* (1860–75; index, 1876).

HOOK, William (1600–1677), Puritan divine; MA, Trinity College, Oxford, 1623; vicar of Axmouth; emigrated to New England, 1640, and became minister at Taunton, Massachusetts, and 'teacher' at Newhaven; sent description of affairs in New England to *Cromwell, 1653; Cromwell's chaplain in England, 1656; published *New England's Teares for Old England's Feares* (1640), and with John *Davenport, *A Catechisme . . . for the . . . Church . . . at New Haven*.

HOOKE, John (1655–1712), serjeant-at-law; of Trinity College, Dublin; barrister, Gray's Inn, 1681; serjeant-at-law, 1700; chief justice of Caernarfon, Merioneth, and Anglesey, c.1703 and 1706; removed for receiving a present, 1707, but subsequently cleared.

HOOKE, Luke Joseph (1716–1796), Roman Catholic divine; son of Nathaniel *Hooke (d. 1763); DD, Sorbonne, 1736; professor of theology, 1742; virtually compelled to resign by Archbishop de Beaumont; when librarian at the Mazarin Library visited by Dr *Johnson, 1775; dismissed from librarianship by Paris Directory, 1791; edited *Memoirs of Duke of Berwick* (1778); died at St Cloud.

HOOKE, Nathaniel, the elder (1664–1738), Jacobite; brother of John *Hooke; of Dublin and Glasgow universities and Sidney Sussex College, Cambridge; sent by *Monmouth to raise London, 1685; pardoned by James II; joined *Dundee and was captured, 1689; served with Jacobites in Ireland and with French in Flanders; undertook secret missions to Scottish Jacobites, 1705 and 1707; corresponded with *Marlborough and *Stair; his correspondence (1703–7) edited by the Revd W. D. Macray, 1870–1.

HOOKE, Nathaniel (or Nathanael), the younger (d. 1763), author; nephew of Nathaniel *Hooke the elder; friend of *Pope and Martha *Blount and disciple of Fénelon; admitted at Lincoln's Inn, 1702; wrote *Account of Conduct of the Dowager Duchess of Marlborough* (1742) at her dictation; published *Roman History* (1738–71), translation of Andrew Michael *Ramsay's *Travels of Cyrus* (1739), and a work denouncing *Chesterfield's *Letters*, published (1791).

HOOKE, Robert (1635–1703), experimental philosopher; educated at Westminster under Busby and at Christ Church, Oxford; MA, 1663; assisted Thomas *Willis in his chemistry and Robert *Boyle with his air-pump; elected curator of experiments to Royal Society, 1662; FRS, 1663; secretary, 1677–82; Gresham professor of geometry, 1665; as surveyor of London designed Montague House, Bethlehem Hospital, and College of Physicians; in his *Micrographia* (1665) pointed out real nature of combustion; proposed to measure force of gravity by swinging of pendulum, 1666; showed experimentally that centre of gravity of earth and moon is the point describing an ellipse round the sun; in astronomy discovered fifth star in Orion, 1664, inferred rotation of Jupiter, 1664, first observed a star by daylight, and made earliest attempts (1669) at telescopic determination of parallax of a fixed star; in optics helped *Newton by hints; first applied spiral spring to regulate watches; expounded true theory of elasticity and kinetic hypothesis of gases, 1678; his anticipation of law of inverse squares admitted by Newton; first asserted true principle of the arch; constructed first Gregorian telescope, 1674; described a system of telegraphy, 1684; invented marine barometer and other instruments; posthumous works edited by R. Waller (1705) and Derham (1726).

HOOKE, Samuel Henry (1874–1968), biblical scholar and oriental linguist; educated at Wirksworth and St Mark's School, Windsor, and Jesus College, Oxford; first class, theology, 1910; second class, oriental languages, 1912; Flavelle associate professor of oriental languages and literature, Victoria College, Toronto, 1913–25; Rockefeller fellow in anthropology studying oriental languages in London, 1926; Samuel Davidson professor of Old Testament Studies, London, 1930–42; master at Blundell's School; examining chaplain to bishop of Coventry; visiting professor, Ghana, 1958; president, Folk-Lore Society, 1936–7; fellow, Society of Antiquaries, 1937; president, Society for Old Testament Study, 1951; hon. DD, Glasgow, 1950; hon. D.Th., Uppsala, 1957; hon. fellow, Jesus College, 1964; editor, *Palestine Exploration Quarterly* for twenty-three years; edited *Myth and Ritual* (1933) and *The Labyrinth* (1935); wrote numerous books on Christian faith and the Old Testament.

HOOKER, John (1526?–1601), alias John Vowell; antiquary; educated at Oxford; visited Cologne and Strasburg; first chamberlain of Exeter, 1555; MP, Athenry (Irish parliament), 1568; contributed to new edition of *Holinshed, 1586; wrote also *The Lyffe of Sir Peter Carewe* and works concerning Exeter.

HOOKER (or HOKER), John (*fl.* 1540), of Maidstone; poet and dramatist; fellow of Magdalen College, Oxford, 1530; MA, 1535; BD, 1540.

HOOKER, Sir Joseph Dalton (1817–1911), botanist and traveller; son of Sir William Jackson *Hooker; graduated MD, Glasgow, 1839; inherited from father a passion for botanical research; naturalist in Sir J. C. *Ross's Antarctic expedition, 1839–43; published botanical results in six volumes (1844–60); became an intimate of Charles *Darwin, and collaborated with him in

researches into the origin of species from 1843; greatly advanced the knowledge of geographical distribution of species; rejected theory of multiple origins in *Flora Antarctica* (1844–7); appointed botanist to Geological Survey, 1845; FRS, 1847; explored Sikkim, part of Eastern Nepal, and passes into Tibet, 1848–9, making observations in geology and meteorology; travelled in Eastern Bengal, 1850–1, collecting plants representing some 700 species; published *Himalayan Journals* (1854) and *Illustrations of Sikkim-Himalayan Plants* (1855); appointed assistant director at Kew, 1855; published in 1860 his *Introductory Essay on the Flora of Tasmania*, in which he adopted the newly propounded Darwin–Wallace theory that species are derivative and mutable; went on scientific expedition to Syria and examined cedar grove on Mt Lebanon, 1860; began with George *Bentham the *Genera Plantarum*, 1862 (last part issued, 1883); succeeded father as director at Kew, 1865; published *Handbook of the New Zealand Flora* (1867) and *Student's Flora of the British Islands* (1870); explored with John *Ball (1818–89) the Great Atlas in Morocco; reached Tagherot Pass; president of Royal Society, 1873–8; visited the Rocky Mountains of Colorado and Utah, 1877; published report of botanical researches, 1881; published *Flora of British India* (7 vols., 1883–97) in which he described nearly 17,000 species; retired from Kew, 1885; edited *Journal* of Sir Joseph *Banks (1896) and wrote on Indian Flora in *Imperial Gazetteer of India* (1904); CB, 1869; KCSI, 1877; GCSI, 1897; OM, 1907; received many honours from English and foreign scientific societies and universities; buried at Kew.

HOOKER, Richard (1554?–1600), theologian; nephew of John *Hooker alias Vowell; admitted at Corpus Christi College, Oxford, by influence of Bishop *Jewel; scholar, 1573; MA and fellow, 1577; deputy Hebrew professor, 1579; intimate at Oxford of (Sir) Edwin *Sandys and George *Cranmer; incumbent of Drayton-Beauchamp, 1584–5; master of the Temple, 1585; rector of Boscombe, Wiltshire, and (1595–1600) of Bishopsbourne, Kent, where the inscription on his monument first calls him 'Judicious'. Five books (four books, 1594, fifth book, 1597) of *The Laws of Ecclesiasticall Politie* appeared in his lifetime, the so-called sixth and the eighth in 1648. The seventh was first included in *Gauden's edition (1662). The sixth book is demonstrably spurious. The whole was reissued, with life by Izaak *Walton, 1666, and frequently re-edited. It was attacked by the Puritans in *A Christian Letter to certaine English Protestants* (1599) but defended by William *Covell, admired by James I and Charles I, and praised for its style by *Fuller and *Swift.

Other works by Hooker were issued at Oxford, 1613.

HOOKER, Sir Stanley George (1907–1984), mathematician, aerodynamicist, and engineer; educated at Borden Grammar School and Imperial College, London; scholar; won BUSK studentship in aeronautics, 1928, and Armourers and Braziers research fellowship, 1930; D.Phil., Brasenose College, Oxford, 1935; served in Scientific and Research Department, Admiralty, 1935–8; in charge of supercharger development, Rolls-Royce, Derby, 1938–48; chief engineer, 1943; working on turbo-props; left Rolls-Royce for Bristol Siddeley, 1948; chief engineer, 1950–70; hon. professor, Peking Institute of Aeronautical Sciences, 1973; FRS, 1962; OBE, 1946; CBE, 1964; knighted, 1974.

HOOKER, Thomas (1586?–1647), New England divine; fellow of Emmanuel College, Cambridge; MA, 1611; rector of Esher, 1620; as lecturer at Chelmsford cited for nonconformity, 1629; withdrew to Holland (1630) to avoid citation of High Commission; sailed for New England, 1633; pastor of the eighth church in Massachusetts, till removal to Hartford, Connecticut, 1636; published theological works, including *A Survey of the Summe of Church Discipline* (1648).

HOOKER, William Dawson (1816–1840), eldest son of Sir William Jackson *Hooker; privately printed *Notes on Norway* (1837).

HOOKER, Sir William Jackson (1785–1865), director of Kew Gardens; formed collection of Norfolk birds; visited Iceland and printed *Recollections* (1811); became acquainted with foreign botanists during tour of 1814; regius professor of botany at Glasgow, 1820; KH, 1836; greatly extended and threw open to the public Kew Gardens, where, with John Stevens *Henslow, he founded a museum of economic botany, 1847; his herbarium purchased by the nation; FLS, 1806; FRS, 1812; LL D, Glasgow; DCL, Oxford, 1845. His works include *Muscologia Britannica* (1818–27), *Flora Boreali-Americana* (1833–40), *Species Filicum* (1846–64).

HOOKES, Nicholas (1628–1712), poet; scholar of Westminster and Trinity College, Cambridge; BA, 1653; published *Amanda* (1653) and other verses.

HOOLE, Charles (1610–1667), educational writer; MA, Lincoln College, Oxford, 1636; master of Rotherham School; rector of Great Ponton, 1642; sequestrated; became known as teacher in London; prebendary of Lincoln and rector of Stock, Essex; published *Terminationes et Exempla* (1650) and other school manuals.

HOOLE, Elijah (1798–1872), orientalist; while Wesleyan missionary in Southern India was member of committee for revising Tamil versions of the Bible; published translations into Tamil, *Personal Narrative* (1820–8), and other works; secretary of Wesleyan Missionary Society, 1836.

HOOLE, John (1727–1803), translator; principal auditor at India House; visited *Johnson in his last illness; his translations of Tasso's *Jerusalem Delivered* (1763) and Ariosto's *Orlando Furioso* (1783) frequently reprinted; published also versions of Metastasio's *Dramas, Life of John Scott of Amwell* (1785), and three tragedies, acted at Covent Garden.

HOOPER, Edmund (1553?–1621), organist of Westminster Abbey, 1606–21, and composer of church music; gentleman of the Chapel Royal, 1603.

HOOPER, Sir Frederic Collins, first baronet (1892–1963), industrialist; educated at Sexey's School, Bruton, and University College, London; commissioned in Dorset Regiment; served on Western Front, 1914–18; recruited to Lewis's of Liverpool by F. J. *Marquis (later the earl of Woolton), 1922; joint managing director, 1940–2; set up Political Research Centre for Conservative party, 1942–3; director of business training, Ministry of Labour, 1945–6; managing director, Schweppes mineral-water company, 1948–63; built up Schweppes's international reputation; published *Management Survey* (1948); member of number of committees and advisory boards; adviser on recruiting to minister of defence, 1960; knighted, 1956; baronet, 1962.

HOOPER, George (1640–1727), bishop of Bath and Wells; scholar of St Paul's and Westminster and student of Christ Church, Oxford; MA, 1663; DD, 1677; classical, Hebrew, and Arabic scholar; chaplain to Bishop *Morley and Archbishop *Sheldon; rector of Lambeth, 1675; precentor of Exeter; as almoner to Princess Mary confirmed her in Anglican principles and offended William of Orange; dean of Canterbury, 1691; prolocutor of the lower house of convocation, 1701; bishop of St Asaph, 1702–3; accepted see of Bath and Wells, 1703, at importunity of his friend *Ken, who dedicated to him his *Hymnarium*; collected edition of his works (issued 1757) includes *Calculation of the Credibility of Human Testimony* and treatise on Tertullian's *De Valentinianorum Haeresi*.

HOOPER, John (d. 1555), bishop of Gloucester and Worcester; BA, Oxford, 1519; said to have been a Cistercian; adopted Protestant views and disputed with *Gardiner; fled from England, 1539, to avoid persecution; while at Zurich, 1547–9, adopted views of John à Lasco (see

LASKI); as chaplain to *Somerset, 1549, led advanced reformers and denounced *Bonner; when nominated to see of Gloucester (1550) refused to wear vestments, and only gave in after committal to the Fleet, 1551; showed great zeal in his diocese and was liberal to the poor; followed Zurich usage in appointing 'superintendents'; member of commission to report on ecclesiastical laws, 1551; bishop of Worcester, *in commendam*, 1552, Gloucester being subsequently made an archdeaconry; opposed attempt to set aside Mary; deprived by Queen Mary and sentenced for heresy; burned at Gloucester. His works consist mainly of homilies and biblical expositions (collected edition issued, 1855).

HOOPER, Robert (1773–1835), medical writer; MA and MB, Pembroke College, Oxford, 1804; MD, St Andrews, 1805; practised in Savile Row, making special study of pathology. His works include *Compendious Medical Dictionary* (1798) and *Anatomist's Vade-Mecum* (1798).

HOOPER, William Hulme (1827–1854), lieutenant in the navy; shared in expedition of the *Plover*, 1848–50, in search of Sir John *Franklin, publishing an account (1853).

HOOPPELL, Robert Eli (1833–1895), antiquary; MA, St John's College, Cambridge, 1858; LL D, 1868; ordained priest, 1859; English chaplain at Menai Bridge, 1859–61; first headmaster of Dr Winterbottom's Nautical College, South Shields, 1861–75; rector of Byers Green, Co. Durham, 1875; published writings relating to excavated Roman camp at South Shields and other antiquarian subjects.

HOOTEN (or HOOTON), Elizabeth (d. 1672), first female Quaker minister; imprisoned at Derby, 1651, York, 1652, and Lincoln, 1654; went to Boston, Massachusetts, 1662; barbarously treated at Cambridge, USA; returned to England; accompanied George *Fox to Jamaica, 1670, and died there.

HOOTON, Charles (1813?–1847), novelist; lived savage life in Texas; journalist in New Orleans, New York, and Montreal; published *Colin Clink* (in *Bentley's Miscellany*, and republished, 1841), *St. Louis's Isle* (1847), and other works.

HOPE, Sir Alexander (1769–1837), general; second son of the second earl of Hopetoun; served in Flanders and Holland, 1794–5, as aide-de-camp to Sir Ralph *Abercromby; wounded while commanding the 14th in attack on Gueldermasen, 1795; major-general, 1808; governor of Royal Military College, Sandhurst, 1812; undertook mission to Sweden, 1813; hon. DCL, Oxford, 1824; lieutenant-governor of Chelsea

Hospital, 1826; MP, Dumfries, 1796, Linlithgowshire, 1802–34; general and GCB.

HOPE (afterwards BERESFORD-HOPE), Alexander James Beresford (1820–1887), politician and author; son of Thomas *Hope (1770?–1831); of Harrow and Trinity College, Cambridge; MA, 1844; DCL, 1848; Tory MP, Maidstone, 1841–52 and 1857–9, Stoke, 1865–8, and Cambridge University, 1868–87; inherited Marshal Lord Beresford's English estates, 1854; prominent opponent of Deceased Wife's Sister Bill, 1859, abolition of church rates, Reform Bill of 1867, and Burials Bill, 1873; privy councillor, 1880; founded missionary college at Canterbury, and built All Saints' Church, Margaret Street, London; established *Saturday Review*, 1855, with John Douglas *Cook as editor; president of Institute of Architects, 1865–7; trustee of British Museum and National Portrait Gallery; published *Hymns of the Church literally translated* (1844), *The English Cathedral of the Nineteenth Century* (1861), works on the American Civil War and on church politics, and two novels.

HOPE, Mrs Anne (1809–1887), authoress; née Fulton; wife and biographer of James *Hope (1801–1841); converted to Romanism, 1850; published *Acts of the Early Martyrs* (1855), lives of St Philip Neri (1859) and St Thomas *Becket (1868), *Conversion of the Teutonic Race* (1872), and *Franciscan Martyrs in England* (1878).

HOPE, Anthony (pseudonym) (1863–1933), novelist. See HAWKINS, Sir ANTHONY HOPE.

HOPE, Archibald, Lord Rankeillor (1639–1706), lord of session, 1689, and of justiciary, 1690; second son of Sir John *Hope, Lord Craighall.

HOPE, Charles, first earl of Hopetoun (1681–1742), supported union with England; created Scots peer, 1703; representative peer from 1722; lord high commissioner of Church of Scotland, 1723.

HOPE, Charles, Lord Granton (1763–1851), president of court of session; eldest son of John *Hope (1739–1785); studied law at Edinburgh University; admitted advocate, 1784; sheriff of Orkney, 1792; lord advocate, 1801; MP, Edinburgh, 1803; lord justice clerk, 1804; president of court of session, 1811–41; privy councillor, 1822; lord justice general from 1836; active colonel of Edinburgh Volunteers.

HOPE, Frederick William (1797–1862), entomologist and collector; MA, Christ Church, Oxford, 1823; presented to the university his collection of insects and prints, and founded professorship of zoology; president of Entomological

Society, 1835 and 1846; published the *Coleopterist's Manual* (1837–40).

HOPE, George (1811–1876), Scottish agriculturist; his holding at Fenton Barns, Haddingtonshire, regarded as model farm; wrote against corn laws and game laws; contributed to Sir A. *Grant's *Recess Studies* (1870).

HOPE, Sir Henry (1787–1863), admiral; served under his cousin (Admiral Sir James *Hope (1808–1881)) in the *Kent*; captured in *Swiftsure*, 1801; commanded cruisers in Mediterranean, 1808–12; while in command of the *Endymion* captured the US ship *President* off Sandy Hook, 1815; rear-admiral, 1846; KCB, 1855; admiral, 1858.

HOPE, Henry Philip (d. 1839), picture and diamond collector; brother of Thomas *Hope (1770?–1831).

HOPE, Sir James (1614–1661), of Hopetoun; lawyer and lead-worker; sixth son of Sir Thomas *Hope, first baronet (d. 1646); general of the cunzie-house, 1642; a lord of session, 1649; member of Committee of Estates; commissioner of justice, 1652; member of English Council of State, 1653.

HOPE (afterwards **HOPE JOHNSTONE**), **James**, third earl of Hopetoun (1741–1816), with Foot Guards at Minden; succeeded to earldom, 1781; representative peer, 1784 and 1794; succeeded to estates of marquis of Annandale and assumed name of Johnstone, 1792; created British baron, 1809, for raising Hopetoun fencibles.

HOPE, James (1764–1846?), United Irishman; cotton-weaver; supported union between Romanists and Presbyterians in Ulster; joined Roughford Volunteer Corps and (1795) the reconstructed United Irish Society; founded branch at Dublin; present at Ballinahinch, 1798; assisted Robert *Emmet and organized rising in Co. Down, 1803, but was amnestied.

HOPE, James (1801–1841), physician; studied at Edinburgh, St Bartholomew's Hospital, and on the continent; early practised auscultation; physician to Marylebone Infirmary, 1831; assistant at St George's Hospital, 1834, full physician, 1839; FRCP, 1840; FRS, 1832; published *Treatise on Diseases of the Heart* (1832) and a work on morbid anatomy (1833–4).

HOPE, Sir James (1808–1881), admiral of the fleet; cousin of Sir Henry *Hope; distinguished in engagement with Obligado batteries, 1845; CB, 1846; commanded the *Majestic* in the Baltic, 1854–6; rear-admiral, 1857; commander-in-chief in China, 1859; repulsed and wounded in attempt to force passage of the Peiho, 1859; took

Taku forts, 1860; created KCB, 1860; wounded while serving against Taipings, 1862; commander in North America, 1863; GCB, 1865; commander at Portsmouth, 1869–72; admiral, 1870; admiral of the fleet, 1879.

HOPE, Sir James Archibald (1785–1871), general; served with 26th in Hanover, 1805–6, and at Copenhagen, 1807; on staff of Sir John *Hope (1765–1836) in Spain, 1808–9, and Walcheren expedition, 1809; aide-de-camp to *Graham at Barossa, 1811, Ciudad Rodrigo, 1812, and Badajoz, 1812; assistant adjutant-general at Salamanca, Vittoria, and St Sebastian, and with *Beresford in France; exchanged into Scots Guards, 1814; major-general in Lower Canada, 1841–7; GCB; general, 1859.

HOPE, James Fitzalan, first Baron Rankeillour (1870–1949), parliamentarian; son of J. R. *Hope-Scott and grandson of fourteenth duke of *Norfolk; educated at Oratory School and Christ Church, Oxford; Conservative MP, Brightside division (1900–6), Central division (1908–29) of Sheffield; junior lord of Treasury, 1916–19; parliamentary and financial secretary to Ministry of Munitions, 1919–21; chairman of ways and means and deputy speaker, 1921–4, 1924–9; prominent Roman Catholic layman; PC, 1922; baron, 1932.

HOPE, Sir John, Lord Craighall (1605?–1654), eldest son of Sir Thomas *Hope, first baronet (d. 1646); lord of session, 1632; knighted, 1632; member of Committee of Estates, 1640; of *Cromwell's judicial committee, 1652; represented Scotland in English parliament, 1653.

HOPE, Sir John (1684?–1766). See BRUCE, Sir JOHN HOPE.

HOPE, John (1725–1786), professor of botany at Edinburgh; grandson of Archibald *Hope, Lord Rankeillor; MD, Glasgow, 1750; professor of botany and materia medica, Edinburgh, 1761; regius professor of medicine and botany, 1768; president, Edinburgh College of Physicians; FRS; founded new Edinburgh botanic gardens, 1776; genus *Hopea* named after him by Linnaeus, whose *Genera Animalium* he edited (1781).

HOPE, John (1739–1785), author; grandson of Charles *Hope, first earl of Hopetoun; MP, Linlithgowshire, 1768–70; published *Letters on Credit* (1784) and other works.

HOPE, John, fourth earl of Hopetoun (1765–1823), general; MP, Linlithgowshire, 1790; adjutant-general under *Abercromby in West Indies, 1796, and in Holland, 1799; wounded at Alexandria, 1801; lieutenant-general, 1808; second-in-command under Sir John *Moore in Sweden and in the Peninsula; commanded left wing at Corunna and directed embarkation; headed division in Walcheren expedition, 1809; succeeded *Graham in the Peninsula; led first division at Nivelle and the Nive, 1813; conducted blockade of Bayonne; wounded and captured in final sortie of Bayonne garrison, 1814; created Baron Niddry; succeeded his half-brother James *Hope, third earl of Hopetoun, 1816; general, 1819.

HOPE, Sir John (1765–1836), lieutenant-general; son of John *Hope (1739–1785); in Dutch service, 1778–82; aide-de-camp to Sir William Erskine in Flanders and Germany, 1792–3; commanded 28th, 1796–9, and 37th, 1799–1804; deputy adjutant-general under *Cathcart at Hanover, 1805, and Copenhagen, 1807; commanded brigade at Salamanca, 1812; lieutenant-general, 1819; knighted, 1821; GCH.

HOPE, John (1794–1858), Scottish judge; eldest son of Charles *Hope (1763–1851); advocate, 1816; summoned to Commons' bar for breach of privilege, 1822; solicitor-general for Scotland, 1822–30; dean of Faculty of Advocates, 1830; lord justice clerk, 1841–58; privy councillor, 1844; edited diary of Sir David *Hume of Crossrig (1828).

HOPE, John Adrian Louis, seventh earl of Hopetoun and first marquess of Linlithgow (1860–1908), first governor-general of the Commonwealth of Australia; succeeded to earldom, 1873; Conservative lord-in-waiting to Queen Victoria, 1885–9; governor of Victoria and GCMG, 1889; paymaster-general, 1895–8; lord chamberlain, 1898; president of Institution of Naval Architects, 1895–1900; first governor-general of Commonwealth of Australia, 1900–2; KT and GCVO, 1900; resigned owing to insufficient salary, May 1902; created marquess of Linlithgow, Oct. 1902; secretary of state for Scotland, 1905; sold Rosyth for naval base to government, 1903; died at Pau; a keen sportsman and huntsman.

HOPE, John Williams (1757–1813), banker and merchant; son of William *Williams; assumed name of Hope on marriage; banker at Amsterdam; one of the eight statesmen of Holland, 1794–1806.

HOPE, Laurence (pseudonym) (1865–1904), poetess. See NICOLSON, ADELA FLORENCE.

HOPE, Sir Thomas (1606–1643), of Kerse; son of Sir Thomas *Hope, first baronet; admitted advocate, 1631; knighted, 1633; commissioner for Clackmannan, 1639–41; colonel of *Leslie's bodyguard, 1639–40; negotiated compromise between Charles I and the estates; lord justice general, 1641–3; wrote the *Law Repertorie*.

HOPE, Sir Thomas, first baronet (d. 1646), lord advocate of Scotland; advocate, 1605; made reputation by defence of John *Forbes (1568?–1634), and other ministers at Linlithgow, 1606; prepared deed revoking James I's grants of church property, 1625; lord advocate, 1626; created Nova Scotia baronet, 1628; conducted case against *Balmerino, 1634; as lord high commissioner to general assembly maintained the king's temporizing policy, 1643; his *Minor Practicks* published by *Bayne (1726).

HOPE, Thomas (1770?–1831), virtuoso and author; of the Hopes of Amsterdam; settled in England, c.1796; collected marbles and sculptures, and deposited them in Duchess Street, London, and at Deepdene, Surrey; patron of Canova, Thorwaldsen, and *Flaxman; caricatured with his wife by Dubost as *Beauty and the Beast*, 1810; published *Anastasius* anonymously (1819), *Household Furniture* (1807), and other works.

HOPE, Thomas Charles (1766–1844), professor of chemistry at Edinburgh; third son of John *Hope (1725–1786); professor of chemistry at Glasgow, 1787–9; professor of chemistry, Edinburgh, 1799–1843; proved that strontian contained a peculiar earth; estimated maximum density point of water; founded chemical prize at Edinburgh.

HOPE, Victor Alexander John, second marquess of Linlithgow (1887–1952), viceroy of India; succeeded father, first marquess of *Linlithgow, 1908; educated at Eton; civil lord of Admiralty, 1922–4; president, Navy League, 1924–31; chairman, Royal Commission on Indian Agriculture, 1926–8, Joint Select Committee on Indian Constitutional Reform, 1933–4; viceroy of India, 1936–43; introduced provincial autonomy, persuading Congress to take office, 1937; ensured stability of North-West Frontier by military operations, 1936–8; organized India for war despite Congress opposition and withdrawal of provincial ministries and country's rejection of *Cripps's constitutional proposals, 1942; expanded his council to fifteen of whom ten were Indians; established National Defence Council and Department of Supply, and initiated Eastern Group Supply Council; chairman, Midland Bank, 1944–52; KT, 1928; GCIE, 1929; PC, 1935; GCSI, 1936; KG, 1943.

HOPE, Sir William Henry St John (1854–1919), antiquary; BA, Peterhouse, Cambridge; carried out excavations at Dale Abbey, Repton Priory, Lewes Priory, and Alnwick Abbey; FSA, 1883; assistant secretary to Society of Antiquaries, 1885–1910; knighted, 1914; writings include numerous ecclesiological and heraldic works and over 200 papers.

HOPE, Sir **William Johnstone** (1766–1831), vice-admiral; son of John *Hope (1739–1785); lieutenant of the *Boreas* under *Nelson, 1787; flag-captain to Rear-Admiral *Pasley in action of 1 June 1794, to *Duncan in the *Venerable* and the *Kent*, 1795–6, and 1798–9; served in Egypt, 1800–1; MP, Dumfries, 1800–4, Dumfriesshire, 1804–30; a lord of the Admiralty, 1807–9; vice-admiral, 1819; member of Admiralty Board, 1820–8; GCB, 1825.

HOPE, William Williams (1802–1855), man of fashion and virtuoso; son of John Williams *Hope.

HOPE-SCOTT, James Robert (1812–1873), parliamentary barrister; third son of Sir Alexander *Hope; travelled in Germany and Italy before going to Eton; at Christ Church, Oxford, became the friend of William Ewart Gladstone and Roundell *Palmer, afterwards earl of Selborne; fellow of Merton, 1833; DCL, 1843; barrister, Inner Temple, 1840; named chancellor of Salisbury, 1840, after arguing before House of Lords against Ecclesiastical Duties and Revenues Bill, 1840; joined Tractarians, becoming *Newman's chief adviser; with *Manning received into Roman Church, 1851; soon obtained immense parliamentary practice; QC, 1849; married John Gibson *Lockhart's daughter, and assumed additional name of Scott, 1853, on becoming possessor of Abbotsford; wrote against Ecclesiastical Titles Act, 1867.

HOPETOUN, earls of. See HOPE, CHARLES, first earl, 1681–1742; HOPE, JAMES, third earl, 1741–1816; HOPE, JOHN, fourth earl, 1765–1823; HOPE, JOHN ADRIAN LOUIS, seventh earl, 1860–1908.

HOPE-WALLACE, Philip Adrian (1911–1979), music and theatre critic; educated at Charterhouse and Balliol College, Oxford; worked for International Broadcasting Co. in France, 1933–4 and Gas Light and Coke Co., 1935–6; began work as critic covering song recitals for *The Times*, 1935; during 1939–45 war worked in Air Ministry press office; became arts critic for the *Daily Telegraph*, 1945–6 and with *Time and Tide*, 1945–9, and later chief drama critic with the *Guardian*, 1946–71; also a mainstay of the *Gramophone*, a member of editorial staff of *Opera*, and a contributor to the *Listener*, the *New Statesman*, and other papers; broadcast with success in such programmes as 'The Critics' and 'Music Magazine'; president of Critics' Circle, 1958; CBE, 1975; regarded himself as spokesman for theatre-goers; his main interest the opera; published *A Key to Opera* (with Frank

Stewart *Howes, 1939), and *A Picture History of Opera* (1959); selection of his notices and essays, *Words and Music*, published posthumously (1981).

HOPKIN, Hopkin (1737–1754), famous dwarf; son of Lewis *Hopkin.

HOPKIN, Lewis (1708–1771), Welsh poet; registered bard, 1760; with Edward *Evans (1716–1798) made rhymed version of Ecclesiastes, 1767; translated 'Chevy Chase', 1770; collected works (*Y Fel Gafod*) edited by J. Miles (1813).

HOPKINS, Charles (1664?–1700?), poet; son of Ezekiel *Hopkins; friend of *Dryden and *Congreve; of Trinity College, Dublin, and Queens' College, Cambridge; BA, Cambridge, 1688; published *Epistolary Poems* (1694), *Whitehall* (1698), and three tragedies.

HOPKINS, Edward (1600–1657), governor of Connecticut; emigrated, 1637; governor of Connecticut, 1640–52 (alternate years); helped to form union of New England colonies, 1643; navy commissioner in England, 1653; MP, Dartmouth, 1656; Hopkinton bought from his donation to Harvard.

HOPKINS, Edward John (1818–1901), organist; organist at Temple Church, London, 1843–98; hon. Mus.Doc., Toronto, 1886; compiled *Temple Church Choral Service Book* (1867) and *Temple Psalter* (1883); wrote *The Organ, its History and Construction* (1855), a standard work.

HOPKINS, Ezekiel (1634–1690), bishop of Derry; of Merchant Taylors' School and Magdalen College, Oxford; MA, 1656; chaplain to Lord Robartes (viceroy of Ireland); archdeacon of Waterford, 1669; bishop of Raphoe, 1670–81; bishop of Derry, 1681–90; left Ireland at Revolution; works edited by Josiah *Pratt (1809).

HOPKINS, Sir **Frederick Gowland** (1861–1947), biochemist; educated at City of London School; articled to consulting analyst; studied chemistry at South Kensington and University College; assistant to (Sir) Thomas *Stevenson; entered Guy's Hospital, 1888; B.Sc., London, 1890; qualified, 1894; assistant in physiology department, 1894–8; lecturer on chemical physiology, Cambridge, 1898; reader, 1902; praelector in biochemistry, Trinity College, 1910–21; professor of biochemistry, 1914; Sir William Dunn professor, 1921–43; in *Journal of Physiology* (1912) published important paper giving precision to ideas about existence of vitamins and methods of exploring them; devoted himself to study of chemistry of intermediary metabolism and establishment of biochemistry as separate discipline; FRS, 1905; shared Nobel Prize, 1929;

president, Royal Society, 1930–5, British Association, 1933; knighted, 1925; OM, 1935.

HOPKINS, George (1620–1666), rector of Evesham (ejected, 1662), and author of *Salvation from Sin* (1655).

HOPKINS, Jane Ellice (1836–1904), social reformer; daughter of William *Hopkins; worked among navvies at Cambridge; removed to Brighton; edited *Life and Letters* of James *Hinton (1875); founded White Cross League, 1886; published *Active Service* (1872–4), *The Power of Womanhood* (1899), and *The Story of Life* (1903).

HOPKINS, John (*fl.* 1700), verse-writer; brother of Charles *Hopkins; MA, Jesus College, Cambridge, 1698; chief works, *Milton's Paradise Lost imitated in Rhyme* (1699) and *Amasia* (1700).

HOPKINS, John (d. 1570), contributor to metrical Psalms; BA, Oxford, 1544; Suffolk schoolmaster; rector of Great Waldingfield, 1561–70; the 'Old Hundredth' psalm often attributed to him.

HOPKINS, John Larkin (1819–1873), organist of Rochester (1841) and Trinity College, Cambridge (1856); Mus.Doc., Cambridge, 1857; composed *Five Glees and a Madrigal* (1842) and church music; published *New Vocal Tutor* (1855).

HOPKINS, Matthew (d. 1647), witch-finder; said to have been a lawyer at Ipswich and Manningtree; made journeys for discovery of witches in eastern counties and Huntingdonshire, 1644–7; procured special judicial commission (1645) under John *Godbolt by which sixty women were hanged in Essex in one year, nearly forty at Bury, and many at Norwich and in Huntingdonshire; published *Discovery of Witches* (1647); exposed by John *Gaule; hanged as a sorcerer; referred to in *Hudibras*.

HOPKINS, Richard (d. 1594?), translator; of St Alban Hall, Oxford, and Middle Temple; studied at Spanish universities, Louvain, Reims, and Paris; translated Spanish religious works.

HOPKINS, Sir Richard Valentine Nind (1880–1955), civil servant; educated at King Edward's School, Birmingham, and Emmanuel College, Cambridge; first class, part i, classical tripos, 1901, and part ii, history tripos, 1902; entered Inland Revenue, 1902; member of Board, 1916; chairman, 1922; transferred to Treasury, controlling finance and supply services, 1927; second secretary, 1932; permanent secretary, 1942–5; withstood challenge to Treasury finance of J. M. (later Lord) *Keynes before Macmillan Committee, 1930; invited him

to Treasury, 1940; CB, 1919; KCB, 1920; GCB, 1941; PC, 1945.

HOPKINS, William (1647–1700), divine; son of George *Hopkins; MA, St Mary Hall, Oxford, 1668; DD, 1692; chaplain to Henry *Coventry (1619–1686) in second embassy to Sweden, 1671; prebendary of Worcester, 1675, and master of St Oswald's Hospital, 1697; published *Book of Bertram or Ratramnus concerning the Body and Blood of the Lord* (1686); assisted Gibson with edition of *Saxon Chronicle* and *Camden in *Britannia*.

HOPKINS, William (*fl.* 1674), stenographer; published *The Flying Pen-Man* (1670).

HOPKINS, William (1706–1786), theological writer; BA, All Souls College, Oxford, 1728; master of Cuckfield School, 1756; as vicar of Bolney, made alterations in the liturgy; published Arian pamphlets attacking liturgy.

HOPKINS, William (1793–1866), mathematician and geologist; of Peterhouse, Cambridge; seventh wrangler, 1827; MA, 1830; as coach, had Stokes, Sir W. Thomson, *Fawcett, and *Todhunter among his pupils; studied geology; Wollaston medallist, 1850; president of Geological Society, 1851, and of British Association, 1853; prize founded in his honour by Cambridge Philosophical Society; published works, including *Elements of Trigonometry* (1833) and *Theoretical Investigations on Motion of Glaciers* (1842).

HOPKINSON, Sir Alfred (1851–1939), lawyer, educationist, and politician; brother of John *Hopkinson; educated at Owens College, Manchester, and Lincoln College, Oxford; called to bar (Lincoln's Inn), 1873; QC, 1892; professor of law, Owens College (1875–89), principal (1898–1904); vice-chancellor, Manchester University, 1900–13; Unionist MP, Cricklade (1895–8), combined English universities (1926–9); knighted, 1910.

HOPKINSON, Bertram (1874–1918), engineer and physicist; son of John *Hopkinson, FRS; BA, Trinity College, Cambridge; professor of mechanism and applied mechanics at Cambridge, 1903–18; FRS, 1910; joined Royal Engineers, 1914; carried out investigations for government on explosives and aircraft equipment; CMG, 1917; killed flying.

HOPKINSON, John (1610–1680), antiquary; of Lincoln's Inn; secretary to *Dugdale during visitation of Yorkshire; made large collections for history of Yorkshire.

HOPKINSON, John (1849–1898), electrical engineer; educated at the Owens College, Manchester, and Trinity College, Cambridge; senior wrangler, 1871; Smith's prizeman; fellow; D.Sc.,

London, 1871; manager and engineer in lighthouse and optical department of Messrs Chance Brothers, Birmingham, 1872–8; consulting engineer in London, 1878; FRS, 1878, and member of council, 1886–7 and 1891–3; patented three-wire system of distributing electricity, 1882; published, with his brother, Edward Hopkinson, paper describing improvements in dynamos, which was foundation of accurate design of dynamos in accordance with theory (1886); professor of electrical engineering, King's College, London, 1890; consulting engineer to contractors of City and South London Railway; member of council of Institute of Civil Engineers, 1895; member of Institution of Electrical Engineers; killed in Alpine accident. A collection of his scientific papers was published (1901).

HOPKINSON, William (*fl.* 1583), divine; BA, St John's College, Cambridge, 1567; published translation from Beza's vindication of Calvin's predestination.

HOPKIRK, Thomas (1785–1841), Glasgow botanist; FLS, 1812; published *Flora Anomoia* (1817).

HOPLEY, Edward William John (1816–1869), painter; exhibited at British Institution and Royal Academy; invented trigonometrical system of facial measurement.

HOPPER, Humphrey (*fl.* 1799–1834), sculptor.

HOPPER, Thomas (1776–1856), architect and surveyor; built Arthur's Club and various mansions.

HOPPNER, John (1758–1810), portrait painter; born in London of German parentage; chorister in Chapel Royal; exhibited at Royal Academy (1780–1809) 168 pictures, mostly portraits, including *A Sleeping Nymph*; RA, 1795; portrait painter to prince of Wales, 1789; *Lawrence's chief rival; *Lady Culling* (Eardley) *Smith and Children* and *Mrs Lascelles* among his finest works.

HOPPUS, John (1789–1875), professor at University College, London; MA, Glasgow; LL D, 1839; Independent minister at Carter Street Chapel, London; first professor of philosophy and logic, University College, London, 1829–66; FRS, 1841; published *Account of Bacon's 'Novum Organon'* (1827), *Thoughts on Academical Education* (1837), and other works.

HOPSON, Charles Rivington (1744–1796), physician to Finsbury Dispensary; educated at St Paul's School and Leiden; MD, 1767; published *Essay on Fire* (1782), and translations from German of J. G. Zimmermann and Wiegleb.

HOPSONN (or HOPSON), Edward (d. 1728), vice-admiral.

HOPSONN, Sir Thomas (1642–1717), vice-admiral; served against Dutch, 1672–3; commanded the *York* at Beachy Head, 1690, and the *St Michael* at Barfleur, 1692; rear-admiral, 1693; commanded squadron off French coast, 1694–5, and Channel squadron, 1699; vice-admiral, 1702; as second-in-command under *Rooke forced boom protecting French and Spanish fleet at Vigo, 1702, and was knighted and pensioned; MP, Newtown (Isle of Wight), 1698–1705.

HOPTON, Arthur (1588?–1614), astrologer and mathematician; of Clement's Inn; friend of *Selden; published prognostications for years 1607–14, *Baculum Geodaeticum* (1610), and similar works.

HOPTON, Sir Arthur (1588?–1650), diplomat; of Lincoln College, Oxford; secretary to Lord *Cottington's embassy in Spain, 1629, ambassador, 1638, and throughout Civil Wars; knighted, 1638.

HOPTON, John (d. 1558), bishop of Norwich; prior of Oxford Dominicans; DD, Oxford, 1532; rector of St Anne's, London, 1539, of Fobbing, Essex, 1548; chaplain to Princess Mary at Copt Hall; bishop of Norwich, 1554–8; persecuted the Protestants.

HOPTON, Ralph, first Baron Hopton (1598–1652), Royalist commander; nephew of Sir Arthur *Hopton; of Lincoln College, Oxford; served under elector palatine and Mansfeld; KB, 1625; MP, Bath, in first parliament of Charles I, and *Somerset in Short Parliament; MP, Wells, 1628–9, and in Long Parliament; supported *Strafford's attainder and presented Grand Remonstrance to king, 1641, but was sent to Tower by parliament for denouncing militia ordinance, 1642; expelled the house; defeated Parliamentarians at Bradock Down and Stratton, Cornwall, 1643; joined *Maurice's attack on *Waller at Lansdown, 1643, and, though wounded, directed defence of Devizes, 1643; created Baron Hopton on resignation of governorship of Bristol to *Rupert, 1643; defeated at Cheriton, 1644; succeeded to command of *Goring's undisciplined force in the west; routed at Torrington, 1646; capitulated at Truro, 1646; left England with Prince Charles, 1648; opposed concessions to Presbyterians and retired to Wesel, 1650; died at Bruges.

HOPTON, Susanna (1627–1709), devotional writer; née Harvey; wife of Richard Hopton, Welsh judge.

HOPWOOD, Charles Henry (1829–1904), recorder of Liverpool, 1886–1904; called to bar,

1853; QC, 1874; treasurer of Middle Temple, 1895; edited *Registration Cases, 1863–72* (3 vols., 1868–79); Liberal MP for Stockport, 1874–85, and for Middleton division of Lancashire, 1892–5; energetic supporter of principle of personal liberty, of trade-unionism, and adult suffrage; opposed severity of punishment and as recorder inflicted short sentences; founded Romilly Society, 1897; edited *Middle Temple Records* (1904).

HOPWOOD, Francis John Stephens, first Baron Southborough (1860–1947), civil servant; educated at King Edward VI School, Louth; admitted solicitor, 1882; entered Board of Trade, 1885; permanent secretary, 1901–7; member, West Ridgeway Committee on Transvaal and Orange River Colony, 1906; permanent under-secretary for colonies, 1907–10; accompanied prince of Wales to Canada (1908) and duke of *Connaught to South Africa (1910); vice-chairman, Development Commission, 1910–12; civil lord of Admiralty, 1912–17; chairman, war trade committees, 1914–18; investigated Austrian peace proposals, 1917; secretary, Irish Convention, 1917–18; chairman, Indian Franchise Committee, 1918–19, and many other committees; KCB, 1901; PC, 1912; baron and GCVO, 1917; KCSI, 1920.

HOPWOOD, James, the elder (1752?–1819), engraver; secretary, Artists' Benevolent Fund.

HOPWOOD, James, the younger (*fl.* 1800–1850), stipple-engraver; son of James *Hopwood the elder.

HOPWOOD, William (1784–1853), engraver; brother of James *Hopwood the younger.

HORBERY, Matthew (1707?–1773), divine; MA, Lincoln College, Oxford, 1733; fellow of Magdalen College, Oxford, 1733; defended *Waterland against John *Jackson (1686–1763); published treatise on *Scripture Doctrine of Eternal Punishment* (1744); canon of Lichfield, 1736; vicar of Hanbury, 1740, of Standlake, 1756; collected works issued (1828).

HORDEN, Hildebrand (d. 1796), actor; member of Drury Lane and Dorset Garden Company, 1695–6; said to have written *Neglected Virtue*; killed in tavern brawl.

HORDER, Percy (Richard) Morley (1870–1944), architect; educated at City of London School; articled to George *Devey; FRIBA, 1904; works include many traditional country houses; at Cambridge, Cheshunt College, Westcott House, and the National Institute of Agricultural Botany; at Oxford, new buildings for Somerville College and the Institute for Research in Agricultural Economics; chemist

shops for Lord *Trent and Nottingham University College.

HORDER, Thomas Jeeves, first Baron Horder (1871–1955), physician; educated at Swindon High School; qualified from St Bartholomew's Hospital, 1896; MD, 1899; FRCP, 1906; house-physician to Samuel *Gee; medical registrar, 1904–11, assistant physician, 1912–21, senior physician, 1921–36, St Bartholomew's; outstanding clinician of his time, combining bedside observation with laboratory investigation; a rationalist and individualist of organized common sense; patients included four successive British sovereigns; organized Fellowship for Freedom in Medicine, 1948; chairman, Empire Rheumatism Council, 1936–53; medical adviser, London Transport, 1940–55; knighted, 1918; baronet, 1923; baron, 1933; KCVO, 1925; GCVO, 1938; held number of honorary degrees.

HORE-BELISHA, (Isaac) Leslie, Baron Hore-Belisha (1893–1957), politician; educated at Clifton and St John's College, Oxford; served in France and Salonika, 1914–18; president of Union, 1919; called to bar (Inner Temple), 1923; Liberal MP, Devonport, 1923–45; organized Liberal National party supporting National government, 1931; its chairman until 1940; parliamentary secretary, Board of Trade, 1931–2; financial secretary to Treasury, 1932–4; minister of transport, 1934–7; introduced 'Belisha beacons' and other well-publicized road-safety measures; transferred trunk roads to care of state and sponsored plans for new arterial roads; secretary for war, 1937; introduced rapid and extensive reforms covering conditions of service, training, mechanization, tactical reorganization, etc.; his personality and methods aroused hostility; his justified anxiety about defences in France caused friction with Lord *Gort and others, and brought offer of transfer; resigned, Jan. 1940; minister of national insurance, caretaker government, 1945; thereafter joined Conservatives but failed to enter parliament; PC, 1935; baron, 1954.

HORE-RUTHVEN, Alexander Gore Arkwright, first earl of Gowrie (1872–1955), soldier and governor-general of Australia; educated at Eton; served in Nile expeditions, 1898–9; VC; military secretary to Lord *Dudley in Ireland and Australia, 1905–10; served in France and Gallipoli, 1914–18; DSO; CB, and CMG; commanded Welsh Guards, 1920–4; 1st Infantry brigade, 1924–8; governor, South Australia, 1928–34, New South Wales, 1935–6; governor-general of Australia, 1936–44; of imperturbable goodwill and common sense; on excellent terms with John *Curtin; deputy constable and lieutenant-governor, Windsor Castle, 1945–53;

KCMG, 1928; GCMG and Baron Gowrie, 1935; PC, 1937; earl, 1945; president, MCC, 1948.

HORMAN, William (d. 1535), vice-provost of Eton; fellow of New College, Oxford, 1477–85; master of Eton, 1485, and fellow, 1502; his Latin aphorisms (*Vulgaria*) printed by *Pynson (1519) and De *Worde (1540); in *Antibossicon* (1521) attacked grammatical works of Robert Whitynton.

HORN, Andrew (d. 1328), chamberlain of London, 1320–8; compiled *Liber Horn*; author or editor of *La Somme appelle Mirroir des Justices* (printed 1624).

HORN, Charles Edward (1786–1849), vocalist and composer; made reputation as Caspar in *Der Freischütz*, at Drury Lane, 1824; subsequently music publisher at New York; director at Princess's, London, 1843–7; conductor of Handel and Haydn Society, Boston, 1848; composed popular airs, including 'Cherry Ripe' and 'I know a bank', operas and oratorios, and glees and pianoforte music; edited *Hindustani Melodies* (1813).

HORNBLOWER, Jabez Carter (1744–1814), engineer; son of Jonathan *Hornblower; employed by Dutch and Swedish governments; patented machine for glazing calicoes.

HORNBLOWER, Jonathan (1717–1780), engineer.

HORNBLOWER, Jonathan Carter (1753–1815), engineer; son of Jonathan *Hornblower; employed by *Watt; his steam engine on the expansion principle (1781) declared infringement of Watt's patent, 1799; contributed to Nicholson's *Journal*.

HORNBLOWER, Josiah (1729?–1809), speaker of New Jersey assembly; brother of Jonathan *Hornblower.

HORNBY, Charles Harry St John (1867–1946), printer and connoisseur; educated at Harrow and New College, Oxford; rowed for Oxford and third class, Lit. Hum., 1890; entered W. H. Smith & Son, 1892; partner, 1894; extended printing business and initiated bookbinding department; from his private Ashendene Press (1895–1935) published forty major works; collected medieval and renaissance manuscripts and printed books.

HORNBY, Sir Geoffrey Thomas Phipps (1825–1895), admiral of the fleet; son of Admiral Sir Phipps *Hornby; entered navy, 1837; lieutenant, 1844; flag-lieutenant to his father in Pacific, 1846; commander, 1850; captain, 1852; at Vancouver's Island, 1858; under Sir William Fanshawe *Martin in Mediterranean, 1861–2;

flag-captain to Rear-Admiral Sidney Colpoys *Dacres in Channel, 1862–5; first-class commodore on west coast of Africa, 1865–7; rear-admiral, 1869; commanded flying squadron, 1869–71, and Channel squadron, 1871–4; lord of Admiralty, 1875–7; vice-admiral, 1875; commander-in-chief in Mediterranean, 1877–80; conducted fleet through Dardanelles to Constantinople during Russo-Turkish War, 1878; KCB, 1878; admiral, 1879; president of Royal Naval College, 1881–2; commander-in-chief at Portsmouth, 1882–5; commanded evolutionary squadron, 1885; GCB, 1885; principal naval aide-de-camp to the queen, 1886; admiral of the fleet, 1888.

HORNBY, James John (1826–1909), provost of Eton; son of Admiral Sir Phipps *Hornby; educated at Eton and Balliol College, Oxford; first-class classic and fellow of Brasenose, 1849; rowed in Oxford eight, 1849 and 1851; MA, 1851; DD, 1869; principal of Bishop Cosin's Hall, Durham, 1853–64; headmaster of Eton, 1868–84; provost, 1884–1909; pioneer of alpine climbing; hon. DCL, Durham, 1882.

HORNBY, Sir Phipps (1785–1867), admiral; midshipman in the *Victory*, 1804; while commanding the *Duchess of Bedford* engaged two privateers off Gibraltar, 1806; in the *Volage* took part in action off Lissa, 1811; CB, 1815; commander in Pacific, 1847–50; a lord of the Admiralty, 1851–2; admiral, 1858; GCB, 1861.

HORNBY, William (fl. 1618), poet; author of *The Scovrge of Drvnkennes* (1618) and *Hornbyes Hornbook* (1622).

HORNE, George (1730–1792), bishop of Norwich; BA, University College, Oxford, 1749; fellow of Magdalen College, Oxford, 1750, and president, 1768–90; MA, 1752; royal chaplain, 1771–81; vice-chancellor, 1776; dean of Canterbury, 1781; bishop of Norwich, 1790–2; allowed John *Wesley to preach in his diocese; defended Hutchinsonian views against *Newton; published *Commentary on the Psalms* (1771), and wrote against *Law, Swedenborg, and *Kennicott.

HORNE, Henry Sinclair, Baron Horne (1861–1929), general; joined Royal Artillery, 1880; served in South African War, 1899–1902; inspector, horse and field artillery, 1912; proceeded to France as brigadier-general commanding Royal Artillery, I Army Corps, 1914; took part in retreat from Mons, battles of Marne, Aisne, and first Battle of Ypres; commanded second division of I Corps, 1915; accompanied Lord *Kitchener to Dardanelles, 1915; commanded XV Corps and took part in Battle of Somme, 1916; commanded First Army, 1916;

assault on Vimy Ridge successfully carried out by First Army, 1917; ridge saved during great German attack, 1918; advance of First Army during 1918 ended with occupation of Mons (Nov.); general, 1919; received thanks of parliament, £30,000, and created baron, 1919; commander-in-chief, Eastern Command, 1919–23; retired, 1926.

HORNE, John (1614–1676), Puritan divine; of Trinity College, Cambridge; incumbent of Sutton St James and All Hallows, Lynn Regis; attacked Quakers, Independents, and Presbyterians; published *The Open Door* (1650) and other devotional works.

HORNE, Richard Henry (or **Hengist**) (1803–1884), author; educated at Sandhurst; in Mexican Navy against Spain; travelled in America and Canada; advocated establishment of Society of Literature and Art, 1833; edited *Monthly Repository*, 1836–7; published *Cosmo de Medici* (1837), *Death of Marlowe* (1837), and other tragedies; corresponded with Mrs *Browning (Miss Barrett), 1839–46; collaborated with her in *New Spirit of the Age* (1844); his epic, *Orion*, published at a farthing (1843); issued *Ballad Romances* (1846) and *The Poor Artist* (1850); in Australia, 1852–69, as commissioner for crown lands, and magistrate; granted civil list pension, 1874; published *Australian Facts and Prospects* (1859).

HORNE, Robert (1519?–1580), bishop of Winchester; fellow of St John's College, Cambridge, 1537; MA, 1540; DD, 1549; rector of All Hallows, Bread Street, 1550; dean of Durham, 1551; removed St *Cuthbert's tomb with his own hands; helped in preparation of Forty-Five Articles; refused see of Durham, 1552; deprived of deanery on accession of Mary; fled to Zurich; chief minister at Frankfort, 1556, at Strasburg, 1557–8; restored at Durham, 1559; led disputations against the Romanists at Westminster; bishop of Winchester, 1560–80; had custody of *Feckenham, and John *Leslie (1527–1596), bishop of Ross; vigorous enforcer of conformity; purged Corpus Christi, Christ's, and St John's colleges, Cambridge, of Romanism; pulled down tabernacle work at New College, Oxford; silenced organs and tried to abolish vestments; assisted in drawing up 'Book of Advertisements', 1564, canons of 1571; in 'Bishops' Bible' (1568), revised Isaiah, Jeremiah, and Lamentations.

HORNE, Robert (1565–1640), divine; probably chaplain of Magdalen Hall, Oxford, 1585–96; MA, Magdalen Hall, Oxford, 1587; published theological works.

HORNE, Robert Stevenson, Viscount Horne of Slamannan (1871–1940), lawyer, politician, and man of business; educated at George Watson's College, Edinburgh, and Glasgow University; advocate, 1896; KC, 1910; Unionist MP, Hillhead division, Glasgow, 1918–37; third civil lord, Admiralty, 1918–19; minister of labour, 1919–20; president, Board of Trade, 1920–1; chancellor of the Exchequer, 1921–2; director, Suez Canal Company, Lloyds Bank, etc.; chairman, Burmah Corporation and (1934–40) Great Western Railway Company; KBE, 1918; PC, 1919; viscount, 1937.

HORNE, Thomas (1610–1654), master of Eton; MA, Magdalen Hall, Oxford, 1633; master of Tunbridge, 1640–8, of Eton, 1648–54; author of classical manuals.

HORNE, Thomas Hartwell (1780–1862), biblical scholar, bibliographer, and polemic; at Christ's Hospital with Samuel Taylor *Coleridge; at Record Office, 1817–19; hon. MA, Aberdeen, 1817; rector of St Edmund and St Nicholas Acons, London, 1833; sub-librarian at Surrey Institution, 1809–23; senior assistant in printed books department, British Museum, 1824–60; FSA, 1828; BD, Cambridge, 1829; his *Introduction to Critical Study and Knowledge of the Holy Scriptures* (1818; Suppl. 1821) frequently reissued and enlarged; fifth volume of seventh edition published separately as *Manual of Biblical Bibliography* (1839); published also *Introduction to Study of Bibliography* (1814), *Deism Refuted* (1819), *Manual of Parochial Psalmody* (1829), and treatises against Romanism, catalogues, and compilations; contributed to *Encyclopaedia Metropolitana*; edited Bishop *Beveridge's *Works* (1824) and other publications.

HORNE, Sir William (1774–1860), master in Chancery; barrister, Lincoln's Inn, 1798; KC, 1818; attorney-general to Queen *Adelaide, 1830; MP, Helston, 1812–18, Bletchingley, Newtown (Isle of Wight), 1831–2, and Marylebone, 1833–4; solicitor-general, 1830; knighted, 1830; attorney-general, 1832; having scruples against pronouncing death-sentence, resigned Exchequer judgeship rather than go on circuit; master in Chancery, 1839–53.

HORNEBOLT (HORNEBAUD, HORENBOUT, HOORENBAULT, or **HOREBOUT), Gerard** (1480?–1540), painter to Henry VIII; came to England from Ghent about 1528.

HORNEBOLT (HORNEBAUD or **HOORENBAULT), Lucas** (d. 1544), king's painter, 1534; relative of Gerard *Hornebolt; instructed *Holbein in miniature painting.

HORNEBOLT, Susanna (1503–1545), illuminator; daughter of Gerard *Hornebolt.

HORNEBY, Henry (d. 1518), master and benefactor of Peterhouse, Cambridge; DD, Clare

Hall, 1495; dean of Wimborne; held various prebends; master of Peterhouse, 1509–18; as secretary and chancellor to Margaret, duchess of Richmond, assisted in opening of St John's College, Cambridge.

HORNECK, Anthony (1641–1697), divine; came to England from Germany, c.1661; MA, Heidelberg (incorporated at The Queen's College, Oxford, 1664); chaplain of The Queen's College, Oxford, and vicar of All Saints, Oxford; preacher at the Savoy, 1671; FRS, 1668; DD, Cambridge, 1681; king's chaplain, 1689; prebendary of Westminster, 1693, and Wells, 1694; popular as preacher and casuist; gave offence by supporting social reform; ancestor of *Goldsmith's 'Jessamy Bride'; devotional works frequently reprinted.

HORNER, Arthur Lewis (1894–1968), miners' leader; left school at 11 to become clerk in railway office; began course of theological training, but abandoned it for politics, 1911; joined Independent Labour party and became known as agitator; conscientious objector, absconded to Ireland, arrested and imprisoned on return; discharged from army for 'incorrigible conduct', 1919; joined British Communist party, 1920; underwent further periods of imprisonment, 1921 and 1932; expelled from South Wales Miners' Federation, 1930; re-entered, 1934; elected president, 1936; political views prevented service on General Council of Trades Union Congress; played leading part in formation of National Union of Mineworkers, 1945; national secretary, 1946–59; received freedom of Merthyr Tydfil, 1959; published autobiography, *Incorrigible Rebel* (1960).

HORNER, Francis (1778–1817), politician; studied at Edinburgh; member of Edinburgh Speculative Society; called to Scottish bar, 1800; joined English bar, 1807; contributed to first number of *Edinburgh Review*, 1802; MP, St Ives, 1806, Wendover, 1807; as chairman of bullion committee (1810) recommended early resumption of cash payments; returned for St Mawes, 1813; took part in debates on corn laws and negro slavery, 1813–15; thanked by common council of the city, 1815; proposed measure to regulate proceedings of Irish grand juries, 1816; spoke ably against ministerial foreign policy, and again advocated cash payments; translated Euler's *Elements of Algebra* (1797); published *Short Account of a late Short Administration* (1807); died at Pisa and was buried at Leghorn.

HORNER, Leonard (1785–1864), geologist and educationalist; studied at Edinburgh University; brother and biographer of Francis *Horner; secretary of Geological Society, 1810; president,

1846; FRS, 1813; organised Whig meetings at Edinburgh, 1821–6; founded Edinburgh School of Arts, 1821; warden of London University, 1827–31; commissioner to inquire into employment of children in factories, 1833, and a chief inspector under Factories Act; anticipated some of *Murchison and *Sedgwick's work on palaeozoic rocks.

HORNER, William George (1786–1837), mathematician; headmaster of Kingswood School (1806–9), and afterwards of Grosvenor Place, Bath (1809–37); discovered method of solving numerical equations by continuous approximation.

HORNE TOOKE, John (1736–1812). See TOOKE.

HORNIMAN, Annie Elizabeth Fredericka (1860–1937), pioneer of the modern theatre repertory movement; daughter of F. J. *Horniman; studied at Slade School; secretary to W. B. *Yeats; subsidized Abbey Theatre, Dublin, 1904–10; founded repertory theatre in Manchester (1907–21) with first-class actors performing wide range of plays, especially by new writers; CH, 1933.

HORNIMAN, Frederick John (1835–1906), founder of the Horniman Museum; joined father's tea-packing business; travelled extensively, making natural history collections; built Horniman's Museum at Forest Hill, 1897, and presented it to London County Council, 1901; Liberal MP for Falmouth and Penryn boroughs, 1895–1904.

HORNSBY, Thomas (1733–1810), astronomer; fellow of Corpus Christi College, Oxford; MA, 1757; Savilian professor of astronomy, 1763; professor of experimental philosophy, 1763–1810; FRS, 1767; first Radcliffe observer, 1772; Radcliffe librarian, 1783; Sedleian professor, 1782; DD, 1785; observed transit of Venus in 1761 and 1769, and deduced solar parallax; edited vol. i of *Bradley's *Astronomical Observations* (1798).

HORRABIN, James Francis (1884–1962), artist, lecturer, cartoonist, and left-wing socialist; educated at Stamford Grammar School and Sheffield School of Art; staff artist on *Sheffield Telegraph*, 1906; art editor, *Yorkshire Telegraph and Star*, 1909; worked on London *Daily News* (later, *News Chronicle*), and the *Star*, 1911–60; created characters of Japhet and Happy, and Dot and Carrie; served in Queen's Westminster Rifles, 1917–18; chosen to illustrate H. G. *Wells's *Outline of History* (1920); also illustrated textbooks and atlases; an advocate of guild socialism, member of executive committee, National Guilds League, 1915; first editor of *Plebs*;

Labour MP, Peterborough, 1929–31; succeeded Arthur Creech *Jones as chairman, Fabian Colonial Bureau, 1945–50; published various books about his cartoon characters, including *Japhet and Fido* (1922) and *The Japhet Book* (1925).

HORRIDGE, Sir Thomas Gardner (1857–1938), judge; solicitor, 1879; called to bar (Middle Temple), 1884; practised in Liverpool; KC, 1901; Liberal MP, East Manchester, 1906–10; judge of King's Bench division, 1910–37; sound, dignified, and expeditious; knighted, 1910; PC, 1937.

HORROCKS, Sir Brian Gwynne (1895–1985), soldier; educated at Uppingham and Royal Military College, Sandhurst; commissioned into Middlesex Regiment, 1914; captured during Battle of Ypres, prisoner of war, 1914–18; and again in 1919–20, captured by Soviets after serving with mission to White Russians; MC, 1919; won British modern pentathlon championship and took part in Olympic Games, 1924; at Staff College, 1933; commanded 2nd battalion, Middlesex Regiment in France, 1939; promoted brigadier during Dunkirk evacuation; summoned by his friend B. L. *Montgomery (later Viscount Montgomery of Alamein) to command XIII Corps and later IX and X Corps in Western Desert, 1942; seriously wounded, 1943; again called on by Montgomery to command XXX Corps in Normandy, 1944; criticized by some commanders for his inaction at time of Arnhem battle and for taking orders direct from Montgomery in the final drive into Germany; CB, 1943; DSO, 1943; KBE, 1945; KCB, 1949; GOC Western Command, 1946; GOC-in-C, British Army of the Rhine, 1948; retired from army with rank of lieutenant-general, 1949; gentleman usher of the Black Rod in House of Lords, 1949–63; became television personality, making some forty programmes; director of Bovis; hon. LL D, Belfast; published autobiography, *A Full Life* (1960, 2nd edn., 1974).

HORROCKS, Jeremiah (1617?–1641), astronomer; sizar at Emmanuel College, Cambridge, 1632–5; commenced acquaintance with William *Crabtree, 1636; observed partial solar eclipse of 1639 with half-crown telescope at Toxteth Park; when curate of Hoole predicted and observed transit of Venus across the sun, 24 Nov. (OS) 1639; began first tidal observations, 1640; obligations for his ascription to moon of an elliptic orbit acknowledged by *Newton; detected 'long inequality' of Jupiter and Saturn, and probably identified solar attraction with terrestrial gravity; marble scroll in his memory, with inscription by Dean *Stanley, in Westminster Abbey, 1875; his *Venus in Sole visa* first printed by Hevelius at

Danzig (1662); *Opera Posthuma* issued by Royal Society, 1672 and 1678.

HORROCKS, John (1768–1804), manufacturer; erected cotton-spinning mill at Preston, 1786; acquired large fortune as muslin-manufacturer; as MP for Preston consulted by Pitt on commercial matters.

HORROCKS, John Ainsworth (1818–1846), Australian explorer and pioneer; grandson of John *Horrocks.

HORSA (d. 455), joint founder of Kent; brother of *Hengist; a Jute; arrived with his brother at Ebbsfleet, Thanet, 449; resisted by *Vortigern; killed at Aylesford.

HORSBRUGH, Florence Gertrude, Baroness Horsbrugh (1889–1969), politician; educated at Lansdowne House, Edinburgh, and St Hilda's, Folkestone; Conservative MP, Dundee, 1931–45; MBE, 1920; CBE, 1939; parliamentary secretary, Ministry of Health, 1939–45; parliamentary secretary, Ministry of Food, 1945; PC, 1945; MP, Moss Side division, Manchester, 1950; minister of education, 1951–4; first woman to hold Cabinet post in a Conservative government, 1953; GBE, 1954; life peer, 1959; delegate, Council of Europe and Western European Union, 1955–61; hon. LL D, Edinburgh, 1946; hon. fellow, Royal College of Surgeons of Edinburgh, 1946.

HORSBURGH, James (1762–1836), hydrographer; when first mate on a trading ship wrecked on Diego Garcia from error in chart, 1786; made charts of Straits of Macassar, of western Philippines, and track from Dampier's Strait to Batavia; published *Directions for Sailing to and from East Indies, China, New Holland, Cape of Good Hope, and interjacent Ports* (1809–11); FRS, 1806; hydrographer to East India Company, 1810.

HORSBURGH, John (1791–1869), historical engraver; executed plates after *Turner; illustrated *Scott's works; engraved Scott's portraits by *Lawrence and Sir John Watson *Gordon.

HORSEY, Sir Edward (d. 1583), naval and military commander; served under the emperor; implicated in *Throckmorton and *Dudley conspiracy, 1556; confidant of *Leicester; served under *Warwick at Havre, 1562–3; captain of Isle of Wight, 1566–83; commanded horse against northern insurgents, 1569; negotiated pacification between French king and Huguenots, 1573; ambassador in Netherlands; knighted, 1577; privy councillor; died in Isle of Wight of the plague.

HORSEY, Sir Jerome (*fl.* 1573–1627), traveller; probably nephew of Sir Edward *Horsey; went to Moscow as clerk in Russia Company,

1573; sent by Tsar Ivan to purchase munitions of war in England, 1580; became esquire of the body to Queen Elizabeth; after return was sent by Tsar Feodor with despatches to Elizabeth, 1585; obtained monopoly of trade for English company, 1587; obliged to leave Russia, 1587; charged with malversation and illegal trading, and refused audience by the tsar, 1590; knighted, 1603; high sheriff of Buckinghamshire, 1610; MP for Cornish boroughs, 1593–1622; account of Russian travels edited by E. A. *Bond (1856).

HORSFIELD, Thomas (1773–1859), naturalist; born and educated in Pennsylvania; served in East Indies under Dutch and English, 1799–1819; keeper of East India Company's Museum, Leadenhall Street, 1820–59; published *Plantae Javanicae rariores* (1838–52) and (with Sir W. *Jardine) *Illustrations of Ornithology* (1830).

HORSFIELD, Thomas Walker (d. 1837), topographer; FSA, 1826; published *History and Antiquities of Lewes* (1824–7) and (with William Durrant *Cooper) *History and Topography of Sussex* (1835).

HORSFORD, Sir Alfred Hastings (1818–1885), general; served with 1st battalion, Rifle Brigade in Kaffir War, 1847–8, and commanded it in war of 1852–3 and the Crimea; led 3rd battalion at Cawnpore and advance on Lucknow; commanded brigade at siege of Lucknow, 1858, and in subsequent operations; deputy adjutant-general at Horse Guards, 1860–6; military secretary, 1874–80; lieutenant-general, 1874; represented England at Brussels Conference, 1874; GCB, 1875; general, 1877.

HORSFORD, Sir John (1751–1817), major-general in Bengal Artillery; of Merchant Taylors' School and St John's College, Oxford; fellow, 1768–71; enlisted under false name; received commission, 1778; served in second Mysore War, 1790–1; commanded artillery under Lake, 1803–5, and brigade at siege of Komanur, 1807; head of Bengal Artillery from 1808; major-general, Bengal Artillery, 1811; directed siege of Hathras, 1817; KCB, 1815; died at Cawnpore.

HORSLEY, Charles Edward (1822–1876), musical composer; son of William *Horsley; studied under Moscheles, Hauptmann, and Mendelssohn; composed instrumental works in Germany, in England three oratorios, ode for opening of Melbourne Town Hall (1870), music to *Comus*, and other music while in America; died at New York; his *Text-book of Harmony* published (1876).

HORSLEY, John (1685–1732), archaeologist; MA, Edinburgh, 1701; Presbyterian minister and schoolmaster at Morpeth; lectured on natural science at Newcastle; FRS, 1730; published *Britannia Romana* (1732); his 'Materials for History of Northumberland' printed in *Inedited Contributions* (1869).

HORSLEY, John Callcott (1817–1903), painter; son of William *Horsley; studied art at Royal Academy, where he exhibited from 1839; opposed to study of nude model; painted domestic scenes, e.g. *Holy Communion, The Gaoler's Daughter, L'Allegro,* and *Il Penseroso*; also painted portraits; ARA, 1855; RA, 1856; treasurer, 1882–97; organized 'Old Masters' exhibitions at Academy, 1875–90; interested in music; friend of Mendelssohn and John *Leech; published *Recollections of a Royal Academician* (1903).

HORSLEY, John William (1845–1921), philanthropist; chaplain to Clerkenwell prison, 1876–86; vicar of Holy Trinity, Woolwich, 1889; rector of St Peter's, Walworth, 1894; mayor of Southwark, 1910; works on social questions include *Jottings from Jail* (1887) and *How Criminals are Made and Prevented* (1912).

HORSLEY, Samuel (1733–1806), bishop of St Asaph; LL B, Trinity Hall, Cambridge, 1758; rector of Newington Butts, 1759–93; FRS, 1767; secretary, Royal Society, 1773; DCL, Oxford, 1774; prebendary of St Paul's, 1783–94, Gloucester, 1787; archdeacon of St Albans, 1781; vicar of South Weald, 1782; bishop of St Davids, 1788, of Rochester, 1793 (with Westminster); member of *Johnson's club at Essex Head, 1783; left Royal Society after dispute of 1783–4; carried on controversy with *Priestley on the Incarnation, 1783–90; edited Sir Isaac *Newton's works, 1779–85; preached impressive sermon on revolutionary spirit before House of Lords, 1793; spoke against Peace of Amiens, 1801; bishop of St Asaph, 1802–6; published mathematical and theological works.

HORSLEY, Thomas (fl. 1631–1653), Roman Catholic agent. See RAMSAY, THOMAS.

HORSLEY, Sir Victor Alexander Haden (1857–1916), physiologist and surgeon; son of John Callcott *Horsley, RA; educated at University College Hospital; professor-superintendent to Brown Institution (University of London), 1884–90; pursued there three main lines of study—action of thyroid gland, protective treatment against rabies, and localization of function in the brain; FRS, professor of pathology, University College, and surgeon to National Hospital for Paralysed and Epileptic, Queen Square, 1886; knighted, 1902; consultant to Mediterranean Expeditionary Force, 1915; died at Amarah; one of the foremost surgeons of his day; a prolific writer.

HORSLEY, William (1774–1858), musical composer; organist of Ely Chapel, Holborn,

1794, of Female Orphans Asylum, 1802–54, of Charterhouse, 1838; Mus.Bac., Oxford, 1800; assisted in founding Philharmonic Society, 1813; published five collections of glees (including 'By Celia's Arbour'), 1801–37, and *The Musical Treasury* (1853); edited *Callcott's *Musical Grammar* (1817) and *Glees, with Memoir* (1824), and *Byrd's *Cantiones Sacrae*.

HORSMAN, Edward (1807–1876), Whig politician; educated at Rugby and Trinity College, Cambridge; MP, Cockermouth, 1836–52, Stroud, 1853–68, and Liskeard, 1869–76; junior lord of Treasury, 1841; chief secretary for Ireland, 1855–7; attacked ecclesiastical commissioners, 1847, and the bishops, 1850; with *Lowe formed 'Cave of Adullam' against Reform Bill of 1866; died at Biarritz.

HORSMAN, Nicholas (*fl.* 1689), divine; fellow of Corpus Christi College, Oxford; MA, 1659; BD, 1667; published *The Spiritual Bee* (1662).

HORT, Fenton John Anthony (1828–1892), scholar and divine; educated at Rugby and Trinity College, Cambridge; MA, 1853; BD, 1875; DD, 1876; fellow of Trinity College, 1852–7; assistant editor of *Journal of Classical and Sacred Philology* from 1854; ordained priest, 1856; examiner for natural sciences tripos, 1856; held living of St Ippolyts cum Great Wymondley, Hertfordshire, 1857–72; Hulsean lecturer, 1871; one of revisers of New Testament, 1870–80; fellow of Emmanuel College, Cambridge, 1871, and lecturer in theology, 1872–6; contributed to *Smith's *Dictionary of Christian Biography* (vol. i published 1877); Hulsean professor of divinity, 1878; published, with Dr Westcott, edition of text of Greek New Testament (1881); Lady Margaret reader, 1887; hon. DCL, Durham, 1890; published religious writings. His *Life and Letters* appeared (1896).

HORT, Josiah (1674?–1751), archbishop of Tuam; educated by Nonconformists; friend of Isaac *Watts; chaplain to John *Hampden, MP; chaplain to Lord *Wharton in Ireland, 1709; dean of Cloyne, 1718, of Ardagh, 1720; bishop of Ferns, 1721, Kilmore and Ardagh, 1727; archbishop of Tuam, 1742–51; mentioned in *Swift's 'Great Storm of Christmas, 1722'.

HORTON, Christiana (1696?–1756?), actress; taken by Barton *Booth from Southwark Fair to Drury Lane, 1714; moved to Covent Garden, 1734; reappeared at Drury Lane, 1752, in benefit performance; distinguished as Millamant (*Way of the World*) and Belinda (*Old Bachelor*); praised by *Steele.

HORTON, Sir Max Kennedy (1883–1951), admiral; joined the training ship *Britannia*, 1898; entered submarine branch; commanding E.9 sank cruiser *Hela* and destroyer S.116 in first two months of war, 1914; DSO; served in Baltic, 1914–15, 1919–20; in home waters commanded new types of submarines; commander, 1914; captain, 1920; rear-admiral, 1932; commanded First Cruiser Squadron, Mediterranean, 1935–6; vice-admiral, 1936; commanded Reserve Fleet, bringing it to war readiness, 1937–9; Northern Patrol, 1939–40; flag officer, submarines, 1940–2; successfully deployed submarines in anticipation of German attack on Norway; admiral, 1941; commander-in-chief, Western Approaches, 1942–5; mounted sea-air offensive of very long-range and long-range aircraft and Support Groups of warships to drive U-boats from mid-Atlantic, 1943; a perfectionist, criticized for ruthlessness of his training methods; a deeply religious man, famous for accuracy of his hunches; CB, 1934; KCB, 1939; GCB, 1945; Bath King of Arms, 1946; received freedom of Liverpool and state funeral there.

HORTON, Percy Frederick (1897–1970), artist; educated at Brighton Municipal School and Brighton College of Art; imprisoned as conscientious objector, 1914; studied at Central School of Arts and Crafts, London, 1918–20; teacher at Rugby School, 1920–2; won royal exhibition to Royal College of Art, South Kensington; ARCA, 1924; art master, Bishop's Stortford College, 1924–9; draughtsman, Royal College of Art, 1929–48; accomplished portraitist; master, Ruskin School of Drawing and Fine Art, Oxford, 1949–64; drew and painted many academic portraits, and landscapes, mainly of Sussex; pictures to be seen in the Tate, the National Portrait Gallery, the Ashmolean, and other galleries.

HORTON, Robert Forman (1855–1934), Congregational divine and theological writer; educated at Tettenhall College, Shrewsbury School, and New College, Oxford; president of Union, 1877; first class, Lit. Hum., 1878; fellow, 1879–86; ordained, 1884; pastor of Lyndhurst Road Congregational Church, Hampstead, 1884–1930; president, National Free Church Council, 1905; great preacher and saintly personality; publications include *The Word of God* (1898) and many devotional pamphlets.

HORTON, Sir Robert John Wilmot, third baronet (1784–1841), politician; assumed name of Horton on death of father-in-law, 1823; of Eton and Christ Church, Oxford; MA, 1815; MP, Newcastle-under-Lyme, 1818–30; took additional name of Horton, 1823; under-secretary for war and colonies, 1821–8; privy councillor, 1827; supported repeal of Test Act, 1828, and Catholic emancipation, 1829; governor of Ceylon, 1831–7; knighted, 1831; succeeded as baronet, 1834; as Lady Leigh's representative destroyed *Byron's 'Memoirs'; published letters and pamphlets.

HORTON, Thomas (b. 1601/2 or 3–d. 1649), regicide; originally falconer to Sir Arthur *Hesilrige; colonel in *Fairfax's army, 1643; defeated *Stradling and *Lingen in South Wales, 1648; signed Charles I's death-warrant; died in Ireland.

HORTON, Thomas (d. 1673), president of Queens' College, Cambridge; fellow of Emmanuel College, Cambridge; MA, 1630; DD, 1649; president of Queens' College, 1647–60; Gresham professor of divinity, London, 1641; petitioned for Presbyterianism; preacher at Gray's Inn, 1647–51; vice-chancellor of Cambridge, 1650; named a trier, 1653; conformed in 1662, and was vicar of St Helen's, Bishopsgate Street, London, 1666–73; his works issued posthumously.

HORTOP, Job (*fl.* 1591), seaman; with Sir John *Hawkins (1532–1595), 1567; escaped in the *Minion* from San Juan de Lua, and travelled from the River Panuco to Mexico; imprisoned at Seville and sent to the galleys at San Lucar; escaped to England, 1590; his narrative in *Hakluyt.

HORWITZ, Bernard (1807–1885), author of *Chess Studies and End-games* (1884) and joint author of *Chess Studies* (1851); came to England from Mecklenburg, 1845.

HOSACK, John (d. 1887), police magistrate at Clerkenwell (1877) and author; of the Middle Temple; legal treatises and books by him defending *Mary Queen of Scots published 1869 and 1888.

HOSE, Charles (1863–1929), civil servant in Sarawak, ethnologist, and naturalist; cadet in Sarawak Civil Service, 1884; rose to be divisional resident; member of Supreme Council and judge of Supreme Court of Sarawak, 1904; established friendly relations with and brought under control warlike natives; retired, 1907; a keen naturalist who enriched zoological and botanical records with many new species, and benefited British national collections; successfully investigated principal cause of disease beri-beri; carried out important ethnographical research among Sarawak tribes; wrote several books on subject; made first reliable map of Sarawak.

HOSIE, Sir Alexander (1853–1925), diplomat and Chinese explorer; joined Chinese Consular Service, 1876; sent on special service to Chungking, Szechwan, 1882; undertook travels in the interior; served in Canton, Wenchow, Chefoo, Amoy, Tamsui, Wuhu; twice in charge of consulate at Newchang; first consul-general at Chingtu, Szechwan, 1903; British delegate at Shanghai International Opium Commission, 1909; retired, having travelled in twenty-one out of twenty-two Chinese provinces, 1912; knighted, 1907; unrivalled in knowledge and presentation of possibilities of Chinese trade; author of many books on China.

HOSIER, Arthur Julius (1877–1963), pioneer farmer, engineer, and inventor; son, grandson, and great-grandson of farmers; as a lad, worked on the farm before walking to school at Bradford on Avon; with his brother took tenancy of farm at 19; invented a side-rake and mechanical milk filter, 1904; worked as engineer, 1904–10; returned to farming with his brother and bought Wexcombe estate, 1910–20; experimented with 'Open-Air Dairying', the 'Hosier System', 1922; designed other equipment, including a portable poultry unit; OBE, 1949; hon. LL D, Cambridge, 1951; Methodist lay preacher throughout his life.

HOSIER, Francis (1673–1727), vice-admiral; lieutenant in *Rooke's flagship at Barfleur, 1693; captured the *Heureux* off Cape Clear, 1710; distinguished in action with Spanish off Cartagena, 1711; suspended as suspected Jacobite, 1714–17; vice-admiral, 1723; died of fever in Jamaica while commanding squadron in West Indies; the event misrepresented in *Glover's ballad.

HOSKEN, James (1798–1885), pioneer of ocean steam navigation; served in Royal Navy; took *Great Western* steamship from Bristol to New York in fifteen days, 1838, and in thirteen days, 1839; commanded the *Great Britain*, 1844–6; chief magistrate at Labuan, 1848–9; commanded *Belleisle* hospital ship in Baltic, 1854–5; captain, 1857; vice-admiral, 1879.

HOSKING, William (1800–1861), architect and civil engineer; worked as builder in Sydney; came to England, 1819; exhibited drawings made in Italy and Sicily at Academy and Suffolk Street, 1826–8; FSA, 1830; FRIBA, 1835; engineer to West London railway; professor of architecture and engineering construction at King's College, London, 1840–61; published *Theory, Practice, and Architecture of Bridges* (1843); claimed to have originated design for British Museum reading-room; contributed to *Encyclopaedia Britannica* (7th and 8th editions).

HOSKINS, Anthony (1568–1615), Jesuit; joined Jesuits, 1593; vice-prefect of English mission in Belgium, 1609, and Spain, 1611; modernized Richard *Whitford's version of *De Imitatione Christi* (1613); translated French works; died at Valladolid.

HOSKINS, Sir Anthony Hiley (1828–1901), admiral; entered navy, 1842; served against Arab slavers in Mozambique; in Kaffir War, 1851–2; in China, 1857–8; commander, 1858; at reduction of Taku forts; commanded in North American, Channel, and Australian waters, 1869–78; CB, 1877; rear-admiral, 1879; lord commissioner of Admiralty, 1880; KCB, 1885; commander-in-chief in Mediterranean, 1889–91; admiral and senior naval lord of Admiralty, 1891; GCB, 1893.

HOSKINS, John (1566–1638), lawyer and wit; of Westminster, Winchester, and New College, Oxford; fellow of New College, 1586; MA, 1592; when MP for Hereford committed to Tower, 1614, for reflections on Scottish favourites; serjeant-at-law, 1623; Welsh judge; said to have revised *Ralegh's History of the World and Ben *Jonson's poems; intimate of *Camden, *Donne, and *Selden; gave information to Aubrey.

HOSKINS, John, the younger (1579–1631), brother of John *Hoskins (1566–1638); fellow of New College, Oxford, 1600–13; DCL, 1613; prebendary of Hereford, 1612; chaplain to James I, and master of St Oswald's Hospital, Worcester, 1614.

HOSKINS, John (d. 1664), miniature painter; painted many contemporary celebrities, including *Falkland, Sir Kenelm *Digby, and *Selden.

HOSKINS (or HOSKYNS), Sir John, second baronet (1634–1705), of Westminster; barrister, Middle Temple; president of Royal Society, 1682–3, and secretary, 1685–7; knighted; master in Chancery and friend of Lord-keeper Guilford; MP, Herefordshire, 1685.

HOSKINS, Samuel Elliott (1799–1888), physician; of Guy's Hospital; FRS, 1843; FRCP, 1859; practised in Channel Islands; published *Stethoscopic Chart* (1830), *Tables of Corrections for Temperature to Barometric Observations* (1842), and works on Channel Islands.

HOSKYNS, Chandos Wren- (1812–1876), writer on agriculture; of Shrewsbury and Balliol College, Oxford; BA, 1834; assumed additional name (1837) on marriage with descendant of *Wren; barrister, Inner Temple, 1838; MP, Hereford, 1869–74; published works, including *Land in England, Ireland, and other Lands* (1869) and *Land Laws of England* (1870).

HOSKYNS, Sir Edwyn Clement, thirteenth baronet (1884–1937), divine; educated at Haileybury and Jesus College, Cambridge; ordained, 1908; dean of chapel (1919–37), librarian and president (1929–37), Corpus Christi College, Cambridge; pioneer of critical, evangelical Anglo-Catholicism; works include

The Riddle of the New Testament (with F. N. Davey, 1931); succeeded father, 1925.

HOSTE, Sir George Charles (1786–1845), colonel, Royal Engineers; educated at Royal Military Academy, Woolwich; lieutenant, Royal Engineers, 1802; captain, 1812; brevet-major, 1814; lieutenant-colonel, 1825; brevet-colonel, 1838; colonel, 1841; served under Lieutenant-General Sir James Henry *Craig, in Italy, 1805–6; in Egypt, 1807, Sicily, 1808–9, and Holland, 1813; at bombardment of Antwerp, and assault of Bergen-op-Zoom, 1814; commanding engineer of 1st Army Corps under prince of Orange at Quatre Bras and Waterloo, assault of Peronne and occupation of Paris, 1815; CB, 1815; gentleman usher of privy chamber to Queen *Adelaide, 1830.

HOSTE, Sir William, first baronet (1780–1828), captain in the navy; served under *Nelson in actions off Toulon (1795), at St Vincent and Santa Cruz; promoted to *Mutine* brig after the Nile, 1798; attained post rank, 1802; with the *Amphion* and other ships (1808–9) took or destroyed 200 French or Venetian vessels in Adriatic; captured Grao, 1808–9, and destroyed 46 sail in 1810; defeated greatly superior squadron at Lissa and took many prizes, but was severely wounded, 1811; with the *Bacchante* captured many gunboats, and assisted Austrians in taking Cattaro and Ragusa, 1813–14; created baronet, 1814; KCB, 1815.

HOTHAM, Beaumont, second Baron Hotham in Irish peerage (1737–1814), educated at Westminster; barrister, Middle Temple, 1758; baron of the Exchequer, 1775–1805; MP, Wigan, 1768–75; commissioner of great seal, 1783; succeeded his brother, William *Hotham, first baron, in Irish peerage.

HOTHAM, Beaumont, third Baron Hotham in Irish peerage (1794–1870), general; grandson of Beaumont Hotham, second Baron *Hotham; wounded at Salamanca, 1812; present at Waterloo, 1815; Tory MP, Leominster, 1820–41, East Riding, Yorkshire, 1841–68.

HOTHAM, Charles (1615–1672?), divine; son of Sir John *Hotham; MA, Christ's College, Cambridge, 1639; fellow of Peterhouse, Cambridge, 1644–51; deprived by parliament, 1651; rector of Wigan, 1653–62; FRS, 1667; minister in the Bermudas; translated Boehme's *Consolatory Treatise of the Four Complexions* (1654).

HOTHAM, Sir Charles (1806–1855), naval commander; as captain in the navy took part in Para expedition against Rosas, 1845; KCB, 1846; governor of Victoria, 1854–5; died at Melbourne.

HOTHAM, Durant (1617?–1691), author of *Life of Jacob Boehme* (1654); MA, Christ's College, Cambridge, 1640; translated (1650) *Ad Philosophiam Teutonicam Manuductio* of his brother Charles *Hotham.

HOTHAM, Sir **Henry** (1777–1833), vice-admiral; youngest son of Beaumont *Hotham, second Baron Hotham; served in Mediterranean operations, 1793–8; commanded *Immortalité* in Bay of Biscay, 1799–1801; with Sir Richard *Strachan, 1805; with the *Defiance* drove ashore three French frigates at Les Sables d'Olonne, 1809; destroyed two frigates and a brig off Lorient, 1812; KCB, 1815; by knowledge of Biscay coast prevented Napoleon's escape to America; a lord of the Admiralty, 1818–22 and 1828–30; vice-admiral, 1825; died at Malta as commander in Mediterranean.

HOTHAM (or HOTHUN), John (d. 1337), bishop of Ely and chancellor; chancellor of Irish Exchequer, 1309; dismissed as one of *Gaveston's stewards, 1311; as chancellor of English Exchequer accompanied Edward II to France, 1312; sent to Ireland, 1314, and Rome, 1317; bishop of Ely, 1316–37; treasurer of Exchequer, 1317–18; lord chancellor, 1318–20 and 1327–8; joined Queen *Isabella, 1326; built octagon tower at Ely.

HOTHAM, John (d. 1645), Parliamentarian; son of Sir John *Hotham; served in Netherlands; MP, Scarborough, 1640; secured Hull for parliament, 1642; joined *Fairfax, 1642; fought at Tadcaster and Sherburn; defeated at Ancaster Heath, 1643; imprisoned at Nottingham on charges of misconduct and suspicion of treachery, 1643; opened negotiations with Charles I's queen and escaped; arrested with his father; tried by court martial and beheaded.

HOTHAM, Sir John, first baronet (d. 1645), Parliamentarian; served under elector palatine and Mansfeld, knighted, 1617; created baronet, 1622; MP, Beverley; as sheriff of Yorkshire levied ship money; after removal from governorship of Hull (1639) went into opposition; committed to the Fleet, 1640; a chief contriver of Yorkshire petition, 1640; as Parliamentary commander of Hull refused to admit Charles I, 1642; recovered Scarborough for parliament, 1643; while negotiating with *Newcastle with a view to rejoining Royalists was arrested, expelled from parliament, and sent to the Tower, 1643; condemned by military commission and executed.

HOTHAM, William, first Baron Hotham in Irish peerage (1736–1813), admiral; educated at Westminster and Naval Academy, Portsmouth; promoted captain for capture of French privateer, 1757; cruised in North Sea, 1758–9; served at Belleisle, 1761; as commodore on North American Station shared in action off St Lucia, 1778, and in action under *Rodney in Apr.–May, 1780; under *Howe at relief of Gibraltar and Battle of Cape Spartel, 1782; vice-admiral, 1790; second-in-command under Lord *Hood, 1793–4; commander in Mediterranean, twice engaging inferior French fleet without result, 1795; created Irish peer, 1797.

HOTHAM, Sir William (1772–1848), admiral; nephew of William, first Baron *Hotham; under *Nelson at Bastia, 1794; commanded the *Adamant* at Camperdown, 1797, and blockade of Mauritius; KCB, 1815; admiral, 1837; GCB, 1840.

HOTHBY, John (d. 1487), Carmelite and writer on music; lived many years at Ferrara; went to Lucca, 1467; invited to England by Henry VII, 1486; works by him in British Museum and at Lambeth; his treatises on *Proportion, Cantus Figuratus*, and *Counterpoint* printed by Coussemaker.

HOTHUM (HODON or ODONE), William of (d. 1298), archbishop of Dublin; graduated in theology at Paris; Dominican; provincial prior in England, 1282–7, reappointed 1290; employed by Edward I on mission to Rome, 1289; provincial of England and Scotland, 1290; summoned to parliament at Norham, 1291; advised the king on Scottish succession; archbishop of Dublin, 1296–8; accompanied the king to Flanders, 1297, and negotiated with French; represented him at Rome when Boniface VIII mediated truce between England and France; wrote scholastic works; died at Dijon.

HOTINE, Martin (1898–1968), geodesist and photogrammetrist; educated at Southend High School and Royal Military Academy, Woolwich; commissioned in Royal Engineers, 1917; saw active service in Persia, Iraq, and India; studied at Magdalene College, Cambridge; research officer, Air Survey Committee, 1925; attached to geographical section, general staff, War Office, 1927–31; published *Surveying from Air Photographs* (1931); worked in Central Africa, 1931–4; served in Ordnance Survey and initiated retriangulation of Great Britain, 1934–9; deputy director of survey, British Expeditionary Force, 1939; director of survey, East Africa; director of military survey, 1941–6; responsible for army maps and aeronautical charts for RAF; director, Directorate of Overseas Surveys, 1946–63; on research staff of United States Coast and Geodetic Survey, 1963–8; published *Mathematical Geodesy* (1969); CBE, 1945; CMG, 1949; awarded Founder's Medal of Royal Geographical Society, 1947, and received other awards and honours.

HOTON (or HOGHTON), Richard of (d. 1307), prior of Durham; probable founder of Durham College, 1289; deposed and imprisoned for resisting visitation of Bishop Antony *Bek I, 1300; reinstated by the pope, 1301, but again suspended; died at Rome.

HOTSPUR (1364–1403). See PERCY, Sir HENRY.

HOTTEN, John Camden (originally John William) (1832–1873), publisher and author; in America, 1848–56; established himself in Piccadilly on his return; first published in England the *Biglow Papers* (1864) and other works of American humour; compiled slang dictionary (1859); published *Handbook of Topography and Family History* (1863) and other compilations.

HOUBLON, Sir James (d. 1700), alderman; knighted, 1692; deputy-governor of the Bank of England, and MP for the city (1698–1700); brother of Sir John *Houblon.

HOUBLON, Sir John (d. 1712), first governor of the Bank of England, 1694; sheriff of London, 1689; knighted, 1689; master of Grocers' Company, 1690–1; lord mayor, 1695; lord of the Admiralty, 1694–9; commissioner of accounts, 1704.

HOUGH, John (1651–1743), bishop of Worcester; MA, Magdalen College, Oxford, 1676; DD, 1687; fellow; elected president, 1687, but ejected by James II; reinstated, 1688; resigned, 1701; bishop of Oxford, 1690–9, of Lichfield and Coventry, 1699–1717, of Worcester, 1717–43; refused primacy, 1715; benefactor to Magdalen College, Lichfield, and Worcester.

HOUGHTON. See also HOTON and HOUTON.

HOUGHTON, first Baron (1809–1885). See MILNES, RICHARD MONCKTON.

HOUGHTON (or HOUTONE), Adam de (d. 1389), bishop of St David's and chancellor of England; LL D, Oxford; bishop of St David's, 1362–89; trier of parliamentary petitions; lord chancellor, 1377; chief negotiator of peace with France, 1377, and with Sir Simon *Burley of marriage of Richard II, 1380; established cathedral school at St David's and founded college or chantry of St Mary's, 1365.

HOUGHTON, Arthur Boyd (1836–1875), book-illustrator and painter; exhibited at Academy, 1860–70, and afterwards at Water-Colour Society; illustrated Dalziel's *Arabian Nights* (1865) and *Don Quixote* (1866).

HOUGHTON, Daniel (1740?–1791), African traveller; left England in employ of African Association, 1790; journeyed from Gambia, 1790, to Medina (capital of Wolli); crossed uninhabited country between Wolli and Bondou and reached Bambouk, where he negotiated a commercial treaty; set out for Timbuctu, but was not heard of again.

HOUGHTON, Henry Hall- (1823–1889), joint founder (with Canon Hall) of biblical prizes at Oxford, 1868–71; of Sherborne School and Pembroke College, Oxford; MA, 1848; benefactor of Church Missionary Society.

HOUGHTON, John (1488?–1535), prior of the London Charterhouse; BA and LL B, Cambridge; prior of Beauvale, 1530; prior of Charterhouse, 1531; imprisoned for refusing oath of allegiance to Princess Elizabeth as heir-apparent, 1534; executed for refusing to accept royal headship of the church; beatified, 1886.

HOUGHTON, John (d. 1705), writer on agriculture and trade; FRS, 1680; first noticed potato plant as agricultural vegetable.

HOUGHTON, Sir Robert (1548–1624), judge; barrister, Lincoln's Inn, 1577; governor of Lincoln's Inn, 1588–1603; serjeant-at-law, 1603; judge of King's Bench, 1613–24; knighted, 1613.

HOUGHTON (or HOGHTON), William Hyacinth (1736–1823), Roman Catholic divine; prefect at Bornhem (Dominican) College, 1758–62, and afterwards procurator; professor of philosophy at Louvain, 1779; returned to England; edited *Catholic Magazine and Reflector*, 1801.

HOUGHTON, William Stanley (1881–1913), dramatist; engaged in father's cloth business in Manchester, 1897–1912; from 1900 made playmaking and acting his hobby; contributed theatrical notices to *Manchester Guardian*, 1905–13; performed dramatic works include *The Dear Departed* (1908), *Independent Means* (1909), *The Younger Generation* and *The Master of the House* (1910), *Fancy-Free* (1911), and *Hindle Wakes* (1912); influenced by Ibsen; portrayed Lancashire life; reached height of his art in *Hindle Wakes*.

HOULDSWORTH, Sir Hubert Stanley, first baronet (1889–1956), chairman of National Coal Board; educated at Heckmondwike Grammar School and Leeds University; first class, physics, 1911; lecturer, 1916–26; called to bar (Lincoln's Inn), 1926; KC, 1937; chairman, Midlands Coal-Selling Control Committee, 1936–42; regional controller, South and West Yorkshire, 1942–4; controller-general, Ministry of Fuel and Power, 1944–5; chairman, East Midland division, National Coal Board, 1946–51; chairman, National Coal Board, 1951–6; knighted, 1944; baronet, 1956; pro-chancellor,

Leeds, 1949–56; hon. LL D, Leeds and Nottingham.

HOULING, John (1539?–1599), Irish Jesuit; established Irish College at Lisbon, 1593, where he died of the plague; his Elizabethan Catholic martyrology printed by Cardinal Moran in *Spicilegium Ossoriense*.

HOULTON, Robert (*fl.* 1801), dramatist and journalist; demy of Magdalen College, Oxford, 1757–65; MA, 1762; practised inoculation in Ireland; MB, Trinity College, Dublin; wrote librettos for operas; editor of *Morning Herald*; with James *Hook (1746–1827) produced *Wilmore Castle* (comic opera) at Drury Lane, 1800.

HOUSE, (Arthur) Humphry (1908–1955), scholar; educated at Repton and Hertford College, Oxford; first class, Lit. Hum., 1929; professor of English, Presidency College, Calcutta, 1936; lecturer, Calcutta University, 1937–8; William Noble fellow, Liverpool, 1940; director of English studies, Peterhouse, Cambridge, 1947–9; university lecturer in English literature, Oxford, 1948–55; senior research fellow, Wadham, 1950–5; publications include *Note-Books and Papers of Gerard Manley Hopkins* (1937), *The Dickens World* (1941), *Coleridge* (1953), and *Aristotle's Poetics* (1956).

HOUSEMAN, Jacob (1636?–1696). See HUYS-MANS.

HOUSMAN, Alfred Edward (1859–1936), poet and classical scholar; educated at Bromsgrove School and St John's College, Oxford; first class, classical moderations (1879); failed to obtain honours in Lit. Hum. through neglecting philosophy and history; worked in Patent Office, 1882–92; professor of Latin, University College, London (1892–1911), Cambridge (1911–36); published at least one classical article or review yearly (1887–1936), restricting himself mainly to Latin after 1892; dealt with most of chief Latin poets from Lucilius to Juvenal; published four masterly papers on manuscripts of Propertius; edited Ovid's a *Ibis* (1894), the five Books of Manilius (with a commentary designed to treat only of 'what Manilius wrote, and what he meant', 1903–30), Juvenal (1905), and Lucan (1926); an intellectually honest and patient classical scholar with a disciplined passion for truth, swift insight, and brilliant power; his lyrics (published in *A Shropshire Lad*, 1896, *Last Poems*, 1922, and *More Poems*, 1936) limited in theme but show great variety of metre and a Horatian felicity of expression; acutely sensitive and very reserved, but when at ease his conversation full of wit and charm; combined declared atheism with an hereditary attachment to high church party; refused almost all honours, but accepted honorary fellowship of St John's College, Oxford, 1911.

HOUSMAN, Laurence (1865–1959), writer; brother of A. E. *Housman whose biography he wrote (1937); educated at Bromsgrove School; studied art in London; encouraged to write by Kegan *Paul; art critic of force and wit, *Manchester Guardian*, 1895–1911; as playwright his unconventionality brought conflict with censor, but *Victoria Regina* (Lyric, 1937) immediately successful; publications include *Green Arras* (poems, 1896), *An Englishwoman's Love-Letters* (anonymously, 1900), *Sheepfold* (novel partly based on life of Mrs *Girling, 1918), *The Little Plays of St. Francis* (1922), *Trimblerigg* (satirical novel, 1924), and autobiography, *The Unexpected Years* (1937); a pioneer feminist, pacifist, and socialist, although too impetuous, insensitive, and muddled to be altogether effective.

HOUSMAN, Robert (1759–1838), divine; intimate when at Cambridge of Charles *Simeon and Henry Venn; BA, 1784; minister of church built by himself at Lancaster, 1795–1836; known as 'the evangelist'; published sermons.

HOUSTON, Dame Fanny Lucy (1857–1936), philanthropist and eccentric; born Radmall; married, secondly, the ninth Lord Byron (d. 1917); thirdly, Sir Robert Paterson Houston, who bequeathed her (1926) four-fifths of his fortune; contributed widely to charity; purchased *Saturday Review*; a strident, combative patriot; financed successful Schneider Trophy team (1931) and flight over Everest (1933); DBE, 1917.

HOUSTON, John (1802–1845), anatomist; curator of Dublin College of Surgeons' Museum, 1824–41; MD, Edinburgh, 1826; surgeon to Dublin Hospital, 1832; lecturer at Part Street School of Medicine, 1837; contributed to medical journals.

HOUSTON, Richard (1721?–1775), mezzotint engraver; pupil of John Brooks; engraved portraits after *Reynolds, *Zoffany, and William *Hoare, and subject-plates after old masters, especially Rembrandt.

HOUSTON (or HOUSTOUN), William (1695?–1733), botanist; MD, Leiden, 1729; with Van Swieten investigated animal respiration; FRS; collected plants in West Indies and Venezuela (*Reliquiae Houstonianae*, catalogue 1781); died in Jamaica.

HOUSTON, Sir William, first baronet (1766–1842), general; commanded 19th Foot in Flanders, 1794, and 58th at Minorca and in Egypt, 1798–1801; brigadier in Egypt, 1801, and Walcheren, 1809; commanded 7th division in

Peninsula, 1811–12; governor of Gibraltar, 1831–35; created baronet, 1836.

HOUTON, John de (d. 1246), justice; archdeacon of Bedford, 1218, of Northampton, 1231–46; represented Henry III in negotiations with Falkes de *Breauté, and at Rome, 1224 and 1228.

HOVEDEN, John (d. 1275), Latin poet; chaplain of Queen *Eleanor and prebendary of Hoveden or Howden, where he built choir; reverenced as saint; his chief poem, *Philomena sive meditacio de nativitate, &c., Domini nostri Jesu Christi*, printed at Ghent (1516), at Luxemburg as *Christias* (1603); his prose treatise *Practica Chilindri* translated by E. Brock.

HOVEDEN (or HOWDEN), Roger of (d. 1201?), chronicler; envoy to Henry II to chiefs of Galloway, 1174; justice for northern forests, 1189; his *Cronica* (732–1201), first printed (1596), and edited by Bishop Stubbs, 1868–71.

HOVELL-THURLOW, Edward, second Baron Thurlow (1781–1829). See THURLOW.

HOVENDEN (or HOVEDEN), Robert (1544–1614), warden of All Souls College, Oxford; fellow of All Souls College, 1565; MA, 1570; DD, 1581; warden, 1571–1614; chaplain to Archbishop *Parker; prebendary of Lincoln, Bath, and Canterbury; vice-chancellor, 1582; admitted poor scholars to the college and recovered property from crown; wrote life of Archbishop *Chichele.

HOW. See also HOWE.

HOW, William Walsham (1823–1897), first bishop of Wakefield; MA, Wadham College, Oxford, 1847; ordained priest, 1847; rural dean of Oswestry, 1854; honorary canon of St Asaph, 1860; suffragan to bishop of London, with title of bishop of Bedford, 1879; prebendary of St Paul's Cathedral; DD, Canterbury, 1879, and Oxford, 1886; bishop of Wakefield, 1888; published religious writings; widely known for his work in connection with the poor in East End of London.

HOWARD, Lady Anne (1475–1513), third daughter of Edward IV, and first wife of Thomas, third duke of *Norfolk.

HOWARD, Bernard Edward, twelfth duke of Norfolk (1765–1842), succeeded his third cousin Charles *Howard, eleventh duke (1746–1815), in dukedom, 1815; though Roman Catholic, he was made earl marshal by parliament, 1824; privy councillor, 1830; KG, 1834; supported Reform Bill.

HOWARD, Bernard Marmaduke Fitz-Alan-, sixteenth duke of Norfolk (1908–1975), earl marshal and hereditary marshal of England; educated at Oratory School, Birmingham; failed to pass examination for entrance to Oxford; succeeded to title, 1917; commissioned into 4th (Territorial) battalion, Royal Sussex Regiment, 1928; served in France and at Dunkirk, 1940; succeeded mother as thirteenth baron Herries, 1945; duties of earl marshal performed from 1929; PC, 1936; official duties began with funeral of George V, 1936, followed by coronation of George VI; KG, 1937; responsible for arrangements, including television, at coronation of Queen Elizabeth II, 1953; regulated state funeral of Sir Winston Churchill, 1965 and investiture of Prince of Wales at Caernarfon, 1969; steward of Jockey Club, 1966–8; vice-chairman, Turf Board, 1965–8; queen's representative at Ascot, 1945–72; won Ascot Gold Cup with Ragstone, 1974; master of Holderness Hunt, 1936; took cricket team to tour West Indies, 1956–7; manager of England team on tour of Australia, 1962–3; mayor of Arundel, 1935–6; lord lieutenant of Sussex, 1949–74; spokesman for Catholic laity of England; chairman, Territorial Army Council, 1956–9; GCVO, 1946; GBE, 1968; Royal Victorian Chain, 1953; succeeded in dukedom by his cousin.

HOWARD, Catherine, Queen (d. 1542). See CATHERINE.

HOWARD, Charles, second Baron Howard of Effingham, first earl of Nottingham (1536–1624), lord high admiral; eldest son of William *Howard, first Baron Howard of Effingham; ambassador to France, 1559; MP, Surrey; commander of horse against northern rebels, 1569, of squadron to watch Spanish fleet, 1570; knighted; succeeded to peerage, 1573; lord chamberlain, 1583–5; lord high admiral, 1585–1618; commissioner for trial of *Mary Queen of Scots, 1586; held chief command against Spanish Armada, 1588, leading mid-channel squadron and ordering and directing attack on the *San Lorenzo*; officially organized 'the chest at Chatham', 1590; colleague of *Essex in Cadiz expedition, 1596; created earl of Nottingham, 1596; commander both by land and sea during alarm of 1599; commissioner at Essex's trial, 1601; commissioner for James I's coronation, 1603; ambassador-extraordinary to Spain, 1605; commissioner for union with Scotland, 1604, and trial of gunpowder plotters, 1606; improbably supposed of recent years to have been a Roman Catholic.

HOWARD, Charles, first earl of Carlisle (1629–1685), great-grandson of Lord William *Howard (1563–1640); rendered distinguished service to Parliamentarians at Worcester, 1651; member of Council of State, 1653; MP, Westmoreland, 1653, Cumberland, 1654, 1656, and

1660; commanded against Scots, 1654; councillor of state for Scotland, 1655; captain of *Cromwell's bodyguard; major-general of Northumberland, Cumberland, and Westmoreland; member of Cromwell's House of Lords, 1657; imprisoned by army leaders, 1659; privy councillor, 1660; lord-lieutenant of Cumberland and Westmoreland, 1660; created earl of Carlisle, 1661; ambassador-extraordinary to Russia, Sweden, and Denmark, 1663–4; governor of Jamaica, 1677–81; lieutenant-general, 1667.

HOWARD, Charles, third earl of Carlisle (1674–1738), statesman; as Viscount Morpeth, MP for Morpeth, 1690–2; succeeded to peerage, 1692; deputy earl marshal, 1701–6; lord-lieutenant of Cumberland and Westmoreland, 1694–1712; first lord of the Treasury, 1701–2 and 1715 (May–Oct.); commissioner for Scottish union; a lord justice, 1714–15.

HOWARD, Sir Charles (d. 1765), general; second son of Charles *Howard, third earl of Carlisle; colonel of 19th Foot ('Green Howards'), 1738; commanded brigade at Dettingen, 1743, and Fontenoy, 1745, and the infantry at Val and Roucoux, 1746; KB, 1749; president of court martial on Lord George Sackville (see GERMAIN, GEORGE SACKVILLE); MP, Carlisle, 1727–61.

HOWARD, Charles, tenth duke of Norfolk (1720–1786), author of *Historical Anecdotes of some of the Howard Family* (1769); a Roman Catholic; succeeded his second cousin, Edward Howard, ninth duke, 1777; FSA and FRS.

HOWARD, Charles, eleventh duke of Norfolk (1746–1815), son of Charles *Howard, tenth duke of Norfolk; became Protestant and a Whig; FRS, 1767; FSA, 1779; MP, Carlisle, 1780–6; a lord of the Treasury under Portland, 1783; dismissed from lord-lieutenancy of the West Riding for democratic speech at Crown and Anchor banquet, 1798; friend of prince of Wales (George IV); lord-lieutenant of Sussex, 1807; president of Society of Arts, 1794.

HOWARD, Sir Ebenezer (1850–1928), originator of the garden-city movement and founder of Letchworth and Welwyn garden cities; clerk in City of London; stenographer in Chicago, 1872–7; influenced by outcome of teaching of Emerson, Lowell, and Whitman; shorthand writer to official reporters to Houses of Parliament; carried on shorthand business of his own until 1920; influenced by Edward Bellamy's *Looking Backward*; published *Tomorrow* (1898); set himself to find remedy for unhealthy conditions produced by overcrowding in great cities and for depopulation of countryside; proposed to build new towns called 'garden cities', both residential and industrial, surrounded by rural belt; formed Garden City Association, 1899; estate of Letchworth, Hertfordshire, bought and development begun, 1903; principle that town should own land adopted in modified form; bought, and subsequently developed, Welwyn Estate, Hertfordshire, 1919; president of International Garden Cities and Town Planning Association, 1909–28; exercised important influence on town planning; knighted, 1927.

HOWARD, Edmund Bernard FitzAlan-, first Viscount FitzAlan of Derwent (1855–1947), son of fourteenth and brother of fifteenth duke of *Norfolk; uncle of Lord *Rankeillour; known as Lord Edmund Talbot, 1876–1921; educated at Oratory School; officer in 11th Hussars; served in South Africa, 1899–1902; DSO; Conservative MP, Chichester, 1894–1921; junior lord of Treasury, 1905; joint parliamentary secretary, 1915–21; chief Conservative whip, 1913–21; viceroy of Ireland, 1921–2; Unionist by conviction but recognized necessity of coming to terms with Sinn Fein; deputy earl marshal, 1917–29; leading Roman Catholic layman; PC, 1918; GCVO, 1919; viscount, 1921; KG, 1925.

HOWARD, Sir Edward (1477?–1513), lord high admiral; second son of Thomas *Howard, second duke of Norfolk; knighted while serving in Scotland, 1497; standard-bearer, 1509; said to have assisted in capturing Robert and Andrew *Barton, 1511; as admiral of the fleet landed and ravaged coast of Brittany, 1512, afterwards defeating and burning many French ships; confirmed as lord high admiral, 1513; lost his life while attempting to cut out French galleys from Whitsand Bay; nominated KG just before his death.

HOWARD, Edward (*fl.* 1669), dramatist; brother of Sir Robert *Howard (1626–1698); published *The Usurper* (tragedy, 1668), *Six Days' Adventure* and *The Women's Conquest* (comedies, 1671); his *United Kingdom* ridiculed in *The Rehearsal*, and *The British Princess* by *Rochester.

HOWARD, Edward, first Baron Howard of Escrick (d. 1675), Parliamentarian; son of Thomas *Howard, first earl of Suffolk; KB, 1616; created peer, 1628; one of the twelve petitioning peers, 1640; represented Carlisle after abolition (1649) of upper house; member of Council of State, 1650; convicted of taking bribes from delinquents, 1651.

HOWARD, Edward (d. 1841), novelist; served in the navy with *Marryat, for whom he sub-edited the *Metropolitan Magazine*; afterwards wrote for *Hood's *New Monthly*; his *Rattlin the Reefer* (1836) wrongly attributed to Marryat; published other maritime novels.

HOWARD, Edward George Fitzalan, first Baron Howard of Glossop (1818–1883), second son of Henry Charles *Howard, thirteenth duke of Norfolk; Liberal MP for Horsham, 1848–53, Arundel, 1853–68; vicechamberlain, 1846–52; created Baron Howard, 1869; chairman of Catholic Poor Schools Committee, 1869–77.

HOWARD, Edward Henry (1829–1892), cardinal; ordained priest in English College, Rome, 1854; archbishop of Neocaesaria *in partibus infidelium*, 1872, and coadjutor bishop of Frascati; cardinal-priest, 1877; arch-priest of basilica of St Peter, and prefect of congregation of St Peter, 1881; cardinal-bishop of Frascati, 1881.

HOWARD, Elizabeth, duchess of Norfolk (1494–1558), daughter of Edward *Stafford, duke of Buckingham; second wife of Thomas *Howard, third duke of Norfolk.

HOWARD, Esme William, first Baron Howard of Penrith (1863–1939), diplomat; educated at Harrow; served in Diplomatic Service, 1885–92; rejoined, 1903; consul-general for Crete, 1903–6; minister to Switzerland (1911–13), Sweden (1913–19); on British delegation to Peace Conference; ambassador to Spain (1919–24), to United States (1924–30); KCMG, 1916; KCB and PC, 1919; GCMG, 1923; GCB, 1928; baron, 1930.

HOWARD, Frank (1805?–1866), painter; son of Henry *Howard (1769–1847); assistant to Sir Thomas *Lawrence; exhibited at British Institution, 1824–43, at the Academy, 1825–33, and later; gained prize for cartoon in Westminster Hall competition, 1843; published *Spirit of Plays of Shakspeare* (plates), 1827–33, and art manuals.

HOWARD, Frederick, fifth earl of Carlisle (1748–1825), statesman; succeeded to earldom, 1758; of Eton and King's College, Cambridge; friend of Charles James *Fox; treasurer of the household, 1777; head of commission to treat with Americans, 1778; president of Board of Trade, 1779; viceroy of Ireland, 1780–2; lord steward, 1782–3; resigned and (1783) moved amendment against the peace; lord privy seal in coalition ministry, 1783; opposed Pitt on Regency question (1788–9), but went over to him with the old Whigs; KG, 1793; Chancery guardian to Lord *Byron; attacked in *English Bards and Scotch Reviewers*; his tragedy *The Father's Revenge* (1783) praised by *Johnson and *Walpole; *Tragedies and Poems* issued (1801).

HOWARD, Sir George (1720?–1796), field marshal; commanded 3rd Buffs at Fontenoy, 1745, Falkirk, 1746, Culloden, 1746, Val, and the Rochefort expedition; commanded brigade in Germany during Seven Years' War; KB, 1763; MP, Lostwithiel, 1762–6, Stamford, 1768–96; governor of Minorca, 1766–8, afterwards of Jersey and Chelsea Hospital; field marshal, 1793.

HOWARD, George, sixth earl of Carlisle (1773–1848), statesman; son of Frederick *Howard, fifth earl; of Eton and Christ Church, Oxford; MA, 1792; DCL, 1799; MP, Morpeth (while Viscount Morpeth), 1795–1806, Cumberland, 1806–28; commissioner for affairs of India in ministry of All the Talents, 1806; advocated Catholic emancipation, 1812; lord-lieutenant of East Riding, 1824; chief commissioner of woods and forests in Canning's Cabinet, 1827; lord privy seal, 1827–8 and 1834; trustee of British Museum; contributed to *Anti-Jacobin*.

HOWARD, George James, ninth earl of Carlisle (1843–1911), amateur artist; grandson of George *Howard, sixth earl; educated at Eton and Trinity College, Cambridge; Liberal MP for East Cumberland, 1879–80, 1881–5; joined Liberal Unionists, 1886; succeeded to earldom, 1889; closed public houses on his Yorkshire and Cumberland estates; skilled water-colour landscape painter; published *A Picture Songbook* (1910); trustee of National Gallery, to which was transferred his Mabuse's *Adoration of the Magi*, 1911; his son, **Charles James Stanley Howard**, tenth earl (1867–1912), was Unionist MP for South Birmingham, 1904–11, and parliamentary whip.

HOWARD, George William Frederick, seventh earl of Carlisle (1802–1864), statesman; eldest son of George *Howard, sixth earl of Carlisle; won prizes for English and Latin verse at Oxford, 1821; MA, Christ Church, Oxford, 1827; as Viscount Morpeth, MP, Morpeth, 1826–30, Yorkshire, 1830–2, the West Riding, 1832–41 and 1846–8; as Irish secretary under Melbourne, 1835–41, carried Irish Tithe, Irish Municipal Reform, and Irish Poor Law bills; admitted to Cabinet, 1839; chief commissioner of woods and forests under Russell, 1846–50; carried Public Health Bill, 1848; chancellor of duchy of Lancaster, 1850–2; viceroy of Ireland, 1855–8 and 1859–64; presided at Shakespeare tercentenary, 1864; published poems, travels, and lectures.

HOWARD, Gorges Edmond (1715–1786), author; educated under Thomas *Sheridan; given freedom of Dublin for public services, 1766; ridiculed for worthless tragedies and occasional verse; published valuable legal works.

HOWARD, Henrietta, countess of Suffolk (1681–1767), mistress of George II; daughter of Sir Henry Hobart, baronet; married to Charles Howard (afterwards ninth earl of Suffolk), with whom she lived at Hanover; followed George I to

England and became bedchamber woman to princess of Wales; her house at Marble Hill, Twickenham, the resort of *Pope, *Arbuthnot, and *Swift; admired by Lord *Peterborough; much courted as mistress of George II; became countess, 1731; retired from court, 1734; married Hon. George Berkeley, 1735; selection from her letters edited by *Croker, 1824.

HOWARD, Henry, earl of Surrey (by courtesy) (1517?–1547), poet; son of Thomas *Howard (afterwards third duke of Norfolk); educated by John *Clerk (d. 1552); proposed as husband for Princess Mary; married Frances Vere, 1532; in France, 1532–3; earl marshal at *Anne Boleyn's trial, 1536; accompanied his father against Yorkshire rebels, 1536; steward of Cambridge University, 1539–40; KG, 1541; imprisoned for a quarrel, 1542, and for annoying London citizens, 1543; with imperial troops at Landrecy, 1543; wounded when marshal before Montreuil, 1544; when commander of Boulogne (1545–6) defeated at St Etienne, 1546; superseded by his enemy, Lord *Hertford, 1546; condemned and executed on frivolous charge of treasonably quartering royal arms and advising his sister to become the king's mistress; his body discovered at Framlingham Church, Suffolk, 1835. Forty poems by Surrey, including 'Description and Praise of his love Geraldine', were printed in *Tottel's *Songes and Sonettes* (1557, reprinted 1867 and 1870). His translations of the *Aeneid* (books ii and iii, reprinted 1814) introduced blank verse in five iambic feet. The poems (with those of *Wyatt) were edited by Dr George Frederick *Nott (1815–16) and others, and for Aldine Poets by James *Yeowell (1866). Surrey first imitated Italian models, especially Petrarch, and (with Wyatt) introduced the sonnet from Italy into England.

HOWARD, Henry, first earl of Northampton (1540–1614), second son of Henry *Howard, earl of Surrey; MA, King's College, Cambridge, 1566; went to court, c.1570; received pension, but failed to gain secure position owing to his relations with *Mary Queen of Scots; sent to the Fleet after publishing work against judicial astrology, 1583; suspected of intrigues with Spain; attached himself to *Essex; gained goodwill of Sir Robert *Cecil; readmitted to court, 1600; corresponded with *James VI of Scotland, advising toleration of Romanists; created earl of Northampton, 1604; warden of Cinque Ports, 1604; KG, 1605; lord privy seal, 1608; chancellor of Cambridge University; commissioner for trials of *Ralegh, 1603, Guy *Fawkes, 1605, and *Garnett, 1606; accused of having secretly apologized to Bellarmine for speech against Catholics; a commissioner of the Treasury, 1612;

supported divorce of grandniece from Essex, 1613, and procured imprisonment of Sir Thomas *Overbury; opposed summoning of parliament, 1614; drew up James I's edict against duelling, 1613; erected monument of Mary Queen of Scots at Westminster; lived and died a Roman Catholic; the most learned noble of his day; built Northumberland House.

HOWARD, Henry, sixth duke of Norfolk (1628–1684), friend of *Evelyn; second son of Henry Frederick *Howard, third earl of Arundel; visited Evelyn at Padua, 1645; entertained by Leopold I at Vienna, 1664; FRS, 1666; presented library to Royal Society and Arundel marbles to Oxford University, 1667; DCL, Oxford, 1668; created Baron Howard of Castle Rising, 1669; envoy to Morocco, 1669; succeeded his brother as duke, 1677.

HOWARD, Henry, seventh duke of Norfolk (1655–1701), son of Henry *Howard, sixth duke; MA, Magdalen College, Oxford, 1668; summoned as Baron Mowbray, 1679; styled earl of Arundel, 1678–84; lord-lieutenant of Norfolk, Berkshire, and Surrey; brought over eastern counties to William III; privy councillor, 1689.

HOWARD, Henry (1684–1720), coadjutor-elect of Bishop Bonaventure *Giffard in London districts, 1720; grandson of Henry *Howard, sixth duke of Norfolk.

HOWARD, Henry, fourth earl of Carlisle (1694–1758), son of Charles *Howard, third earl of Carlisle; MP, Morpeth, 1722, 1727, and 1734–8; KG, 1756.

HOWARD, Henry (1757–1842), of Corby Castle, author of *Memorials of the Howard Family* (1834); friend and correspondent of Louis Philippe.

HOWARD, Henry (1769–1847), painter; went to Italy with introduction from *Reynolds, 1791; exhibited *Dream of Cain* at Royal Academy, 1794; RA, 1808; secretary, Royal Academy, 1811, and professor of painting, 1833; his finest works, *Birth of Venus*, 1819, and *Fairies*, 1818; executed portraits, among others, of *Flaxman and James *Watt.

HOWARD, Henry Charles, thirteenth duke of Norfolk (1791–1856), son of Bernard Edward *Howard, twelfth duke; as earl of Arundel and Surrey, MP, Horsham, 1829–41, and treasurer of the household, 1837–41; master of the horse, 1846–52; KG, 1848; lord steward, 1853–4; though a Romanist, supported Ecclesiastical Titles Bill.

HOWARD, Henry Edward John (1795–1868), dean of Lichfield; youngest son of Frederick *Howard, fifth earl of Carlisle; of Eton and Christ Church, Oxford; MA, 1822; succentor of York, 1822; dean of Lichfield, 1833–68; published translations from Claudian and the Septuagint.

HOWARD, Henry FitzAlan-, fifteenth duke of Norfolk (1847–1917), son of H. G. Fitzalan-*Howard, fourteenth duke; succeeded father, 1860; educated at Oratory School, Edgbaston; as young man took up cause of his co-religionists, especially Irish Catholics; postmaster-general, 1895–1900; maintained close relations with Vatican; as earl marshal largely responsible for coronation ceremonies of Edward VII and George V; great builder of Gothic churches.

HOWARD, Henry Frederick, third earl of Arundel (1608–1652); KB, 1616; son of Thomas *Howard, second earl of Arundel; as Lord Maltravers, MP, Arundel, 1628 and 1640; Irish privy councillor, 1634; created Baron Mowbray, 1640; committed for quarrel with Philip *Herbert, fourth earl of Pembroke, 1641; fought as Royalist in Civil War; succeeded his father as third earl of Arundel and earl marshal, 1646.

HOWARD, Henry Granville Fitzalan-, fourteenth duke of Norfolk (1815–1860), son of Henry Charles *Howard, thirteenth duke; of Trinity College, Cambridge; as Lord Fitzalan (earl of Arundel from 1842) represented Arundel, 1837–50, Limerick, 1850–2; opposed Ecclesiastical Titles Bill, 1850; friend of Montalembert and a zealous Catholic; edited *Lives of Philip Howard, Earl of Arundel, and . . . his wife* (1857).

HOWARD, Hugh (1675–1737), portrait painter and art collector; son of Ralph *Howard (1638–1710); keeper of state papers and paymaster of works belonging to crown; some of his portraits and drawings acquired by British Museum.

HOWARD, James, third earl of Suffolk and third Baron Howard de Walden (1619–1688), eldest son of Theophilus *Howard, second earl of Suffolk; KB, 1626; joint commissioner of the parliament to Charles I, 1646; lord-lieutenant of Suffolk and Cambridgeshire, 1660–82, and gentleman of the bedchamber, 1665.

HOWARD, James (*fl.* 1674), dramatist; brother of Sir Robert *Howard (1626–1698), and brother-in-law of *Dryden; his comedy *All Mistaken, or the Mad Couple* (1672) first acted, 1667; his *English Mounsieur* (1674) played in by Nell *Gwyn and *Hart, 1666.

HOWARD, James (1821–1889), agriculturist; took out patents for agricultural machines, including first iron-wheel plough (1841); president of Farmers' Alliance; mayor of Bedford,

1863–4; MP, Bedford, 1868–74, Bedfordshire, 1880–5; wrote on scientific farming.

HOWARD, John, first duke of Norfolk of the Howard family (1430?–1485), present at Battle of Châtillon, 1453; entered service of his relative, John *Mowbray, duke of Norfolk; knight of the shire for Norfolk, 1455, Suffolk, 1466; named sheriff of Norfolk and Suffolk by Edward IV; constable of Norwich, 1462; served against Lancastrians and in Brittany; envoy to France and Flanders; created Baron Howard by the restored Henry VI, 1470; commanded fleet against Lancastrians, 1471; deputy-governor of Calais, 1471; accompanied Edward IV to France and received pension from Louis XI, 1475; again employed in France, 1477, 1479, and 1480; privy councillor, 1483; created duke of Norfolk and earl marshal by Richard III, 1483; admiral of England, Ireland, and Aquitaine, 1483; commanded vanguard at Bosworth and was slain.

HOWARD, John (1726?–1790), philanthropist; captured on the way to Lisbon and imprisoned in France, 1756; high sheriff of Bedfordshire, though a Dissenter, 1773; visited county and city gaols and bridewells and obtained acts for abolition of gaoler's fees and for sanitary improvements, 1774; inspected Scottish, Irish, French, Flemish, Dutch, German, and Swiss, and revisited British prisons, 1775–6; published *State of the Prisons* (1777), *Appendix to State of Prisons* (1780), translation of *Historical Remarks on the Bastille* (1774); visited Denmark, Sweden, and Russia, 1781; LL D, Dublin, 1782; made third inspection of British prisons, 1783; inspected penal institutions of Spain and Portugal, 1783; issued third enlarged edition of *State of the Prisons* (1784); visited lazarettos in France, Italy, and Turkey, purposely underwent quarantine at Venice, 1785–6, and published an *Account* (1789); died of camp fever while with Russian Army at Kherson.

HOWARD, John (1753–1799), mathematician; self-educated; kept schools at Carlisle and Newcastle; published *Treatise on Spherical Geometry* (1798).

HOWARD, John Eliot (1807–1883), author of *Illustrations of the 'Nueva Quinologia' of Pavon, and Observations on the Barks described* (1862) and *Quinology of the East Indian Plantations* (1869); son of Luke *Howard (1772–1864); FRS, 1874.

HOWARD, Kenneth Alexander, first earl of Effingham of the second creation (1767–1845), general; served with Coldstream Guards in Flanders, 1793–5, Ireland, and Holland, 1799; inspector-general of foreign troops in British service; aide-de-camp to the king, 1805; major-general, 1810; commanded brigades in the Peninsular War from 1811, and first division of army of occupation after Waterloo; KCB, 1815; succeeded as eleventh Baron Howard of Effingham, 1816; deputy earl marshal at coronation of George IV, 1821; general, 1837; created earl, 1837.

HOWARD, Leonard (1699?–1767), compiler of *A Collection of Letters from original Manuscripts of many Princes, great Personages and Statesmen* (1753); DD; rector of St George's, Southwark, 1749–67; chaplain to Augusta, princess dowager of Wales.

HOWARD, Leslie (1893–1943), actor, producer, and film director; acted and produced mainly in America; films included *Berkeley Square, The Scarlet Pimpernel, Pygmalion*, and *Gone with the Wind*; part-producer, British war films *Pimpernel Smith, The First of the Few, The Gentle Sex*, and *The Lamp Still Burns*; shot down in aircraft returning from Portugal.

HOWARD, Luke (1621–1699), Quaker; previously a Baptist; imprisoned at Dover, 1660, 1661, and 1684; wrote against Baptists; his *Journal* prefixed to works issued, 1704.

HOWARD, Luke (1772–1864), pioneer in meteorology; chemist in London in partnership with William *Allen (1770–1843); began to keep meteorological register, 1806; published *Climate of London* (1818–20, enlarged 1830), containing current classification of clouds; FRS, 1821; edited *The Yorkshireman* (Quaker journal), 1833–7; corresponded with Goethe and John *Dalton.

HOWARD, Philip, first earl of Arundel of the Howard family (1557–1595), eldest son of Thomas *Howard III, fourth duke of Norfolk; went to Cambridge with courtesy title earl of Surrey; MA, 1576; court profligate; succeeded to earldom of Arundel, 1580, in right of his mother, Mary Fitzalan (daughter of Henry, twelfth earl); under influence of his wife (Anne Dacre) became Roman Catholic, 1584; after attempting to escape from England, 1585, was fined and rigorously imprisoned for life; condemned to death, 1589, on charge of having mass said for success of the Armada, but, although not executed, remained in Tower till death.

HOWARD, Philip Thomas (1629–1694), known as Cardinal of Norfolk, third son of Henry Frederick *Howard, third earl of Arundel; educated at Utrecht and Antwerp; became a Dominican; studied at Naples and Rennes; ordained priest, 1652; first prior of his own English foundation at Bornhem, East Flanders, 1657; went on secret Royalist mission to England, 1659; promoted marriage of Charles II, 1662, and was first chaplain to Queen *Catherine, and afterwards grand almoner; his appointment as vicar-apostolic in England withdrawn; driven from England by popular feeling, 1674; created cardinal-priest by Clement X, 1675; thenceforth lived at Rome; as cardinal-protector of England and Scotland, 1679, obtained restoration of the episcopate; remonstrated against policy of James II.

HOWARD, Ralph (1638–1710), regius professor of physic at Dublin, 1670–1710; MD, Dublin, 1667.

HOWARD, Ralph, Viscount Wicklow and first Baron Clonmore (d. 1786), grandson of Ralph *Howard (1638–1710); MP, Co. Wicklow, 1761–75; Irish privy councillor, 1770; created Baron Clonmore, 1776, Viscount Wicklow, 1785.

HOWARD, Richard Baron (1807–1848), Manchester physician; MD, Edinburgh; published *Inquiry into Morbid Effects of Deficiency of Food* (1839).

HOWARD, Sir Robert (1585–1653), Royalist; fifth son of Thomas *Howard, first earl of Suffolk; KB, 1616; imprisoned by High Commission and publicly excommunicated, 1625, for intrigue with Frances, Viscountess Purbeck (*Buckingham's brother's wife); MP, Bishop's Castle, 1624–40; voted compensation by Long Parliament, 1640, but expelled for Royalism, 1642; his estates sequestered.

HOWARD, Sir Robert (1626–1698), dramatist; nephew of Sir Robert *Howard (1585–1653); rescued *Wilmot from Parliamentarians at Cropredy Bridge and was knighted, 1644; Whig MP, Stockbridge, 1661, Castle Rising, 1679–98; auditor of the Exchequer; built Ashtead House, Surrey, 1684; privy councillor, 1689; commander of militia horse, 1690; ridiculed as Sir Positive At-All in *Shadwell's *Sullen Lovers*; perhaps the Bilboa of *The Rehearsal*; author of *The Committee* (revived at Covent Garden as *The Honest Thieves*, 1797), published with four other plays (1665), in one of which, the *Indian Queen*, *Dryden assisted; opposed use of rhyme in drama; published also historical works and poems.

HOWARD, Robert (1683–1740), bishop of Elphin; son of Ralph *Howard (1638–1710); fellow of Trinity College, Dublin, 1703; bishop of Killala, 1726, of Elphin, 1729–40.

HOWARD, Rosalind Frances, countess of Carlisle (1845–1921), promoter of women's political rights and of temperance reform; daughter of Edward John, second Baron *Stanley of Alderley; married George *Howard, afterwards ninth earl of Carlisle, 1864; supported home rule; president of National British

Women's Temperance Association (1903) and of Women's Liberal Federation (1891–1901, 1906–14); possessed remarkable business ability.

HOWARD, Samuel (1710–1782), organist and composer; Mus.Doc., Cambridge, 1769; best known by his 'musettes'.

HOWARD, Theophilus, second earl of Suffolk and second Baron Howard de Walden (1584–1640), succeeded his father, Thomas *Howard, first earl of Suffolk, 1626; MA, Magdalene College, Cambridge, incorporated at Oxford, 1605; MP, Maldon, 1605–10; summoned as Baron Howard de Walden, 1610; governor of Jersey, 1610; quarrelled with Lord *Herbert of Cherbury at Juliers, 1610; joint lord-lieutenant of northern counties, 1614; lord-lieutenant of Cambridgeshire, Suffolk, and Dorset, 1626; KG, 1627; warden of Cinque Ports, 1628.

HOWARD, Thomas I, earl of Surrey and second duke of Norfolk of the Howard house (1443–1524), warrior; only son of Sir John *Howard, afterwards first duke of Norfolk; fought for Edward IV at Barnet, 1471; knighted, 1478; earl of Surrey from 1483; became KG, 1483; fought for Richard III at Bosworth, 1485; imprisoned in the Tower by Henry VII, but ultimately recovered his estates; subdued Yorkshire rising, 1489; as lieutenant-general of the north compelled the Scots to retreat, 1497, and negotiated marriage treaty; lord-treasurer, 1501–22; earl marshal, 1510; ousted from power by *Wolsey; when again lieutenant-general of the north won Battle of Flodden, 1513, and was created duke of Norfolk, 1514; vainly opposed Wolsey's foreign policy; put down London apprentices on 'evil May-day', 1517; guardian of the kingdom, 1520; presided as high steward at trial of his friend and connection, *Buckingham, 1521.

HOWARD, Thomas II, earl of Surrey and third duke of Norfolk of the Howard house (1473–1554), eldest son of Thomas *Howard I; as Lord Thomas Howard with his brother, Sir Edward *Howard, captured Andrew *Barton, 1511; lord admiral, 1513; led vanguard at Flodden, 1513; as earl of Surrey (1514–24) strongly opposed *Wolsey; lord-lieutenant of Ireland, 1520–1; raided French coast, 1521–2; lord-treasurer, 1522; as warden-general of the marches devastated Scottish border and forced *Albany to retreat, 1523; pacified *Suffolk insurgents, 1525; as president of the privy council incensed Henry VIII against Wolsey; earl marshal, 1533; acquiesced in execution of his niece, *Anne Boleyn, 1536; put down Pilgrimage of Grace; headed opposition to *Cromwell and brought forward the Six Articles, 1539; again

commanded against the Scots, 1542; lieutenant-general of army in France, 1544; ousted from favour by *Hertford, and condemned to death, but saved by Henry VIII's death; remained in the Tower till accession of Mary (1553), when he was released and restored; presided at *Northumberland's trial, 1553; showed great rashness when commanding against *Wyatt, 1554.

HOWARD, Thomas III, fourth duke of Norfolk of the Howard house (1536–1572), son of Henry *Howard, earl of Surrey; pupil of John *Foxe; KB, 1553; succeeded his grandfather as duke and earl marshal, 1554; employed in Scotland, 1559–60; KG, 1559; privy councillor, 1562; contributed largely towards completion of Magdalene College, Cambridge; quarrelled with *Leicester in Elizabeth's presence, 1565; one of the commissioners to inquire into Scottish affairs at York, 1568; formed project of marriage with *Mary Queen of Scots; imprisoned, 1569–70; involved in *Ridolfi's plot; executed for treason; denied having been a papist.

HOWARD, Lord Thomas, first earl of Suffolk and first Baron Howard de Walden (1561–1626), second son of Thomas *Howard III, fourth duke of Norfolk; as Lord Thomas Howard distinguished himself against Armada, 1588; commanded in attack on Azores fleet, 1591; admiral of the third squadron in Cadiz expedition, 1596; KG and Baron Howard de Walden, 1597; marshal of forces against *Essex and constable of Tower, 1601; created earl of Suffolk by James I, 1603; lord chamberlain, 1603–14; MA, Oxford and Cambridge, 1605; lord-lieutenant of Suffolk, Cambridgeshire, and Dorset; chancellor of Cambridge University, 1614; lord high treasurer, 1614–18; fined and imprisoned for embezzlement, 1619.

HOWARD, Thomas, second earl of Arundel and Surrey (1586–1646), art collector; only son of Philip *Howard, first earl of Arundel; MA, Cambridge, 1605; restored in title and blood, 1604; made first continental tour, 1609–10; KG, 1611; became Protestant, 1615; privy councillor, 1616; president of committee of peers on *Bacon's case, 1621; joint commissioner of great seal, 1621; earl marshal, 1621; imprisoned for hostility to *Buckingham, 1626–8; attempted mediation in debates on Petition of Right, 1628; sent to Vienna to urge restitution of palatinate to Charles I's nephew, 1636; general of army against Scots, 1639; presided at *Strafford's trial, 1641; escorted Queen *Henrietta Maria to the continent, 1642; thenceforward lived at Padua, contributing large sums to royal cause. He formed at Arundel House the first considerable art collection in England, including statues, busts, pictures, and the marbles (described in

*Selden's *Marmora Arundeliana*, 1628), presented to Oxford University, 1667.

HOWARD, Walter (1759–1830?), 'The Heir of Poverty'; claimed kinship with the dukes of Norfolk and received allowances from several; his claim found fictitious; imprisoned, 1812, for importuning the prince regent and the eleventh duke of *Norfolk.

HOWARD, Sir William (d. 1308), judge; justice of assize for northern counties, 1293; summoned to parliament as a justice, 1295; justice of common pleas, 1297.

HOWARD, Lord William, first Baron Howard of Effingham (1510?–1573), lord high admiral; son of Thomas *Howard I, second duke of Norfolk; MA, Trinity Hall, Cambridge, 1564; employed on embassies to Scotland, 1531, 1535, and 1536, and in France, 1537 and 1541; convicted of misprision of treason in connection with Queen *Catherine Howard, but pardoned, 1541; governor of Calais, 1552–4; privy councillor, 1553; lord high admiral, 1553–8; KG, 1554; created peer for defence of London against Wyatt, 1554; remonstrated against harsh treatment of Princess Elizabeth; lord chamberlain, 1558; a negotiator of Treaty of Câteau Cambrésis, 1559; lord privy seal, 1572.

HOWARD, Lord William (1563–1640), *Scott's 'Belted Will'; third son of Thomas *Howard III, fourth duke of Norfolk; married Elizabeth Dacre ('Bessie with the braid apron'), 1577; became a Romanist, 1584; twice imprisoned; restored Naworth Castle; active as commissioner of the borders, being known to contemporaries as 'Bauld Willie'; formed large library, and published edition of *Florence of Worcester's chronicle, 1592; assisted *Camden in *Britannia*; intimate of *Cotton and other antiquaries.

HOWARD, William, first Viscount Stafford (1614–1680), third son of Thomas *Howard, second earl of Arundel and Surrey; KB, 1626; created Viscount Stafford, 1640; remained abroad during rebellion; allowed to return, 1656; discontented with the king, who refused his petition (1664) for restoration of Stafford earldom to his wife; FRS, 1664; member of council of Royal Society, 1672; accused by *Oates of being paymaster of Catholic army, and by others of persuading them to murder Charles II; beheaded for treason, 1680; attainder reversed, 1824.

HOWARD, William, third Baron Howard of Escrick (1626?–1694), second son of Edward *Howard, first Baron Howard; served in Parliamentary army; imprisoned for republican plots, 1657; MP, Winchelsea, in Convention Parliament; succeeded his brother in peerage, 1678;

imprisoned, 1674 and 1681; informed against *Russell and *Sidney, 1683.

HOWARD DE WALDEN, Barons. See HOWARD, Lord THOMAS, first baron, 1561–1626; HOWARD, THEOPHILUS, second baron, 1584–1640; HOWARD, JAMES, third baron, 1619–1688; GRIFFIN (formerly WHITWELL), JOHN GRIFFIN, fourth baron, 1719–1797; HERVEY, FREDERICK AUGUSTUS, fifth baron, 1730–1803; ELLIS, CHARLES AUGUSTUS, sixth baron, 1799–1868; SCOTT-ELLIS, THOMAS EVELYN, eighth baron, 1880–1946.

HOWARD-VYSE, Richard William (1784–1853). See VYSE.

HOWDEN, Barons. See CARADOC, Sir JOHN FRANCIS, first baron, 1759–1839; CARADOC, Sir JOHN HOBART, second baron, 1799–1873.

HOWE, Charles (1661–1742), author of *Devout Meditations* (published 1751); brother of John Grubham *Howe.

HOWE, Clarence Decatur (1886–1960), Canadian minister; born in United States; graduated, civil engineering, Massachusetts Institute of Technology, 1906; taught at Dalhousie University, 1908–13; naturalized, 1913; chief engineer, Board of Grain Commissioners, 1913–16; consulting engineer in Port Arthur, 1916–35; Liberal MP, Port Arthur, 1935–57; minister of transport, 1935–40; established National Harbours Board, 1936, Trans-Canada Airlines, 1937; minister of munitions, 1940–6, of reconstruction, 1944–6, of reconstruction and supply, 1946–8, of trade and commerce, 1948–57, and of defence production, 1951–7; chancellor of Dalhousie, 1957–60; PC, 1946.

HOWE, Edward (pseudonym) (1828–1879), journalist. See ROWE, RICHARD.

HOWE, Emanuel Scrope (d. 1709), diplomat; brother of Scrope *Howe, first Viscount Howe; groom of the bedchamber to William III; MP, Morpeth, 1701–5, Wigan, 1705–8; envoy-extraordinary to Hanover, 1705–9; lieutenant-general, 1709.

HOWE, George (1655?–1710), physician; son of John *Howe (1630–1705); MD, Leiden; censor, Royal College of Physicians, 1707; the Querpo of Garth's *Dispensary*.

HOWE, George Augustus, third Viscount Howe (1725?–1758), grandson of Scrope *Howe, first Viscount Howe, in Irish peerage; succeeded to title, 1735; MP, Nottingham, 1747 and 1754–65; served in Flanders, 1747; colonel, 1757; commanded 60th Foot in Halifax, 1757; killed in skirmish with French at Trout Brook, Lake George.

HOWE, Henry (1812–1896), actor; his real name Henry Howe Hutchinson; appeared at Victoria Theatre, London, 1834; with *Macready at Covent Garden, 1837; at Haymarket for forty years, his parts including Sir Peter Teazle, Malvolio, Jaques, and Macduff; in 1896 accompanied Sir Henry *Irving to America, where he died.

HOWE, James (1780–1836), Scottish animal painter; exhibited at Royal Academy (1816) picture of Waterloo.

HOWE, John (1630–1705), ejected minister; nephew of Obadiah *Howe; entered Christ's College, Cambridge, 1647, where he was an intimate of Henry *More (1614–1687); MA, Magdalen College, Oxford, 1652; fellow and chaplain of Magdalen College; perpetual curate of Great Torrington, 1654–62; as domestic chaplain to *Cromwell preached against fanaticism; befriended *Fuller and Seth *Ward; chaplain to Richard *Cromwell; preached at houses in the west after ejection; joint pastor at Haberdashers' Hall, London, 1676; began controversy on predestination, 1677; answered sermon on schism by *Stillingfleet, 1680; expostulated with *Tillotson, 1680; refused to support dispensing power; advocated mutual forbearance of Conformists and Dissenters, 1689; prominent in 'happy union' of Presbyterians and Congregationalists, 1690; had controversy with *Defoe on occasional conformity, 1700; conferred privately with William III before his death; visited by Richard Cromwell in last illness; chief work, *The Living Temple of God* (1675), included in works, (collected 1724, enlarged 1810–22, 1862–3).

HOWE, John, fourth Baron Chedworth (1754–1804), of Harrow and The Queen's College, Oxford; succeeded his uncle Henry Frederick Howe in title and estates, 1781; left £3,000 to Charles James *Fox; his *Notes upon some of the Obscure Passages in Shakespeare's Plays* issued (1805).

HOWE (or HOW), John Grubham (1657–1722), politician ('Jack How'); forbidden court for slandering duchess of *Richmond, 1679; a strong Whig and vice-chamberlain to Queen Mary, 1689–92; after dismissal a violent Tory, especially denouncing William III's partition treaty (1698) and Dutch favourites; MP, Cirencester, 1689–98, Gloucestershire, 1698–1701 and 1702–5; privy councillor and joint clerk of Privy Council under Anne.

HOWE, Joseph (1804–1873), Nova Scotian statesman; from 1828 edited the *Nova Scotian*; vindicated liberty of the press in successful defence against crown prosecution, 1835; as member for Halifax agitated for responsible government,

1837; member of Executive Council and speaker, 1840; frequently delegate to England; secretary of state for Nova Scotia in Dominion government, 1870; governor of Nova Scotia, 1873.

HOWE, Josias (1611?–1701), divine; fellow of Trinity College, Oxford, 1637–48, restored, 1660; MA, 1638; BD, 1646.

HOWE, Michael (1787–1818), Tasmanian bushranger; transported for highway robbery, 1811; killed while resisting arrest after six years' outlawry.

HOWE, Obadiah (1616?–1683), divine; MA, Magdalen Hall, Oxford, 1638; incumbent of Stickney, Horncastle, and Gedney; vicar of Boston, 1660–83; published controversial works.

HOWE, Richard, Earl Howe (1726–1799), admiral of the fleet; grandson of Scrope *Howe, first Viscount Howe; educated at Eton; sailed in the *Severn* as far as Cape Horn with *Anson, 1740; present at attack on La Guayra, 1743; wounded in action with French frigates off west of Scotland, 1746; by capture of the *Alcide* off mouth of St Lawrence opened Seven Years' War, 1755; MP, Dartmouth, 1757–82; took leading part in Rochefort expedition, 1757; succeeded brother as fourth Viscount (Irish) Howe, 1758; commanded covering squadron in attacks on St Malo and Cherbourg, 1758; distinguished at blockade of Brest and Battle of Quiberon Bay, 1759; a lord of the Admiralty, 1762–5; treasurer of the navy, 1765–70; rear-admiral, 1770; vice-admiral, 1775; as commander-in-chief on North American Station co-operated with his brother, Sir William *Howe; forced passage of Delaware, 1777, and watched French fleet under D'Estaing off Sandy Hook, 1777; resigned command owing to discontent with ministry, 1778, remaining four years in retirement; admiral, 1782; commander in the Channel, 1782; created a British peer, 1782; effected relief of Gibraltar against superior forces, 1782; as first lord of the Admiralty (1783–8) was much attacked in parliament and the press; created Earl Howe, 1788; commanded Channel Fleet, 1790; vice-admiral of England, 1792–6; with Channel fleet won the great victory of 1 June 1794, capturing six French ships; incurred some unpopularity owing to insufficient mention of distinguished officers; admiral of the fleet and general of marines, 1796; KG, 1797; presided over court martial on Vice-admiral *Cornwallis, 1796; after retirement pacified mutineers at Portsmouth, 1797. The signalling code was perfected and refined by him.

HOWE, Scrope, first Viscount Howe (1648–1712), Whig politician; brother of Charles *Howe; knighted, 1663; MP, Nottinghamshire, 1673–98 and 1710–12; active at the Revolution;

groom of the bedchamber, 1689–1702; comptroller of the Exchequer; created Irish viscount, 1701.

HOWE (or HOW), William (1620–1656), botanist; of Merchant Taylors' School and St John's College, Oxford; MA, 1644; published *Phytologia Britannica* (anon. 1650), the earliest work exclusively on British plants.

HOWE, Sir William, fifth Viscount Howe (1729–1814), general; brother of Richard, Earl *Howe; educated at Eton; commanded 58th (later 1st Northampton) Regiment at capture of Louisbourg and defence of Quebec, 1759–60; led forlorn hope at Heights of Abraham, 1759; commanded brigade in Montreal expedition, 1760, and at siege of Belleisle, 1761; adjutant-general at conquest of Havana, 1762; major-general, 1772; lieutenant-general, 1775; MP, Nottingham, 1758–80; commanded at Battle of Bunker Hill, 1775; KB, 1775; succeeded *Gage as commander in American colonies; evacuated Boston and took up position at Halifax, Nova Scotia, 1776; associated with his brother in American Conciliation Commission, 1776; defeated Americans on Long Island, 1776; captured New York and won battles of White Plains and Brandywine, 1776; repulsed attack on Germantown, 1776; failed to draw Washington into further action, 1777; resigned command, 1778; spoke in parliament on American affairs, and obtained (1779) committee of inquiry; published *Narrative* (1780); lieutenant-general of ordnance, 1782–1803; general, 1793; commanded northern, and afterwards eastern, district; succeeded brother in Irish viscountcy, 1799.

HOWEL AB EDWIN (d. 1044), South Welsh prince; descended from *Howel Dda; succeeded in Deheubarth, 1033; expelled by *Gruffydd ab Llywelyn, 1039, and finally defeated and slain by him.

HOWEL AB IEUAV (or HOWEL DDRWG) (d. 984), Howel the Bad; North Welsh prince; expelled *Iago from Gwynedd, and (979) slew his son; slain by Saxon treachery.

HOWEL AB OWAIN GWYNEDD (d. 1171?), warrior and poet; seized part of Ceredigion, 1143; ravaged Cardigan, 1144; with *Gruffydd ab Rhys took Carmarthen Castle, 1145, but afterwards joined the Normans; lost his territory, 1150–2; took part in Henry II's defeat at Basingwerk, 1157; killed by his brother David in Ireland, or in Anglesey; eight of his odes in *Myvyrian Archaeology*.

HOWEL DDA (d. 950), Howel the Good; early Welsh king; doubtfully said to have become king of Gwynedd and all Wales, 915; became directly subject to *Edward the elder, c.918; attested many charters at witenagemots in reign of *Athelstan and Eadred; made pilgrimage to Rome, 928. His 'Laws' survive in Latin manuscripts at Peniarth (twelfth century) and the British Museum (thirteenth century), and the Welsh *Black Book of Chirk* (Peniarth, thirteenth century); they exist only as amended by later rulers, and show traces of English and Norman influence. They were in operation till Edward I's conquest.

HOWELL, David (1831–1903), dean of St David's; held various Welsh livings, 1861–97; dean of St David's, 1897–1903; member of first Cardiff School Board, 1875; well versed in Welsh literature and hymnology; gifted orator of evangelical fervour; mediator between Church and Welsh Nonconformity.

HOWELL, Francis (1625–1679), Puritan divine; MA, Exeter College, Oxford, 1648, fellow, 1648–58; senior proctor, 1652; one of the visitors; professor of moral philosophy, 1654; principal of Jesus College, 1657–60.

HOWELL, George (1833–1910), labour leader and writer; joined Chartists, 1847; prominent in 'nine hours' struggle, 1859; joined 'the Junta' which directed trade-union affairs, 1860; secretary to parliamentary committee of Trades Union Congress, 1871–5; prominent in securing Trade Unions Acts of 1871 and 1876; Liberal MP for Bethnal Green, 1885–95; received civil list pension, 1906; publications include *Trade Unionism New and Old* (1891), *Labour Legislation, Labour Movements and Labour Leaders* (1902); his economic library is in the Bishopsgate Institute.

HOWELL, James (1594?–1666), author; BA, Jesus College, Oxford, 1613; fellow, 1623; travelled through Holland, France, Spain, and Italy; went on diplomatic missions to Spain and Sardinia, and while at Madrid wrote accounts of Prince Charles's courtship of the infanta, 1622–4; MP, Richmond, 1627; secretary to *Leicester's embassy to Denmark, 1632; employed by *Strafford in Edinburgh and London; intimate of Ben *Jonson; corresponded with Lord *Herbert of Cherbury and Sir Kenelm *Digby; published *Dodona's Grove* (political allegory, 1640; 2nd part, 1650), and *Instructions for Forreine Travel* (1642; enlarged 1650; reprinted 1868); Royalist prisoner in the Fleet, 1643–51; wrote in prison Royalist pamphlets, *England's Tears for the present Wars*, a description of Scotland and the Scots (reprinted by Wilkes, 1762), and *Survey of the Seignorie of Venice* (1651); defended *Cromwell against Long Parliament, 1653; advocated Restoration, 1660; historiographer-royal, 1661; his *Cordial for Cavaliers* (1661) attacked by Roger *L'Estrange; *Poems* edited by Payne *Fisher (1663). His reputation rests on

Epistolae Ho-elianae: Familiar Letters, mostly written in the Fleet, and generally to imaginary correspondents (collected 1655, frequently reissued; edited by Mr Joseph Jacobs, 1890–1). His other works include political and historical pamphlets, a revision of *Cotgrave's *French and English Dictionary* (1650), an English–French–Italian–Spanish dictionary (1659–60), with appendix of Welsh proverbs, translations, and an edition of Sir Robert *Cotton's *Posthuma* (1657).

HOWELL, John (1774–1830), Welsh poet (Ioan ab Hywel), fife-major in Carmarthenshire Militia; schoolmaster at Llandovery; published *Blodau Dyfed* (1824).

HOWELL, John (1788–1863), poly-artist, invented 'plough' for cutting edges of books; introduced manufacture of Pompeian plates; published *Life of Alexander Selkirk* (1829); contributed to Wilson's *Tales of the Borders*.

HOWELL, Laurence (1664?–1720), nonjuror; MA, Jesus College, Cambridge, 1688; ordained by George *Hickes, 1712; sentenced to fine, imprisonment, and whipping for his *Case of Schism in the Church of England stated* (1717); died in Newgate. His works include *Synopsis Canonum SS. Apostolorum, et Conciliorum Oecumenicorum et Provincialium*, etc. (1708), *Synopsis Canonum Ecclesiae Latinae* (1710), *View of the Pontificate* (1712).

HOWELL, Thomas (*fl.* 1568), author of *The Arbor of Amitie* (1568), *Newe Sonets and pretie Pamphlets* (1567–8), and *H. His Deuises* (1581).

HOWELL, Thomas (1588–1646), bishop of Bristol; brother of James *Howell; of Jesus College, Oxford; MA, 1612; DD, 1630; chaplain to Charles I; canon of Windsor, 1636; rector of Fulham, 1642; bishop of Bristol, 1644–6; died of effects of maltreatment at siege (1645) of Bristol.

HOWELL, Thomas Bayly (1768–1815), editor of *State Trials* (vols. i–xxi, 1809–15); of Christ Church, Oxford; barrister, Lincoln's Inn, 1790.

HOWELL, Thomas Jones (d. 1858), continuer of *State Trials* (vols. xxii–xxxiii); son of Thomas Bayly *Howell; of Lincoln's Inn.

HOWELL, William (1638?–1683), historian; fellow of Magdalene College, Cambridge; MA, 1655; chancellor of Lincoln; published *An Institution of General History* (1661) and *Medulla Historiae Anglicanae* (1679).

HOWELL, William (1656–1714), devotional writer; MA, New Inn Hall, Oxford, 1676; curate and schoolmaster of Ewelme.

HOWELL, William Gough (1922–1974), architect; educated at Marlborough College; served in Royal Air Force during 1939–45 war;

DFC, 1943; studied architecture at Gonville and Caius College, Cambridge, and Architectural Association School, London; qualified, 1952 and joined architect's department, London County Council; one of group responsible for LCC's Roehampton estate; left LCC to set up private practice, 1956; teacher at Regent Street Polytechnic; set up partnership of Howell, Killick, Partridge and Amis, 1959; received number of commissions for university buildings, including those for St Anne's and St Antony's colleges, Oxford, Downing and Darwin Colleges, Cambridge, and buildings at Birmingham and Reading universities; also played leading part in design of houses for visiting mathematicians at Warwick University and an arts centre for Christ's Hospital, Horsham; appointed professor of architecture, Cambridge, 1973; fellow, Caius College; vice-president, RIBA, 1965–7; ARA, 1974; published (in collaboration with Barbara Jones) *Popular Arts of the First World War* (1972); killed in motor-car accident.

HOWELLS, Herbert Norman (1892–1983), composer, teacher, and writer on music; educated at Lydney Grammar School; pupil of (Sir) A. Herbert *Brewer, organist of Gloucester Cathedral; won open scholarship to Royal College of Music, 1912; pupil of Sir Charles *Stanford and Sir C. Hubert H. *Parry; suffered breakdown of health while assistant organist, Salisbury Cathedral, 1916; taught theory and composition at RCM for over fifty years; editor, RCM magazine; director of music, St Paul's Girls' School, 1936–62; King Edward professor of music, London University, 1955–62; early works include Piano Quartet (1916) and Phantasy String Quartet (1918); also composed three concertos, six quarters, five instrumental sonatas, and large choral works, including *Hymnus Paradisi* (1938); CBE, 1953; CH, 1972; honorary degrees from Cambridge and RAM; D.Mus. Oxford; hon. fellow, St John's College, Cambridge, 1962, and The Queen's College, Oxford, 1977; master of the Worshipful Company of Musicians, 1959; president, Incorporated Society of Musicians, 1952, and Royal College of Organists, 1958–9.

HOWELLS, William (1778–1882), minister at Long Acre Chapel, London, 1817; of Wadham College, Oxford; his *Remains* edited (1833).

HOWEL VYCHAN (d. 825), Howel the Little; Welsh prince; fought with Cynan for Anglesey.

HOWEL Y FWYALL (*fl.* 1356), Howel of the Battle-axe; fought gallantly at Poitiers, 1356; knighted by the Black Prince, 1356; a mess of meat served before his axe and given to the poor till Queen Elizabeth's time.

HOWES, Edmund (*fl.* 1607–1631), continuator of *Stow's Abridgement* (1607 and 1611) and Stow's *Annales* or *Chronicles* (1615 and 1631).

HOWES, Edward (*fl.* 1650), mathematician; rector of Goldanger, Essex, 1659; sent John *Winthrop (1588–1649) tract defining locality of north-west passage; published *A Short Arithmetick* (1659).

HOWES, Francis (1776–1844), translator of Persius and Horace; of Trinity College, Cambridge; eleventh wrangler, 1798; MA, 1804; minor canon of Norwich, 1815; rector of Alderford, 1826–44, Framingham Pigot, 1829–44; his translations collected (1845).

HOWES, Frank Stewart (1891–1974), music critic and author; educated at Oxford High School and St John's College, Oxford, 1910–14; became schoolmaster and conscientious objector during 1914–18 war; studied at Royal College of Music, 1920–2; joined *The Times*, 1925; lectured at RCM, 1938–70; appointed senior music critic of *The Times*, 1943–60; publications include *The Borderland of Music and Psychology* (1926), *William Byrd* (1928), *A Key to Opera* (with P. *Hope-Wallace, 1939), *Full Orchestra* (1942), *The Music of William Walton* (2 vols., 1942–3, revised edn., 1965), *Man, Mind and Music* (1948), *The Music of Ralph Vaughan Williams* (1954), *The Cheltenham Festival* (1965), *The English Musical Renaissance* (1966), *Oxford Concerts* (1969), and *Folk Music of Britain—and Beyond* (1969); editor, *Journal of English Folk Dance and Song Society*, 1927–45; founder of Musica Britannica; president, Royal Music Association, 1948–58; CBE, 1954; hon. fellow, RCM; hon. RAM; hon. freeman, Worshipful Company of Musicians.

HOWES, John (*fl.* 1772–1793), miniature and enamel painter.

HOWES, Thomas (1729–1814), author of *Critical Observations on Books, Ancient and Modern* (1776); BA, Clare Hall, Cambridge, 1746; rector of Morningthorpe, 1756–71, Thorndon, 1771–1814.

HOWES, Thomas George Bond (1853–1905), zoologist; assisted T. H. *Huxley at Royal College of Science, South Kensington, till 1880; succeeded Huxley as professor of zoology, 1895; excellent teacher of biology and skilled draughtsman; published atlases of *Elementary Biology* (1885) and *Zootomy* (1902); made researches into comparative anatomy of the vertebrata; FRS, 1897; LL D, St Andrews, 1898.

HOWGILL, Francis (1618–1669), Quaker; successively churchman, Independent, and Anabaptist; with Anthony *Pearson held first Quaker meetings in London, 1653; preached in Ireland till banished by Henry *Cromwell; sentenced to perpetual imprisonment for refusing oath of allegiance, 1664; published Quaker works.

HOWGILL, William (*fl.* 1794), musical composer.

HOWICK, Viscount, afterwards second Earl Grey (1764–1845). See GREY, CHARLES.

HOWICK OF GLENDALE, first Baron (1903–1973), colonial governor. See BARING, (CHARLES) EVELYN.

HOWIE, John (1735–1793), author of *Scots Worthies* (1774 and 1781–5); farmer of Lochgoin, Ayrshire; published works concerning the Covenanters.

HOWISON (or **HOWIESON), William** (1798–1850), line-engraver; the only engraver ever elected ARSA; best known for engravings of Sir George *Harvey's pictures.

HOWISON, William (*fl.* 1823), author and friend of Sir Walter *Scott.

HOWITT, Alfred William (1830–1908), Australian anthropologist; son of William and Mary *Howitt; left Nottingham for Australia, 1852; explored central Australia, 1859; brought back remains of R. O'Hara *Burke and W. J. *Wills to Melbourne, 1862; police magistrate of Gippsland, 1862–89; made study of Australian aboriginal; admitted a member of the Kurnai tribe; with Lorimer *Fison published *Kamilaroi and Kurnai* (1880) and *The Kurnai Tribe* (1880); secretary of mines in Victoria, 1889, and commissioner of audit, 1896; chairman of Royal Commission on Coal-mining, 1905–6; chief work, *The Native Tribes of South-East Australia* (1904); CMG, 1906; died at Melbourne.

HOWITT, Sir **Harold Gibson** (1886–1969), chartered accountant; educated at Uppingham; articled to chartered accountant, W. R. Hamilton, 1904; qualified, joined W. B. Peat & Co. (later Peat, Marwick, Mitchell & Co.), London, 1909; partner, 1911–61; served in Green Howards, 1914–18; DSO; MC; engaged in many public commissions and inquiries and valuation problems; member, Air Council, 1939–45; chairman and deputy chairman, BOAC, 1943–8; member of council, NAAFI, 1940–6; chairman, Building Materials Board; financial adviser to Ministry of Works, 1943–5; president, Institute of Chartered Accountants in England and Wales, 1945–6; president, International Congress of Accountants, 1952; wrote *History of the Institute of Chartered Accountants in England and Wales 1880–1965* (1966); knighted, 1937; GBE, 1946; hon. DCL, Oxford, 1953; hon. LL D, Nottingham, 1958; chairman, trustees of Uppingham School, 1949–67.

HOWITT, Mary (1799–1888), author; née Botham; married William *Howitt, 1821, and collaborated with him in many works; published translations from Fredrika Bremer and Hans Andersen and successful children's books; other works include *Popular History of the United States* (1859); received civil list pension, 1879; died at Rome.

HOWITT, Richard (1799–1869), poet; brother of William *Howitt; druggist at Nottingham; lived in Australia, 1839–44; published *Impressions of Australia Felix* (1845), *Wasp's Honey* (1868).

HOWITT, Samuel (1765?–1822), painter and etcher; brother-in-law of *Rowlandson; exhibited at Academy, 1785–94, chiefly sporting subjects; published *Miscellaneous Etchings of Animals* (1803) and other works.

HOWITT, William (1792–1879), author; educated at Friends' School, Ackworth; published a poem at 13; published, with his wife, *The Forest Minstrel* and other poems; chemist at Nottingham; published *Book of the Seasons* (1831), *Popular History of Priestcraft* (1833), first series of *Visits to Remarkable Places* (1840; second series, 1842), *Rural and Domestic Life of Germany* (1842), when at Heidelberg; after three years in Australia issued *History of Discovery in Australia, Tasmania, and New Zealand* (1865) and Australian tales; became spiritualist; received civil list pension, 1865; wrote for *Cassell's Popular History of England*, 1856–62; died at Rome.

HOWLAND, Richard (1540–1600), bishop of Peterborough; BA, Christ's College, Cambridge, 1561; fellow of Peterhouse, 1562; MA, 1564; rector of Stathern, 1569; at first an adherent of Thomas *Cartwright (1535–1603), but afterwards a strong opponent; chaplain to Lord *Burghley; master of Magdalene (1576–7), and (1577–86) St John's colleges, Cambridge; vice-chancellor of Cambridge, 1577–8 and 1583–4; bishop of Peterborough, 1584–1600; friend of *Whitgift; attacked by Martin Mar-Prelate.

HOWLAND, Sir William Pearce (1811–1907), Canadian statesman; born in New York; went to Canada, 1830; bought mills near Toronto, 1840; Liberal MP for West York, Ontario, 1857; finance minister, 1862 and 1866; receiver-general, 1863; postmaster-general, 1864–6; at Canadian Federation Conference in London, 1866; minister of inland revenue in first confederation Cabinet, 1867–8; lieutenant-governor of Ontario, 1868–73; KCMG, 1879; promoted building of Canadian Pacific Railway, 1880.

HOWLET, John (1548–1589), Jesuit; fellow of Exeter College, Oxford, 1566; BA, 1566; resided at Douai; died at Wilna.

HOWLETT, Bartholomew (1767–1827), topographical and antiquarian draughtsman and engraver.

HOWLETT, John (1731–1804), political economist; MA, St John's College, Oxford, 1795; BD, 1796; incumbent of Great Dunmow and Great Baddow; published works on enclosures and population combating the views of Price.

HOWLETT, Samuel Burt (1794–1874), military surveyor and inventor; invented an anemometer and method of construction for large drawing-boards; published treatise on perspective (1828).

HOWLEY, Henry (1775?–1803), Irish insurgent; took part in rebellion of 1798, and Robert *Emmet's rising; executed.

HOWLEY, William (1766–1848), archbishop of Canterbury; of Winchester and New College, Oxford (fellow and tutor); MA, 1791; DD, 1805; vicar of Andover, 1802; rector of Bradford Peverell, 1811; canon of Christ Church, Oxford, 1804; regius professor of divinity, Oxford, 1809–13; bishop of London, 1813–28; supported bill of pains and penalties against Queen *Caroline, 1820; archbishop of Canterbury, 1828–48; opposed Catholic emancipation, 1829, parliamentary reform, 1831, and Jewish relief, 1833; carried vote of censure on Lord John Russell's education scheme, 1839.

HOWMAN, John (or FECKENHAM, John de) (1518?–1585). See FECKENHAM, JOHN DE.

HOWSON, John (1557?–1632), bishop of Durham; of St Paul's School and Christ Church, Oxford; MA, 1582; DD, 1601; prebendary of Hereford, 1587, Exeter, 1592; chaplain to Queen Elizabeth and James I; canon of Christ Church, 1601; vice-chancellor, 1602; bishop of Oxford, 1619–28, of Durham, 1628–32; buried in St Paul's.

HOWSON, John Saul (1816–1885), dean of Chester; wrangler, Trinity College, Cambridge; MA, 1841; DD, 1861; principal of Liverpool Collegiate Institution, 1849–66; Hulsean lecturer at Cambridge, 1862; vicar of Wisbech, 1866; dean of Chester, 1867–85; did good service in restoration of Chester Cathedral; active on behalf of Chester educational institutions; with W. J. *Conybeare published *Life and Epistles of St. Paul* (1852); published *Character of St. Paul* (1862) and other Pauline studies; Bohlen lecturer at Philadelphia, 1880; contributed to Smith's *Dictionary of the Bible* and biblical commentaries; wrote also controversial and archaeological works.

HOWTH, Barons. See ST LAWRENCE, ROBERT, third baron, d. 1483; ST LAWRENCE, NICHOLAS, fourth baron, d. 1526; ST LAWRENCE, Sir CHRIS-TOPHER, eighth baron, d. 1589; ST LAWRENCE, Sir NICHOLAS, ninth baron, 1550?–1607; ST LAW-RENCE, Sir CHRISTOPHER, tenth baron, 1568?–1619.

HOY, Thomas (1659–1721?), physician and author; fellow of St John's College, Oxford, 1675; MA, 1684; MD, 1689; regius professor of physic, 1698; published essay on Ovid's *De Arte Amandi* and Musaeus's *Hero and Leander* (1682), and *Agathocles* (poem, 1683); possibly died in Jamaica.

HOYLAND, Francis (*fl.* 1763), poet; BA, Magdalene College, Cambridge, 1748; introduced by *Mason to Horace *Walpole, who printed his *Poems* at Strawberry Hill (1769); published *Odes* (1783).

HOYLAND, Gilbert of (d. 1172). See GILBERT.

HOYLAND, John (1750–1831), Quaker author of *Historical Survey of Customs, Habits, and Present State of the Gypsies* (1816) and euhemeristic *Epitome of History of the World* (1812).

HOYLAND, John (1783–1827), organist at St James's, Sheffield, and at Louth, Lincolnshire; composed sacred music.

HOYLE, Edmond (1672–1769), writer on card games; gave lessons on whist in Queen Square, London, 1741; issued first edition of his *Short Treatise on Whist* (1742) at a guinea, second edition (1743) at two shillings; incorporated in eighth edition (1748) treatises on quadrille, piquet, and backgammon, and in the eleventh edition treatise on chess; Hoyle's *Laws* of 1760 ruled whist till 1864. His book on chess was re-issued (1808).

HOYLE, John (d. 1797?), author of dictionary of musical terms (1770 and 1791).

HOYLE, Joshua (d. 1654), Puritan divine; fellow of Trinity College, Dublin, 1609; DD; master of University College, Oxford, and regius professor of divinity, 1648–54; vicar of Stepney, 1641; member of Westminster Assembly of Divines.

HOYLE, William (1831–1886), Lancashire cotton-spinner and temperance reformer; published *Our National Resources and how they are wasted* (1871) and other works, including temperance hymns and songs.

HUBBARD, John Gellibrand, first Baron Addington (1805–1889), director of Bank of England, 1838; chairman of Public Works Loan Commission, 1853–89; Conservative MP, Buckingham, 1859–68, London, 1874–87; privy councillor, 1874; created Baron Addington, 1887; obtained inquiry into assessment of income tax, 1861; built and endowed St Alban's, Holborn, 1863.

HUBBARD, Louisa Maria (1836–1906), social reformer; born in St Petersburg; her *Work for Ladies in Elementary Schools* (1872), led to the establishment of training college for girls at Chichester, 1873; published *The Englishwoman's Year Book*, 1875–98; advocated nursing, massage, typewriting, and gardening as middle-class women's occupations; helped to form Working Ladies' Guild, 1876, and Teachers' Guild, 1884.

HUBBARD, William (1621?–1704), New England historian; left England, 1635; graduated at Harvard, 1642 (acting president, 1688); pastor of Congregational church, Ipswich, Massachusetts; his *History of New England* printed (1815 and 1848).

HUBBERTHORN, Richard (1628–1662), Quaker writer; officer in Parliamentary army; accompanied *Fox in his journeys in Lancashire and the eastern counties, and with him had interview with Charles II; collaborated with Fox and James *Nayler; died in Newgate.

HUBBOCK, William (*fl.* 1605), chaplain of the Tower; BA, Magdalen College, Oxford, 1581; fellow of Corpus Christi College, Oxford; MA, 1585; cited for Puritanical sermon, 1590; published *Apologie of Infants* (1595).

HUBERT, Sir Francis (d. 1629), poet; clerk in Chancery, 1601; author of *Historie of Edward the Second* (1629) and *Egypt's Favorite* (1631).

HUBERT WALTER (d. 1205), archbishop of Canterbury and statesman; trained under *Glanville; a baron of Exchequer, 1184–5; dean of York, 1186; justice of the curia regis, 1189; bishop of Salisbury, 1189; accompanied Richard I to Palestine and negotiated for him with Saladin; led back English crusaders to Sicily; visited the king in prison and came back to collect ransom; justiciar, 1193; suppressed Prince John's attempt at revolt; archbishop of Canterbury, 1193–1205; officiated at Richard's second coronation, 1194; developed Henry II's judicial and financial system; maintained good relations with Scotland; as legate held council at York, 1195, and London, 1200; unpopular with the clergy for forcing William *Fitzosbert from sanctuary, 1196; negotiated alliance with Flanders, truce with France, and pacification of Richard's quarrel with archbishop of Rouen, 1197; settled succession dispute in South Wales, 1197; caused land tax to be assessed by help of locally elected landowners and representatives of townships and hundreds, 1198; compelled by Innocent III to resign justiciarship, 1198; joined Richard in Normandy; returned as member of regency after his death; asserted elective character of the monarchy at John's coronation, 1199; chancellor, 1199–1205; on missions to France, 1201 and 1203; dissuaded John from expedition against France, 1205; recovered for his see right of coining money. His bones were identified in Canterbury Cathedral, 1890.

HUCHOWN (*fl.* 14th cent.), author of romances in alliterative verse.

HUCK, Richard (1720–1785). See SAUNDERS, RICHARD HUCK-.

HUCKELL, John (1729–1771), poet; BA, Magdalen Hall, Oxford, 1751; curate of Hounslow; his *Avon* printed by *Baskerville (1758).

HUDDART, James (1847–1901), Australian shipowner; joined uncle's shipping firm at Geelong, Australia, 1864; founded intercolonial steamship line, 1870; aimed at 'All Red Route' by starting Canadian-Australian Royal Mail Steamship line between Sydney and Vancouver (1893) and a line between Canada and England (1894); scheme failed through lack of English support.

HUDDART, Joseph (1741–1816), hydrographer and manufacturer; during ten years' service in the East India Company constructed charts of Sumatra and the Indian coast from Bombay to the Godavery; FRS, 1791; made fortune by manufacture of patent cordage.

HUDDESFORD, George (1749–1809), satirical poet; fellow of New College, Oxford, 1771–2; MA, 1780; pupil of Sir Joshua *Reynolds, who painted his portrait in *Two Gentlemen* (National Gallery); vicar of Loxley and incumbent of Wheler's Chapel, Spital Square, London; political satirist; contributed to *Salmagundi* (1791).

HUDDESFORD, William (1732–1772), antiquary; brother of George *Huddesford; fellow of Trinity College, Oxford, 1757; MA, 1756; BD, 1767; keeper of the Ashmolean, 1755–72; vicar of Bishop's Tachbrook, 1761; edited Edward *Lhuyd's *Lithophylacii Britannici Ichnographia* (1760), Martin Lister's *Synopsis Methodica Conchyliorum* (1760), and catalogue of Anthony à *Wood's manuscripts (1761).

HUDDLESTON, Sir Hubert Jervoise (1880–1950), soldier and administrator; educated at Bedford and Felsted; enlisted, 1898; commissioned, 1900; transferred to Egyptian Army, 1910; commanded Camel Corps, 1914–16; brigade in Palestine, 1916–18; chief staff officer and adjutant-general under Sir Lee *Stack, 1923–4; first commandant, Sudan Defence Force, 1925–30; major-general, 1933; commanded districts in India, 1934–8; governor-general, Sudan, 1940–7; DSO, 1917; KCMG, 1940; GCMG, 1947.

HUDDLESTON (or HUDLESTON), John (1608–1698), Benedictine; of Lancashire; while on the English mission was one of those who watched over Charles II at Moseley after Worcester, 1651; joined Benedictines; after Restoration received quarters in Somerset House; chaplain to Queen *Catherine, 1669; received Charles II into Roman Church on his deathbed; his account of Charles II's death reprinted in Foley's Jesuit records.

HUDDLESTON (alias DORMER), John (1636–1700). See DORMER.

HUDDLESTON, Sir John Walter (1815–1890), last baron of the Exchequer; educated in Ireland; barrister, Gray's Inn, 1839 (treasurer, 1859 and 1868); defended Cuffy the Chartist, 1848; with *Cockburn in Rugeley poisoning case; QC, 1857; MP, Canterbury, 1865–8, Norwich, 1874–5; judge-advocate of the Fleet, 1865–75; judge of common pleas, 1875–80; last baron of the Exchequer, 1875; judge of Queen's Bench, 1880–90.

HUDDLESTON (or HUDLESTON), Richard (1583–1655), Benedictine; uncle of John *Huddleston; converted many Yorkshire and Lancashire families; his *Short and Plain Way to the Faith and Church* published by his nephew (1688, reprinted 1844 and 1850).

HUDLESTON (formerly SIMPSON), Wilfred Hudleston (1828–1909), geologist; educated at Uppingham and St John's College, Cambridge; made ornithological collections in Lapland, Algeria, Eastern Atlas, Greece, and Turkey, 1855–60; FGS, 1867; president, 1892–4; FRS, 1884; travelled in India, 1895; published sixty papers dealing with jurassic system and oolite gasteropods, 1887–96, and Indian, Syrian, and African geology.

HUDSON, Charles Thomas (1828–1903), naturalist; BA, St John's College, Cambridge (fifteenth wrangler), 1852; MA, 1855; LL D, 1866; headmaster of Bristol Grammar School, 1855–60; conducted private school at Clifton, 1861–81; devoted leisure to microscopical research and to study of Rotifera; president of Royal Microscopical Society, 1888–90; FRS, 1889; published *The Rotifera: or Wheel-Animalculae* (1886–7).

HUDSON, George (1800–1871), 'railway king'; son of a Yorkshire farmer; made fortune as a draper at York; founded a banking company, and became mayor of York, 1837 and 1846; manager of York and North Midland Railway Company, opened 1839, of the Newcastle and Darlington, 1842, and of the newly formed Midland Railway; MP, Sunderland, 1845–59; chairman of Sunderland Dock Company; owing to questionable business and over-speculation resigned chairmanship of Midland, Eastern Counties, Newcastle and Berwick, and York and North Midland companies, and retired to continent, 1854; annuity bought for him, 1868.

HUDSON, Henry (d. 1611), navigator; made voyage in the *Hopeful* for Muscovy Company to realize *Thorne's scheme of passage across North Pole to 'islands of spicery', 1607; searched for north-east passage by the Waigatz or Kara Strait, 1608; in a voyage for the Dutch East India Company reached Novaya Zemlya, and, by examining the coast from Nova Scotia to Sandy Hook, discredited the notion of a strait across North America in low latitude; afterwards ascended the Hudson River to Albany, 1609; in final expedition to attempt north-west passage (1610), reached Hudson's Strait, and spent some time in the bay beyond; ice-bound in south of James's Bay; after struggle with mutineers was set adrift in a small boat with his son and others, and lost, 1611. Though he explored further than his predecessors, Hudson actually discovered neither the bay, nor straits, nor river called after him.

HUDSON, Henry (*fl.* 1784–1800), mezzotint engraver.

HUDSON, Sir James (1810–1885), diplomat; as private secretary to William IV sent to summon Peel from Rome, 1834; envoy to Rio de Janeiro, 1850, and at Turin, 1851–63; showed great sympathy with the Italian cause; GCB, 1863; died at Strasburg.

HUDSON, Jeffery (1619–1682), dwarf; eighteen inches high till 30; served up in a pie at dinner to Charles I; afterwards reached three feet six or nine inches; entered service of Queen *Henrietta Maria; his capture by Flemish pirates, 1630, celebrated in *D'Avenant's *Jeffreidos*; captain of horse in Civil Wars; went to Paris, 1649; captured by pirates while off the coast of France and carried to Barbary as a slave; managed to escape and return to England; imprisoned for supposed complicity in 'Popish Plot', 1679; released.

HUDSON, John (1662–1719), classical scholar; MA, The Queen's College, Oxford, 1684; fellow and tutor of University College, 1686; Bodley's librarian, 1701; principal of St Mary Hall, 1712; patron of Thomas *Hearne (1678–1735); edited Thucydides (with Latin version of Aemilius Portus, 1696), Dionysius Halicarnassus (1704), *Geographiae veteris Scriptores Graeci minores* (1698–1712), and other classical works.

HUDSON, Sir John (1833–1893), lieutenant-general; lieutenant, 64th Regiment, 1855; served in Persia, 1856–7, and Indian Mutiny, 1857–8;

captain, 43rd Light Infantry, 1858; in Abyssinia, 1867–8; in Afghan War, 1878–80; lieutenant-colonel, 1879; CB, 1881; commanded Indian contingent in Sudan, 1885; KCB, 1885; lieutenant-general, 1892; commander-in-chief in Bombay, 1893.

HUDSON, Mary (d. 1801), organist and composer; daughter of Robert *Hudson (1731–1815).

HUDSON, Michael (1605–1648), Royalist divine; MA, The Queen's College, Oxford, 1628; fellow, *c.*1630; tutor to Prince Charles, who, when king, gave him various livings; his chaplain at Oxford; scoutmaster to northern army, 1643–4; attended Charles I to Newark, 1646; escaped from prison, but was again captured, 1647, and sent to the Tower; again escaped, 1648, and promoted Royalist rising in eastern counties; wrote treatise in defence of divine right (printed 1647), and *Account of King Charles I* (printed 1731); killed while defending Woodcroft, Northamptonshire.

HUDSON, Robert (*fl.* 1600), poet; Chapel Royal musician of James VI; friend of Alexander *Montgomerie; four of his sonnets extant.

HUDSON, Robert (1731–1815), vicar-choral (1756) and master of the children (1773) at St Paul's Cathedral; Mus.Bac., Cambridge, 1784; published *The Myrtle* (songs, 1762) and church music.

HUDSON, Sir Robert Arundell (1864–1927), political organizer; obtained post in National Liberal Federation, Birmingham, 1882; removed with Federation to London, 1886; secretary of Federation and of Liberal Central Association, 1893; influential in guiding party through troublous period; successful chairman of joint finance committee of British Red Cross Society and Order of St John of Jerusalem, 1914; knighted, 1906; GBE, 1918.

HUDSON, Robert George Spencer (1895–1965), geologist, stratigrapher, and palaeontologist; educated at lower school of Lawrence Sheriffe, Rugby; student teacher, Elborrow Boys' School, 1913; entered St Paul's Training College, Cheltenham, 1914; joined Artists' Rifles, 1916; served in France as machine-gunner; entered University College, London, 1918; B.Sc., first class, geology, 1920; part-time demonstrator in geology, University College, 1920–2; M.Sc., 1922; assistant lecturer, Leeds University, 1922–7; lecturer, 1927–39; professor, 1939–40; edited *Transactions of the Leeds Geological Association*, 1927–40; consultant geologist, 1942; involved in petroleum geology; appointed to staff of Iraq Petroleum Company, 1946; hon. lecturer in geology, University College, London,

1947–58; lecturer in palaeontology, Trinity College, Dublin, 1959; professor of geology and mineralogy, 1961–5; important contributor to the palaeontology, stratigraphy, and palaeogeography of the Carboniferous of north of England and the Mesozoic of the Middle East; fellow, Geological Society of London, 1921; vice-president, 1955–7; president, Yorkshire Geological Society, 1940–2; FRS, 1961; fellow, University College, London; president, Irish Geological Association, 1964–5.

HUDSON, Robert Spear, first Viscount Hudson (1886–1957), politician; educated at Eton and Magdalen College, Oxford; in Diplomatic Service, 1911–23; Conservative MP, Whitehaven, 1924–9, Southport, 1931–52; parliamentary secretary, Ministry of Labour, 1931–5, of Health, 1936–7; minister of pensions, 1935–6; secretary, Department of Overseas Trade, 1937–40; minister of agriculture and fisheries, 1940–5; achieved agricultural revolution in production and attitudes, decentralizing powers and introducing guaranteed prices and markets; PC, 1938; CH, 1944; viscount, 1952.

HUDSON, Thomas (*fl.* 1610), poet; probably brother of Robert *Hudson (*fl.* 1600); master of James VI's Chapel Royal, 1586; author of a version of Du Bartas's *Historie of Judith* (1584); contributor to *England's Parnassus* (1600).

HUDSON, Thomas (1701–1779), portrait painter; pupil and son-in-law of Jonathan *Richardson the elder; for two years *Reynolds's master; painted *Handel and George II.

HUDSON, William (d. 1635), lawyer; barrister, Gray's Inn, 1605; bencher, 1623, Lent reader, 1624; opened case against *Prynne, 1633; his *Treatise of the Court of Star Chamber* printed (1792).

HUDSON, William (1730?–1793), botanist; sub-librarian, British Museum, 1757–8; FRS, 1761; *praefectus horti*, Chelsea, 1765–71; original member of Linnean Society, 1791; published *Flora Anglica* (1762, enlarged 1778); genus *Hudsonia* named after him.

HUDSON, William Henry (1841–1922), naturalist and writer; born near Buenos Aires; ran wild on farms and ranches of Rio de la Plata; watched bird life of great plains with care and passion; his career entirely changed by fever, which affected his heart, at age of 15; went to England, 1869; lived for some years in drab London boarding-house surroundings and in considerable poverty; published *The Purple Land that England Lost* (1885), *A Crystal Age* (1887), *Argentine Ornithology* (with Dr P. L. Sclater, 1888–9); *The Naturalist in La Plata* (1892) first book to bring him into prominence; followed it with *Birds*

in a Village (1893); thenceforth his books had increasing sale; awarded civil list pension, 1901; his most interesting book *Far Away and Long Ago* (1918); his philosophy of life based upon observation of animal world; possessed an absolute freedom of spirit and detachment combined with great sensitiveness and receptivity, and an almost mystical sense of natural beauty.

HUEFFER, Ford Hermann (1873–1939). See FORD, FORD MADOX.

HUEFFER, Francis (Franz Hüffer) (1845–1889), musical critic; born at Münster; Ph.D., Göttingen, 1869; came to London, 1869; naturalized, 1882; assistant editor of the *Academy*, c.1871; edited *New Quarterly Magazine* and *Musical World*, 1886; musical critic of *The Times*, 1879; published *Richard Wagner and the Music of the Future* (1874), *The Troubadours* (1878), and other works; translated *Correspondence of Wagner and Liszt* (1888).

HUES, Robert (1553?–1632), geographer; BA, Magdalen Hall, Oxford, 1578; sailed round the world with Thomas *Cavendish; friend of *Chapman; published *Tractatus de Globis et eorum Usu* (1594).

HUET (or HUETT), Thomas (d. 1591), Welsh biblical scholar; BA, Corpus Christi College, Cambridge, 1562; master of Holy Trinity College, Pontefract; precentor of St David's, 1562–88; translated Revelation in Welsh version of New Testament, 1567.

HÜGEL, Friedrich Von, baron of the Holy Roman Empire (1852–1925), theologian. See VON HÜGEL.

HUGESSEN, Edward Hugessen Knatchbull-, first Baron Brabourne (1829–1893). See KNATCHBULL-HUGESSEN.

HUGESSEN, Sir Hughe Montgomery Knatchbull- (1886–1971), diplomat. See KNATCHBULL-HUGESSEN.

HUGFORD, Ferdinando Enrico (1696–1771), monk of Vallombrosa and promoter of the art of scagliola.

HUGFORD, Ignazio Enrico (1703–1778), painter and art critic at Florence; born of English parents at Florence; brother of Ferdinando Enrico *Hugford; compiler of *Raccolta di cento Pensieri diversi di Anton Domenico Gabbiani* (1762).

HUGGARDE (or HOGGARDE), Miles (*fl.* 1557), poet and writer against the Reformation; published *The Abuse of the Blessed Sacrament* (1548), *The Displaying of the Protestants* (1556), and other controversial works in prose and verse.

HUGGINS, Godfrey Martin, first Viscount Malvern (1883–1971), Rhodesian statesman; educated at Malvern College; studied at St Thomas's Hospital, London; MRCS and LRCP, 1906; FRCS, 1908; house surgeon, St Thomas's and medical superintendent, Hospital for Sick Children, Great Ormond Street, London; emigrated to Southern Rhodesia and joined medical partnership in Salisbury, 1911; served during 1914–18 war as surgeon in RAMC; published *Amputation Stumps: Their Care and After-Treatment* (1918); consultant surgeon, leading Rhodesian medical man, 1921; elected as Rhodesia party member for Salisbury North in Legislative Assembly, 1924; left party in protest against economy measures, 1931; became leader of Reform party, 1932; prime minister, 1933–53; Reform party and Rhodesia party joined to form United party, 1934; in favour of closer union of Southern Rhodesia with Northern Rhodesia (Zambia) and Nyasaland (Malawi); Southern Rhodesia made remarkable war effort in British cause, 1939–45; Central African Council set up, 1944; secondary industries developed; Huggins's services recognized with KCMG (1941), CH (1944), PC (1947); abandoned policy of African segregation in favour of Euro-African co-operation; prime minister of Federation of Rhodesia and Nyasaland, 1953–6; initiated construction of Kariba Dam; received number of honorary doctorates; created first Viscount Malvern, 1955; Federation dissolved, 1963; white Rhodesia broke away from British allegiance, 1965; when he died, Malvern was all but forgotten.

HUGGINS, John (*fl.* 1729). See BAMBRIDGE, THOMAS.

HUGGINS, Samuel (1811–1885), architectural writer; president of Liverpool Architectural Society, 1856–8; Society for the Protection of Ancient Buildings largely due to his papers against 'restorations' of cathedrals.

HUGGINS, William (1696–1761), translator of Ariosto's *Orlando Furioso* (1755); MA, Magdalen College, Oxford, 1719; fellow, 1722; wardrobe-keeper at Hampton Court, 1721.

HUGGINS, William (1820–1884), animal painter; brother of Samuel *Huggins; exhibited at Royal Academy from 1846.

HUGGINS, Sir William (1824–1910), astronomer; son of London silk mercer; educated at City of London School; after a few years in business, built observatory at Tulse Hill, 1856; applied to stars the methods of Kirchhoff's researches (1862) into chemical constitution of sun; with William Allen *Miller devised the star spectroscope, and presented to Royal Society results of first investigations with it in 'Lines of

the Spectra of Some of the Fixed Stars' (1863), showing that in structure the stars resemble the sun; FRS, 1865; awarded Royal Medal, 1866; president, 1900–6; president of the Royal Astronomical Society, 1876–8; made observations of nebula in Orion (1865) and of several comets; examined motions of Sirius (1868) and other stars; with refracting telescope determined (1870–5) the velocity of stars; photographed successfully the spectrum of Vega (1876), of larger stars, of the moon, and the planets; method applied to great nebula in Orion, 1882; hon. LL D, Cambridge, 1870; DCL, Oxford, 1871; awarded medals from Royal and Royal Astronomical societies, and from foreign and American societies; awarded civil list pension, 1890; president of British Association, 1891; KCB, 1897; OM, 1902; observed the new star in Auriga, 1892; made valuable researches as to extent and presence of calcium in sun, 1897; published results of work in *An Atlas of Representative Stellar Spectra* (1900) and *The Scientific Papers of Sir William Huggins* (1909); helped much by his wife in his researches.

HUGGINS, William John (1781–1845), marine painter to George IV and William IV.

HUGH (d. 1164), abbot of Reading and archbishop of Rouen; born in Laon; abbot of Reading, 1125; archbishop of Rouen, 1130; founded abbey of St Martin of Aumale; supported Innocent II against the antipope Anacletus; attended Council of Pisa, 1134, and Henry I on his deathbed; supporter of Stephen; reconciled earl of *Gloucester and count of Boulogne; his works in Migne's *Patrologiae Cursus*.

HUGH, William (d. 1549), author of *The Troubled Mans Medicine* (two parts 1546; another edition 1567; reprinted 1831); MA, Corpus Christi College, Oxford, 1543.

HUGH ALBUS (or **CANDIDUS**) (*fl.* 1107?–1155?), chronicler; monk and sometime sub-prior of Peterborough; his (Latin) *History of Peterborough Abbey* to 1155, printed by Joseph *Sparke (1723); authorship of Peterborough English *Chronicle* probably wrongly ascribed to him.

HUGHES, Arthur (1832–1915), painter; studied under Alfred *Stevens at Somerset House School of Design and at Royal Academy Schools; adopted Pre-Raphaelite principles; exhibited at Royal Academy, 1856–1908; chief pictures *The Knight of the Sun* and *Home from Sea*; illustrated poems of *Tennyson, Christina *Rossetti, works of George *MacDonald, etc.

HUGHES, David (1813–1872), Welsh writer; graduated at Glasgow; Independent minister at St Asaph, Bangor, and Tredegar; published

Geiriadur Ysgrythyrol a Duwinyddol ('Scriptural and Theological Dictionary', 1852); edited English–Welsh dictionary of Caerfallwch (see EDWARDS, THOMAS).

HUGHES, David Edward (1830–1900), electrician and inventor; born in London; went to Virginia, 1837; educated at St Joseph's College, Bardstown, Kentucky, and became professor of music, 1849; patented improved type-printing telegraph, 1855; invented microphone almost simultaneously with Lüdtge, 1878; FRS, 1880; received society's Gold Medal, 1885; president of Society of Telegraph Engineers, 1886; manager (1889) and vice-president (1891) of Royal Institution; Albert medallist, Society of Arts, 1898.

HUGHES, Sir Edward (1720?–1794), admiral; at reduction of Porto Bello, 1739, and attempt on Cartagena, 1741; attained post-rank, 1748; commanded the *Somerset* at Louisbourg, 1758, and Quebec, 1759; commander in East Indies, 1773–7; rear-admiral and KB, 1778; vice-admiral, 1780; during second command in East Indies (1778–83) co-operated in capture of Negapatam, 1781, and Trincomalee, 1782, from Dutch, and fought five indecisive battles with French under M de Suffren (1782–3); admiral of the blue, 1793.

HUGHES, Edward (1832–1908), portrait painter; taught by father and by John *Pye; student at Royal Academy Schools; exhibited at Royal Academy from 1847, at first subject pictures, but later portraits; excelled in portraits of ladies, who included Queen *Mary and Queen *Alexandra; idealized sitters; work reproduced in *The Book of Beauty* (1896).

HUGHES, Edward David (1906–1963), organic chemist; educated at Portmadoc Grammar School and University College, Bangor; first class, chemistry, 1927; researched on prototropy, 1927–30; Ph.D., 1930; post-doctoral fellow, University College, London, 1930; worked with Professor (Sir) C. K. *Ingold on the classification of organic mechanisms; M.Sc., 1932; D.Sc. (London), 1936; appointed lecturer, 1937; professor of chemistry, University College, Bangor, 1943–8; professor of chemistry, University College, London, 1948; deputy head of department, 1957; head, 1961; FRS, 1949; fellow, UCL, 1954; vice-president, Chemical Society, 1956–9; published many papers on organic reaction mechanisms.

HUGHES, Edward Hughes Ball (d. 1863); stepson of Sir Edward *Hughes; social celebrity known as the 'Golden Ball'.

HUGHES, George (1603–1667), Puritan divine; MA, Pembroke College, Oxford, 1625; fellow, 1625; lecturer of All Hallows, Bread Street, London, 1631; suspended for nonconformity, 1633; chaplain to Lord *Brooke and rector of Tavistock; vicar of St Andrew's, Plymouth, 1643–62; imprisoned in St Nicholas Island, 1665; published theological works.

HUGHES, Griffith (*fl.* 1750), author of *Natural History of Barbados* (1750); FRS, 1750; rector of St Lucy's, Barbados.

HUGHES, Henry George (1810–1872), Irish judge; of Trinity College, Dublin; Irish barrister, 1834; published *Chancery Practice* (1837); QC, 1844; solicitor-general for Ireland under Russell, 1850–2, and Palmerston, 1858–9; baron of Irish Exchequer, 1859–72.

HUGHES, Hugh (Y Bardd Coch) (1693–1776), Welsh poet, whose works are in *Diddanwch Teuluaidd neu waith Beirdd Môn* (1763); published also translations from English.

HUGHES, Hugh (1790?–1863), Welsh artist and author; expelled by Welsh Calvinistic Methodists for support of Catholic emancipation; joined Plymouth Brethren; drew and engraved *Beauties of Cambria* (1823), and published *Hynaphion Cymreig* (1823) and other works.

HUGHES, Hugh (Tegai) (1805–1864), Welsh poet; Independent minister in Caernarfonshire, at Jackson Street, Manchester, and at (1859) Aberdare; competed at Eisteddfodau; published works on Welsh grammar and composition, poems, and theological works.

HUGHES, Hugh Price (1847–1902), Methodist divine; BA, London, 1869; MA, 1881; from 1884 leader in London of the Methodist 'forward movement'; started *Methodist Times*, 1885, and West London Mission, 1886; promoted Free Church Congress, 1892; first president, National Free Church Council, 1896, and president of Wesleyan Methodist Conference, 1898; magnetic evangelical preacher; a radical in politics, but an imperialist; supported South African War, 1899–1901; opposed Conservative Education Act, 1902; published religious works.

HUGHES, Jabez (1685?–1731), translator of Suetonius' *Lives of the XII Caesars* (1717), parts of Lucan and Claudian, and novels by Cervantes.

HUGHES, James (Iago Trichrug) (1779–1844), Welsh Calvinistic Methodist; author of *New Testament Expositor* (1829–35).

HUGHES, John (1677–1720), poet; brother of Jabez *Hughes; employed in Ordnance Office; secretary to commissions of the peace in court of Chancery, 1717; wrote two volumes of *Kennett's *History of England* (1706); edited *Spenser (1715; reissued, 1750); his *Siege of Damascus* (1720) successfully produced at Drury Lane, and

Calypso and Telemachus at Queen's Theatre, Haymarket, 1712; contributed to *Tatler, Spectator*, and *Guardian*; with Sir Richard *Blackmore wrote *The Lay Monk* (1713–14); friend of Thomas *Britton, at whose concerts he played the violin; his *Venus and Adonis* set by *Handel; *Poems on Several Occasions* edited by his brother-in-law, William *Duncombe (1735); translated works by Fontenelle and others.

HUGHES, John (1776–1843), Wesleyan preacher in Wales and Manchester; author of *Essay on Ancient and Present State of the Welsh Language* (1823) and other works.

HUGHES, John (1787–1860), Welsh divine; vicar of Aberystwyth, 1827; archdeacon of Cardigan, 1859; translated part of *Henry's *Commentary* and Hall's *Meditations* into Welsh.

HUGHES, John (1790–1857), author and artist; of Westminster and Oriel College, Oxford; MA, 1815; published *Itinerary of Provence and the Rhone* (1822); edited *The Boscobel Tracts* (1830 and 1857).

HUGHES, John (1796–1860), Calvinistic Methodist pastor at Liverpool, 1838–60; published *History of Welsh Calvinistic Methodism* (1851, 1854, 1856, 3 vols.), and Welsh theological works.

HUGHES, John (1842–1902), Wesleyan Methodist divine; entered ministry, 1867; an eloquent preacher and writer in Welsh of religious prose and verse under bardic name of 'Glanystwyth'.

HUGHES, John Ceiriog (1832–1887), Welsh poet; farmer, clerk at Manchester, and finally station-master on Cambrian Railway; won prizes at the London Eisteddfod, 1856, at Llangollen, 1858, and Merthyr, 1860; his *Owain Wyn* (1856) the best Welsh pastoral; published about 600 songs, including the original song for which Brinley Richards wrote the air, 'God Bless the Prince of Wales'; contributed to Welsh periodicals.

HUGHES, Joshua (1807–1889), bishop of St Asaph; of St David's College, Lampeter; intimate of Thirlwall; vicar of Llandovery, 1846–70; DD, Lambeth; bishop of St Asaph, 1870–89; promoted Welsh services and higher education.

HUGHES, Lewis (*fl.* 1620), chaplain in the Bermudas; among early settlers, 1612; member of council, 1615; quarrelled with Governor *Tucker; again member of council, 1622; settled in England, *c.*1625; wrote against the church service, 1640–1.

HUGHES, Margaret (d. 1719), actress and mistress of Prince *Rupert; the first recorded Desdemona (1663); original Theodosia of *Dryden's *Evening's Love*, 1668; played in Duke of York's Company, Dorset Garden, in plays by *D'Urfey, *Sedley, and others, 1676–7.

HUGHES, Obadiah (1695–1751), Presbyterian minister; DD, King's College, Old Aberdeen, 1728; secretary to Presbyterian Board, 1738–50; Williams trustee; Salters' Hall lecturer, 1746.

HUGHES, Sir Richard, second baronet (1729?–1812), admiral; took part in reduction of Pondicherry, 1760–1; commander-in-chief at Halifax, Nova Scotia, 1778–80 and 1789–92; rear-admiral, 1780; commanded division in relief of Gibraltar, 1782; commander-in-chief in West Indies, 1784–6; admiral, 1794.

HUGHES, Richard Arthur Warren (1900–1976), novelist, playwright, and poet; educated at Charterhouse and Oriel College, Oxford; published *Gipsy-night, and Other Poems* (1922), and plays, *The Sisters' Tragedy* (1922) and *Danger* (1924), written for radio and produced by (Sir) Nigel *Playfair for the BBC, followed by a best-selling novel, *A High Wind in Jamaica* (1929); further novels are *In Hazard* (1938), *The Fox in the Attic* (1961), and *The Wooden Shepherdess* (1973); books and radio-plays widely translated; appointed Gresham professor of rhetoric, Gresham College; delivered notable lectures on Lady Murasaki's *The Tale of Genji*; edited poems of John *Skelton, 1924; during 1939–45 war worked at Admiralty, OBE, 1946; author (with J. D. Scott) of *The Administration of War Production* (1955) in the Official History of the War; FRSL; hon. D.Litt., University of Wales, 1956.

HUGHES, Robert Ball (1806–1868), sculptor; exhibited busts of Wellington and the duke of *Sussex and other works at the Academy; lived in the United States from 1829; exhibited statue of Oliver Twist at exhibition of 1851.

HUGHES, Robert (Robin Ddu o Fon) (1744?–1785), Welsh poet; his 'Cywydd Molawd Mon' and two Englynion printed in *Diddanwch Teuluaidd* (1817); other poems in *Brython* and other publications.

HUGHES, Sir Sam (1853–1921), Canadian soldier and politician; born in Ontario; represented Victoria County in Federal House as Conservative, 1892–1921; served in South African War, 1899; minister of militia and defence, 1911–16; KCB, 1915; lieutenant-general, 1916.

HUGHES, Thomas (*fl.* 1587), dramatist; fellow of Queens' College, Cambridge, 1576; BA, 1576; of Gray's Inn; chief author of *The Misfortunes of Arthur*, played before Elizabeth at Greenwich, 1588, by members of Gray's Inn.

HUGHES, Thomas (1822–1896), author of *Tom Brown's School Days*; educated at Rugby and

Oriel College, Oxford; BA, 1845; entered Lincoln's Inn, 1845; barrister, Inner Temple, 1848; QC, 1869; bencher, 1870; follower of Frederick Denison *Maurice; assisted in work of Christian Socialism; published anonymously (1857) *Tom Brown's School Days*, which was immediately successful; active in founding and carrying on Working Men's College, Great Ormond Street, being principal, 1872–83; Liberal MP, Lambeth, 1865, Frome, 1868–74; established (1879) in Tennessee a model community which proved unsuccessful; county-court judge, 1882–96. His publications include *The Scouring of the White Horse* (1859) and *Tom Brown at Oxford* (1861), lives of Bishop Fraser (1887), Daniel *Macmillan (1882), *Livingstone (1889), and *Alfred the Great (1869).

HUGHES, Thomas Smart (1786–1847), author; of Shrewsbury and St John's College, Cambridge; MA, 1811; Browne medallist, 1806 and 1807, members' prizeman, 1809 and 1810; Seatonian prizeman, 1817; BD, 1818; described his travels in Sicily, Greece, and Albania, 1820; fellow successively of St John's, Trinity Hall, and Emmanuel colleges; prebendary of Peterborough, 1827; published continuation of *Hume and *Smollett's history from 1760 (3rd edn. 1846) and editions of English divines.

HUGHES, William (d. 1600), bishop of St Asaph; fellow of Christ's College, Cambridge, 1557; MA, 1560; DD, 1575; chaplain to Thomas, fourth duke of *Norfolk; gave offence by sermon at Leicester on the descent into hell, 1567; bishop of St Asaph, 1573–1600; guilty of pluralism and maladministration as bishop, but encouraged the use of Welsh and aided William *Morgan (1540?–1604) in his Welsh Bible.

HUGHES, William (*fl.* 1665–1683), author of *The Complete Vineyard* (1665) and other horticultural works.

HUGHES, William (d. 1798), vicar of St Peter's, Worcester, and from 1741 minor canon of Worcester; published *Remarks upon Church Music* (1763).

HUGHES, William (1793–1825), wood engraver in style of *Thurston.

HUGHES, William (1803–1861), writer on law and angling; nephew of Sir Richard *Hughes; conveyancer, of Gray's Inn; published *Concise Precedents in Modern Conveyancing, Practice of Sales of Real Property*, and books by 'Piscator'.

HUGHES, William Little (1822–1887), translator from English into French; employee in French Ministry of the Interior.

HUGHES, William Morris (1862–1952), Australian prime minister; born in London of Welsh parents; educated at Llandudno Grammar School and St Stephen's, Westminster; emigrated to Queensland, 1884; set up shop in dockside slum, Sydney, 1886; secretary, Sydney Wharf Labourers' Union, 1899–1915; founder and first president, Waterside Workers' Federation, 1902; called to bar, 1903; KC, 1919; Labour member, New South Wales parliament, 1894–1901; member, federal House of Representatives, 1901–52; overcame handicaps of ill health and deafness to become superb orator and dominating figure, nationally known as 'Billy'; minister for external affairs, 1904; attorney-general, 1908–9; favouring strong defence policy, persuaded his party and government of Alfred *Deakin to adopt policy of compulsory military training, serving within Australia, 1909; attorney-general, 1910–13, 1914–21; party leader and prime minister, 1915–17; in England and France, 1916, vigorously advocating total war effort; at home his advocacy of conscription rejected; with Liberals formed Nationalist party, 1917, remaining prime minister until 1923; in England, 1918–19, and at Paris Peace Conference; favoured harsh terms; obtained separate recognition for Australia as signatory to treaty and in League of Nations; lost confidence of Nationalist party as too socialistic; upon coalition with Country party induced to cede leadership and premiership, 1923; voted with Labour to defeat government, 1929; joined United Australia party, 1931; deputy leader, 1939–41, 1943–4; leader, 1941–3; minister, repatriation and health, 1934–5, 1936–7; external affairs, 1937–9; industry, 1939–40; navy, 1940–1; attorney-general, 1939–41; member, War Advisory Council, 1941–4; PC, 1916; CH, 1941.

HUGHES-HALLETT, John (1901–1972), vice-admiral; educated at Bedford School and Royal Naval colleges, Osborne and Dartmouth and for a year after the 1914–18 war at Gonville and Caius College, Cambridge; served in battle cruiser *Lion*, 1918; entered torpedo branch and earned praise for numerous inventions; learnt to fly; secretary to Anglo-German naval conference, 1935; executive officer of cruiser *Devonshire* in Norwegian campaign, 1940; captain; on defence division of naval staff, 1940; chairman, Low-cover Radar Committee; naval adviser to combined operations, 1941; naval commander of Dieppe raid, 1942; DSO, 1942; commander, Force J; lent to organization preparing for invasion of France; responsible for initial naval plan; played major role in conception of artificial harbours; appointed to command cruiser *Jamaica*; in North Cape battle when *Scharnhorst* was sunk, 1943; CB, 1945; commanded torpedo school at HMS *Vernon*; captain, aircraft carrier

Illustrious; rear-admiral, 1950; vice-controller of the navy; commander, heavy squadron, Home Fleet, 1952–3; vice-admiral; resigned, 1954; Conservative MP for Croydon East (later Croydon North-East), 1955–64; British representative to consultative assembly, Council of Europe and to assembly of Western European Union, 1958–60; third parliamentary secretary, Ministry of Transport, responsible for shipping and shipbuilding, 1961; consultant director, British Shipping Council, 1964–9.

HUGH OF AVALON (or LINCOLN), Saint (1135?–1200), bishop of Lincoln; entered Grande Chartreuse, *c*.1160, afterwards becoming bursar; invited to England by Henry II, *c*.1175, to become head of the Carthusian house of Witham, Somerset; adviser of Henry II; liberal to the poor and the lepers; bishop of Lincoln, 1186–1200; excommunicated chief forester in his diocese, and successfully resisted election of royal nominee to a Lincoln prebend; regarded alleged miracles with dislike; went on embassy to France, 1189; joined opposition to *Longchamp, and refused to suspend *Geoffrey of York; excommunicated John, 1194; a leader in first refusal of a money grant, 1198; pacified Richard I in interview at Roche d'Andeli; much courted by John; canonized, 1220, and twice translated. He rebuilt the greater part of his cathedral, where his shrine was much frequented.

HUGH OF AVRANCHES, earl of Chester (d. 1101), perhaps nephew of William I; as viscount of Avranches contributed sixty ships to invasion of England; received earldom of Chester with palatine powers, 1071, and lands in twenty shires; faithful to William II in England, but supported his brother Henry in Normandy, and became one of his chief advisers when king; endowed monastery of St Werburgh's, Chester; carried on savage wars with the Welsh, gaining name of Lupus (the Wolf); conquered Anglesey and North Wales.

HUGH OF BALSHAM (d. 1286). See BALSHAM, HUGH DE.

HUGH OF BUCKLAND, (d. 1119?), sheriff. See BOCLAND, HUGH DE.

HUGH OF CYVEILIOG, palatine earl of Chester (d. 1181); succeeded his father *Randulf II in Chester, Avranches, and Bayeux, 1153; present at Council of Clarendon, 1164; raised Bretons against Henry II, but was forced to surrender at Dol, 1173; imprisoned in England and Normandy, and not restored till 1177; went to Ireland with William *Fitzaldhelm; succeeded by son and four co-heiresses.

HUGH OF EVESHAM (d. 1287). See EVESHAM.

HUGH OF GRANTMESNIL (or GRENTE-MAISNIL) (d. 1094), baron and sheriff of Leicestershire; restored abbey of St Evroul, and became abbot, 1059; expelled by Duke William, 1063; went to Italy; recalled to Normandy; present at Hastings, 1066; left in command of Hampshire, 1067; returned to Normandy, 1068; joined barons against William II, 1088; carried on war against Robert of *Bellême, 1091; died a monk in England.

HUGH OF HERTELPOLL (or HARTLE-POOL) (d. 1302?), Franciscan; one of the two 'proctors' for Balliol College, Oxford, 1282; one of Edward I's proctors to negotiate with France, 1302.

HUGH OF LINCOLN, Saint (1246?–1255), a child supposed to have been crucified by a Jew named Copin at Lincoln after having been tortured or starved. His body was buried near that of *Grosseteste in the cathedral. The story, a frequent theme for poets, is referred to by *Chaucer and *Marlowe.

HUGH OF MONTGOMERY, second earl of Shrewsbury and Arundel (d. 1098), second son of *Roger of Montgomery; helped to hold Rochester Castle against William II, 1088; succeeded to his father's earldoms, 1094; warred with the Welsh; slain in Anglesey by Norse allies of Welsh.

HUGH OF NEWCASTLE (*fl.* 1322). See NEW-CASTLE.

HUGH OF WELLS (d. 1235), bishop of Lincoln; deputy to Chancellor Walter de Grey; archdeacon of Wells, 1204; bishop of Lincoln, 1209–35; having joined *Langton against King John, lived abroad, 1209–13; received favours from King John and supported him against the barons; after John's death acted with the French party and had to pay large sums to recover his see, 1217; justice-itinerant, 1219. As bishop he established vicarages in parishes where the tithes had been appropriated by monastic bodies, and with the help of *Grosseteste made a great visitation; built nave of Lincoln Cathedral and completed hall of the palace, besides establishing future palace at Buckden; co-operated with his brother, *Jocelin (d. 1242), in reorganization of Wells Cathedral and foundation of hospital of St John Baptist.

HUGO, Thomas (1820–1876), historian and Bewick collector; BA, Worcester College, Oxford, 1842; vicar of St Botolph's, Bishopsgate, London, 1852–8; perpetual curate of All Saints, Bishopsgate, 1858–68; rector of West Hackney, 1868–76; high-church preacher and hymnologist; active FSA; published works include *The*

Bewick Collector (1866; supplement 1868), and *Mediaeval Nunneries of Somerset* (1867).

HUICKE, Robert (d. 1581?), physician to Henry VIII, Edward VI, and Elizabeth; fellow of Merton College, Oxford, 1529; MA, 1533; principal of St Alban Hall, 1535; deprived for denunciation of schoolmen, 1535; MD, Cambridge, 1538; five times censor of College of Physicians, and president, 1551, 1552, and 1564.

HUISH, Alexander (1594?–1668), biblical scholar; first graduate of Wadham College, Oxford, 1614; fellow, 1615–29; MA, 1616; BD, 1627; prebendary of Wells, 1627; deprived of benefices in Somerset, but restored, 1660; assisted Brian *Walton in 'Polyglott Bible', collating the Alexandrian MS.

HUISH, Robert (1777–1850), miscellaneous writer; his publications include a *Treatise on Nature, Economy, and Practical Management of Bees* (1815).

HULBERT, Charles (1778–1857), author, cotton manufacturer, and publisher; drew up report on management of factories, 1808; published *History of Salop* (1837) and *Cheshire Antiquities* (1838).

HULBERT, Charles Augustus (1805–1888), divine and parochial annalist; son of Charles *Hulbert; of Shrewsbury and Sidney Sussex College, Cambridge; MA, 1837; incumbent of Slaithwaite, Yorkshire, 1839–67; vicar of Almondbury, 1867–88.

HULBERT, John Norman ('Jack') (1892–1978), actor, producer, and theatre manager; educated at Westminster School and Gonville and Caius College, Cambridge; played leading part in amateur theatre at Cambridge, including 'The Footlights' revue of 1913 for which he wrote most of the sketches, produced, and played the lead; special matinee at Queen's Theatre, London; engaged by theatre manager, Robert Courtneidge, on three-year contract; began sixty-five year partnership with Cicely *Courtneidge, whom he married in 1916; served in army, 1917–19; for joint careers of Hulbert and his wife see COURTNEIDGE, Dame (ESMERALDA) CICELY; between 1931 and 1938 he exclusively devoted himself to acting for cinema; films included *Sunshine Susie, Jack's the Boy, Jack Ahoy, Bull-Dog Jack*, and *Jack-of-all Trades*; successful producer of plays, particularly musical comedies; published autobiography, *The Little Woman's Always Right* (1975).

HULET, Charles (1701–1736), actor; played at Lincoln's Inn Fields, 1722–32, and afterwards at Goodman's Fields; among his best parts,

Macheath, and Henry VIII (*Virtue Betrayed*); played Falstaff in *Henry IV* and the *Merry Wives*.

HULETT, James (d. 1771), engraver.

HULKE, John Whitaker (1830–1895), surgeon; studied at Moravian College, Neuwied, and King's College School and Hospital, London; attached to medical staff of general hospital in Crimea, 1855; FRCS, 1857; surgeon at Middlesex Hospital, 1870, at Royal London Ophthalmic Hospital, Moorfields, 1868–90; president of Royal College of Surgeons, 1893–5; FRS, 1867; president of Geological Society, 1882–4, and Wollaston medallist, 1887.

HULL, John (1761–1843), botanist; MD, Leiden, 1792; physician at Manchester; published *British Flora* (1799) and *Elements of Botany* (1800).

HULL, Robert (d. 1425). See HILL, ROBERT.

HULL, Thomas (1728–1808), actor, dramatist, and author; managed Bath Theatre for John *Palmer; played at Covent Garden forty-eight years; manager for *Colman, 1775–82; first appeared in *Farquhar's *Twin Rivals*, 1759, and last as the uncle in *George Barnwell*; excelled in 'heavy' parts; initiated the Theatrical Fund; his tragedy of *Henry the Second* (1774; first played, 1773) several times revived and reprinted; author of adaptations from Shakespeare and French dramatists, oratorio librettos, two novels, poems, and translations.

HULL, William (1820–1880), artist; educated by the Moravians; travelled on the continent, 1841–4; member of Manchester Academy of Fine Arts and of the Letherbrow Club; friend of *Ruskin. Among his best black-and-white works were views of Oxford and Cambridge, and illustrations to Langton's *Charles Dickens and Rochester*.

HULL, William Winstanley (1794–1873), distinguished writer and hymnologist; son of John *Hull (1761–1843); fellow of Brasenose College, Oxford, 1816–20; BA, 1814; barrister, Lincoln's Inn, 1820; practised at Chancery bar till 1846; friend of *Whately and Dr *Arnold; drew up petition for revision of liturgy, 1840; supported Dr *Hampden, 1836; opposed proceedings against William George *Ward, 1845; published *Occasional Papers on Church Matters* (1848), containing 'Inquiry after the original Books of Common Prayer', hymns, and other works.

HULLAH, John Pyke (1812–1884), musical composer and teacher; organist of the Charterhouse, 1858–84; his *Village Coquettes* (words by *Dickens) produced at the St James's, 1836; began singing-classes on the Wilhem model (tonic sol-fa) at Battersea, 1840; established at St

Martin's Hall, Long Acre, 1850–60; the system awarded medal at Paris Exhibition, 1867; became connected with Academy of Music, 1869; musical inspector of training schools, 1872; LL D, Edinburgh, 1876; composed songs (including settings of Kingsley's lyrics), duets, and motets. His works include manuals on the Wilhem method, lectures on musical history, and *Part Music* (1842–5).

HULLMANDEL, Charles Joseph (1789–1850), lithographer; issued (1818) *Views of Italy*, drawn and lithographed by himself; prepared his *Art of Drawing on Stone*, 1824; defended his improvements against representative of Engelmann; with Cattermole perfected lithotint; supported by James Duffield *Harding and *Faraday.

HULLOCK, Sir John (1767–1829), judge; barrister, Gray's Inn, 1794; serjeant-at-law, 1816; took part in prosecution of Henry *Hunt and Andrew Hardie, 1820; baron of the Exchequer, 1823–9; knighted, 1823; published *Law of Costs* (1792, enlarged 1810).

HULLS (or HULL), Jonathan (*fl.* 1737), author of *Description and Draught of a new-invented Machine for carrying Vessels or Ships . . . against Wind and Tide or in a Calm* (1737, reprinted 1855), detailing his invention of the principle of steam navigation (patented 1736).

HULME, Frederick Edward (1841–1909), botanist and artist; skilful sketcher of plants and flowers; his best work, *Familiar Wild Flowers* (9 vols., 1875–1909); also published works on ornament, heraldry, flower lore, and art students' textbooks; FSA, 1872.

HULME, Frederick William (1816–1884), landscape painter and art teacher; exhibited at British Institution, 1845–62, Royal Academy, 1852–84.

HULME, Nathaniel (1732–1807), physician; MD, Edinburgh, 1765; physician to the Charterhouse, 1774–1807; FRS, 1794; published treatise on scurvy (1768) and puerperal fever (1772); gold medallist, Paris Medical Society, 1787.

HULME, William (1631–1691), founder of Hulme's charity. His original bequest of four exhibitions at Brasenose College, Oxford, was largely extended by increased value of property; as resettled, 1881, it provided for foundation of schools at Manchester, Oldham, and Bury, and grant to The Queen's College.

HULOET, Richard (*fl.* 1552), author of *Abcedarium Anglico-Latinum* (1552).

HULSBERG, Henry (d. 1729), engraver of architectural works; warden of Savoy Lutheran Church.

HULSE, Edward (1631–1711), court physician to prince of Orange; MA, Emmanuel College, Cambridge, 1660; ejected for nonconformity; MD, Leiden; FRCP, 1677, and treasurer, 1704–9.

HULSE, Sir Edward, first baronet (1682–1759), physician to George II; son of Edward *Hulse; MD, Emmanuel College, Cambridge, 1717; leading Whig physician; censor, 1720, and 1750, 1751, and 1753; 'consiliarius' of College of Physicians; created baronet, 1739.

HULSE, John (1708–1790), founder of the Hulsean lectures at Cambridge; BA, St John's College, Cambridge, 1728; bequeathed to his university estates in Cheshire for advancement of religious learning; Hulsean professor substituted for Christian advocate, 1860.

HULSE, Sir Samuel, third baronet (1747–1837), field marshal; grandson of Sir Edward *Hulse; commanded first battalion of 1st Foot Guards in Flanders, 1793, and afterwards as major-general a brigade; in Helder expedition, 1799; general, 1803; governor of Chelsea Hospital, 1820; treasurer, 1820, and vice-chamberlain, 1827, of the household to George IV; privy councillor and GCH; field marshal, 1830.

HULTON, Sir Edward (1869–1925), newspaper proprietor; entered father's newspaper business in Manchester, 1885; produced *Daily Sketch*, 1909; retired, after selling for £6 million his fourteen periodicals to Allied Newspapers Ltd., 1923; baronet, 1921; interests as newspaper proprietor commercial and free from political interference; interested in horse-racing.

HULTON, William Adam (1802–1887), lawyer and antiquary; barrister, Middle Temple, 1827; treasurer of county of Lancaster, 1831–49; county-court judge, 1847; published *Treatise on the Law of Convictions* (1835); edited works for Chetham Society.

HUMBERSTON, Francis Mackenzie (or MACKENZIE, Francis Humberston) first Baron Seaforth and Mackenzie (1754–1815), lieutenant-general; succeeded his brother, Thomas Frederick Mackenzie *Humberston, in estates and hereditary chieftainship, 1783; MP, Ross-shire, 1784; raised 'Ross-shire buffs', 1793–4; created peer, 1797; colonel of 2nd North British Militia (later 3rd Seaforths), 1798; major-general, 1802; lieutenant-general, 1808; as governor of Barbados (1800–6) protected slaves; FRS, 1794; patron of *Lawrence and *West.

HUMBERSTON, Thomas Frederick Mackenzie (1753?–1783), soldier; assumed mother's maiden name (Humberston) on coming of age; served in Dragoon Guards; captain in then 78th (later 1st Seaforth Highlanders), 1778; present at repulse of French attack on Jersey, 1779; commanded newly raised 100th in Cape and India; captured several of Hyder Ali's forts, 1782; repulsed attack of Tippoo Sahib, 1782; commandant of 78th in 1782; captured, mortally wounded, by Mahratta fleets.

HUMBERT, Albert Jenkins (1822–1877), architect; rebuilt Whippingham Church and Sandringham House; designed mausoleums at Frogmore.

HUMBY, Mrs Anne (*fl.* 1817–1849), actress; née Ayre; first appeared at Hull as a singer; at Bath, 1818–20, Dublin, 1821–4; from 1825 at Haymarket and Drury Lane; engaged by *Macready, 1837; at Lyceum, 1849; excelled in light parts.

HUME. See also HOME.

HUME, Abraham (1616?–1707), ejected divine; MA, St Andrews; attended John *Maitland (Lauderdale) on the continent, and (1643) in Westminster Assembly; vicar of Long Benton; banished from England for Royalism; vicar of Whittingham, Northumberland, 1653–62; subsequently Presbyterian minister.

HUME, Sir Abraham, second and last baronet (1749–1838), virtuoso; MP, Petersfield, 1774–80; FRS, 1775; vice-president of Geological Society, 1809–13; a director of British Institution; collected minerals, precious stones, and old masters; published (anonymously) *Notices of Life and Works of Titian* (1829).

HUME, Abraham (1814–1884), antiquarian and social writer; BA, Dublin, 1843; hon. LL D, Glasgow, 1851; vicar of Vauxhall, Liverpool, 1847; explored Chile and Peru for South American Missionary Society, 1867; vice-chairman of Liverpool School Board, 1870–6, and secretary of bishopric committee, 1873–80; FRS; FSA; published *Learned Societies and Printing Clubs of the United Kingdom* (1847, enlarged 1853), *Condition of Liverpool* (1858), and works on Irish dialect and Cheshire antiquities.

HUME (or HOME), Alexander (1560?–1609), Scottish poet; studied law in Paris; graduated at St Andrews, 1597; minister at Logie, 1598–1609; his *Description of the Day Estivall* and poem on defeat of the Armada in *Sibbald's Chronicle,* former also reprinted by *Leyden (1803) and Campbell (1819); *Hymns and Sacred Songs* (1599) reprinted from *Drummond of Hawthornden's copy (1832).

HUME, Alexander (d. 1682), Covenanter; hanged at Edinburgh after capture by Charles Home (eighth earl).

HUME, Alexander, second earl of Marchmont (1675–1740). See CAMPBELL.

HUME, Alexander (1809–1851), poet; brewer's agent in London; published *Poems and Songs* (1845).

HUME, Alexander (1811–1859), poet and composer; cabinet-maker in Edinburgh and Glasgow; chorus-master in Theatre Royal, Edinburgh; edited *Lyric Gems of Scotland* (1856), containing fifty of his own pieces; composed also glees, and music to *Burns's 'Afton Water'.

HUME, Alexander Hamilton (1797–1873), Australian explorer; born at Paramatta; when 17, with his brother, John Kennedy Hume, discovered Bong Bong and Berrima in south-west of New South Wales; shared exploration of Jervis Bay, 1819; discovered Yass Plains, 1821; undertook (with W. H. Hovell) first overland journey from Sydney to Port Philip, 1824, discovering five rivers; granted 1,200 acres; accompanied Captain *Sturt on Macquarie expedition, 1828–9; died at Fort George, Yass.

HUME, Allan Octavian (1829–1912), Indian civil servant and ornithologist; son of Joseph *Hume; joined Bengal Civil Service, 1849; CB for services in Indian Mutiny, 1860; retired, 1882; worked for Indian parliamentary system through Indian National Congress convoked under his guidance, 1885–94; collaborated in standard work on Indian game birds.

HUME, Anna (*fl.* 1644), daughter of David *Hume (1560?–1630?); translated Petrarch's *Triumphs of Love, Chastitie, Death* (1644); superintended publication of her father's *History of House and Race of Douglas and Angus.*

HUME, David (1560?–1630?), historian, controversialist, and Latin poet; studied at St Andrews University; secretary to Archibald *Douglas, eighth earl of Angus, *c.*1583; published part of Latin treatise on the union of Britain, 1605; upheld Presbyterianism against Law, bishop of Orkney, 1608–11, and Cowper, bishop of Galloway, 1613; his *History of House and Race of Douglas and Angus* printed with difficulty by his daughter, owing to opposition of eleventh earl of *Angus; *History of House of Wedderburn* first printed (1839); Latin poems twice issued at Paris (1632 and 1639).

HUME (or HOME), Sir David, of Crossrig, Lord Crossrig (1643–1707), MA, Edinburgh, 1662; studied law at Paris; advocate, 1687; judge, 1689; lord of justiciary, 1690; knighted, 1690; lost his papers in Edinburgh fire of 1700; his *Diary of Parliament and Privy Council of Scotland, 1700–7* printed (1828), *Domestic Details* (1843).

HUME, David (1711–1776), philosopher and historian; studied law; lived in France, 1734–7; his *Treatise of Human Nature* appeared anonymously (1739; ed. Selby-Bigge, 1888); the book neglected; his *Essays Moral and Political* (1741–2) written at Ninewells, Berwickshire, commended by Bishop *Butler and favourably received; unsuccessful candidate for chair of ethics at Edinburgh, 1745; lived with marquis of Annandale at Weldhall, Hertfordshire, 1745–6; judge-advocate to General *Sinclair in expedition against Port L'Orient, 1747; accompanied Sinclair on military embassy to Vienna and Turin, 1748, when his *Philosophical Essays* (including that on miracles) appeared; issued *Enquiry concerning Principles of Morals* (1751); gained reputation by his *Political Discourses* (1752); published *Four Dissertations* (including 'Natural History of Religion'), 1757; unsuccessful candidate for chair of logic at Glasgow, but keeper of the Advocates' Library, Edinburgh, 1752; published first volume of *History of England during reigns of James I and Charles I* (1754), succeeding better with the second (1649–88); issued two volumes on the Tudor period (1759), and the last two (backwards from Henry VII) (1761); secretary to Edinburgh Philosophical Society, 1752; being censured by curators of Edinburgh library for buying La Fontaine's *Contes* and other French works, resigned, 1757; attacked for sceptical views; accompanied Lord *Hertford to Paris, 1763; secretary to the embassy, 1765, and for some months chargé d'affaires; intimate of Comtesse de Boufflers, Madame Geoffrin, D'Alembert, and Turgot, and well received at court; brought home Rousseau and procured him a pension, but afterwards quarrelled with him in consequence of Rousseau's suspicious nature; received a pension and invitation from the king to continue his history; under-secretary to Henry Seymour *Conway, 1767–8; returned to Edinburgh, 1769; made journey (1776) to London and Bath with John *Home, who recorded it. His autobiography (with letter of Adam *Smith) and essays on 'Suicide and Immortality', published (1777), *Dialogues on Natural Religion* (1779). The best edition of his philosophical works is that of T. H. *Green and T. H. Grose (1874–5); abbreviations of his history were edited by (Sir) William *Smith and John Sherren *Brewer. His thoroughgoing empiricism formed a landmark in the development of metaphysics.

HUME, David (1757–1838), judge; nephew of David *Hume (1711–76); sheriff of Berwickshire, 1784, of Linlithgowshire, 1793; professor of Scots law at Edinburgh, 1786; clerk to court of session, 1811; baron of Scottish Exchequer, 1822; published commentaries on Scottish criminal law (1797), and reports from 1781 to 1822 (posthumous, 1839).

HUME, Sir George, earl of Dunbar (d. 1611). See HOME.

HUME, Lady Grizel (1665–1746). See BAILLIE, Lady GRIZEL.

HUME, Hugh, third earl of Marchmont (1708–1794), politician; studied in Dutch universities; as Lord Polwarth represented Berwick, 1734–40; opponent of Walpole; president of court of police in Scotland, 1747; Scottish representative peer, 1750–84; lord keeper of great seal of Scotland, 1764; intimate of *Bolingbroke and *Chesterfield; executor of *Pope and the duchess of *Marlborough; offered information to *Johnson for life of Pope; skilful horticulturist and horseman.

HUME, James (*fl.* 1639), mathematician; son of David *Hume (1560?–1630?); lived in France; published nine mathematical works in Latin, and others in French, including *Algèbre de Viète d'une Méthode nouvelle* (1636).

HUME, James Deacon (1774–1842), free trader; educated at Westminster; consolidated customs laws into ten acts of 1825; thirty-eight years in the customs; joint secretary to Board of Trade, 1828–40; joint founder of Political Economy Club, 1821; deputy-chairman of Atlas Assurance Company; attacked protection in evidence before parliament, 1840.

HUME, John Robert (1781?–1857), physician to Wellington in Peninsula and afterwards in England; MD, St Andrews, 1816; LRCP, 1819; commissioner in lunacy, 1836; inspector-general of hospitals.

HUME, Joseph (1767–1843), clerk at Somerset House; published translation of Dante's *Inferno* (1812) and *A Search into the Old Testament* (1841).

HUME, Joseph (1777–1855), radical politician; entered medical service of East India Company, 1797; army surgeon, interpreter, and paymaster in Mahratta War; returned to England, 1807; travelled; elected Tory member for Weymouth, 1812; Radical MP, Aberdeen, 1818–30, Middlesex, 1830–7, Kilkenny, 1837–41, and Montrose, 1842–55; obtained select committees on revenue collection, 1820, and the combination laws, 1824; moved repeal of corn laws, 1834; carried repeal of combination laws and those prohibiting emigration and export of machinery; devoted himself to question of public expenditure, adding 'retrenchment' to his party's watchwords; privy councillor; FRS; member of Board of Agriculture, and twice lord rector of Aberdeen University.

HUME, Martin Andrew Sharp (1843–1910), author; visited relatives in Spain, 1860; travelled extensively in Central and South America; published *The Courtships of Queen Elizabeth* and *The Year after the Armada* (1896); editor of *Spanish State Papers* at Public Record Office (1898); published histories of Spain (1898) and modern Spain (1899), and other works on Spanish history and literature; later works include *Queens of Old Spain* (1907), *Queen Elizabeth and Her England* (1910); lectured on Spanish history at Cambridge and elsewhere; hon. MA, Cambridge, 1908.

HUME (or HOME), Sir Patrick, second baronet, of Polwarth, first earl of Marchmont and Baron Polwarth (1641–1724), studied law in Paris; elected to Scottish parliament for Berwick, 1665; opposed *Lauderdale's policy; imprisoned for five years and incapacitated from office for petition against council's action against Covenanters, 1675–9; in England joined *Monmouth's party; escaped by Ireland and France to Holland; joined *Argyle's expedition, 1684; being outlawed (1685) in connection with Rye House Plot escaped by Ireland, France, and Geneva, to Utrecht; surgeon at Utrecht under name of Wallace; adviser of William of Orange, accompanying him to England, 1688; privy councillor and Scottish peer (Baron Polwarth), 1689; sheriff of Berwickshire, 1692–1710; extraordinary lord of session, 1693; lord chancellor of Scotland, 1696–1702; created Earl Marchmont, 1697; high commissioner to parliament, 1698, to general assembly, 1702; prevented an act for the abjuration of the Pretender, passed act for security of Presbyterianism, and proposed settlement of succession on house of Hanover; supported union with England; reappointed by George I to sheriffdom and made lord of court of police.

HUME, Patrick (*fl.* 1695), London schoolmaster, and (1695) first commentator on *Milton.

HUME, Thomas (1769?–1850), physician; under Wellesley in Peninsula; BA, Trinity College, Dublin, 1792; MD, 1803; four times censor of College of Physicians.

HUME, Tobias (d. 1645), soldier of fortune and musician; poor brother of the Charterhouse from 1629; published *First Part of Ayres, French, Pollish, and others* (1605) and *Captain Hume's Musicall Humors* (1607).

HUME-ROTHERY, William (1899–1968), first Isaac Wolfson professor of metallurgy in the University of Oxford; great-grandson of Joseph *Hume; educated at Cheltenham College and Magdalen College, Oxford; passed into Royal Military Academy, Woolwich, 1916, but contracted cerebrospinal meningitis and became completely deaf, 1917; first class, natural science, 1922; joined Royal School of Mines; worked under (Sir) H. C. *Carpenter on intermetallic compounds; Ph.D. (London), 1925; research fellow, Oxford, working on constitution of alloys, 1925; D.Sc. (Oxford), 1935; FRS, 1937; fellow, Magdalen College, 1938; lecturer in metallurgical chemistry; reader, 1955; Isaac Wolfson professor of metallurgy, 1958–66; OBE, 1951; honorary degrees, Manchester and Sheffield, 1966; many other academic awards.

HUMFREY, John (1621–1719), ejected minister; MA, Pembroke College, Oxford, 1647; received Presbyterian ordination, 1649; vicar of Frome Selwood till 1662; reordained episcopally; defended his action, but afterwards renounced it; formed Congregational church in Duke's Place, London, afterwards in Petticoat Lane; continued ministry to ninety-ninth year; advocated union of all Protestants; published *Account of the French Prophets* (1708), treatises on justification, and other works.

HUMFREY, Pelham (1647–1674), lutenist and composer; with *Blow and *Turner composed the *Club Anthem*, 1664; studied music in France and Italy, 1665–6; introduced Lully's methods into England; gentleman of Chapel Royal, 1667; master of the children, 1672–4; composer-in-ordinary for violins, 1673; composed anthems, services, and songs, contained in the *Tudway collection and *Boyce's *Cathedral Music*, and other works.

HUMPHREY. See also HUMFREY and HUMPHRY.

HUMPHREY, duke of Gloucester (1391–1447), 'the Good Duke Humphrey'; youngest son of Henry IV; perhaps educated at Balliol College, Oxford; KG, 1400; great chamberlain of England, 1413; created duke of Gloucester, 1414; commanded one of the English divisions in Agincourt expedition; wounded at Agincourt, 1415; as warden of Cinque Ports received Emperor Sigismund, 1416; in Henry V's second expedition took Lisieux, 1417, and Cherbourg, 1418; governor of Rouen, 1419; at siege of Melun, 1420; regent of England, 1420–1; on death of Henry V claimed regency, but was only allowed to act as *Bedford's deputy, with title of protector, 1422; married Jacqueline of Hainault, 1422, and reconquered Hainault, 1424, but allowed Philip of Burgundy to recapture her and her territory, 1425; quarrelled with his uncle, Henry *Beaufort (d. 1447), but was reconciled to him by Bedford; again protector, 1427–29; attempted to give further help to Jacqueline, 1427; his marriage with her having been annulled (1428), married his mistress, Eleanor *Cobham; refused to recognize Beaufort as papal legate,

1428; lieutenant of the kingdom, 1430–2; actively prosecuted quarrel with Beaufort; opposed Beaufort's French policy; went to France as captain of Calais and lieutenant of the new army; appointed count of Flanders, but effected nothing, 1436; returned to denounce Beaufort as the friend of France, 1436; lost influence over the king and was powerless to prevent proceedings (1441) against his wife for witchcraft; vainly advocated Armagnac marriage for Henry VI, and (1445) violation of truce with France; suspected by the king of designs on his life, and arrested; died in custody, popular suspicions of foul play being groundless; owed his name of 'the Good' only to his patronage of men of letters (including Titus Livius of Forli, Leonard Aretino, *Lydgate, and *Capgrave) and to his patriotic sentiment. A strong churchman, he persecuted the Lollards and favoured monasteries, especially St Albans. He read Latin and Italian literature, collected books from his youth, and gave the first books for a library at Oxford; his collection was dispersed in the reign of Edward VI.

HUMPHREY, Sir **Andrew Henry** (1912–1977), marshal of the Royal Air Force; educated at Bradfield and RAF College, Cranwell; posted to No. 266 (Spitfire) Squadron, 1940; on active service in Battle of Britain; transferred to night-fighters; DFC, 1941; experience on Hurricane fighter bombers; rocket-attack instructor, Middle East; AFC, 1943, bars 1945 and 1955; staff work at HQ, No. 106 Group; survey work in Africa with No. 82 Squadron; OBE, 1951; instructor, RAF Flying College, Manby; established new record for Cape Town-to-London flight in twin-jet Canberra bomber Aries IV, 1953; flew same aircraft on first RAF jet-flight to North Pole, 1954; deputy director of operational requirements, Air Ministry, 1957; CB, 1959; commander, RAF station, Akrotiri, Cyprus, 1959–61; served in Ministry of Defence, 1962–5; air officer commanding, Middle East; air vice-marshal, 1965; air member for personnel, MOD; KCB, 1968; air marshal, 1969; commander-in-chief, Strike Command; air chief marshal; GCB, 1974; air ADC to the Queen, 1974–6; chief of air staff, 1974; marshal of the Royal Air Force and chief of defence staff, 1976.

HUMPHREY, Herbert Alfred (1868–1951), engineer; educated at Cowper Street Middle Class School, Finsbury Technical Institute, and City and Guilds Central Institution; with Brunner, Mond & Co., 1890–1901; set up as consulting engineer, 1901; invented gas pump; technical adviser on explosives, 1914–18; member, commission to Synthetic Ammonia Works, Oppau, 1919; consulting engineer and director, Synthetic Ammonia and Nitrates Ltd., Billingham, 1919–26; constructed 40,000 kW electric power-station there; consulting engineer to ICI, 1926–31; died in South Africa.

HUMPHREY (or HUMFREY), Laurence (1527?–1590), president of Magdalen College, Oxford; of Christ's College, Cambridge, and Magdalen College, Oxford; perpetual fellow of Magdalen College; MA, 1552; in Switzerland during reign of Mary; regius professor of divinity at Oxford, 1560; president of Magdalen College, 1561–90; DD, 1562; cited for refusing to wear vestments, 1564; was refused institution to a living by his friend Bishop *Jewel, 1565; after several protests, conformed; dean of Gloucester, 1571, of Winchester, 1580–90; vice-chancellor of Oxford, 1571–6; deputy to diet of Smalcald, 1578; collaborated with Robert *Crowley (1556) in answering *Huggarde's *Displaying of the Protestants*; published Latin *Life of Jewel* (1573), translations from Origen, Cyril, and Philo, and other works.

HUMPHREY, William (1740?–1810?), engraver and printseller.

HUMPHREYS, David (1689–1740), divine; educated at Merchant Taylors' School, Christ's Hospital, and Trinity College, Cambridge; fellow; MA, 1715; DD, 1728; supported *Bentley at Trinity; secretary to the SPG, 1716–40; vicar of Ware, 1730, and Thundridge, 1732; published *Historical Account* (of the SPG, 1730), and translations.

HUMPHREYS, Henry Noel (1810–1879), numismatist, naturalist, and artist; illustrated works on natural history; published miscellaneous works, including treatises on coins and missal painting.

HUMPHREYS, Humphrey (1648–1712), bishop successively of Bangor and Hereford; fellow of Jesus College, Oxford; MA, 1673; DD, 1682; dean of Bangor, 1680; bishop of Bangor, 1689–1701, of Hereford, 1701–12; amplified *Wood's works on Oxford; compiled for Wood catalogue of deans of Bangor and St Asaph.

HUMPHREYS, James (d. 1830), author of *Observations on the Actual State of the English Laws of Real Property, with outlines of a Code* (1826); barrister, Lincoln's Inn, 1800; friend of Charles *Butler (1750–1832).

HUMPHREYS, Leslie Alexander Francis Longmore (1904–1976), organizer for Special Operations Executive (SOE); born in Budapest; educated at Stonyhurst, Faculté des Lettres, Dijon, and Magdalene College, Cambridge; trilingual; fluent in Romanian as well as French and German; served as assistant to his father at

British Legation, Bucharest, for six years; joined Section D, British Secret Service (predecessor of SOE), 1939; liaison officer with French Fifth Bureau, Paris, 1939–40; head of F Section, SOE, charged with organizing subversion in France, 1940; moved to DF Section to work on clandestine communications; designed secret travel-and-supply system through Western Europe; Jacques Mitterand, brother of future president of France, his chief lieutenant in Paris; OBE, 1945; rejoined service under Foreign Office, 1950; served in Frankfurt, Pusan (South Korea), Vienna, and London, 1950–64; on staff of preparatory school for Stonyhurst, 1964–73.

HUMPHREYS, Sir (Richard Somers) Travers (Christmas) (1867–1956), judge; educated at Shrewsbury and Trinity Hall, Cambridge; called to bar (Inner Temple), 1889; bencher, 1922; junior crown counsel, Central Criminal Court, 1908; senior counsel, 1916–28; recorder of Chichester, 1921–6; of Cambridge, 1926–8; judge of King's Bench division, 1928–51; appeared in prosecution of H. H. Crippen, F. H. Seddon, G. J. Smith, Sir Roger *Casement, and Horatio *Bottomley; presided at trials of Mrs Barney (1932), Mrs Rattenbury and George Stoner (1935), and J. G. Haig (1949); knighted, 1925; PC, 1946; published *Criminal Days* (1946), and *A Book of Trials* (1953).

HUMPHREYS, Samuel (1698?–1738), author; published miscellaneous works, including translations from Italian and French, and *Peruvian Tales* (1734).

HUMPHREYS, (Travers) Christmas (1901–1983), judge; educated at Malvern and Trinity Hall, Cambridge; followed his father and grandfather into legal profession; called to bar (Inner Temple), 1924; junior Treasury counsel at Central Criminal Court, 1934; recorder of Deal, 1942–56; deputy chairman, east Kent quarter-sessions, 1947–71; senior Treasury counsel, 1950–9; recorder of Guildford, 1956–68; junior counsel in Japanese war-crimes trials, 1946; bencher of Inner Temple, 1955; QC, 1959; judge at Central Criminal Court, 1962–76; founding president, Buddhist Lodge (later Buddhist Society), 1924; publications include *What is Buddhism?* (1928), and other books on Buddhism and literature, and *Both Sides of the Circle* (autobiography, 1978).

HUMPHRIES, John (d. 1730?), violinist and composer.

HUMPHRY, Sir George Murray (1820–1896), surgeon; studied at St Bartholomew's Hospital, London; MRCS, 1841; LSA, 1842; surgeon at Addenbrooke's College, Cambridge; deputy professor of anatomy, 1847–66; MB,

Downing College, Cambridge, 1852; MD, 1859; professor of human anatomy, Cambridge, 1866–83; professor of surgery, 1883; professorial fellow, King's College, Cambridge, 1884; FRCS, 1844; FRS, 1859; knighted, 1891; published anatomical works; instrumental in procuring for the medical school at Cambridge its high reputation.

HUMPHRY, Ozias (1742–1810), portrait painter; friend of *Romney and *Blake; patronized by duke of *Dorset and others; studied four years in Italy; painted miniatures in India, 1785–8; RA, 1791; abandoned miniature painting for crayon-drawing; lost his eyesight, 1797.

HUMPHRY, William Gilson (1815–1886), divine and author; captain of Shrewsbury School; fellow of Trinity College, Cambridge, 1839; senior classic and second chancellor's medallist, 1837; vicar of St Martin-in-the-Fields, London, 1855–86; member of commissions on clerical subscription, 1865, and ritual, 1869; a New Testament reviser; published, besides Hulsean and Boyle lectures, commentaries on the Acts (1847) and the revised version (1882), *Treatise on Book of Common Prayer* (1853; last edn. 1885), and other works.

HUMPHRYS, William (1794–1865), engraver; in America illustrated poets and engraved banknotes; returned to England, 1822; engraved the queen's head on postage-stamps, and executed plates after old and contemporary masters; died at Genoa.

HUMPSTON (or HUMSTON), Robert (d. 1606), bishop of Down and Connor, 1602–6.

HUNGERFORD, Agnes, Lady (d. 1524), second wife of Sir Edward Hungerford (d. 1522); executed for murder of first husband, John Cotell.

HUNGERFORD, Sir Anthony (1564–1627), controversialist; MA, St John's College, Oxford, 1594; knighted, 1608; brought up by his mother, Bridget Shelley, as a Romanist; deputy-lieutenant of Wiltshire; his treatises in defence of Anglicanism published (1639).

HUNGERFORD, Anthony (d. 1657), Parliamentarian colonel in Ireland; perhaps half-brother of Anthony *Hungerford (d. 1657).

HUNGERFORD, Anthony (d. 1657), Royalist; younger son of Sir Anthony *Hungerford; represented Malmesbury in Short and Long parliaments; fined and imprisoned, 1644, for attending Charles I's parliament at Oxford.

HUNGERFORD, Sir Edward (1596–1648), Parliamentarian; eldest son of Sir Anthony *Hungerford; KB, 1625; sheriff of Wiltshire, 1632; MP, Chippenham, 1620, and in Short and

Long parliaments; occupied and plundered Salisbury, 1643; took Wardour and Farleigh castles.

HUNGERFORD, Sir Edward (1632–1711), founder of Hungerford Market; son of Anthony *Hungerford (d. 1657); KB, 1661; MP, Chippenham, 1660–81, New Shoreham, 1685–90, Steyning, 1695–1702; removed from lieutenancy for opposing the court, 1681; Hungerford Market built to recruit his fortune, 1682, on site of house destroyed by fire (1669). Charing Cross Station was built on site of market house, 1860.

HUNGERFORD, John (d. 1729), lawyer; MA, Cambridge, *per literas regias*, 1683; of Lincoln's Inn; MP, Scarborough, 1692, 1702–5, 1707–29; expelled for receiving a bribe, 1695; counsel for East India Company; defended Francia, 1717, Matthews, 1719, and *Layer, 1722, charged with Jacobitism.

HUNGERFORD, Mrs Margaret Wolfe (1855?–1897), novelist; daughter of Canon Fitzjohn Stannus Hamilton; married Thomas H. Hungerford; published *Molly Bawn* (1878) and more than thirty other novels.

HUNGERFORD, Robert, second Baron Hungerford (1409–1459), eldest surviving son of Sir Walter *Hungerford, first Baron Hungerford (d. 1449); summoned to parliament as baron, 1450–5; acquired large property in Cornwall through mother and wife.

HUNGERFORD, Robert, Baron Moleyns and third Baron Hungerford (1431–1464), son of Robert *Hungerford, second Baron Hungerford; summoned as Baron Moleyns in right of his wife, 1445; quarrelled with John *Paston regarding ownership of manor of Gresham, Norfolk, 1448; while serving with *Shrewsbury in Aquitaine was captured, 1452, and kept prisoner seven years, till 1459; after ransom an active Lancastrian; fled with Henry VI to the north after Towton, 1461, and visited France to obtain help; captured at Hexham and executed.

HUNGERFORD, Sir Thomas (d. 1397), speaker in last parliament of Edward III; MP, Wiltshire, and Somerset, 1357–90; purchased Farleigh, 1369; knighted 1375; steward of *John of Gaunt; first person formally entitled speaker, 1377.

HUNGERFORD, Sir Thomas (d. 1469), eldest son of Robert *Hungerford, third Baron Hungerford; executed as supporter of *Warwick.

HUNGERFORD, Sir Walter, first Baron Hungerford (1378–1449), warrior and statesman; son of Sir Thomas *Hungerford (d. 1397); MP, Wiltshire, 1400, 1404, 1407, 1413, and 1414, Somerset, 1409; speaker, 1414; English envoy at Council of Constance, 1414–15; at Agincourt, 1415, and siege of Rouen, 1418; admiral of fleet, 1418; KG, 1421; executor of Henry V's will and member of *Gloucester's council; steward of household to Henry VI, 1424; first summoned as baron, 1426; treasurer, 1427–32; buried in Salisbury Cathedral in iron chapel erected by himself.

HUNGERFORD, Sir Walter (d. 1516), privy councillor of Henry VII and Henry VIII; son of Robert *Hungerford, third Baron Hungerford; MP, Wiltshire, 1477; knighted; slew Sir Robert *Brackenbury at Bosworth, 1485.

HUNGERFORD, Walter, first Baron Hungerford of Heytesbury (1503–1540), grandson of Sir Walter *Hungerford (d. 1516); squire of the body to Henry VIII; sheriff of Wiltshire, 1533; created peer, 1536; beheaded with Thomas *Cromwell, 1540.

HUNGERFORD, Sir Walter (1532–1596), 'the Knight of Farley'; eldest son of Walter *Hungerford, first Baron Hungerford of Heytesbury; restored to confiscated estate of Farleigh, 1554, his father's attainder being reversed; sheriff of Wiltshire, 1557.

HUNNE, Richard (d. 1514), supposed martyr; found hanged in the Lollards' Tower after prosecution for heresy; verdict of wilful murder brought in against bishop of London's chancellor, Dr Horsey, in civil court.

HUNNEMAN, Christopher William (d. 1793), portrait and miniature painter.

HUNNIS, William (d. 1597), musician and poet; gentleman of Chapel Royal under Edward VI; imprisoned for Protestant conspiracy, 1555; restored by Elizabeth, granted arms, and made master of the children, 1566; published metrical psalms, *A Hyve full of Hunnye* (1578), and other works.

HUNSDON, Barons. See CAREY, HENRY, first baron, 1526–1596; CAREY, GEORGE, second baron, 1547–1603; CAREY, JOHN, third baron, d. 1617.

HUNT, Dame Agnes Gwendoline (1866–1948), pioneer in work amongst cripples; herself crippled by osteomyelitis from age of 10; qualified as queen's nurse and in midwifery; founded first open-air hospital for crippled children at Baschurch, 1900; with Sir Robert *Jones revolutionized treatment; moved hospital to Oswestry as Robert Jones and Agnes Hunt Orthopaedic Hospital, 1921; built up system of after-care and preventive clinics; founded Derwen Cripples' Training College, 1927; DBE, 1926.

HUNT, Alfred William (1830–1896), landscape painter; son of Andrew *Hunt; BA, Corpus

Christi College, Oxford, 1852; fellow, 1853–61; hon. fellow, 1882; member of Liverpool Academy, 1850; exhibited landscapes at Royal Academy, 1854–62, and from 1870; member of Old Water-Colour Society, 1864; disciple of *Turner.

HUNT, Andrew (1790–1861), landscape painter; exhibited at Liverpool.

HUNT, Arabella (d. 1705), vocalist and lutenist; painted by *Kneller and celebrated by *Congreve.

HUNT, Arthur Surridge (1871–1934), papyrologist; educated at Cranbrook, Eastbourne College, and The Queen's College, Oxford; joined B. P. *Grenfell and D. G. *Hogarth in excavations for papyri in the Fayum; lecturer in papyrology (1908), professor (1913–34) at Oxford; many publications with Grenfell and sole editor after 1920 of Egypt Exploration Society's volumes of papyrus texts; FBA, 1913.

HUNT, Frederick Knight (1814–1854), journalist and author; established *Medical Times*, 1839; sub-editor of *Illustrated London News*; editor of *Pictorial Times* and (1851) the *Daily News*, after having been on *Dickens's staff; published *The Fourth Estate* (1850).

HUNT, George Ward (1825–1877), statesman; of Eton and Christ Church, Oxford; MA, 1851; DCL, 1870; barrister, Inner Temple, 1851; bencher, 1873; MP, North Northamptonshire, 1857–77; financial secretary to Treasury, 1866–8; chancellor of the Exchequer, 1868 (Feb.–Dec.); first lord of the Admiralty, 1874–7; died at Homburg.

HUNT, George William (1829?–1904). See under MACDERMOTT, GILBERT HASTINGS.

HUNT, Henry (1773–1835), radical politician; farmed property at Upavon, Wiltshire; fined and imprisoned for challenging colonel of yeomanry, 1800, and for assaulting a gamekeeper, 1810; active in political life of Wiltshire; contested Bristol, 1812, Westminster, 1818, Somerset, 1826; took part in Spa Fields meeting, 1816; published pamphlet against *Burdett (1819); presided at Manchester meeting, 1819, and was sentenced to two years' imprisonment in connection with it; MP, Preston, 1830–3; afterwards a blacking manufacturer; published *Memoirs* (1820).

HUNT, James (1833–1869), ethnologist and writer on stammering; son of Thomas *Hunt (1802–1851); hon. secretary of Ethnological Society, 1859–62; founder and first president of Anthropological Society, 1863–7; edited *Anthropological Review* and (1865) Vogt's *Lectures on Man*; obtained recognition of anthropology as separate section at British Association; defended slavery in paper on 'The Negro's Place in Nature' (Brit. Assoc., 1863); published work on *Stammering and Stuttering* (1861).

HUNT, James Henry Leigh (1784–1859), essayist and poet; named after James Henry Leigh, father of first Lord Leigh; at Christ's Hospital; his verses entitled *Juvenilia* printed (1801); his *Critical Essays on Performers of the London Theatres* and *Classic Tales* reprinted from his brother John's *The News* (1807); began to edit the *Examiner*, 1808, and the *Reflector*, 1810; prosecuted for article against army flogging, but defended by *Brougham and acquitted, 1811; sentenced with his brother to fine and two years' imprisonment, 1813, for reflections on the prince regent; visited in Surrey Gaol by *Byron, Moore, *Bentham, and *Lamb; continued editing the *Examiner* while in prison; entertained *Shelley at Hampstead, and brought about his meeting with *Keats, 1816; introduced Keats and Shelley to the public in *Examiner*, 1816; Shelley's *Cenci* dedicated to him, 1819; published *The Story of Rimini* (1816; subsequently revised and corrected); published *Foliage* (poems, 1818); savagely attacked by *Quarterly* and *Blackwood*; issued *Hero and Leander* (1819); began *The Indicator*, 1819; joined Byron at Pisa, 1822; carried on the *Liberal* with Byron, 1822–3; at Florence, 1823–5, continuing to write; published *Lord Byron and some of his Contemporaries* (1828) and *The Companion* (weekly), 1828; carried on the *Tatler* (daily), 1830–2; introduced by his *Christianism* (privately printed) to *Carlyle; began *Leigh Hunt's Journal*, 1834; published *Captain Sword and Captain Pen* (1835); his play *A Legend of Florence* successfully produced at Covent Garden, 1840; issued critical notices of dramatists (1840), *Imagination and Fancy* and second collective edition of poems (1844), *Wit and Humour* and *Stories from Italian Poets* (1846), *Men, Women, and Books* (1847); received pension, £200, 1847; published *Jar of Honey from Mount Hybla* (1848), *Autobiography* (1850; enlarged 1860), *Table-Talk* (1851), *Old Court Suburb* (1855), and edition of *Beaumont and *Fletcher (1855); bust by Joseph *Durham placed at Kensal Green (where he was buried), 1869. His *Book of the Sonnet* (with S. Adams Lee) appeared posthumously, also (1862) his correspondence. His portrait was painted by *Haydon.

HUNT, Jeremiah (1678–1744), Independent minister; studied at Edinburgh and Leiden; preached at Amsterdam; pastor at Pinners' Hall, Old Broad Street, London, 1707; non-subscriber at Salters' Hall, 1719; hon. DD, Edinburgh, 1729; Williams trustee, 1730; friend of Nathaniel *Lardner; published theological works.

HUNT, Sir **John** (1550?–1615), politician; MP, Sudbury, 1571; knighted, 1611.

HUNT, John (1806–1842), organist of Hereford Cathedral, 1835–42; song-writer.

HUNT, John (1812–1848), Wesleyan missionary and translator of Bible into Fijian.

HUNT, John Higgs (1780–1859), translator; fellow of Trinity College, Cambridge, and Browne medallist; MA, 1804; vicar of Weedon Beck, 1823–59; translated Tasso's *Jerusalem Delivered* (1818).

HUNT, Nicholas (1596–1648), arithmetician and divine; BA, Exeter College, Oxford, 1616; proctor of the arches.

HUNT, Robert (d. 1608?), chaplain to first settlers in Virginia and minister at James Town, 1607; LL B, Trinity Hall, Cambridge, 1606.

HUNT, Robert (1807–1887), scientific writer; president of Royal Cornwall Polytechnic Society, 1859; published first English treatise on photography (1841); keeper of mining records, 1845–78; professor of experimental physics at School of Mines; issued *Mineral Statistics* (1855–84); FRS, 1854; member of Coal Commission, 1866; published handbooks of 1851 and 1862 exhibitions, and other works, including *British Mining* (1884) and three editions of *Ure's Dictionary of Arts*; contributed to this Dictionary.

HUNT, Roger (*fl.* 1433), speaker of the House of Commons; MP, Bedfordshire, 1414 and 1420, and afterwards Huntingdonshire; speaker, 1420 and 1433; baron of Exchequer, 1438.

HUNT, Thomas (1611–1683), schoolmaster; MA, Pembroke College, Oxford, 1636; published works on orthography.

HUNT, Thomas (1627?–1688), lawyer; MA, Queens' College, Cambridge, 1653; fellow of Peterhouse, 1650; of Gray's Inn; counsel for Lord *Stafford, 1680; wrote in support of Exclusion Bill, 1680, bishops' right as peers to judge in capital causes, 1682, and municipal rights of City of London, 1683; ridiculed by *Dryden; outlawed; died in Holland.

HUNT, Thomas (1696–1774), orientalist; fellow of Hart Hall, Oxford; MA, 1721; DD, 1744; Laudian professor of Arabic, 1738; regius professor of Hebrew, 1747; FRS, 1740; FSA, 1757; collaborated with Gregory *Sharpe in preparation of Thomas Hyde's *Dissertations*; quarrelled with him before (1767) publication; edited *Fragment of Hippolytus from Arabic MSS.* (1728) and works of Bishop George *Hooper (1757).

HUNT, Thomas (1802–1851), inventor of a method of curing stammering; of Trinity College, Cambridge.

HUNT, Thomas Frederick (1791–1831), architect.

HUNT, Thornton Leigh (1810–1873), journalist; son of James Henry Leigh *Hunt; director of political department of the *Constitutional*, 1836; helped George Henry *Lewes to establish the *Leader*, 1850; published *The Foster Brother* (1845); edited Leigh Hunt's *Autobiography* (1850), *Poetical Works* (1860), and *Correspondence* (1862).

HUNT, Walter (Latinized **VENANTIUS**) (d. 1478), theologian; perhaps professor at Oxford; represented England at councils of Ferrara and Florence, 1438–9, being a leading exponent of the Latin view as to reunion of western with eastern church; wrote thirty lost Latin treatises.

HUNT, William (1550?–1615). See WESTON.

HUNT, William (1842–1931), historian; educated at Harrow and Trinity College, Oxford; vicar of Congresbury, Somerset, 1867–82; subeditor and contributor of nearly 600 articles to this Dictionary; joint editor of *A History of the English Church* (8 vols., 1899–1910) and *The Political History of England* (12 vols., 1905–10), contributing one volume to each.

HUNT, William Henry (1790–1864), watercolour painter; apprenticed to *Varley; employed in early days by Dr Thomas *Monro and the earl of Essex; exhibited landscapes and interiors at Royal Academy, 1807–11, and a few oils at Old Water-Colour Society; member Society of Painters in Water-Colours, 1826; exhibited 153 drawings (including sixty fisher-folk pieces), 1824–31; excelled in painting still life and in humorous drawings; preferred pure colour to mixed tints; exhibited at Paris, 1855; elected to Amsterdam Academy, 1856.

HUNT, William Holman (1827–1910), painter; born in Wood Street, Cheapside; son of a warehouseman; studied art at British Museum and National Gallery from 1843; at Academy Schools, 1844; made acquaintance of *Millais and D. G. *Rossetti, 1844; exhibited at Academy from 1847; introduced Rossetti to Millais; founded in 1848 with them the Pre-Raphaelite Brotherhood, which was joined subsequently by *Woolner, W. M. *Rossetti, James *Collinson, and F. G. *Stephens; consistently carried on the brotherhood's principles till death; his first Pre-Raphaelite picture, *Rienzi*, hung in Royal Academy, 1849; visited France and Belgium with Rossetti, 1849; removed to Chelsea; found valuable patron in Thomas *Combe; his *Valentine rescuing*

Sylvia from Proteus (1851), attacked by *The Times*, was powerfully defended by John *Ruskin, with whom he became intimate for life; *The Hireling Shepherd* (1852) praised by *Carlyle; exhibited at Academy *Claudio and Isabella* and *Strayed Sheep*, 1853, and in 1854 *The Awakened Conscience* and *The Light of the World* (now at Keble College, Oxford; later replica in St Paul's Cathedral); travelled in Egypt and Palestine, 1854; began at Jerusalem *The Finding of the Saviour in the Temple* (finished, 1860); painted on the Dead Sea *The Scapegoat* (exhibited, 1856); settled at Pimlico, soon removing to Tor Villa, Campden Hill, 1856; refused associateship of the Royal Academy (1856), where he ceased to exhibit after 1874; helped to form Hogarth Club, 1858; designed furniture, setting fashion developed by William *Morris; in Florence, where his first wife died, 1866; painted there *Isabella and the Pot of Basil*; in Holy Land, 1869–71; painted at Jerusalem *The Shadow of Death* (or *The Shadow of the Cross*), 1870–1; after return to London (1871–5) was again in Holy Land, 1875–8; there painted *Nazareth* and *The Triumph of the Innocents*; on voyage out painted *The Ship*, 1875 (now in Tate Gallery); exhibited at the newly founded Grosvenor Gallery from 1877; sent there portraits of his sons, of Sir Richard *Owen (1881), and of Dante Rossetti (1884), as well as *Amaryllis* (1885); executed a water-colour, *Christ among the Doctors* (1886), and *May Morning on Magdalen Tower, Oxford* (1891); painted *The Miracle of Sacred Fire*, 1899; published *Pre-Raphaelitism and the Pre-Raphaelite Brotherhood* (2 vols., 1905); OM and hon. DCL, Oxford, 1905; buried in crypt of St Paul's Cathedral.

HUNTER, Alexander (1729–1809), physician and author; MD, Edinburgh, 1753; studied also at London, Paris, and Rouen; practised at York from 1763; established York Lunatic Asylum; edited *Georgical Essays* in connection with the Agricultural Society, 1770–2; FRS, 1775; FRSE, 1790; honorary member of Board of Agriculture; edited *Evelyn's Sylva* (1776) and *Terra* (1778); published *Culina Famulatrix Medicinae* (1804; reprinted as *Receipts in Modern Cookery*, 1820), and *Men and Manners* (third edn. 1808).

HUNTER, Andrew (1743–1809), professor of divinity at Edinburgh University; studied at Edinburgh and Utrecht; professor of divinity, 1779–1809; minister of Greyfriars, Edinburgh, 1779, of the Tron Church, 1786; DD; moderator of general assembly, 1792.

HUNTER, Anne (1742–1821), poet; sister of Sir Everard *Home; married John *Hunter (1728–1793), 1771.

HUNTER, Sir **Archibald** (1856–1936), general; educated at Glasgow Academy and Sandhurst; gazetted to 4th Foot, 1874; captain, 1882; served with Egyptian Army, 1884–99; commanded Sudan Frontier Force, 1894–6; able commander under Lord *Kitchener, 1896–8; major-general, 1896; KCB, 1898; in South Africa (1899–1901) prominent in defence of Ladysmith and responsible for second great Boer surrender (30 July 1900); assisted Kitchener in reorganizing Indian Army, 1903–8; general, 1905; governor of Gibraltar, 1910–13; held Aldershot command, training New Armies, 1914–17; Conservative MP, Lancaster, 1918–22; GCB, 1911.

HUNTER, Christopher (1675–1757), antiquary; MB, St John's College, Cambridge, 1698; physician successively at Stockton and Durham; published enlarged edition of Davies's *Rites and Monuments of the Church of Durham* (1733); excavated Roman altars; assisted antiquaries; left manuscript topographical collections.

HUNTER, Sir **Claudius Stephen,** first baronet (1775–1851), lord mayor of London; alderman, 1804; sheriff of London, 1808; lord mayor, 1811–12; created baronet, 1812.

HUNTER, Colin (1841–1904), sea painter; after four years in Glasgow shipping office turned to landscape painting, 1861; exhibited 97 pictures, mainly seascapes, at Royal Academy from 1868; his chief works include *Trawlers, waiting for Darkness* (1873), *Their Only Harvest* (1878, in Tate Gallery), and *Signs of Herring* (1899); ARA, 1884; vigorous water-colour artist and etcher.

HUNTER, Donald (1898–1978), physician and authority on occupational medicine; educated at Forest Gate School and London Hospital, 1915–20 (except for one year at sea); MB, BS (Lond.), 1920; MD (Lond.), 1922; MRCP (Lond.), 1923; at Harvard as research fellow studying lead poisoning, 1926; assistant physician, London Hospital, 1927–63; FRCP, 1929; director of Medical Research Council's department for research in industrial medicine, 1943; first editor of *British Journal of Industrial Medicine*, 1944; important lecturer; Sims Commonwealth travelling professor, 1955; published *The Diseases of Occupations* (1955); made great contribution to knowledge of occupational medicine through research into industrial toxicology; CBE, 1957; hon. D.Sc., Durham, 1960; commemorated by Donald Hunter memorial lecture of the Faculty of Occupational Medicine.

HUNTER, Sir **Ellis** (1892–1961), industrialist; articled to firm of accountants after leaving Middlesborough High School; qualified, 1914; worked in steel department, Ministry of Munitions, 1914–18; local partner, W. B. Peat & Co., 1919; general partner, Peat, Marwick, Mitchell & Co., 1928; fellow, Institute of Chartered Accountants, 1927; deputy chairman (and later, managing director), Dorman Long, 1938; chairman, 1948–61; president, Iron and Steel Federation, 1945–53; took leading part in drawing up first post-war development plan; opposed nationalization; knighted, 1948; GBE, 1961.

HUNTER, Sir George Burton (1845–1937), shipbuilder; principal partner of C. S. Swan, Wallsend, 1880; combined as Swan, Hunter & Wigham Richardson, 1903; chairman, 1895–1928; pioneer of system of building within glazed sheds; built the *Mauretania*; KBE, 1918.

HUNTER, George Orby (1773?–1843), translator of *Byron into French; lieutenant, 7th Royal Fusiliers, 1785.

HUNTER, Henry (1741–1802), divine and author; minister of South Leith, 1766, of London Wall (Scottish), 1771; DD, Edinburgh, c.1771; secretary to SPCK in Highlands and islands of Scotland, 1790; DD, Queens' College, Cambridge, incorporated from Trinity College, Dublin, 1795; works include *Sacred Biography* (8th edn. 1820) and translations from Lavater, Euler, and St Pierre.

HUNTER, John (1728–1793), surgeon and anatomist; helped a brother-in-law at Glasgow in cabinet-making; in London assisted his brother *William in dissecting, 1748; pupil of William *Cheselden at Chelsea Hospital and of *Pott at St Bartholomew's; house surgeon at St George's, 1756; surgeon, 1768; student at St Mary Hall, Oxford, 1755–6; in Belleisle expedition, 1761; with army in Portugal, 1762; began to practise in Golden Square, London, 1763; at house in Earl's Court kept dissecting apparatus and wild animals; FRS, 1767; had *Jenner as house pupil in Jermyn Street, London; began lectures on surgery, 1773, having Astley *Cooper and *Abernethy in his class; surgeon-extraordinary to George III, 1776; drew up *Proposals for Recovery of People apparently Drowned* (1776); Croonian lecturer, 1776–82; bought land in Leicester Square and Castle Street, London, and built large museum, 1784–5; first tied femoral artery for popliteal aneurysm, 1785; Copley medallist, 1787; surgeon-general, 1790; died suddenly. His body was removed by College of Surgeons from St Martin's vaults to Westminster Abbey. His chief works were *Treatise on the Blood, Inflammation, and Gunshot Wounds* (1794; edited by Sir Everard *Home, 1812, etc.), *On the Venereal Disease* (1786), *Observations on certain parts of the Animal Oeconomy* (1786), *Observations and Reflections on Geology* (1859), and *Memoranda on Vegetation*

(1860). His manuscripts were destroyed by Sir Everard Home, but his collections were bought by the nation and acquired by the College of Surgeons, 1800, the annual Hunterian oration being first given, 1813. His portrait was painted by *Reynolds.

HUNTER, John (d. 1809), physician; MD, Edinburgh, 1775; superintendent of military hospitals in Jamaica, 1781–3; practised in London; FRCP, 1793; Gulstonian lecturer (on 'softening of the brain'), 1796; Croonian lecturer, 1799–1801; FRS; published *Observations on Diseases of the Army in Jamaica* (1788); his Edinburgh thesis (*De Hominum Varietatibus*) republished in English (1865).

HUNTER, John (1738–1821), vice-admiral; studied at Aberdeen; served in Rochefort expedition (1757) and at capture of Quebec, 1759; served as master in North America under *Hood and *Howe, 1768–78; at the Dogger Bank, 1781, and at relief of Gibraltar, 1782; as captain of the *Sirius* sailed from Port Jackson to the Cape of Good Hope by Cape Horn, 1788–9; wrecked on Norfolk Island, 1789; volunteer; with Howe in action of 1 June 1794; governor of New South Wales, 1795–1801; directed exploration of Terra Australis; wrecked off Paignton, 1804; vice-admiral, 1810.

HUNTER, John (1745–1837), classical scholar; of Edinburgh University; private secretary to Lord *Monboddo; professor of humanity at St Andrews, 1775–1835; LL B; principal of St Salvator's and St Leonard's colleges, 1835–7; published editions of Livy (i–v, 1822), Horace (1797), Caesar (1809), Virgil (1797), and Sallust (1796), and *Ruddiman's *Latin Rudiments*, with additions (1820).

HUNTER, John Kelso (1802–1873), Scottish artist, author, and cobbler; exhibited at Royal Academy portrait of himself as cobbler, 1847; published *Retrospect of an Artist's Life* (1868), a work on *Burns's friends and characters (1870), and *Memorials of West-Country Men and Manners*.

HUNTER, Joseph (1783–1861), antiquary; Presbyterian minister at Bath, 1809–33; member of the 'Stourhead Circle'; sub-commissioner of public records, 1833; assistant keeper, 1838; vice-president, Society of Antiquaries; published *Hallamshire* (1819, enlarged 1869), *South Yorkshire* (1828–31), collections concerning founders of New Plymouth (1854); edited Cresacre More's *Life of More* (1828), *Thoresby's *Diary* (1830), and Dr Thomas Cartwright's *Diary* (1843); wrote also on Robin Hood, *The Tempest*, and other subjects; many of his manuscripts in British Museum.

HUNTER, Leslie Stannard (1890–1983), bishop of Sheffield; educated at Kelvinside Academy, Glasgow, and New College, Oxford; in France with YMCA, 1916; study secretary, Student Christian Movement, 1913–20; ordained, 1916; part-time curacies in Brockley and St Martin-in-the-Fields, London; canonry at Newcastle upon Tyne, 1922–6; vicar of Barking, 1926–30; archdeacon of Northumberland, 1931–9; founded Tyneside Council of Social Service; active in bringing needs of working people of north-east to attention of government; helped to create World Council of Churches; bishop of Sheffield, 1939–62; helped to found William Temple College, Whirlow Grange Conference Centre, and Hollowford Youth Centre; published fourteen books including *The Artist and Religion* (1915), *A Parson's Job* (1931), and *A Mission of the People of God* (1961); honorary degrees, DCL, Durham, 1940, DD, Lambeth, 1949, LL D, Sheffield, 1953, and DD, Trinity College, Toronto; European Bursary Fund set up in his memory.

HUNTER, Sir Martin (1757–1846), general; with 52nd Foot in America, 1775–8, and India; wounded at Seringapatam, 1792; lieutenant-colonel of the 91st, 1794; commanded 60th Royal Americans in West Indies under *Abercromby, troops in Nova Scotia, 1803; general, 1825; KB, GCMG, and GCH.

HUNTER, Philip Vassar (1883–1956), electrical engineer; educated at Wisbech Grammar School and Faraday House; joined C. H. *Merz, 1904; collaborated in evolution of wartime ASDIC submarine detection; CBE, 1920; chief engineer and joint manager, Callender's Cable and Construction, 1919–46; worked on high-voltage power cables; initiated research laboratories, 1934; engineer-in-chief, British Insulated Callender's Cables, 1946; joint deputy chairman, 1947–52; president, British Ice Hockey Association, 1935.

HUNTER, Mrs Rachel (1754–1813), novelist.

HUNTER, Robert (d. 1734), governor of New York; at Blenheim (1704) with Ross's Dragoons; captured by French on voyage to Virginia, 1707; correspondent of *Swift, 1709; as governor of New York (1710–19) took out refugees from the Rhine palatinate and settled them on the Hudson; had constant disputes with the assembly; major-general, 1727; governor of Jamaica, 1729–34.

HUNTER, Robert (*fl.* 1750–1780), portrait painter; exhibited at Dublin; painted portrait of John *Wesley.

HUNTER, Robert (1823–1897), lexicographer and theologian; graduated at Aberdeen, 1840; colleague of Stephen *Hislop at Free Church mission at Nagpore, Central India, 1846–55; resident tutor of Presbyterian Church of England in London, 1864–6; edited *Lloyd's Encyclopaedic Dictionary* (published 1889); LL D, Aberdeen, 1883. His publications include *History of Missions of Free Church of Scotland in India and Africa* (1873).

HUNTER, Sir Robert (1844–1913), solicitor, and authority on commons and public rights; partner in firm of solicitors to Commons Preservation Society, 1869; most notable case, Epping Forest, 1871–4; solicitor to General Post Office, 1882–1913; helped to found National Trust, 1895; knighted, 1894; KCB, 1911.

HUNTER, Samuel (1769–1839), editor of the *Glasgow Herald*, 1803–35.

HUNTER, Thomas (1666–1725), Jesuit; joined Jesuits, 1684; professor at Liège; chaplain to duchess of Norfolk; published *An English Carmelite* (printed 1876); defended Jesuits against Charles *Dodd.

HUNTER, Thomas (1712–1777), author; of The Queen's College, Oxford; master of Blackburn Grammar School, 1737–50; vicar of Weaverham, 1755–78; chief work, *Sketch of the Philosophical Character of Lord Bolingbroke* (1770).

HUNTER, William (1718–1783), anatomist; brother of John *Hunter (1728–1793); educated at Glasgow, Edinburgh, and St George's Hospital; assistant dissector to Dr James *Douglas (1675–1742); assisted by John *Hunter, 1748–59; surgeon-accoucheur to Middlesex, 1748, and British Lying-in Hospital, 1749; MD, Glasgow, 1750; physician-extraordinary to Queen Charlotte, 1764; FRS, 1767; first professor of anatomy, Royal Academy, 1768; FSA, 1768; claimed several of John Hunter's discoveries; president of Medical Society, 1781; his museum acquired by Glasgow University; portrait painted by *Reynolds. His *Anatomical Description of Human Gravid Uterus* (1774, Latin), was edited by *Baillie (1794) and Edward *Rigby (1843). He published *Medical Commentaries* (1762–4) and important papers on *Medical Observations and Inquiries*.

HUNTER, William (1755–1812), orientalist; MA, Marischal College, Aberdeen, 1777; went to India, 1781; published *Concise Account of . . . Pegu* (1785); as surgeon at Agra accompanied Palmer's expedition to Oujein, 1792–3; surgeon to the Marines, 1794–1806; secretary to Asiatic Society of Bengal, 1798–1802 and 1804–11, of Fort William College, 1805–11; published Hindustani–English dictionary (1808); his collection of proverbs in Persian and Hindustani published (1824); died in Java.

HUNTER, William Alexander (1844–1898), lawyer; MA, King's College, Aberdeen, 1864; barrister, Middle Temple, 1867; professor of Roman law, University College, London, 1869–78, of jurisprudence, 1878–82; LL D, Aberdeen, 1882; Liberal MP, North Aberdeen, 1885–96; moved successfully for free elementary education in Scotland, 1890; published legal writings.

HUNTER, Sir William Guyer (1827–1902), surgeon-general; FRCS, 1858; MD, 1867; FRCP, 1875; joined Bengal Medical Service, 1850; civil surgeon in Upper Sind during Mutiny, 1857; professor of medicine in Grant Medical College, Bombay, 1858; principal, 1876; surgeon-general, 1877; vice-chancellor of Bombay University, 1880; KCMG, 1884; hon. LL D, Aberdeen, 1894; member of London School Board, 1886–7; Conservative MP for Central Hackney, 1885–92.

HUNTER, Sir William Wilson (1840–1900), Indian civilian, historian, and publicist; graduated at Glasgow, 1860; entered Indian Civil Service, 1861; assistant-magistrate and collector in Birbhum district; published *Annals of Rural Bengal* (1868), *Orissa* (1872), and *Comparative Dictionary of Non-Aryan Languages of India and High Asia* (1868); appointed by Lord *Mayo to organize statistical survey of Indian empire, 1869; occupied with it twelve years, the compilation reaching 128 volumes, condensed into *The Imperial Gazetteer of India* (9 vols., 1881); his article on 'India' reissued (1895) as *The Indian Empire: its Peoples, History, and Products*; an additional member of Governor-General's Council, 1881–7; settled near Oxford; made extensive collections for a history of India; published first volume of work tracing growth of British dominion in India (1899), second volume (1900); CIE, 1878; CSI, 1884; KCSI, 1887; LL D, Glasgow, 1869; MA, Oxford, by decree of convocation, 1889; hon. LL D, Cambridge, 1887.

HUNTER-WESTON, Sir Aylmer Gould (1864–1940), lieutenant-general. See WESTON.

HUNTINGDON, countess of (1707–1791). See HASTINGS, SELINA.

HUNTINGDON, earls of. See WALTHEOF, d. 1076; SENLIS or ST LIZ, SIMON DE, d. 1109; DAVID I, king of Scotland, 1084–1153; HENRY OF SCOTLAND, 1114?–1152; MALCOLM IV, king of Scotland, 1141–1165; WILLIAM THE LYON, king of Scotland, 1143–1214; HERBERT, WILLIAM, 1460–1491; HOLLAND, JOHN, first earl (of the Holland family), 1352?–1400; HOLLAND, JOHN, second earl (of the Holland family), 1395–1447; HASTINGS, GEORGE, first earl (of the Hastings family),

1488?–1545; HASTINGS, FRANCIS, second earl, 1514?–1561; HASTINGS, HENRY, third earl, 1535–1595; HASTINGS, THEOPHILUS, seventh earl, 1650–1701; HASTINGS, HANS FRANCIS, eleventh earl, 1779–1828.

HUNTINGDON, Gregory of (fl. 1290). See GREGORY.

HUNTINGDON, Henry of (1084?–1155). See HENRY.

HUNTINGFIELD, William de (fl. 1220), justice-itinerant; constable of Dover, 1203; sheriff of Norfolk and Suffolk, 1210–14; one of the twenty-five appointed to enforce Magna Carta; reduced Essex and Suffolk for Louis of France; captured at Lincoln, 1217; licensed to go on crusade, 1219.

HUNTINGFORD, George Isaac (1748–1832), bishop successively of Gloucester and Hereford; fellow of New College, Oxford, 1770; MA, 1776; DD, 1793; warden of Winchester, 1789–1832; bishop of Gloucester, 1802–15, of Hereford, 1815–32; compiled account of his friend Henry *Addington's administration (1802); published also *Short Introduction to Writing of Greek* (frequently reissued), original Latin and Greek verse, and pamphlets.

HUNTINGFORD, Henry (1787–1867), author of editions of Pindar (1814 and 1821) and of Damm's *Pindaric Lexicon* (1814); nephew of George Isaac *Huntingford; fellow of Winchester and New College, Oxford; BCL, 1814; prebendary of Hereford, 1838.

HUNTINGTON, George (1825–1905), rector of Tenby from 1867; his ritualistic sympathies led to controversy with his bishop, 1877; publications include *Church's Work in our Large Towns* (1863), *Random Recollections* (1895), sermons, and addresses.

HUNTINGTON, John (fl. 1553), author of *Genealogy of Heretics* (doggerel, 1540), reprinted and replied to by Bale; Protestant preacher; canon of Exeter, 1560.

HUNTINGTON, Robert (1637–1701), orientalist; MA, Merton College, Oxford, 1663; fellow; chaplain of Levant Company at Aleppo, 1671–81; visited Palestine, Cyprus, and Egypt, acquiring valuable manuscripts and corresponding with Narcissus *Marsh, *Pococke, and *Bernard; provost of Trinity College, Dublin, 1683–92; bishop of Raphoe, 1701; many of his manuscripts in the Bodleian, and library of Merton College, Oxford, and Trinity College, Dublin.

HUNTINGTON, William, SS (i.e. Sinner Saved) (1745–1813), coal-heaver and preacher; preached in Surrey and Sussex; built 'Providence

Chapel', Titchfield Street, London, and preached there, 1783–1810; opened New Providence Chapel, Gray's Inn Lane, London, 1811; had controversies with Rowland *Hill and others; published *God the Guardian of the Poor*, *The Naked Bow*, and other works.

HUNTLEY, Francis (1787?–1831), actor; played Othello to *Kean's Iago at Birmingham; appeared under *Elliston as Lockit, 1809; at Covent Garden, 1811–12; the 'Roscius of the Coburg' (Theatre).

HUNTLEY, Sir Henry Vere (1795–1864), naval captain and colonial governor; cruised successfully against slavers on west African coast; lieutenant-governor of the Gambia, 1839, of Prince Edward Island; knighted, 1841; published *California, its Gold and its Inhabitants* (1856) and other works; died consul at Santos, Brazil.

HUNTLY, earls of. See SETON, ALEXANDER DE, first earl, d. 1470; GORDON, GEORGE, second earl, d. 1502?; GORDON, ALEXANDER, third earl, d. 1524; GORDON, GEORGE, fourth earl, 1514–1562; GORDON, GEORGE, fifth earl, d. 1576.

HUNTLY, marquises of. See GORDON, GEORGE, first marquis, 1562–1636; GORDON, GEORGE, second marquis, d. 1649; GORDON, GEORGE, fourth marquis, first duke of Gordon, 1643–1716; GORDON, ALEXANDER, fifth marquis, second duke of Gordon, 1678?–1728; GORDON, ALEXANDER, seventh marquis, fourth duke of Gordon, 1743–1827; GORDON, GEORGE, eighth marquis, fifth duke of Gordon, 1770–1836; GORDON, GEORGE, ninth marquis, 1761–1853.

HUNTON, Philip (1604?–1682), author of *Treatise of Monarchie* (1643); MA, Wadham College, Oxford, 1629; vicar of Westbury till 1662; provost of *Cromwell's University of Durham, 1657–60.

HUNTSMAN, Benjamin (1704–1776), inventor of cast steel; originally a Doncaster clockmaker; experimented and perfected his invention at Handsworth; removed to Attercliffe, 1770, where his son carried on the business.

HUQUIER, James Gabriel (1725–1805), portrait painter and engraver; came to England from Paris with his father.

HURCOMB, Cyril William, Baron Hurcomb (1883–1975), civil servant; educated at Oxford High School and St John's College, Oxford; entered Civil Service in the Post Office, 1906; transferred to Admiralty, 1914 and to Ministry of Shipping, 1916; deputy director, and later director of commercial services; joined Ministry of Transport, 1919; negotiated regrouping of railway companies, 1921; appointed permanent secretary, 1927; assisted Herbert *Morrison (later Lord Morrison of Lambeth) to introduce legislation establishing London (Passenger) Transport Board and Road Traffic Act of 1930; chairman, Electricity Commission, 1938; director-general, Ministry of Shipping (later War Transport), 1939; chairman, British Transport Commission, 1947–53; chairman, Committee of Bird Sanctuaries in Royal Parks, 1947; chairman, Council of Nature Conservancy, 1961–2; president, Society for the Promotion of Nature Reserves (1950–61), of Field Studies Council (1957), and of Royal Society for the Protection of Birds (1961–6); CBE, 1918; CB, 1922; KBE, 1929; KCB, 1938; GCB, 1946; first Baron Hurcomb, 1950; many foreign decorations; hon. fellow, St John's College, Oxford, 1938; title became extinct when he died, 1975.

HURD, Richard (1720–1808), bishop of Worcester; fellow of Emmanuel College, Cambridge; MA, 1742; DD, 1768; his editions of Horace's *Ars Poetica* (1749) and *Epistola ad Augustum* (1751), praised by *Warburton and translated into German; defended Warburton against *Jortin (1755) and edited (1757) his *Remarks* on *Hume's *Natural History of Religion*; issued *Moral and Political Dialogues* (1759) and *Letters on Chivalry and Romance* (1762); his attacks on *Leland and Jortin reprinted, with caustic preface by *Parr (1789); preacher at Lincoln's Inn, 1765; archdeacon of Gloucester, 1767; Warburtonian lecturer, 1768; bishop of Lichfield and Coventry, 1774–81, of Worcester, 1781–1808; preceptor to prince of Wales, 1776; declined the primacy, 1783; complete works issued (1811).

HURD, Thomas (1757?–1823), hydrographer; lieutenant of the *Unicorn* at capture of *Danaë*, 1779; present at Dominica, 1782; captain, 1802; made first exact survey of Bermuda; hydrographer to the Admiralty, 1808–23.

HURDIS, James (1763–1801), author of *The Village Curate and other Poems* (1788) and friend of *Cowper; BA, Magdalen College, Oxford, 1785; incumbent of Bishopstone, 1791; professor of poetry at Oxford, 1793; attempted to vindicate Oxford from Gibbon's aspersions.

HURDIS, James Henry (1800–1857), amateur artist; son of James *Hurdis; pupil of *Heath and friend of *Cruikshank.

HURLESTON, Richard (*fl.* 1764–1780), painter; with Joseph *Wright in Italy, 1773–80; killed by lightning on Salisbury Plain.

HURLSTONE, Frederick Yeates (1800–1869), portrait and historical painter; grandnephew of Richard *Hurleston; pupil of *Beechey and *Lawrence; began to exhibit at Royal Academy, 1821; exhibited from 1831 chiefly at Society of British Artists, being president,

1840–69; received Gold Medal at Paris Exhibition of 1855, sending *La Mora, Boabdil*, and *Constance and Arthur*.

HURLSTONE, William Yeates (1876–1906), musical composer and pianist; grandson of Frederick Yeates *Hurlstone; composed from age of 9; published orchestral compositions, pianoforte concerto, and cantata.

HURRION, John (1675?–1731), Independent minister of Hare Court Chapel, London, and Merchants' lecturer at Pinners' Hall, London; works edited by Revd A. Taylor (1823).

HURRY, Sir John (d. 1650). See URRY.

HURST, Sir Arthur Frederick (1879–1944), physician; educated at Bradford and Manchester grammar schools and Magdalen College, Oxford; first class, physiology, 1901; BM (Oxon.) from Guy's Hospital, 1904; assistant physician, in charge of neurological department, 1906; full physician, 1918–39; pioneer in clinical science; built up team of colleagues at New Lodge Clinic, Windsor Forest; studied particularly the alimentary tract; edited *Guy's Hospital Reports*, 1921–39; changed name from Hertz, 1916; knighted, 1937.

HURST, Sir Cecil James Barrington (1870–1963), international lawyer; educated at Westminster School and Trinity College, Cambridge; first class, part ii, law tripos, 1891–2; called to bar (Middle Temple), 1893; assistant legal adviser, Foreign Office, 1902; member of arbitration commission to report on *Alsop* claims of United States and Chile, 1910; British agent, British–American Claims Arbitration Tribunal, 1912; KC, 1913; legal adviser to Foreign Office, 1918–29; chief editor, *British Year Book of International Law*, 1919–28; president, Grotius Society, 1940; judge, Permanent Court of International Justice, 1929–46; president, 1934–6; chairman, Home Office panel for appeals against detention under Regulation 18B; first president, War Crimes Commission, 1943–5; CB, 1907; KCB, 1920; KCMG, 1924; GCMG, 1926; treasurer, Middle Temple, 1940; president, Institute of International Law; hon. LL D, Cambridge and Edinburgh.

HURST, Henry (1629–1690), Nonconformist divine; made probationary fellow of Merton College, Oxford, by parliamentary visitors, 1649; MA, 1652; ejected from St Matthew's, Friday Street, London, 1662; preached at conventicles; published religious works.

HURWITZ, Hyman (1770–1844), professor of Hebrew at London University, 1828; born at Posen; acquaintance of *Coleridge; published *Vindiciae Hebraicae* (1820), *Elements of the Hebrew Language* (1829), a Hebrew grammar (2nd edn. 1835), and poems.

HUSBAND, Sir (Henry) Charles (1908–1983), engineer; educated at King Edward VII School, Sheffield, and Sheffield University; B.Eng., 1929; assistant to Sir (Evan) Owen Williams, 1931–3; engineer and surveyor to First National Housing Trust Ltd., 1933–6; founded firm of Husband & Clark, consulting engineers, 1936; involved in variety of public works; senior partner, 1937; during 1939–45 war principal technical officer, Central Register, Ministry of Labour and National Service, 1939–40, and assistant director, Directorate of Aircraft Production Factories, Ministry of Works, 1940–5; post-war, made Husband & Co. one of foremost firms of consulting engineers in UK; constructed Jodrell Bank radio telescope, 1957, and rebuilt Britannia rail-bridge over Menai Strait, 1970; CBE, 1964; knighted, 1975; received Royal Society Royal Medal, 1965; hon. D.Sc., Manchester, 1964, and hon. D.Eng., Sheffield, 1967; awarded number of medals; founder fellow, Fellowship of Engineering; fellow, Institution of Civil Engineers and Mechanical Engineers, and president, Structural Engineers, 1964–5; chairman, Association of Consulting Engineers, 1967.

HUSBAND, William (1823–1887), civil engineer and inventor; superintended erection of Leigh water engine for drainage of Haarlem Lake; became managing partner of Harvey & Co., 1863; patented, 1859, balance valve for waterworks, four-beat pump-valve, the oscillating cylinder stamps called after him, and other inventions; president of Mining Association and Institute of Cornwall, 1881–2.

HUSE, Sir William (d. 1495). See HUSSEY.

HUSENBETH, Frederick Charles (1796–1872), Roman Catholic divine and author; educated at Sedgley Park and Oscott; chaplain at Cossey Hall, Norfolk, from 1820; DD, 1850; vicar-general of Northampton, 1852. His fifty-four works include a defence of Catholicism against Blanco *White (1826), missal and vesper books for the laity, notices of English colleges and convents after the Dissolution, 1849, *Emblems of Saints* (1850; ed. Jessopp, 1882), and a translation of the Vulgate based on the Douay and Rhemish versions.

HUSK, William Henry (1814–1887), writer on music; librarian to Sacred Harmonic Society, 1853–82; published *Account of Musical Celebrations on St. Cecilia's Day* (1857); contributed to *Grove's Dictionary*; edited *Songs of the Nativity* (1868).

HUSKE, Ellis (1700–1755), deputy postmaster-general in America; brother of John *Huske;

reputed author of *Present State of North America* (1755).

HUSKE, John (1692?–1761), general; aide-de-camp to Lord *Cadogan in Holland; major-general for services at Dettingen, 1743; second-in-command at Falkirk, 1746; led second line at Culloden; lieutenant-general, 1747; in Flanders and Minorca; general, 1756; governor of Jersey, 1760.

HUSKISSON, Thomas (1784–1844), captain in the navy; half-brother of William *Huskisson; present in the *Defence* at Trafalgar, 1805; signal-lieutenant to Gambier at Copenhagen, 1807; served in West Indies, attaining post-rank, 1811; paymaster of the navy, 1827–30.

HUSKISSON, William (1770–1830), states-man; privately educated at Paris; private secretary to Lord Gower, English ambassador at Paris; under-secretary at war, 1795; MP, Morpeth, 1796–1802, Liskeard, 1804–7, Harwich, 1807–12, Chichester, 1812–23, and Liverpool, 1823–30; secretary to the Treasury under Pitt, 1804–5, and Portland, 1807–9; resigned with Canning, 1809; supported Canning on the regency and other questions; published pamphlet on *Depreciation of the Currency* (1810); colonial agent for Ceylon, 1811–23; privy councillor, 1814; minister of woods and forests under Liverpool, 1814; took frequent part in debates on corn laws and (1816) bank restriction; member of Finance Committee, 1819; drafted report of committee on agricultural distress, 1821; defeated *Londonderry's proposed relief loan, 1822, but his offer to resign refused by Liverpool; treasurer of the navy and president of Board of Trade, 1823–7; passed measures for regulating the silk manufactures and for removal of restrictions on Scottish linen industry; greatly reduced importation duties on sugar, foreign cotton, woollen goods, glass, paper, and other commodities, 1825; spoke effectively on shipping interest and silk trade; much attacked for his free-trade tendencies; colonial secretary and leader of House of Commons under Goderich and Wellington, 1827–8; disagreed with Wellington on Corn Bill, and resigned on question of redistribution of the disfranchised seats at East Retford and Penrhyn, 1828; supported Catholic emancipation, 1828, and additional representation for Leeds, Liverpool, and Manchester, 1829; gave much attention to Indian questions; killed by being run over at opening of Manchester and Liverpool Railway.

HUSSEY, Bonaventura (d. 1614). See O'HUSSEY, MAELBRIGHDE.

HUSSEY, Christopher Edward Clive (1899–1970), architectural historian and architectural contributor to *Country Life* for fifty years; educated at Eton and Christ Church, Oxford, 1919–21; joined editorial staff, *Country Life*, 1920; contributed nearly 1,400 signed articles in fifty years; editor, 1933–40; publications include *Eton College* (1922), *Petworth House* (1926), *The Picturesque* (1927), *English Country Houses: Early Georgian* (1955), *Mid-Georgian* (1956), and *Late Georgian* (1958), *English Gardens and Landscapes 1700–1750* (1967), and the *Life* of Sir Edwin *Lutyens (1950); president, Society of Architectural Historians, 1964–6; hon. ARIBA, 1935; FSA, 1947; CBE, 1956; associate of the Institute of Landscape Artists.

HUSSEY, Giles (1710–1788), painter; studied under the Venetian, Vincenzo Damini, who while travelling with him decamped with his money; friend and pupil of Ercole Lelli at Rome, where he elaborated and illustrated his theory of beauty in nature, and drew chalk portraits of the Young Pretender; in England painted little.

HUSSEY, Sir John, Baron Hussey (1466?–1537), eldest son of Sir William *Hussey; comptroller of Henry VII's household; employed diplomatically by Henry VIII; chief butler of England, 1521; summoned to House of Lords, 1529; chamberlain to Princess Mary, 1533; executed on charge of complicity in 'Pilgrimage of Grace'.

HUSSEY, Philip (d. 1782), Irish portrait painter.

HUSSEY, Richard (1715?–1770), attorney-general to Queen *Charlotte; barrister, Middle Temple, 1742; MP, St Mawes, 1761–8, East Looe, 1768–70; auditor of duchy of Cornwall, 1768; counsel to East India Company and admiralty; prominent debater.

HUSSEY, Robert (1801–1856), first professor of ecclesiastical history at Oxford; king's scholar of Westminster; double first from Christ Church, 1824; censor, 1835–42; MA, 1827; BD, 1837; professor of ecclesiastical history, 1842–56; edited Socrates (1844), Evagrius (1844); *Bede (1846), and Sozomen (published 1860); established against William *Cureton the accepted view as to Epistles of St Ignatius (1849); published also *Rise of the Papal Power* (1851).

HUSSEY, Thomas (1741–1803), Roman Catholic bishop of Waterford and Lismore; after studying at the Irish College, Salamanca, entered La Trappe; chaplain to Spanish embassy and rector of Spanish Church, London, 1767; undertook confidential political mission to Madrid; FRS, 1792; employed by ministers to check disaffection among Romanists in the public services in Ireland, 1794; president of Maynooth, 1795; bishop of Waterford and Lismore, 1795.

HUSSEY, Walter (1742–1783). See BURGH, WALTER HUSSEY.

HUSSEY (or HUSE), Sir William (d. 1495), chief justice; as attorney-general conducted impeachment of *Clarence; serjeant-at-law, 1478; chief justice of King's Bench, 1481–95; successfully protested against practice of consultation of judges by the crown.

HUSTLER, John (1715–1790), Bradford philanthropist; Quaker and wool-stapler; projected Leeds and Liverpool Canal (opened 1777); advocated in pamphlets (1782 and 1787), prohibition of export of wool.

HUTCHESON, Francis, the elder (1694–1746), philosopher; educated in Ireland and at Glasgow; while keeping a private school in Dublin became acquainted with Lord Carteret, Archbishop *King, and Edward *Synge; as professor of moral philosophy at Glasgow, 1729–46, greatly influenced 'common-sense' school of philosophy; upheld ethical principles of *Shaftesbury against those of *Hobbes and Mandeville; his *System of Moral Philosophy* published by his son (1755).

HUTCHESON, Francis, the younger (*fl.* 1745–1773), also known as Francis Ireland; musical composer; only son of Francis *Hutcheson the elder; MA, Trinity College, Dublin, 1748; MD, 1762; composed part-songs.

HUTCHESON, George (1580?–1639), joint founder of Hutcheson's Hospital, Glasgow.

HUTCHESON, Thomas (1589–1641), joint founder with his brother George *Hutcheson of Hutcheson's Hospital, Glasgow; keeper of register of sasines, Glasgow.

HUTCHINS, Edward (1558?–1629), canon of Salisbury, 1589; fellow of Brasenose College, Oxford, 1581; MA, 1581; BD, 1590.

HUTCHINS, Sir George (d. 1705), king's serjeant; barrister, Gray's Inn, 1667; serjeant-at-law, 1686; king's serjeant, 1689; knighted, 1689; third commissioner of great seal, 1690–3.

HUTCHINS, John (1698–1773), historian of Dorset; BA, Balliol College, Oxford, 1722; MA, Cambridge, 1730; held livings in Dorset; two volumes of his history of Dorset issued (1774); second edition partially destroyed by fire, 1808; two further volumes, edited by Gough (1813 and 1815).

HUTCHINSON, Baron. See HELY-HUTCHINSON, JOHN, afterwards second earl of Donoughmore, 1757–1832.

HUTCHINSON, Mrs Anne (1590?–1643), preacher; née Marbury; followed John *Cotton to Massachusetts, 1634; formed an Antinomian sect; condemned by ecclesiastical synod, 1637, and banished; settled in Aquidneck (Rhode Island), 1638; after death of husband moved to Hell Gate, New York county; murdered there by Indians.

HUTCHINSON, Arthur (1866–1937), mineralogist; educated at Clifton and Christ's College, Cambridge; first classes, natural sciences tripos (1886–8); fellow (1892), assistant tutor (1901–26), master (1928–37), Pembroke College; university demonstrator in mineralogy (1895), lecturer in crystallography (1923), professor of mineralogy, 1926–31; discovered mineral stokesite, 1899; encouraged research in X-ray crystallography; FRS, 1922.

HUTCHINSON, Christopher Hely- (1767–1826). See HELY-HUTCHINSON.

HUTCHINSON, Edward (1613–1675), settler in Massachusetts, son of Mrs Anne *Hutchinson; murdered while negotiating with Nipmuck Indians.

HUTCHINSON, Francis (1660–1739), bishop of Down and Connor; MA, Catharine Hall, Cambridge, 1684; while incumbent of St James's, Bury St Edmunds, published *Historical Essay concerning Witchcraft* (1718); bishop of Down and Connor, 1720–39; published *Life of Archbishop Tillotson* (1718), *Church Catechism in Irish* (1722), *Defence of the Ancient Historians* (1734), and other works.

HUTCHINSON, Francis Ernest (1871–1947), scholar and canon of Worcester; educated at Lancing and Trinity College, Oxford; deacon, 1896; priest, 1897; chaplain, King's College, Cambridge, 1904–12; vicar of Leyland, 1912–20; secretary, delegacy for extra-mural studies, Oxford, 1920–34; chaplain (1928), fellow (1934), All Souls; canon of Worcester, 1934–43; sensitive student of Caroline poetry; FBA, 1944.

HUTCHINSON, Horatio Gordon (Horace) (1859–1932), golfer and author; captained first four Oxford golf teams, 1878–82; amateur champion, 1886, 1887; played for England against Scotland, 1902–7 (except 1905); dashing and characteristic style; published *Hints on the Game of Golf* (1886), and thereafter wrote prolifically on golf, shooting, fishing, etc.

HUTCHINSON, John (1615–1664), regicide; of Peterhouse, Cambridge, and Lincoln's Inn; held Nottingham for the parliament as governor; as member for Nottinghamshire from 1646 attached himself to the Independents; signed the king's death-warrant; member of first two Councils of State, but retired, 1653; took his seat in restored parliament, 1659; worked with *Monck and *Hesilrige against *Lambert; saved from death and confiscation at Restoration by influence of kinsmen, but imprisoned in the Tower and Sandown Castle, 1663–4.

HUTCHINSON, John (1674–1737), author of *Moses's Principia* (1724); while steward to duke of *Somerset employed by *Woodward (his physician) to collect fossils; riding purveyor to George I; invented improved timepiece for determination of longitude; published works of religious symbolism, gaining distinguished adherents.

HUTCHINSON, John (1884–1972), botanist; educated at village school in Northumberland where his father was a gardener; worked as garden boy and attended evening classes at Rutherford College; worked as gardener at Royal Botanic Gardens, Kew, 1904; promoted to post in herbarium, 1905; assistant for India and later for Africa, 1907–16; took charge of African section, 1917–36; keeper of the museums at Kew, 1936–48; published *Flora of Tropical Africa* (1912, 1915), and *Flora of West Tropical Africa* (with J. M. Dalziel, 1937); wrote on the Rhododendron; Victoria Medal of Honour, Royal Horticultural Society, 1945; other publications include *The Families of Flowering Plants* (2 vols., 1926 and 1934; 2nd edn. 1959, 3rd edn. 1973), *Evolution and Phylogeny of Flowering Plants* (1969), *The Genera of Flowering Plants* (2 vols., 1964 and 1967), and popular books such as *Common Wild Flowers* (1945) and *British Wild Flowers* (2 vols., 1955); journeys in southern Africa with General J. C. *Smuts, described in *A Botanist in Southern Africa* (1946); hon. LL D, St Andrews, 1934; fellow, Linnean Society, 1918; Linnean gold medallist, 1965; FRS, 1947; OBE, 1972.

HUTCHINSON, John Hely- (1724–1794). See HELY-HUTCHINSON.

HUTCHINSON, Sir Jonathan (1828–1913), surgeon; educated at York Medical School and St Bartholomew's Hospital, London; assistant surgeon to London Hospital, 1859; full surgeon, 1863; FRCS, 1862; Hunterian professor, 1879–83; FRS, 1882; left staff of London Hospital as emeritus professor of surgery, 1883; president of Royal College of Surgeons, 1889; delivered Hunterian oration, 1891; knighted, 1908; specialist of great repute on ophthalmology, dermatology, and especially on syphilis; works include *Illustrations of Clinical Surgery* (1878–84) and *Archives of Surgery* (1889–1900); formed museum of specimens and drawings.

HUTCHINSON, Lucy (b. 1620), author; daughter of Sir Allen *Apsley; married John *Hutchinson (1615–1664), 1638; in early life made verse translation of Lucretius; adopted Baptist views; exerted herself to save her husband

in 1660. Her *Life of Colonel Hutchinson* was first printed (1806), her treatise *On Principles of the Christian Religion* (1817).

HUTCHINSON (or HUCHENSON), Ralph (1553?–1606), president of St John's College, Oxford; of Merchant Taylors' School, and St John's College, Oxford; MA, 1578; DD, 1602; president, 1590–1606; a translator of New Testament (AV).

HUTCHINSON, Richard Hely-, first earl of Donoughmore (1756–1825). See HELY-HUTCHINSON.

HUTCHINSON, Richard Walter John Hely-, sixth earl of Donoughmore (1875–1948), chairman of committees of the House of Lords. See HELY-HUTCHINSON.

HUTCHINSON, Roger (d. 1555), divine; fellow of St John's College, Cambridge, 1543, and of Eton, 1550; MA, 1544; his works edited by John Bruce.

HUTCHINSON, Thomas (1698–1769), scholar; of Lincoln College and Hart Hall, Oxford; MA, 1721; DD, 1738; vicar of Horsham and Cocking; edited Xenophon's *Anabasis* (1735) and *Cyropaedia* (1727).

HUTCHINSON, Thomas (1711–1780), governor of Massachusetts Bay; descendant of Mrs Anne *Hutchinson; graduated at Harvard, 1727; member of Colonial Legislature; sent on mission to England, 1740; speaker of House of Representatives, 1746–8; judge, 1752; as commissioner to Albany Congress drew up with Franklin plan of union of colonies, 1754; lieutenant-governor of Massachusetts, 1758, and chief justice, 1760; carried out Grenville's policy, after which his house was sacked, 1765; on withdrawal of *Bernard, 1769, acted as governor, being formally appointed, 1771; his removal petitioned for by Massachusetts assembly after disclosure (1773) by Franklin of his correspondence with *Whately; left America, 1774; consulted by George III and ministers; deprecated penal measures against Boston and Massachusetts; DCL, Oxford, 1776. Of his *History of Massachuset's [sic] Bay*, vol. i appeared (1764), vol. ii (1767), vol. iii (written in England) was edited by the Revd John Hutchinson (1828). His *Collection of Original Papers relative to History of Massachusets Bay* (1769) was reissued as *Hutchinson Papers* (1823–5); *Diary and Letters* edited by P. O. Hutchinson (1883–6).

HUTCHINSON, William (1715–1801), mariner and writer on seamanship; dock-master at Liverpool, 1760; published treatise on seamanship (1777), enlarged in fourth edition as *Treatise* *on Naval Architecture*; said to have introduced parabolic reflectors for lighthouses.

HUTCHINSON, William (1732–1814), topographer; FSA, 1781; published histories of Durham, 1785–94, and Cumberland, 1794, *View of Northumberland* (1776–8), and other works.

HUTCHISON, Sir Robert, first baronet of Thurle (1871–1960), physician and paediatrician; educated at the Collegiate School and University, Edinburgh; qualified in medicine, 1893; MD, 1896; FRCP, 1903; on staff of Hospital for Sick Children, Great Ormond Street, and London Hospital, 1900–34; publications include *Clinical Methods* (with H. Rainy, 1897), *Food and the Principles of Dietetics* (1900), and *Lectures on Diseases of Children* (1904); baronet, 1939.

HUTCHISON, Sir William Oliphant (1889–1970), landscape and portrait painter; educated at Kirkcaldy High School, Cargilfield, Rugby, and Edinburgh College of Art; served in Royal Garrison Artillery, 1914–18; practised in London as a portrait painter; exhibited at Royal Academy, 1921–9; director, Glasgow School of Art, 1932–43; moved to Edinburgh, resumed portrait and landscape painting, and became deeply involved with the Royal Scottish Academy, 1943; president, 1950–9; knighted, 1953; returned to London, 1959; president, Royal Society of Portrait Painters, 1965; among his portraits were the Queen, Prince Philip, the Queen Mother, and J. Ramsay MacDonald (now in the House of Commons).

HUTH, Alfred Henry (1850–1910), bibliophile; son of Henry *Huth; travelled in East with Henry Thomas *Buckle, 1861–2; publications include *The Marriage of Near Kin* (1875) and life of Buckle (2 vols., 1880); helped to found Bibliographical Society, 1892; by will left fifty volumes to British Museum; sale of part of collection realized over £108,000 (1911–12).

HUTH, Henry (1815–1878), merchant-banker and bibliophile; travelled in Germany and France; lived some time in the United States and Mexico; finally joined his father's firm in London, 1849; collected voyages, Shakespearian and early English literature, and early Spanish and German books; printed *Ancient Ballads and Broadsides* (1867), *Inedited Poetical Miscellanies, 1584–1700* (1870), *Prefaces, Dedications, and Epistles, 1540–1701* (1874), *Fugitive Tracts, 1493–1700* (1875).

HUTHWAITE, Sir Edward (1793?–1873), lieutenant-general; with Bengal Artillery in Nepal, 1815–16, Oudh, 1817, the Mahratta War of 1817–18, and Cachar, 1824; commanded battery at Bhurtpore, 1825–6, the artillery of the Megwar Field Force, 1840–4, and 3rd brigade,

Bengal Horse Artillery in first Sikh War; brigadier of foot artillery in second Sikh War; major-general, 1857; lieutenant-general, 1868; KCB, 1869.

HUTT, Sir George (1809–1889), artillery officer; brother of Sir William *Hutt; distinguished at Meeanee; commanded artillery in Persian War; KCB, 1886.

HUTT, John (1746–1794), captain in the navy; captured by the French, 1781; distinguished as flag-captain to Sir Alan *Gardner; mortally wounded in *Howe's action of 1 June 1794; his monument in Westminster Abbey.

HUTT, Sir William (1801–1882), politician; nephew of John *Hutt; MA, Trinity College, Cambridge, 1831; MP, Hull, 1832–41, Gateshead, 1841–74; paymaster-general and vice-president of Board of Trade, 1860–5; negotiated commercial treaty with Austria, 1865; KCB, 1865; commissioner for foundation of South Australia; leading member of New Zealand Company.

HUTTEN, Leonard (1557?–1632), divine and antiquary; of Westminster and Christ Church, Oxford; MA, 1582; DD, 1600; sub-dean of Christ Church; vicar of Floore, 1601–32; a translator of the Bible, 1604; prebendary of St Paul's, 1609; published *Answere to . . . A Short Treatise of the Crosse in Baptisme* (1605); his *Antiquities of Oxford* printed (1720).

HÜTTNER, Johann Christian (1765?–1847), author and translator; his account of *Macartney's mission to China surreptitiously published in Germany (1797), and translated into French, anticipating the official narrative; translator to Foreign Office, 1807.

HUTTON, Adam (d. 1389). See HOUGHTON.

HUTTON, Alfred (1839–1910), swordsman; joined 79th Highlanders, 1859; captain, 1868; organized Cameron Fencing Club, for which he published *Swordsmanship* (1862); on retiring from army (1873) practised modern fencing and revived older systems; published *Cold Steel* (1889), *Fixed Bayonets* (1890), *The Swordsman* (1891), *Old Sword Play* (1892), and *The Sword and the Centuries* (1901); FSA, 1894; founder and chairman of Central London Throat and Ear Hospital, 1874; bequeathed collection of fencing literature to Victoria and Albert Museum.

HUTTON, Catherine (1756–1846), author; daughter of William *Hutton (1723–1815); published *Life of W. Hutton* (1816; ed. Llewellyn *Jewitt, 1872), *History of Birmingham* (4th edn. 1819), and novels; left valuable letters (selections published, 1891).

HUTTON, Charles (1737–1823), mathematician; son of a colliery labourer; opened mathematical school at Newcastle upon Tyne, 1760; prepared map of Newcastle, 1770; professor of mathematics at Woolwich Academy, 1773–1807; edited *Ladies' Diary*, 1773–1818; FRS, 1774 (foreign secretary, 1779); Copley medallist, 1778; LL D, Edinburgh, 1779; computed mean density of the earth, 1778; published *Principles of Bridges* (1772), *Mathematical Tables* (1785), and similar works; abridged *Philosophical Transactions* (1809).

HUTTON, Frederick Wollaston (1836–1905), geologist; served in Indian Mercantile Marine; in army, 1855–65; in Crimea and Indian Mutiny; emigrated to New Zealand, 1866; professor of geology in University of New Zealand, 1890–3; curator of museum, 1893; interested in ornithology and ethnology; writings include *Elementary Geology* (1875), *The Lesson of Evolution* (1902), and works on fauna of New Zealand (1904); FRS, 1892.

HUTTON, George Clark (1825–1908), Presbyterian divine; educated at Edinburgh University; hon. DD, 1906; United Presbyterian minister at Paisley from 1851 till death; advocated 'voluntary' movement in religion; strenuously advocated disestablishment of Church of Scotland in speeches and pamphlets; urged state secular education; moderator of synod, 1884; principal of United Presbyterian theological college, 1892; co-principal with G. C. M. *Douglas of United Free Church College, Glasgow, till 1902; moderator of United Free Church general assembly, 1906; a trenchant controversialist.

HUTTON, George Henry (d. 1827), archaeologist; son of Charles *Hutton; lieutenant-general, 1821; LL D, Aberdeen.

HUTTON, Henry (*fl.* 1619), satirical poet; author of *Follie's Anatomie* (1619; edited by E. F. *Rimbault, 1842).

HUTTON, James (1715–1795), founder of the Moravian Church in England; educated at Westminster; became connected with the Methodists and published *Whitefield's Journal*, 1738–9; visited German Moravians, 1739; broke with *Wesley, 1740; 'referendary' of Society for Furtherance of the Gospel; published appreciation of Zinzendorf (1755).

HUTTON, James (1726–1797), geologist; educated at Edinburgh, Paris, and Leiden; MD, Leiden, 1749; studied agriculture and travelled in Holland, Belgium, and Picardy; partner with James Davie in production of sal ammoniac from coal-soot; settled in Edinburgh, 1768; published his *Theory of the Earth* (1795), verified by visits to Glen Tilt, Galloway, Arran, and the Isle of Man;

his *Theory of Rain* attacked by Jean André *Deluc and others; published *Dissertations* (1792) and *Investigations of Principles of Knowledge* (1794); originator of modern theory of formation of the earth's crust and uniformitarian theory of geology; joint editor of Adam Smith's *Essays on Philosophical Subjects* (1795).

HUTTON, John (d. 1712), physician (originally a herd-boy at Caerlaverock); MD, Padua; attended Mary (afterwards queen) in Holland and William III as first king's physician in Ireland; MD, Oxford, 1695; FRS, 1697; first physician to Queen Anne; MP, Dumfries, 1710–12, and local benefactor.

HUTTON, John (1740?–1806), author of *Tour to the Caves . . . of Ingleborough and Settle*, with glossary (2nd edn. 1781); fellow of St John's College, Cambridge; third wrangler, 1763; MA, 1766; vicar of Burton in Kendal.

HUTTON, Luke (d. 1598), reputed author of *Luke Hutton's Repentance* and *The Black Dogge of Newgate* (reprinted 1638); executed at York for robbery.

HUTTON, Matthew (1529–1606), archbishop of York; fellow of Trinity College, Cambridge; MA, 1555; DD, 1565; master of Pembroke Hall, 1562–7; regius professor of divinity, 1562–7; disputed before Elizabeth at Cambridge, 1564; dean of York, 1567; bishop of Durham, 1589; interceded successfully for Lady Margaret Neville, 1594 and 1595; president of the north, 1596–1600; archbishop of York, 1596–1606; founded Warton Grammar School and almshouses.

HUTTON, Matthew (1639–1711), antiquary; great-grandson of Matthew *Hutton (1529–1606); fellow of Brasenose College, Oxford; MA and DD; rector of Aynhoe, Northamptonshire, 1677–1711; friend of Anthony à *Wood; collections of his manuscripts in British Museum.

HUTTON, Matthew (1693–1758), archbishop of York and Canterbury; descended from Matthew *Hutton (1529–1606); MA, Jesus College, Cambridge, 1717; DD, 1728; fellow of Christ's College, Cambridge, 1717; rector of Trowbridge, 1726, of Spofforth, 1729; chaplain to George II; bishop of Bangor, 1743–7; archbishop of York, 1747–57, of Canterbury, 1757–8.

HUTTON, Sir Richard (1561?–1639), judge; of Hutton Hall, Cumberland; studied at Jesus College, Cambridge; barrister, Gray's Inn, 1586; ancient, 1598; member of Council of the North, 1599–1619; serjeant-at-law, 1603; for the defendant in Calvin's case, 1608; knighted, 1617; puisne judge, 1617–39; a grantee of

*Bacon's fine; gave judgment for *Hampden in ship-money case, 1638; some of his reports printed, 1656, and conveyancing precedents (*Young Clerk's Guide*), 1658.

HUTTON, Richard Holt (1826–1897), theologian, journalist, and man of letters; educated at University College school and University College, London; BA, 1845; MA, 1849; studied at Heidelberg and Berlin; prepared for Unitarian ministry at Manchester New College, 1847; principal of University Hall, London; edited Unitarian magazine, *The Inquirer*, 1851–3; studied at Lincoln's Inn; joint editor with Walter *Bagehot of *National Review*, 1855–64; professor of mathematics at Bedford College, London, 1856–65; assistant-editor of *The Economist*, 1858–60; joint editor and part-proprietor of the *Spectator*, 1861–97; definitively abandoned Unitarianism and accepted principles of English Church. His publications include *Essays on some Modern Guides of English Thought* (1887) and *Criticisms on contemporary Thought and Thinkers* (1894).

HUTTON (or **HUTTEN**), **Robert** (d. 1568), divine; of Pembroke Hall, Cambridge; rector of Little Braxted and Wickham Bishops, Essex, and Catterick, Yorkshire; published translation of Spangenberg, called *The Sum of Divinitie* (1548).

HUTTON, Robert Howard (1840–1887), bone-setter; joined his uncle (Richard) about 1869 in London, afterwards setting up for himself; accidentally poisoned.

HUTTON, Thomas (1566–1639), divine; of Merchant Taylors' School and St John's College, Oxford; probationary fellow, 1585; MA, 1591; BD, 1597; vicar of St Kew, rector of North Lew, and prebendary of Exeter, 1616; defended subscription to Prayer-Book, 1605–6.

HUTTON, William (1723–1815), topographer; employed in silk-mills at Derby and Nottingham; bookseller in Birmingham, 1750, opening first circulating library, 1751; opened paper warehouse, 1756; president of local 'Court of Requests', 1787; as friend of *Priestley suffered heavily in riots of 1791; published *History of Birmingham* (1782), *Description of Blackpool* (1789), *History of Derby* (1791), *Dissertation on Juries*, etc. (1789), poems, and other works; an autobiography and family history by him issued posthumously.

HUTTON, William (*c.*1736–1811), antiquary; rector of Beetham, Westmoreland, 1762; his dialect *Bran New Wark* (1785) reprinted (1879).

HUTTON, William (1798–1860), geologist; with John *Lindley prepared *Fossil Flora of Great Britain* (1831–7); his collection of fossils at Newcastle upon Tyne.

HUTTON, William Holden (1860–1930), historian and dean of Winchester; BA, Magdalen College, Oxford, 1882; first class in modern history; fellow of St John's College, Oxford, 1884–1923; deacon, 1885; priest, 1886; archdeacon of Northampton and canon residentiary of Peterborough Cathedral, 1911; university reader in Indian history, 1913–20; dean of Winchester, 1919–30; died at Freiburg im Breisgau; works include lives of *Wellesley (1893), *More (1895), *Laud (1895); *The English Church ... 1625–1714* (1903); and *Lives of the English Saints* (Bampton lectures, 1903).

HUXHAM, John (1692–1768), physician; studied under Boerhaave at Leiden; graduated at Reims, 1717; practised at Plymouth; FRS, 1739; Copley medallist for observations on antimony, 1755; the tincture of cinchona bark in British Pharmacopoeia devised by and named after him; his medical works published in Latin at Leipzig, 1764, 1773, and 1829.

HUXLEY, Aldous Leonard (1894–1963), man of letters; son of Leonard *Huxley, grandson of T. H. *Huxley, great grandson of Dr Thomas *Arnold, and nephew of Mrs Humphrey *Ward; educated at Eton and Balliol College, Oxford; first class, English literature, in spite of damaged eyesight, 1916; met other young writers and painters at the Garsington home of Philip Morrell and Lady Ottoline *Morrell; first novel, *Crome Yellow* (1921), followed by *Antic Hay* (1923), *Those Barren Leaves* (1925), and *Brave New World* (1932); published short stories, such as *Mortal Coils* (1922), and essays and travel books, including *Jesting Pilot* (1926); *Point Counter Point* (1928), best-seller in Britain and America; decided to settle in United States, 1938; eyesight improved; published *The Art of Seeing* (1942); published new series of books, including *The Perennial Philosophy* (1945), *Science, Liberty and Peace* (1946), and *Brave New World Revisited* (1958), and further novels, including *After Many a Summer* (1939), which won the James Tait Black Memorial Prize, and *The Genius and the Goddess* (1955); interested in hypnosis and the use of psychedelic drugs, described in *The Doors of Perception* (1954) and *Heaven and Hell* (1956); Los Angeles home destroyed by fire, 1961.

HUXLEY, Sir Julian Sorell (1887–1975), zoologist, philosopher, and public servant; son of Leonard *Huxley, and grandson of T. H. *Huxley; brother of Aldous *Huxley; King's scholar at Eton; Brackenbury scholar at Balliol College, Oxford; Newdigate Prize for poetry, 1908; first class, natural science (zoology), 1909; with scholarship able to work in Marine Biological Laboratory, Naples, 1909; lecturer in zoology, Balliol, 1910–12; professor of biology, Rice Institute, Texas, 1913–16; worked with Hermann Muller, geneticist; commissioned in Intelligence Unit, ASC, 1917; fellow, New College, Oxford, and senior demonstrator in zoology, 1919; professor of zoology, King's College, London, 1925–7; Fullerian professor of physiology, Royal Institution, 1927–31; secretary, Zoological Society of London, 1935–42; FRS, 1938; published *Problems of Relative Growth* (1932) and *Evolution, the Modern Synthesis* (1942, third edn. 1974); edited *The New Systematics* (1940); member of general committee for *An African Survey* by Lord *Hailey, 1933–8; national figure during 1939–45 as member of BBC 'Brains Trust'; first director-general, Unesco, 1946–8; one of the most influential popularizers of science of his age; published many other books, including *The Science of Life* (in collaboration with H. G. *Wells and G. P. Wells, 1929); leading figure in setting up International Union for the Conservation of Nature, 1948 and the World Wildlife Fund, 1961; president, Association of Scientific Workers; published autobiography, *Memories* (2 vols., 1970 and 1973); knighted, 1958; received Royal Society's Darwin Medal and Frink Gold Medal for British zoologists; honorary degrees and other academic honours from British and foreign universities and societies.

HUXLEY, Leonard (1860–1933), biographer, poet, and editor of the *Cornhill Magazine*; son of T. H. *Huxley; first class, Lit. Hum., Balliol College, Oxford, 1883; assistant master, Charterhouse, 1884–1901; assistant editor, *Cornhill Magazine* (1901), sole editor (1916–33); works include an outstanding biography of his father (1900) and *Anniversaries* (poems, 1920).

HUXLEY, Thomas Henry (1825–1895), man of science; studied at Charing Cross Hospital; announced, 1845, discovery of the layer of cells in root sheath of hair which now bears his name; made as assistant-surgeon on HMS *Rattlesnake*, 1846–50, investigations relating to hydrozoa; established morphological plan dividing hydrozoa into 'Radiata' and 'Nematophora'; sent (1848) to Royal Society memoir 'On the Affinities of the Family of the Medusa'; FRS, 1851; published two memoirs on the Ascidians; lecturer on natural history at Royal School of Mines, 1854; naturalist to Geological Survey, 1855; published writings dealing with subject of fossil forms, including memoirs on cephalaspis and pteraspis (1858), the eurypterina, 1856–9, and the dicynodon, rhamphorhynchus, and other reptiles; read Croonian lecture before Royal Society on 'Theory of the Vertebrate Skull',

1858; published *Zoological Evidences as to Man's Place in Nature* (1863) and *On the Causes of the Phenomena of Organic Nature* (1863); served on royal commissions, including those on sea-fisheries of United Kingdom, 1864–5, Royal College of Science for Ireland, 1866, Administration and Operation of Contagious Diseases Acts, 1870–1, Scientific Instruction and Advancement of Science, 1870–5, on vivisection, 1876, and on Scottish universities, 1876–8; Hunterian professor at Royal College of Surgeons, 1863–9; Fullerian professor at Royal Institution, 1855–8 and 1865–7; published *Manual of the Comparative Anatomy of Vertebrated Animals* (1871), *Elementary Lessons in Physiology* (1866), *Elementary Biology* (in conjunction with H. N. Martin, 1875); an original member of School Board for London, 1870–2, greatly influencing scheme of education finally adopted; president of Royal Society, 1883–5; inspector of fisheries, 1881–5; retired from public work owing to ill health, 1885; delivered Romanes lecture at Oxford on 'Evolution and Ethics', 1893; rector of Aberdeen University, 1872–4; hon. DCL, Oxford, 1885; privy councillor, 1892. His *Collected Essays* were published in nine volumes (1893–4).

HUYSMANS (HOUSEMAN), Jacob (1636?–1696), portrait painter; came to England, *c.*1660; executed portrait of Queen *Catharine of Braganza as a shepherdess, of Izaak *Walton, and others.

HUYSSING (or HYSING), Hans (*fl.* 1700–1735), portrait painter; came to England with Michael *Dahl, 1700; adopted Dahl's manner.

HUYSUM, Jacob van (1687?–1746). See VAN HUYSUM.

HWFA MÔN (1823–1905), archdruid of Wales. See WILLIAMS, ROWLAND.

HYATT, John (1767–1826), minister of the London Tabernacle; published sermons.

HYDE, Barons. See VILLIERS, THOMAS, first baron, 1709–1786; VILLIERS, JOHN CHARLES, third baron, 1757–1838; VILLIERS, GEORGE WILLIAM FREDERICK, fourth baron, 1800–1870.

HYDE, Alexander (1598–1667), bishop of Salisbury; fellow of New College, Oxford; DCL, 1632; sub-dean of Salisbury, 1637; dean of Winchester, 1660; bishop of Salisbury, 1665–7.

HYDE, Anne, duchess of York (1637–1671), eldest daughter of Edward *Hyde, afterwards earl of Clarendon; maid of honour to princess of Orange, 1654, of whom she wrote a 'portrait'; became engaged to James, duke of York, at Breda, 1659; privately married him in London, 1660; of their children only two daughters—

Mary (wife of William III) and (Queen) Anne—survived childhood. She was secretly received into the Roman Church, 1670; many portraits of her were painted by her protegé, *Lely.

HYDE, Catherine, afterwards duchess of Queensberry (d. 1777). See DOUGLAS, CATHERINE.

HYDE, David de la (*fl.* 1580), classical scholar; MA, Merton Colege, Oxford, 1553; probationary fellow, 1549; ejected for denying the queen's supremacy, 1560; wrote learned works.

HYDE, Douglas (1860–1949), Gaelic revivalist, poet, and first president of Eire; graduated in modern literature, Trinity College, Dublin, 1884; LL D, 1888; learnt Irish in his native Roscommon; president, Gaelic League, 1893–1915; conducted successful campaign for revival of Irish language but repudiated any political aim; professor of modern Irish, University College, Dublin, 1908–32; first president of Eire, 1937–45; publications include collected plays (1905), and *Love Songs of Connacht* (1893), *Religious Songs of Connacht* (1906), *The Story of Early Gaelic Literature* (1895), *Literary History of Ireland* (1899), and *Medieval Tales from the Irish* (1899).

HYDE, Edward (1607–1659), Royalist divine; of Westminster and Trinity College, Cambridge; fellow; MA, 1633; DD, Oxford, 1643; rector of Brightwell, 1643–5; dean-elect of Windsor, 1659; published theological works.

HYDE, Edward, first earl of Clarendon (1609–1674), BA, Magdalen Hall, Oxford, 1626; friend of *Falkland, Ben *Jonson, *Selden, and *Waller; barrister, Middle Temple, 1633; keeper of writs and rolls of the common pleas, 1634; as MP for Wootton Bassett in Short Parliament (1640) attacked jurisdiction of the marshal's court, and practically obtained its abolition; represented Saltash in Long Parliament; chairman of committees of investigation into proceedings of councils of the north and of Wales; took prominent part against the judges; helped to prepare impeachment of *Strafford; defended episcopacy, 1641; successfully obstructed Root and Branch Bill, 1641; in second session opposed the Grand Remonstrance, and composed the king's reply; with Falkland and *Colepeper arranged to manage king's parliamentary affairs; kept ignorant of design to arrest the five members, 1642; joined Charles I at York, 1642, and for three years drew up all his declarations; advised adherence to law and constitutional methods, with refusal of further concessions; thwarted by influence of the queen and Lord *Digby; privy councillor and chancellor of the Exchequer, 1643; one of the 'junto' of five; raised loans from

Oxford University and the Catholics; prominent in negotiations, especially at Uxbridge, 1645, refusing real concessions, but endeavouring to win over opposition leaders by personal offers; obtained calling of Oxford parliament as counterpoise to that of Westminster, 1643; leading spirit of Prince Charles's council in the west, 1645; followed him to Scilly and Jersey, 1646, where he began his history; opposed queen's wish for concessions to Scots and plans for using foreign armies; issued reply to Long Parliament's declaration of reasons against further addresses to the king, 1648; captured by corsair on way to Paris; ultimately joined the prince at The Hague; advised him against accepting Scottish proposals; accompanied *Cottington to obtain help from Spain and negotiate alliance between *Ormonde and *O'Neill for recovery of Ireland, 1649–50; after Worcester (1651) Charles II's chief adviser, as secretary of state, and (from 1658) lord chancellor; opposed concessions to Presbyterians and Romanists and isolated movements in England, but favoured negotiations with Levellers; as chancellor and member of secret committee of six became virtual head of the government, 1660; chancellor of Oxford, 1660–7; created Baron Hyde, 1660, and Viscount Cornbury and earl of Clarendon, 1661; forwarded Act of Indemnity; in church matters favoured comprehension rather than toleration; opposed to severe treatment of Nonconformists, but firm in enforcing Act of Uniformity (1662) and subsequent measures; zealous for restoration of episcopacy in Scotland; one of the eight proprietors of Carolina, 1663; tolerant in colonial affairs, but supported navigation laws and measures tending to promote mutual division among the colonies; desired peace policy in foreign affairs, but was forced into war; refused bribe from France, but solicited loan; did not initiate, but carried out, sale of Dunkirk, 1662; deprecated attack on Dutch African possessions, but defended seizure (1664) of New Amsterdam; looked upon as French in his sympathies, though really opposed to French alliance; ill success of Dutch War partly due to his administrative conservatism; overthrown by court intrigues and hostility of parliament, whose authority he had endeavoured to restrict; dismissed, 1667; subsequently impeached; though the Lords declined to commit him, fled to France, 1667; banished; three years at Avignon and Montpellier; removed to Moulins, 1671, and Rouen, 1674, completing his *History* and writing autobiography; died at Rouen; buried in Westminster Abbey. A consistent upholder of constitutional monarchy, he refused to recognize the altered conditions introduced by the Civil War. He took Tacitus and Hooker as models in his *History of the Rebellion*, which is very unequal in its historical and literary value, being a blend of his later written *Life* with an unfinished *History*, the former supplying the more accurate element. *The True Historical Narrative of the Rebellion and Civil Wars in England* was printed from a transcript under supervision of Clarendon's son, *Rochester (1702–4), the original manuscript being first used in *Bandinel's edition (1826); the best text that of W. D. Macray (1888); profits used to build printing-press at Oxford (Clarendon Buildings). A supplement was issued, 1717. The *Life of Clarendon*, by himself, was published (1759), *History of Rebellion and Civil War in Ireland* (1720), and selections from his correspondence (*Clarendon State Papers*), edited by Scrope and Monkhouse (1767–86).

HYDE, Henry, second earl of Clarendon (1638–1709), eldest son of Edward *Hyde, first earl; as Viscount Cornbury represented Wiltshire, 1661–74; private secretary, 1662, and chamberlain, 1665, to Queen *Catherine; intimate of *Evelyn; defended his father in parliament, and on his fall opposed the court and the Cabal; privy councillor by influence of duke of York, 1680; lord privy seal, 1685; viceroy of Ireland, 1685–6, but was thwarted and ousted by *Tyrconnel; high steward of Oxford University, 1686; received pension of £2,000, 1688; adhered to James II for some time; opposed settlement of the crown on William and Mary; imprisoned in the Tower, 1690; implicated in Lord *Preston's plot and again sent to the Tower, 1691; his history of Winchester Cathedral published (1715) and his *Diary and Correspondence* (1828).

HYDE, Henry, Viscount Cornbury and Baron Hyde (1710–1753), friend of *Bolingbroke; grandson of Laurence *Hyde, first earl of Rochester; Jacobite MP for Oxford University, 1732–50; called to the Lords as Baron Hyde, 1650; addressed to *Pope verses upon his *Essay on Man*, 1735 (printed with it, 1739); Bolingbroke's *Letters on the Study of History* (1735) addressed to him; killed by fall from his horse at Paris.

HYDE, Jane, countess of Clarendon and Rochester (d. 1725), mother of Henry *Hyde, Viscount Cornbury; married Henry Hyde, second earl of Rochester, 1693; a celebrated beauty, the Myra of Prior's *Judgement of Venus*.

HYDE, Laurence, first earl of Rochester (1641–1711), statesman; second son of Edward *Hyde, first earl of Clarendon; MP, Newport (Cornwall), 1660–1, Oxford University, 1661–79; master of the robes, 1662–75; warmly defended his father on his impeachment; ambassador-extraordinary to Poland, 1676, and the Congress of Nimeguen, 1677–8; MP, Woot-

ton Bassett, 1679; a commissioner of the Treasury, 1679; privy councillor and first lord of the Treasury in first Tory administration, 1679–85; created Viscount Hyde and earl of Rochester, 1681, negotiated secret subsidy treaty with France, 1681; opposed summoning of new parliament; lord president of the council, 1684; appointed by James II lord high treasurer, 1685; KG, 1685; served (1686) on High Commission, and supported suspension of Bishop *Compton; dismissed for aversion to Roman Catholicism, 1687, though receiving large pension; joined *Halifax in negotiations with William of Orange, 1688, but opposed his accession to the crown and supported a regency; having taken the oaths, was readmitted privy councillor, 1692; head of the church party; opposed *Fenwick's attainder, 1696; named viceroy of Ireland, 1700; retained in office by Queen Anne, but resigned, 1703; adopted non-committal policy as to succession; again president of council, 1710–11; patron of *Dryden, and the Hushai of *Absalom and Achitophel*; wrote prefaces and dedications to *Clarendon's *Rebellion*.

HYDE (or HIDE), Sir Nicholas (d. 1631), chief justice of England; uncle of Edward *Hyde, first earl of Clarendon; barrister, Middle Temple; MP, Andover, 1601, Christchurch, 1603–4; prominent in opposition, but retained for *Buckingham's defence, 1626; knighted, 1627; chief justice of England, 1627–31; died of gaol fever.

HYDE, Sir Robert (1595–1665), chief justice of the King's Bench; nephew of Sir Nicholas *Hyde or Hide; barrister, Middle Temple, 1617; serjeant-at-law, 1640; recorder of Salisbury, 1638–46, and MP in Long Parliament; imprisoned, 1645; deprived of recordership, 1646; sheltered Charles II after Worcester (1651) at Heale; judge of common pleas, 1660; knighted; chief justice of King's Bench, 1663–5; died on the bench.

HYDE, Sir Robert Robertson (1878–1967), founder of the Industrial Welfare Society; educated at Westbourne Park School and King's College, London; studied theology; ordained deacon, 1903; priest, 1904; curate, St Saviour's, Hoxton; warden, Hoxton hostel settlement, founded in memory of F. D. *Maurice, 1907; combined this with the living of parish church of St Mary, 1912–16; asked by Seebohm *Rowntree to take charge of boys' welfare department in Ministry of Munitions, 1916; set up the Boys' Welfare Association, 1918; name changed to Industrial Welfare Society, 1919; co-operated with the duke of York in establishing the Duke of York's camps for boys from industry and from public schools; MVO, 1932; KBE, 1949; retired as director of Industrial Welfare Society, 1950;

published *The Boy in Industry and Leisure* (1921) and *Industry was my Parish* (1968).

HYDE, Thomas (1524–1597), Roman Catholic exile and author of *Consolatorie Epistle to the afflicted Catholikes* (1579); of Winchester and New College, Oxford; fellow, 1543–50; MA, 1549; headmaster of Winchester, 1551–8; imprisoned by Elizabeth, but escaped abroad; died at Douai.

HYDE, Thomas (1636–1703), orientalist; while at King's College, Cambridge, assisted *Walton in Persian and Syriac versions of the Polyglott Bible; Hebrew reader, The Queen's College, Oxford, 1658; MA, Oxford, 1659; Bodley's librarian, 1665–1701; archdeacon of Gloucester, 1673; DD, 1682; Laudian professor of Arabic, 1691; regius professor of Hebrew and canon of Christ Church, 1697; government interpreter of oriental languages; chief work, *Historia religionis veterum Persarum* (1700).

HYDE, William (1597–1651), president of Douai College; graduated at Christ Church, Oxford, under name of Beyard, 1614; MA, 1617; converted to Romanism and admitted at Douai as Hyde, 1623; professor of divinity, Douai; Roman Catholic archdeacon of Worcester and Salop; vice-president of Douai, 1641–5, professor of history, 1649, and president, 1646–51; left money to the college.

HYGDON, Brian (d. 1539), dean of York; brother of John *Hygdon; principal of Broadgates Hall, Oxford, 1505; DCL, 1506; sub-dean of Lincoln, 1511–23; archdeacon of the West Riding, 1515; dean of York, 1516–39; commissioner for peace with Scotland, 1526.

HYGDON (or HIGDEN), John (d. 1533), president of Magdalen College, Oxford, and first dean of Christ Church; brother of Brian *Hygdon; of Westminster and Magdalen College, Oxford, where he became fellow, *c.*1495, dean, 1500–1 and 1503–4, bursar, 1502–3, and president, 1516–25; DD, 1514; founded demyships and fellowships; placed at head of Cardinal College (Christ Church) by *Wolsey, 1525.

HYGEBRYHT (*fl.* 787). See HIGBERT.

HYLL. See HILL.

HYLTON, first Baron (1800–1876). See JOLLIFFE, WILLIAM GEORGE HYLTON.

HYLTON, Jack (1892–1965), dance-band leader, pianist, composer, and impresario; educated at higher grade school, Bolton; learned piano as a child; first professional engagement as pianist and singer with pierrot troupe, 1905; cinema organist at the Alexandra, Stoke Newington, 1913; worked as double act with Tommy *Handley, 1920; became leader of Queen's Hall Roof resident band; made first records, 1921; opened London office and placed dance-bands in Piccadilly Hotel and the Kit-Cat Club, 1925; appeared with his band at London Hippodrome and Palladium, 1927–37; toured in Europe; disbanded his orchestra, 1940; became theatre impresario, 1935; presented number of West-End successes, 1941–6; composed many popular songs; appeared in six Royal Command Variety performances.

HYLTON, Walter (d. 1396). See HILTON.

HYLTON-FOSTER, Sir **Harry Braustyn Hylton** (1905–1965), speaker of the House of Commons; educated at Eton and Magdalen College, Oxford; first class, jurisprudence, 1926; called to bar (Inner Temple), 1928; legal secretary to Viscount *Finlay at Permanent Court of International Justice, 1928; served in RAF Volunteer Reserve and as deputy judge-advocate in North Africa and Italy, 1939–45; recorder of Richmond, 1940–4, Huddersfield, 1944–50, and Kingston upon Hull, 1950–4; chancellor of dioceses of Ripon, 1947–54, and Durham, 1948–54; KC, 1947; Conservative MP, York, 1950–9; MP, Cities of London and Westminster, 1959–65; solicitor-general; knighted, 1954; PC, 1957; speaker of the House of Commons, 1959–65.

HYMERS, John (1803–1887), mathematician; second wrangler, St John's College, Cambridge, 1826; fellow of St John's College, 1827, tutor, 1832, and president, 1848–52; DD, 1841; rector of Brandesburton, 1852–87; caused portrait of *Wordsworth to be painted for the college; left money for foundation of school at Hull; published mathematical treatises.

HYND, John (*fl.* 1606), romancer; probably grandson of Sir John *Hynde; MA, Cambridge, 1599; published *Eliosto Libidinoso* (1606).

HYNDE, Sir **John** (d. 1550), judge of common pleas; educated at Cambridge; barrister, Gray's Inn; reader, 1517, 1527, and 1531; recorder of Cambridge, 1520; serjeant-at-law, 1531; king's serjeant, 1535; prosecuted western rebels, 1536; judge of common pleas, 1545–50; knighted, 1545.

HYNDFORD, earls of. See CARMICHAEL, JOHN, first earl, 1638–1710; CARMICHAEL, JOHN, third earl, 1701–1767.

HYNDLEY, Viscount (1883–1963), business man and administrator. See HINDLEY, JOHN SCOTT.

HYNDMAN, Henry Mayers (1842–1921), socialist leader; on staff of *Pall Mall Gazette*, 1871–80; took lead in forming (Social) Democratic Federation, 1881; agitated among unemployed; opposed South African War; left British Socialist party and formed National Socialist party, 1916; published *England for All* (1881), several books defending political Marxism, and two autobiographical works.

HYSLOP, James (1798–1827), Scottish poet; successively shepherd, schoolmaster, tutor on board ship, reporter in London, and again teacher; died of fever off Cape Verde; his poems collected (1887).

HYWEL. See HOWEL.

I

IAGO AB DEWI (or DAVIES, James) (1648–1722), Welsh bard; translator of English religious works.

IAGO AB IDWAL AB MEIRIG (d. 1039), king of Gwynedd; seized the throne, 1023; killed in battle with *Gruffydd ab Llywelyn.

IAGO AB IDWAL VOEL (*fl.* 943–979), king of Gwynedd; succeeded, 943; at war with sons of *Howel Dda; hanged his brother Ieuav, 967; one of the kings who rowed *Edgar on the Dee, 972; driven from throne by Ieuav's son and the English; captured by Danes, 980.

I'ANSON, Edward (1812–1888), architect; educated at Merchant Taylors' School and the College of Henri IV; designed Royal Exchange Buildings and offices in the City of London; PRIBA, 1886.

IBBETSON, Mrs Agnes (1757–1823), vegetable physiologist.

IBBETSON, Sir Denzil Charles Jelf (1847–1908), lieutenant-governor of the Punjab; passed into Indian Civil Service, 1868; assistant settlement officer at Karnal, 1871; published lucid report on district (1883), containing scholarly research into tribal and agricultural systems; reported on Punjab census of 1881, and based on it *Outlines of Punjab Ethnography* (1883); compiled *Punjab Gazetter* (1883); head of department of public instruction, 1884; his report (1891) on working of Deccan Agriculturists' Relief Act of 1879 led to its amendment in interest of peasantry; CSI, 1896; chief commissioner of Central Provinces, 1898; joined Viceroy's Council, 1902; active in measures for prevention of famine; carried Co-operation Credit Act, 1904; KCSI, 1903; lieutenant-governor of the Punjab, 1907–8; repressed disorders in Lahore and Rawalpindi.

IBBETSON, Sir Henry John Selwin-, seventh baronet, and Baron Rookwood (1826–1902), politician. See SELWIN-IBBETSON.

IBBETSON, Julius Caesar (1759–1817), painter; exhibited at the Academy from 1785; made drawings during a voyage to China, 1788; friend of *Morland; excelled as painter (oil) of cattle and pigs; published *Accidence or Gamut of Painters in Oil and Water-colours* (1803).

IBBOT, Benjamin (1680–1725), divine; BA, Clare Hall, Cambridge, 1699; MA, Corpus Christi College, 1703; Norfolk fellow, 1706–7; chaplain to Archbishop *Tenison and to George I; treasurer of Wells, 1708; rector of St Paul's, Shadwell; prebendary of Westminster, 1724; as Boyle lecturer, 1713–14, replied to Anthony *Collins's *Discourse of Freethinking*.

IBBOTSON, Henry (1816?–1886), Yorkshire botanist and schoolmaster; compiler of *Catalogue of Phaenogamous Plants* (1846–8).

IBHAR (or IBERIUS), Saint (d. 500?), bishop of Begerin (Wexford); locally known as St Ivory; his day, 23 Apr.

ICKHAM, Peter of (*fl.* 1270), reputed author of *Chronicon de Regibus Angliae*; monk of Christ Church, Canterbury.

ICKWORTH, Baron Hervey of (1696–1743). See HERVEY, JOHN.

IDA (d. 559), first Bernician king; began to reign, 547; built Bamborough (Bebbanburch).

IDDESLEIGH, first earl of (1818–1887). See NORTHCOTE, Sir STAFFORD HENRY.

IDRISYN (1804–1887). See JONES, JOHN.

IDWAL AB MEIRIG (d. 997), king of Gwynedd; defeated the usurper *Maredudd ab Owain ab Howel Dda, 995; slain in repelling the Danes.

IDWAL VOEL (d. 943), prince of Gwynedd; succeeded, 915; under-king to *Ethelstan; helped Welsh to regain freedom, 940; killed by English.

IESTIN AB GWRGANT (*fl.* 1093), prince of Gwent and Morganwg; succeeded Howel ab Morgan, 1043; said to have invoked Norman aid against *Rhys ab Tewdwr, but to have been subsequently driven out by Robert *Fitzhamon.

IEUAN AB HYWEL SWRDWAL (*fl.* 1430–1480), Welsh poet and historian of the three principalities; his English ode (1450) printed in *Cambrian Register*.

IEUAN AB RHYDDERCH AB IEUAN LLWYD (*fl.* 1410–1440), Welsh bard and collector of Welsh manuscripts; extracts from his works in *Iolo MSS and in *Cyfrinach y Beirdd*; 'Llyfr Gwyn Rhydderch', preserved at Peniarth, belonged to him.

IEUAN DDU (1795–1871). See THOMAS, JOHN.

IEUAN DDU AB DAFYDD AB OWAIN (*fl.* 1440–1480), poet and bardic patron.

IEUAN DDU O LAN TAWY (1802–1823). See HARRIS, JOHN RYLAND.

IEUAN GWYLLT (1822–1877), Welsh musician. See ROBERTS, JOHN.

IGNATIUS, Father (1837–1908), preacher. See LYNE, JOSEPH LEYCESTER.

ILBERT, Sir **Courtenay Peregrine** (1841–1924), parliamentary draftsman; BA, Balliol College, Oxford; Hertford, Ireland, Craven, and Eldon law scholar; first class, Lit. Hum.; fellow of Balliol, 1864; called to bar (Lincoln's Inn), 1869; joined department for drafting parliamentary bills; law member, Council of Governor-General of India, 1882–6; assistant parliamentary counsel to Treasury, 1886; parliamentary counsel, 1899–1902; clerk of House of Commons, 1902–21; KCSI, 1895; KCB, 1908; GCB, 1911.

ILCHESTER, sixth earl of (1874–1959), landowner and historian. See FOX-STRANGWAYS, GILES STEPHEN HOLLAND.

ILCHESTER, Richard of (d. 1188). See RICHARD.

ILIFFE, Edward Mauger, first Baron Iliffe (1877–1960), newspaper and periodical proprietor; joined father's periodical firm, 1894; with future lords *Camrose and *Kemsley founded Allied Newspapers Ltd., 1924, owning *Sunday Times* and acquiring (1928) *Daily Telegraph*; on dissolution of association, 1937, retained Kelly's Directories; acquired *Birmingham Post* and *Mail*, 1943; Conservative MP, Tamworth, 1923–9; CBE, 1918; knighted, 1922; baron, 1933; GBE, 1946; president, International Lawn Tennis Club of Great Britain, 1945–59.

ILIVE, Jacob (1705–1763), printer, letter-founder, and author; printed his *Layman's Vindication of the Christian Religion* (1730); lectured on religious subjects; imprisoned, 1756–8, for blasphemy in commenting on *Sherlock's sermons; published works on reform of the house of correction, and on management of Stationers' Company.

ILLIDGE, Thomas Henry (1799–1851), portrait painter; exhibited from 1842 at the Academy.

ILLING, Vincent Charles (1890–1969), petroleum geologist; educated at King Edward VI Grammar School, Nuneaton, and Sidney Sussex College, Cambridge; first class, parts i and ii, natural sciences tripos, 1911–12; Harkness scholar, 1914; demonstrator, applied geology, Imperial College of Science and Technology, South Kensington, 1913; developed course in petroleum geology; lecturer, 1915; assistant professor, 1921; professor of oil technology, 1935–55; made first of many visits to Trinidad, 1915; made geological studies in Poland, Romania, and France; published 'The Migration of Oil and Natural Gas' in *Journal of the Institution of Petroleum Technologists*, 1933; published in the United States 'The Role of Stratigraphy in Oil Discovery' (*Bulletin of American Association of Petroleum Geologists*, 1945); petroleum consultant, travelled widely, including making surveys in Venezuela; formed Petroleum Scientific Services Ltd., 1946; changed to V. C. Illing and Partners, 1950; advised Nigerian government on future development of oil resources; adviser to Gas Council on gas exploration in Britain, 1958; member of council, Geological Society, 1927–8; vice-president, Institute of Petroleum, 1942–5 and 1948; hon. member, American Association of Petroleum Geologists; FRS, 1945; fellow, Imperial College, 1958; emeritus professor of oil technology, London University, 1955.

ILLINGWORTH, Cayley (1758?–1823), topographer; MA, Pembroke College, Cambridge, 1787; DD, 1811; archdeacon of Stow, 1808; published *Topographical Account of . . . Scampton* (1808); brother of William *Illingworth.

ILLINGWORTH, William (1764–1845), deputy keeper of the records, 1805–19; attorney of the King's Bench, 1788; published *Inquiry into Laws respecting Forestalling, Regrating and Ingrossing* (1800); transcribed and collated the statutes from Magna Carta to the end of Henry VIII's reign and other important documents; arranged and catalogued Westminster chapter-house records, 1808; gave important (unacknowledged) assistance to Record Commission of 1832, and evidence before Commons' committee, 1836.

ILLTYD (or **ILTUTUS)** (*fl.* 520), Welsh saint ('The Knight'); born in Britanny, where he was a disciple of St *Germanus; came to Glamorganshire and built a monastery at Llantwit Major; had among his scholars St *David and St *Paul de Léon; said to have reclaimed land from the sea.

IMAGE, Selwyn (1849–1930), artist; BA, New College, Oxford; disciple of John *Ruskin; ordained, 1872; Slade professor of fine art at Oxford, 1910–16; best known by his designs for stained glass; also designed decorative title-pages, etc.; produced landscape drawings and water-colours.

IMAGE, Thomas (1772–1856), geologist; MA, Corpus Christi College, Cambridge, 1798; rector of Whepstead, 1798, and Stanningfield,

1807; his fossils acquired by Cambridge University.

IMISON, John (d. 1788), Manchester mechanic and printer; his best work, *The School of Arts* (1785).

IMLAH, John (1799–1846), Scottish poet; published *May Flowers* (1827), *Poems and Songs* (1841); died of fever in Jamaica.

IMLAY, Gilbert (d. 1828), soldier and author; served against British in American War of Independence; lived with Mary *Wollstonecraft, 1793–5, in Le Havre and London; published *Topographical Description of Western Territory of North America* (1792) and the *Emigrants* (1793).

IMMS, Augustus Daniel (1880–1949), entomologist; educated at St Edmund's College and Mason College, Birmingham, and Christ's College, Cambridge; BA, Cambridge, D.Sc., Birmingham, 1907; professor of biology, Allahabad, 1907–11; forest entomologist to Indian government, 1911–13; reader in agricultural entomology, Manchester, 1913–18; chief entomologist, Rothamsted, 1918–31; reader in entomology, Cambridge, 1931–45; publications include *General Textbook of Entomology* (1925) and *Insect Natural History* (1947); FRS, 1929.

IMMYNS, John (d. 1764), founder of Madrigal Society, 1741; active member of Academy of Ancient Music; lutenist to the Chapel Royal.

IMPEY, Sir Elijah (1732–1809), chief justice of Bengal; at Westminster with Warren *Hastings; fellow of Trinity College, Cambridge, 1757; junior chancellor's medallist, 1756; MA, 1759; barrister, Lincoln's Inn, 1756; recorder of Basingstoke, 1766; counsel for East India Company before House of Commons, 1772; went to India, 1774; knighted, 1774; chief justice of Bengal, 1774–89; confirmed committal of Nand Kumar (Nuncomar) for forgery, and condemned and sentenced him to death, 1775; decided for Hastings on question of his resignation of the governor-generalship, 1777; his judicial power restricted as a condition of compromise with Sir Philip *Francis, against whom he awarded damages for criminal conversation, 1779; president of new appeal court over local tribunals, 1780; recalled to defend himself against Francis's charges of illegality, 1783; impeached by the House of Commons; defended himself successfully at bar of House of Commons against six charges, including the Nuncomar proceedings and exercise of extended judicial powers contrary to his patent, 1788; his impeachment dropped, 1788; MP, New Romney, 1790–6.

IMPEY, John (d. 1829), legal writer; attorney of the sheriff's court; published treatises on practice of courts of King's Bench (1782) and common pleas (1784) and other works.

INA (d. 726). See INE.

INCE, Sir Godfrey Herbert (1891–1960), civil servant; educated at Reigate Grammar School and University College, London; first class, mathematics, 1913; joined Ministry of Labour, 1919; chief insurance officer, 1933; advised Australian government on unemployment insurance, 1936–7; in charge of military recruiting department, Ministry of Labour, organizing arrangements for call-up, 1939–41; director-general of manpower under Ernest *Bevin, responsible for all matters affecting call-up to forces and supply of civilian labour, 1941–4; under-secretary, 1940; permanent secretary, 1944–56; concerned with demobilization, resettlement, and Youth Employment Service; chairman, Cable and Wireless, 1956–60; CB, 1941; KBE, 1943; KCB, 1946; GCB, 1951; fellow, University College, London; hon. LL D, London.

INCE, Joseph Murray (1806–1859), landscape painter; pupil of David *Cox the elder.

INCE, William (1825–1910), regius professor of divinity at Oxford; BA, Lincoln College, Oxford (first class, Lit. Hum.), 1846; MA, 1849; DD, 1878; fellow of Exeter College, 1847; tutor, 1850; sub-rector, 1857–78; hon. fellow, 1882; regius professor of divinity and canon of Christ Church, 1878–1910; active in administration of Christ Church; an evangelical and moderate Anglican; published *The Life and Times of St. Athanasius* (1896) and doctrinal pamphlets.

INCHBALD, Mrs Elizabeth (1753–1821), novelist, dramatist, and actress; née Simpson; married Joseph Inchbald, an actor, 1772; appeared as Cordelia to Inchbald's Lear at Bristol, 1772; played other parts with him in Scotland; acted under Tate *Wilkinson in Yorkshire, 1778–80, her husband dying at Leeds; appeared at Covent Garden as Bellario in *Philaster* and other parts, 1780; at the Haymarket and Dublin, 1782; retired from the stage, 1789; her *Mogul Tale* produced at the Haymarket (1784), *I'll tell you what* (1785), *Appearance is against them* at Covent Garden (1785); produced many other comedies and farces, 1786–1805, chiefly adaptations from French; edited *The British Theatre*, 1806–9. Her romances, *A Simple Story* (1791) and *Nature and Art* (1796) have been often reprinted.

INCHBOLD, John William (1830–1888), landscape painter; much admired by *Ruskin and contemporary poets; *The Moorland, The Jungfrau*, and *Drifting* among his chief works; published *Annus Amoris* (1877).

INCHCAPE, first earl of (1852–1932), ship-owner. See MACKAY, JAMES LYLE.

INCHIQUIN, Barons. See O'BRIEN, MURROUGH, first baron, d. 1551; O'BRIEN, MURROUGH, sixth baron, 1614–1674.

INCHIQUIN, earls of. See O'BRIEN, MURROUGH, first earl, 1614–1674; O'BRIEN, WILLIAM, second earl, 1638?–1692; O'BRIEN, JAMES, seventh earl, 1769–1855.

INCLEDON, Benjamin (1730–1796), recorder of Barnstaple and Devonshire genealogist.

INCLEDON, Charles (1763–1826), tenor voca-list; after singing in the Exeter choir spent some time at sea; sang at Southampton, 1784, Bath, 1785, and Vauxhall Gardens, 1786–9; appeared in operas by *Shield and in *Beggar's Opera* at Covent Garden, 1790–1815; sang in sacred con-certs under *Linley, 1792; took part in first per-formance of Haydn's *Creation* at Covent Garden, 1800; unsuccessful at New York, 1817–18; retired, 1822.

INCLEDON, Charles (1791–1865), vocalist; son of Charles *Incledon (1763–1826); died at Bad Tüffer.

INDERWICK, Frederick Andrew (1836–1904), lawyer and antiquary; called to bar (Inner Temple), 1858; QC, 1874; leader in Probate and Divorce division from 1876; commissioner in lunacy, 1903; Liberal MP for Rye, 1880–5; mayor of Winchelsea, 1892–3; FSA, 1894; pub-lished, besides legal and historical works, *Calen-dar of the Inner Temple Records, 1505–1714* (3 vols., 1896–1901).

INDULPHUS (d. 962), king of Alba or Scotland, 954–62; defeated Norse fleet in Buchan.

INE (INI or in Latin **INA)** (d. 726), West Saxon king; chosen king in father's lifetime, 688; invaded Kent, 693, and established his supremacy over all England south of Thames; created see of Sherborne, 705; defeated Gerent, king of the British Dyvnaint, 710, and extended West Saxon territory over western Somerset; fought *Ceolred of Mercia at Wanborough, 715; suppressed rising of the æthelings of the race of Cerdic, 715; made war on South Saxons, 725; his laws (promulgated 690–3) earliest extant West Saxon legislation; benefactor to Glastonbury and Abingdon; abdicated, 726, and died at Rome.

INETT, John (1647–1717), author of *Origines Anglicanae* (1710; ed. Griffiths, 1855); MA, University College, Oxford, 1669; DD, St John's College, Cambridge, 1701; successively incum-bent of St Ebbe's, Oxford, Nuneaton, Tansor, Clayworth, and Wirksworth; precentor of Lin-coln, 1682, and chaplain to William III, 1700; published popular devotional manuals.

INFANS, Roger (*fl.* 1124), chronologer. See ROGER.

ING, (Harry) Raymond (1899–1974), chem-ical pharmacologist; educated at Oxford High School and New College, Oxford; first class, chemistry, 1921; D.Phil. and teacher of chemistry, Wadham College; Ramsay memorial fellow, Owens College, Manchester, 1926; lec-turer, University College, London, 1929; reader in pharmacological chemistry, 1937; fellow, Rockefeller Institute, New York, 1938; on staff of Chemical Research Group, Oxford, 1939–45; reader in chemical pharmacology, Oxford, 1945–66; FRS, 1951.

INGALTON, William (1794–1866), painter and builder.

INGE (or YNGE), Hugh (d. 1528), archbishop of Dublin and lord chancellor of Ireland; scholar at Winchester, 1480; fellow of New College, Oxford, 1488–96; BA; DD; held preferments in dioceses of Bath and Wells, Lincoln, and Wor-cester; at Rome in 1504; promoted by *Wolsey to see of Meath, 1512; archbishop of Dublin, 1521–8; lord chancellor of Ireland, 1527–8; friend of Gerald *Fitzgerald, ninth earl of Kil-dare.

INGE, William Ralph (1860–1954), dean of St Paul's; grandson of Edward *Churton; scholar of Eton and King's College, Cambridge; first class, parts i and ii, classical tripos (1882–3); Bell, Por-son, and Craven scholar, Chancellor's medallist, and Hare prizeman; master at Eton, 1884–8; fel-low and tutor, Hertford College, Oxford, and ordained deacon, 1888; priest, 1892; vicar, All Saints', Ennismore Gardens, 1905; Lady Mar-garet's professor of divinity, Cambridge, and fel-low of Jesus, 1907; BD and DD, 1909; dean of St Paul's, 1911–34; his preaching attracted congre-gations for the originality of his thought; became known as 'the gloomy dean' for criticism of popu-lar illusions in weekly articles in *Evening Stan-dard*, 1921–46; in *Outspoken Essays* (2 vols., 1919–22) expressed his views on theological and political problems; other publications include *Christian Mysticism* (1899), *Faith and its Psychology* (1909), *The Philosophy of Plotinus* (Gifford lec-tures, 2 vols., 1918), *God and the Astronomers* (1933); CVO, 1918; FBA, 1921; KCVO, 1930; several honorary degrees.

INGELEND, Thomas (*fl.* 1560), author of *The Disobedient Child*, interlude (published *c.*1560, reprinted by *Halliwell, 1848).

INGELO, Nathaniel (1621?–1683), divine and musician; MA, Edinburgh (incorporated at Cambridge, 1644); fellow of Queens' College, Cambridge, 1644–6, and of Eton, 1650–83; accompanied *Whitelocke to Sweden as chaplain and 'rector chori', 1653; addressed by *Marvell in a Latin poem; DD, Cambridge, 1658; published *Bentivolio and Urania* (religious romance, 1660); his *Hymnus Eucharisticus* set by Benjamin *Rogers.

INGELOW, Jean (1820–1897), poetess; lived in London, *c.*1863–97. Her works include *A Rhyming Chronicle of Incidents and Feelings* (1850), three series of *Poems* (1863, 1876, and 1885), and novels and stories for children.

INGELRAM (d. 1174), bishop of Glasgow, 1164–74, and chancellor of Scotland under *David and *Malcolm IV; upheld Scottish Church at Norham, 1159.

INGENHOUSZ, John (1730–1799), physician and physicist; came to England from the Netherlands, *c.*1765; went to Vienna to inoculate the Austrian imperial family, 1768, and became body-surgeon and aulic councillor; returned to London, 1779; FRS, 1779; published *Experiments on Vegetables* (1779), also issued at Vienna (1786), containing discovery of respiration of plants.

INGHAM, Albert Edward (1900–1967), mathematician; educated at King Edward VI Grammar School, Stafford, and Trinity College, Cambridge; first class, part ii, mathematics tripos, 1921; Smith's prizeman, 1923; fellow, Trinity College, 1922; research work, 1922–6; reader, Leeds University, 1926; fellow and director of studies, King's College, Cambridge; university lecturer, 1930; FRS, 1945; reader in mathematical analysis, 1953–7; outstanding member of the G. H. *Hardy and J. E. *Littlewood school of mathematical analysis; wrote *The Distribution of Prime Numbers* (1932); edited the papers in number-theory in vol. ii of G. H. Hardy's *Collected Papers* (1967).

INGHAM, Benjamin (1712–1772), Yorkshire evangelist; studied at The Queen's College, Oxford, where he was an active Methodist; BA, 1734; accompanied the Wesleys to Georgia, 1735; on his return joined Moravians and preached extensively in the north; married Lady Margaret Hastings, 1741; gave the Moravians settlement at Fulneck, but separated from them, and in 1760 adopted Sandemanian views.

INGHAM, Charles Cromwell (1796–1863), portrait painter; left Ireland for New York, and became vice-president of National Academy of Design.

INGHAM, Sir James Taylor (1805–1890), police magistrate; MA, Trinity College, Cambridge, 1832; barrister, Inner Temple, 1832; magistrate at Thames Police Court, Hammer-

smith, and Wandsworth; knighted, 1876; chief metropolitan magistrate, 1876–90.

INGHAM, Oliver de, Baron Ingham (d. 1344), seneschal of Aquitaine, 1326 and 1333–43; supported Edward II, and was made justice of Chester; summoned as baron by *Mortimer, 1327; imprisoned by Edward III, 1330.

INGLEBY, Sir Charles (*fl.* 1688), Roman Catholic judge; barrister, Gray's Inn, 1671; acquitted of complicity in Gascoigne plot, 1680; made baron of the Exchequer by James II, 1688, but dismissed by William III; knighted, 1688; resumed practice.

INGLEBY, Clement Mansfield (1823–1886), Shakespearean critic and author; MA, Trinity College, Cambridge, 1850; LL D, 1859; published *Complete View of the Shakespeare Controversy* (1861), closing the Payne *Collier correspondence, *Introduction to Metaphysic* (1864 and 1869), *Revival of Philosophy at Cambridge* (1870), *Shakespeare Hermeneutics* (1875), *Centurie of Prayse* (1875), and *Shakespeare: the Man and the Book* (1877 and 1881); proposed examination of Shakespeare's skull for identification of portrait, 1882; edited *Cymbeline* (1886); vice-president and foreign secretary of Royal Society of Literature.

INGLEFIELD, Sir Edward Augustus (1820–1894), admiral; lieutenant, 1842; flag-lieutenant to his father, Rear-Admiral Samuel Hood Inglefield, then commander-in-chief on South American Station, 1845; commander, 1845; accompanied Lady Franklin's private steamer in expedition to Arctic, 1852; published *A Summer Search for Sir John Franklin* (1853); FRS, 1853; again visited Arctic, 1853 and 1854; captain, 1853; in Black Sea, 1855; in Channel and Mediterranean, 1866–8; rear-admiral, 1869; second-in-command in Mediterranean, 1872–5; knighted, 1877; commander-in-chief on North American Station, 1878–9; admiral, 1879; retired, 1888; KCB, 1887.

INGLEFIELD, John Nicholson (1748–1828), navy captain; served under Sir Samuel (afterwards Viscount) *Hood; at Ushant under Alexander *Hood (1727–1814), 1778; flag-captain to Samuel Hood in actions of 1781–2; one of the survivors of wreck of *Centaur*, 1782; captain of fleet in Mediterranean, 1794; declined flag-rank, but was commissioner of the navy, 1795–1811.

INGLETHORP (or INGOLDSTHORP), Thomas (d. 1291), bishop of Rochester; archdeacon of Middlesex and Sudbury; dean of St Paul's, 1277; bishop of Rochester, 1283–91; had disputes with Rochester monks and abbot of St Augustine's, Canterbury.

INGLIS, Charles (1731?–1791), rear-admiral; present at *Hawke's action with *L'Étenduère*, 1747; commanded a sloop in Rochefort expedition, 1757, and the *Carcass* bomb at *Rodney's bombardment of Havre, 1759; took part in relief of Gibraltar, 1781, and the operations of Sir Samuel (Viscount) *Hood in West Indies, 1782; rear-admiral, 1790.

INGLIS, Charles (1734–1816), first bishop of Nova Scotia; went to America and assisted in evangelical work among the Mohawk Indians; advocated establishment of American episcopate; MA by diploma, Oxford, 1770; DD, 1778; incumbent of Trinity Church, New York, 1777–83; attainted as a Loyalist, 1779; bishop of Nova Scotia, 1787–1816.

INGLIS, Sir Charles Edward (1875–1952), professor of engineering; educated at Cheltenham College and King's College, Cambridge; 22nd wrangler, 1897; first class, part i, mechanical sciences, 1898; trained with Sir John *Wolfe-Barry and (Sir) Alexander *Gibb; fellow of King's and assistant to (Sir) Alfred *Ewing, 1901; to Bertram *Hopkinson, 1903; lecturer in engineering, 1908; professor of mechanical sciences and head of engineering department at time of great expansion, 1919–43; researches included mechanical vibration and bridge stress; published *Applied Mechanics for Engineers* (1951); FRS, 1930; knighted, 1945; hon. LL D, Edinburgh.

INGLIS, Sir Claude Cavendish (1883–1974), civil engineer; educated at St Helen's School, Dublin, Shrewsbury School, and Trinity College, Dublin; BA and BAI, 1905; appointed to India Service of Engineers, 1906; served in Sind; executive engineer, Godaveri canals, Bombay Deccan, 1911; in charge of Niva canals, Poona district, 1913; surveyed half-a-million acres in Bombay Deccan to improve drainage and irrigation conditions; advised on Sukkur Barrage, Sind, 1928; secured selection of Poona Station as central station for whole of India, 1937; appointed its first director; carried out basic studies on barrages, bank protection, river training, and canal intakes; retired, 1945; as independent consulting engineer in England advised on river problems in India, Burma, and Persia; director of research for UK Hydraulic Research Board, 1947; worked for establishment of hydraulic research station at Wallingford, Berkshire, 1955; director up to 1958; CIE, 1936; knighted, 1945; FRS, 1953; awarded James Alfred Ewing Gold Medal by Institution of Civil Engineers, 1958; hon. MAI, 1952.

INGLIS, Elsie Maud (1864–1917), physician and surgeon; born in India; studied medicine at Edinburgh, Glasgow, and Dublin; joint surgeon to Edinburgh Bruntsfield Hospital and Dispensary and private practitioner in Edinburgh; inaugurated there maternity hospice staffed by women, 1901; founded Scottish Women's Suffrage Federation (1906) from which sprang Scottish Women's Hospitals Committee (1914); joined Serbian unit, 1915; remained at post at Krushevatz during German and Austrian invasion, 1915–16; organized two units in aid of Serbian division in Russia, 1916; worked at Braila, Galatz, and Reni, remaining till withdrawal of Serbs (1917).

INGLIS, Henry David (1795–1835), traveller and author of *Tales of the Ardennes* (by Derwent Conway, 1825), *Spain in 1830* (1831), *Ireland in 1834* (fifth edn., 1838), and other books of travel.

INGLIS, Hester (1571–1624). See KELLO.

INGLIS, James (d. 1531), abbot of Culross; clerk of the closet to *James IV; secretary to Queen *Margaret 1515; chancellor of Royal Chapel at Stirling and abbot of Culross, 1527; wrote poems, which are lost; murdered by John Blacater of Tulliallan and William Lothian.

INGLIS, John (1763–1834), Scottish divine; graduated at Edinburgh, 1783; DD, 1804; successor of Principal Robertson at the Old Greyfriars Church; moderator of general assembly, 1804; a dean of Chapel Royal, 1810; originated scheme for evangelization of India, 1824.

INGLIS, John, Lord Glencorse (1810–1891), lord justice-general of Scotland; youngest son of John *Inglis (1763–1834); of Glasgow University and Balliol College, Oxford; MA, Oxford, 1836; advocate, 1835; solicitor-general and afterwards lord advocate of Scotland, 1852 and 1858; carried Universities of Scotland Act 1858; lord justice-clerk, 1858–67; lord justice-general of Scotland, 1867–91; privy councillor, 1859; DCL, Oxford, 1859; elected chancellor of Edinburgh against Gladstone, 1869; rector of Aberdeen, 1857, of Glasgow, 1865; president of Scottish Texts Society; published *Historical Study of Law* (1863).

INGLIS, Sir John Eardley Wilmot (1814–1862), major-general; born in Nova Scotia; grandson of Bishop Charles *Inglis (1734–1816); with the 32nd in Canada, 1837, and the Punjab, 1848–9; succeeded Sir Henry *Lawrence in command at Lucknow; major-general and KCB for his gallant defence of Lucknow, 1857; commander in Ionian Islands, 1860; died at Hamburg.

INGLIS, Mrs Margaret Maxwell (1774–1843), Scottish poetess; née Murray; published

Miscellaneous Collection of Poems, chiefly Scriptural Pieces (1828).

INGLIS, Sir **Robert Harry,** second baronet (1786–1855), Tory politician; of Winchester, and Christ Church, Oxford; MA, 1809; DCL, 1826; of Lincoln's Inn; private secretary to Lord *Sidmouth; FSA, 1816; FRS; MP, Dundalk, 1824–6, Ripon, 1828–9; defeated Peel on the Catholic question at Oxford, 1829; represented Oxford University till 1854; opposed parliamentary reform, Jewish relief, repeal of the corn laws, and (1845) the Maynooth grant; commissioner on public records, 1831; privy councillor, 1854; president of the Literary Club; antiquary of Royal Academy, 1850; edited works by Henry *Thornton and sermon by *Heber.

INGLIS, Sir **William** (1764–1835), general; joined 57th at New York, 1781, and served with it in Flanders, 1793, in St Lucia, 1796, and Grenada, 1797; formed 2nd battalion, 1803; commanded 2nd battalion in Peninsula, holding also a brigade command in *Hill's division; led his regiment with great distinction at Albuera, 1811, where he was wounded; major-general, 1813; distinguished himself at head of first brigade of seventh division, especially at second Battle of Sauroren, 1813, and the action at Vera, 1813, and at Orthez, 1814; lieutenant-general, 1825; colonel of 57th, 1830; KCB.

INGLOTT, William (1554–1621), organist of Norwich Cathedral.

INGMETHORPE, Thomas (1562–1638), schoolmaster; BA, St Mary Hall, Oxford, 1584; MA, Brasenose College, 1586; headmaster of Durham School, *c.*1610; incumbent of Stainton-in-Strata, 1594–1638; learned Hebraist.

INGOLD, Sir **Christopher Kelk** (1893–1970), organic chemist; educated at Sandown Grammar School and Hartley University College (later, Southampton University); B.Sc. (London), 1913; research worker at Imperial College, London, 1913–18; research chemist with Cassel Cyanide Co., Glasgow, 1918–20; lecturer, organic chemistry, Imperial College, 1920; D.Sc. (London), 1921; FRS, 1924; professor, organic chemistry, Leeds University, 1924–30; professor, chemistry, University College, London, 1930–7; director of the laboratories, 1937–61; professor emeritus, 1961; a chemical genius, published 744 papers and a monumental book, *Structure and Mechanism in Organic Chemistry* (1st edn., 1953; 2nd edn., 1969); contributions to chemistry recognized by many honours and awards and numerous honorary degrees; president, Chemical Society, 1952–4; knighted, 1958.

INGOLDSBY, Sir **Henry,** first baronet (1622–1701), Parliamentarian; brother of Sir Richard *Ingoldsby; created baronet by *Cromwell, 1658, and Charles II, 1660.

INGOLDSBY, Sir **Richard** (d. 1685), regicide; admitted to Gray's Inn, 1638; MA, Oxford, 1649; as colonel of a 'new model' regiment took part in storming of Bridgwater and Bristol; signed Charles I's death-warrant under compulsion, as he asserted, 1649; MP, Wendover, 1647, and Buckinghamshire, 1654 and 1656; member of Council of State, 1652, and of *Cromwell's House of Lords, 1657; supported his kinsman, Richard *Cromwell, 1659; seized *Windsor for parliament and suppressed *Lambert's rising, 1659; pardoned and created KB, 1661; MP, Aylesbury, 1660–85.

INGOLDSBY, Richard (d. 1712), lieutenant-general; probably nephew of Sir Richard *Ingoldsby; adjutant-general of the expedition to French coast, 1692; commanded Royal Welch Fusiliers in Flanders under William III; brigadier, 1696; major-general, 1702; lieutenant-general, 1704; second-in-command of first line at Blenheim, 1704; MP for Limerick in Irish parliament from 1703; commander of the forces in Ireland, 1707–12.

INGOLDSBY, Richard (d. 1759), brigadier-general; great-grandson of Sir Richard *Ingoldsby; served in 1st Foot Guards; while commanding a brigade failed to take French redoubt near Fontenoy, 1745, and was dismissed by court martial.

INGRAM, Sir **Arthur** (d. 1642), courtier; comptroller of the customs of London for life, 1607; MP, Stafford, 1609, Romney, 1614, Appleby, 1620, and York, 1623–9; knighted, 1613; secretary of Council of the North, 1612; high sheriff of Yorkshire, 1620; built hospital at Bootham.

INGRAM, Arthur Foley Winnington- (1858–1946), bishop of London. See WINNINGTON-INGRAM.

INGRAM, Sir **Bruce Stirling** (1877–1963), editor of the *Illustrated London News*; grandson of Herbert *Ingram, founder of the paper; educated at Winchester and Trinity College, Oxford; served apprenticeship with the paper, 1897–1900; editor, 1900–63; also editor of the *Sketch*, 1905–46; served in Royal Garrison Artillery during 1914–18 war; MC (1917); OBE (military, 1918); interested in archaeology and collecting pictures; published *Three Sea Journals of Stuart Times* (1936); presented 700 drawings of Dutch marine artists to national Maritime Museum, 1957; presented other paintings to museums and art galleries; hon. keeper of drawings, Fitzwilliam

Museum, Cambridge; vice-president, Society for Nautical Research; vice-president, Navy Records Society; president, Illustrated Newspapers Ltd.; knighted, 1950; Legion of Honour, 1950; hon. D.Litt., Oxford, 1960.

INGRAM, Dale (1710–1793), surgeon; practised in Barbados, 1743–50; surgeon to Christ's Hospital, 1759–91; published *Practical Cases and Observations in Surgery* (1751), containing accounts of early abdominal operations.

INGRAM, Herbert (1811–1860), founder of the *Illustrated London News* (1842); removed to London from Nottingham with Nathaniel Cooke to advertise a pill; purchased *Pictorial Times* and other illustrated papers; attempted a threepenny daily, 1848; MP, Boston, 1856–60; associated with John *Sadleir; while travelling in America, drowned in Lake Michigan.

INGRAM, James (1774–1850), Anglo-Saxon scholar; educated at Westminster and Winchester; scholar of Trinity College, Oxford, 1794, fellow, 1803, president, 1824–50; MA, 1800; DD, 1824; professor of Anglo-Saxon, 1803–8; keeper of the archives, 1815–18; published *Memorials of Oxford* (1832–7); edited the *Saxon Chronicle* (1823) and Quintilian (1809).

INGRAM, John (1721–1771?), line-engraver.

INGRAM, John Kells (1823–1907), scholar, economist, and poet; brother of Thomas Dunbar *Ingram; senior moderator, Trinity College, Dublin, 1842; fellow, 1844; senior fellow, 1884; senior lecturer, 1887; D.Litt., 1891; helped to found Dublin Philosophical Society (1842), and contributed to *Transactions* abstruse papers in pure geometry; contributed sonnets to *Dublin University Magazine*, 1840; composed 'Who fears to speak of Ninety-eight?' which, printed anonymously in *Nation* newspaper (1 Apr. 1843), brought him fame as a popular nationalist poet; member of Royal Irish Academy, 1847; studied mathematics, classics, and metaphysics; visited Comte, 1855, and accepted his beliefs; professor of oratory at Trinity College, 1852–66; regius professor of Greek, 1866–77; librarian, 1879–87; vice-provost, 1898–9; started and edited *Hermathena*, 1874; trustee of the National Library of Ireland, 1881; hon. LL D, Glasgow, 1893; president of Royal Irish Academy, 1892–6; helped to found Dublin Statistical Society, 1847; president, 1878–80; prepared for the society 'Considerations on the State of Ireland', 1863; wrote papers on poor law, 1875–6; vindicated economics as integral branch of sociology; contributed articles to *Encyclopaedia Britannica* (9th edn.), of which those on political economy (1885) and slavery (1887) were separately published; his *History of Political Economy* (1888) was translated

into most European languages and Japanese; he declared his positivist beliefs in *Outlines of the History of Religion* (1900); published other positivist works from 1901 to 1905, and issued *Sonnets and other Poems*, 1900. He distrusted C. S. *Parnell and his nationalist associates; opposed South African War, 1899.

INGRAM, Robert (1727–1804), divine; MA, Corpus Christi College, Cambridge, 1753; vicar of Wormingford and Boxted, Essex; published apocalyptic works.

INGRAM, Robert Acklom (1763–1809), political economist; son of Robert *Ingram; senior wrangler, Queens' College, Cambridge, 1784; fellow; MA, 1787; BD, 1796; rector of Seagrave, 1802–9; chief works *Syllabus of a System of Political Philosophy* (1800) and *Disquisitions on Population* (1808), against *Malthus.

INGRAM, Thomas Dunbar (1826–1901), Irish historical writer and lawyer; LL B, Queen's College, Belfast, 1853; called to bar, 1856; professor of Hindu law in Presidency College, Calcutta, 1866–77; author of *A Critical Examination of Irish History* (2 vols., posthumous, 1904) and other works.

INGRAM, Walter (1855–1888), yeomanry officer; son of Herbert *Ingram; volunteer in Sudan expedition, 1884; killed by an elephant in east Africa.

INGULF (d. 1109), abbot of Crowland or Croyland; secretary to William the Conqueror; entered monastery of St Wandrille under Gerbert; abbot of Crowland, 1086–1109. The 'Crowland History', known by his name, though accepted as genuine by *Spelman, *Dugdale, and *Selden, has been shown to be a forgery (probably of the early fifteenth century) by Sir Francis *Palgrave, *Riley, and others. It was printed by *Savile (1596), *Fulman (1684, with continuations), and by Birch (1883).

INGWORTH, Richard of (*fl.* 1224), Franciscan; came to England with Agnellus, 1224; founded first Franciscan houses in London, Oxford, and Northampton; afterwards custodian of Cambridge and provincial minister of Ireland; died as missionary in Palestine.

INMAN, George Ellis (1814–1840), songwriter and poet; committed suicide in St James's Park.

INMAN, James (1776–1859), writer on nautical science; educated at Sedbergh and St John's College, Cambridge; fellow; MA, 1805; DD, 1820; senior wrangler and first Smith's prizeman, 1800; astronomer with *Flinders in the *Investigator* and *Porpoise*, 1803–4; professor of mathematics at Royal Naval College, Portsmouth, 1808–39; principal of School of Naval Architecture, 1810; published *Navigation and Nautical Astronomy for British Seamen* (1821), the tables of which are still used, *Introduction to Naval Gunnery* (1828), and other works.

INMAN, Thomas (1820–1876), mythologist; MD, London, 1842; physician to Royal Infirmary, Liverpool; published, among other works, *Phenomena of Spinal Irritation* (1858) and *Ancient Faiths embodied in Ancient Names* (vol. i, 1868, vol. ii, 1869).

INMAN, William (1825–1881), founder of the Inman line of steamships; brother of Thomas *Inman; partner of Richardson brothers of Liverpool, 1849, for whom he purchased the *City of Glasgow* (screw steamer) for American voyages, 1850; founded Inman line, 1857; introduced weekly service to New York, 1860; after failure of Collins line carried American mails; launched *City of Berlin*, 1875.

INNERPEFFER, Lord (d. 1650). See FLETCHER, ANDREW.

INNES, Cosmo Nelson (1798–1874), antiquary; educated at King's College, Aberdeen, Glasgow, and Balliol College, Oxford; MA, Oxford, 1824; engaged in peerage cases; sheriff of Moray, 1840–52; principal clerk of session, 1852; professor of civil history at Edinburgh, 1846–74; edited *Rescinded Acts* and assisted in folio edition of *Acts of the Scots Parliament* (1124–1707), besides many works for the Spalding and Bannatyne clubs; published also works on Scottish history.

INNES (or INNES-KER), James, fifth duke of Roxburgh (1738–1823). See KER.

INNES, James John McLeod (1830–1907), lieutenant-general, Royal (Bengal) Engineers; born in Bengal; joined Bengal Engineers, 1848; in Mutiny in charge of Machi Bhowan fort, and of mining operations at defence of Lucknow, which he described in *Lucknow and Oude in the Mutiny* (1895); awarded VC for gallantry at Sutanpur, 1858; accountant-general in Indian Public Works Department, 1870–7; inspector-general of military works, 1882–6; lieutenant-general, 1886; CB, 1907; published *The Sepoy Revolt of 1857* (1907) and lives of Sir Henry *Lawrence (1898) and Sir James Browne (1905).

INNES, Sir James Rose- (1855–1942), chief justice of South Africa. See ROSE-INNES.

INNES, John (d. 1414), bishop of Moray; canon of Elgin, 1389; archdeacon of Caithness, 1396; bishop of Moray, 1406–14; rebuilt Elgin Cathedral and erected part of the palace.

INNES, John (1739–1777), anatomist; dissector under Alexander *Monro secundus at Edinburgh.

INNES, Lewis (1651–1738), principal of the Scots College, Paris, 1682–1713; printed charter establishing the legitimacy of *Robert III, and vindicated its authenticity, 1695; lord-almoner at St Germain, 1714; probably compiled *Life of James II* (printed 1816).

INNES, Thomas (1662–1744), historian and antiquary; brother of Lewis *Innes; studied at Scots College and College of Navarre, Paris; MA, Paris, 1694; three years on Scottish mission; vice-principal of Scots College, 1727; his *Critical Essay on the Ancient Inhabitants of the Northern Parts of Britain* (1729), reprinted in *Historians of Scotland* (1879); his *Civil and Ecclesiastical History of Scotland* edited by George *Grub for Spalding Club (1853).

INNES OF LEARNEY, Sir Thomas (1893–1971), Lord Lyon king of arms; educated at Edinburgh Academy and University; 'passed advocate' to Scots bar, 1922; main interests heraldic; became Carrick pursuivant, 1926; interim Lyon clerk, 1929 and 1939–40; published *Scots Heraldry* (1934); Albany herald, 1935; Lord Lyon king of arms, 1945; KCVO, 1946; secretary to Order of the Thistle, 1945–69; FSA (Scotland); responsible for ceremonial for St Giles service after the coronation of Queen Elizabeth II, and the Silver Jubilee; GCVO, 1967; suggested foundation of Standing Council of Scottish Chiefs; retired in 1969 and became Marchmont herald; knight of St John of Jerusalem; archer of the Queen's Body Guard for Scotland; hon. LL D, St Andrews, 1956; youngest son, Malcolm Innes of Edingight also became Lord Lyon.

INSKIP, Thomas Walker Hobart, first Viscount Caldecote (1876–1947), lawyer and statesman; educated at Clifton and King's College, Cambridge; called to bar (Inner Temple), 1899; KC, 1914; served in Naval Intelligence, 1914–18; Conservative MP, Central Bristol (1918–29), Fareham (1931–9); solicitor-general, 1922–4, 1924–8, 1931–2; attorney-general, 1928–9, 1932–6; strong evangelical; leading adversary of Prayer Book revision, 1927–8; minister for co-ordination of defence, 1936–9; performed thankless and secret task with patience and integrity; obtained transfer of naval aircraft from Air Force to Navy as Fleet Air Arm; secretary of state for dominions, 1939, 1940; lord chancellor, 1939–40; lord chief justice, 1940–6; knighted, 1922; PC, 1932; viscount, 1939.

INSKIPP, James (1790–1868), painter; exhibited at British Institution, Society of British Artists, and Royal Academy.

INSULA, Robert de (or HALIELAND, Robert) (d. 1283), bishop of Durham, 1274–83; refused to admit visitation of Archbishop *Wickwane of York and was excommunicated, 1280.

INVERARITY, Elizabeth (1813–1846), afterwards Mrs Martyn; vocalist and actress.

INVERCHAPEL, Baron (1882–1951), diplomat. See CLARK KERR, ARCHIBALD JOHN KERR.

INVERFORTH, first Baron (1865–1955), shipowner. See WEIR, ANDREW.

INVERKEITHING, Richard (d. 1272), bishop of Dunkeld, 1250–72; chancellor of Scotland, 1255–7.

INVERNAIRN, Baron (1856–1936), shipbuilder. See BEARDMORE, WILLIAM.

INVERNESS, titular earl of (1691–1740). See HAY, JOHN.

INWOOD, Charles Frederick (1798–1840), architect; son of William *Inwood.

INWOOD, Henry William (1794–1843), architect; son of William *Inwood; travelled in Greece; his collection of antiquities purchased by British Museum; published archaeological works.

INWOOD, William (1771?–1843), architect and surveyor; designed (with assistance of his son) St Pancras New Church, 1819–22; published (1811) *Tables for the Purchasing of Estates* (21st edn., 1880).

IOLO GOCH (or the Red) (*fl.* 1328–1405), Welsh bard and lord of Llechryd; real name Edward Llwyd; said to have been made a 'chaired bard' at the Eisteddfod of 1330; friend of Owen *Glendower, for whom he created enthusiasm by his verses; composed also religious poems; eighteen of his poems printed.

IONIDES, Constantine Alexander (1833–1900), public benefactor; entered London Stock Exchange, 1864; bequeathed valuable collections of works of art to South Kensington Museum.

IORWERTH AB BLEDDYN (d. 1112), Welsh prince; being detached from the cause of his lord, Robert of *Bellême, contributed greatly to his defeat, 1102; imprisoned by Henry I, 1103–11; slain by *Madog, his outlawed nephew, and Llywerch at Caereineon.

IQBAL, Sir Muhammad (1876–1938), Indian thinker and poet; educated at Government College, Lahore, Trinity College, Cambridge, and Munich University; called to bar (Lincoln's Inn), 1908; thereafter practised in India; knighted, 1923; president, All-India Moslem League, 1930; delegate, first Round Table Conference, 1930–1; his poems in Persian and Urdu on theme of development of individual personality within idealized Islamic community immensely influential.

IRBY, Charles Leonard (1789–1845), captain in the navy and traveller; present at reduction of Montevideo and Mauritius; commanded the *Thames* in attack on New Orleans; travelled with Captain James *Mangles, *Belzoni, and others up the Nile and through Syria to Jerusalem, 1817–18, their *Travels* being published (1823, reissued, 1844); served in the Levant, 1826–7.

IRBY, Frederick Paul (1779–1844), rear-admiral; brother of Charles Leonard *Irby; present at *Howe's victory of 1 June, 1794, and at Camperdown, 1797; attained post rank, 1802; had four hours' indecisive fight with the *Aréthuse* off Sierra Leone, 1813; CB, 1831; rear-admiral, 1837.

IRBY, Leonard Howard Loyd (1836–1905), lieutenant-colonel and ornithologist; son of Frederick Paul *Irby; entered army, 1854; served at Sevastopol and at Lucknow; at Gibraltar (1864–72) devoted himself to ornithology; retired as lieutenant-colonel, 1874; published *Ornithology of the Straits of Gibraltar* (1875) and *Key List of British Birds* (1888); ardent lepidopterologist.

IRELAND, duke of (1362–1392). See VERE, ROBERT DE.

IRELAND, Alexander (1810–1894), journalist and man of letters; a native of Edinburgh; made acquaintance there of the brothers Chambers, Dr John *Gairdner, and Emerson, for whom (1847–88) he organized lecturing tour in England; one of three persons entrusted by Robert *Chambers with secret of authorship of Chambers's *Vestiges of Creation* (1843); settled in Manchester, 1843; there engaged in business; publisher and business-manager of *Manchester Examiner*, 1846–86. His publications include *The Book-Lover's Enchiridion* (1882) and bibliographies of Leigh *Hunt and *Hazlitt.

IRELAND, Mrs Annie (d. 1893), second wife of Alexander *Ireland; sister of Henry Alleyne *Nicholson; married, 1866; published biography of Jane Welsh *Carlyle (1891).

IRELAND, Francis (*fl.* 1745–1773). See HUTCHESON, FRANCIS, the younger.

IRELAND, John (d. 1808), biographer of *Hogarth; some time a watch-maker in Maiden Lane; published (1786) *Letters and Poems, with Anecdotes*, of his friend, John *Henderson (1747–1785), and *Hogarth Illustrated* (1791), with a biography as supplement (1798).

IRELAND, John (1761–1842), dean of Westminster; son of an Ashburton butcher; friend of William *Gifford (1756–1826); bible-clerk at Oriel College, Oxford, 1779; MA, 1810; DD, 1810; vicar of Croydon and chaplain to Lord Liverpool, 1793–1816; prebendary of Westminster, 1802, sub-dean, 1806, dean, 1816–42; rector of Islip, 1816–35; published *Paganism and Christianity compared* (1809); founded professorship of exegesis and (1825) classical scholarships at Oxford.

IRELAND, John Nicholson (1879–1962), composer, organist, and pianist; son of Alexander and Annie *Ireland; educated at Leeds Grammar School; studied at Royal College of Music, London; studied organ with Sir Walter *Parratt; assistant organist and choirmaster, Holy Trinity Church, Sloane Street, 1896; studied with (Sir) Charles *Stanford, 1897–1901; Mus.B. (Durham), 1908; organist and choirmaster, St Luke's, Chelsea, 1904–26; compositions include Phantasy Trio in A minor (1909), First Violin Sonata in D minor, and Second Violin Sonata (1917); professor of composition, Royal College of Music, 1923–39; FRCM, hon. RAM, 1924; composed Cello Sonata, Piano Sonatina, Piano Concerto in E flat, *A London Overture*, and *These Things Shall Be*, 1924–37; hon. doctorate, Durham, 1932; during war years composed *Sarnia* (1941) and the Epic March (1942); followed by *Satyricon* (1946) and music for the film *The Overlanders* (1947); John Ireland Society formed, 1959.

IRELAND, Samuel (d. 1800), author and engraver; etched plates after *Mortimer, *Hogarth, and Dutch masters; issued *Graphic Illustrations of Hogarth* (2 vols., 1794, 1799) from pictures and prints in his collection, and *Picturesque Tour through France, Holland, Brabant* (1790) and a series of English *Picturesque Views* illustrated from his own drawings. Much of his correspondence respecting the Shakespearean forgeries of his son, William Henry *Ireland, is in British Museum.

IRELAND (alias IRONMONGER), William (1636–1679), Jesuit; educated at St Omer; procurator of the province in London; tried and executed on testimony of *Oates and *Bedloe on charges connected with the 'Popish Plot'.

IRELAND, William Henry (1775–1835), forger of Shakespeare manuscripts; son of Samuel *Ireland; of doubtful legitimacy; partially educated in France; early impressed with story of *Chatterton; had access to Elizabethan parchments at the lawyer's chambers in New Inn, where he was employed; forged deeds and signatures of or relating to Shakespeare, 1794–5;

made in feigned handwriting a transcript of *Lear* and extracts from *Hamlet*; deceived his father and many men of letters and experts, including Dr *Parr, Joseph *Warton, and George *Chalmers; fabricated in forged handwriting pseudo-Shakespearian plays, *Vortigern and Rowena* and *Henry II*, the former being produced unsuccessfully by *Sheridan at Drury Lane, with *Kemble in the cast, Mar. 1796; was caricatured by *Gillray, 1797; authenticity of his documents attacked by *Malone. On the failure of *Vortigern* young Ireland left his father's house and made an avowal of his fraud (*Authentic Account*), afterwards expanded into *Confessions* (1805, reissued, 1872); sold imitations of the forgeries; employed by publishers in London; lived some time in Paris; published ballads, narrative poems, romances, and other works of some literary merit. A collection of his forgeries destroyed by fire at Birmingham Library, 1879. Many specimens are in British Museum.

IRELAND, William Wotherspoon (1832–1909), physician; MD, Edinburgh, 1855; joined East India Company's service, 1856; severely wounded at siege of Delhi, 1856; retired on pension, 1859; medical superintendent of Scottish National Institution for Imbecile Children, 1869; wrote with authority on idiocy and imbecility; applied medico-psychological knowledge to explain lives of celebrated men in *The Blot upon the Brain* (1885) and *Through the Ivory Gate* (1889); wrote also life of Sir Harry *Vane the younger (1905).

IRETON, Henry (1611–1651), regicide; BA, Trinity College, Oxford, 1629; of the Middle Temple; fought at Edgehill, 1642; *Cromwell's deputy-governor of the Isle of Ely; as quartermaster-general in *Manchester's army took part in Yorkshire campaign and second Battle of Newbury, 1644; supported Cromwell's accusation of Manchester; surprised Royalist quarters before Naseby, 1645; as commander of the cavalry of the left wing was wounded and captured in the battle, but afterwards escaped, 1645; at siege of Bristol, 1645; a negotiator of Treaty of Truro, 1646; received overtures from Charles I at Oxford, 1646; married Bridget, Cromwell's daughter, 1646; MP, Appleby, 1645; justified the army petition and consequently quarrelled with *Holles, 1647; one of the four commissioners to pacify the soldiers; sanctioned *Joyce's removal of the king from Holdenby; drew up the 'engagement' of the army and 'Heads of the Army Proposals', 1647, endeavouring to bring about an agreement between king and parliament; opposed the Levellers' constitution and was denounced by them; led conservative party in the Council of the Army till the flight of Charles I to the Isle of Wight, after which he supported his deposition in favour of one of his sons; served under *Fairfax in Kent and Essex, and as commissioner for the surrender of Colchester (1648) defended the execution of *Lucas and *Lisle; with *Ludlow concerted 'Pride's Purge', 1648; attended regularly the High Court of Justice and signed the warrant for Charles I's execution; chief author of the 'Agreement of the People' drawn up by the Council of War, 1649; went to Ireland as Cromwell's second-in-command, 1649, and remained as his deputy; captured Carlow, Waterford, and Duncannon, 1650, and Limerick, 1651; died of fever before Limerick. He carried out the Cromwellian policy with indefatigable industry and honesty. He was buried in Westminster Abbey, but his body was disinterred and dishonoured after the Restoration.

IRETON, John (1615–1689), lord mayor of London, 1658; brother of Henry *Ireton.

IRETON, Ralph (d. 1292), bishop of Carlisle; prior of Guisborough, 1261; elected to see of Carlisle, 1278, but not confirmed by the king and archbishop till after a visit to Rome, where he was consecrated; accused of great extortions in chronicle of Lanercost; with Antony *Bek I or II negotiated Treaty of Brigham, 1290.

IRLAND, Bonaventure (1551–1612?), professor of law at Poitiers; son of Robert *Irland; wrote *Remontrances au roi Henri III* and a philosophical treatise, *De Emphasi et Hypostasi* (1599).

IRLAND, John (*fl.* 1480), Scottish diplomat; sent by Louis XI to Scotland on an anti-English mission, 1480; Scottish ambassador to France, 1484.

IRLAND, Robert (d. 1561), professor of law at Poitiers, 1502–61; went to France, *c.*1496, and was naturalized, 1521.

IRONS, Joseph (1785–1852), Evangelical preacher; minister of Grove Chapel, Camberwell, 1818–52.

IRONS, William Josiah (1812–1883), theological writer; son of Joseph *Irons; MA, The Queen's College, Oxford, 1835; DD, 1854; vicar of Brompton, 1840–70; contributed (1862) to *Replies to Essays and Reviews*; rector of Wadingham, Lincolnshire, 1870; of St Mary Woolnoth, London, 1872–83; Bampton lecturer, 1870; published *Analysis of Human Responsibility* (1869); edited *Literary Churchman*; translated 'Dies Irae'.

IRONSIDE, Edward (1736?–1803), author of *History and Antiquities of Twickenham* (1797).

IRONSIDE, Gilbert, the elder (1588–1671), bishop of Bristol; of Trinity College, Oxford; fellow, 1613; MA, 1612; DD, 1660; rector of Win-terbourne Steepleton, 1618, of Winterbourne Abbas, 1629; bishop of Bristol, 1661–71.

IRONSIDE, Gilbert, the younger (1632–1701), bishop of Bristol and Hereford; son of Gilbert *Ironside the elder; MA, Wadham College, Oxford, 1655; fellow, 1656; DD, 1666; warden of Wadham College, Oxford, 1667–92; as vice-chancellor, 1687–9, resisted James II; bishop of Bristol, 1689–91, of Hereford, 1691–1701.

IRONSIDE, Robin Cunliffe (1912–1965), painter and writer; educated at Bradfield and the Courtauld Institute; assistant keeper, Tate Gallery, 1937–46; assistant secretary, Contemporary Art Society, 1938–45; publications include *Wilson Steer* (1943), *Pre-Raphaelite Painters, British Painting since 1939, David Jones* (1948), and *Andrea del Sarto* (1965); contributed articles to *Horizon*; painted in oils and gouache esoteric subjects such as *Rose being offered in a Coniferous Wood* and *Musical Performance by Patients in a Condition of Hypomania*; exhibited at Redfern Gallery, London, 1944, and later at other galleries in London and New York; made theatrical designs for *Der Rosenkavalier* (1948), *Silvia* (1952), *A Midsummer Night's Dream* (1954), and *La Sylphide* (1960); represented at Tate Gallery, Boston Museum, and Leicester Art Gallery.

IRONSIDE, William Edmund, first Baron Ironside (1880–1959), field marshal; educated at Tonbridge School and Royal Military Academy, Woolwich; commissioned in Royal Artillery, 1899; served in South African War, 1899–1902; in France, 1914–18; DSO, 1915; CMG, 1918; commanded Allied forces in Archangel, 1918–19; major-general and KCB, 1919; commandant, Staff College, Camberley, 1922–6; commander, 2nd division, Aldershot, 1926–8, Meerut District, India, 1928–31; quartermaster-general, India, 1933–6; general, 1935; held Eastern Command, 1936–8; commander-in-chief designate, Middle East, and governor of Gibraltar, 1938–9; GCB, 1938; inspector-general, overseas forces, May 1939; chief of Imperial General Staff, Sept. 1939–May 1940; planned for armies to defeat Hitler on land; commander-in-chief, Home Forces, preparing against invasion, May–July 1940; field marshal, 1940; baron, 1941; hon. LL D, Aberdeen; published *Archangel 1918–19* (1953).

IRVINE, Sir Alexander, of Drum (d. 1658), Royalist; sheriff of Aberdeen, 1634; aided *Huntly in obtaining subscription to Charles I's Covenant, 1638; assisted *Montrose to capture Aberdeen, 1639; surrendered to General *Monro and was fined and imprisoned, 1640–1; released, 1641; several times refused to subscribe the Solemn League and Covenant, and had to submit to plunder of Drum in 1645.

IRVINE, Alexander, tenth laird of Drum (d. 1687), Royalist; son of Sir Alexander *Irvine; outlawed and imprisoned as Royalist, 1644–5; declined earldom of Aberdeen; married as second wife 'the weel-faured May' (Margaret Coutts) of the ballad.

IRVINE, Alexander (1793–1873), botanist; opened school in Chelsea, 1851; accompanied by John Stuart *Mill on botanical excursions; published *London* [so-called] *Flora* (1838) and *Illustrated Handbook of British Plants* (1858); edited *Phytologist*, 1855–63.

IRVINE, Christopher (*fl.* 1638–1685), physician and philologist; ejected from college of Edinburgh for refusing the Covenant, 1638; surgeon in Charles II's camp, 1651, to *Monck's army, 1653–60, and to Horse Guards, 1660–81; published *Bellum Grammaticale* (1658; reprinted, 1698), *Medicina Magnetica* (1656), translations of medical works, and *Historiae Scoticae nomenclatura Latino-vernacula* (1682; reprinted 1817 and 1819).

IRVINE, James (1833–1889), Scottish portrait painter; friend of George Paul *Chalmers.

IRVINE, Sir James Colquhoun (1877–1952), chemist and educationist; educated at Allen Glen's School and Royal Technical College, Glasgow, and St Andrews and Leipzig universities; junior lecturer, St Andrews, 1901; D.Sc., 1903; professor of chemistry, 1909–21; dean of science faculty, 1912–21; researched mainly on carbohydrates; principal, St Andrews, 1921–52; improved and expanded university; chairman, Committee on Indian Institute of Science, 1936, West Indies Higher Education Committee, 1944, Inter-University Council for Higher Education in Colonies, 1946–51; served on Pilgrim Trust and Commonwealth Fund; FRS, 1918; CBE, 1920; knighted, 1925; KBE, 1948.

IRVINE, Robert (d. 1645), Royalist; son of Sir Alexander *Irvine.

IRVINE, William (1741–1804), American brigadier; born in Ireland; surgeon in British Navy during Seven Years' War; settled in Pennsylvania; captured while commanding a regiment of infantry in Canada by the British, 1776; commanded 2nd Pennsylvanian brigade at Staten Island and Bull's Ferry, 1780, and afterwards on western frontier; member of the Continental Congress, 1786; recommended purchase of 'The Triangle', to give Pennsylvania an outlet on Lake Erie.

IRVINE, William (1743–1787), chemist; MD, Glasgow; assisted Joseph *Black in experiments on steam; lecturer in chemistry at Glasgow, 1770–87; his *Essays, chiefly on Chemical Subjects* published (1805).

IRVINE, William (1776–1811), physician to the forces; son of William *Irvine (1743–1787); MD, Edinburgh, 1798; LRCP, 1806; published observations on diseases in Sicily (1810); died at Malta.

IRVINE, William (1840–1911), Mogul historian; joined Indian Civil Service, 1863; magistrate and collector in North-West provinces, 1863–89; published *Rent Digest* (1868); wrote on Mogul history for *Journal of Asiatic Society of Bengal*, 1896–1908; published *The Army of the Indian Moghuls* (1903), and translated and edited N. Manucci's account of India (1658–1707), which was published by the Indian government (1907).

IRVING, David (1778–1860), biographer; MA, Edinburgh, 1801; published *Elements of English Composition* (1801), *Lives of the Scotish Poets* (1804), *Life of George Buchanan* (1805; enlarged, 1817), and *Introduction to Study of the Civil Law* (1837); edited *Selden's *Table-Talk* (1819) and other works; hon. LL D, Aberdeen, 1808; librarian of the Faculty of Advocates, Edinburgh, 1820–48; his *History of Scotish Poetry* edited by Dr John *Carlyle (1861).

IRVING, Edward (1792–1834), founder of the 'Catholic Apostolic Church'; son of a tanner at Annan; MA, Edinburgh, 1809; schoolmaster at Haddington, 1810–12, and afterwards at Kirkcaldy, where he became acquainted with *Carlyle, 1816; assistant to Dr Chalmers at St John's, Glasgow, 1819–22; came to London, 1822, as minister at Hatton Garden Chapel, where his preaching soon made him famous; translated Aben Ezra's (Lacunza) *Coming of the Messiah* (1827); intimate of Henry *Drummond (1786–1860); built new church in Regent Square; issued *Lectures on Baptism* (1828); undertook preaching tour in Scotland, 1828; established the *Morning Watch*, 1829; was compelled to retire from Regent Square on account of his approval of the 'tongues', 1832; title of the 'Holy Catholic Apostolic Church' assumed by his followers, 1832; deprived, by Presbytery of Annan, for heretical views in tract on the Incarnation, 1833; personally laid no claim to supernatural gifts; died at Glasgow. The Irvingite church in Gordon Square was built in 1854.

IRVING, George Vere (1815–1869), Scottish lawyer and antiquary.

IRVING, Sir Henry (1838–1905), actor, whose original name was John Henry Brodribb; born at Keinton Mandeville, Somerset; came of yeoman stock; clerk in London firm of East India merchants, 1852–6; made first appearance as actor at

Lyceum Theatre, Sunderland, as Gaston in *Richelieu*, 1856; in Edinburgh, 1857–9, where his mannerisms were criticized; first appeared in London, 1859; at Manchester under Charles *Calvert, 1860–5; first acted role of Hamlet (his first Shakespearian character), 1864; after much provincial work, he toured with J. L. *Toole, 1866; at Queen's Theatre, London, played Petruchio to (Dame) Ellen *Terry's Katherine, Dec. 1867, and Bill Sikes in *Oxenford's *Oliver Twist*, 1869; made first notable success in London as Digby Grant in *Albery's *Two Roses* at Vaudeville, 1870; joined company of H. L. *Bateman at Lyceum Theatre, 1871; became famous by his acting in *The Bells*, Nov. 1871 to May 1872; took title parts of *Charles I* (1872), *Eugene Aram* (1873), and *Richelieu* (1873); showed originality in conception, but criticized for affectations, monotony, and weakness of voice; scored triumph as Hamlet, 1874; appeared as Macbeth (1875) and Othello (1876), and in *Richard III*, *The Lyons Mail* (1877), and *Louis XI* (1878); became lessee and manager of Lyceum, 1878, and began association—lasting till 1902—with (Dame) Ellen Terry; played Hamlet to her Ophelia, 1878; produced *Merchant of Venice* (1880), *The Corsican Brothers* (1880), *Tennyson's *The Cup* (1881), *Romeo and Juliet* (elaborately mounted), and *Much Ado About Nothing* (1882–3); made first of eight tours to America, 1883–4; on return, produced *Twelfth Night*, May 1884; gave weird and striking impersonation of Mephistopheles in *Wills's *Faust*, 1885–7; revived *Macbeth*, 1888–9; with Ellen Terry he appeared before Queen Victoria at Sandringham, Apr. 1889; produced *Henry VIII* (with splendid staging), Jan. 1892, and *King Lear*, Nov. 1892; Tennyson's *Becket* (Feb. 1893) proved one of Irving's greatest personal and financial triumphs; made fourth and most successful American tour, 1893–4; produced *Waterloo* (1894), *King Arthur* (1895), *Cymbeline* (Sept. 1896), and *Richard III* (Dec.); suffered pecuniary losses; transferred control of Lyceum to a company, 1898; appeared in Sardou's *Robespierre* (1899) and in *Coriolanus* (1901); revived *Faust* and *Merchant of Venice* at Lyceum, 1902; last appearance there, 19 July; produced at Drury Lane Sardou's *Dante*, 1903; made eighth American tour, 1903–4; died in Bradford after acting in *Becket* earlier in the evening, 1905; his ashes buried in Westminster Abbey; contributed to the *Nineteenth Century*, 'An Actor's Notes', 1877–87; superintended the 'Henry Irving Shakespeare', 1888; received honorary degrees from Dublin, Cambridge, and Glasgow; first actor to be knighted, 1895; Rede lecturer at Cambridge, 1898. An intellectual actor, of magnetic personality, but of mannered elocution and gait, he attracted the intelligent playgoer back to the theatre and revived popular interest in Shakespeare. He neglected modern drama and depended much on sumptuous and elaborate mountings, for which he secured assistance from leading artists and composers.

IRVING, Joseph (1830–1891), author and journalist; edited Dumbarton *Herald*, 1854; contributed to *Morning Chronicle* and *Glasgow Herald*; published *History of Dumbartonshire* (1857), *Annals of our Time* (1869), *The Book of Eminent Scotsmen* (1882), and other works.

IRVING, Sir Paulus Aemilius, first baronet (1751–1828), general; served with 47th Foot in America and Canada; captured at Saratoga, 1777; commanded the regiment, 1783–94; major-general, 1794; captured La Vigie in St Vincent, 1795; created baronet, 1809; general, 1812.

IRWIN, Eyles (1751?–1817), traveller and author; superintendent of Madras, 1771; dismissed for protest against deposition of Lord *Pigot, 1776; his journey to England narrated in *Series of Adventures in the course of a Voyage up the Red Sea* etc. (1780, 3rd edn., with suppl., 1787); returned to India, 1780, on reinstatement; revenue officer in Tinnevelly; commissary to negotiate for cession of Dutch settlements, 1785; in China, 1792–4; published poems, political tracts, and *The Bedouins* (comic opera, 1802).

IRWIN, Sir John (1728–1788), general; protégé of Lionel, duke of *Dorset; correspondent of Lord *Chesterfield; lieutenant-colonel of 5th Foot, 1752; served with distinction under Ferdinand of Brunswick, 1760; major-general, 1762; MP, East Grinstead, 1762–83; governor of Gibraltar, 1766–8; commander-in-chief in Ireland, 1775–82; KB, 1779; favourite with George III; general, 1783; obliged by extravagance to retire to the continent; died at Parma.

ISAAC, Samuel (1815–1886), projector of the Mersey Tunnel (opened, 1885); had previously, as army contractor, supplied the Confederates during the American Civil War (1861–5).

ISAACS, Alick (1921–1967), medical scientist; grandson of Lithuanian immigrant; educated at Pollokshields Secondary School and Glasgow University; MB, Ch.B., 1944; studied streptococci bacteria; Medical Research Council student, Sheffield University, 1947; worked on influenza; with Rockefeller fellowship worked on influenza viruses in Melbourne, 1948–50; returned to work at National Institute for Medical Research, Mill Hill, 1951; with Dr J. Lindenmann, discovered 'interferon', of fundamental importance in biology, as well as defence against viruses; worked also with World Influenza Centre under World Health Organization; MD with honours, Glasgow, 1955; head of virus division, Mill Hill, 1961–7; FRS, 1966; hon. MD, Louvain, 1962.

ISAACS, George Alfred (1883–1979), Labour politician; educated at council school at Hoxton, London; entered printing trade as reader's boy; general secretary, National Society of Operative Printers and Assistants, 1909–49; mayor of Southwark, 1919–21; Labour MP for Gravesend, 1923–4, North Southwark, 1929–31 and 1939–50, Southwark division, 1950–9; published *The Story of the Newspaper Printing Press* (1931); served as parliamentary private secretary to secretaries of state for the Colonies, 1924, Dominions, 1929–31, and to first lord of the Admiralty, 1942–5; chairman, TUC General Council, 1945; minister of labour and national service, 1945–51; responsible for placing men and women in suitable employment on release from the forces and from war work; by end of 1947 some five million men and women absorbed into peacetime industry; presided at world conference of trade unions in London, 1945; minister of pensions, 1951; retired from public life, 1959.

ISAACS, Sir Isaac Alfred (1855–1948), chief justice and governor-general of Australia; graduated in law, Melbourne University, and called to Victorian bar, 1880; QC, 1899; member, Victorian Legislative Assembly, 1892–1901; solicitor-general, 1893; attorney-general, 1894–9, 1900–1; MHR, 1901–6; attorney-general, 1905–6; High Court judge, 1906–30; chief justice, 1930–31; his judgements on Australian constitutional law especially important; held Commonwealth legislation to bind the states; first Australian-born governor-general, 1931–6; PC, 1921; KCMG, 1928; GCB, 1937.

ISAACS, Rufus Daniel, first marquess of Reading (1860–1935), lord chief justice of England, ambassador to the United States, and viceroy of India; son of Jewish fruit merchant in Spitalfields; entered family business at 15; ship's boy on *Blair Athole*, 1876–7; jobber on stock exchange, 1880–4; called to bar (Middle Temple), 1887; established busy practice dealing especially with commercial and trade-union law; QC, 1898; in front rank of advocates; triumphs include the Taff Vale litigation (1902) and prosecution of Whitaker *Wright (1904); Liberal MP, Reading, 1904–13; solicitor-general (Mar.), attorney-general (Oct.), 1910; excellent law officer; led in *Rex* v. *Mylius* (1911) and secured conviction of Seddon (1912); PC and KCVO, 1911; entered Cabinet, 1912; implicated (1912–13) in controversy over Marconi Company for which his brother as joint managing director had obtained a Post Office contract; in repudiating the untrue charge that he had exercised influence in favour of his brother, did not think it necessary to state that he himself held shares in the American company which had no interest in the contract; this error of judgement caused him to be fiercely attacked when the fact became known; acquitted by House of acting otherwise than in good faith; lord chief justice, 1913–21; baron, 1914; secured loan of 500 million dollars to be spent in United States, Oct. 1915; viscount, 1916; high commissioner for finance in United States and Canada, Sept.–Nov. 1917; earl, 1917; ambassador and high commissioner in United States, 1918–19; accelerated supplies of food and troops; viceroy of India, 1921–6; watched over early application of Montagu–Chelmsford reforms; approached problems in liberal spirit and showed much patience before resorting to extreme measures; put forward government of India's request for revision of Treaty of Sèvres with result that Lausanne Treaty went far to relieve Moslem anxieties about treatment of Turkey; marquess, 1926; director, later president, Imperial Chemical Industries; took prominent part in Indian Round Table Conference, 1930–1; foreign secretary, Aug.–Oct. 1931; lord warden of Cinque Ports, 1934–5.

ISAACS, Stella, marchioness of Reading and Baroness Swanborough (1894–1971), founder and chairman, Women's Royal Voluntary Service (originally Women's Voluntary Service for Civil Defence—WVS); daughter of Charles Charn; as child, due to spinal ailment studied at home; secretary to Lady Reading, wife of Viceroy of India, Rufus *Isaacs, Earl (later Marquess) of Reading, 1925; later private secretary to Marquess of Reading; married Reading in 1931, one year after death of his first wife; supported her husband devotedly until he died in 1935; invited by home secretary, Sir Samuel *Hoare (later Viscount Templewood), to form a voluntary service for women to cope with dislocation to civil population in time of war, 1938; founder of WVS, mobilizing resources of over a million women by 1942; wartime work notable for evacuation of children from London and other large cities, and provision of wide variety of welfare services for the armed forces, refugees, and victims of enemy bombing; (accolade 'Royal' bestowed in 1966); vice-chairman, Imperial Relations Trust, 1936–68; governor of BBC, 1946–51, vice-chairman, 1947–51; DBE, 1941; GBE, 1944; as Baroness Swanborough, first woman life peer, 1958; number of honorary doctorates; still chairman of WRVS when she died.

ISAACSON, Henry (1581–1654), theologian and chronologer; of Pembroke Hall, Cambridge; friend of Bishop *Andrewes; published *Saturni*

Ephemerides, sive Tabula Historico-Chronologica (1633), a life of Bishop Andrewes (1650), and other works.

ISAACSON, Stephen (1798–1849), author; BA, Christ's College, Cambridge, 1820; translated Bishop *Jewel's Apologia*, with life and preface (1825), which involved him in controversy with Charles *Butler (1750–1832), 1825–6; edited Henry *Isaacson's life of Bishop *Andrewes (1829) with life of the author; rector of St Paul's, Demerara; defended slave proprietors; published also devotional manuals and 'The Barrow Digger', a poem.

ISABELLA (1214–1241), empress; daughter of John, king of England, and *Isabella of Angoulême; married to the emperor Frederic II, 1235; kept in great seclusion; died at Foggia; buried at Andria; called by Matthew *Paris 'the glory and hope of England'.

ISABELLA (1332–1379), eldest daughter of Edward III and *Philippa; proposed as wife for Louis, count of Flanders, who was forced by his subjects to promise assent, but escaped before the day arranged for the ceremony, 1347; after failure of two other matches married Enguerraud VII, lord of Coucy, then a hostage in England, 1365; lived in England during his six years' absence in Italy, and after his final renunciation of English allegiance.

ISABELLA OF ANGOULÊME (d. 1246), queen of John, king of England; daughter of Aymer, count of Angoulême, by Alicia, granddaughter of Louis VI of France; betrothed to Hugh of Lusignan, but married to John, king of England, at Angoulême, 1200; crowned in England, 1201; inherited Angoumois, 1213; imprisoned at Gloucester, 1214; left England, 1217; married Hugh of Lusignan, her old lover, 1220; in alliance with her son (Henry III) made war on Alfonso, count of Poitou, and Louis IX of France, 1241; died at Fontevraud.

ISABELLA OF FRANCE (1292–1358), queen of England; daughter of Philip the Fair of France; married to Edward II at Boulogne, 1308; neglected by her husband for the sake of Piers *Gaveston; helped to mediate between Edward II and the barons, 1313, 1316, and 1321; twice escaped capture by the Scots; deprived of her estates by influence of the Despensers, 1324; went to France, 1325, and formed connection with Roger *Mortimer; raised troops in Germany and the Netherlands; landed in England with Mortimer, John of Hainault, and many exiles, 1326; having obtained the adhesion of London, advanced to Gloucester; joined by armies from the north and Welsh marches, executed the Despensers, deposed Edward II, and had her eldest son proclaimed king as Edward III, 1327; procured her husband's murder, and with Mortimer virtually ruled England; made peace with France, 1327; renounced overlordship of Scotland for money, 1328; alienated the nobility by her own and Mortimer's rapacity, and execution of *Edmund, earl of Kent; arrested with Mortimer at Nottingham by *Lancaster, with the concurrence of Edward III, 1330; compelled to give up her riches, but allowed to live at various places in honourable confinement; took the habit of Santa Clara; buried in the Franciscan Church, Newgate.

ISABELLA OF FRANCE (1389–1409), second queen of Richard II; daughter of Charles VI of France; her marriage in 1396 the pledge of peace between England and France and the prelude to Richard's *coup d'état*; confined by Henry IV at Sonning and not allowed to see her husband, whose death was concealed from her; allowed to return to France, 1401, but her marriage portion withheld; married to Charles of Angoulême (afterwards duke of Orleans), 1406; died in childbirth.

ISBISTER, Alexander Kennedy (1822–1883), educational writer; MA, Edinburgh, 1858; LL B, London, 1866; master of Stationers' Company's School, 1858–82; edited *Educational Times* from 1862; barrister, Middle Temple, 1864; dean of College of Preceptors, 1872; published educational manuals.

ISCANUS, Josephus (*fl.* 1190). See JOSEPH OF EXETER.

ISHAM (or ISUM), John (1680?–1726), composer; Mus.Bac., Merton College, Oxford, 1713; organist of St Anne's, Westminster, 1711, of St Margaret's and St Andrew's, Holborn, London, 1718–26; published (with William Morley) songs.

ISHAM, Sir Justinian, second baronet (1610–1674), Royalist; of Christ's College, Cambridge; imprisoned as delinquent, 1649; forced to compound on succeeding to baronetcy, 1651; MP, Northamptonshire, 1661–74; founded Lamport Hall library.

ISHAM, Sir Thomas, third baronet (1657–1681), son of Sir Justinian *Isham; his Latin diary translated and printed (1875).

ISHAM, Zacheus (1651–1705), divine; MA, Christ Church, Oxford, 1674; DD, 1689; tutor to Sir Thomas *Isham; chaplain to Bishop *Compton, *c.*1685; prebendary of St Paul's, London, 1686; canon of Canterbury, 1691; rector of St Botolph's, London, 1694, and of Solihull, 1701; published sermons.

ISHERWOOD, Sir **Joseph William,** first baronet (1870–1937), ship designer; surveyor to Lloyd's Register, 1896–1907; practised as naval architect; invented 'longitudinal', 'combination', and 'bracketless' systems of ship construction and 'arcform' hull design; baronet, 1921.

ISITT, Dame **Adeline Genée** (1878–1970), ballet dancer. See GENÉE.

ISLES, lords of the. See SUMERLED, d. 1164; MACDONALD, JOHN, first lord, d. 1386?; MAC-DONALD, DONALD, second lord, d. 1420?; MAC-DONALD, ALEXANDER, third lord, d. 1449; MACDONALD, JOHN, fourth lord, d. 1498?.

ISLINGTON, Baron (1866–1936). See POYN-DER, Sir JOHN POYNDER DICKSON-.

ISLIP, John (d. 1532), abbot of Westminster, 1500–32; obtained removal of Henry VI's body from Windsor; built Henry VII's Chapel; privy councillor, 1513; trier of parliamentary petitions; signed letter to the pope in favour of the divorce, 1530; at Westminster raised western tower to level of the roof, filled niches with statues, and built mortuary chapel known by his name.

ISLIP, Simon (d. 1366), archbishop of Canterbury; fellow of Merton College, Oxford, 1307, and doctor of canon and civil law; official of Lincoln, appointed 1334; archdeacon of Canterbury, 1343–6; official of court of Canterbury by 1343; chaplain, secretary, and keeper of the privy seal to Edward III; ambassador to France, 1342; one of the regent's council, 1345; as archbishop (1349–66) issued a canon (1350) ordering chaplains to be content with salaries received before the Black Death; limited rights of friars in favour of secular clergy; arranged compromise with archbishop of York on right of northern primate to carry his cross erect in the southern province, 1353; maintained rights of Canterbury against the prince of Wales, 1357; caused rejection of the king's demand of a clerical tenth for six years, 1356, and by his remonstrance helped to procure statute of 1362, against purveyance; founded at Oxford a college in connection with Christ Church, Canterbury, of mixed monks and seculars, 1361, of which *Wycliffe the reformer may have been the second warden; his foundation monasticized, 1370, and afterwards absorbed in *Wolsey's.

ISLWYN (1832–1878). See THOMAS, WILLIAM.

ISMAIL, Sir **Mirza Mohammad** (1883–1959), Indian administrator and statesman; born in Bangalore; educated with maharaja of *Mysore; BA, Madras, 1905; joined maharaja's staff; private secretary, 1923; dewan, 1926–41; worked with maharaja in perfect accord for development of state with some state socialism; created pleasure gardens and made state famous for its beauty; represented Mysore at Round Table conferences, 1930–2, and Joint Select Committee meetings; prime minister, Jaipur, 1942–6; Hyderabad, 1946–7; CIE, 1924; knighted, 1930; KCIE, 1936; published *My Public Life* (1954).

ISMAY, Hastings Lionel, Baron Ismay (1887–1965), general; educated at Charterhouse and the Royal Military College, Sandhurst; entered Indian Army, 1905; posted to 21st Prince Albert Victor's Own Cavalry, 1907; seconded to King's African Rifles, 1914; served in Somaliland with Camel Corps, 1919–20; DSO; passed through Staff College, Quetta, 1921; posted to RAF Staff College, Andover, 1924; assistant secretary, Committee of Imperial defence, under Sir Maurice (later, Lord) *Hankey, 1925–30; CB, 1931; military secretary to viceroy, Lord *Willingdon, 1931–3; War Office, 1933–6; deputy secretary, Committee of Imperial Defence, 1936–8; succeeded Hankey as secretary, 1938; Churchill's essential link with chiefs of staff; major-general, 1939; lieutenant-general, 1942; full general, 1944; CH, 1945; GCB, 1946; baron, 1947; retired from army, 1946; chief of viceroy's staff under Lord *Mountbatten, 1946–8; chairman of council for Festival of Britain, 1948–51; secretary of state for Commonwealth Relations, 1951; first secretary-general of NATO, 1951–7; PC, 1951; KG, 1957; honorary degrees, Belfast, Bristol, and Cambridge; president, National Institute for the Blind, 1952; deputy lieutenant for Gloucestershire, 1950; published *Memoirs* (1960); known to all as 'Pug'.

ISMAY, Joseph Bruce (1862–1937), shipowner; son of T. H. *Ismay, founder of White Star line; educated at Harrow; partner in Ismay, Imrie & Co. (1891), chairman, 1899; chairman (1904–12), International Mercantile Marine Company; directorships included London, Midland & Scottish Railway; inaugurated cadet ship *Mersey*.

ISMAY, Thomas Henry (1837–1899), shipowner; apprenticed to a firm of shipbrokers in Liverpool, and subsequently started business independently; acquired White Star line of Australian clippers, 1867; formed, with William Imrie, Oceanic Steamship Company, 1868; began to run steamers between Liverpool and America, 1871.

ISRAEL, Manasseh Ben (1604–1657). See MANASSEH BEN ISRAEL.

ITE (d. 569), Irish saint; sometimes called Mary of Munster; founded religious house at Cluaincreadhail (Killeedy in present Co. Limerick); visited St *Comgall when dying.

IVE, Paul (*fl.* 1602), writer on fortification; of Corpus Christi College, Cambridge.

IVE, Simon (1600–1662), musician; eighth minor prebendary of St Paul's, 1661; assisted the brothers Lawes in setting *Shirley's Triumph of Peace*, 1634; composed vocal and instrumental works.

IVE (or IVY), William (d. 1486), theologian; fellow and lecturer at Magdalen College, Oxford; headmaster of Winchester, 1444–54; DD; canon and (1470) chancellor of Salisbury; some time master of Whittington's College at St Michael Royal, London; author of theological works.

IVEAGH, countess of (1881–1966), philanthropist. See under GUINNESS, RUPERT EDWARD CECIL LEE.

IVEAGH, earls of. See GUINNESS, EDWARD CECIL, first earl, 1847–1927; GUINNESS, RUPERT EDWARD CECIL LEE, second earl, 1874–1967.

IVELAW-CHAPMAN, Sir **Ronald** (1899–1978), air chief marshal; educated at Cheltenham College; joined Royal Flying Corps and commissioned as pilot, 1917; served in No. 10 Squadron in France; DFC, 1918; permanently commissioned in RAF; posted to No. 60 Squadron in India, 1920; test-pilot at RAF experimental establishment, 1922; with No. 70 Squadron in Iraq; went to India and took part in Kabul evacuation, first major airlift, 1928; AFC, 1930; served on policy and planning staff, Air Ministry, 1941–3; Bomber Command base commander; shot down over France and made prisoner of war, 1944–5; liberated by American forces; air vice-marshal, commanding No. 38 Group, 1945–6; at Air Ministry and Imperial Defence College, 1947–9; C-in-C, Indian Air Force, 1949–52; air officer commanding-in-chief, Home Command, 1952; deputy chief of air staff, 1952; vice-chief of air staff, air chief marshal, 1953–7; trustee of *Observer*; chairman, RAF Escaping Society; co-author with Anne Baker of *Wings over Kabul* (1976); CBE, 1943; CB, 1949; KBE, 1951; KCB, 1953; GCB, 1957.

IVERS, Mary Ann (1788–1849). See ORGER, MARY ANN.

IVES, Edward (d. 1786), naval surgeon and traveller; served on flagship of Vice-Admiral Charles *Watson, 1753–7, and travelled home overland from India; published description of the campaign of 1755–7, and his own travels (1773).

IVES, Jeremiah (*fl.* 1653–1674), General Baptist; ministered in Old Jewry; imprisoned, 1661; defended adult baptism, and published controversial tracts against Quakers and Sabbatarians.

IVES, John (1751–1776), Suffolk herald extraordinary, 1774; FSA, 1771; FRS, 1772; published *Select Papers chiefly relating to English Antiquities* (1773–5).

IVIE, Edward (1678–1745), author of *Epicteti Enchiridion* in Latin verse (1715, reprinted by Simpson); of Westminster and Christ Church, Oxford; MA, 1702; vicar of Floore, 1717–45.

IVIMEY, Joseph (1773–1834), author of history of English Baptists, 1811–30; pastor of Particular Baptist church, Eagle Street, Holborn, London, from 1805; first secretary of Baptist Missionary Society for Ireland; opposed Catholic emancipation; published miscellaneous works.

IVO OF GRANTMESNIL (*fl.* 1101), crusader; son of *Hugh of Grantmesnil.

IVOR HAEL (or the Generous) (d. 1361), patron of *David ab Gwilym and other Welsh bards; lord of Maesaleg, Y Wenallt, and Gwernycleppa, Monmouthshire.

IVORY, Saint (d. 500?). See IBHAR or IBERIUS.

IVORY, Sir **James** (1765–1842), mathematician; of St Andrews and Edinburgh universities; professor of mathematics at Royal Military College, Marlow, 1805–19; FRS, 1815; Copley medallist, 1814; received the Royal Medal, 1826 (for paper on refractions), and 1839 ('Theory of Astronomical Refractions'); enounced the 'Ivory Theorem', 1809; knighted, 1831; received civil list pension.

IVORY, James, Lord Ivory (1792–1866), Scottish judge; nephew of Sir James *Ivory; admitted advocate, 1816; advocate-depute, 1830; sheriff of Caithness, 1832, of Buteshire, 1833; solicitor-general for Scotland, 1839; lord of session, 1840; lord of justiciary, 1849–66.

IVORY, Thomas (1709–1779), architect; designed buildings at Norwich, including (1757) the theatre.

IVORY, Thomas (d. 1786), master of architectural drawing at Royal Dublin Society's schools, 1759–86; designed Blue Coat Hospital, Dublin.

IWAN-MÜLLER, Ernest Bruce (1853–1910), journalist; BA, New College, Oxford (first class in Lit. Hum.), 1876; editor of the Tory *Manchester Courier*, 1884–93; assistant editor of *Pall Mall Gazette*, 1893–6; leader-writer for *Daily Tele-*

graph, 1896–1910; visited South Africa during Boer War, Ireland (1907), and Paris (1908); well versed in foreign politics; published *Lord Milner in South Africa* (1902) and *Ireland To-day and To-morrow* (1907).

IZACKE, Richard (1624?–1698), antiquary; of Exeter College, Oxford; barrister, Inner Temple, 1650; chamberlain (1653) and town clerk of Exeter (*c*.1682); wrote on antiquities of Exeter, 1677.

J

JACK, Alexander (1805–1857), brigadier; educated at King's College, Aberdeen; with 30th Bengal Native Infantry at Aliwal, 1846; brigadier of the force sent against Kangra, 1846; commanded his battalion in second Sikh War; colonel, 1854; brigadier, 1856; treacherously shot at Cawnpore.

JACK, Gilbert (1578?–1628), metaphysical and medical writer; as professor of philosophy at Leiden, 1604–28, first taught metaphysics there; MD, Leiden, 1611; published physical, metaphysical, and medical *Institutiones*.

JACK, Thomas (d. 1598), master of Glasgow Grammar School, quaestor of the university (1577), and thrice member of general assembly; published dictionary of classical names in Latin verse (1592).

JACK, William (1795–1822), botanist and Bengal army surgeon; MA, Aberdeen, 1811; his contributions to *Malayan Miscellanies* reprinted by Sir W. J. *Hooker; genus *Jackia* named after him.

JACKMAN, Isaac (*fl.* 1795), joint editor of *Morning Post*, 1786–95; author of farces and comic operas.

JACKS, Lawrence Pearsall (1860–1955), Unitarian divine; educated at University School, Nottingham, and Manchester New College, London; MA, 1886; Hibbert scholar, Harvard, 1886; Unitarian minister, Renshaw Street Chapel, Liverpool, 1888; Church of the Messiah, Birmingham, 1894–1903; first editor, *Hibbert Journal*, 1902–47; lecturer in philosophy, Manchester College, Oxford, 1903; principal, 1915–31; publications include *The Education of the Whole Man* (1931); honorary degrees from several universities.

JACKS, William (1841–1907), iron-master and author; started ironworks at Glasgow, 1880; Liberal MP for Leith Burghs, 1885–6, for Stirling, 1892–5; wrote lives of Bismarck (1899) and James *Watt (1901); hon. LL D, Glasgow, 1899; bequeathed £20,000 to Glasgow University for chair of modern languages.

JACKSON, Abraham (1589–1646?), divine and author; BA, Exeter College, Oxford, 1611; MA, Christ Church, Oxford, 1616; prebendary of Peterborough, 1640.

JACKSON, Arthur (1593?–1666), ejected divine; of Trinity College, Cambridge; rector of St Michael's, Wood Street, London, and afterwards of St Faith's under St Paul's, London; fined and imprisoned for refusing to give evidence against Christopher *Love, 1651; Presbyterian commissioner at Savoy Conference, 1661; ejected, 1662; published exegetical works.

JACKSON, Arthur Herbert (1852–1881), composer; professor of harmony and composition at Royal Academy of Music, 1878–81; published orchestral works and vocal and piano pieces.

JACKSON, Sir Barry Vincent (1879–1961), theatre director; son of George Jackson, a wealthy provision merchant who founded the Maypole Dairies; while a boy, developed love for the theatre; founded the amateur theatrical Pilgrim Players with friends, including John *Drinkwater, 1907; the Players developed into the Birmingham Repertory Theatre, 1913; among productions were *The Immortal Hour* (1921), *Back to Methuselah*, and *Cymbeline* (1923); moved to London and presented *The Farmer's Wife* (1924) and *Hamlet* in modern dress (1925); knighted, 1925; planned Malvern summer festival, 1929; worked for three seasons at the Shakespeare Memorial Theatre, 1946–8; concentrated on Birmingham Repertory Theatre, 1948–61; wrote, translated, and adapted plays; hon. MA and D.Litt., Birmingham; LL D, St Andrews; D.Litt., Manchester; director, Royal Opera House, 1949–55.

JACKSON, Basil (1795–1889), lieutenant-colonel; lieutenant, 1813; at St Helena, 1815–21; captain, 1825; assistant-professor of fortification at East India Company's College, Addiscombe, 1835, and of military surveying, 1836–57; lieutenant-colonel, 1846; published work on military surveying.

JACKSON, Brian Anthony (1932–1983), educational reformer, writer, and teacher; educated at Huddersfield College (scholar) and St Catharine's College, Cambridge (exhibitioner); first class, English, 1955; teacher in primary school and supervisor of Cambridge undergraduates; published *Education and the Working Class* (with Dennis Marsden, 1962); on staff of Institute of Community Studies, Bethnal Green;

visiting fellow, department of applied economics, Cambridge, 1962–5; director, Advisory Centre for Education (1962–74) and the National Extension College; started the National Research and Development Trust, 1976; other publications include *Streaming: an Education System in Miniature* (1964), *Working Class Community* (1968), *Child Minder* (with Sonia Jackson, 1979), and *Fatherhood* (1984).

JACKSON, Catherine Hannah Charlotte, Lady (d. 1891), authoress; daughter of Thomas Elliott of Wakefield; became second wife, 1856, of Sir George *Jackson (1785–1861), whose diaries and letters she edited; published works relating to French society.

JACKSON, Charles (1809–1882), antiquary; treasurer of Doncaster from 1838; published *Doncaster Charities* (1881); edited for Surtees Society *Yorkshire Diaries and Autobiographies of 17th and 18th Centuries* (1877).

JACKSON, Cyril (1746–1819), dean of Christ Church, Oxford; educated at Westminster under *Markham; student of Christ Church, Oxford, 1764; canon, 1779; MA, 1771; DD, 1781; subpreceptor to elder sons of George III, 1771–6; preacher at Lincoln's Inn, 1779–83; as dean of Christ Church (1783–1809) had large share in 'Public Examination Statute'; declined offer of several bishoprics; helped to bring about retirement of *Addington from premiership, 1804; his bust by Chantrey in Oxford Cathedral.

JACKSON, Sir Cyril (1863–1924), educationist; BA, New College, Oxford; inspectorgeneral of schools and permanent head of education department, Western Australia, 1896–1903; chief inspector, Board of Education, 1903–6; served on numerous commissions and committees on unemployment, boy labour, etc.; member of London County Council, Limehouse division, 1907–13; chairman of Council, 1915; KBE, 1917.

JACKSON, Derek Ainslie (1906–1982), physicist; educated at Rugby and Trinity College, Cambridge; scholar; first class, natural sciences tripos, part i, 1926; carried out spectroscopic work at Clarendon Laboratory, Oxford; D.Sc., Oxford, 1935; lecturer in spectroscopy, 1934–47; professor, 1947; during 1939–45 war served in RAFVR and worked on interference with German night defences; DFC, 1941; AFC, 1944; OBE, 1945; USA Legion of Merit and chevalier of Legion of Honour; FRS, 1947; worked on spectroscopic work in France from 1952; steeplechase rider who rode twice in Grand National; part-owner of *News of the World*.

JACKSON, Francis James (1770–1814), diplomat; son of Thomas *Jackson (1745–1797);

secretary of legation at Berlin and Madrid, 1789–97; ambassador at Constantinople, 1796; plenipotentiary to France, 1801, Prussia, 1802–6, Washington, 1809–11; envoy to Denmark, 1807.

JACKSON, Sir (Francis) Stanley (1870–1947), cricketer and administrator; son of first Baron *Allerton; educated at Harrow and Trinity College, Cambridge; captain of cricket, 1892–3; played for Yorkshire and England; captained England in test matches against Australia, 1905; raised and commanded 2nd/7th West Yorkshire Regiment, 1914–17; Conservative MP, Howdenshire division, 1915–27; parliamentary and financial secretary, War Office, 1922–3; chairman, Conservative party organization, 1923–7; governor of Bengal, 1927–32; PC, 1926; GCIE, 1927; GCSI, 1932.

JACKSON, Frederick George (1860–1938), explorer, soldier, and big-game hunter; organized Jackson–Harmsworth polar expedition surveying Franz Josef Land, 1894–7; served with distinction in South African and 1914–18 wars; travelled through tropical Africa in search of sport, 1925–6; served on international commission of inquiry into slavery in Liberia (report, 1930).

JACKSON, Sir Frederick John (1860–1929), explorer, naturalist, and administrator; joined service of Imperial British East Africa Company, 1888; first-class administrative assistant, Uganda, 1894; vice-consul, 1895; deputy commissioner, 1896; helped to quell mutiny of Sudanese troops employed in Uganda, 1897; deputy commissioner, East Africa Protectorate, under Sir C. N. E. *Eliot, 1902; lieutenant-governor of Protectorate, 1907; governor of Uganda, 1911–17; formed collection of over 12,000 specimens of birds; CMG, 1902; KCMG, 1913.

JACKSON, Frederick John Foakes (1855–1941), divine; educated at Eton and Trinity College, Cambridge; first class, theology, and deacon, 1879; priest, 1880; chaplain and lecturer in divinity and Hebrew, Jesus College, 1882; fellow, 1886–1941; dean, 1895–1916; Briggs professor of Christian institutions, Union Theological Seminary, New York, 1916–34; honorary canon of Peterborough, 1901–26; publications include *History of the Christian Church* (1891), *A History of Church History* (1939), and first 3 vols. (with Kirsopp *Lake) of *The Beginnings of Christianity* (5 vols., 1920–33).

JACKSON (afterwards DUCKETT), Sir George, first baronet (1725–1822), secretary to Navy Board, 1758; second secretary to Admiralty, 1766–82; judge-advocate of the fleet, 1766; present at court martial (1779) on *Keppel and

*Palliser; MP, Weymouth and Melcombe, 1762–8, Colchester, 1790–6; created baronet, 1791; assumed name of Duckett, 1797; Port Jackson, New South Wales, and Point Jackson, New Zealand, named after him by Captain *Cook.

JACKSON, Sir George (1785–1861), diplomat; brother of Francis James *Jackson; chargé d'affaires in Prussia, 1805–6; secretary of legation to John Hookham *Frere in Spain, 1808–9; accompanied Sir Charles *Stewart to Germany, 1813; minister at Berlin, 1814–15; secretary of embassy at St Petersburg, 1816; special envoy to Madrid, 1822; commissioner at Washington, 1822–7; KCH, 1832; chief commissioner for abolition of slave trade at Rio de Janeiro, 1832–41, Surinam, 1841–5, St Paul de Loando, 1845–59; his *Diaries and Letters* issued (1872–3).

JACKSON, Henry (1586–1662), editor of *Hooker's *Opuscula*; friend and kinsman of Anthony à *Wood; MA, Corpus Christi College, Oxford, 1608; BD, 1617; rector of Meysey Hampton, Gloucestershire, 1630–62; edited Hooker's minor works, 1612–13; supervised Stansby's reprints of Hooker (1618 and 1622); his own recension of the unpublished eighth book of the *Ecclesiastical Polity* utilized by *Keble; published also editions of *Wickliffes Wicket* (1612) and other works.

JACKSON, Henry (1831–1879), author of *Argus Fairbairn* (1874) and other novels.

JACKSON, Henry (1839–1921), regius professor of Greek at Cambridge; BA, Trinity College, Cambridge; fellow, 1864; praelector in ancient philosophy, 1875; vice-master, 1914; regius professor of Greek, 1906; OM, 1908; principal contribution to learning, his doctrine of Plato's 'later theory of Ideas'.

JACKSON, Sir Henry Bradwardine (1855–1929), admiral of the fleet and pioneer of wireless telegraphy; entered navy, 1868; qualified as torpedo lieutenant; conceived idea of employing wireless waves to announce to capital ships approach of friendly torpedo boat, 1890; as commander of *Defiance* successfully experimented with coherers, 1895–6; met Guglielmo Marconi, 1896; contract placed with Marconi Company for supply of wireless installation to many ships of Royal Navy, 1900; communicated important paper on transmission of electric waves to Royal Society, 1902; assistant director of torpedoes, Admiralty, 1902; third sea lord and controller of navy, 1905–8; commanded Third Cruiser Squadron, Mediterranean, 1908; chief of war staff, Admiralty, 1913; first sea lord, 1915; president, Royal Naval College, Greenwich, 1916–19; admiral of the fleet, 1919; chairman, radio research board, Department of Scientific and Industrial Research; FRS, 1901; KCVO, 1906.

JACKSON, Sir Herbert (1863–1936), chemist; successively student, demonstrator, lecturer, professor of organic chemistry (1905), fellow (1907), and Daniell professor of chemistry (1914–18), King's College, London; his 'focustube' (1896) the prototype of later X-ray tubes; determined formulae for many kinds of glass, 1914–15; KBE and FRS, 1917; first director of research, British Scientific Instrument Research Association, 1918–33.

JACKSON, John (d. 1689?), organist of Wells Cathedral from 1676; composed anthems and chants.

JACKSON, John (1686–1763), theological writer; BA, Jesus College, Cambridge, 1707; denied MA degree, 1718, on account of his writings on the Trinity; rector of Rossington, Yorkshire, 1710; expressed Samuel *Clarke's views on the Trinity after 1714; advocated *Hoadly's position on church government; defended infant baptism; succeeded Clarke as master of Wigston's Hospital, Leicester, 1729; wrote treatises against the deists, and compiled *Chronological Antiquities* (1752).

JACKSON, John (*fl.* 1761–1792), actor, manager, and dramatist; played leading parts at Edinburgh, 1761; under *Garrick at Drury Lane, 1762–4, Dublin, 1765; appeared with his wife at the Haymarket, 1775, in his own *Eldred* (1782), also at Covent Garden, 1776; managed theatres in Edinburgh, Glasgow, Dundee, and Aberdeen, 1782–90; again a manager, 1801–9; wrote *History of the Scottish Stage* (published 1793); none of his plays except *Eldred* printed.

JACKSON, John (d. 1807), traveller; FSA, 1787; published account of a journey from India overland (1799); made excavations on site of Carthage and at Udena.

JACKSON, John (1769–1845), pugilist ('Gentleman Jackson'); champion of England, 1795–1803; afterwards kept a boxing-school in Bond Street, London, at which *Byron was a pupil; referred to by Byron and Moore as a popular character.

JACKSON, John (1778–1831), portrait painter; of humble origin; freed from apprenticeship by Lord *Mulgrave and Sir George *Beaumont; studied at Royal Academy with *Haydon and *Wilkie, and introduced them to his patrons; first exhibited, 1804; RA, 1817; made sketching tour in Netherlands with General Phipps, 1816; travelled with *Chantrey in Italy, 1819–20, painting a portrait of Canova and being elected to Academy of St Luke; liberal to his Wesleyan co-religionists. Of his portraits those of Lady Dover and Flaxman are considered the best. He was also a skilful copyist.

JACKSON, John (1801–1848), wood-engraver; apprenticed to Bewick; engraved Northcote's *Fables* and illustrations for the *Penny Magazine*; with William Andrew *Chatto brought out an illustrated history of wood-engraving (1839).

JACKSON, John (1811–1885), bishop successively of Lincoln and London; scholar of Pembroke College, Oxford, 1829; BA, 1833; Ellerton prizeman, 1834; headmaster of Islington Proprietary School, 1836; Boyle lecturer, and vicar of St James's, Piccadilly, London, 1846–53; FRS, 1845; DD, Oxford, 1853; bishop of Lincoln, 1853–68, of London, 1868–85; created diocese of St Albans and suffragan bishopric of East London; contributed section on the pastoral epistles in the *Speaker's Commentary*, and published religious works.

JACKSON, John (1833–1901), professional cricketer; member of Nottinghamshire cricket eleven; leading bowler in England, 1857; played for Players v. Gentlemen, 1859–64; visited America, 1859, and Australia, 1863; often caricatured by John *Leech in *Punch* as 'demon bowler'.

JACKSON, John Baptist (1701–1780?), wood-engraver; worked under Papillon at Paris; during residence in Venice revived colour-engraving, publishing (1745) seventeen engravings of Venetian pictures; established manufactory of chiaroscuro paper-hangings at Battersea; published *Essay on the Invention of Engraving and Printing in Chiaroscuro* and its application to paper-hanging (1754).

JACKSON, John Edward (1805–1891), antiquary; brother of Charles *Jackson; MA, Brasenose College, Oxford, 1830; vicar of Norton Coleparle, Wiltshire, 1846; librarian to marquis of Bath; hon. canon of Bristol, 1855; published topographical monographs; edited *Aubrey's Wiltshire collections (1862).

JACKSON, John Hughlings (1835–1911), physician; studied medicine at York and St Bartholomew's Hospital; MRCS, 1856; MD, St Andrews, 1860; physician at London Hospital (1863–94) and at National Hospital for Epileptics, Queen Square (1862–1906); FRCP, 1868; Gulstonian lecturer, 1869; Croonian lecturer, 1884; Lumleian lecturer, 1890; FRS, 1878; studied speech defect in brain disease, the occurrence of local epileptic discharges (known as Jacksonian epilepsy), and showed that certain regions of the brain were definitely related to certain limb movements; formulated theory of levels in the nervous system, showing that the highest

and most recently developed functions go first in process of disease; also investigated 'uncinate' epilepsy; one of the first to use ophthalmoscope in England in diagnosing eye diseases; published many scientific papers.

JACKSON, John Richardson (1819–1877), engraver in mezzotint of portraits.

JACKSON, Joseph (1733–1792), letter-founder; while apprentice to the elder William *Caslon clandestinely discovered the art of cutting the punches; some years in the navy; in Dorset Street, Salisbury Square, cut Hebrew, Persian, and Bengali letters, 1773; cut fount for Macklin's Bible (1800), and another for Hume's *History* (1806).

JACKSON, Julian (wrongly called **John Richard**) (1790–1853), colonel on the Imperial Russian Staff, and geographer; served in Bengal Artillery, 1808–13; in Russian service with army of occupation in France; colonel on Russian staff, 1829; retired, 1830; secretary of Royal Geographical Society, 1841–7; FRS, 1845; published *Guide du Voyageur* (1822, reproduced as *What to Observe*, 1841), and an edition (with translation) of La Vallée's *Military Geography*, and other works.

JACKSON, Laurence (1691–1772), divine; fellow of Sidney Sussex College, Cambridge; MA, 1716; BD, 1723; prebendary of Lincoln, 1747; published religious works.

JACKSON, Mason (1819–1903), wood-engraver; pupil of brother, John *Jackson (1801–48); art editor to *Illustrated London News*, 1860; published *The Pictorial Press: its Origin and Progress* (1885).

JACKSON, Randle (1757–1837), parliamentary counsel of the East India Company and the corporation of London; MA, Exeter College, Oxford, 1793; barrister, Middle Temple, 1793; bencher, 1828.

JACKSON, Richard (*fl.* 1570), reputed author of the ballad on Flodden Field (first printed, 1664); BA, Clare Hall, Cambridge, 1570; master of Ingleton School, Yorkshire.

JACKSON (or KUERDEN), Richard (1623–1690?), antiquary; BA, Emmanuel College, Cambridge, 1644–5; MA and vice-principal of St Mary Hall, Oxford, 1646; MD, 1663; friend of *Dugdale; left materials for history of Lancashire.

JACKSON, Richard (1700–1782?), founder of Jacksonian professorship at Cambridge; MA, Trinity College, Cambridge, 1731 (incorporated at Oxford, 1739); fellow.

JACKSON, Richard (d. 1787), politician ('Omniscient Jackson'); barrister, Lincoln's Inn, 1744, bencher, 1770, reader, 1779, treasurer, 1780; counsel to South Sea Company and Cambridge University; law officer to Board of Trade; MP, Weymouth, 1762–8, New Romney, 1768–84; secretary to George Grenville, 1765; FSA, 1781; a lord of the Admiralty, 1782–3.

JACKSON, Robert (1750–1827), inspector-general of army hospitals; assistant-surgeon in Jamaica, 1774–80; afterwards served in 71st Regiment; studied at Paris; MD, Leiden, 1786; surgeon to the buffs in Holland and West Indies, 1793–8; overthrew monopoly of College of Physicians in army medical appointments, 1803–9; medical director in West Indies, 1811–15; published *Systematic View of the Formation, Discipline, and Economy of Armies* (1804) and treatises on febrile diseases.

JACKSON (afterwards **SCORESBY-JACKSON**), **Robert Edmund** (1835–1867), nephew and biographer of William *Scoresby (1789–1857); MD, Edinburgh, 1857; FRCS, 1861; FRCP and FRSE, 1862; physician to Edinburgh Royal Infirmary and lecturer in Surgeons' Hall; published *Medical Climatology* (1862), and *Notebook on Materia Medica, etc.* (1866).

JACKSON, Samuel (1786–1861), president of Wesleyan Conference, 1847; brother of Thomas *Jackson (1783–1873).

JACKSON, Samuel (1794–1869), landscape painter; Associate of the Society of Painters in Water-Colours, 1823; founded Bristol Sketching Society, 1833.

JACKSON, Samuel Phillips (1830–1904), water-colour artist; born at Bristol; son of Samuel *Jackson; painted land- and seascapes; exhibited mainly at Royal Water Colour Society; member, 1876; work praised by John *Ruskin; showed preference for Devon and Cornish coast scenes and Thames views; skilful interpreter of west-country atmosphere; an efficient photographer.

JACKSON, Thomas (1579–1640), president of Corpus Christi College, Oxford, and dean of Peterborough; fellow of Corpus Christi College, Oxford, 1606; MA, 1603; DD, 1622; incumbent of St Nicholas, Newcastle upon Tyne, 1623, and Winston, Durham, 1625; president of Corpus Christi College, Oxford, 1630–40; attacked by *Prynne; dean of Peterborough, 1639–40; highly praised by *Pusey; author of *Commentaries on the Apostles' Creed* (twelve books, three posthumous); collective works issued (1672–3 and 1844).

JACKSON, Thomas (d. 1646), prebendary of Canterbury, 1614–33; MA, 1600, and BD, 1608, DD, Emmanuel College, Cambridge, 1615; published sermons.

JACKSON, Thomas (1745–1797), prebendary of Westminster, 1782–92, and canon of St Paul's, 1792; MA, Christ Church, Oxford, 1770; DD, 1783.

JACKSON, Thomas (1783–1873), Wesleyan minister; itinerant preacher; editor of the connectional magazine, 1824–42; president of Conference, 1838–9 and 1849; divinity professor at Richmond College, 1842–61; published life of Charles *Wesley (1841) and other religious biographies, and *The Centenary of Wesleyan Methodism* (1839); edited John *Wesley's *Works* (1829–31) and *Journals* (1864); *Journals, etc.* of Charles Wesley (1849); his *Collection of Christian Biography* published (1837–40); his *Recollections* edited by Revd Benjamin Frankland (1873).

JACKSON, Thomas (1812–1886), divine and author; son of Thomas *Jackson (1783–1873); of St Mary Hall, Oxford, where he wrote *Uniomachia*; MA, 1837; principal of Battersea Training College, 1844; prebendary of St Paul's, London, 1850; nominated to see of Lyttelton, New Zealand, 1850, but not consecrated; rector of Stoke Newington, 1852–86; published miscellaneous works.

JACKSON, Sir Thomas Graham, first baronet (1835–1924), architect; BA, Wadham College; entered office of Sir G. G. *Scott, 1858; contributed greatly towards changing appearance of Oxford; his Oxford buildings include: Examination Schools (foundations laid 1876); new buildings at Brasenose College (1886–9, 1907–11); chapel of Hertford College (finished 1908); his outstanding achievement in buildings connected with schools, such as Giggleswick School Chapel; his buildings especially notable for their ornament; RA, 1896; baronet, 1913.

JACKSON, William (1730–1803), musical composer ('Jackson of Exeter'); organist and lay vicar of Exeter Cathedral, 1777–1803; friend of the Sheridans, Samuel *Rogers, *Wolcot, and *Gainsborough; composed *The Lord of the Manor* (Drury Lane, 1780) and the *Metamorphosis*, 1783 (two operas); set *Lycidas* (1767), *Warton's *Ode to Fancy*, and *Pope's *Dying Christian to his Soul*; composed madrigals, songs, services, and other musical works; published miscellaneous works; posthumous compositions issued (1819).

JACKSON, William (1737?–1795), Irish revolutionist; preacher at Tavistock Chapel, Drury Lane, London; when secretary to the duchess of *Kingston satirized by *Foote as Dr Viper; induced Foote's ex-coachman to make an infamous charge against him; Whig editor of the *Public Ledger* and *Morning Post*; while in France commissioned to ascertain probable success of a French invasion of England and Ireland; betrayed by duchess of Kingston's attorney, and charged with treason in Dublin, 1794; defended by *Curran and *Ponsonby; died in the dock, probably from poison supplied by his wife.

JACKSON, William (1751–1815), bishop of Oxford; brother of Cyril *Jackson; of Westminster and Christ Church, Oxford; MA, 1775; DD, 1799; chancellor's medallist, 1770; regius professor of Greek at Oxford, 1783; preacher at Lincoln's Inn, 1783; dean of Wells, 1799; canon of Christ Church, 1799; bishop of Oxford, 1812–15.

JACKSON, William (1815–1866), musical composer; of Masham, Yorkshire; when a boy worked as a miller; music-seller in Bradford, 1852; organist to St John's Church, Bradford, conducted the Church Union and the Festival Choral Society from 1856; composed oratorios, *Deliverance of Israel from Babylon* (1844–5) and *Isaiah* (1851); *The Year* (cantata, 1859); with glees and other works.

JACKSON, William Lawies, first Baron Allerton (1840–1917), politician; made father's almost bankrupt tanning business one of the largest in England; Conservative MP, North Leeds, 1880; financial secretary to Treasury, 1885–91; PC, 1890; FRS, 1891; chairman of Jameson raid inquiry, 1896–7; baron, 1902; rendered great financial services to Leeds.

JACKSON, Willis, Baron Jackson of Burnley (1904–1970), electrical engineer and educationist; educated at Burnley Grammar School and Manchester University; first class, B.Sc., 1925; M.Sc., 1926; lecturer in electrical engineering, Bradford Technical College, 1926–9; joined Metropolitan-Vickers Company, 1929; further experience at Manchester College of Technology, 1930–3; research at Oxford, 1933–6; D.Phil. (Oxford), D.Sc. (Manchester), 1936; returned to Metropolitan-Vickers; appointed professor, Electrotechnics Department, Manchester University, 1939; professor, electrical engineering, Imperial College of Science and Technology, London, 1946–53; FRS, 1953; director, research and education, Metropolitan-Vickers, 1954; returned to Imperial College, 1961; pro-rector, 1967; member of number of commissions and committees on education and research, including the University Grants Committee; chairman, Industrial Research Committee of FBI (1958–60); published many books, articles, and reports; chairman, Scientific Manpower Committee (1963–4); knighted, 1958; life

baron, 1967; honorary degrees from many universities; president, Institution of Electrical Engineers (1959–60) and the British Association for the Advancement of Science (1967).

JACKSON-COLE, Cecil (1901–1979), business man and charity organizer; born Albert Cecil Cole, changed name by deed poll, 1927; attended council schools; left at 13 to become an office boy, 1914–19; became owner and manager of furnishing business, 1919; studied economics at Balliol College, Oxford, 1928; bedridden with kidney disease, 1930–3; became involved in charitable work through Soldiers and Sailors Home, Watford; concerned with foundation of Oxfam, 1942; first hon. secretary; responsible for growth and expansion of Oxfam, with which he worked until 1979; responsible for setting up autonomous Oxfams in Canada, USA, and Belgium; created a business, Andrews and Partners, 1945, and set up charitable trusts and charities, including Help the Aged, the Anchor Housing Association, and Action Aid; refused national and civil honours.

JACKSON OF LODSWORTH, Baroness (1914–1981), journalist and broadcaster. See WARD, BARBARA MARY.

JACOB, Arthur (1790–1874), oculist; MD, Edinburgh, 1814; while demonstrator of anatomy at Trinity College, Dublin, discovered (1816, announced, 1819) a membrane of the eye; Dublin professor of anatomy, 1826–69; thrice president of Irish College of Surgeons; edited *Dublin Medical Press*, 1839–59; published treatises on inflammation of the eyeball (1849) and on removal of cataract by absorption.

JACOB, Benjamin (1778–1829), organist; organist at Salem Chapel, Soho, at age of 10; chorister at Handel commemoration, 1791; organist at Surrey Chapel, 1794–1825; gave public recitals with the elder Wesley, Crotch, and Salomon the violinist; published settings of Dr *Watts's *Divine and Moral Songs* (c.1800).

JACOB, Sir Claud William (1863–1948), field marshal; educated at Sherborne and Sandhurst; commissioned in Worcestershire Regiment, 1882; transferred to Indian Army, 1884; served mainly on frontier; accompanied Meerut division to France, 1914; commanded Dehra Dun brigade, 1915; Meerut division, 1915; 21st division, 1915–16; II Corps, 1916–19; KCB and lieutenant-general, 1917; chief of General Staff, India, 1920–4; general, 1920; held Northern Command, India, 1924–5; commander-in-chief, 1925; secretary, military department, India Office, 1926–30; field marshal and GCB, 1926; GCSI, 1930.

JACOB, Edgar (1844–1920), bishop of Newcastle and of St Albans; grandson of John *Jacob, Guernsey topographer; educated at Winchester and New College, Oxford; domestic chaplain to Robert *Milman, bishop of Calcutta, 1872–6; vicar of Portsea, 1878–95; bishop of Newcastle, 1896–1903, of St Albans, 1903–19; successfully worked for division of latter see.

JACOB, Edward (1710?–1788), antiquary and naturalist.

JACOB, Edward (d. 1841), editor (1821–3 and 1828) of Chancery reports; son of William *Jacob; fellow of Caius College, Cambridge; senior wrangler and first Smith's prizeman, 1816; MA, 1819; barrister, Lincoln's Inn, 1819; KC, 1834.

JACOB, Sir George le Grand (1805–1881), major-general in the Indian Army; son of John *Jacob (1765–1840); entered 2nd Bombay Native Infantry, 1820; political agent in Kattywar, 1839–43, Sawunt Warree, 1845–51, Kutch, 1851–9; lieutenant-colonel, 31st Bombay Native Infantry, 1853; commanded Native Light Battalion in Persia, 1857; put down the mutiny at Kolapore, 1857; special commissioner of South Mahratta country, 1857–9; retired as major-general, 1861; CB, 1859; KCSI, 1869; early transcriber of Asoka inscriptions; published *Western India before and during the Mutiny* (1871).

JACOB, Giles (1686–1744), compiler of the *Poetical Register* (1719–20) and *New Law Dictionary* (1729); introduced in the *Dunciad*.

JACOB, Gordon Percival Septimus (1895–1984), composer; educated at Dulwich College; served in army and taken prisoner during 1914–18 war; attended School of Journalism, 1919; entered Royal College of Music 1920; member of teaching staff; composed Viola Concerto (1925) and Piano Concerto (1927), symphony (1929), and many orchestrations for Sadler's Wells ballet company; arranged popular tunes for ITMA and other radio programmes during 1939–45 war; awarded Collard fellowship, 1943; retired from Royal College of Music, 1966; composed over 200 works including ballets, symphonies, concertos, and choral works; edited Penguin Scores, 1947–57; publications include *Orchestral Technique* (1931), *How to Read a Score* (1944), and *The Composer and his Art* (1955); D.Mus., London; CBE, 1968.

JACOB, Henry (1563–1624), early Congregationalist; MA, St Mary Hall, Oxford, 1586; precentor of Corpus Christi College, Oxford; retired with Brownists to Holland, 1593; again compelled to take refuge in Holland, 1598; collected congregation at Middelburg; afterwards joined John *Robinson (1575–1625); established in Southwark Congregational church, 1616; formed settlement in Virginia, 1622; died in London; published controversial works.

JACOB, Henry (1608–1652), philologist; son of Henry *Jacob (1563–1624); BA and (1629–48) fellow of Merton College, Oxford; authorship of *Dickinson's *Delphi Phoenicizantes* attributed to him by *Wood.

JACOB, Hildebrand (1693–1739), poet; published *The Curious Maid* (1721), *The Fatal Constancy* (tragedy, 1723), and other poems, collected (1735).

JACOB, Sir Hildebrand, fourth baronet (d. 1790), Hebrew scholar; son of Hildebrand *Jacob.

JACOB, John (1765–1840), Guernsey topographer; son of Edward *Jacob (1710?–1788).

JACOB, John (1812–1858), brigadier-general; cousin of Sir George le Grand *Jacob; commanded artillery in Billamore's Kutchee expedition, 1834–40; published memoir of the campaign (1852); given command of Sind Irregular Horse and political charge of Eastern Kutchee by *Outram, 1841; led his regiment with great distinction at Meanee, 1843, Shah-dad-poor, and other battles; political superintendent of Upper Sind, 1847; CB, 1850; Jacobabad named after him by Dalhousie to commemorate his pacification of the country, 1851; negotiated treaty with khan of Khelat, 1854; acting commissioner in Sind, 1856; commanded cavalry under Outram in Persia, 1857; raised 'Jacob's Rifles' (infantry), 1858, armed with rifle and bullet of his own invention; died suddenly at Jacobabad. He published a reply to *Napier's attack in his *Conquest of Sind* on Outram, *Rifle Practice with Plates* (1855), and several works on the reorganization of the Indian Army.

JACOB, Joseph (1667?–1722), Congregational divine; preacher at Parish Street, Southwark (1698–1702), Turners' Hall, Philpot Lane, and Curriers' Hall, London Wall, London.

JACOB, Joshua (1805?–1877), sectary; disowned by Society of Friends, 1838; founded the 'White Quakers' at Dublin, 1843; imprisoned for contempt of court in connection with Chancery suit; established community at Newlands, Clondalkin, 1849.

JACOB, Robert (d. 1588), physician to Queen Elizabeth; fellow of Trinity College, Cambridge; MA, 1573; MD, Basle (incorporated at Cambridge, 1579); attended the tsarina, 1581; FRCP, 1586; died abroad.

JACOB, William (1762?–1851), statistical writer; FRS, 1807; MP, Rye, 1808–12; comptroller of corn returns, 1822–42; wrote on the corn trade, corn laws, and precious metals, and published *Travels in Spain* (1811).

JACOB, William Stephen (1813–1862), astronomer; brother of John *Jacob (1812–1858); some years in Bombay Engineers; director of Madras Observatory, 1848–59; discovered triplicity of ν Scorpii, 1847; catalogued 244 double stars observed at Poona; re-observed and corrected 317 stars from 'British Association Catalogue'; FRAS, 1849; noticed transparency of Saturn's dusky ring, 1852; died at Poona.

JACOBS, William Wymark (1863–1943), writer; grew up in Wapping; educated at Birkbeck College; Civil Service clerk, 1879–99; wrote short stories relating misadventures of sailormen ashore, ingenuities of artful dodger in country village, and tales of macabre; publications include *Many Cargoes* (1896), *The Skipper's Wooing* (1897), *Light Freights* (1901), *The Lady of the Barge* (1902, containing 'The Monkey's Paw', dramatized by L. N. *Parker), and *Night Watches* (1914); collaborated with Parker in *Beauty and the Barge* (1904); wrote *At Sunwich Port* (1902) and several other novels.

JACOBSEN, Theodore (d. 1772), architect; designed Foundling Hospital (1742) and the Haslar Hospital, Gosport.

JACOBSON, William (1803–1884), bishop of Chester; educated at Homerton Nonconformist College, Glasgow University, and Lincoln College, Oxford; BA, Oxford, 1827; fellow of Exeter College, Oxford, 1829; MA, 1829; vice-principal of Magdalen Hall, 1830; public orator, 1842; regius professor of divinity, 1848; bishop of Chester, 1865–84; published editions of the *Patres Apostolici* (1838, 1840, 1847, 1863), works of Bishop Robert *Sanderson (1854), and *Nowell's *Catechismus* (1835).

JACOMBE, Samuel (d. 1659), Puritan divine; fellow, Queens' College, Cambridge, 1649–51; BD, 1658; incumbent of St Mary Woolnoth, London, 1655.

JACOMBE, Thomas (1622–1687), Nonconformist divine; brother of Samuel *Jacombe; fellow of Trinity College, Cambridge, 1646; MA, 1647; incumbent of St Martin's, Ludgate Hill, London, 1647–62; a trier, 1659; commissioner for review of the Prayer-Book, 1661; imprisoned for holding conventicles in Silver Street, but protected by countess-dowager of Exeter; published sermons.

JAENBERT (JANBRIHT, JAMBERT, GENGBERHT, LAMBERT, or LANBRIHT) (d. 791), archbishop of Canterbury; abbot of St Augustine's 760; archbishop of Canterbury, 766–91; deprived of much of his jurisdiction after Offa's conquest of Kent, Lichfield being made a metropolitan see.

JAFFRAY, Alexander (1614–1673), director of the chancellary of Scotland; bailie of Aberdeen and its representative in Scottish parliament, 1644–50; commissioner for suppressing Royalist rising, 1644, and for treating with Charles II, 1649–50; wounded and captured at Dunbar, 1650; as provost of Aberdeen negotiated with Monck, 1651; director of chancellary, 1652–60; member of Little Parliament, 1653–4; joined Independents, and, in 1661, the Quakers; his *Diary* printed by John Barclay (1833).

JAFFRAY, Andrew (1650–1726), Quaker minister; son of Alexander *Jaffray.

JAGGER, Charles Sargeant (1885–1934), sculptor; learnt silver-engraving with Mappin & Webb; studied at Sheffield School of Art and Royal College of Art; served in 1914–18 war and awarded MC; works include *Artillery* (Hyde Park Corner), *G.W.R.* (Paddington), British Memorial to Belgium (Brussels) and many other war memorials, and stone groups at Imperial Chemical House, Millbank; ARA, 1926.

JAGO, James (1815–1893), physician; BA, St John's College, Cambridge, 1839; incorporated at Wadham College, Oxford, 1843; MD, Oxford, 1859; practised in Truro; FRS, 1870; published medical works.

JAGO, Richard (1715–1781), poet; friend of *Shenstone and *Somerville; MA, University College, Oxford, 1739; vicar of Snitterfield, 1754–81, and Kimcote, 1771–81; his poems in *Chalmers's, *Anderson's, *Park's, and *Davenport's collections.

JAMES I (1394–1437), king of Scotland; third son of *Robert III; placed under guardianship of Henry *Wardlaw at St Andrews, 1403; captured while on his way to France by an English ship, probably in 1406; detained in England 19 years and well educated, but confined first in the Tower, afterwards at Nottingham and Evesham, and, on accession of Henry V, at Windsor, accompanying that king to France in 1420; released, 1423, on condition of his paying a ransom, withdrawing Scottish troops from France, and marrying an English wife; married *Jane, daughter of the earl of Somerset, 1424; returned to Scotland and was crowned, 1424; 27 acts passed in his first parliament, 1424, by the lords of the articles, including confirmation of the privileges of the church, prohibition of private war, and measures strengthening the royal authority, granting the customs to the king, and appointing officers to administer justice to the Commons (the statute-book dates from this parliament); registration of titles to land, parliamentary attendance of prelates, barons and free-holders, punishment of heretics by the secular arm, regulation of weights and measures, and a central judicial court provided for by parliament of 1425–6. James I had the late regent *Albany and his chief adherents tried and executed for misgovernment, 1425; summoned a parliament at Inverness, reducing the Highlands to order, 1427; concluded marriage treaty with France, 1428; renewed truce with England, 1429; made commercial treaty with Flanders, 1429; put down heresy, but reformed clerical abuses and resisted the demands of popes Martin V and Eugenius IV; defeated the Lord of the Isles, 1429; imported cannon from Flanders, 1430; sent representatives to Council of Basle, 1433; sent the Princess *Margaret to marry the dauphin, 1436; held a parliament at Edinburgh; was murdered at Perth by Sir Robert *Graham and conspirators in his own household; buried in the convent of the Carthusians. In spite of his premature attempt to reform the Scottish constitution on the English model he left the monarchy stronger, and improved Scotland's position in Europe. His poem, The Kingis Quair, composed in England, was discovered and printed by Lord *Woodhouselee (1783); other works have also been attributed to him. He was nominal founder and great benefactor of St Andrews University.

JAMES II (1430–1460), king of Scotland; son of *James I; crowned at Holyrood, 1437; removed by queen mother to Stirling, 1439, but kidnapped and brought back to Edinburgh by Sir William *Crichton; regained liberty with help of William *Douglas, eighth earl of Douglas, and Sir Alexander *Livingstone, 1443; captured Edinburgh Castle, 1445; married *Mary of Gueldres, 1449; had Livingstone and his family tried and executed, 1450; re-enacted in parliament of 1450 statutes of James I; proclaimed a general peace, 1450, and afforded protection to tillers of the soil; stabbed Douglas at Stirling, 1452, and wasted his lands, on discovery of the confederacy of Douglas, Crawford, and Ross; forced James, new earl of *Douglas, to submit, his brothers being defeated at Arkinholm, 1455; attainted the Douglases, 1455; annexed the Douglas, Crawford, and other estates to the crown, 1455; proposed joint action with France against England; ravaged Northumberland, 1456, but concluded a two years' truce with Henry VI, afterwards prolonged, 1457; pacified the Highlands; strengthened the crown by marriages of his sisters with a Gordon and a Douglas, 1458; appointed supreme central court to meet at Edinburgh, Perth, and Aberdeen, and established annual circuits of the justiciary court in his parliament of 1458, the burgh courts also being reformed in the interests of the people, and the coinage re-established; favoured the Lancastrians, and received Queen *Margaret and her son after the Battle of Northampton, 1460; killed by accident while besieging Roxburgh Castle; buried at Holyrood.

JAMES III (1451–1488), king of Scotland; son of *James II; crowned at Kelso, 1460; during his minority Henry VI received, Berwick acquired, and truce with England prolonged; his person seized by Sir Alexander Boyd, 1456; his marriage with *Margaret of Denmark, and the cession of Orkney and Shetland, arranged, 1468–9; threw off the Boyds and assumed power, 1469; reduced the Highlands by submission of Ross, 1475, and procured archiepiscopal pall for Scotland; alienated the nobles by partiality to favourites; attacked by an English army, *Albany, his own brother, being in the English camp, 1482, when his forces mutinied, hanged the favourite, Robert *Cochrane, and imprisoned him in Edinburgh Castle, Berwick being finally retaken by the English, 1482; reconciled with Albany, who, however, continued his intrigues with England till driven abroad after the unsuccessful raid of Lochmaben, where Douglas was captured, 1484; was attacked anew owing to his extravagance and choice of fresh favourites by the lowland nobles, including Angus, Gray, and Hume, who put the king's eldest son at their head; was defeated at Sauchieburn and murdered; buried at Cambuskenneth. His portrait is in the altar-piece at Holyrood.

JAMES IV (1473–1513), king of Scotland; son of *James III; crowned at Scone, 1488; did penance for his father's death, but revoked grants made by him; crushed the rebellion of *Lennox, Lyle, and Forbes, 1489; provided for defence of the east coast against English pirates and fostered the navy; passed acts for musters of the forces in each shire and legal reforms, 1491; visited the Western Isles, 1493–5, and began his pilgrimages to Whithern and St Duthac's; received Perkin *Warbeck and married him to Lady Katherine Gordon, 1495; made border raids in Warbeck's favour, 1496–7, but carried on negotiations with the Spanish and French, who endeavoured to detach him from Warbeck; having made a truce for seven years with England and strengthened his hold over the west, agreed to treaty of marriage with *Margaret, daughter of Henry VII, in 1502; married Margaret, 1503; crushed rising of Donald Dubh in the west; introduced royal law into the isles; instituted a daily council to hear civil cases at Edinburgh, confirmed burgh privileges, secured fixity of tenure by the 'feu' statutes, and revoked acts prejudicial to crown and church, 1504; assisted Denmark against the Swedes and Hanse League, 1507 and 1508; sent

James V

embassy to Venice, 1506; favoured English alliance while Henry VII lived, in spite of the national opposition; was asked to enter the League of Cambrai and consulted as to the marriage of Louis XII of France, 1508; sided with Louis XII against the Holy League, 1511; signed treaty with France, 1512, and sent fleet to help Louis against Henry VIII; invaded Northumberland with a large force; took Norham and smaller castles, but was outgeneralled by *Surrey and defeated and slain at Flodden with the flower of his nation, 1513; left several natural children. He was a wise legislator and a good diplomat. He encouraged education, patronized men of letters, and dabbled in astrology and surgery.

JAMES V (1512–1542), king of Scotland; son of *James IV; taken by his mother to Stirling, but brought to Edinburgh after her surrender to the regent *Albany, 1515; educated by Gavin *Dunbar (d. 1547), John *Bellenden, David *Lindsay, and James *Inglis; carried off to Edinburgh by the queen mother and the English party, 1524, and proclaimed competent to rule, 1524; under control of *Angus, 1525–8; prompted by James *Beaton (d. 1539), escaped from Falkland, caused parliament to forfeit the Douglas estates, captured Tantallon and compelled Angus to fly to England, 1528; pacified Western Isles; aided by clergy and Commons crushed power of nobles; established College of Justice, 1532; carried on border raids till peace of 1534; was offered choice of German and French princesses for his wife; received cap and sword of most favoured son of the church and title of 'defender of the faith' from Paul III, 1537; married Madeleine, daughter of Francis I, in France, 1537; on the death of Madeleine married *Mary of Guise, 1538, having meanwhile executed conspirators of the Angus family; persecuted heretics, but forced some reforms on the church, and inspired *Buchanan's works against the friars; refused to follow English advice to support the Reformation; accompanied the fleet, which extorted submission of Western Isles, 1540; annexed to the crown all the isles, and the lands of the Douglases, Crawfords, and other nobles; refused Henry VIII's demand for a conference, 1541, and, after forbidding the discontented barons to cross the borders, collected a force on the west marches; placed Oliver *Sinclair in command instead of Lord *Maxwell, the warden; on hearing of the rout at Solway Moss, 1542, died at Falkland; buried at Holyrood; was succeeded by *Mary Queen of Scots, his only legitimate daughter. Among his natural children were the regent *Moray and the father of Francis Stewart *Hepburn, fifth earl of Bothwell; their legitimation by the pope precipitated the Reformation.

His popularity with the people earned him the name of 'king of the commons'.

JAMES VI, king of Scotland (afterwards **JAMES I,** king of England) (1566–1625); son of *Mary Queen of Scots, and Henry *Stewart, Lord Darnley; crowned on his mother's abdication, 1567; entrusted to *Mar and afterwards to Sir Alexander Erskine; well educated under George *Buchanan (1506–1582); nominally king on first fall of *Morton, 1578; under influence of Lennox (Esmé *Stuart) sanctioned Morton's execution, 1581; seized by Protestant nobles at the raid of Ruthven, 1582, and compelled to proscribe Lennox and *Arran, to reverse their policy, and to submit to the clergy; escaped from Falkland to St Andrews, and took refuge with *Argyll and *Huntly, 1583; recalled Arran, imprisoned Andrew *Melville, and drove the Protestant lords into England; made overtures to the Guises and the pope, 1584; allowed Arran to procure *Gowrie's execution and obtain control of the government; forced by his concern for Protestantism and return of the banished raiders to conclude Treaty of Berwick (1586) with England, receiving pension from Elizabeth; made formal protests and intercessions for his mother, but was incensed at being disinherited by her in favour of Philip II; quickly reconciled himself to his mother's execution in February 1587; married *Anne of Denmark in Norway, 1589; consented to act annulling jurisdiction of the bishops, 1592; intrigued with Spain and Parma; appointed the Octavians to improve the revenue (1596); provoked clergy by recalling northern earls from exile, 1596; made proclamation for removal of the courts of justice, after tumult in Edinburgh caused by his expulsion of discontented Presbyterians, 1596; at the general assemblies of Perth and Dundee (1597) obtained limitation of clerical interference, but agreed to confer with clerical commissioners on church affairs; his proposals for the appointment of parliamentary representatives rejected by further conferences, three bishops only being appointed to seats (1600); his relations with the clergy again embittered after failure of the *Gowrie conspiracy, 1600; before his accession to the English throne (1603) engaged in further intrigues with Rome and secret correspondence with Robert *Cecil and others; after accession made peace with Spain, 1604, and dismissed and imprisoned *Ralegh; called the Hampton Court Conference for discussion of Puritan objections to the liturgy, 1604; issued proclamation (1604) banishing Romanist priests; after the Gunpowder Plot sanctioned a severe Recusancy Act (1606), but modified it in favour of Romanists who rejected papal power of deposition, 1606; thwarted by parliament in his scheme of a union of Great Britain, but obtained from the judges a decision in favour of the *post-nati*, 1608; made defensive league with Dutch republic, 1608; joined France in negotiating truce between it and Spain, 1609; attempted to secure peace by alliance with Catholic powers, 1609; carried on controversy with Bellarmine on the papal power; ordered cessation of common law 'prohibitions' against ecclesiastical courts, 1609; obtained decision (1606) in favour of the right to levy 'impositions', but agreed to abandon the heaviest of them, 1610; dissolved his first parliament after failure of negotiations concerning the great contract, 1611; treated with Spain and Tuscany for the marriage of his eldest son, but betrothed the Princess *Elizabeth to the leader of the German Protestants, making defensive treaty with the Protestant union, 1611; obtained introduction of episcopacy into Scotland, 1610; favoured plantation of Ulster with English and Scotsmen; instituted order of baronets, 1611; dissolved second parliament almost immediately, 1614, imprisoning four members; obtained a benevolence; consulted the judges separately on *Peacham's case, 1615; had to submit to condemnation of his favourite Somerset (Robert *Carr), 1616; renewed negotiations with Spain, 1617; reduced independence of Scottish clergy by appointment of bishops as 'constant moderators' and raising of stipends conditionally upon their acceptance of Articles of Perth (1618); executed Ralegh to please Spain, 1618; refused to support ambitious schemes of his son-in-law Frederick, the elector palatine, 1619; on advice of *Buckingham agreed to redress grievances complained of in his third parliament, and consented to *Bacon's condemnation (1621), but held his own in case of Edward *Floyd; dissolved parliament and punished leading members, 1622; continued negotiations with Spain, agreeing to relieve the English Catholics, 1623, but on the failure of Charles's and Buckingham's mission to Spain was compelled by them to break off the marriage treaty, allow impeachment of *Middlesex and *Bristol, 1624, and consent to a French marriage, with a provision for religious liberty of the Catholics, 1624; failed in attempts on behalf of the Palatinate; buried in Westminster Abbey. Conciliation was the keynote of James I's policy. His chief works were *Basilikon Doron* (1599), *True Law of Free Monarchies* (1603), and *Apology for the Oath of Allegiance* (1607). Collected works published (1616). Portraits of him are in the National Portrait Gallery.

JAMES II (1633–1701), king of England; third son of Charles I; created duke of York; handed over to parliament after the surrender of Oxford, 1646; escaped to Holland, 1648; went to Paris, 1649; left Paris for Holland, 1650; after Battle of Worcester (1651) entered French service as a volunteer, and distinguished himself under Turenne against the Fronde and its allies, 1652–5; took service with the Spanish in Flanders, 1657; in command of Nieuport at *Cromwell's death, 1658; secretly contracted himself to Anne *Hyde at Breda, 1659; created lord high admiral, 1660; received revenues of the Post Office, 1663; dissuaded disbandment of the troops after *Venner's rising, 1661; as head of the Admiralty reconstituted the board, and issued 'Instructions', 1662, which remained in force till beginning of nineteenth century, and memoirs of naval affairs, 1660–73; governor of the Royal Africa Company, *c*.1664; received patent of New York (New Amsterdam), 1664; commanded fleet in first Dutch War, winning Battle of Solebay, 1665, but failed to complete the victory; defended *Clarendon in House of Lords; estranged from Charles II, but early entered into his French policy; probably became Roman Catholic soon after Treaty of Dover (1670); won victory of Southwold Bay over De Ruyter, 1672; ceased to be high admiral after passing of the Test Act, 1673; his second marriage (1673) with Mary *Beatrice of Modena (a Catholic) censured by House of Commons; became increasingly unpopular after discovery of the correspondence with Père La Chaise; at Charles II's request, withdrew to The Hague, and afterwards to Brussels, 1679, the first Exclusion Bill being introduced in his absence; recalled on the king's illness, and afterwards sent to Scotland as high commissioner, 1679; returned, 1680; again forced to retire after a few months, another Exclusion Bill being subsequently passed by the Commons, 1680, who, in spite of its rejection by the Lords, adhered to the plan, 1681; his religious policy in Scotland at first conciliatory, but afterwards more severe; his return to London effected by influence of the duchess of *Portsmouth, 1682; readmitted to the council; regained his powers at the Admiralty (1684), and witnessed Charles's deathbed conversion; ascended the throne on his brother's death, 6 Feb. 1685; during first year of his reign (1685) openly professed Catholicism; appointed the Anglican *Rochester lord treasurer, and banished duchess of Portsmouth, 1685; levied customs duties on his own authority; lost his pension from Louis XIV by summoning a parliament and maintaining good relations with William of Orange, 1685; refused to pardon *Monmouth after Sedgemoor (July 1685); rewarded *Jeffreys for the Bloody Assize (Aug. 1685) with the chief-justiceship; dismissed *Halifax, Oct. 1685; with the help of

*Sunderland, *Petre, and *Talbot (Tyrconnel) remodelled the army; made changes on the bench to ensure a decision in favour of the dispensing power, 1686; revived the High Commission, 1686; dismissed Rochester and Clarendon, 1687; made Roman Catholics officers and justices of the peace; his first declaration of indulgence (preceded by a similar proclamation in Scotland) issued 4 Apr. 1687; publicly received the papal nuncio, 3 July 1687; dissolved parliament, 4 July 1687; by personal influence forced Catholics on Magdalen College, Oxford, 1688; ordered the second declaration to be read in churches (May 1688), the seven bishops petitioning against it being tried for seditious libel, but acquitted (30 June 1688); ordered recall of the six English regiments in the Dutch service (Jan. 1688); accepted money from Louis XIV for equipment of a fleet, Apr. 1688; declined French ships and offer of a joint declaration of war against Holland, Sept. 1688; brought over soldiers from Ireland, and (Sept. 1688) recalled the parliamentary writs; circulated general pardon on same day as William of Orange's declaration (29 Sept. 1688); restored Bishop *Compton, the Protestant fellows, and the charter of London; made formal declaration as to the genuine birth of his son, Oct. 1688; dismissed Sunderland, 1688; augmented the army and navy; marched to Salisbury, but after desertion of his adherents returned to London, 1688; issued writs for a parliament, 1688; named commissioners to meet William, but after the Hungerford Conference secretly left London (11 Dec.), embarked at Sheerness, was brought back to Faversham, and finally escaped with Berwick to France (22–5 Dec. 1688); established by Louis at St Germains; made unsuccessful appeals for help to various powers; landed in Ireland with French force, 1689; held a parliament in Dublin (May 1689), which passed a Toleration Act, transferred tithes to Roman Catholics, and repealed the Act of Settlement; joined his army and was present at the Boyne, 1690, after which he left Ireland; corresponded with *Marlborough and others from St Germains; witnessed defeat of expedition off Cape La Hogue, 1692, and with Berwick prepared another invasion, 1695; rejected proposal of Louis XIV for succession of his son after death of William III, and after Peace of Ryswick (1697) devoted himself to religious exercises; died at St Germains, having received from Louis a promise to recognize his son's title. His remains were reinterred at St Germains in 1824. The manuscript of his 'Original Memoirs' was destroyed during the French Revolution. By Arabella *Churchill he had four natural children and a daughter by Catharine *Sedley, besides issue by both his wives. His talent for business was spoilt by religious and political bigotry. *Kneller painted his portrait (National Portrait Gallery).

JAMES, duke of Berwick (1670–1734). See FITZJAMES, JAMES.

JAMES, Alexander Wilson (1901–1953), footballer; joined Raith Rovers, 1922, Preston North End, 1925; transferred to Arsenal for £9,000, 1929, then the second-highest sum ever paid; an inside forward, his tactical flair made him the mainspring of Arsenal's success in winning the League four times and the Cup twice during his eight seasons; retired, 1937; received eight Scottish caps.

JAMES, Arthur Lloyd (1884–1943), phonetician; graduated in French, University College, Cardiff, 1905; in medieval and modern languages, Trinity College, Cambridge, 1910; taught at Islington Training College, 1910–14; lecturer in phonetics, University College, London, 1920–7; studied West African languages; head of phonetics department, School of Oriental Studies, 1927–41; reader, 1930; professor, 1933; linguistic adviser to BBC, 1929–41.

JAMES, Bartholomew (1752–1827), rear-admiral; in the *Orpheus* at reduction of New York, 1776; captured by French while cruising on the Jamaica Station, 1778; took part in reduction of Omoa, 1779, and defence of Yorktown, 1781; in command of the *Aurora*'s boats at wreck of *Royal George*, 1782; engaged on transport service in connection with capture of Martinique, 1794; afterwards held naval commands in Mediterranean and off Teneriffe.

JAMES, Charles (d. 1821), major and author; travelled through France during the Revolution, which he defended in *Audi alteram Partem* (1793); major of the corps of artillery drivers, 1806; published poems and military manuals, including *Regimental Companion* (1799).

JAMES, David (1839–1893), actor, whose real name was Belasco; appeared at Royalty, 1863, and subsequently played at many London theatres; joint manager, 1870, of the Vaudeville, where his most successful part was Perkyn Middlewick in *Our Boys*, which was played more than a thousand times, 1875–9.

JAMES, Edward (1807–1867), barrister; MA, Brasenose College, Oxford, 1834; barrister, Lincoln's Inn, 1835; assessor of Liverpool court of passage from 1852; QC, 1853; attorney-general of duchy of Lancaster, 1863; MP, Manchester, 1865–7; died in Paris.

JAMES, Edwin John (1812–1882), barrister; admitted, Inner Temple, 1836; defended Dr Simon Bernard, 1858; engaged in the Palmer (1856) and Anderson (1861) cases; QC, 1853;

recorder of Brighton, 1855–61; MP, Marylebone, 1859–61; visited Garibaldi's camp, 1860; became bankrupt and was disbarred for unprofessional conduct, 1861; practised at New York bar and played on the American stage, 1861–72; published *Political Institutions of America and England* (1872); died in London.

JAMES, Eleanor (*fl.* 1715), printer and political writer; wife of Thomas James, a London printer; committed to Newgate for 'dispersing scandalous and reflective papers', 1689; interviewed Charles II and James II, and admonished George I; mentioned by *Dryden.

JAMES, Francis (1581–1621), Latin poet; of Westminster and Christ Church, Oxford; MA, 1605; DD, 1614; rector of St Matthew's, Friday Street, London, 1616.

JAMES, Frank Linsly (1851–1890), African explorer; MA, Downing College, Cambridge, 1881; penetrated the Sudan to Berber, 1877–8; described his subsequent explorations in the Basé country in *Wild Tribes of the Soudan* (1883); ascended the Tchad-Amba, 1883; explored the Somali country to the Webbe Shebeyli, 1884–5, relating his experiences in *The Unknown Horn of Africa* (1888); killed by an elephant near San Benito, West Africa.

JAMES, George (1683–1735), printer to City of London; brother of John *James (d. 1746).

JAMES, George (d. 1795), portrait painter, ARA, 1770; imprisoned during the Revolution at Boulogne, where he died.

JAMES, George Payne Rainsford (1799–1860), novelist and historical writer; grandson of Robert *James; historiographer royal to William IV; British consul in Massachusetts, 1850–2; removed to Norfolk, Virginia, 1852; consul-general at Venice (1856–60), where he died; published, besides historical novels (*Richelieu*, 1829, *Philip Augustus*, 1831, and others), *Memoirs of great Commanders* (1832), *Life of the Black Prince* (1836), and other popular historical works and poems; the style of his romances parodied by *Thackeray.

JAMES, Sir **Henry** (1803–1877), director-general of the Ordnance Survey; entered Royal Engineers, 1826; appointed to Ordnance Survey, 1827; local superintendent of Geological Survey of Ireland, 1843; superintendent of construction at Portsmouth, 1846; director-general of Ordnance Survey, 1854–75; lieutenant-colonel, 1854, colonel, 1857, major-general, 1868, lieutenant-general, 1874, director of topographical department of the War Office, 1857; knighted, 1860; applied photo-zincography to ordnance maps, 1859; published comparisons of standards of lengths in various countries (1866), *Photo-zincography* (1860), and other works.

JAMES, Henry, Baron James of Hereford (1828–1911), lawyer and statesman; interested in cricket; president of MCC, 1889; called to bar, 1852; an excellent criminal advocate; QC, 1869; treasurer of Middle Temple, 1888; Liberal MP for Taunton, 1869–85; solicitor-general under Gladstone, Sept. 1873; attorney-general, Nov. 1873, and 1880–5; drafted and carried Corrupt Practices Bill, 1883; PC, 1885; opposed Gladstone's Irish policy and joined Liberal Unionists; Unionist MP for Bury, 1885–95; resumed private bar practice, appeared for *The Times* before *Parnell Commission, 1888–9, summing up clients' case in a notable twelve days' speech; attorney-general of duchy of Cornwall, 1892–5; hon. LL D, Cambridge, 1892; baron, and joined Unionist Cabinet as chancellor of the duchy of Lancaster, 1895; resigned office, 1902; GCVO, 1902; opposed to A. J. Balfour's education policy and tariff-reform proposals; served on judicial committee of Privy Council from 1896; able chairman of Coal Conciliation Board, 1898–1909; opposed rejection of budget by House of Lords, 1909.

JAMES, Henry (1843–1916), novelist; born in New York; educated in New York, London, Paris, and Geneva; studied law at Harvard; settled in Europe, 1875; lived in London, 1876–98, and at Rye, 1898–1916; found material for novels in society life of London; naturalized, 1915; OM, 1916; work as novelist falls into three 'periods'; in first, chiefly occupied with 'international' subject, impact of American life upon European civilization; novels of this period, *Roderick Hudson* (1875), *The American* (1877), *Daisy Miller* (1879), and *The Portrait of a Lady* (1881); in second period dealt with subjects from English life, social, political, and artistic; novels of this period, *The Tragic Muse* (1890), *The Spoils of Poynton* (1897), *What Maisie Knew* (1897), and *The Awkward Age* (1899); began to develop extremely intricate style to match subtlety of perceptions and discriminations; in third period, which contains *The Wings of the Dove* (1902), *The Ambassadors* (1903), and *The Golden Bowl* (1904), returned to 'international' theme; explored with greater thoroughness than any previous novelist nature and possibilities of art of fiction; in later works subjects appear hardly equal to immense elaboration of treatment; also wrote short stories, plays, and reminiscences.

JAMES, Hugh (1771–1817), surgeon; son of John *James (1729–1785).

JAMES, James (1832–1902), joint composer with his father of 'Land of My Fathers', the

Welsh national anthem, 1856; it attracted public favour at eisteddfodau at Pontypridd, 1857, and Llangollen, 1858, was included in *Gems of Welsh Melody* (1860), and was sung at Bangor National Eisteddfod, 1874, serving thenceforth as Welsh national anthem.

JAMES, John (d. 1661), Fifth-Monarchy man; though not concerned in *Venner's rising (1661), was arrested with his Baptist congregation and executed for treason.

JAMES, John (*c.*1672–1746), architect; son of Eleanor *James; clerk of the works at Greenwich Hospital, 1705–46; surveyor of St Paul's, Westminster Abbey, and (1716) the fifty new churches; master of Carpenters' Company, 1734; designed St George's, Hanover Square, London; rebuilt Twickenham Church and Manor House; wrote on architecture and gardening.

JAMES, John (d. 1772), 'last of old English letter-founders'; nephew of John *James (d. 1746).

JAMES, John (1729–1785), schoolmaster; MA, The Queen's College, Oxford, 1755; DD, 1782; headmaster of St Bees School, 1755–71; rector of Arthuret and Kirk Andrews, 1782–5.

JAMES, John (1760–1786), rector of Arthuret and Kirk Andrews, 1785–6; son of John *James (1729–1785); BA, The Queen's College, Oxford, 1782.

JAMES, John (1811–1867), Yorkshire antiquary; FSA, 1856; published *History and Topography of Bradford* (1841, continued 1866) and other works.

JAMES, John Angell (1785–1859), Independent minister; studied at Gosport Academy; minister at Carr's Lane Chapel, Birmingham, from 1803 (rebuilt, 1820), where he took part in municipal work; chairman of Spring Hill College; a projector of Evangelical Alliance, 1842; published religious works, including *The Anxious Inquirer after Salvation* (1834, often reprinted and translated).

JAMES, John Haddy (1788–1869), surgeon; studied at St Bartholomew's, 1808–12; assistant-surgeon to 1st Life Guards; surgeon to the Devon and Exeter Hospital, 1816–58, and curator of the museum; mayor of Exeter, 1828; hon. FRCS, 1843; won Jacksonian Prize for treatise on inflammation, 1821.

JAMES, John Thomas (1786–1828), bishop of Calcutta; son of Thomas *James (1748–1804); educated at Rugby, Charterhouse, and Christ Church, Oxford; MA, 1810; published *Journal of a Tour in Germany, Sweden, Russia, and Poland, during 1813 and 1814* (1816), works on painting

(1820 and 1822), and *The Semi-Sceptic* (1825); vicar of Flitton-cum-Silsoe, 1816–27; bishop of Calcutta, 1827–8.

JAMES, Montague Rhodes (1862–1936), biblical scholar, antiquary, and palaeographer; scholar of Eton and King's College, Cambridge; first classes, classical tripos (1884–5); assistant, Fitzwilliam Museum (1886), director (1893–1908); fellow of King's (1887) and lecturer in divinity; dean (1889–1900), tutor (1900–2), provost (1905–18); vice-chancellor of Cambridge, 1913–15; provost of Eton, 1918–36; reconstructed painted windows of King's College Chapel and revealed the fifteenth-century wall-paintings in Eton Chapel; catalogued (1895–1932) the Western manuscripts at Cambridge, Eton, Lambeth, Westminster Abbey, John Rylands, and Aberdeen University libraries, and others in private collections; his studies of Apocryphal literature made it a comprehensible documentation of human thought and life; also wrote extensively on medieval arts and literature, translated texts, and wrote ghost stories; FBA, 1903; OM, 1930.

JAMES, Reginald William (1891–1964), physicist; educated at the Polytechnic Day School, Regent Street, the City of London School, and St John's College, Cambridge; first class, parts i and ii, natural sciences tripos, 1911–12; worked in Cavendish Laboratory with (Sir) W. L. *Bragg, 1913–14; joined *Shackleton's Antarctic Expedition as physicist, 1914–16; served in Royal Engineers, 1917–18; appointed physics lecturer, Manchester University, where Bragg was professor, 1919; senior lecturer, 1921; reader in experimental physics, 1934; worked with Bragg on experimental measurements of X-ray reflection; professor of physics, Cape Town, 1936–56; established research in crystallography; published *The Optical Principles of the Diffraction of X-rays* (1948); FRS, 1955; fellow, Cape Town University, 1949–56; president, Royal Society of South Africa, 1950–3; acting principal and vice-chancellor, Cape Town University, 1957.

JAMES, Richard (1592–1638), scholar; nephew of Thomas *James (1573?–1629); scholar and (1615) fellow of Corpus Christi College, Oxford; MA, 1615; BD, 1624; chaplain to Sir Dudley *Digges in Russia, 1618; assisted Selden in examining the Arundel marbles, 1624; librarian to Sir Robert Bruce *Cotton and his son; friend of Ben *Jonson, Sir Kenelm *Digby, and others; published *Anti-Possevinus* (1625), *The Muses Dirge* (1625), and other poems, and a translation of Minucius Felix's dialogue *Octavius* (1636). His manuscripts acquired by the Bodleian (1676) include 'Decanonizatio T. Becket',

'Iter Lancastrense' (poem, ed. Thomas *Corser, 1845), translations, and an Anglo-Saxon dictionary; his *Poems* edited by *Grosart (1880).

JAMES, Robert (1705–1776), physician; educated at Lichfield and St John's College, Oxford; BA, 1726; MD, Cambridge, 1728; LRCP, 1745; friend of Dr *Johnson, who contributed to his *Medical Dictionary* (1743); patented a powder and pill, 1746, recommended in his *Dissertation on Fevers* (1748), and other works.

JAMES, Rolfe Arnold Scott- (1878–1959), journalist, editor, and literary critic. See SCOTT-JAMES.

JAMES, Sidney (1913–1976), comedian; James was probably not his original name and possibly 1913 not his correct date of birth; born in South Africa, son of Jewish music-hall artistes; made first stage appearance at age of 10 as part of family soft-shoe dancing act; had a variety of jobs including stevedore, professional ballroom dancer, skating instructor, and boxer; served with anti-tank regiment in Middle East during 1939–45 war; emigrated to England, 1946; became actor in small parts, appearing in *Kiss Me Kate* (1951); also appeared in films including *It Always Rains on Sunday*, *The Lavender Hill Mob*, *The Titfield Thunderbolt*, *The Deep Blue Sea*, *A Kid for Two Farthings*, and *Trapeze*; joined BBC radio show, 'Hancock's Half-Hour', 1954; perfect foil to Tony *Hancock; appeared in some hundred episodes in the radio version, 1954–9, and sixty in the television show, 1956–61; appeared in first of the 'Carry On' films, *Carry on Constable* (1960), followed by seventeen more up to 1974; continued his TV work in 'Taxi', 'East End, West End' and 'George and the Dragon'; appeared on the stage in *The Solid Gold Cadillac* (1965), *Carry on London* (1974), and *The Mating Game* (1976); probably most enduring TV success 'Bless This House', a series which ran from 1971 to 1975.

JAMES, Thomas (1573?–1629), Bodley's librarian; of Winchester and New College, Oxford; fellow of New College, 1593–1602; MA, 1599; DD, 1614; first librarian of Bodleian, 1602–20; sub-dean of Wells, 1614; rector of Mongeham, 1617; published *Ecloga Oxonio-Cantabrigiensis* (1600), containing list of manuscripts at Oxford and Cambridge, Aungervile's *Philobiblon* (1599), *Wycliffe's treatises against the Begging Friars and (probably) *Fiscus Papalis* (1617); published also, besides the first two Bodleian catalogues (1605 and 1620), patristic and anti-Catholic works.

JAMES, Thomas (1593?–1635?), navigator, of Bristol; set out to discover a north-west passage in the *Henrietta Maria*, 3 May, 1631; sailed round Greenland to the south of Hudson's Bay, met Luke *Fox, and after leaving James's Bay and wintering on an island, arrived in Bristol, with slight loss of crew, 22 Oct., 1633; James's narrative (1633) identified by some as original of Coleridge's *Rime of the Ancient Mariner*.

JAMES, Thomas (1748–1804), headmaster of Rugby; at Eton contributed to *Musae Etonenses*; scholar and fellow (1770) of King's College, Cambridge, of which he wrote an account; MA, 1774; DD, 1786; headmaster at Rugby, 1778–94; raised numbers at Rugby from 52 to 245; rector of Harvington and prebendary of Worcester, 1797–1804.

JAMES, Thomas Smith (1809–1874), author of *History of Litigation and Legislation respecting Presbyterian Chapels and Charities* (1867); son of John Angell *James.

JAMES, William (1542–1617), bishop of Durham; MA, Christ Church, Oxford, 1565; DD, 1574; master of University College, Oxford, 1572; archdeacon of Coventry, 1577–84; dean of Christ Church, 1584; vice-chancellor, 1581 and 1590; chaplain to Leicester; dean of Durham, 1596–1606; bishop of Durham, 1606–17; ordered to receive Arabella Stuart, 1611.

JAMES (or JAMESIUS), William (1635?–1663), scholar; king's scholar at Westminster, 1646; student of Christ Church, Oxford, 1650; MA, 1656; assistant master under *Busby, whom he helped with his *English Introduction to the Latin tongue* (1659); published an introduction to Chaldee (1651).

JAMES, Sir William, first baronet (1721–1783), commodore of the Bombay Marine; of humble birth; entered service of East India Company, 1747; as commander of Bombay Marine (1751–9) captured Severndroog, stronghold of the pirate Angria, 1755, and Gheriah, 1757; carried news of French declaration of war up the Hooghly against north-east monsoon, 1757; returned to England, 1759; created baronet, 1778; MP, West Looe; chairman of directors of East India Company.

JAMES, William (*fl.* 1760–1771), landscape painter; imitator of Canaletto.

JAMES, William (d. 1827), naval historian; practised in Jamaica Supreme Court, 1801–13; detained prisoner in United States, 1812; escaped to Nova Scotia, 1813; published pamphlet on comparative merits of English and American navies (1816); issued in England an account of the war between England and America (naval, 1817, military, 1818); his *Naval History* of the great war (1793–1820) published (1822–4).

JAMES, William (1771–1837), railway projector; solicitor and land-agent in Warwickshire;

afterwards chairman of West Bromwich Coalmasters' Association; removed to London, 1815; partner with *Stephenson, 1821; projected Manchester and Liverpool Railway, and began survey concluded by George Stephenson; drew up plans for various railways; failed, and was imprisoned for debt, 1823.

JAMES, William Henry (1796–1873), engineer; son of William *James (1771–1837); patented locomotives, boilers, and similar appliances.

JAMES, Sir **William Milbourne** (1807–1881), lord justice; MA and hon. LL D, Glasgow; barrister, Lincoln's Inn, 1831, treasurer, 1866; QC, 1853; vice-chancellor of duchy of Lancaster, 1853; engaged in the *Colenso, Lyon v. Home*, and *Martin v. Mackonochie* cases; vice-chancellor of court of Chancery, 1869; knighted, 1869; lord justice, 1870–81; his *British in India* issued (1882).

JAMES, Sir **William Milbourne** (1881–1973), admiral and naval writer; grandson of Sir John Everett *Millais; subject of Millais' painting used by Pears Soap as its famous 'Bubbles' advertisement; educated at Trinity College, Glenalmond, and *Britannia* naval college, Dartmouth, 1895; made progress in Royal Navy and became executive officer of battle cruiser *Queen Mary*, 1913; served in Naval Intelligence Division during 1914–18 war with Sir W. R. ('Blinker') *Hall; director, Royal Naval Staff College, Greenwich, 1925; naval assistant to first sea lord and rear-admiral, 1928; chief of staff to Mediterranean Fleet, 1930; commanded battlecruiser squadron, 1932; vice-admiral, 1933; deputy chief of naval staff, 1935–8; admiral, 1938; commander-in-chief, Portsmouth, 1939–42; chief of naval information; succeeded (Sir) Roger (later Lord) *Keyes as Unionist MP for Portsmouth North, 1943–5; publications include *The British Navy in Adversity* (1926), *Blue Water and Green Fields* (1939), *Admiral Sir William Fisher* (1943), *The British Navies in the Second World War* (1946), *The Portsmouth Letters* (1946), and *The Eyes of the Navy: a Biographical Study of Sir R. Hall* (1955); also published biographies of Nelson (1948), St Vincent (1950), and Admiral Sir Henry Oliver (1956); his autobiography, *The Sky was Always Blue*, appeared in 1951; Lees-Knowles lecturer, Cambridge, 1947; naval editor, Chambers Encyclopaedia; CB, 1919; KCB, 1936; GCB, 1944; freeman of Portsmouth, 1942.

JAMES, William Owen (1900–1978), plant physiologist; educated at Tottenham Grammar School and University College, Reading; first class, B.Sc., London, 1923; did research on plant physiology at Cambridge; Ph.D., 1927; worked at Rothamsted, and then joined staff of (Sir) A. G. *Tansley as demonstrator in botany at Oxford, 1927; reader in botany, 1946–58; suffered from tuberculosis, but recovered; worked on cultivation of medicinal plants during 1939–45 war; editor of *New Phytologist*, 1931–61; FRS, 1952; professor of botany, Imperial College, London, 1959–67; hon. fellow, Imperial College, 1969; published numerous papers and other publications on plant physiology.

JAMES FRANCIS EDWARD STUART (1688–1766), prince of Wales; the Chevalier de St George or 'Old Pretender'; only son of James II by *Mary of Modena; popularly believed to be a supposititious child; at the Revolution secretly conveyed with his mother to France; proclaimed king of England on his father's death at St Germains, 1701; accompanied a French expedition to Scotland, but was prevented by English fleet and bad weather from landing, 1706; served with the French Army and distinguished himself at Oudenarde, 1708, and Malplaquet, 1709; retired to Lorraine at Peace of Utrecht, 1713; on hearing news of Sheriffmuir (1715) sailed in a small privateer from Dunkirk, landed at Peterhead, and being joined by Mar threw off his disguise at Fetteresso, 1715; established a court at Scone, but made bad impression on his army, and, flying before *Argyll to Montrose, embarked with Mar for France, 1716; returned to Bar-le-Duc; dismissed *Bolingbroke, making Mar his chief minister; finally settled in Rome; after failure of Alberoni's attempt in his favour, 1719, returned from Madrid to Rome; married Maria Clementina Sobieski, 1719; appointed John *Hay (1691–1740) his secretary on discovering Mar's treachery, 1724; alienated his followers by neglecting his wife; received papal pension, 1727; gave money for the rising of 1745; buried at St Peter's, where George III employed Canova to erect a monument over his tomb (completed, 1819).

JAMESON, Andrew, Lord Ardwall (1845–1911), Scottish judge; MA, St Andrews, 1865; hon. LL D, 1905; called to Scottish bar, 1870; sheriff of Roxburghshire, 1886, Ross, 1890, and Perthshire, 1891; raised to bench, 1905; frequent arbitrator in industrial disputes; interested in Scottish Free Church affairs.

JAMESON, Anna Brownell (1794–1860), author; eldest daughter of Denis Brownell *Murphy; married Robert Jameson (afterwards speaker and attorney-general of Ontario), 1825, but soon separated from him; published, among other works, *Diary of an Ennuyée* (1826), *Characteristics of Women* (1832), *Visits and Sketches* (1834), *Companion to Public Picture Galleries of London* (1842), and essays, including 'The House of 'Titian' (1846) and 'Sacred and Legendary Art' (1848–52); friend of Ottilie von Goethe and for a time of Lady Byron; devoted much attention to sick nursing.

JAMESON, James Sligo (1856–1888), naturalist and African traveller; discovered the black pern in Borneo, 1877; hunted in Matabeleland and Mashonaland, 1879; shot in Rocky Mountains, 1882; visited Spain and Algeria, 1884; naturalist to Emin Pacha Relief Expedition, 1887; as second-in-command of the rear expedition witnessed and made sketches of a cannibal banquet; after Major *Barttelot's murder (1888) prepared to conduct the rearguard in search of H. M. Stanley, but died of haematuric fever at Bangala; his *Diary of the Emin Expedition* published (1890).

JAMESON, Sir Leander Starr, baronet (1853–1917), South African statesman; born in Edinburgh; MD, London, 1877; went out as doctor to Kimberley, 1878; formed friendship with Cecil John *Rhodes; undertook three missions to Matabele chief, Lobengula, 1889–90; in consequence, effective confirmation of mineral rights concession obtained by British South Africa Company; accompanied, as Rhodes's personal representative, expedition of A. R. Colquhoun, first administrator of Mashonaland, 1890; administrator of Mashonaland, 1891; accompanied force dispatched by company to punish Lobengula for raids by Matabele 'impis' on Mashonas under British protection; Bulawayo occupied, 1893; Matabeleland placed under Jameson's administration, 1894; CB, 1894; carried out famous 'raid' over Transvaal border in 'uitlander' interests, Dec. 1895; surrendered to Boer commandant, P. A. Cronje, Jan. 1896; handed over to British authorities and sent to England for trial; imprisoned in Holloway Jail, but quickly released; entered Cape parliament as member for Kimberley, 1900; succeeded Rhodes as leader of Progressive party at Cape, 1902; prime minister of Cape Colony, 1904–8; attended Imperial Conference in London, and PC, 1907; with General *Botha played chief part in South African National Convention, 1908–9; entered first Union parliament as member for Harbour division of Cape Town, 1910; leader of opposition; baronet, 1911; retired, 1912; died in London.

JAMESON, Robert (1774–1854), mineralogist; studied at Edinburgh University; regius professor of natural history and keeper of the museum at Edinburgh, 1804–54; founded Wernerian Society, 1808; with Sir David *Brewster established *Edinburgh Philosophical Journal*, 1819; published *Mineralogy of the Scottish Isles* (1800) and other works; edited Cuvier's *Theory of the*

Earth (1813, 1817, 1818, and 1827), and Wilson and Bonaparte's *American Ornithology* (1826).

JAMESON, Robert William (1805–1868), journalist and author; nephew of Robert *Jameson; educated at Edinburgh; writer to the signet.

JAMESON, William (*fl.* 1689–1720), blind lecturer on history at Glasgow University, 1692–1720; published *Spicilegia Antiquitatum Aegypti* (1720), *Verus Patroclus* (1689), and anti-Episcopalian treatises.

JAMESON, William (1796–1873), botanist; studied at Edinburgh University; professor of chemistry and botany at Quito, 1827, assayer to Quito Mint, 1832, and director, 1861; published *Synopsis Plantarum Quitensium* (1865); sent home plants, some of which were named after him; died at Quito.

JAMESON, William (1815–1882), pioneer of tea-planting in India; nephew of Robert *Jameson; studied at Edinburgh University; superintendent of Saharunpore garden, 1842–75.

JAMESON, Sir (William) Wilson (1885–1962), professor of public health, medical officer, and medical adviser; educated at Aberdeen Grammar School and King's College, Aberdeen; BA, 1905; transferred to Marischal College and qualified MB, Ch.B., with distinction, 1909; MD (Aberdeen), 1912; worked in London hospitals and in Eastbourne, 1913–14; MRCP (London), 1913; DPH, 1914; served in RAMC, 1915–19; medical officer of health, Finchley, and deputy medical officer of health, Marylebone, 1920; published *Synopsis of Hygiene* (with F. T. Marchant, 1920); called to bar (Middle Temple), 1922; served in further posts as medical officer of health and lecturer, 1925–8; professor of public health, London School of Hygiene and Tropical Medicine, 1929; dean, 1931; part-time medical adviser, Colonial Office, 1940; chief medical officer, Ministry of Health and Board of Education, 1940–50; closely concerned with plans for National Health Service; medical adviser, King Edward's Hospital Fund for London, 1950–60; FRCP, 1930; knighted, 1939; KCB, 1943; GBE, 1949; received many honorary degrees; master of the Society of Apothecaries.

JAMESONE, George (1588?–1644), Scottish portrait painter; perhaps studied under Rubens; visited Italy, 1634; painted James I, Charles I, *Montrose, and other eminent contemporaries.

JAMES THE CISTERCIAN (or THE ENGLISHMAN) (*fl.* 1270), first professor of philosophy and theology in Lexington's college at Paris.

JAMIESON, John (1759–1838), antiquary and philologist; studied at Glasgow University; anti-burgher minister at Forfar, 1781–97, and Nicolson Street, Edinburgh, 1797–1830; friend of Scott; DD, Princeton for his reply to *Priestley's *History of Early Opinions* (1795); edited *Barbour's *Bruce* (1820), and Blind *Harry's *Wallace* (1820); compiled *Etymological Dictionary of the Scottish Language* (1808; ed. *Longmuir and Donaldson, 1879–87).

JAMIESON, John Paul (d. 1700), Roman Catholic divine; DD during residence at the Scots College, Rome; transcribed original documents relating to history of Scotland, some being deposited at Paris.

JAMIESON, Robert (1780?–1844), compiler of *Popular Ballads and Songs* (1806); collaborated with *Scott in *Illustrations of Northern Antiquities* (1814).

JAMIESON, Robert (d. 1861), philanthropist; directed exploration of Niger and other West African rivers; rescued African colonization expedition, 1841; published *Commerce with Africa* (1859).

JAMIESON, Robert (1802–1880), Scottish divine; studied at Edinburgh University; minister of Weststruther, 1830, Currie, 1837, and St Paul's, Glasgow, 1844–80; moderator of general assembly, 1872; published *Eastern Manners illustrative of Old and New Testaments* (1836–8); part author of *Commentary on the Bible* (1861–5).

JAMIESON, Thomas Hill (1843–1876), keeper of the Advocates' Library, Edinburgh, 1871–6; privately printed *Life of Alexander Barclay* (1874); edited *Barclay's version of Brandt's *Ship of Fools* (1874).

JAMRACH, Johann Christian Carl (1815–1891), dealer in wild animals; born in Hamburg.

JANE (or JOHANNA) (d. 1445), queen of Scotland; daughter of John *Beaufort, earl of Somerset; married *James I, 1424, whose love for her is told in the *Kingis Quair*; wounded at James I's assassination; married Sir James Stewart, the knight of Lorne, before 1439; obliged by *Livingstone to surrender custody of *James II, her dowry, and Stirling Castle, 1439.

JANE (1537–1554), queen of England. See DUDLEY, Lady JANE.

JANE, Joseph (fl. 1600–1660), controversialist; mayor and MP for Liskeard in Long Parliament; royal commissioner in Cornwall during Great Rebellion; defended *Eikon Basilike* against *Milton, 1651.

JANE (or JANYN), Thomas (d. 1500), bishop of Norwich; fellow of New College, Oxford, 1454–72; vice-chancellor of Oxford University, 1459–60, 1468–70; doctor of decrees; chancellor's commissary, 1469; archdeacon of Essex, 1480; privy councillor, 1495; canon of Windsor, 1496; dean of Chapel Royal, 1496; bishop of Norwich, 1499–1500.

JANE, William (1645–1707), divine; son of Joseph *Jane; of Westminster and Christ Church, Oxford; MA, 1667; DD, 1674; canon of Christ Church, Oxford, 1669; archdeacon of Middlesex, 1679; regius professor of divinity at Oxford, 1680–1707; framed Oxford declaration in favour of passive obedience, 1683; dean of Gloucester, 1685; prolocutor of the lower house, 1689, procuring defeat of the comprehension scheme in Convocation, 1689.

JANE SEYMOUR (1509?–1537), third queen of Henry VIII; daughter of Sir John Seymour of Wolf Hall, Savernake; lady-in-waiting to *Catherine of Aragon and *Anne Boleyn; resisted dishonourable proposals from the king; privately married to Henry VIII in York Place, 30 May 1536; reconciled Princess Mary to Henry; died soon after the birth of her son (Edward VI); was several times painted by *Holbein.

JANEWAY, James (1636?–1674), Nonconformist divine; brother of John *Janeway; BA, Christ Church, Oxford, 1659; preached in Jamaica Row, Rotherhithe; his *Token for Children* (1671) frequently reprinted.

JANEWAY, John (1633–1657), Puritan; brother of James *Janeway; of St Paul's School and Eton; first scholar of King's College, Cambridge, 1650; fellow, 1654.

JANIEWICZ (afterwards YANIEWICZ), Felix (1762–1848), violinist and composer; native of Wilna; came to London from Paris during the revolution; original member of London Philharmonic Society; published violin and piano music.

JANNER, Barnett, Baron Janner ((1892–1982), parliamentarian, solicitor, and Jewish leader; born in Lithuania; educated at Barry County School and University of Wales; served in Royal Garrison Artillery, 1917–18; solicitor in Cardiff; embraced the Zionist cause; moved law practice to London, 1930; Liberal MP for Whitechapel and St George's, 1931–5; joined Labour party, 1936; Labour MP Leicester (later Leicester North West), 1945–70; vice-president, Leasehold Reform Association, and honorary rents adviser to Labour party; president, board of deputies of British Jews, 1955–64; president, World Confederation of General Zionists; hon. LL D, Leeds, 1957; commander of the Order of Orange Nassau, 1970; knighted, 1961; life peer, 1970.

JANSSEN (or JANSEN), Bernard (fl. 1610–1630), stonemason and tomb-maker; engaged with Nicholas *Stone (1586–1647) on tomb of Thomas *Sutton in the Charterhouse, and of Sir Nicholas *Bacon in Redgrave Church, Suffolk.

JANSSEN (or JONSON) VAN CEULEN, Cornelius (1593–1664?), portrait painter; famous for portrait of Lady Bowyer and groups of the Rushout, Lucy, and Verney families; subsequently practised in Holland.

JANSSEN, Geraert (or Gerard) (fl. 1616), tomb-maker; executed the portrait bust of Shakespeare at Stratford-upon-Avon, 1616.

JANSSEN, Sir Theodore, first baronet (1658?–1748), South Sea director; came to England from Holland, 1680; naturalized, 1685; knighted by William III; created baronet, 1714; MP, Yarmouth, 1714–21; expelled the house, 1721; author of *General Maxims in Trade* (1713).

JAPP, Alexander Hay (1837–1905), author and publisher; at first a tailor's bookkeeper in Edinburgh; attended classes in Edinburgh University, 1860–1; literary adviser in London to Isbister & Co., 1864; assisted in editing *Good Words*, *Sunday Magazine*, and *Contemporary Review*; LL D, Glasgow, 1879; FRS Edinburgh, 1880; wrote much under various pseudonyms, the chief being 'H. A. Page' and 'A. F. Scot'; edited *De Quincey's Posthumous Works* (1891–3) and *De Quincey Memorials* (1891); his works include studies of Hawthorne (1872), of Thoreau (1878), of De Quincey (2 vols., 1877), and R. L. *Stevenson (of whose *Treasure Island* he had negotiated the publication), 1905; he also published verse and studies in German literature, natural history, and anthropology.

JARDINE, Alexander (d. 1799), lieutenant-colonel; captain, Royal Invalid Artillery; went on mission to Morocco, described in *Letters from Morocco* (1790); brevet-lieutenant-colonel, 1793.

JARDINE, David (1794–1860), historical and legal writer; MA, Glasgow, 1813; police magistrate at Bow Street, 1839; published *Narrative of the Gunpowder Plot* (1857); indexed (1828) and (1832–3) abridged *Howell's State Trials*; wrote legal tracts.

JARDINE, Douglas Robert (1900–1958), cricketer; born in Bombay; educated at Winchester and New College, Oxford; qualified as solicitor, 1926; played cricket and tennis for Oxford; became notable Surrey player, heading English averages, 1927, 1928; played 22 tests, 15 as captain, making 1,296 runs, averaging 48; played in all five test matches in Australia, 1928–9; captain, England against New Zealand, 1931; took team to Australia, 1932–3; involved in bitter controversy arising from 'body-line bowling'; took

MCC team to India, 1933–4; published *In Quest of the Ashes* (1933) and *Cricket* (1936).

JARDINE, George (1742–1827), professor at Glasgow; in Paris, 1770–3; professor of Greek at Glasgow, 1774; professor of logic at Glasgow, 1787–1824; secretary of Royal Infirmary.

JARDINE, James (1776–1858), engineer; constructed Union Canal; first to determine mean level of the sea.

JARDINE, John (1716–1766), Scottish divine; minister of Lady Yester's Church, Edinburgh, 1750, of the Tron Church, 1754; DD, St Andrews, 1758; dean of order of the Thistle, 1763; contributed to the first *Edinburgh Review*, 1755.

JARDINE, Sir Robert, first baronet (1825–1905), East India merchant and racehorse owner; partner in uncle's London firm of East India merchants, 1859; succeeded uncle as head of firm, and inherited his property in Perthshire and Dumfriesshire, 1881; Liberal MP for Ashburton, 1865, for Dumfries Burghs, 1868–74 and 1880–92; baronet, 1885; keen agriculturist and breeder of stock; won Two Thousand Guineas and Derby with Pretender (1869), the Cesarewitch (1877), and the Waterloo (coursing) Cup (1873); art collector.

JARDINE, Sir William, seventh baronet (1800–1874), naturalist; succeeded as seventh baronet, 1820; published (with Prideaux *Selby) *Illustrations of Ornithology* (1830); edited *Naturalists' Library*, 1833–45, contributing sections on birds and fish; conducted also *Annals and Magazine of Natural History*; joint editor of *Edinburgh Philosophical Journal*; commissioner on salmon fisheries, 1860.

JARLATH (or IARLATH) (fl. 540), Irish saint; founded a church on site of the modern Tuam; possibly identical with *Jarlath (424–481).

JARLATH (or IARLAITHE) (424–481), third archbishop of Armagh, 464.

JARMAN, Frances Eleanor (1803?–1873), afterwards Mrs Ternan, actress; appeared as a child at Bath, 1815; appeared in Ireland, 1822; played Juliet to Charles *Kemble's Romeo, and Imogen and other parts at Covent Garden, 1827–8; well received at Edinburgh, 1829, in Desdemona and Juliana (*The Honeymoon*); accompanied her husband in American and Canadian tour, 1834–6; at Drury Lane, 1837–8; played Paulina in *Winter's Tale* at the Princess's, 1855; acted blind Alice with Fletcher in *The Bride of Lammermoor*, 1866.

JARRETT, Thomas (1805–1882), linguist; seventh classic at Cambridge, 1827; fellow and lecturer at St Catharine's College, Cambridge,

1828–32; Cambridge professor of Arabic, 1831–54; regius professor of Hebrew, 1854; rector of Trunch, Norfolk, 1832–82; canon of Ely, 1854–82; published *Hebrew–English and English–Hebrew Lexicon* (1848), *New Way of marking sounds of English Words without change of Spelling* (1858), and Sanskrit and Hebrew texts transliterated into Roman characters.

JARROLD, Thomas (1770–1853), physician; MD, Edinburgh; practised at Manchester; published *Anthropologia* (1808), *Instinct and Reason philosophically investigated* (1836), and other works.

JARRY, Francis (1733–1807), military officer; said to have been in Prussian service during Seven Years' War, and to have presided over military school at Berlin under Frederick the Great; adjutant-general in French Army (1791) and maréchal de camp (1792), serving against the Austrians; came to England, 1795; first commandant of the Royal Military College, 1799–1806; his *Employment of Light Troops* issued (1803).

JARVIS, Charles (1675?–1739), portrait painter. See JERVAS.

JARVIS, Claude Scudamore (1879–1953), soldier, administrator, and orientalist; served in South Africa, 1899–1902; in France, Egypt, and Palestine, 1914–18; joined Egyptian Frontiers Administration, 1918; governor of Sinai, 1922–36; settled tribal feuds and became legendary figure for knowledge of Arabic and Bedouin customs and law; publications include *Yesterday and Today in Sinai* (1931); joined staff of *Country Life*; CMG, 1936.

JARVIS, Sir John Layton ('Jack') (1887–1968), racehorse trainer; son and grandson of racehorse trainers; educated at Cranleigh School; apprenticed as jockey to his father; rode winner of Cambridgeshire at age of 16; set up as trainer, 1914; first major success (Ellangowan in the Two Thousand Guineas), 1921; won again in 1928 and 1939; also won One Thousand Guineas three times, the St Leger once, and the Derby twice (Blue Peter, 1939, and Ocean Swell, 1944); trained for the fifth earl of *Rosebery and his son the sixth earl of *Rosebery, 1922–68; keen on shooting and hare-coursing; won the Waterloo Cup; knighted for services to racing, 1967; published autobiography, *They're Off* (1969).

JARVIS, Samuel (*fl.* 1770), blind composer; organist of Foundling Hospital and St Sepulchre's.

JARVIS, Thomas (d. 1789), glass-painter. See JERVAIS.

JASPER OF HATFIELD, earl of Pembroke and duke of Bedford (1431?–1495). See TUDOR, JASPER.

JAY, John George Henry (1770–1849), violinist and composer; Mus.Doc., Cambridge, 1811.

JAY, William (1769–1853), Dissenting minister; stonemason at erection of Fonthill Abbey; preached for Rowland *Hill (1744–1833) at Surrey Chapel, London, 1788; pastor of Argyle Independent Chapel, Bath, from 1791; commended as a preacher by *Sheridan and Beckford; published popular devotional works.

JAYNE, Francis John (1845–1921), bishop of Chester; educated at Rugby and Wadham College, Oxford; first classes in classics and law and modern history; fellow of Jesus College, Oxford, 1868; ordained, 1870; tutor of Keble College, Oxford, 1871; principal of St David's College, Lampeter, 1879–86; vicar of Leeds, 1886–9; bishop of Chester, 1889–1919; a moderate churchman with exceptional administrative talents.

JEACOCKE, Caleb (1706–1786), baker and orator; author of *Vindication of the Moral Character of the Apostle Paul* (1765).

JEAFFRESON, John Cordy (1831–1901), author; BA, Pembroke College, Oxford, 1852; private tutor in London, 1852–8; published many novels, including *Live it Down* (1863); made some repute as an anecdotal anthologist in books 'about doctors' (1860), 'about lawyers' (1866), and 'about the clergy' (1870); called to bar, 1859, but did not practise; inspector of MSS for Royal Historical MSS Commission, 1874–87; author of *The Real Lord Byron* (1883), *The Real Shelley* (1885), *Lady Hamilton and Lord Nelson* (1888), and *The Queen of Naples and Lord Nelson* (1889).

JEAKE, Samuel, the elder (1623–1690), Puritan antiquary; some time town clerk of Rye; detained in London as a Nonconformist, 1682–7; his translation (with annotations) of the charters of the Cinque Ports printed (1728).

JEAKE, Samuel, the younger (1652–1699), astrologer; son of Samuel *Jeake the elder; edited his father's *Logisticelogia* (1696).

JEAN, Philip (1755–1802), miniature painter; native of Jersey.

JEANES, Henry (1611–1662), Puritan divine; MA, New Inn Hall, Oxford, 1633; vicar of Kingston and rector of Chedzoy, Somerset; published theological works and carried on controversies with Dr *Hammond, William *Creed, and Jeremy *Taylor.

JEANS, Sir **James Hopwood** (1877–1946), mathematician, theoretical physicist, astronomer, and popular expositor of physical science and astronomy; educated at Merchant Taylors' and Trinity College, Cambridge; bracketed second wrangler, 1898; fellow, 1901; university lecturer in mathematics (1904–5), Stokes lecturer (1910–12), Cambridge; professor of applied mathematics, Princeton, 1905–9; FRS, 1906; an honorary secretary, Royal Society, 1919–29; president, British Association, 1934; professor of astronomy, Royal Institution, 1935–46; publications include *Dynamical Theory of Gases* (1904), *Theoretical Mechanics* (1906), *The Mathematical Theory of Electricity and Magnetism* (1908), and *Problems of Cosmogony and Stellar Dynamics* (1919); popular scientific works include *The Universe Around Us* (1929), *The Mysterious Universe* (1930), *The Stars in their Courses* (1931), and *Through Space and Time* (1934); knighted, 1928; OM, 1939.

JEAVONS, Thomas (1816–1867), engraver.

JEBB, Ann (1735–1812), contributor to *London Chronicle* ('Priscilla'); wife of John *Jebb (1736–1786).

JEBB, Eglantyne (1876–1928), philanthropist; niece of Sir R. C. *Jebb; educated at Lady Margaret Hall, Oxford; engaged in social work and travel, 1900–14; initiated 'Save the Children Fund', 1919; movement spread into forty countries and sums contributed reached £5½ million; thousands of Greek, Bulgarian, Romanian, Armenian, Polish, and Russian children fed and provided for; work made permanent by League of Nations' Declaration of Geneva (children's charter), 1924; died at Geneva.

JEBB, John (1736–1786), theological and political writer; nephew of Samuel *Jebb; second wrangler, Peterhouse, Cambridge, 1757; fellow, 1761; MA, 1760; as lecturer on the Greek Testament expressed Unitarian views, but held church livings in Suffolk till 1775; engaged actively in movement for abolition of clerical and university subscription, 1771; proposed public examinations at Cambridge, 1773–4; MD, St Andrews, 1777; practised in London; FRS, 1779; his works edited by Dr John *Disney (1787).

JEBB, John (1775–1833), bishop of Limerick; MA, Trinity College, Dublin, 1801; rector of Abington, 1809; archdeacon of Emly, 1820; DD, 1821; bishop of Limerick, 1822–33; defended Irish establishment in House of Lords, 1824; chief work, *Essay on Sacred Literature* (1820); pioneer of Oxford Movement.

JEBB, John (1805–1886), divine; son of Richard *Jebb; of Winchester and Dublin; MA, 1829; BD, 1862; rector of Peterstow, Herefordshire, 1843; canon of Hereford, 1870; published *Literal Translation of the Book of Psalms* (1846), and works on cathedrals and liturgy; Old Testament reviser, but resigned his position.

JEBB, Sir **Joshua** (1793–1863), surveyor-general of convict prisons; with Royal Engineers in Canada and America, 1813–20; surveyor-general of convict prisons, 1837; assisted in construction of 'model prison' at Pentonville; designed prisons at Portland and elsewhere; inspector-general of military prisons, 1844; as chairman of convict prisons developed progressive system; hon. major-general on retiring from the army, 1850; KCB, 1859; published works on prisons, artesian wells, and fortification.

JEBB, Sir **Richard,** first baronet (1729–1787), physician; son of Samuel *Jebb; MD, Aberdeen, 1751; physician to Westminster Hospital, 1754–62, to St George's, 1762–8; attended duke of Gloucester in Italy; FRS and FSA; FRCP, 1771, Harveian orator, 1774, and censor, 1772, 1776, and 1778; created baronet, 1778; physician to prince of Wales, 1780, and to the king, 1786; friend of *Wilkes and Churchill.

JEBB, Richard (1766–1834), Irish judge, 1818–34; brother of John *Jebb (1775–1833); published pamphlet in favour of Union (1799).

JEBB, Sir **Richard Claverhouse** (1841–1905), Greek scholar; born at Dundee; great-nephew of John *Jebb; educated at Charterhouse and Trinity College, Cambridge; Porson scholar, 1859; Craven scholar, 1860; senior classic and first chancellor's medallist, 1862; fellow and classical lecturer, 1863; hon. fellow, 1888; public orator, 1869; helped to found Cambridge Philological Society, 1868; published *The Characters of Theophrastus* (1870) and translations into Greek and Latin verse (1873); professor of Greek at Glasgow, 1875–89; lectured upon modern as well as classical Greek; visited Greece, 1878; wrote *Attic Orators* (2 vols., 1876), *Primer of Greek Literature* (1877), *Modern Greece* (1880), monograph on *Bentley (in 'Men of Letters' series, 1882), and *Homer* (1887); visited America, 1884; hon. LL D, Harvard; regius professor of Greek at Cambridge, 1889–1905; Conservative MP for the university, 1891–1905; served on many education commissions; Rede lecturer, Cambridge, 1890; Romanes lecturer, Oxford, 1899; delivered lectures at Johns Hopkins University (1892) on *The Growth and Influence of Greek Poetry* (published 1893); edited Bacchylides, 1905; chief work was edition of Sophocles (7 vols., 1883–96); an eighth volume containing the Fragments was unfinished; helped to found Society for Promotion of Hellenic Studies, 1879, and the British School of Archaeology at Athens, 1887;

FBA, 1902; close friend of *Tennyson; received honorary degrees from Edinburgh, Dublin, Cambridge, Oxford, and Bologna; professor of ancient history, Royal Academy, 1898; knighted, 1900; trustee of British Museum, 1903; OM, 1905; *Essays and Letters* and *Life and Letters* edited by widow (1907).

JEBB, Samuel (1694?–1772), physician and scholar; BA, Peterhouse, Cambridge, 1713; librarian to Jeremy *Collier; MD, Reims, 1728; practised at Stratford-le-Bow; edited Roger *Bacon's *Opus Majus* (1733) and the works of Aristides (1722 and 1730); published lives of *Mary Queen of Scots and Robert, earl of *Leicester.

JEEJEEBHOY, Sir **Jamsetjee,** first baronet (1783–1859), philanthropist; born at Bombay; made several voyages to China; captured by the French and taken to the Cape; returned, 1807, and made large fortune as a merchant; besides benefactions to his Parsee co-religionists, founded hospital at Bombay (1843), endowed schools at many places, and constructed Mahim–Bandora Causeway, Poona Waterworks, and other public institutions; knighted, 1842; created baronet, 1857; fund established in his name for translations into Gujarat.

JEENS, Charles Henry (1827–1879), engraver.

JEFFCOCK, Parkin (1829–1866), mining engineer; killed by explosion in Oaks Pit Colliery, near Barnsley, while directing rescue operations.

JEFFERIES. See also JEFFREY and JEFFREYS.

JEFFERIES, Richard (1848–1887), naturalist and novelist; son of a Wiltshire farmer; early contributed to Wiltshire papers; after attempts at literature removed to London and wrote for the *Pall Mall Gazette*, in which first appeared his *Gamekeeper at Home* (1877) and *Wild Life in a Southern County* (1879); returned to the country and published, besides other works, *Wood Magic* (1881), *Bevis* (1882), *After London* (1885), and *The Story of my Heart* (1883).

JEFFERSON, Sir **Geoffrey** (1886–1961), neurosurgeon; educated at Manchester Grammar School and Manchester University; qualified, 1909; appointed demonstrator in anatomy under (Sir) Grafton Elliot *Smith, 1911; FRCS, 1911; MS (London), 1913; worked in Anglo-Russian Hospital, Petrograd, 1915–17; worked at Salford on effects of injury on the nervous system, localization of cerebral tumours, and the problem of consciousness; helped to found the Society of British Neurological Surgeons; secretary, 1926–52; worked in Manchester and London, 1926–39; professor, neurosurgery,

Manchester, 1939–51; consultant adviser to ministries of Health and Pensions, 1939; FRS, FRCP, 1947; CBE, 1943; knighted, 1950; member, Medical Research Council, 1948–52; chairman, Clinical Research Board, 1953–9.

JEFFERSON, Samuel (1809–1846), author of *History and Antiquities of Carlisle* (1838); editor of *Carlisle Tracts*, 1839–44.

JEFFERY, Dorothy (1685–1777), Cornish fish-seller; known by her maiden name, Dolly Pentreath; erroneously said to be the last person who spoke Cornish; her monument erected at Paul in 1860 by Prince Louis Lucien Bonaparte.

JEFFERY, George Barker (1891–1957), mathematician and educationist; educated at Strand School, Wilson's Grammar School, Camberwell, and University College, London; B.Sc., 1912; assistant to L. N. G. *Filon, 1912–21; university reader in mathematics, 1921; professor of mathematics, King's College, 1922–4; Astor professor of pure mathematics, University College, 1924–45; published *Relativity for Physics Students* (1924); FRS, 1926; director, Institute of Education, 1945–57; recommended foundation of West African Examinations Council, 1950; dean, College of Handicraft, 1952–7.

JEFFERY, John (1647–1720), archdeacon of Norwich; MA, St Catharine Hall, Cambridge, 1672; DD, 1696; incumbent of St Peter Mancroft, Norwich, 1678; archdeacon, 1694–1720; published devotional works; edited Sir Thomas *Browne's *Christian Morals* (1716).

JEFFERY, Thomas (1700?–1728), Nonconformist divine; minister of Little Baddow; published (1725) reply to the deist *Collins's *Grounds and Reasons*; published *Christianity the Perfection of all Religion* (1728).

JEFFERYS, James (1757–1784), historical painter; studied in Rome; his *Scene before Gibraltar on morning of 14 Sept. 1782*, engraved by *Woollett and John *Emes.

JEFFERYS, Thomas (d. 1771), map engraver; published miscellaneous works.

JEFFREY. See also GEOFFREY.

JEFFREY, Alexander (1806–1874), author of history of Roxburghshire (1836; rewritten, 1853–64).

JEFFREY, Francis, Lord Jeffrey (1773–1850), Scottish judge and critic; educated at the Edinburgh High School and at Glasgow and Edinburgh universities; a few months at The Queen's College, Oxford; admitted to the Scots bar, 1794; obtained little practice for many years owing to his Whiggism; as member of Speculative Society made acquaintance of *Scott and others; joined in foundation of *Edinburgh Review*, 1802, and edited it from 1803 to 1829; himself wrote the Cevallos article (no. 26), after which Scott ceased his contributions, and the review became decidedly Whig; challenged by *Moore for an article on his *Epistles, Odes, and other Poems*, but both duellists arrested at Chalk Farm before fighting, 1806; afterwards became intimate with Moore; from 1807 appeared with success before the general assembly, and gradually extended his practice in the courts; visited New York, 1813; active in British politics, 1821-6; dean of the Faculty of Advocates, 1829; lord advocate, 1830-4; MP for Malton, 1831-2, and after the Reform Bill for Edinburgh; acquainted with *Wordsworth; judge of the court of session, 1834-50, giving a decision for the Free Church at the disruption; became intimate of *Dickens; read proofs of first two volumes of *Macaulay's *History*; an impartial and acute critic. His contributions to the *Edinburgh Review* (selected) appeared (1844 and 1853, 4 vols.).

JEFFREY (or JEFFERAY), John (d. 1578), judge; barrister, Gray's Inn, 1546; queen's serjeant, 1572; judge of Queen's Bench, 1576; chief baron of the Exchequer, 1577.

JEFFREYS, Christopher (d. 1693), musician; son of George *Jeffreys (d. 1685); of Westminster and Christ Church, Oxford; MA, 1666.

JEFFREYS, George (d. 1685), organist to Charles I at Oxford, 1643, and composer; steward to the Hattons of Kirby from 1648; many of his compositions in British Museum and Royal College of Music library.

JEFFREYS, George, first Baron Jeffreys of Wem (1644-1689), judge; educated at Shrewsbury, St Paul's School, and at Westminster; left Trinity College, Cambridge, without graduating; barrister, Inner Temple, 1668; common serjeant, 1671; introduced at court by *Chiffinch; solicitor-general to duke of York, 1677; knighted, 1677; as recorder of London (1678-80) exercised severity in 'Popish Plot' cases; reprimanded by House of Commons for obstructing petitions for the assembling of parliament, and compelled to resign, 1680; his conduct as chief justice of Chester also censured; after his prosecution of *Fitzharris and Colledge created baronet, 1681; active in obtaining *quo warranto* against the City of London and in prosecution of Lord *Russell; named (in spite of Charles II's low estimate of him) lord chief justice, 1682; privy councillor, 1683; conducted the trials of Algernon *Sidney, 1683, and Sir Thomas *Armstrong, 1684; after the accession of James II advised levying of the customs and revival of the High Commission

court; presided at trial of Titus *Oates, 1685; created Baron Jeffreys of Wem, 1685 (an exceptional favour); tried Richard *Baxter, 1685; held 'bloody assize' in the west after suppression of *Monmouth's rebellion, 1685; appointed lord chancellor, Sept. 1685; chief ecclesiastical commissioner, 1686; one of the privy councillors who regulated the municipal corporations, 1687; present at birth of Prince *James Edward, 1688; carried out James II's tardy reforms; member of Council of Five in the king's absence with the army, 1688; arrested in disguise at Wapping, 1688; died in the Tower after petitioning for a pardon. He displayed great acuteness in civil cases, but as a criminal judge was notorious for his brutality.

JEFFREYS, George (1678-1755), poet and dramatist; son of Christopher *Jeffreys; of Westminster and Trinity College, Cambridge; fellow, 1702-9; MA, 1702; published *Edwin* (1724) and *Merope* (1731), two tragedies, acted at Lincoln's Inn Fields; author of *Miscellanies in Verse and Prose* (1754).

JEFFREYS, John, second Baron Jeffreys of Wem (1670?-1702), son of George *Jeffreys, first baron; head of Westminster, 1685; took his seat as peer, 1694; instrumental in obtaining public funeral for *Dryden, 1700.

JEFFREYS, John Gwyn (1809-1885), conchologist; treasurer of Linnean and Geological societies; FRS, 1840; hon. LL D, St Andrews; vice-president of British Association, 1880; conducted dredging operations in the British seas, the Bay of Biscay, the Portuguese coast, Baffin Bay, and the Norwegian coast, and discovered seventy-one unknown species of shells; published *British Conchology* (1862-9); his collection of European molluscs purchased by the American government.

JEFFREYS, Julius (1801-1877), inventor of the respirator; studied medicine at Edinburgh and London; while in the Bengal Medical Service recommended Simla as a health resort; invented respirator, 1836; FRS, 1840; patented various appliances for ships; wrote on diseases of the respiratory organs.

JEGON, John (1550-1618), bishop of Norwich; fellow of Queens' College, Cambridge, 1572; BA, 1572; master of Corpus Christi College, Cambridge, 1590-1603; vice-chancellor, 1596-8, 1600-1; bishop of Norwich, 1602-18.

JEHNER (afterwards JENNER), Isaac (1750-1806?), portrait painter and mezzotint engraver; published *Fortune's Football* (autobiographical, 1806).

JEKYLL, Sir Joseph (1663–1738), master of the Rolls; barrister, Middle Temple, 1687; chief justice of Chester, 1697–1717; king's serjeant, 1700; knighted, 1700; MP, Eye, 1697–1713, Lymington, 1713–22, Reigate, 1722–38; opened the case against Sacheverell, 1710; manager against Lord *Winton, Francia, and Lord *Oxford; master of the Rolls, 1717–38; privy councillor, 1717; prominent in exposing South Sea directors, 1720; steady supporter of Walpole; introduced Gin and Mortmain acts, 1736; left money for relief of the national debt.

JEKYLL, Joseph (d. 1837), wit and politician; great-nephew of Sir Joseph *Jekyll; of Westminster and Christ Church, Oxford; MA, 1777; barrister, Lincoln's Inn, 1778; reader at Inner Temple, 1814, treasurer, 1816; MP, Calne, 1787–1816; contributed Whig pasquinades to *Morning Chronicle* and *Evening Statesman*; attacked in *Jekyll, an Eclogue* (1788); KC and solicitor-general to prince of Wales, 1805; master in Chancery, 1815; compiled *Facts and Observations relating to the Temple Church* (1811), which he restored.

JEKYLL, Thomas (1570–1653), antiquary; secondary of the King's Bench and clerk of the papers; many of his collections for history of Essex, Norfolk, and Suffolk in British Museum.

JEKYLL, Thomas (1646–1700), divine; of Merchant Taylors' School and Trinity College, Oxford; MA, 1670; minister of the New Church in St Margaret, Westminster, 1681–98; instituted free school in Westminster.

JELF, George Edward (1834–1908), master of Charterhouse; son of Richard William *Jelf; educated at Charterhouse and Christ Church, Oxford; BA, 1856; MA, 1859; DD, 1907; honorary canon of St Albans, 1878; residentiary canon of Rochester, 1880–1907; master of Charterhouse, 1907; a moderate high churchman, he exercised considerable influence by his popular devotional publications.

JELF, Richard William (1798–1871), principal of King's College, London; educated at Eton and Christ Church, Oxford; fellow of Oriel College, 1820; MA, 1823; DD, 1839; preceptor to Prince George (afterwards king of Hanover), 1826–39; canon of Christ Church, 1830; Bampton lecturer, 1844; principal of King's College, London, 1844–68; one of the doctors who condemned *Pusey's sermon, 1847; compelled Maurice to resign professorship, 1853; edited *Jewel's works (1848).

JELF, William Edward (1811–1875), divine and scholar; brother of Richard William *Jelf; of Eton and Christ Church, Oxford; tutor, 1836–49, and some time senior censor; MA, 1836; BD, 1844; Bampton lecturer, 1857; vicar of Carleton, 1849–54; published Greek grammar (1842–5) and controversial tracts.

JELLETT, John Hewitt (1817–1888), provost of Trinity College, Dublin; fellow of Trinity College, Dublin, 1840; MA, 1843; DD, 1881; professor of natural philosophy, Dublin, 1848; commissioner of Irish education, 1868; president of Royal Irish Academy, 1869; provost of Trinity College, Dublin, 1881–8; published mathematical and theological works.

JELLICOE, (John) Basil (Lee) (1899–1935), housing reformer; educated at Haileybury and Magdalen College, Oxford; deacon, 1922; priest, 1923; head of Magdalen College mission in Somers Town, 1921–7; largely responsible for formation (1924) of St Pancras House Improvement Society which rehoused some hundreds of families in flats at low but economic rents.

JELLICOE, John Rushworth, first Earl Jellicoe (1859–1935), admiral of the fleet; son of captain in merchant service; passed second into *Britannia* and first out (1874); qualified as gunnery lieutenant and served on staff of *Excellent* gunnery school, 1884–5 (under (Lord) *Fisher) and 1886–9; with Fisher at Admiralty, 1889–92; commander, 1891; commanded *Victoria*, flagship of Sir George *Tryon, 1893; picked up when she was rammed by the *Camperdown* off Tripoli; commanded *Ramillies*, flagship of Sir Michael Culme-Seymour, Mediterranean, 1893–6; captain, 1897; member of Ordnance Committee, 1897–8; flag captain with Sir E. H. *Seymour on China Station, 1898–1901; converted Wei-hai-wei into naval base; chief of staff with International Naval Brigade advancing on Peking (1900) after Boxer Rising; severely wounded in lung; naval assistant to the controller, Admiralty, 1902; commanded *Drake*, 1903–4; director of naval ordnance, 1905–7; stimulated accuracy of long-range gunnery by battle-practice; transferred responsibility for output of naval ordnance from War Office to Admiralty; rear-admiral, 1907; second-in-command, Atlantic Fleet, and KCVO, 1907; controller and third sea lord, 1908–10; secured inclusion of eight battleships in 1909–10 programme; demanded improved armour-piercing shells; vice-admiral commanding Atlantic Fleet, 1910–11; commanded second division of Home Fleet, 1911; second sea lord, 1912–14; commander-in-chief, Grand Fleet, 4 Aug. 1914, with flag in *Iron Duke* based on Scapa Flow; admiral, 1915; kept up vigilant blockade; sent a detached force under (Lord) *Beatty towards the Skagerrak to entice Germans northward (31 May 1916); on learning that contact had been established made all speed south; deployed into single line on his easternmost wing when

German battle fleet reported to westward; crossed the enemy's T, compelling them to alter course and steer parallel to him; thus placed himself between them and Germany; opened fire at 6.23 p.m.; Germans fell back, and reappearing at 7.10 again retreated before devastating fire, launching a torpedo attack which Jellicoe evaded by manœuvre; under cover of night Germans finally succeeded in returning to base with heavy losses; the publication of their claim of victory before receipt of Jellicoe's dispatches resulted in mistaken tradition that Jutland, if not a British defeat, was at least a drawn battle; in fact Jellicoe was correct in thinking that the Germans would not again risk such an encounter; appointed OM, 1916; first sea lord, Dec. 1916; accelerated arming of merchantmen; with entry of United States into war was able to implement convoy system, but was dismissed on Christmas Eve, 1917, Lloyd George having convinced himself that he was the embodiment of what he considered to be Admiralty negligence; viscount, 1918; admiral of fleet, 1919; enthusiastically received during tour of Empire (1919–20) to investigate naval defence; results included formation of naval base at Singapore and establishment of Royal Indian Navy and New Zealand naval division; governor-general, New Zealand, 1920–4; earl, 1925; president of British Legion, 1928–32; lies in St Paul's Cathedral alongside *Nelson and *Collingwood; a selfless character of deep religious convictions; radiated friendliness and sympathy, and inspired deepest devotion in his men who implicitly trusted his leadership; maintained imperturbable calm in battle and made his decisions with lightning speed.

JEMMAT, William (1596?–1678), Puritan divine; BA, Magdalen College, Oxford, 1614; MA; vicar of St Giles's, Reading, 1648–78; author and editor of theological works.

JENISON, Francis, Count Jenison Walworth (1764–1824), diplomat; settled with his family in Heidelberg, 1777; revisited England as ambassador for Hesse-Darmstadt, 1793; high chamberlain of Würtemberg, 1797–1816; died at Heidelberg.

JENISON (or JENNISON), Robert (1584?–1652), Puritan divine; fellow of St John's College, Cambridge, 1607–19; DD; first master of St Mary Magdalen's Hospital, Newcastle upon Tyne, 1619–52; vicar of St Nicholas, Newcastle upon Tyne, 1645–52; author of theological works.

JENISON, Robert (1590–1656), Jesuit; grandson of Thomas *Jenison; of Gray's Inn; seized as 'Beaumont' at Clerkenwell, 1628; rector of house of probation, Ghent, 1645–9.

JENISON, Robert, the younger (1649–1688), informer; grand-nephew of Robert *Jenison (1590–1656); studied at Douai and Gray's Inn; pretended conversion to Catholicism and made revelations concerning the 'Popish Plot'.

JENISON, Thomas (1525?–1587), auditor-general of Ireland and controller of the works at Berwick; bought Walworth, Durham, from Ayscough family.

JENKES, Henry (d. 1697), Gresham professor of rhetoric; MA, Aberdeen, 1646; fellow of Caius College, Cambridge; incorporated MA, Cambridge, 1649; Gresham professor of rhetoric, 1670–6; FRS, 1674; published theological works.

JENKIN, Charles Frewen (1865–1940), first professor of engineering science in the University of Oxford; son of H. C. F. *Jenkin; educated at Edinburgh Academy and University and Trinity College, Cambridge; a practical engineer until 1908; professor at Oxford, 1908–29; reported (1920) for Royal Air Force on materials for aircraft construction; investigations included 'corrosion fatigue'; CBE, 1919; FRS, 1931.

JENKIN, Henrietta Camilla (1807?–1885), novelist; née Jackson; published *Who breaks, pays* (1861) and other novels.

JENKIN, Henry Charles Fleeming (1833–1885), engineer and electrician; son of Henrietta Camilla *Jenkin; MA, Genoa; with Sir William Thomson (Lord Kelvin) made important experiments on the resistance and insulation of electric cables; engaged in fitting out submarine cables, 1858–73; FRS, 1865, and professor of engineering in University College, London, 1867, at Edinburgh, 1868; published *Magnetism and Electricity* (1873) and *Healthy Houses* (1878); invented telpherage (transport of goods by electricity), 1882; his *Miscellaneous Papers* edited by Sidney *Colvin and J. A. *Ewing (1887).

JENKIN, Robert (1656–1727), master of St John's College, Cambridge; fellow of St John's College, Cambridge, 1680–9; MA, 1681; DD, 1709; chaplain to Bishop Lake; refused to take the oaths to William and Mary, but complied under Anne; master of St John's College, Cambridge, 1711–27; Lady Margaret professor of divinity, 1711–27; published *Historical Examination of the Authority of General Councils* (1688; reprinted in Gibson's *Preservative*) and theological works.

JENKINS, David (1582–1663), Welsh judge and Royalist; BA, St Edmund Hall, Oxford, 1600; barrister, Gray's Inn, 1609, ancient, 1622; judge of great sessions for Carmarthen, Pembroke, and Cardiganshire, 1643; indicted Welsh

Parliamentarians; captured at Hereford, 1645; imprisoned till the Restoration; contested right of the parliament to try him, and published several Royalist treatises (collected, 1648), as well as *Eight Centuries of Reports* (1661); bencher of his inn, 1660; patron of Welsh bards in Glamorganshire.

JENKINS, David Llewelyn, Baron Jenkins (1899–1969), judge; educated at Charterhouse and Balliol College, Oxford; Craven scholar; served in Rifle Brigade in France, 1918; called to bar (Lincoln's Inn), 1923; devilled for J. H. Stamp; KC, 1938; served with RASC, 1939–43; transferred to Political Warfare Executive, under Sir Robert Bruce *Lockhart, 1943–5; appointed attorney-general of duchy of Lancaster, 1946; judge, Chancery Court, 1947; Appeal Court judge, 1949–59; lord of appeal in ordinary, 1959; chairman, lord chancellor's Law Reform Committee, and other committees concerned with law reform; bencher, Lincoln's Inn, 1945; hon. fellow, Balliol, 1950; governor, Sutton's Hospital in Charterhouse, 1953–65; chairman, Tancred studentship trustees; knighted, 1947; PC, 1949; life baron, 1959.

JENKINS, Ebenezer Evans (1820–1905), Wesleyan minister and missionary; worked at Madras till 1865; superintendent of the Hackney circuit from 1865; president of the Wesleyan Conference, 1880.

JENKINS, Henry (d. 1670), 'the modern Methuselah'; of Ellerton-upon-Swale, Yorkshire; claimed to have been born about 1501; buried at Bolton-on-Swale.

JENKINS, John (1592–1678), earliest English composer of instrumental music; gave lessons to Roger *l'Estrange and Roger *North; skilful on the lute and lyra-viol; his *Twelve Sonatas for two Violins and a Base, with Thorough Base for the Organ or Theorbo* issued (1660); composed also *Fancies* and *Rants*, and vocal pieces.

JENKINS, John Edward (1838–1910), politician and satirist; born at Bangalore; called to bar (Lincoln's Inn), 1864; retained by Aborigines Protection Society for British Guiana Coolie Commission, 1870; gained repute as author of *Ginx's Baby* (anonymous, 1870), a satire on sectarian education; originated Imperial Federation movement, 1871; first agent-general for Canada, 1874–6; Radical MP for Dundee, 1874–80; wrote other political satires and novels.

JENKINS, Joseph (*fl.* 1730), General Baptist minister.

JENKINS, Joseph (1743–1819), Particular Baptist; educated at King's College, Aberdeen; DD, Edinburgh, 1790; minister at Wrexham,

Blandford Street, London, and (from 1798) at East Street, Walworth, London; published theological tracts.

JENKINS, Joseph John (1811–1885), engraver and water-colour painter; left New Water-Colour Society for the Old, 1847, becoming secretary, 1854–64; introduced private views.

JENKINS, Sir Lawrence Hugh (1857–1928), Indian judge; called to bar (Lincoln's Inn), 1883; judge, High Court of Calcutta, 1896; chief justice, High Court of Judicature, Bombay, 1899–1908; member of Council of India, 1908–9; took large part in drafting Morley–Minto reforms; chief justice of Bengal, 1909–15; dealt with complicated conspiracy cases; member of judicial committee of Privy Council, 1916; knighted, 1899; master of Indian law and custom.

JENKINS, Sir Leoline (1623–1685), civilian and diplomat; travelled with pupils, 1655–8; fellow of Jesus College, Oxford, 1660, LL D, 1661, and principal, 1661–73; assisted *Sheldon in the foundation of his theatre; Sheldon's commissary at Canterbury; deputy-professor of civil law, 1662; judge of the Admiralty court, 1665, and of prerogative court of Canterbury, 1669; knighted, 1670, after he had obtained the setting aside in favour of Charles II of duchess of *Orleans's claims to *Henrietta Maria's personalty; MP, Hythe, 1673–8, and Oxford University, 1679–85; English representative at Congress of Cologne, 1673, at Nimeguen, 1676–9, being alone after Temple's recall; privy councillor, 1680; secretary of state, 1680–4; led opposition to exclusion bills and Hotham's proposal to print parliamentary proceedings, 1681; gave money for enlargement of Jesus College, Oxford, and endowed it with bulk of his property. As a judge he was responsible for the Statute of Distributions and partly for the Statute of Frauds.

JENKINS, Sir Richard (1785–1853), Indian statesman; intimate of Mountstuart *Elphinstone; acting resident at court of Dowlut Rao Scindia, 1804–5, and at Nagpore, 1807; resident of Nagpore, 1810–27; suggested annihilation of Pindaris; distinguished himself at repulse of Appa Sahib's attack on Sitabaldi, 1817; arrested and imprisoned Appa Sahib, 1818; chairman of East India Company, 1839; MP, Shrewsbury, 1830–1 and 1837–41; KCB; hon. DCL, Oxford.

JENKINS, Richard Walter (1925–1984), actor. See BURTON, RICHARD.

JENKINS, Robert (*fl.* 1731–1738), master mariner, the cutting off of whose ear by the Spanish Captain Fandino at Havana, 1731, precipitated war with Spain in 1739.

JENKINS, Thomas (d. 1798), painter; banker in Rome, and dealer in antiquities.

JENKINSON, Anthony (d. 1611), merchant, sea-captain, and traveller; wrote account of entry of Solyman the Great into Aleppo, 1553, and obtained permission to trade in Turkish ports; went to Russia, 1557, as captain-general and agent of the Muscovy Company, sailing round the North Cape and up the Dvina, afterwards sledging to Moscow; after being well received by the tsar went by water to Astrakhan, 1558; visited king of Bokhara, 1558; returned to Moscow, 1559, and England, 1560; being despatched with letters to the tsar and the shah, 1561, attempted to open up trade with Persia, but failed; while in command of a queen's ship captured Wilson, a Scottish pirate, 1565; obtained grant of White Sea trade for Muscovy Company, 1567, and in final mission secured its confirmation, 1571–2; sent on special mission to Embden, 1577; granted arms, 1569; the first Englishman in Central Asia.

JENKINSON, Charles, first earl of Liverpool and first Baron Hawkesbury (1727–1808), statesman; educated at Charterhouse and University College, Oxford; MA, 1752; under-secretary of state, 1761; MP, Cockermouth, 1761–7, Appleby, 1767–72, Harwich, 1772–4, Hastings, 1774–80, Saltash, 1761–86; secretary to the Treasury, 1763–5; led the 'king's friends' after retirement of Bute; privy councillor and vice-treasurer of Ireland, 1772; master of the Mint, 1775; secretary-at-war, 1778; president of Board of Trade, 1786; chancellor of the duchy of Lancaster, 1786; created Baron Hawkesbury, 1786; created earl, 1796; published *Collection of Treaties from 1648 to 1783* (1785); his *Coins of the Realm* reprinted by the bank (1880).

JENKINSON, Charles Cecil Cope, third earl of Liverpool (1784–1851), second son of Charles *Jenkinson, first earl of Liverpool; volunteer in Austrian Army at Austerlitz, 1805; MP, Sandwich, 1807–12, Bridgnorth, 1812–18, and East Grinstead, 1818–28; under-secretary for Home Department, 1807–9, for war, 1809; succeeded to earldom, 1828; lord steward, 1841–6.

JENKINSON, Sir (Charles) Hilary (1882–1961), deputy keeper of the public records; educated at Dulwich College and Pembroke College, Cambridge; first class, classical tripos, 1904; entered the Public Record Office, 1906; in charge of literary search room, 1912; carried out reorganization of this and repairing department and repository, 1912–38; secretary and principal assistant keeper, 1938; deputy keeper, 1947–54; brought in photographic service; served in Royal Garrison Artillery, 1916–18, and at War Office, 1918–20; Maitland memorial lecturer, Cambridge, 1911–35; lecturer, King's College, London, 1920–5, reader in palaeography and archives, 1925–47; publications include *English Court Hand* (with Charles *Johnson, 1915), *Later Court Hands in England from the Fifteenth to the Seventeenth Century* (1927), and *Manual of Archive Administration* (1922); joint secretary (and later vice-president), British Records Association; chairman, the directorate of the National Register; fellow, Society of Antiquaries; president, Jewish Historical Society, and Society of Archivists; CBE, 1943; knighted, 1949; hon. fellow, University College, London; hon. LL D, Aberdeen.

JENKINSON, Francis John Henry (1853–1923), librarian; BA, Trinity College, Cambridge; fellow of Trinity, 1878; university librarian, 1889–1923; specialized in study of incunabula and extended library's acquisitions, particularly among fifteenth-century books; Sandars reader in bibliography at Cambridge, 1907–8; an authority on Lepidoptera; works include edition of *Hisperica Famina* (1908).

JENKINSON, John Banks (1781–1840), bishop of St David's; nephew of Charles *Jenkinson, first earl of Liverpool; of Winchester and Christ Church; MA, 1807; DD, 1817; dean of Worcester, 1817–25, of Durham, 1827–40; bishop of St David's, 1825–40; maintained charity school at Carmarthen.

JENKINSON, Robert Banks, second earl of Liverpool (1770–1828), statesman; eldest son of Charles *Jenkinson, first earl of Liverpool; of Charterhouse and Christ Church, Oxford; in Paris at taking of the Bastille; elected for Appleby, 1790; MP, Rye, 1790–1803; appointed member of the India Board by Pitt; master of the Mint, 1799; as foreign secretary under *Addington, 1801–4, postponed the evacuation of Malta; created Baron Hawkesbury, 1803; reconciled Pitt and Addington, 1804; home secretary and leader in the upper house in Pitt's second ministry, 1804–6; led opposition to Grenville ministry; again home secretary, 1807–9; succeeded to earldom, 1808; secretary for war and the colonies under Perceval, 1809–12; introduced regency resolutions, 1810; proposed measure for strengthening the army, 1811; premier, 1812–27; KG, 1814; opposed to Catholic emancipation, but left it an open question in his Cabinet; vigorously supported Wellington in the Peninsula, carried on war with the United States, sent Napoleon to St Helena, promoted international prohibition of the slave trade; had to suspend Habeas Corpus Act, 1817, and pass six repressive acts, 1819–20; brought in a bill for the divorce of Queen *Caroline; renewed Insurrection Bill in Ireland, 1822; introduced legislation against the Catholic Association in Ireland, 1825; while opposed to the principle of Catholic emancipation favoured minor concessions; supported Canning in his foreign policy, and (1826) prepared to reduce the corn duties.

JENKS, Benjamin (1646–1724), divine; rector of Harley, Shropshire; author of devotional works.

JENKS, Edward (1861–1939), writer on law and history; educated at Dulwich College and King's College, Cambridge; first classes in law (1886) and history (1887); called to bar (Middle Temple), 1887; professor of law, Melbourne (1889–91), Liverpool (1892–6); reader in English law, Oxford, 1896–1903; principal and director of legal studies, Law Society, 1903–24; professor of English law, London, 1924–9; works include *The Government of Victoria (Australia)* (1891) and *Law and Politics in the Middle Ages* (1898); edited *A Digest of English Civil Law* (1905–17); FBA, 1930.

JENKS, Sylvester (1656?–1714), Roman Catholic divine; professor of philosophy at Douai, 1680–6; preacher-in-ordinary to James II; elected vicar-apostolic of northern district, 1713; his *Practical Discourses on the Morality of the Gospel* (1699, reprinted 1817), and *Blind Obedience of a Humble Penitent* (1699, 1872).

JENKYN, William (1613–1685), ejected minister; MA, Emmanuel College, Cambridge, 1635; vicar of Christ Church, Newgate, London, 1643; his living sequestrated, 1650, on account of his remonstrance against the trial of Charles I; imprisoned for participation in plot of Christopher *Love; restored to his living, 1655; ejected, 1662; one of the first 'merchants'' lecturers at Pinners' Hall, 1672; preached in Jewin Street; arrested, 1684; died in Newgate; his *Exposition of the Epistle of Jude* (1652–4) edited by James *Sherman (1840); published controversial works.

JENKYNS, Richard (1782–1854), master of Balliol College, Oxford; fellow of Balliol College, Oxford, 1802, tutor, 1813, bursar, 1814, master, 1819–54; MA, 1806; DD, 1819; vice-chancellor, 1824–8; dean of Wells, 1845–54; inaugurated open competition for scholarships; raised the college to the first rank in Oxford.

JENNENS, Charles (1700–1773), friend of *Handel; a nonjuror; nicknamed 'Solyman the Magnificent'; wrote words for *Saul* (1735), *Messiah* (1742), and *Belshazzar* (1745); printed worthless edition of Shakespeare's tragedies; collected a library at Gopsall.

JENNENS, Sir William (fl. 1661–1690), captain in the navy and Jacobite; knighted; captain of the *Ruby* in action of 3 June 1665, against the Dutch, and in that of 1–4 June 1666; commanded in the second post at the Vlie, 1666; captain of the *Victory* under Prince *Rupert, 1673; entered French Navy and served under Tourville at Beachy Head, 1690.

JENNER, Charles (1736–1774), novelist and poet; great-grandson of Sir Thomas *Jenner; of Prembroke Hall (MA, 1760) and Sidney Sussex College, Cambridge; incumbent of Claybrook and Craneford St John; published *The Placid Man, or Memoirs of Sir Charles Beville* (1770) and other works.

JENNER, David (d. 1691), divine; fellow of Sidney Sussex College, Cambridge; MA, 1662, and BD, 1668, *per literas regias*; prebendary of Salisbury, 1676; chaplain to the king; published *The Prerogative of Primogeniture* (1685).

JENNER, Edward (1749–1823), discoverer of vaccination; pupil of John *Hunter (1728–1793), 1770–2; began to practise at Berkeley, Gloucestershire, 1773; FRS, 1789; MD, St Andrews, 1792 (Oxford, 1813); first vaccinated from cowpox, 1796; published *Inquiry into Cause and Effects of the Variolae Vaccinae* (cowpox, 1798), *Further Observations* (1799), and *Complete Statement of Facts and Observations* (1800); made experiments in transmission of lymph; after parliamentary inquiry received grant of £10,000, 1802, a further sum of £20,000 being voted in 1806; had interviews with the tsar and the king of Prussia, 1814. In 1808 the National Vaccine Establishment was founded. Vaccination was made compulsory in England, 1853, having previously been enforced in Bavaria, Denmark, Sweden, Würtemberg, and Prussia. Statues of Jenner are in Kensington Gardens, Gloucester Cathedral, and at Boulogne and Brünn.

JENNER, Edward (1803–1872), author of *Flora of Tunbridge Wells* (1845).

JENNER, Sir Herbert (1778–1852), dean of the arches. See FUST.

JENNER, Thomas (fl. 1604–1670), author of *Quakerism Anatomiz'd and Confuted* (1670); of Christ's College, Cambridge.

JENNER, Thomas (fl. 1631–1656), author, engraver, and publisher; kept a print shop near the Royal Exchange; published *Soules Solace*, with engravings (1631), which George *Wither answered; also descriptive tracts, with portraits and other works.

JENNER, Sir Thomas (1638–1707), baron of the Exchequer; of Queens' College, Cambridge; barrister, Inner Temple, 1663; recorder of London, 1683; knighted, 1683; king's serjeant, 1684; MP for Rye, 1685–8; baron of the Exchequer, 1686; gave judgment in favour of the dispensing power, 1686; when on the Magdalen Commission opposed expulsion of the fellows; justice of common pleas, 1688; arrested while attempting to escape with James II, and sent to the Tower; resumed practice at the bar.

JENNER, Sir William, first baronet (1815–1898), physician; studied medicine at University College, London; LSA and MRCS, 1837; MD, London, 1844; professor of pathological anatomy at University College, London, 1849; physician to University College Hospital, 1854–76; consulting physician, 1879; Holme professor of clinical medicine at University College, 1860, and professor of principles and practice of medicine, 1863–72; FRCP, 1852, and president, 1881–8; FRS, 1864; hon. DCL, Oxford, 1870; hon. LL D, Cambridge, 1881; hon. LL D, Edinburgh, 1884; physician-extraordinary to Queen Victoria, 1861; physician-in-ordinary to the queen, 1862, and to prince of Wales, 1863; created baronet, 1868; KCB, 1872; GCB (civil), 1889; established the distinct identities of typhus and typhoid fevers; published medical works.

JENNER-FUST, Herbert (1806–1904), cricketer; son of Sir Herbert *Jenner; educated at Eton and Trinity Hall, Cambridge; LL B, 1829; LL D, 1835; called to bar, 1831; captain of first Cambridge cricket XI to meet Oxford, 1827; prominent in first-class cricket till 1836, especially as wicket-keeper; president of MCC, 1833.

JENNINGS, David (1691–1762), Dissenting tutor; pastor of Independent congregation, Wapping New Stairs, London, 1718–62; non-subscriber, 1719; Coward trustee and lecturer, 1743; divinity tutor from 1744; DD, St Andrews, 1749; his *Jewish Antiquities* (1766) edited by Philip *Furneaux.

JENNINGS (afterwards **HAMILTON), Frances** (d. 1730), elder sister of Sarah *Jennings, duchess of Marlborough; mentioned by *Pepys; courted by Richard *Talbot, earl and titular duke of Tyrconnel; married (Sir) George Hamilton.

JENNINGS, Hargrave (1817?–1890), author; some time secretary to Mapleson; published, besides romances, *The Indian Religions* (1858), *The Rosicrucians* (1870), *Phallicism* (1884), and other works of occult learning.

JENNINGS, Henry Constantine (1731–1819), virtuoso; educated at Westminster; resided eight years in Italy, where he bought at Rome the famous marble dog, sold for one thousand guineas (now at Duncombe Park, Yorkshire); while in Chelsea made collections of shells, precious stones, books, and prints; published *Free Inquiry into the Enormous Increase of Attornies* (1785) and other works; died within the rules of the King's Bench.

JENNINGS, John (d. 1723), Nonconformist minister and tutor; brother of David *Jennings; had Philip *Doddridge among his pupils at Kibworth.

JENNINGS, Sir John (1664–1743), admiral; commander-in-chief in the Medway, 1698; with *Rooke at Cadiz, 1702, Vigo, 1702, the capture of Gibraltar, 1704, and Battle of Malaga, 1704; knighted, 1704; rear-admiral, 1705; vice-admiral, 1708; admiral of the white, 1709; commanded off Lisbon, 1708–10; as commander-in-chief in the Mediterranean convoyed allied troops to Italy, 1713; MP, Queensborough, 1705–10, Portsmouth, 1710–11, and Rochester, 1715–34; a lord of the Admiralty, 1714–17 and 1718–27; governor of Greenwich, 1720; commanded fleet of observation on coast of Spain, 1726; rear-admiral of England, 1733.

JENNINGS, Louis John (1836–1893), journalist and politician; special correspondent of *The Times* in India, 1863, and, after Civil War in America, editor of *New York Times*; engaged in literary pursuits in London from 1876; Conservative MP, Stockport, 1885–93; edited *The Croker Papers* (1884).

JENNINGS, Sir Patrick Alfred (1831–1897), premier of New South Wales; born at Newry, Ireland; emigrated to goldfields of Victoria, 1852; settled at St Arnaud, 1855; migrated as squatter to Warbreccan, in Riverina district, New South Wales, 1863; member of legislative council, 1867–9; member of assembly for Murray district, 1869–72; KCMG, 1880; member of assembly for the Bogan, 1880; vice-president of executive council, 1883; colonial treasurer, 1885, and premier, 1886–7; member of legislative council, 1890.

JENNINGS, Sarah, duchess of Marlborough (1660–1744). See CHURCHILL, SARAH.

JENNINGS, Sir (William) Ivor (1903–1965), constitutional lawyer; educated at Bristol Grammar School and St Catharine's College, Cambridge; first class, part i, mathematical tripos, and parts i and ii, law tripos, 1923–5; Holt scholar, Gray's Inn, 1925; Barstow scholar, 1926; called to bar (Gray's Inn), 1928; lecturer in law, Leeds University, 1925–9; lecturer, London School of Economics, and reader in English law, 1930–40; published eleven books, including *Cabinet Government* (1936), *The Law and the Constitution* (1933), *Parliamentary Reform* (1934), *Parliament* (1939), and *A Federation for Western Europe*

(1940); principal, University College, Ceylon; first vice-chancellor, 1940–54; constitutional adviser and chief draughtsman to Pakistan, 1954–5; member, Malayan Constitutional Commission, 1956–7; master, Trinity Hall, Cambridge, 1954; vice-chancellor, 1961–3; Downing professor in the laws of England, 1962; other publications include (with C. M. Young) *Constitutional Laws of the British Empire* (1938), *The Approach to Self-Government* (1956), and *Party Politics* (3 vols., 1960–2); knighted, 1948; KC, 1949; KBE, 1955; FBA, 1955; bencher, Gray's Inn, 1958; honorary degrees in law from many British and overseas universities.

JENOUR, Joshua (1755–1853), author; member of Stationers' Company; author of poems, tales, pamphlets, translations of Boileau (1827), and other works.

JENYE, Thomas (*fl.* 1565–1583), rebel and poet; accompanied Thomas *Randolph (1523–1590) to Scotland, and Sir Henry *Norris to Paris; composed proclamation issued by northern rebels of 1569; was attainted; Spanish agent on the continent; implicated in the *Throckmorton conspiracy, 1584; his *Maister Randolphes Phantasey* (describing Moray's revolt), 1565, first printed (1890); published also (from Ronsard) *The Present Troobles in Fraunce* (1568).

JENYNGES, Edward (*fl.* 1574), poet; author of *Notable Hystory of two faithfull Louers named Alfagus and Archelaus* (1574).

JENYNS, Leonard (1800–1893), naturalist. See BLOMEFIELD.

JENYNS, Soame (1704–1787), author; of St John's College, Cambridge; published *Poems* (1752); MP, Dunwich, 1754–8, Cambridge, 1758–80; a commissioner of trade, 1755–80; his *Free Enquiry into the Nature and Origin of Evil* (1757) reviewed by *Johnson in *Literary Magazine*; *View of the Internal Evidence of the Christian Religion* (1776; 10th edn., 1798), translated into various foreign languages; works collected (1790).

JENYNS, Sir Stephen (d. 1524), lord mayor of London; master of the Merchant Taylors' Company, 1489; sheriff of London, 1498; lord mayor, 1508; knighted, 1509; founded Wolverhampton Grammar School.

JEPHCOTT, Sir Harry, first baronet (1891–1978), pharmaceutical chemist and industrialist; son of train driver; educated at King Edward's Grammar School, Camp Hill, Birmingham; apprenticed to pharmacist; studied at West Ham Technical College; B.Sc., London, with first class in chemistry, 1915; M.Sc., 1918; FRIC, 1920; on staff of Joseph Nathan, Anglo-New Zealand company marketing 'Glaxo', 1919; concerned with process for increasing vitamin D content of foods and marketing of vitamin concentrate, 1924; called to bar (Middle Temple), 1925; general manager, Glaxo department, 1925; managing director, Glaxo Laboratories, 1935; managing director, Glaxo Group, 1939–56; assisted in development of cephalosporin antibiotics, 1955; honorary life-president, Glaxo Group, 1956; during 1939–45 war, adviser to Ministry of Food; chairman, council of school of pharmacy, London University, 1948–69; director, Metal Box Company, 1950–64; chairman, Association of British Chemical Manufacturers, 1947–52 and president, 1952–5; chairman, Council for Scientific and Industrial Research, 1956–61; governor, London School of Economics, 1952–68; president, Royal Institute of Chemistry, 1953–5; knighted, 1946; created baronet, 1962; hon. D.Sc., Birmingham.

JEPHSON, Arthur Jermy Mounteney (1858–1908), explorer; accompanied (Sir) H. M. *Stanley through forests to Lake Albert for relief of Emin Pasha, 1888; imprisoned with Emin at Dufile, Aug. 1888; rejoined Stanley at Kavali (Feb. 1889), and subsequently rescued Emin; queen's messenger, 1895; published *Emin Pasha and the Rebellion at the Equator* (1890), and native folk tales.

JEPHSON, Robert (1736–1803), dramatist and poet; friend of William Gerard *Hamilton; master of the horse in Ireland from 1767; his tragedy *Braganza* (with epilogue by Horace *Walpole) successfully produced at Drury Lane, 1775; his *Conspiracy* acted by *Kemble, 1796; his *Count of Narbonne* played by *Henderson at Covent Garden, 1781 (epilogue by *Malone), and afterwards by John Philip Kemble in Dublin, and his *Julia, or the Italian Lover* performed by Kemble and Mrs *Siddons (Drury Lane, 1787); published also poems and other works.

JEPHSON, William (1615?–1659?), colonel; MP, Stockbridge, in Long Parliament (one of those expelled by Pride); served against rebels in Ireland; lieutenant-governor of Portsmouth, 1644; governor of Bandon, 1646; deserted with Lord *Inchiquin, 1668; as representative of Cork in second protectorate parliament (1656) proposed to offer the crown to *Cromwell; envoy-extraordinary to Sweden, 1657.

JERDAN, William (1782–1869), journalist; came to London from Kelso, 1801; began journalistic career on the *Aurora*, 1806, and the *Pilot*, 1808; joined *Morning Post*; first to seize Perceval's assassin in lobby of House of Commons, 1812; conducted *The Satirist*, 1807–14;

edited *The Sun*, 1813–17; intimate of Canning; in Paris at entry of Louis XVIII, 1814; edited *Literary Gazette*, 1817–50, being sole proprietor from 1843; helped to found Royal Society of Literature, 1821, and Royal Geographical Society, 1830; FSA, 1826; edited for Camden Society, *Rutland Papers* (1842) and *Perth Correspondence*; published *National Portrait Gallery of the Nineteenth Century* (1830–4); obtained civil list pension, 1853; published *Autobiography* (1852–3) and *Men I have known* (1866); figures in *Maclise's *Fraserians*.

JERDON, Thomas Claverhill (1811–1872), zoologist; author of *Birds of India* (1862–4).

JEREMIE, James Amiraux (1802–1872), dean of Lincoln; born in Guernsey; fellow of Trinity College, Cambridge, 1826; MA, 1827; DD, 1850; prebendary of Lincoln, 1834, and dean, 1864–72; professor of classics and literature at Haileybury, 1830–50; dean of Haileybury, 1838; Christian advocate at Cambridge, 1833–4, and regius professor of divinity, 1850–70; founded Septuagint prizes; published *History of the Church in the Second and Third Centuries* (1852).

JEREMIE, Sir **John** (1795–1841), colonial judge; advocate in Guernsey; chief justice of St Lucia, 1824–30; published *Four Essays on Colonial Slavery* (1831); his appointment as procureur-général of the Mauritius resisted by supporters of slavery, 1832–3; judge in Ceylon, 1836; governor of Sierra Leone, 1840–1; knighted, 1840.

JERMAN, Edward (d. 1668), architect of the Royal Exchange (burnt, 1838), Fishmongers' Hall, and other buildings erected after the fire.

JERMIN (or GERMAN), Michael (1591–1659), divine; fellow of Corpus Christi College, Oxford, 1615; MA, 1615; DD, Leiden, and, 1624, Oxford; chaplain to the electress palatine and afterwards to Charles I; rector of St Martin's, Ludgate, 1626–43; ejected as Royalist; published commentaries on Proverbs and Ecclesiastes.

JERMY, Isaac (1789–1848), recorder of Norwich, 1831–48; BA, Christ Church, Oxford, 1812; barrister, Lincoln's Inn, 1814; known as Preston till 1838; his succession to Stanfield Hall forcibly resisted, 1838; murdered there by James Blomfield *Rush.

JERMY, Isaac Jermy (1821–1848), son of Isaac *Jermy; MA, Trinity College, Cambridge, 1848; murdered by James Blomfield *Rush.

JERMY, Seth (d. 1724), captain in the navy; lieutenant of the *Northumberland* at Barfleur, 1692; while on convoy duty at mouth of the Thames, 1707, captured by six French galleys.

JERMYN, George Bitton (1789–1857), antiquary; nephew of Henry *Jermyn (1767–1820); of Caius College and Trinity Hall, Cambridge; LL D, 1826; died in Sardinia; made genealogical collections for history of Suffolk and compiled a family history.

JERMYN, Henry, first earl of St Albans (d. 1684), courtier; vice-chamberlain to Queen *Henrietta Maria, 1628, and her master of the horse, 1639; MP, Liverpool, 1628, Corfe Castle in Short Parliament; after being engaged in 'first army plot', 1641, escaped to France, 1641; returned, 1643; secretary to Queen Henrietta Maria, commander of her bodyguard; created Baron Jermyn, 1643; accompanied Henrietta Maria to France, 1644; governor of Jersey, 1644; proposed to cede Jersey to France in exchange for help; persuaded Charles II to accept the terms offered by the Scots; remained at Paris till the Restoration; created earl of St Albans, 1660; lord chamberlain, 1674; as ambassador at Paris negotiated Charles II's marriage, a treaty with France (1667), and in 1669 preliminaries of Treaty of Dover; planned St James's Square and gave his name to Jermyn Street; the patron of Cowley, but satirized by *Marvell.

JERMYN, Henry, first Baron Dover (1636–1708), nephew of Henry *Jermyn, first earl of St Albans; master of the horse to duke of York, 1660; intrigued with Lady *Castlemaine and Lady Shrewsbury; wounded in duel with Colonel Thomas Howard, 1662; being a Romanist was created Baron Dover by James II, 1685; a commissioner of the Treasury, 1687; entrusted with the prince of Wales at the Revolution; followed James to France; commanded troop at the Boyne, 1690; reconciled to William III; buried at Bruges.

JERMYN, Henry (1767–1820), Suffolk antiquary; of St John's College, Cambridge; barrister, Lincoln's Inn; his manuscript collections in British Museum.

JERMYN, James (d. 1852), philologist; cousin of Henry *Jermyn (1767–1820); author of *Book of English Epithets* (1849) and other works.

JERNINGHAM, Edward (1737–1812), poet and dramatist; friend of *Chesterfield and Horace *Walpole; satirized by Gifford and *Mathias; published *Rise and Progress of Scandinavian Poetry* (poem, 1784) and other verse; his *Siege of Berwick* acted at Covent Garden, 1793, re-edited by H. E. H. Jerningham, 1882; his *Margaret of Anjou* (1777) and *The Welch Heiress* (1795) produced at Drury Lane.

JERNINGHAM (or JERNEGAN), Sir **Henry** (d. 1571); received manor of Costessy, Norfolk, 1547, and founded that branch of the family; first important adherent of Queen Mary, 1553; master of the horse, 1557–8; KB, 1553; privy councillor, vice-chamberlain, and captain of the guard; routed Wyatt, 1554.

JEROME, Jerome Klapka (1859–1927), novelist and playwright; went on the stage and finally took to journalism; a founder of *The Idler* magazine, 1892; his best-known book, *Three Men in a Boat* (1889); his best-known play, *The Passing of the Third Floor Back* (1908).

JEROME, Stephen (*fl.* 1604–1650), author; MA, St John's College, Cambridge, 1607; author of *Origen's Repentance* (1619) and other works.

JERRAM, Charles (1770–1853), Evangelical divine; MA, Magdalene College, Cambridge, 1800; Norrisian prizeman, 1796; successor of Richard *Cecil as vicar of Chobham, 1810; rector of Witney, 1834; published theological works.

JERRAM, Sir (Thomas Henry) Martyn (1858–1933), admiral; entered navy, 1871; served mainly in training ships; commander, 1894; captain, 1899; rear-admiral, 1908; vice-admiral, 1913; commander-in-chief, China Station, 1913–15; KCB, 1914; commanded Second Battle Squadron in Grand Fleet (1915–16) and in *King George V* led battle line at Jutland; KCMG, 1916; admiral and retired, 1917; president of committee on pay scales (1918), of Permanent Welfare Committee (1919), and Naval Prize Tribunal (1925); GCMG, 1919.

JERRARD, George Birch (d. 1863), mathematician; BA, Trinity College, Dublin, 1827; published writings relating to theory of equations.

JERROLD, Douglas Francis (1893–1964), author and publisher; educated at Westminster and New College, Oxford; secretary, Oxford Union; served in Royal Naval Division in Gallipoli and France during 1914–18 war; severely wounded; civil servant in Ministry of Food, 1918, and Treasury, 1920–3; became publisher, first with Benn Brothers, 1923–8, where he collaborated with (Sir) Victor *Gollancz; later director, 1929–45, and chairman, 1945–59, of Eyre and Spottiswoode; also edited the *English Review*, 1930–6, and the *New English Review*, 1945–50; held strongly right-wing views; chairman, Author's Club; prolific writer; publications include a novel, *Storm over Europe* (1930), his autobiography, *Georgian Adventure* (1937), and *An Introduction to the History of England* (of which he finished only the first volume, 1949).

JERROLD, Douglas William (1803–1857), author; appeared on the stage as a child; midshipman, 1813–15; while a printer's assistant began to contribute to papers and magazines; made reputation as playwright with *Black-eyed*

Susan at the Surrey, 1829 (Drury Lane, 1835); his *Bride of Ludgate* acted at Drury Lane, 1831; *Time works Wonders* produced at the Haymarket, 1845; contributed to *Athenaeum, Blackwood*, and other publications; published in *Punch* (1846) *Mrs. Caudle's Curtain Lectures*, and was a constant contributor, 1841–57; started *Douglas Jerrold's Shilling Magazine*, 1845, and *Douglas Jerrold's Weekly Newspaper*, 1846; published *The Story of a Feather* (1844) and several novels; from 1852 till death edited *Lloyd's Weekly Newspaper*; enjoyed great reputation as a wit.

JERROLD, William Blanchard (1826–1884), journalist and author; son of Douglas *Jerrold; contributed to *Douglas Jerrold's Weekly Newspaper* and *Daily News*; Crystal Palace commissioner in Norway and Sweden, 1853; produced *Cool as a Cucumber* at Lyceum, 1851; edited *Lloyd's Weekly* from 1857; collaborated with Gustave Doré in Paris; published *Life of Napoleon III* (1874–82) with help of the empress; also gastronomic manuals, lives of Douglas Jerrold and George *Cruikshank, *History of Industrial Exhibitions* (1862), and novels, including *Cent. per Cent.* (1871); founder and president of English branch of International Association for Assimilation of Copyright Laws.

JERSEY, countess of (1849–1945). See VILLIERS, MARGARET ELIZABETH CHILD-.

JERSEY, earls of. See VILLIERS, EDWARD, first earl, 1656–1711; VILLIERS, WILLIAM, second earl, 1682?–1721; VILLIERS, GEORGE BUSSY, fourth earl, 1735–1805; VILLIERS, GEORGE CHILD-, fifth earl, 1773–1859; VILLIERS, VICTOR ALBERT GEORGE CHILD-, seventh earl, 1845–1915.

JERVAIS (or JARVIS), Thomas (d. 1799), glass-painter; executed *Reynolds's design for New College Chapel, Oxford (1787), and West's for the east window of St George's, Windsor.

JERVAS (or JARVIS), Charles (1675?–1739), portrait painter and translator of *Don Quixote*; studied under *Kneller; copied antiques at Rome; painted portraits of George II and Queen *Caroline; taught *Pope and painted his portrait thrice, as well as those of *Swift, *Arbuthnot, *Newton, and the duchess of *Queensberry; his version of *Don Quixote* (published 1742) frequently reprinted.

JERVIS, John, earl of St Vincent (1735–1823), admiral of the fleet; in West Indies as able seaman and midshipman; lieutenant, 1755; engaged a French privateer off Cape Gata, 1757; led advanced squadron in charge of transports past Quebec, and was entrusted by Wolfe with his last message to his fiancée, 1759; carried important despatches to Lord *Amherst, 1760; exacted satisfaction for seizure of Turkish slaves in the *Alarm* at Genoa, 1769; saved the *Alarm* in violent gale at Marseilles, 1770; with Samuel *Barrington visited Kronstadt, Stockholm, Carlscrona, and Copenhagen, 1774, and the western ports of France, 1775; commanded the *Foudroyant* at Ushant, 1778 (afterwards giving strong evidence in favour of *Keppel) and at the three reliefs of Gibraltar, 1780–2; captured the Pégase, 1782; KB, 1782; MP, Launceston, 1783, Yarmouth, 1784; on fortification commission, 1785–6; rear-admiral, 1787; vice-admiral, 1793; co-operated with Sir Charles (afterwards Earl) Grey in capture of Martinique and Guadeloupe, 1794; admiral, 1795, and commander-in-chief in the Mediterranean; defeated Spanish fleet off Cape St Vincent, 14 Feb. 1797, capturing four ships and disabling many others; received pension of £3,000 and the freedom of the city; created earl of St Vincent, 1797; kept Cadiz sealed and sent *Nelson to Aboukir and *Duckworth to Minorca, 1798; successfully repressed mutiny; censured by the Admiralty for sending home Sir John *Orde, and obliged by failing health to resign his post, 1799; after a few months assumed command of the Channel Fleet, in which he enforced the severe discipline recently applied in the Mediterranean; as first lord of the Admiralty in Addington ministry organized attack on the armed neutrality, 1801, and defence of the coast against French invasion; obtained (1802) commission of inquiry which resulted (1806) in impeachment of *Melville and thorough reform of naval administration; being attacked by Pitt for not building sufficient ships, he undertook no further public service till after Pitt's death; resumed command in Channel, 1806; retired, 1807; admiral of the fleet, 1821.

JERVIS, John (1752–1820), mineralogist; Unitarian minister at Lympstone, 1773–1820; brother of Thomas *Jervis.

JERVIS, Sir **John** (1802–1856), lord chief justice of common pleas; second cousin of John *Jervis, earl of St Vincent; of Westminster, Trinity College, Cambridge, and the Middle Temple; called, 1824; reported in Exchequer court, 1826–32; Liberal MP for Chester, 1832–50; voted against Melbourne on Jamaica Bill, 1839; as attorney-general under Russell (1846–50) introduced the measures (1848) relating to justices of the peace known by his name; knighted, 1846; president of Common Law Pleading Commission, 1850; privy councillor, 1850; lord chief justice of common pleas, 1850–6; contributed to the *Jurist*; published treatise on the office and duties of coroners (1829) and edited *Reports*.

JERVIS, Sir **John Jervis White,** first baronet (1766–1830), author; BA, Dublin, and LL D; barrister-at-law; assumed name of Jervis;

raised volunteer corps, 1796 and 1803; created Irish baronet, 1797; published works, including *Refutation of M. M. de Montgaillard's Calumnies against British Policy* (1812).

JERVIS, Thomas (1748–1833), Unitarian minister and Dr Williams's trustee; successor of *Kippis at Prince's Street, Westminster, 1796; afterwards at Mill Hill, Leeds; contributor to *Gentleman's Magazine* and hymn-writer.

JERVIS, William Henley Pearson- (1813–1883), author of *History of the Church of France* (1872) and *The Gallican Church and the French Revolution* (1882); son of Hugh Nicolas *Pearson; of Harrow and Christ Church, Oxford; MA, 1838; assumed name of Jervis, 1865; rector of St Nicholas, Guildford, 1837.

JERVISE, Andrew (1820–1878), Scottish antiquary; examiner of registers, 1856; published *Epitaphs and Inscriptions from Burial Grounds and Old Buildings in North East Scotland* (vol. i, 1875, vol. ii (posthumous), 1879), and similar works.

JERVISWOODE, Lord (1804–1879). See BAILLIE, CHARLES.

JERVOIS, Sir **William Francis Drummond** (1821–1897), lieutenant-general; second lieutenant, Royal Engineers, 1839; lieutenant, 1841; brevet-major, 1854; lieutenant-colonel, 1862; colonel, 1872; major-general, 1877; lieutenant-general, 1882; colonel-commandant of Royal Engineers, 1893; went to Cape of Good Hope, 1841, and made valuable surveys of many districts; served in Kaffir War; commanded company of sappers and miners at Woolwich and Chatham, 1849–52, and at Alderney, 1852–4; commanding royal engineer of London military district, 1855; assistant inspector-general of fortifications at War Office, 1856; secretary to Royal Commission on Defences of United Kingdom, 1859–60; director of works for fortifications, 1862; CB (civil), 1863; made frequent visits to British colonies to inspect fortifications; KCMG, 1874; governor of Straits Settlements, 1875; appointed adviser to Australian colonies as to defence of chief ports, 1877; governor of South Australia, 1877, and of New Zealand, 1882–9; GCMG, 1878; FRS, 1888; published writings relating to defences.

JESSE, Edward (1780–1868), writer on natural history; deputy-surveyor of royal parks and palaces; friend of *Croker and John *Mitford; published *Gleanings in Natural History* (three series, 1832–4–5), *A Summer's Day at Hampton Court* (1839), and other works; edited *Walton's Angler* and *White's Selborne.*

JESSE, John Heneage (1815–1874), historical writer; son of Edward *Jesse; educated at Eton;

clerk in the Admiralty; author of *Memoirs* of the court of England, of George *Selwyn and his contemporaries (1843), of the Pretenders (1845), of Richard III (1862) and George III (1867), works on London, and *Celebrated Etonians* (published 1875).

JESSEL, Sir George (1824–1883), master of the Rolls; educated at London University, of which he was vice-chancellor, 1881–3; MA, 1844; barrister, Lincoln's Inn, 1847 (treasurer, 1883); practised as conveyancer; leading junior in Rolls court; QC, 1865; Liberal MP for Dover, 1868–73; solicitor-general, 1871–3; master of the Rolls, 1873–83; privy councillor, 1873; working head of the Patent Office, 1873–83; one of the greatest English equity judges; active member of the commission on working of the medical acts, 1881; a baronetcy conferred on his heir after his death, 1883.

JESSEY (or JACIE), Henry (1601–1663), Baptist divine; BA, St John's College, Cambridge, 1623; episcopally ordained, 1627; deprived of vicarage of Aughton for nonconformity, 1634; Independent pastor in Southwark, 1637; adopted Baptist views, 1645; assisted in founding first Welsh Independent Church, 1639; Baptist 'teacher' in Swan Alley, Coleman Street, 1653; a 'trier' and 'expurgator'; collected money for Jews in Jerusalem, 1657; frequently arrested after the Restoration; published annual *Scripture Kalendars* (1645–64) and devotional works, and planned a revision of the Bible.

JESSOP, Constantine (1602?–1658), Presbyterian minister; BA, Trinity College, Dublin, and (1632) MA, Jesus College, Oxford; obtained sequestered benefices of Fyfield, 1643, and St Nicholas, Bristol, 1647; rector of Wimborne Minster, 1654–8; published theological works.

JESSOP, Gilbert Laird (1874–1955), cricketer; educated at Cheltenham Grammar School and Christ's College, Cambridge; captain of cricket, 1899; first played for Gloucestershire, 1894; captain, 1900–13; played in 18 test matches, first playing for England in 1899; nicknamed 'the Croucher', he was a fast scorer with a bewildering variety of strokes; played 5 innings of over 200, in 1903 scoring 286 in 175 minutes; made 53 centuries, 6 of them in less than 1 hour; scored over 1,000 runs in 14 seasons; brilliant fielder and fast bowler; published *A Cricketer's Log* (1922) and *Cricket and How to Play It* (1925).

JESSOPP, Augustus (1823–1914), schoolmaster and historical writer; BA, St John's College, Cambridge; headmaster of King Edward VI's School, Norwich, which he transformed into a modern public school, 1859–79; rector of Scarning, Norfolk, 1879–1911; works include *One Generation of a Norfolk House* (the Walpoles, 1878) and *The Coming of the Friars* (1889); edited *Visitations of Diocese of Norwich, 1492–1532* (1888), etc.

JEUNE, Francis (1806–1868), bishop of Peterborough; MA, Pembroke College, Oxford, 1830; DCL, 1834; fellow of Pembroke College, 1830–7; secretary to Sir John *Colborne in Canada, 1832; headmaster of King Edward's School, Birmingham, 1834–8; dean of Jersey, 1838–43; master of Pembroke College, Oxford, 1843–64; active member of Oxford Commission, 1850; vice-chancellor, 1858–62; dean of Lincoln, 1864; bishop of Peterborough, 1864–8.

JEUNE, Francis Henry, Baron St Helier (1843–1905), judge; eldest son of Francis *Jeune; scholar of Harrow and Balliol College, Oxford; first-class classic, 1865; obtained Stanhope (1863) and Arnold (1867) essay prizes; called to bar, 1868; original fellow of Hertford College, 1874; counsel for Tichborne plaintiff in action of ejectment, 1871–2; had large ecclesiastical practice; counsel for evangelicals in *Mackonochie case; counsel for Louis *Riel in application for leave to appeal; chancellor of several dioceses; QC, 1888; counsel for Edward *King in ritual case, 1889–90; judge of Probate, Divorce, and Admiralty division, and knighted, 1891; president of Probate division, 1892; made court a model of efficiency and dispatch; judge-advocate-general without payment, 1892–1904; KCB, 1897; GCB, 1902; resigned presidency of Probate division through ill health and created peer, Jan. 1905.

JEVON, Thomas (1652–1688), actor and dramatist; brother-in-law of Thomas *Shadwell; played low comedy parts in plays by *D'Urfey, *Shadwell, Mountford's *Dr. Faustus*, and his own play, *The Devil of a Wife* (1686).

JEVONS, Mrs Mary Anne (1795–1845), author of *Sonnets and other Poems, chiefly devotional* (1845); daughter of William *Roscoe; married Thomas Jevons, 1825.

JEVONS, William Stanley (1835–1882), economist and logician; son of Mrs Mary Anne *Jevons; educated at University College, London; assayer, Sydney Mint, 1854–9; published *Remarks on the Australian Goldfields* (1859); returned to England and graduated MA, London, with the Gold Medal for philosophy and political economy, 1862; went to Owens College as tutor, 1863; issued his *Pure Logic* (founded on *Boole's mathematical method, 1864); predicted future exhaustion of British coal supply, 1865; professor of logic, political economy, and philosophy at Owens College, 1866–79; exhibited his reasoning machine in Manchester and Liverpool,

1866; published *Substitution of Similars* (1869), *Elementary Lessons in Logic* (1870), *Studies in Deductive Logic* (1880), and *Principles of Science* (1874); wrote on currency, 1868–9; defended Lowe's match tax, 1871; issued *Theory of Political Economy* (treated as a mathematical science, 1871), with *Primer* (1878); FRS, 1872; hon. LL D, Edinburgh, 1875; professor of political economy, University College, London, 1876–81; published *The State in Relation to Labour* (1882); his *Methods of Social Reform* published posthumously; drowned at Bulverhythe, Sussex; a fund for the encouragement of economic research was founded in his honour.

JEWEL, John (1522–1571), bishop of Salisbury; fellow of Corpus Christi College, Oxford, 1542–53; MA, 1545; trained in biblical criticism by John *Parkhurst (1512?–1575); vicar of Sunningwell, 1551; deprived of his fellowship under Mary; notary to *Cranmer and *Ridley in their disputation, 1554; fled to Frankfort to avoid persecution, 1555, though he had signed Romish articles; joined Richard *Cox against *Knox; afterwards stayed with *Peter Martyr at Strasburg and Zurich; returned to England, 1559; one of the Protestant disputants at the Westminster Conference, 1559; bishop of Salisbury, 1560–71; challenged Romanist antagonists to prove their doctrines; carried on controversies with Henry *Cole and Thomas *Harding (1516–1572); issued in Latin his *Apologia pro Ecclesia Anglicana* (1562) and *Defence of the Apology* (1570); DD, Oxford, 1575; ultimately identified himself with Anglicanism and opposed the Puritans; his answer to *Cartwright and *View of a Seditious Bull* issued posthumously; entrusted by convocation with revision of the articles, 1571; built cathedral library at Salisbury; encouraged education, *Hooker being among his protégés. His complete works have been edited by Fuller (1609), *Jelf (1848), and Eyre (1845–50).

JEWETT, Randolph (or Randal) (d. 1675), composer of anthems and organist of St Patrick and Christ Church, Dublin; Mus.Bac., Trinity College, Dublin; minor canon of St Paul's Cathedral, 1661; organist of Winchester.

JEWITT, Arthur (1772–1852), topographer; author of *History of Lincolnshire* (1817), of Buxton (1810), *The Northern Star, or Yorkshire Magazine* (1817–18), and mathematical handbooks.

JEWITT, Llewellynn Frederick William (1816–1886), antiquary; son of Arthur *Jewitt; executed drawings for Charles *Knight's publications and Parker's architectural works; chief librarian of Plymouth, 1849–53; edited *Derby Telegraph*, 1853–68; established *Reliquary*, 1860; FSA, 1853; published *Ceramic Art of Great Britain*

(1878), *The Wedgwoods* (1865), *Graves, Mounds, and their Contents* (1870), and other works; collaborated with Samuel Carter *Hall in *Stately Homes of England* (1874–7).

JEWITT, Thomas Orlando Sheldon (1799–1869), wood engraver; brother of Llewellynn Frederick William *Jewitt; illustrated Parker's architectural works and other publications.

JEWSBURY, Geraldine Endsor (1812–1880), novelist; friend of the *Carlyles, Helen *Faucit, and William Edward *Forster; published *Zoe* (1845), *The Half-Sisters* (1848), *Marian Withers* (1851), and *Right or Wrong* (1859); and juvenile fiction.

JEWSBURY, Maria Jane (1800–1833), afterwards Mrs Fletcher; authoress; sister of Geraldine Endsor *Jewsbury; contributed to the *Athenaeum*; went to India with her husband; praised by *Wordsworth and Christopher *North; published *Phantasmagoria* (1824), *The Three Histories* (1830), and other works; died of cholera at Poona.

JEX-BLAKE, Sophia Louisa (1840–1912), physician; sister of T. W. *Jex-Blake; medical student at Edinburgh, 1869–72; on being refused, with other women students, right to graduate, founded London School of Medicine for Women, 1874; gained legal right to practise in Great Britain, 1877; practised in Edinburgh, 1878–99.

JEX-BLAKE, Thomas William (1832–1915), schoolmaster and dean of Wells; educated at Rugby and University College, Oxford; fellow of The Queen's College, Oxford, 1855; assistant master at Rugby, 1858–68; principal of Cheltenham College, 1868–74; headmaster of Rugby, which he restored to prosperity, 1874–87; dean of Wells, 1891–1910.

JEZREEL, James Jershom (1840–1885), founder of the 'New and Latter House of Israel', 1876; originally named James White; began life as private in the army; married Clarissa Rogers ('Queen Esther'), 1879, and with her visited America and made converts; published *Extracts from the Flying Scroll* (1879–81); erected extensive building for his sect at Gillingham.

JINNAH, Mahomed Ali (1876–1948), creator of Pakistan; son of Karachi merchant; called to bar (Lincoln's Inn), 1896; practised in Bombay; represented Bombay Moslems on Imperial Legislative Council, 1909–19; joined Moslem League, 1913; resigned from Indian National Congress opposing non-co-operation policy, 1920; led independent party in Legislative Assembly from 1923; powerful in Moslem

League and took lead in seeking Hindu–Moslem unity; attended Round Table Conference, 1930–1; remained in England; returned to India to devote himself to Moslem interests, 1934; inspired Moslem League resolution demanding Pakistan, 1940; took direct action leading to bitter communal fighting, 1946; first governor-general of Pakistan, 1947–8.

JOACHIM, Harold Henry (1868–1938), philosopher; educated at Harrow and Balliol College, Oxford; first class, Lit. Hum., 1890; fellow and tutor in philosophy, Merton, 1897–1919; Wykeham professor of logic, 1919–35; mainly inspired by Hegel; publications include *A Study of the Ethics of Spinoza* (1901), *The Nature of Truth* (1906, presenting the coherence theory), and translation, with commentary, of Aristotle's *De generatione et corruptione* (1922); FBA, 1922.

JOAD, Cyril Edwin Mitchinson (1891–1953), writer and teacher; educated at Blundell's School, Tiverton, and Balliol College, Oxford; first class, Lit. Hum., 1914; with labour exchanges department, Board of Trade (later Ministry of Labour), 1914–30; head, philosophy department, Birkbeck College, 1930–53; D.Litt., 1936; reader in philosophy, 1945–53; stimulating and lucid teacher and prolific writer; Plato and Aristotle his two great loves; lively member of first 'Brains Trust'; moved from agnosticism to Christianity; published *The Recovery of Belief* (1952).

JOAN (JOANNA, JONE, or JANE) (1165–1199), queen of Sicily; third daughter of Henry II of England; married to William II, king of Sicily, 1177; detained after his death (1189) by Tancred, the new king of Sicily, by whom she was given up to her brother Richard, 1190; accompanied him and Queen Berengaria to Palestine, 1191; proposed as wife for Saphadin, brother of Saladin; married Raymond VI, count of Toulouse, 1196; died at Rouen at birth of her second child; buried at Fontevraud, where she was, when dying, veiled as a nun.

JOAN (JOANNA, ANNA, or JANET) (d. 1237), princess of North Wales; according to *Tewkesbury Annals* a daughter of King John; married to *Llywelyn ab Iorwerth, 1206; obtained terms for her husband from King John, 1211; mediated between Henry III and the Welsh; Franciscan house founded in Anglesey at her burial place; her stone coffin now in Baron Hill Park, Beaumaris.

JOAN (or JOANNA) (1210–1238), queen of Scotland; eldest daughter of King John of England; betrothed to the younger Hugh of Lusignan, but (1221) married, at York, *Alexander II of Scotland; died in England; buried at Tarent Nunnery, Dorset.

JOAN (or JOANNA) OF ACRE, countess of Gloucester and Hertford (1272–1307), third daughter of Edward I and *Eleanor of Castile; after five years in Spain was betrothed to Hartmann, son of Rudolf of Habsburg, 1279; married at Westminster Abbey, 1290, Gilbert de *Clare (1243–1295); after his death privately married Ralph de *Monthermer, 1297.

JOAN (1321–1362), queen of Scotland; youngest child of Edward II; married to David *Bruce of Berwick, 1328, both parties being children; crowned at Scone, 1331; accompanied David to France when Baliol seized the crown, 1332; lived at Chateau Gaillard, 1334–41; allowed by Edward III to visit her husband while a prisoner in England; settled in England on account of the infidelity of David, receiving Hertford Castle as a residence; highly popular in Scotland.

JOAN (1328–1385), 'Fair Maid of Kent', daughter of *Edmund of Woodstock, earl of Kent; her marriage with William de *Montacute, second earl of Salisbury, set aside on the ground of pre-contract with Sir Thomas *Holland (d. 1360), 1349; became countess of Kent and Lady Wake of Liddell in her own right, 1352; married, as her second husband, *Edward the Black Prince, 1361; lived with him in Aquitaine, 1362–71; protected *John of Gaunt from the Londoners, 1377; mediated between Richard II and John of Gaunt, 1385.

JOAN (or JOANNA) OF NAVARRE (1370?–1437), queen of Henry IV of England; second daughter of Charles the Bad of Navarre; married first to John IV, duke of Brittany, 1386; when regent married by proxy to Henry IV, 1401, and in person at Winchester, 1403, leaving her Breton children under Burgundy's guardianship; accused of witchcraft, deprived of her revenues and imprisoned at Pevensey, 1419–22; buried at Canterbury.

JOAN, queen of Scotland (d. 1445). See JANE or JOHANNA.

JOAN OF KENT (d. 1550), Anabaptist martyr. See BOCHER, JOAN.

JOBSON, Sir Francis (d. 1573), lieutenant of the Tower, 1564; knighted by Edward VI.

JOBSON, Frederick James (1812–1881), Wesleyan minister; thrice assistant for a three years' term at the City Road Chapel; delegate at Methodist Episcopal Conference, Indianapolis, 1856, and the Sydney Conference, 1862; book steward, 1864; president of Wesleyan Methodist Conference, 1869; published religious works.

JOBSON, Richard (*fl.* 1620–1623), traveller and author; ascended the Gambia, 1620; published *The Golden Trade, or a Discovery of the River Gambia* (1623).

JOCELIN. See also JOSCELYN and JOSSELYN.

JOCELIN (d. 1199), bishop of Glasgow; abbot of Melrose, 1170; bishop of Glasgow, 1175–99; attended Council of Northampton, 1176; sent by *William the Lion to Rome to obtain removal of an interdict, 1181; built crypt and began choir, lady chapel, and central tower, Glasgow Cathedral.

JOCELIN (or **JOSCELIN**) (*fl.* 1200), Cistercian; compiled lives of St Patrick (first printed, 1624; translated by E. L. Swift, 1809) and other saints.

JOCELIN (or **JOSCELINE**) **OF WELLS** (d. 1242), bishop of Bath and Wells; justiciar of fines, 1203–5; bishop of Bath and Glastonbury, 1206–18, of Bath (and Wells) alone, 1206–42; named in preamble of Great Charter; justice-itinerant in western counties, 1218; took part with *Langton against Falkes de *Breauté, 1224; witnessed confirmation of the charter, 1236; buried at Wells, where he built the nave, choir, and west front, as well as the oldest part of the palace.

JOCELIN, Mrs Elizabeth (1596–1622), author of *The Mother's Legacie to her Unborne Childe* (published 1624, 3rd edn., reprinted, 1852); née Brooke; died in childbirth.

JOCELIN DE BRAKELOND (*fl.* 1200), chronicler; monk of Bury St Edmunds. His chronicle of St Edmund's Abbey (1173–1202), translated by T. E. Tomlins (1843) and edited by J. G. *Rokewood (1840) and T. *Arnold (1890), inspired *Carlyle's *Past and Present.*

JOCELYN, Percy (1764–1843), bishop of Clogher; son of Robert *Jocelyn, first earl of Roden; BA, Trinity College, Dublin, 1785; bishop of Ferns and Leighlin, 1809, of Clogher, 1820; deposed for scandalous crime.

JOCELYN, Robert, first (Irish) Viscount Jocelyn (1688?–1756), lord chancellor of Ireland; Irish barrister, 1706; entered Irish parliament, 1725; solicitor-general, 1727; attorney-general, 1730; lord chancellor of Ireland, 1739–56; created Baron Newport, 1743, Viscount Jocelyn, 1755; ten times lord justice.

JOCELYN, Robert, first earl of Roden (1731–1797), auditor-general of Ireland, 1750–97; son of Robert, first Viscount *Jocelyn; created Irish earl, 1771.

JOCELYN, Robert, third earl of Roden (1788–1870), grand master of the Orange Society; MP, Dundalk, 1810–20; created British peer (Baron Clanbrassil), 1821; JP (removed after Dolly's Brae riots, 1849).

JODRELL, Sir Paul (d. 1803), physician; fellow of St John's College, Cambridge; eleventh wrangler, 1769; MA, 1772; MD, 1786; knighted, 1787; physician to the nabob of Arcot, 1787; died at Madras.

JODRELL, Richard Paul (1745–1831), classical scholar and dramatist; brother of Sir Paul *Jodrell; contributed to *Musae Etonenses*; of Hertford College, Oxford; barrister, Lincoln's Inn, 1771; MP, Seaford, 1794–6; FRS and FSA; published *Illustrations of Euripides* (1778), *The Philology of the English Language* (1820), and plays, including *A Widow and no Widow* and *Seeing is Believing*, produced at the Haymarket, 1779 and 1783.

JODRELL, Sir Richard Paul, second baronet (1781–1861), poet; son of Richard Paul *Jodrell; of Eton and Magdalen College, Oxford; MA, 1806; barrister, Lincoln's Inn, 1803; succeeded to baronetcy of his maternal great-uncle, Sir John Lombe, 1817.

JOEL, Jack Barnato (1862–1940), financier and sportsman; career resembled that of his younger brother S. B. *Joel, whom he succeeded as chairman of the Johannesburg Consolidated Investment Company in 1931; won Derby in 1911 and 1921 and headed list of winning owners in 1908, 1913, and 1914.

JOEL, Solomon Barnato (1865–1931), financier and sportsman; nephew of Barnett *Barnato and brother of J. B. *Joel; partner in Barnato Brothers; chairman (from 1898) of Johannesburg Consolidated Investment Company; director of De Beers Consolidated Mines, Standard Bank of South Africa, and many other enterprises; a lavish host; patron of the theatre and of cricket; racing successes included the Two Thousand Guineas, Derby, and St Leger in 1915 with Pommern; headed list of winning owners, 1921.

JOFROI (or **GEOFFROY**) **OF WATERFORD** (*fl.* 1290), translator (Gotafridus).

JOHANNES AEGIDIUS (*fl.* 1230), Dominican and physician. See JOHN OF ST GILES.

JOHANNES DE SACRO BOSCO (*fl.* 1230), mathematician. See HOLYWOOD, JOHN.

JOHN (d. 1147), bishop of Glasgow, 1115; suspended by Archbishop *Thurstan of York, 1122; some time suffragan to the patriarch at Jerusalem; censured by Pope Honorius at Rome, 1125; withdrew to Tiron (Picardy) till 1128; chancellor to *David of Scotland, 1129; rebuilt Glasgow Cathedral.

JOHN (1167?–1216), king of England; youngest son of Henry II; called Lackland in boyhood by his father, whose favourite son he was; declared king of Ireland, 1177; taken to Normandy, 1183; with his brother, *Geoffrey of Brittany, made war on Richard, 1184, who refused to give him Aquitaine; sent to Ireland, 1185, where he alienated the natives by his insolence and the mercenaries by spending their pay; given a command in Normandy, 1187; hastened Henry II's death by his treachery, 1189; married Isabella of Gloucester, 1189, and received from Richard I the counties of Mortain, Derby, Dorset, Somerset, Devon, and Cornwall, the town of Nottingham, and several castles, with full rights of jurisdiction; returned to England, 1191, and kept royal state at Marlborough and Lancaster; headed the opposition to William *Longchamp (chancellor); had himself declared heir to the throne, 1191; with the assistance of the Londoners compelled Longchamp to leave England, 1191; on the news of Richard's imprisonment did homage to his enemy, Philip of France, for his continental dominions, 1193; made raids with foreign mercenaries on Richard's English territory, but was compelled to flee with Philip into France; attempted to prolong Richard I's captivity; excommunicated and deprived of his English lands, but forgiven by Richard through the mediation of their mother, *Eleanor, 1194; made war for him against Philip, and received back some of his lands and a pension, 1195; retired to Brittany on being accused by Philip to Richard, but was declared his brother's heir, 1199; acknowledged in Normandy, but resisted in the Angevin provinces by the adherents of *Arthur of Brittany; crowned at Westminster, 27 May 1199; returned to Normandy and made treaty with Philip of France, being acknowledged king of England and Duke of Normandy, with the homage of Brittany from Arthur; renounced alliance of the emperor and the count of Flanders, and gave his niece, Blanche, in marriage to Louis of France, 1200; divorced his wife, Avice, but retained her inheritance, 1200; married *Isabella of Angoulême, 1200; received homage from *William of Scotland, 1200; proceeded against the Poitevin lords who were allied with Isabella's betrothed, Hugh le Brun; sentenced by the French peers to forfeit all his fiefs for refusing to submit to his suzerain, Philip, his claims to continental possessions, 1202; raised siege of Mirebeau and captured his nephew, *Arthur, Eleanor, his sister, and many French nobles; attempted to blind Arthur, removed him to Rouen, and there probably murdered him, 1203; being defeated in Normandy returned to England, 1204; lost all Normandy and most of Poitou, 1204–5; agreed to a truce for two years, surrendering all territory north of Loire, 1206; refused to accept Stephen *Langton as archbishop, and drove out the monks of Canterbury, in consequence of which the kingdom was laid under interdict, 1208; seized property of bishops who had published it, and confiscated property of the clergy and monks and outlawed them, 1208–9; exacted hostages from William of Scotland and the English nobles; went to Ireland to establish English supremacy, overthrew power of the Lacys, and revenged himself on William de *Braose, 1210; extorted money from the Jews; reduced North Wales, 1211; excommunicated by the pope, 1212; oppressed the nobles, but mitigated forest exactions, and allied himself with the counts of Flanders and Boulogne against France; influenced by rumours of conspiracy surrendered his kingdom to the pope, 1213, promising to pay annual tribute and to receive back the exiled prelates, 1213; after the English naval victory at Damme, 1213, renewed his coronation promises to the returned bishops at Winchester; displeased the barons by appointment of *Peter des Roches as justiciar, Oct. 1213; issued writ for a council at which representatives of counties were to be present, Nov. 1213; sent an embassy to Morocco; filled up vacant benefices; invaded Poitou, and obtained some successes in Anjou, but fled before the dauphin, and after the defeat of his allies at Bouvines (1214) made a truce for five years, and returned to England; compelled, in spite of papal support, to agree to the barons' demands at Runnymede, 15 June 1215; obtaining excommunication of his opponents and aid of mercenaries, caused division among the barons, and took Rochester, Colchester, and many of the northern castles; deserted on landing of Louis of France, 1216, by *Salisbury and other adherents; lost most of England except the west; pursued from Windsor to the east; ravaged the country mercilessly, and after marching north through Lincolnshire, died, possibly poisoned, at Newark; buried in Worcester Cathedral.

JOHN (*fl.* 1215), called Wallensis, Franciscan. See WALLENSIS.

JOHN, Augustus Edwin (1878–1961), artist; attended art school at Tenby and Slade School of Art, London, 1894–8; injured skull in diving accident, 1898; studied under Henry *Tonks; visited Amsterdam, 1898; first one-man exhibition, 1899; travelled abroad with other artists, including (Sir) William *Orpen; art instructor, Liverpool University, 1901–2; began producing succession of masterly works, mainly portraits and landscapes, 1902 up to 1920, when his work deteriorated; paintings in many exhibitions, including the retrospective at the Royal Academy, 1954, and at the National Portrait Gallery,

1975; contributed to the *Journal of The Gypsy Lore Society*; published *Chiaroscuro, Fragments of Autobiography* (1952), and *Finishing Touches* (1964); RA, 1928; OM, 1942.

JOHN, Sir **Caspar** (1903–1984), admiral of the fleet; son of Augustus Edwin *John; educated at Royal Naval colleges, Osborne, and Dartmouth; appointed midshipman in *Iron Duke*, 1920; applied to train as pilot in Fleet Air Arm, 1925; served in aircraft carrier *Hermes*, 1927–9; promoted to lieutenant-commander, 1933, and commander, 1936; in carrier *Courageous*, practised night flying, 1936; transferred to Admiralty naval air division, 1937; second-in-command of cruiser *York*, 1939–41; captain, 1941; at Ministry of Aircraft Production, 1942–3; naval air attaché, British Embassy, Washington, 1943–4; in command of aircraft carriers *Pretoria Castle* and *Ocean*, 1945–6; attended Imperial Defence College, 1947; commanded naval air station, Lossiemouth, 1948; returned to Admiralty as director of air organization and training; promoted rear-admiral, 1951; at Ministry of Supply, 1952–4; vice-admiral, 1954; full admiral, 1957; vice-chief of naval staff to Earl *Mountbatten of Burma, 1957–60; first sea lord, 1960–3; admiral of the fleet, 1962; declined a peerage; CB, 1952; KCB, 1956; GCB, 1960; chairman, Housing Corporation, 1964–6; chairman, Star and Garter Home for disabled servicemen; hon. liveryman of Fruiterers Company; had both legs amputated and spent last six years in a wheelchair, 1978–84.

JOHN, Sir **William Goscombe** (1860–1952), sculptor and medallist; trained at City and Guilds and Royal Academy Schools; ARA, 1899; RA, 1909; academic sculptor compounding realism and romanticism; exhibited annually at Royal Academy for sixty-three years; executed public statues, portrait busts, and medals including Jubilee Medal of George V; collection of works at National Museum of Wales; knighted, 1911.

JOHN BASING (or BASINGSTOKE) (d. 1252), divine. See BASING.

JOHN BEVER (or OF LONDON) (d. 1311), author of *Commendatio lamentabilis in transitum magni Regis Edwardi Quarti* (Edward I); supposed by some to be writer of *Flores Historiarum*; monk of Westminster.

JOHN BOSTON OF BURY (*fl.* 1410), Augustinian monk and bibliographer. See BOSTON BURIENSIS.

JOHN DE LEXINTON (d. 1257), baron. See LEXINTON.

JOHN DE NEWENHAM (d. 1382?), chamberlain of the Exchequer. See NEWENHAM.

JOHN DE ST PAUL (1295?–1362), archbishop of Dublin. See ST PAUL.

JOHN DE SANDALE (d. 1319), bishop of Winchester. See SANDALE.

JOHN DE SANDFORD (d. 1294), poet and grammarian. See SANDFORD.

JOHN DE SHOREDITCH (or SHORDYCH) (d. 1345), diplomat. See SHOREDITCH, Sir JOHN.

JOHN DE THORPE (or THORP), Baron Thorpe (d. 1324), judge. See THORPE.

JOHN DE TREVISA (1326–1402), author. See TREVISA.

JOHN DE TROKELOWE (THROKLOW or THORLOW) (*fl.* 1330), chronicler and monk. See TROKELOWE.

JOHN DE VILLULA (d. 1122), bishop of Bath; originally a physician of Tours; bishop of Somerset, 1088–1122; bought from William II the city of Bath, and removed his see thither; rebuilt the abbey church; destroyed *Gisa's buildings at Wells and forced the canons to live among the laity; present at synod of Westminster, 1102; supposed founder of two baths at Bath.

JOHNES, Arthur James (1809–1871), Welsh county-court judge; studied at London University; barrister, Lincoln's Inn, 1835; advocated legal reforms; published (as 'Maelog') translations from *David ab Gwilym; awarded prize by Cymmrodorion Society for essay on causes of Welsh dissent, 1831; issued *Philological Proofs of original unity and recent origin of the Human Race* (1843).

JOHNES, Basset (*fl.* 1634–1659), physician and grammarian. See JONES.

JOHNES, Thomas (1748–1816), translator of the chronicles of Froissart (1803–5) and Monstrelet (1809), and *Memoirs of de Joinville* (1807); of Shrewsbury, Eton, and Jesus College, Oxford; MP, Cardigan, 1774–80, Radnorshire, 1780–96, Cardiganshire, 1796–1816; FRS, 1809; lord-lieutenant of Cardiganshire.

JOHN GERVAYS (or OF EXETER) (d. 1268), bishop of Winchester, 1262; previously chancellor of York; a baronial negotiator at Brackley, 1264, and with Louis IX; suspended, 1266, after Evesham (1265); died at Rome.

JOHN LLYWELYN (1520?–1616), Welsh bard. See LLYWELYN OF LLANGEWYDD.

JOHN OF BEVERLEY, Saint (d. 721), bishop of York; educated at Canterbury by *Theodore; sometime monk at Whitby (Streonshalch); ordained *Bede; bishop of Hexham, 687; at synod of the Nidd (705) opposed restoration of *Wilfrid, bishop of York, 705–18; retired to monastery built by himself at Beverley, where he died; canonized, 1037, twice translated; his remains discovered, 1664.

JOHN OF BRIDLINGTON (d. 1379), prior of St Mary's, Bridlington, 1360; was formally canonized by Pope Boniface IX on 24 Sept. 1401; the 'prophecies of Bridlington' probably ascribed to him erroneously.

JOHN OF BURY (or JOHN BURY) (*fl.* 1460), Augustinian; provincial at Erfurt, 1459, 1462, and 1476; wrote *Gladius Salomonis* in answer to Bishop Reginald *Pecock's *Repressor of Overmuch Learning*.

JOHN OF CORNWALL (or JOHANNES DE SANCTO GERMANO) (*fl.* 1170); probably of St Germans, Cornwall, but perhaps a Breton; studied at Paris under Peter Lombard, and afterwards lectured there; his only undoubted work, *Eulogium ad Alexandrum Papam III* (printed in Martène's *Thesaurus Novus Anecdotum* and in Migne's *Patrologia*).

JOHN OF DALDERBY (d. 1320), bishop of Lincoln. See DALDERBY, JOHN DE.

JOHN OF ELTHAM, earl of Cornwall (1316–1336), second son of Edward II; regent for Edward III while in France, 1329 and 1331, and Scotland, 1332; commanded first division at Halidon Hill, 1333; died at Perth while commanding in Scotland.

JOHN OF GAUNT, duke of Lancaster (1340–1399), fourth son of Edward III; born at Ghent; created earl of Richmond, 1342; married Blanche of Lancaster and accompanied expedition to France, 1359; succeeded to Lancaster estates in right of his wife, and was created duke, 1362; led first division of the Black Prince's army into Spain, distinguishing himself at Najera, 1367; captain of Calais and Guisnes, 1369; with Black Prince at recapture of Limoges (1370); lieutenant of Aquitaine, 1371; captured Périgord, but resigned his command, July 1371; married (as his second wife) Constance of Castile, assuming title of king of Castile, 1372; accompanied Rochelle expedition, 1372; as captain-general led force from Calais to Bordeaux, but effected nothing, 1373; took part in Bruges negotiations, 1375–6; attacked through his adherents in the Good Parliament, 1376, but on its dissolution, July 1376, reversed its measures; upheld *Wycliffe (his ally against the prelates), and when insulted by the Londoners, obtained dismissal of their officers; on accession of Richard II (1377) retired from court; called upon for advice on French War; incurred great odium by failure of his attempt on St Malo and outrages of his followers, 1378; as commander of the border made truce with Scotland, 1380; acted as jus-

ticiar to inquire into rebellion of 1381; presided over commission to reform the royal household, 1381; negotiated truce with France, 1384; unsuccessfully invaded Scotland, 1384; quarrelled with Richard and fortified Pontefract Castle, but accompanied Richard's Scottish expedition, 1385; in alliance with Portugal possessed himself of part of Galicia, but resigned Castilian claims in favour of his daughter Catharine on her marriage with John of Castile, 1387; lieutenant of Guienne, 1388–9; mediated between Richard II and his opponents; named duke of Aquitaine, 1390; conducted negotiations with France, 1392–4; put down Cheshire revolt, 1393; said to have claimed recognition of his son as heir to the throne; failed to obtain recognition in Aquitaine as duke; married Catharine *Swynford, 1396; presided at trial of *Arundel, 1397; head of the committee of government, 1398; his tomb in St Paul's destroyed during the Commonwealth.

JOHN OF GLASTONBURY (*fl.* 1400), historian of Glastonbury Abbey.

JOHN OF HEXHAM (*fl.* 1180), prior of Hexham; continued Symeon of Durham's *Chronicle* to 1154.

JOHN OF LANCASTER, duke of Bedford (1389–1435), third son of Henry IV; constable of England, governor of Berwick, and warden of the east marches in Henry IV's reign; KG, 1400; created duke, 1414; lieutenant of England during Henry V's first French expedition, 1415, and presided over the succeeding parliament, 1415; relieved Harfleur, 1416; while lieutenant of the kingdom repelled the 'Foul raid' of the Scots, 1417; directed proceedings against Sir John *Oldcastle, 1417; joined Henry V in France, 1419; again lieutenant of England, 1421; assumed command of the army in France during the king's illness, 1422; on Henry's death (1422) became regent of France, and protector of England; negotiated alliance with Burgundy and Brittany against Charles VII of France, himself marrying Philip of Burgundy's sister Anne, 1423; reformed the French coinage, encouraged trade, and promoted good administration; defeated the French and Scots at Verneuil, 1424; forbade his brother, *Humphrey, duke of Gloucester, to proceed with his challenge to Philip of Burgundy; after a visit to England to settle the quarrel between Gloucester and Henry *Beaufort (d. 1447), returned to France, 1427; conducted the war with success till raising of the siege of Orleans, 1429; temporarily resigned the regency to Burgundy; purchased Joan of Arc from her Burgundian captors and caused her to be burnt as a witch at Rouen, 1431; caused Henry VI to be crowned king of France at Notre Dame, 1431;

offended Burgundy by his second marriage with Jacqueline of Luxemburg, 1433; on a visit to England defended his French administration against Gloucester's charges, 1433; forced to send delegates to the peace congress at Arras, 1435; died and was buried at Rouen.

JOHN OF LONDON (*fl.* 1267), mathematician; expounded Roger *Bacon's three chief works to Pope Clement IV, 1267.

JOHN OF OXFORD (d. 1200), bishop of Norwich. See OXFORD.

JOHN OF PADUA (*fl.* 1542–1549), architect. See PADUA, JOHN OF.

JOHN OF PETERBOROUGH (*fl.* 1380), alleged author of *Chronicon Petroburgense* (654–1368); probably an imaginary person.

JOHN OF ST FAITH'S (d. 1359), theological writer. See ST FAITH'S.

JOHN OF ST GILES (*fl.* 1230), Dominican and physician; sometimes called from his birthplace, St Albans; lectured on medicine at Montpellier and on philosophy and theology at Paris; first physician to Philip Augustus, *c.*1209; presented Hôpital de St Jacques to the Dominicans; perhaps the first Englishman of the order; lectured against the Albigenses at Toulouse, 1233–5; invited to England by *Grosseteste; a royal councillor, 1239; attended Grosseteste and Richard de *Clare, earl of Gloucester; his only extant treatise the *Experimenta Joannis de S. Aegidio.*

JOHN OF SALISBURY (d. 1180), bishop of Chartres; called Parvus; born at Salisbury; studied at Paris under Peter Abailard and Alberic of Reims, 1136–8, and at Chartres; returned to Paris (1140) and attended lectures on theology and logic by Gilbert de la Porrée and Robert Pullus; studied and taught with Peter of la Celle at Provins; presented by St Bernard to Archbishop *Theobald at Council of Reims, 1148; attended Pope Eugenius III at Brescia and Rome; came to England probably *c.*1150; at Canterbury till 1164, secretary to Theobald and sent on important missions; intimate of Hadrian IV; obtained bull for the conquest of Ireland, 1155; fell into disgrace with Henry II for denouncing exactions demanded from the church in connection with the Toulouse expedition, 1159; applied to *Becket (then chancellor) to intercede for him; left England, 1164, owing probably to his enthusiastic support of Becket's cause; during residence with Peter of la Celle at abbey of St Remigius, Reims, composed the *Historia Pontificalis*; counselled moderation to Becket in his exile, but firmly upheld his cause, though seeking the good offices of Gilbert *Foliot and others with Henry II; present at meeting of Henry and

Louis VII at Angers, 1166; returned to England after pacification of Fréteval, 1170; with Becket at the time of his murder at Canterbury, 1170; wrote his life and advocated his canonization; named treasurer of Exeter, 1174; as bishop of Chartres (1176–80) excommunicated count of Vendôme, and was present at the peace made between England and France near Ivry, 1177; took active part at Third Lateran Council, 1179; the most learned classical writer of the middle ages. His works (printed by J. A. *Giles, 1848) consist of letters, the *Policraticus* (first printed 1476), the *Metalogicus, Entheticus, Vita Sancti Anselmi,* and other Latin writings.

JOHN OF SCHIPTON (d. 1257), Augustinian prior at Newburgh, 1252; counsellor of Henry III.

JOHN OF THE FAIR HANDS (d. 1203?), bishop. See BELMEIS, JOHN.

JOHN OF TINMOUTH (*fl.* 1366), historian. See TINMOUTH.

JOHN OF WALLINGFORD (d. 1258), compiler or transcriber of a chronicle. See WALLINGFORD.

JOHN OF WALTHAM (d. 1395), bishop of Salisbury. See WALTHAM.

JOHNS, Ambrose Bowden (1776–1858), Devonshire painter; sometime friend of J. M. W. *Turner.

JOHNS, Charles Alexander (1811–1874), author; BA, Trinity College, Dublin, 1841; second master at Helston School under Derwent *Coleridge, afterwards (1843–7) headmaster; FLS, 1836; published popular works of natural history and educational manuals.

JOHNS, Claude Hermann Walter (1857–1920), Assyriologist; BA, Queens' College, Cambridge; rector of St Botolph's, Cambridge, 1892–1909; lecturer in Assyriology at Queens', 1895, and in Assyrian at King's College, London, 1904; master of St Catharine's College, Cambridge, and canon of Norwich, 1909–19; chief work *Assyrian Deeds and Documents* (1898–1923).

JOHNS, David (1794–1843), missionary to Madagascar, 1826–36; published Malagasy dictionary (1835); died at Nossi Be.

JOHNS, William (1771–1845), Unitarian minister at Nantwich and afterwards at Cross Street, Manchester; joint secretary of Manchester Literary and Philosophical Society; published theological and educational works.

JOHNS, William Earl (1893–1968), journalist, and creator of the children's popular fiction character, 'Biggles'; educated at Hertford Grammar School; enlisted in Norfolk Yeomanry; served in Gallipoli and Salonika, 1916–17; transferred to Royal Flying Corps, 1917; shot down and became prisoner of war, 1918; remained in RAF, 1920–7; founder-editor, *Popular Flying*, 1932; first 'Biggles' stories in *The Camels are Coming* (1932); altogether, wrote ninety-six 'Biggles' books; wrote regularly for the *Modern Boy*, *Pearson's Magazine*, and *My Garden* and edited *Flying*; lectured to Air Training Corps, 1939; created 'Worrals of the W.A.A.F.', female counterpart of 'Biggles', and 'Gimlet', a commando; works translated into fourteen languages and issued in braille.

JOHN SCOTUS, Erigena (d. 875), philosopher. See SCOTUS.

JOHNSON. See also JOHNSTON, JOHNSTONE, and JONSON.

JOHNSON, Alan Woodworth (1917–1982), organic chemist and university teacher; educated at King Edward VI's School, Morpeth (scholar) and Imperial College, London (Royal scholar); first-class B.Sc., 1938; laboratory assistant, Swan Hunter & Wigham Richardson Ltd., 1934; analyst, Thomas Hedley & Co. Ltd., 1935–6; Ph.D., 1940; research assistant, dyestuffs division, Imperial Chemical Industries, 1942–6; worked on acetylene chemistry and published *The Chemistry of the Acetyline Compounds* (2 vols. 1946 and 1950); ICI fellow, Cambridge, 1946–8; assistant director of research in organic chemistry, 1948–53; fellow, Christ's College, 1951; worked on vitamin B12; lecturer in organic chemistry, 1953–5; professor of organic chemistry, Nottingham, 1955–68; professor of chemistry and honorary director of Agricultural Research Institute of Invertebrate Chemistry and Physiology, Sussex University, 1968–82; hon. sec., Chemical Society (later the Royal Society of Chemistry), 1958–65; vice-president, 1965–8, and president, 1977–8; FRS, 1965; vice-president, Royal Society, 1981–2; Davy medallist, 1980; member, National Research Development Corporation, 1976, and National Enterprise Board, 1981; in demand as lecturer world-wide.

JOHNSON, Alfred Edward Webb-, Baron Webb-Johnson (1880–1958), surgeon. See WEBB-JOHNSON.

JOHNSON, Amy (1903–1941), otherwise known as Amy Mollison, airwoman; educated at Boulevard Secondary School, Hull; BA, Sheffield, 1925; obtained ground-engineer's licence and full navigation certificate; flew solo to Australia, 1930; made record flights to Tokyo, 1931, Cape Town, 1932, Karachi (with J. A. *Mollison, whom she married, 1932), 1934, Cape and back, 1936; marriage dissolved, 1938; perished ferrying for Air Transport Auxiliary; CBE, 1930.

JOHNSON, Benjamin (1665?–1742), actor; joined Drury Lane company, 1695, and played original parts in plays by *Farquhar, *Vanbrugh, and others; appeared at the Haymarket as Corbaccio (*Volpone*), First Gravedigger (*Hamlet*), and Morose (*Epicoene*), 1706–7; again at Drury Lane, 1708–9; remained there almost continuously from 1710, adding Justice Shallow, Old Gobbo, and many other parts to his repertoire.

JOHNSON, Dame **Celia** (1908–1982), actress; educated at St Paul's Girls' School, Hammersmith; studied at Royal Academy of Dramatic Art; first professional part Sarah in *Major Barbara*, 1928; appeared in London in *A Hundred Years Old*, 1929, and *Cynara*, 1930; played Ophelia in *Hamlet* in USA, 1931; returned to London stage in *The Wind and the Rain*, 1932; married (Robert) Peter *Fleming, 1935; played in *Rebecca*, 1940, and *The Doctor's Dilemma*, 1942; served as auxiliary policewoman during 1939–45 war; postwar, appeared in number of plays by Shakespeare, Chekhov, Robert Bolt, and William Douglas-Home, 1933–77; appeared successfully in films including *In Which We Serve* (1942), *Brief Encounter* (1945), *The Good Companions* (1956), and *The Prime of Miss Jean Brodie* (1969); also appeared in television plays including *Mrs Palfrey at the Claremont* (1973) and *Staying On* (1980); CBE, 1958; DBE, 1981.

JOHNSON, Charles (1679–1748), dramatist; friend of Robert *Wilks; satirized in the *Dunciad*; author of nineteen plays.

JOHNSON, Captain **Charles** (fl. 1724–1736), author of *General History of the Robberies and Murders of the most Notorious Pyrates* (1724) and *General History of the Lives and Adventures of the most famous Highwaymen* (1734).

JOHNSON, Charles (1791–1880), botanist; lecturer at Guy's Hospital; re-edited Smith's (1832) and edited *Sowerby's *English Botany* (1832–46); published monographs on British ferns, poisonous plants, and grasses.

JOHNSON, Charles (1870–1961), assistant keeper of the public records and historian; educated at Giggleswick School and Trinity College, Oxford; first class, Lit. Hum., 1892; entered Public Record Office, 1893; engaged in arrangement and reclassification of ancient miscellanea and files of the Chancery; collaborated with C. G. *Crump and Arthur *Hughes in producing *Dialogus de Scaccario* (1902); largely responsible for Domesday section of the *Victoria History of the County of Norfolk* (1906); with (Sir) C. H. *Jenkinson, produced *English Court Hand* (1915); also published *The Public Record Office* (1918), *The Care of Documents and Management of Archives* (1919), and *The Mechanical Processes of the Histor-*

ian (1922); principal initiator and guide in publication of *Revised Medieval Latin Word-List* (1965); after retirement in 1930 edited some of the basic texts of English medieval history and made frequent contributions to reviews on historical topics; vice-president, Royal Historical Society and Society of Antiquaries, and member of other learned societies; FBA, 1934; CBE, 1951; took charge of records stored for safe-keeping in Culham College, 1939–46.

JOHNSON (or **JONSON**), **Christopher** (1536?–1597), Latin poet and physician; fellow of New College, Oxford, 1555; MA, 1561; headmaster of Winchester, 1560–70; MD, Oxford, 1571; FRCP, 1580, several times censor, and treasurer, 1594–6; his Latin poems in Richard *Willes's *Poemata* (1573).

JOHNSON, Cornelius (1593–1664?), portrait painter. See JANSSEN VAN CEULEN, CORNELIUS.

JOHNSON, Cuthbert William (1799–1878), agricultural writer; barrister, Gray's Inn, 1836; FRS, 1842; published *The Farmers' Encyclopaedia* (1842), *Farmer's Medical Dictionary* (1845), *Life of Sir Edward Coke* (1837); translated Thaër's *Principles of Agriculture* (1844); collaborated with W. *Shaw and his brother, George William *Johnson.

JOHNSON, Daniel (1767–1835), author of *Sketches of Indian Field-Sports* (1822); surgeon in East India Company's service, 1805–9.

JOHNSON, Edward (1599?–1672), author of *History of New England from . . . 1628 untill 1652* ('Wonder-working Providence'); settled in Massachusetts, 1630; represented Woburn in the state assembly from 1643, being speaker, 1655.

JOHNSON, Edward (*fl.* 1601), musical composer; Mus.Bac., Caius College, Cambridge, 1594.

JOHNSON, Sir Edwin Beaumont (1825–1893), general; studied at East India Company's College, Addiscombe; lieutenant, Bengal Artillery, 1845; captain, 1857; lieutenant-colonel, 1865; major-general, 1868; general, 1877; colonel-commandant, Royal (late Bengal) Artillery, 1890; served in Sikh wars, 1845–6 and 1848–9; assistant adjutant-general of artillery in Oudh division, 1855–62; in Indian Mutiny, 1857–8; CB (military), 1858; military secretary for Indian affairs at headquarters of army in London, and extra aide-de-camp to the field marshal commanding-in-chief, the duke of Cambridge, 1865–72; quartermaster-general in India, 1873; returned to England as member of council of secretary of state for India, 1874; KCB, 1875; military member of council of governor-general of India, 1877–80; CIE, 1878; director-general of military education at War Office in London, 1884–6; GCB, 1887.

JOHNSON, Esther (1681–1728), friend of Dean *Swift; an inmate of Sir William *Temple's family, where Swift met her; the 'Stella' of Swift's *Journal to Stella*; possibly, but improbably, married to Swift.

JOHNSON, Francis (1562–1618), Presbyterian separatist; brother of George *Johnson (1564–1605); fellow of Christ's College, Cambridge, 1584; MA, 1585; imprisoned and expelled the university, 1589, for maintaining Presbyterianism to be of divine right; preacher to English merchants at Middelburg, 1589–92; with John *Greenwood (d. 1593) formed Separatist church in London, 1592; several times imprisoned; from 1597 Separatist pastor at Amsterdam; published Brownist treatises and other works.

JOHNSON, Francis (1796?–1876), orientalist; professor of Sanskrit, Bengali, and Telugu, East India Company's college at Haileybury, 1824–55; published *Persian Dictionary* (1829; enlarged, 1852), an edition of the *Gulistan* (1863), and editions of Sanskrit classics.

JOHNSON, George (1564–1605), Puritan; MA, Christ's College, Cambridge, 1588; imprisoned for Separatism, 1593; sailed for America in the company of other Separatists, 1597, but was obliged to return; escaped to Holland; quarrelled with his brother Francis *Johnson (1562–1618) about his wife's fondness for fine clothing and was excommunicated, 1604; returned and prepared an account of the dissensions (Amsterdam, 1603); died in Durham Gaol.

JOHNSON, Sir George (1818–1896), physician; studied medicine at King's College, London; MD, London, 1844; FRCP, 1850; Gulstonian lecturer, 1852; materia medica lecturer, 1853; Lumleian lecturer, 1877; Harveian orator, 1882; vice-president, 1887; assistant physician to King's College Hospital, 1847, physician, 1856, professor of materia medica and therapeutics, 1857–63, of medicine, 1863–76, of clinical medicine, 1876–86, and emeritus professor of clinical medicine and consulting physician, 1886; FRS, 1872; physician-extraordinary to Queen Victoria, 1889; knighted, 1892; published medical works.

JOHNSON, George Henry Sacheverell (1808–1881), dean of Wells; fellow, tutor, and dean of The Queen's College, Oxford; Ireland scholar, 1827; MA, 1833; Savilian professor of astronomy, 1839–42; Whyte professor of moral philosophy, 1842–5; FRS, 1838; member of the Oxford commissions of 1850 and 1854; dean of Wells, 1854–81; edited Psalms for *Speaker's Commentary* (1880).

JOHNSON, George William (1802–1886), writer on gardening; barrister of Gray's Inn, 1836; collaborated with his brother Cuthbert William *Johnson in *Essay on Uses of Salt for Agriculture* (13th edn., 1838), *Outlines of Chemistry* (1828), and an edition of Paley's works (1839); professor of political economy at Hindu College, Calcutta, and editor of the government gazette, 1837–41; published *History of English Gardening* (1829), *Principles of Practical Gardening* (1845; reissued as *Science and Practice*, 1862), and other works; established *The Cottage Gardener* (*Journal of Horticulture*), 1848.

JOHNSON, Gerard (*fl.* 1616), tomb-maker. See JANSSEN, GERAERT.

JOHNSON, Guy (1740?–1788), American loyalist; served against the French, 1757–60; succeeded his uncle, Sir William *Johnson, as superintendent of Indians, 1774; his estates in Tryon county, New York, confiscated by the Americans, against whom he fought in Canada; died in London.

JOHNSON, Harry Gordon (1923–1977), economist; born in Toronto, Canada; educated at University of Toronto schools and Toronto University; served in Canadian armed forces; studied at Jesus College, Cambridge; first class, economics tripos; BA (Toronto); studied economics at Harvard; acquired doctorate; at invitation of (Sir) Dennis *Robertson became assistant lecturer in economics at Cambridge; lecturer, 1950; fellow of King's College, Cambridge; professor of economic theory, Manchester University, 1956; professor of economics, Chicago University, 1959; combined this post with professorship at London School of Economics, 1966–74; returned to Chicago, 1974; combined duties in Chicago with professorship of international economics at University of Geneva, 1976; wrote nineteen books and over 400 papers; publications include *Essays in Monetary Economics* (1967), *Aspects of the Theory of Tariffs* (1971), *Macroeconomics and Monetary Theory* (1972), *The Theory of Income Distribution* (1973), and *On Economics and Society* (1975); editor, *Journal of Political Economy*, 1960–6; founder and co-editor, *Journal of International Economics*; FBA, 1969; fellow of Econometric Society, 1972 and Royal Society of Canada, 1976; officer of the Order of Canada, 1976; awarded number of honorary degrees in Britain and Canada.

JOHNSON, Harry John (1826–1884), watercolour painter; friend and fellow-townsman of the elder David *Cox; member of Institute of Painters in Water-Colours, 1870.

JOHNSON, Henry (1698?–1760), South American traveller and translator from the Spanish.

JOHNSON, Sir Henry, first baronet (1748–1835), general; commanded light battalion of 28th, 1775–8, and the 17th Regiment, 1778–81, during American War; defeated Irish rebels at New Ross, 1798; general, 1809; created baronet, 1818.

JOHNSON, Hewlett (1874–1966), dean successively of Manchester and Canterbury; educated at Macclesfield Grammar School and the Owens College, Manchester; B.Sc., 1894; associate member of Institute of Civil Engineers, 1898; entered Wadham College, Oxford, as theological student; ordained as deacon (1905), and priest (1906), at St Margaret, Altrincham; honorary canon, Chester, 1919; rural dean, Bowden, 1922; edited *The Interpreter*; BD, Oxford, 1917; DD, 1924; dean of Manchester, 1924–31; dean of Canterbury, 1931–63; visited Russia, 1937, and became indefatigable speaker for Left Book Club in association with (Sir) Victor *Gollancz and John *Strachey; published *The Socialist Sixth of the World* (1939); received Stalin Peace Prize, 1951; a controversial figure who came to be known as the 'Red Dean'; chairman, editorial board of the *Daily Worker*; published autobiography, *Searching for Light* (1968).

JOHNSON, Humphry (*fl.* 1713), calligrapher and mathematician.

JOHNSON, Isaac (d. 1630), one of the founders of Massachusetts; MA, Emmanuel College, Cambridge, 1621; accompanied *Winthrop to America, 1630.

JOHNSON, James (1705–1774), bishop of Worcester; of Westminster and Christ Church, Oxford; MA, 1731; DD, 1742; second master at Westminster, 1733–48; rector of Berkhampstead, 1743; canon of St Paul's and chaplain to George II, 1744–52; bishop of Gloucester, 1752–9, of Worcester, 1759–74.

JOHNSON, James (d. 1811), engraver and publisher of *The Scots Musical Museum*, 1787–1803.

JOHNSON, James (1777–1845), physician; naval surgeon during the great war, being at Walcheren in 1809; attended duke of Clarence and became physician-extraordinary (1830) on his accession to the throne as William IV; edited *Medico-Chirurgical Review*, 1818–44; MD, St Andrews, 1821; published *Influence of Tropical Climates on European Constitutions* (1812) and popular medical works.

JOHNSON, John (*fl.* 1641), author of *The Academy of Love* (poem, 1641).

JOHNSON, John, of Cranbrook (1662–1725), divine; BA, Magdalene College, Cambridge, 1681; MA, Corpus Christi College, Cambridge,

1685; vicar of Boughton-under-the-Blean and Hernhill, 1687, of St John's, Margate, and Appledore, 1697; vicar of Cranbrook, Kent, 1707–25; published works of controversial divinity.

JOHNSON, John (1706–1791), Baptist minister; pastor in Stanley Street, Liverpool, 1750–91; founded Johnsonian Baptists; published *Advantages and Disadvantages of the Married State* (5th edn., 1760) and other works; his *Original Letters* issued (1796–1800).

JOHNSON, John (d. 1797), wood engraver.

JOHNSON, John (d. 1804), Dissenting minister of Lady Huntingdon's Connection; pastor of St George's, Rochdale Road, Manchester; published *The Levite's Journal*.

JOHNSON, John (1754–1814), architect; architect and county surveyor for Essex; erected buildings at Chelmsford.

JOHNSON, Sir John, second baronet (d. 1830), superintendent of Indian affairs, 1783–1830, and commander of 'Johnson's Greens'; son of Sir William *Johnson.

JOHNSON, John (1759–1833), divine; of Charterhouse and Oriel College, Oxford; MA, 1782; vicar of North Mimms, Hertfordshire, 1790–1833, and translator.

JOHNSON, John (1769–1833), kinsman and friend of *Cowper; LL D, Caius College, Cambridge, 1803; rector of Yaxham with Welborne, Norfolk, 1800–33; edited Cowper's correspondence (1824) and vol. iii of Cowper's *Poems* (1815), and *Hayley's *Memoirs* (1823).

JOHNSON, John (1777–1848), printer; compositor to Sir Egerton Brydges's private press at Lee Priory; printed at his own office in Brooke Street, Holborn, *Typographia, or the Printer's Instructor* (1824, four sizes).

JOHNSON, John de Monins (1882–1956), printer and scholar; educated at Magdalen College School and Exeter College, Oxford; in Egyptian Civil Service, 1905–7; senior demy, Magdalen College, Oxford, 1908–11; explored in Egypt, 1911, 1913–14; assistant secretary, delegates of Oxford University Press, 1915–25; printer to university, 1925–46; a leader of the renaissance of book printing; his unique collection of printed ephemera moved to Bodleian Library, 1968; published *Print and Privilege at Oxford to the Year 1700* (with S. Gibson, 1946); CBE, 1945.

JOHNSON, John Mordaunt (1776?–1815), diplomat; of Trinity College, Dublin, and Trinity College, Cambridge; chargé d'affaires at Brus-

sels, 1814; afterwards consul at Geneva; died at Florence.

JOHNSON, John Noble (1787–1823), author of *Life of Linacre* (ed. Robert Graves, 1835); MA, Magdalen Hall, Oxford, 1810; MD, 1814; Gulstonian lecturer, 1816; physician to Westminster Hospital, 1818–22.

JOHNSON, Joseph (1738–1809), bookseller and publisher for *Priestley, *Cowper, Horne *Tooke, Erasmus *Darwin, and other authors; fined and imprisoned for issuing pamphlet by Gilbert *Wakefield, 1797; published *Analytical Review*, 1788–99.

JOHNSON, Lawrence (*fl.* 1603), early engraver.

JOHNSON, Lionel Pigot (1867–1902), critic and poet; scholar of Winchester College; edited *The Wykehamist*, 1884–6; BA, New College, Oxford (first class, Lit. Hum.), 1890; entered on literary career in London, 1890, contributing to magazines and reviews; joined Church of Rome, 1891; published his first volume of poems, 1895, in which he gave expression to a 'catholic puritanism'; in *Ireland and other Poems* (1897) he betrayed an intense love for Ireland; also wrote *The Art of Thomas Hardy* (1894) and *Post Liminium: Essays and Critical Papers* (posthumous, 1911).

JOHNSON, Manuel John (1805–1859), astronomer; while in charge of the St Helena Observatory observed solar eclipse of 27 July 1832; catalogued 606 fixed stars in the southern hemisphere (1835); MA, Magdalen Hall, Oxford, 1842; keeper of the Radcliffe Observatory, 1839; made observations and measurements with large heliometer, and (1858) utilized electrical transit-recorder; FRS, 1856; president of Royal Astronomical Society, 1857–8; astronomical prize founded to commemorate him at Oxford, 1862.

JOHNSON, Martin (d. 1686?), seal engraver and landscape painter.

JOHNSON, Maurice (1688–1755), antiquary; founded 'Gentlemen's Society' at Spalding, 1709–10, and the Stamford Society, c.1721; barrister, Inner Temple, 1710; hon. librarian of Society of Antiquaries, 1717; left large manuscript collections relating chiefly to Lincolnshire and Peterborough antiquities; writings by him in Nichols's *Bibliotheca Topographica Britannica*.

JOHNSON, Sir Nelson King (1892–1954), meteorologist; educated at Simon Langton School, Canterbury, and Royal College of Science; B.Sc., 1913; pilot, Royal Flying Corps, 1915–19; joined Meteorological Office, 1919; worked mainly at Chemical Warfare Experimental Station, Porton; researches laid foundation of micro-meteorology; director, Meteorological Office, 1938–53, organizing wartime service, research, and international links; D.Sc., London, 1939; KCB, 1943.

JOHNSON, Pamela Hansford, Lady Snow (1912–1981), novelist, dramatist, and critic; educated at Clapham County Secondary School; worked in bank; won *Sunday Referee's* annual poetry prize, 1934; fell in love with Dylan *Thomas; first novel *This Bed Thy Centre* (1935) immediate success; left bank for full-time writing; married (Gordon) Neil Stewart, 1936; one son and one daughter; divorced, 1949; married Charles Percy (later Lord) *Snow, 1950; one son; published thirty-one novels, including *Too Dear for my Possessing* (1940), *Catherine Carter* (1952), *The Unspeakable Skipton* (1959), *The Humbler Creation* (1959), and *The Honours Board* (1970); published memoirs *Important to Me* (1974); reviewed regularly for *Sunday Times*; wrote radio plays *Six Proust Reconstructions* (1958); fellow, Royal Society of Literature; CBE, 1975; helped to found Migraine Trust, 1969.

JOHNSON, Richard (1573–1659?), romance writer; freeman of London; author of *Famous Historie of the Seaven Champions of Christendom* (c.1597), *The Nine Worthies of London* (1592), *The Crowne Garland of Golden Roses* (1612, reprinted by Percy Society), and *Pleasant Conceites of Old Hobson* (1607; reprinted, 1843).

JOHNSON, Richard (1604–1687), devotional writer. See WHITE.

JOHNSON, Richard (d. 1721), grammarian; BA, St John's College, Cambridge, 1679; headmaster of Nottingham Free School, 1707–18; published *Grammatical Commentaries* (1706), *Aristarchus Anti-Bentleianus* (1717), and other works.

JOHNSON, Robert (*fl.* 1550), musical composer; perhaps chaplain to *Anne Boleyn.

JOHNSON, Robert (d. 1559), canon and chancellor of Worcester, 1544; BCL, Cambridge, 1531 (incorporated at Oxford, 1551); his book against *Hooper published posthumously.

JOHNSON, Robert (1540–1625), archdeacon of Leicester; fellow and steward of Trinity College, Cambridge; MA, 1564 (incorporated at Oxford, 1565); chaplain to Sir Nicholas *Bacon; canon of Peterborough, Rochester, 1569, and Norwich, 1570, and of Windsor, 1572–1625; archdeacon of Leicester, 1591; founded schools at Oakham and Uppingham, and divinity scholarships at Clare, St John's, Emmanuel, and Sidney Sussex colleges, Cambridge.

JOHNSON, Robert (*fl.* 1626), lutenist and composer; musician to Prince *Henry and Charles I; member of Shakespeare's company; first set Ariel's songs in *The Tempest*; composed music for plays by *Beaumont and *Fletcher, *Middleton, and *Jonson; contributed to Leighton's *Teares or Lamentacions* (1614).

JOHNSON, Robert (1770–1796), engraver and water-colour painter; executed drawings for *Bewick's *Fables*.

JOHNSON, Samuel (1649–1702), Whig divine; of St Paul's School and Trinity College, Cambridge; BA, 1669–70; rector of Corringham, Essex, 1670; domestic chaplain to Lord William *Russell; imprisoned and fined, 1683, for his *Julian the Apostate* (tract against the duke of York), 1682; wrote also *Julian's Arts and Methods to undermine and extirpate Christianity* (1683); degraded, pilloried, fined, and whipped for circulating his *Humble and Hearty Address to all the English Protestants in the present Army* (1686); published numerous Protestant pamphlets; received pension and bounty from William III, but declined a deanery as inadequate; the Ben-Jochanan of *Absalom and Achitophel*.

JOHNSON, Samuel (1691–1773), Manchester dancing-master and dramatist; produced in London, 1729, his extravaganza, *Hurlothrumbo*, himself appearing as Lord Flame (satirized in *Fielding's *Author's Farce*), and afterwards *Chester Comics*, *The Mad Lovers*, and other pieces.

JOHNSON, Samuel (1709–1784), lexicographer; son of a Lichfield bookseller; educated at Lichfield, Stourbridge, and Pembroke College, Oxford; usher at Market Bosworth Grammar School; subsequently assisted publisher of the *Birmingham Journal*; married Mrs Porter, 1735; took pupils at Edial, among them being David *Garrick; went up to London with Garrick, 1737; found his first patron in Henry Hervey; contributed to *Gentleman's Magazine*, assisting William *Guthrie (1708–1770) with parliamentary debates, and himself compiling them from July 1741 to Mar. 1744; published *London* through *Dodsley (1738); employed by *Osborne to catalogue library of Edward *Harley, second earl of Oxford, 1742; issued *Life of Savage* (1744); began his *English Dictionary*, 1747; published *The Vanity of Human Wishes* (1749); produced *Irene* at Drury Lane, 1749; formed the Ivy Lane Club, 1749; the *Rambler* written by him with occasional contributions from Mrs *Carter, Samuel *Richardson, and others, 1750–2; lost his wife, 1752; repelled *Chesterfield's tardy offer of patronage, 1755, when his dictionary was published, and he received his MA from Oxford; gained the acquaintance of Dr Charles *Burney (1726–1814) and Bennet *Langton through the *Rambler*, and that of Sir Joshua *Reynolds through the *Life of Savage*; first met *Goldsmith and *Burke in 1761; when arrested for debt, 1756, released by a loan from Richardson; contributed to *Literary Magazine*, 1756–8, reviews of works by *Hanway and Soame *Jenyns; wrote the *Idler* for *Newbery's *Universal Chronicle*, 1758–60, and *Rasselas* (his most popular work), 1759, when he went to live in Inner Temple Lane (now Johnson Buildings); helped to expose the Cock Lane Ghost, 1762; received through *Wedderburn's application a pension of £300 from Lord *Bute, 1762; wrote pamphlets against *Wilkes, 1770, a defence of the government policy in the affair of the Falkland Islands, 1771, and towards America, 1775; became acquainted with *Boswell in May 1763, and probably in the same winter founded his Literary Club held at the Turk's Head in Gerrard Street till 1783; introduced by *Murphy to the *Thrales, 1764, in whose town houses in Southwark and Grosvenor Square and country house at Streatham he was received hospitably; had an interview with George III, 1767, and with Wilkes, 1776; brought out his long-delayed edition of Shakespeare in 1765; wrote Goldsmith's epitaph, 1776; named his own price for *Lives of the Poets* (vols. i–iv, 1779, v–x, 1781); travelled with Boswell in Scotland, 1773 (publishing his *Journey to the Western Isles of Scotland*, 1775); accompanied the Thrales to Wales, 1774, and Paris, 1775; Thrale's executor, 1781; quarrelled with Mrs Thrale on her marriage with Piozzi; formed Essex Head Club, 1783; buried in Westminster Abbey, a monument being erected to him in St Paul's by the club, and statues at Lichfield and Uttoxeter (1878); LL D, Dublin, 1765, and Oxford, 1775, but rarely styled himself 'Dr'; called by *Carlyle the 'last of the tories'. Of the four portraits by Reynolds, one is in the National Gallery. Johnson holds the highest rank among conversationalists, and his style shows some dialectical power. His *Prayers and Meditations, Letters to Mrs. Piozzi*, and an autobiographical fragment appeared posthumously. The best edition of his works is that edited by Professor F. P. Walesby (1825).

JOHNSON, Thomas (d. 1644), botanist and Royalist; published an enlarged and corrected edition of *Gerard's *Herball* (1633), as well as the first local catalogue of plants issued in England (1629), and other works; MD, Oxford, 1643; died from effects of a wound received at defence of Basing House; genus *Johnsonia* named after him; his minor works edited by T. S. Ralph (1847).

JOHNSON, Sir Thomas (1664–1728), founder of the modern Liverpool; bailiff of Liverpool, 1689, mayor, 1695, and MP, 1701–23; purchased site of the old castle for a market, 1707; knighted, 1708; chief promoter of first floating dock at Liverpool, and erection of St Peter's and St George's churches, 1708.

JOHNSON, Thomas (*fl.* 1718), classical scholar; of Eton and King's College, Cambridge; MA, 1692; headmaster of Chigwell School, 1715–18; edited seven plays of Sophocles (collected, 1745), *Gratii Falisci Cynegeticon* (1699), and other works; his compilation, *Novus Graecorum Epigrammatum et Poematiωn Delectus*, still in use at Eton.

JOHNSON, Thomas (d. 1737), classical scholar; fellow of Magdalene College, Cambridge; MA, 1728; one of the editors of Stephens's *Latin Thesaurus* (1734–5); edited Puffendorf's *De Officio Hominis et Civis* (1735).

JOHNSON, Thomas? (1772–1839), smuggler; twice escaped from prison; received pardons for piloting expedition to Holland (1799) and the Walcheren expedition, 1809.

JOHNSON, Thomas Burgeland (d. 1840), author of *The Sportsman's Cyclopaedia* (1831) and other books on field-sports.

JOHNSON, Sir William, first baronet (1715–1774), superintendent of Indian affairs in North America; went to America and established himself south of the Mohawk River, 1738; traded with the Mohawk Indians, and was named Sachem; colonel of the six nations, 1744; commissary for Indian affairs, 1746; member of New York Council, 1750; reconciled the Indians and colonials, 1753; superintendent of Indian affairs, 1755; commanded Crown Point expedition, 1755; received baronetcy and money grant, 1755; as second-in-command carried out successfully Fort Niagara expedition, 1759; led the Indians under Amherst in Canada, 1760; received grant of the 'Kingsland' on north of the Mohawk, and built Johnson Hall, 1764; concluded treaty at Fort Stanwix, 1768; contributed memoir on the Indians to the Philosophical Society (1772).

JOHNSON, William (1784–1864), promoter of education; BD, St John's College, Cambridge, 1827; friend of *Wordsworth and *Southey; had charge of the National Society's model schools in Holborn and Baldwin's Gardens, London, 1812–40; rector of St Clement's, Eastcheap, 1820–64.

JOHNSON, William Ernest (1858–1931), logician; educated at Perse School, Liverpool Royal Institution School, and King's College, Cambridge; eleventh wrangler, 1882; first class, moral sciences tripos, 1883; Sidgwick university lecturer in moral science and fellow of King's, 1902–31; in treatise on *Logic* (3 parts, 1921–4) defined the subject-matter of logic as 'the analysis and criticism of thought' and attached great importance to the 'epistemic' aspect; his treatment of probability similar to that of (Lord) *Keynes; FBA, 1923.

JOHNSON, William Percival (1854–1928), archdeacon of Nyasa, 1896–1928; BA, University College, Oxford; joined Universities' Mission to Central Africa, under Bishop E. *Steere, 1876; deacon, 1876; priest, 1878; worked on and by Lake Nyasa, 1881–1928; made translations in several African languages.

JOHNSON-MARSHALL, Sir **Stirrat Andrew William** (1912–1981), architect; educated at Queen Elizabeth School, Kirby Lonsdale and Liverpool School of Architecture; first-class honours, 1935; ARIBA, 1936; held local-authority posts in Willesden and the Isle of Ely; during 1939–45 war served in Royal Engineers; escaped from Singapore to Colombo in small boat, 1942; worked in Camouflage Development and Training Centre, Farnham, 1943–5; deputy architect, Hertfordshire County Council, 1945–8; chief architect, Ministry of Education, 1948–56; helped to lead revolt of architect members of RIBA during 1950s; vice-president, RIBA, 1964–5; in private practice with (Sir) Robert *Matthew, 1956; pursued ideal of better method of building through prefabrication; major contributions to planning, buildings for York University, Commonwealth Institute, and Central Lancashire New Town; retired, 1978; FRIBA, 1964; CBE,d 1954; knighted, 1971.

JOHNSTON. See also JOHNSON and JOHNSTONE.

JOHNSTON, Sir **Alexander** (1775–1849), reorganizer of the government of Ceylon; barrister, Lincoln's Inn; advocate-general of Ceylon, 1799, chief justice, 1805, and president of the council, 1811–19; knighted, 1811; vice-president of Royal Asiatic Society, 1823; privy councillor, 1832; member of Judicial Committee, 1833.

JOHNSTON, **Alexander** (1815–1891), painter; exhibited at Royal Academy from 1836; his popularity established by the *Gentle Shepherd* (1840) and *Sunday Morning* (1841).

JOHNSTON, Alexander James (1820–1888), colonial judge; barrister, Middle Temple, 1843; chief justice of New Zealand, 1867 and 1886; puisne judge of the Supreme Court, New Zealand, 1860–86; tried native prisoners in Te Kooti and Tito Kowaru wars; member of several legal commissions and author of legal works.

JOHNSTON, Alexander Keith, the elder (1804–1871), geographer; educated at Edinburgh; hon. LL D, 1845; published his first maps, 1830; awarded medal at exhibition of 1851 for first globe of physical geography; Victoria medallist, Royal Geographical Society, 1871; travelled in Palestine, 1863; published at Humboldt's suggestion the first English atlas of physical geography (1848); also *Dictionary of Geography* (1850) and numerous atlases and maps.

JOHNSTON, Alexander Keith, the younger (1844–1879), geographer; son of Alexander Keith *Johnston the elder; studied at Edinburgh and in Germany; geographer to the Paraguay Survey, 1873–5; published maps of Africa (1866) and East Africa (1870) and school geographies; died at Berobero while leading Royal Geographical Society's expedition to head of Lake Nyassa.

JOHNSTON, Alexander Robert Campbell- (1812–1888), colonial official; son of Sir Alexander *Johnston; administrator of Hong Kong, 1841–2; FRS, 1845; died in California.

JOHNSTON, Archibald, Lord Warriston (1610?–1663), Scottish statesman; assisted *Henderson in framing the Scots National Covenant, 1638; procurator of the kirk, 1638; assisted in negotiating pacification of Berwick, 1639, and Treaty of Ripon, 1640; lord of session as Lord Warriston, 1641; as commissioner for Midlothian opposed neutrality in English affairs, 1643; took prominent part in the Westminster Assembly, and became (1644) one of the committee representing Scotland in London; named king's advocate by Charles I, 1646; resisted the 'engagement', 1648, and perhaps drew up the Act of Classes, 1649; lord clerk register, 1649; said to have given *Leslie fatal advice at Dunbar, 1650, after which he lost his offices; as a leading 'remonstrant' renamed by *Cromwell lord clerk register, 1657; member of Oliver and Richard Cromwell's House of Lords; member of Council of State on restoration of the Rump, and on its suppression permanent president of Committee of Safety; arrested at Rouen at the Restoration; tried before Scottish parliament, and hanged at Edinburgh.

JOHNSTON, Arthur (1587–1641), writer of Latin verse; MD, Padua, 1610; intimate of Andrew *Melville (1545–1622) at Sedan; physician at Paris; returned to Scotland after an absence of twenty-four years; patronized by *Laud as a rival to George *Buchanan; rector of King's College, Aberdeen, 1637; published metrical Latin versions of the Psalms (1637) and Solomon's Song (1633), and *Epigrammata* (1632), *Elegia* (1628), and other Latin poems.

JOHNSTON, Christopher Nicholson, Lord Sands (1857–1934), Scottish judge; educated at St Andrews, Edinburgh, and Heidelberg universities; advocate, 1880; advocate-depute, 1892, 1895–9; KC, 1902; sheriff of Perth, 1905–16; Conservative MP, Edinburgh and St Andrews universities, 1916–17; knighted, 1917; senator of College of Justice, 1917–34, with judicial title of Lord Sands; procurator of the Church of Scotland, 1907–18; his memorandum the basis of the Church union of 1929.

JOHNSTON, David (1734–1824), founder of the Blind Asylum, Edinburgh, 1793; minister of North Leith, 1765–1824; hon. DD, Edinburgh, 1781; chaplain-in-ordinary to George III, 1793.

JOHNSTON, Edward (1872–1944), calligrapher and designer of lettering; taught at Central School of Arts and Crafts and Royal College of Art; designed lettering for London Transport; published *Writing and Illuminating, and Lettering* (1906) and *Manuscript and Inscription Letters* (1909); CBE, 1939.

JOHNSTON, Francis (1761–1829), architect; founder of the Royal Hibernian Academy (1813), and frequently president.

JOHNSTON, George (1797–1855), naturalist; surgeon at Berwick; MD, Edinburgh, 1819; hon. LL D, Aberdeen; an editor of *Magazine of Zoology and Botany*; published *Flora of Berwick* (vol. i, 1829, vol. ii, 1831), *History of British Zoophytes* (1838), and other scientific works.

JOHNSTON, George (1814–1889), obstetrician; grandnephew of Francis *Johnston; MD, Edinburgh, 1845; assistant physician to Dublin Lying-in Hospital, 1848–55; master of Rotunda Hospital, 1868–75; president of Dublin College of Physicians, 1880; collaborated with (Sir) Edward B. Sinclair in *Practical Midwifery* (1878).

JOHNSTON, George Lawson, first Baron Luke (1873–1943), man of business and philanthropist; educated at Dulwich and Blair Lodge, Polmont; entered father's firm of Bovril Ltd.; director, 1896; vice-chairman, 1900; chairman, 1916; managing director, 1931; other directorships included *Daily Express*, 1900–17; did much work for hospitals; KBE, 1920; baron, 1929.

JOHNSTON, Sir Harry Hamilton (1858–1927), explorer and administrator; displayed precocious scientific, linguistic, and artistic interests; became interested in problem of partition of Africa, 1879; joined seventh earl of Mayo on expedition through Southern Angola, 1882; penetrated alone into Congo basin, where he won friendship of (Sir) H. M. *Stanley, 1883; undertook scientific and political mission to Mount Kilimanjaro and surroundings, 1884; vice-consul, Cameroon and Niger Delta, 1885; helped to open navigable mouths of Niger to legitimate trade; formed alliance with Cecil *Rhodes; British consul, Portuguese East Africa, 1889; extended British protectorate over Shiré Highlands to include Nyasaland, etc.; British commissioner for South Central Africa, 1891–6; consul-general, Tunisia, 1897–9; special commissioner, Uganda, where he achieved administrative success and pursued geographical, ethnological, and naturalist studies, 1899–1901; occupied with Liberian affairs, 1904–6; KCB, 1896.

JOHNSTON, Henry (d. 1723), Benedictine; brother of Nathaniel *Johnston; on the English mission till 1696; prior of English Benedictines at Paris (St Edmund's), 1697–8 and 1705–10; translated (1685) and defended Bossuet's exposition of Roman Catholic doctrine.

JOHNSTON, Henry Erskine (1777–1830?), actor; (the 'Scottish Roscius'); first appeared at Edinburgh as Hamlet, 1794; at Covent Garden, 1797–1803; acted in *Douglas* and other plays at Drury Lane, 1803–5, 1817–18, and 1821; again at Covent Garden, 1805 and 1816; retired to Edinburgh, 1823.

JOHNSTON (or JOHNSTONE), James (1655–1737), 'Secretary Johnston'; son of Archibald *Johnston, Lord Warriston; studied law at Utrecht and was sent to prepare the way for William of Orange's invasion; envoy to Brandenburg, 1689; secretary of state in Scotland, 1692–6; obtained inquiry (1695) into the Glencoe massacre; dismissed for promoting the African Company Bill, 1696, but given money grant; lord clerk register, 1704–5; afterwards a leader of *squadrone volante*, though living in England.

JOHNSTON, James Finlay Weir (1796–1855), chemist; MA, Glasgow, 1796; studied in Switzerland under Berzelius; reader in chemistry at Durham University, 1833–55; chemist to Agricultural Society of Scotland, 1843; FRS and FRSE; his *Catechism of Agricultural Chemistry* (1844) translated into many European languages. His *Chemistry of Common Life* (1853–5) was continued by George Henry *Lewes (1859) and A. H. Church (1879).

JOHNSTON, James Henry (1787–1851), controller of East India Company's steamers; in Royal Navy till 1815, being at Trafalgar (1805) in the *Spartiate*; proposed plan for establishing steam communication with India by the Mediterranean and Red Sea, 1823; his plan for steam navigation in the Ganges accepted; controller of East India Company's steamers, 1833–50.

JOHNSTON, John (1570?–1611), Scottish poet; studied at King's College, Aberdeen, and abroad, being an intimate of Lipsius at Rostock; co-operated with Andrew *Melville (1545–1622) in Scotland; professor of divinity at St Andrews, c.1593–1611; published *Inscriptiones Historicae Regum Scotorum* (1602), *Heroes* (1603), and other works.

JOHNSTON, Sir John (d. 1690), soldier and criminal; son of a Nova Scotia baronet; hanged at Tyburn for participation in abduction of Mary Wharton.

JOHNSTON, Nathaniel (1627–1705), physician; MD, King's College, Cambridge, 1656; FRCP, 1687; friend of *Thoresby; after the Revolution lived under protection of *Peterborough; chief work, *The Excellency of Monarchical Government* (1686); left collections on Yorkshire antiquities.

JOHNSTON, Pelham (d. 1765), physician; MD, Cambridge, 1728; FRCP, 1732; grandson of Nathaniel *Johnston.

JOHNSTON, Sir Reginald Fleming (1874–1938), scholar, traveller, and administrator; educated at Edinburgh and Oxford universities; entered Hong Kong Civil Service, 1898; made series of journeys into the interior of China; seconded to Wei-hai-wei, 1904; district officer and magistrate, 1906–17; European tutor to last of the Ch'ing emperors, Hsüan T'ung, 1918–25; comptroller of the imperial household, 1924; contrived emperor's flight to the legation quarter, 1924; commissioner, Wei-hai-wei, 1927–30; professor of Chinese, London, 1931–7; KCMG, 1930; to all intents and purposes a Confucianist; highly critical of Christian missionary activities in China; books include *From Peking to Mandalay* (1908), *Lion and Dragon in Northern China* (1910), *Buddhist China* (1913), *Twilight in the Forbidden City* (1934), and *Confucianism and Modern China* (1934).

JOHNSTON, Robert (1567?–1639), historian and friend of George *Heriot; MA, Edinburgh, 1587; clerk of deliveries of the ordnance, 1604; left money for eight scholars at Edinburgh; wrote *Historia Rerum Britannicarum, 1572–1628* (published Amsterdam, 1655); a part of his *History of Scotland during minority of King James* translated (1646).

JOHNSTON, Samuel (1733–1816), American statesman and judge; son of John Johnston of Dundee; member of Continental Congress, 1781–2; governor of North Carolina, 1788–9; US senator, 1789–93; judge of Supreme Court, 1800–3.

JOHNSTON, Thomas (1881–1965), politician and newspaper editor; educated at Lenzie Academy and Glasgow University; launched the socialist weekly, *Forward*, 1906; published *The History of the Working Classes in Scotland* (1920); Labour MP, West Stirlingshire, 1922–4; MP, Dundee, 1925–9, West Stirlingshire, 1929–31 and 1935–45; under-secretary of state for Scotland, 1929; lord privy seal; regional commissioner for Scotland, 1939; secretary of state for Scotland, 1941–5; chairman, North of Scotland Hydro-Electric Board, 1945–59; chairman, Scottish Tourist Board; forestry commissioner; chairman, Broadcasting Council for Scotland; chancellor, Aberdeen University, 1951; president, Scottish History Society, 1950–2; CH, 1953; LL D, Glasgow, 1945; published *Memories* (1952).

JOHNSTON, Sir William, seventh baronet, of Johnston (1760–1844), soldier; descendant of Sir John *Johnston; MP, New Windsor, 1801–6; died at The Hague.

JOHNSTON, Sir William (1773–1844), lieutenant-general; fought in Mediterranean and West Indies; commanded 68th in Walcheren expedition, 1809, and in the Peninsula; seriously wounded at Vittoria, 1813; major-general, 1825; KCB, 1837; lieutenant-general, 1838.

JOHNSTON, William (1800–1874), Presbyterian minister; MA, Glasgow, 1817; minister of Limekilns, 1823–74; moderator of the synod, 1854.

JOHNSTON, Sir William (1802–1888), lord provost of Edinburgh; joined his brother Alexander Keith *Johnston the elder in founding firm of W. & A. K. Johnston at Edinburgh, 1826; high constable of Edinburgh, 1828; engraver to Queen Victoria 1837; bailie, 1840; lord provost, 1848–51.

JOHNSTON, William (1829–1902), Orangeman; BA, Trinity College, Dublin, 1852; MA, 1856; called to Irish bar, 1872; entered Orange order, 1848; proposed institution of triennial council of Orangemen, 1865; imprisoned for organizing and leading a demonstration against Party Processions Act, 1868; Independent Conservative MP for Belfast, 1868–78; inspector of Irish fisheries, 1878; dismissed for violent speeches against Land League and home rule, 1885; MP for South Belfast, 1885 till death; firm advocate of 'the three F's' (fair rent, free sale, fixity of tenure), and of temperance.

JOHNSTONE. See also JOHNSON and JOHNSTON.

JOHNSTONE, Andrew James Cochrane (fl. 1814), adventurer; assumed name of Johnstone on first marriage, 1793; MP for Stirling, 1791–7; lieutenant-colonel of the 79th, 1794; governor of Dominica, 1797–1803; brigadier of Leeward Islands, 1799–1803; his commission suspended for tyranny, 1803; elected MP for Grampound, 1807, unseated, 1808, re-elected, 1812; committed acts of fraud at Tortola, 1807; being found guilty of conspiracy on the Stock Exchange fled the country, and was expelled the House of Commons, 1814.

JOHNSTONE, Bryce (1747–1805), minister of Holywood, Dumfries, 1772–1805; of St Andrews University; agriculturist.

JOHNSTONE, Charles (1719?–1800?), author of *Chrysal, or the Adventures of a Guinea* (1760–5); died at Calcutta.

JOHNSTONE, Mrs Christian Isobel (1781–1857), novelist; assisted her husband, John Johnstone, in editing the *Inverness Courier* and *The Edinburgh Weekly Chronicle*; edited *Tait's Magazine* after its incorporation with Johnstone's *Edinburgh Magazine*, 1834; published *The Cook and Housewife's Manual . . . by Mistress Margaret Dods* (1826), *Clan Albin* (1815), and other works.

JOHNSTONE, Edward (1757–1851), physician; son of James *Johnstone (1730?–1802); MD, Edinburgh, 1799; president of Birmingham Medical School, 1827; first principal of Queen's College, Birmingham.

JOHNSTONE, Edward (1804–1881), claimant of Annandale peerage (1876–81); son of Edward *Johnstone (1757–1851); MA, Trinity College, Cambridge, 1828; barrister, Lincoln's Inn, 1828, and Inner Temple, 1838; joint founder of Literary Association of Friends of Poland, 1832.

JOHNSTONE, George (1730–1787), commodore; distinguished himself in attack on Port Louis, 1748; his appointment as governor of West Florida (1765) attacked in the *North Briton*; MP, Cockermouth, 1768, Appleby, 1774, Lostwithiel, 1781, and Ilchester, 1784; when commissioner to treat with the Americans (1778) tried to win over one of the opposite party by a private arrangement; rewarded for support of government by command of small squadron on the Portuguese coast as commodore, 1779; while leading expedition against the Cape of Good Hope gained some successes, but failed in his objective; elected an East India director, 1783.

JOHNSTONE, James, the younger (1754–1783), physician; son of James *Johnstone the elder; MD, Edinburgh, 1773; died of gaol fever when physician to the Worcester Infirmary.

JOHNSTONE, James (d. 1798), Scandinavian antiquary; chaplain to English envoy in Denmark; translated Danish and Norwegian classics; published *Antiquitates Celto-Scandicae* (1784) and *Antiquitates Celto-Normannicae* (1786), and other works.

JOHNSTONE, James, Chevalier de Johnstone (1719–1800?), Jacobite; aide-de-camp to the Young Pretender in 1745; lay hid after Culloden, eventually escaping to London and Holland; served with the French at Louisbourg and (1759) Quebec, and received the cross of St Louis and a pension; extracts from his memoirs published as *History of the Rebellion of 1745* (1820), the whole being translated (1870).

JOHNSTONE, James, the elder (1730?–1802), physician; MD, Edinburgh, 1750; practised at Kidderminster and Worcester; published essays on the *Malignant Epidemical Fever of 1756* (1758), *Use of the Ganglions of the Nerves* (1771), and other works.

JOHNSTONE, James (1806–1869), physician; son of Edward *Johnstone (1757–1851); MD, Trinity College, Cambridge, 1833; FRCP, 1834; professor of materia medica, Queen's College, Birmingham, and extraordinary physician to Birmingham Hospital, 1841; chief work, *Therapeutic Arrangement and Syllabus of Materia Medica* (1835).

JOHNSTONE, James (1815–1878), proprietor of the *Standard* and *Morning Herald* from 1857; revived *Evening Standard*, 1860.

JOHNSTONE, James Hope, third earl of Hopetoun (1741–1816). See HOPE, JAMES.

JOHNSTONE (or JONSTON), John (1603–1675), naturalist; born in Poland; studied at St Andrews, Cambridge, and Leiden; MD, Leiden, 1632; practised at Leiden; lived on his estate in Silesia from 1655; published scientific treatises; his works on natural history (1649–53) frequently re-edited and translated.

JOHNSTONE, John (1768–1836), physician; brother of Edward *Johnstone (1757–1851); of Merton College, Oxford; MA, 1792; MD, 1800; FRCP, 1805; Harveian orator, 1819; physician to Birmingham General Hospital, 1801–33; author of *Memoirs* of Dr Samuel *Parr (1828); published *Account of Discovery of the Power of Mineral Acid Vapours to Destroy Contagion* (1803).

JOHNSTONE, John Henry (1749–1828), actor and tenor singer; after performing on the Irish operatic stage appeared at Covent Garden, 1783–1803, and at Drury Lane, 1803–20; called 'Irish Johnstone', from his excellence as an exponent of Irish comedy parts.

JOHNSTONE, William, third earl of Annandale and Hartfell, and first marquis of Annandale (d. 1721), of Glasgow University;

succeeded to earldom, 1672; friend of *Monmouth; nominally supported Revolution, but joined 'The Club' of Jacobite malcontents and was imprisoned in connection with *Montgomery plot; restored to favour on making confession; created extraordinary lord of session, 1693, and a lord of the Treasury; pensioned for services in connection with Glencoe inquiry; created marquis, 1701; lord high commissioner to general assembly, 1701 and 1711; lord privy seal (Scotland), 1702; and president of Privy Council, 1702–6; KT, 1704; joint secretary of state, 1705; opposed the Union; Scots representative peer; keeper of the great seal, 1714.

JOHNSTONE, William Borthwick (1804–1868), landscape and historical painter; Royal Scottish Academy, 1848, treasurer, 1850; first curator of National Gallery of Scotland, 1858; painted miniatures and collected works of art and antiquities.

JOHN THE PAINTER (1752–1777), incendiary. See AITKEN, JAMES.

JOHN THOMPSON (THOMSON or TOMSON) (*fl.* 1382), Carmelite. See THOMPSON.

JOHN THORESBY (d. 1373), archbishop of York and chancellor. See THORESBY.

JOHN WELLS (d. 1388), opponent of Wycliffe. See WELLS.

JOHNYS, Sir **Hugh** (*fl.* 1417–1463), knight-marshal of England and France; fought under the eastern emperor against the Turks, 1436–41; suitor for hand of *Elizabeth Woodville, *c.*1452.

JOICEY, James, first Baron Joicey (1846–1936), colliery proprietor; became chairman and managing director of family firm, trading from 1924 as the Lambton, Hetton, and Joicey Collieries, the largest concern in the northern coalfield; Liberal MP, Chester-le-Street division of County Durham, 1885–1906; baronet, 1893; baron, 1906.

JOLIFFE, George (1621–1658), physician. See JOYLIFFE.

JOLIFFE, Henry (d. 1573), dean of Bristol; of Clare Hall and Michaelhouse, Cambridge; MA, 1527; BD; canon of Worcester, 1542; resisted Bishop *Hooper and wrote against *Ridley; dean of Bristol, 1554–8; attended *Cranmer's second trial; lived at Louvain after accession of Elizabeth.

JOLLIE, John, the elder (1640?–1682), ejected minister; brother of Thomas *Jollie the elder; of Trinity College, Dublin; received Presbyterian ordination at Manchester, 1672.

JOLLIE, John, the younger (d. 1725), Nonconformist minister; son of John *Jollie the elder.

JOLLIE, Thomas, the elder (1629–1703), ejected minister; became intimate of Oliver *Heywood at Trinity College, Cambridge; formed a 'gathered church' at Altham, Lancashire, 1649; frequently imprisoned; licensed to preach at Wymondhouses, Whalley, 1672, where he built meeting-houses after the Revolution; one of those who exorcized Richard *Dugdale, 1689–90; joined 'the happy union', 1693; published tracts on the Surrey demoniac (Dugdale).

JOLLIE, Thomas, the younger (d. 1764), Independent minister; son of Timothy *Jollie the elder.

JOLLIE, Timothy, the elder (1659?–1714), Independent tutor; son of Thomas *Jollie (1629–1703); received Presbyterian ordination, 1682; imprisoned at York, 1683; his congregation at Sheffield the largest Nonconformist meeting in Yorkshire; started, 1689, and conducted, 1689–1714, an academy at Attercliffe.

JOLLIE, Timothy, the younger (1692–1757), son of Timothy *Jollie the elder; succeeded his father at Sheffield and Matthew *Clarke (1664–1726) at Miles Lane, Cannon Street, London.

JOLLIFFE, William George Hylton, first Baron Hylton (1800–1876), politician; created baronet, 1821; Conservative MP, Petersfield, 1833–5 and 1837–66; under-secretary for Home Department, 1852; secretary to Treasury and Conservative whip, 1858–9; privy councillor, 1859; created Baron Hylton, 1866.

JOLLY, Alexander (1756–1838), bishop of Moray; educated at Marischal College, Aberdeen; episcopal minister at Turriff, 1777, and Fraserburgh, 1788; coadjutor of Moray and Ross, 1796; bishop of Moray, 1798–1838; hon. DD, Washington College, Connecticut, 1826; published religious works.

JOLOWICZ, Herbert Felix (1890–1954), academic lawyer; educated at St Paul's School and Trinity College, Cambridge; first class, part i, classical tripos (1911), and part i, law tripos (1913); called to bar (Inner Temple), 1919; All Souls reader in Roman law, Oxford, 1920–31; lecturer, 1924; professor, 1931–48, Roman law, University College, London; regius professor of civil law, Oxford, 1948–54; edited *Journal* of Society of Public Teachers of Law, 1924–54; published *Historical Introduction to Roman Law* (1932) and *Roman Foundations of Modern Law* (1957).

JOLY, Charles Jasper (1864–1906), royal astronomer of Ireland; mathematical scholar of Trinity College, Dublin, 1882; obtained studentship, 1886; fellow, 1894–7; made researches in physics, and especially studied the properties of linear vector functions; royal astronomer of Ireland at Dunsink, 1897; edited and enlarged Sir William Rowan *Hamilton's *Elements of Quaternions* (2 vols., 1899–1901); contributed numerous papers on quaternions and kindred subjects to Royal Irish Academy; published *A Manual of Quaternions* (1905); accompanied eclipse expedition to Spain, 1900; FRS, 1904; member of Alpine Club.

JOLY, John (1857–1933), engineer, geologist, and physicist; educated at Rathmines School and Trinity College, Dublin; professor of geology, Dublin, 1887–1933; invented a meldometer, a hydrostatic balance, and a condensation method of calorimetry; reduced aluminium from topaz; propounded (with H. H. *Dixon) the generally accepted cohesion theory of the ascent of sap in trees, 1893; pioneer in colour photography; as a keen yachtsman wrote on synchronous signalling, a collision predictor, floating breakwaters, etc.; paid much attention to radioactivity in geology, advancing in *The Surface History of the Earth* (1925) the radioactive explanation of thermal cycles; chiefly responsible for the building of Trinity College science schools; originated Royal Dublin Society's Radium Institute; FRS, 1892.

JOLY DE LOTBINIÈRE, Sir Henry Gustave (1829–1908), Canadian politician; born at Épernay, France; called to Canadian bar, 1855; Liberal member of Canadian House of Assembly for Lotbinière, 1861; opposed federation movement; member of Quebec Legislative Assembly, 1867–74; QC, 1878; formed government, 1878–9; KCMG, 1895; minister of inland revenue and PC, 1897; lieutenant-governor of British Columbia, 1900–6; promoted interests of agriculture and forestry.

JONES, Lady (1889–1981), novelist and playwright. See BAGNOLD, ENID ALGERINE.

JONES, Adrian (1845–1938), sculptor; qualified as veterinary surgeon; retired from army as captain, 1890; perfectly understood horses, his chief models; monumental sculptures include Royal Marines Monument, St James's Park (1903), *Peace Quadriga*, Constitution Hill (1912), and Cavalry War Memorial, Stanhope Gate (1924).

JONES, (Alfred) Ernest (1879–1958), physician and psychoanalyst; educated at Swansea Grammar School, Llandovery College, and University College, Cardiff; qualified from University College Hospital, London, 1900; MD, 1903; MRCP, 1904; FRCP, 1942; began practising psychoanalysis, 1906; director, psychiatric clinic, Toronto, 1908–12; established London practice, 1913; founded British Psycho-Analytical Society, 1919, and *International Journal of Psycho-Analysis*, 1920; editor until 1939; set up Institute of Psycho-Analysis, 1924, publishing International Psycho-Analytical Library; publications include *Sigmund Freud, Life and Work* (3 vols., 1953–7); hon. D.Sc., Wales.

JONES, Sir Alfred Lewis (1845–1909), man of business; born at Carmarthen; became partner of Messrs Elder, Dempster's shipping firm at Liverpool, 1879; gained monopoly of West African shipping trade; founded Bank of British West Africa, 1897; revivified the Canaries, inaugurating there banana industry (1884) and tourist traffic, and establishing coaling station at Las Palmas; inaugurated new steamship service with Jamaica from Bristol (1901) for banana traffic; helped to found Liverpool School of Tropical Medicine, 1898; KCMG, 1901; hon. fellow of Jesus College, Oxford, 1905.

JONES, Allan Gwynne- (1892–1982), artist. See GWYNNE-JONES.

JONES, Ambrose (d. 1678), bishop of Kildare; son of Lewis *Jones; educated at Dublin; archdeacon of Meath, 1661; bishop of Kildare, 1667–78.

JONES, Arnold Hugh Martin (1904–1970), historian of Greece and Rome; educated at Cheltenham College and New College, Oxford; first class, hon. mods. and Lit. Hum., 1924–6; Craven scholar, 1923; fellow, All Souls, 1926–46; reader in ancient history, Cairo University, 1929–34; lecturer in ancient history, Wadham College, Oxford, 1939–46; served in Ministry of Labour and War Office during 1939–45 war; professor of ancient history, University College, London, 1946, Cambridge, 1951; fellow, Jesus College; publications include *A History of Abyssinia* (with Elizabeth Mouroe, 1935), *The Herods of Judaea* (1938), *The Greek City from Alexander to Justinian* (1940), *Constantine and the Conversion of Europe* (1948), *Athenian Democracy* (1957), *Studies in Roman Government and Law* (1960), *Sparta* (1967), and *Augustus* (1970); FBA, 1947; president, Society for Promotion of Roman Studies, 1952–5; LL D, Cambridge, 1965; DD, Oxford, 1966; hon. fellow, New College.

JONES, Arthur Creech (1891–1964), politician; educated at Whitehall Boys' School, Bristol; worked in solicitor's office, 1905; entered Civil Service as junior clerk; hon. secretary, Dulwich branch of ILP, 1913; organized opposition to conscription; imprisoned, 1916–19; secretary, National Union of Docks, Wharves, and Shipping Staffs, and editor, *Quayside and Office*, 1919–22; national secretary, administrative, clerical, and supervisory group, Transport and General Workers Union, 1922; interested in trade-union organization in colonies; published

Trade Unionism Today (1928); organizing secretary, Workers' Travel Association, 1929; Labour MP, Shipley division of Yorkshire, 1935–50; parliamentary secretary to Ernest *Bevin, minister of labour, 1940–4; founded, with Dr Rita Hinden, Fabian Colonial Bureau, 1940; parliamentary under-secretary of state, Colonial Office, 1945; secretary of state for colonies, 1946–50; contributed much to policy of development and preparing colonies for independence; governor, Ruskin College, 1923–56; governor, Queen Elizabeth House, Oxford, 1954; vice-president, Workers' Educational Association; MP, Wakefield, 1954–64; PC, 1946.

JONES, Avonia (1839?–1867), afterwards Mrs Brooke; actress; native of New York, where she died; married Gustavus *Brooke; played in England, Ireland, America, and Australia.

JONES, Basset (*fl.* 1634–1659), physician and grammarian; of Jesus College, Oxford; author of *Lapis Chymicus Philosophorum Examini subjectus* (1648) and *Hermaeologium* (1659).

JONES, Sir (Bennett) Melvill (1887–1975), professor of aeronautical engineering; educated at Birkenhead School and Emmanuel College, Cambridge, of which he became a scholar; first class, mechanical sciences tripos, 1909; worked in aeronautical department of National Physical Laboratory, 1910–13, and in industry on airship design, 1913; joined Royal Aircraft Factory, Farnborough, 1914, working on aerial gunnery and development of instruments to assist flying in clouds; moved to Air Armament Experimental Station, Orford Ness, 1916; qualified as pilot; served in RFC in France, 1918; AFC; returned to Cambridge as fellow of Emmanuel College, 1919; professor of aeronautical engineering, 1919–52; made detailed study of aeroplane stalling and ways of reducing drag; returned to work for Air Ministry on aerial gunnery, laying foundations of development of gyro gunsight; chairman, Aeronautical Research Committee (later Council), 1943–6; returned to Cambridge and research on drag, 1946–52; part-time consultant at Royal Aircraft Establishment; CBE, 1938; FRS, 1939; knighted, 1942; awarded USA Medal of Freedom, 1947; Gold Medal of Royal Aeronautical Society, 1947; hon. fellow of the Society, 1951.

JONES, Bernard Mouat (1882–1953), chemist, principal of Manchester College of Technology, and vice-chancellor of Leeds University; educated at Dulwich College and Balliol College, Oxford; first class, chemistry, mineralogy, and crystallography, 1904; professor of chemistry, Government College, Lahore,

1906–13; Aberystwyth, 1919–21; DSO, 1917, for work at GHQ central laboratory identifying gases; principal, Manchester College of Technology, 1921–38; vice-chancellor, Leeds, 1938–48; in latter appointments obtained interest and co-operation of industry; honorary degrees, Durham, Leeds, and Wales.

JONES, Charles Handfield (1819–1890), physician; educated at Rugby, Catharine Hall, Cambridge (BA, 1840, MB, 1843), and at St George's; FRCP, 1849, senior censor, 1886, vice-president, 1888; physician to St Mary's Hospital, 1851–90; FRS, 1850; Lumleian lecturer, 1865; published *Manual of Pathological Anatomy* (with Sir E. H. Sieveking, 1854), *Clinical Observations on Functional Nervous Disorders* (1864).

JONES, Charlotte (1768–1847), miniature painter; pupil of *Cosway; exhibited at Royal Academy, 1801–23; chiefly known for her twelve miniatures of Princess *Charlotte, now at Cranmer Hall, Norfolk.

JONES, David (*fl.* 1560–1590), Welsh poet and antiquary; vicar of Llanfair Dyffryn Clwyd.

JONES, David (*fl.* 1676–1720), historical writer and translator; said to have been captain in the Horse Guards; sometime secretary-interpreter to Louvois; author of *Secret History of White Hall from the Restoration . . . to the Abdication of the late King James* (1697), *Compleat History of Europe*, 1705–20 (annual), *History of the Turks, 1655–1701* (1701), and other works.

JONES, David (1663–1724?), eccentric preacher; of Westminster and Christ Church, Oxford; BA, 1685; curate of St Mary Woolnoth and St Mary Woolchurch Haw, London; afterwards vicar of Great Budworth, Cheshire, and Marcham, Berkshire.

JONES, David (1711–1777), Welsh hymn-writer and translator of Dr *Watts's hymns.

JONES, David (Dafydd Sion Dafydd or **Dewi Fardd)** (*fl.* 1750–1780), Welsh poet and antiquary; edited *Blodeugerdd Cymru* (1759) and *Y Cydymaith Dyddan* (1776).

JONES, David (1735–1810), Welsh revivalist; active member of Welsh Methodist 'Association' and preacher at Lady Huntingdon's Chapel; vicar of Llangan, Glamorganshire, 1768, of Maenornawan, Pembrokeshire, 1794; opposed separation from the church.

JONES, David (1765–1816), 'the Welsh Freeholder'; MA, Caius College, Cambridge, 1803; succeeded *Priestley as minister of the New Meeting-House, Birmingham, 1792; practised as a barrister, having been called from Lincoln's Inn, 1800; as 'the Welsh Freeholder' defended

Unitarianism against Bishop Samuel *Horsley, and published tracts in his own name.

JONES, David (1796–1841), missionary to Madagascar; went to Madagascar, 1818; with David *Griffiths and David *Johns settled Malagasy orthography on the phonetic system, 1822; visited the queen at Ambatomanga to petition against persecution of Christians, 1840; died in Mauritius.

JONES, David (1895–1974), painter, poet, and essayist; attended Camberwell School of Art, 1910–14; enlisted in Welch Fusiliers, 1915; wounded on the Somme, 1916; left France with severe trench fever, 1918; studied at Westminster School of Art, 1919–21; became Roman Catholic, 1921; worked under A. Eric R. *Gill; painted the lettering of the war memorial at New College, Oxford; exhibited at Seven and Five Society, 1928; worked as painter, engraver, and sculptor in wood; his poetry published in *In Parenthesis* (1937), *The Anathemata* (1952), and *The Sleeping Lord* (1974); his 'inscriptions', words painted on paper, a new art; work interrupted by eye trouble from 1930 onwards; first retrospective exhibition, National Museum of Wales and the Tate Gallery, 1954–5; CBE, 1955; CH, 1974; hon. D.Litt., University of Wales, 1960; *The Roman Quarry*, with foreword by Harman Grisewood and notes by René Hague, published posthumously, 1981.

JONES, Ebenezer (1820–1860), poet; author of *Studies of Sensation and Event* (1843, reissued 1878) and some maturer lyrics written at the close of life.

JONES, Edward (1641–1703), bishop of St Asaph; of Westminster and Trinity College, Cambridge; fellow, 1667; MA, 1668; while master of Kilkenny School had Swift as pupil; dean of Lismore, 1678; bishop of Cloyne, 1683–92, of St Asaph, 1692–1700; deprived of St Asaph for simony and maladministration, 1701.

JONES, Edward (1752–1824), 'Bardd y Brenin' (the King's Bard); gained repute as a harpist; published *Musical and Poetical Relicks of the Welsh Bards* (1784) and other collections of music.

JONES, Edward (*fl.* 1771–1831), author ('Ned Mon'); of the Gwyneddigion Society; published *Cicero's Brutus* (1776), *Index to Records called the Originalia and Memoranda* (vol. i, 1793, vol. ii, 1795), and *Cyfreithiau Plwyf* (parish laws, 1794).

JONES, Edward (1777–1837), founder of Welsh Wesleyan Methodism.

JONES, Elizabeth Emma (1813–1842), painter. See SOYER.

JONES, Ernest Charles (1819–1869), Chartist and poet; educated abroad; barrister, Middle Temple, 1844; defended Feargus *O'Connor against Thomas *Cooper, 1846; advocated physical force, and suffered two years' imprisonment (1848–50) for seditious speeches; twice contested Halifax and Nottingham; edited *The People's Paper*; published sensational novels, *The Battle Day and other Poems* (1855), political songs, and other verse.

JONES, Evan (Ieuan Gwynedd) (1820–1852), Welsh poet and journalist; Independent minister at Tredegar, 1845–8; published *Facts and Figures and Statements* (1849) defending Welsh Nonconformists against report of commission of 1847 on Welsh education; conducted *Y Gymraes* (magazine for women) and *Yr Adolygydd* (national quarterly), 1850–2; his collected poems edited by the Revd T. Roberts (1876).

JONES, Frederick Edward (1759–1834), manager of Crow Street Theatre, Dublin, 1796–1814, and in 1819; of Trinity College, Dublin; met with persistent opposition and misfortune, and was imprisoned for debt; called 'Buck Jones' from his handsome appearance; Jones Road, Dublin, named after him.

JONES, (Frederic) Wood (1879–1954), anatomist; MB, BS, London Hospital, 1904; professor of anatomy, London School of Medicine for Women, 1912–14; Adelaide University, 1919–27; Rockefeller professor of anthropology, Hawaii, 1927–30; professor of anatomy, Melbourne, 1930–7; Manchester, 1938–45; Royal College of Surgeons, 1945–52; in *Man's Place among the Mammals* (1929) refuted close relationship between man and apes; other publications include works on anatomy of the hand (1920) and the foot (1944); FRS, 1925; FRCS, 1930.

JONES, George (1786–1869), painter; son of John *Jones (1745?–1797); volunteer in the Peninsula; painted views of Waterloo and Vittoria; RA, 1824, librarian, 1834–40, keeper, 1840–50, and acting president, 1845–50; friend of *Turner and *Chantrey; chief adviser of Robert *Vernon.

JONES, George Matthew (1785?–1831), captain in the navy; brother of Sir John Thomas *Jones; lieutenant of the *Amphion* under *Nelson and *Hoste, 1803–8, being severely wounded in the Adriatic; posted, 1818; visited and described in *Travels* (1827) the courts of most of the countries of Europe.

JONES, Sir (George) Roderick (1877–1962), newsagency head; on father's death sent to live in South Africa; became Pretoria journalist in his teens; learned Afrikaans and gained confidence of Paul Kruger; interviewed (Sir) L. S. *Jameson after his capture by Boers; covered South African War as correspondent; arrested by British as a spy; Reuters' senior cable correspondent in Cape Town; chief sub-editor, *Cape Times*; editor, South African desk, London, 1902; succeeded Baron Herbert de Reuter as head of company, 1915; chairman and managing director, 1919–41; travelled widely; received honours from France, Italy, Greece, and China; KBE, 1918; chief executive and director of propaganda, Ministry of Information, 1918; resigned from Reuters after dispute with other directors regarding agreement to accept government financial assistance, 1941; published *A Life in Reuters* (1951); member of council of Royal Institute of International Affairs; delegate to Congress of Europe at The Hague, 1948; chairman of governors of Roedean School, 1950–62; married Enid *Bagnold, novelist and playwright, 1920.

JONES, Giles (*fl.* 1765), brother and collaborator of Griffith *Jones (1722–1786) in *Lilliputian Histories*.

JONES, Griffith (1683–1761), founder of Welsh charity or circulating schools; incumbent of Llandilo Abercowyn, 1711; rector of Llanddowror, 1716; attacked by John Evans, vicar of Eglwys Cymmun, 1752; published *Welsh Piety* (annual, 1737–61) and various theological works in Welsh; said to have 'converted' Daniel *Rowlands of Llangeitho.

JONES, Griffith (1722–1786), writer for the young and editor of the *London Chronicle, Daily Advertiser*, and *Public Ledger*; printed the *Literary* and *British* magazines.

JONES, Sir Harford (1764–1847), diplomat. See BRYDGES, Sir HARFORD JONES.

JONES, Sir Harold Spencer (1890–1960), astronomer; educated at Latymer Upper School, Hammersmith, and Jesus College, Cambridge; first class, parts i and ii, mathematical tripos, 1909–11, and physics in part ii, natural sciences tripos, 1912; research fellow, 1913; appointed to Greenwich, 1913; astronomer, Royal Observatory, Cape of Good Hope, 1923–33; Sc.D., Cambridge, 1925; astronomer royal, Greenwich, 1933–55; organized removal to Herstmonceux Castle and obtained approval for 98-inch telescope; his demonstration of irregularities in rate of rotation of earth led to adoption of concept of Ephemeris Time, 1950; published, 1941, discussions of results of his world-wide programme of observations of Eros (1930–1) to determine value of 'solar parallax'; contributed to time measurement, horology, application of geomagnetism to navigation, and organization of international science; FRS, 1930; knighted, 1943; KBE, 1955; hon. fellow, Jesus College, Cambridge, 1933.

JONES, Sir Harry David (1791–1866), lieutenant-general; brother of Sir John Thomas *Jones; entered Royal Engineers, 1808; served in Walcheren expedition (1809) and Peninsula, being present at capture of Badajoz, 1812, and Battle of Vittoria, 1813; captured severely wounded while leading 'forlorn hope' at San Sebastian (25 July, 1813); again wounded at the Nive, 1813; at New Orleans, 1814, and with the army of occupation after Waterloo; secretary to Irish Railway Commission and first commissioner of boundaries, 1836; chairman of Irish Board of Works, 1845–50; director of engineers at Chatham, 1851; commanded as brigadier land operations in Baltic, 1854; commanding engineer at Sebastopol, 1855, being severely wounded at the unsuccessful assault of 18 June; created KCB, receiving Legion of Honour and other foreign orders; governor of Sandhurst, 1856–66; chairman of Defence Commission of 1859; lieutenant-general, 1860; GCB and DCL of Oxford, 1861.

JONES, Harry Longueville (1806–1870), founder (1846) and first editor of *Archaeologia Cambrensis*; fellow of Magdalene College, Cambridge; thirty-first wrangler, 1828; MA, 1832; proposed formation of a Manchester university, 1836; inspector of schools for Wales, 1849–64; published (with Thomas *Wright) *Memorials of Cambridge* (1841) and other works.

JONES, Henry (1605–1682), bishop of Meath; son of Lewis *Jones; MA, Trinity College, Dublin, 1624 (vice-chancellor, 1646); dean of Ardagh, 1625, of Kilmore, 1637; when prisoner in hands of the rebels presented the Cavan remonstrance, 1641; bishop of Clogher, 1645; engaged on the settlement of Ulster (1653) and other commissions; bishop of Meath, 1661–82; active in procuring evidence of a 'popish plot' in Ireland.

JONES, Henry (d. 1727), abridger of *Philosophical Transactions*, 1700–20; of Eton and King's College, Cambridge; fellow of King's College; MA, 1720; FRS, 1724.

JONES, Henry (1721–1770), poet and dramatist; patronized by *Chesterfield, who assisted him to produce *Poems on Several Occasions* (1749), and by *Cibber; his *Earl of Essex* acted with success at Covent Garden Theatre, 1753; took to drink and was run over in St Martin's Lane, London.

JONES, Henry (1831–1899), known as Cavendish; writer on whist; educated at King's College School; studied at St Bartholomew's Hospital; MRCS and LSA, 1852; practised in London; retired, 1869; an enthusiastic student of whist; published (1862) *Principles of Whist stated* *and explained by Cavendish*; whist editor of the *Field* from 1862; issued works on card games and other pastimes.

JONES, Sir Henry (1852–1922), philosopher; master of Ironworks School, Brynamman, 1873; MA, Glasgow University, 1878; influenced by Edward *Caird; professor of philosophy and political economy, University College of North Wales, Bangor, 1884; professor of logic, rhetoric, and metaphysics, St Andrews, 1891; professor of moral philosophy, Glasgow, 1894–1922; called himself a 'spiritual realist'; fullest statement of his metaphysic given in his last volume, *A Faith that Enquires* (1922); FBA, 1904; knighted, 1912.

JONES, Henry Arthur (1851–1929), dramatist; commercial traveller in London, Bradford, and Exeter districts, 1869–79; thereafter relied for livelihood solely on writing of plays; these include *The Silver King* (1882), *Saints and Sinners* (1884), *Judah* (1890), *The Dancing Girl* (1891), *The Tempter* (1893), *The Case of Rebellious Susan* (1894), *Michael and his Lost Angel* (1896), *The Liars* (1897), *Mrs. Dane's Defence* (1900), *The Hypocrites* (1906), *The Divine Gift* (1913, never produced), *The Lie* (1914); played an important part in revival of English drama; excelled as a craftsman.

JONES, Henry Bence (1814–1873), physician and chemist; of Harrow and Trinity College, Cambridge; MA, 1840; MD, 1849; FRS, 1846; physician to St George's Hospital, 1846–62; FRCP, 1849, afterwards senior censor; secretary to Royal Institution from 1860; studied chemistry under Graham and Liebig; friend and biographer of *Faraday; works include *Lectures on Animal Chemistry* (1860) and *Croonian Lectures on Matter and Force* (1868).

JONES, Henry Cadman (1818–1902), law reporter; educated at Trinity College, Cambridge; second wrangler, second Smith's prizeman, and fellow, 1841; called to bar, 1845; edited Chancery reports from 1857 till 1865.

JONES, Sir Henry Stuart- (1867–1939), classical scholar, Roman historian, and lexicographer; educated at Rossall School and Balliol College, Oxford; first class, Lit. Hum., and fellow of Trinity, 1890; tutor, 1896; director, British School at Rome, 1903–5; engaged upon revision of *Liddell and *Scott's *Greek–English Lexicon*, 1911–39; organized remarkable body of specialists as voluntary collaborators, and although incorporating much new material kept the edition within reasonable bounds; Camden professor of ancient history, Oxford, 1919–27; principal, University College of Wales, Aberystwyth, 1927–34; vice-chancellor, University of Wales, 1929–31; served on representative council of Welsh Church; publications include revision of Thucydides (1898–1900) for Oxford Classical Texts, *Companion to Roman History* (1912), *Fresh Light on Roman Bureaucracy* (1920), and chapters in vol. vii of *Cambridge Ancient History*; FBA, 1915; knighted, 1933.

JONES, Sir Horace (1819–1887), City of London architect; designed Smithfield and reconstructed Billingsgate and Leadenhall markets, the Guildhall Library and museum (1872), and the new council chamber (1884); with Sir J. *Wolfe Barry, made plans for the Tower Bridge; PRIBA, 1882–3; knighted, 1886.

JONES, Sir Hugh (*fl.* 1417–1463), knight-marshal of England and France. See JOHNYS.

JONES, Hugh (1508–1574), bishop of Llandaff, 1567–74; BCL, Oxford, 1541.

JONES, Inigo (1573–1652), architect; son of a Roman Catholic cloth-worker of London; in his youth travelled on the continent at expense of William *Herbert, third earl of Pembroke; summoned from Venice to Denmark by Christian IV; designed shifting scenes, machines, and dresses for many masques by Ben *Jonson, Samuel *Daniel, Aurelian *Townsend, *Heywood, *D'Avenant, and others; quarrelled with Ben Jonson, and was satirized as In-and-In Medlay in his *Tale of a Tub* (1633); surveyor of works to *Henry, prince of Wales, 1610–12; again visited Italy, 1613–15, purchasing works of art for lords *Arundel and *Pembroke; supposed to have designed buildings at Leghorn; surveyor-general of works, 1615; designed the queen's house at Greenwich (1617–35), Lincoln's Inn Chapel (1617–23), west side of Lincoln's Inn Fields, banqueting house at Whitehall (1619–22) as part of a projected new palace; also the water-gate in Buckingham Street, Adelphi, St Paul's Church, Covent Garden (rebuilt from his designs, 1795), and the piazza of Covent Garden, Ashburnham House, Westminster, and other buildings; as surveyor directed extensive repairs to the old St Paul's Cathedral; in Basing House during the siege (1643–5), but on payment of a fine received back his estate; prepared designs for Wilton House, 1648. Large collections of his drawings are at Worcester College, Oxford, and at Chatsworth.

JONES, Isaac (1804–1850), Welsh translator; educated at Aberystwyth, where he was headmaster, 1828–34, and Lampeter (Eldon scholar, 1835); curate in Anglesey, 1840–50; translated into Welsh Gurney's *Dictionary of the Bible* (1835), Adam *Clarke's *Commentary* (1847), and other works; joint editor of *Y Geirlyfr Cymraeg* (Welsh encyclopaedia), 1835.

JONES, James Rhys (1813–1889), Welsh writer and lecturer; known as Kilsby Jones; Independent minister at Kilsby, Northamptonshire, 1840–50; preached at Llandrindod Wells from 1868; edited works of W. Williams of Pantycelyn (Welsh), Welsh versions of the *Pilgrim's Progress*, and other works; contributed to Welsh periodicals; popular lecturer.

JONES, (James) Sidney (1861–1946), composer; wrote song 'Linger Longer Loo' (1892), and operettas, including *A Gaiety Girl* (1893), *An Artist's Model* (1895), *The Geisha* (1896), *A Greek Slave* (1898), *San Toy* (1899), and *A Persian Princess* (1909).

JONES, Jenkin (1700?–1742), Welsh Arminian; founded in 1726 Llwynrhydowen, the first Arminian church in Wales; published and translated theological works.

JONES, Jeremiah (1693–1724), Independent tutor at Nailsworth and biblical critic; nephew of Samuel *Jones (1680?–1719); author of *New and Full Method of settling the Canonical Authority of the New Testament* (published 1726).

JONES, Jezreel (d. 1731), traveller; as clerk to the Royal Society visited Barbary, 1698 and 1701; British envoy to Morocco, 1704; contributed valuable specimens to the Sloane collection.

JONES, John (*fl.* 1579), physician; studied at Oxford and Cambridge; practised at Bath and Buxton; translated *Galens Bookes of Elementes* (1574); published books on baths and other medical works.

JONES, John (in religion **Godfrey Maurice**) (d. 1598), alias John Buckley; Franciscan; went to Pontoise on dissolution of the Greenwich house, 1559, and thence to Rome; arrested in England, 1596; hanged, 1598.

JONES, John (1575–1635), Benedictine ('Leander à Sancto Martino'); educated at Merchant Taylors' School and St John's College, Oxford (fellow); entered abbey of St Martin at Compostella, 1599; DD, Salamanca; professor of theology at Douai; vicar-general of Anglo-Spanish Benedictines, 1612; prior of St Gregory's, Douai, 1621–8 and 1629–33; took the oath of allegiance as papal agent in England, 1634; accusation of dealings with him denied by *Laud, 1643; wrote and edited many theological works; his *Rule of St. Benedict* translated by Canon Francis Cuthbert Doyle (1875); correspondence concerning English Catholics printed in *Clarendon State Papers*.

JONES, John (d. 1660), regicide; colonel, 1646; negotiated surrender of Anglesey to parliament, 1646; helped to suppress Sir John *Owen's rising, 1648; MP, Merionethshire, 1647; signed Charles I's death-warrant; commissioner to assist lord-deputy of Ireland, 1650; was removed for republicanism, but married *Cromwell's sister Catherine; one of Cromwell's peers and governor of Anglesey, 1657; member of Committee of Safety and Council of State, 1659; arrested as supporter of *Lambert, but released on submission, 1659; executed as a regicide.

JONES, John (1645–1709), chancellor of Llandaff; fellow of Jesus College, Oxford; MA, 1670; DCL, 1677; chancellor of Llandaff, 1691–1709; wrote a treatise on intermittent fevers (1683) and invented a clock.

JONES, John (1693–1752), classical scholar; of Merchant Taylors' School and St John's College, Oxford; BA, 1716; BCL, 1720; headmaster of Oundle School, 1718; rector of Uppingham, 1743–52; edited Horace (1736).

JONES, John (1700–1770), controversialist; BA, 1721, and chaplain of Worcester College, Oxford; vicar of Alconbury, Huntingdonshire, 1741–50; rector of Bolnhurst, Bedfordshire, 1750–7; curate at Welwyn, 1757–65; vicar of Sheephall, 1767–70; advocated revision of the liturgy in *Free and Candid Disquisitions relating to the Church of England* (1749).

JONES, John (d. 1796), organist of St Paul's, 1755–96, and composer of chants.

JONES, John (1745?–1797), engraver in mezzotint and stipple.

JONES, John (1766?–1827), Unitarian critic; hon. LL D, Aberdeen, 1818; educated at Christ's College, Brecon, and at Hackney, under Gilbert *Wakefield; Presbyterian minister at Plymouth, 1795–8; minister and tutor at Halifax, 1798–1804; a Williams trustee, 1821; published *Illustrations of the Four Gospels* (1808), *Greek-English Lexicon* (1823), and other works.

JONES, John (*fl.* 1797), sub-director of *Handel Commemoration, 1784, and composer.

JONES, John (1767–1821), Welsh satirical song-writer ('Siôn Glanygors'); active member of the Gwyneddigion Society, which met at the King's Head, Ludgate Hill, London, then owned by him; his humorous pieces collected in *Yr Awen Fywiog* (1858).

JONES, John (*fl.* 1827), author of *Attempts in verse by John Jones, an Old Servant* (1831, introduction by *Southey).

JONES, John (1772–1837), Welsh historian; LL D, Jena; author of *History of Wales* (1824), an original translation into Welsh of the Gospels (1812), and other works.

JONES, John (1788–1858), Welsh verse-writer; served as a sailor in the Napoleonic War; afterwards a cotton-spinner; collected poems issued (1856).

JONES, John (1791–1889), archdeacon of Liverpool; MA, St John's College, Cambridge, 1819; incumbent successively of St Andrew's, Liverpool, and Christ Church, Waterloo, Liverpool; published sermons and expository lectures.

JONES, John (1792–1852), Welsh poet and antiquary and Hebraist ('Tegid'); MA, Jesus College, Oxford, 1821; precentor at Christ Church, Oxford, 1823, and perpetual curate of St Thomas's, Oxford, 1823; incumbent of Nevern, Pembrokeshire, 1841–52; prebendary of St David's, 1848–52; transcribed the *Mabinogion* for Lady Charlotte *Guest; joint editor of *Poetical Works of Lewis Glyn Cothi* (1837–9); upheld etymological system of Welsh spelling; his poems published (1859).

JONES, John (Talsarn) (1796–1857), Welsh preacher; composer of psalm- and hymn-tunes.

JONES, John (1800?–1882), virtuoso; a tailor in Waterloo Place; his pictures, furniture, and objects of vertu bequeathed to South Kensington Museum; benefactor of Ventnor Convalescent Hospital.

JONES, John (1804–1887), Welsh biblical commentator ('Idrisyn'); vicar of Llandyssilio Gogo, Cardiganshire, 1858–87; published *Y Deonglydd Beirniadol* (biblical commentary, 1852).

JONES, John (1810–1869), Welsh poet ('Talhaiarn'); as manager to Sir Joseph *Paxton employed in France; wrote Welsh words to old Welsh airs; published three volumes of poetry (1855, 1862, and 1869).

JONES, Sir John (1811–1878), lieutenant-general; lieutenant-colonel of 1st battalion, 60th Rifles at siege of Delhi, commanding the left attack in Sept. 1857; as brigadier of Roorkhee Field Force acquired name of 'the Avenger'; afterwards in Oudh; KCB; lieutenant-general, 1877; received distinguished-service pension.

JONES, John (1821?–1878), Welsh Baptist ('Mathetes'); contributed to *Seren Gomer*, 1846; minister at Rhymney, Monmouthshire, 1862–77; published *Geiriadur Beiblaidd a Duwinyddol* (biblical dictionary, vol. i, 1864, vol. ii, 1869, vol. iii, 1883), and *Areithfa Mathetes* (sermons, 1873).

JONES, John (1835–1877), geologist and engineer; secretary to Cleveland Ironmasters' Association from 1866; founded Iron and Steel Institute, 1868; chief work, *Geology of South Staffordshire*.

JONES, John Andrews (1779–1863), Baptist minister, and author of *Bunhill Memorials* (1849);

minister in London from 1831 (at 'Jireh Chapel', Brick Lane, till 1861, afterwards at East Street, City Road).

JONES, John Daniel (1865–1942), Congregational minister; son of J. D. *Jones; educated at Towyn Academy, Chorley Grammar School, and Owens College, Manchester; BA, 1886; BD, St Andrews, and ordained to Newland Church, Lincoln, 1889; minister, Richmond Hill Church, Bournemouth, 1898–1937; chairman, Congregational Union, 1909–10, 1925–6; honorary secretary, 1919–42; moderator, Free Church Federal Council, 1921–3; of International Congregational Council, 1930–42; CH, 1927.

JONES, John Edward (1806–1862), sculptor of busts; exhibited at the Academy from 1844.

JONES, Sir John Edward Lennard- (1894–1954), scientist and administrator. See LENNARD-JONES.

JONES, John Felix (d. 1878), captain in the Indian Navy and surveyor; employed in survey of Red Sea, 1829–34, Ceylon, and Mesopotamia; during survey of Euphrates and Tigris discovered site of Opis, 1850; author of *Assyrian Vestiges*; political agent in the Persian Gulf, 1855–8.

JONES, John Gale (1769–1838), radical; educated at Merchant Taylors' School, London; caricatured by *Gillray as a speaker at London Corresponding Society's meeting in Copenhagen Fields, London, 1795; imprisoned for sedition, 1798, and for libel on *Castlereagh, 1810; committed to Newgate by the House of Commons for breach of privilege, 1810.

JONES, Sir John Morris- (1864–1929), Welsh poet and grammarian. See MORRIS-JONES.

JONES, John Ogwen (1829–1884), Welsh biblical scholar; BA, London, 1858; Calvinistic Methodist minister at Liverpool, Oswestry, and Rhyl; published lectures and Welsh commentaries.

JONES, John Paul (1747–1792), naval adventurer; son of a Kirkcudbrightshire gardener named Paul; after five years in the slave trade engaged in smuggling and trading in West Indies; entered American Navy under name of Jones, 1775; while in command of the *Ranger* took the fort at Whitehaven, plundered Lord Selkirk's house on St Mary's Isle, and captured the *Drake* off Carrickfergus, 1778; in the *Bonhomme Richard*, accompanied by three French ships and an American, threatened Edinburgh and captured the *Serapis* while convoying the Baltic trade, 1779; afterwards served in French Navy; present as rear-admiral in the Russian service in

Battle of the Liman, 1788; quarrelled with Potemkin; died at Paris.

JONES, John Pike (1790–1857), antiquary; BA, Pembroke College, Cambridge, 1813; was refused institution to benefices, 1819; vicar of Alton, Staffordshire, 1829, and Butterleigh, Devonshire, 1832; published *Historical and Monumental Antiquities of Devonshire* (1823) and part of *Ecclesiastical Antiquities* (1828), and *Flora Devoniensis* (1829).

JONES, Sir John Thomas, first baronet (1783–1843), major-general; adjutant of Royal Engineers at Gibraltar, 1798–1802; employed on construction of Chelmsford lines of defence, 1804; present at Battle of Maida, 1806, and directed attack on Scylla Castle, which he afterwards refortified; aide-de-camp to General *Leith with Spanish Army, 1808; chief of engineers' staff in Walcheren expedition, 1809; completed the works at Torres Vedras, 1810; brevet-lieutenant-colonel, 1812; disabled at Burgos, 1812; while invalided published a *Journal* of the sieges in Spain, severely criticizing their conduct; named CB after serving on commission to report upon defences of Netherlands, 1815, being sole inspector, 1816, while holding a command at Woolwich; colonel and aide-de-camp to George IV, 1825; created baronet, 1831, for services in the Netherlands; major-general, 1837; KCB, 1838; drew up plans for defence of United Kingdom and of Gibraltar, 1840; his statue erected by Engineers in St Paul's Cathedral, London; published works of contemporary military history; his reports on Netherland fortresses privately circulated among Engineers.

JONES, John Viriamu (1856–1901), physicist; son of Thomas *Jones (1819–82); educated at University College, London (B.Sc. and fellow), and Balliol College, Oxford; first class in mathematics, 1879, and natural science, 1880; first principal of University College of South Wales, Cardiff, 1883; first vice-chancellor of University of Wales, 1893; engaged in physical researches dealing especially with the determination of the ohm; FRS, 1894; member of Alpine Club; died at Geneva.

JONES, John Winter (1805–1881), principal librarian of the British Museum; nephew of Stephen *Jones; educated at St Paul's School, London; travelling secretary to charity commissioners, c.1835–7; entered British Museum, 1837; had principal hand in framing the rules for cataloguing; assistant-keeper of printed books, 1850, keeper, 1856–66, principal librarian, 1866–78; president of Library Association, 1877; edited works for Hakluyt Society;

contributed to *Biographical Dictionary* of Society for the Diffusion of Useful Knowledge.

JONES, Joseph David (1827–1870), Welsh musical composer and schoolmaster; his chief compositions the cantata *Llys Arthur* or *Arthur's Court* (1864) and *Tonau ac Emynau* (hymns and tunes, 1868).

JONES, Joshua (d. 1740), Independent minister at Cross Street, Manchester, 1725–40; brother of Jeremiah *Jones.

JONES, Leslie Grove (1779–1839), soldier and radical politician; in the guards during Peninsular War; commandant at Brussels before Waterloo.

JONES, Lewis (1550?–1646), bishop of Killaloe; fellow of All Souls College, Oxford, 1568; BA, 1568; dean of Ardagh, 1606–25, and of Cashel, 1607–33; bishop of Killaloe, 1633–46; restored Cashel Cathedral.

JONES, Lewis Tobias (1797–1895), admiral; lieutenant, 1822; commander, 1838; under Sir Robert *Stopford on coast of Syria, 1840; captain, 1840; commanded expedition against slavery at Lagos, 1851; CB, 1854; in Black Sea, 1854; rear-admiral, 1859; KCB, 1861; commander-in-chief at Queenstown, 1862–5; retired as admiral, 1871; GCB, 1873.

JONES, Lloyd (1811–1886), advocate of co-operation; supporter of Robert *Owen; joint author of *Progress of the Working Classes* (1867); his life of Robert Owen published (1889).

JONES, Matthew (1654–1717), prebendary of Donoughmore, 1687–1717; brother of Edward *Jones (1641–1703).

JONES, Michael (d. 1649), Irish Parliamentarian; son of Lewis *Jones; of Lincoln's Inn; after fighting for the king against the Irish rebels entered service of parliament and distinguished himself as a cavalry leader in northern England, 1644–5; governor of Chester, 1646; as governor of Dublin, 1647–9, routed the Irish at Dungan Hill, 1647, and *Ormonde at Rathmines, 1649; died of fever when *Cromwell's second-in-command.

JONES, Owen (1741–1814), Welsh antiquary ('Owain Myvyr'); London furrier; founded Gwyneddigion Society, 1770; published *The Myvyrian Archaeology of Wales* (1801–7); joint editor of poems of *David ab Gwilym (1789).

JONES, Owen (*fl.* 1790), president of the Gwyneddigion Society, 1793 ('Cor y Cyrtie'); brother of Edward *Jones (*fl.* 1771–1831).

JONES, Owen (1806–1889), Welsh writer ('Meudwy Môn'); Methodist pastor at Mold, Manchester, and Llandudno, 1866–89; published (in Welsh) works, including a historical, topographical, and biographical dictionary of Wales (1875), and a Welsh concordance and commentary.

JONES, Owen (1809–1874), architect and ornamental designer; son of Owen *Jones (1741–1814); visited Paris and Italy, 1830, Greece, Egypt, and Constantinople, 1833, and Granada, 1834 and 1837; superintendent of 1851 exhibition; joint director of decoration of Crystal Palace; designed St James's Hall, London, and decorated the khedive's palace in Egypt; published works, including *Plans, Elevations, &c., of the Alhambra* (1842–5), *The Polychromatic Ornament of Italy* (1846), and *The Grammar of Ornament* (1856).

JONES, Owen Thomas (1878–1967), geologist; educated at Pencader Grammar School, University College of Wales, Aberystwyth, and Trinity College, Cambridge; first class, parts i and ii, natural sciences tripos, 1902–3; joined Geological Survey of Great Britain, 1903; assisted in mapping part of south-Welsh coalfield; first professor of geology, Aberystwyth, 1910; D.Sc., Wales; professor of geology, Manchester University, 1919; professor, Cambridge, 1930–43; last paper written in Welsh dealt with distribution of the blue stones of Carn Meini of Pembrokeshire; president, Geological Society, 1936–8 and 1950–1; FRS, 1926; vice-president, Royal Society, 1940–1; hon. LL D, University of Wales; honorary fellow of geological societies abroad.

JONES, Paul (1747–1792), naval adventurer. See JONES, JOHN PAUL.

JONES, Philip (1618?–1674), Welsh Parliamentarian governor of Swansea, 1645, and colonel, 1646; with Colonel *Horton defeated the Royalists at St Fagans, 1648; governor of Cardiff; MP, Brecknockshire, 1650, Glamorganshire, 1656; one of Cromwell's peers, 1657; member of the Council of State from 1653; controller of the household to Oliver *Cromwell and Richard *Cromwell; acquired large fortune; charged with corruption by the military party and extreme republicans; governor of the Charterhouse, 1658; made his peace with the king and was sheriff of Glamorgan, 1671; purchased Fonmon Castle, 1664.

JONES, Rhys (1713–1801), Welsh poet and compiler of *Gorchestion Beirdd Cymru* (1773).

JONES (JHONES or JOHNES), Richard (fl. 1564–1602), printer of plays, chapbooks, romances, and popular literature, including Nicholas *Breton's works, *Tamburlaine*, and *Pierce Penilesse*.

JONES, Richard (1603–1673), Welsh Nonconformist divine and author of metrical mnemonic digests of the Bible; MA, Jesus College, Oxford, 1628; ejected from mastership of Denbigh School for nonconformity; translated into Welsh works by Baxter.

JONES, Richard, third Viscount and first earl of Ranelagh (1636?–1712), succeeded as third viscount, 1669; chancellor of the Irish Exchequer, 1668; farmed Irish revenues, 1674–81; as paymaster-general (1691–1702) was convicted of defalcation, but escaped prosecution; sat in the English parliament, 1685–1703; Ranelagh Gardens formed out of his Chelsea estate.

JONES, Richard (1767–1840), animal painter.

JONES, Richard (1779–1851), actor and dramatist ('Gentleman Jones'); appeared at Crow Street, Dublin, under Frederick Edward *Jones, 1799; at Covent Garden, London, 1807–9; afterwards took Lewis's parts at the Haymarket; claimed authorship of *The Green Man* (1818) and *Too Late for Dinner* (1820), in which he acted; collaborated with Theodore *Hook in *Hoaxing*; excelled in eccentric roles.

JONES, Richard (1790–1855), political economist; MA, Caius College, Cambridge, 1819; professor of political economy at King's College, London, 1833–5, at Haileybury, 1835–55; secretary to the Capitular Commission, and a charity commissioner; published essay on *Rent* (1831), attacking *Ricardo; his works collected (1850).

JONES, Richard Roberts (1780–1843), self-educated linguist ('Dick of Aberdaron'); son of a carpenter; acquired a knowledge of Greek, Latin, Hebrew, French, Italian, and Spanish, as well as some Chaldaic and Syriac; compiled a Welsh, Greek, and Hebrew dictionary, but was unable to publish it.

JONES, Robert (fl. 1616), musical composer, poet, and lutenist; published four books of ayres, also madrigals, and (1610) *The Muses' Garden of Delights*; some of his songs reprinted in A. H. Bullen's *Lyrics from Elizabethan Song Books*.

JONES, Robert (1810–1879), writer on Welsh literature; BA, Jesus College, Oxford, 1837; vicar of All Saints, Rotherhithe, London, 1841–79; first editor of *Y Cymmrodor*, 1876; author of *History of the Cymmrodorion*; edited works (with life and correspondence) of Revd Goronwy Owen (1876).

JONES, Sir Robert, first baronet (1857–1933), orthopaedic surgeon; graduated from Liverpool School of Medicine (1878) and specialized in orthopaedic surgery; met (Dame) Agnes *Hunt, and with her developed novel system of surgery, nursing, and after-care for crippled children resulting in establishment of a hospital at Baschurch and (1920) of Central Council for Care of Cripples; widely influential as inspector of military orthopaedics, 1916–19; knighted, 1917; baronet, 1926.

JONES, Sir **Robert Armstrong-** (1857–1943), alienist. See ARMSTRONG-JONES.

JONES, Rowland (1722–1774), philologist; of the Inner Temple; published *The Origin of Language and Nations* (1764), an attempt to prove Welsh the primeval language, also *Hieroglyfic* (1768) and other works.

JONES, Samuel (1628–1697), early Welsh Nonconformist; fellow of Jesus College, Oxford, 1652, and bursar, 1655; MA, 1654; received Presbyterian ordination; incumbent of Llangynwyd, Glamorganshire, 1657–62; established (1689) first Welsh Nonconformist academy (afterwards Presbyterian College, Carmarthen).

JONES, Samuel (1680?–1719), Nonconformist tutor at Gloucester and Tewkesbury; studied at Leiden; had among his pupils *Secker (afterwards archbishop), Joseph *Butler, and Daniel *Scott.

JONES, Samuel (d. 1732), poet; queen's searcher at Whitby, 1709–31; published *Poetical Miscellanies* (1714) and *Whitby: a poem* (1718).

JONES, Stephen (1763–1827), editor of the *Biographia Dramatica*; nephew of Griffith *Jones (1722–1786); educated at St Paul's School; edited *European Magazine* (from 1807) and *Freemasons' Magazine*; compiled *The Spirit of the Public Journals*, 1797–1814 (illustrated by *Cruikshank, 1823–5); published among other works a revised edition of Baker's *Biographia Dramatica* (1812), with a continuation as far as 1811.

JONES, Sir **Theophilus** (d. 1685), scoutmaster-general in Ireland; son of Lewis *Jones; saved Lisburn from the Scots under Robert *Monro, 1644; governor of Dublin, 1649–59; elected to British parliament, 1656; after his dismissal (1659) took part against the commonwealth; privy councillor, 1661; scoutmaster-general in Ireland, 1661–85.

JONES, Theophilus (1758–1812), deputyregistrar of Brecon, and author of *History of County of Brecknock* (1805–9).

JONES, Thomas (1530–1620?), alias Thomas Moetheu; Welsh bard and genealogist ('Twm Shon Catti'); employed by Welsh gentry to draw up pedigrees; claimed kinship with Lord *Burghley; the traditional Welsh Robin Hood.

JONES, Thomas (1550?–1619), archbishop of Dublin and lord-chancellor of Ireland; MA, Christ's College, Cambridge; dean of St Patrick's, 1581–4; bishop of Meath, 1584–1605; archbishop of Dublin and lord chancellor of Ireland, 1605–19; a lord justice, 1613 and 1615.

JONES, Thomas (1618–1665), civilian; fellow of Merton College, Oxford; MA, 1644; DCL, 1659; sometime deputy to Oxford professor of civil law; published *Prolusiones Academicae* (1660); died of the plague.

JONES, Thomas (1622?–1682), Welsh divine; fellow of University College, Oxford, 1648; MA, 1650; rector of Castell Caereinion, 1655–61, of Llandyrnog, 1666–70; as chaplain to duke of York, 1663–6, accused Bishop *Morley of negligence, and was prosecuted by him; wrote against Romanism.

JONES, Sir **Thomas** (d. 1692), chief justice of common pleas; educated at Shrewsbury and Emmanuel College, Cambridge; BA, 1632; barrister, Lincoln's Inn, 1634; king's serjeant, 1671; knighted, 1671; judge of the King's Bench, 1676; chief justice of common pleas, 1683–6; tried Lord *Russell, 1683, and pronounced revocation of the London charter, 1683, but was dismissed (1686) for refusing to declare for the dispensing power; committed by House of Commons, 1689, for judgment against the serjeant-at-arms in 1682.

JONES, Thomas (1743–1803), painter; exhibited Welsh and Italian views at the Society of Artists and the Academy; visited Italy, 1776–84.

JONES, Thomas (1752–1845), promoter of British and Foreign Bible Society; rector of Great Creaton, Northamptonshire, 1828–33; gained great repute as preacher and translator into Welsh of evangelical works; founded prize at Lampeter for Welsh essay.

JONES, Thomas (1756–1807), fellow, 1781, and tutor of Trinity College, Cambridge, 1787–1807; of Shrewsbury and Trinity College, Cambridge; senior wrangler, 1778; MA, 1782; friend of Bishop Herbert *Marsh.

JONES, Thomas (1768–1828), Welsh poet ('Y Bardd Cloff'); London coach-builder; thrice president of the Gwyneddigion Society.

JONES, Thomas (1775–1852), optician; assisted in formation of Astronomical Society, 1820; FRS, 1835.

JONES, Thomas (1810–1875), Chetham librarian, 1845–75; BA, Jesus College, Oxford, 1832; catalogued Neath library, 1842; FSA, 1866.

JONES, Thomas (1819–1882), 'the Welsh poet-preacher'; as 'Jones Treforris' known throughout Wales as an independent preacher and lecturer; preached English sermons at Bedford Chapel, Oakley Square, London; chairman of Congregational Union, 1871–2; pastor of Congregational Church at Melbourne, 1877–80; spent his last years at Swansea; selection of his sermons published (1884) with preface by Robert *Browning, the poet.

JONES, Thomas (1870–1955), civil servant, administrator, and author; educated at Lewis School, Pengam, University College of Wales, Aberystwyth, and Glasgow University; first class, economic science, 1901; joined Independent Labour party and Fabian Society, 1895; assistant in political economy, Glasgow, 1900–9; special investigator, Poor Law Royal Commission, 1906–9; secretary, Welsh campaign against tuberculosis, 1910; first secretary, National Health Insurance Commission (Wales), 1912; as deputy secretary of Cabinet, 1916–30, exercised great influence behind the scenes; a negotiator for Irish treaty, 1921; first secretary, Pilgrim Trust, 1930–45; member, Unemployment Assistance Board, 1934–40; deputy chairman, Arts Council, 1939–42; founder-trustee, *Observer*, 1946; president, University College of Wales, Aberystwyth, 1944–54; principal founder, Coleg Harlech, 1927; 1851 royal commissioner, 1921–55; his lifelong interest in social work enabled him to guide the philanthropy of the wealthy, especially in Wales; publications include biography of Lloyd George (1951) and *A Diary with Letters, 1931–1950* (1954); CH, 1929; honorary degrees from several universities.

JONES, Thomas (Denbigh) (1756–1820), Calvinistic Methodist; printed at Ruthin translation of *Gurnall's *Christian in full Armour* and (1808) of *The Larger Catechism*; published at Denbigh his *History of Martyrs* (1813) and other works.

JONES, Thomas Rupert (1819–1911), geologist and palaeontologist; educated at Ilminster, where he studied geology of district; studied medicine at Newbury; published *Monograph on the Cretaceous Entomostraca of England* (1849) and papers on the geology of Newbury (1854) and of the Kennet valley (1871); assistant secretary of Geological Society, 1851–62; professor of geology at Royal Military College, Sandhurst, 1862; interested in South African geology; FRS, 1872; president of Geologists' Association, 1879–81.

JONES, Thomas Rymer (1810–1880), zoologist; MRCS, 1833; first professor of comparative anatomy at King's College, London, 1836–74; Fullerian professor of physiology at Royal Insti-

tution, 1840–2; chief work, *General Outline of the Animal Kingdom* (1838–41).

JONES, William (1561–1636), author of commentaries on Hebrews and Philemon, 1636; foundation fellow of Emmanuel College, Cambridge; DD, 1597; incumbent of East Bergholt, 1592–1636.

JONES, Sir William (1566–1640), judge; of St Edmund's Hall, Oxford; barrister, Lincoln's Inn, 1595; serjeant, 1617; knighted, 1617; chief justice of the king's bench in Ireland, 1617–20; judge of common pleas in England, 1621, of the King's Bench, 1624–40; member of Irish commissions and of the Council of Wales; gave judgment against *Eliot, *Holles, and *Valentine, 1630, and in favour of ship money, 1638; his *Reports* issued (1675).

JONES, William (b. *c*.1582), chaplain to the countess of Southampton; educated at Eton and King's College, Cambridge; BA, 1604; BD, 1613; fellow, 1602–16; devotional writer.

JONES, Sir William (1631–1682), lawyer; of Gray's Inn; knighted, 1671; KC, 1671; solicitor-general, 1673–5; attorney-general, 1675–9; directed 'Popish Plot' prosecutions; as MP for Plymouth, 1680–2, was manager of *Stafford's trial, 1680, and a strong supporter of the Exclusion Bill; the 'Bull-faced Jonas' of *Absalom and Achitophel*.

JONES, William (1675–1749), mathematician; mathematical tutor to Philip *Yorke (Hardwicke) and the first and second earls of *Macclesfield, living many years with them at Shirburn Castle; friend of *Halley and *Newton; edited some of Newton's mathematical tracts, 1711; FRS, 1712 (afterwards vice-president); published also *Synopsis Palmariorum Matheseos* (1706) and a treatise on navigation.

JONES, William, of Nayland (1726–1800), divine; educated at the Charterhouse and University College, Oxford, where he became the friend of George *Horne; BA, 1749; vicar of Pluckley, Kent; FRS, 1775, delivering the Fairchild 'Discourses on Natural History'; perpetual curate of Nayland, Suffolk, 1777; published, among other works, *The Catholic Doctrine of the Trinity* (1756), *Physiological Disquisitions* (1781), and some church music.

JONES, Sir William (1746–1794), orientalist and jurist; son of William *Jones (1675–1749); educated at Harrow, and at University College, Oxford, where he became fellow, 1766; tutor to Lord Althorp (second Earl Spencer); MA, 1773; published French translation of a Persian life of Nadir Shah (1770), a Persian grammar (1771), and established his reputation by *Poeseos Asiaticae*

Commentariorum Libri Sex (1774); FRS, 1772; member of *Johnson's Literary Club, 1773; intimate of *Burke and *Gibbon; barrister, Middle Temple, 1774; became a commissioner of bankrupts, 1776; published his *Essay on Bailments* (1781, often reprinted both in England and America); judge of the High Court at Calcutta, 1783 till death; knighted, 1783; his version of the Arabic *Moallakat* published (1783); founded Bengal Asiatic Society, 1784; mastered Sanskrit and published *Dissertation on the Orthography of Asiatick Words in Roman Letters* and translations of the *Hitopadesa* and *Sakuntala*, also extracts from the *Vedas*; began publication of *The Institutes of Hindu Law, or Ordinances of Mánu*; his collected works edited by Lord *Teignmouth (1799; reprinted, 1807); monuments erected to him in St Paul's Cathedral, London, and at University College, Oxford (the latter by *Flaxman).

JONES, William (1762–1846), pastor of Scots Baptist Church, Finsbury; author of *History of the Waldenses* (1811) and other works.

JONES, William (1763–1831), optician; FRAS; author of geometrical and graphical essays, and editor (1799 and 1812) of George Adams's works on natural philosophy.

JONES, William (1784–1842), Independent minister at Bolton; wrote religious works for the young.

JONES, Sir **William** (1808–1890), general; created CB for services in command of the 61st during Punjab campaign of 1848–9; commanded third infantry brigade at siege of Delhi, 1857; KCB, 1869; general, 1877; GCB, 1886.

JONES, William Arthur (1818–1873), antiquary; MA, Glasgow, 1841; Unitarian minister at Taunton, 1852–66; founded Taunton School of Science and Art; honorary secretary of the Somerset Archaeological and Natural History Society; with Wadham P. Williams compiled *Glossary of Somersetshire Dialect*.

JONES, William Basil (1822–1897), bishop of St David's; educated at Shrewsbury and Trinity College, Oxford; MA, 1847; Michel scholar, 1845, Michel fellow, 1848, at The Queen's College, Oxford; fellow of University College, Oxford, 1851–7; examining chaplain, 1861, to William *Thomson, then bishop of Gloucester; prebendary of York, 1863; archdeacon of York, 1867; rural dean of Bishopthorpe, 1869; chancellor of York, 1871; canon-residentiary of York, 1873; bishop of St David's and DD by diploma of Archbishop *Tait, 1874; chaplain of House of Lords, 1878–82; visitor of St David's College, Lampeter; brought about the almost total disappearance of non-residence, and effected a very complete organization of diocesan work. His

publications include writings on Welsh antiquities, religious commentaries, and editions of classical authors.

JONES, William Bence (1812–1882), Irish agriculturist; brother of Henry Bence *Jones; educated at Harrow and Balliol College, Oxford; MA, 1836; barrister, Inner Temple; introduced improvements on his estate at Lisselan, Co. Cork; resisted the Land League; published works on the Irish church and an autobiography.

JONES, William Ellis (1796–1848), Welsh poet ('Gwilym Cawrdaf') and printer; won bardic chair at Brecon Eisteddfod, 1822; his collected poetry published as *Gweithoedd Cawrdaf* (1851).

JONES, William Henry Rich (1817–1885), antiquary; Boden Sanskrit scholar at Oxford, 1837; MA, Magdalen Hall, Oxford, 1844; vicar of Bradford-on-Avon, 1851–85; canon of Salisbury, 1872; FSA, 1849. His works include editions of the *Domesday Book for Wiltshire* (1865), the *Registers of St. Osmund* (Rolls Series), and *Fasti Ecclesiae Sarusberiensis* (1879).

JONES, William West (1838–1908), archbishop of Cape Town; BA, St John's College, Oxford, 1860; MA, 1863; fellow, 1859–79; hon. fellow, 1893; hon. DD, 1874; vicar of Summertown, Oxford, 1864–74; bishop of Cape Town, 1874; see elevated to archbishopric, 1897; a strong high churchman, popular with English and Afrikaners alike.

JONES-LOYD, Samuel, Baron Overstone (1796–1883). See LOYD.

JONSON, Benjamin (1573?–1637), dramatist and poet ('Ben Jonson'); of Border descent, but born probably in Westminster; at Westminster School under William *Camden; according to Fuller a member of St John's College, Cambridge; escaped from trade to the army in Flanders; returned to England, *c.*1592; began to work for the Admiral's Company of actors both as player and playwright, 1597; included by *Meres (1598) among English tragedians; killed a fellow-actor in a duel or brawl, but escaped death by benefit of clergy, 1598; became a Roman Catholic during imprisonment, but abjured twelve years later; his *Every Man in his Humour* (with Shakespeare in the cast) performed by the Lord Chamberlain's Company at the Globe, 1598, and *Every Man out of his Humour*, 1599; his *Cynthia's Revels* (1600) and *The Poetaster* (attacking *Dekker and *Marston, 1601), performed by the children of the Queen's chapel; his first extant tragedy, *Sejanus*, given at the Globe by Shakespeare's company, 1603; his first court masque, *Masque of Blacknesse* (with scenery by Inigo *Jones), given on Twelfth Night, 1605; temporarily imprisoned (1605) for his share in *Eastward Ho*, a play reflecting on the Scots; his *Volpone* acted both at the Globe and the two universities, 1605; produced, besides Twelfth Night and marriage masques, five plays (including *Epicoene, The Alchemist*, and *Bartholomew Fayre*) between 1605 and 1615; went on foot to Scotland, 1618–19; was made a burgess of Edinburgh, and entertained by *Drummond of Hawthornden; guest of Richard *Corbet at Oxford, 1619, and created MA; his *Masque of Gypsies* performed, 1621, when he was in high favour with James I; produced *The Staple of News* (last great play), 1625; elected chronologer of London, 1628; wrote *Ode to Himself* after failure of *The New Inn*, 1629; quarrelled with Inigo Jones after production of the masque *Chloridia*, 1630, and withdrew from court; produced *The Magnetic Lady*, 1632, and *Tale of a Tub* (comedies), 1633; his last masques produced, 1633–4; last laureate verses, 1635; buried in Westminster Abbey and celebrated in a collection of elegies entitled *Jonsonus Virbius*. His friends included *Bacon, *Selden, *Chapman, *Fletcher, *Donne, and Shakespeare, and of the younger writers (his 'sons') *Beaumont, *Herrick, *Suckling, Sir Kenelm *Digby, and Lord *Falkland. Among his patrons were the Sidneys, the earl of *Pembroke, and the duke and duchess of *Newcastle. His poems (1616) include *Epigrammes, The Forrest*, and *Underwoods* (epistles and songs), and translations. His chief prose work is *Timber; or Discoveries made upon Men and Matter* (1641). His works have been edited by William *Gifford (1816) and Colonel *Cunningham (1875).

JOPLIN, Thomas (1790?–1847), writer on banking; founded the National and Provincial Bank, 1833; chief work, *Essay on the General Principles and Present Practices of Banking in England and Scotland* (1822), suggesting establishment of a joint-stock bank; died at Böhmischdorf, Silesia.

JOPLING, Joseph Middleton (1831–1884), painter; queen's prizeman at Wimbledon, 1861.

JORDAN, Dorothea (or Dorothy) (1762–1816), actress; née Bland; appeared at Dublin as Phoebe in *As you like it*, 1777, and afterwards at Waterford and Cork under the management of Richard *Daly; ran away to Leeds and, under the name of Mrs Jordan, played Calista and other parts on the York circuit under Tate *Wilkinson, 1782–5; made her début at Drury Lane as Peggy in *The Country Girl*, 1785, and there or at the Haymarket till 1809 played Viola, Rosalind, Miss Tomboy, Hypolita, Sir Harry Wildair, Miss Prue, and original parts in adaptations by *Kemble, and *The Spoiled Child* (a farce attributed to herself); acted at Covent Garden, 1811–14, Lady Teazle being her last part; highly praised by *Hazlitt, *Lamb, Leigh *Hunt, and the elder

*Mathews; had children by Richard Daly and Sir Richard Ford, and was for long mistress of the duke of Clarence (William IV); went to France in 1815, and died at St Cloud, where she was buried.

JORDAN, (Heinrich Ernst) Karl (1861–1959), entomologist; educated at Hildesheim High School and Göttingen University; *summa cum laude*, botany and zoology; entomologist, Tring Zoological Museum, created by future Lord *Rothschild, 1893–1939; director, 1930–3; naturalized, 1911; founded International Congress of Entomology, 1910; secretary until 1948; published large number of papers on his researches, including *Monograph of Charaxes* and *Revision of the Sphingidae*; worked especially on classification of fleas and beetles; FRS, 1932.

JORDAN, John (1746–1809), 'the Stratford poet'; wheelwright near Stratford-upon-Avon; published *Welcombe Hills* (1777); corresponded with Malone; his *Original Collections on Shakespeare and Stratford-on-Avon* and *Original Memoirs and Historical Accounts of the Families of Shakespeare and Hart* printed by Halliwell.

JORDAN, Sir John Newell (1852–1925), diplomat; BA, Queen's College, Belfast; joined Chinese Consular Service in Peking, 1876; appointed to legation in Peking, 1886; assistant Chinese secretary, 1889; full secretary, 1891; consul-general, Seoul, Korea, 1896; chargé d'affaires, 1898; minister-resident, 1901; envoy extraordinary and minister plenipotentiary to Court of Peking, 1906; co-operated with Sir Alexander *Hosie in successful attempt to stop export to China of Indian opium; retired, 1920; KCMG, 1904; KCB, 1909; GCMG, 1920.

JORDAN, Sir Joseph (1603–1685), vice-admiral; rear-admiral on the Irish Station, 1643; retired to Holland, 1648, but was soon readmitted to the service; as vice-admiral of the blue took part in the battles of June and July, 1653, against the Dutch; rear-admiral with *Blake in the Mediterranean, 1654–5; knighted after the battle of 3 June 1665; rear-admiral of the red under *Albemarle, 1–4 June, 1666, and vice-admiral on 25 July 1666; commanded squadron at Harwich, 1667; as vice-admiral of the blue led the van at Solebay, 1672; his portrait by *Lely at Greenwich.

JORDAN, Thomas (1612?–1685), poet; recited a poem before Charles I, 1639; an actor till 1642, and afterwards (1668) in his own *Money is an Ass* (published 1663); wrote numerous dedications, prologues, epilogues, and pamphlets; as poet to the corporation of London devised the lord mayors' shows, 1671–85. Other works include *Poeticall Varieties* (1637), *A Royall Arbour of Loyall*

Poesie (1664), and *Pictures of Passions, Fancies, and Affections* (1665).

JORDAN, Thomas Brown (1807–1890), engineer; secretary of Royal Cornwall Polytechnic after 1839; first keeper of mining records, 1840–5; helped Robert Were *Fox in constructing dipping-needle; invented a declination magnetograph, a self-recording actinometer, and other instruments.

JORDAN, William (*fl.* 1611), Cornish dramatist; supposed author of *Gwreans an Bys, the Creation of the World*.

JORDAN LLOYD, Dorothy (1889–1946), biochemist. See LLOYD.

JORDEN, Edward (1569–1632), physician and chemist; MA, Peterhouse, Cambridge, 1586; MD, Padua; FRCP, 1597; attributed to natural causes a supposed case of demoniacal possession which James I employed him to investigate; published *Discourse of Natural Bathes and Mineral Waters* (1631).

JORTIN, John (1698–1770), ecclesiastical historian; son of Renatus *Jortin; educated at the Charterhouse and Jesus College, Cambridge (fellow), 1721–8; MA, 1722; preacher at chapels of ease in New Street, St Giles, London, and in Oxenden Street, London; Boyle lecturer, 1749; rector of St Dunstan's-in-the-East, London, 1751; vicar of Kensington, 1762; DD, Lambeth, 1755; archdeacon of London, 1764; published *Remarks on Ecclesiastical History* (vol. i, 1751, vol. ii, 1752, vol. iii, 1754; enlarged, 1773), *Life of Erasmus* (1758), and critical and theological tracts; later editions of his works collected as *Various Works* (1805–10).

JORTIN (or JORDAIN), Renatus (d. 1707), Huguenot refugee; gentleman of the privy chamber; secretary successively to Sir Edward *Russell, Sir George *Rooke, and Sir Clowdisley *Shovell, with whom he perished.

JORZ (or JOYCE), Thomas (d. 1310), 'Thomas the Englishman'; prior of Dominicans at Oxford, and provincial of England, 1296–1303; cardinal-priest, 1305; confessor of Edward I; English representative at papal court; one of those appointed to hear the charges brought by Philip IV against the late pope, Boniface VIII; died at Grenoble; author of *Commentarii super quattuor libros Sententiarum* and other works; often confused with Thomas *Wallensis (d. 1350?).

JORZ (or JORSE), Walter (*fl.* 1306), archbishop of Armagh, 1306–7; brother of Thomas *Jorz; fined by Edward I for receiving consecration in Italy.

JOSCELIN. See GOSCELIN and JOCELIN.

JOSCELYN (or JOSSELIN), John (1529–1603), Anglo-Saxon scholar; fellow of Queens' College, Cambridge, 1549–57; MA, 1552; Latin secretary to Archbishop *Parker, 1558; prebendary of Hereford, 1560–77; incumbent of Hollingbourn, Kent, 1577; contributed 'Lives of the Archbishops' to Parker's *De Antiquitate Britannicae Ecclesiae* (1572), and a collection of Anglo-Saxon pieces to his *Paschal Homily of Aelfric Grammaticus* (*c.*1567); his *Historiola Collegii Corporis* printed (1880).

JOSEPH, George Francis (1764–1846), portrait and subject painter; ARA, 1813; painted portraits of Spencer *Perceval, Sir Stamford *Raffles, and Charles *Lamb.

JOSEPH, Horace William Brindley (1867–1943), philosopher; educated at Allhallows, Winchester, and New College, Oxford; first class, Lit. Hum., 1890; fellow, 1891; senior philosophical tutor, 1895–1932; junior bursar, 1895–1919; publications include *An Introduction to Logic* (1906), *The Labour Theory of Value in Karl Marx* (1923), *Some Problems in Ethics* (1931), *Essays in Ancient and Modern Philosophy* (1935, containing the important lecture on 'The Concept of Evolution'), and *Knowledge and the Good in Plato's Republic* (1948); FBA, 1930.

JOSEPH, Sir Maxwell (1910–1982), business man; had little education but learned shorthand and bookkeeping at Pitman's College, London; worked with estate agent; at age of 19 set up his own business with capital of £500 given by his father; during 1939–45 war served as lance-corporal in Royal Engineers; post-war, set up Grand Metropolitan Hotels group; by 1970 had established himself as brilliant financier; took over London brewery group, Truman Hanbury Buxton, 1971; followed by take-over of Watney Mann business; interests soon included hotels in Britain and abroad, beers, wines, and spirits, dairies, industrial catering, and gambling; took over American Liggett drinks-and-tobacco group, and in 1981 bought Intercontinental Hotels from Pan American Airlines; knighted, 1981; retired, 1982; owned famous stamp collection of Cape of Good Hope triangulars.

JOSEPH, Samuel (d. 1850), sculptor; cousin of George Francis *Joseph; best known by his statues of *Wilkie in the National Gallery and of William *Wilberforce in Westminster Abbey.

JOSEPH OF EXETER (*fl.* 1190), Latin poet (Josephus Iscanus); studied at Gueldres; accompanied Archbishop *Baldwin (d. 1190) to Palestine, 1188; his principal poem, *De Bello Trojano*, long current under names of Dares Phrygius and Cornelius Nepos, first published as his own at

Frankfurt (1620), and edited by Jusserand (1877).

JOSI, Christian (d. 1828), engraver and print-dealer; native of Utrecht; studied in London under John Raphael *Smith; practised at Amsterdam; inherited Ploos van Amstel's collections, and catalogued his Rembrandt etchings; settled in Gerrard Street, London, 1819, and published van Amstel's *Collection d'imitations de dessins*, completed by himself (1821).

JOSI, Henry (1802–1845), keeper of prints and drawings, British Museum, 1836–45; born at Amsterdam; son of Christian *Josi; sometime print-seller in Newman Street, London.

JOSSE, Augustin Louis (1763–1841), grammarian and Catholic missioner at Gloucester; born in France; taught French to the Princess *Charlotte, Wellington, and John *Kemble; published Spanish and French grammars and other works.

JOSSELYN, Henry (1606–1683), deputy-governor of Maine, USA, 1645, having gone to New England, 1634; chief justice of Maine, 1668, and justice at Pemaquid until 1683; brother of John *Josselyn.

JOSSELYN, John (*fl.* 1675), author of *New-Englands Rarities discovered* (1672; reprinted, 1865), and *Account of Two Voyages to New-England* (1674; reprinted, 1834 and 1869).

JOUBERT DE LA FERTÉ, Sir **Philip Bennet** (1887–1965), air chief marshal; had French grandfather; educated at Harrow and the Royal Military Academy, Woolwich; commissioned in Field Gunners, 1907; learnt to fly, 1912; attached to Royal Flying Corps (Military Wing), 1913; in France with No. 3 Squadron, 1914; commanded No. 15 Squadron in France, 1915; commanded No. 5 Wing in Egypt, 1916–17; DSO; commanded No. 14 Wing in Italy; commanded RFC in Italy, 1918; permanently commissioned in Royal Air Force, 1918; attended Army Staff College, 1920; group captain, instructor, RAF College, Andover, 1922; first RAF instructor, Imperial Defence College, 1926–9; commandant, RAF Staff College, 1930–3; air vice-marshal; commanded Fighting Area of Great Britain, 1934; air marshal, 1936; AOC-in-C, Coastal Command, 1936; AOC, India, 1937; recalled to England as air adviser on combined operations, 1939; assistant chief of Air Staff, special responsibility for application of radar in the RAF; air chief marshal and AOC-in-C, Coastal Command, 1941–3; inspector-general of the RAF, 1943; deputy chief of staff, South-East Asia Command, 1943–5; director, public relations, Air Ministry, 1946; published

The Third Service (1955); CMG, 1919; CB, 1936; KCB, 1938.

JOULE, James Prescott (1818–1889), physicist; studied under *Dalton; in paper on 'Electromagnetic Forces' (1840) described an attempt to measure an electric current in terms of a unit; elected to Manchester Literary and Philosophical Society, 1842, becoming president, 1860; determined by two distinct methods the physical constant known as Joule's equivalent or 'J', describing his discovery in two papers 'On the Production of Heat by Voltaic Electricity', communicated to Royal Society, 1840, and 'On the Heat evolved during the Electrolysis of Water' in Manchester Society's *Memoirs*; read paper 'On the Calorific Effects of Magneto Electricity and on the Mechanical Value of Heat' before British Association at Cork, 1843; results of further experiments made by him at Whalley Range communicated in paper 'On the Mechanical Equivalent of Heat' to Royal Society by Faraday, 1849; results of his final experiments by direct method of friction communicated, 1878; FRS, 1850; royal medallist, 1852, and Copley medallist, 1860; received honorary degrees from Dublin, Oxford, and Edinburgh; awarded a civil list pension, 1878. Besides the determination of the mechanical equivalent and the discovery of the conservation of energy, he investigated the thermodynamic properties of solids, and suggested improvements in the apparatus for measuring electric currents. He collected his *Scientific Papers* in two volumes (1885, 1887).

JOURDAIN, Francis Charles Robert (1865–1940), ornithologist; BA, Oxford, 1887; ordained, 1890; vicar of Clifton-by-Ashbourne, Derbyshire, 1894–1914, of Appleton, Berkshire, 1914–25; a leading authority on the breeding biology of birds of the palaearctic region; collaborated in *A Practical Handbook of British Birds* (2 vols., 1919–24) and other standard works.

JOURDAIN, Ignatius (1561–1640), mayor and (1625, 1625–6, and 1627–8) MP for Exeter; promoted bills against adultery and swearing.

JOURDAIN, John (d. 1619), captain under East India Company; cousin of Ignatius *Jourdain; visited Surat and Agra, 1609–11; 'president of the English' at Bantam, 1612, and at Jacatra, 1618; president of the council of India, 1618; surprised and slain by the Dutch of Patani.

JOURDAIN (or **JOURDAN**), **Silvester** (*c.*1565–1650), author of *A Discovery of the Bermudas, otherwise called the Ile of Divels* (1610), where he had been wrecked; his *Discovery* probably known to Shakespeare.

JOWETT, Benjamin (1817–1893), master of Balliol College, Oxford, and regius professor of

Greek at Oxford; educated at St Paul's School, London; scholar of Balliol College, Oxford, 1835; obtained Hertford (University) scholarship, 1837; fellow of Balliol College, 1838; MA, 1842; gained Chancellor's Prize for Latin essay, 1841; tutor at Balliol, 1842–70; ordained priest, 1845; public examiner, 1849, 1850, 1851, and 1853; published edition of St Paul's epistles to Thessalonians, Galatians, and Romans, 1855; regius professor of Greek at Oxford, 1855; owing to his having incurred suspicions of heresy by the liberality of his religious opinions, was deprived for ten years of the emoluments of the office; contributed essay on 'Interpretation of Scripture' to *Essays and Reviews* (1860), a liberal work which increased the suspicion of heresy already entertained against Jowett; master of Balliol College, 1870–93; strongly advocated reforms with the object of lessening expense of an Oxford career, and supported claims of secondary education and university extension; published translations of Plato (4 vols., 1871), Thucydides (2 vols., 1881), and Aristotle's *Politics* (1885); vice-chancellor of Oxford, 1882–6; hon. doctor of theology, Leiden, 1875; hon. LL D, Edinburgh, 1884, and hon. LL D, Cambridge, 1890. His essays and translations secured him a high place among the writers of his time, but he definitely identified himself with no party in religion or thought.

JOWETT, Joseph (1752–1813), professor of civil law; fellow, 1773–95, and tutor of Trinity Hall, Cambridge, 1775; LL D, 1780; Cambridge professor of civil law, 1782; vicar of Wethersfield, Essex, 1795.

JOWETT, William (1787–1855), divine and missionary; nephew of Joseph *Jowett; fellow of St John's College, Cambridge; twelfth wrangler, 1810; MA, 1813; missionary in Mediterranean countries and Palestine, 1815–24; secretary of CMS, 1832–40; incumbent of St John, Clapham Rise, London, 1851; works include *Christian Researches in the Mediterranean* (1822) and in Syria and the Holy Land (1825).

JOWITT, William Allen, Earl Jowitt (1885–1957), lord chancellor; educated at Marlborough and New College, Oxford; first class, jurisprudence, 1906; called to bar (Middle Temple), 1909; KC, 1922; Liberal MP, the Hartlepools, 1922–4, Preston, 1929; joined Labour government as attorney-general, knighted, and re-elected for Preston as Labour member, 1929; remained in 'National' government, 1931; defeated as National Labour candidate, Combined English Universities, Oct. 1931; resigned office, Jan. 1932; Labour MP, Ashton-under-Lyne, 1939–45; solicitor-general, 1940–2; paymaster-general, 1942; minister without portfolio, 1943–4; of national insurance, 1944–5; lord chancellor, 1945–51; leader of opposition in House of Lords, 1952–5; baron, 1945; viscount, 1947; earl, 1951; published *The Strange Case of Alger Hiss* (1953), and *Some Were Spies* (1954).

JOY, Francis (1697?–1790), printer, papermaker, and founder (1737) of the *Belfast Newsletter*.

JOY, John Cantiloe (1806–1866), marine painter; collaborated with his brother William *Joy (1803–1867).

JOY, Thomas Musgrave (1812–1866), subject and portrait painter; first exhibited at Royal Academy, 1831.

JOY, William (d. 1734), 'the English Samson'; began to perform at the Duke's Theatre, Dorset Garden, London, c.1699; afterwards a smuggler.

JOY, William (1803–1867), marine painter; brother of John Cantiloe *Joy; government draughtsman.

JOYCE, George (*fl.* 1647), Parliamentarian officer; when cornet in *Fairfax's regiment seized Holmby House and took Charles I to the army at Newmarket, 1647; active in promoting the king's trial; colonel and governor of the Isle of Portland, 1650; imprisoned and cashiered for opposition to *Cromwell, 1653; employed against Royalists, 1659; lived at Rotterdam, 1660–70.

JOYCE, James Augustine (1882–1941), poet, novelist, and playwright; educated at Belvedere College and University College, Dublin; specialized in languages; graduated, 1902; lived in Trieste (1904–14), Zurich (1914–18), Paris (1920–40); died in Zurich; financial independence assured by benefactors after 1918; published *Chamber Music* (poems, 1907), *Dubliners* (1914), *A Portrait of the Artist as a Young Man* (1916); his major work *Ulysses*, the record of a Dublin day, published in Paris, 1922, banned in United States (until 1934) and Great Britain (until 1936); highly influential in style and technique, notably in use of interior monologue; in *Finnegans Wake* (1939), again with central idea of recurrence, created own vocabulary; published also *Exiles* (play, 1918) and *Pomes Penyeach* (1927).

JOYCE, Jeremiah (1763–1816), author of *Scientific Dialogues* (1807) and other educational works; many years secretary of the Unitarian Society; while tutor to Earl Stanhope's sons imprisoned on a charge of treason, but liberated without trial after the acquittal of Hardy and Horne Tooke, 1794.

JOYCE, Sir Matthew Ingle (1839–1930), judge; called to bar (Lincoln's Inn), 1865; junior equity counsel to Treasury, 1886–1900; judge of

High Court and knighted, 1900; PC on resignation, 1915.

JOYCE, Thomas (d. 1310), Dominican prior. See JORZ.

JOYE, George (d. 1553), Protestant controversialist; fellow of Peterhouse, Cambridge, 1517; MA, 1517; being charged with heresy fled to Strasburg, 1527, and published an answer (1527), and a translation of Isaiah (1531); printed at Antwerp translations of Jeremiah and the Psalms; helped *Tyndale in his controversy with Sir Thomas *More, but quarrelled with him after surreptitiously reissuing (1534) his New Testament; returned to England, 1535, but again retired, 1542; carried on controversy with Bishop *Gardiner, 1543–4; issued *Exposicion of Daniel* at Geneva (1545), and *The Conjectures of the ende of the worlde* (translation, 1548); died in England.

JOYLIFFE, George (1621–1658), physician; MA, Pembroke College, Oxford, 1643; MD, Clare Hall, Cambridge, 1652; FRCP, 1658; his discovery of the lymph ducts published by Francis *Glisson, 1654.

JOYNER, William (1622–1706), alias William Lyde; author of *The Roman Empress* (tragedy, acted 1671) and *Some Observations on the Life of Reginaldus Polus* (1686); fellow of Magdalen College, Oxford, 1642–5; MA, 1643; one of the Romanist fellows introduced at Magdalen by James II, 1687; friend of *Hearne and Anthony à *Wood.

JOYNSON-HICKS, William, first Viscount Brentford (1865–1932), statesman. See HICKS.

JUBB, George (1718–1787), professor at Oxford; of Westminster and Christ Church, Oxford; MA, 1742; DD, 1780; chaplain to Archbishop *Herring; archdeacon of Middlesex, 1779; regius professor of Hebrew at Oxford, 1780–7; prebendary of St Paul's, 1781; chancellor of York, 1781.

JUDKIN-FITZGERALD, Sir Thomas, first baronet (d. 1810), high sheriff of Co. Tipperary; notorious for his severity in suppressing the rebellion of 1798; created baronet, 1801.

JUGGE, Joan (*fl.* 1579–1587), widow of Richard *Jugge, whose business she carried on.

JUGGE, John (d. 1579?), printer; probably son of Richard *Jugge.

JUGGE, Richard (d. 1579), printer; of Eton and King's College, Cambridge; original member of the Stationers' Company (1556), being several times master and warden; queen's printer, 1560; famous for his editions of the Bible and New Testament.

JUKES, Francis (1745–1812), aquatint engraver.

JUKES, Joseph Beete (1811–1869), geologist; a favourite pupil of *Sedgwick while at St John's College, Cambridge; BA, 1836; geological surveyor of Newfoundland, 1839–40; naturalist on HMS *Fly* in the survey of the north-east coast of Australia, 1842–6; after employment in North Wales was director of the Irish Survey, 1850–69; FGS; FRS, 1853; member of Royal Commission on Coalfields, 1866. His works include *Excursions in and about Newfoundland* (1842) and manuals of geology.

JULIANA (1343–1443), Norwich anchoret; author of *XVI Revelations of Divine Love* (first printed, 1670; ed. H. Collins, 1877).

JULIEN (or **JULLIEN**), **Louis Antoine** (1812–1860), musical conductor; after some success in Paris gave summer concerts at Drury Lane, 1840, and annual winter concerts, 1842–59, at which classical music was given by the best artists; organised opera season of 1847–8, when Sims *Reeves made his début; became bankrupt; produced an opera by himself at Covent Garden, 1852; arrested for debt, 1859; composed many popular quadrilles; died insane at Neuilly.

JULIUS, Charles (1723–1765), literary forger. See BERTRAM, CHARLES.

JULIUS, Sir George Alfred (1873–1946), consulting engineer; B.Sc., engineering, University of New Zealand, 1896; set up practice in Sydney, 1907; invented automatic race-course totalizator; chairman, Commonwealth Council for Scientific and Industrial Research, 1926–45; of Standards Association of Australia, 1926–40; president, National Research Council, 1932–7; knighted, 1929.

JUMIÈGES, Robert of (*fl.* 1051), archbishop of Canterbury. See ROBERT.

JUMPER, Sir William (d. 1715), navy captain; commanded the *Lennox* at attack on Cadiz, 1703, and reduction of Gibraltar, 1704; wounded in action with *Count of Toulouse* off Malaga, 1704; knighted.

JUNE, John (*fl.* 1740–1770), engraver.

JUNIUS (pseudonym). See FRANCIS, Sir PHILIP, 1740–1818.

JUNIUS, Francis (or **DU JON, François**), the younger (1589–1677), philologist and antiquary; born at Heidelberg; librarian to Thomas *Howard, second earl of Arundel, and tutor to his son, 1621–51; for a time at Amsterdam; presented Anglo-Saxon manuscripts and philological collections to the Bodleian Library; published

De Pictura Veterum (1637), and editions of *Caedmon (1655) and of *Codex Argenteus* of the Moeso-Gothic version of Ulfilas, with glossary (1664–5); his *Etymologicum Anglicanum* (first printed 1743) largely used by Dr *Johnson; buried in St George's Chapel, Windsor.

JUPP, Edward Basil (1812–1877), clerk to the Carpenters' Company, of which he wrote (1848) a historical account; son of Richard Webb *Jupp; FSA; published illustrated catalogues of the Academy, Society of Artists, and the Free Society; collected works of *Bewick.

JUPP, Richard (d. 1799), chief architect and surveyor to the East India Company; an original member of the Architects' Club (1791).

JUPP, Richard Webb (1767–1852), clerk to the Carpenters' Company; son of William *Jupp the elder.

JUPP, William, the elder (d. 1788), architect; brother of Richard *Jupp.

JUPP, William, the younger (d. 1839), architect to the Skinners' and other companies.

JURIN, James (1684–1750), physician; of Christ's Hospital and Trinity College, Cambridge (fellow), 1708; MA, 1709; MD, 1716; FRS, 1717; master of Newcastle Grammar School, 1709–15; president, Royal College of Physicians, 1750; physician to Guy's Hospital, 1725–32; FRS, 1718, secretary, 1721–7; an ardent Newtonian; defended mathematicians against *Berkeley; attended Sir Robert Walpole in his last illness; attempted to make physiology an exact science; edited Varenius's *Geographia Generalis* (1712) and W. *Cowper's *Myotomia Reformata* (2nd edn., 1724).

JUST, John (1797–1852), archaeologist; assistant master at Kirkby Lonsdale, and afterwards at Bury Grammar School; botanical lecturer at Pine Street (Manchester) School of Medicine, 1834–52; wrote for *Transactions* of Manchester Literary and Philosophical Society; compiled Westmorland glossary; deciphered Runic inscriptions in Isle of Man.

JUSTEL, Henri (1620–1693), librarian; born in Paris; succeeded his father as secretary to Louis XIV; left France to avoid persecution as a Protestant; DCL, Oxford, 1675, for gift of valuable manuscripts to the Bodleian; librarian at St James's Palace, 1681–8; published his father's *Bibliotheca Juris Canonici veteris* (1661).

JUSTUS, Saint (d. 627), missionary from Rome, first bishop of Rochester, 604–24, and fourth archbishop of Canterbury, 624–7.

JUSTYNE, Percy William (1812–1883), artist and book-illustrator; lived in Grenada, 1841–8.

JUTSUM, Henry (1816–1869), landscape painter.

JUXON, William (1582–1663), archbishop of Canterbury; educated at Merchant Taylors' School, London, and St John's College, Oxford; BCL, 1603; DCL, 1622; vicar of St Giles, Oxford, 1609–16; rector of Somerton, 1615; president of St John's College, Oxford, 1621–33; vice-chancellor, 1627–8; dean of Worcester, 1627; clerk of the closet on *Laud's recommendation, 1632; as bishop of London, 1633–49, directed the restoration of St Paul's and enforced conformity without giving offence; a lord of the Admiralty, 1636–8; lord high treasurer, 1636–41; summoned as a witness against *Strafford, whose attainder he advised Charles I to veto; attended the king at Newport and during his trial; received his last words on the scaffold; archbishop of Canterbury, 1660–3; buried in the chapel of St John's College, Oxford, to which he left £7,000.

K

KAHN-FREUND, Sir Otto (1900–1979), academic lawyer; born in Frankfurt am Main of Jewish parents; educated at Frankfurt University; became judge of Berlin labour court, 1929; dismissed for opposition to Nazi policy and emigrated to England; student at London School of Economics; assistant lecturer, 1936; professor, 1951; called to bar (Middle Temple), 1936; naturalized, 1940; played important part in establishment of labour law as independent area of legal study; member of Royal Commission on Reform of Trade Unions and Employers' Associations, 1965; one of the editors of sixth to ninth editions of *Dicey*; appointed professor of comparative law, Oxford, and fellow of Brasenose College, 1964; FBA, 1965; hon. bencher, Middle Temple, 1969; QC, 1972; knighted, 1976; list of his publications in his *Selected Writings* (1978).

KALISCH, Marcus (1825–1885), biblical commentator; educated at Berlin and Halle; came to England after 1848 and was secretary to the chief rabbi in London; afterwards tutor to sons of Baron Lionel *Rothschild; published scriptural commentaries, a Hebrew grammar (1862–3), and other works.

KAMES, Lord (1696–1782). See HOME, HENRY.

KANE, John (d. 1834), compiler of Royal Artillery lists; adjutant, late Royal Invalid Artillery, 1799.

KANE, Richard (1666–1736?), brigadier-general; wounded while captain in the 18th (Royal Irish) at Namur, 1695, and at Blenheim (major); commanded regiment at Malplaquet, 1709; lieutenant-governor of Minorca, afterwards of Gibraltar; governor of Minorca, 1730–6; brigadier-general, 1734; wrote narrative of campaigns of William III and Anne and handbook of infantry drill.

KANE, Sir Robert John (1809–1890), Irish man of science; of Trinity College, Dublin; professor of chemistry, Apothecaries' Hall, Dublin, 1831–45, and of natural philosophy to Royal Dublin Society, 1834–47; president of Royal Irish Academy, 1877; FRS, 1849; president of Queen's College, Cork, 1845–73; director of 'Museum of Irish Industry', Dublin, 1846; knighted, 1846; hon. LL D, Dublin, 1868; commissioner of Irish education, 1873; vice-chancellor of Royal University of Ireland, 1880; published *Elements of Chemistry* (1841–3), *Industrial Resources of Ireland* (1844), and other works.

KANE, Robert Romney (1842–1902), writer on Irish land law; son of Sir Robert *Kane; MA, Queen's College, Cork, 1862; hon. LL D, 1882; called to Irish bar, 1865; professor of jurisprudence at King's Inns, Dublin, 1873; legal assistant commissioner under Irish Land Act of 1881, 1881–92; county-court judge, Ireland, 1892.

KAPITZA, Piotr Leonidovich (1894–1984), physicist; born in Kronstadt, Russia; educated at local Realschule, and St Petersburg Polytechnical Institute; appointed to staff, 1918; member of Soviet mission to Cambridge, 1921; invited by Sir Ernest *Rutherford (later Lord Rutherford of Nelson) to work at Cavendish Laboratory; Ph.D., 1923; assistant director of magnetic research and fellow of Trinity College, 1925; FRS, 1929; Royal Society Messel professor, 1931–4; after visit to USSR, refused permission to return to Cambridge; director of Institute for Physical Problems, Moscow, 1934–47; member, Soviet Academy of Sciences, 1939; during thirteen years at Cambridge made important contribution to study of low-temperature and solid-state physics; in Moscow, his work changed to study of behaviour of liquid helium at very low temperatures and techniques of gas liquefaction; dismissed from his post, 1946; continued to work at his private house, but switched from very low-to very high-temperature physics; reappointed to Moscow Institute after death of Stalin in 1953, and continued work on new microwave sources and intense heating of plasma; received many academic honours in USSR and in the West; awarded Nobel Prize, 1978, and hon. fellow, Trinity College, Cambridge, 1966.

KARKEEK, William Floyd (1802–1858), veterinary surgeon and author of essays on agriculture and cattle.

KARLOFF, Boris (1887–1969), actor; born William Henry Pratt; brother of Sir John Thomas Pratt; educated at Merchant Taylors' School, Uppingham, and King's College, London; acted with repertory companies in Canada; adopted name Boris Karloff, 1911; went to Hollywood and played villains in Douglas Fairbanks films; played the mesmerist in *The Bells* (1926) and the convict in *The Criminal Code* (1930); appeared in number of horror films, including *Frankenstein, The Mask of Fu Manchu, The Black Room*, and *Son of Frankenstein*; acted on Broadway stage in plays including *Arsenic and Old Lace* (1941), and *The Linden Tree* (1948); appeared in Hollywood colour films, including *The Secret Life of Walter Mitty* (1947); played in British TV series, including 'The Name of the Game' (1969).

KARSLAKE, Sir **John Burgess** (1821–1881), lawyer; barrister, Middle Temple, 1846; QC, 1861; solicitor-general, 1866; knighted, 1866; attorney-general, 1867–8 and 1874–5; privy councillor, 1876; member of the Judicature Commission.

KAT, Kit (*fl.* 1703–1733), keeper of the 'Cat and Fiddle'. See CAT, CHRISTOPHER.

KATER, Henry (1777–1835), man of science; while serving in the 12th Foot took part in survey of country between Malabar and Coromandel coasts; afterwards in 62nd; FRS, 1815 (sometime treasurer); prepared standard measures for Russian government; made important pendulum and telescopical experiments, and produced a seconds pendulum by application of Huyghen's principle of the reciprocity of the centres of suspension and oscillation; Copley medallist, 1817; Bakerian lecturer, 1820; invented the floating collimator.

KATHARINE (or **KATHERINE).** See CATHERINE.

KATTERFELTO, Gustavus (d. 1799), conjurer and empiric; appeared in London during the influenza epidemic of 1782, exhibiting in Spring Gardens; referred to by Peter *Pindar and *Cowper; gave microscopic and magnetic demonstrations.

KAUFFMANN, Angelica (1741–1807), historical and portrait painter; of Swiss extraction; gained popularity as a portrait painter at Milan; painted *Female Figure allured by Music and Painting*, 1760; studied at Florence and Rome, where she became acquainted with Winckelmann; met English people at Naples and Venice; introduced to London society by Lady Wentworth, 1766; painted Queen Charlotte and Christian VII of Denmark, and decorated the flower room, Frogmore; married the impostor count de Horn, 1767, but separated from him next year; twice painted by Sir Joshua *Reynolds, who was one of her admirers; one of the original Academicians, 1769; exhibited eighty-two pictures, 1769–97; visited Ireland, 1771; after Horn's death married Antonio *Zucchi; left England, 1781; spent the rest of her life at Rome, where she was an intimate of Goethe, and painted pictures for the emperor Joseph II, the tsarina Catherine II, Pope Pius VI, and other potentates; her funeral superintended by Canova, the Academicians of St Luke bearing the pall. Her works were highly esteemed by her contemporaries, and frequently engraved. Her *Religion Surrounded by the Virtues* is in the National Gallery.

KAVANAGH, Arthur MacMorrough (1831–1889), Irish politician and sportsman; though born with only the stumps of arms and legs became an expert angler, shot, huntsman, and yachtsman, and could write legibly and draw well; volunteer scout during movement of 1848; travelled through Russia and Persia to India, 1849–51; for a short time in Survey Department, Poona; succeeded to family estates in Ireland, 1853, becoming a magistrate, railway director, and chairman of Board of Guardians; as Conservative MP for Co. Wexford, 1866–8, and Carlow, 1868–80, opposed Irish disestablishment; supported Land Bill of 1870; after losing his seat in 1880 became lord-lieutenant of Carlow; drew up separate report at close of Bessborough Commission; initiated Irish Land Committee and (1883) Land Corporation; Irish privy councillor, 1886.

KAVANAGH, Cahir Mac Art, lord of St Molyns, baron of Ballyann (d. 1554), took part in rebellion of the Leinster Geraldines, but submitted, 1538; sat in *St Leger's parliament, 1541; defeated Gerald Kavanagh at Hacketstown, 1545, but was obliged to renounce the title MacMurrough, 1550; received lordship of St Molyns, 1543; was created baron, 1554.

KAVANAGH, Julia (1824–1877), novelist and biographical writer; daughter of Morgan Peter *Kavanagh. Her works include *Madeleine* (1848), *Daisy Burns*, and many other stories, and *Woman in France in the Eighteenth Century* (1850); died at Nice.

KAVANAGH, Morgan Peter (d. 1874), poetical writer and philologist.

KAY. See also CAIUS.

KAY, Sir **Edward Ebenezer** (1822–1897), judge; MA, Trinity College, Cambridge, 1847; barrister, Lincoln's Inn, 1847; bencher, 1867; treasurer, 1888; took silk, 1866; knighted and appointed justice of High Court (Chancery division), 1881; lord justice of appeal, 1890; retired, 1897.

KAY, John (*fl.* 1733–1764), of Bury, inventor of the fly-shuttle (1733); removed to Leeds, 1738, but returned to Bury; his invention largely utilized; ruined in consequence of litigation necessary to protect his patent; his house broken into by the Bury mob, 1753; said to have died a pauper in France.

KAY, John (1742–1826), miniature painter and caricaturist; barber at Dalkeith and Edinburgh till 1785; etched nearly 900 plates, including portraits of Adam *Smith and most of chief contemporary Scotsmen; *Series of Original Portraits and Caricature Etchings*, with biographical matter, issued 1837–8 (3rd edn., 1877).

KAY, Joseph (1821–1878), economist; MA, Trinity College, Cambridge, 1849; as travelling bachelor of the university examined and reported upon social and educational condition of the poor in several continental countries, 1845–9; barrister, Inner Temple, 1848; QC, 1869; judge of the Salford Hundred Court of Record, 1862–78; his *Free Trade in Land* issued (1879).

KAY, Robert (*fl.* 1760), inventor of the 'shuttle drop box'; son of John *Kay (1733–1764).

KAY, (Sydney Francis) Patrick (Chippindall Healey) (1904–1983), ballet dancer. See DOLIN, Sir ANTON.

KAY, William (1820–1886), biblical scholar; fellow, 1840, and tutor, 1842, of Lincoln College, Oxford; MA, 1842; Pusey and Ellerton scholar, 1842; principal of Bishop's College, Calcutta, 1849–64; rector of Great Leighs, Essex, 1866–86; Grinfield lecturer, 1869; one of the Old Testament revisers; contributed commentaries on Isaiah (1875) and Hebrews (1881) to the *Speaker's Bible*.

KAYE, John (1783–1853), bishop of Lincoln; educated under Dr Charles *Burney (1757–1817); senior wrangler and senior chancellor's medallist, 1804; MA, Christ's College, Cambridge, 1807; DD, 1815; fellow and tutor of Christ's College, Cambridge, and (1814–30) master; as regius professor of divinity at Cambridge, 1816, revived public lectures; published courses on *The Ecclesiastical History of the Second and Third Centuries* (1825) and some of the fathers; bishop of Bristol, 1820–7, of Lincoln, 1827–53; FRS, 1848; supported repeal of Test and Corporation Acts, 1828; opposed revival of convocation and upheld Gorham judgment; his collected works issued (1888).

KAYE, Sir John William (1814–1876), military historian; educated at Eton and Addiscombe; in Bengal Artillery, 1832–41; entered East India Civil Service, 1856; secretary of India Office, political and secret department, from *Mill's retirement till 1874; KCSI, 1871. His works include *History of the Sepoy War* (3 vols., 1864–76), continued by Colonel *Malleson, and history of the *Administration of the East India Company* (1853).

KAY-SHUTTLEWORTH, Sir James Phillips, first baronet (1804–1877), founder of English popular education; brother of Joseph *Kay; assumed his wife's name, 1842; MD, Edinburgh, 1827; secretary to Manchester Board of Health; published *The Physiology, Pathology, and Treatment of Asphyxia* (1834); assistant poor-law commissioner, 1835; first secretary of the committee of Council on Education, 1839–49; joint founder of Battersea Training College for pupil-teachers, 1839–40; created baronet, 1849; vice-chairman of Central Relief Committee during Lancashire cotton famine (1861–5); high sheriff of Lancashire, 1863; hon. DCL, Oxford, 1870; member of scientific commissions, 1870–3; published two novels and works on education and social questions.

KEACH, Benjamin (1640–1704), Baptist divine; imprisoned for preaching at Winslow, and sentenced to fine and the pillory for his *Child's Instructor* (1664); pastor of Calvinistic Baptists in Tooley Street, London, 1668; caused schism by advocating congregational singing; practised imposition of hands; preached in Goat Yard Passage, Horsleydown, London, from 1672; published expository, controversial, and allegorical works, and religious poems.

KEAN, Charles John (1811?–1868), actor; second son of Edmund *Kean; educated at Eton; appeared at Drury Lane as Young Norval, 1827; played at the Haymarket, Romeo, Mortimer (the *Iron Chest*), and other parts, 1829; successful as Richard III at New York, 1830; acted Iago to his father's Othello at Covent Garden, 25 Mar. 1833; played in Hamburg, 1833, and Edinburgh, 1837; gave Hamlet, Richard III, and Sir Giles Overreach at Drury Lane, 1838; revisited America, 1839 and 1846; first played at Windsor, 1849, and during his management of the Princess's (1850–9) obtained much success in the *Corsican Brothers* and *Louis XI*; produced *Byron's *Sardanapalus* and Charles *Reade's *Courier of Lyons*, besides numerous Shakespearean revivals, which were adversely criticized for their profuse scenic arrangements; visited Australia, America, and Jamaica, 1863–6; acted for the last time at Liverpool, May 1867; excelled only as Hamlet and Louis XI.

KEAN, Edmund (1787–1833), actor; son of an itinerant actress; deserted by his mother; said to have appeared as a child at Her Majesty's and Drury Lane theatres, London, during an adventurous boyhood; received lessons from his uncle, a ventriloquist, and Miss Tidswell, a Drury Lane actress; played Prince Arthur with Mrs *Siddons and *Kemble at Drury Lane, 1801, but ran away to Bartholomew Fair; broke both his legs tumbling in Saunders's Circus; recited before George III at Windsor; in retirement, 1803–6; played subordinate parts at the Haymarket, 1806, and acted at Belfast; married Mary Chambers, 1808, and for six years underwent many hardships, but declined a London engagement as premature; attracted attention of Drury Lane stage-manager while acting at Dorchester, and was engaged by him for three years; on 26 Jan. 1814, in spite of hindrances, made a triumphant appearance as Shylock; increased his reputation with Richard III, and played also Hamlet, Othello, and Iago, being praised by *Hazlitt, Kemble, and *Byron, and invited to her house by Mrs Garrick; first appeared as Macbeth and Sir Giles Overreach, 1814–15; played Barabas, Young Norval, and King John, 1817; he saw Talma at Paris, 1818, and essayed the part of Orestes in emulation; played Leon (*Rule a Wife and have a Wife*) and Rolla (*Pizarro*); failed as Abel Drugger and declined Joseph Surface, 1819; failed as Coriolanus, but triumphed as Lear, 1820; after first visit to America reappeared at Drury Lane as Richard III; gained a success in comedy as Don Felix in the *Wonder*, 1821; played Othello and Cymbeline with Young; after the action of *Cox v. Kean* (1825), when he had to pay damages for crim. con., was badly received in London, Scotland, and America; elected a Huron chief in Canada; reappeared with success at Drury Lane as Shylock, 1827, repeating the part at Covent Garden; played at Paris, 1828, and at Covent Garden, 1829; failed in Henry V at Drury Lane, 1830, playing there for the last time (as Richard III) on 12 Mar. 1833; was taken ill at Covent Garden on 25 Mar. while acting Othello, and died at Richmond on 15 May; unrivalled as a tragedian. Though receiving large sums, he ruined himself by drunkenness and ostentation, but was generous to his friends. A portrait of him as Sir Giles Overreach is at the Garrick Club, London.

KEAN, Ellen (1805–1880), actress; as Ellen Tree played Olivia to the Viola of her sister Maria (Mrs *Bradshaw) at Covent Garden, 1823; appeared at Drury Lane in comedy, 1826–8; at Covent Garden 1829–36, 'created' several parts, and played Romeo to Fanny *Kemble's Juliet; in America, 1836–9; married Charles John *Kean, and played with him in *Tobin's *Honeymoon* the same evening at Dublin, 1842; played leading parts with him at the Princess's Theatre, London; retired on his death. Among her best impersonations were Viola, Constance, Gertrude (*Hamlet*), and Mrs Beverley.

KEAN, Michael (d. 1823), miniature painter and proprietor of the Derby China Factory.

KEANE, John, first Baron Keane (1781–1844), lieutenant-general; aide-de-camp to Lord Cavan in Egypt, 1799–1801; at reduction of Martinique, 1809; led a brigade of the third division at Vittoria, 1813, the Pyrenees, Toulouse,

1814, and other engagements; major-general, 1814; KCB, 1815; directed landing of first troops at New Orleans and led left column in attack of 8 Jan. 1815; commanded troops in Jamaica, 1823–30; lieutenant-general, 1830; commander-in-chief at Bombay, 1834–9; co-operated with Sir Henry *Fane in Sind, 1838–9; took Ghuznee and occupied Kabul, 1839; though adversely criticized, received peerage and pension, 1839; GCH.

KEANE, Joseph B. (d. 1859), Irish architect.

KEARLEY, Hudson Ewbanke, first Viscount Devonport (1856–1934), man of business; founded International Stores, 1880; Liberal MP, Devonport, 1892–1910; parliamentary secretary, Board of Trade, 1905–9; conducted passage of Port of London Bill; became first chairman of the authority, 1909–25; first food controller, 1916–17; baronet, 1908; PC, 1909; baron, 1910; viscount, 1917.

KEARNE, Andreas (*fl.* 1650), sculptor; assisted his brother-in-law, Nicholas *Stone the elder.

KEARNEY, Barnabas (O CEARNAIDH, Brian) (1567–1640), Irish Jesuit; said to have converted Thomas *Butler, tenth earl of Ormonde.

KEARNEY (or CARNEY), John (O CEARNAIDH, Sean) (d. 1600?), Irish Protestant divine; BA, Magdalene College, Cambridge, 1565; sometime treasurer of St Patrick's, Dublin; brought out the first extant work in Irish (*Aibidil air Caiticiosma*, 2nd edn., 1571); his Irish translation of the New Testament not extant.

KEARNEY, John (1741–1813), bishop of Ossory; brother of Michael *Kearney; provost of Trinity College, Dublin, 1799; bishop of Ossory, 1806–13.

KEARNEY, Michael (1733–1814), archdeacon of Raphoe; brother of John *Kearney (1741–1813); fellow of Trinity College, Dublin, 1757; Erasmus Smith professor of history at Dublin, 1769–78; archdeacon of Raphoe, 1798–1814.

KEARNEY, William Henry (1800–1858), water-colour painter; foundation-member and subsequently vice-president of Institute of Painters in Water-Colours.

KEARNS, William Henry (1794–1846), musical composer; played the violin at Ancient Concerts, 1832, and was afterwards first viola; composed *Bachelors' Wives* (operetta, 1817), *Cantata, with Accompaniment* (1823), and arranged works by *Handel, Haydn, Mozart, and others.

KEARSE, Mrs Mary (*fl.* 1794–1830), flower-painter. See LAWRANCE.

KEARY, Annie (1825–1879), author of *Castle Daly* (1875) and other novels; published also children's books, *Heroes of Asgard* (1857), and other educational works.

KEATE, George (1729–1797), author, painter, and friend of Voltaire; exhibited (1766–89) at Royal Academy and Society of Artists; published *Poetical Works* (1781), including 'The Alps' (dedicated to Young) and 'Ferney' (to Voltaire); published *The Distressed Poet* (1787) and an account of Geneva (1761), also dedicated to Voltaire, whom he had met there.

KEATE, Georgiana Jane (1770–1850), afterwards Mrs Henderson; painter; daughter of George *Keate.

KEATE, John (1773–1852), headmaster of Eton; son of William *Keate; fellow of King's College, Cambridge, Browne medallist, and Craven scholar; MA, 1799; DD, 1810; assistant master at Eton, 1797, headmaster, 1809–34; canon of Windsor, 1820; rector of Hartley Westpall, Hampshire, 1824–52; a popular headmaster, but remarkable for severity of his discipline.

KEATE, Robert (1777–1857), surgeon; brother of John *Keate; surgeon at St George's Hospital, 1813–53; sergeant-surgeon to William IV and Queen Victoria; inspector-general of hospitals, 1810; president of College of Surgeons, 1830, 1831, 1839.

KEATE, Robert William (1814–1873), colonial governor; son of Robert *Keate; of Eton and Christ Church, Oxford; governor of Natal, 1867–72, and the Gold Coast, 1872–3.

KEATE, Thomas (1745–1821), surgeon of St George's Hospital, 1792–1813, surgeon-general, 1793; master of the College of Surgeons, 1802, 1809, and 1818; died surgeon to Chelsea Hospital.

KEATE, William (d. 1795), master of Stamford School, afterwards rector of Laverton, Somerset; MA, King's College, Cambridge, 1767.

KEATING, Geoffrey (1570?–1644?), author of 'Foras Feasa ar Eirinn' ('Foundation of Knowledge on Ireland'), a history of Ireland to the English invasion, never printed (except in translation), but widely circulated in manuscript; his *Tri Biorghaoithe an Bhais* printed by R. Atkinson (1890).

KEATING, George (1762–1842), engraver and Roman Catholic bookseller and publisher.

KEATING, Sir Henry Singer (1804–1888), judge; barrister, Inner Temple, 1832; QC, 1849; solicitor-general, 1857–8 and 1859; judge of common pleas, 1859–75; co-editor of *Leading Cases* (3rd edn., 1849, 4th edn., 1856).

KEATING, John (*fl.* 1680), Irish judge; chief justice of common pleas in Ireland, 1679–89, and Irish privy councillor; supported *Clarendon against *Tyrconnel and (1686) advocated renewal of the Commission of Grace; imprisoned by James II; dismissed as a Jacobite.

KEATING, Maurice Bagenal St Leger (d. 1835), lieutenant-colonel; MP, Co. Kildare, 1790 and 1801; lieutenant-colonel, 1793; author of *Travels through France, Spain, and Morocco* (1816–17), and other works.

KEATING, Thomas Patrick (1917–1984), artist, restorer, and faker; educated at Roper Street School, Eltham, Kent, and Dalmain Road School, Forest Hill, London; worked at variety of jobs after leaving school until he joined his father as a house painter; attended evening classes at art school, Croydon and Camberwell; served in Royal Navy during 1939–45 war; invalided from navy and became art student at Goldsmiths' College, London, 1947; joined restoration studio in London, made copies of paintings, and found they were being sold as genuine; decided to flood the market with fakes as a means of striking a blow for impoverished artists against rich dealers; spent twenty-five years as restorer, but at same time painted in his own style and that of artists such as Rembrandt, *Constable, Degas, Renoir, and *Turner; claimed to have put over 2,000 fakes on the market; admitted in *The Times* that he was responsible for thirteen water-colours attributed to Samuel *Palmer, 1976; trial at Old Bailey stopped because of his ill health, 1979; presented on Channel 4 television series 'Tom Keating on Painters', 1982, and awarded Broadcasting Press Guild prize; 135 of his paintings sold at Christie's for £72,000, 1983; published *The Fake's Progress* (with Geraldine and Frank Norman, 1977).

KEATS, John (1795–1821), poet; son of a livery stableman in Moorfields, London; educated at Enfield by John Clarke, with whose son, Charles Cowden *Clarke, he became intimate; acquired a knowledge of Latin and history, and some French, but no Greek; continued his study of literature after being apprenticed to a surgeon; broke his indentures, but continued medical studies at the hospitals; a dresser at Guy's, 1816; soon abandoned surgery; introduced by Clarke to Leigh *Hunt, who printed a sonnet for him in the *Examiner* on 5 May 1816, and in whose house at Hampstead he first met his friend, John Hamilton *Reynolds and *Shelley; published the sonnet on *Chapman's Homer in the *Examiner*, Dec. 1816, and other sonnets, 1817; influenced by

*Haydon and Hunt; with the help of Shelley published (Mar. 1817) *Poems by John Keats*, financially a failure; began *Endymion* during visit to the Isle of Wight; lived with his brothers in Well Walk, Hampstead, London, and became an intimate of Charles Wentworth *Dilke, Charles Armitage *Brown, and Joseph *Severn; finished *Endymion* at Burford Bridge, Surrey, his health having begun to fail; recited a part of the work to *Wordsworth; published *Endymion*, May 1818; on returning from a walking tour with Brown, nursed his brother Tom until the latter's death; pained by the hostile criticism of *Blackwood's Magazine* and the *Quarterly Review*, 1818; commenced *Hyperion* and wrote some lyrics, 1818; finished *The Eve of St. Agnes* early in 1819; wrote his best odes and 'La Belle Dame sans Merci', 1819 (printed in the *Indicator*, 1820); fell meanwhile deeply in love with Fanny Brawne; financially assisted by Brown, who collaborated with him in *Otho the Great*; wrote *Lamia*, broke off *Hyperion* for a time, but afterwards recast it, and lived for a time in Westminster with a view to journalistic work; nursed by Brown, the first overt symptoms of consumption having appeared; his *Lamia and other Poems* (July 1820) praised in the *Edinburgh Review*; nursed first by the Hunts and afterwards by the Brawnes; sailed with Severn from London for Italy, Sept. 1820; landed on the Dorset coast and composed his last poem ('Bright Star'); stayed a fortnight at Naples, and having declined Shelley's invitation to Pisa, reached Rome in November. Here he died, Feb. 1821, and was buried in the Protestant cemetery at Rome, where Severn designed a monument for him. A quarrel between George Keats and the poet's friends delayed the publication of his life, and a false impression as to his character prevailed till the issue of Monckton *Milnes's *Life and Letters of John Keats* (1848).

KEATS, Sir **Richard Goodwin** (1757–1834), admiral; lieutenant of the *Ramillies* at Ushant, 1778; present at relief of Gibraltar, 1780–1; served on the North American Station till end of the war; promoted to post-rank, 1789, and saw service on French coast, 1794–6, and again after the mutiny of 1797 till 1800, sending news of the expedition starting for Ireland in 1798; with *Nelson off Toulon and in West Indies, 1803–5, and at Battle of San Domingo, 1806; rear-admiral, 1807; convoyed *Moore's troops to Gottenburg, 1807; KB for his seizure of Danish ships containing Spanish soldiers, 1807; second-in-command of the expedition to the Scheldt, 1809; commanded squadron defending Cadiz, 1810–11; vice-admiral, 1811; was governor of Newfoundland, 1813–15, and of Greenwich Hospital, 1821; admiral, 1825; a bust, by *Chantrey, erected to his memory at Greenwich Hospital by William IV, his early naval friend.

KEAY, John Seymour (1839–1909), Anglo-Indian politician; went to India to manage branches of government Bank of Bengal, 1862; opened successful banking business and cotton mills at Hyderabad; sympathized with Indian nationalists; Liberal MP for Elgin and Nairn, 1889–95.

KEBLE, John (1792–1866), divine and poet; educated by his father; scholar of Corpus Christi College, Oxford, 1806; fellow of Oriel, 1811, also tutor, 1818–23; BA, 1811; won the university prizes for English and Latin essays, 1812; had Richard Hurrell *Froude and Isaac *Williams among his pupils when curate at Southrop; declined offers of benefices during his father's lifetime; professor of poetry at Oxford, 1831–41; vicar of Hursley, Hampshire, 1836–66. Keble College, Oxford (opened, 1869), was founded in his memory. *Keble's sermon of 1833 on national apostasy initiated the 'Oxford Movement', which he also supported in seven *Tracts for the Times*, by his translation of Irenaeus in 'The Library of the Fathers', and his *Life* and *Works* of Bishop Thomas *Wilson. He also edited *Hooker's works (1836), and helped *Newman with Richard Hurrell Froude's *Remains*. *The Christian Year* appeared anonymously (1827), and attained extraordinary success. His *De Poeticae Vi Medica* (Oxford poetry lectures) appeared (1844), *Lyra Innocentium* (1846), *Sermons Academical and Occasional* (1847), and the treatise *On Eucharistical Adoration* (1857). Chief among the posthumous publications were *Miscellaneous poems* (1869) and *Occasional Papers and Reviews* (1877).

KEBLE, Joseph (1632–1710), author of *Reports in the Court of Queen's Bench* (1685); son of Richard *Keble; fellow of All Souls College, Oxford; BCL, 1654; barrister, Gray's Inn, 1658.

KEBLE (KEEBLE or KEBBEL), Richard (*fl.* 1650), Parliamentary judge in Wales; BA, Corpus Christi College, Cambridge, 1605–6; barrister, Gray's Inn, 1614, Lent reader, 1639; serjeant, 1648; commissioner of the great seal, 1649–54; tried *Lilburne and Christopher *Love, 1651; excepted from the Act of Indemnity.

KEBLE, Thomas (1793–1875), divine; brother of John *Keble; scholar and fellow of Corpus Christi College, Oxford; BA, 1811; rector of Bisley, 1827–75; wrote four *Tracts for the Times* and forty-eight of the *Plain Sermons*, besides translating Chrysostom's *Homilies*.

KEBLE MARTIN, William (1877–1969), botanist. See MARTIN.

KECK, Sir Anthony (1630–1695), second commissioner of the great seal, 1689–90; barrister, Inner Temple, 1659, bencher, 1677; knighted, 1689; MP, Tiverton, 1691.

KEDERMYSTER (or KYDERMINSTRE), Richard (d. 1531?), abbot of Winchcomb, Gloucestershire, 1487; one of the English representatives at the Lateran Council, 1512; defended retention of benefit of clergy as applied to minor orders; some of his Winchcomb register printed in *Dugdale's Monasticon*.

KEDINGTON, Roger (c.1712–1760), divine; of Caius College, Cambridge; MA, 1737; DD, 1749; rector of Kedington, Suffolk; published religious works.

KEEBLE. See also KEBLE.

KEEBLE, Sir Frederick William (1870–1952), botanist, civil servant, and industrial adviser; educated at Alleyn's School, Dulwich, and Caius College, Cambridge; first class, part i, natural sciences tripos, 1891; botany lecturer, 1902, professor, 1907–14, Reading; director, Royal Horticultural Society gardens, Wisley, 1914–19; joined Board of Agriculture, 1914; controller of horticulture, 1917–19; Sherardian professor of botany, Oxford, 1920–7; agricultural adviser to Imperial Chemical Industries, 1927–32; Fullerian professor, Royal Institution, 1938–41; editor, *Gardeners' Chronicle*, 1908–19; married Lillah *McCarthy, 1920; FRS, 1913; CBE, 1917; knighted, 1922.

KEEBLE, John (1711–1786), composer and organist of St George's, Hanover Square, 1737, and at Ranelagh from 1742; published *Theory of Harmonics* (1784).

KEEBLE, Lillah, Lady (1875–1960), actress. See MCCARTHY, LILLAH.

KEEGAN, John (1809–1849), Irish balladwriter.

KEELEY, Mrs Mary Ann (1805?–1899), actress, whose maiden name was Goward; appeared at Lyceum Theatre, London, 1825; married Robert *Keeley, 1829; one of the finest comedians of modern days; last appeared professionally at Lyceum, 1859. Her parts include Jack Sheppard, 1839, Nerissa, Audrey, Maria (*Twelfth Night*), Dame Quickly, and Mrs Page.

KEELEY, Robert (1793–1869), actor; the original Leporello in *Don Giovanni* (Olympic, 1818) and Jemmy Green in *Tom and Jerry* (Adelphi); made a great hit as Rumfit, a tailor in *Peake's Duel, or my two Nephews*, 1823; married Mary Goward and acted with her at Covent Garden, the Lyceum, and other London theatres; with Madame *Vestris at the Olympic, 1838–41, *Macready at Drury Lane 1841–2, Strutt at the Lyceum (Dickens's plays), 1844–7, and Charles John *Kean at the Princess's; retired, 1857, but reappeared, 1861–2.

KEELING, Josiah (*fl.* 1691), conspirator; revealed existence of Rye House Plot and gave evidence against *Russell, *Sidney, and the chief conspirators, 1683; received reward and a place; after Revolution dismissed for Jacobitism; died in prison.

KEELING, William (d. 1620), naval commander and East India Company's agent; captain of the *Susan* in voyage of Sir Henry *Middleton to the Indies, 1604–6; commander in the company's voyage of 1607–10; commander-in-chief in India, 1615–17; afterwards captain of Cowes.

KEELING, William Knight (1807–1886), painter; in early years assisted William *Bradley; exhibited at the New Society; president of the Manchester Academy, 1864–77.

KEENE, Sir Benjamin (1697–1757), diplomat; LL B, Pembroke Hall, Cambridge, 1718; agent for South Sea Company in Spain and consul at Madrid, 1724; ambassador at Madrid, 1727–39 and 1748–57; negotiated Treaty of Seville (1729) and commercial treaty of 1750; member of Board of Trade, 1742–4; envoy to Portugal, 1746–8; KB, 1754; died at Madrid.

KEENE, Charles Samuel (1823–1891), humorous artist; after apprenticeships to an architect and a wood-engraver worked for *Punch* from 1851, and the *Illustrated London News*; illustrated stories in *Once a Week* and *Jerrold's Caudle Lectures*, and contributed plates to the 1879 edition of *Thackeray; gold medallist, Paris Exhibition of 1890.

KEENE, Edmund (1714–1781), bishop of Ely; brother of Sir Benjamin *Keene; of Charterhouse and Caius College, Cambridge (junior fellow, 1736–9); MA, 1737; fellow of Peterhouse, 1739, and master, 1748–54; vice-chancellor, 1749–51; rector of Stanhope, Durham, 1740–70; bishop of Chester, 1752–71, of Ely, 1771–81; sold Ely House, Holborn, London, and built the present residence in Dover Street, London.

KEENE, Henry (1726–1776), architect and surveyor to Westminster Abbey; designed the Radcliffe Infirmary and Observatory and some collegiate buildings at Oxford.

KEENE, Henry George (1781–1864), Persian scholar; grandson of Henry *Keene; while in Madras Army took part in storming of Seringapatam, 1799; afterwards entered Civil Service and studied at Fort William College, Calcutta; BA, Sidney Sussex College, Cambridge, 1815, fellow, 1817; professor of Arabic and Persian at Haileybury, 1824–34; published text and translations of *Akhlak-i-Mahsini* and *Anwas-i-Suhaili*, and *Persian Fables* (edited by his daughter, 1880).

KEEPE, Henry (1652–1688), author of *Monumenta Westmonasteriensia* (1682) and other antiquarian works (one under pseudonym of 'Charles Taylour'); of New Inn, Oxford, and Inner Temple; member of Westminster Abbey choir.

KEEPER, John (*fl.* 1580), poet. See KEPER.

KEETLEY, Charles Robert Bell (1848–1909), surgeon; entered St Bartholomew's Hospital, 1871; LRCP, 1873; FRCS, 1876; on staff of West London Hospital from 1878 till death; introduced there antiseptic methods of surgery; advocated appendicotomy; wrote handbook on orthopaedic surgery (1900) and other medical works.

KEIGHTLEY, Sir Charles Frederic (1901–1974), general; educated at Marlborough and Sandhurst; commissioned into 5th Dragoon Guards, 1921; regiment amalgamated with 6th Inniskilling Dragoons; saw service on North-West Frontier of India; on 1934–5 course at Staff College, Camberley; staff officer to director-general, Territorial Army, 1936; brigade-major to cavalry in Cairo, 1937–8; instructor at Camberley, 1938; assistant adjutant and quarter-master-general, 1st Armoured division in France and Belgium, 1940; major-general, directing Royal Armoured Corps training, 1941; commanded 6th Armoured division in French North Africa; commanded 78th Infantry division in Italian Campaign; director-general of military training, 1946; military secretary, 1948; general, 1951; C-in-C, British Army of the Rhine, 1948–51, Far East land forces, 1951–3, and Middle East land forces, 1953–7; governor and commander-in-chief, Gibraltar, 1957–62; DSO, 1944; American Legion of Merit, 1942; OBE, 1941; CB, 1943; KBE, 1945; KCB, 1950; GCB, 1953; GBE, 1957; grand officer of Legion of Honour, 1958; ADC-general to the queen, 1953–6; colonel of his regiment, 1947–57; colonel commandant, Royal Armoured Corps (Cavalry Wing), 1958–68.

KEIGHTLEY, Thomas (1650?–1719), Irish official; married Frances Hyde, sister of the duchess of York; vice-treasurer of Ireland, 1686; sent by *Clarendon to induce James II to stay in England, 1688; commissioner of Irish revenue, 1692; a lord justice, 1702; commissioner for Irish chancellor, 1710.

KEIGHTLEY, Thomas (1789–1872), author; of Trinity College, Dublin; published *Fairy Mythology* (1828, anon.) and histories, including

one of the war of Greek independence; also editions of Virgil's *Bucolics and Georgics*, and other Latin classics, and of *Milton and Shakespeare; issued *Shakespeare Expositor* (1867); received civil list pension.

KEIGWIN, John (1641–1716), Cornish scholar; his translations of *Pascon Agan Arluth* (mystery play) and of the *Gwreans an Bys* of William *Jordan printed by Davies *Gilbert (1826–7), and re-edited by Whitley Stokes (1860 and 1863).

KEIGWIN, Richard (d. 1690), naval and military commander; present at the four-days' fight of June 1666; took part in capture of St Helena, 1673, and succeeded *Munden as governor; as commandant at Bombay defeated the Mahratta fleet, 1679; headed revolt of 1683 against the company holding Bombay for the king till the arrival of Sir Thomas *Grantham; fell while leading the attack on Basseterre, St Christopher's.

KEILIN, David (1887–1963), biologist; born in Moscow; educated in Warsaw and Liège; studied entomology in Paris, 1905–15; research assistant to George H. F. *Nuttall, first Quick professor, Cambridge, 1915; Beit fellow, 1920–5; lecturer in parasitology, 1925–31; succeeded Nuttall as professor of biology and director, Molteno Institute, 1931–52; published thirty-nine papers between 1914 and 1923 on the reproduction of lice, the life-cycle of the horse bot-fly, the respiratory adaptations in fly larvae, and other subjects; detected pigment in bot-fly which he named cytochrome, an important development in biochemistry; D.Sc. (Sorbonne), 1915; FRS, 1928; hon. fellow, Magdalene College, Cambridge, 1957; honorary degrees and other academic distinctions from number of universities abroad; published *The History of Cell Respiration and Cytochrome* (ed. J. Keilin, 1966).

KEILL, James (1673–1719), physician; hon. MD, Cambridge; practised at Northampton, FRS, 1711; published *Account of Animal Secretion* (1708), enlarged as *Essays on several Parts of the Animal Oeconomy* (1717), the fourth edition containing an account of his controversy with *Jurin.

KEILL, John (1671–1721), mathematician and astronomer; brother of James *Keill; pupil of David *Gregory (1661–1708) at Edinburgh; MA, Edinburgh; incorporated at Oxford, 1694; at Hart Hall, Oxford, gave the first experimental lectures on natural philosophy; as deputy to the Sedleian professor delivered lectures, published as *Introductio ad Veram Physicam*; as 'treasurer of the Palatines' conducted German refugees to New England, 1709; patronized by Harley; 'decypherer' to Queen Anne, 1712; professor of astronomy at Oxford, 1712; FRS, 1701;

defended against Leibniz *Newton's claim to be the inventor of the fluxional calculus; published (1715) Latin editions of Euclid and the elements of trigonometry, and (1718) *Introductio ad Veram Astronomiam*.

KEILWAY (KELLWAY or KAYLWAY), Robert (1497–1581), law reporter; autumn reader at Inner Temple, 1547, and treasurer, 1557–8; serjeant-at-law, 1552; employed by the crown on various commissions; selections from his law reports issued (1602).

KEIMER, Samuel (*fl.* 1707–1738), Quaker printer; while imprisoned in the Fleet wrote *A Brand Pluck'd from the Burning* (containing a letter from *Defoe, 1718); printer in Philadelphia, 1723, with Franklin as foreman; assisted by Franklin in his edition of *Sewel's *History of the Quakers* (1728); published at Bridgetown, Barbados, first newspaper in Caribbean Islands, 1731–8.

KEIR, Sir David Lindsay (1895–1973), university teacher and administrator; educated at Glasgow Academy and University; commissioned in King's Own Scottish Borderers, 1915; wounded on the Somme and at Arras; entered New College, Oxford; first class in history, 1921; fellow, University College; dean, 1925–35; estates bursar, 1933–9; university lecturer in English Constitutional history, 1931–9; published (with F. H. *Lawson) *Cases in Constitutional Law* (1928) and *The Constitutional History of Modern Britain* (1938); vice-chancellor, Queen's University, Belfast, 1939–49; responsible for new building programme and expansion; knighted, 1946; chairman, Northern Ireland Regional Hospitals Board, 1942–9; member, Northern Ireland Planning Advisory Board; master, Balliol College, Oxford, 1949–65; chairman, Advisory Committee on Overseas Colleges of Arts, Science, and Technology, 1954–64; chairman, United Oxford Hospitals Trust, 1950–8; launched Balliol's septcentenary appeal which raised more than a million pounds; recipient of many honorary degrees; hon. fellow of University, Balliol, and New colleges; hon. FRIBA, 1948.

KEIR, James (1735–1820), chemist; studied at Edinburgh; friend of Erasmus *Darwin; issued *Treatise on the different kinds of Elastic Fluids or Gases* (1777); while managing Boulton & Watt's engineering works, patented a metal said to resemble 'Muntz-metal', 1779; with Alexander Blair opened alkali works at Tipton, the method of extraction being Keir's discovery, 1780; established Tividale Colliery; discovered the distinction between carbonic-acid gas and atmospheric air; FRS, 1785; contributed paper concerning experiments and observations on the dissolution of metals in acids, 1790; wrote memoir of Thomas *Day.

KEIR, William Grant (1772–1852), general. See GRANT, Sir WILLIAM KEIR.

KEITH, Viscount (1746–1823). See ELPHINSTONE, GEORGE KEITH.

KEITH, Viscountesses. See ELPHINSTONE, HESTER MARIA, 1764–1857; ELPHINSTONE, MARGARET MERCER, 1788–1867.

KEITH, Alexander (d. 1758), Mayfair parson; excommunicated for celebrating marriages without banns or licence, and afterwards imprisoned for contempt of the church, in the Fleet, where he died.

KEITH, Alexander (1737–1819), of Ravelston; founder of the Keith prizes at Edinburgh; friend and connection of Sir Walter *Scott.

KEITH, Alexander (1791–1880), writer on prophecy; son of George Skene *Keith; DD, Aberdeen, 1833; pastor of St Cyrus, Kincardineshire, 1816–40; visited Palestine and eastern Europe for the Scottish Church, 1839, and in 1844 took daguerrotype views; joined the Free Church; published works of Christian evidences founded on the fulfilment of prophecy.

KEITH, Sir Arthur (1886–1955), conservator of the Hunterian Museum, Royal College of Surgeons; educated at Gordon's College, Aberdeen; qualified from Marischal College, 1888; MD, Aberdeen, and FRCS, 1894; senior demonstrator, later lecturer in anatomy, London Hospital Medical School, 1895–1908; conservator, Hunterian Museum, 1908–33; Fullerian professor of physiology, Royal Institution, 1918–23; president, British Association, 1927; rector, Aberdeen, 1930–3; studied human evolution, claiming higher antiquity for *Homo sapiens* than generally accepted, and involved in controversy over fraudulent Piltdown skull; publications include *Human Embryology and Morphology* (1902), *The Antiquity of Man* (1915), and *A New Theory of Human Evolution* (1948); FRS, 1913; knighted, 1921; honorary degrees from Aberdeen, Durham, Manchester, Birmingham, and Oxford.

KEITH, Arthur Berriedale (1879–1944), Sanskrit scholar and constitutional lawyer; brother of Sir W. J. *Keith; educated at Royal High School and University, Edinburgh, and Balliol College, Oxford; first class, classics, Edinburgh, 1897; oriental languages (1900) and Lit. Hum. (1901), Oxford; called to bar (Inner Temple), 1904; served in Colonial Office, 1901–14; regius professor of Sanskrit and comparative philology, Edinburgh, 1914–44; made important contributions to Vedic and classical Sanskrit studies; published *Responsible Government in the Dominions* (1909, revised, 1912, 1928) and many other books on same subject; *Constitutional History of the First British Empire* (1930) and of *India, 1600–1935* (1936); and works on British constitutional history; FBA, 1935.

KEITH, George, fourth Earl Marischal (1553?–1623), founder of Marischal College, Aberdeen; educated at King's College, Aberdeen, and under Beza at Geneva; succeeded his grandfather in the earldom, 1581; privy councillor of Scotland, 1582; a commissioner for executing laws against Papists; as ambassador-extraordinary to Denmark acted as James VI's proxy in marrying the princess *Anne, 1589; founded Marischal College, Aberdeen, 1593; king's commissioner for apprehension of *Huntly and trial of the Catholic lords, 1593; member of Parliamentary Commission of 1604 for Union with England; royal commissioner to Scottish parliament, 1609; member of the Ecclesiastical Commission.

KEITH, George (1639?–1716), 'Christian Quaker' and SPG missionary; MA, Marischal College, Aberdeen; became a Quaker, 1662; frequently imprisoned for preaching; collaborated with Robert *Barclay (1648–1690), and was imprisoned with him at Aberdeen, 1676; accompanied George *Fox and William *Penn to Holland and Germany on a missionary tour, 1677; after having been twice imprisoned in England, emigrated to Philadelphia, 1689; accused of heresy and interdicted from preaching, 1692; held meetings of 'Christian Quakers'; came to London to defend his views, but was disowned by the 'yearly meeting' of 1694, after which he established a meeting at Turners' Hall, Philpot Lane, London, where, retaining the Quaker externals, he administered baptism and the Lord's Supper, 1695–1700; conformed to the Anglican Church, 1700; conducted a successful mission in America for the SPG, 1702–4; died rector of Edburton, Sussex. Among his chief publications were *The Deism of William Penn and his Brethren* (1699), *The Standard of the Quakers examined* (1702), and *A Journal of Travels* (1706).

KEITH, George, ninth Earl Marischal (1693?–1778), Jacobite and favourite of Frederick the Great; succeeded to earldom, 1712; commanded cavalry at Sheriffmuir, 1715; entertained *James Edward, the Old Pretender, at Newburgh and Fetteresso, 1715; led Spanish Jacobite expedition of 1719, and after Glenshiel escaped to the Western Isles, and thence to Spain; corresponded from Valencia with the Pretender, but took no part in the Forty-five; named Prussian ambassador at Paris, 1751, governor of

Neufchatel, 1752, and ambassador to Madrid, 1758; pardoned by George II, probably for sending intelligence of the Family Compact, 1759; succeeded to the Kintore estates, 1761, but was recalled to Prussia by the king's personal entreaties, 1764; intimate with Voltaire and Rousseau.

KEITH, George Skene (1752–1823), author of *General View of the Agriculture of Aberdeenshire* (1811); graduated at Aberdeen, 1770; DD, Marischal College, Aberdeen, 1803; minister of Keith-Hall and Kinkell, 1778–1822, and Tulliallan, 1822–3; published *Tracts on Weights, Measures, and Coins* (1791); voted £500 by parliament for his experiments in distillation; edited Principal George Campbell's *Lectures on Ecclesiastical History*, with life (1800).

KEITH, James, Baron Keith of Avonholm (1886–1964), judge; educated at Hamilton Academy and Glasgow University; MA; first class, history, 1906; LL B, 1908; admitted to Faculty of Advocates, 1911; commissioned in Seaforth Highlanders, 1914; served in France and the Sudan; KC, 1926; dean, Faculty of Advocates, 1936; lord commissioner of judiciary and senator, College of Justice, with judicial title, Lord Keith, 1937; member, Royal Commission on Marriage and Divorce (the Morton Commission), 1951; succeeded Lord *Normand as lord of appeal in ordinary, 1953–61; life peer, 1953; PC; member of Judicial Committee of Privy Council; honorary bencher, Inner Temple, 1953; trustee, National Library of Scotland, 1925–37; chairman, Scottish Youth Advisory Committee, 1942–6, and of Scottish Probation Council, 1943–9.

KEITH, James Francis Edward (1696–1758), known as Marshal Keith; brother of George *Keith, ninth Earl Marischal; carefully educated under Robert *Keith (1681–1757) and Meston the Jacobite poet; took part in the Fifteen, and escaped with his brother to Brittany; studied mathematics in Paris under Maupertuis; engaged in Alberoni's unsuccessful Jacobite expedition, 1719; served in the Spanish Army; lieutenant-colonel of the tsarina Anne's bodyguard; second-in-command in Polish Succession War, 1733–5, and Russian general, 1737; wounded in Turkish War, 1737; took prominent part in Russo-Swedish War, 1741–3, but fell into disgrace as a foreigner; made field marshal by Frederick the Great, 1747; governor of Berlin, 1749; after sharing in the early victories of the Seven Years' War was mortally wounded at Hochkirch; inventor of Kriegsschachspiel. A marble statue of him was erected at Berlin.

KEITH, Sir John, first earl of Kintore (d. 1714), fourth son of William *Keith, fifth Earl

Marischal; held Dunnottar Castle against *Cromwell, and preserved the regalia, 1650; created knight marischal of Scotland at the Restoration; created earl of Kintore and privy councillor, 1677.

KEITH, Sir Robert (d. 1346), great marischal of Scotland; received lands of Keith from King John *Baliol, 1294; captured by the English, 1300, but released, 1302; one of the four wardens of Scotland till he joined *Bruce, 1308; justiciar of Scotland; led Scottish horse at Bannockburn, 1315; fell at Battle of Durham.

KEITH, Robert (1681–1757), bishop of Fife and historian; at Marischal College, Aberdeen; when coadjutor (1727–33) to Bishop Millar of Edinburgh obtained extinction of project of college of bishops, 1732; bishop of Fife, 1733–43; after his resignation of Fife continued to act as bishop of Orkney and Caithness, and (1743) was chosen 'primus'; published a history of Scotland from the Reformation to 1568 (1734; reprinted, 1844–5), and *Catalogue of the Bishops of Scotland to 1688* (1755; continued by M. *Russell, LL D, 1824).

KEITH, Robert (d. 1774), British ambassador at Vienna, 1748–58, at St Petersburg, 1758–62; friend of *Hume and Robertson.

KEITH, Sir Robert Murray (1730–1795), lieutenant-general and diplomat; son of Robert *Keith (d. 1774); served in Scottish brigade in Dutch service, 1747–52; on staff of Lord George *Sackville at Minden, 1759; as commander of 87th Foot (1759–63) won distinction in the Seven Years' War; British minister in Saxony, 1769–71; while envoy at Copenhagen rescued from the anger of the mob Sophia Matilda of Denmark (sister of George III), and was created KB, 1772; ambassador at Vienna, 1772–92; lieutenant-general, 1781; privy councillor, 1789.

KEITH, Robert William (1787–1846), musical composer and organist at the New Jerusalem Church, Friars Street, London; published sacred melodies and *Musical Vade Mecum* (c.1820).

KEITH, Thomas (1759–1824), mathematical writer and teacher, and accountant to the British Museum.

KEITH, Sir William (d. 1407?), great marischal of Scotland; nephew of Sir Robert *Keith; favourite of David II; built Dunnottar Castle on site of the parish church.

KEITH, William, third Earl Marischal (d. 1581), 'William of the Tower'; succeeded his grandfather in the peerage, 1527; extraordinary lord of session, 1541; privy councillor, 1543; present at Pinkie, 1547; subscribed the confession of faith, 1560, and 'Book of Discipline',

1561; opposed proposal to deprive *Mary Queen of Scots of the mass; retired from affairs after *Darnley's death; the wealthiest Scotsman of his time.

KEITH, William (d. 1608?). See KETHE.

KEITH, William, fifth Earl Marischal (1585?–1635), succeeded George, fourth earl, 1623; captain of three ships on Scottish coast, 1626; fitted out a fleet to help the king of Poland, 1634.

KEITH, William, sixth Earl Marischal (1614–1661), Covenanter; co-operated with *Montrose and twice seized Aberdeen, 1639; chosen a lord of the articles after pacification of Berwick, 1639; again seized Aberdeen and enforced signature of the Covenant, 1640; nominated privy councillor, 1641; attended Covenanting committees in the north, but remained inactive, 1643–4; refused to give up fugitives to Montrose, and was besieged at Dunnottar, 1645; joined *Hamilton's expedition into England, 1648; entertained Charles II at Dunnottar, 1650; arrested and imprisoned in the Tower till the Restoration, when he was appointed keeper of the privy seal of Scotland.

KEITH, Sir William John (1873–1937), administrator in Burma; brother of A. B. *Keith; a dominating influence in Burma secretariat (1896–1928) where he specialized in revenue and finance; leader of house in Legislative Council, and finance member and vice-president of Executive Council, 1923–8; knighted, 1925; KCSI, 1928.

KEITH-FALCONER, Ion Grant Neville (1856–1887), Arabic scholar and bicyclist; educated at Harrow and Trinity College, Cambridge; BA, 1878; Tyrwhitt Hebrew scholar and first class in the Semitic languages tripos; president of the London Bicycle Club, 1877–86; rode from John o' Groat's to Land's End in thirteen days, less forty-five minutes, 1882; studied Arabic at Assiout, 1881–2; published translation from Syriac version of *Fables of Bidpai* (1885); lord almoner's professor of Arabic at Cambridge, 1886; died of fever near Aden, at a station whence he had made excursions to study Somali.

KEKEWICH, Sir Arthur (1832–1907), judge; educated at Eton and Balliol College, Oxford; BA, 1854; fellow of Exeter, 1854–8; called to bar, 1858; QC, 1877; had large junior practice at Chancery bar, but was unsuccessful as leader; judge, 1886; knighted, 1887; expeditious judge, but his judgements were often reversed on appeal; a strong churchman and Conservative.

KEKEWICH, Robert George (1854–1914), major-general; nephew of Sir A. *Kekewich;

entered army, 1874; lieutenant-colonel in Loyal North Lancashires, 1898; during South African War defended Kimberley from Boers, 15 Oct. 1899–15 Feb. 1900; CB, 1900; major-general, 1902.

KELBURN, Sinclare (1754–1802), Irish Presbyterian divine; BA, Trinity College, Dublin, 1774; studied also at Edinburgh; minister at Belfast, 1780–99; imprisoned on suspicion of connection with United Irishmen, 1797; published work on the divinity of Christ (1792).

KELDELETH (or KELDELECH), Robert (d. 1273), chancellor of Scotland; abbot of Dunfermline, 1240–51; of Melrose, 1268–73; chancellor of Scotland, 1250–1; deposed as partisan of Alan Durward.

KELHAM, Robert (1717–1808), attorney in the King's Bench; author of dictionary of Norman–French (1779), index to abridgements of law and equity (1758), and other works.

KELKE, Roger (1524–1576), master of Magdalene College, Cambridge; MA, St John's College, Cambridge, 1547; senior fellow of St John's, 1552; lived at Zurich during reign of Mary; Lady Margaret preacher, 1559 and 1563; master of Magdalene College, 1558–76; vice-chancellor, 1567 and 1571–2; opposed Archbishop *Parker's Advertisements*; archdeacon of Stowe, 1563.

KELLAND, Philip (1808–1879), mathematician; senior wrangler and first Smith's prizeman, Queens' College, Cambridge, 1834; MA, 1837, and tutor; professor of mathematics at Edinburgh, 1838–79; secretary of the Senatus Academicus till 1867; FRS, 1838; president, Edinburgh Royal Society, 1878–9; wrote on mathematics and Scottish education; contributed the article 'Algebra' to *Encyclopaedia Britannica* (ninth edn.).

KELLAWAY, Charles Halliley (1889–1952), scientist; educated at Church of England Grammar School and the University, Melbourne; MB, BS, 1911; served in Europe in Australian Army Medical Corps, 1915–18; Foulerton research student, Royal Society, 1920–3; director, Walter and Eliza Hall Institute for Pathological Research, Melbourne, 1923–44; director of pathology, AAMC, 1939–42; scientific liaison officer to director-general, 1942–4; research director-in-chief, Wellcome Foundation, London, 1944–52; FRCP, 1929; FRS, 1940.

KELLAWE, Richard de (d. 1316), bishop of Durham, 1311–16; refused to receive Gaveston, 1313; his register the earliest extant of the Palatinate.

KELLER, Gottfried (or Godfrey) (d. 1704), harpsichord player and composer; author of a manual of thorough-bass.

KELLETT, Edward (d. 1641), divine; of Eton and King's College, Cambridge; fellow; incorporated MA at Oxford, 1617; DD, 1621; prebendary of Exeter, 1630; friend of *Selden; published *Miscellanies of Divinitie* (1635) and other works.

KELLETT, Sir **Henry** (1806–1875), vice-admiral; named CB for services as surveyor and pilot in Chinese War of 1840; co-operated with *Franklin search expeditions in the *Herald*, 1848–50; went in search of Franklin in the *Resolute*, 1852, but abandoned her under orders, May 1854; commodore at Jamaica, 1855–9; rear-admiral, 1862; vice-admiral, 1868; KCB, 1869; commander-in-chief in China, 1869–71.

KELLEY, Edward (1555–1595), alchemist; said to have studied at Oxford under an alias; pilloried for fraud or coining at Lancaster, 1580; 'skryer' to John *Dee, going with him to Prague and staying with him at the emperor Rudolph II's court; parted from Dee in 1588, but remained in Germany; lost his life in attempting to escape from prison; his Latin treatises on the philosopher's stone issued (1676); mentioned in *Hudibras*.

KELLIE, earls of. See ERSKINE, THOMAS, first earl, 1566–1639; ERSKINE, THOMAS ALEXANDER, sixth earl, 1732–1781.

KELLISON, Matthew (1560?–1642), president of the English College, Douai; professor of scholastic theology at Reims, 1589; rector of the university, 1606; member of Arras College, 1611; as president (1613–42) rid Douai of Jesuit influence; published *The Gagge of the Reformed Gospell* (1623, frequently reprinted as *Touchstone of the Reformed Gospel*), and other works.

KELLNER, Ernest Augustus (1792–1839), musician; played a concerto of *Handel before the royal family when 5 years old; made tours with Incledon as a baritone; sang and played in Switzerland and Germany and at Philharmonic concerts in London, 1820–3; appeared at Venice; gave concerts in Russia and Paris; composed masses and songs.

KELLO, Mrs **Esther (or Hester)** (1571–1624), calligrapher and miniaturist; née English or Inglis (in French Langlois); born in France; perhaps nurse to Prince *Henry; manuscripts written or illuminated by her in British Museum, the Bodleian, and continental libraries.

KELLO, Samuel (d. 1680), rector of Spexall, Suffolk, 1620–80; son of Mrs Esther *Kello;

MA, Edinburgh, 1618; admitted to Christ Church, Oxford.

KELLY, Sir David Victor (1891–1959), diplomat; educated at St Paul's School and Magdalen College, Oxford; first class, history, 1913; became Roman Catholic, 1914; served in France, 1915–19; entered Diplomatic Service, 1919; served in Argentina, Portugal, Belgium, and Sweden; in Foreign Office American department, counsellor, 1931–4; acting high commissioner, and chargé d'affaires, Egypt, 1934–8; head, Foreign Office Egyptian department, 1938–9; minister to Switzerland, 1940–2; ambassador to Argentina, 1942–6, to Turkey, 1946–9, to USSR, 1949–51; advocated co-ordination between foreign policy and financial and economic policy, and cultivation of industrial, financial, and social leaders in countries of his appointment; commentator on Soviet affairs, mainly in *Sunday Times*, 1951–4; chairman, British Council, 1955–9; publications include autobiography, *The Ruling Few* (1952); CMG, 1935; KCMG, 1942; GCMG, 1950.

KELLY, Edward (1555–1595), alchemist. See KELLEY.

KELLY, Edward (1854–1880), bushranger; with his brother and two others held out for two years against the police on the borders of Victoria and New South Wales, occasionally plundering banks; captured and hanged.

KELLY, Sir Fitzroy (1796–1880), lord chief baron; barrister, Lincoln's Inn, 1824; KC, 1834; standing counsel to the Bank and the East India Company; defended Tawell the poisoner, 1845; knighted, 1845; prosecuted Dr Bernard, 1858; appeared in *Gorham case, 1847, and Shrewsbury and Crawford peerage cases; Conservative MP for Ipswich, 1837–41, Cambridge, 1843–7, and east Suffolk, 1852–66; solicitor-general, 1845–6 and 1852, attorney-general, 1858–9; lord chief baron, 1866–80; privy councillor, 1866.

KELLY, Frances Maria (1790–1882), actress and singer; friend of the Lambs; niece of Michael *Kelly; made her first appearance at Drury Lane when 7; impressed by her Arthur (*King John*) *Sheridan, *Fox, and Mrs *Siddons; played at Drury Lane and the Italian Opera, 1800–6; associated with the former from its reopening (1812) till 1835, playing Ophelia to Edmund *Kean's *Hamlet* and other Shakespearean parts; excelled in melodrama; her acting celebrated in two sonnets by *Lamb, who offered her marriage; after her retirement conducted a dramatic school (for which the Royalty was built) and gave readings and monologues.

KELLY, Frederick Septimus (1881–1916), musician and oarsman; born at Sydney; educated at Eton and Balliol; rowed for Oxford; at Henley won Grand Challenge Cup, Stewards' Cup, Diamond Sculls, Wingfield Sculls; one of the greatest scullers of all time; studied pianoforte at Frankfurt-on-Main, 1903–8; left wide range of compositions; joined Royal Naval division, 1914; DSC for gallantry in Gallipoli, 1915; killed in France.

KELLY, George (*fl.* 1736), Jacobite; BA, Trinity College, Dublin, 1706; having acted as Atterbury's amanuensis in his correspondence with the Pretender, was imprisoned in the Tower, 1723–36, but escaped; published translation of Castlenau's *Memoirs of the English Affairs* (1724), of Morabin's *History of Cicero's Banishment* (1725).

KELLY, Sir Gerald Festus (1879–1972), portrait painter; educated at Eton; left early through illness; convalesced in South Africa; entered Trinity Hall, Cambridge, 1897; decided to become painter, without any formal training; moved to Paris, 1901; had many friends there, and became member of Salon d'Automne, 1904; associate of Royal Hibernian Academy, 1908; spent year in Burma; during 1914–18 war served in intelligence department of Admiralty; ARA, 1922; RA, 1930; painted state portraits of King George VI and Queen Elizabeth, 1945; knighted; honorary surveyor of Dulwich College Picture Gallery; involved in controversy over cleaning of paintings in National Gallery; member, Royal Fine Art Commission, 1938–43; president of Royal Academy, 1949–54; KCVO, 1955; RHA, 1914; hon. RSA, 1950; hon. FRIBA, 1950; hon. LL D, Cambridge and Trinity College, Dublin, 1950; paintings include *The Vicar in his Study* (1912), *The Jester* (1911, portrait of W. Somerset *Maugham, both in Tate Gallery, many portraits of his wife and beautiful Asian dancing girls, portraits of Hugh *Walpole (1925), Dr M. R. *James (1937), Sir Malcolm *Sargent (1948), and Dr Ralph *Vaughan Williams (1953).

KELLY, Hugh (1739–1777), playwright and author; came to London as a staymaker, 1760; edited *Court Magazine* and *Ladies' Museum*, and afterwards *The Public Ledger*; published *Memoirs of a Magdalen* (1767) and dramatic criticism; his comedy *False Delicacy* successfully produced by *Garrick at Drury Lane, 1768, in rivalry with Goldsmith's *Good-Natured Man*, and acted at Paris and Lisbon; produced *A Word to the Wise* (1770, revived with prologue by *Johnson at Covent Garden, 1777), and other plays; received pension for political writings; practised as a barrister in his last years.

KELLY, James Fitzmaurice- (1857–1923), historian of Spanish literature. See FITZMAUR-ICE-KELLY.

KELLY, John (1680?–1751), journalist and playwright; of the Inner Temple; works include reprint of *Universal Spectator* (1747) and four plays.

KELLY, John (1750–1809), Manx scholar; transcribed and superintended printing of Manx Bible, 1766–72, revised New Testament, 1775, and with Philip *Moore (1705–1783) the whole Bible, Prayer-Book, and other works, 1776; graduated LL D, St John's College, Cambridge, 1799; vicar of Ardleigh, 1791–1807; rector of Copford, 1807–9; his Manx grammar (1804) reprinted (1859), and part of his *Triglot Dictionary of the Celtic Language* (1866).

KELLY, John (1801–1876), Independent minister at Liverpool, 1829–73; chairman of Congregational Union, 1851.

KELLY, Sir John Donald (1871–1936), admiral of the fleet; entered navy, 1884; captain, 1911; rear-admiral, 1921; fourth sea lord, 1924–7; vice-admiral, 1926; KCB, 1929; admiral, 1930; commander-in-chief, Home Fleet, 1931–3, with task of restoring discipline after Invergordon Mutiny; GCVO, 1932; commander-in-chief, Portsmouth, 1934–6; admiral of the fleet, 1936.

KELLY, Mary Anne ('Eva') (1826–1910), Irish poetess. See O'DOHERTY, MARY ANNE.

KELLY, Matthew (1814–1858), Irish antiquary; professor at the Irish College, Paris, 1839–41, and at Maynooth, 1841–58; made DD by the pope and canon of Ossory, *c.*1854; published *Calendar of Irish Saints* (1857), a translation of Gosselin's *Power of the Popes* (1853), and editions of Irish antiquarian classics; his *Dissertations chiefly on Irish Church History* issued (1864).

KELLY, Michael (1764?–1826), vocalist, actor, and composer; successful treble singer on the Dublin stage; studied at Naples and Palermo, and sang at Florence (1780), Venice, and other Italian cities; when principal tenor in Italian opera at Vienna (1783–6) was prepared by Gluck to sing in *Iphigenia in Tauride* and by Mozart for Basilio in the first performance of *Nozze di Figaro*; sang in Mozart's Sunday concerts; appeared in opera at Drury Lane Theatre, 1787–1808, singing also in oratorios at the Ancient Concerts, 1789–91, in and Scotland and Ireland; as musical director at Drury Lane Theatre and joint director at the King's Theatre, London, composed settings of *Sheridan's *Pizarro*, *Coleridge's *Remorse*, and other plays; last seen on the stage at

Dublin, 1811. His songs include 'Flora Macdonald' and 'The Woodpecker'; his *Reminiscences* written by Theodore *Hook (1826).

KELLY, Patrick (1756–1842), mathematician and astronomer; hon. LL D, Glasgow; master of the 'Mercantile School', Finsbury Square; published *The Universal Cambist and Commercial Instructor* (1811) and other works.

KELLY (or O'KELLY), Ralph (d. 1361), archbishop of Cashel; prolocutor of the Carmelites, 1336; archbishop of Cashel, 1345–61; opposed levy of a subsidy, 1346; assaulted Cradock, bishop of Waterford, 1353.

KELLY, William (1821–1906), Plymouth brother and biblical critic; joined Plymouth Brethren, 1841; edited collected works of John Nelson *Darby (34 vols., 1867–83); seceded from Darbyites on point of church discipline, 1879; a voluminous scriptural commentator and controversialist.

KELLY-KENNY, Sir Thomas (1840–1914), general; joined army, 1858; took sixth division out to South African War, 1900; took part in engagements of Klip Kraal Drift, Paardeberg, Poplar Grove, and Driefontein; left in command in Free State, 1900; KCB, 1902; general, 1905.

KELSEY, Thomas (d. 1680?), Parliamentarian officer; deputy-governor of Oxford, 1646–50; lieutenant of Dover Castle, 1651; a commissioner for the navy and major-general of the Kent and Surrey militia, 1655; MP, Sandwich, 1654, Dover, 1656 and 1659; supported *Fleetwood and *Lambert.

KELTIE, Sir John Scott (1840–1927), geographer; took up journalism; edited *Statesman's Year Book*, 1884–1927; inspector of geographical education for Royal Geographical Society, 1884; produced important report, 1886; librarian and subsequently secretary of Society, publications of which he reorganized; inaugurated and edited *Geographical Journal*, 1893; editor and author of several geographical works; knighted, 1918.

KELTON, Arthur (*fl.* 1546), author of rhymed works on matters of Welsh history.

KELTRIDGE, John (*fl.* 1581), divine; MA, Trinity College, Cambridge, 1575 (incorporated at Oxford, 1579); author of *Exposition and Readynges . . . upon the wordes of our Saviour Christe, that bee written in the xi. of Luke* (1578).

KELTY, Mary Ann (1789–1873), author of a novel, *The Favourite of Nature* (1821), of *Memoirs of the Lives and Persecutions of Primitive Quakers* (1844), and devotional works.

KELVIN, first Baron (1824–1907), scientist and inventor. See THOMSON, WILLIAM.

KELWAY, Joseph (d. 1782), organist and harpsichord player; had Queen *Charlotte and Mrs *Delany among his pupils.

KELWAY, Thomas (d. 1749), organist of Chichester Cathedral, 1726–49; brother of Joseph *Kelway; composed church music.

KELYNG, Sir John (d. 1671), judge; barrister, Inner Temple, 1632; imprisoned for Royalism, 1642–60; serjeant-at-law, 1660; knighted, 1661; MP, Bedford, 1661; employed in drafting Act of Uniformity and in proceedings against the regicides; ridiculed evidence of witchcraft given before Sir Matthew *Hale, 1662; puisne judge, 1663; chief justice of the King's Bench, 1665–71; censured by parliament (1667) for ill treatment of jurors; compelled to apologize for a libel on Lord Hollis, 1671; his reports of pleas of the crown edited by R. Loveland Loveland, 1873.

KELYNG, Sir John (1630?–1680), serjeant-at-law, 1680; knighted, 1679; son of Sir John *Kelyng (d. 1671); barrister, Inner Temple, 1660.

KEM (or KEME), Samuel (1604–1670), Puritan divine; demy of Magdalen College, Oxford, 1624–6; BA, 1625; BD; rector of Albury, Oxfordshire, and vicar of Low Leyton, Essex; chaplain to earl of *Essex; captain in Parliamentary Army; often preached in military dress; spy on Royalists at Rotterdam, 1648; became loyal on the Restoration.

KEMBALL, Sir Arnold Burrowes (1820–1908), general, colonel commandant, Royal Artillery; born in Bombay; joined Bombay Artillery, 1837; present at Ghazni and Kabul; in Persian War, 1856–7; distinguished in expedition against Ahwaz; CB, 1857; consul-general at Baghdad, 1859; KCSI, 1866; accompanied shah of Persia to England, 1873; on international commission for delimiting Turco-Persian frontier, 1875; military commissioner with Turkish Army in Serbo-Turkish and Russo-Turkish wars; lieutenant-general and KCB, 1878; interested in Persian and East African development; advocated construction of Uganda Railway; general, 1880.

KEMBALL-COOK, Sir Basil Alfred (1876–1949), civil servant; scholar of Eton and King's College, Cambridge; second class, classics, 1898; entered transport department, Admiralty, 1900; director, naval sea transport, Ministry of Shipping, 1917–19; assistant British delegate, Reparation Commission, 1921–6; managing director, British Tanker Company, 1927–35; deputy divisional (later divisional) food officer, London, 1942–8; KCMG, 1925.

KEMBLE, Adelaide (1814?–1879), afterwards Mrs Sartoris; vocalist and author; daughter of Charles *Kemble; first sang at the Ancient Concerts, 1835; in Germany and at Paris, 1837–8; had lessons from Pasta and appeared with success at Venice as Norma; sang in Italian opera at Covent Garden, 1841–2; married Edward John Sartoris, 1843; published *A Week in a French Country House* (1867) and other works.

KEMBLE, Charles (1775–1854), actor; son of Roger *Kemble; appeared at Drury Lane as Malcolm in *Macbeth*, 1794, Norval in *Douglas*, 1798, and Alonzo in *Pizarro*, 1799; first appeared as Charles Surface, Falconbridge, and Young Mirabel, 1800; played Hamlet, 1803; joining his brother at Covent Garden, played Romeo, 1803; appeared in adaptations by himself from Kotzebue; after playing at Brussels and in France returned to Covent Garden as Macbeth, 1815; began his management of Covent Garden, 1822, playing Falstaff (1824) and many leading parts; met with little success financially till the appearance of his eldest daughter, Fanny, with whom, in 1832–4, he made a successful tour in America; his Mercutio first seen at Covent Garden, 1829; gave farewell performance as Benedick (Haymarket), 1836, but acted for a few nights at Covent Garden, 1840. He had a greater range than any actor except *Garrick, but was pre-eminent only in comedy.

KEMBLE, Mrs Elizabeth (1763?–1841), actress; née Satchell; appeared at Covent Garden as Polly (*Beggar's Opera*), 1780; played Juliet, Ophelia, and other leading parts next season; Desdemona to Stephen *Kemble's Othello, 1783, marrying him the same year; afterwards eclipsed her husband.

KEMBLE, Frances Anne (generally known as **Fanny)** (1809–1893), afterwards Mrs Butler, actress; daughter of Charles *Kemble and Maria Theresa *Kemble; appeared with great success as Juliet to her father's Mercutio, Covent Garden, 1829; appeared subsequently as Mrs Haller (Stranger), Lady Macbeth, Portia, Beatrice, Constance, Julia, Mariana, and Queen Katherine; visited America, 1833, and married, 1834, Pierce Butler (d. 1867), whom she divorced, 1848; began series of Shakespearean readings, 1848; lived in America, 1849–68, and 1873–8; published poetical and dramatic writings and several autobiographical works.

KEMBLE, Henry (1848–1907), comedian; grandson of Charles *Kemble and nephew of Fanny *Kemble; made professional début at Dublin, 1867; with company of (Sir) John *Hare, 1875; joined the *Bancrofts (1876), with whom he played Dolly Spanker in *London Assurance* and

Sir Oliver Surface in *The School for Scandal*; played Polonius to (Sir) Herbert *Tree as Hamlet, 1891.

KEMBLE, Henry Stephen (1789–1836), actor; son of Stephen *Kemble; of Winchester and Trinity College, Cambridge; after playing in the country appeared at the Haymarket, 1814; acted at Bath and Bristol and played Romeo and other leading parts at Drury Lane, 1818–19; afterwards appeared at minor theatres.

KEMBLE, John (1599?–1679), Roman Catholic priest; missioner in Herefordshire; executed for saying mass; ancestor of Charles *Kemble.

KEMBLE, John Mitchell (1807–1857), philologist and historian; elder son of Charles *Kemble; educated at first under *Richardson, the lexicographer; whilst at Trinity College, Cambridge, intimate of *Tennyson, Richard Chenevix *Trench, and William Bodham *Donne, and one of 'the Apostles'; accompanied Trench to Spain to join a rising against Ferdinand VII, 1830; MA, Cambridge, 1833; studied philology under Jacob Grimm in Germany; edited the poems of Beowulf, 1833, and lectured at Cambridge on Anglo-Saxon; edited *British and Foreign Review*, 1835–44; examiner of stage-plays, 1840; studied prehistoric archaeology at Hanover, making excavations in Lüneburg, and drawings at Munich, Berlin, and Schwerin, 1854–5; died in Dublin. His chief works were *Codex Diplomaticus aevi Saxonici* (1839–48), *The Saxons in England* (1849; ed. Birch, 1876), and *State Papers* illustrating the period 1688–1714.

KEMBLE, John Philip (1757–1823), actor; eldest son of Roger *Kemble; played as a child in his father's company, but was educated for the Roman Catholic priesthood at Sedgley Park and Douai; appeared in Lee's *Theodosius* at Wolverhampton, 1776; produced a tragedy and a poem at Liverpool; played on York circuit under Tate *Wilkinson and lectured at York, 1778–81; appeared at Edinburgh and gained great success at Dublin as Hamlet and Raymond (*Jephson's *Count of Narbonne*), 1781; during engagement at Drury Lane Theatre (1783–1802) presented over 120 characters, beginning with Hamlet; played with Mrs *Siddons (his sister) in *King John, Othello, King Lear*, and many other plays, and also with his wife and Miss *Farren; as manager, from 1788, began to dress characters unconventionally; played Coriolanus and Henry V in arrangements by himself, and gave also Romeo, Petruchio, Wolsey, and Charles Surface (a failure); Macbeth in reopened Drury Lane, 1794, having played meanwhile at the Haymarket; acted in adaptations by himself of many Shakespearean plays, in Ireland's *Vortigern*

(1796), and pieces by Madame D'*Arblay and 'Monk' *Lewis; visited Paris, Madrid, and Douai; manager at Covent Garden from 1803 till 1808, when the theatre was burned down, playing Hamlet, Antonio, Iago, Pierre, Prospero, and original parts in plays by Mrs *Inchbald, *Colman, *Reynolds, and *Morton; reopened Covent Garden Theatre, 1809, with increased prices, thereby occasioning the O.P. riots; played Brutus, 1812, and Coriolanus for his farewell, 1817; went abroad for his health and died at Lausanne; chief founder of the declamatory school of acting; admired by *Lamb and intimate of Sir Walter *Scott.

KEMBLE, Maria Theresa (or Marie Thérèse) (1774–1838), actress; née De Camp; came to England from Vienna, and as Miss De Camp appeared at Drury Lane Theatre, 1786; pleased the public as Macheath in the *Beggar's Opera*, 1792; the original Judith in the *Iron Chest* and Caroline Dormer in the *Heir at Law*, 1797; also played Portia, Desdemona, and Katherine, and in her own *First Faults* (1799); married Charles *Kemble, 1806; acted at Covent Garden Theatre, 1806–19, in her own plays *The Day after the Wedding* (1808) and *Smiles and Tears* (1815), also playing Ophelia, Beatrice, and Mrs Sullen; created Madge Wildfire in *Terry's *Heart of Midlothian*.

KEMBLE, Priscilla (1756–1845), actress; née Hopkins; acted in *Garrick's company at Drury Lane Theatre, 1775; the original Harriet (*The Runaway*), Eliza (*Spleen, or Islington Spa*), and Maria (*School for Scandal*); played secondary parts as Mrs Brereton, 1778–87; married John Philip *Kemble, 1787, and played the Lady Anne (*Richard III*), Hero, Sylvia; retired, 1796.

KEMBLE, Roger (1721–1802), actor and manager; married Sarah Ward (daughter of his manager at Birmingham), 1753, and formed a travelling company, in which his children (Sarah, afterwards Mrs Siddons, John, Charles, Stephen, and others) acted; played Falstaff and in the *Miller of Mansfield* at the Haymarket, 1788.

KEMBLE, Stephen (or George Stephen) (1758–1822), actor and manager, son of Roger *Kemble; first played in Dublin; appeared in Othello and other parts with his wife (Elizabeth Kemble) at Covent Garden Theatre, 1784; played secondary parts at the Haymarket, 1787–91; during his management of the Edinburgh Theatre (1792–1800) engaged John *Kemble and Mrs *Siddons, and brought out Henry Erskine *Johnston, but became involved in litigation and failed financially; after managing theatres in several northern towns, played Falstaff at Covent Garden, 1806, and Drury Lane,

1816, also Sir Christopher Curry (*Inkle and Yarico*), his best part. He published *Odes, Lyrical Ballads, and Poems* (1809).

KEME, Samuel (1604–1670), Puritan divine. See KEM.

KEMP. See also KEMPE.

KEMP, George Meikle (1795–1844), architect of the Scott Monument, Edinburgh (begun, 1840); in early life a shepherd, carpenter's apprentice, and millwright.

KEMP (or KEMPE), John (1380?–1454), lord chancellor and archbishop successively of York and Canterbury; fellow of Merton College, Oxford; practised in ecclesiastical courts; examiner-general, 1413; dean of arches, 1414; archdeacon of Durham, 1417; keeper of the privy seal, 1418; bishop of Rochester, 1419, of London, 1421–6; chancellor of Normandy, 1419–22, being much employed as a diplomat by Henry V; member of Henry VI's council and partisan of Cardinal Beaufort; became archbishop of York and chancellor of England, 1426, holding the secular office till Gloucester recovered power in 1432; supported peace with France, but was prevented by his instructions from effecting anything at Congress of Arras, 1432, or at the Calais conferences in 1439; appointed cardinal-priest by Pope Eugenius IV, 1439; supported Henry VI's marriage with *Margaret of Anjou, but subsequently opposed *Suffolk, on whose fall (1450) he again became chancellor; broke up the Kentish rebellion by temporary concessions; made archbishop of Canterbury by provision, and created cardinal-bishop by Pope Nicholas, 1452; resisted the Yorkists till his death; founded college of secular priests at Wye, Kent (his birthplace), with a grammar school and church.

KEMP, John (1665–1717), antiquary; FRS, 1712; his museum of antiquities described in Ainsworth's *Monumenta vetustatis Kempiana* (1719–20).

KEMP, John (1763–1812), mathematician; MA, Aberdeen, 1781; LL D (America); professor at Columbia College, New York.

KEMP, Joseph (1778–1824), musical composer and teacher; organist of Bristol Cathedral, 1802; Mus.Doc., Sidney Sussex College, Cambridge, 1809; founded musical college at Exeter, 1814; composed songs, glees, and anthems, and the *Jubilee*, 1809; published *New System of Musical Education* (1810–19).

KEMP, Stanley Wells (1882–1945), zoologist and oceanographer; educated at St Paul's School and Trinity College, Dublin; first senior moderator, natural science, 1903; assistant naturalist, fisheries, Irish Department of Agriculture, 1903–10; superintendent, zoological section, Indian Museum (from 1916 Zoological Survey of India), 1910–24; first director, Colonial Office *Discovery* investigations, 1924–36; led voyages, 1925–7, 1929–31; secretary, Marine Biological Association, and director, Plymouth Laboratory, 1936–45; FRS, 1931.

KEMP, Thomas Read (1782–1844), founder of Kemp Town (Brighton); MA, St John's College, Cambridge, 1810; MP, Lewes, 1812–16 and 1826–37, and Arundel, 1823–6; began building Kemp Town, c.1820; founded a religious sect.

KEMP, William (*fl.* 1600), comic actor and dancer; member of the company whose successive patrons were *Leicester, Lord Strange, and Lord *Hunsdon; succeeded to Richard *Tarleton's roles and reputation; chiefly popular for his dancing of jigs accompanied with comic songs; summoned with Richard *Burbage and William Shakespeare to act before Queen Elizabeth at Greenwich, 1594; had parts in plays by Shakespeare and *Jonson, including Peter (*Romeo and Juliet*) and Dogberry; danced a morris dance from London to Norwich, 1599; performed dancing exploits on the continent; played in the Earl of *Worcester's Company at the Rose. *Kemps Nine Daies Wonder* (written by himself, 1600) has been reprinted several times.

KEMP (or KEMPE), William (d. 1601), author of *The Education of Children in Learning* (1588) and *The Art of Arithmeticke* (1592); MA, Trinity Hall, Cambridge, 1584; master of Plymouth Grammar School, 1581–1601.

KEMP, William (1555–1628), of Spains Hall, Finchingfield, Essex; remained silent for seven years as a penance.

KEMPE. See also KEMP.

KEMPE, Alfred John (1785?–1846), antiquary; friend of Charles Alfred *Stothard and Thomas Crofton *Croker; FSA, 1828; formed Society of Noviomagus; on staff of *Gentleman's Magazine*; published works on antiquities of Holwood Hill, Kent, and of St Martin-le-Grand Church, London; edited the Loseley manuscripts, 1836.

KEMPE, Margerie (*c.*1373–*c.*1440), religious writer; of Lynn; the complete manuscript of her 'Book' was discovered in 1934 and edited by S. B. Meech and H. E. Allen for the Early English Text Society, 1940.

KEMPENFELT, Richard (1718–1782), rear-admiral; with *Vernon at Portobello, 1739; as captain of the *Elizabeth* and commodore served in East Indies, 1758; commanded the *Grafton* under *Steevens in expedition of 1759; present at reduction of Pondicherry, 1761; flag-captain to

*Cornish at reduction of Manila, 1762; member of court martial on *Palliser, 1778; rear-admiral, 1780; captured part of a French convoy and dispersed the rest off Ushant, 1781; went down with the *Royal George*; his alteration in signalling system adopted and improved by Lord *Howe.

KEMPT, Sir **James** (1764–1854), general; aide-de-camp to Sir Ralph *Abercromby in Holland, 1799, the Mediterranean, 1800, and Egypt, 1801, and afterwards to *Hely-Hutchinson; commanded light brigade at Maida, 1806; commanded brigade under *Picton in the Peninsula; severely wounded at Badajoz, 1812; commanded brigade of Light Division in 1813–14; succeeded to command of Picton's division on his fall during Battle of Waterloo; GCB, 1815; governor of Nova Scotia, 1820–8; governor-general of Canada, 1828–30; privy councillor, 1830; master-general of the ordnance, 1834–8; general, 1841.

KEMPTHORNE, Sir **John** (1620–1679), vice-admiral; after commanding for Levant company entered Royal Navy, 1664; flag-captain to Prince *Rupert; flag-captain to *Albemarle in the fight off the North Foreland, 1666; rear-admiral of the blue in the action of 27 July 1666; knighted for gallantry against the Algerines, 1670; took part in Battle of Solebay, 1672, and the action of 11 Aug. 1673, after which he was promoted vice-admiral and pensioned.

KEMSLEY, first Viscount (1883–1968), newspaper proprietor. See BERRY, (JAMES) GOMER.

KEMYS, Lawrence (d. 1618), sea captain; accompanied Sir Walter *Ralegh up the Orinoco, 1595–6; imprisoned with Ralegh in the Tower, 1603; as his pilot and captain commanded his last expedition to Guiana, on the failure of which he killed himself.

KEN (or **KENN),** **Thomas** (1637–1711), bishop of Bath and Wells; fellow of Winchester and New College, Oxford; MA, 1664; DD, 1679; rector of Little Easton, Essex, 1663–5, of Brightstone (Isle of Wight), 1667–9, of East Woodhay, Hampshire, 1669–72; chaplain to Bishop *Morley of Winchester; took gratuitous charge of St John in the Soke, Winchester; as chaplain to Princess Mary at The Hague, 1679–80, remonstrated with William of Orange on his unkind behaviour to her; when chaplain to Charles II refused to receive Nell *Gwyn at Winchester, 1683; chaplain to Lord *Dartmouth at Tangier, 1683–4; bishop of Bath and Wells, 1684–91; attended Charles II's deathbed, 2 Feb. 1685; attended *Monmouth in the Tower and at his execution, 1685; interceded with James II on behalf of *Kirke's victims; twice preached at Whitehall against Romish practices; one of the 'seven bishops' who petitioned against the Declaration of Indulgence, 1688; voted for a regency, Jan. 1689, and refused to take the oaths to William and Mary; deprived of his see as a nonjuror; opposed the clandestine consecration of nonjuring bishops, and was offered restoration (1702) by Queen Anne, who gave him a pension; lived chiefly with Lord *Weymouth at Longleat. His prose works include *Manual of Prayers for Winchester Scholars* (edition containing the well-known morning, evening, and midnight hymns, 1695, the hymns being published separately, 1862) and *Practice of Divine Love* (1685–6), translated into French and Italian; his poetical works edited by Hawkins (1721).

KENDAL, duchess of (1667–1743). See SCHULENBURG, Countess EHRENGARD MELUSINA VON DER.

KENDAL, Dame **Margaret Shafto** (1848–1935), better known as Madge Kendal, actress; born Robertson of long line of actors; sister of T. W. *Robertson; first appeared at age of 5; by 17 had played Ophelia and Desdemona with Walter *Montgomery in London; married (1869) W. H. *Kendal whose ostentatious cult of respectability she adopted, becoming increasingly censorious; her character possibly too firm and robust; an accomplished but not a great actress; especially fitted for elderly parts; retired, 1908; DBE, 1926; GBE, 1927.

KENDAL, **William Hunter** (1843–1917), actor-manager, whose original name was William Hunter Grimston; went on professional stage, 1861; partner with Sir John *Hare, first at Court Theatre and later at St James's Theatre; best parts those in *Peril, The Queen's Shilling, Diplomacy, A White Lie*, and *The Elder Miss Blossom*; overshadowed by his wife (see KENDAL, Dame MARGARET SHAFTO).

KENDALE, **Richard** (d. 1431), grammarian.

KENDALL, **Edward Augustus** (1776?–1842), author of books for children, translations from the French, and other works; conducted the *Literary Chronicle*, 1819–28, *The Olio*, 1828–33.

KENDALL, **George** (1610–1663), controversialist; fellow of Exeter College, Oxford, 1630–47; MA, 1633; DD, 1654; rector of Blisland, Cornwall, 1643, and prebendary of Exeter, 1645; rector of Kenton, 1660–2; defended Calvinism in numerous polemics.

KENDALL, **John** (fl. 1476), vicar-choral of Southwell, 1476–86.

KENDALL, **John** (d. 1485), secretary to Richard III and from 1481 a comptroller of public works; said to have fallen at Bosworth.

KENDALL, John (d. 1501?), general of infantry ('Turcopolier') to the knights of St John, 1477–89; prior of the English Hospitallers, 1491; employed diplomatically by Henry VII.

KENDALL, John (1726–1815), Quaker; paid several visits to Holland; founded at Colchester almshouses, a school, and a library; published an abstract of the Bible (1800) and other works; *Memoirs of the Life and Religious Experiences of John Kendall* issued posthumously.

KENDALL, John (1766–1829), architect; author of a work on Gothic architecture (1818).

KENDALL, Sir Maurice George (1907–1983), statistician; educated at Derby Central School and St John's College, Cambridge; scholar; first class, part i, and wrangler, part ii, mathematical tripos, 1927 and 1929; passed into administrative class of Civil Service, 1930; served in Ministry of Agriculture, 1930–41; statistician to British Chamber of Shipping, 1941–9; Sc.D., Cambridge, 1949; professor of statistics, LSE, London University, 1949–61; joined computer consultancy SCICON, 1961–72; scientific director, managing director, and chairman; first director of World Fertility Survey, 1972–80; president, Royal Statistical Society, 1960–2; FBA, 1970; knighted, 1974; degrees from universities of Essex and Lancaster; publications include *An Introduction to the Theory of Statistics* (with George Udny *Yule, 11th edn., 1937), *The Advanced Theory of Statistics* (2 vols., 1943, 1946, revised into 3 vols., 1958, 1961, 1966), and first dictionary of statistical terms (1957).

KENDALL, Thomas Henry (afterwards **Henry Clarence**) (1839–1882), poet of the Australian bush; some time in New South Wales public service; his two chief volumes, *Leaves from an Australian Forest* (1869) and *Songs from the Mountains* (1880); collected works issued (1886).

KENDALL, Timothy (*fl.* 1577), compiler of *Flowers of Epigrammes*; of Eton and Magdalen Hall, Oxford; mentioned by Meres among epigrammatists.

KENDRICK, Emma Eleonora (1788–1871), miniature painter; author of *Conversations on the Art of Miniature-Painting* (1830).

KENDRICK, James (1771–1847), botanist; MD and FLS; president of the Warrington Natural History Society; friend of *Howard the philanthropist.

KENDRICK, James (1809–1882), writer on Warrington antiquities; son of James *Kendrick (1771–1847); MD, Edinburgh, 1833; made excavations at Wilderspool, and collected seals.

KENDRICK, Sir Thomas Downing (1895–1979), director and principal librarian of the British Museum; educated at Charterhouse and Oriel College, Oxford, where he was a scholar; served during 1914–18 war with Warwickshire Regiment; severely wounded; returned to Oriel in 1919 and received diploma with distinction in anthropology, 1921; appointed assistant in department of British and medieval antiquities, British Museum, 1922; assistant keeper, 1928; keeper, 1938; director and principal librarian, 1950–9; KCB, 1951; responsible for display of Sutton Hoo treasure; publications include *The Axe Age* (1925), *The Druids* (1927, reprinted 1966), *The Archaeology of the Channel Islands 1, Bailliwick of Guernsey* (1928: *Jersey* was completed by Jacquetta Hawkes, 1939); *A History of the Vikings* (1930, reprinted 1968), *Anglo-Saxon Art to AD 900* (1938, reprinted 1972), *Late Saxon and Viking Art* (1949, reprinted 1974), and *Archaeology in England and Wales, 1914–1931* (in collaboration with C. F. C. Hawkes, 1932); edited *The County Archaeologies* (7 vols.); also published *British Antiquity* (1950, reprinted 1970), *The Lisbon Earthquake* (1956), *St. James in Spain* (1960), *Mary of Agreda, the Life and Legend of a Spanish Nun* (1967), and a novel, *Great Love for Icarus* (1962); FBA, 1941; secretary, Society of Antiquaries, 1940–50; hon. fellow, Oriel College; hon. FRIBA; other academic distinctions and honorary degrees.

KENEALY, Edward Vaughan Hyde (1819–1880), barrister; of Trinity College, Dublin; BA and LL B, called to Irish Bar, 1840; barrister, Gray's Inn, 1847; QC, 1868; junior counsel for *Palmer the poisoner; imprisoned for cruelty; prosecuted Overend and Gurney, 1869; leading counsel for the Tichborne claimant, 1873, and was disbarred (1874) for his violent conduct of the case (see ORTON, ARTHUR); raised agitation for inquiry into it; MP for Stoke-on-Trent, 1875–80; published poetical translations and other works.

KENINGHALE, John (d. 1451), Carmelite; student at Oxford; provincial, 1430–44; confessor to Richard, duke of York.

KENINGHALE, Peter (d. 1494), Carmelite prior at Oxford, 1466.

KENINGHAM, William (*fl.* 1586), physician, astrologer, and engraver. See CUNINGHAM.

KENMURE, Viscounts. See GORDON, Sir JOHN, first viscount, 1599?–1634; GORDON, WILLIAM, sixth viscount, d. 1716.

KENNARD, Sir Howard William (1878–1955), diplomat; educated at Eton; entered Diplomatic Service, 1901; minister to Yugoslavia, 1925–9, to Sweden, 1929–31, to Switzerland, 1931–5; ambassador to Poland, 1935–9; objected to any Polish support of Hitler's aggression or racialism; British alliance with Poland obtained, 1939; remained with Polish government in exile, 1939–41; CMG and CVO, 1923; KCMG, 1929; GCMG, 1938.

KENNAWAY, Sir **Ernest Laurence** (1881–1958), experimental and chemical pathologist; scholar, New College, Oxford; first class, physiology, 1903; qualified from Middlesex Hospital, 1907; DM, Oxford, 1911; demonstrator in physiology, Guy's Hospital, 1909–14; chemical pathologist, Bland-Sutton Institute, Middlesex Hospital, 1914–21; joined Research Institute, Cancer Hospital, 1921; director and professor of experimental pathology, London, 1931–46; doyen of cancer research; over thirty years inspired research; FRS, 1934; knighted, 1947; hon. fellow, New College, Oxford, and many other academic honours.

KENNAWAY, Sir **John,** first baronet (1758–1836), diplomat; served in the Carnatic, 1780–6; created baronet (1791) for his successful mission to Hyderabad, 1788, where he became first resident; concluded treaty with Tippo Sultan, 1792.

KENNEDY (or **FARRELL),** Mrs (d. 1793), actress and contralto singer; instructed by Dr *Arne; gained great successes in male parts at Covent Garden.

KENNEDY, Alexander (1695?–1785), founder of family of violin-makers.

KENNEDY, Sir **Alexander Blackie William** (1847–1928), engineer; nephew of John Stuart *Blackie; gained first experience in marine-engine construction; professor of engineering, University College, London, where he founded influential school, 1874–89; established pioneer engineering laboratory there, 1878; began practice, which soon became one of largest in country, as consulting engineer at Westminster, 1889; engineer to Westminster Electric Supply Corporation, of which he planned whole system and works, 1889; also engineer to other electric companies; closely connected with development of electric transport; undertook exploration of Petra, 1922; published *Petra; Its History and Monuments*, a valuable monograph (1925); FRS, 1887; knighted, 1905.

KENNEDY, Sir **Arthur Edward** (1810–1883), colonial governor; of Trinity College, Dublin; governor successively of Gambia (1851–2), Sierra Leone (1852–4), West Australia (1854–62), Vancouver's island (1863–7), West Africa (1867–72), Hong Kong (1872–7), and Queensland (1877–83); knighted, 1868.

KENNEDY, (Aubrey) Leo (1885–1965), journalist; educated at Harrow and Magdalen College, Oxford; BA, 1906; joined *The Times*

under G. E. *Buckle, 1910; worked in Paris and in Serbia, Romania, and Albania, 1911–12; served in army during 1914–18 war; MC; returned to *The Times* under Henry Wickham *Steed, 1919; worked in Europe, mainly concerned with power politics; published first book, *Old Diplomacy and New 1876–1922* (1922); founding member of Royal Institute of International Affairs, 1920; foreign leader-writer under G. Geoffrey *Dawson, 1923; published *Britain Faces Germany* (1937); wrote first draft of leading article in *The Times* suggesting that Prague might consider ceding the Sudeten lands, 7 Sept. 1938; later, wrote personal letter to *The Times* warning of dangers of further German expansion; retired after disagreement with new editor, R. M. *Barrington-Ward, 1941; joined European service of BBC, 1941–5; published a life of Lord Salisbury (1953), and edited letters of fourth earl of *Clarendon, 1956.

KENNEDY, Benjamin Hall (1804–1889), headmaster of Shrewsbury and regius professor of Greek at Cambridge; son of Rann *Kennedy; educated at King Edward School, Birmingham, and at Shrewsbury; at St John's College, Cambridge, won numerous distinctions, being senior classic and first chancellor's medallist, 1827; was president of the union and one of 'the Apostles'; fellow of St John's College, Cambridge, 1828–32 and 1885–9; assistant master at Harrow, 1830–6; as head of Shrewsbury (1836–66) became the greatest classical master of the century; canon of Ely, 1867; regius professor of Greek at Cambridge, 1867–89; hon. LL D, Dublin, 1886; a New Testament reviser; the Latin professorship founded at Cambridge from part of his testimonial was held successively by his pupils, Hugh Andrew Johnstone *Munro and J. E. B. *Mayor. The *Public School Latin Primer* generally adopted by the chief schools (1866) was based upon his work of 1843. Besides his Latin primer (revised 1888) and grammar (1871), he published metrical versions of three Greek plays, *Between Whiles* (1877), and other works.

KENNEDY, Charles Rann (1808–1867), lawyer and scholar; brother of Benjamin Hall *Kennedy; educated at Birmingham and Shrewsbury; fellow of Trinity College, Cambridge; senior classic, 1831; Bell and Pitt scholar; Porson prizeman; MA, 1834; barrister, Lincoln's Inn, 1835; engaged in *Stockdale* v. *Hansard*; appeared for the plaintiff in *Swinfen* v. *Swinfen* (failing to recover fees); published translations of Demosthenes and Virgil, poems, and legal treatises.

KENNEDY, David (1825–1886), Scottish tenor singer; gave concerts in Scotland, London, America, South Africa, India, and Australasia; died at Stratford, Ontario.

KENNEDY, Edmund B. (d. 1848), Australian explorer; as second in command of Sir Thomas Livingstone *Mitchell's expedition traced the Barcoo or Victoria River, 1847; killed by natives while exploring Cape York peninsula.

KENNEDY, Gilbert, second earl of Cassillis (d. 1527), partisan of Arran against Angus; afterwards joined Lennox; slain by sheriff of Ayr at instigation of Arran's bastard son.

KENNEDY, Gilbert, third earl of Cassillis (1517?–1558), son of Gilbert *Kennedy, second earl of Cassillis; pupil of *Buchanan in Paris; lord of *James V's secret council, 1538; captured at Solway Moss, 1542; after his release intrigued with the English; lord high treasurer, 1554; one of the seven Scottish commissioners at marriage of *Mary Queen of Scots to the dauphin, 1558; died at Dieppe on his way back.

KENNEDY, Gilbert, fourth earl of Cassillis (1541?–1576), 'King of Carrick'; succeeded his father, Gilbert *Kennedy, third earl of Cassillis, as gentleman of the bedchamber to Henry II of France; fought for *Mary Queen of Scots at Langside, 1568, and subsequently corresponded with her; tortured the abbot of Crosraguel, 1570, in order to obtain a renunciation of his claims, and was imprisoned by the regent *Lennox; obtained liberty by an agreement with *Morton, 1571; privy councillor, 1571.

KENNEDY, Gilbert (1678–1745), Irish Presbyterian minister; moderator of Ulster, 1720; published *New Light set in a Clear Light* (1721) and *Defence of the Principles and Conduct of the General Synod of Ulster* (1724).

KENNEDY, Grace (1782–1825), author of religious tales; German translation of her works issued (1844).

KENNEDY, Harry Angus Alexander (1866–1934), Scottish New Testament scholar; Free Church minister, Callander, 1893–1905; professor of New Testament language and literature, Knox College, Toronto (1905–9), and New College, Edinburgh (1909–25); published *The Sources of New Testament Greek* (1895), *St. Paul's Conceptions of the Last Things* (1904), *St. Paul and the Mystery Religions* (1913), *Philo's Contribution to Religion* (1919), and *The Theology of the Epistles* (1919).

KENNEDY, James (1406?–1465), bishop of St Andrews; while bishop of Dunkeld (1438–1441) attended Council of Florence; bishop of St Andrews, 1441–65; prominent in political affairs during *James II's minority; attempted to mediate in papal schism; founded St Salvator's College (1450) and the Grey Friars monastery at St Andrews; one of the regents during minority of *James III.

KENNEDY, James (1785?–1851), medical writer; MD, Glasgow, 1813; died while compiling a medical bibliography.

KENNEDY, James (1793?–1827), author of *Conversations on Religion with Lord Byron* (1830); garrison physician at Cephalonia, 1823.

KENNEDY (afterwards **KENNEDY-BAILIE**), **James** (1793–1864), classical scholar; fellow of Trinity College, Dublin, 1817; MA, 1819; DD, 1828; published *Fasciculus Inscriptionum Graecarum* (1842–9) and editions of Greek classics.

KENNEDY, James ('Jimmy') (1902–1984), popular song-writer; educated at Trinity College, Dublin; political officer in Colonial Service; turned to song-writing, 1929; first big success, 'Teddy Bears' Picnic', 1932; wrote lyrics for many successful songs including 'Isle of Capri', 'Red Sails in the Sunset', 'Harbour Lights', 'South of the Border', and 'The Siegfried Line'; during 1939–45 war served as captain in Royal Artillery; after the war lived in USA and Switzerland but later returned to Dublin; Ivor Novello Award, 1971; American ASCAP Award, 1976; hon. D.Litt., Ulster, 1978; OBE, 1983; fellow of Royal Geographical Society and Royal Society of Arts; chairman, Songwriters' Guild (later BASCA).

KENNEDY, Sir James Shaw (1788–1865), general; assumed name of Kennedy, 1834; at Copenhagen, 1807, and in the Peninsula, being aide-de-camp to Robert *Craufurd, 1809–12; attached to the quartermaster-general's staff in *Alten's division at Quatre Bras; at Waterloo drew up the division in a novel formation which successfully withstood very severe cavalry attacks; stationed at Calais till 1818; while assistant adjutant-general at Manchester (1826–35) drew up a masterly report concerning methods of keeping order in labour disputes; as inspector-general raised the Irish Constabulary, 1836; appointed to Liverpool command during Chartist alarms, 1848; lieutenant-general, 1854; general, 1862; KCB, 1863; intimate of Sir William *Napier; published *Notes on the Defence of Great Britain and Ireland* (1859) and *Notes on Waterloo*, etc. (1865).

KENNEDY, John, fifth earl of Cassillis (1567?–1615), son of Gilbert *Kennedy, fourth earl; lord high treasurer of Scotland, 1598; killed Gilbert Kennedy of Bargany at Maybole, near Ayr, 1601.

KENNEDY (or KENNEDIE), John (*fl.* 1626), author of *History of Calanthrop and Lucilla* (1626;

reprinted as *The Ladies' Delight*, 1631) and *Theological Epitome* (1629).

KENNEDY, John, sixth earl of Cassillis (1595?–1668), nephew of John *Kennedy, fifth earl of Cassillis; lord justice-general, 1649; joined the Covenanters; privy councillor, 1641 and 1661; opposed the engagement, 1648; took part in the Whiggamores' raid, 1648; commissioner to treat with Charles II, 1649–50; his first wife (Lady Jean Hamilton) sometimes identified with the heroine of *The Gypsy Laddie*.

KENNEDY, John, seventh earl of Cassillis (1646?–1701), opposed Lauderdale's government, and was outlawed; made privy councillor and a lord of the Treasury by William III.

KENNEDY, John (d. 1760), numismatist; MD; lived some time at Smyrna; published *Numismata Selectiora*, describing his coins of *Carausius and *Allectus; his *Dissertation upon Oriuna* (1751), making Oriuna Carausius' guardian-goddess, due to *Stukeley's misreading of 'Fortuna' on a coin of Carausius.

KENNEDY, John (1698–1782), writer on chronology; rector of All Saints, Bradley, 1732–82.

KENNEDY, John (1730?–1816), violin-maker; nephew of Alexander *Kennedy.

KENNEDY, John (1769–1855), Manchester cotton-spinner and friend of *Watt; introduced the 'jack frame' and other improvements.

KENNEDY, John (1789–1833), Scottish poet; author of *Fancy's Tour with the Genius of Cruelty, and other Poems* (1826) and the romance of *Geordie Chalmers* (1830).

KENNEDY, John (1819–1884), Highland divine; MA, King's College, Aberdeen, 1840; hon. DD, 1873; Free Church minister at Dingwall, Ross-shire, 1844; assisted James *Begg in opposing union of the Free and United Presbyterian churches and wrote against disestablishment and instrumental music in churches; preached in Gaelic; published religious works.

KENNEDY, John Clark (1817–1867), colonel. See CLARK-KENNEDY.

KENNEDY, John Pitt (1796–1879), lieutenant-colonel; secretary and director of public works in Cephalonia under Sir Charles *Napier, 1822–8, and sub-inspector of militia in the Ionian Islands, 1828–31; interested in agricultural education in Ireland; inspector-general under Irish National Education Department, 1837–9; secretary to the Devon Commission, 1843; member of Famine Relief Committee, 1845–6; superintended measures for defence of Dublin, 1848; military secretary to Sir Charles Napier in India, 1849–52; consulting engineer

for railways to Indian government, 1850; made the road from Simla to Tibet; lieutenant-colonel, 1853; managing director of Bombay and Central Indian Railway, from 1853; published works on Irish subjects (especially agriculture) and on finance and public works in India.

KENNEDY, Margaret Moore (1896–1967), writer; educated at Cheltenham Ladies' College and Somerville College, Oxford; contemporary of Dorothy *Sayers and Vera *Brittain; published first book, *A Century of Revolution* (1922); first novel, *The Ladies of Lyndon* (1923), followed by the best-seller, *The Constant Nymph* (1924); rewritten as play, and several film versions made; *Escape me Never*, produced at Apollo, with Elisabeth Bergner (1933); other novels include *The Feast* (1950), *Lucy Carmichael* (1951), and *Troy Chimneys* (James Tait Black Memorial Prize, 1953); also published biography of *Jane Austen* (1950) and a study of the art of fiction, *The Outlaws on Parnassus* (1958); fellow, Royal Society of Literature; married (Sir) David Davies, barrister, who became a county court judge, and was knighted in 1952.

KENNEDY, Patrick (1801–1873), Irish writer and Dublin bookseller; author of *Legendary Fictions of the Irish Celts* (1866) and other works.

KENNEDY, Quintin (1520–1564), abbot; son of Gilbert *Kennedy, second earl of Cassillis; educated at St Andrews and Paris; abbot of Crosraguel, 1547; disputed with *Knox at Maybole, 1562; wrote against the Reformation.

KENNEDY, Rann (1772–1851), scholar and poet; intimate with Coleridge at St John's College, Cambridge; MA, 1798; second master at King Edward's School, Birmingham, 1807–36, and incumbent of St Paul's Church, 1817–47; published *The Reign of Youth* (1840) and other poems; assisted his younger son Charles Rann *Kennedy in his translation of Virgil; examples of his work in *Between Whiles*, by his elder son Dr Benjamin Hall *Kennedy.

KENNEDY, Thomas (d. 1754), judge of the Scottish Exchequer, 1714–54.

KENNEDY, Thomas (1784–1870?), violin- and violoncello-maker; son of John *Kennedy (1730?–1816).

KENNEDY, Thomas Francis (1788–1879), politician; grandnephew of Thomas *Kennedy (d. 1754); educated at Harrow and Edinburgh; Whig MP for Ayr, 1818–34; carried bill of 1825 reforming the selection of Scottish juries in criminal cases; chairman of Salmon Fisheries Committee, 1824; prepared Scottish Reform Bill; a lord of the Treasury, 1832–4; paymaster of Irish Civil Service, 1837–50; a commissioner of woods and forests, 1850–4; friend of *Cockburn and *Jeffrey.

KENNEDY, Vans (1784–1846), major-general, Sanskrit and Persian scholar; served as cadet, 2nd Grenadiers, in Malabar district, 1800; Persian interpreter to the Peshwa's subsidiary force at Sirur, 1807; judge advocate-general to Bombay Army, 1817–35; oriental translator to government, 1835–46; published philological writings.

KENNEDY, Walter (1460?–1508?), Scottish poet; nephew of James *Kennedy (1406?–1465); MA, Glasgow, 1478, and an examiner, 1481; probably provost of Maybole, c.1494; a rival of Dunbar; wrote part of the *Flyting*, 1508; most of his poems lost.

KENNEDY, William (1799–1871), poet; secretary to Lord *Durham in Canada, 1838–9; British consul at Galveston, Texas, 1841–7; works include *The Arrow and the Rose* (1830) and a book on Texas (1841); died in Paris.

KENNEDY, William Denholm (1813–1865), painter and friend of *Etty; exhibited at the Academy from 1833.

KENNEDY, Sir William Rann (1846–1915), judge; grandson of Revd Rann *Kennedy; BA, King's College, Cambridge (senior classic); called to bar (Lincoln's Inn), 1871; QC, 1885; judge in Queen's Bench division and knighted, 1892; lord justice of Court of Appeal and PC, 1907; FBA, 1909.

KENNET, first Baron (1879–1960), politician and writer. See YOUNG, EDWARD HILTON.

KENNET, (Edith Agnes) Kathleen, Lady Kennet (1878–1947), sculptor exhibiting as Kathleen Scott; studied at Slade School and Académie Colarossi; influenced by her friend Rodin; married (1908) Robert Falcon *Scott; granted rank of KCB's widow after his death in 1912; married secondly (1922) Edward Hilton *Young (created Baron Kennet, 1935); executed Scott Memorial, Waterloo Place, and many portrait busts and statues remarkably expressive of subject's personality; sitters included Asquith, Lloyd George, Neville Chamberlain, and W. B. *Yeats.

KENNETH I (surnamed **MacALPINE**) (d. 860), founder of the Scottish dynasty; succeeded Alpin in Galloway, 834, and as king of the Dalriad Scots, c.844; finally defeated the Picts and became king of Alban, 846; removed the seat of government from Argyll to Scone, and made Dunkeld the ecclesiastical capital; invaded 'Saxony' (Lothian).

KENNETH II (d. 995), son of Malcolm I; succeeded *Culen in Scottish Pictish monarchy,

971; extended his kingdom north of the Tay and made raids into Northumbria; 'gave the great city of Brechin to the Lord'; probably secured Edinburgh; consolidated central Scotland; said to have been treacherously slain by Fenella. It is improbable that he received Lothian as a fief from *Edgar.

KENNETH III (d. 1005?), nephew of *Kenneth II; succeeded Constantine in Scottish Pictish monarchy, 997; killed in battle, perhaps by *Malcolm II.

KENNETT, Basil (1674–1715), miscellaneous writer; brother of White *Kennett; entered St Edmund Hall, Oxford, 1689; scholar, Corpus Christi College, Oxford, 1690; MA, 1696; fellow and tutor of Corpus Christi College, 1697; chaplain to the British Factory at Leghorn, 1706–13; DD and president of Corpus, 1714; published antiquarian and religious works, of which the most important are *Romae Antiquae Notitia, or the Antiquities of Rome* (1696) and *A Brief Exposition of the Apostles' Creed* (1705). He also translated many French works, among them Pascal's *Thoughts upon Religion* (1704).

KENNETT, Robert Hatch (1864–1932), biblical and Semitic scholar; first class, Semitic languages tripos, Queens' College, Cambridge, 1886; ordained, 1887; fellow, 1888; university lecturer in Aramaic, 1893–1903; regius professor of Hebrew and canon of Ely, 1903–32; bridged gulf between biblical and modern modes of thought; critical work independent and original.

KENNETT, White (1660–1728), bishop of Peterborough; entered St Edmund Hall, Oxford, 1678; began his career as a writer while an undergraduate, and employed by Anthony à *Wood; BA, 1682; MA, 1684; disliked James II's ecclesiastical policy; openly supported the Revolution; tutor and vice-principal, St Edmund Hall, 1691; DD, 1700; prebendary of Salisbury, 1701; acquired reputation as historian and antiquarian, topographer, and philologist; one of the original members of the Society for Propagating the Gospel in Foreign Parts, 1701; published the *Compleat History of England*, his best-known work (1706); chaplain-in-ordinary to Queen Anne; dean of Peterborough, 1708; presented the books and documents collected for a projected history of the propagation of Christianity in the English-American colonies to the Society for Propagating the Gospel; bishop of Peterborough, 1718–28.

KENNEY, Annie (1879–1953), suffragette; born in Yorkshire and became part-time mill worker at 10; met (Dame) Christabel *Pankhurst and Emmeline *Pankhurst, 1905, and became their loyal lieutenant; directed from France by

Christabel in organizing extreme militancy, 1912–14; received several prison sentences; supported Pankhursts' war-work, 1914–18, and retired from public life on granting of women's suffrage, 1918; published *Memories of a Militant* (1924).

KENNEY, Arthur Henry (1776?–1855), controversialist; educated at Dublin University, 1793; MA, 1800; BD, 1806; DD and dean of Achonry, 1812; on account of pecuniary difficulties spent last ten years of his life abroad; died at Boulogne-sur-Mer; edited the fifth edition of Archbishop *Magee's sermons (1834); wrote a memoir of him for the *Works* (1842) and several religious and historical works.

KENNEY, Charles Lamb (1821–1881), journalist and author; born at Bellevue, near Paris; son of James *Kenney, and godson of Charles *Lamb; educated at Merchant Taylors' School; clerk in General Post Office, 1837; wrote for *The Times* and aided in promoting the exhibition of 1851; secretary to Sir Joseph *Paxton during his organization of transport service for Crimea, 1855; barrister, Inner Temple, 1856; secretary to M de Lesseps, 1856–8; advocated Suez Canal in his book *The Gates of the East* (1857); joined staff of *Standard*, 1858; supported International Exhibition at South Kensington, 1862; noted for his impromptu satirical rhyming skits on contemporary celebrities; wrote libretti for some of Offenbach's opera-bouffes.

KENNEY, James (1780–1849), dramatist; his successful farce, *Raising the Wind*, produced 1803, and *Turn him out*, 1812; wrote the popular drama, *Sweethearts and Wives*, 1823; author of many successful and popular farces and comedies; friend of *Lamb and *Rogers.

KENNEY, Peter James (1779–1841), Irish Jesuit; first apprenticed to a coach-builder, then educated at Carlow College and Stonyhurst College; entered Society of Jesus, 1804; Catholic chaplain to the English troops in Sicily; returned to Ireland, 1811; became an eminent preacher and theologian; vice-president of Maynooth College, 1812; mainly instrumental in reviving the Jesuit mission in Ireland; opened Clongowes Wood College, Co. Kildare, since then the leading Catholic lay school in Ireland, 1814; assisted in establishing St Stanislaus College, Tullabeg, and the Jesuit residence of St Francis Xavier, Dublin; assisted Mary *Aikenhead, the foundress of the Irish Sisters of Charity; visitor to the Jesuit mission in the United States, 1819 and 1830; died at Rome.

KENNICOTT, Benjamin (1718–1783), biblical scholar; educated at Wadham College, Oxford; BA (by decree) and fellow of Exeter College,

1747; MA, 1750; Whitehall preacher, 1753; DD, 1761; FRS, 1764; Radcliffe librarian, 1767–83; canon of Christ Church, Oxford, 1770; spent much time in the collation of Hebrew manuscripts; his great work, the *Vetus Testamentum Hebraicum, cum variis lectionibus* (vol. i, 1776, vol. ii, 1780).

KENNINGTON, Eric Henri (1888–1960), artist; educated at St Paul's School; studied at Lambeth School of Art and City and Guilds School; first exhibited at Royal Academy, 1908; a private in France and Flanders, 1914–15; official war artist, 1915–18, 1940–5; art editor, *Seven Pillars of Wisdom* (1926), by T. E. *Lawrence; executed portraits in sculpture and drawing, especially in pastel; British War Memorial at Soissons and 24th Division, Battersea Park; carved decorations on Shakespeare Memorial Theatre, Stratford; ARA, 1951; RA, 1959.

KENNION, Charles John (1789–1853), water-colour painter; son of Edward *Kennion; exhibited landscapes at Royal Academy, 1804 and 1853.

KENNION, Edward (1744–1809), artist; commissary in expedition against Havana, 1762; in Jamaica, 1705–9; engaged in trade in London, 1769; retired to Malvern, 1782; settled in London as teacher of drawing and artist, 1789; exhibited at Royal Academy, 1790–1807; published, as no. 1 of *Elements of Landscape and Picturesque Beauty*, eight etchings of the oak tree, 1790; died before the whole four volumes were completed, but *An Essay on Trees in Landscape* was issued (1815).

KENNISH (or KINNISH), William (1799–1862), Manx poet; entered navy as seaman, 1821; rose to be warrant-officer, and left navy, c.1841; published *Mona's Isle and other Poems* (1844); went to America and became attached to United States Admiralty.

KENNY, Saint (d. 598?). See CAINNECH or CANNICUS, Saint.

KENNY, Courtney Stanhope (1847–1930), legal scholar; BA, Downing College, Cambridge; senior in law and history tripos, 1874; fellow of Downing, 1875; called to bar (Lincoln's Inn), 1881; Liberal MP, Barnsley division of Yorkshire, 1885–8; university reader in English law, Cambridge, 1888; Downing professor of laws of England, Cambridge, 1907–18; FBA, 1909; an outstandingly successful law teacher; his most important work, *Outlines of Criminal Law* (1902, 14th edn., 1932).

KENNY, Elizabeth (1880–1952), nurse; born in Australia; served in Australian Army Nursing Service, 1915–19; advocated non-rigid splinting and early movement for treatment of poliomyelitis paralysis; opened first clinic, 1933; her worldwide demonstrations and untiring fight for acceptance of her technique caused great controversy; although her method gradually superseded orthodox treatment its superiority never openly acknowledged by medical profession; received most acclaim in United States; honorary degrees from American universities; published *And They Shall Walk* (1951).

KENNY, William Stopford (1788–1867), compiler of educational works; kept 'classical establishment' in London; an accomplished chess-player; wrote two books on chess.

KENRICK (or KENDRICK), Daniel (*fl.* 1685), physician and poet; MA, Christ Church, Oxford, 1674; author of several poems, printed in *The Grove* (1721).

KENRICK, George (1792–1874), Unitarian minister; son of Timothy *Kenrick; educated at Glasgow College and Manchester College, York; published sermons and contributed to the *Monthly Repository*.

KENRICK, John (1788–1877), classical scholar and historian; son of Timothy *Kenrick; entered Glasgow University, 1807; MA, 1810; tutor in classics, history, and literature at Manchester College, York (now Manchester College, Oxford); professor of history, 1840–50; the greatest scholar among the Unitarians; wrote historical and philological works.

KENRICK, Timothy (1759–1804), Unitarian commentator; ordained, 1785; opened Nonconformist academy, 1799; his *Exposition of the Historical Writings of the Testament* (published 1807) typical of the older Unitarian exegesis.

KENRICK, William (1725?–1779), miscellaneous writer; libelled almost every successful author and actor; attacked *Goldsmith in the *Monthly Review*, 1759, but recanted with a favourable review of the *Citizen of the World*, 1762; made LL D of Marischal College, Aberdeen for his translation of Rousseau's *Eloisa*; attacked *Garrick, *Fielding, *Johnson, and *Colman.

KENRY, Barons. See QUIN, EDWIN RICHARD WINHAM WYNDHAM, third earl of Dunraven and Mount-Earl in the peerage of Ireland, and first baron, 1812–1871; QUIN, WINDHAM THOMAS WYNDHAM, fourth earl of Dunraven and Mount-Earl in the peerage of Ireland, and second baron, 1841–1926.

KENSINGTON, first Baron (1590–1649). See RICH, Sir HENRY.

KENSIT, John (1853–1902), Protestant agitator; early joined anti-Romanist agitation;

started Protestant book depot in Paternoster Row, 1885; secretary of Protestant Truth Society, 1890; organized 'Wicliffite' itinerant preachers for the denunciation of ritualism, 1898; publicly objected to confirmation of bishops Mandell *Creighton (1897), *Winnington-Ingram and *Gore (1901); fatally wounded in religious riot at Liverpool.

KENSWOOD, first Baron (1887–1963), professional violinist and economist. See WHITFIELD, ERNEST ALBERT.

KENT, countess of (1581–1651). See GREY, ELIZABETH.

KENT, duchesses of. See VICTORIA MARY LOUISA, 1786–1861; MARINA, 1906–1968.

KENT, dukes of. See GREY, HENRY, 1664?–1740; GEORGE EDWARD ALEXANDER EDMUND, 1902–1942.

KENT, earl of. See WILLIAM OF YPRES, d. 1165?, erroneously styled earl of Kent.

KENT, earls of. See ODO, d. 1097; BURGH, HUBERT DE, d. 1243; EDMUND 'OF WOODSTOCK', 1301–1330; GREY, EDMUND, first earl (of the Grey line), 1420?–1489; GREY, GEORGE, second earl, d. 1503; GREY, HENRY, ninth earl, 1594–1651; HOLLAND, Sir THOMAS, first earl (of the Holland line), d. 1360; HOLLAND, THOMAS, second earl, 1350–1397; HOLLAND, THOMAS, third earl, and duke of Surrey, 1374–1400; HOLLAND, EDMUND, fourth earl (of the Holland line), d. 1408; NEVILLE, WILLIAM, d. 1463.

KENT, kings of. See HENGIST, d. 488; HORSA, d. 455; AESC, d. 512?; OCTA, d. 532?; ETHELBERT, 552?–616; EADBALD, d. 640; WIHTRED, d. 725; SIGERED, *fl.* 762; EADBERT, *fl.* 796; BALDRED, *fl.* 823–825.

KENT, Maid of (1506?–1534). See BARTON, ELIZABETH.

KENT, Albert Frank Stanley (1863–1958), scientist; educated at Magdalen College School and Magdalen College, Oxford; demonstrator in physiology, Manchester (1887–9), Oxford (1889–91), St Thomas's Hospital (1891–5); professor of physiology, Bristol, 1899–1918; D.Sc., 1915; director, department of industrial administration, Manchester College of Technology, 1918–22; editor-in-chief, *Journal of Industrial Hygiene*; best known for his work on cardiac physiology.

KENT, James (1700–1776), organist and composer; chorister of the Chapel Royal, 1714; organist to Trinity College, Cambridge, 1731, to Winchester Cathedral and College, 1737–74; published a collection of anthems (1773; republished, 1844).

KENT (or GWENT), John (*fl.* 1348), twentieth provincial of the Franciscans in England; doctor of theology at Oxford; reputed miracle-worker; author of commentary on Peter Lombard's *Sentences*.

KENT, John (Sion Cent) (*fl.* 1400), also called John of Kentchurch, Welsh bard; went to Oxford; parish priest at Kentchurch; said to have lived till the age of 120; perhaps sympathized with *Oldcastle; one of the best of the Welsh poets.

KENT, Nathaniel (1708–1766), scholar; at Eton and King's College, Cambridge; MA, 1733, and fellow of King's College, Cambridge, 1728–66; headmaster of Wisbech School, 1748; his *Excerpta quaedam ex Luciani Samosatensis Operibus* published (1730; 3rd edn., 1757; another edn., 1788).

KENT, Nathaniel (1737–1810), land valuer and agriculturist; secretary to Sir James *Porter at Brussels; studied husbandry of Austrian Netherlands; quitted diplomacy, and returned to England, 1766; published *Hints to Gentlemen of Landed Property* (1775; 3rd edn., 1793); employed as an estate agent and land valuer; did much to improve land management in England.

KENT, Odo of (d. 1200). See ODO.

KENT, Thomas (*fl.* 1460), clerk to the Privy Council, 1444; ambassador to various countries; sub-constable of England, 1445.

KENT, Thomas (d. 1489), mathematician; fellow of Merton College, Oxford, 1480; reputed as an astronomer and as author of a treatise on astronomy.

KENT, William (1684–1748), painter, sculptor, architect, and landscape-gardener; apprenticed to coach-maker, 1698; made attempt at painting in London, 1703; went to Rome, where he met several patrons; brought to England by the earl of *Burlington, with whom he lived for the rest of his life; employed in portrait painting and decoration of walls and ceilings; severely criticized by *Hogarth; excelled only as an architect; published the *Designs of Inigo Jones* (1727); built the Horse Guards and Treasury buildings, and Devonshire House, Piccadilly; executed the statue of Shakespeare in Poet's Corner; principal painter to the crown, 1739.

KENT, William (1751–1812), captain in the navy; nephew of Vice-Admiral John *Hunter (1738–1821); lieutenant, 1781; sailed for New South Wales, 1795; returned to England, 1800; revisited Sydney, 1801; commander, 1802; discovered and named Port St Vincent in New Caledonia, 1802; advanced to post-rank, 1806; died off Toulon.

KENT, (William) Charles (Mark) (1823–1902), author; a strict Roman Catholic; editor and proprietor of the *Sun*, a London evening paper, 1853–71, and editor of the *Weekly Register*, a Roman Catholic periodical, 1874–81; called to bar, 1859, but did not practise; wrote for *Household Words* and *All the Year Round*, and grew intimate with Charles *Dickens, who addressed to him his last letter (8 June 1870, now in British Museum); collected his *Poems* in 1870; prepared popular complete editions of works of great writers, including Charles *Lamb, 1875; received civil list pension, 1887.

KENT AND STRATHERN, Edward Augustus, duke of (1767–1820), fourth son of George III by Queen *Charlotte, and the father of Queen Victoria; educated in England under John *Fisher, successively bishop of Exeter and Salisbury, at Luneburg, Hanover, and Geneva under Baron Wangenheim; brevet-colonel, 1786; ordered to Gibraltar in command of the regiment of foot (Royal Fusiliers); sent to Canada, 1791; major-general, 1793; joined Sir Charles (afterwards Lord) Grey's force in the West Indies, 1794; took part in the subjection of Martinique and St Lucia, 1794; returned to Canada; lieutenant-general, 1796; granted £12,000 a year by parliament, 1799; made duke of Kent and Strathern and earl of Dublin, 1799; general, 1799; commander-in-chief of the forces in British North America, 1799–1800; governor of Gibraltar, 1802–3; field marshal, 1805; keeper of Hampton Court, 1806; the first to abandon flogging in the army, and to establish a regimental school; married in 1818 *Victoria Mary Louisa, widow of Emich Charles, prince of Leiningen, by whom a daughter (afterwards Queen Victoria) was born to him, 1819.

KENTEN (d. 685). See CENTWINE.

KENTIGERN (or MUNGO), Saint (518?–603), the apostle of the Strathclyde Britons; grandson of Loth, a British prince, after whom the Lothians are named; trained in the monastic school of Culross; became a missionary; chosen bishop at Cathures (now Glasgow); driven by persecution to Wales; founded monastery of Llanelwy (afterwards St Asaph's); returned to the north of England, and after reclaiming the Picts of Galloway from idolatry settled at Glasgow, where he died, and was buried in the crypt of Glasgow Cathedral, called after him St Mungo's; many miracles attributed to him.

KENTISH, John (1768–1853), Unitarian divine; minister at various places, 1790–4; at London, 1795; at Birmingham, 1803–44; conservative in religion, but Whig in politics; published memoirs and religious treatises.

KENTON, Benjamin (1719–1800), vintner and philanthropist; educated at a Whitechapel charity school; became a successful tavern-keeper; master of the Vintners' Company, 1776; a liberal benefactor to his old school, to Sir John Cass's School, to the Vintners' Company, and to St Bartholomew's Hospital.

KENTON, Nicholas (d. 1468), Carmelite; studied at Cambridge; chancellor of the University, 1445–6; priest, 1420; chosen provincial, 1444; credited with a commentary on the Song of Songs and theological treatises.

KENULF (or CYNEWULF) (fl. 750), Anglo-Saxon poet. See CYNEWULF.

KENULF (d. 1006), bishop of Winchester. See CENWULF.

KENWEALH (d. 672), king of the West Saxons. See CENWALH.

KENYATTA, Jomo (1890s–1978), African nationalist and first president of Kenya; son of Kikuyu farmer; exact date of birth not known; educated at Scottish mission at Thogota, near Nairobi; held number of jobs in and around Nairobi, 1913–28; became general secretary of Kikuyu Central Association (KCA), 1928; first editor of Kikuyu vernacular monthly, *Muigwithania*, 'The Unifier'; represented KCA in Britain, 1929–30; visited USSR, Germany, France, and Holland; spent fifteen years in Britain, 1931–46; attended Quaker College of Woodbrook, Selly Oak, 1932 and London School of Economics; published *Facing Mount Kenya* (1938) a study of Kikuyu customs and practices; took part in sixth Pan-African Congress, 1946; became president of Kenya African Union (KAU), 1947; accused and convicted unjustly of leading Mau Mau movement; imprisoned, 1953–61; *de facto* leader of Kenya African National Union (KANU), 1960; president of KANU, 1961; led KANU to London Constitutional Conference, 1962; minister of state in transitional coalition government, 1962–3; prime minister, 1963; president, Republic of Kenya, 1964; greatest contribution, building the foundations of a Kenyan state and establishing authority of a national government; life president of KANU, 1974; hon. fellow, LSE; knight of St John, 1972; honorary LL Ds of University of East Africa, 1965 and Manchester University, 1966; published *Suffering Without Bitterness: The Founding of the Kenya Nation* (Nairobi, 1968).

KENYON, Sir Frederic George (1863–1952), scholar and administrator; great-grandson of Baron *Kenyon and grandson of Edward *Hawkins; scholar of Winchester and New College, Oxford; first class, Lit. Hum., 1886; entered manuscripts department, British Museum, 1889; assistant keeper, 1898; director of British Museum, 1909–30; edited Aristotle's treatise on the Athenian constitution, works of Bacchylides and Hyperides, and Chester *Beatty collection of biblical papyri; publications include *The Palaeography of Greek Papyri* (1889), *Greek Papyri in the British Museum* (3 vols., 1893–1907), and *Our Bible and the Ancient Manuscripts* (1895); FBA, 1903, president, 1917–21, secretary, 1930–49; CB, 1911; KCB, 1912; GBE, 1925; hon. fellow, Magdalen and New College, Oxford.

KENYON, George Thomas (1840–1908), politician; educated at Harrow and Christ Church, Oxford; called to bar, 1869; Conservative MP for Denbigh Boroughs, 1885–95, 1900–5; mainly instrumental in passing the Welsh Intermediate Education Act, 1889.

KENYON, John (1784–1856), poet and philanthropist; born in Jamaica; educated at Peterhouse, Cambridge; a friend and benefactor to the Brownings and other men and women of letters; spent his life in society, travel, dilettantism, and dispensing charity; published *A Rhymed Plea for Tolerance* (1833), *Poems* (1838), and *A Day at Tivoli* (1849).

KENYON, Joseph (1885–1961), organic chemist; educated at Blackburn Secondary School; laboratory assistant at age of 14, Municipal Technical School, Blackburn; John Mercer FRS scholar; B.Sc. (London), 1907; D.Sc., 1914; research assistant to (Sir) R. H. *Pickard; made important contributions to stereochemistry; published over 160 papers on stereochemistry and its relation to reaction mechanisms; assistant lecturer, Blackburn Technical College, 1906; lecturer, 1907; worked with W. H. *Perkin in Oxford on dyestuffs chemistry, 1916–20; head of department of chemistry, Battersea Polytechnic, 1920–50; FRS, 1936; member, London University Board of Studies in Chemistry and the senate; vice-president, Chemical Society; fellow, Royal Institute of Chemistry.

KENYON, Dame Kathleen Mary (1906–1978), archaeologist; educated at St Paul's Girls' School and Somerville College, Oxford; joined British Association's expedition to Southern Rhodesia (Zimbabwe), 1929; part of team under (Sir) Mortimer *Wheeler excavating Verulamium (St Albans), 1930; with expedition to Samaria, 1931–4; introduced the 'Wheeler–Kenyon' method; involved with Wheeler in founding the London University Institute of Archaeology, 1937; acting director, 1942–6; directed youth department of British Red Cross Society, 1942–5; lecturer in Palestinian archaeology at Institute of Archaeology, 1948–62; excavated on Phoenician and Roman site of Sabratha, Tripolitania (Libya), 1948–51; honorary director, British School of Archaeology, Jerusalem; excavated mound of Jericho in Jordan Valley, 1952; published *Archaeology in the Holy Land* (1960); excavated in Jerusalem, 1961–7; principal, St Hugh's College, Oxford, 1962–73; CBE, 1954; DBE, 1973; FBA, 1955; FSA; hon. fellow of Somerville, 1960 and St Hugh's, 1973; number of honorary doctorates.

KENYON, Lloyd, first Baron Kenyon (1732–1802), lord chief justice; articled to a Nantwich solicitor, 1749; barrister, Middle Temple, 1756; KC, 1780; chief justice of Chester, 1780; MP, Hendon, 1780; attorney-general, 1782; master of the Rolls, 1784–8; privy councillor, 1784; knighted and created baronet, 1784; chief justice, 1788–1802; raised to the peerage, 1788; lord-lieutenant of Flintshire, 1797.

KENYON-SLANEY, William Slaney (1847–1908), colonel and politician; born at Rajkot, India; educated at Eton and Christ Church, Oxford; joined army, 1867; present at Tel-el-Kebir, 1882; retired with rank of colonel, 1892; Conservative MP for Newport division of Shropshire, 1886–1908; ardent tariff reformer; author of the 'Kenyon-Slaney clause' in Education Act of 1902; PC, 1904.

KEOGH, Sir Alfred (1857–1936), lieutenant-general; educated at Queen's College, Galway; qualified in medicine; entered army, 1880; deputy director-general, Army Medical Services, 1902–5, director-general, 1905–10 and 1914–18; reforms included establishment of Royal Army Medical College, Millbank, army school of hygiene, and central hospitals; brought teaching hospitals into Territorial scheme; rector, Imperial College of Science, 1910–22; KCB, 1906; GCVO and CH, 1918.

KEOGH, John (1650?–1725), Irish divine; MA, Trinity College, Dublin, 1678; led a scholar's life in country livings; left works in manuscript.

KEOGH, John (1681?–1754), divine; second son of John *Keogh (1650?–1725); DD; wrote on antiquities and medicinal plants of Ireland.

KEOGH, John (1740–1817), Irish Catholic leader; instrumental in bringing about Catholic Relief Act of 1793; arrested as one of the United Irishmen, 1796; released; withdrew from public affairs after 1798.

KEOGH, William Nicholas (1817–1878), Irish judge; educated at Trinity College, Dublin; called to the Irish bar, 1840; MP, Athlone, 1847; QC, 1849; solicitor-general for Ireland, 1852; warmly denounced for joining the government after showing sympathy with popular party in Ire-

land; attorney-general and privy councillor for Ireland, 1855; judge of the court of common pleas in Ireland, 1856; on the commission for trial of Fenian prisoners, 1865; hon. LL D, Dublin, 1867; died at Bingen-on-the-Rhine.

KEON, Miles Gerald (1821–1875), novelist and colonial secretary; editor of *Dolman's Magazine*, 1846; joined staff of *Morning Post*, 1848; its representative at St Petersburg, 1850 and 1856; sent to Calcutta to edit the *Bengal Hurkaru*, 1858; colonial secretary at Bermuda, 1859–75; published novels.

KEPER, John (*fl.* 1580), poet; educated at Hart Hall, Oxford; MA, 1569; author of complimentary poems.

KEPPEL, Arnold Joost van, first earl of Albemarle (1669–1718), born in Holland; came to England with William of Orange, 1688; created earl of Albemarle, 1696; major-general, 1697; KG, 1700; confidant of William III, at whose death he returned to Holland; fought at Ramillies, 1706, and Oudenarde, 1708; governor of Tournay, 1709.

KEPPEL, Augustus, first Viscount Keppel (1725–1786), admiral; son of William Anne *Keppel, second earl of Albemarle; educated at Westminster School; entered navy, 1735; accompanied *Anson on a voyage round the world, 1740; commander, 1744; sent to treat with the dey of Algiers, 1748–51; commodore and commander of the ships on the North American Station, 1754; a member of the court martial on *Byng, 1757; rear-admiral, 1762; one of the lord commissioners of the Admiralty, 1766; vice-admiral, 1770; admiral of the blue, 1778; commander-in-chief of the Grand Fleet, 1778; court-martialled for conduct in the operations off Brest, 1779, the charge being pronounced 'malicious and ill-founded'; first lord of the Admiralty, 1782; created Viscount Keppel and Baron Elden, 1782.

KEPPEL, Frederick (1729–1777), bishop of Exeter; son of William Anne *Keppel, second earl of Albemarle; educated at Westminster School and Christ Church, Oxford; MA, 1754; DD, 1762; chaplain-in-ordinary to George II and George III; canon of Windsor, 1754–62; bishop of Exeter, 1762; dean of Windsor, 1765; registrar of the Garter, 1765.

KEPPEL, George, third earl of Albemarle (1724–1772), general; colonel, 3rd Dragoons; eldest son of William Anne *Keppel, second earl of Albemarle; ensign in Coldstream Guards, 1738; captain and lieutenant-colonel, 1745; at Fontenoy, 1745, and Culloden, 1746; MP, Chichester, 1746–54; succeeded to the earldom, 1754; major-general, 1756; lieutenant-general,

1759; privy councillor, 1761; governor of Jersey, 1761; assisted in attack on Havana, 1762; KB, 1764; KG, 1771.

KEPPEL, Sir **George Olof Roos-** (1866–1921), soldier and Anglo-Indian administrator. See ROOS-KEPPEL.

KEPPEL, George Thomas, sixth earl of Albemarle (1799–1891), grandson of George *Keppel, third earl of Albemarle; educated at Westminster School; ensign in the 14th Foot (later Yorkshire Regiment), 1815; present at Waterloo; served in the Ionian Islands, Mauritius, the Cape, and in India; returned home overland, 1823; MP, East Norfolk, 1832; private secretary to Lord John Russell, 1846; succeeded to earldom, 1851.

KEPPEL, Sir **Henry** (1809–1904), admiral of the fleet; entered navy, 1822; commander, 1833; served in West and East Indies, and in China War, 1841–2; senior officer at Singapore, 1842; helped in suppressing Borneo piracy, 1843–4; served with distinction in Baltic campaign, 1854; CB, 1856; second-in-command on China Station, 1856; KCB; groom-in-waiting to Queen Victoria, 1858–60; commander-in-chief on Cape and Brazilian stations, 1860; on China Station, 1866; admiral, 1869; GCB, 1871; commander-in-chief at Devonport, 1872–5; admiral of the fleet, 1877; intimate friend of King Edward VII; published *A Sailor's Life under Four Sovereigns* (3 vols., 1899).

KEPPEL, William Anne, second earl of Albemarle (1702–1754), lieutenant-general; colonel, Coldstream Guards; son of Arnold Joost van *Keppel, first earl of Albemarle; educated in Holland; succeeded as earl, 1718; KB, 1725; governor of Virginia, 1737; brigadier-general, 1739; major-general, 1742; general on the staff at Dettingen, 1743; colonel, Coldstream Guards, 1744; wounded at Fontenoy, 1745; present at Culloden, 1746; ambassador-extraordinary to Paris, and commander-in-chief in North Britain, 1748; KG, 1749; privy councillor, 1750; died in Paris.

KEPPEL, William Coutts, seventh earl of Albemarle and Viscount Bury (1832–1894), son of George Thomas *Keppel, sixth earl of Albemarle; educated at Eton; lieutenant in Scots Guards, 1849; aide-de-camp to Lord Frederick Fitzclarence in India, 1852–3; retired from army; superintendent of Indian affairs in Canada, 1854–7; MP for Norwich, 1857 and 1859, Wick burghs, 1860–5, and Berwick, 1868–74; treasurer of household, 1859–66; KCMG, 1870; raised to peerage as Baron Ashford, 1876; under-secretary at war, 1878–80 and 1885–6;

succeeded to earldom, 1891; published writings relating to Canada and other subjects.

KER. See also KERR.

KER, Sir **Andrew** (d. 1526), of Cessfurd or Cessford; Scottish borderer; fought at Flodden, 1513; warden of the middle marches, 1515; defeated Scott of Buccleuch in a skirmish, but was slain.

KER, Andrew (1471?–1545), of Ferniehirst; border chieftain; succeeded as laird, 1499; captured, 1523; escaped; undertook to serve England, 1544.

KER, Charles Henry Bellenden (1785?–1871), legal reformer; son of John Bellenden *Ker; barrister, Lincoln's Inn, 1814; promoted legal reforms; conveyancing counsel to the courts of Chancery; recorder of Andover; retired from practice, 1860; died at Cannes.

KER, James Innes-, fifth duke of Roxburgh (1738–1823), second son of Sir Harry Innes, fifth baronet; captain of foot, 88th Regiment, 1759, and 58th, 1779; succeeded to baronetcy, 1764; on death of William Ker, fourth duke of Roxburgh (1805), claimed the dukedom; his claims disputed; obtained title, 1812.

KER, John (1673–1726), of Kersland, Ayrshire; government spy; in the pay both of the government and the Jacobites; declared himself instrumental in securing the Hanoverian succession, 1714; died in King's Bench debtors' prison; his memoirs published by Edmund *Curll (1726).

KER, John (d. 1741), Latin poet; master in Royal High School, Edinburgh, *c.*1710; professor of Greek, King's College, Aberdeen, 1717, and of Latin at Edinburgh University, 1734; published *Donaides* (1725) and other Latin poems.

KER, John, fifth earl and first duke of Roxburgh (d. 1741), brother of the fourth earl and second son of the third earl; succeeded his brother, 1696; secretary of state for Scotland, 1704; created duke, 1707; Scots representative peer, 1707, 1708, 1715, and 1722; a member of the Council of Regency; keeper of the privy seal of Scotland, 1714; lord-lieutenant of Roxburgh and Selkirk, 1714; privy councillor, 1714; distinguished himself at Sheriffmuir, 1715; one of the lords justices during George I's absence from England, 1716, 1720, 1723, and 1725.

KER, John, third duke of Roxburgh (1740–1804), book collector; succeeded to dukedom, 1755; lord of the bedchamber, 1767; KT, 1768; groom of the stole and privy councillor, 1796; KG, 1801; his splendid library, including an unrivalled collection of Caxtons, sold for £23,341 in 1812. The Roxburghe Club was inaugurated by the leading bibliophiles on the day of the sale.

KER, John (1819–1886), divine; educated at Edinburgh University, at Halle, and Berlin; ordained, 1845; preacher and platform orator; DD, Edinburgh, 1869; published sermons and pamphlets.

KER, John Bellenden (1765?–1842), botanist, wit, and man of fashion; original name was John Gawler; captain, second regiment of Life Guards, 1790; senior captain, 1793; forced to quit the army in consequence of his sympathy with the French Revolution; claimed unsuccessfully the dukedom of Roxburgh, 1805–12; published many botanical works and first editor of *Botanical Register*, 1812.

KER, Neil Ripley (1908–1982), palaeographer; educated at Eton and Magdalen College, Oxford; first gave classes in palaeography, 1936; appointed lecturer, 1941; elected fellow at Magdalen, 1945; reader in palaeography, 1946–68; during 1939–45 war conscientious objector; worked as porter at Radcliffe Infirmary, Oxford; librarian, Magdalen College, 1955–68; vice-president, 1962–3; hon. fellow, 1975; honorary doctorates from Reading, Leiden, and Cambridge; FBA, 1958; gold medallist of Bibliographical Society, 1975; CBE, 1979; published many catalogues, including *Medieval Libraries of Great Britain* (1941, 2nd edn., 1964), *Catalogue of Manuscripts containing Anglo-Saxon* (1957), and *Medieval Manuscripts of Great Britain* (1969 onwards); published other works including *English Manuscripts in the Century after the Norman Conquest* (1960), lectures given as first Lyell reader in bibliography.

KER, Patrick (*fl.* 1691), poet; probably a Scottish Episcopalian who migrated to London during the reign of Charles II; wrote ultra-loyalist verse; chief work, *The Grand Politician* (1691).

KER, Robert, earl of Somerset (d. 1645). See CARR.

KER, Robert, first earl of Roxburgh (1570?–1650), helped James VI against *Bothwell, 1594–9; member of the privy council of Scotland, 1599; created Baron Roxburgh, 1600; accompanied King James to London, 1603; succeeded to his father's estates, 1606; created earl of Roxburgh, 1616; lord privy seal of Scotland, 1637; subscribed the king's Covenant at Holyrood, 1638; sat in the general assembly at Glasgow, 1638; joined the king's party in the Civil War, 1639; kept the door of the house open at Charles's attempted arrest of the five members, 1642; supported the 'engagement' for the king's rescue, 1648; consequently deprived of the office of privy seal, 1649.

KER, Robert, first earl of Ancrum (1578–1654), grandson of Andrew *Ker of Ferniehirst; succeeded to the family estates on the assassination of his father, 1590; groom of the bedchamber to Prince *Henry and knighted, 1603; gentleman of the bedchamber to Prince Charles in Spain, 1623; lord of the bedchamber, master of the privy purse, 1625–39; created earl of Ancrum at the coronation of Charles in Scotland, 1633; retired from office, 1639; a faithful Royalist, but lived in retirement, 1641–50; died at Amsterdam.

KER, Sir Thomas (d. 1586), of Ferniehirst; succeeded his father, the second son of Andrew *Ker of Ferniehirst, 1562; became a member of the Privy Council at the time of the *Darnley marriage, 1565; joined *Mary Queen of Scots after her escape from Lochleven, 1568; provost of Edinburgh, 1570; believed to have been directly implicated in the murder of Darnley, but pardoned, 1583; warden of the middle marches, 1584; suspected of a plot against the English, 1585; committed to ward in Aberdeen, where he died.

KER, Sir Walter (d. 1584?), of Cessfurd; eldest son of Sir Andrew *Ker of Cessfurd; implicated in murder of Sir Walter Scott of Buccleuch; banished to France, 1552; pardoned, 1553; a leading opponent of *Mary Queen of Scots.

KER, William Paton (1855–1923), scholar and author; educated at Glasgow University and Balliol College, Oxford; assistant to professor of humanity, Edinburgh, 1878–83; fellow of All Souls College, Oxford, 1879–1923; professor of English literature and history, University College of South Wales, Cardiff, 1883; Quain professor of English language and literature, University College, London, 1889–1922; director of department of Scandinavian studies, 1917–23; professor of poetry, Oxford, 1920; died in Italy; his works include *Epic and Romance* (1897), *The Dark Ages* (1904), *English Literature: Medieval* (1912), editions of *Dryden's *Essays* (1900) and of Lord *Berners's translation of Froissart's *Chronicles* (1901–3).

KERCKHOVEN, Catherine, Lady Stanhope and countess of Chesterfield (d. 1667). See KIRKHOVEN.

KERENSKY, Oleg Alexander (1905–1984), consulting bridge engineer; born in St Petersburg (Leningrad), son of Alexander Kerensky, who was briefly prime minister of provisional Russian government in 1917; escaped to London, 1920; attended school in north London and studied engineering at the Engineering College (later the City University); graduated with honours, 1927; joined bridge department of Dorman Long & Co. Ltd. and worked on scheme for Sydney Harbour Bridge and other similar schemes in London, Bangkok, and Cairo; with steel construction firm, Holloway Brothers, 1937–46, working on construction of units for Mulberry harbours and more bridges; moved to consulting firm, Freeman Fox & Partners, 1946, and worked on design for Severn Bridge and Forth Road Bridge; became partner, 1955; responsible for many other bridge designs and highway schemes, including M2 and M5 motorways; president, Institutions of Structural Engineers, 1970–1 and Highway Engineers, 1971–2; received many awards from engineering institutions; FRS, 1970; founder member, Fellowship of Engineering, 1976; hon. D.Sc., City University, 1967; CBE, 1964; president, Welding Institute, and Construction Industry Research and Information Association, 1979; chairman, British Standards Bridge Committee, 1958.

KERMACK, William Ogilvy (1898–1970), biochemist and mathematician; educated at Webster's Seminary, Kirriemuir and Aberdeen University; MA, first class, mathematics and natural philosophy; B.Sc., 1918; served with RAF; worked at Dyson Perrins Laboratory, Oxford, 1919–21, and at the Royal College of Physicians Laboratory, Edinburgh, 1921–49; permanently blinded in laboratory accident, 1924; continued research work; developed methods for synthesis of heterocyclic compounds with anti-malarial activity; also returned to mathematics, and collaborated with A. G. McKendrick on mathematical theory of epidemics; first MacLeod-Smith professor of biological chemistry, Aberdeen, 1949–68; dean, Science Faculty, 1961–4; D.Sc., Aberdeen, 1925; hon. LL D, St Andrews, 1937; FRS, 1944; fellow, Royal Society of Edinburgh, 1924; member of RSE council, 1946–9.

KERNE, Sir Edward (d. 1561), diplomat. See CARNE.

KEROUALLE, Louise Renée de, duchess of Portsmouth and Aubigny (1649–1734), accompanied *Henrietta, duchess of Orleans, the sister of Charles II, to England as maid of honour, 1670; established as Charles II's mistress *en titre*, 1671; naturalized and created duchess of Portsmouth, 1673; granted by Louis XIV, at Charles II's persuasion, the fief of Aubigny, 1674; exerted her influence to keep Charles dependent on France; died at Paris. Her descendants, the dukes of Richmond and Gordon, still bear her motto.

KERR, Archibald John Kerr Clark, Baron Inverchapel (1882–1951), diplomat. See CLARK KERR.

KERR, John (1824–1907), physicist; pupil of Lord *Kelvin at Glasgow University; lecturer in mathematics to Glasgow Free Church Training College for teachers, 1857–1901; made important discoveries in nature of light, 1875–6; author of *An Elementary Treatise on Rational Mechanics* (1867); hon. LL D, Glasgow, 1867; FRS, 1890; royal medallist, 1898; awarded civil list pension, 1902.

KERR, Sir John Graham (1869–1957), zoologist; educated at Royal High School and University, Edinburgh, and Christ's College, Cambridge; first class, parts i and ii, natural sciences tripos, 1894–6; fellow, Christ's College; demonstrator, animal morphology, Cambridge, 1897–1902; regius professor of zoology, Glasgow, 1902–35; devised system for camouflaging ships; MP, Scottish Universities, 1935–50; publications include *Zoology for Medical Students* (1921), *Introduction to Zoology* (1929), *A Naturalist in Gran Chaco* (1950); his collections from expeditions to Chaco region preserved at Glasgow; especially interested in marine biology and Scottish natural history; FRS, 1909; knighted, 1939.

KERR, (John Martin) Munro (1868–1960), obstetrician and gynaecologist; educated at Glasgow Academy and University and Berlin, Jena, and Dublin; MB, CM, 1890; MD, 1909; assistant to midwifery professor, Glasgow, 1894; Muirhead professor, Glasgow, 1911–27; regius professor, 1927–34; published many books on his specialities.

KERR (or KER), Mark (d. 1584), abbot of Newbattle; abbot, 1546; renounced Roman Catholicism, 1560, but continued to hold his benefice; privy councillor, 1569; member of the council to carry on the government after Morton's retirement, 1578.

KERR (or KER), Mark, first earl of Lothian (d. 1609), master of requests; eldest son of Mark *Kerr (d. 1584); master of requests, 1577; made a baron and privy councillor, 1587; created a lord of parliament, 1591; acted as interim chancellor, 1604; created earl of Lothian, 1606, and resigned the office of master of requests, 1606.

KERR, Lord Mark (d. 1752), general; son of Robert *Kerr, fourth earl and first marquis of Lothian; wounded at Almanza, 1707; governor of Guernsey, 1740; general, 1743.

KERR, Norman (1834–1899), physician; MD and CM, Glasgow, 1861; practised in London from 1874; published works relating to temperance, in the advancement of which he was actively interested.

KERR, Philip Henry, eleventh marquess of Lothian (1882–1940), journalist and statesman; educated at Oratory School and New College,

Oxford; first class, modern history, 1904; lost Roman Catholic faith and later became convinced Christian Scientist; youngest member of *Milner's 'kindergarten'; secretary, Transvaal Indigency Commission, 1907; editor of *The State*, 1908–9; co-founder and first editor of the *Round Table*, 1910–16; private secretary to Lloyd George, 1916–21; played important part in dealing with the dominions, India, and United States; largely responsible for document on German nation which forms preface to Treaty of Versailles; secretary to Rhodes trustees, 1925–39; succeeded to title, 1930; as a representative of the Liberal party entered 'National' government as chancellor of the duchy of Lancaster, 1931; under-secretary of state for India, 1931–2; chairman, Indian Franchise Committee, 1932; ambassador to United States, 1939–40; revealed remarkable persuasive powers and statesmanlike qualities; CH, 1920; PC, 1939.

KERR, Robert, fourth earl and first marquis of Lothian (1636–1703), eldest son of William *Kerr, third earl of Lothian; volunteer in the Dutch War, 1673; succeeded his father, 1675; a supporter of the Revolution; privy councillor to William III, and justice-general, 1688; united earldom of Ancrum to his other titles, 1690; commissioner of the king to the general assembly of the Kirk of Scotland, 1692; created marquis, 1701.

KERR, Robert (1755–1813), scientific writer and translator; descendant of Sir Thomas Ker of Redden, brother of Robert *Ker, first earl of Ancrum; studied medicine at Edinburgh University; surgeon to the Edinburgh Foundling Hospital; relinquished medical career for the management of a subsequently unsuccessful paper-mill; FRS Edinburgh, 1805; translated from Lavoisier and Linnaeus.

KERR, Robert (1823–1904), architect; cousin of Joseph *Hume; did much to develop Royal Institute of British Architects; professor of arts of construction, King's College, London, 1861–90; designed many buildings in London and country; published many architectural works.

KERR, Schomberg Henry, ninth marquis of Lothian (1833–1900), diplomat and secretary of state for Scotland; educated at New College, Oxford; attaché at Lisbon, Teheran (1854), Bagdad (1855), and Athens (c.1857); second secretary at Frankfurt (1862), Madrid (1865), and Vienna (1865); succeeded as marquis of Lothian and fourth Baron Ker of Kersheugh, 1870; lord privy seal of Scotland, 1874–1900; privy councillor, 1886; secretary of state for Scotland in Lord Salisbury's adminis-

tration, 1886–92; LL D, Edinburgh, 1882; KT, 1878.

KERR, Lord Walter Talbot (1839–1927), admiral of the fleet; brother of ninth marquess of *Lothian; entered navy, 1853; served in naval brigade throughout Indian Mutiny, 1857–8; captain, 1872; flag captain to Sir Beauchamp Seymour (afterwards Lord Alcester), 1874–7, 1880–1; naval private secretary to Lord George *Hamilton, first lord of Admiralty, 1885; rear-admiral, 1889; fourth naval lord, 1892; second naval lord, 1893–5; vice-admiral commanding Channel Squadron, 1895; first sea lord, 1899–1904; admiral, 1900; admiral of the fleet, 1904; a thorough seaman and wise administrator.

KERR (or KER), William, third earl of Lothian (1605?–1675), eldest son of Robert *Ker, first earl of Ancrum; educated at Cambridge and Paris; accompanied *Buckingham to the Isle of Rhé, 1627; served in expedition against Spain, 1629; created third earl of Lothian, 1631; signed the National Covenant, 1638; governor of Newcastle, 1641; subsequently one of the four commissioners of the Treasury; lieutenant-general of the Scots Army in Ireland; privy councillor; falsely accused of treachery while abroad and imprisoned on his return; released, 1643; in parliament, 1644; joined *Argyll in expedition against *Montrose, 1644; one of the commissioners sent to treat with the king at Newcastle, 1647; accompanied the king to Holmby House, 1647; secretary of state, 1648; one of the commissioners sent by the Scottish parliament to protest against proceeding to extremities against the king, 1649; general of the Scottish forces, 1650; refused to take the abjuration oath, 1662.

KERR, William, second marquis of Lothian (1662?–1722), eldest son of Robert *Kerr, first marquis of Lothian; succeeded to title of Lord Jedburgh, and sat in Scottish parliament, 1692; colonel of dragoons, 1696; succeeded his father, 1703; supporter of the English revolution and of the union of England and Scotland; Scots representative peer, 1708 and 1715; major-general on the North British staff after 1713.

KERR, William Henry, fourth marquis of Lothian (d. 1775), captain in *Cornwallis's Foot, 1739; present at Fontenoy, 1745, and Culloden, 1746; lieutenant-general, 1758; MP, Richmond, 1747, 1754, 1761–3; succeeded his father, 1767; Scots representative peer, 1768; general, 1770.

KERRICH, Thomas (1748–1828), librarian of the university of Cambridge; educated at Magdalene College, Cambridge; MA, 1775; fellow, 1771–5; university taxor, 1793; principal librarian, 1797; prebendary of Lincoln, 1798, and of

Wells, 1812; an antiquarian, painter, draughtsman, and one of the earliest lithographers; bequeathed his collections to the Society of Antiquaries, the British Museum, and the Fitzwilliam Museum, Cambridge.

KERRISON, Sir **Edward** (1774–1853), general; MA, Jesus College, Cambridge, 1835; cornet, 6th Dragoons, 1796; captain, 1798; served in 7th Hussars in Helder expedition, 1799; lieutenant-colonel in campaign of 1808; present at Waterloo, 1815; created baronet, 1821; MP, Shaftesbury, 1812–18, Northampton, 1818–24, Eye, 1824–52; general, 1851.

KERRY, Barons. See FITZMAURICE, THOMAS, sixteenth baron, 1502–1590; FITZMAURICE, PATRICK, seventeenth baron, 1551?–1600; FITZMAURICE, THOMAS, eighteenth baron, 1574–1630.

KERRY, knights of. See FITZGERALD, MAURICE, 1774–1849; FITZGERALD, Sir PETER GEORGE, 1808–1880.

KERSEBOOM, Frederick (1632–1690), painter; born at Solingen; studied painting at Amsterdam; lived at Paris and Rome; settled in England as a portrait painter; painted portraits of Robert *Boyle and of Sophia Dorothea, George I's queen.

KERSEY, John, the elder (1616–1690?), teacher of mathematics in London; published work on algebra at instigation of John *Collins (1625–1683), 1673–4; edited the *Arithmetic* of Edmund *Wingate, 1650–83.

KERSEY, John, the younger (*fl.* 1720), lexicographer; son of John *Kersey the elder; his *Dictionarium Anglo-Britannicum* (1708) used by *Chatterton.

KERSHAW, Arthur (*fl.* 1800), apparently son of James *Kershaw; employed in enlargement of Walker's *Gazetteer.*

KERSHAW, James (1730?–1797), Methodist preacher; converted by Henry *Venn; his poem *The Methodist attempted in Plain Metre* (1780), a sort of Wesleyan epic, determined *Wesley to exercise a censorship over Methodist publications.

KERSLAKE, Thomas (1812–1891), bookseller; a second-hand bookseller at Bristol, 1828–70; wrote articles on antiquarian subjects.

KESWICK, Sir **John Henry** (1906–1982), merchant; chairman of Jardine Matheson & Co. Ltd. of Hong Kong and Mathesons of London; educated at Eton and Trinity College, Cambridge; followed father and grandfather and joined Jardines, at first in New York, then in Shanghai, 1931; travelled widely in China and

learnt Shanghai dialect and Mandarin; during 1939–45 war served on personal staff of Lord Louis *Mountbatten (later Earl Mountbatten of Burma) as political liaison officer in Chungking; returned to Shanghai, 1946; became chairman of British (and international) chambers of commerce; chairman, Jardine Matheson, in Hong Kong, 1952–6; served on legislative and executive councils; returned to Mathesons in England, 1956, but frequently visited China; played leading part in British commercial relations with communist China; president, Sino-British Trade Council, 1963–73; founder member of Great Britain–China Centre; largely instrumental in mounting exhibition of British technology in Beijing, 1964; CMG, 1950; KCMG, 1972.

KETCH, John (commonly known as **Jack)** (d. 1686), executioner; took office probably in 1663; executed Lord *Russell, 1683, and *Monmouth, 1685; notorious for his excessive barbarity; the office of executioner identified with his name by 1702.

KETEL, Cornelis (1548–1616), portrait painter; born at Gouda; worked in London, 1573–81; through Sir Christopher *Hatton obtained a reputation among the nobility; settled at Amsterdam (1581), where he died.

KETEL (or **CHETTLE), William** (*fl.* 1150), hagiographer; a canon of Beverley; wrote a narrative, *De Miraculis Sancti Joannis Beverlacensis,* given in the *Acta Sanctorum.*

KETELBEY, Albert William (1875–1959), composer; composition scholar, Trinity College, London, at 13; organist, St John's Church, Wimbledon, at 16; musical director, Vaudeville Theatre, at 22; his romantic light music included 'In a Monastery Garden', 'In a Persian Market', and atmospheric music for silent films.

KETELBY, Maria Eliza (1745–1828), writer. See RUNDELL.

KETHE, William (d. 1594), Protestant divine; accompanied Ambrose *Dudley, earl of Warwick, to Havre as minister to the English Army, 1563; preacher to the troops in the north, 1569; remembered chiefly for his metrical psalms, first printed in the English Psalter of 1561.

KETT (or **KET), Francis** (*c.*1547–1589), clergyman; educated at Clare College, Cambridge; MA and fellow, Corpus Christi, 1573; condemned for heresy, 1588; burned alive, 1589.

KETT, Henry (1761–1825), miscellaneous writer; entered Trinity College, Oxford, 1777; MA, 1783; fellow, 1784; Bampton lecturer, 1790; BD, 1793; select preacher, 1801–2; classical examiner, 1803–4; drowned himself in a fit of depression.

KETT, Robert (d. 1549), rebel; took the popular side in a local quarrel, and, with 16,000 men, blockaded Norwich, 1549; defeated and executed.

KETTELL, Ralph (1563–1643), third president of Trinity College, Oxford; scholar of Trinity College, Oxford, 1579; fellow, 1583; MA, 1586; DD, 1597; president, 1599; vigilant in dealing with college estates and discipline; rebuilt Trinity College Hall.

KETTERICH (or CATRIK), John (d. 1419), successively bishop of St David's, Lichfield and Coventry, and Exeter; his name also spelt Catryk, Catterich, and Catrik, the latter appearing on his tomb; educated probably at one of the universities; employed on missions abroad, 1406–11; archdeacon of Surrey, 1410–14; king's proctor at the papal court, 1413; bishop of St David's, 1414–15; one of the English representatives at Council of Constance, 1414; bishop of Lichfield and Coventry, 1415; postulated to see of Exeter, 1419; died at Florence.

KETTLE (or KYTELER), Dame Alice (*fl.* 1324), reputed witch of Kilkenny; summoned before the dean of St Patrick's at Dublin; escaped to England.

KETTLE, Edgar Hartley (1882–1936), pathologist; student, pathologist, and ultimately director of Institute of Pathology and Medical Research, St Mary's Hospital; professor of pathology, Welsh National School of Medicine, Cardiff (1924–7), St Bartholomew's Hospital (1927–34), and British Postgraduate Medical School (1934–6); histopathology his special province; published *The Pathology of Tumours* (1916) and (with W. E. Gye) papers on silicosis and its association with pulmonary tuberculosis (1922–34); investigated whole problem of relation of dust to infection; FRS, 1936.

KETTLE, Sir Rupert Alfred (1817–1894), 'Prince of Arbitrators'; articled as attorney in Wolverhampton; barrister, Middle Temple, 1845; bencher, 1882; judge of Worcestershire county courts, 1859–92; advocated arbitration in trade disputes; knighted, 1880, for his public services in establishing a system of arbitration between employers and employed; published works on trade questions.

KETTLE, Tilly (1740?–1786), portrait painter; exhibited at the Free Society of Artists, 1761; at the Society of Artists, 1765; in India, 1770–7; exhibited at Royal Academy, 1779–83; became bankrupt; died at Aleppo on his way to India; his portraits sometimes mistaken for the work of Sir Joshua *Reynolds.

KETTLEWELL, John (1653–1695), nonjuror and devotional writer; educated at St Edmund Hall, Oxford; BA, 1674; fellow and tutor of Lincoln College, Oxford, 1675; MA, 1677; published *The Measures of Christian Obedience* (1681); vicar of Coleshill, 1682 (deprived, 1690); wrote several devotional works.

KETTLEWELL, Samuel (1822–1893), theological writer; licentiate of theology, Durham, 1848; ordained priest, 1849; vicar of St Mark's, Leeds, 1851–70; MA, 1860, and DD, 1892, Lambeth; published works on Thomas à Kempis and other theological writings.

KETTON-CREMER, Robert Wyndham (1906–1969), biographer and historian; educated at Harrow and Balliol College, Oxford; health impaired by rheumatic fever; assisted his father in restoring Felbrigg (near Cromer); inherited the estate, 1933; first book, *The Early Life and Diaries of William Windham* (published 1930); other publications include *Horace Walpole* (1940), *Thomas Gray* (won James Tait Black Memorial Prize, 1955), *Felbrigg: The Story of a House* (1962), and *Norfolk in the Civil War* (1969); published also five volumes of collected essays on Norfolk personalities and events (1944–61); major in Home Guard, 1941–5; chairman, magistrates, 1948–66; high sheriff, 1951; trustee, National Portrait Gallery; FBA, 1968; governor, Gresham's School, Holt; honorary degree, East Anglia University, 1969; fellow-commoner, Christ's College, Cambridge; bequeathed Felbrigg to National Trust.

KEUGH, Matthew (1744?–1798), governor of Wexford; rose during the American War from private to ensign; gazetted, 1763; lieutenant, 1769; retired from the army, 1774; chosen military governor of Wexford by the insurgents, 1798; court-martialled and executed.

KEUX, John Henry le (1812–1896), architectural engraver and draughtsman. See LE KEUX.

KEVIN, Saint (498–618). See COEMGEN.

KEY. See also CAIUS.

KEY, Sir Astley Cooper (1821–1888), admiral; son of Charles Aston *Key; entered navy, 1833; lieutenant, 1842; wounded at Obligado, 1845; promoted commander, 1845; served in the Russian War, 1854–5; commanded battalion of the naval brigade at capture of Canton, 1857; rear-admiral, 1866; director of the new Department of Naval Ordnance, 1866–9; superintendent of Portsmouth Dockyard, 1869; subsequently of Malta Dockyard and second-in-command in Mediterranean; president of the newly organized Royal Naval College, 1873; vice-admiral and KCB, 1873; commander-in-chief on the North

American and West Indian Station, 1876; admiral, 1878; first naval lord of the Admiralty, 1879; FRS, FRGS, and DCL; GCB, 1882; privy councillor, 1884.

KEY, Charles Aston (1793–1849), surgeon; half-brother of Thomas Hewitt *Key; pupil at Guy's Hospital, London, 1814; pupil of Astley *Cooper, 1815; demonstrator of anatomy at St Thomas's Hospital, London; surgeon at Guy's, 1824; gained reputation by successful operations for lithotomy; lecturer on surgery at Guy's, 1825–44; FRS; member of council of Royal College of Surgeons, 1845; surgeon to Prince Albert, 1847; famous operator, and one of the first to use ether as an anaesthetic.

KEY, Sir **John,** first baronet (1794–1858), lord mayor of London; alderman of London, 1823; sheriff, 1824; master of the Stationers' Company, 1830; lord mayor, 1830–1; created baronet, 1831; MP for the city of London, 1833, and chamberlain, 1853.

KEY, Thomas Hewitt (1799–1875), Latin scholar; half-brother of Charles Aston *Key, the surgeon; of St John's and Trinity colleges, Cambridge; MA, 1824; studied medicine, 1821–4; professor of pure mathematics in university of Virginia, 1825–7; professor of Latin in the London University, and joint headmaster of the school attached, 1831; resigned Latin professorship for that of comparative grammar, 1842; sole headmaster, 1842–75; FRS, 1860; his best-known work, his *Latin Grammar* (1846).

KEYES (or KEYS), Roger (d. 1477), architect (1437), and warden of All Souls College, Oxford; one of the original fellows of All Souls; warden, 1443–5; clerk of the works of Eton College, 1448; archdeacon of Barnstaple, 1450; precentor of Exeter Cathedral, by 1467, till death.

KEYES, Roger John Brownlow, first Baron Keyes (1872–1945), admiral of the fleet; entered navy, 1885; promoted commander for services in Boxer Rising, 1900; naval attaché, Rome, 1905–8; captain, 1905; commanded *Venus*, 1908–10; inspecting captain, submarines, 1910; commodore in charge of submarine service, 1912–14; commanded submarines in North Sea, 1914–15; fought at Heligoland Bight; chief of staff to (Sir) John *De Robeck at Dardanelles, 1915; prominent in planning naval operations and army landings; pressed unsuccessfully in Oct. for second naval attempt to force Narrows; DSO; commanded *Centurion* in Grand Fleet, 1916–17; rear-admiral, 1917; director of plans, Admiralty, Oct. 1917–Jan. 1918; planned blockage of Ostend and Zeebrugge; vice-admiral, Dover Patrol, Jan. 1918; implemented audacious operation of storming the German batteries and

sinking blockships at Zeebrugge, 23 April 1918; unsuccessful at Ostend; conducted unremitting offensive against enemy on Belgian coast; KCB, KCVO, 1918; baronet, 1919; commanded Battle Cruiser Squadron, 1919–21; vice-admiral, 1921; deputy chief of naval staff, 1921–5; reached agreement with Royal Air Force on dual control of Naval Air Service; commander-in-chief, Mediterranean, 1925–8; Portsmouth, 1929–31; admiral, 1926; admiral of the fleet and GCB, 1930; Conservative MP, North Portsmouth, 1934–43; liaison officer with king of Belgians, 1940; first director, Combined Operations Command, 1940–1; baron, 1943.

KEYL, Frederick William (Friedrich Wilhelm) (1823–1873), animal painter; born at Frankfurt-on-the-Maine; came to London as pupil of Sir Edwin Henry *Landseer; exhibited at the Royal Academy.

KEYMER (or KEYMOR), John (*fl.* 1610–1620), economic writer; his *Observations upon the Dutch Fishing* first published (1664).

KEYMIS, Lawrence (d. 1618), sea-captain. See KEMYS.

KEYNES, Sir **Geoffrey Langdon** (1887–1982), surgeon, bibliographer, and literary scholar; younger brother of John Maynard (later Lord) *Keynes; educated at Rugby and Pembroke College, Cambridge; first class, part i, natural sciences tripos, 1909; MA, 1913, B.Chir., 1914, MD, 1918, FRCS (Eng.), 1920, FRCP, (Lond.), 1953, FRCOG, 1950, and FRCS (Canada), 1956; Brackenbury scholar in surgery, St Bartholomew's Hospital, 1913; served in RAMC during 1914–18 war; pioneer in blood transfusion; helped to found London Blood Transfusion Service, 1921; published *Blood Transfusion* (1922); returned to Bart's Hospital; assistant-surgeon, 1928; consulting surgeon to RAF during 1939–45 war; acting air vice-marshal, 1944; retired from Bart's, 1952; knighted, 1955; hon. fellow, Pembroke College, 1965; edited letters of Rupert *Brooke (1968); compiled bibliographies of many authors including John *Donne, John *Evelyn, and Sir Thomas *Browne; in addition to bibliography of William *Blake, edited his *Writings* (3 vols., Nonesuch Press, 1925) supplemented by editions of drawings and studies of plates; shorter essays gathered in *Blake Studies* (1949, 2nd edn., 1971); helped establish the Blake Trust; edited volumes by John Donne, John Evelyn, William *Harvey, William *Hazlitt, and Izaak *Walton; compiled bibliographies of Jane *Austen and Hazlitt, and wrote biographies of Rupert Brooke and Siegfried *Sassoon; biography of William Harvey (1966) awarded James Tait Black Memorial

Prize; chairman, National Portrait Gallery, 1958–66; wrote ballet *Job* with music by Ralph *Vaughan Williams, 1931; honorary degrees from Cambridge, Oxford, Edinburgh, Birmingham, Sheffield, and Reading; hon. FBA, 1980.

KEYNES, George (1630–1659), alias George Brett; Jesuit; entered his novitiate at Rome, 1649; studied at St Omer; sailed for China mission, 1654; died in the Philippines; translated the *Roman Martyrology* (2nd edn., 1667).

KEYNES, John (1625?–1697), Jesuit; probably brother of George *Keynes; studied at St Omer and Valladolid; joined Jesuits, 1645; taught philosophy and theology at Spanish universities; as prefect of the higher studies at Liège devoted himself to the plague-stricken English soldiers in the Netherlands; in England till 1679; rector of the college of Liège, 1680; English provincial, 1683–9; established Jesuit college at Savoy Hospital, 1687; died at Watten, near St Omer; author of a pamphlet intended to bring schismatics to the 'true religion', which was translated into Latin (1684), French (1688), and answered by *Burnet (1675).

KEYNES, John Maynard, Baron Keynes (1883–1946), economist; scholar of Eton and King's College, Cambridge; twelfth wrangler and president of Union, 1905; member of 'the Apostles' and later of the 'Bloomsbury group'; in India Office, 1906–8; lecturer in economics, Cambridge, 1908–15; second (1919), first (1924–46) bursar, King's College, Cambridge; editor, *Economic Journal*, 1912–45; member, Royal Commission on Indian Finance and Currency, 1913–14; joined Treasury, 1915; principal representative at Peace Conference, 1919; vigorously disagreed with proposals on frontiers and reparations; resigned, June 1919; wrote *The Economic Consequences of the Peace* (1919) and became centre of controversy on European economics; closely associated with Liberal party; wrote regularly in *Nation and Athenaeum*, 1923–31; collaborated with (Sir) Hubert *Henderson in *Can Lloyd George do it?* (1929); member, Committee on Finance and Industry, 1929–31; his conviction of possibility of curing unemployment and interest in nature of saving and investment and their relation to rising and falling prices resulted in *A Treatise on Money* (2 vols., 1930) and *General Theory of Employment, Interest and Money* (1936); maintained that economic system has no automatic tendency to full employment; expounded new theory of rate of interest and of forms of short-period equilibrium; for a time divided the economists, but his general approach later widely accepted; possessed immense vitality, optimism, and convic-

tion that problems were soluble; by investment and speculation amassed large fortune; collected books and paintings; through marriage (1925) with Lydia *Lopokova interested himself in ballet; built and financed Arts Theatre, Cambridge, 1935; chairman, CEMA, later the Arts Council; wrote *Essays in Persuasion* (1931), *Essays in Biography* (1933), and *Two Memoirs* (1949); returned to Treasury, 1940; chiefly responsible for new concept of budgetary policy, 1941; played leading part at Bretton Woods Conference (1944) from which emerged International Monetary Fund and International Bank; first British governor on both; engaged in negotiations with United States on lend-lease, 1944–5; obtained loan conditional on early establishment of convertibility, 1945; FBA, 1929; baron, 1942.

KEYS, Lady Mary (1540?–1578), third surviving daughter of Henry *Grey, third marquis of Dorset; sister of Lady Jane Grey (see DUDLEY, JANE); secretly married Thomas Keys, Queen Elizabeth's serjeant-porter, 1565; detained in private custody through Queen Elizabeth's anger; released, 1573.

KEYS, Samuel (1771–1850), china-painter; in the old Derby China Factory under William *Duesbury (1725–1786); quitted Derby before the closing of the factory; worked under *Minton at Stoke-upon-Trent; collected materials for the history of the Derby factory, to which his three sons were apprenticed.

KEYSE, Thomas (1722–1800), still-life painter and proprietor of the Bermondsey Spa; self-taught; member of the Free Society of Artists; exhibited at the Royal Academy, 1765–8; opened (c.1770) a tea-garden in Bermondsey near a chalybeate spring.

KEYSER, William de (1647–1692?). See DE KEYSER.

KEYWORTH, Thomas (1782–1852), divine and Hebraist; converted from Unitarianism and became a Congregational minister; interested himself in missionary work; his chief book, *Principia Hebraica* (1817).

KHAMA, Sir Seretse (1921–1980), first president of Botswana; foster-son and nephew of *Tshekedi Khama, acting chief of the Bamangwato people of Bechuanaland; educated at Fort Hare University, South Africa and Balliol College, Oxford; married an English girl, Ruth Williams, 1948; thus aroused opposition of Tshekedi, who had forbidden the wedding; in spite of verdict of tribal gathering at Serowe in his favour, British government exiled him and his family, 1949–56; allowed to return to his homeland having renounced all claim to Bamangwato chieftainship; member of protectorate's executive council, 1961; founded multiracial Democratic party, 1962; won landslide victory in Bechuanaland's first election and became first prime minister, 1965; negotiated independence of renamed Botswana and became first president; established Botswana as a country which could maintain its integrity in black councils; his disclaimer of right of succession to chieftainship set aside by the Bamangwato tribe; OBE, 1963; KBE, 1966; hon. fellow, Balliol College, 1969; chancellor of University of Botswana, Lesotho, and Swaziland, 1967–70.

KHAN SAHIB (1883–1958), Indian politician; educated at Peshawar Government High School and mission college; qualified in medicine; joined brother, Abdul Ghaffar Khan, organizing Red Shirt movement of Muslim Pathans and formed alliance with Congress party; imprisoned, then externed, 1931; chief minister, North-West Frontier Province, 1937; resigned, 1939, but supported war effort; chief minister, 1945; lost office and popularity when Pathans opted for Pakistan, 1947; minister of communications, Pakistan, 1954; chief minister, West Pakistan, 1955–7; assassinated.

KIALLMARK (or KILMARK), George (1781–1835), musical composer; leader of the music at Sadler's Wells; a successful teacher and composer.

KIALLMARK, George Frederick (1804–1887), musician; son of George *Kiallmark; studied under Zimmermann, Kalkbrenner, and Moscheles; distinguished for his rendering of Chopin; opened an academy for the study of the piano in London, 1842.

KIARAN, Saint (516–549). See CIARAN.

KICKHAM, Charles Joseph (1826–1882), journalist; took part in 'Young Ireland Movement', 1848; became a Fenian, 1860; arrested, 1865, and sentenced to fourteen years' penal servitude, but released, 1869; wrote nationalist poems and stories on Irish subjects.

KIDD, Benjamin (1858–1916), sociologist; clerk in Inland Revenue department, 1877–94; published *Social Evolution*, which had remarkable success partly due to its violent attack on socialism, 1894; its main theme is glorification of religion and attack on reason; other works include *Principles of Western Civilization* (1902) and *Science of Power* (posthumous, 1918).

KIDD, James (1761–1834), Presbyterian divine; of humble origin; emigrated to America, 1784; usher to Pennsylvania College; learnt Hebrew and studied at Edinburgh; professor of oriental languages, Marischal College, Aberdeen, 1793;

hon. DD, New Jersey, 1818; author of religious works.

KIDD, John (1775–1851), physician; student, Christ Church, Oxford, 1793; MA, 1800; MD, 1804; studied at Guy's Hospital, London, 1797–1801; pupil of Sir Astley Paston *Cooper; chemical reader, Oxford, 1801; first Aldrichian professor of chemistry, 1803–32; physician to the Radcliffe Infirmary, 1808–26; gave lectures on mineralogy and geology (published, 1809); Lee's reader in anatomy, 1816; FRCP, 1818; regius professor of physic, Oxford, 1822–51; author of Bridgewater treatise *On the Adaptation of External Nature to the Physical Condition of Man* (1833); keeper of the Radcliffe Library, 1834–51; Harveian orator, 1836.

KIDD, Joseph Bartholomew (1808–1889), painter; academician, Royal Scottish Academy, 1829–38; painted Scottish landscapes.

KIDD, Samuel (1804–1843), missionary at Malacca and professor of Chinese at University College, London; entered London Missionary Society's training college at Gosport, 1820; sailed under the auspices of the society to Madras, and thence to Malacca, 1824; published tracts in Chinese, 1826; professor of Chinese in the Anglo-Chinese College, Malacca, 1827, and at University College, London, 1837; author of works on China.

KIDD, Thomas (1770–1850), Greek scholar and schoolmaster; entered Trinity College, Cambridge, 1789; MA, 1797; held various livings; successively headmaster of schools of Lynn, Wymondham, and Norwich; edited tracts on classical scholarship.

KIDD, William (d. 1701), pirate; native of Greenock; lived at Boston, Massachusetts; given the command of a privateer to suppress piracy, 1696; imprisoned for piracy, 1699; sent to England under arrest, 1700; hanged, 1701.

KIDD, William (1790?–1863), painter; exhibitor at Royal Academy, 1817, and at British Institution, 1818.

KIDD, William (1803–1867), naturalist; bookseller in London; published various journals dealing with natural history, 1852–64.

KIDDER, Richard (1633–1703), bishop of Bath and Wells; entered Emmanuel College, Cambridge, 1649; BA, 1652; fellow, 1655; vicar of Stanground, 1659; ejected by the Bartholomew Act, 1662; 'conformed'; rector of Raine, 1664; preacher at the Rolls, 1674; a royal chaplain, 1689; bishop of Bath and Wells, 1691–1703; continually in difficulties with the cathedral chapter and censured by High-Churchmen; wrote on theological questions.

KIDDERMINSTER, Richard (d. 1531?), abbot of Winchcombe. See KEDERMYSTER.

KIDGELL, John (*fl.* 1766), divine; entered Hertford College, Oxford, 1741; MA, 1747; fellow, 1747; fraudulently obtained the proof-sheets of the *Essay on Woman* (probably printed by *Wilkes and written by Thomas *Potter), and then published *A genuine and succinct Narrative of a scandalous, obscene, and exceedingly profane Libel entitled 'An Essay on Woman'* (1763).

KIDLEY, William (*fl.* 1624), poet; BA, Exeter College, Oxford, 1627; composed 'A Poetical Relation of the Voyage of Sᵣ Richard Hawkins' and 'History of the year 1588, wᵗʰ other Historical Passages of these Tymes', 1624 (neither printed).

KIFFIN (or KIFFEN), William (1616–1701), merchant and Baptist minister; said to be apprenticed to John *Lilburne; joined Separatist congregation, 1638; Baptist, 1642; arrested at a conventicle and imprisoned, 1641; parliamentary assessor of taxes for Middlesex, 1647; permitted to preach in Suffolk, 1649; MP, Middlesex, 1656–8; arrested on suspicion of plotting against Charles II; released, 1664; alderman of London, 1687.

KIGGELL, Sir Launcelot Edward (1862–1954), lieutenant-general; born and educated in Ireland; from Sandhurst joined Royal Warwickshire Regiment, 1882; on staff in South Africa, 1899–1904; deputy-assistant-adjutant-general, Staff College, 1904–7; director, staff duties, War Office, 1909–13; commandant, Staff College, 1913–14; at War Office, 1914–15; chief of General Staff to *Haig, Dec. 1915–Jan. 1918; failure of campaigns of 1916–17 due to some extent to his inability to abandon earlier orthodoxies in light of realities of modern warfare; lieutenant-general, 1917; lieutenant-governor, Guernsey, 1918–20; CB, 1908; KCB, 1916; KCMG, 1918.

KILBRACKEN, first Baron (1847–1932), civil servant. See GODLEY, (JOHN) ARTHUR.

KILBURN, William (1745–1818), artist and calico-printer; executed the plates for *Flora Londinensis* of William *Curtis; owned calico-printing factory in Surrey; eminent in Europe as a designer.

KILBURNE, Richard (1605–1678), author of works on the topography of Kent.

KILBYE, Richard (1561?–1620), biblical scholar; BA and fellow, Lincoln College, Oxford, 1578; MA, 1582; rector of Lincoln College, 1590–1620; DD, 1596; prebendary of Lincoln, 1601; regius professor of Hebrew, 1610; and one of the translators of the Authorized Version.

KILDARE, earls of. See FITZTHOMAS, JOHN, first earl, d. 1316; FITZGERALD, THOMAS, second earl, d. 1328; FITZGERALD, MAURICE, fourth earl, 1318–1390; FITZGERALD, THOMAS, seventh earl, d. 1477; FITZGERALD, GERALD, eighth earl, d. 1513; FITZGERALD, GERALD, ninth earl, 1487–1534; FITZGERALD, THOMAS, tenth earl, 1513–1537; FITZGERALD, GERALD, eleventh earl, 1525–1585.

KILDELITH, Robert (d. 1273), chancellor of Scotland. See KELDELETH.

KILHAM, Alexander (1762–1798), founder of the 'Methodist New Connection'; maintained, against the Hull circular (1791), the right of Wesleyan Methodist preachers to administer all Christian ordinances; wrote many pamphlets between 1792 and 1796; 'expelled from the connection', 1796; formed a 'New Methodist Connection', 1798.

KILHAM, Mrs Hannah (1774–1832), missionary and student of unwritten African languages; née Spurr; joined the Wesleyans, 1794; married Alexander *Kilham, 1798; joined the Quakers, 1802; printed anonymously *First lessons in Jaloof* (1820); sailed for Africa, 1823; taught at St Mary's in the Gambia and at Sierra Leone, 1824 and 1832; died at sea.

KILIAN, Saint (d. 697). See CILIAN.

KILKENNY, William de (d. 1256), bishop of Ely and keeper of the seal; archdeacon of Coventry, 1248; keeper of the seal, 1250–5; bishop of Ely, 1255; died at Surgho in Spain.

KILKERRAN, Lord (1688–1759). See FERGUSSON, Sir JAMES.

KILLEARN, first Baron (1880–1964), diplomat. See LAMPSON, MILES WEDDERBURN.

KILLEN, John (d. 1803), Irish rebel; arrested for participation in *Emmet's movement, 1803; tried, unjustly condemned, and executed.

KILLEN, Thomas Young (1826–1886), Irish Presbyterian divine; entered old Belfast College, 1842; licensed to preach, 1848; ordained, 1850; a leader in the Ulster revival, 1859; moderator of the Irish general assembly, 1882; made DD by the Presbyterian theological faculty of Ireland, 1883; published a *Sacramental Catechism* (1874).

KILLEN, William Dool (1806–1902), ecclesiastical historian; after education at Belfast, entered Presbyterian ministry, 1829; minister to Raphoe, Co. Donegal, 1829–41; studied deeply church history; professor of church history at Presbyterian College, Belfast, 1841–89; president of the college, 1869; DD, Glasgow, 1845; LL D, 1901; his voluminous historical works include *The Ancient Church* (1859) and *The*

Ecclesiastical History of Ireland (2 vols., 1875); he also published *Reminiscences of a Long Life* (1901).

KILLIGREW, Anne (1660–1685), poetess and painter; daughter of Henry *Killigrew (1613–1700); maid of honour to *Mary of Modena, duchess of York; her *Poems* published (1686).

KILLIGREW, Catherine (or Katherine), Lady (1530?–1583), a learned lady; fourth daughter of Sir Anthony *Cooke; said to have been proficient in Hebrew, Greek, and Latin; married Sir Henry *Killigrew, 1565.

KILLIGREW, Charles (1655–1725), master of the revels; born at Maestricht; son of Thomas *Killigrew the elder; gentleman of the privy chamber to Charles II, 1670, to James II, 1685, to William and Mary, 1689; master of the revels, 1680; patentee of Drury Lane Theatre, London, 1682.

KILLIGREW, Sir Henry (d. 1603), diplomat and ambassador; educated probably at Cambridge; MP, Launceston, 1553; in exile, 1554–8; employed by Queen Elizabeth on various missions, notably to Scotland, 1558–66, and 1572–91; MP, Truro, 1572; knighted, 1591.

KILLIGREW, Henry (1613–1700), divine; son of Sir Robert *Killigrew; educated under Thomas *Farnaby; of Christ Church, Oxford; MA, 1638; chaplain to the king's army, 1642; DD, 1642; chaplain and almoner to the duke of York, 1660; master of the Savoy, 1663; published sermons and Latin verses, and *The Conspiracy* (play, 1638).

KILLIGREW, Henry (d. 1712), admiral; son of Henry *Killigrew (1613–1700); brother of James *Killigrew; commodore of squadron for suppression of piracy, 1686; vice-admiral of the blue, 1689; commander-in-chief against the French in the Mediterranean, 1689–90; joint admiral with Sir Clowdisley *Shovell and Sir Ralph *Delavall, and a lord commissioner of the Admiralty, 1693; dismissed after the Smyrna disaster, 1693.

KILLIGREW, James (d. 1695), captain in the navy; son of Henry *Killigrew (1613–1700); lieutenant, 1688; captain, 1690; killed in action, 1695.

KILLIGREW, Sir Robert (1579–1633), courtier; of Christ Church, Oxford; MP for various Cornish boroughs, 1601–28; knighted, 1603; famous for his concoctions of drugs and cordials; exonerated (1615) from suspicion of being implicated in Sir Thomas *Overbury's death; protonotary of Chancery, 1618; ambassador to the States-General, 1626; vice-chamberlain to Queen *Henrietta Maria, 1630.

KILLIGREW, Thomas, the elder (1612–1683), dramatist; son of Sir Robert *Killigrew; page to

Charles I, 1633; his best-known comedy, the *Parson's Wedding*, played between 1637 and 1642; arrested for Royalism, 1642; released, 1644; joined Prince Charles at Paris, 1647; appointed resident at Venice, 1651; groom of the bedchamber to Charles II, 1660; built playhouse on site of present Drury Lane Theatre, London, 1663; master of the revels in 1674; folio edition of his *Works* (1664); three of his plays acted; well known as a wit; painted by *Van Dyck with Thomas *Carew.

KILLIGREW, Thomas, the younger (1657–1719), dramatist; son of Thomas *Killigrew the elder; gentleman of the bedchamber to George II when prince of Wales; author of *Chit Chat* (comedy), performed 1719.

KILLIGREW, Sir William (1579?–1622), chamberlain of the Exchequer; groom of the privy chamber to Queen Elizabeth; MP, Helston, 1572, Penryn, 1584 and 1614, Cornwall, 1597, Liskeard, 1604; knighted, 1603; chamberlain of the Exchequer, 1605–6.

KILLIGREW, Sir William (1606–1695), dramatist; eldest son of Sir Robert *Killigrew; entered St John's College, Oxford, 1623; knighted, 1626; MP, Penryn, Cornwall, 1628–9; gentleman usher to Charles I; commander in the king's bodyguard during Civil War; DCL, Oxford, 1642; vice-chamberlain to Charles I's queen, 1660–82; MP, Richmond, Yorkshire, 1664–78; disappeared from court after 1682; published *Three Plays* (1665; reprinted, 1674), and pamphlets in connection with the quarrels concerning the draining of the Lincolnshire fens, 1647–61.

KILLINGWORTH, Grantham (1699–1778), Baptist controversialist; grandson of Thomas *Grantham (1634–1692); published controversial pamphlets.

KILMAINE, Barons. See O'HARA, JAMES, 1690–1773; BROWNE, JOHN FRANCIS ARCHIBALD, 1902–1978.

KILMAINE, Charles Edward Saul Jennings (1751–1799), general in the French Army; went to France, 1762; entered French Army, 1774, and arrested American insurgents; lieutenant-general, 1793; served in Italy under Bonaparte, 1796; died at Paris.

KILMARNOCK, fourth earl of (1704–1746). See BOYD, WILLIAM.

KILMOREY, Viscounts. See NEEDHAM, CHARLES, fourth viscount, d. 1660; NEEDHAM, FRANCIS JACK, twelfth viscount, 1748–1832.

KILMOREY, first earl of (1748–1832). See NEEDHAM, FRANCIS JACK.

KILMUIR, earl of (1900–1967), lord chancellor. See FYFE, DAVID PATRICK MAXWELL.

KILSYTH, first Viscount (1616–1661). See LIVINGSTONE, JAMES.

KILVERT, Francis (1793–1863), antiquary; entered Worcester College, Oxford, 1811; ordained, 1817; MA, 1824; published sermons, memoirs, and papers on the literary associations of Bath.

KILVERT, Richard (d. 1649), lawyer; concerned in the impeachment of Sir John *Bennet, 1621, and in the proceedings of the Star Chamber against Bishop John *Williams, 1634.

KILWARDBY, Robert (d. 1279), archbishop of Canterbury and cardinal-bishop of Porto; studied, and afterwards taught, at Paris; entered the order of St Dominic; teacher of *Thomas of Cantelupe; provincial prior of the Dominicans in England, 1261; archbishop of Canterbury, 1272; crowned Edward I and Queen *Eleanor, 1274; cardinal-bishop of Porto and Santo Rufina, 1278; on going to Italy took away all the registers and judicial records of Canterbury, which were never recovered; died at Viterbo; a voluminous writer on grammatical, philosophical, and theological subjects.

KILWARDEN, Viscount (1739–1803). See WOLFE, ARTHUR.

KIMBER, Edward (1719–1769), novelist and compiler; son of Isaac *Kimber.

KIMBER, Isaac (1692–1755), General Baptist minister; conducted *The Morning Chronicle,* 1728–32; edited *Ainsworth's *Latin Dictionary* (1751); published *Life of Oliver Cromwell* (1724).

KIMBERLEY, first earl of (1826–1902), statesman. See WODEHOUSE, JOHN.

KIMMINS, Dame **Grace Thyrza** (1870–1954), pioneer in work for crippled children; born Hannam; educated at Wilton House School, Reading; founded Guild of the Brave Poor Things, 1894; married C. W. Kimmins, 1897; founded home for cripples at Chailey, 1903, developed into Heritage Craft Schools; remained commandant until transfer to National Health Service, 1948; DBE, 1950.

KINAHAN, George Henry (1829–1908), geologist; entered Irish Geological Survey, 1854; as district surveyor (1869) prepared geological maps; author of *Manual of the Geology of Ireland* (1878), *Economic Geology of Ireland* (1889), and other kindred works.

KINASTON. See KYNASTON.

KINCAID, Mrs **Jean** (1579–1600), murderess; daughter of John Livingstone of Dunipace; wife of John Kincaid of Warriston, an influential man in Edinburgh; procured his murder, 1600; condemned and beheaded.

KINCAID, Sir **John** (1787–1862), of the Rifle Brigade; joined 95th Rifles, 1809; served in Peninsula, 1811–15; severely wounded at Waterloo; captain, 1826; retired, 1831; inspector of factories and prisons for Scotland, 1850; senior exon of the Royal Bodyguard of Yeomen of the Guard and knighted, 1852; published *Adventures in the Rifle Brigade* (1830), *Random Shots of a Rifleman* (1835).

KINCAIRNEY, Lord (1828–1909), Scottish judge. See GLOAG, WILLIAM ELLIS.

KINCARDINE, earls of. See BRUCE, ALEXANDER, second earl, d. 1681; BRUCE, THOMAS, eleventh earl, 1766–1841; BRUCE, JAMES, twelfth earl, 1811–1863.

KINDERSLEY, Barons. See MOLESWORTH, ROBERT, first baron, 1871–1954; MOLESWORTH, HUGH KENYON, second baron, 1899–1976.

KINDERSLEY, Hugh Kenyon Molesworth, second Baron Kindersley (1899–1976), banker and soldier; educated at Eton; served in Scots Guards, 1917–19; MC, 1918; joined Lazard Brothers & Co. Ltd., merchant bankers; appointed a managing director, 1927; joined court of Royal Exchange Assurance, 1928 (governor, 1955); rejoined army, 1939; commanded 3rd battalion, Scots Guards, 1942; commanded 6th Air Landing brigade, 6th Airborne division, 1943; seriously wounded in Normandy landings, 1944; MBE, 1941; CBE, 1945; succeeded father in peerage, 1954; chairman, Lazard Bros., 1953–64; central figure in Bank Rate tribunal, 1957; exonerated from any charge of dishonesty; chairman, Rolls-Royce Ltd., 1957–68; hon. FRCS, 1959; chairman, review body on doctors' and dentists' remuneration, 1962–70; chairman and president, Arthritis and Rheumatism Council; high sheriff of County of London, 1951.

KINDERSLEY, Sir **Richard Torin** (1792–1879), vice-chancellor; born at Madras; of Haileybury and Trinity College, Cambridge; fellow, 1815; MA, 1817; barrister, Lincoln's Inn, 1818; KC, 1825; chancellor of county palatine of Durham, 1847; master in Chancery, 1848; vice-chancellor, 1851; knighted, 1851; retired from the bench and privy councillor, 1866.

KINDERSLEY, Robert Molesworth, first Baron Kindersley (1871–1954), banker and president of the National Savings Committee; educated at Repton; joined Lazard Brothers, 1906; chairman, 1919–53; member, court of Bank of England, 1914–46; chairman, War Savings Committee, 1916; president, National Savings Committee, 1920–46; on Dawes Reparations Committee, 1924; KBE, 1917; GBE, 1920; baron, 1941.

KINDLEMARSH. See KINWELMERSH.

KING, Charles (1687–1748), musical composer; Mus.Bac., Oxford; almoner and 'master of the children' of St Paul's Cathedral, London, 1707; organist of St Benet Finck, Royal Exchange, 1708; vicar-choral of St Paul's, 1730; composed church music.

KING, Charles (fl. 1721), writer on economics; wrote articles in the British Merchant respecting the proposed treaty of commerce with France in 1713; issued the chief numbers as The British Merchant, or Commerce preserved (1721), the volume enjoying high authority for forty years.

KING, Charles William (1818–1888), author of works on engraved gems; entered Trinity College, Cambridge, 1836; BA, 1840; fellow, 1842; took holy orders; formed in Italy a notable collection of antique gems; sold his collection, 1878; published six works on gems between 1860 and 1872.

KING, Daniel (d. 1664?), engraver; executed the engravings in The Vale Royall of England, or the County Palatine of Chester (1656); etched some plates of *Dugdale's Monasticon.

KING, David (1806–1883), Scottish divine; educated at the Aberdeen and Edinburgh universities; studied theology at Glasgow; minister of Greyfriars Secession Church, Glasgow, 1833–55; made LL D, Glasgow University, 1840; active in Evangelical Alliance, 1845; helped to form United Presbyterian Church, 1847; visited Jamaica and United States, 1848; founded Presbyterian congregation in Bayswater, London, 1860; wrote chiefly on religious subjects.

KING, Earl Judson (1901–1962), clinical biochemist; born in Toronto; educated at Brandon College, McMaster University, Ontario, and Toronto University; graduated in chemistry and biology, 1921; Ph.D., 1926; research post, Banting Institute, Toronto, studied biochemistry of silicosis; worked at Lister Institute, London, 1928, and at Kaiser Wilhelm Institute, Munich; associate professor, Banting Institute, 1929; head of biochemical section, 1931; head of chemical pathology department, British Postgraduate Medical School, Hammersmith, 1934–62; reader in chemical pathology, London University, 1935; professor, 1945; continued work on silicosis; demonstrated that silica dissolved to produce toxic action on nearby pulmonary cells; extended research to effects of inhaled asbestos

fibres; during 1939–45 war, developed methods for estimating effects of new anti-malarial drugs, and became consultant in medical biochemistry to Royal and Indian Army Medical Corps; chairman, Biochemical Society, 1957–9; editor, Biochemical Journal; first chairman, International Federation of Clinical Chemists, 1952–60; MD, Oslo and Iceland; books and articles include Microanalysis in Medical Biochemistry (1946).

KING, Sir Edmund (1629–1709), physician; published results of his researches and experiments in the Philosophical Transactions, 1667, 1670, 1686, and 1688; incorporated at Cambridge, 1671; FRS, 1666; knighted, 1686; physician to Charles II, 1676; FRCP, 1687; attended Charles II in his last illness.

KING, Edward (1612–1637), friend of Milton; younger son of Sir John *King (d. 1637); educated at Christ's College, Cambridge; fellow, 1630; praelector and tutor, 1633–4; perished in a shipwreck off the Welsh coast when on the way to Ireland, 1637; commemorated by *Milton in Lycidas.

KING, Edward (1735?–1807), miscellaneous writer; studied at Clare College, Cambridge; barrister, Lincoln's Inn, 1763; FRS, 1767; FSA, 1770; contributed papers to the Archaeologia (reprinted separately, 1774 and 1782); interim PSA, 1784; his most important work, Munimenta Antiqua, or Observations on ancient Castles (1799–1806).

KING, Edward, Viscount Kingsborough (1795–1837), educated at Exeter College, Oxford; MP, Co. Cork, 1818 and 1820–6; promoted and edited Antiquities of Mexico, a magnificent work in nine volumes (published 1830–48).

KING, Edward (1829–1910), bishop of Lincoln; BA, Oriel College, Oxford, 1851; influenced by Tractarian movement and by Charles *Marriott; curate of Wheatley, near Cuddesdon, 1854–8; chaplain of Cuddesdon Theological College, 1858–63; appointed principal of college, and vicar of Cuddesdon, 1863; professor of pastoral theology at Oxford and canon of Christ Church, 1873; exerted much influence on religious life of Oxford; bishop of Lincoln, 1885; specially interested in youth and in confirmations; a High Churchman, he taught real objective presence and practised confession; prosecuted for illegal ritualist practices by the Church Association, 1889; archbishop's judgement (1890) was substantially in King's favour, and was upheld on appeal, 1892; the trial enhanced his popularity in Lincolnshire; a staunch Tory, active in opposition to education bills of Liberal government; favoured Franchise Bill of 1884; had great faculty for sympathy, and perfect refinement of thought and bearing; published many devotional works, sermons, and pamphlets; two churches at Grimsby erected to his memory.

KING, Mrs Frances Elizabeth (1757–1821), author; married Richard *King (1748–1810), 1782; assisted Hannah *More in charitable work; chief work, *Female Scripture Characters* (1813; 10th edn., 1826).

KING, Sir (Frederic) Truby (1858–1938), pioneer of 'mothercraft'; born in New Zealand; qualified in medicine, Edinburgh, 1886; founded Royal New Zealand Society for the Health of Women and Children (Plunket Society), 1907; established training centre, London, 1918; in many countries his mothercraft centres imitated and teaching followed, with notable decrease in infant mortality; director of child welfare, New Zealand, 1921–7; knighted, 1925.

KING, Sir George (1840–1909), Indian botanist; studied medicine and botany at Aberdeen University; MB, 1865; hon. LL D, 1884; entered Indian Medical Service, 1865, Indian Forest Service, 1869; superintendent of Royal Botanic Garden, Calcutta, and of cinchona cultivation in Bengal, 1871; organized Botanical Survey of India; inaugurated economic method of separating quinine from cinchonas, 1887; CIE, 1890; KCIE, 1898; FRS, 1887; made study of flora of Malayan peninsula.

KING, Sir George St Vincent Duckworth (d. 1891), admiral; son of Sir Richard *King the younger; succeeded to baronetcy, 1847; in the Crimean War, 1854–5; rear-admiral, 1863; commander-in-chief in China, 1863–7; vice-admiral, 1867, and admiral, 1875; KCB.

KING, Gregory (1648–1712), herald, genealogist, engraver, and statesman; educated at Lichfield Grammar School; became clerk to Sir William *Dugdale, 1662; Rouge Dragon pursuivant, 1677; registrar of the College of Arms, 1684–94; published heraldic and genealogical works; his *Natural and Political Observations and Conclusions upon the State and Condition of England* published (1696).

KING, Harold (1887–1956), organic chemist; educated at Friar's Grammar School and University College, Bangor; first class, chemistry, 1908; worked for Wellcome Laboratories, 1912–19; chemist, with special responsibility for study of drugs, Medical Research Council, working at National Institute for Chemical Research, 1919–50; chemotherapy research included arsenical drugs, anti-malarial drugs, diamidines, and work leading to discovery of methonium drugs; with Otto *Rosenheim, revised formulation of cholesterol; FRS, 1933; CBE, 1950.

KING, Haynes (1831–1904), genre painter; born at Barbados; exhibited at Royal Academy, 1860–1904; influenced by Thomas *Faed; works include *Looking Out* (1860), *The New Gown* (1892), *Latest Intelligence* (1904).

KING, Henry (1592–1669), bishop of Chichester; son of John *King (1559?–1621); educated at Westminster; MA, Christ Church, Oxford, 1614; prebendary of St Paul's, London, 1616; archdeacon of Colchester, 1617; a royal chaplain, 1617; canon of Christ Church, Oxford, 1624; DD, 1625; dean of Rochester, 1639; bishop of Chichester, 1642; friend of Izaak *Walton, *Jonson, and *Donne; published poems and sermons.

KING, Humphrey (*fl.* 1613), verse-writer; author of *An Halfe-penny-worth of Wit, in a Pennyworth of Paper. Or, the Hermites Tale. The third impression* (1613).

KING, James, first Baron Eythin (1589?–1652), entered service of king of Sweden and was 'general-major' by 1632; joined Rupert and the prince palatine, 1638; recalled to England, 1640; created peer of Scotland as Baron Eythin and Kerrey, 1643; lieutenant-general, 1650; died in Sweden.

KING, James (1750–1784), captain in the navy; entered navy, 1762; lieutenant, 1771; accompanied *Cook as astronomer and second lieutenant, 1776; captain, 1779; advanced to post-rank, 1780; sent to West Indies with convoy of merchant ships, 1781; prepared Cook's journal of the third voyage for the press; FRS, and his *Astronomical Observations* published, 1782; died at Nice.

KING, John (1559?–1621), bishop of London; of Westminster and Christ Church, Oxford; MA, 1583; BD, 1591; prebendary of St Paul's and one of Elizabeth's chaplains, 1599; DD, 1601; dean of Christ Church, Oxford, 1605; vice-chancellor of Oxford, 1607–10; bishop of London, 1611–21; contributed to Oxford collections of poems and printed sermons.

KING, Sir John (d. 1637), Irish administrator; secretary to Sir Richard *Bingham, governor of Connaught, 1585; deputy vice-treasurer, 1605; muster-master-general and clerk of the cheque for Ireland, 1609; privy councillor and knighted, 1609; MP, Co. Roscommon, 1613.

KING, John (1595–1639), divine; son of John *King (1559?–1621); of Westminster and Christ Church, Oxford; MA, 1614; prebendary of St Paul's, 1616; public orator of Oxford, 1622; canon of Christ Church, 1624; DD, 1625; archdeacon of Colchester, 1625; canon of Windsor, 1625; published Latin orations, 1623 and 1625, and poems in the university collections of 1613 and 1619.

KING, John, first Baron Kingston (d. 1676), eldest son of Sir Robert *King; engaged in behalf of parliament in Irish War; knighted, 1658; created an Irish peer, 1660; privy councillor of Ireland, 1660; commissary-general of the horse, 1661; governor of Connaught, 1666.

KING, Sir **John** (1639–1677), lawyer; educated at Eton; of Queens' College, Cambridge; barrister, Inner Temple, 1667; bencher and knighted, 1674; treasurer, 1675; king's counsel and attorney-general to the duke of York.

KING, John (d. 1679), Covenanting preacher; tried for holding conventicles, 1674; outlawed, 1675; executed, 1679.

KING, John (1652–1732), miscellaneous writer; of Exeter College, Oxford; MA, 1680; ordained; DD, Cambridge, 1698; prebendary of York, 1718; published controversial pamphlets.

KING, John (1696–1728), classical writer; eldest son of John *King (1652–1732); of Eton and King's College, Cambridge; MA, 1722, and fellow; published *Euripidis Hecuba, Orestes et Phoenissae* (1726).

KING, John (1788–1847), painter; entered the Royal Academy schools, 1810; exhibited at the British Institution, 1814, Royal Academy, 1817.

KING, John Duncan (1789–1863), captain (1830) in the army and landscape painter; served in the Walcheren expedition, 1809, and the Peninsular War; exhibited at the Royal Academy and British Institution between 1824 and 1858.

KING, John Glen (1732–1787), divine; educated at Caius College, Cambridge; MA, 1763; chaplain to the English Factory at St Petersburg; FSA, FRS, and incorporated MA, Oxford, 1771; DD, Oxford, 1771; published verses in the Cambridge collection of 1752 and antiquarian works.

KING, Matthew Peter (1773–1823), musical composer; composed glees, ballads, pianoforte pieces, and one oratorio; wrote treatise on music, 1800.

KING, Oliver (d. 1503), bishop of Bath and Wells; of Eton and King's College, Cambridge; French secretary to Edward IV, 1476; canon of Windsor, 1480; archdeacon of Oxford, 1482; deprived of secretaryship by Richard III, and imprisoned, 1483; reinstated by Henry VII, 1485; bishop of Exeter, 1493, and of Bath and Wells, 1495.

KING, Paul (d. 1655), Irish Franciscan; in early life captive among the Moors; taught moral theology at Brindisi, 1641; guardian of Kilkenny Convent, 1644; unsuccessfully attempted to betray it to Owen Roe *O'Neill and fled; guard-

ian of St Isidore's, Rome, 1649; published Latin writings; died probably at Rome.

KING, Peter, first Baron King of Ockham in Surrey (1669–1734), lord chancellor; published anonymously *An Enquiry into the Constitution, Discipline, Unity and Worship of the Primitive Church* etc. (1691); barrister, Middle Temple, 1698; MP, Beeralston, Devonshire, 1701; recorder of London and knighted, 1708; assisted at the impeachment of *Sacheverell, 1710; defended William *Whiston on his trial for heresy, 1713; chief justice of common pleas, 1714; privy councillor, 1715; raised to the peerage, 1725; lord chancellor, 1725–33; procured substitution of English for Latin in writs and similar documents. His *History of the Apostles' Creed* (1702) was the first attempt to trace the evolution of the creed.

KING, Peter, seventh Baron King of Ockham in Surrey (1776–1833), great-grandson of Peter *King, first Baron King; educated at Eton and Trinity College, Cambridge; succeeded to the title, 1793; published pamphlet on the currency question (1803, enlarged, 1804, and reprinted, 1844); published *Life of John Locke* (1829).

KING, Peter John Locke (1811–1885), politician; second son of Peter *King, seventh Baron King; of Harrow and Trinity College, Cambridge; MA, 1833; MP, East Surrey, 1847–74; passed the Real Estate Charges Act, 1854; advocated ballot and abolition of church rates; published works on legal reforms.

KING, Philip Gidley (1758–1808), first governor of Norfolk Island, and governor of New South Wales; served in the East Indies and Virginia; lieutenant, 1778; served with Captain Philip in the famous 'first fleet' which sailed for Australia, 1787; commandant of Norfolk Island, 1788; lieutenant-governor, 1790; governor of New South Wales, 1800–6.

KING, Philip Parker (1793–1856), rear-admiral; son of Philip Gidley *King; born at Norfolk Island; entered navy, 1807; lieutenant, 1814; conducted survey of coast of Australia, 1817–22; commander, 1821; FRS, 1824; surveyed the southern coast of South America, 1825; published narrative and charts of the survey of the western coasts of Australia (1827); advanced to post-rank, 1830; published *Sailing Directions to the Coasts of Eastern and Western Patagonia* etc. (1831); settled in Sydney; rear-admiral on retired list, 1855.

KING, Sir **Richard,** the elder, first baronet (1730–1806), admiral; nephew of Commodore Curtis *Barnett; entered navy, 1738; served in the Mediterranean and the East Indies; lieutenant, 1746; in command of the landing party at the capture of Calcutta and Hoogly, 1757; distinguished in action off Sadras, 1782; knighted; rear-admiral, 1787; created baronet and appointed governor and commander-in-chief at Newfoundland, 1792; vice-admiral, 1793; MP, Rochester, 1793; admiral, 1795.

KING, Richard (1748–1810), divine; of Winchester and The Queen's College, Oxford; fellow of New College, 1768; MA, 1776; held livings in Cambridgeshire; wrote, among other things, *Brother Abraham's Answer to Peter Plymley* (1808).

KING, Sir Richard, the younger, second baronet (1774–1834), vice-admiral; son of Sir Richard *King the elder; entered navy, 1788; lieutenant, 1791; commander, 1793; captain, 1794; present at Trafalgar, 1805; succeeded to baronetcy, 1806; rear-admiral, 1812; KCB, 1815; commander-in-chief in East Indies, 1816–20; vice-admiral, 1821.

KING, Richard (1811?–1876), Arctic traveller and ethnologist; educated at Guy's and St Thomas's hospitals, London; MRCS and LSA, 1832; surgeon and naturalist to expedition of Sir George *Back to Great Fish River, 1833–5; published *Narrative of a Journey to the Shore of the Arctic Ocean* (1836); originated the Ethnological Society, 1842; its first secretary, 1844; assistant surgeon to the *Resolute* in expedition to find *Franklin, 1850; received the Arctic Medal, 1857; published summary of his correspondence with the Admiralty concerning the Franklin expedition, 1855; author of works on the Eskimos, Laplanders, and natives of Vancouver Island.

KING, Richard John (1818–1879), antiquary; BA, Exeter College, Oxford, 1841; expert in the literature and history of the West Country; contributed to Murray's handbooks to the English counties and cathedrals, to *Saturday Review, Quarterly Review*, and *Fraser's Magazine*; a selection from his articles published (1874).

KING, Robert (d. 1557), bishop of Oxford; joined the Cistercians; BD, 1507; DD, 1519; prebendary of Lincoln, 1535; bishop of Oseney and Thame, c.1541; bishop of Oxford, 1545–57; sat at *Cranmer's trial.

KING, Sir Robert (1599?–1657), Irish soldier and statesman; eldest son of Sir John *King (d. 1637); muster-master-general and clerk of the cheque in Ireland; knighted, 1621; MP, Boyle, 1634, 1639; MP, Co. Roscommon, 1640; sent to manage the parliament's affairs in Ulster, 1645; member of the Council of State, 1653; sat in *Cromwell's parliament for counties Sligo, Roscommon, and Leitrim, 1654.

KING, Robert (1600–1676), master of Trinity Hall, Cambridge; entered Christ's College, Cambridge, 1617; MA, 1624; fellow of Trinity Hall, 1625; LL D, 1636; master of Trinity Hall, 1660.

KING, Robert, second Baron Kingston (d. 1693), eldest son of John *King, first Baron Kingston; MA, Brasenose College, Oxford, 1670; endowed a college in Co. Roscommon to be called Kingston College.

KING, Robert (*fl.* 1684–1711), composer; member of the band of music to William and Mary, and afterwards to Queen Anne; Mus.Bac., Cambridge, 1696; composed songs.

KING, Robert, second earl of Kingston (1754–1799), as Viscount Kingsborough was MP for Co. Cork, 1783, 1790, and 1798; shot dead (1797) Henry Gerard Fitzgerald, an illegitimate son of his wife's brother, with whom his daughter had eloped; tried and acquitted by House of Lords, 1798.

KING, Samuel William (1821–1868), traveller and man of science; MA, St Catharine's College, Cambridge, 1853; entomologist and geologist; published *The Italian Valleys of the Pennine Alps* (1858); died at Pontresina.

KING, Thomas (d. 1769), portrait painter; pupil of George *Knapton.

KING, Thomas (1730–1805), actor and dramatist; educated at Westminster; bred to the law, which he abandoned for the stage; engaged by *Garrick for Drury Lane Theatre, 1748; acted under *Sheridan at Smock Alley Theatre, Dublin, 1750–8; again at Drury Lane, 1759–1802; the original Sir Peter Teazle in the first representation of the *School for Scandal*, 1777; played Puff in the first performance of the *Critic*, 1779; connected with the management of Drury Lane and Sadler's Wells theatres; played Touchstone, 1789, and Falstaff, 1792; ruined himself by gambling and died in poverty; excellent in parts embracing the whole range of comedy.

KING, Thomas (1835–1888), prize-fighter; served as seaman in navy and merchant service; coached by the ex-champion, Jem Ward; defeated Tommy Truckle of Portsmouth, 1860; defeated William Evans, 1861; defeated by Jem Mace, but won a return match, 1862; defeated American champion John Camel Heenan, the 'Benicia Boy', 1863; retired from prize-ring and set up successfully as bookmaker.

KING, Thomas Chiswell (1818–1893), actor; apprenticed as painter and paper-hanger at Cheltenham; entered theatrical profession; appeared first in London at Princess's, 1850, as Bassanio (in *Merchant of Venice*); leading actor at

Theatre Royal, Dublin, 1851–6; played successfully at Birmingham, 1856, Manchester, 1857, Queen's Theatre, Dublin, 1859, City of London Theatre, 1860, and in various provincial towns, 1861–8; at Drury Lane Theatre, 1869–70, and Adelphi, 1871; appeared at Lyceum Theatre, New York, 1873; toured with success in Canada, giving exclusively Shakespearean plays, 1873–4; lessee of Worcester Theatre, 1878–80; exponent of the school of tragedians which subordinated intelligence to precept and tradition.

KING, William (1624–1680), musician; entered Magdalen College, Oxford, 1648; BA, 1649; probationer-fellow of All Souls College, 1654; incorporated MA at Cambridge, 1655; organist at New College, Oxford, 1664–80; composed church music; set to music *Cowley's *Mistress* (1668).

KING, William (1650–1729), archbishop of Dublin; MA, Trinity College, Dublin, 1673; DD, 1689; dean of St Patrick's, 1689; became an ardent Whig; bishop of Derry, 1691; published his *State of the Protestants of Ireland under the late King James's Government*, a powerful vindication of the principles of the Revolution (1691); his *magnum opus, De Origine Mali*, published (1702); archbishop of Dublin, 1703; founded Archbishop King's lectureship in divinity at Trinity College, Dublin, 1718.

KING, William (1663–1712), miscellaneous writer; of Westminster and Christ Church, Oxford; MA, 1688; DCL and admitted advocate at Doctors' Commons, 1692; published *Dialogues of the Dead* (attack on *Bentley, 1699); judge of the Admiralty court in Ireland, 1701–7; gazetteer, 1711.

KING, William (1685–1763), principal of St Mary Hall, Oxford; entered Balliol College, Oxford, 1701; DCL, 1715; principal of St Mary Hall, 1719; wrote several satires highly praised by *Swift, as well as *The Toast*, a mock-heroic poem (Dublin, 1732); supported Jacobitism; collected editions of his writings published (1760).

KING, William (1701–1769), Independent minister; educated at Utrecht University; returned to England, 1724; ordained, 1725; Merchants' lecturer at Pinners' Hall, 1748.

KING, William (1786–1865), promoter of co-operation; of Peterhouse, Cambridge; MA, 1812; MD, Cambridge, 1819; FRCS, 1820; wrote a monthly magazine, *The Co-operator*, 1828–30, unequalled by any publication of the kind; Harveian orator, 1843; friend and adviser of Lady Byron.

KING, William (1809–1886), geologist and lecturer on geology in the School of Medicine; curator of the Museum of Natural History at Newcastle upon Tyne, 1841; professor of geology at Queen's College, Galway, 1849; and of natural history, 1882–3; D.Sc. of the Queen's University of Ireland, 1870; his chief published work, *Monograph of the Permian Fossils* (1850).

KING, William Bernard Robinson (1889–1963), geologist; educated at Uppingham and Jesus College, Cambridge; first class, part ii, natural sciences tripos, 1912; Harkness scholar; appointed to Geological Survey of Great Britain, 1912; served in Royal Welch Fusiliers and Royal Engineers, 1914–18; OBE (military); demonstrator and assistant to Woodwardian professor of geology, Cambridge, 1920; Yates-Goldsmid professor of geology, University College, London, 1931; Woodwardian professor, 1943–55; fellow, Jesus College, Cambridge, 1920, and Magdalene College, 1922; published over fifty papers concerned mainly with the stratigraphy of Lower Palaeozoic and Quaternary, the Cambrian palaeontology of the Dead Sea and Persian Gulf, the floor of the English Channel, hydrogeology, and military geology; MC, 1940; advised on geological conditions for invasion of Europe, 1941–3; president, Geological Society of London, 1953–5; FRS, 1949; many academic honours both in England and abroad.

KING, William Lyon Mackenzie (1874–1950), Canadian statesman; born in Ontario; grandson of W. L. *Mackenzie; graduated in political science, Toronto, 1895; LL B, 1896; AM, 1898, Ph.D., 1909, Harvard; deputy minister, Canadian Labour Department, 1900–8; MP, 1908–11; minister of labour, 1909–11; director of industrial research, Rockefeller Foundation, 1914–18; elected Liberal party leader and re-entered parliament, 1919; prime minister, 1921–30, 1935–48; minister for external affairs, 1921–30, 1935–46; resigned when refused dissolution by Lord *Byng, 1926; brought down subsequent Conservative government as unconstitutional; won ensuing election as champion of Canadian independence and British constitutional system; steadfastly developed Canadian autonomy; at imperial conferences would not agree that Commonwealth should act as single unit (1923) and adopted middle course on dominion status resulting in Balfour statement (1926); in opposition, 1930–5; obtained overwhelming majority, 1935; repudiated proposal of oil sanctions against Italy by Canadian representative at Geneva, 1935; told Hitler Canada would fight, 1937; increased military appropriations; declared war seven days after Great Britain, 1939, with virtually unanimous support of Commons; pledged not to introduce overseas conscription; returned with record majority, 1940; supplied vast quantities of war material under mutual aid; introduced conscription for home service and wages and prices freeze; made with Roosevelt Ogdensburg agreement on defence (1940) and Hyde Park declaration integrating two economies (1941); conciliated between Roosevelt and Churchill; required resignation of J. L. *Ralston who pressed for conscription, which King introduced three weeks later, 1944; won last election (1945) on programme of reconstruction; completed work for Canadian autonomy with Canadian Citizenship Act (1946); OM, 1947; retired, 1948.

KINGDON-WARD, Francis ('Frank') (1885–1958), plant collector, explorer, and author; son of Harry Marshall *Ward; educated at St Paul's School and Christ's College, Cambridge; became professional plant collector, undertaking some twenty-five expeditions in mountain regions of India, China, Tibet, and Burma; brought back rhododendrons, primulas, gentians, lilies, etc., and notably the blue poppy for cultivation, and material for many books, from *The Land of the Blue Poppy* (1913) to *Return to the Irrawaddy* (1956); contributed to study of plant geography; OBE, 1952.

KING-HALL, (William) Stephen (Richard), Baron King-Hall (1893–1966), writer, and broadcaster on politics and international affairs; educated at Lausanne, and at Osborne and Dartmouth; in action at Jutland in *Southampton*; served in Admiralty, 1919; passed through Royal Naval Staff College, 1920–1; posted to China Squadron, 1922–3; intelligence officer to Sir Roger (later Lord) *Keyes, Mediterranean Fleet, 1925–6; commander, working on Naval Staff, 1928–9; resigned to take research post in Royal Institute of International Affairs, 1929–35; produced in collaboration with Ian *Hay (John Hay Beith) *The Middle Watch*, 1929; made weekly broadcast on current affairs, 1930–7; produced *King-Hall News Letter*, 1936; National Labour MP, Ormskirk, 1939–42; Independent MP, 1942–5; founded Hansard Society, 1944; publications include *Western Civilization and the Far East* (1924), *Imperial Defence* (1926), and *Our Own Times* (1934–5); knighted, 1954; life peer, 1966.

KINGHORN, Joseph (1766–1832), Particular Baptist minister; apprenticed to watch- and clock-making, 1779; clerk in white-lead works at Elswick, 1781; baptized, 1783; entered Baptist academy at Bristol, 1784; minister at Norwich, 1789; published theological works.

KINGHORNE, third earl of (1642–1695). See LYON, PATRICK.

KINGLAKE, Alexander William (1809–1891), historian of the Crimean War; educated at Eton; entered Trinity College, Cambridge, 1828; made the Eastern tour described in *Eothen* (published 1844), 1835; MA, 1836; barrister, Lincoln's Inn, 1837; went to Algiers and accompanied flying column of St Arnaud, 1845; followed the English expedition to the Crimea; present at the Battle of the Alma, 1854; was invited to undertake the history of the campaign by Lady Raglan, 1856; vols. i and ii of the *Invasion of the Crimea* published (1863); vols. iii and iv (1868); vol. v (1875); vol. vi (1880); vols. vii and viii (1887); MP, Bridgewater, 1857–65; his history marked by literary ability and skill in dealing with technical details.

KINGLAKE, Robert (1765–1842), medical writer; MD, Göttingen; also studied at Edinburgh; advocated the cooling treatment in his writings on gout.

KINGSBOROUGH, Viscount (1795–1837). See KING, EDWARD.

KINGSBURGH, Lord (1836–1919), lord justice-clerk of Scotland. See MACDONALD, JOHN HAY ATHOLE.

KINGSBURY, William (1744–1818), Dissenting minister; educated at Merchant Taylors' School and Christ's Hospital, London; 'converted', 1760; preached his first sermon, 1763; published his one controversial work, *The Manner in which Protestant Dissenters perform Prayer in Public Worship vindicated* (1796); a friend of John *Howard (1726?–1790) and John *Newton (1725–1807); published several funeral sermons.

KINGSCOTE, Henry Robert (1802–1882), philanthropist; educated at Harrow; president of the MCC, 1827; instrumental in founding Church of England Scripture Readers' Association and Metropolitan Visiting and Relief Association; published pamphlet letter to the archbishop of Canterbury on the needs of the church (1846); helped in alleviating Irish distress, 1847; sent out supplies to troops in the Crimea, 1854; one of the founders of the British and Colonial Emigration Society, 1868.

KINGSCOTE, Sir Robert Nigel Fitzhardinge (1830–1908), agriculturist; in Scots Fusilier Guards, 1846–56; served in Crimea; CB, 1855; Liberal MP for western division of Gloucestershire, 1852–85; inherited estate at Kingscote, 1861; parliamentary groom-in-waiting to Queen Victoria, 1859–66; extra equerry to King Edward VII when prince of Wales, 1867; commissioner of woods and forests, 1885–95; paymaster-general of the royal household, 1901; KCB, 1889; GCVO, 1902; president of Royal Agricultural Society, 1878; hon. LL D, Cambridge, 1894; member of royal commissions on agriculture, 1879 and 1893.

KINGSDOWN, first Baron (1793–1867). See PEMBERTON-LEIGH, THOMAS.

KINGSFORD, Mrs Anna (1846–1888), doctor of medicine and religious writer; née Bonus; married Algernon Godfrey Kingsford, vicar of Atcham, Shropshire, 1867; wrote stories in the *Penny Post*, 1868–72; turned Roman Catholic, 1870; purchased the *Lady's Own Paper*, 1872; edited it, 1872–3; studied medicine at Paris, 1874; MD, 1880; practised in London; president of the Theosophical Society, 1883; founded Hermetic Society, 1884; published miscellaneous works between 1863 and 1881.

KINGSFORD, Charles Lethbridge (1862–1926), historian and topographer; BA, St John's College, Oxford; Board of Education official, 1890–1912; FBA, 1924; his works include *Henry V* (1901), editions of three unprinted *Chronicles of London* (1905) and of *Stow's Survey of London* (1908), *English Historical Literature in the Fifteenth Century* (1913), *Prejudice and Promise in Fifteenth Century England* (1925), *The Early History of Piccadilly* ... (1925).

KINGSFORD, William (1819–1898), historian of Canada; articled as architect; enlisted in 1st Dragoon Guards, 1836; served in Canada; serjeant; obtained discharge, 1840; qualified as civil engineer at Montreal; obtained post of deputy city surveyor; worked in connection with Grand Trunk and other railways; dominion engineer in charge of harbours of the lakes and the St Lawrence, 1872–9; summarily cashiered by Sir Hector Langevin, 1879; devoted himself to writing *History of Canada* (published 1887–98); LL D, Queen's University, Kingston and Dalhousie; FRS, Canada.

KINGSLAND, Viscounts. See BARNEWALL, NICHOLAS, first viscount, 1592–1663; BARNEWALL, NICHOLAS, third viscount, 1668–1725.

KINGSLEY, Charles (1819–1875), author; student at King's College, London, 1836; entered Magdalene College, Cambridge, 1838; curate of Eversley, Hampshire, 1842; married Fanny Grenfell and accepted living of Eversley, 1844; published *St. Elizabeth of Hungary*, a drama (1848); joined with *Maurice and his friends in their attempt at Christian socialism, 1848; lecturer on English literature at Queen's College, London, 1848–9; contributed, over the signature of 'Parson Lot', to *Politics for the People* (1848) and to the *Christian Socialist*, 1850–1; his *Yeast* published (1848), *Alton Locke* (1850); never sympathized with the distinctively revolutionary movement; published *Hypatia* (1853), *Westward Ho!* (1855), *Two Years Ago* (1857); one of the queen's chaplains-in-ordinary, 1859; professor of modern history at Cambridge, 1860–9; published *Water Babies* (1863); engaged in a controversy with John Henry *Newman, which led Newman to write his *Apologia* (1864); canon of Chester, 1869; visited the West Indies, 1869; published *At Last* (1870); canon of Westminster, 1873; visited America, 1874; his enthusiasm for natural history shown by *Glaucus, or the Wonders of the Shore* (1855) and similar works; a believer in the possibility of reconciling religion and science.

KINGSLEY, George Henry (1827–1892), traveller and author; brother of Charles *Kingsley and of Henry *Kingsley; educated at King's College School, London, and Edinburgh University; MD, Edinburgh, 1846; graduated also at Paris, 1845; his activity during the outbreak of cholera in England in 1848 commemorated by his brother Charles in the character of Tom Thurnall in *Two Years Ago*; adopting foreign travel as his method of treatment of individual patients, explored most of the countries of the world; his most successful book, *South Sea Bubbles by the Earl* [of Pembroke] *and the Doctor* appeared (1872); edited from a manuscript at Bridgewater House, Francis *Thynne's *Animadversions uppon the Annotacions and Corrections of some Imperfections of Impressiones of Chaucer's Workes* (1865).

KINGSLEY, Henry (1830–1876), novelist; brother of Charles *Kingsley and of George Henry *Kingsley; educated at King's College School, London; entered Worcester College, Oxford, 1850; at the Australian goldfields, 1853–8; published *Geoffrey Hamlyn* (1859), *Ravenshoe* (1861); edited *Edinburgh Daily Review* after 1864; correspondent for his paper in the Franco-German War; present at Sedan, 1870; wrote sixteen novels and tales between 1863 and 1876.

KINGSLEY, Mary Henrietta (1862–1900), traveller and writer; daughter of George Henry *Kingsley; lived successively at Highgate and Bexley in Kent (1879), Cambridge (1886), and Addison Road, London; educated at home; made journeys to West Coast of Africa, visiting Ambriz, the Congo River, and Old Calabar, 1893–4, and to Old Calabar, Congo Français, the Ogowé River, Agonjo and Lake Ncovi, ascending the mountain of Mungo Mah Lobeh, 1894–5; formed valuable zoological collections and made careful notes and observations, which she subsequently utilized in published works and lectures; visited Cape Town during Boer War, 1900; attached as nurse to Simon's Town Palace Hospital for sick Boer prisoners; died of enteric fever. Her publications include *Travels in West Africa* (1897).

KINGSLEY, William (1698?–1769), lieutenant-general; cornet, 1721; lieutenant and captain, 1721; captain-lieutenant, 1743; captain and lieutenant-colonel, 1745; present at the battles of Dettingen, 1743 and Fontenoy, 1745, and took part in the 'march to Finchley', 1745; brevet-colonel, 1750; regimental major with the rank of colonel of foot, 1751; colonel, 1756; distinguished himself at Minden, 1759; lieutenant-general, 1760; his portrait painted by *Reynolds.

KINGSMILL, Andrew (1538–1569), Puritan divine; of Corpus Christi College, Oxford; fellow of All Souls, 1558; BCL, 1563; left the study of civil law for the ministry; died at Lausanne; wrote devotional works.

KINGSMILL, Sir Robert Brice, first baronet (1730–1805), admiral; son of Charles Brice; lieutenant, 1756; commander, 1761; took part in the reduction of Martinique and St Lucia, 1762; his wife succeeding to the estates of her grandfather, William Kingsmill, assumed the name of Kingsmill, 1766; fought off Ushant, 1778; MP, Tregony, 1784; rear-admiral, 1793; commander-in-chief on coast of Ireland, 1793–1800; vice-admiral, 1794; admiral, 1799; created baronet, 1800.

KINGSMILL, Thomas (*fl.* 1605), regius professor of Hebrew at Oxford; educated at Magdalen College, Oxford; probationer-fellow, 1559–68; MA, 1564; natural philosophy lecturer, 1563; Hebrew lecturer and public orator, 1565; junior dean of arts, 1567; regius professor of Hebrew, 1570–91; BD, 1572; published pamphlets and sermons.

KINGSNORTH, Richard (d. 1677), Baptist minister; a Kentish farmer.

KINGSTHORPE, Richard (*fl.* 1224), Franciscan. See INGWORTH.

KINGSTON, Barons. See KING, JOHN, first baron, d. 1676; KING, ROBERT, second baron, d. 1693.

KINGSTON, self-styled duchess of (1720–1788). See CHUDLEIGH, ELIZABETH.

KINGSTON, dukes of. See PIERREPONT, EVELYN, first duke, 1665?–1726; PIERREPONT, EVELYN, second duke, 1711–1773.

KINGSTON, earls of, in the peerage of England. See PIERREPONT, ROBERT, first earl, 1584–1643; PIERREPONT, HENRY, second earl, 1606–1680; PIERREPONT, EVELYN, fifth earl, 1665?–1726.

KINGSTON, earl of, in the peerage of Ireland (1754–1799). See KING, ROBERT, second earl.

KINGSTON, Viscount, in the peerage of Scotland. See SETON, ALEXANDER, first viscount, 1621?–1691.

KINGSTON, Sir **Anthony** (1519–1556), provost-marshal in Cornwall; son of Sir William *Kingston; served in Pilgrimage of Grace, 1536–7; knighted, 1537; MP, Gloucestershire, 1545, 1552–3, and 1555; provost-marshal of the king's army in Cornwall, 1549; sent to the Tower on charge of conspiring to put Elizabeth on the throne, but soon discharged, 1555; concerned in plot to rob the Exchequer for the same purpose, 1556; died on his way to trial in London.

KINGSTON, Charles Cameron (1850–1908), Australian statesman; born at Adelaide; admitted to colonial bar, 1873; QC, 1889; Radical member for West Adelaide in House of Representatives of South Australia, 1881–1900; attorney-general, 1884–5 and 1887–9; chief secretary, 1892–3; premier and attorney-general, 1893–9; defeated bills for imposition of land taxes, and for employers' liability; helped to secure woman's suffrage, factory legislation, state banking, protective tariff, and payment of members; represented South Australia at Queen Victoria's Diamond Jubilee; hon. DCL, Oxford, and PC, 1897; took prominent part in securing enactment of Australian Commonwealth Constitution Bill, 1900; elected to Legislative Council of South Australia, 1900; minister of trade and customs in first Commonwealth administration, 1901–3.

KINGSTON, Richard (*fl.* 1700), political pamphleteer; chaplain-in-ordinary to Charles II, 1682; author of controversial pamphlets.

KINGSTON, Sir William (d. 1540), constable of the Tower; fought at Flodden, 1513; knighted, 1513; took part in the Field of the Cloth of Gold; captain of the guard, 1523; constable of the Tower, 1524; brought *Wolsey to London, 1530; received *Anne Boleyn in the Tower, 1536; controller of the household, 1539; KG, 1539.

KINGSTON, William Henry Giles (1814–1880), novelist; grandson of Sir Giles *Rooke; spent much of his youth in sports; wrote newspaper articles which assisted the conclusion of the commercial treaty with Portugal, 1842; received order of Portuguese knighthood and a pension from Donna Maria de Gloria; his first story, 'The Circassian Chief', published (1844); edited *The Colonist* and *The Colonial Magazine and East India Review*, 1844; published *How to Emigrate* (1850); wrote many books for boys, and edited boys' annuals and weekly periodicals.

KINLOCH, Lord (1801–1872). See PENNEY, WILLIAM.

KINLOCH, George Ritchie (1796?–1877), editor of *Ancient Scottish Ballads*; became a lawyer; his *Ancient Scottish Ballads, recovered from Tradition, and never before published* issued (1827);

keeper of the register of deeds in Edinburgh Register House, 1851–69.

KINLOSS, Lord (1549?–1611). See BRUCE, EDWARD.

KINMONT, Willie (*fl.* 1596), border moss-trooper. See ARMSTRONG, WILLIAM.

KINNAIRD, Arthur Fitzgerald, tenth Baron Kinnaird (1814–1887), philanthropist; son of Charles *Kinnaird, eighth Baron Kinnaird; at Eton; attached to English embassy at St Petersburg, 1835–7; partner in banking house of Ransom & Co. in succession to his uncle, Douglas James William *Kinnaird, 1837; MP, Perth, 1837–9 and 1852–78; succeeded his brother, George William Fox *Kinnaird, as Baron Kinnaird, 1878; keenly interested in the well-being of the working classes.

KINNAIRD, Charles, eighth Baron Kinnaird (1780–1826), educated at Edinburgh, Cambridge, and Glasgow universities; MP, Leominster, 1802–5; succeeded to the title, 1805; Scottish representative peer, 1806.

KINNAIRD, Douglas James William (1788–1830), friend of *Byron; younger brother of Charles *Kinnaird, eighth Baron Kinnaird; educated at Eton, Göttingen, and Trinity College, Cambridge; MA, 1811; travelled with John Cam *Hobhouse and William *Jerdan, 1813–14; visited Byron at Venice, 1817; assumed chief management of Ransom's Bank, 1819; MP, Bishops Castle, Shropshire, 1819; author of a comedy and a pamphlet on Indian affairs.

KINNAIRD, George Patrick, first Baron Kinnaird (d. 1689), supporter of Charles II; knighted, 1661; represented Perthshire in Scottish parliament, 1662–3; privy councillor; raised to peerage, 1682.

KINNAIRD, George William Fox, ninth Baron Kinnaird (1807–1878), eldest son of Charles *Kinnaird, eighth Baron Kinnaird; at Eton; entered the army; resigned and succeeded to the Scottish peerage, 1826; created peer of the United Kingdom, 1831; privy councillor, 1840; KT, 1857; lord-lieutenant of Perthshire, 1866; introduced agricultural reforms on his estate; did much to ameliorate condition of the labouring classes.

KINNAIRD, Mary Jane, Lady (1816–1888), philanthropist; née Hoare; wife of Arthur Fitzgerald *Kinnaird, tenth Baron Kinnaird; edited *Servants Prayers* (1848); associated with Lady Canning in sending aid to the wounded in the Crimea; one of the founders of the Young Women's Christian Association.

KINNEAR, Alexander Smith, first Baron Kinnear (1833–1917), judge; advocate at Scots

bar, 1856; QC, 1881; lord ordinary, 1882–90; member of first division, 1890–1913; baron, 1897.

KINNEAR, Sir **Norman Boyd** (1882–1957), ornithologist; educated at Edinburgh Academy and Trinity College, Glenalmond; officer-in-charge, Bombay Natural History Society Museum, 1907–19; organized survey of mammals of India, Burma, and Ceylon; joined zoology department, British Museum (Natural History), 1920; assistant keeper, 1928; deputy keeper in charge of birds, 1936; keeper of zoology, 1945; director of museum, 1947–50; active in work for bird protection, nature reserves, National Trust, etc.; knighted, 1950.

KINNEDER, Lord (1769–1822). See ERSKINE, WILLIAM.

KINNEIR, Sir **John Macdonald** (1782–1830), lieutenant-colonel HEICS, traveller, and diplomat; son of John Macdonald; ensign in Madras Infantry, 1804; lieutenant, 1807; travelled in Persia, Armenia, and Kurdistan, 1813–14; published narrative of his travels; captain, 1818; took his mother's surname of Kinneir; envoy to Persia, 1824–30, and took part in the hostilities with Russia; knighted, 1829.

KINNOULL, earls of. See HAY, Sir GEORGE, first earl, 1572–1634; HAY, GEORGE, seventh earl, d. 1758; HAY, THOMAS, eighth earl, 1710–1787.

KINNS, Samuel (1826–1903), writer on the Bible; Ph.D., Jena University, 1859; rector of Holy Trinity, Minories (1889–99), of which he wrote a history, 1890; published *Moses and Geology* (1882) and *Graven in the Rock* (1891).

KINROSS, first Baron (1837–1905), Scottish judge. See BALFOUR, JOHN BLAIR.

KINSEY, William Morgan (1788–1851), divine and traveller; scholar of Trinity College, Oxford, 1805; MA, 1813; fellow, 1815; dean of his college and BD, 1822; vice-president, 1823; bursar, 1824; travelled in Portugal, 1827; published *Portugal Illustrated* (1828, 2nd edn., 1829); witnessed outbreak of revolution at Brussels, 1830.

KINSIUS (d. 1060), archbishop of York. See KYNSIGE.

KINTORE, first earl of (d. 1714). See KEITH, Sir JOHN.

KINWELMERSH (KYNWELMERSH or **KINDLEMARSH), Francis** (d. 1580?), poet; produced, with the poet George *Gascoigne, a blank-verse rendering of Euripides' *Phoenissae*, entitled *Jocasta*, 1566 (published, 1572); MP, Bossiney, Cornwall, 1572; contributed to the *Paradyse of Daynty Devises* (1576).

KIP, Johannes (1653–1722), draughtsman and engraver; born at Amsterdam; came to London shortly after 1686; employed in engraving portraits; most important work, *Britannia Illustrata*, a series of etchings from drawings by Leonard *Knyff, 1708, of little artistic merit, but great archaeological interest; published a *Prospect of the City of London* (1710, 2nd edn., 1726).

KIPLING, (Joseph) Rudyard (1865–1936), author; born in Bombay; cousin of Stanley Baldwin; out of schooldays at United Services College, Westward Ho!, later wove *Stalky and Co.* (1899); joined staff of Lahore *Civil and Military Gazette*, 1882; wrote especially of the imperial race doing justice and upholding law; became known through stories and verse, including *Departmental Ditties* (1886), *Plain Tales from the Hills*, *Soldiers Three*, and *Wee Willie Winkie* (1888); settled in London (1889) and made much of by the critics; travelled widely; eventually settled at Burwash (1902); published his novel *The Light That Failed* (1891), *Many Inventions* (1893), the two *Jungle Books* (1894–5), and *Captains Courageous* (1897); had now reached height of his fame; himself ranked *Just So Stories for Little Children* (1902) and 'Recessional' (1897) highest among his stories and poems respectively, thus choosing the two poles of family and Empire about which his genius turned; between *Barrack-Room Ballads* (1892) and *The Seven Seas* (1896) became exponent of an imperial ethic; the anti-imperialist reaction to South African War made him less universally popular; maintained his reputation with *Kim* (1901), *Puck of Pook's Hill* (1906), *Rewards and Fairies* (1910), and *A School History of England* (1911), publishing some of his most durable verse besides 'The Glory of the Garden' and 'If'; but his later style became over-mannered and obscure, and his authoritarian political faith unacceptable to many; awarded Nobel Prize for literature, 1907; refused the laureateship (1895) and the OM thrice.

KIPLING, Thomas (d. 1822), dean of Peterborough; fellow of St John's College, Cambridge, 1770; MA, 1771; Lady Margaret's preacher, 1782; DD, 1784; deputy regius professor of divinity, 1787; Boyle lecturer, 1792; promoted prosecution of the Revd William *Frend, 1792; dean of Peterborough, 1798–1802; principal work an edition of the *Codex Bezae* (1793).

KIPPING, Frederic Stanley (1863–1949), chemist; educated at Grammar School and Owens College, Manchester, and Munich (Ph.D.); assistant to W. H. *Perkin, Heriot-Watt College, Edinburgh, 1887–90; collaborated in *Organic Chemistry* (1894–5); chief chemistry demonstrator, Central Technical College, 1890–7; professor of chemistry, University College, Nottingham, 1897–1936; published many papers on organic compounds of silicon and stereochemistry of nitrogen; FRS, 1897.

KIPPING, Sir Norman Victor (1901–1979), director-general, Federation of British Industries; educated at University College School and Birkbeck College, London; junior engineer in General Post Office, 1920; worked in electrical engineering industry, becoming works manager of Standard Telephones & Cables, 1942; set up regional organization of Ministry of Production, 1942; under-secretary, Board of Trade, 1945; knighted, 1946; director-general, FBI, 1946–65; set up Anglo-American Council of Productivity, 1948; joint secretary, British Productivity Council, 1952; active in establishing other organizations for co-operation between government, trade unions, and management, including the National Production Advisory Council, the precursor of the National Economic Development Council; promoted series of British trade exhibitions abroad; active in Council of European Industrial Federations; led trade missions to countries abroad, including Nigeria, Japan, and India; co-author of merger which founded the Confederation of British Industry (CBI), 1965; vice-chairman, Fulton Committee on the Civil Service, 1966–8; KBE, 1962; GCMG, 1966; hon. fellow, British Institute of Management; hon. D.Sc., Loughborough, 1966; director, Joseph Lucas and Pilkingtons.

KIPPIS, Andrew (1725–1795), Nonconformist divine and biographer; classical and philological tutor, Coward Academy, Hoxton, 1763–84; DD, Edinburgh, 1767; FSA, 1778; FRS, 1779; tutor in new Dissenting college at Hackney, 1786; his chief literary work, the preparation of the second edition of the *Biographia Britannica* (five volumes published between 1778 and 1793, first part of a sixth volume printed, 1795); contributed to the *Gentleman's Magazine, Monthly Review*, and *New Annual Register*.

KIPPIST, Richard (1812–1882), botanist; helped to compile the *Tourist's Flora*; librarian of the Linnean Society, 1842–81; specialist in Australian plants.

KIRBY, Elizabeth (1823–1873), authoress, with her sister Mrs Gregg, of stories for children.

KIRBY, John (1690–1753), Suffolk topographer; published *The Suffolk Traveller*, a road book with antiquarian notices (1735, new edn., 1764; reprint, 1800; fourth edn., 1829); issued a *Map of the County of Suffolk* (1736, an improved edition published by his sons 1766); his portrait painted by *Gainsborough.

KIRBY, Joshua (1716–1774), clerk of the works at Kew Palace; eldest son of John *Kirby; coach-

and house-painter at Ipswich, 1738; published twelve drawings for projected history of Suffolk, 1748; lectured on linear perspective; published *Dr. Brook Taylor's Method of Perspective made easy* (1754, reissued, 1755, 1765, and 1768); teacher of perspective to the prince of Wales, afterwards George III; published *The Perspective of Architecture* (1761); secretary to the Incorporated Society of Artists; exhibited with them, 1765–70; president, 1768; portraits of him painted by *Gainsborough and *Hogarth.

KIRBY, Sarah (1741–1810), author. See TRIMMER.

KIRBY, William (1759–1850), entomologist; nephew of John Joshua *Kirby; educated at Caius College, Cambridge; BA, 1781; an original FLS, 1788; published monograph on bees (1802); founded new insect order of *Strepsiptera*, 1811; MA, 1815; his famous *Introduction to Entomology* published in conjunction with William *Spence (1815–26); FRS, 1818; hon. president of the Entomological Society, 1837, to which he bequeathed his collection of insects.

KIRBYE, George (d. 1634), musician; employed by Thomas *East to write new settings for his *Whole Book of Psalms* (1592); published *The First Set of English Madrigalls* (1597, new edn., ed. Arkwright, 1891–2).

KIRK. See also KIRKE.

KIRK, John (1724?–1778?), medallist; produced medals of moderate excellence, 1740–76; member of the Incorporated Society of Artists.

KIRK, John (1760–1851), Catholic divine and antiquary; admitted into the English College at Rome, 1773; priest, 1784; president of Sedgley Park School, 1793; chaplain and private secretary to Dr Charles *Berington, vicar-apostolic of the midland district, 1797; received DD from Pope Gregory XVI, 1841; prepared materials for a continuation of Dodd's *Church History of England*; finally handed work to the Revd Mark Aloysius *Tierney; published historical and theological works.

KIRK, Sir John (1832–1922), naturalist and administrator; MD, Edinburgh University; physician and naturalist to David *Livingstone on second Zambezi expedition, 1858–63; vice-consul, Zanzibar, 1866; assistant political agent, 1868; consul-general, 1873; political agent, 1880; persuaded sultan to abolish slave-trade, 1873; checkmated German designs on Zanzibar; was instrumental in persuading sultan to make great concessions of mainland territory to East African Association, 1887; FRS, 1887; KCMG, 1881.

KIRK, Sir John (1847–1922), philanthropist; entered service of Ragged School Union, 1867; secretary, 1879; knighted and styled director, 1907; largely responsible for survival of Union after 1870 and for increase in activities and annual income.

KIRK, Kenneth Escott (1886–1954), bishop of Oxford; educated at Royal Grammar School, Sheffield, and St John's College, Oxford; first class, Lit. Hum., 1908; deacon, 1912; priest, 1913; chaplain in France and Flanders, 1914–19; tutor, Keble College, Oxford, 1914–22; fellow and chaplain, Trinity, 1922–33; BD, 1922; DD, 1926; reader in moral theology, 1927–33; regius professor of moral and pastoral theology and canon of Christ Church, 1933–7; bishop of Oxford, 1937–54; reorganized administration of diocese and maintained close relationship with university; a leading Anglo-Catholic; publications include *The Vision of God* (1931) and *Commentary on the Epistle to the Romans* (1937); edited *The Study of Theology* (1939) and *The Apostolic Ministry* (1946); hon. fellow, St John's and Trinity colleges, Oxford.

KIRK, Norman Eric (1923–1974), prime minister of New Zealand; left school at age of 12 to find employment in number of odd jobs; joined the Labour party, 1943; elected mayor of Kaiapoi, near Christchurch, 1953; became MP for Lyttelton, 1957–69; vice-president of Labour party, 1963; president, 1964; leader of Parliamentary Labour party, 1965; re-elected, 1968; MP for Sydenham, 1969–74; called for greater New Zealand self-reliance, and led Labour party to sweeping victory, 1972; PC; sought to encourage regional co-operation in neighbouring Pacific and Asian areas; less effective in domestic policy.

KIRK, Robert (1641?–1692), Gaelic scholar; studied at Edinburgh University (MA, 1661) and St Andrews; made first complete translation of the Scottish metrical psalms into Gaelic, 1684; superintended printing of Bedell's Gaelic Bible in London, and added Gaelic vocabulary, 1690.

KIRK, Thomas (1765?–1797), painter and engraver; pupil of Richard *Cosway; painter of historical subjects and of miniatures; exhibited at Royal Academy, 1765–96.

KIRK, Thomas (1777–1845), sculptor; noted for his fine busts and work in relief on mantelpieces, monuments, etc.; member of the Royal Hibernian Academy, 1822; executed statue of *Nelson for memorial column, Dublin; his most important work, the statue of Sir Sidney *Smith at Greenwich Hospital.

KIRKALL, Elisha (1682?–1742), mezzotint engraver; introduced new method of chiaroscuro engraving, 1722.

KIRKBRIDE, Sir Alec Seath (1897–1978), diplomat; educated at Jesuit College in Egypt where he was taught in French and learnt Arabic; enlisted in Royal Engineers, 1916; met T. E. *Lawrence and fought with him; MC; chosen as one of six British officers temporarily administering Transjordan; junior assistant secretary, Palestine government, 1922; assistant secretary, 1926; assistant British resident, Amman, 1927; helped to demarcate Syria–Transjordan boundary; commissioner for Galilee, 1937–9; chief British representative, Transjordan, 1939; first British minister, 1946–51; first British minister, Libya, 1952; negotiated Anglo-Libyan treaty, 1953; ambassador, 1954; OBE, 1932; CMG, 1942; knighted, 1946; KCMG, 1949; CVO when Queen Elizabeth visited Libya in 1954; director, British Bank of the Middle East, 1956–72; published three books of memoirs, *A Crackle of Thorns* (1956), *An Awakening* (1972), and *From the Wings* (1976).

KIRKBY, John (d. 1290), bishop of Ely and treasurer; kept great seal in absence of chancellor, 1272, 1278–9, 1281–3; member of Royal Council, 1276; treasurer, 1284; bishop of Ely, 1286; described unfavourably by contemporary chroniclers.

KIRKBY, John (1705–1754), divine; BA, St John's College, Cambridge, 1726; tutor to Edward *Gibbon, who thought highly of him, 1744; MA, 1745; author of philosophical and theological works, and of a Latin and English grammar.

KIRKBY, John de (d. 1352), bishop of Carlisle; Augustinian canon at Carlisle and afterwards prior of the house; bishop of Carlisle, 1332.

KIRKBY, Richard (d. 1703), captain in the navy; lieutenant, 1689; went to West Indies, 1696; tried for embezzling, plunder, and cruelty, and acquitted, 1698; second-in-command in the West Indies, when he disobeyed his superior's signals to engage the French, 1701; court-martialled and shot.

KIRKCALDY (or KIRKALDY), Sir James (d. 1556), of Grange, lord high treasurer of Scotland; chief opponent of Cardinal *Beaton; mainly procured Beaton's assassination, 1546.

KIRKCALDY, Sir William (d. 1573), of Grange, eldest son of Sir James *Kirkcaldy; assisted in the murder of Cardinal Beaton, 1546; on accession of *Mary entered French service; took part in peace negotiations, 1559; supported the Protestants; opposed marriage of Mary to

*Darnley, 1565; privy to plot against *Riccio, 1566; hostile to *Bothwell, but after his escape joined the queen's party; held Edinburgh town and castle for Queen Mary, 1568–73, when he surrendered it and was executed; an inconsistent politician, but a man of chivalrous honour.

KIRKCUDBRIGHT, first Baron (d. 1639). See MACLELLAN, Sir ROBERT.

KIRKE. See also KIRK.

KIRKE, Edward (1553–1613), friend of Edmund *Spenser; entered Pembroke Hall, Cambridge, 1571; removed to Caius College; MA, 1578; wrote the preface, the arguments, and a verbal commentary to Spenser's *Shepheardes Calender*, under the initials 'E.K.', 1579. Modern critics have, on insufficient grounds, endeavoured to prove that 'E.K.' was Spenser himself.

KIRKE, George (d. 1675?), gentleman of the robes to Charles I and groom of the bedchamber, and keeper of Whitehall Palace to Charles II.

KIRKE, John (fl. 1638), dramatist; author of a popular tragicomedy of small literary merit, *The Seven Champions of Christendome* (published 1638).

KIRKE, Percy (1646?–1691), lieutenant-general, colonel of 'Kirke's Lambs'; son of George *Kirke; served under duke of Monmouth in France, 1673; under Turenne, Luxembourg, and de Creci, 1676–7; lieutenant-colonel, 1680; governor of Tangier, 1682–4; transferred to colonelcy of the old Tangier Regiment, the badge of which was a Paschal Lamb, whence the appellation 'Kirke's Lambs'; brigadier-general, 1685; present at Sedgmoor, 1685, and notorious for his cruelty to the rebels; major-general, 1688; relieved Derry, 1689; lieutenant-general, 1690; died at Brussels.

KIRKE, Percy (1684–1741), eldest son of Lieutenant-General Percy *Kirke, lieutenant-general and colonel of the 'Lambs', 1710–41; keeper of Whitehall Palace; taken prisoner at Almanza, 1708.

KIRKE, Thomas (1650–1706), virtuoso; distant relative and intimate friend of Ralph *Thoresby; formed a fine library and museum; published *A Modern Account of Scotland* (satire, 1679); the 'Journal' of the Scottish journey (made in 1677), printed in *Letters addressed to R. Thoresby*; FRS, 1693.

KIRKES, William Senhouse (1823–1864), physician; studied at St Bartholomew's Hospital, London; MD, Berlin, 1846; FRCP, London, 1855; demonstrator of morbid anatomy at St Bartholomew's, 1848, assistant physician, 1854, and physician, 1864; published (1848), with Sir James *Paget, *Handbook of Physiology*.

KIRKHAM, Walter de (d. 1260), bishop of Durham; of humble parentage; one of the royal clerks; bishop of Durham, 1241; took part in the excommunication of the violators of the charters, 1253.

KIRKHOVEN (or KERCKHOVEN), Catherine, Lady Stanhope and countess of Chesterfield (d. 1667), governess to *Mary, princess royal, daughter of Charles I; married Henry, Lord Stanhope (d. 1634), son and heir to Philip *Stanhope, first earl of Chesterfield, 1628; after refusing *Van Dyck, married John Polyander à Kerckhoven, lord of Heenvliet in Sassenheim, and one of the ambassadors from the States-General to negotiate the marriage between William of Orange and the princess royal, 1641; confidential adviser to the princess; privy to Royalist plots hatched on the continent; arrested in England, 1651; was acquitted and returned to Holland, 1652; created countess of Chesterfield for life, 1660; on the princess's death entered the service of the duchess of *York and married Daniel *O'Neill (d. 1664); lady of the bedchamber to the queen, 1663.

KIRKHOVEN, Charles Henry, first Baron Wotton and earl of Bellomont (d. 1683), son of Catherine *Kirkhoven and John Polyander à Kerckhoven, lord of Heenvliet; created Baron Wotton of Wotton in Kent, 1650; favourite of the princess royal; chief magistrate of Breda, 1659–74; created earl of Bellomont in peerage of Ireland, 1680.

KIRKLAND, Thomas (1722–1798), medical writer; MD, St Andrews, 1769; member of royal medical societies of Edinburgh and London; published medical treatises between 1754 and 1792.

KIRKMAN, Francis (*fl.* 1674), bookseller and author; printed *Catalogue of all the English Stage-playes* (1661, revised edn., 1671); issued *Webster and *Rowley's comedies, *A Cure for a Cuckold* (1661) and *The Thracian Wonder* (1661); a collection of drolls and farces, *The Wits, or Sport upon Sport* (1673); published translations from the French and romances.

KIRKMAN, Jacob (*fl.* 1800), musical composer; esteemed by contemporaries as pianist and composer of pianoforte works.

KIRKMAN, Sir Sidney Chevalier (1895–1982), general; educated at Bedford School and Royal Military Academy, Woolwich; commissioned into Royal Artillery, 1915; served on Western Front and in Italy, twice wounded; MC, 1918; between 1918 and 1939 served in Egypt, Palestine, Malta, and India; attended Staff College, Camberley, 1931–2; commanded 65th Medium Regiment RA (TA), 1940, and 56th division (brigadier), 1941; under General B. L. *Montgomery (later Viscount Montgomery of Alamein) artillery commander, XII Corps, South Eastern Command, and Eighth Army in Western Desert, 1942; brigadier, Royal Artillery 18th Army Group in Tunisia; commander 50th Northumbrian division, 1942–3; commander, XIII Corps, 1944–5, serving under American General Mark Clark; deputy chief, Imperial General Staff, 1945–7; general (1947); quartermaster-general, 1947–50; member of Army Council, 1945–50; special financial representative in Germany, 1951–2; director-general, Civil Defence, 1954–60; OBE, 1941; CBE, 1943; CB, 1944; KBE, 1945; KCB, 1949; GCB, 1951; Croix de Guerre and Legion of Honour; commander, American Legion of Merit; colonel commandant of Royal Artillery, 1947–57.

KIRKPATRICK, Sir Ivone Augustine (1897–1964), diplomat; educated at Downside; commissioned in Royal Inniskilling Fusiliers and served at Gallipoli and in Holland, 1914–18; entered Foreign Service, 1919; served in Western Department, 1920–30; in Rome, 1930–3; head of Chancery, Berlin, 1933–8; served under Sir Eric *Phipps and Sir Nevile *Henderson; foreign adviser to BBC, 1941; controller, European Services, 1941–4; identified Hess, after landing in Scotland, 1941; assistant under-secretary in charge of information work, Foreign Office, 1945–7; deputy under-secretary, 1947–9; permanent under-secretary of German section, 1949–50; worked closely with Ernest *Bevin; high commissioner, Germany, 1950–3; succeeded Sir William (later Lord) *Strang as permanent under-secretary, 1953–6; chairman, Independent Television Authority, 1957–62; CMG, 1939; KCMG, 1948; GCMG, 1953; KCB, 1951; GCB, 1956; published memoirs, *The Inner Circle* (1959), and *Mussolini, Study of a Demagogue* (1964).

KIRKPATRICK, James (d. 1743), Irish Presbyterian divine; educated at Glasgow University; one of the earliest members of the Belfast Society (founded, 1705); minister of the Presbyterian Congregation in Belfast, 1706; moderator of synod of Ulster, 1712; a leader of the non-subscribing party in the north of Ireland, 1720; subsequently MD; public sentiment in Ireland in the time of Queen Anne reflected in his *Historical Essay upon the Loyalty of Presbyterians in Great-Britain and Ireland from the Reformation to this Present Year, 1713*.

KIRKPATRICK, John (1686?–1728), antiquary; a Norwich linen-merchant; accumulated material for the history of Norwich, but his manuscripts never published, and now dispersed;

issued a large north-east prospect of Norwich, 1723.

KIRKPATRICK, William (1754–1812), orientalist; ensign, Bengal Infantry, 1773; lieutenant, 1777; Persian interpreter to the commander-in-chief in Bengal, 1777–9 and 1780–5; in Mysore War, 1790–1; resident with the nizam of Hyderabad, 1795; military secretary to Marquis *Wellesley; resident of Poona; translated Persian works; expert in oriental tongues and the manners, customs, and laws of India.

KIRKPATRICK, William Baillie (1802–1882), Irish Presbyterian divine; MA, Glasgow College; studied theology at the old Belfast College; moderator of the general assembly, 1850; published *Chapters in Irish History* (1875).

KIRKSTALL, Hugh of (*fl.* 1200), historian; received as Cistercian monk at Kirkstall, Yorkshire, between 1181 and 1191; his history of Fountains Abbey printed in *Dugdale's *Monasticon*.

KIRKTON, James (1620?–1699), Scottish divine and historian; MA, Edinburgh, 1647; deprived of his living, 1662; denounced as a rebel for holding conventicles, 1674; in Holland till proclamation of Toleration Act, 1687; minister of the Tolbooth parish, Edinburgh, 1691; published sermons, and left in manuscript 'The Secret and True History of the Church of Scotland from the Restoration to the Year 1678' (printed, 1817).

KIRKUP, Seymour Stocker (1788–1880), artist; admitted student of Royal Academy, 1809; acquainted with William *Blake (1757–1827) and Benjamin Robert *Haydon; present at funeral of *Keats at Rome, 1821, and of *Shelley, 1822; leader of a literary circle at Florence; died at Leghorn.

KIRKWOOD, David, first Baron Kirkwood (1872–1955), politician; trained as engineer on Clydeside; joined Amalgamated Society of Engineers at 20; prominent in union affairs at Parkhead Forge; opposed dilution of labour, increases in rents, etc.; deported to Edinburgh as trouble-maker, 1916–17; Labour MP, Dumbarton Burghs, 1922–50, East Dumbartonshire, 1950–1; the most vehement Clydesider in Parliament; twice suspended; in depression on Clydeside secured resumption of work on *Queen Mary*; PC, 1948; freedom of Clydebank and baron, 1951.

KIRKWOOD, James (1650?–1708), advocate of parochial libraries; MA, Edinburgh, 1670; deprived of living of Minto for refusing to take the test, 1685; migrated to England; rector of Astwick, Bedfordshire, 1685; ejected for not

abjuring, 1702; his tract, *An Overture for founding and maintaining Bibliothecks in every Paroch throughout the Kingdom* printed (1699).

KIRKWOOD, James (*fl.* 1698), Scottish teacher and grammarian; master of the school in Linlithgow burgh, 1675–90; his dismissal (1690) followed by litigation decided in his favour; published account of it (1711); master of Kelso School; again involved in difficulties, of which he published an account (1698); edited Despauter's Latin grammar for use in Scottish schools (1695; 2nd edn., 1700; 3rd, 1711; 4th, 1720).

KIRTON, Edmund (d. 1466), abbot of Westminster; monk of Westminster, 1403; BD, Gloucester Hall (Worcester College), Oxford; prior of the Benedictine scholars at Gloucester Hall, 1423; present at Council of Basle, 1437; abbot of Westminster, 1440–62; a famous orator.

KIRWAN, Francis (1589–1661), bishop of Killala; educated at Galway and Lisbon; ordained, 1614; consecrated bishop of Killala against his will at St Lazaire, 1645; took part in Irish struggles in Connaught; fled, 1652; surrendered, 1654; imprisoned, but (1655) allowed to retire to France; died at Rennes.

KIRWAN, Owen (d. 1803), Irish rebel; a tailor who joined *Emmet's conspiracy and was employed in the manufacture of ammunition; arrested, found guilty, and shot.

KIRWAN, Richard (1733–1812), chemist and natural philosopher; entered Jesuit novitiate at St Omer, 1754; called to the Irish bar, 1766; abandoned law to study science in London; FRS, 1780; Copley medallist, 1782; published *Elements of Mineralogy*, the first English systematic treatise on the subject (1784, 3rd edn., 1810); settled in Dublin, 1787; hon. LL D, Dublin University, 1794; president of Royal Irish Academy, 1799; the 'Nestor of English chemistry'.

KIRWAN, Stephen (d. 1602?), bishop of Clonfert; educated at Oxford and Paris; conformed to the Protestant religion; archdeacon of Annaghdown, 1558; first Protestant bishop of Kilmacduagh, 1573–82; bishop of Clonfert, 1582.

KIRWAN, Walter Blake (1754–1805), dean of Killala; educated at the Jesuit College at St Omer; studied at Louvain; professor of natural and moral philosophy at Louvain, 1777; chaplain to the Neapolitan ambassador at the British court, 1778; became a Protestant; dean of Killala, 1800.

KITCHENER, Horatio Herbert, first Earl Kitchener of Khartoum and of Broome (1850–1916), field marshal; educated at Royal Military Academy, Woolwich; received commission in Royal Engineers, 1871; lent to Palestine Exploration Fund, 1874; sent to survey Cyprus, 1878; second-in-command of Egyptian Cavalry, 1882; served in (Lord) *Wolseley's expedition for relief of General *Gordon, 1884–5; governor-general of Eastern Sudan, 1886; adjutant-general of Egyptian Army, 1888; contributed to defeat of dervishes at Toski, 1889; CB, 1889; sirdar of Egyptian Army, 1892; prepared army for conquest of Sudan, 1892–6; KCMG, 1894; major-general and KCB for services in River War, 1896; well-planned and well-executed campaign resulted in annihilation of Khalifa's army at Omdurman, with great loss of dervishes, and reoccupation of Khartoum, 1898; had interview at Fashoda on White Nile with Major Marchand, leader of small French expedition, resulting in its withdrawal, 1898; baron, 1898; governor-general of Sudan and completed its pacification, 1899; Lord *Roberts's chief of staff in South Africa, 1899; frequently employed as second-in-command and representative of commander-in-chief in his absence; ordered attack and directed preliminary operations at Paardeberg, Feb. 1900; suppressed rebellion of Cape Boers round Priska and cleared southern portion of Orange Free State; as commander-in-chief organized tactics against guerrilla warfare of Boers, Nov. 1900–May 1902; viscount and OM, 1902; commander-in-chief in India, 1902–9; prevailed with (Lord) *Morley, secretary of state for India, to abolish system of dual military control; initiated numerous reforms, including improvement of central administration, redistribution of troops, modernization of system of training, and establishment of Staff College for India; field marshal, 1909; British agent and consul-general in Egypt, 1911; kept Egypt quiet during period of unrest in Near East; earl, 1914; secretary of state for war, 1914; possessed first-hand knowledge of military resources of Empire but had little experience of organization of army at home or of working of War Office and Cabinet; envisaged long war; increased British Army from six regular and fourteen territorial divisions to seventy divisions, 3,000,000 men having voluntarily joined colours, 1914–16; KG, 1915; relations with colleagues in Cabinet sometimes strained; went to Near East and advised abandonment of Dardanelles enterprise, 1915; went down with HMS *Hampshire* off Orkneys on way to Russia.

KITCHIN, Anthony (1477–1566), alias Anthony Dunstan; bishop of Llandaff; a Benedictine monk of Westminster; of Gloucester Hall (now Worcester College), Oxford; BD, 1525; prior of his college, 1526; abbot of Eynsham, Oxford, 1530; surrendered his abbacy on disso-

lution of monasteries, and was appointed king's chaplain; bishop of Llandaff, 1545; was included by Queen Elizabeth in two commissions which she drew for the consecration of *Parker, but refused to act; called Dunstan up to his election as bishop.

KITCHIN, George William (1827–1912), dean of Winchester, 1883–94, and of Durham, 1894–1912; BA, Christ Church, Oxford; censor of Oxford non-collegiate students, 1868–83; wrote *History of France* (1873–7).

KITCHINER, William (1775?–1827), miscellaneous writer; educated at Eton; MD, Glasgow; devoted himself to science; published *Apicius Redivivus, or the Cook's Oracle* (1817, 7th edn., 1827); wrote also on optics and music.

KITCHINGMAN, John (1740?–1781), painter; exhibited at Royal Academy from 1770; painted, among other portraits, one of *Macklin as Shylock.

KITE, Charles (d. 1811), medical writer; author of essays on the 'recovery of the apparently dead' (1788), and on the *Submersion of Animals* (1795).

KITE, John (d. 1537), successively archbishop of Armagh and bishop of Carlisle; educated at Eton and King's College, Cambridge; prebendary of Exeter and sub-dean of the King's Chapel, Westminster, 1510; archbishop of Armagh, 1513–21; accompanied John *Bourchier, second Baron Berners, on embassy to Charles V, 1518; present at the Field of the Cloth of Gold, 1520; bishop of Carlisle, 1521–37; owed his preferments to *Wolsey's influence; renounced the pope's supremacy, 1534.

KITSON, James, first Baron Airedale (1835–1911), iron-master; placed (1854) in charge of father's Monkbridge ironworks, which became limited liability company, 1886; president of Iron and Steel Institute, 1889–91; first lord mayor of Leeds, 1896–7; benefactor to Leeds hospitals and art gallery; hon. D.Sc., 1904; honorary freeman, 1906; president of National Liberal Federation, 1883–90; MP for Colne Valley, 1892–1902; baronet, 1886; PC, 1906; baron, 1907.

KITSON CLARK, George Sidney Roberts (1900–1975), historian; educated at Shrewsbury School and Trinity College, Cambridge; first class, historical tripos, part ii, 1921; research fellow, 1922; college lecturer, 1928; university lecturer, 1929; college tutor, 1933; university reader in English constitutional history, 1954; helped establish New Hall, the third women's college at Cambridge; published *Peel and the Conservative Party: A Study in Party Politics 1832–41* (1929, 2nd edn., 1964); *Peel* (1936), *The Making of Vic-*

torian England (1962), *An Expanding Society, Britain 1830–1900* (1967), *Churchmen and the Condition of England 1832–1885* (1973), and also *The English Inheritance* (1950) and *The Kingdom of Free Men* (1957); Ford's lecturer, Oxford, 1959–60; Birkbeck lecturer, Cambridge, 1967; visiting lecturer at universities of Pennsylvania, 1953–4 and Melbourne, 1964; number of honorary degrees; hon. member of American Academy of Arts and Sciences.

KITTO, John (1804–1854), author of the *Pictorial Bible*; son of a Cornish stonemason; became deaf, 1817; sent to the workhouse, where he learnt shoemaking, 1819; apprenticed to a Plymouth shoemaker, 1821; entered missionary college, 1825; employed by the Church Missionary Society at Malta, 1827–9; with a private mission party in Persia, 1829–33; wrote for periodicals; at suggestion of Charles *Knight (1791–1873) wrote narratives illustrative of life of the deaf and blind, collected as *The Lost Senses* (1845), *Pictorial Bible* completed, 1838, and *Pictorial History of Palestine*, 1840; DD, Giessen, 1844; published *Cyclopaedia of Biblical Literature* (1845); FSA, 1845; edited *Journal of Sacred Literature*, 1848–53; his *Daily Bible Illustrations* published, 1849–54; died at Cannstadt.

KITTON, Frederick George (1856–1904), writer on *Dickens; began life as wood-engraver and etcher; publications include *Dickensiana* (a bibliography, 1886), *Dickens and his Illustrators* (1899), and *The Dickens Country* (1905); his Dickens library presented to Guildhall Library, 1908.

KLEIN, Melanie (1882–1960), psychoanalyst; born in Vienna of Jewish parentage; her marriage to A. S. Klein ended in divorce, 1923; began practise of analysis in Berlin, 1921; developed lay-technique for analysis of very young children; invited to London by Ernest *Jones, 1925, and settled there, 1926; naturalized, 1934; her application of Freudian techniques to child analysis aroused great controversy but influenced social attitudes to child care; publications include *The Psycho-Analysis of Children* (1932) and *Narrative of a Child Analysis* (1961).

KLITZ, Philip (1805–1854), pianist, violinist, and author; printed *Songs of the Mid-watch* (1838) and *Sketches of Life, Character, and Scenery in the New Forest* (1850).

KLOSE, Francis Joseph (1784–1830), musical composer; pianoforte-player and teacher; author of ballads and pianoforte pieces.

KLUGMANN, Norman John ('James') (1912–1977), leading British Communist; son of Jewish parents; educated at Gresham's School, Holt, and Trinity College, Cambridge, where he

was a scholar; first class in French, 1932 and in German, 1934; working for Communist party, 1934–5; secretary, World Student Association against War and Fascism in Paris, 1935–9; visited Balkans, Middle East, India, and China; led student delegation to meet Mao Tse-tung; conscripted into Royal Army Service Corps; transferred to Intelligence Corps; corporal in Cairo HQ of SOE, 1942; commissioned; useful work briefing Special Operations Executive (SOE) agents for Yugoslavia; with Unrra mission to Yugoslavia, 1945–6; head of Communist party education department in England, 1950–60; assistant editor to John *Gollan of *Marxism Today*, 1957; editor, 1963–77; confirmed Marxist; publications include *From Trotsky to Tito* (1951), *History of the Communist Party of Great Britain* (vol. i, 1968, vol. ii, 1969), *What Kind of a Revolution?* (in collaboration with Paul Oestreicher, 1968), and *A Reader's Guide to the Study of Marxism* (an undated pamphlet); edited *Dialogue of Christianity and Marxism* (1968).

KNAPP, John Leonard (1767–1845), botanist; FLS, 1796; FSA; published *Gramina Britannica, or Representations of the British Grasses* (1804, reissued, 1842); contributed to *Time's Telescope*, 1820–30 (reprinted as the *Journal of a Naturalist*, 1829).

KNAPP, William (1698–1768), musical composer; parish clerk of Poole, Dorset, for thirty-nine years; published *A Sett of New Psalm Tunes and Anthems* (1738, 7th edn., 1762); originator of the psalm-tune called 'Wareham'.

KNAPTON, Charles (1700–1760), brother of George *Knapton; assisted in production of volume of imitations of original drawings by old masters (published 1735).

KNAPTON, George (1698–1778), portrait painter; member of and first portrait painter to the Society of Dilettanti, 1750–63; surveyor and keeper of the king's pictures, 1765; a skilful painter of the formal school.

KNAPTON, Philip (1788–1833), musical composer; received his musical education at Cambridge; composer of works for orchestra, piano, and harp.

KNAPWELL, Richard (*fl.* 1286), Dominican. See CLAPWELL.

KNATCHBULL, Sir Edward, ninth baronet (1781–1849), statesman; succeeded to the baronetcy, 1819; MP, Kent, 1819–30 and 1832; opposed corn-law reform and Catholic emancipation; paymaster of the forces and privy councillor, 1834–45.

KNATCHBULL, Sir Norton, first baronet (1602–1685), scholar; BA, St John's College,

Cambridge, 1620; MP, Kent, 1639; knighted, 1641; sat in Long Parliament as a Loyalist, and made a baronet, 1641; published his critical *Animadversiones in Libros Novi Testamenti* (1659, 4th edn., in English, 1692); MP for New Romney, 1661.

KNATCHBULL-HUGESSEN, Edward Hugessen, first Baron Brabourne (1829–1893), son of Sir Edward *Knatchbull, ninth baronet; educated at Eton and Magdalen College, Oxford; MA, 1854; took additional surname of Hugessen, 1849; Liberal MP for Sandwich, 1857; lord of Treasury, 1859–60 and 1860–6; under-secretary for home affairs, 1860 and 1866; under-secretary for colonies, 1871–4; privy councillor, 1873; raised to peerage, 1880; adopted conservative views; published stories for children.

KNATCHBULL-HUGESSEN, Sir Hughe Montgomery (1886–1971), diplomat; educated at Eton and Balliol College, Oxford; entered Foreign Office, 1908; during 1914–18 war worked in Contraband Department; member of British delegation to Peace Conference, 1919; secretary to the legation, The Hague, 1919–23; head of chancery, Paris, 1924–5; counsellor of embassy, Brussels, 1926–30; minister to Estonia, Latvia, and Lithuania, 1930–4; minister, Tehran, 1934–6; succeeded Sir Alexander *Cadogan as ambassador, China, 1936–8; severely wounded by shots from Japanese aeroplane whilst travelling from Nanking to Shanghai and had to spend year recuperating; ambassador, Turkey, 1939–44; his task to counter the efforts of Franz von Papen, the German ambassador, to thwart understanding between Turkey and the Allies; (Sir) Winston Churchill visited Turkey, 1943, but Turks maintained cautious neutrality until 1945 when they declared war on Germany; ambassador's service in Ankara marred by the espionage of his Albanian valet ('Cicero'), who gained access to secret documents and passed information to the Germans; ambassador, Belgium, and minister to Luxemburg, 1944–7; published autobiography, *Diplomat in Peace and War* (1949) and *Kentish Family* (1960), a history of the Knatchbulls; CMG, 1920; KCMG, 1936; during last years, crippled by injury he had suffered in China.

KNELL —— (*fl.* 1586), actor; mentioned by *Nashe and *Heywood, and confused by *Collier with Thomas *Knell the younger.

KNELL, Paul (1615?–1664), divine; BA, Clare Hall, Cambridge, 1635; DD, Oxford, 1643; chaplain in the king's army; published sermons.

KNELL, Thomas, the younger (*fl.* 1560–1581), clergyman; son of Thomas *Knell (*fl.* 1570);

often confused with his father; author of theological treatises.

KNELL, Thomas (*fl.* 1570), divine and versewriter; chaplain to Walter *Devereux, first earl of Essex.

KNELL, William Adolphus (d. 1875), marine painter; exhibited (1826–66) at Royal Academy and British Institution; his *Landing of Prince Albert* purchased for the royal collection.

KNELLER, Sir Godfrey (KNILLER, Gottfried), first baronet (1646–1723), painter; born at Lübeck; studied under Ferdinand Bol at Amsterdam; came to England, 1675; painted portrait of Charles II, 1678; sent by Charles II to paint portrait of Louis XIV; principal painter to William III, and knighted, 1691; painted Peter the Great during his visit to England; his equestrian portrait of William III, one of his best-known works, painted, 1697; retained his dignities under Anne and George I; created baronet, 1715; his monument by *Rysbrack, with inscription by *Pope, erected in Westminster Abbey, 1729. Ten reigning sovereigns sat to Kneller, and almost all persons of importance in his day.

KNELLER (or KNILLER), John Zacharias (1644–1702), painter; brother of Sir Godfrey *Kneller, first baronet; born at Lübeck; travelled with his brother and settled with him in England; painted portraits and scenes containing architecture and ruins.

KNEVET. See also KNYVET and KNYVETT.

KNEVET, Ralph (1600–1671), poet; LL B, Peterhouse, Cambridge, 1624; probably rector of Lyng, Norfolk, 1652–71; published poems between 1628 and 1637.

KNEWSTUBS (or KNEWSTUB), John (1544–1624), divine; fellow, St John's College, Cambridge, 1567; MA, 1568; BD, 1576; preached against the teaching of the Family of Love sect; supporter of Puritan doctrines; took part in the Hampton Court Conference, 1604; published sermons and controversial works.

KNIBB, William (1803–1845), missionary and abolitionist; in printing business at Bristol; master of Baptist Missionary Society's free school at Kingston, Jamaica, 1824; undertook mission of Savannah la Mar, 1828; settled at Falmouth, near Montego Bay, 1830; visited England to advocate abolition of slavery and increased missionary activity, 1832–4, 1840, and 1845; died in Jamaica.

KNIGHT, Charles (1743–1827?), engraver; stated to have been a pupil of Francesco *Bartolozzi, but practised independently; his works often erroneously ascribed to *Bartolozzi.

KNIGHT, Charles (1791–1873), author and publisher; apprenticed to his father, a bookseller of Windsor, 1805; reported, 1812, for the *Globe* and *British Press*; started with his father the *Windsor and Eton Express*, 1812; produced, in conjunction with Edward Hawke *Locker, the *Plain Englishman*, 1820–2; editor and part proprietor of *The Guardian*, a literary and political weekly, 1820–2; publisher in London, 1823; projected a cheap series of books to condense the information contained in voluminous works; published for the Society for the Diffusion of Useful Knowledge; produced *Penny Magazine*, 1832–45, *Penny Cyclopaedia*, 1833–44; published *Pictorial History of England*, in parts, 1837–44; edited and published *Pictorial Shakespere*, 1838–41; began 'Weekly Volumes' series, 1844; began *Half Hours with the Best Authors* and *The Land we live in*, 1847; his *History of the Thirty Years' Peace*, completed by Harriet Martineau, published (1851), and *Passages of a Working Life*, autobiography (1864–5).

KNIGHT, Edward (1774–1826), actor; commonly known as 'Little Knight'; unequalled in the parts of pert footmen, cunning rustics, country boys, and decrepit old men.

KNIGHT, Ellis Cornelia (1757–1837), authoress; companion to Queen *Charlotte, 1805; companion to Princess *Charlotte, 1813–14; her autobiography (published, 1861) valuable as throwing light on court history; wrote romantic tales; published *A Description of Latium, or La Campagna di Roma* (1805); died in Paris.

KNIGHT, Francis (d. 1589), clergyman. See KETT.

KNIGHT, (George) Wilson (1897–1985), literary commentator; educated at Dulwich College, 1909–14; employed in insurance offices, 1914–18; served in Royal Engineers, 1916–20; at St Edmund Hall, Oxford, 1921–3; represented Oxford at chess; master at Hawtreys, Westgate on Sea, 1923–5; English master, Dean Close School, Cheltenham, 1925; Shakespeare studies began with *Myth and Miracle: an Essay on the Mystic Symbolism of Shakespeare* (1929), followed by *The Wheel of Fire: Essays in Interpretation of Shakespeare's Sombre Tragedies* (1936); appointed to Chancellor's chair of English, Trinity College, Toronto University, 1931; published *The Shakespearian Tempest* (1932), *Principles of Shakespearian Production* (1936), *The Crown of Life* (1947), and *The Sovereign Flower* (1958); also produced and acted in Shakespeare's plays; published works on other poets such as *The Starlit Dome* (1941) and published *The Christian Renaissance* (1933), *The Olive and the Sword* (1944), and *Hiroshima* (1946); returned to England, 1940; produced *This Sceptered Isle* in London, 1941; taught at Stowe, 1941–6; reader in English literature, Leeds University, 1946–62; professor, 1956; published further works on *Byron, *Pope, and modern poets; also published *Jackson Knight: a Biography* (1975), the story of his brother; CBE, 1968; hon. fellow, St Edmund Hall, 1965; hon. Litt.D., Sheffield, 1966, and Exeter, 1968.

KNIGHT, Gowin (1713–1772), man of science; first principal librarian of the British Museum; held demyship of Magdalen College, Oxford, 1735–46; MA, 1739; MB, 1742; FRS, 1747; Copley medallist, 1747; his improved compass adopted in Royal Navy, 1752; principal librarian, British Museum, 1756; his papers on magnetism collected and published (1758); rendered important, if unrecognized, services to navigation.

KNIGHT, Harold (1874–1961), painter; educated at Nottingham High School and Nottingham School of Art; won British Institute travelling scholarship, 1895; studied in Paris; exhibited at Royal Academy; married Laura Johnson, 1903, also a painter; careers closely connected. See KNIGHT, Dame LAURA.

KNIGHT, Henrietta, Lady Luxborough (d. 1756), friend of *Shenstone; half-sister of Henry *Saint-John, first Viscount Bolingbroke; married in 1727 Robert Knight of Barrells, Warwickshire, who was created Baron Luxborough in the Irish peerage in 1746; visited Shenstone at Leasowes; corresponded with him (correspondence published, 1775); friend also of the poet William *Somerville; wrote verses.

KNIGHT, Henry Gally (1786–1846), writer on architecture; great-grandson of Henry *Gally; of Eton and Trinity Hall, Cambridge; travelled in Europe, Egypt, and Palestine, 1810–11; his first publications, verses on Greek and oriental themes, 1816–30; MP, Aldborough, 1814–18, Malton, 1830, north Nottinghamshire, 1835 and 1837; works include *Architectural Tour in Normandy* (1836) and *The Ecclesiastical Architecture of Italy* (1842–4).

KNIGHT, James (d. 1719?), Arctic voyager and agent of the Hudson's Bay Company; governor of Fort Albany, 1693; governor of Nelson River settlement, 1714; established Prince of Wales's Fort at mouth of Churchill River, 1717 or 1718; perished in an expedition to discover gold in the far north.

KNIGHT, James (1793–1863), divine; son of Samuel *Knight (1759–1827); scholar of Lincoln College, Oxford, 1812–15; MA, 1817; perpetual curate of St Paul's, Sheffield, 1824 (resigned, 1860); published theological works.

KNIGHT, John (d. 1606), mariner; commanded Danish expedition to coast of Greenland, 1605; employed by East India merchants to discover the North-west Passage, 1606; went ashore after a gale at Labrador and was never again heard of.

KNIGHT, John (*fl.* 1670), mayor of Bristol, 1670; apparently no relation of his namesakes.

KNIGHT, Sir John, 'the elder' (1612–1683), mayor of Bristol; a provision merchant; member of Bristol Common Council till 1680; knighted, 1663; elected mayor, 1663; persecuted Nonconformists and Roman Catholics; MP, Bristol, 1661, 1678, and 1679.

KNIGHT, Sir John, 'the younger' (d. 1718), Jacobite; probably a kinsman of Sir John *Knight 'the elder'; sheriff of Bristol, 1681; zealous against Dissenters; knighted, 1682; mayor of Bristol, 1690; MP, Bristol, 1691; arrested as a suspected Jacobite, 1696; released, 1696.

KNIGHT, Sir John (1748?–1831), admiral; entered navy, 1758; lieutenant, 1770; taken prisoner and exchanged, 1776; sent to West Indies, 1780; took part in action off Martinique, 1781; captain, 1781; present at Camperdown, 1797, and blockade of Brest, 1799–1800; vice-admiral, 1805; admiral, 1813; KCB, 1815.

KNIGHT, John Baverstock (1785–1859), painter; exhibited at Royal Academy; published etchings of old buildings, 1816.

KNIGHT, John Prescott (1803–1881), portrait painter; son of Edward *Knight; student of Royal Academy, 1823; exhibited portraits of his father and Alfred *Bunn, 1824; ARA, 1836; professor of perspective, Royal Academy, 1839–60; exhibited *The Waterloo Banquet*, 1842; RA, 1844; secretary to the Academy, 1848–73; many of his works presentation portraits.

KNIGHT, Joseph (1829–1907), dramatic critic; joined father's business of cloth merchant at Leeds at 19; devoted to literature through life; embarked on journalistic career in London, 1860; dramatic critic of *Athenaeum* from 1867 till death; chief contributor of lives of actors and actresses to this Dictionary; editor of *Notes and Queries* from 1883 to 1907; his numerous literary friends and associates included John Westland *Marston and D. G. *Rossetti, whose life he wrote in 'Great Writers' series, 1887; FSA, 1893; a popular member of the Garrick Club from 1883.

KNIGHT, Joseph (1837–1909), landscape painter and engraver; lost right arm at seven; exhibited mainly Welsh subjects at Royal Academy and elsewhere; fellow of Society of Painter-Etchers, 1883.

KNIGHT, Joseph Philip (1812–1887), composer of songs; published set of six songs under name of 'Philip Mortimer', 1832; composed his famous song, 'Rocked in the cradle of the deep', 1839; took holy orders after 1841; was appointed to the charge of St Agnes, Scilly Isles; composed numerous songs, duets, and trios.

KNIGHT, Dame Laura (1877–1970), painter; educated at Brincliffe School, St Quentin, and Nottingham School of Art; married Harold *Knight, 1903; *A Cup of Tea* by Harold, and *Dutch Interior* by Laura, accepted by RA, 1906; settled at Newlyn, Cornwall; *Daughters of the Sun* exhibited at RA, 1909; moved to London, 1918; Harold now established as portrait painter; Laura worked on ballet scenes; ARA, 1927; introduced by (Sir) Alfred James *Munnings to Bertram *Mills; produced studies of circus scenes; *Charivari* exhibited at RA, 1929; Harold elected ARA, 1928; Laura, DBE, 1929; painted gipsies at Epsom and Ascot; Harold continued to paint fine portraits of celebrities; Laura elected RA, 1936 (first woman to become full member); Harold elected RA, 1937; Laura worked for War Artists' Advisory Committee during 1939–45 war; painted scenes at Nuremberg War Criminals' Trial, 1946; Harold died, 1961; Laura's work shown in retrospective exhibition, Royal Academy, 1965; Harold was ROI (Royal Institute of Oil Painters) and RP (Royal Society of Portrait Painters); his work represented in many public collections in England and abroad; Laura was honoured by many societies of artists, and her works exhibited in numerous galleries, including the Tate and National Portrait galleries; hon. LL D, St Andrews, 1931, hon. D.Litt., Nottingham, 1951; publications include *Oil Paint and Grease Paint* (1936) and *The Magic of a Line* (1965).

KNIGHT, Mary Anne (1776–1831), miniature painter; pupil of Andrew *Plimer; exhibited at Royal Academy from 1807.

KNIGHT, Richard Payne (1750–1824), numismatist; elder brother of Thomas Andrew *Knight; visited Sicily with the German painter, Philipp Hackert, 1777; his diary translated and published by Goethe in his biography of Hackert; began to form collection of bronzes, 1785; MP, Leominster, 1780, Ludlow, 1784–1806; wrote on ancient art; vice-president, Society of Antiquaries; bequeathed his magnificent collection to the British Museum.

KNIGHT, Samuel (1675–1746), biographer; educated at St Paul's School and Trinity College, Cambridge; MA, 1706; fellow and one of the founders of the Society of Antiquaries, 1717; DD, 1717; chaplain to George II, 1731; archdeacon of Berkshire, 1735; prebendary of Lincoln, 1742; published *Life of Dr. John Colet, Dean of St. Paul's* (1724, 2nd edn., 1823) and *Life of Erasmus* (1726).

KNIGHT, Samuel (1759–1827), vicar of Halifax; entered Magdalene College, Cambridge, 1779; BA and fellow, 1783; MA, 1786; published highly popular devotional manuals.

KNIGHT, Thomas (d. 1820), actor and dramatist; intended for the bar; studied elocution under the actor Charles *Macklin, and adopted the stage as profession; married Margaret Farren, sister of the countess of Derby (see FARREN, ELIZABETH), an actress, 1787; lessee and manager of Liverpool Theatre, 1803–20; wrote many pieces, the best being *Turnpike Gate* (farce, 1799); an admirable comic actor, with a repertory similar to that of Edward *Knight.

KNIGHT, Thomas Andrew (1759–1838), vegetable physiologist and horticulturist; brother of Richard Payne *Knight; entered Balliol College, Oxford, 1778; FRS, 1805; Copley medallist, 1806; FLS, 1807; president of the Horticultural Society, 1811–38; awarded first Knightian Medal founded in his honour, 1836; author of *A Treatise on the Culture of the Apple and Pear* (1797), *Pomona Herefordiensis* (1811); a selection of his papers published (1841).

KNIGHT, William (1476–1547), bishop of Bath and Wells; of Winchester School and New College, Oxford; fellow of New College, 1493; sent by Henry VIII on missions to Spain, Italy, and the Low Countries, 1512–1532; chaplain to Henry VIII, 1515; archdeacon of Chester, 1522, of Huntingdon, 1523; canon of Westminster, 1527; archdeacon of Richmond, 1529; bishop of Bath and Wells, 1541.

KNIGHT, William (*fl.* 1612), divine; fellow of Christ's College, Cambridge; MA, 1586; incorporated at Oxford, 1603; rector of Barley, afterwards of Little Gransden; published theological *Concordance Axiomatical* (1610).

KNIGHT, William (1786–1844), natural philosopher; MA, Aberdeen, 1802; professor of natural philosophy, Academical Institution, Belfast, 1816–22; LL D, 1817; published *Facts and Observations towards forming a new Theory of the Earth* (1818); professor, natural philosophy, Aberdeen, 1822–44.

KNIGHT, William Henry (1823–1863), painter; educated for the law, but abandoned it for painting; exhibited pictures of everyday life at the Royal Academy and the Society of British Artists.

KNIGHTBRIDGE, John (*c.*1620–1679), divine; BA, Wadham College, Oxford, 1642; trans-

lated to Peterhouse, Cambridge, and admitted fellow, 1645; DD, 1673; founded by will the Knightbridge professorship in moral theology at Cambridge.

KNIGHT-BRUCE, George Wyndham Hamilton (1852–1896), first bishop of Mashonaland. See BRUCE.

KNIGHT-BRUCE, Sir James Lewis (1791–1866). See BRUCE.

KNIGHTLEY, Sir Edmund (d. 1542), serjeant-at-law; uncle of Sir Richard *Knightley (1533–1615); one of the chief commissioners for the suppression of religious property.

KNIGHTLEY, Sir Richard (1533–1615), patron of Puritans; knighted, 1566; sheriff of Northamptonshire, 1568–9, 1581–2, and 1589; officially attended execution of *Mary Queen of Scots, 1589; MP, Northampton, 1584 and 1585, Northamptonshire, 1589 and 1598; the press at which the Martin Mar-Prelate tracts were printed concealed in his house, 1588; arraigned and released, 1589; fined by Star Chamber and deprived of lieutenancy of Northamptonshire and commission of the peace.

KNIGHTLEY, Richard (d. 1639), member of parliament; grandson of Sir Richard *Knightley (1533–1615); MP, Northamptonshire, 1621, 1624, and 1625; sheriff of Northamptonshire, 1626; refused to subscribe to the forced loan, 1627; acted with *Eliot and *Hampden in Commons, 1628.

KNIGHTLEY, Sir Richard (1617–1661), member of parliament; great-nephew of Sir Richard *Knightley (1533–1615); of Gray's Inn; married Elizabeth, eldest daughter of John *Hampden, *c.*1637; sat in Short Parliament for Northampton; in the Long Parliament, 1640, acted with the opposition; in Richard *Cromwell's parliament, 1659; a member of the council which arranged the recall of Charles II, 1660; KB, 1661.

KNIGHTON (or CNITTHON), Henry (*fl.* 1363), historical compiler; author of *Compilatio de eventibus Angliae* in four books from Edgar to 1366 (based on the seventh book of Cestrensis, i.e. *Higden, and Walter of *Hemingford). Books iii and iv may be original; a fifth book, clearly the work of another hand, is added in the manuscripts, carrying the history down to 1395.

KNIGHTON, Sir William, first baronet (1776–1836), keeper of the privy purse to George IV; studied medicine; assistant-surgeon at the Royal Naval Hospital, Plymouth; studied at Edinburgh, 1803–6; MD, Aberdeen; physician to George IV when prince of Wales, 1813; created baronet, 1812; materially assisted

George IV while prince on matters of business; private secretary to George IV and keeper of the privy purse, 1822; employed on confidential missions abroad, 1823–6; attended George IV during his last illness.

KNILL, Richard (1787–1857), Dissenting minister; volunteered for missionary work, and was in Madras, 1816–19; travelled through the United Kingdom to advocate the claims of foreign missions, 1833–41; published religious works.

KNIPE, Thomas (1638–1711), headmaster of Westminster School; educated at Westminster School and Christ Church, Oxford; MA, 1663; second master at Westminster, 1663; headmaster, 1695; prebendary of Westminster, 1707; compiled two grammars for Westminster scholars.

KNIPP (or KNEP), Mrs (*fl.* 1670), actress; intimate of *Pepys; probably made her début as Epicoene in *Jonson's *Silent Woman* 1664; acted in plays by Jacobean and Restoration dramatists.

KNIVET. See KNYVET.

KNOLLES. See also KNOLLYS and KNOWLES.

KNOLLES, Richard (1550?–1610), historian of the Turks; MA and fellow, Lincoln College, Oxford, 1570; his *Generall Historie of the Turkes* (valuable for its prose style, published, 1604; 2nd edn., 1610; 3rd, 1621; 4th, 1631; 5th, 1638; final and extended edition in three folio vols., 1687–1700).

KNOLLES, Thomas (d. 1537), president of Magdalen College, Oxford; a secular priest, educated at Magdalen College, Oxford; fellow, 1495; sub-dean of York, 1507–29; DD, 1518; president of Magdalen, 1527–35.

KNOLLYS, Charles, called fourth earl of Banbury (1662–1740), son of Nicholas *Knollys, called third earl of Banbury; twice unsuccessfully petitioned for a writ of summons; killed his brother-in-law in a duel, 1692; imprisoned, but subsequently set free in name of earl of Banbury.

KNOLLYS, Edward George William Tyrwhitt, second Viscount Knollys (1895–1966), business man and public servant; son of Francis *Knollys, first viscount; educated at Harrow and New College, Oxford; served in Army and Royal Flying Corps, 1914–18; DFC, MBE, and Croix de Guerre; succeeded his father, 1924; joined Barclays Bank, and worked in Cape Town, 1929–32; director, Employers' Liability Assurance Corporation, 1932; managing director, 1933; first chairman of joint company when Employers' merged with Northern, 1960; governor and commander-in-chief, Ber-

muda; KCMG, 1941–3; first full-time chairman, British Overseas Airways Corporation, 1943–7; represented Britain at International Materials Conference, Washington, 1951; GCMG, 1952; chairman, Vickers Ltd., 1956–62; chairman, English Steel Corporation, 1959–65; FRSA, 1962; chairman, RAF Benevolent Fund; trustee, Churchill College, Cambridge.

KNOLLYS, Sir Francis (1514?–1596), statesman; educated at Oxford; attended *Anne of Cleves on her arrival in England, 1539; MP, Horsham, 1542; knighted, 1547; favoured by Edward VI and Princess Elizabeth; withdrew to Germany on Mary's accession, 1553; privy councillor, 1558; vice-chamberlain of the household and captain of the halberdiers; MP, Arundel, 1559, Horsham, 1544, and Oxfordshire, 1562, 1572, 1584, 1586, 1588, and 1593; governor of Portsmouth, 1563; in charge of the fugitive Queen of Scots, 1568–9; treasurer of the royal household, 1572–96; supported the Puritans; KG, 1593.

KNOLLYS, Francis, first Viscount Knollys (1837–1924), private secretary to King Edward VII; son of General Sir W. T. *Knollys; educated at Royal Military College, Sandhurst; entered Civil Service; private secretary to prince of Wales (afterwards King Edward VII), 1870–1910; joint private secretary to King George V, 1910–13; baron, 1902; viscount, 1911; a strong Liberal; excelled in art of letter-writing.

KNOLLYS, Hanserd (1599?–1691), Particular Baptist divine; educated at Cambridge; became a Separatist and renounced his orders, 1636; fled to New England; returned to London, 1641; gathered a church of his own, 1645; held offices under *Cromwell; fled to Germany at the Restoration; returned to London and resumed his preaching; arrested under the second Conventicle Act, 1670; discharged; author of religious works, and of an autobiography (to 1672).

KNOLLYS, Nicholas, called third earl of Banbury (1631–1674), reputed son of William *Knollys, earl of Banbury, sat in House of Lords in Convention parliament, 1660; his right to sit as peer disputed, 1660; a bill declaring him illegitimate read, 1661, but never carried beyond the initial stage.

KNOLLYS (or KNOLLES), Sir Robert (d. 1407), military commander; knighted, 1351; served under *Henry of Lancaster, 1357; captured Bertrand du Guesclin, 1359; joined the Black Prince in his Spanish expedition, 1367; commander of an expedition to France, 1370; took part in the great expedition under Thomas, earl of Buckingham (see THOMAS OF WOODSTOCK, duke of Gloucester), 1380; active against

Wat *Tyler, 1381; amassed 'regal wealth' in the wars.

KNOLLYS, Robert (d. 1521), usher of the chamber to Henry VII and Henry VIII.

KNOLLYS, William, earl of Banbury (1547–1632), second but eldest surviving son of Sir Francis *Knollys; MP, Tregony, 1572, Oxfordshire, 1584, 1593, 1597, and 1601; accompanied expedition to Low Countries under *Leicester, 1586; knighted, 1586; colonel of foot regiments enrolled to assist the Armada, 1588; MA, Oxford, 1592; a comptroller of the royal household, 1596, and privy councillor, 1596; treasurer of the royal household, 1602; created Baron Knollys of Rotherfield Greys, 1603; commissioner of the Treasury and master of the court of wards, 1614; KG, 1615; promoted to viscountcy of Wallingford, 1616; took leading part in the Lords in the case of *Bacon, 1621; made earl of Banbury by Charles I, 1626; declined to collect ship money, 1628; left will making no mention of children.

KNOLLYS, William, called eighth earl of Banbury (1763–1834), general; lieutenant-governor of St John's, 1818; general, 1819; governor of Limerick; petitioned the crown for his writ as a peer, 1806; declared by the House of Lords, 1813, to be not entitled to the title of earl of Banbury.

KNOLLYS, Sir William Thomas (1797–1883), general; son of William *Knollys, called eighth earl of Banbury; held courtesy title of Viscount Wallingford until 1813; educated at Harrow and Sandhurst; received his first commission, 1813; despatched to the Peninsula; adjutant, 1821; lieutenant-colonel, 1844; regimental colonel, 1850; initiated Prince *Albert into the art of soldiering; major-general, 1854; governor of Guernsey, 1854; organizer of the newly formed camp at Aldershot, 1855; president of the council of military education, 1861; treasurer and comptroller of the household to the prince of Wales, 1862–77; hon. LL D, Oxford, 1862, and hon. LL D, Cambridge, 1864; KCB, 1867; privy councillor, 1871; gentleman usher of the black rod, 1877; published *Some Remarks on the claim to the Earldom of Banbury* (1835) and a translation of the Duc de Fezensac's *Journal of the Russian Campaign of 1812* (1852).

KNOTT, Edward (1582–1656), Jesuit; his real name Matthew Wilson; entered Society of Jesus, 1606; penitentiary in Rome, 1608; professed father, 1618; missioner in Suffolk district, 1625; imprisoned, 1629; released and banished, 1633; English provincial, 1643; author of controversial works.

KNOTT, Ralph (1878–1929), architect; entered office of Sir A. *Webb as draughtsman; won competition for design of new London County Hall on south side of river at Westminster, 1908; two-thirds of building completed and opened, 1922; one of the most successful public buildings of the time; FRIBA, 1921.

KNOWLER, William (1699–1773), divine; educated at St John's College, Cambridge; MA, 1724; LL D, 1728; published, at the request of Thomas Watson Wentworth, afterwards marquis of Rockingham, a selection from the papers of his great-grandfather, Thomas *Wentworth, first earl of Strafford, 1739.

KNOWLES. See also KNOLLYS.

KNOWLES, Sir Charles, first baronet (d. 1777), admiral; reputed son of Charles *Knollys, called fourth earl of Banbury; entered navy as captain's servant, 1718; rated as 'able seaman', 1723–6; lieutenant, 1730; commander, 1732; surveyor and engineer of the fleet against Cartagena, 1741; generally supposed author of *An Account of the Expedition to Carthagena* (1743); governor of Louisbourg, 1746; rear-admiral of the white, 1747; commander-in-chief at Jamaica, 1747; involved in difficulties with those under his command in an engagement off Havana; governor of Jamaica, 1752–6; vice-admiral, 1755; offended the government by his share in the miscarriage of the expedition against Rochefort, 1757; superseded from his command; admiral, 1760; created baronet and nominated rear-admiral of Great Britain, 1765; accepted command in the Russian Navy, 1770; translated De la Croix's *Abstract on the Mechanism of the Motions of Floating Bodies* (1775).

KNOWLES, Sir Charles Henry, second baronet (1754–1831), admiral; only surviving son of Sir Charles *Knowles; entered navy, 1768; lieutenant, 1776; succeeded to baronetcy, 1777; fought in action of St Lucia, 1778, off Grenada, 1779; captain, 1780; present at Battle of Cape St Vincent, 1797; vice-admiral, 1804; admiral, 1810; nominated an extra GCB, 1820; author of pamphlets on technical subjects.

KNOWLES, Dom David (1896–1974), monk and monastic historian. See KNOWLES, MICHAEL CLIVE.

KNOWLES, Sir Francis Gerald William, sixth baronet (1915–1974), biologist; educated at Radley and Oriel College, Oxford; BA, 1936; MA and D.Phil., 1939; awarded Oxford University Naples Scholarship and visited Stazione Zoologica, 1937–8, studying colour change in lampreys and crustaceans; senior biology master, Marlborough College, 1938–58; published *Man and Other Living Things* (1945) and *Biology and*

Man (1950); succeeded father as baronet, 1953; discovered neurosecretion using electron microscopy; lecturer in electron microscopy, department of anatomy, Birmingham University, 1958; reader, 1963; D.Sc., 1963; FRS, 1966; professor of comparative endocrinology, 1967; professor of anatomy, King's College, London, 1967–74; chairman, biological sciences committee, Science Research Council; organized international symposium on neurosecretion, 1973; purchased Avebury Manor, 1955.

KNOWLES, Gilbert (*fl.* 1723), botanist and poet; known only for his *Materia Medica Botanica* (1723).

KNOWLES, Herbert (1798–1817), poet; with *Southey's help, to whom he sent some poems, was elected a sizar at St John's College, Cambridge, 1817, but died a few weeks later. His reputation rests on 'The Three Tabernacles' (better known as 'Stanzas in Richmond Churchyard').

KNOWLES, James (1759–1840), lexicographer; headmaster of English department of Belfast Academical Institution, 1813–16; compiled *A Pronouncing and Explanatory Dictionary of the English Language* (1835).

KNOWLES, James Sheridan (1784–1862), dramatist; son of James *Knowles the lexicographer; tried the army, medicine, the stage, and schoolmastering; his tragedy of *Caius Gracchus* produced at Belfast (1815) and *Virginius* at Covent Garden (1820); his comedy, *The Hunchback* produced at Covent Garden (1832), *The Love Chase* (1837); continued to act till 1843; visited United States, 1834; published also verses, adaptations, novels, and lectures on oratory.

KNOWLES, Sir James Thomas (1831–1908), founder and editor of the *Nineteenth Century*, and architect; joined his father's office as architect; practised his profession for thirty years; designed 'Thatched House Club', St James's Street, 1865; laid out Leicester Square for Albert *Grant, 1874; published *The Story of King Arthur and his Knights* (1862) which attracted *Tennyson and led to a close intimacy with the poet; founded Metaphysical Society (1869) which lasted till 1881, and included leaders of all schools of thought; with Gladstone, who joined the society, Knowles's relations were as close as those with Tennyson; editor of *Contemporary Review* from 1870 to 1877, when he founded the highly successful *Nineteenth Century* with himself as editor; 'signed writing' by eminent persons was Knowles's main editorial principle; KCVO, 1903.

KNOWLES, John (1600?–1685), Nonconformist divine; educated at Magdalene College, Cambridge; fellow of Catharine Hall, Cambridge, 1627; went to New England, and was lecturer at Watertown, Massachusetts, 1639–49; lecturer in the cathedral at Bristol, 1650–60; his preaching made illegal by Act of Uniformity, 1662; given charge of a Presbyterian congregation at the Indulgence of 1672.

KNOWLES, John (*fl.* 1646–1668), anti-Trinitarian; adopted Arianism; joined Parliamentarian army, 1648; apprehended on charge of heresy, 1665; released, 1666; author of controversial pamphlets.

KNOWLES, John (1781–1841), biographer of Henry *Fuseli; chief clerk in the surveyor's department of the navy office, 1806–32; published naval works, an edition of Fuseli's *Lectures on Painting* (1830), and a *Life of Fuseli* (1831); FRS.

KNOWLES, Mrs Mary (1733–1807), Quakeress; née Morris; married Dr Thomas Knowles and travelled abroad; the authenticity of her account of a 'Dialogue between Dr. Johnson and Mrs. Knowles' respecting the conversion to Quakerism of Miss Jane Harry doubted by *Boswell, but established by Miss *Seward (printed in the *Gentleman's Magazine*, 1791).

KNOWLES, Michael Clive (in religion Dom **David)** (1896–1974), monk and monastic historian; educated at Downside and Christ's College, Cambridge, where he was a scholar and took firsts in both parts of the classical tripos, 1919–22; received into monastic community at Downside and became Benedictine monk, 1914; ordained deacon, 1921; priest, 1922; classics master at Downside; completed study of theology at Benedictine house of Sant' Anselmo, Rome, 1922–3; found teaching clashed with life of prayer; formed idea of setting up new community, 1933, but plan rejected at Rome, 1934; moved from Downside to Ealing Priory, 1933, but left community, 1939; cared for by devout Swedish doctor, Dr Elizabeth Kornerup, 1939–74; Litt.D., Cambridge, 1941; elected to teaching fellowship at Peterhouse, 1944–63; professor of medieval history, Cambridge, 1947; regius professor of modern history, 1954–63; publications include *The American Civil War* (1926), *The Monastic Order in England . . . 940–1216* (1940, 2nd edn., 1963), and *The Religious Orders in England* (3 vols., 1948–59); fellow, Royal Historical Society; president, 1956–60; fellow, Society of Antiquaries; FBA, 1947; hon. fellow, Christ's and Peterhouse; honorary doctorates from eight universities.

KNOWLES, Richard Brinsley (1820–1882), journalist; son of James Sheridan *Knowles; barrister, Middle Temple, 1843; produced *The Maiden Aunt* (comedy) at the Haymarket, 1845; converted to Roman Catholicism; became (1849) editor of the *Catholic Standard*, afterwards renamed the *Weekly Register*; edited the *Illustrated London Magazine*, 1853–5; on the staff of the *Standard*, 1857–60; published the *Chronicles of John of Oxenedes* in the Rolls Series (1859); engaged under the Royal Commission on Historical Manuscripts, 1871.

KNOWLES, Thomas (1723–1802), divine; educated at Pembroke Hall, Cambridge; MA, 1747; DD, 1753; prebendary of Ely, 1779; author of religious and controversial works.

KNOWLTON, Thomas (1692–1782), gardener and botanist; entered service of Richard *Boyle, third earl of Burlington, 1728; discoverer of the 'moor-ball', a species of fresh water algae of the conferva family.

KNOX, Alexander (1757–1831), theological writer; descended from the family to which John *Knox the reformer belonged; shown by his correspondence with Bishop *Jebb to have anticipated the Oxford Movement; advocated Catholic emancipation.

KNOX, Alexander Andrew (1818–1891), journalist and police magistrate; educated at Trinity College, Cambridge; BA and barrister, Lincoln's Inn, 1844; on staff of *The Times*, 1846–60; MA, 1847; police magistrate at Worship Street, 1860–2; at Marlborough Street, 1862–78.

KNOX, Andrew (1559–1633), bishop of Raphoe; educated at Glasgow University; MA, 1579; ordained, 1581; helped to frustrate the conspiracy of *Huntly, *Errol, and *Angus, 1592; bishop of the isles, 1600–19; bishop of Raphoe, 1610–33; privy councillor, 1612.

KNOX, Edmund Arbuthnott (1847–1937), bishop of Manchester; brother of Sir G. E. *Knox; first classes, Lit. Hum. (1868), law and modern history (1869), Corpus Christi College, Oxford; fellow (1868), tutor (1875–84) of Merton; ordained priest, 1872; suffragan bishop of Coventry, 1894–1903; bishop of Manchester, 1903–21; a leading evangelical and vigorous critic of Enabling Act (1919).

KNOX, Edmund George Valpy (1881–1971), writer and editor of *Punch*; eldest brother of Dillwyn Knox, Wilfred *Knox, and Ronald *Knox; educated at Rugby and Corpus Christi College, Oxford; taught at North Manchester Preparatory School; contributed to *Punch* under pseudonym 'Evoe'; joined Territorials, 1914; commissioned in Lincolnshire Regiment, 1914; wounded in

France, 1917; worked at Ministry of Labour, 1919–20; joined regular staff of *Punch*, 1921; succeeded Sir Owen *Seaman as editor, 1932; hon. MA, Oxford, 1943; Leslie Stephen lecturer at Cambridge, 1951; wrote number of books and edited an anthology of humorous verse.

KNOX, Sir Geoffrey George (1884–1958), diplomat; born in New South Wales; educated at Malvern College; for the Levant service studied at Trinity College, Cambridge; served in Persia, Egypt, and Salonika; transferred to Diplomatic Service, 1920; served in Berlin, Constantinople, and Madrid; chairman, International Saar Governing Commission, 1932–5; minister to Hungary, 1935–9; ambassador to Brazil, 1939–42; CMG, 1929; KCMG, 1935.

KNOX, Sir George Edward (1845–1922), Indian civil servant; born at Madras; entered Indian Civil Service, 1864; posted to Meerut, 1867; judge of small causes court, Allahabad, 1877; legal remembrancer to local government of North-Western Provinces and Oudh, 1885; judge of High Court of Judicature, Allahabad, 1890; knighted, 1906; died at Naini Tal; his legal and linguistic equipment (Urdu, Sanskrit, Arabic, Persian) outstanding.

KNOX, Isa (1831–1903), poetical writer; born Craig; early contributed to *Scotsman* under name of 'Isa'; married cousin, John Knox, an iron-merchant, 1866; won prize for Burns centenary poem at Crystal Palace, 1858; published verse and fiction.

KNOX, John (1505–1572), Scottish reformer and historian; educated at Haddington School; at Glasgow University, 1522; notary in Haddington and the neighbourhood, 1540–3; called to the ministry and began preaching for the reformed religion, 1547; taken prisoner at capitulation of the castle of St Andrews and sent to France, 1548; released, 1549; appointed a royal chaplain, 1551; fled to Dieppe at accession of Mary Tudor, 1553; met Calvin at Geneva, 1554; pastor of the English congregation at Frankfurt-on-Maine, 1554–5; at Geneva, 1556–8; published six tracts dealing with the controversy in Scotland, one of them the *Blast of the Trumpet against the monstrous regiment of Women* (1558), a work that gave great offence to Queen Elizabeth and permanently affected her attitude to the Scottish Reformation; published *Treatise on Predestination* (1560); had first interview with *Mary Stuart, 1561; issued the Book of Common Order (service-book), 1564; obtained confirmation of Presbyterian reformation in Scottish parliament, 1567; appointed minister at Edinburgh, 1572, where he died; his influence as guiding spirit of the Reformation in Scotland largely due to his power as an orator; his *History of the Reformation of Religioun within the realme of Scotland* first printed (1586–7; best edition in the first two volumes of Laing's edition of Knox's *Works*, 1846–8; new edition by W. C. Dickinson, 1949).

KNOX, John (1555?–1623), Scottish Presbyterian divine; kinsman and adherent of John *Knox (1505–1572); MA, St Andrews, 1575; leader of the resistance to the re-establishment of episcopacy, 1617.

KNOX, John (*fl.* 1621–1654), Scottish divine; said to have been son of John *Knox (1555?–1623); member of the assembly, 1638; minister of Bowden, 1621–54.

KNOX, John (d. 1688), Presbyterian divine; grandson of John *Knox (1555?–1623); MA, Edinburgh, 1641; joined Royalist army; ordained, 1653; deprived of his charge in consequence of his adherence to Presbyterianism, 1662; indulged, 1672; convicted of offences and imprisoned, 1684–5.

KNOX, John (1720–1790), Scottish philanthropist; bookseller in London; improved the fisheries and manufactures of Scotland, 1764–90; published works on Scottish fisheries.

KNOX, Robert (1640?–1720), writer on Ceylon; went to Fort George, 1657; on homeward voyage made prisoner at Ceylon, 1659; escaped, 1679; in the service of the East India Company, 1680–94; published *An Historical Relation of the Island of Ceylon in the East Indies*, the first account of Ceylon in the English language (1681).

KNOX, Robert (1791–1862), anatomist and ethnologist; educated at Edinburgh High School; MD, Edinburgh, 1814; assistant-surgeon in the army, 1815–32; made scientific researches at the Cape, 1817–20; conservator of the museum of comparative anatomy and pathology, Edinburgh College of Surgeons, 1825–31; anatomical lecturer at Edinburgh, 1826; unpopular after 1836 for heterodoxy and for procuring from the 'resurrectionists' his 'subjects' for dissection; fellow of the London Ethnological Society, 1860; hon. curator of its museum, 1862; distinguished anatomical teacher; author of medical works.

KNOX, Robert (1815–1883), Irish Presbyterian divine; MA, Glasgow, 1837; established and edited the *Irish Presbyterian* and published many sermons; founder of the Sabbath School Society for Ireland, and of the Presbyterian Alliance.

KNOX, Robert Bent (1808–1893), archbishop of Armagh; ordained, 1832; MA, Trinity College, Dublin, 1834; chancellor of Ardfert, 1834; prebendary of Limerick, 1841; bishop of Down, Connor, and Dromore, 1849; DD, 1858; archbishop of Armagh, 1886–93; hon. LL D, Cambridge, 1889; chief work, *Ecclesiastical Index* (of Ireland, 1839).

KNOX, Ronald Arbuthnott (1888–1957), Roman Catholic priest and translator of the Bible; son of Revd E. A. *Knox; scholar of Eton and Balliol College, Oxford; Hertford, Ireland, and Craven scholar; president of Union, 1909; first class, Lit. Hum., 1910; deacon, 1911; priest, 1912; fellow (1910), chaplain (1912), Trinity College, Oxford; became Roman Catholic, 1917; ordained, 1919; taught at Ware, 1918–26; Catholic chaplain, Oxford, 1926–39; thereafter undertook translation of Bible, completed in 1955; maintained literary output ranging from detective stories to apologetics; publications include *Absolute and Abithofhell* (1913), *A Spiritual Aeneid* (1918), *Let Dons Delight* (1939), *Enthusiasm* (1950); appointed monsignor, 1936, protonotary apostolic, 1951; member of Pontifical Academy, 1956; hon. fellow of Trinity (1941), Balliol (1953); Romanes lecturer, 1957.

KNOX, Thomas Francis (1822–1882), superior of the London Oratory; educated at Trinity College, Cambridge; BA, 1845; entered the Roman Catholic church, 1845; helped to found the London Oratory, 1849; became its superior; created DD by Pius IX, 1875; published religious and historical works.

KNOX, Sir Thomas George (1824–1887), consul-general in Siam; grandson of William *Knox (1762–1831); ensign, 1840; lieutenant, 1842; interpreter at Bangkok consulate, 1857; acting consul, 1859–60; consul, 1864; consul-general in Siam, 1868; agent and consul-general, 1875–9; KCMG, 1880.

KNOX, Vicesimus (1752–1821), miscellaneous writer; entered St John's College, Oxford, 1771; BA and fellow, 1775; ordained, 1777; published *Essays Moral and Literary* (1778); master of Tunbridge School, 1778–1812; MA, 1779; DD, Philadelphia; remembered as the compiler of the *Elegant Extracts* (1789).

KNOX, Wilfred Lawrence (1886–1950), biblical scholar and divine; son of E. A. *Knox; first class, Lit. Hum., Trinity College, Oxford, 1909; ordained, 1913/14; warden, Oratory House, Cambridge, 1924–40; chaplain (1940), fellow (1946), Pembroke College; studied Hellenistic influence on New Testament writers; FBA, 1948.

KNOX, William (1732–1810), official and controversialist; provost-marshal of Georgia, 1757–61; agent in Great Britain for Georgia and East Florida; dismissed on account of pamphlets written to defend Stamp Act, 1765; under-secretary of state for America, 1770–82; published pamphlets on colonial matters.

KNOX, William (1762–1831), bishop of Derry; entered Trinity College, Dublin, 1778; BA, 1781; chaplain to the Irish House of Commons; bishop of Killaloe, 1794–1803; bishop of Derry, 1803–31; published sermons.

KNOX, William (1789–1825), Scottish poet; became a journalist, 1820; befriended by *Scott and *Wilson; published poems between 1818 and 1825, complete edition (1847).

KNOX-LITTLE, William John (1839–1918), divine and preacher; born in Co. Tyrone; BA, Trinity College, Cambridge; rector of St Alban's, Cheetwood, Manchester, 1875–85; canon of Worcester, 1881; vicar of Hoar Cross, Staffordshire, 1885–1907; enjoyed great popularity as extempore preacher, especially at missions; High Churchman; published sermons and other works.

KNUTSFORD, Viscounts. See HOLLAND, Sir HENRY THURSTAN, first viscount, 1825–1914; HOLLAND, Sir SYDNEY GEORGE, second viscount, 1855–1931.

KNYFF, Leonard (1650–1721), painter; born at Haarlem; settled in London, 1690; devoted himself to topographical drawing and painting; known principally by his series of bird's-eye views of palaces and gentlemen's seats in Great Britain.

KNYVET (or KNEVET), Sir Edmund (d. 1546), sergeant-porter to Henry VIII; younger brother of Sir Thomas *Knyvet; sergeant of the king's gates, 1524; keeper of the king's woods in Rockingham Forest, 1536.

KNYVET (or KNIVETT), Sir John (d. 1381), chancellor of England; serjeant-at-law, 1357; justice of the court of common pleas, 1361; chief justice of the King's Bench, 1365; chancellor, 1372–7.

KNYVET, Sir Thomas (d. 1512), officer in the navy; brother of Sir Edmund *Knyvet; knighted, 1509; master of the horse, 1510; killed in an engagement with the French.

KNYVET, Thomas, Baron Knyvet of Escrick (d. 1622), grandnephew of Sir Edmund *Knyvet; sergeant-porter to Henry VIII; educated at Jesus College, Cambridge; gentleman of the privy chamber to Queen Elizabeth; created MA on her visit to Oxford, 1592; MP, Westminster, 1586, 1588, 1597, 1601, and 1603; knighted, before Sept. 1601; as justice of the peace for Westminster discovered Guy *Fawkes plot, 1605; privy councillor, member of the council of Queen *Anne, and warden of the Mint; created Baron Knyvet of Escrick, 1607.

KNYVETT, Charles (1752–1822), musician; member of the Royal Society of Musicians from 1778; one of the chief singers at the *Handel commemoration, 1784; directed series of oratorio performances at Covent Garden, 1789; established Willis's Rooms concerts, 1791; organist of the Chapel Royal, 1796.

KNYVETT, Charles (1773–1852), musician; eldest son of Charles *Knyvett (1752–1822); educated at Westminster School; organist of St George's, Hanover Square; edited a *Collection of Favourite Glees* (1800); published harmonized airs.

KNYVETT, William (1779–1856), musical composer; third son of Charles *Knyvett (1752–1822); gentleman of the Chapel Royal, 1797; composer of the Chapel Royal, 1802; a fashionable singer in London; conductor of the Concerts of Antient Music, 1832–40; conductor of the Birmingham festivals, 1834–43; of the York Festival, 1835; author of popular vocal works, and of the anthems for the coronations of George IV and Queen Victoria.

KOEHLER, George Frederic (d. 1800), brigadier-general, captain of Royal Artillery; of German birth; second lieutenant in Royal Artillery during siege of Gibraltar, 1780; first lieutenant, 1782; invented a gun-carriage; member of the staff of George Augustus *Eliott, Baron Heathfield; employed in Belgium against the Austrians, 1790; captain-lieutenant, 1793; brevet lieutenant-colonel, 1794; captain, 1796; on service in Egypt, 1798; died at Jaffa.

KOESTLER, Arthur (1905–1983), writer; born in Budapest; educated at Vienna Polytechnic High School and University; in Palestine, Middle East correspondent of Ullstein newspaper chain, 1926; science editor, *Vossische Zeitung*, in Berlin, 1930; joined Communist party and travelled widely in Russia; anti-Nazi exile in Paris; in Spain reporting for *News Chronicle*, 1936–7; captured and imprisoned by Franco's troops; published *Spanish Testament* (1937); left Communist party, 1938; published *The Gladiators* (1939), *Darkness at Noon* (1940), and *Scum of the Earth* (1941); escaped to England and served in Pioneer Corps, 1941–2; naturalized, 1948; interested in parapsychology and published *The Sleepwalkers* (1959), *The Act of Creation* (1964), and *The Case of the Midwife Toad* (1971); left £500,000 to endow chair of parapsychology at Edinburgh University; CBE, 1972; C.Lit., 1974; hon. LL D, Queen's University, Kingston, Ontario, 1968; hon. D.Litt., Leeds, 1977; published autobiographical *Arrow in the Blue* (1952) and *The Invisible Writing* (1954).

KOKOSCHKA, Oskar (1886–1980), painter and author; born in Austria; studied at School of Arts and Crafts, Vienna, 1905–9; early portraits, known as X-ray images, made his reputation; published *Die träumenden Knaben* (The Dreaming Youths), 1908, and wrote first expressionist play, *Mörder, Hoffnung der Frauen* (Murderer, Hope of Woman), 1908–9; other titles include *Hiob* (Job), 1911, and *Der gefesselte Kolumbus* (The Fettered Columbus), 1913; assistant teacher at School of Arts and Crafts, Vienna, 1911, but forced to resign by adverse public opinion; served in Austrian army during 1914–18 war and severely wounded; continued to paint important works; appointed professor at Dresden Art Academy, 1919–23; travelled widely and came to be considered foremost portrait and landscape painter of Europe, 1924–34; painted portrait of president of Czechoslovakia, T. G. Masaryk; all paintings in German museums confiscated and declared degenerate, 1937; fled to London, 1938; acquired British citizenship, 1947; exhibited at Venice Biennale, 1948; exhibited in Germany, Austria, Spain, Greece, Yugoslavia, USA, and Japan, 1950–80; taught at Summer Academy, Salzburg, 1953–63; illustrated Homer's *Odyssey*, Aristophanes' *The Frogs*, and Euripides' *Trojan Women*, 1961–80; created designs for the theatre, including *The Magic Flute* at Salzburg (1955) and Verdi's *Ballo in Maschera* in Florence (1963); painted many portraits of prominent people; published *Schriften* (4 vols., 1973–6) and autobiography, *Mein Leben* (1971, published in English, 1974); CBE, 1959; received other international honours; hon. RA, 1970; hon. D.Litt., Oxford, 1963.

KOLLMAN, August Friedrich Christoph (1756–1829), organist and composer; born at Engelbostel near Hanover; chapel-keeper and schoolmaster at the German Chapel, St James's Palace, London, 1784; author of pianoforte compositions and works on the theory of music.

KOMISARJEVSKY, Theodore (1882–1954), theatrical producer and designer; born in Venice; educated at military academy and Imperial Institute of Architecture, St Petersburg; founded school of acting in Moscow, 1910; became theatrical producer; came to England, 1919; naturalized, 1932; produced widely for societies in the lead of theatrical taste, in a manner unorthodox, provocative, sometimes brilliant, sometimes wayward; brilliant designer of own sets and costumes; required new depth of feeling and understanding from his actors; greatly influenced methods of direction, acting, setting, and lighting.

KOMPFNER, Rudolf (1909–1977), engineer and scientist; born of Jewish parents in Vienna; educated at Technische Hochschule zu Wien; emigrated to London, 1934; managing director of building firm of Roy Franey, 1936–41; studied physics in Patent Office library; first patent, a television-camera tube accepted, 1937; interned as enemy alien, 1940; released after six months and employed by physics department, Birmingham University; invented the travelling-wave tube, 1942; moved to Clarendon Laboratory, Oxford (member of The Queen's College), 1944–51; became British subject, 1947; D.Phil., 1951; principal scientific officer, Admiralty; joined Bell Laboratories as associate director, communication science (systems) research, 1951; became US citizen, 1957; outstanding director of scientific and engineering enterprises; influential in programmes for maser amplifier, superconducting magnets, lasers, and optical communications; his team designed first communication satellite, Echo, 1960, and its successor, Telstar; director of new Crawford Hill Laboratory where much of technology of optical communication was developed; retired from Bell Laboratories, 1973; worked as research professor of applied physics, Stanford, California, and research professor of engineering science, Oxford; fellow of All Souls; received large number of scientific and academic awards in USA and honorary doctorates from Oxford, 1969 and Vienna, 1965.

KONIG (or KÖNIG), Charles Dietrich Eberhard (1774–1851), mineralogist; born in Brunswick; educated at Göttingen; keeper of department of natural history in British Museum, 1813; subsequently keeper of the mineralogical department.

KORDA, Sir Alexander (1893–1956), film producer; born in Hungary; became film director; moved to Vienna, 1919, Berlin, 1923, Hollywood, 1926, Paris, 1930; settled in London, 1931; formed London Film Productions, 1932; completed Denham Studios, 1937, and later studios at Shepperton; films include *The Ghost Goes West* (1935), *The Scarlet Pimpernel* (1935), *Elephant Boy* (1936–7), *The Third Man* (1949), *The Wooden Horse* (1950); naturalized, 1936; knighted, 1942.

KOTZÉ, Sir John Gilbert (1849–1940), South African judge; born at Cape Town; called to bar (Inner Temple), 1874; judge, High Court, Transvaal, 1877–81; chief justice, South African Republic, 1881–98; contested presidency, 1893; in 1897 caused constitutional crisis by reversing his decision (1884) that supreme power was vested in the Volksraad which was not subject to the jurisdiction of the Supreme Court; dismissed, 1898; attorney-general of Southern Rhodesia, 1900; KC, 1902; judge president, Cape eastern districts court, Grahamstown, 1904–13; judge, Cape provincial division, Supreme Court, Cape Town, 1913–20; judge president thereof, 1920–2; judge of appeal, 1922–7; knighted, 1917.

KOTZWARA (or **KOCSWARA**), **Franz** (1750?–1791), musician; born in Prague; assisted in *Handel commemoration, 1784; composer of the popular sonata *Battle of Prague*, for piano, violin, and violoncello; hanged himself accidentally.

KRABTREE. See CRABTREE.

KRATZER, Nicholas (1487–1550?), mathematician; born at Munich; studied at Cologne and Wittemberg; fellow of Corpus Christi College, Oxford, 1517; MA, 1523; skilled constructor of sundials; friend of Erasmus and Hans *Holbein, who painted his portrait, 1528; left in manuscript 'Canones Horopti' and 'De Compositione Horologiorum'.

KRAUSE, William Henry (1796–1852), Irish divine; born in the West Indies; entered the army, 1814; present at Waterloo, 1815; entered Trinity College, Dublin; a noted Evangelical clergyman of Dublin.

KREBS, Sir **Hans Adolf** (1900–1981), biochemist; born at Hildesheim, Germany; educated at Göttingen, Freiburg, and Munich universities; began research in biochemistry, 1925–30; appointed to clinical work at Freiburg, 1931; continued research, and elucidated the process of the formation of urea in the liver; published information which was recognized as milestone in biochemistry, 1932; dismissed from Freiburg as a Jew, 1933; invited to Cambridge by Sir Frederick Gowland *Hopkins; Rockefeller research student, 1933–4; university lecturer in pharmacology, Sheffield, 1935–8; naturalized British subject, 1939; lecturer in biochemistry, Sheffield, 1938–45; professor, 1945–54; FRS, 1947; shared Nobel Prize for medicine, 1953; Whitley professor of biochemistry, Oxford, 1954–67; fellow, Trinity College; received numerous academic honours; knighted, 1958; published more than one hundred papers, 1954–67, and *Reminiscences and Reflections* (1981).

KRONBERGER, Hans (1920–1970), leader in the physics and engineering of nuclear reactors; born in Linz, Austria, of Jewish parents; escaped from Austria, and studied mechanical engineering at King's College, Newcastle; interned, 1940–2; returned to King's College; honours degree in physics, 1944; Ph.D., Birmingham, 1948; joined (Sir) F. E. *Simon's team in 'Tube Alloys' project, 1946; worked with Heinz *London at new atomic-energy establishment, Harwell; research manager, components development laboratory at uranium diffusion plant, Capenhurst, 1951; head of development laboratories, 1953; chief physicist, research and development branch, Industrial Group of Atomic

Energy Authority, 1956; director, 1958; scientist-in-chief, Reactor Group; member, Atomic Energy Authority, 1969; OBE, 1957; CBE, 1966; FRS, 1965.

KRUGER GRAY, George Edward (1880–1943), designer. See GRAY.

KÜCHEMANN, Dietrich (1911–1976), aerodynamicist; born in Göttingen, Germany; educated at the Oberrealschule, Göttingen and Göttingen University, where he studied theoretical aerodynamics; joined the Aerodynamische Versuchsanstalt, Göttingen, 1936; began study of aerodynamics of aircraft propulsion, in collaboration with Dr Johanna Weber, 1940; joined Royal Aircraft Establishment, Farnborough, with Dr Weber, 1946; given permanent appointment, 1951; naturalized, 1953; promoted through grades of scientific officer, 1954–66; head of aerodynamics department, 1966–71; published *Aerodynamics of Propulsion* (with Dr Weber, 1953) and *The Aerodynamic Design of Aircraft* (1978); a gifted cellist; FRS, 1963; CBE, 1964; awarded number of medals and honorary doctorates; visiting professor, department of aeronautics, Imperial College, London, 1972.

KUCZYNSKI, Robert Rene (1876–1947), demographer; born and educated in Germany; director, Statistical Office, Berlin-Schoenberg, 1906–21; research fellow (1933), reader (1938–41), in demography, London School of Economics; adviser to Colonial Office, 1944–7; naturalized, 1946; works include *Fertility and Reproduction* (1932), *Colonial Population* (1937), and *Demographic Survey of the British Colonial Empire* (3 vols., 1948–53).

KUERDEN, Richard (1623–1690?), antiquary. See JACKSON.

KUPER, Sir **Augustus Leopold** (1809–1885), admiral; entered the navy, 1823; lieutenant, 1830; assisted his father-in-law, Captain Sir James John Gordon *Bremer, in forming settlement of Port Essington in North Australia, 1837; commander, 1839; employed in Chinese War, 1840–1; rear-admiral, 1861; commander-in-chief in China, 1862; KCB, 1864; admiral, 1872.

KURZ, Sulpiz (1833?–1878), botanist; born in Munich; entered Dutch service in Java; curator of Calcutta herbarium; explored Burma, Pegu, and the Andaman Islands; published *Forest Flora of Burmah* (1877); died at Penang.

KYAN, Esmond (d. 1798), Irish rebel; commanded rebel artillery at Battle of Arklow, 1798; arrested and executed.

KYAN, John Howard (1774–1850), inventor of the 'Kyanising' process for preserving wood; began experiments to prevent decay of wood,

1812; patented his invention, 1832; his process superseded, c.1835; died at New York.

KYD, Robert (1746–1793), founder of the Botanical Gardens, Calcutta; obtained cadetship, 1764; lieutenant, Bengal Infantry, 1765; major, 1780; lieutenant-colonel, 1782; secretary to Military Department of Inspection, Bengal; laid out Botanical Garden, near Calcutta, 1786; died at Calcutta.

KYD, Stewart (d. 1811), politician and legal writer; educated at King's College, Aberdeen; barrister, Middle Temple, London; friend of Thomas *Hardy (1752–1832); arrested for high treason and discharged, 1794; defended the publisher of *Paine's *Age of Reason*, 1797; wrote legal treatises.

KYD (or KID), Thomas (1557?–1595?), dramatist; educated at Merchant Taylors' School, London; originally a scrivener; *Spanish Tragedy* printed (1594); his *First Part of Ieronimo* published (1605); his *Cornelia* licensed for publication, 1594; often credited with *The rare Triumphs of Love and Fortune* (acted 1582) and *The Tragedye of Solyman and Perseda* (printed 1599); perhaps the author of a pre-Shakespearian play (now lost) on the subject of Hamlet; one of the best-known tragic poets of his time.

KYDERMYNSTER. See KEDERMYNSTER.

KYFFIN, Maurice (d. 1599), poet and translator; published *The Blessednes of Brytaine, or a Celebration of the Queenes Holyday*, a poetical eulogy on the government of Elizabeth (1587; 2nd edn., 1588); translated in prose the *Andria* of Terence (1588); issued his Welsh translation of Bishop *Jewel's *Apologia pro Ecclesia Anglicana* (1594 or 1595).

KYLE, James Francis (1788–1869), Scottish Catholic prelate; ordained, 1812; DD; bishop of Germanicia *in partibus*, and vicar-apostolic of the northern district of Scotland, 1827; collected documents for history of Catholicism in Scotland.

KYLMINGTON (or KYLMETON), Richard (d. 1361), dean of St Paul's and theologian; educated at Oxford; DD before 1339; archdeacon of London, 1348–50; dean of St Paul's, 1353–61.

KYLSANT, Baron (1863–1937), shipowner and financier. See PHILIPPS, OWEN COSBY.

KYME, titular earls of. See UMFRAVILLE, GILBERT DE, 1390–1421; TALBOYS or TAILBOYS, Sir WILLIAM, d. 1464.

KYMER, Gilbert (d. 1463), dean of Salisbury and chancellor of the University of Oxford; educated at Oxford; proctor, 1412–13; principal of Hart Hall, Oxford, 1412–14; dean of Wimborne Minster, 1427; chancellor of Oxford University, 1431–4 and 1447–53; dean of Salisbury, 1449; physician in household of *Humphrey, duke of Gloucester; attended Henry VI, 1455; wrote *Diaetarium de Sanitatis Custodia*.

KYNASTON, Edward (1640?–1706), actor; first appeared at the Cockpit, Drury Lane, 1659; played Epicoene in the *Silent Woman*, 1661; his first important male part, Peregrine in the *Fox*, 1665; played Cassio in *Othello*, 1682; acted with *Betterton, 1682–99; one of the last male actors of female parts.

KYNASTON (or KINASTON), Sir Francis (1587–1642), poet and scholar; entered Oriel College, Oxford, 1601; BA, 1604; MA Oxford, 1611; barrister, Lincoln's Inn, 1611; knighted, 1618; MP, Shropshire, 1621–2; the centre of a brilliant literary coterie at court; founded an academy of learning called the Musaeum Minervae, 1635; published poems and translations.

KYNASTON, Herbert (1809–1878), high master of St Paul's School; educated at Westminster School; entered Christ Church, Oxford, 1827; MA, 1833; ordained, 1834; tutor and Greek reader of his college, 1836; high master of St Paul's School, London, 1838–76; DD, 1849; well known as a schoolmaster and writer and translator of hymns.

KYNASTON (formerly SNOW), Herbert (1835–1910), classical scholar; educated at Eton and St John's College, Cambridge; first Porson scholar and senior classic, 1857; fellow, 1858; MA, 1860; DD, 1882; rowed in university boat, 1856 and 1857; member of Alpine Club; principal of Cheltenham College, 1874–88; canon of Durham and professor of Greek in the University, 1889; edited Theocritus (1869) and *Poetae Graeci* (1879).

KYNASTON, John (1728–1783), author; fellow of Brasenose College, Oxford, 1751; MA, 1752; author of controversial pamphlets; contributor to the *Gentleman's Magazine*.

KYNDER, Philip (*fl.* 1665), miscellaneous writer; educated at Pembroke Hall, Cambridge; BA, 1616; agent for court affairs, 1640–3; published *The Surfeit. To A. B. C.* (1656); many of his works preserved in manuscript in the Bodleian.

KYNEWULF (*fl.* 750). See CYNEWULF.

KYNGESBURY (or KYNBURY), Thomas (*fl.* 1390), Franciscan and DD of Oxford; twenty-sixth provincial minister of English Minorites, 1380–90; encouraged study of science.

KYNNESMAN, Arthur (1682–1770), schoolmaster; entered Trinity College, Cambridge, 1702; MA, 1709; master of Bury St Edmunds

Grammar School, 1715–65; published *A Short Introduction to Grammar* (1768).

KYNSIGE (KINSIUS, KINSI, or **CYNESIGE)** (d. 1060), archbishop of York; monk of Peterborough; a chaplain of *Edward the Confessor; archbishop of York, 1051–60.

KYNTON, John (d. 1536), divinity professor at Oxford; Franciscan friar; DD, 1500; vice-chancellor and *Senior Theologus*, Oxford, at intervals between 1503 and 1513; one of the four doctors of divinity to consult with *Wolsey about the Lutheran doctrines, 1521; Margaret professor of theology (resigned, 1530).

KYNWELMARSH, Francis (d. 1580), poet. See KINWELMERSH.

KYNYNGHAM (or CUNNINGHAM), John (d. 1399), Carmelite; studied at Oxford; twenty-first provincial of his order, 1393; vigorously opposed *Wycliffe.

KYRLE, John (1637–1724), the Man of Ross; educated at the Ross Grammar School and Balliol College, Oxford; student of the Middle Temple, 1657; lived very simply on his estates at Ross; devoted his surplus income to works of charity; eulogized by *Pope, 1732. The Kyrle Society was inaugurated in 1877 as a memorial of him.

KYRTON, Edmund (d. 1466), abbot of Westminster. See KIRTON.

KYTE, Francis (*fl.* 1710–1745), mezzotint engraver and portrait painter; published mezzotint engravings after *Kneller; subsequently devoted himself to portrait painting.

KYTE, John (d. 1537), archbishop of Armagh and bishop of Carlisle. See KITE.

KYTELER, Dame Alice (*fl.* 1324), reputed witch of Kilkenny. See KETTLE.

KYTSON, Sir Thomas (1485–1540), sheriff of London; master of the Mercers' Company, 1535; engaged in extensive mercantile transactions; member of Merchant Adventurers' Company; sheriff of London, 1533; knighted, 1533.

L

LABELYE, Charles (1705–1781?), architect of the first Westminster Bridge; born at Vevey; came to England, c.1725; employed in building Westminster Bridge, 1738–50; naturalized, 1746; published *A Description of Westminster Bridge* (1751); died at Paris.

LABLACHE, Fanny Wyndham (d. 1877), vocalist; née Wilton; wife of Frederick *Lablache; died at Paris.

LABLACHE, Frederick (1815–1887), vocalist; eldest son of Luigi *Lablache; appeared in London in Italian opera, c.1837; sang at Manchester with Mario, Grisi, and Jenny *Lind; withdrew from the stage and devoted himself to teaching, c.1865.

LABLACHE, Luigi (1794–1858), vocalist; born at Naples; sang the solos in Mozart's Requiem on the death of Haydn, 1809; engaged at the San Carlo Theatre, Naples, 1812; at La Scala, Milan, 1817; in London, 1830; a magnificent bass singer and an excellent actor; taught singing to Queen Victoria; died at Naples; buried at Paris.

LABOUCHERE, Henrietta (1841–1910), actress. See HODSON.

LABOUCHERE, Henry, first Baron Taunton (1798–1869); educated at Winchester; BA, Christ Church, Oxford, 1821; Liberal MP, Michael Borough, 1826; MA, 1828; MP, Taunton, 1830; a lord of the Admiralty, 1832; master of the Mint, privy councillor, and vice-president of the Board of Trade, 1835; under-secretary of war and the colonies, Feb. 1839; president of the Board of Trade and admitted to Lord *Melbourne's Cabinet, Aug. 1839–41; again president of the Board of Trade under Lord John *Russell, 1847–52; secretary of state for the colonies under Lord *Palmerston, 1855–8; raised to peerage, 1859; some of his speeches published separately.

LABOUCHERE, Henry Du Pré (1831–1912), journalist and politician; nephew of Henry Labouchere, first Baron *Taunton; educated at Eton and Trinity College, Cambridge; in Diplomatic Service, 1854–64; wrote for *Daily News* and *World*, and established reputation as journalist; founded weekly journal *Truth*, notable for its exposure of fraudulent enterprises, 1876; Liberal MP, Northampton, with Charles *Bradlaugh as his colleague, 1880; held seat till 1906; became one of the most powerful radicals in Commons; attacked home and foreign policy of Whigs, and worked for reorganization of Liberal party; designs frustrated by decision of Joseph *Chamberlain to vote against first Home Rule Bill, 1886; died near Florence.

LACAITA, Sir James Philip (1813–1895), Italian scholar and politician; born at Manduria, Italy; graduated in law at Naples; advocate, 1836; legal adviser to British legation, Naples; assisted Gladstone to collect information about Bourbon misrule, 1850; came to London, 1852; professor of Italian, Queen's College, London, 1853–6; naturalized in England, 1855; secretary to Gladstone's mission to Ionian Islands, 1858; KCMG, 1859; deputy to first Italian legislature, 1861–5; senator, 1876; completed Lord *Vernon's edition of Dante, 1865.

LACEY, Thomas Alexander (1853–1931), ecclesiologist and controversialist; second class, Lit. Hum., Balliol College, Oxford, 1875; ordained, 1876; an accomplished Latinist; with E. Denny composed *Dissertatio Apologetica de Hierarchia Anglicana* (1895); attended commission of inquiry into validity of Anglican orders (1896); on staff of *Church Times*; chaplain (1903), warden (1910–19), London diocesan penitentiary, Highgate; canon of Worcester, 1918–31.

LACEY, William (1584–1673), Jesuit; his real name Wolfe; entered Magdalen College, Oxford, 1600; BA, 1666; became a Roman Catholic; admitted to the English College, Rome, 1608; missioner in England, 1625–73; published controversial pamphlets.

LACHMANN, Gustav Victor (1896–1966), aeronautical engineer; born of Austrian parents at Dresden; educated at the Realgymnasium, Darmstadt; served in German army and air force during 1914–18 war; studied mechanical engineering and aerodynamics, Darmstadt Technical University, 1918–21; became doctor of engineering, Aachen Technical University, for thesis on the slotted wing, 1923; designer, Schneider Aircraft Works, Berlin, 1924; chief designer, Albatross Aircraft Works, Johannisthal, 1925–6; technical adviser, Ishikawajima Aircraft Works, Tokyo, 1926–9; engineer in charge of aerodynamics, Handley Page Ltd., England, 1929–32; chief designer, 1932–6; during 1939–45 war undertook non-military aircraft-design studies; naturalized, 1949; head of Handley Page Research Department, 1953–65; fellow, Royal Aeronautical Society, 1938; publications include *Leichtflugzenbau* (Munich, 1925) and *Boundary Layer and Flow Control* (1961).

LACHTAIN (LAICHTIN, LACHTNAIN, LACHTOC, or MOLACHTOC) (d. 622), Irish saint; claimed descent from a king of Ireland in the second century; a disciple of *Comgall, of Beannchair; founded two churches in Ireland; his day, 19 Mar.

LACK, David Lambert (1910–1973), ornithologist; educated at Gresham's School, Holt, and Magdalene College, Cambridge; schoolmaster, Dartington Hall, 1933–40; visited Tanganyika, 1934 and Kenya, 1935; in Galapagos Islands studying Darwin's finches, 1938–9; published *The Life of the Robin* (1943), and *Darwin's Finches* (1947, reprinted 1983); joined Army Operational Research Group and worked on radar research, 1940–5; director, Edward Grey Institute of Field Ornithology, Oxford, 1945–73; fellow of Trinity College, 1963; did research on robins, tits, and swifts; published *The Natural Regulation of Animal Numbers* (1954); also devout Christian and wrote *Evolutionary Theory and Christian Belief* (1957); Sc.D., 1948; FRS, 1951; president, International Ornithological Congress, 1966; awarded Darwin Medal of Royal Society, 1972.

LACKINGTON, George (1768–1844), bookseller; entered the bookselling business of his relative, James *Lackington, 1779, and became its head, 1798; official assignee of bankrupts.

LACKINGTON, James (1746–1815), bookseller; his shop in Finsbury Square known as the 'Temple of the Muses' and one of the sights of London; published his *Memoirs* (1791), his *Confessions* (1804).

LA CLOCHE, James (*fl.* 1668), natural son of Charles II; born in Jersey; his mother's name unknown; brought up as a Protestant in France and Holland; entered novitiate of Jesuits at Rome; employed by Charles II as a means of secret communication with Rome, 1668.

LACROIX, Alphonse François (1799–1859), missionary; born in the canton of Neuchâtel; became a missionary; agent of the Netherlands Missionary Society at Chinsurah, near Calcutta; transferred his services to the London Missionary Society and became a British subject; removed to Calcutta, 1827; learned Bengali and preached with great success; revised the Bengali scriptures; trained native preachers.

LACY, Edmund (1370?–1455), bishop of Exeter; DD, Oxford; master of University College, Oxford, 1398; prebendary of Hereford, 1412, and of Lincoln, 1414; dean of Chapel Royal under Henry V; bishop of Hereford, 1417, and of Exeter, 1420–55.

LACY, Frances Dalton (1819–1872), actress; first appeared in London at the Haymarket, 1838; joined Madame *Vestris's company at Covent Garden, 1840; married the actor Thomas Hailes *Lacy, 1842.

LACY, Francis Antony (1731–1792), Spanish general and diplomat; of Irish birth; commenced his military career in the Spanish service, 1747; commanded Spanish Artillery at siege of Gibraltar; Spanish minister plenipotentiary at Stockholm and St Petersburg; commandant-general of coast of Grenada; member of Supreme Council of War and commandant-general and sole inspector-general of Artillery and of all ordnance-manufacturing establishments in Spain and the Indies; governor and captain-general of Catalonia, 1789.

LACY, Gilbert de, fourth Baron Lacy (*fl.* 1150), grandson of Walter de *Lacy, first Baron Lacy; supported the Empress *Matilda, 1138, but joined Stephen before 1146; joined the Knights of the Temple and went to the Holy Land; preceptor of his order in the county of Tripoli.

LACY, Harriette Deborah (1807–1874), actress; née Taylor; made her début as Julia in the *Rivals*, 1827; joined *Macready's company and married Walter *Lacy, 1838; among her best performances were Nell *Gwyn in *Jerrold's play and Ophelia; retired from the stage, 1848.

LACY, Henry de, third earl of Lincoln of the Lacy family (1251–1311), grandson of John de *Lacy, first earl of Lincoln; succeeded his father, 1258; knighted, 1272; commanded division in Welsh War, 1276; joint lieutenant of England in Edward I's absence, 1279; accompanied Edward I to Gascony, 1286–9; assisted in the deliberations respecting Scottish succession, 1291 and 1292; in command of the army in France, 1296–8; accompanied Edward I to Scotland and was present at his death, 1307; one of the lords ordainers and guardian of the kingdom in Edward II's absence, 1310.

LACY, Hugh de, fifth Baron Lacy by tenure and first lord of Meath (d. 1186), one of the conquerors of Ireland; doubtless the son of Gilbert de *Lacy, fourth Baron Lacy; went to Ireland with Henry II, 1171; procurator-general of Ireland, 1177–81 and 1185–6; accused of aspiring to the crown of Ireland; assassinated, 1186.

LACY, Hugh de, first earl of Ulster (d. 1242?), earliest Anglo-Norman peer of Ireland; second son of Hugh de *Lacy, fifth Baron Lacy (d. 1186); took part in the fighting in Ireland; created earl of Ulster, 1205; fled to Scotland, and thence to France, 1210; returned to England, 1221; joined *Llywelyn ab Iorwerth in Wales; engaged again in warfare in Ireland.

LACY, John (d. 1681), dramatist and comedian; attached to Charles II's (*Killigrew's) company of actors; his acting commended by *Pepys and Evelyn; his best play, *The Old Troop, or Monsieur Raggou*, written before 1665 (printed 1672); the original Bayes of the *Rehearsal*, 1671.

LACY, John (*fl.* 1737), pseudo-prophet; camisard; published *The Prophetical Warnings of John Lacy* (1707); claimed the power of working miracles; committed to Bridewell, 1737.

LACY, John de (d. 1190), crusader; son of Richard FitzEustace, constable of Chester; assumed cousin's name as heir to the Lacy estates; died at Tyre.

LACY, John de, first earl of Lincoln of the Lacy family (d. 1240), son of Roger de *Lacy; one of the twenty-five barons appointed to see to the maintenance of the Great Charter, 1215; crusader, 1218; created earl of Lincoln, 1232; one of the witnesses of the confirmation of the charters, 1236.

LACY (or DE LACY), Maurice (1740–1820), of Grodno; Russian general; born at Limerick; of the family of Peter *Lacy, Count Lacy; attained general's rank in Russian Army; held command under Suwarrow in campaigns against the French in Switzerland and Italy; governor of Grodno.

LACY, Michael Rophino (1795–1867), violinist and composer; born at Bilbao; studied violin at Paris and in England, 1805; an actor of 'genteel comedy parts', 1808–18; composed balletmusic for Italian opera, London, 1820–3; adapted foreign libretti; composed an oratorio (1833) and minor pieces.

LACY, Peter, Count Lacy (1678–1751), Russian field marshal; entered Russian service, 1697; fought against Danes, Swedes, and Turks, 1705–21; commander-in-chief at St Petersburg and other places, 1725; aided in establishing Augustus of Saxony on the throne of Poland, 1733–5; field marshal, 1736; called by Frederick the Great the 'Prince Eugene of Muscovy'.

LACY, Roger de (d. 1212), justiciar and constable of Chester; son of John de *Lacy (d. 1190); nephew of William de *Mandeville, earl of Essex; constable of Chester, 1190; justiciar, 1209.

LACY, Thomas Hailes (1809–1873), actor and theatrical publisher; first appeared on the London stage, 1828; with *Phelps at Sadler's Wells, 1844–9; theatrical bookseller, 1849; published acting editions of 1,485 dramas between 1848 and 1873; author of several plays.

LACY, Walter (1809–1898), actor; his real name Williams; first appeared on stage in Edinburgh, 1829; played Charles Surface at Haymarket, London, 1838; with Charles *Kean at Princess's, 1852. His parts included Edmund (*Lear*), Benedick, Comus, Faulconbridge, Malvolio, Touchstone, Henry VIII, and Ghost (*Hamlet*).

LACY, Walter de, first Baron Lacy by tenure (d. 1085), said to have fought for the Conqueror at Hastings, 1066.

LACY, Walter de, sixth Baron Lacy by tenure, and second lord of Meath (d. 1241), elder son of Hugh de *Lacy, fifth Baron Lacy (d. 1186); elder brother of Hugh de *Lacy, first earl of Ulster; took part in John's expedition to France, 1214; sheriff of Herefordshire, 1216–23; one of the chief supporters of the young king Henry III.

LACY, William (1610?–1671), Royalist divine; educated at St John's College, Cambridge; MA and fellow, 1636; BD, 1642; associated with John *Barwick (1612–1664) in writing *Certain Disquisitions* against the Covenant; ejected from his fellowship, 1650; became chaplain to Prince *Rupert; taken prisoner, 1645; restored to his fellowship, 1660; DD, 1662.

LACY, William (1788–1871), bass-singer; appeared at concerts in London, 1798–1810; in Calcutta, 1818–25.

LADBROOKE, Henry (1800–1870), landscape painter; second son of Robert *Ladbrooke, landscape painter; acquired reputation for his moonlight scenes; exhibited at various institutions.

LADBROOKE, John Berney (1803–1879), landscape painter; third son of Robert *Ladbrooke, landscape painter; a pupil of John *Crome, whose manner he followed; exhibited at the Royal Academy, 1821–2, at the British Institution and the Suffolk Street Gallery up to 1873.

LADBROOKE, Robert (1768–1842), landscape painter; worked with John *Crome; took a leading part in the establishment of the celebrated Norwich Society of Artists, 1803; vice-president, 1808; exhibitor at Royal Academy between 1804 and 1815; painted chiefly Norfolk scenery.

LADYMAN, Samuel (1625–1684), divine; fellow, Corpus Christi College, Oxford, 1648; MA, 1649; became an Independent; conformed at the Restoration; prebendary of Cashel, 1677;

archdeacon of Limerick; DD; published sermons, 1658.

LAEGHAIRE (or LOEGHAIRE) (d. 458), king of Ireland; succeeded to the throne, 428; baptized by St Patrick, 432; at war with the Leinster men, 453–7; defeated and slain by them.

LAEGHAIRE LORC, mythical king of Ireland; assigned by chroniclers to 595–3 BC.

LAFFAN, Sir **Joseph de Courcy,** first baronet (1786–1848), physician; educated at Edinburgh; MD, Edinburgh, 1808; LRCP, 1808; physician to the forces, 1812; served in Spain and Portugal during the latter part of the Peninsular War; physician-in-ordinary to the duke of Kent; created baronet, 1828; KH, 1836.

LAFFAN, Sir **Robert Michael** (1821–1882), governor of Bermuda; educated at the college of Pont Levoy, near Blois; entered Royal Military Academy, Woolwich, 1835; second lieutenant in Royal Engineers, 1837; first lieutenant, 1839; organized engineering arrangements of expedition for relief of garrison of Natal besieged by the Boer Pretorius; captain, 1846; inspector of railways under the Board of Trade, 1847–52; MP, St Ives, Cornwall, 1852–7; deputy inspector-general of fortifications at the War Office, 1855; brevet-major, 1858; regimental lieutenant-colonel, 1859; commanding royal engineer at Malta, 1860–5; brevet-colonel, 1864; sent to Ceylon as member of commission to report on military expenditure of colony and on its defences, 1865; regimental colonel, 1870; commanding royal engineer at Gibraltar, 1872–7; governor and commander-in-chief of the Bermudas as brigadier-general, 1877; KCMG, 1877; major-general, 1877; lieutenant-general, 1881; died at Mount Langton, Bermuda.

LAFONT, Eugène (1837–1908), science teacher in India; born at Mons, Belgium; was admitted a Jesuit, 1854; inaugurated science teaching in Bengal at St Xavier's College, Calcutta, 1865; rector of the college, 1873–1904; fellow of Calcutta University, 1877; hon. D.Sc., 1908; CIE, 1880; died at Darjeeling.

LAFONTAINE, Sir **Louis Hypolite,** first baronet (1807–1864), Canadian statesman; born at Boucherville, Lower Canada; educated at Montreal; called to bar; member for county of Terrebonne in legislative assembly of Lower Canada, 1830–7; became leader of the *parti prêtre, c.*1839; opposed union of Upper and Lower Canada, 1840; member of parliament of United Provinces for fourth riding of York county, Upper Canada, 1841; leader of French Canadians; attorney-general for lower province in Baldwin–Lafontaine administration, 1842–3; member for Terrebonne, 1844, and for Montreal

city, 1848; premier and attorney-general for Lower Canada, 1848; introduced (1849) Rebellion Losses Bill, which met with extraordinary opposition; retired, 1851; chief justice of Lower Canada, 1853 till death; created baronet, 1854.

LAFOREY, Sir **Francis** (1767–1835), son of Sir John *Laforey, admiral; present at the Battle of Trafalgar, 1805; commander-in-chief at the Leeward Islands, 1811–14; KCB, 1815; admiral of the blue, 1835.

LAFOREY, Sir **John,** first baronet (1729?–1796), admiral; his ancestors Huguenot refugees; lieutenant, 1748; commander, 1755; present at reduction of Martinique, 1762; took part in action off Ushant, 1778; commissioner of the navy at Barbados, with instructions to act as commander-in-chief under special circumstances, 1779; rear-admiral of the red; created baronet, 1789; commander-in-chief at the Leeward Islands, 1789–93 and 1795–6; vice-admiral, 1793; admiral, 1795; Demerara, Essequibo, and Berbice captured during his command; died on the passage home.

LAGUERRE, John (d. 1748), painter and actor; son of Louis *Laguerre; educated for a painter, but became an actor; scene-painter; best known by a series of drawings, *Hob in the Well*, which were engraved.

LAGUERRE, Louis (1663–1721), painter; born at Paris; of Spanish origin; educated at the Jesuits' College, Paris; studied drawing at the school of the French Academy; employed in England as assistant by *Verrio; painted halls, staircases, or ceilings at Burleigh House, Blenheim, Chatsworth, Marlborough House, and elsewhere; employed by William III at Hampton Court; his figure-drawing widely imitated.

LAIDLAW, Anna Robena (1819–1901), pianist; studied music in Edinburgh, Königsberg, and London; made successful appearances in Germany and Austria; praised by Schumann; pianist to queen of Hanover until 1840; settled in London; retired on marriage to George Thomson, 1852.

LAIDLAW, John (1832–1906), Presbyterian divine and theologian; student at Edinburgh University; hon. MA, 1854; hon. DD, 1880; studied theology in Edinburgh and Germany; minister at Perth, 1863–72, and Aberdeen, 1872–81; professor of systematic theology, New College, Edinburgh, 1881–1904; a conservative theologian; author of *The Biblical Doctrine of Man* (1879) and *The Miracles of Our Lord* (1890).

LAIDLAW, Sir **Patrick Playfair** (1881–1940), physician; educated at the Leys School, St John's College, Cambridge, and Guy's Hospital;

worked at Wellcome Physiological Research Laboratories, 1909–13; lecturer in pathology, Guy's Hospital, 1913–22; investigated histamine shock; joined National Institute for Medical Research, 1922, deputy director, 1936–40; concentrated on bacteriological and virus research; developed two methods of inducing immunity to dog distemper; proved human epidemic influenza to be a virus infection; investigated parasitic amoebae and the treatment of amoebic dysentery by alkaloids of ipecacuanha; FRS, 1927; knighted, 1935.

LAIDLAW, William (1780–1845), friend of Sir Walter *Scott; steward to Sir Walter Scott at Abbotsford, 1817; Scott's amanuensis; author of lyrics; compiled, under Scott's direction, part of the *Edinburgh Annual Register* after 1817.

LAING, Alexander (1778–1838), antiquary; published the *Caledonian Itinerary* (1819) and *Scarce Ancient Ballads never before published* (1822); chief work, the *Donean Tourist, interspersed with Anecdotes and Ancient National Ballads* (1828).

LAING, Alexander (1787–1857), the Brechin poet; son of an agricultural labourer; contributed to local newspapers and poetical miscellanies; *Wayside Flowers*, a collection of his poetry, published (1846; 2nd edn., 1850); wrote in lowland Scots.

LAING, Alexander Gordon (1793–1826), African traveller; educated at Edinburgh University; ensign in the Edinburgh Volunteers, 1810; went to Barbados, 1811; lieutenant, 1815; deputy-assistant quartermaster-general in Jamaica; adjutant, 1820; despatched by the governor of Sierra Leone to the Kambian and Mandingo countries to ascertain the native sentiment regarding the slave trade, 1822; frequently engaged with and defeated the Ashantis, 1823; published *Travels in Timmannee, Kooranko, and Soolima, Countries of Western Africa* (1825); undertook expedition to ascertain source and course of Niger, 1825; murdered by Arabs on reaching Timbuctu.

LAING, David (1774–1856), architect; articled to Sir John *Soane, c.1790; surveyor of buildings at the Custom House, London, 1811; designed a new custom house (built 1813–17), the front of which fell down, 1825, much litigation ensuing; wrote on practical architecture.

LAING, David (1793–1878), Scottish antiquary; second son of William *Laing, bookseller; educated at Edinburgh University; became partner in his father's business, 1821, and employed abroad in search of rare books; edited old Scottish ballads and metrical romances; secretary of the Bannatyne Club, 1823–61; fellow of the Society of Antiquaries of Scotland, 1826; issued

first collected edition of the poems of William *Dunbar (1834); librarian to the Signet Library, 1837; edited antiquarian works, 1840–78; hon. professor of antiquities to the Royal Scottish Academy, 1854.

LAING, James (1502–1594), doctor of theology, Paris; educated first in Scotland and then at the University of Paris; procurator of the Scots nation, 1556, 1558, 1560, 1568, 1571; doctor of theology, 1571; a violent enemy of the Reformation; wrote polemical treatises in Latin, 1581 and 1585; died at Paris.

LAING, John (d. 1483), bishop of Glasgow and chancellor of Scotland; king's treasurer, 1470; clerk of the king's rolls and register, 1472; bishop of Glasgow, 1474; founded the 'Greyfriars' of Glasgow, 1476; lord high chancellor, 1482; wrote the oldest extant rolls of the Treasury.

LAING, John (1809–1880), bibliographer; educated at Edinburgh; chaplain to the Presbyterian soldiers at Gibraltar, 1846; afterwards at Malta; librarian of New College, Edinburgh, 1850; completed *A Dictionary of Anonymous and Pseudonymous Literature of Great Britain*, which Samuel *Halkett began (published 1882–8).

LAING, Malcolm (1762–1818), Scottish historian; brother of Samuel *Laing (1780–1868); educated at Edinburgh University; called to the Scottish bar, 1785; published *A History of Scotland from the Union of the Crowns, on the Accession of King James VI to the Throne of England, to the Union of the Kingdoms* (1802; 2nd edn., 1804); published *Poems of Ossian, with Notes and Illustrations* (1805); MP, Orkney and Shetland, 1807–12.

LAING, Samuel (1780–1868), author and traveller; brother of Malcolm *Laing; educated at Edinburgh; in the army and served in Peninsular War, 1805–9; travelled in Norway and Sweden, 1834; wrote on the economic and social condition of Scandinavia; his most considerable work, *The Heimskringla, or Chronicle of the Kings of Norway, translated from the Icelandic* (1844); published three series of *Notes of a Traveller* (1850–2).

LAING, Samuel (1812–1897), politician and author; son of Samuel *Laing (1780–1868); BA; second wrangler and second Smith's prizeman, St John's College, Cambridge, 1831; fellow, 1834; barrister, Lincoln's Inn, 1837; secretary to railway department of Board of Trade, 1842–6; member of Railway Commission, 1845; chairman and managing director of London, Brighton, and South Coast Railway, 1848–55 and 1867–94; Liberal MP for Wick district, 1852–7, 1859, and 1865–8; financial secretary to Treasury, 1859–60; financial minister in India, 1860; MP, Orkney and Shetland, 1872–85; published *Modern Science and Modern Thought* and anthropological works.

LAING, William (1764–1832), bookseller; collector of and authority on best editions and valuable books, both English and foreign; published editions of Thucydides, Herodotus, and Xenophon, as part of a scheme for a worthy edition of the Greek classics.

LAIRD, John (1805–1874), shipbuilder; brother of Macgregor *Laird; managing partner in firm of William Laird & Son till 1861; built a lighter for use on Irish lakes and canals, one of the first iron vessels ever constructed, 1829; the famous *Birkenhead* among the many iron vessels built by him; MP, Birkenhead, 1861–74.

LAIRD, John (1887–1946), regius professor of moral philosophy, Aberdeen; first class, philosophy, Edinburgh, 1908, moral sciences tripos, Trinity College, Cambridge, 1910–11; professor of logic and metaphysics, Queen's University, Belfast, 1913–24; regius professor of moral philosophy, Aberdeen, 1924–46; publications include *Problems of the Self* (1917), *Study in Realism* (1920), *An Enquiry into Moral Notions* (1935), *Theism and Cosmology* (1940), and *Mind and Deity* (1941); FBA, 1933.

LAIRD, Macgregor (1808–1861), African explorer; brother of John *Laird; joined the Company for African Exploration; published narrative of the expedition made by him to the Niger, 1832–4; FRGS; one of the promoters of the British and North American Steam Navigation Company, 1837; fitted out private expedition to Africa, 1854; established trading depots on the Niger.

LAKE, Arthur (1569–1626), bishop of Bath and Wells; brother of Sir Thomas *Lake; educated at Winchester; fellow of New College, Oxford, 1589; MA, 1595; master of St Cross Hospital, Winchester, 1603; DD, 1605; dean of Worcester, 1608; warden of New College, 1613; vice-chancellor of Oxford and bishop of Bath and Wells, 1616–26; his sermons published in 1629 and 1640.

LAKE, Sir Edward, first baronet (1600?–1674), Royalist; BA, Cambridge; BA, Oxford, 1627; BCL, 1628; advocate-general for Ireland; fought and wrote on the king's side; chancellor of diocese of Lincoln at the Restoration; assumed the title of baronet after 1662; account of his interviews with Charles I edited from the original manuscript (1858).

LAKE, Edward (1641–1704), archdeacon of Exeter; entered Wadham College, Oxford, 1658; removed to Cambridge before graduating; chaplain and tutor to the Princesses Mary and Anne;

archdeacon of Exeter, 1676; DD, *per literas regias*, Cambridge, 1676; author of *Officium Eucharisticum*, a popular manual for his royal pupils, published (1673; 30th edn., 1753; republished 1843); his *Diary* in 1677–8 published (1846).

LAKE, Edward John (1823–1877), major-general in the Royal Engineers; born at Madras; second lieutenant, Bengal Engineers, 1840; lieutenant, 1844; fought in Sikh wars, 1845 and 1848–9; assistant of John *Lawrence in trans-Sutlej territory, 1846; captain and brevet-major, 1854; commissioner of the Jalundhur Doab, 1855; secured Kangra in the Mutiny, 1857; lieutenant-colonel, 1861; financial commissioner of the Punjab, 1865; CSI, 1866; colonel, 1868; retired with honorary rank of major-general, 1870; hon. lay secretary of the Church Missionary Society, 1869–76; edited *Church Missionary Record*, 1871–4.

LAKE, Gerard, first Viscount Lake of Delhi and Leswarree (1744–1808), general; descendant of Sir Thomas *Lake; nephew of George *Colman the elder; ensign, 1758; lieutenant and captain, 1762; captain-lieutenant, captain, and lieutenant-colonel, 1776; served in North Carolina, 1781; regimental-major, 1784; major-general, 1790; MP, Aylesbury, 1790–1802; regimental lieutenant-colonel, 1792; served in French War, 1793–4; lieutenant-general, 1797; commander-in-chief and second member of Council in India, 1800; developed military resources of East India Company; assisted Wellesley to break up Mahratta Confederacy, 1803; raised to peerage, 1804; advanced to a viscountcy, 1807.

LAKE, Sir **Henry Atwell** (1808–1881), colonel of the Royal Engineers; educated at Harrow and Addiscombe military college; second lieutenant; went to India, 1826; lieutenant, 1831; brevet-captain, 1840; regimental captain, 1852; brevet-major, 1840; employed principally upon irrigation works; chief engineer at Kars, 1854; lieutenant-colonel, 1855; on the capitulation of Kars sent as prisoner of war to Russia; released, 1856; colonel, 1856; subsequently chief commissioner of police in Dublin; KCB, 1875; author of works on the defence of Kars (published 1856–7).

LAKE, John (1624–1689), bishop of Chichester; educated at St John's College, Cambridge; a Royalist; received holy orders, 1647; vicar of Leeds, 1660; DD, Cambridge, 1661; prebendary of York, 1671; bishop of Sodor and Man, 1683–4; bishop of Bristol, 1684–5; bishop of Chichester, 1685; refused to take the oath of allegiance to William and Mary, 1688; active in the suppression of abuses; wrote life of John *Cleveland the poet (published 1677).

LAKE, Kirsopp (1872–1946), biblical scholar; educated at St Paul's School and Lincoln College, Oxford; second class, theology, 1895; priest, 1896; professor of early Christian literature, Leiden, 1904–14, Harvard, 1914–19; of ecclesiastical history, Harvard, 1919; of history, 1932–8; edited 'Lake Group' of manuscripts, 1902; publications include *The Beginnings of Christianity* (with F. J. Foakes *Jackson, 5 vols., 1920–33).

LAKE, Sir Percy Henry Noel (1855–1940), lieutenant-general; educated at Uppingham; gazetted to 59th Foot, 1873; quartermaster-general (1893–8), chief of the General Staff (1904–8), inspector-general (1908–10), Canadian Militia; lieutenant-general, 1911; chief of General Staff, India, 1912–15; commander-in-chief, Mesopotamia, and unsuccessful in relieving Kut el Amara, 1916; KCMG, 1908; KCB, 1916.

LAKE, Sir Thomas (1567?–1630), secretary of state; brother of Arthur *Lake; educated probably at Cambridge; a member of the Elizabethan Society of Antiquaries; MA, Oxford, 1592; clerk of the signet, c.1600; Latin secretary to James I, 1603; knighted, 1603; keeper of the records at Whitehall, 1604; MP, Bosinney, 1601, Launceston, 1604; privy councillor, 1614; MP, Middlesex, 1614; secretary of state, 1616; charged with defamation of character by the countess of Exeter and found guilty, 1619; fined, imprisoned, and dismissed from his office; MP, Wells, 1625, Wootton Bassett, 1626.

LAKE, William Charles (1817–1897), dean of Durham; educated at Rugby and Balliol College, Oxford; fellow, 1838; took holy orders, 1842; prebendary of Wells, 1860; dean of Durham, 1869–94; greatly assisted in foundation of College of Science, Newcastle, 1871.

LAKINGHETH, John de (d. 1381), chronicler; monk of Bury St Edmunds; surrendered to the insurgents in the peasant rising of 1381, and was beheaded by them; compiled *Kalendare Maneriorum Terrarum . . . ad Monasterium S. Edmundi Buriensis spectantium*.

LALOR, James Finton (d. 1849), politician; brother of Peter *Lalor; contributed to the *Nation*, 1847; prominent in revolutionary circles, 1847–8; edited the *Irish Felon*, 1848.

LALOR, John (1814–1856), journalist and author; entered Trinity College, Dublin, 1831; BA, 1837; one of the principal editors of the London *Morning Chronicle*; joined Unitarians, 1844; edited the *Enquirer* (Unitarian weekly).

LALOR, Peter (1823–1889), colonial legislator; younger brother of James Finton *Lalor; edu-

cated at Trinity College, Dublin; went to the Australian gold mines, 1852; leader among the insurgent miners, 1854; member for Ballarat in the legislative council of Victoria, 1855, and soon afterwards inspector of railways; member for South Grant in the parliament of Victoria, 1856–71 and 1875–7; chairman of committees, 1856; commissioner for customs, 1875; postmaster-general, 1878; speaker, 1880–8; died at Melbourne.

LAMB. See also LAMBE.

LAMB, Andrew (1565?–1634), bishop of Galloway; titular bishop of Brechin, 1607; bishop of Galloway, 1619; supported introduction of episcopacy into Scotland.

LAMB, Benjamin (*fl.* 1715), organist of Eton College and verger of St George's Chapel, Windsor, c.1715; wrote church music and songs.

LAMB, Lady Caroline (1785–1828), novelist; only daughter of the third earl of Bessborough; married William *Lamb, afterwards second Viscount Melbourne, 1805; became passionately infatuated with *Byron; *Glenarvon*, her first novel, containing a caricature portrait of Byron, published anonymously (1816; reprinted as *The Fatal Passion*, 1865); published *A New Canto* (1819); her second novel, *Graham Hamilton*, published (1822), and *Ada Reis; a Tale* (1823); never really recovered from the shock of meeting Byron's funeral procession; separated from her husband, 1825.

LAMB, Charles (1775–1834), essayist and humorist; educated at Christ's Hospital (1782–9), where he formed an enduring friendship with *Coleridge; employed in the South Sea House, 1789–92; a clerk in the India House, 1792–1825; his mother killed by his sister Mary (see LAMB, MARY ANN) in a fit of insanity, 1796; undertook to be his sister's guardian, an office he discharged throughout his life; was himself in an asylum as deranged, 1795–6; contributed four sonnets to Coleridge's first volume, *Poems on Various Subjects* (1796); visited Coleridge at Nether Stowey and met *Wordsworth and others, 1797; with Charles *Lloyd published *Blank Verse* (1798); added to his scanty income by writing for the newspapers; published *John Woodvil*, a blank-verse play of the Restoration period (1802); his farce *Mr. H.* damned at Drury Lane, 1805; *Tales from Shakespeare*, by himself and his sister, published (1807); published a child's version of the adventures of Ulysses (1808) and *Specimens of English Dramatic Poets contemporary with Shakespeare* (1808); a collection of his miscellaneous writings in prose and verse in two volumes published (1818); contributed to the *London Magazine* between Aug. 1820 and

Dec. 1822 twenty-five essays, signed Elia, which showed his literary gifts at their best (reprinted in a volume, 1823); buried in Edmonton Churchyard.

LAMB, Edward Buckton (1806–1869), architect; exhibited at Royal Academy from 1824; published *Etchings of Gothic Ornament* (1830) and *Studies of Ancient Domestic Architecture* (1846).

LAMB, Frederick James, third Viscount Melbourne and Baron Beauvale (1782–1853), third son of first Viscount Melbourne; educated at Eton, Glasgow University, and Trinity College, Cambridge; MA, Trinity College, Cambridge, 1803; entered the Diplomatic Service; secretary of legation at the court of the Two Sicilies, 1811; minister-plenipotentiary *ad interim*, 1812; secretary of legation at Vienna, 1813; minister-plenipotentiary at the court of Bavaria, 1815–20; privy councillor, 1822; minister-plenipotentiary to the court of Spain, 1825–7; civil Grand Cross of the Bath and ambassador at Lisbon, 1827; ambassador to the court of Vienna, 1831–41; created a peer of the United Kingdom with the title of Baron Beauvale, 1839; succeeded as Viscount Melbourne, 1848.

LAMB, George (1784–1834), politician and writer, youngest son of the first Viscount Melbourne; educated at Eton and Trinity College, Cambridge; MA, 1805; barrister, Lincoln's Inn; his comic opera, *Whistle for it*, produced, 1807; his adaptations of *Timon of Athens* produced, 1816; his most important work, a translation of the poems of Catullus (1821; republished, 1854); MP, Westminster, 1819, Dungarvan, 1826; under-secretary of state in the Home Department, 1830.

LAMB, Henry Taylor (1883–1960), painter; son of Sir Horace *Lamb; educated at Manchester Grammar School and Medical School; studied painting in London and Paris; founder-member, Camden Town and London groups; qualified at Guy's Hospital, 1916, and served as medical officer; MC, 1918; at first one-man exhibition, 1922, his portrait of Lytton *Strachey (Tate Gallery) brought him public attention; painted other writers, including Evelyn *Waugh and Lord David Cecil; ARA, 1940; RA, 1949; trustee, Tate Gallery (1944–51) and National Portrait Gallery (1942–60).

LAMB, Henry William, second Viscount Melbourne (1779–1848), statesman; of Eton and Trinity College, Cambridge; MA, 1799; barrister, Lincoln's Inn, 1804; married Lady Caroline Ponsonby (see LAMB, Lady CAROLINE), 1805; Whig MP for Leominster, 1806; MP, Portarlington, 1807; lost his seat for his support of Catholic emancipation, 1812; out of parliament for

four years; MP, Peterborough, 1816–19, Hertfordshire, 1819–26, Newport, Isle of Wight, 1827, Bletchingley, 1827–8; Irish secretary under Canning, 1827, and under Wellington, 1828; succeeded his father, 1829; home secretary under Grey, 1830–4, being thus the Cabinet minister responsible for Ireland; advocated Coercion Bill of 1833; summoned by the king to form a ministry on resignation of Grey, 1834; resigned at the bidding of the king, 1834; again summoned to form a ministry, 1835; remained prime minister for six years; acted as adviser to the young Queen Victoria, 1837–41; resigned office, 1841; universally approved as the political instructor of his young sovereign.

LAMB, Sir **Horace** (1849–1934), mathematician; educated at Stockport Grammar School, Owens College, Manchester, and Trinity College, Cambridge; second wrangler and second Smith's prizeman, 1872; fellow and lecturer, 1872–5; professor of mathematics, Adelaide, Australia, 1875–85; professor of pure (later also of applied) mathematics, Manchester, 1885–1920; honorary (Rayleigh) lecturer, Cambridge, 1920–34; lucid teacher and writer; his special subjects hydrodynamics, sound, elasticity, and mechanics; works include *Hydrodynamics* (1895) and *Infinitesimal Calculus* (1897); FRS, 1884; president of British Association, 1925; knighted, 1931.

LAMB, James (1599–1664), orientalist; educated at Brasenose College, Oxford; MA, 1620; DD and prebendary of Westminster, 1660; bequeathed many of his books to the library of Westminster Abbey; manuscripts by him on oriental subjects in the Bodleian.

LAMB, Sir **James Bland** (1752–1824), politician. See BURGES.

LAMB, John (1789–1850), master of Corpus Christi College, Cambridge, and dean of Bristol; educated at Corpus Christi College, Cambridge; MA, 1814; master of his college, 1822–50; DD, 1827; dean of Bristol, 1837–50; chief works, a continuation of *Masters's History of Corpus Christi College, Cambridge* (1831) and *A Collection of Letters, Statutes, and other Documents from the MS. Library of Corpus Christi College illustrative of the History of the University of Cambridge during the Time of the Reformation* (1838).

LAMB, Lynton Harold (1907–1977), painter, illustrator, and book designer; educated at Kingswood School, Bath, and the Central School of Arts and Crafts, London; joined Oxford University Press to design bindings for prayer-books and bibles, 1930; studied bookbinding at the Central School under Douglas *Cockerell; designed Commemorative Bible for St Giles

Cathedral, 1948 and Coronation Bible, 1953; developed interest in typography and produced covers and wrappers; commissioned into Royal Engineers (Camouflage), 1940; returned to OUP, 1946; collaborated with Geoffrey *Cumberlege in producing Oxford Illustrated Trollopes; did illustrations and wood engravings, including designs for unpublished edition of *Religio Medici* and *Urne Buriall*; designed bookjackets for the World's Classics; member of London Group of painters; first show at Storran Gallery, 1936, last at Radlett Gallery, 1976; head of lithography, Slade School, 1950; lectured at Royal College of Art, 1956–70; president, Society of Industrial Artists and Designers, 1951–3; served on art panel of Arts Council, 1951–4 and Council of Industrial Design, 1952–5; FSIA, 1948; FRSA, 1953; RDI, 1975; publications include *The Purpose of Painting* (1936), *Preparation for Painting* (1954), *Drawing for Illustration* (1962), and *Picture Frame* (1972); also wrote articles for *Graphis* (1950), *Studio* (1951), *Signature* (1947 and 1951), and *Penrose Annual* (1956).

LAMB, Mary Ann (1764–1847), sister of Charles *Lamb; stabbed her mother in a fit of temporary insanity, 1796; assisted her brother in *Tales from Shakespeare*, herself dealing with the comedies, 1807; lived with her brother and with him brought up Emma Isola, an orphan, who married Edward *Moxon.

LAMB, Sir Matthew, first baronet (1705–1768), politician; MP, Stockbridge, 1741, Peterborough, 1741–68; created baronet, 1755.

LAMBARDE, William (1536–1601), historian of Kent; his first work a collection and paraphrase of Anglo-Saxon laws (published, 1568; republished with *Bede's *Historia Ecclesiastica*, 1644); completed first draft of his *Perambulation of Kent*, 1570; printed (1574 and 1576) the earliest county history known, and one considered a model of arrangement and style (2nd edn., 1596; reprinted, 1826); collected materials for a general account of England, but abandoned the design on learning that *Camden was engaged on a similar work; his materials published from the original manuscript (1730); bencher of Lincoln's Inn, 1579; his *Eirenarcha; or of the Office of the Justices of Peace* (1581) long a standard authority (reprinted seven times between 1582 and 1610); keeper of the records at the Rolls Chapel, 1597; keeper of the records in the Tower, 1601.

LAMBART. See also LAMBERT.

LAMBART, Charles, first earl of Cavan (1600–1660), eldest son of Sir Oliver *Lambart, first Baron Lambart in the Irish peerage; succeeded his father, 1618; represented Bossiney, Cornwall, in the English parliaments of 1625 and 1627; created earl of Cavan and Viscount Kilcoursie, 1647.

LAMBART, Frederick Rudolph, tenth earl of Cavan (1865–1946), field marshal; educated at Eton and Sandhurst; gazetted to Grenadier Guards, 1885; succeeded father while serving in South Africa, 1900; retired, 1913; commanded 4th (Guards) brigade (Ypres and Festubert), 1914–15; Guards division (Loos), 1915; XIV Corps (Somme and third Ypres), 1916–17; took Corps to Italy, Nov. 1917; took over command of British troops in Italy, Mar. 1918; repulsed Austrian offensive; commanded small army for final offensive across Piave; elected representative Irish peer, 1915; KP, 1916; KCB, 1918; GCMG, 1919; GOC-in-C, Aldershot Command, 1920–2; headed War Office section, British delegation, Washington Conference, 1921; chief of Imperial General Staff, 1922–6; chief of staff to duke of York touring Australia and New Zealand, 1927; field marshal, 1932; commanded troops at coronation, 1937; GCVO, 1922; GCB, 1926; GBE, 1927.

LAMBART, Sir Oliver, first Baron Lambart of Cavan (d. 1618), Irish administrator; distinguished himself as a soldier in the Netherlands, 1585–92; took part in the expedition against Cadiz and was knighted, 1596; supported the earl of *Essex in Ireland, 1599; privy councillor, 1603; created Baron Lambart of Cavan in the Irish peerage, 1618.

LAMBART, Richard Ford William, seventh earl of Cavan (1763–1836), general; succeeded to the title, 1778; ensign, 1779; lieutenant, 1781; captain-lieutenant, 1790; captain and lieutenant-colonel, 1793; major-general, 1798; commanded a brigade in the Ferrol expedition and before Cadiz, 1800; present at the attack on Alexandria, 1801; commander of the whole army in Egypt; commander in the eastern counties during the invasion alarms of 1803–4; knight of the Crescent and one of the six officers besides *Nelson who received the Diamond Aigrette; general, 1814.

LAMBE. See also LAMB.

LAMBE, Sir Charles Edward (1900–1960), admiral of the fleet; entered navy, 1914; qualified in torpedo and at Naval Staff College; captain, 1937; successively assistant, deputy, and director of plans, Joint Planning Staff, 1940–4; commanded aircraft carrier *Illustrious*, 1944–5; acting rear-admiral, 1945; commander-in-chief, Far East, 1953–4, Mediterranean, 1957–9; second sea lord, 1955–7; first sea lord, 1959–60; admiral of the fleet, 1960; CVO, 1938; CB, 1944; KCB, 1953; GCB, 1957.

LAMBE, John (d. 1628), astrologer; indicted for the practice of 'execrable arts', 1608–23; imprisoned for fifteen years; protected by the duke of *Buckingham, 1623; fatally injured by a mob of apprentices, who denounced him as 'the duke's devil'.

LAMBE, Sir John (1566?–1647), civilian; MA, St John's College, Cambridge, 1590; registrar of diocese of Ely, 1600; chancellor of the diocese of Peterborough; vicar, official, and commissary-general to the bishop of Peterborough, 1615; LL D, 1616; commissary to the dean and chapter of Lincoln, 1617; knighted, 1621; member of the High Commission court and an active supporter of *Laud; dean of the arches court of Canterbury, 1633; chancellor and keeper of the great seal to Queen *Henrietta Maria, 1640.

LAMBE, Robert (1711–1795), author; BA, St John's College, Cambridge, 1734; his chief work, *An Exact and Circumstantial History of the Battle of Flodden, in verse, written about the time of Queen Elizabeth* (1774).

LAMBE (or LAMB), Thomas (d. 1686), philanthropist and sometime Nonconformist; preached in London, 1641–61; returned to the established church, 1658; remarkable for his philanthropic work; published religious works, 1642–56.

LAMBE, William (1495–1580), London merchant and benefactor; gentleman of the Chapel Royal to Henry VIII; master of the Clothworkers' Company, 1569–70; established a free grammar school and almshouses at Sutton Valence, Kent, his native town; an adherent of the reformed religion.

LAMBE, William (1765–1847), physician; educated at St John's College, Cambridge; BA, 1786; fellow, 1788; MD, 1802; FRCP, 1804; censor and frequently Croonian lecturer between 1806 and 1828; Harveian orator, 1818; published medical works.

LAMBERT. See also LAMBART.

LAMBERT (or LANBRIHT) (d. 791), archbishop of Canterbury. See JAENBERHT.

LAMBERT, Aylmer Bourke (1761–1842), botanist; educated at St Mary Hall, Oxford; an original FLS, 1788, and vice-president, 1796–1842; contributed papers on zoology and botany to its *Transactions*; FRS, 1791; *A Description of the genus Cinchona*, his first independent work (1797); chief work, a monograph of the genus *Pinus* (vol. i, 1803, vol. ii, 1824, vol. iii, 1837).

LAMBERT, Brooke (1834–1901), social reformer; student at King's College, London, under F. D. *Maurice; BA, Brasenose College, Oxford, 1858; MA, 1861; BCL, 1863; vicar of St Mark's, Whitechapel, 1866–70; as vestryman and guardian he made thorough study of poor law and local government; in work on pauperism, 1871, anticipated scientific statistical researches of Charles *Booth; resigned through ill health, 1870; went to West Indies to restore health; held living of Tamworth, 1872–8; helped to found London University Extension Society, 1879; vicar of Greenwich, 1880–1901, where he continued his activity in social and educational reform; a prominent freemason; published volumes of sermons.

LAMBERT, Constant (1905–1951), musician; educated at Christ's Hospital and Royal College of Music; his music for ballet includes *Romeo and Juliet, Pomona, Horoscope, Tiresias*, and many arrangements for Sadler's Wells Ballet, of which he was musical director until 1947; other works include *Music for Orchestra*, 'Elegiac Blues', *The Rio Grande*, Piano Sonata and Piano Concerto, *Aubade Héroïque*, and choral masque, *Summer's Last Will and Testament*; frequently conducted at promenade concerts and Covent Garden.

LAMBERT, Daniel (1770–1809), the most corpulent man of whom authentic record exists; keeper of Leicester gaol, 1791–1805; weighed thirty-two stone in 1793; 'received company' daily in London, 1806–7; weighed at death fifty-two and three-quarters stone.

LAMBERT, George (1710–1765), landscape and scene painter; studied under Warner *Hassells and John *Wootton; had a painting loft at Covent Garden Theatre, where distinguished men resorted to sup with him, the Beefsteak Club arising out of these meetings; a friend of *Hogarth, who painted his portrait; exhibited with the Society of Artists of Great Britain, 1761–4.

LAMBERT, George (1842–1915), tennis player; went to Hampton Court Palace tennis court, 1866; head professional at Marylebone Cricket Club court at Lord's, 1869–89; champion, 1870–85.

LAMBERT, George, first Viscount Lambert (1866–1958), yeoman farmer and member of parliament; son of Devon landowner; educated locally, and began farming 800 acres at 19; Liberal MP, South Molton, 1891–1924, 1929–45; on Royal Commission on Agriculture, 1893; civil lord of Admiralty, 1905–15; supported National government of 1931 and became National Liberal; member, Devon County Council, 1889–1952; foundation chairman of

Seale-Hayne Agricultural College, Newton Abbot; PC, 1912; viscount, 1945.

LAMBERT, George Jackson (1794–1880), organist and composer; organist of Beverley Minster, 1818–75; a fine violoncello and violin player; composed overtures, instrumental chamber music, organ fugues, and other works.

LAMBERT, Henry (d. 1813), naval captain; entered navy, 1795; lieutenant, 1801; commander, 1803; captain, 1804; employed in the blockade of Mauritius and in the attack on the French squadron in Grand Port, when he surrendered and was detained as prisoner, 1810; mortally wounded in action off Brazil, 1812; buried at San Salvador.

LAMBERT, James (1725–1788), musician and painter; first painted inn-signs; best known by a series of water-colour drawings illustrating the antiquities of Sussex; exhibited at the Royal Academy and (1761–88) at the Society of Artists; organist of the Church of St Thomas-at-Cliffe, Lewes.

LAMBERT, James (1741–1823), Greek professor at Cambridge; entered Trinity College, Cambridge, 1760; fellow, 1765; MA, 1767; regius professor of Greek, 1771–1780; bursar of his college, 1789–99.

LAMBERT, John (d. 1538), martyr; his real name Nicholson; educated at Cambridge; BA, 1519–20, and fellow of Queens' College, 1521; converted to Protestantism and ordained; suffered persecution and took name of Lambert; chaplain to the English Factory at Antwerp; imprisoned, 1532; released on the death of Archbishop *Warham, 1532; condemned to death by *Cromwell for denying the real presence, and burnt at the stake.

LAMBERT, John (1619–1684), soldier; took up arms for parliament at the beginning of the Civil War; commissary-general of *Fairfax's army, 1644; in command of a regiment in the New Model Army, 1646; assisted *Ireton in drawing up the 'Heads of the Proposals of Army', 1647; commander of the army in the north, 1647; engaged against the Royalist Scottish army, 1648; took part in the Battle of Dunbar, 1650, of Worcester, 1651; deputy lord-lieutenant of Ireland, 1652; president of the council appointed by the officers of the army, 1653; was the leading spirit in the council of officers who offered the post of protector to *Cromwell, and a member of the Protector's Council of State; major-general of the army; a lord of the Cinque Ports; retired on account of a breach with Cromwell about the regal title; MP, Pontefract, 1659; supported Richard *Cromwell and recovered his old position; member of the committee of safety and of the Council of State, 1659; major-general of the army sent to oppose *Monck's advance into England; deprived of his commands, 1660; arrested and committed to the Tower; escaped and collected troops, but without success, 1660; again committed to the Tower, 1661; sent to Guernsey, 1661; tried for high treason and condemned to death, 1662; sent back to Guernsey; imprisoned till death, 1664–84.

LAMBERT, Sir John (1772–1847), general; ensign, 1st Foot Guards, 1791; captain, 1793; lieutenant-colonel, 1801; served in Portugal and Spain, 1808, and in Walcheren expedition, 1809; brevet-colonel, 1810; in Spain, 1811–14; major-general, 1813; KCB, 1815; served with Sir Edward Michael *Pakenham in America, 1815; at Waterloo, 1815; lieutenant-general, 1825; general, 1841; colonel of 10th Regiment, 1824; GCB, 1838.

LAMBERT, John (*fl.* 1811), traveller; visited North America with a view to fostering the cultivation of hemp in Canada, 1806; published *Travels through Lower Canada and the United States of North America, 1806–1808* (1810).

LAMBERT, Sir John (1815–1892), civil servant; mayor of Salisbury, 1854; poor-law inspector, 1857; superintended administration of the Public Works Act, 1865; receiver of the metropolitan common poor fund, 1867; permanent secretary to the Local Government Board, 1871–82; KCB, 1879; privy councillor, 1885; author of *The Modern Domesday Book* (1872) and of several musical publications.

LAMBERT, Mark (d. 1601), Benedictine monk. See BARKWORTH.

LAMBERT, Maurice (1901–1964), sculptor; brother of Constant *Lambert; educated at Manor House School, Clapham; apprenticed to F. Derwent *Wood, 1918–23; first public exhibition, 1925; first one-man exhibition, 1929; alabaster carving accepted by Tate Gallery, 1932; first exhibited at Royal Academy, 1938; ARA, 1941; fellow, Royal Society of British Sculptors, 1938; master, Royal Academy Sculpture School, 1950–8; RA, 1952; works include bronze statue of Dame Margot Fonteyn, equestrian statue of George V, statue of Viscount *Nuffield, and busts of Dame Edith *Sitwell, J. B. *Priestley, and Lord Devlin.

LAMBERTON, William de (d. 1328), bishop of St Andrews; chancellor of Glasgow Cathedral, 1292; bishop of St Andrews, 1297; a supporter of William *Wallace; although swearing fealty to Edward I, 1304, assisted at coronation of Robert the *Bruce, 1306; imprisoned for treason, 1306–8; subsequently worked in the interests of both parties at once.

LAMBORN, Peter Spendelowe (1722–1774), engraver and miniature painter; studied under Isaac *Basire (1704–1768); member of and (1764–74) exhibitor with the Incorporated Society of Artists; executed architectural drawings and etchings.

LAMBORN, Reginald (*fl.* 1363), astronomer; DD, Merton College, Oxford, 1367; entered the Franciscan order at Oxford; two letters (1364 and 1367) of his on astronomical subjects extant in manuscript.

LAMBOURNE, first Baron (1847–1928), politician. See LOCKWOOD, AMELIUS MARK RICHARD.

LAMBTON, John (1710–1794), general; ensign, 1732; lieutenant, 1739; regimental quartermaster, 1742–5; captain and lieutenant-colonel, 1746; colonel, 1758; MP, Durham, 1761–87.

LAMBTON, John George, first earl of Durham (1792–1840), grandson of John *Lambton; educated at Eton; cornet in the dragoons, 1809; lieutenant, 1810; retired from the army, 1811; MP for Durham county, 1813–28; created Baron Durham of the city of Durham and of Lambton Castle; privy councillor and lord privy seal, 1830; assisted in preparation of first Reform Bill; ambassador-extraordinary to St Petersburg, Berlin, and Vienna, 1832; created Viscount Lambton and earl of Durham, 1833; headed the advanced faction of the Whigs; ambassador-extraordinary and minister-plenipotentiary to St Petersburg, 1835–7; GCB, 1837; high commissioner for the adjustment of important questions in Lower and Upper Canada and governor-general of the British provinces in North America, 1838; his high-handed proceedings denounced and disallowed in England; resigned and returned to England, 1838; the policy of all his successors guided by his *Report on the Affairs of British North America* (1839).

LAMBTON, William (1756–1823), lieutenant-colonel, and geodesist; studied mathematics under Dr Charles *Hutton; ensign, 1781–3; lieutenant, 1794; barrack-master at St John's, New Brunswick, till 1795; took part in the capture of Seringapatam, 1799; conducted a survey connecting Malabar and Coromandel coasts, 1800–15; FRS and RAS; died at Hinganghat, near Nagpur; author of papers on geodesy.

LAMBURN, Richmal Crompton (1890–1969), author; known as Richmal Crompton; educated at St Elphin's Clergy Daughters' School, Warrington, at Darley Dale, Derbyshire, and Royal Holloway College, London; BA London, 1914; taught at her old school, 1915–17; classics mistress, Bromley High School for Girls, 1917–24; gave up teaching after attack of polio-myelitis; concentrated on writing short stories; selection of stories about William Brown, schoolboy, published as *Just William* and *More William* (1922); between 1922 and 1969 'William' series ran to thirty-eight titles; translated into many foreign languages; thirty-nine other novels not so successful.

LAMINGTON, Barons. See BAILLIE-COCHRANE, ALEXANDER DUNDAS ROSS WISHART, first baron, 1816–1890; BAILLIE, CHARLES WALLACE ALEXANDER NAPIER ROSS COCHRANE, second baron, 1860–1940.

LAMONT, David (1752–1837), Scottish divine; DD, Edinburgh, 1780; chaplain to the prince of Wales, 1785; moderator of the general assembly, 1822; chaplain-in-ordinary for Scotland, 1824; popular preacher; published sermons.

LAMONT, Johann von (1805–1879), astronomer and magnetician; born at Braemar; educated in mathematics by the prior of the Scottish Benedictine monastery at Ratisbon; extraordinary member of the Munich Academy of Sciences, 1827; director of the observatory of Bogenhausen near Munich, 1835; executed magnetic surveys of Bavaria (1849–52), France and Spain (1856–7), and North Germany and Denmark (1858); professor of astronomy in the university of Munich, 1852; died at Munich; author of important works on terrestrial magnetism.

LAMONT, John (*fl.* 1671), chronicler; his *Diary*, 1649–71 (first published under the title of the *Chronicle of Fife*, 1810), of great value to the Scottish genealogist.

LA MOTHE, Claude Grostête de (1647–1713), theologian; born at Orleans; educated at Orleans University; joined the Paris bar, 1665; abandoned law for theology, and became a Protestant pastor; on revocation of the edict of Nantes came to London, 1685; naturalized, 1688; minister of Savoy Church, 1694–1713.

LA MOTTE, John (1570?–1655), merchant of London; educated at Ghent and probably at Heidelberg University; established a foreign church at Sandtoft, 1636.

LAMPE, Geoffrey William Hugo (1912–1980), theologian; educated at Blundell's School and Exeter College, Oxford; first class, Lit. Hum., 1935 and theology, 1936; ordained deacon, 1937, and priest, 1938; assistant master and assistant chaplain, King's School, Canterbury, 1938–41; chaplain to the forces, 1941–5; MC; chaplain and fellow, St John's College, Oxford, 1945–53; Edward Cadbury professor of theology, Birmingham, 1953–9; Ely professor of divinity, Cambridge, 1959–70; regius professor,

1970–9; fellow, Gonville and Caius College, Cambridge, 1960; BD and DD, Oxford, 1953; hon. DD, Edinburgh, 1959; FBA, 1963; publications include *A Patristic Greek Lexicon* (5 vols., 1961–8) of which he was editor; *The Seal of the Spirit* (1951); Bampton lectures, 1975–6, published as *God as Spirit* (1977); vice-principal, Birmingham University, 1957–9; chairman, board of extra-mural studies, Cambridge; member of general synod of Church of England; advocate of ordination of women and ecumenical co-operation between churches; leading figure in Anglo-Scandinavian conferences; commander of the Northern Star, 1978.

LAMPE, John Frederick (1703?–1751), musical composer; born probably in Saxony; came to London, 1725; one of the finest bassoonists of his time; composer of comic operas and songs; published two works on the theory of music.

LAMPHIRE, John (1614–1688), principal of Hart Hall, Oxford; educated at Winchester and New College, Oxford; fellow of New College, 1636–48; MA, 1642; Camden professor of history, 1660; MD, 1660; principal of New Inn Hall, 1662; of Hart Hall, 1663; owner of many manuscripts, some of which he published.

LAMPLUGH, Thomas (1615–1691), bishop of Exeter and archbishop of York; educated at The Queen's College, Oxford; MA, 1642; DD, 1660; principal of St Alban Hall, 1664–73; archdeacon of London, 1664; dean of Rochester, 1673; bishop of Exeter, 1676–88; archbishop of York, 1688–91; assisted at the coronation of William III, 1689.

LAMPSON, Sir Curtis Miranda, first baronet (1806–1885), advocate of the Atlantic cable; born in Vermont; came to England and set up business as a merchant, 1830; naturalized, 1849; vice-chairman of the company for laying the Atlantic telegraph, 1856–66; created baronet, 1866.

LAMPSON, Miles Wedderburn, first Baron Killearn (1880–1964), diplomat; grandson of Sir Curtis Miranda *Lampson, first baronet; educated at Eton; entered Foreign Office, 1903; served, as secretary to Prince Arthur of Connaught in Japan, and in Peking, 1906–18; acting high commissioner, Siberia, 1919–20; at Washington Conference, 1921–2; head, Central European department, Foreign Office, 1922–6; minister, Peking, 1927–33; high commissioner, Egypt, 1933–6; first British ambassador, Egypt, 1936–46; special commissioner, South-East Asia, 1946–8; CB, 1926; KCMG, 1927; GCMG, 1937; PC, 1941; baron, 1943.

LANARK, earl of (1616–1651). See HAMILTON, WILLIAM, second duke of Hamilton.

LANCASTER, duchess of (1350?–1403). See SWYNFORD, CATHERINE.

LANCASTER, dukes of. See HENRY OF LANCASTER, 1299?–1361; JOHN OF GAUNT, 1340–1399; HENRY IV, king of England, 1367–1413.

LANCASTER, earls of. See LANCASTER, EDMUND, 1245–1296; THOMAS, 1277?–1322; HENRY, 1281?–1345.

LANCASTER, Charles William (1820–1878), improver of rifles and cannon; constructed a model rifle which had great success in 1846; elected associate of the Institution of Civil Engineers, 1852; his carbine adopted for the Royal Engineers, 1855; invented the oval-bored rifle cannon.

LANCASTER, Edmund, earl of (1245–1296), called Crouchback; second son of Henry III and *Eleanor of Provence; styled king of Sicily by the pope, 1255; renounced all claim to the kingdom of Sicily, 1263; crusader, 1271; married Blanche, daughter of the count of Artois, younger son of Louis VIII of France and widow of Henry of Navarre, 1275; took part in the Welsh War, 1277–82; unsuccessfully commanded the English Army in Gascony, 1296; buried in Westminster Abbey.

LANCASTER, Henry Hill (1829–1875), essayist; educated at the High School and University of Glasgow and at Balliol College, Oxford; MA, 1872; passed as an advocate in Edinburgh, 1858; advocate-depute, 1868–74; took active interest in education and contributed to the *North British* and *Edinburgh* reviews; his articles published in a single volume entitled *Essays and Reviews* (with prefatory notice by Professor *Jowett, 1876).

LANCASTER, Hume (d. 1850), marine painter; exhibited, 1836–49, at the Royal Academy, the Society of British Artists, and the British Institution.

LANCASTER, Sir James (c.1554–1618), pioneer of English trade with the East Indies; fought against the Armada, 1588; sailed in the first English voyage to the East Indies, 1591; returned with a rich booty, 1594; appointed to command the first fleet of the East India Company, 1600; knighted, 1603.

LANCASTER, John (c.1570–1619), bishop of Waterford and Lismore; MA, King's College, Cambridge, 1595; bishop of Waterford and Lismore, 1608–19.

LANCASTER, John of, duke of Bedford (1389–1435). See JOHN.

LANCASTER, Joseph (1778–1838), founder of the Lancasterian system of education; joined the Society of Friends; began teaching poor children before 1801, and soon had a free school of a thousand boys; set forth the results of his experience in a pamphlet, *Improvements in Education* (1803); opposed by members of the established church; published *Report of Joseph Lancaster's progress from 1798* (1810); suffered from pecuniary difficulties and went to America, 1818; established a school, which failed, at Montreal; his last pamphlet, *Epitome of some of the chief Events and Transactions in the Life of J. Lancaster, containing an Account of the Rise and Progress of the Lancasterian system of Education* etc., published (1833); public interest in education aroused by his work.

LANCASTER, Nathaniel (1701–1775), author; chaplain to *Frederick, prince of Wales, 1733; DD, Lambeth, 1733; wrote several books on manners between 1746 and 1767.

LANCASTER, Thomas (d. 1583), archbishop of Armagh; probably educated at Oxford; an enthusiastic Protestant; bishop of Kildare, 1549–68; dean of Ossory, 1552; treasurer of Salisbury Cathedral, 1559; a royal chaplain, 1559; accompanied Sir Henry *Sidney to Ireland, 1565; archbishop of Armagh, 1568–83.

LANCASTER, Thomas William (1787–1859), Bampton lecturer; entered Oriel College, Oxford, 1804; fellow of The Queen's College, 1809; MA, 1810; ordained priest, 1812; preached Bampton lectures on 'The Popular Evidence of Christianity', 1831; select preacher to the university, 1832; under-master of Magdalen College School, Oxford, 1840–9; published his Bampton lectures and theological works.

LANCASTER, William (1650–1717), divine; of The Queen's College, Oxford; MA, 1678; fellow, 1679; bursar, 1686–90; DD, 1692; archdeacon of Middlesex, 1705–17; vice-chancellor of Oxford, 1706–10.

LANCE, George (1802–1864), painter; pupil of *Haydon; exhibited from 1824 at the British Institution, the Society of British Artists, and the Royal Academy; a painter of still-life.

LANCEY. See DE LANCEY.

LANCHESTER, Frederick William (1868–1946), engineer; educated at Hartley College, Southampton, South Kensington, and Finsbury Technical College; devised pendulum governor controlling speed of gas-engines and Lanchester gas-starter; produced his first experimental motor car, 1895; second, 1897; formed Lanchester Engine Company, 1899; introduced first real motor car, 1901; consulting engineer, Daimler Motor Company, 1910–30; laid foundations of aircraft design in *Aerial Flight* (2 vols., 1907–8);

member, Advisory Committee on Aeronautics, 1909–20; FRS, 1922.

LANCHESTER, George Herbert (1874–1970), automobile engineer and inventor; educated at Clapham High School, London; apprenticed at 14 to his brother, Frederick William *Lanchester, works manager and designer, Forward Gas Engine Co., Birmingham; works manager, 1893–7; assisted in design of experimental motor cars; works manager, Lanchester Engine Co., 1899–1905; designer and chief engineer and technical director, Lanchester Motor Co., 1909–1936; designed Lanchester cars and armoured cars; joined Alvis Co., 1936; designed Silver Crest car; consultant, Stirling Armament Co., 1939; consultant, Russell Newbery Diesel Engine Co., 1945–52, and part time, 1952–61; fellow, Institution of Mechanical Engineers; president, Institution of Automobile Engineers, 1943–4; consultant editor, *Automobile Engineers' Reference Book*.

LANCRINCK, Prosper Henri (1628–1692), painter. See LANKRINK.

LAND, Edward (1815–1876), vocalist and composer of popular songs.

LANDEL, William (d. 1385), bishop of St Andrews, 1342–85; visited the shrine of St James at Compostella, 1361, Rome, 1362; crowned Robert II, 1370.

LANDELLS, Ebenezer (1808–1860), wood-engraver and projector of *Punch*; apprenticed to Thomas *Bewick, wood-engraver; superintended the fine-art engraving department of the firm of Branston & Vizetelly; contributed chiefly to illustrated periodical literature; conceived the idea of *Punch*, the first number of which appeared 17 July 1841; contributed to the early numbers of the *Illustrated London News*; started the *Lady's Newspaper* (later incorporated with the *Queen*), 1847; Birket *Foster and the *Dalziels among his pupils.

LANDELLS, Robert Thomas (1833–1877), artist and special war correspondent; eldest son of Ebenezer *Landells; educated principally in France; studied drawing and painting in London; special artist for the *Illustrated London News* in the Crimea, 1856, in the war between Germany and Denmark, 1863, in the war between Prussia and Austria, 1866, and in the Franco-German War, 1870; employed by Queen Victoria to paint memorial pictures of several ceremonials attended by her.

LANDEN, John (1719–1790), mathematician; published *Mathematical Lucubrations* (1755); FRS, 1766; discovered a theorem known by his name expressing a hyperbolic arc in terms of two elliptic arcs, 1775; failed to develop and combine his discoveries.

LANDER, John (1807–1839), African traveller; younger brother of Richard Lemon *Lander; accompanied his brother in his exploration of the Niger, 1830–1; his journal incorporated with that of his brother (published 1832).

LANDER, Richard Lemon (1804–1834), African traveller; went to Cape Colony, 1823; accompanied Lieutenant Hugh *Clapperton to Western Africa; published journal and records of Clapperton's last expedition to Africa (1830); made an expedition to explore the Niger, 1830–1; published *Journal of an Expedition to explore the Course and Termination of the Niger* (1832); conducted a second expedition to the Niger, 1832; mortally wounded in a fight with natives at Ingiamma; died at Fernando Po; the question of the course and outlet of the River Niger settled by his exploration.

LANDMANN, George Thomas (1779–1854), lieutenant-colonel, Royal Engineers; son of Isaac *Landmann; entered the Royal Military Academy, Woolwich, 1793; first lieutenant, 1797; employed in construction of fortifications in Canada, 1797–1802; captain, 1806; on active service in the Peninsular War, 1808–12; brevet-major, 1813; lieutenant-colonel, 1814; retired, 1824; author of books on Portugal and on his own adventures and recollections.

LANDMANN, Isaac (1741–1826?), professor of artillery and fortification; held an appointment at the Royal Military School in Paris; professor of artillery and fortification at the Royal Military Academy at Woolwich, 1777–1815; wrote on tactics and fortification.

LANDON, Letitia Elizabeth (1802–1838), afterwards Mrs Maclean; poetess under the initials 'L.E.L.'; her first poem, 'Rome', published in the *Literary Gazette* (1820); her *Fate of Adelaide* published (1821); published poems between 1824 and 1829; contributed to albums and annuals, and edited the *Drawing Scrap Book* from 1832; published novels, 1831 and 1834; her *Traits and Trials of Early Life* (supposed to be autobiographical) brought out (1836), and her best novel, *Ethel Churchill* (1837); married George Maclean, governor of Cape Coast Castle, 1838; arrived at Cape Coast in August; died mysteriously, probably from an accidental overdose of prussic acid, in Oct. Collected editions of her poems published (1850 and 1873).

LANDOR, Robert Eyres (1781–1869), author; youngest brother of Walter Savage *Landor; scholar and fellow of Worcester College, Oxford; author of a tragedy, *Count Arezzi* (1823), which only sold while it was mistaken for a work of

*Byron; published other tragedies between 1841 and 1848.

LANDOR, Walter Savage (1775–1864), author of *Imaginary Conversations*; educated at Rugby; entered Trinity College, Oxford, 1793; rusticated, 1794; lived for three years at Tenby and Swansea; his *Gebir* published (1798); visited Paris, 1802; lived in Bath, Bristol, and Wells, with occasional visits to London; saw some fighting as a volunteer in Spain; published *Tragedy of Count Julian* (1811); bought Llanthony Abbey, Monmouthshire, and married Julia Thuillier, 1811; quarrelled with the authorities at Llanthony; went to Jersey and thence to France, 1814; started for Italy, 1815; lived for three years at Como; insulted the authorities in a Latin poem and was ordered to leave, 1818; at Pisa, 1818–21; at Florence, 1821–35; first two volumes of *Imaginary Conversations* published (1824; 2nd edn., 1826), third volume (1828), fourth and fifth (1829); bought a villa at Fiesole; visited England, 1832; published *Citation and Examination of William Shakespeare . . . touching Deer-stealing* (1834); quarrelled with his wife and left Italy, 1835; published *The Pentameron* (1837); lived at Bath, 1838–58; his collected works published (1846); returned to Florence, 1858; transferred his English estates to his son, and so became entirely dependent on his family; assisted by Robert *Browning, the poet; visited by A. C. *Swinburne, 1864; a classical enthusiast and an admirable writer of English prose; died at Florence.

LANDSBOROUGH, David (1779–1854), naturalist; educated at Edinburgh University; ordained minister of the Church of Scotland, 1811; studied natural history; discovered *Ectocarpus landsburgii* (alga), and contributed to the *Phycologia Britannica* of William Henry *Harvey; joined the Free Kirk and became minister of Saltcoats, 1843; published *Excursions to Arran, Ailsa Craig, and the two Cumbraes* (1847; 2nd series, 1852), *Popular History of British Sea-weeds* (1849; 3rd edn., 1857); published *Popular History of British Zoophytes or Corallines*; said to have discovered nearly seventy species of plants and animals new to Scotland.

LANDSBOROUGH, William (d. 1886), Australian explorer; son of David *Landsborough; an Australian squatter; made explorations chiefly in Queensland between 1856 and 1862; member of the Queensland parliament, 1864; government resident in Burke district, 1865–9; explored the Gulf of Carpentaria; died at Brisbane.

LANDSEER, Charles (1799–1879), historical painter; second son of John *Landseer; entered the Royal Academy schools, 1816; first exhibited at Royal Academy, 1828; RA, 1845; keeper of

Royal Academy, 1851–73; gave £10,000 to Royal Academy for the foundation of Landseer scholarships.

LANDSEER, Sir Edwin Henry (1802–1873), animal painter; youngest son of John *Landseer; entered the Royal Academy schools, 1816; began to exhibit, 1817; visited Sir Walter *Scott at Abbotsford and drew the poet and his dogs, 1824; RA, 1831; excelled in painting portraits of children; frequently painted Queen Victoria and the prince consort and their children between 1839 and 1866; his most famous pictures painted between 1842 and 1850; knighted, 1850; the only English artist who received the large Gold Medal at the Paris Universal Exhibition, 1855; declined presidency of the Royal Academy, 1865; completed the lions for the Nelson monument, Trafalgar Square, 1866; buried in St Paul's Cathedral. He struck out a new path by treating pictorially the analogy between the characters of animals and men; 434 etchings and engravings were made from his works up to 1875.

LANDSEER, Jessica (1810–1880), landscape and miniature painter; daughter of John *Landseer; exhibited at the Royal Academy and the British Institution between 1816 and 1866.

LANDSEER, John (1769–1852), painter, engraver, and author; apprenticed to William *Byrne; delivered lectures on engraving at the Royal Institution, 1806; tried, but without success, to induce the Royal Academy to place engraving on the same footing as in academies abroad; turned his attention to archaeology and published a work on engraved views, 1817; made engravings after drawings and pictures by his son, Sir Edwin Henry *Landseer; FSA; engraver to William IV.

LANDSEER, Thomas (1795–1880), engraver; eldest son of John *Landseer; his life mainly devoted to etching and engraving the drawings and pictures of his brother Sir Edwin Henry *Landseer; ARA, 1868; published *The Life and Letters of William Bewick* (1871).

LANE, Sir Allen (1902–1970), publisher; born Allen Lane Williams; educated at Bristol Grammar School; left school to work at Bodley Head, publishing house of John *Lane, a relative who insisted that he change his name by deed-poll, 1919; director, Bodley Head, 1925; chairman, 1930; published first experimental paperback reprints independently of Bodley Head, 1935; Penguin Books established, resigned from Bodley Head, 1936; first Pelicans issued, 1937; first Penguin Classic, *The Odyssey*, published, 1946; published unexpurgated text of D. H. *Lawrence's *Lady Chatterley's Lover* and won *cause célèbre*, 1960; Penguin Books became public

company, 1960; retired as managing director, 1967; knighted, 1952; CH, 1969; honorary degrees at Birmingham, Bristol, Manchester, Oxford, and Reading; hon. fellow, Royal College of Art.

LANE, Charles Edward William (1786–1872), general in the Indian Army; ensign, 1807; lieutenant, 1812; captain, 1824; major, 1835; lieutenant-colonel, 1841; commanded the garrison of Kandahar, and repulsed an attack of the Afghans, 1842; CB, 1842; colonel, 1852; major-general, 1854; lieutenant-general, 1866; general, 1870.

LANE, Edward (1605–1685), theological writer; educated at St Paul's School, London and St John's College, Cambridge; MA, 1629; incumbent of Sparsholt for fifty years; MA, Oxford, 1639; published *Look unto Jesus* (1663) and *Mercy Triumphant* (1680).

LANE, Edward William (1801–1876), Arabic scholar; went to Egypt for the sake of his health, 1825; made voyages up the Nile, 1826 and 1827; studied the people of Cairo, 1833–5; spoke Arabic fluently and adopted the dress and manners of the Egyptian man of learning; published in two volumes *Account of the Manners and Customs of the Modern Egyptians* (1836), still the standard authority on the subject; published a translation of the *Thousand and one Nights* (the first accurate version, 1838–40); again in Egypt, 1842–9; compiled an exhaustive thesaurus of the Arabic language from native lexicons, published at intervals, 1863–92; the acknowledged chief of Arabic scholars in Europe.

LANE, Sir Hugh Percy (1875–1915), art collector and critic; born in County Cork; picture dealer in London, 1898; formed gallery of modern art in Dublin; knighted, 1909; director of Irish National Gallery, 1914; torpedoed on *Lusitania*; his will caused controversy between Dublin and London national galleries.

LANE, Hunter (d. 1853), medical writer; licentiate of the Royal College of Surgeons, Edinburgh, 1829; MD, Edinburgh, 1830; published his *Compendium of Materia Medica and Pharmacy* (1840); president of the Royal Medical Society of Edinburgh.

LANE, Jane (afterwards Lady **FISHER**) (d. 1689), heroine; distinguished herself by her courage and devotion in the service of Charles II after the Battle of Worcester, 1651; helped Charles to escape his enemies in the disguise of her manservant; fled to France and finally entered the service of the princess of *Orange; rewarded by Charles at the Restoration and her pension continued by William III; married Sir Clement

Fisher, baronet, of Packington Magna, Warwickshire.

LANE, John (*fl.* 1620), verse-writer; friend of *Milton's father; left many poems in manuscript, but only published a poem denouncing the vices of Elizabethan society (1600), and an elegy upon the death of Queen Elizabeth (1603); completed in manuscript *Chaucer's unfinished 'Squire's Tale'.

LANE, John (1854–1925), publisher; clerk in Railway Clearing House, 1869–87; set up as bookseller and then as publisher in Vigo Street with Elkin Matthews, 1887–94; first book under imprint of 'Bodley Head' appeared, 1889; moved to the Albany, 1894; poetry published by firm includes works of Sir William *Watson, Francis *Thompson, and Richard *Le Gallienne; novels include those of W. J. *Locke; produced quarterly *Yellow Book*, to which famous poets, essayists, dramatists, story-tellers, and artists contributed, 1894–7.

LANE, John Bryant (1788–1868), painter; exhibited at Royal Academy, 1808–13; lived at Rome, 1817–27; devoted himself to portrait painting; exhibited at the Royal Academy till 1864.

LANE, Lupino (1892–1959), actor and theatre-manager; born into theatrical family of Lupino; established himself as a leading comedian; played cockney Bill Snibson in and also presented *Twenty to One* (London Coliseum, 1935) and *Me and My Girl* (Victoria Palace, 1937); in latter created 'The Lambeth Walk', the title used when play was filmed.

LANE, Sir Ralph (d. 1603), first governor of Virginia; sailed for North America in the expedition under Sir Richard *Grenville, 1583; governor of colony established at Wokokan, 1585; moved to Roanoke; brought home by Sir Francis *Drake with all the colonists, 1586, the settlement being a failure; employed in carrying out measures for the defence of the coast, 1587–8; muster-master in Drake's Portuguese expedition, 1589; served under *Hawkins, 1590; fought in Ireland, 1592–4; knighted, 1593.

LANE, Sir Richard (1584–1650), lord keeper; barrister, Middle Temple; practised in the court of Exchequer; deputy-recorder of Northampton, 1615; reader to the Middle Temple, 1630; attorney-general to the prince of Wales, 1634; counsel to the University of Cambridge, 1635; treasurer of the Middle Temple, 1637; defended Strafford, 1641; knighted, 1644; lord chief baron, 1644; DCL, Oxford, 1644; lord keeper, 1645; followed Charles II into exile; died at Jersey; author of *Reports in the Court of Exchequer from 1605 to 1612* (first published 1657).

LANE, Richard James (1800–1872), line-engraver and lithographer; elder brother of Edward William *Lane; famous for his pencil and chalk sketches, specially for his portrait of Princess Victoria, 1829; the best examples of his work in lithography, the *Sketches from Gainsborough*; lithographer to Queen Victoria, 1837, and to the prince consort (see ALBERT FRANCIS CHARLES AUGUSTUS EMMANUEL), 1840; helped to obtain the admission of engravers to the honour of full academician in 1865.

LANE, Samuel (1780–1859), portrait painter; studied under Joseph *Farington and under Sir Thomas *Lawrence; contributed to the Royal Academy, 1804–54.

LANE, Theodore (1800–1828), painter; came into notice as a painter of water-colour portraits and miniatures; etched prints of sporting and social life with delicate finish; took up oil-painting, 1825.

LANE, Thomas (*fl.* 1695), civilian; entered St John's College, Cambridge, 1673; BA, 1677; BA, Oxford, 1678; entered Merton College, Oxford, 1680; MA, 1683; DCL, 1686; bursar of Merton, 1688; left suddenly, carrying with him a large sum of money; wounded and taken prisoner at the Battle of the Boyne, 1689; released, 1690; practised as an advocate in Doctors' Commons, 1695.

LANE, William (1746–1819), portrait draughtsman; engraver of gems in the manner of the antique; engraved small copperplates after *Reynolds and *Cosway, 1788–92; became a successful artist in crayon portraits; contributed to the exhibitions, 1797–1815.

LANE, Sir (William) Arbuthnot, first baronet (1856–1943), surgeon; educated in Scotland; entered Guy's Hospital, 1872; MRCS, 1877; FRCS and demonstrator of anatomy, 1882; appointed to staff, 1888; his wonderful manual dexterity brought him to front rank in abdominal surgery; his three main surgical procedures were operation for cleft palate at one day old, for treatment of simple fractures, and for removal of large gut, which he believed to be a focus of sepsis; devised aseptic surgical excellence known as 'Lane technique'; at Hospital for Sick Children, Great Ormond Street, 1883–1916; consulting surgeon, Aldershot Command, 1914–18; during war organized and opened Queen Mary's Hospital, Sidcup, for plastic surgery; retired, 1918; founded New Health Society (1925) as first organized body dealing with social medicine; resigned from medical register (1933) for greater freedom in this work; baronet, 1913; CB, 1917.

LANEHAM, Robert (*fl.* 1575), probably John Laneham, actor; writer on the Kenilworth festivities of 1575; educated at St Paul's School, London; apprenticed to a London mercer; travelled abroad for trade purposes and became efficient linguist; door-keeper of the council chamber; present in this capacity at the entertainment given by *Leicester to Queen Elizabeth, 1575; published anonymously a description of the festivities in a letter dated 1575 (copies in the British Museum and Bodleian libraries). The work was reissued in 1784 and again in 1821.

LANE POOLE, Reginald (1857–1939), historian. See POOLE.

LANE-POOLE, Stanley Edward (1854–1931), orientalist and historian. See POOLE.

LANEY, Benjamin (1591–1675), bishop successively of Peterborough, Lincoln, and Ely; educated at Christ's College, Cambridge; BA, 1611; entered Pembroke Hall; MA, 1615; MA of Oxford, 1617; BD, 1622; DD and master of Pembroke Hall, 1630; vice-chancellor, 1632–3; chaplain to Charles I; deprived of his preferments as a Royalist and High-Churchman; ejected from Cambridge, 1643–4; at Restoration recovered his mastership and other preferments; bishop of Peterborough, 1660, of Lincoln, 1663, of Ely, 1667–75; FRS, 1666. His sermons were published (1668–9), and *Observations* upon a letter of Hobbes of Malmesbury (anon., 1677).

LANFRANC (1005?–1089), archbishop of Canterbury; born at Pavia; educated in the secular learning of the time and in Greek; studied law; set up a school at Avranches, in Normandy, 1039; gained a great reputation as a teacher; became a monk and entered the convent of Herlwin at Bec; prior, 1045; opened school in the monastery, to which scholars flocked from all parts of Europe; took part in the controversy with Berengar on the question of transubstantiation before Pope Leo IX, 1050; confuted Berengar at the Council of Tours, 1055, and in the Lateran Council held by Pope Nicholas II, 1059; abbot of St Stephen's, Caen, 1066; archbishop of Canterbury, 1070–89; worked in full accord with William the Conqueror; rebuilt Canterbury Cathedral after the fire of 1067 in Norman style; crowned William II, 1087; buried in Canterbury Cathedral; his collected works first published by Luc d'Achéry (1648).

LANG, (Alexander) Matheson (1877–1948), actor-manager and dramatist; cousin of Cosmo Gordon *Lang; educated at Inverness College and St Andrews; made first stage appearance, 1897; notably successful as Mr Wu (1913), Matathias in *The Wandering Jew* (1920), and Count Pahlen in *Such Men are Dangerous* (1928); produced *Jew Süss* (1929); repeated many stage successes on the cinema screen.

LANG, Andrew (1844–1912), scholar, folklorist, poet, and man of letters; educated at St Andrews and Glasgow universities and Balliol College, Oxford; fellow of Merton, 1868; settled in London and devoted himself to journalism and letters, 1875; poetical works include *Ballads and Lyrics of Old France* (1872), *xxii Ballades in Blue China* (1880), and *Helen of Troy* (1882); as anthropologist showed that folklore is foundation of higher or literary mythology; works on this subject include *Custom and Myth* (1884), *Myth, Ritual, and Religion* (1887), and *The Making of Religion* (1898); classical works include prose translation of *Odyssey* (with S. H. *Butcher, 1879), of *Iliad* (with Walter *Leaf and Ernest *Myers, 1883), and three books on Homeric question, *Homer and the Epic* (1893), *Homer and his Age* (1896), and *The World of Homer* (1910); historical works include *Pickle the Spy* (1897), *The Companions of Pickle* (1898), *Prince Charles Edward* (1900), and *History of Scotland* (1900–7); also author of *Life and Letters of J. G. Lockhart* (1896), and of essays, novels, and children's books; a founder of Psychical Research Society.

LANG, John Dunmore (1799–1878), writer on Australia; MA, Glasgow, 1820; ordained, 1822; went to New South Wales, 1823; DD, Glasgow, 1825; formed a church at Sydney in connection with the Established Church of Scotland; founded the *Colonist*, a weekly journal which lasted from 1835–40; edited first number of the *Colonial Journal*, 1841; edited the *Press*, 1851–2; encouraged emigration; New Zealand taken possession of for Queen Victoria in consequence of his representations, 1840; one of the six members for Port Phillip district to the legislative council which then ruled New South Wales, 1843–6; lectured in England on the advantages of Australia, 1846–9; represented various constituencies in the parliament of New South Wales, 1850–64; wrote largely on emigration and colonization; died at Sydney.

LANG, Sir John Gerald (1896–1984), secretary of the Admiralty; educated at Haberdashers' Aske's School, Hatcham; entered Admiralty as clerk, 1914; lieutenant in Royal Marine Artillery, 1917–18; promoted to assistant principal, Admiralty, 1930; principal, 1935; assistant secretary, 1939; during 1939–45 war director of labour concerned with organization of dockyard and shipyard work-force; under-secretary concerned with naval personnel, 1946; secretary of the Admiralty, 1947–61; principal adviser to government on sport, 1964–71; governor of Royal Bethlem and Maudsley hospitals, 1961–70; vice-president, Royal Naval Association and Royal Institute of Naval Architects; member, Worshipful Company of Shipwrights and Pepys Club; CB, 1946; KCB, 1947; GCB, 1954.

LANG, John Marshall (1834–1909), principal of Aberdeen University; educated at Glasgow University; hon. DD, 1873; hon. LL D, 1901; minister of East Parish of St Nicholas, Aberdeen, 1856–65, and of Anderston Church, Glasgow, 1865–8; there introduced improvements in ritual, including first organ used in Church of Scotland and psalms chanted in prose version; minister of Morningside, Edinburgh, 1868–73, and Barony of Glasgow, 1873–1901; served on School Board, on Commission for Housing of Poor, and kindred bodies in Glasgow; instituted Sunday evening services in Glasgow; visited Australia, 1897; convener of Assembly's commission of inquiry into religious condition of the people of Scotland, 1890–96; moderator of General Assembly, 1893; promoted Pan-Presbyterian Alliance for union of the Churches; principal of Aberdeen University, 1900–9; CVO, 1906; Baird lecturer at Glasgow, 1901; author of many devotional works.

LANG, (William) Cosmo Gordon, Baron Lang of Lambeth (1864–1945), archbishop of Canterbury; son of J. M. *Lang; educated at Glasgow University and Balliol College, Oxford; president of Union, 1884; second class, Lit. Hum., 1885; first, modern history, 1886; fellow of All Souls, 1888; deacon, 1890; priest, 1891; vicar of St Mary the Virgin, Oxford, 1894–6; of Portsea, 1896–1901; began lifelong association with royal family as a chaplain to Queen Victoria; canon of St Paul's and suffragan bishop of Stepney, 1901–9; archbishop of York, 1909–28; formed diocese of Sheffield, 1914; member of Royal Commission on Divorce, 1909–12; signed minority report; criticized for ill-timed reference to 'sacred memory' of German Emperor, 1914; visited Grand Fleet, 1915, Western Front, 1917, United States and Canada, 1918; took leading part in National Mission of Repentance and Hope, 1916; chairman, Commission on Ecclesiastical Courts and Cathedrals Commission; favoured 1549 communion service as alternative rite but accepted majority decision in Prayer Book discussions; worked closely with Randall *Davidson; succeeded him as archbishop of Canterbury, 1928; obtained 'Appeal to All Christian People' of 1920 Lambeth Conference; visited leading Orthodox ecclesiastics while cruising in Mediterranean; held joint theological commission at Lambeth, 1931; founded Church of England Council on Foreign Relations, 1933; sent delegation to Romanian Church (1935) resulting in Romania joining Jerusalem, Con-

stantinople, Cyprus, and Alexandria acknowledging Anglican orders by 'Economy'; served on Indian Joint Committee, 1933–4; agreed to total 'extinguishment' of tithe, 1936; broadcast on Abdication widely criticized, 1936; GCVO, 1937; resigned and created baron, 1942.

LANG, William Henry (1874–1960), botanist; educated at Dennistoun School and the University, Glasgow; B.Sc., botany and zoology, 1894; qualified in medicine, 1895; D.Sc., 1900; taught by F. O. *Bower and became authority on ferns; under D. H. *Scott acquired interest in fossil botany; lecturer in botany, Glasgow, 1902; Barker professor of cryptogamic botany, Manchester, 1909–40; his investigation, with Robert Kidston, of the 'Rhynie fossils' made unique contribution to evolutionary theory; FRS, 1911; hon. LL D, Manchester and Glasgow.

LANGBAINE, Gerard, the elder (1609–1658), provost of The Queen's College, Oxford; entered The Queen's College, Oxford, 1625; MA and fellow, 1633; keeper of the archives of the university, 1644; provost of Queen's College and DD, 1646; wrote literary and political pamphlets; a zealous Royalist and supporter of Episcopacy; left twenty-one volumes of collections of notes in manuscript to the Bodleian Library.

LANGBAINE, Gerard, the younger (1656–1692), dramatic biographer and critic; son of Gerard *Langbaine the elder; of University College, Oxford; married young and settled in London, where he led a gay and idle life; retired to Oxfordshire; published his best-known work, *An Account of the English Dramatic Poets, or some Observations and Remarks on the Lives and Writings of all those that have published either Comedies, Tragedies, Tragicomedies, Pastorals, Masques, Interludes, Farces, or Operas, in the English tongue*, valuable as a work of reference, but weak in bibliographical details (1691).

LANGDAILE (or LANGDALE), Alban (*fl.* 1584), Roman Catholic divine; educated at St John's College, Cambridge; fellow of St John's, 1534; MA, 1535; proctor, 1539; BD, 1544; took part in disputations concerning transubstantiation, 1549; DD, 1554; archdeacon of Chichester, 1555; chancellor of Lichfield Cathedral, 1559; refused to take oath of supremacy and was deprived of preferments; included in a list of popish recusants, 1561; retired to the continent; published controversial works.

LANGDALE, Barons. See LANGDALE, MARMADUKE, first baron, 1598?–1661; BICKERSTETH, HENRY, 1783–1851.

LANGDALE, Charles (1787–1868), Roman Catholic layman and biographer of Mrs Fitzherbert (see FITZHERBERT, MARIA ANNE); third son of Charles Philip Stourton, sixteenth Lord Stourton; assumed his mother's maiden name of Langdale, 1815; one of the first English Roman Catholics to enter parliament; MP, Beverley, 1834, Knaresborough, 1837–41; published *Memoirs of Mrs. Fitzherbert* (1856) to vindicate her character.

LANGDALE, Marmaduke, first Baron Langdale (1598?–1661); knighted, 1628; opposed ship money, 1639, but adopted the king's cause, 1642; raised regiment of foot, 1643; distinguished as a cavalry commander in the Civil War; routed at Preston and captured, 1648; escaped to the continent and entered the Venetian service; created Baron Langdale by Charles II, 1658.

LANGDON, John (d. 1434), bishop of Rochester; monk of Christ Church, Canterbury, 1398; studied at Oxford; DD, c.1410; one of the twelve Oxford scholars appointed to inquire into *Wycliffe's doctrines, 1411; bishop of Rochester, 1421; engaged on an embassy to France, 1432; died and was buried at Basle.

LANGDON, Richard (1730–1803), organist and composer; organist of Exeter Cathedral, 1753; Mus.Bac., Oxford, 1761; organist of Bristol Cathedral, 1767, of Armagh Cathedral, 1782–94; composed anthems and songs.

LANGDON, Stephen Herbert (1876–1937), Assyriologist; born in Michigan; educated in America and Europe; appointed reader in Assyriology, Oxford, as condition of Shillito foundation, 1908; professor, 1919–37; built up English school of Assyriologists; naturalized, 1913; FBA, 1931.

LANGDON-BROWN, Sir **Walter Langdon** (1870–1946), physician and regius professor of physic, Cambridge; educated at Bedford School and St John's College, Cambridge; first classes, natural sciences tripos, 1892–3; qualified at St Bartholomew's Hospital and house-physician to S. J. *Gee, 1897; medical registrar, 1906; assistant physician, 1913; full physician, 1924–30; assistant physician (1900), full physician (1906–22), Metropolitan Hospital; FRCP, 1908; senior censor, 1934; regius professor of physic, Cambridge, 1932–5; first English physician to relate work of psychologists like Freud, Jung, and Adler to practice of clinical medicine; published *Physiological Principles in Treatment* (1908); knighted, 1935.

LANGEVIN, Sir **Hector Louis** (1826–1906), Canadian statesman; born at Quebec; called to bar of Lower Canada, 1850; mayor of Quebec, 1858–60; member of Canadian Legislative Assembly, 1857–67; QC, 1864; solicitor-general for Lower Canada, 1864–6; postmaster-general, 1866–7; helped to form dominion of Canada; member of dominion House of Commons, 1867–96; secretary of state, 1867–9; minister of public works, 1869–73, 1879–91; postmaster-general, 1878–9; led French-Canadian Conservative party from 1873; KCMG, 1881; died at Quebec.

LANGFORD, Abraham (1711–1774), auctioneer and playwright; produced a ballad-opera, *The Lover his own Rival,* 1736; auctioneer in Covent Garden, 1748; the foremost auctioneer of the period.

LANGFORD, John Alfred (1823–1903), Birmingham antiquary and journalist; contributed to *Howitt's Journal*; joined Unitarians under George *Dawson; carried on printing business at Birmingham, 1852–5; closely associated with *Birmingham Daily Press,* 1855, and *Birmingham Daily Gazette,* 1862–8; an ardent Liberal, he helped in party organization; joined Gladstonian section of party, 1886; author of *Century of Birmingham Life* (2 vols., 1868) and *Modern Birmingham* (2 vols., 1873–7), and poems and dramas.

LANGFORD, Thomas (fl. 1420), historian; a Dominican friar; said to have written a chronicle and other works.

LANGHAM, Simon (d. 1376), archbishop of Canterbury, chancellor of England, and cardinal; became monk of St Peter's, Westminster, c.1335; abbot, 1349; treasurer of England, 1360; bishop of Ely, 1361; chancellor of England, 1363; the first to deliver speeches in parliament in English; archbishop of Canterbury, 1366; removed *Wycliffe from the headship of Canterbury Hall; created cardinal-priest, and forced to resign his archbishopric, 1368; cardinal-bishop of Praeneste, 1373; died at Avignon; buried first at Avignon, but his remains transferred to Westminster Abbey, 1379.

LANGHORNE, Daniel (d. 1681), antiquary; MA, Trinity College, Cambridge, 1657; fellow of Corpus Christi College, Cambridge, 1663; BD, 1664; university preacher, 1664; wrote antiquarian works in Latin and English.

LANGHORNE, John (1735–1779), poet; entered Clare Hall, Cambridge, 1758; commenced writing for the *Monthly Review,* 1764; assistant preacher at Lincoln's Inn, 1765; published *Poetical Works* (1766); translated *Plutarch's Lives* in collaboration with his brother *William (1770; 5th edn., 1792); prebendary of Wells Cathedral, 1777; best remembered as the translator of Plutarch.

LANGHORNE, Richard (d. 1679), one of Titus *Oates's victims; barrister, Inner Temple, 1654; accused by Oates of being a ringleader in the 'Popish Plot' of 1678; tried, condemned, and executed next year.

LANGHORNE, Sir **William,** first baronet (1629–1715), governor of Madras; of the Inner Temple; succeeded to his father's East India trade; created baronet, 1668; governor of Madras, 1670–7.

LANGHORNE, William (1721–1772), poet and translator; brother of John *Langhorne; assisted him in his translation of Plutarch, and published sermons and poetical paraphrases of some books of the Bible.

LANGLAND, John (1473–1547), bishop of Lincoln. See LONGLAND.

LANGLAND, William (1330?–1400?), poet; details of his life chiefly supplied from his one work, *The Vision of Piers the Plowman*; native of the Western Midlands; probably educated at the monastery of Great Malvern; went to London; engaged on his great poem, 1362–92; produced it in at least three versions (first, 1362, second, 1377, third, 1392), treating in them philosophical and social questions in the unrhymed alliterative line of the old English metre; possibly the author of *Richard the Redeless*, a poem written to remonstrate with Richard II.

LANGLEY, Batty (1696–1751), architectural writer; attempted to remodel Gothic architecture by the invention of five orders for that style in imitation of classical architecture; did good work in the mechanical branches of his art; wrote twenty-one works on architecture.

LANGLEY, Edmund de, first duke of York (1341–1402), fifth son of Edward III; accompanied his father to the French wars, 1359; KG, 1361; created earl of Cambridge, 1362; accompanied the Black Prince to Spain, 1367; sent to France, 1369; shared in sack of Limoges, 1370; married Isabel of Castile, daughter of Pedro the Cruel, 1372; king's lieutenant in Brittany, 1374; constable of Dover, 1376–81; member of the Council of Regency to Richard II, 1377; took part in the king's expedition to Scotland, 1385; created duke of York, 1385; regent during the king's absences, 1394–9; went over to the side of Henry of Lancaster (afterwards Henry IV); retired from the court after Henry IV's coronation, 1399.

LANGLEY, Henry (1611–1679), Puritan divine; of Pembroke College, Oxford; MA, 1635; master of Pembroke College, Oxford, 1647–62; canon of Christ Church, 1648; DD, 1649.

LANGLEY, John (d. 1657), grammarian; entered Magdalen Hall, Oxford; MA, 1619; high master of the College School, Gloucester, 1617–27 and 1628–35; of St Paul's School, 1640; a licenser of the press, 1643; published a work on rhetoric for St Paul's School (1644), and an *Introduction to Grammar*.

LANGLEY, John Newport (1852–1925), physiologist; BA, St John's College, Cambridge; fellow of Trinity College, Cambridge, 1877; carried out his first researches on new drug, pilocarpine, and then proceeded to study of secretory process; lecturer at Trinity College and university lecturer in physiology, 1883; professor of physiology, Cambridge University, 1903–25; owned and edited *Journal of Physiology*, 1894–1925; his acquisition of *Journal*, which he thoroughly reformed and made pattern in presentation of scientific work, decisive event for British physiology; climax of his achievement as investigator reached in his research into sympathetic nervous system, 1890–1906; subjected whole of sympathetic ganglionic system to exhaustive analysis; directed energies of workers in newly completed Cambridge physiological laboratory into channels of direct value in time of war, 1914–18; after European war attracted even larger numbers to his school of physiology at Cambridge, which was remarkably productive of distinguished physiologists; FRS, 1883; Croonian lecturer, 1906.

LANGLEY, Thomas (*fl.* 1320?), writer on poetry; monk of St Benet Hulme, Norfolk; author of *Liber de Varietate Carminum in capitulis xviii distinctus cum prologo*, of which ten chapters are preserved in manuscript at the Bodleian.

LANGLEY (or LONGLEY), Thomas (d. 1437), bishop of Durham, cardinal, and chancellor; educated at Cambridge; in his youth attached to the family of *John of Gaunt; canon of York, 1400; dean, 1401; keeper of the privy seal, 1403; chancellor, 1405–7; bishop of Durham, 1406; sent on embassies by the king, 1409, 1410, 1414; cardinal, 1411; again chancellor, 1417 (retiring, 1424); assisted at Henry VI's coronation, 1429; statesman and canonist.

LANGLEY, Thomas (d. 1581), canon of Winchester; BA, Cambridge, 1538; chaplain to Cranmer, 1548; canon of Winchester, 1559–81; BD, Oxford, 1560; chief work, an abridged English edition of Polydore *Vergil's De Inventoribus Rerum* (published 1546).

LANGLEY, Thomas (*fl.* 1745), engraver of antiquities, etc.; brother of Batty *Langley; drew and engraved for his brother's books.

LANGLEY, Thomas (1769–1801), topographer; of Eton and Hertford College, Oxford;

MA, 1794; held livings in Northamptonshire and Buckinghamshire; published *The History and Antiquities of the Hundred of Desborough and Deanery of Wycombe in Buckinghamshire* (1797).

LANGMEAD (afterwards **TASWELL-LANG-MEAD), Thomas Pitt** (1840–1882), writer on constitutional law and history; educated at King's College, London; barrister, Lincoln's Inn, 1863; BA, St Mary Hall, Oxford, 1866; practised as a conveyancer; tutor in constitutional law and legal history at the Inns of Court; joint editor of the *Law Magazine and Review*, 1875–82; professor of constitutional law and legal history at University College, London, 1882; edited for Camden Society (1858) *Sir Edward Lake's Account of his Interviews with Charles I, on being created a Baronet*; published a pamphlet, *Parish Registers: a Plea for their Preservation* (1872), and *English Constitutional History* (1875).

LANGRISH, Browne (d. 1759), physician; extra licentiate of the College of Physicians; FRS, 1734; published *The Modern Theory and Practice of Physic* (1735); delivered the Croonian lectures; graduated MD, 1747.

LANGRISHE, Sir Hercules, first baronet (1731–1811), Irish politician; BA, Trinity College, Dublin, 1753; MP for Knocktopher in the Irish parliament, 1760–1801; commissioner of barracks, 1766–74; supervisor of accounts, 1767–75; commissioner of revenue, 1774–1801; commissioner of excise, 1780–1801; opposed every effort to reform the Irish parliament; created baronet, 1777; privy councillor, 1777; introduced his Catholic Relief Bill, 1792; supported the union scheme, 1799; some of his speeches published.

LANGSHAW, John (1718–1798), organist; employed in London by the earl of *Bute, c.1761; organist of Lancaster Parish Church, 1772.

LANGSHAW, John (*fl.* 1798), organist; son of John *Langshaw (1718–1798); succeeded his father as organist at Lancaster, 1798; published hymns, chants, songs, and pianoforte concertos.

LANGSTON, John (1641?–1704), Independent divine; entered Pembroke College, Oxford, 1655; took out licence to preach, 1672; ministered in Ipswich, 1686–1704; author of two schoolbooks.

LANGTOFT, Peter of (d. 1307?), rhyming chronicler; author of a history of England up to the death of Edward I in French verse, the latter part of which was translated into English by *Robert of Brunne (first published in the Rolls Series, 1866 and 1868).

LANGTON, Bennet (1737–1801), friend of Dr *Johnson; as a lad obtained an introduction to the

doctor, who visited him at Trinity College, Oxford, 1759; member of the Literary Club, 1764; MA, 1765; famous for his Greek scholarship; professor of ancient literature at the Royal Academy, 1788; DCL, Oxford, 1790.

LANGTON, Christopher (1521–1578), physician; educated at Eton and King's College, Cambridge; BA, 1542; published treatises in English on medicine, 1547, 1550, and 1552; MD, Cambridge, 1552; FRCP, 1552–8; expelled for profligate conduct, 1558.

LANGTON, Sir George Philip (1881–1942), judge; educated at Beaumont and New College, Oxford; second class, modern history, 1902; president, OUDS; called to bar (Inner Temple), 1905; specialized in maritime law; director, labour department, commissioner, labour disputes, Ministry of Munitions, 1916–18; controller, demobilization department, Ministry of Labour, 1918–19; secretary and adviser, British Maritime Law Committee, 1922–30; KC, 1925; judge, Probate Divorce and Admiralty division, 1930–42; knighted and bencher, 1930.

LANGTON, John (*fl.* 1390), Carmelite; studied at Oxford, and was bachelor of theology; took part in the trial (1392) of the Lollard Henry *Crump, and wrote an account of it.

LANGTON, John de (d. 1337), bishop of Chichester and chancellor of England; clerk in the Royal Chancery and keeper of the Rolls; chancellor, 1292–1302; treasurer of Wells, 1294; bishop of Chichester, 1305; chancellor, 1307–9; built the chapter-house at Chichester.

LANGTON, Robert (d. 1524), divine and traveller; nephew of Thomas *Langton; educated at The Queen's College, Oxford; prebendary of Lincoln, 1483–1517; archdeacon of Dorset, 1486–1514; DCL, 1501; treasurer of York Minster, 1509–14; prebendary of York, 1514–24.

LANGTON, Simon (d. 1248), archdeacon of Canterbury; brother of Stephen *Langton; shared his brother's exile; returned to England, 1213; adopted the barons' cause; chancellor to Louis of France when he came to claim the English crown, 1216; exiled, 1217–27; archdeacon of Canterbury, 1227; rose into high favour with the king and pope; author of a treatise on the Book of Canticles.

LANGTON, Stephen (d. 1228), archbishop of Canterbury and cardinal; studied at Paris University; became a doctor in arts and theology; went to Rome and was made cardinal-priest, 1206; archbishop of Canterbury, 1207–28; at first rejected by King John, 1207; remained at Pontigny for the next five years after the interdict of 1208; tried to act as peacemaker between John and the pope (Innocent III); visited Dover in the hope of making terms, but had to return into exile, 1209; received by John, 1213; acted as mediator during the business of the Great Charter, which he supported, 1215; held at Osney a church council, which is to the ecclesiastical history of England what the assembly at Runnymede (1215) is to her secular history, 1222; occupied in political affairs during the earlier years of Henry III's reign; a famous theologian, historian, and poet.

LANGTON, Thomas (d. 1501), bishop of Winchester and archbishop-elect of Canterbury; fellow of Pembroke Hall, Cambridge, 1461; BD, Cambridge, 1465–6; also graduated at Bologna; chaplain to Edward IV before 1476; sent on embassies to France, 1467, 1476, 1477, 1478, and 1480; treasurer of Exeter, 1478; prebendary of Wells, 1478; prebendary of Lincoln, 1483; bishop of St David's, 1483; bishop of Salisbury, 1485; provost of The Queen's College, Oxford, 1489–95; bishop of Winchester, 1493–1500; elected archbishop of Canterbury, 22 Jan. 1501; died of the plague, 27 Jan.

LANGTON, Walter (d. 1321), bishop of Lichfield and treasurer; clerk of the king's Chancery; keeper of the king's wardrobe, 1292; a favourite councillor of Edward I; treasurer, 1295; bishop of Lichfield, 1297; accused of various crimes, 1301; formally absolved, 1303; accompanied Edward I to Scotland, and was present at his death, 1307; arrested by Edward II for misdemeanours as treasurer; imprisoned, 1308–12; liberated and restored to office of treasurer, 1312; in the king's council, 1315–18.

LANGTON, William (1803–1881), antiquary and financier; engaged in business in Liverpool, 1821–9; in Messrs Heywood's bank, Manchester, 1829–54; managing director, Manchester and Salford Bank, 1854–76; member of the Chetham Society, editing for it three volumes of miscellanies; an accurate genealogist, herald, and antiquary, philologist, and writer of English and Italian verse.

LANGTON, Zachary (1698–1786), divine; of Magdalen Hall, Oxford; MA, 1724; published anonymously *An Essay Concerning the Human Rational Soul* (1753).

LANGWITH, Benjamin (1684?–1743), antiquary and natural philosopher; educated at Queens' College, Cambridge; MA, 1708; DD, 1717; prebendary of Chichester, 1725; assisted Francis *Drake with his *Eboracum*; published scientific dissertations.

LANIER, Sir John (d. 1692), military commander; governor of Jersey under Charles II; knighted; lieutenant-general, 1688; served in Ireland under William III, 1689–91; one of the king's generals of horse in Flanders, 1692; mortally wounded at Battle of Steinkirk.

LANIER, Nicholas (1568–1646?), etcher; possibly cousin of Nicholas *Lanier (1588–1666).

LANIER (or LANIERE), Nicholas (1588–1666), musician and amateur of art; a musician in the royal household; composed music for masque by *Campion, 1613, for Ben *Jonson's *Lovers made Men*, and the *Vision of Delight*, 1617; master of the king's music, 1625; sent by Charles I to Italy to collect pictures and statues for the royal collection; followed the royal family into exile; reinstated as master of the king's music, 1660.

LANIGAN, John (1758–1828), Irish ecclesiastical historian; ordained at Rome; appointed to the chairs of Hebrew ecclesiastical history and divinity in the University of Pavia; published the first part of his *Institutiones Biblicae* (1793); DD, Pavia, 1794; returned to Ireland, 1796; assistant-librarian, foreign correspondent, and general literary supervisor to the Royal Dublin Society, 1799; assisted to found Gaelic Society of Dublin, 1808; principal work, *An Ecclesiastical History of Ireland, from the first Introduction of Christianity among the Irish to the beginning of the thirteenth Century* (1822).

LANKESTER, Edwin (1814–1874), man of science; articled to a surgeon; studied at London University, 1834–7; MRCS and LSA, 1837; MD, Heidelberg, 1839; secretary of the Ray Society, 1844; FRS, 1845; professor of natural history in New College, London, 1850; joint editor of the *Quarterly Journal of Microscopical Science*, 1853–71; president of the Microscopical Society of London, 1859; examiner in botany to the science and art department, 1862; engaged in important sanitary investigations; medical officer of health for the parish of St James's, Westminster, 1856–74; coroner for Central Middlesex, 1862–74; published works on physiology and sanitary science.

LANKESTER, Sir Edwin Ray (1847–1929), zoologist; son of Edwin *Lankester; BA, Christ Church, Oxford; Radcliffe travelling fellow, 1870; studied marine zoology at Naples, 1871–2; fellow and tutor, Exeter College, Oxford, 1872; Jodrell professor of zoology, University College, London, 1874–91; Linacre professor of comparative anatomy, Oxford, 1891–8; director of natural history departments and keeper of zoology, British Museum, South Kensington, 1898–1907; Fullerian professor of physiology and comparative anatomy, Royal Institution, 1898–1900; FRS, 1875; KCB, 1907; soon recognized as leading British authority on zoology; most distinguished as morphologist; his pioneer researches on embryology of Mollusca have had lasting influence on science of embryology; his researches on protozoan parasites important for study of disease; edited *Quarterly Journal of Microscopical Science*, 1878–1920; founded Marine Biological Association, 1884.

LANKRINK, Prosper Henricus (1628–1692), painter; born in Germany; studied at Antwerp; visited Italy; came to England and was employed by *Lely to paint the accessories in his portraits.

LANQUET (or LANKET), Thomas (1521–1545), chronicler; studied at Oxford and devoted himself to historical research; at his death was engaged on a useful general history, completed by Thomas *Cooper (1517?–1594).

LANSBURY, George (1859–1940), labour leader and politician; elected to Poplar board of guardians, 1892; known as the John Bull of Poplar; a non-smoker, teetotaller, and Anglican, whose socialism and uncompromising pacifism sprang from spiritual conviction; signed minority report as member (1905–9) of Royal Commission on poor laws; Labour MP, Bow and Bromley division, 1910–12, 1922–40; supporter of women's suffrage and defender of conscientious objectors; a founder (1912) and editor (1919–23) of *Daily Herald*; first commissioner of works, 1929–31; established Hyde Park Lido; leader of Labour party opposition, 1931–5; resigned over League of Nations sanctions; PC, 1929.

LANSDOWNE, first Baron (1667–1735), poet and dramatist. See GRANVILLE or GRENVILLE, GEORGE.

LANSDOWNE, marquises of. See PETTY, WILLIAM, first marquis, 1737–1805; PETTY-FITZMAURICE, HENRY, third marquis, 1780–1863; PETTY-FITZMAURICE, HENRY THOMAS, fourth marquis, 1816–1866; PETTY-FITZMAURICE, HENRY CHARLES KEITH, fifth marquis, 1848–1927.

LANT, Thomas (1556?–1600), herald and draughtsman; originally servant to Sir Philip *Sidney; entered College of Arms as Portcullis pursuivant, 1588; Windsor herald, 1597; wrote on heraldry.

LANTFRED (or LAMFRID) (*fl.* 980), hagiographer; author of 'De Miraculis Swithuni', printed partly in the *Acta Sanctorum*, the whole work being contained in the Cotton MSS.

LANYON, Sir **Charles** (1813–1889), civil engineer; surveyor of Co. Antrim, 1836–60; architect of some of the principal buildings in Belfast; mayor of Belfast, 1862; president of the Royal Institute of Architects of Ireland, 1862–8;

MP, Belfast, 1866; knighted, 1868; high sheriff of Co. Antrim, 1876.

LANYON, Sir **William Owen** (1842–1887), colonel and colonial administrator; son of Sir Charles *Lanyon; served in Jamaica during native disturbances, 1865; CMG, 1874; administrator of Griqualand West, 1885–8, of the Transvaal, 1879–81; KCMG, 1880; served in Egyptian campaign, 1882, with Nile expedition, 1884–5; died at New York.

LANZA, Gesualdo (1779–1859), teacher of music; born at Naples; became known in London as a singing-master; delivered lectures and wrote various works on the art of singing.

LAPIDGE, Edward (d. 1860), architect; sent various drawings to the Royal Academy; built a bridge over the Thames at Kingston, 1825–8, and altered and built several churches; FRIBA; surveyor of bridges and public works for Surrey.

LAPORTE, George Henry (d. 1873), animal painter; son of John *Laporte; exhibited sporting subjects at the Academy, British Institution, and Suffolk Street Gallery from 1818; foundation member of the Institute of Painters in Water-Colours.

LAPORTE, John (1761–1839), water-colour painter; drawing-master at the military academy at Addiscombe; exhibited landscapes at the Royal Academy and British Institution from 1785; in conjunction with William Frederick *Wells executed a set of seventy-two etchings from *Gainsborough, 1819; published works on art.

LAPRAIK, John (1727–1807); confined for a time as debtor after the collapse of the Ayr Bank, 1772; conducted a public-house and the village post-office at Muirkirk after 1796; published *Poems on Several Occasions* (1788); three famous 'Epistles' addressed to him by *Burns.

LAPWORTH, Edward (1574–1636), physician and Latin poet; MA, Exeter College, Oxford, 1595; master of Magdalen College School, Oxford, 1598–1610; licensed to practise medicine, 1605; MD, 1611; first Sedleian reader in natural philosophy, 1618; Linacre physic lecturer, 1619–35.

LARCOM, Sir **Thomas Aiskew** (1801–1879), Irish official; educated at Royal Military Academy, Woolwich; employed on Ordnance Survey of England and Wales, 1824–6, of Ireland, 1828–46; published admirable maps of Ireland; census commissioner, 1841; commissioner of public works, 1846; deputy-chairman of the Board of Works, 1850; under-secretary for Ireland, 1853; KCB, 1860; his administration marked by a steady increase of prosperity.

LARDNER, Dionysius (1793–1859), scientific writer; of Trinity College, Dublin; MA, 1819; LL D, 1827; FRS, 1828; took holy orders, but devoted himself to literary and scientific work; professor of natural philosophy and astronomy in London University, now University College, 1827; his principal work, the *Cabinet Cyclopaedia*, completed in 133 volumes (1849); edited the *Edinburgh Cabinet Library*, 1830–44; lectured in the United States and Cuba, 1840–5; settled at Paris, 1845; wrote at Paris works on railway economy and natural philosophy; died at Naples.

LARDNER, Nathaniel (1684–1768), biblical and patristic scholar; preached his first sermon, 1709; lectured on the 'Credibility of the Gospel History', out of which grew his great work, 1723; first two volumes of part i of his *Credibility* published (1727); part ii, vols. i–xii (1733–55); founder of the modern school of critical research in the field of early Christian literature, and remains the leading authority on the conservative side; DD, Marischal College, Aberdeen, 1745.

LARKE, Sir William James (1875–1959), first director of the British Iron and Steel Federation; educated at Colfe's School, Lewisham; joined British Thomson-Houston Company, 1898; executive engineer, 1912–15; joined Ministry of Munitions, 1915; director-general of raw materials, 1919; director, National Federation of Iron and Steel Manufacturers, 1922–34, of British Iron and Steel Federation, 1934–46; OBE, 1917; CBE, 1920; KBE, 1921; hon. D.Sc., Durham.

LARKHAM, Thomas (1602–1669), Puritan divine; MA, Trinity Hall, Cambridge, 1626; in trouble through his Puritan proclivities; fled to New England before 1641; returned, 1642; vicar of Tavistock before 1649; ejected from his benefice, 1662; wrote controversial pamphlets.

LARKIN, Philip Arthur (1922–1985), poet; educated at King Henry VIII School, Coventry and St John's College, Oxford; first class English language and literature, 1943; librarian, Wellington, Shropshire, 1943–6; assistant librarian, Leicester University, 1946–50; sub-librarian, Queen's University, Belfast, 1950–5; librarian, Brynmor Jones Library, Hull University, 1955–85; published novels *Jill* (1946) and *A Girl in Winter* (1947); reviewed jazz records for *Daily Telegraph*, 1961–71; reviews collected in *All What Jazz* (1970); book reviews collected in *Required Writing* (1983); prepared *Oxford Book of Twentieth-Century English Verse* (1973) while a visiting fellow at All Souls, 1970–1; chairman, Poetry Book Society; chairman, Booker Prize judges, 1977; poems collected in *The Less Deceived* (1956); *The Whitsun Weddings* (1964), and *High*

Windows (1974); honorary degrees from Belfast, Leicester, Warwick, St Andrews, Sussex, and Oxford universities; Queen's Gold Medal for poetry and other prizes and awards; hon. fellow, St John's College, Oxford, 1973; CBE, 1975; CH, 1985.

LARKING, Lambert Blackwell (1797–1868), antiquary; educated at Eton and Brasenose College, Oxford; MA, 1823; founder of the university lodge of Freemasons; hon. sec., Kent Archaeological Society, 1857–61; vice-president, 1861; edited volumes for the Camden Society, 1849, 1857, and 1861; the *Domesday Book of Kent* published (1869); made extensive preparations for a revision of *Hasted's *History of Kent*, the first instalment of which—the Hundred of Blackheath—appeared (1886).

LARMOR, Sir Joseph (1857–1942), physicist; graduated at Queen's College, Belfast; senior wrangler and fellow, St John's College, Cambridge, 1880; professor of natural philosophy, Queen's College, Galway, 1880–5; university lecturer in mathematics, Cambridge, 1885–1903; Lucasian professor of mathematics, 1903–32; FRS, 1892, a secretary, 1901–12; knighted, 1909; Unionist MP, Cambridge University, 1911–22; chiefly memorable for conception of matter as consisting entirely of electric particles, 'electrons', moving about in the aether according to electromagnetic laws (*Aether and Matter*, 1900); first to give the formula for rate of radiation of energy from an accelerated electron and to explain effect of a magnetic field in splitting lines of spectrum into multiple lines; edited works of *Cavendish, *Thomson, *Stokes, and *Kelvin, and own collected papers (2 vols., 1929).

LAROCHE, James (*fl.* 1696–1713), singer; appeared while a boy as Cupid in *Motteux's *Loves of Mars and Venus*, 1697; in a musical interlude, *The Raree Show*, 1713.

LAROON (or LAURON), Marcellus, the elder (1653–1702), painter and engraver; born at The Hague; migrated to England; best known by his drawings, *The Cryes of London*; painted draperies for Sir Godfrey *Kneller.

LAROON, Marcellus, the younger (1679–1772), painter and captain in the army; second son of Marcellus *Laroon the elder; studied painting and music; actor and singer at Drury Lane Theatre, London; joined the Foot Guards, 1707; fought at Oudenarde, 1708; deputy quartermaster-general of the English troops in Spain; returned to England, 1712; captain, 1718; a friend and imitator of William *Hogarth; best known for his conversation pieces.

LARPENT, Francis Seymour (1776–1845), civil servant; eldest son of John *Larpent; educated at St John's College, Cambridge; fellow, 1800–9; MA, 1802; called to the bar; deputy judge-advocate-general to the forces in the Peninsula, 1812–14; commissioner of customs, 1814; civil and Admiralty judge for Gibraltar; employed in secret service with reference to the Princess Caroline, 1815 and 1820; chairman of the Board of Audit of the Public Accounts, 1826–43; his *Private Journals* published (1853).

LARPENT, Sir George Gerard de Hochepied, first baronet (1786–1855), politician; son of John *Larpent; entered East India House of Cockerell & Larpent; chairman of the Oriental and China Association; deputy chairman of St Katharine's Docks Company; MP, Nottingham, 1841; created baronet, 1841; wrote pamphlets and edited works by his grandfather and his half-brother, Francis Seymour *Larpent.

LARPENT, John (1741–1824), inspector of plays; educated at Westminster; entered the Foreign Office; secretary to the duke of *Bedford at the Peace of Paris, 1763; inspector of plays, 1778.

LASCELLES, Sir Alan Frederick (1887–1981), royal secretary; educated at Marlborough and Trinity College, Oxford, 1905–9; joined Bedfordshire Yeomanry, 1913, and served with them during 1914–18 war; MC, 1919; aide-de-camp to Sir George Ambrose (later Lord) *Lloyd, governor of Bombay, 1919; assistant private secretary to Prince of Wales (later Edward VIII), 1920–9; private secretary to governor-general of Canada, V. B. *Ponsonby, Earl of Bessborough, 1931–5; CMG, 1933; assistant private secretary to George V, 1935, and to Edward VIII and George VI; private secretary to George VI and Elizabeth II, 1943–52; keeper of royal archives, 1943–53; PC, 1943; MVO, 1926; KCVO, 1939; GCVO, 1947; GCB, 1953; refused peerage; director, Midland Bank; chairman, Pilgrim Trust, 1954–60; chairman, Historic Buildings Council for England, 1953–63; hon. fellow, Trinity College, Oxford, 1948; DCL, Oxford, 1963; hon. LL D, Bristol and Durham.

LASCELLES, Mrs Ann (1745–1789), vocalist. See CATLEY, ANN.

LASCELLES, Sir Frank Cavendish (1841–1920), diplomat; entered Diplomatic Service, 1861; agent and consul-general, Bulgaria, 1879–87; British minister to Romania, 1887, to Persia, 1891; ambassador to Russia, 1894, to Berlin, 1896–1908; worked for Anglo-German amity till 1914; KCMG, 1886; PC, 1892.

LASCELLES, Henry, second earl of Harewood (1767–1841); MP, Yorkshire, 1796, 1802, and 1812, Westbury, 1807, Northallerton, 1818; styled Viscount Lascelles after death of his elder brother (1814), and succeeded his father, the first earl, 1820.

LASCELLES, Henry George Charles, sixth earl of Harewood (1882–1947), educated at Eton and Sandhurst; served with Grenadier Guards, 1915–18; DSO; inherited fortune of marquess of *Clanricarde, 1916; married Princess (*Victoria Alexandra Alice) Mary, only daughter of King George V, 1922; KG, 1922; succeeded father, 1929; GCVO, 1934; chancellor, Sheffield University, 1944–7; interested in the arts, freemasonry, and horse-racing.

LASCELLES, Rowley (1771–1841), antiquary and miscellaneous writer; educated at Harrow; barrister, Middle Temple, 1797; practised at the Irish bar for twenty years; selected by the record commissioners for Ireland (1813) to edit lists of all public officers recorded in Irish court of Chancery from 1540 to 1774, the work appearing as *Liber Munerum Publicorum Hiberniae, ab an. 1152 usque ad 1827* (vol. i, 1824, vol. ii, 1830); prefixed to it a history of Ireland which gave so much offence that the book was suppressed (reissued 1852); author of works on miscellaneous subjects.

LASCELLES, Thomas (1670–1751), colonel; chief engineer of Great Britain and deputy quartermaster-general of the forces; served as volunteer in Ireland, 1689–91; in the expedition to Cadiz, 1702; joined regular army, 1704; present at nearly all *Marlborough's battles; wounded at Blenheim, 1704; employed in the demolition of the fortifications, etc., of Dunkirk, 1713–16, 1720–5, and 1729–32; deputy quartermaster-general of the forces, 1715; director of engineers, 1722; master-surveyor of the ordnance and chief engineer of Great Britain, 1742.

LASKI, Harold Joseph (1893–1950), political theorist and university teacher; educated at Manchester Grammar School and New College, Oxford; first class, modern history, 1914; lecturer, McGill University, 1914–16; at Harvard (forming close friendship with Oliver Wendell Holmes), 1916–20; London School of Economics, 1920–6; professor of political science, 1926–50; after 1931 rejected pluralist theory of state, accepting Marxism; chairman of Labour party and chief target of Conservative electioneers, 1945; publications include *A Grammar of Politics* (1925), *Parliamentary Government in England* (1938), and *Reflections on the Constitution* (1951).

LASKI (or À LASCO), John (1499–1560), reformer; born in Poland; mistakenly claimed descent from Henry de *Lacy, third earl of Lincoln; at Bologna University, 1514–18; canon of Leczyc, 1517, of Cracow and Plock, 1518, and dean of Gnesen, 1521; lived at Basle in Erasmus's house, 1524–5; bishop of Vesprim, 1529; archdeacon of Warsaw, 1538; pastor of a congregation of reformers at Emden in East Frisia, 1542–8; superintendent of the London church of foreign Protestants, 1550; had great influence at Edward VI's court; promoted the Reformation in Poland, 1556–60; an austere Calvinist; published tracts advocating the Reformation.

LASSELL, William (1799–1880), astronomer; educated at a school at Rochdale; apprenticed in a merchant's office at Liverpool, 1814–21; brewer at Liverpool, 1825; built observatory at Starfield, near Liverpool, and erected a nine-inch Newtonian, the first example of the adaptation to reflectors of the equatorial plan of mounting, and with it followed the course of comets further than was possible at any public observatory; invented a new machine mounted at Starfield, 1846; verified discovery of Neptune by its aid, 1847; gold medallist, Royal Astronomical Society, 1849, and FRS, 1849; the first to ascertain clearly the composition of the Uranian system, 1851; removed his observatory to Bradstones, 1854; royal medallist, 1858; constructed a reflecting telescope of four feet aperture, 1859–60; mounted and worked with it at Valetta, 1861–4; set up an observatory near Maidenhead on his return to England; hon. LL D, Cambridge, 1874.

LASSELS, Richard (1603?–1668), Roman Catholic divine; educated probably at Oxford; student of the English College at Douai, 1623; professor of classics at Douai, 1629; ordained priest, 1632; published account of travels in Italy (1670); died at Montpellier.

LAST, Hugh Macilwain (1894–1957), Roman historian and principal of Brasenose College, Oxford; grandson of George *Macilwain; scholar of St Paul's School and Lincoln College, Oxford; first class, Lit. Hum., 1918; fellow, St John's, 1919–36; university lecturer in Roman history, 1927; Camden professor and fellow of Brasenose, 1936–48; principal of Brasenose, 1948–56; president, Roman Society, 1934–7; contributed to *Cambridge Ancient History* but his publications otherwise mainly reviews of works of others; especially successful in supervising young graduates; his main interests Roman Republican constitution, Roman legal system, and early history of Christianity; emeritus fellow, Brasenose.

LÁSZLÓ DE LOMBOS, Philip Alexius (1869–1937), painter; born in poor circumstances in Budapest; studied there and in Munich and Paris; painted Emperor Francis Joseph (1899), Pope Leo XIII (1900), and King Edward VII in 1907, when he moved to London and developed enormous practice among the famous; rapid painter of impeccable likenesses without deep psychological penetration; naturalized, 1914.

LASZOWSKA, (Jane) Emily De (1849–1905), novelist. See GERARD.

LATES, Charles (*fl.* 1794), organist and musical composer; son of John James *Lates; pupil of Dr Philip *Hayes; entered Magdalen College, Oxford, 1793; Mus.Bac., 1794; composed an anthem, and sonatas for the pianoforte.

LATES, John James (d. 1777?), organist; violinist and teacher of the violin at Oxford; probably organist of St John's College, Oxford; composed solos and duets for the violin and violoncello.

LATEWAR, Richard (1560–1601), scholar; educated at Merchant Taylors' School, London; scholar, 1580, and later fellow of St John's College, Oxford; MA, 1588; DD, 1597; accompanied Charles *Blount, eighth Baron Mountjoy, to Ireland, and died of a wound received at Benburb, Co. Tyrone; wrote Latin poems.

LATEY, Gilbert (1626–1705), Quaker; joined the Society of Friends, 1654; suffered imprisonment for his belief; exerted his influence successfully on behalf of the Quakers with James II and William and Mary; by persistently petitioning the king obtained act of 1697 (made perpetual, 1715), by which the Quaker affirmation became equivalent to an oath; author of several religious tracts.

LATEY, John (1842–1902), journalist; art and literary editor of *Penny Illustrated Paper*, 1861–1901; parliamentary reporter to *Illustrated London News* for fifteen years; co-editor (1881–2) with Mayne *Reid of *The Boys' Illustrated News*; edited *Sketch*, 1899–1902; author of *The Showman's Panorama* (1880) and novels.

LATHAM, Charles, first Baron Latham (1888–1970), public servant; changed name from Lathan; left elementary school in Norwich at 14 to work as clerk; after war service during 1914–18, qualified as member of London Association of Accountants; sole Labour member, Hendon Urban District Council, 1926–31; alderman, London County Council, 1928–34 and 1946–7; chairman, finance committee, LCC, 1934; leader, LCC, 1940–7; baron, 1942; chairman, London Transport Executive, 1947–53; lord-lieutenant, Middlesex, 1945–56;

founder member, Administrative Staff College, Henley, 1946–59, and Council of Europe, 1960–2.

LATHAM, Henry (1794–1866), poetical writer; third son of John *Latham (1761–1843); educated at Brasenose College, Oxford; entered the church; published *Sertum Shakesperianum, sub-nexis aliquot inferioris notae floribus* (1863).

LATHAM, Henry (1821–1902), master of Trinity Hall, Cambridge; BA, Trinity College, Cambridge (eighteenth wrangler), 1845; appointed clerical fellow of Trinity Hall, 1847; senior tutor, 1855; broadened aims of the college by destroying its exclusively legal associations; attracted promising men from other colleges; resigned tutorship, 1885; succeeded Sir Henry Sumner *Maine as master, 1888; rebuilt college and reconstructed lodge and hall; published *Pastor Pastorum* (1890) and other devotional works.

LATHAM, James (d. 1750?), portrait painter; called the 'Irish Van Dyck'. Among his sitters were Margaret *Woffington and Bishop *Berkeley.

LATHAM, John (1740–1837), ornithologist; educated at Merchant Taylors' School, London; studied anatomy under *Hunter; MD, Erlangen, 1795; studied archaeology; FSA, 1774; FRS, 1775; assisted to form the Linnean Society, 1788; chief work, *A General History of Birds* (1821–8).

LATHAM, John (1761–1843), physician; entered Brasenose College, Oxford, 1778; BA, 1782; studied at St Bartholomew's Hospital, London, 1782–4; MA, 1784; MB, 1786; physician to the Radcliffe Infirmary, Oxford, 1787; MD, 1788; FRCP, 1789; physician to the Middlesex Hospital, 1789–93, to St Bartholomew's Hospital, 1793–1802; Gulstonian lecturer, 1793; Harveian orator, 1794; Croonian lecturer, 1795; physician-extraordinary to the prince of Wales, 1795; published pamphlet on rheumatism and gout (1796), and works on clinical medicine.

LATHAM, John (1787–1853), poetical writer; eldest son of John *Latham (1761–1843); educated at Brasenose College, Oxford; elected fellow of All Souls College while an undergraduate, 1806; published anonymously a volume of poems (1836); English and Latin poems by him published posthumously (1853).

LATHAM, Peter Mere (1789–1875), physician; second son of John *Latham (1761–1843); educated at Brasenose College, Oxford; BA, 1810; commenced studying at St Bartholomew's Hospital, London, 1810; MA, 1813; MB, 1814; physician to the Middlesex Hospital, 1815–24; MD, 1816; FRCP, 1818; Gulstonian lecturer,

1819; physician to St Bartholomew's Hospital, 1824–41; joint lecturer on medicine in the school of St Bartholomew's Hospital, 1836; physician-extraordinary to Queen Victoria, 1837; Harveian orator, 1839; chief work, *Lectures on Clinical Medicine, comprising Diseases of the Heart* (1845).

LATHAM, Peter Walker (1865–1953), rackets and tennis champion; won World Rackets Championship, 1887; defended title against George Standing (1897) and Gilbert Browne (1902); resigned it 1902; gained British real tennis title, 1895; lost to C. Fairs, 1905; regained it and retired, 1907; for many years from 1888 head professional at Queen's Club.

LATHAM, Robert Gordon (1812–1888), ethnologist and philologist; of Eton and King's College, Cambridge; BA, 1832; studied in Germany, Denmark, and Norway; professor of English language and literature in University College, London, 1839; produced his well-known text-book on the English language, 1841; studied medicine; FRCP, 1846; MD, London; director of the ethnological department of the Crystal Palace, 1852; made protest against the Central Asian theory of the origin of the Aryans, 1862; completed his revision of *Johnson's Dictionary, 1870; published philological and ethnological works, 1840–78.

LATHAM, Simon (fl. 1618), falconer; published *Lathams Falconry or the Faulcons Lure and Cure, in two Bookes* (1615–18).

LATHBERY, John (fl. 1350), Franciscan; famous as a theologian throughout the later Middle Ages; DD, Oxford, after 1350; his best-known work, *Commentary on Lamentations*, one of the earliest books issued by the University Press, printed at Oxford (1482).

LATHBURY, Sir Gerald William (1906–1975), general; educated at Wellington College and Royal Military College, Sandhurst, 1924–5; commissioned into Oxfordshire and Buckinghamshire Light Infantry, 1926; seconded to Gold Coast Regiment, 1928–33; attended Staff College, Camberley, 1937–8; served in France, 1939–40; MBE; commanded 3rd Parachute brigade and then 1st Parachute brigade in North Africa, Sicily, and Italy; DSO, 1943; commanded 1st Parachute brigade at Arnhem, 1944; attended Imperial Defence College, 1948; major-general, commanding 16th Airborne division (TA), 1948; CB, 1950; commandant, Staff College, 1951; vice-adjutant-general, 1954; commander-in-chief, East Africa, 1955, at height of operations against the Mau Mau rebels in Kenya; KCB, 1956; director-general of military training, 1957; GOC-in-C, Eastern Command and promoted general, 1960; quartermaster-general to the forces, 1961–5; governor of Gibraltar, 1965–9; colonel commandant, 1st Royal Green Jackets and Parachute Regiment, 1961–5; ADC-general to the queen, 1962–5; GCB, 1962.

LATHBURY, Thomas (1798–1865), ecclesiastical historian; of St Edmund Hall, Oxford; MA, 1827; vicar of St Simon's, Baptist Mills, Bristol, 1848. His works include a history of Convocation and *A History of the Nonjurors* (1845).

LATHOM, Francis (1777–1832), novelist and dramatist; acted at and wrote for the Norwich Theatre before 1801; wrote several successful comedies and novels between 1795 and 1830.

LATHROP, John (d. 1653), independent divine. See LOTHROPP.

LATHY, Thomas Pike (*fl.* 1820), novelist; published *Memoirs of the Court of Louis XIV* (1819); perpetrated a successful plagiaristic fraud in the *Angler, a poem in ten cantos* (1819), copied from *The Anglers, Eight Dialogues in Verse* (1758); author of *Reparation, or the School for Libertines*, performed at the Boston Theatre, United States, 1800.

LATIMER, Barons. See LATIMER, WILLIAM, first baron of the second creation, d. 1304; LATIMER, WILLIAM, second baron, 1276?–1327; LATIMER, WILLIAM, fourth baron, 1329?–1381; NEVILLE, RICHARD, second baron of the third creation, 1468–1530; NEVILLE, JOHN, third baron, 1490?–1543.

LATIMER, Hugh (1485?–1555), bishop of Worcester; sent to Cambridge, 1500; fellow of Clare Hall and BA, 1510; MA, 1514; took priest's orders; refused to refute Luther's doctrines, 1525; compelled to explain himself before *Wolsey and dismissed, with liberty to preach throughout England; preached his famous sermons 'on the card', 1529; master in theology, Oxford, by 1530; preached before Henry VIII at Windsor, 1530; accused of heresy and brought before convocation by the bishop of London, and absolved on a complete submission, 1532; bishop of Worcester, 1535; preached Jane *Seymour's funeral sermon, 1537; encouraged Puritanism in his diocese; resigned his bishopric because he could not support the Act of the Six Articles, 1539; kept in custody for nearly a year; resumed preaching after eight years' silence and preached his famous sermon 'of the plough', 1548; committed to the Tower on Mary's accession, 1553; sent to Oxford with *Ridley and *Cranmer to defend his views before the leading divines of the university, 1554; condemned as a heretic and burnt at Oxford with Ridley, 1555; his extant writings edited for the Parker Society, 1844–5.

LATIMER, William, first Baron Latimer (d. 1304); served in Wales, 1276 and 1282; took part in the expedition to Gascony, 1292; employed in Scotland; present at the Battle of Stirling, 1297, at the Battle of Falkirk, 1298.

LATIMER, William, second Baron Latimer (1276?–1327), son of William *Latimer, first Baron Latimer; employed in Scotland, 1297–1303; taken prisoner at Bannockburn, 1314; released, 1315; a supporter of *Thomas of Lancaster, but afterwards of Edward II.

LATIMER, William, fourth Baron Latimer (1329?–1381), son of William, third baron; served in Gascony, 1359; governor of Bécherel in Brittany, 1360; KG, 1361; chamberlain of the king's household, 1369; constable of Dover Castle and warden of the Cinque Ports, 1374; in great favour with *John of Gaunt; impeached by the Commons as a bad adviser (this being the earliest record of the impeachment of a minister of the crown by the Commons), 1376; the attempt to bring him to justice unsuccessful; governor of Calais, 1377; served in France, 1380–1.

LATIMER, William (1460?–1545), classical scholar; fellow of All Souls College, Oxford, 1489; studied at Padua; MA, Oxford, by 1503; tutor to Reginald, Cardinal *Pole; prebendary of Salisbury; a great friend of Sir Thomas *More; his *Epistolae ad Erasmum* alone extant.

LA TOUCHE, William George Digges (1747–1803), resident at Bassorah; entered St Paul's School, London, 1757; proceeded to Bassorah, 1764; became British resident there; gained the goodwill of the natives and showed kindness to the principal citizens during the siege, 1775; returned to England, 1784; partner in La Touche's Bank in Dublin.

LATROBE, Charles Joseph (1801–1875), Australian governor and traveller; son of Christian Ignatius *Latrobe; educated for the Moravian ministry, but abandoned the design; travelled in Switzerland, ascending mountains and unexplored passes, 1824–6; travelled in America, 1832–4; superintendent at the time of the gold fever of the Port Phillip district of New South Wales, 1839 (the post converted into the lieutenant-governorship of Victoria, 1851); retired, 1854; CB, 1858; published descriptions of his travels.

LATROBE, Christian Ignatius (1758–1836), musical composer; studied at the Moravian College, Niesky, Upper Lusatia, 1771; teacher in the High School there; returned to England, 1784; secretary to the Society for the Furtherance of the Gospel, 1787, of the Unity of the Brethren in England, 1795; the last to hold the office of 'senior civilis' at the Herrnhut Synod, 1801;

undertook a visitation in South Africa in connection with his church, 1815–16; published an account of his travels (1818); composed anthems, chorales, and some instrumental works; editor of the first English edition of the *Moravian Hymn Tune Book*; chiefly remembered for his *Selection of Sacred Music from the works of the most eminent Composers of Germany and Italy* (1806–25).

LATROBE, John Antes (1799–1878), writer on music; son of Christian Ignatius *Latrobe; educated at St Edmund Hall, Oxford; MA, 1829; took orders; hon. canon of Carlisle Cathedral, 1858; author of *The Music of the Church considered in its various branches, Congregational and Choral* (1831) and of two volumes of hymns.

LATROBE, Peter (1795–1863), Moravian; son of Christian Ignatius *Latrobe; took orders in the Moravian Church and became secretary of the Moravian mission; wrote an *Introduction on the Progress of the Church Psalmody* for an edition of the *Moravian Hymn Tunes.*

LATTER, Mary (1725–1777), authoress; published *Miscellaneous Works in Prose and Verse* (1759); published tragedy, *The Siege of Jerusalem by Titus Vespasian* (1763; accepted for Covent Garden by John *Rich, who died before it could be produced; proved unsuccessful at Reading, 1768).

LATTER, Thomas (1816–1853), soldier and Burmese scholar; born in India; published a Burmese grammar, the first scholarly treatise on the subject (1845); chief interpreter in second Burmese War, and shared in the fighting, 1852; resident deputy-commissioner at Prome, where he was murdered, 1853.

LAUD, William (1573–1645), archbishop of Canterbury; entered St John's College, Oxford, 1589; fellow, 1593; MA, 1598; ordained, 1601; BD, 1604; DD, 1608; president of St John's College, Oxford, 1611; archdeacon of Huntingdon, 1615; dean of Gloucester, 1616; bishop of St David's, 1621–6; became predominant in the Church of England at Charles I's accession, 1625; supported the king in his struggle with the Commons; dean of the Chapel Royal, 1626; bishop of Bath and Wells, 1626–8; privy councillor, 1627; bishop of London, 1628–33; chancellor of the University of Oxford, 1629; archbishop of Canterbury, 1633; adopted the policy of compelling compulsory uniformity of action on the part of churchmen; interfered disastrously with the Scottish Church; impeached of high treason by the Long Parliament, 1640; committed to the Tower, 1641; tried, 1644; condemned and beheaded, 1645. In his ecclesiastical policy he failed to allow for the diversity of the elements which made up the national church. His sermons

were published (1651) and a collected edition of his works appeared (1695–1700).

LAUDER, George (*fl.* 1677), Scottish poet; grandson of Sir Richard *Maitland, Lord Lethington; MA, Edinburgh, *c.*1620; entered the English Army and became a colonel; as a Royalist spent many years on the continent and probably joined the army of the prince of Orange; his poems mainly patriotic and military.

LAUDER, Sir Harry (1870–1950), comedian; born in Portobello; miner; became professional entertainer giving songs with interlude of patter; immediate success in London, 1900; performed notably as rollicking, absurdly-kilted Highlander; usually wrote own words and music, drawing on traditional airs; songs included 'Roamin' in the Gloamin'', 'Stop your tickling, Jock'; frequently ended on serious note with song like 'The End of the Road'; indefatigable recruiter and entertainer in two wars; knighted, 1919.

LAUDER, James Eckford (1811–1869), painter; younger brother of Robert Scott *Lauder; studied at the Trustees' Academy, Edinburgh, 1830–3; contributed to the exhibitions of the Royal Scottish Academy from 1832; studied in Italy, 1834–8; member, RSA, 1846; exhibited at the Royal Academy, 1841–53.

LAUDER, Sir John, of Fountainhall, Lord Fountainhall (1646–1722); MA, Edinburgh, 1664; travelled and studied on the continent, 1665–6; passed advocate at the Scottish bar, 1668; member of the Scottish parliament for Haddingtonshire, 1685, 1690–1702, and 1702–7; a Protestant and supporter of the Revolution; a lord of session with the title of Lord Fountainhall, 1689; opposed the Union; chronicler and diarist; a portion of his diary, entitled *Chronological Notes of Scottish Affairs from 1680 till 1701*, published by Sir Walter *Scott (1822), the full diary printed by the Bannatyne Club (1840).

LAUDER, Robert Scott (1803–1869), subject painter; brother of James Eckford *Lauder; studied at Edinburgh and London, 1822–9; member of the Scottish Academy, 1829; exhibited there and at Royal Academy and British Institution, London, 1827–49; studied in Italy, 1833–8; principal teacher in the Drawing Academy of the Board of Trustees, Edinburgh, 1852–61; his greatest picture the *Trial of Effie Deans.*

LAUDER, Thomas (1395–1481), bishop of Dunkeld; master of the hospital of Soltre or Soltry, Midlothian, 1437; preceptor to James II; bishop of Dunkeld, 1452; finished the church of Dunkeld (begun by his predecessor, James *Kennedy (1406?–1465)), 1464; built bridge over the Tay, 1461; wrote life of Bishop John

Scott, one of his predecessors, and a volume of sermons.

LAUDER, Sir Thomas Dick, seventh baronet (1784–1848), author; son of the sixth baronet of Fountainhall, and a descendant of Sir John *Lauder of Fountainhall; contributed scientific papers to the *Annals of Philosophy* from 1815; succeeded to baronetcy, 1820; his most popular work, *Account of the great Moray Floods of 1829*, published (1830); secretary to the Board of Scottish Manufactures, 1839; encouraged the foundation of technical and art schools; published works on Scotland, 1837–48.

LAUDER, William (d. 1425), lord chancellor of Scotland and bishop of Glasgow; archdeacon of Lothian; bishop of Glasgow, 1408; lord chancellor, 1423–5.

LAUDER, William (1520?–1573), Scottish poet; educated at St Andrews University; took priest's orders; celebrated as a deviser of court pageants, 1549–58; joined the reformers, 1560; appointed minister, c.1563. His published verse, of which there are five separate volumes, consists mainly of denunciation of the immoral practices current in Scotland in his time.

LAUDER, William (d. 1771), literary forger; educated at Edinburgh University; MA, 1695; a good classical scholar and student of modern Latin verse; published (1739) *Poetarum Scotorum Musae Sacrae*; published articles in the *Gentleman's Magazine* to prove that *Paradise Lost* was largely plagiarized from seventeenth-century Latin poets, 1747 (reprinted as *An Essay on Milton's Use and Imitation of the Moderns in his 'Paradise Lost'*, with a preface by Dr *Johnson, 1750). It was proved by John *Douglas, afterwards bishop of Salisbury, that Lauder had himself interpolated in the works of Masenius and Staphorstius (seventeenth-century Latin poets) extracts from a Latin verse rendering of *Paradise Lost*. He confessed and apologized in *A Letter to the Reverend Mr. Douglas* (1751), and emigrated to Barbados, where he died. Incidentally he proved that *Milton had deeply studied the works of modern Latin poets.

LAUDERDALE, duchess of (d. 1697). See MURRAY, ELIZABETH.

LAUDERDALE, duke of (1616–1682). See MAITLAND, JOHN.

LAUDERDALE, earls of. See MAITLAND, JOHN, second earl, 1616–1682; MAITLAND, CHARLES, third earl, d. 1691; MAITLAND, RICHARD, fourth earl, 1653–1695; MAITLAND, JOHN, fifth earl, 1650?–1710; MAITLAND, JAMES, eighth earl, 1759–1839; MAITLAND, ANTHONY, tenth earl,

1785–1863; MAITLAND, THOMAS, eleventh earl, 1803–1878.

LAUGHARNE, Rowland (*fl.* 1648), soldier; took up arms for parliament, 1642; commander-in-chief of the forces in Pembrokeshire; appointed commander-in-chief of the counties of Glamorgan, Cardigan, Carmarthen, and Pembroke, 1646; deserted to the king, 1648; forced to surrender to *Cromwell, 1648; court-martialled; was condemned to death with two others, but escaped through being, with his companions, allowed to cast lots for his life, 1649; pensioned by Charles II, 1660.

LAUGHTON, George (1736–1800), divine; educated at Wadham College, Oxford; MA, 1771; DD, 1771; chief works, *The History of Ancient Egypt* (1774) and *The Progress and Establishment of Christianity, in reply to . . . Mr. Gibbon* (1780).

LAUGHTON, Sir John Knox (1830–1915), naval historian; BA, Caius College, Cambridge; naval instructor in navy, 1853; transferred to Royal Naval College, Portsmouth, 1866; instructor at Greenwich Naval College, 1873–85; lectured there on naval history, 1876–89; professor of history, King's College, London, 1885–1914; founded Navy Records Society, 1893; first secretary, 1893–1912; knighted, 1907; edited *Memoirs relating to Lord Torrington* (1889), Lord *Barham's papers (1907–10), etc.; wrote books on *Nelson, etc.; contributor to this Dictionary.

LAUGHTON, Richard (1668?–1723), prebendary of Worcester; MA, Clare College, Cambridge, 1691; ardently supported the Newtonian philosophy; prebendary of Worcester, 1717.

LAURENCE. See also LAWRENCE.

LAURENCE (or LAWRENCE), Edward (d. 1740?), land surveyor; brother of John *Laurence; an expert on agricultural subjects, and famous for his books of maps; wrote on surveying and farming.

LAURENCE, French (1757–1809), civilian; brother of Richard *Laurence; educated at Winchester School and Corpus Christi College, Oxford; MA, 1781; devoted himself to civil law; DCL, 1787; contributed to the *Rolliad*; helped *Burke in preparing the preliminary case against Warren *Hastings, and was retained as counsel, 1788; friend and literary executor of Edmund Burke; regius professor of civil law at Oxford, 1796; MP, Peterborough, 1796; chancellor of the diocese of Oxford; a judge of the court of Admiralty of the Cinque Ports; his *Poetical Remains* published with those of his brother, Richard Laurence (1872).

LAURENCE, John (c.1668–1732), writer on gardening; entered Clare Hall, Cambridge, 1685; BA, 1688–9; fellow of Clare Hall; prebendary of Sarum; published sermons, and works on gardening.

LAURENCE, Richard (1760–1838), archbishop of Cashel; brother of French *Laurence; educated at Corpus Christi College, Oxford; MA, 1785; entered holy orders; DCL, 1794; deputy professor of civil law, Oxford, 1796; Bampton lecturer, 1804; regius professor of Hebrew and canon of Christ Church, Oxford, 1814; archbishop of Cashel, Ireland, 1822. His writings include Latin and English translations of Ethiopic versions of apocryphal books of the Bible.

LAURENCE, Roger (1670–1736), nonjuror; educated at Christ's Hospital; studied divinity; ordained, 1714; headed a new party among the nonjurors, who objected to lay baptism; author of controversial pamphlets on lay baptism.

LAURENCE, Samuel (1812–1884), portrait painter; executed oil or crayon portraits of contemporary celebrities; exhibited at the Society of British Artists, 1834–53, at the Royal Academy, 1836–82.

LAURENCE, Thomas (1598–1657), master of Balliol College, Oxford; educated at Balliol; fellow of All Souls College before 1618, MA, 1621; MA, Cambridge, 1627; BD, 1629; chaplain to Charles I; master of Balliol, 1637–46; Margaret professor of divinity, 1638–48; received certificate, 1648, attesting that he engaged to preach only practical divinity; appointed to an Irish bishopric by Charles II, but died before he could be consecrated; published three sermons.

LAURENCE O'TOOLE, Saint (1130?–1180), Irish saint and first archbishop of Dublin. See O'TOOLE.

LAURENT, Peter Edmund (1796–1837), classical scholar; born in Picardy; educated at the Polytechnic School, Paris; taught modern languages at Oxford University; French master at the Royal Naval College, Portsmouth; visited Italy and Greece, 1818–19; published Recollections of a Classical Tour (1821).

LAURENTIUS (d. 619), second archbishop of Canterbury. See LAWRENCE.

LAURIE, James Stuart (1832–1904), inspector of schools, 1854–63; held educational posts in Ireland and Ceylon; called to bar, 1871; published school handbooks.

LAURIE, Sir **Peter** (1779?–1861), lord mayor of London; saddler in London, becoming contractor for the Indian Army; sheriff, 1823; knighted, 1824; alderman, 1826; lord mayor, 1832; master of the Saddlers' Company, 1833; chairman of the Union Bank, 1839–61; published two works on prison reform.

LAURIE, Robert (1755?–1836), mezzotint engraver; his earliest portraits in mezzotint, 1771; acted as publisher of engravings, maps, charts, and nautical works, 1794–1812. His plates include both subject pictures and portraits.

LAURIE, Simon Somerville (1829–1909), educational reformer; elder brother of James Stuart *Laurie; MA, Edinburgh University, 1849; secretary to education committee of Church of Scotland at Edinburgh, 1855–1905; his reports as visitor and examiner for Dick Bequest Trust (1856–1907) gave masterly expositions of educational principles and practice; his report on the Edinburgh Merchant Company's 'hospitals' led to their reform by act of parliament, 1869; secretary to Royal Commission on Endowed Schools in Scotland, 1872; first Bell professor of education in Edinburgh University, 1876–1903; president of Teachers' Guild of Great Britain, 1891; hon. LL D of St Andrews, Edinburgh, and Aberdeen universities; wrote on *Training of Teachers* (1882), *Institutes of Education* (1892), and *Educational Opinion from the Renaissance* (1903); his philosophical works include *Metaphysica, Nova et Vetusta* (1884) and *Ethica* (1885); Gifford lecturer in natural theology at Edinburgh, 1905–6; embodied these lectures in *Synthetica* (1906).

LAURIER, Sir **Wilfrid** (1841–1919), Canadian statesman; French Canadian; born near Montreal; elected to Legislature of Quebec, 1871; Liberal member of Canadian parliament for Drummond–Arthabaska, 1874; entered Cabinet of Alexander *Mackenzie, 1877; member for Quebec East, 1877–1919; in opposition, 1878–96; leader of Liberal party in succession to Edward *Blake, 1888; prime minister of Canada, 1896–1911; GCMG, 1897; attacked by Nationalist leader, Bourassa, for sending contingents to help of Great Britain in South African War (1900) and for policy of Canadian Navy (1910); supported Conservative government's war policy, 1914–18, but refused to form coalition, 1917.

LAUTERPACHT, Sir **Hersch** (1897–1960), international lawyer; born in Eastern Galicia; obtained doctorates in law (1921) and political science (1922), Vienna; an active Zionist; LL D, London School of Economics, 1925; assistant lecturer, 1927; naturalized, 1931; reader in public international law, London University, 1935–8; Whewell professor of international law, Cambridge, 1938–55; called to bar (Gray's Inn), 1936; bencher, 1955; KC, 1949; member, United Nations' International Law Commission,

1951–5; judge, International Court of Justice, 1954–60; revised *Manual of Military Law* (1958); edited *British Year Book of International Law*, 1944–54, and *Annual Digest of Public International Cases*, 1929–56; FBA, 1948; knighted, 1956.

LAUWERYS, Joseph Albert (1902–1981), educationist; born in Brussels; came to England, 1914; educated at Leicester and Bournemouth and King's College, London University; first class, B.Sc., 1927; physics master, Christ's Hospital, Horsham, 1928; lecturer in methods of teaching science in schools, London University Institute of Education, 1932; reader in comparative education, 1941; first professor of comparative education, 1947–70; director, Atlantic Institute of Education, Halifax, Nova Scotia, 1970–6; wrote many textbooks and works on science-teaching, and contributed as senior editor of *World Year Book of Education*, 1947–70; published *Science, Morals and Moralogy* (1976); awarded doctorate by Ghent University (1946); commander of Order des Palmes Académiques, 1961; 'professor associé' at the Sorbonne, 1969–71; D.Lit., London, 1958 and fellow, King's College; served on numerous committees and commissions and with Lord *Boyle of Handsworth co-chaired the education committee of the parliamentary group for world government; also interested in Basic English as lingua franca.

LAVENHAM (or LAVYNGHAM), Richard (*fl.* 1380), Carmelite; Carmelite friar at Ipswich; studied at Oxford; prior of the Carmelite house at Bristol; confessor to Richard II; more than sixty treatises ascribed to him.

LAVER, James (1899–1975), museum keeper, author, and broadcaster; educated at Liverpool Institute and New College, Oxford; served in army during 1914–18 war; BA and B.Litt., Oxford, 1921–2; won Newdigate Prize with poem on Cervantes; regular contributor to *Isis*; joined Victoria and Albert Museum, 1922, eventually becoming keeper of departments of engraving, illustration, design, and paintings, 1938–59; ran voluntary classes for the Working Men's College, Camden Town; wrote large number of articles and books, including *A Stitch in Time* (1927); a best-selling novel, *Nymph Errant* (1932), which (Sir) C. B. *Cochran turned into a musical with Gertrude *Lawrence as leading lady, 1933; *Taste and Fashion* (1937), *The First Decadent*, a biography of J. K. Huysmans (1954), and books on J. A. McN. *Whistler (1930), James Tissot (1936), French nineteenth-century painting (1937), and several on costume and fashion; during 1939–45 war helped to promote National Savings Campaign; CBE, 1951; FRSA, FRSL, and hon. RE; became well known as broadcaster

in programmes such as 'The Brains Trust' and 'The Critics'; published autobiography, *Museum Piece* (1963); honorary doctorate, Manchester; died in a fire at his home in Blackheath.

LAVERY, Sir John (1856–1941), painter; born in Belfast; apprenticed to painter-photographer, Glasgow; studied at Glasgow School of Art, Heatherley's, and Académie Julian; influenced for a time by J. A. M. *Whistler; painted Queen Victoria's state visit to Glasgow Exhibition, 1888; thereafter uninterruptedly successful, especially with portraits of women, including *Miss Mary Burrell* (Glasgow) and *Mrs. Lavery Sketching* (Dublin); presented collections of portraits of contemporary statesmen to Dublin and Belfast; also painted conversation pieces and scenes such as *Casement trial; knighted, 1918; RA, 1921.

LAVINGTON, Baron (1738?–1807). See PAYNE, Sir RALPH.

LAVINGTON, George (1684–1762), bishop of Exeter; educated at Winchester and New College, Oxford; fellow of New College, Oxford, 1708; BCL, 1713; DCL, 1732; bishop of Exeter, 1747–62; opponent of Methodism.

LAVINGTON, John (1690?–1759), Presbyterian divine; ordained, 1715; drew up the formula of orthodoxy (1718) that was for thirty-five years the condition of ordination by the Exeter Assembly; instituted a 'Western academy' at Ottery St Mary, 1752; his pamphlets dealing with the Exeter controversy published anonymously (1719–20).

LAVINGTON, John (d. 1764), Nonconformist tutor; son of John *Lavington (1690?–1759); ordained, 1739; principal tutor at the 'Western academy'; published sermons, 1743–59.

LAW, Andrew Bonar (1858–1923), statesman; born in New Brunswick; brought up in Glasgow by his mother's relations from age of 11; educated at Glasgow High School; entered his Kidston relations' firm of merchant bankers, 1874; junior partner in Glasgow firm of William Jacks & Co., iron-merchants, 1885; a director of Clydesdale Bank and chairman of Glasgow Iron Trade Association; Unionist MP, Blackfriars and Hutchesontown division of Glasgow, 1900–6; parliamentary secretary to Board of Trade, 1902; supported Joseph *Chamberlain's scheme of colonial preference and tariff reform, 1903; returned MP, Dulwich, at by-election, 1906; with Austen *Chamberlain now recognized as most effective advocate of fiscal change in Unionist party; denounced Lloyd George's budget of 1909 as socialism 'pure and unadulterated'; again returned for Dulwich, Jan. 1910; failed to capture North-West Manchester, Dec.; returned MP, Bootle division of Lancashire, at by-election, 1911; supported Lord *Lansdowne and Balfour in decision to accept Parliament Bill, 1911; elected leader of opposition in House of Commons, 1911; with Sir Edward *Carson shared leadership of faction which carried opposition to Irish home rule to brink of civil war; on outbreak of European war tendered Asquith support of Unionist party in resisting German aggression, Aug. 1914; relegated to insignificant position of secretary for colonies in first coalition ministry, May 1915; led group in Cabinet which pressed for evacuation of Dardanelles, autumn 1915; took charge of Compulsory Military Service Bill, Jan. 1916; invited by King George V to form administration, Dec.; on failure to secure co-operation first of Lloyd George and then of Asquith, advised king to call on Lloyd George; chancellor of Exchequer and leader of House of Commons in Lloyd George's government; this 'most perfect partnership in political history' profoundly affected fortunes of war; issued series of War Loans on lower interest basis for long terms, one of the greatest achievements in history of British finance; his campaign for national war bonds (Oct. 1917) provided state with continuous flow of money until end of war; introduced war budgets of 1917 and 1918; the 1918 budget unparalleled in demands which it made on nation; throughout these anxious years couched his appeals for sacrifice in markedly sober speeches; supported continuance of coalition, 1918; MP, Central Glasgow, 1918; lord privy seal and leader of House of Commons, 1918; signatory of Treaty of Versailles, 1919; resigned, owing to ill health, March 1921; emerged from retirement in order to recommend Irish treaty, autumn 1921; prime minister, with purely Conservative government, and leader of party, Oct. 1922; outlined programme of negation as best method of securing national recovery; presided at conference of Allied prime ministers on subject of reparations in London (Dec. 1922) and Paris (Jan. 1923); conference broke down owing to failure of English and French to come to agreement over policy with regard to German finance; with utmost reluctance accepted settlement demanded by USA with regard to British debt, Jan. 1923; resigned office, May 1923.

LAW, Augustus Henry (1833–1880), Jesuit; eldest son of William Towry *Law; joined Jesuits, 1854; with the mission in Demerara, 1866–71; joined first missionary staff to the Zambezi, 1879; died at King Umzila's kraal.

LAW, Charles Ewan (1792–1850), recorder of London; second son of Edward *Law, first Baron Ellenborough; educated at St John's College, Cambridge; MA, 1812; barrister, Inner Temple, 1817; a judge of the sheriff's court, 1828; KC,

1829; common serjeant, 1830; recorder of London, 1833–50; MP for Cambridge University, 1835–50; treasurer, Inner Temple, 1839; LL D, Cambridge, 1847.

LAW, David (1831–1901), etcher and water-colour painter; student at Trustees' Academy, Edinburgh, 1845–50; engraver in Ordnance Survey Office, Southampton, 1850–70; helped to found Royal Society of Painter-Etchers, 1880; his etchings after *Turner and Corot were in great demand, 1875–90; best work done in water-colour.

LAW, Edmund (1703–1787), bishop of Carlisle; educated at St John's College, Cambridge; fellow of Christ's College, Cambridge; MA, 1727; published *Essay on the Origin of Evil* (1731), *Enquiry into the Ideas of Space and Time* (1734), *Considerations on the State of the World with regard to the Theory of Religion* (1745); a disciple of *Locke in his philosophical opinions and a Whig in politics; master of Peterhouse, Cambridge, 1756–68; vice-chancellor, 1755–6; librarian of the university of Cambridge, 1760; Knightbridge professor of moral philosophy, 1764; bishop of Carlisle, 1768–87; published anonymously a pamphlet, *Considerations on the Propriety of requiring Subscription to Articles of Faith*, advocating religious tolerance (1774); edited Locke's *Works* (1777).

LAW, Edward, first Baron Ellenborough (1750–1818), lord chief justice of England; fourth son of Edmund *Law; educated at the Charterhouse (1761–7) and Peterhouse, Cambridge; fellow, 1771; MA, 1774; commenced practice as a special pleader, 1775; barrister, Lincoln's Inn, 1780; KC, 1787; retained as leading counsel for Warren *Hastings, 1788; opened the defence, 1792; attorney-general, 1801; serjeant of the county palatine of Lancaster, 1793; counsel for the crown at various state trials, 1794–1802; knighted, 1801; MP for Newtown, Isle of Wight, 1801; lord chief justice of England, created Baron Ellenborough and privy councillor, 1802; speaker of the House of Lords, 1805; admitted to the Cabinet of 'All the Talents' without office, 1806; councillor to George III's queen during the regency, 1811; resigned office, 1818.

LAW, Edward, first earl of Ellenborough (1790–1871), governor-general of India; eldest son of Edward *Law, first Baron Ellenborough; educated at Eton and St John's College, Cambridge; MA, 1809; Tory MP, St Michael's, Cornwall, 1813; succeeded his father as second baron, 1818; lord privy seal, 1828; president of the Board of Control, whence began his connection with Indian affairs, 1828–30, 1834–5, 1841, and 1858; governor-general of India, 1841; successfully contended with great difficulties in China and Afghanistan, 1842; responsible for the annexation of Sind, 1843; unpopular with the civilians; subjugated Gwalior, 1844; recalled and created earl of Ellenborough, 1844; first lord of the Admiralty in Sir Robert Peel's reconstituted ministry, 1846; president of the Board of Control under Lord Derby, 1858.

LAW, Sir **Edward Fitzgerald** (1846–1908), expert in state finance; joined Royal Artillery, 1868; retired, 1872; started business agency in Russia; acting consul at St Petersburg, 1880–1; commercial and financial attaché for Russia, Persia, and Asiatic Turkey, 1888; British delegate for negotiating commercial treaty with Turkey, 1890; reported on Greek finance, 1892–3, and on railway development in Asiatic Turkey, 1895; as commercial secretary at Vienna negotiated commercial treaty with Bulgaria, 1896–7; British delegate at Constantinople for determining Greece's war indemnity to Turkey, 1897; president of international commission on Greek finance, 1898; KCMG, 1898; finance member of government in India, 1900; completed currency reform and reduced arrears of land revenue, income and salt taxes; CSI, 1903; KCSI, 1906; an active champion of imperial preference and tariff reform; represented Great Britain on Cretan Reform Commission, and on committee to found bank of Morocco, 1906; died in Paris; buried at Athens.

LAW, George Henry (1761–1845), bishop successively of Chester and of Bath and Wells; son of Edmund *Law; educated at Charterhouse and Queens' College, Cambridge; fellow, 1781; MA, 1784; DD, 1804; bishop of Chester, 1812–24; bishop of Bath and Wells, 1824–45; FRS and FSA; published sermons, charges, and addresses.

LAW, Henry (1797–1884), dean of Gloucester; son of George Henry *Law; educated at Eton and St John's College, Cambridge; fellow, 1821; MA, 1823; one of the first examiners in the classical tripos, 1824–5; archdeacon of Richmond, 1824, of Wells, 1826; residentiary canon of Wells, 1828; dean of Gloucester, 1862–84; one of the leaders of the Evangelical party in the church; author of *Christ is All*, vols. i–iv, *The Gospel in the Pentateuch* (1854–8), other theological works, and numerous tracts.

LAW, Hugh (1818–1883), lord chancellor of Ireland; educated at Trinity College, Dublin; BA, 1839; called to the bar, 1840; QC, 1860; drafted the Irish Church Act; legal adviser to lord-lieutenant of Ireland, 1868; bencher of the King's Inns, Dublin, 1870; solicitor-general for Ireland, 1872; Irish privy councillor and

attorney-general for Ireland, 1873; MP, Londonderry, 1874; attorney-general again under Gladstone, 1880; lord chancellor for Ireland, 1881; LL D.

LAW, James (1560?–1632), archbishop of Glasgow; graduated at St Andrews, 1581; minister of Kirkliston, 1585; a royal chaplain, 1601; titular bishop of Orkney, 1605; moderator of the general assembly, 1608; bishop of St Andrews, 1611–15; archbishop of Glasgow, 1615; zealously supported James I's ecclesiastical policy.

LAW, James A. B. (1768–1828), general in the French Army; grandnephew of John *Law (1671–1729); a distinguished general in the French Army, a favourite aide-de-camp of Napoleon I; made a marshal of France by Louis XVIII; created comte de Lauriston.

LAW, James Thomas (1790–1876), chancellor of Lichfield; eldest son of George Henry *Law; educated at Christ's College, Cambridge; fellow, 1814–17; took orders, 1814; MA, 1815; prebendary of Lichfield, 1818; chancellor of Lichfield, 1821; commissary of archdeaconry of Richmond, 1824; special commissary of diocese of Bath and Wells, 1840; published works on ecclesiastical law.

LAW, John (1671–1729), of Lauriston; controller-general of French finance; son of the great-grandnephew of James *Law; educated at Edinburgh; migrated to London; killed Edward *Wilson, known as 'Beau' Wilson, in a duel, 1694, and was sentenced to death for murder; escaped from prison and fled to the continent; issued anonymously pamphlets dealing with Scottish finance, 1701 and 1709; established the Banque Générale, the first bank of any kind in France, 1716; his 'Mississippi scheme' incorporated as the 'Western Company', 1717; enlarged its sphere of action, 1718–20; entered the Roman Catholic Church; appointed controller-general of the finances, 1720; fled from France on the fall of the company, 1720; died and was buried at Venice; allowed by French historians to have furthered French industry and commercial enterprise.

LAW, John (1745–1810), bishop of Elphin; son of Edmund *Law; of Charterhouse and Christ's College, Cambridge; MA, 1769; fellow of his college; prebendary of Carlisle, 1773; archdeacon of Carlisle, 1777; DD, 1782; bishop of Clonfert, 1785–7, of Killala, 1787–95, of Elphin, 1795–1810; published two sermons.

LAW, Richard Kidston, first Baron Coleraine (1901–1980), politician; son of Andrew Bonar *Law; educated at Shrewsbury School and St John's College, Oxford; worked as journalist on *Express* and *Morning Post*; Conservative MP for Hull South-West, 1931–45; opposed appeasement; financial secretary, War Office, 1940–1; parliamentary under-secretary of state, Foreign Office, 1941–3; minister of state, Foreign Office, and Cabinet rank, 1943–5; PC, 1943; minister of education, 1945; MP for South Kensington, 1945–50, and for Haltemprice division of Kingston upon Hull, 1950–4; accepted peerage, 1954; served on number of public bodies, including Marshall Scholarship Commission, 1956–65, standing advisory committee on pay of higher Civil Service, 1957–61, and Royal Postgraduate Medical School of London, 1958–71; fellow of Medical School, 1972; chairman of Horlicks; published *Return from Utopia* (1950) and *For Conservatives Only* (1970); succeeded in barony by his elder brother.

LAW, Robert (d. 1690?), Covenanting preacher; grandson of James *Law (1560?–1632); MA, Glasgow, 1646; sided with the protesters against episcopacy, and was deprived of his benefice, 1662; arrested on charge of preaching at conventicles, 1674; accepted the Indulgence of 1679; author of *Memorialls, or the Memorable Things that fell out within this Island of Brittain from 1638 to 1684* (edited 1818).

LAW, Thomas (1759–1834), of Washington; son of Edmund *Law; in the service of the East India Company, 1773–91; went to America, 1793; tried to establish a national currency there; died at Washington; published works on finance.

LAW, Thomas Graves (1836–1904), historian and bibliographer; grandson of Edward *Law, first earl of Ellenborough, and brother of Augustus Henry *Law; educated at Winchester, University College, London, and Stonyhurst; Roman Catholic priest, 1860–78; keeper of Signet Library, Edinburgh, 1879–1904; helped to found Scottish History Society, 1886; hon. LL D, Edinburgh, 1898; wrote much on sixteenth-century religious history; *Collected Essays* were posthumously issued (1904).

LAW, William (1686–1761), author of the *Serious Call*; entered Emmanuel College, Cambridge, 1705; ordained and elected fellow, 1711; MA, 1712; declined to take the oaths of allegiance to George I; attacked *Mandeville's *Fable of the Bees*, 1723; published the first of his practical treatises on *Christian Perfection* (1726); founded school for fourteen girls at Kings Cliffe, 1727; entered family of Edward Gibbon (1666–1736) as tutor to his son, afterwards father of the historian (see GIBBON, EDWARD); published the *Serious Call*, a work of much logical power (1728); became an ardent disciple of the mystic, Jacob Behmen, 1737; retired to Kings Cliffe, 1740; joined by Mrs Hutcheson and Miss Hester

Gibbon (the historian's aunt), who wished to carry out literally the precepts of the *Serious Call*, 1743–4. His works were collected in nine volumes (1762).

LAW, William John (1786–1869), commissioner of insolvent court; grandson of Edmund *Law; educated at Westminster School and Christ Church, Oxford, where he held a studentship, 1804–14; MA, 1810; barrister, Lincoln's Inn, 1813; a commissioner of bankruptcy, 1825; chief commissioner of the insolvent court, 1853–61; published works on the bankruptcy law, also a treatise *On the Passage of Hannibal over the Alps* (1866).

LAW, William Towry (1809–1886), youngest son of Edward *Law, first Baron Ellenborough; MA, Peterhouse, Cambridge, 1834; entered the army, but subsequently took holy orders; chancellor of the diocese of Bath and Wells; joined the church of Rome, 1851.

LAWDER. See LAUDER.

LAWERN, John (*fl.* 1448), theologian; Benedictine monk of Worcester; student at Gloucester Hall (now Worcester College, Oxford). A manuscript volume of sermons and letters by him is in the Bodleian.

LAWES (afterwards **LAWES-WITTE-WRONGE), Sir Charles Bennet,** second baronet (1843–1911), sculptor and athlete; son of Sir John Bennet *Lawes, first baronet, of Rothamsted; educated at Eton and Trinity College, Cambridge; BA, 1866; distinguished oarsman at Cambridge and Henley, runner and cyclist; exhibited sculpture at Royal Academy, 1872–1908; unsuccessful defendant in libel action brought by R. C. Belt, a sculptor, 1882; succeeded to baronetcy and Rothamsted property, 1900.

LAWES, Henry (1596–1662), musician; received his early musical education from Giovanni *Coperario (Cooper); gentleman of the Chapel Royal, 1626; connected with the household of the earl of *Bridgewater, probably before 1633; suggested to *Milton the composition of *Comus* (performed 1634), for which he wrote the music; his edition of *Comus* published (1637); published *Choice Psalmes put into Musick for Three Voices* (1648), *Ayres and Dialogues for One, Two, and Three Voyces* (1653); lost his appointments at outbreak of the Civil Wars; his third book of *Ayres* brought out (1658); restored to his offices in the Chapel Royal, 1660; the first Englishman who studied and practised with success the proper accentuation of words, and made the sense of the poem of paramount importance.

LAWES, Sir John Bennet, first baronet (1814–1900), agriculturist; educated at Eton and Brasenose College, Oxford; studied chemistry; resided on family estate at Rothamsted from 1834; conducted important agricultural experiments and started, 1843, on a regular basis the Rothamsted Agricultural Experiment Station; patented, 1842, and started at Deptford, 1843, manufacture of mineral superphosphate for manure; published independently and with his coadjutor and technical adviser, Dr (Sir) Joseph Henry *Gilbert, numerous reports on experiments; joined Royal Agricultural Society, 1846; vice-president, 1878; FRS, 1854, and gold medallist, 1867; received Albert Medal from Society of Arts, 1877; LL D, Edinburgh, 1877; hon. DCL, Oxford, 1892; hon. Sc.D., Cambridge, 1894; created baronet, 1882; acted on various commissions and committees.

LAWES, William (d. 1645), musical composer; elder brother of Henry *Lawes; gentleman of the Chapel Royal, 1603; wrote the music for *Shirley's masque, *The Triumph of Peace*, performed 1634; lost his life fighting for the Royalists at the siege of Chester.

LAWES, William George (1839–1907), missionary; worked at Niué in South Seas, 1861–72; completed translation of New Testament into Niué, 1886; settled at Port Moresby, New Guinea, 1874–94; with James *Chalmers greatly helped British administration and development of British New Guinea; hon. DD, Glasgow, 1895; settled at Sydney, 1906, where he died.

LAWLESS, John (1773–1837), Irish agitator; commonly known as 'Honest Jack Lawless'; a distant cousin of Valentine Browne *Lawless, second Baron Cloncurry; refused admission to the bar in consequence of his intimacy with the leaders of the United Irish movement; editor of the *Ulster Register*, a political and literary magazine, and subsequently of the *Belfast Magazine*; energetic member of the committee of the Catholic Association; strong opponent of *O'Connell; chief work, *A Compendium of the History of Ireland from the earliest period to the Reign of George I* (1814).

LAWLESS, Matthew James (1837–1864), artist; drew illustrations for *Once a Week*, the *Cornhill*, and *Punch*; his best-known oil-painting, *The Sick Call*, exhibited at the Royal Academy, 1863.

LAWLESS, Valentine Browne, second Baron Cloncurry (1773–1853); BA, Trinity College, Dublin, 1792; sworn a United Irishman; entered the Middle Temple, 1795; published his first pamphlet on the projected union of Great Britain and Ireland (1797); arrested on a charge of suspicion of high treason and discharged, 1798; arrested a second time and committed to the Tower, 1799–1801; for several years took no active part in politics; opponent of *O'Connell during the viceroyalties of Henry William *Paget, marquis of Anglesey, 1828 and 1830–4; published his *Personal Reminiscences* (1849).

LAWLESS, William (1772–1824), French general; born at Dublin; joined the United Irishmen; outlawed; entered the French Army; captain of the Irish Legion, 1803; distinguished himself at Flushing, 1806; decorated by Napoleon with the Legion of Honour and made a lieutenant-colonel; colonel, 1812; wounded at Löwenberg, 1813; placed on half-pay with rank of brigadier-general, 1814; died at Paris.

LAWLEY, Francis Charles (1825–1901), sportsman and journalist; BA, Balliol College, Oxford, 1848; fellow of All Souls, 1848–53; BCL, 1851; Liberal MP for Beverley, 1852; private secretary to Gladstone; lost fortune in gambling and speculation; imputations of dishonesty in stock-exchange dealings led to cancelling of his appointment as governor of South Australia, 1854; settled in America, 1854–65; sent vivid accounts of Civil War to *The Times*; returned to London, 1865; wrote on sport in *Daily Telegraph* and *Baily's Magazine*.

LAWRANCE, Mary (*fl.* 1794–1830), afterwards Mrs Kearse; flower-painter; exhibited at Royal Academy, 1795–1830; published plates illustrating *The Various Kinds of Roses cultivated in England* (1796–9); married Mr Kearse, 1813.

LAWRENCE. See also LAURENCE.

LAWRENCE (or LAURENTIUS) (d. 619), second archbishop of Canterbury; landed in Thanet with *Augustine, 597; archbishop of Canterbury, 604.

LAWRENCE (d. 1154), prior of Durham and Latin poet; a Benedictine monk at Durham; prior, 1147; bishop of Durham, 1153; went to Rome for consecration and died in France on his return journey; wrote Latin poems.

LAWRENCE (d. 1175), abbot of Westminster; a monk of St Albans; abbot of Westminster, *c.*1159; obtained the canonization of *Edward the Confessor from the pope, 1163.

LAWRENCE, Alfred Kingsley (1893–1975), portrait and figure painter; trained at Armstrong College, Newcastle upon Tyne; served in Northumberland Fusiliers during 1914–18 war; studied at Royal College of Art, London; awarded travelling scholarship, 1922 and Prix de Rome, 1923; influenced by works of Piero della Francesca, particularly murals; painted *The Altruists* for basilica of Wembley exhibition, 1924, and other works, including cycle of murals in St Stephen's Hall, Houses of Parliament, and large painting for new Bank of England; member of faculty of painting, British School at Rome, 1926–50; ARA, 1930; RA, 1938; member of Royal Society of Portrait Painters, 1947; made easel paintings of classical subjects and theatrical themes, including *Miss Vivien Leigh as Cleopatra* (1952); also portraits, including *Sir Malcolm Sargent* (1954) and members of the royal family.

LAWRENCE, Alfred Tristram, first Baron Trevethin (1843–1936), lord chief justice of England; educated at Mill Hill and Trinity Hall, Cambridge; first class, law, 1866; called to bar (Middle Temple), 1869; joined Oxford circuit; recorder of Windsor, 1885–1904; QC, 1897; judge, 1904–21; lord chief justice, 1921–2; president, War Compensation Court, 1920–2; baron and PC, 1921.

LAWRENCE, Andrew (1708–1747), engraver; known in France as André Laurent; studied engraving at Paris, where he died. His etchings are mostly after the Flemish seventeenth-century painters.

LAWRENCE, (Arabella) Susan (1871–1947), politician; studied mathematics at University College, London, and Newnham College, Cambridge; member of London County Council (municipal reform), 1910–12 (Labour), 1913–28; elected to Poplar Borough Council, 1919; Labour MP, East Ham North, 1923–4, 1926–31; parliamentary secretary to Ministry of Health, 1929–31; chairman, Labour party, 1929–30.

LAWRENCE, Charles (d. 1760), governor of Nova Scotia; ensign, 1727; captain-lieutenant, 1741; captain, 1742; major, 1747; accompanied his regiment to Nova Scotia; appointed a member of council, 1749; commanded expedition which built Fort Lawrence at the head of the Bay of Fundy, 1750; governor, 1753; brigadier-general, 1757; died at Halifax, Nova Scotia.

LAWRENCE, Charles (1794–1881), agriculturist; brother of Sir William *Lawrence; took leading part in founding and organizing Royal Agricultural College at Cirencester, 1842–5; published his *Handy Book for Young Farmers* (1859); contributed papers to the *Transactions* of the Royal Agricultural Society.

LAWRENCE, David Herbert (1885–1930), poet, novelist, and essayist; schoolmaster at Croydon until 1911; thenceforth devoted himself to literature; passionately sensitive to nature; published novels, *The White Peacock* (1911), *The Trespasser* (1912), and *Sons and Lovers* (1913), and *Love Poems and Others* (1913); by 1914 had won certain reputation as author; indifferent to material success and always possessed simple tastes; his desire to receive sympathetic response to his writings, which he believed to be of value to mankind, defeated by outbreak of European war; felt keenly condemnation for indecency of his novel *The Rainbow*, published 1915; left England, largely because of hostile attitude towards himself and his writings, 1919; lived in Italy, Sicily, and Mexico, and then in Italy again; his later works include *Sea and Sardinia* (1921) and *Lady Chatterley's Lover* (1928, banned until 1960); both prosecutions caused great stir; died at Vence.

LAWRENCE (or LAURENCE), Edward (1623–1695), Nonconformist minister; educated at Magdalene College, Cambridge; BA, 1648; MA, 1654; ejected from his living of Baschurch, Shropshire, 1662; arrested for preaching under the Conventicle Act, 1670; published sermons.

LAWRENCE, Frederick (1821–1867), barrister and journalist; employed in the printed book department of British Museum, 1846–9; barrister, Middle Temple, 1849; practised at the Middlesex sessions and the Old Bailey; contributed to the periodical press; published *The Life of Henry Fielding* (1855).

LAWRENCE, Sir (Frederick) Geoffrey (1902–1967), judge; educated at City of London School and New College, Oxford; BA 1926; violinist; president, Oxford Musical Club; formed Magi String Quartet; called to bar (Middle Temple), 1930; KC, 1950; successfully defended Dr John Bodkin *Adams on murder charge, 1957; recorder, Tenterden, 1948–51; recorder, Canterbury, 1952–62; chairman, West Sussex quarter sessions; chairman, General Council of the Bar, 1960–2; chairman, National Incomes Commission, 1962–4; knighted, 1963; High Court judge, 1965.

LAWRENCE, Frederick William Pethick-, first Baron (1871–1961), social worker and politician. See PETHICK-LAWRENCE.

LAWRENCE, George (1615–1695?), Puritan divine; educated at St Paul's School and New Inn Hall, Oxford; MA, 1639; took the Covenant; minister of the hospital of St Cross, Winchester, before 1650; ejected, 1660; published sermons and pamphlets against the Royalists.

LAWRENCE, George Alfred (1827–1876), author of *Guy Livingstone*; entered Rugby, 1841; Balliol College, Oxford, 1845; BA from New Inn Hall, 1850; barrister, Inner Temple, 1852; abandoned law for literature; published *Guy Livingstone, or Thorough* (1857) and *Sword and Gown* (1859); went to the United States with the intention of joining the Confederate Army, but was imprisoned before he reached the Confederate lines; released on condition of returning to England; recorded the adventure in *Border and Bastile* (1863).

LAWRENCE, Sir George St Patrick (1804–1884), general; brother of Sir Henry Montgomery *Lawrence and of John Laird Mair *Lawrence, first Baron Lawrence; born at Trincomalee; entered Addiscombe College, 1819; joined the 2nd Regiment of Light Cavalry in Bengal, 1822; adjutant, 1825–34; took part in the Afghan War, 1838–9; political assistant and (1839–41) military secretary to Sir William Hay *Macnaghten, the envoy of Afghanistan; in charge of the ladies and children in the retreat from Kabul, 1842; assistant political agent in the Punjab, 1846; taken prisoner during the second Sikh War, 1848; released, 1849; brevet-lieutenant-colonel, 1849; deputy-commissioner of Peshawar, 1849; political agent in Mewar, 1850–7; resident for the Rajputana states, 1857–64; held chief command of the forces there, 1857; CB (civil), 1860; major-general, 1861; KCSI and retired from the army, 1866; hon. lieutenant-general, 1867; published *Forty-three Years in India* (1874).

LAWRENCE, Gertrude (1898–1952), actress; born Klasen, of theatrical parentage; made first stage appearance in pantomime, 1910; became foremost of (Sir) Noël *Coward's leading ladies, especially popular in New York; played notably in *London Calling* (1923), *Private Lives* (1930), and *The King and I* (1952); a fine player of high vitality, keen wit, and style; published *A Star Danced* (1945); died in New York.

LAWRENCE, Giles (*fl.* 1539–1584), professor of Greek at Oxford; member of Corpus Christi College, Oxford, 1539; became fellow of All Souls, *c.*1542; regius professor of Greek, 1550–4 and 1559–84; DCL, 1556; archdeacon of Wiltshire, 1564–78, of St Albans, 1581.

LAWRENCE, Henry (1600–1664), Puritan statesman; of Emmanuel College, Cambridge; MA, 1627; commissioner of plantations, 1648; commissioner for Ireland, 1652; MP, Westmorland, 1646–53, Hertfordshire, 1653, 1654–6; keeper of the library at St James's House, 1653; lord president of the Council of State, 1654–9; MP, Caernarfonshire, 1656–7; published pamphlets on the doctrine of baptism.

LAWRENCE, Sir Henry Montgomery (1806–1857), brigadier-general, chief commissioner in Oudh; brother of Sir George St Patrick *Lawrence and of John Laird Mair *Lawrence, first Baron Lawrence; born at Matura, Ceylon; educated at schools at Londonderry and Bristol; entered Addiscombe College, 1820; second lieutenant in the Bengal Artillery, 1822; reached Calcutta, 1823; first lieutenant and adjutant, 1825; deputy commissary of ordnance at Akyab, 1826; posted to the foot artillery at Kurnaul, 1830; transferred to the horse artillery at Meerut, 1831; assistant revenue surveyor in the North-West Provinces, 1833–5, full surveyor, 1835; captain, 1837; appointed to take civil charge of Ferozepore, 1839; took part in Kabul expedition, 1842; promoted brevet-major; resident of Nepal, 1843–6; founded the Lawrence Asylum for the Children of European Soldiers; governor-general's agent for foreign relations and the affairs of the Punjab and the North-West Frontier, and promoted brevet-lieutenant-colonel, 1846; resident at Lahore, 1847; KCB, 1848; president of the board of administration for the affairs of the Punjab and agent to the governor-general, 1849–53; agent to the governor-general in Rajputana, 1853; colonel, 1854; chief commissioner and agent to the governor-general in Oudh, 1856; at breaking out of Mutiny promoted brigadier-general, with military command over all troops in Oudh, 1857; killed while holding Lucknow successfully against the mutineers; a voluminous contributor to the Indian press.

LAWRENCE, Sir Herbert Alexander (1861–1943), soldier and banker; son of Lord *Lawrence; educated at Harrow and Sandhurst; gazetted to 17th Lancers, 1882; served in South Africa, 1899–1902; retired, 1903; committee member, Ottoman Bank, 1906; joined Glyn's Bank, 1907; a director, Midland Railway, 1913; commanded King Edward's Horse, 1904–9; commanded successively 127th (Manchester) brigade, 53rd and 52nd divisions, Dardanelles; in charge of Cape Helles evacuation; responsible for victory at Romani, Egypt, 1916; took 66th division to France and KCB, 1917; chief of General Staff to (Lord) *Haig from Jan. 1918; general, 1919; on Samuel Commission on Coal Industry, 1925; GCB, 1926; director (1921), chairman (1926), Vickers; chairman of Glyn's, 1934–43.

LAWRENCE, James Henry (1773–1840), miscellaneous writer; a descendant of Henry *Lawrence; educated at Eton and in Germany; published a romance dealing with the Nair caste in Malabar in German (1800); subsequently wrote a French version (an English version published, 1811); arrested in France and detained several years at Verdun, 1803; published *A Picture of Verdun, or the English detained in France* (1810) and a work *On the Nobility of the British Gentry* (1834; 4th edn., 1840).

LAWRENCE, John (1753–1839), writer on horses; began to write for the press, 1787; published his *Philosophical and Practical Treatise on Horses* (1796–8; 3rd edn., 1810); insisted on the duty of humanity to animals.

LAWRENCE, John Laird Mair, first Baron Lawrence (1811–1879), governor-general of India; brother of Sir George St Patrick *Lawrence and of Sir Henry Montgomery *Lawrence; educated at Bristol, Londonderry, Bath, and Haileybury; took up his first appointment under the East India Company at Calcutta, 1830; assistant magistrate and collector at Delhi, 1830–4; in charge of the northern or Paniput division of the Delhi territory, 1834, of the southern or Gurgaon division, 1837; magistrate and collector of the districts of Paniput and Delhi, 1844; administrator of the newly constituted district, the Jullundur Doab, 1846–8; member of the board of administration for the Punjab, 1848–52; chief commissioner for the Punjab, 1853–7; KCB, 1856; the capture of Delhi from the mutineers due to his advice and action, 1857; created baronet, 1858; privy councillor, 1858; in England at the India Office, 1859–62; viceroy of India, 1863–9; sanitation, irrigation, railway extension, and peace the chief aims of his administration; created Baron Lawrence of the Punjab and of Grately, 1869; chairman of the London School Board, 1870–3; opposed the proceedings (by a series of letters in *The Times*) that led to the Afghan War of 1878–9; buried in Westminster Abbey.

LAWRENCE, Sir **Paul Ogden** (1861–1952), judge; educated at Malvern College; called to bar (Lincoln's Inn), 1882; QC, 1896; Chancery judge, 1918–26; lord justice of appeal, 1926–33; helped his sisters found Roedean School, 1885; knighted, 1919; PC, 1926.

LAWRENCE, Richard (*fl.* 1657), author of *Gospel Separation separated from its Abuses* (1657); of Magdalen Hall, Oxford.

LAWRENCE, Richard (d. 1684), Parliamentarian colonel; marshal-general of the horse in *Cromwell's New Model Army, 1645; published pamphlet on ecclesiastical abuses, 1647; employed in Ireland, 1651–9; member of the Council of Trade, 1660–80; published *The Interest of Ireland in its Trade and Wealth stated* (1682).

LAWRENCE, Samuel (1661–1712), Nonconformist divine; nephew of Edward *Lawrence; minister of the Presbyterian congregation of Nantwich, Cheshire, 1688–1712.

LAWRENCE, Sir **Soulden** (1751–1814), judge; son of Thomas *Lawrence (1711–1783); educated at St Paul's School and St John's College, Cambridge; MA and fellow, 1774; barrister, Inner Temple, 1784; serjeant-at-law, 1787; justice of the common pleas and knighted, 1794; transferred to the court of King's Bench; resigned the King's Bench and returned to the common pleas, 1808; retired, 1812.

LAWRENCE, Stringer (1697–1775), major-general; 'father of the Indian Army'; served at Gibraltar, 1727; lieutenant, 1736; served in Flanders, after Fontenoy, 1745, and fought at Culloden, 1746; went to India as 'major in the East Indies only' to command all the company's troops there, 1748; taken prisoner by the French, but released at Peace of Aix-la-Chapelle; civil governor and military commandant of Fort St David, 1749; received local rank of lieutenant-colonel, 1754, and of brigadier-general, 1757; commanded Fort St George during its siege by the French, 1758–9; received local rank of major-general, and left India, 1759.

LAWRENCE, Thomas (1711–1783), physician; educated at Trinity College, Oxford; MA, 1733; studied medicine in London; MD, Oxford, 1740; anatomical reader at Oxford; FRCP, 1744; president, 1767–74; friend and physician of Dr *Johnson; published medical treatises in Latin.

LAWRENCE, Sir **Thomas** (1769–1830), president of the Royal Academy; supported his family at Bath by his pencil, 1779; his studio before he was 12 years old the favourite resort of the beauty and fashion of Bath; entered the schools of the Royal Academy, London, 1787; obtained court patronage; painted George III, 1792; appointed principal portrait painter-in-ordinary to the king, 1792; RA, 1794; painted the poet *Cowper, 1795, and John *Kemble as Hamlet, 1801; knighted, 1815; sent to Aix-la-Chapelle to paint the assembled sovereigns, 1815; visited Vienna and Rome; PRA, 1820; sent by the king to Paris to paint Charles X and the dauphin, 1825; his portraits distinguished for their courtliness and social elegance; formed a fine collection of the drawings of Michaelangelo and Raphael; buried in St Paul's Cathedral.

LAWRENCE, Thomas Edward (1888–1935), known as 'Lawrence of Arabia'; educated at Oxford High School and Jesus College; first class, modern history, 1910; assisted in excavations at Carchemish, 1911–14; served in Arab Bureau, 1914–16; adviser to Faisal (third son of grand sharif of Mecca), whose confidence he won by force of personality, 1916–18; brought Hejaz south of Aqaba, except Medina, under Arab–British control; given half-million pounds by (Lord) *Allenby to raise Arab levies as mobile right wing; broke up Turkish Fourth Army and led Arab troops up to Damascus, 1 Oct. 1918; research fellow, All Souls, 1919; political adviser, Middle Eastern department, Colonial Office, 1921–2; obtained appointment of Faisal as king of Iraq and Abdullah as ruling prince of Trans-Jordan; served in ranks of Royal Air Force, 1922–35, changing name to T. E. Shaw (1927); recorded Arabian exploits in *Seven Pillars of Wis-*

dom (1935; limited edn., 1926; abridged version, *The Revolt in the Desert*, 1927) and early Air Force days in *The Mint* (1955).

LAWRENCE, Sir Walter Roper, first baronet (1857–1940), Indian civil servant; settlement commissioner in Kashmir, 1889–95; private secretary to viceroy (Lord *Curzon), 1898–1903; chief of staff to prince and princess of Wales on Indian visit, 1905–6; works include *The Valley of Kashmir* (1895); KCIE, 1903; baronet, 1906; GCVO, 1918.

LAWRENCE, William (1611?–1681), lawyer; of Trinity College, Oxford; barrister, Middle Temple; commissioner for the administration of justice in Scotland, 1653; MP, Isle of Wight, 1656, Newtown, Dorset, 1659; wrote on divorce, the right of primogeniture in succession, and political affairs.

LAWRENCE, Sir William, first baronet (1783–1867), surgeon; brother of Charles *Lawrence (1794–1881); apprenticed to John *Abernethy, 1799; MRCS, 1805, and FRS, 1813; surgeon to St Bartholomew's Hospital, 1824–65; lecturer on surgery there, 1829–62; president of the College of Surgeons, 1846 and 1855; created baronet, 1867; printed his lectures on anatomy, 1816 and 1819, and on surgery, 1863.

LAWRENSON, Thomas (*fl.* 1760–1777), painter; exhibited at the Society of Artists, 1760–77; fellow of the Society of Incorporated Artists, 1774.

LAWRENSON, William (*fl.* 1760–1780), painter; son of Thomas *Lawrenson; exhibited at the Incorporated Society of Artists, 1762–72; fellow of the Incorporated Society of Artists, 1766; exhibited at Royal Academy, 1774–80.

LAWRIE, William (d. 1700?), tutor of Blackwood; factor to James *Douglas, second marquis of Douglas, 1670–99; imprisoned for befriending Covenanters, 1683–8.

LAWS, Robert (1851–1934), pioneer missionary; studied theology and medicine at Edinburgh, Aberdeen, and Glasgow universities; ordained in United Presbyterian Church of Scotland, 1875; helped to found (1875) Livingstonia Mission Station on Lake Nyasa; in full control, 1877–1927; developed Christian community of 60,000 including African pastors and over 700 schools.

LAWSON, Cecil Gordon (1849–1882), landscape painter; learned elements of painting in the studio of his father, a Scottish portrait painter; exhibited at the Royal Academy, 1870–82; his work influenced by the realistic and impressionist tendencies of his time.

LAWSON, Edward Frederick, fourth Baron Burnham (1890–1963), newspaper proprietor and soldier; educated at Eton and Balliol College, Oxford; reporter on *Daily Telegraph* in Paris and New York, 1913–14; commissioned in Royal Bucks. Hussars, 1914; DSO, MC; returned to *Daily Telegraph*, 1919; hon. colonel, 99th (Bucks. and Berks.) field brigade, Royal Artillery, 1933; brigadier, Royal Artillery 48th (South Midland) division, 1938; fought at Dunkirk, CB, 1940; major-general commanding Yorkshire division, 1941; director, public relations, War Office, and senior military representative, Ministry of Information, 1941–5; succeeded to title, 1943; retired from army, 1945; general manager, *Daily Telegraph*, 1927–39 and 1945–61; vice-chairman, Newspaper Proprietors (later Publishers) Association, 1934–9 and 1945–61; published *Peterborough Court, the Story of the Daily Telegraph* (1955).

LAWSON, Edward Levy-, first Baron Burnham (1833–1916), newspaper proprietor. See LEVY-LAWSON.

LAWSON, Frederick Henry (1897–1983), academic lawyer; educated at Leeds Grammar School and the Queen's College, Oxford; first class, modern history, 1921 and law, 1922, after commission in anti-aircraft regiment (1916–18); called to bar (Gray's Inn), 1923; lecturer in law, University College, Oxford, 1924–5; junior research fellow, Merton College, 1925–30; university lecturer in Byzantine law, 1929–30; tutorial fellow, Merton College, 1930; All Souls reader in Roman law, 1931–48; professor of comparative law, and fellow of Brasenose College, Oxford, 1948–64; lecturer in law, Lancaster University, 1964–77; DCL, 1947; FBA, 1956; honorary doctorates from number of universities in the United Kingdom and abroad; publications include *Cases in Constitutional Law* (with [Sir] David Lindsay *Keir, 1928 and in subsequent editions), *The Rational Strength of English Law* (1951), *A Common Lawyer Looks at the Civil Law* (1955), and *Introduction to the Law of Property* (1958).

LAWSON, George (d. 1678), divine; a supporter of parliament and a valued critic of *Baxter; not identical with George Lawson, the ejected vicar of Mears Ashby; published political and theological works.

LAWSON, George (1749–1820), Scottish associate clergyman; educated at Edinburgh University; ordained pastor of the burgher seceders, 1771; professor of theology in the burgher church of Scotland, 1787–1820; DD, Aberdeen, 1806; published theological works.

LAWSON, George (1831–1903), ophthalmic surgeon; entered King's College Hospital, 1848; MRCS, 1852; FRCS, 1857; joined army as surgeon, 1854; served in Crimea; surgeon at Royal London Ophthalmic Hospital, Moorfields, from 1862; surgeon-oculist to Queen Victoria from 1886; published works on eye diseases.

LAWSON, George Anderson (1832–1904), sculptor; studied at Royal Scottish Academy Schools and in Rome; exhibited at Royal Academy from 1862; works include his popular 'Dominie Sampson', 1868, Burns Memorial at Ayr, and the Wellington Monument at Liverpool.

LAWSON, Sir Harry Lawson Webster Levy-, second baronet, second Baron, and Viscount Burnham (1862–1933), newspaper proprietor; son of first Baron *Burnham; educated at Eton and Balliol College, Oxford; first class, modern history, 1884; Liberal MP, West St Pancras, 1885–92, Cirencester, 1893–5; Unionist MP, Mile End, 1905–6 and 1910–16; succeeded father, 1916; managing proprietor of *Daily Telegraph*, 1903–28; an ideal chairman, notably of the Standing Joint Committee of Teachers and Local Education Authorities which formulated the 'Burnham scales', and of three international labour conferences (1921, 1922, 1926); served on Indian Statutory Commission, 1927–30; CH, 1917; viscount, 1919.

LAWSON, Henry (1774–1855), astronomer; apprenticed at the optical establishment of Edward *Nairne; equipped an observatory at Hereford, 1826; member of the Royal Astronomical Society, 1833; FRS, 1840; published *On the Arrangement of an Observatory for Practical Astronomy and Meteorology* (1844); member of the British Meteorological Society, 1850.

LAWSON, Isaac (d. 1747), physician; MD, 1737; friend of Linnaeus; became a physician to the British Army; died at Oosterhout, Holland.

LAWSON, James (1538–1584), successor to John *Knox in the church of St Giles, Edinburgh; educated at St Andrews; taught Hebrew (the first to do so in Scotland) at St Andrews, 1567 or 1568; sub-principal of King's College, Aberdeen, 1569; leader of the reformed clergy in the north of Scotland; admitted to the ministry of St Giles, Edinburgh, 1572; encouraged a mistaken policy of intolerance.

LAWSON, James Anthony (1817–1887), judge of Queen's Bench, Ireland; BA, Trinity College, Dublin, 1838; Whately professor of political economy, 1840–5; called to the Irish bar, 1840; LL D, Dublin, 1850; QC, 1857; legal adviser to the crown in Ireland, 1858–9; bencher of King's Inn, Dublin, 1861; solicitor-general for Ireland, 1861; attorney-general, 1865; Irish privy councillor, 1865; MP, Portarlington, 1865–8; justice of the common pleas, Ireland, 1868–82; judge of Queen's Bench, 1882–7; DCL, Oxford,

1884; published his lectures on political economy.

LAWSON, Sir John (d. 1665), admiral; in command of ships in parliament's service, 1642–5, 1651–3, 1654–6; dismissed from the public service, apparently on political grounds, 1656; Anabaptist and republican; implicated in the conspiracy of the Fifth-Monarchy men and arrested, 1657; commander-in-chief of the fleet, 1659; co-operated with *Monck in the Restoration, 1660; knighted, 1660; vice-admiral of the red squadron in the war with the Dutch, 1665; died of a wound received in action.

LAWSON, John (d. 1712), traveller; surveyor-general of North Carolina, 1700; recorded his impressions of travel in *A New Voyage to Carolina, etc.* (1709); was murdered by Indians.

LAWSON, John (1712–1759), writer on oratory; MA, Trinity College, Dublin, 1734; senior fellow and first librarian, 1743; DD, 1745; lecturer on oratory and history on the foundation of Erasmus *Smith, 1753; published *Lectures concerning Oratory* (1758); selected sermons published (1764).

LAWSON, John (1723–1779), mathematician; educated at Sidney Sussex College, Cambridge; fellow, 1747; MA and mathematical lecturer, 1749; BD, 1756; published anonymously a *Dissertation on the Geometrical Analysis of the Antients, with a Collection of Theorems and Problems with Solutions* (1774); printed also other mathematical works and some sermons.

LAWSON, John Parker (d. 1852), historical and miscellaneous writer; a minister in the Episcopal Church of Scotland, and for some time a chaplain in the army; wrote works dealing with English and Scottish history for Edinburgh booksellers, 1827–47.

LAWSON, Robert (d. 1816), lieutenant-general; colonel-commandant, Royal Artillery; entered the Royal Military Academy, Woolwich, 1758; lieutenant-fireworker, Royal Artillery, 1759; at the siege of Belle Isle, 1761; second lieutenant, 1766; first lieutenant, 1771; served in America, where he invented a field-carriage for small guns, 1776–83; captain, 1782; in command of the artillery in Jamaica, 1783–6; appointed to command the first formed troop of the Royal Horse Artillery, 1793; lieutenant-colonel, 1794; appointed to command the artillery of the Mediterranean expeditionary force, 1800; colonel, 1801; major-general, 1808; lieutenant-general, 1813.

LAWSON, Thomas (1620?–1695), Independent divine; educated at Catharine Hall, Cambridge; MA; fellow of St John's College, Cambridge;

became a member of the Independent Church at Norwich, 1649.

LAWSON, Thomas (1630–1691), Quaker and botanist; said to have been educated at Cambridge; joined the Quakers, 1653; a noted herbalist; published religious works and left botanical manuscripts.

LAWSON, Sir **Wilfrid,** second baronet (1829–1906), politician and temperance advocate; son of Sir Wilfrid Lawson, an advanced Liberal; keen sportsman, huntsman, angler, and agriculturist; Liberal MP for Carlisle, 1859–65, 1868–85; supported motion for Sunday closing of public houses, 1863; introduced (1864) and frequently reintroduced (1869–74) his 'Permissive', later known as 'Local Veto', Bill; carried resolution for local option in 1880, in 1881, and in 1883; president of United Kingdom Alliance, 1879; succeeded to baronetcy and estates, 1867; supported motion of Sir Charles *Dilke for inquiry into Queen Victoria's expenditure, 1872; advocated Sunday closing in Ireland, 1875–6 (measure carried, 1879); opposed parliamentary 'adjournment for the Derby', 1874; supported claim of Charles *Bradlaugh for religious freedom, 1880; opposed Liberal government's Egyptian policy, 1882–3; MP for Cockermouth, 1886–1900; supported Gladstone's home-rule policy and opposed Balfour's coercion measures; MP for Camborne, 1903, and again for Cockermouth, 1906; passionately denounced South African War and defended free trade; of spontaneous humour, he seasoned his speeches with genial sarcasm and humorous quotation; easy writer of light verse; published *Cartoons in Rhyme and Line* (illustrated by Sir F. C. *Gould, 1905).

LAWSON, William (*fl.* 1618), writer on gardening; published *A New Orchard and Garden, Or the best Way for Planting, Grafting,* etc. (1618), stating it to be the result of forty-eight years' experience.

LAWTHER, Sir **William** (1889–1976), miners' leader; son of coal-miner, and one of family of fifteen children; began work in mine at age of 12; educated at night school; studied at Central Labour College, London, 1911–13; strongly anti-militarist during 1914–18 war; left-wing militant in labour movement post-war; attended his first TUC conference, 1918; served on national executive, 1923–6; leading figure in Durham area during General Strike; served two months in prison, 1926; elected Labour MP for Barnard Castle, 1929–31; treasurer for Durham miners, 1933; vice-president, Mineworkers' Federation, 1934; president, 1939; first president, National Union of Mineworkers; served on General Council of TUC, 1935–54; continued to be on left of labour movement until 1945

when, together with Arthur *Deakin and Tom Williamson, he became bitterly opposed to the left wing and helped keep the right-centre in control of both Labour party and TUC; knighted, 1949; chevalier of Legion of Honour; served as magistrate after retirement in 1954.

LAWTON, Charlwood (1660–1721), friend of William *Penn; educated at Wadham College, Oxford; barrister, Middle Temple, 1688; acted as Penn's agent, 1700; said to have left papers relating to contemporary affairs.

LAWTON, George (1779–1869), antiquary; registrar of the archdeaconry of the East Riding of Yorkshire; served in the ecclesiastical courts under five archbishops of York; ceased practice, 1863; his *Collectio Rerum Ecclesiasticarum* (1840) still an authority.

LAX, William (1761–1836), astronomer; educated at Trinity College, Cambridge; fellow, 1786; MA, 1788; Lowndes's professor of astronomy and geometry, Cambridge, 1795; FRS, 1796; published *Remarks on a supposed Error in the Elements of Euclid* (1807) and *Tables to be used with the Nautical Almanac* (1821).

LAXTON, Sir **William** (d. 1556), lord mayor of London; alderman and sheriff of London, 1540; lord mayor, 1544; founded almshouse and school (still maintained by the Grocers' Company) at Oundle, Northamptonshire.

LAXTON, William (1802–1854), one of the authors of the *Builder's Price Book*; educated at Christ's Hospital, London; surveyed and laid down several lines of railway and constructed waterworks; established *The Civil Engineer and Architect's Journal*, 1837; conducted the *Builder's Price Book*, a standard work in the profession and in the courts of law for thirty years.

LAY. See also LEY.

LAY, Benjamin (1677–1759), eccentric opponent of slavery; emigrated to Barbados and commenced business as a merchant, 1718; became interested in the condition of the slaves; removed to Philadelphia, where he lived in an eccentric manner, 1731; continued there his crusade against slavery. His pamphlets had considerable influence on the younger Quakers of the district.

LAYAMON (*fl.* 1200), author of *Brut*, a poem in English; only known through statements of his own; connected with the church of Areley Regis in North Worcestershire; his poem, based on *Wace's Roman de Brut*, composed 1155, but not completed till beginning of the thirteenth century; an enthusiastic reader and collector of early British legends. The *Brut* is extant in two manuscripts in the British Museum.

LAYARD, Sir Austen Henry (1817–1894), excavator of Nineveh and politician; born in Paris; in solicitor's office in London, 1833–9; travelled in Turkey and Persia; visited Mosul with Emil Botta, then French consul there, who had begun excavations in the mounds near the site of Nineveh; employed by Stratford *Canning (afterwards Viscount Stratford de Redcliffe) to travel unofficially through Western Turkey and report affairs; commissioned by Canning to explore site of Nineveh, 1845; began operations at Nimrud, which was afterwards identified as site of the Assyrian city of Calah; superintended for British Museum excavations at Kal'at Skerkat (site of city of Ashur) and at Kuyunjik, 1846; published *Nineveh and its Remains* (1848–9), incorrectly supposing Nimrud to be within precincts of Nineveh; attaché to embassy at Constantinople, 1849–51; superintended excavations at Kuyunjik and Nebi-Yunus; published *Nineveh and Babylon* (1853); lord rector of Aberdeen University, 1855; Liberal MP for Aylesbury, 1852–7, and for Southwark, 1860; under-secretary for foreign affairs, 1852 and 1861–6; chief commissioner of works, 1868–9; privy councillor, 1868; British minister at Madrid, 1869–77, and Constantinople, 1877–80; GCB, 1878; published *Early Adventures in Persia, Susiana, and Babylonia* (1887) and writings on art.

LAYARD, Daniel Peter (1721–1802), physician; MD, Reims, 1742; hon. DCL, Oxford, 1792; author of medical works.

LAYCOCK, Sir Robert Edward (1907–1968), soldier; educated at Eton and the Royal Military College, Sandhurst; commissioned, Royal Horse Guards, 1927; GSO, Chemical Warfare in France, 1939; lieutenant-colonel in command of 'Layforce' commandos, 1941; fought in Crete and North Africa; commanded Special Service brigade, 1942; fought in Sicily and at Salerno, 1943; DSO; United States Legion of Merit; major-general, succeeding Lord *Mountbatten as chief of combined operations, 1943–7; CB, 1945; governor and commander-in-chief, Malta, 1954–9; KCMG, 1954; high sheriff (1954–5) and lord-lieutenant, Nottinghamshire, 1962; colonel commandant, Special Air Service and Sherwood Rangers Yeomanry, 1960.

LAYCOCK, Thomas (1812–1876), mental physiologist; educated at University College, London; studied anatomy and physiology at Paris, 1834; MRCS, 1835; MD, Göttingen, 1839; published *A Treatise on the Nervous Diseases of Women* (1840); the first to promulgate the theory of the reflex action of the brain, 1844; professor of the practice of physic in Edinburgh University, 1855; published his important work, *Mind and Brain* (1859); contributed to medical journals.

LAYER, Christopher (1683–1723), Jacobite conspirator; barrister, Middle Temple; obtained a large practice; went to Rome and unfolded to the Pretender 'a wondrous plot', 1721; arrested, tried, and condemned to death, 1722; was executed at Tyburn.

LAYER, John (1585?–1641), Cambridge antiquary; educated as lawyer, but devoted himself chiefly to antiquarian pursuits at Shepreth, Cambridgeshire; left manuscripts relating to history of Cambridgeshire.

LAYFIELD, John (d. 1617), divine; educated at Trinity College, Cambridge; fellow, 1585–1603; lector linguae Graecae, 1593; examiner grammatices, 1599; DD; rector of St Clement Danes, London, 1601–17; one of the revisers of the Bible, 1606.

LAYMAN, William (1768–1826), commander in the navy; entered navy, 1782; on the Home Station till 1786; in the West Indies, 1786–8; joined the merchant service and was employed in the East India and China trade; returned to the navy, 1800, and served under *Nelson, 1800–3; commander, 1804; allowed his ship to drift inside the Spanish squadron, 1805; found guilty of carelessness by court martial, and placed at the bottom of the list, 1805; wrote pamphlets on nautical or naval subjects.

LAYTON, Henry (1622–1705), author of pamphlets on the question of the immortality of the soul published anonymously between 1692 and 1704.

LAYTON, Richard (1500?–1544), dean of York and chief agent in the suppression of monasteries; educated at Cambridge; BCL, Oxford, 1522; archdeacon of Buckinghamshire, 1534; clerk to the Privy Council, 1535; made a visitation of the University of Oxford, and instituted many reforms, 1535; began visiting monasteries, 1535; took part in trial of Anne *Boleyn, 1536; master in Chancery, 1538; dean of York, 1539; English ambassador at Brussels, 1543; died at Brussels.

LAYTON, Sir Walter Thomas, first Baron Layton (1884–1966), economist, editor, and newspaper proprietor; educated at King's College School, London, Westminster City School, University College, London, and Trinity College, Cambridge; first class, parts i and ii, economics tripos, 1906–7; lecturer in economics with J. M. (later Lord) *Keynes, 1908; fellow, Gonville and Caius College, 1909–14; Newmarch lecturer, University College, London, 1909–12; worked for Ministry of Munitions during 1914–18 war; member, *Milner Mission to Russia, and Balfour Mission to USA, 1917; CBE, 1917; CH, 1919; published *An Introduction to the Study of Prices* (1920); director, Economic and Financial Section, League of Nations; editor, *The Economist*, 1922–38; refashioned the paper; assisted in publication of Liberal Yellow Book, 1928; chairman, *News Chronicle*, 1930–50, and *Star* 1936–50; director, Reuters, 1945–53; director-general, programmes, Ministry of Supply, 1940–2; chairman, Executive Committee, Ministry of Supply, 1941–2, chief adviser on programmes, Ministry of Production, 1941–3; head, Joint War Production Staff, 1942–3; post-1945, worked for Anglo-American understanding, European unity, and the United Nations; knighted, 1930; baron, 1947; hon. fellow, Gonville and Caius College, 1931; honorary degrees from Columbia and Melbourne universities.

LEA. See LEE, LEGH, LEIGH, and LEY.

LEACH. See also LEECH.

LEACH, Arthur Francis (1851–1915), historical writer; educated at Winchester and New College, Oxford; fellow of All Souls, 1874–81; assistant charity commissioner (endowed schools department), 1884; second charity commissioner, 1906–15; works include *English Schools at the Reformation (1546–1548)* (1896) and *Schools of Medieval England* (1915).

LEACH, Bernard Howell (1887–1979), potter; educated at Beaumont Jesuit College, near Windsor, 1897–1903; studied at Slade School of Art under Henry *Tonks and (Sir) Frank *Brangwyn, 1908–9; went to Japan and exhibited etchings, 1909; experimented with kiln belonging to Kozan Horokawa, 1910; decided to become a potter, 1911; studied with Ogata Kenzen VI; with his friend Shoji Hamada became a great modern potter; published *A Review, 1909–1914* first of long series of books on his ideas with poems, etchings, and designs; returned to England with Hamada and established pottery at St Ives, 1920; Hamada returned to Japan, 1923; Leach trained many pupils at St Ives, including Michael *Cardew; held many one-man exhibitions in England and Japan, and lectured and exhibited in USA, Australia, and South America; among his many publications are *A Potter's Outlook* (1928), *A Potter's Book* (1940), *A Potter in Japan* (1960), *Hamada* (1976), and *Beyond East and West* (1978), an autobiography; two films were produced of Leach's work, *A Potter's World* (BBC, 1960) and an NHK (Japan) TV film (1974); he received many honours, including the Binns Medal of the American Ceramic Society, 1940, hon. D.Litt., Exeter, 1961, CBE, 1962, CH, 1973, and Japanese Foundation Cultural Award, 1974.

LEACH, James (1762–1798), musical composer; member of the king's band; published *A new Sett of Hymn and Psalm Tunes* (1789), *A Second Sett of Hymn and Psalm Tunes* (c.1794); composed anthems and trios for stringed instruments.

LEACH, Sir John (1760–1834), master of the Rolls; educated at Bedford Grammar School; barrister, Middle Temple, 1790; recorder of Seaford, 1795; MP, Seaford, 1806–16; KC, 1807; bencher, 1807; chancellor of the duchy of Cornwall, 1816; chief justice of Chester, 1817; privy councillor, 1817; vice-chancellor of England, 1818; knighted, 1818; master of the Rolls, 1827; deputy-speaker of the House of Lords, 1827; member of judicial committee of Privy Council, 1833.

LEACH, Thomas (1746–1818), legal writer; police magistrate at Hatton Garden, 1790–1818; published legal works.

LEACH, William Elford (1790–1836), naturalist; studied medicine at St Bartholomew's Hospital, London, and at Edinburgh; MD, Edinburgh, 1812; assistant librarian in the British Museum, 1813; published first part of his history of British crustacea, 1815; FRS, 1817; assistant keeper of the natural history department, British Museum, 1821; died in Italy; author of important work on crustacea, his knowledge of them being superior to that of any other naturalist of his time.

LEACOCK, Stephen Butler (1869–1944), professor and humorist; educated at Upper Canada College and Toronto University; graduated in modern languages, 1891; in philosophy, Chicago, 1903; lecturer in political science and history, McGill University, 1903; associate professor, 1905; William Dow professor and head of department of economics and political science 1908–36; publications include many collections of humorous articles, beginning with *Literary Lapses* (1910); also *Elements of Political Science* (1906) and *Our British Empire* (1940).

LEAD (or LEADE), Mrs Jane (1623–1704), mystic; daughter of Schildknap Ward; married William Lead, 1644; deeply impressed by the mystic revelations of Jacob Boehme; recorded her prophetic visions in a spiritual diary entitled 'A Fountain of Gardens', from 1670; published *The Heavenly Cloud* (1681) and *The Revelation of Revelations* (account of her visions, 1683); her disciples styled Philadelphians.

LEADBEATER, Mary (1758–1826), authoress; granddaughter of Abraham *Shackleton; belonged to the Quakers; married William Leadbeater, 1791; corresponded with *Burke; published *Poems* (1808); her best work the *Annals of Ballitore*, an admirable representation of Irish life from 1766–1823 (printed 1862).

LEADBETTER, Charles (*fl.* 1728), astronomer; gauger in the Royal Excise; author of treatises on astronomy and mathematics; one of the first commentators on *Newton.

LEADER, Benjamin Williams (1831–1923), painter; born Williams; brother of Sir E. L. *Williams; entered Royal Academy Schools, 1854; painter of landscapes in Worcestershire and Wales; his pictures include *February Fill-Dyke* (1881) and *In the Evening there shall be Light* (1882); RA, 1898.

LEADER, John Temple (1810–1903), politician and connoisseur; educated at Charterhouse, 1823 and at Christ Church, Oxford, 1828; knew from youth Lord *Brougham, his father's friend; Liberal MP for Bridgwater, 1835; acted with *Grote, *Molesworth, and the philosophical radicals; favoured the Chartists; unsuccessfully contested Westminster at a by-election (May 1837) against Sir Francis *Burdett; MP for Westminster, Aug. 1837–47; prominent in London society; frequent traveller in Italy and France; saw much in London of Louis Napoleon, afterwards Napoleon III; in 1844 his career underwent sudden change, and he left England for permanent residence abroad; at Cannes joined Brougham, and bought property for building; chiefly spent his long exile at Florence, in and near which he bought and restored several old residences, including the gigantic castle of Vincigliata, where he was visited by many distinguished persons, including Queen Victoria (1888) and Gladstone; directed compilation of many archaeological treatises on Vincigliata and adjoining places; wrote, with Giuseppe Marcotti, lives of Sir John *Hawkwood (1889) and Sir Robert *Dudley, duke of Northumberland (1895); left £7,000 for restoration of central bronze door of Duomo at Florence.

LEAF, Walter (1852–1927), classical scholar and banker; educated at Harrow and Trinity College, Cambridge; bracketed senior classic, 1874; entered family business, silks and ribbons dealers, 1875; retired and devoted more attention to banking, 1892; a director of London and Westminster Bank, 1891; chairman, 1918; chairman, Institute of Bankers, 1919; president, International Chamber of Commerce, 1924; his reputation rests chiefly on his work as Homeric scholar; his publications include *Banking* (1926), an edition of the *Iliad* (1886–8, 2nd edn., 1900–2), *Troy . . .* (1912), *Homer and History* (1915), and *Strabo on the Troad* (1923).

LEAHY, Arthur (1830–1878), colonel, Royal Engineers; educated at the Royal Military Academy, Woolwich; lieutenant, 1848; fought through the Crimean War; second captain, 1857; assistant director of the works in the fortifications branch of the War Office, 1864; brevet-lieutenant-colonel, 1868; instructor of field works at the School of Military Engineering at Chatham, 1871; regimental lieutenant-colonel, 1873; brevet-colonel, 1877.

LEAHY, Edward Daniel (1797–1875), portrait and subject painter; exhibited at the Royal Academy and British Institution, 1820–53; resided in Italy, 1837–43; painted portraits of many leading Irishmen.

LEAHY, Patrick (1806–1875), archbishop of Cashel; educated at Maynooth; vice-rector of the Catholic University of Dublin, 1854; archbishop of Cashel, 1857–75; strong advocate of temperance.

LEAKE. See also LEEKE.

LEAKE, Sir Andrew (d. 1704), captain in the navy; took part in Dutch War, 1690; commodore on the Newfoundland Station, 1699–1700; flag captain during the campaign of 1702; knighted, 1702; mortally wounded in attack on Gibraltar.

LEAKE, George (1856–1902), premier of Western Australia; born at Perth, Western Australia; barrister of Supreme Court; crown solicitor, 1883–94; member of Legislative Assembly, 1890–1900; QC, 1898; twice premier of Western Australia, and attorney-general, May 1901–June 1902; died at Perth; a strong advocate of federation.

LEAKE, Sir John (1656–1720), admiral of the fleet; son of Richard *Leake; governor and commander-in-chief at Newfoundland, 1702; knighted, 1704; took part in reduction of Gibraltar, 1704; employed on coast of Spain, 1704–6; admiral of the white, 1708; admiral and commander-in-chief in the Mediterranean, 1708; MP, Rochester, 1708–14; rear-admiral of Great Britain; a lord of the Admiralty, 1709.

LEAKE, John (1729–1792), male midwife; MD, Reims, 1763; LRCP, 1766; author of medical works, addressed rather to women than to physicians, the chief being *The Chronic Diseases of Women* (1777).

LEAKE, Richard (1629–1696), master gunner of England; served in the navy under parliament, in the Dutch Army, and as commander of an English merchant ship; a master gunner of England, 1677.

LEAKE, Stephen Martin (1702–1773), herald and numismatist; son of Captain Martin; assumed surname of Leake on being adopted as the heir of Admiral Leake, 1721; of the Middle Temple; FSA, 1727; FRS; Lancaster herald, 1727, Norroy, 1729, Clarenceux, 1741, Garter,

1754; consistently maintained the rights and privileges of the College of Arms.

LEAKE, William Martin (1777–1860), classical topographer and numismatist; grandson of Stephen Martin *Leake; with his regiment in the West Indies, 1794–8; employed in instructing Turkish troops at Constantinople, 1799; travelled in Asia Minor (his *Journal of a Tour in Asia Minor* published 1824), 1800; engaged in general survey of Egypt, 1801–2, of European Turkey and Greece, 1804–7; resided in Greece, 1808–10; published *Researches in Greece* (1814); his collection of marbles presented to the British Museum, 1839; his vases, gems, and coins purchased by the University of Cambridge. His reputation rests chiefly on the topographical researches embodied in his *Athens* (1821), *Morea* (1830), and *Northern Greece* (1835).

LEAKEY, Caroline Woolmer (1827–1881), religious writer; daughter of James *Leakey; resided in Tasmania; published *Lyra Australis* (1854) and *The Broad Arrow* (1859).

LEAKEY, James (1775–1865), artist and miniaturist; exhibited portraits, landscapes, and interiors at the Royal Academy.

LEAKEY, Louis Seymour Bazett (1903–1972), archaeologist, anthropologist, and human palaeontologist; born in Kenya and brought up there to age of 16; freely associated with Kikuyu boys; educated at Weymouth College, 1919, and St John's College, Cambridge; first class in modern languages tripos (French and Kikuyu) and in archaeology and anthropology, 1926; led four expeditions to East Africa which established sequence of early cultures in Kenya and northern Tanzania, 1926–35; published *The Stone Age Cultures of Kenya Colony* (1931), *The Stone Age Races of Kenya* (1935), and *Stone Age Africa* (1936); Ph.D., 1930; fellow, St John's College, Cambridge, 1929–35; published *Kenya: Contrasts and Problems* (1936) and his autobiographical *White African* (1937); served in special branch of CID, Nairobi, 1939–51; curator of Coryndon Memorial Museum, Nairobi, 1945–61; founder and general secretary, Pan-African Congress on Prehistory, 1947–51; president, 1955–9; warned Kenya government of Mau Mau dangers, 1950; published *Mau Mau and the Kikuyu* (1952) and *Defeating Mau Mau* (1954); court interpreter at trial of Jomo *Kenyatta; found skull of *Proconsul africanus*, and with his wife and son discovered remains of *Australopithecus (Zinjanthropus) boisei*, *Homo habilis*, and *Homo erectus*; researches published in continuing series entitled *Olduvai Gorge*; academic awards included hon. fellowship, St John's College, Cambridge (1966), FBA (1958), and number of honorary doctorates and medals;

published *By the Evidence: Memoirs, 1932–1951* (1974); after his death, Kenya authorities established Louis Leakey Memorial Institute for African Prehistory, and in California the Leakey Foundation was set up.

LEANDER A SANCTO MARTINO (1575–1636), Benedictine. See JONES, JOHN.

LEANERD, John (*fl.* 1679), author of comedies published 1677 and 1678, and perhaps of *The Counterfeits* (1679); described as 'a confident plagiary'.

LEAPOR, Mary (1722–1746), poet; her *Poems on Several Occasions* published (1748, vol. i; and 1751, vol. ii).

LEAR, Edward (1812–1888), artist and author; his *Family of the Psittacidae* one of the earliest volumes of coloured plates of birds on a large scale published in England; gave lessons in drawing to Queen Victoria, 1846; invented *Book of Nonsense* (published 1846) for the grandchildren of his patron, the earl of *Derby, a book of which there have been twenty-six editions; exhibited landscapes at the Suffolk Street Gallery and the Royal Academy; published journals of his travels; died at San Remo.

LEARED, Arthur (1822–1879), traveller; educated at Trinity College, Dublin; BA, 1845; MD, 1860; visited India, 1851, Smyrna and the Holy Land, 1854, Iceland (four times between 1862 and 1874), America, 1870, Morocco, 1872, 1877, and 1879; published *Morocco and the Moors* (1876) and *A Visit to the Court of Morocco* (1879), and some medical treatises.

LEARMONT (or LEIRMOND), Thomas (*fl.* 1220?–1297?), seer and poet. See ERCELDOUNE, THOMAS OF.

LEARMONTH, Sir James Rögnvald (1895–1967), surgeon; educated at Girthon School, Gatehouse of Fleet, Kilmarnock Academy, and Glasgow University; MB, Ch.B., 1921; assistant to Professor Archibald Young, 1922–4; Rockefeller research fellow, Mayo Clinic, 1924–5; dispensary surgeon, Western Infirmary, Glasgow, 1925; Ch.M., 1927; FRCSE, 1928; worked in department of neurosurgery, Mayo Clinic, 1928–32; regius professor of surgery, Aberdeen, 1932–9; specialized in disease of the arteries; professor of surgery, Edinburgh, 1939–56, and regius professor of clinical surgery, 1946–56; expert in peripheral vascular disease; surgeon to royal household in Scotland, 1934; surgeon to the king, 1949; CBE, 1945; KCVO, 1949; chevalier, Legion of Honour, 1950; hon. fellow, American College of Surgeons and Royal Medical Society.

LEASK, William (1812–1884), Dissenting divine; entered Congregational ministry, and held several charges from 1839; edited the *Christian World* and other Nonconformist journals; author of sermons, lectures, and works on theological and moral questions.

LEATE, Nicholas (d. 1631), a London merchant; member of the Levant Company; as the leading merchant in the Turkey trade furnished the government with news from abroad, obtained through his agents and correspondents; master of the Company of Ironmongers, 1616, 1626, and 1627; introduced rare exotics for cultivation in England.

LEATHAM, William Henry (1815–1889), verse-writer and member of parliament; entered his father's bank at Wakefield, 1834; toured on the continent, 1835; published *A Traveller's Thoughts, or Lines suggested by a Tour on the Continent* (1841); MP for Wakefield, 1865–8, for the South-West Riding of Yorkshire, 1880–5; published several volumes of poems, 1841–79.

LEATHERS, Frederick James, first Viscount Leathers (1883–1965), industrialist and public servant; left school at 15 to work with Steamship Owners Coal Association (later merged with William Cory & Sons, Ltd.), 1898, managing director, 1916; concerned also with other companies dealing with coal or shipping services; adviser to Ministry of Shipping, 1914–18 and 1940–1; minister of war transport, 1941; baron, 1941; attended Casablanca, Washington, Quebec, and Cairo conferences, 1943; negotiated lease-lend of American ships to Britain; CH, 1943; accompanied prime minister to Yalta and Potsdam; secretary of state for co-ordination of transport, fuel, and power, 1951–3; viscount, 1954; hon. LL D, Leeds (1946) and Birmingham (1951); hon. member, Institution of Naval Architects; president, Institute of Chartered Shipbrokers.

LEATHES, Stanley (1830–1900), Hebraist; BA, Jesus College, Cambridge, 1852; first Tyrwhitt's Hebrew scholar, 1853; MA, 1855; hon. fellow, 1885; ordained priest, 1857; professor of Hebrew at King's College, London, 1863; member of Old Testament Revision Committee, 1870–85; prebendary of St Paul's Cathedral, 1876; rector of Cliffe-at-Hoo, Kent, 1880–9, and of Much Hadham, Hertfordshire, 1889–1900; published lectures, and theological and other writings.

LEATHES, Sir Stanley Mordaunt (1861–1938), historian and administrator; son of Stanley *Leathes; scholar of Eton and Trinity College, Cambridge; first class, classics, 1882; fellow (1886), history lecturer (1892–1903); joint editor, *Cambridge Modern History* (1901–12); secretary to the Civil Service Commission, 1903, commissioner, 1907, first commissioner, 1910–27; KCB, 1919.

LEAVIS, Frank Raymond (1895–1978), literary critic, editor, and teacher; educated at the Perse School, Cambridge, and Emmanuel College, of which he was a scholar; first class, English tripos, part ii, 1921; during 1914–18 war served on Western Front with Friends' Ambulance Unit; Ph.D., 1924; probationary faculty lecturer in English at Cambridge, 1927–31; published *New Bearings in English Poetry* (1932); director of studies in English, Downing College, 1932; lecturer in English faculty, 1936; reader, 1959–62; married Queenie Dorothy Roth, 1929; together with Denys Thompson, they published *Culture and Environment* (1933); together helped to launch as editor and sub-editor quarterly, *Scrutiny* (1932–53), which established their reputation; other publications include *Revaluations* (1936), *Education and the University* (1943), *The Great Tradition* (1948), *Lectures in America* (1969), *The Living Principle* (1975), and *Thought, Words and Creativity* (1976); hon. fellow, Downing College, 1962–4; Chichele lecturer, Oxford, 1964; visiting professor, York, 1965; Clark lecturer, Cambridge, 1967; visiting professor, University of Wales, 1969, and at Bristol, 1970; CH, 1978; constant controversialist, attacked C. P. (later Lord) *Snow in Richmond lecture, 1962; awarded number of honorary doctorates.

LE BAS, Charles Webb (1779–1861), principal of the East India College, Haileybury; of Trinity College, Cambridge; fellow, 1802; barrister, Lincoln's Inn, 1806; abandoned the law and entered holy orders, 1809; prebendary of Lincoln, 1812; mathematical professor and dean of Haileybury, 1813; principal, 1837–43; the Le Bas Prize at Cambridge for an historical essay founded by his friends, 1848; contributed to the *British Critic*, 1827–38; wrote sermons and biographies of divines.

LE BAS, Edward (1904–1966), painter and collector; educated at Harrow and Pembroke College, Cambridge; studied at Royal College of Art, London; first exhibited at the Royal Academy, 1933; shared first one-man show with Dame Ethel *Walker at Lefevre Galleries, 1936; specialized in still life, landscapes, and figures in interiors; influenced by W. R. *Sickert and Vuillard; became wealthy collector after father's death, including work of young British painters; last one-man exhibition in England, 1939; exhibited annually at Royal Academy; ARA, 1943; RA, 1954; CBE, 1957; exhibited successfully in New York, 1956 and 1961; works to be seen in

Tate Gallery, London, and galleries in York and Leicester, New South Wales, and America.

LE BLANC, Sir Simon (d. 1816), judge; entered Trinity Hall, Cambridge, 1766; LL B, 1773; barrister, Inner Temple, 1773; fellow of his college, 1779; serjeant-at-law, 1787; counsel to his university, 1791; puisne judge of the King's Bench, 1799; knighted, 1799.

LE BLON (or LE BLOND), Jacques Christophe (1670–1741), painter, engraver, and printer in colours; born at Frankfurt-on-Main; studied at Zurich, Paris, and Rome; lived for a time at Amsterdam; came to London; his invention of painting engravings in colour to imitate painting pecuniarily unsuccessful; published an account of his process (1730); the inventor of the modern system of chromolithography.

LE BRETON, Anna Letitia (1808–1885), authoress; daughter of Charles Rochemont *Aikin; married Philip Hemery le Breton, 1833; assisted her husband in his memoirs of Lucy *Aikin, 1864; edited Miss Aikin's correspondence with Dr Channing, 1874; published a memoir of Mrs *Barbauld, and *Memories of Seventy Years* (1883).

LE BRUN, John (d. 1865), Independent missionary in Mauritius; born in Switzerland; ordained for the Congregational ministry, 1813; began to work at Port Louis, Mauritius, under the auspices of the London Missionary Society, 1814; returned to England, 1833, the society subsequently abandoning its efforts in Mauritius in consequence of official opposition; returned on his own account, 1834; reappointed agent of the Society, 1841; died at Port Louis.

LEBWIN (LEBUINUS or LIAFWINE), Saint (*fl.* 755); of English parentage; went as missionary to the Germans; dwelt by the River Ijssel and built two churches; opposed by the heathen Saxons; the collegiate church at Deventer dedicated to him.

LE CAPELAIN, John (1812–1848), painter; native of Jersey; presented drawings of the scenery of Jersey to Queen Victoria; commissioned by her to paint pictures of the Isle of Wight.

LE CARON, Major Henri (1841–1894), government spy. See BEACH, THOMAS.

LE CÈNE, Charles (1647?–1703), Huguenot refugee; born at Caen, Normandy; studied at Sedan, 1667–9, at Geneva, 1669–70, at Saumur, 1670–2; ordained Protestant minister, 1672; came to England at the revocation of the Edict of Nantes, 1685, and retired to Holland, 1691; returned to England, 1699; author of French theological works.

LECHMERE, Edmund (d. 1640?), Roman Catholic divine. See STRATFORD.

LECHMERE, Sir Nicholas (1613–1701), judge; nephew of Sir Thomas *Overbury; BA, Wadham College, Oxford; barrister, Middle Temple, 1641; bencher, 1655; sided with parliament on outbreak of the Civil War; MP, Bewdley, 1648; present at the Battle of Worcester, 1651; MP, Worcester, 1654, 1656, 1658–9; attorney-general to the duchy of Lancaster, 1654; reader at his inn, 1669; serjeant-at-law, 1689; knighted, 1689; judge of the Exchequer Bench, 1689–1700.

LECHMERE, Nicholas, first Baron Lechmere (1675–1727); educated at Merton College, Oxford; barrister, Middle Temple, 1698; MP, Appleby, 1708, for Cockermouth, 1710, 1713, and 1715, and for Tewkesbury, 1717–20; QC, 1708; a collaborator of *Steele in *The Crisis*, 1714; solicitor-general, 1714–18; privy councillor, 1718; attorney-general, 1718–20, and chancellor of the duchy of Lancaster, 1718–27; raised to the peerage, 1721.

LECKY, Squire Thornton Stratford (1838–1902), writer on navigation; served on merchant vessels from age of 14, becoming expert in navigation of Pacific; detected off Rio de Janeiro submerged 'Lecky Rock', 1865; showed many errors in South American charts and surveyed most of South American coast; served in Egyptian War of 1882; chief work on navigation was *Wrinkles in Practical Navigation* (1881, 15th edn., 1898); marine superintendent of Great Western Railway, 1884; younger brother of Trinity House; FRAS and FRGS; died at Las Palmas.

LECKY, William Edward Hartpole (1838–1903), historian and essayist; born near Dublin; of Scottish descent; educated at Cheltenham, 1852–5, and at Trinity College, Dublin, studying desultorily history and philosophy; BA, 1859; MA, 1863; after a volume of poems (1859) he published anonymously *The Religious Tendencies of the Age* (1860) and *Leaders of Public Opinion in Ireland* (1862, revised edn., 1903), which met at first with little success; spent holidays abroad, especially in Spain and Italy; his essay on 'The Declining Sense of the Miraculous' (1863) subsequently formed first two chapters of his abstruse, discursive, but lucid *History of Rationalism* (2 vols., 1865), which brought him his first fame; a Liberal in politics, he condemned Disraeli's Reform Bill of 1867, but supported Irish Church disestablishment and Irish Land Act of 1870; published *History of European Morals* (2 vols., 1869); married in 1871 Elizabeth van Dedem, maid of honour to Queen Sophia of the Netherlands, and settled at 38 Onslow Gardens,

Kensington; meanwhile collected material for his *History of England in the Eighteenth Century*, making extensive researches in Dublin (vols. 1 and 2 appeared in 1878; vols. 3 and 4 in 1882; vols. 5 and 6 in 1887; vols. 7 and 8 in 1890; cabinet edition, 12 vols., 1892; last 5 volumes devoted to History of Ireland); that work, which aimed at refuting *Froude's calumnies of Irish people, was praised by Lord *Acton and American critics. Lecky declined regius professorship of modern history at Oxford, 1892; hon. DCL, Oxford, 1888; Litt.D., Cambridge, 1891; LL D, Dublin (1879), St Andrews (1885), Glasgow (1895); became a Liberal Unionist in 1886; wrote weighty letters to *The Times* and elsewhere (1886, 1892–3) in opposition to home rule; MP for Dublin University, 1895–1902; favoured establishment of a Roman Catholic university in Ireland; supported agricultural policy of Sir Horace *Plunkett there; opposed old-age pensions; favoured international arbitration; a fluent, rapid, but monotonous speaker; his later works were *Democracy and Liberty* (2 vols., 1896; a revised edition of 1899 gave an admirable estimate of Gladstone's work and character); *The Map of Life* (1899), and *Historical and Political Essays* (posthumous, 1908); FBA and OM, 1902; Lecky chair of history founded at Trinity College, Dublin, to which were left all his MSS.

LECLERCQ, Carlotta (1840?–1893), actress; Ariel (*Tempest*), Nerissa (*Merchant of Venice*), Mrs Ford, Mrs Page (*Merry Wives*), and Rosalind (*As You Like It*), among her parts; acted with Charles Albert *Fechter in England and America.

LECLERCQ, Rose (1845?–1899), actress; sister of Carlotta *Leclercq; Mrs Page, and the queen in *La Tosca* among her parts; the best representative of the grand style in comedy.

LECONFIELD, sixth Baron, and first Baron Egremont (1920–1972), civil servant and author. See WYNDHAM, JOHN EDWARD REGINALD.

LE COUTEUR, John (1761–1835), lieutenant-general; of a Jersey family; ensign, 1780; lieutenant and went to India, 1781; taken prisoner by Tippoo Sahib, 1783; released, 1784; captain, 1785; major, 1797; lieutenant-colonel, 1798; inspecting officer of militia and assistant quartermaster-general in Jersey, 1799; lieutenant-governor of Curacoa, 1813; lieutenant-general, 1821; author of two works in French relating his military experiences.

LE DAVIS, Edward (1640?–1684?), engraver; practised his art first in Paris and afterwards in London.

LEDDRA, William (d. 1661), Quaker; emigrated to Rhode Island, 1658; passed to Connecticut, where he was arrested and banished; proceeded to Salem; imprisoned at Boston; condemned and executed on Boston Common; the last Quaker executed in New England.

LEDEREDE (or LEDRED), Richard de (*fl.* 1350), bishop of Ossory; English Franciscan; appointed to see of Ossory, 1316; conducted prosecutions for heresy and sorcery; Latin verses ascribed to him extant in the *Red Book of Ossory*.

LE DESPENCER, Baron (1708–1781), chancellor of the exchequer. See DASHWOOD, Sir FRANCIS.

LEDIARD, Thomas (1685–1743), miscellaneous writer; attached to the staff of the duke of *Marlborough, accompanying him on his visit to Charles XII of Sweden, 1707; returned to England before 1732; produced various historical and biographical works, 1735–6; author of a pamphlet dealing with a scheme for building bridge at Westminster, 1738; FRS, 1742; 'agent and surveyor of Westminster Bridge', 1738–43; author of several works in German and an English opera, *Britannia*.

LEDINGHAM, Sir John Charles Grant (1875–1944), bacteriologist and director of Lister Institute; educated at Banff Academy and Aberdeen University; MA, 1895; B.Sc., 1900; MB, Ch.B., 1902; studied pathology in Leipzig and London; assistant bacteriologist, Lister Institute, 1905; chief bacteriologist, 1909; director, 1931–43; professor of bacteriology, London University, 1920–42; secretary, National Collection of Type Cultures, 1920–30; with (Sir) J. A. *Arkwright wrote *The Carrier Problem in Infectious Diseases* (1912); an associate editor of *System of Bacteriology* (1929–31); FRS, 1921; knighted, 1937.

LEDWARD, Gilbert (1888–1960), sculptor; son of Richard Arthur *Ledward, sculptor; studied at Royal College of Art and Royal Academy School; professor of sculpture, Royal College of Art, 1926–9; war memorials include Guards Memorial, London; other works were direct stone carvings such as *Monolith* (Tate Gallery), portrait busts, and Great Seal of the Realm (1953); ARA, 1932; RA, 1937; OBE, 1956.

LEDWARD, Richard Arthur (1857–1890), sculptor; studied at South Kensington art school; exhibited busts at the Royal Academy, 1882.

LEDWICH, Edward (1738–1823), antiquary; entered Trinity College, Dublin, 1755; BA, 1760; LL B, 1763; became a priest in the established church; published *Antiquities of Ireland* (1790); his best work *A Statistical Account of the Parish of Aghaboe* (published 1796); not identical with the Edward Ledwich (d. 1782) who was dean of Kildare, 1772.

LEDWICH, Thomas Hawkesworth (1823–1858), anatomist and surgeon; grandson of Edward *Ledwich; studied medicine in Dublin; member, Irish College of Surgeons, 1845; a successful lecturer on anatomy; his great work, *The Anatomy of the Human Body*, published (1852).

LEDWIDGE, Francis (1891–1917), poet; engaged in rural occupations in Slane district, County Meath; although a strong nationalist, joined army, 1914; killed in Belgium; wrote about the countryside; *Complete Poems* published posthumously (1919).

LEDYARD, John (1751–1788), traveller; born at Groton in Connecticut, USA; made his way to New York, worked his passage to Plymouth in England, and tramped to London, *c.*1771; enlisted in the Marines, and (1776) accompanied Captain *Cook in the *Resolution*; published account of the voyage (1783); resolved to travel on foot to the east of Asia, as a preliminary to open up trade to the north-west coast of America; reached St Petersburg, 1787; made his way to Yakutsk; returned to London, undertook a journey of exploration in Africa on behalf of the African Association, but died at Cairo.

LEE. See also LEGH, LEIGH, LEY.

LEE, Lord (d. 1674), Scottish judge. See LOCKHART, Sir JAMES.

LEE, Sir **(Albert) George** (1879–1967), engineer-in-chief, General Post Office; educated at Collegiate School, Llandudno; engineering assistant, Post Office Engineering Department, London, 1901; studied part-time at Northampton Institute, Finsbury Technical College, and King's College, London; B.Sc.; increased experience on telephone transmission and promoted to sectional engineer, Bolton, 1908–12; served in Royal Engineers Signal Service during 1914–18; MC; British delegate to Inter-Allied Radio Conference, Paris, 1921; worked on transatlantic telephony, 1923–6; engineer-in-chief, GPO, 1931–9; director, communications, research, and development, Air Ministry, 1939; senior telecommunications officer, Ministry of Supply, 1944; vice-president, Institute of Radio Engineers of America, 1929; president, Institution of Electrical Engineers, 1937–8; OBE, 1927; knighted, 1937.

LEE, Alfred Theophilus (1829–1883), miscellaneous writer; of Christ's College, Cambridge; BA, 1853; held various livings, 1853–68; MA, 1856; hon. LL D, Trinity College, Dublin, 1866; DCL, Oxford, 1867; held various clerical offices in Ireland, 1869–71; preacher at Gray's Inn, 1879; published articles on the church defence question, sermons, and pamphlets.

LEE, Ann (1736–1784), foundress of the American Society of Shakers; factory-hand and afterwards cook in Manchester; joined a band of seceders from the Society of Friends, 1758, who were nicknamed the 'Shaking Quakers' or 'Shakers'; married Abraham Standerin, 1762; discovered celibacy to be the holy state; was sent to prison as a Sabbath-breaker, 1770; resumed preaching on her release; acknowledged by the Shakers as spiritual head; sailed for America, 1774; founded first American Shaker Society, 1776; claimed the power of discerning spirits and working miracles; died at Watervliet, near Albany.

LEE, Arthur Hamilton, Viscount Lee of Fareham (1868–1947), statesman, benefactor, and patron of the arts; educated at Cheltenham College and Woolwich; joined Royal Artillery, 1888; professor at Royal Military College, Kingston, Canada, 1893–8; military attaché, United States Army in Cuba, 1898, Washington, 1899, retired, 1900; Conservative MP, Fareham division, 1900–18; civil lord of Admiralty, 1903–5; parliamentary military secretary, Ministry of Munitions, 1915; personal military secretary to Lloyd George, 1916; director-general of food production, 1917–18; KCB, 1916; presented Chequers estate to nation for use of prime ministers, 1917; baron, 1918; PC, 1919; president of Board of Agriculture, 1919–21; first lord of Admiralty, 1921–2; second British delegate to Washington Conference, 1921–2; viscount, 1922; with Samuel *Courtauld founded Courtauld Institute and brought Warburgh Institute to London.

LEE, Charles (1731–1782), American major-general; ensign, 1746; went to America as lieutenant; present at the disaster at Fort Duquesne; wounded at Ticonderoga, 1758; present at the capture of Montreal; attached to staff of Portuguese Army, 1762; accompanied the Polish embassy to Constantinople, 1766; went to New York, 1773; supported the revolutionary plans; appointed second major-general, 1775; appointed second-in-command to Washington; taken prisoner by the English, 1776; exchanged, 1778; blamed for disaster and court-martialled, 1778; retired, 1779; died at Philadelphia; buried at Washington.

LEE, Cromwell (d. 1602), compiler of an Italian dictionary; brother of Sir Henry *Lee; educated at Oxford, where, after travelling in Italy, he settled and compiled part of an Italian–English dictionary, never printed (manuscript in St John's College library).

LEE, Edward (1482?–1544), archbishop of York; fellow of Magdalen College, Oxford, 1500;

MA, Cambridge, 1504; ordained, 1504; BD, 1515; opposed Erasmus, 1519–20; sent on various embassies, 1523–30; prebendary of York and Westminster, 1530; DD, Louvain and Bologna, incorporated at Oxford, 1530; archbishop of York, 1531; while anxious to avoid displeasing the king, was opposed to the party of the new learning and inclined to Roman usages; author of theological works in Latin and English.

LEE, Edwin (d. 1870), medical writer; MRCS, 1829; awarded the Jacksonian Prize for his dissertation on lithotrity, 1838; MD, Göttingen, 1846; best known by his handbooks to continental health resorts.

LEE, Fitzroy Henry (1699–1750), vice-admiral; entered navy, 1717; lieutenant, 1721; captain, 1728; governor of Newfoundland, 1735–8; commodore and commander-in-chief on the Leeward Islands Station, 1746; rear-admiral, 1747; vice-admiral of the white, 1748; probably the original of *Smollett's Commodore Trunnion.

LEE, Francis (1661–1719), miscellaneous writer; entered St John's College, Oxford, 1679; BA, 1683; MA, 1687; studied medicine at Leiden, 1692; became a disciple of Jane *Lead, 1694; MD; one of the founders of the Philadelphian Society, 1697; LCP London, 1708; died at Gravelines, Flanders; his works (all unclaimed) said to have been very numerous.

LEE, Sir Frank Godbould (1903–1971), civil servant and master of Corpus Christi College, Cambridge; educated at Brentwood School and Downing College, Cambridge, where he was a scholar and gained firsts in part i, English tripos, 1923 and part ii, history tripos, 1924; passed into Indian Civil Service but decided to teach at Brentwood for a year; entered Colonial Office, 1926; spent two years as district officer in Nyasaland; served on supply side of Treasury, 1940; deputy head of Treasury delegation to Washington, 1944; closely associated with Lord *Keynes in Lend-Lease negotiations; deputy secretary, Ministry of Supply, 1946; minister, Embassy in Washington, 1948–9; permanent secretary, Ministry of Food, 1949–51; secretary to Board of Trade, 1951–60; joint permanent secretary, Treasury, 1960–2; master of Corpus Christi College, Cambridge, 1962–71; served on financial board of university and University Appointments Board; governor of Leys School, and vice-chairman of board of Addenbrooke's Hospital; member of council of East Anglia University; governor of London School of Economics; director of Bowaters; CMG, 1946; KCB, 1950; GCMG, 1959; PC, 1962; hon. fellow, Downing College; hon. LL D, London.

LEE, Frederick George (1832–1902), theological writer; educated at St Edmund Hall, Oxford; won Newdigate Prize for English poem, 1854; vicar of All Saints', Lambeth, 1867–99; practised an advanced ritualism; vindicated the validity of Church of England orders, 1870; subsequently questioned their validity and founded Order of Corporate Reunion to restore to Church of England valid orders; consecrated by Catholic prelates 'bishop of Dorchester', 1877; FSA, 1857; historical works, which are partisan and untrustworthy, include *Historical Sketches of the Reformation* (1879) and *The Church under Queen Elizabeth* (3rd edn., 1897); published also *History of Thame* (1886), verse, devotional and antiquarian works; joined Roman Catholic Church, 1901.

LEE, Frederick Richard (1799–1879), painter and royal academician; student of the Royal Academy, 1818; exhibitor at the British Institution from 1822, and at the Royal Academy, 1824–70; painted Devonshire, Scottish, and French landscape; RA, 1838; died in South Africa.

LEE, Sir George (1700–1758), lawyer and politician; brother of Sir William *Lee; entered Christ Church, Oxford, 1720; BCL, 1724; DCL, 1729; MP, Brackley, Northamptonshire, 1733–42; lord of Admiralty, 1742; MP, Devizes, 1742–7, Liskeard, 1747–54; dean of arches, 1751–8; judge of the prerogative court of Canterbury, 1751–8; privy councillor, 1752; knighted, 1752; MP, Launceston, 1754–8.

LEE, George Alexander (1802–1851), musical composer; tenor at the Dublin Theatre, 1825; musical conductor at various London theatres, 1827–51; composed the music to several dramatic pieces, songs, and ballads.

LEE, George Augustus (1761–1826), Manchester cotton-spinner; son of John *Lee (d. 1781); distinguished for his readiness to adopt new inventions in his factories.

LEE, George Henry, third earl of Lichfield (1718–1772), chancellor of Oxford University; created MA, St John's College, Oxford, 1737; MP, Oxfordshire, 1740 and 1741–3; succeeded to the earldom, 1743; privy councillor, 1762; chancellor of Oxford, 1762–72; DCL, 1762; founded by bequest Lichfield clinical professorship at Oxford.

LEE, Harriet (1757–1851), novelist and dramatist; daughter of John *Lee (d. 1781), and sister of Sophia *Lee; published *The Errors of Innocence* (a novel, 1786); her comedy, *The New Peerage*, performed at Drury Lane, 1787; published another novel, *Clara Lennox* (1797); the first two volumes of her chief work, in which her sister

Sophia assisted her, *The Canterbury Tales*, was published (1797–8), and the remaining three volumes (1805); refused offer of marriage from William *Godwin the elder, 1798; a version of her story, 'Kruitzner', dramatized by herself as *The Three Strangers*, performed at Covent Garden (1825), published (1826), the story being dramatized by *Byron in *Werner*, 1822.

LEE, Sir **Henry** (1533–1611), master of the ordnance; educated by his uncle, Sir Thomas *Wyatt; entered service of Henry VIII, 1545; clerk of the armoury, 1549–50; knighted, 1553; MP, Buckinghamshire, 1558 and 1572; personal champion to Queen Elizabeth, 1559–90; master of the ordnance, 1590; visited by Queen Elizabeth at his country house, 1592; KG, 1597; a great sheep-farmer and builder.

LEE, Henry (1765–1836), author of *Caleb Quotem*; became an actor; his farce, *Caleb Quotem*, written 1789, brought out at the Haymarket as *Throw Physic to the Dogs* (1789); charged George *Colman the younger with plagiarizing it in *The Review* (1800); author of some poems, and a volume of desultory reminiscences.

LEE, Henry (1826–1888), naturalist; naturalist to the Brighton Aquarium, 1872; wrote popular account of the octopus, 1874.

LEE, Holm (pseudonym) (1828–1900), novelist. See PARR, HARRIET.

LEE, James (1715–1795), nurseryman; introduced cultivation of the fuchsia in England; translated part of Linnaeus's works into English, 1760.

LEE, James Prince (1804–1869), bishop of Manchester; educated at St Paul's School, London, and Trinity College, Cambridge; fellow, 1829; ordained, 1830; a master at Rugby, 1830–8; MA, 1831; headmaster of King Edward's School, Birmingham, 1838–47; bishop of Manchester, 1847; DD, Cambridge, 1861.

LEE, John (d. 1781), actor and adapter of plays; acted in London under *Garrick (with a short break in 1749–50), 1747–51; manager at Edinburgh, 1752–6; again in London under Garrick, 1761–6; manager of the Bath Theatre, 1778–9; tampered with many of Shakespeare's plays and other dramatic masterpieces.

LEE, John (1733–1793), lawyer and politician; barrister, Lincoln's Inn; attorney-general for county palatine of Lancaster; recorder of Doncaster, 1769; KC, 1780; solicitor-general and MP for Higham Ferrers, Northamptonshire; attorney-general, 1783.

LEE, John (d. 1804), wood-engraver; engraved the cuts for *The Cheap Repository*, 1794–8, and

part of the designs by William Marshall *Craig in *Scripture Illustrated*.

LEE, John (1779–1859), principal of Edinburgh University; entered Edinburgh University, 1794; MD, 1801; licensed as a preacher, 1807; professor of church history at St Mary's College, St Andrews, 1812–21; minister of the Canongate Church, Edinburgh, 1821; DD, St Andrews, 1821; chaplain-in-ordinary to the king, 1830; principal of Edinburgh University, 1840–59; professor of divinity, 1843–59; especially learned in Scottish literary and ecclesiastical history.

LEE, John (1783–1866), collector of antiquities and man of science; son of John Fiott; educated at St John's College, Cambridge; made a tour through Europe and the East collecting objects of antiquity, 1807–10; MA, 1809; assumed name of Lee by royal license, 1815; FSA, 1828; built observatory on his estate, 1830; FRS, 1831; practising member of the ecclesiastical courts till 1858; QC, 1864; published scientific and antiquarian works.

LEE, John Edward (1808–1887), antiquary and geologist; his chief work, *Isca Silurum; or an Illustrated Catalogue of the Museum of Antiquities at Caerleon*, published (1862); translated foreign works on prehistoric archaeology; presented his fine collection of fossils to the British Museum, 1885.

LEE, Joseph (1780–1859), enamel painter; enamel painter to Princess Charlotte of Wales, 1818; occasionally exhibited at the Royal Academy till 1853.

LEE, Matthew (1694–1755), benefactor to Christ Church, Oxford; educated at Westminster School and Christ Church; MA, 1720; MD, 1726; FRCP, 1732; Harveian orator, 1736; physician to *Frederick, prince of Wales, 1739; founded an anatomical lectureship at Christ Church, 1750.

LEE, Nathaniel (1653?–1692), dramatist; educated at Westminster School and Trinity College, Cambridge; BA, 1668; drew the plots of his tragedies mainly from classical history; *Nero*, his earliest effort, produced (1675); wrote *Gloriana* and *Sophonisba*, two rhyming plays, 1676; his best-known tragedy, *The Rival Queens*, produced (1677); collaborated with *Dryden in *Oedipus* (1679) and *The Duke of Guise* (1682); his last tragedy, *Constantine the Great*, produced (1684); lost his reason through intemperance, 1684, and confined in Bethlehem till 1689. Many of his plays (a collected edition appeared in 2 vols. in 1713) long kept the stage, and great actors performed the chief parts.

LEE, Mrs Rachel Fanny Antonina (1774?–1829), heroine of a criminal trial, and the subject of chap. iv of *De Quincey's *Autobiographic Sketches*; a natural daughter of Francis *Dashwood, Lord le Despenser; married Matthew Lee, 1794, but soon separated from him; eloped with Loudoun Gordon, accompanied by his brother Lockhart, 1804; appeared as a witness against the brothers when they were brought to trial for her abduction which resulted in their acquittal, 1804; published *Essay on Government* (1808).

LEE, Rawdon Briggs (1845–1908), writer on dogs; succeeded father as editor of the *Kendal Mercury* till 1885; devoted much time to breeding of dogs; his English setter, Richmond, was sent to Australia to improve the breed; kennel editor of *Field*, 1883–1907; wrote accounts of fox terrier, 1889, and of modern dogs of Great Britain (3 vols., 1894 and 1897).

LEE, Sir Richard (1513?–1575), military engineer; surveyor of the king's works, 1540; knighted for services in Scotland, 1544; employed intermittently in improving the fortifications of Berwick and the Scottish border, 1557–65; received part of the domain of the monastery of St Albans from Henry VIII.

LEE, Richard Nelson (1806–1872), actor and dramatist; acted at the Surrey Theatre, 1827–34; became proprietor of 'Richardson's Show', 1836; author of pantomimes and plays.

LEE, Robert (1793–1877), obstetric physician; educated at Edinburgh University; MD, 1814; physician to Prince Woronzow, governor-general of the Crimea, 1824–6; FRS, 1830; lecturer on midwifery and diseases of women at St George's Hospital, 1835–66; FRCP, 1841; Lumleian lecturer, 1856–7; Croonian lecturer, 1862; Harveian orator, 1864; retired, 1875; made discoveries of permanent value; unfairly treated by the Royal Society; published works on the diseases of women.

LEE, Robert (1804–1868), professor at Edinburgh; educated at St Andrews University; minister of the old Greyfriars Church, Edinburgh, 1843–68; DD, St Andrews, 1844; professor of biblical criticism in Edinburgh University, 1847; dean of the Chapel Royal, Edinburgh, 1847; endeavoured to liberalize the church of Scotland; introduced stained-glass windows, 1857, and an organ, 1864; published *The Reform of the Church in Worship, Government, and Doctrine* (1864); often censured by the Edinburgh Presbytery for his innovations; author of theological works and books of prayers.

LEE, Robert Warden (1868–1958), lawyer; scholar of Rossall School and Balliol College, Oxford; first classes, classics, 1889–91; called to bar (Gray's Inn), 1896; professor, Roman-Dutch law, London University, 1906–14, Oxford (and fellow of All Souls), 1921–56; dean of law faculty, McGill University, Montreal, 1914–21; publications include *Introduction to Roman-Dutch Law* (1915) and *Elements of Roman Law* (1944); FBA, 1933.

LEE (or LEGH), Rowland (d. 1543), bishop of Coventry and Lichfield and lord president of the council in the marches of Wales; educated at Cambridge; ordained priest, 1512; doctor of decrees, 1520; prebendary of Lichfield, 1527; employed under *Wolsey in the suppression of the monasteries, 1528–9; royal chaplain and master in Chancery; bishop of Coventry and Lichfield, 1534–43, and president of the king's council in the marches of Wales, 1534; devoted his energies to suppressing Welsh disorder, 1534–40.

LEE, Samuel (1625–1691), Puritan divine; educated at St Paul's School, London, and Magdalen Hall, Oxford; MA, 1648; fellow of All Souls, 1650; dean of Wadham College, 1653–6; minister of various congregations in London, 1655–60; migrated to New England, 1686; sailed for home from Boston, 1691; taken by the French, his ship being seized, to St Malo, where he died; author of theological works.

LEE, Samuel (1783–1852), orientalist; of humble origin; taught himself Greek, Hebrew, Persian, Hindustani, and other Eastern languages; entered Queens' College, Cambridge, 1814; MA, 1819; professor of Arabic at Cambridge, 1819–31; BD, 1827; regius professor of Hebrew, Cambridge, 1831–48; DD, 1833. His chief works were his editions of the New Testament in Syriac (1816) and of the Old Testament (1823), and a translation of the Book of Job from the original Hebrew (1837).

LEE, Mrs Sarah (1791–1856), artist and authoress; daughter of John Eglinton Wallis; married Thomas Edward *Bowdich, 1813; shared her husband's tastes and travelled with him in Africa, 1814, 1815, and 1823; married Robert Lee as her second husband, 1829; devoted the rest of her life to popularizing natural science; published books on natural history, many illustrated by herself, and *Memoirs of Baron Cuvier* (1833).

LEE, Sir Sidney (1859–1926), Shakespearian scholar and editor of the *Dictionary of National Biography*; educated at City of London School, where interest in Elizabethan literature was stimulated by Dr E. A. *Abbott; BA, Balliol College, Oxford; began his Shakespearian studies as undergraduate with two articles in *Gentleman's Magazine*, 1880; assistant editor to (Sir) Leslie *Stephen, on foundation of *Dictionary of National*

Biography, 1883; his exact and scholarly methods well fitted for organizing editorial work; joint editor, 1890; sole editor, 1891–1901 and 1910–12, retaining general oversight of Dictionary, 1901–16; preserved balance and uniformity of Dictionary; his greatest asset as editor was his personality; Dictionary completed in 63 volumes, 1900; first Supplement issued in 3 volumes, 1901; out of his Dictionary articles developed *Life of William Shakespeare* (1898) and *Queen Victoria* (1902); *Life of Shakespeare*, which passed through fourteen editions, a work of exegesis of first order; furnished reliable basis for sound aesthetic appreciation by his study of origin and formation of Shakespeare's text and influence of foreign literature on Shakespeare's subject-matter; subsequently developed former theme by publishing facsimiles of earliest editions of some of Shakespeare's works; developed latter theme by extensive examination, chiefly in articles and lectures, of foreign influence on Elizabethan literature in general and on Shakespeare in particular; his *Queen Victoria* first serious attempt to present queen's public and private life as whole; although information available, especially on latter part of reign, restricted, as pioneer piece of work remarkably successful; superintended summary of Dictionary which appeared as *Index and Epitome* (1903), volume of *Errata* (1904), and reissue of Dictionary and first Supplement (1909); Clark lecturer in English literature, Trinity College, Cambridge, 1901–2; toured universities and colleges of USA, 1903; edited second Supplement of Dictionary, 1910–12; neither first nor second Supplement preserved exactly standard of selection maintained in main work; first Supplement tended to restrict admission, while second Supplement was far more inclusive than main Dictionary; president (1890) of Elizabethan Literary Society at Toynbee Hall, which he and Frederick Rogers developed into centre of Elizabethan study; a founder of English Association, 1906; president, 1917; appointed to new chair of English language and literature at East London College, London University, 1913; retired, 1924; his last work of importance, *Life of King Edward VII*, undertaken at request of King George V; first volume published, 1925; second, completed by (Sir) S. F. Markham, published, 1927; FBA, 1910; knighted, 1911.

LEE, Sophia (1750–1824), novelist and dramatist; daughter of John *Lee (d. 1781); her comedy, *The Chapter of Accidents*, produced, 1780; conducted a girls' school at Bath, 1781–1803; published *The Recess*, an historical romance (1785), and *Almeyda, Queen of Grenada*, a tragedy in blank verse (produced 1796); helped her sister, Harriet *Lee, in the *Canterbury Tales* (1797).

LEE, Thomas (d. 1601), captain in Ireland and supporter of Robert, earl of *Essex; went to Ireland before 1576; assisted in suppressing rebellions in Ireland, 1581–99; arrested for attempting to procure the release of Essex, 1601; tried and executed, 1601; wrote an historically valuable tract on the government of Ireland (first published 1772).

LEE, Sir Thomas, first baronet (d. 1691), politician; created baronet, 1660; MP for Aylesbury, 1661–81 and 1689–91, and for Buckinghamshire in the Convention Parliament.

LEE, Vernon (pseudonym) (1856–1935), author. See PAGET, VIOLET.

LEE, William (d. 1610?), inventor of the stocking-frame; educated at Christ's and St John's colleges, Cambridge; BA, St John's College, 1583; invented the stocking-frame, 1589; his invention discouraged by Elizabeth and James I; settled at Rouen by invitation of Henri IV of France; died at Paris.

LEE, Sir William (1688–1754), judge; brother of Sir George *Lee; entered the Middle Temple, 1703; barrister, Middle Temple; Latin secretary to George I and George II, 1718–30; recorder of Buckingham, 1722; bencher of the Inner Temple, 1725; MP, Chipping Wycombe, 1727; KC, 1728; attorney-general to *Frederick, prince of Wales, *c.*1728; puisne judge of the King's Bench, 1730; chief justice of King's Bench, 1737; knighted, 1737; privy councillor, 1737.

LEE, William (1809–1865), water-colour painter; member of the Institute of Painters in Water-Colours, 1848; painter of English rustic figures and scenes on the French coast.

LEE, William (1815–1883), archdeacon of Dublin; educated at Trinity College, Dublin; junior fellow, 1839; entered holy orders, 1841; DD, 1857; professor of ecclesiastical history in the University of Dublin, 1857; Archbishop King's lecturer in divinity, 1852; archdeacon of Dublin, 1864; member of the New Testament Revision Company, 1870; author of theological works written from the conservative point of view.

LEECH (LEICH or LEITCH), David (*fl.* 1628–1653), poet; brother of John *Leech (*fl.* 1623); sub-principal of King's College, Aberdeen, 1632; chaplain to Charles II; DD, Aberdeen, 1653; left paraphrases of some of the Psalms in manuscript.

LEECH, Humphrey (1571–1629), Jesuit; educated at Brasenose College, Oxford, and Cambridge; MA, Cambridge (incorporated at Oxford, 1602); entered the English College at Rome,

1609; ordained priest, 1612; joined Jesuits, 1618; missioner in England, 1622–9.

LEECH (or LEACHE), John (1565–1650?), schoolmaster; educated at Brasenose College, Oxford; MA, 1589; published a book of grammar questions (c.1622).

LEECH (or LEITCH; Latinized LEOCHAEUS), John (fl. 1623), epigrammatist; brother of David *Leech; probably related to John *Leech (1565–1650?); MA, Aberdeen, 1614; published Latin epigrams, 1620 and 1623.

LEECH, John (1817–1864), humorous artist; educated at Charterhouse, where he made the acquaintance of *Thackeray; studied medicine by his father's desire; adopted art as a profession; his first work, *Etchings and Sketchings, by A. Pen, Esq.*, published (1835); his first popular hit, a caricature of *Mulready's design for a universal envelope, 1840; contributed to *Punch*, 1841–64; executed for it some 3,000 drawings, 600 being cartoons; illustrated several books, and supplied cuts to a number of magazines; his sporting sketches traceable to his love for hunting.

LEECHMAN, William (1706–1785), divine; studied at Edinburgh University; licensed to preach, 1731; professor of divinity at Glasgow University, 1743; principal, 1761; prefixed a life of the author to *Hutcheson's *System of Moral Philosophy* (1755); published a few sermons.

LEEDES, Edward (1599?–1677), Jesuit. See COURTNEY, EDWARD.

LEEDES, Edward (1627–1707), schoolmaster; educated at Christ's College, Cambridge; MA; master of Bury St Edmunds Grammar School, 1663–1707; author of school-books.

LEEDS, dukes of. See OSBORNE, Sir THOMAS, first duke, 1631–1712; OSBORNE, PEREGRINE, second duke, 1658–1729; OSBORNE, FRANCIS, fifth duke, 1751–1799.

LEEDS, Edward (d. 1590), civilian; educated at Cambridge; MA, 1545; prebendary of Ely, 1559–80; advocate of Doctors' Commons, 1560; master of Clare Hall, Cambridge, 1560–71; LL D, 1569.

LEEDS, Edward (1695?–1758), serjeant-at-law; barrister, Inner Temple, 1718; took the coif, 1742; king's serjeant, 1748–55.

LEEDS, Edward (1728–1803), master in Chancery; son of Edward *Leeds (1695?–1758); barrister, Inner Temple; sheriff of Cambridgeshire, 1768; master in Chancery, 1773; MP, Reigate, 1784–7.

LEE-HAMILTON, Eugene Jacob (1845–1907), poet and novelist; educated at Oriel College, Oxford; held minor diplomatic posts at Paris and Lisbon, 1871–3; disabled for twenty years through nervous disease; lived at Florence and became a centre of intellectual society; published *Imaginary Sonnets* (1888) and *The Sonnets of the Wingless Hours* (1894); was restored to health, 1897; published also a tragedy, two novels, and a metrical translation of Dante's *Inferno* (1898).

LEEKE. See also LEAKE.

LEEKE, Sir Henry John (1790?–1870), admiral; entered navy, 1803; lieutenant, 1810; commander, 1814; knighted, 1835; flag captain, 1845–8; superintendent and commander-in-chief of the Indian Navy, 1852; rear-admiral, 1854; KCB, 1858; vice-admiral, 1860; admiral, 1864.

LEEKE, Laurence (d. 1357), prior of Norwich; appointed prior, 1352; author of *Historiola de Vita et Morte Reverendi domini Willelmi Bateman Norwicensis episcopi.*

LEEMPUT, Remigius Van (1609?–1675), painter. See VAN LEEMPUT.

LEES, Charles (1800–1880), painter; fellow of the Royal Scottish Academy and a regular contributor to its exhibitions; painted portraits, historical and domestic subjects, and landscape.

LEES, Edwin (1800–1887), botanist; began to publish *The Worcestershire Miscellany* (1829); issued his *Botany of the Malvern Hills* (1843) and *Botany of Worcestershire* (1867); one of the first in England to pay regard to the forms of brambles.

LEES, George Martin (1898–1955), geologist; educated at St Andrew's College, Dublin, and Royal Military Academy, Woolwich; served with Royal Flying Corps; DSO; MC; joined Iraq Civil Service, 1919–21; from Royal School of Mines joined Anglo-Persian Oil Company, 1921; chief geologist, 1930–53; initiated search for oil in Britain, 1933, discovering East Midland oilfields, 1939; also successfully explored in Nigeria, Libya, and Abu Dhabi; president, Geological Society, 1951–3; FRS, 1948.

LEES, Sir Harcourt, second baronet (1776–1852), political pamphleteer; MA, Trinity College, Cambridge, 1802; took holy orders; published pamphlets in support of Protestant ascendancy.

LEES, William Nassau (1825–1889), major-general in the Indian Army and orientalist; son of Sir Harcourt *Lees, second baronet; educated at Trinity College, Dublin; ensign, Bengal Native Infantry, 1846; edited Arabic and Persian works between 1853 and 1864; lieutenant, 1853; hon. LL D, Dublin, 1857; captain, 1858; major, 1865; lieutenant-colonel, 1868; member of Royal Asiatic Society, 1872; colonel, 1876; major-general, 1885.

LEESE, Sir **Oliver William Hargreaves,** third baronet (1894–1978), lieutenant-general; educated at Eton; commissioned into Coldstream Guards, 1914; wounded three times during 1914–18 war; DSO, 1916; adjutant, 3rd battalion, Coldstream Guards, 1920–2; adjutant, Eton OTC, 1922–5; at Staff College, Camberley, 1927–8; took command of 1st battalion, Coldstream Guards, 1936; succeeded father as baronet, 1937; chief instructor, Staff College, Quetta, 1938–40; major-general, 1941; lieutenant-general in command, XXX Corps, Eighth Army, at Battle of Alamein; highly regarded by General (later Viscount) *Montgomery; led advance to Tripoli and Mareth and invasion of Sicily; succeeded Montgomery as GOC, Eighth Army, 1943; led army in attack on Monte Cassino and 'Gothic Line'; C-in-C, Allied Land Forces, South-East Asia, 1944; involved in misunderstanding over proposal to move General (later Viscount) *Slim from command of Fourteenth Army; dismissed by Lord Louis *Mountbatten (later Earl Mountbatten); GOC-in-C, Eastern Command; retired from army, 1946, and became expert in horticulture, particularly cacti; national president, British Legion, 1962–70; director, Securicor; lieutenant of Tower of London; president, Warwickshire County Cricket Club, 1959–75; president, MCC, 1965–6; CBE, 1940; CB, 1942; KCB, 1943; awarded Virtuti Militari, highest Polish military honour, Croix de Guerre; commander of Legion of Honour and American Legion of Merit.

LEESON, Spencer Stottesbery Gwatkin (1892–1956), schoolmaster and bishop; scholar of Winchester and New College, Oxford; first class, classical moderations, 1913; war degree, 1916; served in Flanders and naval intelligence, 1915–18; at Board of Education, 1919–24; called to bar (Inner Temple), 1922; assistant master, Winchester, 1924–7; headmaster, Merchant Taylors', 1927–35; moved school to outskirts of London; headmaster, Winchester, 1935–46; chairman, Headmasters' Conference, 1939–45; deacon, 1939; priest, 1940; rector of Southampton, 1946–9; bishop of Peterborough, 1949–56; eloquent speaker and immensely hard worker in educational causes; publications include *Study of the Gospel of Christ* (1941) and *Christian Education* (1947).

LEEVES, William (1748–1828), poet and composer; entered the army, 1764; lieutenant and captain, 1772; took holy orders, 1779; wrote the music to the song 'Auld Robin Gray', by Lady Anne *Barnard; author of other musical compositions, and of occasional poems.

LEE-WARNER, Sir **William** (1846–1914), Indian civil servant and author; BA, St John's College, Cambridge; entered Indian Civil Service, 1867; served in India, 1869–95; secretary of political and secret department at India Office, 1895–1903; KCSI, 1898; GCSI, 1911; works include *Protected Princes of India* (1894), revised as *Native States of India* (1916).

LE FANU, Mrs **Alicia** (1753–1817), playwright; sister of the dramatist Richard Brinsley *Sheridan; married Joseph Le Fanu, brother of Philip *Le Fanu, divine, 1776; author of a comedy, *Sons of Erin*, performed in London, 1812.

LE FANU, Alicia (*fl.* 1812–1826), daughter of Henry Le Fanu, a brother of Philip *Le Fanu; published *Memoirs of Mrs. Frances Sheridan* (1824).

LE FANU, Joseph Sheridan (1814–1873), novelist and journalist; entered Trinity College, Dublin, 1833; devoted himself to journalism from 1839, when he began to issue *The Evening Mail*, a Dublin paper; published *Uncle Silas* (1864), and twelve other novels, 1865–75; edited the *Dublin University Magazine*, 1869–72; stands next to *Lever among modern Irish novelists.

LE FANU, Sir **Michael** (1913–1970), admiral of the fleet; educated at Bedford School and Royal Naval College, Dartmouth; specialized in gunnery, 1938; gunnery officer, *Aurora*, 1939; DSO, 1941; commander, liaison officer to American 3rd and 5th Fleets, 1945; Legion of Merit; captain, 1949; commanded 3rd Training Squadron, Londonderry, 1951; special duty, Admiralty, 1952–3; commanded HMS *Ganges*, 1954; commanded aircraft carrier *Eagle*, 1957–8; rear-admiral, 1958; director-general, weapons, 1958–60; second-in-command, Far East Station, 1960–1; controller of the navy, 1961–5; vice-admiral, 1961; admiral, 1965; commanded three Services in Middle East, Aden, 1965; first sea lord, 1968–9; admiral of the fleet, 1969; CB, 1960; KCB, 1963; GCB, 1968.

LE FANU, Peter (*fl.* 1778), playwright; brother of Philip *Le Fanu; his *Smock Alley Secrets* produced at Dublin, 1778.

LE FANU, Philip (*fl.* 1790), divine; MA, Trinity College, Dublin, 1755; DD, 1776; published translation of the Abbé Guenée's *Lettres de certaines Juives à Monsieur Voltaire* (1777).

LEFEBURE, Nicasius (or **Nicolas**) (d. 1669), chemist. See LE FEVRE.

LEFEBVRE, Roland (1608–1677), painter; born at Anjou; resided at Venice; came to England, 1665; painted mediocre portraits and small history pictures under the patronage of Prince *Rupert.

LEFEVRE, Charles Shaw, first Viscount Eversley (1794–1888). See SHAW-LEFEVRE.

LEFEVRE, Sir George William (1798–1846), physician; studied at Edinburgh and at Guy's and St Thomas's hospitals, London; MD, Aberdeen, 1819; travelled in France, Austria, Poland, and Russia as physician to a Polish nobleman; published *The Life of a Travelling Physician* (1843); afterwards practised at St Petersburg, and became physician to the embassy; knighted; settled in London, 1842; FRCP, 1842; Lumleian lecturer, 1845; committed suicide.

LEFEVRE, Sir John George Shaw (1797–1879), public official. See SHAW-LEFEVRE.

LE FEVRE, Nicasius (or Nicolas) (d. 1669), chemist; studied at Sedan; professor of chemistry to Charles II, and apothecary-in-ordinary to the royal household, 1660; FRS, 1663; published chemical works.

LEFROY, Sir John Henry (1817–1890), governor of Bermuda and of Tasmania; educated at Royal Military Academy, Woolwich; lieutenant, Royal Artillery, 1837; engaged in a magnetic survey, chiefly at St Helena, 1839–42; transferred to observatory at Toronto, 1842; engaged in magnetic survey of extreme north of America, 1843–4; worked at Toronto, 1844–53; captain, 1845; FRS, 1848; founded the Canadian Institute, 1849; compiled *The Handbook of Field Artillery for the use of Officers* (1854); lieutenant-colonel, 1855; inspector-general of army schools, 1857; brevet-colonel, 1858; director-general of ordnance, 1868; retired from the army, 1870; governor and commander-in-chief of the Bermudas, 1871–7; KCMG, 1877; governor of Tasmania, 1880–2; published the diary of his Canadian magnetic survey (1883).

LEFROY, Thomas Langlois (1776–1869), Irish judge; educated at Trinity College, Dublin; BA, 1795; called to the Irish bar, 1797; KC, 1806; king's serjeant, 1808; bencher of the King's Inns, 1819; LL D, 1827; MP, University of Dublin, 1830–41; baron of the Irish court of Exchequer, 1841–52; lord chief justice of the Queen's Bench, 1852–66.

LEFROY, William (1836–1909), dean of Norwich; BA, Trinity College, Dublin, 1863; BD, 1867; DD, 1889; obtained fame as evangelical preacher; incumbent of St Andrew's Chapel, Renshaw Street, Liverpool, 1866; archdeacon of Warrington, 1887; Donnellan lecturer at Dublin, 1887; member of Liverpool School Board from 1876; dean of Norwich, 1889–1909; member of the Alpine Club; helped to build several English churches in Switzerland; died and was buried at Riffel Alp; published theological works.

LE GALLIENNE, Richard Thomas (1866–1947), poet and essayist; educated at Liverpool College; published verse, including *Volumes in Folio* (1889), literary criticisms, and romantic novel, *The Quest of the Golden Girl* (1896); original member, Rhymers' Club; contributor to *Yellow Book*; reader for the Bodley Head; prominently associated with literary movement of nineties; moved to United States, 1901, later to France; published *The Romantic '90s* (1925).

LEGAT, Francis (1755–1809), engraver; historical engraver to the prince of Wales; engraved several pictures in *Boydell's Shakespeare Gallery.

LEGAT, Hugh (*fl.* 1400), Benedictine; studied at Oxford; of St Albans Abbey; studied history, and prepared a commentary on John de *Hauteville's *Architrenius*.

LEGATE, Bartholomew (1575?–1612), the last heretic burned at Smithfield; preacher among the 'Seekers'; denied divinity of Christ, 1604; proceedings taken against him in consistory court of London, 1611; committed to Newgate on charge of heresy; burned at Smithfield.

LEGATE, John, the elder (d. 1620?), printer to Cambridge University; freeman of Stationers' Company, 1586; printer to Cambridge University, 1588–1609; afterwards carried on business in London.

LEGATE, John, the younger (1600–1658), printer to Cambridge University; eldest son of John *Legate the elder; freeman of the Stationers' Company, 1619; succeeded to his father's business, 1620; one of the Cambridge University printers, 1650–5.

LE GEYT, Philip (1635–1716), writer on the laws of Jersey; born at St Helier; educated at Saumur, Caen, and Paris; greffier of the royal court, 1660; jurat, 1665–1710; lieutenant-bailiff, 1676–94; his manuscript collections on the constitution and laws of Jersey published, 1846–7.

LEGG, John Wickham (1843–1921), physician and liturgiologist; MD, University College, London, 1868; joined staff of St Bartholomew's Hospital, London, 1870; abandoned medicine, 1887; FSA, 1875; distinguished student of liturgies; works include editions of Quignon Breviary of 1535 (1888), *Second Recension of Quignon Breviary* (1908, 1912), *Westminster Missal* (1891–7), and *Sarum Missal* (1916), and *English Church Life* [1660–1833] (1914); high churchman.

LEGGE, Edward (1710–1747), commodore; fifth son of William *Legge, first earl of Dartmouth; entered navy, 1726; lieutenant, 1734; captain, 1738; accompanied *Anson's voyage to the Pacific, 1740–2; commodore and commander-in-chief at the Leeward Islands, 1747.

LEGGE, George, first Baron Dartmouth (1648–1691), admiral and commander-in-chief; eldest son of William *Legge (1609?–1670); of Westminster and King's College, Cambridge; lieutenant in Dutch War, 1665–7; captain, 1667; in intervals of war by sea held appointments on land; groom of the bedchamber, 1668; lieutenant-governor of Portsmouth, 1670–83; lieutenant-general of the ordnance, 1672; master of the horse to the duke of York, 1673; commanded in Flanders, 1678; master-general of ordnance, 1682; created Baron Dartmouth, 1682; master of Trinity House, 1683; engaged in Tangier expedition, 1683–4; governor of the Tower, 1685; admiral and commander-in-chief of the fleet, 1688–9; accused of conspiring against William III and committed to the Tower, 1691.

LEGGE, George, third earl of Dartmouth (1755–1810), statesman; son of William *Legge, second earl; educated at Eton and Christ Church, Oxford; MA, 1775; DCL, 1778; MP, Plymouth, 1778, Staffordshire, 1780; privy councillor, 1801; president of the Board of Control, 1801; succeeded his father, 1801; lord chamberlain, 1804.

LEGGE, Heneage (1704–1759), judge; second son of William *Legge, first earl of Dartmouth; barrister, Inner Temple, 1728; raised to the Exchequer bench, 1747.

LEGGE, Henry Bilson- (1708–1764), chancellor of the Exchequer; fourth son of William *Legge, first earl of Dartmouth; MP, East Looe, 1740, Orford, 1741–59; a lord of the Admiralty, 1745–7; a lord of the Treasury, 1746; envoy-extraordinary to the king of Prussia, 1748; chancellor of the Exchequer, 1754–5, 1756–7, 1757–61; MP, Hampshire, 1759–64; had a great reputation as a financier.

LEGGE, James (1815–1897), professor of Chinese at Oxford University; MA, King's College, Aberdeen, 1835; appointed by London Missionary Society to Chinese mission at Malacca, 1839; principal of Anglo-Chinese College at Malacca, 1840, and later at Hong Kong; DD, New York University, 1841; returned to England, 1873; LL D, Aberdeen, 1870, and Edinburgh, 1884; first professor of Chinese at Oxford University and fellow of Corpus Christi College, Oxford, 1875; published numerous writings in Chinese and English, including an edition of Chinese classics.

LEGGE, Thomas (1535–1607), master of Caius College, Cambridge, and Latin dramatist; educated at Trinity College, Cambridge; MA, 1560; fellow of Jesus College, Cambridge, 1568; master of Caius College, 1573–1607; LL D, 1575; regius professor of civil law, Cambridge; vice-chancellor of Cambridge University, 1587–8 and 1592–3; master in Chancery, 1593; his Latin tragedy of *Richard III* acted, 1579.

LEGGE, William (1609?–1670), Royalist; a leader in second army plot, 1641; joined the king's army, 1642; governor of Oxford, 1645; imprisoned for high treason, 1649–53; lieutenant-general of the ordnance, 1660.

LEGGE, William, first earl of Dartmouth (1672–1750), son of George *Legge, first Baron Dartmouth; of Westminster and King's College, Cambridge; MA, 1689; succeeded his father in the Dartmouth barony, 1691; a commissioner of the Board of Trade and Foreign Plantations, 1702; privy councillor, 1702; secretary of state, 1710–13; created earl of Dartmouth, 1711; lord keeper of the privy seal, 1713–14.

LEGGE, William, second earl of Dartmouth (1731–1801), grandson of William *Legge, first earl of Dartmouth; educated at Westminster and Trinity College, Oxford; succeeded to earldom, 1750; MA, 1751; FSA, 1754; DCL, 1756; privy councillor, 1765; president of the Board of Trade and Foreign Plantations, 1765–6; colonial secretary, 1772–5; lord privy seal, 1775–82; high steward of Oxford University, 1786; strongly attached to the Methodists; Dartmouth College in the United States (incorporated 1769) named in his honour.

LEGH. See also LEE, LEIGH, and LEY.

LEGH, Alexander (d. 1501), ambassador; of Eton and King's College, Cambridge; MA; canon of Windsor, 1469; employed on embassies to Scotland, 1474, and later years; temporal chancellor of Durham Cathedral, 1490.

LEGH, Gerard (d. 1563), writer on heraldry; published *The Accedens of Armory* (1562).

LEGH, Sir **Thomas** (d. 1545), visitor of the monasteries; BCL (perhaps of King's College), Cambridge, 1527; DCL, 1531; ambassador to the king of Denmark, 1532–3; 'visited' monasteries, 1535; master in Chancery, 1537; employed in suppressing religious houses, 1538–40; knighted, 1544.

LEGH, Thomas Wodehouse, second Baron Newton (1857–1942), diplomat and politician; educated at Eton and Christ Church, Oxford; entered Foreign Office, 1879; served in Paris, 1881–6; Conservative MP, Newton division, 1886–98; succeeded father, 1898; paymaster-general and PC, 1915; controller, prisoner-of-war department, Foreign Office, 1916–19; obtained exchange of thousands of prisoners;

wrote biographies of Lord *Lyons (1913) and fifth marquess of *Lansdowne (1929).

LEGLAEUS, Gilbertus (*fl.* 1250), medical writer. See GILBERT THE ENGLISHMAN.

LE GRAND, Antoine (d. 1699), Cartesian philosopher; native of Douai; Franciscan Recollect friar; as member of the English mission resided many years in Oxfordshire; provincial of his order, 1698–9; chief work, *Institutio Philosophiae, secundum principia Renati Descartes* (1672; Eng. trans., 1694).

LEGREW, James (1803–1857), sculptor; studied under Sir Francis Legatt *Chantrey and at the Royal Academy schools; exhibited at the Royal Academy from 1826.

LE GRICE, Charles Valentine (1773–1858), friend of *Coleridge and *Lamb; educated at Christ's Hospital, London, and Trinity College, Cambridge; BA, 1796; ordained deacon, 1799, and priest, 1800; MA, 1805; conversationalist and author of small pieces in verse and prose.

LEGROS, Alphonse (1837–1911), painter, sculptor, and etcher; born at Dijon; worked in Paris as scene-painter; exhibited at Salon, 1857; enrolled by Champfleury among the 'Realists'; exhibited *Angelus* (1859), *Ex Voto* (1861), and *Le Lutrin* (1863); earned living by etchings and lithographs; encouraged by J. A. M. *Whistler to come to London, 1863; Slade professor of fine art at University College, London, 1875–92; designed fountains for gardens at Welbeck, 1897; exhibited paintings, etchings, and medals at Royal Academy, 1864–82; fellow of Society of Painter-Etchers, 1880, and hon. fellow of Royal Scottish Academy, 1911; works are in public galleries in Paris, Dijon, London, Manchester, and Liverpool, as well as in private collections.

LE GROS CLARK, Frederick (1892–1977), expert in social and industrial problems. See CLARK.

LE GROS CLARK, Sir Wilfrid Edward (1895–1971), anatomist. See CLARK.

LE GRYS, Sir Robert (d. 1635), courtier and translator; published *John Barclay his Argenis translated out of Latine into English* (1629); knighted, 1629; his translation of *Velleius Paterculus, his Romaine Historie* published (1632); captain of the castle of St Mawes, 1633–4.

LEGUAT, François (1638–1735), voyager and author; born at Bresse, Savoy; Huguenot refugee in Holland, 1689; founded colony of French Protestants in Mascarene Islands, 1691; sailed to Mauritius (1693), where he was imprisoned; transferred to Batavia, 1696; came to England on being released, 1698; published account of his travels (1708).

LE HART, Walter (d. 1472), bishop of Norwich. See LYHERT.

LEHMANN, Rudolf (1819–1905), painter; born near Hamburg; studied art at Paris, Munich, and Rome; first visited London, 1850; exhibited at Royal Academy from 1851, and at other English galleries, mainly subject pictures and portraits of prominent persons; lived in Italy, mostly at Rome, 1856–66; best-known portraits were those of Helen *Faucit, Robert *Browning, Viscount *Goschen; intimate friend of Browning; published *Reminiscences* (1894) and *Men and Women of the Century* (portrait sketches, 1896).

LEICESTER, earls of. See BEAUMONT, ROBERT DE, first earl, 1104–1168; BEAUMONT, ROBERT DE, second earl, d. 1190; MONTFORT, SIMON OF, second earl of the second creation, 1208?–1265; THOMAS, 1277?–1322; DUDLEY, ROBERT, first earl of the fourth creation, 1532?–1588; SIDNEY, ROBERT, first earl of the fifth creation, 1563–1626; SIDNEY, ROBERT, second earl, 1595–1677; SIDNEY, PHILIP, third earl, 1619–1698; TOWNSHEND, GEORGE, first earl of the seventh creation, 1755–1811; COKE, THOMAS WILLIAM, second earl, 1822–1909.

LEICESTER, Sir John Fleming, first Baron de Tabley (1762–1827), art patron; succeeded as fifth baronet, 1770; MA, Trinity College, Cambridge, 1784; collected examples of British art; MP, Yarmouth, Isle of Wight, 1791, Heytesbury, 1796, Stockbridge, 1807; created Baron de Tabley, 1826.

LEICESTER, Lettice, countess of (1541?–1634). See DUDLEY, LETTICE.

LEICESTER, Robert of (*fl.* 1320), Franciscan; DD, Oxford, 1325; author of works on Hebrew chronology, written in 1294 and 1295.

LEICESTER, William de (or WILLIAM DU MONT) (d. 1213), theologian. See WILLIAM.

LEICESTER OF HOLKHAM, earl of (1752–1842). See COKE, THOMAS WILLIAM.

LEICHHARDT, Friedrich Wilhelm Ludwig (1813–1848), Australian explorer; born at Trebatsch, Prussia; studied at Göttingen and Berlin; went to New South Wales, 1841; crossed the Australian continent from east to north, 1844–5; published account of the expedition (1847); explored Sturt's desert in the interior, 1847; started to cross the continent from east to west, 1848, and was never again heard of.

LEIFCHILD, Henry Stormonth (1823–1884), sculptor; studied at the British Museum, the Royal Academy, and (1848–51) at Rome; exhibited at the Royal Academy from 1846.

LEIFCHILD, John (1780–1862), Independent minister; student in Hoxton Academy, 1804–8; minister of several chapels between 1808 and 1854; published religious works.

LEIGH. See also LEE, LEGH, and LEY.

LEIGH, Anthony (d. 1692), comedian; first appeared on the stage, 1672; played many original parts of importance in plays by *Dryden, *Otway, and Mrs *Behn.

LEIGH, Chandos, first Baron Leigh of the second creation (1791–1850), poet and author; descendant of Sir Thomas *Leigh, first Baron Leigh of a former creation; educated at Harrow and Christ Church, Oxford; wrote verses prized by the scholarly few, and took interest in social and political questions; created Baron Leigh of Stoneleigh, 1839; died at Bonn.

LEIGH, Charles (d. 1605), merchant and voyager; made a voyage to the St Lawrence, partly for fishing and trade, and partly for plundering Spanish ships, 1597; sailed for Guiana with a view to establishing a colony to look for gold, 1604–5; died in Guiana.

LEIGH, Charles (1662–1701?), physician and naturalist; great-grandson of William *Leigh; educated at Brasenose College, Oxford; BA, 1683; FRS, 1685; MA and MD, Cambridge, 1689; published an unimportant *Natural History of Lancashire, Cheshire, and the Peak in Derbyshire* (1700).

LEIGH, Edward (1602–1671), miscellaneous writer; MA, Magdalen Hall, Oxford, 1623; his writings mostly compilations, the best-known being *Critica Sacra, or Philologicall and Theologicall Observations upon all the Greek Words of the New Testament* (1639); MP, Stafford, 1644–8, when he was expelled from the house for voting that the king's concessions were satisfactory.

LEIGH, Egerton (1815–1876), writer on dialect; educated at Eton; entered the army, 1833; captain, 1840; edited *Ballads and Legends of Cheshire* (1867); MP for Mid-Cheshire, 1873 and 1874. His *Glossary of Words used in the Dialect of Cheshire* published (1877).

LEIGH, Evan (1811–1876), inventor; became a manufacturer of machinery, 1851; patented nineteen inventions between 1849 and 1870, the most useful for the improvement of the machinery of cotton manufacture; published *The Science of Modern Cotton Spinning* (1871).

LEIGH, Sir Ferdinand (1585?–1654), governor of the Isle of Man; knighted, 1617; deputy-governor of Man, 1625; fought in Civil War on the Royalist side.

LEIGH, Francis, first earl of Chichester (d. 1653), great-grandson of Sir Thomas *Leigh (1504?–1571); created baronet, 1618; MP, Warwick, 1625; created Baron Dunsmore, 1628; privy councillor, 1641; created earl of Chichester, 1644.

LEIGH, Henry Sambrooke (1837–1883), dramatist; son of James Mathews *Leigh; engaged early in literary pursuits; published *Carols of Cockayne* (1869); translated and adapted French comic operas for the English stage, 1871.

LEIGH, James Mathews (1808–1860), painter and author; nephew of Charles *Mathews the elder; exhibited at Royal Academy, 1830–49; published *Cromwell* (historical play, 1838).

LEIGH, Jared (1724–1769), amateur artist; painted chiefly sea-pieces and landscapes; exhibited with the Free Society of Artists, 1761–7.

LEIGH, John (1689–1726), dramatist and actor; played important parts in London, 1714–26; author of a comedy, *The Pretenders* (1720).

LEIGH, Sir Oliph (or Olyff) (1560–1612), encourager of maritime enterprise; brother of Charles *Leigh (d. 1605); keeper of the great park at Eltham; sold the surrender of it, 1609.

LEIGH, Percival (1813–1889), comic writer; studied medicine at St Bartholomew's Hospital; LSA, 1834; MRCS, 1835; abandoned medicine for literature; joined the staff of *Punch*, 1841, to which he contributed till his death; satirized prevailing fashions in *Y^r Manners and Customs of ye Englyshe* (1849).

LEIGH, Richard (b. 1649), poet; educated at The Queen's College, Oxford; BA, 1669; actor in London; attacked *Dryden in pamphlets, published 1673; author of *Poems upon Several Occasions* (published 1675).

LEIGH, Samuel (*fl.* 1686), author of a metrical version of the Psalms; born about 1635; educated at Merton College, Oxford; author of *Samuelis Primitiae, or an Essay towards a Metrical Version of the whole Book of Psalms* (1661).

LEIGH (or LEE), Sir Thomas (1504?–1571), lord mayor of London; warden of the Mercers' Company, 1544 and 1552; master, 1544, 1558, and 1564; alderman, 1552–71; sheriff, 1555; lord mayor and knighted, 1558.

LEIGH, Sir Thomas, first Baron Leigh of the first creation (d. 1671), second son of Sir Thomas *Leigh (1504?–1571); created Baron Leigh of Stoneleigh, 1643; Royalist. The barony became extinct, 1786.

Leigh

LEIGH, Thomas Pemberton, first Baron Kingsdown (1793–1867). See PEMBERTON-LEIGH.

LEIGH, Valentine (*fl.* 1562), miscellaneous writer; published *Death's Generall Proclamation* (1561) and *The most Profitable and Commendable Science of Lands, Tenements, Hereditaments* (1562).

LEIGH, Vivien (1913–1967), actress; born Vivian Mary Hartley; educated at Convent of the Sacred Heart, Roehampton; at 13, travelled with parents abroad, 1926–31; studied at Royal Academy of Dramatic Art; adopted stage name, Vivien Leigh; appeared in film, *Things are Looking Up* (1934); played in *The Mask of Virtue* at Ambassadors Theatre, 1935; signed five-year contract with (Sir) Alexander *Korda; played with Laurence (later Lord) Olivier in *Fire Over England* (1937); played Scarlett O'Hara in *Gone with the Wind* (1939); won an Oscar award; married Laurence Olivier, 1940; toured North Africa with Beatrice Lillie, 1943; toured Australia and New Zealand with Old Vic Company and Olivier, 1948; played Blanche du Bois on stage and in film in *A Streetcar Named Desire* (1949–50); awarded second Oscar; with Olivier at Stratford-upon-Avon in *Titus Andronicus* (1955); last appearance with Olivier, 1957; marriage dissolved, 1960; made new reputation in musical *Tovarich* in New York, 1963; Knight's Cross, Legion of Honour, 1957; died of tuberculosis, 1967; exterior lights of London's West-End theatres darkened for an hour.

LEIGH, William (1550–1639), divine; educated at Brasenose College, Oxford; fellow, 1573; MA, 1578; a popular preacher; BD, 1586; tutor to Prince *Henry, eldest son of James I; published sermons and religious pieces between 1602 and 1613.

LEIGH-MALLORY, Sir Trafford Leigh (1892–1944), air chief marshal; brother of G. L. *Mallory; educated at Haileybury and Magdalene College, Cambridge; served with Royal Flying Corps, 1916–19; DSO and permanent commission, 1919; commanded No. 12 (fighter) group, 1937–40; No. 11 group, 1940–2; AOC-in-C, Fighter Command, 1942–3; air chief marshal and KCB, 1943; air commander-in-chief, Allied Expeditionary Air Force of some 9,000 aircraft, 1943–4; lost flying to take up appointment as Allied air commander-in-chief, South-East Asia.

LEIGHTON, Alexander (1568–1649), physician and divine; studied at St Andrews and Leiden universities; MA, St Andrews; published *Speculum Belli sacri, or the Looking Glass of the Holy War* (1624) and *An Appeal to the Parliament, or Sion's Plea against the Prelacie* (1628); arrested and condemned by Star Chamber to mutilation and life-long imprisonment, 1630; released by Long Parliament, 1640; keeper of Lambeth House, 1642.

LEIGHTON, Alexander (1800–1874), editor of *Tales of the Borders*; edited and helped to write *Tales of the Borders*, 1835–40; re-edited the complete *Tales of the Borders* (1857); published *Romance of the Old Town of Edinburgh* (1867).

LEIGHTON, Charles Blair (1823–1855), artist; painted portraits and figure pieces; occasionally exhibited at the Royal Academy.

LEIGHTON, Sir Elisha (d. 1685), courtier; son of Alexander *Leighton (1568–1649); colonel in the Royalist army; joined Royalist party abroad after Charles I's execution; appointed by Charles II secretary for English affairs in Scotland, 1650; knighted, 1659; FRS, 1663–77; one of the secretaries of the Prize Office, 1664; LL D, Cambridge, 1665; secretary to the lord-lieutenant of Ireland, 1670; recorder of Dublin, 1672.

LEIGHTON, Frederic, Baron Leighton of Stretton (1830–1896), painter and president of the Royal Academy; educated at London and various continental towns; studied art at Florence, Frankfurt, at Paris, again at Frankfurt under Johann Eduard Steinle (1810–86), and at Rome; exhibited *Cimabue's 'Madonna' carried through Streets of Florence* at Royal Academy, 1855; ARA, 1866; exhibited *Venus disrobing for the Bath*, 1866; lived in Holland Park Road from 1866; RA, 1869; made journey, 1873, to the East, which resulted in several oriental pictures; PRA, 1878–96; knighted, 1878; painted two wall pictures in Victoria and Albert Museum, and wall decoration on canvas for Royal Exchange (finished 1895); raised to peerage by patent dated 24 Jan. 1896, the day before his death; hon. DCL, Oxford, LL D, Cambridge and Edinburgh, 1879; buried in St Paul's Cathedral, where an elaborate monument was erected. His *Addresses delivered to students of the Royal Academy* appeared (1896). Among his best works are *Hercules wrestling with Death* and *The Summer Moon* (1871–2), *Athlete struggling with a Python* (1877, sculpture), *The Bath of Psyche* (1890), *Perseus and Andromeda* (1891), *The Garden of the Hesperides* (1892), and *Wedded* (1882).

LEIGHTON, Harcourt Algernon (1903–1967), dancer and ballet master. See ALGERANOFF.

LEIGHTON (LICHTON or LYCHTON), Henry (d. 1440), bishop successively of Moray and Aberdeen; bishop of Moray, 1415, of Aberdeen, 1423; built a great part of Aberdeen Cathedral; employed on diplomatic missions.

LEIGHTON, Henry (d. 1669), French scholar; educated in France; obtained Oxford MA by fraud, 1642; taught French at Oxford; published *Linguae Gallicae addiscendae Regulae* (1659).

LEIGHTON, Robert (1611–1684), archbishop of Glasgow; son of Alexander *Leighton (1568–1649); student at Edinburgh University, 1627; MA, 1631; travelled on the continent; licensed priest, 1641; a famous preacher; principal of Edinburgh University, 1653, and professor of divinity at Edinburgh; bishop of Dunblane, 1661; archbishop of Glasgow, 1669–74; his sermons published, 1692–1708.

LEIGHTON, Robert (1822–1869), Scottish poet; entered the office of his brother, a ship-owner, 1837; went round the world as a super-cargo, 1842–3; managed the business of a firm of seed-merchants, 1854–67; published poems in 1855, 1861, 1866; other poems by him, some in the vernacular, posthumously published.

LEIGHTON, Stanley (1837–1901), politician and antiquary; educated at Harrow and Balliol College, Oxford; BA and MA, 1864; called to bar, 1861; Conservative MP for North Shropshire, 1876–85, and Oswestry, 1885–1901; ardent supporter of the Church in parliament; FSA, 1880; founded Shropshire Parish Register Society, 1897; accomplished amateur artist; wrote and illustrated *Shropshire Houses, Past and Present* (1901).

LEIGHTON, Sir William (*fl.* 1603–1614), poet and composer; published a poem in praise of James I (1603); knighted, 1603; published the *Teares or Lamentations of a sorrowful Soule* (1613) and *Musicall Ayres* (1614).

LEIGHTON, William (1841–1869), Scottish poet, nephew of Robert *Leighton (1822–1869); employed in a Brazilian business house, 1864–9. *Poems by the late William Leighton* appeared (1870), and other volumes in 1872 and 1875.

LEIGHTON, William Allport (1805–1889), botanist; educated at St John's College, Cambridge; BA, 1833; published *Flora of Shropshire* (1841) and other works, including *Lichen Flora of Great Britain* (1871).

LEININGEN, Prince Ernest Leopold Victor Charles Auguste Joseph Emich (1830–1904), admiral, reigning prince of Leiningen; born at Amorbach, Bavaria; entered British Navy, 1849; served in Burmese War, 1851–2; served against Russians on the Danube, 1854; took part in Baltic campaign, 1856; commander and captain from 1858 of royal yacht *Alberta*, which (with Queen Victoria on board) accidentally ran down schooner yacht *Mistletoe* in Stokes Bay, Aug. 1875; vice-admiral, 1881; com-

mander-in-chief at the Nore, 1885–7; admiral, 1887; GCB, 1866; GCVO, 1898; died at Amorbach.

LEINSTER, dukes of. See SCHOMBERG, MEINHARD, first duke of the first creation, 1641–1719; FITZGERALD, JAMES, first duke of the second creation, 1722–1773.

LEINSTER, earl of (1584?–1659). See CHOLMONDELEY, ROBERT.

LEINTWARDEN (or LEYNTWARDYN), Thomas (d. 1421), chancellor of St Paul's Cathedral, London; educated at Oxford; DD, Oxford; chancellor of St Paul's, 1401; provost of Oriel College, Oxford, 1417–21; wrote commentary on St Paul's Epistles.

LEIPER, Robert Thomson (1881–1969), professor of helminthology; educated at Warwick School, Leamington Technical College, Mason College, Birmingham, and Glasgow University; graduated in medicine, 1904; helminthologist, London School of Tropical Medicine, 1905; detected cause of 'Guinea worm' infection, Accra, 1905; and of Calabar swelling, West Africa, 1912; studied wide variety of helminths in the East, 1913; in charge of Bilharzia mission in Egypt, 1914–15; discovered Egyptian species of parasites causing human schistosomiasis; director, prosectorium, Zoological Society, London, 1919–21; professor of helminthology, London University, 1919; founded *Journal of Helminthology*, 1923; director of parasitology, London School of Hygiene and Tropical Medicine, 1924–45; set up Institute of Agricultural Parasitology, 1925; founder and director, Commonwealth Bureau of Helminthology, 1929–58; D.Sc., Glasgow, 1911; MD, 1917; FRS, 1923; FRCP, 1936; CMG, 1941.

LEISHMAN, Thomas (1825–1904), Scottish divine and liturgiologist; MA, Glasgow University, 1843; DD, 1871; Presbyterian minister at Linton, Teviotdale, 1855–95; with G. W. *Sprott published an annotated edition of *The Book of Common Order*; advocated observance of the five great Christian festivals by the Church of Scotland, 1868; helped to found Scottish Church Society, 1892; thrice president; writings include *The Moulding of the Scottish Reformation* (1897); moderator of General Assembly, 1898.

LEISHMAN, Sir William Boog (1865–1926), bacteriologist; MB, CM, Glasgow; entered Army Medical Service, 1887; served in Waziristan campaign, 1894–5; assistant professor of pathology, Army Medical School (Netley), 1900; professor of pathology, Army Medical School (Millbank), 1903–13; War Office expert on tropical diseases, 1914; adviser in pathology to British Expeditionary Force in France, 1914–18; director of pathology, War Office, 1919–23; medical director-general, Army Medical Services, and lieutenant-general, 1923; knighted, 1909; FRS, 1910; famous for his work on anti-typhoid inoculation and kala-azar.

LEITCH, Charlotte Cecilia Pitcairn ('Cecil') (1891–1977), golfer; educated at Carlisle Girls' High School; self-taught, one of five sisters, all championship golfers; reached semi-final of British Ladies' Championship at age of 17, 1908; played for England, 1910; won French championship, 1912; won British Open, 1914, and in 1920 and 1921; defeat in English final by Joyce Wethered (later Lady Heathcoat-Amory), first of many duels between the two; defeated by Wethered at thirty-seventh hole in 1925 British Open, regarded by Cecil Leitch as her greatest match; regained title, 1926; retired in 1928 having won French championship five times, English twice, and Canadian once, and represented England in thirty-three matches of which she lost only three; published *Golf for Girls* (1911), *Golf* (1922), and *Golf Simplified* (1924); chairman, Ladies' Golf Union; served on committees of National Playing Fields Association for nearly fifty years; active member of Embroiderers' Guild; established the Women Golfers' Museum, 1938.

LEITCH, William Leighton (1804–1883), water-colour painter; scene-painter at the Theatre Royal, Glasgow, 1824, and later at the Queen's Theatre, London; a successful teacher of drawing and water-colours; drawing-master to Queen Victoria and the royal family for twenty-two years; member of the Institute of Painters in Water-Colours, 1862; the last of the great English teachers of landscape painting.

LEITH, Alexander (1758–1838), general. See HAY, ALEXANDER LEITH.

LEITH, Sir James (1763–1816), lieutenant-general; educated at Aberdeen and Lille; served in Toulon operations, 1793; colonel, 1794; brigadier-general, 1804; present at the battle of Corunna, 1809; with Peninsular army, 1810–12; KB, 1813; lieutenant-general, 1813; commander of forces in West Indies and governor of the Leeward Islands, 1814; GCB, 1815; died at Barbados.

LEITH, Theodore Forbes (1746–1819), physician; studied at Edinburgh University; MD, 1768; FRS, 1781; LRCP, 1786.

LEITH-ROSS, Sir Frederick William (1887–1968), civil servant and authority on finance; educated at Merchant Taylors' School and Balliol College, Oxford; first class, Lit. Hum., 1909; passed top into Home Civil Service; posted to Treasury, 1909; private secretary to prime minister, H. H. Asquith (later first earl of Oxford and Asquith), 1911; returned to Treasury, 1913; British member, Finance Board, Reparation Commission, 1920–5; deputy controller, finance, Treasury, 1925; settled post-war claims, Egypt, 1929; attended Hague Conference with chancellor of the Exchequer, 1929; chief economic adviser, 1932; worked on currency reform, China, 1935; negotiated revised German Payments Agreement, 1938; director-general, Ministry of Economic Warfare, 1939–42; deputy director-general, European regional office, Unrra; chairman, European Committee, 1945–6; published *UNRRA in Europe* (1946); governor, National Bank of Egypt, 1946–51; director, National Provincial Bank, 1951, deputy chairman, 1952; director, Standard Bank; CB, 1925; KCB, 1933; KCMG, 1930; GCMG, 1937; published autobiography, *Money Talks* (1968).

LEJEUNE, Caroline Alice (1897–1973), film critic; educated at Withington Girls' School; C. P. *Scott, editor, *Manchester Guardian*, friend of family; studied in English school, Manchester University; first-class degree, 1921; already writing for *Manchester Guardian*; decided to become film critic, 1921; had her own film column in *Manchester Guardian*, 1922; married (Edward) Roffe Thompson, 1925 and had one son, Anthony Lejeune, 1928; moved to *Observer* as film critic, and remained for over thirty years; welcomed advent of the 'talkies'; friend of (Sir) Alexander *Korda, (Sir) Alfred *Hitchcock, and (Sir) Michael *Balcon; retired, 1960; hon. D.Litt., Durham, 1961; completed Angela *Thirkell's novel *Three Score and Ten*, 1961; other publications include *Cinema* (1931), collection of her reviews, *Chestnuts in Her Lap* (1947), and autobiography, *Thank You For Having Me* (1964).

LE JEUNE, Henry (1819–1904), historical and genre painter; studied art at Royal Academy Schools; exhibited at Academy, 1840–94, and British Institution, 1842–63; curator of painting school of Royal Academy, 1848–64; ARA, 1863; painted subjects from Bible, Shakespeare, and *Spenser; later devoted himself to painting children, as in *Little Bo-Peep* and *My Little Model*; musician and chess player.

LE KEUX, Henry (1787–1868), engraver; brother of John *Le Keux; apprenticed to James *Basire (1730–1802); engraved for fashionable annuals, 1820–40.

LE KEUX, John (1783–1846), engraver; apprenticed to James *Basire (1730–1802); engraved plates for the architectural publications of John *Britton, Augustus Welby Northmore *Pugin, John Preston *Neale, and similar works.

LE KEUX, John Henry (1812–1896), architectural engraver and draughtsman; son of John *Le Keux; exhibited at Royal Academy, 1853–65; engraved plates for *Ruskin's *Modern Painters* and *Stones of Venice*.

LEKPREVICK, Robert (*fl.* 1561–1588), Scottish printer; principal printer for the reform party in Scotland; king's printer, 1568–88; imprisoned for printing a pamphlet which reflected on the Regent Morton, 1574.

LELAND (or LEYLOND), John, the elder (d. 1428), grammarian; taught as a grammarian at Oxford; wrote grammatical works in Latin.

LELAND (or LEYLAND), John (1506?–1552), the earliest of modern English antiquaries; educated at St Paul's School, London, and Christ's College, Cambridge; BA, 1522; studied at Paris; took holy orders; library-keeper to Henry VIII before 1530; king's antiquary, 1533; made an antiquarian tour through England, 1534–43; intended his researches to be the basis of a great work on the 'History and Antiquities of this Nation'; in *A New Year's Gift* (1545) described to the king the manner and aims of his researches; became insane, 1550. *Leland's Itinerary* was first published at Oxford in nine volumes (1710), and his *Collectanea* in six (1715).

LELAND, John (1691–1766), divine; a Nonconformist minister; DD, Aberdeen, 1739; attacked the deists in *A View of the principal Deistical Writers that have appeared in England during the last and present Century* (1754–6) and other works.

LELAND, Thomas (1722–1785), historian; entered Trinity College, Dublin, 1737; BA, 1741; fellow, 1746; published Latin translation of the *Philippics* of Demosthenes, 1754, and English translation, 1754–61; published the *History of Philip, King of Macedon* (1758); presented the Irish manuscript chronicle, 'Annals of Loch Cé', to Trinity College Library, 1766; vicar of St Anne's, Dublin, 1773; DD; published *History of Ireland from the Invasion of Henry II, with a preliminary Discourse on the ancient State of that Kingdom* (1773).

LELY, Sir Peter (1618–1680), portrait painter; born at Soest by Amersfoort, near Utrecht; studied at Haarlem; came to England, 1641; introduced to Charles I, 1647; painted Charles I's portrait during his captivity at Hampton Court; painted *Cromwell and enjoyed considerable private practice under him; in high favour with Charles II; painted portraits of the beauties of Charles II's court, and of the admirals and commanders in the naval victory at Solebay, 1665; knighted, 1679.

LEMAN, Sir John (1544–1632), lord mayor of London; alderman, 1605; sheriff, 1606; lord mayor, 1616–17, and knighted, 1617.

LEMAN, Thomas (1751–1826), antiquary; educated at Emmanuel College, Cambridge; BA, 1774; fellow of Clare Hall, Cambridge; MA, 1778; Dixie (bye) fellow of Emmanuel College, 1783; chancellor of Cloyne, 1796–1802; visited every Roman and British road and station in Great Britain, and communicated his observations to county historians; FSA, 1788.

LE MARCHANT, Sir Denis, first baronet (1795–1874), politician; son of John Gaspard *Le Marchant; educated at Eton and Trinity College, Cambridge; barrister, Lincoln's Inn, 1823; clerk of the crown in Chancery, 1834; edited a highly successful pamphlet, *The Reform Ministry and the Reform Parliament* (1834); secretary to the Board of Trade, 1836–41; created baronet, 1841; Liberal MP, Worcester, 1846–7; under-secretary for the Home Department, 1847; secretary of the Board of Trade, 1848; chief clerk to the House of Commons, 1850–71; edited Walpole's *Memoirs of the reign of George III* (1845).

LE MARCHANT, John Gaspard (1766–1812), major-general; ensign, 1781; intimate of George III; in Flemish campaigns, 1793–4; major, 1795; devised a system of cavalry sword-exercise, and suggested pattern for improved sword; lieutenant-colonel, 1797; projected schools of instruction for officers, which were the beginnings of Sandhurst; lieutenant-governor of the schools, 1801–10; major-general in the Peninsula, 1810–12; mortally wounded at Salamanca, 1812; wrote on military subjects.

LE MARCHANT, Sir John Gaspard (1803–1874), lieutenant-general, colonial administrator; son of John Gaspard *Le Marchant; ensign, 1820; major in the new 98th Foot, 1832; served at the Cape, 1832; as brigadier-general in the Carlist War, 1835–7; lieutenant-governor of Newfoundland, 1847–52, of Nova Scotia, 1852–7; governor of Malta, 1859–64; GCMG, 1860; commander-in-chief at Madras, 1865–8; KCB, 1865.

LEMASS, Sean Francis (1899–1971), prime minister of the Irish Republic; educated at the Christian Brothers' O'Connell schools, Dublin, and Ross's College; joined Irish Volunteers and took part in 1916 rising; imprisoned, 1920–1; fought against Free State forces; captured and imprisoned, 1922–3; elected to Dáil Eireann, 1924, but abstained from sitting; held Dublin South City, 1924–48 and Dublin South Central, 1948–69; 'defence minister' in clandestine government of Eamon *de Valera, 1924; with de

Valera formed Fianna Fáil Party, 1926; shadow minister for industry and commerce, 1927; youngest minister in de Valera's first government, 1932; held industry and commerce post, 1932–9, 1941–8, 1951–4, and 1957–9; also minister for supplies, 1939–45, and deputy prime minister, 1945–59; pursued policy of protection, and during 1939–45 war created national transport service; also established labour court; prime minister, 1959–66; adopted new policies of free trade, made bid to join EEC, and made gesture of friendship to prime minister of Northern Ireland; carried through reorganization of government; received number of honours and honorary degrees, including the Grand Cross of the Order of Gregory the Great, 1948, the Grand Cross of the Pian Order, 1962, and the Grand Cross of the Order of Merit of the Federal Republic of Germany, 1962.

LEMENS, Balthasar Van (1637–1704), painter. See VAN LEMENS.

LE MESURIER, Havilland (1758–1806), commissary-general; son of John *Le Mesurier; 'adjutant commissary-general of stores, supplies, and storage' to the forces on the continent, 1793; with the army during winter retreat through Holland, 1794–5; served later in Egypt, Malta, Naples, and elsewhere; published pamphlets on commissariat matters.

LE MESURIER, Havilland (1783–1813), lieutenant-colonel; son of Havilland *Le Mesurier (1758–1806); educated at Westminster; ensign, 1801; served under Sir John *Moore in Sweden and at Corunna; brevet-lieutenant-colonel, 1811; commandant of Almeida, 1811; shot in the Battle of the Pyrenees; translated French military works.

LE MESURIER, John (1781–1843), major-general, last hereditary governor of Alderney; nephew of Havilland *Le Mesurier (1783–1813); ensign, 1794; served in Ireland, 1798; at the occupation of Messina, 1799–1800; in Egypt, 1801; governor of Alderney, 1803–24.

LE MESURIER, John (1912–1983), actor; born John Elton Halliday; educated at Sherborne School; articled clerk to solicitors in Bury St Edmunds; adopted mother's name as stage-name and joined Fay Compton Studio of Dramatic Art; worked at Palladium Theatre, Edinburgh and at Oldham; during 1939–45 war served in Royal Armoured Corps; played in numerous minor roles from 1946 onwards; in films, *Private's Progress* (1955) and *I'm All Right Jack* (1959); appeared with A. J. ('Tony') *Hancock on television, and in *The Punch and Judy Man* (1962); also in *Carlton-Brown of the F. O.* (1958), *We Joined the Navy* (1962), *The Pink* Panther (1963), *The Liquidator* (1965), *The Wrong Box* (1966), and *Casino Royale* (1967); most notable part 'Sergeant Wilson' in TV series 'Dad's Army'; played straight parts in plays such as *Traitor* (1971); last appeared in *A Married Man* (1983); published *A Jobbing Actor* (autobiography, 1984).

LE MESURIER, Paul (1755–1805), lord mayor of London; brother of Havilland *Le Mesurier (1758–1806); as a proprietor of the East India Company opposed *Fox's India Bill, 1783; MP, Southwark, 1783; sheriff, 1787; colonel of the Honourable Artillery Company, 1794; lord mayor, 1794.

LEMMENS-SHERRINGTON, Helen (1834–1906), soprano vocalist; studied music at Brussels under Cornelis, 1852; first appeared at London concerts, 1856; married Nicolas Jacques Lemmens, 1857; leading English soprano from 1860, singing in English opera (1860–65) and in Italian opera (1866); showed great power in oratorio music, as in Mendelssohn's *Elijah* and Haydn's *Creation*; sang in first performance in England of Bach's High Mass, 1876; teacher of singing at Brussels Conservatoire, 1881–91; occasionally revisited England; died at Brussels.

LE MOINE, Abraham (d. 1757), theological controversialist; probably son of a Huguenot refugee; chaplain to the French hospital in London, 1723–49, the duke of Portland, 1729; chief work, a *Treatise on Miracles* (reply to Thomas *Chubb, 1747); also published French translations of theological works.

LEMOINE, Henry (1756–1812), author and bookseller; son of a French Protestant refugee; purchased a bookstall in the Little Minories, 1777; contributed to the magazines; published miscellaneous works; started and edited various periodicals; published anonymous books and pamphlets; contributed to the *Gentleman's Magazine*; described as one of the best judges of old books in England, and an authority on foreign and Jewish literature.

LEMON, Sir Ernest John Hutchings (1884–1954), mechanical and railway engineer; trained at Glasgow Technical College and Heriot-Watt College, Edinburgh; chief wagon inspector, Midland Railway, 1911; works superintendent, Derby, 1917; divisional superintendent, LMS, 1923; carriage and wagon superintendent, 1927; chief mechanical engineer, 1931; operating and commercial vice-president, 1932–43; reorganized, modernized, and mechanized; director-general, aircraft production, 1938–40; chairman, post-war Railway Planning Commission; knighted, 1941.

LEMON, George William (1726–1797), master of Norwich School; BA, Queens' College, Cambridge, 1747; took holy orders and held several livings; master of Norwich Free Grammar School, 1769–78; published educational works, 1774–92.

LEMON, Mark (1809–1870), editor of *Punch*; began his career as a playwright, 1835; published farces, melodramas, and operas; contributed to *Household Words*, the *Illustrated London News*, and other periodicals, and edited the *Family Herald* and *Once a Week*; best known as one of the founders and the first editor of *Punch* (first number published 17 July 1841); edited *Punch*, 1841–70; began writing novels late in life with indifferent success; known among his friends as 'Uncle Mark'.

LEMON, Robert (1779–1835), archivist; educated at Norwich Grammar School; under his uncle, George William *Lemon, helped to compile appendix to the *Report on Internal Defence* (1798); deputy-keeper of the State Paper Office, 1818; FSA, 1824.

LEMON, Robert (1800–1867), archivist; son of Robert *Lemon (1779–1835); employed under his father in the State Paper Office; interpreted a certain cipher found in some state papers; FSA, 1836, rearranging society's library, 1846.

LEMPRIERE, Charles (1818–1901), writer and politician; son of John *Lemprière, DD; BCL, St John's College, Oxford, 1842; DCL, 1847; called to bar, 1844; agent of Conservative party from 1850; sent on private mission to Mexico, to watch British interests, 1861; published *The American Crisis Considered* (1861) and *Notes on Mexico* (1862); colonial secretary of the Bahamas, 1867; compelled to resign owing to his Tory opinions; wrote for the American *Tribune*; organized unsuccessful English colony at Buckhorn, West Virginia, 1872.

LEMPRIÈRE, John (1765?–1824), classical scholar; educated at Winchester College and Pembroke College, Oxford; MA, 1792; master of Grammar School at Bolton, Lancashire, 1791; of Grammar School at Abingdon, 1792–1808 (or 1809); DD, Oxford, 1803; master of Exeter Free Grammar School, 1809–c.1823; chief works, *A Classical Dictionary* (1788) and a *Universal Biography . . . of Eminent Persons in all Ages and Countries* (1808 and 1812).

LEMPRIÈRE, Michael (fl. 1640–1660), seigneur of Maufant, and one of the leaders of the Parliamentary party in Jersey; as a jurat of the royal court actively opposed the bailiff of the island, Sir Philip de *Carteret; succeeded de Carteret as bailiff, 1643; royal warrant issued for his arrest, 1643; in exile, 1643–51; on return of Parliamentary party to power resumed his office of bailiff, 1651; removed from the bench of jurats, but allowed to retain his estates, 1660; highly esteemed by *Cromwell.

LEMPRIÈRE, William (d. 1834), traveller and medical writer; entered the Army Medical Service; went to Morocco to attend the emperor's son, 1789, and also attended the ladies of the harem; published account of his travels (1791); army surgeon in Jamaica, 1794–9; published medical pamphlets.

LEMPUT, Remigius Van (1609?–1675), painter. See VAN LEEMPUT.

LENDY, Auguste Frederick (1826–1889), military tutor and author; set up a private military college at Sunbury-on-Thames, c.1854; held a commission in the army, 1859–79; published works on military subjects.

LE NEVE, John (1679–1741), antiquary; of Eton and Trinity College, Cambridge; his greatest work, *Fasti Ecclesiae Anglicanae, or an Essay towards a regular Succession of all the principal Dignitaries*, etc. (published 1716); took holy orders; imprisoned for insolvency, 1722.

LE NEVE, Peter (1661–1729), Norfolk antiquary; entered Merchant Taylors' School, London, 1673; president of the Antiquarian Society, 1687–1724; FRS; Rouge Croix pursuivant, 1689–90; Richmond herald and Norroy king-at-arms, 1704; collected much material, but printed nothing; many of his manuscripts preserved in Bodleian, British Museum, Heralds' College, and elsewhere. His copious notes form the backbone of the history of Norfolk begun by *Blomefield and completed by *Parkin.

LE NEVE, Sir William (1600?–1661), herald and genealogist; Mowbray herald-extraordinary, 1622; York herald and Norroy king, 1633; knighted, 1634; Clarenceux, 1635; sent by Charles I with proclamation to Parliamentarians before Battle of Edgehill, 1642; became insane, 1658.

LENEY, William S. (fl. 1790–1810), engraver; articled to Peltro William *Tomkins; executed five plates for *Boydell's edition of Shakespeare; emigrated to America, 1806; engraved portraits of American celebrities.

LENG, John (1665–1727), bishop of Norwich; educated at St Paul's School, London, and Catharine Hall, Cambridge; fellow, 1688; MA, 1690; a distinguished Latin scholar; DD, 1716; Boyle lecturer, 1717–18; chaplain-in-ordinary to George I; bishop of Norwich, 1723–7; published sermons, his Boyle lectures, and translations from the classics.

LENG, Sir John (1828–1906), newspaper proprietor; sub-editor and reporter of *Hull Advertiser*, 1847–51; editor of bi-weekly *Dundee Advertiser*, 1851; raised paper to high rank; became part proprietor, 1852; issued *Advertiser* daily, 1861; established office in London, 1870; first to attempt illustrations in daily paper; founded first halfpenny daily in Scotland, 1859, the weekly *People's Journal*, 1858, and literary weekly, *People's Friend*, 1869; started *Evening Telegraph*, 1877; Liberal MP for Dundee, 1889–1905; supported railway and factory labour legislation and Home Rule Bill, 1893; knighted, 1893; hon. LL D, St Andrews, 1904; thrice visited America and Canada, India (1896), and Near East; died at Delmonte, California.

LENG, Sir William Christopher (1825–1902), journalist; brother of Sir John *Leng; contributed to *Dundee Advertiser* from 1859; managing editor and owner (1864) of *Sheffield Daily Telegraph*, which became a powerful Conservative organ; first to set up linotype machines; denounced trade-unionist terrorism at Sheffield, 1867, and obtained Royal Commission of Inquiry into his allegations; knighted, 1887.

LENIHAN, Maurice (1811–1895), historian of Limerick; educated at Carlow College; engaged in journalism; editor of *Limerick Reporter*, 1841–3, and of *Tipperary Vindicator*, a paper started in the interests of the repeal movement at Nenagh, 1843; incorporated *Limerick Reporter* with *Tipperary Vindicator*, 1849, and conducted it on moderate nationalist lines; published *Limerick, its History and Antiquities* (1866).

LENNARD, Francis, fourteenth Baron Dacre (1619–1662), succeeded to barony, 1630; sided with parliament against Charles I; lord-lieutenant of Herefordshire, 1641–2; retired from active support of parliament when the supremacy of the army became evident; one of the twelve peers who rejected the bill for Charles I's trial, 1648–9; went abroad, 1655.

LENNARD, Samson (d. 1633), genealogist and translator; accompanied *Sidney to the Netherlands, 1586; entered the College of Arms; Rouge-rose pursuivant-extraordinary, 1615; Bluemantle pursuivant, 1616; author of translations and a devotional work; some of his heraldic visitations printed between 1619 and 1623.

LENNARD-JONES, Sir John Edward (1894–1954), scientist and administrator; educated at Leigh Grammar School and Manchester University; first class, mathematics, 1915; researched and taught at Manchester, Cambridge, and Bristol; professor of theoretical physics, Bristol, 1927; Plummer professor of theoretical chemistry, Cambridge, 1932–53;

principal of University College of North Staffordshire, 1953–4; engaged in armament research, 1939–45; known for work on theory of molecular orbitals and theory of liquids; FRS, 1933; KBE, 1946; Sc.D., Cambridge; hon. D.Sc., Oxford; president, Faraday Society, 1948–50.

LENNIE, William (1779–1852), grammarian; founded bursaries at Edinburgh University; published *Principles of English Grammar* (1816).

LENNON, John (1768–1842?), master mariner; served in the navy during the American War; traded from St Thomas; brought his vessel safely without convoy into the English Channel, 1812.

LENNON, John Winston (1940–1980), musician and composer of popular music; educated at Dovedale Primary and Quarry Bank High School, Liverpool, and Liverpool College of Art, 1957; worked together with (James) Paul McCartney in skiffle group, the Quarrymen; joined later by George Harrison; changed their name to the Beatles, 1960; Ringo Starr became their drummer, 1962; none of them could read or write music; appeared in clubs in Hamburg, 1960–2, and the Cavern, Liverpool, 1961–2; songs written by Lennon and McCartney; successfully auditioned for George Martin who produced their first single disc, 'Love Me Do' (Parlophone, 1962); Beatlemania swept Britain, 1963; 'She Loves You', first single to exceed sales of one-and-a-half million in Britain; six of their records reached top of the charts in USA, 1964; first major pop group to write, play, and sing their own material; earned considerable foreign exchange for Britain; all awarded MBEs, 1965; Lennon returned his as protest against government policy towards Biafra and Vietnam, 1969; published best-selling collection of stories and drawings, *John Lennon in his own Write* (1964) and *A Spaniard in the Works* (1965); Beatles released *Sergeant Pepper's Lonely Hearts Club Band*, considered finest rock music album, 1965; Lennon's first marriage ended in divorce, 1968; married Yoko Ono, Japanese avant-garde artist, 1969; broke with Beatles' group, 1970–1; continued to compose his own songs; after difficulties with immigration authorities permitted to live in USA, 1972; collaborated with Yoko Ono in *Double Fantasy* (1980); shot dead in New York, 1980; fortune at time of death estimated at £100 million.

LENNOX, countess of (1515–1578). See DOUGLAS, Lady MARGARET.

LENNOX, duchess of (1647–1702). See STUART, FRANCES TERESA.

LENNOX, dukes of. See STUART, ESMÉ, first duke, 1542?–1583; STUART, LUDOVICK, second duke, 1574–1624; STUART, JAMES, fourth duke, 1612–1655; STUART, CHARLES, sixth duke, 1639–1672.

LENNOX, earls of. See LENNOX, MALCOLM, fifth earl, 1255?–1333; STEWART, Sir JOHN, first or ninth earl, d. 1495; STEWART, MATTHEW, second or tenth earl, d. 1513; STEWART, JOHN, third or eleventh earl, d. 1526; STEWART, MATTHEW, fourth or twelfth earl, 1516–1571.

LENNOX, Charles, first duke of Richmond (1672–1723), natural son of Charles II by Louise de *Kerouaille, duchess of Portsmouth; created baron of Settrington, Yorkshire, earl of March, and duke of Richmond, Yorkshire, in the peerage of England, and Baron Methuen of Tarbolton, earl of Darnley, and duke of Lennox in the peerage of Scotland, 1675; KG, 1681, and governor of Dumbarton Castle, 1681; master of the horse, 1682–5; aide-de-camp in Flanders, 1693–1702; lord of the bedchamber to George I, 1714; Irish privy councillor, 1715.

LENNOX, Charles, second duke of Richmond, Lennox, and Aubigny (1701–1750), only son of Charles *Lennox, first duke; grandson of Charles II; captain in Royal Regiment of Horse Guards, 1722; MP, Chichester, 1722–3; succeeded to the dukedom, 1723; FRS, 1724; KB, 1725; KG, 1726; lord of the bedchamber, 1727; LL D, Cambridge, 1728; succeeded to dukedom of Aubigny in France on the death of his grandmother, the duchess of Portsmouth (see KEROUALLE, LOUISE DE); master of the horse, 1735; privy councillor, 1735; present at Dettingen, 1743; lieutenant-general, 1745; MD, Cambridge, 1749; PSA, 1750.

LENNOX, Charles, third duke of Richmond and Lennox (1735–1806), third son of Charles *Lennox, second duke of Richmond, Lennox, and Aubigny; educated at Westminster School and Leiden University; graduated at Leiden, 1753; entered the army; FRS, 1755; colonel, 1758; distinguished himself at Minden, 1759; succeeded to the title, 1750; lord-lieutenant of Sussex, 1763; ambassador-extraordinary and minister-plenipotentiary at Paris, 1765; secretary of state for the southern department, 1766–7; denounced ministerial policy with reference to the American colonies; KG, 1782; master general of the ordnance, with a seat in the Cabinet, 1782–95; strongly urged appointment of committee (never formed) upon parliamentary reform, 1782; member of Pitt's Cabinet, 1783; became, in spite of former declarations, strongly opposed to all reform, and consequently extremely unpopular; FSA, 1793. His letter *On the Subject of a Parliamentary Reform*, demanding universal suffrage, together with annual elec-

tions, was published (1783), and passed through a number of editions.

LENNOX, Charles, fourth duke of Richmond and Lennox (1764–1819), eldest son of George Henry *Lennox; fought a duel with the duke of York (see FREDERICK AUGUSTUS, duke of York and Albany), 1789; served in the Leeward Islands; MP, Sussex, 1790; colonel, 1795; lieutenant-general, 1805; succeeded to the title, 1806; privy councillor, 1807; lord-lieutenant of Ireland, 1807–13; general, 1814; gave a ball at Brussels, where he was residing, on the eve of Quatre Bras, 1815; present at Waterloo; governor-general of British North America, 1818; died near Richmond, Canada.

LENNOX, Charles Gordon-, fifth duke of Richmond (1791–1860), eldest son of Charles *Lennox, fourth duke; educated at Westminster School; lieutenant, 1810; assistant military secretary to Wellington in Portugal, 1810–14; lieutenant-colonel, 1816; MP, Chichester, 1812–19; succeeded his father, 1819; KG, 1828; postmaster-general, 1830–4; president, Royal Agricultural Society, 1845–60.

LENNOX, Charles Henry Gordon-, sixth duke of Richmond and first duke of Gordon (1818–1903), lord president of the Council. See GORDON-LENNOX.

LENNOX, Charlotte (1720–1804), miscellaneous writer; daughter of Colonel James Ramsay, lieutenant-governor of New York, where she was born; sent to England, 1735; married one Lennox, c.1748; befriended and flattered by Dr *Johnson; author of *The Female Quixote* (novel, 1752); conducted *The Ladies' Museum Magazine*, 1760–1; her comedy, *The Sister*, acted once, 1769; published novels, poems, and translations from the French.

LENNOX, George Henry (1737–1805), general; son of Charles *Lennox, second duke of Richmond; ensign, 1754; saw service abroad, 1757–63; lieutenant-colonel, 1758; colonel, 1762; brigadier, 1763; MP, Chichester, 1761, Sussex, 1768, 1774, 1780, and 1784; secretary of legation to the court of France, 1765; major-general, 1772; constable of the Tower of London, 1783; privy councillor, 1784; general, 1793.

LENNOX, Lord Henry Charles George Gordon- (1821–1886), son of Charles Gordon-*Lennox, fifth duke of Richmond; MP, Chichester, 1846–85; a lord of the Treasury, 1852 and 1858–9; secretary to the Admiralty, 1866–8; first commissioner of public works, 1874–6.

LENNOX, Malcolm, fifth earl of Lennox (1255?–1333); succeeded to the earldom, 1292; a supporter of *Bruce; killed at Battle of Halidon Hill.

LENNOX, Sir **Wilbraham Oates** (1830–1897), general, Royal Engineers; studied at Woolwich; lieutenant, Royal Engineers, 1854; brevet-major, 1858; brevet-lieutenant-colonel, 1859; first captain, 1863; major, 1872; lieutenant-colonel, 1873; major-general, 1881; lieutenant-general, 1888; general, 1893; served in Crimea, 1854–6; VC (Inkermann), 1854; took conspicuous part in second relief, 1857, and final siege of Lucknow, 1858, and in subsequent campaigns; CB (military), 1867; instructor in field fortification at Chatham, 1866–71; attached officially to German armies in France during Franco-German War, 1870–1; second-in-command of Royal Engineers at Portsmouth, 1873–6; military attaché at Constantinople, 1876–8; commanded garrison of Alexandria, 1884–7; commanded troops in Ceylon, 1887–8; KCB, 1891; director-general of military education at War Office, 1893–5; published writings on military subjects.

LENNOX, Lord **William Pitt** (1799–1881), miscellaneous writer; son of Charles *Lennox, fourth duke of Richmond; at Westminster School, 1808–14; cornet, 1813; present as spectator at Waterloo, 1815; captain, 1822; MP, King's Lynn, 1832–4; published novels of little merit; contributed to the annuals, *Once a Week* and the *Court Journal*; edited the *Review*, newspaper, 1858.

LENNOX-BOYD, **Alan Tindal**, first Viscount Boyd of Merton (1904–1983), politician; educated at Sherborne School and Christ Church, Oxford; president of the Union, 1926; Conservative MP for mid-Bedfordshire, 1931–60; parliamentary secretary, Ministry of Labour 1938–9, Home Security, 1939, and Ministry of Food, 1939–40; served in RNVR, 1940–3; called to bar (Inner Temple), 1941; parliamentary secretary, Ministry of Aircraft Production, 1943–5; became authority on colonial affairs, 1945–51; minister of state, Colonial Office, 1951–2; PC, 1951; minister of transport, 1952–4; secretary of state for the colonies, 1954–9; viscount, 1960; CH, 1960; held directorships; trustee, British Museum and Natural History Museum; concerned with many charitable organizations; killed by car driven by learner driver.

LENO, **Dan** (1860–1904), music-hall singer and dancer, whose true name was George Galvin; made first appearance in London as 'Little George' the contortionist, 1864; took to clog-dancing and singing, 1869; admired by Charles *Dickens at Belfast, 1869; won clog-dancing championship of the world at Leeds, 1880; made first appearance as 'Dan Leno' in London, 1883; appeared in Drury Lane pantomime from 1888–9 annually till death; played at Sandringham before King Edward VII, Nov. 1901; most memorable songs a mixture of song and 'patter'; lavish in charity; wrote burlesque autobiography, *Dan Leno: his Book* (1901).

LE NOIR, **Elizabeth Anne** (1755?–1841), poetess and novelist; daughter of Christopher *Smart, the poet; married Jean Baptiste le Noir de la Brosse, 1795; authoress of novels praised by Dr *Burney and Miss *Mitford, and books of poems.

LENOX-CONYNGHAM, Sir **Gerald Ponsonby** (1866–1956), geodesist; educated at Edinburgh Academy and Royal Military Academy, Woolwich; commissioned in Royal Engineers; transferred to Survey of India, 1889; undertook important longitudinal and gravity measurements; superintendent of trigonometrical survey, 1912–20; colonel, 1914; reader in geodesy, Cambridge, 1922–47; developed department of geodesy and geophysics; FRS, 1918; knighted, 1919.

LENS, **Andrew Benjamin** (fl. 1765–1770), miniature painter; son of Bernard *Lens (1682–1740); re-engraved and published his father's *Granadier's Exercise* (1744); exhibited miniatures with the Incorporated Society of Artists, 1765–70.

LENS, **Bernard** (1631–1708), enamel painter; of Netherlandish origin; practised in London.

LENS, **Bernard** (1659–1725), mezzotint engraver and drawing-master; son of Bernard *Lens (1631–1708); kept a drawing-school with John *Sturt.

LENS, **Bernard** (1682–1740), miniature painter and drawing-master; son of Bernard *Lens (1659–1725); esteemed the best miniature painter in water-colours of his time; limner to George I and George II; taught drawing at Christ's Hospital, London, and drew and engraved plates illustrating *A New and Compleat Drawing-Book*, published posthumously; published etchings illustrating *The Granadier's Exercise* (1735).

LENS, **John** (1756–1825), serjeant-at-law; barrister, Lincoln's Inn, 1781; MA, St John's College, Cambridge, 1782; serjeant-at-law, 1799; king's serjeant, 1806; counsel to the University of Cambridge, 1807.

LENTHALL, Sir **John** (1625–1681), son of William *Lenthall, speaker of the House of Commons; educated at Corpus Christi College, Oxford; MP for Gloucester, 1645; knighted by

*Cromwell, 1658; governor of Windsor, 1660; high sheriff of Oxfordshire, 1672; knighted by Charles II, 1677.

LENTHALL, William (1591–1662), speaker of the House of Commons; entered St Alban Hall, Oxford, 1607; barrister, Lincoln's Inn, 1616; bencher, 1633; reader, 1638; speaker of the Long Parliament, 1640; behaved with discretion and dignity on the occasion of the king's attempt to arrest the five members, 1642; master of the Rolls, 1643; one of the two commissioners of the great seal, 1646–8; chancellor of the duchy of Lancaster, 1647; abandoned his post of speaker, and left London, fearing mob violence, 1647; MP, Oxfordshire, and speaker, 1653; speaker in the restored Long Parliament, 1659; supported *Monck and the Restoration.

LENTON, Francis (*fl.* 1630–1640), court poet and anagrammatist; said to have studied at Lincoln's Inn; styled himself 'Queen's poet'; author of *The Young Gallants Whirligigg, or Youth's Reakes* (1629), *Characterismi, or Lenton's Leasures* (1631), *The Innes of Court Anagrammatist, or the Masquers masqued in Epigrammes* (1666), and other works.

LENTON, John (*fl.* 1682–1718), musician; gentleman of the Chapel Royal extraordinary, 1685; member of the royal band, 1692–1718; composed music for *Venice Preserved* (1682), songs, catches, airs, and 'The Useful Instructor for the Violin' (1694, 1702).

LEOFRIC (Latin **LEURICUS)**, earl of Mercia (d. 1057); witnessed charters as 'minister' or thegn, 1005–26; succeeded his father in the earldom between 1024 and 1032; ranked with *Godwine and *Siward as one of the three great earls among whom the government of the kingdom was divided; his wife *Godgifu the Godiva of legend.

LEOFRIC (Latin **LEFRICUS)** (d. 1072), first bishop of Exeter; educated in Lotharingia; chancellor to *Edward the Confessor, being the first to be so designated; bishop of the united dioceses of Devonshire and Cornwall, 1046; had seat of bishopric removed from Crediton to Exeter, 1050; bestowed lands, money, and books, including the collection of poetry known as the *Liber Exoniensis*, on the church.

LEOFRIC OF BOURNE (*fl.* 1100), monk; said to have written a life of *Hereward.

LEOFWINE (d. 1066), son of Earl *Godwine; acted as governor of Kent, 1049; outlawed; fled to Ireland, 1051; earl of Kent, Surrey, Essex, Middlesex (except London), Hertfordshire, and probably Buckinghamshire, 1057–66; killed at Hastings.

LEOMINSTER, first Baron (d. 1711), connoisseur. See FERMOR, WILLIAM.

LEON, Henry Cecil (1902–1976), county-court judge, and author under name of Henry Cecil; educated at St Paul's School and King's College, Cambridge; called to bar (Gray's Inn), 1923; acquired considerable practice, 1930–9; served with 1/5 battalion, Queen's Royal Regiment, 1939; MC, 1942; resumed career at the bar; county-court judge at Brentford and Uxbridge, 1949–53, and at Willesden, 1953–67; published twenty-four novels and number of short stories, including *Full Circle* (1948), and *Brothers in Law* (1955), made into play and film; also published *Brief to Counsel* (1958), advice to young lawyers, and autobiography, *Just Within the Law* (1975); chairman, British Copyright Council and Society of Authors.

LEONI, Giacomo (1686–1746), architect; Venetian, and architect to the elector palatine; settled in England at beginning of eighteenth century; prepared plates for the English editions of Palladio's *Architecture* (1715); translated Alberti's *De re Aedificatoria* (1726); built various country seats.

LEOPOLD, George Duncan Albert, duke of Albany (1853–1884), fourth and youngest son of Queen Victoria; entered Christ Church, Oxford, 1872; granted an annuity of £15,000, 1874; left Oxford with an hon. DCL, 1876; travelled in Europe and America; president, Royal Society of Literature, 1878; vice-president, Society of Arts, 1879; created duke of Albany, earl of Clarence, and Baron Arklow, 1881; married Princess Helen Frederica Augusta, daughter of HSH George Victor, prince of Waldeck-Pyrmont, 1882; died at Cannes; buried in St George's Chapel, Windsor.

LEPIPRE (or **LE PIPER), Francis** (d. 1698), artist; drew landscapes, humorous compositions, and caricatures, and etched subjects on silver plates; painted twelve small pictures of scenes in *Hudibras*.

LE QUESNE, Charles (1811–1856), writer on the constitutional history of Jersey; contributed articles on commercial questions relating to the Channel Islands to the *Guernsey Magazine*, 1836–8; published *Ireland and the Channel Islands, or a Remedy for Ireland* (1848); jurat of the Royal Court of Jersey, 1850; his *Constitutional History of Jersey* published (1856).

LE ROMEYN, John (d. 1255), ecclesiastic. See ROMANUS.

LE ROMEYN, John (d. 1296), divine. See ROMANUS.

LERPINIERE, Daniel (1745?–1785), engraver; exhibited with the Free Society of Artists, 1773–83; engraved plates, chiefly landscapes, for Messrs Boydell, 1776–85.

LE SAGE, Sir **John Merry** (1837–1926), journalist and managing editor of *Daily Telegraph* for nearly forty years; on staff of *Telegraph*, 1863–1923; sometimes acted as special correspondent abroad; displayed great executive ability; enjoyed confidence of three generations of *Levy family; strongly maintained middle-class traditions of *Telegraph*; less happy after rise of new, twentieth-century journalism; knighted, 1918.

LESIEUR, Sir **Stephen** (*fl.* 1586–1627), ambassador; a Frenchman; came to England, *c.*1575; became secretary of Philip *Sidney; assisted in negotiations for surrender of Antwerp, 1585; naturalized, *c.*1589; sent on embassy to Hamburg, 1597, Denmark, 1602, to the emperor Rudolph II, 1603 and 1612–13, to Florence, 1608 and 1609; knighted 1608.

LESLEY. See also LESLIE and LESLY.

LESLEY, Alexander (1693–1758), Jesuit; studied at Douai and Rome; joined Jesuits, 1712; taught in the Illyrian College of Loreto, 1728; missioner in Aberdeenshire, 1729; taught in colleges of Ancona and Tivoli, 1734; again in England, 1738–44; prefect of studies in the Scots College, Rome, 1744–6; professor of moral theology in the English college, 1746–8; edited a fragment of the *Thesaurus Liturgicus* entitled *Missale mixtum secundum Regulam Beati Isidori dictum Mozarabes* (1755).

LESLEY, William Aloysius (1641–1704), Jesuit; joined Jesuits, 1656; superior of the Scots College at Rome, 1674–83 and 1692–5; DD; published *Vita di S. Margherita, Regina di Scozia* (1675); missioner in Scotland, 1695–1704.

LESLIE. See also LESLEY and LESLY.

LESLIE, Alexander, first earl of Leven (1580?–1661), general; served in the Swedish Army for thirty years; knighted by Gustavus Adolphus, 1626; compelled Wallenstein to raise the siege of Stralsund, 1628; governor of the Baltic district, 1628–30; engaged with the British contingent that aided Gustavus, 1630–2; fought at Lutzen, 1632; besieged and took Brandenburg, 1634; field marshal, 1636; identified himself with the Covenanters; directed the military preparations in Scotland, 1638; lord-general of all the Scottish forces, 1639; victorious at Battle of Newburn, 1640; created earl of Leven and Lord Balgonie, 1641; general of the Scottish Army in Ireland, 1642; sent to the assistance of the English parliament, 1643; present at Marston Moor, 1644; in charge of Charles I at Newcastle, 1645–7; fought for the Royalists at Dunbar, 1650; prisoner of the English parliament, 1651–4.

LESLIE, Andrew, properly fifth, but sometimes called fourth earl of Rothes (d. 1611), eldest son of George *Leslie, fourth earl; succeeded to peerage, 1558; steadfastly supported *Mary Queen of Scots from 1566.

LESLIE, Sir **Bradford** (1831–1926), civil engineer; son of C. R. *Leslie, painter; apprenticed to civil engineer, I. K. *Brunel, 1847; in service of Eastern Bengal Railway Company, acting under W. Purdon as resident engineer in charge of large bridges and viaducts, 1858–62; re-entered service, 1865; chief resident engineer for extension of line in northern delta, 1867–71; this included his first great achievement in India, bridge over Gorai; constructed an original floating bridge over Hugli, 1873–4; municipal engineer of Calcutta, 1873–6; agent and chief engineer, East Indian Railway Company, 1876; superintended construction of bridge over Hugli at Naihati; KCIE, 1887.

LESLIE, Charles (1650–1722), nonjuror and controversialist; son of John *Leslie (1571–1671); MA, Trinity College, Dublin, 1673; took holy orders, 1680; chancellor of Connor, 1686; refused to take the oaths at the Revolution, and was deprived of his office; commenced his series of controversial pamphlets with *An Answer to a Book intituled the State of the Protestants in Ireland under the late King James's Government* (1692); published attack on William III, *Gallienus Redivivus, or Murther will out*, etc. (1695); attacked in various pamphlets the Whig divines, *Burnet, *Tillotson, *Sherlock, as well as the Quakers, deists, and Jews, and defended the sacraments; brought out *The Rehearsal* in opposition to *Defoe's *Review*, 1704–9, carrying on at the same time his ecclesiastico-political pamphlet warfare; warrant issued for his apprehension, 1710; escaped to St Germain, 1711; returned to England, but (1713) accepted a place in the household of the Pretender at Bar-le-duc. A collected edition of his *Theological Works* was published (1721).

LESLIE, Charles Robert (1794–1859), painter; son of American parents; born in London; taken to Philadelphia, 1799; educated at Pennsylvania University; apprenticed to publishers in Philadelphia, 1808; student at the Royal Academy schools, London, 1811; exhibited at the Royal Academy between 1813 and 1839; RA, 1826; taught drawing at the Military Academy at West Point, America, 1833; summoned to Windsor to paint *The Queen receiving the Sacrament at her Coronation*, 1838, and *The Chris-*

tening of the Princess Royal, 1841; published *The Memoirs of John Constable, R.A.* (1845); professor of painting at the Royal Academy, 1848–52; published his lectures as *Handbook for Young Painters* (1855); excelled in depicting quiet humour. His *Autobiographical Recollections*, edited by Tom *Taylor, and his *Life of Reynolds*, completed by the same author, were published (1865).

LESLIE, David, first Baron Newark (d. 1682), military commander; entered service of Gustavus Adolphus; major-general in the Scottish Army under Alexander *Leslie, first earl of Leven, 1643; at Battle of Marston Moor, 1644; defeated *Montrose at Philiphaugh, 1645; commander of the army raised on behalf of Charles II in Scotland in 1651; taken prisoner after Worcester, 1651; imprisoned in the Tower till 1660; created Baron Newark, 1661.

LESLIE, Frank (1821–1880), engraver. See CARTER, HENRY.

LESLIE, Frederick (1855–1892), actor; his real name Frederick Hobson; appeared first in London as Colonel Hardy ('Paul Pry') at the Royalty, 1878, and subsequently took numerous parts in light opera, and, with Miss Ellen Farren at the Gaiety, in burlesque.

LESLIE, George, usually called third, but properly fourth, earl of Rothes (d. 1558); sheriff of Fife, 1529–40; a lord of session, 1541; a lord of the articles, 1544; tried for the murder of Cardinal *Beaton and acquitted, 1547; ambassador to Denmark, 1550; died at Dieppe.

LESLIE (or LESLEY), George (d. 1637), Capuchin friar, known as Father Archangel; scholar in the Scots College, Rome, 1608; preached in Scotland, c.1624–5; fled to France from persecution; returned to Scotland, 1631.

LESLIE, George (d. 1701), divine and poet; works include *Fire and Brimstone, or the Destruction of Sodom* (1675), *Abraham's Faith* (morality play, 1676).

LESLIE, Henry (1580–1661), bishop of Down and Connor; educated at Aberdeen; went to Ireland, 1614; ordained priest, 1617; prebendary of Connor, 1619; dean of Down, 1627; precentor of St Patrick's, Dublin, 1628; prolocutor of lower house in Irish Convocation, 1634; bishop of Down and Connor, 1635; a champion of Laudian episcopacy; withdrew to England after the loss of his property in the Irish rebellion, 1643; went abroad about the time of Charles I's execution; bishop of Meath, 1661.

LESLIE (or LESLEY), John (1527–1596), bishop of Ross; MA, Aberdeen; canon of Aberdeen Cathedral, 1547; studied at Paris and Poitiers, 1549–54; took holy orders, 1558; had a disputation with *Knox and other reformers, 1561; employed in France about the person of Queen Mary; professor of canon law, Aberdeen, 1562; judge of session, 1565; privy councillor, 1565; bishop of Ross, 1566; chief adviser of *Mary Queen of Scots in her ecclesiastical policy; appointed by her ambassador to Queen Elizabeth, 1569; sent to the Tower in connection with the *Ridolfi plot, 1571; set at liberty on condition of leaving England, 1573; went to Paris, 1574, and to Rome to represent Mary's interests, 1575; published there his Latin history of Scotland (1578); suffragan and vicar-general of the diocese of Rouen, 1579; nominated to the bishopric of Coutances by Clement VIII; died at the Augustinian monastery at Guirtenburg, near Brussels.

LESLIE, John (1571–1671), bishop of Clogher; known as 'the fighting bishop'; educated at Aberdeen and in France; with Buckingham at Rhé, 1627; bishop of the Scottish Isles, 1628–33, of Raphoe, 1633–61; a leader in the rebellion of 1641; after the king's execution defended Raphoe against the Cromwellians, and was one of the last Royalists to submit; the only Anglican bishop who remained at his post during the interregnum; bishop of Clogher, 1661; left manuscript treatise on 'Memory'.

LESLIE, John, sixth earl of Rothes (1600–1641), one of the leaders of the Covenanting party; served heir to his grandfather, Andrew *Leslie, fifth (or fourth) earl, 1621; opposed Charles I's ecclesiastical policy in Scotland; chief organizer of the movement against episcopacy, 1638; after pacification of 1640 remained in England at the court of Charles I; author of a *Short Relation of Proceedings concerning the Affairs of Scotland from August 1637 to July 1638* (first published 1830).

LESLIE, John, seventh earl and first duke of Rothes (1630–1681), eldest son of John *Leslie, sixth earl; succeeded his father, 1641; entered the army; taken prisoner at Worcester, 1651; released, 1658; lord of session, 1661; commissioner of the Exchequer, 1661; lord high treasurer, 1663; privy councillor of England, 1663; keeper of the privy seal, 1664; lord chancellor, 1667; created duke of Rothes, 1680.

LESLIE, John, eighth earl of Rothes (1679–1722), eldest son of Charles (Hamilton), fifth earl of Haddington, and Margaret Leslie, elder daughter of John *Leslie, duke of Rothes, who succeeded her father as countess of Rothes, the earldom surname of Leslie passing to her son; privy seal, 1704; aided the Union of 1707; Scots representative peer, 1707–22; vice-admiral of Scotland, 1714; fought against *James Edward, the Old Pretender, in 1715; governor of Stirling Castle, 1716–22.

LESLIE, John, ninth earl of Rothes (1698?–1767), eldest son of John *Leslie, eighth earl; lieutenant-colonel, 1719; succeeded his father, 1722; Scots representative peer, 1723, 1727, 1747, 1754, and 1761; major-general, 1743; present at Dettingen, 1743; lieutenant-general, 1750; KT, 1753; general, 1765; commander-in-chief of the forces in Ireland.

LESLIE, Sir John (1766–1832), mathematician and natural philosopher; educated at St Andrews and Edinburgh universities; his paper 'On the Resolution of Indeterminate Problems' communicated to the Royal Society of Edinburgh, 1788; superintended studies of the Wedgwoods, 1790–2; published, as outcome of his researches, *Experimental Inquiry into the Nature and Properties of Heat* (1804), a work of great scientific value; Rumford medallist, 1805; appointed professor of mathematics at Edinburgh, 1805; published *Elements of Geometry, Geometrical Analysis, and Plane Trigonometry* (1809), *Geometry of Curve Lines* (1813), and *Philosophy of Arithmetic* (1817); the first to achieve artificial congelation; contributed to the *Edinburgh Review* and the *Encyclopaedia Britannica*; professor of natural philosophy, Edinburgh, 1819; published *Elements of Natural Philosophy* (vol. i, 1823); knighted, 1832.

LESLIE, Sir John Randolph ('Shane'), third baronet, of Glaslough, County Monaghan (1885–1971), man of letters, educated at Eton and King's College, Cambridge; cousin of (Sir) Winston Churchill; at Cambridge became Roman Catholic and Irish nationalist; renounced Irish estates and stayed with Leo Tolstoy in Russia, 1907; worked in America and married an American girl; during 1914–18 war served with British Ambulance Corps; *The End of a Chapter* (1916), written in a Malta hospital, made his name; worked in Washington, trying to soften Irish-American hostility to Britain, 1916–17; published a magazine, *Ireland*; interceded unsuccessfully to save leaders of 1916 Easter rising from execution; made lifelong efforts to build bridges of friendship across Irish religious divisions; publications include *Henry Edward Manning, his Life and Labours* (1921), *The Skull of Swift* (1928), *Mrs Fitzherbert* (1928), and *Studies in Sublime Failure* (1932); also three novels, *The Oppidan* (1922), *Doomsland* (1923), and *The Cantab* (1926); wrote in verse *Jutland, a Fragment of Epic* (1930), and produced *The Greek Anthology* (1929), and his autobiographical *The Film of Memory* (1938); served in the Home Guard, 1940–5, and wrote *The Irish Tangle for English Readers* (1946); succeeded to barony, 1944; last

book, *Long Shadows*, published in 1966 when he was over 80.

LESLIE, Norman, master of Rothes (d. 1554), leader of the party who assassinated Cardinal *Beaton; eldest son of George *Leslie, fourth earl of Rothes; sheriff of Fife, 1541; led the conspirators against Beaton, but took no personal part in the act of assassination, 1546; was carried captive to France, but escaped to England and was pensioned by Edward VI; on accession of Mary entered service of Henri II of France; mortally wounded in action near Cambrai.

LESLIE, Thomas Edward Cliffe (1827?–1882), political economist; descended from Charles *Leslie (1650–1722); educated at Trinity College, Dublin; BA, 1847; LL B, 1851; later hon. LL D; professor of jurisprudence and political economy, Queen's College, Belfast, 1853; contributed articles on economic subjects to various periodicals, most of which were reprinted in *Essays on Political and Moral Philosophy* (1879) and *Essays in Political Philosophy* (1888); wrote on land systems and industrial economy.

LESLIE, Walter, Count Leslie (1606–1667), soldier of fortune and diplomat; entered the imperial service and took part in War of Mantuan succession, 1630; served in Germany, 1632–45; instrumental in bringing about the assassination of Wallenstein, 1634; master of the ordnance, 1646; vice-president of the Council of War; warden of the Sclavonian marches, and field marshal, 1650; privy councillor, 1655; invested with Order of Golden Fleece, and ambassador-extraordinary to the Ottoman Porte, 1665; died at Vienna.

LESLIE, William (d. 1654?), principal of King's College, Aberdeen; educated at Aberdeen; regent, 1617; sub-principal, 1623; principal, 1632; with other Aberdeen doctors refused the Covenant, 1639.

LESLIE, William (1657–1727), bishop of Laybach in Styria; educated at Aberdeen; studied at Padua, 1684; converted to Roman Catholicism; professor of theology, Padua; bishop of Waitzen, Hungary, 1716, of Laybach in Styria, 1718.

LESPEC, Walter (d. 1153). See ESPEC.

LESSE, Nicholas (fl. 1550), religious writer; author of *The Apologie of the Worde of God* (1547) and several translations.

LESTER, Frederick Parkinson (1795–1858), major-general, Bombay Artillery; educated at Addiscombe; lieutenant, 1815; captain, 1818; lieutenant-colonel, 1840; major-general, 1854; commander of the southern division of the Bombay Army, 1857–8; instrumental in preventing the Mutiny from extending to Western India, 1857–8.

LESTER, Sean (John Ernest) (1888–1959), secretary-general of the League of Nations; educated at Methodist College, Belfast; became journalist; publicity officer, external affairs department, Irish Free State, 1922–9; Irish representative at League of Nations, 1929; League of Nations' high commissioner, Danzig, 1934–7; deputy secretary-general, 1937; opposed compromise with Nazis; secretary-general, 1940–7; received Woodrow Wilson Award.

LESTOCK, Richard (1679?–1746), admiral; served with Sir Clowdisley *Shovell, 1704–5; with Sir George *Byng, 1717–18; took part in the operations against Cartagena, 1741; vice-admiral, 1743; court-martialled and acquitted (1746) for refusal to obey his superior, Mathews (see MATHEWS, THOMAS) in the action (1744) off Toulon; admiral of the blue, 1746.

LE STRANGE, Guy (1854–1933), orientalist; son of H. L'E. S. *Le Strange; mainly interested in historical geography of Middle Eastern Moslem lands; works include *Palestine under the Moslems* (1890) and *The Lands of the Eastern Caliphate* (1905).

L'ESTRANGE, Hamon (1605–1660), theologian and historian; brother of Sir Nicholas *L'Estrange, first baronet, and of Sir Roger *L'Estrange; published theological works, 1641–59.

L'ESTRANGE, Hamon (1676–1769), grandson of Hamon *L'Estrange (1605–1660); on the Commission of the Peace for sixty-five years; published legal and religious works.

LE STRANGE, Henry L'Estrange Styleman (1815–1862), art amateur and decorative painter; educated at Eton and Christ Church, Oxford; BA, 1837; employed in designing and carrying out the decoration of Ely Cathedral, 1853–62.

LE STRANGE, John (d. 1269), lord marcher; served under King John in Poitou, 1214; defended the Welsh border as a lord marcher.

L'ESTRANGE, John (1836–1877), Norfolk antiquary; clerk in the Stamp Office at Norwich; made large collections for the history of the county of Norfolk, and the city of Norwich; published *The Church Bells of Norfolk* (1874).

LE STRANGE, Sir Nicholas (1515–1580), steward of the manors of the duchess of Richmond, 1547–80; son of Sir Thomas *Le Strange; knighted, 1547; MP, Norfolk, 1547, King's Lynn, 1555, Castle Rising, 1571.

L'ESTRANGE, Sir Nicholas, first baronet (d. 1655), collector of anecdotes; brother of Hamon *L'Estrange (1605–1660); created baronet, 1629; compiled *Merry Passages and Jests*, some of which were printed (1839).

L'ESTRANGE, Sir Roger (1616–1704), Tory journalist and pamphleteer; probably studied at Cambridge; formed a plan to recapture Lynn; seized by the parliament and imprisoned, 1644–8; projected a Royalist rising in Kent; had to flee to Holland; employed while abroad by *Hyde in service of Charles II; returned to England, 1653; published broadsides attacking *Lambert and the leaders of the army, 1659; wrote pamphlets in favour of monarchy, 1660, and to show that the Presbyterians were responsible for the wars and the king's death, 1661–2; advocated a more stringent censorship of the press, 1663; appointed surveyor of printing presses and a licenser of the press, 1663; issued the *Intelligencer* and *The News*, 1663–6; encouraged, perhaps projected, *The City Mercury, or Advertisements concerning trade*, 1675; published pamphlets to meet *Shaftesbury's attack on Charles II and his government, 1679; adversely criticized the evidence for a supposed popish plot, 1680; JP for Middlesex, 1680; had to flee the country owing to the hostility of the promoters of the alleged popish plot; returned to England, 1681; attacked Dissenters and Whigs in his periodical *The Observator*, 1681–7; MP, Winchester, 1685; knighted, 1685; deprived of his office of surveyor and licenser of the press at the Revolution and imprisoned in 1688, 1691, and 1695–6. Besides his pamphlets and periodicals, he issued, among other things, *The Fables of Aesop and other eminent Mythologists, with Moral Reflections* (1692), the most extensive collection of fables in existence, and *The Works of Flavius Josephus compared with the Original Greek* (1702), also translating *Quevedo's Visions* (1667).

LE STRANGE, Sir Thomas (1494–1545), of Hunstanton, Norfolk; attended Henry VIII to the Field of the Cloth of Gold, 1520; knighted, 1529; high sheriff of Norfolk, 1532.

LE SUEUR, Hubert (1595?–1650?), sculptor; born probably at Paris; came to England, 1628; received commission for an equestrian statue of Charles I, 1630, which was not set up at Charing Cross until 1674.

LETCHWORTH, Thomas (1739–1784), Quaker; began preaching, 1758; published verse, 1765, *The Monthly Ledger, or Literary Repository*, an unsectarian periodical, 1766–9; his *Life and Writings of John *Woolman*, published (1775), and a posthumous volume of his sermons (1787).

LETHABY, William Richard (1857–1931), author and architect; worked under R. N. *Shaw; began independent practice, 1891; closely associated with Philip *Webb; an organizer and principal, LCC Central School of Arts and Crafts, 1894; appointed professor of design, Royal College of Art, 1900; surveyor, Westminster Abbey, 1906–28; publications include *Westminster Abbey and the King's Craftsmen* (1906) and *Mediaeval Art . . . 312–1350* (1904).

LETHBRIDGE, Joseph Watts (1817–1885), Dissenting divine; entered Lady Huntingdon's Connection, 1846; migrated to the Independents; published moral and religious works.

LETHBRIDGE, Walter Stephens (1772–1831?), miniature painter; studied at the Royal Academy schools; exhibited miniatures at the Academy, 1801–29.

LETHEBY, Henry (1816–1876), analytical chemist; MB, London, 1842; lecturer on chemistry at the London Hospital; for some years medical officer of health and analyst of foods for the city of London; chief work, *Food, its Varieties, Chemical Composition, etc.* (1870).

LETHERLAND, Joseph (1699–1764), physician; MD, Leiden, 1724; MD, Cambridge, by royal mandate, 1736; physician to St Thomas's Hospital, 1736–58; FRCP, 1737; physician to George III's queen (see CHARLOTTE SOPHIA), 1761; credited with being the first to draw attention in 1739 to the disease of diphtheria.

LETHIEULLIER, Smart (1701–1760), antiquary; MA, Trinity College, Oxford, 1723; formed collections and drawings of antiquities and English fossils; FRS and FSA.

LETHINGTON, Lord (1496–1586), poet, lawyer, and collector of early Scottish poetry. See MAITLAND, Sir RICHARD.

LETHLOBOR (d. 871), Irish king; defeated the Danes, 826; repulsed an invasion made by greater Ulster, 853; became king of all lesser Ulster or Ulidia.

LETT, Sir Hugh, baronet (1876–1964), surgeon; educated at Marlborough College, as pre-clinical student, at Leeds, and the London Hospital; MB, B.Ch. (Victoria), Leeds, 1899, diploma, Royal Colleges, 1901; FRCS, 1902; surgical registrar, London Hospital, 1902; assistant surgeon, 1905; surgical tutor, 1909–12; in charge of urological department; full surgeon, 1915–34; attached to Anglo-American hospital, Wimereux, 1914–15; Belgian Field Hospital, Furnes, 1915; major, RAMC; CBE, 1920; consulting surgeon, London Hospital, 1934; president, Royal College of Surgeons, 1938–41; chairman, Hunterian Museum Trust, 1955–9;

baronet, 1941; KCVO, 1947; president, British Medical Association, 1946–8; hon. fellow, Royal Society of Medicine and Hunterian Society; hon. DCL, Durham, hon. Sc.D., Cambridge.

LETTICE, John (1737–1832), poet and divine; of Sidney Sussex College, Cambridge; MA, 1764; Seatonian prizeman, 1764; chaplain and secretary to British embassy at Copenhagen, 1768–72; published *Letters on a Tour through various parts of Scotland in 1792* (1794) and translations from the Italian and Latin.

LETTOU, John (*fl.* 1480), printer; the first to set up a printing press in the city of London.

LETTS, Thomas (1803–1873), inventor of 'Letts's Diaries'; bookbinder from 1835, devoting himself to the manufacture of diaries; sold several hundred thousand annually. The diary business was purchased by Messrs Cassell & Co. in 1885.

LETTSOM, John Coakley (1744–1815), physician; born in West Indies; brought to England, 1750; studied at St Thomas's Hospital, London; returned to the West Indies, 1767; practised at Tortola; studied at Edinburgh (1768) and at Leiden (1769); commenced practice in London, 1770; LRCP, 1770; FSA, 1770; FRS, 1773; a successful Quaker physician and philanthropist; author of medical, biographical, and philanthropic works.

LETTSOM, William Nanson (1796–1865), man of letters; grandson of John Coakley *Lettsom; educated at Eton and Trinity College, Cambridge; MA, 1822; published *The Fall of the Nebelungers* (1850); edited William Sidney *Walker's *Shakespeare's Versification* (1854) and his *Critical Examination of the Text of Shakespeare* (1860); aided Alexander *Dyce in the preparation of his edition of Shakespeare.

LEVEN, earls of. See LESLIE, ALEXANDER, first earl, 1580?–1661; MELVILLE, DAVID, third earl, 1660–1728.

LEVENS, Peter (*fl.* 1587), scholar and medical writer; educated probably at Magdalen College, Oxford; BA, 1556; fellow, 1559; author of *Manipulus Vocabulorum. A Dictionarie of English and Latine Wordes* (1570), valuable as evidence of contemporary pronunciation.

LEVENS, Robert (1615–1650), royalist. See LEVINZ.

LEVER, Sir Ashton (1729–1788), collector of the Leverian Museum; educated at Corpus Christi College, Oxford; first collected live birds, then shells, fossils, stuffed birds, all kinds of natural objects, savage costumes and weapons; removed his museum to London, 1774;

knighted, 1778; disposed of his museum by lottery in 1788.

LEVER, Charles James (1806–1872), novelist; nephew of Sir Ashton *Lever; entered Trinity College, Dublin, 1822; graduated, 1827; travelled in Holland and Germany, 1828, in Canada, 1829; studied medicine at Dublin; MB, Trinity College, Dublin, 1831; first instalment of *Harry Lorrequer* produced in *Dublin University Magazine*, 1837; practised medicine in Brussels, 1840–2; published *Charles O'Malley*, first in *Dublin University Magazine* (1840), and *Jack Hinton the Guardsman* (1843); returned to Dublin and edited the *Dublin University Magazine*, 1842–5; contributed to that magazine *Tom Burke of Ours* and *Arthur O'Leary* (1844); published *The O'Donoghue* (1845) and the *Knight of Gwynne* (1847); settled at Florence and produced there *Roland Cashel* (1850) and *The Dodd Family Abroad* (1853–4); British consul at Spezzia, 1857; consul at Trieste, 1867–72; his last novel *Lord Kilgobbin* (1872, first issued in *Cornhill Magazine*); died at Trieste; collected edition of his works was issued (1876–8).

LEVER, Christopher (*fl.* 1627), Protestant writer and poet; of Christ's College, Cambridge; published religious poems and prose works, 1607–27.

LEVER, Darcy (1760?–1837), writer on seamanship; nephew of Sir Ashton *Lever; published *The Young Sea Officer's Sheet Anchor, or a Key to the Leading of Rigging and to Practical Seamanship* (1808), for forty years the Navy textbook.

LEVER (or LEAVER), Ralph (d. 1585), master of Sherburn Hospital, Durham; brother of Thomas *Lever; of St John's College, Cambridge; fellow, 1549; MA, 1551; incorporated MA, Oxford, 1560; archdeacon of Northumberland, 1566–73; canon of Durham, 1567; master of Sherburn Hospital, 1577; DD, Oxford, 1578; his work on chess published without his consent (1563); published *The Arte of Reason* (1573), one of the rarest of early English treatises on logic.

LEVER, Sir (Samuel) Hardman, baronet, of Allerton (1869–1947), chartered accountant; educated at Merchant Taylors' School; partner in New York firm of accountants; entered Ministry of Munitions to advise on costing, 1915; financial secretary to Treasury, 1916; Treasury representative in United States, 1917–19; at Ministry of Transport, 1919–21; headed air mission to Canada (1938), Australia and New Zealand (1939); KCB, 1917; baronet, 1920.

LEVER (or LEAVER), Thomas (1521–1577), Puritan divine; brother of Ralph *Lever; MA, St John's College, Cambridge, 1545; fellow, 1543, and college preacher, 1548; a leader of the extreme Protestant reformers at Cambridge; preached at court before Edward VI, 1550; master of St John's College, Cambridge, 1551; BD, 1552; at Mary's accession fled to Zurich, 1553; a hearer of Calvin at Geneva, 1554; minister of the English congregation at Aarau, 1556–9; returned to England, 1559; master of Sherburn Hospital, Durham, 1563; canon of Durham, 1564–7; published sermons and a religious treatise.

LEVER, William Hesketh, first Viscount Leverhulme (1851–1925), soap manufacturer; entered father's grocery business in Bolton, 1867; partner, 1872; with his brother began to trade on his own account, specializing in soap, for which he chose name 'Sunlight', 1884; began to manufacture it, 1885; inaugurated new town, Port Sunlight, on Mersey, near Bebington, Cheshire, as centre for his works and workpeople, 1888; Lever Brothers made limited company, 1890, public company, 1894; by purchase or by interchange of shares exercised wide control over soapmaking trade; Liberal MP, Wirral division of Cheshire, 1906–9; brought and won libel action against *Northcliffe press, 1907; established crushing mills in Nigeria for supply of palm-oil for his soap; assiduous in care for Port Sunlight, on which he lavished many gifts, including art gallery; an enthusiastic collector of pictures, etc.; presented Stafford House (which, as Lancaster House, housed London Museum) to nation; baronet, 1911; baron, 1917; viscount, 1922.

LEVERHULME, first Viscount (1851–1925), soap manufacturer. See LEVER, WILLIAM HESKETH.

LEVERIDGE, Richard (1670?–1758), vocalist, song-writer, and composer; sang at Drury Lane Theatre, 1703–8, at the Haymarket, London, 1708–13, at Lincoln's Inn Fields, 1715–32, at Covent Garden, 1732–51; said to have composed the music to *Macbeth* for the revival of 1702; his best-known songs 'All in the Downs' and 'The Roast Beef of Old England'.

LEVERTON, Thomas (1743–1824), architect; employed in the erection of dwelling-houses in London and the country; exhibited designs at the Royal Academy, 1771–1803.

LEVESON, Sir Richard (1570–1605), vice-admiral of England; volunteer against the Armada, 1588; had command in expedition against Cadiz, 1596; knighted, 1596; destroyed the Spanish fleet off Ireland, 1601; vice-admiral of England, 1604; marshal of the embassy to Spain to conclude the peace, 1605.

LEVESON-GOWER, (Edward) Frederick (1819–1907), politician; son of first Earl *Granville; educated at Eton and Christ Church,

Oxford; BA, 1840; called to bar, 1846; Liberal MP for Derby, 1846–7, Stoke-upon-Trent, 1852–7, and Bodmin, 1859–85; chairman of National School of Cookery, 1874–1903; visited India, 1850–1, and Russia, 1856; a conspicuous figure in society; edited his mother's *Letters* (1894) and published *Bygone Years* (1905).

LEVESON-GOWER, Lord Francis (1800–1857), statesman and poet. See EGERTON, FRANCIS, first earl of Ellesmere.

LEVESON-GOWER, George Granville, first duke of Sutherland (1758–1833); educated at Westminster and Christ Church, Oxford; MP, Newcastle under Lyme, 1778 and 1780; travelled in Europe, 1780–6; MP, Staffordshire, 1787–98; ambassador to Paris, 1790–2; summoned as Baron Gower of Stittenham, Yorkshire, the original barony of his family, 1798; joint postmaster-general, 1799–1810; KG, 1806; became possessed of the greater part of Sutherlandshire through his wife, countess of Sutherland in her own right, 1785; inherited the Bridgewater estates from his uncle, the last duke of *Bridgewater, and by the death of his father, marquis of *Stafford, the estates of Stittenham (Yorkshire), Trentham (Staffordshire), Wolverhampton and Lilleshall (Shropshire), 1803; made 450 miles of roads and built 134 bridges in Sutherlandshire between 1812 and 1832; purchased Stafford House, London, 1827; created duke of Sutherland, 1833.

LEVESON-GOWER, George Granville William Sutherland, third duke of Sutherland (1828–1892); succeeded to the dukedom, 1861; MP, Sutherlandshire, 1852–61; improved his Highland estates; attended coronation of Tsar Alexander II as member of the special mission, 1856; KG, 1864; present at the opening of the Suez Canal, 1869; accompanied Edward VII, when prince of Wales, to India, 1876.

LEVESON-GOWER, Granville, first marquis of Stafford (1721–1803), son of John *Leveson-Gower, first Earl Gower; educated at Westminster and Christ Church, Oxford; MP, Bishop's Castle, 1744, Westminster, 1747 and 1749; lord of the Admiralty, 1749–51; MP, Lichfield, 1754; succeeded to the Upper House, 1754; lord privy seal, 1755–7 and 1785–94; master of the horse, 1757–60; keeper of the great wardrobe, 1760–3; lord chamberlain of the household, 1763–5; president of the council, 1767–79 and 1783–4; KG, 1771; FSA, 1784; created marquis of the county of Stafford, 1786.

LEVESON-GOWER, Lord Granville, first Earl Granville (1773–1846), diplomat; youngest son of Granville *Leveson-Gower, first marquis of Stafford; entered Christ Church, Oxford, 1789; MP, Lichfield, 1795–9; DCL, 1799; MP, Staffordshire, 1799–1815; a lord of the Treasury, 1800; privy councillor, 1804; ambassador-extraordinary at St Petersburg, 1804–5; created Viscount Granville, 1815; minister at Brussels; ambassador at Paris, 1824–41; created Earl Granville and Baron Leveson of Stone, 1833.

LEVESON-GOWER, Granville George, second Earl Granville (1815–1891), statesman; eldest son of Lord Granville *Leveson-Gower, first Earl Granville; of Eton and Christ Church, Oxford; attaché at the British embassy, Paris, 1835; Whig MP, Morpeth, 1837–40; BA, 1839; under-secretary of state for foreign affairs, 1840–1; MP, Lichfield, 1841; succeeded to peerage, 1846; vice-president of Board of Trade in Lord John Russell's ministry, 1848; paymaster of the forces, 1848; minister for foreign affairs, 1851–2 (under Lord John Russell), 1870–4 and 1880–5 (under William Ewart Gladstone); president of the council, 1852–4; chancellor of the duchy of Lancaster, 1854; leader of the House of Lords, when the Liberals were in office, from 1855; chancellor of the University of London, 1856–91; KG, 1857; president of the council, 1855–8 and 1859–66; lord warden of the Cinque Ports and hon. DCL, Oxford, 1865; secretary of state for the colonies, 1868–70 and 1886.

LEVESON-GOWER, Harriet Elizabeth Georgiana, duchess of Sutherland (1806–1868), daughter of George *Howard, sixth earl of Carlisle; married (1823) George Granville Leveson-Gower, Earl Gower, who succeeded his father (see LEVESON-GOVER, GEORGE GRANVILLE) as second duke of Sutherland in 1833; mistress of the robes under Liberal administrations, 1837–41, 1846–52, 1853–8, and 1859–61; a great friend of Queen Victoria.

LEVESON GOWER, Sir Henry Dudley Gresham (1873–1954), cricketer. See GOWER.

LEVESON-GOWER, John, first Baron Gower (1675–1709); MP, Newcastle under Lyme, Staffordshire, 1691–1703; created Baron Gower of Stittenham, 1703; privy councillor, 1703; chancellor of the duchy of Lancaster, 1703–6.

LEVESON-GOWER, John, first Earl Gower (d. 1754), eldest son of John *Leveson-Gower, first Baron Gower; DCL, Oxford, 1732; one of the lords justices of the kingdom, 1740, 1743, 1745, 1748, 1750, and 1752; lord privy seal, 1742–3 and 1744; created Viscount Trentham and Earl Gower, 1746.

LEVESON-GOWER, John (1740–1792), rear-admiral; son of John *Leveson-Gower, first Earl Gower; captain in the navy, 1760; commanded in

Mediterranean, on coast of Guinea, in West Indies, and on the Home and Newfoundland stations between 1760 and 1777; took part in action off Ushant, 1778; a junior lord of the Admiralty, 1783–90; rear-admiral, 1787.

LEVETT, Henry (1668–1725), physician; educated at Charterhouse and Magdalen College, Oxford; fellow of Exeter College, Oxford, 1688; MA, 1694; MD, 1699; FRCP, 1708; physician to the Charterhouse, 1713–25; author of a letter in Latin on the treatment of smallpox, printed in the works of Dr John *Freind, 1733.

LEVETT (or LEVET), Robert (1701?–1782), 'that odd old surgeon whom Johnson kept in his house to tend the out-pensioners'; made *Johnson's acquaintance, c.1746; became a regular inmate of Johnson's house, 1763; had some practice as a surgeon in London.

LEVI, David (1740–1799), Jewish controversialist; published *A Succinct Account of the Rites and Ceremonies of the Jews . . . and the Opinion of Dr. Humphrey Prideaux . . . refuted* (1783); published *Lingua Sacra*, a Hebrew grammar, in weekly parts (1785–7); replied (1787 and 1789) to Joseph *Priestley's *Letters to the Jews*; replied to a fresh antagonist in *Letters to Nathaniel Brassey Halhed, M.P.* (1795); his *Defence of the Old Testament in a Series of Letters addressed to Thomas Paine*, first published in New York (1797). He also published the Pentateuch in Hebrew and English, and an English translation of the prayers used by the London congregations of Jews (1789–93), and *Dissertations of the Prophecies of the Old Testament* (3 vols., published 1793–1800).

LEVI, Leone (1821–1888), jurist and statistician; born in Ancona; settled at Liverpool as a merchant and was naturalized; published pamphlets advocating the establishment in commercial centres of general representative chambers of commerce, 1849–50; hon. secretary, Liverpool Chamber of Commerce; published his great work on commercial law (1850–2); appointed to the newly created chair of commerce at King's College, London, 1852; FSA and published his lectures as *Manual of the Mercantile Law of Great Britain and Ireland* (1854); his chief work on statistics, a periodical summary of parliamentary papers, published in eighteen volumes (1856–68); his *History of British Commerce and of the Economic Progress of the British Nation, 1763–1870* published (1872); vice-president of the Statistical Society, 1885.

LEVICK, George Murray (1876–1956), surgeon and explorer; educated at St Paul's School; qualified from St Bartholomew's Hospital and commissioned as doctor in Royal Navy, 1902; chosen by Captain R. F. *Scott for Antarctic expedition, 1910; spent two years with northern party exploring Victoria Land coast; studied Adélie penguin; surgeon-commander, 1915; retired, 1917; founded Public Schools Exploring Society, 1932, and honorary chief leader of first nine expeditions; recalled to Royal Navy to assist training of commandos, 1939–45.

LÉVIGNAC, Abbé de (1769–1833), Jesuit preacher. See MACCARTHY, NICHOLAS TUITE.

LEVINGE, Sir Richard, first baronet (d. 1724), Irish judge; barrister, Inner Temple, 1678; recorder of Chester, 1686; MP, Chester, 1690–5; solicitor-general for Ireland, 1690–4 and 1704–11; knighted, 1692; MP for Blessington in Irish House of Commons and speaker of the house, 1692–3; MP for Longford, Irish Parliament, 1698–9 and 1703–13; created baronet, 1704; MP, Derby, 1710; attorney-general for Ireland, 1711; MP, Kilkenny, Irish Parliament, 1713–14; lord chief justice of Irish common pleas, 1720–4; his correspondence on *Various Points of State and Domestic Policy*, privately printed (1877).

LEVINGE, Sir Richard George Augustus, seventh baronet (1811–1884), soldier and writer; entered the army, 1828; lieutenant, 1834; served in the Canadian rebellion of 1837–8; lieutenant-colonel in the militia, 1846; succeeded to baronetcy, 1848; high sheriff for Westmeath, 1851; MP for Co. Westmeath, 1857 and 1859; author of *Echoes from the Backwoods* (1846), *Historical Notices of the Levinge Family* (1853), *Historical Records of the Forty-third Regiment, Monmouthshire Light Infantry* (1868), and other works.

LEVINZ, Baptist (1644–1693), bishop of Sodor and Man; brother of Sir Creswell *Levinz; educated at Magdalen Hall and College, Oxford; MA, 1666; White's professor of moral philosophy, Oxford, 1677–82; bishop of Sodor and Man, 1685; prebendary of Winchester, 1691; contributed to *Epicaedia Universitatis Oxoniensis in obitum Georgii Ducis Albemarliae* (1670).

LEVINZ, Sir Creswell (1627–1701), judge; brother of Baptist *Levinz; of Trinity College, Cambridge; barrister, Gray's Inn, 1661; knighted, 1678; king's counsel, 1678; attorney-general, 1679; sat on the bench of common pleas, 1680–6; one of the counsel for the seven bishops, 1688. From manuscripts left by him was published in 1722 *The Reports of Sir Creswell Levinz, Knight.*

LEVINZ (LEVENS or LEVINGE), Robert (1615–1650), Royalist; uncle of Sir Creswell *Levinz, Baptist *Levinz, and William *Levinz; educated at Lincoln College, Oxford; BA, 1634; DCL, 1642; fought for Charles I; employed by Charles II to raise troops in England, 1650;

arrested, condemned by court martial, and hanged.

LEVINZ, William (1625–1698), president of St John's College, Oxford; brother of Sir Creswell *Levinz; educated at Merchant Taylors' School, London, and St John's College, Oxford, 1645; MA, 1649; regius professor of Greek, 1665–98; president of his college, 1673; sub-dean of Wells, 1678; canon, 1682.

LEVIZAC, Jean Pons Victor Lecoutz de (d. 1813), writer on the French language; born in Languedoc; canon in the cathedral of Vabres, and probably vicar-general of the diocese of St Omer; at the Revolution fled to London, where he taught French and published books on the French language, 1797–1808.

LEVY, Amy (1861–1889), poetess and novelist; educated at Newnham College, Cambridge; her *Xantippe and other Poems* published (1881), *A Minor Poet and other Verse* (1884), *A London Plane Tree and other Poems*, and *Reuben Sachs*, a novel (1889); committed suicide.

LEVY, Benn Wolfe (1900–1973), playwright and director; educated at Repton and University College, Oxford; cadet in RAF, 1918; entered publishing, 1923, and became managing director of Jarrolds; his comedy, *This Woman Business*, produced in London (1925) and New York (1926); had number of plays produced between 1928 and 1939, and directed *Springtime for Henry, Hollywood Holiday*, and his adaptation of *Madame Bovary*; worked as writer of dialogue for films, including *Blackmail* (1929), the first 'talkie' directed by (Sir) Alfred *Hitchcock; joined Royal Navy, 1939; wounded and appointed MBE, 1944; Labour MP for Eton and Slough, 1945–50; close friend of Aneurin *Bevan and Jennie Lee (Baroness Lee of Asheridge); directed his plays *Clutterbuck* (1946) and *Return to Tyassi* (1950); also wrote several other plays which he did not direct, including *The Tumbler*, directed by Laurence (later Lord) Olivier (New York, 1960); member of executive committee, Arts Council, 1953–61; wrote for *New Statesman* and *Tribune*; active campaigner for unilateral nuclear disarmament; published *Britain and the Bomb, the Fallacy of Nuclear Defence* (1959).

LEVY, Hyman (1889–1975), mathematician, philosopher, and political activist; educated at George Heriot's School and Edinburgh University; first class, mathematics and physics, 1911; with scholarship and research fellowship studied in Göttingen; escaped from Germany, 1914; worked in aerodynamics division of National Physical Laboratory, 1916–20; published with W. L. Cowley, *Aeronautics in Theory and Experiment* (1918); assistant professor, Royal College of Science, 1920; professor, 1923; head of mathematics department, 1946; dean, 1946–52; published books on numerical analysis and statistics; chairman, Labour party Science Advisory Committee, 1924–30; became well-known publicist for Communist party, 1931–56; visited Moscow and investigated reports of persecution of Jews; denounced injustices revealed by his findings; expelled from Communist party, 1958; published *The Universe of Science* (1932) and broadcast in discussions with (Sir) Julian *Huxley; fellow, Royal Society of Edinburgh, 1916; vice-president, London Mathematical Society, 1931–2.

LEVY, Joseph Moses (1812–1888), founder of the *Daily Telegraph*; purchased a printing establishment; took over the *Daily Telegraph and Courier* and issued it as the *Daily Telegraph*, the first London daily penny paper, 1855.

LEVY-LAWSON, Edward, first Baron Burnham (1833–1916), newspaper proprietor; son of Joseph Moses *Levy; assumed additional surname of Lawson, 1875; began career as dramatic critic to *Sunday Times*; became editor of *Daily Telegraph* shortly after its acquisition by his father, 1855; managing proprietor and sole controller, 1885; humanized his newspaper; paper's support transferred from Gladstone to Beaconsfield, 1879; after 1886, paper definitely Unionist and imperialist; organized appeals to public for national and charitable efforts through *Daily Telegraph* funds; sponsored enterprises such as Assyrian expedition of George *Smith, 1873; baronet, 1892; created baron on retirement from active control of paper, 1903; KCVO, 1904.

LEVY-LAWSON, Sir Harry Lawson Webster, Viscount Burnham (1862–1933), newspaper proprietor. See LAWSON.

LEWES. See also LEWIS.

LEWES, Charles Lee (1740–1803), actor; his first recorded appearance at Covent Garden, 1763; played young Marlow in first performance of *She Stoops to Conquer*, 1773; at Covent Garden as leading comedian till 1783; at Drury Lane, 1783–5; at Edinburgh, 1787; played in Dublin in low comedy, 1792–3; published theatrical compilations.

LEWES, George Henry (1817–1878), miscellaneous writer; grandson of Charles Lee *Lewes; tried various employments, among them that of actor; contributed to the quarterlies (1840–9) and wrote a play and two novels; published *Biographical History of Philosophy* (1845–6); co-operated with Thornton Leigh *Hunt in the *Leader*, 1850; made the acquaintance of Miss Evans (see CROSS, MARY ANN), 1851, and went to Germany with her in 1854, and for the rest of his life lived with her as her husband; his *Life of Goethe*, the standard English work on the subject, published (1855); studied physiology, and published *Seaside Studies* (1858), *Physiology of Common Life* (1859), *Studies in Animal Life* (1862), and *Aristotle*, the first instalment of a projected history of science (1864); edited *Fortnightly Review*, 1865–6; his *Problems of Life and Mind* published at intervals (1873–9); his criticisms on the drama contributed to the *Pall Mall Gazette* published (1875).

LEWGAR, John (1602–1665), Roman Catholic controversialist; MA, Trinity College, Oxford, 1622; published controversial works.

LEWICKE, Edward (*fl.* 1562), poet; author of *The most wonderfull and pleasaunt History of Titus and Gisippus* (1562), a rhymed paraphrase of Sir Thomas *Eliot's prose version of a tale of Boccaccio.

LEWIN, (George) Ronald (1914–1984), military historian and biographer; educated at Heath Grammar School, Halifax, and The Queen's College, Oxford; first class, Lit. Hum., 1936; editorial assistant, Jonathan Cape, publishers, 1937; served during 1939–45 war in Royal Artillery; joined BBC as talks producer, 1946; chief assistant, Home Service, 1954; chief, Home Service, 1963–5; joined Hutchinsons; published *Rommel* (1968), *Montgomery as Military Commander* (1971), *Churchill as War Lord* (1973), *Man of Armour* (1976), *Slim the Standard-Bearer* (1976) which won the W. H. Smith Literary Award (1977), *The Life and Death of the Africa Korps* (1977), *Ultra Goes to War* (1978), and *The Other Ultra* (1982); died before he could finish the one-volume history of World War II commissioned by the Oxford University Press; CBE, 1983; Chesney Gold Medal of Royal United Services Institute, 1982; FRSL and F.R.Hist.S.

LEWIN, John William (*fl.* 1805), naturalist; brother of William *Lewin (d. 1795); settled in Paramatta, New South Wales; published *The Birds of New Holland* (1808–22) and *Prodromus* [sic] *Entomology* (1805), a history of the lepidoptera of New South Wales.

LEWIN, Sir Justinian (1613–1673), master in Chancery; grandson of William *Lewin (d. 1598); of Pembroke College, Oxford; DCL, 1637; official to the archdeacon of Norfolk, 1631; judge marshal of the army in the Scottish expedition, 1639; a master in Chancery, 1641; promoted Charles II's interest in Norfolk; knighted, 1661.

LEWIN, Thomas (1805–1877), miscellaneous writer; educated at Merchant Taylors' School and Worcester and Trinity colleges, Oxford; MA, 1831; conveyancing counsel to the court of Chancery, 1852–77; FSA, 1863; chief works, *Practical Treatise on the Law of Trusts and Trustees*

(1837), an authoritative textbook, *The Life and Epistles of St. Paul* (1851), and archaeological pamphlets.

LEWIN, William (d. 1598), civilian; of Christ's College, Cambridge; MA, 1565; public orator, 1570–1; LL D, 1576; judge of the prerogative court of Canterbury, 1576–98; chancellor of the diocese of Rochester and commissary of the faculties; MP, Rochester, 1586, 1589, and 1593; a master of Chancery, 1593; friend of Gabriel *Harvey; author of the Latin epistle to the Jesuits before Harvey's *Ciceronianus* (1577).

LEWIN, William (d. 1795), naturalist; FLS, 1791; published an unscientific book, *The Birds of Great Britain accurately figured* (7 vols., 1789–95), of which he executed the drawings; and published volume i of *The Insects of Great Britain systematically arranged, accurately engraved, and painted from Nature* (1795).

LEWINS (or LEWENS), Edward John (1756–1828), United Irishman; educated in France; envoy of the Society of United Irishmen at Hamburg, 1797; confidential agent at Paris; banished from Ireland by act of parliament at the Union; inspector of studies at the University of Paris; exercised great influence in France during reign of Charles X.

LEWIS. See also LEWES.

LEWIS, Miss (*fl.* 1715–1737), actress. See THURMOND, Mrs.

LEWIS, Agnes (1843–1926), discoverer of the 'Sinai Palimpsest'; born Smith; married S. S. *Lewis, 1887; with her twin sister, Margaret Gibson, visited St Catherine's Convent, Mount Sinai, 1892; discovered among Syriac manuscripts palimpsest containing ancient text of Gospels; photographed and subsequently (1893) transcribed manuscript.

LEWIS, Andrew (1720?–1781), soldier; volunteer in the Ohio expedition, 1754; major in Washington's Virginia Regiment, 1755; commanded Sandy Creek expedition, 1756; taken prisoner at Fort Duquesne, 1758; brigadier-general, 1774; delegate to the Virginia conventions, 1775; took popular side in the War of Independence and was brigadier-general of the continental army, 1776–7; died in Virginia.

LEWIS, Sir Anthony Carey (1915–1983), musician and founder of *Musica Britannica*; educated at Wellington College (music scholar) and Peterhouse, Cambridge (open scholar); BA and Mus.B., 1935; joined music staff of BBC, 1935; composed *A Choral Overture* which received its première at Queen's Hall Promenade concert, 1938; during 1939–45 war served in Royal Army

Ordnance Corps; helped organize music for troops; returned to BBC and planned music for new Third Programme, 1946; professor of music, Birmingham University, 1947–68; founded *Musica Britannica* and became general editor; hon. secretary, Purcell Society, 1950–76; chairman, Arts Council's music panel, 1954–65, the Purcell–Handel Festival, 1959, and British Council's music committee, 1967–73; dean, Faculty of Arts, Birmingham, 1961–4; president, Royal Musical Association, 1963–9; principal, Royal Academy of Music, 1968; contributed to *The New Oxford History of Music*; president, Incorporated Society of Musicians, 1968; director, English National Opera, 1974–6 and chairman, Purcell Society, 1976–83; CBE, 1967; knighted, 1972; hon. D.Mus., Birmingham, 1970; hon. member, Royal Academy of Music, 1960 and Guildhall School of Music and Drama, 1969; hon. FTCL, 1948, FRCM, 1971, FRNCM, 1974, and FRSAMD, 1980; governor of Wellington College.

LEWIS, Sir Aubrey Julian (1900–1975), psychiatrist; born in Adelaide, Australia; educated at Christian Brothers' College, Adelaide, 1911–17; studied at Adelaide University medical school; MB, B.Ch., 1923; carried out study of Australian aborigines, 1923–6; Rockefeller travelling fellow, 1926; worked in Phipps clinic, Johns Hopkins, and at other hospitals in USA, Germany, and England, including the National, Queen Square, London, 1926–8; joined staff of Maudsley Hospital, London, 1929; MD, Adelaide, 1931; FRCP, 1938; clinical director, Maudsley Hospital, 1936; civilian consultant in psychiatry to RAF, 1945–67; professor of psychiatry, Maudsley Hospital, 1946–66; hon. director, Occupational Psychiatry Research Unit (later Social Psychiatry Unit), 1948; held number of lectureships, including Galton lecturer, Eugenics Society, 1958, and Bertram Roberts lecturer, Yale, 1960; received number of honorary awards; knighted, 1959; published books and papers on psychiatry, including articles in the *British Journal of Sociology* (1953) and in *Price's Textbook of Medicine* (1941).

LEWIS, Bunnell (1824–1908), classical archaeologist; BA, London, 1843; MA, 1849; fellow of University College, London, 1847; professor of Latin, Queen's College, Cork, 1849–1905; FSA, 1865; made researches into surviving Roman antiquities in Europe; contributed to *Archaeological Journal*, 1875–1907; bequeathed library and £1,000 for classical prize to University College.

LEWIS, Cecil Day- (1904–1972), poet laureate and detective novelist. See DAY-LEWIS.

LEWIS, Charles (1753–1795), painter of still life; exhibited at the Society of Artists and Royal Academy, 1772–91.

LEWIS, Charles (1786–1836), bookbinder; brother of Frederick Christian *Lewis (1779–1856) and of George Robert *Lewis; employed by *Beckford on the Fonthill library.

LEWIS, Charles George (1808–1880), engraver; son of Frederick Christian *Lewis (1779–1856); instructed by his father; his best-known plates engraved between 1830 and 1873.

LEWIS, Charles James (1830–1892), painter; his best work in water-colour; painted small domestic subjects and landscapes; member of the Royal Institute of Painters in Water-Colours, 1882.

LEWIS, Clive Staples (1898–1963), writer and scholar; educated at Malvern and University College, Oxford; first class, Lit. Hum., 1922, and English, 1923; fellow, Magdalen College, 1925; published narrative poem *Dymer* under pseudonym, Clive Hamilton, 1926; first allegorical work, *The Pilgrim's Regress* (1933); other publications, while he was lecturing at Oxford, include *The Allegory of Love* (1936) and *The Screwtape Letters* (1942); professor, English medieval and Renaissance literature, Cambridge, 1954–63; fellow, Magdalene College, Cambridge; published *English Literature in the Sixteenth Century* (1954); wrote the Narnia series of children's tales, 1948–56; hon. fellow, Magdalen and University colleges, Oxford, and Magdalene College, Cambridge; other publications include *The Problem of Pain* (1940), *The Four Loves* (1960), and *An Experiment in Criticism* (1961); FBA, 1955; hon. DD, St Andrews, 1948, and D.Litt., Laval, Quebec, 1952.

LEWIS (or LEWES), David (1520?–1584), civilian; educated at All Souls College, Oxford; BCL, 1540; fellow, 1541; principal of New Inn Hall, Oxford, 1545–8; DCL and admitted at Doctors' Commons, 1548; a master in Chancery, 1553; MP, Steyning, 1553; MP, Monmouthshire, 1554–5; judge of the High Court of Admiralty, 1558–75; first principal of Jesus College, Oxford, 1571–2; joint commissioner of the Admiralty, 1575.

LEWIS, David (1617–1679), Jesuit. See BAKER, CHARLES.

LEWIS, David (1683?–1760), poet; probably educated at Westminster and Jesus College, Oxford; BA, 1702; published *Miscellaneous Poems by Several Hands* (1726), *Philip of Macedon* (tragedy, 1727), acted three times, and *Collection of Miscellany Poems* (1730).

LEWIS, Edward (1701–1784), miscellaneous writer; MA, St John's College, Cambridge, 1726; held several livings and wrote and preached against Roman Catholicism.

LEWIS, Erasmus (1670–1754), the friend of *Swift and *Pope; educated at Westminster and Trinity College, Cambridge; BA, 1693; wrote newsletters from Berlin, 1698; secretary to the English ambassador at Paris, 1701, to Robert *Harley, 1704, and secretary at Brussels, 1708; came to London, 1710; MP, Lostwithiel, Cornwall, 1713; intimate of *Prior, *Arbuthnot, Pope, *Gay, and Swift.

LEWIS, Evan (1818–1901), dean of Bangor; BA, Jesus College, Oxford, 1841; MA, 1863; held livings of Aberdare, 1859–66, and Dolgelly, 1866–84; chancellor (1872–6), canon residentiary (1877–84), and dean (1884–1901) of Bangor; influenced by Tractarian movement; his teaching as curate on the sacraments led to a long controversy, 1850–2; his best work was Welsh treatise on apostolic succession (1851); his elder brother, **David Lewis** (1814–1895), vice-principal of Jesus College, Oxford, 1845–6, joined Roman Church, 1846, and translated theological works from Latin and Spanish.

LEWIS, Evan (1828–1869), Independent minister; BA, London; served various Independent chapels; FRGS; fellow of the Ethnological Society; published religious works.

LEWIS, Frederick Christian (1779–1856), engraver and landscape painter; brother of Charles *Lewis (1786–1836); studied under J. C. Stadler and in the schools of the Royal Academy; aquatinted most of *Girtin's etchings of Paris, 1803; made transcripts of drawings by the great masters for *Ottley's *Italian School of Design* (1808–12); executed plates for *Chamberlaine's *Original Designs of the most celebrated Masters in the Royal Collection* (1812); engraved Sir Thomas *Lawrence's crayon portraits; engraver of drawings to Princess *Charlotte, Prince Leopold, George IV, William IV, and Queen Victoria; painted landscapes, chiefly of Devonshire scenery; published several volumes of plates illustrating the Devonshire rivers between 1821 and 1843, and also etchings of the *Scenery of the Rivers of England and Wales* (1845–7).

LEWIS, Frederick Christian (1813–1875), painter; son of Frederick Christian *Lewis (1779–1856); studied under Sir Thomas *Lawrence; went to India, 1834, and painted pictures of durbars for native princes, engraved by his father, and published in England; died at Genoa.

LEWIS, George (1763–1822), Dissenting divine; issued a manual of divinity in Welsh which became very popular (1796), and a valuable

Welsh commentary on the New Testament (1802); head of Abergavenny Theological College, 1812–22.

LEWIS, Sir George Cornewall, second baronet (1806–1863), statesman and author; son of Sir Thomas Frankland *Lewis; of Eton and Christ Church, Oxford; MA, 1831; assistant commissioner to inquire into the condition of the poorer classes in Ireland, 1833, and into the state of religious and other instruction, 1834; joint commissioner to inquire into the affairs of Malta, 1836–8; a poor-law commissioner for England and Wales, 1839–47; Liberal MP, Herefordshire, 1847; secretary to Board of Control, 1847; under-secretary for the Home Department, 1848; financial secretary to the Treasury, 1850–2; editor of the *Edinburgh Review*, to which he contributed eighteen articles, 1852–5; succeeded to baronetcy, 1855; MP for Radnor boroughs, 1855–63; published *Enquiry into the Credibility of the Early Roman History* (1855); chancellor of the Exchequer, 1855–8; home secretary, 1859–61; secretary for war, 1861–3; published, among other works on politics, *A Treatise on the Methods of Observation and Reasoning in Politics* (1852).

LEWIS, Sir George Henry, first baronet (1833–1911), solicitor; joined father's firm of solicitors, 1851; established reputation in connection with Balham mystery, 1876 (see GULLY, JAMES MANBY); obtained monopoly of 'society' cases; unrivalled in knowledge of criminals and in thoroughness of investigation; acted for incriminated nationalists before the Parnell Commission, 1888–9; intimate of King Edward VII; CVO, 1905; knighted, 1892; baronet, 1902; advocate of Criminal Evidence Act of 1898, of court of criminal appeal, 1907, and of Moneylenders Act, 1900.

LEWIS, George Robert (1782–1871), painter of landscapes and portraits; brother of Charles *Lewis (1786–1836); studied at the Royal Academy schools; exhibited landscapes, 1805–7; accompanied Thomas Frognall *Dibdin as draughtsman on his continental journey, and illustrated Dibdin's *Bibliographical and Picturesque Tour through France and Germany* (published 1821); etched *Groups illustrating the Physiognomy, Manners, and Character of the People of France and Germany* (1823); exhibited portraits and landscapes and figure-subjects, 1820–59.

LEWIS, Griffith George (1784–1859), lieutenant-general; colonel-commandant, Royal Engineers; educated at Royal Military Academy, Woolwich; lieutenant, 1803; fought at Maida, 1806; captain, 1807; served in Spanish campaign under Wellington, 1813; served in Newfoundland, 1819–27; lieutenant-colonel, 1825; commanded Royal Engineers at Jersey, 1830–6; at the Cape of Good Hope, 1836–42; in Ireland, 1842–7; at Portsmouth, 1847–51; joint editor of the *Professional Papers of the Corps of Royal Engineers* and of the *Corps Papers*, 1847–54; governor of the Royal Military Academy, Woolwich, 1851–6; lieutenant-general, 1858.

LEWIS, Hubert (1825–1884), jurist; educated at Emmanuel College, Cambridge; BA, 1848; barrister, Middle Temple, 1854; published *Principles of Conveyancing* (1863), *Principles of Equity Drafting* (1865); his *Ancient Laws of Wales* published (1889).

LEWIS, James Henry (1786–1853), stenographer; taught and lectured on writing and stenography in the principal towns of the United Kingdom; his system of shorthand, *The Art of Writing with the Velocity of Speech*, issued anonymously (1814); his *Historical Account of the Rise and Progress of Shorthand* (1816), still the best history of the subject.

LEWIS, John (1675–1747), author; educated at Exeter College, Oxford; BA, 1697; ordained, 1698; vicar of Minster, Kent, 1709–47; MA, Corpus Christi College, Cambridge, 1712; master of Eastbridge Hospital, Canterbury, 1717; chiefly known by his biographies of *Wycliffe (1720 and 1723), *Caxton (1737), *Pecock (1744), and Bishop *Fisher (first printed 1855); published valuable topographical works dealing mainly with Kent; made important contributions to religious history and bibliography.

LEWIS, John Delaware (1828–1884), miscellaneous writer; born at St Petersburg; educated at Eton and Trinity College, Cambridge; published *Sketches of Cantabs* (1849); MA, 1853; barrister, Lincoln's Inn, 1858; MP, Devonport, 1868–74; wrote miscellaneous works in French and English.

LEWIS, John Frederick (1805–1876), painter of Italian, Spanish, and Oriental subjects; son of Frederick Christian *Lewis (1779–1856); painted and exhibited animal subjects, 1820–32; member of the Water-Colour Society, 1829; visited Spain, 1832–4; painted Spanish subjects until about 1841; travelled in the East, 1839–51; painted oriental subjects, 1850–76, based on sketches made during his travels; RA, 1865.

LEWIS, John Spedan (1885–1963), shopkeeper and industrial reformer; educated at Westminster School; at 19, joined father's business in Oxford Street shop, London; took charge of Peter Jones Ltd., acquired by his father, and began experiment of distributing preference shares to employees, 1916–20; became sole partner in John Lewis business, 1928; organized

business on partnership lines for benefit of employees; formed public company, John Lewis Partnership, 1929; completed settlement of business held by trustees on behalf of employees, 1950; retired as chairman, 1955; president, Classical Association, 1956–7; published *Partnership for All* (1948) and *Fairer Shares* (1954).

LEWIS, John Travers (1825–1901), archbishop of Ontario; BA, Trinity College, Dublin, 1848; ordained, 1848; settled in Canada, 1849; first bishop of Ontario, 1861; metropolitan of Canada, 1893, and archbishop of Ontario, 1894; his advocacy (1864) of national council for whole Anglican Church led to first Lambeth Conference, 1867; hon. DD, Oxford, 1897; hon. LL D, Dublin.

LEWIS, Joyce (or Jocasta) (d. 1557), martyr; daughter of Thomas Curzon of Croxall, Staffordshire; married, first, Sir George Appleby, and, secondly, Thomas Lewis; became a Protestant, was imprisoned, 1556, and burned.

LEWIS, Leopold David (1828–1890), dramatist; dramatized *The Bells* from Erckmann-Chatrian's *Le Juif Polonais*, produced 1871; author of *The Wandering Jew* (1873), *Give a Dog a bad Name* (1876), and *The Foundlings* (1881); conducted *The Mask* (1868), and published *A Peal of Merry Bells* (tales, 1880).

LEWIS, Lady Maria Theresa (1803–1865), biographer; granddaughter of Thomas *Villiers, first earl of Clarendon, and sister of George William Frederick *Villiers, fourth earl of Clarendon; married, first, Thomas Henry *Lister, 1830, and, secondly, Sir George Cornewall *Lewis, 1844; published *The Lives of the Friends and Contemporaries of Lord Chancellor Clarendon* (1852); edited *Extracts of the Journals of Miss Berry* (1865).

LEWIS, Mark (fl. 1678), financial and miscellaneous writer; invented a new method of teaching (patented), and published works expounding it between 1670? and 1675?; proposed quack schemes of financial reforms in pamphlets, issued 1676–8.

LEWIS, Matthew Gregory (1775–1818), author of *The Monk*; of Westminster and Christ Church, Oxford; attaché to the British embassy at The Hague, 1794; published *The Monk* (1796), and immediately became famous; MP, Hindon, 1796–1802; brought out the *Castle Spectre* at Drury Lane, 1798; made Walter *Scott's acquaintance (1798), and procured the publication of his translation of *Goetz von Berlichingen* (1799); visited his West Indian property in order to arrange for the proper treatment of the slaves, 1815–16 and 1817–18; died at sea on his way home. His writings are memorable on account of their influence on Scott's early poetical efforts; some of his numerous dramas and tales were translated from the German. His *Journal of a West Indian Proprietor* (1834) is interesting as showing the condition of the negroes in Jamaica at the time.

LEWIS, Owen (also known as **OWEN, Lewis**) (1532–1594), bishop of Cassano; of Winchester and New College, Oxford; BCL, 1559; went to Douai University, 1561; appointed regius professor of law at Douai; canon of Cambrai Cathedral and archdeacon of Hainault; bishop of Cassano, 1588; died at Rome.

LEWIS, Percy Wyndham (1882–1957), writer and artist; son of American father and British mother; educated at Rugby and Slade School; lived mainly in Brittany and Paris, 1901–9; moving to London exhibited with Camden Town and London groups; director, Rebel Art Centre, 1914; published Vorticist review *Blast* (June 1914, July 1915); organized Vorticist exhibition, 1915; served in France as gunner and war artist, 1917–18; edited two issues of *Tyro*, 1921–2, and three of *Enemy*, 1927–9; his enthusiasm for Hitler, subsequently recanted, aroused hostility; his portrait of T. S. *Eliot rejected by Royal Academy, 1938; in United States and Canada, 1939–45; art critic to *Listener*, 1946–51; awarded civil list pension, 1951; hon. Litt.D., Leeds, 1952; *Childermass* presented by BBC, 1951; Tate Gallery exhibition, 'Wyndham Lewis and Vorticism', 1956; became totally blind, 1954; publications include autobiographical and critical works, and among his novels are *Tarr* (1918) and *Self Condemned* (1954); moved from abstract to representational art, notably portraits; a towering, undisciplined, and quarrelsome egotist, his greatest enemy was himself.

LEWIS, Richard (1821–1905), bishop of Llandaff; BA, Worcester College, Oxford, 1843; DD, 1883; travelled in Europe and Near East, 1843–4; ordained, 1844; rector of Lampeter Velfry, 1851–83; archdeacon of St David's, 1875–83; bishop of Llandaff, 1883–1905; inaugurated bishop of Llandaff's church extension fund, for erection of new churches and support of additional curates, thus greatly extending work of diocese; established annual diocesan conference, 1884; a broad and tolerant churchman, but uncompromising on question of church schools; took seat in House of Lords, 1885; unsympathetic with modern Welsh nationalism.

LEWIS, Rosa (1867–1952), hotel owner; went into service at 12; in kitchens of Comte de Paris and Duc d'Orleans learned French cooking and the tastes of King Edward VII; cooked privately for fashionable hostesses; acquired Cavendish Hotel, 1902, and ran it with elegant distinction on Robin Hood tactics until her death.

LEWIS, Samuel, the younger (d. 1862), topographer; son of Samuel *Lewis the elder; author of *Islington as it was and as it is* (1854) and other works.

LEWIS, Samuel, the elder (d. 1865), publisher; his best-known publications, topographical dictionaries and atlases, edited by Joseph *Haydn, 1831–42.

LEWIS, Samuel Savage (1836–1891), librarian of Corpus Christi College, Cambridge; grandson of George *Lewis; educated at the City of London School and St John's College, Cambridge; studied farming in Canada, 1857–60; migrated to Corpus Christi College, Cambridge, 1865, and fellow, 1869; librarian of Corpus Christi College, 1870–91; MA, 1872; FSA, 1872; ordained, 1872; a diligent antiquary; bequeathed his collections of coins, gems, and vases to his college.

LEWIS, Stuart (1756?–1818), Scottish poet; roamed over Scotland as 'the mendicant bard'; produced his poem, *Fair Helen of Kirkconnell* (1796), with an interesting preface on the history of the ballad on the same theme; 'O'er the Muir' the most noteworthy of his lyrics.

LEWIS, Thomas (1689–1749?), controversialist; of Corpus Christi College, Oxford; BA, 1711; ordained, 1713; forced to hide on account of the libellous nature of his periodical publication, *The Scourge, in Vindication of the Church of England*, 1717; continued to issue controversial writings, 1719–35.

LEWIS, Sir Thomas (1881–1945), physician; B.Sc., University College, Cardiff, 1902; MB, BS, University College Hospital, London, 1905; lecturer in cardiac pathology, 1911; assistant physician, 1913; full physician, 1919–45; founded journal *Heart*, 1909; changed scope and title to *Clinical Science*, 1933; remained editor until 1944; changed name of department to that of clinical research and founded Medical Research Society, 1930; transferred control of journal to Society, 1939; investigations included the pulse and respiration, irregularities of heart's action, especially auricular flutter and fibrillation, origin and course of excitation wave, 'soldier's heart' or 'effort syndrome' (for Medical Research Committee), vascular reactions of skin, and pain; FRS, 1918; knighted, 1921.

LEWIS, Sir Thomas Frankland, first baronet (1780–1855), politician; grandson of Sir Thomas *Frankland; of Eton and Christ Church, Oxford; lieutenant-colonel of the Radnorshire Militia, 1806–15; MP, Beaumaris, 1812–26,

Ennis, 1826–8, Radnorshire, 1828–34, Radnor boroughs, 1847–55; member of commission to inquire into Irish revenue, 1821, of commission to inquire into revenue of Great Britain and Ireland, 1822, and of commission on Irish education, 1825–8; joint secretary to the Treasury, 1827; vice-president of the Board of Trade and privy councillor, 1828; treasurer of the navy, 1830; chairman of the Poor-Law Commission, 1834–9; created baronet, 1846.

LEWIS, Thomas Taylor (1801–1858), geologist and antiquary; MA, St John's College, Cambridge, 1828; investigated the Silurian system; edited for the Camden Society the *Letters of Lady Brilliana Harley* (1853).

LEWIS, Titus (1773–1811), Baptist minister; in charge of Baptist church at Carmarthen; published Welsh theological works, 1802–11.

LEWIS, Sir Wilfrid Hubert Poyer (1881–1950), judge; educated at Eton and University College, Oxford; third class, history, 1903; called to bar (Inner Temple), 1908; bencher, 1929; practised in Cardiff until 1914; served with Glamorgan Yeomanry, 1914–18; joined T. W. H. *Inskip (later Viscount Caldecote) in London; built up large and varied practice; junior (common law) counsel to Treasury, 1930; judge of King's Bench division, 1935–50; inherited and devoted leisure to a Pembrokeshire estate; gave much time to affairs of Welsh Church; knighted, 1935.

LEWIS, William (1592–1667), master of the hospital of St Cross, Winchester, and canon of Winchester; educated at Hart Hall, Oxford; BA and fellow of Oriel, 1608; MA, 1612; chaplain to Lord Chancellor *Bacon; provost of Oriel, 1618–21; in the service of George *Villiers, duke of Buckingham, 1627–8; canon of Winchester, 1627; DD, Oxford, 1627; chaplain to Charles I and master of the hospital of St Cross, 1628; DD, Cambridge, 1629; ejected under the Commonwealth; reinstated, 1660.

LEWIS, William (1714–1772), chemist; MA, Christ Church, Oxford, 1737; MB, 1741; MD, 1745; delivered the oration at opening of Radcliffe Library, 1749; chief works, *The New Dispensatory* (1753) and *Experimental History of the Materia Medica* (1761).

LEWIS, William (1787–1870), writer on chess and chess-player, also a teacher of chess; published elementary works on chess between 1814 and 1835.

LEWIS, William Cudmore McCullagh (1885–1956), physical chemist; educated at Bangor Grammar School, Co. Down, and Royal University of Ireland; first class, experimental science, 1905; researched at Liverpool and Heidelberg; demonstrator, later lecturer, University College, London, 1909–13; professor of physical chemistry, Liverpool, 1913–48; published *A System of Physical Chemistry* (2 vols., 1916); studied theory of chemical change, colloid science, and physico-chemical processes possibly underlying malignancy; FRS, 1926.

LEWIS, William Garrett (1821–1885), Baptist minister; obtained clerkship in Post Office, 1840; became a Baptist, and was chosen minister; secretary of the London Baptist Association, which he helped to found, 1865–9, and president, 1870; editor of the *Baptist Magazine* for twenty years.

LEWIS, William Thomas (1748?–1811), called 'Gentleman' Lewis, actor; great-grandson of Erasmus *Lewis; appeared at Dublin, 1770–2, at Covent Garden, London, 1773–1809; played more characters, original and established, than almost any other English comedian; created, among other parts, Faulkland in *The Rivals*, Doricourt in the *Belle's Stratagem*, and Jeremy Diddler in *Raising the Wind*; deputy-manager of Covent Garden, 1782–1804; lessee of the Liverpool Theatre, 1803–11.

LEWIS, William Thomas, first Baron Merthyr (1837–1914), engineer and coal-owner; controller of marquess of Bute's Welsh estates, 1881; main colliery interests latterly in Rhondda Valley and Senghenydd districts; served on royal commissions dealing with coal industry and labour problems; promoted industrial peace; knighted, 1885; baronet, 1896; baron, 1911.

LEWIS, Sir Willmott Harsant (1877–1950), journalist; educated at Eastbourne, Heidelberg, and the Sorbonne; *New York Herald* correspondent during Boxer Rising and Russo-Japanese War; edited *Manila Times*, 1911–17; worked in American Information Service in France, 1917–19; represented *New York Tribune* at Peace Conference, 1919; London *Times* correspondent, Washington, 1920–48; great social figure; politically well informed, especially until advent of Roosevelt administration; KBE, 1931.

LEWIS GLYN COTHI (fl. 1450–1486), Welsh bard; also sometimes called Lewis y Glyn or Llywelyn Glyn Cothi; took the Lancastrian side in the Wars of the Roses; his poems, about 150 of which were published for the Cymmrodorion Society (1837), valuable as illustrating the part played by the Welsh in the Wars of the Roses.

LEWIS MORGANWG, i.e. of Glamorganshire (fl. 1500–1540), Welsh bard; author of a poem on St Iltutus (see ILLTYD or ILTUTUS), entitled

'Cowydd St Illtyd', printed with an English translation in the Iolo MSS.

LEWIS OF CAERLEON (15th cent.). See CAERLEON, LEWIS OF.

LEWSON, Jane (1700?–1816), commonly called Lady Lewson; eccentric centenarian; her maiden name Vaughan; after the death of her husband (1726) lived in close retirement. Her peculiarities possibly suggested *Dickens's character of Miss Havisham.

LEWYS AP RHYS AP OWAIN (d. 1616?), deputy-herald for Wales and bard. See DWNN, LEWYS.

LEXINGTON, Barons. See SUTTON, ROBERT, first baron, 1594–1668; SUTTON, ROBERT, second baron, 1661–1723.

LEXINTON, Henry de (d. 1258), bishop of Lincoln; brother of John de *Lexinton; dean of Lincoln, 1245; bishop of Lincoln, 1253–8.

LEXINTON (or LESSINGTON), John de (d. 1257), baron, judge, and often described as keeper of the great seal; a clerk in Chancery; had custody of great seal for short periods in 1238, 1242, 1247, 1249, 1253; king's seneschal, 1247; chief justice of the forests north of the Trent, and governor of several northern castles, 1255; put in fetters the Jew Copin, supposed murderer, with his co-religionists, of *Hugh of Lincoln, 1255.

LEXINTON, Oliver de (d. 1299), bishop of Lincoln. See SUTTON.

LEXINTON (or LESSINGTON), Robert de (d. 1250), judge; prebendary of Southwell; senior of the justices, 1234; chief of the itinerant justices for the northern division, 1240.

LEXINTON (or LESSINGTON), Stephen de (fl. 1250), abbot of Clairvaux; studied at Paris and Oxford; prebendary of Southwell, 1214; abbot of Savigny, Normandy, 1229; abbot of Clairvaux, 1243–55; founded house in Paris for scholars of his order, 1244.

LEY, Henry George (1887–1962), organist, pianist, and composer; joined choir of St George's, Windsor, 1896; music scholar, Uppingham, 1903; exhibitioner, Royal College of Music, 1904; organ scholar, Keble College, Oxford, 1906; organist, Christ Church, Oxford, 1909; MA, 1913; D.Mus., 1919; university choragus, 1923–6; precentor, St Peter's College, Radley, 1916–18; organ teacher, Royal College of Music, 1919–41; precentor, Eton College, 1926–45; president, Royal College of Organists, 1933–4; president, Incorporated Association of Organists, 1952–3; FRCM, 1928; hon. FRCO, 1920, and hon. RAM, 1942; hon. fellow, Keble College, Oxford.

LEY, Hugh (1790–1837), physician; MD, Edinburgh, 1813; LRCP, 1818; published *An Essay on Laryngismus Stridulus, or Crouplike Inspiration of Infants*, the first work containing a full pathological description of the malady (1836).

LEY, James, first earl of Marlborough (1550–1629), judge; of Brasenose College, Oxford; BA, 1574; barrister, Lincoln's Inn, 1584; MP, Westbury, 1597–8, 1604–5, 1609–11, and 1621; bencher of Lincoln's Inn, 1600; reader, 1602; serjeant-at-law and knighted, 1603; lord chief justice of King's Bench in Ireland, 1604; commissioner of the great seal at Dublin, 1605; commissioner for the plantation of Ulster, 1608; attorney of the court of wards and liveries in England, 1608; governor of Lincoln's Inn, 1609–22; MP, Bath, 1614; created baronet, 1619; lord chief justice of King's Bench, 1621–4; lord high treasurer and privy councillor, 1624, and created Baron Ley of Ley in Devonshire, 1624; earl of Marlborough, 1626; president of the council, 1628; member of Elizabethan Society of Antiquaries.

LEY, James, third earl of Marlborough (1618–1665), naval captain; grandson of James *Ley, first earl of Marlborough; succeeded to the title, 1638; Royalist commander, 1643; established a colony, which soon failed, at Santa Cruz, West Indies, 1645; commanded the squadron which went to the East Indies to receive Bombay from the Portuguese, 1661; nominated governor of Jamaica, 1664; killed in naval action with Dutch, 1665.

LEY, John (1583–1662), Puritan divine; MA, Christ Church, Oxford, 1608; prebendary of Chester, 1627; took the Solemn League and Covenant, 1643; president of Sion College, 1645; a 'trier', 1653; held various rectories, and wrote religious works.

LEYBOURN, Thomas (1770–1840), mathematician; edited the *Mathematical Repository*, 1799–1835; published *A Synopsis of Data for the Construction of Triangles* (1802); teacher of mathematics at the Military College, Sandhurst, 1802–39.

LEYBOURN, William (1626–1700?), mathematician; teacher of mathematics and professional land surveyor; joint author of the first book on astronomy written in English, *Urania Practica* (1648); published *The Compleat Surveyor* (1653), *Arithmetick, Vulgar, Decimal, and Instrumental* (1657), *The Line of Proportion or [of] Numbers, commonly called Gunter's Line, made easie* (1667), *Cursus Mathematicus* (1690), and *Panarithmologia* (1693), the earliest ready-reckoner known in English.

LEYBOURNE (LEYBURN, LEMBURN, or **LEEBURN), Roger de** (d. 1271), warden of the Cinque Ports; accompanied Henry III to Gascony, 1253; served against *Llywelyn of Wales, 1256; sided with the barons, 1258, and was consequently deprived of all his revenues, *c.*1260; took to marauding; associated himself with Simon de *Montfort, 1263; reconciled to the king, 1264; took the king's side in the Battle of Evesham, 1265.

LEYBOURNE, William de (d. 1309), baron; son of Roger de *Leybourne; served in Wales, 1277; constable of Pevensey, 1282; described as 'admiral of the sea of the king of England', 1297; served in Scotland, 1299–1300 and 1304.

LEYBURN, George (1593–1677), Roman Catholic divine; studied at Douai, 1617–25; missioner in England, 1630; chaplain to Queen *Henrietta Maria; forced to retire to Douai, where he taught philosophy and divinity; DD, Reims; returned to England, but during the Civil War retired to France and rendered services to the Royalist party; president of the English College at Douai, 1652–70; died at Châlon-sur-Saône; author of religious works.

LEYBURN, John (1620–1702), Roman Catholic prelate; nephew of George *Leyburn; educated at the English College, Douai; taught classics there; president, 1670–6; DD; vicar-apostolic of all England, 1685–8, and first vicar-apostolic of the London district, 1688; translated Kenelm *Digby's treatise on the soul into Latin (Paris, 1651).

LEYCESTER, John (*fl.* 1639), miscellaneous writer; BA, Brasenose College, Oxford, 1622; works include *A Manual of the Choicest Adagies* (1623) and two poems, one on the death of Hampden (1641) and another entitled *England's Miraculous Preservation* (1646).

LEYCESTER, Sir Peter, first baronet (1614–1678), antiquary; of Brasenose College, Oxford; entered Gray's Inn, 1632; took Royalist side in the Civil War; rewarded with a baronetcy, 1660; author of *Historical Antiquities in two Books* (1673); contributed to the controversy concerning the legitimacy of Amicia, wife of Ralph Mainwaring, his ancestor.

LEYDEN, John (1775–1811), physician and poet; studied at Edinburgh University, 1790–7; contributed to the *Edinburgh Literary Magazine*; contributed to Lewis's *Tales of Wonder* (1801); assisted *Scott with earlier volumes of the *Border Minstrelsy*, 1802; published *Scottish Descriptive Poems* (1802); MD, St Andrews; assistant-surgeon at Madras, 1803–5; settled at Calcutta, 1806; published his essay on the Indo-Persian, Indo-Chinese, and Deccan languages (1807); commissioner of the court of requests, Calcutta, 1809; assay-master of the Mint, Calcutta, 1810;

accompanied Lord *Minto to Java, 1811; translated into English the *Sejarah Malayu* ('Malay Annals', published 1821), and *Commentaries of Baber* (published 1826); died at Cornelis, Java.

LEYEL, Hilda Winifred Ivy (Mrs C. F. Leyel) (1880–1957), herbalist; born Wauton; married C. F. Leyel, 1900; studied Nicholas *Culpeper and other herbalists; published *The Magic of Herbs* (1926) and many other similar works; opened Culpeper House (Baker Street, 1927) and others elsewhere; founded Society of Herbalists.

LEYLAND, Joseph Bentley (1811–1851), sculptor; his most important works a statue of Dr Beckwith of York, in York Minster, and a group of African bloodhounds.

LEYSON, Thomas (1549–1608?), poet and physician; of Winchester and New College, Oxford; fellow, 1569–86; MA, 1576; MB and proctor, 1583; practised physic at Bath; wrote Latin verses.

LHUYD. See also LLOYD, LLWYD, and LOYD.

LHUYD, Edward (1660–1709), Celtic scholar and naturalist; entered Jesus College, Oxford, 1682; keeper of the Ashmolean Museum, 1690–1709; published catalogue of the figured fossils in the Ashmolean (1699); MA, 1701; volume i of his *Archaeologia Britannica* published (1707); FRS, 1708; superior beadle of divinity in Oxford University, 1709.

LIAFWINE, Saint (*fl.* 755). See LEBWIN.

LIAQAT ALIKHAN (1895–1951), first prime minister of Pakistan; born in East Punjab; educated at Muhammad Anglo-Oriental College and Exeter College, Oxford; honours in jurisprudence, 1921; called to bar (Inner Temple), 1922; member, United Provinces Legislative Council, 1926; deputy president, 1931; general-secretary, All-India Muslim League and member, Parliamentary Board, 1936; became loyal associate of M. A. *Jinnah; member, Central Legislative Assembly, and deputy leader, Muslim League party, 1940; finance minister, 1946; prime minister, Pakistan, 1947–51; assassinated.

LIARDET, Francis (1798–1863), captain in the navy; entered navy, 1809; served on the coast of Africa and on the North American Station, 1810–14; lieutenant, 1824; on the South American Station, 1833–8; commander and serving in the Mediterranean, 1838–40; obtained post-rank, 1840; New Zealand Company's agent at Taranaki, 1841–2; published *Professional Recollections on Points of Seamanship, Discipline*, etc. (1849) and *The Midshipman's Companion* (1851); one of the captains of Greenwich Hospital, 1856; published *Friendly Hints to the Young Naval Lieutenant* (1858).

LIART, Matthew (1736–1782?), engraver; apprenticed to Simon François *Ravenet; published engravings after Benjamin *West, PRA.

LIBBERTOUN, Lord (d. 1650), Scottish judge. See WINRAM, GEORGE.

LIBERTY, Sir Arthur Lasenby (1843–1917), fabric manufacturer; opened business in Regent Street, London (afterwards Liberty & Co.), 1875; dealt in oriental fabrics and produced British machine-made stuffs which equalled handmade products of Asia; friend of Pre-Raphaelite painters; knighted, 1913.

LICHFIELD. See also LITCHFIELD.

LICHFIELD, earls of. See STUART, BERNARD, titular earl, 1623?–1645; LEE, GEORGE HENRY, third earl of the Lee family, 1718–1772.

LICHFIELD, Leonard (1604–1657), printer and author; printer to the University of Oxford; printed public papers for Charles I, 1642–6.

LICHFIELD, Leonard (d. 1686), printer; son of Leonard *Lichfield (1604–1657); printed at Oxford *The Oxford Gazette*, a folio half-sheet, containing the government's official notices, the earliest English periodical of the kind (1665–6), which was continued in London as *The London Gazette*.

LICHFIELD, William (d. 1447), divine and poet; BA, 1404, and DD, Peterhouse, Cambridge; rector of All Hallows the Great, London; a famous preacher; left 3,083 sermons written in English with his own hand.

LIDDEL, Duncan (1561–1613), mathematician and physician; educated at Aberdeen; studied mathematics and physic at Frankfurt-on-Oder; professor of mathematics at Helmstadt, 1591–1603; MD, Helmstadt, 1596, and dean of the faculty of philosophy, 1599; prorector, 1604; returned to Scotland, 1607; endowed a professorship of mathematics in the Marischal College, Aberdeen, 1613; published medical works.

LIDDELL, Edward George Tandy (1895–1981), physiologist; educated at Harrow and Trinity College, Oxford; first class, physiology, 1918; qualified BM, B.Ch. (Oxon.), at St Thomas's Hospital, London, 1921; lecturer and research fellow, Trinity College, Oxford, and assistant to (Sir) Charles *Sherrington, 1921–40; part-author with Sherrington and others of *Reflex Activity of the Spinal Cord* (1932); FRS, 1939; Waynflete professor of physiology, 1940–60; published *The Discovery of Reflexes* (1960); member of council of Royal Society; chairman, Oxford Eye Hospital.

LIDDELL, Henry George (1811–1898), dean of Christ Church, Oxford; of Charterhouse and

Christ Church, Oxford; MA, 1835; DD, 1855; tutor, 1836, and censor, 1845, of Christ Church, Oxford; White's professor of moral philosophy, 1845; domestic chaplain to Prince *Albert, 1846; headmaster of Westminster School, 1846–55; published (1843), with Robert *Scott (1811–1887), *Greek–English Lexicon*, which he revised alone for 7th edition (1883); member of first Oxford University Commission, 1852; dean of Christ Church, 1855–91; took prominent part in administrative reforms at Christ Church; vice-chancellor, 1870–4; hon. LL D, Edinburgh, 1884; hon. DCL, Oxford, 1893; his publications include *A History of Ancient Rome* (1855).

LIDDELL, Henry Thomas, first earl of Ravensworth (1797–1878); educated at Eton and St John's College, Cambridge; MP, North-umberland, 1826, North Durham, 1837–47, Liverpool, 1853–5; succeeded his father as second Baron Ravensworth (of a second creation), 1855; created earl of Ravensworth and Baron Eslington, 1874; published original poems, and translations from Horace and Virgil.

LIDDELL, Sir John (1794–1868), director-general of the medical department of the Royal Navy, 1854–64; MD, Edinburgh; entered the navy as assistant-surgeon, 1812; LRCS, 1821; director of the hospital at Malta, 1831; inspector of fleets and hospitals, 1844; FRS, 1846; deputy inspector-general of Haslar Hospital; inspector-general of Royal Hospital, Greenwich; knighted, 1848; honorary physician to Queen Victoria, 1859; KCB, 1864.

LIDDELL HART, Sir Basil Henry (1895–1970), military historian and strategist. See HART.

LIDDERDALE, William (1832–1902), governor of the Bank of England; born at St Petersburg; son of a Russian merchant; director (1870), deputy governor (1887), and governor (1889) of Bank of England; concerned in reduction of interest on national debt by G. J. (later Viscount) *Goschen, 1888; by his firm action liquidated Messrs Baring's affairs and increased the City's confidence in the Bank, 1890; PC, 1891; concluded negotiations with government which took shape in Bank Act of 1892.

LIDDESDALE, knight of (1300?–1353). See DOUGLAS, Sir WILLIAM.

LIDDIARD, William (1773–1841), miscellaneous writer; entered University College, Oxford, 1792; in the army, 1794–6; BA, Trinity College, Dublin, 1803; author of poems and a book of travels.

LIDDON, Henry Parry (1829–1890), canon of St Paul's Cathedral, London, and preacher; of

King's College School, London, and Christ Church, Oxford; BA, 1850; ordained, 1853; joined *Pusey and *Keble; vice-principal of Bishop *Wilberforce's Theological College, Cuddesdon, 1854–9; vice-principal of St Edmund Hall, Oxford, 1859; on the Hebdomadal Board three times between 1864 and 1875; Bampton lecturer, 1866; BD, DD, and hon. DCL, 1870; Ireland professor of exegesis, 1870–82; canon of St Paul's Cathedral, 1870; chancellor of St Paul's Cathedral, 1886; his sermons at St Paul's for twenty years a central fact of London life; most of his sermons published; left ready for publication three volumes of a 'Life of Pusey'.

LIDELL, (Tord) Alvar (Quan) (1908–1981), BBC broadcaster; son of Swedish parents; educated at King's College School, Wimbledon, and Exeter College, Oxford; joined BBC as chief announcer at Birmingham, 1935; deputy chief announcer in London, 1936; read announcement of King Edward VIII's abdication, 1936, and ultimatum to Germany, 1939; served in RAF Intelligence, 1943; returned to work at BBC, 1944; appointed chief announcer on new Third Programme, 1946; returned to news-reading, 1952; MBE, 1964; retired, 1969; published influential article in the *Listener* on deteriorating standards of speech, 1979; in demand as narrator for works such as *Façade* by (Sir) William *Walton and (Dame) Edith *Sitwell; dedicated reader of 'Books for the Blind'; baritone singer of distinction.

LIDGETT, John Scott (1854–1953), theologian and educationist; educated at Blackheath Proprietary School and University College, London; MA, logic and philosophy, 1875; entered Wesleyan Methodist ministry, 1876; founder, 1891, and warden, 1891–1949, Bermondsey Settlement providing social and educational amenities; member, LCC Education Committee, 1905–28; leader of Progressive party, 1918–28; member, London University Senate, 1922–46; vice-chancellor, 1930–2; president, National Council of Evangelical Free Churches, 1906; of Wesleyan Methodist Conference, 1908; of United Church, 1932; moderator, Free Church General Council, 1923–5; founder member, British Council of Churches, 1942; sought unity of English Christendom; editor, *Methodist Times*, 1907–18; joint editor, *Contemporary Review*, 1911–53; publications include *The Spiritual Principle of the Atonement* (1897), *The Fatherhood of God* (1902), *The Christian Religion, its Meaning and Proof* (1907), and *God in Christ Jesus* (1915); CH, 1933; honorary degrees from Aberdeen, Oxford, and London.

LIFARD, Gilbert of, Saint (d. 1305), bishop of Chichester. See GILBERT.

LIFFORD, first Viscount (1709–1789), lord chancellor of Ireland. See HEWITT, JAMES.

LIGHT, Edward (1747–1832), professor of music and inventor of musical instruments; organist of St George's, Hanover Square, 1794; invented the harp-guitar and the lute-harp, 1798, and the harp-lyre, lute-harp, and dital-harp, 1816; published *A First Book on Music* (1794), *Lessons and Songs for the Guitar* (1795 and 1800), and instructions for lute-playing (1800 and 1817).

LIGHT, William (1784–1838), colonel; surveyor-general of South Australia and founder of the city of Adelaide; lieutenant, 1809; served in the Peninsula; captain, 1821; employed in navy of Mehmet Ali, pasha of Egypt; surveyor-general of South Australia, 1836; selected site for city of Adelaide, 1836; died at Port Adelaide; author of *A Trigonometrical Survey of Adelaide*.

LIGHTFOOT, Hannah (fl. 1768), the beautiful Quakeress; said by scandal to have been secretly married to George, prince of Wales, afterwards George III.

LIGHTFOOT, John (1602–1675), biblical critic; entered Christ's College, Cambridge, 1617; took holy orders and held various cures; his first work, *Erubhim, or Miscellanies, Christian and Judaical* (1629); master of Catharine Hall, Cambridge, 1650; DD, 1652; vice-chancellor of his university, 1654; prebendary of Ely, 1668; aided in *Walton's Polyglot Bible, 1657; the first collected edition of his works published (1684).

LIGHTFOOT, John (1735–1788), naturalist; MA, Pembroke College, Oxford, 1766; in holy orders, holding several cures; published the *Flora Scotica* (1778); FRS, 1781; member of the Linnean Society.

LIGHTFOOT, Joseph Barber (1828–1889), bishop of Durham, divine and scholar; educated at King Edward's School, Birmingham, and Trinity College, Cambridge; BA, 1851; fellow of Trinity College, 1852–79; edited *Journal of Classical and Sacred Philology*, 1854–9; ordained, 1858; member of the 'council of senate', 1860; Hulsean professor of divinity, 1861; chaplain to Queen Victoria, 1862; member of the New Testament Company of Revisers, 1870–80; Lady Margaret professor of divinity, 1875; bishop of Durham, 1879–89; published many valuable works on biblical criticism and early post-biblical Christian history and literature.

LIGHTWOOD, John Mason (1852–1947), conveyancing counsel and legal writer; educated at Kingswood School, Bath, and Trinity Hall,

Cambridge; bracketed eighth wrangler and fellow, 1874; called to bar (Lincoln's Inn), 1879; practised as conveyancer and draftsman; conveyancing counsel to the Court, 1932–47; wrote copiously on property law for legal journals; legal editor, *Law Journal*, 1925–39; publications include *Possession of Land* (1894).

LIGONIER, Edward, first Earl Ligonier in the peerage of Ireland (d. 1782), lieutenant-general; son of Francis *Ligonier; entered the army, 1748; present at Minden, 1759; succeeded his uncle, Earl Ligonier (see LIGONIER, JOHN), in the Irish viscountcy, 1770; created Earl Ligonier, 1776; lieutenant-general, 1777; KB, 1781.

LIGONIER, Francis (otherwise **François Auguste)** (d. 1746), colonel in the British Army; brother of John *Ligonier, first Earl Ligonier; entered the army, 1720; present at Dettingen, 1743; colonel, 1745.

LIGONIER, John (otherwise **Jean Louis),** first Earl Ligonier (1680–1770), field marshal in the British Army; born at Castres, France; educated in France and Switzerland; came to Dublin, 1697; fought under *Marlborough at Blenheim, 1704, Ramillies, 1706, Oudenarde, 1708, Malplaquet, 1709; governor of Fort St Philip, Minorca, 1712; adjutant-general of the Vigo expedition, 1718; colonel of the Black Horse (now 7th Dragoons), 1720–49; major-general and governor of Kinsale, 1739; present at Dettingen, 1743; KB and lieutenant-general, 1743; commanded the British Foot at Fontenoy, 1745; commander-in-chief in the Austrian Netherlands, 1746–7; MP, Bath, 1748; governor of Jersey, 1750, of Plymouth, 1752; commander-in-chief and created Viscount Ligonier of Enniskillen, Co. Fermanagh, 1757; master-general of the ordnance, 1759–62; his title altered to Viscount Ligonier of Clonmell, 1762; created Baron Ligonier in peerage of Great Britain, 1763; created Earl Ligonier of Ripley, Surrey, 1766; field marshal, 1766.

LILBURNE, John (1614?–1657), political agitator; accused before the Star Chamber of printing and circulating unlicensed books, 1637; imprisoned, 1638–40; fought for parliament, 1642–5; left the service, because he would not take the Covenant, 1645; expressed his distrust of the army leaders in pamphlets, 1648–9; sent to the Tower, tried, and acquitted, 1649; advocated release of trade from the restrictions of chartered companies and monopolists, 1650; exiled for supporting his uncle, George Lilburne, in his quarrel with Sir Arthur *Hesilrige, 1652–3; allowed to return to England, but on refusing to promise compliance with the government was

confined in Jersey and Guernsey, and at Dover Castle till 1655; joined the Quakers.

LILBURNE, Robert (1613–1665), regicide; brother of John *Lilburne; entered the Parliamentary Army; signed Charles I's death-warrant, 1649; served in *Cromwell's Scottish campaigns, 1651–2; MP for the East Riding of Yorkshire, 1656; acted with *Lambert, 1659; condemned to lifelong imprisonment, 1660.

LILFORD, fourth Baron (1833–1896), ornithologist. See POWYS, THOMAS LITTLETON.

LILLICRAP, Sir **Charles Swift** (1887–1966), naval constructor; educated at Stoke School, Devonport, Royal Naval Engineering College, Keyham, and Royal Naval College, Greenwich; first-class professional certificate, 1910; joined Royal Corps of Naval Constructors, 1910; appointed to Naval Construction Department, Admiralty, 1914; constructor, responsible for cruiser design, 1917; lecturer in naval architecture, Royal Naval College, 1921; made special survey of welding, 1930; assistant director, naval construction, 1936; director, 1944–51; MBE, 1918; CB, 1944; KCB, 1947; officer of the Légion d'Honneur; president, Institute of Welding, 1956–8; vice-president, Royal Institution of Naval Architects, 1945; fellow, Imperial College of Science and Technology, 1964; hon. D.Sc. (Eng.), Bristol, 1951; president, Johnson Society, 1955–6.

LILLINGSTON, Luke (1653–1713), brigadier-general; served in Ireland under William III; in the Martinique expedition, 1693; in Jamaica, 1695; brigadier-general, 1704; ordered to Antigua, 1707, whither his regiment had been sent in 1706; deprived of command for unreadiness, 1708.

LILLO, George (1693–1739), dramatist; his famous tragedy, *The London Merchant, or the History of George Barnwell*, first acted, 1731; his *Christian Hero* acted, 1735; his *Fatal Curiosity* produced, 1736, and *Elmerick, or Justice Triumphant* after his death, 1740; helped to popularize the 'domestic drama' in England.

LILLY. See also LILY and LYLY.

LILLY, Christian (d. 1738), military engineer; commenced his military career in service of the dukes of Zelle and Hanover, 1685; entered service of William III, 1688; engineer of the Office of Ordnance, 1692; employed in the West Indies as engineer, 1693 and 1694–5; chief engineer at Jamaica, 1696; third engineer of England, 1701–15; chief engineer in West Indies, 1704–38.

LILLY, Edmond (d. 1716), portrait painter; executed indifferent portraits of enormous dimensions; his best-known work a portrait of Queen Anne, 1703.

LILLY, Henry (d. 1638), Rouge-dragon pursuivant; educated at Christ's Hospital; Rouge-rose pursuivant, 1634; Rouge-dragon pursuivant, 1638; left in manuscript 'Pedigrees of Nobility' and 'The Genealogie of the Princelie Familie of the Howards'.

LILLY, John (1554?–1606), dramatist and author of *Euphues*. See LYLY.

LILLY, William (1602–1681), astrologer; wrote a treatise on *The Eclipse of the Sun in the eleventh Degree of Gemini, 22 May 1639* (1639); published his first almanac, *Merlinus Anglicus Junior, the English Merlin revived* (1644), and henceforth prepared one every year till his death; began to issue pamphlets of prophecy, 1644; published *Christian Astrology modestly treated in three Books*, long an authority in astrological literature (1647); while ostensibly serving parliament endeavoured to aid Charles I, 1647–8; claimed scientific value for his *Annus Tenebrosus, or the dark Year, together with a short Method how to judge the Effects of Eclipses* (1652); studied medicine; granted a licence to practise, 1670. His published writings consist mainly of astrological predictions and vindications of their correctness; his chief non-professional work is his *True History of King James I and King Charles I* (1651).

LILLYWHITE, Frederick William (1792–1854), cricketer; a bricklayer by trade; in middle life took a foremost place among professional cricketers; played his first match at Lord's, 1827; known as the 'Nonpareil Bowler'; bowler for the MCC, 1844–54.

LILY, George (d. 1559), Roman Catholic divine; son of William *Lily; educated at Magdalen College, Oxford; domestic chaplain to Cardinal *Pole; canon of Canterbury, 1558; author of some Latin historical works.

LILY (or LILLY), Peter (d. 1615), archdeacon of Taunton; grandson of William *Lily; educated at Jesus College, Cambridge; fellow; MA and DD; prebendary of St Paul's, 1599; archdeacon of Taunton, 1613; *Conciones Duae* and *Two Sermons* published (1619).

LILY, William (1468?–1522), grammarian; entered Magdalen College, Oxford, 1486; graduated; made a pilgrimage to Jerusalem; studied Greek and Latin and classical antiquities in Italy; engaged in teaching in London; high master of St Paul's School, London, 1512–22; contributed a short Latin syntax, with the rules in English, under the title of *Grammatices Rudimenta*, to Colet's *Aeditio* (first printed 1527).

LIMERICK, countess of (1897–1981), leader of the British and International Red Cross movements. See PERY, ANGELA OLIVIA.

LIMERICK, first earl of the second creation (1758–1845). See PERY, EDMUND HENRY.

LIMPUS, Richard (1824–1875), founder of the College of Organists, 1864; secretary, 1864–75; composed sacred and secular music.

LINACRE, Thomas (1460?–1524), physician and classical scholar; educated at Oxford; fellow of All Souls College, Oxford, 1484; went to Italy, c.1485–6; MD, Padua, 1496; returned to England about 1496; one of Henry VIII's physicians, 1509; lectured at Oxford, 1510; received many ecclesiastical preferments, 1509–20; mainly instrumental in founding College of Physicians, 1518; Latin tutor to the princess Mary, 1523, for whom he composed a Latin grammar, *Rudimenta Grammatices*; founded lectureships in medicine at Oxford and Cambridge; wrote grammatical and medical works, and translated from the Greek, especially from Galen.

LINCHE (or LYNCHE), Richard (*fl.* 1596–1601), poet; author of *The Fountaine of English Fiction* (1599) and *An Historical Treatise of the Travels of Noah into Europe* (1601), both so-called translations from the Italian; supposed to be the 'R.L. gentleman' who published (1596) a volume of sonnets entitled *Diella*.

LINCOLN, earls of. See ROUMARE, WILLIAM DE, *fl.* 1140; LACY, JOHN DE, first earl of the Lacy family, d. 1240; LACY, HENRY DE, third earl, 1251–1311; THOMAS, 1277?–1322; POLE, JOHN DE LA, 1464?–1487; CLINTON, EDWARD FIENNES DE, first earl of the Clinton family, 1512–1585; CLINTON, HENRY FIENNES, ninth earl, 1720–1794.

LINCOLN, Hugh of, Saint (1246?–1255). See HUGH.

LINCOLNSHIRE, marquess of (1843–1928), politician. See WYNN-CARRINGTON, CHARLES ROBERT.

LIND, James (1716–1794), physician; surgeon in the navy; served at Minorca (1739) and in the West Indies, Mediterranean, and Channel; MD, Edinburgh, 1748; fellow of the College of Physicians of Edinburgh, 1750; physician to the Naval Hospital, Haslar, 1758–94; published *An Essay on Diseases incidental to Europeans in Hot Climates* (1768) and other medical works; discovered lemon-juice to be a specific for scurvy at sea.

LIND, James (1736–1812), physician; MD, Edinburgh, 1768; fellow of the Edinburgh College of Physicians, 1770; made a voyage to Iceland, 1772; FRS, 1777; settled at Windsor and became physician in the royal household; interested in astronomy and science; had a private press at which he printed mysterious little books, and (1795) Sir Robert *Douglas's *Genealogy of the Families of Lind and the Montgomeries of Smithson.*

LIND (afterwards **LIND-GOLDSCHMIDT), Johanna Maria ('Jenny')** (1820–1887), vocalist, known as Madame Jenny Lind-Goldschmidt; born at Stockholm; began to study singing at the Royal Theatre, Stockholm, 1830; first appearance at the theatre, 1838; appointed court singer, 1840; studied in Paris under Garcia; visited professionally Finland and Copenhagen, 1843, Dresden and Berlin, and other German cities, 1844–5, and Vienna, 1846–7; first appeared in London, 1847; retired from the operatic stage, but continued to sing at concerts, 1849; made tours in America, 1850–2; married Otto Goldschmidt of Hamburg, 1852, and lived at Dresden, 1852–5; made tours in Germany, Austria, and Holland, 1854–5, in Great Britain, 1855–6; became a naturalized British subject, 1859; made her last appearance in public, 1883; professor of singing at the Royal College of Music, 1883–6.

LIND, John (1737–1781), political writer; MA, Balliol College, Oxford, 1761; went to Warsaw and became tutor to Prince Stanislaus Poniatowski; appointed governor of an institution for educating 400 cadets; FSA; returned to England, 1773; published his *Letters concerning the Present State of Poland* (1773); FRS, 1773; barrister, Lincoln's Inn, 1776; wrote also on the American War.

LINDEMANN, Frederick Alexander, Viscount Cherwell (1886–1957), scientist and politician; born in Baden Baden of naturalized British father of French Alsatian Catholic origin and American mother; educated at Blair Lodge, Polmont, and Darmstadt Hochschule; Ph.D., Physikalisch-Chemisches Institut, Berlin, 1910; worked on low-temperature physics; contributed to theory of solids; devised a fibre electrometer; also became excellent pianist and tennis player; at Royal Aircraft Factory, Farnborough, 1915–19; learned to fly and solved problem of 'spin'; Dr Lee's professor of experimental philosophy, Oxford, and fellow of Wadham, 1919–56; obtained new Clarendon Laboratory and made it a leading physics department; elected student of Christ Church, 1921, where he lived from 1922; became close friend of Churchill who obtained his membership of Tizard Committee on Air Defence, 1935–6; his unorthodox methods of obtaining his objectives caused committee's break up; personal assistant to Churchill and head of his statistics section, 1940–5; provided useful checks on departmental statistics; advised Churchill on many subjects, producing some

2,000 minutes for him; introduced 'bending' of wireless beams used by German night bombers; encouraged research into microwave radar; over-estimated effectiveness of massive area bombing; sceptical of existence of German rocket bombs; nevertheless made immense contribution to war effort, combining scientific expertise with clarity and brilliance of mind; paymaster-general, 1942–5 and 1951–3; a vegetarian, teetotaller, and non-smoker, his background was wealthy, his contacts aristocratic, and his views extreme right-wing; aggressive in the cause of science and unable to suffer fools, he aroused friction but could be an amusing if cynical controversialist; FRS, 1920; baron, 1941; PC, 1943; CH, 1953; viscount, 1956.

LINDESAY, Thomas (1656–1724), archbishop of Armagh; of Wadham College, Oxford; MA, 1678; fellow, 1679; DD, 1693; dean of St Patrick's, Dublin, 1693; bishop of Killaloe, 1693–1713, and of Raphoe, 1713–14; archbishop of Armagh, 1714.

LINDEWOOD, William (1375?–1446), civilian, canonist, and bishop of St David's. See LYNDWOOD.

LINDLEY, Sir Francis Oswald (1872–1950), diplomat; son of Lord *Lindley; educated at Winchester and Magdalen College, Oxford; third class, jurisprudence, 1893; entered Diplomatic Service, 1896; counsellor of embassy, Petrograd, 1915–18; consul-general for Russia, 1918–19; high commissioner, Vienna, 1919–20, minister, 1920–1; Athens, 1921–2; Oslo, 1923–9; ambassador, Lisbon, 1929–31, Tokyo, 1931–4; KCMG, 1926; PC, 1929; GCMG, 1931.

LINDLEY, John (1799–1865), botanist and horticulturist; published his first book, a translation of Richard's *Analyse du Fruit* (1819); assistant librarian to Sir Joseph *Banks; published *Rosarum Monographia* (1820); FLS and FGS, 1820; assistant secretary to the Horticultural Society, 1822–41; FRS, 1828; professor of botany in the University of London, 1828–60; lecturer on botany to the Apothecaries' Company, 1836–53; vice-secretary, 1841–58; hon. secretary and member of the council, 1858–62; helped to found the *Gardeners' Chronicle*, 1841. His chief work was *The Vegetable Kingdom* (1846).

LINDLEY, Nathaniel, Baron Lindley (1828–1921), lord of appeal; son of John *Lindley, FRS; educated at University College School, London; called to bar (Middle Temple), 1850; published *A Treatise on the Law of Partnership . . .*, publicly noticed by judges (1860); career assured by success as junior for Overend, Gurney & Co., in City financial crisis, 1866; reputation enhanced by case of *Knox* v. *Gye* (1871) and action concerning 'Frou-frou'; QC, 1872; judge of common pleas and knighted, 1875; lord justice of appeal, 1881; master of the rolls, 1897; FRS, 1897; lord of appeal in ordinary, 1900–5; life peer, 1900; remarkable for impartiality and versatility.

LINDLEY, Robert (1776–1855), violoncellist; principal violoncello at the opera, 1794–1851; professor of the Royal Academy of Music, 1822; the greatest violoncellist of his time.

LINDLEY, William (1808–1900), civil engineer; engineer-in-chief to Hamburg and Bergedorf Railway, 1838–60; designed Hamburg sewerage and waterworks, and drainage and reclamation of the 'Hammerbrook' district; consulting engineer to city of Frankfurt-on-Main, 1865–79.

LINDON, Patrick (d. 1734), Irish poet; some of his songs, which were very popular while Irish was spoken in the district of the Fews, Co. Armagh, are extant in manuscript.

LINDRUM, Walter Albert (1898–1960), billiards player; born in Western Australia; son and grandson of billiards champions; in a career lasting from 15 to 50 broke all billiards records, including one break of 4,137 (1932), six of 3,000-odd, and twenty-nine of 2,000-odd; twice won World Championship (1933, 1934); made four tours of Britain, 1929–33; active in charitable work; OBE, 1958.

LINDSAY, Alexander, fourth earl of Crawford (d. 1454), surnamed the Tiger Earl, and also Earl Beardie; hereditary sheriff of Aberdeen, 1446; warden of the marches, 1451; engaged in quarrels with other Scottish nobles, 1445–52; received king's pardon, 1453.

LINDSAY, Alexander, first Baron Spynie (d. 1607), fourth son of the tenth earl of *Crawford; brother of David *Lindsay, eleventh earl of Crawford; vice-chamberlain to James VI; created Baron Spynie, 1590; accused of harbouring the earl of *Bothwell, 1592; tried and acquitted; slain 'by a pitiful mistake' in a brawl in his own house.

LINDSAY, Alexander (d. 1639), bishop of Dunkeld; bishopric bestowed on him, 1607; deposed, 1638.

LINDSAY, Alexander, second Baron Spynie (d. 1646), eldest son of Alexander *Lindsay, first Baron Spynie; commander-in-chief in Scotland, 1626–46; served under Gustavus Adolphus, 1628–33; supported Charles I against the Covenanters.

LINDSAY, Alexander, second Baron Balcarres and first earl of Balcarres (1618–1659), eldest son of David Lindsay, first Baron Balcarres, and grandson of John *Lindsay, Lord Menmuir; succeeded his father, 1641; present at Marston Moor, 1644; declared for the king, severing his connection with the Covenanting party, 1648; admitted to parliament, 1649; a commissioner of the Exchequer, 1650; created earl of Balcarres and hereditary governor of Edinburgh Castle, 1651; visited France to advise the king, 1653 and 1654; finally resided at the court of Charles II; died at Breda.

LINDSAY, Alexander, sixth earl of Balcarres (1752–1825), eldest son of James Lindsay, fifth earl of Balcarres, and grandson of Colin *Lindsay, third earl; succeeded to peerage, 1768; studied at Göttingen, 1768–70; captain, 1771; major, 1775; present at Ticonderoga, 1777; compelled to surrender and a prisoner till 1779; lieutenant-colonel, 1782; Scots representative peer, 1784–1825; colonel, 1789; major-general and commander of the forces in Jersey, 1793; governor of Jamaica, 1794–1801; lieutenant-general, 1798; general, 1803; completed the *Memoirs of the Lindsays* begun by his father, and left manuscript 'Anecdotes of a Soldier's Life'.

LINDSAY, Sir **Alexander** (1785–1872), general; colonel-commandant, Royal (late Bengal) Artillery; educated at the Royal Military Academy, Woolwich; received his first Indian commission as first lieutenant, 1804; on active service, 1806–18; captain, 1813; major, 1820; lieutenant-colonel, 1824; colonel and colonel-commandant, 1835; superintendent of telegraphs and agent for the manufacture of gunpowder; served in first Burmese War; major-general, 1838; lieutenant-general, 1851; general, 1859; KCB, 1862.

LINDSAY, of Luffness, Sir **Alexander de** (*fl.* 1283–1309), high chamberlain of Scotland under *Alexander III; wavered in his allegiance, sometimes supporting the English, sometimes the Scottish sovereign.

LINDSAY, Alexander Dunlop, first Baron Lindsay of Birker (1879–1952), educationist; son of T. M. *Lindsay; educated at University of Glasgow, 1899; first class, Lit. Hum., University College, Oxford, 1902; president of Union, 1902; Clark philosophy fellow, Glasgow, 1902–4; Shaw fellow, Edinburgh, 1904–9; fellow and classical tutor, Balliol College, Oxford, 1906–22; deputy controller of labour in France and lieutenant-colonel, 1917–19; CBE; professor, moral philosophy, Glasgow, 1922–4; master of Balliol, 1924–49; welcomed opening of Oxford to wider social classes; his democratic theories were outcome of his Christian beliefs and his moral fervour made him a national figure; adviser on education to Labour party and Trades Union Congress; chairman, committee on work of Protestant colleges in India, 1930; unsuccessfully contested Oxford City on anti-Munich platform, 1938; vice-chancellor, Oxford University, 1935–8; sponsored appeal for funds; piloted schemes for expansion of science departments, including new Clarendon Laboratory and absorption of Nuffield benefactions, including Nuffield College; first principal, University College of North Staffordshire which he had worked to create, 1949–52; publications include *The Essentials of Democracy* (1929) and *Religion, Science and Society in the Modern World* (1943); baron, 1945; hon. fellow, Balliol College; hon. LL D, Glasgow, St Andrews, and Princeton.

LINDSAY, Alexander William Crawford, twenty-fifth earl of Crawford and eighth earl of Balcarres (1812–1880), of Eton and Trinity College, Cambridge; MA, 1833; travelled and collected books; succeeded to the earldoms, 1869; died at Florence; chief works, *Lives of the Lindsays* (1840) and *Sketches of the History of Christian Art* (1847).

LINDSAY, Lady Anne (1750–1825), authoress of 'Auld Robin Gray'. See BARNARD.

LINDSAY, Colin, third earl of Balcarres (1654?–1722), second son of Alexander *Lindsay, second Baron Balcarres and first earl of Balcarres; succeeded his brother in the earldom, 1662; went to sea with the duke of York and distinguished himself at Solebay, 1672; privy councillor, 1680; a commissioner of the Treasury, 1686; was connected with the Montgomery plot for James II's restoration; left the country, 1690; settled at Utrecht; returned to Scotland, 1700; privy councillor, 1705; supported the Union, 1707; published his *Memoirs touching the Revolution in Scotland* (1714), a valuable narrative of proceedings and negotiations of 1688–90; joined Prince Charles Edward, 1715.

LINDSAY, Colin (1819–1892), founder of English Church Union; fourth son of James Lindsay, twenty-fourth earl of Crawford; educated at Trinity College, Cambridge; founder and president of Manchester Church Society, which developed (1860) into English Church Union; president, 1860–7; joined Roman Catholic Church, 1868; published theological writings.

LINDSAY, Sir David, first earl of Crawford (1365?–1407), chiefly celebrated for his successful tournament with Lord Welles at London Bridge, 1390; succeeded as tenth Baron Crawford, 1397; created earl of Crawford, 1398; deputy-chamberlain north of the Forth, 1406.

LINDSAY, David, fifth earl of Crawford and first duke of Montrose (1440?–1495), eldest son of Alexander *Lindsay, fourth earl of Crawford; succeeded to the earldom, 1454; ward of

Sir James *Hamilton of Cadzow, first Baron Hamilton, whose daughter he married, 1459; sheriff of Forfar, 1466; lord high admiral, 1476; master of the household, 1480; lord chamberlain, 1483; joint high justiciary of the north of Scotland, 1488; created duke of Montrose, 1488, the first time such a dignity was conferred on a Scotsman not a member of the royal family; privy councillor, 1490.

LINDSAY (or LYNDSAY), Sir David (1490–1555), Scottish poet and Lyon king of arms; entered the royal service as equerry; usher to Prince James (afterwards *James V), 1512–22; his first poem, *The Dreme*, written 1528, not printed till after his death; Lyon king-of-arms, 1529; circulated *The Complaynt to the King*, 1529, and *The Testament and Complaynt of our Soverane Lordis Papyngo*, 1530; his first embassy as Lyon king to the court of the emperor Charles V, 1531; his principal poem, *Ane Satyre of the Three Estaits*, a drama, produced 1540; his *Register of Arms of the Scottish Nobility and Gentry* (unpublished till 1821), the best source for early Scottish heraldry, completed 1542; printed *Ane Dialog betuix Experience and ane Courteour* (1552) and *The Monarchy* (1554); a satirist of abuses in church and state and the poet of the Scottish Reformation. Repeated editions of the poems were published from 1558 to 1870.

LINDSAY, David, tenth earl of Crawford (d. 1574); succeeded to earldom, 1558; supporter of *Mary Queen of Scots, joining the association for her defence, 1568.

LINDSAY, David (1531?–1613), bishop of Ross; one of the twelve original ministers nominated to the 'chief places in Scotland', 1560; one of the recognized leaders of the kirk; as chaplain of James VI of Scotland accompanied him to Norway to fetch home his bride, 1589; bishop of Ross, 1600; privy councillor, 1600.

LINDSAY, David, eleventh earl of Crawford (1547?–1607), eldest son of David *Lindsay, tenth earl of Crawford; lived abroad, 1579–82; master stabler to the king and provost of Dundee, 1582; converted to Roman Catholicism and associated himself with the schemes of the Romanist nobles; convicted of treason and condemned to confinement, 1589.

LINDSAY, Sir David, of Edzell, Baron Edzell (1551?–1610), eldest son of the ninth earl of Crawford; succeeded to the Edzell estates on death of his father, 1558, the earldom of Crawford passing to David *Lindsay, tenth earl, son of Alexander Lindsay the 'wicked master', son of David Lindsay, eighth earl; educated on the continent with his brother, John *Lindsay, Lord Menmuir, under care of John *Lawson;

knighted, 1581; lord of session as Lord Edzell, 1593; privy councillor, 1598; in seeking to avenge the murder of Sir Walter *Lindsay of Balgavie indirectly occasioned the death of Alexander *Lindsay, first Baron Spynie, 1607.

LINDSAY, David, twelfth earl of Crawford (d. 1621); slew his kinsman, Sir Walter *Lindsay of Balgavie, 1605; ultimately placed under surveillance in Edinburgh Castle.

LINDSAY, David (1566?–1627), Presbyterian divine; possibly son of David *Lindsay (1531?–1613); MA, St Andrews, 1586; published theological works.

LINDSAY, David (d. 1641?), bishop of Edinburgh; graduated at St Andrews, 1593; master of Dundee Grammar School, 1597–1606; member of the High Commission, 1616; supported the 'king's articles' at Perth Assembly, 1618; rewarded with the bishopric of Brechin, 1619; crowned Charles I at Holyrood, 1633; bishop of Edinburgh and one of the lords of Exchequer, 1634; deposed by the Glasgow Assembly, 1638.

LINDSAY, David (1856–1922), explorer; born in South Australia; entered South Australia Survey Department, 1873; led expedition for scientific exploration of interior of Western Australia, financed by Sir Thomas Elder, 1891; results fell short of expectations, but auriferous area revealed.

LINDSAY, David Alexander Edward, twenty-seventh earl of Crawford and tenth earl of Balcarres (1871–1940), politician and art connoisseur; educated at Eton and Oxford; succeeded father, James Ludovic *Lindsay 1913; Conservative MP, Chorley division, 1895–1913; party whip, 1903–13; lord privy seal, 1916–19; first commissioner of works, 1921–2; trustee, British Museum, National Gallery, etc.; chairman, Royal Fine Art Commission; chancellor of Manchester University from 1923; PC, 1916; KT, 1921; FRS, 1924.

LINDSAY, David Alexander Robert, Lord Balniel, Baron Wigan, twenty-eighth earl of Crawford, and eleventh earl of Balcarres (1900–1975), connoisseur of the arts; educated at Eton and Magdalen College, Oxford; honorary attaché at British Embassy, Rome; active with Kenneth (later Lord) *Clark in organization of Burlington House exhibition of Italian art, 1200–1900 (1931); Conservative MP for Lonsdale division of Lancashire, 1924–40; trustee of National Gallery, 1935–60; chairman, 1938–9 and 1946–8; succeeded to earldom, 1940; on board of British Museum, 1940–73; chairman, Royal Fine Art Commission (1943–57), National Library of Scotland (1944–74), National Trust (1945–65), National Art Collection Fund

(1945–70), and National Gallery of Scotland (1952–72); Pilgrim trustee, 1949; GBE, 1951; KT, 1955; DCL, Oxford, 1951; LL D, Cambridge, 1955; rector, St Andrews University, 1952–5; hon. fellow, Magdalen College, Oxford, 1975.

LINDSAY, George, third Baron Spynie (d. 1671), second son of Alexander *Lindsay, second Baron Spynie; succeeded to the estates, 1646; supporter of Charles I; taken prisoner at the Battle of Worcester, 1651, and committed to the Tower; reinstated in his possessions, 1660; became chief representative of the Lindsays on the death of Ludovic *Lindsay, sixteenth earl of Crawford.

LINDSAY, George Mackintosh (1880–1956), major-general; educated at Sandroyd and Radley; commissioned in Rifle Brigade, 1900; served in South African War, 1900–2; instructor, Musketry School, Hythe, 1913–15; in France, 1916–18, and moving spirit in creation of Machine-Gun Corps after 1915; chief inspector, Royal Tank Corps Centre, 1923–5; inspector, Royal Tank Corps, 1925–9; foremost advocate of mobile armoured warfare; brigadier, General Staff, Egypt, 1929–32; commanded 7th Infantry brigade (motorized), 1932–4; major-general, 1934; commander, Presidency and Assam District, India, 1935–9; colonel-commandant, Royal Tank Regiment, 1938–47; CMG, 1919; CB, 1936; CBE, 1946.

LINDSAY, Sir James, ninth Baron Crawford, of Lanarkshire (d. 1396), son of Sir James Lindsay, eighth Baron Crawford; probably succeeded his father, 1357; fought at Otterburn, 1388; founded a convent of Trinity friars, Dundee, 1392; at feud with other Scottish nobles.

LINDSAY, James, seventh Baron Lindsay (d. 1601), son of Patrick *Lindsay, sixth Baron Lindsay of the Byres; chiefly responsible for the Protestant tumult in the Tolbooth, 1596.

LINDSAY, James Bowman (1799–1862), electrician and philologist; apprenticed as handloom weaver at Carmyllie, Forfarshire; studied at St Andrews University; lecturer on mathematics and physical science at Watt Institution, Dundee, 1829; patented, 1854, a wire-less system of telegraphy by which water was to be utilized as conductor of the electric current; devoted much time to compiling a Pentecontaglossal dictionary, which he left incomplete in MS.

LINDSAY, James Gavin (1835–1903), colonel, RE; joined Madras Engineers, 1854; served in Indian Mutiny; as engineer-in-chief constructed Northern Bengal Railway, 1872; showed capacity in dealing with Bengal famine, 1873–4; colonel, 1882; built Sukkur–Sibi Railway in Second Afghan War, 1879–80; took part in relief of Kandahar; finished Southern Mahratta Railway, 1891.

LINDSAY, James Ludovic, twenty-sixth earl of Crawford and ninth earl of Balcarres (1847–1913), astronomer, collector, and bibliophile; son of Alexander William *Lindsay, twenty-fifth earl; erected Dunecht Observatory, near Aberdeen, 1872; succeeded father, 1880; collector of French Revolution documents, etc.; published *Bibliotheca Lindesiana* (1883–1913); FRS, 1878; KT, 1896.

LINDSAY, John (d. 1335), bishop of Glasgow; probably appointed, 1321; held office till 1329; a supporter of the house of Bruce; the year and manner of his death a matter of dispute.

LINDSAY, John, fifth Baron Lindsay of the Byres, Haddingtonshire (d. 1563), descended from William, son of Sir David Lindsay of Crawford (d. 1355?); succeeded to the title on death of his grandfather, Patrick, fourth Lord Lindsay, 1526; present at the death of *James V, 1542; one of the four noblemen entrusted with the custody of the infant Princess Mary (see MARY QUEEN OF SCOTS), 1543; subscribed the 'Book of Discipline', 1561.

LINDSAY, John, Lord Menmuir (1552–1598), secretary of state in Scotland; brother of Sir David *Lindsay, Baron Edzell; studied at Paris and Cambridge; adopted the profession of the law; lord of session as Lord Menmuir, 1581; privy councillor, 1589; lord keeper of the privy seal and secretary of state, 1595; advised the king to establish episcopacy, 1596.

LINDSAY (afterwards **CRAWFORD-LINDSAY), John,** tenth Baron Lindsay of the Byres, first earl of Lindsay, seventeenth earl of Crawford (1596–1678); created earl of Lindsay, 1633; leader of the Covenanters; lord of session and commissioner of the Treasury, 1641; distinguished himself at Marston Moor, and title and dignities of earl of Crawford ratified on him, 1644; president of the parliament, 1645; took part in attempt to rescue Charles I from Carisbrook, 1646; joined the coalition for Charles II's restoration, 1650; taken prisoner, 1652; released, 1660; lord high treasurer, 1661; refusing to abjure the Covenant resigned his offices and retired from public life, 1663.

LINDSAY, John (1686–1768), nonjuror; published historical and religious works.

LINDSAY, John, twentieth earl of Crawford (1702–1749), military commander; educated at the universities of Glasgow and Edinburgh and the Military Academy of Vaudeuil, Paris; entered the army, 1726; Scots representative peer, 1733;

captain, 1734; joined the Imperial Army under Prince Eugène, 1735; served in the Russian Army, 1738–41; adjutant-general at Dettingen, 1743; brigadier-general at Fontenoy, 1745; engaged in suppressing the rebellion of 1745; lieutenant-general, 1747.

LINDSAY, Sir **John** (1737–1788), rear-admiral; served in Rochefort expedition, 1757, in expedition against Havana, 1762; knighted, 1763; in West Indies, 1764–5; commodore and commander-in-chief in East Indies, 1769–72; KB, 1771; took part in engagement off Ushant, 1778; commodore and commander-in-chief in the Mediterranean, 1783; rear-admiral, 1787.

LINDSAY, John (fl. 1758), chaplain of the *Fougueux* with Keppel at the Goree expedition; published *A Voyage to the Coast of Africa in 1758* (1759).

LINDSAY, (John) Seymour (1882–1966), designer and metalworker; educated at home; apprenticed to Leonard Ashford, designer and draughtsman, London, 1889; designer of electrical fittings for Higgins and Griffiths; served in London Rifle Brigade, DCM, 1914–16; returned to Higgins and Griffiths, 1919; started own ironwork business and worked for Sir Herbert *Baker, Sir Edwin *Lutyens, and (Sir) Albert *Richardson; work included ironwork in Bank of England, 1921–37, light-fittings and ironwork, Government Buildings, New Delhi, and iron staircase and weathervane, Trinity House, Tower Hill; designed silver altar-rails and plate for altar, Battle of Britain Memorial Chapel, Westminster Abbey, 1947; published articles in the *Architect, Iron and Brass Implements of the English House* (1927), and *An Anatomy of English Wrought Iron* (1964); fellow, Society of Antiquaries, 1942; fellow, Royal Society of Arts, 1949.

LINDSAY, Ludovic, sixteenth earl of Crawford (1600–1652?); succeeded his brother Alexander Lindsay, fifteenth earl, 1639; entered Spanish service; connected with the 'Incident' plot, 1641; joined Charles I's standard, 1642; fought at Newbury, 1643; at Marston Moor, 1644; exiled, 1646; subsequently served in Spain and France; died probably in France.

LINDSAY, Sir **Martin Alexander,** first baronet, of Downhill (1905–1981), soldier, explorer, politician, and author; educated at Wellington and Royal Military College, Sandhurst; commissioned in Royal Scots Fusiliers, 1925; seconded to Nigeria Regiment at Ibadan, 1927; travelled across Africa through Ituri forest in the Belgian Congo, 1929; surveyor on Greenland expedition, led by H. G. ('Gino') *Watkins, 1930–1; awarded King's Polar Medal; published

Those Greenland Days (1932); led expedition across Greenland ice-cap and mapped 350 miles of mountainous country, 1934; described expedition in *Sledge* (1935); awarded medals by French, Belgian, and Swedish geographical societies; appointed to command 1st battalion, Gordon Highlanders, and fought in north-west Europe; DSO, 1945; published *So Few Got Through* (1946); Conservative MP for Solihull, 1945–64; CBE, 1952; baronet, 1962; member of Queen's Body Guard for Scotland; vice-chairman, standing council of the baronetage, 1973–9, of which he wrote a history (1979).

LINDSAY, Patrick, sixth Baron Lindsay of the Byres (d. 1589), supporter of the reformers in Scotland; eldest son of John *Lindsay, fifth baron of the Byres; succeeded to title, 1563; supporter of the plot to murder David *Riccio or Rizzio, 1566; supported the king's party, 1570–2; concerned in *Ruthven raid, 1582, and in Gowrie conspiracy, 1584.

LINDSAY, Patrick (1566–1644), archbishop of Glasgow; educated at St Andrews; supported the episcopalian schemes of James I; bishop of Ross, 1613–33; privy councillor of Scotland, 1615; archbishop of Glasgow, 1633; deposed by the general assembly, 1638.

LINDSAY, Patrick (d. 1753), lord provost of Edinburgh; served in Spain until Peace of Utrecht, 1713; lord provost of Edinburgh, 1729 and 1733; published work on the economic resources of Scotland (1733); MP, Edinburgh, 1734–41; governor of the Isle of Man, 1741.

LINDSAY, Robert (1500?–1565?), of Pitscottie, Scottish historian; his *History*, covering a period of Scottish history about the earlier part of which, from the death of *James I to that of *James III, very little is known, first published (1728).

LINDSAY (afterwards **LOYD-LINDSAY), Robert James,** Baron Wantage (1832–1901), soldier and politician; joined Scots Guards, 1850; retired as lieutenant-colonel, 1859; served with distinction in Crimea; received VC, 1857; assumed name of Loyd-Lindsay on marriage, 1858; a pioneer of Volunteer movement, 1859; Conservative MP for Berkshire, 1865–85; financial secretary to War Office, 1877–80; represented Red Cross Aid Society, which he helped to found (1870), in Franco-Prussian and Turko-Serbian wars; KCB, 1881; baron, 1885; a prominent freemason; leading agriculturist in Berkshire; discriminating art patron; helped to found Reading University College (afterwards Reading University).

LINDSAY, Sir Ronald Charles (1877–1945), diplomat; son of twenty-sixth and brother of twenty-seventh earl of *Crawford; educated at Winchester; entered Diplomatic Service, 1899; under-secretary, Egyptian Ministry of Finance, 1913–19; assistant under-secretary, Foreign Office, in charge, Near Eastern affairs, 1921–4; 'representative', Constantinople, 1924; ambassador, 1925–6; negotiated Treaty of Angora, 1926; ambassador, Berlin, 1926–8; permanent under-secretary, Foreign Office, 1928–30; ambassador, Washington, 1930–9; KCMG and PC, 1925; GCB, 1939.

LINDSAY, Thomas Martin (1843–1914), historian; educated at Glasgow and Edinburgh universities; entered ministry of Free Church of Scotland, 1869; professor of church history at Free Church theological college, Glasgow, 1872; principal, 1902; interested in missions and social problems; chief works, *Luther and the German Reformation* (1900) and *A History of the Reformation in Europe* (1906–7).

LINDSAY, Wallace Martin (1858–1937), classical scholar; brother of T. M. *Lindsay; educated at Glasgow University and Balliol College, Oxford; first class, Lit. Hum., 1881; fellow of Jesus; tutor, 1884–99; professor of humanity, St Andrews, 1899–1937; established reputation with *The Latin Language* (1894); other works include editions of Martial (1903), Plautus (1904–5), and Terence (1926), and *Early Latin Verse* (1922) and *Glossaria Latina* (5 vols., 1926–32); FBA, 1905.

LINDSAY, Sir Walter (d. 1605), of Balgavie, Forfarshire, Roman Catholic intriguer; acquired property of Balgavie, 1584; converted to Roman Catholicism, and constantly charged with conspiring against Presbyterianism; escaped the vengeance of the kirk by fleeing to Spain; there published *An Account of the present State of the Catholic Religion in the Realm of Scotland* (1594); returned to Scotland, 1598; took part in all the feuds of the Lindsays; barbarously murdered by his kinsman, David *Lindsay, twelfth earl of Crawford.

LINDSAY, William, eighteenth earl of Crawford and second earl of Lindsay (d. 1698), eldest son of John *Lindsay, tenth Baron Lindsay of the Byres, seventeenth earl of Crawford, and first earl of Lindsay; succeeded to the earldoms, 1678; a zealous Presbyterian; president of the Convention parliament, 1689; a commissioner of the Treasury, 1690; one of the commissioners for settling the government of the church.

LINDSAY, William (1802–1866), United Presbyterian minister; studied at Glasgow University and the Theological Hall at Paisley; ordained, 1830; appointed professor of exegetical theology and biblical criticism by the relief synod; DD, Glasgow, 1844; professor of sacred languages and biblical criticism on the staff of the United Presbyterian Hall, Glasgow, 1847, and professor of exegetical theology, 1858; published *The Law of Marriage* (1855), *Exposition of Epistle to the Hebrews* (edited 1867), and other works.

LINDSAY, William Lauder (1829–1880), botanist; educated at Edinburgh High School and University; MD, Edinburgh, 1852; combined geological and botanical studies with his practice of medicine; published *The History of British Lichens* (1856); visited New Zealand, 1861–2; published *Contributions to New Zealand Botany* (1868) and *Memoirs on the Spermogenes and Pycnides of Lichens* (1870). Of his works on medical subjects, the chief is *Mind in the Lower Animals in Health and Disease* (1879).

LINDSAY, William Schaw (1816–1877), merchant and shipowner; began a seafaring life, 1831; captain in the merchant service, 1830–40; fitter to the Castle Eden Coal Company, Hartlepool, 1841; established firm of W. S. Lindsay & Co., one of the largest shipowning concerns in the world; MP, Tynemouth and North Shields, 1854–9, Sunderland, 1859–65; published a valuable *History of Merchant Shipping and Ancient Commerce* (1874–6); author of other works on kindred subjects, and of *Log of my Leisure Hours*.

LINDSELL, Augustine (d. 1634), bishop of Hereford; MA, Clare Hall, Cambridge; fellow of Clare Hall, 1599; DD, 1621; dean of Lichfield, 1628; bishop of Peterborough, 1633, of Hereford, 1634; his edition of Theophylact's *Commentaries on St. Paul's Epistles* published (1636).

LINDSELL, Sir Wilfrid Gordon (1884–1973), lieutenant-general; educated at Birkenhead School, Victoria College, Jersey, and Royal Military Academy, Woolwich; commissioned into Royal Garrison Artillery, 1903; served in administrative posts in Malta and Australia, 1909–14; ADC to GOC, 7th division in France, 1914; served in regimental and staff appointments, 1915–18; MC, 1916; Croix de Guerre, 1918; DSO, 1918; OBE, 1919; served in War Office, 1920–1; instructor at School of Military Administration, 1921–3; produced first edition of *Military Organization and Administration* (1923) which, after many editions, was republished as *Lindsell's Military Organization and Administration* (1948); instructor at Staff College, Camberley, 1925–8; major-general, Southern Command, 1938; quartermaster-general (temporary lieutenant-general), British Expeditionary Force, 1939; seconded to Ministry of Supply as senior military adviser for re-equipment of the army, 1941; lieutenant-general in charge of administration in Middle East, 1942; principal administration officer, Fourteenth Army, 1943; attached to Board of Trade, 1945; chairman, Ely Breweries (later Watney Mann), 1946–55; KBE, 1940; CB, 1942; KCB, 1943; GBE, 1946; hon. LL D, Aberdeen.

LINDSEY, earls of. See BERTIE, ROBERT, first earl, 1582–1642; BERTIE, MONTAGUE, second earl, 1608?–1666.

LINDSEY, Theophilus (1723–1808), Unitarian; educated at St John's College, Cambridge; fellow, 1747; held several livings, but his views becoming Unitarian, resigned, 1773; opened a temporary chapel (established permanently, 1778) in London, 1774, and issued his *Apology*; *A Sequel to the Apology* (1776), his most valuable contribution to dogmatic theology; his *Historical View of the State of the Unitarian Doctrine and Worship from the Reformation to our own Time* published (1783); took leave of his pulpit, 1793; published *Conversations on the Divine Government* (1802) and a liturgy adapted for Unitarian congregations.

LINE, Francis (1595–1675), Jesuit and scientific writer, alias Francis Hall; joined Jesuits, 1623; ordained, 1628; professed of the four vows, 1640; professor of Hebrew and mathematics in the Jesuit college, Liège; missioner in England, 1656–69; constructed a sundial set up in the king's private garden at Whitehall, 1669; returned to Liège, 1672, where he died; author of several scientific works written between 1660 and 1675 on such subjects as squaring the circle, sundials, and the barometer.

LINES, Samuel (1778–1863), painter, designer, and art instructor; worked as designer to a clock-dial enameller, papier-mâché maker, and die engraver; began to teach drawing at Birmingham, 1807; set up in conjunction with others a life academy there, 1809; helped to found Birmingham School of Art, 1821; treasurer and curator of the Birmingham Society of Artists.

LINES, Samuel Restell (1804–1833), painter; son of Samuel *Lines (1778–1863); studied under his father; occasionally exhibited at the Royal Academy.

LINFORD, Thomas (1650–1724), divine. See LYNFORD.

LINGARD, Frederick (1811–1847), musician; organist, choirmaster, teacher of music, and composer; lay-vicar of Durham Cathedral, 1835; published *Antiphonal Chants for the Psalter* (1843) and a *Series of Anthems*.

LINGARD, John (1771–1851), Roman Catholic historian of England; studied at the English College at Douai, 1782–93; ordained and appointed vice-president of Crookhall College, near Durham, 1795–1811; published *The Antiquities of the*

Anglo-Saxon Church (1806); began his *History of England* when missioner at Hornby, near Lancaster, 1811; DD; visited Rome, 1817 and 1825; took part in the jurisdiction of the Roman Church in Great Britain; created doctor of divinity and of the canon and civil law by Pius VII, 1821; volumes i, ii, and iii of the *History* published (1819); the remainder followed at intervals (1820–30). It had five editions before 1851, and remains the authority for the Reformation from the side of the enlightened Roman Catholic priesthood.

LINGARD (or LYNGARD), Richard (1598?–1670), dean of Lismore; ordained, 1622; archdeacon of Clonmacnoise, 1639; professor of divinity, Dublin University, 1662–70; vice-provost, 1662; DD, 1664; dean of Lismore, 1666.

LINGEN, Sir Henry (1612–1662), Royalist; raised troops and fought for Charles I, 1643–8; knighted, 1645; temporarily imprisoned, 1648; MP, Hereford, 1660 and 1661.

LINGEN, Ralph Robert Wheeler, Baron Lingen (1819–1905), civil servant; educated at Trinity College, Oxford; friend of *Jowett, *Froude, and Frederick *Temple; Ireland and Hertford scholar (1838–9); BA, 1840; won Latin essay (1843) and Eldon scholarship (1846); fellow of Balliol, 1841; hon. DCL, 1881; hon. fellow of Trinity, 1886; called to bar, 1847; secretary to Education Office, 1849–69; worked harmoniously under Lord *Granville and Robert *Lowe (Lord Sherbrooke); issued code advocating payment by results in accordance with report of Newcastle Commission of Inquiry, 1861; code severely criticized by Lord Robert *Cecil (Lord Salisbury) and W. E. *Forster; CB, 1869; permanent secretary of the Treasury, 1869–85; vigilant guardian of public purse; KCB, 1878; baron, 1885; alderman of first London County Council, 1889–92.

LINKLATER, Eric Robert Russell (1899–1974), novelist; educated at Aberdeen Grammar School and Aberdeen University, 1918–25; first class in English; MA; served with Black Watch, 1917–18; wounded; assistant editor of *Times of India* in Bombay, 1925–7; assistant to professor of English, Aberdeen, 1927–8; Commonwealth fellow at Cornell and Berkeley Universities, USA, 1928–30; established reputation as novelist with *Juan in America* (1931); settled in Orkney; commanded Orkney Fortress company, Royal Engineers, 1939–41; served in War Office, 1942–3, and in Italy, 1944–5; published *Private Angelo* (1946); rector, Aberdeen University, 1945; hon. LL D, 1946; published semi-official history of *The Campaign in Italy* (1951); CBE, 1954; deputy lieutenant, Ross and Cromarty,

1968–73; fellow, Royal Society of Edinburgh, 1971; also published autobiographical *The Man on My Back* (1941), *A Year of Space* (1953), and *Fanfare for a Tin Hat* (1970).

LINLEY, Elizabeth Ann, afterwards Mrs Sheridan (1754–1792), vocalist. See SHERIDAN.

LINLEY, Francis (1774–1800), organist and composer; blind from birth; organist at St James's Chapel, Pentonville, London, *c.*1790; carried on business as a music-seller, 1796; composed sonatas and airs for pianoforte and flute, and wrote a practical introduction to the organ (12th edn., *c.*1810).

LINLEY, George (1798–1865), verse-writer and musical composer; composed fashionable and popular ballads, 1830–47; author of farces and satirical poems, including *Musical Cynics of London, a satire* (1862), a savage onslaught on *Chorley; his operetta *The Toymakers* performed, 1861, and *Law versus Love* (comedietta), 1862.

LINLEY, George (d. 1869), son of George *Linley; published *The Goldseeker and other poems* (1860), *Old Saws newly set* (1864).

LINLEY, Maria (1763–1784), singer at the Bath concerts and in oratorio; daughter of Thomas *Linley the elder.

LINLEY, Mary (1758–1787), afterwards Mrs Tickell; vocalist; daughter of Thomas *Linley the elder, musician; first appeared in public, 1771; married Richard *Tickell, pamphleteer and commissioner of stamps, 1780.

LINLEY, Ozias Thurston (1766–1831), organist; son of Thomas *Linley the elder; educated at Corpus Christi College, Oxford; BA, 1789; minor canon of Norwich, 1790; organist, Dulwich College, 1816.

LINLEY, Thomas, the elder (1732–1795), musical composer; set up at Bath as a singing-master and carried on the concerts in the Bath Assembly Rooms; became joint manager of the Drury Lane oratorios, 1774; composed with his son Thomas the music for *Sheridan's *Duenna*, 1775; directed the music at Drury Lane, 1776–81; member of the Royal Society of Musicians, 1777. His compositions include the music to various dramatic pieces, and separate songs, glees, and canzonets.

LINLEY, Thomas, the younger (1756–1778), violinist and composer; son of Thomas *Linley the elder; studied violin under his father, and at Florence under Nardini; leader of the orchestra and solo-player at his father's concerts at Bath, 1773, and at the Drury Lane oratorios, 1774; drowned through the capsizing of a pleasure boat off the Lincolnshire coast; his compositions include songs for *The Duenna* (1775), songs for

The Tempest (1776), and a short oratorio, *The Song of Moses*.

LINLEY, William (1771–1835), author and musical composer; son of Thomas *Linley the elder; educated at St Paul's School, London, and Harrow; writer under the East India Company, sailing for Madras, 1790; deputy-secretary to the Military Board, 1793; returned to England, and brought out at Drury Lane *Harlequin Captive, or Magic Fire*, 1796; produced *The Honeymoon* (comic opera), 1797, and *The Pavilion* (entertainment), 1799; returned to Madras, 1800; paymaster at Nellore, 1801; sub-treasurer and mint-master to the presidency, Fort St George, 1805; settled in London, 1806; collected Shakespeare's dramatic lyrics, with music by various composers and himself (2 vols., 1816); composed songs and wrote novels and verse.

LINLITHGOW, earls of. See LIVINGSTONE, ALEXANDER, first earl, d. 1622; LIVINGSTONE, GEORGE, third earl, 1616–1690; LIVINGSTONE, GEORGE, fourth earl, 1652?–1695.

LINLITHGOW, marquesses of. See HOPE, JOHN ADRIAN LOUIS, first marquess, 1860–1908; HOPE, VICTOR ALEXANDER JOHN, second marquess, 1887–1952.

LINNECAR, Richard (1722–1800), dramatist; postmaster at Wakefield; coroner for the West Riding of Yorkshire, 1763; published *Miscellaneous Works*, containing two insipid comedies and other efforts (1789).

LINNELL, John (1792–1882), portrait and landscape painter; entered the Royal Academy schools, 1805; first exhibited at the Academy, 1807; member of the Society of Painters in Oil and Water-Colours, 1812, exhibiting, 1813–20; treasurer, 1817; became intimate of William *Blake (1757–1827), 1818; drew, painted, and engraved portraits; exhibited over a hundred portraits and ten or twelve landscapes at the Royal Academy, 1821–47; subsequently exhibited landscapes; put down his name for the ARA, 1821; withdrew it in disgust, 1842; declined membership when offered in later life.

LINNETT, John Wilfrid (1913–1975), chemist; educated at King Henry VIII School, Coventry, and St John's College, Oxford, of which he was a scholar; first class, chemistry, 1935; D.Phil., 1938; Henry fellow, Harvard, working on infra-red and Raman spectroscopy, 1937–8; junior research fellow, Balliol College, Oxford, 1939–45; university demonstrator in inorganic chemistry, 1944; fellow and praelector in chemistry, The Queen's College, Oxford, 1945; dean, 1945–8; FRS, 1955; published *Wave Mechanics and Valency* (1960); reader, 1962; succeeded R. G. W. *Norrish as professor of phys-

ical chemistry, Cambridge, 1965; fellow of Emmanuel College; master, Sidney Sussex College, Cambridge, 1970; vice-chancellor, 1973; produced survey of 'useful' research in Cambridge, 1975; president, Faraday Society, 1971–3; hon. D.Sc., Warwick, 1973; Coventry Award of Merit, 1966; hon. fellow, St John's College, Oxford, 1968; fellow, New York Academy of Sciences.

LINSKILL, Mary (1840–1891), novelist; contributed, under pseudonym of Stephen Yorke, *Tales of the North Riding* to *Good Words* (published 1871); author of four other novels, 1876–87, and of some short stories.

LINSTEAD, Sir (Reginald) Patrick (1902–1966), experimental organic chemist and university administrator; educated at City of London School and Imperial College; first class, chemistry, 1923; Ph.D., 1926; demonstrator, and later lecturer, Imperial College, 1929; Firth professor of chemistry, Sheffield University, 1938; professor, organic chemistry, Harvard, 1939–45; deputy director of scientific research, Ministry of Supply, 1942; director, Government Chemical Research Laboratory, Teddington, 1945–9; professor, organic chemistry, Imperial College, 1949; dean, Royal College of Science, 1953; rector, 1955; D.Sc., London, 1930; hon. MA, Harvard, 1942; hon. D.Sc., Exeter, 1965; CBE, 1946; knighted, 1959; FRS, 1940; vice-president, Royal Society, 1959–65; trustee, National Gallery, 1962; member, Central Advisory Council for Education, 1956–60, and Committee on Higher Education, 1961–4; revised Cain and Thorpe's *The Synthetic Dyestuffs* (with Thorpe, 1933), and published *A Course in Modern Techniques of Organic Chemistry* (with J. A. Elridge and M. Whalley, 1955) and *A Guide to Qualitative Organic Chemical Analysis* (with B. C. L. Weedon, 1956).

LINTON, Eliza Lynn (1822–1898), novelist and miscellaneous writer; daughter of the Revd James Lynn, and granddaughter of Samuel *Goodenough; established herself in London, 1845, as a woman of letters; published *Azeth the Egyptian* (1846), *Amymone* (1848), and *Realities* (1851), none of which were very successful; member of staff of *Morning Chronicle*, 1848–51; newspaper correspondent at Paris, 1851–4; contributed to *All the Year Round*; married, 1858, William James *Linton, from whom she subsequently separated amicably; returned to fiction and achieved considerable success, two of her works, *Joshua Davidson* (1872) and *Autobiography of Christopher Kirkland* (1885), the latter in a large measure her own autobiography, being especially notable; contributed to *Saturday Review* from

1866. Her works include *The Girl of the Period, and other Essays* (1883) and *George Eliot* (1897).

LINTON, William (1791–1876), landscape painter; first exhibited at Royal Academy, 1817; helped to found the Society of British Artists, 1824; visited the continent, 1828; published in two folio volumes, *Sketches in Italy*, drawn on stone, with descriptive text (1832); resigned membership of the Society of British Artists, 1842; well versed in chemistry of colours; published *Ancient and Modern Colours, from the earliest periods to the present time; with their Chemical and Artistical Properties* (1852); ceased to exhibit at Royal Academy after 1859, at Society of British Artists after 1871.

LINTON, Sir William (1801–1880), army physician; educated at Edinburgh University; LRCS and entered Army Medical Department, 1826; MD, Glasgow, 1834; staff surgeon of the first class, 1848; served in Canada, the Mediterranean, and the West Indies; deputy-inspector of hospitals in the Crimea; present in every action up to Balaclava; in charge of barrack hospital, Scutari, from 1854 till return of British forces; proceeded to India as inspector-general of hospitals, 1857; held offices throughout the Mutiny; retired from the active list, 1863; KCB, 1865.

LINTON, William James (1812–1898), engraver, poet, and political reformer; apprenticed as wood-engraver; became associated with John Orrin *Smith; adopted advanced views in religion and politics; established, 1839, *The National*, designed as a vehicle for reprints from publications inaccessible to working men; editor of *The Illuminated Magazine*, 1845; formed intimate friendship with Mazzini; took part in founding 'International League' of patriots of all nations, 1847; supported 'The Friends of Italy'; founded and conducted, 1850–5, *The English Republic* periodical; gained wide reputation as wood-engraver; married Eliza Lynn (see LINTON, ELIZA LYNN), 1858; engraved covers of *Cornhill* and *Macmillan's* magazines; went to America (1866) and established himself at Appledore, near New Haven, Connecticut, where he engaged privately in printing and engraving, and issued several books; died at New Haven. His publications include *A History of Wood Engraving in America* (1882), *Masters of Wood Engraving* (1890), some volumes of verse, and *Memories*, an autobiography (1895).

LINTOT, Barnaby Bernard (1675–1736), publisher; apprentice at Stationers' Hall, 1690; free of the company, 1699; published poems and plays for *Pope, *Gay, *Farquhar, *Parnell, *Steele, and *Rowe, 1702–8; published Fenton's *Oxford and Cambridge Miscellany Poems* (1709)

and *Miscellaneous Poems and Translations* (containing Pope's *Rape of the Lock* in its first form, 1712); published Pope's *Iliad* (1715–20), *Odyssey* (1725–6); under-warden of the Stationers' Company, 1729–30.

LINTOT, Henry (1703–1758), publisher and, from 1730, partner with his father, Barnaby Bernard *Lintot.

LINWOOD, Mary (1755–1845), musical composer and artist in needlework; imitated pictures in worsted embroidery; exhibited at the Society of Artists, 1776 and 1778, and in London and the chief provincial towns, 1798–1835; composed an oratorio and some songs; published *Leicestershire Tales* (1808).

LINWOOD, William (1817–1878), classical scholar; entered Christ Church, Oxford, 1835; MA, 1842; public examiner at Oxford, 1850–1; his best-known works, *A Lexicon to Aeschylus* (1843) and *Sophoclis Tragoediae* (1846).

LIONEL OF ANTWERP, earl of Ulster and first duke of Clarence (1338–1368), third son of Edward III; born at Antwerp; guardian and lieutenant of England during his father's absence, 1345 and 1346; created earl of Ulster, 1347; married Elizabeth (d. 1362), daughter of William de *Burgh, third earl of Ulster, 1352; knighted, 1355; king's lieutenant in Ireland, 1361; created duke of Clarence, 1362; met the parliament which drew up statute of Kilkenny, 1367; married at Milan, as his second wife, Violante, daughter of Galeazzo Visconti, lord of Pavia, 1368; died at Alba.

LIPSCOMB, Christopher (1781–1843), first bishop of Jamaica, 1824; son of William *Lipscomb.

LIPSCOMB, George (1773–1846), historian of Buckinghamshire; studied surgery; house surgeon of St Bartholomew's Hospital, London, 1792; captain commandant of the Warwickshire Volunteer Infantry, and deputy recorder of Warwick, 1798; MD, Aberdeen, 1801; joint editor of the *National Adviser*, 1811; contributed to the *Gentleman's Magazine*; his great work, *The History and Antiquities of the County of Buckingham*, published in eight parts (1831–47); published medical works.

LIPSCOMB, William (1754–1842), miscellaneous writer; cousin of George *Lipscomb; educated at Winchester and Corpus Christi College, Oxford; MA, 1784; published *Poems* (including translations of Italian sonnets, 1784), and *The Canterbury Tales of Chaucer completed in a Modern Version* (1795).

LIPSON, Ephraim (1888–1960), economic historian; grievously deformed by childhood accident; scholar of Sheffield Royal Grammar School and Trinity College, Cambridge; first class, parts i and ii, historical tripos, 1909–10; migrated as private tutor to Oxford; reader in economic history and fellow of New College, 1922–31; left Oxford embittered by non-election as first Chichele professor of economic history; published vol. i, *Economic History of England* (The Middle Ages, 1915); vols. ii and iii (The Age of Mercantilism, 1931).

LIPTON, Sir Thomas Johnstone, baronet (1850–1931), grocer and yachtsman; born in Glasgow tenement; worked for five years in United States; opened in Glasgow (1871) first of series of grocery shops which, by publicity backed by sound stock at fair prices, made him a millionaire by 1880; lavish host and generous contributor to charity; spent a fortune on yacht-racing; made unsuccessful attempts to win the America's Cup with successive *Shamrocks* (1899–1930); knighted, 1898; KCVO, 1901; baronet, 1902.

LISGAR, first Baron (1807–1876). See YOUNG, Sir JOHN.

LISLE, Viscounts. See PLANTAGENET, ARTHUR, 1480?–1542; DUDLEY, JOHN, 1502?–1553; SIDNEY, ROBERT, first viscount of the Sidney family, 1563–1626; SIDNEY, ROBERT, second viscount, 1595–1677; SIDNEY, PHILIP, third viscount, 1619–1698.

LISLE, Alice (1614?–1685), victim of a judicial murder; daughter of Sir White Beckenshaw; married John *Lisle, 1630; tried before *Jeffreys for sheltering *Monmouth's supporters at her house at Moyles Court; found guilty and beheaded at Winchester.

LISLE, Sir George (d. 1648), Royalist; received his military education in the Netherlands; fought for Charles I in battles of Newbury, 1643 and 1644, Cheriton, 1644, and Naseby, 1645; governor of Faringdon, 1644–5; hon. DCL, Oxford, 1645; knighted, 1645; defended Colchester, but was forced to surrender and shot as a rebel, 1648.

LISLE, James George Semple (*fl.* 1799), adventurer. See SEMPLE.

LISLE, John (1610?–1664), regicide; educated at Magdalen Hall, Oxford; BA, 1626; barrister, Middle Temple, 1633; bencher, 1649; MP, Winchester, 1640; master of St Cross Hospital, Winchester, 1644–9; one of the managers in Charles I's trial; appointed one of the commissioners of the great seal, and placed on the Council of State, 1649; MP, Southampton, 1654; held various offices in parliaments of 1654–9; commissioner of the Admiralty and navy, 1660; at Restoration fled to Switzerland;

murdered at Lausanne by an Irishman known as Thomas Macdonnell, really named Sir James Fitz Edmond Cotter. Alice *Lisle was his second wife.

LISLE, Samuel (1683–1749), successively bishop of St Asaph and of Norwich; MA, Wadham College, Oxford, 1706; received holy orders, 1707; chaplain to the Levant Company, 1710–19; archdeacon of Canterbury, 1724; prebendary of Canterbury, 1728; prolocutor of the Lower House of Convocation, 1734 and 1741; warden of Wadham College, Oxford, 1739–44; DD, 1739; bishop of St Asaph, 1744–8, of Norwich, 1748–9; printed a few sermons and collected inscriptions during his Levant chaplaincy, printed in the *Antiquitates Asiaticae* of Edmund *Chishull, 1728.

LISLE, Thomas (d. 1361), bishop of Ely; called Lyle, Lylde, and Lyldus; educated in the Dominican house, Cambridge; joined the order of Predicant friars, and acquired celebrity as a preacher; bishop of Ely, 1345; built churches in his diocese, and rendered material services to the University of Cambridge; at feud with Blanche, daughter of *Henry, earl of Lancaster, and compelled to flee; died a refugee at Avignon.

LISLE (or L'ISLE), William (1569?–1637), Anglo-Saxon scholar; of Eton and King's College, Cambridge; MA, 1592; lived at Cambridge; a pioneer in the study of Anglo-Saxon; printed for the first time, with an English translation, the *Treatise on the Old and New Testament*, by *Ælfric Grammaticus; published a rhymed version of Heliodorus's *Aethiopica* (1631).

LISTER, Arthur (1830–1908), botanist; son of Joseph Jackson *Lister; published *A Monograph of the Mycetozoa* (1894) and *Guide to the British Mycetozoa* (1895); FRS, 1898.

LISTER, Edward (1557–1620), physician; brother of Sir Matthew *Lister; of Eton and King's College, Cambridge; MA, 1583; MD, 1590; FRCP, 1594, and treasurer, 1612–18; physician-in-ordinary to Queen Elizabeth and to James I.

LISTER, Joseph (1627–1709), Puritan autobiographer; by turns trader, manservant, and small farmer; his autobiography edited by Thomas *Wright (1842).

LISTER, Joseph, first Baron Lister (1827–1912), founder of antiseptic surgery; son of Joseph Jackson *Lister, FRS; educated at Grove House School, Tottenham, and University College, London; especially influenced during his medical studies by Wharton Jones, professor of ophthalmic medicine and surgery, and William *Sharpey, professor of physiology; after taking

MB (1852) carried out researches on physiological problems; went to Edinburgh to study method of James *Syme, celebrated surgeon, 1853; settled in Edinburgh; assistant surgeon to Royal Infirmary, 1856; professor of surgery, Glasgow University, and FRS, 1860; surgeon to Glasgow Infirmary, 1861; professor of clinical surgery, Edinburgh, 1869–77; at King's College, London, 1877–92; baronet, 1883; president of Royal Society, 1894–1900; baron, 1897; OM, 1902; devoted himself to prevention of mortality from injuries and wounds by studying inflammation and suppuration; influenced by researches of Louis Pasteur; employed carbolic acid to destroy germs and prevent septic infection; successfully applied treatment to cases of compound fracture; invented new operations and improved technique of old ones by introducing use of absorbable ligatures and drainage tubes; reduction of septic diseases caused practice of surgery to undergo complete revolution and enormously enlarged its field.

LISTER, Joseph Jackson (1786–1869), discoverer of the principle of the modern microscope; occupied in the wine trade; attempted to improve the object glass, 1824; continued his investigations, 1826–7; discovered principle of construction of modern microscope, 1830; the first to ascertain the true form of the red corpuscle of mammalian blood, 1834; aided opticians in the construction of the microscope. His law of the aplanatic foci remains the guiding principle of microscopy.

LISTER, Martin (1638?–1712), zoologist; nephew of Sir Matthew *Lister; of St John's College, Cambridge; fellow, 1660; MA, 1662; FRS, 1671; practised medicine at York till 1683; removed to London, 1684; MD, Oxford, 1684; published *Historia sive Synopsis Methodica Conchyliorum* (1685–92); FRCP, 1687; censor, 1694; accompanied earl of *Portland on his embassy to Paris, and published an account of his journey (1698). His contributions to the *Philosophical Transactions* (extending over nos. 25–585) treat of plants, spiders, meteorology, minerals, molluscs, medicine, and antiquities.

LISTER, Sir Matthew (1571?–1656), physician; MA, Oriel College, Oxford, 1595; MD, Basle, incorporated at Oxford, 1605, at Cambridge, 1608; FRCP, 1607; physician to *Anne, queen of James I, and to Charles I; knighted, 1636.

LISTER, Philip Cunliffe-, first earl of Swinton (1884–1972), politician. See CUNLIFFE-LISTER.

LISTER, Samuel Cunliffe, first Baron Masham (1815–1906), inventor; brother carried on worsted mill at Manningham till 1889; took out over 150 patents for inventions; evolved Lister-Cartwright (1845), the 'square motion' (1846), and 'square nip' (1850) wool-combing machines, which cheapened cloth, advanced Bradford's prosperity, and created Australian wool trade; successfully converted silk waste into silk velvets, poplins, and the like; invented (1848) a compressed-air brake for railways; purchased Ackton Colliery in Yorkshire, where the works were destroyed in coal strike of 1893; early advocated tariff reform; presented Lister Park to Bradford city; baron, 1891; hon. LL D, Leeds University; ardent art collector and sportsman; published account of his inventions (1905).

LISTER, Thomas (1559–1626?), alias Thomas Butler; Jesuit; entered the English College at Rome, 1579; joined Jesuits, 1583; DD, Pont-à-Mousson, 1592; missioner in England, 1596; imprisoned at time of Gunpowder Plot; banished, 1606; again in England, and professed of the four vows, 1610; superior of the Oxford district, 1621; author of a 'Treatise of Schism', widely circulated in manuscript.

LISTER, Thomas (1597–1668), Parliamentarian colonel; admitted to Gray's Inn, 1616; lieutenant-colonel in the Parliamentary Army and deputy-governor of Lincoln; MP, Lincoln, 1647–56, and in 1659; member of the Council of State, 1651; forbidden to hold office from 1660.

LISTER, Thomas (1810–1888), poet and naturalist; assisted his father, a Quaker gardener and small farmer; published *Rustic Wreath*, a collection of fugitive verses (1834); visited the continent, 1838; postmaster of Barnsley, 1839–70; an enthusiastic naturalist, and constant attendant and contributor of papers at the British Association meetings.

LISTER, Thomas Henry (1800–1842), novelist and dramatist; of Westminster and Trinity College, Cambridge; commissioner for inquiring into state of religious and other instruction in Ireland, 1834, into the opportunities of religious worship and means of religious instruction in Scotland, 1835; the first registrar-general of England and Wales, 1836; works include *Granby* (novel, 1826), *Epicharis* (a tragedy performed at Drury Lane, 1829), and *The Life and Administration of Edward, first Earl of Clarendon* (1837–8).

LISTON, Henry (1771–1836), writer on music; studied for the ministry at Edinburgh University; minister of Ecclesmachan, Linlithgowshire, 1793–1836; inventor of the 'Eucharmonic' organ, 1811; published *Essay on Perfect Intonation* (1812); conjunct clerk of the synod of Lothian and Tweeddale, 1820.

LISTON, John (1776?–1846), actor; master at the Grammar School of St Martin's, Leicester Square, London, 1799; his first efforts as an actor made in company with Stephen *Kemble in north of England; played comic parts at Haymarket Theatre, London, 1805, at Covent Garden, London, 1808–22, at Drury Lane, London, 1823, subsequently at Olympic, London; retired from the stage, 1837; played, among other parts, Polonius, Slender, Sir Andrew Aguecheek, Bottom, and Cloten.

LISTON, Sir Robert (1742–1836), diplomat; educated at Edinburgh University; tutor to the sons of Sir Gilbert *Elliot (1722–1777); minister-plenipotentiary at Madrid, 1783–8; LL D, Edinburgh, 1785; envoy-extraordinary at Stockholm, 1789–92; ambassador-extraordinary and plenipotentiary, Constantinople, 1793–6; ambassador-extraordinary and minister-plenipotentiary, Washington, 1796–1800; envoy-extraordinary and plenipotentiary to the Batavian republic, 1802–3; ambassador-extraordinary and plenipotentiary, Constantinople, 1811–20; privy councillor, 1812; GCB (civil), 1816.

LISTON, Robert (1794–1847), surgeon; son of Henry *Liston; entered Edinburgh University, 1808; assistant to Dr John *Barclay (1758–1826); house surgeon at Royal Infirmary, Edinburgh, 1814–16; MRCS, 1816; worked in Edinburgh as teacher of anatomy and operating surgeon, 1818–28; surgeon to the hospital attached to the London University, 1834; professor of clinical surgery, University College, London, 1835; FRS, 1841; a skilful operator; best known in connection with the 'Liston splint'; chief works, *The Elements of Surgery* (1831–2) and *Practical Surgery* (1837).

LITCHFIELD. See also LICHFIELD.

LITCHFIELD, Mrs Harriett (1777–1854), actress; née Hay; made her first appearance on the stage, 1792; married John Litchfield (d. 1858) of the Privy Council Office, 1794; acted at Covent Garden from 1797; retired after 1812; her best part Emilia in Othello.

LITHGOW, Sir James, first baronet, of Ormsary (1883–1952), shipbuilder and industrialist; educated at Glasgow Academy and in Paris; apprenticed in family shipyard; partner, 1906; with younger brother assumed management on death of father, 1908; director, merchant shipbuilding, Admiralty, 1917–18; rationalized post-war Scottish shipbuilding; appointed chairman, 1930, National Shipbuilders' Security Ltd. to buy out uneconomic shipyards; chairman, Scottish National Development Council, 1931; rescued number of Scottish industries, including Beardmores and Fairfields;

president, Federation of British Industries, 1930–2; controller, merchant shipbuilding and member, Board of Admiralty, 1940–6; president, Iron and Steel Federation, 1943–5; baronet, 1925; GBE, 1945; CB, 1947.

LITHGOW, William (1582–1645?), traveller; made voyages to the Orkneys and Shetlands; travelled in Germany, Bohemia, Helvetia, and the Low Countries; claimed to have tramped over 36,000 miles in Europe, Asia, Africa, 1610–13; made other journeys, 1614–19 and 1620–2; walked from London to Edinburgh, 1627; journeyed in England, Scotland, and Holland, 1628–44; chief work, *The Totall Discourse of the Rare Aduentures and painfull Peregrinations of long nineteene Yeares* (1614).

LITLINGTON (or **LITTLINGTON**), **Nicholas** (1316?–1386), successively prior and abbot of Westminster Abbey; prior of Westminster, 1352; abbot, 1362; built the Jerusalem Chamber; assisted at the coronation of Richard II, 1377.

LITSTER (or **LE LITESTER**), **John** (d. 1381), 'king of the commons'; led the 'rustics and ribalds' of Norfolk, 1381; assumed the royal title as 'king of the commons', 1381; taken at the Battle of North Walsham and hanged, beheaded, and quartered at the command of Henry le *Despenser, bishop of Norwich.

LITTLE, Andrew George (1863–1945), historian; educated at Clifton and Balliol College, Oxford; first class, modern history, 1886; at Dresden and Göttingen; lecturer in history, University College of South Wales, Cardiff, 1892; professor, 1898–1901; visiting lecturer (reader from 1920) in palaeography, Manchester, 1903–28; founded (1902) a society which became (1907–37) the British Society of Franciscan Studies; works include *The Grey Friars in Oxford* (1892), *Studies in English Franciscan History* (1917), and (with F. Pelster, SJ) *Oxford Theology and Theologians c.A.D. 1282–1302* (1934); FBA, 1922.

LITTLE, Sir Charles James Colebrooke (1882–1973), admiral; joined HMS *Britannia*, 1897; served in submarines, 1903–18; CB (civil), 1917; commanded cruiser *Cleopatra* in Baltic campaign against Bolsheviks, 1918; CB (military), 1919; served in Admiralty, 1921; member, British delegation to Washington Naval Conference, 1921; held number of posts between 1922 and 1931, when he returned to submarines as rear-admiral; deputy chief of naval staff, Admiralty, 1932–5; KCB, 1935; commander-in-chief, China station, 1936–8; admiral, 1937; second sea lord, responsible for personnel, 1938–41; undertook mobilization of the fleet, 1938 and 1939; head of British Admiralty delegation,

Washington, 1941–2; commander-in-chief, Portsmouth, 1942–5; involved with operational planning for invasion of Europe; retired, GCB, 1945; Bronze Medal of Royal Humane Society for life-saving; grand officer, Legion of Honour; commander, USA, Legion of Merit; Grand Cross, Order of Orange Nassau; Order of St Olaf (Norway); vice-president, Navy Records Society and Royal United Services Institution.

LITTLE, Sir Ernest Gordon Graham Graham- (1867–1950), physician, and member of parliament for London University. See GRAHAM-LITTLE.

LITTLE, William John Knox- (1839–1918), divine and preacher. See KNOX-LITTLE.

LITTLEDALE, Sir Joseph (1767–1842), judge; MA, St John's College, Cambridge, 1790; barrister, Gray's Inn, 1798; counsel to the University of Cambridge, 1813; edited *Skelton's *Magnyfycence, an Interlude* (1821); judge in the court of King's Bench, 1824–41; knighted, 1824; privy councillor, 1841.

LITTLEDALE, Richard Frederick (1833–1890), Anglican controversialist; MA, Trinity College, Dublin, 1858; LL D, 1862; held curacies in England, but devoted himself mainly to literary work; published works in support of Anglicanism in opposition to Roman Catholicism, 1857–89.

LITTLER, Sir John Hunter (1783–1856), lieutenant-general, Indian Army; lieutenant, 10th Bengal Infantry, 1800; served in the campaigns under Lord *Lake, 1804–5; in Java, 1811–16; captain, 1812; commissary-general in the marquis of *Hastings's army, 1816–24; major, 1824; colonel, 36th Bengal Native Infantry, 1839–56; major-general, 1841; commander of the Agra division of the Bengal Army, 1843; KCB, 1844; served in the Sikh War, 1845; GCB and deputy governor of Bengal, 1849; lieutenant-general, 1851.

LITTLER, Sir Ralph Daniel Makinson (1835–1908), barrister; BA, London, 1854; called to bar, 1857; QC, 1873; treasurer of Middle Temple, 1900–1; CB, 1890; knighted, 1902; chairman of Middlesex Sessions and County Council from 1889 to death; was often criticized for long sentences on habitual criminals.

LITTLETON. See also LYTTELTON.

LITTLETON, Adam (1627–1694), lexicographer; educated at Westminster and Christ Church, Oxford; second master at Westminster, 1658; rector of Chelsea, 1669; chaplain to Charles II, 1670; published *A Latin Dictionary in four parts* (1673); prebendary of Westminster, 1674.

LITTLETON, Sir Edward, first Baron Littleton (1589–1645); educated at Christ Church, Oxford; BA, 1609; barrister, Inner Temple, 1617; chief justice of North Wales, 1621; MP, Leominster, 1625–6 and 1627–8; helped to frame the Petition of Right, 1628; bencher of his inn, 1629; recorder of London, 1631; reader to the Inner Temple, 1632; solicitor-general, 1634; knighted, 1635; chief justice of the common pleas, 1640; lord keeper, 1641; created Baron Littleton, 1641; DCL, Oxford, 1643.

LITTLETON, Edward (*fl.* 1694), agent for the island of Barbados; educated at Westminster and St Mary Hall, Oxford; BA, 1644; fellow of All Souls College, Oxford, 1647; MA, 1648; senior proctor, 1656; barrister, Lincoln's Inn, 1664; went to Barbados as secretary to Lord *Willoughby of Parham, 1666; judge, 1670–83; elected member of the assembly, 1674; agent for Barbados, 1683; published tracts on the colonies, finance, and general politics, 1664–94.

LITTLETON, Edward (d. 1733), divine and poet; educated at Eton and King's College, Cambridge; BA, 1720; LL D, *comitiis regiis*, 1728; assistant master at Eton, 1720; MA, 1724; a royal chaplain, 1730; his poems published in *Dodsley's *Collection* (edited 1782), the most celebrated being 'On a Spider'; two volumes of sermons published (1735).

LITTLETON, Edward John, first Baron Hatherton (1791–1863); of Rugby and Brasenose College, Oxford; MP, Staffordshire, 1812–32; created DCL, Oxford, 1817; supported Reform Bill; MP, South Staffordshire, 1832 and 1835; chief secretary to the lord-lieutenant of Ireland, 1833; privy councillor, 1833; supported new Coercion Bill, 1834, but resigned office in consequence of having made indiscreet communications to *O'Connell, 1834; created Baron Hatherton of Hatherton, 1835; began his political career as member of the Independent Country party, and ended it as a Whig.

LITTLETON, Henry (1823–1888), music publisher; entered music publishing house of *Novello, 1841; manager, 1846; partner, 1861; sole proprietor, 1866; retired, leaving largest business of the kind in the world, 1887.

LITTLETON, James (d. 1723), vice-admiral; grandnephew of Sir Thomas *Littleton (1647?–1710); present as first lieutenant at the Battle of La Hogue, 1692; captain, 1693; on the Newfoundland Station, 1696–7; in the East Indies acting against pirates, 1699; present at Alicante, 1706; in the West Indies, 1709–12; resident commissioner and commander-in-chief at Chatham, 1715; rear-admiral of the red, 1716; vice-admiral of the blue, 1717; MP, Queensborough, 1722.

LITTLETON, Sir Thomas (1422–1481), judge and legal author; sheriff of Worcestershire, 1447; serjeant-at-law, 1453; king's serjeant, 1455; justice of the common pleas, 1466; KB, 1475. His fame rests on his treatise on *Tenures*, written in law-French, and his text, with Coke's comment (see COKE, Sir EDWARD), long remained the principal authority on English real property law; the *editio princeps* is a folio published in London without date or title.

LITTLETON, Sir Thomas, third baronet (1647?–1710), speaker of the House of Commons and treasurer of the navy; educated at St Edmund Hall, Oxford; entered Inner Temple, 1671; succeeded to his father's baronetcy, 1681; MP, Woodstock, 1689–1702; an active Whig; a lord of the Admiralty, 1697; speaker of the House of Commons, 1698–1700; treasurer of the navy, 1701–10; MP, Castle Rising, Norfolk, 1702, Chichester, 1707, Portsmouth, 1708–10.

LITTLEWOOD, John Edensor (1885–1977), mathematician; educated at St Paul's School, London, and Trinity College, Cambridge; scholar, 1903; senior wrangler, 1905; first class, mathematical tripos, part ii, 1906; Richardson lecturer, Manchester, 1907–10; Smith's prizeman and fellow of Trinity College, Cambridge, 1908; succeeded A. N. *Whitehead as lecturer at Trinity, 1910; began his thirty-five-year collaboration with G. H. *Hardy, 1912; commissioned in Royal Garrison Artillery, 1914–18; employed on problems such as calculation of trajectories of anti-aircraft missiles; Cayley lecturer, Cambridge, 1920–8; Rouse Ball professor of mathematics, 1928–50; publications include *The Theory of Real Functions* (1926), and *Lectures on the Theory of Functions* (1944); enunciated with R. E. A. C. Paley ten *Theorems on Fourier Series and Power Series* (1931); completed details of proofs, 1937, four years after Paley's death; wrote many papers with G. H. Hardy and other mathematicians; also published *A Mathematician's Miscellany* (1953); FRS, 1916; received Royal (1929), Sylvester (1943), and Copley (1958) medals; awarded other medals and prizes and academic honours abroad; honorary degrees from Liverpool, St Andrews, and Cambridge.

LITTLEWOOD, Sir Sydney Charles Thomas (1895–1967), solicitor and principal architect of England's legal aid system in civil proceedings; worked as office boy in solicitor's office and as a police constable; served in army and RFC during 1914–18 war; prisoner of war;

admitted as solicitor, 1922; partnership with Wilkinson Howlett & Co., 1928; member, Council of Law Society, 1940; member, Committee on Legal Aid, 1944; chairman, Legal Aid Committee; knighted, 1951; president, Law Society, 1959; president, London Rent Assessment Panel, 1965–7.

LITTLEWOOD, William Edensor (1831–1886), miscellaneous writer; of Merchant Taylors' School and Pembroke College, Cambridge; BA, 1854; ordained, 1858; MA, 1859; published theological and historical works.

LITTLINGTON, William of (d. 1312), theological writer. See WILLIAM.

LITTON, Marie (1847–1884), actress; her real name Lowe; first appeared on the stage, 1868; managed the Court Theatre, 1871–4, the Imperial Theatre, 1878, and the Theatre Royal, Glasgow, 1880; made her reputation in old comedy in such parts as Lady Teazle, Lydia Languish, and Miss Hardcastle.

LIULF (or LIGULF) (d. 1080), Anglo-Saxon nobleman; friend of *Walcher, bishop of Durham; excited envy of bishop's chaplain, Leobwine, by whom he was murdered.

LIVEING, George Downing (1827–1924), chemist; BA, St John's College, Cambridge; eleventh wrangler, 1850; senior in new natural sciences tripos, 1851; fellow of St John's, 1853–60 and 1880–1924; professor of chemistry, Staff College and Royal Military College, Sandhurst, 1860; professor of chemistry, Cambridge, 1861–1908; carried out in collaboration with (Sir) James *Dewar spectroscopic investigations, 1878–1900; subjects investigated include the reversal of the lines of metallic vapours, the spectrum of carbon, ultraviolet spectra, and sun-spots; seventy-eight joint papers republished in a single volume, 1915; superintended erection of new university chemical laboratory from 1888; FRS, 1879; published *Chemical Equilibrium the Result of the Dissipation of Energy* (1885).

LIVELY, Edward (1545?–1605), Hebrew professor at Cambridge; MA, Trinity College, Cambridge, 1572; regius professor of Hebrew, 1575; prebendary of Peterborough, 1602; one of the translators of the Authorized Version, 1604; published *A true Chronologie of the . . . Persian Monarchie* (1597) and other works.

LIVENS, William Howard (1889–1964), soldier and inventor; educated at Oundle and Christ's College, Cambridge; commissioned in Royal Engineers, 1914; joined the Special brigade, formed to retaliate for German gas attacks; designed Livens gas-flame projector and phosgene bomb; MC, DSO, worked in Ministry of Supply, 1939–45.

LIVERPOOL, earls of. See JENKINSON, CHARLES, first earl, 1727–1808; JENKINSON, ROBERT BANKS, second earl, 1770–1828; JENKINSON, CHARLES CECIL COPE, third earl, 1784–1851.

LIVERSEEGE, Henry (1803–1832), painter; lived chiefly in Manchester; painted subject pictures.

LIVESAY, Richard (d. 1823?), portrait and landscape painter; exhibited portraits and domestic subjects at Royal Academy, 1776–1821; copied pictures at Windsor for Benjamin *West, and taught some of the royal children drawing, 1790; drawing-master to the Royal Naval College, Portsmouth, 1796.

LIVESEY, Sir George Thomas (1834–1908), promoter of labour co-partnership; joined South Metropolitan Gas Company, 1848; assistant manager, 1857; engineer and secretary, 1871; chairman of board of directors, 1885; adopted principle of sliding scale, 1876; admitted foremen (1886) and workmen (1889) to share in profits; capitalized bonus of workmen, who became shareholders (1894) and were admitted to board of directors (1898); sat on Labour Commission, 1891–4; knighted, 1902; erected Livesey Library, Camberwell; Livesey professorship of coal gas and fuel industries was founded at Leeds University.

LIVESEY, James (1625?–1682), divine; vicar of Great Budworth, Cheshire, 1657–82; published some scholarly sermons.

LIVESEY, Joseph (1794–1884), temperance advocate and philanthropist; brought out *The Moral Reformer*, a magazine, 1831–3 and 1838–9; issued the *Preston Temperance Advocate*, the first teetotal publication in England, 1834; managed the *Preston Guardian*, 1844–59, the *Teetotal Progressionist*, 1851–2, *The Staunch Teetotaler*, 1867–9; published an autobiography (1881).

LIVESEY, Sir Michael, first baronet (1611–1663?), regicide; created baronet, 1627; MP, Queensborough, Kent, 1645; signed Charles I's death-warrant; commissioner of the Admiralty and navy, 1660; escaped to the Low Countries at the Restoration.

LIVING (LYFING, ELFSTAN, or ETHELSTAN) (d. 1020), archbishop of Canterbury; bishop of Wells, 999; appointed to Canterbury by *Ethelred the Unready, 1013; crowned *Edmund Ironside, 1016, and *Canute, 1017.

LIVING (or LYFING) (d. 1046), bishop of Crediton; abbot of Tavistock, Devonshire; accompanied *Canute to Rome, and brought back his famous letter to the English people; bishop of Crediton, 1027; bishop of Worcester, holding the see in plurality, 1038, the see of Cornwall being merged with that of Crediton, c.1043.

LIVINGSTONE, Sir Alexander (d. 1450?), of Callander; guardian of *James II of Scotland; aided *James I of Scotland's widow in foiling Sir William *Crichton, 1439 and 1443; justiciary of Scotland, 1449; fell into disgrace and was imprisoned.

LIVINGSTONE, Alexander, seventh Baron Livingstone and first earl of Linlithgow (d. 1622), eldest son of William *Livingstone, sixth Baron; supported *Mary Queen of Scots; lord of the bedchamber, 1580; succeeded his father, 1592; commissioner of taxation, 1594; guardian of Princess Elizabeth, 1596–1603; privy councillor, 1598; created earl of Linlithgow, Lord Livingstone and Callander, 1600.

LIVINGSTONE, Charles (1821–1873), missionary and traveller; brother of David *Livingstone; emigrated to America and became a missionary, 1840; joined his brother in his African expeditions, 1857–63; appointed English consul at Fernando Po, 1864; the Bights of Benin and Biafra added to his district, 1867; died near Lagos.

LIVINGSTONE, Charlotte Maria, countess of Newburgh (d. 1755). See RADCLIFFE or RADCLYFFE, CHARLOTTE MARIA.

LIVINGSTONE, David (1813–1873), African missionary and explorer; educated himself while working at a cotton factory near Glasgow; attended the medical class at Anderson College and lectures at Glasgow University, 1832; entered the service of the London Missionary Society, studied medicine and science in London; embarked as a missionary for the Cape of Good Hope, 1840; made journeys into the interior, 1841, 1842, and 1843; discovered Lake Ngami, 1849, and the Zambezi in the centre of the continent, 1851; made great exploring expedition from Cape Town northwards through West-Central Africa to Loanda and back to Quilimane, 1852–6; visited England, 1856; DCL Oxford, and FRS; published his missionary travels, and severed his connection with the London Missionary Society, 1857; consul at Quilimane, 1858–64; commanded expedition to explore Eastern and Central Africa, 1858; discovered lakes Shirwa and Nyasa, 1859; lost his wife at Shupanga, 1862; visited England, 1864; published *The Zambesi and its Tributaries* (1865); started on expedition to solve the question of the Nile basin, 1865; discovered Lake Bangweolo, 1868; reached Ujiji, 1869; explored the cannibal country, enduring great sufferings, and returned, almost dying, to Ujiji, where he was rescued by Stanley, 1871; reached Unyanyembe, 1872; made further explorations to discover the sources of the Nile, and died at a village in the country of Ilala; buried in Westminster Abbey, 1874.

LIVINGSTONE, George, third earl of Linlithgow (1616–1690), eldest son of Alexander Livingstone, second earl of Linlithgow; MP, Perthshire, 1654–5; privy councillor, 1660; major-general of the forces in Scotland, 1677–9; justice-general, 1684; deprived of the justice-generalship at the Revolution.

LIVINGSTONE, George, fourth earl of Linlithgow (1652?–1695), eldest son of George *Livingstone, third earl of Linlithgow; supported his father against the Covenanters; attempted to support King James, 1689; succeeded his father, 1690; privy councillor and commissioner of the Treasury, 1692.

LIVINGSTONE, Sir James, of Barncloich, first Viscount Kilsyth (1616–1661), a devoted Royalist; raised to the peerage of Scotland as Viscount Kilsyth and Lord Campsie, 1661.

LIVINGSTONE, Sir James, of Kinnaird, first earl of Newburgh (d. 1670); gentleman of the bedchamber to Charles I, and created Viscount Newburgh, 1647; joined Charles II at The Hague, 1650; accompanied Charles's expedition to England, 1651; escaped to France after the Battle of Worcester, 1651; captain of the guards, 1660; created earl of Newburgh, Viscount Kinnaird, and Baron Livingstone of Flacraig, 1660.

LIVINGSTONE, James, first earl of Callander (d. 1674), third son of Alexander *Livingstone, first earl of Linlithgow; saw military service abroad; knighted before 1629; created Baron Livingstone of Almond, 1633; accepted office from the Covenanters, but secretly favoured Charles I, who created him earl of Callander, Baron Livingstone and Almond, 1641; appointed lieutenant-general of the 'Engagement' army raised to liberate the king; escaped to Holland on its failure; took an active part in parliament, 1661–72.

LIVINGSTONE, John (1603–1672), Scottish divine; educated at Glasgow University; licensed to preach, 1625; banished at the Restoration, 1660; died at Rotterdam; his *Life* first published (1754).

LIVINGSTONE, Sir Richard Winn (1880–1960), educationist; scholar of Winchester and New College, Oxford; first class, hon. mods. and Lit. Hum., 1901–3; fellow, tutor, and librarian, Corpus Christi College, until 1924; vice-chancellor, Queen's University, Belfast, 1924–33; president of Corpus, 1933–50; vice-chancellor,

Oxford University, 1944–7; originator and general editor, Clarendon Series of Greek and Latin authors; helped to found Denman College; publications include *A Defence of Classical Education* (1916); knighted, 1931; honorary degrees from ten universities.

LIVINGSTONE, Sir Thomas, first viscount of Teviot (1652?–1711), lieutenant-general; born in Holland; succeeded as second baronet; came to England with William of Orange, 1688; appointed colonel of the (present) Royal Scots Greys, 1688; commander-in-chief in Scotland and privy councillor, 1690; major-general on the English establishment, 1696; created viscount of Teviot in the peerage of Scotland, 1696; lieutenant-general, 1704.

LIVINGSTONE, William, sixth Baron Livingstone (d. 1592), partisan of Queen Mary; succeeded to barony, 1553; fought for *Mary Queen of Scots at Langside, and accompanied her in her flight, 1568; Mary's agent in England, 1570; advised the king to abolish the regency, 1577.

LIVINGUS (d. 1046), bishop of Crediton. See LIVING.

LIVINUS, Saint (d. 656?), known as the 'Apostle of Brabant'; the proof of his existence rests on an epistle and epitaph which he is said to have written; according to late authorities he was of Scottish or Irish race, and an archbishop of Ireland, who went to Ghent, 633, and was martyred at Escha.

LIVIUS, Titus (*fl.* 1437), historian; called himself Titus Livius de Frulovisiis, of Ferrara; came to England and found a patron in *Humphrey, duke of Gloucester; naturalized, 1437; his *Vita Henrici Quinti, Regis Invictissimi* edited by *Hearne (1716).

LIXNAW, Barons. See FITZMAURICE, THOMAS, 1502–1590; FITZMAURICE, PATRICK, 1551?–1600; FITZMAURICE, THOMAS, 1574–1630.

LIZARS, John (1787?–1860), surgeon; educated at Edinburgh University; his best-known work, *A System of Anatomical Plates of the Human Body, with Descriptions* (1822); professor of surgery in the Royal College of Surgeons, Edinburgh, 1831.

LIZARS, William Home (1788–1859), painter and engraver; brother of John *Lizars; learnt engraving from his father; studied painting at Trustees' Academy, Edinburgh; carried on the engraving business after his father's death, 1812; perfected method of etching for book illustration.

LLANDAFF, Viscount (1826–1913), lawyer and politician. See MATTHEWS, HENRY.

LLANOVER, first Baron (1802–1867), politician. See HALL, Sir BENJAMIN.

LLEWELLIN, John Jestyn, Baron Llewellin (1893–1957), politician and first governor-general of the Federation of the Rhodesias and Nyasaland; educated at Eton and University College, Oxford; called to bar (Inner Temple), 1921; Conservative MP, Uxbridge, 1929–45; civil lord of Admiralty, 1937–9; parliamentary secretary, Ministry of Supply (1939–40), Aircraft Production (1940–1), Transport (1941–2); minister, Aircraft Production, May–Nov. 1942; minister resident for supply, Washington, 1942–3; minister of food, 1943–5; first governor-general, Federation of the Rhodesias and Nyasaland, 1953–7; PC, 1941; baron, 1945; CBE, 1939; GBE, 1953.

LLEWELLYN, Richard (pseudonym) (1906–1983), novelist and dramatist. See LLOYD RICHARD DAFYDD VIVIAN LLEWELLYN.

LLEWELLYN, Sir (Samuel Henry) William (1858–1941), artist and president of Royal Academy of Arts; studied at South Kensington and in Paris; began exhibiting at Royal Academy, 1884; ARA, 1912; RA, 1920; president, 1928–38; negotiated and supervised arrangements for exhibitions of Dutch, Italian, Persian, French, Chinese, and Scottish art; also exhibition of industrial art, 1935; his portraits sincere and graceful rather than character-searching presentations; sitters included Queen *Mary, seventeenth earl of *Derby, and Archbishop *Lang; KCVO, 1918; GCVO, 1931.

LLEWELYN. See also LLUELYN and LLYWELYN.

LLEWELYN, David (d. 1415), Welsh warrior. See GAM.

LLEWELYN, Thomas (1720?–1793), Baptist minister; published an *Historical Account of the British or Welsh Versions and Editions of the Bible* (1768); prominent in establishment of Baptist mission in North Wales, 1776.

LLEWELYN DAVIES, Richard, Baron Llewelyn-Davies (1912–1981), architect; educated privately in Ireland and at Trinity College, Cambridge; studied at École des Beaux Arts, Paris; gained diploma, with honours, Architectural Association, London, 1937; ARIBA, 1939; during 1939–45 war worked on programme of factory-building with Sir Alexander Gibb & Partners; developed system for prefabricating railway stations for London, Midland, and Scottish Railway, 1942; developed influential programme of hospital design with Nuffield Foundation, 1948; FRIBA, 1956; professor of architecture, University College, London, 1960; developed new curriculum based on application of a science subject and mathematics to architecture; created life peer, 1963; professor of urban planning, University College, 1969–75; member, Royal Fine Art Commission, 1961–72; first chairman, Centre for Environmental Studies, 1967; formed partnership in new firm, Llewelyn-Davies Weeks, 1960, concerned with town-planning; responsible for development plan of Milton Keynes; many buildings designed by the firm, including the London Stock Exchange, but personally noted for his design of houses.

LLEYN, Sion (1749–1817), Welsh poet. See SION.

LLEYN, William (1530?–1587), Welsh poet. See OWEN.

LLOYD. See also LHUYD, LLWYD, and LOYD.

LLOYD, Bartholomew (1772–1837), provost of Trinity College, Dublin; educated at Trinity College, Dublin; MA, 1796; DD, 1808; Erasmus Smith's professor of mathematics, 1813; regius professor of Greek, 1821, 1823, and 1825; Erasmus Smith's professor of natural and experimental philosophy, 1822; king's lecturer in divinity, 1823 and 1827; provost, 1831–7; president of the Royal Irish Academy, 1835; 'Lloyd Exhibitions' founded in his memory, 1839.

LLOYD (or FLOYD), Sir Charles (d. 1661), Royalist; brother of Sir Godfrey *Lloyd or Floyd; quartermaster-general of the king's army, 1644; knighted, 1644.

LLOYD, Charles (1735–1773), secretary to George *Grenville; of Westminster and Christ Church, Oxford; MA, 1761; secretary to George Grenville, 1763; deputy-teller of the Exchequer, 1767; published political pamphlets in Grenville's interest, 1763–7.

LLOYD, Charles (1748–1828), Quaker; philanthropist; banker of Birmingham; a pioneer in the movement for the emancipation of slaves; published translations from Homer and Horace.

LLOYD, Charles (1766–1829), Dissenting minister and schoolmaster; held ministries in England till 1793; pastor in Cardiganshire and Suffolk; LL D, Glasgow, 1809; opened school in London, 1811; chief work, *Particulars in the Life of a Dissenting Minister* (autobiography, 1813).

LLOYD, Charles (1775–1839), poet; son of Charles *Lloyd (1748–1828); published poems, 1795; lived with *Coleridge, 1796–7; his poems appended to an edition of Coleridge's poems, along with verses by Charles *Lamb, 1797; cultivated Lamb's society; his *Desultory Thoughts in London* published (1821); became insane; died at Chaillot near Versailles.

LLOYD, Charles (1784–1829), bishop of Oxford; of Eton and Christ Church, Oxford; MA, 1809; mathematical lecturer, tutor, and censor, Christ Church, Oxford; preacher of Lincoln's Inn, 1819–22; regius professor of divinity, Oxford, 1822–9; bishop of Oxford, 1827–9; the first to publish the 'Book of Common Prayer' with red-lettered rubrics (1829).

LLOYD, Charles Dalton Clifford (1844–1891), servant of the crown; grandson of Bartholomew *Lloyd; educated at Sandhurst; in police force in British Burma, 1862–72; resident magistrate for Co. Down, 1874; employed to restore order in Co. Longford, 1881; concerted scheme (1881) for vigorous administration of Protection of Person and Property Act; inspector-general of reforms to khedive of Egypt, 1883; under-secretary at the Home Office in Egypt; resigned (1884) because his schemes for prison reform were not supported; again resident magistrate in Ireland, 1885; lieutenant-governor of Mauritius, 1885–7; consul for Kurdistan, 1889; died at Erzeroum, 1891; his *Ireland under the Land League, a Narrative of Personal Experiences* published (1892).

LLOYD, David (1597–1663), author of the *Legend of Captain Jones*; educated at Hart Hall, Oxford; BA, 1615; fellow of All Souls College, Oxford, 1618; DCL, 1628; canon of Chester, 1639; remembered by his popular *jeu d'esprit, The Legend of Captain Jones*, a burlesque on the adventures of an Elizabethan sea-rover named Jones (1631).

LLOYD, David (1635–1692), biographer; MA, Merton College, Oxford, 1659; reader in Charterhouse, London, 1659; chaplain to Isaac *Barrow, bishop of St Asaph; published *The Statesmen and Favourites of England since the Reformation* (1665 and 1670); his memoirs of Royalist sufferers published (1668).

LLOYD, David (d. 1714?); captain in the navy, 1677; employed by James II as agent and emissary during the reign of William III; retired into private life after James's death.

LLOYD, David (1752–1838), divine and poet; took holy orders, 1778; his *Characteristics of Men, Manners, and Sentiments, on the Voyage of Life* (1812) an imitation of *Young; published *Horae Theologicae* (1823).

LLOYD, Dorothy Jordan (1889–1946), biochemist; first classes, natural sciences tripos, 1910–12, Newnham College, Cambridge; fellow, 1914–21; joined British Leather Manufacturers' Research Association, 1920, director,

1927–46; planned and contributed to *Progress in Leather Science, 1920–45* (3 vols., 1946–8).

LLOYD, Edward (d. 1648?). See FLOYD.

LLOYD, Edward (*fl.* 1688–1726), coffee-house keeper, from whom the great commercial corporation known as 'Lloyd's' derives its name; his coffee-house in Lombard Street the centre of ship-broking and marine-insurance business, 1692; issued *Lloyd's News*, a shipping and commercial chronicle, 1696–7, revived as *Lloyd's Lists*, 1726, and still continued.

LLOYD, Edward (d. 1847), captain of the Gambia River; captain in the Royal African Corps, 1804–12; regarded as the founder of the Gambia River settlement, where he died.

LLOYD, Edward (1815–1890), founder of *Lloyd's Weekly London Newspaper*; sold books and published cheap literature in London; issued *Lloyd's Penny Weekly Miscellany*, 1842–4, continued as *Lloyd's Entertaining Journal* till 1847; first issued *Lloyd's Weekly London Newspaper*, 1842; bought the *Daily Chronicle*, 1876.

LLOYD, Edward Mayow Hastings (1889–1968), British and international civil servant, and world food expert; educated at Rugby and Corpus Christi College, Oxford; entered Home Civil Service and posted to Department of Inland Revenue, 1913; transferred to War Office, 1914–17; Ministry of Food, 1917–19; seconded to League of Nations Secretariat, 1919–21; Ministry of Agriculture, 1921–6; assistant secretary, Empire Marketing Board, 1926; secretary, Market Supply Committee, 1933; assistant director, Food (Defence Plans) Department, 1936; principal assistant secretary, general department, Ministry of Food, 1939; unhappy relationship with permanent secretary; transferred as economic adviser to Minister of State, Middle East, 1942; worked with Food and Agriculture Organization, 1946–7; under-secretary, Ministry of Food, 1947–53; president, Agricultural Economics Society, 1956; consultant to Political and Economic Planning, 1958–64; publications include *Stabilisation* (1923), *Experiments in State Control* (1924), and *Food and Inflation in the Middle East, 1940–1945* (1956); CMG, 1945; CB, 1952.

LLOYD, Evan (1734–1776), poet; MA, Jesus College, Oxford, 1757; published *The Powers of the Pen*, an attack on *Warburton and *Johnson (1765), *The Curate* (1766), and *The Methodist*, for which latter satire he underwent imprisonment for libel; friend of *Wilkes and *Garrick.

LLOYD, George (1560–1615), bishop of Chester; fellow of Magdalene College, Cambridge; rector of Heswell-in-Wirrall, Cheshire, and divinity reader in Chester Cathedral; bishop of

Sodor and Man, 1600, of Chester, 1604; held livings in addition to his sees.

LLOYD, George Ambrose, first Baron Lloyd (1879–1941), statesman; educated at Eton and Trinity College, Cambridge; coxed winning Cambridge boat, 1899, 1900; Conservative MP, West Staffordshire, 1910–18, Eastbourne, 1924–5; attached to Arab Bureau, 1916–17; DSO, 1917; governor of Bombay, 1918–23; initiated Bombay development scheme and Lloyd Barrage across Indus; GCIE, 1918; GCSI and PC, 1924; high commissioner in Egypt and baron, 1925; his views increasingly divergent from government; virtually compelled to resign by Arthur *Henderson, 1929; published *Egypt since Cromer* (2 vols., 1933–4); chairman, British Council, 1937–40; secretary of state for colonies, 1940–1; flew to Bordeaux in unsuccessful attempt to persuade French government to continue fighting, 1940.

LLOYD (or **FLOYD**), Sir **Godfrey** (*fl.* 1667), military engineer; brother of Sir Charles *Lloyd or Floyd; captain in the Dutch service; knighted by Charles II, 1657; chief engineer of ports, castles, and fortifications in England, 1661–7.

LLOYD, Hannibal Evans (1771–1847), philologist and translator; son of Henry Humphrey Evans *Lloyd; settled at Hamburg, 1800; held appointment in London Foreign Office, 1813–47; published annals of Hamburg for 1813 (1813); his *Theoretisch-praktische Englische Sprachlehre für Deutsche* (1833) long the standard grammar in several German universities; published translations from various European languages.

LLOYD, Henry (or **Henry Humphrey Evans**) (1720?–1783), historian and soldier; engineer in the Young Pretender's (see CHARLES EDWARD LOUIS PHILIP CASIMIR) expedition to Scotland, 1745; distinguished himself at the siege of Bergen-op-Zoom, 1747, and was made major in the French Army, 1747; served first on Austrian side, and afterwards on Prussian side, in the Seven Years' War; in the Russian service, 1774; occupied himself with literary work, 1779–83; died at Hay, Belgium; chief works, *History of the War between the King of Prussia and the Empress of Germany and her Allies* (vol. i, 1766, vols. ii and iii, 1782) and *A Political and Military Rhapsody on the Defence of Great Britain* (1779).

LLOYD, Hugh (1546–1601), master of Winchester College; educated at Winchester and New College, Oxford; BA, 1566; chancellor of Rochester, 1578; master of Winchester, 1580–7; DCL, 1588; Latin phrase-book by him published (1654).

LLOYD, Hugh (1586–1667), bishop of Llandaff; MA, Oriel College, Oxford, 1614; held various livings in Wales, 1617–44; DD, 1638; a staunch Royalist; his benefices sequestered during the Civil Wars; canon and archdeacon of St David's, 1644; bishop of Llandaff, 1660–7.

LLOYD, Sir Hugh Pughe (1894–1981), air chief marshal; educated at King's School, Worcester, and Peterhouse, Cambridge; enlisted as private in Royal Engineers, 1915; commissioned in Royal Flying Corps, 1917; bomber reconnaissance pilot; MC, Croix de Guerre, and DFC, 1918; permanently commissioned in RAF, 1919; flight commander with No. 28 Squadron in India, 1920–4; passed through RAF Staff College; promoted squadron leader; chief flying instructor, No. 2 Flying Training School; took Staff College course at Quetta, 1931–2; on air staff, HQ No. 1 Indian Group, Peshawar, 1933–5; senior RAF instructor, Staff College, Camberley, 1936–8; commanded bomber station, Marham, as group captain, 1939; senior air staff officer, No. 2 (Bomber) Group, 1940–1; air vice-marshal commanding RAF Mediterranean, Malta, 1941–2; Senior air staff officer, RAF Middle East, 1942–3; commanded North-West African Coastal Air Forces, 1943–4; CBE, 1941; CB and KBE, 1942; officer of French Legion of Honour, 1943, and commander, 1945; officer of US Legion of Merit, 1944; acting air marshal commanding Tiger Force long-range RAF bomber group, 1945; RAF instructor, Imperial Defence College, 1946; commander RAF in Far East, 1947–9; head of Bomber Command, 1950–3; air chief marshal and KCB, 1951; president, Polish Air Force Association and RAF Association, Wales; honorary degree, University of Wales; published *Briefed to Attack* (1949).

LLOYD, Humphrey (1610–1689), bishop of Bangor; educated at Jesus and Oriel colleges, Oxford; MA, 1635; prebendary of York, 1660; dean of St Asaph, 1663–74; bishop of Bangor, 1674–89.

LLOYD, Humphrey (1800–1881), provost of Trinity College, Dublin, and man of science; son of Bartholomew *Lloyd; BA, Trinity College, Dublin, 1819; junior fellow, 1824; MA, 1827; Erasmus Smith's professor of natural and experimental philosophy, 1831–43; president of Royal Irish Academy, 1846–51; hon. DCL, Oxford, 1855; vice-provost, 1862; provost, 1867; published treatises on optics and magnetism, embodying his discoveries.

LLOYD, Jacob Youde William (1816–1887), genealogist; son of Jacob William Hinde, but assumed name of Lloyd on succeeding to estates,

1857; MA, Wadham College, Oxford, 1874; convert to Roman Catholicism; served in the pontifical Zouaves; published genealogical works.

LLOYD (FLOYD or FLUD), John (d. 1523), composer; took a musical degree at Oxford; attended Henry VIII at the Field of the Cloth of Gold, 1520; his extant compositions in the British Museum Add. MSS.

LLOYD, John (1558–1603), classical scholar; brother of Hugh *Lloyd (1546–1601); of Winchester and New College, Oxford; perpetual fellow, 1579–96; MA, 1585; edited, with Latin translation and notes, *Flavii Josephi de Maccabaeis liber* (1590); DD, 1595; vicar of Writtle, Essex, 1598–1603.

LLOYD, John (d. 1682), poet; brother of Nicholas *Lloyd; MA, Wadham College, Oxford, 1669; published a *Paraphrase* of the Song of Solomon (1682).

LLOYD, John (1638–1687), bishop of St David's; of Merton College, Oxford; MA, 1662; precentor of Llandaff, 1672; principal of Jesus College, Oxford, 1673; DD, 1674; vice-chancellor of Oxford 1682–5; bishop of St David's, 1686.

LLOYD, John Augustus (1800–1854), engineer and surveyor; served on the staff of Simon Bolivar, the liberator of Colombia, as a captain of engineers; surveyed Isthmus of Panama, 1827; FRS, 1830; colonial civil engineer and surveyor-general in Mauritius, 1831–49; British chargé d'affaires, Bolivia, 1851; died at Therapia.

LLOYD, Sir John Edward (1861–1947), historian; educated at University College of Wales, Aberystwyth, and Lincoln College, Oxford; first class, modern history, 1885; lecturer, Aberystwyth, 1885–92; lecturer in Welsh history (1892–9), Bangor; registrar (1892–1919); professor of history, 1899–1930; first chairman, Board of Celtic Studies, 1919–40; publications include *History of Wales to the Edwardian Conquest* (2 vols., 1911); FBA, 1930; knighted, 1934.

LLOYD, John Selwyn Brooke, Baron Selwyn-Lloyd (1904–1978), politician; educated at Fettes College, Edinburgh, and Magdalene College, Cambridge; president of the Union, 1927; called to the bar (Gray's Inn), 1930 and practised on northern circuit; served during 1939–45 war in the Royal Horse Artillery; OBE, 1943; CBE, 1945; Conservative MP for Wirral, 1945–76; KC, 1947; recorder of Wigan, 1948–51; minister of state, Foreign Office, 1951–4; minister of supply, 1954–5; entered Cabinet as minister of defence, 1955; foreign secretary, 1955–60; involved in Suez crisis; unaware of secret military agreement between Britain, France, and Israel, 1956, but loyally supported Anthony Eden (later earl of Avon) in policy towards Egypt in spite of his own misgivings; concerned with restoring good Anglo-American relations and improving Anglo-Soviet relations; opened negotiations for Britain's entry to European Economic Community, 1959; chancellor of the Exchequer, 1960–2; introduced 'pay pause'; dismissed by Harold Macmillan (later earl of Stockton) in 'the night of the long knives', 1962; CH, 1962; deputy lord lieutenant, Chester, 1963; hon. fellow, Magdalene College; returned to government as leader of House of Commons, 1963–4; resigned from shadow Cabinet, 1966; accepted company directorships; elected speaker of House of Commons, 1971–6; created life peer, 1976; published *Mr Speaker Sir* (1976) and *Suez 1956* (1978); received number of honorary degrees.

LLOYD, Julius (1830–1892), divine and author; MA, Trinity College, Cambridge, 1855; canon of Manchester, 1891; author of sermons and essays.

LLOYD, Ludovic (Lodowick or **Lewis)** (*fl.* 1573–1610), poet and compiler; 'Seargeant at Armes' to Queen Elizabeth and James I; author of *The Pilgrimage of Princes*, compiled from Greek and Latin authors (1573), and other compilations and poems, mainly treating of 'Collectanea Curiosa'.

LLOYD, Marie (pseudonym) (1870–1922), music-hall comedian. See WOOD, MATILDA ALICE VICTORIA.

LLOYD, Sir Nathaniel (1669–1741), master of Trinity Hall, Cambridge; son of Sir Richard *Lloyd (1634–1686); of St Paul's School, London, and Trinity College, Oxford; fellow of All Souls College, Oxford, 1689; DCL, 1696; member of the College of Advocates, 1696; knighted, 1710; master of Trinity Hall, Cambridge, 1710–35; vice-chancellor, 1710–11; king's advocate, 1715–27.

LLOYD, Nicholas (1630–1680), historical compiler; educated at Winchester and Hart Hall and Wadham College, Oxford; MA, 1658; university rhetoric reader, 1665; sub-warden of Wadham College, 1666 and 1670; published a *Dictionarium Historicum* (1670).

LLOYD, Richard (1595–1659), Royalist divine; educated at Oriel College, Oxford; BD, 1628; on outbreak of Civil War deprived of his preferments and imprisoned.

LLOYD, Sir Richard (1606–1676), Royalist; entered Inner Temple, 1631; attended Charles I in the north, 1639; attorney-general for North Wales and knighted, 1642; justice of Glamorganshire, Brecknockshire, and Radnorshire, 1660; MP, Radnorshire, 1661.

LLOYD, Sir Richard (1634–1686), judge; fellow of All Souls College, Oxford; DCL, 1662; advocate at Doctors' Commons, 1664; Admiralty advocate, 1674–85; chancellor of the dioceses of Llandaff and Durham; knighted, 1677; MP, Durham, 1679–81 and 1685; dean of the arches, 1684–6; judge of the High Court of Admiralty, 1685–6.

LLOYD, Richard (d. 1834), divine; educated at Magdalene College, Cambridge; MA and fellow, 1790; published theological works.

LLOYD, Richard Dafydd Vivian Llewellyn (1906–1983), novelist and dramatist under name of Richard Llewellyn; educated at schools in south Wales and London; worked in hotels in London and in Italy, and enlisted in 1926 and served in army in India and Hong Kong; returned to Britain, 1931; film reporter *Cinema Express*; had successful run with play *Poison Pen* (1937); obtained instant celebrity and assured income with novel *How Green was my Valley* (1939), filmed under direction of John Ford (1941); subsequent novels include *None but the Lonely Heart* (1943), *A Few Flowers for Shiner* (1960), *A Man in a Mirror* (1964), *Bride of Israel, my Love* (1973), *A Hill of Many Dreams* (1974), each set in England, Italy, Kenya, Israel, and other countries in which Llewellyn had travelled; two further novels about the Welsh of Patagonia, *Up, Into the Singing Mountain* (1963) and *Down where the Moon is Small* (1966), were followed by *Green, Green My Valley Now* (1975); in all wrote twenty-three novels and four stage plays.

LLOYD, Ridgway Robert Syers Christian Codner (1842–1884), physician and antiquary; MRCS and LSA, 1866; published *An Account of the Altars, Monuments, and Tombs in St. Albans Abbey* (1873), and wrote many archaeological papers.

LLOYD, Robert (1733–1764), poet; of Westminster and Trinity College, Cambridge; MA, 1758; published *The Actor* (1760) and a collection of poems (1762); edited the *St. James's Magazine*, 1762–3; imprisoned for debt; drudged for the booksellers; his comic opera, *The Capricious Lovers*, performed, 1764; friend of *Churchill, *Garrick, and *Wilkes.

LLOYD, Simon (1756–1836), Welsh Methodist; MA, Jesus College, Oxford, 1779; associated himself with the Calvinistic Methodist movement after 1785; edited the Welsh magazine *Y Drysorfa*, 1814; published a biblical chronology (1816) and a commentary on the Apocalypse (1828), both in Welsh.

LLOYD, Thomas (1784–1813), colonel; served in the Egyptian campaign, 1801; at Gibraltar, 1802; captain, 1803; served at Copenhagen and throughout the Peninsular campaigns, 1808–10; major, 1810; killed at Battle of Nivelle.

LLOYD, Sir Thomas Ingram Kynaston (1896–1968), civil servant; educated at Rossall School and Gonville and Caius College, Cambridge; served in Royal Engineers in 1914–18 war; entered Home Civil Service and posted to Ministry of Health, 1920; transferred to Colonial Office, 1921; private secretary to permanent under-secretary of state, 1929; secretary, Palestine Commission, 1929; Colonial Service Department, 1930–8; secretary, Royal Commission on West Indies, 1938; assistant secretary, 1939; head of Defence Department, 1942; assistant under-secretary, West African and Eastern Departments, 1943; permanent under-secretary of state, 1947–56; CMG, 1943; KCMG, 1947; KCB, 1949; GCMG, 1951; director, Harrisons and Crosfield Ltd.; governor and member, Rossall School Council, 1956–68.

LLOYD, William (1627–1717), successively bishop of St Asaph, of Lichfield and Coventry, and of Worcester; son of Richard *Lloyd (1595–1659); of Oriel and Jesus colleges, Oxford; MA, 1646; MA, Cambridge, 1660; prebendary of Ripon, 1663; DD, 1667; prebendary of Salisbury, 1667; archdeacon of Merioneth, 1668–72; dean of Bangor and prebendary of St Paul's, 1672; bishop of St Asaph, 1680; tried with the six other bishops on the charge of publishing a seditious libel against the king and acquitted, 1688; bishop of Lichfield and Coventry, 1692, of Worcester, 1700; being half crazed by excessive study of the apocalyptic visions prophesied to Queen *Anne, *Harley, *Evelyn, and *Whiston; a staunch supporter of the Revolution and an excellent scholar; engaged *Burnet to undertake *The History of the Reformation of the Church of England* and gave him valuable assistance; published sermons and controversial pamphlets.

LLOYD, William (1637–1710), nonjuring bishop of Norwich; MA, St John's College, Cambridge; DD, *per literas regias*, 1670; chaplain to the English Merchants' Factory, Portugal; prebendary of St Paul's, 1672–6; bishop of Llandaff, 1675–9, of Peterborough, 1679–85, of Norwich, 1685–91; deprived of his office for refusing the oath of allegiance to William III, 1691.

LLOYD, William Forster (1794–1852), mathematician; of Westminster and Christ Church, Oxford; MA, 1818; Greek reader, 1823; mathematical lecturer at Christ Church, Oxford, 1824; Drummond professor of political economy, 1832–7; FRS, 1834; published professorial lectures.

LLOYD, William Watkiss (1813–1893), classical and Shakespearian scholar; partner in tobacco-manufacturing business in London; retired, 1864; member of Society of Dilettanti, 1854; published *History of Sicily, to the Athenian War* (1872), *The Age of Pericles* (1875), *The Moses of Michael Angelo* (1863), *Homer, his Art and Age* (1848), *Shakespeare's 'Much Ado about Nothing'* . . . *in fully recovered Metrical Form* (1884—he contended that Shakespeare's prose was disguised blank verse), and other miscellaneous works.

LLOYD GEORGE, David, first Earl Lloyd-George of Dwyfor (1863–1945), statesman; brought up at Llanystumdwy, Caernarfonshire, by widowed mother and her shoemaker brother; attendance at church school developed his hostility to English privilege; qualified as solicitor with honours, 1884; established reputation as fearless advocate and made mark as speaker on religious, temperance, and political subjects; elected Liberal MP for Caernarfon Boroughs, 1890; retained seat until 1945; became leading Welsh political figure; his opposition to South African War made him notorious; escaped mob in Birmingham disguised as policeman, 1901; opposed rate-aid to voluntary schools, started revolt schools in Wales, and added to his reputation as champion of Welsh causes; became less single-minded after taking office; obtained a Welsh department in the Board of Education, but his delays over Welsh Church disestablishment (not effected until 1920) irritated his followers; president of Board of Trade and PC, 1905; a patient negotiator in settling strikes; promoted Merchant Shipping Act, 1906, Port of London Act, 1908; chancellor of Exchequer, 1908; introduced first ('the People's') budget (1909) providing funds for social services and setting up road and development funds; most controversial measure the taxes on unearned increment in land values (abolished, 1920); rejection of budget by House of Lords led to general election, Jan. 1910, after which it was passed; on appearance of *Panther* at Agadir, 1911, warned Germany that Britain would resist interference with her international interests; established contributory scheme of health and unemployment insurance, 1911; ill-judged investment in American Marconi shares when government was concluding contract with British company (1912) led to investigation by select committee which cleared his honour; after German violation of Belgian frontier (1914) handled immediate crisis with courage and skill; introduced first war budget, Nov. 1914; doubled income-tax; increased tea and beer duties; in conduct of war favoured 'sideshows' and was never content with policy of maximum concentration in west; minister of munitions, May 1915–July 1916; secretary of state for war, July 1916; deeply agitated by progress of war; his resignation (5 Dec. 1916) precipitated crisis; succeeded Asquith as prime minister 7 Dec.; obtained support of Conservative, Labour, and some Liberal members; made immediate impact as most widely known, dynamic, and eloquent figure then in British politics; set up War Cabinet of five; summoned dominion ministers to Imperial War Conference and War Cabinet; persisted in urging convoy system on Admiralty; in land campaign fought for pooling of resources, unified conception of front from Flanders to Mesopotamia with attack at weakest points, and unity of command in France; his dislike of offensives in west increased by events of 1917; obtained establishment of Supreme War Council, Nov. 1917; appointment of Foch as commander-in-chief of Allied armies in France, April 1918; at home (1917) set up Irish Convention, forecast responsible government for India, and enthusiastically supported Balfour declaration on national home for Jews; took extreme measures to reinforce army during German offensive, 1918; persuaded Commons that charges of issuing misleading statements on military matters were unfounded, May 1918; with Bonar Law, appealed to country as coalition, 1918; returned with large Unionist majority but only 133 Liberal supporters; OM, 1919; spent five months in Paris negotiating peace treaty, 1919; sought pacification and economic survival of Europe at this and subsequent conferences, culminating in Genoa Conference, 1922; negotiated treaty with Ireland, 1921; averted war by firm handling of Chanak crisis, 1922, but gave Conservatives opportunity to end coalition; resigned Oct. 1922; returned at head of fifty-five National Liberals; controlled party fund believed acquired by traffic in honours; increased it by journalism and investment in and skilful management of *Daily Chronicle* and other periodicals; used fund to investigate social problems on which he produced series of able reports; Liberal party reunited by general election, 1923; differences with Asquith ended in separation over General Strike, 1926; after Asquith's resignation (1926) worked hard as chairman of parliamentary party to restore liberalism; advocated expansionist remedies for unemployment; despite lavish expenditure, returned with only fifty-nine followers, 1929; opposed general election of 1931 and returned with family party of four; declined to stand again for party leadership; developed agricultural estate at Churt; settled there and wrote *The Truth About Reparations and War-Debts* (1932), *War Memoirs* (6 vols., 1933–6), and *The Truth About the Peace Treaties* (2 vols., 1938); launched unsuccessful programme for 'new deal' and Council of Action for Peace and Reconstruction, 1935; had become increasingly hostile to France and partial to Germany; visited Hitler, who much impressed him, 1936; as he gradually recognized the German menace, urged co-operation with Russia and attacked Chamberlain's policy of appeasement; owing to declining health refused invitation to enter (Sir) Winston Churchill's government and the ambassadorship in Washington, 1940; created earl, 1945; buried on bank of River Dwyfor.

LLOYD GEORGE, Frances Louise, Countess Lloyd-George of Dwyfor (1888–1972), political secretary; daughter of John Stevenson; educated at Clapham High School and Royal Holloway College, London; appointed private tutor in French and music to *Megan, younger daughter of David Lloyd George, chancellor of the Exchequer, 1911; became mistress of Lloyd George and his personal secretary, 1913; worked closely with him throughout his political career as minister of munitions and prime minister; CBE, 1918; together they arranged purchase of estate at Churt, Surrey, 1921; declined suggestion, when Bonar Law became prime minister, that she should stay on as civil servant; daughter, Jennifer, born, 1929; involved in research and writing of Lloyd George's *War Memoirs* (6 vols., 1933–6); Margaret, wife of Lloyd George died, 1941; Frances and Lloyd George married, 1943; lived briefly at Criccieth during which time Lloyd George became Earl Lloyd-George of Dwyfor, 1945; after his death in 1945 and quarrels with his children, she lived quietly at Churt; published *The Years that are Past* (1967); A. J. P. Taylor edited and published her diary from 1914 to 1944 (1971).

LLOYD-GEORGE, Gwilym, first Viscount Tenby (1894–1967), politician; son of David Lloyd George, prime minister; educated at Eastbourne College and Jesus College, Cambridge; served in army during 1914–18 war; National Liberal MP, Pembrokeshire, 1922–4; managing director, United Newspapers, 1925–6; MP, Pembrokeshire, 1929–50; parliamentary secretary, Board of Trade, 1939–41; parliamentary secretary, Ministry of Food, 1941–2; Minister of Fuel and Power, 1942–5; National Liberal and Conservative MP, Newcastle upon Tyne (North), 1951–7; Minister of Food, 1951–4; home secretary, 1954–7; viscount, 1957; president, Fleming Memorial Fund for Medical Research, 1961; hon. fellow, Jesus College, Cambridge, 1953.

LLOYD GEORGE, Lady Megan (1902–1966), politician; daughter of David Lloyd George, prime minister; educated at Garratts' Hall, Banstead, and in Paris; Liberal MP, Anglesey, 1929–51; served on wartime consultative committees for ministries of Health and Labour; member of Speaker's Conference on Electoral Reform, 1944; deputy leader, Liberal Parliamentary party, 1949; after 1951 much involved with Welsh affairs; joined Labour party, 1955; Labour MP, Carmarthen, 1957–66; CH, 1966; superb speaker in Welsh or English; member, BBC Advisory Council; bard of National Eisteddfod, 1935; first woman member of Welsh Church Commissioners, 1942.

LLOYD-GREAME, Philip, first earl of Swinton (1884–1972), politician. See CUNLIFFE-LISTER.

LLOYD JAMES, Arthur (1884–1943), phonetician. See JAMES.

LLUELYN. See also LLEWELYN and LLYWELYN.

LLUELYN (or LLUELLYN), Martin (1616–1682), poet, physician, and principal of St Mary Hall, Oxford; of Westminster and Christ Church, Oxford; MA, 1643; joined the royal army; published *Men Miracles, with other Poems* (1646); ejected from Oxford, 1648; physician in London; MD, Oxford, 1653; FRCP, 1659; principal of St Mary Hall, 1660–4; physician at High Wycombe after 1664; mayor of High Wycombe, 1671.

LLWYD. See also LHUYD, LLOYD, and LOYD.

LLWYD, Edward (*fl.* 1328–1405), Welsh bard and lord of Llechryd. See IOLO GOCH.

LLWYD, Sir Gruffydd (*fl.* 1322), Welsh hero; grandson of *Ednyved Vychan; knighted, 1284; rebelled against the English and was defeated and imprisoned.

LLWYD, Gruffydd (*fl.* 1370–1420), Welsh poet; family bard to Owen *Glendower. Two poems by him published.

LLWYD, Hugh (or Huw) (1533?–1620), Welsh poet; held commission in the English Army and saw service abroad; his best-known production, a 'Poem on the Fox', printed in *Cymru Fu* (i. 357).

LLWYD, Humphrey (1527–1568), physician and antiquary; of Brasenose College, Oxford; MA, 1551; MP, East Grinstead, 1559, Denbigh boroughs, 1563–7; author of antiquarian works, among them, *Commentarioli Descriptionis Britannicae Fragmentum,* published at Cologne (1572; an English translation, *The Breviary of Britain,* published in London, 1573), and *Cambriae Typus,* one of the earliest known maps of Wales.

LLWYD (or LLOYD), John (1558?–1603), of Winchester and New College, Oxford; fellow of New College, 1579; MA, 1585; DD, 1595; author of an edition of Josephus's *De Maccabaeis*

(1590); edited Barlaamus's *De Papae Principatu* (1592).

LLWYD, Morgan (1619–1659), Welsh Puritan divine and mystic writer; grandson or nephew of Hugh *Llwyd; served with the Parliamentary army in England; founded a Nonconformist church at Wrexham, and became its first minister, c.1646. His published works rank among the Welsh prose classics.

LLWYD, Richard (1752–1835), poet; known as 'the Bard of Snowdon'; 'Beaumaris Bay', his best-known poem, published (1800); published other poems, 1804.

LLYWARCH AB LLYWELYN (*fl.* 1160–1220), Welsh bard, otherwise known as Prydydd y Moch; the most illustrious Welsh bard of the middle ages; some of his poems, all of which are historically valuable, printed in the *Myvyrian Archaiology of Wales*.

LLYWARCH HEN, or the Aged (496?–646?), British chieftain and bard; not mentioned till several centuries after his death; ancient form of his name Loumarc; probably spent some time at *Arthur's court. Twelve poems, six of an historical character and the remainder on moral subjects, are ascribed to him, and were first published with an English translation (1792).

LLYWELYN. See also LLEWELYN and LLUELYN.

LLYWELYN AB GRUFFYDD (d. 1282), prince of Wales; son of *Gruffydd ab Llywelyn (d. 1244); succeeded (with his elder brother, Owain the Red) his uncle, Davydd ab Llywelyn (see DAVYDD II), as ruler of Wales, 1246; did homage to Henry III, and gave up to him all lands east of the Conway, 1247; allied himself with Simon of *Montfort, 1262; took the offensive against Prince Edward and forced him to a truce, 1263; after renewal of hostilities (1265) agreed to hold the principality of Wales subject to the crown of England, 1267; neglected to do homage to Edward I, 1272; quarrelled with *Gruffydd ab Gwenwynwyn and *Davydd III and drove them to England, 1274; signed Treaty of Conway, 1277; married to Eleanor of *Montfort (d. 1282), 1278; revolted against English rule and was slain in a skirmish, 1282; the last champion of Welsh liberty.

LLYWELYN AB IORWERTH (called LLYWELYN THE GREAT) (d. 1240), prince of North Wales, afterwards called prince of Wales; son of *Owain Gwynedd; brought up in exile, probably in England; drove his uncle Davydd ab Owain (see DAVYDD I) from his territory, 1194; made peace with *Gwenwynwyn, 1202; married *Joan (d. 1237), King John's illegitimate daughter, 1206; with John's help extended his power to South Wales, 1207; opposed by John with some success, 1208–11; regained his possessions and conquered South Wales, 1212–15; prince of all Wales not ruled by the Normans, 1216; did homage to Henry III, 1218; fought against the English, 1228; submitted to Henry III, 1237; the greatest of the native rulers of Wales.

LLYWELYN AB RHYS (commonly called LLYWELYN BREN) (d. 1317), Welsh rebel; held high office under Gilbert de *Clare (1291–1314); revolted against one of the English overlords, 1314; surrendered, 1316; tried, condemned, and hung.

LLYWELYN AB SEISYLL (or SEISYLLT) (d. 1023?), king of Gwynedd; took possession of the throne of North Wales, c.1018.

LLYWELYN OF LLANGEWYDD (or LLEWELYN SION) (1520?–1616), Welsh bard; disciple of Thomas Llewelyn of Rhegoes; gained his living by transcribing Welsh manuscripts; several of his compositions published in the Iolo MSS.

LOATES, Thomas (1867–1910), jockey; first rode a winner, 1883; won Derby, 1889; headed list of winning jockeys, 1889, 1890, and 1893; won on Isinglass the Two Thousand Guineas, Derby, and St Leger, 1893, and on St Frusquin the Two Thousand Guineas, 1896; a resourceful rider; amassed large fortune.

LOBB, Emmanuel (1594–1671), provincial of English Jesuits and dramatist. See SIMEON, JOSEPH.

LOBB, Stephen (d. 1699), Nonconformist divine; imprisoned for complicity in the Rye House Plot, 1683; published controversial pamphlets.

LOBB, Theophilus (1678–1763), physician; son of Stephen *Lobb; educated for the ministry; studied medicine and practised while acting as Nonconformist minister; MD, Glasgow, 1722; FRS, 1729; applied himself wholly to medicine from 1736; LRCP, 1740; published religious and medical works.

LOBEL, Edgar (1888–1982), Greek scholar; educated at Manchester Grammar School and Balliol College, Oxford; first class, classical hon. mods. (1909) and Lit. Hum. (1911); assistant in humanity, Edinburgh University, 1911–12; Craven fellow, Oxford, studying papyri, 1912–13; research student, The Queen's College, 1914; during 1914–18 war worked in military intelligence; sub-librarian, Bodleian Library, 1919–34; continued work on papyri and produced edition of Sappho (1925) and Alcaeus (1927); supernumerary fellow. The Queen's College, 1927; keeper of western manuscripts, Bodleian Library, 1931–8; editor, literary papyri in Oxyrhynchus series, 1934; reader in papyrology, Oxford, 1936; senior research fellow, The Queen's College, 1938–59; edited texts of Hesiod, Aeschylus, Sophocles, and other Greek authors; hon. Litt.D., Cambridge, 1954; hon. fellow, Balliol, 1959, and Queen's, 1959.

LÖBEL, Hirsch (1721–1800), chief rabbi. See LYON, HART.

LOCH, Sir Charles Stewart (1849–1923), social worker; born in Bengal; BA, Balliol College, Oxford; influenced by T. H. *Green and Arnold *Toynbee; secretary to council of Charity Organisation Society, 1875–1914; his enthusiastic idealism, combined with common sense and efficiency, infected paid staff and volunteers; made influence of Society felt in social legislation and in institution of hospital almoners; member of several royal commissions, 1893–1909; majority report on poor laws largely his work; Tooke professor of economic science and statistics, King's College, London, 1904–8; knighted, 1915.

LOCH, David (d. 1780), writer on commerce; inspector-general of the woollen manufactures of Scotland, 1776, and afterwards of the fisheries; author of pamphlets advocating the abolition of the wool duties (1774) and of *Essays on the Trade, Commerce, Manufactures, and Fisheries of Scotland* (1775).

LOCH, Granville Gower (1813–1853), captain in the navy; son of James *Loch; entered the navy, 1826; commander, 1837; attained post rank and went to China as a volunteer, 1841; published *The Closing Events of the Campaign in China* (1843); employed at Nicaragua, 1848; CB, 1848; took prominent part in the second Burmese War, 1852–3; shot while attacking Donabew; buried at Rangoon.

LOCH, Henry Brougham, first Baron Loch of Drylaw (1827–1900); gazetted to 3rd Bengal Cavalry, 1844; aide-de-camp to Lord *Gough in Sutlej campaign, 1845; adjutant of Skinner's (irregular) Horse, 1850; served in Crimean War; attached to staff of embassy to China, 1857; private secretary to Lord *Elgin when plenipotentiary in China, 1860; seized by Chinese officials, imprisoned, and tortured; returned to England in charge of Treaty of Tientsin, 1860; private secretary to Sir George *Grey (1799–1882); governor of Isle of Man, 1863–82; KCB, 1880; commissioner of woods and forests and land revenue, 1882–4; governor of Victoria, 1884–9; governor of the Cape and high commissioner in South Africa, 1889–95; raised to peerage, 1895; took leading share in raising and equipping 'Loch's Horse' for service in South Africa, 1899; published *Personal Narrative of . . . Lord Elgin's second Embassy to China* (1869).

LOCH, James (1780–1855), economist; admitted an advocate in Scotland, 1801; barrister, Lincoln's Inn, 1806; abandoned law and assumed management of several noblemen's estates; MP for St Germans, Cornwall, 1827–30, for Wick burghs, 1830–52.

LOCHINVAR, first Baron (1599?–1634). See GORDON, Sir JOHN, first Viscount Kenmure.

LOCHORE, Robert (1762–1852), Scottish poet; published poems in Scottish vernacular, 1795–6 and 1815; edited the *Kilmarnock Mirror*, c.1817.

LOCK. See also LOCKE and LOK.

LOCK, Walter (1846–1933), warden of Keble College, Oxford, and professor of divinity; educated at Marlborough and Corpus Christi College, Oxford; first class, Lit. Hum., 1869; priest, 1873; tutor (1870), sub-warden (1881), warden (1897–1920), Keble College; held Dean Ireland's (1895–1919) and Lady Margaret (1919–27) professorships.

LOCKE. See also LOK.

LOCKE, John (1632–1704), philosopher; educated at Westminster and Christ Church, Oxford; MA, 1658; Greek lecturer at Oxford, 1660; lecturer on rhetoric, 1662; censor of moral philosophy, 1663; wrote *An Essay concerning Toleration*, which contains his views on religion, 1667; became physician to Anthony Ashley *Cooper (afterwards the first earl of Shaftesbury) and settled in his house, 1667; FRS, 1668; MB, 1675; secretary to the 'lords' proprietors of Carolina, 1669–72; secretary of presentations under Shaftesbury as lord chancellor, 1672; secretary to the reconstructed Council of Trade, 1673–5; in France, 1675–9; subsequently resided in Oxford until expelled for supposed complicity in Shaftesbury's plots, 1684; lived in Holland, where he became known to the prince of Orange, 1685–9; commissioner of appeals, 1689–1704; his first letter on *Toleration* published in Latin and then in English (1689); published *An Essay concerning Human Understanding* (1690; 2nd edn., 1694; 3rd, 1695); his second letter on *Toleration* published (1690; a third in 1692, a fourth left unpublished at his death); lived with the Masham family at Oates, Essex, 1691; published treatise *On Education* (1693), on the *Reasonableness of Christianity* (1695), and on the currency question (1695); member of the new Council of Trade, 1696–1700; his *Paraphrases of St. Paul's Epistles* published (1705–7); first edition of his collected works (1714); called by John Stuart *Mill the 'unquestioned founder of the analytic philosophy of mind'.

LOCKE, John (1805–1880), legal writer and politician; of Dulwich College and Trinity College, Cambridge; MA, 1832; barrister, Inner Temple, 1833; bencher, 1857; QC, 1857; MP, Southwark, 1857–80; introduced and passed bill (1861) for the admission of witnesses in criminal cases to the same right of substituting an affirmation for an oath as in civil cases; published two legal works.

LOCKE, Joseph (1805–1860), civil engineer; aided George Stephenson in construction of the railway between Manchester and Liverpool (opened 1830); constructed various lines on his own account in Great Britain, France, Spain, and Germany, 1835–52; FRS, 1838; MP, Honiton, 1847–60; president of the Institution of Civil Engineers, 1858 and 1859; designer of the 'Crewe engine'.

LOCKE, Matthew (1630?–1677), musical composer; assisted in the composition of the music for *Shirley's masque, Cupid and Death, 1653, and *D'Avenant's Siege of Rhodes, 1656; created 'composer in ordinary to his majesty' (Charles II), 1661; organist to Queen *Catherine's Roman Catholic establishment at Somerset House; composed music for *Macbeth, 1666 and 1669, and for The Tempest; published Melothesia, or Certain General Rules for Playing on a Continued Bass, with a choice collection of Lessons for the Harpsichord or Organ of all sorts* (1673).

LOCKE (or LOCK), William, the elder (1732–1810), art amateur and collector of works of art.

LOCKE, William, the younger (1767–1847), amateur artist; son of William *Locke the elder; painted historical and allegorical subjects.

LOCKE, William (1804–1832), captain in the Life Guards and amateur artist; published illustrations to *Byron's works; drowned in the lake of Como.

LOCKE, William John (1863–1930), novelist; born in British Guiana; BA, St John's College, Cambridge; schoolmaster; secretary, Royal Institute of British Architects, 1897–1907; died in Paris; his novels include *The Morals of Marcus Ordeyne* (1905), *The Beloved Vagabond* (1906), *The Glory of Clementina Wing* (1911), and *The Joyous Adventures of Aristide Pujol* (1912).

LOCKER, Arthur (1828–1893), novelist and journalist; son of Edward Hawke *Locker; educated at Charterhouse School and Pembroke College, Oxford; BA, 1851; journalist in Victoria, 1852; returned to England, 1861; editor of the *Graphic*, 1870–91.

LOCKER, Edward Hawke (1777–1849), commissioner of Greenwich Hospital; son of William *Locker; educated at Eton; entered the Navy Pay Office, 1795; civil secretary to Sir Edward *Pellew (afterwards Viscount Exmouth), 1804–14; secretary to Greenwich Hospital, 1819; civil commissioner, 1824–44; joint editor of *The Plain Englishman*, 1820–3; published *Views in Spain* (1824) and *Memoirs of celebrated Naval Commanders* (1832). He established the gallery of naval pictures at Greenwich, 1823.

LOCKER, John (1693–1760), miscellaneous writer; educated at Merchant Taylors' School, London, and Merton College, Oxford; admitted of Gray's Inn, 1719; translated the last two books of Voltaire's *Charles XII*, and wrote the preface (1731); collected original or authentic manuscripts of *Bacon's works, now in the British Museum; FSA, 1737.

LOCKER, William (1731–1800), captain in the navy; son of John *Locker; educated at Merchant Taylors' School, London; entered the navy, 1746; fought at Quiberon Bay, 1759; commander, 1762; served at Goree and in West Indies, 1763–6; advanced to post rank, 1768; lieutenant-governor of Greenwich Hospital, 1793–1800; compiled materials for a naval history, which he handed over to John *Charnock.

LOCKER-LAMPSON, Frederick (1821–1895), poet; more commonly known as Frederick Locker; son of Edward Hawke *Locker; clerk in Somerset House (1841) and the Admiralty (1842), where he became deputy-reader and précis writer; left government service, c.1850; published (1857) *London Lyrics*, which he extended and rearranged in subsequent editions, of which the last is dated 1893; took name of Lampson, 1885 (his second wife's maiden name). He compiled *Lyra Elegantiarum*, a collection of light verse (1867), *Patchwork*, a volume of prose extracts (1879), and a catalogue of his choice library at Rowfant (1886). His *Confidences* appeared posthumously (1896).

LOCKEY, Charles (1820–1901), tenor vocalist; sang in Rossini's *Stabat Mater*, 1842, and created tenor part in Mendelssohn's *Elijah* at Birmingham, 1846.

LOCKEY, Rowland (fl. 1590–1610), painter; mentioned in Francis *Meres's *Wit's Commonwealth* (1598).

LOCKEY, Thomas (1602–1679), librarian of the Bodleian and canon of Christ Church, Oxford; educated at Westminster School and Christ Church, Oxford; MA, 1625; prebendary of Chichester, 1633–60; DD; librarian of the Bodleian, 1660–5; designed the catalogue of *Selden's books; canon of Christ Church Cathedral, Oxford, 1665–79.

LOCKHART, David (d. 1846), botanist; assistant naturalist in *Tuckey's Congo expedition, 1816; in charge of the gardens at Trinidad, 1818–46; died at Trinidad.

LOCKHART (or LOKERT), George (*fl.* 1520), professor of arts at the college of Montaigu, Paris, 1516; a Scotsman; author of *De Proportione et Proportionalitate* (1518) and of *Termini Georgii Lokert* (1524).

LOCKHART, Sir George (1630?–1689), of Carnwath, lord president of the court of session; son of Sir James *Lockhart, laird of Lee; admitted advocate, 1656; MP, Lanarkshire (in the English parliament), 1658–9; knighted, 1663; dean of the Faculty of Advocates, 1672; MP, Lanarkshire (Scottish parliament), 1681–2 and 1685–6; lord president of the court of session, 1685; privy councillor, 1686; commissioner of the Exchequer, 1686; shot in Edinburgh by a man in favour of whose wife's claim for aliment he had decided.

LOCKHART, George (1673–1731), of Carnwath; Jacobite and author; son of Sir George *Lockhart; MP for Edinburgh, 1702–7 and 1708–10, for Wigton burghs, 1710–13 and 1713–15; arrested during the rebellion of 1715; imprisoned, but liberated without a trial; confidential agent to Prince *James Edward in Scotland, 1718–27; detected and forced to flee to Holland; permitted to return to Scotland, 1728; killed in a duel. His *Memoirs of the Affairs of Scotland from Queen Anne's Accession . . . to the commencement of the Union . . . 1707* was published anonymously (1714). His *Papers on the Affairs of Scotland*, the most valuable sources of the history of the Jacobite movement, appeared (1817).

LOCKHART, Sir James, laird of Lee (d. 1674), Scottish judge; gentleman of the privy chamber to Charles I, by whom he was knighted; commissioner for Lanarkshire in parliaments of 1630, 1633, 1645, 1661, 1665, and 1669; lord of the articles, 1633; ordinary lord of session, 1646; fought for Charles I, 1648; deprived of his office, 1649; superintended levy for Charles II's invasion of England; imprisoned in the Tower, 1651; restored to his offices, 1661; lord justice clerk, 1671–4.

LOCKHART, John Gibson (1794–1854), biographer of *Scott; educated at the High School and University of Glasgow, and Balliol College, Oxford; advocate, 1816; began to contribute to *Blackwood's Magazine*, 1817; met Sir Walter Scott, 1818; published *Peter's Letters to his Kinsfolk*, a description of Edinburgh society (1819); married Scott's daughter Sophia, 1820; edited the *Quarterly Review*, 1825–53; published his *Life of Burns* (1828); published his famous *Life of Scott* (1838); wrote several novels, the most notable being *Some Passages in the Life of Adam Blair* (1822); edited *Motteux's Don Quixote* (1822); translated *Ancient Spanish Ballads* (1823).

LOCKHART, Laurence William Maxwell (1831–1882), novelist; nephew of John Gibson *Lockhart; educated at Glasgow University and Caius College, Cambridge; BA, 1855; entered the army, 1855; served before Sebastopol, 1856; MA, 1861; captain, 1864; retired, 1865; published three novels, *Doubles and Quits*, *Fair to See*, and *Mine is Thine*, in *Blackwood's Magazine*; *Times* correspondent for the Franco-German War, 1870; died at Mentone.

LOCKHART, Philip (1690?–1715), Jacobite; brother of George *Lockhart; taken prisoner at the Battle of Preston, 1715; condemned to death as a deserter, having been previously a half-pay officer in Lord Mark Ker's regiment.

LOCKHART, Sir Robert Hamilton Bruce (1887–1970), diplomat and writer; educated at Fettes College and in Berlin and Paris; rubber planter, Malaya; entered Consular Service; vice-consul, Moscow, 1912; acting consul-general, 1914–17; headed special mission to Russia, 1918; imprisoned and exchanged for Litvinov, 1918; commercial secretary, Prague, 1919; left Foreign Service, 1922; editor, Londoner's Diary, *Evening Standard*, 1928–37; rejoined Foreign Office, 1939; British representative, provisional Czechoslovak Government in exile, 1940; deputy under-secretary of state, in charge of Political Warfare Executive, 1941–5; knighted, 1943; publications include *Memoirs of a British Agent* (1932), *Retreat from Glory* (1934), and *Comes the Reckoning* (1947).

LOCKHART, Sir William (1621–1676), of Lee; soldier and diplomat; son of Sir James *Lockhart, laird of Lee; entered the French Army and rose to be captain; lieutenant-colonel of *Lanark's regiment during the Civil War; knighted, 1646; went over to *Cromwell's side; a commissioner for the administration of justice in Scotland, 1652; MP, Lanark, 1653, 1654–5, and 1656–8; English ambassador in Paris, 1656–8, 1673–6; commanded the English forces at Dunkirk and was made governor after the town's surrender, 1658; deprived of the office, 1660.

LOCKHART, William (1820–1892), Roman Catholic divine; BA, Exeter College, Oxford, 1842; follower of John Henry *Newman; received into the Roman communion, 1843; entered the Rosminian Order of Charity at Rome, 1845, and became its procurator-general; edited *Outline of the Life of Rosmini* (1856); wrote second volume of a *Life of Antonio Rosmini-Serbati* (1886); edited the *Lamp*.

LOCKHART, William Ewart (1846–1900),
subject and portrait painter; studied art in Edinburgh; RSA, 1878; commissioned by Queen Victoria to paint *Jubilee Celebration in Westminster*,
1887; subsequently devoted himself principally
to portraiture. His best works are Spanish and
Majorca subjects.

**LOCKHART, Sir William Stephen Alex-
ander** (1841–1900), general; nephew of Sir
John Gibson *Lockhart; lieutenant, 44th Bengal
Native Infantry, 1859; major, 1877; brevet-colonel, 1883; lieutenant-general, 1894; general,
1896; served in Indian Mutiny, 1858–9, Bhutan
campaigns, 1864–6, Abyssinian expedition,
1867–8, expedition to Hazara Black Mountains,
1868–9; quartermaster-general in Northern
Afghanistan, 1878–80; CB (military), 1880;
deputy quartermaster-general in intelligence
branch at headquarters in India, 1880–5; brigadier-general in Burmese War, 1886–7; KCB and
CSI, 1887; assistant military secretary for Indian
affairs at Horse Guards, London, 1889–90;
commanded Punjab Frontier Force, 1890–5;
KCSI, 1895; commanded force sent to quell rising of tribes of the Tirah, 1897; GCB; commander-in-chief in India, 1898.

LOCKHART-ROSS, Sir John, sixth baronet
(1721–1790), vice-admiral. See ROSS.

LOCKIER, Francis (1667–1740), dean of
Peterborough and friend of *Dryden and *Pope;
entered Trinity College, Cambridge, 1683; MA,
1690; chaplain to the English Factory at Hamburg; DD, 1717; dean of Peterborough, 1725;
his reminiscences of Dryden and Pope in
*Spence's *Anecdotes* (ed. 1820).

LOCKMAN, John (1698–1771), miscellaneous
writer; author of occasional verses intended to be
set to music for Vauxhall; wrote for the *General
Dictionary*, 1734–41; translated French works;
contributed to the *Gentleman's Magazine*.

LOCKWOOD, Amelius Mark Richard, first
Baron Lambourne (1847–1928), politician;
joined army, 1866; Conservative MP, Epping,
1892–1917; baron, 1917; exercised considerable
independent influence in House of Commons;
vice-president, Royal Society for Prevention of
Cruelty to Animals; served on Royal Commission
on Vivisection, 1906–8; a noted horticulturist;
PC, 1905; lord-lieutenant of Essex, 1919.

LOCKWOOD, Sir Frank (1846–1897), solicitor-general; graduated at Caius College, Cambridge, 1869; barrister, Lincoln's Inn, 1872;
joined old midland circuit; defended the burglar
and murderer Charles Peace, 1879; QC, 1882;
recorder of Sheffield, 1884; Liberal MP for
York, 1885–97; solicitor-general, 1894–5;

several of his sketches reproduced in *The Frank
Lockwood Sketch-Book* (1898).

LOCKWOOD, Sir John Francis (1903–1965),
university administrator; educated at Preston
Grammar School and Corpus Christi College,
Oxford; assistant lecturer, Manchester University, 1927; senior assistant classics lecturer,
University College, London, 1927; lecturer in
Greek, 1930–40; tutor to arts students, University College, and London University reader in
classics, 1940; professor of Latin, 1945; dean of
faculty of arts, 1950–1; chairman, governing
delegacy, Goldsmiths' College, 1951–8; master,
Birkbeck College, 1951–65; public orator, Lon-
don University, 1952–5; chairman, Collegiate
Council, 1953–5; deputy vice-chancellor,
1954–5; vice-chancellor, 1955–8; member,
United States–United Kingdom Educational
Commission, 1956–61; chairman, Secondary
School Examinations Council, 1958–64; chairman, Colonial Office working party on higher
education in East Africa, 1958–9; chairman,
West African Examinations Council, 1960–4;
knighted, 1962; chairman, Voluntary Societies'
Committee for Service Overseas, 1962.

LOCKYER, Sir (Joseph) Norman (1836–
1920), astronomer; clerk in War Office, 1857;
made pioneer observations of spectrum of sun-
spot, 1866, and of solar prominences, 1868;
coined terms 'chromosphere' and 'helium',
1868; secretary to Royal Commission on Scientific Instruction and Advancement of Science,
1870; transferred to science and art department,
South Kensington, 1875; director of Solar Physics Observatory and professor of astronomical
physics, Royal College of Science, 1890–1913;
FRS, 1869; Rumford medallist, 1874; CB, 1894;
KCB, 1897; wrote numerous astronomical
books.

LOCKYER, Nicholas (1611–1685), Puritan
divine; BA, New Inn Hall, Oxford, 1633; incorporated at Cambridge, 1635; MA, Emmanuel
College, Cambridge, 1636; took the Covenant
and became a powerful preacher; BD, Oxford,
1654; provost of Eton, 1659–60; compelled to
leave the country for disregarding Uniformity
Act, 1666 and 1670; published theological works.

LOCOCK, Sir Charles, first baronet (1799–
1875), obstetric physician; MD, Edinburgh,
1821; FRCP, 1836; first physician-accoucheur
to Queen Victoria, 1840; discovered the efficacy
of bromide of potassium in epilepsy; created baronet, 1857; FRS; hon. DCL, Oxford, 1864.

LODER, Edward James (1813–1865), musical composer; son of John David *Loder; studied
in Germany; his opera *Nourjahad* produced,
1834; author of musical compositions, including

operas and a cantata, and *Modern Pianoforte Tutor*.

LODER, George (1816?–1868), musician; nephew of John David *Loder; went to America, 1836; principal of the New York Vocal Institute, 1844; published *Pets of the Parterre*, a comic operetta (1861), and *The Old House at Home*, a musical entertainment (1862); died at Adelaide.

LODER, John David (1788–1846), violinist; professor of the Royal Academy of Music, London, 1840; leader at the Ancient Concerts, 1845; author of a standard work of instruction for the violin (1814).

LODER, John Fawcett (1812–1853), violinist; played the viola in Dando's quartet, 1842–53.

LODGE, Edmund (1756–1839), biographer; Bluemantle pursuivant-at-arms at the College of Arms, 1782; FSA, 1787; Lancaster herald, 1793, Norroy, 1822, Clarenceux, 1838. His chief work is the series of 'biographical and historical memoirs', attached to *Portraits of Illustrious Personages of Great Britain, engraved from authentic pictures* (1821–34).

LODGE, Eleanor Constance (1869–1936), historian and principal of Westfield College, London; sister of Sir *Oliver and Sir Richard *Lodge; studied history at Lady Margaret Hall, Oxford; librarian, 1895; history tutor, 1899–1921; vice-principal, 1906–21; principal of Westfield College, 1921–31; works include *The English Rule in Gascony* (1926); CBE, 1932.

LODGE, John (1692–1774), archivist; entered St John's College, Cambridge, 1716; MA, 1730; deputy clerk and keeper of the rolls, 1759; chief work, *The Peerage of Ireland* (1754).

LODGE, John (1801–1873), amateur musical composer. See ELLERTON, JOHN LODGE.

LODGE, Sir Oliver Joseph (1851–1940), scientist and first principal of Birmingham University; brother of Sir Richard *Lodge and Eleanor Constance *Lodge; studied at Royal College of Science and University College, London; D.Sc., 1877; professor of physics, Liverpool, 1881–1900; made fundamental contributions to wireless and experiments on relative motion of matter and ether; as first principal (1900–19) shaped development of Birmingham University; actively interested in, and especially influential as philosopher of, psychical research; concluded that mind survives death and expounded instrument theory of relation between body and mind; works include *The Ether of Space* (1909), *Advancing Science* (1931), *Raymond* (1916), and *My Philosophy* (1933); FRS, 1887; knighted, 1902; president, British Association, 1913.

LODGE, Sir **Richard** (1855–1936), historian and teacher; brother of Sir Oliver *Lodge and Eleanor Constance *Lodge; educated at Christ's Hospital and Balliol College, Oxford; first class, modern history, 1877; fellow of Brasenose, 1878; vice-principal, 1891; professor of modern history, Glasgow (1894–9), Edinburgh (1899–1925); dean of faculty of arts, 1911–25; works include *A History of Modern Europe* (1885) and *Richelieu* (1896); knighted, 1917.

LODGE, Sir **Thomas** (d. 1584), lord mayor of London; alderman, 1553; sheriff of London, 1556; master of the Grocers' Company, 1559; chartered ships to 'sail and traffic in the ports of Africa and Ethiopia', a voyage said to have inaugurated the traffic in slaves countenanced by Elizabeth, 1562; lord mayor and knighted, 1562.

LODGE, Thomas (1558?–1625), author; son of Sir Thomas *Lodge, lord mayor of London; educated at Merchant Taylors' School, London, and Trinity College, Oxford; BA, 1577; student of Lincoln's Inn, 1578; MA, 1581; abandoned law for literature; published *A Defence of Plays*, a reply to *School of Abuse* of Stephen *Gosson (1580); published *An Alarum against Usurers* (1584), and his first romance, *The Delectable Historie of Forbonius and Prisceria* (1584); sailed to the islands of Terceras and the Canaries, 1588, and to South America, 1591; issued *Scillaes Metamorphosis* (verse, 1589, reissued as *A most pleasant Historie of Glaucus and Scilla*, 1610); issued his second and best-known romance *Rosalynde. Euphues Golden Legacie* (1590), written during his voyage to the Canaries; his work praised by *Spenser and *Greene; his chief volume of verse, *Phillis: honoured with Pastorall Sonnets, Elegies, and amorous Delights* issued (1593); published *A Fig for Momus* (1595), *The Divel Conjured* (1596), *A Margarite of America* (romance of the Euphues pattern, 1596), *Wits Miserie and Worlds Madnesse* (1596); converted to Roman Catholicism; studied medicine; MD at Oxford, 1603; published a laborious volume, *The Famous and Memorable Workes of Josephus* (1602); issued *A Treatise of the Plague* (1603); published *The Workes, both Morrall and Natural, of Lucius Annaeus Seneca* (1614); his last literary undertaking, *A learned Summary upon the famous Poeme of William of Saluste, lord of Bartas, translated out of the French* (published 1625); excelled as a lyric poet.

LODGE, William (1649–1689), amateur artist and engraver; of Jesus College, Cambridge, and Lincoln's Inn; translated Giacomo Barri's *Viaggio Pittoresco d'Italia* (1679); a prolific draughtsman and etcher mainly of topography; painted a portrait of Oliver *Cromwell.

LODVILL (or LUDVILLE), Philip (d. 1767), divine; published *The Orthodox Confession of the Catholic and Apostolic Eastern Church* (1762), the first authoritative work in English on the subject.

LOE, William (d. 1645), divine; MA, St Alban Hall, Oxford, 1600; prebendary of Gloucester, 1602; DD, 1618; pastor of the English Church at Hamburg; published *Songs of Sion* (religious verse, 1620) and quaint prose writings, 1609–23.

LOE, William (d. 1679), compiler; son of William *Loe (d. 1645); of Westminster School and Trinity College, Cambridge; BD, 1636; contributed to the university collections of Latin and Greek verses on the birth of Princess *Elizabeth, 1635, and of Princess Anne, 1637; compiled from his father's papers *The Merchants Manuell*, etc. (1628).

LOEGHAIRE (d. 458), king of Ireland. See LAEGHAIRE.

LOEWE, Louis (1809–1888), linguist; born at Zülz, Prussian Silesia; educated at Berlin, where he graduated Ph.D.; accompanied Sir Moses *Montefiore as his secretary to the Holy Land and other places thirteen times between 1839 and 1874; first principal of Jews' College, 1856; examiner in oriental languages to Royal College of Preceptors, 1858; principal and director, Judith Theological College, Ramsgate, 1868–88; published English translation of J. B. Levinsohn's *Efes Dammim*, conversations between a patriarch of the Greek Church and a chief rabbi of the Jews, 1841; translated first two conversations in David *Nieto's *Matteh Dan*, 1842; edited the *Diaries of Sir Moses and Lady Montefiore* (published 1890).

LOEWENTHAL (or LÖWENTHAL), Johann Jacob (1810–1876), chess-player; born at Budapest; expelled from Austro-Hungary as a follower of Kossuth, 1849; settled in London, 1851; chess editor of the *Illustrated News of the World* and of the *Era*; published *Morphy's Games of Chess* (1860); edited *Chess Player's Magazine*, 1863–7; manager of the British Chess Association, 1865–9; became a naturalized Englishman.

LOFFT, Capell, the elder (1751–1824), miscellaneous writer; educated at Eton and Peterhouse, Cambridge; barrister, Lincoln's Inn, 1775; settled at Turin, 1822; died at Moncalieri; author of poems and works on miscellaneous subjects and translations from Virgil and Petrarch, published between 1775 and 1814.

LOFFT, Capell, the younger (1806–1873), classical scholar, poet, and miscellaneous writer; son of Capell *Lofft the elder; of Eton and King's College, Cambridge; MA, 1832; barrister,

Middle Temple, 1834; published an ethical *Self-Formation, or the History of an Individual Mind* (1837); published *Ernest*, an epic poem (1839), representing the growth, struggles, and triumphs of Chartism; died at Millmead, Virginia, USA.

LOFTHOUSE, Mary (1853–1885), water-colour painter; née Forster; associate of the Royal Society of Painters in Water-Colours, 1884; married Samuel H. S. Lofthouse, 1884.

LOFTIE, William John (1839–1911), antiquary; ordained, 1865; assistant chaplain, Chapel Royal, Savoy, 1871–95; FSA, 1872; frequent contributor to reviews; travelled much in Egypt; a keen Egyptologist; wrote much on British art and architecture; specially interested in London history and London buildings; chief works were *Memorials of the Savoy* (1878) and *A History of London* (2 vols., 1883–4).

LOFTING (or LOFTINGH), John (1659?–1742), inventor; native of Holland; naturalized in England, 1688; patented a fire-engine, 1690; engaged in the manufacture of fire-engines.

LOFTUS, Adam (1533?–1605), archbishop of Armagh and Dublin; educated at Cambridge, probably at Trinity College; archbishop of Armagh, 1563; dean of St Patrick's, 1565; DD, Cambridge, 1566; archbishop of Dublin, 1567; lord keeper, 1573–6, 1579, and 1581; lord chancellor, 1581–1605; lord justice, 1582–4, 1597–9, and 1600; assisted in foundation of Trinity College, Dublin; appointed first provost, 1590.

LOFTUS, Adam, first Viscount Loftus of Ely (1568?–1643), lord chancellor of Ireland; nephew of Adam *Loftus (1533?–1605); MA, Jesus College, Cambridge, 1589; prebendary of St Patrick's, Dublin, 1592; judge of the Irish marshal court, 1597; master of Chancery, 1598; knighted, c.1604; Irish privy councillor, 1608; MP, King's County, 1613; lord chancellor, 1619; created Viscount Loftus of Ely, 1622; lord justice, 1622–5, 1629–33, 1636.

LOFTUS, Lord Augustus William Frederick Spencer (1817–1904), diplomat; son of second marquess of Ely; attaché to British legation at Berlin, 1837–44; at Stuttgart and Baden Baden, 1844–71; joined Sir Stratford *Canning in special mission to European courts and witnessed revolutionary incidents in Germany and Austria, 1848; secretary of legation at Berlin, 1853; reported on British consulates on German shores of Baltic after Crimean War; envoy extraordinary to emperor of Austria, 1858; warned Austrian government of England's friendship to Italy, 1859; transferred to Berlin (1860), where he favoured Denmark's claims in Schleswig-Holstein crisis; at Munich, 1863–6; returned to Berlin, 1866; GCB, 1866; PC, 1868; managed *solde de captivité* for French prisoners of war in Germany, 1870; at St Petersburg, 1871–9; attended Tsar Alexander on visit to England, 1874; conferred with Prince Gortchakoff with a view to prevent Russo-Turkish War, 1876; suggested Anglo-Russian understanding, which was brought about by Lord *Salisbury and the Russian ambassador in London; governor of New South Wales, 1879–85; published *Diplomatic Reminiscences* (4 vols., 1892–4).

LOFTUS, Dudley (1619–1695), jurist and orientalist; great-grandson of Adam *Loftus (1533?–1605); educated at Trinity College, Dublin; BA, 1638; incorporated BA at Oxford, 1639; MA, University College, Oxford, 1640; MP for Naas in Irish House of Commons, 1642–8; deputy judge advocate, 1651; commissioner of revenue and judge of Admiralty, 1654; master in Chancery, 1655; MP, Co. Kildare and Co. Wicklow, 1659, Bannow, 1661, Fethard, 1692; supplied the Ethiopic version of the New Testament in *Walton's Polyglott Bible (1657) and published several translations from the Armenian and Greek, 1657–95.

LOFTUS, William Kennett (1821?–1858), archaeologist and traveller; educated at Cambridge; geologist to the Turco-Persian Frontier Commission, 1849–52; at Babylon and Nineveh on behalf of the Assyrian Excavation Fund, 1853–5; published *Travels and Researches in Chaldaea and Susiana* (1857); died on the voyage home from India, where he had been appointed to the Geological Survey.

LOGAN, George (1678–1755), controversialist; MA, Glasgow, 1696; moderator of the general assembly, 1740; published ecclesiastical and political works.

LOGAN, James (1674–1751), man of science and *Penn's agent in America; accompanied Penn to Pennsylvania as secretary, 1699; secretary to the province, commissioner of property, receiver-general and business agent for the proprietor, 1701; member of the Provincial Council, 1702–47; a justice of common pleas, 1715; presiding judge in court of common pleas and mayor of Philadelphia, 1723; published *The Antidote* (1725) and *A Memorial from James Logan in behalf of the Proprietor's family and of himself* (1726); chief justice and president of the council, 1731–9; governor, 1736–8; published scientific works and translations from the classics; died at Philadelphia.

LOGAN, James (1794?–1872), author of the *Scottish Gael*; studied at Marischal College, Aberdeen; published his *Scottish Gael, or Celtic Manners as preserved among the Highlanders* (1831).

LOGAN, James Richardson (d. 1869), scientific writer; settled at Penang; rendered important services to the struggling settlement; contributed geological papers to *Journal of the Asiatic Society of Bengal*, 1846; started and edited the *Journal of the Indian Archipelago and Eastern Asia*, 1847–57; published his articles as *The Languages* [and Ethnology] *of the Indian Archipelago* (1857); started and edited the *Penang Gazette*; died at Penang.

LOGAN, John (1748–1788), divine and poet; entered Edinburgh University, 1762; ordained, 1773; member of the Committee for the Revision of Paraphrases and Hymns in Use in Public Worship, 1775; lectured on history in Edinburgh, 1779–80 and 1780–1; published analysis of lectures as *Elements of the Philosophy of History* (1781); his tragedy *Runnamede* acted, 1783; his chief poem, the 'Ode to the Cuckoo', pronounced by *Burke the most beautiful lyric in the language, although it has also been ascribed to Michael *Bruce (1746–1767).

LOGAN, Sir Robert (d. 1606), of Restalrig; supposed Gowrie conspirator; supported the cause of *Mary Queen of Scots. After his death, George *Sprott confessed knowledge of letters written by Logan in connection with the Gowrie plot, and on that evidence his bones were exhumed (1609) and sentence of forfeiture for high treason passed against him.

LOGAN, Sir William Edmond (1798–1875), Canadian geologist; born in Montreal; graduated at Edinburgh, 1817; head of the Geological Survey of Canada, 1842–70; FRS, 1851; knighted, 1856; his *Geology of Canada* published (1863).

LOGGAN, David (1635–1700?), artist and engraver; born at Danzig; came to England before 1653; engraver to Oxford University, 1669, naturalized and published his *Oxonia Illustrata* (1675), *Cantabrigia Illustrata* (1676–90); engraver to Cambridge University, 1690.

LOGGON, Samuel (1712–1778?), writer; MA, Balliol College, Oxford, 1736; author of a popular schoolbook, *M. Corderii Colloquia* (21st edn., 1830).

LOGIER, John Bernard (1780–1846), musician; born at Kaiserslautern in the Palatinate; came to England, *c.*1790; invented the 'chiroplast', an apparatus to facilitate the position of the hands on the piano; established chiroplast school at Berlin by invitation of the Prussian government, 1821.

LOGUE, Michael (1840–1924), cardinal; entered Maynooth College, 1857; deacon, 1864; priest and professor of dogmatic theology, Irish College, Paris, 1866; curate of Glenswilly,

Co. Donegal, 1874; dean at Maynooth, 1876; professor of theology, Maynooth, 1878; bishop of Raphoe, 1879; archbishop of Armagh, 1887; cardinal, with title of Santa Maria della Pace, 1893; exercised great influence in Irish politics, largely contributing to eventual deposition of C. S. *Parnell from leadership of Nationalist party; a great church builder; mediated between Irish people and British government, 1919–21.

LOHMANN, George Alfred (1865–1901), Surrey cricketer; won great success as medium-pace bowler for Surrey from 1885 to 1890; thrice visited Australia; played for Players v. Gentlemen, 1886–96; a good hitting batsman and first-class fieldsman; raised Surrey cricket to leading position.

LOINGSECH (d. 704), king of Ireland; first mentioned in the annals, 672; slain in battle.

LOK (LOCK or LOCKE), Henry (1553?–1608?), poet; grandson of Sir William *Lok; educated probably at Oxford; contributed sonnet to the *Essayes of a Prentice* by James VI of Scotland, 1591; his *Ecclesiasticus . . . paraphristically dilated in English Poesie . . . whereunto are annexed sundrie Sonets of Christian Passions* printed by Richard *Field (1597).

LOK, Michael (*fl.* 1615), traveller; son of Sir William *Lok; 'travelled through almost all the countries of Christianity'; governor of the Cathay Company, 1577; consul for the Levant Company at Aleppo, 1592–4; translated into English part of Peter Martyr's *Historie of the West Indies* (1613).

LOK, Sir William (1480–1550), London merchant; sent Henry VIII and *Cromwell letters of intelligence from Bergen-op-Zoom and Antwerp, 1532–7; sheriff of London, 1548; knighted, 1548.

LOLA MONTEZ, countess von Landsfeld (1818–1861), adventuress. See GILBERT, MARIE DOLORES ELIZA ROSANNA.

LOMBARD, Adrian Albert (1915–1967), aero-engineer; educated at John Gulson Central Advanced School, Coventry, and Coventry Technical College; joined Rover Co., in drawing office, 1930; transferred to Morris Motors, 1935; returned to Rover Co., 1936; one of design-team making Whittle W2B jet engine suitable for production, 1940; joined Rolls-Royce when they took over Whittle engine, 1943; supervised production of W2B engine, Derwent I, Nene, Derwent V, and Avon engines, 1944–5; chief designer (projects), Rolls-Royce Co.; chief designer (aero), 1952; chief engineer, 1954; supervised production of Conway and Spey engines; director, engineering (aero) and director, Rolls-Royce Co., 1958; served on Council,

Royal Aeronautical Society, Air Registration Board, Aeronautical Research Council; CBE, 1967.

LOMBARD, Daniel (1678–1746), divine; born at Angers; naturalized in England, 1688; of Merchant Taylors' School, London, and St John's College, Oxford; fellow, 1697–1718; BA, 1698; chaplain at Hanover to the princess Sophia and the embassy, 1701; DD, 1714; chaplain to *Caroline, princess of Wales, 1714; chief work, *Succinct History of Ancient and Modern Persecutions* (published 1747).

LOMBARD, Peter (d. 1625), Irish Roman Catholic prelate; educated at Westminster and Louvain University; DD, 1594; provost of Cambrai Cathedral; archbishop of Armagh and primate of all Ireland, 1601; died at Rome; author of *De Regno Hiberniae, Sanctorum Insula Commentarius* (published 1632).

LOMBART, Pierre (1620?–1681), engraver and portrait painter; born at Paris; came to England, *c*.1640; returned to France after 1660; died at Paris.

LOMBE, John (1693?–1722), half-brother of Sir Thomas *Lombe; sent by his brother to Italy to make himself acquainted with the processes of silk-throwing; said to have been poisoned by jealous Italian workmen.

LOMBE, Sir Thomas (1685–1739), introducer of silk-throwing machinery into England; patented his new invention, 1718; sheriff of London and knighted, 1727.

LONDESBOROUGH, first Baron (1805–1860). See DENISON, ALBERT.

LONDON, Heinz (1907–1970), physicist; born at Bonn, Germany; educated at Bonn, Berlin, and Munich; studied low-temperature physics at Breslau University; Ph.D., Breslau, 1933; moved to Oxford, 1933, and to Bristol, 1936; studied high-frequency resistance problem; interned, 1939; released to work on atom bomb project at Bristol, Birmingham, Imperial College, ICI Witton and Winnington, and Ministry of Supply, Mold, 1940–4; naturalized, 1942; leader of Birmingham team, 1944; principal scientific officer, Harwell, 1945; senior principal scientific officer, 1950; deputy chief scientist, 1958; worked on isotope separation; invented 'dilution refrigerator'; awarded first Simon Memorial Prize, 1959; FRS, 1961.

LONDON, Henry of (d. 1228). See LOUNDRES, HENRY DE.

LONDON, John (1486?–1543), visitor of monasteries; educated at Winchester and New College, Oxford; fellow of New College, 1505–18; DCL and prebendary of York, 1519; treasurer of Lincoln Cathedral, 1522; warden of New College, 1526; attached himself to *Cromwell; a commissioner for the visitation of monasteries, 1535–8; after Cromwell's death (1540) attached himself to Stephen *Gardiner, and became canon of Windsor; convicted of perjury, stripped of his dignities, and committed to prison, where he died.

LONDON, John of (fl. 1267), mathematician. See JOHN OF LONDON.

LONDON, John of (d. 1311). See JOHN OF LONDON.

LONDON, Richard of (fl. 1190–1229). See RICHARD DE TEMPLO.

LONDON, William (fl. 1658), bibliographer; his Catalogue of the most vendible Books in England (1658) and Catalogue of New Books by way of Supplement to the former (1660) the earliest bibliographical catalogues of value.

LONDONDERRY, earls of. See RIDGEWAY, Sir THOMAS, first earl, 1565?–1631; PITT, THOMAS, first earl of the second creation, 1688?–1729.

LONDONDERRY, marquises of. See STEWART, ROBERT, first marquis, 1739–1821; STEWART, ROBERT, second marquis, 1769–1822; STEWART, CHARLES WILLIAM, third marquis, 1778–1854; VANE-TEMPEST-STEWART, CHARLES STEWART, sixth marquis, 1852–1915; VANE-TEMPEST-STEWART, CHARLES STEWART HENRY, seventh marquis, 1878–1949.

LONG, Amelia, Lady Farnborough (1762–1837), daughter of Sir Abraham *Hume of Wormleybury, Hertfordshire; married Charles *Long, afterwards first Baron Farnborough, 1793; art connoisseur and horticulturalist.

LONG, Ann (1681?–1711), granddaughter of Sir James *Long; a celebrated beauty; acquainted with *Swift.

LONG, Lady Catharine (d. 1867), novelist and religious writer; daughter of Horatio Walpole, third earl of Orford; married Henry Lawes Long, 1822; her novel Sir Roland Ashton (1833) directed against the Tractarian movement; published religious works, 1846–63.

LONG, Charles, first Baron Farnborough (1761–1838), politician; of Emmanuel College, Cambridge; MP, Rye, 1789–96, Midhurst, 1796, Wendover, 1802, and Haslemere, 1806–26; joint secretary to the Treasury, 1791–1801; FRS, 1792; a lord commissioner of the Treasury, 1804; privy councillor, 1802, and for Ireland, 1805; secretary of state for Ireland, 1806; joint paymaster-general, and subsequently sole occupant of the office, 1807–26; GCB (civil), 1820; created Baron Farnborough, 1826; assisted

George III and George IV in the decoration of the royal palaces.

LONG, Charles Edward (1796–1861), genealogist and antiquary; grandson of Edward *Long; of Harrow and Trinity College, Cambridge; MA, 1822; published works, including Royal Descents (1845).

LONG, Dudley (1748–1829), politician. See NORTH.

LONG, Edward (1734–1813), author; of Gray's Inn; in Jamaica as private secretary to Sir Henry *Moore, the lieutenant-governor, and subsequently judge of the vice-Admiralty court, 1757–69; his chief work, The History of Jamaica, issued anonymously (1774).

LONG, Edwin Longsden (1829–1891), painter and royal academician; RA, 1881; excelled as a painter of oriental scenes.

LONG, George (1780–1868), police magistrate; barrister, Gray's Inn, 1811; magistrate at Great Marlborough Street police court, 1839–41; recorder of Coventry, 1840–2; magistrate at Marylebone police court, 1841–59; published legal works.

LONG, George (1800–1879), classical scholar; BA, Trinity College, Cambridge, 1822; fellow of Trinity College, Cambridge, 1823; professor of ancient languages in the University of Virginia at Charlottesville, 1824–8; professor of Greek, University College, London, 1828–31; edited Quarterly Journal of Education, 1831–5; hon. secretary of the Royal Geographical Society (which he helped to found in 1830), 1846–8; edited Penny Cyclopaedia, 1833–46; professor of Latin, University College, London, 1842–6; published Two Discourses on Roman Law, in which subject he surpassed all his English contemporaries (1847); established and edited the Bibliotheca Classica, 1851–8; published his translation of Marcus Aurelius (1862), of the Discourses of Epictetus (1877).

LONG, Sir James, second baronet (1617–1692), Royalist; nephew of Sir Robert *Long; served in the Royalist army; succeeded to baronetcy, 1673.

LONG, James (1814–1887), missionary; went to India in the service of the Church Missionary Society, 1846; wrote a preface, adversely criticizing the English press at Calcutta, to an English version of Niladarpana Nataka, a sort of oriental Uncle Tom's Cabin (1861); indicted for libel and imprisoned; author of various books, pamphlets, and contributions to periodical literature dealing with Anglo-Indian questions.

LONG, John (1548–1589), archbishop of Armagh; of Eton and King's College, Cambridge; archbishop of Armagh and primate of all Ireland, 1584; Irish privy councillor, 1585.

LONG, John St John (1798–1834), empiric; studied drawing and painting at Dublin, 1816–22; set up practice in London and became fashionable, 1827; twice tried for manslaughter through the deaths of his patients; chief work, *A Critical Exposure of the Ignorance and Malpractice of Certain Medical Practitioners in their Theory and Treatment of Disease* (1831).

LONG, Sir **Lislebone** (1613–1659), speaker of the House of Commons; educated at Magdalen Hall, Oxford; BA, 1631; barrister, Lincoln's Inn, 1640; MP (Parliamentarian), Wells, 1645–53, 1654–5, and 1659, Somerset, 1656–8; knighted, 1655; recorder of London, a master of requests, and treasurer of Lincoln's Inn, 1656; appointed speaker, 9 Mar. 1659, but died 16 Mar.

LONG, Sir **Robert** (d. 1673), auditor of the Exchequer; MP, Devizes, 1625, Midhurst, 1640; knighted, 1660; chancellor of the Exchequer, 1660–7; MP, Boroughbridge, 1661; auditor of the Exchequer, 1662; privy councillor, 1672.

LONG, Robert Ballard (1771–1825), lieutenant-general; son of Edward *Long (1734–1813); educated at Harrow and Göttingen University; captain, serving in Flanders, 1793–4; deputy adjutant-general, 1794–5; lieutenant-colonel, 1798; colonel on the staff in Spain, 1808, present at Corunna, 1809; brigadier-general in Wellington's army in Portugal, 1810–11; lieutenant-general, 1821.

LONG, Roger (1680–1770), divine and astronomer; of Pembroke Hall, Cambridge; fellow, 1703; MA, 1704; DD, 1728; FRS, 1729; master of Pembroke Hall, 1733; vice-chancellor of the university, 1733; published instalments of an important work on astronomy, 1742–64 (completed by Richard *Dunthorne); first Lowndean professor of astronomy and geometry, 1750.

LONG, Samuel (1638–1683), speaker of the Jamaica House of Assembly; served in the expedition which conquered Jamaica, 1655; clerk of the House of Assembly, 1661; speaker, 1672–4; chief justice, 1674; died at St Katherine, Jamaica.

LONG, Thomas, the elder (1621–1707), divine; educated at Exeter College, Oxford; BA, 1642; BD, 1660; prebendary of Exeter, 1661–1701; a voluminous controversial writer.

LONG, Thomas, the younger (1649–1707), son of Thomas *Long the elder; educated at Corpus Christi College, Oxford; MA, 1670; prebendary of Exeter, 1681; deprived at the Revolution.

LONG, Walter Hume, first Viscount Long of Wraxall (1854–1924), statesman; educated at Harrow and Christ Church, Oxford; Conservative MP, North Wiltshire, 1880–5, East Wiltshire, 1885–92, West Derby division of Liverpool, 1893–1900, South Bristol, 1900–6; South County Dublin, 1906–10, Strand division of Middlesex, 1910–18, St George's, Westminster, 1918–21; belonged to 'country party' on entry into parliament, 1880; parliamentary secretary to Local Government Board, 1886–92; took large part in framing and getting through House of Commons Local Government Act, which created county councils throughout Great Britain, 1888; president of Board of Agriculture, with seat in Cabinet, 1895–1900; popularity of his appointment soon impaired by his vigorous and successful measures to stamp out rabies, which met with violent opposition; president of Local Government Board, 1900–5; secured passing of Metropolitan Water Act, in teeth of bitter opposition, 1902; successful chief secretary for Ireland, 1905; created Union Defence League, 1907; president of Local Government Board, 1915–16; secretary of state for colonies, 1916–18; first lord of Admiralty, 1919–21; FRS, 1902; created viscount, 1921.

LONG, William (1817–1886), antiquary; educated at Balliol College, Oxford; MA, 1844; FSA; published *Stonehenge and its Burrows* (1876).

LONGBEARD, William (d. 1196), demagogue. See FITZOSBERT, WILLIAM.

LONGCHAMP, William of (d. 1197), bishop of Ely and chancellor to Richard I; chancellor of the kingdom, 1189; bishop of Ely, 1189; justiciar, 1190; joined Richard I while in prison in Germany, 1193; Richard I's intermediary in England, France, Germany, and at home, 1194–5; a faithful servant to Richard I; died at Poitiers.

LONGDEN, Sir **Henry Errington** (1819–1890), general; educated at Eton and the Royal Military College, Sandhurst; entered the army, 1836; captain, 1843; served in the Sikh wars, 1845–6 and 1848–9, in the Indian Mutiny, 1857–8; colonel, 1859; adjutant-general in India, 1866–9; major-general, 1872; lieutenant-general, 1877; retired with honorary rank of general, 1880; KCB and CSI.

LONGDEN, Sir **James Robert** (1827–1891), colonial administrator; acting colonial secretary in the Falkland Islands, 1845; president of the Virgin Islands, 1861; governor of Dominica, 1865; governor of British Honduras, 1867; governor of Trinidad, 1870; KCMG, 1876; governor of Ceylon, 1876–83; GCMG, 1883.

LONGESPÉE (or LUNGESPÉE), i.e. Longsword, **William de,** third earl of Salisbury (d. 1226), natural son of Henry II by an unknown mother; according to a late tradition by Rosamond *Clifford ('Fair Rosamond'); received earldom of Salisbury, 1198; lieutenant of Gascony, 1202; warden of the Cinque Ports, 1204–6; warden of the Welsh marches, 1208; counselled King John to grant the Great Charter, 1215; joined the dauphin Louis, 1216, but returned to the English allegiance, 1217; faithfully served his nephew, Henry III, 1218–26.

LONGESPÉE (LUNGESPÉE, LUNGESPEYE, or LUNGESPERE), William de, called earl of Salisbury (1212?–1250), son of William de *Longespée (d. 1226); knighted, 1233; witnessed the confirmation of the Great Charter, 1236; accompanied Earl *Richard of Cornwall to the crusade, 1240; accompanied Henry III to Gascony, 1242; went again to the crusades, 1247; killed at the battle near Mansourah, 1250.

LONGFIELD, Mountifort (1802–1884), Irish judge; MA, Trinity College, Dublin, 1828; LL D, 1831; professor of political economy at Trinity College, 1832–4; regius professor of feudal and English law, Dublin University, 1834–84; QC, 1841; judge of the landed estates court, 1858–67; Irish privy councillor, 1867.

LONGHURST, Henry Carpenter (1909–1979), golf journalist and television broadcaster; educated at Charterhouse and Clare College, Cambridge; golf blue, captain of university team; winner of German amateur championship, 1936, and runner-up in French, 1937 and Swiss, 1938; like Bernard *Darwin, became golf journalist; associated with *Sunday Times* from 1932 for over forty-five years; also wrote for *Tatler* and *Evening Standard*; during 1939–45 war served with Home Guard as anti-aircraft gunner officer; Conservative MP for Acton, 1943–5; pioneer of presentation of golf on BBC television; also became well known in USA; won Walter Hagen Award 'for furtherance of golfing ties between Great Britain and America', 1973; CBE, 1972; hon. life member, Royal and Ancient Golf Club, St Andrews, 1977; wrote twelve light-hearted books, including autobiography, *My Life and Soft Times* (1971).

LONGHURST, William Henry (1819–1904), organist and composer; chorister (1828), assistant organist (1836), and organist (1873–98) of Canterbury Cathedral; Mus. Doc., 1875; published church music.

LONGLAND, John (1473–1547), bishop of Lincoln; educated at Magdalen College, Oxford; principal of Magdalen Hall, Oxford, 1505; DD, 1511; dean of Salisbury, 1514; canon of Windsor, 1519; bishop of Lincoln, 1521; chancellor of the university of Oxford, 1532–47; printed sermons (1517, 1536, and 1538) and *Tres Conciones* (1527).

LONGLAND, William (1330?–1400?), poet. See LANGLAND.

LONGLEY, Charles Thomas (1794–1868), archbishop of Canterbury; educated at Westminster School and Christ Church, Oxford; student, 1812; MA, 1818; DD, 1829; headmaster of Harrow, 1829–36; bishop of Ripon, 1836–56, of Durham, 1856–60; archbishop of York, 1860–2, of Canterbury, 1862–8; published sermons and addresses.

LONGLEY, Thomas (d. 1437), bishop of Durham, cardinal, and chancellor. See LANGLEY.

LONGMAN, Thomas (1699–1755), founder of the publishing house of Longman; bought a bookseller's business, 1724; increased his business by the purchase of shares in sound literary properties.

LONGMAN, Thomas (1730–1797), publisher; nephew of Thomas *Longman (1699–1755); taken into partnership, 1753; succeeded to the business, 1755.

LONGMAN, Thomas (1804–1879), publisher; son of Thomas Norton *Longman; educated at Glasgow; became partner in the firm, 1834, and its head, 1842; published for *Macaulay and Disraeli.

LONGMAN, Thomas Norton (1771–1842), publisher; son of Thomas *Longman (1730–1797); succeeded to the business, 1797; took Owen *Rees into partnership, on which the firm became one of the greatest in London; published for *Wordsworth, *Southey, *Scott (*Lay of the Last Minstrel*), and *Moore; became sole proprietor of *Edinburgh Review*, 1826.

LONGMAN, William (1813–1877), publisher; son of Thomas Norton *Longman; became a partner in the business, 1839; compiled *A Catalogue of Works in all Departments of English Literature, classified, with a general Alphabetical Index* (2nd edn., 1848); promoted the publication of *Peaks, Passes, and Glaciers*, 1859–62; published his *History of the Life and Times of Edward III* (1869); president of the Alpine Club, 1871–4; published *A History of the three Cathedrals dedicated to St. Paul in London* (1873).

LONGMATE, Barak (1738–1793), genealogist and heraldic engraver; published fifth edition of John *Collins's *Peerage* (1779) and a *Supplement* (1784); edited *Pocket Peerage of England, Scotland, and Ireland* (1788).

LONGMATE, Barak (1768–1836), compiler; son of Barak *Longmate (1738–1793); edited

Pocket Peerage (1813); assisted John *Nichols and other antiquaries in their researches.

LONGMORE, Sir **Arthur Murray** (1885–1970), air chief marshal; educated at Benges School, Hertford, and Foster's Academy, Stubbington; entered *Britannia* as naval cadet, 1900; commissioned in Royal Navy, 1904; attended course of flying instruction at Eastchurch, 1910; awarded Royal Aero Club certificate No. 72; commanded Cromarty Air Station, and later, Experimental Seaplane Station, Calshot; commanded No. 1 Squadron, Royal Naval Air Service, 1914–16; lieutenant-commander, *Tiger*, present at Battle of Jutland, 1916; wing-captain, RNAS, Malta; lieutenant-colonel, Royal Air Force, 1918; commanded Adriatic Group at Taranto; DSO, 1919; group captain, Iraq, 1923; CB, 1925; commandant, RAF College, Cranwell; air vice-marshal, 1931; air marshal, 1933; commandant, Imperial Defence College, 1934; KCB, 1935; commander-in-chief, Training Command, 1939–40; initiated Empire air-training scheme; AOC-in-C, Middle East, 1940–1; inspector-general, RAF, 1941–2; GCB; member, Post-Hostilities Planning Committee, 1943–4; published autobiography, *From Sea to Sky* (1946).

LONGMUIR, John (1803–1883), Scottish antiquary; studied at Marischal College, Aberdeen; MA; LL D, 1859; his most important work a revised edition of *Jamieson's *Scottish Dictionary* (1879–82); published verse and two guidebooks.

LONGSTAFF, Tom George (1875–1964), mountain explorer; educated at Eton and Christ Church, Oxford; MB, B.Ch., 1903; MD, 1906; qualified, St Thomas's Hospital, 1903; climbed in Caucasus, 1903; explored eastern approaches to Nanda Devi, Himalayas, 1905; explored western approaches to Nanda Devi, climbed Trisul, and explored glaciers of Kamet group, 1907; explored Karakoram, continental watershed between Indus and Tarim Basin of Chinese Turkestan, 1909; climbed in Canadian Rockies, 1910–11; served in India during 1914–18 war; joined expeditions to Everest, Spitsbergen, and Greenland, 1922–34; hon. secretary, Royal Geographical Society, 1930–4; vice-president, 1934–7; president, Alpine Club, 1947; published autobiography, *This My Voyage* (1950).

LONGSTROTHER, John (d. 1471), lord treasurer of England; a knight of the Order of St John of Jerusalem; castellan of Rhodes, 1453; English prior of the Order of St John, 1460; lord treasurer to Henry VI, 1470; tried and beheaded after the Battle of Tewkesbury.

LONGSWORD. See LONGESPÉE.

LONGUEVILLE, William (1639–1721), friend of the poet Samuel *Butler; barrister, Inner Temple, 1660, and treasurer, 1695; a six-clerk in Chancery, 1660–78; *Farquhar indebted to him for part of his *Twin Rivals*.

LONGWORTH, Maria Theresa (1832?–1881), authoress and plaintiff in the Yelverton case; married to William Charles *Yelverton, afterwards fourth Viscount Avonmore, by a priest at the Roman Catholic chapel, Rostrevor, Ireland, 1857; the marriage repudiated by Yelverton (who afterwards married the widow of Professor Edward *Forbes, 1858); the validity of Miss Longworth's marriage established in the Irish court, 1861, but annulled in the Scottish court, 1862; the Scottish judgment confirmed in the House of Lords, 1864; published several novels, 1861–75, and *The Yelverton Correspondence* etc. (1863).

LONSDALE, earls of. See LOWTHER, JAMES, first earl, 1736–1802; LOWTHER, WILLIAM, first earl of the second creation, 1757–1844; LOWTHER, WILLIAM, third earl, 1787–1872; LOWTHER, HUGH CECIL, fifth earl, 1857–1944.

LONSDALE, Viscounts. See LOWTHER, Sir JOHN, first viscount, 1655–1700; LOWTHER, HENRY, third viscount, d. 1751.

LONSDALE, Frederick (1881–1954), playwright; original name Lionel Frederick Leonard; son of seaman; educated locally in St Helier; wrote musical comedies and plays with brilliant dialogue about the wealthy and well-bred, a subject which eventually became outdated; productions included *The King of Cadonia* and *The Early Worm* (1908), *The Balkan Princess* (1910), *The Maid of the Mountains* (a notable success, with José *Collins as Teresa, 1927), *Aren't We All?* (1923), and *The Last of Mrs. Cheyney* (1925); moved to America (1938), then to France (1950).

LONSDALE, Henry (1816–1876), biographer; studied medicine at Edinburgh, 1834; became partner of Dr Robert *Knox (1791–1862), 1840; fellow of the Royal College of Physicians, Edinburgh, 1841; published biographies, including *The Worthies of Cumberland* (1867–75), *A Sketch of the Life and Writings of Robert Knox, the Anatomist* (1870).

LONSDALE, James (1777–1839), portrait painter; first exhibited at Royal Academy, 1802; helped to found Society of British Artists; portrait painter-in-ordinary to Queen *Caroline.

LONSDALE, James Gylby (1816–1892), son of John *Lonsdale (1788–1867); educated at Eton and Balliol College, Oxford; fellow, 1838–64; took holy orders, 1842; professor of classical literature, King's College, London,

1865–70; published with Samuel Lee prose translation of Virgil (1871) and of Horace (1893).

LONSDALE, John (1788–1867), bishop of Lichfield; educated at Eton and King's College, Cambridge; fellow of King's College, 1809; prebendary of Lincoln, 1827, of St Paul's, 1828; principal of King's College, London, 1839; archdeacon of Middlesex, 1842; bishop of Lichfield, 1843; prepared for press, in conjunction with Archdeacon *Hale, *The Four Gospels, with Annotations* (1849).

LONSDALE, Dame Kathleen (1903–1971), crystallographer; daughter of Harry Frederick Yardley and Jessie Cameron; educated at Ilford County High School for Girls, and Bedford College, London; headed university list in honours B.Sc. exam, 1922; joined research team of Sir W. H. *Bragg; married Thomas Jackson Lonsdale, 1927; worked on structure of crystals at Leeds University, 1929–31; research assistant to Sir W. H. Bragg at Royal Institution, 1931; one of first two women to be elected FRS, 1945, for her research in crystallography; reader in crystallography, University College, London, 1946; professor of chemistry, 1949; general editor, *International Tables for X-Ray Crystallography* (1946); became a Quaker, 1935; imprisoned for reasons of conscience as pacifist, 1943; publications include *Crystals and X-rays* (1948), *Is Peace Possible?* (1957), and *Removing the Causes of War* (Swarthmore lecture, 1953); president at Moscow Congress of International Union of Crystallography, 1966; first woman president of British Association, 1968; DBE, 1956; honorary degrees from eight universities.

LONSDALE, William (1794–1871), geologist; entered the army, 1812; fought at Waterloo, 1815; retired soon after 1815 and studied geology; curator and librarian to the Geological Society, 1829–42; joint originator with *Murchison and *Sedgwick of the theory of the independence of the Devonian system.

LOOKUP, John (*fl.* 1740), theologian; a disciple of John *Hutchinson (1674–1737); published an essay on the Trinity (1739) and a translation of Genesis (1740).

LOOSEMORE, George (*fl.* 1660), organist and composer; son of Henry *Loosemore; organist of Trinity College, Cambridge; Mus.Doc., 1665; composed anthems.

LOOSEMORE, Henry (1600?–1670), organist at King's College, Cambridge, 1627–70, and composer; Mus.Bac., Cambridge, 1640; organist of Exeter Cathedral, 1660; composed litanies and anthems.

LOOSEMORE, John (1613?–1681), organbuilder; brother of Henry *Loosemore; designed organ for Exeter Cathedral; also made virginals.

LOOTEN (LOTEN), Jan (1618–1681), landscape painter; native of Amsterdam; came to London early in Charles II's reign.

LOPES, Henry Charles, first Baron Ludlow (1828–1899), judge; educated at Winchester and Balliol College, Oxford; BA, 1849; barrister, Inner Temple, 1852; bencher, 1870; treasurer, 1890; QC, 1869; Conservative MP for Launceston, 1868–74, and Frome, 1874; justice in High Court, 1876; knighted, 1876; sat successively in common pleas and Queen's Bench divisions, and was advanced to court of appeal, 1885; privy councillor, 1885; raised to peerage, 1897.

LOPES, Sir Lopes Massey, third baronet (1818–1908), politician and agriculturist; educated at Winchester and Oriel College, Oxford; BA, 1842; MA, 1845; Conservative MP for Westbury, 1857–68, for South Devon, 1868–85; urged grievance of burden of local taxation; helped to carry Agricultural Ratings Act, 1879; civil lord of the Admiralty, 1874–80; PC, 1885; alderman of Devonshire County Council, 1888–1904; a scientific farmer, he spent much money on improving his estates.

LOPES, Sir Manasseh Masseh, first baronet (1755–1831), politician; descended from a family of Spanish Jews; born in Jamaica; conformed to Church of England; MP, Romney, 1802; created baronet, 1805; MP, Barnstaple, 1812; imprisoned for bribery and corruption, 1819; MP, Westbury, 1823 and 1826–9.

LOPEZ, Roderigo (d. 1594), Jewish physician; native of Portugal; settled in England, 1559; first house physician at St Bartholomew's Hospital; member of Royal College of Physicians before 1569; chief physician to Queen Elizabeth, 1586; implicated in the plot to murder Antonio Perez and Queen Elizabeth; tried, found guilty, and executed at Tyburn, 1594; possibly the original of Shakespeare's Shylock.

LOPOKOVA, Lydia Vasilievna, Lady Keynes (1892–1981), ballerina; born at St Petersburg (Leningrad); educated at Imperial Ballet School; joined Imperial Ballet, 1909; toured with Diaghilev Company, 1910; danced with Nijinsky in *Firebird* and *Carnaval*; danced in ballet groups in USA until 1916 when she rejoined Diaghilev's Ballets Russes as leading ballerina; toured in Europe and made first appearance in London in 1918; starred in Diaghilev's 1921 London production of *Sleeping Beauty*; married (John) Maynard (later Lord) *Keynes, 1925, and dedicated her life to him between his first serious illness until his death,

1937–46; gave much help to burgeoning British Ballet.

LORAINE, Sir **Percy Lyham,** twelfth baronet (1880–1961), diplomat; educated at Eton and New College, Oxford, 1899; served in South African War; entered Foreign Office, 1904; served in Constantinople, 1904, Tehran, 1907, Rome, 1909, Peking, 1911, Paris, 1912, and Madrid, 1916; attached to Peace Conference Delegation, 1918–19; minister, Tehran, 1921; Greece, 1926–9; high commissioner, Egypt and Sudan, 1929–33; Ankara, 1933–9; PC; ambassador, Italy, 1939–40; succeeded to baronetcy, 1917; CMG, 1921; KCMG, 1925; GCMG, 1937.

LORAINE, Violet Mary (1886–1956), actress; chorus girl in Drury Lane pantomime, 1902; principal boy there, 1911; played notably opposite (Sir) George *Robey in *The Bing Boys are Here* (1916), with songs such as 'If you were the only girl in the world'; married and retired, 1921.

LORD, Henry (*fl.* 1630), traveller; of Magdalen Hall, Oxford; English chaplain at Surat, 1624; published *A Display of two forraigne Sects in the East Indies*, etc. (1630).

LORD, John Keast (1818–1872), naturalist; entered the Royal Veterinary College, London, 1842; received his diploma, 1844; served in the Crimea as veterinary surgeon to the artillery of the Turkish contingent, 1855–6; naturalist to the boundary commission sent to British Columbia, 1858; employed in archaeological and scientific researches in Egypt; first manager of the Brighton Aquarium, 1872; author of *The Naturalist in Vancouver's Island* (1866) and a *Handbook of Sea-Fishing*.

LORD, Percival Barton (1808–1840), diplomatic agent; BA, Dublin, 1829; MB, 1832; studied medicine at Edinburgh; assistant surgeon under East India Company, 1834; accompanied the 'commercial mission' under Sir Alexander *Burnes to Kabul, penetrated into Tartary, 1837; political assistant to William Hay *Macnaghten, 1838; killed in action at Purwan, 1840; author of *Popular Physiology* (1834) and *Algiers, with Notices of the neighbouring States of Barbary* (1835).

LORD, Thomas (*fl.* 1796), ornithologist; published *Lord's Entire New System of Ornithology* (1791–6).

LORD, Thomas (1808–1908), Congregational minister; held Midland pastorates (1834–79) till he settled at Horncastle, where he preached in his 101st year; original member of Peace Society; published devotional works.

LOREBURN, Earl (1846–1923), lord chancellor. See REID, ROBERT THRESHIE.

LORIMER, James (1818–1890), jurist and political philosopher; educated at the universities of Edinburgh, Berlin, Bonn, and the academy of Geneva; member of the Faculty of Advocates of Scotland, 1845; published *Political Progress not necessarily Democratic* (1857) and the sequel *Constitutionalism of the Future* (1865); appointed to the chair of 'The Law of Nature and of Nations', Edinburgh, 1865; published *The Institutes of Law* (1872) and *The Institutes of the Law of Nations* (1883–4).

LORIMER, Peter (1812–1879), Presbyterian divine; entered Edinburgh University, 1827; professor of theology in the English Presbyterian College, London, 1844, and principal, 1878; chief work, *John Knox and the Church of England* (1875).

LORIMER, Sir **Robert Stodart** (1864–1929), architect; son of Professor James *Lorimer; apprenticed to Sir Rowand Anderson, architect, 1885; entered office of G. F. *Bodley, 1889; returning to Edinburgh, began long series of restorations, which were among his most pleasing works, 1892; designed many large Scottish country houses; his churches include St Peter's (Roman Catholic), Morningside, Edinburgh (1906); designed chapel of Order of the Thistle, St Giles' Cathedral, Edinburgh, 1909–11; recognized as leading architect of Scotland, 1914–18; after European war chiefly occupied on memorials, most important being Scottish National War Memorial, Edinburgh (1918–27); knighted, 1911; saviour of crafts in Scotland; restored to Scotland vital and characteristic architecture.

LORING, Sir **John Wentworth** (1775–1852), admiral; born in America; entered the navy, 1789; lieutenant, 1794; present in actions off Toulon, 1795; employed off France, 1805–13; CB, 1815; lieutenant-governor of the Royal Naval College, Portsmouth, 1819–37; KCB, 1840; vice-admiral, 1840; admiral, 1851.

LORKIN, Thomas (1528?–1591), regius professor of physic at Cambridge; educated at Pembroke Hall, Cambridge; MA, Peterhouse, 1555; MD, 1560; fellow of Queens' College, of Peterhouse, 1554–62; published *Recta Regula et Victus ratio pro studiosis et literatis* (1562); regius professor of physic, 1564.

LORKYN, Thomas (d. 1625); MA, Emmanuel College, Cambridge, 1604; secretary to the embassy at Paris, 1623; drowned at sea, 1625.

LORRAIN, Paul (d. 1719), ordinary of Newgate, 1698–1719; compiled the official accounts of the dying speeches of criminals; published *The Dying Man's Assistant* (1702) and a translation of Muret's *Rites of Funeral* (1683).

LORT, Michael (1725–1790), antiquary; MA, Trinity College, Cambridge, 1750; senior fellow, 1768; FSA, 1755; regius professor of Greek at Cambridge, 1759–71; FRS, 1766; DD and prebendary of St Paul's, 1780. The results of his antiquarian researches appeared in works like *Chalmers's *Biographical Dictionary* and *Nichols's *Literary Anecdotes*.

LORTE, Sir **Roger,** first baronet (1608–1664), Latin poet; BA, Wadham College, Oxford, 1627; published *Epigrammatum liber primus* (1646); created baronet, 1662.

LORYNG, Sir **Nigel (or Nele)** (d. 1386), soldier; knighted for bravery at Sluys, 1340; one of the original knights of the Garter, 1344; present at Poitiers, 1356; served in France and Spain, 1364–9.

LOSINGA, Herbert de (1054?–1119), first bishop of Norwich and founder of the cathedral church; his native place and the signification of his surname a matter of dispute; educated in the monastery at Fécamp, Normandy; Benedictine monk, *c.*1075; prior of Fécamp, 1088; abbot of Ramsey, 1088; bishop of Thetford, 1091; removed the see from Thetford to Norwich, 1094; his sermons and letters edited and translated by *Goulburn and *Symonds (1878).

LOSINGA (or DE LOTHARINGIA), Robert (d. 1095), bishop of Hereford; a native of Lotharingia or the southern Netherlands; doubtless a relative of Herbert de *Losinga; wrote astronomical works; crossed to England and became one of the royal clerks; bishop of Hereford, 1079.

LOTBINIÈRE, Sir **Henry Gustave Joly De** (1829–1908), Canadian politician. See JOLY DE LOTBINIÈRE.

LOTHIAN, earls of. See KERR, MARK, first earl, d. 1609; KERR, WILLIAM, third earl, 1605?–1675; KERR, ROBERT, fourth earl, 1636–1703.

LOTHIAN, marquises of. See KERR, ROBERT, first marquis, 1636–1703; KERR, WILLIAM, second marquis, 1662?–1722; KERR, WILLIAM HENRY, fourth marquis, d. 1775; KERR, SCHOMBERG HENRY, ninth marquis, 1833–1900; KERR, PHILIP HENRY, eleventh marquis, 1882–1940.

LOTHIAN, William (1740–1783), divine and historian; DD, Edinburgh, 1779; published a history of the Netherlands (1780).

LOTHROPP (LATHROP or LOTHROP), John (*c.*1584–1653), Independent divine; MA, Queens' College, Cambridge, 1609; sailed for Boston, 1634; died at Barnstaple, Massachusetts, where he ministered, 1639–53.

LOUDON, earls of. See LOUDOUN.

LOUDON, Charles (1801–1844), medical writer; MRCS, 1826; MD, Glasgow, 1827; published medical works, 1826–42.

LOUDON, Jane (1807–1858), horticultural and miscellaneous writer; née Webb; published *The Mummy, a Tale of the Twenty-second Century* (1827), which may have furnished some of the ideas of *Lytton's *Coming Race*; married John Claudius *Loudon, 1830; published *The Ladies' Companion to the Flower Garden* (1841) and other horticultural works.

LOUDON, John Claudius (1783–1843), landscape-gardener and horticultural writer; FLS, 1806; his *Encyclopaedia of Gardening* published (1822), *Encyclopaedia of Agriculture* (1825), *Encyclopaedia of Plants* (1829); edited *Gardener's Magazine*, 1826–43; began to compile the *Encyclopaedia of Cottage, Farm, and Villa Architecture*, 1832; began to publish his *Arboretum et Fruticetum Britannicum* (1833); established *Architectural Magazine*, 1834, *Suburban Gardener and Villa Companion*, 1836; published *Encyclopaedia of Trees and Shrubs* (1842).

LOUDOUN, earls of. See CAMPBELL, JOHN, first earl, 1598–1663; CAMPBELL, HUGH, third earl, d. 1731; CAMPBELL, JOHN, fourth earl, 1705–1782.

LOUGH, John Graham (1806–1876), sculptor; first exhibited at Royal Academy, 1826.

LOUGHBOROUGH, Barons. See HASTINGS, HENRY, d. 1667; WEDDERBURN, ALEXANDER, earl of Rosslyn, 1733–1805.

LOUGHBOROUGH, first Baron Hastings of (d. 1573). See HASTINGS, Sir EDWARD.

LOUGHER, Robert (d. 1585), civilian; fellow of All Souls College, Oxford, 1553; BCL, 1558; principal of New Inn Hall, 1564–70 and 1575–80; DCL and regius professor of civil law, 1565; MP, Pembroke, 1572; master in Chancery, 1574.

LOUIS, Sir **Thomas,** first baronet (1759–1807), rear-admiral; entered the navy, 1770; on active service, 1778–80; advanced to post rank, 1783; present at the Battle of the Nile, 1798; acted under *Nelson, 1799–1802; rear-admiral, 1804; performed brilliant service at Battle of St Domingo, 1806; rewarded with a baronetcy; died off the coast of Egypt.

LOUIS ALEXANDER, Prince, of Battenburg (1854–1921). See MOUNTBATTEN, LOUIS ALEXANDER.

LOUISE CAROLINE ALBERTA (1848–1939), princess of Great Britain and Ireland, duchess of

Argyll; sixth child of Queen Victoria; married (1871) the marquess of Lorne (later ninth duke of *Argyll); a gifted sculptress; made home an artists' rendezvous; wrote magazine articles as 'Myra Fontenoy'; first president of National Union for the Higher Education of Women.

LOUISE VICTORIA ALEXANDRA DAG-MAR (1867–1931), princess royal of Great Britain and Ireland, duchess of Fife; third child of prince and princess of Wales; married (1889) the sixth earl of Fife, created duke on his marriage; declared princess royal, 1905; rescued from shipwreck off Cape Spartel, 1911.

LOUND, Thomas (1802–1861), amateur painter; occasionally exhibited at the Royal Academy.

LOUNDRES, Henry de (d. 1228), archbishop of Dublin from 1212; papal legate to Ireland, 1217–20; justiciary in Ireland, 1219–24.

LOUTH, first earl of (d. 1328), lord justice of Ireland. See BERMINGHAM, Sir JOHN.

LOUTH, Gilbert of (d. 1153?), abbot of Basingwerk, Flintshire. See GILBERT.

LOUTHERBOURGH (LOUTHERBOURG), Philip James (Philippe Jacques) de (1740–1812), painter and royal academician; born at Fulda, Germany; studied at Paris under Francis *Casanova; exhibited at the Salon, 1763; member of the Académie Royale, 1767; came to England, 1771; assisted *Garrick as designer of scenery and costume; exhibited at Royal Academy, 1772; RA, 1781; painted landscapes, marine subjects, and battle pieces.

LOVAT, Barons. See FRASER, SIMON, twelfth baron, 1667?–1747; FRASER, SIMON JOSEPH, 1871–1933.

LOVATT EVANS, Sir Charles Arthur (1884–1968), physiologist. See EVANS.

LOVE, Augustus Edward Hough (1863–1940), mathematician and geophysicist; second wrangler (1885), fellow (1886–99), St John's College, Cambridge; FRS, 1894; Sedleian professor of natural philosophy, Oxford, 1898–1940; investigated theory of elasticity of solids in its mathematical setting and its application to problems of the earth's crust; discovered 'Love waves', 1911; formulated a theory of bi-harmonic analysis, 1929; his *Treatise on the Mathematical Theory of Elasticity* (1892–3) a standard work.

LOVE, Christopher (1618–1651), Puritan minister; of New Inn Hall, Oxford; MA, 1642; tried, condemned, and executed for plotting against the Commonwealth, 1651; published controversial pamphlets and sermons.

LOVE, David (1750–1827), pedlar-poet; issued verses in single sheets and chapbooks; wrote the *Life, Adventures, and Experience of David Love* (3rd edn., 1823).

LOVE, James (1722–1774), comedian. See DANCE.

LOVE, Sir James Frederick (1789–1866), general; entered the army, 1804; served in the Corunna retreat, 1809; captain, 1811; present at Ciudad Rodrigo, 1812; wounded at Waterloo, 1815; saved Bristol during the riots of 1831; lieutenant-colonel, 1834; British resident at Zante, 1835–8; colonel, 1838; governor of Jersey, 1852–6; inspector-general of infantry, 1857–62; general, 1864; GCB and KH.

LOVE, John (1695–1750), grammarian and controversialist; educated at Glasgow University; master of Dumbarton Grammar School, 1721; issued *Two Grammatical Treatises* (1733); published, in conjunction with others, an edition of *Buchanan's Latin version of the Psalms (1737); rector of Dalkeith Grammar School, 1739.

LOVE, John (1757–1825), Presbyterian divine; educated at Glasgow University; founded the London Missionary Society, 1795; DD, Aberdeen, 1816; letters, sermons, and addresses by him published posthumously.

LOVE, Nicholas (1608–1682), regicide; educated at Wadham College, Oxford; MA, 1636; barrister, Lincoln's Inn, 1636; MP, Winchester, 1645; one of the judges at Charles I's trial, but did not sign the death-warrant; MP, Winchester, in the Rump Parliament of 1659; escaped to Switzerland at the Restoration; died at Vevey.

LOVE, Richard (1596–1661), dean of Ely; fellow of Clare Hall, Cambridge, before 1628; DD, 1630, and prebendary of Lichfield, 1634; master of Corpus Christi College, Cambridge, 1632; vice-chancellor, 1633–4; Lady Margaret professor of divinity, 1649; dean of Ely, 1660; contributed commendatory verses to *Quarles's *Emblems*.

LOVE, William Edward (1806–1867), polyphonist; mimicked sounds made by musical instruments, beasts, birds, and insects; gave public performances in England, Scotland, France, United States, West Indies, and South America, 1826–56.

LOVEDAY, John (1711–1789), philologist and antiquary; MA, Magdalen College, Oxford, 1734; collected pictures, books, and antiquities, and assisted in literary researches.

LOVEDAY, John (1742–1809), scholar; son of John *Loveday (1711–1789); educated at Magdalen College, Oxford; assisted Dr *Chandler in the preparation of *Marmora Oxoniensia* (1763); DCL, 1771.

LOVEDAY, Robert (*fl.* 1655), translator; studied at Cambridge; translated into English the first three parts of La Calprenéde's *Cleopatra* as *Hymen's Praeludia, or Love's Master-Piece*, 1652-4-5.

LOVEDAY, Samuel (1619-1677), Baptist minister and author of religious pamphlets.

LOVEGROVE, William (1778-1816), actor; first appeared in London, 1810.

LOVEKYN, John (d. 1368), lord mayor of London; traded in salted fish; sheriff of London, 1342; MP for the City, 1347-8 and 1365; lord mayor, 1348, 1358, 1365, and 1366.

LOVEL. See also LOVELL.

LOVEL, Philip (d. 1259), treasurer and justice; treasurer, 1252; justice-itinerant, 1255; prebendary of St Paul's.

LOVELACE, second earl of (1839-1906), author of *Astarte*. See MILBANKE, RALPH GORDON NOEL KING.

LOVELACE, Francis (1618?-1675?), governor of New York; deputy-governor of Long Island, 1664 or 1665; governor of New York and New Jersey, 1668; his paternal, but autocratic government not relished by the Dutch, and city surrendered to the Dutch fleet in his absence, 1673; arrested at Long Island, sent back to England, and examined; died shortly afterwards.

LOVELACE, John, third Baron Lovelace of Hurley (1638?-1693); MA, Wadham College, Oxford, 1661; MP, Berkshire, 1661-70; succeeded to barony, 1670; arrested on account of the Rye House Plot, 1683; embraced the cause of William III; overpowered and imprisoned by James II's supporters, 1688; captain of the Gentlemen Pensioners, 1689.

LOVELACE, John, fourth Baron Lovelace of Hurley (d. 1709), cousin of John *Lovelace, third baron; entered House of Lords, 1693; guidon of the Horse Guards, 1699; governor of New York and New Jersey, 1709; died at New York.

LOVELACE, Richard (1618-1658), cavalier and poet; educated at Charterhouse School and Gloucester Hall, Oxford; MA, 1636 (incorporated at Cambridge, 1637); wrote *The Scholar, a comedy*, 1636; contributed to *Musarum Oxoniensium Charisteria*, 1638; repaired to court, and served in the Scottish expeditions, 1639; wrote his famous song, 'Stone walls do not a prison make', when imprisoned (1642) for supporting the 'Kentish Petition'; rejoined Charles I, 1645; served with the French king, 1646; again imprisoned, 1648; while in prison prepared for press his *Lucasta; Epodes, Odes, Sonnets, Songs, etc.* (published 1649); known almost exclusively by a few lyrics.

LOVELL. See also LOVEL.

LOVELL, Daniel (d. 1818), journalist; proprietor and editor of the *Statesman*, 1806-18; imprisoned for libel, 1810-15; heavily fined, 1817, for traducing the ministerial journal, the *Courier*.

LOVELL, Francis, first Viscount Lovell (1454-1487?), descended from Philip *Lovel; son of John, eighth Baron Lovell of Tichmarsh, Northamptonshire; knighted, 1480; summoned to parliament as ninth Baron Lovell of Tichmarsh, 1482; supporter of Richard III; created Viscount Lovell, privy councillor, and KG, 1483; lord chamberlain, 1483-5; attainted, 1485; fought for Lambert *Simnel, 1487, and seems to have escaped to his own house, where he died of starvation.

LOVELL, George William (1804-1878), dramatic author; his first play, *The Avenger*, produced 1835; his most famous play, *The Wife's Secret*, originally produced at New York, 1846, brought out in London, 1848.

LOVELL (formerly BADCOCK), Sir Lovell Benjamin Badcock (1786-1861), major-general; descended from Sir Salathiel *Lovell; educated at Eton; entered the army, 1805; served in the Montevideo expedition, 1807, in the Peninsular campaign, 1809-14; captain, 1811; lieutenant-colonel, 1826; one of the military reporters at the siege of Oporto and in the Miguelite war in Portugal; published *Rough Leaves from a Journal in Spain and Portugal* (1835); KH, 1835; assumed surname of Lovell, 1840; major-general, 1854; KCB, 1856.

LOVELL, Maria Anne (1803-1877), actress and dramatist, née Lacy; first appeared on the stage, 1818; represented Belvidera at Covent Garden, London, 1822; married George William *Lovell, 1830; retired from the stage; her *Ingomar the Barbarian* produced at Drury Lane, 1851, and *The Beginning and the End* at the Haymarket, 1855.

LOVELL (or LOVEL), Robert (1630?-1690), naturalist; brother of Sir Salathiel *Lovell; MA, Christ Church, Oxford, 1659; published his *Enchiridion Botanicum* (1659) and *A Compleat History of Animals and Minerals* (1661).

LOVELL, Robert (1770?-1796), poet; son of a Quaker; probably engaged in business at Bristol; made acquaintance of *Southey (with whom he published *Poems by Bion and Moschus*, 1794) and *Coleridge, and participated in their project for a pantisocratic colony on the banks of the Susquehanna.

LOVELL, Sir **Salathiel** (1619–1713), judge; brother of Robert *Lovell (1630?–1690); barrister, Gray's Inn, 1656; ancient, 1671; serjeant-at-law, 1688; recorder of London, 1692–1708; knighted, 1692; king's serjeant, 1695; judge on the Welsh circuit, 1696; fifth baron of the Exchequer, 1708.

LOVELL, Sir **Thomas** (d. 1524), speaker of the House of Commons; probably related to Francis, first Viscount *Lovell; fought at Bosworth on side of Henry Tudor, afterwards Henry VII, 1485; created chancellor of the Exchequer for life, 1485; MP, Northamptonshire, 1485; speaker, 1485–8; knighted, 1487; president of the council, 1502; KG, 1503; constable of the Tower, 1513–24; high steward of the universities of Cambridge, 1509, and Oxford, 1509–24.

LOVER, Samuel (1797–1868), song-writer, novelist, and painter; applied himself to portraiture, especially miniature painting; secretary to Royal Hibernian Academy, 1830; produced the best-known of his ballads, *Rory o' More*, 1826; published *Legends and Stories of Ireland*, illustrated by himself (1831); helped to found the *Dublin University Magazine*, 1833; miniature painter in London, 1835; associated with *Dickens in founding *Bentley's Magazine*; published a novel, *Rory o' More, a National Romance* (1837); dramatized it and wrote other plays; published *Songs and Ballads* (1839), and his second and best-known novel, *Handy Andy* (1842); gave an entertainment called 'Irish Evenings' in England, Canada, and (1846) United States; produced selection of Irish lyrics, 1858; produced parodies entitled *Rival Rhymes* (1859); *Volunteer Songs* (1859).

LOVETT, Richard (1692–1780), author of works on electricity; declared himself able to cure disease by the aid of electricity (1758).

LOVETT, Richard (1851–1904), author; spent boyhood (1858–67) in United States; BA London, 1873; MA, 1874; book editor of Religious Tract Society, 1882; secretary, 1899; wrote centenary history of London Missionary Society, 1899; wrote lives of James Gilmour (1892) and James *Chalmers (1902); author of *The Printed English Bible* (1895).

LOVETT, William (1800–1877), Chartist; secretary of the British Association for Promoting Co-operative Knowledge, 1830; arrested and tried for rioting, 1832; assisted in drafting parliamentary petitions and bills, 1836–8; arrested for his manifesto against the police, tried, and imprisoned, 1839–40; opened a bookseller's shop, and published *Chartism; a new Organisation*

of the People, the best book on the organization of the Chartist party (1841); member of the council of the Anti-Slavery League, 1846; published schoolbooks on elementary science.

LOVIBOND, Edward (1724–1775), poet; entered Magdalen College, Oxford, 1739; contributed well-known articles to the *World*, a weekly newspaper started by Edward *Moore; his best-known piece, 'The Tears of Old Mayday', published, 1754; his *Poems on several occasions* published by his brother (1785).

LOW, Alexander, Lord Low (1845–1910), Scottish judge; BA, St John's College, Cambridge, 1867; passed to Scottish bar, 1870; raised to bench, 1890; his decision against minority's claim to 'Free Church' property (1900) was reversed by House of Lords, 1904.

LOW, David (1768–1855), bishop of Ross, Moray, and Argyll; educated at Marischal College, Aberdeen; bishop of the united dioceses of Ross, Argyle, and the Isles, to which Moray was added (1838), 1819–50; LL D, 1820; effected separation of Argyll and the Isles from Ross and Moray, 1847; DD, Hartford College, Connecticut, and Geneva College, New York, 1848.

LOW, David (1786–1859), professor of agriculture; educated at Edinburgh University; published *Observations on the Present State of Landed Property and on the Prospects of the Landholder and the Farmer* (1817); established *Quarterly Journal of Agriculture* (1826), editing it, 1828–32; professor of agriculture in Edinburgh University, 1831–54; formed an agricultural museum; published *The Breeds of the Domestic Animals of the British Islands* (1842), and works on agriculture.

LOW, Sir **David Alexander Cecil** (1891–1963), cartoonist and caricaturist; born in New Zealand; educated at Christchurch Boys' High School; political cartoonist, *Spectator* and *Canterbury Times*; joined Sydney *Bulletin*, 1911; resident cartoonist, 1914; William M. *Hughes, his target for pictorial wit; cartoons published in *The Billy Book* (Sydney, 1918); arrived in London, 1919; political cartoonist, the *Star*, 1919–26; *Evening Standard*, 1926–49; derided Hitler and Mussolini; joined *Daily Herald*, 1950–3; *Manchester Guardian*, 1953; created 'Colonel Blimp'; selections published in book form include *Lloyd George & Co.* (1921), *Low's Political Parade* (1936), and *Low Visibility: A Cartoon History, 1945–53* (1953); other publications include *British Cartoonists, Caricaturists and Comic Artists* (1942), and *Low's Autobiography* (1956); knighted, 1962; hon. LL D, New Brunswick, 1958.

LOW, George (1747–1795), naturalist; educated at Aberdeen and St Andrews universities; studied the natural history and antiquities of the

Orkney Isles; his manuscripts never printed, but freely used by other antiquaries.

LOW, James (d. 1852), lieutenant-colonel, Madras Army; Siamese scholar; captain, 1826; retired as lieutenant-colonel, 1845; in civil charge of Province Wellesley; published *A Dissertation on the Soil and Agriculture of Penang* (1828), a grammar of the Siamese language, and treatises on Siamese literature.

LOW, Sir John (1788–1880), general in the Indian Army and political administrator; educated at St Andrews University; lieutenant, Madras Native Infantry, 1805; captain, 1820; resident of Cawnpore; political agent at Jeypore, 1825, at Gwalior, 1830, at Lucknow, 1831; governor-general's agent in Rajputana and commissioner at Ajmere and Mhairwar, 1848–52; resident to the nizam at Hyderabad, 1852; member of the council, 1853; major-general, 1854; gave valuable assistance in Indian Mutiny, 1857–8; KCB, 1862; general, 1867; GCSI, 1873.

LOW, Sir Robert Cunliffe (1838–1911), general; son of Sir John *Low; joined Indian Army, 1854; served in Indian Mutiny at Delhi and Lucknow; lieutenant-colonel, 1878; director of the Transport Service on march from Kabul to Kandahar; CB, 1880; actively engaged in Upper Burma, 1886–7; KCB, 1887; commander-in-chief of Chitral Relief Expedition, 1895; lieutenant-general and GCB, 1896; commanded Bombay Army, 1898–1909; general, 1900; keeper of crown jewels at Tower of London, 1909–11.

LOW, Sampson (1797–1886), publisher; brought out first number of *Publishers' Circular*, 1837 (his sole property, 1867); issued the *English Catalogue*, 1853–82; retired from business, 1875.

LOW, Sir Sidney James Mark (1857–1932), author and journalist; educated at King's College School and Balliol College, Oxford; first class, modern history, 1879; brilliant editor of *St. James's Gazette*, 1888–97; ardent imperialist and friend of *Rhodes, *Cromer, *Curzon, *Milner, etc.; works include *The Governance of England* (1904) and *A Vision of India* (1906); knighted, 1918.

LOW, William (1814–1886), civil engineer; engaged under *Brunel in construction of Great Western Railway; colliery engineer; MICE, 1867.

LOWDER, Charles Fuge (1820–1880), vicar of St Peter's, London Docks; educated at Exeter College, Oxford; MA, 1845; joined the mission at St George's-in-the-East, 1856; riots in the congregation being produced by his high-church views, built a new church, St Peter's, London Docks (consecrated 1866); known as 'Father

Lowder'; published accounts of his ministry at St George's; died at Zell-am-See, Salzburg, Austria.

LOWE, Sir Drury Curzon Drury- (1830–1908), lieutenant-general. See DRURY-LOWE.

LOWE, Edward (d. 1682), composer and organist; organist of Christ Church, Oxford, 1630–56; one of the organists at the Chapel Royal, London, 1660–82; published *A Short Direction for the performance of Cathedrall Service*, etc. (1661); professor of music at Oxford, 1661; composed anthems.

LOWE, Edward William Howe de Lancy (1820–1880), major-general; son of Sir Hudson *Lowe; educated at Royal Military College, Sandhurst; entered the army, 1837; captain, 1845; served in second Sikh War, 1848–9, in Indian Mutiny, 1857–8; lieutenant-colonel, 1858; CB, 1859; major-general, 1877.

LOWE, Eveline Mary (1869–1956), first woman chairman of the London County Council; born Farren; educated at Milton Mount College; trained as teacher at Homerton College; lecturer, 1893; vice-principal, 1894–1903, Homerton College; married G. C. Lowe, a Bermondsey veterinary surgeon, later a doctor, 1903; Labour member, LCC, for West Bermondsey, 1922–46; member (1919–49), chairman (1934–7), LCC Education Committee; deputy chairman, LCC, 1929–30; chairman, Council's jubilee year, 1939–40; hon. LL D, London.

LOWE, Sir Hudson (1769–1844), lieutenant-general and governor of St Helena; gazetted ensign, 1787; captain, 1795; served at Toulon and in Corsica, Elba, Portugal, Minorca, and Egypt; served in Italy, 1805–12; served with Blücher; knighted, 1817; major-general, 1814; served in Italy, 1815; while governor of St Helena (1815–21) had custody of Napoleon; KCB, 1816; his treatment of Napoleon the subject of an attack by Barry Edward *O'Meara, at one time Napoleon's medical attendant at St Helena, 1822; governor of Antigua, 1823; on the staff in Ceylon, 1825–30; lieutenant-general, 1830. The 'Lowe Papers', which supplied the materials for *Forsyth's *Captivity of Napoleon at St. Helena* (1853), are in the British Museum.

LOWE, James (d. 1865), journalist and translator; edited *The Critic of Literature, Science, and the Drama*, 1843–63; projected a *Selected Series of French Literature* (one volume issued, 1853).

LOWE, James (d. 1866), a claimant to the invention of the screw-propeller; patented 'improvements in propelling vessels', 1838 and

1852. His propeller was used in the navy, but he never obtained any compensation for it.

LOWE, John (d. 1467), bishop successively of St Asaph and Rochester; prior of Augustinian eremites at London and provincial for England, 1428; bishop of St Asaph, 1433, of Rochester, 1444.

LOWE, John (1750–1798), Scottish poet; entered Edinburgh University, 1771; went to the United States, 1773; took orders and obtained a living as a clergyman of the church of England; his chief lyric, 'Mary's Dream'.

LOWE, Mauritius (1746–1793), painter; one of the first students in the school of the Royal Academy; gold medallist, 1769; obtained the travelling allowance for study at Rome, 1771; exhibited at Royal Academy and Society of Artists; befriended by Dr *Johnson.

LOWE, Peter (1550?–1612?), founder of the Faculty of Physicians and Surgeons of Glasgow; studied at Paris; published the *Whole Course of Chirurgerie* (1597); settled in Glasgow, 1598; founded the Glasgow Faculty, 1599.

LOWE, Richard Thomas (1802–1874), naturalist; educated at Christ's College, Cambridge; BA, 1825; English chaplain at Madeira, 1832–52; rector of Lea, Lincolnshire, 1852–74; published *A Manual Flora of Madeira* (1857–72); drowned in the wreck of the *Liberia*, in which he was returning to Madeira.

LOWE, Robert, first Viscount Sherbrooke (1811–1892), politician; educated at Winchester and University College, Oxford; MA, 1836; barrister, Lincoln's Inn, 1842; went to Sydney, where he practised, 1842; in the legislative council for New South Wales, 1843–50; returned to England and became leader-writer in *The Times*, 1850; MP, Kidderminster, 1852–9; joint secretary of the Board of Control, 1852–5; vice-president of Board of Trade and paymaster-general, 1855–8; privy councillor, 1855; MP, Calne, 1859–67; vice-president of the committee of Council on Education, 1859–64; his best speeches made during the reform debates, 1866–7; first MP for London University, 1868–80; chancellor of the Exchequer, 1868–73; DCL, Oxford, 1870; home secretary, 1873–4; created Viscount Sherbrooke of Sherbrooke in Warlingham, Surrey, 1880; published *Poems of a Life* (1884); GCB, 1885.

LOWE, Thomas (d. 1783), vocalist and actor; first appeared at Drury Lane, London, 1740; associated with the production of Handel's oratorios, 1742–50; lessee and manager of Marylebone Gardens, London, 1763–8; at Sadler's Wells, 1772–83.

LOWER, Mark Anthony (1813–1876), antiquary; son of Richard *Lower (1782–1865); mainly instrumental in founding the Sussex Archaeological Society, 1846; author of *Patronymica Britannica. A Dictionary of Family Names of the United Kingdom* (1860) and antiquarian works on Sussex.

LOWER, Richard (1631–1691), physician and physiologist; brother of Thomas *Lower; educated at Westminster School and Christ Church, Oxford; student, 1649; MA, 1655; MD, 1665; FRS, 1667; FRCP, 1675; the most noted physician of his time in London; the first to perform the operation of direct transfusion of blood from one animal into the veins of another; author of three medical treatises, the chief being *Tractatus de Corde* (1669).

LOWER, Richard (1782–1865), Sussex poet; his best-known production, *Tom Cladpole's Jurney to Lunnon*, printed as a sixpenny pamphlet (1830); published *Stray Leaves from an Old Tree* (1862).

LOWER, Thomas (1633–1720), Quaker sufferer; brother of Richard *Lower (1631–1691); educated at Winchester College; became a Quaker; imprisoned, with occasional periods of liberty, 1673–86; married a stepdaughter of George *Fox (1624–1691).

LOWER, Sir William (1600?–1662), dramatist; published *The Phoenix in her Flames. A Tragedy* (1639); fought for Charles I, 1640–5; knighted, 1645; lived in Cologne and Holland, 1655–61; published *The Enchanted Lovers; a Pastoral* (1658); published a sumptuous *Relation . . . of the Voyage and Residence which the most mighty . . . Prince Charles II . . . hath made in Holland* (1660).

LOWICK, Robert (d. 1696), conspirator; fought for James II, 1689; implicated in the 'Assassination plot', tried, and executed.

LOWIN, John (1576–1659), actor; his name spelt Lowine, Lowen, Lowyn, and Lewen; joined the King's Company, 1603; acted with Shakespeare, *Burbage, John *Heming, *Condell, etc., 1603–11; shared with *Taylor the management of the King's Players, 1623–42; acted in the chief plays of Shakespeare, *Jonson, *Beaumont and *Fletcher, and *Massinger.

LOWKE, Wenman Joseph Bassett- (1877–1953), model maker. See BASSETT-LOWKE.

LOWMAN, Moses (1680–1752), Nonconformist divine; studied at Leiden and Utrecht; chief work, *Dissertation on the Civil Government of the Hebrews* (1740).

LOWNDES, Thomas (1692–1748), founder of the Lowndes chair of astronomy in Cambridge; provost-marshal of South Carolina, 1725–7,

1730–3; entrusted his duties to a deputy and never visited the colony, but advanced schemes for its improvement; published pamphlet advocating a project for supplying the navy with salt, 1746; left his property to found a chair of astronomy in Cambridge University.

LOWNDES, William (1652–1724), secretary to the Treasury; first connected with the Treasury, 1679; secretary, 1695; MP, Seaford, 1695–1714, St Mawes, 1714, East Looe, 1722–4; credited with originating the phrase, 'ways and means'.

LOWNDES, William Thomas (d. 1843), bibliographer; published *The Bibliographer's Manual*, the first systematic work of the kind in England (1834), and *The British Librarian* (1839–42).

LOWRIE alias **WEIR, William** (d. 1700?). See LAWRIE.

LOWRY, (Clarence) Malcolm (1909–1957), author; educated at Leys School and St Catharine's College, Cambridge; established lifelong reputation as writer and drinker; married twice and lived variously in United States, Mexico, Canada (1940–54), and England; based *Ultramarine* (1933) on voyage 'before the mast' to China Seas, 1927; *Under the Volcano* (1947), claimed as work of genius, describes last day in life of drunken consul and wife in Mexico on Day of the Dead; *Lunar Caustic* and *Dark as the Grave* published posthumously (1968).

LOWRY, Henry Dawson (1869–1906), author; wrote Cornish stories for *National Observer* from 1891; on staff of *Pall Mall Gazette*, 1895, and *Morning Post*, 1897; published novels and *The Hundred Windows* (poems, 1904).

LOWRY, John (1769–1850), mathematician; contributed to Thomas *Leybourn's *Mathematical Repository* (1799–1819); his tract on spherical trigonometry appended to volume ii of *Dalby's *Course of Mathematics*.

LOWRY, Joseph Wilson (1803–1879), engraver; son of Wilson *Lowry; illustrator of scientific works; engraver to the Geological Survey of Great Britain and Ireland; FRGS.

LOWRY, Laurence Stephen (1887–1976), painter; educated at Victoria Park School, Manchester; began work with firm of accountants, 1905; attended evening classes at Manchester Municipal College of Art, 1905–15 and at Salford School of Art, 1915–20; rent-collector and clerk with Pall Mall Property Co. in Manchester, 1910–52, kept job a closely guarded secret; many pictures painted by artificial light at night, hence the absence of shadows; his imagination haunted by the Stockport Viaduct and other industrial scenes; Manchester City Art Gallery purchased (1930) *An Accident* (1926); elected to Royal

Society of British Artists, 1934; his work discovered by art-dealer A. J. McNeil Reid of Lefevre Gallery, London, 1938; first one-man exhibition, 1939; hon. MA, 1945 and LL D, 1961, Manchester University; ARA, 1955; RA, 1962; received freedom of City of Salford, 1965; GPO issued stamp reproducing one of his industrial scenes, 1967; main collection of his work owned by City Art Gallery, Salford, including self-portrait (1925) and *The Cripples* (1949).

LOWRY, Thomas Martin (1874–1936), chemist; educated at Kingswood School, Bath, and Central Technical College, South Kensington; assistant there to H. E. *Armstrong, 1896–1913; head of chemical department, Guy's Hospital Medical School, 1913–20; professor of physical chemistry, Cambridge, 1920–36; mainly investigated optical rotatory power; FRS, 1914.

LOWRY, Wilson (1762–1824), engraver; studied in the Royal Academy schools; engraver of architecture and mechanism, devising ingenious instruments for the work; discovered the secret of biting in steel successfully; the first to use diamond points for ruling; executed the plates for Dr *Rees's *Cyclopaedia*; FRS, 1812.

LOWSON, Sir Denys Colquhoun Flowerdew, first baronet of Westlaws (1906–1975), financier; educated at Winchester and Christ Church, Oxford; called to bar (Inner Temple), 1930; worked in banks before setting up own business in 1935; set out to dominate unit-trust movement; gained control of National Group of Unit Trusts and used this success to obtain control of investment companies until he controlled financial empire worth some £200 million in 1972; surreptitiously bought management company of National Group of Unit Trusts for less than £500,000 and six months later sold it for £6½ million; exposed and disgraced; served with indictment summons but died before case could be heard; lord mayor of London, 1950–1; created baronet, 1951; gave freely to charities; church commissioner for England, 1948; grand warden of United Grand Lodge of England; life governor, Dundee University; one of Britain's leading philatelists.

LOWTH (or LOUTH), Robert (1710–1787), bishop of London; son of William *Lowth; educated at Winchester College and New College, Oxford; MA, 1737; professor of poetry at Oxford, 1741–50; archdeacon of Winchester, 1750; published his lectures on Hebrew poetry (1753); created DD, Oxford, 1753; prebendary of Durham, 1755; FRS, 1765; bishop of Oxford, 1766–77; bishop of London, 1777; dean of the Chapel Royal, 1777; privy councillor, 1777; wrote a life of William *Wykeham (1758), a short introduction to English grammar (1762), and a new translation of Isaiah (1778).

LOWTH, Simon (*c.*1636–1720), nonjuring clergyman; MA, Clare Hall, Cambridge, 1660; DD, 1689; deprived of his livings, 1690; wrote in defence of the nonjuring schism and an episcopal succession against any right of deposition by a civil magistrate.

LOWTH, William (1660–1732), theologian; educated at Merchant Taylors' School, London, and St John's College, Oxford; fellow; MA, 1683; BD, 1688; prebendary of Winchester, 1696; best-known work, *Commentary on the Prophets* (1714–25).

LOWTHER, Sir Gerard (d. 1624), Irish judge; third son of Sir Richard *Lowther (1529–1607); judge of the common pleas in Ireland from 1610 till death; knighted, 1618.

LOWTHER, Sir Gerard (1589–1660), Irish judge; godson of the elder Sir Gerard *Lowther, being natural son of the elder Sir Gerard's brother, Sir Christopher Gerard; educated at The Queen's College, Oxford; barrister, Gray's Inn, 1614; baron of the Irish Exchequer, 1628; knighted, 1631; chief justice of the common pleas in Ireland, 1634; at first on Charles I's side, but subsequently joined the parliament; commissioner of the great seal in Ireland, 1654.

LOWTHER, Henry, third Viscount Lonsdale (d. 1751), son of Sir John *Lowther, first Viscount Lonsdale; lord of the bedchamber; constable of the Tower, 1726; lord privy seal, 1733–5.

LOWTHER, Hugh Cecil, fifth earl of Lonsdale (1857–1944), sportsman; educated at Eton; succeeded brother, 1882; master in turn of Woodland Pytchley, Blankney, Quorn, and Cottesmore hounds; won St Leger (1922) but normally unsuccessful as racehorse owner; notable boxer and yacht-racer; maintained splendid establishments and endeared himself to populace as sporting grandee; friend of circus folk and London costermongers; with Eric *Parker edited 'The Lonsdale Library of Sports, Games & Pastimes'; lord-lieutenant of Cumberland, 1917–44; GCVO, 1925; KG, 1928.

LOWTHER, James, earl of Lonsdale (1736–1802); MP, Cumberland, 1757–61, 1762, 1768, 1774–84, Westmorland, 1761, Cockermouth, 1769; created earl of Lonsdale, 1784, and Viscount and Baron Lowther of Whitehaven, 1797; unrivalled in the art of electioneering.

LOWTHER, James (1840–1904), politician and sportsman; educated at Westminster and Trinity College, Cambridge; BA, 1863; MA, 1866; called to bar, 1864, but did not practise;

Conservative MP for York City, 1865–80, for North Lincs., 1881–5, for Isle of Thanet, 1888–1904; parliamentary secretary to the Poor Law Board under Disraeli, 1867–8; opposed Irish Land Bill, 1870; under-secretary for the colonies, 1874–8; chief secretary to lord-lieutenant of Ireland, 1878–80; PC, 1878; opposed establishment of county councils (1888); advocated protection; took part in Yorkshire local affairs; bred racehorses from 1873; senior steward of Jockey Club, 1889.

LOWTHER, James William, first Viscount Ullswater (1855–1949), speaker of the House of Commons; educated at Eton and Trinity College, Cambridge; third class, law, 1878; called to bar (Inner Temple), 1879; Conservative MP, Rutland, 1883; Penrith division, 1886–1921; charity commissioner, 1887; chairman of ways and means and deputy speaker, 1895; PC, 1898; speaker, 1905–21; handled series of difficult situations in House with tact, fairness, and humour; GCB and viscount, 1921; thereafter served on royal commissions and other public bodies.

LOWTHER, Sir John, first Viscount Lonsdale (1655–1700), educated at The Queen's College, Oxford; succeeded to baronetcy, 1675; barrister, Inner Temple, 1677; MP, Westmorland, 1676–96; actively supported William of Orange; vice-chancellor and privy councillor, 1689; first lord of the Treasury, 1690–2; created Baron Lowther and Viscount Lonsdale, 1696; lord privy seal, 1699; his *Memoirs of the Reign of James II* privately printed (1808).

LOWTHER, Sir Richard (1529–1607), lord warden of the west marches; knighted, 1566; assisted *Mary Queen of Scots, 1568–72; lord warden of the west marches, 1591.

LOWTHER, William, first earl of Lonsdale of the second creation (1757–1844); succeeded his third cousin, James *Lowther, earl of Lonsdale, as Viscount Lowther by special patent, 1802, and created earl of Lonsdale, 1807; patron of *Wordsworth.

LOWTHER, William, third earl of Lonsdale of the second creation (1787–1872); of Harrow and Trinity College, Cambridge; MA, 1808; FRS, 1810; MP, Cockermouth, 1808–13, Westmorland, 1813, 1818, 1820, 1826, and 1832, and Dunwich, 1832; junior lord of the Admiralty, 1809; on the Treasury board, 1813–26; first commissioner of woods and forests, 1828; president of Board of Trade, 1834–5; postmaster-general, 1841; summoned to the House of Lords in his father's (see LOWTHER, WILLIAM) barony, 1841; succeeded to the earldom, 1844; president of council, 1852.

LÖWY, Albert (or Abraham) (1816–1908), Hebrew scholar; born in Moravia; studied at Vienna University; helped to found 'Die Einheit', a society for promoting welfare of Jews; came to London for support of scheme, 1840; with Jewish reformers in London founded West London Synagogue, 1842, and became first minister, 1842–92; helped to form Anglo-Jewish Association, 1870; secretary, 1875–89; catalogued Lord *Crawford's Samaritan literature, 1872, and Hebrew books of City of London, 1891; founded Society of Hebrew Literature, 1870; hon. LL D, St Andrews, 1893.

LOYD. See also LHUYD, LLOYD, and LLWYD.

LOYD, Samuel Jones, first Baron Overstone (1796–1883); of Eton and Trinity College, Cambridge; MP, Hythe, 1819–26; MA, 1822; became a partner in his father's banking business (London and Westminster Bank, founded 1834), 1844; hon. DCL, Oxford, 1854; created Baron Overstone of Overstone and Fotheringay, 1850; authority on banking and finance; the Bank Act of 1844 substantially based on his principles; influenced current politics on the financial side.

LOYD-LINDSAY, Robert James, Baron Wantage (1832–1901), soldier and politician. See LINDSAY.

LUARD, Henry Richards (1825–1891), registrary of the university of Cambridge; fellow of Trinity College, 1849; MA, 1850; vicar of Great St Mary's, Cambridge, 1860–87; registrary of the university, 1862; contributed a 'Life of Porson' to the *Cambridge Essays*, 1856, and to the ninth edition of the *Encyclopaedia Britannica*; contributed to the Master of the Rolls series; a frequent contributor of articles on medieval and classical scholars to this Dictionary (vols. i–xxxii).

LUARD, John (1790–1875), lieutenant-colonel; author of the *History of the Dress of the British Soldier*; served in the navy, 1802–7; in the army through the Peninsular campaigns, 1810–14; as lieutenant fought at Waterloo, 1815; retired as major, 1834; published *Views in India, St. Helena, and bar Nicobar* (1835) and *History of the Dress of the British Soldier* (1852).

LUARD, John Dalbiac (1830–1860), artist; son of John *Luard; educated at Sandhurst; in the army, 1848–53; studied art, and exhibited paintings at Royal Academy, 1855–8.

LUARD, Sir William Garnham (1820–1910), admiral; of Huguenot origin; joined navy, 1835; served in China War, 1841; commander, 1850; took part in capture of Rangoon and of Pegu (1852) and in operations in Japan in Straits of Shimonoseki, 1864; CB, 1864; captain superintendent of Sheerness Dockyard, 1870–5;

superintendent of Malta Dockyard, 1878–9; vice-admiral, 1879; president of Royal Naval College, Greenwich, 1882–5; admiral, 1885; KCB, 1897.

LUBBOCK, Sir John, fourth baronet, and first Baron Avebury (1834–1913), banker, scientist, and author; son of Sir J. W. *Lubbock, third baronet; educated at Eton, but early installed in his father's bank; succeeded father, 1865; Liberal MP, Maidstone, 1870 and 1874, London University, 1880–1900; secured passage of Bank Holidays Act (1871), Act for Preservation of Ancient Monuments (1882), Early Closing Act (1904), etc.; PC, 1890; baron, 1900; held leading position in banking world; his researches on ants his most valuable contribution to science; FRS, 1858; author of numerous scientific and ethical works.

LUBBOCK, Sir John William, third baronet (1803–1865), astronomer and mathematician; of Eton and Trinity College, Cambridge; partner in his father's bank, 1825; FRS, 1829; treasurer and vice-president of the Royal Society, 1830–5 and 1838–47; Bakerian lecturer, 1836; first vice-chancellor of London University, 1837–42; succeeded to baronetcy, 1840; compared in detail tidal observations with theory; mainly directed his researches in physical astronomy towards the simplification of methods; foremost among English mathematicians in adopting Laplace's doctrine of probability.

LUBBOCK, Percy (1879–1965), author; educated at Eton and King's College, Cambridge; first class, classical tripos, 1901; Pepys librarian, Magdalene College, Cambridge, 1906–8; contributed to *The Times Literary Supplement*, 1908–14; publications include *Elizabeth Barrett Browning in her Letters* (1906), *Samuel Pepys* (1909), *The Craft of Fiction* (1921), *Earlham* (1922), *Roman Pictures* (1923), *The Region Cloud* (1925), *Shades of Eton* (1929), and *Portrait of Edith Wharton* (1947); CBE, 1952.

LUBY, Thomas (1800–1870), mathematician; educated at Trinity College, Dublin; MA, 1825; DD, 1840; senior fellow, 1867; filled various college offices; wrote mathematical textbooks.

LUBY, Thomas Clarke (1821–1901), Fenian; BA, Trinity College, Dublin, 1845; abandoned theological studies for nationalist propaganda; planned risings in Ireland, 1848–9; captured and imprisoned; went to Australia; on return started with James *Stephens Fenian movement, 1853; founded Irish Republican Brotherhood, 1858; sent as envoy from Ireland to America to collect funds, 1863; on return revived waning enthusiasm, and launched *Irish People* newspaper as organ of party (Nov. 1863–Sept. 1865); sentenced to twenty years' penal servitude for treason-felony, 1865; set at liberty, 1871; settled in New York and engaged in journalism; distrusted home-rule movement under C. S. *Parnell; wrote *Lives of . . . Representative Irishmen* (1878).

LUCAN, countess of (d. 1814), amateur painter. See BINGHAM, MARGARET.

LUCAN, titular earl of (d. 1693). See SARSFIELD, PATRICK.

LUCAN, third earl of (1800–1888), field-marshal. See BINGHAM, GEORGE CHARLES.

LUCAR, Cyprian (*fl.* 1590), mechanician and author; of Winchester and New College, Oxford; fellow of New College before 1564; entered Lincoln's Inn, 1568; issued work on artillery (1588) and *A Treatise named Lucar Solace*, dealing with mensuration, geometry, and practical mechanics (1590).

LUCAS, eighth Baron (1876–1916), politician and airman. See HERBERT, AUBERON THOMAS.

LUCAS, Anthony (1633–1693), Jesuit; studied at St Omer; joined Jesuits, 1662; professor of theology in the college at Liège, 1672; rector of the English College at Rome, 1687; provincial of his order, 1693; involved in a controversy with Sir Isaac *Newton respecting the prismatic spectrum.

LUCAS, Sir **Charles** (d. 1648), Royalist; knighted, 1639; taken prisoner at Marston Moor, 1644; lieutenant-general of the cavalry, 1645; played foremost part in defence of Colchester, and on its capitulation was condemned to death by court martial, 1648.

LUCAS, Charles (1713–1771), Irish patriot; published *Pharmacomastix* (1741); interested himself in municipal reform in Dublin and issued *Divelina Libera: an Apology for the Civil Rights and Liberties of the Commons and Citizens of Dublin* (1744); behaved during his candidature for the parliamentary representation of Dublin city in such a way as to cause the government to prevent his going to the poll, to declare him an enemy of his country, and to condemn him to imprisonment, 1748; escaped to London; studied medicine at Paris, Reims, and Leiden; MD, Leiden, 1752; published a successful *Essay on Waters* (1756); LRCP, 1760; MP, Dublin, 1761–71; contributed to the *Freeman's Journal* from 1763; 'the Wilkes of Ireland'.

LUCAS, Charles (1769–1854), miscellaneous writer and divine; educated at Oriel College, Oxford; published novels and poems between 1795 and 1810.

LUCAS, Charles (1808–1869), musical composer; principal of the Royal Academy of Music, 1859–66; composed an opera, symphonies, string quartets, anthems, and songs.

LUCAS, Sir **Charles Prestwood** (1853–1931), civil servant and historian; educated at Winchester and Balliol College, Oxford; first class, Lit. Hum., 1876; headed Civil Service list, 1877; assistant under-secretary (1897), first head of dominions department (1907–11) of Colonial Office; KCMG, 1907; KCB, 1912; wrote many books on British Empire; fellow of All Souls, 1920–7.

LUCAS, Edward Verrall (1868–1938), journalist, essayist, and critic; cultivated effortless manner of communicating his delight in art, travel, and letters; publications include a life of his idol Charles *Lamb (1905), travel essays, short books on painters, collections of light essays, and anthologies; prolific contributor to and on staff of *Punch*; chairman of Methuen's, 1924–38; CH, 1932.

LUCAS, Frank Laurence (1894–1967), author and scholar; educated at Colfe's Grammar School, Lewisham, Rugby, and Trinity College, Cambridge; first class, classical tripos; served on Western Front in 1914–18 war; fellow, classics, King's College, Cambridge; employed at Government Codes and Cyphers headquarters, Bletchley Park, 1939–45; reader, Cambridge University, 1947–62; CBE, 1946; publications include *Seneca and Elizabethan Tragedy* (1922), *Euripides and his Influence* (1924), *The River Flows* (1926), *Tragedy in Relation to Aristotle's Poetics* (1927), *Time and Memory* (1929), *Cécile* (1930), *Studies French and English* (1934), *The Decline and Fall of the Romantic Ideal* (1936), *Delights of Dictatorship* (1938), *Greek Poetry for Everyman* (1951), *Greek Drama for Everyman* (1954), *The Art of Living* (1959), and *The Drama of Chekhov, Synge, Yeats and Pirandello* (1963).

LUCAS, Frederick (1812–1855), Roman Catholic journalist and politician; brother of Samuel *Lucas (1811–1865); brought up as a Quaker; student at University College, London; barrister, Middle Temple, 1835; became a Roman Catholic, 1839, and published *Reasons for becoming a Roman Catholic*; started the *Tablet*, 1840; MP, Co. Meath, 1852; identified himself with the Nationalist party; at the suggestion of Pope Pius IX began to write a 'Statement' of the condition of affairs in Ireland (1854), which appears in the second volume of Lucas's *Life* by his brother.

LUCAS, Henry (d. 1663), founder of the Lucasian professorship; MA, St John's College, Cambridge, 1636; MP, Cambridge University, 1640; left money to endow a professorship of the mathematical sciences at Cambridge.

LUCAS, Henry (*fl.* 1795), poet; son of Charles *Lucas (1713–1771); educated at Trinity College, Dublin; MA, 1762; wrote occasional verse.

LUCAS, Horatio Joseph (1839–1873), artist; exhibited at the Royal Academy and the Salon, Paris; excelled in the art of etching.

LUCAS, James (1813–1874), 'the Hertfordshire hermit'; led an eccentric life at his house near Hitchin, abjured washing, slept on cinders, associated mainly with tramps, but was visited out of curiosity by many well-known persons.

LUCAS, John (1807–1874), portrait painter; apprenticed to Samuel William *Reynolds (1773–1835); began to exhibit at Royal Academy, 1828; painted contemporary celebrities and court beauties.

LUCAS, John Templeton (1836–1880), artist; son of John *Lucas (1807–1874); exhibited landscapes at the Royal Academy, the British Institution, and the Suffolk Street Gallery, 1859–76; published a farce and (1871) a volume of fairy tales.

LUCAS, Keith (1879–1916), physiologist; BA, Trinity College, Cambridge; fellow of Trinity, 1904; science lecturer, 1908; Croonian lecturer of Royal Society, 1912; FRS, 1913; researched on muscle and nerve problems; services enlisted for Royal Aircraft Factory, Farnborough, 1914; killed flying.

LUCAS, Louis Arthur (1851–1876), African traveller; educated at University College, London; started to explore the Congo, 1875; reached Khartoum, 1876; arrived at Lardo; not permitted by *Gordon to undertake so difficult an expedition, which was likely to be certain destruction; navigated the northern portion of Lake Albert Nyanza; died on the steamboat voyage from Suakim to Suez; buried at Jeddah.

LUCAS, Margaret Bright (1818–1890), sister of John *Bright (1811–1889); married Samuel *Lucas (1811–1865), 1839; aided her husband in his public projects; visited America and began to take interest in temperance reform and women's suffrage, 1870; president of the British Women's Temperance Association.

LUCAS, Richard (1648–1715), prebendary of Westminster; MA, Jesus College, Oxford, 1672; DD, 1691; prebendary of Westminster, 1697; published his *Enquiry after Happiness*, a popular devotional work (1685), and other religious works.

LUCAS, Richard Cockle (1800–1883), sculptor; exhibitor at the Royal Academy, 1829–59; his best works medallion portraits, executed in marble, wax, and ivory; published *An Essay on Art, especially that of Painting* (1870).

LUCAS, Robert (1748?–1812), divine and poet; of Trinity College, Cambridge; DD, 1793; held a living in Worcestershire, and others in Northamptonshire; published *Poems on Various Subjects* (1810), containing a translation of the Homeric hymn to Ceres (Demeter).

LUCAS, Samuel (1805–1870), amateur painter; exhibited at the Royal Academy, 1830.

LUCAS, Samuel (1811–1865), journalist and politician; brother of Frederick *Lucas; married Margaret Bright (see LUCAS, MARGARET BRIGHT), sister of John *Bright, 1839; member of the Anti-Corn-Law League; published *Plan for the Establishment of a General System of Secular Education in the County of Lancaster* (1847); edited the *Morning Star*, 1856–65.

LUCAS, Samuel (1818–1868), journalist and author; educated at The Queen's College, Oxford; MA and barrister, Inner Temple, 1846; started the *Shilling Magazine*, 1865; published essays and poems.

LUCAS, Theophilus (*fl.* 1714), biographer; author of an entertaining work entitled *Memoirs of the Lives, Intrigues, and Comical Adventures* of famous gamblers and sharpers from Charles II to Anne (published 1714).

LUCAS, Sir Thomas (d. 1649), brother of Sir Charles *Lucas (d. 1648); distinguished himself on the king's side in Ireland in the Civil War; knighted, 1628; Irish privy councillor, 1642.

LUCAS, William? (*fl.* 1789), African explorer; three years a slave at Morocco, having been captured when a boy; vice-consul at Morocco till 1785; travelled in Africa in the service of the newly formed Association for Promoting African Exploration, 1788–9; published his account of Africa in the *Reports* of the African Association.

LUCIUS, a legendary hero; called the first Christian king in Britain; supposed to have lived in the second century. No record of his existence appears till three or four centuries after his supposed death. His legend owes its detail to *Geoffrey of Monmouth.

LUCKOCK, Herbert Mortimer (1833–1909), dean of Lichfield; educated at Shrewsbury and Jesus College, Cambridge; BA, 1858; MA, 1862; DD, 1879; won university theological prizes and scholarships; fellow, 1860; vicar of All Saints', Cambridge, 1862–3, 1865–75; principal of Ely Theological College, 1876–87; residentiary canon of Ely, 1875–92; dean of Lichfield, 1892–1909; a high churchman, he exerted influence through his devotional writings, which included *After Death* (1879) and *The Intermediate State* (1890).

LUCKOMBE, Philip (d. 1803), miscellaneous writer and conchologist; edited dictionaries and cyclopaedias, and wrote on printing.

LUCY, Charles (1814–1873), historical painter; studied at Paris and at the Royal Academy, London; exhibited his first historical painting, *The Interview between Milton and Galileo*, 1840; painted historical subjects and some portraits, frequently engraved.

LUCY, Godfrey de (d. 1204), bishop of Winchester; son of Richard de *Lucy; became a royal clerk and received many ecclesiastical preferments; archdeacon of Derby, 1182; canon of York and archdeacon of Richmond; justice-itinerant for the district beyond the Trent and the Mersey, 1179; bishop of Winchester, 1189–1204.

LUCY, Sir Henry William (1843–1924), journalist; employed by various newspapers and engaged in freelance journalism, 1864–72; engaged by *Daily News*, 1872; manager of its parliamentary staff and writer of parliamentary summary; as 'Toby, MP', wrote 'Essence of Parliament' for *Punch*, 1881–1916; knighted, 1909; his close personal relations with prominent politicians made his work first-hand.

LUCY, Sir Richard, first baronet (1592–1667), son of Sir Thomas *Lucy (1532–1600); BA, Exeter College, Oxford, 1611; created baronet, 1618; MP for Old Sarum in the Long Parliament, 1647, for Hertfordshire in *Cromwell's parliament, 1654 and 1656.

LUCY, Richard de (d. 1179), chief justiciary; maintained the cause of Stephen in Normandy against Geoffrey of Anjou; recalled to England, 1140; chief justiciary jointly with Robert de *Beaumont, earl of Leicester (1104–1168), 1153–66; sole chief justiciary, 1166–79; excommunicated by *Thomas Becket in 1166 and 1169 for his share in drawing up the constitutions of Clarendon (1164); commanded for Henry II in the insurrection of 1173.

LUCY, Sir Thomas (1532–1600), owner of Charlecote, Warwickshire; educated by John *Foxe, the martyrologist, whose Puritan sentiments he adopted; inherited the great Warwickshire estate, 1552; rebuilt his manor house at Charlecote, 1558–9; knighted, 1565; MP, Warwick, 1571 and 1584; alleged to have prosecuted Shakespeare for deer-stealing, 1585; Shakespeare's Justice Shallow.

LUCY, Sir Thomas (1585–1640), grandson of Sir Thomas *Lucy (1532–1600); of Magdalen College, Oxford; student of Lincoln's Inn, 1602; knighted, 1614; MP, Warwickshire, 1614, 1621, 1624, 1625, 1626, 1628, and 1640; friend of Lord Herbert of Cherbury (see HERBERT, EDWARD, first Baron Herbert of Cherbury).

LUCY, William (1594–1677), bishop of St David's; of the Charlecote family; educated at Trinity College, Oxford; BA, 1615; entered Caius College, Cambridge, 1615; BD, 1623; bishop of St David's, 1660; inhibited the archdeacon of Brecon from holding visitations in his diocese; published controversial works.

LUDERS, Alexander (d. 1819), legal writer; probably of German extraction; barrister, Inner Temple, 1778; bencher, 1811; author of historico-legal writings, published, 1785–1818.

LUDFORD, Simon (d. 1574), physician; Franciscan; at dissolution of the monasteries became an apothecary; MD, Oxford, 1560; FRCP, 1563.

LUDLAM, Henry (1824–1880), mineralogist; bequeathed his fine collection of minerals to the Geological Museum, Jermyn Street, London.

LUDLAM, Isaac (d. 1817), rebel; prominent in the 'Derbyshire insurrection' promoted by Jeremiah *Brandreth, 1817; arrested, tried, and executed.

LUDLAM, Thomas (1727–1811), theologian and essayist; brother of William *Ludlam; MA, St John's College, Cambridge, 1752; attacked Calvinistic writers in the *Orthodox Churchman's Review*; most of his essays included in *Essays, Scriptural, Moral, and Logical*, by William and Thomas Ludlam (1807).

LUDLAM, Thomas (1775–1810), governor of Sierra Leone; son of William *Ludlam; retired, 1807; died at Sierra Leone.

LUDLAM, William (1717–1788), mathematician; brother of Thomas *Ludlam (1727–1811); MA, St John's College, Cambridge, 1742; BD, 1749; Sadlerian lecturer, 1746–69; Linacre lecturer in physic, 1767–9; published mathematical and theological works; his *Rudiments of Mathematics* (1785) still used at Cambridge in 1815.

LUDLOW, Baron (1828–1899), judge. See LOPES, HENRY CHARLES.

LUDLOW, Edmund (1617?–1692), regicide; BA, Trinity College, Oxford, 1636; fought at Edgehill, 1642; MP, Wiltshire, 1646; one of the chief promoters of Pride's Purge, 1648; one of the king's judges who signed the death-warrant; member of Council of State, 1649 and 1650; lieutenant-general of the horse in Ireland and a commissioner for the civil government of Ireland, 1650–5; after the proclamation of *Cromwell as protector refused to acknowledge his authority or to give security for peaceable behaviour, 1656; allowed to retire to Essex; MP, Hindon, 1659; on the recall of the Long Parliament (7 May 1659) made member of the committee of safety, of the Council of State, and commander-in-chief of the Irish Army; impeached by the restored parliament, 1660; surrendered to proclamation summoning all Charles I's judges to surrender, 1660; allowed his liberty by providing sureties; escaped to Switzerland; came to England in hope of being employed by William III, 1689; proclamation published by William III for his arrest; escaped abroad and died at Vevey. Ludlow's *Memoirs*, the composition of his exile, were first printed (1698–9). Their chief value lies in their account of the Republican party's opposition to Cromwell and of the factions which caused the overthrow of the republic after its restoration in 1659.

LUDLOW, George (1596–1655), younger brother of Roger *Ludlow; a prominent and influential colonist; held large grants of land in Massachusetts; member of the council, 1642–55.

LUDLOW, George James, third and last Earl Ludlow (1758–1842), general; entered the army, 1778; captain, serving in America, 1781–2; served in Flanders, where he lost his left arm, 1793–4; in the Vigo expedition (1801), the Egyptian campaign (1801), the Hanover expedition (1805), and the Copenhagen expedition (1807); succeeded his brother in the peerage (of Ireland), 1811; general, 1814; GCB, 1815; created Baron Ludlow (peerage of United Kingdom), 1831.

LUDLOW, John Malcolm Forbes (1821–1911), social reformer; born at Nimach, India; educated in Paris; called to bar, 1843; practised as conveyancer, 1843–74; advocate of reforms in India and of abolition of slavery; member of Anti-Corn-Law League; in Paris during revolution of 1848; friend of F. D. *Maurice, Charles *Kingsley, and Tom *Hughes; one of founders of Christian Socialist movement; promoted labour co-partnership, 1850; founded and edited weekly *Christian Socialist*, 1850; helped to found Working Men's College (1854), lecturing there on law and English and Indian history; wrote historical works, including *Popular Epics of the Middle Ages* (2 vols., 1865); secretary to Royal Commission on Friendly Societies, 1870–4; chief registrar of friendly societies, 1875–91; CB, 1887.

LUDLOW, Roger (*fl.* 1640), deputy-governor of Connecticut; of Balliol College, Oxford; assistant of the Massachusetts colony, 1630–4; deputy-governor, 1634–5; deputy-governor of Connecticut, 1639; appointed to codify the laws of Connecticut, 1646; his code established, 1650; commissioner in the congress of the United Colonies of New England, 1651, 1652, and 1653; said to have finally settled in Ireland.

LUDLOW-HEWITT, Sir **Edgar Rainey** (1886–1973), air chief marshal; educated at Radley and Sandhurst; commissioned into Royal Irish Rifles, 1905; learnt to fly and joined Royal Flying Corps, 1914; gained reputation as able and courageous pilot; MC, 1916; commanded No. 3 Squadron and then took over III Corps Wing; chevalier of Legion of Honour, 1917; DSO, 1918; commandant, RAF Staff College, Andover, 1926–30; air officer commanding in Iraq, 1930–2; director of operations and intelligence, Air Ministry, 1933–5; AOC, India, 1935–7; air chief marshal, 1937 and AOC, Bomber Command, 1937–40; realized that Bomber Command was ill-prepared for war; pressed Air Ministry in vain for a Bombing Development Unit; his pessimism confirmed in disasters of early offensive operations; superseded by Sir C. F. A. *Portal (later Viscount Portal of Hungerford), 1940; inspector-general of the RAF, 1940–5; CMG, 1919; CB, 1928; KCB, 1933; GBE, 1943; GCB, 1946; principal air ADC to the king, 1943–5; chairman of board of College of Aeronautics, 1945–53; Christian Scientist.

LUGARD, Frederick John Dealtry, Baron Lugard (1858–1945), soldier, administrator, and author; educated at Rossall School and Sandhurst; commissioned in 95th Foot (Norfolk Regiment); joined second battalion in India, 1878; skilled big-game hunter; seconded to Military Transport Service, 1884; served in Sudan (1885) and Burma (1886); DSO, 1887; commanded force sent by African Lakes Company to defend Karongwa against slave raiders, 1888–9; sent to Uganda by Imperial British East Africa Company, 1890; secured treaty with Kabaka of Buganda and established some sort of order; the Company being unable to maintain its position, he returned to England (1892) to persuade government to undertake responsibility of administration; influential in securing dispatch of Sir Gerald *Portal, resulting in British protectorate, 1894; published *The Rise of Our East African Empire* (2 vols., 1893); sent by Royal Niger Company to Nikki; arrived ahead of the French and secured treaty with Borgu, 1894; CB, 1895; explored mineral concession in Ngamiland for British West Charterland Company, 1896–7; HM commissioner for Nigerian hinterland, 1897; raised and commanded West African Frontier Force, 1897–9; lieutenant-colonel, 1899; high commissioner, Northern Nigeria, 1900–6; KCMG, 1901; brought area under administrative control with minimum use of force and realistic and statesmanlike conception of relations between his administration and chiefs as dependent rulers to be guided and when necessary controlled; governor, Hong Kong, 1907–12; largely responsible for creation of Hong Kong University, 1911; GCMG, 1911; governor of North and South Nigeria, 1912–14; carried out amalgamation of two protectorates; governor-general of Nigeria, 1914–19; conspicuously developed system of indirect rule; regarded traditional native institutions as surest foundation upon which to build; published *The Dual Mandate in British Tropical Africa* (1922); acknowledged authority on colonial administration; member of Permanent Mandates Commission of League of Nations (1922–36) and Colonial Advisory Committee on Education (1923–36); chairman of International Institute of African Languages and Cultures from 1926; PC, 1920; baron, 1928.

LUGHAIDH (d. 507), king of Ireland; ardrigh after the Battle of Ocha, 484.

LUGID (or MOLUA), Saint (554?–608?), first abbot of Clonfertmulloe, alias Kyle, in Queen's County; his name also spelt Lua, Luaid, Luanus, Lugdach, Lugdaigh, Lughaidh, Lugidus, Lugeth, and Moluanus; trained under St *Comgall at Bangor; the Bollandists' and Fleming's life of him both untrustworthy.

LUKE, first Baron (1873–1943), man of business and philanthropist. See JOHNSTON, GEORGE LAWSON.

LUKE, Sir **Harry Charles** (1884–1969), colonial administrator; educated at Eton and Trinity College, Cambridge; appointed private secretary (1908) and aide-de-camp (1909) to the governor of Sierra Leone; second-lieutenant, London Yeomanry, 1909–11; private secretary to high commissioner, Cyprus, 1911; assistant secretary to government, 1912; political officer with Royal Navy in Eastern Mediterranean, 1915–16; commissioner, Famagusta, Cyprus, 1918; British chief commissioner, Georgia, Armenia, and Azerbaijan, 1920; assistant governor, Jerusalem, 1920; colonial secretary, Sierra Leone, 1924–8; chief secretary, Palestine, 1928–30; lieutenant-governor, Malta, 1930–8; governor, Fiji, and high commissioner, Western Pacific, 1938–43; CMG, 1926; knighted, 1933; KCMG, 1939; D.Litt., Oxford, 1938; hon. LL D, Malta; publications include *The Fringe of the East* (1913) and *Cities and Men* (3 vols., 1953–6).

LUKE, Jemima (1813–1906), hymn writer; born Thompson; enthusiastic Non-conformist; author of children's hymn, 'I think when I read that sweet story of old' (1840) and autobiography (1900).

LUKE, Sir **Samuel** (d. 1670), Parliamentarian; knighted, 1624; MP, Bedford, 1640; belonged to the Presbyterian section of the popular party;

present at Edgehill, 1642, and Chalgrove Field, 1643; scoutmaster-general of the army of the earl of *Essex, 1643–5; took no part in public affairs during the Commonwealth and protectorate; the supposed original of *Butler's Sir Hudibras.

LUKE, Stephen (1763–1829), physician; studied medicine at London and Paris; MD, Aberdeen, 1792; mayor of Falmouth, where he practised, 1797; LRCP, 1815; MD, Cambridge, 1821; physician-extraordinary to George IV, 1828; contributed to Thomas *Beddoes's *Contributions to Physical and Medical Knowledge* (1799).

LUKIN, Henry (1628–1719), Nonconformist divine; published religious works.

LUKIN, Sir **Henry Timson** (1860–1925), major-general; served in Zulu War, 1879, South African War, 1899–1902; commandant-general, Cape Colonial forces, 1904–12; inspector-general, Permanent Force, Union of South Africa, 1912; commanded 1st South African infantry brigade in Egypt, gaining victory at Agagiya, 1916; commanded brigade in France, April; major-general, commanding 9th division, 1916–18; KCB, 1918.

LUKIN, Lionel (1742–1834), inventor of lifeboats; invented an 'unsubmergible' boat, 1785; his boat in little demand; published a description of his lifeboat (1790).

LULACH (LUTHLACH, LULAG, LAHOULAN, DULACH, or **GULAK)** (d. 1058), king of Scots; son of Gilcomgan, mormser of Moray; his mother probably Gruoch, the wife, after Gilcomgan's death, of *Macbeth; succeeded to the mormaership of Moray, 1057; set up as king by the people of Alban; slain by treachery; buried at Iona.

LUMBY, Joseph Rawson (1831–1895), author and divine; MA, Magdalen College, Cambridge, 1861; DD, 1879; ordained priest, 1860; Tyrwhitt Hebrew scholar, 1861; classical lecturer at Queens' College, Cambridge, 1861; member of Old Testament Revision Company, 1873; fellow and dean of St Catharine's College, Cambridge, 1874; vicar of St Edward's, Cambridge, 1875; Norrisian professor of divinity, 1879; prebendary of York, 1887; Lady Margaret professor of divinity, 1892; helped to found Early English Text Society; edited literary, historical, and religious works.

LUMISDEN. See also LUMSDEN.

LUMISDEN (or LUMSDEN), Andrew (1720–1801), Jacobite; private secretary to Prince *Charles Edward, 1745; present at Culloden, 1746; included in the Act of Attainder; escaped to France; under-secretary to the Chevalier de St George at Rome, 1757; principal secretary, 1762–6; allowed to return to England, 1773; pardoned, 1778; published work on the antiquities of Rome (1797).

LUMLEY, Benjamin (1811–1875), author and manager of the opera in London; solicitor, 1832; superintended the finances of Her Majesty's Theatre, 1836–41; took over the management, 1842; his position shaken by the opening of the Royal Italian Opera House, Covent Garden, 1847; saved for a time from disaster by the engagement of Jenny Lind (see LIND, JOHANNA MARIA), 1847–9; his theatre closed, 1853–5, re-opened, 1856, closed, 1858; returned to the practice of the law; published a standard book, *Parliamentary Practice on Passing Private Bills* (1838), and *Sirenia* (1862) and *Another World, or Fragments from the Star City of Montallayah by Hermes* (1873), romances; published *Reminiscences* (1864).

LUMLEY, George, fourth Baron Lumley (d. 1508), grandnephew of Marmaduke *Lumley; fought on the Yorkist side; knighted, 1462; MP, Northumberland, 1467; knight-banneret, 1481; submitted to Henry VII, 1485.

LUMLEY, George (d. 1537), son of John *Lumley, fifth (or sixth) Baron Lumley; took part with his father in the northern insurrection of 1536; surrendered, arraigned, and executed.

LUMLEY, Henry (1658?–1722), general and governor of Jersey; brother of Richard *Lumley, first earl of Scarborough; entered the army, 1685; colonel, 1692; brigadier-general, 1693; at siege of Namur, 1695; major-general, 1696; MP, Sussex, 1701 and 1702; lieutenant-general and governor of Jersey, 1703; fought at Blenheim, 1704, Ramillies, 1706, Oudenarde, 1708, and Malplaquet, 1709; general, 1711; MP, Arundel, 1715; resigned his command, 1717.

LUMLEY, John, fifth (or sixth) Baron Lumley (1493–1544); fought at Flodden, 1513; summoned to parliament, 1514; present at the Field of the Cloth of Gold, 1520; a leader in the Pilgrimage of Grace, 1536.

LUMLEY, John, first Baron Lumley of the second creation (1534?–1609), son of George *Lumley (d. 1537); of Queens' College, Cambridge; KB, 1553; high steward of Oxford University, 1559; implicated in the *Ridolfi Plot; imprisoned, 1569–73; founded a surgery lectureship in the Royal College of Physicians, 1583; member of the Elizabethan Society of Antiquaries; collected portraits and books.

LUMLEY, Lawrence Roger, eleventh earl of Scarbrough (1896–1969), public servant; educated at Eton, Sandhurst, and Magdalen College, Oxford; served with 11th Hussars on Western Front, 1916–18; Conservative MP, Hull East, 1922–9; York, 1931–7; governor of Bombay, 1937–43; succeeded uncle as eleventh earl, 1945; hon. colonel, Yorkshire Dragoons, 1956–62; hon. major-general, 1946; parliamentary under-secretary of state for India and Burma, 1945; chairman, Commission on Oriental, Slavonic, East European, and African studies, 1945–6; president, Royal Asiatic Society, 1946–9, the East India Association, 1946–61, the Royal Asian Society, 1954–60; chairman, School of Oriental and African Studies, 1951–9; chairman, Commonwealth Scholarship Committee, 1960–3; lord-lieutenant, West Riding of Yorkshire and of the City of York, 1948; chancellor, Durham University, 1958; hon. DCL, Durham; LL D, Sheffield, Leeds, and London; high steward, York Minster, 1967; GCIE, 1937; GCSI, 1943; KG, 1948; lord chamberlain, 1952–63; permanent lord in waiting, 1963; PC, 1952; GCVO, 1953; Royal Victorian Chair, 1963.

LUMLEY, Marmaduke (d. 1450), bishop successively of Carlisle and Lincoln; educated at Cambridge; precentor of Lincoln, 1425; archdeacon of Northumberland, 1425; chancellor of Cambridge University, 1427; master of Trinity Hall, 1429–43; bishop of Carlisle, 1429–50; lord high treasurer of England, 1447; bishop of Lincoln, 1450.

LUMLEY, Richard, first Viscount Lumley of Waterford (d. 1661?), grandson of Anthony Lumley, brother of John *Lumley, fifth (or sixth) Baron Lumley; knighted, 1616; created Viscount Lumley of Waterford (peerage of Ireland), 1628; Royalist in the Civil War.

LUMLEY, Richard, first earl of Scarborough (1650?–1721), grandson of Richard *Lumley, first Viscount Lumley of Waterford; educated with Richard *Lassels; master of the horse to Queen *Catherine, 1680–2; created Baron Lumley of Lumley Castle, 1681; treasurer to Charles II's queen, 1684; *Monmouth captured by his troop of horse, 1685; signed the invitation to William of Orange, 1688; privy councillor, 1689; created Viscount Lumley, 1689, and earl of Scarborough, 1690; fought at the Boyne, 1692; major-general, 1692; lieutenant-general, 1694; retired from active service, 1697; chancellor of the duchy of Lancaster, 1716–17; joint vice-treasurer of Ireland, 1717.

LUMLEY, Sir William (1769–1850), general; educated at Eton; entered the army, 1787; lieutenant-colonel, 1795; served during the Irish rebellion, 1798, and in Egypt, 1801; major-general, 1805; took part in recapture of Cape of Good Hope, 1806, in the operations in South America, 1806–7; joined Wellington's army in the Peninsula, 1810; lieutenant-general, 1814; governor and commander-in-chief at Bermuda, 1819–25; GCB, 1831; general, 1837.

LUMSDEN. See also LUMISDEN.

LUMSDEN, Sir **Harry Burnett** (1821–1896), lieutenant-general; ensign, 1838; interpreter and quartermaster to 33rd Bengal Native Infantry, 1842; lieutenant, 59th, 1842; served in Sutlej campaign, 1845; assistant to (Sir) Henry Montgomery *Lawrence, then resident at Lahore, 1846; charged with formation of corps of guides for frontier service; introduced khaki uniform into Indian Army; captain, 1853; went on mission to Kandahar, 1857–8; lieutenant-colonel, 1858; CB (civil), 1859; severed connection with guides, and as brigadier-general commanded Hyderabad contingent, 1862; colonel, 1862; left India, 1869; major-general, 1868; KCSI, 1873; retired as hon. lieutenant-general, 1875.

LUMSDEN, Sir **James** (1598?–1660?), military commander; entered the service of Gustavus Adolphus; in England soon after 1639; taken prisoner at Dunbar, 1650; set free, 1652.

LUMSDEN, Matthew (1777–1835), orientalist; professor of Persian and Arabic in Fort William College, India, 1808; published *A Grammar of the Persian Language* (1810); secretary to the Calcutta Madressa, 1812; published *A Grammar of the Arabic Language* (vol. i, 1813); in charge of the company's press at Calcutta, 1814–17; secretary to the stationery committee, 1818; travelled through Persia, Georgia, and Russia to England, 1830.

LUMSDEN, Robert (d. 1651), brother of Sir James *Lumsden; served under Gustavus Adolphus and in the Civil War; killed at storming of Dundee.

LUMSDEN, William (fl. 1651), brother of Sir James *Lumsden; served under Gustavus Adolphus and in the Civil War; present at Marston Moor, 1644, and at Dunbar, 1650.

LUNARDI, Vincenzo (1759–1806), 'first aerial traveller in the English atmosphere'; born probably at Lucca; secretary to the Neapolitan ambassador in England; made his first balloon ascent, 1784; published *An Account of Five Aerial Voyages in Scotland* (1786).

LUND, John (fl. 1785), humorous poet.

LUNDGREN, Egron Sellif (1815–1875), water-colour painter; born at Stockholm; studied at Stockholm and Paris; accompanied Sir Colin *Campbell's relief expedition on the campaign in Oudh, and made sketches on the spot, 1857; member of the Society of Painters in Water-Colours, 1865; settled in Sweden; published *Letters from Spain and Italy*, and *Letters from India* (1870); died at Stockholm.

LUNDIE, John (d. 1652?), poet; professor of humanity, Aberdeen, 1631; author of Latin poems.

LUNDIN, Sir **Alan,** earl of Atholl (d. 1268). See DURWARD, ALAN.

LUNDY, Robert (fl. 1689), governor of Londonderry; supported William III, 1689, yet advised the surrender of Londonderry to James II; turned out by the citizens who undertook their historic defence under George *Walker (1618–1690); his conduct found 'faulty' by the House of Commons; excepted from William's Act of Indemnity, 1690.

LUNN, Sir **Arnold Henry Moore** (1888–1974), ski pioneer, and Christian controversialist; son of medical missionary and travel agent; educated at Harrow and Balliol College, Oxford; founded Oxford University Mountaineering Club and Alpine Ski Club; edited *The Isis*; served in France with Quaker ambulance unit, 1915; worked at Mürren on behalf of British and French internees; invented modern slalom in 1922 at Mürren which his father, Sir Henry *Lunn, had made into a well-known ski resort; gained Olympic recognition of downhill and slalom racing; organized first world championships, 1931; introduced these races into Olympic Games, 1936; crossed Bernese Oberland on skis and made first ski ascent of the Dom; shattered right leg in fall in Welsh mountains, 1909, but made first ski ascent of the Eiger, 1924; wrote many books on mountaineering and skiing, and edited *British Ski Year Book*, 1919–71; also published number of books in religious controversy with Ronald *Knox, C. E. M. *Joad, J. B. S. *Haldane, and G. G. *Coulton; during 1939–45 war press correspondent in Balkans, Chile, and Peru, and attached to Ministry of Information; carried out anti-Nazi and anti-communist lecture tours in USA and elsewhere; knighted, 1952; received many foreign civic and academic awards; commemorated in annual Arnold Lunn memorial lecture of the Ski Club of Great Britain and the Alpine Ski Club.

LUNN, Sir **Henry Simpson** (1859–1939), founder of the travel agency which bears his name; Indian medical missionary (Methodist), 1887–8; founded *The Review of the Churches*, 1891; devoted himself to cause of reunion; founded his firm (1909) as result of arranging religious conferences; knighted, 1910.

LUNN, Joseph (1784–1863), dramatic author; his burlesque, *The Sorrows of Werther*, produced at Covent Garden, 1818; his *Family Jars, Fish out of Water, Hide and Seek*, and *Roses and Thorns*, produced at the Haymarket between 1822 and 1825; adapted other plays from the French.

LUNSFORD, Henry (1611–1643), brother of Sir Thomas *Lunsford; lieutenant-colonel, 1640; killed at the siege of Bristol.

LUNSFORD, Sir Herbert (*fl.* 1640–1665), brother of Sir Thomas *Lunsford; captain, 1640; present at Edgehill, 1642; knighted, 1645.

LUNSFORD, Sir Thomas (1610?–1653?), Royalist colonel; committed a murderous assault upon Sir Thomas Pelham, 1633; outlawed for failing to appear to receive judgment, 1637; pardoned, 1639; joined Charles I's army, 1639; lieutenant of the Tower, 1641; removed on petition from the Commons; knighted, 1641; made prisoner at Edgehill, 1642; released, 1644; went to Virginia, 1649, where he died.

LUNY, Thomas (1759–1837), marine painter; studied under Francis *Holman; exhibited at the Society of Artists, 1777–8, at the Royal Academy, 1780–93.

LUPO (or LUPUS), Thomas, the elder (d. 1628?), musician; member of the royal band, 1579.

LUPO, Thomas, the younger (*fl.* 1598–1641), probably first cousin of Thomas *Lupo the elder; one of her majesty's violins, 1598; in Prince *Henry's band of musicians, 1610; many compositions assigned to him, some possibly by the elder Thomas Lupo.

LUPSET, Thomas (1498?–1532), divine; of St Paul's School, London, and Pembroke Hall, Cambridge; BA, Paris; read the rhetoric and humanity lecture founded by *Wolsey at Corpus Christi College, Oxford, 1520; MA, Oxford, 1521; helped *More, Erasmus, and *Linacre to prepare their works for the press, and himself produced religious works and translations.

LUPTON, Donald (d. 1676), miscellaneous writer; chaplain to the English forces in the Low Countries and Germany; hack author in London, 1632; published *Emblems of Rarieties* (1636) and biographical and other works, 1632–58.

LUPTON, Joseph Hirst (1836–1905), scholar and schoolmaster; BA, St John's College, Cambridge (fifth classic), 1858; MA and fellow, 1861; ordained, 1859; DD, 1896; sur-master in St Paul's School, 1864–99; published *Wakefield Worthies* (1864); published *Life of Dean Colet* (1887) and edited and translated many of *Colet's works; Hulsean lecturer (1887) and Seatonian prizeman (1897) of Cambridge; other works were life of St John of Damascus (1882) and an edition of *More's *Utopia* (1895).

LUPTON, Roger (d. 1540), provost of Eton and founder of Sedbergh School in Yorkshire; B.Can.L., Cambridge, 1483; canon of Windsor, 1500; provost of Eton, 1504–35; founded a free school in his native town of Sedbergh, 1523–5, and scholarships and fellowships at St John's College, Cambridge, 1528 and 1536.

LUPTON, Thomas (*fl.* 1583), miscellaneous writer; best-known work, *A Thousand Notable Things of Sundry Sortes*, a variety of enigmatic and grotesque recipes and nostrums (1579).

LUPTON, Thomas Goff (1791–1873), engraver; studied mezzotint engraving under George *Clint; exhibited crayon portraits at Royal Academy, 1811–20; mainly responsible for the introduction of steel for mezzotint engraving; employed by *Turner on the *Liber Studiorum*; engraved the plates for *The Harbours of England*, with text by *Ruskin (published 1856).

LUPTON, William (1676–1726), divine; fellow of Lincoln College, Oxford, 1698; MA, The Queen's College, Oxford, 1700; DD, 1712; preacher of Lincoln's Inn and afternoon preacher at the Temple, 1714; prebendary of Durham, 1715; published single sermons.

LUPUS, Hugh, earl of Chester (d. 1101). See HUGH OF AVRANCHES.

LUSCOMBE, Michael Henry Thornhill (1776–1846), bishop; of Catharine Hall, Cambridge; MA, 1805; incorporated at Oxford and DCL, 1810; consecrated to a continental bishopric by the bishops of the Scottish Episcopal Church, and appointed embassy chaplain at Paris, 1825; helped to found the *Christian Remembrancer*, 1841; published *The Church of Rome Compared with the Bible, the Fathers of the Church and the Church of England* (1839) and sermons; died at Lausanne.

LUSH, Sir Charles Montague (1853–1930), judge; son of Sir Robert *Lush; BA, Trinity College, Cambridge; called to bar (Gray's Inn), 1879; KC, 1902; judge, King's Bench division and knighted, 1910; retired, 1925; an eloquent advocate, but hesitant judge; wrote *Law of Husband and Wife* (1884).

LUSH, Sir Robert (1807–1881), lord justice; entered Gray's Inn, 1836; published an edition of *The Act for the Abolition of Arrest on Mesne Process* (1838); barrister, Gray's Inn, 1840; published *The Practice of the Superior Courts of Common Law at Westminster in Actions and Proceedings over which they have a common Jurisdiction*, which became the standard book on common-law practice (1840); QC and bencher, 1857; succeeded to the court of Queen's Bench, 1865; privy councillor, 1879; succeeded to the court of appeal, 1880.

LUSHINGTON, Charles (1785–1866), brother of Stephen *Lushington; in the service of the East India Company in Bengal, 1800–27; MP, Ashburton, 1833–41, Westminster, 1847–52; published a *History of Calcutta's Religious Institutions* (1824) and *Dilemmas of a Churchman* (1838).

LUSHINGTON, Edmund Law (1811–1893), Greek scholar; of Charterhouse and Trinity College, Cambridge; senior classic and senior chancellor's medallist, 1832; professor of Greek at Glasgow, 1838–75; hon. LL D, Glasgow, 1875; lord rector of Glasgow University, 1884; he married (1842) Cecilia Tennyson, sister of Lord *Tennyson, the epilogue to whose *In Memoriam* is an epithalamium on the marriage.

LUSHINGTON, Henry (1812–1855), chief secretary to the government of Malta; of Charterhouse and Trinity College, Cambridge; fellow, 1836; MA, 1837; barrister, Inner Temple, 1840; chief secretary to the government of Malta, 1847–55; published verse and prose works, 1828–55; died at Paris.

LUSHINGTON, Sir James Law (1779–1859), general; brother of Stephen Rumbold *Lushington; entered the Madras Army, 1797; rose to be general; chairman of the East India Company, 1838–9; MP successively for Petersfield, Hastings, and Carlisle.

LUSHINGTON, Stephen (1782–1873), civilian; educated at Eton and Christ Church, Oxford; BA and fellow of All Souls College, Oxford, 1802; MA; barrister, Inner Temple, 1806; MP, Great Yarmouth, 1806–8, Ilchester, 1820–6, Tregony, Cornwall, 1826–30, Winchelsea, 1830–1, Tower Hamlets, 1832–41; judge of the consistory court of London, 1828, of the High Court of Admiralty, 1838–67; privy councillor, 1838; dean of arches, 1858–67; reformer and abolitionist; some of his speeches and judgments published separately.

LUSHINGTON, Sir Stephen (1803–1877), admiral; nephew of Stephen *Lushington (1782–1873); entered navy, 1816; present at Navarino, 1827; distinguished at the reduction of Kastro Morea, 1828; superintendent of the Indian Navy, 1848–52; commanded naval brigade at Sebastopol, 1854; KCB and rear-admiral, 1855; lieutenant-governor of Greenwich Hospital, 1862–5; admiral, 1865; GCB, 1867.

LUSHINGTON, Stephen Rumbold (1776–1868), Indian official; educated at Rugby; assistant in Military, Political, and Secret Department, Madras, 1792; translator to Board of Revenue, 1793; deputy Persian translator to government, and Persian translator to Revenue Board, 1794; secretary to Board of Revenue, 1798; left the service, 1807; MP, Rye, 1807–12, Canterbury, 1812–30 and 1835–7; privy councillor, 1827; governor of Madras, 1827–35; hon. DCL, Oxford, 1839; published life of his father-in-law, Lord Harris (1840).

LUSHINGTON, Thomas (1590–1661), divine; educated at Oxford; MA, Lincoln College, Oxford, 1618; prebendary of Salisbury, 1631; DD, 1632; published a commentary on the Epistle to the Hebrews (1646), *Logica Analytica de Principiis* (1650).

LUSK, Sir Andrew, baronet (1810–1909), lord mayor of London; started grocery business in Greenock, 1835; founded business in London, 1840; chairman of Imperial Bank from 1862; lord mayor of London, 1873; raised £150,000 for relief of Bengal famine; baronet, 1874; Liberal MP for Finsbury, 1865–85; became Liberal Unionist, 1886.

LUSKA, Sidney (pseudonym) (1861–1905), novelist. See HARLAND, HENRY.

LUTHULI, Albert John (1898?–1967), president-general of the African National Congress; born in Southern Rhodesia; educated at Ohlange Institute and Methodist Institution, Edenvale; appointed as teacher, 1918; became lay preacher; awarded bursary to Adams College, Durban; became teacher trainer; elected chief of Umvoti Mission Reserve, 1936; served on advisory board to South African Sugar Association, delegate to International Missionary Conference in Madras, 1938; lecture tour on missions, United States, 1948; member, executive, African National Congress, 1945; president of Congress in Natal, 1951; led Defiance Campaign against apartheid, 1952; deposed from chieftainship by South African Government; president-general, ANC, 1952; banned from attending public gatherings, 1953–6; arrested on charge of treason, 1956; discharged, 1957; banned again, 1959; arrested again, 1960; prison sentence suspended on health grounds; awarded Nobel Peace Prize for 1960, 1961; under house arrest, 1964–7; killed by a freight train, 1967; awarded United Nations Human Rights Prize, 1968.

LUTTERELL, John (d. 1335), theologian; DD, Oxford; chancellor of Oxford University, 1317–22; prebendary of Salisbury, 1319, of York, 1334; said to have written theological, philosophical, and mathematical works; died at Avignon.

LUTTICHUYS, Isaac (1616–1673), painter; brother of Simon *Luttichuys; removed from London to Amsterdam before 1643, where he died.

LUTTICHUYS, Simon (1610–1663?), painter of portraits and still life; removed before 1650 from London to Amsterdam, where he died.

LUTTRELL (or LUTTEREL), Edward (*fl.* 1670–1710), crayon painter and mezzotint engraver; invented a method of laying a ground on copper on which to draw in crayons; one of the earliest of English mezzotint engravers.

LUTTRELL, Henry (1655?–1717), colonel; brother of Simon *Luttrell; assisted James II, but subsequently joined William III; enlisted Irish papists for the Venetian republic, 1693; shot dead in Dublin.

LUTTRELL, Henry (1765?–1851), wit and poet of society; a natural son of Henry Lawes *Luttrell, second earl of Carhampton; MP, Clonmines, Co. Wexford, in the Irish parliament, 1798; introduced to London society through the duchess of Devonshire; famous as a conversationalist and diner-out; published *Advice to Julia, a Letter in Rhyme* (1820; third and improved edition as *Letters to Julia in Rhyme*, 1822) and *Crockford House*, a satire on high play (1827).

LUTTRELL, Henry Lawes, second earl of Carhampton (1743–1821), soldier and politician; entered the army, 1757; deputy adjutant-general to the forces in Portugal, 1762; MP, Bossiney, 1768–9 and 1774–84, Middlesex, 1769–74; major-general, 1782; MP, Old Leighton, in the Irish parliament, 1783; succeeded his father in the (Irish) peerage, 1787; lieutenant-general of the ordnance in Ireland, 1789; MP, Plympton Earls, 1790–4; commander of the forces in Ireland, 1796–7; master-general of the ordnance, 1797–1800; MP, Ludgershall, 1817–21.

LUTTRELL, James (1751?–1788), captain in the navy; brother of Henry Lawes *Luttrell, second earl of Carhampton; MP for Stockbridge, Hampshire, 1775–84; engaged on active service, 1782; surveyor-general of the ordnance, 1783–8; MP, Dover, 1784.

LUTTRELL (afterwards **LUTTRELL-OLMIUS), John,** third earl of Carhampton (d. 1829), brother of Henry Lawes *Luttrell, second earl of Carhampton; captain in the navy, 1762; a commissioner of the excise, 1784; took the name and arms of Olmius, 1787; succeeded to peerage, 1821.

LUTTRELL, Narcissus (1657–1732), annalist and bibliographer; educated at St John's College, Cambridge; MA, 1675; collected valuable manuscripts and fugitive poetical tracts, broadsides, and slips relative to his own time; compiled in manuscript 'A Brief Historicall Relation of State Affairs from September 1678 to April 1714', printed (1857).

LUTTRELL, Simon (d. 1698), colonel; brother of Henry *Luttrell (1655?–1717); an adherent of James II; MP, Co. Dublin, in Irish parliament, 1689; served in Italy as brigadier under Catinat, and in Catalonia under the Duke of Vendôme.

LUTTRELL, Temple Simon (d. 1803), third son of Simon Luttrell, first earl of Carhampton; MP, Milborne Port, Somerset, 1774–80; arrested at Boulogne, 1793; imprisoned in Paris, 1793–5; died in Paris.

LUTWYCHE, Sir Edward (d. 1709), judge; barrister, Gray's Inn, 1661; ancient, 1671; king's serjeant, 1684; knighted, 1684; judge of the common pleas, 1686–8; prepared *Reports of Cases in the Common Pleas*, 1704 (published 1718).

LUTWYCHE, Thomas (1675–1734), lawyer; son of Sir Edward *Lutwyche; of Westminster School and Christ Church, Oxford; barrister, Inner Temple, 1697; treasurer, 1722; MP, Appleby, 1710–22, Callington, 1722–7, Agmondesham, 1728–34.

LUTYENS, (Agnes) Elizabeth (1906–1983), composer; daughter of (Sir) Edwin Landseer *Lutyens architect; educated at Worcester Park School, Westgate on Sea and École Normale, Paris; entered Royal College of Music, London, 1926; with Anne Macnaghton-Lemare concerts, 1931; compositions include a hundred film scores and a hundred musical commissions for radio as well as settings for ballet, chamber concertos, string quartets, and *O Saisons, O Châteaux!*, op. 13, 1946, for soprano and strings, and an opera 'charade', *Time Off? Not a Ghost of a Chance!*, op.68, 1967–8, staged at Sadler's Wells theatre, 1972; CBE, 1969; hon. D.Mus., York, 1977; published autobiography, *A Goldfish Bowl* (1972).

LUTYENS, Sir Edwin Landseer (1869–1944), architect; studied at South Kensington and under (Sir) Ernest *George; set up London practice, 1888; built brilliant series of romantic country houses; architect for British Pavilion, Paris Exhibition, 1900; FRIBA, 1906; consulting architect, Hampstead Garden Suburb, 1908–9; designed British Pavilion for International Exhibition, Rome, Rand War Memorial, and Johannesburg Art Gallery, 1909–11; joint architect with Sir Herbert *Baker for New Delhi, 1913–30; in the viceroy's house and ancillaries created one of the finest palaces in architectural history, characterized by extraordinary fertility of invention and aristocratic restraint; appointed to Imperial War Graves Commission, 1917; designed the Cenotaph (1919) and many war memorials, including that to 'the Missing of the

Somme' at Thiepval; his work romantic in inspiration, classic in discipline, yet abstract in design; buildings include Britannic House, Finsbury Circus (1920–2), Midland Bank, Poultry (1924–37), British Embassy, Washington (1926–9), Campion Hall, Oxford (1934); collaborated on many large blocks of flats including Grosvenor House, Park Lane; his magnificent designs for Liverpool Roman Catholic Cathedral (1929–43) proved impracticable to complete in post-war conditions; ARA, 1913; RA, 1920; president, 1938–44; knighted, 1918; KCIE, 1930; OM, 1942.

LUTZ, (Wilhelm) Meyer (1829–1903), musical composer; born in Bavaria; settled in England, 1848; toured provinces with Italian operatic singers; conductor of Gaiety Theatre, 1869–96, and organist of St George's Cathedral, Southwark; composed, besides church music, operettas for the Gaiety Theatre.

LUXBOROUGH, Henrietta, Lady (d. 1756). See KNIGHT, HENRIETTA.

LUXFORD, George (1807–1854), botanist; published *Flora of Reigate* (1838); sub-editor of the *Westminster Review*; edited the *Phytologist*, 1841–54; lecturer on botany in St Thomas's Hospital, 1846–51.

LUXMOORE, Sir (Arthur) Fairfax (Charles Coryndon) (1876–1944), judge; educated at King's School, Canterbury, and Jesus College, Cambridge; played Rugby for Cambridge and England; called to bar (Lincoln's Inn), 1899; KC, 1919; bencher, 1922; judge of Chancery division, 1929–38; lord justice of appeal, 1938–44; possessed unrivalled knowledge of trademark and patent law; chairman, Committee on Post-War Agricultural Education, 1941–3; active man of Kent and president of county cricket club; knighted, 1929; PC, 1938.

LUXMOORE, Charles Scott (1792–1854), dean of St Asaph; son of John *Luxmoore (1756–1830); MA, St John's College, Cambridge, 1818; a notable pluralist; dean of St Asaph and chancellor of the diocese; prebendary of Hereford, and holder of three rectories at the same time.

LUXMOORE, John (1756–1830), bishop successively of Bristol, Hereford, and St Asaph; of Eton and King's College, Cambridge; MA, 1783; DD, Lambeth, 1795; dean of Gloucester, 1799–1808; bishop of Bristol, 1807, of Hereford, 1808, of St Asaph, 1815.

LYALL. See also LYELL and LYLE.

LYALL, Alfred (1795–1865), philosopher and traveller; brother of George *Lyall; educated at Eton and Trinity College, Cambridge; BA, 1818; edited the *Annual Register*, 1822–7; published *Rambles in Madeira and Portugal* (1827) and *Principles of Necessity and Contingent Truth* (1830); vicar of Godmersham, 1839; rector of Harbledown, 1846; criticized John Stuart *Mill in *Agonistes*, 1856; contributed to the 'History of the Mediaeval Church' in vol. xi of the *Encyclopaedia Metropolitana*.

LYALL, Sir Alfred Comyn (1835–1911), Indian civil servant and writer; son of Alfred *Lyall; educated at Eton and Haileybury; joined Indian Civil Service, 1856; actively served in Mutiny, 1857–8; made commissioner of West Berar (1867), home secretary to Indian government (1873), and governor-general's agent in Rajputana (1874); foreign secretary to Indian government, 1878–81; took part in negotiations at Kabul and Kandahar, 1880, and advocated definite treaty with Russia in regard to Afghanistan, 1881; CB, 1879; KCB, 1881; lieutenant-governor of North-West Provinces and Oudh, 1882–7; founded new University of Allahabad; returned to England, 1887; member of India Council in London, 1887–1902; KCIE, 1887; GCIE, 1896; PC, 1902; filled distinguished place in English society; Rede lecturer at Cambridge, 1891; Ford's lecturer at Oxford, 1908; published *Verses Written in India* (1889), *Asiatic Studies* (2 series, 1882 and 1899), *Rise of British Dominion in India* (1893), and life of the marquess of *Dufferin (2 vols., 1905); hon. DCL, Oxford, 1889, LL D, Cambridge, 1891; FBA, 1903; trustee of British Museum, 1911; a Liberal Unionist, free trader, and opponent of women's suffrage.

LYALL, Sir Charles James (1845–1920), Indian civil servant and orientalist; entered Indian Civil Service, 1865; held secretariats, etc., in India, 1867–94; chief commissioner of Central Provinces, 1895; KCSI, 1897; secretary of judicial and public department, India Office, 1898–1910; works include series on early Arabic literature.

LYALL, Edna (pseudonym) (1857–1903), novelist. See BAYLY, ADA ELLEN.

LYALL, George (d. 1853), politician and merchant; succeeded to his father's shipowning and merchant's business, 1805; assisted to reform *Lloyd's Register* of shipping, 1834; MP for the City of London, 1833–5 and 1841–7; chairman of the East India Company, 1841.

LYALL, Robert (1790–1831), botanist and traveller; MD, Edinburgh; spent many years in Russia; published *The Character of the Russians and a detailed History of Moscow* (1823) and narrative of travel (1825); British agent in Madagascar,

1826–8; collected plants and specimens; died at Mauritius.

LYALL, William Rowe (1788–1857), dean of Canterbury; educated at Trinity College, Cambridge; MA, 1816; conducted the *British Critic*, 1816–17; reorganized the *Encyclopaedia Metropolitana*, 1820; Warburtonian lecturer, 1826; helped to edit the *Theological Library* (vols. i–xiv, 1832–46); archdeacon of Maidstone, 1841; dean of Canterbury, 1845.

LYDE, William (1622–1706). See JOYNER.

LYDGATE, John (1370?–1451?), poet; ordained priest, 1397; celebrated civic ceremonies in verse at the request of the corporation of London; began his *Troy Book* (finished 1420) at request of the prince of Wales (afterwards Henry V), 1412; acted as court poet, and found a patron in *Humphrey, duke of Gloucester, from 1422; rewarded with lands and money; spent the later part of his life at Bury Monastery; describes himself as *Chaucer's disciple; shows to best advantage in his shorter poems on social subjects. His chief poems are *Falls of Princes*, written between 1430 and 1438 (first printed 1494), *Troy Book*, written between 1412 and 1420 (first printed 1513), *The Story of Thebes*, written *c.*1420 (first printed *c.*1500). He wrote also devotional, philosophical, scientific, historical, and occasional poems, besides allegories, fables, and moral romances. One prose work, *The Damage and Destruccyon in Realmes*, written in 1400, is assigned to him.

LYDIAT, Thomas (1572–1646), divine and chronologer; educated at Winchester and New College, Oxford; fellow of New College, 1593; MA, 1599; chronographer and cosmographer to *Henry, prince of Wales, to whom he dedicated his *Emendatio Temporum* (1609); in Dublin, becoming fellow of Trinity College and MA, 1609–11; first contrived the octodesexcentenary period; published chronological works in Latin, 1605–21; some of his manuscripts printed after his death.

LYE, Edward (1694–1767), Anglo-Saxon and Gothic scholar; educated at Hart Hall, Oxford; BA, 1716; ordained, 1717; published, with additions, the *Etymologicum Anglicanum* of Francis *Junius, and prefixed to it an Anglo-Saxon grammar (1743); published *Sacrorum Evangeliorum Versio Gothica*, with a Latin translation and a Gothic grammar (1750); his Anglo-Saxon and Gothic dictionary published (1772).

LYE (LEE or LEIGH), Thomas (1621–1684), Nonconformist minister; BA, Wadham College, Oxford, 1641; migrated to Emmanuel College, Cambridge; MA, 1646; refused to sign the engagement, 1651; ejected from All Hallows, Lombard Street, London, 1662; a popular and successful instructor of children; wrote educational works for children.

LYELL. See also LYALL and LYLE.

LYELL, Charles (1769–1849), botanist and student of Dante; educated at St Andrews and Peterhouse, Cambridge; MA, 1794; studied mosses; published translations of Dante, 1835, 1842, and 1845.

LYELL, Sir Charles, first baronet (1797–1875), geologist; son of Charles *Lyell (1769–1849); MA, Exeter College, Oxford, 1821; studied geology under Dr *Buckland; began the series of continental tours which formed the foundation of his best-known works, 1818; entered Lincoln's Inn, 1819; secretary of the Geological Society, 1823–6; FRS, 1826; published volume i of his *Principles of Geology* (1830, vol. ii, 1832, vol. iii, 1833, whole work in four smaller volumes, 1834), finally discrediting the catastrophic school of geologists; professor of geology, King's College, London, 1831–3; president of the Geological Society, 1835–6 and 1849–50; published *Elements of Geology*, supplementary to the *Principles*, and more a descriptive textbook (1838; 6th edn., 1865); lectured in the United States, 1841 and 1852; published *Travels in North America, with Geological Observations* (1845); knighted, 1848; published *A Second Visit to the United States of North America* (1849); hon. DCL, Oxford, 1854; published *The Antiquity of Man* (1863); created baronet, 1864; published *The Student's Elements of Geology* (1871).

LYFORD, William (1598–1653), Nonconformist divine; educated at Magdalen College, Oxford; BA, 1618; BD, 1631; held Calvinistic views; author of theological works.

LYGON, Frederick, sixth Earl Beauchamp (1830–1891); of Eton and Christ Church, Oxford; MA, 1856; fellow of All Souls College, Oxford, 1852–6; MP, Tewkesbury, 1857–63; a lord of the Admiralty, 1859; MP, Worcestershire, 1863–6; succeeded to earldom, 1866; DCL, Oxford, 1870; lord steward of the household, 1874–80; privy councillor, 1874; paymaster of the forces, 1885–6 and 1886–7; helped to found Keble College, Oxford.

LYGON, William, first Earl Beauchamp (1747–1816); of Christ Church, Oxford; MP, Worcester, 1775–1806; created Baron Beauchamp of Powycke, Worcestershire, 1806, and Viscount Elmley and Earl Beauchamp, 1816.

LYGON, William, seventh Earl Beauchamp (1872–1938), politician; educated at Eton and Christ Church, Oxford; succeeded father, Frederick *Lygon, 1891; governor of New South Wales, 1899–1902; PC, 1906; lord president of the Council, 1910, 1914–15; first commissioner of works, 1910–14; leader of Liberal party in the Lords, 1924–31; KG, 1914.

LYHERT (LYART, LE HERT, or LEHART), Walter (d. 1472), bishop of Norwich; fellow of Exeter and Oriel colleges, Oxford; provost of Oriel College, Oxford, 1435; bishop of Norwich, 1446; when English ambassador to Savoy prevailed on the antipope, Felix V, to resign his claim to the papacy, 1449.

LYLE. See also LYALL and LYELL.

LYLE, Charles Ernest Leonard, first Baron Lyle of Westbourne (1882–1954), industrialist and politician; educated at Harrow, Trinity Hall, Cambridge, and Kahlsruhe University; international lawn-tennis player; entered family sugar-refining firm; chairman, Tate & Lyle, 1922–37; president, 1937–54; vigorous opponent of nationalization of his industry; Conservative MP, Stratford, West Ham (1918–22), Epping (1923–4), Bournemouth (1940–5); knighted, 1923; baronet, 1932; baron, 1945.

LYLE, David (*fl.* 1762), stenographer; MA, Glasgow, 1755; his *The Art of Short-hand improved* (1762) of little practical value.

LYLE, Robert, second Baron Lyle (d. 1497?), justiciary of Scotland; engaged on embassies to England, 1472, 1484, and 1485; a lord in council, 1485; great justiciary of Scotland, 1488; ambassador to Spain, 1491; an auditor of the Exchequer, 1492.

LYLE, Thomas (1792–1859), Scottish poet; educated at Glasgow University; took the diploma of surgeon, 1816; remembered solely for the song, 'Let us haste to Kelvin Grove', first published (1820).

LYLY, John (1554?–1606), dramatist and author of *Euphues*; of Magdalen College, Oxford; MA, 1575; studied also at Cambridge, being incorporated MA, 1579; published, in London, the first part of his *Euphues, the Anatomy of Wit* (1579), and the second part, *Euphues and his England* (1580); wrote light plays to be performed at court by the children's acting companies of the Chapel Royal and St Paul's, London, including *Campaspe* and *Sapho and Phao*, produced 1584; championed the cause of the bishops in the Martin Mar-Prelate controversy in a pamphlet, *Pappe with an Hatchet* (1589); MP, Hindon, 1589, Aylesbury, 1593 and 1601, Appleby, 1597; his *Euphues* interesting for its prose style, which is characterized by a continuous straining after antithesis and epigram, and received the name of 'Euphuism'. Lyly's style became popular and influenced some writers, while it was ridiculed by others, Shakespeare among them. His best plays

are *Alexander and Campaspe* (1584), *Midas* (1592), and *Endymion* (1591); they contain attractive lyrics, which were first printed in *Blount's collected edition of the plays (1632).

LYNAM, Robert (1796–1845), miscellaneous writer; of Christ's Hospital and Trinity College, Cambridge; MA, 1821; assistant chaplain and secretary to the Magdalene Hospital, London, 1832; wrote a history of the reign of George III and of the Roman emperors, but is chiefly remembered as an editor of such authors as Rollin, *Skelton, Paley, and *Johnson. His most complete compilation was *The British Essayist* (30 vols., 1827).

LYNCH, Arthur Alfred (1861–1934), author, soldier, and politician; born in Australia; Paris correspondent, *Daily Mail*, 1896–9; fought for Boers, 1900; sentenced to death for high treason, 1903; pardoned, 1907; qualified and practised medicine in North London, 1908–34; MP, Galway City (1901), West Clare (1909–18); works include *Principles of Psychology* (1923).

LYNCH, Dominic (d. 1697?), Dominican friar; joined the order of St Dominic; lived for many years in the convent of St Paul at Seville; professor of theology in the College of St Thomas, 1674; published a scholastic work in Latin (1666–86).

LYNCH, Henry Blosse (1807–1873), Mesopotamian explorer; brother of Thomas Kerr *Lynch; volunteer in the Indian Navy, 1823; employed on the survey of the Persian Gulf; Persian and Arabic interpreter to the gulf squadron, 1829–32; second-in-command of the expedition under Francis Rawdon *Chesney to explore the Euphrates route to India, 1834; in full command of it, 1837; decorated by the shah, 1837; assistant to the superintendent of the Indian Navy, 1843–51; captain, 1847; master attendant in Bombay Dockyard, 1849; distinguished himself in second Burmese War, 1851–3; CB, 1853; retired and settled at Paris, 1856; conducted the negotiations with Persia that led to the Treaty of Paris, 1857; died at Paris.

LYNCH, James (1608?–1713), Roman Catholic archbishop of Tuam; educated at the English College, Rome; archbishop of Tuam, 1669; accused of violating the statute of præmunire and forced to retire to Spain; returned to Ireland, 1685; settled at Paris, 1691; died at the Irish College, Paris.

LYNCH, John (1599?–1673?), Irish historian; educated by the Jesuits; secular priest, 1622; archdeacon of Tuam; died probably at St Malo; author of Latin works on Irish history, including *Cambrensis Eversus* (trans. 1795 and 1848–52).

LYNCH, Patrick Edward (d. 1884), lieutenant-general in the English Army; brother of Thomas Kerr *Lynch; entered the Indian Army, 1826; employed in Persia and Afghanistan, 1840–1 and 1858; lieutenant-general and retired, 1878.

LYNCH, Richard (1611–1676), Jesuit; educated in Irish College of Compostella; joined Jesuits, 1630; rector of the Irish College of Seville, 1637; published *Universa Philosophia Scholastica* (1654) and Latin sermons.

LYNCH, Theodora Elizabeth (1812–1885), poetical and prose writer; daughter of Arthur Foulks; married, in Jamaica, Henry Mark Lynch, 1835; returned to England after her husband's death and wrote seventeen volumes (1846–65) of poems and fiction for young people, frequently with a West Indian setting.

LYNCH, Sir Thomas (d. 1684), governor of Jamaica; great-grandson of John *Aylmer, bishop of London; served in Jamaica expedition, 1655; provost-marshal of Jamaica, 1661; member of council, 1663; president, 1664; lieutenant-governor and knighted, 1670; recalled, 1674; sent out again, 1682; died in Jamaica.

LYNCH, Thomas Kerr (1818–1891), Mesopotamian explorer; educated at Trinity College, Dublin; accompanied his brother, Henry Blosse *Lynch, in second Euphrates expedition, 1837–42; travelled extensively in Mesopotamia and Persia; consul-general for Persia in London; published *A Visit to the Suez Canal* (1866).

LYNCH, Thomas Toke (1818–1871), hymn-writer; his *Hymns for Heart and Voice: the Rivulet* (1855) attacked as pantheistic; composed several tunes for them, and other works both in prose and verse.

LYNCHE, Richard (fl. 1596–1601), poet. See LINCHE.

LYND, Robert Wilson (1879–1949), journalist and essayist; educated at Royal Academical Institution and Queen's College, Belfast; assistant literary editor (1908), literary editor (from 1912) of *Daily News* (after 1930 the *News Chronicle*); essayist as 'Y.Y.' in *New Statesman*, 1913–45; publications include *Dr. Johnson and Company* (1927).

LYNDE, Sir Humphrey (1579–1636), Puritan controversialist; of Westminster School and Christ Church, Oxford; BA, 1600; knighted, 1613; MP, Brecknock, 1626; wrote numerous controversial works, including *Via Tuta, the Safe Way* (1628).

LYNDHURST, first Baron (1772–1863), lord chancellor. See COPLEY, JOHN SINGLETON.

LYNDSAY, Sir David (1490–1555), Scottish poet and Lyon king of arms. See LINDSAY.

LYNDWOOD, William (1375?–1446), civilian, canonist, and bishop of St David's; his name is variously spelt Lyndewode, Lindewood, Lyndwood, and Lindwood; educated at Gonville Hall, Cambridge; fellow of Pembroke Hall; removed to Oxford, where he took DCL degree; prebendary of Salisbury, 1412, of Hereford, 1422; official of the court of Canterbury by 1417, and still in 1431; archdeacon of Oxford, 1438–42; keeper of the privy seal, 1433; bishop of St David's, 1442; completed his *Provinciale*, a digest of the synodal constitutions of the province of Canterbury from Stephen *Langton to Henry *Chichele, the principal authority for English canon law, 1433 (first printed c.1470–80).

LYNE, Joseph Leycester (in religion Father **Ignatius)** (1837–1908), preacher; educated at St Paul's School and Trinity College, Glenalmond; ordained, 1860; developed advanced views; curate to George Rundle *Prynne at Plymouth; studied Benedictine order at Bruges, 1861; on return to London replaced A. H. *Mackonochie as curate of St George's-in-the-East; resigned on assuming Benedictine habit; formed a monastic community at Claydon, near Ipswich, 1862; removed to Elm Hill, near Norwich, 1863–6, where he frequently came into conflict with the bishop; built Llanthony Abbey, 1869; the community dwindled owing to quarrels; an eloquent preacher; made missionary tour through Canada and America, 1890–1.

LYNE, Richard (fl. 1570–1600), painter and engraver; one of the earliest native artists in England whose works have been preserved; employed by Matthew *Parker; drew and engraved map of the University of Cambridge, published, 1574; mentioned by *Meres in *Palladis Tamia* (1598) as among the leading painters of the time.

LYNE, Sir William John (1844–1913), Australian politician; born in Tasmania; entered New South Wales Legislative Assembly, 1880; premier, 1899; minister of home affairs in first Commonwealth ministry, 1901; minister of trade and customs, 1903–4 and 1905–7; treasurer, 1907–8; KCMG, 1900; protectionist with rather narrowly Australian outlook.

LYNEDOCH, first Baron (1748–1843), general. See GRAHAM, THOMAS.

LYNFORD (or **LINFORD), Thomas** (1650–1724), divine; of Christ's College, Cambridge; MA, 1674; fellow of Christ's College, 1675; canon of Westminster, 1700; archdeacon of Barnstaple, 1709–24; published sermons and

Some Dialogues between Mr. Godden and others etc. (1687).

LYNGARD, Richard (1598?–1670), dean of Lismore. See LINGARD.

LYNN, George, the elder (1676–1742), astronomer and antiquary; communicated his astronomical observations and meteorological registers to the Royal Society, 1724–40.

LYNN, George, the younger (1707–1758), barrister, Inner Temple; son of George *Lynn the elder; FSA, 1726.

LYNN, Samuel Ferris (1836–1876), sculptor; exhibited at the Royal Academy, 1856–75; member of the Institute of Sculptors, 1861; associate of the Royal Hibernian Academy.

LYNN, Thomas (1774–1847), writer on astronomy; in the naval service of the East India Company; examiner in nautical astronomy to the company's officers; author of *Solar Tables, Star Tables, Astronomical Tables, A new Method of finding the Longitude* (1826), and *Practical Methods for finding the Latitude* (1833).

LYNN, Walter (1677–1763), medical writer and inventor; brother of George *Lynn the elder; BA, Peterhouse, Cambridge, 1698; MB, 1704; published medical works; chiefly remembered by his proposed improvements on the steam-engine, described in *The Case of Walter Lynn, M.B.* (1726).

LYNNE, Nicholas of (*fl.* 1360). See NICHOLAS.

LYNNE, Walter (*fl.* 1550), printer and translator; an ardent reformer; printed and translated about nineteen religious works; patronized by *Cranmer.

LYNSKEY, Sir **George Justin** (1888–1957), judge; educated at St Francis Xavier's College and the University, Liverpool; LL B, 1907; admitted solicitor, 1910; called to bar (Inner Temple), 1920; KC, 1930; judge, Salford Hundred Court of Record, 1937–44, of King's Bench division, 1944–57; chairman, Board of Trade inquiry, 1948; knighted, 1944.

LYON, Mrs **Agnes** (1762–1840), Scottish poetess; née L'Amy; married the Revd Dr James Lyon, 1786; solely remembered by the song, 'You've surely heard of famous Niel'.

LYON, Claude George Bowes-, fourteenth earl of Strathmore and Kinghorne (1855–1944), See BOWES-LYON.

LYON, George Francis (1795–1832), captain in the navy and traveller; entered the navy, 1808; travelled in Africa in the interests of the government, 1818–20; published *A Narrative of Travels in North Africa* (1821); took part in *Parry's Arctic

expedition, 1821–3, publishing a narrative (1824); unsuccessfully attempted to reach Repulse Bay, 1824; hon. DCL, Oxford, 1825; went to Mexico and South America; died at sea.

LYON (LÖBEL or **LEWIN), Hart (Hirsch)** (1721–1800), chief rabbi; born at Resha, Poland; chief rabbi of the London congregation of German and Polish Jews, 1757–63; subsequently rabbi of Halberstadt, Mannheim, and Berlin; died at Berlin.

LYON, Sir **James Andrew Hamilton** (1775–1842), lieutenant-general; born on a homeward-bound transport from America after Bunker's Hill, where his father was killed; entered the army, 1791; lieutenant, 1794; in Egypt as major, 1801; as lieutenant-colonel in the Peninsula, 1808–11; KCB, 1815; GCH, 1817; commander of the troops in the Windward and Leeward Islands, 1828–33; lieutenant-general, 1830.

LYON, Janet, Lady Glammis (d. 1537). See DOUGLAS, JANET.

LYON, John, seventh Baron Glammis (1510?–1558), son of John, sixth Lord Glammis, by Janet *Douglas; tried for conspiring to effect the death of James V, 1537; imprisoned, 1537–40; held a command in the Scottish Army, 1545.

LYON, John, eighth Baron Glammis (d. 1578), lord high chancellor of Scotland; son of John, seventh Baron *Glammis; partisan and kinsman of the regent *Morton; lord chancellor of Scotland, 1573; accidentally slain in a street brawl.

LYON, John (1514?–1592), founder of Harrow School; obtained charter for the foundation of a free grammar school for boys in Harrow, 1572; drew up statutes and course of study for the school, 1590.

LYON (or LYOUN), John (*fl.* 1608–1622), of Auldbar, the supposed author of *Teares for the Death of Alexander, Earle of Dunfermeling* (first printed 1622); son of Sir Thomas *Lyon (d. 1608).

LYON, John (1702–1790), antiquary; MA, Trinity College, Dublin, 1732; minor canon of St Patrick's, Dublin, 1740; published nothing; reputed a learned ecclesiologist; took care of *Swift in his last illness.

LYON, John (1734–1817), historian of Dover; took holy orders; his principal work is a *History of the Town and Port of Dover* (1813–14); published works on electricity, 1780–96.

LYON, John, ninth earl of Strathmore (1737–1776), married Mary Eleanor *Bowes, a member of a distinguished border family, 1767; took his wife's surname; Scots representative peer.

LYON, Sir **Patrick** of Carse (d. 1695?), lord of session; second cousin of Patrick *Lyon, first earl of Strathmore; professor of philosophy at St Andrews; member of the Faculty of Advocates, 1671; lord of session as Lord Carse, 1683–8; a lord justiciary, 1684–8; deprived of both offices at the Revolution, 1688.

LYON, Patrick, first earl of Strathmore and third earl of Kinghorne (1642–1695), succeeded to his estates, 1660; restored the fortunes of his family by a course of self-denial; privy councillor, 1682; lord of session, 1686–9; took the oath to King William III, 1690.

LYON, Sir **Thomas** of Balduckie and Auldbar, master of Glammis (d. 1608), lord high treasurer of Scotland; son of John *Lyon, seventh Baron Glammis; a main contriver of the raid of Ruthven of 1582; escaped to Ireland, 1583; pardoned, 1585; lord high treasurer, 1585–96; lord of session, 1586; knighted, 1590; deprived of his office for favouring *Bothwell, 1591; reappointed, 1593.

LYON, William (d. 1617), bishop of Cork, Cloyne, and Ross; educated at Oxford; first Protestant bishop of Ross, 1582; bishop of Cork and Cloyne, 1584 (three sees united, 1587); foiled machinations of Jesuits and friars; recommended the strict exclusion of foreign priests.

LYONS, Sir **Algernon McLennan** (1833–1908), admiral of the fleet; born at Bombay; entered navy, 1847; served on China and Mediterranean stations; distinguished himself in Crimean War; promoted commander, 1858; commodore in charge at Jamaica, 1875–8; rear-admiral, 1878; commander-in-chief in Pacific, 1881; in command of North America and West Indies Station, 1886; admiral, 1888; commander-in-chief at Plymouth, 1893–6; admiral of the fleet, 1897; KCB, 1889; GCB, 1897.

LYONS, Edmund, first Baron Lyons (1790–1858), admiral; entered the navy, 1803; present at the passing of the Dardanelles, 1807; saw active service in East Indies, 1810–11; commander, 1812; employed in the Mediterranean, 1828–33; KCH and minister-plenipotentiary at Athens, 1835; created baronet, 1840; minister to the Swiss Confederation, 1849–51; rear-admiral, 1850; minister at Stockholm, 1851–3; second-in-command of the Mediterranean Fleet, 1853–5; commander-in-chief, 1855–8; military GCB, 1855; created Baron Lyons of Christchurch, 1856; rear-admiral, with temporary rank of admiral, while in command in the Mediterranean, 1857.

LYONS, (Francis Stewart) Leland (1923–1983), historian; educated at Dover College and Trinity College, Dublin; first class, modern history and political science, 1945; lecturer in history, Hull University, 1947; fellow, Trinity College, Dublin, 1951–64; W. B. Rankin memorial lecturer on *The Burden of our History*, 1978; first professor of modern history, University of Kent, 1964–74; provost, Trinity College, Dublin, 1974–81; publications include *The Irish Parliamentary Party 1890–1910* (1951), *The Fall of Parnell* (1960), *Internationalism in Europe 1815–1914* (1963), *John Dillon* (1968) which won Heinemann Award of Royal Society of Literature, *Ireland since the Famine* (1971), and *Charles Stewart Parnell* (1977); appointed official biographer of W. B. *Yeats, 1974; Ford lecturer at Oxford, 1977–8 (published as *Culture and Anarchy in Ireland 1890–1939*, 1979, won Wolfson Literary Award, 1980); member, Royal Irish Academy, 1962; FBA, 1974; F.R.Hist.S. and FRSL; hon. fellow, Oriel College, Oxford, 1975; honorary doctorates of universities of Pennsylvania, 1975; Hull, Kent, and Queen's, Belfast, 1978, Ulster, 1980, and St Andrews 1981.

LYONS, Sir **Henry George** (1864–1944), geographer and scientist; educated at Wellington College and Woolwich; gazetted to Royal Engineers, 1884; posted to Cairo, 1890; transferred to organize Geological Survey of Egypt, 1896; director, Combined Geological and Cadastral Survey Department, 1901–9; originated an observatory and meteorological office; entered Science Museum, South Kensington, 1912; director, 1920–33; created Royal Engineers' meteorological service and directed Meteorological Office, 1914–18; fellow (1906), foreign secretary (1928), treasurer (1929–39), Royal Society; wrote *The Royal Society, 1660–1940* (1944); knighted, 1926.

LYONS, Israel, the elder (d. 1770), Hebraist; a Polish Jew settled at Cambridge; instructed members of the university in Hebrew; author of *The Scholar's Instructor: an Hebrew Grammar, with Points* (1735).

LYONS, Israel, the younger (1739–1775), mathematician and botanist; son of Israel *Lyons the elder; published *A Treatise of Fluxions* (1758) and *Fasciculus Plantarum circa Cantabrigiam* (1763); lectured on botany at Oxford, 1764; appointed by the Board of Longitude to accompany Captain *Phipps as principal astronomer in his Arctic expedition, 1773.

LYONS, John Charles (1792–1874), antiquary and writer on gardening; educated at Pembroke College, Oxford; published a *Treatise on the Management of Orchidaceous Plants* (2nd edn., 1845); interested in local antiquities and literature, publishing *The Grand Juries of Westmeath from 1727 to 1853, with an Historical Appendix* (1853).

LYONS, Joseph Aloysius (1879–1939), prime minister of Australia; born in Tasmania; a Roman Catholic; became schoolteacher; Labour member of Tasmanian parliament, 1909–29; treasurer and minister for education and for railways, 1914–16; leader of opposition, 1916–23; premier, 1923–8; member of Commonwealth parliament, 1929–39; postmaster-general, 1929–31; acting-treasurer, 1930–1; opposed bringing Commonwealth Bank under Treasury control and expelled from Labour party; joined with Nationalists to form United Australia party and won elections, 1931; prime minister, 1932–9; treasurer, 1932–5; pledged to carry out the 'Premier's Plan', combining deflationary with some expansionist measures; his recovery policy successful; establishment of independent department of external affairs (1935) one of few positive achievements of later years; PC, 1932; CH, 1936.

LYONS, Richard Bickerton Pemell, second Baron and first Earl Lyons (1817–1887), diplomat; son of Edmund *Lyons, first Baron Lyons; of Winchester College and Christ Church, Oxford; MA, 1843; unpaid attaché at Athens, 1839; paid attaché, 1844; transferred to Dresden, 1852; appointed to Florence, 1853; secretary of that legation, 1856; British minister at Washington, 1858–65; KCB, 1860; GCB, 1862; ambassador at Constantinople, and privy councillor, 1865–7, at Paris, 1867–87; created Viscount Lyons of Christchurch, 1881, and Earl Lyons, 1887.

LYONS, Robert Spencer Dyer (1826–1886), physician; educated at Trinity College, Dublin; MB, 1848; licentiate, Royal College of Surgeons in Ireland, 1849; chief pathological commissioner to the army in the Crimea, 1855; investigated pathological anatomy of Lisbon yellow fever, 1857; joined St George's Hospital, Dublin; professor of medicine in the Roman Catholic University medical school; MP, Dublin, 1880–5; published two medical works and a book on forestry.

LYONS, Sir William (1901–1985), founder of Jaguar Cars Ltd.; educated at Arnold House (later Arnold School), Blackpool; at 17 became trainee with Crossley Motors Ltd.; in partnership with William Walmsley, opened factory in Blackpool for production of Swallow motor-cycle sidecars, 1922; extended business to Swallow Sidecar and Coach Building Company making bodywork for Austin Swallow and Morris Cowley Swallow cars; moved to larger works in Coventry, 1928; on retirement of Walmsley, became chairman and managing director of SS Cars Ltd., 1935; produced first Jaguar car; during 1939–45 war manufactured spare parts for bomber and fighter aircraft; post-war changed name to Jaguar Cars Ltd.; new sports Jaguar won Le Mans twenty-four hours race, 1951, 1953, 1955, 1956, and 1957; after fire damaged works, cars withdrawn from motor racing, 1957; took over Daimler Company, 1960, and Guy Motors of Wolverhampton and Coventry Climax Engines Ltd., 1961; merged with British Motor Corporation Ltd., 1966; merged in British Leyland, 1968; retired from executive position, 1968; knighted, 1956; president, Society of British Motor Manufacturers and Traders; honorary degree, Loughborough University, 1969; RDI, 1954.

LYSAGHT, Edward (1763–1811), Irish songwriter; educated at Trinity College, Dublin, and St Edmund Hall, Oxford; MA, 1788; called to the English and Irish bars, 1788; practised first in England and afterwards in Ireland; commissioner of bankruptcy in Ireland and police magistrate for Dublin; wrote poems (published posthumously 1811), political squibs, and pamphlets.

LYSARDE, Nicholas (d. 1570), sergeant-painter. See LYZARDE.

LYSONS, Daniel (1727–1800), physician; MA, Magdalen College, Oxford, 1751; fellow and BCL of All Souls College, Oxford, 1755; MD, 1769; published medical works.

LYSONS, Daniel (1762–1834), topographer; nephew of Daniel *Lysons (1727–1800); of St Mary Hall, Oxford; MA, 1785; his principal work, *The Environs of London* (1792–6); held family living of Rodmarton, 1804–33; in conjunction with his brother Samuel *Lysons (1763–1819) began a *Magna Britannia . . . Account of the . . . Counties of Great Britain*, dealing with ten counties from Bedfordshire to Devonshire, in alphabetical order, 1806–22.

LYSONS, Sir Daniel (1816–1898), general; son of Daniel *Lysons (1762–1834); ensign, 1834; lieutenant, 1837; served in Canada; received company in 3rd West India Regiment, 1843; brigade-major of 23rd Welsh Fusiliers in Barbados, 1845–7, and in Halifax, Nova Scotia, 1847–8; major, 1849; in Crimea, 1854–5; lieutenant-colonel, 1854; brevet-colonel and CB, 1855; assistant adjutant-general at headquarters in England, 1856; in Canada in connection with the 'Trent' affair, 1861; major-general, 1868; quartermaster-general at headquarters, 1876; lieutenant-general and KCB, 1877; general, 1879; commanded Aldershot division, 1880–3; GCB, 1886; constable of the Tower, 1890; published *Instructions for Mounted Rifle Volunteers* (1860).

LYSONS, Samuel (1763–1819), antiquary; FSA, 1786; FRS, 1797; barrister, Inner Temple,

1798; keeper of the Tower of London records, 1803; vice-president and treasurer of the Royal Society, 1810; antiquary professor in the Royal Academy, 1818; assisted his brother, Daniel *Lysons (1762–1834), on the *Magna Britannia*. His greatest work, *Reliquiae Britannico-Romanae, containing Figures of Roman Antiquities discovered in England*, with plates, was published (1801–17).

LYSONS, Samuel (1806–1877), antiquary; son of Daniel *Lysons (1762–1834); BA, Exeter College, Oxford, 1830; hon. canon of Gloucester Cathedral, 1867; published antiquarian works connected with Gloucestershire, 1832–68.

LYSTER, Sir Richard (d. 1554), chief justice of the court of King's Bench; reader at the Middle Temple, 1515; solicitor-general, 1522–6; chief baron of the Exchequer, 1529; knighted, 1529; chief justice of the King's Bench, 1546–52.

LYTE, Henry (1529?–1607), botanist and antiquary; student at Oxford, c.1546; published a translation through the French of the *Cruydeboeck* of Rembert Dodoens, with the title, *A niewe Herball or Historie of Plantes* (1578); published *The Light of Britayne; a Recorde of the honorable Originall and Antiquitie of Britaine* (1588).

LYTE, Sir Henry Churchill Maxwell (1848–1940), deputy keeper of the public records and historian; educated at Eton and Oxford and wrote their histories; deputy keeper of the public records, 1886–1926; instituted series of *Calendars of the Chancery Rolls*; edited *Book of Fees* (2 parts, 1920–3); KCB, 1897; FBA, 1902.

LYTE, Henry Francis (1793–1847), hymnwriter; lineal descendant of Henry *Lyte; educated at Trinity College, Dublin; took holy orders; published *Poems, chiefly Religious* (1833) and other works; chiefly remembered for his hymns, the best of which appear in most hymnals; died at Nice.

LYTE, Thomas (1568?–1638), genealogist; educated at Sherborne School; drew up the 'most royally ennobled Genealogy' of James I, now lost, which he presented to the king, 1610; compiled Lyte pedigrees.

LYTTELTON, Alfred (1857–1913), lawyer and statesman; son of fourth Baron *Lyttelton; educated at Eton and Trinity College, Cambridge; practised successfully at bar, 1881–1903; Liberal Unionist MP, Leamington, 1895; chairman of commission to South Africa, 1900; colonial secretary, 1903–5; sanctioned, in face of opposition, introduction of Chinese coolies into Rand, 1904; prepared way for development of imperial conference; MP, St George's, Hanover Square, 1906; first-class cricketer and for long amateur tennis champion.

LYTTELTON, Arthur Temple (1852–1903), suffragan bishop of Southampton; son of fourth Baron *Lyttelton; educated at Eton and Trinity College, Cambridge; BA, 1874; MA, 1877; DD, 1898; tutor of Keble College, Oxford, 1879–82; first master of Selwyn College, Cambridge, 1882–93; Hulsean lecturer, 1891; vicar of Eccles, Lancashire, 1893–8; suffragan bishop of Southampton, 1898–1903; a high churchman; published *Modern Poets of Faith, Doubt, and Unbelief* (1904).

LYTTELTON (or **LITTLETON),** Sir **Charles,** second baronet (1629–1716), governor of Jamaica; son of Sir Thomas *Lyttelton (1596–1650); fought in the Royalist army; escaped to France, 1648; cupbearer to Charles II, 1650; knighted, 1662; governor of Jamaica, 1662–4; founded first town of Port Royal; summoned the first legislative assembly, 1664; major of the yellow-coated 'maritime' regiment, the precursor of the marine forces; governor of Harwich and Landguard Fort at time of great seafight with the Dutch, 1672; MP, Bewdley, 1685–9; succeeded his brother as second baronet, 1693.

LYTTELTON, Charles (1714–1768), antiquary and bishop of Carlisle; grandson of Sir Charles *Lyttelton; of Eton and University College, Oxford; barrister, Middle Temple, 1738; ordained, 1742; FRS, 1743; DCL, 1745; FSA, 1746; dean of Exeter, 1747; bishop of Carlisle, 1762; president of the Society of Antiquaries, 1765; contributed to the *Philosophical Transactions* (1748 and 1750), and to *Archaeologia* (vols. i–iii).

LYTTELTON, Sir Edward, first Baron Lyttelton of Munslow (1589–1645). See LITTLETON.

LYTTELTON, Edward (1855–1942), schoolmaster, divine, and cricketer; son of fourth Baron *Lyttelton; educated at Eton and Trinity College, Cambridge; captained Eton (1874) and Cambridge (1878) elevens; deacon, 1884; priest, 1886; master at Eton, 1882–90; headmaster of Haileybury, 1890–1905; of Eton, 1905–16; dean of Whitelands Training College, Chelsea, 1920–9; honorary canon of Norwich from 1931.

LYTTELTON, George, first Baron Lyttelton (1709–1773), descended from William, son of Sir Thomas *Littleton (1422–1481); educated at Eton and Christ Church, Oxford; MP, Okehampton, 1735–56; opposed Walpole; a lord of the Treasury, 1744–54; with his connections, Pitt and the Grenvilles, composed 'Cobhamite' party; succeeded to baronetcy, 1751; privy councillor, 1754; chancellor of the Exchequer for a short period, 1756; created Baron Lyttelton of

Frankley, 1756; opposed the repeal of the Stamp Act, 1766; friend of *Pope and a liberal patron of literature; his best poem, the monody on the death of his wife, 1747; published, among numerous other works, *Dialogues of the Dead* (1760) and *The History of the Life of Henry the Second, and of the Age in which he lived* (1767–71).

LYTTELTON, George William, fourth Baron Lyttelton of Frankley of the second creation (1817–1876), son of William Henry *Lyttelton, third Baron Lyttelton; educated at Eton and Trinity College, Cambridge; succeeded to peerage, 1837; MA, 1838; hon. LL D, 1862; hon. DCL, Oxford, 1870; the centre of the intellectual life of Worcestershire from 1839; FRS, 1840; principal of Queen's College, Birmingham, 1845; under-secretary of state for the colonies, 1846; chairman of the Canterbury Association, a church of England corporation which established Canterbury, New Zealand, 1850; first president of the Birmingham and Midland Institute, 1853; chief commissioner of endowed schools, 1869; privy councillor, 1869; KCMG, 1869; killed himself in an attack of constitutional melancholia; published, together with Gladstone, a volume of translations (1863).

LYTTELTON, Sir Henry, second baronet (1624–1693), son of Sir Thomas *Lyttelton (1596–1650); educated at Balliol College, Oxford; taken prisoner at the Battle of Worcester, 1651; MP, Lichfield, 1678–9.

LYTTELTON, James (d. 1723), vice-admiral. See LITTLETON.

LYTTELTON, Sir Neville Gerald (1845–1931), general; son of fourth Baron *Lyttelton; educated at Eton; joined Rifle Brigade, 1865; commander-in-chief, South Africa, 1902–4; chief of the General Staff, 1904–8; general, 1906; built up Expeditionary Force concentrating especially on training of staff and formation of Officers' Training Corps; commander-in-chief, Ireland, 1908–12; governor, Chelsea Hospital, 1912–31; KCB, 1902; GCVO, 1911.

LYTTELTON, Sir Thomas (1422–1481), judge and legal author. See LITTLETON.

LYTTELTON, Sir Thomas, first baronet (1596–1650), Royalist; educated at Balliol College, Oxford; BA, 1614; created baronet, 1618; MP, Worcester, 1621–2, 1624–5, 1625, 1626, 1640; colonel of the Worcestershire Horse and Foot, 1642; imprisoned, 1644–6.

LYTTELTON, Sir Thomas (1647?–1710), speaker of the House of Commons and Treasurer of the navy. See LITTLETON.

LYTTELTON, Thomas, second Baron Lyttelton (1744–1779), commonly called the wicked Lord Lyttelton; son of George, first Baron *Lyttelton; educated at Eton and Christ Church, Oxford; MP, Bewdley, 1768–9; took his seat in the House of Lords, 1774; prominent in debates on American affairs, 1774–8; warned in a dream (24 Nov. 1779), which was exactly fulfilled, that he would die in three days; a notorious profligate.

LYTTELTON, William Henry, first Baron Lyttelton of Frankley of the second creation (1724–1808); educated at Eton College and St Mary Hall, Oxford; barrister, Middle Temple, 1748; MP, Bewdley, 1748–55 and 1774–6; governor of South Carolina, 1755–62, of Jamaica, 1762–6; ambassador to Portugal, 1766–71; created Baron Westcote of Balamare, Co. Longford (Irish peerage), 1776; a commissioner of the Treasury, 1776–82; hon. DCL, 1781; created Baron Lyttelton of Frankley (peerage of Great Britain), 1794; chief published work *An Historical Account of the Constitution of Jamaica* (1792).

LYTTELTON, William Henry, third Baron Lyttelton of Frankley of the second creation (1782–1837), son of William Henry *Lyttelton, first Baron Lyttelton of the second creation; educated at Christ Church, Oxford; MA, 1805; MP, Worcestershire, 1807–20; DCL, 1810; succeeded to the title on death of his half-brother, George Fulke, second baron, 1828; a Whig and an eloquent orator.

LYTTELTON, William Henry (1820–1884), canon of Gloucester; son of William Henry *Lyttelton, third Baron Lyttelton; of Winchester College and Trinity College, Cambridge; MA, 1841; hon. canon of Worcester, 1847; canon of Gloucester, 1880; published religious works.

LYTTELTON, Oliver, first Viscount Chandos (1893–1972), politician and business man; educated at Eton and Trinity College, Cambridge; gold blue; joined Grenadier Guards, 1914; DSO, 1916; MC; wounded, 1918; joined merchant bankers as clerk; became manager and managing director, British Metal Corporation; controller, non-ferrous metals, 1939; president, Board of Trade, 1940; Conservative MP for Aldershot, 1940–54; joined War Cabinet as minister of state, Cairo, 1941; minister of production, 1942; responsible for initiating with USA the Combined Production and Resources Board; chairman, Associated Electrical Industries (AEI), 1945; colonial secretary, 1951–4; dealt with problems of rebellion in Malaya and Kenya and constitutional reform in Nigeria; supported Sir Andrew *Cohen in dispute with Kabaka, in Uganda; retired from AEI, 1963; PC, 1940; created Viscount Chandos, 1954; KG, 1970; president, Institute of Directors, 1954–63;

trustee of colleges in Oxford and Cambridge and of National Gallery; chairman, National Theatre, 1962–71; published *Memoirs* (1962) and *From Peace to War, a Study in Contrast: 1857–1918* (1968).

LYTTON, earls of. See LYTTON, EDWARD ROBERT BULWER, first earl, 1831–1891; BULWER-LYTTON, VICTOR ALEXANDER GEORGE ROBERT, 1876–1947.

LYTTON, Edward George Earle Lytton Bulwer-, first Baron Lytton (1803–1873), novelist; educated at private schools under a tutor, and then successively at Trinity College and Trinity Hall, Cambridge; published a small volume of poems; chancellor's medallist, 1825; BA, 1826; frequented the fashionable circles of London and Paris; married Rosina Wheeler, 1827 (see LYTTON, ROSINA BULWER-LYTTON, Lady); supported himself by energetic literary labour; wrote for all kinds of periodicals, from *Quarterly Reviews* to *Keepsakes*; published *Falkland* (1827), *Pelham*, one of his best novels (1828), and *The Disowned* (1828); published *Devereux* (1829), *Paul Clifford* (1830); edited the *New Monthly*, 1831–2; MP, St Ives, Huntingdonshire, 1831, Lincoln, 1832–41; a reformer in politics and a steady supporter of authors' copyrights and the removal of taxes upon literature; published *Eugene Aram* (1832), *Godolphin* (1833), *The Last Days of Pompeii* (1834), and *Rienzi* (1835); separated from his wife (legal separation, 1836), who spent her remaining years (d. 1882) in lawsuits directed against her husband, and in publishing a long series of attacks upon him; the *Lady of Lyons* produced at Covent Garden (1838), and *Richelieu* (1839); produced *Money* at the Haymarket (1840); undertook, in conjunction with others, *The Monthly Chronicle*, 1841; published *The Last of the Barons* (1843) and *The New Timon*, a romantic story in heroic couplets (1846); brought out *Harold* (1848); joined the Conservatives and returned to politics; MP, Hertfordshire, 1852–66; published *My Novel* (1853); lord rector of Glasgow University, 1856 and 1858; secretary for the colonies, 1858–9; created baronet, 1838, and Baron Lytton of Knebworth, 1866; published anonymously *The Coming Race*, an ingenious prophecy of the society of the future (1871), and *The Parisians* (1873).

LYTTON, Edward Robert Bulwer, first earl of Lytton (1831–1891), statesman and poet; son of Edward George Earle Lytton Bulwer-*Lytton, first Baron Lytton; educated at Harrow and Bonn; private secretary to his uncle,

Lord *Dalling, at Washington and Florence; paid attaché at The Hague and Vienna; published *Clytemnestra, The Earl's Return*, and other poems, under the pseudonym of Owen Meredith (1855); published *The Wanderer*, a volume of lyrics (1857), and *Lucile*, a poem (1860); consul-general at Belgrade; second secretary at Vienna, 1862; secretary of legation at Copenhagen, 1863; transferred to Athens, 1864, and to Lisbon, 1865; employed successively at Madrid and Vienna, 1868–72; published *Chronicles and Characters* (1868); *Orval, or the Fool of Time*, the sole representative in English literature of the great Polish school of mystical poetry (1869); secretary to the embassy at Paris, 1872–4; British minister at Lisbon, 1872; succeeded to his father's title, 1873; published *Fables in Song* (1874); viceroy of India, 1876–80; proclaimed Queen Victoria empress of India at Delhi, 1877; did admirable work in famine of 1877–8; responsible for the Afghan War, 1879; effected memorable internal reforms, but his administration regarded at home as a failure; ambassador at Paris, an office in which he won great popularity, 1887–91; *King Poppy*, his most original and best poem, published 1892; takes high rank as a prose writer in his minutes and despatches.

LYTTON, Sir **Henry Alfred** (1865–1936), actor, whose original name was Henry Alfred Jones; played with D'Oyly Carte Opera Company (1884, 1887–1903, 1908–34) and became its mainstay; played thirty characters, including Jack Point in *The Yeomen of the Guard*, Reginald Bunthorne in *Patience*, and Ko-Ko in *The Mikado*; possessed a light, pleasant voice with crystal-clear diction, and excellent sense of comedy and timing; knighted, 1930.

LYTTON, Rosina Bulwer-Lytton, Lady (1802–1882), novelist; née Wheeler; married to Edward George Earle Lytton Bulwer-*Lytton, first Baron Lytton, against his mother's wishes, 1827; a woman of excitable temperament; became estranged from her husband (1836) and was legally separated from him; wrote a long series of attacks upon him, publishing (1839) *Cheveley, or the Man of Honour*, a novel in which she made her husband the villain.

LYVEDEN, first Baron (1800–1873). See SMITH, ROBERT VERNON.

LYZARDE, Nicholas (d. 1570), sergeant-painter; painter to the court in time of Henry VIII and Edward VI; sergeant-painter to queens Mary and Elizabeth.

M

MAAS, Joseph (1847–1886), vocalist; studied at Milan, 1869–71; public singer in London, 1871; principal tenor at her majesty's opera; created the part of the Chevalier des Grieux in Massenet's *Manon* at Drury Lane, 1885.

MAB (or **MABBE**), **James** (1572–1642?), Spanish scholar; grandson of John *Mab; fellow of Magdalen College, Oxford, 1594–1633; MA, 1598; secretary to Sir John *Digby, ambassador at Madrid, 1611–13; published translations from the Spanish, including *The Rogue, or the Life of Guzman de Alfarache* (1622) and some *Devout Contemplations, by Fr. Ch. de Fonseca* (1629).

MAB (or **MABBE**), **John** (d. 1582), chamberlain of London; freeman of the Goldsmiths' Company; chamberlain of London, 1577–82; wrote *Remembrances, faithfullie printed out of his own hand writing, etc.* (licensed 1583).

MABERLY, Catherine Charlotte (1805–1875), novelist; née Prittie; married William Leader *Maberly, 1830; wrote eight novels, published between 1840 and 1856.

MABERLY, Frederick Herbert (1781–1860), politician; of Westminster School and Trinity College, Cambridge; MA, 1809; led by his fanatical zeal against Catholic emancipation into eccentric and violent conduct, which caused the magistrates and the home secretary anxiety about the public peace, 1812–35.

MABERLY, William Leader (1798–1885), secretary of the General Post Office; entered the army, 1815; lieutenant-colonel; MP, Westbury, 1819–20, Northampton, 1820–30, Shaftesbury, 1831–2, Chatham, 1832–4; joint secretary of the General Post Office, 1836–54; opposed all Rowland *Hill's schemes of reform; transferred to the Board of Audit, 1854, where he remained till 1866; retired from the army, 1881.

MABS. See MAB, JOHN.

MACADAM, John (1827–1865), chemist; studied medicine at Glasgow University and chemistry at Edinburgh; MD, Glasgow; lecturer on chemistry and natural science in the Scottish College, Melbourne, 1855; member of the Legislative Assembly of Victoria, 1859–64; postmaster-general, 1861; lecturer in chemistry in Melbourne University, 1861–2; died at sea on his way to New Zealand.

McADAM, John Loudon (1756–1836), the 'macadamizer' of roads; began experiments in road-making in Ayrshire; continued them at Falmouth, where he resided after 1798 as agent for revictualling the navy in the western ports; arrived at the conclusion that roads should be constructed of broken stone; surveyor-general of the Bristol roads, 1815; published *Present State of Road-making* (1820); general surveyor of roads, 1827; his process adopted in all parts of the civilized world, his name becoming the synonym for the invention.

MACALISTER, Arthur (1818–1883), Australian politician; emigrated to Australia, 1850; represented Ipswich in the first Queensland parliament, 1860; secretary for lands and works, 1862; premier and colonial secretary, 1866–7, 1874–6; speaker, 1870–1; agent-general for Queensland in London, 1876–81.

MacALISTER, Sir Donald, first baronet (1854–1934), physician, principal and vice-chancellor, and later, chancellor of Glasgow University; educated at Liverpool Institute and St John's College, Cambridge; senior wrangler and fellow, 1877; MD, 1884; president, General Medical Council, 1904–31; played large part in preparing *British Pharmacopœia* (1898, 1914); principal of Glasgow University, 1907–29; chancellor, 1929–34; activities in country's university business included chairmanship of vice-chancellors' committee; KCB, 1908; baronet, 1924.

MacALISTER, Sir (George) Ian (1878–1957), secretary of the Royal Institute of British Architects; scholar of St Paul's School; exhibitioner, Merton College, Oxford; secretary, Royal Institute of British Architects, 1908–43; widened its influence in provinces and Commonwealth; obtained Architects Registration Acts, 1931, 1938; organized new headquarters in Portland Place and knighted, 1934.

McALL, Robert Stephens (1792–1838), Congregational minister; ordained, 1823; a brilliant preacher; published sermons and poems.

MACALLUM, Hamilton (1841–1896), painter; studied at Royal Academy, where he exhibited between 1876 and 1896.

McALPINE, (Archibald) Douglas (1890–1981), neurologist; educated at Kirton College, Edinburgh, at Cheltenham, and Glasgow

University; MB, Ch.B., 1913; during 1914–18 war served in RAMC and Royal Navy; worked on post-encephalitic Parkinsonism at the National Hospital, Queen Square, London; MRCP, 1921; MD, 1923; physician for nervous diseases, Middlesex Hospital, 1924; in charge of new neurological unit, 1930; FRCP, 1932; during 1939–45 war adviser in neurology in Middle East, India, and South-East Asia; post-war, returned to Middlesex Hospital as consultant physician; published clinical data on his speciality *Multiple Sclerosis* (1955); initiated the formation of the Multiple Sclerosis Society of Great Britain, 1951–3; first recipient of Charcot Award of the International Federation of Multiple Sclerosis Societies, 1969.

MACALPINE (MACCABEUS, MACHA-BEUS, MACCABE, or MACHABE), John (d. 1557), Scottish reformer and professor of theology at Copenhagen; prior of Dominicans at Perth, 1532–4; imbibed Reformation principles and fled to England; passed to the continent; professor in Copenhagen, 1542; assisted to translate Luther's Bible into Danish, 1550; author of Latin theological works; died at Copenhagen.

MACAN, Sir Arthur Vernon (1843–1908), gynaecologist and obstetrician; BA, Trinity College, Dublin, 1864; MB and M.Ch., 1868; MAO, 1877; studied medicine at Berlin, 1869–72; served as volunteer in Prussian Army, 1870; fellow of King and Queen's College of Physicians, Ireland; master of the Rotunda Hospital, Dublin, 1882; introduced newer obstetric methods despite opposition; applied Listerian principles in midwifery; president of Royal College of Physicians, Ireland, 1902–4; knighted, 1903; contributed to Dublin scientific journals.

MACANWARD, Hugh Boy (1580?–1635), Irish historian; belonged to a clan, eight of whom, flourishing between 1587 and 1696, were poets; studied at the Franciscan convent of Donegal, at Salamanca, and in Paris; first professor of theology in the Irish College of St Anthony at Louvain, 1616; made collections for a complete Irish martyrology and hagiology, which John *Colgan used for his *Acta Sanctorum Hiberniae*; died at Louvain.

MACARA, Sir Charles Wright, first baronet (1845–1929), cotton spinner; managing partner of Henry Bannerman & Sons, cotton spinners and merchants, of Manchester, 1880; president, Federation of Master Cotton Spinners' Associations, 1894–1914; founded International Federation of Master Cotton Spinners' and Manufacturers' Associations, 1904; chairman, 1904–15; baronet, 1911.

MACARDELL, James (1729?–1765), mezzotint engraver; studied under John *Brooks; engraved over forty plates after Sir Joshua *Reynolds and twenty-five after *Hudson.

MACARIUS SCOTUS (d. 1153), abbot; migrated to Germany from Scotland, 1139; abbot of the Benedictine monastery of St James, near Würzburg; author of *De Laude Martyrum*.

McARTHUR, Charles (1844–1910), politician and writer on marine insurance; won repute by *The Policy of Marine Insurance Popularly Examined* (1871); established own business as an average adjuster at Liverpool, 1874; president of Liverpool Chamber of Commerce, 1892–6; Liberal Unionist MP for Exchange division of Liverpool, 1897–1906, and for Kirkdale, 1907–10; championed shipping and Protestant Church interests in parliament; wrote on *Evidences of Natural Religion* (1880).

MACARTHUR (or McARTHUR), Sir Edward (1789–1872), lieutenant-general; son of John *Macarthur (1767–1834); born in England; lived as a boy at Parramatta, near Sydney; entered the army, 1808; saw action in the Peninsula, 1812–14, in Canada, 1814; captain, 1821; assistant adjutant-general in Ireland, 1837; deputy adjutant-general in the Australian colonies, 1841–55; commander of the troops in Australia, with rank of major-general, 1855–60; acting governor of Victoria, 1856; KCB, 1862; lieutenant-general, 1866.

MACARTHUR, Hannibal Hawkins (1788–1861), nephew of John *Macarthur (1767–1834); born in England; emigrated to New South Wales, 1805; engaged in the wool trade; police magistrate at Parramatta; member of the legislative council, 1843.

MACARTHUR, James (1798–1867), son of John *Macarthur (1767–1834); born at Camden, New South Wales; published *New South Wales, its Present State and Future Prospects* (1838); member of the legislative council of New South Wales, 1839, 1848, and 1851; engaged in the exploration of Gippsland, 1840.

McARTHUR, John (1755–1840), author; entered navy, 1778; secretary to Lord *Hood, 1791; published *A Treatise of the Principles and Practice of Naval Courts-Martial* (1792; the second edn., 1805, entitled *Principles and Practice of Naval and Military Courts-Martial*, long the standard work); commenced publication, in conjunction with James Stanier *Clarke, of the *Naval Chronicle* (1799); chief work, *Life of Lord Nelson*, also in conjunction with Clarke (1809).

MACARTHUR, John (1767–1834), 'the father' of New South Wales; born in England; entered the army, 1788; accompanied the New South Wales corps to Sydney, 1790; commandant at Parramatta, 1793–1804; turned his attention to agriculture and to improving the colonial breed of sheep; tried at Sydney for high misdemeanors in connection with the liquor traffic and acquitted, 1808; planted the first vineyard in the colony, 1817; member of the first legislative council of New South Wales, 1825–31; created the Australian wool and wine trade.

MACARTHUR, John (1794–1831), son of John *Macarthur (1767–1834); of Caius College, Cambridge; appointed chief justice of New South Wales; died before assuming office.

MACARTHUR, Mary Reid (1880–1921), women's labour organizer. See ANDERSON.

MACARTHUR, Sir William (1800–1882), son of John *Macarthur (1767–1834); born at Parramatta; member of New South Wales legislative council, 1849 and 1864; knighted, 1855.

McARTHUR, Sir William (1809–1887), lord mayor of London; a woollen draper of Londonderry; commenced exporting woollen goods to his brother in Sydney; transferred headquarters of his business to London, 1857; MP, Lambeth, 1868–85; sheriff of London, 1867; alderman, 1872; lord mayor, 1880; one of the founders of the London Chamber of Commerce, 1881; KCMG, 1882.

MacARTHUR, Sir William Porter (1884–1964), director-general of the Army Medical Services; educated at Queen's University, Belfast; MB, B.Ch. (RUI), 1908; DPH, Oxon, 1910; MD, Belfast, 1911; FRCP, Ireland, 1913; DTM & H, Cantab., 1920; FRCP, London, 1937; joined RAMC, 1909; served in Mauritius, 1911–14; in France, 1915–16; DSO; commanding officer and chief instructor, Army School of Hygiene, 1919–22; professor, tropical medicine, RAM College, London, 1922–9 and 1932–4; consulting physician to the army, 1929–34; director of studies and commandant, RAM College, 1935–8; deputy director-general, Army Medical Services, 1934–5; director-general, 1938–41; CB, 1938; KCB, 1939; hon. physician to the king, 1930–41; colonel commandant, RAMC, 1946–51; consultant in tropical diseases, Royal Masonic Hospital; additional member, faculty of medicine, Oxford; editor, *Transactions* of Royal Society of Tropical Medicine and Hygiene; lifelong hobby, the study of medical history; contributed to various journals and published numerous lectures.

MACARTNEY, George (1660?–1730), general. See MACCARTNEY.

MACARTNEY, George, first Earl Macartney (1737–1806), diplomat and colonial governor; MA, Trinity College, Dublin, 1759; envoy-extraordinary at St Petersburg, 1764–7; MP, Antrim, in Irish House of Commons; chief secretary for Ireland, 1769–72; captain-general and governor of the Caribbean Islands, 1775–9; created Baron Macartney of Lissanoure (Irish peerage), 1776; governor and president of Fort St George (Madras), 1780–6; Irish privy councillor, 1788; created Earl Macartney and Viscount Macartney of Dervock in the Irish peerage, 1792; ambassador-extraordinary and plenipotentiary to Peking, 1792–4; governor of the Cape of Good Hope, 1796–8; wrote 'An Account of an Embassy to Russia', 'A Political Account of Ireland', and 'Journal of the Embassy to China', all published in *Barrow's Memoir* of him (vol. ii).

MACARTNEY, Sir George (1867–1945), consul-general at Kashgar; son of Sir Samuel Halliday *Macartney and his Chinese wife; educated at Dulwich College and in Paris; B. ès. L., 1886; entered Indian Foreign Department, 1888; sent to Kashgar, 1890; position regularized as first British consul in Chinese Turkestan, 1908; consul-general, 1910–18; KCIE, 1913.

MACARTNEY, James (1770–1843), anatomist; apprenticed as surgeon in Dublin; studied at Hunterian school of medicine, London, and at Guy's, St Thomas's, and St Bartholomew's hospitals; MRCS, 1800; FRS, 1811; MD, St Andrews, 1813; professor of anatomy and surgery, Dublin University, 1813–37; hon. FRCP, Ireland, 1818; MD incorporated from Trinity College, Dublin, Cambridge, 1833; published anatomical works.

MACARTNEY, Sir Samuel Halliday (1833–1906), official in the Chinese Service; studied medicine at Edinburgh University, 1852–5; joined medical staff in Crimean War, 1855; MD, 1858; served in Indian Mutiny (1859) and in China (1860–2); entered Chinese Service, 1862; commanded Chinese troops co-operating with C. G. *Gordon; took Fung Ching and Seedong, 1863; mediated between Gordon and Li Hung Chang regarding murder of Taiping leaders at Soochow, 1864; in charge of arsenal at Nanking, 1865–75; secretary to the Chinese legation in London, 1877–1906; adviser of Chinese government; CMG, 1881; KCMG, 1885.

MACASSEY, Sir Lynden Livingston (1876–1963), industrial lawyer; educated at Upper Sullivan School, Holywood, County Down, Bedford School, Trinity College, Dublin, and London University; trained as engineer; called to bar (Middle Temple), 1899; lecturer on economics and law, London School of Economics, 1901–9;

KC, 1912; secretary to Royal Commission on London Traffic, 1903–6; Board of Trade arbitrator in shipbuilding and engineering disputes, 1914–16; head of Dilution Commission to the Clyde, 1916; director of shipyard labour, Admiralty, 1917–18; member, War Cabinet committees on Labour and on Women in Industry, 1917–19; labour assessor for British government, Permanent Court of International Justice, 1920; KBE, 1917; bencher (1922) and treasurer (1935), Middle Temple; hon. fellow, chairman of governors, Queen Mary College, London University; president, Institute of Arbitrators; president, Scottish Amicable Life Assurance Society, Ltd.; published *Labour Policy—False and True* (1922).

MACAULAY, Aulay (1758–1819), miscellaneous writer; brother of Zachary *Macaulay; MA, Glasgow, 1778; took orders; published sermons and miscellaneous essays (1780).

MACAULAY (afterwards **MACAULAY GRAHAM), Mrs Catharine** (1731–1791), historian and controversialist; née Sawbridge; married George Macaulay, MD (d. 1766), 1760; published volume i of her *History of England* (1763); settled at Bath, 1774; married William Graham, brother of James *Graham (1745–1794), the quack doctor, 1778; visited North America, 1784; stopped ten days with Washington, 1785; her most famous production, *The History of England from the Accession of James I to that of the Brunswick Line* (i, 1763, ii, 1766, iii, 1767, iv, 1768, v, 1771, vi and vii, 1781, viii, 1783), now almost forgotten.

MACAULAY, Colin Campbell (1799–1853), son of Aulay *Macaulay; educated at Rugby; contributed to the transactions of the Leicester Literary and Philosophical Society.

MACAULAY, Dame (Emilie) Rose (1881–1958), author; educated at Oxford High School and Somerville College, Oxford; wrote twenty-three novels, many exposing current absurdities with gentle irony; they include *Dangerous Ages* (Femina Vie Heureuse Prize, 1921), *The Towers of Trebizond* (James Tait Black Memorial Prize, 1956), *Keeping up Appearances* (1928), and *Going Abroad* (1934); other writings were a biography of *Milton, a study of *Some Religious Elements in English Literature* (1931), *Personal Pleasures* (essays, 1935), and travel books, such as *Pleasure of Ruins* (1953); contributed prolifically to periodicals; DBE, 1958; hon. D.Litt., Cambridge, 1951.

MACAULAY, James (1817–1902), author; MA and MD, Edinburgh, 1838; a strenuous opponent of vivisection; tutor in Italy and Spain, and Madeira; FRCS Edinburgh, 1862; edited *Leisure Hour, Sunday at Home*, and the Religious Tract Society's periodicals; helped to found *Boy's Own Paper* and *Girl's Own Paper*, 1879; published accounts of travels in America, 1871, and Ireland, 1872; wrote narratives of adventure for boys and girls.

MACAULAY, Sir James Buchanan (1793–1859), Canadian judge; born at Niagara, Ontario; lieutenant, Glengarry Fencibles, 1812, serving during the American War; admitted to the Canadian bar, 1822; judge of the court of King's Bench, Canada, 1829; chief justice of court of common pleas, 1849–56, subsequently judge of the court of error and appeal; chairman of commission to revise and consolidate statutes of Canada and Upper Canada; CB, 1858; knighted, 1859.

MACAULAY, John (d. 1789), divine; minister successively of South Uist, 1746, Lismore, 1756, Inverary, 1765, and Cardross, 1775; mentioned in *Boswell's account of *Johnson's *Tour to the Hebrides in 1773*.

MACAULAY, Kenneth (1723–1779), alleged author of a *History of St. Kilda*; MA, Aberdeen, 1742; minister of Harris in the Hebrides and other places in Scotland; sent by the kirk on a special mission to St Kilda, 1759; published *History of St. Kilda* as his own composition (1764); doubts thrown on his authorship by Dr Johnson; probably did no more than supply the materials to Dr John *Macpherson of Skye, the real author.

MACAULAY, Thomas Babington, first Baron Macaulay (1800–1859), historian; son of Zachary *Macaulay; educated at private schools and Trinity College, Cambridge; fellow of Trinity College, 1824; barrister, Lincoln's Inn, 1826; his first article (on *Milton) published in the *Edinburgh Review* (1825); became a mainstay of the *Edinburgh Review*; a commissioner in bankruptcy, 1828; Liberal MP, Calne, 1830, Leeds, 1832–4; a commissioner of the Board of Control, 1832, secretary, 1833; member of the Supreme Council of India, 1834–8; president of the commission for composing a criminal code for India, 1835 (published 1837, becoming law 1860); returned to London and engaged in literature and politics, 1838; began his *History of England*, 1839; MP, Edinburgh, 1839–47, and 1852–6; secretary of war, 1839–41; published *Lays of Ancient Rome* (1842); a collective edition of the *Edinburgh* essays published (1843); proposed and carried the Copyright Bill of forty-two years; paymaster of the forces, 1846–7; published volumes i and ii of the *History* (1848), volumes iii and iv (1855); lord rector of Glasgow University, 1849; created Baron Macaulay of Rothley, 1857; buried in Westminster Abbey. His writings were largely coloured by his Whig sympathies and dislike of speculation. His complete works appeared in eight volumes (1866).

MACAULAY, Zachary (1768–1838), philanthropist; son of John *Macaulay; when manager of an estate in Jamaica, became deeply impressed with the miseries of the slave population; governor of Sierra Leone, 1793–9; secretary to the Sierra Leone Company, 1799–1808; edited the *Christian Observer*, an organ specially devoted to the abolition of the British slave-trade, and to the destruction of the slave-trade abroad, 1802–16; secretary to the African Institute, 1807–12; helped to form Anti-Slavery Society, 1823; did much for the abolitionist cause. His works, consisting chiefly of papers issued by the societies to which he belonged, are anonymous.

McAULEY, Catharine (1787–1841), foundress of the Order of Mercy; founded the 'House of our Blessed Lady of Mercy' in Dublin, 1827, which became a flourishing (Roman Catholic) order of Sisters of Mercy, and spread to England, 1839, Newfoundland, 1842, United States, 1843, Australia, 1845, Scotland and New Zealand, 1849, and South America, 1856.

M'AVOY, Margaret (1800–1820), blind lady; became blind, 1816; could distinguish colours and decipher printed or clearly written manuscript forms of letters by her touch.

MACBAIN, Alexander (1855–1907), Celtic scholar; graduate of King's College, Aberdeen, 1880; rector of Raining's School, Inverness, from 1881; published *Celtic Mythology and Religion* (1885) and a Gaelic dictionary (1896); edited many Celtic and Gaelic works; hon. LL D, Aberdeen, 1901; awarded civil list pension, 1905.

MACBAIN, Sir James (1828–1892), Australian statesman; born in Scotland; migrated to Melbourne, 1853; partner in Gibbs, Ronald & Co., a firm of mercantile and squatting agents which was bought by the Australian Mortgage Land and Finance Company; of that company Macbain was chairman of Australian directorate, 1865–90; member of the legislative assembly, 1864; member of the Cabinet, without portfolio, 1881–3; president of the legislative council, 1884; knighted, 1886; KCMG, 1889; died at Toorak.

MACBEAN, Alexander (d. 1784), one of the six amanuenses whom *Johnson employed on the *Dictionary*; assisted when starving by Johnson, who wrote a preface for his *Dictionary of Ancient Geography* (1773); admitted to the Charterhouse, 1780.

MACBEAN, Forbes (1725–1800), lieutenant-general, Royal Artillery; educated at Royal Military Academy, Woolwich; present at Fontenoy, 1745; adjutant at Woolwich, 1755–9; distinguished himself at Minden, 1759, at Warburg, 1760, and at Fritzlar, 1761; inspector-general of Portuguese Artillery, 1765–9; served in Canada, 1769–73, and 1778–80; lieutenant-general, 1798; left valuable manuscript notes relating to the earlier history of the Royal Artillery.

MACBETH (d. 1057), king of Scotland; commander of the forces of *Duncan, king of Scotland, whom he slew, and whose kingdom he took, 1040; defeated by *Siward, earl of Northumbria, 1054; defeated and slain by *Malcolm III, Canmore, 1057.

MACBETH, Norman (1821–1888), portrait painter; studied in the Royal Academy schools, London, and in Paris; exhibited at the Royal Scottish Academy from 1845; RSA, 1880.

MACBETH, Robert Walker (1848–1910), painter and etcher; son of Norman *Macbeth; studied at schools of Royal Scottish Academy and of Royal Academy; frequent exhibitor at Academy; an able etcher of pictures by Velázquez and Titian; ARA, 1883; RA, 1903.

McBEY, James (1883–1959), etcher and painter; educated at Newburgh Village School; bank clerk in Aberdeen and Edinburgh, 1899–1910; taught himself etching; travelled and studied work of Rembrandt and *Whistler; obtained London recognition as etcher and became much sought-after during twenties; official artist, Egyptian Expeditionary Force, 1917–19; collections of his works are at Aberdeen Art Gallery, Boston Public Library (Mass.), and Washington National Gallery; became American citizen, 1942; died in Tangier.

MACBRADY, Fiachra (*fl.* 1712), Irish poet; author of poems in Irish, printed in the *Anthologia Hibernica*.

MACBRADY, Philip (*fl.* 1710), Irish scholar; a Protestant clergyman and famous wit; translated sermons into Irish and wrote Irish poems.

MACBRIDE, David (1726–1778), medical writer; son of Robert *McBride; studied in Edinburgh and London; secretary to the Medico-Philosophical Society, Dublin, 1762; published *Experimental Essays* (1764); suggested a method for treating scurvy by an infusion of malt, and advocated the use of lime-water in certain parts of the process of tanning; published *Introduction to the Theory and Practice of Physic* (Dublin lectures, 1772).

McBRIDE, John (1651?–1718), Irish Presbyterian divine; graduated at Glasgow, 1673; received Presbyterian ordination, 1680; minister of Belfast, 1694–1718; moderator of general synod of Ulster, 1697; refused oath of abjuration, 1703, in consequence of which his ministry was often interrupted; an able preacher; published controversial tracts.

MACBRIDE, John (d. 1800), admiral; son of Robert *McBride; entered the navy, 1754; lieutenant, 1761; took part in the action off Ushant, 1776, off Cape St Vincent, 1780; MP, Plymouth, 1784; rear-admiral and commander-in-chief in the Downs, 1793; admiral, 1799.

MACBRIDE, John Alexander Paterson (1819–1890), sculptor; worked in the studio of Samuel *Joseph; exhibited at the Liverpool Academy from 1836; executed chiefly portrait busts and monuments for Liverpool Institution.

MACBRIDE, John David (1778–1868), principal of Magdalen Hall, Oxford; son of John *Macbride (d. 1800); educated at Exeter College, Oxford; fellow, 1800; MA, 1802; interested in oriental literature; both principal of Magdalen Hall (named Hertford College, 1874) and lord almoner's reader in Arabic, 1813–68; his principal literary work, *The Mohammedan Religion explained* (1857).

McBRIDE, Robert (1687–1759), son of John *McBride (1651?–1718); ordained minister of Ballymoney, 1716; took the side of subscription in the synodical controversies of 1720–6.

MACBRUAIDEDH, Maoilin (d. 1602), Irish historian and poet, commonly called Maoilin the younger; belonged to a family of hereditary historians; *ollamh* (chief chronicler) to the chiefs of the O'Gradys and the O'Gormans; author of a number of Irish poems, some in a very difficult metre called *dan direch*.

MACBRUAIDEDH, Tadhg (1570–1652), Irish poet; called by Irish writers Tadhg MacDaire; *ollamh* to Donough *O'Brien, fourth earl of Thomond, 1603; president of Munster, 1605; author of numerous Irish poems, some of them in defence of the northern Irish poetry against southern; flung over a cliff and killed by a Cromwellian, to whom his estate had been granted.

MacBRYDE, Robert (1913–1966), painter of still-life and figure subjects. See under COLQUHOUN, ROBERT.

MACCABE, Cathaoir (d. 1740), Irish poet and harper; name written MacCaba in Irish; friend of the poet *O'Carolan.

M'CABE, Edward (1816–1885), cardinal and Roman Catholic archbishop of Dublin; educated at Maynooth; ordained, 1839; bishop of Gadara as assistant to Cardinal *Cullen, 1877; archbishop of Dublin, 1879; created cardinal, 1882; denounced agrarian agitation.

McCABE, Joseph Martin (1867–1955), rationalist; educated at Roman Catholic Elementary School, Gorton, Manchester; solemnly professed as Franciscan at 21; ordained priest, 1890; left order and Church, 1896; publications include *Twelve Years in a Monastery* and *Modern Rationalism* (1897); a founder of Rationalist Press Association, 1899; lecturer, journalist, and author in rationalist cause.

MACCABE, William Bernard (1801–1891), author and historian; connected with the Irish press from 1823; became member of the staff of the London *Morning Chronicle*, 1833; published *A Catholic History of England* (3 vols., closing with the Norman Conquest, 1847–54); wrote historical romances; edited Dublin *Telegraph*, 1852.

M'CABE, William Putnam (1776?–1821), United Irishman; went about Ireland as an organizer; joined French invaders, and on their capitulation escaped to Wales; assumed name of Lee (his real name having been inserted in the Irish Banishment Act), and started cotton mill near Rouen; encouraged by Napoleon; visited England and Ireland on business, and is said to have had hairbreadth escapes from arrest.

MACCAGHWELL, Hugh (1571–1626), sometimes known as Aodh mac aingil, Roman Catholic archbishop of Armagh; went to Salamanca, where he was famous as a reader in theology; taught at the Irish Franciscan College of St Anthony of Padua at Louvain, 1616; reader in theology at the convent of Ara Coeli, Rome, 1623; consecrated archbishop of Armagh at Rome, 1626; died just as he was prepared to go to Ireland; published Latin theological works.

MACCALL, William (1812–1888), author; MA, Glasgow, 1833; joined the Unitarian ministry; wrote for the press and published works of individualist ethics.

MacCALLUM, Andrew (1821–1902), landscape painter; apprenticed to Nottingham hosiery business; studied art at Nottingham; art teacher in Manchester and Stourbridge, 1850–4; exhibited at Royal Academy, 1850–86; went to Italy, 1854; painted landscapes in Windsor Forest, in Switzerland, Germany, Italy, Paris, and Egypt; lectured on art; work represented in Tate Gallery, Victoria and Albert Museum, and in Nottingham Art Gallery.

McCALLUM, Ronald Buchanan (1898–1973), historian and master of Pembroke College, Oxford; educated at Paisley Grammar School and Trinity College, Glenalmond; served in Labour Corps of BEF in France, 1917–19; read modern history at Worcester College, Oxford; first class, 1922; fellow and tutor in history, Pembroke College, Oxford, 1925; senior proctor, 1942–3; master of Pembroke, 1955–67; pro-vice-chancellor, 1961; university member of Oxford City Council, 1958–67; played part in creation of Nuffield College; senior treasurer of the Union; edited the *Oxford Magazine*; under his mastership Pembroke expanded and developed; lifelong Liberal; publications include a life of Asquith (1936), *The Liberal Party from Earl Grey to Asquith* (1963), *Public Opinion and the Last Peace* (1944) and *The British General Election of 1945* (in collaboration with Alison Readman, 1947); principal of St Catharine's, Cumberland Lodge, Windsor Great Park, 1967–71; hon. fellow, Pembroke, 1968 and Worcester, 1961; hon. LL D, Dundee, 1967.

McCALMONT, Harry Leslie Blundell (1861–1902), sportsman; joined army, 1881; inherited some £4 million, 1894; won £57,455 with horse Isinglass, which won the Two Thousand Guineas, Derby, and St Leger in 1893, and was sire of Cherry Lass and Glass Doll, winners of the Oaks, 1905 and 1907; Conservative MP for Newmarket, 1895–1902; CB for services in South African War.

McCANCE, Sir Andrew (1889–1983), industrialist and scientist; educated at Morrison's Academy, Crieff, and Allan Glen's School, Glasgow; graduated in mining at Royal School of Mines, London, 1910; joined W. Beardmore & Co., Glasgow; D.Sc., London, 1916; started Clyde Alloy Steel Company, Motherwell, 1919; general manager, Clyde Alloy and Colvilles Ltd., 1930; succeeded (Sir) John *Craig as chairman, 1956–65; introduced number of innovations to Ravenscraig complex; published scientific papers on steel processes; FRS, 1943; knighted, 1947; president, West of Scotland Iron and Steel Institute, 1933–7; chairman, Royal Technical College (which later became Strathclyde University), 1950; hon. D.Sc., 1965; president, Institute of Engineers and Shipbuilders in Scotland, 1951–2; president, British Iron and Steel Federation, 1957 and 1958; received number of other academic honours.

McCARDIE, Sir Henry Alfred (1869–1933), judge; called to bar (Middle Temple), 1894; joined Midland circuit; judge of King's Bench division, 1916–33; remarkable for the learning, careful phraseology, and prolixity of his judgements; convinced that a judge should consider social problems; criticized for his comments thereon; his removal sought after he recorded his opinion that action of R. E. H. *Dyer in Amritsar was right; cases included the trials for murder (1922) of Henry Jacoby and Ronald True; committed suicide.

McCARRISON, Sir Robert (1878–1960), medical scientist; first-class honours, medicine, Queen's College, Belfast, 1900; entered Indian Medical Service, 1901; served in Chitral, 1902–4, Gilgit, 1904–11; assigned to special study of goitre, 1913, and of deficiency diseases, 1918; on active service, 1914–18; first director, Nutrition Research Laboratories, Coonor, 1929–35, having persisted in research despite official discouragement; combined laboratory and field-work; retired as major-general, 1935, and settled in Oxford; deputy regional adviser, Emergency Medical Service, 1939–45; first director, postgraduate medical education, 1945–55; FRCP, 1914; CIE, 1923; knighted, 1933; hon. LL D, Belfast, 1919.

MACCARTAIN, William (*fl.* 1703), Irish poet; Roman Catholic and royalist; wrote a poetical address to Sir James FitzEdmond Cotter, the real murderer of John *Lisle; author of Irish poems.

M'CARTHY, Sir Charles (1764–1824), governor of Sierra Leone; served in the West Indies with the Irish brigade, 1794–6; lieutenant-colonel, Royal African Corps, 1811; governor of Sierra Leone, 1812–24; knighted, 1820; mortally wounded in a battle with the Ashantis.

MacCARTHY, Sir (Charles Otto) Desmond (1877–1952), literary and dramatic critic; educated at Eton and Trinity College, Cambridge; an 'Apostle' with talent for criticism and conversation; became literary journalist; covered Vedrenne–Barker seasons at Royal Court Theatre for *Speaker* published as *The Court Theatre 1904–1907* (1907); edited *New Quarterly*, 1907–10; on staff of *New Statesman*, 1913–28, as dramatic critic and literary editor (1920–7), reviewing as 'Affable Hawk'; senior literary critic, *Sunday Times*, 1928–52; editor, *Life and Letters*, 1928–33; seven volumes of collected writings published in lifetime, including *Portraits* (1931) and *Shaw* (1951); reviewed from background of wide reading and knowledge; knighted, 1951; president, PEN in England, 1945; hon. LL D, Aberdeen, 1932.

MACCARTHY, Cormac Laidhir Oge (d. 1536), Irish chieftain and lord of Muskerry.

MACCARTHY, Denis Florence (1817–1882), poet; a descendant of the Irish sept of Maccauras; espoused the repeal movement and contributed political verse to the *Nation*; published admirable translations of Calderón's plays (1848–73), *Ballads, Poems, and Lyrics* (1850), and *The Bell-founder*, and *Under-glimpses* (1857).

MACCARTHY (or MACCARTY), Donough, fourth earl of Clancarty (1668–1734), sent by his mother, his guardian after his father's death, to Christ Church, Oxford, 1676; decoyed to

London by his uncle, Justin *MacCarthy, titular Viscount Mountcashel; married at the age of 16; became a Roman Catholic, 1685; espoused James II's cause in Ireland; member of the Irish House of Lords, 1689; made prisoner at the capitulation of Cork, 1690; escaped from the Tower of London, 1694; went to St Germains; arrested in London, and committed to Newgate, 1698; pardoned; resided on an island in the Elbe, near Altona; died at Praals-Hoff.

McCARTHY, Dame (Emma) Maud (1858–1949), army matron-in-chief; born in Sydney; trained at London Hospital; served in South Africa, 1899–1902; in Queen Alexandra's Imperial Military Nursing Service, 1902–10; principal matron at War Office, 1910–14; matron-in-chief, British Armies in France, 1914–19, Territorial Army Nursing Service, 1920–5; GBE, 1918.

MACCARTHY, John George (1829–1892), Irish land commissioner and author; MP, Mallow, 1874–80; one of the two commissioners for carrying out the Land Purchase Act, 1885; published legal pamphlets and works dealing with Irish questions.

MACCARTHY, Justin, titular Viscount Mountcashel (d. 1694), uncle of Donough *MacCarthy, fourth earl of Clancarty; served under *Tyrconnel in Ireland, 1687; took Bandon, disarmed the Protestants in Cork, and was created Viscount Mountcashel by James II, 1689; taken prisoner at the Battle of Newtown Butler, 1689; escaped to France though on parole; commanded with distinction the Irish regiments sent to France at the demand of Louis XIV; died at Barèges.

M'CARTHY, Justin (1830–1912), Irish politician, historian, and novelist; leader-writer on *Daily News*, 1871; MP, County Longford, 1879, Derry City, 1886, North Longford, 1892–1900; chairman of anti-Parnellite Nationalist party, 1890–6; wrote *History of Our Own Times* (1877), *Dear Lady Disdain* (1875), *Miss Misanthrope* (1878), etc.

McCARTHY, Lillah (1875–1960), actress; studied elocution (with Hermann *Vezin), and voice production; acted with Wilson *Barrett, 1896–1904; at Court Theatre 1905–6 in plays by G. B. *Shaw who 'blessed the day' when he found her; married Harley *Granville-Barker, 1906; played title-role in *Masefield's *Nan*, Lady Sybil in *Barrie's *What Every Woman Knows* (1908), and Margaret Knox in *Fanny's First Play* (1911); with husband made historic Shakespearian productions at Savoy, 1912–14; played Lavinia in *Androcles and the Lion* (1913); divorced husband, 1918; married (Sir) Frederick *Keeble,

1920; published autobiography, *Myself and My Friends* (1933).

MACCARTHY, Nicholas Tuite, called the Abbé de Lévignac (1769–1833), Jesuit preacher; born in Dublin; taken to Toulouse, 1773; studied at Paris and received the tonsure; ordained, 1814; joined Jesuits, 1820; one of the most eloquent of French preachers; died at Annécy.

MACCARTHY, Robert, Viscount Muskerry and titular earl of Clancarty (d. 1769), son of Donough *MacCarthy, fourth earl of Clancarty; entered the navy; governor of Newfoundland, 1733–5; unsuccessfully attempted to recover the family estates (forfeited by his father's attainder); left the navy; went over to France and devoted himself to the Stuart cause, 1741; excluded from the Act of Indemnity, 1747; died at Boulogne.

MACCARTHY REAGH, Florence (Fineen) (1562?–1640?), Irish chieftain; served on the side of the crown during *Desmond's rebellion; suspected of intriguing with Spain, and committed to the Tower, 1589; liberated, 1591; returned to Ireland, 1593; again charged with disloyalty and plotting, arrested, sent to England and imprisoned, 1601–14, 1617–19, and 1624–6; wrote during his imprisonment a treatise on the history of Ireland in prehistoric times (published, 1858).

MACCARTNEY (or MACARTNEY), George (1660?–1730), general; accompanied his regiment to Flanders, 1706, and afterwards to Spain, commanding a brigade at Almanza, 1707; distinguished himself at Malplaquet, 1709; major-general and acting engineer at the siege of Douai, 1710; dismissed from his appointments on *Marlborough's fall; second to Charles *Mohun, fifth baron, in his duel with James *Douglas, fourth duke of Hamilton; accused of giving the murderous thrust which caused the duke's death, 1712; escaped to Holland; surrendered and arraigned for murder, and found guilty as an accessory, 1716; immediately restored to his military rank and promoted lieutenant-general.

MACCARWELL (or MACCERBHAILL), David (d. 1289), archbishop of Cashel; dean of Cashel; elected archbishop, 1253; involved in disputes with the crown, 1266–81; founded the Cistercian abbey of the Rock of Cashel, c.1270.

M'CAUL, Alexander (1799–1863), divine; BA, Trinity College, Dublin, 1819; MA, 1831; DD, 1837; missionary in Poland under the London Society for promoting Christianity among the Jews, 1821–32; settled in London; published *Old Paths*, a weekly pamphlet on Jewish ritual, 1837–8; principal of the Hebrew College, 1840; professor of Hebrew and rabbinical literature at

King's College, London, 1841, and of divinity also, 1846; prebendary of St Paul's, 1845; published a *Hebrew Primer* (1844) and religious works.

McCAUSLAND, Dominick (1806–1873), religious writer; BA, Trinity College, Dublin; called to the Irish bar, 1835; LL D, 1859; QC, 1860; published religious works, the most popular being *Sermons in Stones* (1856).

McCHEYNE, Robert Murray (1813–1843), Scottish divine; educated at Edinburgh University; licensed as a preacher, 1835; a member of the committee sent to Palestine by the Church of Scotland to collect information about the Jews, 1839; published (jointly with Dr Andrew *Bonar) *Narrative of a Mission of Inquiry to the Jews* (1842); a fine preacher; several of his hymns constantly used in the Scottish churches.

McCLEAN, Frank (1837–1904), civil engineer and amateur astronomer; BA, Trinity College, Cambridge (27th wrangler), 1859; partner in father's engineering firm, 1862–70; built private observatory near Tunbridge Wells; designed a star spectroscope; published results of systematic survey of spectra of stars brighter than magnitude $3\frac{1}{2}$, 1898; FRAS, 1877; hon. LL D, Glasgow, 1894; FRS, 1895; bequeathed large sums of money to Cambridge and Birmingham universities for physical research.

MACCLESFIELD, earls of. See GERARD, CHARLES, first earl, d. 1694; GERARD, CHARLES, second earl, 1659?–1701; PARKER, THOMAS, first earl of the second creation, 1666?–1732; PARKER, GEORGE, second earl, 1697–1764.

McCLINTOCK, Sir Francis Leopold (1819–1907), admiral; entered navy, 1831; served under Sir James Clark *Ross, 1848, Sir Erasmus *Ommanney, 1850, and Sir Edward *Belcher, 1852, in Arctic voyages; commanded expedition in search of Sir John *Franklin, 1857–9; published account of his voyage and fate of Franklin and his companions, 1859; knighted, 1860; commodore in charge at Jamaica, 1865–8; admiral superintendent of Portsmouth Dockyard, 1872–7; vice-admiral, 1877; admiral, 1884; KCB, 1891.

McCLUER, John (d. 1794?), commander in the Bombay Marine and hydrographer; surveyed Persian Gulf, the bank of soundings off Bombay, the Pelew Islands, the Sulu Archipelago, and part of the New Guinea coast, 1785–93; settled in the Pelew Islands, 1793; sailed for China, taken ill at Macao, eventually sailed for Calcutta, and was never again heard of.

McCLURE, Sir John David (1860–1922), schoolmaster; BA, London and Trinity College,

Cambridge; professor of astronomy, Queen's College, London, 1889–94; headmaster, Mill Hill School, 1891–1922; raised it from being comparatively unknown Nonconformist school of sixty boys to status of successful public school with over three hundred boys; knighted, 1913; contributed to educational, musical, and religious life of his time.

McCLURE, Sir Robert John le Mesurier (1807–1873), vice-admiral; educated at Eton and Sandhurst; entered navy, 1824; made an Arctic voyage, 1836–7; lieutenant, 1837; served in Canada, 1838–9, the West Indies, 1839–48; commander in the search for Sir John *Franklin, 1850–4; discovered the north-west passage, but had to abandon his ship, 1854; court-martialled and honourably acquitted; knighted and made captain; served in China and the Straits of Malacca, 1856–61; CB, 1859; vice-admiral on the retired list, 1873.

McCOAN, James Carlile (1829–1904), author and journalist; called to bar, 1856; practised in supreme consular court at Constantinople till 1864; published *Egypt as it is* (1877) and *Egypt under Ismail* (1889); wrote sympathetically of the Turks in *Turkey in Asia* (2 vols., 1879); Protestant home ruler MP for Wicklow County, 1880–5.

MACCODRUM, John (d. 1779), Gaelic poet; last bard of the Macdonalds; his satirical and political verses, the most popular being 'Old Age' and 'Whisky', never collected.

MACCOISSE, Erard (or **Urard**) (d. 1023), Irish chronicler; poet to *Maelsechlainn or Malachy II (949–1022); five poems and one prose composition in Irish, partly historical, attributed to him; sometimes confused with another MacCoisse, who wrote a poem preserved in the *Book of Leinster*.

MacCOLL, Dugald Sutherland (1859–1948), painter, critic, and art-gallery director; educated at Glasgow Academy, University College School, University College, London, and Lincoln College, Oxford; studied art under Frederick *Brown; exhibited regularly at New English Art Club; art critic successively on *Spectator*, *Saturday Review*, and *Week-end Review*; editor, *Architectural Review*, 1901–5; keeper, Tate Gallery, 1906–11, Wallace Collection, 1911–24; energetic administrator and controversialist; publications include *Nineteenth Century Art* (1902) and biography of P. Wilson *Steer (1945).

MacCOLL, Malcolm (1831–1907), high-church divine and author; ordained, 1856; attracted notice of Gladstone, who presented him to City living of St George's, Botolph Lane, 1871–91, and to canonry of Ripon, 1884; took frequent part in ecclesiastical and political controversies; supported Gladstone's Irish Church and home-rule policies; visited Eastern Europe with Canon *Liddon, 1876, and denounced Bulgarian atrocities; hon. DD, Edinburgh, 1899.

MacCOLL, Norman (1843–1904), editor of the *Athenaeum* and Spanish scholar; BA, Downing College, Cambridge, 1866; MA, 1869; fellow, 1869; called to bar, 1875; editor of *Athenaeum*, 1871–1900; published *Select Plays of Calderon* (1888), and translations of Cervantes' *Exemplary Novels* (2 vols., 1902), and of his *Miscellaneous Poems* (posthumous, 1912); endowed MacColl lectureship in Spanish and Portuguese at Cambridge.

McCOMB, William (1793–1873), poet; bookseller in Belfast, 1828–64; established *McComb's Presbyterian Almanac*, 1840; his *Poetical Works* collected (1864).

McCOMBIE, William (1805–1880), cattle-breeder; educated at Aberdeen University; reformed cattle-breeding, and was one of the largest farmers in Aberdeenshire; MP, West Aberdeen, 1868–76; published *Cattle and Cattle-Breeders* (1867).

McCOMBIE, William (1809–1870), journalist; began to write while a farm labourer, 1835; joined *North of Scotland Gazette*, 1849; edited *Aberdeen Daily Free Press*, 1853–70; published miscellaneous works, 1838–69.

MACCONMIDHE, Gillabrighde (*fl.* 1260), historian and poet; hereditary poet to the O'Neills; his chief work a lament on the death of Brian O'Neill (first printed with an English translation, 1849). Other literary members of the family lived between 1420 and 1583.

McCONNELL, William (1833–1867), humorous-book illustrator.

MACCORMAC, Henry (1800–1886), physician; studied at Dublin, Paris, and Edinburgh; MD, Edinburgh, 1824; in charge of the Belfast hospitals during the cholera, 1832; retired from practice, 1866; author of medical works, many of which advocate the fresh-air treatment of consumption.

MacCORMAC, Sir William, first baronet (1836–1901), surgeon; BA, Queen's University, Belfast, 1855; MA, 1858; MD, 1857; hon. M.Ch., 1879; D.Sc., 1882; hon. MD and M.Ch., Dublin, 1900; studied surgery in Berlin; MRCS, 1857; FRCS Ireland, 1864; volunteered for surgical service in Franco-German War, 1870; lecturer on surgery at St Thomas's Hospital, 1873–93; chief surgeon to National Aid Society in Turco-Serbian War; knighted for services as secretary to Seventh International Medical Congress, 1881; baronet, 1897; KCVO, 1898; pres-

ident of the Royal College of Surgeons, 1896–1900; government consulting surgeon to the Field Force in South African War, 1899–1900; KCB, 1901; publications include account of his work at Sedan (1870) and *Surgical Operations* (1885–9).

McCORMICK, Charles (1755?–1807), historian and biographer; educated at St Mary Hall, Oxford; BCL, 1794; abandoned law for literature; continued *Hume and *Smollett's histories to 1783, and wrote a *Memoir of Edmund Burke*, famous for its party virulence (1797).

MACCORMICK, Joseph (1733–1799), Scottish divine; MA, St Andrews University, 1750; ordained, 1758; DD, 1760; edited the *State Papers and Letters addressed to William Carstares, to which is prefixed the Life of William Carstares* (1774); moderator to the general assembly, 1782; principal of the United College of St Andrews, 1783; dean of the Chapel Royal, London, 1788.

McCORMICK, Robert (1800–1890), naval surgeon, explorer and naturalist; entered the navy as assistant-surgeon, 1823; served on various stations; accompanied the Antarctic expedition commanded by Captain Sir James Clark *Ross, 1839–43; conducted a search for Sir John *Franklin, 1852; published *Narrative of a Boat Expedition up the Wellington Channel* (1854); deputy-inspector of hospitals, 1859; published *Voyages of Discovery in the Arctic and Antarctic Seas and round the World* (2 vols., 1884).

McCORMICK, William Patrick Glyn (1877–1940), vicar of St Martin-in-the-Fields, London; educated at St John's College, Cambridge; deacon, 1900; priest, 1901; vicar in Cleveland (1903–10), Belgravia, Johannesburg (1910–14); of Croydon (1919–27), St Martin-in-the-Fields (1927–40); army chaplain, 1914–19; DSO, 1917.

McCORMICK, Sir William Symington (1859–1930), scholar and administrator; grandson of Revd William *Symington; MA, Glasgow University; professor of English literature, University College, Dundee, 1890; first secretary of Carnegie Trust for Universities of Scotland, 1901; connected with every important government step to aid university education from 1906 onwards; chairman of Advisory Council for Scientific and Industrial Research, 1915; of Treasury University Grants Committee, 1919; knighted, 1911; FRS, 1928; died at sea; works include *The MSS. of Chaucer's Canterbury Tales* (posthumous, 1933).

McCOSH, James (1811–1894), philosopher; educated at Glasgow and Edinburgh; MA, Edinburgh, 1834; licensed by Presbytery of Ayrshire; officiated at Arbroath, 1835–8, and Brechin,

1838–50; adopted 'free-kirk' principles; published *Method of the Divine Government* (1850); professor of logic at Queen's College, Belfast, 1851–68; president of Princeton College, New Jersey, 1868–88, and professor of philosophy, 1868, till death; LL D, Aberdeen, 1850, and Harvard, 1868; D.Lit., Royal University of Ireland, and DD. His publications include *Intuitions of the Mind inductively investigated* (1860), *Laws of Discursive Thought* (1870), *Scottish Philosophy* (1874), and *Psychology* (1886–7).

McCOY, Sir **Frederick** (1823–1899), naturalist and geologist; studied medicine at Dublin; employed by Sir Richard John *Griffith to make palaeontological investigations required for the *Geological Map of Ireland*; professor of mineralogy and geology, Queen's College, Belfast, 1850; of natural science in new University of Melbourne, 1854; founded National Museum of Natural History and Geology, Melbourne; FGS, 1852; FRS, 1880; hon. D.Sc., Cambridge, 1887; KCMG, 1891. He arranged and issued (1854) description of fossils in Woodwardian Museum, Cambridge, and published zoological and palaeontological works.

McCRACKEN, Henry Joy (1767–1798), United Irishman; helped to form the first society of United Irishmen in Belfast, 1791; commanded the rebels in Co. Antrim, 1798; tried and executed.

MACCREERY, John (1768–1832), printer and poet; wrote and printed in Liverpool *The Press: a poem published as a specimen of Typography* (1803), second part published in London, 1827); removed to London, where he printed the *Bibliomania* for *Dibdin; died in Paris.

McCREERY, Sir **Richard Loudon** (1898–1967), general; educated at Eton and Sandhurst; commissioned in 12th Royal Lancers, 1915; served in France, 1915–18; MC; fine horseman; attended Staff College, 1928; brigade-major, cavalry brigade; commanded 12th Lancers, 1935–8; colonel, 1938; commanded 2nd Armoured Brigade; DSO, 1940; major-general; commanded armoured division in England, 1940–2; chief of staff to General *Alexander (later Earl Alexander of Tunis), Cairo, 1942; lieutenant-general; commanded X corps, 1943; CB, KCB, 1943; commanded Eighth Army, 1944–5; commanded British Forces of Occupation, Austria, 1945–6; KBE, 1945; full general, 1946; commanded British Army of the Rhine, 1946–8; British Army representative, UN Military Staff Committee, 1948–9; GCB, 1949; colonel commandant, RAC, 1947–56.

McCRIE, Thomas, the elder (1772–1835), Scottish seceding divine and ecclesiastical historian; entered Edinburgh University, 1788; ordained, 1796; ejected from his pastorate, 1809; published his *Life of John Knox* (1812), a work of genius and erudition; DD, 1813; professor of divinity, Edinburgh, 1816–18; published a history of the Reformation in Italy (1827), in Spain (1829), and other biographical and historical works.

McCRIE, Thomas, the younger (1797–1875), Scottish divine and author; son of Thomas *McCrie the elder; educated at Edinburgh University; ordained, 1820; DD, Aberdeen, and LL D, Glasgow before 1850; professor of church history and systematic theology at the London College of the English Presbyterian Church, 1856–66; published historical and religious works, 1840–72.

MACCUAIRT, James (*fl.* 1712), Irish poet; became blind early; composed Irish poems and songs.

McCUDDEN, James Thomas Byford (1895–1918), airman; joined Royal Flying Corps, 1913; went to France as air mechanic, 1914; learned to fly, 1916; became leading British fighting pilot; brought down fifty-four enemy aeroplanes; MC and DSO, 1917; VC, 1918; killed flying in France.

McCULLAGH, James (1809–1847), mathematician; educated at Trinity College, Dublin; professor of mathematics, Dublin University, 1836; secretary of council to the Royal Irish Academy, 1840–2, and secretary to the Academy, 1842–6; professor of natural philosophy, 1843; FRS, 1843; committed suicide. The most important of his scanty remains is the memoir on surfaces of the second order, read to the Royal Irish Academy, 1843.

MACCULLOCH, Horatio (1805–1867), landscape painter; pupil of William Home *Lizars; associate of the Scottish Academy, 1834; academician, 1838; the most popular landscape painter of his day in Scotland; exhibited only once at Royal Academy, London, 1844.

McCULLOCH, Sir **James** (1819–1893), Australian politician; opened a branch of Messrs Dennistoun & Co.'s business in Melbourne, 1853; nominee member of the Victoria Chamber, 1854; member of the first elective legislative assembly, 1857; formed a government, of which he held the portfolio of trades and customs, 1857; resigned, and was elected member for East Melbourne, 1858; treasurer, 1859–60; member for Mornington, 1862; premier, 1863–8, 1868–9, 1870–1, 1875–7; knighted, 1869; agent-general in London, 1872–3; KCMG, 1874; settled finally in England, 1877.

MACCULLOCH, John (1773–1835), geologist; studied medicine at Edinburgh; MD, 1793; chemist to the Board of Ordnance, 1803; LRCP, 1808; gave up practice as a physician, 1811; geologist to the Trigonometrical Survey, 1814; president of the Geological Society, 1816–17; FRS, 1820; commissioned to prepare a geological map of Scotland (published shortly after his death), 1826; chief works, *A Description of the Western Isles of Scotland, including the Isle of Man*, still a classic in geology (1819), *A Geological Classification of Rocks* (1821), and *Highlands and Western Isles of Scotland* (1824).

McCULLOCH, John Ramsay (1789–1864), statistician and political economist; educated at Edinburgh University; devoted himself to the study of economics and wrote the articles on that subject for the *Scotsman*, 1817–27; edited the *Scotsman*, 1818–20; contributed to the *Edinburgh Review*, 1818–37; delivered the Ricardo memorial lectures in London, 1824; published *Principles of Political Economy* (1825); professor of political economy, London University, 1828–37; expounded the celebrated 'wages' fund theory in an *Essay on the Circumstances which determine the Rate of Wages and the Condition of the Labouring Classes* (1826); published *A Dictionary, Practical, Theoretical, and Historical, of Commerce and Commercial Navigation* (1832), and a number of statistical and economical works between 1841 and 1860; comptroller of the Stationery Office, 1838–64.

McCULLOCH, William (1816–1885), resident at Manipur; son of John Ramsay *McCulloch; entered the army, 1834; employed in India, 1835–67; political agent at Manipur, 1845–63, and 1864–7; retired from the army as lieutenant-colonel, 1861; published *Account of the Valley of [Manipur or] Munnipore and the Hill Tribes* (1859).

MacCUNN, Hamish (James) (1868–1916), musical composer; studied at Royal College of Music; orchestral and choral works include *Land of the Mountain and Flood* (1887), *Ship o' the Fiend*, *Dowie Dens o' Yarrow*, *Lord Ullin's Daughter*, *Lay of the Last Minstrel*, and *Bonny Kilmeny* (all 1888); composed operas.

MACCURTIN (in Irish **MacCRUITIN**), **Andrew** (d. 1749), Irish poet; hereditary *ollamh* to the O'Briens; two of his poems, one in praise of Sorley MacDonnell (written, *c.*1720), the other an address to a fairy chief, still remembered in Clare.

MACCURTIN, Hugh (1680?–1755), Irish antiquary; succeeded his cousin, Andrew *MacCurtin, as *ollamh* to the O'Briens; studied in France; tutor for seven years to the dauphin; returned to Ireland, 1714; works include *The Elements of the Irish Language* (1728) and an *English–Irish Dictionary*, a valuable record of the vernacular of its day (1732).

MacDERMOT, Hugh Hyacinth O'Rorke, the MacDermot (1834–1904), attorney-general for Ireland; called to bar (King's Inns, Dublin), 1862; bencher, 1884; counsel in leading political cases in Ireland; succeeded father as titular 'Prince of Coolavin', 1873; Liberal solicitor-general for Ireland, May–July 1885 and Feb.–Aug. 1886; attorney-general and PC, 1892–5.

MACDERMOTT, Gilbert Hastings (1845–1901), music-hall singer, whose real surname was Farrell; made some position as an actor and writer of melodramas, which included *Driven from Home*, 1871; leaped into fame (1878) by singing on music-hall stage the patriotic song by George William Hunt (1829?–1904), 'We don't want to fight', which became popular watchword of war-party in England during Russo-Turkish War and gave the political terms 'jingo' and 'jingoism' to the English language; last 'lion comique' of English music-hall.

MacDERMOTT, John Clarke, Baron Macdermot (1896–1979), lord chief justice, Northern Ireland; educated at Campbell College, Belfast and Queen's University of which he was a scholar, 1914; served in Machine Gun battalion (51st Highland division) in France; MC, 1918; graduated LL B (with first class and the Dunbar Barton Prize), 1921; first-class honours in bar final at King's Inns, Dublin; called to bar in both Dublin and Belfast; busy practice; also lecturer in jurisprudence at Queen's University, 1931–5; KC, 1936; Unionist MP in Northern Ireland Parliament, 1938; major, RA, 1939; minister of public security, 1940; PC (NI), 1941; attorney-general, 1941; High Court judge, 1944; PC and first lord of appeal appointed from Northern Ireland, 1947; life peer, 1947; lord chief justice, 1951–71; hon. bencher, Gray's Inn, 1947; hon. bencher, King's Inn and hon. LL D, Queen's University, Edinburgh, and Cambridge; chairman of number of important committees; governor of Campbell College, 1934–59; pro-chancellor, Queen's University, 1951–69; unfinished autobiography, *An Enriching Life*, privately published (1980).

MacDERMOTT, Martin (1823–1905), Irish poet and architect; wrote occasional verse for *Nation* from 1840; delegate to Paris to obtain French republican support for Young Ireland movement, 1848; chief architect to Egyptian government in Alexandria from 1866; retired to London, 1878; prepared anthology of Irish poetry, 1894.

MacDIARMID, Hugh (pseudonym) (1892–1978), poet and prose writer. See GRIEVE, CHRISTOPHER MURRAY.

MACDIARMID, John (1779–1808), journalist and author; studied at Edinburgh and St Andrews universities; settled in London, 1801; edited the *St. James's Chronicle*; author of two works on military topics, published in 1805 and 1806.

M'DIARMID, John (1790–1852), Scottish journalist; editor of the *Dumfries and Galloway Courier*, 1817; published his *Scrap-Book* (1820); started the *Dumfries Magazine*, 1825; became owner of the *Courier*, 1837; edited, with memoirs, *Cowper's Poems (1817) and *Goldsmith's *Vicar of Wakefield* (1823).

MACDONALD, Alexander, third lord of the Isles and tenth earl of Ross (d. 1449), eldest son of Donald *Macdonald, second lord of the Isles; imprisoned as a rebel, 1427–9; destroyed Inverness, but was eventually defeated by *James I of Scotland and again imprisoned, 1429; later gave loyal obedience to the king; justiciar of Scotland north of the Forth, 1438.

MACDONALD (or MACDONNELL), Alexander (or Alaster) (d. 1647), general; joined the insurgents, 1641; with *Montrose in Scotland, 1644–5; being defeated, escaped to Ireland, 1647; killed by treachery.

MACDONALD, Alexander (or MACIAN OF GLENCOE) (d. 1692), chief of his clan; joined *Claverhouse, 1689; took part in the rising of the northern Highlands; bidden to take the oath of allegiance within a stipulated time; when that period had almost elapsed, made a vain effort to find a magistrate to administer the oath; finally persuaded Sir Colin Campbell to administer the oath five days later; his tardy action ignored and the clan destroyed in their home in the valley of Glencoe, 1692. An inquiry was made, but, although the massacre of Glencoe was condemned, none of the agents were brought to justice.

MACDONALD, Alexander (or ALESTAIR OF GLENGARRY) (d. 1724), Jacobite. See MACDONELL.

MACDONALD, Alexander (or ALASDAIR MacMHAIGHSTIR ALASDAIR) (1700?–1780?), Gaelic poet; educated at Glasgow University; assisted the Society for Propagating Christian Knowledge in the Highlands; published an *English and Gaelic Vocabulary* (1741); became a Roman Catholic and joined the Chevalier (see JAMES FRANCIS EDWARD STUART), 1745; became the 'sacer vates' of the rebellion of 1745; served through the campaign, 1745–6; his collected poems, a fine contribution to martial literature, published as *Ais-eiridh na Sean Chanoin Albannaich* (1751).

MACDONALD, Alexander (1736–1791), Scottish Catholic prelate; entered the Scots College, Rome, 1754; ordained, 1764; joined the mission in Scotland and was stationed at Barra, 1765–80; vicar-apostolic of the Highland district, 1780.

MACDONALD, Alexander (1755–1837), Gaelic scholar; educated at the Roman Catholic seminary of Bourblach and at the Scots College, Rome; ordained, 1778; returned to Scotland, 1782; published *Phingateis, sive Hibernia Liberata* (1820); contributed to the Gaelic dictionary published under the direction of the Highland Society of Scotland (1828).

MACDONALD, Alexander (1791?–1850), Scottish antiquary; employed in the Register House, Edinburgh; principal keeper of the register of deeds and probate writs, 1836; supplied notes for the *Waverley Novels*; editor of the Maitland Club publications.

MACDONALD, Andrew (1755?–1790), dramatist and verse-writer; educated at Edinburgh University; ordained to the Scottish Episcopal Church, 1775; resigned his charge and came to London; his most successful tragedy, *Vimonda*, produced 1787 (published 1788). His *Miscellaneous Works* appeared (1791).

MACDONALD, Angus (1834–1886), medical writer; MD, Edinburgh, 1864; practised and lectured in Edinburgh; published medical works.

MACDONALD, Archibald (1736–1814), author; a Benedictine monk and Roman Catholic pastor; published defence of the authenticity of *Macpherson's *Ossian* (1805).

MACDONALD, Sir Archibald, first baronet (1747–1826), judge; lineal descendant of the old lords of the Isles; student of Christ Church, Oxford, 1764; BA, 1768; barrister, Lincoln's Inn, 1770; MA, 1772; KC, 1778; MP, Hindon, 1777, Newcastle-under-Lyme, 1780–93; solicitor-general, 1784–8; knighted, 1788; attorney-general, 1788–92; lord chief baron of the Exchequer, 1793–1813; privy councillor, 1793; created baronet, 1813.

MACDONALD, Sir Claude Maxwell (1852–1915), soldier and diplomat; joined army, 1872; minister at Peking, 1896; organized defence of legations during Boxer Rising, 1900; minister at Tokyo, 1900; ambassador, 1905–12; promoted Anglo-Japanese friendship; KCB, 1898; military KCB, 1901; PC, 1906.

MACDONALD, Donald, second lord of the Isles and ninth earl of Ross (d. 1420?), eldest son of John *Macdonald, first lord of the Isles; made permanent alliance with Henry IV, 1405; claimed the earldom of Ross, but after the Battle of Harlaw (1411) surrendered his claim and became vassal to the Scottish throne, 1412.

MACDONALD, Duncan George Forbes (1823?–1884), agricultural engineer and miscellaneous writer; son of John *Macdonald (1779–1849); published *What Farmers may do with the Land* (1852); member of the Government Survey staff in British North America; published *British Columbia and Vancouver's Island* (1862); drainage engineer of improvements to the enclosure commissioners for England and Wales; engineer-in-chief to the inspector-general of Highland destitution.

MACDONALD, Flora (1722–1790), Jacobite heroine; daughter of Ranald Macdonald, farmer at Milton, South Uist (Hebrides); while in 1746 on a visit to the Clanranalds in Benbecula (Hebrides), met Prince *Charles Edward in flight after Culloden; helped the prince to reach Skye; imprisoned in the Tower of London after Prince Charles Edward's escape; released by the Act of Indemnity, 1747; married Allan Macdonald, 1750; emigrated to North Carolina, 1774; returned to Scotland, 1779.

MacDONALD, George (1824–1905), poet and novelist; MA, King's College, Aberdeen, 1845; hon. LL D, 1868; settled in Manchester, 1853; published narrative poem, *Within and Without* (1855, admired by *Tennyson and Lady Byron), and *Phantastes* (1858), a faerie romance in prose; thenceforth largely engaged in prose fiction— either of mystical character, as *David Elginbrod* (1863), or descriptive of Scottish humble life, as *Alec Forbes* (1865) and *Robert Falconer* (1868); long preached as a layman at Manchester; settled in London for life, 1860; friend of F. D. *Maurice, *Browning, *Ruskin, *Carlyle, William *Morris, and Tennyson; lectured in London and in America, 1872; granted civil list pension, 1877; spent part of each year at Bordighera, 1881–1902; his works include the children's stories *At the Back of the North Wind* (1871) and *The Princess and the Goblin* (1872), and *Unspoken Sermons* (3 vols., 1867–89) and *Letters from Hell* (1884); a collected edition, excluding novels, appeared in 1886 (10 vols.), and his *Poetical Works* (2 vols.) in 1893.

MACDONALD, Sir George (1862–1940), numismatist, classical scholar and archaeologist, and civil servant; first class, Lit. Hum., Balliol College, Oxford, 1887; lecturer in Greek, Glasgow, 1892–1904; assistant secretary, Scottish Education Department (1904), secretary, 1922–8; catalogued Greek and Roman coins in Hunterian collection, Glasgow; authority on Romano-British history; FBA, 1913; KCB, 1927.

MACDONALD, Sir Hector Archibald (1853–1903), major-general; joined army as private in Gordon Highlanders, 1870; served with distinction in Second Afghan War, 1879–80; won sobriquet of 'Fighting Mac'; promoted second lieutenant, 1880; displayed heroism at Battle of Majuba, 1881; shared in Nile expedition (1885), and in reorganization of Egyptian Army; distinguished in Sudan campaign, 1888–91; commanded brigade of Egyptian infantry in expedition to Dongola (1896) and at Atbara (1898); displayed successful adroitness at Omdurman, Sept. 1898; CB, 1897; brigadier-general in Punjab, 1899–1900; major-general, Jan. 1900; in South African War prepared way for relief of Kimberley by seizure of Koodoesberg, Feb. 1900; engaged in actions which led to surrender of generals Cronje and Prinsloo, Feb.–May 1900; KCB, 1900; placed in command of Belgaum district, 1901, and of troops in Ceylon, 1902; owing to opprobrious accusation, he shot himself in Paris.

MACDONALD, Hector Munro (1865–1935), mathematical physicist; educated at Aberdeen University and Clare College, Cambridge; fourth wrangler, 1889; fellow, 1890–1908; made life study of radiation, transmission, and reflection of electric waves; publications include *Electric Waves* (1902) and *Electro-magnetism* (1934); FRS, 1901; professor of mathematics, Aberdeen, 1904–35; member of university court from 1907, especially interested in oversight of university lands and buildings.

MACDONALD, Hugh (1701–1773), Scottish Catholic prelate; ordained, 1725; vicar of the Highland district and bishop of Diana in Numidia, 1731; escaped to Paris after the rebellion of 1745; returned to Scotland, 1749; apprehended, 1755; sentenced to banishment, but sentence not carried out, 1756.

MACDONALD, Hugh (1817–1860), Scottish poet; wrote verses in the *Glasgow Citizen*, joining its staff, 1849; joined the *Glasgow Sentinel*, 1855; edited the *Glasgow Times*; wrote, for those journals, *Rambles round Glasgow* and *Days at the Coast*, afterwards published in book form; literary editor of the *Morning Journal* (Glasgow), 1858–60.

MacDONALD, James Ramsay (1866–1937), labour leader and statesman; born illegitimately at Lossiemouth, Morayshire, of farming stock; educated locally and became pupil teacher;

joined Social Democratic Federation (1885) and Fabian Society (1886); experienced some years of extreme poverty and intensive study in London; defeated as Independent Labour party candidate, Southampton, 1895; earned living by journalism and contributed to this Dictionary; obtained financial independence, opportunity for world-wide travel, and upper middle-class background through marriage (1896) to Margaret Ethel (d. 1911), daughter of John Hall *Gladstone, a distinguished scientist and active social worker; secretary, Labour Representation Committee (later the Labour party) 1900–12; treasurer, 1912–24; MP, Leicester, 1906–18; early showed himself a natural parliamentarian; his books (among them *Socialism and Society*, 1905, and *Socialism*, 1907) marked him also as a theorist; chairman (1906–9) and for long a leading figure in Independent Labour party, in which he implanted his own instinct for moderation; chairman, Parliamentary Labour Group, 1911; unsupported in opposing a war credit and resigned, 5 Aug. 1914; his view that although war must be won Britain had been wrong to embark on it and must preserve a generous temper for sake of future peace widely misunderstood and misrepresented; became greatly mistrusted; heavily defeated at Leicester, 1918; his courage in face of bitter attack gained his party's respect; persuaded both Independent Labour party and Labour party to reject communism, 1920; MP, Aberavon division, 1922–9; became chairman of Parliamentary Labour party and leader of opposition, 1922; PC, first Labour prime minister, and foreign secretary, Jan. 1924; his diplomacy more successful than his domestic policy; defeated over Campbell case, Oct. 1924; sought to avert, but acquiesced in, General Strike, 1926; MP, Seaham division, and prime minister for second time, 1929; chiefly interested in foreign affairs; brought about and presided over London Naval Conference, 1930; presided over Indian Round Table Conference, 1930; tendered resignation of government, 23 Aug. 1931, after failure of Cabinet to agree on reduction in payments to unemployed in face of financial crisis; formed all-party government in conjunction with Conservative and Liberal leaders; breach with his own party became permanent; on winning election, Oct. 1931, formed fourth administration; pressed on with programme of retrenchment and reform; continued to regard European situation key to domestic recovery and believed in personal diplomacy; after rise of Hitler realized necessity of rearmament and drafted White Paper on national defence, 1935; resigned premiership and became lord president of the Council, June 1935; defeated at Seaham, 1935; MP for Scottish Universities, 1936–7.

MACDONALD, Sir **James Ronald Leslie** (1862–1927), major-general; gazetted to Royal Engineers, 1882; attached to military works department, India, 1885–91; chief engineer on preliminary survey for projected Uganda railway; acting commissioner, Uganda protectorate, 1893; largely instrumental in securing its safety from rebels, 1897–9; director of balloons (afterwards of railways) for China Expeditionary Force, 1900; commanded military escort of political mission dispatched to Tibet under (Sir) Francis *Younghusband, 1903–4; major-general, 1908; general officer commanding in Mauritius, 1909–12; KCIE, 1904.

MACDONALD, John, of Isla, first lord of the Isles (d. 1386?), joined Edward de *Baliol, 1335; transferred his allegiance to *David II, 1341; joined Baliol again when the king objected to his assumption of the title of lord of the Isles; persuaded to take an oath of obedience, 1369.

MACDONALD, John, fourth and last lord of the Isles and eleventh earl of Ross (d. 1498?), son of Alexander *Macdonald, third lord of the Isles; rebelled against King *James II of Scotland, but came to terms, and was made one of the wardens of the marches, 1457; one of the ambassadors who helped to bring about the treaty with the English signed at Westminster, 1463; summoned to answer for treasonable acts, and sentence of attainder passed against him, 1475; pardoned, 1476; finally retired to the monastery of Paisley.

MACDONALD, John (1620?–1716?), known in the Highlands as Ian Lom, Gaelic poet and warrior; assisted *Montrose, 1645–50; composed a 'Lament' in his honour, 1650; became absorbed in local politics; pensioned by the government, 1660; present at Killiecrankie, 1689; celebrated the triumph of the Highlanders in his poem, 'Rinrory'.

MACDONALD, John (1727–1779), Scottish Catholic prelate; nephew of Hugh *Macdonald (1701–1773); entered the Scots College, Rome, 1743; ordained, 1752; returned to Scotland, 1753; vicar-apostolic of the Highland district of Scotland, 1773–9.

MACDONALD, John (b. 1741), gentleman's servant; became known as Beau Macdonald; spent some years in Bombay, and travelled in India and Europe with his employers, 1768–78; settled at Toledo, 1778; published *Travels in Various Parts* (1790).

MACDONALD, John (1759–1831), lieutenant-colonel and military engineer; son of Flora *Macdonald; as ensign, Bengal Engineers, surveyed the Dutch settlements in Sumatra, 1783; remained there as military and civil engineer until

1796; employed in England during the French wars; FRS, 1800; author of military and technical engineering works, and of a book on Anglo-Indian administration.

MACDONALD, John (1779–1849), called the 'Apostle of the North'; MA, King's College, Aberdeen, 1801; ordained missionary minister, 1806; visited Ireland, 1824; joined the Secession party, 1843; author of sermons (published 1830) and a volume of Gaelic verse (1848).

MACDONALD, Sir **John** (1782–1830), lieutenant-colonel, traveller, and diplomat. See KINNEIR.

MACDONALD, Sir John (d. 1850), adjutant-general at the Horse Guards; a connection of Flora *Macdonald; entered the army, 1795; served in Ireland and Egypt and on the continent; held important staff appointments during the Peninsular campaign; deputy adjutant-general at the Horse Guards, 1820–30; adjutant-general, 1830–50; GCB, 1847.

MACDONALD, John (1818–1889), Scottish Catholic prelate; at the Scots Seminary, Ratisbon, 1830–7; at the Scots College, Rome, 1837–40; vicar-apostolic of the northern district of Scotland, 1869; bishop of Aberdeen, 1878.

MACDONALD, Sir John Alexander (1815–1891), the organizer of the dominion of Canada; born in Glasgow; settled in Kingston, Canada, 1820; admitted to the bar, 1836; member for Kingston in the House of Assembly, 1844–54; commissioner for crown lands, 1847; attorney-general for Upper Canada, 1854; leader of the House of Assembly, 1856–91; premier, 1857; succeeded, despite strong opposition, in making Ottawa the capital, 1859; led the federation movement, and went to England as a delegate, 1866; mainly responsible for the British North America Act, 1867; KCB, 1867; first prime minister of the Dominion, 1867; one of the commissioners of the Treaty of Washington, 1871; privy councillor of the United Kingdom, 1872; premier and minister of the interior, 1878–91; also president of the council and superintendent of Indian affairs, 1883; GCB, 1884.

McDONALD, John Blake (1829–1901), Scottish artist; painted, largely in chiaroscuro, dramatic episodes of Jacobite romance, and later landscape; ARSA, 1862; RSA, 1877.

MACDONALD, Sir John Denis (1826–1908), inspector-general of hospitals and fleets, 1880–6; joined navy as assistant surgeon, 1849; engaged in microscopic study and deep-sea investigations; FRS, 1859; professor of naval hygiene at Netley, 1872; KCB, 1902; published *Outlines of Naval Hygiene* (1881).

MACDONALD, John Hay Athole, Lord Kingsburgh (1836–1919), lord justice-clerk of Scotland; called to Scottish bar, 1859; solicitor-general for Scotland, 1876–80; QC, 1880; lord advocate, 1885–6, 1886–8; lord justice-clerk and assumed judicial title, 1888; presided over second division of Court of Session, 1888–1915; specialized in criminal law; PC, 1885; KCB, 1900; FRS.

MACDONALD, Lawrence (1799–1878), sculptor; entered the Trustees' Academy, Edinburgh, 1822; went to Rome, and helped to found the British Academy of Arts there, 1823; returned to Edinburgh, 1827; exhibited at the Royal Academy from 1829; member of the Scottish Academy, 1829–58; died at Rome; noted for his portrait busts.

MacDONALD, Malcolm John (1901–1981), politician, diplomat, and writer; son of James Ramsay MacDonald; educated at Bedales and The Queen's College, Oxford; toured United States, Canada, and Australia with Oxford debating team, 1924–5; member of LCC, 1927–30; Labour MP for Bassetlaw division of Nottinghamshire, 1929–35, and Ross and Cromarty, 1936–45; parliamentary under-secretary, Dominions Office, 1931; secretary of state and Cabinet minister, 1935–40; PC 1935; minister of health in Churchill government, 1940; high commissioner to Canada, 1941–6; governor-general, Malaya and Singapore, 1946–8; commissioner-general, South-East Asia, 1948–55; high commissioner in India, 1955–60; co-chairman and leader of British delegation at international conference on Laos, Geneva, 1961–2; governor of Kenya, 1963; governor-general, Kenya, 1963–4; high commissioner, 1964–5; special representative of British government in Africa, 1967–9; president, Royal Commonwealth Society, 1971, Great Britain–China Centre, 1972, Federation of Commonwealth Chambers of Commerce, 1971, VSO 1975, Caribbean Youth Development Trust, 1977, and Britain–Burma Society, 1980; OM, 1969; hon. fellow, The Queen's College, Oxford; number of honorary doctorates and other honours; Rhodes trustee, 1948–57; chancellor, University of Malaya, 1949–61; visitor, University College of Kenya, 1963–4; senior research fellow, University of Sussex, 1971–3; published books on birds of Ottawa, Delhi, and Kenya.

MacDONALD, Sir Murdoch (1866–1957), engineer; educated at Dr Bell's Institution, Inverness; apprenticed with Highland Railway; joined Sir Benjamin *Baker as assistant engineer, Aswan Dam, 1898; remained in Egyptian government service until 1921, responsible for heightening Aswan Dam, construction of Esna

Barrage, and schemes for Sennar and Gebel Aulia dams; founded London consulting firm, 1921; Liberal (later National Liberal) MP for Inverness, 1922–50; CMG, 1910; KCMG, 1914; CB, 1917; president, Institution of Civil Engineers, 1932.

MACDONALD, Patrick (1729–1824), amateur musician; educated at Aberdeen University; ordained missionary, 1756; chief work, *A Collection of Highland Vocal Airs never hitherto published* (1784).

MACDONALD, Ranald (1756–1832), Scottish Catholic prelate; educated at the Scots College, Douai; returned to Scotland, 1782; DD; vicar-apostolic of the Highland district, 1819, and of the western district, 1827.

MACDONALD, William Bell (1807–1862), linguist; educated at Glasgow University; graduated, 1827; surgeon on a flagship in the Mediterranean, 1828–31; famous linguist; published miscellaneous works.

MACDONALD, William Russell (1787–1854), miscellaneous writer; editor of, part proprietor of, and contributor to, various periodicals; later wrote books for the young.

MACDONELL, Alastair Ruadh (1725?–1761), known as Pickle the Spy; thirteenth chief of Glengarry; went to France, 1738, and joined Lord Drummond's regiment of Royal Scots Guards, 1743; employed by Highland chiefs on secret mission to Prince *Charles, 1745; captured by English and imprisoned in Tower of London, 1745–7; acted, under pseudonym of 'Pickle', as spy on Charles, 1749–54; succeeded as chief of clan, 1754.

MACDONELL (or MACDONALD), Alexander (or Alestair) of Glengarry (d. 1724), Jacobite; surnamed 'Dubh' from his dark complexion; joined *Claverhouse, 1689; one of the leaders at Killiecrankie, 1689; reluctantly took the oath to William III, 1691; joined *Mar and fought at Sheriffmuir, 1715; a trustee for managing the Chevalier's (see JAMES FRANCIS EDWARD STUART) affairs in Scotland, 1720.

MACDONELL, Alexander (1762–1840), first Roman Catholic bishop of Upper Canada; educated at the Scots College, Valladolid; ordained, 1787; while missionary priest, helped to form Romanist peasants into the 1st Glengarry Fencibles (disbanded, 1801); obtained a grant of land in Canada for the men; again raised a regiment of Glengarry Fencibles, which did good service for Upper Canada in the United States war, 1812; organized the colony, and devoted himself to missionary work in Upper Canada; vicar-apostolic of Upper Canada, 1819; bishop of Regiopolis

or Kingston, 1826; died at Dumfries; was buried in Kingston Cathedral, Canada.

MACDONELL (or MACDONNELL), Alexander Ranaldson, of Glengarry (d. 1828), colonel, Highland chieftain; brother of Sir James *Macdonell; major in the Glengarry Fencibles Infantry, 1795–1801; lived in feudal style; the original, to some extent, of *Scott's Fergus MacIvor in *Waverley*; perished by shipwreck.

MACDONELL, Arthur Anthony (1854–1930), Sanskrit scholar; born in India; educated at Dresden and Göttingen; BA, Corpus Christi College, Oxford; deputy to Boden professor of Sanskrit at Oxford and keeper of Indian Institute, 1888; succeeded to these offices and to professorial fellowship at Balliol College, 1899; retired, 1926; raised funds for critical edition of Sanskrit epic, *Mahā-Bhārata*; visited India, 1907–8 and 1922–3; FBA, 1906; as Sanskrit scholar worked chiefly in Vedic field; works include editions of *Sarvānukramaṇī* (1886) and *Bṛhad-devatā* (1904), *Vedic Mythology* (1897), and *Vedic Grammar* (1910).

MacDONELL, Sir Hugh Guion (1832–1904), soldier and diplomat; served in British Kaffraria with Rifle Brigade, 1849–53; after holding several minor diplomatic posts (1858–85) was British envoy at Rio, 1885, Copenhagen, 1888, and Lisbon, 1893–1902; tactfully dealt with Anglo-Portuguese difficulties in South African War; KCMG, 1892; GCMG, 1899; PC, 1902.

MACDONELL, Sir James (d. 1857), general; brother of Alexander Ranaldson *Macdonell of Glengarry; fought in Naples, Sicily, and Egypt, 1804–7; lieutenant-colonel, 1809; in the Peninsula, 1812–14; present at Waterloo, and KCB, 1815; commanded in Canada, 1838–41; lieutenant-general, 1841; general, 1854; GCB, 1855.

MACDONELL, James (1842–1879), journalist; on the staff of the *Daily Review* in Edinburgh, 1862; editor of the Newcastle *Northern Daily Express*; on the staff of the *Daily Telegraph*, 1865–75; special correspondent in France, 1870–1; leader-writer on *The Times*, 1875; made a special study of French politics; his *France since the First Empire* published (1880).

MACDONELL, Sir John (1845–1921), jurist; brother of James *Macdonell; MA, Aberdeen; called to bar (Middle Temple), 1873; master of Supreme Court, 1889; senior master and king's remembrancer, 1912–20; Quain professor of comparative law, University College, London, 1901–20; knighted, 1903; KCB, 1914; FBA, 1913; writer on legal subjects.

MACDONELL, Sir Philip James (1873–1940), colonial judge; son of James *Macdonell; educated at Clifton and Brasenose College, Oxford; first class, modern history, 1894; president of Union, 1895; called to bar (Gray's Inn), 1900; war correspondent of *The Times* in South Africa, 1900–2; secretary, Transvaal Native Commission, 1903; public prosecutor (1908–18), high court judge (1918–27), Northern Rhodesia; chief justice, Trinidad and Tobago (president, West Indian Court of Appeal), 1927–30, of Ceylon, 1930–6; knighted, 1925; PC, 1939.

MACDONLEVY, Cormac (*fl.* 1459), physician; called in Irish MacDuinntshleibhe; translated 'Gualterus' and other medical works into Irish; hereditary physician to the O'Donnells, like other members of the family (1200–1586).

MACDONNELL, Alexander (or Alaster) (d. 1647), general. See MACDONALD.

MACDONNELL, Alexander, third earl of Antrim (d. 1696?), brother of Randal *Macdonnell, second earl of Antrim; joined the rebellion in Ireland; represented Wigan at intervals, 1660–83; succeeded to the earldom, 1683; marched to the relief of Londonderry, but was mistaken for the enemy, 1689.

McDONNELL, Sir Alexander, first baronet (1794–1875), commissioner of national education in Ireland; educated at Westminster and Christ Church, Oxford; student till 1826; MA, 1820; barrister, Lincoln's Inn, 1824; renounced the bar and became chief clerk in the Chief Secretary's Office, Ireland; resident commissioner of the Board of Education, Ireland, 1839–71; privy councillor of Ireland, 1846; created baronet, 1872.

MACDONNELL, Alexander (1798–1835), chess-player; merchant at Demerara, 1820–30; secretary to the West India Committee of Merchants, 1830; studied chess under William *Lewis (1787–1870); admitted the best English player from 1833; beaten by the French player, Labourdonnais, 1834.

MacDONNELL, Antony Patrick, Baron MacDonnell (1844–1925), statesman; BA, Queen's College, Galway; entered Indian Civil Service, 1865; accountant-general and later revenue secretary to provincial government, Calcutta, 1881; largely responsible for Tenancy Act, 1885; home secretary to central government, 1886–9; chief commissioner, Central Provinces, 1890; lieutenant-governor, North-Western Provinces and Oudh, 1895; his period of office marked by severe visitations of plague and famine, which he combated with notable energy and ability; chairman of important famine commission, 1901; permanent under-secretary of state, Ireland, 1902–8; attempted to lift long-standing Irish quarrel above bitterness of party warfare, but his administration regarded with suspicion by both parties in Ireland; helped George *Wyndham, chief secretary for Ireland, to prepare and shape Irish Land Purchase Bill, 1903; unjustly censured by Cabinet for his assistance to Lord *Dunraven and Irish Reform Association in preparing scheme of 'devolution' for Ireland; secured support of (Lord) *Bryce when he became chief secretary for Ireland, 1905–7; his new scheme of devolution, which formed basis of Irish Council Bill (1907), approved by Bryce; unsupported by A. *Birrell in his devolution scheme and in attempts to suppress disorder; after resignation continued to take part in public life; created baron, 1908.

MACDONNELL, John (1691–1754), Irish poet; began a translation of Homer into Irish and a *History of Ireland*; some of his Irish poems printed.

MACDONNELL, Sir Randal, first Viscount Dunluce and first earl of Antrim (d. 1636), called 'Arranach'; son of Sorley Boy *Macdonnell; joined *O'Neill's rebellion, 1600; submitted to *Mountjoy, the lord-deputy, 1602; created Viscount Dunluce, 1618, and earl of Antrim, 1620.

MACDONNELL, Randal, second Viscount Dunluce, second earl and first marquis of Antrim (1609–1683), son of Sir Randal *Macdonnell, first Viscount Dunluce and first earl of Antrim; introduced at court, 1634; married the duke of *Buckingham's widow, 1635; sent by the king to raise forces in Scotland, 1639; took his seat in the Irish House of Lords, 1640; frequently imprisoned as a suspect, 1642–5; ordered to lay down his arms, 1646; retired to Ireland; allowed to return to England, 1650; pardoned, 1663.

McDONNELL, Randal John Somerled, eighth earl of Antrim (1911–1977), chairman of the National Trust; educated at Eton and Christ Church, Oxford; succeeded to earldom, 1932; clerk in House of Lords, 1933–4; served in Royal Naval Volunteer Reserve during 1939–45 war; chairman, National Trust's committee for Northern Ireland, 1948; chairman, National Trust, 1965–77; supervised reorganization and modernization of the Trust which greatly expanded during his chairmanship; overcame by tact and firmness considerable controversy and enhanced the reputation of the Trust; chairman, new Ulster Television station, 1959; chairman, St Peter's group of hospitals in London, 1966;

member of Sports Council, 1972–4; KBE, 1970; hon. FRIBA; D.Litt., University of Ulster.

MACDONNELL, Sir Richard Graves (1814–1881), colonial governor; educated at Trinity College, Dublin; MA, 1836; called to the Irish bar, 1838; barrister, Lincoln's Inn, 1841; chief justice of the Gambia, 1843; LL B, 1845; governor of the British settlements on the Gambia, 1847–52; governor of St Lucia, 1852–3; CB, 1852; administrator and captain-general of St Vincent, 1853–5; governor of South Australia, 1855–62; knighted, 1856; lieutenant-governor of Nova Scotia, 1864–5; governor of Hong Kong, 1865–72; KCMG, 1871; died at Hyères.

McDONNELL, Robert (1828–1889), surgeon; BA and MB, Trinity College, Dublin, 1850; volunteered as civil surgeon in Crimean War, 1855; medical superintendent of Mountjoy Government Prison, 1857–67; FRS, 1865; president of Academy of Medicine in Ireland, 1885–8.

McDONNELL, Sir Schomberg Kerr (1861–1915), civil servant; principal private secretary to marquess of *Salisbury, 1888–92, 1895–9, 1900–2; secretary to Office of Works, 1902–12; KCB, 1902; died of wounds in Flanders.

MACDONNELL, Sorley Boy (in Latin Carolus Flavus) (1505?–1590), Scoto-Irish chieftain, lord of the Route and constable of Dunluce Castle; appointed to lordship of Route district, 1558; made overtures to Elizabeth regarding the Scottish settlement on the Antrim coast, 1560; worsted by Shane *O'Neill, 1564–7; defeated by earl of *Essex, 1575; after some success was forced to escape to Scotland, 1585; admitted his lack of legal right in Ulster, 1586, and submitted to government.

MACDOUGALL, Allan (1750?–1829), Gaelic poet; published Gaelic verses (1798); family bard to Colonel MacDonald, laird of Glengarry.

MACDOUGALL, Sir Duncan (1787–1862), lieutenant-colonel, 79th Cameron Highlanders; ensign, 1804; served at the Cape of Good Hope, in the Peninsula; and in the American War, 1814–15; entrusted, as commander of 79th Foot at Halifax, Nova Scotia, with organization of colonial militia, 1825; quartermaster-general and second in command of British Auxiliary Legion of Spain, 1835; a prominent figure in the Volunteer movement; buried in St Paul's Cathedral.

McDOUGALL, Francis Thomas (1817–1886), bishop of Labuan and Sarawak; studied medicine at Malta University, King's College, London, and London University; subsequently entered Magdalen College, Oxford; BA, 1842; ordained, 1845; missionary in Borneo, 1847–67;

bishop of Labuan, 1855–68; archdeacon of Huntingdon, 1870; canon of Ely, 1871, of Winchester, 1873; archdeacon of the Isle of Wight, 1874.

MACDOUGALL, Sir John (1790–1865), vice-admiral; entered the navy, 1802; repeatedly in boat actions, 1803–9; lieutenant, 1809; commander, 1820; captured the Bogue Ports, Canton, 1847; KCB, 1862; vice-admiral, 1863.

MACDOUGALL, Sir Patrick Leonard (1819–1894), general; educated at Military Academy, Edinburgh, and at Sandhurst; lieutenant, 36th Foot, 1839; major, 1849; major-general, 1868; lieutenant-general, 1877; colonel, 2nd battalion, West India Regiment, 1881; and of Leinster Regiment, 1891; general, 1883; served in Canada, 1844–54; superintendent of studies at Sandhurst, 1854–8, but served in Crimea, 1854–5; adjutant-general of Canadian Militia, 1865–9; deputy inspector-general of auxiliary forces at headquarters, 1871; head of intelligence branch of War Office, 1873–8; KCMG, 1877; commander in North America, 1877–83; retired, 1885; principal work, *The Theory of War* (1856).

McDOUGALL, William (1871–1938), psychologist; educated at Owens College, Manchester, St John's College, Cambridge (fellow, 1897), and St Thomas's Hospital; Wilde reader in mental philosophy, Oxford, 1903; professor of psychology, Harvard (1920), Duke University, North Carolina, 1927–38; works include his influential *Introduction to Social Psychology* (1908), and *An Outline of Psychology* (1923) and *Abnormal Psychology* (1926); powerful advocate of the idealistic outlook; investigated inheritance of acquired characteristics; FRS, 1912.

MACDOWALL, Andrew, Lord Bankton (1685–1760), Scottish judge; educated at Edinburgh University; admitted advocate, 1708; became judge, with the title Lord Bankton, 1755; author of *An Institute of the Laws of Scotland in Civil Rights* (1751–3).

M'DOWALL, William (1815–1888), journalist and antiquary; appointed to the editorial staff of the *Scottish Herald*, 1843; edited *Dumfries and Galloway Standard*, 1846–88; published *History of Dumfries* (1867), *The Man of the Woods and other Poems* (1844), and *Mind in the Face* (1882).

McDOWELL, Benjamin (1739–1824), Presbyterian divine; born at Elizabethtown, New Jersey; educated at Princeton and Glasgow universities; joined the Established Church of Scotland; ordained, 1766; influential in Dublin Presbyterianism; DD, Edinburgh, 1789; author of controversial works.

MACDOWELL, Patrick (1799–1870), sculptor; exhibited at the Royal Academy, 1822 and 1826–9; entered the Academy Schools, 1830; RA, 1846; executed, among other works, *Girl going to the Bath* (1841), and *Europa* for the Albert Memorial (1870).

MACDOWELL, William (1590–1666), diplomat; educated at St Andrews University; professor of philosophy at Groningen, 1614; LL D, Groningen, 1625; president of the Council of War in Groningen and Friesland, 1627; ambassador to England, 1629, 1630, and 1636; Charles II's resident agent at The Hague, 1650; defeated the proposals of the envoys of the English parliament to the assembly of the States-General, 1651; his *Answer to English envoys* published (1651).

MACDUFF, thane or earl of Fife (*fl.* 1056?), a half or wholly mythical personage; advanced the cause of *Malcolm Canmore against the usurper *Macbeth, 1057.

MACE, Daniel (d. 1753), textual critic; Presbyterian minister; published anonymously *The New Testament in Greek and English . . . corrected from the Authority of the most authentic Manuscripts*, a precursor of the modern critical texts (1729).

MACE, James ('Jem') (1831–1910), pugilist; at first a showman and circus performer; became best boxer of his generation; middleweight champion, 1860; beat Thomas *King and Joe Goss for championship, 1862–6; last surviving representative of old prize ring.

MACE, Thomas (1619?–1709?), musician; an accomplished lutenist, though deaf; devised a lute of fifty strings, 1672; published *Music's Monument* (1676).

MACEACHEN, Evan (1769–1849), Gaelic scholar; entered the Scots College, Valladolid, 1788; ordained there, 1798; missioner in Scotland, 1798–1838; his most important work, 'Gaelic Translation of the New Testament' (unpublished).

MACEGAN (MACEGGAN, MACEOGAN, or MACKEGAN), Owen (or Eugenius) (d. 1603), bishop-designate of Ross, Co. Cork; probably educated at an Irish Roman Catholic seminary in Spain; encouraged rebellion in Ireland, 1600; went to Spain again and gained influence with Philip III, persuading him to assist *Tyrone's rebellion, 1601; as a reward for this made vicar-apostolic by the pope; prevented Charles *Blount, eighth Baron Mountjoy, from entirely crushing the rebellion, 1602; exercised great power, but was slain in an encounter with the English at Cladach.

MACERONI, Francis (1788–1846), aide-de-camp to Murat and mechanical inventor; aide-de-camp to Murat, king of Naples, 1814; Murat's envoy in England, 1815; settled in England, 1816; published a biography of Joachim Murat, king of Naples (1817); meddled in American, Spanish, and Neapolitan politics, 1819–25. A 'steam-coach', his most important invention, experimented with, 1833.

McEVOY, Arthur Ambrose (1878–1927), painter; entered Slade School of Fine Art, 1893; began as painter of poetical landscapes and restful interiors; later became popular as portrait painter; executed series of portraits in Imperial War Museum; capable of rendering masculine qualities, but his subjective treatment of women's portraits gave him unique place among contemporary English portrait painters.

McEVOY, Harry (1902–1984), industrialist; educated at Bradford Grammar School; worked in father's grocery business; studied at Columbia University, USA; degree in business methods and administration, 1930; joined export division of American Kellogg Company, manufacturers of cereal foods; assistant to manager of new Kellogg Company of Great Britain, 1933; managing director, 1934–67; selected Stretford, Manchester, as site for factory in Britain, 1938; assisted Ministry of Food during 1939–45 war when cereal foods were rationed; arranged for manufacture of all-bran from home-grown wheat; postwar, planned extension of Stretford factory and greatly increased turnover of breakfast cereal products; founder member and chairman of Association of Cereal Food Manufacturers, 1955–67; outstandingly successful in influencing trend to natural cereal-based diet in Europe.

McEWEN, Sir John Blackwood (1868–1948), principal of Royal Academy of Music; MA, Glasgow, 1888; entered Royal Academy of Music, 1893; professor of harmony and composition, 1898–1924; principal, 1924–36; pioneer of renascence of chamber-music composition; knighted, 1931.

M'EWEN, William (1735–1762), Scottish Secessionist; ordained, 1754; published religious works.

MACEWEN, Sir William (1848–1924), surgeon; BM, CM, Glasgow University; assistant surgeon, Royal Infirmary, Glasgow, 1875; full surgeon, 1877; regius professor of surgery, Glasgow, 1892–1924; FRS, 1895; knighted, 1902; his most important contributions to surgery made in brain surgery and bone surgery; first surgeon deliberately to operate for brain disorders; laid basis of modern brain surgery, especially in mastoid disease; introduced method of implanting small grafts to replace missing parts of limbbones and new method of rectifying knock-knee.

McFADYEAN, Sir **Andrew** (1887–1974), civil servant, business man, and political publicist; educated at University College School, London, and University College, Oxford; first class, Lit. Hum., 1909; entered Treasury, 1910; private secretary to six financial secretaries, 1913–17; served under J. M. (later Lord) *Keynes, 1917–19; Treasury representative at Paris Peace Conference; secretary to British delegation to Reparation Commission, 1920–2; succeeded Sir Arthur *Salter as general secretary of the commission; agreed with Keynes's *The Economic Consequences of the Peace* (1919), and was closely concerned with the Dawes Plan; knighted, 1925; started new career in City of London, 1930; chairman of S. G. Warburg and Co. Ltd., 1934–52, director, 1952–67; president, Liberal party, 1949–50; published *The Liberal Case* (1950); member of council, Royal Institute of International Affairs, 1933–67, president, 1970; in favour of European union; helped to found the Liberal International, vice-president, 1954–67; president, Free Trade Union, 1948–59; edited *The History of Rubber Regulation, 1934–1943* (1944); also published *Reparation Reviewed* (1930) and *Recollected in Tranquility* (1964), and translated R. N. Coudenhove-Kalergi's *The Totalitarian State Against Man* (1938) and *Europe Must Unite* (1940).

MACFADYEN, Allan (1860–1907), bacteriologist; MB, CM, Edinburgh University, 1883; MD, 1886; B.Sc. in hygiene, 1888; lecturer on bacteriology at College of State Medicine, subsequently amalgamated with Lister Institute of Preventive Medicine, from 1889; director, 1891; secretary, 1903; planned and organized Lister Institute; Fullerian professor of physiology at Royal Institution, 1901–4; lectures published as *The Cell as the Unit of Life* (posthumous, 1908).

MACFADYEN, Sir **Eric** (1879–1966), rubberindustry pioneer; educated at Lynams (the Dragon) School, Oxford, Clifton College, and Wadham College, Oxford; president of the Union, 1902; served in South African War, 1901–2; entered Malayan Civil Service, 1902; resigned and became rubber planter, 1905; senior partner, Macfadyen Wilde & Company; chairman, Planters' Association; member, Federal Council, Federated Malay States, 1911–16 and 1919–20; joined board of Harrisons & Crosfield Ltd., East India merchants, 1919, director, 1919–55; Liberal MP, Devizes, 1923–4; chairman, Ross Institute, 1946–58; chairman, Letchworth Garden City; knighted, 1943; life president, Imperial College of Agriculture, Trinidad.

McFADYEN, John Edgar (1870–1933), Scottish biblical scholar; educated at Glasgow University, Balliol College, Oxford, and the Free Church College, Glasgow; professor of Old Testament literature and exegesis, Knox College, Toronto, 1898–1910; of Old Testament language, literature, and theology, Trinity College, Glasgow, 1910–33.

MACFAIT, Ebenezer (d. 1786), Greek scholar, mathematician, physician, and miscellaneous writer.

MACFARLAN, James (1800–1871), Presbyterian minister; son of John *Macfarlan (d. 1846); licensed, 1831; published an English version of the *Prophecies of Ezekiel* (1845).

MACFARLAN, James (1832–1862), poet; a professional pedlar; walked from Glasgow to London to publish a volume of lyrics (1853); published other volumes of poems (1854, 1855, and 1856); contributed to *Household Words*.

MACFARLAN, James (1845–1889), Presbyterian minister; son of James *Macfarlan (1800–1871); educated at Edinburgh Academy and University, 1858–64; minister of Ruthwell, 1871–89.

MACFARLAN, John (d. 1846), Scottish advocate; brother of Patrick *Macfarlan; friend of Sir Walter *Scott; author of two religious pamphlets.

MACFARLAN, Patrick (1780–1849), Scottish divine; brother of John *Macfarlan; licensed, 1803; joined Secessionists, 1843; moderator of the Free General Assembly, 1845; published religious works.

MACFARLAN, Walter (d. 1767), antiquary; devoted himself to Scottish antiquarian research; his materials used by Douglas in his *Peerage of Scotland*.

MACFARLANE, Mrs (*fl.* 1716–1719), murderess; née Straiton; married John Macfarlane, writer to the signet; for some unknown reason shot Captain Cayley at her house in Edinburgh, 1716; not appearing to stand her trial (1717), was outlawed and remained in hiding, probably till her death.

MACFARLANE, Charles (d. 1858), miscellaneous writer; travelled in Italy, 1816–27; in Turkey, 1827–9; settled in London and supported himself by literary work, 1829; again travelled abroad, 1847–8; nominated a poor brother of the Charterhouse, 1857; his best works *Civil and Military History of England* (8 vols., 1838–44) and *The Book of Table Talk* (1836).

MACFARLANE, Duncan (1771–1857), principal of Glasgow University; educated at Glasgow University; ordained, 1792; DD, 1806;

principal of Glasgow University, 1824; as moderator, defended the Established Church in the disruption year, 1843.

MACFARLANE, Sir (Frank) Noel Mason- (1889–1953), lieutenant-general. See MASON-MACFARLANE.

MACFARLANE, John (1807–1874), Scottish divine; educated at Edinburgh and Glasgow universities; ordained, 1831; LL D, 1842; promoted Presbyterian church extension in England; published religious works.

MACFARLANE, Patrick (1758–1832), Gaelic scholar; translated religious books into Gaelic for the Society in Scotland for the Propagation of Christian Knowledge; published a collection of Gaelic poems (1813) and a vocabulary of Gaelic and English (1815).

MACFARLANE, Robert (1734–1804), miscellaneous writer; MA, Edinburgh; editor of the *Morning Chronicle* and *London Packet*; accidentally run over and killed; author of a Latin translation of the first book of Ossian's *Temora* (1769), and of volumes i and iv of a *History of George III* (1770 and 1796).

MACFARLANE, Robert, Lord Ormidale (1802–1880), senator of the College of Justice; educated at Glasgow and Edinburgh; writer to the signet, 1827; advocate at Edinburgh, 1838; sheriff of Renfrewshire, 1853; lord of session as Lord Ormidale, 1862; wrote on procedure of court of session.

MACFARREN, George (1788–1843), dramatist and theatrical manager; his first play performed, 1818; produced a play almost every year after 1818; took the Queen's Theatre, London, 1831; stage-manager of the Surrey Theatre, and then of the Strand Theatre, London; first suggested the Handel Society; editor and proprietor of the *Musical World*, 1841.

MACFARREN, Sir George Alexander (1813–1887), musical composer; son of George *Macfarren; studied at the Royal Academy of Music, 1829–36; his Symphony in C performed, 1830; other compositions performed, 1830–7; professor of harmony and composition at the Royal Academy of Music, 1837–46 and 1851–75; the *Devil's Opera*, one of his best dramatic works, produced, 1838; founded the Handel Society, 1844; conductor at Covent Garden, 1845; became blind, 1860; composed operas, 1860–73; his first oratorio, *St. John the Baptist*, performed 1873; principal of the Royal Academy of Music, and professor of music, Cambridge, 1875–87; knighted, 1883.

MACFARREN, Walter Cecil (1826–1905), pianist and composer; brother of Sir George A.

*Macfarren; studied at Royal Academy of Music; sub-professor of pianoforte there from 1846; composed pianoforte pieces in style of Mendelssohn, vocal works, church services, and overtures; published *Scale and Arpeggio Manual* (1882) and autobiographical *Memories* (1905).

MACFIE, Robert Andrew (1811–1893), free-trade advocate; educated at Leith and Edinburgh; engaged in business as sugar refiner at Edinburgh and Liverpool, where he assisted in founding Chamber of Commerce; MP, Leith Burghs, 1868–74; FRCI and FRSE; published works dealing with patents, copyright, and political questions.

MACFIRBIS, Duald (1585–1670), Irish historian; composed a treatise on Irish genealogy, finished 1650; in Dublin translating Irish manuscripts for Sir James *Ware, 1655–66; stabbed at Dunflin while on his way to Dublin; the last of the hereditary sennachies of Ireland.

MACFLYNN, Florence (or Flann) (d. 1256), archbishop of Tuam; also called Fiacha O'Flyn; consecrated archbishop, 1250; went to England to plead the cause of the Irish church, 1255.

M'GAULEY, James William (d. 1867), professor of natural philosophy to the Board of National Education in Ireland, 1836–56; in Canada, 1856–65; on the council of the Inventors' Institute, and editor of the *Scientific Review*; published scientific works.

M'GAVIN, William (1773–1832), controversialist; partner in a firm of cotton merchants, 1813; Glasgow agent for the British Linen Company's bank, 1822; belonged to the Anti-Burgher Communion; contributed controversial letters to the *Glasgow Chronicle* under the title of the 'Protestant', 1818–22, afterwards issued in book form; author of other controversial works.

McGEE, Thomas D'Arcy (1825–1868), Irish-Canadian statesman and poet; emigrated to America, 1842; edited *Boston Pilot*; London correspondent for the *Nation*; secretary to the committee of the Irish Confederation, 1847; escaped to America on the rout of the 'Young Ireland' party, 1848; founded the *American Celt*, and conducted it, 1850–7; started the *New Era* at Montreal; member for Montreal in legislative assembly, 1858–62; president of the council, 1864; a warm advocate of federation; member for Montreal West, and minister of agriculture and emigration, 1867; openly denounced Irish disloyalty, and was shot in Ottawa; chief work, *Popular History of Ireland* (1862).

MACGEOGHEGAN, Conall (*fl.* 1635), Irish historian. See MAGEOGHEGAN.

MACGEOGHEGAN, James (1702–1763), historian; related to Conall *Macgeoghegan; educated in France, becoming an abbé; published *Histoire de l'Irlande* (vol. i, 1758, vol. ii, 1762, vol. iii, 1763); died at Paris.

MACGEOGHEGAN, Roche (also called **ROCHUS DE CRUCE**) (1580–1644), Irish Dominican and bishop of Kildare; studied at the Irish College, Lisbon; Dominican provincial of Ireland, 1622; bishop of Kildare, 1629–44; constantly persecuted and forced to live in hiding.

MACGEORGE, Andrew (1810–1891), antiquarian writer and historian; educated at Glasgow University; practised as an ecclesiastical lawyer, 1836–89; caricaturist and author of works on heraldry and antiquarian subjects.

MACGILL, Hamilton Montgomery (1807–1880), United Presbyterian divine, educated at Glasgow University; ordained, 1837; home mission secretary of the United Presbyterian Church, 1865–8; foreign mission secretary, 1868–80; DD, Glasgow, 1870; author of *Songs of the Christian Creed and Life* (1876).

MACGILL, Stevenson (1765–1840), professor of theology at Glasgow; educated at Glasgow University; ordained, 1796; DD, Aberdeen and Marischal College, 1803; professor of theology, Glasgow, 1814; moderator of the general assembly, 1828; dean of the Chapel Royal, London, 1835.

M'GILL, William (1732–1807), Scottish divine; MA, Glasgow College; ordained, 1761; published essay on *The Death of Christ* (1786); the discussion of his supposed heterodoxy by the Presbytery gave rise to *Burns's satire, *The Kirk's Alarm*.

MACGILLIVRAY, Charles R. (1804?–1867), MD, 1853; lecturer in Gaelic at the Glasgow Institution, 1859; translated the *Pilgrim's Progress* into Gaelic (published 1869).

MacGILLIVRAY, Sir Donald Charles (1906–1966), colonial administrator; educated at Sherborne School and Trinity College, Oxford, 1920–9; entered Colonial Administrative Service, 1928; posted to Tanganyika, 1929; district officer, 1930–4; private secretary to governor, Sir Harold A. *MacMichael, 1935–8; posted to Palestine with Sir Harold, 1938–42; district officer, Galilee, and then Samaria, 1942–4; under-secretary, Palestine Government; colonial secretary, Jamaica, 1947–52; deputy high commissioner, Malaya, 1952–4; civil high commissioner, Malaya, 1954–7; retired to Kenya; chairman, Council of Makerere College, Uganda, 1958–61; chairman, Council of East Africa University, 1961–4; director, UN Special Fund for East Africa Livestock Development Survey, 1964; MBE, 1936; CMG, 1949; KCMG, 1953; GCMG, 1957.

MACGILLIVRAY, John (1822–1867), naturalist; son of William *Macgillivray; studied medicine at Edinburgh; naturalist on various government surveying expeditions, 1842–55; after 1855 studied natural history in Australasian islands; died at Sydney.

MACGILLIVRAY, William (1796–1852), naturalist; MA, Aberdeen, 1815; dissector to the lecturer on comparative anatomy, Aberdeen; assistant and secretary to the regius professor (Robert *Jameson) of natural history, Edinburgh, 1823; conservator of the Royal College of Surgeons' Museum, Edinburgh, 1831–41; professor of natural history, Aberdeen, 1841; best-known work, *A History of British Birds* (1837–52).

MAC GIOLLA CUDDY (1618–1693), Irish Jesuit. See ARCHDEKIN, RICHARD.

McGLASHAN, Alexander (d. 1797), Scottish violinist; edited *A Collection of Scots Measures, Hornpipes, Jigs* etc. (1781).

McGLASHAN, John (d. 1866), legal author; an Edinburgh solicitor; went to New Zealand, 1855, where he died; published legal works, 1831–44.

McGOWAN, Harry Duncan, first Baron McGowan (1874–1961), business man; educated at Huthesontown School and Allan Glen's School, Glasgow; at 15 joined Nobel's Explosives Co. as office boy; became assistant to general manager; assisted in constructing Canadian Explosives Ltd., later Canadian Industries Ltd., largest chemical business in Canada, 1909–11; chairman and managing director, Explosives Trades Ltd., 1918; joined board, British Dye-stuffs Corporation, 1919; agreed with Sir Alfred *Mond (later Lord Melchett) on merger of British chemical firms and formed ICI, 1926; chairman and sole managing director, ICI, 1930–50; KBE, 1918; baron, 1937.

MACGOWAN, John (1726–1780), Baptist minister; pastor of the meeting-house, Devonshire Square, 1766–80; chief work, *Infernal Conferences, or Dialogues of Devils, by the Listener* (1772).

MACGRADOIGH, Augustin (1349–1405), also called Magraidin; Irish chronicler; canon-regular of St Austin; continued the O'Brian annals to 1405.

McGRATH, Sir Patrick Thomas (1868–1929), statesman and journalist; born in Newfoundland; editor of Newfoundland *Evening Herald*, 1894–1907; assistant clerk, Newfoundland House of Assembly, 1897–1900, chief clerk,

1900–11; president, Legislative Council, 1915–19, 1925–9; KBE, 1918.

MACGREGOR, Sir Charles Metcalfe (1840–1887), major-general; educated at Marlborough; took part in the suppression of the Indian Mutiny, 1857–8; served in China, 1860–1; took part in the Abyssinian expedition, 1867–8; compiled the *Gazetteer of Central Asia* for the Indian government, 1868–73; made expeditions to obtain information about the Afghan frontier, 1875; served in the second Afghan War, 1878–9; KCB, 1881; quartermaster-general of India, 1880; general officer commanding the Punjab frontier force, 1885; major-general, 1887; published accounts of his travels in Afghanistan and Beluchistan (1879 and 1882), and works suppressed by the Indian government, 1884 and 1885–6; died at Cairo.

MacGREGOR, Sir Evan (1842–1926), civil servant; entered Admiralty, 1860; private secretary to successive senior naval lords, 1869–79; principal clerk in secretariat and head of military branch which dealt with fleet operations and political work, 1880; permanent secretary of Admiralty, 1884–1907; his period of office one of immense development both in fleet and in administration of navy, witnessing almost entire rebuilding of navy, construction of new harbours, barracks, and dockyards, reforms in naval education and training and in distribution and organization of Fleet, and construction of new Great Fleet; KCB, 1892.

MACGREGOR, Sir Gregor (*fl.* 1817), calling himself His Highness Gregor, cacique of Poyais, South American adventurer; said to have served in youth in British Army; went to Caraccas to aid in the struggle for South American independence, 1811; general of brigade, Venezuelan Army, 1812; distinguished himself in the campaign of 1813–21; general of division, 1817; assumed the title of cacique and settled among the Poyais Indians, 1821; failed in his schemes for colonizing the mosquito territory; restored to the rank of general of division, Venezuelan Army, 1839; died probably at Caraccas.

MACGREGOR, James (d. 1551), dean of Lismore; notary public, 1511; dean of Lismore, 1514; collected Gaelic poetry (selection edited, 1862).

MacGREGOR, James (1832–1910), moderator of the General Assembly of the Church of Scotland, 1891; student at St Andrews University, 1848–55; hon. DD, 1870; served churches at Paisley, Glasgow, and Edinburgh; first minister of St Cuthbert's, Edinburgh, 1873–1910; a fervent and popular preacher; visited Canada, 1881, and Australia, 1889.

MACGREGOR, John (1797–1857), statistician and historian; emigrated to Canada and settled in Prince Edward Island; member of the House of Assembly; high sheriff, 1823; travelled over America collecting statistics; joint secretary of the Board of Trade in London, 1840; MP, Glasgow, 1847; promoter of the Royal British Bank, 1849; absconded shortly before it stopped payment; died at Boulogne; best-known works, *My Note-book* (1835) and *The Resources and Statistics of Nations* (1835).

MACGREGOR, John (1825–1892), also known as Rob Roy; philanthropist and traveller; entered Trinity College, Dublin, 1839; proceeded to Trinity College, Cambridge, 1842; BA, 1847; MA, 1850; barrister, Inner Temple, 1851; travelled widely, 1848–57; went for his first solitary cruise in his *Rob Roy* canoe, 1865; published *A Thousand Miles in the Rob Roy Canoe* (1866); made other cruises, 1866, 1867, and 1868; member of the London School Board, 1870 and 1873; actively promoted philanthropic schemes in London.

McGREGOR, John James (1775–1834), historian and topographer; edited *Munster Telegraph*, and subsequently *Church Methodist Magazine*; literary assistant to the Kildare Place Education Society, Dublin, 1829.

MACGREGOR (or CAMPBELL), Robert (commonly called **ROB ROY**) (1671–1734), Highland freebooter; nominally a grazier, though deriving his principal income from cattle-lifting and exacting money for affording protection against thieves; a man of some education; penal acts enforced against him and his clan for their conduct at the Revolution, 1693; accused of fraudulent bankruptcy, 1712; followed with his men in the wake of the rebel army, but did not join it, 1715; surrendered to the duke of *Atholl, 1717; escaped and continued his depredations; apprehended and sentenced to be transported to Barbados, but pardoned, 1727; eventually became a Roman Catholic and a peaceful subject. Authentic particulars of his life are to be found in *Scott's introduction to *Rob Roy*.

MacGREGOR, Sir William (1846–1919), colonial governor; MD, Aberdeen, 1874; chief medical officer for Fiji, 1875; first administrator (styled lieutenant-governor, 1895) of British New Guinea, 1888; promoted policy of peaceful penetration and exploration; governor of Lagos, where he carried on campaign against malaria, 1899; governor of Newfoundland, 1904; organized and conducted important scientific expedition to Labrador; governor of Queensland, 1909–14; KCMG, 1889; GCMG, 1907; PC, 1914.

McGRIGOR, Sir James, first baronet (1771–1858), army surgeon; studied medicine at Aberdeen and Edinburgh universities; MA, Aberdeen, 1788; surgeon to de Burgh's regiment (Connaught Rangers), 1793; saw service in Flanders, West Indies, and India; superintending surgeon to the European and Indian troops going to Egypt, 1801; MD, Marischal College, Aberdeen, 1804; inspector-general of hospitals, 1809; chief of the medical staff of Wellington's army in the Peninsula, 1811; knighted, 1814; director-general of the Army Medical Department, 1815–51; FRS, 1816; created baronet, 1830; hon. LL D, Edinburgh; KCB, 1850; author of medical reports.

McGRIGOR, James (1819–1863), lieutenant-colonel in the Indian Army; nephew of Sir James *McGrigor; distinguished himself in the Indian Mutiny, 1857–8; major, 1858; lieutenant-colonel, 1862; drowned while bathing at Aden.

McGRIGOR, Sir Rhoderick Robert (1893–1959), admiral of the fleet; during 1914–18 war, served in destroyers in Dardanelles campaign, and in *Malaya* at the Battle of Jutland; commanded *Renown*, 1940–1, in *Bismarck* action and bombardment of Genoa; rear-admiral, 1941; assistant chief of naval staff (weapons), 1941–3; force commander for capture of Pantelleria and invasion of Sicily; naval commander, southern Italy, 1944; commanded First Cruiser Squadron, Scapa Flow, 1944–5; vice-chief of naval staff, 1945–7; admiral, 1948; commander-in-chief, Home Fleet, 1948–50, Plymouth, 1950–1; first sea lord, 1951–5; CB, 1944; KCB, 1945; GCB, 1951; admiral of the fleet, 1953.

MACGUIRE. See MAGUIRE.

MACHABE, John (d. 1557), Scottish reformer and professor of theology at Copenhagen. See MACALPINE.

MACHADO, Roger (d. 1511?), diplomat and Clarenceux king-of-arms; present at Edward IV's funeral, 1483; Richmond herald and Norroy king-of-arms, 1485; Clarenceux king-of-arms, 1494; employed on diplomatic missions in France, 1494–6.

MACHALE, John (1791–1881), archbishop of Tuam; educated at Maynooth; lecturer on theology there, 1814; coadjutor bishop of Killala, 1825; visited Rome, 1831; archbishop of Tuam, 1834; induced by his dislike of everything English to oppose *Newman; quarrelled with Archbishop *Cullen; translated the Pentateuch into Irish, 1801, also some of Moore's melodies and part of the *Iliad*, 1844–71.

MACHELL, James Octavius (1837–1902), owner and manager of racehorses; joined army, 1854; retired as captain, 1863; won Derby with Hermit, 1867; superintended training of Isinglass (see MCCALMONT, HARRY) and of many other winning horses; his own horses won 540 races, 1864–1902; a good athlete.

MACHEN, Thomas (1568–1614), MA, Magdalen College, Oxford, 1592, and fellow; student of Lincoln's Inn, 1589; MP, Gloucester, 1614.

McHENRY, James (1785–1845), poet and novelist; emigrated to the United States, 1817; settled in Philadelphia, 1824; United States consul in Londonderry, 1842–5; best known by his novel, *O'Halloran, or the Insurgent Chief* (1824).

MACHIN (or MACHYN), Henry (1498?–1563?), diarist; kept a valuable diary of the years 1550–63 (published by the Camden Society, 1848).

MACHIN, John (1624–1664), ejected Nonconformist; converted after entering Jesus College, Cambridge, 1645; BA, 1649; received Presbyterian ordination, 1649; lectured at different towns, 1650–61; ejected from curacy of Whitley Chapel, Great Budworth, Cheshire, 1662.

MACHIN, John (1679?–1751), astronomer; FRS, 1710; professor of astronomy at Gresham College, London, 1713–51; left unpublished writings.

MACHIN, Lewis (*fl.* 1608), author, in collaboration with Gervase *Markham, of a comedy, *The Dumbe Knight* (1608).

MACHIN (or MACHAM), Robert (*fl.* 1344), legendary discoverer of Madeira; supposed to have fled from England with Anna Dorset, daughter of an English noble, and landed on an island at a port which he called Machico; Madeira was discovered by Genoese sailors in the Portuguese service prior to the date of Machin's voyage.

MACHLINIA, William de (*fl.* 1482–1490), printer; probably a native of Mechlin; printer in England after 1482; about twenty-two books assigned to his press.

MACHON, John (1572–1640?), BA, Magdalen College, Oxford, 1594; canon of Lichfield, 1631.

MACHRAY, Robert (1831–1904), archbishop of Rupert's Land; of Presbyterian parentage; MA, Aberdeen, 1851; BA, Sidney Sussex College, Cambridge, 1855; MA, 1858; vicar of Madingley, 1862–5; bishop of Rupert's Land, 1865; reorganized St John's College, Winnipeg; chancellor of Manitoba University, 1877–1904; subdivided diocese into eight sees; metropolitan of Canada, 1875; archbishop of Rupert's Land and primate of all Canada, 1893.

M'IAN, Robert Ronald (1803–1856), historical painter; while studying art, was on the stage till 1839; exhibited at the Royal Academy from 1836; associate of the Royal Scottish Academy, 1852; painted chiefly pictures of Highland life and history.

MACIAN OF GLENCOE (d. 1692), chief of his clan. See MACDONALD, ALEXANDER.

MACILWAIN, George (1797–1882), medical writer; studied under Abernethy at St Bartholomew's Hospital, London; FRCS, 1843; held various surgical appointments in London; published *Memoirs of John Abernethy* (1853) and medical treatises.

McILWRAITH, Sir **Thomas** (1835–1900), premier of Queensland; educated as engineer at Glasgow University; went (1854) to Victoria, where he found employment on railways; engaged in pastoral pursuits in Queensland; member of legislative assembly for Maranoa, 1869; minister for works and mines, 1874; member for Mulgrave, 1878; premier, 1879–83; colonial treasurer, 1879–81; colonial secretary, 1881–3; KCMG, 1882; annexed New Guinea to Queensland, 1883; came to Great Britain; hon. LL D, Glasgow, 1883; member for North Brisbane, 1888; premier, colonial secretary, and treasurer, 1888; resigned premiership, 1888, but retained seat in Cabinet without portfolio; colonial treasurer, 1890; premier, 1893; returned (1893) to England, where he died.

McINDOE, Sir **Archibald Hector** (1900–1960), plastic surgeon; educated at Otago High School and University, New Zealand; MB, Ch.B., 1924; postgraduate, Mayo Clinic; MS (Rochester), 1930; joined cousin, Sir Harold *Gillies, in London; FRCS (England), 1932; appointed consultant in plastic surgery to Royal Air Force, 1939; organized centre at Queen Victoria Hospital, East Grinstead, for treatment and rehabilitation; on council, Royal College of Surgeons, 1948–60; a founder, British Association of Plastic Surgeons; skilful surgeon and powerful and independent personality; CBE, 1944; knighted, 1947.

MACINTOSH. See also MACKINTOSH.

MACINTOSH, Charles (1766–1843), chemist and inventor of waterproof fabrics; studied chemistry while a counting-house clerk; started the first alum works in Scotland, 1797; connected with the St Rollox Chemical Works till 1814; patented his waterproof invention, 1823, and started works in Manchester (still continued); FRS, 1824.

MACINTOSH, Donald (1743–1808), Scottish nonjuring bishop; clerk for the Gaelic language to the Scottish Society of Antiquaries, 1785–9; ordained, 1789; acted as a missionary or untitled bishop of Jacobite episcopacy; Gaelic translator and keeper of Gaelic records to the Highland Society of Scotland, 1801; the last representative of the nonjuring Scottish Episcopal Church; compiled *A Collection of Gaelic Proverbs*, the first ever made.

McINTOSH, William Carmichael (1838–1931), zoologist; MD, Edinburgh, 1860; medical superintendent, Perth District Asylum, 1863–82; professor of zoology (1882–1917), St Andrews, where established first marine laboratory in United Kingdom; works include *Monograph of the British Marine Annelids* (4 vols., 1873–1923) and report on the polychaete worms obtained by *Challenger* expedition (1885); FRS, 1877.

MACINTYRE, Donald (1831–1903), major-general, Bengal Staff Corps; won VC for gallantry in Lushai expedition, 1871–2; commanded 2nd Prince of Wales's Own Ghurkhas with Khyber Column in Afghan War, 1878–9, and in Bazar valley expeditions; major-general, 1880; published account of travel and sport in Himalayas, 1889.

MACINTYRE, Donald George Frederick Wyville (1904–1981), naval officer and historian; educated at Osborne and Dartmouth Royal Naval colleges; became Fleet fighter pilot, 1927–35; in command of HMS *Venomous* at outbreak of war, 1939; distinguished war career in convoy escort duties; sank two notable submarines, 1941; DSO; further successes against submarines, 1942–3; two bars to DSO, and DSC; officer of American Legion of Merit; commander, 1940; captain, 1945; commanded third training flotilla, 1948–50; retired, 1955; published numerous books on naval history including *U-Boat Killer* (1956), and a biography of Admiral Lord *Rodney; associated with Naval Historical Branch, 1964–72.

MACINTYRE, Duncan Ban (1724–1812), Gaelic poet; joined the Hanoverian forces, 1745; present at the Battle of Falkirk, 1746; published the first edition of his poems (1786; other editions, 1790 and 1804); some of his poems translated into English; vividly described Highland scenery.

MacIVER, David Randall- (1873–1945), archaeologist and anthropologist. See RANDALL-MACIVER.

MACKAIL, Hugh (1640?–1666), Scottish martyr; educated at Edinburgh University; ordained, 1661; apprehended for his preaching, 1662; escaped to Holland; joined a Covenanters' rising in Scotland, 1666; tortured and hanged in Edinburgh.

MACKAIL, John William (1859–1945), classical scholar, literary critic, and poet; educated at Ayr Academy, Edinburgh University, and Balliol College, Oxford; first class, Lit. Hum., 1881; fellow, 1882; entered Education Department (later Board of Education), 1884; assistant secretary, 1903–19; professor of poetry, Oxford, 1906–11 (lectures published in 3 vols., 1909–11); other publications include translation of the *Aeneid* (1885), of the *Eclogues* and *Georgics* (1889), *Select Epigrams from the Greek Anthology* (1890), *Latin Literature* (1895), *Life of William Morris* (1899), translation of the *Odyssey* (3 vols., 1903–10), *Virgil and his Meaning to the World of To-day* (1923), *Approach to Shakespeare* (1930), and an edition of the *Aeneid* (1930); fellow (1914), president (1932–6), British Academy; OM, 1935.

MACKAIL (or MACKAILLE), Matthew (*fl.* 1657–1696), medical writer; MD, Aberdeen, 1696; published medical works.

MACKAIL, Matthew (d. 1734), son of Matthew *Mackail (*fl.* 1657–1696); studied medicine at Leiden; professor of medicine, Aberdeen, 1717.

MACKARNESS, John Fielder (1820–1889), bishop of Oxford; educated at Eton and Merton College, Oxford; BA, 1844; hon. canon of Worcester, 1854–8; prebendary of Exeter, 1858; bishop of Oxford, 1870–88; a liberal in politics.

MACKARNESS, Mrs Matilda Anne (1826–1881), author; daughter of James Robinson *Planché; published her best-known story, 'A Trap to Catch a Sunbeam', 1849; married the Revd Henry S. Mackarness (d. 1868), brother of John Fielder *Mackarness.

MACKAY, Æneas James George (1839–1911), legal and historical writer; BA, University College, Oxford, 1862; MA, 1865; admitted to Scottish bar, 1864; professor of constitutional law, Edinburgh University, 1874; advocate depute, 1881; sheriff principal of Fife and Kinross, 1886–1901; LL D, Edinburgh, 1882; works include *The Practice of the Court of Session* (2 vols., 1877–9), *William Dunbar* (1889), and *A History of Fife and Kinross* (1896).

MACKAY, Alexander (1808–1852), journalist; barrister, Middle Temple, 1847; on the staff of the *Morning Chronicle* till 1849; sent to India by the chambers of commerce of the big cities in the north to inquire into the cultivation of cotton, 1851; his *Western World, or Travels in the United States in 1846–7* (1849) long the most complete work on the subject.

MACKAY, Alexander (1815–1895), educational writer; MA, King's College, Aberdeen, 1840; LL D, 1866; first Free Church minister of Rhynie, Aberdeenshire, 1844–67; studied local geology, and was FRGS, 1859; published educational works, including *Manual of Modern Geography* (1861).

MACKAY, Alexander (1833–1902), promoter of education in Scotland; MA, St Andrews; LL D, 1891; developed educational methods and organization as schoolmaster at Torryburn; editor of *Educational News*, 1878; president of Educational Institute of Scotland, 1881; member of Edinburgh School Board, 1897; published educational works.

MACKAY, Alexander Murdoch (1849–1890), missionary; studied engineering subjects at Edinburgh University; draughtsman in an engineering firm at Berlin, 1873–5; joined the mission to Uganda, 1876, and gained great influence over the natives; died at Usambiro.

MACKAY, Andrew (1760–1809), mathematician; keeper of Aberdeen Observatory, 1781; LL D, Aberdeen, 1786; mathematical examiner to the Trinity House (1805–9) and to the East India Company; chief works, *The Theory and Practice of finding the Longitude at Sea or on Land* (1793), *A Collection of Mathematical Tables* (1804), and *The Complete Navigator* (1804).

MACKAY, Angus (1824–1886), colonial journalist and politician; taken by his parents to New South Wales, 1827; editor of the *Atlas*, 1847; represented the *Empire* at the goldfields, 1851; member for Sandhurst burghs, Victoria, 1868–79 and 1883–6; minister of mines, 1870; launched the *Sydney Daily Telegraph*, 1879; died at Sandhurst burghs.

McKAY, Archibald (1801–1883), poet and topographer; his most popular poems 'My First Bawbee', 'My ain Couthie Wife', and 'Drouthy Tam', 1828; author of *A History of Kilmarnock* (1848).

MACKAY, Charles (1814–1889), poet and journalist; educated at Brussels; private secretary to William *Cockerill, 1830–2; assistant sub-editor of the *Morning Chronicle*, 1834–44; editor of the *Glasgow Argus*, 1844–7, of the *Illustrated London News*, 1852–9; special correspondent of *The Times* at New York, 1862–5; wrote his song, 'The Good Time Coming', 1846, of which 400,000 copies were circulated; published songs at intervals from 1834–90 (collected, 1859 and 1868), his 'Gossamer and Snowdrift', being posthumous (1890); LL D of Glasgow, 1846; published numerous prose works.

MACKAY, Sir Donald, of Far, first Baron Reay (1591–1649), succeeded to the headship of the clan, 1614; knighted, 1616; created baronet, 1627; served the king of Denmark with distinction, 1627–9; created Baron Reay, 1628; transferred his regiment to Gustavus Adolphus, 1629; present at the battles of Leipzig (1631) and Lutzen (1633); returned to Denmark, 1643; joined King Charles I, 1644; captured at Newcastle, 1644; set free, 1645; retired to Denmark (1648), where he died.

MACKAY, Donald James, eleventh Baron Reay (1839–1921), governor of Bombay (1885–90), and first president of British Academy (1902–7); born at The Hague; educated at Leiden; entered Dutch Foreign Office; settled in England, 1875; naturalized, 1877; created baron of United Kingdom, 1881; under-secretary of state for India, 1894–5; interested in international law and politics.

MACKAY, Hugh (1640?–1692), of Scourie, general; served with his regiment abroad, 1660–73; transferred his services to the States-General, 1673; colonel of Scots Dutch regiments, 1680; summoned to England to aid against *Monmouth, 1685; privy councillor of Scotland; returned to Holland, remaining there on the recall of the regiment by James II, 1687; in command of the English and Scots division in the expedition of William of Orange, 1688; commander-in-chief of the forces in Scotland, 1689; defeated by *Claverhouse at Killiecrankie, 1689; induced the surrender of the forces of Cannon, Claverhouse's successor, 1689; led the attack at Steinkirk, where he was slain.

MACKAY, James Lyle, first earl of Inchcape (1852–1932), shipowner; joined staff of Mackinnon, Mackenzie & Co., Calcutta, 1874; became senior partner; served on Bengal Legislative Council, 1891–3; returned to take charge of London office of British India Company, 1893; chairman, 1914; carried through fusion with P. & O. and other companies into a group with capital of £23 million and nearly 2 million tonnage; director and chairman of numerous shipping and banking concerns; thrice president of UK Chamber of Shipping; negotiated commercial treaty with China, 1901–2; served on Council of India, 1897–1911, Imperial Defence Committee, 1917, and Geddes Economy Committee, 1921–2; chairman, Indian Retrenchment Committee, 1922–3; disposed of wartime shipping for government for £35 millions at expense of £850; ardent free trader; crossed from Liberal to Conservative benches, 1926; KCIE, 1894; baron, 1911; viscount, 1924; earl, 1929.

MACKAY, James Townsend (1775?–1862), botanist; curator of the botanical garden, Trinity College, Dublin, 1806–62; published his *Flora Hibernica* (1836); LL D, Dublin University, 1850; discovered plants new to the British isles.

MACKAY, John, second Baron Reay (*fl.* 1649–1654), son of Sir Donald *Mackay of Far, first Baron Reay; took part in Royalist insurrections in Scotland, 1649 and 1654.

MACKAY, Mackintosh (1800–1873), Gaelic scholar; educated for the ministry; superintended the printing of the Gaelic dictionary of the Highland and Agricultural Society (1828); published the *Poems* of Robert *Mackay, Rob Donn, 1829; at the disruption joined the Free Church; minister of the Gaelic Church at Melbourne, 1854, and Sydney, 1856; returned to Scotland.

MACKAY, Mary (1855–1924), novelist; known as Marie Corelli; daughter of Charles *Mackay; showed precocious talent for piano-playing; published her first article, signed 'Marie Corelli', 1885; published her first novel, 1886; achieved popularity with *Barabbas* (1893) and *The Sorrows of Satan* (1895) which secured hysterical triumph and marked climax of her career as popular novelist in Great Britain, and reinforced her determination to flout critics; later works include *The Mighty Atom* (1896); voiced mass-sentiment of pre-war bourgeoisie; settled in Stratford-upon-Avon, to which she was a benefactress, 1901.

MACKAY, Robert (commonly called **ROB DONN** or the Brown) (1714–1778), Gaelic poet; acted as herd, gamekeeper, and boman; in the Reay Fencibles, 1759–67; wrote poems, chiefly elegies and satires, in the Sutherlandshire dialect.

MACKAY, Robert William (1803–1882), philosopher and scholar; educated at Winchester and Brasenose College, Oxford; MA, 1828; published *The Progress of the Intellect as exemplified in the Religious Development of the Greeks and Hebrews* (1850) and other learned works.

McKECHNIE, William Sharp (1863–1930), constitutional historian; MA, Glasgow University; solicitor in Glasgow, 1890–1915; lecturer in constitutional law and history, Glasgow University, 1894; professor of conveyancing, Glasgow, 1916–27; his chief work, *Magna Carta* (1905), in which the Charter is represented as a feudal document only accidentally serving interests of others than the baronial class; others include *The State and the Individual* (1896) and *The New Democracy and the Constitution* (1912).

MACKELLAR, Mary (1834–1890), Highland poetess; née Cameron; married John Mackellar, captain of a coasting vessel; obtained judicial separation from him; settled in Edinburgh, c.1786; her *Poems and Songs, Gaelic and English*, contributed to newspapers and periodicals, published (1880); translated into Gaelic the second series of Queen Victoria's *Leaves from our Journal in the Highlands*.

MACKELLAR, Patrick (1717–1778), colonel, military engineer; clerk in the Ordnance Service, 1735; employed in Minorca, 1739–54 and 1763–78; engineer-in-ordinary, 1751; served in *Braddock's campaign in North America, 1754; chief engineer of the frontier forts, 1756; taken prisoner and confined in Quebec and Montreal, 1756–7; second and then chief engineer at the capture of Louisburg, 1758; chief engineer to *Wolfe, 1759; in the expedition against Martinique, 1761–2, and the attack on Havannah, 1762; director of engineering and colonel at Minorca, 1777.

MACKELVIE, William (1800–1863), United Presbyterian divine; studied for the ministry as a Secessionist at Edinburgh University; ordained, 1829; promoted union of secession and relief churches; best-known work *Annals and Statistics of the United Presbyterian Church* (published 1873).

MACKEN, John (1784?–1823), poet; merchant at Ballyconnell; joint editor of the *Enniskillen Chronicle*, 1808; in London, 1818; assisted in compiling *Huntingdon Peerage* (1821); returned to Ireland and resumed his joint editorship of the *Enniskillen Chronicle*, 1821; published verse.

MACKENNA, John (Juan) (1771–1814), Chilean general; left Ireland and entered the Royal Academy of Mathematics at Barcelona, 1784; entered an Irish engineer corps in the Spanish Army, 1787; served against the French, 1787–8 and 1794; went to Peru, 1796; governor of Osorno, 1797–1808; joined revolution, 1810; provisional governor of Valparaiso and commander-in-chief of artillery and engineers, 1811–14; brigadier-general, 1813; banished, 1814; killed in a duel at Buenos Aires.

MACKENNA, Nial (*fl.* 1700), Irish poet and harper; author of the celebrated song, 'Little Celia Connellan'.

McKENNA, Reginald (1863–1943), statesman and banker; scholar of Trinity Hall, Cambridge; senior optime, 1885; rowed for Cambridge, 1887; called to bar (Inner Temple), 1887; Liberal MP, North Monmouthshire, 1895–1918; financial secretary to the Treasury, 1905–7; PC, 1907; president of Board of Education, 1907–8; first lord of the Admiralty, 1908–11; convinced of German danger, obtained construction of eight *Dreadnoughts* in 1909 and five each in 1910–11; refused to give way to War Office on question of strategy and transferred to Home Office (1911–15); attempted to solve suffragette problem by 'Cat and Mouse Act', 1913; chancellor of Exchequer, May 1915–Dec. 1916; obtained 40 million securities from Prudential Assurance Company for new American con-

tracts, 1915; by increasing income-tax and imposing import and other taxes met running cost of war in two budgets, Sept. 1915 and April 1916; opposed conscription but remained in office until Asquith's resignation; refused chancellorship of Exchequer, 1922; director (1917), chairman (1919–43), Midland Bank; published *Post-War Banking Policy* (1928).

MACKENNA, Theobald (d. 1808), Irish Catholic writer; secretary to the Catholic Committee in Ireland; the mouthpiece of the seceders after 1791; opposed Wolfe *Tone's views in a pamphlet, 1793; disappointed with the results of the Union; suggested raising the Irish Catholic Church to an establishment, 1805; issued political pamphlets.

MACKENNAL, Alexander (1835–1904), Congregational minister; educated at Glasgow University, 1851–4; hon. DD, 1887; BA, London, 1857; minister at Bowdon, Cheshire, 1877 to death; chairman of Congregational Union, 1887; frequently visited America from 1889; advocated co-operative union of Churches; secretary (1892–8) and president (1899) of National Free Church Council; published many theological works, and life of J. A. Macfadyen, DD, 1891.

MACKENNAL, Sir (Edgar) Bertram (1863–1931), Australian sculptor; studied in Melbourne and Paris; works include obverse of new coinage (1910); King Edward VII Memorial, St George's Chapel, Windsor (1921), and equestrian statue, Waterloo Place; war memorial, members of both Houses of Parliament, St Stephen's Hall; brilliant all-round sculptor, particularly in marble; ARA, 1909; RA, 1922; KCVO, 1921.

MACKENZIE, first baron of Kintail (1754–1815), lieutenant-general. See HUMBERSTON, FRANCIS MACKENZIE, first Baron Seaforth and Mackenzie.

MACKENZIE, Sir Alexander (1755?–1820), North American explorer; explored the then-unknown north-west, 1789; started from Fort Chippewayan, a trading port at the head of Lake Athabasca, with the object of reaching the Pacific coast, 1792; published an account of his voyages (1801); knighted, 1802; resided in Canada and represented Huntingdon county in the provincial parliament; returned to Scotland, where he died.

MACKENZIE, Alexander (1822–1892), first Liberal premier of the Canadian Dominion; emigrated to Canada, 1842; builder and contractor at Sarnia, 1848; edited *Lambton Shield*, 1852; member for Lambton in the provincial parliament, 1861–7, and in the Dominion House of Commons, 1867; premier and minister of public works, 1873–8; resigned the leadership of the opposition, 1880; member for East York, 1882–92; died at Toronto; upheld the connection between Canada and Great Britain.

MACKENZIE, Sir Alexander (1842–1902), lieutenant-governor of Bengal; joined Indian Civil Service, 1862; under-secretary to local government, Bengal, 1866; home secretary to government of India, 1882; helped to shape Bengal Tenancy Act of 1885; CSI, 1886; chief commissioner of Central Provinces, 1887–90, and of Burma, 1890–5; KCSI, 1891; suppressed hill-tribe raids and restored order, 1892; lieutenant-governor of Bengal, 1895–8; made sanitary survey of Calcutta; enlarged powers of Bengal municipalities; co-operated with Assam in Lushai expedition of 1895–6; expedited land settlement operations in Bihar and Orissa; dealt efficiently with the famine of 1896–7 and the plague; published *History of the Relations of Government with the Hill Tribes of the North-East Frontier of Bengal* (1884).

McKENZIE, Alexander (1869–1951), professor of chemistry; educated at Dundee High School and St Andrews; B.Sc., chemistry and natural philosophy, 1891; lecture assistant, 1891–3; university assistant, 1893–8; Ph.D., Berlin, 1901; assistant lecturer, chemistry, Birmingham, 1902; head, chemistry department, Birkbeck College, London, 1905–13; professor of chemistry, Dundee, 1914–38; researched in stereochemical field; FRS, 1916; hon. LL D, St Andrews, 1939.

MACKENZIE, Sir Alexander Campbell (1847–1935), composer and principal of the Royal Academy of Music; studied there; violinist, organist, and conductor in Edinburgh, 1866–81; lived in Florence, 1881–8; principal, Royal Academy of Music, 1888–1924; broadened its musical education; with Royal College of Music founded an examining body in the Associated Board; conductor, Philharmonic Society's concerts, 1892–9; president, International Musical Society, 1908–12; compositions include operas *Colomba* and *The Cricket on the Hearth*; oratorio *Rose of Sharon, The Cotter's Saturday Night* for chorus and orchestra; cantata *The Bride*; Scottish rhapsodies; overture *Cervantes*; knighted, 1895; KCVO, 1922.

MACKENZIE, Charles Frederick (1825–1862), bishop of Central Africa; brother of William Forbes *Mackenzie; educated at Caius College, Cambridge; MA, 1851; fellow; accompanied John William *Colenso to Natal as his archdeacon, 1855; chaplain to the troops round Durban, 1858; head of the universities' mission to Central Africa, 1860; consecrated bishop at Cape Town, 1861; settled at Mago-

mero in the Manganja country; often resorted to force to help the Manganja; died at Malo.

MACKENZIE, Colin (1753?–1821), colonel in the Madras Engineers, Indian antiquary and topographer; served in the Madras Engineers against Tippoo Sahib, 1790–2 and 1799; surveyed Mysore, 1799–1806; surveyor-general of Madras, 1807; commanding engineer in Java, 1811–15; CB, 1815; surveyor-general of India, 1819; made valuable collections of Indian antiquities, inscriptions, and manuscripts.

MACKENZIE, Colin (1806–1881), lieutenant-general in Indian Army; cadet of infantry on Madras establishment, 1825; served in Coorg campaign, 1834, and in Straits of Malacca, 1836; assistant political agent at Peshawar, 1840; served with distinction at Kabul; brevet-captain; attended conference between Akbar Khan and Sir William Hay *Macnaghten and was taken prisoner; on being released, chosen by Akbar Khan as one of the hostages to be given up to him; raised Sikh regiment during the last Sikh campaign; brigadier-general in command of Ellichpur division of Hyderabad contingent, 1853; dangerously wounded at Bolarum in mutiny of a cavalry regiment against orders which the government subsequently condemned as ill judged, 1855; returned temporarily to England; agent to governor-general with Nawab Nazim of Bengal; CB, 1867; failed to obtain divisional command owing to censure in Bolarum case, and finally left India, 1873.

MACKENZIE, Dugal (d. 1588?), Scottish author; educated at Aberdeen and Paris universities; some Latin poems and epigrams attributed to him.

MACKENZIE, Sir (Edward Montague) Compton (1883–1972), writer; brother of Fay *Compton, the actress; educated at St Paul's School and Magdalen College, Oxford; member of Bohemian family, meeting artists and writers; first book, a volume of poems, published in 1907; first novel in 1911, followed by *Carnival* (1912) and *Sinister Street* (1913); served with Royal Naval Division in Dardanelles, 1915; invalided and appointed military control officer, Athens, 1916; director, Aegean Intelligence Service, 1917; work in Secret Service led to *Gallipoli Memories* (1929), *Athenian Memories* (1931), and *Greek Memories* (1932—withdrawn—reissued, 1940); stayed on Capri and published *Vestal Fire* (1927) and *Extraordinary Women* (1928); literary critic of *Daily Mail*, 1931–5; rector of Glasgow University, 1931–4; editor of the *Gramophone*, 1923–61; stayed on Barra during 1939–45 war and published *Whisky Galore* (1947), made into very successful film; wrote enchanting children's books as well as novels and published autobiography, *My Life and Times* (10 vols., 1963–71); passion for islands and for cats; life president, Siamese Cat Club; president, Croquet Association, 1954–66, Songwriters' Guild, 1956, Poetry Society, 1961–4, and Dickens Fellowship, 1939–46; OBE, 1919; knighted, 1952; C.Lit., 1968; FRSL, hon. RSA, and hon. LL D of Glasgow and St Francis Xavier University.

MACKENZIE, Eneas (1778–1832), topographer; became Baptist minister and ultimately printer and publisher; founded the Mechanics' Institution, Newcastle; published several topographical works.

MACKENZIE, Frederick (1788?–1854), water-colour painter and topographical draughtsman; employed in making topographical and architectural drawings; exhibited at the Royal Academy, 1804–28; member of the Society of Painters in Water-Colours, 1823.

MACKENZIE, George, second earl of Seaforth (d. 1651), succeeded, 1633; of Royalist inclination, but with the Covenanters, 1639–40; sometimes supported and sometimes opposed *Montrose, 1640–6; joined Charles II in Holland, 1649; died at Schiedam.

MACKENZIE, George, first Viscount Tarbat, first earl of Cromarty (1630–1714), statesman; educated at St Andrews and Aberdeen universities; succeeded to family estates, 1654; as a Royalist had to remain in exile till 1660; lord of session as Lord Tarbat; planned *Lauderdale's downfall by means of the 'act of billeting', 1662; deprived of office, 1664; appointed lord justice-general of Scotland, 1678; chief minister of the king in Scotland, 1682–8; created Viscount Tarbat, 1685; joined the new government, 1689; secretary of state, 1702–4; created earl of Cromarty, 1703; advocated the Union; published miscellaneous pamphlets.

MACKENZIE, Sir George (1636–1691), of Rosehaugh, king's advocate; studied at St Andrews, Aberdeen, and Bourges universities; called to the bar at Edinburgh, 1659; distinguished himself in the trial of the marquis of *Argyll, 1661; knighted; MP, Ross, 1669; king's advocate, 1677; privy councillor, 1677; called 'Bloody' from his severe treatment (1679–86) of the Covenanters; resigned for a short time, 1686; again in office, 1688; opposed the dethronement of James II, and to escape the consequences retired from public life; founded the library of the Faculty of Advocates, opened 1689; author of moral essays and legal and historical works of a bigoted character.

MACKENZIE, George (1669–1725), Scottish biographer; son of George *Mackenzie, second earl of Seaforth; studied medicine at Aberdeen, Oxford, and Paris; MD, Aberdeen; chief work, *Lives and Characters of the most Eminent Writers of the Scots Nation* (vol. i, 1708, vol. ii, 1711, and vol. iii, 1722).

MACKENZIE, George, third earl of Cromarty (d. 1766), succeeded, 1731; joined Prince *Charles Edward, 1745; taken prisoner, tried, and sentenced to death, 1746; pardoned, 1749.

MACKENZIE, George (1741–1787), brother of John *Mackenzie, Baron Macleod; present at the defence of Gibraltar, 1780; lieutenant-colonel, 1783; died at Wallajabad.

MACKENZIE, George (1777–1856), meteorologist; began a register of atmospheric changes, 1802; formed his 'primary cycle of the winds', 1819; author of reports or *Manuals* of the weather.

MACKENZIE, Sir George Steuart, seventh baronet (1780–1848), of Coul, mineralogist; succeeded to baronetcy, 1796; discovered identity of diamond and carbon, 1800; FRS; studied mineralogy and geology in Iceland, 1810; in the Faroe Islands, 1812; joint author of *Travels in Iceland* (1811); wrote geological and miscellaneous works.

MACKENZIE, Sir George Sutherland (1844–1910), explorer and administrator; born at Bolarum, India; as representative of a London firm of East India merchants (1866) opened up trade route through Persian interior from Persian Gulf; pioneer explorer of Persian interior; managing director of Imperial British East Africa Company, 1888; developed East Africa, and explored interior as far as Uganda; CB, 1897; KCMG, 1902.

MACKENZIE, Henry (1745–1831), novelist and miscellaneous writer; educated at Edinburgh High School and University; attorney for the crown in Scotland; his novels, *The Man of Feeling* (1771), *The Man of the World* (1773), and *Julia de Roubigné* (1777), published anonymously; produced a successful tragedy, *The Prince of Tunis* (1773); superintended the periodicals *The Mirror*, 1779–80, and *The Lounger*, 1785–7; wrote on contemporary politics, 1784–93; comptroller of taxes for Scotland, 1804–31; his *Works* issued (1807 and 1808); called by *Scott the 'Northern *Addison'.

MACKENZIE, Henry (1808–1878), bishop suffragan of Nottingham; educated at Merchant Taylors' School, London, and Pembroke College, Oxford; ordained, 1834; MA, 1838; prebendary of Lincoln, 1858; sub-dean and canon-residentiary, 1864; archdeacon of Nottingham,

1866; DD, 1869; bishop suffragan of Nottingham, 1870–8.

MACKENZIE, James (1680?–1761), physician; studied at Edinburgh and Leiden universities; published *The History of Health and the Art of preserving it* (1758).

MACKENZIE, Sir James (1853–1925), physician and clinical researcher; MA, Edinburgh University, 1878; practised at Burnley, 1879–1907; consulting practitioner, London, 1907; FRS, 1915; knighted, 1915; best known for his researches into the nature of irregularities of heart's rhythm; his works include *The Study of the Pulse* (1902) and *Diseases of the Heart* (1908).

MACKENZIE, James Archibald Stuart-Wortley-, first Baron Wharncliffe (1776–1845), statesman. See STUART-WORTLEY-MACKENZIE.

MACKENZIE, John (1648?–1696), Irish divine; ordained Presbyterian minister, 1673; chaplain of *Walker's regiment during the siege of Londonderry, 1689; wrote narrative of siege, 1690.

MACKENZIE, John, Baron Macleod, Count Cromarty in the Swedish peerage (1727–1789), major-general in the British Army; great-grandson of George *Mackenzie, first Viscount Tarbat and first earl of Cromarty; joined Prince *Charles Edward, 1745; captured, 1746; pardoned, but deprived of his title and estates, 1748; joined a Swedish regiment, 1750; present at the Battle of Prague as a volunteer in the Prussian Army and aide-de-camp to Marshal Keith (see KEITH, JAMES FRANCIS EDWARD), 1757; returned to England, 1777; raised Highland Regiment, and as its colonel embarked with it for India, 1779; served in India till 1783; major-general, 1783; his estates restored, 1784.

MACKENZIE, John (1806–1848), Gaelic scholar; collected popular songs; bookkeeper in Glasgow University printing-office, 1836; published *Beauties of Gaelic Poetry* (1841); translated theological works into Gaelic.

M'KENZIE, Sir John (1836–1901), minister of lands in New Zealand; emigrated from Rossshire to New Zealand, 1860; minister of lands and immigration, 1881–1900; successfully purchased and divided large estates among small farmers; passed Lands for Settlement Act, 1894; member of Legislative Council and KCMG, 1901.

MACKENZIE, John Kenneth (1850–1888), medical missionary; obtained medical diplomas, London and Edinburgh, 1874; sent by the London Missionary Society to Hankow as a medical missionary, 1875; founded a medical school for native students at Tien-tsin; died at Tien-tsin.

MACKENZIE, John Stuart (1860–1935), philosopher; educated at Glasgow High School and University and Trinity College, Cambridge; first class, moral sciences tripos, 1889; fellow, 1890–96; professor of logic and philosophy, University College, Cardiff, 1895–1915; works include *Manual of Ethics* (1893), *Elements of Constructive Philosophy* (1917), *Outlines of Social Philosophy* (1918), *Fundamental Problems of Life* (1928), and *Cosmic Problems* (1931); a neo-Hegelian idealist; FBA, 1934.

MACKENZIE, Kenneth, fourth earl of Seaforth (d. 1701), succeeded to the earldom, 1678; followed James II to France, 1689; served in the siege of Londonderry, 1689; created by James titular marquis of Seaforth; failed to make terms with William III's government, 1690; imprisoned till 1697; died in Paris.

MACKENZIE, Kenneth (1754–1833), lieutenant-general. See DOUGLAS, Sir KENNETH.

MACKENZIE, Kenneth Douglas (1811–1873), colonel; ensign in the Gordon Highlanders, 1831; captured William Smith *O'Brien in the Irish insurrection, 1848; served in Crimea, 1854–6; went to India, 1857; employed in the expedition to China, 1860; colonel, 1869; assistant quartermaster-general at the Horse Guards, 1870.

MACKENZIE, Maria Elizabeth Frederica Stewart-, Lady Hood (1783–1862). See STEWART-MACKENZIE.

MACKENZIE, Sir Morell (1837–1892), physician; studied medicine at the London Hospital, at Paris, Vienna, and Pesth; specialized on throat diseases; MD, London, 1862; helped to found the Hospital for Diseases of the Throat, Golden Square, London, 1863; summoned to Berlin to attend the crown prince of Germany, afterwards the Emperor Frederick III, 1887; knighted, 1887; justified his conduct in regard to the German physicians and his general treatment of the case in *Frederick the Noble* (1888), an injudicious work, for which he was censured by the Royal College of Surgeons, 1889; published *Manual of Diseases of the Throat and Nose* (vol. i, 1880, vol. ii, 1884).

McKENZIE, Murdoch, the elder (d. 1797), hydrographer; surveyed the Orkney and Shetland isles, 1749; Admiralty surveyor till 1771; FRS, 1774; published *A Treatise on Marine Surveying* (1774) and the results of his work on the Scottish and Irish coasts (1776).

McKENZIE, Murdoch, the younger (1743–1829), commander in the navy; nephew of Murdoch *McKenzie the elder; Admiralty surveyor, 1771–88; commander, 1814.

MACKENZIE, Robert (1823–1881), miscellaneous writer; journalist and author of historical works.

MACKENZIE, Robert Shelton (1809–1880), miscellaneous writer; contributed poems to the *Dublin and London Magazine*, published *Lays of Palestine*, 1828; journalist in London after 1830; engaged in literary work in New York, 1852; settled at Philadelphia (1857), where he died; remembered chiefly for his compilations, including valuable editions of the *Noctes Ambrosianae* (1861–3) and of *Maginn's *Miscellaneous Works* (1855–7).

McKENZIE, (Robert) Tait (1867–1938), Canadian sculptor and expert in physical culture; BA (1889), MD (1892), McGill University; practised as orthopaedic surgeon in Montreal; professor of physical education, university of Pennsylvania, 1904–31; exhibited sculpture giving direct plastic expression to his ruling passion for bodily fitness; other work included the Scottish-American (Princes Street, Edinburgh) and Cambridge war memorials.

McKENZIE, Robert Trelford (1917–1981), political scientist and broadcaster; born in Vancouver; educated at King Edward High School, Vancouver, and University of British Columbia; lecturer there, 1937; served in Canadian Army, 1943–6; worked for doctorate at London School of Economics, 1946; lecturer, sociology department, 1949; professor of sociology, 1964; visiting lecturer on politics, Harvard and Yale, 1958–9; honorary degree, Simon Fraser University, Vancouver, 1969; political commentator and interviewer on television; known to public for the 'swingometer', a device, pre-computers, for determining how swing of votes as early election results are known translates to shift in parliamentary seats; published *British Political Parties: the Distribution of Power Within the Conservative and Labour Parties* (1955), and *Angels in Marble: Working Class Conservatism in Urban England* (with Allan Silver, 1968).

MACKENZIE, Samuel (1785–1847), portrait painter; studied in *Raeburn's studio at Edinburgh; contributed to the exhibitions of Associated Artists, Edinburgh, 1812–16, and to the Royal Institution, Edinburgh, 1821–9; member of the Scottish Academy, and contributed to its exhibitions, 1829–46; especially successful in his female portraits.

MACKENZIE, Sir Stephen (1844–1909), physician; brother of Sir Morell *Mackenzie; student at London Hospital, 1866; MRCS, 1869; MB, Aberdeen, 1873; MD, 1875; FRCP, 1879; physician at London Hospital, 1886, and at London Ophthalmic Hospital, 1884; made original researches into skin diseases and ophthalmology; knighted, 1903.

MACKENZIE, Thomas, Lord Mackenzie (1807–1869), Scottish judge; studied at St Andrews and Edinburgh universities; called to the Scottish bar, 1832; solicitor-general, 1851; raised to the bench with the title Lord Mackenzie, 1854; retired, 1864; author of *Studies in Roman Law, with Comparative Views of the Laws of France, England, and Scotland* (1862).

MACKENZIE, William, fifth earl of Seaforth (d. 1740), joined the Pretender (see JAMES FRANCIS EDWARD STUART), 1715; served throughout the war and escaped to France, 1716; accompanied George *Keith, tenth Earl Marischal, in his expedition to the Highlands, 1719; again escaped to France; pardoned and returned to Scotland, 1726.

MACKENZIE, William (1791–1868), ophthalmic surgeon; studied chiefly at Glasgow and Vienna; Waltonian lecturer, Glasgow University, 1828; surgeon-oculist to the queen in Scotland, 1838; helped to raise ophthalmic surgery to a high place among the special branches of medical science; his most important work, *Practical Treatise on the Diseases of the Eye* (1830).

MACKENZIE, Sir William (1849–1923), Canadian financier and railway builder; born in Upper Canada; became contractor, 1871; partner with (Sir) Donald Mann, 1886; their first line, Lake Manitoba Railway; Canadian Northern Railway Company incorporated, 1899; line completed from Port Arthur to Winnipeg, 1902; from Winnipeg to Edmonton, 1905; by 1915 trains were running from Montreal to Vancouver; financed all these operations; knighted, 1911; died at Toronto.

MACKENZIE, William Bell (1806–1870), of Magdalen Hall, Oxford; MA, 1837; published religious works.

MACKENZIE, William Forbes (1807–1862), of Portmore, Peeblesshire, politician; brother of Charles Frederick *Mackenzie; called to the bar, 1827; MP, Peeblesshire, 1837–52; lord of the Treasury, 1845–6; author of the Forbes Mackenzie Act (for the regulation of public-houses in Scotland), 1852.

MACKENZIE, William Lyon (1795–1861), leader of Canadian insurgents; a native of Dundee; emigrated to Canada, 1820; conducted the *Colonial Advocate* at Toronto, 1824–34; member of the Upper Canada legislative assembly for the county of York, 1828–30, and 1834–6; mayor of Toronto, 1834; led an insurrection (1837) which failed, and ended in his imprisonment for a year, but which drew the attention of the home government to colonial abuses; member of the United Provinces legislature, 1850–8.

MACKENZIE, William Warrender, first Baron Amulree (1860–1942), lawyer and industrial arbitrator; educated at Perth Academy and Edinburgh University; called to bar (Lincoln's Inn), 1886; KC, 1914; a chairman of committee on production, 1917–19; first president, Industrial Court, 1919–26; chairman, Railway National Wages Board, 1920–6, royal commissions on licensing (1929–31) and Newfoundland (1933), and many committees; secretary of state for air, 1930–1; KBE, 1918; baron, 1929; PC, 1930.

MACKENZIE KING, William Lyon (1874–1950), Canadian statesman. See KING.

MACKERELL, Benjamin (d. 1738), Norfolk antiquary; librarian of the Norwich Public Library, 1724–31.

McKERROW, John (1789–1867), Presbyterian divine; educated at Glasgow University; ordained by the Secession Church, 1813; published works on the history of his church.

McKERROW, Ronald Brunlees (1872–1940), scholar and bibliographer; educated at Harrow, King's College, London, and Trinity College, Cambridge; joint honorary secretary, Bibliographical Society, from 1912; founded and edited (1925–40) *Review of English Studies*; published *Introduction to Bibliography for Literary Students* (1927), an edition of Thomas *Nashe (1904–10), and prepared substantial portion of the Oxford Shakespeare; FBA, 1932.

McKERROW, William (1803–1878), Presbyterian divine; educated at Glasgow University; ordained and ministered in Manchester, 1827–69; supported Manchester liberal movements; started the Manchester *Examiner and Times*, 1846; member of the first Manchester School Board, 1870.

MACKESON, Frederick (1807–1853), lieutenant-colonel; in the East India Company's service; commissioner at Peshawar; received a Bengal cadetship, 1825; accompanied Sir Alexander *Burnes to Kabul, 1837; distinguished himself in the Sikh wars; commissioner at Peshawar, 1851–3; employed in quieting the frontier tribes; assassinated by a native.

McKEWAN, David Hall (1816–1873), watercolour painter; studied under David *Cox the elder; member of the Royal Institute of Painters in Water-colours, 1850; painted landscapes and interiors.

MACKGILL (or MACGILL), James (d. 1579), of Nether Rankeillour, clerk register of Scotland; educated at St Andrews University; admitted advocate, 1550; appointed clerk register and an ordinary lord of session, 1554; at first adhered to Queen *Mary, but was concerned in *Riccio's murder, 1565, and afterwards became her opponent; member of the new council, 1578.

McKIE, Douglas (1896–1967), historian of science; educated at Tredegar Grammar School, Sandhurst, and University College, London; served in France, 1915–17; severely wounded, 1917, and left army, 1920; first class, chemistry, B.Sc., 1923; Ph.D., 1928; part-time assistant in department of history and philosophy of science, University College, 1925; lecturer, 1934; reader, 1946; professor, 1957; emeritus professor, 1964; publications include *The Discovery of Specific and Latent Heat* (with N. H. de V. Heathcote, 1935), *The Essays of Jean Ray* (1951), and books on Lavoisier (1935 and 1952), for which he was made chevalier of the Legion of Honour; also contributed to the *New Cambridge Modern History*; founded and edited the *Annals of Science*, 1936–67; FRS, Edinburgh, 1958; fellow, University College, London, Royal Institute of Chemistry, Royal Society of Arts, and Society of Antiquaries.

McKIE, James (1816–1891), *Burns collector; bookseller at Kilmarnock; started the *Kilmarnock Journal* and the *Kilmarnock Weekly Post*; collected rare editions of Burns, and published facsimiles; author of works connected with Burns.

MACKIE, John (1748–1831), physician; studied at Edinburgh University; spent much time abroad, where he occasionally practised; published a *Sketch of a New Theory of Man* (1819).

McKIE, Sir William Neil (1901–1984), organist, choirmaster, and church musician; educated at Melbourne Grammar School, Australia, Royal College of Music, and Worcester College, Oxford; organ scholar; B.Mus., 1924; music teacher, Radley College, 1923–6; director of music, Clifton College, 1926–30; city organist, Melbourne, 1931–8; organist and choirmaster, Magdalen College, Oxford, 1938–41; organist and master of choristers, Westminster Abbey, 1941–63, but served in RAFVR during 1941–5; director of music, coronation service, 1953; taught at Royal Academy of Music, 1946–62; president, Royal College of Organists, 1956–8; hon. D.Mus., Oxford; MVO, 1948; knighted, 1953; FRSM, FRCM, FRCO, FTCL., and hon. RAM; hon. fellow, Worcester College, 1954; composed church music.

MACKINDER, Sir Halford John (1861–1947), geographer and politician; educated at Epsom College and Christ Church, Oxford; first class, natural science and president of Union, 1883; second class, history, 1884; called to bar

(Inner Temple), 1886; reader in geography, 1887–1905; principal, University College, Reading, 1892–1903; director, London School of Economics, 1903–8; taught economic geography, London University, 1895–1925; Unionist MP, Camlachie division, Glasgow, 1910–22; British high commissioner, South Russia, 1919–20; chairman, Imperial Shipping Committee, 1920–45, of Imperial Economic Committee, 1925–31; knighted, 1920; PC, 1926.

MacKINLAY, Antoinette (1843–1904), contralto singer. See STERLING.

McKINLAY, John (1819–1872), Australian explorer; emigrated to New South Wales, 1836; left Adelaide to trace the fate of O'Hara, *Burke, and *Wills, and to explore, 1861; proved that Lake Torrens did not exist; struck the coast at Gulf Carpentaria, 1862; headed another expedition to explore the northern territory, 1865.

MACKINNON, Daniel (1791–1836), colonel and historian of the Coldstream Guards; brother of William Alexander *Mackinnon; entered the guards, 1804; on the continent, 1805–14; wounded at Waterloo, 1815; colonel, 1830; published a famous *Origin and History of the Coldstream Guards* (1832).

MACKINNON, Daniel Henry (1813–1884), soldier and author; BA, Trinity College, Dublin; entered the army, 1836; served in Afghanistan, 1838–9; in the Sikh War, 1846; major-general, 1878; published *Military Services and Adventures in the Far East* (1849).

MacKINNON, Sir Frank Douglas (1871–1946), judge and author; educated at Highgate School and Trinity College, Oxford; second class, Lit. Hum., 1894; called to bar (Inner Temple), 1897; pupil and close associate of Sir T. E. *Scrutton; KC, 1914; bencher, 1923; treasurer, 1945; regular leader in commercial cases; judge of King's Bench division, 1924–37; sat frequently in commercial court and went regularly on circuit; lord justice of appeal, 1937–46; especially interested in eighteenth century; publications include edition of *Evelina* (1930), *The Murder in the Temple and other Holiday Tasks* (1935), *Grand Larceny* (1937), *On Circuit* (1940), and the lives of a number of lawyers in this Dictionary; knighted, 1924; PC, 1937.

MACKINNON, Sir William, first baronet (1823–1893), founder of British East Africa Company; engaged in mercantile firm in Glasgow; went to India, 1847, and with a partner founded firm of Mackinnon, Mackenzie & Co. for coasting trade in Bay of Bengal; took great part in founding Calcutta and Burma (after 1862, British India) Steam Navigation Company, 1856;

negotiated with Sultan Seyyid Barghash, 1878, for lease of land now called German East Africa (sanction declined by British government); chairman of Imperial British East Africa Company, 1888–95; territory taken over by British government, 1895; shared largely in promoting Sir H. M. *Stanley's expedition for relief of Emin Pasha, 1886; founded East African Scottish Mission, 1891; CIE, 1882; created baronet, 1889.

MACKINNON, William Alexander (1784–1870), legislator; brother of Daniel *Mackinnon; MA, St John's College, Cambridge, 1807; MP, Dunwich, 1819–20, 1830–1, Lymington, 1831–2, 1837–52, Rye, 1853, 1857, and 1859–65; published *On Public Opinion in Great Britain and other Parts of the World* (1828); rewritten as *History of Civilisation* (1846); FRS, 1827.

MACKINNON, Sir William Henry (1852–1929), general; appointed to Grenadier Guards, 1870; colonel commandant, City of London Imperial Volunteers, Dec. 1899; took unit out to South Africa, Jan. 1900; its most outstanding experiences battles of Doornkop (29 May) and Diamond Hill (12 June), but all its achievements completely justified faith of its commandant, whose military reputation was enhanced by its exploits; director-general of newly formed Territorial Force, 1908; general officer commanding-in-chief, Western Command, 1910; full general, 1913; KCB, 1908.

MACKINTOSH. See also MACINTOSH.

MACKINTOSH, Sir Alexander (1858–1948), parliamentary correspondent; educated at Macduff and Aberdeen University; on *Aberdeen Free Press*, 1879–1922; joined London parliamentary staff, 1881; London editor, 1887; political correspondent, *Liverpool Daily Post*, 1923–38; knighted, 1932.

MACKINTOSH, Charles Rennie (1868–1928), architect and painter; studied art and architecture in Glasgow; won competition for new building of Glasgow School of Art (1894) of great originality; Mackintosh exhibitions held in Venice, Munich, Dresden, Budapest, and Moscow; extremely influential on continent and founder of foreign school (*Jugendstil*); subsequently devoted himself with great success to water-colours.

MACKINTOSH, Harold Vincent, first Viscount Mackintosh of Halifax (1891–1964), man of business and public servant; educated at Halifax New School and private grammar school; worked in family confectionary business in Germany, 1909–11; served in RNVR during 1914–18 war; chairman, family firm, 1920; president, Advertising Association, 1942–6; involved in negotiations for Halifax building societies amalgamation into 'The Halifax', 1928; chairman, National Savings Committee, 1943; president, National Sunday School Union, 1924–5; president, World Council of Christian Education and Sunday School Association, 1928–58; acquired A. J. Caley, chocolate business, Norwich; chairman, promotion committee, East Anglia University, 1959; president, Yorkshire Agricultural Society, 1928–9; president, Royal Norfolk Agricultural Society, 1960; published *Early English Figure Pottery* (1938); JP, 1925; deputy lieutenant, West Riding of Yorkshire, 1945; hon. LL D, Leeds, 1948; knighted, 1922; baronet, 1935; baron, 1948; viscount, 1957.

MACKINTOSH, Hugh Ross (1870–1936), Scottish theologian; educated at George Watson's College and Edinburgh University; studied theology at New College, Edinburgh, and in Germany; ordained to Free Church ministry, 1897; professor of systematic theology, New College, Edinburgh, 1904–36; works include *The Doctrine of the Person of Jesus Christ* (1912) and *The Christian Experience of Forgiveness* (1927).

MACKINTOSH, Sir James (1765–1832), philosopher; educated at Aberdeen University; studied medicine at Edinburgh; obtained his diploma, 1787; moved to London, 1788; became a regular contributor to the *Oracle* belonging to John *Bell (1745–1831); published *Vindiciae Gallicae* (1791) in answer to *Burke's *Reflections on the French Revolution*; on becoming known to Burke, adopted his view of the French Revolution; barrister, Lincoln's Inn, 1795; lectured on 'The Law of Nature and Nations', 1799; recorder of Bombay, 1804–6; judge in the vice-Admiralty court, Bombay, 1806–11; MP, Nairn, 1813, Knaresborough, 1819; professor of 'law and general politics' at Haileybury, 1818–24; published *Dissertation on the Progress of Ethical Philosophy* (1830); commissioner of the Board of Control, 1830; wrote *History of England* in Lardner's *Cabinet Cyclopaedia* (1830), *History of the Revolution in England in 1688* (published 1834), and other historical works.

MACKINTOSH, James Macalister (1891–1966), public-health teacher and administrator; educated at Glasgow High School and Glasgow University; MA, 1912; served in France with 6th Cameron Highlanders, wounded; graduated MB, Ch.B., 1916; returned to France in RAMC, 1918; DPH, 1920; MD, 1923; called to bar (Gray's Inn) 1930; served as public-health officer in Dorset, Burton-on-Trent, and Leicestershire, 1920–30; county medical officer, Northampton, 1930–7; expert on rural housing; chief medical officer, Department of Health for Scotland, 1937–41; professor, public health, Glasgow,

1941–4; professor, public health, London, 1944–56, and dean, London School of Hygiene and Tropical Medicine, 1944–9; active in international field under World Health Organization; director WHO division of education and training, 1958–60; FRCP, London and Edinburgh, 1943; hon. LL D, Glasgow, 1950, and Birmingham, 1961; publications include *Housing and Family Life* (1952), *Teaching of Hygiene and Public Health in Europe* (with Professor Fred Grundy, 1957), and *Topics in Public Health* (1965).

MACKINTOSH, John (1833–1907), Scottish historian; published *History of Civilization in Scotland* (4 vols., 1878–88); LL D, Aberdeen, 1880.

MACKINTOSH, John Pitcairn (1929–1978), politician and political scientist; educated at Melville College, Edinburgh, and Edinburgh University; first class, history, 1950; studied for PPE at Balliol College, Oxford, 1951–2, but disliked Oxford; Sir John Dill memorial fellow, Princeton, USA, 1952–3; junior lecturer in history, Glasgow University, 1953–4; lecturer at Edinburgh, 1954–61; unsuccessful as Labour candidate for Pentlands division of Edinburgh, 1959; professor, Ibadan University, Nigeria, 1961–3; published *The British Cabinet* (1962); senior lecturer in politics, Glasgow, 1963–5; professor of politics, University of Strathclyde, 1965–6; published *The Devolution of Power: Local Democracy, Regionalism and Nationalism* (1968); Labour MP for Berwick and East Lothian, 1966; persuasive parliamentary orator who did not always agree with his Labour colleagues; served on select committees on agriculture and Scottish affairs; chairman, Hansard Society, 1974–8; contributed articles to many papers, including *The Times* and the *Scotsman*.

MACKINTOSH, William (1662–1743), of Borlum, Inverness-shire; brigadier in *James Edward the Old Pretender's service; educated at King's College, Aberdeen; prominent in the Jacobite rising, 1714; confined in Newgate, 1715; escaped to France, 1716; returned to Scotland probably in 1719; again captured and imprisoned for life in Edinburgh Castle; published work on tillage in Scotland (1729).

MACKLIN, Charles (1697?–1797), actor and stage-manager; played in London at Lincoln's Inn Theatre, 1730, at Drury Lane, 1733–44, and 1744–8; made his reputation by his interpretation of the character of Shylock; appeared in Dublin (under *Sheridan's auspices), 1748–50, and again, 1761 and 1763–70; at Covent Garden, London, 1750–3, 1761, 1772, 1775, 1781–9; retired from the stage, 1789. Of his dramatic productions, *Love à la Mode*, a farce (1759) and

The Man of the World (1781), one of the best comedies of the century, are the most notable.

MACKLIN, Maria (d. 1781), actress; daughter of Charles *Macklin; appeared first at Drury Lane in *Richard III*, 1743; left the stage, 1777; Portia, Desdemona, and Rosalind among her parts.

MACKNESS, James (1804–1851), medical writer; passed the College of Surgeons, 1824; MD, St Andrews, 1840; member of the council of the British Medical Association, 1847; published medical works.

MACKNIGHT, James (1721–1800), biblical critic; educated at Glasgow and Leiden universities; ordained, 1753; published a *Harmony of the Gospels* (1756), which became celebrated; DD, Edinburgh, 1759; main promoter of the declaratory Act of Assembly, 1782; issued a *Translation of all the Apostolical Epistles* (1795).

MACKNIGHT, Thomas (1829–1899), political writer; studied medicine at King's College, London; editor (1866–99) of Belfast *Northern Whig*, which became mainstay of Liberal party in Ireland, though it opposed home rule; published *Life and Times of Edmund Burke* (1858–60) and other political and historical works.

MACKONOCHIE. See also MACONOCHIE.

MACKONOCHIE, Alexander Heriot (1825–1887), divine; of Wadham College, Oxford; ordained, 1849; MA, 1851; adopted advanced ritualistic views, and was subjected to a series of lawsuits promoted by the Church Association, 1867–82.

McKOWEN, James (1814–1889), Ulster poet; employed in bleach-works at Belfast; contributed racy poems to various Irish newspapers; his 'Ould Irish Jig' known throughout Ireland.

MACKRETH, Sir Robert (1726–1819), club proprietor; at first a billiard-marker, and then a waiter, at White's Club; proprietor of White's, 1761; bookmaker and usurer; MP for Castle Rising through the nomination of the earl of Orford, his debtor, 1774–1802; proceeded against and found guilty for taking advantage of a minor, 1786, and for assaulting John *Scott (afterwards Lord Eldon), 1792; knighted for his services in parliament, 1795.

MACKULLOCH, Magnus (*fl.* 1480), reputed continuator of *Fordun's *Scotichronicon*; copied for the archbishop of St Andrews the *Scotichronicon*, 1483–84; probably wrote the additions at the end, which bring the narrative down to 1460.

MACKWORTH, Sir Humphry (1657–1727), politician and capitalist; of Magdalen College, Oxford; barrister, Middle Temple, 1682; knighted, 1683; MP, Cardiganshire, 1701, 1702–5 and 1710–13; deputy-governor of a large mining company; accused of peculation and found guilty by the House of Commons, 1710; one of the founders of the Society for Promoting Christian Knowledge; author of political and financial pamphlets.

MACKWORTH-YOUNG, Gerard (1884–1965), Indian civil servant and archaeologist; eldest son of (Sir) William Mackworth *Young; educated at Eton and King's College, Cambridge; first class, part i, classical tripos, 1906; entered Indian Civil Service, 1907; journeyed in western Tibet, 1912; under-secretary, Punjab government, 1913; under-secretary, home department, Government of India, 1916–19; deputy-commissioner, Delhi, 1921; deputy secretary, army department, Government of India, 1924; secretary, 1926; CIE, 1929; retired from ICS, 1932; published *The Epigrams of Callimachus* (1934) and *Archaic Marble Sculpture from the Acropolis* (with Humfry *Payne, 1936); enrolled as student, British School of Archaeology, Athens, 1932; director, 1936–9; returned to India during 1939–45 war, joint secretary, War Department; director, British School of Archaeology, Athens, 1945–6; published *What Happens in Singing* (1953).

MACKY, John (d. 1726), government agent or spy; discovered James II's intended expedition to England, 1692; inspector of the coast from Dover to Harwich, 1693; published *A View of the Court of St. Germains from the Year 1690 to 1695* (1696); directed the packet-boat service from Dover to France and Flanders, 1697–1702, and 1706–8; suspected by the government and imprisoned; released at accession of George I; died at Rotterdam. His *Memoirs of the Secret Services of John Macky, Esq.* (published 1733) is an important contribution to contemporary history.

MACLACHLAN, Ewen (1775–1822), Gaelic poet and scholar; educated at Aberdeen University; headmaster of Aberdeen Grammar School, 1819–22; author of some Gaelic poems, also *Attempts in Verse* (1807) and *Metrical Effusions* (1816).

MACLACHLAN, Lauchlan (d. 1746), fifteenth chief of the ancient Argyllshire clan; succeeded his father, 1719; joined Prince *Charles Edward, 1745; killed at Culloden, 1746.

McLACHLAN, Robert (1837–1904), entomologist; published *Catalogue of British Neuroptera* (1870) and *Synopsis of the Trichoptera of the European Fauna* (1874–84); FRS, 1877; president of Entomological Society, 1885–6, and editor from 1864 and proprietor (1902) of *Entomological Monthly Magazine*.

McLACHLAN, Thomas Hope (1845–1897), landscape painter; BA, Trinity College, Cambridge, 1868; barrister, Lincoln's Inn, 1868; abandoned law for art, 1878. His picture, *Ships that pass in the Night*, is in the National Gallery.

MACLAGAN, Christian (1811–1901), Scottish archaeologist; devoted time and money to removal of slums in Stirling; made valuable researches into and published works on prehistoric remains in Scotland; prepared skilful rubbings from sculptured stones; lady associate of Scottish Society of Antiquaries, 1871.

MACLAGAN, Sir Eric Robert Dalrymple (1879–1951), director of the Victoria and Albert Museum; son of W. D. *Maclagan, archbishop of York; educated at Winchester and Christ Church, Oxford; joined Victoria and Albert Museum in textiles department, 1905; transferred to architecture and sculpture, 1909; director of museum, 1924–45; popularized it and organized special exhibitions including English medieval art (1930) and William Morris centenary (1934); publications include *Guide to English Ecclesiastical Embroideries* (1907), catalogues of *Italian Plaquettes* (1924) and *Italian Sculpture* (with Margaret Longhurst, 1932), and *The Bayeux Tapestry* (King Penguin, 1943); CBE, 1919; knighted, 1933; KCVO, 1945; hon. LL D, Birmingham, 1944; hon. D.Litt., Oxford, 1945.

MACLAGAN, William Dalrymple (1826–1910), successively bishop of Lichfield and archbishop of York; studied law at Edinburgh University; an officer in 51st Regiment Madras Native Infantry, 1847–9; BA, Peterhouse, Cambridge, 1857; ordained, 1856; served curacies in London until 1869; rector of Newington, 1869–75, of St Mary Abbots, Kensington, 1875–8; bishop of Lichfield, 1878–91; interested in unity of Christendom; attended conference of Old Catholics at Bonn, 1887; archbishop of York, 1891–1908; established training college for clergy at York, 1892; discouraged advanced ritual; inaugurated Poor Benefices Fund; responsible with Archbishop Frederick *Temple for reply to Pope Leo XIII's bull denying validity of Anglican orders, 1896; crowned Queen *Alexandra, 1902; resigned archbishopric, 1908; composed hymns (including 'The Saints of God') and hymn tunes.

MACLAINE, Archibald (1722–1804), divine; brother of James *Maclaine; MA, Glasgow, 1746; DD, Glasgow, 1767; co-pastor to the English church at The Hague, 1747–96; translated Mosheim's *Ecclesiastical History*, 1765 (last reprint, 1825).

MACLAINE (or MACLEAN), James (1724–1750), 'gentleman highwayman'; spent his patrimony and took to the highway, 1748; arrested, 1750; tried and hanged.

MACLAREN, Alexander (1826–1910), Baptist divine; student at Glasgow University; BA, London, 1845; successful minister at Southampton, 1846–58, and Union Chapel, Manchester, 1858–1903; rebuilt Union Chapel (1869) and added schools (1880); built new churches and missions in poor districts; exerted great influence as preacher of sermons showing both literary and exegetical skill; president of Baptist Union, 1875 and 1901, and of Baptist World Congress in London, 1905; hon. DD, Edinburgh, 1877, Glasgow, 1907; Litt.D., Manchester, 1902; visited Australia, 1883, and Italy, 1865 and 1903; published devotional works and scripture expositions; edited in *Expositor's Bible*, Colossians and Ephesians (1887) and the Psalms (3 vols., 1893–4).

MACLAREN, Archibald (1755–1826), dramatist; entered the army, 1755; served in the American War; returned to Scotland; on his discharge joined a troop of strolling players; joined Dumbartonshire Highlanders, 1794; discharged after serving in Guernsey and Ireland; author of numerous dramatic pieces, two prose works describing the Irish rebellion, 1798–1800, and a few poems.

MacLAREN, Archibald Campbell (1871–1944), cricketer; captained Harrow, 1890; first played for Lancashire, 1890; his 424 against Somerset (1895) long remained record innings; played for England in Australia, 1894, 1897–8, and (captain) 1901–2; captained England in fourteen home matches against Australia (1899, 1902, 1909), winning only twice; captained MCC in Australia and New Zealand, 1922–3.

MACLAREN, Charles (1782–1866), editor of the *Scotsman*; established the *Scotsman*, 1817; editor, 1820–45; edited the sixth edition of the *Encyclopaedia Britannica* (1823); published geological works.

McLAREN, Charles Benjamin Bright, first Baron Aberconway (1850–1934), barrister and man of business; son of Duncan *McLaren and half-brother of John, Lord *McLaren; educated at Edinburgh, Bonn, and Heidelberg universities; called (Lincoln's Inn, 1874) and practised at Chancery bar until 1897 when turned to direction of industrial concerns; chairman, John Brown & Co., Metropolitan Railway Co., steel and colliery undertakings; Liberal MP, Stafford (1880–6), Bosworth division (1892–1910); QC, 1897; baronet, 1902; PC, 1908; baron, 1911.

McLAREN, Duncan (1800–1886), politician; member of the Edinburgh Town Council, 1833, provost, 1851–4; MP, Edinburgh, 1865–81; wrote on political questions.

McLAREN, Henry Duncan, second Baron Aberconway (1879–1953), industrialist; son of first Baron *Aberconway; succeeded father, 1934; educated at Eton and Balliol College, Oxford; Liberal MP, West Staffordshire, 1906–10; Bosworth division, 1910–22; served in Ministry of Munitions during 1914–18 war; succeeded father as chairman of John Brown & Co.; formed and chairman, English Clays Lovering Pochin & Co., 1932; his garden at Bodnant given to National Trust, 1949; president, Royal Horticultural Society, 1931–53.

MACLAREN, Ian (pseudonym) (1850–1907), Presbyterian divine and author. See WATSON, JOHN.

McLAREN, John, Lord McLaren (1831–1910), Scottish judge; son of Duncan *McLaren; passed to Scottish bar, 1856; helped to reorganize Scottish Liberals and arrange Gladstone's 'Midlothian campaign', 1879–80; MP for Wigton, 1880; appointed lord advocate (Apr.), losing seat on seeking re-election; elected for Edinburgh, Jan. 1881; accepted Scottish judgeship under pressure from Gladstone and Sir William *Harcourt, 1881; an eminently successful judge; edited works on Scottish law; a student of astronomy and mathematics; hon. LL D, Edinburgh, 1882, Glasgow, 1883, and Aberdeen, 1906.

McLAREN, William (1772–1832), Scottish poet; weaver, manufacturer, and tavern-keeper; published verse (1817 and 1827).

MACLAUCHLAN, Thomas (1816–1886), Scottish Presbyterian divine, and Gaelic scholar; MA, Aberdeen, 1833; ordained, 1837; supported the non-intrusionists at the disruption, 1843; LL D, Aberdeen, 1864; moderator of the Free Church Assembly, 1876; maintained the authenticity of *Macpherson's *Ossian*; edited the *Book of the Dean of Lismore* (1862).

MACLAURIN, Colin (1698–1746), mathematician and natural philosopher; educated at Glasgow; professor of mathematics in the Marischal College, Aberdeen, 1715–26; FRS, 1719; deputy-professor at Edinburgh University, 1725; organized the defence of Edinburgh against the rebels, 1745; the one mathematician of first rank trained in Great Britain in the eighteenth century. His most noted works are *Geometria Organica, sive Descriptio Linearum Curvarum Universalis* (1720), *A Treatise of Fluxions* (1742), *A Treatise of Algebra, with an Appendix De Linearum Geometricarum Proprietatibus Generalibus* (published 1748), and *An account of Sir Isaac Newton's Philosophy* (published 1748).

MACLAURIN, John (1693–1754), Presbyterian divine; brother of Colin *Maclaurin; studied at Glasgow and Leiden; ordained, 1719; a leader of the 'intrusionists'; a famous preacher and controversialist; his *Sermons and Essays* published (1755).

MACLAURIN, John, Lord Dreghorn (1734–1796), Scottish judge; son of Colin *Maclaurin; educated at Edinburgh High School and University; advocate, 1756; senator of the College of Justice, with the title Lord Dreghorn, 1788–96; published satirical poems and legal works.

MACLAY, Joseph Paton, first Baron Maclay (1857–1951), shipowner and shipping controller; educated in Glasgow; established tramp-ship firm with T. W. McIntyre, 1885, to become one of largest shipping concerns on Clyde; active in Scottish evangelical and philanthropic life; appointed shipping controller and head of new Ministry of Shipping, 1916; requisitioned all British shipping and co-ordinated with Americans; this with convoys and control of imports overcame shipping shortage; baronet, 1914; PC, 1916; baron, 1922.

MACLEAN. See also MACLAINE.

MACLEAN, Alexander (1840–1877), painter; studied at Rome, Florence, and Antwerp; exhibited at the Royal Academy, 1872–7.

MACLEAN, Allan (1725–1784), colonel; in the Scots Brigade in the Dutch service; taken prisoner, 1747; served in America, 1757–83; commanded the operations against Quebec, 1776–7; colonel, 1782.

McLEAN, Archibald (1733–1812), Baptist minister; a printer and bookseller by trade; successively a Presbyterian and Sandemanian; became a Baptist minister, 1768; author of religious and controversial works (collected, 1823).

MACLEAN, Charles (*fl.* 1788–1824), medical and political writer; entered the service of the East India Company; appointed surgeon to East Indiamen voyaging to Jamaica and India; settled in Bengal, 1792; ordered to leave India for making an insinuation in an Indian newspaper against a magistrate, 1798; went to Hamburg and was forcibly detained by Napoleon, 1803; left the service on failing to obtain promotion; travelled for the Levant Company, 1815–17; lecturer on the diseases of hot climates to the East India Company; published medical works.

McLEAN, Sir Donald (1820–1877), New Zealand statesman; emigrated to Sydney, c.1837; went to New Zealand and devoted himself to the study of the Maori language; local protector for the Taranaki district; employed in difficult negotiations with the Maoris from 1844; resident magistrate for the Taranaki district, 1850; entered the legislative assembly, 1866; obtained the admittance of Maoris to the assembly, 1867; native minister and minister for colonial defence, 1869–76; brought about a final peace with the natives, 1870; KCMG, 1874; died in New Zealand.

MACLEAN, Sir Donald (1864–1932), politician; educated at Haverfordwest and Carmarthen grammar schools; admitted solicitor, 1887; practised in Cardiff and London; Liberal MP, Bath, 1906–10, Peebles, 1910–22, North Cornwall, 1929–32; deputy speaker, 1911–18; influential in formation (chairman, 1919–22) of Liberal Parliamentary party; president, Board of Education, 1931–2; PC, 1916; KBE, 1917.

MACLEAN, Donald Duart (1913–1983), British diplomat and Soviet spy; third son of (Sir) Donald *Maclean; educated at Gresham's School, Holt, and Trinity Hall, Cambridge; first class, part ii, modern languages tripos, 1934; associated with Guy Burgess, Anthony *Blunt, and H. A. R. ('Kim') Philby, all recruited to the Soviet NKVD (later KGB); entered the Diplomatic Service; third secretary, Paris embassy, 1938; first secretary, Washington, 1944; joint secretary, Anglo-American-Canadian Combined Policy Committee, 1947, with access to American Atomic Energy Commission; counsellor and head of Chancery, Cairo, 1948; sent back to London and treated psychiatrically for alcoholism and homosexuality; thought to have recovered, appointed head of American department, Foreign Office, 1950; investigation of earlier leakages in Washington pointed to Maclean as prime suspect; warned by Philby and Burgess, defected to USSR, 1951; taught graduate courses in international relations in Moscow; published *British Foreign Policy since Suez* (London, 1970); awarded doctorate of Institute of World Economics and International Relations; caused lasting damage to Anglo-American relations arising from American criticism of laxity of British security.

MACLEAN, Sir Harry Aubrey De Vere (1848–1920), soldier; served in army, 1869–76; kaid of infantry and instructor to forces attached to court of sultans of Morocco, 1877–1909; CMG, for services rendered to British legation at Tangier, 1898; KCMG, 1901; kidnapped and held to ransom by rebel sherif, Raisuli, 1907; died at Tangier.

MACLEAN, James Mackenzie (1835–1906), journalist and politician; educated at Christ's Hospital; edited *Newcastle Chronicle*, 1855–8; a leader-writer for *Manchester Guardian*, 1859; edited *Bombay Gazette*, 1859–61; proprietor from 1864; an independent critic both of Indian aspirations and of Indian government; greatly influenced public opinion in Bombay; appointed a magistrate, 1862; helped in creation of semi-elective municipal corporations, 1872; returned home, 1879; had interest in and regularly contributed to *Western Mail*, Cardiff, from 1882; supporter of Lord Randolph *Churchill; Conservative MP for Oldham, 1885–92, and for Cardiff, 1895–1900; opposed South African War, 1899; supported free trade, 1903; broke with Conservative party, and wrote for Liberal journals; published *Recollections of Westminster and India* (1902).

MACLEAN, Sir John (1811–1895), archaeologist; entered ordnance department of War Office, 1837; keeper of ordnance records in Tower of London, 1855–61, and deputy chief auditor of army accounts, 1865–71; knighted, 1871; works include *Parochial and Family History of Deanery of Trigg Minor* (1868–79).

MACLEAN, John (1828–1886), first bishop of Saskatchewan; MA, Aberdeen, 1851; ordained, 1858, and went to Canada under the Colonial and Continental Church Society, 1858; archdeacon of Assiniboia, 1866; bishop of Saskatchewan, 1874; founder of the Alberta University.

MACLEAN, John (1835?–1890), actor; first appeared on the stage at Plymouth, 1859; in London, 1861; thenceforth acted constantly at the Gaiety and other theatres.

MACLEAN, Mrs Letitia Elizabeth (1802–1838), poetess. See LANDON.

McLEAN, Norman (1865–1947), orientalist; educated at Edinburgh High School and University, and Christ's College, Cambridge; first class, classics (1888), Semitic languages (1890); fellow, 1893; tutor, 1911; master, 1927–36; university lecturer in Aramaic, 1903–31; with A. E. *Brooke prepared larger Cambridge edition of Septuagint; FBA, 1934.

MACLEAR, George Frederick (1833–1902), theological writer; BA, Trinity College, Cambridge, 1855; first class in theological tripos, 1856; MA, 1860; DD, 1872; reader at the Temple, 1865–70; assistant at (1860–6) and headmaster of (1867–80) King's College School, London; warden of St Augustine's Missionary College, Canterbury, 1880–1902; honorary canon of Canterbury Cathedral, 1885; works include lucid textbooks on Bible history (1862) and *The Conversion of the West* (4 vols., 1878).

MACLEAR, John Fiot Lee Pearse (1838–1907), admiral; son of Sir Thomas *Maclear; born at Cape Town; entered navy, 1851; commander, 1868; went as commander of *Challenger* with Sir George *Nares on a voyage of discovery round the world, 1872–6; surveyed Straits of Magellan in *Alert*, 1879–82; on surveying service, 1883; admiral, 1907; died at Niagara.

MACLEAR, Sir **Thomas** (1794–1879), astronomer; studied medicine in London; MRCS, 1815; FRS, 1831; studied astronomy; royal astronomer at Cape of Good Hope, 1834–70; occupied with the re-measurement and extension of Lacaille's arc, 1837–47; made valuable astronomical, meteorological, magnetic, and tidal observations; knighted, 1860; became blind, 1876; his more important observations recorded in the 'Cape Catalogues'; died at Mowbray, Cape Town.

MACLEAY, Alexander (1767–1848), entomologist and colonial statesman; chief clerk in the Prisoners-of-war Office, London, 1795; secretary of the Transport Board, 1806–18; FRS, 1809; colonial secretary for New South Wales, 1825–37; first speaker in the first legislative council, 1843–6; died at Sydney; possessed a fine collection of insects.

MACLEAY, Sir **George** (1809–1891), Australian explorer and statesman; son of Alexander *Macleay; explored South Australia with *Sturt; speaker of the legislative council of New South Wales, 1843–6; KCMG, 1875.

MACLEAY, James Robert (1811–1892), of the Foreign Office; son of Alexander *Macleay; secretary and registrar to the British and Portuguese commission at the Cape of Good Hope for the suppression of the slave trade, 1843–58.

MACLEAY, Kenneth, the younger (1802–1878), miniature painter; son of Kenneth *Macleay the elder; entered the Trustees' Academy, Edinburgh, 1822; one of the original members of the Royal Scottish Academy, founded, 1826; employed by Queen Victoria to paint figures illustrative of the Highland clan costumes (selection published as *Highlanders of Scotland*, 1870).

MACLEAY, Kenneth, the elder (*fl.* 1819), antiquary; physician in Glasgow; published *Historical Memoirs of Rob Roy and the Clan MacGregor* (1818).

MACLEAY, Sir **William** (1820–1891), Australian statesman and naturalist; nephew of Alexander *Macleay; emigrated to Australia, 1839; member of the legislative assembly, 1854–74; formed a valuable entomological museum, afterwards presented to the New South Wales University; member of the legislative council; knighted, 1889.

MACLEAY, William Sharp (1792–1865), zoologist; son of Alexander *Macleay; educated at Westminster and Trinity College, Cambridge; MA, 1818; secretary to the board for liquidating British claims in France on the peace of 1815; commissary judge in Havana, 1830–7; went to New South Wales, 1839, where he enlarged his father's collection of insects; chief work, *Horae Entomologicae*, propounding the circular or quinary system of classification (2 vols., 1819 and 1821).

MACLEHOSE, Mrs **Agnes** (1759–1841), the 'Clarinda' of Robert *Burns; née Craig; grandniece of Colin *Maclaurin; married James Maclehose, a Glasgow lawyer, 1776; separated from him, 1780; moved to Edinburgh, 1782; first met Burns, 1787; entered into a familiar correspondence with him and sent him verses; her ambiguous relations with Burns were interrupted for a while by his marriage to Jean Armour, 1788, but were continued till 1791. Mrs Maclehose went to Jamaica to join her husband, but soon returned, 1792; corresponded with Burns till 1794; the whole correspondence between Burns and herself published (1843).

McLELLAN, Archibald (1797–1854), coach-builder and amateur of works of art; a leading Glasgow citizen. His collection of pictures forms the nucleus of the Corporation Galleries of Art at Glasgow.

MACLELLAN, John (1609?–1651), of Kirkcudbright; Covenanting minister; MA, Glasgow, 1629; after ordination ministered in Ireland and Scotland; supposed to possess the gift of prophecy; prophesied the disaster of *Hamilton's force in England, 1648; member of the assemblies' commissions, 1642, 1645, and 1649.

MACLELLAN, Sir **Robert,** of Bombie, first Baron Kirkcudbright (d. 1639), succeeded his father as baron of Bombie, 1608; gentleman of the bedchamber to James I and Charles I; knighted by James I and created baronet by Charles I; created Baron Kirkcudbright (Scottish peerage), 1633; representative elder to the general assembly, 1638.

McLENNAN, Sir **John Cunningham** (1867–1935), Canadian physicist; first-class honours, physics, Toronto, 1892; assistant demonstrator in physics, 1892, demonstrator, 1899, associate professor, 1902, director of physics laboratory, 1904, professor, 1907–32, dean of graduate studies, 1930–2; worked in England on anti-submarine measures, 1917–19, on radium treatment of cancer, 1932–5; authority on radioactivity and cosmic rays; succeeded in liquefying helium, 1923; reproduced 'auroral green line', 1925; FRS, 1915; KBE, 1935.

McLENNAN, John Ferguson (1827–1881), sociologist; educated at Aberdeen University and

Trinity College, Cambridge; 25th wrangler, 1853; wrote for the *Leader* for two years; called to the Scottish bar, 1857; contributed the article on 'Law' to the *Encyclopaedia Britannica* (8th edn.), 1857; parliamentary draughtsman for Scotland, 1871; LL D, Aberdeen, 1874; author of *Primitive Marriage* (1865), a book that gave immense impetus to research, and other works; originated theory that exogamy was the primitive form of marriage, polyandry and monandry being successive developments.

MACLEOD, Alexander (1817–1891), Presbyterian divine; educated at Glasgow University; ordained, 1844; DD, 1865; moderator of the Presbyterian Church of England, 1889; author of articles and essays on religious subjects.

MACLEOD, Allan (d. 1805), political writer; editor and owner of the *London Albion Journal*; author of virulent pamphlets.

McLEOD, Sir Donald Friell (1810–1872), Indian administrator; son of Duncan *McLeod; born at Calcutta; came to England, 1814; educated at Haileybury; returned to Calcutta, 1828; after holding subordinate posts became commissioner of the Trans-Sutlej states, 1849–54; at Lahore during the Mutiny, 1857–8; lieutenant-governor of the Punjab, 1865–70; KCSI, 1866.

McLEOD, Duncan (1780–1856), lieutenant-general; relative of Neil *Macleod; second-lieutenant, Bengal Engineers, 1795; chief engineer for Bengal; lieutenant-general, 1851.

MACLEOD, Fiona (pseudonym) (1855–1905), romanticist. See SHARP, WILLIAM.

MACLEOD, Sir George Husband Baird (1828–1892), surgeon; son of Norman *Macleod the elder; studied medicine at Glasgow (MD, 1853), Paris, and Vienna; senior surgeon of the civil hospital at Smyrna during the Crimean War; regius professor of surgery, Glasgow, 1869; knighted, 1887.

MACLEOD, Henry Dunning (1821–1902), economist; BA, Trinity College, Cambridge, 1843; MA, 1863; called to bar, 1849; published *The Theory and Practice of Banking* (1856); lectured on banking at Cambridge, London, Edinburgh, and Aberdeen, 1877–82; made valuable contributions to historical side of economic science; in *Elements of Political Economy* (1858) first applied term 'Gresham's Law' to principle that 'bad money drives out good'; awarded civil list pension, 1892; also wrote *The Theory of Credit* (2 vols., 1889–91) and *The History of Banking in Great Britain* (1896).

MACLEOD, Iain Norman (1913–1970), politician; educated at Fettes College and Gonville and Caius College, Cambridge; president, Cam-

bridge Bridge Club; fought in France, 1939–40 and 1943–4; joined Conservative parliamentary secretariat, 1946; wrote weekly bridge column for *Sunday Times*; published *Bridge is an Easy Game* (1952); Conservative MP, Enfield, 1950; minister of health, 1952–5; PC, 1952; minister of labour, 1955–9; secretary of state for colonies, 1959–61; accelerated movement towards independence of African colonies; chancellor of duchy of Lancaster and leader of House of Commons; chairman, Conservative party organization, 1961–3; editor of the *Spectator*, 1963–5; chancellor of the Exchequer, 1970; published *Neville Chamberlain* (1961).

McLEOD, (James) Walter (1887–1978), bacteriologist; educated at Mill Hill School, London, and Glasgow University; MB, Ch.B., 1908; blue for athletics; Coates scholar, 1909; Carnegie scholar, 1910–11 in department of pathology, Glasgow; assistant lecturer in pathology, Charing Cross Medical School, 1912, working on streptococci and spirochaetes; served in RAMC, 1914–18, working on trench fever, bacillary dysentery, and other diseases; OBE (military), 1919; lecturer in bacteriology, department of pathology, Leeds, 1919; Brotherton professor of bacteriology, Leeds, 1922–52; professor emeritus; worked on problems of diphtheria, and studies of sulphonamides and penicillin; continued laboratory work after retirement from his chair, studying infections of the urinary tract; FRS, 1933; fellow, Royal Society of Edinburgh, 1957; hon. fellow, Royal College of Pathologists, 1970; president, Society for General Microbiology, 1949–52; received honorary degrees and other academic distinctions.

MACLEOD, John (1757–1841), Presbyterian divine and Gaelic scholar; educated at Aberdeen University; ordained, 1779; DD, 1795; superintended publication of Gaelic Bible, 1826; general editor of Gaelic dictionary, 1828.

McLEOD, John (1777?–1820), naval surgeon and author; surgeon in the navy, 1801; on the *Trusty*, a slave-trade boat, 1803; concerned in the capture of a French ship and tried for piracy; employed on foreign service till 1817; MD, St Andrews, 1818; surgeon to the *Royal Sovereign* yacht, 1818–20; published *Narrative of a Voyage in His Majesty's late Ship* Alceste *to the Yellow Sea, along the coast of Corea* (1817) and *A Voyage to Africa* (1820).

MACLEOD, John James Rickard (1876–1935), physiologist and biochemist; educated at Aberdeen Grammar School and Marischal College; MB, Ch.B., 1898; professor of physiology, Western Reserve University, Cleveland, Ohio, 1903–18, Toronto, 1918–28, Aberdeen,

1928–35; from 1905 interested in diabetes; provided facilities, advice, and co-operation for experiments of (Sir) F. G. *Banting and C. H. Best which resulted in discovery of insulin; shared Nobel Prize with Banting, 1923; carried out research in many fields but most influential as a teacher and director of research; FRS, 1923.

MACLEOD, Sir John Macpherson (1792–1881), Indian civilian; educated at Haileybury and Edinburgh University; writer in Madras Civil Service, 1811; commissioner (1832) for government of Mysore, of which province he organized the financial and political administration; KCSI, 1866; privy councillor, 1871.

MACLEOD, Mary (1569–1674), Gaelic poetess; called 'Poetess of the Isles'; her poems chiefly panegyrics of the Macleods.

MACLEOD, Neil, eleventh of Assynt (1628?–1697?), betrayed *Montrose to his enemies, 1650; imprisoned for having delivered up Montrose, 1660–6; pardoned, 1666; again imprisoned in consequence of a feud with the Mackenzies, 1672; tried on four charges, although acquitted on two; was deprived of his estates, 1690.

MACLEOD, Sir Norman (fl. 1650), founder of the Macleods of Bernera and Muiravonside; joined forces of Charles II, 1650; present at the Battle of Worcester, 1651, and tried for high treason; escaped; was made lieutenant-colonel and employed by Charles II to carry information to his adherents; knighted at the Restoration.

MACLEOD, Norman, the elder (1783–1862), clergyman of the church of Scotland; ordained, 1806; DD, Glasgow, 1827; moderator of the general assembly, 1836; chaplain-in-ordinary to Queen Victoria, 1841; author of religious works in Gaelic and English.

MACLEOD, Norman, the younger (1812–1872), Scottish divine; son of Norman *Macleod the elder; studied divinity at Edinburgh, 1831; ordained, 1838; remained in the church at the disruption, 1843; one of the founders of the Evangelical Alliance, 1847; editor of the Edinburgh *Christian Instructor*, 1849; chaplain to Queen Victoria, 1857–72; DD, Glasgow, 1858; editor of *Good Words*, 1860–72; made a tour in Palestine and published an account of it, entitled *Eastward* (1866); visited the mission stations in India, 1867; published *Peeps at the Far East* (1871).

MACLEOD, Roderick (d. 1852), physician; educated at Edinburgh University; MD, 1816; FRCP, 1836; Gulstonian lecturer, 1837; consiliarius, 1839; editor and proprietor of the *London Medical and Physical Journal* (1822).

MACLIAC, Muircheartach (d. 1015), Irish poet; chief poet to *Brian (926–1014); present at the Battle of Clontarf, 1014; a legend of Carn Conaill in the *Book of Leinster* is attributed to him and considered genuine.

McLINTOCK, Sir William, first baronet (1873–1947), chartered accountant; educated at Dumfries Academy and Glasgow High School; qualified as chartered accountant; senior partner, Thomson McLintock & Co., Glasgow; opened London office, 1912; overhauled finances of royal household after war; a financial adviser at Imperial Wireless and Cable Conference, 1928; served on Economic Advisory Council, Industrial Arbitration Court, and many other bodies; CVO and KBE, 1922; GBE, 1929; baronet, 1934.

McLINTOCK, William Francis Porter (1887–1960), geologist; educated at George Heriot's and University, Edinburgh; B.Sc., distinction in botany, 1907; assistant curator, Museum of Practical Geology, London, 1907–11; curator of geology, Royal Scottish Museum, Edinburgh, 1911–21; D.Sc., 1915; curator, Museum of Practical Geology, 1921–5; planned new Geological Museum, South Kensington, opened 1935, on lines of popular exposition of science; deputy director, 1937–45; director, 1945–50; reopened museum, 1947; reorganized Geological Survey to advise on water and fuel resources; CB, 1951.

MACLISE, Daniel (1806–1870), historical painter; first studied art at the Cork Academy, 1822; unobserved made a clever drawing of Sir Walter *Scott, while in a bookshop at Cork; opened a studio as a portrait painter; went to London, 1827; came into notice in London by his portrait of Charles *Kean, 1827; entered the Academy schools, 1828; exhibited at the Royal Academy, 1829–70; contributed series of character portraits, including all the great literary men and women of the time, under the pseudonym of Alfred Croquis, to *Fraser's Magazine*, 1830–8; RA, 1840; occupied in painting the two frescos in the Royal Gallery in the House of Lords, *Wellington and Blücher at Waterloo* and *The Death of Nelson*, 1857–66; refused presidency of Royal Academy; designed book illustrations for *Tennyson (1860), and for some of his friend *Dickens's Christmas books; his frescos the greatest historical paintings of the English school.

MACLONAN, Flann (d. 896), Irish historian and poet; author of a poem contained in the *Book of Leinster*; two other poems attributed to him.

MACLURE, Edward Craig (1833–1906), dean of Manchester; BA, Brasenose College, Oxford, 1856; MA, 1858; DD, 1890; vicar of

Rochdale, 1877–90; dean of Manchester, 1890–1906; chairman of Manchester School Board, 1891–1903; member of Royal Commission on Secondary Education, 1894; hon. LL D, Victoria University, Manchester, 1902.

MACLURE, Sir John William, first baronet (1835–1901), brother of E. C. *Maclure; secretary of Lancashire Cotton Relief Fund, 1862; Conservative MP for Stretford, 1886–1901; baronet, 1898.

McMAHON, Sir (Arthur) Henry (1862–1949), military political officer; son of C. A. *McMahon; educated at Haileybury and Sandhurst; entered Indian Political Department, 1890; demarcated Baluchistan–Afghanistan boundary; arbitrator on Persian–Afghan boundary, 1903–5; agent in Baluchistan, 1905–11; foreign secretary to Indian government, 1911–14; negotiated treaty with China and Tibet, 1913–14; high commissioner, Egypt, 1914–16; conducted 'McMahon–Husain correspondence'; KCIE, 1906; GCVO, 1911; GCMG, 1916.

MACMAHON, Sir Charles (1824–1891), captain; son of Sir William *MacMahon; in the army, 1842–51; served in India and Canada, and (1851) attained a captaincy; entered the Melbourne Police, 1853; chief commissioner till 1858; member of the legislative assembly at Melbourne, 1861–86; speaker, 1871–7 and 1880; knighted, 1875.

McMAHON, Charles Alexander (1830–1904), general and geologist; joined Indian Army, 1847; commanded troops in Sialkot district during Indian Mutiny; Punjab commissioner, 1872–85; lieutenant-general, 1892; edited *Records of Geological Survey of India*, vol. x (1877); pioneer in study of petrology and in metamorphism and foliation of rocks; FGS, 1879; Lyell medallist, 1899; FRS, 1898.

MACMAHON, Heber (Ever or Emer, usually Latinized as **Emerus Mattheus)** (1600–1650), bishop of Clogher and general in Ulster; educated at the Irish College, Douai, and at Louvain; ordained priest 1625; bishop of Clogher, 1643; a leader among the Confederate Catholics; general of the Ulster Army against *Cromwell, 1650; defeated at Scariffhollis, taken prisoner, and executed.

MACMAHON, Hugh Oge (1606?–1644), Irish conspirator; joined the northern conspiracy, 1641; planned the assault on Dublin Castle, was betrayed by an accomplice, and arrested; imprisoned in Dublin and in the Tower of London; escaped, 1644; retaken, tried, and executed.

MACMAHON, John Henry (1829–1900), scholar; MA, Trinity College, Dublin, 1856; took holy orders, 1853; chaplain to lord-lieutenant, and, from 1890, to Mountjoy Prison; published classical translations and other works.

MacMAHON, Percy Alexander (1854–1929), mathematician; born in Malta; educated at the Royal Military Academy, Woolwich; served with Royal Artillery in India; mathematical instructor, Royal Military Academy, 1882; professor of physics, Ordnance College, 1890–7; retired from army to devote himself to mathematical and scientific pursuits, 1898; deputy warden of standards, 1904–20; FRS, 1890; president, London Mathematical Society, 1894–6; chiefly studied theory of algebraic forms; his works include *Combinatory Analysis* (1915).

M'MAHON, Thomas O'Brien (*fl.* 1777), Irish miscellaneous writer.

MACMAHON, Sir Thomas Westropp, third baronet (1813–1892), general; entered the army, 1829; served in the Sutlej campaign, 1846; major, 1847; served through the Crimean War; succeeded to baronetcy, 1860; general, 1880.

MACMAHON, Sir William, first baronet (1776–1837), Irish judge; called to the Irish bar, 1799; master of the Rolls, 1814–37; received a baronetcy, 1814.

MACMANUS, Terence Bellew (1823?–1860), Irish patriot; member of the '82 club, 1844; joined the 'physical force' movement, 1848; took part in the Tipperary Civil War; arrested and transported to Van Diemen's Land, 1849; escaped (1852) to San Francisco, where he died.

MacMICHAEL, Sir Harold Alfred (1882–1969), colonial civil servant; educated at Bedford Grammar School and Magdalene College, Cambridge; first class, part i, classical tripos, 1904; first class, Arabic examination for Sudan Political Service, 1905; entered Sudan Political Service, 1905; served in Kordofan province and Blue Nile province, 1905–15; senior inspector, Khartoum province, 1915–16; political officer to expedition to Darfur, 1916; DSO; assistant civil secretary, Khartoum, 1919–26; civil secretary, 1926; governor of Tanganyika, 1933–7; high commissioner and commander-in-chief, Palestine, 1938–44; Jewish terrorism increased; attempt to murder high commissioner and his wife; Lady MacMichael slightly wounded, 1944; worked on constitution for Malaya, 1945–6; and Malta, 1946; publications include *Sudan Notes and Records* (1918), *A History of the Arab in the Sudan* (2 vols., 1922), *The Anglo-Egyptian Sudan* (1934), and *The Sudan* (1954); CMG, 1927; KCMG,

1932; GCMG, 1941; hon. fellow, Magdalene College, Cambridge, 1939.

MACMICHAEL, William (1783–1839), physician; of Christ Church, Oxford; MA, 1807; Radcliffe travelling fellow, 1811; MD, 1816; FRCP, 1818; censor, 1822, registrar, 1824–9; published (1819) *Journey from Moscow to Constantinople*, an account of his travels, 1814–17; published *The Gold-headed Cane* (1827); physician-in-ordinary to William IV, 1831; published also medical works.

MACMILLAN, Angus (1810–1865), discoverer of Gippsland, Australia; emigrated to Australia, 1829; explored the country south-west of Sydney, afterwards called Gippsland, 1839–41; died in Australia.

MACMILLAN, Daniel (1813–1857), bookseller and publisher; founder of the firm of Macmillan & Co., London; took service with a Cambridge bookseller, 1833–7, and with Messrs Seeley of Fleet Street, London, 1837–43; set up for himself with his brother Alexander, at first in London, but soon resettled at Cambridge, 1843; added publishing to the bookselling business at Cambridge, 1844; published *Kingsley's Westward Ho!* (1855), and *Tom Brown's School Days* (1857).

MACMILLAN, Sir Frederick Orridge (1851–1936), publisher; son of Daniel *Macmillan; educated at Uppingham; entered family business and built up world-wide organization; took lead in establishing 'net book agreement', 1890; knighted for hospital work, 1909.

MACMILLAN, Hugh (1833–1903), religious writer; Free Church minister at Glasgow (1864–78) and Greenock (1878–1901); made wide fame through *Bible Teachings in Nature* (1867) and *The Ministry of Nature* (1871); hon. LL D, St Andrews, 1871; hon. DD, Edinburgh, 1879, and Glasgow; FRS, Edinburgh, and FSA, Scotland; Cunningham (1894) and Gunning (1897) lecturer at Edinburgh; moderator of General Assembly of Free Church, 1897; voluminous author of works mainly dealing with relations of religion and science.

MACMILLAN, Hugh Pattison, Baron Macmillan (1873–1952), judge; son of Revd Hugh *Macmillan; educated at Collegiate School, Greenock, and Edinburgh (first class, philosophy, 1893) and Glasgow (LL B, 1896) universities; advocate, 1897; KC, 1912; lord advocate in Labour government, 1924; established London chambers; standing counsel, Canada (1928), Australia (1929); lord of appeal in ordinary, 1930–9, 1941–7; minister of information, 1939–40; chairmanships included Treasury Finance and Industry Committee, 1929–31;

Royal Commission on Canadian banking and currency, 1933; Pilgrim Trust, 1935–52; Political Honours Committee, 1935–52; court of London University, 1929–43; BBC Advisory Council, 1936–46; PC, 1924; life peer, 1930; GCVO, 1937; published autobiography, *A Man of Law's Tale* (1952).

MACMILLAN, John (1670–1753), founder of the Reformed Presbyterian church; studied at Edinburgh University; ordained, 1701; deposed for schismatical practices, 1703; retained his church and manse; resigned in order to terminate the insults to which his appointed successor was subjected, 1715; minister to the 'remnant' afterwards called Macmillanites, 1706–43; first pastor of the 'Reformed Presbyterians', 1712; published controversial pamphlets.

McMILLAN, Margaret (1860–1931), educationist; educated at Inverness High School; joined Independent Labour party, Bradford, 1893; obtained first elementary school medical inspection, 1899; with Rachel McMillan, established children's clinic at Deptford, 1910 and pioneer open-air nursery school, 1917; built new Rachel McMillan Training College, 1930; CBE, 1917; CH, 1930.

McMILLAN, William (1887–1977), sculptor; trained at Gray's School of Art, Aberdeen and Royal College of Art, 1908–12; served during 1914–18 war in France with Oxfordshire and Buckinghamshire Light Infantry; exhibited at Royal Academy, 1917–71; designed the Great War Medal and Victory Medal; ARA, 1925; RA, 1933; associate member, Royal Society of British Sculptors, 1928; full member, 1932; master of sculpture school, Royal Academy Schools, 1929–40; between 1940 and 1966 involved in series of important public sculptures, including bronze group for Beatty Memorial Fountain, Trafalgar Square, 1948, *King George VI*, 1955, and *Alcock and Brown*, 1966; other works include *Statuette* carved in green slate, 1927 and *Birth of Venus* in Portland stone, 1931; CVO, 1956; freeman of Aberdeen; hon. degree, Aberdeen University; badly injured after assault and robbery and died shortly afterwards at age of 90; works exhibited in Tate Gallery.

MACMOYER, Florence (d. 1713), last keeper of the Book of Armagh, written in 807; schoolmaster; pledged the 'Book of Armagh', of which he was custodian, as a member of the Clan Mac-Moyre, to pay his expenses to London, 1680; a witness, probably perjured, at trial of Oliver *Plunket, 1681; imprisoned till after 1683; the 'Book of Armagh' was ultimately sold to Trinity College, Dublin.

MACMURCHADA, Diarmaid (or Mac-MURROUGH, Dermod) (1110?–1171), king of Leinster, succeeding 1126; claimed the south of Ireland, 1134; ravaged the south with great cruelty and abducted Dervorgill, wife of the lord of Breifne, 1152; was defeated and banished by a combination of chieftains, 1166; his offer to become Henry II's vassal, if assisted in the restoration of his kingdom, accepted; returned to Ireland, 1167, having prevailed on Richard de *Clare (Strongbow) to assist him, Henry II being unwilling to afford him direct help; took Waterford and Dublin with the aid of various Norman nobles; claimed to be king of all Ireland.

McMURDO, Sir William Montagu Scott (1819–1894), general; studied at Sandhurst; lieutenant, 22nd Foot, 1841; quartermaster-general in Sind, 1842–7; aide-de-camp to Sir Charles James *Napier, 1849; served against Afridis, 1851; brevet-lieutenant-colonel, 1853; organized transport service in Crimea; aide-de-camp to Queen Victoria and brevet-colonel, 1855; CB, 1857; colonel commandant of military train, 1857; lieutenant-general, 1876; general, 1878; KCB, 1881.

MACMURRAY, John (1745–1793), editor and publisher; lieutenant of marines, 1762–8; purchased bookselling business of William Sandby, Fleet Street, London, 1768; stopped using prefix; started editing and publishing as well as bookselling; father of John *Murray (1778–1843).

McMURRICH, James Playfair (1859–1939), Canadian anatomist; BA, Toronto, 1879; professor of anatomy, 1907–30, dean of graduate studies, 1922–30; wrote extensively on morphology, embryology, and the history of anatomy; leading authority on sea-anemones; FRS, Canada, 1909.

MACMURROGH (or MACMURCHAD), Art (1357–1417), styled also Cavanagh; Irish chief; descended from Donall, illegitimate son of Diarmaid or Dermod *MacMurchada; frequently in arms against the English government for private reasons; a reward offered for his capture by Richard II.

MACNAB, Sir Allan Napier, first baronet (1798–1862), Canadian soldier and politician; born at Newark, now Niagara, Ontario; joined the army and then the navy at the time of the American invasion, 1813–15; called to the Canadian bar, 1826; member of the House of Assembly, 1830, and speaker, 1837–41, 1844–8, and 1862; with the militia in the rebellion, 1837–8; knighted, 1838; created baronet, 1858.

MACNAB, Henry Gray (or Grey) (1761–1823), publicist; studied medicine at Montpellier; prepared an educational scheme on Owenite lines, but died at Paris before it was put into practice; published works on education.

McNAB, William Ramsay (1844–1889), botanist; MD, Edinburgh, 1866; professor of botany, Dublin Royal College of Science, 1872–89; scientific superintendent of Royal Botanic Gardens, Glasnevin, and Swiney lecturer on geology at British Museum; author of botanical papers and textbooks.

MACNAGHTEN, Sir Edward, fourth baronet, and Baron Macnaghten (1830–1913), judge; educated at Trinity College, Dublin, and Trinity College, Cambridge; bracketed senior classic, 1852; fellow of Trinity, Cambridge, 1853; called to bar (Lincoln's Inn), 1857; equity junior, 1857–80; QC, 1880; Conservative MP, County Antrim, 1880, North Antrim, 1885; lord of appeal in ordinary and life peer, 1887; GCMG, 1903; GCB, and succeeded brother in baronetcy, 1911; took active part in both Houses in debates on Irish questions; as judge possessed remarkable power of combining learning, style, and humour.

MACNAGHTEN (or MACNAUGHTON), John (d. 1761), criminal; educated at Dublin University; sought to marry Miss Knox, an heiress of Prehen, Londonderry, and persuaded her to go through the ceremony with him; being forbidden to communicate with her by her family, he and his accomplices attacked the coach by which she was travelling to Dublin, and shot her; captured, tried, and hanged at Strabane.

MACNAGHTEN, Sir William Hay, first baronet (1793–1841), diplomat; educated at Charterhouse School; went to India in the East India Company's service, 1809; studied Hindustani, Persian, and other Asiatic tongues; judge and magistrate of Shahabad, 1820; registrar of the Sudder Dewanny Adawlut for nine years; published works on Indian law, 1825–9; secretary to Lord William *Bentinck, 1830–3; in charge of the secret and political departments of the secretariat, 1833–7; accompanied Lord *Auckland to the North-West Provinces, 1837; appointed envoy and minister to the Afghan court at Kabul, 1 Oct. 1838; accompanied expedition which placed Shah Soojah on Afghan throne; found difficulty in acting with the military authorities; created baronet and a provisional member of the Council of India, 1840; nominated governor of Bombay, 1841; meanwhile rebellion broke out anew in Afghanistan, and Macnaghten unsuspectingly accepted the terms of the insurgents, which were not adhered to; he was shot at Kabul by Akbar Khan, the deposed amir's son, at a meeting with the chiefs to discuss the situation.

McNAIR, Arnold Duncan, first Baron McNair (1885–1975), university teacher and international judge; educated at Aldenham School and Gonville and Caius College, Cambridge; president of the Union, 1909; BA, LL B, 1909; LL M, 1913; MA, 1919; LL D, 1925; fellow of Caius College, 1912 (later senior tutor); called to bar (Gray's Inn), 1917; reader, University of London, 1926–7; taught in Cambridge until 1935; Whewell professor in international law, 1935–7; vice-chancellor, Liverpool University, 1937–45; professor of comparative law, Cambridge, 1945; KC, 1945; judge of International Court of Justice in The Hague, 1946; president 1952–5; first president of European Court of Human Rights, 1959–65; publications include *Legal Effects of War* (1920, 2nd edn., 1944; 3rd and 4th edn., with A. D. Watts, 1948, 1966), *The Law of the Air* (1932, 2nd edn., with M. R. E. Kerr and R. A. MacCrindle, 1953), *Roman Law and Common Law* (with W. W. *Buckland, 1936), and *The Law of Treaties* (1938 and a new volume, 1961); also edited the fourth edition of *International Law* by L. F. L. *Oppenheim (1926–8); CBE, 1918; FBA, 1939; knighted, 1943; first baron, 1955; number of honorary doctorates; master of bench of Gray's Inn, 1936, treasurer, 1947; president, Institut de Droit International, 1949–50.

McNAIR, John Frederick Adolphus (1828–1910), colonial official; joined Madras Artillery, 1845; at Singapore efficient superintendent of convicts, 1858; controller of convicts, 1867, colonial secretary, 1868; member of the Executive Council of Straits Settlements from 1869, and surveyor-general from 1873; lieutenant-governor of Penang, 1881–4; chief commissioner in Perak, 1875–6; CMG, 1878; wrote accounts of Perak (1878) and Singapore Convict Prison (1899).

McNAIR, William Watts (1849–1889), traveller; joined Indian Survey Department, 1867; accompanied Aghan Field Force, 1879–80; attempted to visit Kafristan disguised as native doctor, but failed, 1883; continued his survey work; died at Mussooree.

MACNALLY, Leonard (1752–1820), playwright and political informer; called to the Irish bar, 1776; barrister, Middle Temple, 1783; edited *The Public Ledger* and wrote plays; joined the United Irishmen, but secretly betrayed them to the government, 1794–1820; took briefs for the defence in government prosecutions, and disclosed their contents to the crown lawyers; his conduct only discovered after his death; author of dramatic pieces, legal works, and the song, 'Sweet Lass of Richmond Hill'.

MacNALTY, Sir Arthur Salusbury (1880–1969), expert in public health; educated at Hartley College, Southampton, St Catherine's Society, Oxford, and Corpus Christi College, Oxford; BM, 1907; DM, 1911; MRCP, 1925; DPH, 1927; FRCP, 1930; special interest in pulmonary tuberculosis; joined Local Government Board, as specialist to promote 'sanatorium' and 'dispensary' service, 1913; transferred to Ministry of Health; deputy chief medical officer, 1919; chief medical officer, 1935–40; editor-in-chief, official medical history of 1939–45 war (1940–69); KCB, 1936.

MACNAMARA, James (1768–1826), rear-admiral; entered the navy, 1782; served on foreign stations; commander, 1793; served under *Nelson, 1795–6; tried for manslaughter, having mortally wounded Colonel Montgomery in a duel, but was acquitted, 1803; served in the North Sea; rear-admiral, 1814.

McNAMARA, Thomas (1808–1892), Irish Catholic divine; helped to establish Castleknock College, Co. Dublin, 1834, and acted as its superior, 1804–8; rector of the Irish College in Paris, 1868–89; wrote works for the Catholic clergy.

MACNAMARA, Thomas James (1861–1931), politician; Liberal MP, North Camberwell, 1900–24; parliamentary and financial secretary to Admiralty, 1908–20; minister of labour, 1920–2; organizer and platform speaker for Lloyd George; PC, 1911.

McNAUGHTON, Andrew George Latta (1887–1966), Canadian soldier, scientist, and public servant; born at Moosomin, Saskatchewan; educated at Bishop's College School, Lennoxville, Quebec, and McGill University; honours, electrical engineering, 1910; M.Sc., 1912; lecturer at McGill; served in Canadian Army in France and Belgium, 1914–18; DSO, 1917; CMG, 1919; hon. LL D, McGill University, 1920; director of military training, acting brigadier-general; attended Staff College, 1921; deputy chief, Canadian General Staff, 1923; attended Imperial Defence College, 1927; major-general, chief, Canadian General Staff, 1929–35; president, Canadian National Research Council; commanded Canadian troops in Britain, 1939–43; retired from army with rank of full general, 1944; Canadian minister of defence, 1944–5; chairman, Canadian section, Canada–United States Permanent Joint Board on Defence, 1945–59; president, Atomic Energy Control Board of Canada, 1946–8; Canadian representative, UN Atomic Energy Commission, 1946–50; permanent Canadian delegate to UN, 1948–9; chairman, Canadian section, International Joint Commission, 1950–2; PC (Canada), 1944; CB, 1935; CH, 1946.

MACNAUGHTON, John (d. 1761), criminal. See MACNAGHTEN.

MACNEE, Sir **Daniel** (1806–1882), portrait painter; employed by William Home *Lizars; an academician of the newly founded Royal Scottish Academy, 1830; portrait painter at Glasgow, 1832; exhibited at the Royal Academy, 1840–81; president of the Royal Scottish Academy, 1876; knighted, 1877.

McNEE, Sir **John William** (1887–1984), professor of medicine; educated at Royal Grammar School, Newcastle upon Tyne, and Glasgow University; MB, Ch.B. with honours, 1909; research scholar, Freiburg, Germany; MD with gold medal, 1914; during 1914–18 war served in RAMC; DSO, 1918; member of teaching medical unit, University College Hospital, London, doing research on the liver; D.Sc., 1920; published *Diseases of the Liver, Gall-Bladder, and Bile Ducts* (third edn. with Sir Humphry *Rolleston, 1929); Rockefeller medical fellow, Johns Hopkins University, Baltimore, 1924; FRCP (Lond., 1925, Edn., 1943) and FRSE, 1940; consulting physician UCH; Lettsomian lecturer (1931); Croonian lecturer (1932); regius professor of practice of medicine, Glasgow, 1936–53; consultant physician to Royal Navy, 1935; served as surgeon rear-admiral during 1939–45 war; physician to the King in Scotland (1937–52) and the Queen (1952–4); had many medical appointments and honours and honorary medical degrees; president of British Medical Association in Glasgow, 1954–5; knighted, 1951; other publications include the *Textbook of Medical Treatment* (1st edn., 1939, 6th edn., 1955) with (Sir) Derrick *Dunlop and (Sir) L. Stanley P. *Davidson.

MacNEICE, (Frederick) Louis (1907–1963), writer; educated at Marlborough and Merton College, Oxford; first class, Lit. Hum., 1930; edited *Oxford Poetry* with Stephen Spender; published first book of poems, *Blind Fireworks* (1930); lecturer in classics, Birmingham University, 1930–6; lecturer in Greek, Bedford College, London, 1936–40; lecturer at Cornell University, USA, 1940; joined BBC Features Department, 1941; director, British Institute, Athens, 1950; left BBC, 1961; hon. doctorate, Queen's University, Belfast, 1957; CBE, 1958; publications include *Poems* (1935), *Letters from Iceland* (with W. H. *Auden, 1937), *The Earth Compels* (1938), *Autumn Journal* (1939), *The Last Ditch* (1940), *Springboard* (1944), *The Poetry of W. B. Yeats* (1941), *Collected Poems 1925–1948* (1949), *Autumn Sequel* (1954), *Visitations* (1957), and *The Strings are False* (1965).

McNEIL, Hector (1907–1955), journalist and politician; educated at Glasgow secondary schools and University; joined *Scottish Daily Express*, becoming night news editor and finally leader-writer; Labour MP, Greenock, 1941–55; parliamentary private secretary to Philip *Noel-Baker, 1942–5; minister of state, foreign affairs, 1946–50; forceful speaker at United Nations general assemblies; Scottish secretary, 1950–1; PC, 1946; died in New York.

McNEILE, (Herman) Cyril (1888–1937), soldier, and novelist under the pseudonym of Sapper; educated at Cheltenham and Woolwich; officer in Royal Engineers, 1907–19; wrote series of thrillers beginning with *Bulldog Drummond* (1920).

McNEILE, Hugh (1795–1879), dean of Ripon; MA, Trinity College, Dublin, 1821; DD, 1847; ordained, 1820; canon of Chester, 1845–68; dean of Ripon, 1868–75; a strong evangelical; published sermons and religious works.

McNEILL, Duncan, first Baron Colonsay and Oronsay (1793–1874), Scottish judge; educated at St Andrews and Edinburgh universities; called to the Scottish bar, 1816; solicitor-general for Scotland, 1834–5, 1841–2; MP, Argyllshire, 1843–51; lord advocate, 1842–6; ordinary lord of session as Lord Colonsay and Oronsay, 1851; lord justice-general, 1852–67; created Baron Colonsay and Oronsay, 1867.

MACNEILL, Hector (1746–1818), Scottish poet; filled a succession of subordinate posts with commercial firms in West Indies, 1761–76; assistant secretary on board flagships in naval expeditions, 1780–6; subsequently failed to obtain remunerative employment; lived with friends, in Scotland and Jamaica; wrote, among other poems, 'Scotland's Scaith, or the History of Will and Jean' (1795) and 'The Waes o' War, or the Upshot of the History of Will and Jean' (1796).

McNEILL, James (1869–1938), Indian and Irish civil servant; an Ulster Catholic; educated at Belvedere, Dublin, and Emmanuel College, Cambridge; served in Bombay presidency, 1890–1915; joined Mr *de Valera's political movement, 1916; helped to draft Irish Free State constitution, 1922; high commissioner in London, 1923–8; governor-general, Irish Free State, 1928–32; challenged efforts to reduce his position to obscurity and forced Executive Council to obtain his removal.

McNEILL, Sir **James McFadyen** (1892–1964), shipbuilder; educated at Clydebank High School and Allan Glen's School, Glasgow; apprenticed with John Brown & Co. Ltd., 1908; Lloyd's scholar in naval architecture, Glasgow

University; B.Sc., 1915; served in Royal Field Artillery in 1914–18 war; MC, 1918; assistant naval architect, Clydebank, 1922–8; principal naval architect and technical manager, 1928; collaborated with Cunard Company in producing *Queen Mary* and *Queen Elizabeth*; delivered classic paper on launching to Institution of Naval Architects, 1935; managing director, Clydebank Yard, 1948; CBE, 1950; deputy chairman, 1953–62; on completion of Royal Yacht *Britannia*, KCVO, 1954; retired from executive duties, 1959; director of number of other firms; hon. LL D, Glasgow, 1939; FRS, 1948; vice-president, Institution of Naval Architects; president, Institution of Engineers and Shipbuilders in Scotland, 1947–9; president, Shipbuilding Conference, 1956–8.

McNEILL, Sir John (1795–1883), diplomat; brother of Duncan *McNeill, first Baron Colonsay; MD, Edinburgh, 1814; surgeon on the East India Company's Bombay establishment, 1816–36; envoy and minister-plenipotentiary to the shah at Teheran, 1836; failed to prevent the shah from attacking the Afghans, 1838; eventually brought about treaty of commerce between Great Britain and Persia, 1841; chairman of the Board of Supervision of the working of the Scottish Poor Law Act, 1845–78; on commission of inquiry into the commissariat department and general organization of troops in Crimea, 1855; privy councillor, 1857; died at Cannes.

MacNEILL, John (otherwise **Eoin)** (1867–1945), Irish scholar and politician; brother of James *McNeill; BA, Royal University of Ireland, 1888; entered Civil Service; a founder (1893) and first secretary, Gaelic League; first professor of early Irish history, University College, Dublin, 1908–45; leader of extreme Irish nationalists, 1914; countermanded mobilization on learning of plans for Easter Rising, 1916; released from life imprisonment, 1917; MP, National University, 1918–22; member of the Dail, 1921–7, speaker, 1921–2; minister of education, 1922–5; Free State representative, Ulster Boundary Commission, 1924; resigned after newspaper forecast of contents of award, 1925; publications include *Phases of Irish History* (1919) and *Celtic Ireland* (1921).

MACNEILL, Sir John Benjamin (1793?–1880), civil engineer; one of *Telford's chief assistants in road and bridge making; made known his plan of 'sectio-planography', 1837; professor of civil engineering at Trinity College, Dublin, 1842–52; knighted, 1844; constructed railway lines in Scotland, and was surveyor to the Irish railway commission; on becoming blind withdrew from professional pursuits; author of works on engineering.

McNEILL, Sir John Carstairs (1831–1904), major-general; joined Bengal Native Infantry, 1850; served with distinction at Lucknow, 1857–8; won VC in Maori War, 1864; on staff of Red River expedition, 1870; CMG, 1876; chief of staff in Ashanti War, 1873–4; CB, 1874; KCMG, 1880; major-general and KCB, 1882; commanded second infantry brigade in Sudan campaign, 1885; criticized for lack of caution; retired, 1890; GCVO, 1901.

MacNEILL, John Gordon Swift (1849–1926), Irish politician and jurist; closely connected with Protestant Ireland; BA, Christ Church, Oxford; called to Irish bar, 1875; professor of constitutional and criminal law, King's Inns, Dublin, 1882–8; joined Home Government Association founded by Isaac *Butt, 1870; Nationalist MP, South Donegal, 1887–1918; had real veneration for parliament; professor of constitutional law, National University of Ireland, 1909–26.

McNEILL, Ronald John, Baron Cushendun (1861–1934), politician; educated at Harrow and Christ Church, Oxford; editor, *St. James's Gazette*, 1900–4; assistant editor, eleventh edition *Encyclopaedia Britannica*, 1906–11; MP, East Kent, 1911–27; parliamentary under-secretary, foreign affairs, 1922–4–5; financial secretary to Treasury, 1925–7; chancellor, duchy of Lancaster, 1927–9; diehard Conservative of impulsive temper; PC, 1924; baron, 1927.

MACNEVEN (or **MACNEVIN), William James** (1763–1841), United Irishman; educated at Prague; studied medicine there and practised in Dublin, 1784; joined the United Irishmen, 1797; urged French intervention, and, his memorial falling into the hands of the English, was arrested, 1798; to allay the severity with which the government suppressed the rebellion, disclosed the conspiracy and offered to submit to banishment for life; eventually confined in Fort George, Scotland, till 1802; physician in New York, 1805; held various medical appointments in the College of Physicians and Surgeons there, 1808–39; champion of the Irish in America; died at New York.

MACNICOL, Donald (1735–1802), Presbyterian divine and author; graduated at St Andrews, 1756; published a defence of the Highlands against Dr *Johnson's *Journey to the Hebrides* (1779).

MACNISH, Robert (1802–1837), author and physician; MD, Glasgow, 1825; contributed his one masterpiece in fiction, *The Metempsychosis*, to *Blackwood*, 1826; published *The Philosophy of Sleep* (1830).

MACONOCHIE (afterwards MACONOCHIE-WELWOOD), Alexander, Lord Meadowbank (1777–1861), Scottish judge; son of Allan *Maconochie; admitted advocate, 1799; solicitor-general, 1813; lord-advocate, 1816; MP, Yarmouth, Isle of Wight, 1817–18, Kilrenny district of burghs, 1818–19; raised to the Scottish bench as Lord Meadowbank, 1819; resigned, 1843; assumed the additional surname of Welwood on succeeding to his cousin's estates, 1854.

MACONOCHIE, Allan, Lord Meadowbank (1748–1816), Scottish judge; educated at Edinburgh University; admitted advocate, 1770; professor of public law, Edinburgh, 1779–96; took his seat on the Scottish bench as Lord Meadowbank, 1796; author of legal and agricultural works.

MACPHAIL, James (*fl.* 1785–1805), gardener; invented a new method of growing cucumbers; published horticultural works.

MACPHAIL, Sir (John) Andrew (1864–1938), pathologist and author; graduated in medicine at McGill University, 1891; professor of medical history, 1907–37; edited *Canadian Medical Journal* and *University Magazine*; translated *Marie Chapdelaine* (1921); other publications include *The Master's Wife* (1939); knighted, 1918.

MACPHERSON, David (1746–1816), historian and compiler; deputy keeper in London of public records; edited *Wyntoun's Orygynal Cronykil of Scotland* (1795); assisted in preparing for publication *Rotuli Scotiae* (vol. i and part of vol. ii).

MACPHERSON, Duncan (d. 1867), army surgeon and writer; surgeon to the army in Madras, 1836, in China, 1840–2, in Russia, 1855; inspector-general of the Medical Service of Madras, 1857; chief work, *Antiquities of Kertch and Researches in the Cimmerian Bosphorus* (1857); died at Merkara, Coorg.

MACPHERSON, Ewen (d. 1764), of Cluny; Jacobite; before the outbreak of the rebellion supported the government, but on being pressed joined Prince *Charles Edward, 1745; helped the prince to escape; fled to France, 1755; died at Dunkirk.

MACPHERSON, Ewen (1804–1884), grandson of Ewen *Macpherson (d. 1764); captain in the 42nd Highlanders; interested himself in the Highland Volunteer movement; CB.

MACPHERSON, Sir Herbert Taylor (1827–1886), major-general, Bengal Staff Corps; served under *Havelock at Lucknow, gaining the VC, 1857; transferred to the Indian Army, 1865; commanded a division in the Afghan War, 1878–9; KCB, 1879; major-general and present at Tel-el-Kebir, 1882; commander-in-chief at Madras, 1886; sent to organize the pacification of Burma, 1886; fell ill and died on his way from Prome to Rangoon.

MACPHERSON, James (d. 1700), the Banff freebooter; of gypsy parentage; wandered about Scotland with his mother till captured, 1700; executed on the charge of 'going up and doune the country armed'; said to have played a 'rant' before his execution, the words of which are—probably wrongly—attributed to him.

MACPHERSON, James (1736–1796), the alleged translator of the Ossianic poems; studied at Aberdeen and Edinburgh universities; said to have composed over 4,000 verses while at college; published *The Highlander* (1758) and *Fragments of Ancient Poetry collected in the Highlands* (1760); issued two epic poems, *Fingal* (1762) and *Temora* (1763), which he alleged to be translated from the Gaelic of a poet called *Ossian; was generally believed to have wholly invented the poems; never seriously rebutted the charge of forgery; attacked by Dr *Johnson in his *Journey to the Western Islands of Scotland* (1775); secretary to the governor of Pensacola, West Florida, 1764–6; published *Original Papers containing the Secret History of Great Britain from the Restoration till the Accession of George I* (1775); employed by North's ministry to defend their American policy, from 1766; MP, Camelford, 1780–96; London agent to Mohammed Ali, nabob of Arcot, 1781. After Macpherson's death a committee was appointed by the Highland Society of Scotland to investigate the Ossianic poems, 1797. They reported that while a great legend of Fingal and Ossian existed in Scotland, Macpherson had liberally edited his originals and inserted passages of his own. Subsequent investigation has confirmed the committee's conclusions.

MACPHERSON, (James) Ian, first Baron Strathcarron (1880–1937), educated at George Watson's College and Edinburgh University; called to bar (Middle Temple), 1906; Liberal MP, Ross and Cromarty, 1911–35; under-secretary for war, 1916–18; vice-president, Army Council, 1918–19; chief secretary for Ireland, 1919–20; minister of pensions, 1920–2; recorder of Southend, 1931–7; PC, 1918; KC, 1919; baronet, 1933; baron, 1936.

MACPHERSON, John (1710–1765), Presbyterian minister; MA, Aberdeen, 1728; DD, 1761; work on the *Ancient Caledonians* published (1768).

MACPHERSON, Sir John, first baronet (1745–1821), governor-general of India; educated at Edinburgh University; writer under the East India Company at Madras, 1770–6; dismissed in consequence of his conduct while on a secret mission to England for the nabob of the Carnatic in 1768, 1777; reinstated, 1781; MP, Cricklade, 1779–82, Horsham, 1796–1802; member of the Supreme Council at Calcutta, 1782; governor-general of India, 1785–6; created baronet, 1786.

MACPHERSON, John (1817–1890), physician; brother of Samuel Charters *Macpherson and of William *Macpherson; MA and hon. MD, Aberdeen; studied medicine in London and abroad, 1835–9; member Royal College of Surgeons, 1839; in the East India Company's service, 1839–64, becoming inspector-general of hospitals; published medical works.

MACPHERSON, Sir John Molesworth (1853–1914), Anglo-Indian legislative draftsman; son of John *Macpherson, MD; born in Calcutta; called to English bar, 1876; deputy secretary to Indian government in Legislative Department, 1877; permanent secretary, 1896–1911; knighted, 1911.

MACPHERSON, Paul (1756–1846), Scottish abbé; studied at the Scots colleges in Rome and Valladolid; procurator of the mission in Scotland, 1791; agent of the Scottish clergy at Rome, 1793–8 and 1800–11; first Scottish rector of the Scots College in Rome, 1820–6 and 1834–46; died at Rome.

MACPHERSON, Samuel Charters (1806–1860), political agent in India; brother of John *Macpherson (1817–1890) and of William *Macpherson; studied at Edinburgh University and at Trinity College, Cambridge; entered the Indian Army, 1827; despatched to obtain information about the Khonds in Gumsur, 1837–9; principal assistant to the agent, completely reforming the tribe, 1842–4; governor-general's agent for suppression of human sacrifice in Orissa, 1845; agent at Gwalior; prevented Gwalior tribes from joining the Mutiny, 1857; died in India.

MACPHERSON, William (1812–1893), legal writer; brother of John *Macpherson (1817–1890), and of Samuel Charters *Macpherson; of Charterhouse School and Trinity College, Cambridge; barrister, Inner Temple, 1837; MA, 1838; master of equity in the Supreme Court, Calcutta, 1848–59; edited the *Quarterly Review*, 1860–7; secretary to the Indian Law Commission, 1861–70; in the India Office as legal adviser, 1874–9, and as secretary in the judicial department, 1879–82; chief work, *Procedure of the Civil Courts of India* (1850).

MACQUARIE, Lachlan (d. 1824), major-general and governor of New South Wales; entered the army, 1777; served in America and Jamaica, 1777–84, India, China, and Egypt, 1787–1807; governor of New South Wales, 1809–21; personally encouraged exploration in the colony; his administration attacked at home for his efforts on behalf of the convict population.

MACQUEEN, James (1778–1870), geographer; manager of a sugar plantation in the West Indies, 1796; a student of African geography; edited *Glasgow Courier*, 1821; wrote in London on politics, geography, economics, and general literature.

MACQUEEN, John Fraser (1803–1881), lawyer; barrister, Lincoln's Inn, 1838; bencher, 1861; official reporter of Scottish and divorce appeals in the House of Lords, 1860–79; compiled 4 volumes of appellate reports, 1801–5; QC, 1861; published legal works.

McQUEEN, Sir John Withers (1836–1909), major-general; born in Calcutta; joined 27th Bengal Native Infantry, 1854; recommended for VC for bravery at the Secundarabagh, 1857; commanded 5th Punjab Rifles in Jowaki expedition, 1877–8; of great service in Afghan War, 1878–80; CB, 1879; brigadier-general in command of Hyderabad contingent, 1885; commanded expedition against Black Mountain tribes, 1888; KCB, 1890; major-general, 1891; GCB, 1907.

MACQUEEN, Robert, Lord Braxfield (1722–1799), Scottish judge; educated at Edinburgh University; admitted advocate, 1744; ordinary lord of session as Lord Braxfield, 1776; lord of justiciary, 1780; lord justice clerk, 1788; expert in feudal law.

MACQUEEN-POPE, Walter James (1888–1960), theatre manager, publicist, and historian; educated at Tollington School; business-manager for Sir Alfred Butt at the Queen's, St James's, Lyric, and other theatres; manager, Alexandra Palace (1922–5); manager, number of other West-End theatres; public relations officer for ENSA during 1939–45 war; wrote books and lectured on the history of particular theatres.

MACQUIN, Ange Denis (1756–1823), abbé and miscellaneous writer; born at Meaux; professor of belles-lettres and rhetoric at Meaux; came to England, 1792; heraldic draughtsman to the College of Arms, 1793; published works on heraldry and other subjects.

MACRAE, James (1677?–1744), governor of Madras; went to sea, 1692; subsequently served under the East India Company; governor of Madras, 1725; effected reforms in the fiscal administration; settled in Scotland, 1731.

MACREADY, Sir (Cecil Frederick) Nevil, first baronet (1862–1946), general; son of

W. C. *Macready; educated at Marlborough, Cheltenham, and Sandhurst; joined Gordon Highlanders, 1881; served in Egyptian campaign, 1882, and South Africa, 1899–1902; director of personal services, War Office, 1910–14; major-general, 1910; reported on administration in Dublin and Belfast, 1913; GOC, Belfast, 1914; adjutant-general, British Expeditionary Force, 1914–16; adjutant-general to the forces, 1916–18; commissioner, Metropolitan Police, 1918–20; GOC-in-C, Ireland, 1920–3; lieutenant-general, 1916; general, 1918; KCB, 1912; KCMG, 1915; GCMG, 1918, baronet, 1923.

MACREADY, William Charles (1793–1873), actor; educated at Rugby; made his first appearance at Birmingham as Romeo, 1810; acted in the provinces with his father's company, at Newcastle playing with Mrs *Siddons; first appeared at Covent Garden, London, 1816; raised by his Richard III to the undisputed head of the theatre, 1819; quarrelled with the management of Covent Garden, and began to play at Drury Lane, 1823; acted in America, 1826–7, and in Paris, 1828; manager of Covent Garden, 1837–9; produced the *Lady of Lyons*, 1838; at the Haymarket, 1839–41; manager of Drury Lane, 1841–3; visited America, 1843; played in Paris with Miss Helen *Faucit; while in America (1848) was involved in an unfortunate quarrel with the actor Forrest, which caused a riot; obliged to leave the country in consequence; took leave of the stage as Macbeth at Drury Lane, 1851; called by *Talfourd 'the most romantic of actors'; his impersonation of King Lear still held to be unrivalled.

MACRO, Cox (1683–1767), antiquary; educated at Christ's College, Cambridge (LL B, 1710), and Leiden University; chaplain to George II; DD, Cambridge, 1717; collected valuable antiquities, books, paintings, coins, and medals.

MACRORIE, William Kenneth (1831–1905), bishop of Maritzburg; BA, Brasenose College, Oxford, 1852; MA, 1855; consecrated, by Bishop *Gray of Cape Town, bishop of Maritzburg in Natal in opposition to Bishop *Colenso, 1869; an uncompromising high churchman; resigned bishopric, 1891; canon of Ely and assistant bishop, 1892.

MACSPARRAN, James (d. 1757), writer on America; MA, Glasgow, 1709; ordained, 1720; sent as a missionary to Narragansett, Rhode Island, 1721, and ministered there till his death; visited England, 1736 and 1754–6; made DD Oxford as a recognition of his efforts against the Dissenters, 1737; warned intending colonists against emigrating to America in *America Dissected* (1753).

MACSWINNY, Owen (d. 1754), playwright. See SWINNY.

MACTAGGART, John (1791–1830), encyclopaedist and versifier; studied at Edinburgh; clerk of works to Rideau Canal, Canada, 1826–8; published *Scottish Gallovidian Encyclopedia* (1824) and *Three Years in Canada* (1829).

M'TAGGART, John M'Taggart Ellis (1866–1925), philosopher; BA, Trinity College, Cambridge; first class in moral sciences tripos, 1888; prize fellow of Trinity, 1891; college lecturer in moral sciences, 1897–1923; FBA, 1906; an atheist who believed in human immortality; his earlier work devoted to expounding and defending method and some results of Hegel's *Logic* in *Studies in the Hegelian Dialectic* (1896), *Studies in Hegelian Cosmology* (1901), *Commentary on Hegel's Logic* (1910); other works include *Some Dogmas of Religion* (1906) and *The Nature of Existence* (2 vols., 1921–7).

McTAGGART, William (1835–1910), artist; fellow student at Trustees' Academy, Edinburgh, with (Sir) W. Q. *Orchardson, Tom *Graham, and John *MacWhirter; ARSA, 1859; RSA, 1870; exhibited at Royal Academy, 1866–75; vice-president of the Royal Scottish Water-Colour Society, 1878; early engaged in portraiture, genre pictures, and land- and seascape; later confined his work to landscape and the sea.

MacTAGGART, Sir William (1903–1981), painter; grandson of William *McTaggart, landscape painter; because of ill health educated privately; attended Edinburgh College of Art, 1918–21; influenced by William Crozier (1893–1936); went regularly to South of France for sake of health, 1922–9; held exhibition in Cannes, 1924; first one-man show in Edinburgh, 1929; president, Society of Scottish Artists, 1933–6; taught at Edinburgh College of Art, 1933–58; elected to Royal Scottish Academy, 1937; president, 1959–69; painted landscapes of East Lothian and influenced by Rouault exhibition at Musée d'Art Moderne, Paris, 1952; 'window' theme, views seen through an open window, repeated often during 1960s; ARA, 1968; RA, 1973; knighted, 1962; chevalier of Legion of Honour, 1968; hon. LL D, Edinburgh, 1961.

MACVICAR, John Gibson (1800–1884), author; educated at St Andrews and Edinburgh universities; lecturer in natural history at St Andrews, 1827; pastor of the Scottish Church in Ceylon, 1839–52; published scientific works.

MACWARD (or MACUARD), Robert (1633?–1687), Covenanting minister; studied at St Andrews University; ordained, 1654; preached in support of the Covenant, 1661; banished to

Holland; died at Rotterdam; published religious pamphlets.

McWHIRTER, (Alan) Ross (1925–1975), editor and litigant; twin brother of Norris McWhirter; educated at Marlborough College and Trinity College, Oxford; athletics blue; served in Royal Naval Volunteer Reserve (minesweeping), 1944–5; established agency to provide information to press and publishers (with his brother Norris), 1951; tennis and rugby correspondent of London evening *Star*; twin brothers published *Get To Your Marks* (1951), on history of athletics; Ross involved in number of law cases, the first against the National Union of Journalists, 1954; fought and won further law suits in 1967 and 1968; sued James Callaghan, home secretary, on his failure to implement recommendations of boundary commissions, 1969; sued Independent Broadcasting Authority regarding transmission of subliminal messages and succeeded in getting this activity stopped, 1970; also brought cases against Edward Heath, prime minister, and the Eagle Ferry and National Union of Seamen; final case settled after his death when European Court of Human Rights declared against the coercion of compulsory unionism, 1981; co-edited (with Norris) the *Guinness Book of Records* (1954); published the *Centenary History of Oxford University Rugby Club* (1969) and the *Centenary History of the Rugby Football Union* (1971); hon. press officer for the Victoria Cross and George Cross Association; campaigned against IRA terrorists and was shot by two of them and killed, 1975; Ross McWhirter Foundation established as memorial.

MacWHIRTER, John (1839–1911), landscape painter; fellow student with William *McTaggart at Trustees' Academy, Edinburgh; made direct study of nature; annually visited continent; ARSA, 1867; removed to London, 1869; ARA, 1879; hon. RSA, 1892; RA, 1893; published *Landscape Painting in Water Colours* (1901); painted popular landscapes and studies of trees; his best-known work, *June in the Austrian Tyrol*, in Tate Gallery.

McWILLIAM, James Ormiston (1808–1862), medical officer to the Niger expedition; surgeon in the navy, 1830; MD, Edinburgh, 1840; appointed senior surgeon (1840) on the *Albert*, one of the ships which joined the Niger expedition; practically saved his own ship when a fever broke out among the members of the expedition at the mouth of the Niger and their return was necessary, 1841; published his *Medical History of the Niger Expedition* (1843); sent to the Cape de Verde islands to study the yellow fever; medical officer to the Custom House, 1847–62; FRS, 1848.

MADAN, Martin (1726–1790), author of *Thelyphthora*; educated at Westminster School and Christ Church, Oxford; BA, 1746; barrister, 1748; adopted Methodist principles after hearing a sermon by *Wesley; ordained; became chaplain of the Lock Hospital, 1750–80; in close connection with Lady *Huntingdon; corresponded with John Wesley; published *Thelyphthora*, a book in favour of polygamy (1780), which excited public indignation, the poet *Cowper being among its assailants; author of religious works.

MADAN, Spencer (1729–1813), bishop successively of Bristol and Peterborough; younger brother of Martin *Madan; of Westminster and Trinity College, Cambridge; MA, 1753; fellow, 1752; DD, 1766; chaplain-in-ordinary to the king, 1761–87; bishop of Bristol, 1792–4, of Peterborough, 1794–1813.

MADAN, Spencer (1758–1836), translator of Grotius; son of Spencer *Madan (1729–1813); of Westminster School and Trinity College, Cambridge; MA, 1778; chaplain-in-ordinary to the king, 1788; prebendary of Peterborough, 1800; DD, 1809; published translation of Grotius's *De Veritate* (1782).

MADARIAGA, Salvador De (1886–1978), writer, professor of Spanish and diplomat; born at Corunna, Spain; educated in Madrid and Paris; worked as mining engineer in Spain, 1911; married British wife, 1912; abandoned engineering career for writing, 1916; moved to London and reported on 1914–18 war for Spanish press; published *Shelley and Calderón* (1920); member of press section, League of Nations secretariat, Geneva, 1921; director, disarmament section, 1922–7; professor of Spanish, Oxford, 1928–31; published *Disarmament* (1929), *Englishmen, Frenchmen, Spaniards* (1928), and *Spain* (1930); Spanish ambassador to Washington, 1931 and Paris, 1932; permanent Spanish delegate at League of Nations; returned to London, 1936, and Oxford, 1939; published *Christopher Columbus* (1939), *Hernan Cortes* (1941), *Bolivar* (1952), *The Rise of the Spanish American Empire* (1947), and *The Fall of the Spanish American Empire* (1947); also published novels, including *The Heart of Jade* (1944) and an essay 'On Hamlet' (1948); broadcast weekly for nine years from BBC to Spanish America; fervent promoter of European unity; founded and presided over European College of Bruges, 1949–64; founder and president of Liberal International; hon. president, Congress of Liberty of Culture, Paris, 1950; received numerous academic honours, decorations, and prizes; considered himself a citizen of the world; published *Morning Without Noon, Memoirs* (1974).

MADDEN, Sir Charles Edward, first baronet (1862–1935), admiral of the fleet; entered navy, 1875; specialized in torpedo; staff officer in the *Vernon*, torpedo school, 1893–6, 1899–1901; naval assistant to (Sir) H. B. *Jackson, 1905, and to (Lord) *Fisher, 1906–7, at Admiralty at time of great reforms; captain of the *Dreadnought* and chief of staff, Home Fleet, 1907–8; fourth sea lord, 1910–11; rear-admiral, 1911; chief of staff to (Lord) *Jellicoe, 1914–16; commander, First Battle Squadron, and second-in-command to (Lord) *Beatty, 1916–19; commander-in-chief, Atlantic Fleet, 1919–22; admiral, 1919; admiral of the fleet, 1924; first sea lord, 1927–30; assented under protest to reduced figure of fifty cruisers agreed at London Naval Conference, 1930; KCB and KCMG, 1916; baronet, 1919; GCVO, 1920; OM, 1931.

MADDEN, Sir Frederic (1801–1873), antiquary and palaeographer; nephew of Sir George Allan *Madden; collated manuscripts of *Cædmon for Oxford University, 1825; engaged on the British Museum *Catalogue*, 1826–8; assistant-keeper of manuscripts, 1828; head of the department, 1837–66; FRS, 1830; an original member of the Athenaeum Club, 1830; knighted, 1833; edited *Layamon's Brut* (1847) and *Wyclif's Bible* (1850).

MADDEN, Frederic William (1839–1904), numismatist; assistant in coin department of British Museum, 1859–68; chief librarian at Brighton Public Library, 1888–1902; published *The Coins of the Jews* (1881) and a manual of Roman coins (1861).

MADDEN, Sir George Allan (1771–1828), major-general in the British and Portuguese armies; entered the army, 1788; served in Italy, Corsica, and Portugal, 1793–5; in Egypt, 1801; tried by court martial for perjury, 1801; had to resign his commission, 1802; brigadier-general in the Portuguese Army, 1809; served with the Spanish troops, 1810–13; reinstated in the British Army, 1813; knighted, 1816; major-general in the British Army, 1819.

MADDEN, Katherine Cecil (1875–1911), novelist. See THURSTON.

MADDEN, Richard Robert (1798–1886), miscellaneous writer; studied medicine at Paris, Naples, and London; one of the special magistrates appointed to administer statute abolishing slavery in Jamaica plantations, 1833–41; superintendent of liberated Africans, and judge-arbitrator in the mixed court of commission, Havana, 1836–40; special commissioner on the west coast of Africa, 1841–3; special correspondent of the *Morning Chronicle*, 1843–6; colonial secretary of Western Australia, 1847–50; secretary to the Loan Fund Board, Dublin Castle, 1850–80; FRCS, 1855; best-known work, *The United Irishmen, their Lives and Times* (7 vols., 1843–6).

MADDEN, Samuel (1686–1765), miscellaneous writer and philanthropist; BA, Dublin, 1705; DD, 1723; ordained and held cures; organized the system of premiums in Dublin University, 1730; chief work, *Reflections and Resolutions proper for the Gentlemen of Ireland as to their conduct for the service of their country* (1738).

MADDEN, Thomas More (1844–1902), Irish gynaecologist; MRCS, 1862; raised Irish Ambulance Corps in Franco-Prussian War, 1870; master of the National Lying-in Hospital, Dublin, 1878; FRCS Edinburgh, 1882; recognized as a foremost gynaecologist; voluminous writings include *Uterine Tumours* (1887), *Clinical Gynaecology* (1893), and accounts of his family.

MADDISON (or MADDESTONE), Sir Ralph (1571?–1655?), economic writer; knighted, 1603; member of the Royal Commission on the Woollen Trade, 1622; held office in the Mint during the Commonwealth; author of *England's Looking in and out: presented to the High Court of Parliament now assembled*, a clear statement of the theory of the balance of trade (1640).

MADDOCK, Henry (d. 1824), legal author; educated at St John's College, Cambridge; barrister, Lincoln's Inn, 1801; died at St Lucia in the West Indies; chief work, *A Treatise on the . . . High Court of Chancery* (2 vols., 1815).

MADDOX, Isaac (1697–1759), bishop of Worcester; MA, Edinburgh, 1723; ordained, 1723; BA, The Queen's College, Oxford, 1724; MA, Queens' College, Cambridge, 1728; published his best-known work, a *Vindication* of the Elizabethan settlement of the Church of England (1733); dean of Wells, 1734; bishop of St Asaph, 1736, of Worcester, 1743.

MADDOX, Willis (1813–1853), painter; exhibited at the Royal Academy, 1844–52; invited to Constantinople to paint the sultan; died at Pera.

MADDY, Watkin (d. 1857), astronomer; of St John's College, Cambridge; MA, 1823; fellow, 1823; BD, 1830; joined Cambridge Astronomical Society; published *The Elements of the Theory of Plane Astronomy* (1826).

MADERTY, first Baron (1540?–1623), 'commendator' of Inchaffray. See DRUMMOND, JAMES.

MADGETT (or MADGET), Nicholas (*fl.* 1799), Irish adventurer; in the French Foreign Office, 1794; supported scheme for French expedition to Ireland, 1796; member of a 'secret committee for managing the affairs of Ireland and Scotland', 1798; wrongly identified with another Maget, an Irish priest.

MADOCKS, William Alexander (1774–1828), philanthropist; MA, Christ Church, Oxford, 1799; reclaimed marsh land in Caernarfonshire and founded the town of Tremadoc; MP, Boston, Lincolnshire, 1802–20, Chippenham, 1820–8; died in Paris.

MADOG (*fl.* 1294–1295), leader of the North Welsh rebellion; in consequence of heavy taxation rose in rebellion with many of the Welsh, 1294; forced to submit by Edward I, 1295.

MADOG AB OWAIN GWYNEDD (1150–1180?), supposed discoverer of America; said in a Welsh poem of the fifteenth century to have gone to sea in ten ships and never returned. Dr David *Powell, who published *Llwyd's translation of the *Brut y Tywysogion* (1584), with additions of his own, declared that Madog, after leaving Ireland to the north, came to a land which must have been Florida or New Spain. The story, which is unsupported by evidence, is the subject of *Southey's poem of *Madoc*.

MADOG AP GRUFFYDD MAELOR (d. 1236), prince of Northern Powys; ruler of Northern Powys, 1197; an ally of *Llywelyn ab Iorwerth; founded Valle Crucis Abbey, 1200.

MADOG AP MAREDUDD (d. 1160), prince of Powys; nephew of *Iorwerth ab Bleddyn; prince of Powys during the reign of Stephen; allied himself with the English to protect his own domains; defeated in battle by the prince of Gwynedd; probably had a secret understanding with Henry II.

MADOG BENFRAS, i.e. Greathead (*fl.* 1350), Welsh poet; prominent with his brothers in the revival of Welsh poetry.

MADOX, Thomas (1666–1727), legal antiquary; sworn clerk in the Lord-Treasurer's Office; joint clerk in the Augmentation Office, and published his *Formulare Anglicanum* (1702), his *History and Antiquities of the Exchequer of the Kings of England* (1711), one of his best-known works; historiographer royal, 1714.

MAEL, Saint (d. 487), Irish saint. See MEL.

MAEL-DUBH (d. 675?), Scottish or Irish teacher. See MAILDULF.

MAELGARBH (d. 544), king of Ireland. See TUATHAL.

MAELGWN GWYNEDD (d. 550?), British king; possibly the 'Maglocune' of *Gildas; according to tradition succeeded to the throne by overthrowing an uncle; probably died of the 'yellow pestilence'.

MAELMURA (d. 886), Irish historian; monk of Fahan; one of his historical poems preserved in the *Book of Leinster*.

MAELSECHLAINN I (d. 863), king of Ireland; succeeded his father, 842; defeated the Danes, 844 and 847; thrice invaded Munster; again defeated the Danes, 859.

MAELSECHLAINN II (949–1022), king of Ireland; chief of his clan, 979; became king of all Ireland, 980; defeated the Danes, 980 and 1000; recognized the superiority of *Brian (926–1014) as king, 1002; regained his kingship on Brian's death in the Battle of Cluantarbh (Clontarf), in which the Danes were finally overthrown, 1014.

MAFFEY, John Loader, first Baron Rugby (1877–1969), public servant; educated at Rugby and Christ Church, Oxford; entered Indian Civil Service, 1899; transferred to political department, 1905; served with Mohmand Field Force, 1908; political agent, Kyber, 1909–12; deputy commissioner, Peshawar, 1914–15; chief political officer with forces in Afghanistan, 1919; deputy secretary, foreign and political department, Government of India, 1915–16; private secretary to the viceroy, 1916–20; chief secretary to duke of *Connaught, 1920–1; chief commissioner, North-West Frontier Province, 1921–4; organized rescue of Mollie Ellis from tribesmen; disagreed with British government frontier policy, and resigned from ICS, 1924; governor-general, Sudan, 1926–33; permanent under-secretary of state, Colonial Office, 1933–7; first British representative in Eire, 1939–49; director, Rio Tinto Company and Imperial Airways; CIE, 1916; CSI, 1920; KCVO, 1921; KCMG, 1931; KCB, 1934; GCMG, 1935; baron, 1947.

MAGAN, Francis (1772?–1843), Irish informer; graduated at Trinity College, Dublin, 1794; admitted to the Irish bar, 1793; acted as government spy on Lord Edward *Fitzgerald (1763–1798), 1798; elected member of the committee of United Irishmen on the night of Fitzgerald's arrest; commissioner for enclosing waste lands and commons, 1821; had a secret pension from government until 1834.

MAGAURAN, Edmund (1548–1593), Roman Catholic archbishop of Armagh; educated abroad; sent on a mission to the pope by the Irish chiefs, 1581; bishop of Ardagh, 1581; archbishop of Armagh and primate of all Ireland, 1587; went to Spain and obtained from Philip II a promise of help for the Irish against Queen Elizabeth, 1592; instigated a rebellion; killed in an engagement with Elizabeth's troops.

MAGEE, James (d. 1866), Irish journalist; son of John *Magee (d. 1809); conducted the *Dublin Evening Post* from 1815; was subsequently a Dublin police magistrate.

MAGEE, John (d. 1809), Irish journalist and colliery broker; proprietor and printer of *Magee's Weekly Packet*, 1777, of the *Dublin Evening Post*, 1779; opposed government measures in his paper; tried for libel on Francis *Higgins (1746–1802) and found guilty, 1789; imprisoned in Newgate, Dublin.

MAGEE, John (*fl.* 1814), son of John *Magee (d. 1809); carried on the *Dublin Evening Post*; convicted of libel and imprisoned, 1813 and 1814; defended by Daniel *O'Connell.

MAGEE, Martha Maria (d. 1846), foundress of the Magee College, Londonderry; daughter of Mr Stewart of Lurgan, Co. Armagh; married (1780) William Magee (d. 1800), Presbyterian minister; inherited a fortune from her brothers; left £20,000 to erect and endow a college for the education of the Irish Presbyterian ministry (Magee College, opened, 1865).

MAGEE, William (1766–1831), archbishop of Dublin; educated at Trinity College, Dublin; BA, 1785; fellow, 1788; ordained, 1790; Donnellan lecturer, 1795; professor of mathematics, Trinity College, Dublin, 1800; published sermons, delivered (1798 and 1799) in Trinity College Chapel as *Discourses on the Scriptural Doctrines of Atonement and Sacrifice* (1801); dean of Cork, 1813–19; bishop of Raphoe, 1819–22; archbishop of Dublin, 1822–31; rendered considerable services to the Irish church; his *Works* published (1842).

MAGEE, William Connor (1821–1891), successively bishop of Peterborough and archbishop of York; grandson of William *Magee; entered Trinity College, Dublin, 1835; MA, 1854; ordained, 1845; held various livings in England and Ireland, 1845–64; DD, Dublin, 1860; dean of Cork, 1864–8; Donnellan lecturer at Trinity College, Dublin, 1865; dean of the Chapel Royal, Dublin, 1866–8; bishop of Peterborough, 1868–91; opposed Irish disestablishment; hon. DCL, Oxford, 1870; archbishop of York, 1891; one of the greatest orators and most brilliant controversialists of his day; published speeches, addresses, and sermons.

MAGELLAN (or MAGALHAENS), Jean Hyacinthe de (1723–1790), scientific investigator; descendant of the Portuguese navigator who discovered Magellan Straits in 1520; born probably at Talavera; Augustinian monk; abandoned monastic life for scientific research, 1763; reached England, 1764; FRS, 1774; published work on English reflecting instruments, 1775; engaged in perfecting the construction of scientific instruments; published descriptions of them, and the memoirs of his friend the Hungarian Count de Benyowsky (posthumous, 1791).

MAGEOGHEGAN, Conall (*fl.* 1635), Irish historian; translated *The Annals of Clonmacnois* (1627).

MAGHERAMORNE, first Baron (1823–1890). See HOGG, Sir JAMES MACNAGHTEN MCGAREL.

MAGILL, Robert (1788–1839), Irish Presbyterian clergyman; MA, Glasgow, 1817; licensed to preach, 1818; his best-known work, *The Thinking Few* (1828).

MAGINN, Edward (1802–1849), Irish Catholic prelate; educated at the Irish College, Paris; ordained priest, 1825; agitated for the repeal of the Union, 1829; coadjutor to the bishop of Derry and nominated bishop of Ortosia in the archbishopric of Tyre, *in partibus infidelium*, 1845; DD.

MAGINN, William (1793–1842), poet, journalist, and miscellaneous writer; educated at Trinity College, Dublin; BA, 1811; LL D, 1819; contributed to *Blackwood's Magazine*, 1819–28 and 1834–42; in Edinburgh, 1821–3; settled in London, 1823; joint editor of the *Standard*; contributed to the *Age*; established *Fraser's Magazine*, 1830, his 'Gallery of Literary Characters' being its most popular feature; his masterpiece in humorous fiction, *Bob Burke's Duel with Ensign Brady* (1834); published his *Homeric Ballads* in *Fraser* (1838); published reproductions of Lucian's dialogues in the form of blank-verse comedies (1839); his health ruined after imprisonment for debt; the original of *Thackeray's 'Captain Shandon'.

MAGLORIUS, Saint (495?–575), second bishop of Dol in Brittany; educated in the college of St *Illtyd at Llantwit Major; placed at the head of one of the religious communities of St *Samson, near Dol; ordained priest and bishop; episcopal abbot there; retired to Jersey, where his hermitage grew into a monastery; his relics removed to Paris in the tenth century.

MAGNUS, Thomas (d. 1550), ambassador; archdeacon of the East Riding of Yorkshire, 1504; employed on diplomatic missions, 1509–19 and 1524–7; present at the Field of the Cloth of Gold, 1520; privy councillor, *c.*1520; incorporated in a doctor's degree at Oxford, 1520; canon of Windsor, 1520–49; prebendary of Lincoln, 1522–48; paymaster of the forces and treasurer of the wars in the north, 1523; custodian of St Leonard's Hospital, York, 1529.

MAGRAIDIN, Augustin (1349–1405), Irish chronicler. See MACGRADOIGH.

MAGRATH, John Macrory (*fl.* 1459), in Irish Eoghan MacRuadhri MacCraith, Irish historian; one of a family of hereditary men of letters; chief historian to the Dal Cais in Thomond; author of *Cathreim Thoirdhealbhaigh*, a history of the wars of Thomond, of which the best existing copy is by Andrew *MacCurtin.

MAGRATH, John Richard (1839–1930), provost of The Queen's College, Oxford; born in Guernsey; BA, Oriel College, Oxford; fellow of Queen's College, 1860; ordained, 1863; tutor of Queen's, 1864, dean, 1864–77; chaplain, 1867–78, bursar, 1874–8, pro-provost, 1877, provost, 1878–1930; member of Hebdomadal Council, 1878–99; curator of University Chest, 1885–1908; delegate of University Press, 1894–1920; vice-chancellor, 1894–8; alderman, 1889–95; supported movement for higher education of women; greatly interested in northern schools linked with Queen's, particularly St Bees; identified himself with reforms of statutory commission of 1877; a keen sportsman; his works include *The Queen's College* (1921).

MAGRATH, Meiler (1523?–1622), archbishop of Cashel; became a Franciscan friar; lived, when young, in Rome; bishop of Clogher, 1570–1; archbishop of Cashel and bishop of Emly, 1571; attacked by James Fitzmaurice *Fitzgerald (d. 1579) for imprisoning friars, 1571–80; continued to serve the government, though intriguing with rebels; bishop of Waterford and Lismore, 1582–1607; received sees of Killala and Achonry, 1611; according to Sir John *Davies, 'a notable example of pluralities'.

MAGUIRE, Cathal Macmaghnusa (1439–1498), Irish historian; archdeacon of Clogher, 1483; collected a fine library of manuscripts, and compiled *The Historical Book of Ballymacmanus* ('Annals of Ulster', AD 60–1498); according to Paul *Harris, author of additions to the *Felire* of Oengus and annotations to the *Register of Clogher*.

MAGUIRE, Connor (or Cornelius), second baron of Enniskillen (1616–1645), succeeded to peerage, 1634; inveigled by Roger *More into taking part in Catholic conspiracy, 1641, which was discovered through the folly of Hugh Oge *MacMahon; imprisoned in the Tower of London and subsequently in Newgate; tried and sentenced to be hanged, drawn, and quartered.

MAGUIRE, Hugh, lord of Fermanagh (d. 1600), implicated in a plot with Hugh *O'Neill, second earl of Tyrone; succeeded to estates of Fermanagh, 1589; declared by the lord-deputy of Ireland to be a traitor; invaded Connaught; driven back by Sir Richard *Bingham; slain in Tyrone's expedition into Munster and Leinster.

MAGUIRE, James Rochfort (1855–1925), president of British South Africa Company; BA, Merton College, Oxford; friend of Cecil *Rhodes; Parnellite MP, North Donegal, 1890;

MP, West Clare, 1892–5; one of the emissaries sent by Rhodes to obtain mineral concessions from Matabele chief, Lobengula, at Bulawayo, 1883; vice-president, British South Africa Company, 1906; president, 1923.

MAGUIRE, John Francis (1815–1872), Irish politician; called to the Irish bar, 1843; journalist; founded (1841) and conducted *Cork Examiner*; MP, Dungarvan, 1852, Cork, 1865–72; acted with the Independent Irishmen; took prominent part in debates on the Irish land question; upheld the papacy and published *Rome and its Ruler*, for which the pope named him knight commander of St Gregory, 1856; issued third edition as *The Pontificate of Pius IX* (1870); published also miscellaneous works.

MAGUIRE, Nicholas (1460?–1512), bishop of Leighlin; educated at Oxford; bishop of Leighlin, 1490; completed the *Chronicon Hiberniae* and *Vita Milonis Episcopi Leighlinensis*.

MAGUIRE, Robert (1826–1890), controversialist; educated at Trinity College, Dublin; clerical secretary to the Islington Protestant Institute, 1852; MA, 1855; DD, 1877; a popular preacher and lecturer; published addresses and sermons.

MAGUIRE, Thomas (1792–1847), Roman Catholic controversialist; educated at Maynooth College; ordained, 1816; held various livings; engaged in platform discussions, of which *Authenticated Reports* appeared in 1827 and 1839.

MAGUIRE, Thomas (1831–1889), classical scholar and metaphysician; first Roman Catholic fellow of Trinity College, Dublin; educated at Trinity College; BA, 1855; obtained law studentship at Lincoln's Inn, 1861; barrister, Lincoln's Inn, 1862; LL D, Dublin, 1868; after 'Fawcett's Act' of 1873 was elected to a fellowship at Trinity College, Dublin, 1880; professor, classical composition (chair specially created), till 1882; professor of moral philosophy, 1882–9; took part in discussion concerning the 'Pigott letters' (see PIGOTT, RICHARD); published philosophical works, including *Essays on the Platonic Idea* (1866) and translations.

MAHAFFY, Sir John Pentland (1839–1919), provost of Trinity College, Dublin; born in Switzerland; BA, Trinity College, Dublin (first senior moderator in classics and logics), 1859; fellow, and ordained, 1864; first professor of ancient history at Dublin, 1869; provost of Trinity, 1914–19; GBE, 1918; reputation chiefly rests on works dealing with life, literature, and history of ancient Greeks; these include *Prolegomena to Ancient History* (1871), *Greek Social Life from Homer to Menander* (1874), *History of Classical Greek Literature* (1880), *Story of Alexander's*

Empire (1887), *Greek Life and Thought from Alexander to the Roman Conquest* (1887), *The Greek World under Roman Sway* (1890), and *Problems in Greek History* (1892); turned his attention to papyri, 1890; produced *Flinders Petrie Papyri* (1891, etc.) and *The Empire of the Ptolemies* (1895); a remarkably versatile writer of great shrewdness and sagacity.

MAHOMED, Frederick Henry Horatio Akbar (1849–1884), physician; son of the keeper of a Turkish bath; studied at Guy's Hospital, London; MRCS, 1872; resident medical officer at the London Fever Hospital; medical tutor at St Mary's Hospital, London, 1875; MD, Brussels; medical registrar at Guy's, London; entered Caius College, Cambridge, going up to Cambridge every night to keep his term; FRCP, 1880; MB, Cambridge and assistant physician to Guy's Hospital, London, 1881; contributed to medical periodicals.

MAHON, Viscount (1805–1875), historian. See STANHOPE, PHILIP HENRY, fifth Earl Stanhope.

MAHON, Sir **Bryan Thomas** (1862–1930), general; gazetted to 8th Hussars, 1883; served in Egypt, playing active part in operations in Dongola (1896) and Nile valley (1897) which led to final destruction of dervish power, 1893–1900; left Egypt for South Africa on special service, Jan. 1900; commanded column which achieved relief of Mafeking, on which his reputation chiefly rests, 17 May; governor of Kordofan, 1901–4; commanded district of Belgaum, India, 1904–9; Lucknow division, 1909–13; appointed to command 10th (Irish) division of new armies, 1914; took division to Gallipoli, 1915; commander-in-chief, Salonika Army, 1915–16; commander-in-chief, Ireland, 1916–18; military commander, Lille, 1918–19; KCB, 1922.

MAHON, Charles James Patrick (1800–1891), better known as The O'Gorman Mahon; Irish politician; educated at Trinity College, Dublin; MA, 1826; urged *O'Connell to wrest Clare from William Vesey *Fitzgerald when Fitzgerald became president of the Board of Trade in 1828; failed to gain the seat himself in 1831, quarrelling with O'Connell in consequence; MP, Ennis, 1847–52; lived a life of adventure under many flags 1852–71; as a supporter of Charles Stewart *Parnell was MP for Clare, 1879–85; sat for Carlow, 1887–91, repudiating Parnell in 1890.

MAHONY, Connor (Cornelius or **Constantine)** (*fl.* 1650), called also Cornelius à Sancto Patricio; Irish Jesuit; author of *Disputatio Apologetica de Jure Regni Hiberniae pro Catholicis Hibernis adversus haereticos Anglos*, urging the Irish to elect a Roman Catholic king for themselves (1645).

MAHONY, Francis Sylvester (1804–1866), humorist best known by his pseudonym of Father Prout; educated at the Jesuit colleges of Clongoweswood, Co. Kildare, and of St Acheul, Amiens, and at Rome; admitted Jesuit; master of rhetoric at the Clongoweswood Jesuits' College, August 1830; dismissed from the order, Nov. 1830; abandoned the priesthood for literary life in London; befriended by William *Maginn; contributed entertaining papers, over signature 'Father Prout', to *Fraser's Magazine*, 1834–6 (published collectively, 1836); contributed poems to *Bentley's Miscellany*, 1837; correspondent at Rome to the *Daily News*, 1846; Paris correspondent to the *Globe*, 1858–66; died in Paris.

MAIDMENT, James (1795?–1879), Scottish antiquary; called to the Scottish bar, 1817; advocate; much engaged in disputed peerage cases; interested in historical and antiquarian research; edited works for the Bannatyne, Maitland, Abbotsford, and Hunterian clubs, and for the Spottiswoode Society. One of his most valuable works is the *Dramatists of the Restoration* (1877).

MAIDSTONE (or MAYDESTONE), Clement (*fl.* 1410), theologian and historical writer; probably a Trinitarian friar; author of ecclesiastical works.

MAIDSTONE, Ralph of (d. 1246), bishop of Hereford. See RALPH.

MAIDSTONE (or MAYDESTONE), Richard (d. 1396), Carmelite; educated at Oxford; DD, and confessor to *John of Gaunt; prominent opponent of *Wycliffe; manuscripts by him preserved in the Bodleian Library, British Museum, and elsewhere.

MAIHEW, Edward (1570–1625), Benedictine; educated in the English College at Douai, and subsequently at Rome; took orders; secular priest in England; Benedictine in the abbey of Westminster, 1607; prior of the monastery of St Laurence at Dieulwart in Lorraine, 1614–20; died at Cambrai; author of some religious treatises.

MAILDULF (or MAILDUF) (d. 675?), Scottish or Irish teacher; gave his name to the town of Malmesbury; according to *William of Malmesbury, opened a school in 'the spot now called Malmesbury', which *Aldhelm attended, and where he took the tonsure later.

MAIMBRAY (or MAINBRAY), Stephen Charles Triboudet (1710–1782), electrician and astronomer. See DEMAINBRAY.

MAIN, James (1700?–1761), philologist. See MAN.

MAIN, Robert (1808–1878), astronomer; brother of Thomas John *Main; fellow of Queens' College, Cambridge; took orders; MA, 1837; chief assistant at the Royal Observatory, 1835; gold medallist, Astronomical Society, 1858; FRS, 1860; Radcliffe observer, 1860; edited first Radcliffe catalogue and compiled second, 1860; collected materials for a third, with the Redhill transit circle purchased (1861) from Richard Christopher *Carrington; published astronomical treatises and addresses.

MAIN, Thomas John (1818–1885), mathematician; younger brother of Robert *Main; senior wrangler, St John's College, Cambridge, 1838; took orders; MA, 1841; naval chaplain; placed on retired list, 1869; for thirty-four years professor of mathematics at the Royal Naval College, Portsmouth; published works on applied mathematics.

MAINE, Sir Henry James Sumner (1822–1888), jurist; of Christ's Hospital, London, and Pembroke College, Cambridge; senior classic, 1844; junior tutor at Trinity Hall, Cambridge, 1845–7; regius professor of civil law, 1847–54; called to the bar, 1850; reader in Roman law and jurisprudence at the Inns of Court, 1852; contributed to the *Saturday Review* from its start in 1855; published *Ancient Law: its Connection with the Early History of Society and its Relations to Modern Ideas* (1861); legal member of the Council of India, 1862–9; Corpus professor of jurisprudence, Oxford, 1869–78; published lectures as *Village Communities* (1871), *Early History of Institutions* (1875), and *Dissertations on Early Law and Customs* (1883); KCSI and appointed to a seat on the Indian Council, 1871; master of Trinity Hall, Cambridge, 1877–88; Whewell professor of international law, Cambridge, 1887–8; died at Cannes; one of the earliest to apply the historical method to the study of political institutions.

MAINE, Jasper (1604–1672), archdeacon of Chichester and dramatist. See MAYNE.

MAINWARING (or **MAYNWARING**), **Arthur** (1668–1712), auditor of imprests; entered Christ Church, Oxford, 1683, and the Inner Temple, 1687; at first opposed, but subsequently served the Revolution government; auditor of imprests, 1705–12; MP, Preston, 1706–10, West Looe, 1710–12; started the *Medley*, 1710; in his writings attacked *Sacheverell, defended *Marlborough, and arraigned the French policy.

MAINWARING, Everard (1628–1699?), medical writer. See MAYNWARING.

MAINWARING, Matthew (1561–1652), romancist; published *Vienna*, an adaptation of a romance of Catalonian origin, *c.*1618.

MAINWARING, Sir Philip (1589–1661), secretary for Ireland; BA, Brasenose College, Oxford, 1613; MP, Boroughbridge, 1624–6, Derby, 1628–9, Morpeth, 1640, Newton, Lancashire, 1661; knighted, 1634; secretary to the lord-lieutenant of Ireland, the earl of *Strafford, 1634; returned to London and was imprisoned as a delinquent, 1650–1.

MAINWARING, Roger (1590–1653), bishop of St David's. See MANWARING.

MAINWARING, Rowland (1783–1862), naval commander and author; present at the Battle of the Nile, 1798, at the blockade of Copenhagen, 1801; captain, 1830; author of *Instructive Gleanings . . . on Painting and Drawing* (1832) and *Annals of Bath* (1838).

MAINWARING, Sir Thomas, first baronet (1623–1689), author of the *Defence of Amicia*; entered Brasenose College, Oxford, 1637, and Gray's Inn, 1640; took Parliamentary side in Civil War, but at the Restoration gained favour at court; created baronet, 1660. His *Defence of Amicia*, to prove that his ancestor Amicia was the lawful daughter of Earl Hugh of Cyveiliog (see HUGH, d. 1181) (published, 1673), led to a controversy with his relative Sir Peter *Leycester.

MAINZER, Joseph (1801–1851), teacher of music; born at Trèves; ordained, 1826; singing-master to the college at Trèves; being compelled to leave Germany on account of his political opinions, went to Brussels, 1833; proceeded to Paris and came to England, 1839; best-known work, *Singing for the Million* (1841).

MAIR, John (1469–1550), historian and scholastic divine. See MAJOR, JOHN.

MAIR, William (1830–1920), Scottish divine; served ministries in established church, 1861–1903; moderator of General Assembly, 1897; pioneer in cause of Church reunion and authority on Scottish ecclesiastical law.

MAIRE, Christopher (1697–1767), Jesuit; educated at St Omer; joined Jesuits, 1715; professed, 1733; rector of the English College at Rome, 1744–50; died at Ghent; author of Latin theological and astronomical works.

MAIRE, William (d. 1769), Roman Catholic prelate; educated at the English College, Douai; ordained priest, 1730; served the Durham mission, 1742–67; coadjutor to the vicar-apostolic of the northern district of England, 1767–9.

MAITLAND, Agnes Catherine (1850–1906), principal of Somerville College, Oxford; published *The Rudiments of Cookery* (35th thousand, 1910) and other cookery books and novels; principal of Somerville College, Oxford, 1889–1906; largely increased numbers and extended buildings; developed tutorial system, and had college library erected.

MAITLAND, Anthony, tenth earl of Lauderdale (1785–1863), admiral of the red; son of James *Maitland, eighth earl of Lauderdale; served under *Nelson, 1801, and Lord *Exmouth, 1826; GCB and GCMG; last Baron Lauderdale.

MAITLAND, Sir Arthur Herbert Drummond Ramsay-Steel-, first baronet (1876–1935), politician and economist. See STEEL-MAITLAND.

MAITLAND, Charles, third earl of Lauderdale (d. 1691), brother of John *Maitland, first duke of Lauderdale; master-general of the Scottish Mint; privy councillor, 1661; commissioner to parliament for the shire of Edinburgh, and lord of the articles, 1669; treasurer-depute, 1671; created baronet, 1672; assisted his brother in the management of Scottish affairs, 1674–81; accused of perjury and deprived of his position, 1681; succeeded as earl of Lauderdale, 1682.

MAITLAND, Charles (1815–1866), author; nephew of Sir Peregrine *Maitland; MD, Edinburgh, 1838; studied theology and graduated BA, Magdalen Hall, Oxford, 1852; held various curacies; author of the first popular book on the *Catacombs of Rome* (1846).

MAITLAND, Edward (1824–1897), mystical writer; BA, Caius College, Cambridge, 1847; went to California, 1849, became a commissioner of crown lands in Australia, and returned to England, 1857; published romances, including *The Pilgrim and the Shrine* (largely autobiographical, 1867); collaborated with Anna *Kingsford in *Keys of the Creeds* (1875), and joined her in crusade against materialism, animal food, and vivisection; declared (1876) that he had acquired a new sense, that of 'spiritual sensitiveness', which enabled him to see the spiritual condition of people; published, with Anna Kingsford, *The Perfect Way; or the Finding of Christ* (1882), and founded with her the Hermetic Society, 1884; founded Esoteric Christian Union, 1891. His publications include *Anna Kingsford. Her Life, Letters, Diary, and Work* (1896).

MAITLAND, Edward Francis, Lord Barcaple (1803–1870), Scottish judge; brother of Thomas *Maitland, Lord Dundrennan; LL D, Edinburgh; advocate, 1831; solicitor-general for Scotland, 1855–8 and 1859–62; lord of session as Lord Barcaple, 1802–70.

MAITLAND, Frederick (1763–1848), general; grandson of Charles Maitland, sixth earl of Lauderdale; entered the army, 1779; present as lieutenant at the relief of Gibraltar, 1782; served chiefly in the West Indies; lieutenant-colonel, 1795; major-general, 1805; lieutenant-governor of Grenada, 1805–10; lieutenant-general, 1811; second-in-command in the Mediterranean, 1812; lieutenant-governor of Dominica, 1813; general, 1825.

MAITLAND, Frederick Lewis (d. 1786), captain of the Royal Navy; son of Charles Maitland, sixth earl of Lauderdale; commanded the royal yacht, 1763–75; served under *Rodney, 1782; rear-admiral, 1786.

MAITLAND, Sir Frederick Lewis (1777–1839), rear-admiral; son of Frederick Lewis *Maitland (d. 1786); served in the Mediterranean and off the French and Spanish coasts; commanded on the Halifax and West India stations, 1813–14; as commander of the *Bellerophon* took Napoleon to England, 1815; CB, 1815; KCB and rear-admiral, 1830; admiral superintendent of Portsmouth Dockyard, 1832–7; commander-in-chief in the East Indies and China, 1837–9; died at sea.

MAITLAND, Frederic William (1850–1906), Downing professor of the laws of England at Cambridge; son of John Gorham *Maitland; educated at Eton and Trinity College, Cambridge; senior in moral sciences tripos, 1872; Whewell international law scholar, 1873; president of Union; obtained blue for running; BA, 1873; MA, 1876; hon. LL D, 1891; called to bar, 1876; reader in English law at Cambridge, 1884; Downing professor, 1888–1906; founded Selden Society for encouraging study of history of English law, editing several volumes, 1887; literary director, 1895; published *Bracton's Note-Book* (3 vols., 1887) and *History of English Law before the time of Edward I* (with Sir Frederick *Pollock, 2 vols., 1895); traced Roman influence in English law in thirteenth century in *Bracton and Azo* (Selden Soc., 1895) and in *Roman Canon Law in the Church of England* (1898); made researches into legal effect of the Reformation; edited and translated MSS of Year Books in old legal Anglo-French, *temp.* Edward II (4 vols., 1903–7); advocated simplification and codification of English law; ardent alpinist; Ford's lecturer, Oxford, 1897; Rede lecturer, Cambridge, 1901; hon. DCL, Oxford, 1899, LL D, Glasgow, Cracow, and Moscow; original FBA, 1902; hon. fellow, Trinity College, Cambridge; died at Las Palmas; other publications include *Life and Letters of Leslie Stephen* (1906) and posthumously *The Constitutional History of England* (1908) and *Collected Works* (1911).

MAITLAND, James, eighth earl of Lauderdale (1759–1839), studied at Edinburgh High School and University, Trinity College, Oxford (1775), and Glasgow University; admitted to Lincoln's Inn, 1777; member of the Faculty of Advocates, 1780; MP, Newport, Cornwall, 1780, Malmesbury, 1784; succeeded to the title, 1789; Scots representative peer, 1790; strenuously opposed Pitt's government; published his *Inquiry into the Nature and Origin of Public Wealth* (1804); created Baron Lauderdale of Thirlestane in the county of Berwick (peerage of Great Britain and Ireland, 1806); lord high keeper of the great seal of Scotland, 1806; privy councillor, 1806; resigned, 1807; turned Tory after 1821; retired from public life after 1830.

MAITLAND, Sir John, first Baron Maitland of Thirlestane (1545?–1595), lord high chancellor of Scotland; son of Sir Richard *Maitland, Lord Lethington; brother of William *Maitland of Lethington; lord privy seal, 1567; favoured the queen and was rigorously treated by *Morton, 1569–78; privy councillor, 1583; secretary of state, 1584; vice-chancellor, 1586; acquired great influence over the king; created Baron Maitland of Thirlestane, 1590; responsible for the act which established the kirk on a strictly Presbyterian basis; wrote verse.

MAITLAND, John, second earl and first duke of Lauderdale (1616–1682), grandson of Sir John *Maitland; grand-nephew of William *Maitland of Lethington; regarded as a rising hope of the ultra-Covenanting party; commissioner for the Solemn League and Covenant, 1643–6; one of the commissioners who obtained the famous 'Engagement'; with Charles II in Holland, 1649; followed him to Worcester and was taken prisoner, 1651; kept a prisoner till 1660; secretary for Scottish affairs, 1660–80; aimed at making the crown absolute in Scotland both in state and church; had complete influence over Charles; created duke of Lauderdale and marquis of March in the Scottish peerage, 1672; placed upon the commission for the Admiralty, 1673; made a privy councillor and a peer of England as earl of Guildford and Baron Petersham, 1674; supported by Charles II against attacks from the English parliament.

MAITLAND, John, Lord Ravelrig, and fifth earl of Lauderdale (1650?–1710), brother of Richard *Maitland, fourth earl of Lauderdale; passed advocate at the Scottish bar, 1680; concurred in the Revolution, a lord of session as Lord Ravelrig, 1689; succeeded to the earldom of Lauderdale, 1695; supported the Union.

MAITLAND, John Alexander Fuller- (1856–1936), musical critic and connoisseur; educated at Trinity College, Cambridge; musical critic, *Pall Mall Gazette,* 1882–4, *Guardian,* 1884–9, *The Times,* 1889–1911; contributed vol. iv (*The Age of Bach and Handel,* 1902) to *Oxford History of Music* and edited second edition of *Grove's Dictionary of Music and Musicians* (1904–10).

MAITLAND, John Gorham (1818–1863), civil servant; son of Samuel Roffey *Maitland; fellow of Trinity College, Cambridge; secretary to the Civil Service Commission; FRS, 1847; published pamphlets.

MAITLAND, Sir Peregrine (1777–1854), general and colonial governor; entered the army, 1792; served in Flanders, 1794–8; in Spain, 1809 and 1812; major-general, 1814; present at Waterloo, 1815; KCB, 1815; lieutenant-governor of Upper Canada, 1818–28, of Nova Scotia, 1828–34; commander-in-chief of the Madras Army, 1836–8, and at the Cape of Good Hope, 1844–7; general, 1846; resigned governorship of Cape of Good Hope, 1847; GCB, 1852.

MAITLAND, Sir Richard, Lord Lethington (1496–1586), poet, lawyer, and collector of early Scottish poetry; educated at St Andrews University; studied law at Paris; employed by *James V and Queen *Mary; an ordinary lord of session and privy councillor, 1561; keeper of the great seal, 1562–7; a selection from his collection of early Scottish poems, with additions by himself, published (1786).

MAITLAND, Richard, fourth earl of Lauderdale (1653–1695), Jacobite; son of Charles *Maitland, third earl of Lauderdale; privy councillor and joint general of the Mint with his father, 1678; lord justice general, 1681–4; declined to agree to the Revolution settlement; for a time in exile at the court of St Germains; outlawed, 1694; died at Paris; author of a verse translation of Virgil (published 1737).

MAITLAND, Richard (1714?–1763), captor of Surat; enlisted in Royal Artillery, 1732; lieutenant-fireworker, 1742; fought at Fontenoy as first lieutenant, 1745; served under *Clive in India; commanded the expedition for capturing Surat, 1759; major, 1762; died at Bombay.

MAITLAND, Samuel Roffey (1792–1866), historian and miscellaneous writer; educated at St John's and Trinity colleges, Cambridge; barrister, Inner Temple, 1816; entered holy orders, 1821; published his elaborate monograph on the Albigenses and Waldenses (1832); commenced contributing to the *British Magazine,* 1835, the remarkable papers afterwards published as *The Dark Ages* (1844) and *Essays on Subjects connected with the Reformation in England* (1849); librarian and keeper of the manuscripts at Lambeth, 1838;

FRS, 1839; editor of the *British Magazine*, 1839–49; contributed to *Notes and Queries*; author of thirty-seven works, mainly historical and ecclesiastical.

MAITLAND, Sir **Thomas** (1759?–1824), lieutenant-general; commander-in-chief in the Mediterranean; served in India, both ashore and afloat, till 1790; in San Domingo, 1794–8; MP, Haddington burghs, 1794–6 and 1800–6; brigadier-general, 1797; employed in the secret expedition against Belle Isle, 1799; major-general, 1805; lieutenant-general and commander-in-chief in Ceylon, 1806–11; major-general, 1811; governor of Malta, 1813; lord high commissioner of the Ionian Islands and commander-in-chief in the Mediterranean, 1815; died at Malta; an able administrator, though nicknamed 'King Tom' from his eccentricities and arbitrary conduct.

MAITLAND, Thomas, Lord Dundrennan (1792–1851), Scottish judge; studied at Edinburgh; called to the Scottish bar, 1813; solicitor-general, 1840–1 and 1846–50; MP, Kirkcudbrightshire, 1845–50; lord of session as Lord Dundrennan, 1850; studied antiquarian literature; his fine library sold in 1851.

MAITLAND, Thomas, eleventh earl of Lauderdale (1803–1878), admiral of the fleet; entered the navy, 1816; served on the South American Station, 1826, the West Indian, 1832–3, the north coast of Spain, 1835–7; advanced to post rank, 1837; shared in the operations in the Persian Gulf, 1839; served during the first Chinese War, 1840–1; knighted, 1843; rear-admiral, 1857; commander-in-chief in the Pacific, 1860–3; succeeded to earldom on the death of his cousin (see MAITLAND, ANTHONY), 1863; admiral, 1868; admiral of the fleet on the retired list, 1877.

MAITLAND, William (1528?–1573), of Lethington, known as the 'Secretary Lethington'; son of Sir Richard *Maitland; educated at St Andrews and on the continent; in the service of the queen-regent (see MARY OF GUISE) of Scotland, 1554–9; entered into close relations with *Cecil, 1560; secretary and entrusted with *Mary's foreign policy, 1561; pursued a conciliatory policy towards England; supported the *Darnley marriage, 1564–5; said to have been a party to Darnley's murder, 1567; tried to reconcile the two Scottish factions, 1570; surrendered Edinburgh Castle to the English commander, 1573; died in prison at Leith.

MAITLAND, William (1693?–1757), topographer; published topographical compilations, 1739–57, of ephemeral reputation.

MAITLAND, William Fuller (1813–1876), picture-collector; of Trinity College, Cambridge; MA, 1839; formed a fine collection of early Italian masters and of English landscape paintings, some of which were bought after his death by the National Gallery.

MAITTAIRE, Michael (1668–1747), classical scholar and writer on typography; born in France; educated at Westminster School; 'canoneer' student of Christ Church, Oxford; MA, 1696; second master of Westminster, 1695–9; began to publish (*c.*1706) works consisting principally of editions of the Latin classics; published *Annales Typographici* (5 vols., 1719–41).

MAJENDIE, Henry William (1754–1830), bishop of Chester and Bangor; of Charterhouse and Christ's College, Cambridge; BA, 1776; fellow, 1776; preceptor to Prince William, afterwards William IV; canon of Windsor, 1785–98; DD, 1791; canon of St Paul's Cathedral, 1798; bishop of Chester, 1800–9, of Bangor, 1809–30.

MAJOR, Henry Dewsbury Alves (1871–1961), theologian; educated at home and St John's College, Auckland, New Zealand; BA, 1895; ordained as deacon, 1895; priest, 1896; curate, St Mark's, Remuera, 1895–9; MA, first class in natural sciences, 1896; acting vicar, Waitotara, 1899; vicar, St Peter's, Hamilton, 1900–2; entered Exeter College, Oxford, 1903; first class, theology, 1905; chaplain, Ripon Clergy College, 1906; vice-principal, 1906; joined Churchman's Union (later the Modern Churchmen's Union); became fanatical advocate of modernism, 1910; founded and edited *Modern Churchman*, 1911–56; rector, Copgrove, 1915–18; principal, Ripon Hall, Oxford, 1919–46; vicar, Merton, 1929–61; DD, Oxford, 1924; publications include *Life and Letters of W. B. Carpenter* (1925), *The Gospel of Freedom* (1912), *A Resurrection of Relics* (1922), *English Modernism; its Origin, Methods, Aims* (1927), *Reminiscences of Jesus by an Eye-Witness* (1925), and *The Roman Church and the Modern Man* (1934).

MAJOR (or MAIR), John (1469–1550), historian and scholastic divine; studied at Cambridge and Paris; MA, 1496; taught at Paris in arts and scholastic philosophy; published his first work on logic (1503); DD, 1505; began to lecture on scholastic divinity at the Sorbonne, Paris, 1505; published *A Commentary on the Four Books of Peter the Lombard's 'Sentences'*, at intervals (1509–17); professor of philosophy and divinity, Glasgow, 1518; published *History of Greater Britain, both England and Scotland* (1521); taught philosophy and logic in St Andrews University, 1522; taught again at Paris University, 1525–31; returned to

St Andrews, 1531; provost of St Salvator's College there, 1533–50; with William *Manderston founded and endowed chaplaincy at St Andrews, 1539; championed the doctrinal system of Rome; wrote entirely in Latin.

MAJOR, John (1782–1849), bookseller and publisher; a supporter of *Dibdin's publications; failed in business through becoming entangled in Dibdin's speculations; well known by his beautiful edition of *Walton and Cotton's *Complete Angler* (first published 1823); published verse, including squibs on current politics.

MAJOR, John Henniker-, second Baron Henniker (1752–1821), antiquary. See HENNIKER-MAJOR.

MAJOR, Joshua (1787–1866), landscape-gardener; author of important works on gardening, published 1829–1861.

MAJOR, Richard Henry (1818–1891), geographer; keeper of the department of maps and plans, British Museum, 1867–80; his chief work, *The Life of Prince Henry of Portugal, surnamed the Navigator* (1868); edited ten works for the Hakluyt Society (hon. secretary, 1849–58), 1847–73.

MAJOR, Thomas (1720–1799), engraver; resided and worked for some time in Paris; returned to England, 1753; issued a series of his prints, 1754 (2nd edn., 1768); first English engraver to be elected ARA, 1770; engraver to the king and to the Stamp Office.

MAKARIOS III (1913–1977), archbishop and first president of Cyprus, whose real name was Michael Mouskos; born near Paphos, son of a peasant farmer; educated at monastery of Kykko and Pan-Cypriot High School, Nicosia; studied theology and law in Athens; ordained as deacon, 1938 taking the name Makarios; priest, 1946; studied at Massachusetts University, 1948; elected bishop of Kition, 1948; member of Cypriot Ethnack and campaigner for *enosis* (union with Greece); succeeded as archbishop, 1950; discussed active measures for *enosis* with Colonel George Grivas, 1952; sanctioned campaign of sabotage by Cypriot Fighters (EOKA), 1955; spurned British offers of self-government for Cyprus; deported to Seychelles, 1956; released and settled in Athens, 1957; accepted independence, 1958; independent republic established excluding *enosis* and partition between Greek and Turkish Cypriots, 1959; Makarios elected president, with Turkish vice-president; communal fighting broke out, 1963; UN intervened with peace-keeping force; Makarios rebuffed UN mediators and sought help from USSR; military coup in Athens threatens position of Makarios, 1967; attempts on his life, 1970; re-elected to presidency, 1968 and 1973; after fleeing from Cyprus to escape terrorist attacks, addressed UN in New York, 1974; returned to Cyprus, 1974; Turks occupied two-fifths of island and proclaimed 'Turkish Federated State', 1975; discussions at UN and between Turkish and Greek Cypriots failed up to time of his death.

MAKELSFELD, William (d. 1304), cardinal. See MYKELFELD.

MAKEMIE, Francis (1658–1708), Irish divine; studied at Glasgow University; missionary to America, 1682; worked in Virginia, Maryland, and Barbados; formed at Philadelphia the first presbytery in America, 1706, and the father of Presbyterianism in America; died in Accomac, Virginia.

MAKIN, Bathsua (*fl.* 1673), the most learned Englishwoman of her time; sister of John *Pell (1611–1685); tutoress to Charles I's daughters; probably kept a school at Putney, 1649; wrote on female education, 1673.

MAKITTRICK, James (1728–1802). See ADAIR, JAMES MAKITTRICK.

MAKKARELL (or MACKARELL), Matthew (d. 1537), abbot of Barlings, Lincolnshire; DD, Paris (incorporated at Cambridge, 1516); abbot of Gilbertines or Premonstratensians at Alnwick; subsequently of Barlings or Oxeney, Lincolnshire; suffragan bishop of Lincoln, 1535; a leader in Lincolnshire rebellion, 1536; taken prisoner and executed, 1537.

MAKYN, David (d. 1588?), Scottish author. See MACKENZIE, DUGAL.

MALACHY I (d. 863), king of Ireland. See MAELSECHLAINN I.

MALACHY MACAEDH (d. 1348), archbishop of Tuam; bishop of Elphin, 1307–12; archbishop of Tuam, 1312–48; often confused with *Malachy (*fl.* 1310).

MALACHY MOR (949–1022), king of Ireland. See MAELSECHLAINN II.

MALACHY OF IRELAND (*fl.* 1310), Franciscan; probably author of *Libellus septem peccatorum mortalium* (Paris, 1518), remarkable for its denunciation of the government of Ireland.

MALACHY O'MORGAIR, Saint (1094?–1148), in Irish, Maelmaedhoig Ua Morgair; archbishop of Armagh; gained a great reputation for sanctity and learning; head of the abbey of Bangor, Co. Down; bishop of Connor, 1124; established monastery of Ibrach in south of Ireland after the destruction of the seat of his bishopric by a northern chieftain; archbishop of Armagh, 1132–6; bishop of Down, 1136; visited St Bernard, his future biographer, at Clairvaux; died at Clairvaux on his way to Rome.

MALAN, Cesar Jean Salomon (calling himself later **Solomon Caesar**) (1812–1894), oriental linguist and biblical scholar; born at Geneva; educated at St Edmund Hall, Oxford; Boden (Sanskrit) scholar, 1834; Pusey and Ellerton (Hebrew) scholar, 1837; BA, 1837; classical lecturer at Bishop's College, Calcutta, 1838; deacon, 1838; returned to England, 1840; priest and MA, Balliol College, 1843; held living of Broadwindsor, Dorset, 1845–85; travelled in the East, and published numerous translations from oriental literature; joined John William *Burgon in attacking Revised Version of New Testament, 1881. His works include *Notes on Proverbs* (1892–3).

MALAN, Daniel François (1874–1959), South African prime minister; obtained MA in philosophy, Stellenbosch, and doctorate in divinity, Utrecht; Dutch Reformed Church minister, 1906–15; editor, *Die Burger*, 1915–24; leader, Cape Nationalist party, 1915–53; MP, Calvinia, 1919–38; Piketberg, 1938–54; minister, interior public health and education, 1924–33; made Afrikaans second official language; reformed Senate and Civil Service; gave South Africa her own flag; broke with J. B. M. *Hertzog and became leader of 'purified' Nationalists, 1934, which party gradually increased in parliamentary strength; further break with Hertzog and N. C. Havenga brought him Nationalist leadership, 1940; made election agreement with Havenga and became prime minister, 1948; formed government exclusively Afrikaner and republican; abolished dual citizenship and appeal to Privy Council, but wished to remain within Commonwealth; introduced apartheid despite world opinion; resigned as Cape leader, 1953, and as prime minister, 1954.

MALAN, François Stephanus (1871–1941), South African statesman; BA, Victoria College, Stellenbosch, 1892; LL B, Cambridge, 1894; called to Cape bar; editor, *Ons Land*, 1895–1908; minister for agriculture and education, 1908–10; member, National Convention, 1908–9; MP, Malmesbury, 1910–24; minister for education (1910–21), agriculture (1919–21), mines and industries (1912–24); acting minister, native affairs, 1915–21; elected to senate, 1927; president, 1940–1; PC, 1920.

MALARD, Michael (*fl.* 1717–1720), French Protestant divine; born at Vaurenard; educated for the Roman Catholic priesthood; came to England, *c.*1700; embraced Protestantism, 1705; published pamphlets against the French committee for the distribution of the money charged upon the civil list for the benefit of the French Protestants, 1717–20; author of manuals of French accidence.

MALBY, Sir Nicholas (1530?–1584), president of Connaught; served in France, Spain, and Ireland; stationed at Carrickfergus, 1567–9; collector of customs of Strangford, Ardglass, and Dundrum, 1571; made unsuccessful efforts to colonize part of Down, 1571–4; knighted and appointed military governor of Connaught, 1576; president of Connaught, 1579; engaged in suppressing rebellions, 1579–81; his services ignored by Queen Elizabeth.

MALCOLM I (surnamed **MACDONALD**) (d. 954), king of Scotland; succeeded, 943; made treaty with *Edmund, the West Saxon king, 945; lost Northumbria, 954; slain in a border skirmish.

MALCOLM II (surnamed **MACKENNETH**) (d. 1034), king of Scotland; son of *Kenneth II; succeeded, 1005?, by defeating and killing *Kenneth III; defeated Eadulf Cudel, 1018, thereby causing the cession of Lothian to the Scottish kingdom, Cambria north of the Solway becoming also an appanage of the same; did homage to *Canute, 1031.

MALCOLM III (called **CANMORE**) (d. 1093), king of Scotland; succeeded his father *Duncan I in consequence of the defeat of *Macbeth by Earl Edward of Northumbria, 1054; defeated and slew Macbeth at Lumphanan; crowned at Scone, 1057; married *Margaret (d. 1093), sister of *Edgar Atheling; did homage to the English kings, 1072 and 1091; treacherously slain while invading Northumberland.

MALCOLM IV (called the **MAIDEN**) (1141–1165), king of Scotland; grandson of *David I; succeeded his grandfather, 1153; surrendered Northumberland and Cumberland to Henry II, 1157; served as English baron in the expedition against Toulouse, 1159; engaged in suppressing rebellions in Scotland, 1160–4.

MALCOLM, Sir Charles (1782–1851), vice-admiral; brother of Sir Pulteney *Malcolm; entered the navy, 1795; employed in the East Indies till 1802; on the coast of France and Portugal, 1806–9; chiefly in the West Indies, 1809–19; knighted while in attendance on the Marquis *Wellesley, lord-lieutenant of Ireland, 1822–7; superintendent of the Bombay Marine (name afterwards changed to the Indian Navy), 1827–37; rear-admiral, 1837; vice-admiral, 1847.

MALCOLM, Sir Dougal Orme (1877–1955), scholar and imperialist; educated at Eton and New College, Oxford; first class, Lit. Hum.,

1899; fellow, All Souls, 1899–1955; Lord Mallard, 1928–55; entered Colonial Office, 1900; joined *Milner's 'kindergarten' as private secretary to Lord *Selborne in South Africa, 1905–10; assisted with memorandum on South African Union, foundation of *Round Table*, and *The Problem of the Commonwealth* (1916) by Lionel *Curtis; private secretary to Lord *Grey in Canada, 1910–11; transferred to Treasury, 1912; retired, 1912, on nomination as director of British South Africa Company in charge of its affairs in Rhodesia; president, 1937–55; ceded political functions to colonial governments, 1923; sold railways, 1947; negotiated new mining rights, 1950; opposed federation with Nyasaland; KCMG, 1938.

MALCOLM, Sir **George** (1818–1897), general; born at Bombay; ensign in East India Company's service, 1836; lieutenant, 1840; served in Sind and second Sikh War; lieutenant-colonel, 1854; in Persian War, 1856–7, and Indian Mutiny, 1857–8; CB, 1859; brevet-colonel, 1860; major-general, 1867; in Abyssinian expedition, 1868; general, 1877; GCB, 1886.

MALCOLM, **James Peller** (1767–1815), topographer and engraver; born in Philadelphia; came to London and studied in the Royal Academy; chief work, *Londinium Redivivum* (history and description), with forty-seven plates (published 1802–7).

MALCOLM, Sir **John** (1769–1833), Indian administrator and diplomat; entered the service of the East India Company, 1782; preferring diplomacy to fighting, studied Persian, and was appointed Persian interpreter to the nizam of the Deccan, 1792; secretary to Sir Alured *Clarke, commander-in-chief, 1795–7, and to his successor, General George, Lord *Harris, 1797–8; assistant to the resident of Hyderabad, 1798; chosen by Lord *Wellesley, the governor-general, as envoy to Persia, 1799–1801; private secretary to Wellesley, 1801–2; political agent to General Wellesley during the Mahratta War, 1803–4; sent on a mission to Teheran, 1808–9, and 1810; published his *Political History of India* (1811), his *History of Persia* (1815); KCB, 1815; as brigadier in the army of the Deccan took part in the new Mahratta War, 1817–18; after assisting in the reclamation of Malwah, returned to England and occupied himself with literary work, 1822; governor of Bombay, 1826–30; MP, Launceston, 1831–2; his *Administration of India* published (1833), and his life of *Clive (completed by another hand), posthumously published (1836).

MALCOLM, Sir **Pulteney** (1768–1838), admiral; entered the navy, 1778; served in West Indies, Quebec, East Indies, and China seas; under *Nelson in the Mediterranean, 1804–5; rear-admiral, 1813; KCB, 1815; commander-in-chief on the St Helena Station, 1816–17; vice-admiral, 1821; commander-in-chief in the Mediterranean, 1828–31 and 1833–4.

MALCOLM, **Sarah** (1710?–1733), criminal; charwoman in the Temple, London; murdered Mrs Duncomb, her employer, and her two servants, 1733; condemned to death and executed; painted by *Hogarth while in the condemned cell.

MALCOLME, **David** (d. 1748), philologist; ordained as Presbyterian minister, 1705; deposed for deserting his charge, 1742; specialized in Celtic philology; chief work, *Letters, Essays, and other Tracts illustrating the Antiquities of Great Britain and Ireland . . . Also Specimens of the Celtic, Welsh, Irish, Saxon, and American Languages* (1744).

MALCOM, **Andrew George** (1782–1823), Irish Presbyterian divine and hymn-writer; MA, Glasgow; ordained, 1807; ministered at Newry, Co. Down; DD, Glasgow, 1820; composed hymns.

MALCOME, **John** (1662?–1729), Presbyterian polemic; MA, Glasgow; ordained, 1687; adhered to the subscription and invented the phrase 'new light', 1720; published theological works.

MALDEN, **Daniel** (d. 1736), prison-breaker; adopted street-robbery as a profession; condemned and ordered to be executed, 1736; escaped from prison twice, but was retaken and hanged.

MALDEN, **Henry** (1800–1876), classical scholar; of Trinity College, Cambridge; fellow, 1824; MA, 1825; professor of Greek at University College, London, 1831–76; headmaster of University College School with Thomas Hewitt *Key, 1831–42.

MALDON, **Thomas** (d. 1404), Carmelite; DD, Cambridge; prior of the convent at Maldon; Latin works, now lost, ascribed to him by *Leland and *Bale.

MALEBYSSE, **Richard** (d. 1209), justiciar; one of the leaders in an attack on and massacre of the Jews at York, 1190; justice-itinerant for Yorkshire, 1201; sat to acknowledge fines at Westminster, 1202; employed in enforcing payment of aids, 1204.

MALET, Sir **Alexander**, second baronet (1800–1886), diplomat; son of Sir Charles Warre *Malet; educated at Winchester and Christ Church, Oxford; BA, 1822; entered Diplomatic Service, 1824; minister-plenipotentiary to the Germanic Confederation at Frankfurt, 1849–66;

KCB, 1866; published *The Overthrow of the Germanic Confederation by Prussia in 1866* (1870).

MALET, Arthur (1806–1888), Indian civilian; son of Sir Charles Warre *Malet; educated at Winchester, Addiscombe, and Haileybury; appointed to the Bombay Civil Service, 1824; chief secretary for the political and secret departments to the Bombay government, 1847; member of the legislative council of India, 1854; of the government council of Bombay, 1855–60; published *Notices of an English Branch of the Malet Family* (1885).

MALET, Sir Charles Warre, first baronet (1753?–1815), Indian administrator and diplomat; descendant of William *Malet (d. 1071) of Graville; resident minister at Poonah, 1785–91; created baronet for his services, 1791; acting governor at Bombay till 1798; retired and returned to England, 1798.

MALET, Sir Edward Baldwin, fourth baronet (1837–1908), diplomat; born at The Hague; son of Sir Alexander *Malet, second baronet; attaché to his father at Frankfort, 1854; served under Lord *Lyons, at Washington, 1862–5, and Paris, 1867–71; negotiated meeting of Jules Favre and Bismarck at Ferrières, 1870; in charge of embassy at Paris, Mar.–June 1871; CB, 1871; secretary of legation at Peking, 1871, Rome, 1875, and Constantinople, 1878; British agent and consul-general in Egypt, 1879–83; KCB, 1881; helped to restore financial stability and soothe native unrest in Egypt; reconstituted government machinery, and developed scheme of reorganization, 1882–3; British envoy at Brussels, 1883, and Berlin, 1884–95, where he settled rival British and German claims in the Congo and in Samoa; PC and GCMG, 1885; GCB, 1886; a British member of the International Court of Arbitration at The Hague, 1899; succeeded brother, 1904; author of *Shifting Scenes* (1901) and an unfinished memoir of his service in Egypt (posthumous, 1909).

MALET, George Grenville (1804–1856), lieutenant-colonel; son of Sir Charles Warre *Malet; entered the Indian Army, 1822; political superintendent of Mellanee, Rajputana, 1839; engaged in the Afghan War, 1842, and in the war with Persia, 1856; superintendent of the Guicowar Horse, 1856; killed in action.

MALET, Lucas (pseudonym) (1852–1931), novelist. See HARRISON, MARY ST LEGER.

MALET (or MALLET), Robert (d. 1106?), baron of Eye; son of William *Malet (d. 1071) of Graville; endowed a Benedictine monastery at Eye; supported Robert against Henry I; supposed to have been killed at the Battle of Tinchebrai.

MALET (or MALLETT), Sir Thomas (1582–1665), judge; descendant of William *Malet (d. 1071) of Graville; barrister, Middle Temple, 1606; reader, 1626; sat in the first two parliaments of Charles I; serjeant, 1635; raised to the King's Bench, 1641; knighted, 1641; supported the royal policy and prerogative; imprisoned in the Tower, 1642–4; again on the bench, 1660–3.

MALET (or MALLET), William (d. 1071), of Graville in Normandy; companion of the Conqueror; his exploits at Hastings celebrated by *Wace in his *Roman de Rou* (ll. 13,472–84); sheriff of York, 1068; taken prisoner at capture of York, 1069, but subsequently released.

MALET (or MALLET), William (*fl.* 1195–1215), baron of Curry Mallet and Shepton Mallet, Somerset; descended from Gilbert, son of William *Malet (d. 1071) of Graville; in Normandy with Richard I, 1195; sheriff of Dorset and Somerset, 1211; joined barons in their struggle with King John, 1215.

MALGER (d. 1212), bishop of Worcester. See MAUGER.

MALHAM, John (1747–1821), miscellaneous writer; Northamptonshire curate; acted as schoolmaster; employed by London booksellers in the issue of a number of illustrated bibles, prayer-books, and popular historical works, 1782–1812; edited edition of *Harleian Miscellany* (1808–11).

MALIM, William (1533–1594), schoolmaster; educated at Eton and King's College, Cambridge; fellow, 1551; MA, 1556; headmaster of Eton, 1561–71; prebendary of Lincoln, 1569; high master of St Paul's, 1573–81; his extant pieces chiefly commendary Latin verses and letters prefixed to the works of friends.

MALINS, Sir Richard (1805–1882), judge; educated at Caius College, Cambridge; BA, 1827; barrister, Inner Temple, 1830; QC, 1849; MP, Wallingford, 1852–65; a vice-chancellor, 1866–81; knighted, 1867; privy councillor, 1881.

MALKIN, Benjamin Heath (1769–1842), miscellaneous writer; of Harrow and Trinity College, Cambridge; MA, 1802; headmaster of Bury St Edmunds Grammar School, 1809–28; DCL, St Mary Hall, Oxford, 1810; professor of history, ancient and modern, London University, 1829; FSA; author of some antiquarian and historical works, 1795–1825, and of a translation of *Gil Blas* (1809).

MALLABY, Sir (Howard) George (Charles) (1902–1978), public servant and teacher; educated at Radley College, and Merton College, Oxford; assistant master at Clifton College, 1923–4, and at St Edmund's School, Oxford,

1924–6; taught at Diocesan College, Rondebosch, South Africa, 1926; returned to St Edmunds, 1927–35; housemaster, 1931; headmaster, St Bees School, Cumberland, 1935–8; district commissioner for Special Area of West Cumberland, 1938–9; worked in directorate of military operations, War Office, 1940–2; secretary, Joint Planning Staff, 1943; attended Cairo, Quebec, and Potsdam conferences; OBE, 1945; US Legion of Merit, 1946; secretary, National Trust, 1945–6; assistant secretary, Ministry of Defence, 1946–8; secretary-general, Brussels Treaty Defence Organization, 1948–50; under-secretary, Cabinet Office, 1950–4; undertook delicate negotiations in Kenya at time of Mau Mau rebellion, 1954; deputy secretary, University Grants Committee, 1955–7; UK high commissioner in New Zealand, 1957–9; first Civil Service commissioner, 1959–64; CMG, 1953; KCMG, 1958; fellow, Churchill College, Cambridge, 1964; published selection of Wordsworth's poems (1932), *Wordsworth: a Tribute* (1950), and edited *Poems by William Wordsworth* (1970); also published reminiscences, *From my Level* (1965) and *Each in his Office* (1972), and *Local Government Councillors—their Motives and Manners* (1976); governor, St Edward's School; chairman of Council of Radley College; chairman of number of committees including special committee of the Rugby Football Union which proposed change in the rules covering kicking to touch, 1972–3.

MALLESON, George Bruce (1825–1898), colonel and military writer; educated at Winchester; ensign, 1842; lieutenant, 33rd BNI, 1847; assistant military auditor-general, 1856; captain, 1861; major, Bengal Staff Corps, 1863; lieutenant-colonel, 1868; colonel in army, 1873; guardian of young maharajah of Mysore, 1869–77; CSI, 1872; wrote on military history.

MALLESON, John Philip (1796–1869), Unitarian minister and schoolmaster; graduated at Glasgow, 1819; became minister of a Presbyterian congregation; adopted Arian views and resigned, 1822; Unitarian minister at Brighton, 1829; conducted a school at Brighton.

MALLESON, (William) Miles (1888–1969), actor, dramatist, and stage director; educated at Brighton College, Emmanuel College, Cambridge, and the (Royal) Academy of Dramatic Art; acted at the Court Theatre under J. B. *Fagan, and at the Lyric, Hammersmith, under (Sir) Nigel *Playfair; a most resourceful stage clown; wrote serious plays, including *The Fanatics* (1927) and *Six Men of Dorset* (1938); first chairman, Screen Writers' Association, 1937; played with Old Vic Company, 1945–6, and 1949–50; played the main part in Molière's *The Miser* (his

own adaptation); translated series of Molière plays.

MALLET (originally **MALLOCH**), **David** (1705?–1765), poet and miscellaneous writer; studied at Edinburgh University (1721–2, 1722–3) and formed a friendship with James *Thomson, author of *The Seasons*; composed a number of short poems, 1720–4; produced *Eurydice* (tragedy) at Drury Lane, London, 1731; studied at St Mary Hall, Oxford; MA, 1734; produced *Mustapha* (tragedy) at Drury Lane, London, 1739; with Thomson wrote the masque of *Alfred*, 1740; under-secretary to *Frederick, prince of Wales, 1742; received inspectorship of exchequer-book in the outports of London for his political writings, 1763; author of *William and Margaret* (1723), a famous ballad. The national ode, 'Rule Britannia', sometimes ascribed to him, was more probably written by Thomson.

MALLET, Sir Louis (1823–1890), civil servant and economist; of Huguenot origin; clerk in the Audit Office from 1839; transferred to the Board of Trade, 1847; private secretary to the president, 1848–52 and 1855–7; employed chiefly in the work of extension of commercial treaties, 1860–5; CB, 1866; knighted, 1868; nominated to the Council of India in London, 1872; permanent under-secretary of state for India, 1874–83; privy councillor, 1883; after *Cobden's death (1865) the principal authority on questions of commercial policy, and the chief official representative of free-trade opinion; his occasional writings, which set forth the 'free-trade' doctrine, published as *Free Exchange* (1891).

MALLET, Robert (1810–1881), civil engineer and scientific investigator; BA, Trinity College, Dublin, 1830; MA, 1862; assumed charge of the Victoria Foundry, Dublin, 1831; conducted many engineering works in Ireland, among them the building of the Fastnet Rock lighthouse, 1848–9; FRS, 1854; consulting engineer in London, 1861; edited the *Practical Mechanic's Journal*, 1865–9; contributed to *Philosophical Transactions*, and published works on engineering subjects.

MALLETT, Francis (d. 1570), dean of Lincoln; BA, Cambridge, 1522; MA, 1525; DD, 1535; master of Michaelhouse, 1542; vice-chancellor, 1536 and 1540; chaplain to Thomas *Cromwell, 1538; canon of Windsor, 1543; prebendary of Wells, 1544; chaplain to the Princess Mary, 1544; prebendary of Westminster, 1553–8, and dean of Lincoln, 1554–70; master of the Hospital of St Katherine by the Tower, London, 1554–60.

MALLOCH, David (1705?–1765), poet and miscellaneous writer. See MALLET.

MALLOCK, William Hurrell (1849–1923), author; nephew of Richard Hurrell *Froude,

William *Froude, and James Anthony *Froude; BA, Balliol College, Oxford; his satires include *The New Republic* (1877), in which he seeks to demonstrate impossible position of undogmatic belief; his novels include *The Old Order Changes* (1886); his political writings include *Social Equality* (1882), in which he refutes erroneous ideas about distribution of wealth, especially ownership of land.

MALLON, James Joseph (1875–1961), warden of Toynbee Hall; educated at the Owens College, Manchester; did social work in Ancoats Settlement, Manchester; secretary, National League to Establish a Minimum Wage, 1906; hon. secretary, Trade Boards Advisory Council; warden, Toynbee Hall, 1919–54; helped to found Toynbee Hall Theatre and the Children's Theatre; governor, BBC, 1937–9 and 1941–6; member, executive committee, British Empire Exhibition, 1924; member, executive committee, and hon. treasurer, Workers' Educational Association; wrote articles on social and economic subjects for *Observer*, *Daily News*, and *Manchester Guardian*; published (with E. C. T. Lascelles), *Poverty Yesterday and Today* (1930); hon. doctorate, Liverpool University, 1944; CH, 1939; awarded Margaret McMillan Medal, 1955.

MALLORY, George Leigh (1886–1924), mountaineer; educated at Winchester, where R. L. G. Irving introduced him to climbing; BA, Magdalene College, Cambridge; assistant master, Charterhouse, 1910–15; returned there after serving in European war, 1919; lecturer and assistant secretary, board of extra-mural studies, Cambridge, 1923; took part in Mount Everest expeditions, 1921, 1922, and 1924; perished in attempt on summit, 1924.

MALLORY (or MALLERY), Thomas (*fl.* 1662), ejected minister; vicar of St Nicholas, Deptford, 1644; ejected from lectureship of St Michael's, Crooked Lane, London, 1662; mentioned by *Evelyn.

MALLORY (or MALLORIE), Thomas (1605?–1666?), divine; of New College, Oxford; MA, 1632; incumbent of Northenden, 1635; ejected as a loyalist, 1642; canon of Chester and DD, 1660.

MALLORY, Sir Trafford Leigh Leigh- (1892–1944), air chief marshal. See LEIGH-MALLORY.

MALLOWAN, Sir Max Edgar Lucien (1904–1978), archaeologist; educated at Lancing and New College, Oxford; assistant to (Sir) C. Leonard *Woolley at Ur of the Chaldees, 1925; married (Dame) Agatha *Christie, 1930; field director in series of expeditions jointly sponsored by the British Museum and the British School of Archaeology in Iraq; made important discoveries at Arpachiyah, 1933, and later at Chagar Bazar and Tell Brak, 1937; served in RAFVR in North Africa, 1940–5; reactivated School of Archaeology in Iraq after 1939–45 war; director of British School, Iraq, 1947–61, and professor in western Asiatic archaeology, London University, 1947–62; carried out most important work at Nimrud, described in *Nimrud and Its Remains* (2 vols., 1966); fellow of All Souls, Oxford, 1962; FBA; FSA; president, British Institute of Persian Studies, 1961; vice-president, British Academy, 1961–2; CBE, 1960; knighted, 1968; trustee, British Museum, 1973–8; editor of *Iraq*, 1948–71; advisory editor, *Antiquity*; editor of Penguin books Near-Eastern and Western Asiatic Series, 1948–65; other publications include *Twenty-five Years of Mesopotamian Discovery, 1932–1956* (1956) and *Mallowan's Memoirs* (1977).

MALMESBURY, earls of. See HARRIS, JAMES, first earl, 1746–1820; HARRIS, JAMES HOWARD, third earl, 1807–1889.

MALMESBURY, Godfrey of (*fl.* 1081). See GODFREY.

MALMESBURY, Oliver of (*fl.* 1066), astrologer and mechanician. See OLIVER.

MALMESBURY, William of (d. 1143?), historian. See WILLIAM.

MALONE, Anthony (1700–1776), Irish politician; educated at Christ Church, Oxford; called to the Irish bar, 1726; MP, Co. Westmeath, 1727–60 and 1769–76, Castlemartyr, 1761–8, in the Irish parliament; LL D, Trinity College, Dublin, 1737; prime serjeant-at-law, 1740–64; chancellor of the Exchequer, 1757–61.

MALONE, Edmond (1741–1812), critic and author; son of Edmund *Malone (1704–1774); BA, Trinity College, Dublin; entered the Inner Temple, 1763; called to the Irish bar soon after 1767; settled permanently in London as a man of letters, 1777; joined the Literary Club, 1782; intimate with *Johnson, *Reynolds, Bishop Percy, *Burke, and *Boswell; a supporter of the union with Ireland; published *Attempt to ascertain the Order in which the Plays of Shakespeare were written* (1778); edited Shakespeare (1790); collected materials for a new edition, which he left to James *Boswell the younger, who published it in 21 volumes (1821; the 'third variorum' edition of works of Shakespeare, and generally acknowledged to be the best); edited works of *Dryden (1800).

MALONE, Edmund (1704–1774), judge; called to the English bar, 1730; practised in the

Irish courts after 1740; MP for Granard in the Irish parliament, 1760–6; judge of the court of common pleas, 1766.

MALONE, Richard, Lord Sunderlin (1738–1816), elder brother of Edmond *Malone (1741–1812); BA, Trinity College, Dublin, 1759; MP in Irish House of Commons, 1768–85; raised to Irish peerage, 1785.

MALONE, Sylvester (1822–1906), Irish ecclesiastical historian; vicar-general of Kilrush, 1872–1906; canon and archdeacon; made valuable researches in his *Church History of Ireland, 1169–1532* (1867); promoter of preservation of Irish language.

MALONE, William (1586–1656), Jesuit; joined Jesuits at Rome, 1606; joined the mission of the society in Ireland; issued *The Jesuits' Challenge*, *c.*1623 (answered by *Ussher, Protestant bishop of Armagh, 1624); issued *A Reply to Mr. James Ussher, his answere* (1627); president of the Irish College at Rome, 1635–47; superior of the Jesuits in Ireland, 1647; taken prisoner by the Parliamentarians and banished, 1648; rector of the Jesuit College at Seville, where he died.

MALORY, Sir Thomas (*fl.* 1470), author of *Le Morte Arthur*; Malory translated, 'from the Frensshe', 'a most pleasant jumble and summary of the legends about *Arthur', in twenty-one books, finished between Mar. 1469 and Mar. 1470. The translation was printed by *Caxton (1485). Malory's *Le Morte Arthur* greatly influenced the English prose of the sixteenth century.

MALTBY, Edward (1770–1859), bishop of Durham; educated at Winchester and Pembroke Hall, Cambridge; MA, 1794; DD, 1806; preacher at Lincoln's Inn, 1824–33; bishop of Chichester, 1831, of Durham, 1836–56; FRS and FSA; published a useful *Lexicon Graeco-prosodiacum* (1815) and some sermons.

MALTBY, Sir Paul Copeland (1892–1971), air vice-marshal; educated at Bedford School and Royal Military College, Sandhurst; commissioned in Royal Welch Fusiliers; served in India and France, 1911–14; joined Royal Flying Corps, 1915; DSO, 1917; took permanent commission in RAF, 1919; commanded squadron at Quetta, 1920–4; attended RAF Staff College and Imperial Defence College, 1926–7 and 1931; commandant Central Flying School, 1932–4; commanded RAF in Mediterranean; wing commander, 1925; group captain, 1932; air commodore, 1936; air vice-marshal, 1938; posted to Singapore for special duties at GHQ Far East, 1941; deputy to air commander in Malaya, Air Vice-Marshal C. W. H. Pulford; after Pulford's death, Maltby flown to Java to reorganize de-

pleted squadrons; captured by Japanese, 1942; prisoner of war, 1942–5; in charge of compilation of reports on Malaya; sergeant-at-arms (Black Rod), 1946–62; AFC, 1919; CB, 1941; KBE, 1946; KCVO, 1962; grand officer of the Order of Orange Nassau; deputy lieutenant, county of Southampton, 1956.

MALTBY, William (1763–1854), bibliographer; cousin of Edward *Maltby (1770–1859); educated at Gonville and Caius College, Cambridge; principal librarian of the London Institution, 1809–34.

MALTHUS, Thomas Robert (1766–1834), political economist; was educated by his father, at Warrington Dissenting Academy and Jesus College, Cambridge; MA, 1791; fellow, 1793; curate at Albury, Surrey, 1798; published *Essay on Population* (1798), in which he laid down that population increases in geometrical, and subsistence in arithmetical proportion only, and argued necessity of 'checks' on population in order to reduce vice and misery; travelled abroad, 1799 and 1802; professor of history and political economy at Haileybury College, 1805; published *The Nature and Progress of Rent* (1815), in which he laid down doctrines generally accepted by later economists; FRS, 1819, and member of foreign academies; supported factory acts and national education; disapproved of the poor laws; as exponent of new doctrine had great influence on development of political economy.

MALTON, James (d. 1803), architectural draughtsman and author; son of Thomas *Malton the elder.

MALTON, Thomas, the elder (1726–1801), architectural draughtsman and writer on geometry.

MALTON, Thomas, the younger (1748–1804), architectural draughtsman; son of Thomas *Malton the elder; exhibited at Academy chiefly architectural views of great accuracy of execution; published *A Picturesque Tour through . . . London and Westminster* (1792).

MALTRAVERS, Sir John (1266–1343?), knighted, 1306; conservator of the peace for Dorset, 1307, 1308, and 1314; served in Scotland between 1314 and 1322, 1327 and 1331; sent to serve in Ireland, 1317, in Guienne, 1325.

MALTRAVERS, John, Baron Maltravers (1290?–1365), knighted, 1306; knight of the shire for Dorset, 1318; sided with *Thomas of Lancaster and Roger *Mortimer; fled abroad after Battle of Boroughbridge, 1322; keeper of Edward II, 1327, whom he is said to have harshly treated; justice in eyre and keeper of the forests; accompanied Edward III to France as steward,

1329; concerned in death of *Edmund, earl of Kent, 1330; summoned to parliament as Baron Maltravers, 1330; constable of Corfe Castle, 1330; on fall of Mortimer was condemned to death for his share in the murder of the earl of Kent, and fled abroad; allowed to return, 1345; subsequently employed by the king.

MALVERN, first Viscount (1883–1971), Rhodesian statesman. See HUGGINS, GODFREY MARTIN.

MALVERN, William of (d. 1539), alias William Parker; last abbot of St Peter's, Gloucester, 1514; DCL, 1508, and DD, 1515, Gloucester Hall, Oxford; attended parliament; added largely to the abbey buildings.

MALVERNE, John (d. 1414?), historian; prior of Worcester; author of continuation of *Higden's *Polychronicon*, 1346–94.

MALVERNE, John (d. 1422?), physician and priest; prebendary of St Paul's Cathedral, 1405; wrote *De Remediis Spiritualibus et Corporalibus*.

MALVOISIN, William (d. 1238), chancellor of Scotland and archbishop of St Andrews; chancellor, 1199–1211; bishop of Glasgow, 1200; corresponded with archbishop of Lyons; archbishop of St Andrews, 1202; energetically vindicated rights of his see; founded hospitals and continued building of cathedral; visited Rome; treated with King John in England, 1215.

MALYNES (MALINES or DE MALINES), Gerard (*fl.* 1586–1641), merchant and economic writer; commissioner of trade in Netherlands, *c.*1586, for establishing par of exchange, 1600, and on Mint affairs, 1609; consulted by council on mercantile questions; attempted unsuccessfully development of English lead and silver mines; ruined by undertaking farthing coinage; proposed system of pawnbroking under government control to relieve poor from usurers; published *A Treatise of the Canker of England's Commonwealth* . . . (1601), *Consuetudo vel Lex Mercatoria* . . . (1622), and other important works; one of the first English writers to apply natural law to economic science.

MAN, Henry (1747–1799), author; deputy secretary of the South Sea House and colleague of Charles *Lamb; contributed essays to *Morning Chronicle*; his works collected (1802).

MAN (or MAIN), James (1700?–1761), philologist; MA, King's College, Aberdeen, 1721; exposed errors in *Ruddiman's edition of *Buchanan in *A Censure* (1753).

MAN, John (1512–1569), dean of Gloucester; of Winchester College and New College, Oxford; fellow, 1531; MA, 1538; expelled for heresy, but (1547) made president of White Hall, Oxford;

warden of Merton College, Oxford, 1562; dean of Gloucester, 1566–9; ambassador to Spain, 1567; published *Common places of Christian Religion* (1563).

MANASSEH BEN ISRAEL (1604–1657), Jewish theologian and chief advocate of readmission of Jews into England; studied at Amsterdam; became minister of the synagogue there; formed friendships with Isaac *Vossius and Grotius; established press for Hebrew printing, 1626; published *Spes Israelis* (1650); sent petition to the Long Parliament for return of Jews into England; was encouraged by sympathy of *Cromwell, but his request was refused by Council of State, 1652; subsequently he petitioned Cromwell again and wrote in defence of his cause, 1655, after which Jews were tacitly allowed to settle in London and opened a synagogue; received pension of £100 from Cromwell; published theological works.

MANBY, Aaron (1776–1850), engineer; ironmaster at Wolverhampton and founder of Horseley Ironworks, Tipton; took out patent for (but did not invent) 'oscillating engine', 1821; built the *Aaron Manby*, 1822, first iron steamship to go to sea and first vessel to make voyage from London to Paris; founded Charenton Works, 1819; obtained concession with others for lighting Paris with gas, 1822; bought Creusot Ironworks, 1826.

MANBY, Charles (1804–1884), civil engineer; son of Aaron *Manby; assisted his father in England and France; manager of Beaufort Ironworks, South Wales, 1829; civil engineer in London, 1835; secretary to Institution of Civil Engineers, 1839–56; FRS, 1853.

MANBY, George William (1765–1854), inventor of apparatus for saving life from shipwreck; brother of Thomas *Manby; schoolfellow of *Nelson at Durham; joined Cambridgeshire militia; barrack-master at Yarmouth, 1803; invented apparatus for firing line from mortar to wreck, successfully used, 1808, and afterwards extensively employed; invented other life-saving apparatus; FRS, 1831; published miscellaneous works.

MANBY, Peter (d. 1697), dean of Derry; MA, Trinity College, Dublin; chancellor of St Patrick's, 1666; dean of Derry, 1672; turned Roman Catholic, but was authorized by James II to retain deanery, 1686; retired to France after Battle of the Boyne; published controversial religious works.

MANBY, Peter (*fl.* 1724), son of Peter *Manby (d. 1697); Jesuit.

MANBY, Thomas (*fl.* 1670–1690), landscape painter.

MANBY, Thomas (1769–1834), rear-admiral; brother of George William *Manby; entered navy, 1783, and served on various ships and stations; convoyed ships to West Indies, on the *Bordelais*, 1799, and engaged in small successful fight with French ships, 1801; convoyed ships again to West Indies, 1802, on the *Africaine*, a third of the crew dying from yellow fever on the voyage home; commanded small squadron on voyage to Davis Straits, 1808; rear-admiral, 1825.

MANCHESTER, dukes of. See MONTAGU, CHARLES, first duke, 1660?–1722; MONTAGU, GEORGE, fourth duke, 1737–1788; MONTAGU, WILLIAM, fifth duke, 1768–1843.

MANCHESTER, earls of. See MONTAGU, Sir HENRY, first earl, 1563?–1642; MONTAGU, EDWARD, second earl, 1602–1671; MONTAGU, ROBERT, third earl, 1634–1683; MONTAGU, CHARLES, fourth earl, 1660?–1722.

MANDERSTOWN, William (*fl.* 1515–1540), philosopher; studied at Paris University; rector, 1525; published philosophical works.

MANDEVIL, Robert (1578–1618), Puritan divine; MA, St Edmund's Hall, Oxford, 1603; wrote *Timothies Taske* (published 1619).

MANDEVILLE, Bernard (1670?–1733), author of the *Fable of the Bees*; native of Dort, Holland; MD, Leiden, 1691; settled in England, where he was known for his wit and advocacy of 'dram drinking'; published 'The Grumbling Hive' (poem, 1705), republished with *Inquiry into the Origin of Moral Virtue* and *The Fable of the Bees, or Private Vices Public Benefits* (1714), and again with *Essay on Charity and Charity Schools* and a *Search into the Nature of Society* (1723). His *Fable*, maintaining the essential vileness of human nature, was widely controverted.

MANDEVILLE, Geoffrey de, first earl of Essex (d. 1144), rebel; constable of the Tower of London; detained there Constance of France after her betrothal to Eustace, son of King Stephen; created earl of Essex before 1141; got possession of vast lands and enormous power by giving treacherous support to the king and the Empress *Maud and betraying both; arrested by Stephen, 1143, and deprived of the Tower and other castles; raised rebellion in the fens, but was fatally wounded in fighting against Stephen at Burwell.

MANDEVILLE, Sir John (d. 1372?), was the ostensible author of a book of travels bearing his name, composed soon after middle of the fourteenth century, purporting to be an account of his own journeys in the east, including Turkey, Tartary, Persia, Egypt, India, and Holy Land, but really a mere compilation, especially from William of Boldensele and Friar Odoric of Pordenone, and from the *Speculum* of Vincent de Beauvais; his work written originally in French, from which English, Latin, German, and other translations were made. The author of this book of travels certainly died 1372, and was buried in the church of the Guillemins at Liège in the name of John Mandeville. Probably this name was fictitious, and its bearer is to be identified with Jean de Bourgogne or Burgoyne, chamberlain to John, baron de *Mowbray, who took part in rising against *Despensers, and on Mowbray's execution (1322) fled from England.

MANDEVILLE (or MAGNAVILLA), William de, third earl of Essex and earl or count of Aumâle (d. 1189), son of Geoffrey de *Mandeville, first earl of Essex; knighted by Philip of Flanders and brought up at Philip's court; became earl of Essex on death of his brother, 1166; came over to England, 1166; accompanied Henry II abroad and remained faithful during rebellion, 1173–5; took part in crusade with Philip of Flanders, 1177–8; married heiress of Aumâle, 1180, and received lands and title; ambassador to Emperor Frederic I, 1182; took part with Henry II in his French wars; remained with Henry till the last; made a chief justiciar by Richard I, 1189; died at Rouen; founded several religious houses.

MANDUIT, John (*fl.* 1310), astronomer. See MAUDUITH.

MANECKJI BYRAMJI DADABHOY, Sir (1865–1953), Indian lawyer, industrialist, and parliamentarian. See DADABHOY.

MANFIELD, Sir James (1733–1821), lord chief-justice of common pleas. See MANSFIELD.

MANGAN, James (commonly called **James Clarence**) (1803–1849), Irish poet; lawyer's clerk; later employed in library of Trinity College, Dublin, and Irish Ordnance Survey Office; contributed prose and verse translations and original poems to various Irish journals and magazines; wrote for the *Nation* and *United Irishman*, but was prevented from keeping regular employment by his indulgence in drink; probably the greatest of the poets of Irish birth; published *German Anthology* (1845) and other volumes.

MANGEY, Thomas (1688–1755), divine and controversialist; MA, St John's College, Cambridge, 1711; fellow, 1715, and DD; held livings of St Nicholas, Guildford, Ealing, and St Mildred's, Bread Street, London; canon of Durham, 1721; edited *Philonis Judaei Opera* (1742).

MANGIN, Edward (1772–1852), miscellaneous writer; of Huguenot descent; MA, Balliol College, Oxford, 1795; prebendary of Killaloe; lived at Bath and devoted his time to literary study; published, among other works, *An Essay on Light Reading* (1808).

MANGLES, James (1786–1867), captain, RN, and traveller; saw much service abroad; travelled with Charles Leonard *Irby, 1816, their letters being published in *Murray's *Home and Colonial Library* (1844); published a few miscellaneous works.

MANGLES, Ross Donnelly (1801–1877), chairman of East India Company; educated at Eton and East India Company's College at Haileybury; writer in Bengal Civil Service, 1819; deputy secretary in General Department, 1832; secretary to government of Bengal in judicial and revenue departments, 1835–9; Liberal MP for Guildford, 1841–58; director of East India Company, 1847–57; chairman, 1857–8; member of Council of India, 1858–66; published writings on Indian affairs.

MANGNALL, Richmal (1769–1820), schoolmistress of Crofton Hall, Yorkshire; works include *Historical and Miscellaneous Questions* (1800).

MANING, Frederick Edward (1812–1883), the Pakeha Maori; his father an emigrant to Van Diemen's Land, 1824; went to New Zealand, 1833; married Maori wife and settled among the natives; a judge of the native lands court, 1865–81; author of *Old New Zealand* (1863) and *History of the War . . . in 1845*.

MANINI, Antony (1750–1786), violinist; played and taught in provinces and at Cambridge as leading violinist; taught Charles *Hague.

MANISTY, Sir Henry (1808–1890), judge; solicitor, 1830; barrister, Gray's Inn, 1845; QC, 1857; judge, 1876; knighted, 1876.

MANLEY, Mrs Mary De La Riviere (1663–1724), author of the *New Atalantis*; daughter of Sir Roger *Manley; drawn into false marriage with her cousin, John Manley, his wife being then alive; lived with duchess of *Cleveland; subsequently brought out *Letters* (1696), several plays, some of which were acted with success, and fell into disreputable course of life; published *The New Atalantis* (1709), in which Whigs and persons of note were slandered, and was arrested, but escaped punishment; published *Memoirs of Europe . . . written by Eginardus* (1710) and *Court Intrigues* (1711); attacked by *Swift in the *Tatler* (no. 63); succeeded Swift as editor of the *Examiner*, 1711, and was assisted by him; wrote several political pamphlets and defended herself from attacks by *Steele in the *Guardian*; brought out *Lucius* at Drury Lane, 1717; pub-

lished works, including *The Power of Love* (1720); mistress for some years of Alderman Barber.

MANLEY, Norman Washington (1893–1969), Jamaican statesman and lawyer; born in Jamaica, his father part Negro, part English, his mother part Irish descent; educated at Jamaica College and Jesus College, Oxford; Rhodes scholar; enlisted in Royal Field Artillery, 1915; MM; returned to Oxford, 1919; BA, 1921; BCL, called to bar (Gray's Inn), 1921; practised in Jamaica, 1922; KC, 1932; founded Jamaica's first political party, the People's National party, 1938; MP, 1949; chief minister, 1955–62; retired from politics, 1969; hon. LL D, Howard University, 1946, and University of the West Indies (posthumously, 1970).

MANLEY, Sir Roger (1626?–1688), Cavalier; fought for the king, but was exiled to Holland, 1646–60; lieutenant-governor of Jersey, 1667–74; subsequently governor of Landguard Fort; published *History of Late Warres in Denmark* (1670) and *De Rebellione* (1686).

MANLEY, Thomas (1628–1690), author; barrister, Middle Temple, c.1650; KC, 1672; published several legal works and a pamphlet, *Usury at Six per cent*, against *Culpeper's tract, *Usury* (1669), as well as *The Present State of Europe . . . found languishing, occasioned by the greatness of the French Monarchy* (1689).

MANLEY, William George Nicholas (1831–1901), surgeon-general; MRCS, 1851; joined Army Medical Staff, 1855; present at Sevastopol; won VC in New Zealand War, 1863–6; in charge of division of British Ambulance Corps in Franco-Prussian War, 1870; at siege of Paris, 1870; in Afghan War, 1878–9; principal medical officer in Egyptian War, 1882; surgeon-general, 1884; CB, 1894.

MANLOVE, Edward (*fl.* 1667), poet and lawyer; wrote *Liberties and Customs of the Lead Mines* (1653, in verse) and other works.

MANLOVE, Timothy (d. 1699), Presbyterian divine and physician; probably grandson of Edward *Manlove; minister at Leeds; published religious works.

MANN, Arthur Henry (1850–1929), organist; chorister at Norwich Cathedral; B.Mus., New College, Oxford, 1874; organist of King's College, Cambridge, 1876–1929; with his active co-operation lay clerks replaced by choral scholars and a residential school for choirboys established; his Festival Choir, which continued under his name until 1912, established 1887; it presented a fine series of works by *Elgar, Beethoven, Brahms, etc.; rearranged Handel MSS at

Fitzwilliam Museum, 1889–92; fellow of King's, 1922.

MANN, Arthur Henry (1876–1972), journalist; educated at Warwick School; apprenticed to *Western Mail*, Cardiff; played cricket for Glamorgan; sub-editor, *Birmingham Daily Mail*, 1900–5; editor, *Birmingham Evening Dispatch*, 1905–12; London editor, *Manchester Daily Dispatch*, 1912–15; editor, *Evening Standard*, 1915–19; started Londoner's Diary; editor, *Yorkshire Post*, 1919–39; saw steady growth in prestige of the paper; published leader on bishop of Bradford's address and precipitated crisis leading to abdication of Edward VIII, 1936; resolutely opposed policy of appeasement, 1938–9; insisted on his right as editor to dictate paper's line on important issues; declining circulation led to clash with business managers; merger of *Yorkshire Post* with *Leeds Mercury* led to Mann's resignation, 1939; CH, 1941; hon. LL D, Leeds; governor of BBC, 1941–6; trustee of *Observer*, 1945–56; chairman of Press Association, 1937–8; director, Argus Press, 1946.

MANN, Cathleen Sabine (1896–1959), painter; daughter of portrait painter Harrington Mann; studied with him, at Slade School, and with (Dame) Ethel *Walker; exhibited at Royal Academy and with Royal Society of Portrait Painters; official war artist (mainly portraitist), 1939–45; her marriage (1926) to tenth marquess of Queensberry dissolved, 1946; took own life.

MANN, Gother (1747–1830), general, inspector-general of fortifications, colonel-commandant, RE; served in Dominica, 1775–8; employed in tour of survey of north-east coast of England, 1781; commanding RE in Canada, 1785–91 and 1794–1804; served under duke of *York in Holland, 1793; colonel-commandant, RE, 1805, and general, 1821; inspector-general of fortifications, 1811; several of his plans for fortifying Canada still preserved.

MANN, Sir Horace (or Horatio), first baronet (1701–1786), British envoy at Florence; friend of Horace *Walpole and made by Sir Robert Walpole assistant to Fane, envoy at Florence, 1737, becoming Fane's successor, 1740–86; communicated with government principally on subject of Young Pretender (see CHARLES EDWARD LOUIS PHILIP CASIMIR), who resided at Florence; kept up artificial correspondence, extending to thousands of letters, with Horace Walpole, 1741–85, valuable as illustrating Florentine society; created baronet, 1755; KB, 1768.

MANN, Sir James Gow (1897–1962), master of the Armouries of the Tower of London and director of the Wallace Collection; educated at Winchester and New College, Oxford; BA, 1920; B.Litt., 1922; assistant keeper of fine arts, Ashmolean Museum, Oxford, 1922–3; assistant to keeper of Wallace Collection, 1924–32; deputy director, Courtauld Institute, London University, 1932–6; keeper, Wallace Collection, 1936–46; director, 1946–62; master of the Armouries, Tower of London, 1939; director, Society of Antiquaries of London, 1944; president, 1949–54; surveyor of Royal Works of Art, 1946–62; trustee, British Museum and the College of Arms; knighted, 1948; KCVO, 1957; FBA, 1952; publications include *The Wallace Collection Catalogue of Sculpture* (1931) and *Catalogue of the European Arms and Armour* of the Wallace Collection (1962).

MANN, Nicholas (d. 1753), master of the Charterhouse, 1737; MA, King's College, Cambridge, 1707, and fellow; scholar, antiquarian, and author.

MANN, Robert James (1817–1886), scientific writer; educated for the medical profession at University College, London; practised in Norfolk, but soon devoted himself more especially to literature; published series of scientific textbooks which had large circulation; contributed to various publications; MD, St Andrews, 1854; superintendent of education in Natal, 1859; emigration agent for Natal in London, 1866; member of numerous learned societies.

MANN, Theodore Augustus (1735–1809), man of science, historian, and antiquary called the Abbé Mann; sent to London to study for legal profession, 1753; proceeded, unknown to his parents, to Paris, 1754, read Bossuet and turned Roman Catholic; on outbreak of war went to Spain, 1756, and was given commission in O'Mahony's dragoons; became monk in the English Chartreuse, Nieuport, 1759, and prior, 1764; appointed imperial minister of public instruction at Brussels, 1776; wrote memoirs on various practical projects for imperial government and numerous educational primers; travelled; secretary and treasurer of Brussels Academy, 1786; FRS, 1788; retired to England, 1792, during French irruption; at Prague, 1794; published works in French and English, miscellaneous papers, and catalogues, reports, and letters.

MANN, Thomas (1856–1941), trade-unionist and Communist; known as Tom Mann; engineer in Birmingham and London; joined Amalgamated Society of Engineers, 1881, Social Democratic Federation, 1885; demanded shorter working hours; helped in London dock strike, 1889; first president, Dockers' Union, 1889–93; member of Royal Commission on Labour,

1891–4; signed minority report; secretary, Independent Labour party, 1894–7; a founder and first president of International Federation of Ship, Dock, and River Workers, 1896; largely responsible for launching Workers' Union, 1898; labour organizer in Australia, 1902–10; edited *Industrial Syndicalist* (1910–11) advocating direct action; imprisoned for inciting to mutiny, 1912; joined British Socialist party, 1916; founder-member, British Communist party, 1920; chairman, National Minority Movement, 1924–32; paid four visits to Russia; general secretary, Amalgamated Society of Engineers (1919–20), Amalgamated Engineering Union (1920–1).

MANN, William (1817–1873), astronomer; grandson of Gother *Mann; assistant at Royal Observatory, Cape of Good Hope; erected transit-circle with native aid, 1855, and made valuable observations.

MANNERS, Mrs Catherine, afterwards Lady Stepney (d. 1845), novelist. See STEPNEY.

MANNERS, Charles, fourth duke of Rutland (1754–1787), eldest son of John *Manners, marquis of Granby; MA, Trinity College, Cambridge, 1774; MP, Cambridge, 1774; opposed government policy in America; succeeded to dukedom, 1779; lord-lieutenant of Leicestershire, 1779; KG, 1782; lord-steward, 1783; privy councillor, 1783; resigned on formation of coalition government, but lord privy seal in Pitt's ministry; lord-lieutenant of Ireland, 1784, advocated union and passed, with some concessions, Pitt's commercial propositions through Irish parliament; gave magnificent entertainments and made a tour through the country, 1787; died at Phoenix Lodge, Dublin, from fever.

MANNERS, Charles Cecil John, sixth duke of Rutland (1815–1888), MP; strong protectionist, and supporter of George *Bentinck; succeeded to title, 1857; KG, 1867.

MANNERS, Edward, third earl of Rutland (1549–1587), son of Henry *Manners, second earl of Rutland; displayed great devotion to Elizabeth; filled numerous offices; lord-lieutenant of Nottinghamshire and Lincolnshire; KG, 1584; commissioner to try *Mary Queen of Scots, 1586; lord-chancellor designate, Apr. 1587, dying the same month.

MANNERS, Francis, sixth earl of Rutland (1578–1632), brother of Roger *Manners, fifth earl; travelled abroad; took part in *Essex's plot, 1601; KB, 1605; MA, Christ's College, Cambridge, 1612; succeeded to earldom, 1612; lord-lieutenant of Lincolnshire and Northamptonshire; held several offices; KG, 1616; privy councillor, 1617; admiral of the fleet to bring home Prince Charles from Spain, 1623.

MANNERS, George (1778–1853), editor and founder of the *Satirist*, 1807, a scurrilous periodical; consul at Boston, USA, 1819–39; published miscellaneous works.

MANNERS, Henry, second earl of Rutland (d. 1563), son of Thomas *Manners, first earl of Rutland; succeeded to earldom, 1543; knighted, 1544; made chief justice of Sherwood Forest, 1547; took part in Scottish operations; attended embassy to France, 1551; belonged to the extreme reformers' party; lord-lieutenant of Nottinghamshire, 1552, of Rutland, 1559; imprisoned at Mary's accession, 1553; admiral, 1556; general in French War, 1557; favourite of Elizabeth; KG, 1559; lord president of the north, 1561, and ecclesiastical commissioner for York.

MANNERS, John, eighth earl of Rutland (1604–1679), descended from Thomas *Manners, first earl of Rutland; MA, Queens' College, Cambridge, 1620–1; succeeded to earldom, 1642; moderate Parliamentarian; took Covenant, 1643; filled various offices; at the Restoration rebuilt Belvoir, which had been dismantled; lord-lieutenant of Leicestershire, 1667.

MANNERS, John (1609–1695), Jesuit. See SIMCOCKS.

MANNERS, John, ninth earl and first duke of Rutland (1638–1711), son of John *Manners, eighth earl of Rutland; succeeded to earldom, 1679; lord-lieutenant of Leicestershire, 1677, dismissed, 1687, and restored, 1689; assisted in raising forces for William of Orange in Nottinghamshire; created marquis of Granby and duke of Rutland, 1703.

MANNERS, John, marquis of Granby (1721–1770), lieutenant-general; colonel of Royal Horse Guards (blues); eldest son of John Manners, third duke of Rutland (1696–1779); of Eton and Trinity College, Cambridge; travelled with his tutor, John *Ewer; MP for Grantham, 1741, 1747, Cambridgeshire, 1754, 1761, and 1768; colonel of 'Leicester blues' at Jacobite invasion, 1745; served in Flanders, 1747; colonel of the blues, 1758; lieutenant-general, 1759; commanded blues at Minden, 1759, where his advance was stayed by orders of Lord George Sackville (see GERMAIN); succeeded latter as commander-in-chief of British contingent, 1759; performed brilliant services at Warburg, 1760, Fellinghausen, 1761, Gravenstein, Wilhelmstahl, heights of Homburg, and Kassel, 1762; master-general of the ordnance, 1763; twelfth commander-in-chief, 1766; savagely assailed by *Junius; retired from office, 1770; lord-lieutenant of Derbyshire.

MANNERS, Lord John James Robert, seventh duke of Rutland (1818–1906), politician; brother of Charles *Manners, sixth duke; MA, Trinity College, Cambridge, 1839; published verse account of foreign travel in 1839-40, *England's Trust and other Poems* (1841, containing a couplet on English nobility which obtained permanent currency), *English Ballads and other Poems* (1850), and notes of Irish and Scottish tours (1848-9); Conservative MP for Newark, 1841-7; under Disraeli's influence joined 'Young England' party; freely criticized Peel's administration, 1843-4; advocated public holidays, 1843, factory reform, 1844, and a general system of allotments; with Disraeli and George *Smythe (later Viscount Strangford) toured through industrial districts of Lancashire, 1844; figures in *Coningsby* (1844), *Sybil* (1845), and *Endymion* (1880); advocated disestablishment of the Irish Church and supported proposed grant to Maynooth, 1845; differences of opinion on religious and free-trade questions led to dissolution of 'Young England' party, 1847; unsuccessfully contested as Protectionist Liverpool, 1847, and City of London, 1849; Conservative member for Colchester, 1850-7, North Leicestershire, 1857-85, and Melton, 1885-8; PC, 1852; first commissioner of works, and Cabinet minister, Feb.-Dec. 1852, 1858-9, and 1866-8; accepted Disraeli's Reform Bill of 1867; postmaster-general, 1874-80 and 1885-6; reduced minimum telegram charge to sixpence, Oct. 1885; opposed extension of franchise without redistribution, 1884-5; chancellor of duchy of Lancaster, 1886-92; succeeded to dukedom, 1888; KG, 1891; made Baron Roos of Belvoir, 1896; hon. LL D, Cambridge, 1862, DCL, Oxford, 1876; GCB, 1880.

MANNERS, Sir Robert (d. 1355?), MP, Northumberland, 1340; constable of Norham before 1345; fought at Neville's Cross, 1346.

MANNERS, Sir Robert (1408-1461), sheriff, 1454, and MP for Northumberland, 1459.

MANNERS, Lord Robert (1758-1782), captain, RN; son of John *Manners, marquis of Granby; served under *Rodney and *Hood and took part in actions off Ushant, 1778, Cape St Vincent, 1779, Cape Henry, 1781, and Dominica, 1782, where he was fatally wounded.

MANNERS, Roger, fifth earl of Rutland (1576-1612), son of fourth earl; educated at Queens' and Corpus Christi colleges, Cambridge; MA, 1595; travelled abroad, *Profitable Instructions* being written for him, probably by *Bacon; knighted by *Essex in Ireland, 1599; steward of Sherwood Forest, 1600; took part in Essex's conspiracy, 1601, and was heavily fined; KB, 1603; lord-lieutenant of Lincolnshire, 1603.

MANNERS, Thomas, first earl of Rutland and thirteenth Baron Ros (d. 1543), became Baron Ros on his father's death, 1513; took part in French expedition, 1513; present at Field of the Cloth of Gold, 1520; favourite of Henry VIII, receiving numerous grants and offices; warden of the east marches and of Sherwood Forest; KG, 1525; created earl of Rutland, 1525; took active part against northern rebels, 1536; constable of Nottingham Castle, 1542.

MANNERS-SUTTON, Charles (1755-1828), archbishop of Canterbury; brother of Thomas *Manners-Sutton, first Baron Manners; fifteenth wrangler, 1777, and MA, Emmanuel College, Cambridge, 1780; DD, 1792; rector of Averham-with-Kelham and Whitwell, 1785; dean of Peterborough, 1791; bishop of Norwich, 1792-1805; dean of Windsor, 1794; favourite of royal family; archbishop of Canterbury, 1805-28; active in church revival.

MANNERS-SUTTON, Charles, first Viscount Canterbury (1780-1845), speaker of the House of Commons; son of Charles *Manners-Sutton, archbishop of Canterbury; of Eton and Trinity College, Cambridge; MA, 1805; LL D, 1824; barrister, Lincoln's Inn, 1806; Tory MP for Scarborough and subsequently for Cambridge University; judge advocate-general, 1809; privy councillor, 1809; opposed inquiry into state of Ireland, 1812, and Catholic claims, 1813; passed Clergy Residence Bill, 1817; speaker, 1817-35, when he was accused of partisanship and his candidature defeated; refused office several times; GCB and received pension, 1833; created Baron Bottesford and Viscount Canterbury, 1835.

MANNERS-SUTTON, John Henry Thomas, third Viscount Canterbury (1814-1877), son of Charles *Manners-Sutton, first Viscount Canterbury; MA, Trinity College, Cambridge, 1835; MP, Cambridge, 1841-7; under home secretary (1841-6) in Peel's administration; lieutenant-governor of New Brunswick, 1854-61; governor of Trinidad, 1864-6, and Victoria, 1866-73; KCB, 1866; succeeded to title, 1869; GCMG, 1873; published *Lexington Papers* (1851).

MANNERS-SUTTON, Thomas, first Baron Manners (1756-1842), lord chancellor of Ireland; grandson of the third duke of Rutland; fifth wrangler, Emmanuel College, Cambridge, 1777; MA, 1780; barrister, Lincoln's Inn, 1780; obtained large Chancery practice; MP, Newark-upon-Trent, 1796-1805; Welsh judge, 1797; KC, 1800, and solicitor-general to prince of Wales, 1800; solicitor-general, 1802; knighted, 1802; serjeant-at-law and baron of Exchequer,

1805; created Baron Manners and privy councillor, 1807; lord chancellor of Ireland, 1807–27; removed O'Hanlon from bench for supporting Catholic claims; took active part in proceedings against Queen *Caroline, 1820; opposed Catholic claims, 1828.

MANNHEIM, Hermann (1889–1974), criminologist; born in Berlin; studied law and political science at Munich, Freiburg, Strasburg, and Königsberg Universities; during 1914–18 war served in German artillery in Russia and France; judge of the Kammergericht in Berlin, 1932; professor of law faculty, Berlin University; gave up professorship when Nazis came to power; moved to London, 1934; became naturalized British subject, 1940; appointed honorary part-time lecturer in criminology, London School of Economics, 1935; Leon fellow, 1936; full-time lecturer, 1944; reader in criminology, 1944–55; published many books and articles, including *The Dilemma of Penal Reform* (1939), *Criminal Justice and Social Reconstruction* (1946; 2nd impr., 1949), *Group Problems in Crime and Punishment* (1955), and *Comparative Criminology* (2 vols., 1965; translated into Italian and German); also wrote for the *British Journal of Criminology*; founding editor of *British Journal of Delinquency* (later *British Journal of Criminology*); closely associated with Howard League for Penal Reform; recognized by government of Federal German Republic, 1952; OBE, 1959; received hon. doctorates from Utrecht and University of Wales; hon. fellow, LSE, 1965.

MANNIN, Ethel Edith (1900–1984), writer; educated at council school in Clapham; stenographer in Charles F. Higham's advertising agency, 1915; associate editor, *Pelican* magazine, 1917; first successful novel, *Sounding Brass* (1925); published nearly one hundred books, including six autobiographical volumes from *Confessions and Impressions* (1930) to *Sunset over Dartmoor* (1977); published novels include *Men Are Unwise* (1934), *At Sundown, the Tiger . . .* (1951), and *The Living Lotus* (1956); travel books include *Bavarian Story* (1950), *Jungle Journey* (1950), *Moroccan Mosaic* (1953), and *Land of the Crested Lion* (1955); also published memoir of her father, *This Was a Man* (1952).

MANNIN, James (d. 1779), flower painter.

MANNING, Anne (1807–1879), miscellaneous writer; sister of William Oke *Manning; contributed to *Sharpe's Magazine* (1849) *The Maiden and Married Life of Mistress Mary Powell* (frequently reprinted); was known thenceforward as the 'author of Mary Powell'; her best works are historical tales of the sixteenth century.

MANNING, Bernard Lord (1892–1941), scholar; first classes, history (1914–15), Jesus College, Cambridge; fellow, 1919; bursar, 1920–33; senior tutor, 1933–41; university lecturer in medieval history, 1930–41; publications include *The Making of Modern English Religion* (1929) and chapters in vol. vii of *Cambridge Medieval History*.

MANNING, Henry Edward (1808–1892), cardinal-priest; educated at Balliol College, Oxford, under Charles *Wordsworth, and with William Ewart Gladstone; MA, 1833; obtained post in Colonial Office, 1830; fellow, Merton College, 1832; curate of Woollavington-cum-Graffham, 1832, and rector, 1833; rural dean, 1837; archdeacon of Chichester, 1840; select preacher at Oxford, 1842; published *The Unity of the Church*, an able exposition of Anglo-Catholic principles, and *Sermons* (1844); disapproved of *Tract XC* and preached anti-papal sermon at Oxford on Guy Fawkes' day, 1843; voted against William George *Ward's degradation by the Oxford convocation, 1845; travelled abroad and (1848) visited Pius IX; supported resistance to government grants in aid of elementary schools, 1849; protested against *Gorham judgment, 1850, and wrote *The Appellate Jurisdiction of the Crown in Matters Spiritual* denying the jurisdiction; resigned archdeaconry and became Roman Catholic, 1851; published *The Grounds of Faith* (1852); superior of 'Congregation of the Oblates of St Charles', at Bayswater, 1857; occupied himself in preaching, education, mission work, and literary defence of papal temporal power; appointed at Rome domestic prelate and monsignore, 1860; published letters *To an Anglican Friend* (1864) and on *The Workings of the Holy Spirit in the Church of England*, addressed to *Pusey; nominated Roman Catholic archbishop of Westminster, 1865; published *The Temporal Mission of the Holy Ghost* (1865 and 1875); as archbishop was autocratic and a thorough Ultramontane; established Westminster Education Fund, 1866; supported infallibility of the pope, and published *Petri Privilegium* (1871) and *National Education* (1872) in favour of voluntary teaching; contributed articles to various papers defending his orthodoxy and Ultramontane theory; published *The Vatican Decrees* (1875), in answer to William Ewart Gladstone; published in the *Daily Telegraph* letters on the infallibility of the Roman Church, in answer to Lord *Redesdale, 1875 (reprinted, 1875); cardinal, 1875; carried on crusade against drink; a zealous philanthropist; sat on royal commissions on housing of the poor, 1884–5, and Education Acts, 1886–7, and published articles on those topics; favoured Gladstone's domestic politics in later life; great preacher and ecclesiastical statesman; of ascetic temper; a subtle but unspeculative controversialist; published in late years *The Eternal Priesthood* (1883), sermons, and other works.

MANNING, James (1781–1866), serjeant-at-law; barrister, Lincoln's Inn, 1817; leader of western circuit; learned especially in copyright law; recorder of Sudbury, 1835–66, and Oxford and Banbury, 1857–66; serjeant-at-law, 1840, and queen's ancient serjeant, 1846; judge of Whitechapel County Court, 1847; published legal works.

MANNING, John Edmondson (1848–1910), Unitarian divine; BA, London, 1872; MA, 1876; minister at Upper Chapel, Sheffield, 1889–1902, of which he wrote a history, 1900; tutor at Unitarian Home Missionary College, Manchester.

MANNING, Marie (1821–1849), murderess; née de Roux; native of Lausanne; married Frederick George Manning, publican, 1847, and with him murdered O'Connor at Bermondsey, 1849, both being condemned and executed.

MANNING, Olivia Mary (1908–1980), novelist; unhappy childhood portrayed later in her novels; educated at Portsmouth Grammar School, and then studied art; worked in architect's office in Portsmouth and as a typist in London; produced first novels under pseudonym Jacob Morrow; first literary novel, *The Wind Changes* (1937), followed after a twelve-year interval by *Artist Among the Missing* (1949) and then *The Doves of Venus* (1955); married Reginald Donald Smith, lecturer with the British Council, 1939; travelled with him to Romania and Greece; appointed press officer at US Embassy, Cairo, 1942; press assistant, Public Information Office, Jerusalem 1943–4 and with British Council in Jerusalem, 1944–5; published the Balkan trilogy, *The Great Fortune* (1960), *The Spoilt City* (1962), and *Friends and Heroes* (1965), followed by the Levant trilogy, two further novels, *The Play Room* (1969) and *The Rain Forest* (1974), and one volume of stories, *A Romantic Hero* (1967); also *The Danger Tree* (1977), *The Battle Lost and Won* (1978), and *The Sum of Things* (1980), war in the Middle East being the centre-piece of her canvas; CBE, 1976.

MANNING, Owen (1721–1801), historian of Surrey; MA, Queens' College, Cambridge, 1744; BD, 1753; fellow, 1742–55; incumbent of St Botolph, Cambridge, 1749–60; obtained several other preferments; rector of Godalming, 1763–1801; prebendary of Lincoln, 1757–1801; FRS, 1767; collected materials for history of Surrey, afterwards published with additions by

William *Bray (1736–1832), 1804–9–14; completed *Lye's Saxon dictionary (1772) and annotated *The Will of King Alfred* (1788).

MANNING, Robert (d. 1731), Roman Catholic controversialist; professor at Douai English College; missioner in England; works include *The Shortest Way to end disputes about religion* (1716).

MANNING, Samuel, the younger (*fl.* 1846), sculptor; son of Samuel *Manning (d. 1847).

MANNING, Samuel (d. 1847), sculptor; executed bust of Warren *Hastings's statue in Westminster Abbey; exhibited statuary at Royal Academy.

MANNING, Samuel (1822–1881), Baptist minister at Sheppard's Barton, Somerset, 1846–61; editor of the *Baptist Magazine*; general book editor of Religious Tract Society, 1863, and joint secretary, 1876.

MANNING, Thomas (1772–1840), traveller and friend of Charles *Lamb; scholar of Caius College, Cambridge, and private tutor; studied mathematics and made acquaintance with *Porson and Lamb; studied Chinese at Paris, 1800–3; studied medicine and left for Canton, 1807, but failed to penetrate into China; went to Calcutta, 1810, and travelled from Rangpur to Lhasa, 1811, the first Englishman to enter Lhasa; returned to Canton, 1812; accompanied Lord *Amherst to Peking as interpreter, 1816; returned to England, 1817; considered first Chinese scholar in Europe; wrote mathematical works.

MANNING, William (1630?–1711), ejected minister; BA, Caius College, Cambridge, 1650–1; perpetual curate of Middleton, Suffolk; ejected, 1662; took out licence as 'congregational teacher' at Peasenhall, 1672; became Socinian; published sermons.

MANNING, William Oke (1809–1878), legal writer; nephew of James *Manning (1781–1866); published *Commentaries on Law of Nations* (1839).

MANNINGHAM, John (d. 1622), diarist; BA, Magdalene College, Cambridge, 1596; student of Middle Temple and utter barrister, 1605; his diary (1602–3), of considerable value, was first printed by the Camden Society (1868).

MANNINGHAM, Sir Richard (1690–1759), man-midwife; son of Thomas *Manningham; LL B, Cambridge, 1717; MD; FRS, 1720; knighted, 1721; chief man-midwife of the day; attended Mary *Toft, and published *Exact Diary* on the case (1726); published *Artis Obstetricariae Compendium* (1740) and other works.

MANNINGHAM, Thomas (1651?–1722), bishop of Chichester; scholar of Winchester College and New College, Oxford; fellow, 1671–81; MA, 1677; DD, Lambeth, 1691; obtained various preferments; dean of Windsor, 1709; bishop of Chichester, 1709; published sermons.

MANNINGHAM-BULLER, Reginald Edward, fourth baronet, and first Viscount Dilhorne (1905–1980), lord chancellor; educated at Eton and Magdalen College, Oxford; called to bar (Inner Temple), 1927; served in judge advocate-general's department during 1939–45 war; KC, 1946; Conservative MP for Daventry, 1943–50, reorganized as southern division of Northamptonshire, 1950–62; solicitor-general, 1951; PC, 1954 and attorney-general, 1954–62; succeeded father as fourth baronet, 1954; lord chancellor, 1962–4; concerned with appointment of earl of Home (later Lord Home of the Hirsel) as prime minister; first viscount, 1964; deputy lieutenant of Northamptonshire, 1967; lord of appeal in ordinary, 1969; honorary degrees from McGill University, Canada, and Southern Methodist University, Dallas, Texas.

MANNOCK, John (1677–1764), Benedictine monk; made profession at Douai, 1700; chaplain to Canning family; procurator of southern province, 1729; published religious works.

MANNS, Sir August (1825–1907), conductor of the Crystal Palace concerts from 1855 to 1901; born at Stolzenburg, Pomerania; bandmaster in von Roon's Regiment at Königsberg, 1851; came to England, 1854; transformed wind band at Crystal Palace into full orchestra; conducted Saturday concerts there for forty years; introduced works by Schumann, Schubert, and Brahms; frequently (from 1861) devoted programme to living English composers; conducted Handel triennial festivals, 1883–1900.

MANNY (or MAUNY), Sir Walter de, afterwards Baron de Manny (d. 1372), military commander and founder of the Charterhouse, London; native of Hainault; esquire to Queen *Philippa; knighted, 1331; distinguished himself in Scottish wars; was rewarded with lands and governorship of Merioneth (1332) and Harlech Castle (1334); admiral of northern fleet, 1337, capturing Guy de Rickenburg in the Scheldt; according to Froissart took French castle of Thun l'Evêque with only forty lances on defiance of French king, 1339; served throughout campaign and won distinction at Sluys, 1340; sent by Edward III to assist countess of Montfort against Charles of Blois, 1342; accompanied earl of Derby in successful Gascony campaigns; according to Froissart conducted siege of Calais, and

was summoned to parliament as baron, 1345; sent to negotiate in France, 1348, and in Netherlands, 1351; received grants of land; accompanied Edward III to Artois, 1355; present at siege of Berwick, 1355; took part in Edward's French campaigns, 1359–60, and negotiated in his name; a guarantor of Treaty of Bretigni and guardian of King John of France at Calais, 1360; KG, 1359; ordered to Ireland, 1368; accompanied *John of Gaunt in invasion of France, 1369; obtained licence to found house of Carthusian monks, i.e. the Charterhouse in London, 1371; one of the ablest of Edward III's soldiers.

MANNYNG, Robert (*fl.* 1288–1338), poet also known as Robert de Brunne; native of Bourne, Lincolnshire; entered Sempringham Priory, 1288; wrote *Handlyng Synne* (edited, 1862), the *Chronicle of England* (first part edited by Dr Furnivall, second part by *Hearne), neither original works, but of great literary value; also probable author of *Meditacyuns* (edited, 1875).

MANSBRIDGE, Albert (1876–1952), founder of Workers' Educational Association; left Battersea Grammar School at 14; obtained clerical work; cashier, Co-operative Permanent Building Society, 1901–5; a director, 1910; student and teacher at evening classes; founded Workers' Educational Association, 1903; general secretary, 1905–14; founded branches throughout country and obtained co-operation of universities in providing tutorial classes for study at university level; founded Central Library for Students (later National Central Library), 1916; World Association for Adult Education, 1918; Seafarers' Educational Service, 1919; British Institute of Adult Education, 1921; member, Royal Commission on Oxford and Cambridge, 1919–22; appointed to Oxford Statutory Commission, 1923; publications include *The Kingdom of the Mind* (1944); hon. MA, Oxford, 1912; hon. LL D, Manchester, 1922, Cambridge, 1923; CH, 1931.

MANSEL, Charles Grenville (1806–1886), Indian official; filled various posts at Agra; member of Punjab administration, 1849, resident of Nagpur, 1850.

MANSEL, Henry Longueville (1820–1871), metaphysician; educated at Merchant Taylors' School, London, where he wrote verses; scholar of St John's College, Oxford; obtained 'double first', 1843; tutor, and ordained, 1844; strong Tory and High-Churchman; 'professor fellow', 1864; reader in theology at Magdalen College, Oxford, from 1855; wrote article on metaphysics in *Encyclopaedia Britannica*, 1857; Bampton lecturer, 1858; engaged in controversy with *Maurice, Goldwin Smith, and *Mill; select preacher, 1860–2, and 1869–71; professor of ecclesiastical history, 1866–8; lectured on 'The Gnostic Heresies', 1868; dean of St Paul's, 1868–71; published *Phrontisterion* (1850), *Prolegomena Logica* (1851), *The Limits of Demonstrative Science* (1853), *Man's Conception of Eternity* (1854), and other metaphysical works; contributed to *The Speaker's Commentary* and to *Aids to Faith*; follower of Sir William *Hamilton, and, with *Veitch, edited his lectures, 1859.

MANSEL (or MAUNSELL), John (d. 1265), keeper of the seal and counsellor of Henry III; son of a country priest; obtained post at Exchequer, 1234; accompanied Henry III on expedition to France, 1242–3, and greatly distinguished himself; keeper of the great seal, 1246–7, and subsequently; ambassador to Brabant, 1247; had considerable influence with Henry III; sent on missions to Scotland, Brabant, France, Germany, and Brittany; concerned in Edward's marriage to *Eleanor of Castile, 1254, in the election of *Richard, king of the Romans, 1257, and in the abandonment of English claims on Normandy, 1258; member of the Committee of Twenty-Four and Council of Fifteen, 1258; followed Henry III to France; the king compelled to dismiss him, 1261; obtained papal bull releasing Henry III from his obligations, 1262; accompanied Henry III to France, 1262; on civil war breaking out, escaped to Boulogne, 1263; present at mise of Amiens, 1264; died in France in great poverty; said to have held three hundred benefices; by supporting the king's measures acquired much odium, but was a capable and diligent administrator.

MANSEL, William Lort (1753–1820), bishop of Bristol; fellow, Trinity College, Cambridge, 1775; MA, 1777; DD, 1798; tutor; master, 1798; vice-chancellor, 1799–1800; held livings of Bottisham and Chesterton; appointed bishop of Bristol by *Perceval, a former pupil, 1808; well-known wit and writer of epigrams; author of sermons.

MANSELL, Francis (1579–1665), principal of Jesus College, Oxford; MA, Jesus College, Oxford, 1611; fellow of All Souls College, Oxford, 1613; DD, 1624; principal of Jesus College, 1620; after expelling several fellows retired from office; again principal, 1630–47; treasurer of Llandaff and prebendary of St David's, 1631; benefactor of the college; assisted Royalists in Wales, 1643–7; ejected from Jesus College, 1647; reinstated, 1660.

MANSELL, Sir Robert (1573–1656), admiral; served in Cadiz expedition and was knighted, 1596; took part in 'the Islands' Voyage', 1597; held commands off Irish coast, 1599–1600; active in arresting accomplices of *Essex and captured Hansa ships, 1601; MP, King's Lynn, 1601, Carmarthen, 1603, Carmarthenshire, 1614, Glamorganshire, 1623–5, Lostwithiel, 1626, and Glamorganshire, 1628; intercepted Portuguese galleys, 1602; 'vice-admiral of the Narrow Seas', 1603; treasurer of the navy, 1604; accompanied earl of *Nottingham on Spanish mission, 1605; imprisoned in the Marshalsea for alleged political disaffection, 1613; vice-admiral of England, 1618; commanded unsuccessful expeditions against Algiers, 1620–1; obtained glass monopoly, 1615.

MANSELL, Sir Thomas (1777–1858), rear-admiral; present at actions off Lorient, 1795, Cape St Vincent, 1797, and Battle of the Nile, 1798; promoted lieutenant by *Nelson; held various commands and captured 170 ships; KCH, 1837; rear-admiral, 1849.

MANSEL-PLEYDELL, John Clavell (1817–1902), Dorset antiquary; BA, St John's College, Cambridge, 1839; built Milborne Reformatory, 1856; founded Dorset Natural History Club, 1875; made valuable geological finds in Dorsetshire; published the *Flora* (1874), *Birds* (1888), and *Mollusca* (1898) of Dorsetshire.

MANSERGH, James (1834–1905), civil engineer; worked in Brazil, 1855–9; practised at Westminster from 1866 till death; specialized in water and sewage works; constructed reservoirs and aqueduct from valleys of Elan and Cherwen rivers to Birmingham, 1894–1904; carried out sewage disposal for several midland towns; prepared schemes for sewerage of Lower Thames valley; on Royal Commission on Metropolitan Water Supply, 1892–3; FRS, 1901; president of Institution of Civil Engineers, 1900–1.

MANSFIELD, earls of. See MURRAY, WILLIAM, first earl, 1705–1793; MURRAY, DAVID, second earl, 1727–1796.

MANSFIELD, Charles Blackford (1819–1855), chemist and author; MA, Clare Hall, Cambridge, 1849; discovered method of extracting benzol from coal tar, 1848, and published pamphlet; joined *Maurice and *Kingsley in efforts for social reform (1848–9), and contributed to *Politics for the people* and *Christian Socialist*; published *Aerial Navigation* (1850) and delivered lectures at Royal Institution on chemistry of metals, 1851–2; visited Buenos Aires and Paraguay, 1852–3; published *Theory of Salts* (1855); died from accident by burning.

MANSFIELD, Henry de (d. 1328). See MAUNSFIELD.

MANSFIELD (originally MANFIELD), Sir James (1733–1821), lord chief justice of common pleas; fellow, King's College, Cambridge,

1754; MA, 1758; barrister, Middle Temple, 1758; adviser of *Wilkes, 1768, duchess of *Kingston, and others; KC, 1772; MP, Cambridge University, 1779–84; solicitor-general, 1780–2, and in coalition ministry, 1783; chief justice of common pleas and knighted, 1804.

MANSFIELD, Sir John Maurice (1893–1949), vice-admiral; entered navy, 1906; chief of staff to commander-in-chief, Western Approaches, 1941–3; rear-admiral, 1943; commanded Cruiser Squadron, Mediterranean, 1943–5; supported landings in Italy and southern France; commanded British naval forces liberating Greece; DSO, 1945; flag officer, Ceylon (1945–6), submarines (1946–8); vice-admiral, 1946; KCB, 1948.

MANSFIELD, Katherine (pseudonym) (1888–1923), writer. See MURRY, KATHLEEN.

MANSFIELD, Robert Blachford (1824–1908), author and oarsman; brother of Charles Blachford *Mansfield; educated at Eton and University College, Oxford; BA, 1846; called to bar, 1849; pioneer of English golf, 1857; rowed in university boat-race, 1843; pioneer of English rowing in Germany; recorded his German experiences in *The Log of the Water-Lily* (1851) and *The Water-Lily on the Danube* (1852).

MANSFIELD, Sir William Rose, first Baron Sandhurst (1819–1876), general; grandson of Sir James *Mansfield; joined 53rd Foot, 1835; distinguished himself in first Sikh War, Punjab War, 1849, and under Sir Colin *Campbell on Peshawar frontier; military adviser to British ambassador at Constantinople, 1855; consul-general at Warsaw, 1856; chief of the staff to Sir Colin Campbell in Indian Mutiny, 1857; present at relief and siege of Lucknow and fight at Cawnpore, when his conduct was much criticized; served in campaigns in Rohilcund, Oudh, and other operations; commander of Bombay presidency, 1860; commander-in-chief in India, 1865; in Ireland, 1870; general, 1872; KCB, 1857; created Baron Sandhurst, 1871; GCSI, 1866; GCB, 1870; DCL, Oxford, 1870; Irish privy councillor, 1870.

MANSHIP, Henry (*fl.* 1562), topographer; directed construction of Yarmouth harbour; his *Greate Yermouthe* printed (1847).

MANSHIP, Henry (d. 1625), topographer; son of Henry *Manship; town clerk of Yarmouth, 1579–85; dismissed from corporation, 1604; managed Yarmouth affairs in London, again falling into disgrace, 1616; published *History of Great Yarmouth* (1619); died in poverty.

MANSON, David (1726–1792), schoolmaster; began life as farmer's boy at Cairncastle, Co. Antrim; opened school there and afterwards (1755) one at Belfast and also a brewery; published school-books.

MANSON, George (1850–1876), Scottish artist; executed woodcuts for *Chambers's Miscellany*; disciple of Bewick and painter of homely subjects.

MANSON, James Bolivar (1879–1945), painter and director of Tate Gallery; educated at Alleyn's School, Dulwich; studied at Heatherley's and Académie Julian, Paris; admirer of Impressionists; most successful in landscape and still life; first secretary, Camden Town (1911) and London (1913) groups; assistant (1912), assistant keeper (1917), director (1930–7), Tate Gallery.

MANSON, Sir Patrick (1844–1922), physician and parasitologist; MB, CM, Aberdeen, 1865; medical officer for Formosa to Chinese Imperial Maritime Customs, 1866; at Amoy, 1871–83; while working on elephantoid diseases discovered developmental phase in life of *filaria* worms in tissues of the blood-sucking insect, mosquito; settled in Hong Kong, where he instituted school of medicine which developed into university and medical school of Hong Kong, 1883–9; physician to Seamen's Hospital, London, 1892; propounded his mosquito-malaria theory, which was confirmed by other researchers; physician and adviser to Colonial Office, 1897; instrumental in foundation of London School of Tropical Medicine, 1899; FRS, 1900; KCMG, 1903; the 'father of tropical medicine'; published works on tropical diseases.

MANSON, Thomas Walter (1893–1958), biblical scholar; educated at Tynemouth High School and Glasgow University; MA, 1917; entered Westminster and Christ's colleges, Cambridge; first class, part ii, oriental languages tripos (Hebrew and Aramaic), 1923; ordained in Presbyterian Church of England, 1925; minister, Falstone, Northumberland, 1926–32; Yates professor of New Testament Greek, Mansfield College, Oxford, 1932–6; Rylands professor of biblical criticism, Manchester, 1936–58; served on New Testament and Apocrypha panels for New English Bible; publications include *The Church's Ministry* (1948) and *The Servant-Messiah* (1953); FBA, 1945.

MANT, Richard (1776–1848), bishop of Down, Connor, and Dromore; scholar of Winchester College and Trinity College, Oxford; fellow of Oriel College, Oxford, 1798; gained Chancellor's Prize with essay 'On Commerce', 1799; MA, 1801; DD, 1815; vicar of Coggeshall, Essex, 1810; Bampton lecturer, 1811; chaplain to the archbishop of Canterbury, 1813; rector of St

Botolph's, 1815, and East Horsley, 1818; bishop of Killaloe and Kilfenoragh, 1820; translated to Down and Connor, 1823, Dromore being added, 1842; built many new churches; published poetical, theological, miscellaneous, and historical works, including *History of the Church of Ireland* (1840).

MANT, Walter Bishop (1807–1869), divine; son of Richard *Mant; archdeacon of Down, antiquarian, and author of works in prose and verse.

MANTE, Thomas (*fl.* 1772), military writer; author of *History of the late War in America* (1772) and other works.

MANTELL, Gideon Algernon (1790–1852), geologist; son of a shoemaker; articled to, and finally partner of Lewes surgeon; devoted himself to natural history and geology and made noted collection; removed to Brighton, 1833, and lectured; published *The Wonders of Geology* (1838) and other geological works, besides papers published by Royal and Geological societies, setting forth his extensive investigations and discoveries; FRS, 1825; hon. FRCS, 1844.

MANTELL, Joshua (1795–1865), surgeon and horticultural writer; brother of Gideon Algernon *Mantell.

MANTELL, Sir Thomas (1751–1831), antiquary; FSA, 1810; surgeon at Dover and mayor; knighted, 1820; published *Cinque Ports* (1828) and other works.

MANTON, John (d. 1834), gun-maker; brother of Joseph *Manton.

MANTON, Joseph (1766?–1835), gun-maker; took out several patents for improvements in guns, 1792–1825, and other inventions; bankrupt, 1826.

MANTON, Sidnie Milana (1902–1979), zoologist; educated at the Froebel Educational Institute School, St Paul's Girls' School, Hammersmith, and Girton College, Cambridge; first class, both parts of natural sciences tripos, 1923 and 1925; top in zoology; Cambridge swimming captain, 1923 and hockey blue, 1924; Alfred Yarrow student, Imperial College, London; university demonstrator in comparative anatomy, Cambridge, 1927; supervisor in zoology, director of studies (1935–42), staff fellow (1928–35 and 1942–5), and research fellow (1945–8), Girton College; Ph.D., 1928; Sc.D., 1934; visited Tasmania and joined Great Barrier Reef expedition, 1928; reader in zoology, King's College, London, 1949–60; eminent in fields of arthropod embryology and functional morphology, her findings elucidating problems of evolution; work summarized in *The Arthropods. Habits,*

Functional Morphology and Evolution (1977); also published (with J. T. Saunders) *A Manual of Practical Vertebrate Morphology* (1931) and *Colourpoint, Himalayan and Longhair Cats* (1971, 2nd edn., 1979); FRS, 1948; Gold Medal for Zoology of Linnean Society, 1963 and Frink Medal of Zoological Society, 1977; hon. fellow, Queen Mary College, London; married Dr John Philip Harding, 1937.

MANTON, Thomas (1620–1677), Presbyterian divine; BA, Hart Hall, Oxford, 1639; ordained, 1640; lecturer at Cullompton and (*c.*1645) obtained living of Stoke Newington; one of the scribes to Westminster Assembly; disapproved of Charles I's execution; attended Christopher *Love on the scaffold and preached funeral sermon, 1651; rector of St Paul's, Covent Garden, London, 1656; drew up with *Baxter and others 'Fundamentals of Religion', 1658; one of the deputies to Breda, and chaplain to Charles II; took part in religious conferences and was created DD, Oxford, 1660; left St Paul's, Covent Garden, 1662, and held meetings elsewhere in London; arrested, 1670; preacher at Pinners' Hall, London, 1672; discussed 'accommodation' with *Tillotson and Stillingfleet, 1674; the most popular of the Presbyterians; published religious works.

MANUCHE (or MANUCCI), Cosmo (*fl.* 1652), dramatist; of Italian origin; probably member of household of James Compton, third earl of Northampton; captain and major of foot in king's army during Civil War; subsequently obtained employment under the protector. Twelve plays have been assigned to him, three of which were published, *The Just General* (1652), *The Loyal Lovers* (1652), and *The Bastard* (issued anonymously, 1652); of the remaining nine plays which were formerly in manuscript at Castle Ashby only one is still known there.

MANWARING (or MAYNWARING), Roger (1590–1653), bishop of St David's; DD, All Souls College, Oxford; rector of St Giles'-in-the-Fields, London, 1616; chaplain to Charles I; preached sermons before Charles I on 'Religion' and 'Allegiance', 1627, asserting 'peril of damnation' of those who resisted taxation levied by royal authority; on being sentenced to imprisonment, fine, and suspension, made retractation; received several preferments; dean of Worcester, 1633; bishop of St David's, 1635; was deprived of vote in House of Lords by Short Parliament, 1640; imprisoned and persecuted by Long Parliament.

MANWOOD, John (d. 1610), legal author; relative of Sir Roger *Manwood; barrister, Lincoln's Inn; justice of the New Forest; published

A Brefe Collection of the Lawes of the Forest (1592; enlarged, 1615).

MANWOOD, Sir Peter (d. 1625), antiquary; son of Sir Roger *Manwood; student of the Inner Temple, 1583; represented between 1588 and 1621 Sandwich, Saltash, Kent, and New Romney; sheriff of Kent, 1602; KB, 1603; patron of learned men at St Stephen's, near Canterbury, and mentioned with great respect by Camden; published part of *Williams's *Actions of the Lowe Countries* (1618).

MANWOOD, Sir Roger (1525–1592), judge; barrister, Inner Temple, 1555; recorder of Sandwich, 1555–66, and steward of Chancery and Admiralty courts, Dover; MP, Hastings, 1555, Sandwich, 1558; granted by Elizabeth manor of St Stephen's, Kent; friend of Sir Thomas *Gresham and Archbishop *Parker, and founded with the latter grammar school at Sandwich; supported Treason Bill, 1571; judge of common pleas, 1572–8; with bishops of London and Rochester convicted of Anabaptism two Flemings, who were burnt, 1575; showed himself severe towards enemies of the government; knighted, 1578; chief baron of the Exchequer, 1578–92; member of Star Chamber, which sentenced Lord *Vaux of Harrowden, 1581; member of commission at Fotheringay, 1586; rebuked by Elizabeth for sale of office, 1591; accused of various malpractices and arraigned before privy council, 1592.

MAP (or MAPES), Walter (*fl.* 1200), medieval author and wit; probably native of Herefordshire; studied in Paris under Girard la Pucelle; clerk of royal household and justice-itinerant; accompanied Henry II abroad, 1173 and 1183; sent to Rome, 1179; canon of St Paul's Cathedral, Lincoln, and Hereford; precentor, and, later, chancellor of Lincoln; archdeacon of Oxford from 1197; author of *De Nugis Curialium*, a collection of anecdotes and legends of considerable interest and of satirical purport (edited, 1850); probably also author, or largely author, of *Lancelot*, and perhaps of some of the satirical Goliardic verse; specimens of his wit preserved by *Giraldus.

MAPLE, Sir John Blundell, baronet (1845–1903), merchant and sportsman; joined (1862) father's furnishing firm in Tottenham Court Road, which was converted into limited liability company, with Maple as chairman, 1891; Conservative MP for Dulwich, 1887–1903; knighted, 1892; baronet, 1897; racehorse breeder and owner; won 544 races; headed list of winning owners, 1891; won Cesarewitch, 1894, and Two Thousand Guineas, 1895; rebuilt University College Hospital, 1897–1906.

MAPLESON, James Henry (1830–1901), operatic manager; studied violin and pianoforte at Royal Academy of Music, 1844, and singing in Italy; managed Italian opera season from 1858 variously at Drury Lane, Lyceum Theatre, and Covent Garden; produced Gounod's *Faust* (1863) and Bizet's *Carmen* (1878); from 1878 took touring companies to America in winter; engaged Adelina Patti, 1881–5; his repertory of Italian opera lost vogue from 1887; published *Memoirs* (2 vols., 1888).

MAPLET, John (d. 1592), miscellaneous writer; fellow of Catharine Hall, Cambridge, 1564; MA, 1567; vicar of Northolt, Middlesex, 1576; wrote *A Greene Forest* (natural history, 1567) and *The Diall of Destinie* (1581).

MAPLET, John (1612?–1670), physician; MA, 1638, and MD, 1647, Christ Church, Oxford; principal of Gloucester Hall, Oxford, 1647; travelled in France with third Viscount Falkland and went to Holland; ejected from Oxford appointments; practised medicine at Bath; reinstated at Oxford, 1660; author of miscellaneous works in Latin, prose and verse.

MAPLETOFT, John (1631–1721), physician and divine; nephew of Robert *Mapletoft; educated at Westminster School; scholar and fellow (1653) of Trinity College, Cambridge; MA, 1655, and MD, 1667 (incorporated at Oxford, 1669); tutor to earl of *Northumberland's son; practised medicine in London with *Sydenham and became intimate with John *Locke; travelled abroad; Gresham professor of physic, 1675–9; successively rector of Braybrooke and St Lawrence Jewry, London; lecturer at Ipswich, 1685, and St Christopher's, London, 1685; DD, Cambridge, 1690; FRS, 1676; works include *The Principles and Duties of the Christian Religion* (1710).

MAPLETOFT, Robert (1609–1677), dean of Ely; MA, Pembroke College, Cambridge, 1632; fellow of Pembroke College, 1631; chaplain to Bishop *Wren; rector of Bartlow, 1639; ejected, 1644; officiated privately at Lincoln; DD at Restoration by royal mandate; sub-dean of Lincoln, 1660; master of Spital Hospital, 1660, reviving the charity; rector successively of Clayworth and Soham; master of Pembroke, 1664–77; vice-chancellor, 1671–2; dean of Ely, 1667–77; founded educational institutions.

MAPOTHER, Edward Dillon (1835–1908), surgeon; MD, Queen's University, Dublin, 1857; FRCS, Ireland, 1862; surgeon of St Vincent's Hospital, Dublin, 1859; professor of hygiene in Royal College of Surgeons, 1864; professor of anatomy and physiology, 1867; president, 1879; first medical officer of health for

Dublin; wrote much on diseases of the skin and public health.

MAPPIN, Sir Frederick Thorpe, first baronet (1821–1910), benefactor to Sheffield; head of father's cutlery business, 1841–59; senior partner in firm of Turton & Sons, steel manufacturers, 1859–85; mayor of Sheffield, 1877–8; a founder and benefactor of Sheffield Technical School; largely endowed Sheffield University; first senior pro-chancellor, 1905; director of Midland Railway, 1869–1900; enthusiastic Volunteer; Whig MP for East Retford, 1880–5, and for Hallamshire, 1885–1906; baronet, 1886; added 80 pictures to Mappin Art Gallery, founded by uncle; first honorary freeman of Sheffield, 1900.

MAPSON, Leslie William (1907–1970), biochemist; educated at Cambridge and County High School, and Fitzwilliam House (later College), Cambridge, 1928–30; began research in biochemistry under (Sir) F. G. *Hopkins and J. B. S. *Haldane; studied nutrition and enzyme catalysis; Ph.D., 1934; lecturer in biochemistry, Portsmouth College of Technology, 1934–8; scientific officer, Food Investigation Board, DSIR, 1938; seconded to Dunn Nutritional Laboratory, MRC, Cambridge, 1939; principal scientific officer, DSIR, 1950; senior principal scientific officer, 1956–67; FRS, 1969; hon. professor, East Anglia University.

MAR, earls of. See ERSKINE, JOHN, first or sixth earl of the Erskine line, d. 1572; ERSKINE, JOHN, second or seventh earl, 1558–1634; ERSKINE, JOHN, sixth or eleventh earl, 1675–1732; STEWART, ALEXANDER, earl of Mar, 1375?–1435; STEWART, JOHN, earl of Mar, 1457?–1479?; COCHRANE, ROBERT, earl of Mar, d. 1482; STEWART, Lord JAMES, earl of Mar, 1531?–1570.

MAR, Donald, tenth earl of (d. 1297), son of William *Mar, ninth earl of Mar; supported Edward I's suzerainty over Scotland; revolted, 1294, but returned to allegiance after battle of Dunbar, 1296.

MAR, Donald, twelfth earl of (1293?–1332), grandson of Donald *Mar, tenth earl of Mar, and nephew of Robert *Bruce; brought to England, 1306; was exchanged, 1314, after Bannockburn, but returned, preferring England; received grants; keeper of Newark Castle, 1321; joined Scots in raid, 1327; regent of Scotland, 1332; defeated by Baliol at Dupplin Moor and slain.

MAR, Thomas, thirteenth earl of (d. 1377), son of Donald *Mar, twelfth earl of Mar; Scottish commissioner to treat for peace with England, 1351, and hostage chamberlain of Scotland, 1358; entered service of Edward III, 1359; his castle seized by *David II, 1361, and

himself imprisoned, 1370; present at coronation of *Robert II, 1371.

MAR, William, ninth earl of (d. 1281?), one of the regents of Scotland, 1249, and great chamberlain, 1252–5; commanded expedition to reduce chiefs of Western Isles, 1263.

MARA, Mrs Gertrude Elizabeth (1749–1833), vocalist; née Schmeling; native of Kassel; violinist, but became singer; studied under Paradisi and Hiller; a better vocalist than actress; engaged by Frederick II at Berlin, 1771; married Johann Mara, who ill-treated her; escaped from Berlin, 1778, and toured on the continent; did not please Mozart; sang in London, 1784–7 and 1790–1802, chiefly in *Handel's music; settled at Moscow till 1812; ruined by the burning of Moscow, 1812; sang again in London, 1816; died at Revel; Goethe sent her a poem for her birthday, 1831.

MARA, William de (*fl.* 1280), Franciscan; studied at Paris under Bonaventura and Roger *Bacon; wrote *Correctorium* (criticism of Thomas Aquinas), first printed at Strasburg (1501), and other works.

MARBECK (or MERBECK), John (d. 1585?), musician and theologian; lay-clerk and afterwards organist of St George's Chapel, Windsor, 1541; Calvinist; arrested for possessing heretical writings, 1543; sentenced to be burnt, but pardoned through Gardiner's instrumentality, 1544; published his *Concordāce* (1550, the earliest concordance of whole English Bible), *The Boke of Common Praier noted* (1550), adaptation of plainchant to liturgy of 1549, and several other works, besides musical compositions.

MARBECK (MARKBEEKE or MERBECK), Roger (1536–1605), provost of Oriel College, Oxford, and physician; son of John *Marbeck; student of Christ Church, Oxford; MA, 1558; senior proctor and public orator; elegant Latinist, and twice pronounced oration before Elizabeth; prebendary of Hereford and canon of Christ Church; provost of Oriel, 1565; resigned all Oxford offices on account of discreditable marriage; MD, 1573; fellow and registrar of London College of Physicians and physician to Queen Elizabeth; accompanied *Howard in Cadiz expedition, 1596, and wrote account.

MARCET, Alexander John Gaspard (1770–1822), physician; MD, Edinburgh, 1797; physician and chemical lecturer at Guy's Hospital, London; professor of chemistry at Geneva, 1819; FRS, 1815; published medical and chemical papers.

MARCET, Mrs Jane (1769–1858), writer for the young; formerly Haldimand; of Swiss birth;

married Alexander John Gaspard *Marcet, 1799; wrote popular scientific textbooks, which obtained large circulation; her *Conversations on Political Economy* (1816) praised by *Macaulay.

MARCH, earls of, in the Scottish peerage. See DUNBAR, PATRICK, second earl, 1285–1369; STEWART, ALEXANDER, 1454?–1485; DOUGLAS, WILLIAM, third earl of the Douglas family, 1724–1810.

MARCH, earls of, in the English peerage. See MORTIMER, ROGER (IV) DE, first earl, 1287?–1330; MORTIMER, ROGER (V) DE, second earl, 1327?–1360; MORTIMER, EDMUND (II) DE, third earl, 1351–1381; MORTIMER, ROGER (VI) DE, fourth earl, 1374–1398; MORTIMER, EDMUND (IV) DE, fifth earl, 1391–1425.

MARCH, Mrs (1825–1877). See GABRIEL, MARY ANN VIRGINIA.

MARCH, John (1612–1657), legal writer; employed by Council of State during Commonwealth in various capacities; justice in Scotland, 1652; wrote *Actions for Slander* (1648), *Reports* (1648), *Amicus Reipublicae* (1651), and other works.

MARCH, John (1640–1692), vicar of Newcastle upon Tyne; educated at The Queen's College and St Edmund Hall, Oxford; MA, 1664; BD, 1674; tutor and (1664–72) vice-president of St Edmund Hall; vicar successively of Embleton, 1672–9, and Newcastle upon Tyne, 1679–92, and proctor for Durham; strong churchman and defended passive obedience; published sermons and a *Vindication* (1689).

MARCH, Samuel (1780–1862), legal writer. See PHILLIPPS, SAMUEL MARCH.

MARCH (DE LA MARCHE or DE MARCHIA), William (d. 1302), treasurer, and bishop of Bath and Wells; clerk of the Chancery, clerk of the king's wardrobe, c.1285; treasurer, 1290–5; prominent official during Edward I's absence; received various preferments; bishop of Bath and Wells, 1293; became unpopular through Edward I's exactions; removed from Treasury, 1295; built chapter-house at Wells; much venerated, 'miracles' being wrought at his tomb.

MARCHANT, Nathaniel (1739–1816), gem-engraver and medallist; studied under Edward *Burch and at Rome; exhibited at Royal Academy; RA, 1809; FSA; assistant engraver at the Mint, 1797; produced intaglios of great merit and delicacy; published catalogue (1792).

MARCHI, Giuseppe Filippo Liberati (1735?–1808), painter and engraver; assistant to Sir Joshua *Reynolds; excelled as a mezzotint engraver and copyist.

MARCHILEY, John (d. 1386?). See MARDISLEY.

MARCHMONT, earls of. See HUME, Sir PATRICK, first earl, 1641–1724; CAMPBELL, ALEXANDER, second earl, 1675–1740; HUME, HUGH, third earl, 1708–1794.

MARCKANT, John (*fl.* 1562), contributor to *Sternhold and *Hopkins's *Metrical Psalter* (1562); vicar of Clacton-Magna, 1559, and Shopland, 1563–8; wrote other works.

MARCUARD, Robert Samuel (1751–1792?), engraver.

MARDELEY, John (*fl.* 1548), clerk of the Mint and author.

MARDISLEY, John (d. 1386?), Franciscan; provincial minister; DD, Oxford before 1355; denied pope's temporal power in council at Westminster, 1374.

MARE, Sir Peter De La (*fl.* 1370). See DE LA MARE.

MARE, Thomas de la (1309–1396), abbot of St Albans; entered St Albans, 1326; prior of Tynemouth, 1340; abbot of St Albans, 1349; skilful administrator; member of Edward III's council; zealous defender of rights of abbey against exactions of the pope and of powerful courtiers, including Alice *Perrers, as well as against recalcitrant tenants; his abbey threatened in Peasant Rising, 1381, when tenants extorted privileges, afterwards withdrawn; benefactor of the abbey; spent much on the maintenance of scholars at Oxford.

MAREDUDD AB BLEDDYN (d. 1132), prince of Powys; brother of *Iorwerth and *Cadwgan; led resistance to invasion of Henry I, 1121; eventually became lord of all Powys.

MAREDUDD AB OWAIN (d. 999?), Welsh prince; son of Owain ap Hywel Dda, whom he succeeded, 988.

MARETT (or MARET), Philip (1568?–1637), attorney-general of Jersey, 1609; became involved in complicated feud with John *Herault, the bailiff, ordered to make submission by privy council, and imprisoned on refusal; lieutenant-governor, 1632.

MARETT, Sir Robert Pipon (1820–1884), attorney-general and bailiff of Jersey; descendant of Philip *Marett; distinguished judge; edited manuscripts of Philip *Le Geyt, 1847; wrote poems in Jersey patois.

MARETT, Robert Ranulph (1866–1943), anthropologist; son of Sir R. P. *Marett; educated at Victoria College, Jersey, and Balliol College, Oxford; first class, Lit. Hum., 1888; studied philosophy, Berlin University; fellow, Exeter College, Oxford, 1891; tutor in philosophy, 1893; sub-rector, 1893–8; rector, 1928–43; secretary, committee for anthropology, 1907–27; reader in social anthropology, 1910–36; developed the conception of 'Präanimismus'; publications include *Faith, Hope and Charity in Primitive Religion* (1932) and *Sacraments of Simple Folk* (1933); FBA, 1931.

MARFELD, John (*fl.* 1393). See MIRFELD.

MARGARET, Saint (d. 1093), queen of Scotland and sister of *Edgar Atheling; went to Scotland with him soon after Conquest, and married *Malcolm III, *c.*1067; had Roman use introduced into Scotland; reformed manners and customs; educated her sons with great care; died after hearing of slaughter of Malcolm her husband, and her eldest son; canonized, 1250.

MARGARET (1240–1275), queen of Scots; eldest daughter of Henry III of England; married *Alexander III of Scotland, 1251; was treated unkindly, but eventually was provided with proper household; her tyrannical guardians, Robert de Ros and John Baliol, punished, English influence being restored, 1255; visited England with her husband, 1256 and 1260; gave birth to eldest child, Margaret, 1261, to Alexander, 1264, and David, 1270; visited Henry III, 1268, and attended Edward I's coronation, 1274.

MARGARET (1282?–1318), queen of Edward I; daughter of Philip III of France; married Edward, as his second wife, 1299; gave birth to three children: *Thomas, 1300, *Edmund, 1301, and Margaret, 1306; crossed to Boulogne to be present at Edward II's marriage, 1308.

MARGARET, the Maid of Norway (1283–1290), queen of Scotland; daughter of Eric II of Norway and Margaret, daughter of *Alexander III of Scotland (1241–85), by his queen *Margaret, daughter of Henry III; acknowledged by nobles as heir of kingdom of Scotland, 1284; affianced to Prince Edward, son of Edward I, 1287; died in the Orkneys while on voyage from Bergen to England. A woman declaring herself to be Margaret was burned at Bergen, 1301, by King Hakon V, and was reverenced as a saint by many who believed her story.

MARGARET, duchess of Burgundy (1446–1503), sister of Edward IV; married Charles, duke of Burgundy, at Damme, 1468, thus cementing alliance between houses of York and Burgundy; reconciled *Clarence to his brother, Edward IV, the latter having been compelled to take refuge in Burgundy, 1470; patroness of *Caxton; visited England, 1480; on Henry VII's accession received discontented Yorkists at her

court, and encouraged the pretenders, Lambert *Simnel and Perkin *Warbeck; apologized to Henry VII, 1498; died at Mechlin.

MARGARET BEAUFORT, countess of Richmond and Derby (1443–1509). See BEAUFORT.

MARGARET OF ANJOU (1430–1482), queen consort of Henry VI; daughter of René of Anjou; brought up by her grandmother, Yolande of Aragon in Anjou; truce of Tours confirming her betrothal to Henry VI signed, 1444; married by proxy at Nancy, 1445, these events being brought about by Beaufort and the peace party; entered London and crowned at Westminster Abbey in same year, 1445; devoted her abilities towards identifying herself and Henry VI with one faction, the Beaufort-*Suffolk party; brought about Henry's surrender of possessions in Maine, 1445; appropriated greedily part of Duke *Humphrey's estates on his death, 1447; on fall of Suffolk (1449) transferred her confidence to Somerset, who incurred unpopularity by his loss of Normandy and Guienne; liberated Somerset from prison, 1450, and drove *Richard, duke of York, into violent courses; displayed covetousness and high-handedness; founded, with Andrew *Doket, Queens' College, Cambridge, 1448; gave birth to son *Edward, 1453; failed to secure regency on Henry's prostration, but on his recovery (1455) tried to crush York; defeated at St Albans, 1455, when *Somerset was killed, on which York again became protector; left Henry in disgust, 1456; was seemingly reconciled to York, 1458, but forthwith stirred up country against his party; communicated secretly with Brezé, seneschal of Normandy; on Henry's defeat at Northampton, 1460, fled with the prince into Cheshire, and after many adventures took refuge successively at Harlech Castle, at Denbigh, and in Scotland; signed treaty at Lincluden consenting to Edward's marriage with Mary of Scotland and surrendering Berwick, 1461; after victory at Wakefield (1460) marched to London and defeated *Warwick at St Albans, 1461; showed great brutality in execution of her enemies; after defeat at Towton (Mar. 1461) retired again to Scotland with Henry, surrendering Berwick to the Scots; went to Brittany and Anjou and appealed to Louis XI, 1462; invaded Northumberland with Brezé and French troops, but failed, 1462; protected by a robber; landed at Sluys, 1463, almost destitute; took refuge in Flanders and finally with her father; sent Jasper *Tudor to raise revolt in Wales, 1468; made treaty with Warwick at Angers, 1470; landed at Weymouth with forces, 1471, though meanwhile Warwick had been killed at Barnet (1471) and Henry was again a prisoner; marched north gathering contingents, but being blocked by Edward IV turned towards Wales; defeated at Tewkesbury and captured, her son being slain on the field and her husband being murdered soon after, 1471; remained imprisoned till released by Treaty of Pecquigny, 1476; was conveyed abroad and pensioned by Louis XI, but compelled to surrender all rights of succession to French territory; lived in extreme poverty and isolation in Anjou, and was buried at Angers; commemorated by Chastellain and Drayton. Shakespeare probably little responsible for the portrait of her in *King Henry VI*.

MARGARET OF DENMARK (1457?–1486), queen of James III of Scotland; daughter of Christian I of Denmark, Norway, and Sweden; married James III, 1469; part of her dowry being the Orkney and Shetland Isles; gave birth to heir (afterwards *James IV of Scotland), 1472.

MARGARET OF SCOTLAND (1425?–1445), wife of the dauphin Louis (afterwards Louis XI of France); daughter of *James I of Scotland; married Louis at Tours, 1436, and was treated badly by him; wrote poetry.

MARGARET TUDOR (1489–1541), queen of Scotland; eldest daughter of Henry VII; married *James IV of Scotland at Holyrood, 1503; crowned, 1504; gave birth to six children, two of whom survived, *James (afterwards James V) and Alexander; supported English party against the French; on James IV's death at Flodden, 1513, became regent and guardian of young king, but met with great opposition; secured peace with England, 1514; married Archibald *Douglas, sixth earl of Angus, 1514, whereby she strengthened French party; was besieged in Stirling and compelled to give up regency and young king to John *Stewart, duke of Albany, 1515; escaped to England and gave birth to Lady Margaret *Douglas, afterwards countess of Lennox; returned to Edinburgh, 1517, but the promise made her of dower, rents, and access to her son never fulfilled; quarrelled with her husband, Angus, 1518; joined French party; was allowed access to the king, but constantly changed sides; allied herself with Albany, 1521; was accused of 'over-tenderness' for him, and caused withdrawal of her husband, Angus, to France; played with both parties; carried off her son James to Edinburgh, and abrogated Albany's regency, but alienated support by rash actions, 1524; fired on Angus when he broke into Edinburgh, but admitted him to the regency, 1525; regained influence over her son James, but retired to Stirling on his refusal to allow return of Henry *Stewart, first Lord Methven, her favourite; obtained divorce from Angus, 1527, and married Stewart, and together with him became James's chief adviser on fall of Angus, 1528; helped to bring about

peace with England, 1534; accused by James of taking bribes from England, and treated with coldness by Henry VIII; interceded with Henry VIII for her daughter, Lady Margaret Douglas, 1536; endeavoured unsuccessfully to procure divorce from Henry Stewart; attempted to escape into England, but was overtaken, 1537; troubled Henry VIII with various complaints; died at Methven Castle; buried in the church of St John at Perth.

MARGARY, Augustus Raymond (1846–1875), traveller; interpreter in Chinese consular establishment; filled various appointments in China; travelled through south-western provinces to Yunnan to meet Colonel Browne, 1875, being the first Englishman to accomplish the journey; murdered at Manwein; obtained medals for saving life at Formosa, 1872.

MARGESSON, (Henry) David (Reginald), first Viscount Margesson (1890–1965), politician; educated at Harrow and Magdalene College, Cambridge; served with 11th Hussars during 1914–18 war; MC; Conservative MP, Upton division of West Ham, 1922–3; MP, Rugby, 1924–42; junior lord of the Treasury, 1926; parliamentary secretary to the Treasury, 1931; PC, 1933; government chief whip, 1931–40; secretary of state for war, 1940–2; displaced by his permanent under-secretary Sir (P.) James *Grigg; viscount, 1942.

MARGETSON, James (1600–1678), archbishop of Armagh; educated at Peterhouse, Cambridge; chaplain to Wentworth in Ireland, 1633; dean of Waterford, 1635; successively rector of Armagh and Galloon or Dartry; prebendary of Cork and dean of Derry, 1637; dean of Christ Church, Dublin, 1639; refused to use directory instead of Prayer-Book, 1647; fled to England, and was imprisoned; archbishop of Dublin, 1661–3; privy councillor, 1661; archbishop of Armagh, 1663–78, and vice-chancellor of Dublin University, 1667; rebuilt Armagh Cathedral.

MARGOLIOUTH, David Samuel (1858–1940), classical scholar and orientalist; scholar of Winchester and New College, Oxford; first class, Lit. Hum., 1880; won Hertford, Ireland, Craven, Derby, Boden Sanskrit, Pusey and Ellerton Hebrew, and Kennicott Hebrew scholarships; fellow, 1881; Laudian professor of Arabic, 1889–1937; ordained, 1899; works include an edition of *The Poetics of Aristotle* (1911), *Arabic Papyri of the Bodleian Library* (1893), *A Compendious Syriac Dictionary* (with his wife, 1896–1903), *Lines of Defence of the Biblical Revelation* (1900), *The Synoptic Gospels as Independent Witnesses* (1903), *Mohammed and the Rise of Islam* (1905), *Mohammedanism* (1911), and catalogue of Arabic papyri in the John Rylands Library, 1933; his editions of Arabic texts include Yāqūt's *Dictionary of Learned Men* (1907–27); his translations, *The Eclipse of the Abbasid Caliphate* (7 vols., 1920–1); FBA, 1915.

MARGOLIOUTH, Moses (1820–1881), divine; Jewish native of Suwalki, Poland; entered Church of England, 1838; taught Hebrew and other subjects; entered Trinity College, Dublin, 1840; ordained to curacy of St Augustine, Liverpool, 1844; incumbent of Glasnevin, 1844; examining chaplain to bishop of Kildare, 1844; served several curacies; visited the Holy Land, 1847; vicar of Little Linford, 1877–81; published *The Fundamental Principles of Modern Judaism* (1843) and other works.

MARHAM, Ralph (*fl.* 1380), historian; DD, Cambridge; prior of King's Lynn; wrote *Manipulus Chronicorum*.

MARIANUS SCOTUS (1028–1082?), chronicler; native of Ireland; his true name Moelbrigte; pupil of Tigernach; entered Cologne monastery, 1056; 'recluse' successively at Fulda and Mentz; wrote universal chronicle.

MARIANUS SCOTUS (or MUIREDACH) (d. 1088), first abbot of St Peter's, Ratisbon; famous for his calligraphy.

MARIE LOUISE, Princess (1872–1956), whose full names were Franziska Josepha Louise Augusta Marie Christiana Helena, daughter of Prince and Princess Christian and granddaughter of Queen Victoria; married Prince Aribert of Anhalt, 1891; marriage annulled, 1900; returned to England and devoted life to charitable, social, and artistic causes; published *My Memories of Six Reigns* (1956); GBE, 1919; GCVO, 1953.

MARILLIER, Henry Currie (1865–1951), journalist and expert on tapestries; born in South Africa; educated at Christ's Hospital and Peterhouse, Cambridge; joined *Pall Mall Gazette*, 1893; Swan Electric Engraving Co., 1896; Merton Abbey Tapestry Works of William *Morris, 1905; developed craft of tapestry repair; wound up company, 1940; published history of its tapestries, 1927; compiled subject-index and illustrated catalogue of European tapestries given to Victoria and Albert Museum, 1945; publications include *The Liverpool School of Painters 1810–67* (1904).

MARINA, duchess of Kent (1906–1968), youngest daughter of Prince and Princess Nicholas of Greece; educated in Paris; married Prince *George, fourth son of King George V and Queen *Mary, 1934; eldest son, Prince Edward, born, 1935; Princess Alexandra born, 1936; Prince Michael born, 1942; Prince George killed

in flying accident, 1942; commandant (later chief commandant), WRNS, 1940; president, Royal National Lifeboat Institution; president, All England Lawn Tennis Club; chancellor, Kent University; patron, National Association for Mental Health; colonel-in-chief, Queen's Own Royal West Kent Regiment and the Corps of Royal Electrical and Mechanical Engineers; CI and GBE, 1937; GCVO, 1948.

MARINER, William (*fl.* 1800–1860), traveller; detained in friendly captivity in the Tonga Islands, 1805–1810; communicated to John *Martin (1789–1869) materials for his *Account . . . of the Tonga Islands* (1817).

MARISCHAL, earls of. See KEITH, WILLIAM, fourth earl, d. 1581; KEITH, GEORGE, fifth earl, 1553?–1623; KEITH, WILLIAM, sixth earl, d. 1635; KEITH, WILLIAM, seventh earl, 1617?–1661; KEITH, GEORGE, tenth earl, 1693?–1778.

MARISCO, Adam de (d. 1257?). See ADAM.

MARISCO (MARISCIS, MAREYS, or **MARES), Geoffrey de** (d. 1245), justiciar or viceroy of Ireland; nephew of John *Comyn, archbishop of Dublin; powerful in South Munster and Leinster; received large grants of land in Ireland; defeated Hugh de *Lacy (d. 1242?) at Thurles; conquered Connaught, 1210; made protestation of loyalty to King John, 1211; justiciar of Ireland, 1215–21, 1226–8, and 1230–2; visited Henry III at Oxford and made agreement with him, leaving one of his sons as hostage, 1220; carried on private wars; treacherously brought about death of Richard *Marshal, 1234; being suspected of having plotted assassination of Henry III, 1238, fled to *Alexander II of Scotland; expelled from Scotland, 1244; died in poverty in France.

MARISCO, Hervey de (*fl.* 1169–1176). See MOUNT-MAURICE.

MARISCO (or MARSH), Richard de (d. 1226), bishop of Durham and chancellor; clerk of the Exchequer; held various preferments; advised King John's persecution of Cistercians, 1210; archdeacon of Northumberland before 1212, and Richmond, 1213; sheriff of Dorset and Somerset, 1212; suspended for officiating during interdict, 1212; visited Rome; justiciar; 1213–14; accompanied King John abroad, 1214; chancellor, 1214; sent on missions abroad, 1215; bishop of Durham, 1217–26; justice-itinerant, 1219; engaged in violent dispute with his monks; one of John's worst advisers.

MARJORIBANKS, Edward, second Baron Tweedmouth (1849–1909), politician; educated at Harrow and Christ Church, Oxford; a keen sportsman through life; toured round world,

1872–3; abandoned law for politics; Liberal MP for North Berwickshire, 1880–94; comptroller of Queen Victoria's household and PC, 1886; parliamentary secretary to the Treasury and chief Liberal whip under Gladstone, 1892; succeeded to peerage, 1894; joined Lord Rosebery's Cabinet as lord privy seal and chancellor of the duchy of Lancaster, 1894–5; married (1873) Lady Fanny (d. 1904), sister of Lord Randolph *Churchill, a successful society and political hostess; suffered financial losses, 1904; first lord of the Admiralty in Campbell-Bannerman's ministry, 1905–8; maintained policy of England's naval supremacy; incurred public censure for alleged premature disclosure of naval estimates to German Emperor, 1908; KT, 1908; lord president of Council under Asquith, 1908; died of cerebral malady.

MARKAUNT, Thomas (d. 1439), antiquary; BD; fellow of Corpus Christi College, Cambridge; proctor, 1417; said to have first collected the privileges, statutes, and laws of Cambridge University.

MARKHAM, Mrs (1780–1837). See PENROSE, ELIZABETH.

MARKHAM, Sir Albert Hastings (1841–1918), admiral and Arctic explorer; entered navy, 1856; commanded *Alert* in Arctic expedition of Sir G. S. *Nares, 1875–6; record of latitude reached without dogs lasted until 1895; rear-admiral, 1891; KCB, 1903.

MARKHAM, Sir Clements Robert (1830–1916), geographer and historical writer; cousin of Sir A. H. *Markham; served in navy, 1844–51; entered Civil Service, 1853; in charge of geographical work of India Office, 1867–77; CB, 1871; FRS, 1873; accompanied Arctic expedition of Sir G. S. *Nares, 1875; president of Hakluyt Society, 1889–1909, and of Royal Geographical Society, 1893–1905; KCB, 1896; promoted Antarctic exploration.

MARKHAM, Francis (1565–1627), soldier and author; brother of Gervase *Markham; fought in several campaigns abroad; muster-master at Nottingham; works include *Five Decades of Epistles of War* (1622).

MARKHAM, Frederick (1805–1855), lieutenant-general, son of John *Markham (1761–1827); joined 32nd Foot, 1824; imprisoned for acting as second in fatal duel, 1830; served in Canada and was wounded, 1837; commanded divisions in Punjab campaign, 1848–9, including victory at Gujerat; CB and aide-de-camp to the queen; adjutant-general in India, 1854; commanded division at attack on the Redan, 1855; published *Shooting in the Himalayas* (1854).

MARKHAM, Gervase (or **Jervis)** (1568?–1637), author; brother of Francis *Markham; fought in the Netherlands; a scholar acquainted with various languages; agricultural writer and reformer; said to have imported first Arab horse into England; 'earliest English hackney writer'; author of works and compilations, including *The most Honorable Tragedie of Sir Richard Grinvile* (1595), *The English Arcadia* (1607), *Discourse on Horsemanshippe* (1593), *Country Contentments* (1611), *The Souldier's Accidence* (1625), and *The Faithfull Farrier* (1635); collaborated in writing plays; styled 'a base fellow' by Ben *Jonson.

MARKHAM, Sir Griffin (1564?–1644?), soldier and conspirator; cousin of Francis and Gervase *Markham; served in Netherlands; with *Essex in France, where he was knighted, and in Ireland; concerned in the 'Bye' plot, 1603, convicted of high treason, but respited at moment of execution; banished and his estates confiscated; retired abroad.

MARKHAM, John (d. 1409), judge of common pleas, 1396; member of commission which carried out change of dynasty, 1399.

MARKHAM, Sir John (d. 1479), chief justice of England; son of John *Markham (d. 1409); serjeant-at-law, 1440; judge, 1444; KB and chief justice of King's Bench, 1461; deprived, 1469; famous for his impartiality.

MARKHAM, John (1761–1827), admiral; son of William *Markham; entered navy, 1775; served on North America and West Indies stations; nearly wrecked and murdered when in charge of prize ship, 1777; cashiered for firing upon a French cartel, 1782, but reinstated by *Rodney and promoted post-captain, 1783; commanded *Sphynx* in Mediterranean, 1783–6; travelled, 1786–93; served under Lord *St Vincent at reduction of Martinique, 1793, off Cadiz, 1797, in Mediterranean, 1799, and off Brest, 1800; colleague of St Vincent at Admiralty Board, 1801–4, and of *Howick and *Grenville, 1806–7; MP, Portsmouth, 1807–26 (except 1818–20).

MARKHAM, Peter (*fl.* 1758), writer on adulteration of bread, 1758; MD.

MARKHAM, Violet Rosa (1872–1959), public servant; granddaughter of Sir Joseph *Paxton; daughter of Chesterfield colliery owner; made home in London meeting place for notable people in politics, the arts, and social service; joined Liberal party; served from 1914 on, and for many years chairman of, Central Committee on Women's Training and Employment; member, executive committee, National Relief Fund; member, Industrial Court, 1919–46; joined Assistance Board, 1934; deputy chairman,

1937–46; member, Appeals Tribunal on Internment, 1939–45; chairman, Investigation Committee on Welfare of Service Women, 1942; mayor of Chesterfield, 1927; married (1915) Lt.-Col. James Carruthers (d. 1936); published autobiography, *Return Passage* (1953); CH, 1917; hon. Litt.D., Sheffield, 1936; hon. LL D, Edinburgh, 1938.

MARKHAM, William (1719–1807), archbishop of York; descended from John *Markham (d. 1409); educated at Westminster School; student of Christ Church, Oxford; BA, 1742; MA, 1745; DCL, 1752; one of the best scholars of the day; published Latin verse; headmaster of Westminster School, 1753–65; chaplain to George II, 1756; prebendary of Durham, 1759; dean of Rochester, 1765; vicar of Boxley, 1765; dean of Christ Church, Oxford, 1767; bishop of Chester, 1771; preceptor to George, prince of Wales and Prince Frederick, 1771, but dismissed, 1776; archbishop of York, 1777; lord high almoner and privy councillor, 1777; denounced by Chatham and others for preaching 'pernicious' doctrines; attacked by Gordon rioters, 1780; used intemperate language in defence of Warren *Hastings, which was brought under notice of parliament, 1793; at one time intimate friend of *Burke.

MARKLAND, Abraham (1645–1728), master of St Cross Hospital, Winchester; scholar and fellow of St John's College, Oxford; MA, 1689; DD, 1692; master of St Cross, Winchester, 1694–1728; held several livings, and Winchester prebend; published poems and sermons.

MARKLAND, James Heywood (1788–1864), antiquary; London solicitor, 1808 and 1839; FSA, 1809; parliamentary agent to West Indian planters, 1814; student, Inner Temple, 1814; FRS, 1816; edited for Roxburghe Club, which (1813) he joined, *Chester Mysteries* (1818); assisted and contributed to various publications, including papers for the *Archaeologia*; wrote *On the Reverence due to Holy Places* (1845) and several other works.

MARKLAND, Jeremiah (1693–1776), classical scholar; of Christ's Hospital, London, and St Peter's College, Cambridge; MA, 1717; fellow and tutor, 1717; contributed poetry to *Cambridge Gratulations* (1724); engaged in private tuition; settled finally at Milton Court, near Dorking; published *Epistola Critica* (on Horace, 1723), *Remarks on the Epistles of Cicero* (1745), and other works.

MARKS, David Woolf (1811–1909), Goldsmid professor of Hebrew at University College, London, from 1844 to 1898; secretary to the Hebrew congregation at Liverpool, 1833; first minister with Albert *Löwy of newly established West London congregation, 1842–95; prepared reformed prayer book, and obtained licence for marriages, 1857; hon. DD, Cincinnati; published lectures on Mosaic law.

MARKS, Henry Stacy (1829–1898), artist; employed in his father's coach-building business to paint heraldic devices on carriages; studied art under James Mathews *Leigh; entered Royal Academy schools, 1851; exhibited at Royal Academy from 1853; executed wall-paintings, representing the Canterbury pilgrims, in Eaton Hall, Cheshire, 1876–8; RA, 1878; member of Royal Water-Colour Society, 1883. His earlier pictures were largely humorous Shakespearian subjects; in later years he specialized in natural-history subjects (principally birds), but produced also land- and seascapes.

MARKS, Simon, first Baron Marks of Broughton (1888–1964), retailer and business innovator; son of Jewish immigrant from Poland who founded Marks and Spencer Ltd.; educated at Manchester Grammar School; studied languages and business methods in Europe; joined father's firm, 1907; director, 1911; chairman, 1916–64; joined by his friend and brother-in-law, Israel (later Lord) *Sieff, 1915; joined Royal Artillery during 1914–18 war; seconded to Chaim *Weizmann, to set up Zionist headquarters in London, 1917; Marks and Spencer incorporated as public company, 1926; registered 'St Michael', the firm's brand name, 1928; deputy chairman, London and South Eastern Regional Production Board and adviser to Petroleum Warfare Department during 1939–45 war; one of first directors, British Overseas Airways; benefactor to Royal College of Surgeons, University College, London, Manchester Grammar School, British Heart Foundation, and the cause of Israel; knighted, 1944; baron, 1961; vice-president, Zionist Federation; hon. D.Sc. (Economics), London; LL D, Manchester; Ph.D., Hebrew University, Jerusalem; hon. fellow, Royal College of Surgeons, Weizmann Institute of Science, and University College, London.

MARKWICK (or MARKWICKE), Nathaniel (1664–1735), divine; MA, St John's College, Oxford, 1690; BD (as Markwith), 1696; prebendary of Bath and Wells, 1699; works include *Stricturae Lucis* (1728).

MARLBOROUGH, dukes of. See CHURCHILL, JOHN, first duke, 1650–1722; SPENCER, CHARLES, third duke, 1706–1758; SPENCER, GEORGE, fourth duke, 1739–1817; SPENCER, GEORGE, fifth duke, 1766–1840; CHURCHILL, JOHN WINSTON SPENCER, seventh duke, 1822–1883.

MARLBOROUGH, earls of. See LEY, JAMES, first earl, 1550–1629; LEY, JAMES, third earl, 1618–1665.

MARLBOROUGH, Henry of (*fl.* 1420). See HENRY.

MARLBOROUGH, Sarah, duchess of (1660–1744). See CHURCHILL, SARAH.

MARLEBERGE, Thomas de (d. 1236), abbot of Evesham; learned in canon and civil law; taught at Oxford; monk of Evesham, 1199 or 1200; engaged in dispute with bishop of Worcester concerning right of visitation of monastery; went to Rome and obtained verdict of exemption, 1205; quarrelled with Abbot *Norris; expelled and attacked with his companions, 1206, but beat off assailants; effected deposition of Norris, 1213; made abbot, 1229; paid off the abbey's debts and carried out numerous and important restorations and adornments; architect, mechanical workman, painter, and embroiderer; wrote *Chronicon Abbatiae de Evesham* and other works.

MARLOW, William (1740–1813), water-colour painter; member of Society of Artists; exhibited there and at Academy; painted mostly English country seats and scenes; worked also in oil.

MARLOWE, Christopher (1564–1593), dramatist; son of a Canterbury shoemaker; educated at King's School, Canterbury, and Corpus Christi College, Cambridge; MA, 1587; attached himself to earl of Nottingham's theatrical company, which produced most of his plays; acquainted with leading men of letters, including *Ralegh; wrote, not later than 1587, *Tamburlaine* (published 1590), in which he gave new development to blank verse; wrote *The Tragedy of Dr Faustus* (first entered on *Stationers' Register*, 1601, but not apparently published till 1604), which was well received; produced after 1588, *The Jew of Malta* (first published 1633), *Edward II*, the best-constructed of his plays, 1593 (first published 1594), and two inferior pieces, the *Massacre at Paris* (probably published 1600) and *Tragedy of Dido* (joint work of Marlowe and *Nashe), published 1594; pointed to as part author of Shakespeare's *Titus Andronicus* by internal evidence; wrote much of the second and third parts of *Henry VI*, which Shakespeare revised and completed, and of *Edward III*; translated Ovid's *Amores* (published with Sir John *Davies's *Epigrammes and Elegies*, *c.*1597); paraphrased part of Musaeus's *Hero and Leander* (completed by George *Chapman and published 1598); translated *The First Book of Lucan*['s Pharsalia] (published 1600); wrote the song 'Come live with me and be my love' (published in *The Passionate Pilgrim*, 1599, and in *England's Helicon*); held and propagated atheistical opinions, and a warrant issued for his arrest, 1593; killed in a drunken brawl at Deptford; probably not guilty of the blasphemy and gross immorality often ascribed to him; spoken of with affection by Edward *Blount, Nashe, and Chapman; his 'mighty line' spoken of by Ben *Jonson; quoted and apostrophized by Shakespeare in *As you like it*. Marlowe excelled in portraying human ambition and exerted much influence over Shakespeare. His collected works were first published (1826).

MARLOWE, Thomas (1868–1935), journalist; educated at Queen's College, Galway; joined the *Star* (1888), *Evening News* (1894); managing editor, *Daily Mail*, 1899–1926.

MARMION, Philip (d. 1291), grandson of Robert Marmion (d. 1218); sheriff of Warwickshire and Leicestershire, 1249, of Norfolk and Suffolk, 1261; taken prisoner fighting for the king at Lewes, 1264.

MARMION, Robert (d. 1143), carried on war during anarchy in Stephen's reign; killed in fight with earl of *Chester at Coventry.

MARMION, Robert (d. 1218), justice-itinerant and reputed king's champion; descended from lords of Fontenay le Marmion in Normandy, grandson of Robert *Marmion (d. 1143); sheriff of Worcester, 1186; attended Richard I and King John in Normandy; sided with barons against King John; benefactor of Kirkstead Abbey, Lincolnshire.

MARMION, Shackerley (1603–1639), dramatist; MA, Wadham College, Oxford, 1624; soldier for a short time in the Netherlands; settled in London and was patronized by Ben *Jonson, whose dramatic work he imitated; convicted of stabbing, 1629; joined *Suckling's expedition to Scotland, 1638; wrote *A Morall Poem intituled the Legend of Cupid and Psyche*, 1637 (in heroic couplets); contributed poetry to *Annalia Dubrensia* (1636) and to *Jonsonus Virbius* (1638); produced the comedies *Hollands Leaguer* (1632), *A Fine Companion* (1633), and *The Antiquary* (published 1641).

MARNOCK, Robert (1800–1889), landscape-gardener; laid out botanical gardens in Sheffield and Regent's Park, London, becoming curator; carried out designs at Greenlands, Henley-on-Thames, Taplow Court, San Donato, near Florence, and Alexandra Park, Hastings; his designs distinguished by good taste and 'picturesqueness'; edited *Floricultural Magazine* (1836–42) and other gardening publications, and wrote with Deakin first volume of *Florigraphia Britannica* (1837).

MAROCHETTI, Carlo (1805–1867), sculptor, baron of Italy; studied at Paris and Rome; executed statue of Emmanuel Philibert of Savoy for Turin, and other work; made baron by Carlo Alberto, later patronized by Louis-Philippe; executed at Paris statue of duke of Orleans, relief of *Assumption* in the Madeleine, and other sculptures; given Legion of Honour, 1839; patronized by Queen Victoria and Prince *Albert after 1848; exhibited *Sappho* and other work at Academy, and statue of Richard Cœur de Lion at Great Exhibition, 1851; executed statues of Queen Victoria, the duke of Wellington, and others, the Inkerman monument in St Paul's Cathedral, and other monuments and busts; RA, 1866; advocate of polychromy in sculpture.

MARPLES, (Alfred) Ernest, Baron Marples (1907–1978), politician; educated at council school and grammar school in Manchester suburb of Stretford; qualified as chartered accountant, 1928; entered building industry, 1929 and established Marples, Ridgway, and Partners, building contractors; served in Royal Artillery during 1939–45 war; Conservative MP for Wallasey, 1945; parliamentary secretary to Ministry of Housing and Local Government, 1951–4; supervised housing campaign; joint parliamentary secretary, Ministry of Pensions and National Insurance, 1954–5; postmaster-general, 1957–9; identified with introduction of Ernie premium bonds; entered Cabinet as minister of transport, 1959; concerned with motorways, seat-belts, yellow lines, parking meters, and other innovations, 1959–64; also concerned with Beeching Report on railways, and defence of British shipping interests; shadow minister for technology, 1964; PC, 1957; freeman of Wallasey, 1970; life peer, 1974.

MARQUAND, Hilary Adair (1901–1972), economist and politician; educated at Cardiff High School and University College, Cardiff, where he was a state scholar; first class, history, 1923 and economics, 1924; spent two years in USA with Laura Spelman Rockefeller Foundation fellowship; lecturer in economics, Birmingham University, 1926–30; professor of industrial relations, Cardiff, 1930; studied industrial relations in USA, 1932–3; visiting professor, University of Wisconsin, 1938–9; published *The Dynamics of Industrial Combination* (1931) and *Industrial Relations in the United States of America* (1934); editor and co-author of *Organized Labour in Four Continents* (1939); also published *Industrial Survey of South Wales* (1931) and *South Wales Needs a Plan* (1936); temporary civil servant during 1939–45 war; Labour MP for Cardiff East, 1945–50 and for Middlesborough East, 1950–61; secretary for overseas trade, 1945–7; paymaster-general, 1947–8; minister of pensions, 1948–51; PC, 1949; succeeded Aneurin *Bevan as minister of health, 1951; chief opposition spokesman on Commonwealth affairs, 1959; director, Institute of Labour Studies, ILO, Geneva, 1961–5; deputy chairman, Prices and Incomes Board, 1965–8.

MARQUIS, Frederick James, first earl of Woolton (1883–1964), politician and business man; educated at Manchester Grammar School and Manchester University; B.Sc., 1906; schoolteacher, 1906–10; research fellow, Manchester University, 1910; MA, 1912; warden, David Lewis Hotel and Club Association, Liverpool, and warden, University Settlement, 1912; secretary, Leather Control Board, 1914; secretary, Federation of the Boot Industry; joined board of Lewis's, Liverpool; joint managing director, 1928; chairman, 1936–51; member, advisory councils to Overseas Development Committee, 1928–31, Board of Trade, 1930–4, and Post Office, 1933–47; president, Retail Distributors Association, 1930–3; chairman, 1934; director-general, Ministry of Supply, 1939; minister of food, 1940; minister of reconstruction, 1943–5; joined Conservative party, 1945; party chairman, 1946–55; lord president of the Council, 1951–2; chancellor of the duchy of Lancaster, 1952–5; minister of materials, 1953–4; knighted, 1935; baron, 1939; PC, 1940; CH, 1942; viscount, 1953; earl, 1956; chairman, executive committee, British Red Cross Society, 1943–63; chancellor, Manchester University, 1944; honorary degrees, Manchester, Liverpool, Cambridge, McGill, and Hamilton College.

MARR, John Edward (1857–1933), geologist; educated at Lancaster Grammar School and St John's College, Cambridge; first class, natural sciences tripos (geology), 1878; fellow, 1881–1933; university lecturer in geology, 1886–1917; professor, 1917–30; authority on the palaeozoic strata; influential teacher; FRS, 1891.

MARRABLE, Frederick (1818–1872), architect; superintending architect to Metropolitan Board of Works, 1856–62; constructed offices in Spring Gardens, besides other important London buildings.

MARRAS, Giacinto (1810–1883), singer and musical composer; born at Naples and studied music there; came to England, 1835; sang at, and gave, concerts with Grisi, *Lablache, *Balfe, and others; visited Russia, 1842, and Vienna and Naples later; was in Paris, 1844; settled in England, 1846; published songs and other works; sang in public; instituted *après-midis musicales* at his own house; visited India, 1870–3, and the Riviera, 1879; possessed immense repertoire of oratorio, opera, and chamber music; as composer belongs to Italian school; published also *Lezioni di Canto* and *Elementi Vocali* (1850), valuable treatises on singing.

MARRAT, William (1772–1852), mathematician and topographer; contributed to mathematical serials; printer and publisher at Boston, Lincolnshire, and teacher of mathematics; works include *An Introduction to the Theory and Practice of Mechanics* (1810) and *The History of Lincolnshire* (1814–16).

MARREY (or MARRE), John (d. 1407), Carmelite; scholastic theologian, disputant, and preacher; head of Doncaster Convent; wrote scholastic treatises and other works.

MARRIAN, Guy Frederic (1904–1981), biochemist; educated at Tollington School, London, and University College, London; B.Sc., (Hons.), 1925; research student working on pregnanediol and oestriol, 1925–31; D.Sc., 1930; FRIC, 1931; continued research at Toronto University, Canada, 1933–9; FRS (Canada), 1937; professor of chemistry in relation to medicine, Edinburgh, 1939–59; during 1939–45 war studied poison gas, arsine; FRSE, 1940; FRS, 1944; director of research, Imperial Cancer Research Fund, 1959–68; made important contribution to steroid endocrinology; fellow, University College, London, 1946; CBE, 1969; hon. DM, Edinburgh, 1975; recipient of number of academic awards.

MARRIOTT, Charles (1811–1858), divine; son of John *Marriott (1780–1825); scholar of Balliol College, Oxford; BA, 1832; fellow, mathematical lecturer, and tutor of Oriel College, Oxford, 1833; principal of Theological College, Chichester, 1839; sub-dean of Oriel College, Oxford, 1841; disciple of *Newman till Newman went over to Rome; had great influence among younger men at Oxford; vicar of St Mary the Virgin, 1850–8; member of Hebdomadal Council; published sermons and pamphlets, and edited with *Pusey and *Keble 'The Library of the Fathers', 1841–55, also *The Literary Churchman* from 1855, and other publications.

MARRIOTT, Sir James (1730?–1803), lawyer and politician; scholar and (1756) fellow of Trinity Hall, Cambridge; LL D, 1757; patronized by duke of *Newcastle; advocate-general, 1764; master of Trinity Hall, 1764; vice-chancellor, 1767; judge of Admiralty court, 1778; knighted, 1778; MP, Sudbury, 1781–4 and 1796–1802; declared America to be represented in the English parliament by the member for Kent, the thirteen provinces being described in their charters as part and parcel of the manor of Greenwich,

1782; published poems and legal and political works.

MARRIOTT, John (d. 1653), 'the great eater', known as 'Ben Marriott'; celebrated in *The Great Eater of Graye's Inn* (pasquinade, 1652), where his insatiable appetite is described in detail.

MARRIOTT, John (1780–1825), poet and divine; student, Christ Church, Oxford; MA, 1806; tutor to Lord Scott, 1804–8, and intimate of Sir Walter *Scott, who addressed to him the second canto of *Marmion*; rector of Church Lawford, Warwickshire, 1807; held curacies in Devonshire; contributed poems to Scott's *Minstrelsy of the Scottish Border* and author of several others, including 'Marriage is like a Devonshire Lane', and hymns, also of sermons.

MARRIOTT, Sir John Arthur Ransome (1859–1945), historian, educationist, and politician; educated at Repton and New College, Oxford; lecturer, modern history, Worcester College, 1885–1920; secretary, Oxford University Extension Delegacy, 1895–1920; Conservative MP, Oxford City, 1917–22, York, 1923–9; successful popularizer and voluminous writer on history, biography, and politics; knighted, 1924.

MARRIOTT, Wharton Booth (1823–1871), divine; scholar of Trinity College, Oxford, 1843–6; fellow of Exeter College, Oxford, 1846–51; BCL, 1851; MA, 1856; BD, 1870; university preacher, 1868; Grinfield lecturer, 1871; assistant-master at Eton, 1850–60; FSA, 1857; published *Vestiarium Christianum* (1868) and other works.

MARRIOTT, Sir William Thackeray (1834–1903), judge-advocate-general; BA, St John's College, Cambridge, 1858; curate of St George's, Hulme, 1858; renounced orders, 1861; called to bar, 1864; acquired lucrative practice in railway and compensation cases; QC, 1877; Liberal MP for Brighton, 1880–4; re-elected for Brighton as Conservative, 1884–93; PC, 1885; judge-advocate-general, 1885–92; knighted, 1888; chancellor of Primrose League, 1892; counsel for ex-Khedive Ismail Pasha in claims against Egyptian government, 1887–8; made unsuccessful financial speculations; died at Aix-la-Chapelle.

MARRIS, Sir William Sinclair (1873–1945), Indian civil servant; educated at Wanganui, Canterbury College, New Zealand, and Christ Church, Oxford; posted to North-West Provinces and Oudh, 1896; under-secretary, Indian Home Department, 1901; deputy secretary, 1904–6; lent to Transvaal government, 1906–8; intimately associated with *Milner's 'kindergarten' and member of Round Table group; joint secretary, Home Department, India, 1917;

drafted Montagu–Chelmsford Report, Nov. 1917–April 1918; reforms commissioner, 1919–21; governor of Assam, 1921–2, of United Provinces, 1922–7; principal, Armstrong College, Newcastle upon Tyne, 1929–37; advocated union of two Newcastle colleges; translated Horace (1912), Catullus (1924), and Homer (*Odyssey* 1925, *Iliad* 1934) into English verse; KCIE, 1919; KCSI, 1921.

MARROWE, George (*fl.* 1437), alchemist.

MARRYAT, Florence (1838–1899), successively Mrs Church and Mrs Lean; novelist; daughter of Frederick *Marryat; married, firstly, T. Ross Church, afterwards colonel in Madras Staff Corps, 1854, and secondly, Colonel Francis Lean of Royal Marine Light Infantry, 1890; published from 1865 many novels, works dealing with spiritualism, and *Life and Letters of Captain Marryat* (1872).

MARRYAT, Frederick (1792–1848), captain, RN, and novelist; grandson of Thomas *Marryat; served under Lord *Cochrane in the *Impérieuse*, which performed several brilliant actions, including attack on French fleet in Aix Roads, 1809; took part in Walcheren expedition, 1809; served on Mediterranean, West Indies, North America, and St Helena stations; commanded the *Larne* in first Burmese War, 1823; senior naval officer at Rangoon, 1824; commanded successful expedition up Bassein River, 1825; appointed to the *Tees*, 1825, and *Ariadne*, 1828; CB, 1826; gold medallist, Royal Humane Society, for saving life at sea; adapted Popham's signalling system to mercantile marine; FRS, 1819; member of Legion of Honour, 1833; published *The Naval Officer* (1829) and series of well-known novels of sea-life, including *Peter Simple* (1834) and *Mr Midshipman Easy* (1836), largely autobiographical; published children's books and other works, and (1832–5) edited *Metropolitan Magazine*; lived for some time at Brussels and in Canada and the United States.

MARRYAT, Thomas (1730–1792), physician and wit; belonged to poetical club which met at the Robin Hood, Butcher Row, Strand; was educated for Presbyterian ministry; MD, Edinburgh; practised in London, America, Ireland, and elsewhere, finally settling at Bristol; administered strange remedies; published *The Philosophy of Masons, Therapeutics* (1758), and verses, and other works.

MARSDEN, Alexander Edwin (1832–1902), surgeon; son of William *Marsden; MRCS, 1854; MD, St Andrews, 1862; FRCS, Edinburgh, 1868; served as surgeon at Scutari and Sevastopol; surgeon to Royal Free Hospital,

1853–84; and to Brompton Cancer Hospital; published works on cancer.

MARSDEN, Sir Ernest (1889–1970), atomic physicist and science administrator; educated at Queen Elizabeth's Grammar School, Blackburn, and Manchester University; worked with (Lord) *Rutherford on radioactivity, 1907–9; John Harling fellow, Manchester University, 1911; lecturer and research assistant, 1912–13; professor of physics, Victoria University College, Wellington, New Zealand, 1914; served in France, 1914–18; MC, 1919; returned as teacher and administrator to Victoria College, 1919; assistant director of education, 1922–6; permanent secretary, New Zealand Department of Scientific and Industrial Research, 1926–47; trained in England in radar production, 1939; scientific adviser to New Zealand fighting services (lieutenant-colonel); attended Empire Scientific Congress, 1946; New Zealand scientific liaison officer, London, 1947–54; CBE, 1935; FRS, CMG, 1946; knighted, 1958; honorary degrees, Oxford (1946), Manchester (1961), and Victoria University, Wellington (1965).

MARSDEN, John Buxton (1803–1870), historical writer; MA, St John's College, Cambridge, 1830; vicar of Great Missenden, Buckinghamshire, 1844; perpetual curate of St Peter, Dale End, Birmingham, 1851; works include *The History of the Early Puritans* (1850), *The History of the Later Puritans* (1852), *History of Christian Churches* (1856).

MARSDEN, John Howard (1803–1891), antiquary; scholar of St John's College, Cambridge, and Bell scholar; Seatonian prizeman, 1829; MA, 1829; BD, 1836; select preacher, 1834, 1837, and 1847; Hulsean lecturer, 1843 and 1844, and Disney professor of archaeology, 1851–65; rector of Great Oakley, Essex, 1840–89, and rural dean; published religious, archaeological, and historical works, and verses.

MARSDEN, Samuel (1764–1838), apostle of New Zealand; tradesman's son; studied at Magdalene College, Cambridge; chaplain in New South Wales, 1793; had charge of convicts; while on visit to London in 1807 obtained audience of George III, who presented him with five Spanish sheep, the progenitors of extensive Australian flocks; made several visits to New Zealand, and was one of the chief settlers of that country; endeavoured to improve the standard of morals; was attacked by authorities, but defended himself successfully before commission, 1820; died at Parramatta.

MARSDEN, William (1754–1836), orientalist and numismatist; entered East India Company's service, 1770; secretary to government at Sumatra; established agency business in London, 1785; second secretary, 1795, and secretary, 1804, to Admiralty; FRS, 1783; subsequently treasurer and vice-president; member of various learned societies; DCL, Oxford, 1786; published *History of Sumatra* (1783), *Dictionary and Grammar of the Malayan Language* (1812), *Numismata Orientalia* (1823–5), and other works; presented his collection of oriental coins to British Museum, 1834.

MARSDEN, William (1796–1867), surgeon; worked under Abernethy at St Bartholomew's Hospital; MRCP, 1827; founded Royal Free Hospital, London, where poor were admitted immediately without formalities, and Brompton Cancer Hospital; MD, Erlangen, 1838; published *Symptoms and Treatment of . . . Asiatic . . . Cholera* (1834).

MARSH. See also MARISCO.

MARSH, Alphonso, the elder (1627–1681), musician to Charles I; gentleman of the Chapel Royal, *c.*1661; composed songs.

MARSH, Alphonso, the younger (1648?–1692), musician; son of Alphonso *Marsh the elder; gentleman of the Chapel Royal, 1676.

MARSH, Charles (1735–1812), clerk in War Office; fellow of Trinity College, Cambridge; MA, 1760; FSA, 1784; buried in Westminster Abbey.

MARSH, Charles (1774?–1835?), barrister, Lincoln's Inn; practised at Madras; MP, East Retford, 1812; distinguished himself by knowledge of Indian affairs and denounced Wilberforce's attempt to force Christianity on natives; contributed to various publications and wrote able pamphlets.

MARSH, Dame (Edith) Ngaio (1899–1982), detective novelist and theatre director; born in Christchurch, New Zealand; educated at St Margaret's College and Canterbury University School of Art, Christchurch; joined Allan Wilkie Shakespeare Company, 1920–3; theatrical producer, 1923–7; worked as interior decorator in England, 1928–32; published first of thirty-one detective novels, *A Man Lay Dead* (1934), creating character of Roderick Alleyn of Scotland Yard; during 1939–45 war served as driver for Red Cross transport unit; produced Shakespeare's plays in New Zealand, 1944–52; in London directed Pirandello's *Six Characters in Search of an Author* at Embassy Theatre, 1950; published autobiography, *Black Beech and Honeydew* (1966, revised 1981); OBE, 1948; DBE, 1966; hon. Dr.Litt., Canterbury University, 1956; Ngaio Marsh Theatre founded there, 1962.

MARSH, Sir Edward Howard (1872–1953), civil servant, scholar, and patron of the arts; great grandson of Spencer *Perceval; educated at Westminster and Trinity College, Cambridge; first class, parts i and ii, classical tripos, 1893–5; an 'Apostle'; entered Colonial Office, 1896; worked for (Sir) Winston Churchill at Colonial Office, 1906–8, Board of Trade, 1908–10, Home Office, 1910–11, Admiralty, 1911–15, Munitions, 1917, War Office, 1919–21, Colonial Office, 1921–2, and Treasury, 1924–9; in Dominions Office, 1930–7; retired, 1937; corrected proofs of Churchill's literary writings from *Marlborough* (4 vols., 1933–8) onwards; also sixteen works by Somerset *Maugham; began collecting pictures, 1896; acquired Horne collection, 1904; became patron of contemporary British painting and literature; edited five volumes of *Georgian Poetry*, 1912–22; literary executor of Rupert *Brooke, whose collected poems he published, 1918; translations include La Fontaine's Fables (2 vols., 1931) and *Odes of Horace* (1941); published reminiscences, *A Number of People* (1939); trustee of Tate Gallery; governor of Old Vic; chairman, Contemporary Art Society, 1936–52; KCVO, 1937.

MARSH, Francis (1627–1693), archbishop of Dublin; MA, Emmanuel College, Cambridge, 1650; fellow of Caius College, Cambridge, 1651; praelector rhetoricus, 1651–2 and 1654–7; dean of Connor, 1660; dean of Armagh and archdeacon of Dromore, 1661; bishop of Limerick, Ardfert, and Aghadoe, 1667; translated to Kilmore and Ardagh, 1672; archbishop of Dublin, 1682; opposed *Tyrconnel; withdrew to England, 1689, and was included in Act of Attainder; returned after Battle of the Boyne, 1690.

MARSH, George (1515–1555), Protestant martyr; farmer; matriculated from Christ's College, Cambridge, 1551; lived at Cambridge and also acted as curate in Leicestershire and London; preached in Lancashire and was imprisoned at Lancaster, 1554, and Chester; burnt at Spital Boughton, his character and sufferings giving rise to marvellous traditions.

MARSH, Sir Henry, first baronet (1790–1860), physician; descended from Francis *Marsh; BA, 1812, and MD, 1840, Dublin; professor of medicine at Dublin College of Surgeons, 1827; president of the Irish College of Physicians, 1841, 1842, 1845, and 1846; physician to the queen, 1837; created baronet, 1839; clinical teacher and medical author.

MARSH, Herbert (1757–1839), successively bishop of Llandaff and Peterborough; educated at King's School, Canterbury; scholar of St John's College, Cambridge, 1775; second wrangler and second Smith's prizeman, 1779; fellow, 1779; MA, 1782; DD (by royal mandate), 1808; FRS, 1801; studied at Leipzig; returned to Leipzig after prosecution of William *Frend; published translation of Michaelis's *Introduction to the New Testament*, with original notes (1793–1801), which aroused a great controversy; supported English national credit by publishing translation of an essay by Patje (president of the Board of Finance at Hanover), 1797; his *History of the Politics of Great Britain and France* widely read, 1799; given pension by Pitt and proscribed by Napoleon; Lady Margaret professor at Cambridge, 1807; gave several courses on biblical criticism, which were attended by crowded audiences; preached anti-Calvinistic sermons before university, 1805; opposed establishment of Bible Society in Cambridge; wrote various pamphlets and was answered by *Simeon and *Milner; published *Comparative View of the Churches of England and Rome* (1814) and *Horae Pelasgicae* (1815); bishop of Llandaff, 1816, of Peterborough, 1819; endeavoured to exclude Evangelical clergy from diocese by his notorious 'eighty-seven questions'; successfully defended himself in House of Lords; denounced by Sydney *Smith; opposed hymns in services and Catholic emancipation; foremost divine at Cambridge; a vigorous but often coarse pamphleteer; introduced German methods of research into biblical study.

MARSH, James (1794–1846), chemist; practical chemist at Woolwich Arsenal and assistant to *Faraday at Military Academy, 1829; invented electromagnetic apparatus and Marsh arsenic test; gained gold and silver medals from Society of Arts; wrote papers.

MARSH, John (1750–1828), musical composer; wrote works on musical theory; compiled chartbooks; composed various pieces.

MARSH, John Fitchett (1818–1880), antiquary; solicitor and town-clerk of Warrington; contributed to various societies papers on *Milton and other subjects; his *Annals of Chepstow Castle* printed (1883).

MARSH, Narcissus (1638–1713), archbishop of Armagh; BA, Magdalen Hall, Oxford, 1658; fellow of Exeter, 1658; DD, 1671; incumbent of Swindon, 1662–3; preached at Oxford; chaplain to bishop of Exeter and Clarendon; principal of St Alban Hall, Oxford, 1673; provost of Trinity College, Dublin, 1679; encouraged maintenance of Irish language, and prepared, with Robert *Boyle, Irish translation of Old Testament; enthusiastic mathematician; joined in founding Royal Dublin Society, contributing essay on sound, 1683; learned orientalist; built new hall

and chapel; bishop of Ferns and Leighlin and rector of Killeban, 1683; fled to England, 1689, and obtained preferment; returned, 1690; archbishop of Cashel, 1691; gave *Swift prebend of Dunlavin, 1700; established library at St Sepulchre's, for which he purchased *Stillingfleet's books; several times lord justice of Ireland; translated to Armagh, 1703; benefactor of Armagh diocese; published miscellaneous works.

MARSH, William (1775–1864), divine; MA, St Edmund Hall, Oxford, 1807; DD, 1839; curate of St Lawrence, Reading, 1800; impressive Evangelical preacher; friend and correspondent of Charles *Simeon; held livings successively of Nettlebed, Basildon, and Ashampstead, St Peter's, Colchester, St Thomas, Birmingham, St Mary, Leamington, and Beddington, Surrey; canon of Worcester, 1848; published religious works.

MARSHAL, Andrew (1742–1813), physician and anatomist; private tutor; later studied medicine in London; surgeon at Jersey to 83rd Regiment, 1778–83; MD, Edinburgh, 1782; successful teacher of anatomy in London; devoted himself to medical practice, 1800; wrote papers on madness.

MARSHAL, Anselm, sixth and last earl of Pembroke and Striguil (d. 1245), son of William *Marshal, first earl of Pembroke and Striguil.

MARSHAL, Ebenezer (d. 1813), historian; Presbyterian minister; published *The History of the Union of Scotland and England* (1799), and other works.

MARSHAL, Gilbert, fourth earl of Pembroke and Striguil (d. 1241), son of William *Marshal, first earl of Pembroke and Striguil; took minor orders; joined opposition to Henry III's foreign favourites; received fatal injuries in a tournament.

MARSHAL, John (d. 1164?), warrior; was besieged by Stephen at Marlborough, 1139; supported Empress Maud; present at siege of Winchester, 1141; took refuge in Wherwell Abbey; with the empress *Matilda at Oxford, 1142; given lands by Henry II on his accession; present at Council of Clarendon, 1164; appealed to the king for justice against *Becket, 1164.

MARSHAL, John, first Baron Marshal of Hingham (1170?–1235), nephew of William *Marshal, first earl of Pembroke and Striguil; accompanied his uncle on Flanders campaign, 1197–8; had charge of Falaise, 1203; received grant of lands; steward for his uncle in Ireland, 1204; marshal of Ireland, 1207; given charge of various counties and castles; received large grants of land; supported King John against the barons; went to Rome on mission for John, 1215; accompanied him north, 1216; fought against the French at Lincoln, 1217, and prepared for arrival of French fleet; sheriff of Hampshire, 1217; justice of the forest and justice-itinerant, and for assize of arms, 1230; sent on various missions to Ireland; sent abroad, 1225.

MARSHAL, Richard, third earl of Pembroke and Striguil (d. 1234), son of William *Marshal, first earl; lived at first in France; on death of elder brother came to England and obtained possession of earldom, 1231; defended Hubert de *Burgh, 1232, and opposed *Peter des Roches; as head of baronage appealed in vain to Henry III to dismiss foreigners, 1233; engaged in war with *Llywelyn ab Iorwerth, 1233; being warned of intended treachery refused to come to council, 1233; proclaimed traitor and deprived of marshalship, 1233; made alliance with Llywelyn and captured several castles; defeated foreign mercenaries and royal army, 1234, and secured dismissal of Peter des Roches and Poitevins, 1234; went to Ireland to make war against enemies stirred up by Peter des Roches; treacherously betrayed and fatally wounded in Kildare.

MARSHAL, Walter, fifth earl of Pembroke and Striguil (d. 1245), son of William *Marshal, first earl of Pembroke and Striguil.

MARSHAL, William, first earl of Pembroke and Striguil (d. 1219), regent of England; son of John *Marshal (d. 1164?); hostage in Stephen's hands, 1152; trained in Normandy; accompanied his uncle, Earl Patrick, to Poitou, 1168, but was wounded and captured; ransomed by Queen *Eleanor; guardian of Prince *Henry, 1170; sided with the prince in his rebellion against his father; left the court, 1182; went to France; recalled, 1183; on death of young Henry started for the Holy Land to bear Henry II's cross to the holy sepulchre and performed great exploits there; returned, c.1187; became member of king's household; present at Conference of Gisors, 1188, and volunteered to fight as champion; promised the hand of the heiress of Pembroke and Striguil; failed in mission to King Philip of France at Paris, 1189; took part in engagements; spared Prince Richard's life in battle; remained faithful to Henry II to the last at Chinon; joint marshal at Richard I's coronation, 1189; subordinate justiciar under Longchamp; subsequently joined in opposition to Longchamp; received Nottingham Castle to hold for Richard I, 1191; associated in government with Walter de *Coutances and excommunicated by *Longchamp; retained Richard I's favour; took up arms against Earl John, brother of Richard I, 1193; accompanied Richard to Normandy, 1194,

and took part in fighting; made treaties with counts of Boulogne and Flanders, 1196; appointed custodian of Rouen by Richard before his death, 1199; declared for King John, and with *Hubert secured his peaceful succession in England, 1199; invaded Wales, 1204; with John's consent did homage to King Philip of France for his Norman lands, 1204; refused to accompany John's projected expedition to Poitou, 1205; entrusted with defence of England in John's absence, 1206; visited his estates in Ireland, 1207; recalled to England, and his Irish lands ravaged by John's direction; returned to Ireland, 1208, and obtained full possession; received William de *Braose, 1208; compelled to give hostages to John; protested against papal encroachments, 1212; returned to England, 1213; became John's chief adviser, 1213; witnessed charter of resignation to pope, 1213; made guardian of John's eldest son, and guardian of England, 1214, during John's absence abroad; one of John's envoys to the barons, but also one of the counsellers of Magna Carta, 1215; sent to France to avert threatened invasion, end of 1215; executor of John's will, 1216; regent, 1216; republished Great Charter with omissions, 1216; took Lincoln, 1217, while Hubert defeated French fleet; effected Treaty of Lambeth (1217) with Louis, and made himself responsible for payment of 10,000 marks; established order in the kingdom; took habit of a Templar before his death at Caversham, near Reading; possessed lands in Ireland, England, Wales, and Normandy.

MARSHAL, William, second earl of Pembroke and Striguil (d. 1231), son of William *Marshal, first earl; hostage in King John's hands, 1205–12; joined barons and was one of twenty-five executors of Magna Carta, 1215; excommunicated by the pope; joined Louis of France, 1216, but abandoned him later; fought with his father at Lincoln, 1217; succeeded to earldom and estates, 1219, and surrendered Norman lands to his brother Richard *Marshal; forced *Llywelyn of Wales to make terms, 1223; justiciar in Ireland (1224), where he compelled submission of Hugh de *Lacy, 1224; lived alternately in England and Ireland; married as second wife Henry III's sister Eleanor, 1224; high in Henry III's favour, though supporting *Richard of Cornwall, 1227; accompanied Henry III into Brittany, 1230, and fought in Normandy and Anjou.

MARSHALL, Alfred (1842–1924), economist; educated at Merchant Taylors' School and St John's College, Cambridge; second wrangler, 1865; fellow of St John's, 1865–77, 1885–1908; came into intellectual circle of which Henry

*Sidgwick was chief, 1867; passed from study of metaphysics to that of political economy; lecturer in moral science, St John's, 1868; first principal of University College, Bristol, 1877–81; professor of political economy, Bristol, 1877–83; fellow and lecturer in political economy, Balliol College, Oxford, 1883–5; professor of political economy, Cambridge, 1884–1908; served on royal commissions on labour, 1891–4, the aged poor, 1893, and local taxation, 1899; on Indian Currency Committee, 1899; his works include *The Economics of Industry* (1879), *Principles of Economics* (1890), *Industry and Trade* (1919), and *Money, Credit, and Commerce* (1923).

MARSHALL, Arthur Milnes (1852–1893), naturalist; BA, London, 1870, and St John's College, Cambridge, 1874; lectured with Francis Maitland *Balfour on zoology at Cambridge, 1875; D.Sc., London, and fellow of St John's College, Cambridge, 1877; MA, 1878; MD, 1882; professor of zoology, Owens College, Manchester, 1879–93; secretary, and subsequently chairman of board of studies of the Victoria University; killed accidentally while on Scafell; FRS, 1885; published important memoirs on origin and development of nervous system in higher animals and other subjects.

MARSHALL, Benjamin (1767?–1835), animal painter; exhibited thirteen pictures, chiefly portraits of racehorses and their owners, at Royal Academy, 1801–12 and 1818–19.

MARSHALL, Charles (1637–1698), Quaker; 'chymist' and 'medical practitioner'; devoted his life to preaching throughout the country; was frequently imprisoned, fined, and prosecuted for non-payment of tithes; worked hard to counteract divisions; published *The Way of Life Revealed* (1674), *A Plain and Candid Account of . . . certain experienced Medicines* (c.1681) and a journal, and other works.

MARSHALL, Charles (1806–1890), scenepainter; executed very successful work under *Macready at Covent Garden and Drury Lane, London, especially in some of Shakespeare's plays; employed also at the opera; painted landscapes and other pictures.

MARSHALL, Charles Ward (1808–1876), tenor singer; brother of William *Marshall (1806–1875).

MARSHALL, Edward (1578–1675), statuary and master-mason; master-mason to Charles II; executed monuments.

MARSHALL, Emma (1830–1899), novelist; daughter of Simon Martin, banker at Norwich; married Hugh George Marshall, 1854; settled at Clifton; published numerous novels, the stories of which are generally woven round some historical character.

MARSHALL, Francis Albert (1840–1889), dramatist; of Harrow and Exeter College, Oxford; clerk in Audit Office and later contributor to the press and dramatic critic; wrote several plays and some other works; edited the 'Henry Irving Edition' of Shakespeare (8 vols., 1888–90).

MARSHALL, George (*fl.* 1554), poet; wrote *A Compendious Treatise in metre* describing growth of Christianity till Mary's reign from Catholic point of view (reprinted, 1875).

MARSHALL, George William (1839–1905), genealogist; LL B, Peterhouse, Cambridge, 1861; LL M, 1864; LL D, 1874; called to bar, 1865; founded *The Genealogist*, 1877; works include *The Genealogist's Guide* (1879) and *Handbook to the Ancient Courts of Probate* (1889); FSA, 1872; helped to found Parish Register Society, 1896; Rouge Croix pursuivant of arms, 1887; York herald, 1904; made for College of Arms unique collection of parish registers.

MARSHALL, Sir Guy Anstruther Knox (1871–1959), entomologist; born in Amritsar; grandson of Sir Jonathan Frederick *Pollock; educated at Charterhouse; followed various employments in Natal and Rhodesia; encouraged as amateur entomologist by Sir Edward *Poulton; scientific secretary, Entomological Research Committee (Tropical Africa), 1909–13; director, Imperial Bureau (later the Commonwealth Institute) of Entomology, 1913–42; made is centre of information on insect pests; specialized on beetles of the family Curculionidae; FRS, 1923; CMG, 1920; knighted, 1930; KCMG, 1942; hon. D.Sc., Oxford.

MARSHALL, Henry (1775–1851), inspectorgeneral of army hospitals; surgeon's mate in navy, 1803; served with army later; served in South America, Cape, and Ceylon; MD; held various posts in England; drew up valuable report with *Tulloch concerning health of West Indian troops, 1836; hon. MD, New York, 1847; founder of military medical statistics; wrote on military and medical topics.

MARSHALL, James (1796–1855), divine; Presbyterian minister, but subsequently joined English Church; held livings successively of St Mary-le-Port, Bristol, 1842, and Christ Church, Clifton, 1847–55; published sermons and other works.

MARSHALL, Sir James (1829–1889), colonial judge; son of James *Marshall, vicar of Christ Church, Clifton; graduated from Exeter College, Oxford; was ordained, but turned Roman Catholic, 1857; barrister, Lincoln's Inn, 1866; chief magistrate of Gold Coast, 1873; chief justice, 1877–82; knighted, 1882; CMG, 1886.

MARSHALL (or MARISHALL), Jane (*fl.* 1765), novelist and dramatist; imitator of *Richardson.

MARSHALL, John (1534–1597). See MAR-TIALL.

MARSHALL, John (1757–1825), village pedagogue; educated at Newcastle upon Tyne Grammar School; schoolmaster successively in Lake District and Freeman's Hospital, Newcastle; published *The Village Pedagogue, a poem* (1817).

MARSHALL, John (1783–1841), statistical writer; employed at the Home Office; chief work, *A Digest of all the Accounts relating to . . . the United Kingdom* (1833).

MARSHALL, John (1784?–1837), lieutenant, RN (1815) and author; published the *Royal Naval Biography* (1823–35).

MARSHALL, John, Lord Curriehill (1794–1868), judge of the court of session as Lord Curriehill, 1852–68.

MARSHALL, John (1818–1891), anatomist and surgeon; entered University College, London, 1838; FRCS, 1849; assisted Robert *Liston and practised; demonstrator of anatomy at University College, London, 1845; professor of surgery, 1866, subsequently professor of clinical surgery; consulting surgeon, University College Hospital, 1884; Hunterian (1885) and Morton (1889) lecturer; FRS, 1857; president of several medical societies; LL D, Edinburgh; hon. MD, Dublin, 1890; professor of anatomy at Royal Academy, 1873–91; Fullerian professor of physiology at Royal Institution; introduced galvano-cautery and excision of varicose veins; published *The Outlines of Physiology* (1867) and several valuable works.

MARSHALL, Sir John Hubert (1870–1958), archaeologist; educated at Dulwich College and King's College, Cambridge; first class, parts i and ii, classical tripos, 1898–1900; at British School at Athens, 1898–1901; director-general of archaeology, India, 1902–28; on special duties, 1928–34; organized Archaeological Survey of India; prepared Antiquities Law; gave first attention to conserving upstanding structures and recreated original beauty of setting by restoring gardens; notable explorations included ancient Taxila, near Rawalpindi (published in 3 vols., 1951) and Indus Valley Civilization (3 vols., 1931); restored Buddhist site of Sanchi, Central India (3 vols., with A. Foucher, 1940); CIE,

1910; knighted, 1914; FBA, 1936; hon. fellow, King's College, Cambridge, 1936.

MARSHALL, Joshua (1629–1678), statuary and master-mason; son of Edward *Marshall.

MARSHALL, Julian (1836–1903), art collector and author; in family flax-spinning business at Leeds, 1855–61; formed collection of engravings embracing leading works of ancient and modern schools, of musical autographs, and of bookplates; contributed to *Grove's Dictionary of Music*; wrote *Annals of Tennis* (1878) and other kindred works.

MARSHALL, Nathaniel (d. 1730), divine; LL B, Emmanuel College, Cambridge, 1702; took orders; preacher in London and George I's chaplain, 1715; rector of St Vedast and St Michael-le-Querne, London, 1715; DD, Cambridge, by royal mandate, 1717; canon of Windsor, 1722; works include *A Defence of the Constitution*, etc. (1717).

MARSHALL, Stephen (1594?–1655), Presbyterian divine; son of a poor Huntingdonshire glover; BA, Emmanuel College, Cambridge; BD, 1629; vicar of Finchingfield, Essex; reported for 'want of conformity', 1636; a great preacher; influenced elections for Short Parliament, 1640, and delivered series of eloquent sermons before the Commons of great political influence; advocated liturgical and episcopal reform; supported ministers' 'petition' and 'remonstrance', 1641, and wrote with other divines *Smectymnuus* (1641); supported bill for abolishing episcopacy, 1641; appointed preacher at St Margaret's, Westminster, 1642; chaplain to regiment of third earl of *Essex, 1642; summoned to Westminster Assembly, 1643; sent to Scotland and took part in discussions with Scottish delegates; waited on *Laud before execution, 1645; attended Uxbridge Conference, 1645; parliamentary commissioner at Newcastle upon Tyne, 1647; chaplain to the king at Holmby House and in the Isle of Wight; prepared with others the 'shorter catechism', 1647; town preacher at Ipswich, 1651; commissioner to draw up 'fundamentals of religion', 1653; a 'trier', 1654; buried in Westminster Abbey, but exhumed at Restoration. His sermons, especially the funeral sermon for Pym, 1643, helped to guide the course of events, and his influence was esteemed by *Clarendon greater than that of Laud's on the other side.

MARSHALL, Sir Stirrat Andrew William Johnson- (1912–1981), architect. See JOHNSON-MARSHALL.

MARSHALL, Thomas (1621–1685), dean of Gloucester; BA, Lincoln College, Oxford, 1645; served in king's army; preacher in Holland to merchant adventurers, 1650–76; published

Observations on Anglo-Saxon and Gothic versions of the Gospel (1665) and other works; DD, Oxford, 1659; rector of Lincoln College, 1672; chaplain to the king; rector of Bladon, 1680–2; dean of Gloucester, 1681–5; left estate for maintenance of scholars at his college, and books and manuscripts to university library.

MARSHALL, Thomas Falcon (1818–1878), portrait, landscape, genre and history painter.

MARSHALL, Thomas Humphrey (1893–1981), sociologist; educated at Rugby School and Trinity College, Cambridge; first class, part i, historical tripos, 1914; interned in Germany during 1914–18 war; fellow, Trinity College, 1919; assistant lecturer in social science, London School of Economics, 1925–9; reader, 1930; helped to launch the *British Journal of Sociology*; during 1939–45 war in charge of section of research department of Foreign Office; professor of social institutions, LSE, 1944; educational adviser to British High Commission in Germany, 1949–50; Martin White professor of sociology, 1954–6; director, social sciences department, Unesco, 1956–60; publications include *Citizenship and Social Class* (1950), *Sociology at the Crossroads* (1963), *Social Policy in the Twentieth Century* (1967), and *The Right to Welfare* (1981); CMG, 1947; president, International Sociological Association, 1959–62; hon. fellow, LSE; honorary degrees from Southampton, Leicester, York, and Cambridge.

MARSHALL, Thomas William (1818–1877), Catholic controversialist; BA, Trinity College, Cambridge, 1840; took orders, but (1845) turned Roman Catholic; inspector of schools; lectured in United States, 1873; published *Christian Missions* (1862) and controversial works.

MARSHALL, Walter (1628–1680), Presbyterian divine; scholar of Winchester; MA and fellow, New College, Oxford, 1650; fellow of Winchester, 1657–61; incumbent of Hursley, but ejected, 1662; later, minister at Gosport; his *Gospel Mystery of Sanctification* published (1692).

MARSHALL, William (*fl.* 1535), reformer, printer, and translator; enthusiastic Protestant reformer, and *Cromwell's agent; published several anti-Catholic works, including translation of Erasmus's *Maner and Forme of Confession, The Defence of Peace* (translation from Marsilio of Padua, 1535), and *Pyctures and Ymages* (1535).

MARSHALL, William (*fl.* 1630–1650), early English engraver; illustrated books, and executed portraits of historical interest.

MARSHALL, William (1745–1818), agriculturist and philologist; traded in West Indies; subsequently took farm near Croydon, 1774; agent in Norfolk to Sir Harbord Harbord, 1780; published *Minutes of Agriculture* (1778, submitted to Dr *Johnson), *General Survey of the Rural Economy of England* (1787–98); originated Board of Agriculture, 1793; published vocabulary of Yorkshire dialect in his *Economy of Yorkshire.*

MARSHALL, William (1748–1833), violinist and composer, and factor (1790) to the duke of *Richmond and *Gordon; published *Marshall's Scottish Airs* (1821).

MARSHALL, William (1806–1875), organist at Christ Church, Oxford, and St John's College, Oxford, 1825, and St Mary's, Kidderminster, 1846; Mus.Doc., Oxford, 1840; composer and compiler.

MARSHALL, William (1807–1880), Scottish divine and controversialist; studied at Glasgow and Edinburgh universities; Secessionist minister at Coupar-Angus, Perthshire, 1830; champion of 'the voluntary principle'; zealous advocate of free trade and abolitionism; instrumental in effecting union between Relief and Secession churches, 1847; moderator of Presbyterian synod, 1865; published historical and other works.

MARSHALL, William Calder (1813–1894), sculptor; studied at Trustees' Academy, Edinburgh, and at Royal Academy, London; ARSA, 1840; RA, 1852; retired, 1890; his works include the group symbolic of *Agriculture* on the Albert Memorial, Hyde Park.

MARSHALL, Sir William Raine (1865–1939), lieutenant-general; educated at Repton and Sandhurst; commissioned in the Sherwood Foresters, 1885; captain, 1893; served with distinction at Bothaville, 1900; commanded a brigade at Gallipoli landings, 1915; promoted major-general commanding a division; commanded III (Indian) Corps, Mesopotamia, 1916–17; commander-in-chief, Mesopotamia, 1917–19; enforced surrender of Turks on upper Tigris, Oct. 1918; lieutenant-general, 1919; held Southern Command, India, 1919–23; KCB, 1917; KCSI, 1918; GCMG, 1919.

MARSHALL-CORNWALL, Sir James Handyside (1887–1985), soldier, linguist, and author; born James Cornwall; educated at Rugby and Royal Military Academy, Woolwich; commissioned into Royal Field Artillery, 1907; passed examinations as first-class interpreter in German, French, Norwegian, Swedish, Dutch, and Italian; served in Intelligence Corps, 1914–17; head of MI3 section of Military Intelligence Directorate, War Office, 1918; MC, 1916; DSO, 1917; *ex officio* member, general staff delegation at peace conference, 1919; served in Middle East, 1920–5; studied Turkish and modern Greek; brigade major, Royal Artillery (Shanghai defence force), 1927; learnt Chinese; inherited Scottish estate from his uncle and assumed name Marshall-Cornwall, 1927; military attaché, Berlin, 1928–32; commanded 51st Highland division, Royal Artillery, 1932–4; promoted to major-general; head of British Military Mission to Egypt, 1937–8; qualified in colloquial Arabic; promoted to lieutenant-general, 1938; in charge of air defence of Great Britain; served in France and Turkey, 1940–1; took over Western Command, 1941–2; served with Special Operations Executive (SOE) and MI6, 1942–5; retired as full general, 1945; editor-in-chief, captured German archives, attached Foreign Office, 1948–51; president, Royal Geographical Society, 1954–8; publications include autobiography, *Wars and Rumours of Wars* (1984); CBE, 1919; CB, 1936; KCB, 1940.

MARSHALL HALL, Sir **Edward** (1858–1927), lawyer. See HALL.

MARSHAM, Sir **John,** first baronet (1602–1685), writer on chronology; MA, St John's College, Oxford, 1625; travelled abroad; Chancery clerk, 1638; followed Charles I to Oxford; compounded, 1646, and retired to his seat at Cuxton, Kent; MP, Rochester, 1660; reinstated in Chancery and knighted, 1660; created baronet, 1663; published *Chronicus Canon . . .* (1672) and other works; according to *Wotton, the first to make the Egyptian antiquities intelligible.

MARSHAM, Thomas (d. 1819), entomologist; published *Coleoptera Britannica* (1802).

MARSH-CALDWELL, Mrs **Anne** (1791–1874), novelist; née Caldwell; married Arthur Cuthbert Marsh, 1817; published *Two Old Men's Tales* (1834), followed by *Emilia Wyndham* (1846) and other novels.

MARSHE, George (1515–1555). See MARSH.

MARSHMAN, John Clark (1794–1877), author of *History of India*; son of Joshua *Marshman; accompanied his father to Serampur, 1800, and directed mission; subsequently undertook secular work; started first paper mill in India, and (1818) first paper in Bengali, and first English weekly, the *Friend of India*, 1821; published *Guide to the Civil Law*, long the civil code of India; established Serampur College for education of natives; official Bengali translator; published his *History of India* (1842), the *History of Bengal* (1848), and other works; CIE, 1868.

MARSHMAN, Joshua (1768–1837), orientalist and missionary; weaver; master of Baptist School at Broadmead, Bristol, 1794; Baptist missionary to Serampur, 1799; took prominent part in translating scriptures into various dialects, and with

his son, John Clark *Marshman, established newspapers and Serampur College; published first complete Chinese Bible and other works, including translation of Confucius (1809).

MARSTON, Barons. See BOYLE, CHARLES, first baron, 1676–1731; BOYLE, JOHN, second baron, 1707–1762.

MARSTON, John (1575?–1634), dramatist and divine; belonged to Shropshire Marstons; BA, Brasenose College, Oxford, 1594; incumbent of Christchurch, Hampshire, 1616–31; published *The Metamorphosis of Pigmalion's Image* (1598) and *The Scourge of Villanie* (1598 and 1599, satires); issued *History of Antonio and Mellida*, a tragedy (1602), which was ridiculed by Ben *Jonson; wrote a series of comedies: *The Malcontent*, with additions by *Webster (1604), *Eastward Ho* (comedy, 1605) with Jonson and *Chapman, for which latter they were imprisoned, *The Dutch Courtezan* (1605), and *Parasitaster* (1606); finally published a tragedy on Sophonisba (1606), *What You Will* (comedy, 1607), and *The Insatiate Countess* (tragedy, 1613), the last sometimes assigned to William Barksteed.

MARSTON, John Westland (1819–1890), dramatic poet; solicitor's clerk; joined mystical society of James Pierrepont *Greaves; edited *Psyche*, a mystical periodical; wrote *Gerald . . . and other Poems* (1842) and several plays, including the *Patrician's Daughter* (1841), *Strathmore* (historical drama, 1849), *Marie de Méranie* (1850), 'a stirring tragedy'; his *Hard Struggle* (1858) much praised by *Dickens, and the most successful of all his pieces; *Donna Diana* (1863) his best play; from about 1863 contributed poetical criticism to the *Athenaeum*, including celebrated review of *Atalanta in Calydon*; published *Our Recent Actors . . .* (1888); contributed to this Dictionary; chief upholder of poetical drama on English stage; praised for his elegant diction and well-constructed plots.

MARSTON, Philip Bourke (1850–1887), poet; son of John Westland *Marston; lost his sight at early age; wrote *Song-Tide and other Poems* (1871), *All in All* (1875), and *Wind Voices* (1883); the subject of an elegy by *Swinburne. There were published posthumously, *For a Song's Sake* (1887, a collection of short stories), *Garden Secrets* (1887), and *A Last Harvest* (1891).

MARTEL, Sir **Giffard Le Quesne** (1889–1958), lieutenant-general; educated at Wellington College and Royal Military Academy, Woolwich; commissioned in Royal Engineers, 1909; army and combined Services welterweight champion, 1912–13, army champion, 1920, Imperial Services champion, 1921–2; served in France, 1914–16; at tanks headquarters in

France, 1916–18; major, 1917; DSO, MC; returned to Royal Engineers experimental establishment; devised a box-girder bridge; built a tankette; commanded first mechanized RE field company, 1926–9; devised a 'stepping-stone' bridge and a 'mat bridge'; recognized in Germany as pioneer of new type of warfare; instructor, Quetta Staff College, 1930–3; assistant director, mechanization, War Office, 1936, deputy director, 1938–9; commanded 50th Northumbrian division, 1939–40; improvised counter-attack at Arras, May 1940; commander, Royal Armoured Corps, 1940–2; lieutenant-general, 1942; head of Military Mission, Moscow, 1943–4; CB, 1940; KBE, 1943; KCB, 1944.

MARTEN. See also MARTIN, MARTINE, and MARTYN.

MARTEN, Sir (Clarence) Henry (Kennett) (1872–1948), provost of Eton; educated at Eton and Balliol College, Oxford; first class, modern history, 1895; returned to Eton as history master; vice-provost, 1929, provost, 1945–8; entrusted with Princess Elizabeth's historical education, 1938; KCVO, 1945.

MARTEN, Sir Henry (1562?–1641), civilian; fellow of New College, Oxford, 1582; DCL, 1592; king's advocate, 1609; sent on mission to Palatinate, 1613; chancellor of London diocese, 1616; knighted, 1617; judge of Admiralty court, 1617–41; member of High Commission, 1620–41; dean of arches and judge of Canterbury prerogative court, 1624; was superseded as dean of arches in 1633 by Sir John *Lambe; MP, St Germans, 1625 and 1626, Oxford University, 1628, and St Ives, Cornwall (Short Parliament), 1640; supported attack on Buckingham; prominent in debates on Petition of Right, 1628; unsuccessfully appealed to king against writs impeding his administration of Admiralty court, 1630; argued before privy council against 'new canons', 1640.

MARTEN, Henry (or Harry) (1602–1680), regicide; son of Sir Henry *Marten; BA, University College, Oxford, 1619; admitted to Gray's Inn, 1618; lived a dissipated life; refused to subscribe to loan for Scottish War, 1639; MP, Berkshire, 1640; supported *Strafford's attainder and supremacy of parliament; raised regiment of horse; served on Committee of Safety; specially excepted from pardon by Charles I, 1642; governor of Reading, which he soon evacuated; conducted himself with great violence; seized the king's private property, and was expelled House and imprisoned for advocating destruction of royal family, 1643; governor of Aylesbury, 1644; commanded at siege of Dennington

Castle, 1645–6; readmitted to parliament, 1646; leader of extreme party; opposed Scottish influence and claims; proposed motion that no more addresses should be sent to Charles I, 1647; sided with army against parliament, and was supported by the Levellers; said to have desired *Cromwell's assassination; raised troop of horse on his own authority to prevent restoration of Charles I, 1648; extremely active in bringing king to trial and in establishing republic; signed death-warrant, 1649; member of first, second, and fourth Councils of State, and granted lands, 1649; influential speaker in parliament; became hostile to Cromwell and *Bradshaw; gave offence by his immorality and lost support of army; disappeared from political life at expulsion of Long Parliament; outlawed and imprisoned for debt, 1655–7; resumed seat in Long Parliament, 1659; surrendered at Restoration and conducted his defence with great courage and ability; escaped death and was imprisoned for life; published speech and pamphlets, including *The Independency of England ... Maintained* (1647).

MARTEN, Maria (d. 1827), murdered by her lover, William *Corder.

MARTIAL (or MARSHALL), Richard (d. 1563), dean of Christ Church, Oxford; MA, Corpus Christi College, Oxford, 1540; DD, 1552; Roman Catholic and Protestant alternately in reigns of Henry VIII, Edward VI, Mary, and Elizabeth; witness against *Cranmer; vice-chancellor of Oxford University, 1552; dean of Christ Church, 1553–63.

MARTIALL (or MARSHALL), John (1534–1597), Roman Catholic divine; perpetual fellow of New College, Oxford, 1551; BCL, 1556; usher of Winchester School, but being Roman Catholic left England at Elizabeth's accession; one of the founders of English College, Douai; BD, Douai, 1568; canon of St Peter at Lille; published theological treatises.

MARTIN. See also MARTEN, MARTINE, and MARTYN.

MARTIN, Lady (1817–1898). See FAUCIT, HELENA SAVILLE.

MARTIN (d. 1241). See CADWGAN.

MARTIN, Alexander (1857–1946), Presbyterian theologian and church leader; son of Hugh *Martin; educated at George Watson's College, the University, and New College, Edinburgh; first class, philosophy, 1880; minister, Morningside Free Church, 1884–97; professor, apologetics and practical theology, New College, 1897–1927; principal, 1918–35.

MARTIN, Ann (1757–1830), authoress. See TAYLOR.

MARTIN, Anthony (d. 1597), miscellaneous writer; gentleman sewer, c.1570, and cup-bearer to Queen Elizabeth; keeper of royal library at Westminster, 1588–97; published translations and other works.

MARTIN, (Basil) Kingsley (1897–1969), editor; educated at Hereford Cathedral School, Mill Hill, and Magdalene College, Cambridge; first class, historical tripos, parts i and ii, 1920–1, after serving in France with Friends' Ambulance Unit, 1917–18; bye-fellow, Magdalene, 1920; assistant lecturer in politics, London School of Economics, 1924; leader-writer, *Manchester Guardian*, 1927–30; editor, *New Statesman* (later *New Statesman and Nation*), 1931–60; co-founder (with W. A. *Robson) and joint editor, *Political Quarterly*; publications include *The Triumph of Lord Palmerston* (1924), *French Liberal Thought in the Eighteenth Century* (1929), *Father Figures* (1966), and *Editor* (1968).

MARTIN (or MARTYN), Bendal (1700–1761), son of Henry *Martin or Martyn; MA, King's College, Cambridge, 1726; fellow, 1722; entered of the Temple; treasurer of excise, 1738–61.

MARTIN, Benjamin (1704–1782), mathematician, instrument maker, and general compiler; schoolmaster and travelling lecturer; published *Philosophical Grammar* (1735), *Bibliotheca Technologica* (1737); invented and made optical and scientific instruments; settled in Fleet Street, 1740; published *An English Dictionary* (1749), *Martin's Magazine*, 1755–64, and some not very original works; became bankrupt and hastened his death by attempted suicide.

MARTIN, Sir Charles James (1866–1955), physiologist and pathologist; educated at Birkbeck and King's colleges and St Thomas's Hospital, London; B.Sc., 1886; MRCS, LSA, 1889; MB, 1890; demonstrator in physiology, Sydney, 1891–7; Melbourne, 1897–1901; professor, 1901–3; director, Lister Institute of Preventive Medicine, 1903–30; professor of experimental pathology, London, 1912–30; investigations included bubonic plague in India, vitamins and deficiency diseases; pathologist, Third Australian General Hospital, Lemnos, 1915–18; identified cause of enteric fever; devised vitamin 'soup cube', creating nutrition division at Institute; director, nutrition division and professor of biochemistry and general physiology, Adelaide, 1931–3; at Cambridge continued investigations, including myxomatosis and wartime food problems; FRS, 1901; CMG, 1919; knighted, 1927;

FRCP, 1913; fellow, King's College, London; several honorary degrees.

MARTIN, David (1737–1798), painter and engraver; studied under Allan *Ramsay (1713–1784); successful engraver in mezzotint and in line and portrait painter in Ramsay's style.

MARTIN, Sir David Christie (1914–1976), scientist and administrator; educated at Kirkcaldy High School and Edinburgh University; B.Sc. with first class in chemistry, 1937; Ph.D., 1939; assistant secretary, Royal Society of Arts, London, 1939–45; seconded to department of research and development, Ministry of Supply, 1945; general secretary, Chemical Society, 1945–7; assistant secretary (later executive secretary), Royal Society, 1947–76; played leading part in organizing International Geophysical Year, 1957 and arrangements for Royal Society's tercentenary, 1960; played crucial role in starting the Society's European exchange programme; chairman, BBC Consultative Group; CBE, 1960; knighted, 1970; FRSE, 1956; honorary degrees from Edinburgh and Newcastle upon Tyne; David Martin annual lecture inaugurated by British Association of Young Scientists, 1977.

MARTIN, Sir Douglas Eric ('Deric') Holland- (1906–1977), admiral. See HOLLAND-MARTIN.

MARTIN, Edward (d. 1662), dean of Ely; MA, Queens' College, Cambridge, 1612; MA, 1617; chaplain to *Laud, 1627; preached at St Paul's Cross, London, against Presbyterianism; received several livings; president of Queens' College, Cambridge, 1631; DD by royal mandate, 1631; sent college plate to Charles I, 1642, and thereupon was imprisoned in the Tower and ejected; drew up famous mock petition, *Submission to the Covenant*; escaped to Suffolk, 1648, but was again imprisoned; released, 1650; reinstated, 1660; a manager at Savoy Conference; dean of Ely, 1662; published controversial works.

MARTIN, Elias (1740?–1811), painter and engraver; born in Sweden; exhibited at Academy landscapes, views of country seats, engravings, and other work; ARA, 1771; court painter to king of Sweden, 1780.

MARTIN, Francis (1652–1722), Augustinian divine; studied at Louvain; lector in theology at convent of St Martin; professor of Greek at Collegium Buslidianum; supported Ultramontane party; visited England, 1687 or 1688, and suggested to papal nuncio assassination of William of Orange, 1688; doctor of theology at Louvain, 1688; involved in various controversies; regius professor of holy scripture and canon of St Peter's at Louvain, 1694; works include *Scutum*

Fidei contra Haereses hodiernas (1714), in answer to *Tillotson.

MARTIN, Frederick (1830–1883), miscellaneous writer; secretary to Thomas *Carlyle after 1856; inaugurated the *Statesman's Year-Book*, 1864; given pension by Lord Beaconsfield, 1879.

MARTIN, Sir George (1764–1847), admiral of the fleet; great-nephew of William *Martin (1696?–1756); present under his uncle, Joshua *Rowley, at actions off Ushant, 1778, and Martinique, 1780, and Battle of Grenada, 1779; served in Jamaica and commanded ships in various stations; present in the *Irresistible* at Battle of Cape St Vincent, 1797; captured the *Ninfa* and was warmly commended by Lord *St Vincent, 1797; assisted in capture of the *Généreux*, 1800; took part in action off Cape Finisterre, 1805; rear-admiral, 1805; held important commands; knighted, 1814; GCB, 1821; GCMG, 1836; admiral of the fleet, 1846.

MARTIN, George William (1828–1881), musical composer; chorister at St Paul's Cathedral; first organist of Christ Church, Battersea; established National Choral Society, 1860; composed glees and hymns.

MARTIN, Gregory (d. 1582), biblical translator; scholar of St John's College, Oxford; MA, 1565; tutor to sons of Thomas *Howard, fourth duke of Norfolk; escaped to Douai, 1570; ordained priest, 1573; lectured on Hebrew and the scriptures; went to Rome to help organize the new English College there, 1577; returned to Douai and removed with the Douai College to Reims, 1578; translated the Bible (the 'Douay version') with some assistance from Richard *Bristow and other theologians, the New Testament being published 1582, and the Old Testament, 1610. Martin's translation was revised by Bishop *Challoner, 1749–50. Martin also published religious works.

MARTIN, Harriet Letitia (1801–1891), writer of tales; daughter of Richard ('Humanity') *Martin.

MARTIN (or MARTYN), Henry (d. 1721), essayist; lawyer; wrote in *Spectator* and *Guardian*; praised by *Steele; largely caused by his writings rejection of commercial treaty with France, 1714; inspector-general of imports and exports of customs.

MARTIN, Herbert Henry (1881–1954), secretary of the Lord's Day Observance Society; educated at Alderman Norman's Endowed School, Norwich; a 'Wycliffe preacher' of Protestant Truth Society, attacking Roman Catholicism, 1898–1923; worked for Imperial Alliance for Defence of Sunday, 1923–5; secretary, Lord's Day Observance Society, 1925–51; opposed Sunday opening of cinemas (unsuccessfully, 1931) and theatres (1941).

MARTIN, Hugh (1822–1885), minister of Scottish Free Church; MA, Aberdeen, 1839; minister at Panbride, 1844–58, at Free Greyfriars, Edinburgh, 1858–65; mathematical examiner at Edinburgh University, 1866–8; DD, Edinburgh, 1872; his works mostly religious.

MARTIN, Hugh (1890–1964), ecumenical student leader and publisher; educated at Glasgow Academy, Royal Technical College, Glasgow, and Glasgow University; MA, 1913; studied theology at Baptist Theological College of Scotland, 1909–14; assistant secretary, Student Christian Movement, 1914; treasurer, World Students' Christian Federation, 1928–35; chairman, preparatory committee for 1924 Conference on Politics, Economics, and Citizenship; organized 'SCM Press', 1929; set up Religious Book Club, 1937; director, Religious Division, Ministry of Information, 1939–43; managing director, SCM Press, 1943; Free Church leader, British Council of Churches; vice-president, 1950; moderator, Free Church Federal Council, 1952–3; edited *Baptist Hymn Book Companion* (1962); hon. DD, Glasgow University, 1943; CH, 1955.

MARTIN, James (*fl.* 1577), philosophical writer; professor of philosophy at Paris; published *De prima simplicium & concretorum corporum Generatione . . . disputatio* (1577) and other treatises.

MARTIN, Sir James (1815–1886), chief justice of New South Wales; taken by his parents to New South Wales, 1821; member of legislative council, 1848, and of first parliament under responsible government, 1856; attorney-general, 1856 and 1857; premier, 1863, 1866–8, and 1870–2; knighted, 1869; chief justice, 1873–86; published *The Australian Sketch-book* (1838).

MARTIN, Sir James Ranald (1793–1874), surgeon; surgeon on Bengal medical establishment, 1817; served in first Burmese War; presidency surgeon, 1830, and surgeon to Calcutta Hospital; wrote with Dr James *Johnson *On the Influence of Tropical Climates on European Constitutions* (1841), and published memoirs and pamphlets; FRCS, 1843; FRS, 1845; inspector-general of army hospitals; CB, 1860; knighted, 1860.

MARTIN, John (1619–1693), divine; BA, Oriel College, Oxford, 1640; MA; obtained living of Compton Chamberlayne, Wiltshire, seat of the Penruddockes, 1645, but was ejected; arrested after *Penruddocke's rising, 1654; given living of Melcombe Horsey, Dorset, at Restoration; prebendary of Salisbury, 1668 and 1677; nonjuror; published religious works.

MARTIN, John (1741–1820), Baptist minister; called to various places, finally (1795) to Keppel Street, London; offended his congregation by his opinions, and was ejected from communion of Particular Baptists; published various works, including autobiography (1797).

MARTIN, John (1789–1854), historical and landscape painter; apprenticed to coach-painter and subsequently to china-painter; exhibited at the Royal Academy, 1812; exhibited *Joshua*, 1816, which obtained prize from British Institution; sent other pictures to British Institution, including *The Fall of Babylon* (1819) and *Belshazzar's Feast* (1821), considered his finest work, which obtained premium of £200; exhibited *The Fall of Nineveh* at Brussels, 1833; elected member of Belgian Academy and given order of Leopold; died while engaged on a series of three large pictures of Apocalypse, 1853; his artistic work marked by wild imaginative power.

MARTIN, John (1789–1869), meteorologist; MD; London physician; made meteorological charts; published *An Account of the Natives of the Tonga Islands* (1817); died at Lisbon.

MARTIN, John (1791–1855), bibliographer; London bookseller; librarian at Woburn, 1836; wrote description of Bedfordshire churches in local papers; published *Bibliographical Catalogue of Books privately printed* (1834), *History . . . of Woburn* (1845), and other works; FSA and FLS.

MARTIN, John (1812–1875), Irish nationalist; BA, Trinity College, Dublin, 1834; travelled abroad; member of Repeal Association; subsequently joined secession of Young Ireland party; took prominent part in meetings of Irish confederation, and contributed to Mitchel's *United Irishman*; on arrest of Mitchel, 1848, issued *The Irish Felon* and was arrested; exhorted people from Newgate to retain arms in spite of proclamation, 1848; convicted of treason-felony and transported to Van Diemen's Land, 1849; allowed to return, 1856; prosecuted for violent speech at funeral at Dublin of 'Manchester Martyrs', 1867; home-rule MP, Co. Meath, 1871–5; secretary to Home Rule League; known in Ireland as 'Honest John Martin'.

MARTIN, John Frederick (1745–1808), engraver; brother of Elias *Martin.

MARTIN, Jonathan (1715–1737), organist to Chapel Royal, London, 1736, and once chorister; composed 'To thee, O gentle sleep', in *Tamerlane*.

MARTIN, Jonathan (1782–1838), incendiary; brother of John *Martin (1789–1854), the painter; apprentice to a tanner; pressed for the navy, 1804; subsequently farm labourer, Wesleyan, and disturber of church services; confined in asylum for threatening to shoot bishop of Oxford, 1817; escaped, and was excluded from Methodist societies; wrote his biography, 1826; set fire to York Minster, 1829; tried and confined as a lunatic.

MARTIN, Josiah (1683–1747), Quaker; classical scholar; published *A Letter from one of the People called Quakers to Francis de Voltaire* (1741) and other works.

MARTIN, Leopold Charles (1817–1889), miscellaneous writer; son of John *Martin (1789–1854), the painter; published with his brother *Civil Costumes of England* (1842) and other works; skilful artist and authority on costume and numismatics.

MARTIN, Martin (d. 1719), author; visited Western Islands of Scotland; published *Voyage to St. Kilda* (1698) and *A Description of the Western Islands of Scotland* (1703).

MARTIN, Mary Letitia (1815–1850), novelist; 'Mrs Bell Martin' of Ballinahinch Castle, Co. Galway; married Arthur Gonne Bell, 1847; became impoverished; published *Julia Howard* (1850) and other works; died at New York.

MARTIN, Matthew (1748–1838), naturalist and philanthropist; Exeter tradesman; member of Bath Philosophical Society; published works on natural history; investigated and wrote report on London mendicity, 1803.

MARTIN, Peter John (1786–1860), geologist; received medical education at London hospitals and Edinburgh; MRCS; joined his father in practice at Pulborough; wrote *Geological Memoir on a part of Western Sussex* (1828), and contributed geological, archaeological, and gardening articles to various publications.

MARTIN, Sir Richard (1534–1617), master of the Mint and lord mayor of London; goldsmith to Queen Elizabeth; warden, 1560–95, and (1581–1617) master of the Mint; as master of the Mint, issued report, 1601; lord mayor, 1581, 1589, and 1594; removed from aldermanship for debt, 1602; knighted by Queen Elizabeth; president of Christ's Hospital, London, 1593–1602.

MARTIN, Richard (1570–1618), recorder of London; commoner of Broadgates Hall, Oxford; expelled from Middle Temple for riot, 1591; MP, Barnstaple, 1601; barrister, 1602; recorder of London, 1618; celebrated as a wit.

MARTIN, Richard (1754–1834), 'Humanity Martin'; of Harrow and Trinity College, Cambridge; Irish MP for Jamestown, 1776–83, Lanesborough, 1798–1800, Galway (first united parliament), 1801–12 and 1818–26; owned extensive estates at Connemara; supported Union; friend of George IV; supported Catholic emancipation; succeeded in carrying 'first modern legislation for protecting animals', 1822; a founder of Royal Society for Prevention of Cruelty to Animals, 1824; worked to abolish death penalty for forgery, and to secure counsel for prisoners charged with capital crimes; declined peerage; elected to parliament, 1826, but his name erased, 1827; withdrew to Boulogne, where he died.

MARTIN, Robert Montgomery (1803?– 1868), historical writer and statistician; travelled as botanist and naturalist in Ceylon, Africa, Australia, and India; took part in naval expedition as surgeon 'off coasts of Africa, Madagascar, and South-Eastern Islands', 1823; energetic member of court of East India Company; treasurer of Hong Kong, 1844–5; on mission to Jamaica, 1851; published *The History of the British Colonies* (1834) and other important works.

MARTIN, Sir Samuel (1801–1883), baron of the Exchequer; MA, Trinity College, Dublin, 1832; hon. LL D, 1857; barrister, Middle Temple, 1830; QC, 1843; Liberal MP for Pontefract, 1847; baron of Exchequer, 1850–74; knighted, 1850.

MARTIN, Samuel (1817–1878), congregational minister; architect; subsequently minister at Cheltenham and afterwards at Westminster; attracted enormous congregations and worked successfully for improvement of bad neighbourhood; took active part in management of Westminster Hospital, London; chairman of Congregational Union, 1862; published sermons and other works.

MARTIN, Sarah (1791–1843), prison visitor; dressmaker and Sunday school teacher; visited the notorious Yarmouth Gaol and Workhouse; preached and gave instruction, 1819–41; exerted great influence over the criminals; wrote poems and journals.

MARTIN, Sir Theodore (1816–1909), man of letters; educated at Edinburgh High School and University, 1830–3; hon. LL D, 1875; practised as solicitor in Edinburgh until 1846, when he migrated to London to become parliamentary agent; his parliamentary work the main occupation of his life; contributed before leaving Edinburgh humorous prose and verse to *Tait's* and *Fraser's* magazines under pseudonym of Bon Gaultier; soon collaborated with William Edmondstoune *Aytoun; together they published *Bon Gaultier Ballads* (1845, 16th edn., 1903), a notable collection of witty parodies; devoted to the drama; was fascinated by the act-

ing of Helen *Faucit, for whom he adapted from the Danish *King René's Daughter*, 1849; married Miss Faucit at Brighton, 1851, and settled for life at 31 Onslow Square, Kensington; acquired in 1861 country residence Bryntysilio; wrote on dramatic themes in *Fraser's Magazine*, 1858–65, the *Quarterly Review*, and *Blackwood*; translated Oehlenschläger's German romantic dramas *Aladdin* (1854) and *Correggio* (1857), the works of Horace (1860, 1882) and of Catullus (1861), Dante's *Vita Nuova* (1862), Goethe's *Faust* (pt. i, 1865, pt. ii, 1866), poems and ballads of Heine (1878), and the *Aeneid*, i–vi (1896); on recommendation of his friend Sir Arthur *Helps, Martin prepared for Queen Victoria a life of the Prince Consort (See ALBERT FRANCIS CHARLES AUGUSTUS EMMANUEL) (5 vols., 1875–80); CB, 1878; KCB, 1880; KCVO, 1896; wrote life of Lord *Lyndhurst, 1883; lord rector of St Andrews University, 1881; privately circulated *Queen Victoria as I knew her*, 1901 (published, 1908); a trustee of Shakespeare's birthplace from 1889 till death, and an active member of the Royal Literary Fund from 1868.

MARTIN, Thomas (1697–1771), antiquary; 'Honest Tom Martin of Palgrave'; clerk to his brother Robert, attorney; settled at Palgrave, Suffolk, 1723; FSA, 1720; his collections afterwards published by Richard *Gough as *The History of Thetford* (1779).

MARTIN, Sir Thomas Acquin (1850–1906), industrial pioneer in India and agent-general for Afghanistan; founded engineering firm in Calcutta, which took over Bengal Iron and Steel Company (1889) and worked iron deposits at Manharpur; pioneer of light railways in India; built many jute mills and controlled large collieries and engineered water supplies in Bengal; appointed agent to amir of Afghanistan (1887), for whom he built an arsenal, a mint, and various factories; accompanied amir's son to England on diplomatic mission, and knighted, 1895.

MARTIN, Thomas Barnewall (d. 1847), MP, Co. Galway, 1832–47; son of Richard ('Humanity') *Martin.

MARTIN, Sir Thomas Byam (1773–1854), admiral of the fleet; 'captain's servant' in the *Pegasus*, 1786; captured the *Tamise*, 1796, and while commanding various ships off Irish and French coasts, and in West Indies, the *Immortalité*, 1798, and large number of privateers and other ships; had large share in capture of Russian ship *Sewolod*, 1808; received Swedish Order of the Sword; rear-admiral, 1811; took part in defence of Riga, 1812; comptroller of the navy, 1816–31; MP, Plymouth, 1818–31; GCB, 1830; admiral of the fleet, 1849.

MARTIN, Violet Florence (1862–1915), novelist under the pseudonym of Martin Ross; member of ancient Galway family; wrote books in collaboration with her cousin, E. A. Œ. *Somerville, describing Anglo-Irish life; best-known novels *The Real Charlotte* (1894) and *The Irish R.M.* series (begun 1899).

MARTIN, William (1696?–1756), admiral; entered navy, 1708; served on various ships and stations; commanded squadron which enforced neutrality of Naples, 1742, and protected Italy against Spaniards; vice-admiral, 1744; commanded fleet at Lisbon and in North Sea; retired, 1747; linguist and classical scholar.

MARTIN, William (*fl.* 1765–1821), painter; assistant to *Cipriani; exhibited Shakespearian and classical subjects and portraits at the Royal Academy.

MARTIN, William (1767–1810), naturalist; actor and, later, drawing-master; FLS, 1796; published *Figures and Descriptions of Petrifications collected in Derbyshire* (1793) and other works.

MARTIN, William (1772–1851), natural philosopher and poet; brother of John *Martin (1789–1854) and of Jonathan *Martin (1782–1838); rope-maker; announced discovery of perpetual motion and collapse of Newtonian system; gained medal from Society of Arts for spring weighing machine, 1814, and exhibited other inventions; affected great singularity of dress and founded 'Martinean Society', 1814, in opposition to Royal Society; works include *W. M.'s Challenge to the whole Terrestrial Globe* (1829).

MARTIN, William (1801–1867), writer for the young; woollen-draper's assistant at Woodbridge and subsequently schoolmaster at Uxbridge; returned to Woodbridge, 1836, and gained livelihood by writing and lecturing; author of *Peter Parley's Annual*, 1840–67, various books of simple instruction, and household tracts.

MARTIN, Sir William (1807–1880), scholar and first chief justice of New Zealand; fellow of St John's College, Cambridge, 1831; MA, 1832; gained classical and mathematical distinctions; barrister, 1836; chief justice of New Zealand, 1841; supported rights of natives and protested against Lord *Grey's instructions, 1847; hon. DCL, Oxford, 1858; knighted, 1860.

MARTIN, William Charles Linnaeus (1798–1864), writer on natural history; son of William *Martin (1767–1810); superintendent of museum of Zoological Society, 1830–8; wrote several volumes in 'Farmer's Library'.

MARTIN, Sir William Fanshawe, fourth baronet (1801–1895), admiral; son of Sir Thomas Byam *Martin; entered navy, 1813; lieutenant, 1820; commander, 1823; served with distinction at Callao at time of civil war; post captain, 1824; in Mediterranean, 1826–31; commodore in command of Lisbon squadron, 1849–52; rear-admiral, 1853; superintendent of Portsmouth Dockyard, 1853–8; vice-admiral, 1858; lord of Admiralty, 1859; commanded with great rigour on Mediterranean Station, 1860–3; admiral, 1863; succeeded to baronetcy on a cousin's death, 1863; commander-in-chief at Portsmouth, 1866–9; GCB, 1873; rear-admiral of United Kingdom, 1878.

MARTIN, William Keble (1877–1969), botanist; educated at Marlborough, Christ Church, Oxford, and Cuddesdon Theological College; ordained, 1902; curate, Beeston, Ashbourne, and Lancaster, 1902–9; vicar, Wath-upon-Dearne, near Rotherham, 1909–17; temporary chaplain to the forces, 1917; rector, Haccombe and Coffinswell, near Torquay, 1921; Great Torrington, North Devon, 1934–43; Combe-in-Teignhead with Milber, 1943–9; a keen botanist and flower artist; edited (with Gordon T. Fraser), *The Flora of Devon* (1939); published *A History of the Ancient Parish of Wath-upon-Dearne* (1920) and *Concise British Flora in Colour* (1965); fellow, Linnean Society, 1928; hon. D.Sc., Exeter, 1966; four stamps issued with his designs, 1967.

MARTINDALE, Adam (1623–1686), Presbyterian divine; tutor and schoolmaster; later deputy quartermaster; took 'Covenant', 1643; became preacher at Manchester and vicar of Rostherne, Cheshire, 1648; sympathized with rising of George *Booth (1622–1684); deprived, 1662; preached and taught mathematics; chaplain to Lord Delamer (Sir George Booth) at Dunham, 1671; took out licence, 1672; imprisoned on groundless suspicions, 1685; works include controversial publications and an autobiography.

MARTINDALE, Cyril Charlie (1879–1963), priest and scholar; educated at Harrow and Campion Hall, Oxford; entered Jesuit novitiate, 1897; first class, Lit. Hum., 1905; ordained, 1911; taught at Stoneyhurst, 1913–16; classics lecturer, Oxford, 1916–27; joined staff of Farm Street Church, Mayfair, 1927; noted preacher and broadcaster; unable to leave Denmark, 1940–5; returned to Farm Street, 1945–53; published over eighty books and hundreds of pamphlets, including biographies of R. H. *Benson and C. D. *Plater, *Waters of Twilight* (1914), and *The Goddess of Ghosts* (1915).

MARTINDALE, Hilda (1875–1952), civil servant; educated in Germany, at Brighton High School, Royal Holloway College, and Bedford College; studied hygiene and sanitary sciences;

appointed temporary factory inspector, 1901; senior lady inspector, 1908; served in Ireland, Birmingham, and London; superintending inspector, 1921; deputy chief inspector, 1925; director, women establishments, Treasury, 1933–7; CBE, 1935; publications include *Women Servants of the State* (1938).

MARTINDALE, Miles (1756–1824), Wesleyan minister; preacher in Cheshire; governor of Woodhouse Grove school, 1816; published sermons, poems, and other works.

MARTINDELL (or MARTINDALL), Sir Gabriel (1756?–1831), major-general in East India Company's service; ensign in Bengal Native Infantry, 1776; distinguished himself in Mahratta War, 1804–5; held commands in India; major-general, 1813; KCB, 1815; commander of field army, 1820.

MARTINE. See also MARTEN, MARTIN, and MARTYN.

MARTINE, George, the elder (1635–1712), historian of St Andrews; commissary clerk, but deprived for refusing to take oath, 1690; secretary to Archbishop *Sharp; his *Reliquiae divi Andreae* published (1797).

MARTINE, George, the younger (1702–1741), physician; son of George *Martine the elder; MD Leiden, 1725; accompanied Cathcart's American expedition, 1740, and various expeditions against Carthagena; published scientific works.

MARTINEAU, Harriet (1802–1876), miscellaneous writer; daughter of Norwich manufacturer and sister of James *Martineau; of Huguenot origin; Unitarian; suffered from feeble health and deafness; attracted by philosophical books; contributed article on 'Female Writers on Practical Divinity' to the *Monthly Repository* (1821), followed by other papers, and published short tales; went through long illness and was left penniless, 1829; published successful works, *Illustrations of Political Economy* (1832–4), *Poor Law and Paupers Illustrated* (1833), and *Illustrations of Taxation* (1834); came to London; became acquainted with literary celebrities, and was consulted by Cabinet ministers; visited America, 1834–6, and wrote *Society in America* (1837) and a *Retrospect of Western Travel* (1838); published *Deerbrook*, a novel (1839); visited Venice and returned seriously ill; published *The Playfellow* series and other books; tried mesmerism and recovered, 1844; friend of *Wordsworth; travelled in Egypt and Palestine, and published *Eastern Life* (1848) and *History of England during the Thirty Years' Peace* (1849); published Atkinson's *Letters on the Laws of Man's Social Nature and Development* (1851), containing anti-theological views; brought out condensed translation of Comte's *Philosophie Positive* (1853); contributed to the *Daily News* and *Edinburgh Review*, and wrote, among other works, an autobiography, which was published posthumously.

MARTINEAU, James (1805–1900), Unitarian divine; educated at Norwich Grammar School under Edward *Valpy, and at Bristol under Lant *Carpenter; apprenticed as civil engineer, 1821; studied divinity at Manchester College, York, 1822–7; assistant in Lant Carpenter's school at Bristol, 1827; assistant pastor of Eustace Street congregation, Dublin, 1828; ordained, 1828; chief promoter and first secretary of 'Irish Unitarian Christian Society', 1830; colleague with John *Grundy (1782–1843) at Paradise Street Chapel, Liverpool, 1832, and sole pastor, 1835, continuing in that office despite other appointments elsewhere till 1857 (the chapel removed to Hope Street, 1849); published *Rationale of Religious Enquiry* (1836); professor of mental and moral philosophy and political economy from 1840 to 1857 at Manchester New College (removed from Manchester, 1853, to University Hall, Gordon Square, London); joint editor with John James *Tayler and Charles Wicksteed of *Prospective Review*, 1845–54, and contributed (1855–64) much to *National Review*, which Richard Holt *Hutton and Walter *Bagehot edited; professor of mental, moral, and religious philosophy at Manchester New College, 1857–69; colleague with Tayler in charge of Little Portland Street Chapel, London, 1859, and sole pastor, 1860–72; principal of Manchester New College, 1869–85; DD, Edinburgh, 1884; DCL, Oxford, 1888; Litt.D., Dublin, 1892. His publications include *Ideal Substitutes for God* (1879), *Study of Spinoza* (1882), *Types of Ethical Theory* (1885), *Study of Religion* (1888), *Seat of Authority in Religion* (1890), and two volumes of hymns.

MARTINEAU, Robert Braithwaite (1826–1869), painter; educated at University College, London; first exhibited at Royal Academy, 1852.

MARTINEAU, Russell (1831–1898), orientalist; son of James *Martineau; educated at Heidelberg and University College, London; MA, London, 1854; joined staff of British Museum Library, 1857, and was assistant keeper, 1884–98; lecturer on Hebrew language and literature at Manchester New College, London, 1857–1866, and professor, 1866–74; published philosophical and other writings.

MARTIN-HARVEY, Sir John Martin (1863–1944), actor-manager; with Sir Henry *Irving at Lyceum, 1882–96; outstandingly successful with *The Only Way* (adaptation of *Tale of Two Cities*) first produced at Lyceum, 1899; produced *Hamlet* (1904), *Richard III* (1910), and *The Taming of the Shrew* (1913); rakish vigour of his 'The Rat' in *The Breed of the Treshams* (1903) contrasted with sensitive study as Count Skariatine in *A Cigarette Maker's Romance* (1901); his *Œdipus Rex* (1912) profoundly impressive; knighted, 1921.

MARTIN OF ALNWICK (d. 1336), Franciscan; member of minorite convent at Oxford; DD; took part at Avignon in controversy between conventual and spiritual Franciscans, 1311.

MARTYN. See also MARTEN, MARTIN, and MARTINE.

MARTYN, Benjamin (1699–1763), miscellaneous writer; nephew of Henry *Martin; examiner at the Custom House, secretary to Society for Colony of Georgia, and (1733) published account; original member of Society for Encouragement of Learning, 1736; instrumental in erecting Shakespeare's monument in Westminster Abbey; composed life of first earl of *Shaftesbury, unsatisfactory and suppressed; produced *Timoleon* (tragedy) at Drury Lane, 1730.

MARTYN, Elizabeth (1813–1846). See INVERARITY.

MARTYN, Francis (1782–1838), Roman Catholic divine; published *Homilies on the Book of Tobias* (1817) and other works.

MARTYN, Henry (1781–1812), missionary; senior wrangler and Smith's prizeman, St John's College, Cambridge; fellow, 1802; MA, 1804; curate to *Simeon at Holy Trinity, Cambridge, 1803; chaplain on Bengal establishment, 1805; opened church at Cawnpore for natives; translated New Testament and Prayer-Book into Hindustani, New Testament and Psalms into Persian, and Gospels into Judaeo-Persic; visited Persia, and died at Tokat from fever; left *Journals and Letters* (edited 1837).

MARTYN, John (1699–1768), botanist; translated Tournefort's works, *The Compleat Herbal* and *History of Plants growing about Paris*; made excursions in country and collected botanical specimens; became secretary to botanical society meeting at Rainbow Coffee-house; FRS, 1727; contributed to *Bailey's *Dictionary*, 1725, and lectured in London and at Cambridge, and practised as apothecary; published *Historia Plantarum rariorum* (1728–37), and, with Dr Alexander *Russel, *The Grub Street Journal* (styling himself 'Bavius'), 1730–7; entered Emmanuel College, Cambridge, 1730; Cambridge professor of botany, 1732–62; corresponded with *Sloane, Linnaeus, and others; collected material for an English dictionary; contributed to *Philosophical* *Transactions*; published editions of Virgil's *Georgicks* (1741) and *Bucolicks* (1749), and other works.

MARTYN (or MARTIN), Richard (d. 1483), bishop of St David's; B.Can.L., Oxford, 1449; probably D.Can.L., Cambridge; archdeacon of London, 1469, and member of king's council before 1471; prebendary of St Paul's Cathedral, 1471, and Hereford, 1472; chancellor of the marches, 1471; served on commissions; master in Chancery, 1472–7; perhaps bishop of Waterford and Lismore, 1472; archdeacon of Hereford and king's chaplain, 1476; chancellor of Ireland and ambassador to Castile, 1477; bishop of St David's, 1482–3.

MARTYN (or MARTIN), Thomas (d. 1597?), civilian and controversialist; fellow of New College, Oxford, 1538–53; member of College of Advocates, 1555; chancellor to *Gardiner, bishop of Winchester and master in Chancery; wrote treatise against marriage of priests, 1553; took active part against *Cranmer, *Hooper, and others; went to Calais, 1555; master of requests, 1556; sent on mission to King Philip at Ghent, 1556; member of Council of the North, 1557; commissioner to settle matters between England and Scotland, 1557; miscellaneous writer.

MARTYN, Thomas (1735–1825), botanist; son of John *Martyn; studied at Emmanuel College, Cambridge, and gained scholarships; fellow of Sidney Sussex College, Cambridge; MA, 1758; tutor, 1760–74; Cambridge professor of botany, 1762–1825; lectured and introduced Linnaean system; published *Plantae Cantabrigienses* (1763), and travelled abroad; BD, 1766; incumbent of Ludgershall, Buckinghamshire, 1774, and Little Marlow, 1776; travelled abroad with a ward, 1778–80; purchased Charlotte Street Chapel, Pimlico; published translation and continuation of Rousseau's *Letters on the Elements of Botany* (1785); edited *Miller's *Gardener's Dictionary* on Linnaean system, 1807, and other works; rector of Pertenhall, 1804; FRS, 1786; FLS, 1785.

MARTYN, Thomas (*fl.* 1760–1816), natural-history draughtsman and pamphleteer; established academy in Great Marlborough Street, London, where his books on natural history were prepared; published also political pamphlets.

MARTYN, William (1562–1617), lawyer and historian; barrister, Middle Temple, 1589; MP, Exeter, 1597–8; recorder of Exeter, 1605–17; published *The Historie and Lives of the Kings of England* (1615 and 1638) and *Youth's Instruction* (1612).

MARVELL, Andrew, the elder (1586?–1641), divine; MA, Emmanuel College, Cambridge, 1608; 'minister' of Flamborough, 1610; incumbent of Winestead, 1614–24; master of Grammar School, Hull, 1624; master of the Charterhouse and lecturer at Holy Trinity Church, *c.*1624; drowned in the Humber; described by *Fuller as excellent preacher.

MARVELL, Andrew, the younger (1621–1678), poet and satirist; son of Andrew *Marvell the elder; educated under his father at Hull Grammar School; scholar of Trinity College, Cambridge; BA, 1638; contributed verses to *Musa Cantabrigiensis*, 1637; travelled abroad; wrote poems, including satire on death of Thomas *May; tutor to Mary, daughter of Lord *Fairfax, *c.*1650; wrote poems in praise of gardens and country life, and became ardent republican; recommended unsuccessfully to Council of State by *Milton to be his assistant in the secretaryship for foreign tongues, 1653; resided at Eton, in house of John *Oxenbridge, as tutor of William Dutton, Cromwell's ward, 1653; became Milton's colleague in Latin secretaryship, 1657; wrote several poems in the protector's honour, including 'Horatian Ode upon Cromwell's Return from Ireland', 1650, his greatest achievement (first printed, 1776) and elegy upon his death; thrice elected MP, Hull, 1660 and 1661; guarded vigilantly interests of his constituents and corresponded with corporation; went to Holland, 1663; accompanied earl of *Carlisle, ambassador to northern powers, as secretary, 1663–5, publishing an account of the mission (1669); vigorously defended Milton; opposed Bill for Securing the Protestant Religion, 1677; became disgusted at management of public affairs, and wrote, for private circulation, bitter satires, first attacking ministers, but afterwards Charles II himself, and advocating republic; wrote the *Rehearsal Transprosed*, 1672 and 1673, against Samuel *Parker, afterwards bishop of Oxford, a leading champion of intolerance; took part also in controversy about predestination, 1678; wrote, anonymously, *Account of the Growth of Popery and Arbitrary Government in England* (1677), which produced great sensation; according to his biographer, Cooke, refused court favours; an intimate of James *Harrington and Milton; wrote prefatory lines extolling the 'mighty poet' to second edition of *Paradise Lost*, and rebuked *Dryden for attempting to convert it into a rhyming opera; as pamphleteer was admired by *Swift; his work as poet belongs to pre-Restoration period.

MARVIN, Charles Thomas (1854–1890), writer on Russia; resided in Russia, 1870–6; while writer at foreign office disclosed secret treaty with Russia to the *Globe*, 1878, and published an account of the secret treaty of 1878; sent to Russia by Joseph *Cowen, 1882; wrote

several books on Russia, including *The Russians at the Gates of Herat* (1885).

MARWICK, Sir **James David** (1826–1908), legal and historical writer; founded legal firm of Watt & Marwick in Edinburgh, 1855; town clerk of Edinburgh, 1860–73, and of Glasgow, 1873–1903; extended city of Glasgow by annexing fourteen suburban burghs, 1881–91; FRS, Edinburgh, 1884; hon. LL D, Glasgow, 1878; knighted, 1888; helped to found Scottish Burgh Records Society, Edinburgh, editing its publications from 1868 to 1897.

MARWOOD, William (1820–1883), public executioner; introduced the 'long drop'.

MARY I (1516–1558), queen of England and Ireland; third but only surviving child of Henry VIII and *Catherine of Aragon; tentatively betrothed to son of Francis I, and subsequently to the emperor Charles V; made princess or governor of Wales at Ludlow Castle, 1525; studied Greek, Latin, French, Italian, science, and music, and read Erasmus's *Paraphrases* and *More's *Utopia*; attended by countess of Salisbury, mother of Reginald *Pole; was separated from her mother on Queen Catherine's divorce, 1532, but boldly avowed sympathy with her; was declared illegitimate, 1533, but refused to give up title of princess; sent to Hatfield to reside there with her half-sister Princess Elizabeth, under care of Lady Shelton, aunt of Anne Boleyn; ill-treated, denounced by Henry, and her life threatened; received much public sympathy and had a protector in the emperor Charles V; after Queen *Anne Boleyn's execution was reconciled with Henry VIII on acknowledging her illegitimacy and the king's ecclesiastical supremacy; chief mourner at funeral of Queen *Jane Seymour, 1537; proposed in marriage to Duke Philip of Bavaria, 1539; declared capable of inheriting crown after Henry's legitimate children, 1544; translated Erasmus's Latin paraphrase of St John; on friendly terms with her half-brother Edward and her half-sister Elizabeth after her father's death and Edward's succession to the throne, 1547; received proposal of marriage from Lord Seymour; refused to give up mass on passing of Act of Uniformity, 1549; was supported by Charles V, who prepared for her escape to the continent; on Edward VI's death and proclamation as queen of Lady *Jane Grey, took refuge at Framlingham Castle, Suffolk, 1553; on country declaring for her accession to the throne, journeyed to London, and was proclaimed queen 16 July; released duke of Norfolk, Stephen *Gardiner, and other prisoners in the Tower of London; first queen regnant of England; announced her intention abroad to reintroduce Roman Catholicism, but promised in England that religion should be settled by common consent; restored Gardiner and *Bonner to their sees and made Gardiner chancellor and chief adviser, 1553; executed the duke of *Northumberland, but for the time spared Lady Jane Grey; crowned with great splendour, 1 Oct. 1553; in first parliament abolished new treasons and felonies and Edward VI's religious laws; had her legitimacy declared; announced (contrary to Gardiner's and to the French ambassador's wishes) intention of marrying her cousin *Philip of Spain, a suitor agreeable to her on account of his fanatical Roman Catholicism; evoked by her steadfast pursuit of this project three insurrections, 1554; showed courage in rebellion of Sir Thomas *Wyatt, who marched into London but was defeated in the city; executed Wyatt, duke of *Suffolk, Lady Jane Grey and her husband, and many others, and imprisoned Princess Elizabeth; began campaign against Protestantism and expelled married clergy; married Philip of Spain at Winchester, 25 July, 1554, and pardoned Elizabeth; with Philip opened parliament which reversed Cardinal Pole's attainder and passed acts restoring papal power; imagined herself to be pregnant; gave consent to re-enactment of statute against Lollardy and set on foot great persecution, ninety-six Protestants suffering death, including Bishop *Hooper, during 1555, and 300 before end of the reign; restored some of the property taken by the crown from the church and re-established many monasteries; had disputes with her husband, who left the country (Aug. 1555); suffered from continued ill health and grief caused by Philip's absence; received Philip at Greenwich, 1557; agreed to join in his schemes of war with France; said farewell to Philip, July 1557; successfully resisted appointment by the pope of new legate in place of Pole, 1557; demanded forced loans to support war against France and Scotland; lost Calais, Jan. 1558; took measures during her last days to secure accession of Elizabeth; buried in Westminster Abbey. Religious devotion to the Catholic faith was the central feature of Mary's life, inducing her to marry Philip, one of the great errors of her reign, and to persecute her Protestant subjects. Owing mainly to her persecution of the Protestants, her personal character has been assailed with fanatical animosity.

MARY (1631–1660), princess royal of England and princess of Orange; eldest daughter of Charles I and Queen *Henrietta Maria; celebrated for her beauty and intelligence; married William, son of Frederick Henry, prince of Orange, 1641; went to Holland, 1642, and welcomed Charles and James, 1648; gave birth to son, afterwards William III of England, after death of her husband, 1650; made guardian of young prince, 1651; disliked by the Dutch, whose sympathies were with *Cromwell; received Charles II secretly, 1651, and helped her brothers and their adherents liberally; finally forbidden by the Dutch States to receive them on outbreak of war between England and Holland, 1652; her son William formally elected stadtholder by Zealand and several northern provinces, but excluded from his father's military dignities; visited Charles II at Cologne and Paris, 1656; courted by Buckingham and others; became sole regent, 1658, opposed by Dona, governor of town of Orange; invoked help of Louis XIV of France, who took Orange, 1660; took part in festivities at The Hague on Charles's restoration; visited England and died there of smallpox.

MARY II (1662–1694), queen of England, Scotland, and Ireland; eldest child of James II and Anne *Hyde, lived with her grandfather, *Clarendon, at Twickenham, and later at Richmond Palace; brought up a Protestant; received religious instruction from *Compton, bishop of London; married William of Orange, the marriage being part of *Danby's policy for pacifying parliament; left with her husband for Holland, 1677; at first neglected by William; received visits from the duke and duchess of York and from Monmouth, 1679; received the latter again, 1685; obtained great popularity among the Dutch by her noble and amiable character; became estranged from English court on expedition of Monmouth; promised William that he should always bear rule, 1686; obliged to dismiss *Burnet, 1687; joined with William in protesting against Declaration of Indulgence; received proselytizing letters from her father, James II, 1687–8; identified herself completely with William in subsequent events; believed birth of prince of Wales a fraud, 1688; repudiated idea of reigning as sole sovereign (suggested by Danby); arrived in England, 1689; accepted crown with William and assented to Declaration of Rights; interfered little in public affairs, but was very popular; settled at Hampton Court and Kensington Palace; endeavoured to improve social morals, and in accordance with her Puritan opinions abolished singing of prayers at the Chapel Royal, Whitehall; became estranged from her sister, Princess Anne; governed England during William's absence, and in a time of great crisis, 1690–1; exercised wise patronage in church matters, and endeavoured to obtain lenient treatment for nonjuring bishops; alarmed by conspiracy of Anne and the *Marlboroughs, 1692; administered government, 1692; disturbed by fears of a French invasion, conspiracies against her life and that of William, and William's defeats in Holland; addressed letter of confidence to the navy; issued orders to magistrates for enforcing law against vice; resumed regency, 1693 and 1694; requested and obtained loan from city of London of £300,000; died of smallpox, to the great grief of William and England and Holland, her scheme of Greenwich Hospital being carried out by William in memory of her; buried in Henry VII's Chapel, Westminster Abbey. Obliged by fate to choose between father and husband, she chose the latter, making devotion to William III's interests almost a religious duty, but retaining kindly feelings for James II till his connivance in Grandvaal's attempt on William's life, 1692. She endowed William and Mary Missionary College, Virginia, and supported SPCK.

MARY (1723–1772), princess of Hesse; daughter of George II and Queen *Caroline; married Frederic, hereditary prince, afterwards landgrave of Hesse-Kassel, 1740; separated from him on his turning Roman Catholic, 1754, and resided with her children at Hanau.

MARY, duchess of Gloucester and Edinburgh (1776–1857), princess; fourth daughter of George III; mentioned by Miss Burney; married William *Frederick, second duke of Gloucester, 1816.

MARY (1867–1953), whose full names were Victoria Mary Augusta Louise Olga Pauline Claudine Agnes, queen consort of King George V; born in Kensington Palace; only daughter of duke and duchess of Teck; devoted sister of earl of *Athlone; known until marriage as Princess May; extended her education beyond drawing-room accomplishments with help of governess, but mainly by own determination with aid of excellent memory; proficient in French, German, European history, and knowledge of art; engaged to duke of *Clarence, 1891; after his death to duke of York, 1893; married in St James's Palace Chapel, 6 July 1893; had five sons and one daughter; with husband set new pattern of family life, providing simple and sensible upbringing for children whom she protected from occasional over-harsh discipline from their father; travelled with duke in *Ophir* for first opening of Australian Federal Parliament, 1901, and extended tour of Empire; became princess of Wales, 1901; made arduous tour of India with husband, 1905–6; with his succession to throne became known as Queen Mary, 1910; with king visited India (1911–12), Berlin (1913), Paris (1914); toured industrial areas of Great Britain with genuine interest and sympathetic understanding; indefatigable during war of 1914–18; thereafter supported the king through difficult post-war years

in execution of duties for which he was physically unfitted, especially after his illness in 1928–9 during which she was a tower of strength; after his death (1936) moved to Marlborough House; sustained abdication of eldest son with calm dignity; attended coronation of King George VI, 1937; pursued her interest in art collection and cultural and industrial projects; her eyesight injured in car accident, May 1939; removed to Badminton during war of 1939–45; attended funeral of her fourth and favourite son, duke of *Kent, 1942; returned to London, 1945, and resumed public engagements until after death of King George VI in 1952; died at Marlborough House, 24 Mar. 1953; buried beside her husband in St George's Chapel, Windsor; possessed of great physical strength, self-discipline, and mental vigour; formidable in her rigidity of conduct, she yet exercised great practical sympathy; a great queen consort, selflessly loyal to monarchy, she won respect and affection of nation by her devotion to duty and refusal to be deflected from it by personal griefs.

MARYBOROUGH, first baronet. See WELLESLEY-POLE, WILLIAM, 1763–1845.

MARYBOROUGH, Viscounts. See MOLYNEUX, Sir RICHARD, first viscount, 1593–1636; MOLYNEUX, Sir RICHARD, second viscount, 1617?–1654?; MOLYNEUX, CARYLL, third viscount, 1621–1699.

MARY OF BUTTERMERE (*fl.* 1802). See ROBINSON, MARY.

MARY OF FRANCE (1496–1533), queen of Louis XII, king of France; daughter of Henry VII by *Elizabeth of York; betrothed to Charles, prince of Castile (afterwards Emperor Charles V), 1508, but contract subsequently broken off, 1514; married by Henry VIII to Louis XII at Abbeville, 1514; on his death (1515) married in France Charles *Brandon, first duke of Suffolk, to the annoyance of Henry VIII, who was, however, pacified by large gifts of money; gave birth to a son, 1516, and to two daughters, one, Frances, being mother of Lady *Jane Grey; present at Field of the Cloth of Gold, 1520; disliked *Anne Boleyn, and refused to go with her and Henry to meeting with Francis I, 1532.

MARY OF GUELDRES (d. 1463), queen of James II of Scotland; daughter of Arnold, duke of Gueldres; brought up by Philip the Good of Burgundy; married James II, 1449; on death of James at Roxburgh, 1460, set out for the camp with the infant king and took the castle; regent of Scotland during James III's minority; received *Margaret and Henry VI after defeat at Towton, 1461.

MARY OF GUISE (1515–1560), queen of *James V of Scotland, and mother of *Mary

Queen of Scots; daughter of Claude, count of Guise; married Louis of Orleans, 1534, and gave birth to a son, Francis, 1535; sought in marriage by Henry VIII on death of her husband, 1537; married *James V of Scotland at Paris, 1538, and brought him as dower 150,000 livres; after giving birth to two princes, who died, became mother of a daughter, *Mary, 1542; almost at the same time received news of disaster of Solway Moor and death of James; failed in preventing nomination to regency of James *Hamilton, second earl of Arran and duke of Châtelherault, who as next heir after the infant princess was regent according to constitutional precedent, but being a Protestant and supporter of English interests came under her displeasure; carried off by David *Beaton, her chief adviser, with her daughter to Stirling, 1543; accused of too great familiarity with Beaton; accepted French offers of help against England, on which war was declared; desired to marry her daughter in France, but was opposed by Arran and Beaton; secured support of the *Douglases, 1544, and was left leading figure in Scotland by murder of Beaton, 1546; resisted *Somerset's attempts to force Mary's marriage with Edward VI; showed great courage in subsequent disasters; obtained consent of nobles and parliament to Mary's marriage with the dauphin, 1548; sent the princess to France; made peace, 1550; went to France and was received with great honour; on her way back to Scotland visited Edward VI, 1551; became regent of Scotland, 1554; bent on bringing Scotland into line with policy of her family, the Guises; but in order to promote French marriage was obliged to temporize with Protestant party; provoked war with England, 1557, but failed to raise force for invasion; succeeded in bringing about marriage of Mary and dauphin, 1558, and subsequently (1559) treated reformers with severity, with the result that civil war broke out; received help from France, while the Protestants were encouraged by *Cecil, by English money, and the aid of Arran; fortified Leith with French help; on approach of English force to besiege Leith, took refuge in Edinburgh Castle and died there.

MARY OF MODENA (1658–1718), queen of James II of England; only daughter of Alfonso IV, duke of Modena; brought up religiously and strictly; intended becoming a nun; married James, duke of York, through influence of Louis XIV, who aimed at England's conversion and subservience to French policy, 1673; received with great honours on her way to England at Versailles and elsewhere; found favour at court and was attached to her husband's daughters, Mary and Anne, but shared unpopularity of James with

the public; gave birth to five children, 1675–82, who all died young; visited Mary in Holland, 1678; her secretary, Edward *Coleman (d. 1678), fatally involved in the 'Popish Plot', though she herself was innocent; accompanied James, on his withdrawal from England, to the Netherlands, 1679, and to Scotland; returned with him to England, 1680, and again to Scotland; finally came to London with him, 1682; on accession of James II to the throne became identified with aggressive Roman Catholic faction; became ill and distressed by the king's infidelities, 1685; announced her pregnancy, 1687; gave birth to prince of Wales, 1688, an event beyond question, but then commonly disbelieved, suspicion being greatly increased by absence of the proper witnesses; fled to France, followed soon afterwards by James; in contrast with James made very favourable impression on French court; supported schemes for invasion of England and for exciting religious war; corresponded with Jacobites; resided at St Germains Palace, retiring frequently to nunnery at Chaillot; gave birth to Princess Louisa, 1692; received with James pension of 50,000 crowns a month from Louis, and after his death, 1701, annuity of 100,000 francs; buried at Chaillot; was praised by St Simon and Madame de Sévigné, but was always unpopular in England.

MARY QUEEN OF SCOTS (1542–1587), third child and only daughter of *James V of Scotland and *Mary of Guise; queen in infancy on her father's death, 1542; sent to France, 1548, the agreement for her marriage with the dauphin of France (Francis II) being ratified by the estates; educated with royal children of France; brought up strict Roman Catholic, and taught various accomplishments, but not English; famous for her beauty and grace; the great hope of Catholicism; married Francis, 1558, and made secret treaty delivering Scotland to France in case of her death without heir; laid claim to English throne on death of Mary I, 1558, as great-granddaughter of Henry VII; styled herself queen of England; was prostrated by her husband Francis II's death, 1560; entertained various proposals of marriage which were brought forward by the Guises, but obstructed by Catherine de Medici; determined to return to Scotland; arrived, 1561, accompanied by Brantôme, Chastelard, and others; heard mass in her chapel; had stormy interview with *Knox, who had denounced the 'idolatry'; informed the pope of her determination to restore Catholicism; carried on negotiations with Elizabeth for a reconciliation, 1562; entered into sports of the nobles and life of the people, and disarmed hostility; conferred on the Protestant Lord James *Stewart, afterwards earl of Moray (1531?–1570), the title of earl of Mar, and sanctioned expedition against George *Gordon, fourth earl of Huntly, 1562; sent *Maitland to England to claim right of succession to Elizabeth, 1563; showed imprudent partiality for Chastelard, who was executed, after being found concealed in her bedroom, 1563; her project of marriage with Don Carlos of Spain thwarted by the French; pretended to be guided in choice of a husband by Elizabeth, who proposed the earl of Leicester, 1563; married in 1565 Henry *Stewart, earl of Darnley, thus strengthening her claims as heir-presumptive and defying Elizabeth; marched with a force to Glasgow to capture *Moray and rebellious lords, on which Moray took refuge in England; determined to make herself absolute and to impose Roman Catholicism on the country; quarrelled with Darnley, who was supported by the nobles; her favourite, *Riccio, murdered, 1566; determined on revenge, but for the time was reconciled to her husband; fled to Dunbar with Darnley and entered Edinburgh with a powerful force; gave birth to a prince (afterwards James I of England), 1566; became finally estranged from Darnley and showed more marked favour to James *Hepburn, fourth earl of Bothwell; visited Darnley at Glasgow, 1567; persuaded him to accompany her to Edinburgh, and was met by Bothwell, who conveyed them to a house in Kirk-o'-Field, which was blown up in her temporary absence, Darnley being killed; was probably actuated, in conniving at the murder, by motives of revenge and love for Bothwell; co-operated with Bothwell and others in making trial of murderers a fiasco, and left for Seton with Bothwell and others implicated; was carried off to Dunbar, probably at her own instigation; refused offer of a rescue; married to Bothwell at Edinburgh with Protestant rites, 1567; consented to prohibition of cathedral services throughout Scotland, 1567; joined Bothwell, who had escaped from Borthwick Castle, and rode with him to Dunbar; delivered herself to the lords at Carberry Hill, and was imprisoned at Lochleven, 1567; was allowed to choose between a divorce, a trial at which the Casket letters were to be adduced as evidence, and abdication; chose the last and nominated Moray regent; escaped from Lochleven (1568) with George Douglas to Hamilton Palace, where she was joined by nobles and 6,000 men; watched the Battle of Langside, and seeing all was lost escaped to England, 1568; guarded closely at Carlisle and denied interview by Elizabeth till she had cleared herself of Darnley's murder; refused to allow Elizabeth's jurisdiction when conferences meeting at York and Westminster finally reached a formal verdict that nothing had been proved against either party; was nevertheless kept for life a prisoner by Elizabeth;

removed to care of earl of *Shrewsbury, 1569, to Tutbury, and to Wingfield; accepted proposal of marriage with *Norfolk, and joined plot formed for her escape and for a Catholic rising, 1569; on advance of *Northumberland and *Westmorland to Tutbury was removed to Coventry; approved of Moray's assassination, 1570; obtained papal bull dissolving marriage with Bothwell, 1570; was transferred to Chatsworth and then to Sheffield; her death contemplated by Elizabeth after Ridolfi plot, 1572, and the massacre of St Bartholomew; made plans for escape, but achieved nothing by treating with both parties; proposed to pope and Philip conquest of England, and superintended details of projected invasion under the duke of Guise; was accused unjustly by countess of Shrewsbury of criminal intrigues with Shrewsbury, and removed once more to Wingfield; was ignored by her son James VI in negotiations between England and Scotland, 1584, on which she bequeathed her crown to Philip II of Spain; was removed to Tutbury and then to Chartley, 1586; involved herself, through facilities afforded her by *Walsingham, in the *Babington conspiracy; was removed to Fotheringay; put on her trial there, 1586, condemned to death, and was at length executed, 1587, Elizabeth maintaining that she had never intended the execution to take place. A woman of much cultivation, she wrote verse of no great merit. 'Adieu plaisant pays de France', sometimes ascribed to her, was really written by Meusnier de Querlon.

MARZAI, Stephen de (d. 1193). See STEPHEN.

MASCALL, Edward James (d. 1832), collector of customs for port of London, 1816; published works on the customs.

MASCALL, Leonard (d. 1589), author and translator; clerk of the kitchen to Archbishop *Parker; possibly author of *A Booke of the Arte . . . howe to plant and graffe all sortes of trees* (1572) and works on poultry, cattle, fishing, and 'remedies'; drew up *Registrum parochiae de Farnham* (1573).

MASCALL, Robert (d. 1416), bishop of Hereford; distinguished himself at Oxford in philosophy and theology; confessor to Henry IV, c.1400; bishop of Hereford, 1404; took part in condemnation of *Cobham, 1413; delegate to Council of Constance, 1415; *De Legationibus suis lib. i.* and sermons attributed to him.

MASCARENE, Paul (1684–1760), lieutenant-governor of Nova Scotia; of Huguenot family; educated at Geneva; nationalized in England, 1706; commanded Grenadiers at storming of Port Royal; brevet major; lieutenant-governor of Annapolis, 1740, and of province, 1744; defended fort against Indians and French, 1744, in spite of state of garrison and neglect by authorities; sent on mission to New England by Cornwallis, 1751; major-general, 1758; his services inadequately recompensed.

MASCHIART, Michael (1544–1598), Latin poet; perpetual fellow of New College, Oxford, 1562; DCL, 1573; vicar of Writtle, Essex, 1572–98; reputed author of *Poemata Varia*.

MASEFIELD, John Edward (1878–1967), poet laureate; educated at King's School, Warwick, and in the *Conway*, where he learnt seamanship; travelled and worked in the United States; returned to England and contributed to the *Outlook*, the *Academy*, and the *Speaker*, 1897–1906; published *Salt Water Ballads* (1902); worked on *Manchester Guardian*, 1907; published first major poem, *The Everlasting Mercy* (1911), followed by *Reynard the Fox* (1919); wrote naval histories, and criticism, including *William Shakespeare* (1911); also novels and plays, including *Lost Endeavour* (1910) and *Good Friday* (1916), and children's books such as *The Box of Delights* (1935); appointed poet laureate, 1930; OM, 1935; wrote *The Nine Days Wonder* on Dunkirk (1940); honorary degrees from Oxford, Liverpool, and St Andrews; C.Lit., 1961; president, Society of Authors, 1937, and National Book League, 1944–9.

MASERES, Francis (1731–1824), mathematician, historian, and reformer; of Huguenot family; BA, Clare College, Cambridge, 1752; first Newcastle medallist, 1752; MA, 1755; fellow, 1756–9; barrister, Inner Temple, 1750, and later, bencher and treasurer; attorney-general of Quebec, 1766–9; cursitor baron of Exchequer, 1773–1824; senior judge of London sheriffs' court, 1780; zealous Protestant and Whig; Unitarian; inherited great wealth, which he generously employed; FRS, 1771; published several mathematical works, and rejected negative quantities; wrote several books on Quebec, and on social and political questions, including translations from French writers; edited reprints of historical works, and supplied funds for other publications.

MASHAM, Baron (1815–1906). See LISTER, SAMUEL CUNLIFFE.

MASHAM, Abigail, Lady Masham (d. 1734), daughter of Francis Hill, first cousin of Sarah, duchess of Marlborough (see CHURCHILL, SARAH), and related to *Harley; entered service of Lady Rivers, and subsequently lived with the duchess of Marlborough; made bedchamber woman to Queen Anne by the latter's influence; sympathized with Anne's opinions on church and state matters, and gradually supplanted the duchess in Anne's favour; married privately Samuel *Masham (1679?–1758), groom of the bed-

chamber to Prince *George of Denmark, 1707; kept queen's favour in spite of the duchess's indignation; medium of Harley's communications with Anne after his fall, 1708; given care of privy purse on dismissal of the duchess, 1711, and her husband made peer; procured Harley's dismissal, and sided with *Bolingbroke and the Jacobites, 1714; lived in retirement after death of Anne; much esteemed by *Swift.

MASHAM, Damaris, Lady Masham (1658–1708), theological writer; daughter of Ralph *Cudworth; studied under her father and Locke; married Sir Francis Masham, third baronet, of Oates, Essex, 1685; gave birth to a son, 1686; adopted the views of John *Locke, who resided at Oates from 1691 till his death in 1704; published *A Discourse concerning the Love of God* (1696), *Occasional Thoughts* (c.1700), and account of Locke in *Great Historical Dictionary*.

MASHAM, Samuel, first Baron Masham (1679?–1758), son of Sir Francis Masham, third baronet; successively page, equerry, and groom of the bedchamber to Prince *George of Denmark; married Abigail Hill, 1707 (see MASHAM, ABIGAIL, Lady); brigadier-general, 1710; MP, Ilchester, 1710, Windsor, 1711; cofferer of household to Queen Anne, 1711; one of twelve Tory peers created, 1712; remembrancer of the Exchequer, 1716; belonged to famous Society of Brothers.

MASHAM, Samuel, second Baron Masham (1712–1776), son of Samuel *Masham, first Baron Masham; auditor-general of household of George, prince of Wales; given pension by George III, 1761; lord of the bedchamber, 1762; hated by *Swift.

MASKELL, William (1814?–1890), medievalist; MA, University College, Oxford, 1838; extreme high churchman; attacked Bishop *Stanley of Norwich for his support of relaxation of subscription, 1840; rector of Corscombe, Dorset, 1842–7; vicar of St Mary Church, near Torquay, 1847–50; published *Ancient Liturgy of the Church of England* (1844) and other works, which placed him in front rank of English ecclesiastical historians; chaplain to bishop of Exeter; published *Holy Baptism* (1848) and other works; questioned jurisdiction of Privy Council in Gorham case (see GORHAM, GEORGE CORNELIUS); became Roman Catholic, 1850; acquiesced unwillingly in dogma of papal infallibility; lived in retirement and devoted himself to literature and collecting medieval service books and objects; JP and deputy lieutenant for Cornwall.

MASKELYNE, Mervyn Herbert Nevil Story- (1823–1911), mineralogist. See STORY-MASKELYNE.

MASKELYNE, Nevil (1732–1811), astronomer royal; wrangler, Trinity College, Cambridge, 1754; fellow, 1757; MA, 1757; DD, 1777; obtained livings of Shrawardine, 1775, and North Runcton, 1782; assisted *Bradley; sent by Royal Society to observe transit of Venus at St Helena, 1761; was unsuccessful, but made other useful observations; astronomer royal, 1765; established the *Nautical Almanac*, 1766; made about 90,000 observations, published, 1776–1811, with one assistant only; perfected method of transit-observation, 1772; obviated effects of parallax; invented prismatic micrometer (in part anticipated); Copley medallist for *Observations on the Attraction of Mountains* (1775); edited *Mason's correction of Mayer's *Lunar Tables* (1787) and other works; wrote essay on *Equation of Time*; member of French Institute, 1802; FRS, 1758.

MASON, Alfred Edward Woodley (1865–1948), novelist; educated at Dulwich and Trinity College, Oxford; provincial actor, 1888–94; Liberal MP, Coventry, 1906–10; secret-service agent, 1914–18; wrote *The Four Feathers* (1902) and other adventure stories, historical novels, including *Musk and Amber* (1942), Inspector Hanaud detective series, and several plays.

MASON, Arthur James (1851–1928), theological scholar and preacher; BA, Trinity College, Cambridge; fellow of Trinity, 1873; assistant tutor, 1874; honorary canon and diocesan missioner, Truro, 1878; vicar of All Hallows, Barking, 1884–95; honorary canon of Canterbury, 1893; Lady Margaret's professor of divinity and fellow of Jesus College, Cambridge, 1895; master of Pembroke College, Cambridge, 1903; withdrew to Canterbury, 1912; the trusted adviser and helper of successive archbishops in current ecclesiastical affairs; belonged to older school of high churchmen; wrote theological and historical works.

MASON, Charles (1616–1677), Royalist divine; of Eton and King's College, Cambridge; BA, 1635; fellow, 1635–44; DD Oxford, 1642, Cambridge, 1660; deprived of fellowship, 1644; rector of Stower Provost, Dorset, 1647; rector of St Mary Woolchurch, London, 1660–6, and of St Peter-le-Poor, London, 1669–77, and prebendary of St Paul's, London, 1663, and of Salisbury, 1671; published sermons and verse.

MASON, Charles (1730–1787), astronomer; assistant to *Bradley at Greenwich; with Dixon observed transit of Venus at Cape of Good Hope, 1761; settled boundary between Pennsylvania and Maryland, 1763–7; measured an arc of the meridian, 1764; employed by Royal Society on mission at Cavan, Ireland, 1769; observed second transit of Venus and other phenomena; corrected Mayer's *Lunar Tables*; died at Philadelphia.

MASON, Francis (1566?–1621), archdeacon of Norfolk; fellow of Merton College, Oxford, 1586; BA, Brasenose College, Oxford, 1587; MA, Merton College, Oxford, 1590; BD, 1597; obtained rectory of Sudbourn, with chapel of Orford in Suffolk, 1599; wrote *Of the Consecration of the Bishops in the Church of England* (1613), proving validity of their consecration, and exciting several answers from Roman Catholics; published Latin and enlarged editions, and other works.

MASON, Francis (1837–1886), surgeon; FRCS, 1862; filled posts of surgeon and lecturer at Westminster and St Thomas's hospitals and elsewhere; president of Medical Society, 1882; published medical works.

MASON, George (1735–1806), miscellaneous writer; of Corpus Christi College, Oxford; barrister, Inner Temple, 1761; collector of scarce books; published *A Supplement to Johnson's 'English Dictionary'* (1801), *Life of Richard Earl Howe* (1803), and other works.

MASON, George Heming (1818–1872), painter; travelled to Rome through France and Switzerland with his brother, mostly on foot, 1843–5, and earned livelihood by painting portraits of English visitors or settlers and their pet animals; tended the wounded during Italian war; painted cattle in the Campagna; formed friendships with Frederic Lord *Leighton and *Costa; painted *Ploughing in the Campagna*, 1856, and similar pictures; visited Paris exhibition, 1855; returned to England, married, and settled in family mansion at Whitby Abbey, 1858; painted *Wind on the Wolds*, followed by series of English idylls; exhibited at Academy and Dudley Gallery several fine pictures, including *The Cast Shoe* (1865) and the *Harvest Moon* (his last, 1872); ARA, 1869.

MASON, George Henry Monck (1825–1857), British resident at Jodhpore; nephew of Henry Joseph Monck *Mason; distinguished himself as assistant to agent in Rajputana from 1847, and as political agent at Kerowlee; resident at Jodhpur, 1857; provided for safety of Europeans on mutiny of the Jodhpur legion; accompanied troops to meet Sir George St Patrick *Lawrence, and was murdered by the rebels.

MASON, Henry (1573?–1647), divine; brother of Francis *Mason (1566?–1621); MA, Corpus Christi College, Oxford, 1603; BD, 1610; obtained several livings, including (1613) that of St Andrew Undershaft, London; chaplain to

Mason

bishop of London; prebendary of St Paul's, London, 1616; works include *The New Art of Lying, covered by Jesuits* (1624).

MASON, Henry Joseph Monck (1778–1858), miscellaneous writer; brother of William *Monck; scholar and gold medallist, Trinity College, Dublin; BA, 1798; Irish barrister, 1800; examiner to prerogative court; subsequently librarian of King's Inns, 1815; corresponded with Robert Southey; organized societies for giving religious instruction to the Irish-speaking population, and for improvement of prisons; instrumental in founding Irish professorship and scholarships at Dublin University; LL D, Dublin, 1817; works include *Essay on the Antiquity and Constitution of Parliaments in Ireland* (1820).

MASON, James (*fl.* 1743–1783), landscape engraver; executed plates from pictures by Claude, Poussin, and contemporary English artists.

MASON, James (1779–1827), miscellaneous writer; supporter of *Fox; advocated abolition of slavery and Catholic emancipation; published political pamphlets and *The Natural Son* (tragedy, 1805), *Literary Miscellanies* (1809), and other works.

MASON, James Neville (1909–1984), actor; educated at Marlborough College, and Peterhouse, Cambridge; first class in architecture, 1931; acted in Marlowe Society production of *The White Devil*; no formal training as actor; made professional début at Theatre Royal, Aldershot, 1931, and first London appearance at the Arts Theatre, 1933; worked with Old Vic Company and Gate Theatre, Dublin, 1934–7; first film part in *Late Extra*, 1935; during 1939–45 war worked in films, appearing in *The Man in Grey* (1943), *Fanny by Gaslight* (1944), and *The Wicked Lady* (1945); established as film star by *The Seventh Veil* (1945) and *Odd Man Out* (1946); starred in Hollywood films, *Rommel, Desert Fox* (1951) and *Julius Caesar* (1953); nominated for Oscar in *A Star is Born*, 1954; appeared in over a hundred films during fifty years as screen actor; retired to Switzerland; published autobiography, *Before I Forget* (1981).

MASON, Sir John (1503–1566), statesman; son of a cowherd at Abingdon; fellow of All Souls College, Oxford; MA, 1525; king's scholar at Paris; obtained living of Kyngeston, 1532; travelled abroad on the king's service for several years; secretary to Sir Thomas *Wyatt (1503?–1542); gained reputation as diplomat; clerk to Privy Council, 1542; master of the posts, 1544, and French secretary; knighted by Edward VI, 1547; searched registers to establish English suzerainty over Scotland, 1548; dean of Winchester, 1549; ambassador to France, 1550–1, and corresponded with council; master of requests and clerk of parliament, 1551; commissioner to collect 'church stuff', 1552; obtained some of *Somerset's lands; MP, Reading, 1551 and 1552, Taunton, 1552–3; chancellor of Oxford University, 1552–6 and 1559–64; witness to Edward VI's will, 1553; signed letter to Mary announcing proclamation of *Jane, but soon afterwards arranged with lord mayor proclamation of Mary, 1553; gave up ecclesiastical offices, but, favoured by Mary, was made treasurer of the chamber, 1554; ambassador to the emperor Charles V at Brussels, 1553–6, and present at his abdication; reinstated in chancellorship and deanery at Elizabeth's accession; directed foreign policy and negotiated with France, 1559 and 1564.

MASON, John (1586–1635), founder of New Hampshire; matriculated from Magdalen College, Oxford, 1602; assisted in reclamation of the Hebrides, 1610; governor of Newfoundland, 1615; completed first English map of the island, 1625, and wrote *A Briefe Discourse of the Newfoundland* (1620); received various patents for lands in New England; returned to England, 1624; treasurer and paymaster of the army, 1627; received new patents and sailed again, 1629; associated with Sir Ferdinando *Gorges and six London merchants, obtained land on Piscataqua River, 1631 (colony afterwards known as New Hampshire); returned, 1634; was appointed captain of Southsea Castle and inspector of forts and castles on south coast; nominated to council for New England, 1633, and 'vice-admiral of New England', 1635; zealous churchman and Royalist.

MASON, John (*fl.* 1603), fellow of Corpus Christi College, Oxford; MA, 1603; BD; brother of Francis *Mason (1566?–1621).

MASON, John (1600–1672), New England commander; served in Netherlands under Sir Thomas, afterwards Baron *Fairfax (1612–1671); went to Dorchester, Massachusetts, 1630, and obtained military command; assisted migration to Windsor, New Connecticut, 1635; with help of friendly Indians exterminated the Pequots, 1637; major-general of colonial forces, 1638–70; deputy-governor of Connecticut, 1660, and chief judge of colonial county court, 1664–70; prepared *Brief History of the Pequot War*.

MASON, John (1646?–1694), enthusiast and poet; MA, Clare Hall, Cambridge, 1668; vicar of Stantonbury, 1668–74, and rector of Water Stratford, 1674; Calvinist and enthusiastic preacher on the millenium, which he announced was beginning at Water Stratford; preached,

1690, and published sermon on the ten virgins, which made some stir; attracted noisy encampment of followers to the village, who remained unconvinced of his mortality after his exhumed corpse had been shown to them; wrote 'A living stream as crystal clear', and other familiar hymns.

MASON, John (1706–1763), Nonconformist divine and author; grandson of John *Mason (1646?–1694); tutor and chaplain in family of Governor Feaks; Presbyterian minister at Dorking, 1729, and at Cheshunt, 1746; published *Plea for Christianity* (1743) and other works, and trained students for ministry.

MASON, John Charles (1798–1881), marine secretary to Indian government; solicitor's clerk; later employed in important affairs in secretary's office at East India House; compiled *An Analysis of the Constitution of the East India Company* (1825–6); marine secretary, 1837; introduced great improvements; arranged for transport of 50,000 troops on outbreak of Mutiny, 1857.

MASON, John Monck (1726–1809), Shakespearian commentator; MA, Trinity College, Dublin, 1761; Irish barrister, 1752; Irish MP, Blessington, 1761 and 1769, St Canice, 1776, 1783, 1790, and 1798; made commissioner of public works, 1771, and of revenue of Ireland, 1772; became supporter of government in Ireland; Irish privy councillor; voted for Union in last Irish parliament; works include *Comments on the last Edition of Shakespeare's Plays* (1785).

MASON, Sir Josiah (1795–1881), pen manufacturer and philanthropist; was successively fruit-seller in the streets, shoemaker, carpenter, blacksmith, house-painter, and manufacturer of imitation gold jewellery and split rings; made split rings by machinery; manufactured pens for Perry; joined the Elkingtons in electroplate business, 1844, and in smelting works; acquired great wealth; founded almshouses and orphanage at Erdington and the Mason College at Birmingham; knighted, 1872.

MASON, Martin (*fl.* 1650–1676), Quaker; continually imprisoned for his opinions, 1650–71; concerned in schism of John *Perrot; wrote *An Address* (to Charles II), and another to parliament, 1660; liberated, 1672; published controversial tracts.

MASON, Richard (pseudonym) (1601–1678), Franciscan. See ANGELUS À SANCTO FRANCISCO.

MASON, Robert (1571–1635), politician and author; of Balliol College, Oxford, and Lincoln's Inn; MP, Ludgershall, Wiltshire, 1626, Winchester, 1628; opponent of the court; assistant to managers of *Buckingham's impeachment, 1626; one of the framers of the Petition of Right,

1628; defended *Eliot, 1630; recorder of London, 1634; author of *Reason's Monarchie* (1602) and of other writings.

MASON, Sir Robert (1589?–1662), secretary to duke of *Buckingham; fellow of St John's College, Cambridge, and LL D; knighted, 1661.

MASON, Thomas (1580–1619?), divine; of Magdalen College, Oxford; vicar of Odiham, 1614–19; published *Christ's Victorie over Sathan's Tyrannie* (1615) and *A Revelation of the Revelation* (1619).

MASON, Thomas (d. 1660), Latin poet; demy, 1596, and fellow, 1603–14; of Magdalen College, Oxford, MA, 1605; DD, 1631; prebendary of Salisbury, 1624; rector of North Waltham, 1623, and Weyhill, 1624; ejected during rebellion; wrote Latin verses.

MASON, William (*fl.* 1672–1709), stenographer; London writing-master; published three treatises on shorthand (1672, 1682, and 1707), embodying three systems, the last and best, with modifications, being still in use; greatest stenographer of seventeenth century; celebrated for his skill in minute handwriting.

MASON, William (1724–1797), poet; scholar of St John's College, Cambridge; MA, Pembroke, 1749; wrote 'monody' on *Pope's death (published 1747); elected fellow of Pembroke College, Cambridge, through *Gray's influence, 1747; composed 'Isis' (poem denouncing Oxford Jacobitism), 1748, and ode upon duke of Newcastle's installation, 1749, and 'Elfrida', dramatic poem, 1752; became acquainted with *Hurd and *Warburton; rector of Aston, Yorkshire, 1754, and chaplain to Lord *Holderness; visited Germany, 1755; king's chaplain, 1757; canon of York, 1762; published odes (1756), *Caractacus* (1759), and 'elegies' (1762); maintained close friendship with Gray, and was his literary executor; published *An Heroic Epistle* to Sir William *Chambers, a sharp satire (1773); published Gray's *Life and Letters* (1775); corresponded with Horace *Walpole; prominent in political agitation for retrenchment and reform, 1780, but later became follower of Pitt; his *Sappho* (lyrical drama) first printed (1797); imitator of Gray, and, in satire, follower of Pope; composed church music, and invented an instrument, the 'Celestina'; his *Works* collected (1811).

MASON, William Monck (1775–1859), historian; brother of Henry Joseph Monck *Mason; 'land waiter for exports' at Dublin, 1796; published *The History and Antiquities of the . . . Church of St. Patrick* (1819), portion of much larger projected work, and a pamphlet, *Suggestions relative to . . . a Survey . . . of Ireland* (1825).

MASON, William Shaw (1774–1853), statist; BA, Dublin, 1796; remembrancer, 1805, and secretary to commissioners for public records in Ireland, 1810; published *A Statistical Account . . . of Ireland* (1814, 1816, 1819) and other works.

MASON-MACFARLANE, Sir **(Frank) Noel** (1889–1953), lieutenant-general; educated at Rugby and Royal Military Academy, Woolwich; gazetted to Royal Artillery, 1909; served in 1914–18 and Afghan (1919) wars; military attaché, Berlin, 1937–9; believed war inevitable and advocated choosing time unfavourable to Hitler; major-general and director of military intelligence, BEF in France, 1939–40; improvised 'MacForce', 1940; DSO; deputy governor, Gibraltar, 1940; head, British Military Mission, Moscow, 1941–2; governor, Gibraltar, 1942–4; chief commissioner, Allied Control Commission, Italy, 1944; Labour MP, North Paddington, 1945–6; CB, 1939; KCB, 1943.

MASQUERIER, John James (1778–1855), painter; studied at Paris and in London; exhibited a picture of *Napoleon reviewing the Consular Guards*, 1801, which caused him to be bitterly attacked as a spy by *William Cobbett; painted, among others, portraits of Emma, Lady *Hamilton, Harriot *Mellon, afterwards duchess of St Albans, Miss *O'Neil, and Warren *Hastings; intimate with Sir Francis *Burdett, Baroness Burdett Coutts, John *Wilkes, Michael *Faraday, and Thomas *Campbell.

MASSEREENE, second earl of. See SKEFF-INGTON, CLOTWORTHY, 1742–1805.

MASSEREENE, Viscounts. See CLOT-WORTHY, Sir JOHN, first viscount, d. 1665; SKEFFINGTON, Sir JOHN, second viscount, d. 1695; SKEFFINGTON, JOHN SKEFFINGTON FOS-TER, tenth viscount, 1812–1863.

MASSEY, (Charles) Vincent (1887–1967), diplomat, patron of education and arts, and first Canadian-born governor-general of Canada; born in Toronto; educated at St Andrews College, Toronto, University of Toronto, and Balliol College, Oxford; lecturer in modern history, Toronto University, 1913; dean of residence, Victoria College, 1913–15; served in Canadian Army (lieutenant-colonel), 1914–18; president of family business, Massey-Harris, 1921–5; set up Massey Foundation to encourage the arts; first diplomatic representative to United States of ministerial rank, 1926; president, National Liberal Federation, 1932–5; high commissioner, London, 1935–46; trustee, National Gallery, London, 1941–6; chairman, 1943–6; trustee, Tate Gallery, 1942–6; chairman, board of trustees, National Gallery of Canada, 1948–52; governor-general of Canada, 1952–9; PC, 1941;

CH, 1946; hon. DCL, Oxford, and honorary degrees from other universities; hon. fellow, Royal Society of Canada; publications include *The Sword of Lionheart and Other Wartime Speeches* (1943) and *What's Past is Prologue, Memoirs* (1963).

MASSEY, Sir **Edward** (1619?–1674?), major-general; Royalist, 1642; joined Parliamentarians; general of the Western Association, 1645; co-operated with Fairfax in reducing the west, 1645–6; MP, Wootton Bassett, 1646; commander-in-chief of the London forces; impeached by the army, 1647; fled to Holland; returned, 1648; excluded from the House of Commons by *Pride's Purge, 1648, and imprisoned with *Waller; again escaped to Holland and joined the king, 1649; lieutenant-general, 1651; wounded at Worcester, taken prisoner, and lodged in the Tower, 1651; again escaped to Holland; negotiated with English Presbyterians, 1654, 1655, and 1660; appointed governor of Gloucester by Charles and knighted, 1660; MP, Gloucester, 1661–74.

MASSEY, Eyre, first Baron Clarina (1719–1804), general; served in West Indies, 1739; ensign, 1741; commanded Niagara expedition, 1759; routed the French at La Belle Famille and gained possession of all the Upper Ohio; commanded Grenadiers at Montreal, 1760, Martinique, 1761, Havana, 1762, New York and Quebec, 1763–9; Halifax, 1776–80, and Cork, 1794–6; raised to peerage of Ireland, 1800.

MASSEY, Gerald (1828–1907), poet; after scanty education was put to work at Tring at age of 8; studied for himself; published at Tring *Poems and Chansons* (1848); joined Chartists; helped to edit *The Spirit of Freedom*, 1849; soon turned to Christian socialism; wrote for the *Christian Socialist*; brought out *Voices of Freedom and Lyrics of Love* (1850), and *The Ballad of Babe Christabel and other Poems* (1854); his lyrical impulse was widely acknowledged; other volumes of verse followed; complete poetical works, Boston (1857), London (1861); a selection, *My Lyrical Life*, appeared in 1899; his career suggested that of Felix Holt to George *Eliot; he became a journalist and popular lecturer, living for a time at Edinburgh, and from 1862 to 1877 near Little Gaddesden in a farmhouse provided by Lord Brownlow; wrote on Shakespeare's sonnets, 1866 (reissued, 1888); thrice lectured in America; developed faith in spiritualism and finally took to writing on old Egyptian civilization.

MASSEY, Sir **Harrie Stewart Wilson** (1908–1983), physicist; born in Melbourne, Australia; educated at University High School, Melbourne, and Melbourne University; M.Sc.,

BA; studied wave mechanics for M.Sc.; awarded Aitchison scholarship to study at Cavendish Laboratory, Cambridge, 1929–33; attached to Trinity College; Ph.D., 1932; published *Theory of Atomic Collisions* (in collaboration with Nevill Mott, 1933); lecturer in mathematical physics, Queen's University, Belfast, 1933–8; Goldsmid professor of mathematics, University College, London, 1938–40; worked on magnetic mines in Admiralty research department, 1940; FRS, 1940; deputy chief scientist, 1941; chief scientist, 1943; worked on Manhattan Project at Berkeley, California, USA, 1943–5; Quain professor of physics, University College, London, 1950; vice-provost, 1969–73; chairman, British national committee on space research, 1959; president, council of European Space Research Organization, 1964; physical secretary, Royal Society, 1969–78; chairman, Council for Scientific Policy, 1965–9; received many honorary doctorates and other academic honours; published more than 200 scientific papers and many books; knighted, 1960.

MASSEY, John (1651–1715), Roman Catholic divine; fellow of Merton College, Oxford, 1672; MA, Magdalen Hall, Oxford, 1676; senior proctor, 1684; became a Roman Catholic, 1685; dean of Christ Church, Oxford, 1686; one of the founders of the Oxford Chemical Society, 1683; fled to France, 1688; died in Paris.

MASSEY, William (1691–1764?), miscellaneous writer and translator; published *Origin and Progress of Letters* (1763) and translations.

MASSEY, William Ferguson (1856–1925), prime minister of New Zealand; born County Derry; emigrated to New Zealand and took up farming, 1870; Conservative MHR, 1894–1925; chief opposition whip, 1895–1903; leader of Conservative opposition, 1903–12; prime minister, as leader of 'Reform party', 1912–25; formed national government, 1915; led New Zealand very ably through European war.

MASSEY, William Nathaniel (1809–1881), politician and historian; recorder of Portsmouth, 1852, Plymouth, 1855; MP, Newport, Isle of Wight, 1855–7, Salford, 1857–63; financial member of government of India, 1863–8; MP, Tiverton, 1872–81; published history of George III's reign, 1855–63.

MASSIE, James William (1799–1869), Independent minister; missionary in India, 1822–39; secretary to Home Missionary Society; advocated free trade and emancipation of slaves.

MASSIE, Joseph (d. 1784), writer on trade and finance; formed collection of 1,500 treatises on economics, 1557–1763; compiled statistics to illustrate the growth of British trade and published works on political economy.

MASSIE, Thomas Leeke (1802–1898), admiral; entered navy, 1818; lieutenant, 1827; commander, 1838; captain, 1841; served in Burmese War, 1849; on North American Station, 1855–6; rear-admiral, 1860; admiral, 1872.

MASSINGBERD, Sir Archibald Armar Montgomery- (1871–1947), field marshal. See MONTGOMERY-MASSINGBERD.

MASSINGBERD, Francis Charles (1800–1872), chancellor of Lincoln; went to Italy with Dr Arnold and William Ralph *Churton, 1824; MA, Magdalen College, Oxford, 1825; prebendary of Lincoln, 1847; chancellor and canon, 1862; active member of Convocation; proctor for parochial clergy, 1857, for the chapter, 1868; published *English History of the Leaders of the Reformation* (1842).

MASSINGER, Philip (1583–1640), dramatist; entered at St Alban Hall, Oxford, 1602; came to London, 1606; soon became a famous playwright; collaborated with Nathaniel *Field, Robert *Daborne, Cyril *Tourneur, and *Dekker; wrote regularly in conjunction with *Fletcher, 1613–30; associated with the King's Company of actors, 1616–23 and 1625–40; with the Cockpit Company, 1623–5; remarkable for his skill in the working out of plots and his insight into stage requirements. Among his patrons were the *Herbert family, the earl of *Carnarvon, Sir Warham *St Leger, Sir Francis Foljambe, Sir Thomas Bland, Sir Aston *Cokayne, and Lord *Mohun; the fifteen plays entirely written by him are *The Duke of Milan* (1623), *The Unnatural Combat* (1639), *The Bondman* (1624), *The Renegado* (1630), *The Parliament of Love* (licensed for the Cockpit, 1624), *A New Way to pay Old Debts* (1632), *The Roman Actor* (1629), *The Maid of Honour* (1632), *The Picture* (1630), *The Great Duke of Florence* (1635), *The Emperor of the East* (1631), *Believe as you list* ('Stationers' Registers', 1653), *The City Madam* (1658), *The Guardian* (1655), and *The Bashful Lover* (1655). In collaboration with Fletcher he wrote, among others, portions of *Henry VIII* (1617) and of *Two Noble Kinsmen* (1634), in both of which a large share is attributed to Shakespeare. His political views inclined to the popular party; in *The Bondman* he supported the Herberts in their quarrel with *Buckingham, whom he denounced under the guise of Gisco. Thinly veiled reflections on current politics figure in other plays.

MASSINGHAM, Harold John (1888–1952), author and journalist; son of H. W. *Massingham; educated at Westminster and The Queen's College, Oxford; contributed on literary and natural history topics to *Nation* and *Athenaeum*, 1916–24, *Field*, 1938–51; books on English countryside include *English Downland* (1936) and *Cotswold Country* (1937); other publications include *Downland Man* (1926), *The English Countryman* (1942), and edition of *The Writings of Gilbert White of Selborne* (1938).

MASSINGHAM, Henry William (1860–1924), journalist; joined staff of *Eastern Daily Press*, 1877; went to London, 1883; editor of *Star*, 1890, of *Labour World*, 1891; occupied various positions on staff of *Daily Chronicle*, 1892–5; editor, 1895; resigned because of his opposition to South African War, 1899; editor of *The Nation*, 1907–23; formed this Liberal weekly journal into powerful organ of advanced but independent opinion; joined Labour party and transferred his 'Wayfarer's Diary' to *New Statesman*, 1923; showed passionate energy for human welfare.

MASSON, David (1822–1907), biographer and editor; MA, Aberdeen University, 1839; studied divinity at Edinburgh, 1839–42, but abandoned thoughts of entering ministry; visited London, 1843; introduced by Thomas *Carlyle to editor of *Fraser's Magazine*, 1844; wrote for W. & R. Chambers textbooks on Roman, ancient, medieval, and modern history, 1847–56; removed to London, 1847; an intimate of the Carlyles, *Thackeray, Douglas *Jerrold, and Mark *Lemon; professor of English literature at University College, London, 1853–65; published *Essays, chiefly on English Poets* (1859); started (1859) *Life of Milton* (6 vols., 1859–80), the standard authority; started, 1859, and edited till 1867, *Macmillan's Magazine*; professor of rhetoric and English literature at Edinburgh University, 1865–95; a popular teacher; supporter of women's higher education; edited *Privy Council Register of Scotland* (1880–99); Rhind lecturer, 1886; historiographer royal for Scotland, 1896; hon. RSA, 1896; hon. LL D, Aberdeen, Litt.D, Dublin; voluminous writings include editions of *Goldsmith (1869), *Milton (3 vols., 1874), and *De Quincey (14 vols., 1889–90), biographies of *Drummond of Hawthornden (1873) and De Quincey (1878), *Edinburgh Sketches and Memories* (1892), and (posthumously) *Memories of London in the Forties* (1908) and *Memories of Two Cities* (1911).

MASSON, Sir David Orme (1858–1937), chemist; son of David *Masson; educated at Edinburgh Academy and University; research fellow in chemistry, 1882–6; professor of chemistry, Melbourne, 1886–1923; president, Australasian Association for Advancement of Science, 1911–13; influential in founding and served on Commonwealth Council for Scientific and Industrial Research; initiated Australian

Chemical Institute, the Australian National Research Council (with Sir T. W. E. *David), and other bodies; FRS, 1903; KBE, 1923.

MASSON, Francis (1741–1805), gardener and botanist; sent, by the authorities at Kew Gardens, to collect plants and bulbs at the Cape, 1772; in 1776 to the Canaries, Azores, Madeira, and the West Indies, and to Portugal and Madeira, 1783; again sent to the Cape, 1786–95, and to North America, 1798; genus *Massonia* named after him by Linnaeus.

MASSON, George Joseph Gustave (1819–1888), educational writer; educated at Tours; B. ès L., Université de France, 1837; came to England as private tutor, 1847; French master at Harrow, 1855–88; Vaughan librarian from 1869; published works on French literature and history, and edited French classics.

MASSUE DE RUVIGNY, Henri de, second marquis de Ruvigny, first earl of Galway (1648–1720), born in Paris; entered the army and served in Portugal; aide-de-camp to Marshal Turenne, 1672–5; sent by Louis XIV to England to detach Charles II from the Dutch alliance and elected deputy-general of the Huguenots, 1678; endeavoured unsuccessfully to avert their persecution; retired to England, 1688; as major-general of horse in the English service served in Ireland under William III, 1691; commander-in-chief of the forces in Ireland, 1692; created Viscount Galway and Baron Portarlington, 1692; joined the army in Flanders, 1693; envoy-extraordinary to Turin, 1694; created earl of Galway, 1697; appointed one of the lords justices of Ireland, 1697; retired from government of Ireland, 1701; sent on a mission to the elector of Cologne, 1701; commander of the English forces in Portugal, 1704; badly wounded while besieging Badajoz, 1705; reduced fortresses of Alcantara and Ciudad Rodrigo, and entered Madrid, 1706; compelled to retreat to Valentia, 1706; defeated at Almanza through the cowardice of the Portuguese, 1707; collected 14,600 troops in less than five months; envoy-extraordinary to Lisbon, 1708; displayed great personal bravery at the Battle on the Caya, 1709; recalled, 1710; appointed lord justice in Ireland, in view of Jacobite rising, 1715; retired, 1716.

MASSY, William Godfrey Dunham (1838–1906), lieutenant-general; BA, Trinity College, Dublin, 1859; LL D, 1873; entered army, 1854; served at the Redan, where his gallantry earned him the sobriquet of 'Redan' Massy; commanded Royal Irish Lancers, 1871–9; prominent in Battle of Charasiab (Oct. 1879), in Afghan War; cut off by Afghans at Killa Kazi, Dec. 1879; removed from command for rash advance, 1880; CB,

1887; in command of troops in Ceylon, 1888–93; lieutenant-general, 1893.

MASTER, John (*fl.* 1654–1680), physician; BA, Christ Church, Oxford, 1657, and MD, 1672; MA, St Mary Hall, Oxford, 1659; hon. FRCP, 1680, and assisted Dr Thomas *Willis (1621–1675) in his medical publications.

MASTER, Richard (d. 1588), physician; fellow of All Souls, Oxford, 1533; MA, 1537; FCP, 1554; MD, Christ Church, Oxford, 1554; physician to Queen Elizabeth, 1559; president, College of Physicians, 1561; prebendary of York, 1563.

MASTER, Streynsham (1682–1724), naval captain; brother-in-law of George *Byng; captain, 1709; as captain of the *Superbe* at the Battle of Cape Passaro, 1718, captured the Spanish commander-in-chief.

MASTER, Thomas (1603–1643), divine; fellow of New College, Oxford, 1624; MA, 1629; BD, 1641; rector of Wykeham, 1637; assisted Edward *Herbert, Baron Herbert of Cherbury, in his *Life of Henry VIII*, and translated Herbert's work into Latin.

MASTER, Sir William (d. 1662), high sheriff of Gloucestershire; grandson of Richard *Master; member of the Inner Temple, 1612; knighted, 1622; MP, Cirencester, 1624; high sheriff of Gloucestershire, 1627; at first a Parliamentarian, but (1642) forced to contribute to the royal garrison of Cirencester; submitted to parliament, 1644, but his estate sequestered for entertaining Charles I, 1644.

MASTER, William (1627–1684), divine; son of Sir William *Master; bachelor-fellow of Merton College, Oxford, 1651; MA, 1652; vicar of Preston, near Cirencester, 1658; rector of Woodford, Essex, 1661; prebendary of St Paul's, London, 1663; rector of Southchurch, 1666, for a year; prebendary of Cadington Major, 1667; rector of St Vedast, Foster Lane, London, 1671; published moral essays.

MASTERMAN, Charles Frederick Gurney (1874–1927), politician, author, and journalist; BA, Christ's College, Cambridge; Liberal MP, West Ham (North), 1906–11, for South-West Bethnal Green, 1911–14; under-secretary, Local Government Board, 1908; under-secretary of state, Home Department, 1909; financial secretary to Treasury, 1912; chancellor, duchy of Lancaster, with seat in Cabinet, 1914–15; director, Wellington House (propaganda department), 1914–18; MP, Rusholme division of Manchester, 1923–4; works include *The Condition of England* (1909).

MASTERMAN, Sir John Cecil (1891–1977), academic and intelligence officer; educated at Osborne and Dartmouth as naval cadet, but abandoned naval career and won a scholarship to Worcester College, Oxford, 1909; first class in modern history, 1913; lecturer at Christ Church; interned in Germany during 1914–18 war; elected student of Christ Church, 1919; junior censor, 1921–4; senior censor, 1925–6; represented England at lawn tennis, 1920 and 1925, and at hockey, 1927; toured Canada with MCC, 1937; published a detective story (1933), novel (1935), and play (1937); joined army, 1940; chairman, XX committee of MI5, concerned with supply of false information to Germany, 1941–5; elected provost of Worcester College, Oxford, 1946; published *To Teach the Senators Wisdom* (1952); on governing bodies of five public schools; vice-chancellor, Oxford University, 1957–8; raised Oxford Historic Buildings' Fund; chairman of committee to examine restrictions on political activities of civil servants, 1947–8; chairman, Army Education Advisory Board, 1952–6; member of BBC General Advisory Council, 1952–9; on retirement from Worcester College (1961), adviser to Birfield Group of engineering companies; member of Educational Advisory Committee for Associated Television; published *The Double-Cross System in the War of 1939 to 1945* (1972) and autobiography, *On the Chariot Wheel* (1975); OBE, 1944; knighted, 1959; received honorary degrees; hon. fellow, Worcester College, Oxford, St Catharine's College, Cambridge, and hon. student of Christ Church.

MASTERS, John (1914–1983), soldier and author; born at Calcutta; educated at Wellington and Sandhurst; joined 4th Prince of Wales's Own Gurkha Rifles, 1935; served on North-West Frontier, 1936–8; Baluchistan, 1939; Iraq, Syria, and Persia (Iran), 1941; at Staff College, Quetta, 1942–3; commanded brigade of Chindits in Burma, 1944–5; chief of staff, 19th Indian Infantry division; DSO, 1944; OBE, 1945; at GHQ, Army in India, 1945–7; instructor, Staff College, Camberley, 1947–8; unhappy in England, resigned commission, and emigrated to USA, 1948; wrote article accepted by *Atlantic Monthly*; first novel, *Nightrunners of Bengal*, rejected by many publishers until accepted by Viking Press; became immediate success, 1951; followed by *The Deceivers* (1952), *The Lotus and the Wind* (1953), and *Bhowani Junction* (1954) which was filmed, 1955; further novels published as 'Loss of Eden' trilogy, *Now God be Thanked* (1979), *Heart of War* (1980), and *By the Green of the Spring* (1981); last novel, *Man of War* (1983) based on his army experiences; also published autobiographical *Bugles and a Tiger* (1956), *The Road Past Mandalay* (1961), and *Pilgrim Son* (1971).

MASTERS, Mrs Mary (d. 1771), poetess; acquainted with Dr *Johnson; wrote hymns.

MASTERS, Maxwell Tylden (1833–1907), botanist; MRCS, 1856; MD, St Andrews, 1862; lecturer on botany at St George's Hospital Medical School, 1855–68; published valuable researches in his *Vegetable Teratology* (1869); principal editor of *Gardeners' Chronicle*, 1865; active supporter of Royal Horticultural Society; wrote much on passion flowers and conifers in botanical works and journals; revised *Henfrey's *Elementary Course of Botany* (1870) and wrote *Botany for Beginners* (1872) and *Plant Life* (1883); FRS, 1870.

MASTERS, Robert (1713–1798), historian; grandson of Sir William *Master; fellow of Corpus Christi College, Cambridge, 1738–58; MA, 1738; BD, 1746; FSA, 1752; rector of Landbeach, 1756, and of Waterbeach, 1759; resigned his rectories in favour of relations; published *History of Corpus Christi College* (1753; with appendix of lives of its members, 1755).

MASTERTOWN, Charles (1679–1750), Presbyterian divine; MA, Edinburgh, 1697; ministered at Connor, Co. Antrim, 1704–23; moderator of the general synod at Dungannon, and installed at Third Belfast, 1723, where the non-subscription controversy was in active progress; established an orthodox congregation; published expository and polemical works.

MATCHAM, George (1753–1833), traveller and Indian civil servant; wrote account of part of his overland journey home from India in 1783; patented apparatus for preserving vessels from shipwreck, 1802.

MATCHAM, George (1789–1877), civil lawyer; son of George *Matcham (1753–1833); LL D, St John's College, Cambridge, 1820; advocate in Doctors' Commons, 1820; contributed to *Hoare's *History of Wilts* (1825).

MATHER, Cotton (1663–1728), New England divine; son of Increase *Mather; minister at Boston, Mass., 1684–1728; DD, Glasgow, 1710; FRS, 1714; linguist and author of *Magnalia Christi Americana* (1702).

MATHER, Increase (1639–1723), president of Harvard College; son of Richard *Mather; MA and fellow of Harvard, 1656; came to England, 1657; MA, Trinity College, Dublin, 1658; ordained at Boston, Massachusetts, 1664; presided at Boston synod, 1680; procured refusal to give up Boston charter, 1683; president of Harvard, 1684–1701; conveyed (1688) thanks of colony to James II for declaration of liberty of conscience, 1687; DD; gained an enlarged charter from William III for Massachusetts; published religious writings.

MATHER, Nathanael (1631–1697), Congregational divine; son of Richard *Mather; MA, Harvard, 1647; vicar of Harberton, 1655, of Barnstaple, 1656; pastor of English Church, Rotterdam, 1660, and at New Row, Dublin, 1671, and Paved Alley, Lime Street, London, 1688; joined the 'happy union', 1691, but aided in its disruption; Pinners' Hall lecturer, 1694.

MATHER, Richard (1596–1669), Congregational divine; originally a schoolmaster; ordained minister at Toxteth, 1618; suspended, 1633, for not using ceremonies; emigrated to New England, 1635; accepted call from Dorchester, Massachusetts; his plan to check Presbyterianism (the 'Cambridge platform') adopted by the Cambridge synod, 1648; wrote principally on church government.

MATHER, Robert Cotton (1808–1877), missionary; went to India, 1833; built schools and churches at Mirzapore, 1838–73; revised and edited the Bible in Hindustani; LL D, Glasgow, 1862; returned to England, 1873; published a New Testament commentary in Hindustani.

MATHER, Samuel (1626–1671), Congregational divine; son of Richard *Mather; MA and fellow, Harvard, 1643; chaplain of Magdalen College, Oxford, 1650; attended parliamentary commissioners to Scotland, 1653; incorporated MA, Cambridge and (1654) Dublin; senior fellow of Trinity College, Dublin, 1654; ordained, 1656; curate of Burtonwood, 1660; ejected, 1662; erected meeting house in New Row, Dublin, 1662; published religious works.

MATHER, William (*fl.* 1695), author; Quaker from 1661; schoolmaster and surveyor of highways at Bedford; chief work, *Young Man's Companion* (1681), reaching twenty-four editions.

MATHESON, George (1842–1906), theologian and hymn-writer; known as 'the blind preacher'; blind from boyhood; BA, Glasgow University, 1861; MA, 1862; minister of Innellan Church, 1868–86, and of St Bernard's Parish Church, Edinburgh, 1886–99; issued popular theological and devotional works which had a wide vogue; they include *The Growth of the Spirit of Christianity* (2 vols., 1877), *The Psalmist and the Scientist* (1887), *Sacred Songs* (1890, 3rd edn., 1904), and studies of representative men and women of the Bible (4 ser., 1902–7); DD, Edinburgh, 1879; LL D, 1902; FRS, Edinburgh, 1902.

MATHETES (1821?–1878). See JONES, JOHN.

MATHEW. See also MATTHEW.

MATHEW, David James (1902–1975), archbishop of Apamea in Bithynia; educated at Osborne and Dartmouth and served as midshipman, 1918; entered Balliol College, Oxford, 1920; attracted to Carthusian life, studied at Beda College, Rome; ordained, 1929, but found unsuitable for the religious life; curate at St David's Cathedral, Cardiff; Litt.D., Trinity College, Dublin, 1933; published (in collaboration with his brother Gervase) *The Reformation and the Contemplative Life* (1934), having published in 1933 *The Celtic Peoples and Renaissance Europe*; chaplain to Roman Catholics, London University, 1934–44; published *Catholicism in England 1535–1935* (1936); bishop auxiliary of Westminster, 1938–45; apostolic visitor to Ethiopia, 1945; delivered Ford lectures at Oxford, 1945–6, published as *The Social Structure in Caroline England* (1948); in Mombasa as archbishop of Apamea, 1946–53; published trilogy of novels, 1950–3; bishop-in-ordinary (RC) to HM Forces, 1954–63; in retirement published light biographies, *James I* (1967), *Lord Acton and his Times* (1968), *The Courtiers of Henry VIII* (1970), and *Lady Jane Grey* (1972); devoted to his brother, **Anthony** (1905–1976), scholar, who received name Gervase when he entered the Dominican Order, 1928; studied at Balliol College, Oxford, 1925–7; ordained priest, 1934, at Blackfriars, Oxford, where he spent the rest of his life; university lecturer in Byzantine studies, 1947–71; took part in archaeological investigations in East Africa and Southern Arabia; edited (with Roland Oliver) first volume of *History of East Africa* (1963); also published *Byzantine Aesthetics* (1963); collaborated in his brother David's work.

MATHEW, Sir James Charles (1830–1908), judge; senior moderator, Trinity College, Dublin, 1850; called to bar (Lincoln's Inn), 1851; had vast City practice as a junior; among Treasury counsel on prosecution of the Tichborne claimant, 1873; made judge of Queen's Bench division and knighted, 1881; obtained institution of commercial court, 1895; as first judge, gave concise and terse judgements; as chairman of Royal Commission of Inquiry into evictions in Ireland, created precedent of refusing to allow cross-examination by counsel, which led to resignation of many members of commission, 1892; judge of Court of Appeal, 1901–5; ready, facile, and humorous speaker; an ardent radical and devout Roman Catholic.

MATHEW, Theobald (1790–1856), apostle of temperance; Roman Catholic priest, 1841; sent to small chapel in Cork; opened free school for boys and another for girls; signed total abstinence pledge, 1838; visited the principal cities of Ireland with wonderful effect; his preaching in London described by Mrs Carlyle, 1843; worked energetically during the Irish famine; preached in the United States, 1849; returned to Ireland, 1851.

MATHEW, Theobald (1866–1939), lawyer and wit; son of Sir J. C. *Mathew and brother-in-law of John *Dillon; educated at the Oratory School and Trinity College, Oxford; called to bar (Lincoln's Inn), 1890; bencher, 1916; practised as junior on common-law side; recorder of Margate, 1913–27, Maidstone, 1927–36; joint-editor of *Commercial Cases* (1896); contributed 'Forensic Fables' to *Law Journal* (collected in 4 vols., 1926–32).

MATHEW, Sir Theobald (1898–1964), director of public prosecutions; educated at the Oratory School, London; served with Irish Guards during 1914–18 war; MC, 1918; called to bar (Lincoln's Inn), 1921; admitted solicitor and partner in Charles Russell & Co., 1928; joined Home Office, 1941; head of criminal division, 1942–4; director of public prosecutions, 1944–64; KBE, 1946.

MATHEWS. See also MATTHEWS.

MATHEWS, Basil Joseph (1879–1951), writer and teacher on the missionary and ecumenical movement; educated at Oxford High School and University; editor for London Missionary Society, 1910–19; head, Press Bureau of Conference of British Missionary Societies, 1920–4; literary secretary, World's Committee, YMCA, Geneva, 1924–9; visiting lecturer, later professor, Christian world-relations, Boston, 1932–44; Union College, University of British Columbia, 1944–9; wrote over forty books; hon. LL D, British Columbia, 1949.

MATHEWS, Charles (1776–1835), comedian; went to Ireland, 1794; played at Dublin, Cork, and Limerick; left Ireland, 1795; played in Wales, 1795–7; joined Tate *Wilkinson, and became a popular actor on the York circuit; appeared at the Haymarket, 1803, 1805–7, and 1812–17; at Drury Lane, London, 1804 and 1807; accompanied the burnt-out actors of Drury Lane to the Lyceum, London, 1809–11; instituted at entertainments, called 'At Homes', a series of sketches, the first called *The Mail Coach* (1808); produced numerous other 'At Homes'; went on tour in America, 1822–3; undertook with Frederick Henry *Yates the management of the Adelphi, 1828; played with Yates in Paris, 1829; again visited America, 1834; compelled to return by the failure of his voice; played 400 different parts; praised by Leigh Hunt, Horace *Smith, and Lord *Byron; intimate of *Coleridge and the *Lambs; his collection of pictures, largely consisting of theatrical portraits, bought for the Garrick Club, 1836.

MATHEWS, Charles Edward (1834–1905), alpine climber and writer; solicitor at Birmingham from 1856; clerk of the peace, 1891–1905; founded Children's Hospital there, 1864; lifelong friend of Joseph *Chamberlain; helped to found Alpine Club, 1857; president, 1878–80; prominent in conquest of Alps; wrote critical and exhaustive *Annals of Mont Blanc* (1898).

MATHEWS, Charles James (1803–1878), actor and dramatist; son of Charles *Mathews; articled to Augustus Charles *Pugin, 1819; visited with Pugin, York, Oxford, and Paris; amateur actor, 1822; went to Ireland to build a house for Lord Blessington, 1823, whom he accompanied to Italy; entered the employ of John *Nash; again in Italy, 1827, where he acted at a private theatre built by Lord *Normanby; returned home, 1830; district surveyor at Bow, London; took to the stage, 1835; joined *Yates in management of the Adelphi, London; appeared at the Olympic, London, 1835, after the failure of the Adelphi; married his manageress, Lucia Elizabeth *Mathews or Vestris, 1838; unsuccessful in American tour, 1838, and management of Covent Garden, London, 1839–42; produced over a hundred pieces at Covent Garden, London; opened the Lyceum, London, 1847; resigned, in consequence of heavy debts, though his management was remunerative; bankrupt, 1856; revisited America, 1856; played in London, 1858–63, in Paris, 1863 and 1865; appeared at Melbourne, 1870, leaving Australia, 1871; visited Auckland, Honolulu, San Francisco, and New York; took *Wallack's Theatre, New York, 1872; acted in London, 1872–7, except for a season in Calcutta (1875); successful chiefly in comedy and farce; wrote various light pieces, mostly adaptations.

MATHEWS, Sir Charles Willie, baronet (1850–1920), lawyer; called to bar (Middle Temple), 1872; director of public prosecutions, 1908–20; appeared in criminal trials and notorious civil cases; knighted, 1907; baronet, 1917.

MATHEWS, Sir Lloyd William (1850–1901), general and prime minister of Zanzibar; entered navy, 1863; served in Ashanti campaign, 1873–4; retired with rank of lieutenant, 1881; in command of Zanzibar Army, with rank of brigadier-general, 1877; obtained abolition of slavery in Zanzibar, 1890; Zanzibar declared British protectorate, 1890; prime minister and treasurer of reconstituted government, 1891; introduced modern agricultural methods; CMG, 1880; KCMG, 1894; died at Zanzibar.

MATHEWS (also known as **VESTRIS, Madame), Lucia Elizabeth (or Elizabetta)** (1797–1856), actress; daughter of Gaetano Stefano *Bartolozzi; first appeared in Italian opera, 1815; acted at Paris, 1816; appeared frequently at Drury Lane, Covent Garden, and the Haymarket, London, as well as in Ireland and the provinces, 1820–31; opened the Olympic, London, with Maria *Foote, 1831; married Charles James *Mathews, 1838, and went with him to America; aided him in his management of Covent Garden, London, 1839–42, and the Lyceum, 1847–54; unrivalled as a stage singer.

MATHEWS, Thomas (1676–1751), admiral; entered the navy, 1690; lieutenant, 1699; captain, 1703; assisted in capture of Spanish flagship at Cape Passaro, 1718; blockaded Messina unsuccessfully; commanded squadron in East Indies against pirates, 1722–4; virtually retired, 1724; but was appointed commissioner of the navy at Chatham, 1736; vice-admiral of the red, 1742; commander-in-chief in the Mediterranean, and plenipotentiary to the king of Sardinia and the States of Italy, 1742; to prevent the allies slipping away to the south fought without waiting for the rear division to close up, on which a panic seized the English fleet and the blockade off Toulon was fairly broken; resigned, 1744; charged by Richard *Lestock with having neglected to give necessary orders, and having fled from the enemy and given up the chase, though there was every chance of success; dismissed, after a trial of unprecedented length, 1747; regarded the sentence as merely the outcome of parliamentary faction.

MATHEWS, Dame Vera Laughton (Elvira Sibyl Maria) (1888–1959), director of the Women's Royal Naval Service; daughter of Sir John Knox *Laughton; educated at convents and King's College, London; served with Women's Royal Naval Service, 1917–19; first editor, *Time and Tide*; married Gordon Dewar Mathews (d. 1943), 1924; director, Women's Royal Naval Service, 1939–46; CBE, 1942; DBE, 1945.

MATHIAS, Benjamin Williams (1772–1841), divine; MA, Trinity College, Dublin, 1799; ordained to the curacy of Rathfryland, 1797; chaplain of Bethesda Chapel, Dorset Street, Dublin, 1805–35; published theological works.

MATHIAS, Thomas James (1754?–1835), satirist and Italian scholar; major-fellow, Trinity College, Cambridge, 1776; MA, 1777; sub-treasurer to George III's queen, 1782; afterwards treasurer; FSA and FRS, 1795; librarian at Buckingham Palace, 1812; lost heavily over his edition of *Gray's works (1814); went to Italy,

1817; published the *Pursuits of Literature* (1794), a reckless satire on authors, which went through sixteen editions and provoked many replies; the best English scholar in Italian since *Milton; translated English poets into Italian and Italian works into English; published *Poesie Liriche* (1810) and *Canzoni Toscane*.

MATHIESON, William Law (1868–1938), historian; educated at Edinburgh Academy and University; historian of *Politics and Religion . . .* [in Scotland] (1902), of *English Church Reform . . .* (1923) and *British Slavery and its Abolition . . .* (1926).

MATILDA (d. 1083), queen of William the Conqueror; daughter of Baldwin V of Flanders, descendant of *Alfred; forbidden to marry Duke William of Normandy by the Council of Reims, 1049; married at Eu, 1053, dispensation being granted by Nicolas II, 1059; built abbey at Caen as a penance; ruled Normandy in William's absence; crowned at Westminster, 1067; resided much in Normandy superintending the affairs of the duchy; sent quantities of valuables to her son *Robert, 1079, during his quarrel with his father; founded the abbey of St Mary de Pré at Rouen; benefactor of French religious houses.

MATILDA (MAUD, MAHALDE, or MOLD) (1080–1118), first wife of Henry I of England; daughter of *Malcolm III of Scotland and great-granddaughter of Edmund Ironside; educated at Romsey; left Scotland on her father's death; went to her uncle *Edgar Aetheling, 1094; married Henry I, 1100; crowned at Westminster, 1100; corresponded with Bishop Hildebert of Le Mans, and *Anselm, whose return she welcomed, 1106; built a leper hospital at St Giles-in-the-Fields, London, and a bridge over the Lea at Stratford; founded Austin priory, Aldgate, 1108.

MATILDA (MAUD, MOLD, ÆTHELIC, or AALIZ) (1102–1167), empress; daughter of Henry I; married to Henry V of Germany, and crowned at Mainz, 1114; after her husband's death (1125) returned to England, 1126; recognized as Henry I's successor by the barons and bishops, 1126, 1131, and 1133; on her father's death (1135) entered Normandy, which, as well as England, chose her cousin Stephen for its king; gained nothing by an appeal to Rome, 1136; landed in England, 1139; Stephen brought captive to her at Gloucester, 1141; acknowledged by a council at Winchester as 'Lady of England and Normandy', 1141; went to London, but, her confiscations and demands for money irritating the citizens, was driven from the city; besieged Winchester, but, being in turn besieged by Stephen's wife, *Matilda (1103?–1152), cut her way out and fled to Gloucester; besieged by Stephen in Oxford Castle, 1142; escaped from Oxford, but had no further hope of success, 1142; conjointly with her husband, who held Normandy as a conqueror, ceded the duchy to her son Henry (afterwards Henry II), 1150; induced Henry II not to invade Ireland, 1155; founded several religious houses.

MATILDA, duchess of Saxony (1156–1189), daughter of Henry II of England; married Henry the Lion, duke of Saxony, at Minden, 1168; Brunswick besieged by the emperor in consequence of her husband's refusal to submit to the forfeiture of his lands, 1180, but the siege raised on her appeal to his chivalry; sought refuge in England with her husband, who, however (1181), had submitted, returning to Brunswick, 1185; her husband again exiled, 1189.

MATILDA OF BOULOGNE (1103?–1152), wife of Stephen, king of England; daughter of Eustace III of Boulogne; married, before 1125, Stephen of Blois, who seized the crown on Henry I's death, 1135; crowned at Westminster, 1136; made treaty with *David of Scotland, 1139; secured alliance of France, 1140; her husband a prisoner, 1141; regained London for her husband; besieged the Empress *Matilda (1102–1167), who was besieging Winchester, and compelled her to withdraw, soon effecting Stephen's release, 1141.

MATON, Robert (1607–1653?), divine; MA, Wadham College, Oxford, 1630; took orders; 'millenary' and believer in the literal meaning of scriptural prophecy; published *Israel's Redemption* (1642); replied to controversy thereby excited, in *Israel's Redemption Redeemed* (1646).

MATON, William George (1774–1835), physician; MA, The Queen's College, Oxford, 1797; FLS, 1794, subsequently vice-president; physician to Westminster Hospital, London, 1800–8; MD Oxford, 1801; FRCP, 1802; Gulstonian lecturer, 1803; Harveian orator, 1815; physician-extraordinary to Queen *Charlotte, 1816, to the duchess of Kent, and the infant princess Victoria, 1820; published (1797) account of tour in Dorset, Devonshire, Cornwall, and Somerset.

MATTHEW. See also MATHEW.

MATTHEW, Sir Robert Hogg (1906–1975), architect; educated at Melville College, Edinburgh, and Edinburgh University; studied at the School of Architecture and was concerned with slum housing and the social role of architecture; joined Department of Health for Scotland and worked with (Sir) L. Patrick *Abercrombie on wartime Clyde Valley regional plan; impressed by co-operative housing in Sweden; chief architect and planning officer, Health Department for Scotland, 1945; member of RIBA's reconstruction committee; chief architect to London County Council, 1946–53; introduced the 'mixed development' type of housing exemplified by Ackroyden estate on Putney Heath, and also initiated LCC's permanent contributions to 1951 Festival of Britain, including the Royal Festival Hall; appointed Forbes professor of architecture, Edinburgh, and set up, with (Sir) Stirrat *Johnson-Marshall, private practice known as RMJM, 1953; designed Turnhouse Airport, Cockenzie Power Station, Stirling University, and international pool, Edinburgh; succeeded Sir William (later Lord) *Holford as president of RIBA, 1962; president, International Union of Architects, 1961–5 and of Commonwealth Association of Architects, 1965–8; hon. fellow of architectural institutes in America, Canada, and New Zealand; RIBA Royal Gold medallist, 1970; CBE, 1952; knighted, 1962.

MATTHEW, Tobie (or Tobias) (1546–1628), archbishop of York; BA, University College, Oxford, 1564; MA, Christ Church, Oxford, 1566, and student; DD, 1574; ordained, 1566; attracted Queen Elizabeth's notice at Oxford, 1566; public orator, 1569–72; canon of Christ Church, 1570; prebendary of Salisbury, 1572; president of St John's College, Oxford, 1572–7; dean of Christ Church, 1576; vice-chancellor, 1579; preached a Latin sermon defending the Reformation, 1581; dean of Durham, 1584; vicar of Bishop's Wearmouth, 1590; acted as political agent in the north; bishop of Durham, 1595; active against recusants; prominent in the Hampton Court Conference, 1604; archbishop of York, 1606; entrusted with the detention of Lady *Arabella Stuart, who, however, escaped, 1611; frequently opposed the royal policy.

MATTHEW, Sir Tobie (1577–1655), courtier, diplomat, and writer; son of Tobie or Tobias *Matthew; MA, Christ Church, Oxford, 1597; admitted of Gray's Inn, 1599; MP, Newport, Cornwall, 1601, St Albans, 1604; travelled in Italy, 1604–6; converted to Roman Catholicism at Florence, 1606; returned to England and was committed to the Fleet on account of his religion; allowed to leave prison on parole in consequence of the plague, 1608; obtained leave to go abroad, 1608; ordained priest at Rome, 1614; returned to London, 1617; exiled on refusing to take the oath of allegiance, 1619; allowed to return, 1621; acquainted government with a scheme for erecting titular Roman Catholic bishoprics in England, 1622; sent to Madrid to advise Charles and *Buckingham, 1623; knighted on his return, 1623; member of abortive Academy Royal, 1624; in Paris and Brussels, 1625–33; secretary to

*Strafford in Ireland, 1633; soon returned to court, where the Puritans suspected him of being a papal spy; retired to Ghent, both houses of parliament having petitioned for his banishment, 1640; *Bacon's later work submitted by the author to his criticism; translated Bacon's *Essays* into Italian (1618); wrote an account of his conversion (never printed); died at Ghent; a collection of letters made by him published (1660).

MATTHEW PARIS (d. 1259). See PARIS.

MATTHEWS. See also MATHEWS.

MATTHEWS, Alfred Edward (1869–1960), actor; son of original Christy Minstrel; became touring, then West-End actor; in demand for plays by *Pinero, *Galsworthy, and *Barrie; skilled in technique of light comedy acting; became star as Lord Lister in *The Chiltern Hundreds* (1947) and its sequel (1954); OBE, 1951.

MATTHEWS, Henry (1789–1828), judge and traveller; son of John *Matthews; of Eton and King's College, Cambridge; fellow of King's College; MA, 1815; advocate-fiscal of Ceylon, 1821–7; judge, 1827; published *Diary* of continental travels, 1820 (5th edn., 1835); died in Ceylon.

MATTHEWS, Henry, Viscount Llandaff (1826–1913), lawyer and politician; son of Henry *Matthews; born in Ceylon; educated at universities of Paris and London; called to bar (Lincoln's Inn), 1850; QC, 1868; Conservative MP, Dungarvan, 1868–74, East Birmingham, 1886–95; home secretary, 1886–92; baron, 1895; a founder of Westminster Cathedral.

MATTHEWS, Jessie Margaret (1907–1981), actress; educated at Pulteney Street School for Girls, Soho; trained as ballet dancer and chorus girl; made first London appearance in *Bluebell in Fairyland*, 1919; went to New York in chorus of *André Charlot's Revue of 1924*; took over part of Gertrude *Lawrence; starred with Sonnie Hale in *One Dam Thing After Another* (1927), and in *This Year of Grace* (1928), *Wake Up and Dream* (1929), and *Ever Green* (1930); starred in fourteen films, including, *The Good Companions* (1933), *Friday the Thirteenth* (1933), and *Ever Green* (1934); had series of nervous breakdowns, including one in New York which prevented her appearance in *The Lady Comes Across* (1941); returned to London stage in Jerome Kern's *Wild Rose* (1942), followed by appearances in *Pygmalion* (1952) and *Private Lives* (1954); played role of Mary Dale in BBC radio serial 'The Dales', 1963–9; made last appearance in *Night of One Hundred Stars*, 1980; OBE, 1970; published autobiography *Over My Shoulder* (with Muriel Burgess, 1974).

MATTHEWS, John (1755–1826), physician and poet; MA, Merton College, Oxford, 1779; MD, 1782; physician to St George's Hospital, London, 1781–3; FRCP, 1783; Gulstonian lecturer, 1784; mayor of Hereford, 1793; MP, Herefordshire, 1803–6; composed prose and verse; parodied *Pope's Eloisa* (1780).

MATTHEWS (or MATHEWS), Lemuel (*fl.* 1661–1705), archdeacon of Down; son of Marmaduke *Matthews; MA, Lincoln College, Oxford, before 1667; rector of Lenavy and chaplain to Jeremy *Taylor, bishop of Down; prebendary of Carncastle, 1667; archdeacon of Down, 1674; chancellor of Down and Connor, 1690; held nine livings; attainted by Irish parliament, 1689; found guilty and suspended by the Lisburn visitation, 1694, for maintenance, non-residence, and neglect of duties; agitated in a series of fourteen appeals; restored only to his prebend.

MATTHEWS, Marmaduke (1606–1683?), Welsh Nonconformist; MA, All Souls, Oxford, 1627; inhibited by the bishop of St David's; fled to West Indies; 'teaching-elder' at Maldon, New England; appointed to St John's, Swansea, 1658; ejected, 1662; licensed to preach, 1672.

MATTHEWS, Thomas (pseudonym) (1500?–1555). See ROGERS, JOHN.

MATTHEWS, Thomas (1805–1889), actor and pantomimist; coached by *Grimaldi; clown at Sadler's Wells, Theatre, 1829; in pantomimes in London, Paris, and Edinburgh; retired, 1865.

MATTHEWS, Walter Robert (1881–1973), dean of St Paul's and theologian; educated at Wilson's Grammar School, Camberwell, and, after five years as clerk in Westminster bank, at King's College, London; ordained, 1907; lecturer in the philosophy of religion, King's College, 1908–18; professor and dean of the college, 1918–32; chaplain to Gray's Inn, 1920; preacher to the Inn, 1929; chaplain to the King, 1923–31; dean of Exeter, 1931–4; succeeded W. R. *Inge as dean of St Paul's, 1934–67; prolific writer on theological subjects; publications include *Studies in Christian Philosophy* (1921), *God in Christian Thought and Experience* (1930), and *The Problem of Christ in the Twentieth Century* (1950); contributed Saturday sermons to *Daily Telegraph* over period of twenty-four years; KCVO, 1935; CH, 1962; hon. DD, Cambridge, St Andrews, Glasgow, Trinity College, Dublin, and Trinity College, Toronto; hon. bencher, Gray's Inn; published autobiography, *Memories and Meanings* (1969).

MATTHEWS, Sir William (1844–1922), civil engineer; pupil in office of Sir John *Coode, harbour engineer; partner in Coode's firm, consulting engineers to crown agents for colonies, 1892; frequently employed by Admiralty on works at naval bases; KCMG, 1906.

MATTHEW WESTMINSTER. See WESTMINSTER.

MATTHIAS. See MATHIAS.

MATTHIESSEN, Augustus (1831–1870), chemist and physicist; studied at Giessen, 1852, and at Heidelberg, 1853; returned to London and studied with Hofmann, 1857; FRS, 1861; lecturer on chemistry at St Mary's Hospital, London, 1862–8, at St Bartholomew's, London, 1868; worked chiefly on the constitution of alloys and opium alkaloids.

MATTOCKS, Isabella (1746–1826), actress; daughter of Lewis Hallam, a comedian; played children's parts, 1753; chief support of Covent Garden, at which she played an immense variety of parts, 1761 till her retirement, 1808; also appeared at Portsmouth and Liverpool, where her husband became manager; especially shone in the role of chambermaid.

MATURIN, Basil William (1847–1915), Catholic preacher and writer; BA, Trinity College, Dublin; ordained, 1870; member of Society of St John the Evangelist, Cowley, 1873–97; received into Roman Church, 1897; ordained, 1898; torpedoed on *Lusitania* returning from third visit to America.

MATURIN, Charles Robert (1782–1824), novelist and dramatist; BA, Trinity College, Dublin, 1800; curate of St Peter's, Dublin; set up a school and took to literature, 1807; compelled to give up the school, 1813; his manuscript tragedy *Bertram*, recommended by *Scott to *Kemble, who declined it; produced by *Kean, on *Byron's recommendation, at Drury Lane, 1816, with great success; produced two unsuccessful tragedies; published, besides other novels, *Montorio* (1807), which Scott reviewed with appreciation, *The Milesian Chief* (1812), imitated by Scott in *The Bride of Lammermoor*, and *Melmoth* (1820), his masterpiece; had great influence on the rising romantic school of France.

MATURIN, William (1803–1887), divine; son of Charles Robert *Maturin; MA and DD, Dublin, 1866; was made perpetual curate of Grangegorman, 1844; librarian in Archbishop Marsh's library, Dublin, 1860; Tractarian.

MATY, Matthew (1718–1776), physician, writer, and principal librarian of the British Museum, born near Utrecht; Ph.D. and MD, Leiden, 1740; physician in London, 1741; published *Journal Britannique*, 1750–5, which reviewed English publications in French; FRS, 1751; appointed under-librarian on the establishment of the British Museum, 1753; foreign secretary, Royal Society, 1762; principal secretary, 1765; LRCP, 1765; principal librarian of the British Museum, 1772; disliked by Dr *Johnson, but intimate of other literary men of the day.

MATY, Paul Henry (1744–1787), assistant librarian of the British Museum; son of Matthew *Maty; of Westminster School and Trinity College, Cambridge; MA, 1770, and travelling fellow; FRS, 1771; chaplain to Lord Stormont, English ambassador at Paris; assistant librarian at the British Museum, 1776; foreign secretary, Royal Society, 1776 (principal secretary, 1778); protested strongly against Dr Charles Hutton's dismissal and resigned his secretaryship, 1784; started the *New Review*, 1782.

MAUCLERK, Walter (d. 1248), bishop of Carlisle; sent to Ireland, 1210, and to Rome, to urge the royal complaints, 1215; justice of the northern counties, 1221; sheriff of Cumberland and constable of Carlisle, 1222; bishop of Carlisle, 1223; employed on diplomatic missions; treasurer, 1227–33; councillor during Henry III's absences, 1243 and 1245; resigned bishopric, 1248.

MAUD. See MATILDA.

MAUD, John Primatt Redcliffe, Baron Redcliffe-Maud (1906–1982), public servant; educated at Eton and New College, Oxford; first class, Lit. Hum., 1928; junior research fellow in politics, University College, Oxford, 1929; tutorial fellow, 1932; dean, 1933; master, Birkbeck College, London, 1939; principal private secretary, Ministry of Food, 1940; deputy secretary, 1941; second secretary, 1944; second secretary, Ministry of Reconstruction, 1944–5; permanent secretary, Ministry of Education, 1945–52; Ministry of Fuel and Power, 1952–9; British high commissioner, South Africa, 1959; ambassador, 1961–3; master, University College, Oxford, 1963–76; chairman, royal commission on English local government, 1966–9; CBE, 1942; KCB, 1946; GCB, 1955; life peer, 1967; honorary degrees from Witwatersrand, 1960, Natal, 1963, Leeds, 1967, Nottingham, 1968, and Birmingham, 1968; FRCM, 1964; hon. fellow, New College, 1964, and University College, Oxford, 1976; publications include *Local Government in Modern England* (1932), *English Local Government Reformed* (with Bruce Wood, 1974), *Training Musicians* (1978), and *Experiences of an Optimist* (memoirs, 1981).

MAUD CHARLOTTE MARY VICTORIA (1869–1938), princess of Great Britain and Ireland, queen of Norway; fifth child of prince and princess of Wales (later Edward VII and Queen

*Alexandra); married (1896) Prince Christian Frederick Charles George Valdemar Axel (second son of crown prince of Denmark), elected to throne of Norway as King Haakon VII, 1905.

MAUDE, Aylmer (1858–1938), translator and expounder of Tolstoy's works; educated at Christ's Hospital and in Moscow, where he lived until 1897; close friend of Tolstoy, whom he translated jointly with his wife (21 vols., 1928–37); wrote *Life of Tolstoy* (2 vols., 1908–10).

MAUDE, Sir (Frederick) Stanley (1864–1917), lieutenant-general; born at Gibraltar; educated at Eton and Sandhurst; joined 2nd Coldstream Guards, 1884; entered Staff College, Camberley, 1895; served in South African War, 1899–1901; DSO, 1901; military secretary to earl of *Minto, governor-general of Canada, 1901–5; CMG, 1905; held staff appointments in England and Ireland, 1906–14; served in France, Aug. to Nov. 1914; CB, 1915; major-general and appointed to command thirteenth division at Dardanelles, 1915; took prominent part in evacuation of Suvla and Helles, 1915–16; took division to Mesopotamia, 1916; assumed command of army in Mesopotamia and created KCB, 1916; recovered Kut and captured Baghdad, 1917; died of cholera at Baghdad.

MAUDE, Thomas (1718–1798), minor poet and essayist; surgeon on board the *Barfleur*, 1755; steward of the Yorkshire estates of his commander, Lord Harry *Paulet, at whose court martial (1755) he had given favourable evidence, 1765–94; wrote verses descriptive of Yorkshire dales; contributed to Grose's *Antiquities*.

MAUDLING, Reginald (1917–1979), politician; educated at Merchant Taylors' School and Merton College, Oxford, where he was a scholar and obtained a first in Lit. Hum., 1938; called to bar (Middle Temple), 1940; during 1939–45 war commissioned in RAF intelligence; private secretary to Sir Archibald *Sinclair (later Viscount Thurso); worked for Conservative Parliamentary Secretariat (amalgamated with Research Department in 1948); assistant secretary to group which produced the Industrial Charter; Conservative MP, Barnet, 1950–79; economic secretary to Treasury, 1952; minister of supply and PC, 1955; recommended abolition of the ministry; paymaster-general, 1957; promoted to Cabinet; led British delegation at discussions to negotiate European free-trade area; argued in Commons against membership of Common Market, 1959; later changed his mind, but opposed joining European monetary system; president, Board of Trade, 1959; colonial secretary, 1961–2; succeeded J. S. B. (later Lord) *Selwyn-Lloyd as chancellor of the Exchequer, 1962–4; regarded incomes policy as indispensable to achievement of sustained growth; narrowly defeated by Edward Heath in first Conservative leadership election, 1965; became deputy leader; home secretary, 1970; resigned in 1972 owing to association with John Poulson; select committee of Commons reported that Maudling should have declared to the House his interest in a contract for a hospital when aid to Malta had been debated; left public life for three years but returned briefly to shadow Cabinet in 1975; published *Memoirs* (1978).

MAUDSLAY, Henry (1771–1831), engineer; entered Woolwich Arsenal; employed by *Bramah, 1789–98; set up business in London and made improvements in the lathe and marine engines; Sir Joseph *Whitworth and James *Nasmyth among his pupils.

MAUDSLAY, Joseph (1801–1861), engineer, son of Henry *Maudslay; originally a shipbuilder; patented marine engines, which were extensively used; built the engines of the first Admiralty screw steamship, 1841.

MAUDSLAY, Thomas Henry (1792–1864), engineer; son of Henry *Maudslay; greatly contributed to the success of his father's firm, which constructed engines for Royal Navy for over twenty-five years; gave evidence before a House of Commons committee on steam navigation, 1831.

MAUDUIT, Israel (1708–1787), political pamphleteer; preached at The Hague and other Protestant churches; partner in a woollen-draper's business, London; FRS, 1751; appointed customer of Southampton and agent in England for Massachusetts, 1763; witness for the defence at Governor *Hutchinson's trial; declared for American independence, 1778; published pamphlets on the American War, and *Considerations on the present German War* (1760), the latter, according to *Walpole, having enormous influence.

MAUDUIT, William, earl of Warwick (1220–1268), became earl of Warwick, in right of his mother, 1263; sided with the barons, but afterwards joined Henry III; surprised and taken prisoner at Warwick Castle, 1264.

MAUDUITH (or MANDUIT), John (*fl.* 1310), astronomer; fellow of Merton College, Oxford, by 1309, till 1319; famous as physician, astronomer, and theologian; his mathematical tables well known in Leland's time.

MAUFE, Sir Edward Brantwood (1883–1974), architect; younger son of Henry Muff; educated at Wharfedale School, Ilkley; pupil of

London architect, William A. Pite, 1899–1904; entered St John's College, Oxford, 1904–8; changed name from Muff to Maufe, 1909; ARIBA, 1910; set up practice and received first large commission, Kelling Hall, Norfolk, 1912; other work included decoration of St Martin-in-the Fields and alterations at All Saints, Southampton, and St John, Hackney; during 1914–18 war served in Royal Artillery; fellow, RIBA, 1920; designed palace of industry for Wembley Exhibition, 1924; made reputation as designer of churches notable for their affinities with modern Swedish architecture; designed interiors for houses such as Yaffle Hill, Broadstone, Dorset, and for studies such as that for religious services at Broadcasting House; also designed branch banks for Lloyds; won competition for new Guildford Cathedral, 1932; other works include buildings for Trinity and St John's colleges, Cambridge, and Balliol and St John's colleges, Oxford (hon. fellow, 1943); also designed Festival Theatre, Cambridge, and Playhouse, Oxford, and rebuilding in neo-Georgian style of Middle Temple and Gray's Inn (hon. master of the bench, 1951); principal architect UK and then chief architect and artistic adviser to Imperial (later Commonwealth) War Graves Commission, 1943–69; designed many memorials including RAF record cloister and Canadian record building, Brookwood military cemetery, 1947, and RAF memorial, Cooper's Hill, Runnymede, 1950–3; ARA, 1938; RA, 1947, treasurer, 1954–9; member of Royal Fine Art Commission, 1946–53; Royal Gold medallist for architecture, 1944; knighted, 1954; one of assessors who chose design for Coventry Cathedral by (Sir) Basil *Spence.

MAUGER (d. 1212), bishop of Worcester; physician to Richard I and archdeacon of Evreux; bishop of Worcester, 1199; urged King John to submit to the pope; pronounced the interdict, 1208; fled to France; attempted reconciliation with King John, 1208 and 1209; died at Pontigny.

MAUGHAM, Frederick Herbert, first Viscount Maugham (1866–1958), lord chancellor; born in Paris; grandson of Robert *Maugham; educated at Dover College and Trinity Hall, Cambridge; senior optime, 1888; rowed for Cambridge, 1888–9; president of Union, 1889; called to bar (Lincoln's Inn), 1890; KC, 1913; Chancery judge (knighted), 1928–34; lord justice of appeal (PC), 1934; lord of appeal in ordinary (life peer), 1935–8, 1939–41; lord chancellor, 1938–9; made solid contribution to English law, especially in patents and trademarks; publications include *The Tichborne Case* (1936), *The Truth About the Munich Crisis* (1944), *U.N.O. and War Crimes* (1951), and *At the End of* *the Day* (1954); viscount, 1939; hon. fellow, Trinity Hall, 1928.

MAUGHAM, Robert (d. 1862), first secretary to the Incorporated Law Society, of which he urged the formation, 1825, establishment, 1827, and incorporation, 1831; sole proprietor and editor of the *Legal Observer*, 1830–56; promoted Attorneys Act, 1843, and Solicitors Act, 1860; published legal works.

MAUGHAM, William Somerset (1874–1965), writer; educated at King's School, Canterbury, and Heidelberg University; medical student, St Thomas's Hospital, London, 1892–5; MRCS, LRCP, 1897; published first novel, *Liza of Lambeth* (1897); first stage-play success, *Lady Frederick* (1907); served in Intelligence Department during 1914–18 war; published *Of Human Bondage* (1915), *The Moon and Sixpence* (1919), *The Painted Veil* (1925), and *Cakes and Ale* (1930); settled in South of France, 1928–40; returned there in 1945; published *The Summing Up* (1938) and *The Razor's Edge* (1944); founded the Somerset Maugham Award for young writers, 1947; CH, 1954; C.Lit., 1961; fellow, Royal Society of Literature; commander of the Legion of Honour; hon. D.Litt., Oxford and Toulouse.

MAULE, Fox, second Baron Panmure of the United Kingdom, and eventually eleventh earl of Dalhousie in the peerage of Scotland (1801–1874), in the army, 1820–32; MP, Perthshire, 1835–7, Elgin burghs, 1838–41, and Perth, 1841–52; under-secretary of state, 1835–41; secretary at war, 1846–52 and 1855–8; succeeded to earldom, 1860.

MAULE, Harry, titular earl of Panmure (d. 1734), joined Jacobite rising, 1715; fought at Sheriffmuir, rescuing his brother, James *Maule, fourth earl of Panmure, under perilous circumstances, 1715; fled to Holland, 1716; corresponded with leading Jacobites; collected at Kelly Castle, chronicles, chartularies, and historical documents of Scotland; compiled a family history, 1733.

MAULE, James, fourth earl of Panmure (1659?–1723), Jacobite; privy councillor to James II, 1686–7; proclaimed the Old Pretender king at Brechin, 1715; taken prisoner at Sheriffmuir and rescued by his brother, Harry *Maule, titular earl of Panmure; escaped to the continent, 1716; his estates confiscated, 1716; twice declined their restoration at the price of swearing allegiance to George I; died at Paris.

MAULE, Patrick, first earl of Panmure (d. 1661), gentleman of the bedchamber, 1603; keeper of Eltham and sheriff of Forfarshire, 1625; endeavoured to reconcile the king and the Covenanters; created Baron Maule of Brechin and Man and earl of Panmure, 1646; fined by *Cromwell.

MAULE, Sir **William Henry** (1788–1858), judge; senior wrangler, Trinity College, Cambridge, 1810; fellow, 1811; barrister, Lincoln's Inn, 1814; joined Oxford circuit; KC, 1833; counsel to Bank of England, 1835; MP, Carlow, 1837; baron of the Exchequer and knighted, 1839; transferred to court of common pleas, 1839; member of judicial committee of Privy Council.

MAULE, William Ramsay, Baron Panmure (1771–1852), cornet, 11th Dragoons, 1789; Whig MP, Forfarshire, 1796 and 1805–31; created Baron Panmure (peerage of Great Britain), 1831.

MAULEVERER, John (d. 1650), colonel; parliamentary governor of Hull, 1646; colonel of foot regiment in Scots War, 1650.

MAULEVERER, Sir **Richard** (1623?–1675), Royalist; son of Sir Thomas *Mauleverer (d. 1655); admitted of Gray's Inn, 1641; knighted, 1645; fined by parliament, 1649; his estates sequestered, 1650; declared outlaw, 1654; taken prisoner, 1655; escaped to The Hague; gentleman of the privy chamber, 1660; MP, Boroughbridge, 1661.

MAULEVERER, Sir **Thomas,** first baronet (*c.*1599–1655), regicide; admitted of Gray's Inn, 1617; MP, Boroughbridge, 1640; created baronet, 1641; raised two foot regiments and a troop of horse for parliament; fought at Atherton Moor, 1643; attended the king's trial and signed the death-warrant.

MAULEVERER, Sir **Thomas** (1643?–1687), eldest son of Sir Richard *Mauleverer; MP, Boroughbridge, 1679; commanded a troop of horse in *Monmouth's rebellion, 1685.

MAULEY, Peter de (d. 1241), favourite of King John; took charge of treasure and prisoners at Corfe Castle, 1215; sheriff of Somerset and Dorset, 1216; summoned to bring regalia to coronation, 1220; arrested for treason, 1221; given charge of Sherborne Castle, 1221; died a crusader in the Holy Land.

MAUND, Benjamin (1790–1863), botanical writer; at once chemist, bookseller, printer, and publisher; FLS, 1827; on committee of Worcestershire Natural History Society; started monthly botanical publications.

MAUNDER, Samuel (1785–1849), compiler; assisted his partner, William *Pinnock, in the *Catechisms*, 1837–49; published the *Literary Gazette*; compiled educational dictionaries.

MAUNDRELL, Henry (1665–1701), oriental traveller; MA, Exeter College, Oxford, 1688; BD, 1697; fellow, 1697; chaplain to the Levant merchants at Aleppo, 1695; travelled in the Holy Land, spending Easter at Jerusalem, 1697; his narrative of the expedition (published, 1703) frequently reprinted, and translated into French, Dutch, and German.

MAUNSELL, Andrew (d. 1595), bibliographer and publisher; brought out Martin's translation of Peter Martyr's *Commonplaces* (1583); designed a classified catalogue of English books, the first two parts (divinity and science) published (1595).

MAUNSELL, John (d. 1265). See MANSEL.

MAUNSFIELD (MAUNNESFELD, MAM-MESFELD, or MAYMYSFELD), Henry de (d. 1328), dean of Lincoln; chancellor of Oxford University, 1309 and 1311; dean of Lincoln, 1314; declined bishopric of Lincoln, 1319; canon of Carlisle, 1324.

MAUNY, Sir Walter, afterwards baron de Manny (d. 1372). See MANNY.

MAURICE (*fl.* 1210), called Morganensis and Morganius, epigrammatist; wrote a volume of epigrams; probably identical with *Meyrig (*fl.* 1250), treasurer of Llandaff.

MAURICE (d. 1107), bishop of London, chaplain and chancellor to William the Conqueror; bishop of London, 1086; controversy with *Anselm as to the right to consecrate Harrow Church decided against him, 1094; crowned Henry I in Anselm's absence, 1100; commenced building St Paul's Cathedral.

MAURICE, Prince (1620–1652), son of the elector palatine Frederick V and Elizabeth, daughter of James I; landed in England, 1642, to aid the Royalist cause; commissioned to protect Gloucestershire, 1643; forced his way to Oxford for reinforcements, 1643; Exeter and Dartmouth surrendered to him, 1643; abandoned the siege of Plymouth in consequence of illness, 1643; lieutenant-general of the southern counties, 1644; present at the second Battle of Newbury, 1644; unable to keep order in Wales, 1645; relieved by his brother, Prince *Rupert, at Chester, 1645; fought on the right wing at Naseby, 14 June 1645; besieged in Oxford, 1646; banished by parliament, 26 June 1646; joined Rupert in his piracy, 1648; lost at sea off the Anagadas.

MAURICE, Sir Frederick Barton (1871–1951), major-general; son of (Major-General Sir) John Frederick *Maurice; educated at St Paul's School and Sandhurst; married Helen Margaret Marsh, sister of (Sir) Edward *Marsh, 1899; commissioned in Derbyshire Regiment, 1892; served in Tirah campaign, 1897–8, South African War, 1899–1902; instructor to Staff College under Sir William *Robertson, 1913; served in France, 1914–15; director, military operations, War Office, under Robertson, Dec. 1915–18; resigned Apr. 1918, and wrote to newspapers accusing Lloyd George's government of deceiving parliament about strength of British Army in France; Lloyd George defeated censure motion, quoting War Office figures that he knew to be inaccurate; Army Council retired Maurice from army and refused inquiry; principal, Working Men's College, 1922–33; professor of military studies, London University, 1927; principal, East London College, 1933–44; member of London University senate, 1946; president, British Legion, 1932–47; published works include military biographies, *Forty Days in 1914* (1919), *Governments and War* (1926), and a *History of the Scots Guards* (2 vols., 1934); KCMG, 1918; hon. LL D, Cambridge, 1926.

MAURICE, Godfrey (d. 1598). See JONES, JOHN.

MAURICE, Henry (1648–1691), divine; MA, Jesus College, Oxford, 1671; DD, 1683; fellow; gained, as curate of Cheltenham, 1669, great reputation in a controversy with the Socinians; chaplain to Sir Leoline *Jenkins at Cologne, 1673–6; domestic chaplain to Sancroft, 1680–91; treasurer of Chichester, 1681; rector of Newington, Oxfordshire, 1685; represented Oxford at Westminster Convocation, 1689; Margaret professor of divinity at Oxford, 1691; published controversial works; well versed in canon law.

MAURICE, James Wilkes (1775–1857), rear-admiral; entered navy, 1789; lieutenant, 1797; went to West Indies, 1802; commander, 1804; held Diamond Rock, Martinique, for more than a year, 1805; governor of Marie Galante, 1808; advanced to post-rank, 1809; governor of Anholt, 1810–12, where he defeated the Danes, 1811; retired rear-admiral, 1846.

MAURICE, Sir John Frederick (1841–1912), major-general; son of F. D. *Maurice; joined Royal Artillery, 1862; served in War Office and in Ashanti, South Africa, Egypt, and Sudan, 1873–85; professor of military art and history at Staff College, 1885; commanded artillery, Woolwich district, 1895; major-general, 1895; KCB, 1900; works include prize essay which greatly influenced army reform; edited first two volumes of official *History of the War in South Africa, 1899–1902* (1906–7).

MAURICE, John Frederick Denison (1805–1872), divine; went up to Cambridge, 1823; with *Sterling founded the 'Apostles' Club'; with Whitmore edited the *Metropolitan*

Quarterly Magazine for a year, 1825; first class in 'civil law classes', Trinity Hall, Cambridge, 1827; edited the *London Literary Chronicle* until 1830; went up to Oxford to take orders, 1830; joined the 'Essay Society' and met William Ewart Gladstone; curate of Bubbenhall, 1834; published *Subscription no Bondage*, against abolishing subscription to the Thirty-nine Articles; chaplain at Guy's Hospital, London, 1836–46, lecturing on moral philosophy; married Anna, sister-in-law of John *Sterling, 1837; published *Letters to a Quaker* (1837); edited the *Education Magazine*, 1839–41; professor of English literature and history at King's College, London, 1840; Boyle lecturer and Warburton lecturer, 1845; chaplain of Lincoln's Inn, 1846; resigned chaplaincy of Guy's Hospital, London, 1846; helped to found Queen's College, London, 1848; married Julius *Hare's half-sister, 1849; edited for a few weeks the paper of the 'Christian Socialists', and had his attention drawn to co-operation and trade associations; called upon by the principal of King's College to clear himself of charges of heterodoxy brought against him in the *Quarterly Review*, 1851; cleared by a committee of inquiry, 1852; asked to retire by the council of King's College after the publication of his *Theological Essays*, 1853; strongly advocated abolition of university tests, 1853; inaugurated (1854) the Working Men's College in Red Lion Square, London (afterwards removed to Great Ormond Street), of which he was chosen principal; accepted the chapel of St Peter's, Vere Street, London, 1860–9; professor of moral philosophy at Cambridge, 1866; incumbent of St Edward's, Cambridge, 1870–2; Cambridge preacher at Whitehall, 1871.

MAURICE, Thomas (1754–1824), oriental scholar and historian; MA, University College, Oxford, 1808; while at Oxford translated *Oedipus Tyrannus*, for which Dr *Johnson wrote the preface; vicar of Wormleighton, 1798; assistant-keeper of manuscripts in the British Museum, 1798; obtained pension, 1800; vicar of Cudham, 1804; a voluminous author, and the first to popularize Eastern history and religions.

MAURICE, William (*fl.* 1640–1680), collector and transcriber of Welsh manuscripts; his collection preserved at Wynnstay.

MAVOR, Osborne Henry (1888–1951), better known as playwright James Bridie; educated at Glasgow Academy and Glasgow University; fellow student of Walter *Elliot; qualified in medicine, 1913; served in Royal Army Medical Corps, 1914–18 war; consulting physician, Victoria Infirmary; professor of medicine, Anderson College, Glasgow; wrote some forty plays, including *Tobias and the Angel* (1930), *The Anatomist* (1931),

Mr Bolfry (1943), *Daphne Laureola* (1949); established Citizens' Theatre, Glasgow, 1943; hon. LL D, Glasgow, 1939; CBE, 1946.

MAVOR, William Fordyce (1758–1837), compiler of educational works; schoolmaster at Woodstock; ordained, 1781; vicar of Hurley and LL D, Aberdeen, 1789; rector of Stonesfield, Oxfordshire, which he exchanged (1810) for Bladon-with-Woodstock; chief compilation, *English Spelling Book* (1801).

MAWBEY, Sir Joseph, first baronet (1730–1798), politician; inherited property in Surrey, 1754; sheriff, 1757; MP, Southwark, 1761–74; created baronet, 1765; MP, Surrey, 1775–90; chairman of Surrey quarter sessions for twenty-seven years; contributed to the *Gentleman's Magazine*.

MAWDSLEY, James (1848–1902), trade-union leader; secretary of Amalgamated Society of Cotton Spinners, 1878; developed trade-union policy in Lancashire; negotiated conciliation scheme—the Brooklands agreement—referring trade disputes to arbitration, 1893; member of Royal Commission on Labour Questions, 1891–4.

MAWE, John (1764–1829), mineralogist; a sailor for fifteen years; collected minerals in England and Scotland for the king of Spain; blockaded in Cadiz, 1804; imprisoned at Montevideo, 1805–6; visited the interior of Brazil, 1809–10; opened a shop in the Strand, 1811; wrote books on mineralogy and his South American travels.

MAWE (or MAW), Leonard (d. 1629), bishop of Bath and Wells; fellow of Peterhouse, Cambridge, 1595; MA (incorporated at Oxford, 1599); master of Peterhouse, Cambridge, 1617; vice-chancellor of Cambridge University, 1621; prebendary of Wells, and chaplain to Charles, prince of Wales; joined him in Spain, 1623; master of Trinity College, Cambridge, 1625; bishop of Bath and Wells, 1628.

MAWER, Sir Allen (1879–1942), scholar; graduated in English, London (1897) and Cambridge (1904); lecturer in English, Sheffield, 1905–8; professor, Armstrong College, Newcastle upon Tyne, 1908–21; Liverpool, 1921–9; provost, University College, London, 1930–42; published *The Vikings* (1913), *Place-Names of Northumberland and Durham* (1920), and chiefly responsible for English Place-Name Society publications, 1924–43; FBA, 1930; knighted, 1937.

MAWSON, Sir Douglas (1882–1958), scientist and explorer; born at Shipley, Yorkshire; educated at Fort Street School and University of

Sydney, Australia; BE, mining, 1902; B.Sc., 1905; lecturer in mineralogy and petrology, Adelaide, 1905; D.Sc., Adelaide, 1909; professor of geology and mineralogy, 1920–52; physicist on Antarctic expedition of (Sir) Ernest *Shackleton, 1907; climbed Mount Erebus, 1908; reached South Magnetic Pole, 1909; led Australian Antarctic expedition, 1914–18; organized Banzare expedition, 1929–31, which led to annexation for Australia of two-and-a-half million square miles between the Ross Dependency and Enderby Land; made important mineral discoveries in South Australia, including uranium; knighted, 1914; OBE, 1920; FRS, 1923.

MAWSON, Matthias (1683–1770), bishop of Ely; of St Paul's School, London, and Corpus Christi College, Cambridge; fellow, 1707; MA, 1708; DD, 1725; master of Corpus Christi College, Cambridge, 1724–44; vice-chancellor, 1730; bishop of Llandaff, 1738; transferred to Chichester, 1740; bishop of Ely, 1754; founded twelve scholarships at Corpus Christi College, Cambridge, 1754.

MAXEY, Anthony (d. 1618), dean of Windsor; MA, Trinity College, Cambridge, 1585; DD, 1608; chaplain to James I; dean of Windsor and registrar of the Order of the Garter, 1612; made the highest bid for the vacant see of Norwich, 1618.

MAXFIELD, Thomas (d. 1616), Roman Catholic priest; educated at Douai; missioner in England, 1615; arrested; refused the oath of allegiance, and was executed.

MAXFIELD, Thomas (d. 1784), Wesleyan; converted by John *Wesley, 1739; travelled with Charles *Wesley, 1740; left in charge of the Foundery Society by John Wesley, 1742; seized by the press gang, 1745; transferred to the army; on his discharge, became one of Wesley's chief assistants and chaplain to the countess of Huntingdon; separated from the Wesleys, 1763; preached in Moorfields, 1767; at his secession became Wesley's enemy; unsuccessfully negotiated for a reunion, 1772 and 1779.

MAXIM, Sir Hiram Stevens (1840–1916), engineer and inventor; born in Maine, USA; chief engineer to United States Electric Lighting Company, 1878; came to England and opened workshop in London, c.1882; naturalized, 1900; knighted, 1901; chief inventions electrical pressure regulator (1881), rapid-firing gun with completely automatic action (adopted by British army, 1889, and navy, 1892), steam-driven flying-machine (1889–94), and maximite, a smokeless powder (1889).

MAX MÜLLER, Friedrich (1823–1900), orientalist and philologist; son of the poet Wilhelm Müller (1794–1827); born at Dessau; educated at Leipzig; Ph.D., 1843; studied under Franz Bopp and Schelling at Berlin and under Eugène Burnouf at Paris; obtained introduction to Baron Bunsen, then Prussian minister in London; came to England, 1846, and was commissioned by board of directors of East India Company to bring out edition of the Sanskrit classic *Rigveda*, with Sayana's commentary (published, 1849–73); settled at Oxford, 1848; deputy Taylorian professor of modern European languages, 1850; hon. MA and member of Christ Church, 1851; full MA and Taylorian professor, 1854–68; curator of Bodleian Library, 1856–63 and 1881–94; fellow of All Souls College, Oxford, 1858; unsuccessfully opposed (Sir) Monier *Monier-Williams as candidate for professorship of Sanskrit at Oxford, 1860; studied comparative philology and was first professor of that subject at Oxford, 1868 till death, though he retired from the active duties of the chair, 1875; devoted much attention to comparative mythology and the comparative study of religions; edited, from 1875, 'Sacred Books of the East', a series of English translations of oriental works of a religious character. He was a privy councillor and obtained numerous honours from British and foreign courts and learned bodies. Though much in his works and methods may already be superseded, his writings exercised an extraordinary stimulating influence in many fields. They fall under the heads of Sanskrit, Pali, science of religion, comparative mythology, comparative philology, philosophy, biography, and writings in German. A collected edition of his essays entitled *Chips from a German Workshop* appeared (1867–75). A full collected edition of his works began to appear (1898).

MAXSE, Frederick Augustus (1833–1900), admiral and political writer; brother of Sir Henry Berkeley Fitzhardinge *Maxse; lieutenant, RN, 1852; captain, 1855; retired as admiral, 1867; wrote on social questions. George *Meredith's novel, *Beauchamp's Career*, is largely a study of his character.

MAXSE, Sir (Frederick) Ivor (1862–1958), general; son of Admiral Frederick Augustus *Maxse; educated at Rugby and Sandhurst; commissioned, 1882; captain, Coldstream Guards, 1891; seconded to Egyptian Army, 1897–9; fought at Atbara and Khartoum; DSO, 1898; in South African War, on staff of Lord *Roberts, 1899–1902; brigadier-general, 1st Guards brigade, 1910; major-general with brigade in France, 1914; commanded 18th division in France, 1915–17; lieutenant-general in command, XVIII Corps, 1917–18; inspector-general of training in France, Apr. 1918; held Northern

Command in Britain, 1919–23; general, 1923–6; took up commercial fruit growing after retirement from army; CB, 1900; CVO, 1907; KCB, 1917.

MAXSE, Sir Henry Berkeley Fitzhardinge (1832–1883), governor of Heligoland; army captain, 1854; served through Crimean War (medals); lieutenant-colonel, 1863; governor of Heligoland, 1864–81, during which time the constitution was reformed, 1868, the gaming-tables abolished, 1870, and telegraphic communication established; governor of Newfoundland, 1881–3; died at St John's, Newfoundland.

MAXSE, Leopold James (1864–1932), journalist and political writer; son of F. A. *Maxse; educated at Harrow and King's College, Cambridge; owned and edited *National Review*, 1893–1932; convinced imperialist and democrat; lover of France; foresaw both German wars; considered League of Nations useless and advocated armaments and plain speaking with Germany.

MAXTON, James (1885–1946), politician; educated at Hutcheson's Grammar School and the University, Glasgow; elementary school-teacher and spare-time expositor of socialism; persuasive platform orator of burning eloquence; called for general strike on Clyde and imprisoned for sedition, 1916; organizer, Independent Labour party, 1919; chairman, 1926–31, 1934–9; MP, Bridgeton division of Glasgow, 1922–46; published *Lenin* (1932) and *If I were Dictator* (1935).

MAXWELL, Sir Alexander (1880–1963), civil servant; educated at Plymouth College and Christ Church, Oxford; first class, Lit. Hum., 1903; entered Home Office, 1904; acting chief inspector, reformatory and industrial schools, 1917; assistant secretary, 1924; chairman, Prison Commission, 1928; deputy under-secretary of state, Home Office, 1932; permanent under-secretary, 1938–48; CB, 1924; KBE, 1936; KCB, 1939; GCB, 1945; member, Royal Commission on Capital Punishment, 1949; governor, Bedford College, 1948–50.

MAXWELL, Caroline Elizabeth Sarah, Lady Stirling (1808–1877). See NORTON.

MAXWELL, Gavin (1914–1969), writer and conservationist; educated at Stowe and Hertford College, Oxford; strong interest in natural history; served with Scots Guards, 1939–44; bought island of Soay off Skye; worked in London as portrait painter, 1949–52; visited Sicily, 1953; travelled in southern Iraq, 1956; president, British Junior Exploration Society; fellow, Royal Society of Literature, Royal Geographical Society, and Royal Zoological Society (Scotland); publications include *Harpoon at a Venture* (1952),

God Protect me from my Friends (1956), a study of Sicilian life, *A Reed Shaken by the Wind* (1957), a study of marsh Arabs, *Ring of Bright Water* (1962), his first study of relationship between man and otter, *The House of Elrig* (1965), an autobiography, and *Lords of the Atlas*, a history of the Moroccan house of Glaoua.

MAXWELL, Sir George Clerk (1715–1784). See CLERK-MAXWELL.

MAXWELL, Sir Herbert Eustace, seventh baronet, of Monreith (1845–1937), country gentleman, politician, and writer; succeeded father, 1877; Conservative MP, Wigtownshire, 1880–1906; lord-lieutenant, 1903–35; works include *Memories of the Months* (1897–1922), *Life of Wellington* (1899); edited the *Creevey Papers*, 1903; PC, 1897; FRS, 1898; KT, 1933.

MAXWELL, James (*fl.* 1600–1640), author; MA, Edinburgh, 1600; went abroad; returned to England and published numerous works, including poems on Charles I and Prince Henry, and works in defence of the English church; nicknamed by Laud 'Mountebank Maxwell'.

MAXWELL, James (1708?–1762), of Kirkconnel; Jacobite; joined the rebellion of 1745; escaped to France after Culloden; published *Narrative of Charles Prince of Wales's Expedition in 1745*.

MAXWELL, James (1720–1800), 'Poet in Paisley'; followed numerous trades; received assistance from Paisley Town Council, 1787; author of doggerel religious publications.

MAXWELL, James Clerk (1831–1879). See CLERK-MAXWELL.

MAXWELL, Sir John of Terregles, master of Maxwell, and afterwards fourth Baron Herries (1512?–1583), partisan of *Mary Queen of Scots; held Lochmaben Castle, 1545; warden of the west marches, 1552–3; reappointed warden of the west marches, 1561; endeavoured to mediate between Mary and *Moray, 1565; after *Riccio's murder joined Mary with a strong force at Dunbar, 1566; became Baron Herries, 1566; one of the assize who acquitted *Bothwell; entreated Mary not to marry Bothwell; submitted to Moray's regency, 1567; commanded Mary's horse at Langside, 1568; commissioner to England, 1568; joined a revolt against Moray, 1569; submitted to the regent on finding that Elizabeth would not aid Mary; assisted in depriving *Morton, 1578; member of the new Privy Council; on Morton's return to power sent to Stirling to maintain quiet; subsequently supported *Lennox.

MAXWELL, John, seventh or eighth Baron Maxwell and earl of Morton (1553–1593), attended Perth Convention, 1569; voted for *Mary's divorce from *Bothwell, 1569; his territories invaded and castles demolished by Lord Scrope, 1570; came to terms with *Morton, 1573; imprisoned at Edinburgh on claiming (1577) the earldom of Morton, which he obtained on Morton's execution, 1581; denounced as rebel after *Lennox's overthrow, 1582 and 1585, when the earldom of Morton and its adjuncts were revoked; assisted in the capture of Stirling Castle, 1585; granted indemnity, 1585; imprisoned for causing mass to be celebrated; exiled; returned without permission, was again exiled, the earldom of Morton being ratified by parliament to the earl of *Angus, 1587; assembled his followers to help Spanish invasion, 1588; captured and brought prisoner to Edinburgh; appointed, under title of earl of Morton, warden of the west marches, 1592; subscribed Presbyterian confession of faith, 1593; slain in an encounter with the laird of Johnstone's followers.

MAXWELL, John, eighth or ninth Baron Maxwell (1586?–1612), son of John *Maxwell, seventh or eighth Baron Maxwell; at feud with Johnstone on account of his father's death, and with the *Douglases regarding the earldom of Morton; constantly called before the council to answer for his plots against Johnstone, 1598–1603; reconciled, 1605; committed to Edinburgh Castle for his feud with the earl of Morton, 1607; escaped, 1607; denounced as rebel; shot Johnstone and escaped to the continent, 1608; in his absence found guilty of acts of treason, including Johnstone's murder, 1608; condemned to death; on his return, 1612, apprehended and beheaded at Edinburgh.

MAXWELL, John (1590?–1647), archbishop of Tuam; MA, St Andrews, 1611; advocated the restoration of liturgical forms in Scotland; bishop of Ross, 1633; privy councillor and extraordinary lord of session, 1636; assisted in compilation of new service-book, using it at Fortrose, 1637–8; deposed and excommunicated by the assembly, 1638; appealed, 1639; DD, Trinity College, Dublin, 1640; bishop of Killala and Achonry, 1640; left for dead in the rebellion, 1641; finally went to Oxford and acted as royal chaplain; appointed archbishop of Tuam, 1643.

MAXWELL, Sir John Grenfell (1859–1929), general; grandson of Vice-Admiral J. P. *Grenfell and cousin of first Baron *Grenfell; gazetted to 42nd Foot, 1879; served in Egypt, 1882–1900; present at Battle of Tel-el-Kebir, 1882; accompanied Lord *Wolseley on his fruitless attempt to relieve General *Gordon, 1884–5; took part in Sudan frontier operations, 1885–9; served under Lord *Kitchener in reconquest of Sudan,

1896–8; proceeded to Cape, Feb. 1900; appointed military governor of Pretoria, June; chief staff officer to duke of *Connaught in Ireland, London, and Malta, 1902–8; commanded British troops in Egypt, 1908–12; resumed command, 1914–16, an important and exacting position; commander-in-chief in Ireland, 1916; commander-in-chief, Northern Command, 1916–19; full general, 1919; KCB, 1900; died at Cape Town.

MAXWELL, John Hall (1812–1866), agriculturist; called to Scottish bar, 1835; secretary to Highland Agricultural Society; collected stock and crop statistics; CB, 1856.

MAXWELL, Mary Elizabeth (1837–1915), better known as Miss Braddon, novelist; sister of Sir Edward N. C. *Braddon; her best-known novel, *Lady Audley's Secret* (1862), had an immediate and very great success and made her fortune; published about eighty novels between 1862 and 1911; also wrote many plays, edited several magazines, and contributed to periodicals; plots of novels concerned with crime, but not a mere sensationalist; married John Maxwell, publisher, 1874.

MAXWELL, Sir Murray (1775–1831), naval captain; entered navy, 1790; lieutenant, 1796; commander, 1802; took part in capture of Tobago, Demerara, and Essequibo, 1803; of Berbice and Surinam, 1804; CB, 1815; after landing Lord *Amherst at Pei-ho, 1816, explored the Gulf of Pechili, the west coast of Corea, and the Loo-Choo islands, an account of which was published (1818) by Captain Basil *Hall; wrecked in the Straits of Gaspar, with Lord Amherst on board, 1817, and was in charge of the crew (all saved) on Pulo Leat; acquitted by court martial, 1817; knighted, 1818; FRS, 1819; lieutenant-governor of Prince Edward's Island, 1831.

MAXWELL, Sir Peter Benson (1817–1893), chief justice of Straits Settlements; BA, Trinity College, Dublin, 1839; barrister, Middle Temple, 1841; recorder of Penang, 1856–66, and of Singapore, 1866–71; chief justice of Straits Settlements, 1867–71; knighted, 1856.

MAXWELL, Robert, fifth Baron Maxwell (d. 1546), warden of the west marches, 1517; lord provost of Edinburgh on the removal of the king there, 1524; councillor, 1526; extraordinary lord of session, 1533; one of the regents, 1536; taken prisoner at Solway Moss, 1542; sent to London, but released on *James V's death; intrigued with Henry VIII; taken prisoner at Glasgow, 1544; set free on approach of the English; imprisoned in the Tower of London for supposed treachery; released, 1545; taken prisoner by Beaton, but granted remission on stating he only made terms with Henry VIII under compulsion; chief justice of Annandale and warden of the west marches, 1546.

MAXWELL, Robert (1695–1765), writer on agriculture; experimented in farming; member of the Society of Improvers in the Knowledge of Agriculture in Scotland, 1723; insolvent, 1749; land-valuer; published agricultural works.

MAXWELL, William, fifth Baron Herries (d. 1603), son of Sir John *Maxwell, fourth Baron Herries; gentleman of the chamber, 1580; privy councillor, 1583; warden of the west marches, 1587; called before the council to answer for his feud with the Johnstones, whom he attacked unsuccessfully (1595) with 300 men; submitted the feud to arbitration, 1599.

MAXWELL, William, fifth earl of Nithsdale (1676–1744), Jacobite; joined the English Jacobites, 1715; taken prisoner at Preston, 1715; sent to the Tower of London; condemned to death; escaped by the aid of his wife Winifred *Maxwell; joined the Chevalier *James Edward at Rome, where he died.

MAXWELL, William (1732–1818), friend of Dr *Johnson; MA, Trinity College, Dublin, 1755; DD, 1777; first met Dr Johnson, c.1755; assistant preacher at the Temple, London; rector of Mount Temple, Co. Westmeath, 1775–1808; copied Dr Johnson's appearance and manner; furnished *Boswell with collectanea.

MAXWELL, Sir William Edward (1846–1897), governor of the Gold Coast; son of Sir Peter Benson *Maxwell; educated at Repton; qualified at local bar in Singapore and Penang, 1867; assistant resident of Perak and member of State Council, 1878; barrister, Inner Temple, 1881; CMG, 1884; British resident of Selangor, 1889; colonial secretary of Straits Settlements, 1892, and acting governor, 1893–5; governor of Gold Coast, 1895; KCMG, 1896; died at sea.

MAXWELL, William Hamilton (1792–1850), Irish novelist; graduate, Trinity College, Dublin; served in Peninsular campaign and at Waterloo; rector of Ballagh, 1820–44; originated a rollicking style of fiction, which culminated in *Lever.

MAXWELL, Sir William Stirling-, ninth baronet (1818–1878). See STIRLING-MAXWELL.

MAXWELL, Winifred, countess of Niths-dale (d. 1749), daughter of William Herbert, first marquis of Powis; married William *Maxwell, fifth earl of Nithsdale, 1699; fruitlessly petitioned George I (1716) for the life of her husband, who had been sentenced to death for his share in the rebellion of 1715; enabled him to escape from the Tower of London, 1716, and joined him at Rome; wrote a narrative of his escape, first published in the *Transactions of the Society of Antiquaries of Scotland* (vol. i).

MAXWELL FYFE, David Patrick, earl of Kilmuir (1900–1967), lord chancellor. See FYFE.

MAXWELL-INGLIS, Mrs Margaret (1774–1843). See INGLIS.

MAXWELL LYTE, Sir Henry Churchill (1848–1940), deputy keeper of the public records and historian. See LYTE.

MAY. See also MEY.

MAY, Baptist (1629–1698), keeper of the privy purse to Charles II; registrar in Chancery court, 1660; keeper of the privy purse, 1665; MP, Mid-hurst, 1670; clerk of the works at Windsor Castle, 1671; with *Lely and *Evelyn recommended Grinling *Gibbons to Charles II, 1671; MP, Thetford, 1690.

MAY, George Augustus Chichester (1815–1892), Irish judge; of Shrewsbury School and Magdalene College, Cambridge; MA, 1841; fellow; called to Irish bar, 1844; QC, 1865; legal adviser at Dublin Castle, 1874; attorney-general, 1875; lord chief justice of Ireland and privy councillor, 1877; president of the Queen's Bench division, 1878, retaining title of lord chief justice of Ireland; withdrew from presiding at *Parnell's trial on being accused of partiality, 1881; resigned, 1887.

MAY, George Ernest, first Baron May (1871–1946), financial expert; educated at Cranleigh; entered Prudential Assurance Company, 1887; secretary, 1915–31; made its American investments available to government, 1915; manager, American Dollar Securities Committee, 1915–19; deputy quartermaster-general in charge of canteen administration, 1916–19; chairman of Committee on National Expenditure which recommended economies, mainly in social services, amounting to over £96½ million and brought about downfall of Labour government, 1931; chairman, and specially responsible for iron and steel industry, Import Duties Advisory Committee, 1932–41; KBE, 1918; baronet, 1931; baron, 1935.

MAY, Sir Humphrey (1573–1630), statesman; of St John's College, Oxford, and the Middle Temple; BA, 1592; groom of the king's privy chamber, 1604; MP, Beeralston, 1605–11, Westminster, 1614, Lancaster, 1621–2, Leicester, 1624–5, Lancaster, 1625, and Leicester, 1626 and 1628–9; pensioned and knighted, 1613; surveyor of the court of wards, 1618; chancellor of the duchy of Lancaster, 1618; privy councillor, 1625; defended Charles and *Buckingham in the House of Commons against the attacks of the opposition; attempted to rescue Speaker *Finch from violence, 1629.

MAY, John (d. 1598), bishop of Carlisle; brother of William *May; fellow of Queens' College, Cambridge, 1550; MA, 1553; master of Catharine Hall, Cambridge, 1559; held various rectories; canon of Ely, 1564–82; Lent preacher at court, 1565; archdeacon of East Riding of Yorkshire, 1569; vice-chancellor of Cambridge, 1570; bishop of Carlisle, 1577.

MAY, John (*fl.* 1613), economic writer; deputy aulnager, c.1606; published (1613) an account of the means by which woollen manufacturers evaded the statutes.

MAY, Philip William ('Phil'), (1864–1903), humorous draughtsman; a caricature by him of *Irving, *Bancroft, and *Toole (1883) attracted notice of Lionel *Brough, who introduced him to editor of *Society*, for which he executed drawings; in Australia, 1885–8, contributing to the *Sydney Bulletin*; studied art in Paris; made sketches for *St. Stephen's Review*; from 1892 issued *Phil May's Winter Annual*; made reputation as comic artist of low life in *Daily Graphic* and other illustrated papers; published *Phil May's Sketch Book: Fifty Cartoons* (1895) and his vivid *Guttersnipes: Fifty Original Sketches* (1896); member of the *Punch* table from 1896 to death; a rapid cartoonist of vigour and vivacity; sociable and generous to a fault; his *Picture Book* edited with life by G. R. Halkett (1903).

MAY, Thomas (1595–1650), author; BA, Sidney Sussex College, Cambridge, 1612; admitted to Gray's Inn, 1615; prevented by defective utterance from practising law; unsuccessful as a playwright; his translations of the classics praised by Ben *Jonson; wrote two narrative poems, one on Henry II, 1633, the other on Edward III, 1635, by the king's command; unsuccessful candidate for laureateship, 1637; adopted Parliamentary cause; secretary for the parliament, 1646; his *History of the Long Parliament* (1647) considered by *Chatham 'honester and more instructive than *Clarendon's'.

MAY, Sir Thomas Erskine, first Baron Farnborough (1815–1886), constitutional jurist; assistant librarian of the House of Commons, 1831; barrister, Middle Temple, 1838; examiner of petitions for private bills and taxing-master for both houses of parliament, 1847–56; clerk of the House of Commons, 1871–86; KCB, 1866; president of the Statute Law Revision Committee, 1866–84; privy councillor, 1885; created Baron Farnborough, 1886; wrote historical works and on parliamentary procedure.

MAY (MEY or MEYE), William (d. 1560), archbishop-elect of York; brother of John *May (d. 1598), bishop of Carlisle; D.Civ.L., Cambridge, 1531; fellow of Trinity Hall; energetically supported the Reformation; chancellor of Ely, 1532; vicar-general of Ely, 1533; signed the Ten Articles, 1536; assisted in the *Institution of a Christian Man*, 1537; president of Queens' College, Cambridge, 1537–53, 1559–60; prebendary of Ely, 1541; prebendary of St Paul's, London, 1545; saved the Cambridge colleges from dissolution by his favourable report, 1546; dean of St Paul's, 1546; a prominent ecclesiastic in Edward VI's reign; dispossessed on Queen Mary's, restored on Queen Elizabeth's, accession; died on the day of his election to the archbishopric of York.

MAY, Sir William Henry (1849–1930), admiral of the fleet; entered navy, 1863; navigating officer of the *Alert* in Arctic expedition led by Sir G. S. *Nares, 1875–6; joined torpedo-school ship *Vernon*, 1877–80; captain, 1887; naval attaché to European states, 1891–3; rear-admiral, 1901; third sea lord and controller of navy, 1901–5; during his controllership *Dreadnought* policy initiated; commander-in-chief, Atlantic Fleet, 1905–7; second sea lord, 1907–9; successfully protested against reduction in naval expenditure, 1907; commander of Home Fleet, 1909–11; devoted his attention to reforms in naval tactics; commander-in-chief, Devonport, 1911–13; admiral of the fleet, 1913; member of Dardanelles Commission, 1916–17; KCVO, 1904.

MAYART, Sir Samuel (d. 1660?), Irish judge; appointed justice of Irish common pleas, having offered £300 to anyone who should procure him the office, 1625; knighted, 1631; wrote on constitutional relations between England and Ireland, 1643.

MAYBURY, Sir Henry Percy (1864–1943), civil engineer; educated at Upton Magna School; county engineer, Kent, 1904–10; joined Road Board, 1910; director of roads in France, 1917–19; director-general of roads, Ministry of Transport, 1919–28; consulting engineer to minister, 1928–32; chairman, London Traffic Advisory Committee, 1924–33; KCMG, 1919; GBE, 1928.

MAYDESTONE, Richard (d. 1396). See MAIDSTONE.

MAYER, John (1583–1664), biblical commentator; MA, Emmanuel College, Cambridge, 1605; DD, 1627; published a biblical commentary, 1627–59, and other theological works.

MAYER, Joseph (1803–1886), antiquary and collector; first studied Greek coins; sold his cabinet of Greek coins to the French government, 1844; presented his collection, which included Egyptian antiquities and Saxon remains (valued at £80,000), to the corporation of Liverpool, 1867; purchased some spurious papyri of the scriptures from Simonides (published, 1861); acquired many thousands of drawings, engravings, and autograph letters on the history of art in England, including the collections of William *Upcott and Thomas *Dodd; founded the Historic Society of Lancashire and Cheshire; president, 1866–9; established a free library at Bebington, 1866.

MAYER, Sir **Robert** (1879–1985), business man, patron of music, and philanthropist; born at Mannheim, Germany; educated at Mannheim Gymnasium and Conservatoire; settled in Britain, 1896; entered non-ferrous metal business; naturalized, 1902; served in British army, 1917–19; with his daughter, Dorothy, a soprano singer, instituted Robert Mayer Concerts for Children, 1923; retired from business, 1929; co-founder with Sir Thomas *Beecham of London Philharmonic Orchestra, 1932; knighted for services to music, 1939; established Youth and Music, 1954; interested in problems of juvenile delinquency; published *Young People in Trouble* (1945); supported Elizabeth Fry Fund, the Transatlantic Foundation, and Anglo-Israel Foundation; strong supporter of British membership of European Community; CH, 1973; published autobiography, *My First Hundred Years* (1979); KCVO, 1979; hon. fellow or member, Royal Academy of Music, Royal College of Music, Guildhall School of Music, and Trinity College, London; honorary doctorates from Leeds, the City University, London, and Cleveland, Ohio; awarded Albert Medal of Royal Society of Arts, 1979; other honours from Germany and Belgium.

MAYER, **Samuel Ralph Townshend** (1840–1880), miscellaneous writer; secretary of the Free and Open Church Association, 1866–72; one of the founders of the Junior Conservative Club, 1870; editor of various magazines.

MAYERNE, Sir **Theodore Turquet de** (1573–1655), physician; MD, Montpellier, 1597; royal district physician at Paris, 1600; his treatise on chemical remedies condemned by the College of Physicians at Paris, 1603; came to England, 1603; physician to James I's queen; returned to Paris, but after 1611 resided entirely in England, attending the royal family and nobility; knighted, 1624; made chemical and physical experiments; drew up a series of precautions against plague, 1644; wrote an historically valuable account of the typhoid fever, of which Prince

*Henry died, 1612; twenty-three volumes of his notes on cases in the British Museum.

MAYERS, **William Frederick** (1831–1878), Chinese scholar; went to China as student-interpreter, 1859; secretary of legation at Peking, 1872; FRGS, 1861; FRAS, 1861; wrote on Chinese subjects.

MAYHEW, **Augustus Septimus** (1826–1875), author; brother of Henry *Mayhew and Horace *Mayhew; wrote popular fiction with his brother Henry Mayhew; with Henry Sutherland Edwards wrote six plays.

MAYHEW, **Edward** (1570–1625). See MAIHEW.

MAYHEW, **Henry** (1812–1887), author; brother of Augustus Septimus *Mayhew and Horace *Mayhew; educated at Westminster; started *Figaro in London*, 1831–9; collaborated with Augustus Septimus *Mayhew; an originator of *Punch*, 1841; started philanthropic journalism on the subject of the London poor, 1862; published *German Life and Manners in Saxony* (1864), humorous works, and plays.

MAYHEW, **Horace** (1816–1872), author; brother of Augustus Septimus *Mayhew and Henry *Mayhew; wrote farces and tales; contributed to *Cruikshank's *Table-book* (1845) and *Lloyd's Weekly News*, 1852; sub-editor of *Punch*; many of his books illustrated by Cruikshank.

MAYMYSFELD (MAUNNESFELD or **MAUNSFIELD), Henry de** (d. 1328). See MAUNSFIELD.

MAYNARD, **Edward** (1654–1740), antiquary; fellow of Magdalen College, Oxford, 1678–94; MA, 1677; DD, 1691; canon and precentor of Lichfield, 1700; edited *Dugdale's *History of St. Paul's Cathedral* (1716).

MAYNARD, Sir **John** (1592–1658), courtier, Presbyterian, and Royalist; entered the Inner Temple, 1610; partisan of Buckingham; MP, Chippenham, 1624; KB and servant of the privy chamber, 1625; MP, Calne, 1628; raised troops in Surrey for parliament, 1642; MP, Lostwithiel, 1647; leader of the Presbyterian party and charged with disaffection by Fairfax, 1647; re-admitted to the house and placed on the Committee of Safety, 1647; committed to the Tower and impeached, 1648; protested against the Lords' jurisdiction over the Commons, 1648; resumed his seat, 1648.

MAYNARD, **John** (*fl.* 1611), lutenist; one of the first to use the lyra-viol; wrote *The Twelve Wonders* (songs), 1611.

MAYNARD, **John** (1600–1665), divine; BA, The Queen's College, Oxford, 1620; MA, Magdalen Hall, 1622; incumbent of Mayfield, 1624; became a Puritan; chosen one of the Westminster Assembly; preached before the Long Parliament, 1644, 1646, and 1648; Sussex commissioner for ejecting scandalous ministers and schoolmasters, 1654; ejected, 1662; published sermons.

MAYNARD, Sir **John** (1602–1690), judge; barrister, Middle Temple, 1626; MP, Totnes, in Short and Long parliaments; framed *Strafford's impeachment; deputy lieutenant of militia under parliament, 1642; member of the Westminster Assembly; advocated abolition of feudal wardships; protested against the king's deposition, 1648; serjeant-at-law, 1654; imprisoned for hinting *Cromwell's government a usurpation, 1655; MP, Plymouth, 1656–8; protector's serjeant, 1658; solicitor-general on Richard *Cromwell's accession; one of the first serjeants called at the Restoration; king's serjeant and knighted, 1660; appeared for the crown at most of the state trials at the Restoration, and at most of the Popish Plot prosecutions; MP, Plymouth, in the convention, 1689; lord commissioner of the great seal, 1689; left such an obscure will that a private act of parliament was passed, 1694, to settle the disputes to which it gave rise; his legal manuscript collections preserved in Lincoln's Inn Library.

MAYNARD, Walter (pseudonym) (1828–1894). See BEALE, THOMAS WILLERT.

MAYNE, Cuthbert (d. 1577), first seminary priest executed in England; chaplain of St John's College, Oxford; MA, 1570; went to Douai, 1573; ordained Roman Catholic priest, 1575; chaplain to Francis Tregian, 1576; discovered and imprisoned, 1577; executed.

MAYNE, Jasper (1604–1672), archdeacon of Chichester and dramatist; student of Christ Church, Oxford, 1627; MA, 1631; DD, 1646; wrote *City Match* (comedy), 1639, and *The Amorous War* (tragicomedy), 1648; in middle life abandoned poetry and (1639) became rector of Cassington; preached before Charles I at Oxford and wrote controversial pamphlets; ejected from his studentship and from Cassington, but made rector of Pyrton, 1648; ejected from Pyrton, 1656; reinstated in his benefices at the Restoration and appointed canon of Christ Church, Oxford, archdeacon of Chichester, and chaplain-in-ordinary to the king.

MAYNE, John (1759–1836), Scottish poet; printer; subsequently proprietor and joint editor of the *Star*; wrote poems for magazines; praised by *Scott and *Burns.

MAYNE, Perry (1700?–1761), vice-admiral; entered navy, 1712; captain, 1725; present at reduction of Portobello, 1739; unsuccessfully

attacked Cartagena, 1741; rear-admiral, 1745; presided at the trials of Vice-Admiral Richard *Lestock, 1746, and Admiral Thomas *Mathews, 1747; vice-admiral, 1747.

MAYNE, Sir **Richard** (1796–1868), police commissioner; BA, Trinity College, Dublin, 1818; MA, Trinity College, Cambridge, 1821; barrister, Lincoln's Inn, 1822; commissioner to institute metropolitan police, 1850; KCB, 1851.

MAYNE, Richard Charles (1835–1892), admiral; educated at Eton; entered navy, 1847; commanded survey expedition to the Straits of Magellan, 1866–9, the results of which he published (1871); rear-admiral, 1879; CB, 1879; vice-admiral, 1885; MP, Pembroke and Haverfordwest, 1886.

MAYNE, Simon (1612–1661), regicide; student at Inner Temple, 1630; MP, Aylesbury, 1645; judge at Charles I's trial, signing the warrant; attainted, 1660; died in the Tower of London.

MAYNE, Thomas (1818–1883), novelist. See REID, MAYNE.

MAYNE, William (1818–1855), colonel and brigadier of the Hyderabad contingent; ensign in East India Company's service, 1837; lieutenant, 1841; distinguished himself at Julgar, 1840, Jellalabad, and Istiliff, 1842; suppressed disturbances in the Deccan, 1851–4; brevet-colonel and aide-de-camp to Queen Victoria, 1854.

MAYNE, Zachary (1631–1694), religious writer; fellow of Magdalen College, Oxford, 1654; MA, 1654; convened before the vice-chancellor for a sermon preached in St Mary's Church, Oxford, 1660; expelled from his fellowship, 1660; schoolmaster at Dalwood, 1671–90; master of Exeter Grammar School, 1688–94; published religious treatises.

MAYNWARING. See also MAINWARING and MANWARING.

MAYNWARING, Arthur (1668–1712). See MAINWARING.

MAYNWARING, Everard (1628–1699?), medical writer; MB, St John's College, Cambridge, 1652; visited America; MD, Dublin, 1655; began to practise in London, 1663; condemned violent purgatives and blood-letting; had charge of Middlesex Pest-House during the plague, 1665; published medical works.

MAYO, sixth earl of (1822–1872). See BOURKE, RICHARD SOUTHWELL.

MAYO, Charles (1750–1829), historian; MA, The Queen's College, Oxford, 1774; BCL, 1779; incumbent of Huish, 1775, Beechingstoke, 1779; wrote a European (1793) and a universal, history (1804); founded two scholarships at Oxford.

MAYO, Charles (1767–1858), professor of Anglo-Saxon at Oxford; son of Herbert *Mayo (1720–1802); of Merchant Taylors' School, London; fellow of St John's College, Oxford, 1788; MA, 1793; professor of Anglo-Saxon, 1795–1800; BD, 1796; Whitehall preacher, 1799; FSA, 1820; FRS, 1827.

MAYO, Charles (1792–1846), educational reformer; of Merchant Taylors' School, London, and St John's College, Oxford; DCL, 1822; headmaster of Bridgnorth Grammar School, 1817–19; English chaplain to Pestalozzi's establishment at Yverdun, 1819; introduced Pestalozzi's system at Epsom, 1822, and at Cheam, 1826; published school-books and *Memoirs of Pestalozzi* (1828).

MAYO, Charles (1837–1877), army surgeon; of Winchester School; fellow of New College, Oxford, 1856; MA, 1863; MD, 1871; MRCS, 1861; LRCP, 1869; university coroner, 1865–9; in Medical Service Corps under Grant, 1862; with the German Army, 1870; with the Dutch in Sumatra, 1873–4; published *History of Wimborne Minster* (1860); died at sea.

MAYO, Daniel (1672?–1733), Presbyterian minister; son of Richard *Mayo; educated at Glasgow (MA) and Leiden; Presbyterian minister at Kingston upon Thames, where he kept a school, 1698; Presbyterian pastor in London; published sermons.

MAYO, Elizabeth (1793–1865), educational reformer; with her brother, Charles *Mayo (1792–1846), at Epsom and Cheam; published school-books.

MAYO, Henry (1733–1793), Dissenting minister; pastor of Independent church, Wapping, 1762; DD and LL D; acquainted with Dr *Johnson, and known as the 'Literary Anvil'.

MAYO, Herbert (1720–1802), divine; fellow of Brasenose College, Oxford, 1740; MA, 1745; DD, 1763; rector of Middleton Cheney, 1764, of St George's, London, 1764–1802; JP for Middlesex.

MAYO, Herbert (1796–1852), physiologist; son of John *Mayo; pupil of Sir *Charles Bell, 1812–15; MD, Leiden; MRCS, 1819; discovered the real function of the nerves of the face, 1822; surgeon of Middlesex Hospital, 1827–42; professor of anatomy and surgery to Royal College of Surgeons, 1828–9; FRS, 1828; professor of anatomy at King's College, London, 1830–6; FGS, 1832; founded medical school at the Middlesex Hospital, 1836; physician to hydropathic establishment at Boppart, 1843, after-

wards at Bad Weilbach; published medical works.

MAYO, John (1761–1818), physician; fellow of Oriel College, Oxford, 1784; MA, 1785; MD, 1788; FRCP, 1788; censor, 1790, 1795, 1804, and 1808; Harveian orator, 1795; physician to Foundling Hospital, London, 1787–1809, Middlesex Hospital, 1788–1803; physician-in-ordinary to Caroline, princess of Wales.

MAYO, Paggen William (1766–1836), physician; son of Herbert *Mayo (1720–1802); medical fellow, St John's College, Oxford, 1792; MD, 1795; physician to Middlesex Hospital, 1793–1801; FRCP, 1796; censor, 1797; Gulstonian lecturer, 1798; Harveian orator, 1807.

MAYO, Richard (1631?–1695), ejected divine; vicar of Kingston-on-Thames, 1648; ejected, 1662; Presbyterian minister in London; merchants' lecturer, 1694; published theological works.

MAYO, Thomas (1790–1871), president of the Royal College of Physicians; son of John *Mayo; fellow of Oriel College, Oxford, 1813; MA, 1814; MD, 1818; FRCP, 1819; censor, 1835, 1839, 1850; FRS, 1835; Lumleian lecturer, 1839, 1842; physician to Marylebone Infirmary, 1841; Harveian orator, 1841; Croonian lecturer, 1853; president, RCP, 1857–62; wrote on mental diseases.

MAYOR, John Eyton Bickersteth (1825–1910), classical scholar and divine; revelled in classical literature from age of 6; educated at Christ's Hospital, at Shrewsbury, and St John's College, Cambridge; third classic, 1848; fellow, 1849; master at Marlborough, 1849–53; prepared edition of Juvenal, (1853, 3rd edn., 1881); classical tutor at St John's from 1853; an accomplished linguist; published lives of Nicholas *Ferrar (1855), Matthew *Robinson (1856), Ambrose *Bonwicke (1870), and William *Bedell (1870), and edited *Ascham's *Scholemaster* (1863); edited transcript of admissions to St John's College; published Thomas *Baker's *History of St. John's College* (2 vols., 1869); university librarian, 1864–7; completed catalogue of MSS; university professor of Latin, 1872 to death; edited (with J. R. *Lumby) *Bede's *Ecclesiastical History*, bks. iii and iv (1878); visited Leiden and Rome, 1875; advocate of vegetarian diet from middle life; president of St John's, 1902; hon. DCL, Oxford, 1895, LL D, Aberdeen, 1892, and St Andrews, 1906, DD, Glasgow, 1901; original FBA, 1902; had power of accumulating knowledge but small faculty of construction; projected uncompleted commentary on Seneca and a Latin dictionary; edited works by Cicero, Pliny, Homer, Quintilian, and volumes for the Rolls and Early English Text societies; published also *A Bibliography of Latin Literature* (1875), a *First Greek Reader* (1868), and *First German Reader* (1910).

MAYOW (MAYOUWE or MAYO), John (1643–1679), physiologist and chemist; fellow of All Souls, Oxford, 1660; DCL, 1670; published tract on respiration, 1668 (republished at Leiden, 1671), in which he discovered the double articulation of the ribs with the spine, and put forward views (still discussed) on the internal intercostals, developed in *Tractatus quinque* (1674, translated into French, German, and Dutch); discussed the chemistry of combustion, and described muscular action; FRS, 1678.

MAZZINGHI, Joseph, Count (1765–1844), composer; pupil of John Christian Bach, Bertolini, Sacchini, and Anfossi; organist at the Portuguese Chapel, London, 1775; composer and director of music at the Italian opera, 1785–92; arranged Carlton House and Nobility concerts, 1791; partner in Goulding, D'Almaine & Co., 1790; composed stage pieces, pianoforte sonatas, and other works.

MEAD (or MEDE), Joseph (1586–1638), biblical scholar; MA, Christ's College, Cambridge, 1610; fellow, 1613; appointed to the Greek lectureship, 1619; philologist, historian, mathematician, and physicist; botanist and practical anatomist; studied astrology, Egyptology, and the origin of Semitic religions; chief work, *Clavis Apocalyptica* (1627).

MEAD (or MEADE), Matthew (1630?–1699), Independent divine; of King's College, Cambridge, 1649–51; contested the rectorship of Great Brickhill, 1653; appointed by *Cromwell to St Paul's, Shadwell, 1658; ejected, 1662; went to Holland, 1664; in London during the plague, 1665; minister at Stepney, 1671; guardian of James *Peirce, the Exeter heretic, 1680; suspected of complicity in the Rye House Plot, but discharged, 1683; assisted in amalgamation of the Presbyterian and Congregationalist bodies, 1690; published sermons.

MEAD, Richard (1673–1754), physician; son of Matthew *Mead; educated at Utrecht under Graevius, and at Leiden under Paul Herman and Archibald *Pitcairne; travelled in Italy, 1695; MD, Padua, 1695; began practice at Stepney, 1696; published *Mechanical Account of Poisons* (an account of venomous snakes, 1702); FRS, 1703; physician to St Thomas's Hospital, 1703–15; published a treatise on the influence of the sun and moon on human bodies (1704); on the council of the Royal Society, 1705 and 1707–54; vice-president, 1717; MD, Oxford, 1707; FRCP, 1716; censor, 1716, 1719, and 1724; anatomy

lecturer to the Barber-Surgeons, 1711–15; collected objects of vertu; procured the release of Dr *Freind from the Tower; attended Sir Isaac *Newton, Bishop *Burnet, George I, and Sir Robert Walpole; friend of Richard *Bentley (1662–1742); drew up a statement concerning the prevention of the plague, 1720; successfully inoculated seven condemned criminals, 1721; Harveian orator, 1723; physician to George II, 1727; financially assisted various literary projects.

MEAD, Robert (1616–1653), poet; contributed, while at Westminster School, to *Cowley's *Poetical Blossomes* (1633); as an undergraduate of Christ Church, Oxford, wrote a comedy, *The Combat of Love and Friendship*; contributed to *Jonsonus Virbius* (1638); MA, 1641; Royalist captain at the siege of Oxford and assault on Abingdon, 1646; Charles II's envoy to Sweden, 1649–51.

MEAD, William (1628–1713), Quaker; originally captain of a train band; joined the Quakers, 1670; imprisoned with William Penn, 1670; jury committed to Newgate for acquitting him and *Penn, 1670; wrote in defence of the Quakers.

MEADE, John (1572–1653). See ALMEIDA.

MEADE, Richard Charles Francis Christian, third earl of Clanwilliam (Irish peerage) and first Baron Clanwilliam (peerage of United Kingdom) (1795–1879), educated at Eton; succeeded to earldom, 1805; attended Lord Castlereagh at Vienna Congress, 1814; *Castlereagh's private secretary, 1817–19; foreign under-secretary, 1822; with Wellington at Verona Congress, 1822; minister at Berlin, 1823–7; GCH, 1826; created Baron Clanwilliam, 1828.

MEADE, Richard James, fourth earl of Clanwilliam in the Irish peerage, and second Baron Clanwilliam in the peerage of the United Kingdom (1832–1907), admiral of the fleet; entered navy, 1845; served in Russian War, 1852; wounded at storming of Canton, 1857; junior sea lord, 1874–80; CB, 1877; succeeded to earldom, 1879; commanded flying squadron, 1880–2; KCMG, 1882; commander-in-chief on North America Station, 1885–6, and at Portsmouth, 1891–4; admiral, 1886; KCB, 1887; admiral of the fleet and GCB, 1895.

MEADE, Sir Robert Henry (1835–1898), civil servant; second son of Richard Charles Francis *Meade, third earl of Clanwilliam; of Eton and Exeter College, Oxford; MA, 1860; entered Foreign Office, 1859; accompanied prince of Wales (later Edward VII) on tour in Palestine and Eastern Europe, 1861–2; groom of bedchamber to prince of Wales, 1862; private secretary to Earl

*Granville as president of council, 1864–6, and in Colonial Office, 1868; assistant under-secretary of state in Colonial Office, 1871–92, and permanent under-secretary, 1892–6; GCB, 1897.

MEADE-FETHERSTONHAUGH, Sir Herbert (1875–1964), admiral; entered *Britannia*, 1889; lieutenant, served in *Iphigenia* in China, 1897; severely injured in cable accident in *Venerable*, 1904; in Admiralty yacht, *Enchantress*, 1906, commander, 1908; divisional leader in destroyer, *Goshawk*, 1912; in Heligoland Bight action, 1914; DSO; captain, 1914; in Dogger Bank action, 1915; in *Caroline* at Battle of Jutland, 1916; chief of staff to commander-in-chief, Rosyth, 1919; commanded *Renown* on prince of Wales's visit to India, China, and Japan, 1921; CVO, 1922; captain, Royal Naval College, Dartmouth, 1923; rear-admiral, CB, 1925; commanded Mediterranean destroyer flotillas, 1926–8; KCVO, 1929; vice-admiral, 1930; admiral, 1934; GCVO, extra equerry to the king, 1934; sergeant at arms, House of Lords, 1939–46.

MEADLEY, George Wilson (1774–1818), biographer; banker's apprentice, 1788–93; founded Sunderland Subscription Library, 1795; met Paley, whose *Memoirs* he wrote, 1809; made mercantile voyages to the Levant, 1796, to Danzig, 1801, and to Hamburg, 1803; became a Unitarian; published biographies of Algernon Sidney (1813), and others.

MEADOWBANK, Lords. See MACONOCHIE, ALLAN, 1748–1816; MACONOCHIE, afterwards MACONOCHIE-WELWOOD, ALEXANDER, 1777–1861.

MEADOWCOURT, Richard (1695–1760), divine and author; fellow of Merton College, Oxford, 1718; MA, 1718; controversy caused by his sermon on calumny in religious polemics, 1722; vicar of Oakley, 1727; canon of Worcester, 1734; incumbent of Quinton, 1738, of Lindridge, 1751; published *Critique on Paradise Regained* (1732) and similar works.

MEADOWE, John (1622–1697). See MEADOWS.

MEADOWS. See also MEDOWS.

MEADOWS, Alfred (1833–1887), obstetric physician; entered King's College medical school, 1853; MD, London, 1858; FRCP, 1873; house-physician, 1856, and assistant physician, 1860, at King's College Hospital, London; physician to Hospital for Women, Soho Square, London, 1863–74; physician accoucheur and lecturer to St Mary's Hospital, London, 1871–87; first president of British Gynaecological Society, 1884; his *Manual of Midwifery* (3rd edn., 1876) translated into Japanese.

MEADOWS, Drinkwater (1799–1869), actor; acted at Covent Garden, 1821–44; at the Lyceum, London, under the Keeley management, 1844–7; joined *Kean and *Keeley in the management of the Princess's, London, where he remained under *Harris until his retirement, 1862; most successful in eccentric comedy.

MEADOWS (or MEADOWE), John (1622–1697), ejected minister; fellow of Christ's College, Cambridge, 1644; MA, 1646; rector of Ousden, 1653; ejected, 1662; licensed as a Presbyterian, 1672.

MEADOWS, John (1676–1757), divine; son of John *Meadows (1622–1697); Presbyterian minister at Needham Market, 1701; published *Apostolic Rule of Ordination* (1738).

MEADOWS, Joseph Kenny (1790–1874), draughtsman; produced an illustrated edition of Shakespeare, 1839–43; exhibited occasionally at the Royal Academy and the Society of British Artists; received civil list pension, 1864.

MEADOWS, Sir Philip, the elder (1626–1718), diplomat; MA, Queens' College, Cambridge; appointed Latin secretary to *Cromwell's council to relieve *Milton, 1653; represented Cromwell at Lisbon, 1656; envoy to Frederick III of Denmark at the Treaty of Roskild, 1658; knighted, 1662; ambassador to Sweden, 1658; published in retirement an account of the wars between Sweden and Denmark (1675), also a book on naval supremacy and marine jurisdiction (1689); commissioner of public accounts, 1692; member of the Council of Trade, 1696; commissioner of trade, 1708.

MEADOWS, Sir Philip, the younger (d. 1757), son of Sir Philip *Meadows the elder; commissioner of excise, 1698–1700; knight-marshal of the king's household and knighted, 1700; envoy to Holland, 1706; sent on a mission to the emperor, 1707; controller of army accounts, 1707.

MEAGER, Leonard (1624?–1704?), gardener; published *English Gardener* (1670, 11th edn., c.1710).

MEAGHER, Thaddeus (or Thadee) de (1670–1765), soldier of fortune; left Ireland and served in the French Army; chamberlain to Frederick Augustus II, king of Poland and elector of Saxony, 1739; lieutenant-general in the Polish Army, 1752; despatched to negotiate with Frederick the Great, 1756; died at Dresden.

MEAGHER, Thomas Francis (1823–1867), Irish nationalist; studied at Dublin for the bar, 1844; made a brilliant speech against peace with

England, 1846, which led *Thackeray to dub him 'Meagher of the Sword'; founded the Irish Confederation, 1847; arrested for sedition, 1848; found guilty of high treason for endeavouring to raise an insurrection in Ireland, 1848; transported to Van Diemen's Land, 1849; escaped to America, 1852; admitted to the New York bar, 1855; founded the *Citizen*, 1854, and *Irish News*, 1856; volunteer in the Civil War, becoming brigadier-general, 1862; secretary of Montana territory, 1865; temporary governor, 1866; drowned in the Missouri.

MEAKIN, James Edward Budgett (1866–1906), historian of the Moors; edited *Times of Morocco*, founded (1884) by his father; visited Mohammedan settlements in Asia and Africa, 1893; settled down to journalism in England, 1897; helped to found British Institute of Social Service, 1905; published *The Moorish Empire* (1899), *The Land of the Moors* (1901), and *The Moors* (1902).

MEANS, Joseph Calrow (1801–1879), General Baptist minister; on General Baptist Assembly committee, 1823; entered University College, London, 1828; afternoon preacher at Worship Street, London, 1829–39; secretary to General Baptist Assembly, 1831; edited *General Baptist Advocate*, 1831–6; minister at Chatham, 1843–55; headmaster of Chatham Proprietary School; returned to Worship Street, London, 1855.

MEARA, Dermod (or Dermitius) (*fl.* 1610), author and physician; studied at Oxford; physician in Ireland; published Latin poem on the earl of *Ormonde, 1615, and treatise on hereditary diseases, 1619.

MEARA (or O'MEARA), Edmund (d. 1680), physician; son of Dermod *Meara; MD, Reims, 1636; hon. FRCP, 1664; defended in his *Examen* (1665) Thomas *Willis (1621–1675), and was attacked by Richard *Lower (1631–1691).

MEARES. See also MERES.

MEARES, John (1756?–1809), naval commander and voyager; entered navy, 1771; lieutenant, 1778; went to India, 1783; formed a company for trading with north-west America, and (1786) explored Prince William Sound; obtained promise of monopoly of Nootka Sound trade, 1788; returned to India, 1788, leaving at Nootka Sound the *Iphigenia*, which was seized by the Spaniards; appealed to government, 1790, war being only averted by Spain acceding to the British demands; his accounts of his voyages disputed by George *Dixon (d. 1800?).

MEARNS, Duncan (1779–1852), professor of theology; MA, Aberdeen, 1795; minister of Tarves, 1799; professor of divinity, Aberdeen, 1816; moderator of the general assembly, 1821; one of George IV's chaplains for Scotland, 1823.

MEARS (or MAIRS), John (1695?–1767), Irish Presbyterian divine; studied divinity, Glasgow; MA, 1713; licensed to Newtownards, 1720; non-subscriber; formed a separate congregation, 1723; minister at Clonmel, 1735–40, at Stafford Street, Dublin, 1740–67; his *Catechism* (1732) long in use.

MEARS, William (*fl.* 1722), publisher; foreman of the Stationers' Company, 1707; issued in 1722 editions of *Holinshed, *Defoe's *Moll Flanders* (3rd edn.) and *Ludlow's *Memoirs*; imprisoned for publishing *Philosophical Dissertation on Death* by de Passereau and Morgan, 1732; mentioned in the *Dunciad*.

MEATH, twelfth earl of (1841–1929), diplomat and philanthropist. See BRABAZON, REGINALD.

MEATH, lords of. See LACY, HUGH DE, first lord, d. 1186; LACY, WALTER DE, second lord, d. 1241.

MECHI, John Joseph (1802–1880), agriculturist; clerk in the Newfoundland trade, 1818; cutler; made a fortune by his 'magic razor strop'; purchased a farm, 1841; effected improvements in agriculture; sheriff of London, 1856; alderman, 1857; published agricultural works.

MEDBOURNE, Matthew (d. 1679), actor and dramatist; of the Duke's Theatre company; imprisoned on *Oates's information, 1678; wrote and translated plays.

MEDD, Peter Goldsmith (1829–1908), theologian; BA, University College, Oxford, 1852; MA, 1855; fellow, 1852–77; rector of North Cerney, Cirencester, 1876–1908; honorary canon of St Albans, 1877; Bampton lecturer, Oxford, 1882; edited Lancelot *Andrewes's *Greek Devotions* (1892); wrote *The One Mediator* (1884) and other theological works.

MEDE, Joseph (1586–1638). See MEAD.

MEDHURST, George (1759–1827), projector of the atmospheric railway; clockmaker; subsequently engineer; patented windmill for compressing air, 1799, 'Aeolian engine', 1800, and compound crank, 1801; machinist and iron-founder in London; invented balance scales; suggested 'pneumatic dispatch' for conveying letters and goods in tubes by compressed air, 1810; extended his suggestion to passengers, 1812, developing it into a project for a carriage on rails in the open air, 1827.

MEDHURST, Walter Henry (1796–1857), missionary, of St Paul's School, London; went to China as missionary printer, 1816; learnt Malay and Chinese; ordained, 1819; translated the Bible into Chinese, and published English and Japanese (1830) and Chinese and English (1842–3) dictionaries.

MEDHURST, Sir Walter Henry (1822–1885), British consul in China; son of Walter Henry *Medhurst; entered office of Chinese secretary, 1840; sent to Hong Kong, 1841; present at Amoy and Chusan (gaining medal), 1841; consular interpreter at Shanghai, 1843; vice-consul at Amoy and (1854) at Foo-chow-foo, also at Tang-chow and Shanghai; mentioned in war despatches, 1861; consul at Hankow, 1864; defended British treaty rights, 1868; removed to Shanghai, 1868–77; knighted, 1877; promoted formation of British North Borneo Company, 1881.

MEDINA, John (1721–1796), painter; grandson of Sir John Baptist *Medina; restored the Holyrood pictures; made copies of the 'Ailsa' portrait of *Mary Queen of Scots; exhibited at Royal Academy, 1772 and 1773.

MEDINA, Sir John Baptist (1659–1710), portrait painter; born at Brussels; went to Scotland, 1688, where he was known as 'the Kneller of the North'; last knight made in Scotland before the Union, 1707.

MEDLAND, Thomas (d. 1833), engraver and draughtsman; drawing-master at Haileybury College, 1806; exhibited at Royal Academy; illustrated various works.

MEDLEY, Henry (d. 1747), vice-admiral; entered navy, 1703; lieutenant, 1710; captain, 1720; rear-admiral of the white, 1744; vice-admiral, 1745; commander-in-chief in the Mediterranean, 1745; vice-admiral of the red, 1747.

MEDLEY, John (1804–1892), first bishop of Fredericton, New Brunswick; MA, Wadham College, Oxford, 1830; vicar of St John's, Truro, 1831; prebendary of Exeter, 1842; DD, 1845; bishop of Fredericton, 1845; metropolitan of Canada, 1879; hon. LL D, Cambridge and DD, Durham, 1889; published theological works.

MEDLEY, Samuel (1738–1799), Baptist minister and hymn-writer; wounded off Cape Lagos and discharged from the navy, 1759; schoolmaster, 1762–6; Baptist minister at Watford, 1767, at Byrom Street, Liverpool, 1772; worked among the seamen; wrote hymns and devotional works.

MEDLEY, Samuel (1769–1857), painter; son of Samuel *Medley (1738–1799); painted portraits, 1792–1805; assisted in founding University College, London, 1826.

MEDLICOTT, Henry Benedict (1829–1905), geologist; BA in civil engineering, Trinity College, Dublin, 1850; MA, 1870; joined Italian geological survey, 1854; professor of geology at Rurki from 1862; volunteer in Indian Mutiny; made study of structure of Himalayas; superintendent of Indian survey, 1876; FRS, 1877; president of Asiatic Society of Bengal, 1879–81; wrote on geology of Punjab (1874) and of India (2 vols., 1879, with W. T. *Blanford).

MEDOWS. See also MEADOWS.

MEDOWS, Sir William (1738–1813), general; grandson of Sir Philip *Meadows (d. 1757); entered the army, 1756; served in Germany, 1760–4; lieutenant-colonel, 1764; distinguished himself at Brandywine, 1776, and against Santa Lucia, 1778; colonel, 1780; sent to Cape of Good Hope, 1781; commander-in-chief and governor of Bombay, 1788; led unsuccessful campaign against Tippoo, sultan of Mysore, 1790; distinguished himself at Nandidrug, 1791, and Seringapatam, 1792; KB, 1792; lieutenant-general, 1793; general and governor of the Isle of Wight, 1798; commander-in-chief in Ireland, 1801.

MEDWALL, Henry (*fl.* 1486), writer of interludes; B.Civ.L., King's College, Cambridge, 1492; chaplain to *Morton, archbishop of Canterbury; his extant interlude, *Nature* (printed *c.*1515), performed before Morton in Henry VII's reign.

MEDWIN, Thomas (1788–1869), biographer of Shelley and author of *Conversations of Lord Byron*; lieutenant, 24th Dragoon Guards, 1813; served in India; introduced by his cousin *Shelley to *Byron at Pisa, 1821; took notes of his conversation, which he published on Byron's death (1824); expanded his memoir of Shelley, issued in *Shelley Papers* (1833) into a life (1847).

MEDWYN, Lord (1776–1854). See FORBES, JOHN HAY.

MEE, Anne (1775?–1851), miniature painter; eldest child of John *Foldsone; received much royal and aristocratic patronage; exhibited at the Royal Academy, 1815–37.

MEE, Arthur Henry (1875–1943), journalist; on staff of Lord *Northcliffe; productions included a *Self-Educator, History of the World, Natural History*, and *Popular Science* (between 1905 and 1913), and *I See All* (1928–30) and *Arthur Mee's Thousand Heroes* (1933–4); first issued *Children's Encyclopædia*, 1908; edited monthly *My Magazine*, 1908–33, and weekly *Children's Newspaper*, 1919–43.

MEEHAN, Charles Patrick (1812–1890), author and translator; educated at Ballymahon and Rome; Roman Catholic curate of Rathdrum, 1834; member of Royal Irish Academy; published translations and historical compilations in connection with Irish Roman Catholic subjects.

MEEK, Charles Kingsley (1885–1965), anthropologist and colonial administrator; educated at Rothesay Academy, Bedford School, and Brasenose College, Oxford; BA, 1910; entered Colonial Administrative Service; posted to Nigeria, 1912; commissioner, decennial census, 1921; published *The Northern Tribes of Nigeria* (1925); government anthropologist, Nigeria, 1924–9; resident, Southern Nigeria, 1929–33; resigned due to ill health; Heath Clark lecturer, London University, 1938–9; senior research fellow, Brasenose College, 1943; advised Colonial Office on 'Devonshire' courses, training programme, 1947; tutor and supernumerary fellow, Brasenose, 1950; publications include *A Sudanese Kingdom* (1931), *Tribal Studies in Northern Nigeria* (1931), *Law and Authority in a Nigerian Tribe: a study in indirect rule* (1937), and *Land Tenure and Land Administration in Nigeria and the Cameroons* (1957).

MEEK, Sir James (1778–1856), public servant; entered Commissariat Department, 1798; collected supplies for Egyptian expedition, 1800; comptroller of the victualling and transport services, 1830; collected information (1841) for Peel's free-trade measures; knighted, 1851.

MEEKE, Mrs Mary (d. 1816?), novelist; published novels, from 1795, in her own name and under the pseudonym 'Gabrielli'.

MEEN, Henry (d. 1817), classical scholar; fellow of Emmanuel College, Cambridge; MA, 1769; BD, 1776; minor canon of St Paul's, London, 1792; prebendary of St Paul's, London, 1795; published *Remarks on the Cassandra of Lycophron* (1800).

MEESON, Alfred (1808–1885), architect and surveyor; superintended construction of houses of parliament under Sir Charles *Barry, 1842, and other public buildings.

MEETKERKE, Edward (1590–1657), divine; of Westminster School; student and tutor of Christ Church, Oxford, 1610; MA, 1613 (incorporated at Cambridge, 1617); regius professor of Hebrew, 1620–6; DD, 1625; prebendary of Winchester, 1631; deprived of his stall under parliament; wrote poems in Hebrew and Latin.

MEGGOT (or MEGGOTT), Richard (d. 1692), dean of Winchester; MA, Queens' College, Cambridge, 1657; DD, 1669; incumbent of Twickenham, 1668–86–7, and St Olave's, Southwark, 1662; canon of Windsor, 1677; dean of Winchester, 1679; entertained James II at Winchester, 1685.

MEGGOTT, John (1714–1789). See ELWES.

MEGHNAD SAHA (1893–1956), scientist; educated at Government Collegiate School, Dacca, Dacca College, and Presidency College, Calcutta; B.Sc., 1913; M.Sc., 1915; lecturer in mathematics, University College of Science, Calcutta, 1916; studied astrophysics, 1918–25; published paper on physical theory of stellar spectra, 1921; worked in London with Alfred *Fowler, and in Berlin with W. Nernst; professor, Allahabad University, 1923–38; concerned with spectroscopic and ionospheric studies, 1925–38; Palit professor, Calcutta, 1938–55; concerned mainly with nuclear physics; established Institute of Nuclear Physics, Calcutta, 1948; member of National Planning Commission, 1939–41, and of Indian Education Commission, 1948; published numerous scientific papers in Indian and foreign journals; FRS, 1927.

MEIDEL, Christopher (*fl.* 1687–1708), Quaker; of Norwegian birth; chaplain to Prince *George of Denmark in England, *c.*1683; minister of Danish congregation, 1687; joined Quakers, 1699; accompanied *Claridge, preaching in Herefordshire and Buckinghamshire, 1705; imprisoned, 1706; visited Holstein; arrested in France, 1608; published Danish translations of Quaker books.

MEIGANT (MAUGANTIUS, MEUGAN, or MEUGANT) (*fl.* 6th cent.), Welsh saint or druid; president of the college of St *Illtyd at Llantwit; subsequently moved to the establishment of St *Dubricius.

MEIGHEN, Arthur (1874–1960), Canadian statesman; educated at St Mary's Collegiate Institute and Toronto University; first class, mathematics, 1896; admitted to Manitoba bar, 1903; Conservative MP, 1908–26; solicitor-general in ministry of (Sir) Robert *Borden, 1913–17; secretary of state, 1917; minister of interior, 1917–20; his concern with conscription and public ownership of railways in wartime government made him a leading figure; prime minister, 1920–1 and 1926; member of Senate, 1932–41; minister without portfolio in government of R. B. (later Viscount) *Bennett, 1932–5; resumed leadership, Conservative party, 1941; retired from public life, 1942.

MEIKLE, Andrew (1719–1811), millwright and inventor of the thrashing-machine; millwright near Dunbar; patented machine for dressing grain, 1768; unsuccessful with first thrashing-machine, 1778; invented drum thrashing-machine, 1784; manufactured thrashing-machines, 1789; subscription raised for his benefit, 1809.

MEIKLE, George (d. 1811), millwright; son of Andrew *Meikle; invented a water-raising wheel, used to drain Kincardine Moss, 1787.

MEIKLE, James (1730–1799), surgeon and devotional writer; passed at Surgeons' Hall, London; second surgeon's mate to the Portland, 1758; present at Cape Lagos, 1759; promoted first mate, 1759; obtained discharge, 1762; published religious meditations.

MEIKLEJOHN, John Miller Dow (1836–1902), writer of school books; MA, Edinburgh, 1858; war correspondent in Danish-German War, 1864; first professor of education in St Andrews University, 1876; raised standard of school books in his *English Language* (1886), *The British Empire* (1891), *The Art of Writing English* (1899), and *English Literature* (1904).

MEILAN, Mark Anthony (*fl.* 1812), miscellaneous writer; resigned situation in Post-Office; schoolmaster at Hoxton, 1776; curate of St John, Wapping, 1809; published dramatic works and religious books for children.

MEILYR BRYDYDD (i.e. the Poet) (d. 1140?), Welsh bard; chief bard of *Gruffydd ab Cynan; once acted as envoy; three poems by him preserved in *Myvyrian Archaiology*.

MEL (d. 487), Irish saint; nephew of St *Patrick; founded see of Ardagh, *c*.454.

MELBA, Dame Nellie (1861–1931), prima donna; born Helen Porter Mitchell; born, educated, and trained in Melbourne, Australia; came to London 1886; studied in Paris under Mme Mathilde Marchesi and adopted name 'Melba'; her appearance in *Rigoletto* in Brussels (1887) extraordinary triumph; sang regularly at Covent Garden and in the capitals of the world, 1888–1926; helped in her acting by Sarah Bernhardt; studied *Faust* and *Roméo et Juliette* with Gounod, *Otello* with Verdi, *La Bohème* with Puccini; introduced Nedda in *Pagliacci* at Covent Garden (1893) at request of Leoncavallo; first sang *Hélène*, composed for her by Saint-Saëns, at Monte Carlo, 1904; her voice extraordinarily fresh and beautiful, with power of expansion, and perfectly even through $2\frac{1}{2}$ octaves; DBE, 1918; GBE, 1927.

MELBANCKE, Brian (*fl.* 1583), euphuistic writer; BA, St John's College, Cambridge, 1579; imitated *Lyly's *Euphues* in *Philotimus* (1583); alludes to story of Romeo and Juliet as well known.

MELBOURNE, Viscounts. See LAMB, HENRY WILLIAM, second viscount, 1779–1848; LAMB, FREDERICK JAMES, Baron Beauvale, third viscount, 1782–1853.

MELCHETT, Barons. See MOND, ALFRED MORITZ, 1868–1930; MOND, JULIAN EDWARD ALFRED, 1925–1973.

MELCHETT, first Baron (1868–1930), industrialist, financier, and politician. See MOND, ALFRED MORITZ.

MELCOMBE, first Baron (1691–1762). See DODINGTON, GEORGE BUBB.

MELDOLA, Raphael (1754–1828), Jewish theologian; born at Leghorn; 'rabbi' of the Spanish and Portuguese Jews in London, 1804; restored synagogue, 1824; endeavoured to maintain sanctity of Sabbath; wrote devotional books in Hebrew.

MELDRUM, Charles (1821–1901), meteorologist; MA, Marischal College, Aberdeen, 1844; professor of mathematics, Royal College of Mauritius, 1848; founded Mauritius Meteorological Society, 1851; in charge of Mauritius Government Observatory, 1862–96; studied laws of cyclones in Indian Ocean; FRS, 1876; CMG, 1886.

MELDRUM, George (1635?–1709), rector of Marischal College, Aberdeen, and professor of divinity at Edinburgh; minister of Aberdeen, 1658; MA, Aberdeen; suspended, 1662–3; elected rector of Marischal College ten times; deprived, 1681, for refusing the test; minister of Kilwinning, 1688, of Tron Church, Edinburgh, 1692; moderator of the general assembly, 1698 and 1703; professor of divinity, Edinburgh, 1702; published sermons and treatises on church matters.

MELDRUM, Sir John (d. 1645), soldier; assisted in plantation of Ulster, 1610–17; served in the Low Countries; knighted, 1622; took part in Rochelle expedition and French War; patentee for erecting lighthouses on north and south Foreland, 1635; wrote to the king justifying his conduct in joining the parliament; fought at Edgehill, 1642, and the siege of Reading, 1643; raised siege of Hull, 1643; captured Gainsborough, Cawood Castle, and the fort of Airemouth, 1643; forced to a disadvantageous capitulation at Newark by *Rupert, 1644; mortally wounded at Scarborough.

MELFORT, first earl and titular duke of (1649–1714). See DRUMMOND, JOHN.

MELIA, Pius (1800–1883), Roman Catholic divine; professor of literature in the Jesuits' College, Rome; missioner in England, 1848; almoner of the Italian Benevolent Society, 1862; published doctrinal works.

MELITON (MILITON or MILTON), William of (d. 1261), Franciscan; fifth master of the Friars Minors, Cambridge, 1250; DD; finished

*Alexander of Hales's *Summa Theologiae*, 1252; died in Paris; his commentaries extant among the National Library manuscripts, Paris.

MELL, Davis (*fl.* 1650), violinist; musician to Charles I; considered the first violinist in England; entertained at Oxford, 1658; leader of Charles II's band, 1660; some of his compositions contained in Simpson's *Division Violin* (1684).

MELLANBY, Sir Edward (1884–1955), medical scientist and administrator; brother of John *Mellanby; educated at Barnard Castle School and Emmanuel College, Cambridge; first class, part ii, natural sciences, 1905; research student under (Sir) Frederick Gowland *Hopkins, 1905–7; qualified in medicine at St Thomas's Hospital, 1909; lecturer and then professor of physiology, King's College for Women, 1913–20; MD, Cambridge, 1915; professor of pharmacology, Sheffield, and honorary physician, Royal Infirmary, 1920–33; secretary, Medical Research Council, 1933–49; Fullerian professor, Royal Institution, 1936–7; his research established main cause of rickets as deficiency of vitamin D, 1919; expert in biochemistry and physiology; chairman of international conferences on vitamins and nutrition; concerned with schemes for wartime diet, 1939–45; KCB, 1937; GBE, 1948; FRS, 1925; FRCP, 1928; hon. FRCS, Ed., 1946.

MELLANBY, John (1878–1939), physiologist; educated at Emmanuel College, Cambridge; MD, 1907; lecturer (from 1920 professor in London University) in charge of physiological department, St Thomas's Hospital Medical School, 1909–36; Waynflete professor of physiology, Oxford, 1936–9; obtained valuable results in work on the proteins of the blood, coagulation, and the secretion of the pancreas; FRS, 1929.

MELLENT, count of (1104–1166). See BEAUMONT, WALERAN DE.

MELLIS, John (*fl.* 1588), mathematician; Southwark schoolmaster; published works on arithmetic and bookkeeping.

MELLISH, Sir George (1814–1877), lord justice of appeal; educated at Eton and University College, Oxford; MA, 1839; hon. fellow, 1872; barrister, Inner Temple, 1848; QC, 1861; lord justice of appeal, 1870; knighted and privy councillor, 1870; hon. DCL, Oxford, 1874.

MELLITUS (d. 624), first bishop of London and third archbishop of Canterbury; sent from Rome by Pope Gregory to reinforce *Augustine, 601; consecrated bishop by Augustine, and sent to preach to the East Saxons; won the support of *Ethelbert, king of Kent, who built St Paul's

Church, London; attended a council at Rome, 610; brought back decrees and letters from the pope; banished, 616; returned to Kent, 617, on *Eadbald's conversion; archbishop of Canterbury, 619–24.

MELLON, Alfred (1820–1867), musician; leading violinist of the Royal Italian Opera, London; musical director at the Haymarket and Adelphi Theatres; his opera *Victorine* produced at Covent Garden, London, 1859.

MELLON, Harriot, duchess of St Albans (1777?–1837), actress; first appeared, 1787; at Drury Lane, 1795–1815, playing an extensive round of characters; married Thomas *Coutts, the banker, 1815, and after his death, William Aubrey de Vere, ninth duke of St Albans, 1827.

MELLON, Sarah Jane (1824–1909), actress; born Woolgar; made début at Plymouth, 1836; long associated with Adelphi from 1843; original Lemuel there in *Buckstone's *Flowers of the Forest* (1847); at Lyceum appeared as Florizel in burlesque of *Perdita* (1856) and as Ophelia (1857); married Alfred *Mellon, 1858; played Catherine Duval at Adelphi in *The Dead Heart* (1859), Mrs Cratchit in *The Christmas Carol* (1860), and Anne Chute in *The Colleen Bawn* (1860); subsequently lost vogue; reappeared as Mrs O'Kelly in *The Shaughraun*, and created Miss Sniffe in *A Bridal Tour* (1880); retired, 1883; versatile actress in tragedy, comedy, burlesque, or farce.

MELLOR, Sir John (1809–1887), judge; barrister, Inner Temple, 1833; QC, 1851; recorder of Warwick, 1849–52, of Leicester, 1855–61; MP, Great Yarmouth, 1857, Nottingham, 1859; justice of the Queen's Bench and knighted, 1861; tried the Fenians at Manchester, 1867, and Arthur *Orton for perjury, 1873; privy councillor, 1879; published a life of Selden.

MELMOTH, Courtney (1749–1814). See PRATT, SAMUEL JACKSON.

MELMOTH, William, the elder (1666–1743), religious writer and lawyer; barrister, 1693; member of Lincoln's Inn, 1699; corresponded anonymously with Archbishop *Tenison, 1705; bencher, 1719; treasurer (1730) of Lincoln's Inn; published anonymously the *Great Importance of a Religious Life* (1711), which was generally assigned to John *Perceval, first earl of Egmont.

MELMOTH, William, the younger (1710–1799), author and commissioner of bankrupts; son of William *Melmoth the elder; abandoned law, 1739; commissioner of bankrupts, 1756; derided by Dr *Johnson; knew Mrs *Thrale at Bath, 1780; wrote *Letters on Several Subjects* (1742), under the pseudonym Sir Thomas Fitz-osborne; translated Pliny's *Letters* (1746), Cicero's *Ad Familiares* (1753) and *De Senectute* (1773).

MELROSE, first earl of (1563–1637). See HAMILTON, THOMAS.

MELTON, Sir **John** (d. 1640), politician and author; read law; knighted, 1632; traded in saltpetre and coal; secretary to the Council of the North, 1635; MP, Newcastle upon Tyne, 1640; published *Sixefolde Politician* (1609) and *Astrologaster* (1620).

MELTON, William de (d. 1340), archbishop of York; held posts in the king's household; received ecclesiastical preferments; keeper of the privy seal, 1307; accompanied Edward II to France as secretary, 1308; commissioner to the Cinque Ports, 1312; archbishop of York, 1316; commissioner to treat with Scotland, 1318, 1321, and 1323; routed by the Scots at Myton-on-Swale ('Chaptour of Mytoun'), 1319; treasurer of England, 1325–7; officiated at Edward III's marriage, 1328; acquitted of complicity in the earl of *Kent's plot, 1329; treasurer, 1330; empowered to open parliament at York, 1332; keeper of the great seal, 1333–4; asserted his right to bear the cross in the southern province.

MELTON, William de (d. 1528), chancellor of York; MA, Cambridge, 1479; DD, 1496; master of Michaelhouse, Cambridge, 1495; chancellor of York, 1496; author of *Sermo Exhortatorius*, published by Wynkyn de *Worde (1494); sometimes confounded with three namesakes.

MELUN, Robert de (d. 1167). See ROBERT.

MELVILL, Henry (1798–1871), canon of St Paul's Cathedral; sizar of St John's College, Cambridge, 1817; second wrangler, 1821; fellow and tutor of Peterhouse, 1822–9; MA, 1824; BD, 1836; chaplain at the Tower of London, 1840; principal of Haileybury College, 1843–57; chaplain to Queen Victoria, 1853; canon of St Paul's, 1856–71; rector of Barnes, 1863–71; published numerous sermons.

MELVILL, Sir **James Cosmo** (1792–1861), brother of Henry *Melvill; entered home service of East India Company, 1808, became financial secretary, 1834, and was chief secretary, 1836, till termination of company's existence as governing body, 1858; government director of Indian railways, 1858; FRS, 1841; KCB, 1853.

MELVILL, Thomas (1726–1753), experimental philosopher; divinity student at Glasgow, 1748–9; read before Edinburgh Medical Society 'Observations on Light and Colours', containing fundamental experiments in spectrum analysis, 1752, 'Refrangibility of the Rays of Light' before Royal Society, 1753.

MELVILLE, Viscounts. See DUNDAS, HENRY, first viscount, 1742–1811; DUNDAS, ROBERT SAUNDERS, second viscount, 1771–1851; DUNDAS, HENRY, third viscount, 1801–1876.

MELVILLE (or MELVILL), Andrew (1545–1622), Scottish Presbyterian leader and scholar; educated at Montrose Grammar School under Pierre de Marsiliers, 1557–9, and St Mary's College, St Andrews; went to Paris, 1564; studied Greek, oriental languages, mathematics, and law; influenced by Peter Ramus; went to Poitiers, 1566; helped to defend Poitiers during the siege, 1568; professor of humanity, Geneva, 1568; met Beza, Joseph Scaliger, and Francis Hottoman; returned to Scotland, 1573; appointed head of Glasgow College, 1574; introduced an enlarged curriculum and established chairs in languages, science, philosophy, and divinity, confirmed by royal charter, 1577; assisted in the organization of the Scottish Church in the Presbyterian mould, which was set forth in the 'second book of discipline', sanctioned, 1581; assisted in the reconstitution of Aberdeen University, 1575, and the reformation of St Andrews, 1579; became principal of St Mary's College, St Andrews, 1580, where he promoted the study of Aristotle, and created a taste for Greek letters; moderator of the general assembly at St Andrews, 1582, at which the order for the excommunication of Montgomery (whom he prosecuted as a 'tulchan' bishop) caused open war between the assembly and the court; his party placed in power by the 'raid of *Ruthven', 1582; charged with treason, 1584; escaped to England, and was well received in Oxford, Cambridge, and London; returned to Scotland on Arran's fall, 1585; effected a compromise, 1586; rector of St Andrews University, 1590; unsuccessfully claimed the right to sit in the assembly at Dundee, 1598, and at Montrose, 1600; deprived of the rectorship in a visitation of St Andrews, but made dean of the faculty of theology, 1599; protested on behalf of the leaders of a general assembly constituted at Aberdeen, 1605, in defiance of the king's messenger; summoned to London, 1606, where he made two long uncompromising speeches on behalf of freedom of assemblies; confined in the Tower for a bitter epigram on Anglican ritual, 1607; his release at last obtained, 1611, by Henri de la Tour, duc de Bouillon, who wished him to become professor of biblical theology in the University of Sédan; wrote controversial prose works; ranked by Isaac *Walton next to *Buchanan as a Latin poet; died at Sédan.

MELVILLE, Andrew (1624–1706), soldier of fortune; studied languages at Königsberg; joined Presbyterian troops, 1647; joined Charles II at Breda; escaped after Worcester (1651) to Holland; fought for France, Sweden, and Branden-burg; sent by the duke of Celle to congratulate Charles II, 1660; appointed commandant of Gif-horn, 1677; published an autobiography (1704); died at Gifhorn.

MELVILLE, Arthur (1855–1904), artist; stu-died at Royal Scottish Academy and in Paris, 1878; travelled in Egypt, Persia, and Turkey, 1881–3; moulded the Glasgow artistic move-ment; exhibited several oil portraits at Edin-burgh, including *The Flower Girl* (1883) and *Portrait of a Lady*, before settling in London, 1888; visited Spain, 1889–92 and 1904, and Venice, 1894; ARSA, 1886; member of Royal Water Colour Society, 1900; works include *A Moorish Procession, Christmas Eve, The Capture of a Spy*, and *The Little Bull Fight*.

MELVILLE, David, third earl of Leven, second earl of Melville (1660–1728), son of George *Melville, first earl of Melville; military commander; became earl of Leven, 1681; confidential agent to the prince of Orange; raised regiment of Scottish refugees, 1688; dis-tinguished himself at Killiecrankie (1689) and in the Irish campaign; served in Flanders, 1692; major-general of the Scottish forces, 1703; mas-ter of ordnance, 1705; commander-in-chief of the Scots forces, 1706; suppressed Jacobite ris-ing, 1708; deprived of all offices by Tory admin-istration, 1712.

MELVILLE, Elizabeth (*fl.* 1603). See COL-VILLE.

MELVILLE, George, fourth Baron and first earl of Melville (1634?–1707), welcomed Charles II in London, 1660; joined Monmouth against the Covenanters, 1679, and endeavoured to avoid a conflict; fled on discovery of the Rye House Plot and joined the prince of Orange, 1683; secretary of state for Scotland, 1689; com-missioner to the parliament (1690) which estab-lished Presbyterianism; trusted by the king to propitiate the Presbyterians; created earl of Mel-ville, Viscount Kirkcaldy, 1690; lord privy seal, 1691; president of the Privy Council and member of the Committee for the Security of the King-dom, 1696; deprived of his offices, 1702.

MELVILLE, Captain George John Whyte- (1821–1878). See WHYTE-MELVILLE.

MELVILLE, Sir James (1535–1617), of Hall-hill; autobiographer; son of Sir John *Melville; page to *Mary Queen of Scots, 1549; wounded at St Quentin, 1557; sent to discover the designs of Lord James *Stewart, earl of Moray, 1557; endeavoured to win Queen Elizabeth's approval of Mary Stuart's marriage to *Darnley; sent to offer the regency to Moray; entrusted with diplo-matic missions throughout James VI's minority;

knighted; privy councillor; manuscript of his autobiography first discovered 1660, last edited 1827.

MELVILLE (or MELVILL), James (1556–1614), Scottish reformer; nephew of Andrew *Melville (1545–1622); educated at St Andrews (BA, St Leonard's College, 1571) and Glasgow; professor of Hebrew and oriental languages at St Mary's College, St Andrews, 1580; seconded his uncle in his views on Presbyterianism; fled to Berwick, 1584; prohibited from preaching; attacked Bishop *Adamson at the synod of Fife, 1586; ordained to a charge in Fifeshire, 1586; moderator of the general assembly, 1589; pre-sented petitions on ecclesiastical matters to *James VI of Scotland, who sent him to collect subscriptions from the Presbyterians to pay for the expedition against *Bothwell; opposed James VI's proposal of a parliamentary vote for minis-ters, 1598; summoned to London on ecclesiast-ical affairs, 1606; ordered to confine himself within ten miles of Newcastle, 1607; died at Ber-wick on his way back to Scotland; published numerous poems; *Diary* printed (1829).

MELVILLE, Sir John (d. 1548), laird of Raith; engaged in the disputes of the regency during James V's minority; master of artillery, 1526; fol-lowed James V in his border expeditions; assisted in the trial of Janet *Douglas, Lady Glamis, 1537; captain of Dunbar Castle, 1540; a reformer, supporting the 'English' party in Scot-land; convicted of treason and executed.

MELVILLE, Robert, first Baron Melville (1527–1621), son of Sir John *Melville; in the French service; returned to Scotland, 1559; opposed *Mary Stuart's marriage to *Darnley; visited Mary Stuart in Lochleven Castle, 1567; taken prisoner at Langside, but released as a noncombatant, 1568; declared traitor, 1573; his forfeiture rescinded, 1580; knighted, 1581; clerk and treasurer depute, 1581; privy councillor, 1582; entreated Queen Elizabeth for Mary Stuart's life; acted as chancellor, 1589; sent to negotiate with Queen Elizabeth, 1593; extraord-inary lord of session as Lord Murdocairnie, 1594; resigned his offices, 1600; accompanied James VI to England, 1603; commissioner for the Union, 1605; created Baron Melville of Moni-mail, 1616.

MELVILLE, Robert (1723–1809), general and antiquary; studied at Glasgow and Edinburgh universities; ensign, 1744; served in Flanders; captain, 1751; major, 1756; lieutenant-governor of Guadeloupe, 1759, governor, 1760; governor of the ceded islands, 1763–70; sent to France to solicit certain indulgences for the British in Tobago; suggested a new theory of Hannibal's route across the Alps; invented a naval gun, 1759 (used until the middle of the nineteenth century); FRS; FSA.

MELVIN, James (1795–1853), Latin scholar; educated at Aberdeen Grammar School and Marischal College, Aberdeen; MA, 1816; LL D, 1834; master at Aberdeen Grammar School, 1822, rector, 1826; 'lecturer on humanity' at Marischal College; published Latin grammar (1822), exercises (posthumous, 1857); collected classical and medieval Latin literature.

MENASSEH BEN ISRAEL (1604–1657), Jewish theologian. See MANASSEH.

MENDELSOHN, Eric (1887–1953), architect; born in East Prussia of German-Jewish parents; educated at the Gymnasium, Allenstein; graduated in architecture at Munich, 1912; served in German Army, 1914–18; designed buildings in steel and concrete, including Einstein Observatory, Potsdam, 1920, and numerous factories, stores, houses, and flats in Berlin and other German cities; after advent of Hitler, moved to London, 1933; in partnership with Serge Chermayeff, designed De La Warr Pavilion, Bexhill, 1934; naturalized, 1938; FRIBA, 1939; left England for Palestine, 1939; moved to United States, 1941; set up practice in San Francisco, 1945; built many hospitals, synagogues, and community centres; one of first architects to realize potentialities of steel, concrete, and glass.

MENDES, Fernando (d. 1724), physician; born in Portugal; MD, Montpellier, 1667; attended *Catherine of Braganza to England; physician-in-ordinary to Catherine of Braganza, 1669; attended Charles II; FRCP, 1687.

MENDES, Moses (d. 1758), poet and dramatist; grandson of Fernando *Mendes; successful stockbroker; bon vivant and wit; wrote dramatic pieces set to music by *Boyce and *Burney, and poems and songs in imitation of Spenser.

MENDHAM, Joseph (1769–1856), controversialist; MA, St Edmund Hall, Oxford, 1795; incumbent of Hill Chapel in Arden, 1836; wrote against Romish doctrine and organization; his library presented to the Incorporated Law Society.

MENDIP, first Baron (1713–1802). See ELLIS WELBORE.

MENDL, Sir Charles Ferdinand (1871–1958), press attaché; educated at Harrow; in business in Paris until outbreak of war, 1914; served as interpreter with 25th Infantry brigade; invalided out, 1915; worked in Intelligence in Paris for the Admiralty, 1918; Paris representative of Foreign Office news department, 1920; knighted, 1924; press attaché, Paris Embassy,

1926–40; served five ambassadors, including Lord *Tyrrell and Sir Eric *Phipps; cultivated wide contacts with the social and political world; enjoyed close friendship with Pertinax of the *Echo de Paris*.

MENDOZA, Daniel (1764–1836), pugilist; successfully united sparring with boxing; encountered 'the Bath butcher', 1787; at times acted as officer of the sheriff of Middlesex; made tours in Ireland, 1791, and England; retired, 1820; published the *Art of Boxing* (1789).

MENDOZA Y RIOS, Joseph de (1762–1816), astronomer; born at Seville; educated at the Royal College of Nobles, Madrid; served in the Spanish Navy with distinction; commissioned by government to form a maritime library at Madrid; travelled in France; made his home in England after being elected FRS, 1793; published works on nautical astronomy, which revolutionized that science, and on navigation.

MENDS, Sir Robert (1767?–1823), commodore; entered navy, 1779; lost right arm at the defence of York town, 1781; wounded at Battle of Dominica; lieutenant, 1789; severely burnt by an explosion in action off Lorient, 1795; captain, 1800; distinguished himself on Spanish coast, 1810; superintendent of Portsmouth harbour, 1811–14; knighted, 1815; appointed commodore and commander-in-chief on the west coast of Africa, 1821; died on board his ship at Cape Coast, 1823.

MENDS, Sir William Robert (1812–1897), admiral; nephew of Sir Robert *Mends; studied at Royal Naval College, Portsmouth; served under Captain Henry John *Rous on the *Pique*, 1835; lieutenant, 1835; commander, 1846; post-captain, 1852; in Mediterranean, 1853; distinguished at bombardment of Odessa, 1854; flag-captain to Sir Edmund (afterwards Lord) *Lyons, 1854–7; CB, 1855; deputy controller-general of coastguard at Admiralty, 1861–2; director of transports, 1862–83; rear-admiral, 1869; vice-admiral, 1874; admiral, 1879; GCB, 1882; his *Life* published by his son, Bowen Stilon Mends (1899).

MENKEN, Adah Isaacs (formerly **McCORD, Adelaide)** (1835–1868), actress and writer; acted at New Orleans and in Texas; journalist; taught French, Greek, and Latin in a school at New Orleans; married Alexander Isaac Menken, 1856; became a Jewess; acted in the States, New York, and (1864) London; became acquainted with *Dickens, Charles *Reade, and *Swinburne; met the elder Dumas and Gautier in Paris, 1866; published *Infelicia* (poems, 1868); was married four and divorced three times; died in Paris.

MENMUIR, Lord (1552–1598), secretary of state in Scotland. See LINDSAY, JOHN.

MENNES, Sir **John** (1599–1671), admiral; recommended by Sir Alexander Brett for command, 1626; served in the Narrow Seas; raised troop of carabineers, 1640; knighted, 1642; governor of North Wales for Charles I, 1644; commander of the king's navy, 1645; comptroller of the navy, 1661, 'though not fit for business', according to *Pepys; commander-in-chief in the Downs and admiral, 1662; published, with Dr James *Smith, *Wits Recreations* (1640) and *Musarum Deliciae* (1655).

MENON, Vapal Pangunni (1894–1966), Indian public servant and author; educated at Ottopalam High School; employed by Imperial Tobacco Company, and as contractor in Kolar gold-fields; clerk in Home Department, Government of India, 1914; transferred to Reforms Office, 1930; on secretarial staff, Round Table Conference, London, 1931; assistant secretary, Reforms Office, 1933; under-secretary, 1934; deputy secretary, 1936; CIE, 1941; reforms commissioner, 1942; CSI, 1946; KCSI, 1948; secretary, States Department; governor, Orissa, 1951; member, Finance Commission; retired, 1952; published *The Story of the Integration of the Indian States* (1956), *The Transfer of Power in India* (1957), and *An Outline of Indian Constitutional History* (1965).

MENON, Vengalil Krishnan Kunji-Krishna (1896–1974), Indian politician; born at Calicut; educated at Madras Presidency College, 1918, London School of Economics (B.Sc. first class honours, 1927, M.Sc. in political science), and University College, London (MA in psychology, 1930); called to bar (Middle Temple), 1934; editor for Bodley Head; with (Sir) Allen *Lane started Penguin and Pelican books, 1935; founded India League and other means of propagating the cause of India's freedom; secretary to Labour fact-finding mission on civil disobedience movement, 1932; Labour member, St Pancras Borough Council, 1934–48; close friend of Jawaharlal *Nehru; first high commissioner for independent India in London, 1947–52; leader of Indian delegation to UN, 1946; made many powerful enemies in India but defence of India at UN on Kashmir and Goa issues made him immensely popular with Indian public; anti-colonial hostility contributed to India's brief entente with China and the Bandung Conference, 1955; minister without portfolio in Nehru's government, 1956–7; defence minister in Nehru's Cabinet, 1957–62; held responsible for débâcle in India's war with China, 1962; career never recovered from this set-back; hon. fellow, LSE.

MENTEITH, earls of. See COMYN, WALTER, d. 1258; GRAHAM, WILLIAM, seventh earl, 1591–1661.

MENTEITH, Sir **John de** (d. after 1329), Scottish knight; imprisoned for resistance to Edward I, 1296; released, 1297; warden of castle, town, and sheriffdom of Dumbarton, 1304; captured *Wallace at Glasgow and took him to London; nominated one of the Scots barons in the united parliament; on the Scottish council and created earl of Lennox; joined *Bruce in his revolt, 1307; commissioned to treat for truce, 1316 and 1323; present at Arbroath parliament, 1320; last recorded grants to him, 1329.

MENTEITH (MENTET or MONTEITH), Robert (*fl.* 1621–1660), author of *Histoire des Troubles de la Grande Bretagne*; MA, Edinburgh, 1621; professor of philosophy at Saumur; presented to the kirk of Duddingston, 1630; fled to Paris, 1633; denounced as rebel; became Roman Catholic and secretary to De Retz till (1652) the cardinal's arrest; canon of Notre-Dame; his *Histoire* published (1660).

MENZIES, Archibald (1754–1842), botanical collector; studied at Edinburgh; naval surgeon; accompanied fur-trading voyage of discovery to north-west coast of America and China, 1786–9; as naturalist and surgeon went with Vancouver to the Cape, New Zealand, and north-west America, 1790–5; ascended Wha-ra-rai and Mauna Loa in Hawaii, determining their altitude by the barometer; brought back various plants, cryptogams, and natural-history objects; FLS, 1790.

MENZIES, Sir **Frederick Norton Kay** (1875–1949), medical officer of health; educated at Llandovery College; MB, Edinburgh, 1899; MD, 1903; public-health diploma, 1905; lecturer in public health, University College, London, and deputy medical officer of health, Stoke Newington, 1907; a medical officer, London County Council, 1909–24; county medical officer, 1926–39; welded hospitals of Metropolitan Asylums Board and Boards of Guardians into integrated service on their transfer to the Council; KBE, 1932.

MENZIES, John (1624–1684), Scottish divine and professor; graduate and regent, Marischal College, Aberdeen; professor of divinity, Marischal College, Aberdeen, and pastor of Greyfriars Church, Aberdeen, 1649; became an Independent, 1651; 'trier' in Scotland, 1654; returned to Presbyterianism; reluctantly conformed to episcopacy; engaged in controversy with Roman Catholics and Quakers; professor of divinity, King's College, Old Aberdeen, 1679, but soon resigned; reinstated professor at Marischal College, Aberdeen, 1679; deprived on refusing the test, 1681; gave way, and was reinstated, 1682; published theological works.

MENZIES, John (1756–1834), founder of Blairs College, Kincardineshire; educated at Dinant; conveyed to Bishop *Paterson his estate of Blairs for the education of secular priests, 1827; benefactor of St Margaret's Convent, Edinburgh, opened, 1835; acquainted with *Scott.

MENZIES, Michael (d. 1766), advocate and inventor; advocate, 1719; invented a thrashing-machine, 1734, a machine for conveying coal to the shaft, 1750, and a machine for draining coal-mines, 1761, which came into partial use.

MENZIES, Sir Robert Gordon (1894–1978), prime minister of Australia; educated at schools in Ballarat and Melbourne and Melbourne University; first-class honours in law, 1916; called to Victorian bar, 1918; built up successful practice, 1918–28; Nationalist member of Upper House, Victorian parliament, 1928; member, Victoria Legislative Assembly; KC, 1929; deputy premier, attorney-general, and minister for railways, Victoria, 1932; United Australian party member for Kooyong, Melbourne, in Commonwealth House of Representatives, 1934–66; deputy leader, UAP, attorney-general, and minister for industry, 1934–8; succeeded to leadership of UAP, 1939; formed government, 1939 and led Australia into war; increasingly anxious about Japan's intentions; visited London and attended meetings of British War Cabinet, 1941; resigned, and Labour government came into power, 1941–9; built up united anti-socialist party and returned to power, 1949; defection of Vladimir Petrov detrimental to Labour-party opposition and 1954 election won by Menzies; in 1951 he sent Australian forces to Korea, in 1954 he successfully negotiated the Anzus treaty and South-East Asia Defence Treaty, and in 1956 negotiated comprehensive trade treaty with Japan; regular contributor to Commonwealth conferences; saw communism as main threat to peace in South Pacific; saw with anxiety negotiations for entry of Britain into EEC; attended prime ministers' conference in London, 1956; led delegation to Egypt with plan for international control of Suez Canal but his mission failed; supported USA in Vietnam with an infantry battalion; won further election, 1962; encouraged development of Canberra, the capital city; retired from office, 1966; published *Afternoon Light* (1967) and *The Measure of the Years* (1970); PC, 1937; CH, 1951; knight of the Thistle, 1963; knight of the Order of Australia, 1976; many honorary degrees; FRS, 1965.

MENZIES, Sir Stewart Graham (1890–1968), head of the Secret Intelligence Service; educated at Eton; joined Grenadier Guards, 1909; transferred to Life Guards, 1910; served in France, 1914; assigned to Intelligence, 1915; DSO, MC; military liaison officer with MI6, Secret Intelligence Service, 1919; colonel, 1932; retired from Life Guards, 1939; appointed 'C', head of MI6, 1939; responsible also for supervision of Government Code and Cypher School, which broke the German 'Enigma' code; in charge of SIS throughout 1939–45 war and with the cold-war period up to 1951; CB, 1942; KCMG, 1943; KCB, 1951.

MEOPHAM (or MEPEHAM), Simon (d. 1333), archbishop of Canterbury; fellow of Merton College, Oxford; DD; prebendary of Llandaff, 1295; canon of Chichester; archbishop of Canterbury, 1327; consecrated at Avignon; mediated between *Henry, earl of Lancaster, and *Mortimer, 1328; enthroned at Canterbury, 1329; crowned Queen *Philippa, 1329; held several church councils; irritated his suffragans by a series of systematic visitations; contested right of archbishop of York to have his cross borne erect before him in the southern province; called on the monks of St Augustine's Abbey to justify their rights to their Kentish churches, 1329; refused to appear before the papal nuncio on the monks' appeal, 1332; pronounced contumacious, fined £700, and excommunicated for non-payment.

MERBECKE, John (d. 1585?), musician and theologian. See MARBECK.

MERBURY (or MARBURY), Charles (fl. 1581), author; BA, Oxford, 1570; entered Gray's Inn, 1571; went to Italy; entered household of earl of *Sussex; in France on official business, 1583; corresponded with Anthony *Bacon and *Walsingham; published defence of absolute monarchy (1581).

MERCER, Andrew (1775–1842), poet and topographer; gave up theology for miniature painting; wrote for magazines in Edinburgh; settled at Dunfermline and taught drawing; wrote poems and *History of Dunfermline* (1828).

MERCER, Cecil William (1885–1960), novelist under name of Dornford Yates; first cousin of 'Saki' (H. H. *Munro); educated at Harrow and University College, Oxford; president, OUDS, 1906–7; called to bar (Inner Temple), 1909; assisted (Sir) Travers *Humphreys in Crippen case; commissioned in 3rd County of London Yeomanry in 1914–18 war; settled at Pau in South of France, 1919; wrote many romantic comedies and thrillers, including *The Brother of Daphne* (1914), *Berry and Co.* (1921), *Jonah and*

Co. (1922), and *She Fell Among Thieves* (1925); after 1939–45 war lived at Umtali, Southern Rhodesia; published *As Berry and I Were Saying* (1952) and *B-Berry and I Look Back* (1958).

MERCER, Hugh (1726?–1777), American brigadier-general; medical student at Aberdeen; surgeon's mate in the pretender's army; went to America, 1747; lieutenant-colonel of provincials, 1758; in command at the new Fort Du Quesne; doctor at Fredericksburg; drilled the Virginian Militia; colonel, 1775; brigadier-general, 1776; died of wounds received at Princeton.

MERCER, James (1734–1804), poet and soldier; second cousin to Hugh *Mercer; MA, Aberdeen, 1754; went to Paris; appointed ensign, 25th regiment, 1758; distinguished himself at Minden, 1759, and in Ireland; major, 1769; sold out of the army, 1772; major in the 'Gordon Fencibles', 1777; an intimate of *Beattie, Dr Reid, Sir William *Forbes, and Robert Arbuthnot; his *Lyric Poems* (1797) republished (1804 and 1806).

MERCER, James (1883–1932), mathematician; bracketed senior wrangler, Cambridge, 1905; mathematical lecturer, Christ's College, 1912–26; FRS, 1922; contributed striking theorems to theories of integral equations and orthogonal series and to modern theory of divergent series.

MERCER, John (1791–1866), calico-printer and chemist; bobbin-winder and hand-loom weaver; experimented in dyeing; studied mathematics and chemistry; discovered dyes suitable for printing calico in orange, yellow, and bronze; chemist at Messrs Fort Brothers' print-works, 1818; partner, 1825; propounded theory of 'catalytic' action at British Association meeting, 1842; joined Chemical Society, 1847; discovered process of 'Mercerizing', 1850; FRS, 1852; read paper on ferro-cyanides at British Association, 1858; made other discoveries connected with dyeing processes.

MERCER, William (1605?–1675?), lieutenant-colonel and poet; served in Denmark and Sweden; granted prebend of Glenholme, 1630; officer in Ireland, 1638; lieutenant-colonel in Parliamentarian army, 1646; swore allegiance at the Restoration; published poems, including *Angliae Speculum* (1646) and *News from Parnassus* (1682).

MERCHISTON, lords of. See NAPIER, ARCHIBALD, first lord, 1574–1645; NAPIER, ARCHIBALD, second lord, d. 1660.

MERCIA, earl of (d. 1057). See LEOFRIC.

MERCIANS, kings of. See PENDA, 577?–655; PEADA, under-king of the South Mercians, d.

656; WULFHERE, d. 675; COENRED, *fl.* 704–709; CEOLRED, d. 716; ETHELBALD, d. 757; OFFA, d. 796; BEORNWULF, d. 826; WIGLAF, d. 838; BEORHTWULF, d. 852; BURHRED, *fl.* 852–874.

MERCIER, Honoré (1840–1894), premier of Quebec; born at Ste-Athanase, Lower Canada; educated at Jesuit College, Montreal; edited *Le Courier*, called to Montreal bar, 1867; member of House of Commons for Rouville in province of Quebec, 1872; solicitor-general, 1878–9; member for Ste-Hyacinthe and Liberal leader in provincial house, 1883; premier of Quebec, 1887–92. His measures included the consolidation of provincial statutes and the establishment of an agricultural department. In 1891 investigations, begun in the senate, traced to Mercier or his agents sums which the provincial house had voted to the Baie des Chaleurs Railway; a royal commission was issued and the ministry dismissed; a prosecution against him, 1892, on an indictment of conspiracy to defraud the province, failed. Subsequently he again took an active part in politics.

MERCIER, Philip (1689–1760), portrait painter; born at Berlin; studied under Antoine Pesne; visited Italy, France, and Hanover; painted the then prince of Wales's portrait; settled in London, 1716; appointed principal painter (1727) and librarian to *Frederick, prince of Wales.

MERDDIN WYLLT (*fl.* 580?). See MYRDDIN.

MEREDITH, Edward (1648–1689?), Roman Catholic controversialist; educated at Westminster School and Christ Church, Oxford; accompanied Sir William *Godolphin to Spain as secretary; became Roman Catholic; went abroad, 1688; published controversial works; died in Italy.

MEREDITH, George (1828–1909), novelist and poet; grandson of Melchizedek Meredith (d. 1804), a prosperous tailor and naval outfitter of Portsmouth (the Lymport of the novel *Evan Harrington*); was privately educated at Portsmouth and Southsea and at the Moravian school at Neuwied, where he became an adept at German, 1843–4; was articled to a London solicitor of Bohemian tastes, 1845; soon turning to journalism, he contributed poems to *Household Words* and to *Chambers's Journal*; making acquaintance of a son of Thomas Love *Peacock, he married Peacock's daughter, 9 Aug. 1849; boarding at Weybridge he came to know there Sir Alexander and Lady *Duff Gordon, and afterwards settled in a cottage at Lower Halliford. In 1858 he was deserted by his wife (d. 1861), who had borne him a son, Arthur Gryffdh (1853–90). Meanwhile, besides writing for *Fraser's Magazine*, he published *Poems* (with dedication to Peacock, 1851), *The Shaving of Shagpat: an Arabian Entertainment* (1855), and *Farina, a Legend of Cologne* (1857). *The Ordeal of Richard Feverel*, the first of his great novels, came out in 1859; the book introduced him to *Swinburne and the Pre-Raphaelite group, while through the Duff Gordons his acquaintance with other notable people quickly grew, but few copies of the book were sold, and his means were long scanty and precarious. He worked regularly for the *Ipswich Journal*, 1859–75; contributed to *Once a Week* six poems, 1859, and a new novel, *Evan Harrington*, serially through 1860; made his residence at Copsham near Esher, 1860, where his intimate circle soon included Frederick Augustus *Maxse, J. A. Cotter *Morison, and others; found his chief recreation in long walks in Surrey and occasionally in France and Switzerland; lodged for a time with *Rossetti and Swinburne at the Queen's House, Chelsea, 1861–2; published *Modern Love and Poems of the English Roadside* (1862); became contributor to the *Morning Post*, 1862; was reader to Chapman & Hall from 1862 to 1894; brought out in 1864 *Emilia in England* (later renamed *Sandra Belloni*); married his second wife, Sept. 1864, and after some years at Norbiton finally settled for life at Flint Cottage facing Boxhill, 1867. There his second wife died, 17 Sept. 1889, leaving a son and daughter. He published *Rhoda Fleming* (1865); contributed serially to *Fortnightly Review* in 1866 *Vittoria*, a sequel to *Emilia*, which was expanded in separate issue; went to Italy as special correspondent for *Morning Post* during war with Austria, 1866; contributed serially to the *Cornhill*, *The Adventures of Harry Richmond* (separately issued in 1871); published *Odes in Contribution to the Song of French History* (1871), *Beauchamp's Career* (1876, after serial issue in condensed form in the *Fortnightly*, 1875), and *The Egoist* (1879, after serial issue in *Glasgow Weekly Herald*); delivered (1 Feb. 1877) at London Institution a characteristic lecture on 'The Idea of Comedy and the Uses of the Comic Spirit' (printed in *New Quarterly Magazine*, 1877, and separately, 1897); published *The Tragic Comedians*, embodying the love story of Ferdinand Lassalle, the German socialist, in Dec. 1880 (after serial issue in *Fortnightly*), and *Poems and Lyrics of the Joy of Earth* (1883). Though both his novels and poetry won growing appreciation from critical circles, the public showed small interest until publication of *Diana of the Crossways* (1885, after serial issue in the *Fortnightly*). There followed *Ballads and Poems of Tragic Life* (1887), *A Reading of Earth* (1888), two of his most characteristic volumes of verse; and the last three novels, *One of Our Conquerors* (1891), *Lord Ormont and his Aminta* (serially issued in *Pall Mall*

Magazine, 1894), and *The Amazing Marriage*, begun in 1879 and serially issued in *Scribner's Magazine* through 1895. In his last years he published many expressions of opinion on public questions, but was from 1893 disabled from active exercise by paraplegia. He received in old age many marks of public regard. Addresses were presented by his admirers on both his seventieth and eightieth birthdays. He was president of the Society of Authors from 1892 to death, and was admitted to Order of Merit, 1905. He died at Flint Cottage, 18 May, and was buried in Dorking Cemetery, 23 May 1909; a memorial service was held in Westminster Abbey on day of funeral. There appeared posthumously *Celt and Saxon*, an unfinished story (*Fortnightly*, 1910), and *The Sentimentalists*, a conversational comedy, was produced at Duke of York's Theatre, Mar. 1910; *Last Poems* came out in 1910. Two collections were made of his work: the edition de luxe (36 vols., 1896–1911) and the memorial edition (27 vols., 1909–11). A collection of his letters appeared in 1912.

MEREDITH, Richard (1550?–1597), bishop of Leighlin and Ferns; MA, Jesus College, Oxford, 1575; held several ecclesiastical appointments in Wales; chaplain to Sir John *Perrot, lord deputy of Ireland, 1584; dean of St Patrick's, Dublin, 1584; bishop of Leighlin, 1589; accused of complicity in Perrot's treasonable designs; tried in the Star Chamber, 1590; imprisoned and fined, 1591 and again, 1594; died in Dublin.

MEREDITH, Richard (1559–1621), dean of Wells; educated at Westminster School and New College, Oxford (fellow, 1578); BCL, 1584; BD, 1606; royal chaplain and dean of Wells, 1607.

MEREDITH, Sir William, third baronet (d. 1790), politician; DCL, Christ Church, Oxford, 1749; MP, Wigan, 1754–61, Liverpool, 1761–80; a Whig and follower of Lord Rockingham; Admiralty lord, 1765; protected Lord North from the mob, 1771; his bill for repealing a clause in the Nullum Tempus Act rejected, 1771; failed in attempt to abolish subscription for members of the universities, 1773; comptroller of the household and privy councillor, 1774; resigned, 1777; sold his property, 1779; wrote on political subjects; died at Lyons.

MEREDITH, Sir William Ralph (1840–1923), Canadian politician; born Upper Canada; called to bar of Upper Canada; represented London as Conservative in Legislative Assembly of Ontario, 1872; leader of opposition, 1878; retired from politics and appointed chief justice, common pleas division of Ontario High Court of Justice, 1894; chief justice of Ontario, 1912; took important part in codifying laws of province and in affairs of Toronto University.

MEREDYDD (d. 999?). See MAREDUDD AB OWAIN.

MEREDYDD AB BLEDDYN, prince of Powys (d. 1132). See MAREDUDD.

MEREDYTH, first Baron. See SOMERVILLE, Sir WILLIAM MEREDYTH, 1802–1873.

MERES, Francis (1565–1647), divine and author; MA, Pembroke College, Cambridge, 1591; incorporated at Oxford, 1593; rector and schoolmaster at Wing, 1602; author of *Gods Arithmeticke* (1597), *Palladis Tamia* (1598), and *Wits Treasury* (1598); translated works by Luis de Granada.

MERES (or **MEERES**), **John** (1698–1761), printer and journalist; printer's apprentice, 1712; partner and manager with Richard Nutt; owner of the *London Evening Post* and *Daily Post*; imprisoned, 1740, for remarks on an act of parliament; compiled a catalogue of English plays, 1713 (with continuation, 1715) and 1734.

MERES, Sir **Thomas** (1634–1715), knighted, 1660; barrister, Inner Temple, 1660; Whig MP, Lincoln, 1660–87, 1701–10; commissioner of the Admiralty, 1679–84; tried to pass a bill compelling foreigners in England to adopt the English liturgy, 1685.

MEREWETHER, Henry Alworth (1780–1864), serjeant-at-law; barrister, 1809; serjeant-at-law, 1827; DCL, Oxford, 1839; town clerk of London, 1842–59; QC, 1853; recorder of Reading; attorney-general to *Adelaide, queen-dowager; chief work, *History of Boroughs and Municipal Corporations* (1835).

MEREWETHER, John (1797–1850), dean of Hereford; BA, The Queen's College, Oxford, 1818; DD, 1832; incumbent of New Radnor, 1828; dean of Hereford, 1832; deputy clerk of the closet to William IV, 1833; opposed election of *Hampden to see of Hereford, 1847; FSA, 1836; assisted in the restoration of Hereford Cathedral.

MEREWETHER, Sir **William Lockyer** (1825–1880), Indian military officer and administrator; son of Henry Alworth *Merewether; educated at Westminster School; entered Bombay Army, 1841; distinguished himself during Sind campaign, 1843; commandant of the frontier force, 1859; CB, 1860; political agent at Aden, 1865; commanded the pioneer force in Abyssinia, 1867; KCSI, 1868; chief commissioner in Sind, 1867; member of the Council of India, 1876.

MERFYN FRYCH (i.e. Freckled) (d. 844), Welsh prince; became lord of Anglesey, 825. His descendants became princes of North and South Wales.

MERICK. See MERRICK and MEYRICK.

MERITON (or **MERYTON**), **George** (d. 1624), dean of York; graduated MA from St John's College, 1588; fellow of Queens' College, Cambridge, 1589; rector of Hadleigh, 1599; dean of Peterborough, 1612; chaplain to James I's queen; dean of York, 1617; published sermons.

MERITON (or **MERRITON**), **George** (1634–1711), author; grandson of George *Meriton (d. 1624); lawyer at Northallerton; went to Ireland, 1684; LL D, of Dublin, 1700; published legal works and a curious poem in 'Praise of Yorkshire Ale' (1683).

MERITON, John (1636–1704), divine; sizar of St John's College, Cambridge; recommended by *Cromwell to St Nicholas Acons, London, 1656; MA, Cambridge, by royal mandate, 1660, and DD, 1669; rector of St Michael's, Cornhill, 1663; remained at his post during the plague, 1665; assisted in uniting and rebuilding churches after the fire, 1666; published devotional works.

MERITON, Thomas (*fl.* 1658), dramatist; grandson of George *Meriton (d. 1624); MA, St John's College, Cambridge, 1669; published *Love and War* (1658) and *The Wandring Lover* (1658), two tragedies.

MERIVALE, Charles (1808–1893), dean of Ely; son of John Herman *Merivale; of Harrow and St John's College, Cambridge; MA, 1833; BD, 1840; rowed for university in first contest with Oxford at Henley, 1829; fellow of St John's College, Cambridge, 1833; rector of Lawford, Essex, 1848; chaplain to speaker of House of Commons (John Evelyn *Denison), 1863–9; Hulsean lecturer, 1862; Boyle lecturer, 1864–5; dean of Ely, 1869; hon. DCL, Oxford, 1866; published *History of the Romans under the Empire* (1850–64) and other historical writings, sermons, and lectures, besides numerous Latin poems, including a translation of *Keats's *Hyperion*.

MERIVALE, Herman (1806–1874), undersecretary for India; son of John Herman *Merivale; was educated at Harrow and Oxford; BA, Trinity College, Oxford, 1827; fellow of Balliol College, 1828; barrister, Inner Temple, 1832; professor of political economy at Oxford, 1837; assistant under-secretary of state for the colonies, 1847; permanent under-secretary, 1848; transferred to the India Office and CB, 1859; DCL, Oxford, 1870; principal works, *Lectures on

Colonisation (1841), *Historical Studies* (1865), and *Life of Sir Henry Lawrence* (1872).

MERIVALE, Herman Charles (1839–1906), playwright and novelist; son of Herman *Merivale; educated at Harrow and Balliol College, Oxford; BA, 1861; called to bar, 1864; edited *Annual Register*, 1870–80; collaborated in *All for Her* (1875) and *Forget Me Not* (1879), plays which attained great success; his *The White Pilgrim* (1883) shows high qualities of poetic drama; skilful adapter of foreign dramas; wrote excellent farces and burlesques, including *The Butler* (1886), and *The Don* (1888), written for J. L. *Toole; published novel, *Faucit of Balliol* (3 vols., 1882), and a children's fairy tale, *Binko's Blues* (1884); lost fortune through default of trustee and awarded civil list pension, 1900.

MERIVALE, John Herman (1779–1844), scholar and minor poet; grandson of Samuel *Merivale; of St John's College, Cambridge; barrister, Lincoln's Inn, 1804; practised in Chancery and bankruptcy; Chancery commissioner, 1824; bankruptcy commissioner, 1831; published law reports and translations from Greek and Italian poetry.

MERIVALE, Samuel (1715–1771), Presbyterian minister at Sleaford, 1737, and Tavistock, 1743; tutor at Exeter Presbyterian Theological Seminary, 1761; published devotional works.

MERKE, Thomas (d. 1409), bishop of Carlisle; educated at Oxford; DD; monk of Westminster; appointed bishop of Carlisle, 1397; ambassador to the German princes, 1397; present in parliament, 1397; commissioner for Queen *Isabella's dowry, 1398; accompanied Richard II to Ireland, 1399; protested against Henry IV's treatment of Richard; committed to the Tower of London, 1400; found guilty and deprived of his bishopric; received conditional pardon, 1401; acted occasionally as deputy to *Wykeham; commissioned to perform episcopal functions in the diocese of Winchester during its vacancy; sided against the pope at Lucca, 1408.

MERLAC, Daniel of (*fl.* 1170–1190), astronomer. See MORLEY.

MERLE (or MORLEY), William (d. 1347), meteorologist; rector of Driby, 1331; kept systematic record of the weather for seven years, preserved in Digby MS, Merton College, Oxford.

MERLIN AMBROSIUS (or MYRDDIN EMRYS), legendary enchanter and bard; brought before *Vortigern as a child; foretold the king's death and the triumph of Aurelius Ambrosius; made ruler of the western part of Britain by *Vortigern; advised Aurelius, as a memorial of his triumph, to send for the stones called 'Giants' Dance' from Ireland; defeated the Irish by his art, and the 'Dance' was set up (Stonehenge). One legend represents Merlin to have gone to sea in a glass vessel and disappeared. Welsh tradition recognizes another Merlin, Merlin Silvester, or Myrddin Wyllt, who lived *c.*570, was connected with the fatal Battle of Arderydd, 573, and subsequently became insane and lived in the forest. The Merlin legend is common to Scotland, Wales, Cornwall, and Brittany. The popular French romance of *Merlin*, by Robert de Borron (thirteenth century), was founded on *Geoffrey of Monmouth. Sir Thomas *Malory borrowed much from Borron's *Merlin* in his *Morte d'Arthur*.

MERLIN CELIDONIUS (or SILVESTER). See MYRDDIN WYLLT.

MERRET (or MERRETT), Christopher (1614–1695), physician; MD, Gloucester Hall, Oxford, 1643; FRCP, 1651; Gulstonian lecturer, 1654; censor seven times between 1657 and 1670; first librarian at Royal College of Physicians, which was destroyed, 1666, and his services dispensed with; expelled from his fellowship for non-attendance, 1681; published works on natural history and medicine.

MERREY, Walter (1723–1799), numismatist; Nottingham manufacturer; published a history of English coinage (1789).

MERRICK, James (1720–1769), poet and scholar; MA, Trinity College, Oxford, 1742; fellow, 1745; ordained, but lived in college; published poems, including *The Chameleon*; translated from the Greek and advocated the compilation and amalgamation of indexes to the principal Greek authors; versified the Psalms, several editions of which were set to music.

MERRICK, Rice (d. 1587), historian of Glamorgan; clerk of the peace; his history printed (1825 and 1887).

MERRIFIELD, Charles Watkins (1827–1884), mathematician; entered the Education Department, 1847; barrister, 1851; FRS, 1863; held offices in the London Mathematical Society and the Royal Institution of Naval Architects; principal of Royal School of Naval Architecture and Marine Engineering, 1867–73; served on royal commissions; wrote books and papers in periodicals on mathematics and hydraulics.

MERRIMAN, Brian (1757–1808), Irish poet; schoolmaster at Kilclerin; wrote a poem, 'Midnight Court', 1780; composed songs.

MERRIMAN, Frank Boyd, Baron Merriman (1880–1962), judge; educated at Winchester; called to bar (Inner Temple), 1904; served with Manchester Regiment, 1914–18; OBE, 1918;

KC, 1919; recorder of Wigan, 1920–8; Conservative MP, Rusholme division, Manchester, 1924–33; solicitor-general, 1928–9 and 1932–3; president, Probate, Divorce, and Admiralty Division of the High Court, 1933; PC, 1933; bencher, Inner Temple, 1927; chairman, bishop of London's Commission on City churches, 1941–6; hon. LL D, McGill University; knighted, 1928; baron, 1941; GCVO, 1950.

MERRIMAN, Henry Seton (pseudonym) (1862–1903), novelist. See SCOTT, HUGH STOWELL.

MERRIMAN, John (1774–1839), surgeon; first cousin to Samuel *Merriman (1771–1852); MRCS and MSA; general medical attendant on the duchess of Kent; apothecary extraordinary to Queen Victoria, 1837.

MERRIMAN, John Xavier (1841–1926), South African statesman; son of N. J. *Merriman; taken to South Africa, 1848; educated in England; returned to Cape, where he practised as land surveyor, 1861; elected to Cape House of Assembly, 1869; joined Cabinet of (Sir) J. C. *Molteno as commissioner of crown lands and public works, 1875–7; secretary of war during Kaffir War, 1877–8; associated with J. W. Sauer, 1881–1913; commissioner of public works, Scanlen ministry, 1881–4; treasurer-general, Rhodes ministry, 1890–3, Schreiner ministry, 1898–1900; prime minister, 1908–10; concerned with hastening South African union and restoring finances of Cape Colony.

MERRIMAN, Nathaniel James (1810–1882), bishop of Grahamstown, South Africa; educated at Winchester College and Oxford; MA, Brasenose College, Oxford, 1834; archdeacon of Grahamstown, 1848; undertook a Kaffir mission, 1850; one of Bishop *Colenso's accusers, 1863; bishop of Grahamstown, 1871; wrote on South Africa.

MERRIMAN, Samuel (1731–1818), physician; MD, Edinburgh, 1753; settled in London, 1757; specialized in midwifery.

MERRIMAN, Samuel (1771–1852), physician; studied medicine under his uncle, Samuel *Merriman (1731–1818); hon. MD, Marischal College, Aberdeen; physician-accoucheur, Westminster General Dispensary, London, 1808–15, to Middlesex Hospital, London, 1809–26, where he lectured on midwifery, 1810–25; published medical works, some on obstetrics.

MERRIOT, Thomas (1589–1662), grammarian; fellow of New College, Oxford, 1610–24; BCL, 1615; vicar of Swalcliffe, 1624;

where he taught grammar; sequestered, 1646; published grammatical works in Latin.

MERRITT, Henry (1822–1877), picture cleaner and art critic; came to London, 1846; cleaned pictures for the National Portrait Gallery, London, Hampton Court, and Marlborough House; acquainted with Gladstone and *Ruskin, with whom he corresponded; published *Robert Dalby* (autobiographical romance, 1865); art critic to the *Standard*, 1866.

MERRIVALE, first Baron (1855–1939), judge and politician. See DUKE, HENRY EDWARD.

MERRY, Robert (1755–1798), dilettante; educated at Harrow; left Christ's College, Cambridge, without graduating; entered Lincoln's Inn; purchased a commission in the Horse Guards, which he sold on account of gambling debts; settled at Florence, 1784; wrote for the *Arno* and *Florence Miscellany*, 1785; member of the Della Cruscan Academy; left for London, 1787; carried on a sentimental correspondence in verse in the *World* with Mrs Hannah *Cowley, 1787; sympathized with the French Revolution; visited Paris, 1789, 1791, and 1792; went to America, 1796, where his wife, Elizabeth Brunton, acted in the chief cities in the States; wrote several unsuccessful plays; died at Baltimore.

MERRY, William Walter (1835–1918), classical scholar; BA, Balliol College, Oxford; fellow and classical tutor, Lincoln College, 1859–84; rector, 1884–1918; ordained, 1860; public orator, 1880–1910; completed large edition of *Odyssey* begun by James *Riddell; edited plays of Aristophanes, etc.

MERRY DEL VAL, Rafael (1865–1930), cardinal; studied for priesthood at Ushaw College, Durham (1883–5), and in Rome (1885–91); ordained priest, 1888; secretary to Papal Commission on Anglican Orders, 1896; apostolic delegate to Canada, 1897; consistorial secretary, 1903; pontifical secretary of state, 1903–14; cardinal priest with titular church of Santa Prassede, 1903; archpriest of St Peter's, 1914; secretary of Holy Office, 1914–30; died in Rome.

MERRYFELLOW, Dick (1723–1781), author. See GARDINER, RICHARD.

MERSEY, first Viscount (1840–1929), judge. See BIGHAM, JOHN CHARLES.

MERSINGTON, Lord (1625?–1700), Scottish judge. See SWINTON, ALEXANDER.

MERTHYR, first Baron (1837–1914), engineer and coal-owner. See LEWIS, WILLIAM THOMAS.

MERTON, Sir Thomas Ralph (1888–1969), scientist; educated at Farnborough School, Eton, and Balliol College, Oxford; B.Sc., 1910;

lieutenant, RNVR, in the secret service, 1916; D.Sc., Oxford, 1916; lecturer in spectroscopy, King's College, London; research fellow, Balliol, reader in spectroscopy, 1919; professor, 1920; FRS, 1920; retired to his Herefordshire estate, 1923; member, Air Defence Committee; experiments with cathode rays contributed to radar; other research included paint to reduce light reflected from bombers by searchlights; post-war research in methods of ruling diffraction gratings led to production of cheap infra-red spectrometers; treasurer, Royal Society, 1939–56; became collector of Renaissance paintings; member, scientific advisory board, National Gallery; chairman, 1957–65; trustee, National Gallery and National Portrait Gallery, 1955–62; knighted, 1944; KBE, 1956.

MERTON, Walter de (d. 1277), bishop of Rochester and founder of Merton College, Oxford; probably a pupil of *Adam de Marisco, at Mauger Hall, Oxford; founded a hospital at Basingstoke in memory of his parents; protonotary of Chancery; negotiated with the pope about the grant of Sicily to Edmund, the king's son, 1258; chancellor, 1261–3; justiciar, 1271; again chancellor, 1272–4; bishop of Rochester, 1274. He obtained charters, 1261, 1263, 1264, 1270, 1274, to assign various manors for the support of scholars at Oxford who should form a corporate body under a warden.

MERVIN (or MERVYN), Sir Audley (d. 1675), soldier, lawyer, and politician; acquired lands in Ulster; MP, Tyrone, 1640; lieutenant-colonel against the rebels, 1641; governor of Derry, 1644; taken prisoner by parliamentarians, 1648; co-operated against Sir Charles *Coote, but afterwards withdrew from the Royalist party, 1649; admitted of King's Inns at Dublin, 1658; assisted in the restoration of Charles II in Ireland; knighted, 1660; serjeant-at-law in Ireland, 1660; commissioner of lands and for the settlement of Ireland, 1661; speaker of the Irish House of Commons, 1661–6.

MERYCK, Sir William (d. 1668), civilian. See MEYRICK.

MERYON, Charles Lewis (1783–1877), physician and biographer of Lady Hester *Stanhope; educated at Merchant Taylors' School, London, St John's College, Oxford, and St Thomas's Hospital, London; MA, 1809; MD, 1817; accompanied Lady Hester Stanhope as medical attendant, 1810; revisited her in Syria; FRCP, 1821; published *Memoirs* (1845) and *Travels* (1846) of Lady Hester Stanhope.

MERZ, Charles Hesterman (1874–1940), electrical engineer; educated at Bootham School, York, and Armstrong College, Newcastle; estab-lished a consultative firm with William McLellan, 1902; designed Neptune Bank Power Station, Wallsend (1902), first station in Britain to generate 3-phase current at voltage of 5,500; electrified railway between Newcastle and Tynemouth (1902) and Melbourne suburban railways (1912); organizer and first director of Admiralty department of experiment and research; chairman of committee whose report resulted in the 'grid' system; superb expert witness.

MESSEL, Oliver Hilary Sambourne (1904–1978), artist and stage designer; educated at Eton, 1917–21; studied at Slade School of Art with his contemporary Rex *Whistler under Henry *Tonks; designed head-masks for student parties; held exhibition of these at Claridge Galleries, London, 1925; designed masks for ballet, *Zephyr and Flora*, directed by Georges Braque; engaged by (Sir) C. B. *Cochran to design masks for *Cochran's Revue*, 1926; contributed designs for costume and scenery for succession of Cochran revues, and for more ambitious ventures such as the revival of *Helen*, directed by Max Reinhardt, and *The Miracle* (1932); recognized as one of foremost stage designers in Britain; designed for opera and ballet including *The Magic Flute* (1947), *Queen of Spades* (1950), *Der Rosenkavalier* (1959), *Francesca da Rimini* (1937), and *Sleeping Beauty* (1946); also contributed designs for costumes and backgrounds for films, notably *Romeo and Juliet* (1936), *Caesar and Cleopatra* (1945), and *Suddenly Last Summer* (1959); other examples of his work include the Oliver Messel Suite in the Dorchester Hotel, London; fellow, University College, London, 1956; CBE, 1958; his nephew, earl of Snowdon, lent Oliver Messel Collection to Victoria and Albert Museum, 1982; served in army during 1939–45 war; published *Stage Designs and Costumes* (1933).

MESSERVY, Sir Frank Walter (1893–1973), general; educated at Eton and Royal Military College, Sandhurst; commissioned into Indian Army, 1913; served during 1914–18 war with Hodson's Horse in France, Palestine, Syria, and Kurdistan; attended Staff College, Camberley, 1925–6; served on North-West Frontier of India; instructor at Staff College, Quetta; commanded 13th Duke of Connaught's Own Lancers, 1938–9; saw them through mechanization; general staff officer, 5th Indian Infantry division, 1939–40, in Sudan; commanded 9th Infantry brigade, 1941 and 4th Indian division in Western Desert, 1941; DSO; commanded 7th Armoured division in North Africa; captured by Rommel's troops; pretended to be batman and escaped; posted to India; major-general, 1943; fought in Arakan and at Kohima and Imphal; commanded IV Corps under W. J. (later Viscount) *Slim; led

IV Corps to Rangoon; appointed general officer commanding-in-chief, Malaya, 1945; GOC-in-C, Northern Command, India, 1946; first C-in-C of independent Pakistan, 1947; retired with honorary rank of general, 1948; colonel, 16th Light Cavalry, 1946–9 and Jat Regiment, 1947–55; CB, 1942; bar to DSO, 1944; KBE, 1945; KCSI, 1947; commander of US Legion of Merit.

MESSING, Richard (d. 1462?), Carmelite. See MISYN.

MESTON, James Scorgie, first Baron Meston (1865–1943), Indian civil servant and man of affairs; educated at Aberdeen Grammar School and University and Balliol College, Oxford; posted to North-Western Provinces and Oudh, 1885; financial secretary, 1899–1903; financial secretary to Indian government, 1906–12; lieutenant-governor, United Provinces, 1912–18; influential in preparing way for political advance; finance member, Viceroy's Executive Council, 1918–19; chairman, committee on financial adjustments between provinces and centre, 1920; with Lionel *Curtis main designer of Royal Institute of International Affairs; first chairman of governors, 1920–6; chancellor, Aberdeen University, 1928–43; president, Liberal party organization, 1936–43; KCSI, 1911; baron, 1919.

MESTON, William (1688?–1745), burlesque poet; educated at Marischal College, Aberdeen, and (1715) regent; governor of Dunnottar Castle during Jacobite rising, 1715; schoolmaster at Elgin and Turriff; published *The Knight of the Kirk* (imitation of *Hudibras*, 1723).

METCALF, John (1717–1810), commonly known as 'Blind Jack of Knaresborough'; became blind when 6 years old; distinguished athlete and dealer in horses; rode several races successfully; walked from Knaresborough to London and back; recruiting-serjeant, 1745; fought at Falkirk, 1746, and Culloden, 1746; set up a stage-coach between York and Knaresborough, 1754; a pioneer road-maker and bridge-builder; constructed about 180 miles of turnpike road; retired to a small farm, 1792.

METCALFE, Sir Charles Herbert Theophilus, sixth baronet (1853–1928), civil engineer; born at Simla; great-nephew of Baron *Metcalfe; BA, University College, Oxford; succeeded father Sir Theophilus *Metcalfe, 1883; apprenticed to engineering firm of Fox & Sons; his most important work accomplished in South Africa, where he lived more and more frequently, 1882–1914; friend of Cecil *Rhodes, whose dreams of northward expansion in Africa he realized by his railway work; together with firm of Fox, consulting engineer for various lines constituting Rhodesia railway system, Benguela Railway through Portuguese West Africa, etc.

METCALFE, Charles Theophilus, first Baron Metcalfe (1785–1846), provisional governor-general of India; educated at Eton; appointed to a Bengal writer-ship, 1800; political agent successively to generals *Lake, *Smith, and *Dowdeswell; sent on a mission to Lahore, 1808; resident of Delhi, 1811–20; developed the industrial resources of Delhi territory; resident of Hyderabad, 1820–7; member of the Supreme Council, 1827; provisional governor-general, 1835–6; GCB and lieutenant-governor of the North-West Provinces, 1836–8; as governor of Jamaica, 1839–42, smoothed matters between proprietors and negroes; governor-general of Canada, 1843–5, where his tact won the general election, 1844, for the government; created Baron Metcalfe, 1845; retired, 1845.

METCALFE, Frederick (1815–1885), Scandinavian scholar; BA, St John's College, Cambridge, 1838; fellow of Lincoln College, Oxford, 1844–85; MA, 1845; published works on Norway, Sweden, and Iceland.

METCALFE, James (1817–1888), lieutenant-colonel, Indian Army; natural son of Charles Theophilus *Metcalfe, first Baron Metcalfe; entered Bengal Regiment, 1836; adjutant, 1839–46; aide-de-camp to the marquis of Dalhousie, 1848–53; interpreter to Sir Colin *Campbell during the Mutiny; CB, 1860.

METCALFE, Nicholas (1475?–1539), archdeacon of Rochester; BA Michaelhouse, Cambridge, 1494; DD, 1507; archdeacon, 1515; master of St John's College, Cambridge, 1518–37; opposed Henry VIII's divorce from *Catherine and royal supremacy in doctrinal matters; founded scholarships at Cambridge.

METCALFE, Robert (1590?–1652), fellow of Trinity College, Cambridge; fellow of St John's College, Cambridge, 1606; regius professor of Hebrew, Cambridge, till 1648; fellow, 1645, and vice-master of Trinity College, Cambridge; benefactor of Beverley School.

METCALFE, Theophilus (fl. 1649), stenographer; teacher of shorthand; published stenographic system, 1635; on lines of *Shelton's *Tachygraphy* (frequently reprinted and used by Isaac *Watts).

METCALFE, Sir Theophilus John (1828–1883), joint magistrate at Meerut; nephew of Charles Theophilus *Metcalfe, first Baron Metcalfe; entered Bengal Civil Service, 1848; joint magistrate at Meerut and deputy collector at

Futtepur, 1857; joined army before Delhi; CB, 1864.

METEYARD, Eliza (1816–1879), author; contributed to periodicals, published novels, *Life of Josiah Wedgwood* (1865–6), besides other works on *Wedgwood's friends and ware.

METFORD, William Ellis (1824–1899), inventor; apprenticed as engineer; employed on Wilts, Somerset, and Weymouth Railway, 1846–50; associate of Institution of Civil Engineers, 1856; held appointment on East India Railway, 1857–8; an explosive rifle bullet invented by him adopted by government, 1863; the pioneer of substitution of shallow grooving and a hardened cylindrical bullet expanding into it for deep grooving and soft bullets of lead; produced his first match rifle, 1865, and his first breech-loading rifle, 1871. A rifle which combined the Metford bore with the bolt-action and detachable magazine invented by the American, James P. Lee, was selected for British use, 1888.

METHOLD, Sir William (1560?–1620), chief baron of the Exchequer in Ireland; entered Lincoln's Inn, 1581 (bencher, 1608); serjeant, 1611; chief baron of the Exchequer in Ireland, 1612; privy councillor and knighted, 1612; lord chief justice in Ireland and joint keeper of the great seal, 1619.

METHOLD, William (d. 1653), nephew of Sir William *Methold; entered East India Company, 1615; visited Golconda, 1622; director, 1628; sent on a mission to Persia, 1633; deputy-governor of the East India Company, 1650; published travels.

METHUEN, Sir Algernon Methuen Marshall, baronet (1856–1924), publisher, whose original name was Algernon Stedman; BA, Wadham College, Oxford; private schoolmaster, 1880–95; opened publishing office in London as Methuen & Co., 1889; firm's range catholic, but specialized in educational and topographical works; firm's authors included *Kipling, *Corelli, *Belloc, J. B. *Bury, *Chesterton, *Conrad, Anthony *Hope, E. V. *Lucas; baronet, 1916.

METHUEN, John (1650?–1706), lord chancellor of Ireland; son of Paul *Methuen (d. 1667); educated at St Edmund Hall, Oxford; barrister, Inner Temple; master in Chancery, 1685; MP, Devizes, 1690; envoy to Portugal, 1691; lord chancellor of Ireland, 1697; again sent to Portugal, 1702; ambassador-extraordinary to Portugal, 1703; concluded 'Methuen Treaty' (commercial treaty with Portugal), 1703; died at Lisbon; buried in Westminster Abbey.

METHUEN, Paul (*fl.* 1566), Scottish reformer; a Dundee baker; converted to Protestantism; escaped arrest and preached publicly during the war, 1556; found guilty of usurping ministerial office, 1559; nominated to Jedburgh Church, 1560; deposed and excommunicated for adultery, 1562; fled to England; commanded by the assembly to repent publicly at Edinburgh, Dundee, and Jedburgh, 1566; partly obeyed and returned to England.

METHUEN, Paul (d. 1667), Bradford clothier; obtained spinners from Holland.

METHUEN, Sir Paul (1672–1757), diplomat; son of John *Methuen; entered Diplomatic Service, 1690; envoy to king of Portugal, 1697–1705; minister at Turin, 1705; ambassador to Portugal, 1706–8; MP, Devizes, 1708–10, Brackley, 1713–47; lord of the Admiralty, 1714–17; ambassador to Spain and Morocco and privy councillor, 1714; comptroller of the household, 1720; KB, 1725; retired, 1730; collected pictures.

METHUEN, Paul Sanford, third Baron Methuen (1845–1932), field marshal; educated at Eton; joined Scots Fusilier Guards, 1864; commanded Methuen's Horse in Bechuanaland, 1884–5; succeeded father, 1891; commanded Home district, 1892–7; lieutenant-general, 1898; commanded 1st division in South Africa, 1899–1902; unjustly criticized for miscarriage of his attack at Magersfontein, 11 Dec. 1899; obtained many minor successes; wounded and captured at Tweebosch, 7 March 1902; general, 1904; held Eastern Command, 1905–8; GOC-in-C, South Africa, 1908–12; field marshal, 1911; governor and commander-in-chief, Malta, 1915–19; constable of the Tower, 1919–32; KCVO, 1897; KCB, 1900; GCB, 1902; GCVO, 1910; GCMG, 1919.

METHVEN, first Baron (1495?–1551?). See STEWART, HENRY.

METHVEN, Lord (1746–1801), Scottish judge. See SMYTHE, DAVID.

METHVEN, Sir (Malcolm) John (1926–1980), director-general of Confederation of British Industry; educated at Mill Hill School and Gonville and Caius College, Cambridge; first class, part ii, law tripos, 1949; admitted solicitor, 1952; solicitor with Birmingham Corporation, 1952–7; in legal department of metals division of ICI, 1957–68; head of central purchasing department, 1968; deputy chairman, Mond division, 1970–3; first director-general, Office of Fair Trading, 1973–6; as first consumer watch-dog brought about changes in standards, especially in advertising; director-general, CBI, 1976; responsible for increased prestige and efficiency; knighted, 1978.

MEUDWY MÔN (1806–1889), Welsh writer. See JONES, OWEN.

MEULAN, counts of. See BEAUMONT, ROBERT DE, d. 1118; BEAUMONT, WALERAN DE, 1104–1166.

MEURYG (*fl.* 1250), treasurer of Llandaff. See MEYRIG.

MEUX (formerly **LAMBTON),** Sir **Hedworth** (1856–1929), admiral; entered navy, 1870; captain, 1889; naval private secretary to first lord of Admiralty, 1894–7; landed with naval brigade in time to join garrison in Ladysmith, Oct. 1899; rear-admiral, 1902; commanded cruiser division of Mediterranean Fleet, 1904–6; vice-admiral, 1908; commander-in-chief, China, 1908–10; changed his name to Meux on coming into large fortune under will of Lady Meux, 1911; admiral, 1911; commander-in-chief, Portsmouth, 1912–16; admiral of the fleet, 1915; secured safe passage of transports conveying British Expeditionary Force to France; Conservative MP, Portsmouth, 1916–18; KCVO, 1906; KCB, 1908.

MEVERALL, Othowell (1585–1648), physician; BA, Christ's College, Cambridge; MD, Leiden, 1613; FRCP, 1618; censor for eight years, registrar, 1639–40, president, 1641–4; lecturer on anatomy, 1638; lecturer to the Barber-Surgeons, 1638; notes of his lectures still extant.

MEW, Charlotte Mary (1869–1928), poet; lived nearly all her life in Bloomsbury; published poems, stories, essays, studies in periodicals, and two volumes of verse (1915 and, posthumous publication, 1929).

MEWS, Peter (1619–1706), bishop of Winchester; educated at Merchant Taylors' School, London, and St John's College, Oxford; MA, 1645; served in the king's army, 1642; retired to Holland, 1648; acted as Royalist agent; went to Scotland as secretary to *Middleton, 1654; served in Flanders; rewarded at the Restoration; president of St John's College, Oxford, 1667–73; vice-chancellor of Oxford University, 1669–73; bishop of Bath and Wells, 1672, of Winchester, 1684; opposed *Monmouth at Sedgmoor, 1685; upheld the fellows of Magdalen College, Oxford, in their contention with James II, 1687; took the oaths to William and Mary.

MEY, John (d. 1456), archbishop of Armagh; official of the court of Meath; archbishop of Armagh, 1444; as deputy lord-lieutenant was unsuccessful in maintaining order.

MEY, William (d. 1560). See MAY.

MEYER, Frederick Brotherton (1847–1929), Baptist divine; BA, London University;

served Baptist ministries in York and Leicester; Melbourne Hall, Leicester, built for his pastorate after 1878; later, minister at Regent's Park Chapel and Christ Church, Westminster Bridge Road, London; a prolific writer; travelled widely for religious purposes.

MEYER, Henry (1782?–1847), portrait painter and engraver; nephew of John *Hoppner; pupil of *Bartolozzi; worked in mezzotint and painted portraits in oil and water colours; foundation member of the Society of British Artists, 1824; president, 1828.

MEYER, Jeremiah (1735–1789), miniature painter; born at Tübingen; pupil of *Zincke; his profile of George III used on the coinage, 1761; original director of Incorporated Society of Artists; foundation member of Royal Academy.

MEYER, Philip James (1732–1820), musician; born at Strasburg; improved the harp; visited England, 1772; returned to Paris, but finally settled in England, 1784; composer and teacher of the harp.

MEYER, Sir **William Stevenson** (1860–1922), Indian civil servant; born in Moldavia; joined Indian Civil Service in Madras, 1881; deputy secretary, finance department, Government of India, 1898; Indian editor, *Imperial Gazetteer of India*, 1902–5; financial secretary, Government of India, 1905; secretary of military finance, 1906; finance member, Government of India, 1913–18; his administration of military finance unjustly criticized for parsimony; first high commissioner of India, 1920–2; largely instrumental in procuring open market for government requirements not available in India; KCIE, 1909.

MEYNELL, Alice Christiana Gertrude (1847–1922), poet, essayist, and journalist; born Thompson; joined Roman Church, *c.*1872; married Wilfrid Meynell, 1877; her first volume of poems, *Preludes*, published 1875, of essays, *The Rhythm of Life*, 1893; championship of Coventry *Patmore and George *Meredith, and poems addressed to her by Francis *Thompson, did much to secure early prestige for her writings; a marked difference noticeable between her earlier and later poems; published several further volumes of essays and edited various anthologies; admirer of seventeenth-century poetry.

MEYNELL, Charles (1828–1882), Roman Catholic divine; professor of metaphysics at St Mary's College, Oscott; missioner of Caverswall, 1873; published controversial works.

MEYNELL, Sir **Francis Meredith Wilfrid** (1891–1975), typographer, publisher, and poet; educated at Downside and Trinity College,

Dublin; entered publishing firm, Burns & Oates, and, with Stanley *Morison, shared interest in typography and good book design; manager of the *Herald* (later in 1919 the *Daily Herald*), 1913–20; conscientious objector during 1914–18 war; editor, the *Communist*, 1921; founded the Pelican Press, 1916 and quickly earned reputation for quality of printing; published *Typography* (1923); founded the Nonesuch Press, 1923; productions included John Donne's *Love Poems* (1923), William Blake's *Poetry and Prose* (1927), two selections of Blake's drawings (1927 and 1956), Blake's Rosetti Notebook (1935), and editions of Congreve (1924), Wycherley (1924), Rochester (1926), Otway (1927), Vanbrugh (1928), Farquhar (1930), and Dryden (1931), and also two of John Evelyn's works, John Donne's *Complete Poetry and Selected Prose* (1929), the *Anacreon* of Stephen *Gooden (1923), *Genesis* of Paul *Nash (1924) and E. McKnight-Kauffer's pictures for Burton's *Anatomy of Melancholy* (1925); edited (in collaboration with his wife Vera) an anthology, *The Weekend Book* (1924), and published *The Nonesuch Century* (in collaboration with A. J. A. Symons and Desmond Flower, 1936); after short period in which Nonesuch Press was taken over by George Macy, resumed publication in association with The Bodley Head, published a coronation Shakespeare and a new series of children's classics, the Nonesuch Cygnets (1963); published his own *Poems and Pieces 1911–1961* (1961) and *My Lives* (1971); while engaged with Nonesuch Press also worked in advertising agencies and with the *News Chronicle*; adviser to Board of Trade, 1940; director, Cement and Concrete Association, 1946–58; knighted, 1946; Royal Designer for Industry, 1945; member, Royal Mint Advisory Committee, 1954–70; hon. typographic adviser, HM Stationery Office, 1945–66; hon. D.Litt., Reading, 1964; vice-president, Poetry Society, 1960–5.

MEYRICK, Edward (1854–1938), entomologist; educated at Marlborough and Trinity College, Cambridge; first class, classics, 1877; a classical master at Marlborough, 1887–1914; reclassified whole order Lepidoptera and described some 20,000 new species; published *A Handbook of British Lepidoptera* (1895); FRS, 1904.

MEYRICK, Frederick (1827–1906), divine; BA, Trinity College, Oxford, 1847; MA, 1850; fellow, 1847; travelled in Europe; founder and secretary of Anglo-Continental Society, 1853; rector of Blickling, Norfolk, 1868–1906; non-residentiary canon of Lincoln, 1869; helped to organize Bonn conferences on reunion, 1874–5; an ardent evangelical controversialist; wrote several anti-Roman pamphlets, as well as *The Church in Spain* (1892) and *Memories of Life at Oxford* (1905).

MEYRICK, Sir Gelly (or Gilly) (1556?–1601), conspirator; son of Rowland *Meyrick; attended *Essex to Flushing, 1585; steward in Essex's household; accompanied him to Portugal, 1589, Normandy, 1591, and Cadiz, 1596, where he was knighted; with Essex in the Islands voyage, 1597, and accompanied him to Ireland, 1599; defended Essex House, 1601; surrendered at Essex's bidding; hanged at Tyburn.

MEYRICK, John (1538–1599), bishop of Sodor and Man; scholar of Winchester College, 1550; scholar, 1555, and fellow, 1557, of New College, Oxford; MA, 1562; vicar of Hornchurch, 1570; bishop of Sodor and Man, 1575.

MEYRICK, Sir John (d. 1638), English ambassador to Russia; agent for the London Russia Company at Jaroslavl, 1584, and at Moscow, 1592; forwarded political intelligence from Russia, 1596–7; visited England, 1600; ambassador to the tsar, 1602; secured protection for English merchants from successive Russian tsars; reappointed ambassador and knighted, 1614; took part in peace negotiations between Russia and Sweden, 1615; obtained commercial treaty, 1623; governor of Russia Company, 1628.

MEYRICK, Sir John (d. 1659), Parliamentarian general; grandson of Rowland *Meyrick; fought under *Essex in Flanders, 1620; served in the United Provinces, 1624, and Spain, 1625; knighted; wounded before Maestricht, 1632; MP, Newcastle under Lyme, 1640; president of the Council of War; general of ordnance, 1643; after Lostwithiel fled with Essex to Plymouth, withdrew from public affairs, 1649.

MEYRICK, Rowland (1505–1566), bishop of Bangor; principal of New Inn Hall, Oxford, 1534–6; DCL, Oxford, 1538; precentor of Llandewy-Velfrey, 1541; chancellor of Wells, 1547; canon and chancellor of St David's, 1550; led the struggle between the chapter and Bishop Robert *Ferrar; ejected from St David's on his marriage, 1554; bishop of Bangor, 1559.

MEYRICK, Sir Samuel Rush (1783–1848), antiquary; MA, 1810, DCL, 1811, The Queen's College, Oxford; ecclesiastical and Admiralty lawyer; FSA, 1810; consulted on the arrangement of the armour at the Tower of London and Windsor Castle, 1826; knighted, 1832; high sheriff of Herefordshire, 1834; principal works, a history of Cardiganshire (1810) and of arms and armour (1824), and an edition of Lewis *Dwnn's *Heraldic Visitations of Wales* (1840).

MEYRICK (or MERICKE), Sir William (d. 1668), civilian; scholar of Winchester College, and fellow of New College, Oxford, 1616–26; DCL, New College, Oxford, 1627; advocate, 1628; judge of the prerogative court of Canterbury, 1641; joined the king; ejected, 1648; reinstated and knighted, 1660.

MEYRIG (or MEURYG) (*fl.* 1250), treasurer of Llandaff; probably identical with the epigrammatist *Maurice (fl.* 1210); wrote various Welsh works (none traced), including 'Y Cwtta Cyfarwydd' (existing copy, *c.*1445, possibly borrowed from an older manuscript).

MIALL, Edward (1809–1881), politician; Independent minister at Leicester, 1834; established and edited the *Nonconformist* (weekly), 1841; endeavoured to amalgamate with the Chartists, 1842; procured a conference on disestablishment in London, 1844, which founded the 'British Anti-State Church Association'; MP, Rochdale, 1852–7; commissioner on education, 1858; MP, Bradford, 1869–74; endeavoured to bring forward disestablishment, 1871 and 1872; retired from public life, 1874; published pamphlets on disestablishment.

MICHAEL, Blaunpayn (*fl.* 1250), also called Michael the Cornishman and Michael the Englishman, Latin poet; possibly studied at Oxford and Paris; traditionally dean of Utrecht; wrote a satirical Latin poem, *c.*1250.

MICHEL, Sir John (1804–1886), field marshal; educated at Eton; entered the army, 1823; lieutenant, 1825; passed his examinations, 1832; major, 1840; lieutenant-colonel, 1842; served in the Kaffir wars, 1846–7 and 1852–3 (medal and CB); brevet-colonel, 1854; chief of the staff of the Turkish contingent in the Crimean War (medals); sent to the Cape, 1856; transferred to China; wrecked and carried to Singapore, 1857; placed on the Bombay staff, 1858; major-general, 1858; defeated the rebels at Beorora, Mingrauli, and Sindwaha, 1858 (KCB and medal); commanded at Sinho and Peking, 1860 (GCB and medal); lieutenant-general, 1866; general, 1874; Irish privy councillor and commander of the forces in Ireland, 1875–1880; field marshal, 1885.

MICHELBORNE, Sir Edward (d. 1609), adventurer; served in the Low Countries, 1591; MP, Bramber, 1593; accompanied *Essex on Islands voyage, 1597; served in Ireland and was knighted, 1599; subscriber to the East India Company, 1600; implicated in Essex's rebellion, 1601; sailed for the East, 1604, nominally to trade; returned, after plundering a Chinese ship, 1606.

MICHELBORNE, Edward (1565–1626), Latin poet; of St Mary and Gloucester halls, Oxford; friend of Charles *Fitzgeffrey and Thomas *Campion, contributing to the works of both.

MICHELBORNE (MITCHELBURN or MICHELBURNE), John (1647–1721), governor of Londonderry; served under Percy *Kirke (1646?–1691) at Tangier, 1680–3; acted as military governor during the siege of Londonderry after Governor Baker's death, 1689; sole governor after the relief, 1689; petitioned for arrears of pay, 1691 (paid, 1703); his sword and saddle preserved at Londonderry.

MICHELL. See also MICHEL, MITCHEL, and MITCHELL.

MICHELL, Anthony George Maldon (1870–1959), engineer; born in London; educated at Perse School, Cambridge, and Melbourne University; BCE, 1895; MCE, 1899; set up practice, centred on hydraulic engineering, 1903; invented Michell thrust-block, 1905, and 'crankless engine', 1922; published *Lubrication: its principles and practice* (1950); FRS, 1934; Kernot Memorial Medal of Melbourne University, 1938; James Watt International Medal of Institution of Mechanical Engineers, London, 1942.

MICHELL, Charles Cornwallis (1793–1851), lieutenant-colonel; entered army, 1809; distinguished himself in Peninsular War; lieutenant, 1813; captain, 1817; on the staff of Marshal *Beresford in Lisbon; accompanied Beresford to the Brazils, 1820; master at Sandhurst, 1824, and Woolwich, 1825; major, 1826; superintendent of works at the Cape, 1828–48; assistant quartermaster-general during Kaffir War, 1833–4; lieutenant-colonel, 1841.

MICHELL, Edward Thomas (1786–1841), brigadier-general; lieutenant, 1803; commanded artillery in Peninsular War; served in Holland, 1813–14; brevet-major, 1814; lieutenant-colonel, 1838; CB, 1838; British commissioner in Spain, 1839–40; sent as brigadier-general to Syria; present at Medjdel, 1841; died of fever at Jaffa.

MICHELL, Sir Francis (*fl.* 1621), commissioner for enforcing monopolies; educated at Magdalen Hall, Oxford; secured reversion of clerk of the market, 1603; commissioner for enforcing gold and silver thread patents, 1618; knighted, 1620; tried for corruption; sentenced to degradation from knighthood and imprisoned, 1621; released immediately; subsequently petitioned for financial assistance.

MICHELL, Henry (1714–1789), scholar; fellow of Clare Hall, Cambridge; MA, 1739; vicar of

Brighton, 1744; assisted in development of Brighton; wrote on classical antiquities.

MICHELL, John (1724–1793), astronomer; fellow of Queens' College, Cambridge, 1749–64; MA, 1752; BD, 1761; lectured on Hebrew, arithmetic, geometry, and Greek; FRS, 1760; Woodwardian professor of geology, 1762; rector of Thornhill, 1767; wrote on artificial magnets, 1750, earthquakes, 1760, longitude, 1767, and fixed stars, 1767; invented apparatus for weighing the earth with torsion-balance.

MICHELL, Sir **Lewis Loyd** (1842–1928), South African banker and politician; joined London and South African Bank, 1863; sent to Port Elizabeth, Cape Colony, 1864; manager, Standard Bank of South Africa and Port Elizabeth, c.1872; transferred to Cape Town, 1885; sole general manager of Standard Bank, South Africa, 1895–1902; executor and trustee of Cecil *Rhodes; directed financing of British army's requirements during South African War, 1899–1902; chairman, De Beers Consolidated Mines and director, British South Africa Company, 1902; member, Cape House of Assembly, 1902; minister without portfolio, in Sir Leander *Jameson's Cabinet, 1903–5; knighted, 1902; wrote life of Rhodes (1910).

MICHELL (or MITCHELL), Matthew (d. 1752), commodore; lieutenant, 1729; commanded the *Gloucester*, the only ship besides *Anson's which doubled Cape Horn, 1740; commodore of a squadron off Flanders coast; MP, Westbury, 1747.

MICHELL, Nicholas (1807–1880), miscellaneous writer; encouraged by *Campbell; author of poems and novels in prose and verse.

MICHELL, Richard (1805–1877), first principal of Hertford College, Oxford; educated at Wadham College, Oxford; MA, 1827; DD, 1868; fellow of Lincoln College, 1830; first praelector of logic, 1839; Bampton lecturer, 1849; public orator, 1848–77; vice-principal, 1848; principal, 1868, of Magdalen Hall, Oxford, 1848; agitated for its formation into a college; the Hall endowed with fellowships and scholarships by T. C. Baring, MP, and called Hertford College, 1874.

MICHIE, Alexander (1833–1902), writer on China; prominent in Chinese commerce at Hong Kong and Shanghai from 1853; helped in negotiations with Taiping rebels, 1861; explored Yangtze valley and Szechuan, 1869; special correspondent to *The Times* in Sino-Japanese war, 1895; wrote *The Englishman in China* (2 vols., 1900) and *China and Christianity* (1900).

MICKLE, William Julius (1735–1788), poet; owner of a brewery in Edinburgh, 1757; failed, 1763; corrector to Clarendon Press, Oxford, 1765–71; author of *The Concubine* (1767) and *Voltaire in the Shades* (1770); translated the *Lusiad* of Camoens (1775, reprinted, 1778, 1798, and 1807); as secretary to George *Johnstone (1730–87) sailed to Portugal, 1779; received share of naval prizes; wrote the ballad *Cumnor Hall*; credited with the song 'There's na'e luck about the hoose'.

MICKLEM, Nathaniel (1888–1976), theologian and church leader; educated at Rugby School and New College, Oxford; president of the Union, 1912; studied theology at Mansfield College, Oxford; ordained Congregational minister, 1914; worked with YMCA near Dieppe, 1916–18; chaplain, Mansfield College, 1918–21; professor of Old Testament, Selly Oak, Birmingham, 1921–7; professor of New Testament, Queen's Theological College, Kingston, Ontario, 1927–31; professor of dogmatic theology, Mansfield College, and principal, 1932–53; publications include *A Book of Personal Religion* (1938), *The Creed of a Christian* (1940), *Prayers and Praises* (1941), and *The Idea of Liberal Democracy* (1957); president, Liberal party in Oxford, 1957–8; also interested in law, and published *Law and the Laws* (1952); worked for union of Congregationalists and Presbyterians in England; chairman, Congregational Church, 1944–5; published autobiography, *The Box and the Puppets (1888–1953)* (1957) and book of verse, *The Labyrinth* (1945); honorary degrees from Queen's University, Ontario, and Glasgow; hon. fellow, Mansfield College, 1972; CH, 1974.

MICKLETHWAITE, Sir **John** (1612–1682), physician; studied at Leiden, Padua, and Oxford; MA, Queens' College, Cambridge, 1634; physician at St Bartholomew's Hospital, London, 1653; FRCP, 1643; Gulstonian lecturer, 1644; censor seven times; president, 1676–81; attended Charles II; knighted, 1681.

MICKLETHWAITE, John Thomas (1843–1906), architect; pupil of George Gilbert *Scott, 1862; partner with fellow pupil, Somers Clarke, 1876–92; churches designed by him include St Hilda, Leeds, St Peter, Bocking, and St Bartholomew, East Ham; executed much internal decoration, chancels, and screens; architect to St George's Chapel, Windsor, 1900; surveyor to dean and chapter of Westminster Abbey, 1898; restored south transept and west front; FSA, 1870; vice-president, 1902; helped to found Alcuin Club and Henry Bradshaw Society; published *Ornaments of the Rubric* (1897).

MIDDIMAN, Samuel (1750–1831), engraver; engraved Shakespearean scenes for *Boydell.

MIDDLE ANGLES, earl of (d. 1049). See BEORN.

MIDDLEMORE, George (d. 1850), lieutenant-general; entered the army, 1793; lieutenant, 1794; major, 1804; served at the Cape and in India, Egypt, and Portugal (Talavera Medal); CB, 1815; lieutenant-colonel, 1815; major-general, 1830; commanded in West Indies, 1830–5; governor of St Helena, 1836; Napoleon's remains removed during his governorship; lieutenant-general, 1841.

MIDDLESEX, earls of. See CRANFIELD, LIONEL, first earl, 1575–1645; SACKVILLE, CHARLES, first earl of the second creation, 1638–1706.

MIDDLETON. See also MYDDELTON.

MIDDLETON, Charles, second earl of Middleton and titular earl of Monmouth (1640?–1719), secretary of state to James II; eldest son of John *Middleton, first earl of Middleton; accompanied his father abroad, 1653; envoy-extraordinary at Vienna, 1680; privy councillor and joint secretary of Scotland, 1682; privy councillor and secretary of state for England, 1684; MP, Winchelsea, 1685; endeavoured to induce James to abandon his flight and summon parliament, 1688; remained in England; apprehended, 1692; released; chief adviser of the exiled king at St Germain; created earl of Monmouth by *James Edward the Old Pretender, 1701; became a Roman Catholic, 1703; responsible for the abortive expedition to Scotland, 1707; resigned office of secretary of state for England, 1713, and returned to St Germain.

MIDDLETON, Charles, first Baron Barham (1726–1813), admiral; on convoy service; cruised in West Indies, 1761; comptroller of the navy, 1778–90; created baronet, 1781; MP, Rochester, 1784; rear-admiral, 1787; vice-admiral, 1793; admiral, 1795; lord commissioner of the Admiralty, 1794; first lord of the Admiralty, 1805, and created Baron Barham, 1805.

MIDDLETON, Christopher (1560?–1628), translator and poet; translated Digby's *Art of Swimming* (1595); published works, including *The Famous Historie of Chinon* (1597) and *The Legend of Humphrey, Duke of Glocester* (1600).

MIDDLETON, Christopher (d. 1770), naval commander and Arctic voyager; employed by the Hudson's Bay Company, 1720; observed variation of magnetic needle, 1721; discovered how to obtain true time at sea with *Hadley's quadrant, c.1737; FRS, 1737; commander in the navy; set out to discover the North-West Passage, 1741; arrived in Hudson Bay too late in the sea-son for discovery, 1741; examined the coast to the northward and entered a river inlet, 1742; returned to England, 1742; stationed off Scottish and Flemish coasts, 1745.

MIDDLETON, Conyers (1683–1750), divine; MA, Trinity College, Cambridge, 1706; fellow of Trinity College, Cambridge, 1706; known for his musical tastes; one of thirty fellows who petitioned against *Bentley, the master of Trinity, 1710; DD on George I's visit to Cambridge, 1717; involved in a bitter dispute with Bentley about the fees, 1717; an action for a libel contained in *The Present State of Trinity College* (1719) brought against him by Bentley, a compromise resulting; 'Protobibliothecarius' of the university library, 1721; in Italy, 1724–5; published *Letter from Rome* (1729); Woodwardian professor, 1732–4; engaged in a controversy with *Waterland on the historical accuracy of the Bible, for which he was threatened with the loss of his degrees; published a *Life of Cicero* (1741), mainly plagiarized from William *Bellenden (d. 1633?); excited much criticism by his latitudinarian treatise on *Miracles* (1748).

MIDDLETON, David (d. 1615), merchant and sea-captain; younger brother of John and Sir Henry *Middleton; joint commander in a voyage to West Indies, 1601; made successful voyages to East Indies, 1604–6, 1607–8, and 1609–11; wrecked on the coast of Madagascar, 1615.

MIDDLETON, Erasmus (1739–1805), author; of St Edmund Hall, Oxford; expelled, 1768, for publicly praying and preaching; curate in London; rector of Turvey, 1804; published theological works.

MIDDLETON, Henry (d. 1587), printer; probably son of William *Middleton (*fl.* 1541–1547); admitted to the Stationers' Company, 1567; partner with Thomas *East, 1567–72; under-warden of the Stationers' Company, 1587.

MIDDLETON, Sir Henry (d. 1613), merchant and sea-captain; promoted captain during the first voyage of the East India Company, 1602; commanded the second voyage, 1604–6; knighted, 1606; commanded the sixth voyage, 1610–13; escaped from imprisonment at Mocha; attempted (1611–12) to trade at Surat and Dabul; died in Java.

MIDDLETON, Sir Hugh (1560?–1631), projector of New River. See MYDDELTON.

MIDDLETON, James Smith (1878–1962), secretary of the Labour party; educated at elementary schools; worked in his father's printing establishment, Workington; secretary, Workington Trades Council and local branch of ILP; moved to London, 1902; assistant secretary,

Labour party, 1904; close friendship with Mr and Mrs Ramsay MacDonald; secretary, War Emergency Workers' National Committee, 1914–18; secretary, Labour party, 1934–44.

MIDDLETON, Jane (1645–1692), the great beauty of Charles II's time. See MYDDELTON.

MIDDLETON, John, first earl of Middleton (1619–1674), pikeman in *Hepburn's regiment in France; major in Covenant army, 1639; lieutenant-general in Parliamentary army; second-in-command at Philiphaugh, 1645; negotiated *Montrose's submission, 1646, suppressed Royalist rising, 1647; as lieutenant-general of the Scottish cavalry distinguished himself at Preston, 1648; wounded and taken prisoner at Worcester, 1651; escaped from the Tower to France; captain-general of a Highland force, dispersed by Monck, 1654; joined the king at Cologne; created an earl by Charles II, 1656 (the creation confirmed at the Restoration); commander-in-chief, governor of Edinburgh Castle, and lord high commissioner to the Scottish parliament, 1660; urged restoration of episcopacy in Scotland, 1661; accused of withholding letters from the king, consenting to measures without authority, and taking bribes, 1663; deprived of his offices; subsequently became governor of Tangier, where he died.

MIDDLETON, John (1827–1856), landscape painter.

MIDDLETON, John Henry (1846–1896), archaeologist and architect; educated at Cheltenham College and Exeter College, Oxford; studied art and archaeology; travelled abroad; practised as architect at Westminster till 1885; FSA, 1879, vice-president, 1894; contributed to *Encyclopaedia Britannica* (9th edn.); Slade professor of fine art at Cambridge, 1886; MA, 1886, and Litt.D., 1892, King's College, Cambridge; MA, 1887, and DCL, 1894, Oxford; director of Fitzwilliam Museum, Cambridge, 1889–92; art director at South Kensington Museum, London, 1892–6; published works on artistic and archaeological subjects.

MIDDLETON, Joshua (1647–1721), Quaker; early joined the Quakers and travelled as a minister.

MIDDLETON, Marmaduke (d. 1593), bishop of Waterford and St David's; left Oxford without a degree; obtained preferment in Ireland; bishop of Waterford, 1579; accused of plundering the cathedral, but acquitted; translated to St David's, 1582; DD, Oxford, 1583; fined by the Star Chamber, 1589, and handed over to the High Commission court for degradation, which took place at Lambeth House.

MIDDLETON, Patrick (1662–1736), Scottish nonjuring divine; MA, St Leonard's College, St Andrews, 1680; summoned 1689, 1692, 1716, and 1717 for not praying for William III and George I; published theological works.

MIDDLETON, Richard (*fl.* 1280), Franciscan; BD, 1283, and DD, Paris; one of the fifteen chief doctors of his order; wrote works of theology and canon law.

MIDDLETON, Richard (d. 1641), divine; BA, Jesus College, Oxford, 1586; prebendary of Brecon, 1589; archdeacon of Cardigan, 1589–1629; published theological works.

MIDDLETON, Sir Thomas (1550–1631), lord mayor of London. See MYDDELTON.

MIDDLETON, Thomas (1570?–1627), dramatist; entered at Gray's Inn, 1593; became connected with the stage, 1592; collaborated with *Dekker, *Rowley, *Munday, *Drayton, *Webster, and others; turned his attention to satirical comedies of contemporary manners, 1607–8; wrote pageants and masques for city ceremonials; city chronologer, 1620; wrote a political drama, *A Game at Chess* (1624), for which he and the players were censured on the representations of the Spanish ambassador. His plays (which were very popular) include *The Old Law* (1656, in collaboration with *Massinger and Rowley), *Michaelmas Terme* (1607), *A Trick to catch the Old One* (1608), *The Familie of Love* (1608), *A Mad World, my Masters* (1608), *The Roaring Girle* (1611, with Dekker), *A Faire Quarrell* (1617, with Rowley), *More Dissemblers besides Women* (1657), *A Game at Chess* (1624), *A Chast Mayd in Cheapeside* (1630), *No Wit, no Help like a Woman's* (1657), *Women beware Women* (1657), *The Witch* (not published until 1778), *Anything for a Quiet Life* (1662), *The Widdow* (1652, with Ben *Jonson and *Fletcher). His pageants and masques include *The Triumphs of Truth* (1613), *Civitatis Amor* (1616), *The Tryumphs of Honor and Industry* (1617), *The Inner Temple Masque* (1619), *The Triumphs of Love and Antiquity* (1619), *The World Tost at Tennis* (1620), *The Triumphs of Honor and Virtue* (1622), *The Triumphs of Integrity* (1623), *The Triumphs of Health and Prosperity* (1626). He is supposed to have also written some miscellaneous verse and prose.

MIDDLETON, Sir Thomas (1586–1666), parliamentarian. See MYDDELTON.

MIDDLETON, Thomas Fanshaw (1769–1822), bishop of Calcutta; of Christ's Hospital and Pembroke College, Cambridge; MA, 1795; DD, 1808; curate of Gainsborough, 1792; edited *The Country Spectator*, 1792–3; rector of Tansor, 1795, of Bytham, 1802; prebendary of Lincoln, 1809; edited *British Critic*, 1811; FRS, 1814;

bishop of Calcutta, 1814; organized schools, 1815, and established the Bishop's Mission College, Calcutta, 1820; died at Calcutta.

MIDDLETON (or MYDDYLTON), William (*fl.* 1541–1547), printer; succeeded to *Pynson and *Redman's press; printed legal, medical, and other learned works.

MIDDLETON, William (d. 1613), Protestant controversialist; of Queens' College, Cambridge; BA, 1571; fellow, 1572–90; denied Cambridge MA; MA, Oxford; deprived of fellowship for not taking his MA; restored by Lord *Burghley, chancellor of Cambridge University; incorporated MA, Cambridge, 1576; BD, 1582; elected master of Corpus Christi College, Cambridge, in place of John *Jegon, who was subsequently restored; published defence of Protestantism (1606).

MIDDLETON, William (1556?–1621), Welsh poet and seaman. See MYDDELTON.

MIDDLETON, William of (d. 1261), Franciscan. See MELITON.

MIDGLEY, Robert (1653–1723), alleged author of the *Turkish Spy*; MB, Christ's College, Cambridge, 1676; MD, 1687; candidate of the College of Physicians, 1687; licenser of the press, 1686; remembered chiefly as the 'editor' of *Letters writ by a Turkish Spy*, 1687–93 (probably written in French by a Genoese, Giovanni Paolo Marana, translated by Bradshaw and edited by Midgley).

MIDLANE, Albert (1825–1909), hymn-writer; tinsmith and ironmonger; joined Plymouth Brethren; wrote over 800 hymns, the best known, 'There's a Friend for Little Children', being composed in 1859; hymns marked by religious emotion and love of children; published several volumes of verse.

MIDLETON, Viscounts. See BRODERICK, ALAN, first viscount, 1660?–1728; BRODERICK, (WILLIAM) JOHN (FREMANTLE), ninth viscount, 1856–1942.

MIDNIGHT (MARY). Pseudonym of NEWBERY, JOHN, and SMART, CHRISTOPHER.

MIEGE, Guy (1644–1718?), miscellaneous writer; native of Lausanne; came to London, 1661; under-secretary to Charles *Howard, first earl of Carlisle; ambassador-extraordinary to Russia, Sweden, and Denmark, 1663; published account of the embassy (1669); best-known work, the *New State of England* (1691), Scotland and Ireland being subsequently added; published also French and English dictionaries and grammars.

MIERS, Sir Anthony Cecil Capel (1906–1985), submariner; educated at Edinburgh Academy and Wellington College; entered Royal Navy, 1924; joined submarine service, 1929; commanded L54, 1936–7; while in command of HMS *Torbay* decorated twice with DSO (1941 and 2) and with VC (1942); submarine liaison officer with American Pacific Fleet, 1942–4; officer of Legion of Merit; commander S/M, eighth submarine flotilla, Perth, Western Australia, 1944; promoted to captain, 1946; commanded naval air station HMS *Blackcap*, 1948–50, HMS *Forth*, and first submarine squadron, 1950–2, RN College, Greenwich, 1952–4, and aircraft carrier HMS *Theseus*, 1954–5; promoted to rear-admiral, 1956 and appointed flag officer, Middle East, 1956–9; CB, 1958; KBE, 1959; burgess and freeman of Inverness, 1955; freeman of City of London, 1966; president, RN Lawn Tennis Association and RN Squash Racket Association; national president, Submarine Old Comrades' Association.

MIERS, Sir Henry Alexander (1858–1942), mineralogist, administrator, and scholar; grandson of John *Miers; scholar of Eton and Trinity College, Oxford; second class, mathematics, 1881; studied crystallography and mineralogy in Strasburg; first-class assistant, mineralogy department, British Museum, South Kensington, 1882–95; instructor in crystallography, Central Technical College, 1886–95; Waynflete professor of mineralogy, Oxford, 1895–1908; fellow of Magdalen, 1908–42; principal, London University, 1908–15; vice-chancellor and professor of crystallography, Manchester, 1915–26; member, royal and standing commissions on museums; published *Mineralogy: an Introduction to the Scientific Study of Minerals* (1902); mineral miersite named after him; FRS, 1896; knighted, 1912.

MIERS, John (1789–1879), engineer and botanist; accompanied Lord *Cochrane to Chile, 1818; made collections of birds, insects, and plants; settled in London, 1836; FLS, 1839; FRS, 1843; published *Travels in Chile and La Plata* (1825) and botanical works.

MILBANKE, Mark (1725?–1805), admiral; entered navy, 1737; lieutenant, 1744; promoted to command the *Serpent*, 1746; commissioner to Morocco, 1759; rear-admiral of the white, 1779; sat on the court martial of Admiral *Keppel; vice-admiral of the blue, 1780; port-admiral at Plymouth, 1783–6; commander-in-chief in Newfoundland, 1790–2; admiral, 1793; commander-in-chief at Portsmouth, 1799–1803.

MILBANKE, Ralph Gordon Noel King, second earl of Lovelace (1839–1906), author of *Astarte*; grandson of poet *Byron; spent a year in Iceland, 1861; a bold alpinist and accomplished linguist; his privately printed *Astarte* (1905), vindicating his grandmother, Lady Byron, from aspersions cast on her, and incriminating Lord Byron, provoked replies from (Sir) John *Murray (1851–1928) and Richard Edgcumbe.

MILBOURN, John (*fl.* 1773–1790), portrait painter; exhibited at the Royal Academy, 1772–4.

MILBOURNE, Luke (1622–1668), ejected Nonconformist divine; BA, Emmanuel College, Cambridge, 1637–8; perpetual curate of Honiley; Royalist; in retirement at Kenilworth, 1645–60; ejected, 1662; schoolmaster at Coventry; compelled to leave by the Five Mile Act, 1666.

MILBOURNE, Luke (1649–1720), poet; son of Luke *Milbourne (1622–1668); of Pembroke Hall, Cambridge; held chaplaincies at Hamburg, Rotterdam, and Harwich; rector of St Ethelburga's, London, 1704; supported Dr Sacheverell; attempted an English rendering of Virgil; chiefly remembered by his subsequent strictures on *Dryden's translations of Virgil, and the retaliation made by Dryden and *Pope.

MILBURG (MILDBURGA or MILDBURH) (d. 722?), saint and abbess; reputed miracle-worker; built nunnery at Winwick or Wenlock, 680, restored by the earl of *Shrewsbury, 1080; her day 23 Feb.

MILDMAY, Sir Anthony (d. 1617), ambassador; son of Sir Walter *Mildmay; was educated at Peterhouse, Cambridge; entered at Gray's Inn, 1579; knighted, 1596; ambassador to Henry IV of France, 1596–7.

MILDMAY, Anthony Bingham, second Baron Mildmay of Flete (1909–1950), gentleman rider; educated at Eton and Trinity College, Cambridge; with Baring Brothers, 1930–3; thereafter devoted himself to becoming successful amateur steeplechase jockey; rode 21 winners in 1937–8 and 32 in 1946–7; took third and fourth places respectively in Grand National in 1948 and 1949; beloved by racecourse crowds for his courage and skill; member, National Hunt Committee, 1942–50; succeeded father, 1947; drowned while bathing.

MILDMAY, Sir Henry (d. 1664?), master of the king's jewel house; BA, Emmanuel College, Cambridge, 1612; knighted, 1617; master of the king's jewel house, 1620; MP, Maldon, 1620, Westbury, 1624, Maldon again, 1625–60; attended Charles I to Scotland, 1639; deserted the king, 1641; revenue commissioner, 1645–52; left as hostage in Scotland, 1646; present at Charles I's trial; member of state councils, 1649–52; attempted escape when called on to account for the king's jewels, 1660; degraded and sentenced to imprisonment for life; warrant issued for his transportation to Tangier, 1664; died at Antwerp on the way.

MILDMAY, Sir **Walter** (1520?–1589), chancellor of the Exchequer and founder of Emmanuel College, Cambridge; educated at Christ's College, Cambridge; entered Gray's Inn, 1546; surveyor-general of the court of augmentation, 1545; knighted, and appointed revenue commissioner, 1547; examiner of the Mint accounts, 1550; MP, Lostwithiel, 1545, Lewes, 1547, Maldon, 1552, Peterborough, 1553, Northamptonshire, 1557, 1558, 1563, 1571, 1572, 1584, 1586, and 1588; after Elizabeth's accession directed the issue of a new coinage, 1560; chancellor of the Exchequer and auditor of the duchy of Lancaster, 1566; a commissioner at the trial of *Mary Queen of Scots, 1586; founded Emmanuel College, Cambridge, 1585; benefactor of Christ's Hospital, London, Christ's College, Cambridge, and other educational institutions.

MILDRED (or MILDRYTH) (d. 700?), saint and abbess; sister of *Milburg; instructed in ecclesiastical learning at Chelles, near Paris; being persecuted by the abbess, escaped to England and succeeded her mother as abbess of Minster, St Augustine's, and St Gregory's, Canterbury. The two latter houses claimed possession of her body.

MILES. See also MILLES.

MILES, Charles Popham (1810–1891), divine; son of William Augustus *Miles; midshipman in the navy; MA, Caius College, Cambridge, 1851; chaplain of the Sailors' Home, London Docks, 1838; principal of Malta Protestant College, 1858–67; rector of Monkwearmouth, 1867–83; edited his father's correspondence and published religious treatises.

MILES, Edward (d. 1798), miniature painter; copied some of *Reynolds's pictures; exhibited at the Royal Academy, 1775–97.

MILES, George Francis (known as **Frank)** (1852–1891), painter; known for a series of pretty female heads; student of Japanese art and botany.

MILES, Henry (1698–1763), dissenting minister and scientific writer; FRS, 1743; communicated scientific papers to *Philosophical Transactions*, 1741–53.

MILES, John (1621–1684), founder of Welsh Baptist churches. See MYLES.

MILES, Mrs Sibella Elizabeth (1800–1882), poetess; née Hatfield; kept boarding school at

Penzance; married Alfred Miles, 1833; published poems and prose works.

MILES, William (d. 1860), major-general, Indian Army; entered army, 1799; lieutenant, 1800; captain, 1815; concluded treaty with raja of Rodanpur, 1820; major, 1821; lieutenant-colonel, 1824; captured Mergui; concluded treaty with Suigam chiefs, 1826; political resident at Pallampur, 1829; brevet-colonel, 1829; translated oriental works.

MILES, William Augustus (1753?–1817), political writer; held appointment in Ordnance Office, 1770; served under *Rodney in West Indies; prisoner of war in St Lucia; settled at Seraing, near Liège, 1783; corresponded with Pitt; met all the leading French politicians at Paris, 1790; pensioned, 1791; suggested a Suez canal, 1791; author of political tracts and two comic operas; published pamphlet on the then prince of Wales's debts (1795) which went through thirteen editions; died at Paris, where he was collecting materials for a history of the French Revolution.

MILES DE GLOUCESTER, earl of Hereford (d. 1143). See GLOUCESTER.

MILEY, John (1805?–1861), Roman Catholic divine; educated at Maynooth and Rome; DD; endeavoured to reconcile the Young Ireland party and Daniel *O'Connell, 1846; accompanied O'Connell to Italy, 1847; rector of the Irish College, Paris, 1849–59; vicar of Bray, 1859; wrote on ecclesiastical history.

MILFORD, David Sumner (1905–1984), world open rackets champion and international hockey player; educated at Rugby and New College, Oxford; master at Marlborough, 1928–63; British amateur rackets champion, 1930; won singles championship seven times and doubles eleven times; won world championship, 1937, and remained champion until 1947; awarded hockey blue, 1927; played against Cambridge three times; chosen to play for England, 1930; wrote two books on hockey; also good cricketer and lawn-tennis player.

MILFORD, Sir Humphrey Sumner (1877–1952), publisher; grandson of Charles Richard *Sumner, bishop of Winchester; scholar of Winchester and New College, Oxford; first class, Lit. Hum., 1900; assistant to Charles *Cannan, secretary to the delegates of Oxford University Press, 1900; transferred to London office, 1906; manager of London business and publisher to the University of Oxford, 1913–45; under his management, the Oxford University Press became one of the three or four largest publishers in the country; originator of the *Oxford Dictionary of Quotations*; editor of the *Oxford Book*

of English Verse of the Romantic Period; hon. D.Litt., Oxford, 1928; knighted, 1936.

MILFORD HAVEN, first marquess of (1854–1921), admiral of the fleet. See MOUNTBATTEN, LOUIS ALEXANDER.

MILL, Henry (1683?–1771), engineer; engineer to the New River Company, 1720; carried out Houghton Hall water supply; possibly invented a typewriter, 1714.

MILL, Hugh Robert (1861–1950), geographer and meteorologist; educated privately owing to tubercular illnesses; B.Sc., Edinburgh, 1883; fellow, Scottish Marine Station, 1884; FRSE, 1885; D.Sc., 1886; lecturer in geography and physiography, Heriot-Watt College, Edinburgh, 1887–92; librarian, Royal Geographical Society, 1892–1900; university extension lecturer, 1887–1900; director, British Rainfall Organization, 1901–19; established it on strictly scientific basis; rainfall expert to Metropolitan Water Board, 1903–19; confidant and inspirer of many polar explorers; edited geographical material for eleventh edition of *Encyclopaedia Britannica*; publications include *The Siege of the South Pole* (1905), biography of Sir Ernest *Shackleton (1923), and *Record of the Royal Geographical Society, 1830–1930* (1930).

MILL (or MILLE), Humphrey (*fl.* 1646), verse-writer.

MILL, James (*fl.* 1744), Indian colonel; captain and second-in-command of the East India Company's military in Bengal, 1743; submitted project for the conquest of India to Francis, duke of Lorraine, 1744.

MILL, James (1773–1836), utilitarian philosopher; educated at Edinburgh by Sir John Stuart of Fettercairn; licensed to preach, 1798; came to London, 1802; became editor of the *Literary Journal*, 1803, and the *St. James's Chronicle*, 1805; wrote for the *Edinburgh Review*, 1808–13; met *Bentham, 1808; promulgator of Benthamism in England; supported his family by writing, at the same time working at his history of India; abandoned theology after his acquaintance with Bentham; took active part in *Bell and *Lancaster educational controversy, supporting the Lancasterian institution; formed an association to set up a 'Chrestomathic' school for superior education on the same lines, 1814, the outcome being the formation of the London University, 1825; published *History of India* (1818); assistant to the examiner of India correspondence, 1819; second assistant, 1821; assistant-examiner, 1823; examiner, 1830; encouraged *Ricardo to publish his political economy; took part in meetings at Ricardo's house, which resulted in the Political Economy

Club, founded 1820; contributed utilitarian articles to the *Encyclopaedia Britannica*, 1816–23, and to the *Westminster Review*, started (1824) as the official Benthamite organ; wrote in the *London Review*, 1835. He published an essay on the export of grain (1804), *Commerce Defended* (1808), *History of India* (1818), *Elements of Political Economy* (1821), *Analysis of the Phenomena of the Human Mind* (1829), and *Fragment on Mackintosh* (1835).

MILL, John (1645–1707), principal of St Edmund Hall, Oxford; MA, The Queen's College, Oxford, 1669; DD, 1681; speaker of the 'Oratio Panegyrica' at the opening of the Sheldonian Theatre, 1669; prebendary of Exeter, 1677; rector of Bletchington and chaplain to Charles II, 1681; elected principal of St Edmund Hall, Oxford, 1685; prebendary of Canterbury, 1704; collated all the readings of the principal manuscripts in England and on the continent in his edition of the New Testament in Greek (1707).

MILL, John Stuart (1806–1873), philosopher; son of James *Mill (1773–1836); educated entirely by his father; before he was 14 had studied classical literature, logic, political economy, history, general literature, and mathematics; visited France, 1820; junior clerk in the India House, 1823; formed the Utilitarian Society, which met to read essays and discuss them, 1823–6; edited *Bentham's *Treatise upon Evidence* (1825); assisted in the formation of the Speculative Society, 1826; visited Paris, 1830; contributed to the *London Review*, started (1835) as an organ of philosophical radicalism; was its proprietor, 1837–40; published his *Logic* (1843) and *Political Economy* (1848); retired with a pension on the dissolution of the East India Company, 1858; MP, Westminster, 1865–8; a follower of William Ewart Gladstone; rector of St Andrews University, 1866; returned to literary pursuits, 1868. His works, devoted to the humanizing and widening of utilitarian teaching, include *A System of Logic* (1843), essays on *Political Economy* (1844), *Principles of Political Economy* (1848), *On Liberty* (1859), *Thoughts on Parliamentary Reform* (1859), *Representative Government* (1861), *Utilitarianism* (1863), *Examination of Sir William Hamilton's Philosophy* (1865), *Auguste Comte and Positivism* (1865), *The Subjection of Women* (1869), *Chapters and Speeches on the Irish Land Question* (1870), *Autobiography* (1873), and *Three Essays on Religion*, posthumously published (1874).

MILL, Walter (d. 1558), martyr. See MYLNE.

MILL, William Hodge (1792–1853), orientalist; sixth wrangler, Trinity College, Cambridge; 1813; fellow, 1814; MA, 1816; first principal of Bishop's College, Calcutta, 1820; vice-president, Bengal Asiatic Society, 1833–7; regius professor of Hebrew at Cambridge, with canonry at Ely, 1848; chief work, *Christa-Saṅgītā* (1831), the Gospel story in Sanskrit.

MILLAIS, Sir **John Everett** (1829–1896), painter, and president of Royal Academy; a native of Southampton; lived during various periods of early life in Jersey and Brittany; came to London, 1838; studied art under Henry *Sass; entered Royal Academy schools, 1840, and obtained gold medal for painting *The Young Men of Benjamin seizing their Brides*, 1846; first exhibited at Royal Academy *Pizarro seizing the Inca of Peru*, 1846; originated (1848), with Holman *Hunt, the Pre-Raphaelite movement, soon joined by Dante Gabriel *Rossetti, who exerted influence on some of Millais's subsequent work; his most successful Pre-Raphaelite picture, *Isabella*, 1849; great hostility aroused by his *Christ in the House of his Parents*, 1850, owing to the unconventional treatment of a scene in the life of the Holy Family; among the most notable of his works at this period are *The Return of the Dove to the Ark* and *Mariana of the Moated Grange* (1851), *The Huguenot* and *Ophelia* (1852), *The Proscribed Royalist* and *The Order of Release* (1853); ARA, 1853; married, 1855, Euphemia Chalmers, daughter of George Gray, who had obtained a decree of the 'nullity' of her marriage with John *Ruskin; exhibited *Autumn Leaves* and *Peace concluded* (1856), *Sir Isumbras at the Ford* and *The Escape of a Heretic* (1857), *Apple Blossoms* and *The Vale of Rest* (1859); deviated from the Pre-Raphaelite manner in his *Black Brunswicker* (1860); RA, 1863; exhibited *The Eve of St. Agnes* (1863), *Jephthah* (1867), *Rosalind and Celia* (1868), *The Boyhood of Raleigh*, *The Knight Errant* (1870), and *Victory, O Lord*, *Chill October*, his first exhibited pure landscape (1871); after 1870 devoted himself mainly to portrait and landscape, and to single figures of children and pretty girls under fancy titles such as *Cherry Ripe*; exhibited *The North-West Passage* (1874), *A Yeoman of the Guard* (1877), *The Princes in the Tower* (1878), and *The Princess Elizabeth* (1879); painted his own portrait for the Uffizi Gallery, Florence, 1880; created baronet, 1885; the last subject-picture exhibited by him, *The Forerunner*, PRA, 1896.

MILLAR. See also MILLER and MÜLLER.

MILLAR, Andrew (*fl.* 1503–1508), the first Scottish printer. See MYLLAR, ANDREW.

MILLAR, Andrew (1707–1768), publisher; published *Johnson's *Dictionary*, *Thomson's *Seasons*, *Fielding's works, and the histories of Robertson and Hume.

MILLAR, Gertie (1879–1952), actress; first success at 14 years of age in Manchester pantomime; played in London theatres in *The Toreador* (1901), and other musical comedies, including *Our Miss Gibbs* (1909), *The Quaker Girl* (1910), and *A Country Girl* (1914); married in 1902 Lionel Monckton, who composed the music for her shows; regarded as the Gaiety Girl *par excellence*; after Monckton's death, married second earl of *Dudley, 1924.

MILLAR, James (1762–1827), physician and miscellaneous writer; educated at Glasgow; MD and FRCP, Edinburgh; chaplain to Glasgow University; edited the fourth and part of the fifth editions of the *Encyclopaedia Britannica* (1810–17), also the *Encyclopaedia Edinensis* (1827).

MILLAR, John (1733–1805), medical writer; MD, Edinburgh; physician, Westminster General Dispensary, London, 1774; published medical works.

MILLAR, John (1735–1801), professor of law; educated under Adam *Smith at Glasgow; intimate of James *Watt; an advocate, 1760; professor of law at Glasgow, 1761; lectured on civil law, jurisprudence, Scottish and English law; member of the Literary Society; sympathized with the French Revolution and opposed the slave trade; published *The Origin of the Distinction of Ranks* (1771) and *Historical View of the English Government* (1787).

MILLAR, William (d. 1838), lieutenant-general; colonel commandant, Royal Artillery; son of John *Millar (1735–1801); second lieutenant, Royal Artillery, 1781; first lieutenant, 1787; captain-lieutenant, 1794; captain, 1799; major, 1806; lieutenant-colonel, 1806; colonel, 1814; major-general, 1831; colonel commandant, 1834; lieutenant-general, 1837; originated the 10-inch and 8-inch shell-guns; inspector-general of artillery, 1827; director-general of the field-train department, 1833.

MILLER. See also MILLAR and MÜLLER.

MILLER, Andrew (d. 1763), mezzotint engraver, mainly of portraits.

MILLER, Anna, Lady (1741–1781), verse-writer; née Riggs; married John Miller of Ballicasey, 1765; travelled in Italy, 1770–1, publishing an account; her husband created an Irish baronet, 1778; instituted a literary salon at Batheaston, at which each guest was invited to contribute an original poem; four volumes of the compositions published.

MILLER, Edward (1731–1807), organist and historian of Doncaster; trained by Dr *Burney at King's Lynn; organist of Doncaster, 1756–1807;

created Mus.Doc., Cambridge, 1786; set the Psalms to music, 1774; published *Thorough Bass and Composition* (1787), *History and Antiquities of Doncaster* (1804); taught Francis *Linley.

MILLER, George (1764–1848), divine; MA, Trinity College, Dublin, 1789; fellow, 1789; DD, 1799; assistant professor of modern history, Dublin, 1799–1803; headmaster of the Royal School, Armagh, 1817; as vicar-general of the diocese of Armagh (1843) settled important points in law of marriage and divorce; member of the Royal Irish Academy; published two pamphlets on the Athanasian Creed, 1825 and 1826, besides sermons and miscellanea; *Newman's *Tract XC* partly elicited by his *Letter* to *Pusey (1840).

MILLER, Hugh (1802–1856), man of letters and geologist; stonemason by trade; accountant in the Commercial Bank at Cromarty, 1834; contributed to Mackay Wilson's *Tales of the Borders*; became editor of the *Witness*, 1840, the non-intrusionists' organ; his *Old Red Sandstone* (published serially in the *Witness*) republished (1841); chief works, *Footprints of the Creator* (1847), *My Schools and Schoolmasters* (1852), and *The Testimony of the Rocks* (1857).

MILLER, James (1706–1744), playwright; of Wadham College, Oxford; lecturer at Trinity Chapel, Conduit Street, London; took to dramatic writing to enlarge his income, but by his supposed representation of the keepers of Temple coffee-house caused the templars to ruin his subsequent pieces; his principal plays, *Humours of Oxford* (1730), *The Man of Taste* (1735, an adaptation of Molière, to be distinguished from a like-named piece attacking *Pope), *Universal Passion* (1737), *The Coffee-house* (1737), and *Mahomet the Impostor* (1744).

MILLER, James (1812–1864), surgeon; educated at St Andrews and Edinburgh universities; LRCS, 1832; assistant to Robert *Liston; 1842; surgeon-in-ordinary to Queen Victoria, 1848; published surgical works.

MILLER, Sir James Percy, second baronet (1864–1906), sportsman; joined army, 1888; served in South Africa, 1900–1; won Derby with Sainfoin, 1890; purchased mare Roquebrune (1894), who, mated with Sainfoin, produced Rock Sand, winner of Two Thousand Guineas, Derby, and St Leger in 1903; headed list of winning owners, 1903 and 1904.

MILLER, John (*fl.* 1780), architect; studied in Italy; practised in London; published books on architecture, with designs.

MILLER, John Cale (1814–1880), Evangelical divine; MA, Lincoln College, Oxford, 1838;

DD, 1857; curate of Park Chapel, Chelsea; incumbent of St Martin's, Birmingham, 1846; most successful among the working classes; canon of Rochester, 1873; published theological works. The Miller Hospital of Greenwich was opened (1884) as a memorial to him.

MILLER, John Frederick (*fl.* 1785), draughtsman; son of John *Miller (1715?–1790?); accompanied Sir Joseph *Banks to Ireland, 1772; published *Various Subjects of Natural History* (1785).

MILLER (MÜLLER), John (Johann Sebastian) (1715?–1790?), draughtsman and engraver; born at Nuremberg; came to England, 1744; published *Illustration of the Sexual System in Plants* (1777), arranged according to the system of Dr Linnaeus; also executed other plates, including those for Lord *Bute's *Botanical Tables* (1785).

MILLER, Joseph (or **Josias;** commonly called **Joe**) (1684–1738), actor and reputed humorist; joined Drury Lane Company, 1709; a prominent member of the company; temporarily engaged at Goodman's Fields, London, 1731; returned to Drury Lane, London, 1732; described as a natural spirited comedian. After his death a collection of jests by John *Mottley was published, unwarrantably entitled *Joe Miller's Jests* (1739), which became a standard book.

MILLER, Josiah (1832–1880), hymnologist; MA, London, 1855; Independent minister and missionary secretary; wrote biographical sketches of hymn-writers and hymns.

MILLER, Mrs Lydia Falconer (1811?–1876), authoress; née Fraser; married Hugh *Miller, 1837; assisted him in the management of the *Witness* and edited his works after his death; published stories for the young under the pseudonym of Harriet Myrtle.

MILLER, Patrick (1731–1815), projector of steam navigation; brother of Sir Thomas *Miller; Edinburgh merchant, 1760; a director of the Bank of Scotland, 1767; deputy-governor, 1790; shareholder in Carron Iron Company; purchased estate of Dalswinton, 1785; devoted himself to agricultural improvements and shipbuilding experiments; his first idea, a ship with two or three hulls propelled by paddle-wheels placed between the hulls and worked by men from capstans on deck; subsequently experimented with a double boat fitted with a steam engine made by Symington, 1788 and 1789; lost heart at not meeting with James *Watt's approval; introduced fiorin grass into Scotland, 1810; numbered among his friends *Burns and the Nasmyths.

MILLER, Philip (1691–1771), gardener; began business as a florist; appointed gardener of the Chelsea Botanical Garden on Sir Hans *Sloane's recommendation, 1722; discovered the method of flowering bulbous plants in bottles filled with water, 1730; visited Holland between 1723 and 1730; experimented in fertilization, 1751; grew rare plants; chief works, *The Gardener's and Florist's Dictionary* (1724, translated into German, Dutch, and French), *Gardener's Kalendar* (1732), and *Method of Cultivating Madder* (1758).

MILLER, Ralph Willett (1762–1799), naval captain; born in New York; came to England and entered the navy; promoted lieutenant by *Rodney, 1781; posted to command the *Mignonne*, 1796; became flag-captain to *Nelson, 1796; with Nelson at Cape St Vincent (1797) and the Nile (1798); served under Sir Sidney *Smith off the coast of Egypt and Syria; killed during the defence of St Jean d'Acre by the accidental bursting of some shells.

MILLER, Sir Thomas, Lord Glenlee, first baronet (1717–1789), lord-president of the College of Justice; educated at Glasgow University; advocate, 1742; solicitor of the excise in Scotland, 1755; solicitor-general, 1759; lord advocate, 1760; MP, Dumfries, 1761; rector of Glasgow University, 1762; lord justice clerk, 1766, as Lord Glenlee; lord president of the College of Justice, 1788; created baronet, 1789.

MILLER, Thomas (1731–1804), bookseller; brother of Edward *Miller; combined grocery and bookselling, 1755; formed collections which comprised a nearly complete series of Roman and English silver and brass coins.

MILLER, Thomas (1807–1874), poet and novelist; apprenticed to a basket-maker; encouraged by Thomas *Bailey to publish *Songs of the Sea Nymphs* (1832); bookseller in London, 1841; noticed by W. H. Harrison; granted a pension by Disraeli; published novels, poems, and children's books.

MILLER, William (1740?–1810?), painter; exhibited at the Society of Artists, 1780–3, and the Royal Academy, 1788–1803.

MILLER, William (d. 1815), lieutenant-colonel; second son of Sir William *Miller, Lord Glenlee; mortally wounded at Quatre-Bras; referred to by *Scott.

MILLER, Sir William, Lord Glenlee, second baronet (1755–1846), Scottish judge; son of Sir Thomas *Miller, Lord Glenlee; advocate, 1777; principal clerk in the High Court of Justiciary; MP, Edinburgh, 1780; unseated, 1781; succeeded to baronetcy, 1789; lord of session as Lord Glenlee, 1795–1840.

MILLER, William (1769–1844), publisher; son of Thomas *Miller (1731–1804); placed in

Hookham's publishing house, 1787; commenced publishing on his own account, 1790; succeeded by John *Murray, 1812; Fox's *James II* and *Scott's edition of *Dryden among his publications.

MILLER, William (1795–1861), general in Peruvian Army; assistant-commissary in (British) Royal Artillery, 1811; served in the Peninsula and North America; went out to La Plata and repeatedly distinguished himself in Chile and Peru; governor of Potosi, 1825; became grand marshal; left Chile owing to political changes, 1839; British consul-general in the Pacific, 1843; died at Callao.

MILLER, William (1796–1882), line-engraver; educated in England and Edinburgh; landscape engraver in Edinburgh, 1821; acquired fame as an interpreter of the works of *Turner; engraved plates after Clarkson, *Stanfield, and other artists.

MILLER, William (1810–1872), Scottish poet; contributed to *Whistle Binkie*, 1832–53; wrote 'Wee Willie Winkie' and other nursery lyrics.

MILLER, William (1864–1945), historian and journalist; educated at Rugby and Hertford College, Oxford; first class, Lit. Hum., 1887; *Morning Post* correspondent for Italy and Balkans, 1903–37; publications include *Mediaeval Rome* (1901), *The Latins in the Levant* (1908), *The Ottoman Empire, 1801–1913* (1913), *Essays on the Latin Orient* (1921), and *Greece* (1928); FBA, 1932.

MILLER, William Allen (1817–1870), chemist; studied at Birmingham General Hospital and King's College, London; worked in Liebig's laboratory, 1840; chemical demonstrator, King's College, London; MD, London, 1842; professor of chemistry at King's College, London, 1845; FRS, 1845; experimented in spectrum analysis, on which he read papers at the British Association, 1845 and 1861; with Dr (Sir William) Huggins investigated the spectra of heavenly bodies and procured the first trustworthy information on stellar chemistry, 1862; assayer to the Mint and Bank of England; hon. LL D, Edinburgh, 1860; hon. DCL, Oxford, 1868; hon. LL D, Cambridge, 1870; published *Elements of Chemistry* (1855–7).

MILLER, William Hallowes (1801–1880), mineralogist; of St John's College, Cambridge; fifth wrangler, 1826; fellow, 1829; MD, 1841; professor of mineralogy, 1832–80; developed system of crystallography adapted to mathematical calculation, 1838; commissioner for standard weights and measures; member of the International Commission, 1870; LL D, Dublin, 1865; hon. DCL, Oxford, 1876; foreign secretary, Royal Society, 1856–73; royal medallist, 1870; published scientific works.

MILLER, William Henry (1789–1848), book collector; MP, Newcastle under Lyme, 1830–41; formed a library at Britwell Court, unrivalled among private collections for its examples of early English and Scottish literature.

MILLES, Isaac, the elder (1638–1720), divine; of St John's College, Cambridge; vicar of Chipping Wycombe, 1674, of Highclere, 1680; taught the sons of Thomas *Herbert, eighth earl of Pembroke.

MILLES, Isaac, the younger (*fl.* 1701–1727), son of Isaac *Milles the elder; BA, Balliol College, Oxford, 1696; MA, Sidney Sussex College, Cambridge, 1701; treasurer of the diocese of Waterford, 1714; prebendary of Lismore, 1716.

MILLES, Jeremiah (1675–1746), son of Isaac *Milles the elder; fellow and tutor of Balliol College, Oxford, 1696–1705; rector of Duloe, 1704–46.

MILLES, Jeremiah (1714–1784), antiquary; son of Jeremiah *Milles (1675–1746); of Eton and Corpus Christi College, Oxford; MA, 1735; DD, 1747; travelled through Europe, 1733–7; treasurer of Lismore, 1735–45; precentor of Waterford, 1737–44; FSA, 1741; FRS, 1742; member of the Egyptian Club; son-in-law of Archbishop *Potter; precentor and prebendary of Exeter, 1747, dean, 1762; PSA, 1768; collected materials for a history of Devonshire; maintained the antiquity of *Chatterton's Rowley poems; his library sold, 1843.

MILLES, Thomas (d. 1627?), customer of Sandwich; bailiff of Sandwich, 1579; accompanied *Randolph on his mission to Edinburgh, 1586; customer of Sandwich, 1587; sent to Brittany to report on the forces there, 1591; prize commissioner at Plymouth, 1596; secretary to Lord *Cobham, lord warden of the Cinque Ports, 1598; obtained reversion of keepership of Rochester Castle, 1598; wrote books on economics in support of the staple system; edited the manuscripts of his brother-in-law, Robert *Glover, Somerset herald.

MILLES, Thomas (1671–1740), bishop of Waterford and Lismore; eldest son of Isaac *Milles (1638–1720); MA, Wadham College, Oxford, 1695; BD, 1704; chaplain of Christ Church, Oxford, 1694; vice-principal of St Edmund Hall, Oxford, 1695–1707; regius professor of Greek, 1707; bishop of Waterford and Lismore, 1708; published tracts and sermons and edited the works of St Cyril of Jerusalem (1703).

MILLHOUSE, Robert (1788–1839), weaver and poet; wrote his first verses, 1810; received grant from the Royal Literary Fund, 1822; assistant at a savings bank, 1832; published poems.

MILLIGAN, George (1860–1934), Scottish divine and biblical scholar; son of William *Milligan and brother of Sir William *Milligan; studied at Aberdeen, Edinburgh, Göttingen, and Bonn; ordained, 1887; minister, Caputh, Perthshire, 1894–1910; regius professor of biblical criticism, Glasgow, 1910–32; clerk to the senate, 1911–30; works include *The Vocabulary of the Greek Testament* (1914–29); moderator of General Assembly, 1923.

MILLIGAN, William (1821–1893), Scottish divine; MA, St Andrews, 1839; ordained minister of Cameron, Fifeshire, and of Kilconquhar, 1850; first professor of biblical criticism, Aberdeen University, 1860–93; member of company formed for revision of English New Testament, 1870; moderator of general assembly, 1882; principal clerk of general assembly, 1886; took prominent part in formation of Scottish Church Society, 1892 (first president); published theological and other writings, including article on 'Epistle to Ephesians' in *Encyclopaedia Britannica* (1879).

MILLIGAN, Sir William (1864–1929), laryngologist and otologist; son of William *Milligan; grandson of D. M. *Moir; MD, Aberdeen University; successful aural surgeon and laryngologist in Manchester; advocate of radium; knighted, 1914.

MILLIKEN (or MILLIKIN), Richard Alfred (1767–1815), poet; admitted attorney; volunteered on the outbreak of the Irish rebellion; chiefly remembered for 'The Groves of Blarney' and other lyrics, sung by the elder Charles *Mathews on the stage.

MILLINGEN, James (1774–1845), archaeologist; brother of John Gideon *Millingen; educated at Westminster School; banker's clerk, 1790; obtained post in French Mint; arrested as a British subject, 1792; partner in Sir Robert Smith & Co., 1794; resided in Italy; granted civil list pension; FSA and member of many learned societies in Europe; compiled valuable works on coins, medals, Etruscan vases, and kindred subjects in English, French, and Italian; died in Florence.

MILLINGEN, John Gideon (1782–1862), physician and writer; brother of James *Millingen; obtained a medical degree in Paris; assistant surgeon in the British Army, 1802; served in the Peninsular campaigns and at Waterloo (medal) and the surrender of Paris; retired, 1823; physician to the military asylum at Chatham and Hanwell, 1837; published medical and other works.

MILLINGEN, Julius Michael (1800–1878), physician and writer; son of James *Millingen; studied at Rome and Edinburgh, 1817; MRCS, Edinburgh, 1821; went to Corfu, 1823; attended Byron in his last illness; surgeon in Greek Army, 1824; settled in Constantinople, 1827; court physician to five successive sultans; instrumental in introducing Turkish baths into England; discovered ruins of Aczani and excavated site of temple of Jupiter Urius on the Bosphorus; published memoirs; died in Constantinople.

MILLINGTON, Gilbert (d. 1666), regicide; member of Lincoln's Inn, 1614; BA, Peterhouse, Cambridge, 1616; barrister, 1621; MP, Nottingham, in Long Parliament; deputy lieutenant for Nottingham, 1642; agent of communication between the governor, John *Hutchinson (1615–1664), and parliament; energetic at Charles I's trial; signed the king's death-warrant, 1649; condemned to death, 1660; his sentence commuted to life imprisonment; died in Jersey.

MILLINGTON, James Heath (d. 1873), painter; curator of the Royal Academy School of Painting.

MILLINGTON, John (1779–1868), engineer; professor of mechanics at the Royal Institution, London, 1817–29; engineer of some Mexican mines, 1829; professor of chemistry at Williamsburg, 1837, where he died; wrote on scientific subjects.

MILLINGTON, Sir Thomas (1628–1704), physician; of Westminster School and Trinity College, Cambridge; BA, 1648–9; MD, Oxford, 1659; fellow of All Souls College, Oxford; original member of the Royal Society; Sedleian professor of natural philosophy, Oxford, 1675; FRCP, 1672, treasurer, 1686–90, president, 1696–1704; court physician and knighted, 1680; alleged discoverer of sexuality in plants.

MILLINGTON, William (d. 1466?), first provost of King's College, Cambridge; probably educated at Clare Hall, Cambridge; rector, St Nicholas House, 1441; provost, 1443, of King's College; deprived by royal commissioners; assisted in drawing up Queens' College statutes, 1448; vice-chancellor, 1457.

MILLNER. See also MILNER.

MILLNER, John (*fl.* 1712), served throughout *Marlborough's campaigns in royal regiment of foot of Ireland; serjeant; served under Marlborough; published journal of Marlborough's marches (1701–12), 1733.

MILLS, Alfred (1776–1833), draughtsman.

MILLS, Bertram Wagstaff (1873–1938), circus proprietor; worked until 1914 exhibiting carriages built by his father; put on circus at Olympia every Christmas, 1920–37; started a touring circus, 1929; member of the London County Council, 1928–38.

MILLS, Charles (1788–1826), historical writer; abandoned law for literature; published *History of Muhammedanism* (1817), *History of the Crusades* (1820), and other works.

MILLS, Sir Charles (1825–1895), first agent-general for Cape Colony; born at Ischl, Hungary; private in 98th Regiment, 1843; with his regiment in China; staff clerk in adjutant-general's office; served in Punjab, 1849; ensign and adjutant, 1851; lieutenant, 1854; brigade-major in Crimea, 1855; in charge of military settlement of Germans on east border of British Kaffraria, 1858; retired on its incorporation with Cape Colony, 1865; member of Cape parliament for Kingwilliamstown, 1866; chief clerk for finance, 1867; permanent under-secretary, 1872; in colonial secretary's office; agent-general in London for Cape Colony, 1882; KCMG, 1885; CB, 1886.

MILLS, George (1792?–1824), medallist; gained three Gold Medals from the Society of Arts; exhibited at the Royal Academy, 1816–23; engraved for Mudie's *National Medals*.

MILLS, George (1808–1881), shipbuilder, journalist, and novelist; as shipbuilder began to build iron steamers, 1838; stockbroker, 1848–50; started *Glasgow Advertiser and Shipping Gazette*, 1857; started the Milton Chemical Works, 1866; started *The Northern Star* in Aberdeen, 1869; literary critic of the *Glasgow Mail*; wrote three novels.

MILLS, John (d. 1736), actor; acted at Drury Lane Theatre, London, for forty years, and occasionally at the Haymarket, London.

MILLS, John (d. 1784?), writer on agriculture; translated French agricultural works; FRS, 1766; first foreign associate of the French Agricultural Society, 1767–84; author of *System of Practical Husbandry* (1767).

MILLS, John (1812–1873), author and Calvinistic Methodist minister; extended musical culture in Wales; visited the Holy Land, 1855 and 1859; published Welsh miscellaneous works.

MILLS, Percy Herbert, first Viscount Mills (1890–1968), politician and industrialist; educated at North Eastern County School, Barnard Castle; left school at 15 and articled to chartered accountants in London, 1905; entered W. & T. Avery Ltd. (later Averys Ltd.), 1919; general manager, 1924; managing director, 1933–55;

deputy director, ordnance factories, 1939; controller-general, machine tools, 1940–4; head of production division, Ministry of Production, 1943–4; knighted, 1942; head of economic subcommission of British element of Control Commission, Germany, 1945; ignored instructions and blew up submarine yards of Bloehm & Voss; KBE, 1946; president, Birmingham Chamber of Commerce, 1947; chairman, National Research Development Corporation, 1949–55; hon. adviser on housing to Harold Macmillan; baronet, 1953; baron, 1957; Conservative minister of power, 1957–9; paymaster general, 1959–61; minister without portfolio and deputy leader, House of Lords, 1961–2; viscount, 1962; chairman, electronic subsidiary, Electric and Musical Industries, 1962–8.

MILLS, Richard (1809–1844), Welsh musician; published Congregational tunes.

MILLS, Sir William (1856–1932), engineer; trained as marine engineer; invented a boat-disengaging gear; established first British aluminium foundry, Sunderland, 1885; introduced (1915) and manufactured (Birmingham) hand grenades known by his name; knighted, 1922.

MILLS, William Hobson (1873–1959), organic chemist; educated at Uppingham and Jesus College, Cambridge; first class, part i, natural sciences tripos, 1896, and part ii, chemistry, 1897; fellow of Jesus College, 1899; head of chemical department, Northern Polytechnic Institute, London, 1902–12; demonstrator to Jacksonian professor of natural philosophy, Cambridge, Sir James *Dewar, 1912–19; university lecturer in organic chemistry, 1919; reader in stereochemistry, 1931–8; president, Jesus College, 1940–8; worked mainly on stereochemistry and cyanine dyes; after retirement, studied sub-species of British bramble and donated collection to university botany department; FRS, 1923.

MILLWARD. See MILWARD.

MILLYNG, Thomas (d. 1492), bishop of Hereford; DD, Gloucester Hall, Oxford; prior of Westminster, 1465, abbot, 1469; received (1470) *Elizabeth, queen of Edward IV, into sanctuary at Westminster, where her son Edward was born; bishop of Hereford, 1474.

MILMAN, Sir Francis, first baronet (1746–1821), physician; MA, Exeter College, Oxford, 1767; MD, 1776; Radcliffe fellow, 1771; physician to Middlesex Hospital, 1771–9; FCP, 1778; Gulstonian lecturer, 1780; Croonian lecturer, 1781; Harveian orator, 1782; president, 1811 and 1812; created baronet, 1800; physician to George III, 1806; published medical works.

MILMAN, Henry Hart (1791–1868), dean of St Paul's; son of Sir Francis *Milman; of Eton and Brasenose College, Oxford; MA, 1816; DD, 1849; Newdigate prizeman, 1812; chancellor's English essay prizeman, 1816; fellow of Brasenose, 1814; incumbent of St Mary's, Reading, 1818; professor of poetry at Oxford, 1821–31; Bampton lecturer, 1827; rector of St Margaret's, Westminster, 1835; dean of St Paul's, 1849; published *Fazio* (1815, acted in London, 1818), *Samor* (epic, 1818), *The Fall of Jerusalem* (1820), *The Martyr of Antioch* (1822), *Belshazzar* (1822), and *Anne Boleyn* (1826), *History of the Jews* (1830), *History of Christianity under the Empire* (1840), and *Latin Christianity* (1855); edited *Gibbon (1838); a history of St Paul's Cathedral published by his son (1868).

MILMAN, Robert (1816–1876), bishop of Calcutta; grandson of Sir Francis *Milman; educated at Westminster School, and Exeter College, Oxford; MA and DD, 1867; vicar of Chaddleworth, 1840, of Lambourn, 1851, of Great Marlow, 1862; bishop of Calcutta, 1867; published devotional works and a life of Tasso (1850).

MILN, James (1819–1881), archaeologist; entered navy, 1842; merchant in China and India; interested in astronomy, archaeology, and small arms; excavated at Carnac and Kermario, accounts of which he published.

MILN, Walter (d. 1558). See MYLNE.

MILNE, Alan Alexander (1882–1956), author; educated at Westminster and Trinity College, Cambridge; editor, the *Granta*; assistant editor, *Punch*, under (Sir) Owen *Seaman, 1906; during 1914–18 war served as signalling officer in Royal Warwickshire Regiment; left *Punch* to work on stage comedies, 1919; *Mr Pim Passes By* (1920), *The Truth About Blayds* (1921), *The Dover Road* (1922), *To Have the Honour* (1924), *The Fourth Wall* (1928), *Toad of Toad Hall*, a dramatization of *The Wind in the Willows* by Kenneth *Grahame (1929); wrote verses for children, *When We Were Very Young* (1924), and stories, *Winnie-the-Pooh* (1926) and *The House at Pooh Corner* (1928).

MILNE, Sir Alexander, first baronet (1806–1896), admiral of the fleet; son of Sir David *Milne; lieutenant, 1827; commander, 1830; served in West Indies, North America, and Newfoundland, 1836–41; flag-captain to his father at Devonport, 1842–5; junior lord of Admiralty, 1847–59; rear-admiral and civil KCB, 1858; commanded in West Indies and North American Station, 1860; military KCB, 1864; junior naval lord of Admiralty, 1866–8 and 1872–6; com-

mander-in-chief in Mediterranean, 1869–70; GCB, 1871; created baronet, 1876.

MILNE, Sir (Archibald) Berkeley, second baronet (1855–1938), admiral; son of Sir Alexander *Milne; entered navy, 1869; commander, 1884; captain, 1891; succeeded father, 1896; spent eight years between 1882 and 1900 in royal yachts; in command, HM yachts, 1903–5; rear-admiral, 1904; second-in-command, Atlantic Fleet (1905–6), Channel Fleet (1908–9); admiral, 1911; commander-in-chief, Mediterranean, 1912–14; on outbreak of war obtained Admiralty authority to concentrate his force at Malta; criticized for allowing German battle cruiser *Goeben* and cruiser *Breslau* to escape eastwards to Dardanelles, but his conduct and dispositions subsequently received public approval of Admiralty; retired, 1919; KCVO, 1904; KCB, 1909; GCVO, 1912.

MILNE, Colin (1743?–1815), divine and botanist; educated at Marischal College, Aberdeen; LL D, Aberdeen; rector of North Chapel, Sussex; founded Kent Dispensary (Miller Hospital), Greenwich, 1783; promoted the Royal Humane Society; published botanical works.

MILNE, Sir David (1763–1845), admiral; entered navy, 1779; in the East India service until 1793; lieutenant, 1794; commander, 1795; served on various stations abroad; in command of Forth district of Sea Fencibles, 1803–11; captain, 1814; served with distinction against Algiers, 1816; KCB, 1816; commander-in-chief in North American waters; MP, Berwick, 1820; vice-admiral, 1825; GCB, 1840; admiral, 1841; commander-in-chief at Plymouth, 1845.

MILNE, Edward Arthur (1896–1950), mathematician and natural philosopher; educated at Hymers College, Hull, and Trinity College, Cambridge; served in munitions inventions department, Ministry of Munitions, 1916–19, and on Ordnance Board, 1939–44; assistant director, Solar Physics Observatory, Cambridge, 1920–4; devoted himself to theory of stellar atmospheres; university lecturer in astrophysics, 1922–5; Beyer professor of applied mathematics, Manchester, 1925–8; Rouse Ball professor and fellow of Wadham College, Oxford, 1929–50; worked on theory of stellar structure and development of kinematic relativity; FRS, 1926.

MILNE, George Francis, first Baron Milne (1866–1948), field marshal; educated at the Gymnasium, Old Aberdeen; gazetted from Woolwich to Royal Artillery, 1885; with Lord *Kitchener on Nile (1898) and in South Africa (1899–1902); DSO, 1902; served in France, 1914–15; assumed command, British forces in Salonika, 1916 (in final offensive the first Allies to enter Bulgaria); commanded in Constantinople until Nov. 1920; GOC-in-C, Eastern Command, 1923–6; chief of Imperial General Staff, 1926–33; colonel commandant, Royal Artillery, 1918–48; master gunner, St James's Park, 1929–46; general, 1920; field marshal, 1928; KCB, 1918; baron, 1933; founder and head of Old Contemptibles and Salonika Reunion Association.

MILNE, John (1850–1913), mining engineer and seismologist; educated at King's College, London, and Royal School of Mines; professor of geology and mining, Imperial College, Tokyo, 1875; first professor of seismology, Imperial University, Tokyo; established seismic survey of Japan; secretary to seismological committee of British Association, 1895–1913; devised seismograph; travelled widely.

MILNE, Joshua (1776–1851), actuary to the Sun Life Assurance Society, 1810; compiled *Treatise on the Valuation of Annuities . . . the Probabilities and Expectations of Life* (1815), which revolutionized actuarial science.

MILNE, William (1785–1822), missionary; ordained, 1812; settled at Malacca; founded and became principal of an Anglo-Chinese college; DD, Glasgow, 1820.

MILNE, William Charles (1815–1863), Chinese missionary at Macao, Canton, and Shanghai; son of William *Milne; assistant Chinese secretary to the Peking legation; wrote books on China.

MILNE-HOME, David (1805–1890), founder of Scottish Meteorological Society; son of Sir David *Milne; proposed Ben Nevis as an observatory, 1877.

MILNER. See also MILLNER.

MILNER, Alfred, Viscount Milner (1854–1925), statesman; born in Hesse-Darmstadt; educated at Tübingen, King's College, London, and Balliol College, Oxford; obtained first classes in classical moderations (1874) and Lit. Hum. (1876); won Hertford (1874), Craven (1877), Eldon (1878), and Derby (1878) scholarships; president of Union, 1875; in society of his Oxford friends developed passion for public work, political and social; fellow of New College, Oxford, 1876; called to bar (Inner Temple), 1881; joined staff of *Pall Mall Gazette*, 1882–5; in London maintained association with his Oxford friends, notably Arnold *Toynbee, by whom he was profoundly influenced; took part in University Extension Society founded by S. A. *Barnett; co-operated in foundation of Toynbee Hall, Whitechapel, 1884; private secretary to G. J. (afterwards Viscount) *Goschen, whose ideas on

social reform and foreign and imperial policy coincided with his own, 1884; actively co-operated with Goschen in forming Liberal Unionist Association, 1886; secretary to Goschen as chancellor of Exchequer, 1887–9; director-general of accounts, Egypt, 1889; under-secretary for finance, Egypt, 1890–2; rendered great services to Great Britain's task in Egypt, especially by his book, *England in Egypt* (1892); chairman, Board of Inland Revenue, 1892–7; had large share in introducing new form of death duties devised by Sir William *Harcourt; high commissioner for South Africa, 1897–1905; went out with open mind as to rights in dispute between Boers and Britons and resolved to form judgement on spot; learned Dutch; attempted to effect friendly and informal relations with President Kruger; came to understanding with Cecil *Rhodes; concluded that there was no solution of political troubles of South Africa except reform in Transvaal or war, 1898; warned Cape Dutch against disloyalty; although his objects and those of Joseph *Chamberlain, secretary of state for colonies, were identical in South Africa, namely to secure justice and reasonable liberty for uitlanders and to ensure Great Britain's right to be alone responsible for whole of South Africa's foreign relations, his forward policy was somewhat distrusted by Chamberlain; forwarded to Chamberlain petition of uitlanders recounting their grievances, Mar. 1899; himself set out grievances in famous cable pronouncing case for intervention by British government to be overwhelming, May; met Kruger at abortive conference at Bloemfontein, 31 May; over-hasty in breaking off conference; on outbreak of war (Oct.) British colonies, in spite of his urgent representations, almost defenceless; Mafeking and Kimberley enabled to hold out largely through his insistence; his months of anxiety relieved by Lord *Roberts's capture of Pretoria and resignation of ministry of W. P. *Schreiner, June 1900; administrator of Orange River Colony and Transvaal, 1900; went to England, where he was received with extraordinary honour, May 1901; while there made preparations for starting his schemes of reorganization and social reform in new colonies; with Lord *Kitchener signed Treaty of Vereeniging on behalf of British government, May 1902; differed from Kitchener in his greater rigidity; immediately set about task of repatriating Boers on their farms; organized permanent system of education; succeeded, in spite of Boer opposition, in establishing English as medium of instruction; greatly encouraged improved methods and results in farming; stimulated land settlement by British farmers in order to introduce English ideas into country districts; set before him ultimate aim of union of all South

African colonies and early secured co-operative measures; aroused controversy by sympathy with idea of suspending Cape constitution; visited by Chamberlain, now in general accord with his South African policy, 1902; obtained consent of Alfred *Lyttelton, secretary of state for colonies, to import Chinese labour into Rand, 1904; policy aroused violent opposition, especially from Liberal party; acquiesced in grant of representative institutions to Transvaal, 1905; left South Africa, 1905; in spite of his very real success in repairing ravages of South African War, failed to touch hearts or win confidence of Boers; took little part in politics for some time after return, but carried on remunerative work in City and occupied himself with Rhodes Trust; supported movements for national service and tariff reform; opposed Lloyd George's budget (1909), which he advised Lords to reject, Parliament Bill (1911), and home rule; during European war successfully presided over committee to increase food production of country; member of Lloyd George's small War Cabinet, 1916; accompanied him to Allied Conference in Rome, Jan. 1917; sent to Amiens front in order to report on serious state of affairs owing to great German attack and breakdown of co-operation between two Allied commands, March 1918; took upon himself responsibility for momentous decision of enforcing unity of command; owing to his initiative, General Foch placed in supreme command of Allied armies on Western Front, thereby procuring turning-point of war; secretary of state for war, 1918; his great reform in administration, inauguration of army education branch; his sane utterances with regard to peace absurdly denounced as pro-German; secretary of state for colonies, 1918–21; visited Egypt in order to report on her future relations with Great Britain, 1919–20; chancellor-elect of Oxford University, 1925; baron, 1901; viscount, 1902; KG, 1921; a great public servant, whose chief contribution to contemporary political thought was conviction of need for imperial unity.

MILNER, Isaac (1750–1820), mathematician and divine; brother of Joseph *Milner; sizar of Queens' College, Cambridge, 1770; BA, 1774; fellow, 1776; FRS, 1780; rector of St Botolph's, Cambridge, 1778–92; first professor of natural philosophy at Cambridge, 1783–92; president of Queens' College, Cambridge, 1788–1820; dean of Carlisle, 1791; vice-chancellor, 1792 and 1809; Lucasian professor of mathematics, 1798–1820; intimate of William *Wilberforce; wrote on chemistry and mathematics; edited his brother's theological works.

MILNER, James (d. 1721), merchant of London; traded extensively with Portugal; wrote several articles on the Methuen treaty and Portuguese trade, 1713, and on the South Sea Company, 1720; MP, Minehead, 1717.

MILNER, James, first Baron Milner of Leeds (1889–1967), politician and lawyer; educated at Easingwold Grammar School, Leeds Modern School, and Leeds University; LL B, 1911; served in the army in France during 1914–18 war; MC with clasp; returned to family firm, J. H. Milner & Son, Leeds; joined Labour party; served on City Council, 1923–9; deputy lord mayor and president, Leeds Labour party, 1928–9; Labour MP, South-East Leeds, 1929–51; parliamentary private secretary to Christopher (later Viscount) *Addison; member, Select Committee on Capital Punishment, 1931; member, Indian Franchise Committee, 1932; chairman, Committee of Ways and Means, deputy speaker, 1943; PC, 1945; chairman, British group, Inter-Parliamentary Union; baron, deputy speaker, House of Lords, 1951; hon. LL D, Leeds; deputy-lieutenant, West Riding of Yorkshire; vice-president, Association of Municipal Corporations and Building Societies Association.

MILNER, John (1628–1702), nonjuring divine; of Christ's College, Cambridge; curate of Beeston, 1660; BD, 1662; vicar of Leeds, 1673; prebendary of Ripon, 1681; joined nonjurors, 1688; retired to St John's College, Cambridge; published theological and controversial works.

MILNER, John (1752–1826), bishop of Castabala and vicar-apostolic of the western district of England; educated at the English College, Douai, 1766–77; ordained Roman Catholic priest, 1777; missioner in England; established at Winchester the Benedictine nuns who fled from Brussels during the French Revolution; FSA, 1790; successfully opposed the suggested oath of allegiance in the Catholic Relief Bill, 1791; bishop of Castabala, 1803; steadily opposed the right of English government to 'veto' appointment of Roman Catholic bishops. He published *The History, Civil and Ecclesiastical, and Survey of the Antiquities of Winchester* (1798–1801), *The End of Religious Controversy* (1818), and other theological works.

MILNER, Joseph (1744–1797), Evangelical divine; brother of Isaac *Milner; MA, 1773, Catharine Hall, Cambridge; headmaster at Hull Grammar School; afternoon lecturer at Holy Trinity, Hull, 1768; subsequently vicar of North Ferriby; his chief work, *The History of the Church of Christ* (1794–7) edited and continued by his brother Isaac *Milner.

MILNER, Thomas (1719–1797), physician; MD, St Andrews, 1740; physician to St Thomas's Hospital, London, 1759–62; wrote on electricity.

MILNER, Violet Georgina, Viscountess Milner (1872–1958), editor of the *National Review*; daughter of Admiral Frederick Augustus *Maxse and sister of (Sir) Ivor and Leo *Maxse; married, first, Lord Edward *Cecil, 1894 (d. 1918); secondly, Sir Alfred (later Viscount) *Milner, 1921; edited *National Review*, 1932–48; brilliant raconteuse; published autobiography, *My Picture Gallery 1886–1901* (1951).

MILNER-GIBSON, Thomas (1806–1884), statesman. See GIBSON, THOMAS MILNER-.

MILNER HOLLAND, Sir **Edward** (1902–1969), lawyer. See HOLLAND.

MILNES, Richard Monckton, first Baron Houghton (1809–1885), son of Robert Pemberton *Milnes; educated at Trinity College, Cambridge, where he was an 'Apostle' and intimate of *Tennyson, *Hallam, and *Thackeray; MA, 1831; travelled, 1832–6; Conservative MP, Pontefract, 1837; did much to secure the Copyright Act; became a Liberal on Peel's conversion to free trade; assisted in preparation of *The Tribune*, 1836; visited Egypt and the Levant, 1842–3; established Philobiblon Society, 1853; interested himself in Florence *Nightingale's fund during the Crimean War; advocated mechanics' institutes and penny banks; created Baron Houghton, 1863; supported reform of franchise; visited Canada and United States, 1875; trustee of the British Museum; president of the London Library, 1882–5; hon. DCL, Oxford; published poems of a meditative kind, and political and social writings; died at Vichy.

MILNES, Robert Offley Ashburton Crewe-, second Baron Houghton, and marquess of Crewe (1858–1945), statesman. See CREWE-MILNES.

MILNES, Robert Pemberton (1784–1858), entered Trinity College, Cambridge, 1801; MP, Pontefract, 1806; resided chiefly in Milan and Rome after 1829.

MILNE-WATSON, Sir **David Milne,** first baronet (1869–1945), man of business; educated at Merchiston Castle, and Edinburgh, Oxford, and Marburg universities; joined Gas Light and Coke Company, 1897; general manager, 1903; managing director, 1916; governor and managing director, 1918–45; made it world's biggest gas company; encouraged new developments, established research laboratories, and maintained good labour relations; president, National Gas Council, 1919–43; chairman, Joint Industrial Council for Gas Industry, 1919–44; knighted, 1927; baronet, 1937.

MILO OF GLOUCESTER (d. 1143), sheriff of Gloucestershire and Staffordshire. See GLOUCESTER, MILES DE, earl of Hereford, d. 1143.

MILRED (or **MILRET)** (d. 775), bishop of the Hwiccas (Worcester); succeeded Wilfrith, 743; visited *Boniface and Lullus in Germany, 754.

MILROY, Gavin (1805–1886), medical writer and founder of the 'Milroy lectureship' at the Royal College of Physicians; MD, Edinburgh, 1828; assisted in founding Hunterian Society; co-editor of Johnson's *Medico-Chirurgical Review*, 1844–7; superintendent medical inspector of the General Board of Health, 1849–50; inspected sanitary condition of Jamaica, 1852; sanitary commissioner to the army during the Crimean War, 1855–6; left £2,000 to the London College of Physicians to found a lectureship.

MILTON, Lord (1692–1766), lord justice clerk. See FLETCHER, ANDREW.

MILTON, Sir **Christopher** (1615–1693), judge; brother of the poet John *Milton; of St Paul's School and Christ's College, Cambridge; barrister, Inner Temple, 1639; deputy recorder of Ipswich, 1674; invested with the coif, knighted, and raised to Exchequer bench, 1686; transferred to common pleas, 1687.

MILTON, John, the elder (1563?–1647), musician; of Christ Church, Oxford; scrivener in London, 1595; admitted to Scriveners' Company, 1600; composed motets, madrigals, and melodies.

MILTON, John (1608–1674), poet; son of John *Milton the elder; of St Paul's School and Christ's College, Cambridge, 1625; BA, 1629; MA, 1632; at Cambridge wrote Latin poems on university events, an *Ode on the Nativity* (1629), the sonnet to Shakespeare, 1630, and English poems; lived at Horton with his father, reading classics, 1632–8; wrote 'L'Allegro' and 'Il Penseroso', 1632, and *Arcades* (1633) and *Comus* (1634), two masques, for which *Lawes wrote the music; wrote *Lycidas*, 1637 (published 1638); travelled abroad, chiefly in Italy, 1637–9; on his return became tutor to his two nephews, Edward and John *Phillips; published three pamphlets against episcopacy (1641), to which Bishop *Hall replied acrimoniously; defended himself in his *Apology* (1642), bitterly abusing Hall; abandoned intention of taking orders, and married Mary Powell, 1643, who returned to her father's house after a month; immediately published pamphlet on 'doctrine and discipline of divorce', which made him notorious; published *The Judgment of Martin Bucer on Divorce* (1644), being attacked by the Stationers' Company for publishing these two pamphlets without licence; wrote *Areopagitica* (1644); reconciled to his wife, 1645; gave up pupils, 1647, and employed himself on the *History of Britain*; published, after Charles I's execution, *Tenure of Kings and Magistrates* (1649); Latin secretary to the newly formed Council of State, 1649, officially replying to *Eikon Basilike* with *Eikonoklastes* (1649), and to Salmasius with *Pro Populo Anglicano Defensio* (1650), also to du Moulin's *Clamor* with *Defensio Secunda* (1654), which contains autobiographical passages; being blind, was assisted in his secretarial duties successively by Georg Rudolph *Weckherlin, Philip *Meadows, and Andrew *Marvell (1621–1678); retained his post until the Restoration; married, as his second wife, Catharine Woodcock, 1656 (d. 1658); concealed himself at the Restoration; arrested during the summer, but fined and released; married his third wife, Elizabeth Minshull, 1662; his *Paradise Lost* said by *Aubrey to have been finished 1663 (begun, 1650), but agreement for his copyright not signed till 1667; received £10 for it, his widow afterwards settling all subsequent claims for £8; sold 1,300 copies by 1688; his last poems, *Paradise Regained* and *Samson Agonistes* published together (1671); published his Latin grammar and *History of Great Britain*, 1669 (written long before), a compendium of Ramus's *Logic* (1672), a tract on *True Religion* (1673), *Familiar Letters* (1674), and *College Exercises* (1674); died from 'gout struck in'; buried, beside his father, in St Giles's, Cripplegate, London.

MILTON, John (*fl.* 1770), painter; descendant of Sir Christopher *Milton.

MILTON, John (d. 1805), medallist; assistant engraver at the Royal Mint, 1789–98; exhibited at the Royal Academy, 1785–1802; FSA, 1792; executed the Isle of Man penny, 1786, and the Barbados penny and halfpenny.

MILTON, Thomas (1743–1827), engraver; son of John *Milton (*fl.* 1770); engraved *Views of Seats in Ireland* (1783–93) and *Views in Egypt* (1801); unique in his power of distinguishing the foliage of trees.

MILTON, William of (d. 1261), Franciscan. See MELITON.

MILVERLEY, William (*fl.* 1350), Oxford schoolman; wrote scholastic works in Latin.

MILVERTON, first Baron (1885–1978), colonial governor. See RICHARDS, ARTHUR FREDERICK.

MILVERTON, John (d. 1487), Carmelite; studied at Oxford, where he became prior; English provincial, 1456–65 and 1469–82; opposed by William *Ive or Ivy; excommunicated and imprisoned by the bishop, 1464; went to Rome;

possibly chosen bishop of St David's; imprisoned by Paul II for three years; acquitted of heresy.

MILWARD, Edward (1712?–1757), physician; of Trinity College, Cambridge; created MD, Cambridge, 1741; FRS, 1742; FRCP, 1748; censor and Harveian orator, 1752; published essay on Alexander Trallianus (1733); collected materials for a history of British medical writers and for a treatise on gangrene.

MILWARD, John (1556–1609), divine; BA, St John's College, Cambridge, subsequently of Christ Church, Oxford, 1582; MA and DD, Oxford, 1584; vicar of Bovey Tracey, 1596; rector of Passenham, 1605, of St Margaret Pattens, Billingsgate, London, 1608; chaplain to James I, *c.*1603; sent to Scotland to aid the establishment of episcopacy, 1609.

MILWARD, John (1619–1683), Nonconformist divine; BA, New Inn Hall, Oxford, 1641; fellow of Corpus Christi College, Oxford, and MA, 1648; ejected from living of Darfield, Yorkshire, 1660.

MILWARD, Matthias (*fl.* 1603–1641), divine; brother of John *Milward (1556–1609); scholar of St John's College, Cambridge; rector of East Barnet, 1603; member of Gray's Inn, 1624; rector of St Helen's, Bishopsgate, London.

MILWARD, Richard (1609–1680), editor of Selden's *Table Talk*; sizar of Trinity College, Cambridge, 1625; BA, 1628; MA, 1632; DD by royal mandate, 1662; rector of Great Braxted in Essex, 1643–80; canon of Windsor, 1666; vicar of Isleworth, 1678–80; amanuensis to John *Selden; arranged Selden's *Table Talk* for publication (published 1689).

MIMPRISS, Robert (1797–1875), Sunday-school worker; went to sea; became a merchant's clerk; studied art; devised system of instruction for Sunday schools based on *Greswell's *Harmony of the Gospels*, and published devotional works.

MINETT, Francis Colin (1890–1953), veterinary pathologist; educated at King Edward's School, Bath, and the Royal Veterinary College, London; MRCVS, 1911; B.Sc. (veterinary science), London, 1912; Royal Army Veterinary Corps, 1914–24; research officer, Ministry of Agriculture Laboratory, Weybridge, working on foot-and-mouth disease, 1924–7; director of research institute in animal pathology, Royal Veterinary College, 1927–39; D.Sc., London, 1927; combined duties as director with those of professor, pathology, 1933–9; director, Imperial Veterinary Research Institute, Mukteswar, India, 1939–47; animal husbandry commissioner, Government of Pakistan, 1947–50; director, farm livestock research station, Animal Health Trust, 1950–3; CIE, 1945.

MINIFIE, Susannah (1740?–1800), novelist. See GUNNING.

MINNAN, Saint (d. 875?), missionary to Fifeshire. See MONAN.

MINNES, Sir **John** (1599–1671), admiral. See MENNES.

MINNS (or MINGH), Sir **Christopher** (1625–1666), vice-admiral. See MYNGS.

MINOT, Laurence (1300?–1352?), lyric poet; probably a soldier; his poems (terminating abruptly in 1352) remarkable for their personal devotion to Edward III and savage triumph in the national successes.

MINSHEU, John (*fl.* 1617), lexicographer; taught languages in London; published Spanish dictionaries and a grammar (1599), also a *Guide into Tongues* (1617), the first book published by subscription, which contained equivalents in eleven languages.

MINSHULL (or MYNSHUL), Geffray (1594?–1668), author; admitted at Gray's Inn, 1612; occupied himself, when imprisoned for debt, by writing a series of prison 'characters' (published 1618).

MINTO, earls of. See ELLIOT, Sir GILBERT, first earl, 1751–1814; ELLIOT, GILBERT, second earl, 1782–1859; ELLIOT, GILBERT JOHN MURRAY KYNYNMOND, fourth earl, 1845–1914.

MINTO, Lord. See ELLIOT, Sir GILBERT, 1651–1718; ELLIOT, Sir GILBERT, 1693–1766.

MINTO, William (1845–1893), critic; MA, Aberdeen, 1865; assistant to Dr Alexander *Bain at Aberdeen; edited the *Examiner* in London, 1874–8; leader-writer to the *Daily News* and *Pall Mall Gazette*; professor of logic and literature, Aberdeen, 1880–93; wrote three novels, books on logic, and works on literature; edited *Scott's works.

MINTON, Francis John (1917–1957), artist; educated at Reading School; studied at St John's Wood Art School; collaborated with Michael *Ayrton on costumes and decor for (Sir) John Gielgud's production of *Macbeth* (1942); leading figure among post-war romantic painters; taught at Camberwell Art School, the Central School of Arts and Crafts, and the Royal College of Art; produced large number of paintings reflecting his travels in Spain, the West Indies, and Morocco; exhibited regularly at Royal Academy from 1949; elected member of the London Group, 1949; from 1950 felt himself to be out of contact with international fashion; died from overdose of drugs.

MINTON, Herbert (1793–1858), manufacturer of pottery and porcelain; partner with his father, 1817–36; sole proprietor from 1836; manufactured, among other things, majolica and Palissy ware.

MIRFIELD, John (*fl.* 1393), writer on medicine; Augustinian canon of St Bartholomew's, Smithfield; wrote *Breviarium Bartholomaei*.

MIRK, John (*fl.* 1403?), prior of Lilleshall in Shropshire; wrote *Liber ffestialis, Manuale Sacerdotum,* and *Instructions to Parish Priests*.

MIRZA MOHAMMAD ISMAIL, Sir (1883–1959), Indian administrator and statesman. See ISMAIL.

MISAUBIN, John (d. 1734), physician; born in France; MD, Cahors, 1687; LRCP, 1719; mentioned in *Tom Jones*.

MISSELDEN, Edward (*fl.* 1608–1654), merchant and economic writer; deputy-governor of the Merchant Adventurers' Company at Delft, 1623–33; commissioner at Amsterdam for the East India Company to negotiate a Dutch treaty, 1624, and to obtain satisfaction for the Amboyna outrages, 1624–8; endeavoured to thrust the Prayer-Book on the Merchant Adventurers at Delft, 1633; published *Free Trade* (1622) and *The Circle of Commerce* (1623).

MISSON, Francis Maximilian (1650?–1722), traveller and author; French refugee; became tutor to Charles Butler, afterwards earl of Arran, 1685; published *Voyage d'Italie* (1691), *Mémoires et Observations* (1698), and *Théâtre Sacré des Cévennes* (1707). His *Observations* form a humorous descriptive dictionary of London in Queen Anne's reign.

MIST, Nathaniel (d. 1737), printer; originally a sailor; became a printer and started the *Weekly Journal,* 1716, afterwards the organ of the Jacobites; twice arrested for libel, 1717, but discharged; assisted by Daniel *Defoe, a secret agent of the Whig government, who became 'translator of foreign news' for the *Journal,* 1717; twice examined, 1718, but discharged through Defoe's intervention; found guilty of scandalously reflecting on George I's interposition in favour of Protestants abroad, 1720; was sentenced to the pillory and three months' imprisonment; arrested and fined for printing libels on the government, 1723, 1724, 1727; retired to France, 1728; died at Boulogne.

MISYN, Richard (d. 1462?), Carmelite; probably bishop of Dromore, 1457, and suffragan of York; translated *Rolle's *De Emendatione Vitae* and *Incendium Amoris* into English.

MITAN, James (1776–1822), line-engraver; exhibited at Royal Academy, 1802–5 and 1818.

MITAN, Samuel (1786–1843), line-engraver; brother of James *Mitan; engraved plates of French scenery, 1822.

MITAND, Louis Huguenin du (*fl.* 1816), educational writer; born in Paris; taught languages in London, 1777; published *New Method of Teaching Languages* (1778), and Greek and French grammars; edited Boyer's *French Dictionary* (1816).

MITCH, Richard (*fl.* 1557), lawyer; educated at Cambridge; fellow of St John's College, Cambridge, 1543; MA, 1544; subsequently of Trinity Hall, Cambridge; advocate of Doctors' Commons, 1559; active opponent at Cambridge of the reformed religion in Mary's reign; subsequently went abroad.

MITCHEL. See also MICHELL and MITCHELL.

MITCHEL, John (1815–1875), Irish nationalist; matriculated at Trinity College, Dublin, 1830; solicitor, 1840; aided Repeal Association, 1843–6; employed on staff of the *Nation*, 1845–7; started the *Weekly Irishman*, 1848; tried for sedition and transported, 1848; escaped to San Francisco, 1853; started the *Citizen* at New York, 1854; farmer and lecturer, 1855; edited the *Southern Citizens*, 1857–9; strenuously opposed abolition; edited the New York *Daily News*, 1864–5; financial agent of the Fenians in Paris, 1865–6; started and conducted *Irish Citizen*, 1867–72; elected MP for Tipperary, 1875, but a new writ ordered on the ground that Mitchel was a convicted felon; was again returned by a large majority, but died soon after.

MITCHEL, Jonathan (1624?–1668), New England divine; went to America, 1635; graduated at Harvard, 1647; fellow, 1650; pastor of Cambridge, Massachusetts, 1662; drew up petition to Charles II respecting the colony's charter, 1664; published theological works.

MITCHEL, William (1672–1740?), pamphleteer; the 'Tinklarian Doctor'; tinsmith in West Bow, Edinburgh, and town lamplighter, 1695–1707; issued from 1712 illiterate pamphlets dealing with religion and church politics.

MITCHELBURN. See MICHELBORNE.

MITCHELL. See also MICHELL and MITCHEL.

MITCHELL, Alexander (1780–1868), civil engineer; invented in 1842 the Mitchell screw-pile and mooring, a simple means of constructing durable light houses in deep water on shifting sands, extensively used in India and the breakwater at Portland.

MITCHELL, Alexander Ferrier (1822–1899), Scottish ecclesiastical historian; MA, St Mary's College, St Andrews, 1841; DD, 1862; ordained to Presbyterian ministry of Dunnichen, 1847; member of general assembly, 1848; professor of Hebrew, St Mary's College, 1848, and of divinity and ecclesiastical history, 1868–94; moderator of Church of Scotland, 1885; hon. LL D, Glasgow, 1892; published works on Scottish ecclesiastical history.

MITCHELL, Sir Andrew (1708–1771), diplomat; educated at Edinburgh and Leiden; barrister, Middle Temple, 1738; under-secretary of state for Scotland, 1741–7; MP, Aberdeenshire, 1747, Elgin burghs, 1755 and 1761; British envoy to Frederick the Great, 1756; accompanied Frederick during the Seven Years' War; KB, 1765; died at Berlin.

MITCHELL, Sir Andrew (1757–1806), admiral; entered navy, 1771; lieutenant, 1777; rear-admiral, 1795; vice-admiral, 1799; served in expedition to Holland, 1799; KB, 1800; commanded in Channel Fleet, 1800 and 1801; president of the court martial for mutiny in the Channel Fleet, 1801; commander-in-chief on the North American Station, 1802; died at Bermuda.

MITCHELL, Sir Arthur (1826–1909), Scottish commissioner in lunacy (1870–95) and antiquary; MA, Aberdeen, 1845; MD, 1850; hon. LL D, 1875; member of English Commission on Criminal Lunacy, 1880; FSA Scotland, 1867; made study of superstition in Scottish Highlands; first Rhind lecturer in archaeology, Edinburgh; CB, 1886; KCB, 1887; hon. FRCP, Ireland, 1891; published *The Past in the Present* (1880) and edited *Macfarlane's Topographical Collections* (3 vols., 1906–8).

MITCHELL, Cornelius (d. 1749?), naval captain; entered navy, 1709; lieutenant, 1720; captain, 1731; met convoy off Cape Nicolas and failed to engage it, 1746; court-martialled, 1747, and cashiered.

MITCHELL, Sir David (1650?–1710), vice-admiral; pressed into the navy, 1672; lieutenant, 1678; commander, 1683; captain of the fleet, 1691; groom of the bedchamber; convoyed William III to Holland, 1693; rear-admiral of the blue, 1693; knighted, 1694; vice-admiral, 1695; convoyed Peter the Great to England, 1698; lord commissioner of the Admiralty, 1699–1702; visited Holland, 'to negotiate matters relating to the sea', 1709.

MITCHELL, Sir Godfrey Way (1891–1982), leading figure in construction industry; educated at Haberdashers' Aske's School, Hatcham; worked in father's quarry business; during 1914–18 war served in Royal Engineers; purchased small insolvent contracting business from George Wimpey, 1919; built up civil engineering side of George Wimpey & Co. Ltd.; started private house building, 1927; became one of the largest London-based house builders; during 1939–45 war built airfields, docks, and army camps; controller of building materials, Ministry of Works; knighted, 1948; post-war, created highly efficient overseas contracting organization; in Britain built over 300,000 houses; major private-house builder in Britain; chairman of Wimpey's, 1930–73; executive director, 1973–9; life president, 1979–82; chairman, Federation of Civil Engineering Contractors, 1948; master of Worshipful Company of Paviors; hon. fellow, Institution of Civil Engineers, 1968 and Institute of Building, 1971.

MITCHELL, Graham Russell (1905–1984), deputy director-general, Security Service; educated at Winchester and Magdalen College, Oxford; in spite of suffering from poliomyelitis, excelled at golf, sailed for the university, and won Queen's Club men's doubles tennis championship (1930); played chess for Oxford and correspondence chess for Great Britain; worked as journalist for *Illustrated London News* and research department of Conservative Central Office; joined Security Service, MI5, 1939; posted to F division, responsible for monitoring subversion; promoted to director, F division, 1945–52; transferred to D branch, dealing with counter-espionage; on appointment of (Sir) Roger *Hollis as director-general of MI5, became his deputy, 1956–63; at time of retirement under suspicion as Soviet spy; Hollis also suspected; both interrogated but nothing proved against either of them.

MITCHELL, Hugh Henry (1770–1817), colonel; ensign, 1782; lieutenant, 1783; lieutenant-colonel, 1805; colonel, 1815; CB, 1815; served with distinction at Waterloo.

MITCHELL (or MITCHEL), James (d. 1678), fanatic; graduated at Edinburgh, 1656; joined Covenanter rising, 1666; escaped to Holland, 1667; returned to Edinburgh, 1668; fired at James *Sharp, archbishop of St Andrews, 1668, but again escaped; returned, 1673; confessed on receiving promise of his life, but denied his guilt before the justiciary court, 1674; imprisoned, and, in 1677, tortured, but persisted in his denial; tried and executed.

MITCHELL, James (1786?–1844), scientific writer; MA, University and King's College, Aberdeen, 1804; created LL D, Aberdeen; secretary to insurance companies; served on factory, weaving, and colliery commissions; collected Scottish antiquities and published scientific works.

MITCHELL, James (1791–1852), line-engraver.

MITCHELL, James Alexander Hugh (1939–1985), publisher; educated at Winchester College, and Trinity College, Cambridge; sales assistant, Hatchards bookshop, Piccadilly, London; editor at Constable & Co., 1961; editorial director, Thomas Nelson & Sons, 1967; there met John Beazley, production director; started publishing business with Beazley as partner, 1969; published Patrick Moore's *Moon Flight Atlas* (1969) and *Atlas of the Universe* (1970); also Hugh Johnson's *The World Atlas of Wine* (1971); all best-sellers; Mitchell Beazley Ltd. given Queen's Award to Industry (1975); published illustrated encyclopaedia, *The Joy of Knowledge* (ten vols., 1977–8), and sold translation rights into twenty-three languages; other publications included Alex Comfort's *The Joy of Sex* (1974); John Beazley died, 1977; Mitchell sold firm to American Express Publishing, retaining chairmanship, 1980; bought it back again, 1983.

MITCHELL (or MYCHELL), John (*fl.* 1556), printer; at Canterbury, compiled *A breviat Cronicle* of the kings from Brut to the year 1551; printed other works.

MITCHELL, John (d. 1768), botanist; emigrated to Virginia, *c.*1700, and discovered several new species of plants; returned to England, 1746; FRS, 1748; published, besides botanical works, *A Map of the British and French Dominions in North America* (1755).

MITCHELL, John (1785–1859), major-general; ensign, 1803; captain, 1807; served in the Peninsula and Holland; major, 1821; colonel, 1851; major-general, 1855; published works, including *The Life of Wallenstein* (1837) and *The Fall of Napoleon* (1845).

MITCHELL, Sir John (1804–1886), field marshal. See MICHEL.

MITCHELL, John (1806–1874), theatrical manager; introduced various foreign plays, actors, and musicians into England.

MITCHELL, John Mitchell (1789–1865), antiquary; brother of Sir Thomas Livingstone *Mitchell; Leith merchant; acted as consul-general for Belgium; published miscellaneous works, including *Mesehowe: Illustrations of the Runic Literature of Scandinavia* (1863).

MITCHELL, John Murray (1815–1904), Presbyterian missionary and orientalist; MA, Marischal College, Aberdeen, 1833; hon. LL D, 1858; missionary in Bombay, 1838; made many converts among Marathis; founded flourishing Free Church Mission at Poona, 1843; in Bengal, 1867–73; formed 'Union Church' at Simla; minister of Scottish Church at Nice, 1888–98; Duff missionary lecturer at Edinburgh, 1903;

published *Hinduism Past and Present* (1885), *The Great Religions of India* (posthumous, 1905), and metrical translations from Indian poets.

MITCHELL, Joseph (1684–1738), dramatist; settled in London under the patronage of Sir Robert Walpole; published dramas and lyrics.

MITCHELL, Leslie Scott Falconer (1905–1985), actor, pioneer television announcer, and commentator; educated at King's School, Canterbury, and Chillon College on Lake Geneva; worked as an actor, 1923–34; joined BBC as general announcer and transferred to compèring dance-band music; announced launch of first public-service television, 1936; conducted interviews for *Picture Page*, a TV magazine; during 1939–45 war worked on Allied Expeditionary Forces Radio; post-war visited USA to study publicity methods; returned to free-lance activities as writer, commentator, and producer, 1948; television commentator at wedding of Princess Elizabeth and Duke of Edinburgh; prominent in launch of commercial television, 1955; published autobiography, *Leslie Mitchell Reporting . . .* (1981); first honorary member of Royal Television Society, 1983; freeman of City of London, 1984.

MITCHELL, Peter (1821–1899), Canadian politician; born at Newcastle, New Brunswick; called to New Brunswick bar, 1848; member of provincial assembly for Northumberland, 1858; member of New Brunswick legislative council, 1860; delegate to meeting at Quebec for union of British America, 1864; provincial premier and president of council, 1866; strongly advocated federation, and on proclamation of the dominion (1867) became privy councillor of Canada and dominion minister of marine and fisheries; member of senate, 1867–72; conducted fisheries negotiations with United States, 1869–71; edited *Herald* newspaper, Montreal, 1873; inspector of fisheries, 1897.

MITCHELL, Sir Peter Chalmers (1864–1945), zoologist; MA, Aberdeen, 1884; first class, natural science, Christ Church, Oxford, 1888; university demonstrator in comparative anatomy, 1888–91; lecturer in biology, Charing Cross Hospital, 1892, London Hospital, 1894; secretary, Zoological Society of London, 1903–35; made it the leading institution of its kind; mainly responsible for creation of Whipsnade Zoological Park; biological editor, eleventh edition, *Encyclopaedia Britannica*; scientific correspondent of *The Times*; publications include biography of T. H. *Huxley (1900); FRS, 1906; knighted, 1929.

MITCHELL, Sir Philip Euen (1890–1964), colonial administrator; educated at St Paul's School and Trinity College, Oxford; joined Colonial Service, 1912; assistant resident, Nyasaland; served in King's African Rifles, 1914–18; MC; district officer, Tanganyika, 1919–26; assistant secretary, native affairs, 1926; secretary, 1928; chief secretary, 1934; governor, Uganda, 1935–40; deputy chairman, Governors' Conference, 1940; on staff of Sir A. P. (later Earl) *Wavell, major-general, 1941; governor, Fiji, 1942; Kenya, 1944–52; CMG, 1933; KCMG, 1937; GCMG, 1947.

MITCHELL, Reginald Joseph (1895–1937), aircraft designer; trained as an engineer; joined Supermarine Aviation works, Southampton, 1916; chief engineer and designer, 1919–37; designed high-speed float-seaplanes for Schneider Trophy races (1922–31) and the Spitfire fighter aircraft used in the 1939–45 war; CBE, 1931.

MITCHELL, Robert (*fl.* 1800), architect; exhibited at the Royal Academy, 1782–98; wrote on perspective, 1801.

MITCHELL, Robert (1820–1873), mezzotint engraver; son of James *Mitchell (1791–1852); etched plates after *Landseer.

MITCHELL, Thomas (*fl.* 1735–1790), marine-painter and naval official; assistant-surveyor of the navy; exhibited at the Royal Academy, 1774–89.

MITCHELL, Thomas (1783–1845), classical scholar; of Christ's Hospital and Pembroke College, Cambridge; MA, 1809; fellow of Sidney Sussex College, Cambridge, 1809–12; translated plays of Aristophanes into English verse, 1820–2; edited plays of Aristophanes, 1834–8, and Sophocles.

MITCHELL, Sir Thomas Livingstone (1792–1855), Australian explorer; brother of John Mitchell *Mitchell; served as a volunteer in the Peninsula; lieutenant, 1813; captain, 1822; major, 1826; surveyor-general to New South Wales, 1828; surveyed road to western plains and Bathurst, 1830; made four explorations into the interior of Australia, in the third of which he proved the junction of the Murray with the Darling and struck the Glenelg, which he followed to the sea, 1836; knighted, 1839; endeavoured to find an overland route to the Gulf of Carpentaria and discovered sources of Barcoo, 1845–7; DCL of Oxford and FRS; published accounts of his explorations; died at Darling Point.

MITCHELL, Sir William (1811–1878), maritime writer; chief proprietor and editor of the *Shipping and Mercantile Gazette*, 1836; introduced international code of signals for ships; knighted, 1867.

MITCHELL, Sir William Gore Sutherland (1888–1944), air chief marshal; born in Australia; educated at Wellington College; with Royal Flying Corps, 1914–18; wing commander, RAF, 1919; director of training, 1929–33; commandant, Cranwell, 1933–4; AOC, Iraq, 1934–7; air member for personnel, 1937–9; AOC-in-C, Middle East, 1939–40; inspector-general of RAF, 1940–1; air chief marshal, 1939; KCB, 1938.

MITCHELL, Sir William Henry Fancourt (1811–1884), Australian politician; became writer in the colonial secretary's office in Tasmania, 1833, and assistant colonial secretary, 1839; head of the police in the gold districts of Victoria, 1853; postmaster-general of Victoria, 1857–8; commissioner of railways, 1861–3, and president of the council, 1870–84; knighted, 1875.

MITFORD, Algernon Bertram Freeman-, first Baron Redesdale in the second creation (1837–1916), diplomat and author; great-grandson of William *Mitford, the historian; educated at Eton and Christ Church, Oxford; entered Foreign Office, 1858; attaché in Japan, 1866–70; resigned from Diplomatic Service, 1873; secretary to Board of Works, 1874–86; as heir to cousin assumed additional name and arms of Mitford and went to live at Batsford Park, Gloucestershire, 1886; Conservative MP, Stratford-upon-Avon division of Warwickshire, 1892–5; baron, 1902; works include *Tales of Old Japan* (1871) and his autobiography, *Memories* (1915).

MITFORD, John (1781–1859), miscellaneous writer; BA, Oriel College, Oxford, 1804; combined the livings of Benhall, Weston St Mary's, and Stratford St Andrew; formed an extensive library, principally of English poetry, at Benhall; devoted to landscape gardening; edited the *Gentleman's Magazine*, 1834–50, *Gray's Works* (1814), and many of the Aldine editions of the poets; published original poems; his collections sold, 1859.

MITFORD, John (1782–1831), miscellaneous writer; entered navy, 1795; commanded revenue cutter on Irish coast, 1804–6; employed by Lady Perceval, who had promised to secure him a lucrative appointment in the civil service, to write in the *Star* and *News* in support of *Caroline, princess of Wales; placed in a private lunatic asylum, 1812–13; falsely accused of perjury and acquitted, 1814; took to journalism; became a drunkard and fell into poverty.

MITFORD, John Freeman-, first Baron Redesdale (1748–1830), brother of William *Mitford; barrister, Inner Temple, 1777; practised at the Chancery bar; MP, Beeralston, 1788; KC, 1789; Welsh judge, 1789; solicitor-general and knighted, 1793; attorney-general, 1799; speaker of the House of Commons, 1801; privy councillor, 1801; lord chancellor of Ireland, 1802; created Baron Redesdale, 1802; unpopular in Ireland through his opposition to Catholic emancipation; dismissed from the chancellorship, 1806; opposed repeal of Test and Corporation Acts; supported restrictions on corn; FSA, 1794; FRS, 1794; published treatise on pleadings in Chancery (1780) and other works, chiefly on Catholic emancipation.

MITFORD, John Thomas Freeman-, first earl of Redesdale (1805–1886), son of John Freeman-*Mitford, first Baron Redesdale; educated at Eton and New College, Oxford; MA, 1828; DCL, 1853; interested himself in the detail of parliamentary bills; chairman of committees, 1851; carried on a controversy in the press with Cardinal *Manning, 1875; opposed the divorce laws and Irish disestablishment; created earl of Redesdale, 1877.

MITFORD, Mary Russell (1787–1855), novelist and dramatist; published *Poems* (1810); wrote much for magazines; contributed *Our Village* (sketches of country life) to the *Lady's Magazine*, 1819, thereby originating a new branch of literature; published *Rienzi*, a tragedy (1828); published *Belford Regis* (1835) and *Recollections of a Literary Life* (1852); *Atherton* (1854); won high praise from *Ruskin; conversationalist and letter-writer.

MITFORD, Nancy Freeman- (1904–1973), novelist and biographer; eldest of six daughters of second Baron Redesdale; education sketchy as father did not believe in education for girls; avid reader of biographies, memoirs, and letters; studied at Slade School of Art; broke away from her family and lived with Evelyn *Waugh and his first wife, 1928, supporting herself by articles for *Vogue* and *Harper's Magazine*; first novel, *Highland Fling*, published in 1931, followed by *Christmas Pudding* (1932) and *Wigs on the Green* (1935); married Peter Murray Rennell Rodd, 1933; divorced, 1958; became ARP driver, 1939; published *Pigeon Pie* (1940); assistant in Heywood Hill's Curzon Street Bookshop, 1942–6; on retirement became partner in firm; published fifth novel, *The Pursuit of Love* (1945), a best-seller; fell in love with Gaston Palewski, a follower of General de Gaulle, and introduced him in *Pursuit of Love* and other books; settled in Paris and published further successful novels, *Love in a Cold Climate* (1949) and *The Blessing* (1951); highly popular in Paris; turned to biography, and published *Madame de Pompadour* (1953), *Voltaire in Love* (1957), *The Sun King* (1966), and *Frederick the Great* (1970); other works include *The Ladies of Alderley* (1938), one of whom was her great-grandmother, *The Stanleys of Alderley* (1939), *Noblesse Oblige* (1956), and *The Water Beetle* (1962); awarded Legion d'Honneur and CBE, 1972.

MITFORD, William (1744–1827), historian; brother of John Freeman-*Mitford, first Baron Redesdale; matriculated from The Queen's College, Oxford, 1761; colonel of the South Hampshire Militia with *Gibbon; wrote at Gibbon's suggestion *History of Greece* (published 1784–1810), which became very popular; MP, Newport, Cornwall, 1785–90; Beeralston, 1796–1806, New Romney, 1812–18; published some miscellaneous works.

MIVART, St George Jackson (1827–1900), biologist; studied at King's College, London; joined Roman Catholic church and proceeded to St Mary's College, Oscott; barrister, Lincoln's Inn, 1851; member of Royal Institution, 1849; FRS, 1858; lecturer on comparative anatomy in St Mary's Hospital, London, 1862; FLS, 1862; secretary, 1874–80, and vice-president, 1892; FRS, 1869; professor of biology at Roman Catholic University College, Kensington, 1874; received degree of Ph.D. from the pope, 1876; MD, Louvain, 1884; professor of philosophy at Louvain, 1890–3; excommunicated by Cardinal *Vaughan in consequence of several articles contributed to the *Nineteenth Century* and *Fortnightly Review* (1885–1900) in which he repudiated ecclesiastical authority; published biological, philosophical, and other works.

MOBERLY, George (1803–1885), bishop of Salisbury; of Winchester College and Balliol College, Oxford; gained the English Essay Prize, 1826; fellow and tutor at Balliol, 1826; MA, 1828; DCL, 1836; select preacher, 1833, 1858, and 1863; Bampton lecturer, 1868; headmaster of Winchester College, 1835–66; canon of Chester, 1868; bishop of Salisbury, 1869; objected to the damnatory clauses in the Athanasian Creed, 1872; opposed confession, 1877; published sermons and charges.

MOBERLY, Robert Campbell (1845–1903), theologian; son of George *Moberly; scholar of Winchester and New College, Oxford; BA, 1867; won Newdigate Prize, 1867; MA, 1870; DD, 1892; a senior student of Christ Church, 1867–80; principal of diocesan theological college, Salisbury, 1878; honorary canon of Chester, 1890; regius professor of pastoral theology at Oxford and canon of Christ Church, 1892–1903; contributed 'The Incarnation as the Basis of Dogma' to *Lux Mundi* (1889); chief work was *Atonement and Personality* (1901).

MOBERLY, Sir **Walter Hamilton** (1881–1974), philosopher and vice-chancellor; educated at Winchester and New College, Oxford, of which he was a scholar; first class, Lit. Hum., 1903; fellow of Merton College, 1904; lecturer in political science, Aberdeen, 1904–6; fellow of Lincoln College, Oxford, and lecturer in philosophy, 1906; during 1914–18 war served in France and Belgium with Oxford and Bucks Light Infantry; DSO, 1917; professor of philosophy, Birmingham University, 1921–4; principal, University College, Exeter, 1924–6; succeeded Sir Henry *Miers as vice-chancellor, Manchester, 1926; chairman, University Grants Committee, 1935–49; principal, St Catherine's, Cumberland Lodge, 1949–65; played important part in Oxford conference on 'Church, Community, and State', 1937; chairman, Christian Frontier Council, 1942; published *Responsibility* (1956, his Riddell memorial lectures at Durham, 1951), and *The Ethics of Punishment* (1968); honorary degrees from Belfast, Manchester, Nottingham, and Keele; hon. fellow of Lincoln, Merton, and New colleges, Oxford; knighted, 1934; KCB, 1944; GCB, 1949.

MOCATTA, Frederic David (1828–1905), Jewish philanthropist; in father's bullion broker's business, 1843–74; promoter of Charity Organisation Society, 1869; interested in housing of working classes and liberal benefactor of London hospitals; organized Board of Guardians of the Jewish Poor (founded 1859); generous supporter of Jewish charities; encouraged Jewish literature and research; FSA, 1889; published *The Jews and the Inquisition* (1877).

MOCHAEI (d. 497), saint and bishop of Aendruim; known also as Cailan; baptized and ordained by St *Patrick; built a church of wattles on Mahee Island; his monastery also a school.

MOCHAEMOG (or PULCHERIUS), Saint (d. 655), studied under St *Comgall, and was sent as a missionary to Tipperary; granted site for a monastery on Lake Lurgan; had great influence over local chieftains; credited with curing blindness.

MOCHUA (or CRONÁN), Saint (580?–637), educated by St *Comgall; travelled through Armagh and Westmeath into Galway; effected many cures during the yellow plague; miraculously created a road connecting Inishlee with the mainland.

MOCHUDA (d. 636). See CARTHACH, Saint, the younger.

MOCKET (MOKET or MOQUET), Richard (1577–1618), warden of All Souls College, Oxford; BA, Brasenose College, Oxford, 1595; fellow of All Souls College, Oxford, 1599; MA, 1600; DD, 1609; held several livings; licensed books for entry at Stationers' Hall, 1610–14;

warden of All Souls College, Oxford, 1614; said to have written a tract, *God and the King*, 1615, which was ordered to be bought by every householder in England and Scotland; published a volume of theological tracts (including one on ecclesiastical jurisdiction, 1616), which was condemned to be burnt, 1617.

MOCKET, Thomas (1602–1670?), Puritan divine; MA, Queens' College, Cambridge, 1631; incorporated MA, Oxford, 1639; chaplain to John *Egerton, first earl of Bridgewater; rector of Gilston, 1648–60; resigned Gilston to the sequestered rector, 1660; published theological works.

MOCKLER-FERRYMAN, Eric Edward (1896–1978), soldier; educated at Wellington College, and Royal Military Academy, Woolwich; commissioned into Royal Artillery, 1915; fought in France and Flanders, 1915–18; MC, 1919; on duty in Dublin, 1921–2; passed through Staff College, 1928; instructor there, 1933–5; chief staff officer to 4th Australian division, 1937–9; served in military intelligence, War Office, 1939–40; head of intelligence branch, GHQ Home Forces, 1940–2; head of intelligence branch under General Eisenhower in Algiers, 1942–3; sent back to London, and recruited by (Sir) Colin *Gubbins for Special Operations Executive (SOE), 1943; concerned with sabotage of German heavy-water production in Norway and of communications in German rear areas during Normandy invasion; CBE, 1941; CB, 1945; French and Belgian Croix de Guerre, and other foreign decorations; hon. MA (London); with Allied Control Commission in Hungary, 1945–6; after retirement became expert botanist.

MODESTUS, Saint (*fl.* 777), missionary to the Carinthians and regionary bishop; of Irish birth; disciple of St *Fergil of Salzburg; founded three churches in Carinthia; said to have baptized St Domitian; his day 5 Dec.

MODWENNA (or MONINNE), Saint (d. 518), an Irish princess baptized by St *Patrick; travelled with other maidens to England and Scotland, founding churches; died at Dundee; buried at Burton-on-Trent.

MODYFORD, Sir James, baronet (d. 1673), merchant; colonial agent and deputy-governor of Jamaica; brother of Sir Thomas *Modyford; served the Turkey Company; knighted, 1660; created baronet, 1661; visited Jamaica and sent home a survey and description of the island, 1663; agent for the colony, 1664–6; deputy governor and chief judge of the Admiralty court of Jamaica, 1667; died in Jamaica.

MODYFORD, Sir Thomas, baronet (1620?–1679), governor of Jamaica; brother of Sir James *Modyford; barrister, Lincoln's Inn; went to Barbados, 1647; a zealous royalist, afterwards going over to the parliamentarians; governor of Barbados, 1660; resigned to become speaker of the assembly; created baronet, 1664; governor of Jamaica, 1664, this island prospering under his rule; accused of encouraging piracy and sent home under arrest, 1671; he returned to Jamaica, where he died.

MOELES, Baldwin of (d. 1100?). See BALDWIN.

MOELMUD, Dyfnwal (*fl.* 500), northern British prince; in legend the primitive legislator of the Britons; probably a mythical personage.

MOELS (or MOLIS), Nicholas de (*fl.* 1250), seneschal of Gascony; constantly sent abroad as a royal messenger, 1215–28; sheriff of Hampshire and custos of Winchester Castle, 1228–32; sheriff of Yorkshire, 1239–41; seneschal of Gascony, 1243–5; when warden, established the Carmelites in Oxford Castle, 1254; warden of Cinque Ports, 1258; had charge of Sherborne Castle, 1261, and of Corfe Castle, 1263.

MÖENS, William John Charles (1833–1904), Huguenot antiquary; settled in Hampshire, devoting himself to yachting and antiquarian research; held captive in South Italy by brigands for four months, 1865; published experiences in *English Travellers and Italian Brigands* (1866); helped to found Huguenot Society of London, 1885; president, 1899–1902; edited for society registers of Walloons at Norwich (1887–8), of French church, Threadneedle Street (1896), and of Dutch church, Colchester (1905); FSA, 1886.

MOERAN, Ernest John (1894–1950), composer; educated at Uppingham and Royal College of Music; studied under Dr John *Ireland; compositions include many songs, folk-song arrangements, and choral pieces; chamber music; G minor Symphony (1937), Sinfonietta (1945), Violin Concerto (1942), Cello Concerto (1945) and Sonata (1947).

MOETHEU, Thomas (1530–1620?), Welsh bard and genealogist. See JONES, THOMAS.

MOFFAT, Robert (1795–1883), missionary; was accepted by the London Missionary Society, 1816; sent to Namaqualand, he converted the chief, Afrikaner; married Mary Smith, 1819; appointed superintendent at Lattakoo, 1820; discovered that the Mantatees were on their way to take Lattakoo, and secured assistance from the Griquas; compelled by the restlessness of the natives to seek refuge at Griquatown, 1824, the mission station being moved to Kuruman, 1825; commenced learning the Sechwana language; gained many converts; completed his translation of the New Testament, 1839, and visited England, 1839–43; met, and secured for the Bakwana mission, David *Livingstone, who (1844) married his daughter, Mary Moffat; established (1859) a mission station among the Matabeles, but was obliged by failing health to leave Africa, 1870; translated into Sechwana the Old and New testaments and *Pilgrim's Progress*, and compiled a Sechwana hymn-book, besides writing books on South African mission work, of which he was the pioneer.

MOFFATT, James (1870–1944), divine; educated at Glasgow Academy, University, and Free Church of Scotland College; ordained, 1896; professor of Greek and New Testament exegesis, Mansfield College, Oxford, 1911–15, of church history, Glasgow Free Church College (1915–27) and Union Theological Seminary, New York (1927–39); publications include *The Historical New Testament* (1901), *Introduction to the Literature of the New Testament* (1911), and translations of New (1913) and Old (1924) Testaments; edited 'Moffatt New Testament Commentary'.

MOFFATT, John Marks (d. 1802), antiquary and dissenting minister; published a history of Malmesbury (1805).

MOFFETT, Peter (d. 1617), divine; brother of Thomas *Moffett; MA, Trinity College, Cambridge, 1582; rector of Fobbing, 1592–1617; published scripture commentaries.

MOFFETT (MOUFET or MUFFET), Thomas (1553–1604), physician and author; brother of Peter *Moffett; educated at Merchant Taylors' School, London; matriculated at Trinity College, Cambridge, 1569, but BA, Caius College, 1572; MA, Trinity College, Cambridge, 1576, and expelled from Caius College, Cambridge; studied medicine at Cambridge and Basle; MD, Basle, 1578; visited Italy, Spain, and Germany, 1579–82; published *De Jure et Præstantia Chemicorum Medicamentorum Dialogus Apologeticus* (1584); practised at Ipswich and afterwards in London; FRCP, 1588; attended Anne, duchess of Somerset, widow of the protector, 1586, and attested her will; patronized by Henry *Herbert, second earl of Pembroke, who induced him to settle at Wilton; MP, Wilton, 1597; published an interesting poem on the silkworm (1599); two scientific works by him published (1634 and 1655).

MOGFORD, Thomas (1809–1868), portrait and landscape painter; exhibited at the Royal Academy, 1838–46.

MOGRIDGE, George (1787–1854), miscellaneous writer; published, under his own name and various pseudonyms, tales and religious books for children, and religious tracts and ballads.

MOHL, Madame Mary (1793–1883), née Clarke; educated in a convent school; visited Madame Récamier, 1831–49, and Chateaubriand; married Julius Mohl, the orientalist, 1847; her receptions in Paris attended by most literary and other celebrities for nearly forty years.

MOHUN, Charles, fourth Baron Mohun (1675?–1712), duellist; fought his first recorded duel, 1692; arrested for being concerned in the death of William *Mountfort, but acquitted before his peers, 1693; volunteered for the Brest expedition, 1694; made captain of horse, 1694; distinguished himself in Flanders; fought a duel with Captain Richard Cook, 1699; became a staunch supporter of the Whigs; attended Charles *Gerard, second earl of Macclesfield, as envoy-extraordinary to Hanover, 1701; entered on a complicated dispute with James *Douglas, fourth duke of Hamilton, concerning Macclesfield's real estate, and challenged the duke to a duel, in which both combatants were mortally wounded, 1712. This duel forms an incident in *Thackeray's *Esmond*.

MOHUN, John, first Baron Mohun (1592?–1640), Royalist and politician; BA, Exeter College, Oxford, 1608; student at the Middle Temple, 1610; MP, Grampound, 1623–4 and 1625; created Baron Mohun, 1628.

MOHUN, John de (1270?–1330), baron; lord of Dunster in Somerset; great-grandson of Reginald de *Mohun; a prominent figure in the reigns of Edward I and II; granted charters to Dunster and Bruton priories.

MOHUN, John de (1320–1376), baron; lord of Dunster; grandson of John de *Mohun (1270?–1330); served in Scotland and France; an original KG; gave a charter to the monks of Dunster.

MOHUN, Michael (1620?–1684), actor; performed under Beeston at the Cockpit; entered the Royalist army; went to Flanders and attained the rank of major; resumed acting at the Restoration, joining *Killigrew's company; many of his parts original; played second to *Hart.

MOHUN (MOUN or MOYUN), Reginald de (d. 1257), sometimes called earl of Somerset; great-grandson of William de *Mohun (*fl.* 1141); sat among the king's justices, 1234; founded Newnham Abbey, 1246; said to have received his title earl of Somerset from the pope; benefactor of Cleeve Abbey and other religious houses.

MOHUN (or MOION), William de (*fl.* 1066), baron and sheriff of Somerset; a Norman who followed William the Conqueror to England, 1066; received manors in the west of England, was sheriff of Somerset, and (*c.*1095) founded Dunster Priory.

MOHUN (MOION or MOYNE), William de, earl of Somerset or Dorset (*fl.* 1141), son of William de *Mohun; rose against Stephen, 1138; marched to the siege of Winchester, 1141, with Matilda, who created him earl of Dorset or Somerset; founded Bruton Priory, 1142.

MOINENNO, Saint (d. 570), suffragan bishop of Clonfert; a disciple of St *Brendan.

MOIR, David Macbeth (1798–1851), physician and author; known as Delta (Δ); obtained his surgeon's diploma, 1816; practised in Musselburgh; became a regular writer of essays and serious verse for a number of magazines and of *jeux d'esprit* for *Blackwood's*, for which he wrote *The Autobiography of Mansie Wauch* (republished 1828); published works, including *Outlines of the Ancient History of Medicine* (1831).

MOIR, Frank Lewis (1852–1904), song composer; composed ballads, church music, and organ voluntaries; best-known songs were 'Only Once More', 1883, and 'Down the Vale', 1885.

MOIR, George (1800–1870), advocate and author; advocate, 1825; became acquainted with Sir William *Hamilton, 1788–1856 and Thomas *Carlyle; professor of rhetoric and *belles lettres* at Edinburgh, 1835–40; sheriff of Ross and Cromarty, 1855–9; sheriff of Stirlingshire, 1859; professor of Scots law, 1864; wrote on Scots law and translated Schiller's *Piccolomini* and *Wallenstein* (1827) and *Thirty Years' War* (1828).

MOIRA, earl of. See HASTINGS, FRANCIS RAWDON-, second earl, 1754–1826.

MOISES, Hugh (1722–1806), schoolmaster; BA, Trinity College, Cambridge, 1745; fellow of Peterhouse, Cambridge; MA, 1749; headmaster (1749–87) of Newcastle upon Tyne Grammar School, which he raised to a high state of efficiency; rector of Greystoke, 1787.

MOIVRE, Abraham de (1667–1754), mathematician; born at Vitry; educated at Sedan and Namur; devoted himself to mathematics in Paris under Ozanam; came to London, 1688; FRS, 1697; commissioner to arbitrate on the claims of *Newton and Leibniz to the invention of the infinitesimal calculus, 1712; wrote on fluxions, 1695, on the doctrine of chances, 1711 and 1718, and on life annuities, 1725; published *Miscellanea Analytica* (1730), in which his method of recurring series created 'imaginary trigonometry'.

MOLAGA (or MOLACA) (*fl.* 650), Irish saint; baptized by St Cuimin; travelled through Ulster, Scotland, and Wales; cured the king of Dublin, who gave him a town in Fingal, where he erected a church; confessor to the king of Tulachmin, at which place he founded a sanctuary and arrested the yellow plague.

MOLAISSI (533–563), Irish saint; founded a church on an island in Loch Erne; made pilgrimage to Rome.

MOLE, John (1743–1827), mathematician; farm labourer; opened school at Nacton, 1773; removed to Witnesham, 1793; wrote books on algebra (1788 and 1809).

MOLE, John Henry (1814–1886), water-colour painter; vice-president of the Royal Institute of Painters in Water-Colours, 1879.

MOLESWORTH, John, second Viscount Molesworth (1679–1726), ambassador in Tuscany and Turin; son of Robert *Molesworth, first Viscount; commissioner of trade and plantations, 1715.

MOLESWORTH, John Edward Nassau (1790–1877), vicar of Rochdale; great-grandson of Robert *Molesworth, first Viscount; graduated MA, Trinity College, Oxford, 1817; DD, 1838; curate of Millbrook, 1812–28; vicar of Rochdale, 1840; started and edited *Penny Sunday Reader*; opposed *Bright on the abolition of church rates; promoted the Rochdale Vicarage Act, 1866, which converted thirteen chapels of ease into parish churches; had a misunderstanding with Bishop Prince *Lee of Manchester; published pamphlets and sermons.

MOLESWORTH, Hon. Mary (d. 1715), poetess. See MONCK.

MOLESWORTH, Richard, third Viscount Molesworth (1680–1758), field marshal; son of Robert *Molesworth, first Viscount; abandoned law to join the army in Holland; present at Blenheim, 1704; saved *Marlborough's life at Ramillies, 1706; lieutenant-colonel, 1707; colonel, 1710; lieutenant of the ordnance in Ireland, 1714; MP, Swords, 1714; served against the Jacobites, 1715; succeeded as Viscount Molesworth, 1731; Irish privy councillor, 1735; major-general, 1735; lieutenant-general, 1742; general of horse, 1746; commander-in-chief in Ireland, 1751; field marshal, 1757.

MOLESWORTH, Robert, first Viscount Molesworth (1656–1725), educated at Dublin; supported the prince of Orange in Ireland, 1688; sent on missions to Denmark, 1689 and 1692, where he gave serious offence; returned to Ireland, 1695; MP, Dublin, 1695, Swords (Irish parliament), 1703–5, Lostwithiel and East Retford (English parliament), 1705–8; Irish PC, 1697; after George I's accession sat for St Michael's; created Baron Molesworth of Philipstown and Viscount Molesworth of Swords, 1719; published pamphlets and an *Account of Denmark* (1692).

MOLESWORTH, Sir **William,** eighth baronet (1810–1855), politician; educated at Offenbach near Frankfurt; entered at Trinity College, Cambridge, but, offering to fight a duel with his tutor, was expelled; finished his education at Edinburgh; travelled in the south of Europe; MP, East Cornwall, 1832 and 1835; started *London Review*, 1835; supported all measures for colonial self-government; MP, Leeds, 1837, Southwark, 1845; first commissioner of the Board of Works in Lord Aberdeen's government, 1853; colonial secretary in Lord Palmerston's government, 1855; first opened Kew Gardens on Sunday; edited *Hobbes's Works* (1839–45).

MOLESWORTH, William Nassau (1816–1890), historian; son of John Edward Nassau *Molesworth; BA, Pembroke College, Cambridge, 1839; MA, 1842; incumbent of St Clement's, Spotland, near Rochdale, 1844–89; hon. canon of Manchester, 1881; hon. LL D, Glasgow, 1883; chief work, *History of England from 1830* (1871–3).

MOLEYNS, Baron. See HUNGERFORD, ROBERT, 1431–1464.

MOLEYNS, Adam de (d. 1450), bishop of Chichester. See MOLYNEUX.

MOLINES (or MULLEN), Allan (d. 1690), anatomist; MD, Dublin, 1686; FRS, 1683; went to Barbados, 1690; wrote on human and comparative anatomy; made discoveries in connection with the eye; died in Barbados.

MOLINES, Edward (d. 1663), surgeon; son of James *Molines (d. 1639); surgeon to St Thomas's and St Bartholomew's hospitals, London; fought in the Royalist army and was expelled from his offices; restored, 1660.

MOLINES, James (*fl.* 1675), surgeon; cousin of James *Molines (1628–1686); left manuscript notes on the surgical practice at St Thomas's Hospital, London.

MOLINES (MOLEYNS or **MULLINS), James** (d. 1639), surgeon; warden of the Barber-Surgeons' Company, 1625; master, 1632; surgeon to St Bartholomew and St Thomas's hospitals, London.

MOLINES, James (1628–1686), surgeon; son of Edward *Molines; surgeon to St Thomas's Hospital, London, 1663; surgeon-in-ordinary to Charles II and James II; MD, Oxford, 1681.

MOLINES (MOLYNS or **MOLEYNS),** Sir **John de** (d. 1362?), soldier; assisted William de *Montacute to arrest *Mortimer, 1330; received grants of land from Edward III; served in the Scottish wars, 1336–8; apprehended, 1340; escaped from the Tower of London; pardoned, 1345; served against the French, 1346–7; steward to Queen *Philippa, 1352; probably died in Cambridge Gaol; benefactor of St Mary Overy, Southwark, and St Frideswide's, Oxford.

MOLINES, William (*fl.* 1680), author of *Myotomia*, a manual of dissection (1680).

MOLINEUX, Thomas (1759–1850), stenographer; writing master at Macclesfield Grammar School, 1776; published works on *Byrom's shorthand.

MOLINS, Lewis du (1606–1680). See MOULIN.

MOLL, Herman (d. 1732), geographer; of Dutch nationality; came to London, 1698; published works on geography and maps of all parts of the world.

MOLLINEUX, Henry (d. 1719), Quaker; imprisoned in Lancaster Castle, 1684 and 1690; wrote in defence of Quaker principles.

MOLLING (d. 696), Irish saint and bishop. See DAIRCELL.

MOLLISON, Amy (1903–1941), airwoman. See JOHNSON.

MOLLISON, James Allan (1905–1959), airman; educated at Glasgow and Edinburgh academies; held short service commission in RAF, 1923–8; became airline pilot in Australia; assisted by Lord *Wakefield with aeroplanes for record-breaking flights; solo flight from Australia to England, 1931; England to the Cape, 1932; east–west North Atlantic, 1932; married Amy *Johnson, 1932; flew South Atlantic east to west, 1933; awarded Britannia Trophy, 1933; made further record flights with his wife, 1934; MBE, for work with Air Transport Auxiliary, 1946; published *Death Cometh Soon or Late* (1932) and *Playboy of the Air* (1937).

MOLLOY, Charles (1646–1690), legal writer; entered Lincoln's Inn, 1663; migrated to Gray's Inn, 1669; published treatise on maritime law and commerce (1676).

MOLLOY, Charles (d. 1767), journalist and dramatist; author of three comedies; adopted Whig journalism and contributed to *Fog's Weekly Journal* and *Common Sense*, 1737–9.

MOLLOY (or O'MAOLMHUAIDH), Francis (*fl.* 1660), theologian and grammarian; appointed theological professor at St Isidore's College, Rome; acted as Irish agent at the papal court;

wrote on theology and compiled a grammar of the Irish language in Latin (1677).

MOLLOY, Gerald (1834–1906), rector of the Catholic University of Dublin from 1883 till death; professor of theology at Maynooth, 1857; professor of natural philosophy, Catholic University, Dublin, 1874; rector, 1883; D.Sc., Royal University of Ireland, 1879; commissioner of inquiry into educational endowments in Ireland, 1885–94; vice-chancellor of Royal University, 1903; published *Geology and Revelation* (1870) and *Gleanings in Science* (1888).

MOLLOY, James Lynam (1837–1909), composer; MA, Catholic University, Dublin, 1858; called to English bar, 1863; composed songs (of which 'Darby and Joan', 'The Kerry Dance', 'Love's Old Sweet Song' had wide vogue) and operettas; wrote *Our Autumn Holiday on French Rivers* (1874).

MOLLOY, Joseph Fitzgerald (1858–1908), miscellaneous writer; published *Songs of Passion and Pain* (1881), *London under the Four Georges* (4 vols., 1882–3), and *London under Charles II* (2 vols., 1885), lives of Margaret (Peg) *Woffington (2 vols., 1884) and Edmund *Kean (2 vols., 1888), *Romance of the Irish State* (2 vols., 1897), and many novels.

MOLONY, Sir Thomas Francis, first baronet (1865–1949), lord chief justice of Ireland; thrice law prizeman, and senior moderator (1886), history and political science, Trinity College, Dublin; called to Irish (1887) and English (1900) bar; QC, 1899; second serjeant-at-law, 1911; solicitor-general for Ireland, 1912; attorney-general, 1913; judge, 1913–15; lord justice of appeal, 1915–18; lord chief justice of Ireland, 1918–24; baronet, 1925; vice-chancellor, Dublin University, 1931–49.

MOLTENO, Sir John Charles (1814–1886), South African statesman; went to Cape Town, where he was employed in public library, 1831; started commercial business, 1837; engaged in wool trade in the great Karoo, 1841–52; burgher and commandant in Kaffir War, 1846; returned to mercantile pursuits, 1852; first member for Beaufort in Cape legislative assembly, 1854; advocated responsible government and became first Cape premier, 1872; came into conflict on questions of policy and administration with Sir Henry Bartle Edward *Frere, who dismissed him from office, 1878; colonial secretary, 1881–2; KCMG, 1882.

MOLUA, Saint (554?–608?), first abbot of Clonfertmulloe. See LUGID.

MOLYNEUX (MOLEYNS or **MOLINS), Adam de** (d. 1450), bishop of Chichester; clerk of the council, 1436–41; archdeacon of Taunton, 1440; prebendary of St Paul's Cathedral, 1440; archdeacon of Salisbury, 1440; employed on diplomatic missions abroad; keeper of the privy seal, 1444; bishop of Chichester, 1446–50; considered responsible for the unpopular peace negotiations which led to the surrender of Maine and Anjou; mortally wounded in a riot over the payment of the sailors at Portsmouth.

MOLYNEUX, Caryll, third Viscount Maryborough (1621–1699), son of Sir Richard *Molyneux, second Viscount Maryborough; Royalist in Civil War; lord-lieutenant of Lancashire; arrested on charge of treason, 1694, but acquitted.

MOLYNEUX, Sir Edmund (d. 1552), judge; BA, Oxford, 1510; entered Gray's Inn, 1510; serjeant-at-law, 1542; KB, 1547; on the council of the north, 1549; justice of common pleas, 1550.

MOLYNEUX, Edmund (*fl.* 1587), biographer; son of Sir Edmund *Molyneux; accompanied Sir Henry *Sidney to Ireland; acted as clerk to the council there; reported on state of Ireland, 1578; contributed biographies of the Sidneys to *Holinshed's *Chronicles* (ed., 1587).

MOLYNEUX, Sir Richard (d. 1459), soldier; chief forester of West Derbyshire, 1446; constable of Liverpool, 1446; sided with Henry VI in the Wars of the Roses; fell at Bloore Heath.

MOLYNEUX, Sir Richard, first Viscount Maryborough (1593–1636), receiver-general of the duchy of Lancaster; created Viscount Molyneux of Maryborough (Irish peerage), 1628.

MOLYNEUX, Sir Richard, second Viscount Maryborough (1617?–1654?), son of Sir Richard *Molyneux, first Viscount Maryborough; raised two Royalist regiments; defeated at Whalley, 1643, and at Ormskirk, 1644; escaped after Battle of Worcester, 1651.

MOLYNEUX, Sir Robert Henry More- (1838–1904), admiral. See MORE-MOLYNEUX.

MOLYNEUX, Samuel (1689–1728), astronomer and politician; son of William *Molyneux; MA, Trinity College, Dublin, 1710; visited England and Holland; sent to Hanover; FRS, 1712; secretary to George, prince of Wales; MP, Bossiney, 1715, St Mawes, 1726, and Exeter (British parliament), 1727; MP, Dublin University (Irish parliament), 1727; successfully experimented on construction of reflecting telescopes, 1724; endeavoured to determine stellar annular parallax; lord of the Admiralty, 1727; privy councillor of England and Ireland.

MOLYNEUX (or MOLINEL), Sir Thomas (1531–1597), chancellor of the Exchequer in

Ireland; born at Calais; surveyor of victuals for the army in Ireland, 1578; chancellor of the Irish Exchequer, 1590.

MOLYNEUX, Sir Thomas, first baronet (1661–1733), physician; brother of William *Molyneux; MA and MB, Trinity College, Dublin, 1683; visited London, Cambridge, and Oxford; corresponded with *Locke; entered Leiden University, 1683; MD, Dublin, 1687; FRS, 1687; practised in Dublin; president, Irish College of Physicians, 1702, 1709, 1713, and 1720; professor of medicine, Dublin, 1717; created baronet, 1730; several of his zoological papers the first upon their subjects.

MOLYNEUX, Sir William (1483–1548), soldier; a leader at Flodden Field, 1513, where he took two Scottish banners; joined Derby's Sallee expedition, 1536.

MOLYNEUX, William (1656–1698), philosopher; brother of Sir Thomas *Molyneux (1661–1733); BA, Trinity College, Dublin; entered Middle Temple, 1675; studied philosophy and applied mathematics; surveyor-general of the king's buildings, 1684–8; FRS, 1685; commissioner for army accounts, 1690; MP, Dublin University, 1692 and 1695; wrote on philosophy and optics; best known as the author of *The Case of Ireland's being bound by Acts of Parliament in England stated* (1698).

MOLYNS, John (d. 1591), divine; MA, Magdalen College, Oxford, 1545; DD, 1566; reader in Greek at Frankfurt during Queen Mary's reign; canon of St Paul's Cathedral, 1559; archdeacon of London, 1559; endowed two scholarships at his college, Oxford.

MOMERIE, Alfred Williams (1848–1900), divine; educated at City of London School and Edinburgh University; MA, 1875; D.Sc., 1876; entered St John's College, Cambridge, 1875; BA, 1878; MA, 1881; ordained priest, 1879; fellow of his college, 1880; professor of logic and mental philosophy, King's College, London, 1880–91; published sermons and works on philosophy of Christianity.

MOMPESSON, Sir Giles (1584–1651?), politician; MP, Great Bedwin, 1614; suggested creation of licensing commission, 1616; made one of the commissioners and knighted, 1617; charged exorbitant fees and exacted heavy fines; gold and silver thread commissioner, 1618; surveyor of the New River Company profits, 1619; received charcoal licence, 1620; committed to the care of the serjeant-at-arms, the House of Commons having ordered an investigation of the licensing patent, 1621; escaped to France; his sentence, degradation from knighthood, imprisonment for life, and a fine of £10,000; permitted to return to England on private business, 1623, and lived in retirement in Wiltshire; possibly the original of *Massinger's Sir Giles Overreach.

MOMPESSON, William (1639–1709), hero of the 'plague at Eyam'; MA, Peterhouse, Cambridge, 1662; rector at Eyam, Derbyshire, 1664; persuaded the people to confine themselves to the village, plague infection having reached Eyam, 1665, receiving necessaries in exchange for money placed in running water; rector of Eaking, 1669; prebendary of Southwell (1671) and York.

MONAHAN, James Henry (1804–1878), Irish judge; BA, Trinity College, Dublin, 1823; called to the Irish bar, 1828; QC, 1840; solicitor-general for Ireland, 1846; attorney-general, 1847; Irish privy councillor, 1848; conducted revolutionary prosecutions, 1848; chief justice of common pleas, 1850; LL D, Dublin, 1860; commissioner of national education, 1861.

MONAMY, Peter (1670?–1749), marine painter; native of Jersey; devoted himself in London to drawing shipping; painted parts of the decorative paintings at Vauxhall, London.

MONAN, Saint (d. 875?), missionary in Fifeshire; is said to have preached in Fifeshire, and been martyred by the Danes in the Isle of May in the Firth of Forth.

MONASH, Sir John (1865–1931), Australian general; educated at Scotch College and Melbourne University; practised as a civil engineer specializing after 1900 in reinforced concrete construction; commissioned in Australian Citizen Forces, 1887; colonel, 1913; commanded 4th Infantry brigade at Gallipoli, 1915; 3rd Australian division (1916–18) at Messines, Passchendaele, Ypres, and Amiens; Australian Army Corps, 1918; lieutenant-general; withstood German offensive; launched Allied offensive, Aug. 1918; brilliant planner; director-general, Australian repatriation and demobilization; general and retired, 1930; chairman, Victorian Government State Electricity Commission, 1920–31; vice-chancellor, Melbourne University, 1923–31; president, Australasian Association for Advancement of Science, 1924–6; KCB, 1918; GCMG, 1919.

MONBODDO, Lord (1714–1799). See BURNETT, JAMES.

MONCK. See also MONK.

MONCK, Sir Charles Stanley, fourth Viscount Monck in Irish peerage and first Baron Monck in peerage of United Kingdom (1819–1894), BA, Trinity College, Dublin, 1841; LL D, 1870; called to Irish bar at King's Inn, Dublin, 1841; succeeded as viscount, 1849;

Liberal MP for Portsmouth, 1852; lord of Treasury, 1855–8; captain-general and governor-in-chief of Canada and governor-general of British North America, 1861; received renewal of appointment, with title of governor-general of Dominion of Canada, 1866; privy councillor of Canada, 1867; resigned office, 1868, after inaugurating the federation; created Baron Monck of Ballytrammon, 1866; GCMG and privy councillor, 1869; on commission to carry out provisions of new Irish Land Acts, 1882–4.

MONCK, Christopher, second duke of Albemarle (1653–1688), son of George *Monck, first duke of Albemarle; succeeded to title, 1670; KG, 1670; colonel of foot regiment, 1673; lord-lieutenant of Devonshire and joint lord-lieutenant of Essex, 1675, and Wiltshire, 1681; colonel of the 1st Horse Guards and captain of all king's guards of horse, 1679; chancellor of Cambridge University, 1682; raised Devon and Cornwall militia against Monmouth, 1685; governor-general of Jamaica, 1687; died in Jamaica.

MONCK (or MONK), George, first duke of Albemarle (1608–1670), volunteered for Cadiz expedition, 1625; distinguished himself at Breda, 1637, and in the Scottish troubles, 1640; served against the Irish rebels in command of a foot regiment; returned with Irish troops to help Charles I; taken prisoner by *Fairfax at Nantwich, 1644, and imprisoned in the Tower of London; offered command in Ireland by the parliament on condition of taking the negative oath, after which he became adjutant-general and governor of Ulster, 1647; captured Robert *Monro, commander of the Royalist Scots in Ireland, 1648; as governor of Carrickfergus, concluded a cessation of arms with *O'Neill, 1649; thereupon forced by his discontented soldiers to surrender Dundalk, 1649; proceeded to England and was censured by parliament, 1649; went with *Cromwell to Scotland, a new regiment having been formed (which became the Coldstream Guards), 1650; appointed lieutenant-general of the ordnance and left commander-in-chief in Scotland, 1651; completed conquest of Scotland, 1652; admiral (1652), fighting in the three great battles which practically ended the Dutch War; resumed command of army in Scotland, 1654; extended powers of civil government granted him and his council, 1655; much trusted by Oliver Cromwell; sent Richard *Cromwell a letter of valuable advice on Oliver's death; received Royalist overtures, 1659; promised support to the parliament, a breach with the army seeming imminent, and, on hearing of the parliament's expulsion, expostulated with *Lambert and *Fleetwood; after parliament had again resumed its place at Westminster, marched slowly towards London,

besieged by addresses from all parts of England; ordered to make the City of London indefensible; the quarrel between the City and parliament having come to a head, roused the indignation of the soldiers against the parliament by obeying this order, Feb. 1660; demanded the issue of writs for a new parliament, and ordered the guards to admit the secluded members; elected head of a new council, Feb. 1660; general-in-chief of the land forces and joint commander of the navy; refused to listen to the suggestions offered by *Heselrige and others of supreme power; had entered into direct communication with Charles II, but the precise date at which he resolved to restore the king much disputed; his suggestions practically adopted by the king in the Declaration of Breda, 4 Apr. 1660; received from the king a commission as captain-general, authority to appoint a secretary of state, and letters for the city, the council, and parliament, the king's letters being presented to parliament, 1 May, and the restoration of the monarchy voted the same day; knighted on the king's arrival, made KG, and (July 1660) created Baron Monck, earl of Torrington, and duke of Albemarle; had much influence in military affairs, his own regiments being retained as king's guards; had less influence in purely political and none in ecclesiastical questions; his advice of weight in the settlement of Scotland, but the withdrawal of English garrisons carried out against his wishes; lord-lieutenant of Ireland, but (1661) withdrew in favour of *Ormonde; remained in London throughout the plague, 1665, maintaining order and superintending preventive measures; largely responsible for the conduct of the Dutch War; put to sea with *Rupert as his colleague, 1666; defeated by the Dutch off the North Foreland, 1666, but later in the same year gained a victory, facilitated by the jealousy between Tromp and De Ruyter; called to restore order in the city after the great fire, 1666, the large ships being subsequently harboured; his orders on the appearance of the Dutch, 1667, in the Thames being neglected, eight great ships burnt in the Medway and the *Royal Charles* captured; first lord of the Treasury, 1667; retired, 1668.

MONCK, Mary (d. 1715), poetess; daughter of Robert *Molesworth, first Viscount Molesworth; married George Monck of Dublin; her *Marinda, Poems, and Translations* published (1716).

MONCK (or MONK), Nicholas (1610–1661), provost of Eton and bishop of Hereford; brother of George *Monck, first duke of Albemarle; MA, Wadham College, Oxford, 1633; rector of Plymtree, 1646; incumbent of Kilhampton, Cornwall, 1653; sent to Scotland to discover his brother's intentions, 1659, but failed to do so; made

Provost of Eton after the Restoration; DD, Oxford, 1660; bishop of Hereford, 1660.

MONCKTON, Mary, afterwards countess of Cork and Orrery (1746–1840), daughter of John Monckton, first Viscount Galway; became known as a 'blue-stocking'; her mother's house a rendezvous of persons of genius and talent; married Edmund Boyle, seventh earl of Cork and Orrery, 1786; as Lady Cork entertained, among many notable people, including the prince regent, Canning, *Byron, *Scott, *Sheridan, Lord John Russell, and Sir Robert Peel; possibly the 'Lady Bellair' of Beaconsfield's *Henrietta Temple* and 'Mrs Leo Hunter' of *Pickwick Papers.*

MONCKTON, Sir Philip (1620?–1679), Royalist; distinguished himself at Atherton Moor, 1643, and Naseby, 1645; wounded at Rowton Heath; knighted, 1644; shared command of the Yorkshire Cavaliers; defeated and taken prisoner at Willoughby Field, 1648; after five months' imprisonment received a pass to the continent; controller of the excise and customs of Dunkirk, 1661; MP, Scarborough, 1670; sheriff of Yorkshire, 1675; committed to the Tower for writing defamatory letters, 1676; held various military appointments.

MONCKTON, Robert (1726–1782), lieutenant-general; commissioned to serve in Flanders, 1742; captain, 1744; major, 1747; lieutenant-colonel, 1751; MP, Pontefract, 1752; sent to Nova Scotia, 1752, and appointed lieutenant-governor of Annapolis Royal, 1754; reduced forts Beauséjour and Gaspereau in the 1755 campaign; second-in-command of *Wolfe's expedition to Quebec, 1759, where he was wounded; major-general, 1761; governor of New York, 1761; sailed with *Rodney, 1762; after surrender of Martinique, Grenada, St Lucia, and St Vincent returned to England, 1763; governor of Berwick-on-Tweed, 1765; lieutenant-general, 1770; governor of Portsmouth, 1778; MP, Portsmouth, 1779–1782.

MONCKTON, Walter Turner, first Viscount Monckton of Brenchley (1891–1965), lawyer and politician; educated at Harrow and Balliol College, Oxford; president of the Union, 1913; served in France during 1914–18 war; MC, 1919; called to bar (Inner Temple), 1919; KC, 1930; recorder, Hythe, 1930–7; chancellor, diocese of Southwell, 1930–6; attorney-general to prince of Wales, 1932–6; constitutional adviser to nizam of Hyderabad and nawab of *Bhopal, 1933–6; attorney-general, duchy of Cornwall, 1936–51; close confidant of Edward VIII during Abdication crisis, 1936; KCVO, knighted, 1937; chairman, Aliens Advisory Committee, 1939; director-general, Press and Censorship Bureau; deputy-director, and then director-general, Ministry of Information, 1940; director-general, Propaganda and Information Services, Cairo, 1941; acting minister of state, 1942; solicitor-general, 1945; visited Hyderabad and negotiated with government of India on behalf of nizam, 1946–8; Conservative MP, Bristol West, 1951–7; minister of labour and national service, 1951–5; minister of defence, 1955–6; paymaster-general, 1956–7; viscount; president, MCC, 1957; chairman, Midland Bank, 1957–64; chairman, Iraq Petroleum Company, 1958–65; governor, Harrow; standing counsel, Oxford University (1938–51); honorary degrees, Oxford, Bristol, and Sussex; hon. fellow and visitor, Balliol, 1957; first chancellor, Sussex University, 1963; KCMG, 1945; PC, 1951; GCVO, 1964.

MONCREIFF (afterwards WELLWOOD) Sir Henry (afterwards Henry Moncreiff), eighth baronet, of Tulliebole (1750–1827), Scottish divine; educated at Glasgow and Edinburgh Universities; ordained minister at Blackford, 1771; appointed to one of the charges of St Cuthbert's, Edinburgh, 1775; moderator of the assembly and DD of Glasgow, 1785; chaplain to George III, 1793; published sermons and religious biographies.

MONCREIFF, Henry James, second Baron Moncreiff (1840–1909), Scottish judge; son of James *Moncreiff, first baron; BA and LL B, Trinity College, Cambridge, 1861; passed to Scottish bar, 1863; Whig advocate depute, 1865–6; reappointed under Gladstone, 1868 and 1880; joined Liberal Unionists, 1886; sheriff of Renfrew and Bute, 1881; Scottish judge, 1888–1905.

MONCREIFF, Sir Henry Wellwood, tenth baronet (1809–1883), Scottish divine; son of Sir James Wellwood *Moncreiff, afterwards Lord Moncreiff; BA, New College, Oxford, 1831; studied divinity under Dr Chalmers; minister of East Kilbride, 1837–52; joined Free Church at disruption, 1843; succeeded to baronetcy, 1851; minister of Free St Cuthbert's, Edinburgh, 1852; joint principal clerk (1855) and moderator (1869) of the free general assembly; DD, Glasgow, 1860; wrote vindications of the Free Church.

MONCREIFF, James, first Baron Moncreiff of Tulliebole (1811–1895), lord justice-clerk of Scotland; son of Sir James Wellwood *Moncreiff; educated at Edinburgh; called to Scottish bar, 1833; MP for Leith Burghs, 1851–9, Edinburgh, 1859–68, and Glasgow and Aberdeen universities, 1868; solicitor-general for Scotland, 1850; lord advocate, 1851–2, 1852–8, 1859–66, and 1868–9; lord justice-clerk, 1869–88; dean of

Faculty of Advocates, 1858–69; LL D, Edinburgh, 1858; rector of Glasgow University, 1868–71, and LL D, 1879; privy councillor, 1869; created baronet, 1871, and baron of United Kingdom, 1874; succeeded as eleventh baronet of Tulliebole, 1883.

MONCREIFF, Sir James Wellwood, Lord Moncreiff (1776–1851), Scottish judge; son of Sir Henry Wellwood *Moncreiff of Tulliebole; called to the Scottish bar, 1799; BCL, Balliol College, Oxford, 1800; sheriff of Clackmannan and Kinross, 1807; dean of the Faculty of Advocates, 1826; judge of the session, 1829; favoured Catholic emancipation and strongly opposed patronage; joined Free Church at disruption.

MONCREIFFE OF THAT ILK, Sir (Rupert) Iain (Kay), eleventh baronet (1919–1985), herald and genealogist; educated at Stowe School, Heidelberg University, and Christ Church, Oxford; served in Scots Guards throughout 1939–45 war; attaché at British Embassy, Moscow; LL B Edinburgh, 1950; admitted to Faculty of Advocates, 1950; took silk, 1980; joined court of Lord Lyon king of arms as Falkland pursuivant, 1952; Kintyre pursuivant (in ordinary), 1953; Unicorn pursuivant, 1955; Albany herald, 1961; CVO, 1980; published, in collaboration with heraldic artist Don Pottinger, *Simple Heraldry* (1953), *Simple Custom* (1954), and *Blood Royal* (1956); also published *The Highland Clans* (1967), but most of his best work remains unpublished, including Edinburgh University Ph.D. thesis (1958).

MONCRIEFF, Alexander (1695–1761), Presbyterian minister; studied at St Andrews and Leiden; minister of Abernethy, 1720; agitated against patronage; being suspended by the assembly, helped to form the Secession Church of Scotland, 1733; professor of divinity, 1742; published vindication of Secession Church (1750).

MONCRIEFF, Sir Alexander (1829–1906), colonel and engineer; joined army, 1855; served in Crimea; colonel, 1878; invented Moncrieff system of raising and lowering guns, and devised means of laying and sighting them when thus mounted; designed hydro-pneumatic carriage for similar purposes, 1869; FRS, 1871; CB, 1880; KCB, 1890; a keen sportsman, amateur artist, and golfer.

MONCRIEFF, James (1744–1793), military engineer; entered Woolwich, 1759; practitioner engineer and ensign, 1762; served in West Indies; sub-engineer and lieutenant, 1770; engineer-extraordinary and captain-lieutenant, 1776; distinguished himself at the defence of Savannah, 1779 (promoted brevet-major), and at the capture of Charleston, 1780 (promoted brevet-lieutenant-colonel); quartermaster-general to the allies in Holland, 1793; chief engineer at Valenciennes, 1793; promoted lieutenant-colonel of the Royal Engineers, 1793; mortally wounded at the siege of Dunkirk and buried at Ostend with military honours.

MONCRIEFF, William Thomas (1794–1857), dramatist; clerk in a solicitor's office, 1804; associated with Robert William *Elliston, 1815, William *Oxberry, 1824, and Charles *Mathews the elder, whom he assisted in his entertainments; opened a music shop in Regent Street, 1828; gradually became blind, and on Queen Victoria's presentation became a Charterhouse brother, 1844; *Tom and Jerry,* dramatization of *Egan's Life in London,* 1821, the most successful of his numerous dramatic pieces.

MOND, Alfred Moritz, first Baron Melchett (1868–1930), industrialist, financier, and politician; son of Ludwig *Mond; educated at Cheltenham, Cambridge, and Edinburgh; called to bar (Inner Temple), 1894; managing director of father's chemical business; advocated and worked for principles of co-ordination and co-operation as bases of industrial enterprise; became prominent for number and importance of enterprises with which he was connected, and for scale of amalgamations incorporated in firm of Imperial Chemical Industries, Ltd., 1926; instituted Mond–Turner Conference to discuss problems arising between employers and employed, 1927; Liberal MP, Chester, 1906, Swansea, 1910–23, Carmarthen, 1924–8; first commissioner of works, 1916–21; minister of health, 1921–2; became protectionist after European war; convert to Conservatism, 1926; an enthusiastic Zionist; baronet, 1910; baron, 1928; PC, 1913; FRS, 1928.

MOND, Julian Edward Alfred, third Baron Melchett (1925–1973), merchant banker and first chairman of the British Steel Corporation; grandson of Alfred *Mond; educated at Eton; served in Fleet Air Arm (RNVR), 1942–5; joined merchant bankers M. Samuel & Co., 1947; succeeded to barony, 1949; formed and chaired farming company, British Field Products Ltd.; adviser to Export Credits Guarantee Department and British Transport Docks Board, 1959; director, Guardian Assurance Company and Anglo-American Shipping Co. Ltd.; director of banking and overseas departments of Philip Hill, Higginson & Erlanger Ltd. after merger with M. Samuel & Co., 1965; on council of Confederation of British Industry and National Economic Development Council; saw British Field Products Ltd. grow into one of largest companies of its kind in Britain; appointed chairman of British Steel Corporation by Labour government, 1967–73; arranged for retraining of redundant workers and introduced worker-directorships; secured agreement of Conservative government to long-term development plan, 1972; announced profit, 1973; non-executive director, Orion Bank, 1972.

MOND, Ludwig (1839–1909), chemical technologist, manufacturer, and art collector; born and educated at Cassel; employed in soda works near Cassel, 1859; in England (1862) took out patent for recovery of sulphur from Leblanc alkali waste; joined firm at Widnes to push process, 1867; bought English patent of ammonia-soda process, and with (Sir) J. T. Brunner started alkali works at Winnington near Northwich, 1873; firm became Brunner, Mond & Co. (1881; with Mond as managing director (in 1909 employing 4,000 workmen); invented Mond producer-gas plant (patented 1883) for the production of ammonia and cheap producer-gas; his efforts to recover chlorine wasted in ammonia-soda process, and his use of nickel compounds to purify producer-gas, led to discovery of nickel carbonyl, and of a method for extracting metallic nickel from its ores; Mond formed Mond Nickel Company, with mines in Canada and works near Swansea, 1888; active in founding Society of Chemical Industry and its *Journal*, 1881; FRS, 1891; received honorary doctorates from Padua, Heidelberg, Manchester, and Oxford; left fortune of over £1 million; took out forty-nine patents and published many scientific papers; founded Davy–Faraday laboratory for chemical research at Royal Institution, 1896; left large sums to Royal Society and Heidelberg for research; benefactor to town of Cassel and to Jewish charities; bequeathed (contingently on wife's death) art collection, mainly early Italian pictures, to National Gallery.

MOND, Sir Robert Ludwig (1867–1938), chemist, industrialist, and archaeologist; son of Ludwig *Mond and brother of first Lord *Melchett; carried out and encouraged others in research in father's firm; honorary life secretary, Davy–Faraday laboratory, Royal Institution; financed, organized, and published results of archaeological expeditions in Egypt, Palestine, etc.; knighted, 1932; FRS, 1938.

MO-NENNIUS (*fl.* 500), bishop of Whithorn; protégé of St *Ninian; bishop of Whithorn before 497; master or abbat of a celebrated school at Whithorn called Monasterium Rosnatense; fell a victim to his own plot for the death of Finian, one of his pupils; author of 'Hymn of Mugint' (parts of which are embodied in the Anglican church service).

MONEY, John (1752–1817), aeronaut and general; entered army, 1762; captain, 1770; brevet-lieutenant-colonel, 1790; colonel, 1795; major-general, 1798; lieutenant-general, 1805; general, 1814; one of the earliest English aeronauts, making two ascents, 1785.

MONGRÉDIEN, Augustus (1807–1888), political economist and miscellaneous writer; born in London of French parents; gradually withdrew from business and devoted himself to literary pursuits; joined National Political Union, 1831; member of Cobden Club, 1872; received a civil list pension; wrote on free trade and botanical subjects.

MONIER-WILLIAMS, Sir Monier (1819–1899), orientalist; born at Bombay; came to England, 1822; educated at King's College School, London, and Balliol College, Oxford; received writership in East India Company's civil service, 1839; studied at Haileybury, 1840, but abandoned intention of going to India and entered University College, Oxford; studied Sanskrit; Boden scholar, 1843; BA, 1844; professor of Sanskrit, Persian, and Hindustani at Haileybury, 1844–58; Boden professor of Sanskrit at Oxford, 1860; conceived plan of Indian Institute, which was founded at Oxford largely owing to his exertions, 1883; fellow of Balliol College, 1882–8; hon. fellow of University College, Oxford, 1892; keeper and perpetual curator of Indian Institute; hon. DCL, Oxford, 1875; knighted, 1886; KCIE, 1887, when he assumed additional surname of Monier; published Sanskrit texts and translations and other works, including a *Sanskrit–English Dictionary* (1872).

MONK. See also MONCK.

MONK, James Henry (1784–1856), bishop of Gloucester and Bristol, educated at Charterhouse School and Trinity College, Cambridge; MA, 1807; DD, *per literas regias*, 1822; fellow of Trinity College, Cambridge, 1805; regius professor of Greek, 1808–23; dean of Peterborough, 1822; assisted in restoration of Peterborough Cathedral; canon of Westminster, 1830; consecrated bishop of Gloucester, 1830, the see of Bristol being amalgamated with Gloucester, 1836; wrote on classical subjects.

MONK, Richard (*fl.* 1434), chronologer; an Oxford chaplain who compiled chronological tables.

MONK, William Henry (1823–1889), composer; organist and professor of music at King's College, London, 1874, and Bedford College, 1878; lectured at London Institute, Manchester, and Edinburgh; musical editor of *Hymns Ancient and Modern* and many other collections.

MONK-BRETTON, first Baron. See DODSON, JOHN GEORGE, 1825–1897.

MONKHOUSE, William Cosmo (1840–1901), poet and critic; clerk in Board of Trade, 1856; assistant secretary to finance department at death; published poems, *A Dream of Idleness* (1865) and *Corn and Poppies* (1890); a novel, 1868; *Masterpieces of English Art* (1869); lives of *Turner (1879) and *Tenniel (1901), and *Earlier English Water Colour Painters* (1890).

MONKSWELL, first Baron (1817–1886). See COLLIER, ROBERT PORRETT.

MONMOUTH, duke of (1649–1685). See SCOTT, JAMES.

MONMOUTH, titular earl of. See MIDDLETON, CHARLES, 1640?–1719.

MONMOUTH, earls of. See CAREY, ROBERT, first earl, 1560?–1639; CAREY, HENRY, second earl, 1596–1661; MORDAUNT, CHARLES, first earl of the second creation, 1658–1735.

MONMOUTH, Geoffrey of (1100?–1154). See GEOFFREY.

MONMOUTH (or MONEMUE), John de (1182?–1247?), lord marcher; actively supported King John against the barons; negotiated with the barons, 1215; justice-itinerant in Gloucestershire, 1221; built Cistercian abbey of Grace Dieu in Wales, 1226; negotiated truce with *Llywelyn, 1231; justiciar and commander of the foreign mercenaries in South Wales; defeated by Richard *Marshal, 1233; witnessed confirmation of Magna Charta and rebuilt abbey of Grace Dieu, 1236; chief bailiff of Cardigan, Carmarthen, and South Wales, 1242; defeated *Davydd, 1244.

MONMOUTH, John de (*fl.* 1320), partisan of Roger *Mortimer, first earl of March.

MONNINGTON, Sir **(Walter) Thomas** (1902–1976), artist; developed heart trouble at age of 12 and set himself to draw and paint; entered Slade School, 1918, and came under influence of Henry *Tonks; won scholarship in decorative painting offered by British School at Rome 1922; in Italy, 1922–5; influenced by Piero della Francesca; made reputation with large tempera *Allegory*, purchased by Contemporary Art Society; taught part-time at Royal College of Art and Royal Academy Schools; involved, with other artists, in major decorative schemes for St Stephen's Hall, Westminster, and the Bank of England, 1926–37; completed *Supper at Emmaus* for reredos of Bolton parish church; received commissions for portraits of eminent contemporaries; ARA, 1931; RA, 1938; designed camouflage for aircraft-production airfields, 1939–43; flew with RAF as official war artist, 1943; and served in

Holland, drawing pioneer mobile-radar equipment, 1944–5; taught at Camberwell School of Art, 1946–9, then at Slade, 1949–67; produced geometric paintings, 1951–76, including large painted ceiling for Bristol Council House symbolizing progress in nuclear physics, electronics, aeronautics, and biochemistry, 1956; fellow, University College, London, 1957; president, Royal Academy, 1966; knighted, 1967; chiefly responsible for opening treasures of Academy's private rooms to the public; member, executive committee, National Art Collections Fund, 1941–76.

MONNOYER, Antoine (d. 1747), flower painter; called 'Young Baptiste'; son of Jean Baptiste *Monnoyer; died at St Germain-en-Laye.

MONNOYER, Jean Baptiste (better known as BAPTISTE, Jean) (1634–1699), flower painter; born at Lille; decorated the French royal palaces; accompanied Ralph *Montagu, afterwards duke of Montagu, to England, 1678; painted panels at Hampton Court, Kensington Palace, London, and elsewhere.

MONRO. See also MUNRO.

MONRO, Alexander (d. 1715?), principal of Edinburgh University; educated at St Andrews University; DD and professor of divinity, St Andrews, 1682; principal of Edinburgh University, 1685; forced to demit his office at the Revolution.

MONRO, Alexander, *primus* (1697–1767), physician; MD, Edinburgh; studied at London, Paris, and (1718) Leiden; professor of anatomy and surgery to the Surgeons' Company, Edinburgh, 1719; first professor of anatomy, Edinburgh University, 1720; attended the wounded at Prestonpans, 1745; published *Osteology* (1726); edited *Transactions* of the Medico-Chirurgical Society (1732).

MONRO, Alexander, *secundus* (1733–1817), anatomist; son of Alexander *Monro *primus*, entered Edinburgh University, 1752; coadjutor to his father as professor of anatomy and surgery; MD, Edinburgh, 1755; studied at London, Paris, Leiden, and Berlin; lectured in Edinburgh, 1759–1808; the communication between the lateral ventricles of the brain called the 'foramen of Monro' from his description, 1783; described accurately the bursae mucosae, 1788, and wrote other medical works.

MONRO, Alexander, *tertius* (1773–1859), anatomist; son of Alexander *Monro *secundus*; MD, Edinburgh, 1797; studied at London and Paris; joint professor with his father, 1800; published no works of permanent value.

MONRO, Sir Charles Carmichael, baronet (1860–1929), general; grandson of Alexander *Monro, tertius (1773–1859); gazetted to 2nd Foot, 1879; served in South African War, 1899–1900; chief instructor, Hythe School of Musketry, 1901–3; commandant, 1903–7; virtually responsible for evolution of new system of infantry fire-tactics; commanded 13th infantry brigade, Ireland, 1907–12; major-general, 1910; commanded 2nd division, Aldershot, 1914; proceeded to France, Aug.; received command of I Corps, Dec.; commanded Third Army, with rank of general, July 1915; placed in command of Mediterranean Expeditionary Force at Gallipoli, Oct.; successfully advocated and effected (Jan. 1916) complete withdrawal from peninsula; commanded First Army in France, 1916; commander-in-chief, India, 1916–20; successfully developed Indian military power, 1917–18; ably handled unrest in India following war; governor of Gibraltar, 1923–8; KCB, 1915; baronet and Bath king of arms, 1921.

MONRO, Charles Henry (1835–1908), author; educated at Harrow; BA, Caius College, Cambridge (first class, classics), and fellow, 1857; law lecturer, 1872–96; planned but left unfinished a complete translation of Justinian's *Digest* (2 vols., 1904–9); memorial fellowship and Celtic lectureship founded at Caius College.

MONRO, Sir David (1813–1877), colonial politician; son of Alexander *Monro *tertius*; member of first general assembly in New Zealand, 1854; speaker, 1861, 1862–70; knighted, 1862.

MONRO, David Binning (1836–1905), classical scholar; educated at Glasgow University and Balliol College, Oxford; BA (first-class classic), 1858; Ireland scholar, 1858; fellow of Oriel, 1858; vice-provost, 1874; provost, 1882; vice-chancellor of university, 1901–4; published a Homeric grammar, 1882 (an authoritative work), a school edition of the *Iliad* (2 vols., 1884–9), and *Odyssey* xiii–xxiv (1901); edited complete text, 1896; sought in philology the solution of Homeric problems; founded Oxford Philological Society, 1870; original FBA, 1902; hon. DCL, Oxford, 1904, LL D, Glasgow, 1883, Litt.D., Dublin, 1892; died in Switzerland.

MONRO, Donald (*fl.* 1550), known as High Dean of the Isles; parson of Kiltearn; transferred on account of his ignorance of Gaelic to Lymlair, 1574; published narrative of travels through the Western Isles (1549).

MONRO, Donald (1727–1802), medical writer; son of Alexander *Monro *primus*; MD, Edinburgh, 1753; army physician; LRCP, 1756; physician to St George's Hospital, London, 1758–86; FRS, 1766; FRCP, 1771; censor,

1772, 1781, 1785, and 1789; Croonian lecturer, 1774–5; Harveian orator, 1775; published works on medicine and soldiers' health.

MONRO, Edward (1815–1866), divine and author; brother of Henry *Monro (1817–1891); educated at Harrow and Oriel College, Oxford; BA, 1836; perpetual curate of Harrow Weald, 1842–60; established college for poor boys at Harrow Weald, which was pecuniarily unsuccessful; vicar of St John's, Leeds, 1860–6; published stories, allegories, and religious works.

MONRO (or MUNRO), Sir George (d. 1693), of Culrain and Newmore; Royalist general; served under Gustavus Adolphus; commanded troops in Ireland, 1644; recalled to Scotland, 1648; followed *Hamilton into England, 1648, but was not present at Preston; disbanded his troops and went to Holland; appointed lieutenant-general under John *Middleton, first earl of Middleton to promote a rising on behalf of Prince Charles, 1654; MP, Ross-shire, 1661–3, 1680–6, and 1689–93, and Sutherland, 1669–74; KB; supported the Revolution.

MONRO, Harold Edward (1879–1932), poet, editor, and bookseller; educated at Radley and Gonville and Caius College, Cambridge; published several volumes of verse and founded *Poetry Review* (1912), Poetry Bookshop, Bloomsbury (1913–32), *Poetry and Drama* (1913–14), and (*Monthly*) *Chapbook* (1919–25).

MONRO (MONROE or MUNRO), Henry (1768–1798), United Irishman; entered the linen business, 1788; joined the United Irishmen, 1795; chosen to command the rebels, 1798; routed at Ballinahinch; tried by court martial and hanged.

MONRO, Henry (1791–1814), portrait and subject painter; son of Thomas *Monro (1759–1833); exhibited at the Royal Academy and British Institution.

MONRO, Henry (1817–1891), physician and philanthropist; brother of Edward *Monro; BA, Oriel College, Oxford, 1839; MD, 1863; FRCP, 1848; president of the Medical Psychological Society, 1864; physician of Bethlehem Hospital, London, 1848; chief work, *Remarks on Insanity* (1851).

MONRO, Sir Horace Cecil (1861–1949), civil servant; educated at Repton and Clare College, Cambridge; second class, classics, 1883; entered Local Government Board, 1884; private secretary to successive presidents; an assistant secretary to the Board, 1897; permanent secretary, 1910–19; KCB, 1911.

MONRO, James (1680–1752), physician; son of Alexander *Monro (d. 1715?); MA, Balliol College, Oxford, 1708; MD, 1722; FRCP, 1729; studied insanity; physician to Bethlehem Hospital, London, 1728–52.

MONRO, John (1715–1791), physician; son of James *Monro; of Merchant Taylors' School, London, and St John's College, Oxford; MA, 1740; Radcliffe travelling fellow, 1741; studied insanity at Edinburgh and on the continent; physician to Bethlehem Hospital, 1751; FRCP, 1752.

MONRO, Matt (1930–1985), singer of popular music; born Terence Parsons; began singing during service in army, 1947–53; worked at numerous jobs from lorry driver to builder's mate and bus driver; met pianist Winifred Atwell and changed name to Matt Monro; singer with Radio Luxembourg, 1956; recording contract with Decca; 'Portrait of my Love' entered list of British best-selling records, 1960; best-known albums include *Walk Away*, *I Have Dreamed*, *My Kind of Girl*, *The Late Late Show*, and *Softly*; travelled widely, covering some 150,000 miles a year; regarded as 'a singer's singer' by Frank Sinatra, Tony Bennett, and Bing Crosby; one of best singers of popular music Britain has produced.

MONRO (or MUNRO), Robert (d. 1633), styled the Black Baron; joined the Scottish corps in the German wars, 1626; colonel under Gustavus Adolphus; died at Ulm of a wound.

MONRO (or MUNRO), Robert (d. 1680?), general; cousin of Robert *Monro, the 'Black Baron'; served for seven years on the continent; sided with the Scots against Charles I; sent to Ireland as major-general on the outbreak of the Irish rebellion; dispersed Lord Iveagh's forces near Moira, 1642, sacked Newry, 1642, and (1642) captured Randal *Macdonnell, second earl of Antrim, who subsequently escaped; relieved Sir John *Clotworthy, gained a dubious advantage over Owen Roe *O'Neill, and recaptured Antrim, 1643; surprised Belfast, 1644; defended Ulster against *Castlehaven, 1644; defeated by O'Neill at Benburb, 1646; came to an understanding with the Royalist party, but was taken prisoner by *Monck and sent to England, 1648, where he was imprisoned till 1654; he thenceforth lived in Ireland.

MONRO (or MUNRO), Sir Robert, twenty-seventh Baron and sixth baronet of Foulis (d. 1746), served in Flanders; MP, Wick, 1710–41; assisted *Sutherland against Jacobites, 1715; commissioner for forfeited estates of Highland chiefs, 1716; lieutenant-colonel of the 'Black Watch', 1739; distinguished at Fontenoy, 1745; ordered to Scotland at the outbreak of the rebellion; killed at Falkirk.

MONRO, Thomas (1759–1833), physician and connoisseur; son of John *Monro; educated under Dr Samuel *Parr and at Oriel College, Oxford; MA, 1783; MD, 1787; FRCP, 1791, censor, 1792, 1799, and 1812; Harveian orator, 1799; physician at Bethlehem Hospital, London, 1792–1816; a patron of young artists, including Joseph Mallord William *Turner and John *Linnell.

MONRO, Thomas (1764–1815), miscellaneous writer; educated under Dr Samuel *Parr and at Magdalen College, Oxford; MA, 1791; rector of Little Easton, 1800–15; projector and editor of *Olla Podrida*, 1787; with William *Beloe translated *Alciphron's Epistles* (1791).

MONSARRAT, Nicholas John Turney (1910–1979), writer; educated at Winchester and Trinity College, Cambridge; articled to firm of Nottingham solicitors but determined to live by his pen; published three novels between 1934 and 1937, but first of any significance, *This is the Schoolroom*, published in 1939; during 1939–45 war served in RNVR on a corvette in the Atlantic; during this period published *Three Corvettes* (1945); director, UK Information Service, Johannesburg, 1946–53; published *Depends what you mean by Love* (1947) and *My Brother Denys* (1948), followed by his best-seller *The Cruel Sea* (1951), of which his English publishers alone had sold 1,330,000 copies in hardback by 1981; British Information Officer, Ottawa, 1953–6; held various public offices, including governor of Stratford Festival of Canada; wrote many other books, including *The Tribe that lost its Head* (1956), *The Ship that died of Shame* (1959), *The White Rajah* (1961), *The Kapillan of Malta* (1973), and *The Master Mariner* (vol. i, 1978, vol. ii, 1980); also wrote autobiography, *Life is a Four-Letter Word* (2 vols., 1966 and 1970); three films made of his major works; won Heinemann Foundation Prize for Literature, 1951; fellow of Royal Society of Literature.

MONSELL, John Samuel Bewley (1811–1875), hymn-writer; BA, Trinity College, Dublin, 1832; LL D, 1856; successively chancellor of the diocese of Connor, vicar of Egham, and rector of St Nicholas, Guildford; a popular writer of hymns and religious verse.

MONSELL, William, Baron Emly (1812–1894), politician; of Winchester College and Oriel College, Oxford; moderate Liberal MP, Limerick, 1847–74; clerk of ordnance, 1852–7; president of Board of Health, 1857; privy councillor, 1855; vice-president of Board of Trade and paymaster-general, 1866; under-secretary for colonies, 1868–70; postmaster-general,

1871–3; raised to peerage, 1874; vice-chancellor of Royal University of Ireland, 1885.

MONSEY, Messenger (1693–1788), physician; BA, Pembroke College, Cambridge, 1714; LRCP, 1723; physician to Chelsea Hospital and chief medical adviser of the Whigs; eccentric and rough in his manner.

MONSON, Sir Edmund John, first baronet (1834–1909), diplomat; educated at Eton and Balliol College, Oxford; BA (first class in history), 1855; MA and fellow of All Souls, 1858; held various minor posts in Diplomatic Service, 1856–65; consul in Azores, 1869–71; consul-general at Budapest, 1871; British representative at Cetinje during war of Serbia and Montenegro with Turkey, 1876–7; CB, 1878; employed in Uruguay (1879–84), Buenos Aires (1884), Copenhagen (1884–8), Athens (1888), and Brussels (1892); KCMG, 1886; GCMG, 1892; ambassador at Vienna and PC, 1893, and Paris, 1896–1904; GCB, 1896; tactfully settled disputes with French in Newfoundland, New Hebrides, and East and West Africa; hon. DCL, Oxford, 1898, LL D, Cambridge, 1905; GCVO, 1903; baronet, 1905; received grand cross of Legion of Honour.

MONSON, George (1730–1776), Indian officer and opponent of Warren *Hastings; son of Sir John *Monson, first Baron Monson; entered the army, 1750; lieutenant, 1754; MP, Lincoln, 1754–68; groom of the bedchamber to George, prince of Wales, 1756; major, 1757; went to India, 1758; distinguished himself at Pondicherry, 1760, and Manila, 1762; brigadier-general, 1763; colonel and aide-de-camp to George III, 1769; one of the Supreme Council of Bengal, 1773; united with *Clavering and *Francis against Warren Hastings; died in India.

MONSON, Sir John, second baronet (1600–1683), Royalist; son of Sir Thomas *Monson; studied law; MP, Lincoln, 1625; KB, 1626; undertook to reclaim some of the fens, 1638; succeeded to baronetcy, 1641; DCL, Oxford, 1642; negotiated surrender of Oxford to *Fairfax, 1646; signed the engagement to the Commonwealth, 1652; refused to pay decimation tax, 1655; imprisoned in his own house, 1655–7; endowed a free school in South Carlton, and a hospital in Burton; published religious works.

MONSON, Sir John, first Baron Monson (1693–1748), educated at Christ Church, Oxford; MP for Lincoln, 1722 and 1727; KB, 1725; succeeded to baronetcy, 1727; created Baron Monson of Burton, 1728; commissioner of trade and plantations and privy councillor, 1737.

MONSON, John, second Baron Monson (1727–1774), son of Sir John *Monson, first Baron Monson; created LL D, Cambridge, 1749; warden and chief justice in eyre of the forests south of the Trent, 1765; resigned with Portland.

MONSON, Robert (d. 1583), judge; educated at Cambridge; barrister, Lincoln's Inn, 1550; MP, Dunheved, 1553 and 1558, Looe, 1554, Newport-juxta-Launceston, 1554, Lincoln, 1559 and 1563, Totnes, 1572; serjeant-at-law and justice of the common pleas, 1572; a commissioner for examination of Anabaptists, 1575.

MONSON, Sir Thomas, first baronet (1564–1641), master of the armoury at the Tower of London; brother of Sir William *Monson (1569–1643); educated at Magdalen College, Oxford, knighted, 1588; MP, Lincolnshire, 1597, Castle Rising, 1603, Cricklade, 1614; created MA, Oxford, 1605; master falconer; keeper of the armoury at Greenwich; master of the armoury at the Tower of London, 1611; created baronet, 1611; accused of complicity in the *Overbury poisoning case, 1615; remained in the Tower of London till 1617; clerk for the king's bills before the Council of the North, 1625.

MONSON, Sir William (1569–1643), admiral; brother of Sir Thomas *Monson; matriculated from Balliol College, Oxford, 1581; went to sea, 1585; lieutenant, 1588; commanded the *Margaret* in the voyage to the Azores and the Canaries, 1589; prisoner in Spain, 1591–3; distinguished himself in Cadiz expedition and was knighted by *Essex, 1596; commanded in the narrow seas and the Downs; vice-admiral of squadron sent to intercept a Spanish treasure fleet, 1602; admiral of the narrow seas, 1604; enforced proclamation prohibiting nations from offering violence one to another within the compass of a line drawn from headland to headland, 1605; arrested Lady *Arabella Stuart as she was escaping to France, 1611; suppressed the pirates of Broad Haven in Ireland, 1614; suspected of complicity in the *Overbury murder, 1615, and in consequence deprived of his command; vice-admiral of the fleet under *Lindsey, which restored the sovereignty of the narrow seas to the English, 1635; author of *Naval Tracts*.

MONSON, Sir William, first Viscount Monson of Castlemaine (d. 1672?), regicide; son of Sir Thomas *Monson; created Viscount Monson of Castlemaine (Irish peerage), 1628; knighted, 1633; MP, Reigate, 1640; nominated one of the king's judges, but only attended three sittings; sentenced by Parliament to degradation from his honours and titles and to be imprisoned for life, 1661; died in the Fleet.

MONSON, William (1760–1807), Indian officer; son of John *Monson, second Baron Monson; went to India with his regiment, 1780; captain, 1785; served against Tippoo, sultan of Mysore; major, 1795; lieutenant-colonel, 1797; obliged to retreat before the Mahratta chief, 1804, but employed in the final operations against him; MP, Lincoln, 1806.

MONT (MOUNT, MUNDT, or MONTABOR-INUS), Christopher (d. 1572), English agent in Germany; entered *Cromwell's service, 1531; sent to Germany to report on the political situation, 1533; continued to act as agent in Germany during Edward VI's reign; recalled under Queen Mary; regained his position on Queen Elizabeth's accession; died at Strasburg.

MONT, William du (d. 1213), theologian. See WILLIAM DE LEICESTER.

MONTACUTE, Baron (1492?–1539). See POLE, HENRY.

MONTACUTE (or MONTAGU), John de, third earl of Salisbury (1350?–1400), nephew of William de *Montacute, second earl of Salisbury; knighted before Bourdeille, 1369; held a command in Ireland, 1394–5; privy councillor; advocated Richard II's marriage with *Isabella of France, 1396; succeeded as earl of Salisbury, 1397; KG; commissioner for discharging the functions of parliament, 1398; deputy marshal of England for three years, 1398; joint ambassador to France, 1398; accompanied Richard II to Ireland, 1399; accused on Henry IV's accession of complicity in *Gloucester's death; entered into a conspiracy, 1400, and beheaded at Cirencester by the anti-Lollard mob; author of ballads and songs, not now extant.

MONTACUTE, Nicholas (fl. 1466), historian; wrote accounts in verse of the popes, and of the kings and bishops of England, the first only extant.

MONTACUTE, Simon de, first Baron Montacute (d. 1317), served in the Welsh wars, 1277 and 1282; broke through the French fleet blockading Bordeaux, 1296; summoned to an assembly of the lay estates at York, 1298; served in the Scottish wars; signed the barons' letter to the pope, 1301; governor of Beaumaris Castle, 1308; admiral of the fleet, 1310; employed against the Scots, 1310; guarded the northern frontier, 1315–16.

MONTACUTE, Simon de (d. 1345), son of William de *Montacute, second Baron Montacute; studied at Oxford; archdeacon of Canterbury; bishop of Worcester, 1334, of Ely, 1337.

MONTACUTE (or MONTAGUE), Thomas de, fourth earl of Salisbury (1388–1428), son of John de *Montacute, third earl of Salisbury; KG, 1414; joint commissioner to treat with France concerning Henry V's rights, 1414; served against France in command of the rear division of Henry V's army, and was appointed lieutenant-general of Normandy and created earl of Perche, 1419; besieged Meulan, Frénay, and Melun, 1420; marched into Maine and Anjou, 1421; governor of Champagne and Brie, 1422; distinguished himself in the relief of Crevant, 1423, and the siege of Montaguillon, which latter surrendered, 1424; completed the subjugation of Champagne and Maine, 1425; went to England to obtain reinforcements and petition for the payment of arrears, 1427; returned to France, 1428; after gaining many victories besieged Orleans, 1428; died at Meung of injuries received from a cannon ball at Tourelles.

MONTACUTE, William de, second Baron Montacute (d. 1319), son of Simon de *Montacute, first Baron Montacute; served continually against the Scots; commanded an expedition into Wales, 1316; seneschal of Aquitaine and Gascony, 1318; died in Gascony.

MONTACUTE (or MONTAGU), William de, third Baron Montacute and first earl of Salisbury (1301–1344), son of William de *Montacute, second Baron Montacute; knighted, 1325; accompanied Edward III to Scotland, 1327, and abroad, 1329; assisted in arrest of *Mortimer, 1330; rewarded with some of Mortimer's forfeited lands; present at the siege of Berwick and Battle of Halidon Hill, 1333; left in command with Arundel, 1335; blockaded Dunbar Castle and concluded a truce in Scotland, 1336; created earl of Salisbury, 1337; sent to declare Edward III's claim to the French crown and to organize a league against France, 1337; marshal of England, 1338; served in Flanders and taken prisoner to Paris, 1340; conquered and was crowned king of the Isle of Man, 1341; sent on an embassy to Carlisle, 1343; benefactor of the church.

MONTACUTE (or MONTAGU), William de, second earl of Salisbury (1328–1397), son of William de *Montacute, first earl of Salisbury; served in France and was knighted, 1346; KG, 1350; constable of Edward III's army in France, 1354; distinguished himself at Poitiers, 1356; served in France, 1357, 1359, 1360, and 1369; commander to guard the coast, 1373; joint commissioner to treat for peace with France, 1375; captain against the rebels in Somerset and Dorset, 1381; commissioner to treat with France, 1389 and 1392.

MONTAGU, Baron (1492?–1538). See POLE, HENRY.

MONTAGU, marquis of (d. 1471). See NEVILLE, JOHN.

MONTAGU (or **MONTAGUE**), first Viscount (1526–1592). See BROWNE, ANTHONY.

MONTAGU, Basil (1770–1851), legal and miscellaneous writer; of Charterhouse and Christ's College, Cambridge; MA, 1793; an intimate of *Coleridge and *Wordsworth at Cambridge; barrister, Gray's Inn, 1798; commissioner in bankruptcy, 1806; KC, 1835; accountant-general in bankruptcy, 1835; suggested radical reform in the existing bankruptcy procedure, and wrote on bankruptcy; published *Essays* and pamphlets; edited *Bacon, 1825–37; died at Boulogne.

MONTAGU, Charles, first duke of Manchester (1660?–1722), diplomat; son of Robert *Montagu, third earl of Manchester; educated at Trinity College, Cambridge, and abroad; succeeded to title and estates, 1683; raised troop for prince of Orange; fought in Ireland, 1690; ambassador-extraordinary at Venice, 1697, Paris, 1699, Venice again, 1707.

MONTAGU, Charles, first earl of Halifax (1661–1715), brother of Sir James *Montagu; educated at Westminster School and Trinity College, Cambridge, where he formed friendship with Sir Isaac *Newton; MA and fellow of Trinity College, Cambridge; high steward of Cambridge University, 1697; PRS, 1695–8; MP, Maldon, 1689–95; clerk of the Privy Council, 1689; a lord of the Treasury, 1692; the national debt originated by his proposal (1692) to raise a million by life annuities; introduced bill establishing the Bank of England, which became law, 1694; chancellor of the Exchequer and privy councillor, 1694; MP, Westminster, 1695; supported bill for regulating trials in cases of high treason; introduced Recoinage Bill, 1695; issued the first Exchequer bills to provide credit for the government when the old coins had been withdrawn; carried his scheme for the formation of a consolidated fund to meet the interest on the various government loans, 1696; first lord of the Treasury, 1697; resigned his offices of chancellor of the Exchequer and first lord of the Treasury, 1699; auditor of the Exchequer, 1700; created Baron Halifax of Halifax, 1700; impeached by the House of Commons, 1701, on account of grants obtained from William III in the names of Railton, Seager, and Montagu, in trust for himself, and for advising and promoting the conclusion of the second Partition Treaty, but his impeachment dismissed for want of prosecution; resisted Occasional Conformity Bill, 1703; next charged (1703) with neglect of his duties as auditor of the Exchequer; continued out of office during Anne's reign; first lord of the Treasury on George I's accession; created KG and Viscount Sunbury and earl of Halifax, 1714; lord-lieutenant of Surrey.

MONTAGU, Sir **Edward** (d. 1557), judge; educated at Cambridge; barrister, Middle Temple; serjeant-at-law, 1531; knighted, 1537; chief justice of the King's Bench, 1539; assisted in the examination of the duchess of *Norfolk, 1541; transferred to the common pleas, 1545; member of the Council of Regency appointed by Henry VIII's will; drafted the clauses in Edward VI's will in favour of Lady Jane *Grey, for which he was fined £1,000 on Queen Mary's accession.

MONTAGU, Edward, first Baron Montagu of Boughton (1562–1644), grandson of Sir Edward *Montagu; BA, Christ Church, Oxford, 1579; student of the Middle Temple, 1580; MP, Brackley, 1601, Northamptonshire, 1603–4, 1614, 1620–1–2; KB, 1603; created Baron Montagu of Boughton, 1621; imprisoned as a Royalist in the Tower of London, 1642; died in the Tower of London.

MONTAGU, Edward, second earl of Manchester (1602–1671), son of Sir Henry *Montagu, first earl of Manchester; of Sidney Sussex College, Cambridge; MP, Huntingdon, 1623 and 1625; KB and created Baron Montagu of Kimbolton, but known as Viscount Mandeville on his father being created earl of Manchester, 1626; took command of a foot regiment in *Essex's army, 1642; lord-lieutenant of Huntingdonshire and Northamptonshire, 1642; succeeded as earl of Manchester, 1642; major-general of the associated counties, 1643; joined *Cromwell and *Fairfax in winning Horncastle fight and Lincoln, 1643; directed to 'regulate' the university of Cambridge, 1644; secured Lincolnshire for the parliament, 1644; marched to Fairfax's assistance at York, 1644; palpably negligent at the second Battle of Newbury, 1644; charged by Cromwell in the House of Commons with neglect and incompetency in the prosecution of the war, 1644; resigned his commission, 1645; opposed the ordinance for the king's trial, 1649; retired from public life when the formation of a commonwealth became inevitable; chancellor of the University of Cambridge, 1649–51; welcomed Charles II; one of the commissioners of the great seal, 1660; restored to his lord-lieutenancy and chancellorship, 1660; privy councillor and lord chamberlain, 1660; inclined to leniency on the trial of the regicides, 1660; KG, 1661; made a general when the Dutch appeared in the Channel, 1667; FRS, 1665.

MONTAGU, Edward, second Baron Montagu of Boughton (1616–1684), son of Edward

*Montagu, first Baron Montagu; of Sidney Sussex College, Cambridge; MP, Huntingdon, 1640; treated for the surrender of Newark, 1646; conducted Charles I to Holmby House and attended him till his escape, 1647.

MONTAGU (or MOUNTAGU), Edward, first earl of Sandwich (1625–1672), admiral and general at sea; raised foot regiment in Cambridgeshire and joined Parliamentarian army, 1643; distinguished himself at Naseby, 1645, and the storming of Bristol, 1645; member of the Council of State, 1653; conjoint general at sea with *Blake, 1656; commanded in the Downs, 1657; supported Richard *Cromwell, but on his fall listened to overtures from Charles II; resigned his command, 1659, but was reappointed jointly with *Monck, 1660; sailed to Holland to convey Charles II to England; nominated KG and created Viscount Hinchinbroke and earl of Sandwich, 1660; admiral of the narrow seas, lieutenant-admiral to the duke of York and master of the wardrobe, 1660; negotiated the marriage between Charles II and *Catherine of Braganza, receiving the surrender of Tangier and conducting the queen to England, 1661; distinguished himself in a battle with the Dutch fleet off Lowestoft, 1664; captured some Dutch East Indiamen, 1665, and fell into general disfavour by his manner of dealing with the cargo; ambassador-extraordinary to Madrid, concluding a treaty with Spain, 1666; president of the Council of Trade and Plantations, 1670; second-in-command of the English Fleet on the outbreak of the Dutch War, 1672; blown up in his ship when the fleet were surprised by the Dutch in Solebay, 1672; his body found near Harwich and buried in Westminster Abbey; Samuel *Pepys was his secretary.

MONTAGU, Edward (1635–1665), son of Edward *Montagu, second Baron Montagu; of Westminster School, Christ Church, Oxford, and Sidney Sussex College, Cambridge; created MA Oxford, 1661; MP, Sandwich, 1661–5; killed at Bergen.

MONTAGU, Edward (1755–1799), Indian officer; son of John *Montagu (1719–1795); went out to Bengal, 1770; lieutenant-fireworker, 1772; first lieutenant, 1777; served in the Mahratta campaign, 1781, and in the Carnatic, 1782; captain, 1784; took prominent part in invasion of Mysore, 1791; lieutenant-colonel, 1794; commanded the Bengal Artillery at Seringapatam, where he was shot.

MONTAGU, Edward Wortley (1713–1776), author and traveller; son of Lady Mary Wortley *Montagu; was sent to Westminster School, from which he ran away several times, and then to the continent in charge of a keeper; studied Arabic and European languages; cornet in *Cope's (7th) Dragoons, 1743; captain-lieutenant, Royal Scots, 1745; MP, Huntingdon, 1747; secretary at the Congress of Aix-la-Chapelle, 1748; MP, Bossiney, 1754–62; travelled in Italy, 1762, and Egypt and the Holy Land; returned to Italy, 1775, and died at Padua; published *Reflections on the Rise and Fall of the Antient Republics* (1759), a historical didactical essay.

MONTAGU, Edwin Samuel (1879–1924), statesman; son of first Baron *Swaythling; BA, Trinity College, Cambridge; president of Union, 1902; Liberal MP, Chesterton division, Cambridgeshire, 1906–22; private secretary to Asquith, 1906–10; parliamentary under-secretary of state for India, 1910–14; financial secretary to Treasury, 1914–16; chancellor of duchy of Lancaster with seat in Cabinet, 1915; minister of munitions, 1916; resigned, Dec. 1916; secretary of state for India, June 1917–March 1922; his first task, declaration of goal of British policy regarding constitutional change in India, namely 'progressive realization of responsible government' in India, Aug. 1917; toured provinces of India with small delegation, Nov. 1917–May 1918; outcome of this delegation, drafting of *Report on Indian Constitutional Reforms* (1918); handled his problems with elasticity and resilience, and by pertinacity, drive, and determination rallied bulk of opinion to his scheme, which passed into law as Government of India Act, 1919; central feature, extension of self-government operating through 'dyarchy'; forced to resign owing to divergences with his colleagues over Turkish policy.

MONTAGU, Mrs Elizabeth (1720–1800), authoress and leader of society; née Robinson; married Edward Montagu, grandson of the first earl of Sandwich, 1742; sought to make her husband's house 'the central point of union' for all the intellect and fashion of the metropolis, 1750; held evening assemblies, at which literary topics were discussed; the epithet 'blue stocking' applied to her; lost her husband, 1775; built a mansion at Sandleford after plans by *Wyatt, 1781, and Montagu House at the corner of Portman Square, London, designed by James ('Athenian') *Stuart, where she entertained George III and his queen, 1791; she contributed three dialogues to *Lyttleton's *Dialogues of the Dead* (1760), and attacked Voltaire in *An Essay on the Writings and Genius of Shakespear* (1769); four volumes of her letters published by her nephew (1809 and 1813).

MONTAGU, Ewen Edward Samuel (1901–1985), judge and deception planner; elder brother of Ivor *Montagu; educated at Westminster School, Harvard, and Trinity College, Cambridge, 1920–3; called to bar (Middle Temple), 1924; practised on Western circuit, 1924–39; QC, 1939; commissioned in Royal Naval Volunteer Reserve, 1939; ran NID 17(M), sub-branch of naval intelligence division of Admiralty, 1941–5; responsible for Operation Mincemeat, a plot to mislead the Abwehr as to the landing-place for invasion of Italy, 1943; judge advocate of the fleet, 1945–73; recorder of Devizes, 1944–51; recorder of Southampton, 1951–60; deputy lieutenant, Hampshire, 1953; chairman, quarter-sessions for Middlesex, 1965–9; bencher, Middle Temple, 1948; treasurer, 1968; published *The Man Who Never Was* (1953, made into film, 1955), and *Beyond Top Secret U* (1977); president, United Synagogue, 1954–62; OBE, 1944; CBE, 1950; Order of the Crown of Yugoslavia, 1943.

MONTAGU, Frederick (1733–1800), politician; of Eton and Trinity College, Cambridge; barrister, Lincoln's Inn, 1757; bencher, 1782; MP, Northampton, 1759–67, Higham Ferrers, 1768–90; lord of the Treasury, 1782 and 1783; member of the committee which prepared the articles of Warren *Hastings's impeachment, 1787; privy councillor, 1790; retired from public life, 1790.

MONTAGU, George, second earl of Halifax (1716–1771). See DUNK.

MONTAGU, George, fourth duke of Manchester (1737–1788), MP, Huntingdonshire, 1761; succeeded to dukedom, 1762; appointed lord-lieutenant of the county and collector of the subsidies of tonnage and poundage in London, 1762; lord of the bedchamber, 1763–70; sided with the colonies in the disputes preceding the American War of Independence, but opposed the Roman Catholic Relief Bill of 1778; lord chamberlain and privy councillor, 1782; named ambassador to France to treat for peace, 1783; resisted Pitt's commercial treaty, 1786.

MONTAGU, Sir George (1750–1829), admiral; son of John *Montagu (1719–1795); lieutenant in navy, 1771; commander, 1773; served with distinction on the North American Station; rear-admiral, 1794; unsuccessfully attempted to intercept the French provision convoy, 1794; vice-admiral, 1795; admiral, 1801; commander-in-chief at Portsmouth, 1803; GCB, 1815.

MONTAGU, George (1751–1815), writer on natural history; captain in the army during the war with the American colonies; devoted himself at Easton Grey to scientific study; chief works, *The Sportsman's Directory* (1792), *Ornithological Dictionary* (1802), and *Testacea Britannica* (1803).

MONTAGU (formerly BRUDENELL), George Brudenell, duke of Montagu of a new creation, and fourth earl of Cardigan (1712–1790), succeeded his father as fourth earl of Cardigan, 1732; on the death of his father-in-law, John *Montagu, second duke of Montagu, 1749, took name and arms of Montagu; KG, 1762; received dukedom of Montagu, 1766; appointed governor to the prince of Wales, 1776; master of the horse, 1776; governor of Windsor Castle; privy councillor and lord-lieutenant of Huntingdon.

MONTAGU, Sir Henry, first earl of Manchester (1563?–1642), judge and statesman; of Christ's College, Cambridge; barrister, Middle Temple; MP, Higham Ferrers, 1593, 1597–8, London, 1604 and 1614; recorder of London and knighted, 1603; KC, 1607; serjeant-at-law and king's serjeant, 1611; opened case against earl and countess of Somerset (see CARR, ROBERT, earl of Somerset), 1616; as chief justice of the King's Bench condemned Sir Walter *Ralegh, 1618; lord high treasurer of England, 1620; created Baron Montagu of Kimbolton and Viscount Mandeville, 1620; appointed master of the court of wards and placed at the head of the Virginian Commission, 1624; created earl of Manchester, 1626; on the legislative council for the colonies, 1634; a commissioner of the Treasury, 1635; one of the guardians of the realm during Charles I's absence, 1641; published *Contemplatio Mortis et Immortalitatis* (1631); high steward of Cambridge University, 1634–42.

MONTAGU, Ivor Goldsmid Samuel (1904–1984), film producer and writer; educated at Westminster School, Royal College of Science, London, and King's College, Cambridge; published *Table Tennis Today* (1924); founded English Table Tennis Association and the Film Society; wrote film reviews for the *Observer*; directed films *Bluebottles* (1928), *Daydreams* (1929), and *The Tonic* (1930); visited USSR and joined British Communist party; met Russian film director Sergei Eisenstein and assisted him in Hollywood; worked as associate producer for (Sir) Michael *Balcon on five British feature films, including *The Thirty-Nine Steps* (1935); produced left-wing documentary films; during 1939–45 war worked on editorial staff of the *Daily Worker* and produced for the Central Office of Information *Man, One Family* (1946); co-wrote *Scott of the Antarctic* (1948); worked for the Peace Movement; awarded Lenin Peace Prize, 1959; published autobiographical *Film World* (1964), *With Eisenstein in Hollywood* (1968), and *The Youngest Son* (1970).

MONTAGU (or MOUNTAGUE), James (1568?–1618), bishop of Winchester; brother of Sir Henry *Montagu, first earl of Manchester; of Christ's College, Cambridge; first master of Sidney Sussex College, Cambridge, 1595; dean of Lichfield, 1603; dean of Worcester, 1604; bishop of Bath and Wells, 1608–16; bishop of Winchester, 1616; edited and translated the works of James I (1616).

MONTAGU, Sir James (1666–1723), judge; MA, Trinity College, Cambridge, 1698; barrister, Middle Temple; MP, Tregony, 1695, Beeralston, 1698, Carlisle, 1705–13; knighted, 1705; QC, 1705; solicitor-general, 1707; attorney-general, 1708–10; first baron of the Exchequer, 1722.

MONTAGU, James (1752–1794), navy captain; son of John *Montagu (1719–1795); lieutenant, 1771; commander, 1773; carried home despatches announcing capture of Rhode Island, 1776; served in Channel and East Indies, 1782, and with the Grand Fleet, 1793–4; killed in the battle off Ushant.

MONTAGU, John (1655?–1728), divine; son of Edward *Montagu, first earl of Sandwich; educated at Trinity College, Cambridge; MA, *jure natalium*, 1673; DD, *per literas regias*, 1682; fellow, 1674; master of Sherburn Hospital, Durham, 1680; prebendary of Durham, 1683; master of Trinity College, Cambridge, 1683; vice-chancellor of Cambridge University, 1687; dean of Durham, 1699.

MONTAGU, John, second duke of Montagu (1688?–1749), courtier; son of Ralph *Montagu, first duke of Montagu; succeeded as second duke, 1709; KG, 1719; was granted the islands of St Vincent and St Lucia, 1722, but failed in his attempt to establish a footing; grand master of the Order of the Bath, 1725; master-general of the ordnance, 1740; raised regiment of horse ('Montagu's Carabineers'), 1745 (disbanded after Culloden).

MONTAGU, John, fourth earl of Sandwich (1718–1792), educated at Eton and Trinity College, Cambridge; toured on the continent and in the East, 1737–9; FRS, 1740; lord commissioner of the Admiralty, 1744; appointed captain in duke of *Bedford's foot regiment; aide-de-camp and colonel in the army, 1745; plenipotentiary at Breda, 1746, and at Aix-la-Chapelle, 1748; first lord of the Admiralty, 1748; with *Anson's help detected abuses and instituted stringent reforms; dismissed, 1751; again nominated first lord of the Admiralty and one of the principal secretaries of state, 1763; his reputation permanently sullied by the part he took in the prosecution of *Wilkes; postmaster-general, 1768; returned to his post at

the Admiralty, 1771, and began to employ the vast patronage of the office as an engine for bribery and political jobbery, in consequence of which, when war broke out, 1778, the navy was found inadequate and the naval storehouses empty; Sandwich Islands named after him; retired from public life on the fall of the North administration, 1782.

MONTAGU, John (1719–1795), admiral; lieutenant in the navy, 1741; commander, 1745; rear-admiral, 1770; commander-in-chief on the North American Station, 1771–4; vice-admiral and commander-in-chief at Newfoundland, 1776; admiral of the blue, 1782; commander-in-chief at Portsmouth, 1783–6; admiral of the red, 1787.

MONTAGU, John (1797–1853), colonial official; son of Edward *Montagu (1755–1799); ensign, 1814; lieutenant, 1815; captain, 1822; private secretary, 1824–7, to (Sir) George *Arthur when lieutenant-governor of Van Diemen's Land; was clerk of excise and legislative councils, 1827–9; colonial treasurer, 1832; colonial secretary, 1834; suspended from office owing to difference with the governor, Sir John *Franklin, 1842; colonial secretary at Cape of Good Hope, 1843 till death; left colony owing to ill health, 1851; died in London. He greatly improved the financial condition of Cape Colony.

MONTAGU, Lady Mary Wortley (1689–1762), writer of *Letters*; daughter of Evelyn *Pierrepont, afterwards fifth earl and first duke of Kingston; taught herself Latin at an early age; married (1712) Edward Wortley *Montagu, MP for Huntingdon, commissioner (1714–15) of the Treasury, and ambassador to Constantinople, 1716; went to Constantinople with her husband, and on her return to England (1718) introduced the practice of inoculation for smallpox; became a leader of society; quarrelled with *Pope, who had professed a special admiration for her; her favour courted by *Young; on good terms with Sarah, duchess of *Marlborough; went to Italy, 1739; settled in Avignon, 1742; moved to Brescia, 1746; finally settled at Venice; returned to England on her husband's death, 1761; author of *Town Eclogues*, privately published as *Court Poems* (1716), and *Letters from the East*, posthumously published.

MONTAGU, Ralph, first duke of Montagu (1638?–1709), son of Edward *Montagu, second Baron Montagu of Boughton; master of the horse to the duchess of *York; ambassador-extraordinary to Louis XIV, 1669; purchased the mastership of the great wardrobe, 1671; privy councillor, 1672; again ambassador-extraordinary to Louis XIV, 1676; unsuccessfully intrigued for the post of secretary of state; being denounced by the duchess of *Cleveland, returned to England without permission, to find himself struck out of the Privy Council (1678) and superseded as ambassador; negotiated with the French ambassador, offering to procure *Danby's fall within six months; his papers seized; produced two letters, which were voted as sufficient ground for Danby's impeachment, 1678; escaped arrest after the dissolution of parliament, 1678; unsuccessfully endeavoured to get *Monmouth declared prince of Wales; retired to France, 1680; succeeded as Baron Montagu, 1684, and returned to England on the accession of James II; took up William's cause at the Revolution; privy councillor and created Viscount Monthermer and earl of Montagu, 1689; the mastership of the wardrobe restored to him; several lawsuits concerning the Albemarle property caused by his marriage with Elizabeth Cavendish, widow of Christopher *Monck, second duke of Albemarle, 1692; became marquis of Monthermer and duke of Montagu, 1705.

MONTAGU (or MOUNTAGUE), Richard (1577–1641), controversialist and bishop; of Eton and King's College, Cambridge; MA, 1602; BD, 1609; assisted Sir Henry *Savile in his literary work; fellow of Eton, 1613; dean of Hereford, 1616; exchanged deanery for a canonry of Windsor, 1617; archdeacon of Hereford and chaplain to James I, 1617; prepared an answer to Baronius, issued as *Analecta Ecclesiasticarum Exercitationum* (1622); published *Diatribæ upon the first part of the late History of Tithes* (1621); answered Matthew *Kellison's *Gag for the New Gospel* with *A New Gagg* (1624), in *Appello Caesarem* (1625); vindicated his teaching from the charge of Arminianism and popery; committed to the custody of the serjeant-at-arms in consequence of a hot debate in the House of Commons; his punishment petitioned for by the House of Commons; appointed by Charles I bishop of Chichester, 1628; a bitter pamphlet against him addressed to the House of Commons, 1629; endeavoured to recover the alienated estates of his diocese; diligent in procuring obedience to church discipline; published a book on the Eucharistic Sacrifice (1638); according to Panzani, considered reunion with the Roman Church quite possible; bishop of Norwich, 1638.

MONTAGU, Robert, third earl of Manchester (1634–1683), son of Edward *Montagu, second earl of Manchester; MP, Huntingdonshire, 1660 and 1661; sent on a mission to France, 1663; gentleman of the bedchamber, 1666; died at Montpellier.

MONTAGU, Lord Robert (1825–1902), politician and controversialist; MA, Trinity College, Cambridge, 1849; Conservative MP for Huntingdonshire, 1859–74; champion of church rates and trade unions; vice-president of the Committee of Council on Education, charity commissioner, and PC, 1867; criticized Education Bill of 1870; Conservative home rule MP for Westmeath 1874–80; condemned Conservative policy in Afghan War; joined Church of Rome, 1870, but rejoined English Church on ethical and political grounds, 1882, and attacked Romanists in published volumes.

MONTAGU, Samuel, first Baron Swaythling (1832–1911), foreign-exchange banker and Jewish philanthropist; founded with brother and brother-in-law the foreign-exchange and banking firm of Samuel Montagu & Co., 1853; acquired large exchange business and helped to make London the clearing house of the international money market; engaged in large transactions in silver; Liberal MP for Whitechapel, 1885–1900; chief author of Weights and Measures Act, 1897; ardent supporter of bimetallism; member of Select Committee on Alien Immigration, 1888; took leading part in Jewish religious, social, and charitable work; founded Jewish Working Men's Club, 1870; formed federation of smaller East End synagogues, 1887; gave to London County Council £10,000 for Tottenham housing scheme, 1903; travelled abroad in interests of oppressed Jews; visited Russia to investigate condition of Jews (1886), but was expelled; president of Russo-Jewish Committee, 1896–1909; collector of works of art and of old English silver; FSA, 1897; baronet, 1894; baron, 1907.

MONTAGU, Walter (1603?–1677), abbot of St Martin near Pontoise; son of Sir Henry *Montagu, first earl of Manchester; educated at Sidney Sussex College, Cambridge, and on the continent; employed by *Buckingham on a secret mission to France, 1624 and 1625; continued in secret service in France, 1627–33; became Roman Catholic, 1635; collected Catholic contributions to the Royalist army; imprisoned in the Tower of London, 1643–7; exiled, 1649; became abbot of St Martin near Pontoise; resigned in favour of Cardinal Bouillon at the request of the French government, 1670, but continued to enjoy the revenues; published a comedy, verses, and theological and political works.

MONTAGU, William (1619?–1706), judge; son of Edward *Montagu, first Baron Montagu of Boughton; educated at Sidney Sussex College, Cambridge; barrister, Middle Temple, 1641; MP, Huntingdon, 1640; Cambridge University, 1660; attorney-general to Charles II's queen, 1662; serjeant-at-law and lord chief baron of the Exchequer, 1676; removed from the bench on his refusal to give an unqualified opinion in favour of the prerogative of dispensation, 1686; assessor to the convention, 1689.

MONTAGU, William (1720?–1757), naval captain; brother of John *Montagu, fourth earl of Sandwich; lieutenant, 1740; commander, 1744; distinguished in the action of 3 May 1747; MP, Huntingdon, 1745, Bossiney, 1752.

MONTAGU, William, fifth duke of Manchester (1768–1843), governor of Jamaica; son of George *Montagu, fourth duke of Manchester; gazetted lieutenant, 1787; colonel in the army, 1794; lord-lieutenant of Huntingdonshire, 1793; governor of Jamaica, 1808; reforms made in the law courts and post office during his governorship, 1814; alleviated the distress caused by the hurricane and floods, 1815; the Jamaica slaves pacified by his personal influence during the insurrection of the slaves in Barbados; returned to England, 1827; postmaster-general, 1827–30; voted against the Reform Bill; died in Rome.

MONTAGU-DOUGLAS-SCOTT, Lord **Charles Thomas** (1839–1911), admiral. See SCOTT.

MONTAGU-DOUGLAS-SCOTT, Lord **Francis George** (1879–1952), soldier, Kenya farmer, and political leader. See SCOTT.

MONTAGUE. See also MONTAGU.

MONTAGUE, Baron (1492?–1539). See POLE, HENRY.

MONTAGUE, Charles Edward (1867–1928), man of letters and journalist; BA, Balliol College, Oxford; on staff of *Manchester Guardian*, 1890–1914, 1919–25; second-in-command, 1898; a brilliant, many-sided journalist; made his mark as dramatic critic; served in European war, 1914–19; works include *A Hind Let Loose* (1910), *Disenchantment* (1922), *Fiery Particles* (1923), *The Right Place* (1924), *Rough Justice* (1926), *Action* (1928).

MONTAGUE, Francis Charles (1858–1935), historian; brother of C. E. *Montague; first class, Lit. Hum., Balliol College, Oxford, 1879; professor of history, University College, London, and lecturer at Oriel College, Oxford, 1893–1927.

MONTAGUE, Henry James (1843?–1878), actor; his real name Mann; held an appointment in the Sun Fire office; appeared in London at Astley's Theatre, 1863, the St James's, 1864, the Prince of Wales's, 1867, and the Princess's, 1868; partner in the Vaudeville, 1870–1; sole lessee of the Globe, 1871–4; excelled in juvenile parts; went to America and died at San Francisco.

MONTAGU OF BEAULIEU, second Baron (1866–1929), pioneer of motoring. See DOUGLAS-SCOTT-MONTAGU, JOHN WALTER EDWARD.

MONTAIGNE (or MOUNTAIN), George (1569–1628), archbishop of York; MA, Queens' College, Cambridge, 1593; fellow, 1591; attended *Essex as chaplain to Cadiz, 1596; professor of divinity at Gresham College, London, 1607; master of the Savoy and chaplain to James I, 1608; incumbent of Cheam, 1609; dean of Westminster, 1610; bishop of Lincoln, 1617; lord high almoner, 1619; bishop of London, 1621; enthusiastic supporter of *Laud; bishop of Durham, 1627; said to have secured the primacy of York by a witty remark, 1628. He founded two scholarships at Queens' College, Cambridge.

MONTALBA, Henrietta Skerrett (1856–1893), sculptor; first exhibited at the Royal Academy, 1876; devoted herself mainly to portrait or fancy busts, and worked mostly in terracotta; died at Venice.

MONTE, Robert de (1110?–1186), chronicler. See ROBERT.

MONTEAGE, Stephen (1623?–1687), merchant and accountant; agent to Christopher *Hatton, first Viscount Hatton; did much to bring double entry into general use; published books on double entry.

MONTEAGLE, Barons. See STANLEY, EDWARD, first baron, 1460?–1523; PARKER, WILLIAM, fourth baron, 1575–1622.

MONTEAGLE OF BRANDON, first Baron. See SPRING-RICE, THOMAS, 1790–1866.

MONTEATH, George Cunningham (1788–1828), physician and oculist; studied in Glasgow; licensed by the RCS; surgeon to Northumberland militia, 1809–13; physician and oculist in Glasgow; published *Manual of the Diseases of the Human Eye* (1821).

MONTEATH, Sir James (1847–1929), Indian civil servant; passed Indian Civil Service examination, 1868; appointed to Bombay presidency, 1870; chief secretary to government of Bombay, 1896; successfully dealt with Bombay famines, 1896–7 and 1899–1902; introduced Land Revenue Code Amendment Bill, which greatly benefited Bombay agriculturists, 1901; KCSI, 1903.

MONTEATH, Sir Thomas (1787–1868), general. See DOUGLAS, Sir THOMAS MONTEATH.

MONTEFIORE, Claude Joseph Goldsmid- (1858–1938), Jewish biblical scholar and philanthropist; first class, Lit. Hum., Balliol College, Oxford, 1881; joint editor, *Jewish Quarterly Review*, 1888–1908; joint-founder, Jewish

Religious Union for the Advancement of Liberal Judaism and Liberal Jewish Synagogue, London; president, Anglo-Jewish Association (1896–1921) and University College, Southampton (1915–34); works include *The Synoptic Gospels* (2 vols., 1909) and *Rabbinic Literature and Gospel Teachings* (1930).

MONTEFIORE, Sir Moses Haim, first baronet (1784–1885), philanthropist and centenarian; amassed a fortune as a stockbroker and retired, 1824; sheriff of London and knighted, 1837; secured a firman from the sultan placing Jews on the same footing as all other aliens, 1840; obtained abrogation of ukase for removal of Jews into the interior of Russia, 1846; received baronetcy, 1846; collected and distributed fund for relief of sufferers by Syrian famine, 1855; founded girls' school and hospital at Jerusalem, 1855; raised funds for the Jewish and Christian refugees at Gibraltar, 1860; obtained from the sultan of Morocco an edict giving equality to the Jews, 1864; interceded on behalf of the Moldavian Jews, 1867; visited Jerusalem for the seventh time, 1875; wrote a narrative of his visit for private circulation.

MONTEITH, Robert (*fl.* 1621–1660), author. See MENTEITH.

MONTEITH, William (1790–1864), lieutenant-general, Indian Army, diplomat, and historian; lieutenant in Madras Engineers, 1809; captain, 1817; colonel, 1839; accompanied Sir John *Malcolm's embassy to Persia, 1810; commanded against Russians, 1810–13; employed to ascertain the boundary between Persia and Turkey, 1821, and between Persia and Russia, 1828; left Persia, 1829; chief engineer at Madras, 1832; major-general, 1841; retired from service, 1847; lieutenant-general, 1854; wrote books on geography and the Russian campaigns of 1808–9 and 1826–8.

MONTEZ, Lola (1818–1861), adventuress. See GILBERT, MARIE DOLORES ELIZA ROSANNA.

MONTFICHET, Richard de (d. 1268), justiciar; one of the twenty-five barons appointed to enforce Magna Charta; justice-itinerant for Essex and Hertfordshire, 1225; baron of the Exchequer, 1234; justice of the forest for nineteen counties, 1237; sheriff of Essex and Hertfordshire, 1242–6.

MONTFORT, Almeric of (d. 1292?), son of Simon of *Montfort, earl of Leicester; canon and treasurer of York, 1265; lost these preferments on his father's fall, 1265; went to Italy, 1268; chaplain to the pope; assumed title of earl of Leicester, his brother Guy being an outlaw, 1272; refused permission to return to England, 1273; sued Edmund Mortimer, the treasurer of York,

before the official of Paris, 1274; captured at Bristol, 1276; imprisoned for six years and liberated on condition of abjuring the realm, 1282.

MONTFORT, Eleanor of (1252–1282), daughter of Simon of *Montfort, earl of Leicester; exiled to France, 1265; married by proxy to *Llywelyn ab Gruffydd, prince of Wales, 1275; captured and imprisoned till 1278; married to Llywelyn on his submission to Edward I, 1278.

MONTFORT, Guy of (1243?–1288?), son of Simon of *Montfort, earl of Leicester; shared command at Lewes, 1264; wounded and taken prisoner at Evesham, 1265; escaped to France, 1266; governor of Tuscany, 1268; with his brother Simon murdered *Henry of Cornwall at Viterbo, 1271, in revenge for his father's death; excommunicated and outlawed, 1273; bought his freedom, 1274; captain-general of the papal forces, 1283; captured at Catania, 1287; died in a Sicilian prison.

MONTFORT, Henry of (1238–1265), son of Simon of *Montfort, earl of Leicester; accompanied his father to Gascony, 1252; knighted by Prince Edward, 1260; represented barons at Mise of Amiens, 1264; commanded on Welsh border, 1264; seized Worcester, 1264; led van at Lewes, 1264; constable of Dover Castle, governor of the Cinque Ports, and treasurer of Sandwich, 1264; fought and fell at Evesham.

MONTFORT, Simon of, earl of Leicester (1208?–1265), son of Simon IV of Montfort l'Amaury (Normandy); born in Normandy; agreed with his elder brother Almeric to exchange his share in their continental patrimony for the earldom of Leicester, the heritage of their English grandmother; went to England, 1229; found that the estates had been given to the earl of *Chester, who, however, acknowledged Simon's right to them and petitioned the king to restore them, 1231; unable to support the rank and dignity of an earl, although he officiated as grand seneschal at the queen's coronation, 1236, an office belonging to the earldom of Leicester; married Eleanor, sister of Henry III, 1238; went to Rome to obtain the pope's dispensation, the marriage being an ecclesiastical offence, as Eleanor had taken a vow of perpetual widowhood; formally invested with the earldom of Leicester, 1239; quarrelled with Henry III concerning a debt, 1239; crusader, 1240; returned to Europe, 1242, and helped Henry III in Poitou; commissioner to answer the king's demand for money, 1244; induced (1248) to undertake the government of Gascony on condition of having absolute control; his high-handed severity, at first successful, followed by a rising in Gascony, 1251; besieged chief malcontents at Castillon and took the town, forcing the rebel leaders one by one to make their peace; after a second rising Henry III heard complaints against Simon at Westminster; he was accused of all sorts of oppression and violence; denied some of the charges and claimed that his severity was justified by the utter lawlessness of the Gascons; the accusers agreeing to no settlement, Simon was acquitted; returned to Gascony to find the truce broken and prepared to fight Gaston de Béarn, 1252; yielded to Henry III's demand that he should resign his governorship, 1252; withdrew to France; his help in quelling the revolt requested by Henry III, 1253; envoy to Scotland, 1254, to France, 1255, 1257, and 1258, and to Italy, 1257; one of the commissioners of administrative reform, who drew up the 'Provisions of Oxford', 1258; attacked by Henry III in council, 1260; withdrew to France, 1261, Henry having proclaimed his intention of ruling as he pleased; summoned to England as its leader by the parliament, which had denounced the king as false to his oath and proclaimed war on all violators of the 'Provisions', 1263; agreed with the other barons to refer the dispute to the arbitration of St Louis of France, whose decision, the 'Mise of Amiens' (1264), quashed the 'Provisions', but recognized popular rights; defeated the royalists and captured the king at the Battle of Lewes (14 May 1264); being the 'Mise of Lewes' virtually governor of the king and kingdom summoned (1264) a parliament (Jan. 1265), not only of churchmen, barons, and knights, but also two citizens from every borough in England; quarrelled with Gilbert de *Clare, the young (ninth) earl of Gloucester, who thereupon joined Prince Edward and the marcher lords; killed in the resulting battle at Evesham, 4 Aug. 1265. He was not the inventor of the representative system, nor the creator of the House of Commons, but a champion of righteousness rather than a reformer of government, a hero rather than a statesman.

MONTFORT, Simon of, the younger (1240–1271), son of Simon of *Montfort, earl of Leicester; knighted by Prince Edward, 1260; defended Northampton, 1264, but was captured by Henry III; released after Lewes (1264), but reached Evesham after the battle and withdrew to Kenilworth, 1265, where he was forced to submit; escaped over sea, 1266; took part with his brother Guy of *Montfort in the murder of *Henry of Cornwall at Viterbo, 1271; died at Siena.

MONTGOMERIE. See also MONTGOMERY.

MONTGOMERIE, Alexander (*fl.* 1568–1589), Scottish poet; brother of Robert *Montgomerie (d. 1609); held office in the Scottish court, 1577; styled captain; became laureate of the court; travelled on the continent, 1586; imprisoned abroad and his pension withheld, a protracted lawsuit resulting; wrote, besides miscellaneous poems, *The Cherrie and the Slae,* (first edition printed 1597), which has long been popular; his *Flyting betwixt Montgomery and Polwart* published by Andro *Hart (1621).

MONTGOMERIE (or SETON), Alexander, sixth earl of Eglinton (1588–1661), originally known as Sir Alexander Seton; succeeded his cousin Hugh, fifth earl of Eglinton, who, having no issue, made a resignation and settlement of the earldom and entail on him, provided he took the name and arms of Montgomerie, 1612 (confirmed by the king, 1615); petitioned against the Prayer-Book and assisted in the preparations of the National Covenant; privy councillor of Scotland, 1641; commanded Scottish regiment of horse for the English parliament; distinguished himself at Marston Moor, 1644; on the execution of Charles I supported the recall of Charles II and the policy of *Argyll; betrayed to *Cromwell, 1651; detained in Edinburgh Castle, but afterwards allowed the liberty of Berwick; his estates sequestered for two years; included in Cromwell's Act of Grace.

MONTGOMERIE, Alexander, ninth earl of Eglinton (1660?–1729), grandson of Hugh *Montgomerie, seventh earl of Eglinton; educated at St Andrews University; privy councillor and a lord of the Treasury under William III; succeeded as ninth earl, 1701; Scottish representative peer, 1710 and 1713; supported bill for resuming bishops' revenues in Scotland and applying them to the episcopal clergy; raised and disciplined the Ayrshire Fencibles, 1715.

MONTGOMERIE, Alexander, tenth earl of Eglinton (1723–1769), son of Alexander *Montgomerie, ninth earl of Eglinton; purchased the sheriffship of Renfrew, 1748; governor of Dumbarton Castle, 1759; lord of the bedchamber to George III; strongly opposed to the optional clause in the Scottish Bank Act and to the accumulation of the public debt; published *Inquiry into the Origin and Consequences of the Public Debt* (1754); representative peer for Scotland, 1761 and 1768; shot by Mungo Campbell, an excise officer, perhaps accidentally.

MONTGOMERIE, Sir Alexander de, of Ardrossan, first Baron Montgomerie (d. 1470?), grandson of Sir John *Montgomerie; privy councillor, 1425; joint-governor of Cantyre and Knapdale, 1430; commissioner to England and sent on various important embassies; keeper of Brodick Castle, 1444; lord of parliament, 1445.

MONTGOMERIE, Archibald, eleventh earl of Eglinton (1726–1796), son of Alexander *Montgomerie, ninth earl of Eglinton; raised regiment of Highlanders and was appointed lieutenant-colonel commandant, 1757; served in America; colonel, 1769; succeeded to earldom, 1769; lieutenant-general, 1777.

MONTGOMERIE, Archibald William, thirteenth earl of Eglinton and first earl of Winton in the peerage of the United Kingdom (1812–1861), born at Palermo; succeeded his grandfather, Hugh *Montgomerie, twelfth earl of Eglinton, 1819; lord-lieutenant of Ayrshire, 1842; one of the whips of the protection party, 1846; lord-lieutenant of Ireland, 1852; privy councillor, 1852 (Feb. to Dec.) and 1858–9; KT, 1853; created earl of Winton, 1859; held tournament at Eglinton Castle, 1839, described in Disraeli's *Endymion*; lord rector of Aberdeen and Glasgow, 1852; president of the Burns Commemoration, 1844; DCL, Oxford, 1853.

MONTGOMERIE, Hugh, third Baron Montgomerie and first earl of Eglinton (1460?–1545), grandson of Sir Alexander *Montgomerie, first Baron Montgomerie; was privy councillor, 1489; created earl of Eglinton, 1506; guardian of the infant *James V, 1513; justice-general of the northern parts of Scotland, 1527; one of the Council of Regency, 1536.

MONTGOMERIE, Hugh, third earl of Eglinton (1531?–1585), great-grandson of Hugh *Montgomerie, first earl of Eglinton; student of St Mary's College, St Andrews, 1552; visited *Mary Stuart in France and returned in her train, 1560; supported Mary's Roman Catholic policy; had no connection with *Darnley's murder; opposed Mary's marriage to *Bothwell; joined her after her escape from Lochleven; fought for her at Langside, 1568; subscribed his obedience to the regent, 1571; endeavoured to secure toleration for Romanists, 1573; privy councillor, 1578; subscribed order for prosecution of the Hamiltons, 1579; one of the assize for *Morton's trial, 1581; formally approved Ruthven raid, 1582.

MONTGOMERIE, Hugh, seventh earl of Eglinton (1613–1669), son of Alexander *Montgomerie, sixth earl of Eglinton; student of Glasgow University, 1628; opposed Charles I's ecclesiastical policy; colonel under *Leslie at Newburn; failed to seize Tynemouth, 1640; engaged in northern campaign under *Middleton, 1646; defeated by *Huntly at Aberdeen, 1646; disqualified for public service until 1650 for being accessory to the 'engagement'; taken prisoner, 1651; excepted from *Cromwell's Act of Grace, 1654.

MONTGOMERIE, Hugh, twelfth earl of Eglinton (1739–1819), captain in the army during the American War; major in the Western Fencibles, 1788; MP, Ayrshire, 1780–9; inspector of military roads in Scotland, 1789; colonel of West Lowland Fencibles, 1793; succeeded to earldom, 1796; representative peer of Scotland, 1798 and 1802; created Baron Ardrossan of Ardrossan in the United Kingdom, 1806; KT; lord-lieutenant of Ayrshire; commenced a harbour for Ardrossan, 1806; composed popular airs.

MONTGOMERIE, Sir John, ninth of Eaglesham and first of Eglinton and Ardrossan (d. 1398?), succeeded his father, c.1380; obtained baronies of Eglinton and Ardrossan by his marriage; distinguished himself at Otterburn, 1388.

MONTGOMERIE, Robert (d. 1609), titular archbishop of Glasgow; brother of Alexander *Montgomerie (1556?–1610?); minister at Cupar, 1562, Dunblane, 1567, and Stirling, 1572; presented to the archbishopric of Glasgow, 1581; censured and interdicted from taking the office by the general assembly; having entered Glasgow church with an armed force, was excommunicated by the Presbytery of Edinburgh; his excommunication was declared void by parliament, 1584; resigned bishopric, 1587; pastor of Symington, 1588, of Ayr, 1589.

MONTGOMERIE, Robert (d. 1684), Parliamentary and afterwards Royalist officer; son of Alexander *Montgomerie, sixth earl of Eglinton; educated at Glasgow University; fought at Marston Moor, 1644; commanded under *Middleton, 1646; joined western whigamores in march on Edinburgh, 1648; after the recall of Charles II, 1650, was employed on the Royalist side; fought as major-general and captured at Worcester, 1651; escaped from the Tower of London, 1654; arrested and confined in Edinburgh Castle; again escaped, 1657; lord of the bedchamber to Charles II; imprisoned for his Presbyterian sympathies, 1665–8.

MONTGOMERIE, Robert Archibald James (1855–1908), rear-admiral; entered navy, 1869; served in Egyptian War, 1882; in charge of naval transport in Nile expedition, 1885–6; commanded field battery in Vitu expedition, 1890; CB, 1892; conducted bombardment of Puerto Cabello, 1903; inspecting captain of boys' training ships, 1904; CMG, 1904; rear-admiral, 1905; CVO, 1907; champion heavyweight boxer of navy.

MONTGOMERIE, Thomas George (1830–1878), colonel, Royal Engineers, and geographer; second lieutenant, Bengal Engineers, 1849; assisted in surveying plain of Chach, 1853, and Karachi, 1854–5; first lieutenant, 1854; given charge of the trigo-topographical survey of Janin and Kashmir, 1855–64; captain, 1858; appointed to the Himalayan survey in Kumaon and Gurhwal, 1867; trained natives, who passed freely to and fro as traders, it being impossible for European officers to extend the survey without the risk of political complications; responsible for the survey of the route to Yarkand, 1863, and the discovery of the upper valley and source of the Brahmaputra; officiated as superintendent of the great trigonometrical survey of India, 1870–3; major, 1872; lieutenant-colonel, 1874; retired as colonel, 1876; FRS; contributed to scientific periodicals papers on the native explorers' travels and the geography of India.

MONTGOMERY, countess of. See CLIFFORD, ANNE, 1590–1676.

MONTGOMERY, earls of. See HERBERT, PHILIP, first earl, 1584–1650; HERBERT, HENRY, sixth earl, 1693–1751; HERBERT, HENRY, seventh earl, 1734–1794; HERBERT, GEORGE AUGUSTUS, eighth earl, 1759–1827; HERBERT, GEORGE ROBERT CHARLES, ninth earl, 1850–1895.

MONTGOMERY, Bernard Law, first Viscount Montgomery of Alamein (1887–1976), field marshal; grandson of Frederic Farrar, Dean of Canterbury and author of *Eric, or Little by Little*; educated at St Paul's School, London, and Royal Military College, Sandhurst; commissioned in 1st Royal Warwickshire Regiment and posted to North-West Frontier of India, 1908; returned to England, passed out top of musketry course and played hockey for army, 1912; during 1914–18 war served on Western Front, was seriously wounded at first Battle of Ypres; DSO, 1914, and Croix de Guerre; went to Staff College, Camberley, 1920; served in Ireland; returned to Staff College as instructor, 1926; served with his regiment in Middle East and India; chief instructor at Staff College, Quetta, 1934–7; major-general commanding division in Palestine, 1938; commanded 3rd division of British Expeditionary Force under Alan *Brooke (later Viscount Alanbrooke) 1939–40; after evacuation from Dunkirk, appointed C-in-C South-Eastern Command; acquired reputation as strict disciplinarian; CB, 1940; appointed to command Eighth Army at El Alamein, North Africa, 1942; defeated attack by Rommel, the German commander; refused to mount counter-attack until he was sure of success; achieved one of most decisive victories of the war and carried out advance that cleared Germans out of whole of North Africa; KCB and full general, 1942; fought with Eighth Army in Sicily and Italy under General Eisenhower, Supreme Allied Commander, but frequently disagreed with American tactics; returned to England as commander, 21st Army Group, in preparation for invasion of Europe, 1943; C-in-C of all ground forces for landings in Normandy, 1944, on understanding that, once bridgehead was established, Eisenhower would take over; handed over reluctantly, particularly as he did not agree with Americans about next steps to be taken; in command of British forces pushing forward through Belgium and Holland, uncharacteristically made hurried attempt to secure bridges over Rhine and suffered defeat at Arnhem; called upon by Eisenhower to command American units taken by surprise by German counter-attack in Ardennes; succeeded in pushing back Germans, but further exacerbated his relations with American allies by his overbearing attitude; on German surrender, appointed C-in-C of British Forces of Occupation; field marshal, 1944; GCB, 1945; succeeded Alanbrooke as Chief, Imperial General Staff, 1946–8; viscount and KG, 1946; his controversial attitudes as CIGS did not commend him to politicians, and in 1948 he became military chairman of the Western Union Commanders'-in-Chief Committee until 1951, when he was appointed deputy supreme commander under Eisenhower of the Allied forces of NATO in Europe; he retired from this post in 1958, and published in that year his controversial *Memoirs*; he visited the Soviet Union, 1959 and India and China, 1960, and also toured Africa and Central America, publishing an account of these travels in *Three Continents* (1962); among his other publications is the *History of Warfare* (1968); he was not renowned for self-restraint, but had a flair for inspiring confidence in the troops under his command.

MONTGOMERY, Henry (1788–1865), founder of the Remonstrant Synod of Ulster; MA, Glasgow, 1807; pastor of Dunmurry, near Belfast, 1809; headmaster of Belfast Academical Institution, 1817–39; moderator of the synod, 1818; strongly opposed Henry *Cooke's attempt to render Presbyterian discipline more stringent; adopted a 'remonstrance', 1829, the first meeting of the Remonstrance Synod being held, 1830; advocated Catholic emancipation and Irish disestablishment; elected by the combined Remonstrance Synod, Antrim Presbytery, and Munster Synod professor of ecclesiastical history and pastoral theology, 1838; an original editor of the *Bible Christian*; contributed *Outlines of the History of Presbyterianism in Ireland* to the *Irish Unitarian Magazine*, 1846–7.

MONTGOMERY, Sir Henry Conyngham, second baronet (1803–1878), Madras civil servant; educated at Eton and Haileybury; went to India, 1825; succeeded to baronetcy, 1830; sent on special commission to Rajahmundry district, 1843, and recommended utilization of waters of the Godavery for irrigation (see COTTON, Sir ARTHUR THOMAS); secretary to government in Revenue and Public Works Department, 1843–50; chief secretary, 1850; member of governor's council, 1855–7; original member of new Council of India in London, 1858–76; privy councillor, 1876.

MONTGOMERY, Hugh, third Viscount Montgomery of the Ards and first earl of Mount Alexander (1623?–1663), succeeded his father as viscount, and was appointed to command his father's regiment, 1642; commander-in-chief of the Royalist army in Ulster, 1649; seized successively Belfast, Antrim, and Carrickfergus; surrendered to Cromwell, and was banished to Holland; life master of ordnance in Ireland, 1660; created earl of Mount Alexander, 1661.

MONTGOMERY, Hugh of, second earl of Shrewsbury (d. 1098). See HUGH.

MONTGOMERY (or MONTGOMERIE), Sir James, tenth baronet of Skelmorlie (d. 1694), politician; imprisoned for harbouring Covenanters, 1684; visited Holland in connection with the invitation to William, prince of Orange; MP, Ayrshire, 1689; organized The Club political society; went to London with his confederates, but William III having declined to listen to their complaints, joined the Jacobites in the Montgomery plot; confessed on promise of indemnity; was imprisoned for writing against the government, but escaped to Paris, 1694; died at St Germain.

MONTGOMERY, Sir James, first baronet (1721–1803), Scottish judge; called to the Scottish bar, 1743; sheriff of Peeblesshire, 1748; joint solicitor-general, 1760; sole solicitor-general, 1764; lord advocate, 1766; MP, Dumfries burghs, 1766, Peeblesshire, 1768; introduced measure for reform of entails, 1770; created lord chief baron of the Scottish Exchequer, 1775; resigned his judgeship and was created baronet, 1801.

MONTGOMERY, James (1771–1854), poet; clerk and bookkeeper to the *Sheffield Register*, 1792, becoming a contributor to and finally editor of the paper, which was renamed the *Sheffield Iris*, and became Montgomery's property, 1795; imprisoned for libel, 1795 and 1796; sold his paper, 1825; lectured on poetry at the Royal Institution, 1830 and 1831. His best-known hymns include 'For ever with the Lord', 'Songs of praise the Angels sang', and 'Go to dark Gethsemane', and among his poems are 'The Wanderer of Switzerland' (1806), 'The West Indies'

(1809), 'The World before the Flood' (1812), 'Greenland' (1819), and 'The Pelican Island' (1826).

MONTGOMERY, Jemima (1807–1893), novelist. See TAUTPHOEUS, Baroness von.

MONTGOMERY, Philip of (d. 1099). See PHILIP.

MONTGOMERY, Richard (1736–1775), major-general; of St Andrews and Trinity College, Dublin; entered the army, 1756; captain, 1762; served in Canada, 1759, and Cuba, 1762; sold out of the army, 1772; settled on the Hudson river; became brigadier-general in the American army, 1775; took (1775) Fort Chamblai and St John's, but was killed in an attack on Quebec.

MONTGOMERY, Sir Robert, eleventh baronet of Skelmorlie (1680–1731), projector of a scheme for colonization in America; served in War of Spanish Succession, 1702–13; granted land in South Carolina, 1717; recommended as governor, 1718.

MONTGOMERY, Robert (1807–1855), poetaster; wrote religious poems (including 'The Omnipresence of the Deity', 1828, and 'Satan', 1830) which were extravagantly praised in the press, and severely criticized by *Macaulay in the *Edinburgh Review*, 1830; BA, Lincoln College, Oxford, 1833; MA, 1838; curate of Whittington, 1835; incumbent of St Jude's, Glasgow, 1836; minister of Percy Chapel, St Pancras, London, 1843.

MONTGOMERY, Sir Robert (1809–1887), Indian administrator; appointed to the Bengal Civil Service, 1827; transferred to the Punjab; commissioner of the Lahore division, 1849; disarmed the sepoys at Lahore and Mean Meer, 12 May 1857, and warned Ferozepore, Mooltan, and Kangra of the Mutiny; chief commissioner of Oudh, 1858; lieutenant-governor of the Punjab, 1859–65; KCB, 1859; GCSI, 1866; member of the Council of State for India, 1868.

MONTGOMERY, (Robert) Bruce (1921–1978), detective novelist under pseudonym of Edmund Crispin, and composer; educated at Merchant Taylors' School and St John's College, Oxford; wrote nine detective novels, including *The Case of the Gilded Fly* (1944), *The Moving Toyshop* (1946), and *The Glimpses of the Moon* (1977); also published short stories, edited anthologies, and reviewed crime literature; earliest published music, a choral *Ode on the Resurrection of Christ* (1947); another important work, *An Oxford Requiem* for chorus and orchestra (1951); in mid 1960s concentrated on film music.

MONTGOMERY, Roger of, earl of Shrewsbury and Arundel (d. 1093?). See ROGER.

MONTGOMERY, Walter (1827–1871), actor; his real name Richard Tomlinson; born at Long Island, America; acted in London, 1863; acted with Helen *Faucit and Mrs Kendal; made some reputation in America and Australia; committed suicide.

MONTGOMERY, William (1633–1707), historian; educated at Glasgow and Leiden universities; MP, Newtownards, 1661; high sheriff of Down, 1670; chief works, *Incidentall Remembrances of the two Ancient Families of the Savadges* (first printed 1830), *The Narrative of Gransheogh, Memoires of William Montgomery of Rosemount, co. Down,* and *Memoirs of the Montgomerys of England and Scotland* (first printed 1869).

MONTGOMERY-MASSINGBERD, Sir **Archibald Armar** (1871–1947), field marshal; educated at Charterhouse and Woolwich; commissioned in Royal Artillery, 1891; served in South Africa, 1899–1902; chief of staff to (Lord) *Rawlinson in France, 1914–18; GOC-in-C, Southern Command, 1928–31; general, 1930; adjutant-general to the forces, 1931–3; chief of the Imperial General Staff, 1933–6; field marshal, 1935; KCMG, 1919; KCB, 1925; GCB, 1934.

MONTHERMER, Ralph de, earl of Gloucester and Hertford (d. 1325?), a squire of Gilbert de *Clare, earl of Gloucester, whose widow he married, 1297, and whose titles he bore in right of his wife; served in Scotland, 1298, 1303, 1304, and 1306; received earldom of Athol, 1306, but surrendered it, 1307; keeper of castles in Wales, 1307; warden and lieutenant for Edward II in Scotland, 1311 and 1312; taken prisoner at Bannockburn, 1314; warden of the royal forest south of the Trent, 1320.

MONTJOY. See MOUNTJOY.

MONTMORENCY, Hervey de (fl. 1169–1176), invader of Ireland. See MOUNT-MAURICE.

MONTMORENCY, James Edward Geoffrey de (1866–1934), legal scholar. See DE MONTMORENCY.

MONTMORENCY, Raymond Harvey de, third Viscount Frankfort de Montmorency (1835–1902), major-general. See DE MONTMORENCY.

MONTRESOR, James Gabriel (1702–1776), director and colonel, Royal Engineers; matross, 1727; practitioner-engineer, 1731; ensign, 1732; lieutenant, 1737; engineer-extraordinary, 1742; engineer at Port Mahon, 1743–7; chief engineer at Gibraltar, 1747–54; chief engineer of the expedition to North America under Major-General *Braddock, 1754; prepared roads over the Alleghany mountains, 1755; surveyed Lake Champlain and strategic vicinity, 1756; major, 1757; director and lieutenant-colonel, 1758; designed and constructed Fort George, 1759; superintended erection of new powder magazines at Purfleet, 1763–5; chief engineer at Chatham, 1769; colonel, 1772.

MONTRESOR, John (1736–1788?), major, Royal Engineers; son of James Gabriel *Montresor; born at Gibraltar; accompanied his father to North America, 1754; wounded at Battle of Du Quesne, 1755; sub-engineer, 1759; took part in reduction of Canada; captain-lieutenant, 1765; chief engineer in America, 1775; captain and engineer-in-ordinary, 1776; constructed Philadelphia lines of defence; retired, 1779.

MONTROSE, dukes of. See LINDSAY, DAVID, first duke, 1440?–1495; GRAHAM, JAMES, first duke of the second creation, d. 1742; GRAHAM, JAMES, third duke, 1755–1836; GRAHAM, JAMES, fourth duke, 1799–1874.

MONTROSE, earls of. See GRAHAM, JOHN, third earl, 1547?–1608; GRAHAM, JAMES, fifth earl, 1612–1650.

MONTROSE, marquises of. See GRAHAM, JAMES, first marquis, 1612–1650; GRAHAM, JAMES, second marquis, 1631?–1669; GRAHAM, JAMES, fourth marquis, d. 1742.

MONYPENNY, William Flavelle (1866–1912), journalist, and biographer of Disraeli; joined editorial staff of *The Times,* 1893; chosen to undertake authoritative biography of Lord Beaconsfield; published first volume, 1910, second, 1912; work completed by G. E. *Buckle.

MOODIE, Donald (d. 1861), commander, Royal Navy, and colonial secretary in Natal; entered navy, 1808; lieutenant, 1816; emigrated to Cape Colony, 1816; resident magistrate at Fort Francis, 1825, at Graham's Town, 1828; protector of slaves in the eastern district, 1830–4; superintendent of the government bank, Cape Town, 1840; secretary and colonial treasurer of Natal, 1845–51; published works on the history of the Cape; died at Pietermaritzburg.

MOODIE, John Wedderburn Dunbar (1797–1869), soldier; brother of Donald *Moodie; second lieutenant, 1813; first lieutenant, 1814; wounded at Bergen-op-Zoom, 1814; joined his brothers James and Donald in South Africa, 1814–24; emigrated to Upper Canada; captain of militia on the Niagara frontier, 1837; sheriff of Vittoria, Ontario, 1839; wrote on the wars in Holland, 1814; published *Ten Years in South Africa* (1835).

MOODIE, Mrs Susannah (1803–1885), authoress; sister of Agnes *Strickland; married John Wedderburn Dunbar *Moodie; published poems, stories, and (with her husband's assistance) *Roughing it in the Bush* (1852).

MOODY, Harold Arundel (1882–1947), medical practitioner and founder (1931) of the League of Coloured Peoples; negro, born in Jamaica; MB, BS, King's College, London, 1912; practised in Peckham; sought to improve status of coloured people; prominent Congregationalist.

MOODY, John (1727?–1812), actor; his real name Cochran; first acted in Jamaica; in London, 1759; acted chiefly at Drury Lane; retired, 1796; excelled in comic characters.

MOODY, Richard Clement (1813–1887), colonial governor; born in Barbados; entered Woolwich, 1827; second lieutenant in the Royal Engineers, 1830; for some years at St Vincent; first lieutenant, 1835; professor of fortification at Woolwich, 1838; first governor of the Falkland Islands, 1841; captain, RE, 1847; returned to England, 1849; lieutenant-colonel, 1855; brevet-colonel, 1858; lieutenant-governor of British Columbia, 1858; colonel, 1863; returned home, 1863, retired as major-general, 1866.

MOON, Sir Francis Graham, first baronet (1796–1871), print-seller and publisher; placed with the book and print-seller Tugwell, whose business he subsequently purchased; joined the firm Moon, Boys & Graves in Pall Mall, 1825; reproduced some of the finest works of *Wilkie, *Eastlake, *Landseer, and others; sheriff of London, 1843; alderman, 1844; lord mayor, 1854; created baronet, 1855.

MOON, William (1818–1894), inventor of Moon's embossed type for the blind; became totally blind, 1840; taught blind children, and constructed (1845) a system of embossed type differing from former systems in almost entirely discarding contractions; issued several publications, including the Bible, in his system, which he extended to foreign languages, beginning with Irish and Chinese; FRGS, 1852; fellow of Society of Arts, 1859; LL D, Philadelphia, 1871; advocated and assisted in forming home teaching societies and lending libraries for the blind.

MOONE, Peter (fl. 1548), poet; author of *A short Treatise of certayne Thinges abused in the Popysh Church*.

MOOR. See also MOORE and MORE.

MOOR, Edward (1771–1848), writer on Hindu mythology; cadet under the East India Company, 1782; lieutenant, 1788; served with the Mahratta Army, 1790–1; wounded at Doridroog and Gadjmoor, 1791; brevet-captain, 1796; garrison storekeeper at Bombay, 1799–1805; member of the Asiatic Society of Calcutta, 1796; FRS, 1806; FSA, 1818; wrote principally on Hindu mythology and other Indian subjects.

MOOR, Sir Frederick Robert (1853–1927), South African statesman; born in Natal; Kimberley diamond digger, 1872–9; afterwards farmer in Natal; represented Weenen County in Natal Legislative Assembly, 1886; on grant of responsible government (1893) held portfolio of native affairs until 1897, and again 1899–1903; prime minister, 1906–10; worked wholeheartedly for unification of South Africa; held portfolio of commerce and customs in federal ministry of Louis *Botha, 1910; senator, 1910–20; knighted, 1911.

MOOR, James (1712–1779), professor of Greek; distinguished himself in classics and mathematics at Glasgow University; private tutor; librarian of Glasgow University, 1742; professor of Greek, Glasgow, 1745–74; vice-rector, 1761; LL D, 1763; edited classical authors for the Foulis Press, and wrote on classical subjects.

MOOR, Michael (1640–1726), provost of Trinity College, Dublin; studied at Nantes and Paris; prebendary of Tymothan, 1685; provost of Trinity College, Dublin, 1689; his deposition procured by the Jesuits; censor of books at Rome; rector of Paris University, 1702; principal of the Collège de Navarre; professor of Greek and Latin philosophy at the Collège de France; helped to remodel the university, and to found the college, of Cambrai; wrote against the Cartesian philosophy; died in Paris.

MOOR, Sir Ralph Denham Rayment (1860–1909), first high commissioner of Southern Nigeria, 1900–3; commandant of constabulary in Oil Rivers protectorate, 1891; vice-consul, 1892; consul, 1896; commissioner and consul-general of newly formed Niger Coast protectorate, 1896–1900.

MOOR, Robert (1568–1640), chronographer; of Winchester College and New College, Oxford; MA, 1595; DD, 1614; perpetual fellow of New College, 1589–97; rector of West Meon and vicar of East Meon, 1597; prebendary of Winchester, 1613; published a long Latin poem intended as a universal chronology (1595).

MOOR, Sir Thomas de la (fl. 1327–1351), alleged chronicler. See MORE.

MOORCROFT, William (1765?–1825), veterinary surgeon and traveller; studied veterinary science in France; settled in London, where he realized an ample fortune, but lost it over patents; veterinary surgeon to the Bengal Army, 1808;

crossed the Himalaya and examined the sources of the Sutlej and Indus, 1811–12; explored Lahore and Cashmere, 1819–22; visited Bokhara, 1825; died at Andekhui; a summary of his travels published (1841); wrote also on veterinary surgery.

MOORE. See also MOOR and MORE.

MOORE, Albert Joseph (1841–1893), painter; son of William *Moore (1790–1851); exhibited natural-history subjects at the Royal Academy, 1857–9, and sacred subjects, 1861–5; devoted himself entirely to decorative pictures from 1865; noted for his diaphanous draperies.

MOORE, Ann (*fl.* 1813), the 'fasting woman of Tutbury'; née Pegg; married a farm servant, James Moore, who deserted her; arrived at Tutbury, *c.*1800; originally compelled to fast by poverty, she afterwards traded on her fame as a 'fasting woman'; confessed the fraudulence of her fasts in 1813.

MOORE, Arthur (1666?–1730), economist and politician; born in Ireland; studied trade questions; MP, Grimsby, 1695–1715; high steward of Grimsby, 1714–30; director of the South Sea Company; comptroller of army accounts, 1704; lord commissioner of trade and plantations, 1710; responsible for the reciprocal tariff clauses in the treaty of commerce, 1712, which were eventually cancelled; charged before the South Sea Company with being privy to clandestine trade, 1714; censured and declared incapable of further employment, 1714; held advanced views on trade questions.

MOORE, Arthur William (1853–1909), Manx antiquary; educated at Rugby and Trinity College, Cambridge; second in historical tripos, 1875; MA, 1879; won blue for Rugby football; speaker of House of Keys, 1898–1909; championed House in disputes with governor; wrote on meteorology of the island; CVO, 1902; founded Manx Language Society, 1899; wrote on Manx folk-lore (1891), music (1896), and records (1905); his *History of the Isle of Man* (1900) is an authoritative work.

MOORE, Aubrey Lackington (1848–1890), writer on theology; of St Paul's School, London, and Exeter College, Oxford; MA, 1874; fellow of St John's College, Oxford, 1872–6; rector of Frenchay, 1876–81; tutor of Keble College, Oxford, 1881; select preacher at Oxford, 1885–6, Whitehall, 1887–8; hon. canon of Christ Church, Oxford, 1887; contributed to *Lux Mundi* (1889); published scientific and philosophical works.

MOORE, Sir Charles, second Viscount Moore of Drogheda (1603–1643), son of Sir Garret *Moore, Viscount Moore of Drogheda; succeeded his father, 1627; energetically set about repairing the fortifications of Drogheda, and endeavoured to procure assistance from government against the rebels, 1641; distinguished himself at the siege and was active in suppressing the Meath rebellion, 1642; commissioner to hear the grievances of the confederate Catholics, 1643; advanced against Owen *O'Neill at Portlester, where he was killed.

MOORE, Charles, sixth earl and first marquis of Drogheda (1730–1822), entered the army, 1755; MP, St Canice, 1756–8; succeeded as earl, 1758; governor of Meath, 1759; lieutenant-colonel, 1759; colonel, 1762; secretary to the lord-lieutenant, 1763; lord justice, 1766; governor of Queen's County, 1767; lieutenant-general, 1777; general, 1793; field marshal, 1821; MP, Horsham, 1776–80; KP, 1783; created marquis of Drogheda, 1791; joint post-master-general, 1797–1806.

MOORE, Charles (1815–1881), geologist; FGS, 1854; discovered the Rhaetic beds and founded the Museum at Bath Institute; contributed papers to geological and scientific societies.

MOORE, David (1807–1879), botanist; migrated to Ireland, 1828; assistant in Dublin University Botanic Garden; director of Glasnevin Botanic Garden, 1838; published botanical papers.

MOORE, Dugald (1805–1841), Scottish poet; bookseller in Glasgow; published lyrical poems, including *The African* (1829) and *The Bard of the North* (1833).

MOORE, Sir Edward (1530?–1602), constable of Philipstown; went to Ireland, *c.*1559; sheriff of Louth, 1571; constable of Philipstown, 1576; commissioner for concealed lands and ecclesiastical causes, 1577; knighted, 1579; Irish privy councillor, 1589; negotiated with the earl of *Tyrone and acted as commissioner for the preservation of the peace of Leinster, 1599 and 1601.

MOORE, Edward (1712–1757), fabulist and dramatist; failed as a linen-draper; patronized by George *Lyttelton, first Baron Lyttelton, and Henry *Pelham; editor of *The World*, a satirical periodical, 1753–7; published *Fables for the Female Sex* (1744), *The Trial of Selim the Persian* (1748), *The Foundling* (1748), *Gil Blas* (1751), and *The Gamester* (1753); probably assisted by *Garrick.

MOORE, Edward (1835–1916), principal of St Edmund Hall, Oxford, and Dante scholar; BA, Pembroke College, Oxford; fellow of Queen's, 1858; principal of St Edmund Hall, 1864–1913;

preserved its independence; canon of Canterbury, 1903; works include *Contributions to the Textual Criticism of the 'Divina Commedia'* (1889) and *Oxford Dante* (1894).

MOORE, Edwin (1813–1893), water-colour painter; son of William *Moore (1790–1851); taught painting at York.

MOORE, Eleanora (or Nelly) (d. 1869), actress; most successful at the Haymarket Theatre, London, with Sothern.

MOORE, Sir Francis (1558–1621), law reporter; commoner of St John's College, Oxford, 1574; member of New Inn; entered Middle Temple, 1580; autumn reader, 1607; counsel and under-steward of Oxford University, 1612; created MA, Oxford, 1612; serjeant-at-law, 1614; knighted, 1616; MP, Boroughbridge, 1588–9, Reading, 1597–8, 1601, 1604–11, and 1614; invented the conveyance known as lease and release. His law reports (1663) extend from 1512 to 1621.

MOORE, Francis (1657–1715?), astrologer and almanac-maker; physician, astrologer, and schoolmaster in Lambeth; published an almanac prophesying the weather (1699), to advertise his pills; published the *Vox Stellarum* (*Old Moore's Almanac*, 1700).

MOORE, Francis (*fl.* 1744), traveller; entered service of Royal African Company, 1730; factor at Joar, 1732; assisted in establishing the colony of Georgia, 1735–6 and 1738–43; wrote descriptions of the interior of Africa and Georgia.

MOORE, Sir Garret, first Baron Moore of Mellifont, first Viscount Moore of Drogheda (1560?–1627), son of Sir Edward *Moore; commissioner for arranging matters with *Tyrone, 1594, 1596, and 1598; constable of Philipstown, 1602; Irish privy councillor, 1604; accused of complicity in Tyrone's schemes by *Howth, 1607; fully acquitted, 1609; undertaker in the Ulster plantation; MP, Dungannon, 1613; created Baron Moore, 1615, and Viscount Moore, 1621.

MOORE, Sir George (1563–1632), lieutenant of the Tower of London. See MORE.

MOORE, George (1803–1880), physician and author; studied at Paris with Erasmus Wilson; MRCS, 1829; MD, St Andrews, 1841; MRCP, 1859; physician in London; published *The Lost Tribes and the Saxons* (1861) and other works of religious and medical character.

MOORE, George (1806–1876), philanthropist; came to London, 1825; traveller for a lace house; partner in Groucock, Copestake & Moore, 1829; devoted himself to philanthropic work; died from the effects of an accident at Carlisle.

MOORE, George Augustus (1852–1933), novelist; son of G. H. *Moore; born and brought up in Ireland; educated at Oscott College, Birmingham; lived in London (1880–1901), in Dublin (1901–11), and at 121 Ebury Street, London (1911–33); works include *A Modern Lover* (1883), *A Mummer's Wife* (1885), *Confessions of a Young Man* (1888), *Esther Waters* (1894), *Hail and Farewell*, candid and intimate autobiography (3 vols., 1911–14), *The Brook Kerith* (1916), *A Story-Teller's Holiday* (1918), *Avowals* (1919), *Héloïse and Abélard* (1921), *Conversations in Ebury Street* (1924); sought lucidity and 'the melodic line', treating epic themes in prose beautiful and dignified yet preserving illusion of a story melodiously spoken.

MOORE, George Belton (1806–1875), painter; drawing master at the Royal Military Academy, Woolwich; wrote on perspective.

MOORE, George Edward (1873–1958), philosopher; grandson of George *Moore (1803–80); educated at Dulwich College and Trinity College, Cambridge; first class, part i, classical tripos, 1894; Craven scholarship, 1895; first class, part ii, moral sciences tripos, 1896; fellow of Trinity, 1898; university lecturer in moral science, 1911–25; professor of philosophy, 1925–39; editor of *Mind*, 1921–47; close friend at Cambridge of Bertrand (later Earl) *Russell; published *Principia Ethica* in same year as Russell's *Principles of Mathematics* (1903); leading figure in twentieth-century revolution in philosophy, insisting that philosophy should adhere to common sense; outstanding teacher and lecturer; published *Ethics* (1912), *Philosophical Studies* (1922), and *Some Main Problems of Philosophy* (1953); FBA, 1918; OM, 1951.

MOORE, George Henry (1809–1870), Irish politician; educated at Oscott College, Birmingham, and Christ's College, Cambridge; MP, Co. Mayo, 1847; a leader of the tenant-right movement; unseated, 1857; elected unopposed, 1868.

MOORE, Sir Graham (1764–1843), admiral; son of John *Moore (1729–1802); entered navy, 1777; lieutenant, 1782; commander, 1790; seized four treasure ships off Spanish coast, 1803; escorted Portuguese royal family to Brazil, 1807; served in Walcheren expedition, 1809; rear-admiral, 1812; KCB, 1815; lord of the Admiralty, 1816–20; vice-admiral, 1819; commander-in-chief in the Mediterranean and GCMG, 1820; GCB, 1836; admiral, 1837; commander-in-chief at Plymouth, 1839–42.

MOORE, Sir Henry, first baronet (1713–1769), colonial governor; born in Vere, Jamaica; studied at Leiden; trained in the militia; lieutenant-governor of Jamaica, 1755–62; allayed quarrels between the two houses of legislature; suppressed slave rising, 1760; created baronet, 1762; governor of New York, 1765; suspended the Stamp Act; tried unsuccessfully to determine the question of boundary with Massachusetts, 1767; died at New York.

MOORE, Henry (1732–1802), Unitarian minister and hymn-writer; became minister successively of Dulverton, 1756, Modbury, 1757, and Liskeard, 1787; secured by *Priestley as a contributor to his *Commentaries and Essays*; wrote essays, lyrical poems, and hymns.

MOORE, Henry (1751–1844), Wesleyan minister and biographer; originally a wood-craver; converted to Methodism, 1777; John Wesley's assistant, travelling companion, and amanuensis, 1784–6 and 1788–90; one of John *Wesley's literary executors, and entrusted by him with joint authority at City Road Chapel; with Thomas *Coke wrote a life of John Wesley (1792); after obtaining access to Wesley's private papers published a more valuable biography (1824–5).

MOORE, Henry (1831–1895), marine painter; son of William *Moore (1790–1851), by whom he was taught painting; exhibited at Royal Academy from 1853, British Institution, 1855–65, and at Suffolk Street gallery from 1855; RA, 1893.

MOORE, James (1702–1734), playwright. See SMYTHE, JAMES MOORE.

MOORE, James (or James Carrick) (1763–1834), surgeon; son of John *Moore (1729–1802); studied medicine in Edinburgh and London; MCS, 1792; director of the National Vaccine Establishment, 1809; wrote two accounts of his brother, Sir John *Moore (1761–1809), and medical works.

MOORE, John (d. 1619), divine; of University College, Oxford; rector of Knaptoft, 1586, of Shearsby, 1615; published *A Target for Tillage* (1612) and a theological work.

MOORE, John (1595?–1657), son of John *Moore (d. 1619); of Exeter College, Oxford; rector of Knaptoft, 1638, of Lutterworth, 1647; preached and wrote against enclosures.

MOORE, Sir John (1620–1702), lord mayor of London; gained wealth in East India trade; alderman, 1671; sheriff of London and knighted, 1672; lord mayor, 1681; supported the court party in London; MP, City of London, 1685; benefactor to City charities and to Christ's Hospital (president, 1681); founded and endowed Appleby Grammar School, 1697; rebuilt Grocers' Company's Hall, London, 1682, of which company he was master.

MOORE, John (*fl.* 1669), author of *Moses Revived* (1669).

MOORE, John (*fl.* 1696), curate of Brislington; published Episcopalian sermons.

MOORE, John (1642?–1717), Dissenting minister; of Brasenose College, Oxford; curate of Long Burton, Dorset, 1662; became a Dissenter, 1667; pastor of Christ Church Chapel, Bridgwater, 1676.

MOORE, John (1646–1714), bishop successively of Norwich and Ely; grandson of John *Moore (1595?–1657); MA, Clare College, Cambridge, 1669; DD, 1681; incorporated MA, Oxford, 1673; fellow of Clare College, 1667–77; canon of Ely, 1679; held two rectories in London; bishop of Norwich, 1691–1707, of Ely, 1707; presided, as visitor of Trinity College, Cambridge, at *Bentley's trial, a draft sentence of deprivation being found among his papers. His library, which was famous throughout Europe, was bought by George I and presented to Cambridge University. He was a munificent patron of Clare College Library.

MOORE, John (*fl.* 1721), Dissenting minister; kept a seminary at Bridgwater and wrote a defence of the *Deity of Christ* (1721).

MOORE, Sir John, first baronet (1718–1779), admiral; entered navy, 1729; lieutenant, 1738; commander, 1743; distinguished himself in the action with *L'Etenduère*, 1747; commodore and commander-in-chief on the Leeward Islands Station, 1756; convoyed General Hopton to Martinique, 1759; assisted in the reduction of Guadeloupe, 1759; rear-admiral, 1762; commander-in-chief in the Downs; created baronet, 1766; KB, 1772; admiral, 1778.

MOORE, John (1729–1802), physician and man of letters; studied at Glasgow; surgeon's mate in the duke of *Argyll's regiment serving in Holland, 1747; studied at Paris and London; practised in Glasgow, 1751; MD, Glasgow, 1770; travelled with Douglas, eighth duke of Hamilton, 1772–8; published *A View of Society and Manners in France, Switzerland, and Germany* (1779) and *A View of . . . Italy* (1781); published *Zeluco* (1786), *Edward* (1796), and *Mordaunt* (1800), three novels; in France, 1792; published journal of Paris disturbances (1793 and 1794); published an account of the French Revolution (1795); edited the works of his friend and patient, *Smollett, with memoir (1797).

MOORE, John (1730–1805), archbishop of Canterbury; MA, Pembroke College, Oxford, 1751; private tutor to the sons of the second duke of Marlborough; prebendary of Durham, 1761; canon of Christ Church, Oxford, 1763; dean of

Canterbury, 1771; bishop of Bangor, 1775–83; archbishop of Canterbury, 1783–1805.

MOORE, John (1742–1821), biblical scholar; of Merchant Taylors' School, London, and St John's College, Oxford; BA, 1763; LL B; prebendary of St Paul's, London, 1766; rector of Langdon Hill, Essex, 1798; assisted Kennicott in collating Hebrew manuscripts of the Old Testament; published works on the Old Testament.

MOORE, Sir John (1761–1809), lieutenant-general; son of John *Moore (1729–1802); ensign, 1776; captain-lieutenant, 1778; served in the American War, 1779; MP, Linlithgow, Selkirk, Lanark, and Peebles burghs, 1784–90; major, 1785; lieutenant-colonel, 1790; sent to Corsica to interview General *Paoli; assisted in the reduction of the French garrisons there; adjutant-general, 1794; recalled to England by reason of disputes between the military and naval forces, 1795; brevet-colonel, with local rank of brigadier-general; sent to the West Indies, 1796; under Sir Ralph *Abercromby attacked St Lucia, 1796; left in command of the island; re-established order and security; major-general, 1798; ordered to Holland, 1799; wounded at Egmont-op-Zee, 1799; colonel-commandant, second battalion, 52nd Foot, 1799; served in Mediterranean, 1800, and Egypt, 1801; distinguished himself before Alexandria and Cairo, 1801; colonel of 52nd Foot, 1801; introduced a new system of drill and manœuvre in the Shorncliffe camp; KB, 1804; lieutenant-general, 1805; held Mediterranean command, 1806; sent under Sir Harry *Burrard to Portugal, 1808; commander-in-chief on Burrard's recall; decided to transport his troops by land from Lisbon to Corunna, 1808; decided, partly in consequence of want of supplies, to retreat into Portugal, when he was requested by Sir Charles Stuart (1808) to come to the defence of Madrid; effected junction with *Baird at Majorga, 20 Dec. 1808, and had advanced to within a march of the enemy when an intercepted letter brought news that Napoleon had already entered Madrid and cut off his own retreat into Portugal, commenced his historic retreat over difficult country in midwinter to Corunna, arriving there on 13 Jan. 1809, and began the embarkation 16 Jan.; mortally wounded, on the arrival of the French, who soon appeared; lived to hear that the French were defeated; buried at midnight in the citadel of Corunna, 16 Jan. 1809. A temporary monument placed over his grave by the Spanish commander, marquis de la Romana, was converted into a permanent one by the prince regent, 1811.

MOORE, John Bramley (1800–1886), chairman of Liverpool docks. See BRAMLEY-MOORE.

MOORE, John Collingham (1829–1880), painter; son of William *Moore (1790–1851); exhibited at the Royal Academy Italian scenes and portraits of children.

MOORE, John Francis (d. 1809), sculptor; native of Hanover; executed monuments to Mrs Catherine *Macaulay, Earl Ligonier, Robert, Earl Ferrers, and others.

MOORE, Sir John Henry, second baronet (1756–1780), poet; son of Sir Henry *Moore; born in Jamaica; of Eton and Emmanuel College, Cambridge; MA, 1776; acquainted with Edward *Jerningham and Lady *Miller of Bath Easton; published *The New Paradise of Dainty Devices* (1777).

MOORE, Sir Jonas (1617–1679), mathematician; clerk to Dr Burghill, chancellor of Durham; mathematical tutor to the duke of York, 1647; surveyor of Fen drainage system, 1649, publishing an account (1685); sent to report on fortifications of Tangier, 1663; knighted; surveyor-general of the ordnance, 1663; published *Arithmetick* (1650), a *New System of the Mathematicks* (posthumous, 1681), and other works.

MOORE, Jonas (1691?–1741), military engineer; probably grandson of Sir Jonas *Moore; probationer-engineer, 1709; sub-engineer at Gibraltar, 1711; chief engineer and commander-in-chief of artillery train, 1720; sub-director of engineers and major, 1722; distinguished himself at siege of Gibraltar, 1727; chief engineer of expedition to Spanish America, 1740; mortally wounded during attack on Carthagena.

MOORE, Joseph (1766–1851), Birmingham benefactor; acquired wealth in the button trade at Birmingham; founded a dispensary; established Birmingham Oratorio Choral Society, 1808; agitated for erection of the town hall (1832–4); induced Mendelssohn to compose *St Paul* (given at the festival, 1837) and *Elijah* (performed, 1846).

MOORE, Joseph (1817–1892), medallist and die-sinker; die-sinker's apprentice in Birmingham; partner in a business which manufactured papier-mâché and metal articles, 1844–56; executed numerous prize and commemoration medals; his medal, bearing *Salvator Mundi* of Da Vinci on the obverse and *Christus Consolator* of Scheffer as the reverse (1846) much praised by Scheffer.

MOORE, Mary (1861–1931), actress and theatre manager. See WYNDHAM, MARY, Lady.

MOORE, Peter (1753–1828), politician; amassed a fortune in the East India Company; Radical MP, Coventry, 1803; known as the most adroit manager of private bills; lent his name as director to companies with such freedom that he was obliged to fly to Dieppe to escape arrest, 1825; gave up nearly all his property; died at Abbeville.

MOORE, Philip (*fl.* 1573), medical writer; practised physic and chirurgery; wrote on medicinal herbs; published *Almanack and Prognostication for xxxiiii. yeares* (1573).

MOORE, Philip (1705–1783), Manx scholar; rector of Kirk Bride and master of Douglas School; revised the Manx translation of the Bible and Prayer-Book and religious pieces.

MOORE, Richard (1619–1683), Nonconformist divine; BA, Magdalen Hall, Oxford, 1640; preached at Worcester and Alvechurch; published sermons.

MOORE, Richard (1810–1878), politician; originally a wood-carver, began young to take part in radical politics; acquainted with and assisted Robert *Owen, Sir Francis *Burdett, *Lovett, Collins, Henry *Hetherington, and James *Watson; worked for the promotion of electoral purity, the Chartist cause, and the abolition of newspaper stamps.

MOORE, Robert Ross Rowan (1811–1864), political economist; BA, Trinity College, Dublin, 1835; barrister, Gray's Inn, 1837; intimate of *Cobden and *Bright; joined the Anti-Corn-Law League; a valuable speaker in favour of free trade in England, Scotland, and Ireland; unsuccessfully contested Hastings, 1844.

MOORE, Samuel (*fl.* 1680–1720), draughtsman and engraver; drew plates of the coronation of James II and of William and Mary.

MOORE, Stuart Archibald (1842–1907), legal antiquary; FSA, 1869; called to bar, 1884; published volumes (1888 and 1903) on the history and law relating to foreshore and fishery rights; keen yachtsman; edited antiquarian works for Camden Society and Roxburghe Club.

MOORE, Temple Lushington (1856–1920), architect; pupil (1875–8) of George Gilbert Scott, junior, with whom he maintained close professional association, 1878–90; employed pure Gothic style; designs include seventeen important new churches (1885–1917), nave of Hexham Abbey (1902–8), Anglican cathedral, Nairobi (1914), chapels of Pusey House, Oxford, and Bishop's Hostel, Lincoln, and several houses.

MOORE, Sir Thomas (d. 1735), playwright; admitted at Gray's Inn, 1670; of Corpus Christi College, Oxford, 1674; knighted, 1716; his tragedy, *Mangora, King of the Timbusians*, acted, 1717.

MOORE, Thomas (d. 1792), teacher of psalmody; taught music at Manchester, 1750; precentor and psalmody teacher at Glasgow, 1755–87; kept a bookseller's shop in Glasgow; edited collections of psalms.

MOORE, Thomas (1779–1852), poet; entered at Trinity College, Dublin, 1794, and Middle Temple, 1799; Admiralty registrar at Bermuda, 1803; discovered the office to be a sinecure, and travelled through the States on his way back to London; became the national lyrist of Ireland by his publication of *Irish Melodies* (1807–34), with music by Sir John *Stevenson; inspired by the failure of the prince of Wales as regent to support Catholic emancipation to write airily malicious lampoons in verse, which were collected into a volume called *The Twopenny Post Bag* (1813); acquainted with *Byron and Leigh *Hunt; acquired a European reputation by his *Lalla Rookh* (1817); rendered liable for £6,000 by the defalcations of his deputy at Bermuda; took refuge abroad, visiting Italy with Lord John Russell; given his memoirs by Byron at Venice; returned to England, the debt to the Admiralty being paid, 1822; excited much reprehension by his *Loves of the Angels* (1823); destroyed Byron's memoirs, and on his death wrote a graceful life of Byron (1830); edited Byron's works; received a literary pension, 1835, to which a civil list pension was added, 1850; his last work, *The History of Ireland* for *Lardner's *Cabinet Cyclopaedia* (1846). Moore also wrote *Poems by the late Thomas Little* (1801), *Odes and Epistles* (1806), *National Airs* (1815), *Sacred Song* (1816), *The Fudge Family in Paris* (1818), *The Fudges in England* (published 1835), and *Rhymes on the Road* and *Fables for the Holy Alliance* (1823), the last four under the pseudonym of Thomas *Brown the younger; first collective edition (1840–1).

MOORE, Thomas (1821–1887), gardener and botanist; assisted in laying out Regent's Park gardens, London; curator of the Apothecaries' Company's garden, Chelsea, 1840; edited numerous botanical publications; FLS, 1851; wrote chiefly on British ferns.

MOORE, William (1590–1659), librarian; MA, Gonville and Caius College, Cambridge, 1613; fellow, 1615–47; university librarian, 1653; contributed to the *Obsequies to the Memorie of Mr. Edward King* (1638).

MOORE, William (1790–1851), portrait painter; successful as a portrait painter in oils, water-colour, and pastel.

MOORE-BRABAZON, John Theodore Cuthbert, first Baron Brabazon of Tara (1884–1964), aviator and politician. See BRABAZON, JOHN THEODORE CUTHBERT MOORE-.

MOOREHEAD, Alan McCrae (1910–1983), author and journalist; educated at Scotch College, Melbourne, and Melbourne University; reporter on *Melbourne Herald*, 1930–6; star reporter and war correspondent for *Daily Express*, 1936–46; published *African Trilogy* (1944) and biography of *Montgomery (1946); settled in Italy; published *The Villa Diana* (1951), *The Traitors: the Double Life of Fuchs, Pontecorvo, and Nunn May* (1952), *Gallipoli* (1956), *The Russian Revolution* (1958), *No Room in the Ark* (1959), *The White Nile* (1960), *The Blue Nile* (1962), *Cooper's Creek* (1963), *The Fatal Impact* (1966), and *A Late Education* (autobiography, 1970); OBE, 1946; CBE, 1968; Royal Society of Literature Award, 1964.

MOOREHEAD, John (d. 1804), violinist and composer; brought to London by Thomas *Dibdin, 1794; engaged at Sadler's Wells; at Covent Garden Theatre, 1798; became insane; was sailor, afterwards bandmaster, on board H.M.S. *Monarch*; with Attwood, *Reeve, and Braham composed theatre music; committed suicide.

MOORHOUSE, James (1826–1915), bishop of Melbourne and afterwards of Manchester; BA, St John's College, Cambridge; prebendary of St Paul's, 1874; bishop of Melbourne, 1876–86; presided over synod at Sydney which framed constitution of Church in Australia; bishop of Manchester, 1886–1903.

MOORSOM, Constantine Richard (1792–1861), vice-admiral; brother of William Scarth *Moorsom; entered navy, 1809; lieutenant, 1812; commander, 1814; devised a new mortar for bombs, first used in the bombardment of Algiers (1816); received post-rank, 1818; senior officer at Mauritius; flag-captain to his father, then commander-in-chief at Chatham, 1825–7; rear-admiral, 1851; vice-admiral, 1857; director and chairman of London and North Western Railway; published *Principles of Naval Tactics* (1843).

MOORSOM, William (1817–1860), cousin of Constantine Richard *Moorsom; served as lieutenant in the first China War, as captain in the Black Sea and Crimea; CB; inventor of the Moorsom shell with percussion fuse, and of the 'director' for concentrating a ship's broadside; published two naval works.

MOORSOM, William Robert (1834–1858), son of William Scarth *Moorsom; ensign, 1852; lieutenant, 1853; served in the siege of Lucknow as aide-de-camp to Havelock; helped forward the relief of Lucknow by his skilful plans; killed at Lucknow.

MOORSOM, William Scarth (1804–1863), captain; civil engineer; brother of Constantine

Richard *Moorsom; ensign, 1821; lieutenant, 1825; captain, 1826; served in Nova Scotia; deputy quartermaster-general; sold out of the army, 1832; employed in laying out many railway systems in England and Ireland; his plans for the railway bridge over the Rhine at Cologne adopted, 1850; sent to Ceylon to report on the feasibility of a railway to the highlands of Kandy, 1856; published an account of Nova Scotia and papers on engineering.

MOR, Anthonis (1512?–1576?), portrait painter. See MORE, Sir ANTHONY.

MORAN, first Baron (1882–1977), physician and writer. See WILSON, CHARLES MCMORAN.

MORAN, Patrick Francis (1830–1911), cardinal archbishop of Sydney; nephew of Cardinal *Cullen; educated at Rome; priest, 1853; vice-principal of St Agatha's College, Rome, 1856–66; private secretary to Cardinal Cullen, 1866–72; archbishop of Sydney, 1884; cardinal, 1885; militant churchman and a keen controversialist; built many Roman Catholic institutions in New South Wales; prominent in Australian politics; advocated home rule, and supported Australian federation; publications include *The Catholic Archbishops of Dublin* (1864) and *The Catholics of Ireland . . . in the 18th Century* (1899).

MORAN, Samuel (pseudonym) (1828?–1865), Australian bushranger. See MORGAN, DANIEL.

MORANT, Geoffrey Miles (1899–1964), anthropologist and statistician; educated at Battersea Secondary School and University College, London; B.Sc. (applied statistics), 1920; M.Sc., 1922; D.Sc., 1926; joined staff of the Department of Applied Statistics; leader of biometric school of physical anthropologists; papers on 'Tibetan skulls' (1923) and 'Racial History of Egypt' (1925); published *The Races of Central Europe*, with preface by J. B. S. *Haldane (1939); joined Ministry of Information, 1939; assisted Medical Research Council's Army Personnel Research Committee, 1942; worked at Physiological Laboratory (later RAF Institute of Aviation Medicine), 1944–59; OBE, 1952.

MORANT, Philip (1700–1770), historian of Essex; born in Jersey; BA, Pembroke College, Oxford, 1721; curate of Great Waltham, Essex, 1724; MA, Sidney Sussex College, Cambridge, incorporated from Oxford, 1730; chaplain to the English Church at Amsterdam, 1732–4; patronage conferred on him by the bishop of London; held cures of Colchester and Aldham conjointly; FSA, 1755; prepared for the press the ancient records of parliament (1278–1413); chief works, *The History and Antiquities of Colchester* (1748) and *History and Antiquities of the County of Essex*

(1760–8); published also theological and historical works.

MORANT, Sir **Robert Laurie** (1863–1920), civil servant; BA, New College, Oxford; assistant director of special inquiries and reports, Education Department, 1895; assistant private secretary to eighth duke of *Devonshire, 1902; passing of Education Act (1902) largely due to him; permanent secretary, Board of Education, which he entirely remodelled, 1903–11; chairman, National Health Insurance Commission, which he organized, 1911–19; first secretary, Ministry of Health, which he constructed, 1919–20; CB, 1902; KCB, 1907.

MORAY. See MURRAY.

MORAY (or MURRAY), earls of. See RANDOLPH, Sir THOMAS, first earl of the Randolph family, d. 1332; RANDOLPH, JOHN, third earl, d. 1346; STEWART, JAMES, first earl of the Stewart family, 1499?–1544; STEWART, JAMES, first earl of a new creation, 1531?–1570; STEWART, JAMES, second earl, d. 1592; STEWART, ALEXANDER, fifth earl, d. 1701.

MORAY, Gilbert of (d. 1245), bishop of Caithness. See GILBERT.

MORCAR (or MORKERE) (*fl.* 1066), earl of the Northumbrians; son of *Aelfgar; stirred up a revolt against Earl *Tostig, 1065; chosen earl by the Northumbrians, an election which *Harold eventually recognized, 1065; defeated, with his brother Edwin, by the Norsemen at the Battle of Fulford Gate, near York, the invaders being soon defeated by Harold at Stamford Bridge; submitted to William the Conqueror and remained at court; joined in a rebellion against William the Conqueror, 1068; made submission and was pardoned; joined insurgents in Isle of Ely; on its surrender committed to the custody of Roger de Beaumont in Normandy; transferred to Winchester Prison, 1087.

MORDAF HAEL (i.e. The Generous) (*fl.* 550?), North British prince; one of the three princes who went to avenge upon Arfon the death of Elidyr Mwynfawr.

MORDAUNT, Charles, third earl of Peterborough and first earl of Monmouth of the second creation (1658–1735), admiral, general, and diplomat; son of John *Mordaunt, Viscount Mordaunt (1627–1675); served in the Mediterranean, 1674–7 and 1678–9, and on shore at Tangier, 1680; active member of the parliamentary opposition, 1680–6; went to Holland and intrigued against James II; commanded Dutch squadron in West Indies, 1687; privy councillor on William III's accession, 1689; made lord of the bedchamber, 1689, and first lord of the Treasury, 1689; created earl of Monmouth, 1689; one of the queen's 'council of nine', 1689; accompanied William III to Holland, 1691 and 1692; endeavoured to incriminate *Marlborough, Russell, and *Shrewsbury in Sir John *Fenwick's plot, 1696; ordered to the Tower of London for three months; succeeded his uncle as third earl of Peterborough, 1697; advocated the impeachment of *Somers; declined command of an inadequate expedition to Jamaica, 1702; helped Somers (1702) to translate the *Olynthiacs* and *Philippics* of Demosthenes; appointed joint commander with Sir Clowdisley *Shovell of the expeditionary force to Spain, 1705; surprised Montjuich and compelled the surrender of Barcelona, deemed impregnable, 1705, on which the Archduke Charles made a formal entry and was proclaimed king of Spain, 12 Oct. 1705; proceeded to Valencia, leaving Barcelona at the mercy of the French Marshal de Tessé, who was, however, obliged to abandon the siege on the arrival (1706) of the English fleet; remained at Valencia; ordered by King Charles, who had turned aside towards Aragon, to join him with every available man; having no means of transport, arrived with only four hundred dragoons; decided to go to Italy to arrange with the duke of Savoy for a combined attack on Toulon, Sept. 1706; negotiated a loan at ruinous interest without authority; returned to Spain, but was recalled to England to explain his conduct, 1707; charges against him at the official inquiry not adopted by the House of Lords, 1708; ordered to render an account of money received and expended; inquiry into his conduct renewed without effect, 1711; sent on special embassies to Vienna, Frankfurt, and Italy, 1712; KG, 1713; ambassador-extraordinary to Italian princes, 1713; recalled on the accession of George I, 1714; travelled for the sake of his health; said to have married Anastasia *Robinson, the singer, 1722; corresponded with and addressed verses to Mrs Howard; patron of letters and science; numbered among his friends *Swift, *Pope, *Arbuthnot, and *Gay; died at Lisbon.

MORDAUNT, Henry, second earl of Peterborough (1624?–1697), Cavalier; educated at Eton; served in the Parliamentary army; deserted to Charles I, 1643; raised the royal standard at Dorking, 1647, but was defeated and wounded; escaped to Antwerp, 1647; governor of Tangier, 1661; resigned, 1662; escorted *Mary of Modena to England, 1673; privy councillor, 1674; suspected of complicity in the Popish Plot; KG, 1685; became a Roman Catholic, 1687; impeached, 1689, but released on bail, 1690; published a book on the genealogies of his family under the pseudonym 'Robert Halstead' (1685).

MORDAUNT, Henry (1681?–1710), navy captain; son of Charles *Mordaunt, third earl of Peterborough; captain, 1703; ran his ship ashore, landed his men, and burnt the ship on being attacked between Barcelona and Genoa by the French, 1707; tried by court martial and honourably acquitted, 1709; MP, Malmesbury, 1705.

MORDAUNT, Sir John (d. 1504), speaker of the House of Commons; chosen speaker, 1487, being MP for Bedfordshire; serjeant-at-law and king's serjeant, 1495; chief justice of Chester, 1499; knighted, 1503; high steward of Cambridge University, 1504; chancellor of the duchy of Lancaster, 1504; privy councillor; benefactor of the church.

MORDAUNT, John, first Baron Mordaunt of Turvey (1490?–1562), courtier; son of Sir John *Mordaunt (d. 1504); sheriff of Bedfordshire and Buckinghamshire, 1509; knighted, 1520; privy councillor, 1526; general surveyor of the king's woods, 1526; supported the Reformation; made Baron Mordaunt of Turvey, 1532; engaged in trial of Lord *Dacre, 1534, of *Anne Boleyn, 1536.

MORDAUNT, John, afterwards first earl of Peterborough (d. 1642), ward of Archbishop *Abbot; educated at Oxford; KB, 1616; created earl of Peterborough, 1628; general of the ordnance under *Essex in the Parliamentary army.

MORDAUNT, John, first Baron Mordaunt of Reigate in Surrey, and Viscount Mordaunt of Avalon in Somerset (1627–1675), Cavalier and conspirator; son of John *Mordaunt, first earl of Peterborough; educated in France and Italy; planned an insurrection in Sussex; arrested and committed to the Tower, 1658; acquitted; raised to the peerage in anticipation of another insurrection in the king's favour, 1659; escaped to Calais on its suppression; messenger of King Charles II to the city of London, Apr. 1660; constable of Windsor Castle, 1660; lord-lieutenant of Surrey, 1660; impeached for arbitrary acts, 1667, but pardoned.

MORDAUNT, Sir John (1697–1780), general; nephew of Charles *Mordaunt, third earl of Peterborough; entered the army, 1721; colonel, 1741; brigadier-general, 1745; served in Scotland and Holland; major-general and colonel, 1747; MP, Cockermouth, 1754–67; lieutenant-general, 1754; commanded the futile expedition against Rochefort, 1757; censured by a court of inquiry, but acquitted by court martial; general, 1770; KB and governor of Berwick.

MORDELL, Louis Joel (1888–1972), mathematician; born in Philadelphia, USA, the son of Lithuanian immigrants; educated at Central High School, Philadelphia, and St John's College, Cambridge, which he entered as a scholar, 1906; third wrangler, part i, mathematical tripos, 1909; first class, part ii, 1910; interested in theory of numbers; Smith's prizeman; lecturer, Birkbeck College, London, 1913; lecturer, Manchester College of Technology, 1920; reader, University of Manchester, 1922; Fielden professor of pure mathematics, 1922–45; FRS, 1924; became naturalized British subject, 1929; succeeded G. H. *Hardy as Sadleirian professor at Cambridge, 1945–53; fellow of St John's College; interested in geometry of numbers; awarded Sylvester Medal of Royal Society, 1949, and other prizes; president, London Mathematical Society, 1943–5; number of honorary doctorates and other academic honours in Britain and abroad.

MORDEN, Sir John, first baronet (1623–1708), founder of Morden's College, Blackheath; acquired wealth as a Levant merchant; created baronet, 1688; on the committee of the East India Company; excise commissioner, 1691; MP, Colchester, 1695–8; founded a 'college' at Blackheath for twelve decayed merchants (the number increased after his death to forty).

MORDEN, Robert (d. 1703), geographer; commenced business as a map and globe maker in London, 1668; went into partnership with Thomas Cockerill at the Atlas in Cornhill, 1688; published astronomical, navigation, and geographical maps and terrestrial and celestial globes.

MORDINGTON, fourth Baron. See DOUGLAS, GEORGE, d. 1741.

MORE, Alexander (1616–1670), Protestant divine and antagonist of *Milton; born of Scots parents at Castres; educated at Castres and Geneva; professor of Greek at Geneva, 1639, and of theology at Geneva, 1642–8, at Middelburg, 1649; professor of ecclesiastical history, Amsterdam, 1652–9; pastor of Charenton, 1659; violently attacked by Milton as the supposed author of *Regii Sanguinis Clamor ad Coelum adversus Parricidas Anglicanos* (1652); a reply to his rejoinder published by Milton.

MORE, Sir Anthony (properly **MOR, Anthonis;** also known as **MORO, Antonio)** (1512?–1576?), portrait painter; was born in Utrecht; admitted to the guild of St Luke in Antwerp, 1547; in Italy, 1550 and 1551; employed at the court at Madrid, 1552; sent to England, 1553, to paint Queen Mary's portrait for *Philip of Spain; knighted; remained in England until 1555; went to the Netherlands; visited Madrid, 1559; settled at Antwerp, 1568; one of the chief portrait painters of the world; Sir Thomas *Gresham and Sir Henry *Lee are probably his only genuine portraits of English patrons.

MORE, Cresacre (1572–1649), biographer (1631) and grandson of Sir Thomas *More.

MORE, Edward (1479–1541), divine; scholar of Winchester College, 1492; New College, Oxford; fellow, 1498–1503; headmaster of Winchester, 1508–17; canon of Chichester; rector of Cranford, 1521–41; eighth warden of Winchester, 1526.

MORE, Edward (1537?–1620), grandson of Sir Thomas *More; wrote a poem in defence of women, 1560.

MORE (or MOORE), Sir George (1553–1632), lieutenant of the Tower of London; of Corpus Christi College, Oxford; entered the Inner Temple, 1574; MP, Guildford, 1584–5, 1586–7, 1593, 1604–11, and 1624–5, Surrey, 1597–8, 1614, and 1621–2; knighted, 1597; sheriff of Surrey and Sussex, 1598; chamberlain of receipt of the Exchequer, 1603; visited by James I, 1603 and 1606; created MA, Oxford, 1605; chancellor of the order of the Garter, 1611–29; lieutenant of the Tower of London, 1615–17; induced Robert *Carr, earl of Somerset, to appear for trial; collector of loans in Surrey, 1625.

MORE, Gertrude (1606–1633), daughter of Cresacre *More; originally Helen, took the veil as Gertrude, and became a nun of Cambrai, 1623.

MORE, Hannah (1745–1833), religious writer; acquired Italian, Spanish, and Latin at her sister's boarding school in Bristol, 1757; published a pastoral drama, *The Search after Happiness* (1762), intended for school children; engaged to a Mr Turner of Belmont, but the match was broken off; visited London, 1774; intimate of *Garrick and his wife; met *Burke, *Reynolds, Dr *Johnson, Mrs *Montagu, Mrs *Delany, Mrs *Carter, Mrs *Chapone, and Mrs Boscawen; her tragedy *Percy* produced by Garrick, 1777; her *Fatal Falsehood* produced, 1779; came to think playgoing wrong after Garrick's death; published *Sacred Dramas* (1782); became acquainted with Dr *Kennicott, Dr *Horne, Bishop *Porteus, John *Newton, and *Wilberforce, and published *Thoughts on the Importance of the Manners of the Great to General Society* (1788), which met with great success; induced by the general ignorance and distress in Cheddar to institute Sunday schools in the neighbourhood, 1789; involved (1800–2), in the 'Blagdon controversy', which originated in a complaint of the curate of Blagdon that the master of the school she had started there (1795) was holding a kind of conventicle; wrote, during the excitement caused by the French Revolution, a tract called *Village Politics* (1792); emboldened by its success, she issued series of cheap tracts called *Cheap Repository Tracts*, which appeared regularly, and the venture being supported by committees all over the kingdom, led (1799) to the formation of the Religious Tract Society; published her most popular work, *Coelebs in Search of a Wife* (1809); continued writing her moral and religious treatises until 1819; during illness compiled her *Spirit of Prayer* (1825); left about £30,000 in legacies to charitable institutions and religious societies.

MORE, Henry (1586–1661), Jesuit; son of Edward *More (1537?–1620); studied at St Omer and Louvain; professed of the four vows, 1622; missioner in London; vice-provincial of his order; author of *Historia Missionis Anglicanae Societatis Jesu* (1649) and other theological works; died at Watten, Belgium.

MORE, Henry (1614–1687), theologian; of Eton and Christ's College, Cambridge; MA, 1639; fellow, 1639; received holy orders, but refused all preferment, including two bishoprics, and shrank from theological and political disputes; benevolent to the poor; one of the Cambridge Platonists; published theological and philosophical works in verse and prose, including *Psychodia Platonica* (verse, 1642), *Philosophicall Poems* (1647), *Enthusiasmus Triumphatus* (prose, 1656), and *Divine Dialogues* (prose, 1668); FRS, 1664; believed to have written *Philosophiae Teutonicae Censura* (1670); supposed to have edited *Glanvill's *Saducismus Triumphatus* (1681); his writings valued by John *Wesley and *Coleridge.

MORE, Jacob (1740–1793), landscape painter, known as 'More of Rome'; born in Edinburgh; went to Italy, 1773; employed by Prince Borghese; sent views of Italian scenery to English exhibitions; his paintings praised by Goethe; died in Rome.

MORE, Sir John (1453?–1530), judge; butler of Lincoln's Inn and subsequently barrister; serjeant-at-law, 1503; mentioned as judge of the common pleas, 1518, and judge of the King's Bench, 1523.

MORE, John (d. 1592), the 'Apostle of Norwich'; BA, Christ's College, Cambridge, 1562; fellow; incumbent of St Andrew's, Norwich, till death; refused to wear a surplice, 1573; entered into a controversy with Andrew *Perne, 1573; suspended (1576–8) for objecting to the imposition of ceremonies; his works (theological and chronological) published by Nicholas *Bownde.

MORE, John (1630–1689). See CROSS.

MORE, Richard (d. 1643), Puritan; burgess of Bishop's Castle, 1610; JP and MP for Bishop's Castle, in the Short and Long parliaments; supported Parliamentary cause in Shropshire;

published *A true Relation of the Murders of Enoch ap Evan* (printed 1641, though a licence had been refused before) and a translation of *Mead's Clavis Apocalyptica* (1641).

MORE, Richard (1627–1698), lawyer; son of Samuel *More; admitted of Gray's Inn, 1646; commissioner for compounding, 1646–59; serjeant of Gray's Inn; MP, Bishop's Castle, 1680–98.

MORE, Robert (1671–1727?), writing master; master of Colonel John *Ayres's school at St Paul's Churchyard, London; published *The Writing Master's Assistant* (1696) and similar works.

MORE, Robert (1703–1780), botanist; grandson of Samuel *More; FRS.

MORE, Roger (*fl.* 1620–1652). See O'MORE, RORY.

MORE, Samuel (1594–1662), Parliamentarian; son of Richard *More (d. 1643); member of the 'committee of parliament for Shropshire'; governor of Montgomery Castle, 1645–7, Monmouth, 1645, Ludlow Castle, 1646, and Hereford Castle, 1647; accused of complicity in an attempt to depose *Cromwell; MP, Bishop's Castle, 1658.

MORE, Saint **Thomas** (1478–1535), lord chancellor of England and author; son of Sir John *More; educated at St Anthony's School, Threadneedle Street, London; placed, 1491, in the household of John *Morton, archbishop of Canterbury, on whose recommendation he entered Canterbury Hall, Oxford, 1492; pupil of *Linacre and *Grocyn; entered at New Inn, 1494; removed to Lincoln's Inn, 1496, and was called to the outer bar; appointed reader at Furnival's Inn; devoted his leisure to literature and became an intimate (1497) of *Colet, *Lily, and Erasmus, who afterwards stayed frequently at his house; contemplated becoming a priest, but at the end of four years returned to secular affairs; brilliantly successful at the bar; began to study politics; member of parliament, 1504; successfully opposed Henry VII's demand for an aid of three-fifteenths on his daughter *Margaret Tudor's marriage, 1503; visited Louvain and Paris, 1508; bencher of Lincoln's Inn, 1509; reader, 1511 and 1516; under-sheriff of London, 1510; nominated one of the envoys to Flanders to secure by treaty fuller protection of English commerce, 1515; during his absence sketched his description of the imaginary island of 'Utopia', which he completed and published (1516); included in the Commission of the Peace for Hampshire, 1515 and 1528; a member of a new embassy to Calais to arrange disputes with French envoys, 1516; impressed Henry VIII with the necessity of making him an officer of the crown by the adroitness of his arguments in a Star Chamber case against the claim of the crown to seize a ship belonging to the pope; master of requests and privy councillor, 1518; treated by Henry VIII with exceptional familiarity, affability, and courtesy during his residence at court; frequently chosen as spokesman of the court at ceremonial functions; welcomed *Campeggio, 1518; present at the Field of the Cloth of Gold, 1520, when he met William Budé or Budaeus, the greatest Greek scholar of the age; knighted, 1521; under-treasurer of England, 1521; accompanied *Wolsey to Calais and Bruges, 1521; received grants of land in Oxfordshire and Kent, 1522 and 1525; as speaker of the House of Commons pleaded privilege of the House against Wolsey, 1523; high steward of Cambridge University, 1525, and Oxford University, 1524–32; chancellor of the duchy of Lancaster, 1525; took part in important negotiations with Wolsey at Amiens, 1527, and with *Tunstall at Cambrai, 1529; completed his *Dialogue*, his first controversial book in English (directed mainly against *Tyndale's writings), 1528; succeeded Wolsey as lord chancellor, 1529; unrivalled in the rapidity with which he despatched Chancery business; vexed the king by his opposition to the relaxation of the heresy laws, and (1532) resigned the chancellorship; attacked by Protestants for having used undue severity to persons charged with heresy; lived for some time after his resignation in complete retirement, mainly engaged in religious controversy with Tyndale and *Frith; on the arrest of the 'Holy Maid of *Kent', 1533, was included as guilty of misprision of treason in the bill of attainder aimed at the nun's friends, 1534; summoned before four members of the council (1534) to explain why he declined to acknowledge the wisdom of Henry VIII's attitude to the pope; his name struck out of the bill in consequence of his personal popularity; although willing to swear fidelity to the new Act of Succession, refused to take any oath that should impugn the pope's authority, or assume the justice of the king's divorce from Queen *Catherine, 1534, and was committed to the Tower of London with John *Fisher, bishop of Rochester, who had assumed a like attitude; during the first days of his imprisonment prepared a *Dialogue of Comfort against Tribulation* and treatises on Christ's passion; examined from time to time, but without result; indicted of high treason in Westminster Hall, 1 July 1535; denied that he had maliciously opposed the king's second marriage, or advised Fisher to disobey the Act of Supremacy; found guilty and sentenced to be hanged at Tyburn; executed, 6 July 1535, the sentence having been commuted to decapitation; his body buried in St Peter's in the Tower, London, and his head exhibited on London Bridge. Catholic Europe was shocked by the news, and English ambassadors abroad were instructed to declare that More and Fisher had been found traitors by due course of law.

More was a critic and a patron of art, and *Holbein is said to have stayed three years in his house at Chelsea; he painted portraits of him and his family. For two centuries he was regarded in Catholic Europe as one of the glories of English literature; his Latin verse and prose are scholarly and fluent, while his epigrams embody much shrewd satire. The English prose in his controversial tracts is simple and direct, and his devotional works are noticeable for their sincerity. The *Utopia*, his greatest literary effort, was written in Latin in two books, the second in 1515 and the first in 1516. It describes the social defects of England, and suggests remedies in the account of the social and political constitution of the imaginary island of 'Utopia', where communism is the law of the land, a national system of education is extended to men and women alike, and the freest toleration in religion is recognized. The *Utopia*, however, does not contain his own personal and practical opinions on religion and politics. The book at once became popular and was translated into French (1530), into English (1551), into German (1524), into Italian (1548), and into Spanish (1790). More's other chief English works are his *Life of John Picus, Earl of Mirandula* (printed by Wynkyn de *Worde, 1510), his *History of Richard III* (printed imperfectly in *Grafton's *Chronicle*, 1543, used by Hall, and printed fully by *Rastell in 1557), *A Dyaloge of Syr Thomas More* (1528), *Supplycacyon of Soulys* (1529), *Confutacyon of Tyndale's Answere* (1532), and *An Apologye of Syr Thomas More* (1533). His English works were collected (1557). His Latin publications included two dialogues of Lucian, epigrammata and controversial tracts in divinity. Collections of his Latin works are dated 1563, 1565, 1566, and 1689. Canonized, 1935.

MORE, Thomas (1587–1623?), Jesuit; son of Edward *More (1537?–1620); translated into Latin (1620) *God and the King*, by John *Floyd.

MORE, Thomas (d. 1685), author; of Merton College and St Alban Hall, Oxford; barrister, Gray's Inn, 1642; joined the Parliamentary army and afterwards took Anglican orders; published *The English Catholike Christian* and *True old News*, both in 1649; died of drink.

MORE, Thomas (1722–1795), Jesuit; descendant of Cresacre *More; provincial of the English Jesuits, 1769–73.

MORE (or MOORE), Sir Thomas de la (fl. 1327–1351), alleged chronicler; passed for three centuries as the author of *Vita et Mors Edwardi Secundi*, which is really nothing but an extract from the chronicle of Geoffrey *Baker; MP, Oxfordshire, 1340, 1343, and 1351; possibly constable or vice-warden of Porchester Castle, 1370.

MORE, William (d. 1540), suffragan bishop of Colchester; studied at Oxford and Cambridge; B.Can.L., 1531–2; rector of Bradwell and of West Tilbury, 1534, prebendary of Lincoln, 1535, bishop of Colchester, 1536 (suffragan to Ely); master in Chancery and archdeacon of Leicester.

MORE, William (1472–1552), prior of Worcester; entered Worcester Priory, 1488, sub-prior, 1507, prior, 1518; spent much on repairs, books, and plate for the monastery and on churches on its estates; JP, Worcestershire, 1532; resigned the priory, 1535.

MORECAMBE, Eric (1926–1984), actor and comedian; born in Morecambe (John) Eric Bartholomew; educated at Euston Road Elementary School; became child actor at 13; formed double act with Ernie Wise (Ernest Wiseman), 1941; drafted as 'Bevin Boy' in the mines; resumed partnership with Ernie Wise in *Lord George Sanger's Variety Circus*, billed as Morecambe and Wise, 1947; first television series with 'Running Wild' (BBC 1954); toured Australia, 1958; in Val Parnell's 'Sunday Night at the London Palladium'; became established with 'The Morecambe and Wise Show' on ATV, 1961–8; moved to BBC, 1968; appeared on 'Ed Sullivan Show' in New York and several Royal Command Performances; in three films for Rank Organization; had to undergo open-heart surgery and turned author, 1979; published novel, *Mr Lonely* (1981), and children's books *The Reluctant Vampire* (1982) and *The Vampire's Revenge* (1983); also published posthumously *Eric Morecambe on Fishing*; director Luton Town Football Club, 1969–75; supported many charitable organizations, including the British Heart Foundation; OBE and freeman of City of London, 1976; hon. D.Litt., Lancaster, 1977; published (with Ernie Wise) *Eric and Ernie* (1973).

MOREHEAD, Charles (1807–1882), Bombay medical officer; brother of William Ambrose *Morehead; studied at Edinburgh and Paris; MD, Edinburgh; went to India, 1829; first principal and professor of medicine, Grant Medical College, Bombay; retired, 1862; CIE, 1881; FRCP; published *Researches on the Diseases of India* (1856).

MOREHEAD, William (1637–1692), divine; of Winchester College and New College, Oxford; MA, 1663; fellow, 1658–72; incumbent of Buck-nell, 1670; published *Lachrymae Scotiae* (1660), on the departure from Scotland of his uncle, General *Monck.

MOREHEAD, William Ambrose (1805–1863), Indian official; brother of Charles *Morehead; entered Madras Civil Service, 1825; as sub-collector at Cuddapah, 1832, restored order and brought to justice the murderers of Macdonald, the head assistant collector; judge of the court of Sadr Adalut, 1846; member of the council of the governor of Madras, 1857–1862.

MORELL, Sir Charles (pseudonym), (1736–1765). See RIDLEY, JAMES.

MORELL, John Daniel (1816–1891), philosopher and inspector of schools; MA, Glasgow, 1841; studied at Bonn, 1841; Congregational minister at Gosport, 1842–5; inspector of schools, 1848–76; published works dealing with English grammar and spelling, and a *Historical and Critical View of the Speculative Philosophy of Europe in the Nineteenth Century* (1846).

MORELL, Thomas (1703–1784), classical scholar; of Eton and King's College, Cambridge; MA, 1730; DD, 1743; incorporated MA at Oxford, 1733; rector of Buckland, 1737; FSA, 1737; chaplain to Portsmouth garrison, 1775; compiled *Thesaurus Graecae Poeseos* (1762); supplied libretti for *Handel's oratorios, including the well-known lines, 'See the Conquering Hero comes'; edited *Chaucer (1737) and *Spenser (1747), and published miscellaneous writings.

MOREMAN, John (1490?–1554), divine; fellow of Exeter College, Oxford, 1510–22; MA, 1513; DD, 1530; principal of Hart Hall, Oxford, 1522–7; vicar of Menheniot, 1529; canon of Exeter, 1544; opposed Henry VIII's divorce from *Catherine of Aragon; imprisoned during Edward VI's reign.

MORE-MOLYNEUX, Sir Robert Henry (1838–1904), admiral; joined navy, 1852; served in Crimea, 1854; on West Coast of Africa, 1859; commander, 1865; on North America and West Indies Station, 1867; commanded *Ruby* in Russian War, 1877–8; at bombardment of Alexandria; CB; protected Suakin till arrival of Sir Gerald *Graham; KCB, 1885; captain superintendent of Sheerness Dockyard, 1885–8; admiral, 1899; president of Royal Naval College, Greenwich, 1900–3; GCB, 1902; died at Cairo.

MORES, Edward Rowe (1731–1778), antiquary; of Merchant Taylors' School, London, and The Queen's College, Oxford; FSA, 1752; MA, 1753; started Society for Equitable Assurances, 1761; purchased John *James's collection of printing materials, 1772; composed a valuable *Dissertation upon English Typographical Founders*

and Founderies (published 1778); collected materials for histories of Merchant Taylors' School, London, and Oxford; his books, manuscripts, engravings, and printing types now in the Bodleian and the British Museum.

MORESBY, Sir Fairfax (1786–1877), admiral of the fleet; entered navy, 1799; lieutenant, 1806; commander, 1811; received post-rank, 1814; CB, 1815; suppressed slave trade at Mauritius, 1821–3; rear-admiral, 1849; DCL, Oxford, 1854; vice-admiral, 1856; admiral, 1864; GCB, 1865; admiral of the fleet, 1870.

MORESBY, John (1830–1922), admiral and explorer; son of Sir Fairfax *Moresby; entered navy, 1842; took part in suppression of Taiping Rebellion, 1861; commanded paddle sloop *Basilisk* on Australia Station, 1871; with *Basilisk* carried out important explorations in Torres Straits and on New Guinea coasts, 1872–4; his surveys covered 1,200 miles of unknown coastline and about 100 islands; senior naval officer, Bermuda Dockyard, 1878–81; rear-admiral and assessor to Board of Trade, 1881; vice-admiral, 1888; admiral, 1893.

MORESIN, Thomas (1558?–1603?), physician and diplomatist. See MORISON.

MORET, Hubert (*fl.* 1530–1550), goldsmith and jeweller; a Paris merchant; friend of *Holbein; visited London and sold jewels to Henry VIII.

MORETON, Edward (1599–1665), Royalist divine; educated at Eton and Cambridge; prebendary of Chester, 1637; his property sequestered, 1645, but restored, 1660.

MORETON, Henry George Francis, second earl of Ducie (1802–1853), educated at Eton; MP, Gloucestershire, 1831, East Gloucestershire, 1832–4; succeeded his father, 1840; lord-in-waiting to the queen, 1846–7; charity commissioner, 1847; advocated free trade; agriculturist and breeder of shorthorns.

MORETON, William (1641–1715), bishop successively of Kildare and Meath; son of Edward *Moreton; MA, Christ Church, Oxford, 1667; BD, 1674; accompanied the duke of *Ormonde (lord-lieutenant) to Ireland as chaplain, 1677; dean of Christ Church, Dublin, 1677; bishop of Kildare, 1682; Irish privy councillor, 1682; translated to Meath, 1705.

MOREVILLE, Hugh de (d. 1204), murderer of *Thomas Becket. See MORVILLE.

MORFILL, William Richard (1834–1909), Slavonic scholar; BA, Oriel College, Oxford, 1857; MA, 1860; travelled much in Slavonic countries, studying their history and literature; university reader in Russian at Oxford, 1889;

Ph.D., Prague; FBA, 1903; wrote grammars of Polish (1884), Serbian (1887), Russian (1889), Czech (1889), and Bulgarian (1897), and histories of Russia (1885 and 1902), Poland (1893), and of Slavonic literature (1883); he also knew Welsh, Old Irish, and Turkish; bequeathed Slavonic library to The Queen's College, Oxford.

MORGAN (*fl.* 400?–418), heresiarch. See PELAGIUS.

MORGAN (*fl.* 1294–1295), leader of rebels in Glamorgan, 1294; submitted to Edward I, 1295.

MORGAN, Abel (1673–1722), Baptist minister; pastor of Blaenau Gwent, 1700–11; emigrated to Pennsylvania; compiled the first *Concordance of the Welsh Bible* (published 1730).

MORGAN, Mrs Alice Mary (1850–1890), painter; née Havers; studied at South Kensington; married Frederick Morgan, 1872; exhibited (1873–89) at the Society of British Artists, the Royal Academy, and the Salon.

MORGAN, Anthony (*fl.* 1652), Royalist; served the earl of Worcester, 1642; his estates sequestered.

MORGAN, Anthony (d. 1665), Royalist; knighted, 1642; fought at Edgehill, 1642; succeeded to his half-brother's estates, which were sequestered, 1646; being a 'papist delinquent' was unable to compound, 1650.

MORGAN, Sir Anthony (1621–1668), soldier; BA, Magdalen College, Oxford, 1641; first a Royalist captain; then a Parliamentarian, 1645; captain in *Ireton's horse in Ireland, 1649; major, 1652; MP, Wicklow and Kildare, 1654, Meath and Louth, 1659, in *Cromwell's united parliament; knighted, 1656, and again by Charles II, 1660; commissioner of the English auxiliaries in France; an original FRS, 1663.

MORGAN, Augustus de (1806–1871), mathematician. See DE MORGAN.

MORGAN, Sir Charles (1575?–1642), soldier; served in the Netherlands; knighted, 1603; commanded the English at Bergen, 1622, and Breda, 1625; compelled through want and disease to surrender Stade, 1628; helped to besiege Breda, 1637; governor of Bergen; died at Bergen.

MORGAN, Sir Charles (1726–1806), judge advocate-general. See GOULD.

MORGAN, Charles Langbridge (1894–1958), novelist, critic, and playwright; served in Royal Navy, 1907–13; entered at Brasenose College, Oxford, 1913, rejoined navy on outbreak of war, 1914; took part in Antwerp expedition, interned in Holland, 1914–17; published *The Gunroom* (1919); returned to Oxford University, 1919–21; president, OUDS; joined editorial staff, *The Times*, 1921; succeeded A. B. *Walkley as dramatic critic, 1926–39; published *My Name is Legion* (1925), *Portrait in a Mirror* (1929, Femina Vie Heureuse Prize, 1930), *The Fountain* (1932, Hawthornden Prize, 1933), *Epitaph on George Moore* (1935), and *Sparkenbroke* (1936); successful play, *The Flashing Stream* (produced in London, 1938); served with the Admiralty during 1939–45 war; published further novels, *The Voyage* (1940, James Tait Black Memorial Prize), *The Empty Room* (1941), *The Judge's Story* (1947), *The River Line* (1949), *A Breeze of Morning* (1951), and *Challenge to Venus* (1957); last play, *The Burning Glass* (produced, 1953); his books translated into nineteen languages; member of Institute of France, 1949; president, International PEN, 1953–6.

MORGAN, Charles Octavius Swinnerton (1803–1888), antiquary; grandson of Sir Charles *Gould; of Westminster School and Christ Church, Oxford; MA, 1832; MP, Monmouthshire, 1841–74; deputy lieutenant and JP, Monmouthshire; president of Caerleon Antiquarian Association, to whose papers he contributed, as also to the Society of Antiquaries.

MORGAN, Conwy Lloyd (1852–1936), comparative psychologist and philosopher; studied at School of Mines and Royal College of Science, London; professor of geology and zoology (from 1910 of psychology and ethics), Bristol, 1884–1919; principal, 1887–1909; first vice-chancellor, Bristol University, 1909–10; a pioneer in study of animal psychology; works include *Animal Life and Intelligence* (1890–1) and *Instinct and Experience* (1912); FRS, 1899.

MORGAN, Daniel (1828?–1865), or Samuel Moran, Australian bushranger; a stockrider for whose apprehension £500 reward was offered, 1864; increased to £1,500, 1865, in consequence of murders; captured and shot at Peechalba Station.

MORGAN, Edward Delmar (1840–1909), linguist and traveller; lived in St Petersburg; travelled in Persia, 1872, Little Russia, and Lower Congo, 1883; honorary secretary of Hakluyt Society, 1886–92, editing Anthony *Jenkinson's travels, 1886; translated works by the Central Asian explorer Przhevalsky, 1876–9.

MORGAN, Sir Frederick Edgworth (1894–1967), lieutenant-general; educated at Clifton College and Royal Military Academy, Woolwich; commissioned in Royal Artillery, 1913; served in India and France during 1914–18 war; served in India, 1919–35; Staff College, Quetta, 1927–8; commanded support group, 1st Armoured division in France, 1940; commanded I Corps, 1943; chief of staff to supreme allied commander, 1943–4; prepared plan for invasion of Europe; criticized by General Sir B. L. *Montgomery (later Viscount Montgomery of Alamein); deputy chief of staff to General Eisenhower, 1944–5; chief of operations to Unrra in Germany, 1945–6; retired from army, 1946; controller, atomic energy, 1951; controller, atomic weapons, Atomic Energy Authority, 1954–6; CB, 1943; KCB, 1944; commander, US Legion of Merit and French Legion of Honour; colonel commandant, Royal Artillery, 1948–58; publications include *Overture to Overlord* (1950), *Memoirs* (1958), and *Peace and War, a Soldier's Life* (1961).

MORGAN, George Cadogan (1754–1798), scientific writer; brother of William *Morgan (1750–1833); was educated at Jesus College, Oxford; Unitarian minister at Norwich, 1776; tutor at Hackney College, 1787–91; took private pupils at Southgate, Middlesex, 1791; wrote on electricity and chemistry.

MORGAN, Sir George Osborne, first baronet (1826–1897), lawyer and politician; born at Gothenburg, Sweden; educated at Shrewsbury School and Balliol College, Oxford; gained Craven scholarship while at school, 1844; scholar of Worcester College, Oxford, 1847; BA, 1848; Eldon law scholar, 1851; barrister, Lincoln's Inn, 1853; joint editor of the *New Reports*; Liberal MP for Denbighshire, 1868; introduced Burials Bill, 1870, and Places of Worship (sites) Bill, which became law, 1873; QC and bencher of Lincoln's Inn, 1869, and treasurer, 1890; chairman of Select Committee on Land Titles and Transfer, 1878–9; judge advocate-general, 1880–5; privy councillor, 1880; introduced successfully annual Army Discipline Bill, 1881; took charge of Married Women's Property Bill, 1882; MP, East Denbighshire, 1885, 1886, and 1892; parliamentary under-secretary for colonies, 1886; founded Emigration Inquiry Office; created baronet, 1892; published translation of Virgil's *Eclogues* in English hexameters, and other writings.

MORGAN, Sir Gilbert Thomas (1872–1940), chemist; educated at Finsbury Technical College and Royal College of Science; professor of chemistry, Royal College of Science, Dublin (1912–16), at Finsbury (1916–19), at Birmingham (1919–25); director, Chemical Research Laboratory, 1925–37; mainly interested in chemical reactions under high pressures and synthetic resins; FRS, 1915; knighted, 1936.

MORGAN, Hector Davies (1785–1850), theological writer; assumed the name of Morgan in addition to Davies, 1800; MA, Trinity College, Oxford, 1815; curate of Castle Hedingham, 1809–46; opened savings bank there, 1817; chief work, *The Doctrine and Law of Marriage, Adultery, and Divorce* (1826).

MORGAN, Henry (d. 1559), bishop of St David's; became an Oxford student, 1515; DCL, 1525; principal of St Edward's Hall, Oxford, c.1525; admitted at Doctors' Commons, 1528; obtained much clerical preferment, 1530–51; bishop of St David's, 1554–9.

MORGAN, Sir Henry (1635?–1688), buccaneer; lieutenant-governor of Jamaica; commanded a privateer, 1663; sailed with Edward Mansfield, and was elected 'admiral' of the buccaneers on Mansfield's death, 1666; on a rumoured Spanish invasion of Jamaica (1668) received commission to sail towards the mainland, where he attacked Porto Bello and utterly sacked it; unsuccessfully attacked by the president of Panama; reproved on his return for exceeding his commission; forced the entrance to Lake Maracaybo, 1669, sacked the town and proceeded to the head of the lake and sacked Gibraltar; after ravaging the coast of Cuba and the mainland of America, resolved to take Panama, 1670; the castle of Chagre being successfully stormed, proceeded over the ridge on foot, dispersed the Spaniards after two hours' fighting, and took possession of the city of Panama; received the formal thanks of Jamaica, but was sent to England to answer for his conduct, 1672; in disgrace for a short time; knighted, 1675, and appointed lieutenant-governor of Jamaica, senior member of the council, and commander-in-chief of the forces; died at Port Royal.

MORGAN, J. (*fl.* 1739), historical compiler; projected and edited *Phoenix Britannicus*, 1732 (discontinued after six months); compiled oriental biographies, 1739.

MORGAN, James (1799–1873), Irish Presbyterian divine; studied at Glasgow and Belfast; minister of Carlow, 1820, Lisburn, 1824, Fisherwick Place, Belfast, 1828; moderator of the general assembly, 1846; DD, Glasgow, 1847; published devotional works.

MORGAN (or YONG), John (d. 1504), bishop of St David's; doctor of laws at Oxford; a counsellor of Sir *Rhys ap Thomas; bishop of St David's, 1496.

MORGAN, John Hartman (1876–1955), lawyer; educated at Caterham School, University College of South Wales, and Balliol College, Oxford; MA, London, 1896; on literary staff, *Daily Chronicle*, and postgraduate student at London School of Economics, 1901–3; leaderwriter for *Manchester Guardian*, 1904–5; Home Office representative with British Expeditionary Force to inquire into conduct of Germans in the field, 1914; called to bar (Inner Temple), 1915; attended Peace Conference as assistant adjutant-general, 1919; member of Inter-Allied Council of Central Commission for Disarmament of Germany; retired from army with rank of brigadier-general, 1923; convinced that Germany had no intention of disarming; counsel for defence of Sir Roger *Casement, 1916; professor of constitutional law, University College, London, 1923–41; KC, 1926; reader in constitutional law, Inns of Court, 1926–36; legal adviser to American War Crimes Commission, 1947–9; published *The House of Lords and the Constitution* (1910), *War, its Conduct and Legal Results* (with T. Baty, 1915), *Gentlemen at Arms* (1918), *Viscount Morley, an Appreciation* (1924), *Assize of Arms* (1945), and *The Great Assize* (1948).

MORGAN, John Minter (1782–1854), miscellaneous writer; devoted himself to philanthropy; founded National Orphan Home, 1849; tried to form a self-supporting village, 1850; wrote principally on the education and condition of the lower classes.

MORGAN, Macnamara (d. 1762), dramatist; his *Philoclea* (based on Sidney's *Arcadia*), acted 1754, and *Florizel and Perdita* (based on *Winter's Tale*), 1754; possibly wrote (1742) *The Causidicade* and (1746) *The Processionade*, satires on William *Murray, afterwards earl of Mansfield.

MORGAN, Matthew (1652–1703), versewriter; MA, St John's College, Oxford, 1674; DCL, 1685; vicar of Wear, 1693; translated Plutarch's *Morals* (1684); wrote biographies and elegies.

MORGAN, Sir Morien Bedford (1912–1978), aeronautical engineer; educated at schools in Bridgend, Oxford, Cardiff, and London; skilled pianist and organist; entered St Catharine's College, Cambridge, 1931; first class, mechanical sciences tripos (aeronautics), 1934; awarded John Bernard Seely Prize in aeronautics, 1934; appointed junior scientific officer at Royal Aircraft Establishment, Farnborough, 1935; research worker with Aero Flight; head of new guided-weapons department, 1948–53; deputy director (A) in charge of aircraft, 1954–9; scientific adviser to Air Ministry, 1959; deputy controller of aircraft (research and development), Ministry of Aviation, 1960–3; controller of aircraft, 1963–6; controller of guided weapons and electronics, 1966–9; director, RAE, 1969–72; directed scientific investigation in public inquiry into Comet accidents that demonstrated metal fatigue as cause; also directed research into feasibility of supersonic civil aircraft culminating in Concorde; appointed master of Downing College, Cambridge, 1972; CB, 1958; knighted, 1969; president, Royal Aeronautical Society, 1967–8; awarded society's Gold Medal, 1971;

hon. fellow, 1976; hon. fellow, St Catharine's College, Cambridge, 1972; FRS, 1972; founder fellow of Fellowship of Engineering, 1976; hononary doctorates at Cranfield and Southampton, 1976; member of Airworthiness Requirements Board and chairman of its research committee, 1973; chairman of Air Traffic Control Board, 1975.

MORGAN, Philip (d. 1435), bishop successively of Worcester and Ely; D.Can. and CL by 1404; continually sent on foreign missions, 1414–18; prebendary of Lincoln, 1416; bishop of Worcester, 1419; privy councillor, 1419; constantly attended the council during Henry VI's minority; unanimously elected archbishop by the chapter at York, 1423, but was instead translated by the pope to Ely, 1426; arbitrator between *Gloucester and *Beaufort, 1426; vigilant in putting down clerical abuses.

MORGAN, Philip (d. 1570). See PHILIPPS, MORGAN.

MORGAN, Sir Richard (d. 1556), judge; barrister, Lincoln's Inn, 1529; reader, 1542 and 1546; serjeant-at-law, 1546; recorder and MP for Gloucester, 1545–7 and 1553; chief justice of common pleas, 1553; knighted, 1553.

MORGAN, Robert (1608–1673), bishop of Bangor; MA, Jesus College, Cambridge, 1630; incumbent of Llanwnol, 1632, Llangynhafal, Llanfair, 1637, and Efenechtyd, 1638; BD, 1638; bought the lease of the tithes of Llandyvnan, 1642, but was ejected from his other preferments; archdeacon of Merioneth, 1660; bishop of Bangor, 1666; gave an organ to, and effected considerable restorations in, Bangor Cathedral.

MORGAN, Sydney, Lady Morgan (1783?–1859), novelist; daughter of Robert *Owenson; published sentimental verse, 1801; took to fiction, 1804; made her reputation by *The Wild Irish Girl* (1806); married Sir Thomas Charles *Morgan, 1812; attacked in the *Quarterly Review* for her patriotic novels *O'Donnel* (1814) and *Florence M'Carthy* (1816); induced by the popularity of her *France* (1817) to publish a similar book on Italy (1821), and the *Life of Salvator Rosa* (1823); published *The O'Briens and the O'Flahertys* (1827); visited France a second time, 1829, and Belgium, 1835; received a government pension, 1837; came to live in London, 1839; subsequently gave her whole attention to society.

MORGAN, Sylvanus (1620–1693), armspainter and author; published 'London', a poem (1648), *Horologiographia Optica* (1652), and two books on heraldry (1661 and 1666).

MORGAN, Sir Thomas (d. 1595), 'the warrior'; appointed captain of a band of English volunteers under William of Orange, 1572; served in Holland, 1572–3, in Ireland, 1574; returned to the Low Countries, 1578; conspicuous for his bravery at Kowenstyn Dyke, 1585; governor of Flushing for a short time, then commander of the fortress of Rheinberg; ousted as governor of Bergen-op-Zoom, 1586, by Peregrine *Bertie, Baron Willoughby de Eresby; decision given in his favour by Elizabeth and the States-General; knighted, 1587; deprived of his governorship, 1593; returned to England.

MORGAN, Thomas (1543–1606?), Roman Catholic conspirator; became secretary to the earl of *Shrewsbury, 1569, in order to serve *Mary Queen of Scots; dismissed unpunished after ten months' imprisonment on a charge of conspiracy, 1572; secretary to James *Beaton, Mary Stuart's ambassador in Paris, 1573; Queen Elizabeth having applied for his extradition, he was sent to the Bastille, 1583; corresponded with Mary Stuart through Gilbert *Gifford, who betrayed him; helped to organize the *Babington plot, 1586, and advised Mary Stuart to send Babington a letter of approval; released, 1590, and again imprisoned for three years in Flanders; visited Italy and returned to Paris.

MORGAN, Sir Thomas (d. 1679?), soldier; served in the Low Countries, and under *Fairfax in the Thirty Years' War; parliamentary governor of Gloucester, 1645; took Chepstow Castle and Monmouth, 1645; besieged Raglan Castle, 1646; assisted *Monck in Scotland, 1651–7, becoming major-general; second-in-command in Flanders, 1657; knighted on his return, 1658; rejoined Monck in Scotland, and played a conspicuous part in the Restoration in Edinburgh; governor of Jersey, 1665; repaired Jersey forts and reorganized militia; a pamphlet narrating his acts in France and Flanders (1657 and 1658), said to be by himself, published (1699).

MORGAN, Thomas (d. 1743), deist; of humble origin; Independent minister of Burton, 1716, and Marlborough; dismissed for heterodoxy, 1720; studied medicine; MD; described himself as a 'Christian deist'; published pamphlets in opposition to Samuel *Chandler, John *Chapman, Thomas *Chubb, Samuel *Fancourt, and John *Leland.

MORGAN, Sir Thomas Charles (1783–1843), philosophical and miscellaneous writer; of Eton and Peterhouse, Cambridge; MD, 1809; FRCP, 1810; knighted in Ireland, 1811; physician to the Marshalsea prison; a commissioner of Irish fisheries, 1835, supplying an appendix to the first report; published *Sketches of the Philosophy of Life* (1818) and *Sketches of the Philosophy of Morals* (1822).

MORGAN, Sir William (d. 1584), soldier; volunteered in the Huguenot army, 1569; assisted in capture of Valenciennes, 1572, and defence of Mons, 1572; took part in the colonization of Ireland under *Essex, 1573; knighted, 1574; governor of Dungarvan, 1579–82; displayed great activity against the rebels in South Munster.

MORGAN, William (1540?–1604), bishop of St Asaph; sizar of St John's College, Cambridge; MA, 1571; DD, 1583; university preacher, 1578; incumbent of Llanrhaiadr Mochnant, 1578, of Llanfyllin, 1579; summoned before Archbishop *Whitgift to justify his pretensions to translate the Bible into Welsh, 1587; bishop of Llandaff, 1595–1601, and of St Asaph, 1601.

MORGAN, William (1623–1689), Jesuit; of Westminster School and Trinity College, Cambridge; exiled after Naseby; professed of the four vows, 1666; missioner in Wales, 1670; rector of the English College at Rome, 1683; provincial of his order, 1689.

MORGAN, William (1750–1833), actuary; brother of George Cadogan *Morgan; assistant (1774), afterwards chief (1775–1830) actuary to the Equitable Assurance Society; published *Doctrine of Annuities* (1779), upon the basis of which new tables of mortality were constructed; vigorously denounced the accumulation of the National Debt in many pamphlets; wrote life of his uncle, Richard *Price (1723–1791), 1816; intimate of Horne *Tooke, Sir Francis *Burdett, Samuel *Rogers, and Tom *Paine.

MORGAN, Sir William (1829–1883), South Australian statesman; emigrated to Australia, 1848, and became head of a leading mercantile house; member of the legislative council, 1869; intercolonial delegate, 1871, and chief secretary of the legislative council, 1875–6 and 1877–8; premier, 1878–81; KCMG, 1883.

MORGANENSIS (*fl.* 1210), epigrammatist. See MAURICE.

MORGAN HEN, i.e. the Aged (d. 973), regulus of Glamorgan; chief prince of the region between the Towy and the Wye; attended the courts of *Edgar, *Athelstan, *Edred, and *Edwy.

MORGAN MWYNFAWR (d. 665?), regulus of Glamorgan; owned lands in Gower, Glamorgan, and Gwent; granted lands to the church of Llandaff, and was proceeded against by *Oudoceus for murdering his uncle, Ffriog.

MORGANN, Maurice (1726–1802), commentator on the character of Sir John Falstaff; undersecretary of state, 1782; secretary to the embassy for peace with America, 1782; chief work, *Essay* *on the Dramatic Character of Sir John Falstaff* (vindication of Falstaff's courage, 1777).

MORGANWG, Iolo (1746–1826), Welsh bard. See WILLIAMS, EDWARD.

MORGANWG, Lewis (*fl.* 1500–1540), Welsh bard. See LEWIS.

MORI, Francis (1820–1873), composer; son of Nicolas *Mori; composed *Fridolin* and *The River Sprite* (1865); died at Chamant.

MORI, Nicolas (1797–1839), violinist; born in London; pupil of *Barthélemon and Viotti; leader of the Philharmonic orchestra, 1816; published *The Musical Gem* (annual); member of the first board of professors of the new Academy of Music, 1823; principal orchestral leader of festivals.

MORIARTY, David (1814–1877), bishop of Kerry; educated at Boulogne-sur-Mer and Maynooth; bishop of Kerry, 1856; opposed treasonable movements and home rule.

MORIARTY, Henry Augustus (1815–1906), captain in the navy; prepared vessels for bombardment of Sveaborg, 1855; navigated *Great Eastern* when employed for laying Atlantic cables, 1865–6; CB, 1866; Queen's harbourmaster, Portsmouth, 1869–74; captain, 1874; nautical expert before parliamentary committees; published volumes of sailing directions, 1887–93.

MORICE. See also MORRIS.

MORICE, Humphry (1640?–1696), son of Sir William *Morice; auditor of the Exchequer; probably secretary to the embassy to the Dutch, 1667.

MORICE, Humphry (1671?–1731), governor of the Bank of England; son of Humphry *Morice (1640?–1696); a Turkey merchant; MP, Newport, 1713–22, Grampound, 1722–31; steadily supported Walpole; director of the Bank of England, 1716; deputy-governor, 1725–6; governor, 1727–8; discovered, after his death, to have drawn fictitious bills and to have appropriated trust funds.

MORICE, Sir Humphry, fourth baronet (1723–1785), politician; son of Humphry *Morice (1671?–1731); succeeded to his cousin's baronetcy and estates, 1750; MP, Launceston, 1754 and 1757; clerk-comptroller of the household of George II, 1757; went abroad, 1760; his household appointment not renewed till 1761; privy councillor, 1763; lord warden of the stannaries, 1763; high steward of the duchy of Cornwall, 1763; recorder of Launceston, 1771; retired from parliament, 1780; resigned the recordership, 1782; ousted from the stannaries, 1783; died at Naples.

MORICE, Ralph (*fl.* 1523–1570), secretary to Archbishop *Cranmer; MA, Cambridge, 1526; Cranmer's secretary, 1528; bailiff for some crown lands, 1537; registrar to the commissioners for Rochester, Canterbury, Chichester, and Winchester, 1547; was imprisoned in Queen Mary's reign, but escaped; supplied information to *Foxe and others.

MORICE, William (*fl.* 1547), brother of Ralph *Morice; gentleman-usher to Henry VIII; imprisoned for heresy, but released on Henry's death; MP.

MORICE, Sir William (1602–1676), secretary of state and theologian; BA, Exeter College, Oxford, 1622; JP, 1640; MP, 1648, 1654, and 1656; excluded in *Pride's Purge; high sheriff of Devonshire, 1651; MP, Newport, 1658, Plymouth, 1660; related to *Monck; assisted in the Restoration; secretary of state, 1660; knighted, 1660; privy councillor, 1660; resigned secretaryship, 1668; published treatise on the administration of the sacrament to all church members (1657).

MORIER, David (1705?–1770), painter; born at Berne; came to England, 1743; exhibited equestrian portraits at the Society of Artists, 1760, 1762, 1765, and 1768; died in the Fleet.

MORIER, David Richard (1784–1877), diplomat; son of Isaac *Morier; born at Smyrna; entered the Diplomatic Service, 1804; served in south-east Europe, Egypt, Dardanelles, and Constantinople, till 1812; assisted in the 'settlement of Europe', 1813–15; consul-general for France, 1815–32; minister-plenipotentiary to the Swiss States, 1832–47; published two religious pamphlets and *Photo*, a tale of modern Greece (1857).

MORIER, Isaac (1750–1817), consul-general of the Levant Company; born at Smyrna; naturalized in England, 1803; consul-general of the Levant Company at Constantinople, 1804; his post converted into a British consulship, 1806; died of plague at Constantinople.

MORIER, James Justinian (1780?–1849), diplomat, traveller, and novelist; son of Isaac *Morier; born at Smyrna; entered Persian Diplomatic Service, 1807; travelled home by Turkey in Asia, 1809, publishing an account (1812); returned from Tehran through Asia Minor, 1815, and published a second book (1818); published oriental romances, *Hajji Baba* (1824) being the best.

MORIER, John Philip (1776–1853), diplomat; son of Isaac *Morier; born at Smyrna; became attached to Constantinople embassy, 1799; sent to Egypt, 1799; published account of the Egyptian campaign (1800); consul-general in Albania, 1803; secretary of legation at Washington, 1810; under-secretary for foreign affairs, 1815; envoy-extraordinary to court of Saxony, 1816–25.

MORIER, Sir **Robert Burnett David** (1826–1893), diplomat; son of David Richard *Morier; born in Paris; BA, Balliol College, Oxford, 1849; entered Diplomatic Service, 1851; held various appointments at German courts, 1853–76, and acquired an unrivalled intimacy with German politics; minister at Lisbon, 1876–81, Madrid, 1881–4; ambassador at St Petersburg, 1884–93; KCB, 1882; privy councillor, 1885; GCMG, 1886; GCB, 1887; DCL, Oxford, 1889; displayed exceptional ability in the conduct of British relations with Russia, especially in 1885; died at Montreux.

MORIER, William (1790–1864), admiral; son of Isaac *Morier; born at Smyrna; entered navy, 1803; served in Mediterranean and North Sea, 1825; post captain, 1830; rear-admiral, 1855; vice-admiral, 1862.

MORINS, Richard de (d. 1242), historian; canon of Merton; became prior of Dunstable, 1202; went to Rome, 1203 and 1215; arbitrated between the bishop of London and the abbey of Westminster, 1222; compiled the early portion of the *Dunstable Annals* (Rolls Ser., 1866).

MORISON. See also MORRISON and MORYSON.

MORISON, Sir **Alexander** (1779–1866), physician; MD, Edinburgh, 1799; FRCP, 1841; knighted, 1838; wrote on mental diseases.

MORISON, Douglas (1814–1847), painter and lithographer; associate of the New Society of Painters in Water-Colours, 1836–8.

MORISON, George (1757–1845), son of James *Morison (1708–1786); graduated at Aberdeen; minister of Banchory-Devenick, 1785; DD, Aberdeen, 1824; wrote on the Scottish Church.

MORISON, James (1708–1786), of Elsick; elected provost of Aberdeen, 1744; forced by John Hamilton to hear the Pretender proclaimed king, but declined to drink his health, 1745.

MORISON, James (1762–1809), theologian; Perth bookseller; seceded from the Glassites; founded a new sect, and published theological works.

MORISON, James (1770–1840), self-styled 'the Hygeist'; merchant; cured himself of ill health and became a vendor of 'Morison's pills', 1825, of which he wrote puffs; died in Paris.

MORISON, James (1816–1893), founder of the Evangelical Union; educated at Edinburgh University; embodied his views of the atonement being for all mankind in a tract (1840); minister of Kilmarnock, 1840; suspended by the Presbytery, 1841; being joined by other suspended ministers formed 'Evangelical Union', 1843; established a theological college, 1843, of which he was first principal; left Kilmarnock for Glasgow, 1853; DD, Michigan, 1862, Glasgow, 1883; retired from the ministry, 1884; published New Testament commentaries.

MORISON, James Augustus Cotter (1832–1888), author; son of James *Morison (1770–1840); lived in Paris, 1834–40; MA, Lincoln College, Oxford, 1859; contributed to *Saturday Review*; wrote *Life of St. Bernard* (1863), *Gibbon* (1878), and *Macaulay* (1882) in 'Men of Letters' series; published *Service of Man* (positivist essay, 1887); contemplated a history of Louis XIV's reign.

MORISON, John (1750–1798), Scottish divine and poet; MA, King's College, Aberdeen, 1771; minister of Canisbay, 1780; contributed to *Scottish Paraphrases* (1781) and *Chalmers's *Caledonia*.

MORISON, John (1791–1859), Congregational minister; pastor at Chelsea, 1815–16, at Trevor Chapel, London, 1816–59; edited *Evangelical Magazine*, 1827–57; DD, Glasgow, 1830; published devotional works.

MORISON, Sir **Richard** (d. 1556), ambassador; BA, Oxford, 1528; visited Italy; prebendary of Salisbury, 1537; ambassador to the Hanse towns, 1546; commissioner to visit Oxford, 1549; knighted before 1550; ambassador to Charles V, 1550–3, with *Ascham as his secretary; studied with Peter Martyr at Strasburg, 1554–6; published a defence of Henry VIII against Cochlaeus (1537) and other works; died at Strasburg.

MORISON, Robert (1620–1683), botanist; MA and Ph.D., Aberdeen, 1638; studied science at Paris; MD, Angers, 1648; physician to Gaston, duke of Orleans, 1649; senior physician and king's botanist to Charles II, 1660; professor of botany at Oxford, 1669; published *Praeludia Botanica* (1669) and *Historia Plantarum Oxoniensis* (1680), containing a clear conception of genus, species, and family; his name perpetuated by the genus *Morisonia*; died from the effects of an accident.

MORISON, Stanley Arthur (1889–1967), typographer; educated at Owen's School, Islington; left school at 14; clerk with London City Mission, 1905–12; assistant, the *Imprint*, 1913–14; joined staff of Burns & Oates, Roman Catholic publishers; conscientious objector, imprisoned, 1916; typographer, Cloister Press, 1921–2; free-lance consultant; part-time consultant, Monotype Corporation, 1922–54; part-time typographical adviser, Cambridge University

Press, 1923–59; typographical adviser to *The Times*, 1930–60; edited *The History of The Times* (1935–52), edited *The Times Literary Supplement* (1945–7); member, editorial board, *Encyclopaedia Britannica*, 1961; James P. R. Lyell reader in bibliography, Oxford, 1956–7; Litt.D., Cambridge, 1950; Litt.D., Marquette (Wisconsin, USA) and Birmingham; FBA, 1954; Royal Designer for Industry, 1960; published *Block-letter Text* (1942); his collection of books in 'Morison Room' at Cambridge University Library.

MORISON, Sir Theodore (1863–1936), educationist and writer; son of J. A. C. *Morison; educated at Westminster and Trinity College, Cambridge; professor, Mohammedan Anglo-Oriental College, Aligarh, 1889, principal, 1899–1905; member, Council of India, 1906–16; principal, Armstrong College, Newcastle upon Tyne, 1919–29; director, British Institute, Paris, 1933–6; KCIE, 1910; KCSI, 1917.

MORISON (or MORESIN), Thomas (1558?–1603?), physician and diplomat; born in Scotland; MD, Montpellier; visited Frankfurt; after his return to Scotland (1593) became one of *Essex's intelligencers; wrote against alchemists and astrologers (1593); published a history of the papacy (1594).

MORISON, Thomas (d. 1824), army surgeon; son of James *Morison (1708–1786); brought into notice the medicinal properties of Strathpeffer springs.

MORLAND, George (1763–1804), painter; son of Henry Robert *Morland; exhibited when 10 years old at the Royal Academy; copied Flemish and Dutch pictures; early developed a taste for dissipation; his original picture, *The Angler's Repast*, was engraved by William Ward and published by John Raphael *Smith, 1780; married Anne, sister of William *Ward (1766–1826), 1786, his marriage having for a time a steadying effect; again fell into bad habits, and was arrested for debt, 1799; released, 1802; died in a sponging-house, his own epitaph on himself being 'Here lies a drunken dog'. He was a master of genre and animal painting, and his most characteristic pictures are faithful reflections of lowly life in England. His total production is estimated at 4,000 pictures.

MORLAND, George Henry (d. 1789?), genre painter; assisted by the Incorporated Society of Artists, 1760; his works engraved by *Watson and Philip *Dawe.

MORLAND, Sir Henry (1837–1891), Indian official; entered Indian Navy, 1852; fourth lieutenant, 1857; lieutenant, 1859; transferred to the marines, 1863; transport officer at Bombay, 1865; superintended Abyssinian expedition,

1867; organized commissariat and transport of Afghan War; conservator of the port of Bombay and registrar of shipping, 1873; knighted, 1887; died in Bombay.

MORLAND, Henry Robert (1730?–1797), portrait painter; son of George Henry *Morland; picture dealer; exhibited (1760–91) portraits and domestic subjects at the Royal Academy and Society of Artists.

MORLAND, Sir Samuel, first baronet (1625–1695), diplomat, mathematician and inventor; of Winchester School and Magdalene College, Cambridge; fellow and tutor, 1649; supported Parliamentarians; accompanied *Whitelocke's embassy to Sweden, 1653; assistant to Secretary *Thurloe, 1654; sent to remonstrate with the duke of Saxony on the Waldensian cruelties, 1655; published history of Waldensian Church (1658); became acquainted with Sir Richard Willis's plot, and from that time endeavoured to promote the Restoration; joined Charles II at Breda, May 1660; created baronet and gentleman of the privy chamber, 1660; visited France 'about the king's waterworks', 1682; became blind, 1692. He invented two arithmetical machines and a speaking trumpet, and by the 'plunger-pump' raised water to the top of Windsor Castle, 1675. Besides this, he endeavoured to use high-pressed steam as a power, and suggested it for the propulsion of vessels. He wrote on mathematics and hydrostatics. One of Morland's calculating machines is now at South Kensington, and a speaking trumpet is preserved at Cambridge.

MORLAND, Sir Thomas Lethbridge Napier (1865–1925), general; born at Montreal, Canada; gazetted into King's Royal Rifle Corps, 1884; transferred to West African Frontier Force, 1898; took part in six minor campaigns in Nigeria, 1898–1903; inspector-general, West African Frontier Force, 1905–9; major-general, 1913; commanded 5th division, 1914; X Army Corps, 1915–18; XIII Army Corps, 1918–19; commander-in-chief, army of occupation, Cologne, 1920–2; at Aldershot, 1922–3; general, 1922; KCB, 1915; died at Montreux.

MORLEY, Barons. See PARKER, HENRY, eighth baron, 1476–1556; PARKER, HENRY, ninth baron, d. 1577.

MORLEY, earls of. See PARKER, JOHN, first earl, 1772–1840; PARKER, EDMUND, second earl, 1810–1864; PARKER, ALBERT EDMUND, third earl, 1843–1905.

MORLEY, Christopher Love (*fl.* 1700), physician; MD, Leiden, 1679; studied under Schacht, Drelincourt, Maëts, Marggraff, and Le

Mort; hon. FCP, 1680; published *De Morbo Epidemico* (1679) and *Collectanea Chemica Leydensia* (1684).

MORLEY (MERLAI, MERLAC, or MARLACH), Daniel of (*fl.* 1170–1190), astronomer; said to have studied at Oxford, Paris, and Toledo; author of *Philosophia Magistri Danielis de Merlac* or *Liber de Naturis inferiorum et superiorum.*

MORLEY, George (1598–1684), bishop of Winchester; of Westminster School and Christ Church, Oxford; MA, 1621; DD, 1642; met at Oxford Robert *Sanderson, Gilbert *Sheldon, Edward *Hyde, afterwards earl of Clarendon, and subsequently Edmund *Waller and John *Hampden; canon of Christ Church, 1641; rector of Mildenhall, 1641; preached before the House of Commons, 1642; ejected, 1648; went abroad and performed service for the English Royalists wherever he stayed; sent to England to win over the Presbyterians to the Restoration; regained his canonry, became dean of Christ Church, Oxford, and in October bishop of Worcester, 1660; preacher of the coronation sermon, 1661; translated to Winchester, 1662; frequently entertained the duke of York at Farnham Castle; signified to Clarendon the king's wish that he should leave the country, 1667; of Calvinistic leanings; benefactor of Winchester diocese, St Paul's Cathedral, and Christ Church and Pembroke College, Oxford; published controversial works.

MORLEY, Henry (1822–1894), author; educated at King's College, London; editor of *Dickens's periodicals, 1850–65, and the *Examiner*; evening lecturer at King's College, London, 1857; professor of literature at University College, London, 1865, and Queen's College, London, 1878; principal of University Hall, Gordon Square, London, 1882–89; edited 'Morley's Universal Library' and 'Cassell's National Library'; wrote on English literature and biographies.

MORLEY, Herbert (1616–1667), colonel; educated at Lewes with John *Evelyn; entered the Inner Temple, 1634; MP, Lewes, 1640; colonel in the Parliamentary army; put Sussex in a state of defence, 1642; assisted in the recapture of Arundel and at Basing House, 1644; refused to act as one of the king's judges; opposed *Cromwell as long as possible and (1653) withdrew into private life; MP, Sussex, 1654, 1656, 1659, Lewes, 1659; one of the Council of State, 1650–1, 1651–3, 1659, and 1660; Admiralty commissioner, 1659; collected troops and opposed Lambert, Oct. 1659; restored parliament, Dec. 1659; refused to negotiate for the king's return; purchased pardon, 1660; was elected MP for Rye, but probably did not sit.

MORLEY, John (1656–1732), known as 'Merchant Morley'; agent and land-jobber of Halstead, Essex; a butcher who became agent to Edward *Harley, afterwards second earl of Oxford, and negotiated his marriage (1713) with Lady Henrietta Holles.

MORLEY, John (d. 1776?), medical writer; grandson of John *Morley (1656–1732); published an essay on scrofula (1767).

MORLEY, John, Viscount Morley of Blackburn (1838–1923), statesman and man of letters; educated at Cheltenham College and Lincoln College, Oxford; free-lance journalist in London, 1860–3; joined staff of *Saturday Review*, 1863; became acquainted with George *Meredith and John Stuart *Mill, to both of whom he owed much; editor of *Fortnightly Review*, which he made influential organ of liberal opinion, 1867–82; in close sympathy with Frederic *Harrison, who assisted him with *Fortnightly*, leading positivists; published his first study of *Burke, 1867; attempted unsuccessfully to enter parliament, 1868–9; admirer of T. H. *Huxley; his studies of Frenchmen of the Revolution and their precursors including *Voltaire* (1872) and *Rousseau* (1873) conveyed a message of rationalism and progress to his generation; through his radical opinions and views on national education, brought into contact with Joseph *Chamberlain; worked with Chamberlain and Sir Charles *Dilke at programme of disestablishment, secular education, land reform, and progressive taxation; adopted pacific outlook on foreign and imperial policy; published *Burke* ('English Men of Letters' series), 1879; editor of *Pall Mall Gazette*, which he changed from conservatism and imperialism to radicalism and Cobdenism, 1880; again attempted unsuccessfully to enter parliament, 1880; published *Life of Cobden*, one of his best writings and a classic among English political biographies (1881); MP, Newcastle upon Tyne, 1883–95; although only moderately successful as speaker, his moral leadership gave him position of independence and influence; broke with Chamberlain over Irish question; chief secretary for Ireland, 1886; took leading part in Round Table Conference, the object of which was to bring about concordat with Chamberlain and Sir G. O. *Trevelyan on Irish question, 1887; during years of opposition his energies largely absorbed in denouncing Lord Salisbury's policy of coercion; one of the most popular orators on Liberal platforms; edited 'English Men of Letters' series; published *Walpole* in 'Twelve English Statesmen' series (1889); chief secretary for Ireland, 1892–5; achieved his main task of helping Gladstone to prepare and carry through House of Commons second Home Rule Bill; MP, Montrose Burghs, 1896–1908; with Sir William *Harcourt resisted policy which found expression in South African War; published *Oliver Cromwell* (1900); published *Life of Gladstone*, his most important work (3 vols., 1903); secretary of state for India, 1905–10; planned series of reforms which aimed at gradually associating people of India with civil administration and government; created viscount, 1908; helped to conduct Parliament Bill limiting Lords' veto through Upper House, 1911; with John *Burns resigned from Cabinet on government's decision to intervene in European war, 1914; in retirement occupied himself with affairs of Manchester University, of which he had been elected chancellor (1908); OM, 1902; remained to end of his life agnostic, Liberal, and individualist.

MORLEY, Robert de, second Baron Morley (1296?–1360), summoned to parliament, 1317; served in Ireland, 1331; admiral of the fleet; gained the victory of Sluys, 1340; commanded the fleet, 1341, 1348, and 1354; served in the French wars, 1341, 1346, 1347, and 1359.

MORLEY, Samuel (1809–1886), politician; amassed a fortune in the hosiery business; active in religious, philanthropic, and temperance movements; MP, Nottingham, 1865; unseated on petition, 1866; became proprietor of the *Daily News*; MP, Bristol, 1868–85; consistently followed Gladstone; supported Irish disestablishment, and was converted to state education; on the London School Board, 1870–6; took part in all movements for the abolition of tests and Dissenters' burial grievances; munificent builder of chapels; pensioned his employees at a cost of £2,000 annually.

MORLEY, Thomas (1557–1604?), musician; pupil of William *Byrd; Mus.Bac., Oxford, 1588; organist of St Paul's Cathedral, 1591–2; gentleman of the Chapel Royal, 1592; wrote *Plaine and Easie Introduction to Practicall Musicke* (1597); composed graceful madrigals (including the well-known 'It was a Lover and his Lass') and church music.

MORLEY, William (d. 1347), meteorologist. See MERLE.

MORLEY, William Hook (1815–1860), orientalist; barrister, Middle Temple, 1840; discovered (1838) a missing manuscript of Rashidudin Jam'ia Tawarikh; librarian of Royal Asiatic Society.

MORLEY HORDER, Percy (Richard) (1870–1944), architect. See HORDER.

MORNINGTON, Barons. See WELLESLEY, RICHARD COLLEY, first baron, 1690?–1758; WELLESLEY, GARRETT, second baron, 1735–1781.

MORNINGTON, earls of. See WELLESLEY, GARRETT, first earl, 1735–1781; WELLESLEY, RICHARD COLLEY, second earl, 1760–1842; WELLESLEY-POLE, WILLIAM, third earl, 1763–1845; WELLESLEY, WILLIAM POLE TYLNEY LONG-, fourth earl, 1788–1857.

MORO, Antonio (1512?–1576?), portrait painter. See MORE, Sir ANTHONY.

MORPETH, Viscount (1773–1848). See HOWARD, GEORGE, sixth earl of Carlisle.

MORPHETT, Sir **John** (1809–1892), pioneer and politician of South Australia; emigrated, 1836; general merchant; nominated for the legislative assembly, 1843; speaker, 1851–5; chief secretary, 1861; president of the council, 1865–73; knighted, 1870; died in Australia.

MORRAH, Dermot Michael Macgregor (1896–1974), journalist and Arundel herald extraordinary; educated at Winchester and New College, Oxford, where he was a mathematical scholar; served in Royal Engineers in Palestine and Egypt, 1916–18; returned to Oxford; first class, modern history, 1921; received into Roman Catholic Church, 1922; fellow of All Souls, 1921–8; worked in Mines Department, 1922–8; assisted G. E. *Buckle with history of *The Times*, and joined staff of *Daily Mail*; member of staff of *The Times*, 1932–61; wrote stories and plays and books on the royal family; appointed Arundel herald extraordinary and took part in coronation of Queen Elizabeth II; editor of *Round Table*, 1944; leader writer of *Daily Telegraph*; member of Commonwealth Press Union; chairman, Wine Society, 1959–63; chairman, Circle of Wine Writers, 1964–6.

MORRELL, Hugh (d. 1664?), woollen merchant; was engaged in export trade between Exeter and France; obtained patents to regulate manufactures in Herefordshire, 1624, and Devonshire, 1626; having had his goods at Rouen seized by the French, petitioned the king for satisfaction, 1627; made efforts to improve trade, 1633, 1638, 1647; surveyor of customs at Dover, 1642; employed by government in commercial negotiations with France, 1650.

MORRELL, Lady **Ottoline Violet Anne** (1873–1938), half-sister of sixth duke of Portland; married Philip Edward Morrell, 1902; centre and patroness of distinguished literary and artistic circle in London, at Garsington Manor, Oxfordshire (1913–24), and after 1924 at 10 Gower Street, London.

MORRELL, William (*fl.* 1625), New England poet; BA, Magdalene College, Cambridge, 1614–15; an Anglican clergyman who remained a year in Massachusetts, 1623; wrote Latin hexameters and English verse on New England, 1625.

MORREN, Nathaniel (1798–1847), Scottish divine; MA, Marischal College, Aberdeen, 1814; minister at Greenock, 1823, and Brechin, 1843; wrote *Annals of the General Assembly* and other ecclesiastical works.

MORRES, Hervey Montmorency (1767–1839), United Irishman; entered the Austrian service; returned to Ireland, 1795; became a United Irishman, 1796; chosen county representative for Tipperary, 1797; adjutant-general of Munster; escaped to Hamburg after the capitulation of the French at Ballinamuck, 1798; arrested and extradited, 1799; prosecuted, but without result; released, 1801; entered the French service, *c.*1811, and became adjutant-commandant, with the rank of colonel, 1812; obtained letters of naturalization, 1816; wrote on Irish topography and the Montmorency genealogy; died at St Germain-en-Laye.

MORRES, Hervey Redmond, second Viscount Mountmorres (1746?–1797), BA, Christ Church, Oxford, 1766; created MA, 1766; DCL, 1773; supported Pitt strongly in Ireland, 1788; wrote on political questions; shot himself in a fit of insanity.

MORRICE. See MORICE and MORRIS.

MORRIS. See also MORICE.

MORRIS, (Alfred) Edwin (1894–1971), fifth archbishop of Wales; educated at St David's College School, Lampeter; served in RAMC during 1914–18 war; senior scholar, St David's College, Lampeter; first class, theology, 1924; exhibitioner, St John's College, Oxford; professor of Hebrew and theology, Lampeter, 1924; ordained deacon, 1924; priest, 1925; examining chaplain to bishop of Bangor, 1925–8, and to bishop of Llandaff, 1931–4; Lloyd Williams fellow, St David's College, Lampeter, 1931–45; BD, 1932; bishop of Monmouth, 1945; published *The Church in Wales and Nonconformity* (1949), *The Problem of Life and Death* (1950), and *The Catholicity of the Book of Common Prayer* (1952); DD (Lambeth), 1950; hon. DD (University of Wales), 1971; archbishop of Wales, 1957–67; hon. fellow, St John's College, Oxford, 1958; an Englishman in Wales who enjoyed controversy.

MORRIS, Charles (1745–1838), song-writer; entered 17th Foot, 1764; served in America; exchanged into the 2nd Life Guards; punchmaker and bard of the Beefsteak Society, 1785, at which he sang many of his wittiest songs; visited frequently at Carlton House; his songs published as *Lyra Urbanica* (1840).

MORRIS (MORES or **MORICE),** Sir **Christopher** (1490?–1544), master of ordnance; gunner in the Tower, 1513; served on the coast of France, 1522–4; master of ordnance, 1537; master-gunner of England, and knighted, 1537; with Hertford in Scotland, 1544; mortally wounded at Boulogne.

MORRIS, Corbyn (1710–1779), commissioner of customs; provoked controversy on the national income by a *Letter from a Bystander* (1742); made proposals for regulating the Highlands, 1745; secretary of the customs in Scotland, 1751; suggested a census to the duke of Newcastle, 1753; FRS, 1757; commissioner of customs in England, 1763; published economic works.

MORRIS, Edward (d. 1689), Welsh poet; wrote carols, ballads, and 'englynion'; translated an English ecclesiastical work into Welsh.

MORRIS, Edward Patrick, first Baron Morris (1859–1935), premier of Newfoundland; born at St John's, Newfoundland; educated at Ottawa University; MP, St John's West, 1885–1919; entered Cabinet, 1889; leader of Independent Liberal party, 1898–1900; attorney-general and minister of justice under Sir Robert *Bond, 1902–7; leader of 'People's' party, 1908; premier, 1909–18; brought Newfoundland prominently into councils of the Empire; knighted, 1904; PC, 1911; KCMG, 1913; baron, 1918.

MORRIS, Francis Orpen (1810–1893), naturalist; grandson of Roger *Morris; BA, Worcester College, Oxford, 1833; incumbent of Nafferton, 1844, of Nunburnholme, 1854; antivivisectionist; wrote against Darwinianism and on religion and natural history; chief work, *History of British Birds* (1851–7).

MORRIS, Sir Harold Spencer (1876–1967), president of the Industrial Court; educated at Westminster, Clifton, and Magdalen College, Oxford; called to bar (Inner Temple), 1899; member, south-eastern circuit; commissioned in Coldstream Guards, 1916; transferred to Flying Corps as deputy assistant adjutant-general, 1918; MBE, 1919; KC, 1921; recorder of Folkestone, 1921–6; National Liberal MP, East Bristol, 1922–3; chairman, court of investigation into dispute in the woollen industry, 1925; chairman, Railways National Wages Board, 1925; president, Industrial Court, 1926–45; knighted, 1927; chairman, Coal Wages Board, 1930–5; published *The Barrister* (1930) and *Back View* (1960).

MORRIS (or MORUS), Huw (1622–1709), Welsh poet; composed carols, ballads, and occasional verse; Royalist; wrote satires on the Parliamentary party; collected edition of his poems published (1823).

MORRIS, Sir James Nicoll (1763?–1830), vice-admiral; joined navy before 1778; lieutenant, 1780; commander, 1790; served in the Channel and Mediterranean, and with Nelson off Cadiz; wounded at Trafalgar, 1805; rear-admiral, 1811; third-in-command in the Baltic, 1812; KCB, 1815; vice-admiral, 1819.

MORRIS, John (1617?–1649), soldier; brought up in the household of Thomas *Wentworth, first earl of Strafford; after Strafford's death became major, 1643; threw up his commission, 1644; colonel in the Parliamentary army; ousted from command by the New Model Army; took Pontefract Castle by stratagem, 1645 (castle retaken by Parliamentarians, 1649); imprisoned in Lancaster Castle; escaped, but was retaken and executed.

MORRIS, John (1810–1886), geologist; originally a pharmaceutical chemist; professor of geology, University College, London, 1854–77; FGS, 1845; published *Catalogue of British Fossils* (1845) and, in conjunction with John Lycett, *Great Oolite Mollusca*.

MORRIS, John (1826–1893), Jesuit; son of John Carnac *Morris; born at Ootacamund; entered Trinity College, Cambridge, 1845; became a Roman Catholic, 1846; ordained to the English mission, 1849; vice-rector of the English College, Rome, 1852–5; secretary to Cardinal *Wiseman; professed of the four vows, 1877; rector at Roehampton, 1880–6; FSA, 1889; published works on ecclesiastical history.

MORRIS, John Brande (1812–1880), theological writer; MA, Balliol College, Oxford, 1837; fellow and Hebrew lecturer, Exeter College, Oxford, 1837; joined Church of Rome, 1846; priest, 1849; held various charges; published mystic and devotional works.

MORRIS, John Carnac (1798–1858), Telugu scholar; midshipman, 1813–15; entered Madras Civil Service, 1818; FRS, 1831; Telugu translator to government, 1832; accountant-general, 1834; established bank in Madras, 1834; returned to England, 1846, and engaged in commercial enterprise; published an *English–Telugu Dictionary* (1835); died at St Heliers.

MORRIS, John Humphrey Carlile (1910–1984), academic lawyer; educated at Charterhouse and Christ Church, Oxford; Holford history scholar; first class, jurisprudence, 1931 and in BCL, 1932; Eldon law scholar, 1933; called to the bar (Gray's Inn), 1934; fellow, Magdalen College, 1936–77; served in Royal Naval Volunteer Reserve, 1940–5; All Souls lecturer in pri-

vate international law, 1939–51; reader in the conflict of laws, 1951–77; visiting professor at Harvard, 1950–1; author or contributor to twenty-seven volumes of legal works, including *The Rule against Perpetuities* (1956, 2nd edn., 1962, with W. Barton Leach), *Cases on Private International Law* (1939–68), *Cases and Materials on Private International Law* (with P. M. North, 1984), and three editions of students' textbook, *The Conflict of Laws* (1971–84); edited five editions of A. V. *Dicey and Morris, *The Conflict of Laws* (1949–80), three editions of *Theobold on the Law of Wills* (1939–54), and 22nd edition of *Chitty on Contracts* (1961); DCL, 1949; FBA, 1966; hon. fellow, Magdalen College, 1977; hon. bencher, Gray's Inn, 1980; QC, 1981; associate member, Institute of International Law, 1954, and of American Academy of Arts and Sciences, 1960; Arthur Goodhart visiting professor of legal science and fellow of Gonville and Caius College, Cambridge, 1978–9; an ardent sailor; published *Thank You, Wodehouse*, 1981.

MORRIS, John Webster (1763–1836), Baptist minister and author; pastor of Clipstone, 1785, of Dunstable, 1803–9; set up as a printer, and published the works of Sutcliffe, *Fuller, and Hall; chief works, *Sacred Biography* and *Memoirs of . . . Andrew Fuller* (1816).

MORRIS, John William, Baron Morris of Borth-y-Gest (1896–1979), lawyer and public servant; educated at Liverpool Institute; served in Royal Welch Fusiliers in France, 1914–18; MC; studied at Trinity Hall, Cambridge; president of the Union; LL B, 1920; studied at Harvard, 1920–1; called to bar (Inner Temple), 1921; joined the northern circuit; KC, 1935; judge of King's Bench division, 1945; CBE and knighted, 1945; lord justice of appeal, 1951; PC, 1951; lord of appeal in ordinary, 1960–75; baron, 1960; CH, 1975; bencher, Inner Temple, 1943; treasurer, 1967; chairman of number of committees including Home Office Committee on Jury Service, 1963–4; member of Pilgrims' Society and University Grants Committee; chairman, board of governors of Charing Cross Hospital, 1948–68; honorary standing counsel to University of Wales, 1938–45; pro-chancellor, 1956–74; member of Gorsedd of Bards; vice-president, Honourable Society of Cymmrodorion; president, London Welsh Association, 1951–3; number of honorary degrees; hon. fellow, Trinity Hall, Cambridge, 1951.

MORRIS (or MORYS), Lewis (1700–1765), Welsh poet; philologist and antiquary; originally a land surveyor; collector of customs at Holyhead, 1729; surveyed the Welsh coast, 1737–48; superintendent of crown lands and mines in Wales, 1750; retired to Penbryn, 1761; published poetry and works on Welsh history and antiquities; author of a dictionary of Celtic mythology, history, and geography, completed 1760, published (1878).

MORRIS, Sir Lewis (1833–1907), poet and Welsh educationist; born at Carmarthen; BA (first class, Lit. Hum.), Jesus College, Oxford, 1856; MA, 1858; Chancellor's Prize for English essay, 1858; fellow, 1877; called to bar, 1861; practised as conveyancer in London till 1880; published anonymously *Songs of Two Worlds*, sonorous and optimistic verse (3 series, 1871, 1874, 1875, republished in one vol., 1878); imitated *Tennyson's *Tithonus* in a series of blank-verse monologues, collected as *The Epic of Hades* (1877), which was popular with the middle classes and reached a 45th edition; there followed *Gwen: a Drama in Monologue* (1879), *The Ode of Life* (descriptive poems, 1880), *Songs Unsung* (1883, the first volume issued under author's name), *Gycia: a tragedy* (1886), and *Songs of Britain* (1887); collected editions appeared in 1882 (3 vols.) and 1890; *A Vision of Saints* in 1890, and subsequently other collections of lyrics; his work was ridiculed in *Saturday Review*; published a volume of essays, *The New Rambler* (1905); honorary secretary (1878), honorary treasurer (1889), and vice-president (1896) of University College of Wales, Aberystwyth; helped in establishing University of Wales, 1893; hon. D.Lit., 1906; knighted, 1895; an advanced Liberal; failed in attempts to enter parliament.

MORRIS, Michael, Baron Morris and Killanin (1826–1901), lord chief justice of Ireland; senior moderator in ethics and logic, Trinity College, Dublin, 1846; hon. LL D, 1887; called to Irish bar, 1849; recorder of Galway, 1857–65; QC, 1863; Independent Conservative MP for Galway, 1865; solicitor-general for Ireland, July 1866; attorney-general, Nov.; Irish PC; puisne judge of court of common pleas, 1867; lord chief justice of Ireland, 1887; baronet, 1885; member of judicial committee of English Privy Council, receiving life peerage, 1889; bencher of Lincoln's Inn, 1890; commissioner of Irish national education; vice-chancellor of Royal University, Ireland, 1899; made hereditary baron of Killanin, 1900; an opponent of home rule, but a caustic critic of English rule in Ireland.

MORRIS, Morris Drake (*fl.* 1717), biographer; of Trinity College, Cambridge; assumed surname Morris, 1717; compiled biographies of famous men, 1715–16.

MORRIS, Philip Richard (1836–1902), painter; won travelling studentship at Royal Academy Schools, 1858; exhibited at Academy, 1858–1901; ARA, 1877; early painted sea pictures, later religious subjects; best-known works were *Sons of the Brave* and *The First Communion*.

MORRIS, Sir Philip Robert (1901–1979), educationist; educated at Tonbridge School, St Peter's School, York, and Trinity College, Oxford; teacher's diploma, London, 1924; lecturer in history and classics, Westminster Training College, 1923–5; joined Kent education authority as administrative officer; director, 1938–43; CBE, 1941; director-general of army education, 1944–6; knighted, 1946; vice-chancellor, Bristol University, 1946–66; chairman, Vice-chancellors' Committee, 1955–8; served on McNair Committee on Supply and Training of Teachers, 1943–4, and on Robbins Committee on Higher Education, 1961–4; chairman, Secondary Schools Examination Council; governor, BBC, 1952–60; vice-chairman, 1954–60; chairman, Bristol Old Vic Trust, 1946–71; KCMG, 1960; FRSA, 1961; hon. FRCS, 1966; many honorary degrees.

MORRIS (or MORYS), Richard (d. 1779), Welsh scholar; brother of Lewis *Morris; clerk of foreign accounts in Navy Office; supervised editions of the Welsh Bible (1746 and 1752) and of the Prayer-Book.

MORRIS, Richard (1833–1894), philologist; Winchester lecturer on English language and literature at King's College School, 1869; ordained, 1871; headmaster of Royal Masonic Institution for Boys, Wood Green, London, 1875–88; LL D, Lambeth, 1870; hon. MA, Oxford, 1874; published educational works on English grammar, besides editions of texts for the Early English Text Society and Pali Text Society.

MORRIS, Robert (*fl.* 1754), architect; supervised building of Inverary Castle, 1745–61, Richmond Park Lodge, Brandenburgh House, c.1750, Wimbledon House, and Kirby Hall, c.1750; published architectural works.

MORRIS, Roger (1727–1794), lieutenant-colonel; American Loyalist; captain in 48th Foot, 1745; went to America, 1755; aide-de-camp to Major-General *Braddock and major, 1758; wounded at Quebec; lieutenant-colonel, 1760; retired, 1764; returned to England, 1776, after his wife's property on the Hudson River was confiscated and she was attainted.

MORRIS, Thomas (1660–1748), nonjuror; minor canon of Worcester and vicar of Claines; MA, King's College, Cambridge, 1688; deprived, 1689; buried in Worcester Cathedral as 'Miserimus' (*sic*), without name or date, a fact which called forth poems from *Wordsworth and others, and a novel by Frederic Mansel *Reynolds, 1832. The epitaph was nearly obliterated in 1829, but renewed as 'Miserrimus'.

MORRIS, Thomas (*fl.* 1780–1800), engraver; pupil of *Woollett; confined himself to line-engravings of landscapes after *Gilpin and *Garrard.

MORRIS, Captain **Thomas** (*fl.* 1806), song-writer; brother of Charles *Morris; of Winchester College and Jesus College, Oxford; BA, 1753; served with 17th Foot in America; published songs and verses.

MORRIS, Tom (1821–1908), golfer; apprenticed to Allan Robertson, golfer of St Andrews and golf-ball maker; won Open Golf Championship, 1861–2–4–6; green keeper to St Andrews Golf Club, 1863–1903.

MORRIS, Sir William (1602–1676), secretary of state and theologian. See MORICE.

MORRIS, William (1834–1896), poet, artist, manufacturer, and socialist; of Marlborough School and Exeter College, Oxford; formed friendship with (Sir) Edward Coley *Burne-Jones; BA, 1856; articled as architect to George Edmund *Street, 1856; followed profession of painter, 1857–62; one of originators of *Oxford and Cambridge Magazine*, to which he contributed tales, essays, and poems; assisted in painting frescos in Oxford Union, 1857; published *Defence of Guenevere and other Poems* (1858); helped to found manufacturing and decorating firm of Morris, Marshall, Faulkner & Co. (dissolved, 1874), in which *Rossetti, *Burne-Jones, Madox *Brown, and Philip Webb were also partners; published *Life and Death of Jason* (1867) and *Earthly Paradise* (1868–70); travelled in Iceland, 1871; acquired Kelmscott Manor House, near Lechlade; published *Love is Enough* (1872); produced numerous illuminated manuscripts, including two of *Fitzgerald's *Omar Khayyam*; published *Aeneids of Virgil* (an English verse translation, 1875), *Three Northern Love Stories* (1875), and the epic, *Sigurd the Volsung and the Fall of the Niblungs* (1876); studied practical arts of dyeing and carpet-weaving; founded Society for the Protection of Ancient Buildings, 1877; treasurer of National Liberal League, 1879; joined, 1883, Democratic Federation, the doctrine of which, largely under his leadership, developed into socialism, and on its disruption, 1884, became head of the seceders, who organized themselves as the Socialist League; published English verse translation of *Odyssey* (1887), *Dream of John Ball* (1888), *House of the Wolfings* (1889), *The Roots of the Mountains* (1890), *Story of the Glittering Plain* (1890), *News from Nowhere* (1891), *The Wood beyond the World* (1894), *Child Christopher* (1895), *The Well at the World's End* (1896), and *The Water of the Wondrous Isles* and *Story of the Sundering Flood*, posthumously (1897 and 1898 respectively); started, 1890, at Hammersmith, the Kelmscott Press, for which he designed founts of type and ornamental letters and borders, and from which were issued fifty-three books, comprising (1) Morris's own works, (2) reprints of English classics, and (3) various smaller books, originals or translations.

MORRIS, William O'Connor (1824–1904), Irish county-court judge and historian; BA, Oriel College, Oxford, 1848; called to Irish bar, 1854; professor of common and criminal law in King's Inns, Dublin, 1862; contributed to *Edinburgh Review*, and wrote articles on land tenure in *The Times*, 1870; county-court judge for Louth, 1872, and Kerry, 1878; disapproved of Land Act of 1881; transferred as judge for Sligo and Roscommon, 1886; published superficial but independent studies of Hannibal (1890), Napoleon (1890), Moltke (1893), *Nelson (1898), and Wellington (1904); *Ireland from 1494 to 1868* (1894) and *Ireland from '98 to '98* (1898).

MORRIS, William Richard, Viscount Nuffield (1877–1963), industrialist and philanthropist; educated at village school, Cowley; started making bicycles at 16 with capital of £4; designed motor cycle, 1902; produced Morris-Oxford car at Motor Show, 1912; acquired property in Cowley for expansion; Cowley factory produced mainly munitions during 1914–18 war; OBE, 1917; Morris Motors Ltd. incorporated, 1919; produced 50,000 cars a year, 1926; established Pressed Steel Company, Cowley, and Morris Motors (1926) Ltd.; produced Morris-Minor, 1931; acquired Wolseley, MG, and SU Carburettor companies; endowed chair of Spanish studies, Oxford, 1926; endowed medical school at Oxford, 1936; aided financially the Royal College of Surgeons, 1948, Oxford hospitals, Guy's, St Thomas's, Great Ormond Street, and hospitals in Birmingham, Coventry, and Worcester; provided Nuffield Orthopaedic Centre, Oxford, Nuffield Fund for Cripples (1935–7), and fund for orthopaedic services in Australia, New Zealand, and South Africa (1935–45); financed Nuffield Provincial Hospitals Trust, 1939; founded Nuffield College, 1937, and Nuffield Foundation to promote research, 1943; manufactured tanks and aircraft from 1937/8; merged Morris Motors with Austin Motor Company to form British Motor Corporation, 1952; baronet, 1929; baron, 1934; viscount, 1938; GBE, 1941; CH, 1958; hon. DCL, Oxford, 1931; MA, 1937; FRS, 1939; hon. FRCS, 1948; hon. fellow, St Peter's, Pembroke, Worcester, and Nuffield colleges, Oxford.

MORRIS AND KILLANIN, Baron (1826–1901), lord chief justice of Ireland. See MORRIS, MICHAEL.

MORRIS-JONES, Sir **John** (1864–1929), Welsh poet and grammarian; educated at Christ College, Brecon; BA, Jesus College, Oxford; turned from mathematics to devote himself wholly to study of Welsh; a founder of Dafydd ap Gwilym Society at Oxford; specialized in philology and Welsh verse; lecturer in Welsh, Bangor University College, 1889; professor of Welsh, 1895–1929; by his series of adjudications at national eisteddfod, Llandudno, raised standard of poetic diction; his chief works, *Cerdd Dafod* (1925) and *Welsh Grammar* (1913); knighted, 1918.

MORRISON, Alfred (1821–1897), collector of works of art; son of James *Morrison; made at his houses at Fonthill and Carlton House Terrace, London, collections of works of art and autographs. The autographs comprised many valuable manuscripts, including the papers of Sir Richard *Bulstrode, which he printed for the first time.

MORRISON, Charles (*fl.* 1753), first projector of the electric telegraph; a Greenock surgeon who emigrated to Virginia; in a letter to the *Scots Magazine*, 1753, he suggested conveying messages by electricity; died in Virginia.

MORRISON, George (1704?–1799), general; gunner, 1722; served in Flanders, 1747; employed in surveying and constructing roads in the Highlands, 1745–50; captain and engineer-in-ordinary, 1758; engaged in descents on the French coast, 1758; lieutenant-colonel, 1761; quartermaster-general, 1763; equerry to the duke of York, 1764; colonel, 1777; lieutenant-general, 1782; general, 1796.

MORRISON, Herbert Stanley, Baron Morrison of Lambeth (1888–1965), Labour Cabinet minister; left school at 14 to become an errand boy; worked as shop assistant and switchboard operator; circulation manager for first official Labour paper, the *Daily Citizen*, 1912–15; part-time secretary, London Labour party, 1915; mayor of Hackney, 1919; member, London County Council, 1922–45, leader, 1934–40; Labour MP, Hackney South, 1923–4 and 1929–31; minister of transport, 1929; created London Passenger Transport Board; lost parliamentary seat, 1931; re-elected for Hackney South, 1935–45; Clement Attlee preferred for Labour leadership; minister of supply in National government, 1940; home secretary and minister of home security, 1940; created National Fire Service; played notable part in preparing for Labour victory, 1945; MP, Lewisham East, 1945–51, and South Lewisham, 1951–9; lord president of the Council, 1945–7; leader, House of Commons, 1947–51; CH, 1951; foreign sec-

retary, 1951; not so successful as in previous ministries; overridden by Attlee in proposal for direct action against Mossadeq in Persia; deputy prime minister, 1945–51; strong claims to succeed Attlee as leader, but Hugh *Gaitskell elected, 1955; visiting fellow, Nuffield College, Oxford, 1947; publications include *Socialization and Transport* (1933), *Government and Parliament, a Survey from the Inside* (1954), and *An Autobiography* (1960); life peer, 1959; president, British Board of Film Censors, 1960; great leader of the London Labour party and LCC, and a fine parliamentarian.

MORRISON, James (1790–1857), merchant and politician; amassed a fortune as a draper; MP, St Ives, 1830; voted for the Reform Bill; MP, Ipswich, 1831–7, Inverness burghs, 1840–7; endeavoured to improve railway legislation, and published pamphlets on the subject.

MORRISON, John Robert (1814–1843), officiating colonial secretary of Hong Kong; son of Robert *Morrison; born at Macao; translator to the Canton merchants, 1830; secretary and interpreter to the British government, 1834–42; officiating colonial secretary of Hong Kong; published the *Chinese Commercial Guide* (1833); died at Hong Kong.

MORRISON, Sir **Richard** (1767–1849), architect; knighted, 1841; built, among other public works, the Roman Catholic cathedral at Dublin.

MORRISON, Richard James (1795–1874), inventor and astrologer; known by his pseudonym of 'Zadkiel'; entered navy, 1806; served in the Adriatic and on the North Sea, Baltic, and Cork stations; lieutenant, 1815; coastguard, 1827–9; presented plan to the Admiralty (1824) for registering merchant seamen, and another (1835) for providing seamen without impressment; brought out the *Herald of Astrology* (1831, continued as *Zadkiel's Almanac*); wrote on astrology and astronomy.

MORRISON, Robert (1782–1834), Chinese missionary; originally a shoemaker; studied in England, 1801–7; went to China, 1807; translator to the East India Company, 1809; interpreter to Lord *Amherst, 1817; DD, Glasgow, 1817; established the Anglo-Chinese College at Malacca, 1818; FRS, 1825; published *Dictionary of the Chinese Language* (1815–23) and translated the Bible into Chinese; died at Macao.

MORRISON, Thomas (d. 1835?), medical writer; MRCS; practised in Chelsea, 1798; moved to Dublin, 1806. His medical works include *An Examination into the . . . Brunonian System* (1806).

MORRISON, Walter (1836–1921), man of business and philanthropist; educated at Eton and Balliol; Liberal MP, Plymouth, 1861–74; Liberal Unionist MP, Skipton division of Yorkshire, 1886–92, 1895–1900; inherited large fortune which he increased; entertained many eminent friends at Malham Tarn, Yorkshire; benefactions include gifts to northern universities, Giggleswick School, King Edward's Hospital Fund (annual contribution for many years £10,000), Palestine Exploration Fund, Oxford University (£30,000), and Bodleian Library (£50,000).

MORRISON, William Shepherd, first Viscount Dunrossil (1893–1961), speaker of the House of Commons; educated at George Watson's College and Edinburgh University; MA, 1920; served in Royal Field Artillery, MC, during 1914–18 war; called to bar (Inner Temple), 1923; Conservative MP, Cirencester and Tewkesbury, 1929–59; chairman, 1922 Committee, 1932–6; KC, 1934; recorder, Walsall, 1935; financial secretary to the Treasury, 1935; minister of agriculture and fisheries, 1936; PC, 1936; chancellor, duchy of Lancaster, and minister of food, 1939–40; postmaster-general, 1940–2; minister, town and country planning, 1943–5; speaker of the House of Commons, 1951–9; governor-general, Australia, 1960–1; viscount, GCMG, 1959.

MORRISON, William Vitruvius (1794–1838), architect; son of Sir Richard *Morrison; made tour through Europe, 1821; assisted his father.

MORRITT, John Bacon Sawrey (1771–1843), traveller and classical scholar; MA, St John's College, Cambridge, 1798; travelled in Greece and Asia Minor, 1794–6; surveyed the scene of the *Iliad*; maintained historical existence of Troy against Jacob *Bryant; MP, Beverley, 1799–1802, Northallerton, 1814–18, Shaftesbury, 1818–20; exchanged visits with *Scott; 'arch-master' of the Dilettanti Society; a founder of the Travellers' Club, 1819.

MORS, Roderick (d. 1546), satirist. See BRINKELOW, HENRY.

MORSE, Henry (1595–1645), Jesuit; known as Claxton and Warde; studied at Douai and Rome; missioner in England, 1624; Jesuit, 1625; three times arrested and imprisoned in England, and finally executed at Tyburn; his diary in the British Museum.

MORSE, Robert (1743–1818), general; employed in descents on the French coast, 1758; served in the West Indies, 1759, and in the expedition against Belle Isle, 1761; in Germany, 1762–3; captain-lieutenant and engineer-extra-ordinary, 1763; commanded in the West Indies; chief engineer in America, 1782; lieutenant-colonel, 1783; colonel, 1788; commanding engineer at Gibraltar, 1791; major-general, 1793; lieutenant-general, 1799; inspector-general of fortifications, 1802; general, 1808; author of report on Nova Scotia and plans.

MORSE, William (d. 1649), Jesuit; brother of Henry *Morse; missioner in England.

MORSHEAD, Henry Anderson (1774?–1831), colonel, Royal Engineers; entered artillery, 1790; served in Flanders; transferred to the engineers, 1794; first lieutenant, 1796; captain-lieutenant, 1801; captain, 1805; assumed name of Morshead, 1805; served in Madeira, 1808–12; lieutenant-colonel, 1813; commanding Royal Engineer of western district, 1815; colonel, 1825; commanding engineer at Malta, 1829; died at Valetta.

MORSHEAD, Sir Leslie James (1889–1959), lieutenant-general; born in Australia; educated at Mount Pleasant State School, Ballarat, and the Teachers' Training College, Melbourne; schoolmaster up to 1914; commissioned in First Australian Imperial Force, 1914; landed at Anzac, 1915; invalided home with enteric fever, and on recovery commanded 33rd battalion (3rd division) in France, 1916–18; DSO, CMG; on demobilization became sheep farmer, and then joined the Orient Steam Navigation Company; on outbreak of 1939–45 war commanded 18th Australian brigade; promoted major-general and commanded 9th Australian division, 1941; besieged in Tobruk; lieutenant-general in command, Australian Imperial Force, Middle East, 1942; at El Alamein battle; commanded 1st Australian Corps in recapture of Borneo; KBE and KCB, 1942; general manager in Australia, Orient Steam Navigation Company, 1948.

MORT, Thomas Sutcliffe (1816–1878), a pioneer of commerce in New South Wales; went to Australia, 1838; promoted steam navigation, 1841; started public wool sales, 1843; promoted first railway in New South Wales, 1849; encouraged pastoral development; commenced dock at Port Jackson, 1863; originated frozen meat trade, 1875; died in Australia.

MORTAIN, Robert of, count of Mortain, in the diocese of Avranches (d. 1091?), brother of *Odo of Bayeux; uterine brother of William the Conqueror; received from William the county of Mortain, 1049; accompanied William to England and received many grants; held Pevensey Castle against William Rufus (William II), 1088.

MORTEN, Thomas (1836–1866), painter and book-illustrator; occasionally exhibited at the

Royal Academy; illustrated works, including *Gulliver's Travels* (1846).

MORTIMER, (Charles) Raymond (Bell) (1895–1980), literary and art critic and editor; educated at Malvern College, and Balliol College, Oxford; worked in hospital in France, 1915–18; cipher clerk in Foreign Office, 1918; published novel, *The Oxford Circus* (in collaboration with Hamish Miles, 1922); reader for *Vogue*, the *Nation*, and the *New Statesman*; took over from T. S. *Eliot London letter to New York periodical, the *Dial*; reviewer of literature and the visual arts for *New Statesman*; published *The New Interior Decoration* (with Dorothy Todd, 1929); also published *The French Pictures, a Letter to Harriet* (1932) and *Duncan Grant* (1944); member of Royal Fine Art Commission; literary editor, *New Statesman*, 1935–47 (but at Ministry of Information, 1940–1); moved to *Sunday Times*, 1948; became chief reviewer, 1952–80; selected pieces published in *Channel Packet* (1942) and *Try Anything Once* (1976); CBE, 1955, and officer of French Legion of Honour; awarded Prix de l'Académie Française, 1977.

MORTIMER, Cromwell (d. 1752), physician; son of John *Mortimer; MA, Cambridge, *comitiis regiis*, 1728; studied under Boerhaave at Leiden; MD, Leiden, 1724; LRCP, 1725; assistant to Sir Hans *Sloane, 1729–40; issued account of his system of payments, 1744; FRS, 1728 (secretary, 1730–52); promoted incorporation of Society of Antiquaries, 1750; edited Royal Society's *Transactions*; wrote on chemistry.

MORTIMER, Edmund (II) de, third earl of March (1351–1381), son of Roger de *Mortimer (V), second earl of March; succeeded to earldom, 1360; married Philippa, daughter of *Lionel, second son of Edward III, 1368, and handed on to the house of York the claim to the throne, which resulted in the Wars of the Roses; marshal of England, 1369–77; ambassador to France and Scotland, 1373; led the constitutional and popular party in opposition to the court and *John of Gaunt in the Good Parliament, 1376; bore the sword and spurs at Richard II's coronation, 1377; elected on the king's new council; commissioner to treat with Scotland and inspect the fortifications in the north, 1378; lieutenant of Ireland, 1379; established himself in eastern Ulster; attempted to gain possession of Connaught and Munster; died at Cork.

MORTIMER, Sir Edmund (III) de (1376–1409?), son of Edmund de *Mortimer (II), third earl of March; adhered to Henry of Lancaster's rising fortunes, 1399; assisted to put down revolt of Owen *Glendower, but, on being taken prisoner at Brynglas, 1402, joined with Glendower,

married his daughter, and possibly assisted in the triple partition treaty, 1405; perished during the siege of Harlech.

MORTIMER, Edmund (IV) de, fifth earl of March and third earl of Ulster (1391–1425), son of Roger de *Mortimer (VI), fourth earl of March; succeeded his father and was recognized as heir-presumptive by Richard II, 1398; honourably treated, but strictly guarded on the Lancastrian revolution; his estates restored, 1413; KB and summoned to parliament, 1413; founded college of secular canons at Stoke-by-Clare, 1414; retained Henry V's friendship, divulging a plot formed in his favour against the king, and served with him in France, 1415–21; lieutenant of Ireland, 1423, sending a deputy there; obliged by the unsettled state of Ireland to go there in person, 1424, and negotiate with the native septs, but he died suddenly of plague.

MORTIMER, Mrs Favell Lee (1802–1878), authoress; née Bevan; corresponded with Henry Edward *Manning; married Thomas Mortimer, 1841; wrote educational works for the young, including *Peep of Day* (last edn., 1891), *Line upon Line* (1837), and *Reading without Tears* (1857).

MORTIMER, George Ferris Whidborne (1805–1871), schoolmaster and divine; BA, The Queen's College, Oxford, 1826; headmaster of Newcastle Grammar School, 1828, Brompton Proprietary School, 1833, and the City of London School, 1840–65; hon. prebendary of St Paul's Cathedral, 1864.

MORTIMER, Hugh (I) de (d. 1181), lord of Wigmore and founder of Wigmore Priory; son of Ralph de *Mortimer (I); during Stephen's reign devoted himself to strengthening his local position and fortifying Bridgnorth, Cleobury, and Wigmore castles; resisted Henry II, 1155; his castles taken; subsequently allowed to retain his castles and lands, which he held free from military service, aids, and scutages; established Wigmore Priory (consecrated, 1174).

MORTIMER, John (1656?–1736), writer on agriculture and merchant; chief work, *The whole Art of Husbandry* (1707; sixth edn., 1761).

MORTIMER, John Hamilton (1741–1779), historical painter; studied under *Cipriani, Robert Edge *Pine, and *Reynolds; won, in competition with *Romney, the prize for an historical picture, with *St Paul converting the Britons*, 1763; vice-president of the Incorporated Society of Arts, 1773; RA, 1779; painted historical and allegorical pictures.

MORTIMER, Ralph (I) de (d. 1104?), Norman baron; son of Roger de *Mortimer (*fl.* 1054); received forfeited estates, including Wigmore, in the middle marches of Wales, 1074; probably seneschal of the earl of Shrewsbury; joined in the rising of 1088; as a partisan of William Rufus (William II) joined the barons of Caux in repelling the French, 1089; received fresh estates, 1102; upheld Henry I in Normandy against *Robert, 1104.

MORTIMER, Robert Cecil (1902–1976), bishop of Exeter; educated at St Edward's School, Oxford (entrance scholar), and Keble College, Oxford; first class, hon. mods., 1923 and Lit. Hum., 1925; studied at Wells Theological College, 1926; ordained deacon, 1926; lecturer in theology, Christ Church, Oxford, 1929; student, 1930; specialized in study of canon law; published *The Origins of Private Penance in the Western Church* (1939); member of Archbishops' Commission for Revision of the Canon Law, 1939–47; published *The Elements of Moral Theology*, 1947; DD; proctor in convocation, Oxford University, 1943–73; chancellor of diocese of Blackburn, 1948; bishop of Exeter, 1949–73; published *Christian Ethics* (1950), *The Duties of a Churchman* (1951), and *Western Canon Law* (1953); introduced to House of Lords, 1955; chairman of group which produced *Putting Asunder*, which became the basis of the Divorce Reform Bill of 1969; hon. fellow, Keble, 1951; hon. student, Christ Church, 1968.

MORTIMER, Roger de (*fl.* 1054–1074), son of Hugh, bishop of Coutances; assumed the name of Mortimer from Mortemer-en-Brai, where he won a victory, 1054; transferred his chief seat to Saint-Victor-en-Caux and erected an abbey there, 1074.

MORTIMER, Roger (II) de, sixth baron of Wigmore (1231?–1282), succeeded to his father's estates and married Matilda de Braose, 1247; knighted, 1253; on the outbreak of the struggle between Henry III and the barons, 1258, sided with the barons and was elected to various councils; after the compromise of 1261 became a strong Royalist; fought against *Llywelyn with varying success, 1262 and 1263; returned to Wales after the Battle of Lewes, 1264, and was exiled to Ireland, when de *Montfort marched to subdue the marcher lords, who were obliged to surrender; did not leave England, but prepared for fresh resistance; assisted Prince Edward in his escape from de Montfort, 1265, commanded the rear-guard at Evesham, 1265, and assisted the siege of Kenilworth, 1266; remained Prince Edward's close friend, and was one of the guardians of his children, 1270 and 1271, and of the realm, 1272; he took a conspicuous part in Edward I's early struggles with Llywelyn.

MORTIMER, Roger (III) de, lord of Chirk (1256?–1326), son of Roger de *Mortimer (II); assisted his brothers to entice *Llywelyn of Wales to his doom, 1282; granted the lordship of Chirk, 1282; raised troops of Welsh infantry for Edward I's wars in Gascony, 1294 and 1297, and in Scotland, 1300, 1301, and 1303; king's lieutenant and justice of Wales, 1307–21; served in the Bannockburn campaign and in those of 1319–20; joined in the attack on the Despensers, 1321, and finally surrendered to Edward II at Shrewsbury, 1322; remained in the Tower of London until his death.

MORTIMER, Roger (IV) de, eighth baron of Wigmore and first earl of March (1287?–1330), succeeded his father, Edmund de Mortimer, seventh baron, *c.*1304; knighted, 1306; acquired large estates in Ireland through his wife, Joan de Genville; went to Ireland, 1308, and defeated his kinsfolk, the Lacys; defeated at Kells, 1316, by Edward *Bruce, whom the Lacys had invited to assist them; appointed lieutenant of Ireland, 1316; drove Bruce to Carrickfergus, 1317; defeated the Lacys and the Leinster clans, 1317; justiciar of Ireland, 1319; helped his uncle Roger (of Chirk) to establish in Wales the independent position of house of Mortimer, which was threatened by the Despensers, 1320; obliged, on the appearance of Edward II in the west, to submit, and was sent to the Tower of London, 1322; escaped, after two years' imprisonment, with the help of *Orleton, bishop of Hereford, to Paris, 1324; became chief adviser to Queen *Isabella, his paramour, and with her and her son Edward landed at Orwell, 1326; employed his agent, Orleton, to obtain Edward II's deposition in parliament, 1327; after Edward III's election as king virtually ruled the realm for four years through his influence over Queen Isabella; appointed justiciar of Wales and the border counties, 1327; became earl of March, 1328, and received palatine jurisdiction in Trim, Meath, and Louth; popularly regarded as responsible for Edward II's murder, the failure of the Scots expedition, 1327, and the 'Shameful Peace' with Scotland, 1328; his position assailed by Henry of Lancaster (1328), who was, however, ultimately obliged to accept mediation; formed a plot, which resulted in the execution for treason of the king's uncle, *Edmund, earl of Kent, 1330; seized by William de *Montacute, who had been joined by Edward III, and taken to the Tower of London; accused before parliament of causing dissension between Edward II and his queen, of usurping royal power, procuring Edward II's murder, and the execution of Edmund, earl of Kent; hanged, drawn, and quartered like a common malefactor at Tyburn.

MORTIMER, Roger (V) de, second earl of March (1327?–1360), grandson of Roger *Mortimer (IV), first earl of March; was gradually restored to the family estates and honours; accompanied Edward III to France, 1346; knighted, 1346; KG and summoned to parliament, 1348; obtained the reversal of his grandfather's sentence and the remainder of the Mortimer inheritance, 1354; received various offices; fought in France, 1355 and 1359; died suddenly at Rouvray.

MORTIMER, Roger (VI) de, fourth earl of March and Ulster (1374–1398), son of Edmund *Mortimer (II), third earl of March; succeeded his father, 1381; brought up as a royal ward and proclaimed heir-presumptive, 1385; married Eleanor Holland, the king's niece, 1388; knighted, 1390; accompanied Richard II to Ireland, 1394; lieutenant of Ulster, Connaught, and Meath, 1395, and of Ireland, 1397; waged war against native septs without notable result; summoned to attend parliament, his growing popularity having aroused Richard II's suspicions; by his caution or duplicity deprived Richard of any opportunity of attacking him; returned to Ireland and was slain in battle at Kells.

MORTIMER, Thomas (1730–1810), author; grandson of John *Mortimer; vice-consul of the Austrian Netherlands, 1762–8; man of letters and private tutor in England; wrote on economic subjects, and published *The British Plutarch* (1762).

MORTON, earls of. See DOUGLAS, JAMES, fourth earl, d. 1581; DOUGLAS, Sir WILLIAM, of Lochleven, sixth or seventh earl, d. 1606; DOUGLAS, WILLIAM, seventh or eighth earl, 1582–1650; DOUGLAS, JAMES, fourteenth earl, 1702–1768; and MAXWELL, JOHN, 1553–1593.

MORTON, Sir Albertus (1584?–1625), secretary of state; of Eton and King's College, Cambridge; accompanied his half-uncle, Sir Henry *Wotton, to Venice as secretary, 1604; minister to Savoy, 1612; clerk of the council, 1615; secretary to the electress palatine, 1616; knighted, 1617; clerk of the council, 1619–23; ambassador to France, 1624; secretary of state, 1625; returned as MP for both Kent and Cambridge University, 1625.

MORTON, Andrew (1802–1845), portrait painter; brother of Thomas *Morton (1813–1849); exhibited portraits of distinguished people at the Royal Academy and the British Institution, 1821–45.

MORTON, Charles (1627–1698), Puritan divine; MA, Wadham College, Oxford, 1652 (incorporated at Cambridge, 1653); rector of Blisland, 1655; ejected, 1662; master of the Dissenters' school at Stoke Newington; went to New England and became minister of the first church at Charlestown, 1686; prosecuted for seditious sermon, but acquitted, 1687; wrote on social and theological questions; approved the prosecutions for witchcraft at Salem; died at Charlestown.

MORTON, Charles (1716–1799), principal librarian of the British Museum; MD, Leiden, 1748; practised in London; under-librarian of the British Museum, 1756; secretary to the trustees and principal librarian, 1776; FRS, 1752; secretary to the Royal Society, 1760–74; FSA; edited *Whitelocke.

MORTON, Sir Desmond John Falkiner (1891–1971), soldier, intelligence officer, and public servant; educated at Eton and Royal Military Academy, Woolwich; joined Royal Horse and Royal Field Artillery, 1911; served through 1914–18 war, surviving bullet wound in heart; MC; aide-de-camp to Field-Marshal Douglas (later Earl) *Haig; came to notice of (Sir) Winston Churchill; entered Foreign Office as intelligence officer, 1919; head of Committee of Imperial Defence's Industrial Intelligence Centre, 1929–39; kept Churchill briefed on German rearmament and assisted him with *The World Crisis* (5 vols., 1923–31); principal assistant secretary, Ministry of Economic Warfare, 1939; personal assistant to Churchill, 1940; filtered information to Churchill received from breach of the German 'Enigma' cipher; his role reduced as flow of information increased and required more systematic handling; served on economic survey mission, Middle East, 1949; seconded to ministry of Civil Aviation, 1950–3; CMG, 1937; CB, 1941; KCB, 1945; Croix de Guerre with palms; officer of Legion of Honour; Knight's Grand Cross of Orange Nassau; governor of Hammersmith group of hospitals; correspondence published in R. W. Thompson's *Churchill and Morton* (1976) reveals him as disappointed man.

MORTON, Fergus Dunlop, Baron Morton of Henryton (1887–1973), lord of appeal in ordinary; educated at Kelvinside Academy and St John's College, Cambridge; foundation scholar, 1908; first class, part ii, law tripos, 1910; called to bar (Inner Temple), 1912; joined Lincoln's Inn, 1914; served in Highland Light Infantry in German East Africa during 1914–18 war; MC; at War Office, 1918–19; returned to Chancery bar, 1919; KC, 1929; knighted and appointed High Court judge (Chancery division), 1938; promoted to Court of Appeal and PC, 1944; life peer and lord of appeal in ordinary, 1947–59; deputy chairman, Contraband Committee at Ministry of Economic Warfare, 1939, and chairman, Black List Committee, 1941–6;

chairman, Council of Legal Education, 1949–53; chairman, Royal Commission on Marriage and Divorce, 1951–5; played golf for Cambridge University; succeeded Bernard *Darwin as president, Oxford and Cambridge Golfing Society, 1953; received honorary degrees from Cambridge, Glasgow, St Andrews, and Sydney; hon. fellow, St John's, 1940; deputy high steward, Cambridge University; hon. member of Faculty of Advocates, 1953; treasurer, Lincoln's Inn, 1953; Grand Cross of Order of Orange Nassau and US Medal of Freedom (with silver palms).

MORTON, George Highfield (1826–1900), geologist; house decorator at Liverpool; formed valuable collection of fossils; FGS, 1858, and Lyell medallist, 1892; lecturer on geology, Queen's College, Liverpool; chief work, *Geology of Country round Liverpool* (1863).

MORTON, John (1420?–1500), archbishop of Canterbury and cardinal; DCL, Balliol College, Oxford; principal of Peckwater Inn in 1448 and still in 1453; practised as a canon lawyer in the court of arches; given much ecclesiastical preferment; followed the Lancastrian party in their wanderings and was attainted; submitted after the Battle of Tewkesbury, on which his attainder was reversed; prebendary of St Paul's Cathedral, 1472; master of the Rolls, 1473; went on an embassy to Hungary, 1474; helped to negotiate the Treaty of Picquigny, 1475; elected bishop of Ely, 1479; present at Edward IV's death and funeral, 1483; arrested, 1483, and imprisoned, first in the Tower of London, and afterwards at Brecknock Castle, where he encouraged *Buckingham to revolt; escaped to Ely and thence to Flanders, where he remained till summoned home (1485) by Henry VII; privy councillor; archbishop of Canterbury, 1486–1500; lord chancellor, 1487; cardinal, 1493; chancellor of Oxford, 1495. He was a great builder and repairer, and Morton's Dyke in the Fens perpetuates his memory.

MORTON, John (1671?–1726), naturalist; MA, Emmanuel College, Cambridge, 1695; rector of Great Oxendon, 1706; FRS, 1703; published *The Natural History of Northamptonshire, with some Account of the Antiquities* (1712).

MORTON, John (1781–1864), agriculturist; agent on Lord *Ducie's Gloucestershire estates, where he conducted the 'Whitfield Example Farm'; invented the 'Uley cultivator' and other agricultural appliances; wrote *On Soils* (1838).

MORTON, John Cameron Andrieu Bingham Michael (1893–1979), humorist who wrote under pseudonym, Beachcomber; educated at Harrow and Worcester College, Oxford; served in Suffolk Regiment during 1914–18 war; wounded on the Somme, and worked in intelligence; published *The Barber of Putney* (1919), a novel based on his experiences in the trenches; columnist on *Sunday Express*, 1919; took over Beachcomber column from D. B. Wyndham Lewis, 1924–75; built up cast of comic characters such as Dr Smart-Allick, Dr Strabismus (Whom God Preserve) of Utrecht, and Prodnose; colossal output, running to millions of words; some of his work reprinted in Beachcomber Collections, illustrated by Nicolas *Bentley; friend of Hilaire *Belloc and became Roman Catholic, 1922; publications include *The Bastille Falls* (1936), *The Dauphin* (1937), *St. Therese of Lisieux, the Making of a Saint* (1954), and *Hilaire Belloc* (1955).

MORTON, John Chalmers (1821–1888), agriculturist; son of John *Morton (1781–1864); editor of the *Agricultural Gazette*, 1844; commissioner for inquiry into the pollution of rivers, 1868–74; wrote and edited works on agriculture.

MORTON, John Maddison (1811–1891), dramatist; son of Thomas *Morton (1764?–1838); educated in France; held clerkship in Chelsea Hospital, London, 1832–40; Charterhouse brother, 1881; wrote farces and showed exceptional facility in suiting French dialogues to English tastes; his most popular piece, *Box and Cox* (1847).

MORTON, Nicholas (*fl.* 1586), papal agent; MA, Cambridge, 1545; fellow of Trinity College, Cambridge, 1546; BD, 1554; withdrew to Rome on Queen Elizabeth's accession, 1558; DD, Rome; came to England and promoted the northern rebellion of 1569; again intrigued against Queen Elizabeth at Reims, 1580.

MORTON, Richard (1637–1698), ejected minister and physician; MA, Magdalen Hall, Oxford, 1659; vicar of Kinver, 1659; ejected, 1662; MD, Oxford, 1670; FRCP, 1678; incorporated MD, Cambridge, 1680; censor of the College of Physicians, 1690, 1691, and 1697; physician to the king; published *Phthisiologia* (1689) and *Pyretologia* (1692).

MORTON, Richard (1669–1730), physician; son of Richard *Morton (1637–1698); entered Catharine Hall, Cambridge, 1688; MD, 1695; FRCP, 1707; physician to Greenwich Hospital, 1716.

MORTON, Richard Alan (1899–1977), biochemist; son of an engine driver; educated at Oulton School, Liverpool, and Liverpool University; first class, chemistry, 1922; Ph.D.; lecturer in spectroscopy, 1924–44; Johnston professor of biochemistry, Liverpool, 1944–66; FRS, 1950; carried out research into vitamins; served under Sir Jack *Drummond, scientific adviser to the Ministry of Food, during 1939–45 war; reported on 'Vitamin A requirements of human adults'; post-war research included biochemistry of vision; served on many university committees; chairman of publications board of Royal Society, 1961–2; chairman, Biochemical Society, 1959–61; editor, *Biochemical Journal*, 1947–53; hon. member of American Institute of Nutrition, 1969; honorary degrees from University of Wales, Trinity College, Dublin, and Coimbra University, Portugal; biennial Morton lectureship established by Biochemical Society, 1978.

MORTON, Robert (d. 1497), bishop of Worcester; nephew of John *Morton (1420?–1500); master of the Rolls, 1479; deprived during Richard III's reign, but reinstated by Henry VII; canon of Windsor, 1481–6; collated archdeacon of Gloucester, 1482; bishop of Worcester, 1487.

MORTON, Thomas (d. 1646), author of *New English Canaan*; an attorney of Clifford's Inn; landed in New England, 1622; established himself at Merry Mount, Massachusetts Bay, 1626; traded with the Indians; arrested and sent home, 1628; returned to New England as Isaac Allerton's secretary, 1629; again banished, 1630; successfully prosecuted a suit at law repealing the Massachusetts Company's patent, 1635; returned to New England, 1643, and died in poverty at Acomenticus, 1646; published *New English Canaan*, a descriptive work (1637).

MORTON, Thomas (1564–1659), bishop successively of Chester, Lichfield, and Durham; MA, St John's College, Cambridge, 1590; DD, 1606; fellow; university lecturer in logic; rector of Long Marston, 1598; devoted himself to the plague-stricken sufferers at York, 1602; accompanied Lord Eure, ambassador-extraordinary to Germany and Denmark, 1602; one of James I's chaplains and dean of Gloucester, 1606; transferred to deanery of Winchester, 1609, and collated to canonry at York, 1610; bishop of Chester, 1616; on his translation to Lichfield and Coventry, 1618, continued his endeavours to win over Nonconformists and recusants; appointed, 1632, to the see of Durham, which he held canonically until his death, although parliament claimed to deprive him of it, 1647; impeached, 1641, but released after four months' imprisonment without trial; imprisoned, 1645, for refusing to surrender the seal of Durham; driven from Durham House, Strand, 1648; resided ultimately at Easton-Mauduit with Sir Christopher Yelverton; patron and friend of learned men. The larger portion of his writings were devoted to the exposure of Romish fallacies; his three chief works are *Apologia Catholica* (1605), *Catholic Appeal* (1609), and *Causa Regia* (1620).

MORTON, Thomas (1764?–1838), dramatist; entered Lincoln's Inn, 1784; wrote a considerable number of comedies, in which John *Emery, Charles and John *Kemble, and *Macready appeared; honorary member of the Garrick Club, 1837.

MORTON, Thomas (1781–1832), inventor of the 'patent slip' for docking vessels; shipwright; invented a cheap substitute for a dry dock, 1819, which was later in nearly all harbours (extension of patent refused, 1832).

MORTON, Thomas (1813–1849), surgeon; brother of Andrew *Morton; studied at University College Hospital, London, 1832; MRCS, 1835; demonstrator of anatomy, 1836; surgeon, 1848, at University College Hospital, London; wrote on surgical anatomy; committed suicide.

MORTON, Sir William (d. 1672), judge; MA, Sidney Sussex College, Cambridge, 1625; barrister, Inner Temple, 1630; MP, Evesham, 1640; fought on the Royalist side; knighted; imprisoned in the Tower of London, 1644; serjeant-at-law, 1660; king's serjeant, 1663; justice of the King's Bench, 1665.

MORVILLE, Hugh de (d. 1162), constable of Scotland under *David I; assisted in making William Cumin bishop of Durham, 1140; founded Kilwinning Abbey, 1140, and Melrose Abbey, 1150.

MORVILLE, Hugh de (d. 1204), one of the murderers of St *Thomas of Canterbury; attached to the court from the beginning of the reign of Henry II; itinerant justice for Cumberland and Northumberland, 1170; kept back the crowd with his sword while St Thomas was murdered; did penance in the Holy Land, and soon regained royal favour.

MORVILLE, Richard de (d. 1189), son of Hugh de *Morville (d. 1162); constable of Scotland, 1162; adviser of *William the Lyon; commanded part of the Scottish army before Alnwick, 1174; benefactor of Melrose Abbey.

MORWEN (MORING or MORVEN), John (1518?–1561?), divine; was placed under a relative, Robert *Morwen; president of Corpus Christi College, Oxford; MA, 1543; BD, 1552; secretary to Bishop *Bonner; prebendary of St Paul's Cathedral, 1558; deprived on Queen Elizabeth's accession; charged with scattering libel, 1561; a famous Greek scholar.

MORWEN (MORWENT or MORWINGE), Peter (1530?–1573?), translator; BA, Magdalen College, Oxford, 1550; fellow, 1552; MA, 1560; went to Germany, 1553; received various livings; prebendary of Lichfield, 1567; translated Joseph

Ben Gorion's *History of the Jews* (1558) and two medical works.

MORWEN (MORWENT or **MORWYN), Robert** (1486?–1558), president of Corpus Christi College, Oxford; BA, Oxford, 1507; fellow of Magdalen College, Oxford, 1510; MA, 1511; vice-president of the newly founded Corpus Christi College, 1517; president, 1537; conformed outwardly during Edward VI's reign, but carefully preserved the Roman Catholic vessels and vestments; on *Pole's commission for visiting the university, 1556.

MORYS (or MORIZ), Sir **John** (*fl.* 1346), deputy of Ireland; MP, Bedford, 1322–40; commissioner of array for Bedfordshire and Buckinghamshire, 1322 and 1324; knighted and acting deputy in Ireland, 1341; held parliament in Dublin, 1341; again deputy, 1346.

MORYSINE, Sir **Richard** (d. 1556), ambassador. See MORISON.

MORYSON, Fynes (1566–1630), traveller; BA, Peterhouse, Cambridge; fellow, 1586; MA, 1587; obtained licence to travel, 1589; visited Germany, the Low Countries, Denmark, Poland, Italy, Switzerland, and France, 1591–5; visited the Holy Land, Constantinople, and Scotland, 1598; went to Ireland, 1600; became chief secretary to Sir Charles *Blount, 1600, and helped to suppress Tyrone's rebellion; published an account of his travels and a history of Tyrone's rebellion (1617).

MORYSON, Sir **Richard** (1571?–1628), vice-president of Munster; brother of Fynes *Moryson; sailed in the Islands voyage, 1597; colonel with *Essex in Ireland, 1599; knighted by Essex, 1599; governor of Waterford and Wexford, 1604; vice-president of Munster, 1609; MP, Bandon (Irish parliament), 1613; lieutenant-general of the ordnance in England, 1616–28; MP, Leicester, 1621.

MOSELEY. See also MOSLEY.

MOSELEY, Benjamin (1742–1819), physician; studied at London, Paris, and Leiden; practised in West Indies; returned to England, 1784; MD, St Andrews, 1784; visited continental hospitals; LRCP, 1787; physician to the Royal Hospital, Chelsea, 1788; wrote chiefly on tropical diseases.

MOSELEY, Henry (1801–1872), mathematician; MA, St John's College, Cambridge, 1836; DCL *hon. causa*, Oxford, 1870; professor of natural and experimental philosophy and astronomy, King's College, London, 1831–44; FRS, 1839; one of the first inspectors of schools, 1844; canon of Bristol, 1853; published works on mechanics.

MOSELEY, Henry Gwyn Jeffreys (1887–1915), experimental physicist; son of Professor Henry Nottidge *Moseley; BA, Trinity College, Oxford; physics lecturer, Manchester University, 1910–14; carried out important researches on X-ray spectra of elements; killed in action at Gallipoli.

MOSELEY, Henry Nottidge (1844–1891), naturalist; son of Henry *Moseley; of Harrow and Exeter College, Oxford; BA, 1868; Radcliffe travelling fellow, 1869; joined government expedition to Ceylon, 1871, and Challenger expedition, 1872–6; fellow of Exeter College, Oxford, 1876; went to California and Oregon, 1877; FRS, 1877; FZS, 1879; assistant registrar to the University of London, 1879; Linacre professor of human and comparative anatomy at Oxford, 1881; published *Notes by a Naturalist on the Challenger* (1879) and other scientific works.

MOSELEY, Humphrey (d. 1661), bookseller; warden of the Stationers' Company, 1659; published the first collected edition of *Milton's *Poems* (1645) and early editions of *Crashaw, *D'Avenant, and others, also translations of Spanish, Italian, and French romances.

MOSER, George Michael (1704–1783), chaser and enameller; born at Schaffhausen; came to England; distinguished for compositions in enamel on watches and bracelets; drawing master to George III; engraved George III's first great seal; assisted in establishing the Royal Academy, 1767; elected the first keeper.

MOSER, Joseph (1748–1819), artist, author, and magistrate; nephew of George Michael *Moser; exhibited at the Royal Academy, 1774–82; magistrate for Westminster, 1794; published political pamphlets, dramas, and fiction.

MOSER, Mary (d. 1819), flower painter; daughter of George Michael *Moser; foundation member of the Royal Academy, contributing to its exhibitions till 1802; married Captain Hugh Lloyd of Chelsea, 1793.

MOSES, Henry (1782?–1870), engraver; obtained great reputation for his outline plates.

MOSES, William (1623?–1688), serjeant-at-law; of Christ's Hospital, London, and Pembroke College, Cambridge; MA; master, 1655–60; counsel to the East India Company; serjeant-at-law, 1688.

MOSES, William Stainton (1840–1892), spiritualist; MA, Exeter College, Oxford, 1865; English master at University College School, London, 1872–90; a 'medium', writing and editing spiritualistic literature.

MOSLEY. See also MOSELEY.

MOSLEY, Charles (d. 1770?), engraver; employed by *Hogarth.

MOSLEY, Nicholas (1611–1672), author and Royalist; his estates sequestered, 1643, but restored, 1646; headed the Manchester procession on coronation day, 1661; published *The Soul of Man* (1653).

MOSLEY, Sir Oswald Ernald, sixth baronet (1896–1980), politician and Fascist leader; educated at Winchester and Sandhurst; commissioned into 16th Lancers, 1914; joined Royal Flying Corps as observer, but in consequence of an escapade was returned to 16th Lancers; invalided out and worked in Ministry of Munitions and Foreign Office, 1916–18; Conservative MP for Harrow division of Middlesex, 1918–22; married Lady Cynthia Blanche, daughter of Sir George Nathaniel *Curzon (later Marquess Curzon of Kedleston), 1920; opposed Government's Irish policy and became secretary of Peace with Ireland Council; crossed to opposition bench and stood as Independent at Harrow, 1922; returned with large majority; joined the Labour party, 1924; Labour MP for Smethwick, 1926; succeeded to baronetcy, 1928; returned for Smethwick, 1929, and his wife became Labour MP for Stoke-on-Trent; chancellor of Duchy of Lancaster; strong disagreement with J. H. *Thomas and Philip (later Viscount) *Snowdon regarding solution to unemployment problem; Cabinet rejected his proposals for recovery, 1930; Mosley resigned, and set about planning New party; party launched, 1931, but twenty-four candidates all defeated; visited Italy and planned a British Fascist movement; launched British Union of Fascists, 1932; his supporters turned to extremism, violence, and anti-Semitism, 1934; Mosley lost middle-class support and became influenced by Nazism; movement became 'British Union of Fascists and National Socialists', 1936; Lady Cynthia died, 1933; Mosley married the Hon. Mrs Diana Guinness, sister of Nancy *Mitford, 1936; mounted peace campaign; Mosley and his wife detained under Regulation 18B, 1940–3; after end of war Mosley attempted to justify his pre-war attitudes in *My Answer* (1946) and *My Life* (1968); led Union movement for European unity, 1948–66; failed to get elected to parliament, 1959 and 1966; died in France, 1980.

MOSLEY, Samuel (*fl.* 1675–1676), New England settler; served in the war against the Indian chief 'King Philip', and distinguished himself in the capture and destruction of Canonicut, 1675.

MOSS, Charles (1711–1802), bishop successively of St David's and of Bath and Wells; nephew of Robert *Moss; MA, Caius College, Cambridge, 1735; fellow, 1735; received much preferment from *Sherlock, bishop of Salisbury; bishop of St David's, 1766–74, of Bath and Wells, 1774.

MOSS, Charles (1763–1811), bishop of Oxford; son of Charles *Moss (1711–1802); BA, Christ Church, Oxford, 1783; DD, 1797, received preferment from his father; bishop of Oxford, 1807–11.

MOSS, Joseph William (1803–1862), bibliographer; MA, Magdalen Hall, Oxford, 1827; MB, 1829; practised in Dudley; FRS, 1830; published *Manual of Classical Bibliography* (1825).

MOSS, Robert (1666–1729), dean of Ely; MA, Corpus Christi College, Cambridge, 1688; fellow, 1686–1714; hon. DD, 1705; chaplain-in-ordinary to William III, Anne, and George I; dean of Ely, 1713; his sermons collected and published (1736).

MOSS, Thomas (d. 1808), poet; BA, Emmanuel College, Cambridge, 1761; perpetual curate of Brinley Hill Chapel; published *Poems on several Occasions* (1769), including the well-known 'Beggar's Petition'.

MOSSE, Bartholomew (1712–1759), philanthropist; travelled through England, France, and Holland to perfect himself in midwifery and surgery; rented a house in Dublin for poor lying-in women, 1745; erected the Rotunda Hospital (incorporated, 1756, opened, 1757).

MOSSE (or MOSES), Miles (*c.*1558–1615), divine; educated at Cambridge (DD, 1595); vicar of St Stephen, Norwich, 1585; published *A Catechism* (1590) and various sermons with a Calvinistic tendency.

MOSSES, Alexander (1793–1837), artist; taught drawing at Liverpool Royal Institution; exhibited portraits at the Liverpool Academy, 1811–36.

MOSSMAN, George (*fl.* 1800), medical writer; physician at Bradford; wrote on the use of digitalis in consumption and scrofula.

MOSSMAN, Thomas Wimberley (1826–1885), divine; BA, St Edmund Hall, Oxford, 1845; held several livings; became a Roman Catholic during his last illness; published controversial works.

MOSSOM, Robert (d. 1679), bishop of Derry; MA, Peterhouse, Cambridge, 1638; used the Prayer-Book, notwithstanding its prohibition, at St Peter's, Paul's Wharf, London, 1650–5; dean of Christ Church, Dublin, 1660; bishop of Derry, 1666; published religious works.

MOSSOP, Henry (1729?–1774?), actor; appeared in Dublin, 1749; acted with *Garrick in

London, 1751–9, where he was most successful as Richard III; returned to Dublin, 1759; acted with *Barry at Crow Street, Dublin; opened Smock Alley Theatre, Dublin, in opposition to Barry, 1760, Barry being ruined, 1768; tried to manage both theatres, but broke down under troubles, vexations, and debt; arrested for debt, 1771; became bankrupt; admirable in heroic parts.

MOSSOP, William (1751–1804), medallist; a die-sinker who prepared numerous seals for public bodies in Ireland, and engraved a large number of portraits on medals.

MOSSOP, William Stephen (1788–1827), medallist; son of William *Mossop; studied under Francis West; followed his father's method of making a wax model before cutting the steel die; made dies for the Stamp Office, Dublin; projected a series of portrait-medals of distinguished Irishmen.

MOSTYN, John (1710–1779), general; son of Sir Roger *Mostyn (1675–1739); of Westminster School and Christ Church, Oxford; captain, 2nd Foot Guards, 1743; major-general, 1757; governor and commander-in-chief of Minorca, 1758; MP, Malton, 1747, 1754, and 1761; governor of Chelsea Hospital, 1768; general, 1772.

MOSTYN, Sir Roger, first baronet (1625?–1690), Royalist; took up arms for Charles I; sacked the houses of Parliamentarians in Chester, 1642 and 1643; governor of Flint Castle, but (1643) forced to surrender it; captured Hawarden Castle and went to Chester; raised recruits in Ireland, 1645; arrested, 1658, but immediately released on parole; created baronet, 1660.

MOSTYN, Sir Roger, third baronet (1675–1739), politician; grandson of Sir Roger *Mostyn, first baronet; Tory MP for Cheshire, 1701, for Flintshire, 1705–34, except 1713, when he sat for Flint borough; paymaster of the marines, 1711; teller of the Exchequer, 1714–16.

MOSTYN, Savage (d. 1757), vice-admiral; son of Sir Roger *Mostyn (1675–1739); lieutenant in navy, 1734; commander, 1739; post-captain, 1739; failed to engage two French ships off Ushant, 1745; acquitted by court martial, but his conduct unfavourably commented on; MP, Weobley, 1747; comptroller of the navy, 1749; vice-admiral and second-in-command on the North American Station, 1755; junior lord of the Admiralty, 1757.

MOTHERBY, George (1732–1793), medical writer; a Highgate physician; compiled a *New Medical Dictionary* (1775).

MOTHERWELL, William (1797–1835), poet; sheriff-clerk depute of Renfrewshire, 1819–29;

editor of *Paisley Advertiser*, 1828–30, and *Glasgow Courier*, 1830; issued *Poems, Narrative and Lyrical* (1832); collaborated with Hogg in an edition of *Burns (1835).

MOTT, Sir Basil, first baronet (1859–1938), civil engineer; trained at Royal School of Mines; constructed first (Monument–Stockwell, 1890) and second (Bank–Shepherd's Bush, 1900, with Sir Benjamin *Baker) deep-level tubes; responsible with his partners for many tube extensions, bridge schemes, and the Mersey Tunnel (opened 1934); introduced escalators into Great Britain; chairman, St Paul's Preservation Works Committee, 1925; baronet, 1930; FRS, 1932.

MOTT, Sir Frederick Walker (1853–1926), neuropathologist; MD, University College, London; held various posts at Charing Cross Hospital School, from 1884; pathologist to London County Council asylums, 1895–1923; best known for his determination of association between syphilitic infection and other bodily changes and mental disorders; did notable work on shell-shock during European war; FRS, 1896; KBE, 1919; his numerous honours include Croonian lectureship (1900), Lettsomian lectureship (1916), and Harveian oratorship (1925) of Royal College of Physicians, London; his works include *Archives of Neurology and Psychiatry*.

MOTTE, Andrew (d. 1730), mathematician; lecturer in geometry at Gresham College, London, before 1727; published treatise on *Motion* (1727); translated *Newton's *Principia* (1729).

MOTTE, Benjamin (d. 1738), bookseller and publisher; brother of Andrew *Motte; edited an abridgment of the Royal Society's *Transactions*, 1700–21; succeeded to Benjamin Tooke's business with the Tories; published *Gulliver's Travels* (1726); acted as London agent to *Swift.

MOTTERSHEAD, Joseph (1688–1771), Dissenting minister; studied under Timothy *Jollie and Matthew *Henry; minister at Cross Street, Manchester, 1717; published religious discourses.

MOTTEUX, Peter Anthony (1660–1718), translator and dramatist; born at Rouen; came to England, 1685; edited *Gentleman's Journal*, 1692–3; continued and completed the work of Sir Thomas *Urquhart in bringing out an edition of Rabelais, 1693–1708; wrote comedies and masques; clerk in the foreign department of the Post Office, 1703–11; published a free translation of *Don Quixote* (1712); became an East India merchant, 1712.

MOTTISTONE, first Baron (1868–1947), politician and soldier. See SEELY, JOHN EDWARD BERNARD.

MOTTLEY, John (1692–1750), dramatist and biographer; clerk in the Excise Office, 1708–20; wrote two dull pseudo-classical tragedies, but was more successful with comedies; published *Joe Miller's Jest-book* (1739); wrote the life of Peter I of Russia (1739), of Catherine of Russia (1744).

MOTTRAM, Charles (1807–1876), engraver; exhibited at the Royal Academy from 1861; engraved after *Landseer, Rosa Bonheur, and Holman *Hunt.

MOTTRAM, Ralph Hale (1883–1971), writer; born in Gurney's Bank house, Norwich, where his father, like his grandfather and great grandfather, was resident chief clerk; educated at a private school and in Lausanne; entered the bank, 1899–1927 (except for the years 1914–18 when he served in Flanders in the Norfolk Regiment and was made responsible for investigating complaints of damage done to crops and property by British troops); encouraged by John *Galsworthy and his wife to write; published *The Spanish Farm*, based on his wartime experiences, 1924; at first unacceptable to publishers, but when published, awarded Hawthornden Prize and became best-seller; filmed as *Rose of Picardy* (1927), and televised, 1968; published *Sixty-four Ninety-four* (1925) and *The Crime at Vanderlyndens* (1926); the three parts reissued as *The Spanish Farm Trilogy* (1927); retired from bank and published number of other novels and books on banking, Norwich, and East Anglia, including *Our Mr Dormer* (1927) and *John Crome of Norwich* (1931); also published poems; in great demand as lecturer; supporter of Octagon Chapel (Unitarian) in Norwich and trustee of Manchester College, Oxford; secretary of Norwich Society for twenty years; member of local societies; fellow, Royal Society of Literature; lord mayor of Norwich, 1953; hon. D.Litt., East Anglia University, 1966; published *Autobiography with a Difference* (1938) and *The Window Seat* (1954), *Another Window Seat* (1957), and *Vanities and Verities* (1958), 3 vols. of autobiography; memorial overlooks city of Norwich.

MOTTRAM, Vernon Henry (1882–1976), physiologist and nutritionist; educated at Caterham School, St Olave's Grammar School, London, and Trinity College, Cambridge, where he was a scholar and took firsts in both parts of the natural sciences tripos, 1903–5; fellow, Trinity College, 1907; physiology demonstrator under (Sir) Frederick Gowland *Hopkins; senior demonstrator, Liverpool University with (Sir) C. S. *Sherrington, 1911–14; lecturer at McGill University, Montreal, and at Toronto, 1914–15; senior science master, Caterham School, and engaged in biological research for Lever Bros., 1918–20; succeeded (Sir) Edward *Mellanby as professor of physiology, King's College of Household and Social Science, London, 1921–44; publications include *A Manual of Histology* (1923), *Food and the Family* (1925), *The Functions of the Body* (1926), *Manual of Modern Cookery* (with Jessie Lindsay, 1927), and *Properties of Food* (with W. M. Clifford, 1929); organized postgraduate dietetics course at King's College, 1936; brought out booklets and lectures on nutrition during 1939–45 war; further publications include *The Physical Basis of Personality* (1944) and *Human Nutrition* (1948), which has been reprinted many times; first president, Cambridge Fabian Society.

MOUFET, Thomas (1553–1604), physician and author. See MOFFETT.

MOULE, George Evans (1828–1912), missionary bishop in mid-China; second son of Revd Henry *Moule; BA, Corpus Christi College, Cambridge; went as missionary to China, 1857; first bishop of mid-China, 1880–1906.

MOULE, Handley Carr Glyn (1841–1920), bishop of Durham; eighth son of Revd Henry *Moule; BA, Trinity College, Cambridge; principal of Ridley Hall, Cambridge, 1880–99; Norrisian professor of divinity, 1899–1901; bishop of Durham, 1901–20; an evangelical; wrote theological and devotional works.

MOULE, Henry (1801–1880), divine and inventor; MA, St John's College, Cambridge, 1828; vicar of Fordington, 1829; exerted himself unweariedly during the cholera, 1849–54; invented dry-earth system, 1860; wrote on sanitary science, gardening, and religious topics.

MOULE, Thomas (1784–1851), writer on heraldry and antiquities; bookseller, 1816–23; clerk in the Post Office and chamber-keeper in the lord-chamberlain's department and member of the Westminster Society; published *Bibliotheca Heraldica Magnae Britanniae* (1822) and antiquarian works.

MOULIN, Lewis du (1606–1680), Nonconformist controversialist; son of Pierre du *Moulin; born at Paris; MD, Leiden; graduated at Cambridge, 1634, and Oxford, 1649; LRCP, 1640; Camden professor of ancient history, Oxford, 1648–60; published violent attacks on Anglican theologians.

MOULIN, Peter du (1601–1684), Anglican divine; son of Pierre du *Moulin; born at Paris; studied at Sedan, Leiden, and Cambridge; DD, Cambridge; incumbent of St John's, Chester,

1625; published *Regii Sanguinis Clamor* anonymously; DD, Oxford, 1656; chaplain to Charles II, 1660; prebendary of Canterbury, 1660.

MOULIN, Pierre du (1568–1658), French Protestant divine; born at Buhy; studied at Sedan and Cambridge, 1588–92; professor of philosophy, Leiden, 1592–8; Protestant minister at Charenton, 1599; assisted James I in his *Regis Declaratio pro Jure Regio*, and received prebend at Canterbury, 1615; professor of theology at Sedan, 1620–8; died at Sedan.

MOULLIN, Eric Balliol (1893–1963), professor of electrical engineering; educated privately and at Downing College, Cambridge; first class, mechanical sciences tripos, 1916; lecturer, Royal Naval College, Dartmouth, 1917–19; teacher and research worker, Cambridge Engineering Laboratory, assistant director of studies, King's College, 1919–29; Donald Pollock reader in engineering, Oxford University, 1929–39; fellow, Magdalen College, 1931; joined Admiralty Signals Establishment, Portsmouth, 1939; transferred to Metropolitan Vickers Electrical Co. Ltd., Manchester, 1942; professor, electrical engineering, Cambridge, 1945–60; professorial fellow, King's College, 1946; Sc.D., Cambridge, 1939; hon. LL D, Glasgow, 1958; president, Institution of Electrical Engineers, 1949–50; member, radio research board, Department of Scientific and Industrial Research, 1934–42; publications include *The Theory and Practice of Radio Frequency Measurements* (1926), *The Principles of Electromagnetism* (1932), *Spontaneous Fluctuations of Voltage* (1938), *Radio Aerials* (1949), and *Electromagnetic Principles of the Dynamo* (1955).

MOULTON, James Hope (1863–1917), classical and Iranian scholar and student of Zoroastrianism; son of W. F. *Moulton; BA, King's College, Cambridge; Greenwood professor of Hellenistic Greek and Indo-European philology, Manchester, 1908; works include *Prolegomena* to unfinished *Grammar of New Testament Greek* (1906) and *Early Zoroastrianism* (1913); torpedoed in Mediterranean returning from India.

MOULTON, John Fletcher, Baron Moulton (1844–1921), lord of appeal in ordinary; brother of W. F. *Moulton; BA, St John's College, Cambridge (senior wrangler with highest total of marks ever gained), 1868; fellow of Christ's, Cambridge, 1868–75; called to bar (Middle Temple), 1874; QC, 1885; specialized in patent actions; Liberal MP, Clapham division of Battersea, 1885–6, South Hackney, 1894–5, Launceston division of Cornwall, 1898–1906; lord justice of appeal, knight, and PC, 1906; lord of appeal in ordinary and life peer, 1912; created KCB, 1915;

GBE, 1917, for brilliant organization of explosives supply department, 1914–18.

MOULTON, Thomas (*fl.* 1540?), Dominican; called himself 'Doctor of Divinity of the order of Friar Preachers'; his *Myrour or Glasse of Helthe* published (*c*.1539).

MOULTON, William Fiddian (1835–1898), biblical scholar; MA, London, 1856; entered Wesleyan ministry, 1858; classical tutor at Wesley College, Richmond, Surrey, 1858–74; published (1870) translation of Winer's *Grammar of New Testament Greek*; member of Committee of Revisers of New Testament, 1870; first headmaster of the Leys School, Cambridge, 1874–98; DD, Edinburgh, 1874; hon. MA, Cambridge, 1877; published *History of the English Bible* and other writings relating to the Bible.

MOULTRIE, Gerard (1829–1885), devotional writer; son of John *Moultrie; BA, Exeter College, Oxford, 1851; vicar of Southleigh and warden of St John's College there, 1873; wrote hymns and religious verse.

MOULTRIE, John (1799–1874), poet; educated at Eton under Dr Keate, and at Trinity College, Cambridge; MA, 1826; abandoned law for the church; went to reside at Rugby as rector, 1828, Thomas *Arnold being headmaster at the school; *My Brother's Grave* (1820) and *Godiva* (1820) his best work, which he never afterwards surpassed; collected works published (1876).

MOUNDEFORD, Thomas (1550–1630), physician; fellow of King's College, Cambridge, 1571; MA, 1576; MD; studied medicine; censor seven times and president of the Royal College of Physicians, 1612, 1613, 1614, 1619, 1621, 1622, and 1623; published *Vir Bonus* (1622).

MOUNSEY, Messenger (1693–1788), physician. See MONSEY.

MOUNSLOW, Baron Littleton of (1589–1645). See LITTLETON, Sir EDWARD.

MOUNSTEVEN, John (1644–1706), politician; BA, Christ Church, Oxford, 1671; secretary to the earl of *Sunderland and undersecretary of state; MP, Bossiney, 1685–8, West Looe, 1695, 1701, and 1705–6; committed suicide.

MOUNT, Christopher (d. 1572), English agent in Germany. See MONT.

MOUNT, William (1545–1602), master of the Savoy; BA, King's College, Cambridge, 1567; fellow, 1566; master of the Savoy, 1594; wrote on distilled waters.

MOUNTAGU. See MONTAGU.

MOUNTAGUE, Frederick William (d. 1841), architect; son of William *Mountague;

made many architectural improvements in London.

MOUNTAGUE, William (1773–1843), architect and surveyor; clerk of works to City of London, 1816.

MOUNTAIGNE (or MOUNTAIN), George (1569–1628). See MOUNTAIGNE.

MOUNTAIN, Armine Simcoe Henry (1797–1854), adjutant-general in India; son of Jacob *Mountain; born at Quebec; entered army, 1815; lieutenant, 1818; captain, 1825; major, 1826; went to India, 1829; military secretary to Sir Colin *Halkett, 1832; served throughout the China War as deputy adjutant-general; CB; colonel and aide-de-camp to Queen Victoria, 1845; military secretary to Lord *Dalhousie, 1847; brigadier-general; served in the second Sikh War; adjutant-general, 1849; died at Futtyghur.

MOUNTAIN, Didymus (pseudonym) (*fl.* 1590). See HILL, THOMAS.

MOUNTAIN, George Jehoshaphat (1789–1863), Protestant bishop of Quebec; son of Jacob *Mountain; BA, Trinity College, Cambridge, 1810; DD, Lambeth, 1817; rector of Quebec and bishop's official, 1817; suffragan bishop of Montreal, 1836; bishop of Quebec, 1850; published sermons and journals.

MOUNTAIN, Jacob (1749–1825), Protestant bishop of Quebec; MA, Caius College, Cambridge, 1777; fellow, 1779; DD, 1793; prebendary of Lincoln, 1788; first bishop of Quebec, 1793.

MOUNTAIN, Mrs Rosoman (1768?–1841), vocalist and actress; née Wilkinson; taught by *Dibdin; performed at Hull, York, Leeds, Liverpool, and Doncaster, 1784; appeared at Covent Garden, London, 1786–98, chiefly in musical pieces; married John Mountain, violinist, 1787; one of the first vocalists of the day; retired, 1815.

MOUNTAIN, Thomas (d. 1561?), divine; MA, Cambridge; partisan of Lady *Jane Grey; imprisoned, 1553; went abroad, but returned on Queen Elizabeth's accession; rector of St Pancras, Soper Lane, London; his narrative used by *Strype and *Froude.

MOUNT ALEXANDER, first earl of. See MONTGOMERY, HUGH, 1623?–1663.

MOUNTBATTEN, Edwina Cynthia Annette, Countess Mountbatten of Burma (1901–1960), daughter of Colonel W. W. *Ashley, PC, MP, later Baron Mount Temple, granddaughter of Sir Ernest *Cassel, and great-granddaughter of the seventh earl of *Shaftesbury; at age of 19 inherited large fortune from her grandfather; married Lieutenant Lord Louis

*Mountbatten, RN, 1922; undertook numerous charitable activities; on outbreak of 1939–45 war, served with Order of St John; superintendent-in-chief, St John Ambulance Brigade, 1942; inaugurated welfare services for Allied prisoners of war and internees, 1943–5, when her husband was supreme allied commander, South-East Asia; accompanied Lord Mountbatten to India when he was appointed last viceroy and first governor-general of independent India, 1947–8; chairman, St John and Red Cross Services Hospitals, 1948; superintendent-in-chief, St John Ambulance Brigade Overseas, 1950; CI, 1947; GBE, 1947; DCVO, 1946; GCSt.J, 1945.

MOUNTBATTEN, Louis Alexander, first marquess of Milford Haven, formerly styled Prince Louis Alexander of Battenberg (1854–1921), admiral of the fleet; son of Prince Alexander of Hesse; born at Graz, Austria; naturalized and entered British Navy, 1868; director of Naval Intelligence, 1902–5; rear-admiral, 1904; commander-in-chief Atlantic Fleet, 1908–10; vice-admiral, 1910; first sea lord, 1912; resigned, Oct. 1914; relinquished German titles and created marquess, 1917; admiral, 1919.

MOUNTBATTEN, Louis Francis Albert Victor Nicholas, first Earl Mountbatten of Burma (1900–1979), admiral of the fleet; son of Prince Louis of *Battenberg; related to British royal family; educated at Osborne and Dartmouth naval colleges; served in *Lion* and *Queen Elizabeth* during 1914–18 war; father abandoned German title and Battenberg became Mountbatten; spent year at Christ's College, Cambridge, 1919; accompanied his cousin Edward, prince of Wales, on tour of Australasia, 1920 and India and Japan, 1921–2; married Edwina Ashley (*see* *Mountbatten), 1922; during next fifteen years served in destroyers, and in 1939 took over destroyer *Kelly* as captain; served in Mediterranean until sinking of *Kelly* in which he nearly lost his life; *Kelly*'s achievements remembered in film *In Which We Serve* made by (Sir) Noël *Coward.

Appointed chief of Combined Operations, 1942; responsible for attack on dry dock at St Nazaire and raid on Dieppe; contributed to plans for invasion of Europe; in favour of Normandy landings, and supported devices such as Mulberry, the floating harbour, and Pluto (pipeline under the ocean); at Quebec Conference, 1943; appointed supreme commander, South-East Asia, with rank of admiral; favoured amphibious strategy; Japanese attack on Imphal forestalled his plans, 1944; General W. J. (later Viscount) *Slim, with Mountbatten's full support, defeated Japanese and recaptured Rangoon, 1945; attended Potsdam Conference and was told of atom bomb; received formal surrender of Japanese at Singapore, 1945; created viscount; favoured nationalist movements in Burma and Malaya, and left South-East Asia with reputation of liberal committed to decolonization.

Succeeded Viscount (later Earl) *Wavell as viceroy of India, 1946; endeavoured to maintain unity of India but defeated by intransigence of Mohammed Ali *Jinnah, who was determined to secure separate Pakistan; established lasting rapport with Jawaharlal *Nehru; announced that independence would be granted on 15 August 1947; tried to persuade princely states to give up independence; on partition became governor-general of India; created first Earl Mountbatten of Burma, with special remainder to his daughter Patricia, 1947; persuaded Indian government not to withhold money owing to Pakistan from division of assets, 1948; postponed war between India and Pakistan over Kashmir; left India, 1948. Returned to sea as rear-admiral, commanding first cruiser squadron in Mediterranean; promoted vice-admiral, 1949; fourth sea lord, 1950; admiral, 1951, in command of Mediterranean fleet; Supreme Allied Commander, NATO Mediterranean Command (SACMED), 1953; first sea lord, 1954; in Suez crisis appealed to prime minister to turn back invasion fleet; offered resignation but told to stay on; promoted admiral of the fleet, 1956; chief of defence staff (CDS), 1959; attempted to impose unification on Services; central role of CDS strengthened, but his ideas repugnant to chiefs of staff; believed independent British nuclear deterrent essential and preferred Polaris missile; tenure of office as CDS extended to 1964; left Ministry of Defence, 1965.

In retirement undertook enquiry into prison security and was actively associated with 179 organizations, including the United World Colleges and the electronics industry; first chairman, National Electronic Research Council; governor of Isle of Wight, 1965; colonel of the Life Guards, 1965; concerned with filming of television series 'The Life and Times of Lord Mountbatten', 1966–7; honours included MVO, 1920; KCVO, 1922; GCVO, 1937; DSO, 1941; CB, 1943; KCB, 1945; KG, 1946; PC, 1947; GCSI, 1947; GCIE, 1947; GCB, 1955; OM, 1965; and FRS, 1966, together with number of honorary degrees; killed by IRA bomb, 1979; succeeded by his elder daughter, Patricia Edwina Victoria Knatchbull, who became Countess Mountbatten of Burma.

MOUNTCASHEL, Viscount. See MACCARTHY, JUSTIN, d. 1694.

MOUNT-EDGCUMBE, earls of. See EDG-CUMBE, GEORGE, first earl, 1721–1795; EDG-CUMBE, RICHARD, second earl, 1764–1839.

MOUNTENEY (or MOUNTNEY), Richard (1707–1768), Irish judge and classical scholar; fellow, King's College, Cambridge, 1728; MA, 1735; admitted Lincoln's Inn, 1725; called to the bar, 1732; baron of the Irish Exchequer, 1741–68; edited Demosthenes (1731).

MOUNTEVANS, first Baron (1880–1957), admiral. See EVANS, EDWARD RATCLIFFE GARTH RUSSELL.

MOUNTFORD, Edward William (1855–1908), architect; won open competition for Sheffield Town Hall, 1890; designed several London buildings, including the Central Criminal Court, Old Bailey; style developed from Renaissance to classic method.

MOUNTFORT, Mrs Susanna (1667?–1703). See VERBRUGGEN.

MOUNTFORT, William (1664?–1692), actor and dramatist; joined Dorset Garden company, 1678; married Mrs Susanna *Verbruggen, 1686; wrote an unsuccessful tragedy, *The Injur'd Lovers*, 1688; his comedies, *Successful Strangers* (1690), *King Edward the Third* (1691), and *Greenwich Park* (1691), well received; intimate of Judge *Jeffreys; stabbed by Captain Richard Hill; praised by Cibber as an affecting lover in tragedy.

MOUNTGARRET, third Viscount. See BUTLER, RICHARD, 1578–1651.

MOUNTIER, Thomas (fl. 1719–1733), vocalist; lay vicar and preceptor of Chichester, 1719–32; sang in London, 1732; joined Italian opera troupe, 1733.

MOUNTJOY, Barons. See BLOUNT, WALTER, first baron, d. 1474; BLOUNT, Sir JOHN, third baron, d. 1485; BLOUNT, WILLIAM, fourth baron, d. 1534; BLOUNT, CHARLES, fifth baron, d. 1545; BLOUNT, CHARLES, eighth baron, 1563–1606; BLOUNT, MOUNTJOY, ninth baron, 1597?–1665.

MOUNTJOY, first Viscount. See STEWART, Sir WILLIAM, 1653–1692.

MOUNT-MAURICE, Hervey de (fl. 1169–1176), invader of Ireland; probably served in France; sent by his nephew, Earl Richard, called Strongbow (see CLARE, RICHARD DE, d. 1176), to Ireland, 1169, to report on affairs there; was victorious at Wexford, and received grants of land; shared in Raymond *FitzGerald's victory at Waterford; arranged matters between Earl Richard and Henry II, 1171; commanded in Ireland, 1173; constable of Leinster; probably advised the disastrous expedition into Munster, 1174; returned to England after Earl Richard's death, 1176, and became a monk; benefactor of the church and one of the four principal conquerors of the Irish.

MOUNTMORRES, second Viscount. See MORRES, HERVEY REDMOND, 1746?–1797.

MOUNTNEY, Richard (1707–1768), Irish judge and classical scholar. See MOUNTENEY, RICHARD.

MOUNTNORRIS, Barons. See ANNESLEY, Sir FRANCIS, first baron, 1585–1660; ANNESLEY, RICHARD, seventh baron, 1694–1761.

MOUNTRATH, first earl of. See COOTE, Sir CHARLES, d. 1661.

MOUNT STEPHEN, first Baron (1829–1921), financier and philanthropist. See STEPHEN, GEORGE.

MOUNT TEMPLE, Barons. See COWPER, WILLIAM FRANCIS, 1811–1888; ASHLEY, WILFRID WILLIAM, 1867–1938.

MOUSKOS, Michael (1913–1977), archbishop and first president of Cyprus. See MAKARIOS III.

MOUTRAY, John (d. 1785), naval captain; lieutenant, 1744; commander, 1759; advanced to post-rank, 1758; convoyed a valuable fleet for the East and West Indies, 1780, nearly the whole of which was captured by the Franco-Spanish fleet; tried by court martial and censured; resident commissioner of the navy at Antigua, 1783; recalled, 1785.

MOWAT, Sir Oliver (1820–1903), Canadian statesman; born at Kingston, Ontario; called to bar of Upper Canada, 1841; leader of chancery bar at Toronto; QC, 1856; on commission to consolidate statutes of Upper Canada; Radical member of Legislative Assembly, 1857; advocated federation of Upper and Lower Canada, and representation by population, 1859; as postmaster-general carried out considerable economies, 1863; took part in conference for federation, 1864; vice-chancellor of Ontario, 1864–72; premier, 1872–96; responsible for Ballot Act, 1874, Manhood Suffrage Act, 1888, and Acts to simplify and cheapen judicial procedure; championed provincial rights in matters of legal appointments, regulation of companies, and control of liquor traffic; gained victory for Ontario over Manitoba in delimitation of boundaries, 1884; KCMG, 1892; GCMG, 1893; as dominion minister of justice, 1896–7, suggested compromise with Roman Catholics in Manitoba school question; lieutenant-governor of Ontario, 1897; advocated reciprocity with America.

MOWATT, Sir Francis (1837–1919), civil servant; clerk in Treasury, 1856; assistant secretary, 1888; permanent secretary, 1894–1903; raised reputation of department for promptness and efficiency; owing to misunderstanding offered to resign, 1900; served on numerous royal commissions and committees; CB, 1884; KCB, 1893; GCB, 1901; PC, 1906.

MOWBRAY, John (I) de, eighth Baron Mowbray (1286–1322), great-grandson of William de *Mowbray, fourth Baron Mowbray; succeeded his father, 1298; knighted, 1306; ordered to arrest Percy for permitting *Gaveston's death, 1312; involved in a dispute with the Despensers (1320) about the lordship of Gower, which his father-in-law, William de Brewes, had granted him; joined by the other lords-marchers, who harried Glamorgan, 1321; pardoned with them on the fall of the Despensers, 1321; taken prisoner at Boroughbridge, 1322, Edward II having recourse to arms, and executed at Pontefract.

MOWBRAY, John (II) de, ninth Baron Mowbray (d. 1361), son of John (I) de *Mowbray; released from the Tower of London and his father's lands restored to him, 1327; involved in litigation through the De Brewes's inheritance, 1338–47; served frequently against the Scots, 1327–37 and 1347–55; justiciar of Lothian and governor of Berwick, 1340; fought at Neville's Cross, 1346; JP, 1359; commissioner of array at Leicester, 1360.

MOWBRAY, John (III) de (1328?–1368), son of John (II) de *Mowbray; killed by the Turks near Constantinople on his way to the Holy Land.

MOWBRAY, John (V), second duke of Norfolk (1389–1432), son of Thomas *Mowbray (I), first duke of Norfolk; earl-marshal and fourth earl of Nottingham on the execution of his brother, Thomas *Mowbray (II), 1405; commissioner to investigate the earl of *Cambridge's plot, 1415; prominent in the French wars, 1417–21, 1423–4, and 1430; KG, 1421; nominated one of the Protector's Council, 1422; restored to the dukedom of Norfolk, 1425; assisted in the arbitration between *Gloucester and *Beaufort, 1426; marshal at Henry VI's coronation, 1429; attended parliament, 1432.

MOWBRAY, John (VI), third duke of Norfolk, hereditary earl marshal of England, and fifth earl of Nottingham (1415–1461), son of John (V) *Mowbray; knighted, 1426; succeeded his father, 1432; summoned to the council, 1434; warden of the east march, 1437; inquired into the Norwich disturbances, 1441; went on a pilgrimage, 1446; supported *Richard, duke of York (his uncle by marriage), in his struggle for the direction of the royal policy; his influence with York overshadowed by that of the Nevilles; took the oath to the Lancastrian succession, 1459; renewed his allegiance to the Yorkist cause, 1460; shared *Warwick's defeat at St Albans, 1461; accompanied Edward, duke of York, to his enthronement and fought at Towton, 1461; rewarded with the offices of steward and chief justice of the royal forests south of Trent, and made constable of Scarborough Castle, 1461.

MOWBRAY, John (VII), fourth duke of Norfolk (1444–1476), son of John (VI) *Mowbray, third duke of Norfolk; figures in the *Paston Letters*; besieged and took Caistor Castle in support of his father's baseless claim, 1469 (recovered by the Pastons, 1476); transferred his Gower and Chepstow estates to William *Herbert, first earl of Pembroke (d. 1469), in exchange for manors in Norfolk and Suffolk.

MOWBRAY (formerly **CORNISH**), Sir **John Robert,** first baronet (1815–1899), 'father of the House of Commons'; son of Robert Stribling Cornish; educated at Westminster School and Christ Church, Oxford; MA, 1839; barrister, Inner Temple, 1841; married (1847) daughter of George Isaac Mowbray, whose name he assumed; Conservative MP for Durham city, 1853–68, and for Oxford University, 1868–99; made baronet and privy councillor, 1880; chairman of House of Commons committee of selection and committee of standing orders, 1874–99; became 'father of the house' on death of Charles Pelham *Villiers, 1898; his *Seventy Years at Westminster* published posthumously (1900).

MOWBRAY, Robert de, earl of Northumberland (d. 1125?), nephew of *Geoffrey (d. 1093), bishop of Coutances; became earl of Northumberland, c.1080; sided with *Robert against William Rufus (William II), 1088; ejected a Durham monk from St Oswine's and bestowed the church on the Benedictines, c.1091; surprised and slew *Malcolm of Scotland at Alnwick, 1093; joined a conspiracy to transfer the crown to Count Stephen of Aumâle, 1095; taken prisoner and deprived of his earldom and possessions; remained a prisoner at Windsor until his death, or possibly until he became a monk of St Albans.

MOWBRAY, Roger (I) de, second Baron (d. 1188?), ward of the crown; went on crusades, 1147 and 1164; joined the Scottish king in the rebellion of 1174, but surrendered on the collapse of the rising in the midlands; his Yorkshire castles demolished; went on a third crusade, 1186; according to one tradition buried at Tyre; according to another tradition he returned to England and was buried in Byland Abbey; benefactor of the church and credited with the foundation of thirty-five monasteries and nunneries, as well as the leper hospital at Burton.

MOWBRAY, Thomas (I), twelfth Baron Mowbray and first duke of Norfolk (1366?–1399), son of John de *Mowbray (III); succeeded

his brother John (IV), 1383; KG, 1383; summoned as earl of Nottingham, 1383; served against the Scots, 1384, and shared with *Arundel the glory of the naval victory, 1387; joined the revolted lords and assisted (1388) in the prosecution of Richard II's friends in the Merciless Parliament; conciliated by Richard II after that king had thrown off the yoke of the appellants; made warden of the Scottish marches, 1389; exchanged wardenship for the captaincy of Calais, 1391; accompanied Richard II to Ireland, 1394; assisted in negotiating the marriage of Richard with *Isabella of France, 1396; confirmed his ancestor's grants to various monasteries, and founded a Carthusian priory at Epworth, 1396; helped to arrest *Gloucester, Arundel, and *Warwick, and received Gloucester into his custody at Calais; present at the trial of Arundel, 1397; when called upon to produce Gloucester for trial asserted that he had died in prison; possibly responsible for Gloucester's death; received part of Arundel's estates, and was created duke of Norfolk, 1397; being accused of treason by Hereford, 1398, denied the charges, but in the end was banished and his estates forfeited; reached Venice, 1399, and made preparations to visit Palestine, but died at Venice.

MOWBRAY, Thomas (II), earl marshal and third earl of Nottingham (1386–1405), son of Thomas *Mowbray, first duke of Norfolk; smarting under his exclusion from his father's honours, entered into the treasonable movements of 1405, and marched with Archbishop *Scrope to join *Northumberland; seized with Scrope at Shipton Moor, and along with him beheaded without trial.

MOWBRAY, William de, fourth Baron Mowbray (d. 1222?), one of the executors of Magna Charta; grandson of Roger (I) de *Mowbray, second Baron Mowbray; prominent among John's opponents, 1215; executor of Magna Charta; assisted in driving William of Aumâle from Bytham, 1221; benefactor of the church.

MOWSE (or **MOSSE**), **William** (d. 1588), civilian; LL D, Cambridge, 1552; master of Trinity Hall, Cambridge, 1552–3; deprived, 1553; reinstated, 1555; regius professor of civil law at Oxford, 1554; deprived on Queen Elizabeth's accession; prebendary of Southwell, 1559, of York, 1561; liberal donor to his college.

MOXON, Edward (1801–1858), publisher and verse-writer; came to London from Wakefield, 1817; entered the service of Messrs Longman, 1821; published a volume of verse (1826); set up as a publisher, 1830, his first publication being *Lamb's *Album Verses*; married Lamb's adopted daughter Emma Isola, 1833; published for Barry

*Cornwall, *Southey, *Wordsworth, *Tennyson, Monckton *Milnes, *Landor, and Coventry *Patmore; published *Sordello, Bells and Pomegranates*, and *Cleon*, and *The Statue and the Bust*, by Browning; accompanied Wordsworth and Crabb Robinson to Paris, 1837; visited Wordsworth at Rydal Mount, 1846; commenced a series of single-volume editions of poets, 1840. He wrote a second volume of sonnets (1837), and the two were republished together (1843 and 1871).

MOXON, George (*c*.1602–1687), Congregational divine; of Sidney Sussex College, Cambridge; perpetual curate of St Helens, Lancashire; pastor of Springfield, Massachusetts, 1637–53; returned to England, 1653; ejected from Rushton, 1662; licensed to preach, 1672.

MOXON, George (*fl.* 1650–1660), ejected minister; son of George *Moxon (1603?–1687); rector of Radwinter, 1650; ejected, 1660; chaplain to Samuel Shute, sheriff of London.

MOXON, Joseph (1627–1700), hydrographer and mathematician; visited Holland; settled in London, 1657; sold mathematical and geographical instruments and maps; nominated hydrographer to the king, 1660; published *Mechanick Exercises* (1678) and works on astronomy, geography, architecture, mathematics, and typography.

MOXON, Walter (1836–1886), physician; gave up commerce to enter Guy's Hospital, London, 1854; MD, London, 1864; FRCP, 1868; physician, 1873; lecturer on medicine, 1882, at Guy's Hospital, London; Croonian lecturer, 1881; contributed to many medical papers; poisoned himself.

MOYLAN, Francis (1735–1815), bishop of Cork; educated at Paris, Montpellier, and Toulouse; bishop of Kerry, 1775; translated to Cork, 1786; actively engaged in the establishment of Maynooth College and in the 'veto' controversy.

MOYLE, John (1592?–1661), friend of Sir John *Eliot; met Eliot at Exeter College, Oxford; wounded by him in a temporary fit of rage, caused by his having represented to Eliot's father his son's extravagance; sheriff of Cornwall, 1624; MP, East Looe, 1649.

MOYLE, John (d. 1714), naval surgeon; served in various naval engagements; wrote four works on his surgical experiences.

MOYLE, Matthew Paul (1788–1880), meteorologist; MRCS, 1809; practised at Helston; wrote on the atmosphere and temperature of mines.

MOYLE, Sir Thomas (d. 1560), speaker of the House of Commons; grandson of Sir Walter *Moyle; Lent reader, Gray's Inn, 1533; knighted, 1537; receiver, afterwards chancellor of the court of augmentations, 1537; MP, Kent, 1542, and chosen speaker; first speaker to claim privilege of freedom of speech; MP, Rochester, 1544, 1553, and King's Lynn, 1554.

MOYLE, Sir Walter (d. 1470?), judge; reader at Gray's Inn and serjeant-at-law, 1443; king's serjeant and judge of the King's Bench, 1454; knighted, 1465.

MOYLE, Walter (1672–1721), politician and student; grandson of John *Moyle (1592?–1661); left Exeter College, Oxford, without taking a degree; studied constitutional law and history at the Middle Temple, 1691; frequented Will's Coffee-House; became acquainted with *Congreve, *Wycherley, and others; MP, Saltash, 1695–8; issued, with John *Trenchard, a pamphlet against a standing army (1697); contributed to *Dryden's issue of Lucian (1711); studied botany and ornithology; wrote on the forms and laws of government; his works edited (1726), reprinted (1727).

MOYNE, first Baron (1880–1944), statesman and traveller. See GUINNESS, WALTER EDWARD.

MOYNE, William de, earl of Somerset or Dorset (*fl.* 1141). See MOHUN.

MOYNIHAN, Berkeley George Andrew, first Baron Moynihan (1865–1936), surgeon; qualified MB (London, 1887) from Leeds Medical School; FRCS, 1890; MS, 1893; professor of clinical surgery, Leeds, 1909–26; assistant surgeon, Leeds General Infirmary, 1896; surgeon, 1906–26; considered the most accomplished surgeon in England; advocated gentleness in manipulation; studied medical care before and after operation; made advances in asepsis and introduced use of rubber gloves; set out his surgical doctrine in *Abdominal Operations* (1905); wrote also on surgical treatment of diseases of the stomach, pancreas, gastric and duodenal ulcers, and gallstones; founded 'Chirurgical Club' for visiting surgical clinics, 1909; instigated *British Journal of Surgery*, 1913; member, Army Medical Advisory Board, 1917–36; president, Royal College of Surgeons, 1926–32; knighted, 1912; KCMG, 1918; baronet, 1922; baron, 1929.

MOYSIE (MOISE, MOYSES, or MOSEY), David (*fl.* 1582–1603), author of *Memoirs of the Affairs of Scotland, 1577–1603*, the record of an eye-witness, since he was clerk of the Privy Council, 1582, and (1596) in the office of the king's secretary.

MOYUN, Reginald de (d. 1257). See MOHUN.

MOZEEN, Thomas (d. 1768), actor and dramatist; forsook the bar for the stage, and appeared at Drury Lane, London, 1745; acted in Dublin,

1748–9; wrote a farce, verses, and fables in verse; with one Owen Bray wrote the song 'Kilruddery'.

MOZLEY, Anne (1809–1891), author; sister of James Bowling *Mozley; reviewed books; contributed to the *Saturday Review* and *Blackwood's Magazine*; edited her brother's *Letters* (1885) and those of *Newman (1891).

MOZLEY, James Bowling (1813–1878), regius professor of divinity at Oxford; MA, Oriel College, 1838; DD, 1871; gained the English essay, 1835; fellow of Magdalen College, Oxford, 1840; took part in the Oxford Movement; joint editor of the *Christian Remembrancer*; incumbent of Old Shoreham, 1856; agreed with the *Gorham decision (1850), and wrote three works on the subject of dispute; his Bampton lectures on *Miracles* published (1865); canon of Worcester, 1869; regius professor of divinity, 1871; his lectures and collected works published after his death.

MOZLEY, John Kenneth (1883–1946), divine; scholar of Pembroke College, Cambridge; first classes, classics (1905), theology (1906); ordained, 1909–10; fellow of Pembroke, 1907–19; dean, 1909–19; principal, Leeds Clergy School, 1920–5; lecturer, Leeds Parish Church, 1920–30; canon (1930–41), chancellor (1931–41), St Paul's Cathedral; publications include *The Doctrine of the Atonement* (1915) and *The Impassibility of God* (1926).

MOZLEY, Thomas (1806–1893), divine and journalist; BA, Oriel College, Oxford, 1828; fellow, 1829; married *Newman's sister, Harriet Elizabeth, 1836; rector of Cholderton, 1836–47; took part in the Tractarian movement; editor of the *British Critic*, 1841–3; wrote leaders for *The Times* from 1844; rector of Plymtree, 1868–80; attended the oecumenical council at Rome as *The Times* correspondent, 1869–70. His *Reminiscences* (1882) contain a valuable account of Oxford during the Tractarian movement.

MUCKLOW, William (1631–1713), Quaker controversialist; seceded from the Quakers before 1673; carried on a controversy with William *Penn and George *Whitehead, but finally rejoined the connection.

MUDD, Thomas (*fl.* 1577–1590), musical composer; MA, Pembroke, Cambridge, 1584; fellow of Pembroke Hall, Cambridge; composed church music and pieces for four viols.

MUDDIMAN, Sir Alexander Phillips (1875–1928), Indian civil servant; joined Indian Civil Service, 1899; secretary to government and nominated official member of Central Legislature, 1915; president of Council of State, 1921; ordinary member of Governor-General's Council in charge of home department, 1924; governor of United Provinces, 1928; knighted, 1922; KCSI, 1926; died in India.

MUDFORD, William (1782–1848), author and journalist; originally assistant, then editor, of the *Courier*, supporting Canning; editor and proprietor of the *Kentish Observer*; succeeded *Hook as editor of the *John Bull*, 1841; published tales, essays, and translations, and an account of the Waterloo campaign (1815).

MUDGE, Henry (1806–1874), temperance advocate; studied at St Bartholomew's; MRCS, 1828; practised in Bodmin, where he was twice mayor; published works advocating strict temperance.

MUDGE, John (1721–1793), physician; son of Zachariah *Mudge; studied at Plymouth Hospital and practised at Plymouth; published *Dissertation on Small-pox* (1777); FRS and Copley medallist, 1777; made two large telescopes, one of which passed from Count *Brühl to the Gotha Observatory; intimate of Sir Joshua *Reynolds, Dr *Johnson, John *Smeaton, James *Ferguson, and James *Northcote.

MUDGE, Richard Zachariah (1790–1854), lieutenant-colonel, Royal Engineers; son of William *Mudge (1762–1820); second lieutenant, 1807; first lieutenant, 1807; fought at Talavera, 1809; second captain, 1813; employed on Ordnance Survey; went to Dunkirk, 1819, and the north of France, 1821; FRS, 1823; lieutenant-colonel, 1837; commissioner to report on the boundary between Maine and New Brunswick, 1838.

MUDGE, Thomas (1717–1794), horologist; son of Zachariah *Mudge; apprenticed to a watchmaker, 1731; constructed an elaborate chronometer for Ferdinand VI of Spain; went into partnership with William Dutton, 1750; retired to Plymouth, 1771; devoted himself to improving maritime chronometers; king's watchmaker, 1776; completed his first maritime chronometer, and submitted it to Nevil *Maskelyne to test for the government award, 1776–7; rewarded, after some discussion, by government, 1792.

MUDGE, Thomas (1760–1843), horologist; son of Thomas *Mudge (1717–1794); barrister, Lincoln's Inn; successfully advocated his father's claims to government award; wrote on the improvement of time-keepers.

MUDGE, William (1762–1820), major-general, Royal Artillery; son of John *Mudge; a godson of Dr *Johnson; commissioned, 1779; first lieutenant, 1781; director of Ordnance Survey and FRS, 1798; major, 1801; lieutenant-colonel,

1804; lieutenant-governor of Woolwich, 1809; superintended the extension of the meridian line into Scotland, and was promoted colonel, 1813; commissioner of Board of Longitude, 1818; major-general, 1819; wrote geodetic works.

MUDGE, William (1796–1837), naval commander; son of William *Mudge (1762–1820); employed (1821–5) on survey of the east coast of Africa; conducted (1825–37) survey of the coast of Ireland; wrote on hydrography.

MUDGE, Zachariah (1694–1769), divine; second master in John (grandfather of Sir Joshua) *Reynolds's school, becoming intimately acquainted with three generations of the Reynolds family; master of Bideford Grammar School, 1718; left Nonconformists and joined the Church of England and became incumbent of Abbotsham, 1729, of St Andrew's, Plymouth, 1732; prebendary of Exeter, 1736; acquainted with Dr *Johnson, John *Smeaton, and Edmund *Burke; author of sermons and a new version of the Psalms (1744).

MUDGE, Zachary (1770–1852), admiral; son of John *Mudge; entered the navy, 1780; lieutenant, 1789; commander, 1797; advanced to post-rank, 1800; his ship reduced to a wreck by a small French squadron, 1805; rear-admiral, 1830; vice-admiral, 1841; admiral, 1849.

MUDIE, Charles Edward (1818–1890), founder of Mudie's Lending Library, London; stationer and bookseller, 1840; commenced lending books, 1842; published Lowell's poems in England (1844); advertised extensively, and by his knowledge of public requirements made his library successful; published verse (1872).

MUDIE, Charles Henry (1850–1879), philanthropist; son of Charles Edward *Mudie; devoted himself to work among the poor.

MUDIE, Robert (1777–1842), miscellaneous writer; professor of Gaelic and drawing, Inverness Academy, 1802; master at Dundee High School, c.1808; removed to London; reporter to the *Morning Chronicle*, 1821; subsequently edited the *Sunday Times*; wrote for a Winchester bookseller, 1838; described George IV's visit to Edinburgh in *Modern Athens* (1824); wrote mostly on natural history.

MUDIE, Thomas Molleson (1809–1876), composer; pianoforte professor at the Royal Academy of Music, 1832–44, and at Edinburgh, 1844–63.

MUFFET, Thomas (1553–1604), physician and author. See MOFFETT.

MUGGLETON, Lodowicke (1609–1698), heresiarch; apprenticed to a tailor; journeyman to his cousin William Reeve, a strong Puritan, 1631;

had inward revelations, 1651–2; declared by Reeve to have been appointed with himself messenger of a new dispensation, 1652; identified himself and Reeve as the 'two witnesses' and made some converts of position; imprisoned for blasphemy, 1653; his authority twice disputed, 1660 and 1670, the ringleaders returning to their allegiance; had controversies with the Quakers; arrested for blasphemous writings and fined £500, 1677; prepared an autobiography and wrote an abundance of doctrinal letters, published after his death; in some points anticipated Swedenborg. Reeve and Muggleton's 'commission book', the *Transcendent Spirituall Treatise*, was published (1652).

MUILMAN, Richard (1735?–1797), antiquary. See CHISWELL, TRENCH.

MUIR, Edwin (1887–1959), writer; educated at Kirkwall Grammar School; office boy and clerk in Glasgow and Greenock; contributed verses to *New Age* (1913); published *We Moderns* (1918); assistant to A. R. *Orage on *New Age*, 1919; published voluminous work as critic and novelist, 1924–42, including a life of John *Knox (1929); came to poetry late in life; worked for British Council, 1942–50; warden of Newbattle Abbey, 1950–5; Charles Eliot Norton professor, Harvard, 1955–6; published *An Autobiography* (1954); collected poems published (1960); CBE, 1953; honorary degrees from Prague, 1947, Edinburgh, 1947, Rennes, 1949, Leeds, 1955, and Cambridge, 1958.

MUIR, John (1810–1882), orientalist; entered service of East India Company, 1829, principal of Queen's College, Benares, 1844; judge at Fatehpur, 1845; retired, 1853; DCL, Oxford, 1855; LL D, Edinburgh, 1861; wrote Sanskrit works dealing with Indian history, Christian apologetics, and biography; founded Sanskrit and comparative philology professorship, Edinburgh, 1862.

MUIR, (John) Ramsay (Bryce) (1872–1941), historian and politician; educated at University College, Liverpool, and Balliol College, Oxford; first classes, Lit. Hum., 1897, and modern history, 1898; lecturer (1899), professor of modern history, Liverpool, 1906–13; at Manchester, 1914–21; director, Liberal summer school, from 1921; Liberal MP, Rochdale, 1923–4; chairman (1931–3), president (1933–6), National Liberal Federation; chairman, Education and Propaganda Committee, and vice-president, Liberal party organization, 1936–41; publications include *Short History of the British Commonwealth* (2 vols., 1920–2).

MUIR, Sir Robert (1864–1959), pathologist; educated at Teviot Grove Academy and Edinburgh University; MA, 1884; MB, CM, first-class honours, 1888; assistant pathologist, Edinburgh, 1892–8; lecturer on pathological bacteriology, 1894–8; wrote *Manual of Bacteriology* with James Ritchie (1897); professor of pathology, St Andrews, 1898; professor of pathology, Glasgow, 1899–1936; published *Textbook of Pathology* (1924); served on Medical Research Council, 1928–32; FRS, 1911; knighted, 1934; did outstanding work on diseases of the blood cells, immunology, and cancer.

MUIR, Thomas (1765–1798), parliamentary reformer; MA, Edinburgh, 1782; advocate, 1787; assisted to found a society for obtaining parliamentary reform, 1792; arrested for sedition, 1793, and sentenced to fourteen years' transportation to Botany Bay; escaped, 1796, and after a variety of adventures was severely wounded on board a Spanish frigate at Cadiz; died at Chantilly.

MUIR, William (1787–1869), divine; minister of St George's, Glasgow, 1810; transferred to Edinburgh, 1822; moderator of the general assembly, 1838; at the disruption remained with the established church; dean of the Thistle, 1845, and chaplain to Queen Victoria.

MUIR, William (1806–1888), engineer; apprenticed at Kilmarnock; came to London, 1831; became acquainted with James *Nasmyth and Joseph *Whitworth; worked for *Maudslay, *Holtzapffel, and Bramah, and at Manchester for *Whitworth; started business at Manchester as a maker of lathes and machine-tools, 1842.

MUIR, Sir William (1819–1905), Indian administrator and principal of Edinburgh University; brother of John *Muir; joined East India Company's service, 1837; head of intelligence department at Agra during Mutiny, 1857; related experiences in *Agra in the Mutiny* (1896); secretary to Lord *Canning's government at Allahabad, 1858; foreign secretary under Lord *Lawrence and KCSI, 1867; lieutenant-governor of North-West Provinces, 1868–74; founded Muir College and University at Allahabad; financial member of Lord *Northbrook's Council, 1874–6; member of Council of India in London, 1876–85; principal of Edinburgh University, 1885–1905; president of Royal Asiatic Society, 1884; hon. DCL, Oxford, 1882, LL D, Edinburgh and Glasgow, Ph.D., Bologna, 1888; published standard *Life of Mahomet* (4 vols., 1858–61), *Annals of the Early Caliphate* (1883), and *Mameluke Dynasty of Egypt* (1896); Rede lecturer at Cambridge, 1881; with his brother, endowed Shaw professorship of Sanskrit at Edinburgh, 1862.

MUIRCHEARTACH (d. 533), king of Ireland; victorious in battles at Ocha, 482, Kellistown, 489, and Indemor, 497, and in the Curlieu Hills, 504; made king of Ireland, 517; he attacked and conquered the Oirghialla; fought against the Leinstermen and the Connaughtmen, 524.

MUIRCHEARTACH (d. 943), king of Ailech; won important battles over the Danes, 921 and 926, and (938) plundered their territory; made an expedition to the Hebrides, 941; his most famous campaign ('Moirthimchell Eireann', or great circuit of Ireland) described in a poem by Cormacan, son of Maolbrighde; killed in battle at Ardee.

MUIRCHEARTACH (d. 1166), king of Ireland. See O'LOCHLAINN, MUIRCHEARTACH.

MUIRCHU MACCU MACHTHENI, Saint (*fl.* 697), only known as the author of the life of St Patrick in the *Book of Armagh*; identified the author of the *Confession* with the popular saint.

MUIRHEAD, George (1715–1773), MA, Edinburgh, 1742; ordained, 1746; professor of oriental languages at Glasgow, 1752, and of humanity, 1754–73.

MUIRHEAD, James (1742–1808), songwriter; minister of Urr, 1770; replied to a satire of *Burns, 1795; naturalist and mathematician; author of *Bess the Gawkie* (1776).

MUIRHEAD, James (1831–1889), jurist; barrister, Inner Temple, 1857, and admitted advocate, 1857; professor of civil law, Edinburgh, 1862; sheriff in Chancery, 1885; wrote on Roman law.

MUIRHEAD, James Patrick (1813–1898), biographer of James Watt; educated at Glasgow College and Balliol College, Oxford; BA, 1835; MA, 1838; admitted advocate, 1838; became acquainted with James *Watt, son of the great engineer, who entrusted him with the task of writing his father's life; published *Life of James Watt* (1858), several works relating to Watt's inventions, and other writings.

MUIRHEAD, John Henry (1855–1940), philosopher; educated at Glasgow Academy and University, Balliol College, Oxford, Manchester New College, London; lecturer in mental and moral science, Royal Holloway College, 1888–96; professor of philosophy, Birmingham, 1896–1922; editor, 'Library of Philosophy', 1888–1940; a founder (1891) of Ethical Society; works include *The Elements of Ethics* (1892) and *Coleridge as Philosopher* (1930); prominent representative of British school of idealists; FBA, 1931.

MULCASTER, Sir Frederick William (1772–1846), lieutenant-general; second lieutenant, 1792; first lieutenant, 1793; captain-lieutenant, 1798; judge of the vice-admiralty court in the Mediterranean, 1799–1801; under-secretary to Chatham, 1801; major, 1810; lieutenant-colonel, 1811; colonel and KCH 1817; major-general, 1825; inspector-general of fortifications, 1834; lieutenant-general, 1838.

MULCASTER, Richard (1530?–1611), school-master and author; educated at Eton under Udall, and at Christ Church, Oxford; BA, Cambridge, 1553–4; MA, 1556; first headmaster of Merchant Taylors' School, London, 1561–86; vicar of Cranbrook, 1590; prebendary of Salisbury, 1594; high master at St Paul's School, London, 1596–1608; rector of Stanford Rivers, 1598; wrote chiefly on the training of children; masques frequently performed at court by his pupils.

MULGRAVE, Barons. See PHIPPS, CONSTANTINE JOHN, second baron, 1744–1792; PHIPPS, HENRY, third baron, 1755–1831.

MULGRAVE, earls of. See SHEFFIELD, EDMUND, first earl, 1564?–1646; SHEFFIELD, EDMUND, second earl, 1611?–1658; SHEFFIELD, JOHN, third earl, 1648–1721; PHIPPS, HENRY, first earl of the second creation, 1755–1831; PHIPPS, Sir CONSTANTINE HENRY, second earl, 1797–1863.

MULHALL, Michael George (1836–1900), statistical compiler; born in Dublin; educated at Irish College, Rome; went to South America; founded (1861) Buenos Aires *Standard*, with which he remained connected till 1894; published *Dictionary of Statistics* (1883) and other statistical works.

MULHOLLAND, Andrew (1791–1866), cotton and linen manufacturer; set up flax-spinning machinery in Belfast, 1828; mayor of Belfast, 1845; subsequently JP, deputy-lieutenant, and high sheriff of Down and Antrim.

MULLEN, Allan (d. 1690), anatomist. See MOLINES.

MULLENS, Joseph (1820–1879), missionary; BA, London, 1841; worked at Bhowanipore in India, 1842–58; foreign secretary to the London Missionary Society, 1865; visited America, 1870, Madagascar, 1873, and Central Africa, 1879; wrote on missionary work; died at Chakombe.

MÜLLER, Ernest Bruce Iwan- (1853–1910), journalist. See IWAN-MÜLLER.

MÜLLER, Friedrich Max (1823–1900), orientalist and philologist. See MAX MÜLLER.

MÜLLER, George (1805–1898), preacher and philanthropist; born at Kroppenstadt, near Halberstadt; educated at Halle; came to London, 1829; pastor of congregation at Teignmouth,

1830; adopted (1830) principle that trust in God is sufficient for all purposes temporal and spiritual, and thenceforth depended for support on free-will offerings; lived (1832 till death) at Bristol, where he conducted philanthropic work, which gradually grew to immense proportions; published *The Lord's Dealings with George Müller* (1845).

MÜLLER, Johann Sebastian (1715?–1790?), draughtsman and engraver. See MILLER, JOHN.

MULLER, John (1699–1784), mathematician; born in Germany; headmaster and professor of fortification and mathematics at Woolwich, 1741; wrote on mathematics and fortification.

MÜLLER, William (d. 1846), writer on military and engineering science; a Hanoverian officer; instructor in military science at Göttingen University; came to England, 1807; lieutenant of engineers in George III's German legion, 1807; captain of engineers in the reformed Hanoverian Army, 1816; wrote military and engineering works in German and English; KH; died at Stade.

MÜLLER, William John (1812–1845), land-scape painter; studied under Pyne at Bristol; travelled in Germany, Switzerland, and Italy, 1833; Greece and Egypt, 1838; and Lycia, 1841; painted in oil and water-colour; exhibited at the Royal Academy, 1833–45, his best-known work, *The Ammunition Waggon*.

MULLINER, Thomas (*fl.* 1550?), musician; possibly master of St Paul's (Cathedral) choir school before 1559; collected virginal music.

MULLINS, Edwin Roscoe (1848–1907), sculptor; studied art at Lambeth, Royal Academy, and Munich; executed works such as *Cain*, *Innocence*, *Rest*, and several portraits, including Dr Martineau (bust), Gladstone (statuette), Queen Victoria, William *Barnes (statues); decorated many London buildings; published *A Primer of Sculpture* (1892).

MULLINS, George (*fl.* 1760–1775), painter; an Irishman; exhibited landscapes at the Royal Academy, 1770–5.

MULLINS, James (d. 1639), surgeon. See MOLINES.

MULLINS, John (d. 1591), divine. See MOLYNS.

MULOCK, Dinah Maria (1826–1887), after-wards Mrs Craik; authoress; came to London, c.1846; at first wrote children's books; her chief novel, *John Halifax, Gentleman* (1857); published latterly didactic essays; married (1865) George Lillie Craik, a partner in the house of Macmillan & Co.

MULREADY, William (1786–1863), genre painter; showed early a tendency towards art, and received tuition through the kindness of Thomas Banks; admitted as a student of the Royal Academy, 1800; entered the house of John *Varley as pupil teacher, and married Varley's sister, 1803; taught drawing, illustrated children's books, and exhibited at the Royal Academy figure subjects and domestic scenes of the Wilkie type; RA, 1816; illustrated *The Vicar of Wakefield, c.*1840; designed the first penny-postage envelope issued by Rowland *Hill, 1840 (caricatured by John *Leech in *Punch*); his *Choosing the Wedding Gown* (1846) celebrated for its technical merits in the representation of textures.

MULSO, Hester (1727–1801), essayist. See CHAPONE.

MULTON (or MULETON), Thomas de (d. 1240?), justiciar; sheriff of Lincolnshire, 1206–8; accompanied King John to Ireland, 1210; sided with the barons, 1215; imprisoned at Corfe, 1215–17; justice-itinerant in the north, 1219; after 1224 sat continually at Westminster; witnessed confirmation of Magna Charta, 1225; endowed various religious foundations.

MULVANY, Charles Pelham (1835–1885), minor poet and journalist; BA, Trinity College, Dublin, 1856; naval surgeon; subsequently emigrated to Canada, 1868; curate in Ontario, contributing to newspapers and magazines.

MULVANY, George F. (1809–1869), painter; son of Thomas James *Mulvany; keeper of the Royal Hibernian Academy, 1845; director of the Irish National Gallery, 1854.

MULVANY, Thomas James (d. 1845?), painter; advocated incorporation of Irish artists (charter obtained, 1823); academician on the foundation of the Royal Hibernian Academy, 1823; keeper, 1841.

MUMFORD, James (1606–1666), Jesuit; professed at St Omer, 1641; remained abroad till 1650, when he was sent to Norwich, seized by Parliamentary soldiers and imprisoned; his theological works frequently reprinted and translated.

MUMMERY, Albert Frederick (1855–1895), author of works relating to economical questions and to climbing in the Alps and Caucasus.

MUN, Thomas (1571–1641), economic writer; engaged in mercantile affairs in Italy and the Levant; a director of the East India Company, 1615; declined the deputy-governorship, 1624; published *A Discourse of Trade, from England unto the East Indies* (1621), defending the East India Company from the complaints that the scarcity of specie was due to the company's exportation of it. His second book, *England's Treasure by Forraign Trade* (written *c.*1630, published 1664), defines the balance of trade, makes interesting reference to the customs revenue in relation to trade with India and other countries, and deplores the neglect of the English fishing trade.

MUNBY, Alan Noel Latimer (1913–1974), bibliographical historian, librarian, and book collector; educated at Clifton, and King's College, Cambridge, 1933–5; formed collection of eighteenth-century English verse while at Cambridge; worked in antiquarian bookshop of Bernard *Quaritch, 1935–7; book cataloguer at Sotheby's, 1937–9; served in Queen Victoria's Rifles and captured at Calais, 1940; prisoner of war, 1940–5; returned to Sotheby's, 1945; librarian, King's College, Cambridge, 1947; fellow, 1948; secured collections of papers of many authors, including Rupert *Brooke and E. M. *Forster; co-founder of Cambridge Bibliographical Society, 1949; publications include *English Poetical Autographs* (with Desmond Flower, 1938), wartime verse, *Lyra Catenata* (1948), ghost stories, *The Alabaster Hand* (1949), *Phillipps Studies* (5 vols., 1951–60), and *Cambridge College Libraries* (1960); praelector of King's, 1951–60, and domus bursar, 1964–67; other appointments included Lyell readership in bibliography at Oxford, 1962–3 and Sandars readership at Cambridge, 1969–70; lectures at Cambridge published as *Connoisseurs and Medieval Miniatures 1750–1850* (1972) and lectures at King's College, London, as *The Cult of the Autograph Letter in England* (1962); Litt.D., Cambridge, 1962; trustee, British Museum, 1969; president, Bibliographical Society; general editor of series of reprints, *Sale Catalogues of Libraries of Eminent Persons* and joint author, with Lenore Coral, of *British Book Sale Catalogues 1676–1800* (1977); part of his own collection of sale catalogues and other bibliographical material acquired by Cambridge University Library and Trinity College, Cambridge; remembered by Munby fellowship at Cambridge University Library.

MUNBY, Arthur Joseph (1828–1910), poet and civil servant; BA, Trinity College, Cambridge, 1851; MA, 1856; called to bar, 1855; in ecclesiastical commissioners' office, 1858–88; published poetic idylls, *Benoni* (1852), *Verses New and Old* (1865), and *Dorothy* (1880); work praised by *Browning for craftsmanship; later works include *Poems, chiefly Lyric and Elegiac* (1901) and *Relicta* (1909); FSA; supporter of Working Men's College.

MUNBY, Giles (1813–1876), botanist; studied medicine at Edinburgh, London, and Paris; travelled in the south of France, 1836; lived at Algiers, 1839–44, collecting plants; returned to England, 1860; wrote on the flora of Algeria.

MUNCASTER, Barons. See PENNINGTON, Sir JOHN, first baron, 1737–1813; PENNINGTON, LOWTHER, second baron, 1745–1818.

MUNCASTER, Richard (1530?–1611), schoolmaster. See MULCASTER.

MUNCHENSI, Warine (II) de (d. 1255), baron; served in Wales, 1223, and Poitou, 1225; distinguished himself at the Battle of Saintes.

MUNCHENSI, William de (d. 1289), baronial leader; son of Warine (II) de *Munchensi; taken prisoner with the younger Simon de *Montfort at Kenilworth, 1265; made submission, 1267, but was not fully pardoned until 1279; served in Wales and was killed at the siege of Dyryslwyan Castle.

MUNDAY, Anthony (1553–1633), poet and playwright; apprenticed to John *Allde, stationer, 1576; went to Rome, 1578; described the arrangements at the English College, the carnival, and matters likely to excite Protestants, in *The English Romayne Lyfe* (1582); on his return, 1579, tried the stage; published an anti-Catholic work narrating the circumstances of *Campion's capture, 1581; employed for a short time in guarding and taking bonds of recusants; concerned in eighteen plays (1584–1602), of which only four are extant, *John a Kent and John a Cumber* (1595), *The Downfall of Robert, Earl of Huntingdon* (produced 1599), *The Death of Robert Earle of Huntingdon* (with *Chettle), and the *True and Honourable History of the Life of Sir John Oldcastle, the good Lord Cobham* (1600, with *Drayton, *Hathway, and Wilson); accompanied Pembroke's players on a foreign tour to the exclusion of Ben *Jonson, 1598; ridiculed by Ben Jonson as Antonio Balladino in *The Case is Altered* (1599); was also a ballad-writer, all his pieces being lost, unless 'Beauty sat bathing in a Springe', by 'Shepherd Tonie', in *England's Helicon*, can be assigned to him; wrote (1592–1623) most of the city pageants, and was keeper of the properties of the show; best known for his voluminous translation of popular romances, including *Palladino of England* (1588) and *Amadis de Gaule* (1589–95); as literary executor produced *Stow's *Survey of London* (1618). In some cases he uses the pseudonym 'Lazarus Piot' or 'L.P.', and some miscellaneous pieces bear his motto, 'Honos alit artes'.

MUNDAY, Henry (1623–1682), physician; BA, Merton College, Oxford, 1647; headmaster of Henley-on-Thames Grammar School, 1656; his Βιοχρησιτολογία, published (Oxford, 1680 and 1685, London, 1681, Frankfurt, 1685, Leipzig, 1685, Leiden, 1715).

MUNDEFORD, Osbert (or Osbern) (d. 1460), treasurer of Normandy; English representative at various foreign conferences;

treasurer of Normandy, 1448; taken prisoner at Pont Audemer, 1449; beheaded at Calais.

MUNDELLA, Anthony John (1825–1897), statesman; entered partnership with Messrs Hine & Co., hosiery manufacturers at Nottingham, 1848; took part in local politics; formed 'Nottingham board of conciliation in glove and hosiery trade', 1866; Radical MP for Sheffield, 1868–85, and for Brightside division of Sheffield, 1885–97; brought about the passing of Mr (afterwards Viscount) Cross's Factories Act, 1874; largely responsible for procuring Education Act, 1870; privy councillor, 1880; vice-president of committee of Council for Education, 1880–5; introduced important educational reforms, including Compulsory Education Act, 1881; president of Board of Trade, 1886 and 1892–4; created Labour Department, 1886; chairman of Departmental Committee on Poor-Law Schools, 1894–5.

MUNDEN, Sir John (d. 1719), rear-admiral; brother of Sir Richard *Munden; lieutenant, 1677; commander, 1688; rear-admiral and knighted, 1701; fully acquitted by court martial for failing to intercept a French squadron, 1702, but cashiered by government.

MUNDEN, Joseph Shepherd (1758–1832), actor; joined a company of strolling players; gradually became a leading comic actor in the northern towns; came to London, 1790; acted at Covent Garden, with occasional appearances at the Haymarket, till 1811, gradually becoming the most celebrated comedian of his day; acted at Drury Lane, 1813–24. His appearance and merits are described by *Lamb, *Hazlitt, Leigh *Hunt, and *Talfourd.

MUNDEN, Sir Richard (1640–1680), naval captain; brother of Sir John *Munden; first appears as commander, 1666; captain, 1672; knighted for capturing St Helena from the Dutch, 1673; convoyed the trade to the Mediterranean, 1677–80.

MUNDY, Sir George Rodney (1805–1884), admiral of the fleet; grandson of George Brydges *Rodney, first Baron Rodney; lieutenant, 1826; commander, 1828; advanced to post-rank, 1837; engaged against the Borneo pirates, 1846, publishing an account of his operations (1848); rear-admiral, 1857; CB, 1859; protected British interests at Palermo and Naples, 1859–60, and published a history of the revolution (1863); KCB, 1862; vice-admiral, 1863; admiral, 1869; commander-in-chief at Portsmouth, 1872–5; GCB, 1877; admiral of the fleet, 1877.

MUNDY, John (d. 1630), organist and composer; son of William *Mundy; Mus.Bac., Oxford, 1586; Mus.Doc., 1624; organist of St

George's Chapel, Windsor *c*.1586–*c*.1630; composed songs and church music.

MUNDY, Peter (1596?–1667), traveller; went to Rouen, 1608; rose to independent circumstances after being cabin boy on a merchant ship; kept journals of his voyages to India, China, and Japan, 1628–36; visited Denmark, Russia, and Prussia, 1639–48.

MUNDY, Sir Robert Miller (1813–1892), colonial governor; entered the army, 1833; joined the Horse Artillery, 1841; lieutenant-colonel, 1856; lieutenant-governor of Grenada, 1863, of British Honduras, 1874; KCMG, 1877.

MUNDY, William (*fl.* 1564), musical composer; member of St Paul's (Cathedral) choir; gentleman of the Chapel Royal, 1564; composed church music, songs, and Latin motets in parts.

MUNGO, Saint (518?–603), apostle of the Strathclyde Britons. See KENTIGERN.

MUNK, William (1816–1898), physician; educated at University College, London; MD, Leiden, 1837; FRCP, 1854; Harveian librarian, 1857–98; published *Roll of Royal College of Physicians of London* (1861) and other works relating to eminent physicians.

MUNN, Paul Sandby (1773–1845), water-colour painter; godson of Paul *Sandby; exhibited at the Royal Academy and other exhibitions from 1798.

MUNNINGS, Sir Alfred James (1878–1959), painter; educated at Redenhall Grammar School and Framlingham College; apprenticed to lithographers at Norwich and studied at Norwich School of Art; blinded in right eye, 1898; designed posters for Caley's chocolates and crackers; specialized in painting and drawing horses; joined Newlyn group around Stanhope *Forbes, 1911; official war artist with Canadian cavalry brigade, 1917; produced many equestrian portraits, 1919–59, including Lord *Harewood, with the princess royal, and Lord *Birkenhead; immortalized many famous racehorses, including Humorist, Hyperion, and Brown Jack; ARA, 1919; RA, 1925; president, RA, 1944–9; knighted, 1944; KCVO, 1947.

MUNNU, Saint (d. 634), founder of a monastery. See FINTAN.

MUNRO. See also MONRO.

MUNRO, Alexander (1825–1871), sculptor; employed on stone-carving at the Houses of Parliament, 1848; exhibited portrait busts of celebrities at the Royal Academy from 1849; died at Cannes.

MUNRO, Sir Hector (1726–1805), general; received his commission, 1747; lieutenant, 1754;

captain, 1756; major, 1759; served in India; effectively suppressed mutiny at Patna, 1764; routed the confederate princes of Hindustan at Buxar, 1764; lieutenant-colonel, 1765; MP, Inverness burghs, 1768–1801; local major-general to command the army in Madras, 1777; captured Pondicherry, 1778; KB, 1779; commanded right division of Coote's army at Porto Novo, 1781; captured Negapatam, 1781; returned home; major-general, 1782; lieutenant-general, 1793; general, 1798.

MUNRO, Hector Hugh (1870–1916), writer of fiction; born in Burma; took up journalism in London; works include *The Westminster Alice* (political sketches, 1902), *Reginald* (1904), *Reginald in Russia* (1910), *Chronicles of Clovis* (1911), *Beasts and Super-Beasts* (1914), all short stories, and *The Unbearable Bassington* (1912), a novel; employed pseudonym 'Saki'; killed in action in France.

MUNRO, Hugh Andrew Johnstone (1819–1885), classical scholar and critic; of Shrewsbury School and Trinity College, Cambridge; BA, 1842; fellow, 1843; collated Vatican and Laurentian manuscripts of Lucretius, examined those at Leiden, and in 1860 edited the text; published text of *Aetna* (1867), of Horace (1868); first Kennedy professor of Latin, 1869 (resigned, 1872); published *Criticisms and Elucidations of Catullus* (1878); his translations into Latin and Greek verse privately printed (1884); died at Rome.

MUNRO, Innes (d. 1827), of Poyntzfield; lieutenant-colonel; fought (1780–4) against Hyder Ali, publishing an account of the campaigns (1789); left the army, 1808; published *A System of Farm Book-keeping* (1821).

MUNRO, James (1832–1908), premier of Victoria, Australia; emigrated to Victoria, 1858, working as printer till 1865; founded Federal Banking Company, 1882, and Real Estate Bank, 1887; Liberal minister of public instruction, Aug.–Oct. 1875; treasurer and premier, 1890–1902; agent-general in London, 1902; temperance advocate.

MUNRO, Sir Thomas, first baronet (1761–1827), major-general; governor of Madras; educated at Glasgow; infantry cadet at Madras, 1780; served against Hyder Ali, 1780–4; assisted in forming the civil administration of the Baramahal, 1792–9; after Seringapatam, secretary to the commission for the administration of Mysore; contracted a lasting friendship with Colonel Wellesley, the future duke of Wellington; in administrative charge of Canara, but soon transferred to the ceded districts south of the Tungabhadra, 1800, where he introduced and developed the ryotwar system of land tenure and revenue;

left India for England, 1807, and informed the government on internal Indian administration, on trade questions, and on the organization of the Indian Army; returned to India, 1814, on a special commission to reorganize the judicial and police departments; brigadier-general during the second Mahratta War; KCB; nominated governor of Madras, 1819; created baronet for services in connection with first Burma War; died of cholera while on a farewell tour through the ceded districts.

MUNRO, William (1818–1880), general and botanist; entered the army, 1834; commanded 39th Foot at Sebastopol; CB; served in India, the Crimea, Canada, and Bermuda; general, 1878; wrote on botany, specializing on grasses.

MUNRO-FERGUSON, Ronald Crauford, Viscount Novar (1860–1934), politician. See FERGUSON.

MUNROW, David John (1942–1976), early-woodwind instrumentalist; educated at King Edward VI School, Birmingham, where he became proficient on bassoon and recorder, and Pembroke College, Cambridge, 1961–4, where he was president of the University Music Club (1964) and was encouraged by Thurston *Dart; lecture-recitals demonstrated many species of woodwind instrument; MA, Birmingham, 1964; member of wind band of Royal Shakespeare Company, 1966–8; founded the Early Music Consort of London (James Bowman, Oliver Brookes, Christopher Hogwood, and later, James Tyler); début in Louvain, 1967; first appearance in London, 1968; made frequent international tours, annual series of London concerts, and regular recordings which attracted major awards; hon. ARAM, 1970; part-time lecturer, music department, Leicester University, 1967–74; professor of recorder, Royal Academy of Music, London, 1968–75; virtuoso exponent of repertoire for baroque recorder; recorded and arranged music for television and cinema in such films as *The Six Wives of Henry VIII, Elizabeth R.*, and *A Man for All Seasons*; with Consort gave number of first performances; published *Instruments of the Middle Ages and Renaissance* (1976); devised and presented radio and television programmes such as BBC Radio 3 series, 'Pied Piper', 1971–6; committed suicide, 1976.

MUNSON, Lionel (d. 1680), Roman Catholic priest. See ANDERSON.

MUNSTER, first earl of. See FITZCLARENCE, GEORGE AUGUSTUS FREDERICK, 1794–1842.

MUNSTER, kings of. See O'BRIEN, DONOUGH, d. 1064; O'BRIEN, TURLOUGH, 1009–1086; O'BRIEN, MURTOUGH, d. 1119; O'BRIEN, DOMHNALL, d. 1194; O'BRIEN, DONOGH CAIRBRECH, d. 1242; O'BRIEN, CONCHOBHAR, d. 1267; O'BRIEN, BRIAN RUADH, d. 1276.

MUNTZ, George Frederick (1794–1857), political reformer; went into his father's metal works; took out patents, 1832 and 1846, in connection with Muntz's metal; actively supported the repeal of the Test and Corporation Acts, Catholic emancipation, and political reform; MP, Birmingham, 1840–57; induced the adoption of perforated postage-stamps; opposed church rates.

MÜNTZ, John Henry (fl. 1755–1775), painter; of Swiss origin; employed by Horace *Walpole as painter and engraver; published *Encaustic* (1760).

MURA (d. 645?), Irish saint; founded Fahan Abbey, becoming the first abbot; received lands from Aodh Uairidhneach, king of Ireland; possibly wrote a poem on St Columcille; founded church of Banagher; his staff and bell still preserved.

MURCHISON, Charles (1830–1879), physician; born in Jamaica; studied at Aberdeen, Edinburgh (MD, 1851), Turin, Dublin, and Paris; went to India, 1853; professor of chemistry at Calcutta; served in Burma, 1854; settled in London, 1855; attached to several London hospitals; a prominent figure in many scientific societies; wrote principally on *Continued Fevers* and *Diseases of the Liver*; FRCP, 1859; Croonian lecturer, 1873; FRS, 1866; LL D, Edinburgh, 1870.

MURCHISON, Sir Roderick Impey, first baronet (1792–1871), geologist; entered the army, 1807; served in Portugal, Sicily, and Ireland; sold out of the army, 1814; became acquainted with Sir Humphry *Davy, 1823; studied secondary rocks, making summer geological tours, 1825–31; FRS, 1826; subsequently devoted himself to the older masses underlying the old red sandstone, to which, in 1835, he assigned the name Silurian; published *The Silurian System* (1838); travelled extensively in Germany, Russia, Scandinavia, and Finland, and collaborated with Von Keyserling and De Verneuil in *The Geology of Russia and the Ural Mountains* (1845); director-general of the Geological Survey, 1855; attempted to unravel the complicated structure of the Scottish Highlands; president of the Royal Geographical Society, 1843; received Russian orders; knighted, 1846; KCB, 1863; created baronet, 1866; hon. DCL, Oxford; hon. LL D, Cambridge and Dublin.

MURCOT, John (1625–1654), Puritan divine; BA, Merton College, Oxford, 1647; went to Ireland, 1651; preacher to the lord-deputy and attached to Dr *Winter's Independent congregation; wrote on religious topics.

MURDAC (or MURDOCH), second duke of Albany (d. 1425). See STEWART.

MURDAC, Henry (d. 1153), archbishop of York; Cistercian monk; first abbot of Vauclair, 1135, and third abbot of Fountains in Yorkshire, 1143; five daughter houses founded during his abbacy; elected archbishop of York, 1147, on the deprivation of William Fitzherbert, King Stephen's nephew, whom Stephen upheld; refused admission into the city of York by the citizens; interdicted the citizens and complained to the pope, on which a reconciliation followed, and he was magnificently received at York, 1151; refused to recognize the election of Hugh of Puiset to the see of Durham, 1153, and excommunicated the offenders, but finally absolved them.

MURDOCH, John (1747-1824), miscellaneous writer; friend and fellow-pupil of *Burns at Ayr School; visited Paris; taught languages in London; corresponded with Burns, and wrote on the pronunciation of French and English.

MURDOCH, Patrick (d. 1774), author; distinguished himself at Edinburgh in mathematics; after acting as travelling tutor became rector of Stradishall, 1738; FRS, 1745; published memoirs of Colin *Maclaurin (1748) and of Thomson (1762); published *Mercator's Sailing* (1741) and geographical works.

MURDOCH, Sir Thomas William Clinton (1809-1891), civil servant; entered Colonial Office, 1826; in Canada, 1839-42; chairman of the Colonial Land and Emigration Commission, 1847; special commissioner to Canada, 1870; KCMG, 1870.

MURDOCH, William Lloyd (1855-1911), Australian cricketer; born in Victoria, Australia; practised as solicitor; played cricket for New South Wales, 1875-84; known as 'W. G. Grace of Australia'; acquired fame first as wicketkeeper and finally as batsman; member (1878) and captain (1880-2, 1884, 1890) of Australian teams to England; made record Australian individual score (211) against England, 1884; visited America, 1878, and South Africa, 1891-2; settled in England, 1891; captained Sussex team, 1893-9; died at Melbourne; published handbook of cricket, 1893.

MURDOCK, William (1754-1839), engineer and inventor of coal-gas lighting; obtained employment under Boulton & Watt at Soho, 1777; commenced making experiments on the illuminating properties of gases produced by distilling coal, wood, peat, etc., 1792; put up experimental gas apparatus at Soho, 1800, the foundry being regularly lighted with gas, 1803; Rumford gold medallist for paper which he read before the Royal Society, 1808; issued a *Letter to a Member of Parliament . . . in Vindication of his Character and Claims*, answering the charge of plagiarism (1809), gas-lighting having fallen into the hands of company promoters; sometimes supposed to have invented the steam locomotive, but wrongly, since, though he made three steam engines, his experiments led to no results; originated the 'sun and planet motion' and the 'bell-crank engine'. He took out a patent for making stone pipes, 1810, and the invention of 'iron cement' is also attributed to him.

MURE, Sir William (1594-1657), poet; probably educated at Glasgow; MP, Edinburgh, 1643; wounded at Marston Moor, 1644; commanded his regiment at Newcastle, 1644; left numerous manuscript verses, some of which occur in *Lyle's *Ancient Ballads and Songs*.

MURE, William (1718-1776), baron of the Scots Exchequer; studied at Edinburgh and Leiden; MP, Renfrewshire, 1742-1761; baron of the Scots Exchequer, 1761; lord rector of Glasgow, 1764 and 1765; the friend of John *Stuart, third earl of Bute, and of David *Hume (1711-1766).

MURE, William (1799-1860), classical scholar; grandson of William *Mure (1718-1776); educated at Edinburgh and Bonn; travelled in Greece, 1838; MP, Renfrewshire, 1846-55; rector of Glasgow, 1847-8; chief work, *A critical History of the Language and Literature of Ancient Greece* (1850-7).

MURFORD, Nicholas (*fl.* 1638-1652), poet; salt merchant at Lynn; travelled widely for business purposes; petitioned parliament, 1638, on the infringement of his patent method of manufacture; imprisoned for debt, 1652; produced two volumes of pedestrian verse.

MURGATROID, Michael (1551-1608), author; fellow, Jesus College, Cambridge, 1577-1600; MA, 1580; secretary to Archbishop *Whitgift and commissary of the faculties; wrote on Greek scholarship and on Whitgift's archiepiscopate.

MURIMUTH, Adam (1275?-1347), historian; DCL, Oxford, before 1312; agent at Avignon for Oxford University, for the chapter of Canterbury, and Edward II, 1312-17; and again for Edward II, 1319 and 1323; sent on a mission to Sicily, 1323; prebendary of St Paul's Cathedral and vicar-general for Archbishop *Reynolds, 1325; exchanged precentorship of Exeter for rectory of Wraysbury, 1331; author of *Continuatio Chronicarum* (from 1303 to 1347); the continuation of the *Flores Historiarum* sometimes ascribed to him.

MURISON, Alexander Falconer (1847–1934), jurist and author; first class, classics, Aberdeen; called to bar (Middle Temple), 1881; professor, Roman law (1883), jurisprudence (1901), deputy professor, Roman-Dutch law (1913), concurrently until 1925, University College, London; dean of law faculty, 1912–24; deputy professor, civil law, Oxford, 1916–19; KC, 1924; left unfinished manuscript collation of codices of Justinian's *Institutes*; editor, *Educational Times*, 1902–12; translated into verse Horace, Pindar, and some of Virgil and Homer.

MURLIN, John (1722–1799), Methodist preacher; converted to Methodism, 1749; itinerant preacher in England and Ireland; resided at Bristol and (1784) at Manchester; published religious verse and doctrinal letters.

MURPHY, Alfred John (1901–1980), metallurgist; educated at Altrincham High School and Manchester University; first class, chemistry, 1920; involved in metallurgical research at University College, Swansea, 1920–3; at National Physical Laboratory, 1923–31; chief metallurgist, J. Stone and Co., Light Metal Forgings Ltd., 1931–49; chairman, Stone-Fry Magnesium Ltd., 1946; professor of industrial metallurgy, Birmingham University, 1950; director of departments of metallurgy, 1953; principal, College of Aeronautics, Cranfield, Bedfordshire, 1955; campaigned successfully to obtain degree-awarding status for the college; first vice-chancellor, Cranfield Institute of Technology, 1970; president, Institution of Metallurgists, Institute of Metals, and British Cast Iron Research Association; chairman, Inter-Service Metallurgical Research Council, 1949–55; fellow, Royal Aeronautical Society; CBE, 1964; edited *Non-Ferrous Foundry Metallurgy* (1954).

MURPHY, Arthur (1727–1805), author and actor; educated at St Omer; became a merchant's clerk; published the *Gray's Inn Journal*, 1752–4; took to the stage, 1754; refused admission to the Middle Temple, 1757, because he was an actor, but admitted at Lincoln's Inn; a commissioner of bankrupts and granted a pension, 1803; invariably took his plots from previous writers; edited *Fielding's works (1762), and wrote an *Essay on the Life and Genius of Samuel Johnson* (1792), a *Life of David Garrick* (1801), and miscellaneous works.

MURPHY, Denis (1833–1896), historical writer; trained in various Jesuit colleges in England, Germany, and Spain; entered Society of Jesus; professor of history and literature at University College, Dublin; published *Cromwell in Ireland* (1883) and other historical writings; vice-president of Royal Irish Academy.

MURPHY, Denis Brownell (d. 1842), miniature painter; settled in London, 1803; commanded by Princess *Charlotte to copy in miniature *Lely's *Beauties* (purchased by Sir Gerard Noel and published as *Beauties of the Court of King Charles II*, 1833).

MURPHY (or MORPHY), Edward (or Dominic Edward) (d. 1728), bishop of Kildare and Leighlin, 1715–24; archbishop of Dublin, 1724–8.

MURPHY, Francis (1795–1858), first Roman Catholic bishop of Adelaide; educated at Maynooth; went to New South Wales, 1838; bishop of Adelaide, 1844; established twenty-one churches and commenced a cathedral.

MURPHY, Sir Francis (1809–1891), first speaker of the legislative assembly of Victoria; studied medicine at Trinity College, Dublin; district surgeon for Bungonia, Argyle county, 1837–40; on the separation of Victoria became member for Murray and chairman of committees, 1851; speaker, 1856–60; knighted, 1860.

MURPHY, Francis Stack (1810?–1860), serjeant-at-law; MA, Trinity College, Dublin, 1832; called to the English bar; contributed to *Fraser's Magazine*, 1834; MP, Co. Cork, 1837–53; serjeant-at-law, 1842; commissioner of bankruptcy, 1853.

MURPHY, James (1725–1759), dramatic writer; brother of Arthur *Murphy; barrister, Middle Temple; adopted the surname French; wrote a comedy and a farce; died at Kingston, Jamaica.

MURPHY, James Cavanah (1760–1814), architect and antiquary; consulted as to additions to the House of Commons, 1786; made drawings of Batalha church and monastery, 1788; studied Moorish architecture at Cadiz, 1802; wrote on Portugal and on Arabian antiquities.

MURPHY, Jeremiah Daniel (1806–1824), boy linguist; cousin of Francis Stack *Murphy.

MURPHY, John (1753?–1798), Irish rebel; DD, Seville; assistant priest at Boulavogue, 1785; raised the standard of revolt, 1798; established a camp on Vinegar Hill, 1798; failed to take Arklow, and after the Battle of Vinegar Hill escaped to Wexford; attacked and routed by Sir Charles *Asgill at Kilcomney Hill; beheaded and his body burnt.

MURPHY, John (fl. 1780–1820), engraver; engraved historical subjects after contemporary painters and old masters.

MURPHY, Marie Louise (1737–1814), mistress of Louis XV; an Irish shoemaker's daughter; born at Rouen; first occupant of the Parc aux Cerfs, 1753; dismissed for aiming at supplanting Madame de Pompadour; married Major Beaufranchet d'Ayat, 1755, François-Nicolas Le Normant, 1757, and Louis Philippe Dumont, who obtained a divorce in 1799.

MURPHY, Michael (1767?–1798), Irish rebel; officiating priest of Ballycanew; joined the rebellion, 1798; shot while leading the attack at Arklow.

MURPHY, Patrick (1782–1847), weather prophet; accurately predicted in the *Weather Almanack* that 20 Jan. 1838 would be the coldest day of winter; wrote also on natural science.

MURPHY, Robert (1806–1843), mathematician; BA, Gonville and Caius College, Cambridge; fellow, 1829; dean, 1831; examiner in mathematics in London University, 1838; wrote on the theory of equations and electricity.

MURRAY (or MORAY), earls of. See RANDOLPH, THOMAS, first earl of the Randolph family, d. 1332; RANDOLPH, JOHN, third earl, d. 1346; STEWART, JAMES, first earl of the Stewart family, 1499?–1544; STEWART, JAMES, first earl of a new creation, 1531?–1570, the regent; STEWART, JAMES, second earl, d. 1592; STEWART, ALEXANDER, fourth earl, d. 1701.

MURRAY, Adam (d. 1700), defender of Londonderry; raised troop of horse against *Tyrconnel, 1688; leader of the No-Surrender party, and chosen to command the horse; distinguished by his bravery and was badly wounded.

MURRAY, Alexander (d. 1777), Jacobite; actively supported Sir George Vandeput, the anti-ministerial candidate at the Westminster election, 1750; tried by the House of Commons as the ringleader of a mob, and committed to Newgate, 1751; released after five months' imprisonment; went to France; recalled from exile, 1771.

MURRAY, Alexander, Lord Henderland (1736–1795), Scottish judge; called to the Scottish bar, 1758; solicitor-general for Scotland, 1775; lord of session and a commissioner of the court of justiciary, 1783.

MURRAY, Alexander (1775–1813), linguist; taught himself Latin, Greek, Hebrew, French, German, and some Abyssinian; translated Drackenburg's German lectures on Roman authors; student at Edinburgh; studied the languages of western Asia and north-east Africa and Lappish; wrote the biography and edited the works of James *Bruce the Abyssinian traveller; minister of Urr, 1806; translated an Ethiopic letter for George III, 1811; professor of oriental languages at Edinburgh, 1812; wrote *History of European Languages*, edited by Dr Scott (1823).

MURRAY, Alexander Stuart (1841–1904), keeper of Greek and Roman antiquities in the British Museum from 1886; brother of G. R. M. *Murray; MA, Edinburgh University; assistant at British Museum, 1867; as keeper, reorganized galleries of Greek and Roman antiquities; frequently visited classical sites; LL D, Glasgow, 1891; FSA, 1889; FBA, 1903; independent works include *A History of Greek Sculpture* (2 vols., 1880–3), *Handbook of Archaeology* (1892), *Greek Bronzes* (1898), and *The Sculptures of the Parthenon* (1903).

MURRAY, Amelia Matilda (1795–1884), writer; daughter of Lord George *Murray (1761–1803); maid of honour to Queen Victoria, 1837–56; abolitionist; published *Letters from the United States* (1856) and *Recollections from 1803–37* (1868).

MURRAY (or MORAY), Sir Andrew (d. 1338), of Bothwell; warden of Scotland; led a rising, 1297; joined with *Wallace in command of the Scottish raiders, 1297; elected warden by *David II's adherents, 1332; opposed the English, 1334; relieved Kildrummie, 1335; again made warden, 1335; captured and sacked St Andrews and marched to Carlisle, 1337; returned to invest Edinburgh; claimed the victory at Crichton, but raised the siege.

MURRAY, Sir Andrew, first Baron Balvaird (1597?–1644), minister of Abdie; MA, St Andrews, 1618; presented to Abdie, 1622; knighted, 1633; created peer, 1641.

MURRAY, Andrew (1812–1878), naturalist; abandoned law and took up natural science; FRS, Edinburgh, 1857; president of Edinburgh Botanical Society, 1858; secretary of the Royal Horticultural Society, 1860; FLS, 1861, and its scientific director, 1877; wrote on botany and entomology.

MURRAY, Andrew Graham, Viscount Dunedin (1849–1942), judge; educated at Harrow, Trinity College, Cambridge, and Edinburgh University; admitted advocate, 1874; senior advocate depute, 1888–90; sheriff of Perthshire, 1890–1; solicitor-general for Scotland, 1891–2, 1895–6; lord advocate, 1896–1903; QC, 1891; PC, 1896; Conservative MP, Buteshire, 1891–1905; secretary for Scotland with seat in Cabinet, 1903–5; lord justice-general of Scotland and lord president of the Court of Session, 1905–13; infused animation and efficiency into every branch of the court's activities; lord of appeal in ordinary, 1913–32; admirable exponent of legal doctrine; especially interested in patent law and feudal law; keeper of the Great Seal of the principality of Scotland, 1900–36; KCVO, 1908; GCVO, 1923; baron, 1905; viscount, 1926.

MURRAY, Sir Archibald James (1860–1945), general; educated at Cheltenham and Sandhurst; gazetted to 27th Regiment (Royal Inniskilling Fusiliers), 1879; served with distinction in South Africa, 1899–1902; DSO; director of military training, 1907–12; inspector of infantry, 1912–14; chief of the General Staff, British Expeditionary Force, Aug. 1914–Jan. 1915; deputy chief of the Imperial General Staff, Feb.–Sept. 1915; chief of the Imperial General Staff, Sept.–Dec. 1915; commanded forces in Egypt, Jan. 1916–June 1917; advanced to Palestine frontier; suffered serious defeat in second attempt to capture Gaza with insufficient forces and superseded; GOC-in-C, Aldershot, 1917–19; general, 1919; KCB, 1911; GCB, 1928.

MURRAY, Lord Charles, first earl of Dunmore (1660–1710), son of John *Murray, first marquis of Atholl; lieutenant-colonel of Dalyell's regiment of horse, 1681; served in Flanders, 1684; created earl of Dunmore, 1686; imprisoned at the Revolution; privy councillor, 1703; examiner of public accounts, 1704; supported the union; governor of Blackness Castle, 1707.

MURRAY, Lord Charles (d. 1720), Jacobite; son of John *Murray, first duke of Atholl; taken prisoner at Preston in the 1715 rebellion, but ultimately pardoned.

MURRAY, Charles (1754–1821), actor and dramatist; son of Sir John *Murray of Broughton (1718–1777); abandoned surgery and acted in York, Bath, Norwich, and elsewhere; came to Covent Garden, London, 1796; commended in role of dignified old man; wrote *The Experiment* (1779) and possibly the *New Maid of the Oaks* (1778).

MURRAY, Charles Adolphus, seventh earl of Dunmore (1841–1907), explorer; joined army, 1860; lord-in-waiting to Queen Victoria, 1874–80; explored Kashmir and Tibet, 1892; published account in *The Pamirs* (1893); wrote *Ormisdale*, a novel (1893); joined Christian Scientists late in life.

MURRAY, Sir Charles Augustus (1806–1895), diplomat and author; second son of George Murray, fifth earl of Dunmore (1762–1836); of Eton and Oriel College, Oxford; BA and fellow of All Souls College, Oxford, 1827; MA, 1832; entered Lincoln's Inn, 1827; travelled in America, 1834, and published *Travels in North America* (1839); groom-in-waiting to Queen Victoria, 1838; master of household, 1838–44; secretary of legation at Naples, 1844;

consul-general in Egypt, 1846–53; minister to Swiss Confederation at Berne, 1853; envoy and minister-plenipotentiary to court of Persia, 1854–9; charged by the grand vizier, Sadr Azim, with odious offences, on which, the charges not being withdrawn, war was declared by Great Britain, 1856; minister at court of Saxony, 1859; CB, 1848; KCB, 1866; minister at Copenhagen, 1866, and subsequently at Lisbon till 1874; privy councillor, 1875.

MURRAY, Daniel (1768–1852), archbishop of Dublin; studied at Dublin and Salamanca; coadjutor to the archbishop of Dublin, 1809; succeeded to the see, 1823; corresponded with John Henry *Newman.

MURRAY, Sir David (1567–1629), of Gorthy, poet; held various court appointments, 1600–15; received the estate of Gorthy from Charles I; published *The Tragicall Death of Sophonisba* and *Coelia* (1611).

MURRAY, Sir David, of Gospertie, Baron Scone and afterwards Viscount Stormont (d. 1631), comptroller of Scotland and captain of the king's guard; brought up at the court of James VI; knighted and admitted privy councillor, 1599; comptroller of the royal revenues, 1599; provost of Perth, 1600; attended James VI of Scotland to England, 1603; invested with the lordship of Scone, 1605; James I's commissioner at the synods of Perth and Fife, 1607, and the conference at Falkland, 1609; re-chosen privy councillor and appointed justice of Fife, Kinross, and Perth, 1610; James I's commissioner at the general assembly at Perth, 1618, when sanction was given to the 'five articles'; created Viscount Stormont, 1621.

MURRAY, David, second earl of Mansfield (1727–1796), diplomat and statesman; succeeded his father as Viscount Stormont, 1748; attaché at the British embassy, Paris, 1751; envoy-extraordinary to Saxony, 1756–9; privy councillor, 1763; envoy-extraordinary to Austria, 1763–72; transferred to Paris, 1772; recalled, 1778; entered the Cabinet as secretary of state for the northern department, 1779–82; succeeded his uncle William *Murray as second earl of Mansfield, 1793; president of the council in the coalition ministry, 1783, and again from 1794 to 1796.

MURRAY, David Christie (1847–1907), novelist and journalist; reporter to *Birmingham Morning News* till 1865; parliamentary reporter for *Daily News*, 1871; contributed articles to *Referee*, collected as *Guesses at Truth* (1908); travelled much on continent and in colonies; represented *The Times* in Russo-Turkish War, 1877–8; a prolific and vigorous novelist; novels include *Rainbow Gold* (1885) and *Aunt Rachel* (1886); he published also *A Novelist's Notebook* (1887) and *Recollections* (posthumous, 1908).

MURRAY, Elizabeth, countess of Dysart and afterwards duchess of Lauderdale (d. 1697), succeeded her father, William *Murray, first earl of Dysart, 1650; her title confirmed by Charles II, 1670; married Sir Lionel Tollemache, 1647; married John *Maitland, duke of Lauderdale, 1672; a prominent beauty in the court of Charles II.

MURRAY, Mrs Elizabeth Leigh (d. 1892), daughter of Henry *Lee (1765–1836); married Henry Leigh *Murray, 1841; accompanied him to London, 1845, and became famous as a singer in domestic comedy.

MURRAY, Gaston (1826–1889), his real name Garstin Parker Wilson; brother of Henry Leigh *Murray; essayed his brother's parts.

MURRAY, Mrs Gaston (d. 1891), actress; née Hughes; married Gaston *Murray, the actor.

MURRAY, Lord George (1700?–1760), Jacobite general; son of John *Murray, first duke of Atholl; fought in the rebellion of 1715 and the Highland expedition, 1719; acquired a high reputation in the Sardinian Army; joined Prince *Charles Edward, 1745; made lieutenant-general; advanced from Edinburgh and defeated Sir John *Cope at Prestonpans, Sept. 1745; marched into England and besieged Carlisle, which surrendered 18 Nov.; during the retreat from Derby attacked *Cumberland's dragoons and successfully checked his pursuit of Prince Charles Edward; led the right wing at Falkirk and completely routed *Hawley's forces, 17 Jan. 1746; after the Highlanders' retreat to Inverness, attempted to free the Atholl country and Blair Castle from the royal troops, but was recalled to Inverness; averse to making a stand at Culloden; commanded the right wing at the battle, 1746; retired to France, failing to persuade Prince Charles Edward to remain in Scotland; travelled on the continent and died at Medenblik in Holland.

MURRAY, Sir **George** (1759–1819), vice-admiral; entered navy, 1772; lieutenant, 1778; wrecked on the Breton coast; prisoner in France till 1781; served in East Indies; took part in battle off Cape St Vincent, 1797; wrecked off the Scilly Islands, 1798, but acquitted by court martial; distinguished himself at Copenhagen, 1801; captain of the fleet to Nelson, 1803–5; vice-admiral, 1809; KCB, 1815.

MURRAY, Lord **George** (1761–1803), bishop of St David's; son of John *Murray, third duke of Atholl; BA, New College, Oxford, 1782; DD by

diploma, 1800; archdeacon of Man, 1787; director of the telegraph at the Admiralty, 1796; consecrated bishop of St David's, 1801.

MURRAY, Sir **George** (1772–1846), general and statesman; of Edinburgh University; entered the army, 1789; served in Flanders; lieutenant-colonel, 1799; served in Egypt, the West Indies, 1802, and Ireland, 1804; quartermaster-general in the Peninsular War; major-general, 1812; KCB, 1813; lieutenant-general and governor of Canada, 1814; with the army of Flanders after Waterloo, 1815–18; governor of the Royal Military College at Sandhurst, 1819–24; MP, Perth, 1823; commander-in-chief in Ireland, 1825–8; privy councillor and colonial secretary, 1828–30; master-general of the ordnance; general, 1841; edited Marlborough's despatches, 1845.

MURRAY, George (1784–1860), bishop; son of Lord George *Murray (1761–1803); MA, Christ Church, Oxford, 1810; DD by diploma, 1814; archdeacon of Man, 1808; bishop of Sodor and Man, 1814; bishop of Rochester, 1827–54; dean of Worcester, 1828–54.

MURRAY, Sir **(George) Evelyn (Pemberton)** (1880–1947), civil servant; son of Sir G. H. *Murray; educated at Eton and Christ Church, Oxford; entered Civil Service, 1903; secretary to the Post Office, 1914–34; chairman, Board of Customs and Excise, 1934–40; KCB, 1919.

MURRAY, (George) Gilbert (Aimé) (1866–1957), classical scholar and internationalist; born in Sydney, son of (Sir) Terence *Murray; educated at Merchant Taylors' School and St John's College, Oxford; first class, Lit. Hum.; fellowship, New College, 1888; described by Sir Richard *Jebb as 'the most accomplished Greek scholar of the day'; professor of Greek, Glasgow University, 1889–99; returned to New College, Oxford, 1905; regius professor of Greek, Oxford, 1908–36; FBA, 1910; founder of the League of Nations Union and chairman of the executive council, 1923–38; publications include *Rise of the Greek Epic* (1907), *Four Stages of Greek Religion* (1912), extended in 1925 to *Five Stages*, *Euripides and his Age* (1913), and *Foreign Policy of Sir Edward Grey* (1915); OM, 1941.

MURRAY, Sir **George Herbert** (1849–1936), civil servant; educated at Harrow and Christ Church, Oxford; entered Foreign Office, 1873; transferred to Treasury, 1880; chairman, Board of Inland Revenue, 1897–9; secretary, Post Office, 1899–1903; permanent secretary, Treasury, 1903–11; KCB, 1899; GCB, 1908; PC, 1910; GCVO, 1920.

MURRAY, George Redmayne (1865–1939), physician; educated at Eton, Trinity College, Cambridge, and University College Hospital,

London; MB (Camb.), 1889; discovered cure for myxoedema by hypodermic injection of animal thyroid, 1891; professor of comparative pathology, Durham, 1893–1908; of medicine (and physician to Royal Infirmary), Manchester, 1908–25; physician, Royal Victoria Infirmary, Newcastle upon Tyne, 1898–1908.

MURRAY, George Robert Milne (1858–1911), botanist; assistant at British Museum, 1876; keeper of botanical department, 1895–1905; director of scientific staff of Antarctic expedition of Captain R. F. *Scott, 1901; FRS, 1897; made special study of marine algae; wrote works on *Cryptogamic Botany* (1889) and on seaweeds (1895); edited *Phycological Memoirs* (1892–5).

MURRAY, Sir Gideon, Lord Elibank (d. 1621), deputy-treasurer and lord of session; imprisoned for killing a man in a quarrel, 1586; justiciary for the borders, 1603; knighted, 1605; commissioner for establishing peace on the borders, 1607; privy councillor and commissioner of the Exchequer, 1610; MP, Selkirkshire, 1612; treasurer-depute, 1612; lord of session as Lord Elibank, 1613; held in high esteem by James I; committed suicide in a fit of insanity caused by an accusation of malversation as treasurer-depute.

MURRAY, Grenville (1824–1881), journalist; his full name Eustace Clare Grenville Murray; sent as attaché to Vienna, 1851; correspondent to the *Morning Post*, 1851; vice-consul at Mitylene, 1852; consul-general at Odessa, 1855–68; publicly horsewhipped by Lord Carrington, 1869; published several novels, but was more successful in satirical essays and sketches for the London and American press; died at Plassy.

MURRAY, Henry Leigh (1820–1870), actor; his original name Wilson; made his début under Hooper on the York circuit, 1839; acted in Scotland; appeared in London at the Princess's Theatre, 1845; acted with *Macready, 1846, and Miss *Faucit (Lady Martin), 1848; became stage-manager at the Olympic Theatre, London, under Spicer, Davidson, and William *Farren; a painstaking and natural actor.

MURRAY, Hugh (1779–1846), geographer; clerk in the Edinburgh Excise Office; FRS, Edinburgh, 1814; editor of the *Scots Magazine*; FRGS; brought out *Encyclopaedia of Geography* (1834), to which Hooker, Wallace, and Swainston contributed.

MURRAY, James (d. 1596), of Pardovis; opponent of the earl of *Bothwell; brother of Sir William *Murray of Tullibardine; helped Bothwell to return to Scotland, 1564, but accused him of *Darnley's murder by placards affixed on the

Tolbooth, Edinburgh; escaped arrest, offered proofs of Bothwell's guilt and challenged him.

MURRAY, Sir James, Lord Philiphaugh (1655–1708), lord register of Scotland; succeeded his father as sheriff of Selkirk; accused of remissness in proceeding against conventicles and deprived, 1681; concerned in the Rye House Plot, 1683; confessed and witnessed against the chief contrivers, 1684 and 1685; lord of session as Lord Philiphaugh, 1689; political associate of Queensberry; clerk-register, 1702–4 and 1705–8.

MURRAY, James, second duke of Atholl (1690?–1764), lord privy seal; son of John *Murray, first duke of Atholl; succeeded his father, 1724, in consequence of the attainder of his elder brother William *Murray, marquis of Tullibardine; lord privy seal, 1733–63; keeper of the great seal and lord justice general, 1763.

MURRAY, James (1702–1758), Presbyterian divine; published *Aletheia*, an ethical work (1747).

MURRAY, James (1719?–1794), general; governor of Quebec and Minorca; brother of Alexander *Murray (d. 1777); entered the army, c.1728; served in West Indies, Flanders, and Brittany; major, 1749; lieutenant-colonel, 1751; distinguished himself at Louisburg, 1758, and in the expedition against Quebec, 1759; left in command of Quebec after its surrender, 1759; defended Quebec against the French, who retired disheartened to Montreal, 1760; governor of Quebec, 1760; major-general, 1762; governor of Canada, 1763–6, where his efforts to alleviate discontent met with only partial success; lieutenant-general, 1772; governor of Minorca, 1774; Sir William *Draper sent as his lieutenant-governor when war broke out with Spain, 1779; was obliged to capitulate (1782) after Minorca was blockaded by De Crillon, and sickness broke out in the garrison; acquitted by court martial (1783) of charges brought against him by Sir William Draper; general, 1783.

MURRAY, James (1732–1782), author of *Sermons to Asses*; studied at Edinburgh; minister at Alnwick, 1761; removed to Newcastle upon Tyne, 1764; opposed the Catholic Relief Bill and the American War, of which he wrote a history (1778); published, besides his *Sermons to Asses* (1768), various theological works.

MURRAY (afterwards **MURRAY-PULTENEY), Sir James,** seventh baronet, of Clermont, Fifeshire (1751?–1811), general; entered the army, 1762; succeeded to baronetcy, 1771; served in America and the West Indies; lieutenant-colonel, 1780; aide-de-camp to the king, 1789; major-general, 1793; assumed the name

Pulteney on his marriage with Henrietta Laura Pulteney, Baroness Bath, 1794; major-general, 1798; lieutenant-general, 1799; general, 1808; accompanied *Abercromby to Holland; temporarily occupied the heights of Ferrol, 1800; MP, Weymouth, 1790–1811; died from the effects of the bursting of a powder-flask.

MURRAY, Sir **James** (1788–1871), discoverer of fluid magnesia; MD, Edinburgh, 1829; published *Heat and Humidity* (1829); resident physician to the lord-lieutenant of Ireland; knighted; hon. MD, Dublin, 1832; inspector of anatomy in Dublin; established manufactory for fluid magnesia; suggested electricity as a curative agent; published *Observations on Fluid Magnesia* (1840).

MURRAY, James (1831–1863), architect; executed several works with Edward Welby *Pugin; published two works on architecture.

MURRAY, Sir **James Augustus Henry** (1837–1915), lexicographer; educated at Cavers and Minto schools; headmaster of Hawick Subscription Academy, 1857; took up study of languages; on staff of Mill Hill School, 1870–85; BA, London University, 1873; editor of *New English Dictionary on Historical Principles* projected by Clarendon Press, 1879; removed to Oxford in order to devote himself to this work, 1885; conceived plan and settled scope of greatest lexicographical achievement of present age, although his editorial responsibility only covers half of it (A–D, H–K, O, P, T); also edited Sir David Lyndesay's *Works*, part v, *The Complaynte of Scotlande*, and *The Romance and Prophecies of Thomas of Erceldoune*; wrote *Dialect of the Southern Counties of Scotland* (1873); FBA, 1902; knighted, 1908.

MURRAY, Sir **James Wolfe** (1853–1919), lieutenant-general; entered army from Woolwich, 1872; engaged for many years in staff and extra-regimental service; KCB, for services in South African War, 1901; quartermaster-general in India and major-general, 1903; lieutenant-general, 1909; chief of Imperial General Staff, 1914–15.

MURRAY, John (d. 1510), laird of Falahill; sheriff of Selkirk, 1501; according to the ballad held possession of Ettrick Forest, but finally swore fealty on being made hereditary sheriff; slain by Andrew Ker.

MURRAY (or MORAY), John (1575?–1632), Scottish divine; brother of Sir David *Murray of Gorthy; MA, Edinburgh, 1595; opposed Episcopacy, and in consequence of an 'impertinent sermon' on Galatians 3: 1 was imprisoned at Edinburgh, 1608–9; minister at Dunfermline, 1614; summoned to answer for nonconformity,

1621; ordered to confine himself within his native parish of Fowlis Wester, 1624.

MURRAY, John, first earl of Annandale (d. 1640), accompanied James VI to England, 1603; keeper of the privy purse, received many grants of land, those in Scotland being erected into the earldom of Annandale, 1625; frequently engaged on judicial border commission.

MURRAY, John, second earl and first marquis of Atholl (1635?–1703), Royalist; supported a Highland rising, 1653; exempted from the Act of Grace, 1654; privy councillor, 1660; sheriff of Fifeshire, 1660; justice-general of Scotland, 1670–8; succeeded as earl of Tullibardine, 1670; created marquis of Atholl, 1676; severed himself from *Lauderdale on account of the excesses committed in the western raid, 1678; lord-lieutenant of Argyll, 1684; captured the earl of *Argyll, 1685; irresolute at the Revolution, but probably had no desire to further the interests of William of Orange, and his clan declared for Dundee during his absence at Bath; concerned in intrigues, 1691; subsequently appointed to negotiate the pacification of the Highlands.

MURRAY, John, second marquis and first duke of Atholl (1659/60–1724), son of John *Murray, first marquis of Atholl; unsuccessfully endeavoured to prevent clan joining Dundee during his father's absence, 1689; a secretary of state for Scotland, 1696–8; created earl of Tullibardine, 1696; became privy councillor, lord privy seal, and duke of Atholl, 1703; exasperated at his treatment by the Whigs in connection with the Queensberry plot; strongly opposed the Union, 1705, and was suspected of Jacobite sympathies; proclaimed George I at Perth, 1714, but was deprived nevertheless of his office of lord privy seal; sided with the government in the 1715 rebellion, and displayed great activity in collecting arms from the rebels; captured Rob Roy *Macgregor, 1717.

MURRAY, Lord **John** (1711–1787), of Banner Cross, Yorkshire, general; son of John *Murray, first duke of Atholl; entered army, 1727; colonel of Black Watch, 1745–87; major-general, 1755; lieutenant-general, 1758; general, 1770; MP, Perth, 1741, 1747, and 1754; died in Paris.

MURRAY, Sir **John,** baronet (1718–1777), of Broughton, secretary to Prince *Charles Edward during the rebellion of 1745; educated at Edinburgh University; visited Prince Charles Edward in Rome, 1742, and Paris, 1743; joined Prince Charles Edward on his arrival and acted as his secretary; too ill to be present at Culloden, but was arrested at Polmood and sent to London, where he turned king's evidence, and was one of the chief witnesses against Simon *Fraser, twelfth Lord Lovat; succeeded to baronetcy, 1770; a client of Sir Walter *Scott's father.

MURRAY, John, third duke of Atholl (1729–1774), son of Lord George *Murray (1700?–1760); successfully claimed the dukedom on the death of his uncle, second duke of Atholl, 1764, whose daughter he had married; representative peer, 1764 and 1768; sold the sovereignty of the Isle of Man to the Treasury, 1765; KT, 1767.

MURRAY, John, fourth earl of Dunmore (1732–1809), succeeded to peerage, 1756; governor of New York and Virginia, 1770; nearly provoked armed resistance by his removal of some powder to a man-of-war, 1775; withdrew to a warship during a riot, 1775; returned to England, 1776; governor of the Bahama islands, 1787.

MURRAY, John (d. 1820), chemist and physicist; MD, St Andrews, 1814; lectured at Edinburgh on chemistry, materia medica, and pharmacy, on which he wrote; FRCP, Edinburgh; FRS, Edinburgh; FGS.

MURRAY, Sir John, eighth baronet, of Clermont (1768?–1827), general; half-brother of Sir James *Murray (1751?–1811); entered the army, 1788; captain, 1793; lieutenant-colonel, 1794; commanded in the Red Sea, 1798–1800; quartermaster-general of the Indian Army, 1801–5; major-general, 1805; served in Sweden and Portugal; succeeded to baronetcy, 1811; lieutenant-general, 1812; appointed to the army in Sicily, 1812; court-martialled, after long delay (1815), for sacrificing stores and guns at Tarragona, 1813, and neglecting Wellington's instructions; acquitted with an admonition; general, 1825; died at Frankfurt-on-Maine.

MURRAY, John (1778–1843), publisher; son of John MacMurray; London agent for Constable of Edinburgh, 1803, sharing in *Marmion* and other joint publications (business relations broken off, 1808, and though resumed, 1810, finally terminated, 1813); started *Quarterly Review* on Tory principles, with *Gifford as editor, 1809, *Scott and *Southey being among the contributors; moved to Albemarle Street, 1812, and became acquainted with *Byron; published for Jane *Austen, *Crabbe, *Lyell, *Borrow, and many others; published Mrs Mariana *Starke's *Guide for Travellers on the Continent* (1820), which led to the publication of Murray's guide-books; involved in the controversy about Byron's 'Memoirs' which resulted in their destruction in 1824; Murray's project of *The Representative*, a daily newspaper, suggested by Disraeli, proved a failure, and was discontinued after six months, 1826. His chief literary advisers were *Lockhart,

who became editor of the *Quarterly* in 1824, *Milman, Barrow, and Lady *Callcott.

MURRAY, John (1786?–1851), scientific writer and lecturer; became well known as a scientific lecturer at mechanics' institutions; exhibited at his lectures an experimental safety-lamp; FLS, 1819; FSA, 1822; FGS, 1823; FHS, 1824; contributed to scientific journals and periodicals.

MURRAY, John (1798–1873), man of science; son of John *Murray (d. 1820); edited his father's works; died in Melbourne.

MURRAY, John (1808–1892), publisher; son of John *Murray (1778–1843); of Charterhouse School and Edinburgh University; MA, 1827; present when *Scott acknowledged the authorship of the Waverley Novels, 1827; travelled on the continent, 1829–32; wrote guide-books on Holland, France, South Germany, and Switzerland; published for Layard, Grote, Dr (Sir William) *Smith, Milman, *Darwin, Dean Stanley, Dr Smiles, and many others; inaugurated series of illustrated books of travel by Mrs Bird, Mr Whymper, and others.

MURRAY, Sir John (1841–1914), marine naturalist and oceanographer; born at Cobourg, Ontario; came to Scotland to complete his education, 1858; naturalist in charge of collections on *Challenger* expedition directed by (Sir) C. W. *Thomson, 1872–6; chief assistant in 'Challenger Office', Edinburgh, 1876; director of office and editor of *Report on the Scientific Results of the Voyage of H.M.S. Challenger* (1880–95), 1882–95; explored Faroe Channel, 1880–2; carried out bathymetrical survey of Scottish freshwater lochs, 1897–1909; leased, explored, and financed scientific expeditions to Christmas Island; explored North Atlantic, 1910; FRS, 1896; KCB, 1898; works include *On the Origin and Structure of Coral Reefs and Islands* (1880), *Deep Sea Deposits* (1891), and *Depths of the Sea* (1912), the two latter in collaboration.

MURRAY, Sir John (1851–1928), publisher; son of John *Murray (1808–92); entered father's publishing house, Albemarle Street, London; head of firm, 1892; edited *Quarterly Review*, 1922–8; KCVO, 1926; his works include editions of *Gibbon's *Autobiography* (1897) and *Byron's *Correspondence* (1922).

MURRAY, John (1879–1964), educationist and politician; educated at Robert Gordon's College, Aberdeen, Aberdeen University, and Christ Church, Oxford; first class, Lit. Hum., 1905; prize fellow, Merton College, 1905; student and tutor, Christ Church, 1908–15; joined labour department, Ministry of Munitions, 1915; assistant commissioner, Labour Adviser's Department; Coalition Liberal MP, Leeds West,

1918–23; principal, University College of the South West, Exeter, 1926–51; hon. LL D, Aberdeen, 1930; Litt.D., Columbia, NY, 1939; D.Litt., Exeter, 1956; member, de la Warr Committee on Higher Education in East Africa, 1936–7; contributed to *Hibbert Journal* and *Contemporary Review*.

MURRAY, Sir John Archibald, Lord Murray (1779–1859), Scottish judge; son of Alexander *Murray, Lord Henderland; contributed to the *Edinburgh Review* from its commencement; promoted the (1832) Reform Bill; MP, Leith, 1832; lord advocate, 1835; knighted and appointed judge as Lord Murray, 1839.

MURRAY, John Fisher (1811–1865), Irish poet and humorist; son of Sir James *Murray (1788–1871); MA, Trinity College, Dublin, 1832; contributed satirical sketches to *Blackwood's Magazine*, the *Nation*, and the *United Irishman*.

MURRAY, Sir (John) Hubert (Plunkett) (1861–1940), Australian administrator of Papua; born in Sydney; son of Sir T. A. *Murray; first class, Lit. Hum., Magdalen College, Oxford, 1885; called to bar (Inner Temple), 1886; practised as a barrister in Australia; commanded New South Wales Irish Rifles in South African War; chief judicial officer, British New Guinea, 1904–40; lieutenant-governor, 1908–40; built up strong and enduring administration with native welfare as object, based upon an understanding of native mentality; insisted upon exclusion of Asiatic immigration; by land ordinance restricted purchase of land from natives to government; prescribed areas for the competing missions and placed education in their hands with government subsidy; undertook extensive patrols throughout country and insisted upon justice and mutual understanding; his government recognized as model administration of a native community and fully appreciated by Papuans; KCMG, 1925.

MURRAY, Mrs Leigh (d. 1892), singer. See MURRAY, Mrs ELIZABETH LEIGH.

MURRAY, Lindley (1745–1826), grammarian; born in Pennsylvania; called to the bar at New York, where he practised; settled in England, 1784; published religious works and an *English Grammar* (1795), *Reader* (1799), and *Spelling Book* (1804), which went through many editions, and were used in schools to the exclusion of any others; introduced system into grammar; styled the 'father of English grammar'.

MURRAY, Margaret Alice (1863–1963), Egyptologist; born in Calcutta; educated privately in England and Germany; entered Calcutta General Hospital as 'lady probationer',

1883; returned to England, 1886; entered University College, London, to study Egyptology under (Sir) Flinders *Petrie, 1894; junior lecturer, 1899; assistant, 1909; lecturer, 1921; senior lecturer and fellow, University College, 1922; assistant professor, 1924–35; D.Litt., 1931; assisted Petrie in excavation at Abydos, 1902; excavated in Malta, 1920–3, Minorca, 1930–1, and Petra, 1937; joined Petrie's expedition to ancient Gaza and concentrated on Hyksos cities; published over eighty books and articles on ancient Egypt, including *Ancient Egyptian Legends* (1904), *Elementary Egyptian Grammar* (1905), *Index of Names and Titles in the Old Kingdom* (1908), *Egyptian Temples* (1931), *The Splendour that was Egypt* (1949), and *The Genesis of Religion* (1963); interested in folklore and witchcraft; president, Folklore Society, 1953–5; fellow, Royal Anthropological Institute, 1926; published *The Witch-cult in Western Europe* (1921) and autobiography, *My First Hundred Years* (1963).

MURRAY, Matthew (1765–1826), engineer; worked at Marshall's, Leeds, 1789–95, and made many improvements in flax-spinning; set up in partnership with Fenton and Wood at Leeds, 1795; patented improvements in the steam-engine, notably the 'short D-slide valve'; built four railway engines, 1812–13, and fitted up a steamboat, 1813.

MURRAY, Mungo (d. 1770), author of a treatise on shipbuilding, 1754; appointed to the Magnanime as schoolmaster, 1758–62; published *Rudiments of Navigation* (1760).

MURRAY, Sir Oswyn Alexander Ruthven (1873–1936), civil servant; son of Sir J. A. H. *Murray; educated at High School and Exeter College, Oxford; first class, Lit. Hum. (1895), jurisprudence (1896); entered Admiralty, 1897; as director of victualling and clothing (1905–11) made drastic reforms; assistant secretary, 1911–17; permanent secretary, 1917–36; influential in preserving adequate navy; KCB, 1917; GCB, 1931.

MURRAY, Patrick, fifth Baron Elibank (1703–1778), brother of James *Murray (1719–1794); advocate, 1722; lieutenant-colonel in the army; succeeded his father, 1736; wrote on currency, entails, and the state of the Scottish peerage.

MURRAY, Patrick Aloysius (1811–1882), Roman Catholic theologian; professor of belles-lettres at Maynooth, 1838, of theology, 1841–82; published *Tractatus de Ecclesia Christi* (1860–6).

MURRAY (or MORAY), Sir Robert (1608?–1673), one of the founders of the Royal Society; served in the French Army; knighted by Charles

I, 1643; negotiated between France and Scotland on Charles's behalf, and unsuccessfully planned his escape from Newcastle, 1646; joined Charles II in Paris, 1654, after the collapse of the Highland rising; lord of Exchequer for Scotland and deputy-secretary, 1663; assisted in the foundation of the Royal Society, 1661; learned in geology, chemistry, and natural history.

MURRAY, Robert (1635–1725?), writer on trade; took up his freedom in the Clothworkers' Company, 1660; invented ruled copybooks; originated the idea of penny post in London, 1681; possibly clerk to the Irish revenue commissioners; appointed paymaster of the 1714 lottery; published various proposals for the advancement and improvement of trade and raising of revenue.

MURRAY, the Hon. Mrs **Sarah** (1744–1811). See AUST.

MURRAY, Sir **Terence Aubrey** (1810–1873), Australian politician; went to New South Wales, 1827; represented Murray in the legislature, 1843–56, and Argyle, 1856–62; appointed to the upper house, 1862; secretary for lands and works, 1856 and 1857–8; speaker, 1860–73; knighted, 1869.

MURRAY, Thomas (1564–1623), provost of Eton; tutor to Charles, duke of York, afterwards Charles I; secretary to Charles when prince of Wales, 1617; provost of Eton, 1622.

MURRAY, Sir **Thomas** (1630?–1684), of Glendoick, clerk-register; advocate, 1661; lord clerk-register, 1662–81; senator, with the title of Lord Glendoick, 1674; created baronet, 1676; received licence to print the statutes, 1679.

MURRAY (or **MURREY), Thomas** (1663–1734), portrait painter; painted faces only, others supplying the accessories.

MURRAY, Thomas (1792–1872), printer and miscellaneous writer; intimate of *Carlyle and Alexander *Murray at Edinburgh; established a printing business in Edinburgh, 1841; published biographical works; contributed to *Brewster's Cyclopaedia*.

MURRAY, Sir **William** (d. 1583), of Tullibardine; comptroller of Scotland; supported the marriage of *Mary Queen of Scots with *Darnley; comptroller and privy councillor, 1565; joined the confederate lords after the queen's marriage to *Bothwell; attended the coronation of the young king James VI; was ready to help the queen after Bothwell's flight, and (1569) voted for her divorce; joint governor of the young king James VI, 1572; joined conspiracy against *Morton, 1578.

MURRAY, William, first earl of Dysart (1600?–1653?), nephew of Thomas *Murray (1564–1623); educated with Charles, prince of Wales; gentleman of his bedchamber, 1626; negotiated between Charles I and the leading Covenanters; created earl of Dysart, 1643; on the outbreak of Civil War negotiated for the king with Scotland, foreign powers, and the pope; arrested as a spy, 1646; joined Charles at Newcastle on his release; went to Charles II at The Hague, 1649; accused by Burnet of duplicity.

MURRAY, Lord **William,** second Baron Nairne (d. 1724). See NAIRNE, WILLIAM.

MURRAY, William, marquis of Tullibardine (d. 1746), son of John *Murray, first duke of Atholl; attainted for taking part in the 1715 rebellion; commanded in the Highland expedition, 1719, and in 1745; gained a large number of Atholl men and accompanied the Pretender into England; delivered himself up after the defeat at Culloden, 1746; died in the Tower of London.

MURRAY, William, first earl of Mansfield (1705–1793), judge; MA, Christ Church, Oxford, 1730; barrister, Lincoln's Inn, 1730; KC, 1742; MP, Boroughbridge, 1742; solicitor-general, 1742; proved himself an able defender of the government; attorney-general, 1754; serjeant-at-law, 1756; privy councillor, 1756; lord chief justice, 1756; created Baron Mansfield of Mansfield, 1756; reversed *Wilkes's outlawry on account of a technical flaw, discovered by himself, and substituted a sentence of fine and imprisonment, 1768; gained more and more unpopularity over the cases of seditious libel arising out of Junius's *Letter to the King* (1770) and the case of the dean of St Asaph, 1784, holding in both cases that if the jury were satisfied of the fact of publication or sale they ought to find for the crown, as the question of libel or no libel was matter of law for the court to decide (this view was technically correct until *Fox's Libel Act, 1792); created earl of Mansfield, 1776; his house sacked and burned during the Gordon Riots, 1780; he resigned office, 1788; instrumental in the improvement of mercantile law, the law of evidence, and the procedure of courts; termed by *Macaulay 'the father of modern toryism'. As a parliamentary debater he was second only to Chatham, but as a statesman his fame is tarnished by his adhesion to the policy of coercing America.

MURRAY, William Henry Wood (1790–1852), actor and manager; son of Charles *Murray; played minor parts at Covent Garden, London, 1803–4; appeared in Edinburgh, 1809; took up the management of the Theatre Royal, Edinburgh, on the death of his brother-in-law, Henry

*Siddons, 1815, after which Mrs *Siddons reappeared, and Miss *O'Neill, *Kemble, Charles *Mathews, *Kean, *Yates, and *Mackay were engaged; acquired both theatres in Edinburgh, and was for one year in partnership with Yates; retired, 1848; a good actor in comedy and 'character' parts; wrote many dramas for a temporary purpose and without literary aim.

MURRELL, John (*fl.* 1630), writer on cookery; improved his knowledge of his art by foreign travel; published two books on cookery, which passed through seven editions.

MURRY, John Middleton (1889–1957), author; educated at Christ's Hospital and Brasenose College, Oxford; wrote for *Westminster Gazette*, 1912–13, and then for the *Times Literary Supplement*; worked in political intelligence department of War Office, 1916; chief censor, 1919; OBE, 1920; married Katherine *Mansfield, 1918; editor of *Athenaeum*, 1919–21; founded the *Adelphi*; controlled it, 1923–48; published works include studies of Shakespeare, *Keats, *Blake, D. H. *Lawrence, and Jonathan *Swift, *Unprofessional Essays* (1956), and *Love, Freedom and Society* (1957).

MURRY, Kathleen (1888–1923), writer under the pseudonym of Katherine Mansfield; born in New Zealand; educated in England; married John Middleton *Murry, the critic, 1918; died in France; her works include collections of short stories: *In a German Pension* (1911), *Prelude* (1918), *Je ne parle pas français* (1919), *Bliss* (1920), *The Garden Party* (1922), and two posthumous volumes; *Poems* (1923), *Journal* (1927), *Letters* (1928).

MUSCHAMP, Geoffrey de (d. 1208). See GEOFFREY.

MUSGRAVE, Sir Anthony (1828–1888), administrator; student at the Inner Temple, 1851; governor of Newfoundland, 1864, of British Columbia, 1869; lieutenant-governor of Natal, 1872; governor of South Australia, 1873, of Jamaica, 1877, of Queensland, 1888; KCMG, 1875; published *Studies in Political Economy* (1875).

MUSGRAVE, Sir Christopher, fourth baronet (1632?–1704), politician; son of Sir Philip *Musgrave; BA, The Queen's College, Oxford, 1651; student of Gray's Inn, 1654; a captain in Carlisle garrison; mayor of Carlisle, 1672; governor of Carlisle Castle, 1677; lieutenant-general of ordnance, 1681–7; MP, Carlisle, 1661–90, Westmoreland, 1690–5, 1700–1, and 1702–4, Appleby, 1695–8, Oxford University, 1698–1700, Totnes, 1701–2; fiercely opposed Sir John Lowther in parliamentary contest and was well rewarded for supporting the crown; a teller of the Exchequer, 1702.

MUSGRAVE, George Musgrave (1798–1883), divine and topographer; MA, Brasenose College, Oxford, 1822; incumbent of Bexwell, 1835–8, of Borden, 1838–54; travelled, principally in France; author of *Cautions for Travellers* (1863) and of seven volumes narrating his rambles; published instructive books for his parishioners.

MUSGRAVE, Sir James, baronet (1826–1904), benefactor of Belfast; established firm of iron-founders in Belfast; chairman of Belfast Harbour Commission, 1887–1903; greatly improved harbour and constructed 'Musgrave Channel' and docks; founded Musgrave chair of pathology in Queen's College, Belfast, 1901; baronet, 1897.

MUSGRAVE, John (*fl.* 1654), pamphleteer; captain in Parliamentary army; wrote three virulent pamphlets during his imprisonment for contempt of court, 1644–7; made various attempts to induce parliament to redress his grievances, and charged the Cumberland commissioners with disaffection; published apologetic pamphlets.

MUSGRAVE, Sir Philip, second baronet (1607–1678), Royalist; MP, Westmoreland, 1640; governor of Carlisle, 1642; taken prisoner at Rowton Heath, 1644; intrigued for the king with the Scots; capitulated at Appleby, 1648; withdrew to the Isle of Man, 1649; engaged in Royalist conspiracies, 1653, 1655, and 1659; again governor of Carlisle, 1660; MP for Westmoreland in Charles II's Long Parliament.

MUSGRAVE, Sir Richard, first baronet (1757?–1818), Irish political writer; MP, Lismore, 1778; created baronet, 1782; wrote on contemporary political events; attached to the English connection, but opposed to the Act of Union.

MUSGRAVE, Samuel (1732–1780), physician and classical scholar; BA, Corpus Christi College, Oxford, 1754; MA, 1756; Radcliffe travelling fellow, 1754; went to Holland and France; FRS, 1760; MD, Leiden, 1763; published pamphlets accusing three persons of rank of having sold the peace of 1763 to the French; MD, Oxford, 1775; FRCP, 1777; Gulstonian lecturer and censor, 1779; had few superiors as a Greek scholar; published medical works and edited and collated various plays of Euripides; his notes on Sophocles bought by Oxford University after his death and inserted in the 1800 edition.

MUSGRAVE, Thomas, Baron Musgrave (d. 1384), summoned to parliament, 1341–4 and 1350–73; warden of Berwick, 1373–8; taken prisoner at Melrose, 1377; released, 1378, and his ransom paid, 1382.

MUSGRAVE, Sir **Thomas** (1737–1812), general; entered the army, 1754; lieutenant, 1756; major, 1775; lieutenant-colonel, 1776; distinguished himself at Philadelphia, 1777; appointed colonel of the 'Hindustan' Regiment, 1787; served on the staff at Madras; lieutenant-general, 1797; general, 1802.

MUSGRAVE, Thomas (1788–1860), successively bishop of Hereford and archbishop of York; fellow, Trinity College, Cambridge, 1812; MA, 1813; professor of Arabic, 1821; dean of Bristol and bishop of Hereford, 1837–47; archbishop of York, 1847–60.

MUSGRAVE, William (1655?–1721), physician and antiquary; fellow of New College, Oxford, 1677–92; BCL, 1682; MD, 1689; FRS, 1684; secretary of the Royal Society, 1685; FRCP, 1692; practised at Exeter; published three treatises on arthritis (1703, 1707, 1776) and four volumes of *Antiquitates Britanno-Belgicae* (1719–20).

MUSH, John (1552–1617), Roman Catholic divine; educated at Douai and Rome; opposed George *Blackwell's appointment as arch-priest, and urged the grievances of the secular clergy at Rome, 1602; assistant to the arch-priest; spiritual director of Mrs Margaret *Clitheroe, whose biography he wrote, 1586; published defence of the secular clergy in their conflicts with the Jesuits and Blackwell (1601).

MUSHET, David (1772–1847), metallurgist; authority on iron and steel; discovered the economic value of black-band ironstone, 1801; his chief invention the preparation of steel from bar iron by a direct process, 1800; wrote papers on iron and steel.

MUSHET, Robert (1782–1828), officer of the Royal Mint, brother of David *Mushet; entered the Mint, 1804; wrote and gave evidence to a parliamentary committee on currency questions, 1819.

MUSHET, Robert (1811–1871), officer of the Royal Mint, nephew of David and Robert *Mushet (1782–1828); senior clerk and melter at the Mint, 1851; wrote on symbols and coinage.

MUSHET, Robert Forester (1811–1891), metallurgist; son of David *Mushet; discovered the value of spiegeleisen in restoring the quality of 'burnt iron', which discovery he applied to the Bessemer process and produced cast steel, but neglected to secure his patent rights; invented 'special steel' for engineers' tools, 1870; Sir Henry *Bessemer paid Mushet an annuity, but steadily refused him any royalty; Mushet stated his own case in the 'Bessemer-Mushet Process', 1883.

MUSHET, William (1716–1792), physician; MD, King's College, Cambridge, 1746; FRCP, 1749; Gulstonian lecturer, 1751; physician-in-chief to the forces; fought at Minden, 1759.

MUSKERRY, Lord of. See MACCARTHY, COR-MAC LAIDHIR OGE, d. 1536.

MUSKERRY, Viscount. See MACCARTHY, ROBERT, d. 1769.

MUSKET, George (1583–1645), alias George Fisher; Roman Catholic divine; converted to Roman Catholicism, 1597; educated at Douai and Rome; missioner in England, 1608; held a disputation with Dr Daniel *Featley and Dr Thomas *Goad, 1621; imprisoned under Charles I; chosen president of the English College at Douai, 1640; released and banished, 1641; took up duties at Douai, 1641; possibly wrote *The Bishop of London, his Legacy* (1624).

MUSPRATT, James (1793–1886), founder of the alkali industry in Lancashire; apprenticed to a wholesale chemist; went to Spain; enlisted as a midshipman, 1812, but deserted, 1814; started Leblanc Soda Works in Liverpool, 1823, opening other works in St Helens, Widnes, and Flint; helped to found the Liverpool Institute.

MUSPRATT, James Sheridan (1821–1871), chemist; son of James *Muspratt; entered Liebig's laboratory, 1843; founded the Liverpool College of Chemistry, 1848; partner in his father's business, 1857; edited a dictionary of chemistry, 1854–60.

MUSS, Charles (1779–1824), enamel and glass painter; copied the works of the old masters.

MUSTERS, George Chaworth (1841–1879), 'King of Patagonia', commander, Royal Navy; born at Naples; entered navy, 1854; lieutenant, 1861; travelled from Magellan Straits to the Rio Negro with a horde of Patagonian aborigines; published an account of the experience (1871); visited Vancouver Island, British Columbia, and Bolivia.

MUTFORD, John de (d. 1329), judge; justice for ten counties, 1306; a justice of common pleas, 1316.

MUTRIE, Annie Feray (1826–1893), artist; sister of Martha Darley *Mutrie; exhibited paintings of flowers and fruit at the Royal Academy, 1851–82.

MUTRIE, Martha Darley (1824–1885), artist; sister of Annie Feray *Mutrie; exhibited paintings of flowers and fruit at Manchester and the Royal Academy, 1853–78.

MUYBRIDGE, Eadweard (1830–1904), investigator of animal locomotion, whose original name was Edward James Muggeridge; born at Kingston-on-Thames; emigrated to America; as government director of photographic surveys, he proved that the trotting horse has at times all feet off the ground, 1872; published researches in *The Horse in Motion* (1878); invented the 'zoopraxiscope', 1881, which projected animated pictures on a screen; published further researches in *Animal Locomotion* (profusely illustrated, 1887, abridged as *Animals in Motion*, 1899) and other works; led way to invention of cinematograph; bequeathed £3,000, with his zoopraxiscope and lantern slides, to Kingston Public Library.

MWYNFAWR (d. 665?). See MORGAN MWYNFAWR.

MYCHELBOURNE. See MICHELBORNE.

MYCHELL, John (*fl.* 1556), printer. See MITCHELL.

MYDDELTON. See also MIDDLETON.

MYDDELTON (or MIDDLETON), Sir Hugh, first baronet (1560?–1631), projector of New River; brother of Sir Thomas *Myddelton (1550–1631) and of William *Myddelton; traded as a goldsmith, banker, and clothmaker; alderman of Denbigh, 1597; MP, Denbigh, 1603, 1614, 1620, 1623, 1625, and 1628; the London corporation having obtained authority from parliament to bring in a stream from Chadwell and Amwell, offered to execute the work; compelled by the opposition and demands of the landlords to apply to James I for money, on which James paid half the cost on condition of receiving half the profits (the canal, which was about thirty-eight miles long, ten feet wide, and four feet deep, completed, 1613); obtained large profits from some lead and silver mines in Cardiganshire, 1617; began reclaiming Brading harbour, 1620; created baronet, 1622.

MYDDELTON (or MIDDLETON), Jane (1645–1692), 'the great beauty of Charles II's time'; daughter of Sir Robert Needham; married to Charles Myddelton, 1660; attracted many lovers, including the chevalier de Grammont, Ralph, duke of *Montagu, the duke of York, and Edmund *Waller; menaced the supremacy of the countess of Castlemaine, 1665; received pension from James II.

MYDDELTON (or MIDDLETON), Sir Thomas (1550–1631), lord mayor of London; brother of Sir Hugh *Myddelton; admitted to the Grocers' Company, 1582; MP for Merionethshire, 1597–8, for the City of London, 1624–6; original member of the East India Company, 1600, the New River Company, 1613, and member of the Virginia Company, 1623; alderman, sheriff, and knighted, 1603; lord mayor, 1613.

MYDDELTON, Sir Thomas (1586–1666), Parliamentarian; son of Sir Thomas *Myddelton; of The Queen's College, Oxford; student of Gray's Inn, 1607; knighted, 1617; MP, Weymouth, 1624–5, and Denbigh, 1625 and 1640–8; was appointed (1643) sergeant-major-general for North Wales, but after taking several strongholds hastily retreated before Irish reinforcements; finally crushed the Royalists of North Wales at Montgomery, 1644; took up arms in behalf of Charles II, 1659, but was defeated by Lambert.

MYDDELTON, William (1556?–1621), Welsh poet and seaman; brother of Sir Hugh *Myddelton; served under *Cumberland off Portugal, 1591; sent to the Azores to warn Lord Thomas *Howard of the impending Spanish attack, 1591; wrote on Welsh prosody (1593) and published a metrical version of the Psalms (1603); died in Antwerp.

MYERS, Charles Samuel (1873–1946), psychologist; first classes, natural sciences tripos, Gonville and Caius College, Cambridge, 1893–5; MB, 1898; successively demonstrator, lecturer, and (1921–2) reader in experimental psychology, Cambridge; professor, King's College, London, 1906–9; consultant psychologist, British armies in France, 1916–18; with H. J. Welch founded National Institute of Industrial Psychology, 1921; editor, *British Journal of Psychology*, 1911–24; publications include *Text-Book of Experimental Psychology* (1909) and *Mind and Work* (1920); FRS, 1915.

MYERS, Ernest James (1844–1921), poet and translator; son of Revd Frederic *Myers and brother of F. W. H. *Myers; BA, Balliol College, Oxford; works include four volumes of verse (1877–1904), and prose translations of Pindar's *Odes* (1874) and of last eight books of *Iliad* (in collaboration, 1882); enthusiast for Greece.

MYERS, Frederic (1811–1851), author and divine; son of Thomas *Myers; BA, Clare Hall, Cambridge, 1833; fellow; perpetual curate of St John's, Keswick, 1838; published *Catholic Thoughts* (1834–48), and sermons and *Lectures on Great Men* (1848).

MYERS, Frederic William Henry (1843–1901), poet and essayist; son of Frederic *Myers; educated at Cheltenham, where he displayed a remarkable taste for poetry; first minor scholar of Trinity College, Cambridge, 1860; BA, 1864; fellow, 1864; classical lecturer, 1865–9; on Education Department's permanent staff of school inspectors, 1872–1900; published, 1867–82, several volumes of poems including 'St. Paul'

(1867); his *Essays Classical and Modern* published (1883); contributed monograph (1881) on *Wordsworth to the 'English Men of Letters' series, and wrote on *Shelley (1880) for Ward's 'English Poets'; began to give much attention to the phenomena of mesmerism and spiritualism, *c*.1870; one of the founders of the Society for Psychical Research, 1882; joint author of *Phantasms of the Living* (1886), which embodied the first considerable results of the society's labours; contributed to the society's *Proceedings* on the 'Subliminal Self'.

MYERS, Leopold Hamilton (1881–1944), novelist; son of F. W. H. *Myers; educated at Eton and Trinity College, Cambridge; published *The Orissers* (1923), *The Clio* (1925), and four philosophical novels set in India (1929–40) republished collectively as *The Near and the Far* (1943).

MYERS, Thomas (1774–1834), mathematician and geographer; professor at Woolwich, 1806; wrote on geography, mathematics, and astronomy.

MYKELFELD (MAKELSFELD, MACLESFELD, or MASSET), William (d. 1304), cardinal; BD, Paris; fellow of Merton College, Oxford, 1291; DD, Oxford; cardinal, 1303; wrote theological works.

MYLES (or MILES), John (1621–1684), founder of Welsh Baptist churches; of Brasenose College, Oxford; formed the first Baptist church, 1649; obtained the sequestered rectory of Ilston; emigrated to New England, 1663, and was preacher at Rehoboth, Barrington, and Swansea, Massachusetts; died at Swansea, Massachusetts.

MYLLAR, Androw (*fl.* 1503–1508), the first Scottish printer; a bookseller, who published Joannes de Garlandia's *Multorum vocabulorum equiuocorum interpretatio* (1505) and *Expositio Sequentiarum* (1506), both of which were printed abroad; in partnership with Walter *Chepman set up a printing press in Edinburgh, 1507; issued *The Maying or Disport of Chaucer* (1508).

MYLNE (or MYLN), Alexander (1474–1548?), abbot of Cambuskenneth and president of the court of session in Scotland; graduated from St Andrews, 1494; canon of Aberdeen; dean of Angus; abbot of Cambuskenneth, 1517; lord of the articles, 1532–42; president of the court of session, 1532–48; wrote a history of the bishops of Dunkeld, and collected the records of Cambuskenneth.

MYLNE, Alexander (1613–1643), sculptor; son of John *Mylne (d. 1657); assisted his brother, John *Mylne (1611–1667).

MYLNE, James (d. 1788), poet; his *Poems, consisting of Miscellaneous Pieces and two Tragedies* published (1790).

MYLNE (or MYLN), John (d. 1621), mason; great-nephew of Alexander *Mylne (1474–1548?); master-mason in Scotland before 1584; repaired the Dundee Harbour Works; built bridge over the Tay, 1604–17 (destroyed, 1621).

MYLNE, John (d. 1657), mason; son of John *Mylne (d. 1621); engaged on the present steeple of the Tolbooth at Aberdeen, 1622–9, on fortifications at Dundee, 1643–51; master-mason, 1631–6.

MYLNE, John (1611–1667), mason; son of John *Mylne (d. 1657); principal master-mason, 1636; designed Tron Church (opened, 1647), partly built Heriot's Hospital, 1643–59, and Edinburgh College, 1646–7; served with the Covenanters, 1640; master-gunner of Scotland, 1646; sat on Edinburgh Town Council, 1655–64; MP, Edinburgh, 1662–3.

MYLNE, Robert (1633–1710), mason; son of Alexander *Mylne (1613–1643); master-mason, 1668; reclaimed the foreshore and constructed the sea-wall at Leith, 1669–85; superintended building of Holyrood Palace, 1670–9; erected many stone buildings in the principal streets of Edinburgh, and built 'Mylne's Mount', one of the bastions in Edinburgh Castle.

MYLNE, Robert (1643?–1747), writer of pasquils and antiquary; collected public records; notorious for his bitter political squibs against the Whigs.

MYLNE, Robert (1734–1811), architect and engineer; son of Thomas *Mylne; studied at Rome, 1754–8; travelled through Switzerland and Holland, 1759; constructed Blackfriars Bridge, 1760–9; engaged in many architectural and engineering works in England and Scotland; designed the Gloucester and Berkeley Canal, and an improvement to the fen level drainage by the Eau Brink Cut; surveyor of St Paul's Cathedral, 1766; engineer to the New River Company, 1770–1811; FRS, 1767; original member of the Architects' Club, 1791.

MYLNE, Robert William (1817–1890), architect, engineer, and geologist; son of William Chadwell *Mylne; engineer to the Limerick Water Works; wrote on artesian wells and the geology of London.

MYLNE, Thomas (d. 1763), city surveyor of Edinburgh; son of William *Mylne (1662–1728).

MYLNE (or MILN), Walter (d. 1558), martyr; imbibed Protestant doctrines in Germany, and was condemned as a heretic before 1546; fled abroad, but in 1558 was burnt as a heretic at St Andrews.

MYLNE, William (1662–1728), master-mason; son of Robert *Mylne (1633–1710).

MYLNE, William (d. 1790), architect; son of Thomas *Mylne; architect to city of Edinburgh, 1765; built the North Bridge, Edinburgh, 1765–72.

MYLNE, William Chadwell (1781–1863), engineer and architect; son of Robert *Mylne (1734–1811); engineer to the New River Company, 1811–61; much engaged in engineering projects in connection with water-supply and drainage; FRAS, 1821; FRS, 1826; FRIBA, 1834; MICE, 1842.

MYNGS, Sir Christopher (1625–1666), vice-admiral; entered the navy when young; captain, 1653; captured a fleet of Dutch merchant vessels, 1653; served in Jamaica, 1655–64; knighted, 1665; led the van on the fourth day of the battle off the North Foreland, 1–4 June 1666, and was mortally wounded.

MYNN, Alfred (1807–1861), cricketer; originally a hop merchant; became a cricketer, 1832; played for the Gentlemen, Kent, and All England; the first fast round-arm bowler of eminence.

MYNORS, Robert (1739–1806), surgeon; practised at Birmingham; wrote on surgery.

MYNSHUL, Geffray (1594?–1668), author. See MINSHULL.

MYRDDIN EMRYS. See MERLIN AMBROSIUS.

MYRDDIN-EVANS, Sir Guildhaume (1894–1964), civil servant; educated at Llandovery and Christ Church, Oxford; first class, mathematical mods., 1914; served in South Wales Borderers, 1914–17; invalided from army, joined prime minister's secretariat, 1917; assistant secretary to the Cabinet, 1919; assistant principal, Treasury, 1919–29; transferred to Ministry of Labour, 1929; head of International Labour Division, 1938–59; led most of the British delegations to international labour conferences; representative of British government on governing body of ILO, 1945; chairman for three periods of office; first civil servant to be elected president of International Labour Conference, 1949; CB, 1945; KCMG, 1947; published (with (Sir) Thomas Chegwidden) *The Employment Exchange Service of Great Britain* (1934).

MYRDDIN WYLLT (i.e. the Mad) (*fl.* 580?), legendary Welsh poet; erroneously credited with six poems printed in the *Myvyrian Archaiology*; has been improbably identified with Merlin Ambrosius and Merlin 'Silvester' or 'Celidonius' (see MERLIN).

MYRES, Sir John Linton (1869–1954), archaeologist and historian; scholar of Winchester and New College, Oxford; first class, Lit. Hum., 1892; fellow of Magdalen College, Oxford, 1892–5; Craven fellow, 1892; excavated in Crete and Cyprus; lecturer in classical archaeology, Oxford, 1895–1907; professor of Greek, Liverpool University, 1907–10; Wykeham professor in ancient history, Oxford, 1910–39; FBA, 1923; general secretary, British Association, 1919–32; knighted, 1943; publications include *History of Rome* (1902), *Dawn of History* (1911), *Who were the Greeks?* (1930), *Herodotus, Father of History* (1953), and *Geographical History in Greek Lands* (1953).

MYSORE, Sir Shri Krishnaraja Wadiyar Bahadur, maharaja of (1884–1940); succeeded father as head of the state, 1895; invested with full administrative powers, 1902; introduced a system of popular government (1922) and later a system approaching constitutional monarchy; welcomed prospect of federal India; a strictly orthodox Hindu; GCSI, 1907; GBE, 1917.

MYTENS, Daniel (1590?–1642), portrait painter; born at The Hague; member of the Guild of St Luke, 1610; came to England before 1618; became 'king's painter' on Charles I's accession; painted portraits of the court and nobility and copied old masters; returned to Holland, 1630, and died there.

MYTTON, John (1796–1834), sportsman and eccentric; of Westminster School; served in the army, 1816–17; MP, Shrewsbury, 1818–20; high sheriff for Shropshire and Merionethshire; a great sportsman; ran through a fortune and died of delirium tremens in the King's Bench Prison.

MYTTON, Thomas (1597?–1656), Parliamentarian; of Balliol College, Oxford; student of Lincoln's Inn, 1616; a prominent parliamentarian in Shropshire; seized, and became governor of, Wem, 1643, and Oswestry, 1644, and captured Shrewsbury, 1645; commander-in-chief and vice-admiral in North Wales, 1645; recovered Anglesea from the Royalists, 1648–9; member of the court martial which condemned the earl of Derby, 1651; represented Shropshire in *Cromwell's first parliament.

MYVYR, Owain (1741–1814), Welsh antiquary. See JONES, OWEN.